2001

WOMEN IN WORLD HISTORY

A Biographical Encyclopedia

Women in World History

A Biographical Encyclopedia

VOLUME
2
Ba-Brec

Anne Commire, Editor
Deborah Klezmer, Associate Editor

YORKIN PUBLICATIONS

GALE GROUP
Detroit
San Francisco
London
Boston
Woodbridge, CT

Yorkin Publications

Anne Commire, *Editor*
Deborah Klezmer, *Associate Editor*
Barbara Morgan, *Assistant Editor*

Eileen O'Pasek, Gail Schermer, Patricia Coombs, James Fox,
Catherine Cappelli, Karen Rikkers, *Editorial Assistants*
Karen Walker, *Assistant for Genealogical Charts*

Special acknowledgment is due to Peg Yorkin who made this project possible.

Thanks also to Karin and John Haag, Bob Schermer, and to
the Gale Group staff, in particular Dedria Bryfonski, Linda Hubbard, John Schmittroth, Cynthia Baldwin,
Tracey Rowens, Randy Bassett, Christine O'Bryan, Rebecca Parks, and especially Sharon Malinowski.

The Gale Group

Sharon Malinowski, *Senior Editor*
Rebecca Parks, *Editor*
Linda S. Hubbard, *Managing Editor, Multicultural Team*

Margaret A. Chamberlain, *Permissions Specialist*
Mary K. Grimes, *Image Cataloger*

Mary Beth Trimper, *Production Director*
Evi Seoud, *Assistant Production Manager*

Cynthia Baldwin, *Product Design Manager*
Tracey Rowens, *Cover and Page Designer*

Barbara Yarrow, *Graphic Services Manager*
Randy Bassett, *Image Database Supervisor*
Robert Duncan and Michael Logusz, *Imaging Specialists*
Christine O'Bryan, *Graphics Desktop Publisher*

Gale Group, Inc.
27500 Drake Road
Farmington Hills, MI 48331-3535

Library of Congress Catalog Card Number 99-24692
A CIP record is available from the British Library

ISBN 0-7876-4061-1
Printed in the United States of America.

Library of Congress Cataloging-in-Publication Data

Women in world history : a biographical encyclopedia / Anne Commire, editor, Deborah Klezmer, associate editor.
p. cm.
Includes bibliographical references and index.
ISBN 0-7876-3736-X (set). — ISBN 0-7876-4080-8 (v. 1). —
ISBN 0-7876-4061-1 (v. 2) — ISBN 0-7876-4062-X (v. 3) — ISBN 0-7876-4063-8 (v. 4)
1. Women—History Encyclopedias.2. Women—Biography Encyclopedias.
I. Commire, Anne. II. Klezmer, Deborah.
HQ1115.W6 1999 99-24692
920.72'03—DC21

10 9 8 7 6 5 4 3 2 1

Bâ, Mariama (1929–1981)

Senegalese novelist who won Africa's first Noma Award. *Name variations: Ba or Baâ. Born to Muslim parents in Dakar, Senegal, in 1929; died after a long illness in Dakar in 1981; daughter of a civil servant; attended the École Normal for girls in Rufisque; married a Senegalese politician (divorced); children: nine.*

After suffering the loss of her mother at an early age, Mariama Bâ grew up under the traditional tutelage of her well-to-do maternal grandparents. Her father, believing in the importance of a French education, then sent her off to the École Normal in Rufisque. There she was considered a brilliant student and began writing. Upon graduation, she worked as a secretary before becoming a grade-school teacher in 1947. Forced to resign after 12 years because of ill health, she joined various Senegalese women's organizations and wrote essays on such topics as polygamy and clitoridectomy. In 1979, in her epistolary first novel *Une Si longue lettre* (*So Long a Letter*), Bâ wrote of her chosen profession: "Teachers—at kindergarten level, as at university level—form a noble army accomplishing daily feats, never praised, never decorated. An army forever on the move, forever vigilant. An army without drums, without gleaming uniforms. This army, thwarting traps and snares, everywhere plants the flag of knowledge and morality." The novel won the first Noma Award for Publishing in Africa. Bâ also authored *Le Chant écarlate* (*Scarlet Song*) but did not live to see its publication. Married and divorced, Mariama Bâ was the mother of nine children.

Ba Trieu (225–248 CE)

Vietnamese resistance fighter who, at 19, led an insurrection against Chinese invaders and now serves as an inspiration for national defiance against foreign domination. *Name variations: Trieu Thi Chinh, Trieu Thi Trinh, Trieu Tring Nuong, Lady Trieu; Trieu Au (used by Chinese, though considered disrespectful by Vietnamese). Pronunciation: Bah Tcheel. Born around 225 CE; lived in the Nui Nua, Thanh Hoa province, Vietnam; committed suicide on Tung Mountain at age 23 in 248 CE; sister of Trieu Quoc Dat, a headman in Quang An, Thanh Hoa (northern Vietnam).*

Since its birth, Vietnam has been a country in struggle, constantly facing natural calamities and foreign invaders. Ten centuries under the domination of neighboring China, and one hundred years of French colonialism, have forged the will of the Vietnamese to live independently and to preserve their national identity. The first significant insurrections against foreign rule were led by women: first the ***Trung sisters** and later by Trieu Thi Trinh, more popularly known as Ba Trieu. Western scholars and historians call Ba Trieu the Vietnamese Joan of Arc, a woman of strength, courage, and conviction. She is a national hero in Vietnam and a role model for generations of Vietnamese women.

Vietnam traces its origins to a legendary kingdom reigned by mythical monarchs. According to legend, the lord Lac Long Quan married the princess Au Co, and she gave birth to a hundred sons. Lac Long Quan announced one day that he was a dragon and she a fairy, which meant, he reasoned, that they could not remain together. Au Co took 50 of the sons to the mountains; the other 50 followed their father to the sea. The bravest of Lac Long Quan's sons became the founder of the Hung Dynasty, which gave the country 18 successive rulers. According to Vietnamese ancient history, the first state was called Van Lang, a federation of 15 tribes in the northern part of current-day Vietnam. Toward the end of the 3rd century BCE, An Duong Vuong (also known as Thuc Phan), seized Van Lang and named it Au Lac. He established his capital at Co Loa, about 20 miles north of present-day Ha Noi (Hanoi). A model for later fortresses, his fortified citadel had three spiraling walls, the outer one measuring 9,000 yards. An Duong Vuong's forces were armed with crossed bows, which released ten bronze-tipped arrows at a time. In 1959, some 10,000 of these bronze arrowheads were discovered in Co Loa, evidence that it was once the scene of heavy fighting. An Duong Vuong waged a ten-year struggle of national resistance to preserve his kingdom. In the beginning of the 3rd century, Trieu Da, a renegade Chinese general, conquered Au Lac and proclaimed it the independent state of Nam Viet (Southern Viet). However, his successors could not hold out against the powerful armies of the Chinese Han.

In 111 BCE, the Han annexed Nam Viet into their empire and made it a Chinese province called Giao Chi. The occupation marked the beginning of a policy of political and cultural assimilation. Chinese settlers began moving into the province, bringing Confucian ideology, Chinese customs, and written characters, which were used until the 17th century. The Han heavily taxed their Vietnamese subjects and administered a tribute policy that required the population to turn over precious stones, metals, and rare goods, such as elephant tusks, rhinoceros horns, and tortoise shells. They confiscated land to set up ranches and monopolized the salt and metal markets, making the Vietnamese economically dependent.

Although there were many attempts to resist Chinese rule, the first successful insurrection was led by the spirited Trung sisters. They took power in 39 CE and ruled Vietnam for two years. After their defeat by the Chinese armies, the sisters committed suicide by drowning themselves in the River Hat in 43 CE. They are honored at the Den Hai Ba Trung (The Two Trung Sisters Temple) outside Ha Noi.

Dau cuong nhuoc co luc khac nhau,
Song hao kiet doi nao cung co
[Although we have been at times strong, at times
weak,
We have at no time lacked heroes.]

—Nguyen Trai, *Binh Ngo Dai Cao*, 1428

Over the next two centuries, the Chinese intensified their campaign to assimilate the Vietnamese. Chinese lords replaced many of the local officials with their own administrators in order to form a loyal base of support. The Chinese referred to the country as An Nam, meaning the pacified south. But the country was not placated and would not remain conquered. Resistance to Chinese rule persisted; revolts were continuous. Some rebellions succeeded long enough to give the Vietnamese short periods of independence. It was after one of these periods of freedom, in the 3rd century, that Ba Trieu made her mark on the history and psyche of the Vietnamese people.

Ba Trieu was the sister of Trieu Quoc Dat, a powerful headman in Quan An, Cuu Chan District. Her parents died when she was a young girl, and Ba Trieu went to live with her brother. She was described as "physically strong, witty and visionary." At age 19, she rallied 1,000 fighters and trained them for battle on Nua Mountain. Denouncing the crimes of the Chinese Wu Dynasty, Ba Trieu appealed to the citizens to take up arms to save the country. People in the region wholeheartedly followed her call. When her brother advised her to get married rather than revolt, she replied:

> I want to ride the storm, tread the dangerous waves,
> Kill fierce sharks in the open sea, drive out the Ngo aggressors,
> Reclaim our country, break the yoke of slavery.
> I will not bow my head and be a concubine of man.

Her brother led an uprising against the Chinese in Cuu Chan District, and Ba Trieu came to his aid. His soldiers admired Ba Trieu's brave command to such a degree that they pronounced her their leader. When Trieu Quoc Dat died in battle, Ba Trieu took over, leading her troops in 30 battles. She commanded fearlessly, riding atop an elephant in a coat of armor, adorned with golden hairpins and ivory clogs. Her troops won many battles, and they succeeded in killing the governor of Giao Chau. People in Giao Chi and Cuu Chan soon joined the revolt. Chinese Wu history of the period is a testament to Ba Trieu's effectiveness: "In 248, the whole region of Giao Chau was shaken."

The Wu Dynasty sent its famous general, Luc Dan, and another 8,000 troops to suppress the uprising. After six months of fierce fighting, Ba Trieu's troops were crushed, but her courage earned her the respect and awe of the Chinese soldiers:

> Clad in a golden robe with a gold pin through her hair, wearing ivory shoes, she was always seen on her elephant, on the front line.
> It is easy to handle a spear to attack a tiger, but facing the Queen, how it is difficult to fight.

At age 23, Ba Trieu killed herself on Tung Mountain, rather than give in to the enemy. During the early Ly Dynasty in the 6th century,

King Nam De commended Ba Trieu for her loyalty and bravery and ordered the construction of a temple in her honor. He gave her the highest title in the country: *Bat chinh anh liet hung tai trinh nhat phu nhan* (Truest and Bravest First Lady). Her tomb and the temple still stand. In the late 20th century, a bronze sword was discovered on Mount Nua in Thanh Hoa province, where the insurrection led by Lady Trieu took place. The carving on the sword's handle shows an aristocratic Vietnamese woman wearing a turban and magnificent clothing.

Ru con con ngu cho lanh
De me ganh nuoc rua banh con voi
Muon coi len nui ma coi
Co ba Trieu tuong cuoi voi banh vang!

Sleep, sleep tight my child
So that I can fetch water to wash the gilded saddle of the elephant.
Climb the hill if you want to watch
Lady General Trieu on her golden gilded seat.

—Vietnamese folk song

Even though Ba Trieu's attempt to overthrow the Chinese failed, Vietnamese resistance did not die. The Vietnamese finally won their freedom in the year 939 and remained an independent state for the next 1,000 years. Despite the campaign of forced assimilation by the Chinese, Vietnamese language, culture, and customs survived. Although Vietnamese women were oppressed under Chinese rule, their status was always higher than women in other Asian nations, and they never suffered the ordeal of having their feet bound. For a brief period in the 15th century, the Chinese managed to occupy Vietnam once again and tried to rule as they had in the past. This time, however, they could not turn back the clock, and Vietnam maintained its sovereignty.

By the late 16th century, two ruling clans dominated the country: the Trinh in the north and the Nguyen in the south. In 1771, a peasant insurrection known as the Tay Son Rebellion led to the unification of Vietnam. Again, a woman figured prominently in the struggle. ⊳ **Bui Thi Xuan**, wife of the Tay Son general Tran Quang Dieu, was herself a general celebrated for her courage and heroism. Mounted atop an elephant, she led 5,000 troops in an attack on Dong Hoi, a fortified line dividing north and south. The assault almost succeeded, but the forces of Nguyen Anh in the South prevailed. By 1802, his armies had defeated the emperor Quang Trung (also known as Nguyen Hue), and Nguyen Anh viciously retaliated against his enemies. Bui Thi Xuan, Tran Quang Dieu, and their 14-year-old daughter were executed. It has been written that Bui Thi Xuan "died as she lived; when faced with the elephant which was about to trample her to death, she remained calm and brave. She expressed her disdain for the enemy and maintained her commanding and majestic posture."

Before the end of the 19th century, Vietnam was again subjugated, this time by the French. Many resistance groups formed to fight colonial rule and women were leaders of this struggle as well. A woman named **Lady Dinh** worked clandestinely for the Duy Tan (Reformation) campaign, a nonviolent movement led by two scholars. Lady Dinh was arrested and tortured by the French, but she never disclosed the whereabouts of her compatriots, nor revealed the movement's operations. The night before she was killed, Lady Dinh invoked the memory of another female resistance fighter, writing this poem on the prison wall:

In the other world, I will wipe my tears in meeting Lady Trung
Soaked in blood and lamented like the soul of the Quyen bird
A bow to Buddha: If I was ever reincarnated
I would want a thousand arms with a thousand swords.

It was not until 1954 that the French were defeated by the guerrilla fighters—known as the Viet Minh—in the historic battle at Dien Bien Phu. The peace agreement between the two sides divided Vietnam into North and South. Elections were supposed to unify the country in 1956, but they never happened. Vietnam was soon pushed into another war for independence, this time against the United States. Not surprisingly, women again took up arms, fighting valiantly alongside the men. Scores of women—peasants and intellectuals alike—joined the so-called "long-haired" army. They faced separation from their families, brutal torture, and terrible hardships. Their lives and sacrifices are memorialized in the Women's Museum in Ho Chi Minh City.

⊳ **Bui Thi Xuan** (d. 1771)

Vietnamese heroine. *Executed around 1771; married Tran Quang Dieu, a Tay Son general; children: a daughter.*

Bui Thi Xuan, a famous general in Vietnamese history, was captured for leading 5,000 rebels in a peasant insurgence, known as the Tay Son Rebellion. Following her execution, the new emperor had her heart, arms, liver, and lungs fed to his troops. He believed that by ingesting small segments of this fearless woman his armies would gain courage. A street in Hanoi bears the name Bui Thi Xuan.

The dauntless spirit of Ba Trieu and other brave Vietnamese women who gave themselves for their country are kept alive today. Their temples are lovingly cared for, fragrant with daily freshenings of incense and symbols of respect. Schools and streets throughout Vietnam bear their names. Their heroics are reenacted in plays, poems, songs, and traditional operas. Their spirit lives.

SOURCES:

Hodgkin, Thomas. *The Revolutionary Path*. London: Macmillan, 1981.

Karnow, Stanley. *Vietnam: A History*. NY: Viking, 1983.

Lamb, Helen. *Vietnam's Will to Live*. NY: Monthly Review Press, 1972.

Le, Thi Nham Tuyet, and Thi Tu Mai. *Women in Viet Nam*. Ha Noi: Foreign Languages Publishing House, 1978.

Lich Su Viet Nam. Ha Noi: Nha Xuat Ban Khoa Hoc, 1971.

Mus, Paul and John T. McAlister. *The Vietnamese and Their Revolution*. NY: Harper Torchbooks, 1970.

Tran, Trong Kim. *Lich Su Viet Nam, Tap 1*. Saigon.

Doan Thi Nam-Hau, freelance writer;
and **Willa Seidenberg**, co-author of
A Matter of Conscience: GI Resistance During the Viet Nam War

Baard, Francina (1920—)

South African activist. *Name variations: Mrs. Frances Baard. Born in Port Elizabeth, South Africa, in 1920; married (husband died in 1953); children.*

A left-wing member and one-time leader of the African National Congress (ANC), Francina Baard was also a leading member of the Food and Canning Workers' Union and the South African Congress of Trade Unions (SACTU) Local and Management Committees. Baard, a former domestic servant and teacher, had joined the ANC in 1948 and was involved in organizing the ANC's Women's League. By 1952, she was secretary of the Women's League in Port Elizabeth.

In 1956, Baard was among the ANC's 156 members and allies—including Nelson Mandela, Walter Sisulu, ***Lilian Ngoyi, Florence Matomela, *Ida Mntwana, Bertha Mkize, *Annie Silinga, Gert Sibande**, and ***Ruth First**—caught up in a government sweep backed by Afrikaner Nationalists. Accused of being members of a conspiracy inspired by international communism to overthrow the South African state by violence, they faced a preliminary Treason Trial that started on December 19, 1956, and dragged on until September 11, 1957. The Treason Trial then opened in Pretoria on August 1, 1958, with 91 accused. By April of that year, of the 156 arrested, only 30 remained on trial until March 29, 1961. Eventually release was won for all, but only temporarily. In 1963, Baard was again charged under the Suppression of Communism Act (which had made the Communist Party illegal) and held in jail in solitary confinement for one year before her trial; after which, she was imprisoned for five more years. Released in 1969, she was "endorsed out" to Mabopane. A South African government euphemism for driving Africans out of urban areas to reserves, "endorsed out" also meant splitting up families. Baard's children, who had remained behind in Port Elizabeth, were soon evicted from the city.

Baarova, Lida (1914—)

German actress. *Born in Prague, Czechoslovakia, on September 7, 1914 (one source cites May 12, 1910); lived in Salzburg, Austria; daughter of a civil servant; simultaneously attended secondary school and the dramatic arts school of the State Conservatory of Prague; married Gustav Fröhlich (a celebrated actor and star of* Metropolis, *who had been married earlier to* ***Gitta Alpar**); married Jan Kopecky (a theatrical agent), 1947 (divorced 1956).*

Filmography: Kariéra Pavla Camrdy *(The Career of Pavla Camrdy, Czech, 1931);* Madla z sihelny *(Madla of the Brickyard, Czech, 1932);* Okénko *(Scatterbrain, Czech, 1933);* Jeji Lekai *(Her Doctor, Czech, 1933);* Barbarole *(German, 1935);* Ein Teufelskerl *(A Devilish Fellow, German, 1935);* Einer zuviel an Bord *(One Too Many on Board, German, 1935);* Die Stunde der Versuchung *(The Hour of Temptation, German, 1936);* Verräter *(Traitor, German, 1936);* Unter Ausschluss der Öffentlichkeit *(Public Excluded, German, 1937);* Patrioten *(Patriots, German, 1937);* Panenstvi *(Virginity, Czech, 1937);* Der Spieler *(The Gambler, German, 1937);* Divka v Modrem *(The Girl in Blue, German, 1938);* Moskovana milenka *(The Masked Mistress, German, 1938);* Ohnivé léto *(Exciting Summer, German, 1939);* La Fornarina *(The Baker Maid, Italy, 1942);* Il cappello del prete *(The Priest's Hat, Italy, 1942);* Ti conosco, mascherina! *(You Can't Fool Me!, Italy, 1942);* L'ippocampo *(Hippocampus, with Vittorio De Sica and* **Maria Mercader**, *Italy, 1943);* La bisarca *(The Great-grandmother, Italy);* Gli amanti di Ravello *(The Lovers of Ravello, Italy);* Casa sul lago *(A House by the Lake, Italy);* Carne inquieta *(Restless Flesh, Italy); Frederico Fellini's* I vitelloni *(The Young and the Passionate, Italy, 1953).*

Following a stint at the National Theater in Prague, Lida Baarova moved on to the world of film, first in Prague, then in Berlin. She soon found stardom in Germany with *Barbarole, Ein*

Lida Baarova

Teufelskerl, Einer zuviel an Bord, and *Die Stunde der Versuchung*. In two of these, Baarova co-starred with her husband Gustav Fröhlich, who would cause an early end to her German career. When he learned that Joseph Goebbels, the Nazi minister of propaganda, had an interest in his wife, Fröhlich reputedly slapped Goebbels' face, a move that cost Fröhlich temporary internment in a concentration camp. With the help of compatriots, Fröhlich had his revenge. In 1938, the New York *Daily News* reported that Goebbels was "beaten almost to death," when he was "surprised in the flat of a glamorous film star by a group of her husband's friends." To avoid scandal, Hitler stepped in, and Baarova was banished from German films and sent back to Prague. In 1942, she made four films in Italy before Mussolini fell from power.

Accused of collaboration with the Axis in 1945, Baarova was interned in the Pankrac Prison in Prague until December 1946. Upon release, she married a theatrical agent and moved to Argentina, then Spain. She would make a few more films in Italy, including Frederico Fellini's *I vitelloni* in which she played Giulia, a role that would earn her a Silver Ribbon at the 1953 Venice Film Festival. Following a divorce in 1956, she moved to Salzburg, Austria, where she remained and successfully returned to the stage. In 1983, Baarova's autobiography *Escapes* was published in Toronto, Canada, where she had briefly lived.

SOURCES:

Romani, Cinzia. *Tainted Goddesses: Female Film Stars of the 3rd Reich.* NY: Sarpedon, 1992.

Babashoff, Shirley (1957—)

American swimmer who set world freestyle records for the 200 and 400 meters. *Pronunciation: BA-buh-shoff. Born Shirley Frances Babashoff in Whittier, California, on January 31, 1957; daughter of Vera (Slevkoff) and Jack Babashoff.*

Won Olympic silver medals in the 200-meter and 100-meter freestyle and the gold medal in the 4x100-meter freestyle relay in Munich, 1972; won silver medals in the 200-meter, 400-meter, and 800-meter freestyle, and 4x100-meter relay, and the gold medal in the 4x100-meter relay in Montreal, 1976.

In the 1972 Munich Olympics, 19 participants came from towns in Southern California, including Mission Viejo, a planned community

Shirley Babashoff

intent on providing children with athletic opportunities. One of those participants was Shirley Babashoff. After beginning competitive swimming at age nine, Shirley Babashoff swam at the Mission Viejo Swimming Complex under Coach Mark Schubert. At 13, she attained national championship status.

In 1974, Babashoff set world freestyle records: 2:2.94 in the 200 meters and 4:15.77 in the 400 meters. For three successive years, from 1973 to 1975, she won the 200-meter freestyle Amateur Athletic Union (AAU) outdoor championship. In 1975, she defeated ***Kornelia Ender** of East Germany, the world recordholder, in the 200-meter freestyle. Later that year, Babashoff won the 400-meter freestyle in 4:14.76—another world record.

In the 1972 Munich Olympics, Babashoff earned a gold medal in the 4x100 freestyle relay and a silver in both the 100- and 200-meter freestyle events. (***Sandra Neilson** of the U.S. placed first in the 100, while ***Shane Gould** of Australia took gold in the 200.) In Montreal in 1976, Babashoff again earned a gold medal in the 4x100 freestyle relay, silver medals in the 200-, 400-, and 800-meter freestyle events, and a silver in the 400-meter relay. (Gold medals were won by East Germany's Kornelia Ender in the 200, and **Petra Thuemer** in the 400 and 800.) In 1987, Babashoff was named to the U.S. Olympic Hall of Fame.

Karin L. Haag, Athens, Georgia

Babcock, Maud May (1867–1954)

First woman professor at the University of Utah, whose blend of classes in oratory, speech, and physical education became the basis for the earliest university theater in the U.S. *Born Maud May Babcock in East Worcester, Otsego County, New York, on May 2, 1867; died on December 31, 1954, in Salt Lake City, Utah; daughter of William Wayne Babcock (a doctor) and* ***Sarah Jane (Butler) Babcock****; graduated from high school in Binghamton, New York; granted B.A., Welles College, 1884; B.E. in elocution, Philadelphia National School of Oratory, 1886; attended Harvard University, 1890–92; granted diploma, American Academy of Dramatic Art, 1890; pupil of Albert Ayres, 1891; studied in London and Paris one year, and University of Chicago, 1901; never married; no children.*

Taught in the public schools, New York City (1888–89); was visiting professor of oratory and speech, Rutgers College; taught at School of Physical Education of Harvard University (1890–92); accepted position of professor of oratory, speech, and physical education at the University of Utah in Salt Lake City, Utah Territory (1892); with brother, Dr. William Wayne Babcock, joined in providing $2,500 for equipment for first women's gymnasium in Utah (1893); directed first public performance (1893); produced Eleusthenia *(1895); guest director for the Washington Square and Provincetown Players (1916); conducted first university Little Theatre west of the Mississippi (1917); made world tour (1928–29); manager of Utah Theatre (now Playhouse) and other theatrical companies performing in the intermountain region; member of executive council of National Association of Teachers of Speech; instigated Theta Alpha Phi dramatic fraternity at the University of Utah and was national president for two years; served on board of trustees of State School for Deaf and Blind (1897–1917), and was board president for 12 years, the first woman to preside over the trustees of a state institution.*

Selected writings: The Handbook for Teachers of Interpretation, Interpretative Selection for High Schools, Interpretative Selection for College, *and* Interpretation of the Printed Page *(all text books); contributed to* Quarterly Journal for Speech Education.

A fetching photograph made in 1892 suggests something of the nature of the independent-minded woman known to decades of students at the University of Utah as "Miss B." A slender young woman with round, prominent eyes in an oval face stands staring into the camera, while one shapely leg points to the side in a ballet-second position. Above her black stockings, navy blue bloomers end just below the knee, and a long-sleeved navy blouse is filled in at the neck, sailor-suit style, by a striped dickey, while a sash wrapped around her slim waist adds a touch of flair. This innovative "bloomer-suit," introduced at the University of Utah in the year of May Babcock's arrival was for women to wear while playing basketball, a sport the new teacher introduced to her female students shortly after its invention back in Springfield, Massachusetts. Before this outfit, revealing hitherto "undisclosed knee and well-turned ankle," could be introduced, the innovative teacher had to ride out the protests of some students' mothers, but Babcock's activity costume prevailed. With typical aplomb, she then went on to other things. While women's basketball competition remained under her direction until 1900 (a full decade before the men's first games), Miss B's main interest was in the theater.

Born on May 2, 1867, in East Worcester, Otsego County, New York, Maud May Babcock was the daughter of Sara Jane Butler and physician William Wayne Babcock. The family moved to Binghamton when Babcock was ten; there, she completed high school. In later years, she gave credit to an elderly, doting neighbor who played "audience" to her earliest impulses, heartily applauding her dramatic portrayals. At age 15, she gave a stirring Daniel Webster oration at school that won her encouragement to become an elocutionist.

After graduation from Welles College in 1884, Babcock studied elocution widely, first at the Philadelphia National School of Oratory, then the American Academy of Dramatic Art, where she received a diploma in 1890; she also studied in London and Paris for a year and spent the summers from 1890–92 at Harvard University. Apparently a sickly child, she grew stronger from doing light calisthenics and performing the Delsarte system of exercise required in her oratory classes. Her most valued training came under the Shakespearean dramatist Alfred Ayers, whom she often quoted as saying, "If you can read Shakespeare properly, you can read anything."

In 1888–89, Babcock taught in the public schools of New York City and was a visiting professor of oratory at Rutgers University. In the summer of 1892, while directing a summer school of physical education for women at Harvard University, she impressed a young woman student, **Susa Young Gates**, a daughter of Brigham Young, who encouraged her to consider teaching at the University of Utah. Accustomed only to established communities but curious about life in a frontier area that was not yet a state, the adventurous Babcock decided to move west, at age 25, with her handmade shoes, gloves, and Eastern ladies' regalia.

Enchanted by the welcome she received, Babcock quickly made Salt Lake City her home. Nestled downtown, the University of Utah would relocate at the turn of the century to the foothills of the eastern Rocky Mountains bordering Salt Lake; meanwhile, she became its first woman educator appointed in the new but promising field of physical education and elocution; 12 years later, she would be made a full professor.

Blending physical culture and oratory, Babcock presented her first public production on May 23, 1893. It was described as "largely a demonstration of drills with dumbbells, wands, Indian clubs, and dances" but possessing dramatic elements. That same year, she joined with her brother Dr. William Wayne Babcock, a specialist in spinal surgery and author of specialty medical texts, in providing the school with what was then the lordly sum of $2,500 for equipment to set up the first women's gymnasium in Utah in the remodeled Social Hall. This became the basis for a physical education summer program featuring other outstanding visiting professionals in the field, and led to a blending of physical culture and oratory that was to become the first university theater in the United States.

On June 6, 1895, Babcock produced and directed *The Eleusthenia*, based on the Greek harvest festival and the myths of Demeter and Persephone, as the university's first dramatic production, at the Salt Lake Theater. Acclaimed as "sensational" by the local press, it received praise from the university's new president, James E. Talmadge, who wrote, "I was so enchanted with *Eleusthenia* that the critical faculty was entirely subdued in me." A new play followed each year, and, after the school's relocation in 1900, a dramatic club was organized, and both a freshman play and a varsity play were performed annually. Miss B took the best productions to smaller communities in Utah and Idaho, bringing Shaw, Ibsen, Barrie, and Shakespeare to the outlying regions.

In 1920, the Utah Alpha chapter of the national dramatic fraternity Theta Alpha Phi was installed at the university, opening a new epoch of college theater, in which alumni members added maturity to the productions and became devoted troupers, building scenery and contributing costumes and props. By the early 1930s, the construction of Kingsbury Hall included a theater, giving the campus a permanent performance setting. Under Babcock's direction, one to three full-length plays were put on each year over the 46 years of her professorial career.

When he entered the university, Herbert Maw, the future governor of Utah, approached Babcock, describing his insecurity and need to improve his confidence in order to succeed in his chosen field: law. Babcock encouraged him to enroll in her drama class and try out for a play. As he sat through an evening listening to his betters in the tryouts, the shy student hoped to land a part of perhaps 10–12 words, but at the next meeting Babcock announced that Maw was to take the role of king. Thus followed "six or eight weeks of torture" in which he learned to "stress lines," said Maw. "The worst of it was my walking. . . . [S]he had to teach me to walk with dignity—the dignity of a king." Instructing him to walk with his head held high and shoulders straight, Miss B would remind him, "You *are* the king. . . . Don't walk like a nincompoop." By opening night, Maw could walk on stage with the queen at his side, feeling that he was indeed the king. Then, for her production of *Twelfth Night*, the wily professor cast him as the drunken fool, explaining, "You need ease while performing." When he was cast as Pete Swallow, a tombstone salesman, she said it was because "he needed a little more freedom to weave things into his acting on the impulse of the moment."

Babcock was also a champion of women's rights, insisting that "our women must and are freeing themselves from the false ideals of our grandmothers that little girls should 'sit still,' 'be quiet,' 'fold their hands,' and grow up 'little ladies.'" She blessed "gumption" feeling the soul was devoid without it. She insisted on literary excellence in oratory and interpretation of the printed page, expecting any reading to be done "with brains—one would *understand* the thought, *hold* the thought, and *give* the thought, and then could perform skillfully." She claimed "literature was written to be spoken. . . . A poem is not truly a poem until it is voiced by an accomplished artist."

In 1916, Babcock was guest director for the Washington Square and Provincetown Players; the following year, she conducted the first University Little Theatre west of the Mississippi; meanwhile, she was largely responsible for the University of Utah being among the first colleges to offer undergraduate classes in dramatic production. She traveled widely in the U.S., doing dramatic readings from her vast repertory of literary and theatrical works that drew large audiences. In 1928–29, she traveled around the world, and she managed the Utah Theatre (now the Playhouse), a professional company, for one year, as well as other theater companies that performed in the Intermountain Region.

In her home, Babcock was a gracious hostess, surrounded by objects collected in her travels. She was especially fond of treasures from the ancient Chinese culture, and she set her table with a delicate hand-embroidered linen cloth that was complemented by pieces of ancient carved ivory and jade from her Oriental collection, with hand-painted dishes, and imported gold-rimmed crystal that had been her mother's. Large bowls of steaming rice would be topped with her special recipe of chicken chow mein, while her Chinese Chow dog Chi Mu would rest at her feet and Loreeta, a mimicking parrot from South America, added bits of jargon. Hand-carved chests of Chinese camphorwood, imported Chinese nesting tables, objects of cloisonne and carved ivory memorabilia stood in rooms lined with shelves of her professorial books. On her desk, she kept a long letter from Madame Chiang-Kai-Shek (***Song Meiling**) thanking Babcock for her interest in the Chinese people and contributions for the aid of Chinese victims of the Sino-Japanese war. She answered her phone with a perfunctory "yes," voicing a slight upswing, and penned her notes and comments to students and friends in purple ink; she was an institution.

In June 1939, Miss B became Doctor Babcock, awarded an honorary doctorate at commencement. In November 1950, she gave what proved to be her final address, in response to a special request from the National Speech Association, which she had served as president in 1936. She had been one of a very small group who brought about the recognition of speech as an academic discipline on the college level, making her program at Utah one of the first to achieve departmental status anywhere in the country. She has been credited with starting the now widespread practice among American colleges and universities of presenting dramatic productions with regularity. The Pioneer Memorial Theatre has now been named the Babcock Theatre. In her last years, Maud May Babcock suffered from Alzheimer's disease; she died December 31, 1954, at age 87, in her beloved Salt Lake City.

SOURCES:

Babcock, Maud May, Litt. D. *Interpretation of the Printed Page: Mental Technique of Speech.* NY: Prentice-Hall, 1940.

Chamberlain, Ralph Vary. *The University of Utah: A History of Its First Hundred Years, 1850–1950.* Salt Lake City, 1960.

Gates, Susa Young. "Maud May Babcock, B.E.," in *The Young Woman's Journal, The Organ of the Y.L.M.I. Associations.* June 1894.

Glade, Earl J. *Utah's Distinguished Personalities.* Vol I. Compiled and edited by Ralph B. Simmons. Salt Lake City, UT: Personality Publishing, 1933.

"Maud May Babcock celebration," presented by the Maud May Babcock Reading Arts Society in cooperation with the University of Utah Theater Department, October 8, 1981.

Price, Raye. "Utah's Leading Ladies of the Arts," in *Utah Historical Quarterly.* Volume 38, no. 1. Winter 1970, pp. 77–82.

Harriet Horne Arrington, women's biographer, Salt Lake City, Utah

Babilenska, Gertruda (1902–1997)

Polish-born Gentile who, during World War II, raised a Jewish boy as her own after his mother died. *Name variations: Babilinska. Born near Danzig (Gdansk), Poland, in 1902; died in 1997; one of a family of eight children; children: adopted son Michael Stolowitzky.*

Though pre-1939 Poland was a land permeated with often virulent anti-Semitic politics and prejudices, many Polish men and women risked their lives during World War II to save endangered Jews. Born in 1902 near Danzig (Gdansk) into a family of eight children, Gertruda Babilenska would become such a woman. Her father worked in the local post office, and the family was religious in a practical fashion. Raised by a mother who was concerned about others, Gertruda Babilenska was armed with a simple and strong moral education. An untutored Polish domestic, she worked for 15 years for a wealthy Jewish family named Stolowitzky, raising their two children, a daughter and a son named Michael. After the father was sent to Auschwitz and the daughter died, Babilenska moved with the mother and son to Warsaw, but conditions were poor there and they left for Vilna-Vilnius, Lithuania.

When circumstances in Vilna proved no better, Mrs. Stolowitzky made Babilenska promise to take care of her son if anything happened to her. Despite the dangers of life in Vilna—Babilenska was hit by an anti-Semite and the local Nazis gave poisoned candy to children—she stayed with the family. After Mrs. Stolowitzky died of illness, the Catholic, single, 40-year-old Babilenska decided to raise the boy as her own. When Michael took ill and she had to risk taking him to a German doctor, she told the physician that he was her brother. After Michael recovered, she inquired as to the doctor's fee, but he refused to allow her to pay, saying, "No, you have made me feel like a man"; it was clear that he was aware of the boy's identity.

After the war, Babilenska took Michael to Palestine, soon to be Israel, and they arrived under extremely difficult conditions on the legendary ship *Exodus*. The boy's relatives in Israel were hostile to her and threatened to withhold funds for his schooling if she remained in Israel. The issue was resolved by Michael, who demanded he remain with Babilenska.

In Israel, Babilenska lived in a tiny room with no water and no toilet. She labored as a maid to pay for the room and to purchase items for Michael, who grew up to work as a travel agent, first in Israel and then in the United States. After her son's departure, she remained in Israel. Visited often by her son, she was immensely proud that he became "such a good Jew." In her final years, Michael took care of her until she died at age 95.

SOURCES:

Block, Gay, and Malka Drucker. *Rescuers: Portraits of Moral Courage in the Holocaust*. New York and London: Holmes & Meier Publishers, 1992.

RELATED MEDIA:

Her story, entitled "Mamusha," appeared on "Rescuers: Stories of Courage," on "Showtime" cable network, starring **Elizabeth Perkins** and Fraser McGregor, October 5, 1997.

John Haag, Associate Professor,
University of Georgia, Athens, Georgia

Baby Peggy (b. 1917).

See Montgomery, Peggy.

Baccelli, Giovanna (c. 1753–1801)

Italian ballerina. *Born Giovanna Zanerini in Venice, around 1753; died in London, England, in 1801.*

Giovanna Baccelli was born in Venice around 1753. On November 19, 1774, age 21, she made her London debut at the King's Theatre, Haymarket, in the role of Rose in Jean Lany's *Le Ballet des Fleurs*. Remaining in London, Baccelli was the mistress of the third duke of Dorset for 15 years, then of the earl of Pembroke. During her career, she danced with Gaetan Vestris and Charles Le Picq. Her portrait was rendered by Sir Joshua Reynolds and Thomas Gainsborough.

Bacciocchi, Elisa (1777–1820).

See Bonaparte, Elisa.

Bacewicz, Grazyna (1909–1969)

Polish violinist and composer, widely considered the most gifted composer of her time. *Born in Lodz, Poland, on February 5, 1909; died in Warsaw on January 17, 1969; one of four children; studied at the Lodz Conservatory, Warsaw Conservatory, and Warsaw University as well as with Nadia Boulanger, the famed French teacher; married Andrzej Biernacki (a physician, professor of medicine, and secretary of the Polish Academy of Science); children: one daughter, Alina.*

Began performing at age seven; won first prize at the Young Composers' Competition for a wind quintet in Paris (1933); won second prize for her Trio *at the Publishing Polish Music Society in Warsaw (1936); recorded* Overture *(1946); premiered her* Concerto for String Orchestra *in U.S. (1952); published* Music for Strings, Trumpets, and Percussion *(1958) which was played throughout the world; received the gold medal from the Belgian government at the International Composers' Competition (1965). Two streets have been named after her in Poland, one in Warsaw and one in Gdansk.*

In an age when women's works were rarely performed and even more rarely recorded, almost 20 recordings of Grazyna Bacewicz's compositions were made. Her work marked a new trend in the field for women.

When her talent was recognized at a young age, Bacewicz studied music with the famous ***Nadia Boulanger**, who accepted only the most gifted students. In 1933, Bacewicz won the first prize at the Young Composers' Competition in Paris. A gifted violinist as well as a composer, she toured Europe widely as a concert artist. Many of her compositions are for string ensembles, and her violinistic expertise enabled her to compose seven violin concertos. Surviving World War II, she was also forced to survive artistically under Communist rule in Poland; still, she maintained her integrity and creativity, winning numerous prizes throughout Europe. In Poland, composers depended upon government subsidies in order to survive. Although this imposed some burden, Bacewicz was able to perfect her form. Her *Music for Strings, Trumpets, and Percussion*, published in 1958, was enthusiastically received throughout the world. Performed by the BBC Orchestra in 1961, it was also recorded. Grazyna Bacewicz died unexpectedly in 1969, cutting short her remarkable career as the most celebrated female composer of contemporary Poland. Also a respected author, she published novels and short stories in her last years.

John Haag, Athens, Georgia

Bach, Anna Magdalena

(1701–1760)

German musician and artistic collaborator of husband Johann Sebastian Bach. *Born Anna Magdalena Wilcken (or Wilcke) on September 22, 1701, in Zeitz, Germany; died in poverty in February 1760; daughter of Johann Caspar Wilcken and Margaretha Elisabeth Liebe; became second wife of Johann Sebastian Bach (1685–1750), on December 3, 1721; children: 13, including Johann Christoph Friedrich; Johann Christian (the "London" Bach); and seven who died in infancy.*

The great German composer Johann Sebastian Bach was almost as prolific at fathering children—20 in all—as he was at completing concertos and cantatas. A man of cheerful, even temperament, he was fortunate in both of his marriages. His first wife was his cousin **Maria Barbara Bach**, whom he married on October 17, 1707. Johann Sebastian and Maria Barbara Bach had seven children, four of whom would live to maturity. Of these, Carl Philipp Emanuel and Wilhelm Friedemann became distinguished composers. Maria Barbara Bach died in July 1720, while her husband was away on a tour in Karlsbad. Although he had four young children at home at the time of his wife's death, Bach did not remarry immediately, as was the custom of the day. He waited 18 months before marrying Anna Magdalena Wilcken on December 3, 1721.

Like Bach, Wilcken was descended from a long line of Thuringian musicians. Her father Johann Caspar Wilcken was the court trumpeter at Zeitz and later at Weissenfels. Her mother **Margaretha Elisabeth Liebe** was part of a musically gifted family; Margaretha's mother was the daughter of an organist as well as the sister of an organist who was also a noted trumpeter. Anna Magdalena had an excellent soprano voice; at the time she met Bach, she held a position as a "princely singer" at the small but culturally active court of Anhalt-Zerbst. After their marriage, she retained her singing post, drawing a salary equal to half of her husband's. A week after her own wedding, she was called upon to perform at the festive wedding of Prince Leopold of Anhalt-Zerbst. Her singing was much admired by churchgoers for its sincerity and beauty, and Johann Sebastian praised the "excellent clarity" of his wife's voice.

Although his several posts would keep Bach extremely busy, the couple enjoyed a happy marriage of almost 30 years. With her voice in mind, he wrote a number of church cantatas, and she often sang these parts. Now the stepmother of four children, Anna Magdalena would give birth to 13 more, while remaining musically active. She often assisted her husband with the laborious chores of copying his scores so that the instrumental parts were available in time for Sunday church services, and her musical talent flourished as her husband taught her to play the clavichord and harpsichord.

During the first years of their marriage, Johann Sebastian Bach wrote several notebooks; only the one written for his son Wilhelm Friedemann and the one written in 1722 for Anna Magdalena have survived. The music of this first *Clavierbüchlein* ("Little Clavier Book for Anna Magdalena"), although often technically demanding, is permeated with a sense of great joy. Much of the music in this book was written as technical exercises, or to entertain the Bach family. Some of the pieces may have been composed by Anna Magdalena, and many are certainly the result of their happy collaboration. A second, much larger *Clavierbüchlein* was finished in 1725 and offers glimpses into the private life of the couple. Several poems, probably written by Bach himself, celebrate the pleasures of settled domestic life, including the pleasures of his pipe. Another poem expresses his love for his young wife:

> If thou be near, I go rejoicing
> To peace and rest beyond the skies,
> Nor will I fear what may befall me;
> For I will hear thy sweet voice call me,
> Thy gentle hand will close my eyes.

As was common for the times, of the 13 children borne to Anna Magdalena, seven died in infancy. Their children's genetic predisposition toward musical talent revealed itself in the careers of Johann Christoph Friedrich Bach and Johann Christian Bach (the "London" Bach). When Johann Sebastian Bach died at age 65 on July 28, 1750, he was survived by nine of his children and his beloved wife. Without a will, most of his possessions (including household furniture and 19 musical instruments) were auctioned off for the modest sum of 1,122 thalers and 22 groschen, which had to be divided among the children. Little was left to support the widow. During those years, Anna Magdalena was forced to sell many of his manuscripts for tiny sums. Some were literally used in the shops of Leipzig as wrapping paper; others ended up as wrappings for fruit trees, smeared with tar to ward off insects. Anna Magdalena Bach died in an almshouse in 1760, having lived her final years in abject poverty.

SOURCES:

Chiapusso, Jan. *Bach's World.* Bloomington: Indiana University Press, 1968.

David, Hans T., and Arthur Mendel, eds. *The Bach Reader: A Life of Johann Sebastian Bach in Letters and Documents.* Rev. ed. NY: W.W. Norton, 1966.

Dowley, Tim. *Bach: His Life and Times.* Tunbridge Wells, Kent: Midas Books, 1981.

John Haag, Associate Professor, University of Georgia, Athens, Georgia

Bach, Maria (1896–1978)

Austrian composer, pianist, violinist, and artist. *Born in Vienna, Austria, on March 11, 1896; died in Vienna on February 26, 1978; related to Johann Sebastian Bach; one of four daughters of* ***Lenore von Bach*** *(a well-known soprano and concert singer) and Robert Freiherr von Bach (a violinist and government official); studied with Josef Marx and Ivan Boutnikoff.*

Maria Bach began her musical career at age six when she entered the Grimm Piano School in Baden bei Wien, a suburb of Vienna. She won five of the school's six prizes during her tenure there and gave her first concert at age ten. At first, she studied violin under Arnold Rose but returned to the piano and studied under Paul de Conne. She was 19 when she wrote *Flohtanz*, a piece for piano which attracted the attention of influential critic Julius Korngold. Bach decided to study composition with Josef Marx and instrumentation under the conductor Ivan Boutnikoff. Her *Narrenlied* composed in 1924 established her reputation in Vienna as an up-and-coming composer. In 1962, she won the Premio Internationale para Compositores Buenos Aires prize. An orchestral, chamber, and piano composer, she set the works of Hesse, Rilke, Rimbaud, Nietzsche and others to music.

John Haag, Athens, Georgia

Bachauer, Gina (1913–1976)

Greek pianist who gave hundreds of performances for the Allied troops during World War II. *Born in Athens, Greece, on May 21, 1913; died of a heart attack in Athens on August 22, 1976; daughter of an Austrian father and Italian mother; married second husband Alec Sherman (a conductor).*

Gina Bachauer began serious piano instruction at age five, studying in Athens and then in Paris with Alfred Cortot. When she was 20, her infectious Romanticism earned her the Medal of Honor at the 1933 Vienna international competition. Bachauer's concerto debut took place in Athens in 1935 with the brilliant Dmitri Mitropoulos conducting, and, in 1937, she repeated that triumph in Paris under the baton of Pierre Monteux. During the second World War, she lived in Alexandria, Egypt, and showed her solidarity with the Allied cause by giving hundreds of performances for soldiers throughout the Middle East. Her 1946 London debut was with the conductor Alec Sherman, who became her second husband. Though Bachauer's New York recital debut in October 1950 was poorly attended, the major critics unanimously praised her bravura performance. Projecting a muscular and Romantic pianism, she was linked in the minds of some veteran concert-goers to the blood-and-thunder tradition established generations earlier by ***Teresa Carreño** (1853–1917). Bachauer's profound enthusiasm for the virtuoso warhorse concertos of Liszt, Tchaikovsky, and Rachmaninoff was obvious from the first note of all her performances and recordings. The extraordinary range of her interests is evident in her huge repertoire, which included the major works of Mozart down through the spiky modernists like Igor Stravinsky. Bachauer died suddenly of a heart attack in her native Athens on August 22, 1976. The important Gina Bachauer International Competition, held in Salt Lake City, Utah, is dedicated to her memory. On the fifth anniversary of her death, in 1981, Greece issued a special commemorative postage stamp in her honor.

SOURCES:

"Miss Gina Bachauer," in *The Times* [London]. August 24, 1976, p. 12.

John Haag, Athens, Georgia

Bache, Sarah (1743–1808)

American patriot. *Born on September 11, 1743; died in 1808; only daughter of Benjamin Franklin and Deborah Read Rogers (his common-law wife); married Richard Bache (a Philadelphia merchant); children: eight.*

On September 1, 1730, Benjamin Franklin "took to wife" ➧ **Deborah Read**, whose first husband had deserted her. Not wanting to be saddled with the departed husband's debts, the always frugal Franklin never worked to formalize this common-law union. Especially during the early years of their relationship, Deborah Read proved to be a loving wife and valuable companion. While Franklin ran the newspaper and print shop, his wife handled the business of running the adjacent stationary shop. To this marriage Franklin brought his illegitimate son William (born in 1729 or early 1730 to an unidentified mother), and the couple had two children of their own: Francis Folger (born 1732), who died of smallpox, and Sarah (born 1743).

Sarah, who married Richard Bache and raised a family of eight children, was a source of pride and comfort to her father, especially in his old age. In 1780, during the Revolutionary War, when many soldiers of George Washington's Continental Army were barefoot and half-clad, Sarah Bache led an effort whereby over 300,000 Continental dollars were collected by Philadelphia women for soldiers' relief and allocated for dry goods. Her home was a gathering place for women who sewed while discussing financial strategy; in all, more than 2,000 women were employed by her in sewing uniforms for the army. On many occasions, she also served in the hospitals. The Marquis de Chastellux, then visiting in Philadelphia, recommended her to the ladies of Europe as a model of "domestic virtues and feminine patriotism."

During the last few years of his life, Franklin lived with his daughter and his numerous grandchildren in a large house on Market Street in Philadelphia. There, Sarah was hostess to many prominent government leaders.

Bacheracht, Therese von (1804–1852)

German novelist and travel writer. *Born in 1804; died in 1852; daughter of a diplomat; married a Russian consul; later became lover of the writer Karl Gutzkow.*

Therese von Bacheracht, distinguished for her expert depiction of character, wrote of the upper classes. Contemporaries considered her best novels to be *Falkenberg* (1843), *Lydia* (1844) and *Heinrich Burkart* (1846). At the urging of her lover, writer Karl Gutzkow,

Sarah Bache

➧ **Read, Deborah** (1707–1774)

American colonial. *Name variations: Deborah Read Rogers, Deborah Franklin. Born Deborah Read in 1707; died of a stroke in December 1774; married a man named Rogers; common-law wife of Benjamin Franklin from 1730 to 1774; children: Francis Folger (b. 1732, died of smallpox) and *Sarah Bache (1743–1808).*

Deborah Read was courted and jilted in Philadelphia by a younger Benjamin Franklin before she entered into a common-law marriage with him in 1730, long before he had gained fame. Married previously, and unable to divorce her deserting husband, Read could not wed legally, but when her daughter Sarah Bache was born 13 years later, the baby was deemed legitimate by Philadelphia society.

Ben Franklin's attitudes toward women veered from amicable to patronizing. Before settling down with Read, he had been a bonvivant with two previous children born out of wedlock. One of them, William Franklin (a future governor of New Jersey), became a part of the household, though a coldness separated stepmother and stepchild. Franklin was dispatched to England in 1757 to present a case of the Pennsylvania assembly; he was there five years. On his return, he contemplated settling in England, "provided," he said, "we can persuade the good woman to cross the seas." But Read was fearful of the long voyage and preferred to stay at home. When Franklin again departed for London in 1764, it was with his son William. Deborah Read died of a stroke in December 1774 before her husband's return.

she also published her diaries and letters concerning her travels to Russia and the Far East: *Briefe aus dem Süden* (Letters from the South, 1841) and *Menschen und Gegenden* (People and Places, 1845). She is credited for publishing Wilhelm von Humboldt's *Letters to a Friend* (1847).

Bachmann, Ingeborg (1926–1973)

One of the 20th century's most significant German-language authors. *Pronunciation: ING-a-borg BOCK-mun. Born Ingeborg Bachmann on June 25, 1926, in Klagenfurt in Carinthia, southern Austria; died on October 17, 1973, in Rome from burns suffered in a house fire and complications resulting from a drug withdrawal; daughter of Mathias Bachmann (a teacher) and Olga (Haas) Bachmann; studied philosophy and law in Innsbruck and Graz, 1945–46; continued her studies in Vienna, minoring in Germanistik and psychology, 1946–50; wrote her Ph.D. dissertation on the reception of Martin Heidegger's existential philosophy and was awarded her doctorate, 1950; never married but had long-term relationships with the composer Hans Werner Henze and the writer Max Frisch; no children.*

Born the eldest of three children; left Klagenfurt to study in Innsbruck and Graz; published her first story at 20 and her first poems three years later; traveled to Paris and London (1950); after returning to Vienna, worked as a script writer and editor for the radio station Red-White-Red (until 1953); invited to a meeting of Gruppe 47 (1952) and later received the Gruppe 47 prize; supported herself as a writer (1953–73); moved to Italy; invited to Harvard (1955); published several volumes of poetry and a number of radio plays; worked as a dramaturg for Bavarian Television (1957–58); lived on and off in Rome and Zurich; wrote several opera libretti; awarded numerous prizes; made guest professor of poetics at the University of Frankfurt (1959); invited to spend a year in Berlin (1963); traveled to Prague, Egypt, and the Sudan; moved to Rome permanently (1965); published her novel Malina *(1971) and a volume of stories* Simultan *(1972).*

Awards: The Gruppe 47 prize for her volume of poetry Die gestundete Zeit *(Borrowed Time; 1953); made a member of the German Academy of Language and Literature (1957); among other awards, given the radio-play prize of the War Blind for "Der gute Gott von Manhattan" (The Good God of Manhattan, 1962), the Georg Büchner prize (1964) and the Austrian State Prize (1968).*

Selected publications: "Die Fähre" (The Ferry, story, 1946); "Ein Geschäft mit Träumen" (A Business with Dreams, radio play, 1952); Die gestundete Zeit *(Borrowed Time, volume of poetry, 1953); "Die Zikaden" (The Cicadas, radio play, 1955);* Anrufung des Grossen Bären *(Invocation of the Great Bear, volume of poetry, 1957); "Der gute Gott von Manhattan" (The Good God of Manhattan, radio play, 1958);* Der Prinz von Homburg *(The Prince of Homburg, opera libretto, 1960);* Das dreissigste Jahr *(The Thirtieth Year, volume of stories, 1961); "Der junge Lord" (The Young Lord, opera libretto, 1965); "Der Fall Franza" (The Case of Franza, novel fragment, 1966);* Malina *(Malina, novel, 1971);* Simultan *(Three Paths to the Lake, volume of stories, 1972).*

Ingeborg Bachmann's life was punctuated by political upheaval and violence. Though she was born in 1926 during the brief period of stability between the first and second World Wars, the relative harmony of her Carinthian childhood would be interrupted by an event that was to have far-reaching repercussions. In March of 1938, with the war machine in full-swing, Hitler invaded Austria. The invasion of Czechoslovakia would follow, and, by the next year, Britain and France would declare war on Germany. Although the annexation of Bachmann's country was accomplished with the support of many of her fellow Austrians, and German troops were met by cheering crowds, for Ingeborg Bachmann the influx of National Socialism signified a moment of unmitigated terror. She later reported: "There was a particular event that shattered my childhood. It was the moment Hitler's troops marched into Klagenfurt. It was something so horrible, that my memory begins with this day. . . . You could sense the hideous brutality, this bellowing, singing and marching—it was the first time I felt afraid of death."

The confluence of private terror and political turmoil would generate her most prevalent theme, human beings engaged in a "constant state of war." Her work would also explore the basis of fascism, not as a political phenomenon, but as a manifestation of everyday life. From childhood on, for Bachmann, war—whether begun by the Nazis, or perpetuated between the sexes—was "no longer declared, only continued."

With Austria now under the sway of National Socialism, the 11-year-old Bachmann left her coeducational high school in 1938 to attend an all-girls school from which she graduated in 1944. Although she hated practicing, she loved music, and from an early age wrote and played music with a friend. As **Karen Achberger** relates, the young Bachmann wrote her first poems because she needed texts for her songs; indeed, from this point on, all of Bachmann's material exhibits an intensely musical quality.

After the war, Bachmann went to university in Innsbruck (1945) and Graz (summer of 1946), studying law, philosophy, psychology and Germanistik. In 1949, she completed her doctorate on the reception of Martin Heidegger's existentialist philosophy at the University of Vienna, but, because of the conservative nature of academia at the time, she ruled out the possibility of a university career. As she later pointed out, jobs were not easy to come by in postwar Vienna. After she graduated, she was glad simply to have a job working in an office in order to support herself while writing. In 1950, Bachmann took her first trips abroad—first to Paris, where she met the poet Paul Celan, and then to London for a reading of her work and a meeting with the writer Elias Canetti, who was highly impressed by the originality of her work. As her predilection for radio plays might suggest, the early '50s saw her working as a scriptwriter and editor for the Austrian radio station Rot-Weiss-Rot (Red-White-Red). Her writing career received a further boost when, in 1952, she met Hans Werner Richter, the doyen of Gruppe 47, a preeminent group of postwar German writers, in Vienna. This meeting prompted an invitation the following year to appear before the Gruppe 47 in Niendorf, where she gave a reading during which she was said to have spoken "very quietly, almost whispered." But the quietude of this appearance met with an inverse degree of public approbation: she won the Gruppe 47 prize and found herself launched on her career as a freelance writer. Almost immediately, however, she abandoned the German-speaking world, and, although she returned periodically to visit, she departed for Italy to begin her life as an itinerant.

According to Mark Anderson in his afterward to *Malina*, it was the attention she received as a young poet that impelled her into exile. Her inability to deal with the fame generated by her appearance before Gruppe 47—coupled with the acclaim she received for her poetry collection *Die gestundete Zeit* (Borrowed Time, 1953), her winning of the Gruppe 47 prize, and the cover story that appeared about her in the German news weekly *Der Spiegel*—set her adrift and created the defining feature of her life and work, her ephemerality.

Aside from public acclaim, Bachmann's appearance before Gruppe 47 had personal ramifications, occasioning an invitation to Italy and the beginning of a relationship with the composer Hans Werner Henze. She wrote opera libretti for

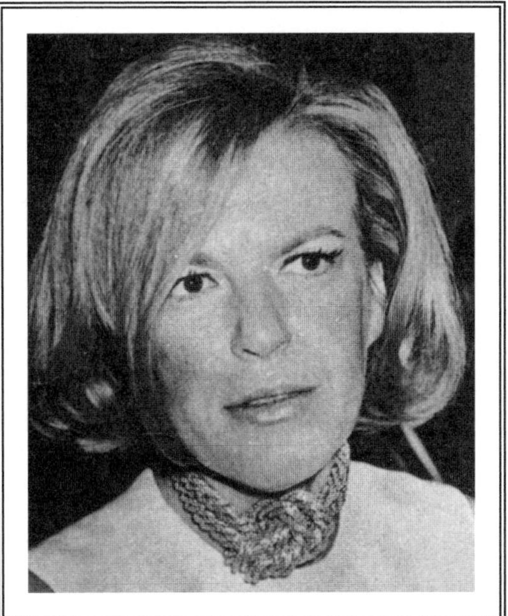

Ingeborg Bachmann

him, including *Der Prinz von Homburg* (The Prince of Homburg, 1958) and *Der junge Lord* (The Young Lord, 1964), and he wrote the music to her radio play "Die Zikaden" (The Cicadas, 1955), among other works. Ultimately, however, earning a living in Italy as a writer proved difficult for Bachmann. Her infatuation with the country, which she regarded as a kind of spiritual home, was thus interrupted by a stint in Munich working for Bavarian Television during the late 1950s. This sojourn in Germany was accompanied by professional accolades. In 1957, she was made a member of the Deutsche Akademie für Sprache und Dichtung (The German Academy for Language and Poesy); in 1959, she received the Radio Prize of the War Blind, and thereafter was invited to lecture on poetry at Frankfurt University. In 1964, she received the prestigious Georg Büchner Prize and a grant from the Ford Foundation at the Akademie der Künste (Academy of Arts) in Berlin.

In Munich, she also met the Swiss writer Max Frisch with whom she quickly became romantically involved. They lived together intermittently in Zurich and Rome, and in 1959 he proposed to her. Wanting to maintain her independence, she declined, finally ending the relationship in 1963. Max Frisch documented the vagaries of their relationship in his book *Montauk*.

Vienna, Naples, Rome, Munich, Zurich, Berlin—whatever the cause of her mobility, Bachmann never stayed anywhere for very long. She incorporated this trait into her writing, illustrating women's sense of displacement in the world, their disenfranchisement, alienation, and ultimate erasure. Her postwar poem "Exil" (Exile) remarks,"*Ein Toter bin ich der wandelt/ gemeldet nirgends mehr/ unbekannt im Reich des Präfekten/ überzählig in den goldenen Städten und im grünenden Land// abgetan lange schon/ und mit nichts bedacht*" (I am a dead man who wanders/ registered nowhere/ unknown in the prefect's realm/ unaccounted for in the golden cities/ and the greening land// long since given up/ and provided with nothing).

Linked to the theme of itinerancy in her writing is the issue of borders, dividing lines and the spaces between people. Unlike many of her contemporary male authors who provide a monolithic account of human existence, she stresses differentiation. For Bachmann, people are not all the same; though they might be subjected to similar determinants, men and women experience things differently. But disharmony between the sexes is not just a product of men and women's divergent experiences and competing interests. Disharmony, Bachmann tells us, arises because difference is not recognized. In her works, the male characters disallow women to express their own individuality and, in so doing, neglect the needs and identities of their female companions. They fail to recognize that in bowing to a patriarchal order the women must truncate their own existence. In the nameless main character of *Malina*, for example, this leads to death.

Although primarily concerned with manifestations of loss and alienation, Bachmann's work also represents the attempt to overcome loss and, as such, has a certain utopian quality. In contradistinction to their author, whose youthfulness reportedly conveyed a sense of fragility and vulnerability, Bachmann's characters embody a degree of indefatigability. They seem to know that though their situation is ultimately hopeless, and the ending dismal, there are, nonetheless, moments of redemption, and they persevere with their endeavors as if there were the possibility that things might end differently. In this world of short-term consolation in the face of long-term uncertainty, pleasure is gleaned from the prosaic, a doorbell announcing the arrival of a lover, for example, as in "A Type of Loss" in *Songs in Flight*.

Bachmann draws on images from her rural childhood, and in descriptions of nature and domestic life. We find dirty teacups, folded newspapers, stale cigarette smoke, stones and autumn leaves as she juxtaposes the reality of the everyday against larger aesthetic and moral considerations: the issue of female subjectivity, the imperative to create a new language and to preserve the social function of art.

For Bachmann, the main obstacle to communion between human beings is language. Following Ludwig Wittgenstein's assertion about the limitations of language in the *Tractatus* ("The limitations of my language imply the limitations of my world"), Bachmann calls for a new language, and in particular a language that can express the ineffable. She gives voice to this theme in the main character of "Everything," a man who tries to raise a child capable of articulating a new reality:

> And I suddenly knew it is all a question of language and not merely of this language of ours that was created with others in Babel to confuse the world. For underneath it there smolders another language that extends to gestures and looks, the unwinding of thoughts and the passage of feelings, and in it is all our misfortune. It was all a question of whether I could preserve the child from our language until he had established a new one and could introduce a new era. . . . Teach him the language of stones! . . . Teach him the language of leaves!

After achieving acclaim as one of the most important poets of the postwar period (accolades included being invited to Harvard in the summer of 1955 and winning numerous prizes), Bachmann published a second and final volume of poetry in 1956, *Anrufung des Grossen Bären* (Invocation of the Great Bear), and then turned to prose. In 1961, five years after the so-called "turning point" in Bachmann's literary oeuvre, she published the volume of stories entitled *Das dreissigste Jahr* (The Thirtieth Year). Although initially not well-received, her subsequent novel *Malina* (1971), part of the larger uncompleted work called *Todesarten* (Ways of Dying), established her, in Mark Anderson's words, as "one of the truly original, influential prose writers of contemporary German literature."

In 1965, Bachmann returned to Rome. Although relieved to be back in Italy, she suffered profoundly from depression and an increasing dependence on prescription drugs. As Beicken points out, the political engagement of her Berlin years was superseded by a sense of personal isolation and resignation. Despite this, she received for the first time acclaim in her homeland, receiving the Austrian State Prize in 1968. Ever the political person, she used this occasion to speak out against contemporary political and social occurrences. Her changing attitude toward Austria, and her final acceptance there, may have represented an end to her exile, but this was to be short-lived. Within a few years, she would be dead.

Ironically, the uncompleted *Todesarten* with its allusion to Brecht, foreshadowed Bachmann's own death. "There are many ways to kill," wrote Brecht. "You can stick a knife into someone's belly, take away their bread, not heal them from a disease, stick them in a bad apartment, work them to death, drive them to commit suicide, send them off to war, etc. Only a few of these things are forbidden in our country." After falling asleep while smoking in bed, Bachmann was consumed by fire and suffered serious burns. She languished in the hospital for a time and then finally died, not as a consequence of her injuries but from convulsions brought on by her withdrawal from the drugs she had been taking.

Aged 11 when the war came to Klagenfurt, Bachmann belonged to the generation of writers who were old enough to suffer the second World War but too young to affect its course. As such, her work can be seen as an effort to comprehend the horrors of Austria's National Socialist past and to search for new ways of going on. While transgressing Adorno's dictum that after Auschwitz the writing of poetry was an impossibility, Bachmann used her work as a vehicle for exploring the private and interpersonal manifestations of the political. In so doing, she demonstrated the need for remembering, for the disenfranchised to find a voice, and above all for a new language of hope.

SOURCES:

Achberger, Karen R. *Understanding Ingeborg Bachmann.* Columbia: South Carolina University Press, 1995.

Bachmann, Ingeborg. *Malina.* Translated by Philip Boehm. Afterward by Mark Anderson. London: Holmes and Meier, 1990.

———. *Songs in Flight: The Collected Poems of Ingeborg Bachmann.* Translated and introduction by Peter Filkins. NY: Marsilio, 1994.

———. *The Thirtieth Year.* Translated by Michael Bullock. NY: Knopf, 1964.

Beicken, Peter. *Ingeborg Bachmann.* Munich: C.H. Beck, 1988.

Koschel, Christine, ed. *Ingeborg Bachmann: Werke.* Munich: R. Piper, 1978, pp. 418–423.

Lutz, Bernd. "Ingeborg Bachmann," in *Metzler Autoren Lexikon.* Edited by Bernd Lutz. Stuttgart: Metzler 1994, pp. 38.

SUGGESTED READING:

Bartsch, Kurt. *Ingeborg Bachmann.* Sammlung Metzler 242. Stuttgart: J.B. Metzler, 1988.

Lennox, Sarah. "The Feminist Reception of Ingeborg Bachmann," in Jeanette Clausen and Sara Friedrichsmeyer, eds., *Women in German Yearbook 8: Feminist Studies in German Literature and Culture.* Lincoln: Nebraska University Press, 1993, pp. 73–111.

Modern Austrian Literature. Vol. 18, no. 3–4, 1985.

Weigel, Sigrid. *Die Stimme der Medusa: Schreibweisen in der Gegenwartsliteratur von Frauen.* Dülmen-Hiddingsel: tende, 1987.

COLLECTIONS:

Correspondence, papers and memorabilia located in Vienna, Austria.

RELATED MEDIA:

"Der ich unter Menschen nicht leben kann: Auf der Suche nach Ingeborg Bachmann," television film, directed by Peter Hamm (FS 2), 1980.

"Die Wahrheit ist dem Menschen zumutbar: Leben und Werk von Ingeborg Bachmann" (44 min.), television documentary directed by **Gerda Haller** (ZDF), 1974.

"Zu Gast bei Ingeborg Bachmann" (25 min.), television film directed by Karl Stanzl, 1968.

Vanessa Agnew, author of *Red Feathers, White Paper, Blue Beads: A Natural History of the Colony*

Bacinetti-Florenzi, Marianna

(1802–1870)

Italian philosopher and translator. *Name variations: Marchesa Marianna Bacinetti-Florenzi Waddington. Born into a wealthy family in Ravenna, Italy, in 1802; died in April 1870; educated privately in Faenza by Torrigiani; married the Marquis Lodovico e Carlotta (died); married Evelino Waddington; children: (first marriage) two.*

Selected works: Italian translations of the works of German philosophers Friedrich Wilhelm Joseph von Schelling and Gottfried Wilhelm Leibniz; annotations of the works of Giordano Bruno; Taluui Pensieri *(1843);* Letters filesofiche *(1848);* Alcune Riflessioni sopra il Socialismo ed il Comunismo *(1860);* Filosofemini di Cosmologia e di Antologia *(1863);* Saggi di Psicologia e di Logica *(1864);* Saggio sulla Natura *(*Dante, il poeta del pensiero, *1866);* Saggio sulla filosofia dello spirito *(1867);* Della Immortalita dell'Anima Umana *(1868);* La Facolta di Sentire *(1868);* Corrispondenza inedita di Vittorio Cousin con la marchesa Florenzi *(1870).*

Marianna Bacinetti-Florenzi was born in 1802 to an illustrious family in Ravenna, Italy, who sent her to study with the distinguished philosopher Torrigiani in Faenza. At age 15, she left school and married the Marquis Lodovico e Carlotta. During her marriage and the birth of two children, she continued to read Italian and German philosophy, but she was soon widowed.

Known far and wide for her philosophical writing and her deft interpretations of other philosophers, Bacinetti-Florenzi astonished Friedrich Schelling, whose philosophy she was instrumental in introducing to Italy. She translated much of his work into Italian, including the conversion, commissioned by King Maximilian of Bavaria, of some of Schelling's unpublished writings. Particularly interested in Schelling's work, she ignited the movement of scientific philosophy in Italy. Bacinetti-Florenzi became known for her insight as well as for the beauty and clarity of her prose. She was generally well-loved in her community, and her work was so admired that many sought her correspondence. Her own philosophy, however, received some opposition from the Catholic Church, and she was disturbed by the philosophical writings of Bini, a monk and professor in Perugia. Although troubled by his lack of attention to human emotion, she tried to reconcile some of his understandings with her own, seeking help from her correspondents. Bacinetti-Florenzi married an Englishman, Evelino Waddington, who became an Italian citizen out of love for her. She died, greatly missed by her community, in April 1870.

Catherine Hundleby, M.A. Philosophy,
University of Guelph, Guelph, Ontario, Canada

Bacinskaite-Buciene, S. (1904–1945).

See Neris, Salomeja.

Backer, Harriet (1845–1932)

Norwegian painter whose luminous interiors evoked great acclaim. *Born on January 21, 1845, in Holmestrand, on the Oslofjord, Norway; died in February 1932; second of four daughters, one of whom was* ****Agathe Backer-Grondahl,*** *of Consul Nils Backer (a shipowner) and Sophie (Petersen) Backer (originally the Backer family came to Norway from Holland in the 17th century; another branch of Backer's relatives originated in Denmark, emigrating in the 19th century); studied in Germany and Italy, as well as Paris with Bonnat.*

> **Kielland, Kitty L.** (1843–1914)
>
> ***Norwegian painter.*** *Born in Stavanger, Norway, in 1843; died in 1914; studied at the art academies of Karlsruhe and Munich; also studied in Paris.*
>
> After a few drawing lessons in her hometown of Stavanger, Norway, Kitty Kielland attended the art academy in Karlsruhe before entering Munich's art academy in 1875 where one of her tutors was fellow Norwegian Eilif Peterssen. In 1879, she and artist ***Harriet Backer** moved to Paris. For the next nine years, they worked there and took field trips. They also spent the summers of 1886 and 1887 in Fleskum, Norway, with a group of Norwegian painters. Influenced by Impressionism in her treatment of atmosphere, light, and air, Kielland concentrated on plein-air painting, a style developed chiefly in France in the mid-19th century.

Known for her paintings of interiors from all levels of society—Paris salons, Breton and Norwegian farmhouses, her own background, and in particular the interiors of Norwegian churches—all of them with figures, mainly of women: By Lamplight *(1890);* Blue Interior *(1892);* Baptism at Tanum Church *(1892, at Washington University, St. Louis.); also known for her studio in Christiania where she taught younger painters (1889–1912); a torchlight procession in her honor on the occasion of her 85th birthday was organized by the Artists' Society (1930); was decorated with the Order of St. Olav.*

Harriet Backer was born at Holmestrand, a shipping center at the Christianiafjord, as the second of four daughters. Unusually well educated for her time, she began drawing lessons at age six. When the family moved to Christiania (now Oslo) in 1857, her parents encouraged her artistic aspirations and enrolled her in Johan Fredrik Eckersberg's school from 1861 to 1865. Subsequently, she became a student at Christian Brun's institute from 1867 to 1868 and at Knut Bergslien's painting academy from 1872 to 1874. She spent several winters in Berlin and Weimar and in 1870 had traveled to Italy to copy old masters. She also studied in Munich in 1874 and 1875.

Inspired by French Naturalism, Backer moved to Paris in 1878, where she would stay for ten years and receive not only instruction but four large scholarships. She made her debut in the Paris Salon in 1880. The following decade was divided between France and Norway. In Norway, she was in the circle of leading Norwegian painters (such as Erik Werenskiold and Ludvig Munthe) and the foremost Norwegian writers of the day. She returned to Norway for good in 1888, painting during the summer in the valleys north of Christiania with another Norwegian artist **Kitty Kielland**, and spending the rest of the year teaching young artists at her own painting school which she ran until 1912.

Backer's production is relatively small, but her Norwegian interiors are famous for their luminous quality. *Blue Interior*, for example, painted in Paris in 1883 and shown in the Christiania Exhibition the same year, was a great success. It represents a sitting woman suffused in light from an unseen window; light falls on her white knitting, the red chest, the leaves of a plant, a painting on the wall, and her figure in blue. Critics praised its "courageous harmony of blue color and blue light" which imbued the painting with a mood of contemplation and silence.

Blue Interior *by Harriet Backer.*

Backer had spent the summers of 1886 and 1887 with a group of Norwegian Naturalist painters at Christian Skredsvig's farm at Fleskum. Unlike her colleagues who concentrated on painting the summer night, Backer continued to focus on interiors. In the summer of 1890, she painted a group of superb small canvases, among them *By Lamplight* (1890) which hangs in the National Gallery in Oslo. Again she shows a self-absorbed woman, this time reading a book. Outside is darkness, but the kerosine lamp on the table where the woman sits lights up her face, along with one blue and one white wall, the wood stove, and the back of a wooden chair. As with *Blue Interior*, the painting has been said to show "the inaccessibility and introspection" of Backer's female subjects.

To paint, to paint! For that I was born and came into the world.

—Harriet Backer, 1927.

SOURCES:

Haug, Kristian. "Norway's Great Woman Artist," in *American-Scandinavian Review* (illus.). Vol. 13, 1925, pp. 735–40.

Kielland, Else Christie. *Harriet Backer.* Oslo, Norway: Aschehoug, Oslo, 1958.

Lange, Marit. *Harriet Backer.* Oslo: Gyldendal, 1995.

Store Norske Leksikon. Oslo: Kunnskapsforlaget, 1991.

Vanedoe, Kirk. *Northern Light.* New Haven and London: Yale University Press, 1988.

COLLECTIONS:

Many of Backer's paintings are in the collections of the National Gallery, Oslo, and the Rasmus Meyer Gallery, Bergen, Norway; her papers are deposited at the University Library, Oslo.

Inga Wiehl, Yakima, Washington,
and **Elizabeth Rokkan**, translator, formerly Associate Professor, Department of English, University of Bergen, Norway

Backer-Grondahl, Agathe (1847–1907)

Norwegian concert artist and composer who wrote many works she performed. *Born in Holmestrand, on the Oslofjord, Norway, on December 1, 1847; died in Ormoen near Christiana, Norway, on June 16, 1907; one of four daughters, one of whom was* ****Harriet Backer****, of Consul Nils Backer (a much-traveled shipowner) and Sophie (Petersen) Backer; married with two sons who retained her name and were well-known: Fridtjof, a pianist and composer, and Nils, a professor of medicine at the University of Bergen.*

A student of Theodor Kullak and Hans von Bülow, Agathe Backer-Grondahl was well regarded in her lifetime. Contemporary accounts speak of her as an extraordinary musician. Wrote George Bernard Shaw: "A great artist—a serious artist—a beautiful, incomparable unique artist! She morally regenerated us all." Her repertoire was a large one, and her own piano compositions, effectively written in the style of Mendelssohn and Schumann, are warmly Romantic, imaginative, and more pianistically idiomatic than those of her fellow Norwegian Edvard Grieg.

SUGGESTED READING:

Christensen, Inga Hoegsbro. *Biography of the Late Agathe Backer-Grondahl.* NY: Roy Press, 1913.

John Haag, Athens, Georgia

Backhouse, Elizabeth (1917—)

Australian author of fiction and drama. *Born Elizabeth Backhouse in Northam, Western Australia, in 1917; daughter of Hilda (Booth) Backhouse and William Backhouse; educated in public schools; never married; no children.*

Selected works: In Our Hands *(1940);* The Sky Has Its Clouds *(1943);* Death Came Uninvited *(1957);* Death Climbs a Hill *(1963);* The Web of Shadows *(1966);* The Thin Line *(1968);* The Fourth Picture *(1974);* KAL *(ballet, 1979);* Against Time and Place *(1990). Author of eleven novels, four plays, a children's book, television drama, ballet, and a family anecdotal history which portrays early 1900s Australian life.*

Though Britons first settled in Australia in the late 1700s, the heaviest migration came in the early and mid-1900s. Elizabeth Backhouse's father William, a violinist, was among those who endured the long voyage in hopes of a new climate and opportunities in unchartered territory. Since Australia could not claim a strong musical community, he took a fair-paying job on the Australia railroad and, once he had earned enough money, sent for his fiancée Hilda. They married the day she arrived. In Northam, the couple bought a country house whose walls were made of hessian, a tightly stretched fabric or hide, on which pictures and other decorations were hung by stitching. It was surrounded by gardens, with a giant mulberry tree that stooped close to the rear porch.

Elizabeth Backhouse was born at home in 1917, two years after her brother Clive. Raised on music, the Backhouse children learned violin from William and piano from Hilda. Then, while their parents gave lessons to local children, Elizabeth and Clive slipped out the back door to explore their neighborhood. Always an eager student, Elizabeth attended public schools, even during an extended visit to England with Hilda's family in 1924.

When Elizabeth was nine, a sexual assault crippled her childhood. On her way home from school, she encountered an older man who asked directions to the park. Next, he demanded that she walk him there, then forced her into a public restroom and molested her. Elizabeth escaped by kicking him. The following day, she was struck blind and began to stutter. Later, in her 1990 memoir *Against Time and Place*, she wrote, "Sometimes I would finish a whole sentence. Sometimes I would speak normally for a whole day and be able to say nothing on the following day. I could say nothing at all if I did not have a firm grip on my right ankle. I had used my right foot to kick the man."

Backhouse stayed home from school with her mother, who read to her, and her father, who played the violin to soothe her. Thinking it might be therapeutic if she could play, her parents encouraged her toward music. Sometimes the attempts worked, but more often she was struck with paralyzing panic and her fingers would not move. Six months after the assault, when she had seen several doctors who could find nothing physically wrong with her, Elizabeth's sight was instantaneously restored. Her speech remained stilted, however, aided only by a grip on her ankle. Only as an adult, with the help of a public-speaking class, would she resume more normal speech.

The stutter ruined school for Backhouse. Since she refused all oral presentations and examinations, her grades suffered and the Backhouses saw university hopes fade. "You can educate yourself," Backhouse recalled her father saying, "through books. All education, all learning, all instruction, all wisdom and truth come from men's and women's minds. Read books. Sift everything, distill everything and see what rises from it."

Backhouse joined the Women's Auxiliary Australian Air Force at the start of World War II and served for four years stationed near Melbourne. She wrote her first three books during off-duty hours in a small, abandoned hut. Based on these early successes, she went to England after the war and for five years lived abroad and worked for Korda Films. Within a year of her 1951 return to her parents' new home in Perth, William Backhouse died. With a friend, Elizabeth bought a house nearby and made daily visits to her mother. When Hilda's health began to fail at age 70, Elizabeth had rooms built onto her own home for her mother. The two lived together for 23 years; Hilda was bedridden for the last ten.

Elizabeth Backhouse published novels throughout the 1950s and into the 1960s. After the 1966 release *The Web of Shadows*, she focused her literary attentions on the stage and television. Published in 1990, her most recent work, *Against Time and Place*, provides an anecdotal history of the Booth and Backhouse families, several of whose members emigrated from England. The memoir is an unusual account of the experiences they had in a newly flourishing country.

SOURCES:

Backhouse, Elizabeth. *Against Time and Place*. Fremantle, Western Australia: Fremantle Arts Centre Press, 1990.

Wilde, William H., Joy Horton, and Barry Andrews, ed. *Oxford Companion to Australian Literature*. Melbourne: Oxford University Press, 1994.

Crista Martin, freelance writer,
Boston, Massachusetts

Baclanova, Olga (1899–1974)

Russian actress. *Pronunciation: Bah-CLAHN-ova. Born in Moscow, Russia, on August 19, 1899; died on September 6, 1974, in Vevey, Switzerland; studied at the Cherniavsky Institute and the Moscow Art Theater; married a man named Zoppi (divorced); married Nicholas Soussanin; married Richard Davis (a film exhibitor and distributor); children: (second marriage) Nicholas Soussanin, Jr. (also known as Nicholas Saunders).*

Filmography: Symphony of Love and Death *(Russia, 1914);* Wanderer Beyond the Grave *(Russia, 1915);* He Who Gets Slapped *(Russia, 1916);* The Flowers Are Late *(Russia, 1917);* The Dove *(U.S., 1928);* Street of Sin *(U.S., 1928);* Forgotten Faces *(U.S., 1928);* Docks of New York *(U.S., 1928);* Three Sinners *(U.S., 1928);* The Man Who Laughs *(U.S., 1928);* Avalanche *(U.S., 1928);* A Dangerous Woman *(U.S., 1929);* The Wolf of Wall Street *(U.S., 1929);* The Man I Love *(U.S., 1929);* Are You There? *(U.S., 1930);* Cheer Up and Smile *(U.S., 1930);* The Great Lover *(U.S., 1931);* Freaks *(also known as* Nature's Mistakes, Forbidden Love, The Monster Show, *U.S., 1932);* Billion Dollar Scandal *(U.S., 1933);* Claudia *(U.S., 1943).*

At age 16, Olga Baclanova made her stage debut at the famed Moscow Art Theater and was soon appearing in leading roles as one of the company's top draws. While on a 1923 tour in America with *Lysistrata*, she decided to stay and snagged a minor role opposite ***Norma Talmadge** in the film *The Dove. Baclanova* moved on to more significant, though unsympathetic, parts in two Josef von Sternberg films: *The Docks of New York* (as Lou) and *Street of Sin*, both opposite Emil Jannings. Her most prominent leading role, however, was as the cruel and conniving trapeze artist Cleopatra opposite Wallace Ford in Tod Browning's cult classic *Freaks*. When the film was released, it was greeted with such repulsion by critics that it lost over $164,000 in a matter of weeks and was withdrawn by Metro-Goldwyn-Mayer. It was also banned in Eng-

Olga Baclanova

land for over 30 years (though MGM continued to release it under a number of aliases). "Baclanova's memorable performance was shockingly realistic," writes Charles Stumpf. "At long last she had proven her dramatic ability. Her stardom should have been assured. But she returned to Paramount for one final long forgotten flop—*The Billion Dollar Scandal.*" In the 1930s, Baclanova appeared on Broadway with Bela Lugosi in *Murder at the Vanities*, a "whodunit with music"; she also hosted her own radio program. The actress continued to work in theater, on tour and in stock, then returned to Broadway as Madame Daruscha in *Claudia*, repeating the role in the film version. Following her retirement, she lived with her third husband in a villa in Vevey, Switzerland.

SOURCES:

Stumpf, Charles. "Olga Baclanova: Miscast Legend," in *Classic Images*. No. 276. June 1998.

Bacon, Albion Fellows (1865–1933)

American housing reformer. *Born on April 8, 1865, in Evansville, Indiana; grew up in McCutchanville; died in Evansville, on December 10, 1933; daughter of Albion (a Methodist minister) and Mary (Erskine) Fellows; younger sister of Annie Fellows Johnston (1863–1931); married Hilary E. Bacon (a banker and merchant), in October 1888; children: four.*

In October 1888, after graduating from high school in Evansville, Indiana, Albion Fellows married Hilary Bacon. It was a double ceremony. That same day, her sister ***Annie Fellows (Johnston)**, who would go on to author "The Little Colonel" series, married William L. Johnston. A small, fragile woman, Albion Bacon's next few years were marked by periods of confinement because of a lengthy illness and the birth of four children.

By chance, she became aware of the riverfront slums of Evansville and became involved with the Evansville Civic Improvement Society. Over the years, Bacon organized the Men's Circle of Friendly Visitors, the Flower Mission for poor working girls, a Working Girls' Association, an Anti-Tuberculosis League, and the Monday Night Club which was composed of influential denizens with a charitable bent. Convinced that the chief cause of slums was substandard housing, Bacon struggled for years before she managed to have a tenement-house law included in the cities' building codes (1909) for Evanston and Indianapolis. In 1913, the Indiana Housing Association, which she had helped organize, pushed through a bill that pertained to the entire state. Bacon published an account of the campaign in her autobiographical *Beauty for Ashes* (1914). She was also responsible for another 1917 law involving the condemnation of unsafe or unsanitary buildings.

Bacon, Anne Cooke (1528–1610)

English writer. *Born in 1528 in England; died in 1610 in England; daughter of Anthony Cooke (a scholar and tutor) and Anne Fitzwilliam Cooke; married Nicholas Bacon, in 1556; children: two sons, Anthony and Francis Bacon (1561–1626, the theologian).*

Born into an affluent family, Anne Cooke and her sisters were given an unusually thorough education by their father Anthony Cooke, who was the tutor of King Henry VIII's only son, Edward (later King Edward VI). The young girl showed a remarkable aptitude for learning and would eventually speak and write in several languages, including Latin and possibly Greek. A devoted follower of the new Protestant faith, she employed her facility with foreign languages to produce many English translations of Protestant works and thus contribute to the spread of Protestantism in England. When she was only 22, her translations from the Italian of works by Barnadine Ochine were published. Six years later, she married Nicholas Bacon, another Reformation scholar, but marriage and subsequent motherhood did not deter her from her studies and writing. One of her more important translations appeared in 1564, an English edition of the Latin "Apology in Defense of the Church of England" by John Jewett. Anne Cooke Bacon, who died about age 82, lived long enough to see her younger son, Sir Francis Bacon (born 1561), gain international renown for his theological writings on the new faith.

Laura York, Anza, California

Bacon, Delia Salter (1811–1859)

American author who advanced the theory that English philosopher Francis Bacon wrote the plays of William Shakespeare. *Born Delia Salter Bacon on February 2, 1811, in Tallmadge, Ohio; died on September 2, 1859, in Hartford, Connecticut; daughter of Alice (Parks) Bacon and Reverend David Bacon (a congregationalist missionary); educated at public school, Harriet Parson's School, and Catharine Beecher's School; never married; no children.*

Selected works: Tales of the Puritans *(1831);* The Bride of Fort Edward *(play) (1839);* Philosophy of the Plays of Shakespeare Unfolded *(1857).*

As the first person ever to theorize publicly that Francis Bacon was the true author of Shakespeare's plays, educator Delia Salter Bacon staked her life—psychological, physical, and financial—on this premise. If her theory proved true, she would be a literary revolutionary and legend. Anything less made her a footnote in history. The latter was her fate, and the failure drove Bacon literally insane with disappointment. She died in an institution for the mentally ill two years after her theory was published and roundly dismissed by critics and literary scholars.

The Bacons came to America as British colonists, first settling in Dedham, Massachusetts. Through the years, they migrated to Connecticut, where David Bacon was born and met his wife Alice Parks. As missionaries, the couple traveled west into Ohio. In 1811, Delia was born there, the fifth of seven children, but the Bacons ran out of money and returned to Connecticut. Reverend David Bacon struggled to feed his family and cope with his disappointment. Ill and depressed, he died in poverty on August 29, 1817, and Delia was sent to live with her namesake, her mother's old school friend **Delia Williams**, in Hartford. Delia's brother Leonard, attending theological school at Yale in New Haven, was her nearest relative.

Delia Bacon

Delia was allowed to attend public schools in Hartford and kept contact with her own family by way of letters. In 1821, she saw her mother Alice again; shortly thereafter, she was sent to live with her. Religion became an omnipresent force for Delia with Leonard's 1824 ordination in the ministry. In April of 1825, Bacon returned to the Williams family, attending a new school run by ***Catharine Beecher**. One of Delia's classmates was Beecher's sister, Harriet, who would become Bacon's lifelong rival.

In 1826, Delia's schooling was complete, making employment a necessity. Anxious to avoid housework, she recruited her older sister **Julia** and established a boarding school in Jamaica, New York. For the next four years, Delia and Julia taught young girls, often learning subjects as they were teaching them. Their school proved initially successful until both sisters succumbed to malaria during an epidemic, and Delia nearly died. Ever after, her health would be frail. When the sisters recovered, their debt was so great that they had to sell the furniture and close down the school. In April 1830, they moved to New Haven to live with Leonard and his wife.

In her suitcase, Bacon packed a secret passion—a book of stories she had written during private hours. One year later, with Leonard's help, the highly sentimental *Tales of the Puritans* was published anonymously, but the author's identity soon leaked out. Proud of her efforts, Delia was hurt when an embarrassed Leonard dismissed the book as foolishness. Though she made little money from it, *Tales of the Puritans* brought attention to Delia. A compelling speaker and tireless learner, she was soon a welcome house or party guest.

For two years, she traveled and studied. By the time she returned to Leonard's home in 1833, Delia determined to offer "classes" for women which would parallel the men's Yale experience. Leonard's mentor, Nathaniel Taylor, head of the theology department at Yale, helped Delia fill her brother's sitting room with women to whom she taught literature, philosophy, sciences, and history. Through her contacts at the university, Bacon invited professors to speak to her group. The venture was a success, and she enjoyed the opportunity to earn a living and still study. At the recommendation of her brother, she took up the works of Francis Bacon.

In 1935, having proved herself in Connecticut, Delia was drawn to the challenge of New York. Though she taught only one year, she stayed on to write the historical and sentimental play *The Bride of Fort Edward*, published in July of 1839. She received little financial reward and a harsh critique from her brother. Ill from stress, she withdrew to her sister's home in Canandaigua, New York, for a year. By the fall of 1841, Delia had returned to Leonard and her sitting-room classes.

Though Bacon had suitors, she paid them little mind until she met Alexander MacWhorter, a Yale theologian ten years her junior. With MacWhorter, Delia first shared her suspicion that Francis Bacon had penned Shakespeare's plays. She studied their writings at length. She also had it on good authority from her New York friend Samuel Morse that Francis Bacon developed a secret code and used ciphered messages in his work.

As gossip about Delia and the young minister surfaced, Delia tried to break off the relationship; but MacWhorter pleaded for her company and affection, and they continued courting. In the fall of 1846, suffering from exhaustion, Delia withdrew to a spa where she met up with her erstwhile teacher, Catharine Beecher, and her former schoolmate, ***Harriet Beecher Stowe**, who was now a published writer. The encounter renewed Bacon's rivalry but also her friendship with the sisters. MacWhorter made a surprise visit to the spa, and Bacon confided to the sisters that he had proposed.

Both Beecher and MacWhorter preceded Delia back to Connecticut. When Bacon arrived, scandal was brewing. Beecher had announced MacWhorter's proposal, but he denied it. Deeply hurt, Delia wrote to MacWhorter. He then announced that she had proposed to him, been denied, and now was vengeful. When suggestions of impropriety began to damage Delia's reputation, Leonard called for an investigation by a religious council. Leonard's one-time mentor Nathaniel Taylor took MacWhorter's side in the argument, and Delia Bacon's personal anguish turned into a political dispute between Leonard and Taylor, theological rivals battling for control of New Haven. It took a year for the hearing, which ruled that Alexander MacWhorter behaved questionably. Delia's assertion of his proposal could not be proved, and, her reputation tattered, she went into seclusion.

Afterward, Bacon traveled as the guest of **Myra Clark Gaines** and her husband, General Edmund Gaines, traversing the Eastern states from New Orleans, Louisiana, to Saginaw, Michigan. Back in New Haven a year later, Bacon was still an object of curiosity. Hoping to teach a class in Boston, she contacted Catharine Beecher, only to discover—to her horror—that Beecher was writing an account of the MacWhorter incident. Because she had announced Bacon's engagement without her consent, Beecher felt compelled to assist Bacon in clearing her name. Mediocre at best, *Truth Stranger Than Fiction* appeared in June 1850.

The book haunted Bacon when she arrived in Boston in October to begin her classes. In a casual encounter with a young woman in a bookstore, Bacon admitted the book was about her. The young woman, ***Elizabeth Palmer Peabody**, turned out to be Nathaniel Hawthorne's sister-in-law. Through her connections, Peabody encouraged Boston's elite to attend Bacon's first lecture. Delia turned in a winning performance which gained her a full classroom for six months. In the summer of 1851, she withdrew to work on her Baconian theory until illness, once more, deterred her.

In Boston that winter, Bacon sought support for what was now an obsession, but her ideas were most often met with shock and dismissal. Ralph Waldo Emerson, however, became a patron. Bacon reminded many New Englanders of another intellectual, ***Margaret Fuller**, who had died tragically in 1850. Her physical and intellectual resemblance to Fuller won friends where resistance seemed likely. In June of 1851, rival Stowe's most popular work, *Uncle Tom's Cabin*, began to appear in serial form (the book's character of Miss Ophelia was based on Delia).

Pressured to publish her theory lest anyone else attempt it, Bacon felt compelled to go to England. There, she thought she would find solid proof of the plays' authorship. With Emerson's support, she went to New York City. Unable to earn her passage to England, she turned to Charles Butler, a New York lawyer, who provided for her trip. Without advising Leonard, Bacon set sail on May 14, 1853. When she arrived in England, advance letters from Emerson had already found her friends. Soon, Bacon was so immersed in research that she rarely saw anyone and declined all invitations.

Bacon decided that publication of her work in America and England simultaneously would be best. Acting as her agent in the states, Emerson had little success. To his dismay, her theory remained unsubstantiated by any evidence. Shakespeare's manuscripts, the ultimate proof, she believed to be buried with him; Francis Bacon had said so himself, she maintained, in a ciphered message from his works. In August of 1855, publisher Phillips, Sampson offered a $200 advance and ten percent of the royalties for her book. Feeling the offer to be inadequate, Bacon hedged; instead, she accepted an offer from *Putnam's Magazine* to serialize her theory. The first piece, "William Shakespeare and His Plays: An Inquiry Concerning Them," appeared in January of 1856. Greeted with scorn, the theory nevertheless inspired some interest. But when *Putnam*'s discovered that the second article offered no conclusive proof—as was promised in chapter one—they rescinded their offer.

Bacon stopped seeking help from America. Instead, she wrote to Nathaniel Hawthorne who was then American consul in Liverpool. Describing her work and her need for money, she warned Hawthorne that if he denied her plea and she were unable to pursue her theory, the president of the United States would lose the honor of the discovery and hold Hawthorne responsible. "I am determined it shall not be my fault if this thing is lost to us." Hawthorne, who knew of Bacon but was surprised by her tone, agreed to read her work. As their friendship developed, she wrote: "I have given up this world entirely, and if I had my choice, I don't know as I should ever see anyone again while I live. . . . I used to be somebody . . . whereas now I am nothing but this work, and don't wish to be. I would rather be this than anything else."

Hawthorne became, if not a believer, at least an agent for her in England. In June 1856, Emerson wrote that several of her chapters, while crossing the Atlantic, were lost. Bacon considered them the most pivotal to her book, and she did not have copies. In despair, she went to Stratford, Shakespeare's birthplace, to begin the task once more. Unbeknownst to her, Hawthorne wrote to Leonard and asked him to reconsider support of his sister. Leonard responded with a letter to Delia, accusing her of being "delusional" and "misguided." Bacon was devastated. Feeling forced to provide some tangible evidence, she made her way one September night to Trinity Church and Shakespeare's grave. Resolved to rob the grave of the manuscripts, she was not strong enough to lift the covering stones; instead, she spent the night sitting in the dark church contemplating the possibility that no evidence existed. In a formal plea to the church vicar, she was granted the right to examine the grave. But Delia did not show up. She had lost faith.

> What she may have suffered before her intellect gave way, we had better not try to imagine. No author had ever hoped so confidently as she; none ever failed more utterly.
>
> —**Nathaniel Hawthorne**

At this time, an agent, Francis Bennoch, acting at Hawthorne's direction, found a placement for the book. An alternate author had produced a pamphlet espousing a Baconian theory, and Hawthorne was concerned. certain she would kill herself if another published the theory first, Hawthorne secretly arranged with a publisher to pay all printing costs and write a preface. A printing of 1,000 was agreed upon, and Hawthorne contracted for 500 of them to bear Ticknor and Fields' imprint for U.S. sale. The next six months were spent on proofs and a title. Hawthorne wrote an uninspired preface; Bacon pronounced it awful and rewrote it. Before printing in April 1857, the original publisher withdrew and another publisher was arranged. The whole affair cost Hawthorne $1,100 and *Philosophy of the Plays of Shakespeare Unfolded* was finally printed.

Bacon, who suddenly had nothing to do, fell ill. For two months no reviews were forthcoming, then the silence was broken in June when her book was fiercely denounced. Delia's tenuous hold on sanity snapped. She began to falsely claim Francis Bacon as a distant relative. American astronomer ***Maria Mitchell** visited Bacon, entirely unaware of her situation, and found her so disturbed that she wrote to Leonard and asked him to retrieve her. In November, David Rice, doctor and mayor of Stratford, had Delia Bacon committed to the nearby sanitarium Henley-in-Arden. The Bacons, unable to fund Delia's return, could only exchange letters with Rice, who had grown close to Delia.

Delia Bacon was finally rescued when Leonard's son George passed through England on his way home from China. Unaware of his aunt's state, he stopped in Stratford and discovered her plight. George sold all his belongings and treasures from the Orient, and the pair returned to America on April 13, 1858. She had been away almost five years.

By July, Bacon was committed to the Hartford Retreat, an asylum. More lucid in her last days than she had been for years, she died on September 2, 1859, and was buried in the family plot at Grove Street cemetery in New Haven. While her theory was taken up by others, it has never been proven.

SOURCES:

Bacon, Theodore. *Delia Bacon: A Biographical Sketch.* Boston, MA: Houghton Mifflin, 1888.

Blain, Virginia, Pat Clements, and Isobel Grundy, eds. *The Feminist Companion to Literature in English.* New Haven, CT: Yale University Press, 1990.

Hart, James D. *Oxford Guide to American Literature.* NY: Oxford University Press, 1995.

Hopkins, Vivian C. *Prodigal Puritan: A Life of Delia Bacon.* Cambridge, MA: Harvard University Press, 1959.

Kunitz, Stanley and Howard Haycraft. *American Authors, 1600–1900.* NY: H.W. Wilson, 1938.

Crista Martin, freelance writer,
Boston, Massachusetts

Bacon, Josephine Dodge

(1876–1961)

American writer of juvenile and adult satire. *Name variations: Josephine Dodge Daskam. Born Josephine Dodge Daskam on February 17, 1876, in Stamford, Connecticut; died on July 29, 1961, in Tannersville, New York; daughter of Anne (Loring) and Horace Sawyer Daskam; graduated Smith College, 1898; married Selden Bacon (a lawyer), on July 25, 1903; children: Anne, Deborah, and Selden, Jr.*

Selected works: Smith College Stories *(1900);* Sister's Vacation and Other Girls' Stories *(1900);* The Imp and the Angel *(1901);* Fables for the Fair *(1901);* The Madness of Philip *(1902);* The Memoirs of a Baby *(1904);* The Inheritance *(1912);* Square Peggy *(1919);* Truth o' Women *(1923);* Counterpoint *(1927);* Kathy *(1933);* Girl Wanted! *(1936);* Cassie-on-the-Job *(1937);* The House By the Road *(1937);* The World in His Heart *(1941).*

According to Josephine Dodge Bacon, no societal ill was more insidious nor more treatable than the breakdown of a family due to inferior homemaking. "The only 'cause' which interests me at all in connection with women is the systematic education for duties and responsibilities inevitably assumed by the great majority of them," she wrote in *Good Housekeeping* (October 1911). Maintaining that attention to such details would eliminate moral disintegration in other areas of the family, Bacon directed the majority of her writing to this cause, and her work was called feminist for its focus on women's efforts to find a place in the world.

Raised in middle- to upper-class Stamford, Connecticut, Bacon never lived outside the Northeast. In Massachusetts, she attended Smith College and graduated in 1898. She then moved to New York City and wrote stories for magazines and journals, most notably the *Saturday Evening Post.* The year 1900 marked her first major success, with the publication of *Smith College Stories*, a collection of short fiction. Early work, under the name Josephine Dodge Daskam, was prolific, approximately two books a year. Her July 25, 1903, marriage to prominent New York attorney Selden Bacon slowed her pace and changed her name, but the year following their marriage was her most successful. *The Memoirs of a Baby* (1904), a satire on child rearing, was a bestseller; no other Bacon work would equal its popularity, though her subject matter remained similarly concerned with women and family.

The Bacons moved to suburban Westchester, New York, where they raised three children, two of whom became physicians. While her daughters were of Scouting age, Josephine went to work for the national Girl Scouts, an organization which she felt provided an early and vital introduction to home-economics skills. From 1915 to 1925, Bacon served on the executive committee of the Girl Scouts, and as editor of the official handbook and the *Girl Scout Magazine.* Summering in Tannersville, New York, she became a lifelong participant in the Onteora Club, an amateur theatrical group; she also coordinated a permanent collection for Onteora, "A Hundred Years of American Art," which featured Catskills painters. Further free time was spent on recording books for the Lighthouse for the Blind. All the while, Bacon wrote. She would publish more than 35 books in 60 years.

In 1946, on their 43rd wedding anniversary, Selden Bacon died. Shortly after, Josephine made a new winter home at 130 East 57th Street in New York City. She was summering in Tannersville when she died at age 86.

Crista Martin, freelance writer, Boston, Massachusetts

Bacon, Mary (1948–1991)

American jockey and one of the first women to earn a place on the American racetrack who, in two decades of thoroughbred racing, won 286 races. *Born in Chicago to a carnival family in 1948; committed suicide in Fort Worth, Texas, on June 8, 1991; completed high school and studied stable management, veterinary medicine, and steeplechase riding at Porelock Vale Riding School in Somerset, England; married Johnny Bacon (a jockey), in 1968; children: Susan Michaela Bacon (b. March 4, 1969); a son (died at birth, 1970).*

After attending Porelock Vale Riding School, awarded a certificate as a British Horse Society Assistant; began professional career racing thoroughbreds the first year women were licensed as jockeys in the U.S. (1969); named Most Courageous Athlete of the Year by the Philadelphia Sports Writer Association (1973).

The lot of a jockey is never easy, regardless of gender. In most states, a jockey is "bound" to a boss, who determines whether the apprentice works five days a week or seven, what mounts will be ridden, and what salary given. But Mary Bacon's childhood did much to prepare her for the world of thoroughbred racing. Born to a father who came from a carnival family and a mother who grew up illiterate on a small horse and cattle farm, the skillful and tough-willed Bacon described herself, in the jargon of the horse-raising world, as "a carny out of a hillbilly." Her itinerant childhood took her from Oklahoma to Illinois, to New Mexico, Minnesota, and Michigan, and her father's al-

Mary Bacon

coholism led to his frequent unemployment while her mother tried to hold the family together. Mary's high school years were lonely and friendless; she was often in trouble, sometimes for stealing watermelons and chickens, sometimes for stealing cars. By age 12, she was a foster child of **Maryann Wanatick** in New Mexico. Though Bacon felt loved, she missed her own mother and was still at sea; she ended up in reform school, the first of several times. Wrote Bacon:

> It was the first time in my life that I had a dress on. The dress was the kind with two big holes in front for your arms and it wrapped around and tied in the back. I used to lie on my cot in that stupid cell and count the blocks. There were 247 blocks up and 283 blocks wide. I used to watch the cockroaches go up the walls. You get schooled awful fast. I learned to lie and to steal and to cheat and to fight.

In Bacon's life, horses represented stability. She began riding in horse shows at age five, and at age nine she was racing quarter horses and Appaloosas on backwood bush tracks in Oklahoma, where girls were a rarity in the competition. "I had one horse that I used to tell all my problems to. At night I'd lie down in the stall and sleep on his neck." Reunited with her family, she ran away many times, always to a stable. "I cheated all the way through" high school. "I don't know why they ever passed me," she said. But "sometimes not a top stud produces a real runner," and it was the depth of her love of horses that gave her life its unexpected dimensions.

At age 16, Bacon saw the Walt Disney movie *The Horsemaster* while at the Porelock Vale Riding School in Somerset, England. Though the world of steeplechase racing described in the film was alien to her Western world of rodeos and quarterhorse racing, she became obsessed with acquiring steeplechase training, which involves jumping hedges, fences, and ditches in the course of a race. To earn money, she worked during the day as a lifeguard and rode in meets at night, did odd jobs at a country club, galloped racehorses in training from 5–8:30 AM at Porelock Vale, and even worked as a model and singer.

After a year of study in stable management, veterinary medicine, and steeplechase riding, she passed the horsemanship examination administered by the British government, and received a certificate as a British Horse Society Assistant. She returned to the U.S., where she was hired at the Grosse Pointe Hunt Club, outside Detroit, Michigan, to teach riding to wealthy socialites such as **Christina Ford**, of the Ford automobile family. In 1968, Bacon was galloping horses for Pete Maxwell, one of the country's top trainers, when she became reacquainted with Johnny Bacon, one of Maxwell's apprentice jockeys, whom she had known as a teenager in Oklahoma. Three weeks after their second meeting, the couple eloped to Canadian, Texas.

The following year, Bacon was pregnant with her first child when the U.S. racing world was changed forever. The Maryland Racing Commission had turned down the application for a jockey's license by ***Kathy Kusner**, who sued the commission on the basis of sexual discrimination, and in 1969, Judge Ernest A. Loveless ruled in Kusner's favor. As one woman followed another at the starting gate and sometimes crossed the finish line first, Bacon grew more eager to become a professional jockey in thoroughbred horseracing.

On March 4, 1969, she gave birth to a daughter, Susan Michaela; seven days later, she was back on horseback. Unfortunately, Suzy's birth had resulted in numerous stitches, internal and external, and Bacon was soon back in the hospital for painful restitching. In May, she received her license, ran her first race, and signed a three-year contract as a jockey for Pete Maxwell. Shortly after, she was thrown from a horse, hospitalized with a broken back, and spent four days paralyzed from the waist down. After six weeks of recovery, however, she was back on the track.

A fearless rider, Bacon worked as many tracks as she could, riding days in Cleveland and nights at Waterford Park, West Virginia, or days in Lexington, Kentucky, and nights at the Latonia Racetrack in nearby Florence. A good jockey has to have superior reflexes, split-second timing, and excellent nerve control, as the pressure of a race is intense. She has to be able to recognize not only the speed of the mount, but the pace of the competition as well. A good jockey knows not to exhaust her horse before the final stretch, and must be able to bob and weave, leading the animal in and out of small holes in the pack to find the opening to maneuver in front during the final stretch. By the end of 1969, even though she had not begun racing until May, Mary Bacon had ridden in three times as many races as any other female jockey in the country, with three times as many wins.

But her life was still troubled. Paul Corley Turner, a drifter who worked at a stables, became obsessed with Bacon; one day, he manhandled her agent and attacked her. When the attempted rape made the local news, Bacon found herself portrayed in a weekly tabloid as sex-starved. At this time, her marriage was also strained and would end in divorce.

Through all this Bacon seemed driven. In 1970, she became pregnant a second time but hid her condition and continued to race into her seventh month, while gaining only five pounds. The day of her son's birth, she was scheduled for five mounts but rode only three before she went into labor. Born two months premature, the baby lived only a few hours. Bacon was out of the hospital and had returned to riding when the stalker Turner was released after four months' imprisonment. In short order, he threatened to kill her. In 1972, he snuck into her motel room and fired at her directly, but the gun jammed. Arrested once more, he was sentenced to 12 years in prison.

In the next few years, Bacon, an attractive woman, promoted the Charlie line of cosmetics for Revlon. Glad for the publicity and the additional income, she saw both as a means of staying on horseback. In 1971, a race at Ellis Park in Owensboro, Kentucky, resulted in a concussion, a broken collarbone, contusions of the lung and several broken ribs. After 13 days, she slipped out of the hospital and went to the Latonia Racetrack, where she cut off her shoulder cast with a butcher knife and rode once more. The following September, she suffered another serious accident at Pitt Park in Pennsylvania. Thrown by her mount after it clipped the heels of another horse, she landed on her head and lay so still that she was thought to be dead. Held for a week in intensive care, she noticed after a few days that a nice young man stopped by every morning to inquire about her progress. When she asked who he was, her mother replied that he was the undertaker. Eleven days later, she was released from the hospital and advised to stay away from the track for awhile, but it was useless advice. In 1973, Bacon was voted the Most Courageous Athlete of the Year by the Philadelphia Sports Writer Association.

When she and jockey **Joan Phipps** won the Daily Double at New York's Aqueduct, they became the first women to do so. Although women had won the right to compete on thoroughbred tracks, it took some time before many rode on a daily basis, and Bacon was one of the first to ride as regularly as her male counterparts. But in her early 40s, Bacon learned she had cancer. As she grew progressively weaker she was able to ride less and grew despondent. In June 1991, she was 43 years old and knew she would never ride again when she took her own life in Fort Worth, Texas. Her body was cremated, and, according to her wishes, her ashes were scattered at the finish line at Belmont Park.

SOURCES:

"Bacon is Dead," in *Washington Post.* June 15, 1991, p. G7.

Blue, Adrianne. *Grace Under Pressure: The Emergence of Women in Sport.* London: Sidgwick & Jackson 1987.

"For the Record," in *Sports Illustrated.* Vol. 74, no. 24. June 24, 1991, p. 88.

Golden, Flora. *Women in Sports: Horseback Riding.* NY: Harvey House, 1978.

Haney, Lynn. *The Lady is a Jock.* NY: Dodd, Mead, 1973.

"Patient in Silks: Wind Her Up, She Talks," in *The New York Times Biographical Service.* July 1973, p. 1084.

Roach, Margaret. "Mary Bacon: Independent," in *The New York Times Biographical Service.* February 1977, p. 183.

Ryan, Joan. "Life Wasn't Living Without Riding," in *San Francisco Chronicle.* June 23, 1991, p. C1.

Schuster, Julie. "For Mary Bacon, 'Riding Was Living,'" in *Houston Post.* June 29, 1991, p. A25.

Karin L. Haag, freelance writer,
Athens, Georgia

Bacon, Peggy (1895–1987)

American artist and illustrator, much admired for the wit, charm and plainspoken honesty in her drypoint caricatures and satirical glimpses of New Yorkers. *Name variations: Peggy B. Brook (legally since 1920). Born Margaret Frances Bacon on May 2, 1895, in Ridgefield, Connecticut; died on January 4, 1987, in Kennebunk, Maine; daughter of Elizabeth (Chase) Bacon and Charles Roswell Bacon (both artists); graduated from Kent Place School, Summit, New Jersey, 1913; attended School of Applied Arts for Women, New York, 1913–14; New York School of Fine and Applied Arts, 1914–15; studied painting at Art Students' League, New York, 1915–20; studied painting under various instructors at Provincetown, Massachusetts, and Woodstock, New York; married Alexander Brook, in 1920 (divorced 1940); children: Belinda Bacon (b. 1920), Alexander "Sandy" Brook (b. 1922).*

Taught at Art Students League, New York (1935, 1949–51), School of the Corcoran Gallery of Art, Washington, D.C. (1942–44), Fieldston Ethical Cultural School, Bronx (1933–38), Moore College of Art, Philadelphia (1963–64), and other schools. Works are in the collections of Metropolitan Museum of Art, Whitney Museum of American Art, Museum of Modern Art, New York; Brooklyn Museum, Brooklyn; Art Institute of Chicago, Chicago, and many other museums and private collections.

Awards: bronze medal, Philadelphia Sesquicentennial Exposition, Department of Fine Arts (1926); John Simon Guggenheim Memorial Foundation fellowship (1934); National Academy of Arts and Letters grant (1944); named an Associate of the National Academy of Design (1947); first prize, Second Annual Exhibition of Contemporary American Drawings; American Artists Group Alan Dunn Prize from the Society of American Graphic Artists at 36th Annual Exhibition (1952); Edgar Allan Poe Special Award for mystery novel, The Inward Eye *by the Mystery Writers of America (1953); American Artists Prize, Butler Institute (Youngstown, Ohio, 1955); elected to the National Institute of Arts and Letters (1956); certificate of merit, National Academy of Design (1963); honorary degree of DFA, Moore College of Art, Temple University, Philadelphia (1964); honorary degree, Nasson College, Springvale, Maine (1975); gold medal, American Academy and Institute of Arts and Letters (1980).*

Selected publications—author-illustrator: The True Philosopher and Other Cat Tales, Funerealities, The Lion-Hearted King, Mercy and the Mouse, The Ballad of Tangle Street, The Terrible Nuisance and Other Tales, Animosities, Mischief in Mayfield, Off With Their Heads!, Cat-Calls, The Mystery at East Hatchett, Starting from Scratch, The Inward Eye, The Good American Witch, The Oddity, The Ghost of Opalina, *and* The Magic Touch. *Illustrator: T. Robinson's* Buttons *(Viking, 1938); T.S. Eliot's* The Hollow Men *(1925); Carl Sandberg's* Rootabaga Country *(1929), and many others; illustrations published in* The New Yorker, Vanity Fair, Town and Country, *among others.*

Peggy Bacon

An author, illustrator, poet, and writer, Peggy Bacon was most well known for her satirical, though affectionate, caricatures of the famous and not-so-famous in and around New York, including some of Manhattan's toughest alley cats. By the time she published *Off With Their Heads* in 1934, she had gained a reputation as a sharp wit, publishing her illustrations in such popular magazines as *The New Yorker*, *Vanity Fair*, and *Town and Country.* But Bacon could just as easily turn her pen on herself. Consider this self-description in that 1934 book:

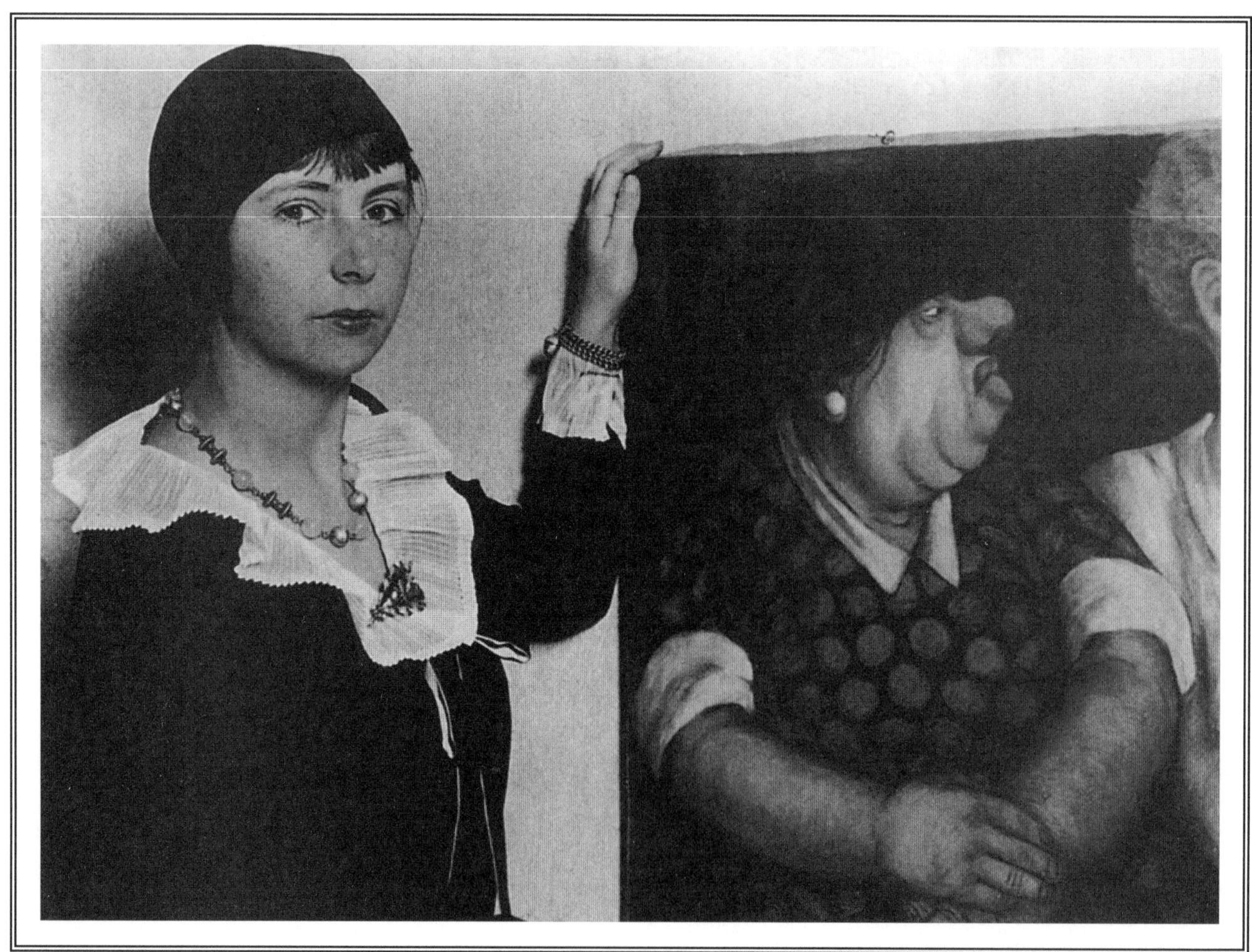

> Pin head, parsimoniously covered with thin dark hair, on a short dumpy body. Small features, prominent nose, chipmunk teeth and no chin, conveying the sharp, weak look of a little rodent. Absent-minded eyes with a half glimmer of observation. Prim, critical mouth and faint coloring. Personality lifeless, retiring, snippy, quietly egotistical. Lacks vigor and sparkle.

One writer felt that Bacon put forth this unflattering self-portrait "purely in self defense—a weapon of words to ward off potential howls of protest from others described in the book." By 1935, she no longer did scathing caricatures because of the reaction of those depicted; she was not comfortable causing discomfort to others. "I couldn't stand getting under people's skins," she told an interviewer in 1943, "the caricatures made them smart so."

Born the daughter of two artists on May 2, 1895, in Ridgefield, Connecticut, Peggy Bacon enjoyed a childhood of imaginative and varied experiences. Her father Charles Roswell Bacon was a painter of landscapes, figures and murals, having studied in New York, Paris, and Giverny, France. Her mother **Elizabeth Chase Bacon,** who met her husband while studying at the Art Students League in New York, was a painter of miniatures. Peggy was raised as an only child; her two younger brothers died in infancy. Neither parent taught Bacon to paint but provided the materials and experiences to foster her talent. According to family lore, Peggy began to draw at 18 months, before she was able to talk. Early on, she included illustrations and drawings with her poems and letters to her family, foreshadowing the descriptive imagery and reportorial style associated with her mature work.

As the child of working artists who were forever searching for new subjects to paint, Bacon traveled a great deal in her early years. Her family lived in Nassau, Bahamas, during the winter of 1902–03, when it was still a lush, unspoiled tropical island. From Nassau, the Bacons traveled to New Hampshire for the summer, where Peggy met and was encouraged in her art by ❧▸ **Lucia Fairchild Fuller,** a noted artist of that time. Bacon's father was a lover of all things French and returned there with his family in 1904 to live for two years at Montreuil-Sur-Mer. At this time, Peggy attended a French school, traveled briefly to London, and sketched. In 1909, back in America, she attended boarding school at Kent Place School in Summit, New Jersey, while her parents lived and worked in New York City. Bacon excelled in French, Latin, and Greek, and creative writing.

In February 1913, she attended the Armory Show in New York City with her father. This exhibit was a turning point in American art and the public's initial rejection of the contemporary styles was astounding. Both Bacons enjoyed the work of the Impressionists but were baffled by some of the other paintings and sculptures. Neither felt the "moderns" had much to offer. As time passed, Bacon's work would take a contemporary turn in style, becoming far more abstract in line and color.

That June, Bacon was accepted at Smith College in Massachusetts where she planned to continue her classical studies; later that summer, however, she decided she would rather follow her compulsion to study art. Writes biographer **Roberta Tarbell:** "Her parents wept; as artists themselves they understood the hardships that she would face." Bacon started her higher education at the School for Applied Arts for Women in New York. Shortly thereafter, on October 9, depressed by the lack of patrons and the dearth of critical attention to his paintings, Charles Bacon killed himself in his studio. It took courage for Peggy to return to her art studies, but in November she reappeared in her classes, her expenses paid by friends of the family.

In 1914–15, Bacon studied life drawing with George Graecen and illustration with Howard Giles at the New York School of Fine and Applied Arts (later known as the Parson's School of Design). During the summer of 1914, she also studied oil painting with the artist Jonas Lie in Port Jefferson, Long Island. Though Lie commented on her rapid progress, pleasing de-

❧▸ Fuller, Lucia Fairchild (1870–1924)

American artist. *Name variations: Mrs. Henry Brown Fuller. Born Lucia Fairchild in 1870; died in 1924; grew up in Madison, Wisconsin; attended Cowles Art School in Boston, studying under Dennis Bunker; studied in New York with William Merritt Chase and H. Siddons Mowbray; married Henry Brown Fuller (an artist), in 1893 (separated); children: two.*

Known for her talent and originality, Lucia Fairchild Fuller helped rekindle the dying art of miniature painting around the turn of the century, a medium suffering from the advent of photography. In 1899, she co-founded the American Society of Miniature Painters, along with William Baer, I.A. Josephi, and **Laura Coombs Hill.** Fuller had also created a mural for the Woman's Building of the World's Columbian Exposition in Chicago in 1893.

Illustration by Peggy Bacon from Rootabaga Country *by Carl Sandburg.*

signs, and "luscious colors," she destroyed these oils and none survive. That fall, Bacon worked in gouache and tempera (water-based painting mediums) in a private class with Lie in New York. The following year, Lie sponsored her first one-woman show, which sold out, and would finance her first year of study at the Art Students League in 1915–16.

Bacon spent part of the next three summers in Provincetown, Massachusetts, a well-known summer art colony, studying painting with

Charles Hawthorne, and B.J.O. Norfeldt. She was enthusiastic about Norfeldt's work, even though she, like most people, were still not thrilled with the "moderns." She was stimulated by the presence of older and well-established artists at the colony, such as Marsden Hartley and Charles Demuth, and attended performances of the newly formed Provincetown Players, initiated by Eugene O'Neill, ***Edna St. Vincent Millay**, John Reed and ***Louise Bryant**. In 1917, Bacon studied landscape painting with E. Ambrose Webster and became acquainted with the works of Monet, an artist who greatly influenced her father but whose work she found "flat, uninteresting, and out of date." She thought Manet and Degas, however, were "modern in spirit."

A student at the Art Students League from October 1915 through May 1920, Bacon studied with many of America's foremost artists of the 20th century: George Bellows, John Sloan, Max Weber, and Kenneth Hayes Miller. Her drypoint of 1918, *The Bellows Class* (Guild Hall collection, East Hampton, New York), shows a sympathy with the avant-garde of the New York art world, through her use of physical distortion of figures, and large, flat areas of light and dark. Though she preferred caricatures to standard portrait painting, Bellows' portraiture class focused her attention; she found the art form in harmony with her own temperament and pursued it for over 20 years. John Sloan's influence was in life drawing, sketches, and composition. Since her reporting style and candid humor was similar to Sloan's philosophy, she was enthusiastic about his work and his teaching. Several of her drypoint prints are scenes of his classes, such as *John Sloan's Lecture (Guild Hall)* and *John Sloan's Night Class*.

Back then, printmaking was not being taught at the Art Students League, so Bacon taught herself the drypoint technique, using a heavy steel needle to cut a line into a zinc plate which, when inked, makes duplicate prints. She and another student used an old press in one of the drawing studios and made prints, working the press together. This medium became the primary expression of her ideas. In 1920–21, she took a class in etching in order to have access to the printing presses, primarily working alone, with occasional critiques by faculty members.

In 1919, Bacon's drypoints had been exhibited in two national shows and reproduced for the first time in *World Magazine*. A Boston publisher, Four Seas, printed her first book *The True Philosopher and other Cat Tales*, which she had written in 1915 while sick with the measles. Though the majority of her training was in painting, her drypoints had been published, exhibited, and were recognized more often. Bacon had discovered that her best arena was in the humorous representation of human interaction. She told Tarbell that her ambition was to show what the world looked like around her, a goal realized as early as 1920.

In 1918, Peggy Bacon had met her future husband, Alexander Brook, in the lunchroom of the Art Students League, the scene of many of her early prints. They married in New York in early 1920 and left for England that August, living for the next nine months in Chelsea, London. Their first child Belinda was born in December of 1920. The following spring, the couple traveled to Paris with friends and spent their time in galleries and museums, but neither of their styles seemed to be changed by the modern art they saw there. Bacon found she could not work as well in Europe, as her work needed American friends and subject matter to give it life. She wrote to her family that she was looking forward to returning home to paint but, in reality, did not paint again for over 30 years. Her husband, who was a painter with a developed sense of color and form, was highly critical of her painting. Since her drypoint technique was so successful, she stuck with it and continued to create and publish more artwork. A notable print from this period is *The Promenade Deck*, the result of various sketches made on board the S.S. *New Amsterdam*, drawings of "people who amused her with their individual ways." Her composition began with curving lines that outlined the 40 people, including her husband and herself on deck, then areas of fabric patterns were placed in the interior spaces, resulting in flattened figures that are less angular than in her earlier work. The print was purchased in 1924 by the *New Republic* for a subscriber promotion.

The Brooks family returned from Europe to a farm outside Woodstock, New York, purchased for them by Bacon's mother, but the distance to the village and the lack of childcare prevented Peggy from associating with the local artists until an automobile allowed more freedom of movement. The art community in Woodstock was large and diverse, and both Bacon and her husband were active in showing their work in the town's galleries; they were also the subject of monographs published by William Murrell in his Younger Artists series in 1922. That year, they moved into the town where their second child Alexander was born.

In 1924, the family moved to New York, where Peggy had several one-woman shows over the next two years. She was then writing and publishing poems and fine line-drawings with a dreamlike quality, the most noted being *Funerealities* in 1925. She also began to publish stories for children, building on the storytelling tradition gleaned from her father. Among these were *The Lion-hearted Kitten* (1927) and *The Ballad of Tangle Street* (1929). For many years, Bacon was one of the foremost American illustrators, not only of children's literature, but also for adult magazines such as *Vanity Fair* and *The New Yorker*. Her work included groups of people involved in daily life as it had while she was in school, but now the compositions had more open space and were more softly drawn satirical interpretations. In the summer of 1926, the family purchased a home in Westchester County, New York, where they spent summers until 1937. Her work of this period often depicted friends in their homes and gatherings of artists, such as *A Few Ideas* (1927).

In 1928, Bacon began to make lithographs, using a technique of lithograph pencil on specially coated paper that is transferred to a zinc plate, inked and printed. These transfer lithos do not usually have the texture or rich tone of a lithograph drawn directly on stone, but her drawings retained their witty character. According to Tarbell, "The cat she shows in *Lunch No. 1-Hors D'Oeuvres*, 1928, is one of the funniest felines in the history of art—it evokes the spontaneous amusement that accompanies Peggy Bacon's best works." Bacon also made etchings, a technique employing a fine line that is etched into the surface of a metal plate using an acid bath, inking the plate and printing. Her etching, *Peter Platt Printing* (1929), shows a sensitive modulated line with a narrow range of values. Each December, Bacon would display her work in the *American Printmakers* Exhibit in New York.

Both professionally successful, Bacon and Brook were not affected financially by the Depression of the '20s. Bacon had household help and her children attended private school. In 1931, Bacon traveled to Europe with her husband who was awarded a Guggenheim Traveling Fellowship, enabling them to spend weeks in the vast museums studying masterworks. Her drypoint and lithograph, both entitled *Aesthetic Pleasure*, published in 1936 (Guild Hall), poke fun at American tourists in a European gallery; even in Europe, Bacon's arena was the American view. From 1933 to 1935, she taught children drawing and composition at one of the most progressive schools in the country, the Fieldston Ethical Cultural School in the Bronx, New York.

From 1927 to 1945, Bacon worked in pastel, her first foray into color since her painting days as a student. She felt that pastel was a natural extension of her drawing and printmaking, enabling her to use color without having to deal with a totally different medium. She did not follow the techniques of those pastellists she considered the greatest, such as Degas, but began working in neutral colors to emphasize the character of the portrait rather than the beauty. She progressed to some monochromatic themes, working from one color-range only. Her group of 100 caricatures done between 1927 and 1934 are "unique in American art," writes Tarbell, "representing the highest level of her brilliant combination of penetrating and devastating wit and fine draftsmanship." Between 1919 and 1966, Peggy Bacon illustrated more than 60 books, 17 of which she wrote herself.

In 1934, a John Simon Guggenheim fellowship resulted in 39 satirical portraits in black-and-white pastel of artists, politicians, and notables in the news, accompanied by written vignettes. *Off With Their Heads*, her best-known publication, established her reputation as America's leading caricaturist. Bacon felt that a successful caricature "heightens and intensifies to the point of absurdity all the subject's most striking attributes; . . . a comic interpretation of a person not only recognizable to those familiar with the subject but also convincing to those who are not."

After 1937, Bacon began to do genre pictures in pastel. Divided into four areas, the 60 scenes include *Manhattan Genre* (scenes of New York), *Manhattan Cats*, *Life on the Maine Coast*, and *Summer Folks, Provincetown*. The portraits of scrawny *Manhattan Cats* are some of Bacon's finest and most original works, but the scenes are soft anecdotes, not the biting satire of her pastel portraits. As popular as her portraits were, these pastel drawings may be her most important contribution to the history of American art.

After Bacon and Brook separated in 1938 and divorced in 1940, she began to spend her summers in Maine or at Cape Cod. She taught more extensively than she had in the past, at such schools as the Art Students League, Temple University in Philadelphia, and the Corcoran Gallery in Washington, D.C. She exhibited less often but had a major retrospective of her work staged by The Associated American Artists in

1942, called *Pens and Needles*, a title that Bacon truly felt "identified the biting and subtle innuendoes of her work, in which she poked fun for a quarter of a century at her friends, herself, and the great mass of American men and women."

Abandoning drypoint and prints, Bacon returned to painting in the 1950s and limited herself to painting after 1955. In 1960, she was honored by the American Academy and Institute of Arts and Letters with their gold medal in recognition, said *The New York Times*, of "her long and impressive career as a graphic artist and illustrator." She also found a new venue. Her book *The Inward Eye*, a highly successful mystery novel, received the Edgar Allan Poe Mystery Award in 1953.

In later years, Bacon's work moved to landscapes and abstractions of familiar scenes. Laughter was no longer a primary goal, though many humorous details remained. The paintings have a quality of fantasy, as can be seen in both *The Wraith* (1961), a depiction of an apparition in a cemetery, and *A Quiet Street* (1971), a street scene where the few figures have no interaction. In 1975, the artist was recognized with a yearlong retrospective exhibit, *Peggy Bacon: Personalities and Places*, at the Smithsonian Institution National Collection of Fine Arts in Washington, D.C.

In 1961, Bacon had moved to Cape Porpoise, Maine, to be closer to her son, an editor and owner of a newspaper in Kennebunk. Late in her life, though nearly blind, she had continued to paint in a well-lit room during the day, using a magnifying glass. "It was so natural to her it was like breathing," noted Tarbell. Peggy Bacon died, age 91, on January 4, 1987, in Kennebunk, Maine.

SOURCES:

Murrell, William, ed. *Peggy Bacon* (Young Artists Series) Woodstock, NY: William M. Fisher, 1922.

The New York Times (obituary). January 7, 1987.

"Peggy Bacon," in *Current Biography*, 1987. NY: H.W. Wilson, 1988.

Tarbell, Roberta K. *Peggy Bacon: Personalities and Places.* Washington, D.C.: Smithsonian Institution Press, no. 6151, 1975.

COLLECTIONS:

Major holdings of prints with annotations by Alexander Brook in Guild Hall, East Hampton, New York.

Correspondence, papers and memorabilia located in the George Arents Research Library, Syracuse University, Syracuse, New York.

Peggy Bacon papers in the Archives of American Art, Smithsonian Institution; Peggy Bacon papers, letters and lists of work in the National Collection of Fine Arts, Smithsonian Institution, Washington, D.C.

Laurie Twist Binder, Library Media Specialist, Buffalo Public Schools, Buffalo, New York, and freelance graphic artist and illustrator

Badarzewski-Baranowska, Tekla (1834–1861)

***Polish composer known chiefly for her piece* The Maiden's Prayer.** *Born in Warsaw, Poland, in 1834; died in Warsaw on September 24, 1861.*

Tekla Badarzewski-Baranowska wrote one of the first musical pieces to sell on the international music market. Originally published in 1856, *The Maiden's Prayer* appeared throughout the world. By 1859, over 80 publishers had printed versions of the 22-year-old composer's work. This world bestseller appeared in over 140 editions and reprints, and hundreds of thousands of copies were printed. The work was transcribed for almost every instrument and even for full orchestra. *The Maiden's Prayer* was a popular rather than a classical work, a salon composition of a type common in the 19th century. Although Badarzewski-Baranowska wrote other works, she never duplicated her first success. Her career was cut short when she died at the young age of 27.

John Haag, Athens, Georgia

Baddeley, Angela (1904–1976)

English actress. *Born Madeleine Angela Clinton-Baddeley on July 4, 1904, in London, England; died in 1976; daughter of W.H. Clinton-Baddeley and Louise (Bourdin) Clinton-Baddeley; sister of actress* ****Hermione Baddeley*** *(1906–1986); married Stephen Kerr Thomas (divorced); married Glen Byam Shaw.*

Angela Baddeley made her stage debut at the Old Vic on November 22, 1915, as the little Duke of York in *Richard III*. A popular stage actress in England, Baddeley frequently appeared as Jenny Diver in *The Beggar's Opera* during a successful three-year run (1920–23). She also played Anne Boleyn in ***Sybil Thorndike**'s revival of *Henry VIII* (1925); the title role in *Marigold* (1927); the title role in *Sadie Dupont* (1928); Phyllis Richmond in *Thunder on the Left* (1928); Phoebe in *Quality Street* (1929); Lady Teazle in *The School for Scandal* (1929); Mary Barker in *To Account Rendered* (1931); Lisa de Montorio in *The Love Pirate* (1932); Jennie Warwick in *Night of the Garter* (1932); Sylvette in *The Fantasticks* (1933); Schatze in *The Greeks Had a Word for It* (1934); Olivia Grayne in *Night Must Fall* (1935); Elizabeth Bennett in *Pride and Prejudice* (1936); Lady Anne in *Richard III* at the Old Vic (1937); Natasha in *Three Sisters* (1938); Grace Fenning in *Dear Octopus* (1938); Cattrin in *The Light of Heart* (1940); Miss Prue in *Love for Love* (1943); Catherine Winslow in *The*

Hermione Baddeley

Winslow Boy (1946); Constance in *The Mad Woman of Chaillot* (1951); Mae Peterson in *Bye Bye Birdie* (1961); Madame Ranevsky in *The Cherry Orchard* (1965); Zinaida Savishna in *Ivanov* (1965).

Baddeley made her U.S. stage debut in *Night Must Fall* at the **Ethel Barrymore* Theater on September 28, 1936. She was also a member of the Old Vic Company (1949–50), and the Shakespeare Memorial Theatre Company at Stratford-on-Avon (1955, 1958, 1959). Her British television appearances included "Play of the Week" and "Armchair Theatre." She also played Mrs. Bridges, the cook, in the highly successful British television production "Upstairs, Downstairs." Her movies include: *The Speckled Band* (1931), *Arms and the Man* (1932), *The Ghost Train* (1932), *The Safe* (1932), *Those Were the Days* (1934), *The Citadel* (1938), *Quartet* (1948), *Zoo Baby* (1957), and *Tom Jones* (1963).

Baddeley, Hermione (1906–1986)

English actress. *Born Hermione Clinton-Baddeley on November 13, 1906, in Broseley, Shropshire, Eng-*

*land; died in 1986; daughter of W.H. Clinton-Baddeley and Louise (Bourdin) Clinton-Baddeley; sister of actress *****Angela Baddeley** *(1904–1976); educated privately; married David Tennant (divorced); married Captain J.H. Willis.*

Hermione Baddeley began acting at age six. At age twelve, on March 11, 1918, she made her London debut as Le Nègre in *La Boîte à Joujoux* at the Court Theatre, but it was not until 1923 that she scored her first notable success as Florrie Small in *The Likes of Her* at the St. Martin's Theatre. In 1959, Baddeley made her New York debut at the Booth Theater when she took over the part of Helen in **Shelagh Delaney**'s *A Taste of Honey*. That same year, Baddeley was nominated for an Oscar for her best supporting performance in *Room at the Top*. On television, she appeared in the series "The Good Life" (1971) and played the part of Mrs. Naugatuck, the tart-tongued housekeeper in the series "Maude" (1974–77). Her films include *A Daughter in Revolt* (1926), *The Guns of Loos* (1928), *Caste* (1930), *Royal Cavalcade* (1935), *Kipps* (1941), *It Always Rains on Sunday* (1947), *Brighton Rock* (*Young Scarface*, 1947), *Quartet* (1948), *No Room at the Inn* (1948), *Dear Mr. Prohack* (1949), *Passport to Pimlico* (1949), *The Woman in Question* (1950), Mrs. Cratchit in *Scrooge* (*A Christmas Carol*, 1951), *Tom Brown's School Days* (1951), *Time Gentlemen Please* (1952), *The Pickwick Papers* (1952), *The Belles of St. Trinian's* (1954), *Room at the Top* (1959), *Expresso Bongo* (1959), *Midnight Lace* (1960), *The Unsinkable Molly Brown* (1964), *Mary Poppins* (1964), *Harlow* (1964), *Marriage on the Rocks* (1965), *Do Not Disturb* (1965), *The Happiest Millionaire* (1967), *The Black Windmill* (1974), *C.H.O.M.P.S.* (1979), *There Goes the Bride* (1980), and voiceover for *The Secret of Nimh* (1982).

Baden, grand duchess of.

See Stephanie de Beauharnais (1789–1860).
See Sophia of Sweden (1801–1865).
See Louise of Baden (1838–1923).
See Margaret of Baden (b. 1932).

Baden, margravine of.

See Marie Louise (1879–1948).
See Theodora Oldenburg (1906–1969).

Baden, princess of.

See Amalie of Hesse-Darmstadt (1754–1832).
See Elizabeth of Wurttemberg (1802–1864).
See Louise of Baden (1811–1854).

Baden-Durlach, margravine of.

See Christina Casimir.
See Augusta Maria of Holstein-Gottorp (1649–1728).

Baden-Powell, Agnes (1858–1945).

See Baden-Powell, Olave for sidebar.

Baden-Powell, Olave (1889–1977)

Organizer of the English Girl Guides and leader of the international Girl Scout movement. *Born Olave St. Clair Soames in Chesterfield, Derbyshire, England, on February 22, 1889; died in 1977; youngest daughter of Harold Soames; married Sir Robert Stephenson Smyth Baden-Powell (founder of the Boy Scout movement and chief scout, who was made a baronet, and, in 1929, elevated to the peerage as the first Baron Baden-Powell of Gilwell), in 1912; children: Peter (b. 1913);* ***Heather Baden-Powell*** *(b. 1915);* ***Betty Baden-Powell*** *(b. 1917).*

Delaney, Shelagh. See Littlewood, Joan for sidebar.

The daughter of an independently wealthy world traveler and student of Norwegian history, Olave (feminine of Olaf) St. Clair Soames spent her childhood in 17 different homes. With the exception of violin lessons, her formal education ended at the age of 12. After her society debut, in 1912, she accompanied her father on a trip to the West Indies. Aboard ship, she met Sir Robert Baden-Powell, 32 years her senior, who was known as "the Scout Man" for founding of the Boy Scout movement. According to a letter to her mother, he was "the only interesting person on board." The couple married in the fall of that year. Settling in Sussex, England, Baden-Powell tended to her growing family and helped her husband with the burgeoning Scout movement. During World War I, she also ran a YMCA canteen in Calais.

Around 1909, in response to the large number of young girls who wanted to be scouts, Sir Robert had approved a Scout movement for girls which he put in the hands of his sister **Agnes Baden-Powell**. While Agnes organized the Girl Guides in England, ***Juliette Gordon Low** established the Girl Scouts in the United States. In 1916, Olave Baden-Powell was asked by the Girl Guide Association to become guide commissioner of Sussex. Making the most of an outgoing, charismatic personality, she organized, publicized, and solicited leadership for the new movement. Through letters and personal visits, she encouraged involvement, stressing that "training girls to be good citizens was important war work." With the Boy Scout organization as a model, she set up local committees in each town

See sidebar on the following page

Baden-Powell, Agnes (1858–1945)

English co-founder of the Girl Guides. *Born in 1858; died in 1945; daughter of Baden Powell (1796–1860, Savilian professor of geometry, known for his research on optics and radiation); sister of George Smyth Baden-Powell (1847–1898, Conservative MP), and Robert Stephenson Smyth, 1st baron Baden-Powell (1857–1941).*

to encourage organization. In the various districts, she selected commissioners to direct activities and provide a liaison with headquarters. Becoming chief commissioner in 1917, she extended the network of organizations to every county in Great Britain, as well as overseas, and brought the units together in a strong unified society. Using her experience as a commissioner, in 1917 she published *Training Girls as Guides*, a manual for leaders.

Baden-Powell was unanimously elected permanent chief guide in 1918. She began plans for an International Council which would function as an information center on the world Scouting movement, and as a means to further integrate the many groups. With the help and cooperation of colleagues abroad, the meeting of the first International Council was held in February 1920 with representatives from 20 nations. In July of that year, the Council organized an International Conference for the exchange of ideas at St. Hugh's College, Oxford. Leadership delegates from Belgium, Denmark, Italy, Poland, Sweden, the British dominion, Switzerland, and the United States were in attendance. This led to formulation of a World Association in 1926, with a permanent headquarters and staff. As a tribute to her leadership, Baden-Powell was made chief guide of the world at the 1930 World Conference.

Olave Baden-Powell

Another important aspect of the Scouting movement was the establishment of international camps, the first of which were held in Switzerland and Normandy. In 1924, 1,100 Guides and Girl Scouts—half from overseas—spent the summer camping at Foxlease, England. The girls from foreign countries were distributed among 30 groups of English girls, allowing all nationalities to mingle.

As chief guide and chief scout, the Baden-Powells became world travelers, making numerous journeys to visit their scattered troops. In 1919, they undertook a trip around the world, followed by two more in the '30s. They also arranged for several hundred leaders in their organizations to travel and observe the scouting movement in other countries; in 1933, they led a group on a good-will cruise of the Baltic ports, followed in 1934 by a trip to the Mediterranean region. Olave Baden-Powell documented her travels in two books, *Travelogues* and *Guide Links*.

Due to Sir Robert's failing health, the couple retired in 1938 to Kenya, East Africa. After her husband's death in 1941, Baden-Powell returned to England to lend her expertise to the World Bureau, headquartered in London. During World War II, both the Girl Guides and the Girl Scouts in Allied countries were involved in every aspect of the war effort, from selling bonds to working in hospitals and canteens. By 1946, the international Scouting movement had reached remote parts of Africa and even the minute island of Tristan da Cunha in the South Atlantic. During a visit to the United States, Baden-Powell called the growth "reinspired," and cited the movement as significant in promoting world peace and fellowship.

In 1932, Olave Baden-Powell was made a Dame of the Grand Cross of the Order of the British Empire. Her years of service brought countless other honors from many countries, including the Order of the White Rose from Finland and the Order of the Sun from Peru. In 1973, she published her autobiography, *Window on My Heart*. At the time of her death in 1977, the World Association of Girl Guides and Girl Scouts had 6.5 million members.

SOURCES:

Rothe Anna, ed. *Current Biography*, 1946. NY: H.W. Wilson, 1947.

SUGGESTED READING:

Baden-Powell, Olave St. Clair with Mary Drewery. *Window on My Heart* (autobiography), 1973.

Barbara Morgan, Melrose, Massachusetts

Badia, Baahissat el (1886–1918).

See Malak Hifni Nassif in entry titled "Egyptian Feminism."

Badiya, Bahithat al- (1886–1918).

See Malak Hifni Nassif in entry titled "Egyptian Feminism."

Badlesmere, Elizabeth (fl. 1315–1342)

***Countess of Northampton.** Flourished from 1315 to 1342; daughter of Bartholomew Badlesmere (d. 1322), Lord Badlesmere, and *__Margaret de Clare__ (fl. 1280–1322); married Edmund Mortimer (d. around 1331), 3rd baron of Wigmore; married William Bohun (c. 1312–1360), 1st earl of Northampton; children: (first marriage) Roger Mortimer (1328–1359), 2nd earl of March; (second marriage) *__Elizabeth Fitzalan__ (d. 1385); Humphrey Bohun (1342–1372), earl of Hereford, Essex, and Northampton.*

Badlesmere, Lady (fl. 1280–1322).

See Siege Warfare and Women for sidebar on Margaret de Clare.

Badlesmere, Maud (d. 1366)

***Countess of Oxford.** Name variations: Maud de Vere. Born around 1312; died on May 24, 1366, in Earls Colne; interred at Earls Conne; daughter of Bartholomew Badlesmere (d. 1322), Lord Badlesmere, and *__Margaret de Clare__ (fl. 1280–1322); married John de Vere, 7th earl of Oxford, before March 27, 1336; children: John de Vere (b. around 1335); *__Margaret de Vere__; Thomas de Vere (c. 1337–1371), 8th earl of Oxford; Aubrey (c. 1340–1400), 10th earl of Oxford; Robert de Vere; Maud de Vere; Elizabeth de Vere.*

Baels, Liliane (1916—)

***Queen of the Belgians.** Name variations: Mary Liliane Baels. Born on November 28, 1916, in Highbury, London, England; became second wife of Leopold III, king of the Belgians (r. 1934–1951), on September 11, 1941; children: Alexandre (b. 1942); Marie Christine (b. 1951, who married Paul Druker); Marie Esmeralda (b. 1956).*

Baesinger, Barbara (d. 1497).

See Fugger, Barbara Baesinger.

Baffa, Sultana (d. 1603).

See Safiye Sultana in Reign of Women.

Bagenal, Mabel (c. 1571–1595)

***Irish noblewoman.** Born around 1571; died at Dungannon in December 1595; daughter of Marshal Bagenal, leader of the army in Ireland; sister of Henry Bagenal (c. 1556–1598); married Hugh O'Neill (1550–1616), 3rd Baron Dungannon and 2nd earl of Tyrone, in August 1591.*

When Henry Bagenal, marshal of the army in Ireland, refused to allow his 20-year-old sister Mabel to marry the twice-married Hugh O'Neill, she and the 41-year-old O'Neill defied him and eloped in August 1591. Henry then set out to prove that O'Neill was not legally severed from his first wife, whom O'Neill had divorced in 1574 (his second wife died in 1591). For two years, Henry held back Mabel's dowry left to her by her father. Early historians often made Mabel Bagenal the cause of ill will between O'Neill and Bagenal, calling her the "Helen" of the Elizabethan Bagenal wars, though this simplistic theory has been discredited. When O'Neill, in his own words, "affected two other gentlewomen," the marriage quickly disintegrated. Mabel left him and entered a complaint to the Council. When she died in December of 1595, O'Neill married his fourth wife **Catherine Magennis**.

Bagley, Sarah (b. 1806)

***American labor leader.** Born Sarah George Bagley in Meredith, New Hampshire, on April 29, 1806; died after 1847 (date, place, and cause of death unknown); daughter of Nathan (a farmer and entrepreneur) and Rhoda (Witham) Bagley.*

Entered the Hamilton Manufacturing Corporation as an operative (1837); was founder and president, the Lowell Female Reform League 1844–47); active in the Ten-Hour Day movement (1844–45); was founder and member, Lowell Union of Associationists (1844–47), vice-president (1846); organizer of the Lowell Industrial Reform Lyceum (1845); edited Voice of Industry *(1846); chosen delegate to the National Industrial Congress, Boston, and the National Reform Convention, Worcester (both 1846); served as superintendent of the Lowell telegraph office and became the first woman telegraph operator in U.S. (1846). Publications: several articles in* Lowell Offering, Factory Tracts, *and* Voice of Industry.

Sarah Bagley was born in Meredith, New Hampshire, on April 29, 1806, the daughter of Rhoda and Nathan Bagley, a farmer and small businessman. Educated in local schools, Sarah lived in the nearby towns of Candia and Laconia, New Hampshire, before heading for Lowell, Massachusetts, at age 31. When New England agriculture was in decline and the country was in the midst of a severe economic depression, she entered one of the weaving rooms of the Hamilton Manufacturing Company in the fall of 1837. The mill owners, known collectively as the Boston Associates, operated their mills in a paternalistic manner. At the time, it was most unusual for a woman to live outside of a family, potentially threatening her moral reputation. Therefore, the mill owners required all women workers to live in corporation boarding houses, obey a curfew, and attend church every Sunday. Despite these parameters and a 12-hour day, many women still found time to attend lectures, visit local libraries, and shop for the latest fashions—activities unavailable in the rural farm communities they had left behind. With the backing of the mill owners, the "mill girls," as they were called, even established their own newspaper, the *Lowell Offering*, in 1840. Sarah Bagley was a frequent contributor. Apparently, she was initially pleased with her life in Lowell, indicated by one of her pieces entitled "The Pleasures of Factory Life."

Yet, beginning in the early 1840s, there came a growing discontent with mill work as wages declined at the same time that speed-ups—increases in the pace of production—occurred. Simultaneously, women's boarding fees grew, and the number of women went from four to six, sometimes eight, per room. Many, including Bagley, could no longer find pleasure in factory life. As discontent turned into an organized movement, Sarah Bagley emerged as one of its most articulate leaders.

In December 1844, she founded the Lowell Female Labor Reform League which joined with the New England Workingmen's Association in demanding a ten-hour day. Having presented a petition with over 2,000 signatures, her own at the top, Bagley testified before the Massachusetts legislature in February 1845, citing her own declining health as an indication of the harsh conditions of factory life. Soon, she left her mill job and became a full-time organizer, helping to establish Female Labor Reform Leagues in Waltham and Fall River, Massachusetts, as well as in Dover, Manchester, and Nashua, New Hampshire. In print, Bagley attacked not only the mill owners but also those workers who appeared to cooperate with the paternalistic system. Particularly outraged by the pro-corporation stance of the *Lowell Offering*, she called it and its editor, ***Harriet Farley**, "a mouthpiece of the corporation."

Interest in the *Offering* dwindled in 1845 at the same time the much more radical *Voice of Industry* came to Lowell. Published by the New England Workingmen's Association, the *Voice* became the property of the Female Labor Reform League in March 1846, and for several months Bagley served as chief editor. Feeling that most of the lectures in Lowell were also sponsored by the mill owners, Bagley organized the Industrial Reform Lyceum in 1845. Topics included women's rights, abolitionism, and labor reform; speakers included Horace Greeley and William Lloyd Garrison. However, in spite of this increased awareness of labor's demands, the Massachusetts legislature turned down the mill workers' request for a ten-hour day. After that decision, in March 1846, the mill owners felt free to attack the ten-hour movement by accusing one of the male leaders of immoral behavior. Bagley, while not involved, was tainted by association and slowly moved out of the New England labor movement.

In 1846, Bagley briefly ran a dressmaking and millinery business with another woman in Lowell. She also took a job as a superintendent in Lowell's recently established telegraph office, thus becoming the first American woman telegrapher. No longer so involved with the cause of labor, Bagley devoted more of her time to the Lowell Union of Associationists, an organization based on the utopian social thought of Fournier. She had helped establish the Lowell chapter in 1844, and in 1846 she became its vice-president. Perhaps for financial reasons, Bagley returned to the weaving room at the Hamilton mill in 1848. After only five months in the mill, the now 42-year-old woman was called home to Laconia, New Hampshire, to help care for her father who was dying of typhus.

When Sarah Bagley left Lowell in 1848, she also left the historical record. Historians have found no trace of Bagley after her departure. Yet, in a few short years, she had established herself as an articulate advocate for the cause of labor reform. Her accomplishments are even more impressive given that, in her day, it was deemed inappropriate for women to speak in public, much less speak out against the power of the Boston Associates. Nonetheless, Sarah Bagley had accomplished the goal she expressed in the *Lowell Offering*: to show the world "that there is 'mind among the spindles,' but also to show that the minds here are not all spindles."

SOURCES:

Dublin, Thomas. *Women at Work: The Transformation of Work and Community in Lowell, Massachusetts, 1826–1860*. NY: Columbia University Press, 1979.

Selden, Bernice. *The Mill Girls: Lucy Larcom, Harriet Hanson Robinson, and Sarah G. Bagley*. NY: Atheneum, 1983.

Kathleen Banks Nutter, Department of History, University of Massachusetts at Amherst

Bagnold, Enid (1889–1981)

***English author and socialite whose versatile career encompassed the popular children's novel* National Velvet, *as well as the immensely successful play* The Chalk Garden.** *Name variations: Lady Jones; (pseudonym) "A Lady of Quality." Born Enid Algerine Bagnold on October 27, 1889, in Rochester, Kent, England; died in St. John's Wood, London, on March 31, 1981; daughter of Arthur Henry (a colonel in the Royal Engineers) and Ethel (Alger) Bagnold; tutored at home; attended Prior's Field, as well as finishing schools in Germany, Switzerland, and France; studied painting and drawing in London with British impressionist artist Walter Sickert; married Sir George Roderick Jones, on July 8, 1920; children: Laurian (b. 1921); Timothy Angus (b. 1924); Richard Bagnold (b. 1926); Dominick (b. 1930).*

Awards: Arts Theatre Prize, Fellow of the Royal Society of Literature (resigned 1979), Commander of the British Empire, American Academy of Arts and Letters silver medal.

Selected publications: A Diary Without Dates *(Heinemann, 1918);* The Sailing Ship and Other Poems *(Heinemann, 1918);* The Happy Foreigner *(Heinemann, 1920);* Serena Blandish *(Heinemann, 1924);* Alice and Thomas and Jane *(Heinemann, 1930); (translator)* Alexander of Asia *(Heinemann, 1935);* National Velvet *(Heinemann, 1935);* The Squire *(Heinemann, 1938);* The Loved and Envied *(Doubleday, 1950);* Two Plays: Lottie Dundas and Poor Judas *(Heinemann, 1951);* The Chinese Prime Minister *(Random House, 1964);* Enid Bagnold's Autobiography *(Heinemann, 1969);* Four Plays: The Chalk Garden, The Last Joke, The Chinese Prime Minister, Call Me Jacky *(Heinemann, 1970);* A Matter of Gravity *(Heinemann, 1978);* Letters to Frank Harris and Others *(Whittington Press and Heinemann, 1980);* Poems *(Whittington Press, 1978).*

"If you want to do creative, imaginative work—*never* interest yourself in politics, welfare, or the conditions in which people live. Only in their aspects, their hearts and minds, and *what they are.*" It was advice given to an awkward teenaged schoolgirl by the great Irish poet and playwright William Butler Yeats. Enid Bagnold never forgot Yeats' words, quoting them many years later in her autobiography. Hers was in fact to be a life filled with people—the gifted, the rich, the exotic, as well as her beloved family—and filled, of course, with writing. "I was not a born writer, but I was born a writer," she said with that hint of enigma which was to characterize much of her work.

Enid Algerine Bagnold's birthplace was Borstal Cottage, Rochester, Kent. The date was October 27, 1889. Her parents, married only ten months, were **Ethel Alger Bagnold** and Arthur Henry Bagnold, then an instructor at the School of Military Engineering, Chatham. Arthur was brilliant; Ethel was beautiful. Enid was proud of her father's distinguished military lineage; she never doubted his loyalty and love, but it was her mother who adored her without qualification.

Enid's brother Ralph was born when she was six years old. Bagnold felt that the baby—who would grow up to be a gifted engineer like their father—came too late for her. Her childhood world was bounded by "Daddy, Mummie and me" and by her own adventurous and daring nature.

The family moved often, following Arthur Bagnold's rising military career. Posted in a variety of locations around the south of Britain, they went out in 1889 to the most glamorous assignment of all. Lt. Colonel Bagnold became commanding of-

Enid Bagnold

ficer of the Royal Engineers in sun-drenched Kingston, Jamaica. "This was the first page of my life as someone who can 'see.' It was like a man idly staring at a field suddenly finding he had Picasso's eyes," Bagnold would later recall.

The family home for three magical years was Coldspring House, a coffee plantation high on a hill above the city of Kingston. It was a setting of exquisite beauty where Bagnold learned to ride, managed to escape almost all formal instruction from her governess, read very little—she would never be a great reader—but discovered that she liked to write poetry and began imagining herself in love. Colonel Bagnold, who disapproved of the poetry and flew into a rage when he discovered his daughter's love letters, was pacified only when Enid vehemently assured him that the lover was nonexistent. Otherwise the adoring parents seem not to have been greatly concerned about their daughter's unconventional education.

On the family's return to England, more definite steps were taken. Enid was sent for five years to Prior's Field, a small but growing girls' school whose headmistress was **Julia Arnold Huxley**, daughter of the famous headmaster Thomas Arnold of Rugby and mother of Aldous and Julian, who visited at Prior's Field often. For its day, Prior's Field was an unusually lenient school with a strong emphasis on art, literature, and theater. Bagnold was exceedingly happy there, a plump clown who struggled for attention and played a variety of audacious pranks which included keeping grass snakes in her desk and exploring the tile roofs of her dormitory by moonlight. To her intense delight, she won the school poetry prize and was taken by Julia Huxley, whom she adored, to London for her memorable encounter with Yeats. Bagnold was confirmed in the Church of England but was already beginning her lifelong rebellion against organized religion. Her silent prayer in church at this period was, so she reported later, "Give me fame."

At 17, with little academic accomplishment and her beloved Julia Huxley dead, Bagnold left Prior's Field. In an attempt to give their self-willed daughter some final polish, her parents sent her to the Continent—first to a finishing school in Switzerland where she was miserable and contemptuous of her dull-spirited classmates, then to Villa Leona in Paris where for a year she was once again blissfully happy. Her great love—this time not fictional but distant—was the dazzling actress ***Sarah Bernhardt**.

Still plump and awkward yet filled with a splendid vitality, Bagnold returned to England to her parents' home Warren Wood and was taken by her mother to the requisite provincial dances where, so it was hoped, she would find a husband. The project met with no success. Terrified by her first proposal of marriage and even more frightened by her first kiss, she fled. Despite her awkwardness, Bagnold had other dreams. She was beginning to write. A poem was published in the magazine *English Illustrated*, another in *New Age*. Her father equipped a Tower Room up a winding stair from his own dressing room where she could work in private. "Who wants to become a writer?" she would later ask. "And why? Because it's the answer to everything. To 'Why am I here?' It's the streaming reason for living."

Yet even the Tower Room did not offer enough freedom. At last, in 1912, Bagnold persuaded her reluctant father to let her take a flat in London with a new friend, a general's daughter named **Dolly Tylden**. Her allowance was to be £75, not enough to provide an affluent lifestyle but enough to make her far more comfortable than her new bohemian friends. The gifted and penniless young sculptor Henri Gaudier did a bust of her in clay, a striking portrait reflecting the strong personality of the sitter. The bust was later cast in bronze.

Bagnold took art lessons from the impressionist painter Walter Sickert, then turned to journalism, serving on Frank Harris' short-lived magazine *Home and Hearth* for which she recklessly turned out reams of both original and plagiarized copy. Harris' second magazine *Modern Society* ended in disaster, with Harris discredited and briefly jailed. Disillusioned, Bagnold fled home to her relieved parents and to her Tower Room. In 1917, her first book *The Sailing Ship and Other Poems* was published. World War I brought its own tragic opportunities. Enid joined the Red Cross and served as a nurse's aide in the Royal Herbert Hospital to which the wounded were brought from the battlefields of France. *A Diary Without Dates*, published in 1918, recounted that experience in a fresh, impressionistic style. Its frankness caused Bagnold's dismissal from the hospital for "breaching military discipline." She joined a corps of ambulance drivers in France and from this experience drew material for *The Happy Foreigner*, her first novel, published in 1920. Bagnold's writing was always closely linked to events and people in her life. She is even said to have used real life names for her characters in first drafts of her novels, changing only in final drafts to the fictional names.

Her love affair with Prince Antoine Bibesco, Rumanian diplomat and friend of Proust, set new and demanding literary standards for her. Bibesco would call Bagnold's novel *Serena Blandish*, published in 1924, his "spiritual child." It was, however, her marriage in 1920 to Sir Roderick Jones, head of the great news agency Reuter, which brought her into a glittering world of wealth and power. The marriage also brought her motherhood which would prove to be an immensely important aspect of her life. Within six years, she gave birth to a daughter Laurian and three sons, Timothy, Richard, and Dominick. These children, about whom she kept extensive records, would scarcely be mentioned in her autobiography. The omission was not the result of indifference but rather, it would seem, respect for their privacy.

In 1930, Heinemann published *Alice and Thomas and Jane*, a children's book based on the activities of the Jones family at North End House, their home in the seaside village of Rottingdean. In 1935, *Alexander of Asia*, a translation of *Alexandre Asiatique* by ***Marthe Bibesco** appeared, as well as Bagnold's great popular success, *National Velvet*, a traditional narrative reflecting the author's and her children's love of horses. In the novel, Velvet, daughter of a small-town butcher, trains a piebald horse and wins the Grand National with him, an award withdrawn when the rider is discovered to be a girl. The characters were closely patterned after citizens of Rottingdean and caused some resentment in the village. Elsewhere, the book was highly acclaimed, and Hollywood producers jockeyed for movie rights. In the end, Paramount won out and cast a beautiful 13-year-old who had the appropriate English accent and loved horses. With *National Velvet*, **Elizabeth Taylor** became a star. Bagnold sold the rights for an initial fixed sum and earned no royalties from the film's success.

Writing of situations so close to her own experience, Bagnold obeyed Yeats' dictum never to write about politics or public life. For a time, she worked enthusiastically for the Babies Club, the first private welfare clinic in London, but otherwise never took part in organized charity despite much personal generosity. Her brief schoolgirl flirtation with the cause of women's suffrage

From the movie National Velvet, *starring Elizabeth Taylor and Mickey Rooney, 1944.*

faded quickly. Now, in 1938, she made her only—and unfortunate—foray into the world of public affairs. In an article published by Reuter, she lauded Hitler, finding Germany a vibrant and healthy contrast to Europe's pallid Western democracies. She was not, however, interned with Sir Oswald Mosley and other leading Nazi sympathizers when World War II broke out, and she spent the war years caring for her homes and family in London and Rottingdean. One son, Timothy, lost a leg fighting in Italy. She admitted after the war that there were "great gaps" in her intelligence, but she seems never to have apologized explicitly for her Nazi leanings.

I shall continue to explore—the *astonishment* of living!

—Enid Bagnold, *The Chalk Garden*

Bagnold wrote one more novel, *The Loved and the Envied*, first published in 1950, with a heroine based on her great friend Lady **Diana Duff Cooper**. With this single exception, Bagnold's postwar career was devoted to the theater. There she met with both disaster and success, and there she fought ferociously to preserve the integrity of her own artistic vision. She also made dear and lasting friends, **Irene Selznick**, Alfred Lunt, ***Lynn Fontanne**, and ***Katharine Hepburn** among them.

Both *Dottie Dundass*, an English murder mystery play which opened in California in 1941, and *Poor Judas*, 1946, explore the lives of failed artists with central characters that are unsympathetic. Both plays also had a limited success. Bagnold's skill with language was perhaps their major strength. *Gertie*, later renamed *The Little Idiot*, followed in 1951. Bagnold, in a humorous article printed in the *Atlantic Monthly* later that year, called the play "a flop."

Cooper, Diana Duff (1892–1986)

English actress. *Name variations: Lady Diana Duff Cooper; Lady Duff Cooper; Lady Diana Manners. Born in 1892; died in 1986; daughter of the 8th duke of Rutland; sister of Lady* ***Violet Charteris****; married Alfred Duff Cooper (1890–1954), 1st viscount Norwich (a politician, diplomat, and author), in 1919.*

As an actress, Diana, Lady Duff Cooper, used the stage name of Lady Diana Manners. She appeared as the madonna in *The Miracle*, her most notable role.

Now, however, came her greatest theatrical success. With the creative help of Irene Selznick, Bagnold wrote *The Chalk Garden*, which was first produced by Selznick at the ***Ethel Barrymore** Theatre in New York in October 1955 and starred ***Siobhan McKenna** and ***Gladys Cooper**. The play met with instant critical acclaim and wide public acceptance. At its London opening in 1956, the critic for the London *Observer* declared, "On Wednesday night a wonder happened. The West End Theatre justified its existence." *The Chalk Garden* came directly from Bagnold's life. The setting is a manor house in a Sussex "village by the sea." Bagnold even insisted in the original production that the garden, seen upstage from the manor, be a replica of her own garden at Rottingdean. The characters are wealthy, upper class. The plot is slight, the characterization strong in a manner somewhat akin to that of the Russian playwright Anton Chekhov. Subtly comic, the play is notable for its elegant and expressive dialogue. It had a splendid filming in England in 1964 with a cast including **Hayley Mills**, ***Deborah Kerr**, and ***Edith Evans**.

In 1962, Roderick Jones died after a lengthy and distressing illness through which Bagnold nursed him faithfully. Theirs had been a long marriage, marked by loyalty and respect rather than strict fidelity, wrote Bagnold, but satisfying and necessary to both. Bagnold's life as a playwright continued, though never again with the dazzling success of *The Chalk Garden. The Last Joke*, produced two years before Sir Roderick's death, had a noted cast which included John Gielgud and Ralph Richardson, but received exceedingly bad reviews. *The Chinese Prime Minister*, the story of an aging actress coming to the end of her career, starring ***Margaret Leighton**, was a hit in New York in 1964. *Call Me Jacky* opened in 1968 at the Oxford Playhouse. A revised version, entitled *A Matter of Gravity*, produced in New York in 1976 starred Katharine Hepburn. The strong-willed actress and the strong-willed playwright liked and understood each other at first meeting, and Hepburn gave a dazzling performance. The 86-year-old Bagnold joyously attended opening night but returned to England to serious illness. A later hip replacement, performed when the procedure was still new, failed to relieve her pain, and during her remaining years she became strongly addicted to cocaine. She died on March 31, 1981, feeling, according to her biographer, that her children, not her written works, were her major achievement.

Enid Bagnold was a woman of immense energy, possessed of a true gift with words and a fierce loyalty to friends, family, and her own vision. *National Velvet*, *The Chalk Garden*, and *The Chinese Prime Minister* are likely to have their admirers for many years.

SOURCES:

Arkin, Marian. *Longmans' Anthology of World Literature by Women.* White Plains, NY: Longmans, 1989.

Bagnold, Enid. *Enid Bagnold's Autobiography.* Boston, MA: Little, Brown, 1969.

———. *Four Plays.* Boston, MA: Little, Brown, 1970.

Friedman, Lenemaja. *Enid Bagnold.* Boston, MA: Twayne, 1986.

Sebba, Anne. *Enid Bagnold.* NY: Taplinger, 1986.

COLLECTIONS:

The Henry W. and Albert G. Berg Collection of English and American Literature in the New York Public Library; The Beinecke Rare Book and Manuscript Library, Yale University, Connecticut; The Humanities Research Center, University of Texas at Austin; the McFarlin Library, University of Tulsa, Oklahoma; Department of Special Collections, University of California at Los Angeles.

RELATED MEDIA:

Chalk Garden, film produced in England by Universal, starring Deborah Kerr, Hayley Mills, and Edith Evans, directed by Ronald Neame, 1964.

National Velvet, film produced by MGM, starring Elizabeth Taylor and Mickey Rooney, screenplay by ***Helen Deutsch** and Theodore Reeves, 1944.

International Velvet (125 min.), screenplay by Bryan Forbes, starring **Tatum O'Neal** and Anthony Hopkins, MGM, 1978.

Margery Evernden,
Professor Emerita, English Department,
University of Pittsburgh, and freelance writer

Bagryana, Elisaveta (1893–1991)

Bulgarian poet who became her nation's most popular female poet in the post World War I era. *Name variations: Yelisaveta Bagryana, Elizaveta Bagriana; (real name) Elisaveta Lyubomirova Belcheva Likov. Born Elisaveta Lyubomirova Belcheva on April 16, 1893, in Sofia, Bulgaria; died on March 23, 1991; daughter of Maria and Lyubomir Belchev; educated at the University of Sofia; married Ivan Shapkarev, in 1919 (divorced 1925); married Aleksandur Likov, in 1944 (died 1954); children: (first marriage) son Lyubomir (b. 1919).*

Selected works: Vechnata i svyatata *(*The Eternal and the Sacred*) (1927);* Zvezda ne moryaka *(*The Mariner's Star*) (1932);* Pet zvezdi *(*Five Stars*) (1953);* Ot bryag do bryag *(*From Shore to Shore*) (1963);* Counterpoint *(1970).*

Bulgarian native Elisaveta Bagryana was a world traveler and romantic who claimed "a husband in every country." Renowned for her international affairs, she was in fact a woman whose greatest loves slipped away before they had had much time to mature. Projecting the image of an explorer, she was most praised in Bulgaria for her visions of her homeland, its traditions and its peasant life, and earned a place as one of Bulgaria's greatest poets.

Elisaveta was the firstborn of Maria and Lyubomir Belchev's seven children. The family moved among small villages following Lyubomir's work. Attending schools in Sliven and Veliko Turnovo, Elisaveta graduated from a Sofia high school in 1910. After one year teaching in the village of Autanè, she enrolled at the University of Sofia where she studied Slavonic philology. But Bagryana was filled with a passion for both reading and writing poetry, which had seen its beginnings in her adolescence.

> Can you restrain me then—I'm self-willed, wandering, free—true sister of the wind, of the water, of the wine, lured on to boundless spaces, to what cannot yet be reached, dreaming always of those pathways ungained and still untried—can you restrain me now?
>
> **—Elisaveta Bagryana, *Elements***

Poet Yordan Yovkov, who first encouraged her to publish, guided two of her poems to press in 1915. A noted perfectionist, Bagryana did not enjoy seeing her work in print and withdrew again to high school teaching. Her working-class roots have been credited for helping her develop a keen eye for realistic, traditional life, a vision which would later win her a faithful Bulgarian readership. In 1919, Bagryana married army captain Ivan Shapkarev, the son of Bulgaria's famous folklorist Kuyman Shapkarev; that same year, their own son was born. She started writing regularly and, in October of 1922, first published under the pseudonym Elisaveta Bagryana. The marriage soon soured. By the time of her divorce in April of 1925, her work was coming to national and European attention.

While Bagryana's popularity rose, her productivity decreased as she dedicated herself to writer Boyan Penev, her former teacher and constant companion, who was already married. After a three-year, open relationship, Penev died suddenly in June 1927. Bagryana resumed writing and before year's end released her first volume of poetry *The Eternal and the Sacred*, one of the most celebrated collections in Bulgarian poetry.

Ostensibly promoting her work, she fled to France and Italy for two years. On her return to

Bulgaria in 1929, she secured a lifetime arrangement with publisher Khemus which assured her a monthly stipend. Back to the rails, she crisscrossed the Continent for another decade before meeting and marrying publicist and critic Aleksandur Likov. During World War II, they were in their home in Sofia when a bomb demolished the house. Though both escaped, fire destroyed most of Bagryana's personal papers. After ten years of marriage, Likov died, and Bagryana once again took to traveling, roaming well into her 80s. She died at age 98 in 1973. Her work has been translated and published internationally.

SUGGESTED READING:

Bagryana, Elisaveta, and Peter Dinekov. *Ten Poems.* Sofia: Sofia Press, 1970.

Crista Martin, freelance writer, Boston, Massachusetts

Bahissat el Badia, or Bahithat al-Badiya (1886–1918).

See Malak Hifni Nassif in entry titled "Egyptian Feminism."

Bahr-Mildenburg, Anna (1872–1947)

Austrian soprano. *Born Anna Mildenburg on November 29, 1872, in Vienna, Austria; died on January 27, 1947, in Vienna; studied with Rosa Papier-Paumgartner; married Hermann Bahr (the writer), in 1909.*

Debuted in Hamburg as Brünnhilde in a performance conducted by Gustav Mahler (1895); began a relationship with Mahler; appeared with Mahler in Vienna (1898–1916) and at Bayreuth (1897–1914).

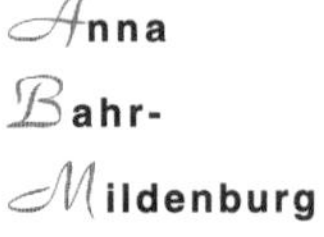

In the musical world, Anna Bahr-Mildenburg's name is inextricably linked with that of Gustav Mahler. Born in Vienna on November 29, 1872, she did not choose singing early and was already 19 when she began to study with **Rosa Papier-Paumgartner**, an influential teacher. Four years later, Anna auditioned for Pollini, the director of the Hamburg Opera. Recognizing her great talent, Pollini engaged her immediately, and she appeared shortly thereafter as Brünnhilde in *Die Walküre*, one of opera's most demanding roles. During rehearsals, Bahr-Mildenburg met Gustav Mahler, and he took over the direction of her career. Under his training, she became an outstanding dramatic soprano. During their years in Hamburg, Bahr-Mildenburg and Mahler had a passionate affair which ended by the time she first performed in Vienna in 1898. Their professional relationship continued, however, after Papier-Paumgartner suggested the former lovers renew their professional collaboration when Mahler became director of the Vienna Hofopera. Bahr-Mildenburg joined the peerless Mahler ensemble and was on the Hofopera staff until 1917, nearly 20 years.

Bahr-Mildenburg also appeared on the international stage. She was at Covent Garden in 1906 and would appear in the first London performance of Richard Strauss' *Elektra* in 1910. By 1907, some said her voice was in decline, perhaps because she had assumed the heaviest dramatic roles which taxed her capabilities. The sole recording which documents her talents was made in 1905; it demonstrates that hers was a powerful, penetrating voice with a superb attack. As a singer, she did not hold herself back, an approach which may explain the decline of her voice but also explains why Mahler and Pollini were so excited by their discovery of her.

SUGGESTED READING:

Bahr-Mildenburg, Anna, and Hermann Bahr. *Bayreuth and das Wagnertheater.* Leipzig, 1910.

John Haag, Athens, Georgia

Bai, Lakshmi (c. 1835–1858).

See Lakshmibai.

Bai, Putli (1929–1958).

See Phoolan Devi for sidebar.

Bailey, Abigail Abbott (1746–1815)

American memoirist who documented her family's struggle against domestic abuse and incest. *Born Abigail Abbott on February 2, 1746, in Rumford, Connecticut; died on February 11, 1815, in Bath, New Hampshire; daughter of Deacon James Abbott; married Major Asa Bailey, in 1767; children: 17, including Samuel, Asa, Abigail, Caleb and Anna (twins), Chloe, Amos, Olive, Phinehas, Judith, and Patience. Author of* Memoirs of Mrs. Abigail Bailey *(1815).*

When she was 22 years old, Abigail Abbott hoped that marriage would join her with a lifelong "friend" and "companion." The spiritual woman, whose father was a deacon, sought peace and partnership in her union to New Hampshire native Asa Bailey. The couple bought a farm in Landaff, New Hampshire.

For the first three years, the marriage went smoothly, though Asa had a temper. In 1770, they hired a woman for live-in help. By September of that year, Asa appeared to have seduced this employee. Abigail, perceiving the indiscretion, fired the woman, then confronted her husband and commanded him to repent. For several years he seemed a changed man. But in July of 1773, he again committed adultery with another hired woman. Though Abigail acted as she had before, this second affair did not escape public notice. The young woman in question was brought up on charges in another incident, and her relationship with Asa Bailey was presented as evidence against her character. All of Landaff knew of the scandal.

These accounts, offered in the *Memoirs of Mrs. Abigail Bailey*, foreshadow what would be Abigail's greatest trial with her husband. The memoirs, begun some time after 1789, were a response to her discovery that Asa was sexually abusing one of their elder daughters. Abigail never intended the texts for publication; she was writing them for her church. After her death, however, it was the decision of the congregation and pastor that the memoirs provided a compelling example of the disgraces committed by Asa Bailey and of his wife's stalwart faith in God and self which had seen her through the difficulties.

In the years following the 1773 trial, Asa Bailey came closer to religion. His volatile temper, however, remained, and it was not uncommon for him to explode if Abigail questioned his actions. Meanwhile, their family expanded. In 1787, they welcomed their sixth son, who was their fourteenth child.

In 1788, Asa went on a trip west, and Abigail was relieved to see him go. When he returned in December, he told Abigail he had resolved to move the family west to Ohio. Initially, he would take a son and a daughter to care for him on the journey and help him establish the homestead; then he would send for Abigail and the rest of the children. As one of his companions, he set his sights on an elder Bailey daughter. His actions toward the daughter, never named, seemed seductive. When Abigail questioned him, his defensive response told Abigail that Asa had sexually assaulted his own child.

Because the daughter would not corroborate her suspicions, Abigail had no recourse. Finally, on September 15, 1789, Abigail challenged Asa. As before, he promised to turn to God, while denying the charges. A truce held for several weeks, until a Sunday, with Abigail at church, when he again assaulted their daughter. Soon after this second incident, as soon as the daughter turned 18, she fled the Bailey home.

Around the same time, Abigail gave birth to twins—a boy who lived only a short time and a girl who was healthy. Almost a year later, the other children—who had witnessed their father's assault on their sibling—told their mother. Abigail then went to her daughter, who was living with relatives, and pleaded until the girl admitted the abuse. On September 7, 1790, Abigail ordered her husband to leave the family and helped pack his bags. Asa Bailey departed the next morning. Though rejected, he promised to divide their property and provide support for the children. During these months, Landaff learned of Asa Bailey's abuse, and he was disgraced. Shortly after, Abigail gave birth to her final child, a daughter.

> I clearly saw that Mr. B. entertained the most vile intentions relative to his own daughter. Whatever difficulty attended the obtaining of legal proof, yet no remaining doubt existed in my mind relative to the existence of his wickedness.
>
> **—Abigail Abbott Bailey**

Asa arranged to trade his farmland in Landaff for his brother's farm in Bradford, Vermont. In theory, the exchange would allow the Baileys to sell the Vermont property and split the money. Thus, in February of 1792, the family moved to Bradford, Vermont. The following month, Asa and Abigail left, ostensibly to travel to Connecticut, where Asa claimed he had a buyer for the Vermont farm. Instead, he led her to Whitestown, New York, where he planned to settle, convinced that Abigail would be unable to find her way back to Vermont.

For two months, Abigail was thus detained. In May, Asa set out for Bradford on foot to sell the family property and return with the children. He had, however, underestimated his wife. Abigail determined to follow a short distance behind him. Assisted by townspeople, she was drawn a map and given contacts along the way. Never having traveled 20 miles alone, Abigail, barely recovered from smallpox, set out on horseback to make the over 200-mile journey.

In the first week of June, Abigail arrived in Vermont and had a warrant sworn against Asa.

Asa initially refused to yield to court demands to settle their property. When Abigail threatened to haul him to New Hampshire, where charges of incest would surely prevent his gaining any of their estate, he settled quickly and left for New York, taking their remaining eldest son. Abigail petitioned for, and was granted, a divorce in 1792, after 25 years of marriage.

Because she did not have enough money to support them, Abigail Bailey had to find families with whom her children could live. She took lodging with Deacon Andrew Crook in Piermont, Vermont. In 1804, Abigail moved to Bath, New Hampshire, to live with the family of her son Asa. In 1815, on her way to a religious lecture, she caught cold, and several weeks later, she died of what was described as lung fever. She was 70 years old. Her memoirs, published that same year, are a rare account of sexual abuse from an era when women were under the dominance of husbands and fathers. Notes **Claire Buck**: "*The Memoirs of Mrs Abigail Bailey* constitutes one of the few explicit early American accounts of domestic violence recorded by a woman."

SOURCES:

Buck, Claire, ed. *The Bloomsbury Guide to Women's Literature.* NY: Prentice Hall, 1992.

Smith, Ethan, ed. *Memoirs of Mrs. Abigail Bailey.* Boston, MA: Samuel T. Armstrong, 1815.

Crista Martin, freelance writer, Boston, Massachusetts

Bailey, Angela (1962—)

Canadian runner. *Born in Coventry, England, of Jamaican parentage, on February 28, 1962.*

Winner of the silver medal in the 4x400-meter relay in the 1984 Olympic Games and a finalist in the 100- and 200-meter races in the 1983 World Championships.

At 16, coached by John Mumford at the University of Ontario, Angela Bailey first came to attention as a runner while competing in the 1978 Commonwealth Games. Later, she attended the University of California at Los Angeles (UCLA) in the United States. In 1983, Bailey was a finalist in the 100 and 200 meters in the World Championships. In the 1984 Olympics, she was a finalist in the 100 meter (***Evelyn Ashford** took the gold) and won a silver medal in the 4x400-meter relay. She had bests of 11.17 (100 meters), 22.64 (200), and 51.96 (400).

Karin L. Haag, Athens, Georgia

Bailey, Ann (1742–1825)

Legendary frontier scout. *Name variations: "White Squaw of the Kanawha" and Mad Ann. Born Ann Hennis in Liverpool, England, in 1742; died in Gallia County, Ohio, on November 22, 1825; came to America, probably as an indentured servant, in 1761; married Richard Trotter (d. 1774); married John Bailey; children: one son.*

Legend has become inextricably bound to the adventuresome life of Ann Bailey. We know that she arrived in America from England in 1761. Her marriage to Richard Trotter, a Shenandoah valley settler, ended with his death in the battle of Point Pleasant on October 10, 1774. The widow then donned male attire, armed herself with a tomahawk and rifle, and forged a new life as a frontier scout, "Indian fighter," messenger, and spy.

Known as the "White Squaw of the Kanawha," or Mad Ann, she married her second husband John Bailey, and moved to Clendenin's Settlement, now the site of Charleston, West Virginia. In 1791, when the settlement's Fort Lee was under attack by Native Americans, Mad Ann pulled off her most famous exploit. Volunteering to ride through dangerous forest and enemy lines to replace a dwindling supply of gun powder, she accomplished the 200-mile trek to and from Fort Union—now Lewisburg—in less than three days. After the death of her second husband, Bailey lived with her son in Ohio. She died there on November 22, 1825.

Barbara Morgan, Melrose, Massachusetts

Bailey, Carolyn Sherwin (1875–1961)

Author and editor of children's books. *Born October 25, 1875, in Hoosick Falls, New York; died on December 24, 1961, in Concord, Massachusetts; one of two daughters of Charles Henry (a scientist and traveler) and Emma Frances (Blanchard) Bailey (a teacher and writer); educated at home until age 12; attended Lansingburgh Academy, near Albany, New York; graduated from Teachers College, Columbia University, 1896; attended Montessori School (Rome), and the New York School of Social Work; married Eben Clayton Hill, in 1936.*

Selected works: Daily Programs of Gift and Occupation Work *(1904);* For the Children's Hour *(1906);* The Jungle Primer *(1906);* Firelight Stories *(1907);* For the Story Teller *(1913);* Every Child's Folk Songs and Games *(1914);* Montessori Children

(1915); Letting in the Gang *(1916);* The Way of the Gate *(1917);* Once Upon a Time Animal Stories *(1918);* The Outdoor Story Book *(1918);* Broad Stripes and Bright Stars *(1919);* Folk Tales and Fables *(1919);* Legends from Many Lands *(1919);* The Enchanted Bugle and Other Stories *(1920);* The Torch of Courage *(1921);* Flint, The Story of a Trail *(1922);* When Grandfather Was a Boy *(1923);* Boys and Girls of Pioneer Days *(1924);* In the Animal World *(1924);* Stories from an Indian Cave *(1924);* The Wonderful Tree and Golden Day Stories *(1925);* Boys and Girls of Discovery Days *(1926);* The Wonderful Window *(1926);* Garden, Orchard and Meadow Stories *(1929);* The Wonderful Days *(1929);* Children of the Handcrafts *(1935);* Tops and Whistles, Stories of Early American Toys and Children *(1937);* From Moccasins to Wings *(1938);* L'il Hannibal *(1938);* Pioneer Art in America *(1944);* The Little Rabbit Who Wanted Red Wings *(1945);* Miss Hickory *(1946);* Merry Christmas Book *(1948);* Old Man Rabbit's Dinner Party *(1949);* Enchanted Village *(1950);* A Candle for Your Cake *(1952);* Finnegan II *(1953);* The Little Red Schoolhouse *(1957);* Flickertail *(1962).*

Carolyn Sherwin Bailey was taught at home by her mother, a teacher and writer of children's books, until the age of 12. Following in her mother's footsteps, Bailey's first success as a storyteller came at age five, when a narrative she dictated to her mother won the $25 second prize in a magazine contest. Bailey later enrolled at Lansingburgh Academy, and, after graduating from Teachers College, Columbia University, she attended the Montessori School in Rome and the New York School of Social Work. She worked as a public-school teacher, as a kindergarten principal in Springfield, Massachusetts, and did resident social work at Warren Goddard House in New York. Some of her early collections of short stories and poems grew out of her work at Warren Goddard House. One collection, *For the Children's Hour*, written in 1906, would remain in print for over 40 years. Editorial accomplishments included the children's department of *Delineator*, of which she served as editor, many collections for use in educational settings, and *American Childhood* which she edited for a number of years.

In 1936, Bailey married Dr. Eben Clayton Hill, a research specialist in radiology at Johns Hopkins. The couple bought a 150-year-old house in Temple, New Hampshire, complete with 135 acres of timberland and an apple orchard, which they undertook to restore. Bailey discovered the house's cache of books, old furniture, and toys, which inspired a series of books about pioneer arts and crafts. The resulting four volumes, *Children of the Handcrafts* (1935), *Tops and Whistles, Stories of Early American Toys and Children* (1937), *Homespun Playdays* (1940), and *Pioneer Art in America* (1944), are thought by some critics to be her finest achievements. Cited for their meticulous research into "genealogical records, personal letters and diaries, rare village and county records, and a study of old maps," the books were praised for bringing American arts and crafts vividly into focus for young readers.

A less characteristic work, *Miss Hickory*, received the 1947 Newbery award from the American Library Association and remains a favorite among children. Bailey's title character, inspired by a doll made for her by her grandmother, is an old New England spinster with a twig body, a hickory nut head, and a sharp tongue. The *Atlantic* called the work "a skillful blending of fact, fantasy, and woody detail told in prose as clear and delicate as an etching." A dramatization of *Miss Hickory* was adapted by Ray Fowler and Barrett Clark as a Viking recorded book in 1972.

Calling storytelling "a real force for mental and moral good," Bailey believed that to be effective, a children's story must be developmentally appropriate. Reviewers marveled at her continuing "freshness," and her ability to improve in imaginative depth and technique with each succeeding work. She continued writing until her death on December 24, 1961.

SOURCES:

Commire, Anne. *Something about the Author.* Vol. 14. Detroit, MI: Gale Research.

Mainiero, Lina, ed. *American Women Writers.* NY: Frederick Ungar, 1979.

Rothe, Anna. *Current Biography.* NY: H.W. Wilson, 1948.

Barbara Morgan,
Melrose, Massachusetts

Bailey, Chris (1972—).

See Team USA: Women's Ice Hockey at Nagano.

Bailey, Florence (1863–1948)

American ornithologist and nature writer. *Born Florence Augusta Merriam in Locust Grove, New York, on August 8, 1863; died in Washington, D.C., on September 22, 1948; youngest of four children of Clinton (a banker) and Caroline (Hart) Merriam; sister of Clinton Hart, first chief of the United States Biological Survey; attended Mrs. Piatt's, a private school in Utica, New York; attended Smith College, Northampton, Massachusetts, as a special student, 1882–86,* *granted B.A., 1921; married Vernon Bailey (a naturalist), on December 16, 1899.*

Selected writings: Birds Through an Opera Glass *(1889);* My Summer in a Mormon Village *(1894);* A-Birding on a Bronco *(1896);* Birds of Village and Field *(1898);* Handbook of Birds of the Western United States *(1902);* Birds of New Mexico *(1928);* Among the Birds in the Grand Canyon National Park *(1939).*

Florence Merriam Bailey, who grew up on the family country estate of Homewood in Locust Grove, New York, showed an interest in natural history at an early age. While at Smith College as a non-degree student (she would be awarded a B.A. in 1921), she became interested in ornithology and began birding expeditions with friends and classmates in the Northampton countryside. Some early articles she prepared for *Audubon Magazine* and other publications on birds were later revised to form the basis of her first book *Birds Through an Opera Glass*, published in 1889. During these early years, Bailey also dabbled in social work. In the summer of 1891, she spent a month at a school for Chicago working girls (a branch of ***Jane Addams**' Hull House), and in the winter of that year she took a job in one of ***Grace Hoadley Dodge**'s working girls' clubs in New York City.

Diagnosed with tuberculosis in 1893, Bailey embarked on a trip to the curative climate of the Southwest, traveling in Utah, California, and Arizona, while producing a number of books. Upon her return to Washington, D.C., in 1896, she took up residence with her brother Clinton, then chief of the U.S. Biological Survey. Clinton introduced her to a colleague, Vernon Bailey, who was also a naturalist with the Biological Survey. The two had much in common and married in 1899. During the next 30 years, Bailey often accompanied her husband on arduous field expeditions in Texas, California, Arizona, the Pacific Northwest, and the Dakotas. While he pursued his studies of mammals, birds, reptiles, and plants, she concentrated on birdlife. Bailey's *Handbook of Birds of the Western United States* appeared in 1902, as she continued to regularly publish articles and papers on her observations. A counterpart to Frank M. Chapman's *Handbook of Birds of Eastern North America* (1895), Bailey's *Handbook* became a standard and went through many printings. She also contributed sections on birds to a number of her husband's books, notably *Wild Animals of Glacier National Park* (1918) and *Cave Life of Kentucky* (1933).

In 1928, Bailey finished a comprehensive study of the birdlife of the Southwest. The resulting book, *Birds of New Mexico*, was awarded the 1931 Brewster Medal of the American Ornithologists' Union, making Bailey the first woman to receive that award. This particular work was acknowledged again in 1933, when she received an honorary degree from the University of New Mexico. Bailey's last work of note, *Among the Birds in the Grand Canyon National Park*, was published when she was past 75 years of age, a mark of her incredible vitality.

Keeping a home in Washington, Bailey remained active as a founding member of the Audubon Society of the District of Columbia when not in the field and often taught classes in basic ornithology. As the first woman associate member of the American Ornithologists' Union (1885), she became its first woman fellow in 1929. Throughout her life, Bailey retained her strong social conscience and held memberships in groups like the Playground and Recreation Association of America, the National Housing Association, and the National Child Labor Committee. She served on the board of managers of the Working Boys' Home in Washington for many years.

Surviving her husband by six years, Florence Bailey died at age 85. Perhaps the greatest of her many honors was bestowed in 1908, when a variety of chickadee from the mountains of southern California was named *Parus gambeli baileyae*. Florence Bailey is remembered as one of the most literary ornithologists of her time.

Barbara Morgan, Melrose, Massachusetts

Bailey, Hannah Johnston

(1839–1923)

American suffragist, philanthropist, and superintendent of the Woman's Christian Temperance Union's department of peace and arbitration. *Pronunciation: BAY-lee. Born Hannah Clark Johnston on July 5, 1839, in Cornwall-on-the-Hudson, New York; died in Portland, Maine, on October 23, 1923; daughter of David Johnston (a tanner, farmer, and Quaker minister) and Letitia (Clark) Johnston; attended public schools and Friends boarding school; married Moses Bailey, on October 13, 1868 (died 1882); children: Moses Melvin.*

Worked as a school teacher (1858–67); undertook religious mission to New England (1867); named superintendent of the National Woman's Christian Temperance Union's department of peace and arbitration (1887), and of the World WCTU's comparable department (1889); began publishing peace journals, The Acorn *and* Pacific Banner *(1889); elected presi-*

dent of Maine Equal Suffrage Association (1891–97); resigned as superintendent of national WCTU department of peace and arbitration (1915); joined Woman's Peace Party (1915) and Woman's International League for Peace and Freedom (1918).

In 1887, Hannah Johnston Bailey of Winthrop Centre, Maine, accepted a new challenge. ***Frances Willard**, national president of the Woman's Christian Temperance Union (WCTU), asked Bailey to become the first superintendent of the recently created WCTU department of peace and arbitration. Upon assuming this position, Hannah Bailey quickly transformed the department into the most active separate women's peace agency in the United States. Within three years, she convinced 30 state auxiliaries of the WCTU to create their own peace departments, began publishing two periodicals, and founded the peace department of the World WCTU. Drawing in part from her considerable personal wealth, as well as from WCTU funds, she published and distributed a large volume of peace literature. Bailey also wrote extensively for the popular press, met frequently with leading politicians, and addressed countless women's and gender-mixed groups. In sum, she became one of the most effective publicists in the United States dedicated to the cause of peace and internationalism.

The eldest in a family of seven children, Hannah Clark Johnston was born at Cornwall-on-the Hudson, New York, in 1839. Her father David Johnston was a tanner and farmer who, like her mother Letitia, was an active member of the Society of Friends. Hannah attended a Friends' boarding school and public schools near her home in Plattekill, Ulster County, where she would continue to live for the first 30 years of her life. From the time Hannah was a young girl growing up in the Hudson River Valley, her faith and extensive Christian learning influenced every aspect of her life. As a Quaker, she was devoted to serving God by undertaking good works within and beyond her community. As she recorded in her diary, "It is [God's] blessing alone which prospers me in my labors. Without that I would be a useless drone on earth."

In keeping with the Quaker peace testimony, Hannah Johnston viewed war as evil. But like many other Friends, she faced a great trial in 1861 as the Civil War began. Her brother Frank, only 19, was one of only a few hundred Quaker men who enlisted to fight. Hannah supported his decision because, as she told him, "our Country has called you . . . to aid your fellow countrymen in putting down rebellion and slavery and instituting freedom and peace in a permanent reign over a land so long noted for its freedom." A year later, her 17-year-old brother Joseph also joined the Union army. Critically wounded at the battle of the Wilderness, Joseph died in November 1864, an event that certainly intensified Hannah's hatred of war.

Hannah worked as a school teacher until 1867, then left her position to accompany a Quaker preacher on a six-month mission to New England. She attended Friends meetings and visited various Protestant churches, almshouses, prisons, and asylums. She offered public prayer and sought, in various ways, to administer to the needs of the most unfortunate members of society. At one of her last stops, in Winthrop Centre, Maine, she met Moses Bailey, a recently widowed Friend and wealthy manufacturer. A deep mutual affection developed quickly between the two. They married on October 13, 1868, then took up residence in Winthrop Centre, where Hannah would live the rest of her life. Consistent with prevailing attitudes regarding married women, Hannah Bailey gave up missionary work but, in spite of chronic ill health during the 1870s, remained a very active member of the Society of Friends. The Baileys had one son, Moses Melvin ("Melvie"), born in 1869.

> The subject of peace is one of vital importance to women. It is her mission to bring life, not death, to this world.
>
> —Hannah Johnston Bailey

The elder Moses also experienced poor health dating from about the time he married Hannah, and in 1882 he died after a long battle with lung disease. Hannah inherited substantial wealth, which she used in part to fund various philanthropic projects. But she became much more than a monied benefactor, devoting tremendous energy to a number of causes. Like many other leading female political activists of the 19th century, Bailey's career as a reformer began in earnest only upon the death of her husband. She also managed Moses' businesses: a large farm in Winthrop, an oil-cloth factory in New Jersey (until selling it in 1889), and a retail carpet store in Portland, Maine, which her son took over in 1891. She taught Sunday school, served on countless Friends committees, and acted as treasurer of the Women's Foreign Missionary Society of the New England Yearly Meeting of Friends. In 1883, she joined the Women's

Christian Temperance Union (WCTU), the leading anti-drink organization in the country. Four years later, in 1887, she assumed leadership of the department of peace and arbitration.

Long active in Quaker Meeting and a successful manager of three businesses, Hannah Bailey brought administrative experience and confidence to her new position. She transformed her department into one of the most active in the WCTU. By the early 1900s, the various WCTU state departments of peace and arbitration were reporting a yearly distribution of up to a million pages of peace literature, the presentation of thousands of lectures and sermons, and a wide variety of other activities. Though occasionally concerned with lobbying government officials, Bailey's efforts usually targeted women and children. She argued, for instance, against the participation of children in "military drills." She saw such activities as harmful because they instilled in young people the sense that fighting is natural and even desirable. To Bailey, "peace" was not simply an absence of war but a state of mind. This explains why she also hoped to abolish prize fighting, capital punishment, and military parades.

Bailey's WCTU department also agitated against the manufacture and use of military toys. As she argued, playing with "toy soldiers, drums, swords or guns . . . may create or foster in the little people a love for such things, and skill in handling them, which will culminate in a desire for real ones and a spirit of war." Her department produced volumes of literature attacking military toys. But Bailey went even further. She wrote to company owners (and encouraged others to do the same), calling upon them to voluntarily abandon the manufacture of such toys.

As the WCTU crusade against military drills and toys indicated, a primary focus of the WCTU peace effort was to influence the development of children's attitudes about war and peace. Bailey encouraged local WCTU chapters to create "children's peace bands" who would meet regularly. In her suggested outline of duties and ideas, children were to elect officers of the band or club (an adult would serve as the "general superintendent," an advisory position), sing and recite peace-oriented verse at meetings, "pledge themselves to keep from quarreling," write letters to disabled soldiers, and "carry flowers, reading matter, [and] fruit to the sick or unfortunate." According to the annual reports of the WCTU department, many local temperance unions encouraged the formation of children's peace bands.

Beginning in 1889, Bailey began publishing and editing *The Acorn*, a monthly periodical for children. In her first editorial, she explained to her young readers the purpose of the journal. "While I want you all to be happy and cheerful and enjoy a free-hearted childhood," she wrote, "I want you also to be my helpers in a cause which will make you individually happier. And I tell you the name of the Cause. It is 'Peace and Arbitration.'" In subsequent issues, the *Acorn* included short stories, poetry, letters from children, and a variety of information about many subjects. Bailey encouraged her readers to secure new subscribers by offering prizes, cash included, for convincing others to buy the journal.

In many ways, the efforts of the Woman's Christian Temperance Union were consistent with Victorian notion's about gender differences. Not only did WCTU literature concentrate on building support among women, it often referred to their "special" nature. Its rhetoric focused on women's unique hatred of war, and women's natural role as peacemakers. Like many of her WCTU colleagues, Bailey, who served as president of Maine's Equal Suffrage Association from 1891 to 1897, worked from the assumption that women were morally superior to men. She claimed, "The subject of peace is one of vital importance to women. It is [their] mission to bring life, not death, to this world." She also noted that women, who "have more feeling than men," find it "simply inconceivable . . . to realize how men can heartlessly engage in warfare." She accepted without question that women tended to view some issues differently than men, and that it was their duty as the nation's "moral housekeepers" to take the lead in eradicating evils such as intemperance and warfare.

At age 75, Hannah Bailey joined the Woman's Peace Party in 1915 and later became a member of the Women's International League for Peace and Freedom. She remained superintendent of the national WCTU department of peace and arbitration until 1916 and head of the World WCTU's comparable department even longer. With her health failing somewhat, though, she rarely left southern Maine as she approached her 80th birthday. But thousands of old friends and colleagues visited her at her summer home, the Pine Bluff Chalet, on Belle Isle in Lake Cobbosseccontee, before her death in 1923 at the age of 83.

It was fitting that Hannah Bailey joined the Woman's Peace Party and Women's International League for Peace and Freedom in the decade before her death. Her work in molding the

WCTU department of peace and arbitration into the most successful separate women's peace agency in the United States paved the way for these groups. Believing that the "motherhood half of humanity" had a special obligation to help bring an end to war, Bailey and her female colleagues constructed an effective crusade for peace. If it was not in their power to end war, their effort was notable.

SOURCES:

Craig, John M. "Hannah Johnston Bailey: Publicist for Peace," in *Quaker History.* Vol. 84. Spring 1995, pp. 3–16.

Tyrell, Ian. *Woman's World, Woman's Empire: The Woman's Christian Temperance Union in International Perspective, 1880–1930.* Chapel Hill, NC: University of North Carolina Press, 1991.

SUGGESTED READING:

Alonso, Harriet Hyman. *Peace as a Women's Issue: A History of the U.S. Movement for World Peace and Women's Rights.* Syracuse, NY: Syracuse University Press, 1993.

Bordin, Ruth. *Woman and Temperance: The Quest for Power and Liberty, 1873–1900.* Philadelphia, PA: Temple University Press, 1981.

COLLECTIONS:

Papers of Hannah Johnston Bailey, Swarthmore College Peace Collection, Swarthmore, Pennsylvania.

John M. Craig, Professor of History, Slippery Rock University, Slippery Rock, Pennsylvania, author of *Lucia Ames Mead and the American Peace Movement* and numerous articles on activist American women

Bailey, Mary (1890–1960)

British pilot. *Name variations: Lady Mary Bailey; Dame Mary Bailey. Born in England in 1890; died in 1960; daughter of 5th Lord Rossmore; married Sir Abe Bailey, in 1911.*

After obtaining a pilot's license in 1927, Lady Mary Bailey made a solo flight from Croydon, England, to Cape Town, South Africa, from March 1928 to January 1929. She was awarded the Britannia Trophy and Dame of the British Empire (DBE) in 1930.

Bailey, Mildred (1903–1951)

American jazz singer and first white female to be completely accepted in jazz circles. *Born Mildred Rinker in Tekoa, near Seattle, Washington, on February 27, 1903; died in Poughkeepsie, New York, on December 12, 1951; sister of Al Rinker, who sang with Paul Whiteman's Rhythm Boys; married second husband Red Norvo (bandleader and xylophonist), in 1933 (divorced 1945).*

Sang with Paul Whiteman's Band (1929–33), Ben Berney's Orchestra (1934), Red Norvo and his Orchestra (1936–39), the Dorsey Brothers' and Benny Goodman's orchestras (from 1939 on); devoted to jazz, she helped move the genre into the American mainstream.

Mildred Bailey

Born and raised in Washington State, Mildred Bailey loved jazz. While she was in high school, her brother Al Rinker had a six-piece band called the Musicaladers, with a fellow named Bing Crosby as its featured vocalist. "Mildred would get some great records from the East," wrote Crosby, and the band would copy them. Listening carefully to the singers, Mildred would mimic the Southern enunciation she heard, producing a perfect blues inflection. She listened so carefully that, after hearing her recordings, those who didn't know her voice often responded erroneously that she was African American. Bailey lent credence to the notion that impersonation is the highest form of compliment; she loved the blues and wanted to be a part of the culture to which the art form was inextricably bound. ***Bessie Smith** was her idol. While Bailey and her fellow musicians wanted to reproduce the sounds they were hearing in black nightclubs, the general public was still not ready for this style of music. For people like Mildred Bailey, the music in white theaters and dance bands couldn't compare to black jazz.

Bailey began to sing in clubs. Crosby would later remember hearing her in a Spokane nightspot named Charlie Dale's Cabaret when he was in college. After she married and moved to Los Angeles, Crosby and her brother Al, who followed a year later, were soon listening to her at a plush club in Bakersfield called The Swede's. "She had a way of talking that was unique," wrote Crosby. "Even then I can recall her describing a town that was nowhere as 'tiredsville,' or a singer who was a little zingy as 'twenty dash eight dash four.'" Bailey was interested in all kinds of popular music—blues, pseudo-blues, gospel, pseudo-gospel, Tin Pan Alley, and show tunes. Every song she performed, she sang idiomatically, and an ability to move effortlessly from one kind of popular music to another spurred her career.

Her brother and Crosby became Paul Whiteman's original Rhythm Boys, a connection that would soon prove useful for Bailey. In 1929, hired as Whiteman's first featured female singer at $75 a week, she moved to New York, the center of the jazz world and the Whiteman radio broadcasts. The performers she recorded with read like a Who's Who of early swing—Bunny Berigan, Chu Berry, Jimmy and Tommy Dorsey, Coleman Hawkins, Johnny Hodges, Gene Krupa, and Teddy Wilson. She also met Red Norvo who became her second husband.

Meanwhile, Bailey's home functioned as a kind of clearinghouse for jazz musicians. Benny Goodman was a friend; his famous trio was hatched when he met Teddy Wilson at her home on Pilgrim Circle in Forest Hills, Long Island. Fats Waller, Jess Stacy, Hugues Panassié, Spike Hughes, Lee Wiley, Alec Wilder, and Red Nichols all hung out there, and Bessie Smith and her husband were frequent guests. Mildred and Bessie, both enormously overweight, loved to make jokes about their grand size. When Bessie arrived at Mildred's, one of them would continue a joke that never grew old: "Look, I've got this brand-new dress, but it's too big for me, so why don't you take it?" Bailey's love of jazz and her adulation of Bessie Smith grew into a treasured friendship.

Passionate about jazz, food, and life, Bailey sang with the top bands of the era from Benny Goodman's to the Dorsey Brothers'; she headlined the top nightclubs: Café Society, the Famous Door, and the Blue Angel. She made many recordings which are considered classics and was especially known for her recording of Hoagy Carmichael's "Ol' Rockin' Chair." Some have compared her voice to a horn, because, when she sang, she seemed more like a member of the band than a solo vocalist. Bailey adopted the black musician's way with a phrase and the pronounced nasal resonance which characterizes the singing of Bessie Smith, **Aretha Franklin**, and other great black female jazz singers. Her voice was always fresh, her technical mastery superb. "Oh Daddy!," "Down Hearted Blues," and "Sweet Mama, Where Did You Stay Last Night" were some of her favorites.

Though Bailey's career prospered in the 1920s and 1930s, she struggled with an addiction to food and a fierce temper. While she claimed her weight problem was glandular, her friends claimed "overeating," but no one seemed to diagnose an underlying cause. When she became diabetic, she was put on a diet, reputedly commenting at meals: "Now I've ate the diet, so bring on the food." Her rages were as monumental as her appetite. Her husband Red Norvo recalled a time when he had gone fishing with Benny Goodman and stayed longer than he'd planned:

> When I got home, I could tell that Mildred was hacked. Things were cool, but I didn't say anything, and a night or two after, when we were sitting in front of the fire—I was on a love seat on one side and she was on one on the other side—Mildred suddenly got up and took this brand-new hat she had bought me at Cavanaugh's and threw it in the fire. So I got up and threw a white fox stole of hers in the fire, and she got a Burberry I'd got in Canada and threw that in. By this time she was screaming at me and I was yelling at her, so finally I picked up a cushion from one of the love seats, and in it went. The fire was really burning. In fact, it was licking right out the front and up the mantel, and that was the end of the fight because we had to call the Fire Department to come and put it out.

Convinced she would never be the star she wanted to be, Bailey gave it all up in the late 1940s. She had watched as her career was eclipsed by singers whom she had clearly influenced, like ***Peggy Lee** and ***Ella Fitzgerald.** In 1949, a combination of diabetes, heart trouble, hardening of the arteries, and disappointment forced her to retire to a farm outside of New York. When Jimmy Van Heusen found her living out her days in a Poughkeepsie hospital, he—along with Frank Sinatra and Crosby—paid for a private room. For a short time, Lee Wiley paid for Bailey to live in a Beverly Hills apartment, but it wasn't long before Bailey moved back East, made a few more appearances in 1950, and died penniless on December 12, 1951, at the age of 48.

For a time, Mildred Bailey was forgotten, but many recordings documented her marvelous abilities and increasingly informed jazz lovers sought them out. As Leonard Feather pointed out, in the history of jazz, she was a pivotal figure:

> Jazz singing, until the late 1920s was largely confined to the Negro artists, and, despite occasional exceptions . . . was limited in substance to the form of the blues. The break on both levels may have been completed with the advent of Mildred Bailey. Where earlier white singers with pretensions to a jazz identification had captured only the surface qualities of the Negro styles, Mildred contrived to invest her thin, high pitched voice with a vibrato, an easy sense of jazz phrasing that might almost have been Bessie Smith's overtones.

SOURCES:

Hemming, Roy, and David Hajdu. *Discovering Great Singers of Classic Pop*. Newmarket Press, 1991.

Pleasants, Henry. *The Great American Popular Singers*. NY: Simon and Schuster, 1974.

John Haag, Associate Professor, University of Georgia, Athens, Georgia

Bailey, Pearl (1918–1990)

African-American jazz singer, Tony Award-winning actress, author, and tireless campaigner for world peace who served as an American delegate to the United Nations. *Born in Newport News, Virginia, on March 29, 1918; died on August 17, 1990; youngest of four children of Joseph James Bailey (an evangelical preacher) and Ella Mae Bailey; married a drummer (the marriage lasted only 18 months); married a soldier just returned from overseas during World War II (divorced); married John Randolph Pinkett, Jr., on August 31, 1948 (divorced, March 1952); married Louis Bellson, Jr. (a drummer and bandleader), in 1952.*

After winning an amateur contest (1933), began touring with several bands, singing and dancing; first appeared on Broadway (1946) and was named most promising newcomer; won the Tony Award (1968) for her performance in the all-black version of Hello, Dolly!*; appeared in feature films and had her own television show (early 1970s); appointed by President Gerald Ford to U.S. Mission to the U.N. (1975); awarded the Medal of Freedom by President Ronald Reagan (1988).*

Films: Variety Girl *(1947);* Isn't It Romantic? *(1948);* Carmen Jones *(1955);* That Certain Feeling *(1956);* St. Louis Blues *(1958);* Porgy and Bess *(1959);* All The Fine Young Cannibals *(1960);* The Landlord *(1970);* Norman . . . Is That You? *(1976).*

On a sunny spring day in 1978, Pearl Bailey donned the robes and mortarboard of a college graduate and was welcomed to the podium at Washington's prestigious Georgetown University to receive an honorary degree from the school's president. Though she had barely finished high school and had spent most of her life in show business, it seemed entirely appropriate to everyone gathered for the ceremony that "Pearlie Mae" should be honored that day. For the past 20 years, Bailey had been a frequent guest at the White House, had sat as part of the United States' contingent at the UN, had toured the Middle East and Europe as an ambassador of goodwill, and had been a public advocate for harmonious relations among all the world's peoples. But Bailey had one more surprise in store that day. Holding her honorary degree, she told the audience: "Who knows, folks. One day I may be coming to this school." A year later, when she was 61, Pearl Bailey's name appeared on the freshmen rolls.

Bailey had been surprising people all her life, starting on the day of her birth, March 29, 1918, in Newport News, Virginia. Her parents had been expecting a boy and had even chosen "Dick" as their new son's name—a nickname Pearl would bear for most of her childhood. The daughter of Joseph James Bailey, an evangelical preacher, and Ella Mae Bailey, she was the youngest of four children, with two sisters, Virgie and Eura, and a brother Willie. Bailey remembered little about Newport News, since the family moved to Washington, D.C., when she was only four. But she would never forget the church services at Washington's House of Prayer, where her father, as an elder of the church, preached every Sunday.

The African-American congregation was one of the largest in the capital, and the Sunday morning service was filled with rollicking gospel music, singing, dancing, and joyful shouting. The Bailey children were quick to notice that when the congregation began to enthusiastically praise the Lord, money would often shake loose from their pockets and fall to the floor. That was when, Bailey recalled, "we got extremely happy, started to shout, fell under the Power, but on top of money." A more permanent benefit of Elder Bailey's occupation was Pearl's early and constant exposure to the church meeting's harmony and rhythm, which she believed were the foundations for all later forms of popular music. "Just listen to the beat [of pop music] and go to one of the churches and see if you don't hear the same thing," she would tell her fans.

Sunday was also what Pearl called "Argument Day," the day her parents seemed to pick for their fights. After one particularly heated dispute, her mother Ella Mae Bailey left the household, taking the children with her. She moved first to another neighborhood, then to Philadelphia, where she eventually remarried.

At 15, Bailey went to work housecleaning for families across town in the affluent white sections of Philadelphia. Her brother Willie, on the other hand, seemed to have found a much more exciting way to make a living. He had gained some notoriety as a gifted tap dancer and had begun appearing at local black theaters, sharing bills with such established entertainers as the Berry Brothers, Jigsaw Jackson, and **Ada Ward**. Willie had seen Pearl singing and dancing around the Bailey home and suggested she enter an amateur-night competition at one of the theaters. The prize, after all, was five dollars and a week's work—better than cleaning houses and a lot more fun. With her mother's approval, Pearl entered the contest singing "Talk of the Town" and "Poor Butterfly," was declared the winner, and offered $30 for a week's work. At the end of the first week, she was offered a second week and another $30, the grand sum of $60 to be paid at the end. She accepted, but the theater went broke and closed before the second week was over. "Never start the second week until you've been paid for the first one" was the advice her mother gave her.

Despite the financial setback, Bailey was fascinated by show business, especially after a summer trip to New York with Willie, who took her to the Cotton Club, the famous Apollo, and the Harlem Opera House, where they watched a young singer named ***Ella Fitzgerald** win a singing contest. Now determined to follow Willie on the stage, Bailey took a job at the old Howard Theater in Philadelphia as a chorine with bandleader Noble Sissle's act. America had now slipped into the Depression, and the $22 a week she was paid seemed like a fortune. She traveled with the act back to New York, this time as a show-business professional rather than a spectator. "I simply danced my fanny off, and ate like a horse," she remembered. "Some weeks, I ate the whole salary, except for rent money."

Not long after returning to Philadelphia, Bailey was offered a long-term contract to play the "coal circuit"—a dreary round of Pennsylvania coal towns where many blacks had gone to find work in the mines. Pearl's first stop was Pottstown, where she played the Manhattan Café, ducking flying beer bottles during the occasional brawl and steering clear of the pimps who looked her over for employment. It was a rough and tumble world, but Bailey held her own, touring through Scranton and Wilkes-Barre and a string of sooty, grimy camp towns. Along the way, she married a drummer—the first of four marriages, this one lasting only 18 months. Her mother visited her at one of the stops on the tour and gave her another piece of advice Bailey never forgot: "I want you to live in the best place you can afford, eat well, and if there's anything left, send it to Mama."

Her contract finally came to an end, and Bailey returned to Washington and a somewhat more genteel lifestyle. She was hired to sing with the Royal Sunset Band, playing established theaters in Washington, Baltimore, and Boston; when war broke out in 1941, Bailey traveled with the band for the USO, to places she would never have dreamed of seeing—Texas, Florida, Arizona, and California. This time it wasn't coal towns, but boot camps, and all of them strictly segregated. It was Bailey's first real exposure to the frictions between blacks and whites.

At Camp Hood, in Texas, she watched as a white woman, a fellow entertainer, flew into a screaming fit when she discovered a black man in her room. Another entertainer on the tour had mistaken the room for his and was taking a nap. The post MP's had to be called, and while they calmed the woman down and explained the error, they made a point of removing the bed from her room and replacing it with a new one, "as if," Bailey said, the man "had germs." At another stop in Texas, she emerged from the train tired and hungry to find that the only "colored" restaurant in town had closed. She walked boldly into the whites-only diner and, before they could tell her to leave, placed her order and told them she'd take it outside to eat. Though she was allowed to sit at the end of the counter, the stares and murmurs around her were impossible to ignore. Not long after, back in the North, Bailey visited a New Jersey club to see a hot new singer she'd heard about named Frank Sinatra. After the show, she was grabbed by two white men in the lobby. No one tried to help her as she broke free and ran back into the club, but the two men caught up with her and began beating her until a waiter ran up and chased them off. She suffered severe cuts and bruises about the head and neck. When the police repeatedly asked if her attackers were white, she replied that she "didn't give a dern if they were purple." But she later wrote, "They represented for me all the miserable people who go around looking at skin. How could a man hate someone he had never met before, just because he had a different color skin? What is he really afraid of?"

Bailey stayed on the USO circuit throughout most of the war and married for the second time, a soldier just returned from overseas. As with her first husband, Pearl never publicly revealed his name, and wrote many years later that she felt the marriage ended after only a few months

Pearl Bailey

because her husband had difficulty adjusting to civilian life after so many years in combat. They were divorced in Washington.

The year 1944 found Bailey back in New York, where she appeared at two of the city's most famous jazz clubs, the Village Vanguard and the Blue Angel. It was the New York jazz world that would open so many doors for her, professionally and personally. For one thing, jazz audiences in New York were white as well as black, so different from the strict segregation Pearl had experienced up until now. For another, she was playing quality clubs in which those audiences regularly included show-business luminaries, from movie stars to directors to agents. It was in New York that she signed her first recording contract, with Columbia, and recorded her first hit, "Tired," in 1945. (Its opening line—"Honey, aren't you tired?"—became her trademark.) She also met and formed a long-lasting friendship with Sinatra, with whom she would record "A Little Learning Is a Dangerous Thing"; auditioned for Cab Calloway's band and opened with him at the Strand Theater to rave reviews; and snagged her first job in a Broadway musical, *St. Louis Woman*, with music by Harold Arlen and lyrics by Johnny Mercer. It was during this dynamic time in her career that Bailey developed her distinctive style—an almost off-hand delivery, with a subtle variation in phrasing and intonation interspersed with droll, comical asides.

Man has nothing to do but be beautiful. But, Lord, he makes such a chore of it!

—Pearl Bailey

Her third marriage—to a wealthy Washington playboy—was effectively over in two years. This time Bailey discovered her ex-husband had left her with $70,000 in debts, all of which she was able to pay off by selling their home in the capital and appearing in two more Broadway productions—*Arms And The Girl*, a Revolutionary War musical review in which she co-starred with **Nanette Fabray**, and *House of Flowers*, again singing Harold Arlen's music.

The income from her first movie contract also came in handy. In 1946, she was offered $25,000 to appear in Paramount's *Variety Girl*, a musical review about the Variety Clubs formed by the film industry after the war as a means to raise money for charities. She had only one scene and only three weeks' work, but Bailey remembered her mother's advice and made sure she was paid by the week. She took her first check to the bank, asked for the cash in a brown paper sack, and took the money back to her hotel room to see what that much money looked like.

Bailey's scene called for her to walk into a Variety Club rehearsal dressed in a fancy gown designed by ***Edith Head**, drape herself around a column, and tell the chorus girls assembled there, in song, how to keep their man. "Dear, dear, I am the worst draper," Bailey recalled. "With my feet killing me, I just get across a room and when I find a post, I don't drape, I lean." When it became obvious the scene wasn't working, it was Pearl's idea to shed the gown and appear in a housecoat and slippers, carrying a feather duster; and instead of the Frank Loesser number she was supposed to sing, she sang "Tired." It became the film's most memorable scene, and Paramount immediately offered her parts in some of its more prestigious films. Among them were two of the most popular African American-cast movies of the day, *Carmen Jones* and *Porgy and Bess*, both directed by Otto Preminger, featuring the likes of Harry Belafonte, Sidney Poitier, Sammy Davis Jr., and ***Dorothy Dandridge.**

In 1952, Bailey met and married her fourth husband, drummer and bandleader Louis Bellson. The marriage drew some harsh remarks from the press, since Bellson was white, but Bailey brushed them off. "There is only one race," she said, "the human race." The couple were married in London, where she was appearing as part of a government-sponsored goodwill tour; this marriage would last a lifetime. Their home was near Victorville, California, Bailey's beloved Apple Valley Ranch, where she would spend what little time she had between films or tours.

Shortly before marrying Bellson, Bailey accepted an invitation that would open up a new career for her. Former actor George Murphy, now a U.S. senator and a good friend of Bailey's from his show-business days, asked her to appear at a Press Club luncheon in Washington for then-president Dwight Eisenhower. She sang her current popular hit, "Won't You Come Home, Bill Bailey," an old 1890's ragtime tune she'd discovered and brought up to date. She soon became the toast of the capital's social circuit, was invited to Eisenhower's second inauguration, and was dispatched on the first of a long series of overseas tours as part of America's growing cultural presence in the postwar world, rubbing elbows easily with heads of state, diplomats, and educators.

The recognition was not without its critics, however. With the civil-rights movement beginning to gather steam, Bailey was seen by some African-American leaders and political liberals as tied to an administration that was painfully slow in empowering the nation's black population. As usual, she spoke her mind, pointing out to Northern liberals that civil rights was not just a Southern issue. "The North has merely lived under a thin veil of liberalism," she wrote. She also told those who challenged her lack of membership in civil-rights organizations, "I don't have to join an organization to care. I care about everyone, and that's more important than caring about one." She pointed to her profession as an example of what she meant: "We have no chips on our shoulders, no burden to carry, because we all have a thing in common, a cause." To the white press that had made such a fuss about her marriage to a white man but now took her to task for failing to march for integration, she said that she "marched in her heart every day." She might have also pointed out that she was one of a handful of black entertainers to have played to integrated audiences in the '40s and '50s. She would later appear in two films with strong racial themes, *All The Fine Young Cannibals* and *The Landlord*.

In 1965, after returning to Apple Valley from a particularly grueling tour, Bailey complained of being "in a fog," with no energy and low spirits. Taken to a hospital for tests, she was diagnosed with heart disease, confined to bed for three weeks, and told to slow down. Making good use of the time, she took notes for an autobiography she was planning to write (published in 1968) and found she had a penchant for poetry. Her verses were about everyday things, especially about families, for she felt that a disintegration in family life was responsible for the problems confronting the nation's youth. In one poem, she wrote:

> There's nobody home
> Upstairs or downstairs.
> Mom is out of work, looking,
> John is in or out of school
> Who knows, who cares.
> Mary is—now let me see. . . .

Finally given medical clearance, Bailey returned to work in one of her most successful roles, as Dolly Levi in Jerome Robbins' all-black version of *Hello, Dolly!*, which opened on Broadway in 1967. It was one of the proudest moments of her career, a culmination of her years of hoofing and singing. Broadway would recognize that fact by awarding her the Tony the following year for her performance. "At last I can sing, dance, say intelligent words on stage, love and be loved, and deliver what God gave me—and I'm dressed up besides!" she told reporters. *The New York Times* review was typical of the show's critical reception: "For Miss Bailey, this was a Broadway triumph for the history books. . . . The audience would have elected her governor if she'd only named her choice of state."

The critic wasn't far off the mark with his political analogy, although it wasn't an elected office that came Bailey's way. After touring with *Dolly* nationally and overseas, her second career as a diplomat and goodwill ambassador accelerated. She toured the Middle East in the early 1970s, shaking hands with the Shah of Iran before his downfall and with Anwar Sadat just months before his assassination. In 1975, President Gerald Ford named her as the public delegate to the United States Mission to the U.N., where she participated in debates on solutions to the Israeli-Arab conflict to such effect that she was reappointed to three more terms, first by Jimmy Carter and then by Ronald Reagan, who awarded her the Medal of Freedom. On her retirement, she told a U.N. press conference that she had done nothing of which she was happier or more proud. U.N. Ambassador Vernon Walters called her a "national treasure."

Bailey accomplished all this while continuing the studies she announced that June Day at Georgetown University, graduating with a degree in theology and a Dean's Award in 1985, at the age of 67. By now, no one was surprised at what Pearlie Mae from Newport News could accomplish. Before the heart disease diagnosed 30 years earlier caused her death on August 17, 1990, she had brightened the lives of the millions who had heard her sing, watched her dance, or been moved by her dramatic performances on stage, screen, and television. She had also broken down racial barriers long before the civil-rights movement came to the fore; published six books; toured the world with her message of human kindness and understanding; and participated in the search for peace at the highest levels of government.

"The way we're going to get understanding," Bailey once wrote, "is for each man to open his heart and open his mind and look within himself as he looks at his neighbor." Anyone who was familiar with Pearl Bailey recognized that that was exactly what she'd been doing all along.

SOURCES:

Bailey, Pearl. *The Raw Pearl.* NY: Harcourt, Brace, 1968.

———. *Between You And Me: A Heartfelt Memoir Of Learning, Loving, And Living.* NY: Doubleday, 1989.

Brandt, Keith. *Pearl Bailey: With A Song In Her Heart.* NY: Troll Associates, 1993.

Null, Gary. *Black Hollywood: The Black Performer In Motion Pictures.* NY: Citadel Press, 1975.

Norman Powers, writer-producer,
Chelsea Lane Productions, New York, New York

Bailey, Temple (c. 1869–1953)

American romance author whose many novels were serialized in popular magazines before publication.

Born Irene Temple Bailey in Petersburg, Virginia, around 1869; died on July 6, 1953, in Washington, D.C.; daughter of Emma (Sprague) and Milo Varnum Bailey; educated at private schools in Richmond, Virginia; never married; no children.

Selected works: Judy *(1907);* Glory of Youth *(1913);* Adventures in Girlhood *(1917);* The Blue Window *(1926);* Little Girl Lost *(1932);* Fair As the Moon *(1935);* I've Been to London *(1937);* The Pink Camellia *(1942);* Red Fruit *(1945).*

Among her estimated three million books sold, Temple Bailey could count at least 5,200 which had been bought by department-store magnate John Wannamaker. The businessman was so enamored of her work that he purchased 200 copies of each of Bailey's 26 books, passing them out to friends and associates. The size of Bailey's fees and royalties were legendary. Noted as the highest paid author of her time, she earned $60,000 from *McCall's* for a single serial, and *Cosmopolitan* paid $325,000 for the right to three serials and several short stories. While all her serials were ultimately published as books, readers—primarily women and young girls—clamored for the next installments and their appearance guaranteed high magazine sales.

Raised in Washington, D.C., in a well-to-do family, Bailey enjoyed a protected upbringing and education in private Virginia schools. That privacy accompanied her into adulthood, when she moved in elite Washington circles and counted many influential people among her friends. Bailey never married, pouring her romantic notions instead into her work, which depicted innocent heroines, happy endings, and high drama.

Crista Martin, freelance writer, Boston, Massachusetts

Baillie, Grizel (1665–1746)

Scottish songwriter. *Name variations: Grisell, Grizelda, Lady Grizel Baillie, Lady Grizel Hume. Born Grizel Hume at Redbraes Castle, Berwickshire, on December 25, 1665; died on December 6, 1746; eldest daughter of Sir Patrick Hume (or Home) of Polwarth, afterwards earl of Marchmont; married George Baillie, in 1602; children: two daughters, Grizel (who married Sir Alexander Murray of Stanhope and was known as* ***Lady Murray of Stanhope****) and* ***Rachel, Lady Binning****.*

In 1677, the 12-year-old Grizel carried letters from her father Sir Patrick Hume to the imprisoned Scottish patriot Robert Baillie of Jerviswood. Hume's friendship with Baillie made him a suspect of treason, and the troops of England's King Charles II took over Hume's Redbraes Castle. Hume remained in hiding for some time in a nearby churchyard, where his daughter supplied him with food. When he heard of the execution of Robert Baillie in 1684, Hume fled to Holland. Though his family soon joined him, they returned to Scotland after the successful invasion of William of Orange in 1688.

In 1692, Lady Grizel married George Baillie, son of the executed patriot. She had two daughters, Lady Murray of Stanhope and Rachel, Lady Binning. At the time of Lady Grizel's death, Lady Murray possessed a manuscript of her mother's in prose and verse. Some of the songs had been printed in Allan Ramsay's *Tea-Table Miscellany*. The most famous of Lady Grizel's songs, "And werena my heart light I wad dee," originally appeared in the 1725 *Orpheus Caledonius. Memoirs of the Lives and Characters of the Right Hon. George Baillie of Jerviswood and Lady Grisell Baillie, by their daughter, Lady Murray of Stanhope*, were printed in 1822. Two decades later, in 1842, George Baillie's *Correspondence (1702–1708)* was edited by Lord Minto for the Bannatyne Club. "The Legend of Lady Grizelda Baillie" forms one of ***Joanna Baillie**'s *Metrical Legends of Exalted Character.*

Baillie, Isobel (1895–1983)

Scottish soprano. *Name variations: Dame Isobel Baillie. Born in Hawick, Scotland, in 1895; died in 1983; attended Manchester High School and studied with Guglielmo Somma in Milan, 1925–26.*

Known for her high, pure tone, Scottish soprano Dame Isobel Baillie made her first public appearance at age 15. Following her inaugural London season in 1923, she was one of England's most sought after singers for the works of Handel, Haydn, Brahms, and Elgar, and especially noted for her singing in Handel's *Messiah*, Gluck's *Orphée*, and her recording of "I Know That My Redeemer Liveth." Baillie was also one of the first British opera stars to sing at the Hollywood Bowl (1933). She gave many performances of Gounod's *Faust* in New Zealand; made frequent appearances with the Royal Choral Society; and sang for 26 years with the Hallé orchestra. Though she retired from the stage in the late 1950s, Baillie went on to teach at the Royal College of Music (1955–57, 1961–64), Cornell University (1960–61), and Manchester College of Music. Named Commander of the British Empire (CBE) in 1951, she was also made Dame of the British Empire (DBE) in 1978. Her autobiography *Never Sing Louder than Lovely* was published in 1982.

Baillie, Jane Welsh (1801–1866).

See Carlyle, Jane Welsh.

Baillie, Joanna (1762–1851)

English dramatist and poet who was famous for her **Plays on the Passions,** ***which, along with several other of her plays, were produced in leading theaters in England, Scotland, Ireland, and the U.S.*** *Born September 11, 1762, in Bothwell, Lanarkshire, Scotland; died on February 23, 1851, at Hampstead Heath; daughter of Reverend Dr. Baillie (a descendant of the Scottish patriot William Wallace) and Dorothea Hunter; received little formal education: tutored by her father, spent five or six years at Miss McDonald's boarding school in Glasgow; never married; no children.*

Educated in Glasgow until her father's death (1778); lived in London, published her first book of poems, and began writing drama (1779–91); moved to Hampstead and published three volumes of Plays on the Passions, *as well as several poems (1791); enjoyed close friendship with Sir Walter Scott (1808–1851); published religious pamphlet defending the human nature of Christ (1831); published complete works in London (1851). Honors: honorary member of the Historical Society of Michigan (1840); honorary member of the Whittington Club (1846).*

Selected publications: Fugitive Verses *(1790);* Plays on the Passions, *vol. I (1798);* Plays on the Passions, *vol. II (1802);* Miscellaneous Plays *(1802);* The Family Legend *(1810);* Plays on the Passions, *vol. III (1812);* A Collection of Poems, chiefly Manuscript and From Living Authors, Edited for the Benefit of a Friend by Joanna Baillie *(1823);* A View of the General Tenor of the New Testament regarding the Nature and Dignity of Jesus Christ *(1831);* Miscellaneous Plays *(1836).*

Joanna Baillie was a well-known poet and dramatist of the early 19th century, who published 28 plays, seven of which were professionally produced. She also published two volumes of poetry, entitled *Fugitive Verses* and *Metrical Legends*, which were highly praised by her contemporaries. Her works, many of which dealt with human emotions or "passions," were extremely appealing to the early 19th-century literary world. These plays were considered both aesthetically appealing and comfortingly moral during the opening years of the English Romantic movement.

Joanna was born September 11, 1762, at the manse in Bothwell, Lanarkshire, Scotland, to a minister, Dr. Baillie, and **Dorothea Hunter Baillie.** Two of her siblings survived infancy: **Agnes,** born 1760, and Matthew, born 1761. Joanna's family was supportive but not openly affectionate. Her parents discouraged open emotion or affection, and Joanna grew up to be a quiet woman, more inclined to listen than to talk. She was later described as a small woman, "with a mean, shuffling gait," but with impeccably well-bred manners.

Joanna Baillie

Baillie's relatively carefree childhood was spent engaged in more play than work. In later life, she recalled being fond of riding and other outdoor sports. Her early education came from her father, who tutored her in ethics but little else. According to her memories as well as those of Agnes, Joanna was not able to read well until she was 11 years old.

At that age, Joanna was sent to boarding school in Glasgow, where she quickly remedied her deficiencies in education. She proved to be especially gifted in the areas of mathematics, drawing, and music. She enjoyed telling stories of her own design and making up little dramas for the other students to act out. When, in 1776, Baillie's father was appointed professor of Divinity at the University of Glasgow, the whole family moved into a home provided by the university.

> If I had to present any one to a foreigner as a model of an English Gentlewoman, it would be Joanna Baillie.
>
> —William Wordsworth

This period of togetherness was short-lived. In 1778, Baillie's father suddenly died, leaving her mother with few resources to provide for her three children. Dorothea Baillie turned to her family for help, and her brother, William Hunter, a physician, invited Dorothea, Agnes, and Joanna to live with him. Hunter also helped send Joanna's brother Matthew to medical school.

When Dr. Hunter died in 1783, he willed his house in London and his family estate in Scotland to Matthew. Matthew accepted the house but later conveyed the estate in Scotland to his uncle, John Hunter, William's younger brother.

Joanna, Agnes, and Dorothea moved to London in 1783 to keep house for Matthew. It was in London that Joanna made her first forays into serious writing. The result was a collection of poems, later titled *Fugitive Verses*, which she published anonymously in 1790. The book was not a commercial success, and Baillie turned to drama, writing her first tragedy, *Arnold*, which was later lost.

In 1791, Matthew married **Sophia Denman**, and his mother and sisters moved from London to Hampstead, where they lived for the remainder of their lives. The three women were greeted warmly in Hampstead and were immediately received into the town's literary circle. Joanna's enthusiasm for writing was rekindled by her new circle of acquaintances, and she soon devised a plan for producing a complete set of dramas on the human passions. She originally envisioned producing both a tragedy and a comedy which focused on each of the preeminent passions, highlighting each particular desire as the primary motivation for action of the main character. Although she never completed her plan, she would eventually produce three volumes of *Plays on the Passions*, which included both comedies and tragedies. She treated the passions of jealousy, love, hate, remorse, ambition, and fear, and avoided emotions which she considered unfit for public performance, or emotions, like revenge, which she believed had been treated fully by previous authors.

In 1798, Baillie anonymously published the first volume of her *Plays on the Passions*, which included three dramas: *Basil, a tragedy on Love; The Tryal, a comedy on Love;* and *De Montfort, a tragedy on Hatred.* This created an immediate stir in the literary community. Critics received them favorably, and many assumed that they had been written by a man. They sold readily; five editions of the three plays were published by 1806.

The literary success of the *Plays on the Passions*, however, was not matched by success on stage. *De Montfort* was performed at Drury Lane Theater in London with John Kemble and ***Sarah Kemble Siddons**, two of the most famous actors of the day, but the play was universally considered a failure on stage. Critics considered the plays too intellectual and philosophical to work on stage. Baillie insisted upon using the dramas as a warning to the audience to avoid excessive passions, but she also expected her heroes to appeal to their sympathies. The overwhelming force of the passion, by which her heroes were driven against their will, gave a mixed message which tended to confuse. Audiences were unsure whether to sympathize with the hero or to condemn him. In her introduction to the first volume of plays, Baillie acknowledged "man's" inability, "amidst [passion's] wild uproar, [to] listen to the voice of reason, and save ourselves from destruction," but was quick to note that "we can foresee its coming, we can . . . shelter our heads from the coming blast." She cautioned her audiences to avoid rising passion, before it grew to the extent that it could overcome one's self-control, as in the case of her protagonists. Although the rest of Joanna's plays were not produced at Drury Lane, at least five were produced by other theaters in Liverpool, Dublin, and Edinburgh, where they were more favorably received.

Despite their initial lack of success on the London stage, her plays remained popular items in their written form. In 1802, Baillie followed up on her initial literary forays with a flurry of publication. She was paid £300 by her publisher for the second volume of *Plays on the Passions*, which included a comedy on Hatred entitled *The Election*, and two dramas dealing with Ambition: *The Ethwald* and *The Second Marriage.* She also published in 1802 a collection of *Miscellaneous Plays*, which included, among others, the dramas *Constantine Paleologue*, *The Country Inn*, and *Rayner*. Both of these new volumes were very popular, and Joanna was praised for the philosophical and moral nature of her plays, which depicted human nature through the lens of the early 19th-century audience's fascination with psychology and behavioral expectation.

During this period, she also spent a great deal of time caring for her mother, who had become sick and blind. Dorothea died in 1808. Joanna became known as a great philanthropist, donating one-half of her slender annuity, and much of the profit from her writing, to those who had fallen upon misfortune or were in need of funds for education or business ventures.

In 1808, Baillie met Sir Walter Scott, who had been impressed by her plays. She and Agnes were invited to visit at his house in Edinburgh, and the sisters, recently freed from the need for caring for their mother, were able to accept the invitation. Baillie and Scott became lifelong friends. During this first visit, she was flattered that Scott asked for her honest opinion of his newest work, *House of Aspen*. At his request, Joanna wrote out a careful, but insightful, critique of the book.

When Baillie returned to Hampstead, she continued her dramatic writing, producing in 1810 *The Family Legend*, followed in 1812 by the third volume of *Plays on the Passions*, which included three dramas on Fear: *Orra*, *The Dream*, and *The Siege*, plus a musical drama, *The Beacon*. During this period, she also continued writing short poems, a few of which were published in the *Edinburgh Annual Register* and the *British Critic*. In 1817, she began a new project, *Metrical Legends of Exalted Characters*, a collection of poems and dramatic ballads in the ancient style on famous personages in Scottish history.

Baillie continued to make contacts with the leading lights of the British literary community, and she persuaded her friends to assist her philanthropic efforts. In 1823, she published *A Collection of Poems, chiefly Manuscript and From Living Authors, Edited for the Benefit of a Friend by Joanna Baillie*. The book included contributions by Sir Walter Scott, Robert Southey, and William Wordsworth, and many other of Joanna's contemporaries, including five women, among them ***Susan Edmonstone Ferrier**. In addition to her literary work, Joanna remained on close and affectionate terms with her brother and sister-in-law, whom she and Agnes visited frequently. When, in 1823, Matthew became seriously ill, Joanna traveled to London to help care for him and was devastated when he died on September 23.

Throughout her writing career, Baillie never lost hope that her plays would one day be a success on stage, and she was overjoyed by the occasional news that one of her dramas had been produced on some obscure English or Scottish stage. During the 1830s, she wrote a series of 12 plays, which she intended to have released posthumously to small London theaters for production but, by 1836, convinced that they would probably not succeed on any London stage, she agreed to allow them to be published. This latest collection included two dramas on Jealousy: *Romiero* and *The Alienated Manor; a play on Remorse, Henriquez, and a tragedy on Religion, The Martyr*. The collection was well-received by critics, who marvelled at the continued output of a literary figure nearing 80.

During her later years, Joanna also turned her attention and her pen to religion. Throughout her life, she had been deeply religious. Her belief in the power of prayer and personal immortality are evident in her dramas. She became increasingly interested in the issue of the human nature of Christ, which she treated in a pamphlet entitled "A View of the General Tenor of the New Testament regarding the Nature and Dignity of Jesus Christ." She released her religious treatise privately, and it received mixed reviews, even from her close friends. Scott cautioned Baillie against miring herself in a debate she was ill-equipped to argue. She did succeed, however, in starting up a lively correspondence with the bishop of Salisbury, who disagreed with her views but admired her intellect.

Baillie remained remarkably active in the literary community well into her 80s. Although in 1832 she had been stricken with what she described as "a very heavy disease" which curtailed her physical activity, she and Agnes continued to host social engagements in their home. Baillie remarked in a letter to a friend, "Ladies of four score and upwards cannot expect to be robust, and need not be gay. We sit by the fireside with our books, . . . and receive the visits of our friendly neighbors very contentedly, and I trust I may say, very thankfully."

During the last decade of her life, Baillie still received visitors from Britain, America, and Europe, and was considered a leading light of the British literary community. She was recognized for her contributions by two learned societies. In 1840, she was made an honorary member of the Historical Society of Michigan, and in 1846 she was made an honorary member of the Whittington Club, a newly established lodge with a library and reading room, designed to provide meals and lectures on literature, science, art, music, and mathematics. An even greater honor to Baillie was the printing of a volume of her complete works shortly before her death in 1851 by Longman, Browne, Green, and Longman in London, which Joanna happily referred to as "my great monster book." Her dramas and poems continued to be popular reading material throughout the 19th century.

The last years of Baillie's life were plagued by physical infirmity, and by 1844 she was complaining of memory loss. She and Agnes continued to receive visitors even when she was no longer able to leave her house. After retiring to bed on February 22, 1851, she slipped into a coma and died early on the morning of February 23, at 88 years of age. Her sister Agnes survived her by a decade, dying in 1861 at the age of 100.

During her lifetime and afterwards, Joanna Baillie has been praised for her firm morality and her literary achievements, and she has been compared favorably with William Shakespeare (although even her admirers admitted that she never succeeded in throwing herself fully into the emotions of her characters) and with Sir

Walter Scott, her lifelong friend. Throughout the 19th century, her tragedies, despite their lack of success on the stage, were considered the best ever written by a woman. Baillie was praised by contemporaries for her "clear, masculine and unaffected eloquence." Her ability to maintain cordial relationships with her peers and avoid "literary feuds" was ascribed soon after her death to the fact that she "never bated a jot of the dignity of the lady, that she might gain the laurels of a poet." Modern literary scholars have marvelled at how a woman so lacking in education and worldly experience could ever produce such convincing portrayals of some of humanity's basest passions, and she is considered a pioneer in the development of a new style of drama which examined "motives and personality . . . what makes some people self-defeating and destructive while others are benevolent and virtuous," and thus laid the foundation for a secular morality that defined psychological imbalance as a person's separation from self, rather than a person's separation from God. Baillie's virtuous personal life helped to give her plays tremendous moral force, and her life was considered to exemplify both great literary talent and the best of virtuous 19th-century womanhood.

SOURCES:

Baillie, Joanna. *The Dramatic and Poetical Works of Joanna Baillie.* London: Longman, Brown, Green, & Longman, 1851.

Carhart, Margaret S. *The Life and Work of Joanna Baillie.* New Haven, CT: Yale University Press, 1923.

Gaull, Marilyn. *English Romanticism: The Human Context.* NY: Norton, 1988.

Gilfillan, George. *Galleries of Literary Portraits,* Vol. 1. Edinburgh: James Hogg, 1856.

Hughes, Laurie B. "Joanna Baillie: Drama, Morality and Passion," Master's Thesis, University of Tennessee, Knoxville, 1990.

Kimberly Estep Spangler,
Assistant Professor of History and Chair of the Division of Religion and Humanities at Friends University, Wichita, Kansas

Bajer, Matilde (1840–1934)

Danish feminist. *Name variations: Mathilde. Born in 1840; died in 1934; married Frederik Bajer (an influential Member of Parliament).*

When John Stuart Mill's *Subjection of Women* was translated into Danish by leading Danish literary figure Georg Brandes in 1869, the book's subject matter was not lost on Matilde Bajer. In his essay, Mill argued that women were only different from slaves because their masters demanded that they be willing slaves. A leading feminist in the late 19th century, Matilde Bajer, together with her husband Frederik, founded the Society of Danish Women to "improve the intellectual, moral and economic status of women, and make them an active and independent member of the family and the nation." As the Bajers primary goal was to increase economic opportunities for women, they opened a women's trade school in Copenhagen in 1872. In 1886, Matilde founded the Danish Women's Progress Association, a harbinger of the suffrage movement. Members included **Marie Rovsig**, journalist **Caroline Testmann**, and **Elizabeth Grundtvig**, editor of the journal *Kvinden og Samfundet* (*Women and Society*).

Baker, Augusta (1911–1998)

Storyteller and librarian who pioneered efforts to bring an honest portrayal of ethnic groups to children's literature. *Born Augusta Braxton in Baltimore, Maryland, on April 1, 1911; died after a long illness on February 22, 1998; daughter of Winfort J. and Mabel (Gough) Braxton (both teachers); attended University of Pittsburgh, 1927–29; graduated New York State College, Albany, New York, A.B., 1933, B.S. in Library Science, 1934; married James Baker (divorced); married Gordon Alexander, on November 23, 1944; children: (first marriage) James Baker III.*

During a 37-year career as a children's librarian and storyteller with the New York Public Library, Augusta Baker influenced the lives of several generations of children. Groundwork for her mission was perhaps laid during her childhood in a family that valued education above all else. The only child of teachers, Baker came from a close-knit family which included a grandmother who enchanted the young Baker with stories that had been handed down from generation to generation. Baker credits these storytelling sessions with both strengthening her imagination and increasing her vocabulary. "I learned new words—long, difficult, beautiful words—for my grandmother did not know about vocabulary control and short sentences."

After graduating from the all-black high school where her father taught, 16-year-old Baker enrolled at the University of Pittsburgh. Entering this predominantly white environment in 1927 presented a new challenge for the black teenager, one she was to face many times. At the end of her sophomore year, she married James Baker, a graduate student in social work. The couple had a son and later divorced. Baker remarried in 1944.

After deciding against a teaching career, Baker went on to receive a library science degree. In 1937, she was hired as assistant to the children's librarian at the New York Public Library's 135th Street branch which served Harlem's black community. Her first survey of the children's collection revealed an appalling lack of material about black history and culture. Harlem's children had little knowledge of their own history, a situation made worse by the often deplorable depictions of blacks in literature. Recalled Baker: "Most of the books which included black characters represented them as shiftless, happy, grinning, dialect-speaking menials. This was what was being written for children and what they read. I was distressed and frustrated."

Realizing she was not alone in her concern, she enlisted the support and financial backing of those who could help and, in 1939, founded the James Weldon Johnson Memorial Collection, a body of children's books selected for their "unbiased, accurate, well rounded picture of Negro life in all parts of the world." Baker also initiated a number of new services and programs, including concerts, reading clubs, and guest appearance of black artists, writers, diplomats, and other role models. She also began storytelling. Her grandmother's folktales made their way to the ears of a new generation.

Instrumental in expanding her programs into the community, Baker shared her educational values with parents, teachers, and allied agencies. Using her opportunities to speak with publishers and editors of children's books, she shared her concerns about stereotypical representations of blacks in juvenile literature and the lack of substantive material. Through the years, some publishing houses began to respond to the problem.

In 1953, Baker was promoted to assistant coordinator of Children's Services (she later became coordinator), and in 1955 was invited to Trinidad to organize children's library service at the Trinidad Public Library. She also became a visiting lecturer in the school of library service at Columbia University. She continued her program on storytelling, training others in the technique through workshops and lectures, and she produced several reference guides for storytellers, including *Stories: A List of Stories to Tell and to Read Aloud*, *The Talking Tree*, and *Golden Lynx*. In 1971, she published a bibliography, *The Black Experience in Children's Books*, a listing of books highly rated for their value in intercultural education which has been revised every five years since 1974. In November of that year, she also began a series of weekly broadcasts, "The World of Children's Literature," on WNYC-Radio.

Throughout her career, Augusta Baker was active in numerous professional associations and agencies, and she received countless awards, including the Parent's Magazine Medal Award (1966) for "outstanding service to the Nation's children"; the American Library Association Grolier Award (1968) for "outstanding achievement in guiding and stimulating the reading of children and young people"; the Women's National Book Association Constance Lindsay Skinner Award (1971); and the Catholic Library Association's Regina Medal (1981). In 1989, she became the first recipient of the ***Zora Neale Hurston** Award, presented by the Association of Black Storytellers.

Augusta Baker retired in March 1974. "The black child needs the image of a black librarian—and white children need this image also," she once wrote. "The community needs the black children's librarian who will relate to it and understand the unique problems."

SOURCES:

Commire, Anne. *Something about the Author.* Vol. 3. Detroit, MI: Gale Research.

Smith, Jessie Carney. *Notable Black American Women.* Detroit, MI: Gale Research, 1992.

SUGGESTED READING:

Baker, Augusta. "My Years as a Children's Librarian," in *The Black Librarian in America.* Edited by E.J. Josey. Metuchen, NJ: Scarecrow Press, 1970.

Baker, Augusta, selector. *The Black Experience in Children's Books.* NY: The New York Public Library, 1971.

RELATED MEDIA:

A taped interview with Baker is in the Black Oral History Collection, Special Collections, Fisk University Library.

Barbara Morgan,
Melrose, Massachusetts

Baker, Bea (b. 1929).

See Baker, LaVern.

Baker, Belle (c. 1895–1957)

American actress, singer, and entertainer. *Born Bella Becker in New York, New York, around 1895; died in Los Angeles, California, on April 28, 1957.*

Belle Baker first appeared on the stage as a boy in the Jacob Adler production of *The Homecoming*. Her deep, resonant singing voice and commanding stage presence caught the attention of vaudeville agents, and she soon had star billing at New York's Palace Theatre. Baker's Broadway debut came in 1911 in *Vera Violetta*, and in 1926 she performed the starring role in the short-lived *Betsy*, in which she introduced the Irving Berlin song, "Blue Skies." During her vaudeville days, she popularized a number of other songs, including "All of Me" and "My Yiddische Mama," which came to be associated with her friend *Sophie Tucker. She also appeared in two movies: *The Song of Love* (1929) and *Atlantic City* (1944).

One of Baker's most unusual roles was as the first host of a radio variety program transmitted from a B&O train in 1932. The broadcast from the train, which ran throughout the state of Maryland, helped demonstrate the versatility and mobility of radio broadcasting. Baker played the Palace one last time in 1950. Five years later, she was featured on the television show "This is Your Life."

Barbara Morgan,
Melrose, Massachusetts

Baker, Bonnie (b. 1917)

American singer of the 1940s, whose greatest hit was "Oh Johnny, Oh Johnny." *Name variations: called Wee Bonnie Baker because of her height. Born Evelyn Nelson in Orange, Texas, on April 1, 1917; married*

Belle Baker

Billy Roger (her accompanist), in 1950; children: one daughter, Sharon.

With a baby voice that matched her diminutive size—4'5''—Bonnie Baker rose to fame with her recording of the old song "Oh Johnny, Oh Johnny," and hit her stride in the 1940s. During her heyday, one critic called her sound "sex in a high chair."

Born Evelyn Nelson and raised in Texas, Baker learned to sing on her own, gaining her early experience at school proms and parties. After struggling along on the professional club circuit, her big break came in 1936, when she was hired by bandleader Orrin Tucker as his vocalist. He changed her name to Bonnie Baker, and, after some teasing from the musicians about her size, the "Wee" was added. In 1939, while on tour, Baker sang the 1917 song "Oh Johnny, Oh Johnny" and recorded it during an engagement at Chicago's Palmer House. Returning from a month of one-nighters, she found that the recording had swept the East Coast. Tucker and Baker were then signed for spots on the popular radio show "Your Hit Parade" and were featured in the 1941 movie *You're the One.*

After a number of other hits, including "Billy," "My Resistance Is Low," and "You'd Be Surprised," Baker left Tucker and went solo, singing with such notables as Stan Kenton and Tony Pastor. She toured for the USO with an all-girl band and in 1943 appeared in a second movie, *Spotlight Scandals.* After the war, she joined "Ken Murray's Blackouts," where she met and became good friends with comedienne **Marie Wilson.**

Baker married her accompanist Billy Rogers in 1950, and the couple had a daughter. Though she continued to tour, the musical tastes of the country were changing and quality bookings became harder to find. She cut a final album for Warner Bros. in 1958. After a major heart attack in 1963, Baker retired for good and moved to Fort Lauderdale, Florida.

SOURCES:

Lamparski, Richard. *Whatever Became of. . . ?* 4th Series. NY: Crown, 1973.

Barbara Morgan,
Melrose, Massachusetts

Baker, Dorothy (1907–1968)

***American novelist known for her depiction of an aging jazz trumpeter in* Young Man with a Horn.**

Born Dorothy Dodds on April 21, 1907, in Missoula, Montana; died of cancer on June 17, 1968, in Terra Bella, California; daughter of Raymond Branson Dodds and Alice (Grady) Dodds; educated at Occidental College and Whittier College; granted B.A., 1929, M.A., 1933, University of California, Los Angeles; married Howard Baker, on September 2, 1930; children: Ellen (b. 1940) and Joan (b. 1943).

Selected works: Young Man with a Horn *(1938);* Trio *(1943);* Our Gifted Son *(1948);* The Street *(1951); (with Howard Baker)* The Ninth Day *(1967);* Cassandra at the Wedding *(1962).*

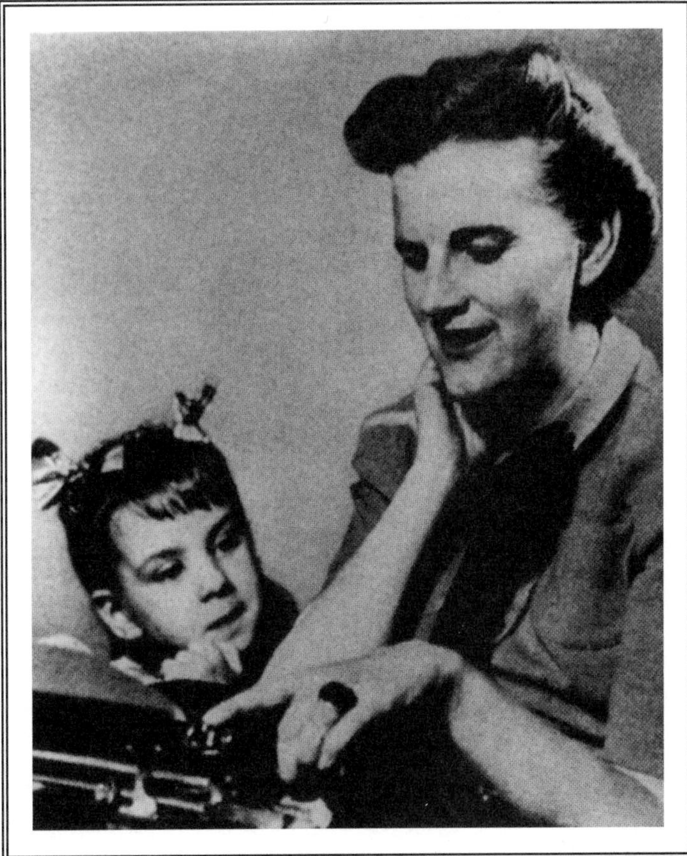

Dorothy Baker

Though childhood study of the violin provided Dorothy Baker a musical background from which to build her novel *Young Man with a Horn,* no amount of training could account for what critics called an uncanny capacity to describe music and the emotional response it inspires. Loosely based on the life of jazz legend "Bix" Beiderbecke, *Young Man* marked a debut that Baker would struggle to equal for the remainder of her literary life.

She was born Dorothy Dodds on April 21, 1907, in Missoula, Montana. Railroad dispatcher Raymond Dodds moved his wife and daughter to California early in Dorothy's life so he could pursue the oil business. Encouraged toward music, Dorothy studied the violin throughout her childhood and shared her father's interest in jazz. Her penchant was more for languages, however, and she attended college at Occidental and Whittier before settling at the University of California, Los Angeles. After graduation in 1929, she began work on a master's degree in French. While studying in Paris in 1930, she met and married poet Howard Baker and wrote the first draft of a book she called *Trio*, but, once back home in California, she shelved the manuscript. While completing her master's degree, she began teaching at a small private school. Inspired by her experiences as a teacher, she wrote a short story, "A Glance Around," that *The Magazine* published in 1934. Encouraged, she quit her job to write full time.

Howard Baker's work as a literature professor led the couple to Cambridge, Massachusetts, where Dorothy began writing about an aging jazz trumpeter. One hundred pages of the story earned her a 1937 Houghton Mifflin fellowship, which guaranteed publication. In 1938, *Young Man with a Horn* appeared to rave reviews. With critics and the reading public clamoring for her next effort, Baker dusted off *Trio* and began to revise it. Simultaneously, she worked on a movie script for *Young Man*, which had been sold to Hollywood. Actor Burgess Meredith was secured to play the lead, but the movie never received adequate funding and was abandoned. A similar fate awaited a theatrical version of the book. (However, in 1950, *Young Man with a Horn*, starring Kirk Douglas, ***Doris Day**, and **Lauren Bacall**, was made into a successful film, famed for its extraordinary jazz soundtrack.)

In 1943, the response to the publication of *Trio*—the story of a college woman's rescue from her lesbian affair with a professor by a dashing young man—was decidedly cold, with critics maintaining that Baker had fallen far short of her obvious talent. Nevertheless, the Bakers retooled *Trio* for the stage and opened at the Belasco Theatre in New York City. Plagued by finances and controversy, *Trio* shut down.

The Bakers returned to California where they collaborated on the 1957 television drama *The Ninth Day*, and Dorothy wrote three more novels. Her last, *Cassandra at the Wedding*, again characterized a gay woman, whose twin sister is her personal and philosophical opposite. The book provoked debate for a second time in Baker's career but was successful enough to renew the author's reputation.

SOURCES:

"Dorothy Baker," in *Current Biography*. NY: H.W. Wilson, 1943.

Evory, Ann, ed. *Contemporary Authors New Review Series*, Vol. 1. Detroit: Gale Research, 1981.

"Houghton Mifflin Awards 1937 Fellowships," in *Publisher's Weekly*. Vol. 12. June 1937.

Kunitz, Stanley, ed. *Twentieth Century Authors*. NY: H.W. Wilson, 1955.

RELATED MEDIA:

Young Man with a Horn, (111 min.) film starring Kirk Douglas, Doris Day, and Lauren Bacall, produced by Warner Bros., 1950.

Crista Martin, freelance writer, Boston, Massachusetts

Baker, Ella (1903–1986)

Civil-rights activist, consumer advocate, community organizer, founder of Student Nonviolent Coordinating Committee, and theorist of participatory democracy. *Name variations: Ella Jo or Ella Josephine Baker. Born Ella Josephine Baker on December 13, 1903, in Norfolk, Virginia; died on December 13, 1986, in Harlem, New York; daughter of Blake (worked as a waiter on a steamship ferry running between Norfolk, Va. and Washington, D.C.) and Georgianna (a schoolteacher before marriage) Baker; attended primary school in Littleton, North Carolina; attended secondary school at Shaw University academy; earned bachelors degree at Shaw, 1927; married T.J. Roberts, late 1930s (though married for over a decade, she kept her own name); children: none of her own, but in 1946 she took in her young niece and raised her as a daughter through her college years.*

Moved from Norfolk to rural Littleton, North Carolina (1912); graduated as valedictorian from Shaw University, Raleigh, North Carolina (1927), then moved to New York City; did editorial work for American West Indian News *and* National News *(1929 and early 1930s); founded (with black writer George Schuyler) the Young Negro Cooperative League, organizing consumer food co-ops during the Great Depression (1932); also worked for WPA (Works Progress Administration) consumer education project; began an association with the National Association for the Advancement of Colored People (NAACP, 1938); named NAACP national field secretary (1941); named national director of branches (1943); resigned position to raise niece (1946); ran unsuccessfully for N.Y. City Council on Liberal Party ticket (1951); named president of New York City branch of NAACP and began working to end de facto segregation in New York City schools (1954); inspired by Montgomery bus boycott in Alabama, formed "In Friendship" with Bayard Rustin*

Ella Baker

and Stanley Levison to raise funds and provide encouragement to Montgomery boycotters (1956); went to Atlanta to help found the SCLC (Southern Christian Leadership Conference) with Dr. Martin Luther King, Jr. (1957); set up SCLC office in Atlanta and became associate director (1958); worked to register African-American voters during "Crusade for Citizenship" (1958–60); named executive director of SCLC (1959); "midwifed" birth of a student-controlled civil-rights group, the Student Nonviolent Coordinating Committee (SNCC), convening a meeting of student leaders at her alma mater (1960); set up SNCC office in Atlanta (August 1960); helped focus SNCC on voter registration, culminating in the successful "Freedom Summer" (1964), which influenced passage of the Voting Rights Act of 1965; presented keynote address at the Mississippi Freedom Democratic Party convention in Jackson, Mississippi (July 1964), and organized an MFDP office in Washington, D.C.; joined the staff of the interracial social justice group Southern Conference Education Fund (SCEF, 1967); continued activism through the 1970s and into the '80s, as vice-chair of the Mass Party Organizing Committee (1972), as national board member of the Puerto Rican Solidarity Committee, and as public speaker and advisor to human-rights groups.

By the spring of 1960, Ella Baker was becoming frustrated with the leadership of the Southern Christian Leadership Conference (SCLC); to her, everything revolved around Martin Luther King's personality. Rank and file members were permitted to contribute little toward the development of the organization's goals and policies. Baker disagreed with this style of command. She felt that political movements should be built around "group-centered leadership" in order to help the members develop their self-sufficiency. Accordingly, she opposed the focus on a strong church organization, led by a charismatic preacher. Baker had been pushing the ministers to set up "citizenship classes" so that their people could meet official reading-and-writing voting requirements and become better informed. But this did not become a priority for SCLC until after Baker had left the organization. Apparently, there was a strong element of sexism within the SCLC hierarchy. Aldon Morris maintains that the ministers ignored organizational rules and were perennially late for meetings, but expected women workers to put in long hours and be available for work on demand. She was 20 years older than King, with far more experience in civil-rights work, yet Baker's advice on policy was largely ignored. She found herself relegated mainly to the administrative and clerical work of running the office.

> My theory is, strong people don't need strong leaders.
>
> —**Ella Baker**

This, in itself, was not the cause of Baker's frustration. Though she was responsible for setting up the office of the Southern Christian Leadership Conference in 1958, she had never been one to seek the limelight or the reins of power. As she told **Ellen Cantarow**: "The kind of role that I tried to play was to pick up pieces or put together pieces out of which I hoped organization might come. My theory is, strong people don't need strong leaders."

However, by 1959, Baker was convinced that SCLC was limiting its effectiveness and hindering the black community's quest for freedom and equality. She found it especially aggravating to witness discrimination within the organization against its female members. Baker stands as an example of how, as Charles Payne has argued, "men led, but women organized" the civil-rights activities in the South, just as they kept the pews filled in the preachers' churches. Thus, she began pushing the SCLC leaders to involve both women and young people at all levels of the organization. In 1959, she insisted "the participation of women and youth in the southern civil-rights struggle must be promoted," and criticized the lack of women's involvement on the SCLC Executive Board. She also strongly approved of the new student activism signaled by the wave of sit-ins that began in February of 1960. Thus, she induced the SCLC to allocate the funding and convinced the president of her alma mater, Shaw University in Raleigh, N.C., to provide the space for a gathering of campus sit-in leaders on the Easter weekend of April 16–18, 1960. Baker's invitation, sent to campuses around the country, explained that the conference would be "youth centered," with an expressed purpose being "TO SHARE experience gained in recent protest demonstrations and TO HELP chart future goals" and also to provide "training and action in Nonviolent Resistance."

Prior to the conference, there was much talk, as well as speculation in the press, that SCLC was planning to bring the student movement under their direction and control. When SCLC leaders arrived in Raleigh, they attempted to implement their agenda. Remembering that day, Baker told Cantarow:

> The Southern Christian Leadership Conference felt they could influence how things went. They were interested in having the students become an arm of SCLC. . . . So when it was proposed that the leadership could influence the direction . . . I was outraged. I walked out.

It was a momentous decision. Had she been so inclined, Baker probably could have convinced the students to accept King and the ministers' leadership. However, she refrained from this, and the next day, April 17, students voted to create an independent organization, the Student Non-violent Coordinating Committee (SNCC), with Marion Barry as chair. "Snick," as it was called, became, in **Anne Braden**'s words, the biggest "single factor that shaped Southern history in the early 1960s" as it harnessed the vitality and enthusiasm of youth to an ambitious voter registration drive that changed the political character of the South forever.

Though Ella Baker was born in Norfolk, Virginia, most of her reminiscences involve the rural community of Littleton, North Carolina, where she moved with her family when she was eight years old. An ethic of caring pervades Baker's stories. Memories of her childhood are replete with examples of generosity and the sharing of food, work, and home. Her mother took in the sick, her aunt raised other's children during hard times, her grandfather mortgaged his farm to buy food for families who lost their crops when the Roanoke River flooded. The charity she describes was a way of life in the small, intimate community where she grew up.

Out of that experience came her life's mission: to extend to others the feelings of security and human connectedness that get lost when communities transform and people relocate to the urban areas. As Baker told Cantarow, "Whatever deep sense of community that may have been developed . . . didn't always carry over to the city when they migrated. They lost their roots. When you lose that, what will you do next? You *hope* that you begin to think in terms of the *wider* brotherhood."

Ella Baker had two siblings, her older brother Curtis and her younger sister Margaret. Her father Blake Baker was frequently away from home because he worked as a waiter on a ferry between Washington, D.C., and Norfolk. Her maternal grandparents, Mitchell and Josephine Elizabeth Ross, had been born slaves but gained their freedom after the Civil War. Her grandfather was able to buy a portion of the plantation estate he had worked as a slave, and on that 20-acre or so plot of land he provided for his family. On Sundays, he was the Baptist preacher, and Baker remembered feeling important as she sat next to him in a big chair in front of the congregation. She understood Christianity to mean that "your relationship to human beings was more important than your relationship to the amount of money that you made."

Littleton provided no secondary school that Ella could attend, so in 1918 her mother, a schoolteacher before she married, sent her to a boarding school in Raleigh, North Carolina, an academy run by Shaw University and the American Baptist Home Mission Society. After completing the secondary course, Baker enrolled at the university. Unlike most schools for African-Americans which emphasized vocational skills, the Shaw curriculum was liberal arts. Studying philosophy, languages, mathematics, and sociology, Baker excelled at Shaw and was named valedictorian of the class of 1927. She hoped to go on to graduate study in sociology at the University of Chicago (one of the few graduate schools then that would enroll African-Americans), but she couldn't afford to live there: "You can't go to Chicago and make it as easily with nothing as you could in New York." Instead, she went to New York City and moved in with her cousin.

Though Baker had excellent credentials, she was also a black woman; consequently, she was unable to find anything except unskilled employment in New York until 1929. She took factory work and waited tables as she had during her college years until she landed an editorial position with the *American West Indian News*, and then with the *National News* in 1932. This brought her in contact with many black writers, including Pittsburgh *Courier* writer George Schuyler, who had written about the need to develop food cooperatives to help the poor during the Great Depression. Intrigued with this idea, Baker worked with Schuyler to develop the Young Negroes' Cooperative League (YNCL) and was elected its national director in 1931. She traveled the Eastern states and helped set up co-ops in a number of cities. The YNCL embodied an organizational structure that was non-hierarchical and egalitarian, which provided Baker with her standard.

When the Works Progress Administration (WPA) was created as part of Roosevelt's New Deal programs, Baker signed on with the Workers' Education Project (WEP). Using her formal education and her YNCL experience, she wrote brochures and offered classes on consumer issues. In the later '30s, Baker progressed from consumer advocacy to full-time civil-rights work. Joining the NAACP in 1938, she became its national field secretary in 1941 and embarked on a campaign to increase membership. Leaving her New York home in mid-February, Baker spent six months on the road in the South. This work put her in touch with many leaders in the black communities, important contacts for future civil-rights work. Speaking effectively to laborers and black professionals alike, she emphasized the need to connect black communities to one another through the NAACP branches.

Named the national director of NAACP branches in 1943, Baker initiated a series of regional leadership conferences designed to encourage inexperienced members to develop their potential. ***Rosa Parks**, who later became famous for initiating the Montgomery bus boycott, attended one of those conferences in 1944.

In 1946, Baker resigned from the NAACP. Her stated reason was that she had accepted responsibility for raising her young niece and could no longer travel for six months of the year. There were apparently other contributing factors, however. As she later did with King, Baker clashed with other NAACP leaders on matters of policy and strategy. At the time that Baker was national director of branches, the NAACP had 400,000 members, who were used mainly as a source of funds to support the lobbyists and legal teams. As Mueller has written, Baker wanted the members to become more "meaningfully involved in the program." In addition, she favored direct action politics over the NAACP's traditional reliance on law suits.

After resigning from her position, she worked at fund-raising with the National Urban League Service Fund and with several national health organizations. She joined other progressive causes, including the opposition to McCarthyism and the unsuccessful battle to prevent passage of the harsh McCarran-Walters Act, which allowed the deportation of any immigrant believed to be involved in "Communist" or "Communist-front" activities. In 1951, Baker campaigned unsuccessfully for a seat on the New York City Council as a member of the Liberal Party. Also in the early 1950s, she joined the New York City branch of the NAACP, becoming advisor to its Youth Council and then its president.

After the 1954 Supreme Court decision outlawing segregation in public schools and other public facilities, Baker tackled the New York City school system. Statistical evidence showed that black children's levels of achievement deteriorated once they entered the schools. She argued that the pervasive inequality in New York schools resulted from the de facto segregation in housing, and that school integration could be achieved only by ending segregated neighborhoods. For her efforts, she was named to Mayor Robert F. Wagner's Commission On School Integration. She spent the summer of 1957 organizing "Parents in Action for Quality Education," because she believed that parental involvement in school policy decisions would improve the performance and accountability of the school system.

The Montgomery bus boycott of 1956 inspired Baker, and New York activist-intellectuals Bayard Rustin and Stanley Levison, to work with King to continue the direct-action approach in other areas. The Southern Christian Leadership Conference (SCLC) emerged from this collaboration. So Baker went South in late 1957 to run the SCLC office in Atlanta and stayed on for over two years. Her first SCLC assignment was the "Crusade for Citizenship," aimed at doubling the number of Southern black voters in one year (a goal that would not be met). The Crusade was launched in a series of meetings held across the South on Lincoln's Birthday, 1958; 13,000 attended, despite its being one of the coldest evenings in many years. The organizing of the Crusade was hard, hands-on work. It involved traveling to churches and other meeting places of local communities, speaking to the people, distributing literature, setting up voter clinics, and the like. Other SCLC leaders did not become involved in the work to the extent Baker had hoped they would.

Baker left SCLC in August of 1960 to work for SNCC, where she remained a champion of grass-roots, group-centered leadership. The students of SNCC enthusiastically embraced this idea, which came to be called "participatory democracy." "She was much older in terms of age," remarked future SNCC chair John Lewis, "but I think in terms of ideas and philosophy and commitment she was one of the youngest persons in the movement." The concept of group-centered leadership spread to young white political protestors like Tom Hayden, who had worked with Baker and SNCC before writing the Port Huron Statement of the Students for a Democratic Society (SDS). Participatory democracy became a central tenet of the New Left.

With Baker's backing, SNCC commenced the difficult and dangerous task of organizing the politically powerless Southern blacks. They encountered violent resistance from the white political establishment. For example, in 1961, SNCC's Bob Moses attempted to register the black voters of McComb, Mississippi, a community of 13,000. That campaign failed after Moses was beaten by segregationists, McComb activist Herbert Lee was murdered, and other SNCC volunteers were arrested on trumped-up charges. Despite the severity of this repression, SNCC held together.

In 1961, SNCC joined with the older civil-rights organization Congress Of Racial Equality (CORE) to sponsor integrated bus rides through the most dangerous areas of the South. Segregation on busses had been outlawed by the Federal courts, but the South had ignored the rulings. Freedom rides, as they were called, drew intense opposition from segregationists, resulting in firebomb attacks and mob violence against the riders. This induced the Kennedy Administration to put its weight behind the civil-rights activists. Attorney General Robert Kennedy sent in 400 Federal marshals to protect the riders and persuaded Alabama Governor Patterson to mobilize the national guard for further protection.

The most ambitious SNCC project occurred in 1964, an all-out effort to register black voters in Mississippi. The strategy for the "Mississippi Thrust" came after intense sessions among SNCC members. One tactic, Baker told Cantarow, was to invite many white students to join the Freedom Summer campaign.

> They were very aware that when a black person got brutalized for attempting to register to vote, this was nothing new, it had been done before. But when the son of a governor or the daughter of a congressman or the daughter and son of people up North who could give money and who had some political clout got involved, it was a challenge to the powers that be.

Freedom Summer suffered a setback with the shocking murder of three SNCC activists, James Chaney, Andrew Goodman, and Michael Schwerner. Goodman and Schwerner were white, a fact that drew national attention to the murders, and ultimately strengthened the voter drive. Additionally, the conservatives' filibuster of the 1964 Civil Rights bill, strongly pushed by the Johnson Administration but stalled in the Senate since early February, was broken during the week of the murders.

By mid-summer, thousands of new voters had been registered in Mississippi. Because these black voters were excluded from the whites-only primary elections, they formed their own political party, open to all regardless of race or creed. They called it the Mississippi Freedom Democratic Party (MFDP). The new party began readying itself to send delegates to the national Democratic convention being held in Atlantic City that year. At the state-wide MFDP convention in Jackson on August 7, Baker gave the keynote address.

In Atlantic City, the MFDP presented the credentials committee with proof that they ought to be seated, in place of the white Mississippi delegation, for two reasons. They had received more votes than the regular (white) party delegates, and their primary had not been restricted by race qualifications. Despite the support of a number of individuals, the seating challenge failed, largely because President Lyndon Johnson held the convention under his tight control, and he feared losing the votes of white Southern Democrats if the white delegation was expelled. The MFDP reached a national audience, however, when *__Fannie Lou Hamer__'s testimony about the brutality she and others had experienced was broadcast by the television networks.

Congress soon passed another civil-rights bill, the Voting Rights Act of 1965, which sent government inspectors into the South to end discriminatory voter registration practices. Enactment of that law came largely as a result of the efforts of Ella Baker and the other voting rights activists who had brought the issue to national prominence.

Involvement with SNCC was the culmination of Baker's life work, which reveals her to be an advocate not only for African-Americans but for women, the poor, and for any oppressed group. Her career as an activist and organizer spanned five decades. Because she preferred to work behind the scenes, she never attained fame, but her accomplishments are widely known and highly regarded among civil-rights leaders and progressive activists.

In 1967, Ella Baker joined the staff of the Southern Conference Educational Fund (SCEF), an organization formed by Carl and **Anne Braden** to encourage the races to work together. In 1972, Baker was elected vice-chair of the Mass Party Organizing Committee. She was a national board member of the Puerto Rican Solidarity Committee and supported freedom struggles in Third World nations like Zimbabwe and South Africa. Her life story has been the subject of a film *"Fundi"—the Story of Ella Baker* (1981), produced by **Joanne Grant.** Ella Josephine Baker died on December 13, 1986, on her 83rd birthday.

SOURCES:

Braden, Anne. "The Southern Freedom Movement in Perspective," in *We Shall Overcome: The Civil Rights Movement in the United States in the 1950's and 1960's.* Vol. I. Brooklyn, NY: Carlson, 1989.

Britton, John. Interview with Ella Baker, June 19, 1968. Civil Rights Documentation Project. Moorland-Spingarn Research Center, Howard University.

Cantarow, Ellen. *Moving the Mountain: Women Working for Social Change.* Old Westbury, NY: The Feminist Press, 1980.

Carson, Clayborne. *In Struggle: SNCC and the Black Awakening of the 1960s.* Cambridge, MA: Harvard University Press, 1981

Clinton, Catherine. "Ella Baker," in *Portraits of American Women: From Settlement to the Present.* Edited by G.J. Barker-Benfield and Catherine Clinton. NY: St. Martin's, 1991.

Fairclough, Adam. *To Redeem the Soul of America: The Southern Christian Leadership Conference and Martin Luther King, Jr.* Athens, GA: University of Georgia Press, 1987.

Hine, Darlene Clark, ed. *Black Women in United States History: Trailblazers and Torchbearers, 1941–1965.* Brooklyn: Carlson, 1990.

———, ed. *Black Women in America*, Vol. I. Brooklyn: Carlson, 1993.

Lerner, Gerda. "Developing Community Leadership," in *Black Women in White America: A Documentary History.* NY: Vintage Books, 1992.

McAdam, Doug. *Freedom Summer.* NY: Oxford University Press, 1988, pp. 119–120.

Mills, Kay. *This Little Light of Mine: The Life of Fannie Lou Hamer.* NY: Dutton, 1993.

Morris, Aldon D. *The Origins of the Civil Rights Movement: Black Communities Organizing for Change.* NY: The Free Press, 1984.

Sitkoff, Harvard. *The Struggle for Black Equality, 1954–1992.* NY: Hill and Wang, 1993 (revised ed.).

Stoper, Emily. *The Student Nonviolent Coordinating Committee: The Growth of Radicalism in a Civil Rights Organization.* Brooklyn, NY: Carlson, 1989.

SUGGESTED READING:

Baker, Ella. "Bigger than a Hamburger," in *Southern Patriot.* June 1960.

Grant, Joanne. *Ella Baker: Freedom Bound.* Foreword by Julian Bond. Wiley, 1998.

COLLECTIONS:

Ella Baker Oral History, Civil Rights Documentation Project, Moorland-Spingarn Research Center, Howard University.

RELATED MEDIA:

Fundi—the Story of Ella Baker (VHS; 48 minutes), New Day Films, 1981.

"Salute to Ella Baker" (audio cassette; 60 minutes), Pacifica Tape Library, Los Angeles, no date.

Michael D. Cary, Chair,
Department of History and Political Science,
Seton Hill College, Greensburg, Pennsylvania

Baker, Irene Bailey (1901–1994)

Irene Bailey Baker

U.S. Representative, Republican of Tennessee, 88th Congress, March 10, 1964–January 3, 1965. *Born Edith Irene Bailey, in Sevierville, Tennessee, on November 17, 1901; died in Loudon, Tennessee, on April 2, 1994; married Howard H. Baker (Congressman 1951–1964); stepson Howard H. Baker, Jr., served as U.S. senator from Tennessee (1967–1985) and as chief of staff to President Ronald Reagan (1987–1988).*

Irene Baker grew up and was educated in Sevier County, Tennessee, where she also gained experience in local government, working as a court clerk. After her marriage to Howard Baker, she helped in his political campaigns and also chaired a state Republican committee to recruit new women voters. During her husband's seven terms in the House, she worked her way up in the party, serving as Republican National Committeewoman from Tennessee from 1960 to 1964.

After her husband's death in January 1964, Baker won Tennessee's Second District Republican endorsement as a candidate in the special election to determine his successor. With a campaign promise to continue her husband's work to balance the budget, protect jobs in the district's nuclear laboratories and coal mines, and support the Tennessee Valley Authority, she defeated her Democratic rival, Knoxville newspaperman Willard Yarborough.

During her tenure in the House of Representatives, Baker served on the Committee on Government Operations. She supported a Social Security cost of living increase and was critical of what she called the Democratic administration's excessive government spending.

When her term ended, Baker did not seek reelection, but returned to Knoxville, where she was director of public welfare from 1965 to 1971. Her stepson, Howard H. Baker, Jr., followed his parents into politics, serving as U.S. senator from Tennessee from 1967 to 1985, and as President Ronald Reagan's chief of staff from 1987 to 1988.

SOURCES:

Office of the Historian. *Women in Congress, 1917–1990.* Commission on the Bicentenary of the U.S. House of Representatives, 1991.

Baker, Janet (1933—)

British mezzo-soprano and one of the great lieder artists of her day, particularly known for her performances of Benjamin Britten's operas. *Name variations: Dame Janet Baker. Born Janet Abbott Baker on August 21, 1933, in York, England; daughter of May Pollard and Robert Abbott Baker (an engineer); studied with Helene Isepp and Meriel St. Clair; studied at the Mozarteum in Salzburg, Austria; attended master classes with Lotte Lehmann; married James Keith Shelly, in 1956.*

Sang in church and school choirs; left College for Girls in York at 17 to clerk in a bank in Leeds; trans-

ferred to London by the bank manager for better opportunities to study singing; won the Kathleen Ferrier Prize (1956); joined the Glyndebourne Festival chorus (1956); began operatic career (1957); won the Queen's Prize from the Royal College of Music (1959); awarded an Arts Council grant for further study (1960); toured the British Isles, Sweden, France, and the Soviet Union with Benjamin Britten's English Opera Group (early 1960s); made American debut at New York's Town Hall (1966); performed mainly with the English Opera Company, the Glyndebourne Opera, and Covent Garden in London (1970s); awarded an honorary D.Mus. by the University of Birmingham (1968); named a Commander of the Order of the British Empire (1970), Dame Commander (1976); retired from opera (1982); continued to concertize until 1989. Baker's varied operatic roles included the Sorceress in Purcell's Dido and Aeneas; *Pippo in Rossini's* La Gazza Ladra; *Lucretia in Britten's* The Rape of Lucretia, *and Polly Peachum in Britten's* The Beggar's Opera.

Selected discography: Britten's A Midsummer Night's Dream *(Angel, 1961); Elgar's* The Dream of Gerontius *(Angel, 1964);* Lieder Recital *(Saga, 1965);* A Pageant of English Song *(Angel, 1967);* A Tribute to Gerald Moore *(Angel, 1968);* A Schubert Evening *(His Master's Voice, 1970); Britten's* Owen Wingrave *(London, 1970); Cavalli's* La Calisto *(Argo, 1971); Donizetti's* Mary Stuart *(Angel, 1983); Gluck's* Orfeo ed Euridice *(RCA-Erato, 1983); Mahler's* Lieder und Gesänge aus der Jugendzeit *(Hyperion, 1985); Elgar's* Sea Pictures *(Angel-EMI, 1986); Fauré's* La Chanson d'Éve *(Hyperion, 1990); Berlioz's* Les nuits d'été *(Virgin Classics, 1991); Brahms'* Alto Rhapsody *(Virgin Classics, 1991); Mendelssohn's* Infelice *(concert aria);* Psalm 42 for Soprano, Chorus and Orchestra *(Virgin Classics, 1991).*

Selected videos: Christmas at Ripon Cathedral *(Home Vision, 1987);* A Time There Was . . . : A Profile of Benjamin Britten *(Kultur, 1987); Gluck's* Orfeo ed Euridice *(Home Vision, 1988).*

Janet Baker's love of music began in churches like York's famous cathedral, where the notes soared round the high arches until they disappeared heavenward. Growing up with the best English church music, she later noted, "the long phrases of the plainsong soaked in." Born in Yorkshire on August 21, 1933, Baker was exposed early to English culture. Her father Robert Abbott Baker was an engineer who loved music. Her mother **May Pollard Baker** was a theater buff who took her to repertory performances each week. Since the Bakers had limited means, piano and music lessons for their daughter were out of the question. Janet's exposure to music came from performing in school and church choirs, going to local concerts, and listening to the BBC. From the beginning, Baker could distinguish between a good performance and a poor one, a rare ability in a young child.

Until she was 15, Baker sang high soprano, then her voice "broke," she recalled. "It went rocky. I didn't sing for two years. When it came back, I was a mezzo." At age 17, Baker left the College for Girls in York, uncertain about her vocal goals. A father-daughter dialogue in 1952 helped define her course. Wrote Baker:

> My father said to me, "You've got to make up your mind whether you want to do this seriously or just mess around." I was working in a York bank and the sympathetic manager got me a transfer to a London branch. There I began studying with **Helene Isepp**, the mother of Martin Isepp.

She also studied with **Meriel St. Clair.** At the bank, Baker was assigned to the coin-sorting

machine in a back room so that she could practice while she worked. In addition to singing at weddings and funerals, she began giving recitals in small towns in England and Wales under the sponsorship of the Arts Council. Baker recalled:

> I made a pact with myself when I began, that if, by the end of six years, I wasn't doing what I thought I ought to be, or if anything was stopping me, I would go back and live where I always wanted to—in the North of England. Then, in 1956, before the time was up, I won the *Daily Mail*'s Kathleen Ferrier award. It was a big national do and winning was very useful because it gave me a lot of publicity at the right sort of time—the name began to register. But I've always been grateful to my agents for letting me come up the slow, hard way, you know, sending me out to the wilds of Wales for the Arts Council and finding out about audiences and learning my job.

Recognition gave Baker the opportunity to study at the Mozarteum in Salzburg, to join the Glyndebourne Festival chorus, and to take a master class with ***Lotte Lehmann**. During that same time, she married James Keith Shelley who eventually became her business manager. Wrote Baker:

> My husband is an executive in the national driving school and he can't tour with me.... When I get back and say, "Look, they probably want me to go back in January," he'll not complain about it, but say, "How marvelous," because that's the kind of man he is. When we got married 10 years ago my father told him, "You're going to have to give a great deal more than you take," and he has with a very good grace.

Bowing to the demands of a singing profession, the couple chose not to have children.

Because her natural talents had been carefully nurtured, Baker's career continued to advance. But it was her recorded performance as Dido in Purcell's *Dido and Aeneas* that put her on the map. She noted:

> Anthony Lewis, who is a professor at Birmingham, out of the blue, asked me to sing Dido. Of course, I was shocked to the core, knowing I'd been the Sorceress and a Witch in "Dido" and had done about everything else in it in my time—I'd been in the Glyndebourne chorus since 1956—but this was entirely new. I told him, "If you think I can do it, I'll have a go." It opened up a completely new world.

In 1962, Baker made her debut with the English Opera Group at Aldeburgh, an environment dominated by the English composer Benjamin Britten and his companion Peter Pears. They both had a great influence on Baker. "The debt I owe those two wonderful men is incalculable," she wrote:

> Most performers who went through the experience of Aldeburgh must have known this feeling of being burned at the sacred fire. We survived the ordeal or we did not; but if we did, we were always changed, and I feel I was changed for the better. Ben and Peter gave us standards which turned us from national to international performers, and the alteration in status which British performers are now accorded, the respect we are unreservedly given all over the world, is due in large measure to them.

The Aldeburgh association was important not only because her standards were raised, but also because she became increasingly known for her performance of Britten's operas. Some felt when Britten composed *The Rape of Lucretia* in 1946, he had a voice exactly like Baker's in mind. A critic described her performance in the title role: "Few singers have managed to suggest a Lucretia whose internal temperature is drastically higher than her cool exterior. Though she came on looking as wholesome as an English garden, Baker did just that. She seemed aquiver with passion, then overwhelmed with shame at her own suddenly revealed sexuality."

Well established as a singer of oratorios and lieder, Baker began to take the opera world by storm. Whether she portrayed the compliant Dorabella in Mozart's *Cosi fan tutte* or Polly in Britten's realistic *The Beggar's Opera*, her enormous talent impressed opera lovers. When she made her American debut in 1966, critics and audiences were ecstatic. Howard Klein wrote in *The New York Times*, "She can do just about anything vocally and dramatically in a variety of contexts, and she does it all with a communicative radiance and personal warmth that borders on magic."

At this point in her career, her parents' contribution to her stardom was clearly visible. Her father's love of music revealed itself in her impeccable musicianship. Her enunciation, the subtlety and acuity of her phrasing, and her ability to "color sound" made Janet Baker an exceptional singer. Wrote J.B. Steane: "Her art is insistent: . . . to take the song to her heart and communicate it to her never-forgotten listeners." But opera is the most demanding of the arts and more than musicianship is required. It must be coupled with theatrical aptitude. Years of watching theatrical performances with her mother played a critical role in Baker's stage manner. "I'm not *projecting* a picture of the 'Junge Nonne' or Gretchen or Dido," wrote

Janet Baker in Orfeo and Euridice, *1982, at Glyndebourne.*

Baker, "I *am* her. I am her *totally*. Every fiber of my body is this person. I don't think, 'I am the young nun.' It's not like that at all." Her pure mezzo-soprano, musical interpretation, and acting ability made Janet Baker an international opera star.

In 1967, Baker made her first appearance in London's Covent Garden as Hermia in Mendelssohn's *A Midsummer Night's Dream.* Then, under difficult circumstances, Baker was asked to replace **Josephine Veasey** as Dido in the Berlioz opera *Les Troyens* when Veasey fell ill.

Although Baker knew the role, she had sung it only in English at the Scottish Opera. So while the rest of the cast sang *Les Troyens* in the original French, Baker sang her part in English, a difficult task which earned rave reviews.

In the 1970s, Baker reached a new level of stardom performing with three companies: Glyndebourne, Covent Garden, and the English National Opera. In 1971, she performed *Calisto*, *Damnation de Faust*, and *L'Incoronazione di Poppea*. That same year, she appeared in a six-week tour of the United States in solo concerts and in a joint recital with Dietrich Fischer-Dieskau, accompanied by Daniel Barenboim directing the New York Philharmonic. During this decade, she recorded 30 disks, including Berlioz's *Les Nuits d'été*, Vaughan Williams' *Hodie, A Christmas Cantata*, Elgar's *The Dream of Gerontius*, and Ravel's *Shéhérazade*, and gave a televised appearance in Britten's opera *Owen Wingrave*. Baker also proved to be one of the century's great lieder artists, excelling in Schubert and Schumann.

One may well ask if any man-made instrument can pierce the heart so directly as the human voice . . . as Janet's does.

—Gerard Moore

Never a prima donna, Baker had a clear vision of her role as a performer. "In singing a song," she said, "one must be willing to stand aside all the time and not use the song as a vehicle for the personality, which is a dangerous temptation. It *is* a vehicle, but it must be for the right reason." Gerald Moore, a close friend who frequently accompanied the singer when she concertized, concurred: "She has the capacity to thoroughly understand and *hear* her own voice, a faculty that is surprisingly uncommon among singers." He went on to describe his friend:

> There is generosity of nature, her love for her neighbour, her ardent wish to be of service to others, there is her directness and honesty. She is not frivolous, her conviviality and humour are not manifested to all and sundry for she is a serious person and takes herself seriously. I would choose wisdom as her outstanding characteristic, wisdom in her exact assessment of her own powers as a singer, wisdom in her attitude toward life.

Moore, who accompanied many of the 20th century's most celebrated singers, said in a 1970 interview: "My idea of a great singer is one who can do everything: baroque, modern, Italian, German, opera, oratorio. Janet can do all that with absolute ease and conviction. She and baritone Dietrich Fischer-Dieskau are two of the greatest singers in the world today." As Baker's international fame grew, honors followed. She was awarded an honorary D.Mus. by the University of Birmingham in 1968. In 1970, she was named a Commander of the Order of the British Empire and a Dame Commander in 1976. As the honors accumulated, she continued to make highly acclaimed recordings.

In 1982, Dame Janet Baker decided to retire from the operatic stage, though she continued to concertize until 1989. She knew of too many divas whose performances were painful to witness in their waning years. That June, she gave her last performance as Euridice in Gluck's *Orfeo ed Euridice* at Glyndebourne where she had begun her career in the chorus.

Throughout the years, Baker's Yorkshire sensibility never left her. "There's always somebody as good as you and better," she once said, "I try not to bother myself about it. I know I'll never satisfy the masses the way Sutherland does or Callas did. I could never do that sort of thing." But Baker had a clear notion of what her gift meant personally:

> Whether we do it with the written word or with the spoken word . . . we're all desperately trying to talk to each other. We all feel so totally alone, so isolated, and we've got to get through to each other in some way, and music is one of these. . . . Fame and fortune and all the lovely things that happen if you make a name—they're terrific, marvelous, and to have a successful career is a wonderfully fulfilling life. But it's a by-product of the fact that one is doing what one was born to do. I wish everybody could have something so certain.

SOURCES:

Baker, Janet. *Full Circle: An Autobiographical Journal.* London: Julia MacRae, 1982.

Blyth, Alan. *Janet Baker.* London: Ian Allen, 1973.

Carpenter, Humphrey. *Benjamin Britten: A Biography.* London: Faber and Faber, 1992.

Freed, Richard, "Dame Janet Baker's Operatic Farewells," in *Stereo Review.* Vol. 48, no. 6. June 1983, pp. 116–117.

Graeme, Roland. "Janet Baker Sings Berlioz," in *Opera Quarterly.* Vol. 7, no. 1. Spring 1990, pp. 225–227.

Klein, Howard. "If You Think I Can Do It, I'll Have a Go," in *The New York Times.* December 18, 1966, pp. D 19, D 28.

LaRue, C. Steven, ed. *International Dictionary of Opera.* 2 vols. London: St. James Press, 1993.

Moore, Gerald. *Furthermoore: Interludes in an Accompanist's Life.* London: Hamish Hamilton, 1983.

Mordden, Ethan. *Demented: The World of the Opera Diva.* NY: Simon & Schuster, 1990.

———. *Opera Anecdotes.* Oxford: Oxford University Press, 1985.

"Passion and Purity," in *Time.* Vol. 96, no. 12. September 21, 1970, pp. 68, 73.

Reiner, Joseph. "Janet Baker," in *Contemporary Musicians*. Vol. 14, pp. 12–14.

Reinthaler, Joan. "Janet Baker's Classic Elegance," in *Washington Post*. May 12, 1989, p. D3.

Rosenthal, Harold. "Glyndebourne—Contrasted Pleasures," in *Opera*. Vol. 33, Festival Issue. Autumn 1982, pp. 26–30.

Steane, J.B. *The Grand Tradition: Seventy Years of Singing on Record*. 2nd ed. Portland, OR: Amadeus Press, 1993.

Wadsworth, Stephen. "Sense and Sensibility. Janet Baker, Dame Commander of the British Empire" (cover story), in *Opera News*. Vol. 42, no. 1. July 1977, pp. 8–13.

John Haag, Associate Professor of History, University of Georgia, Athens, Georgia

Baker, Josephine (1906–1975)

African-American singer, dancer, music-hall entertainer, civil-rights activist, who took Paris by storm. *Born in St. Louis, Missouri, on June 3, 1906; died in Paris, France, on April 14, 1975; illegitimate child of Carrie McDonald and Eddie Carson; married Willie Wells, in 1919; married William Howard Baker, 1921; married Jean Lion, in 1937; married Jo Bouillon, in 1947; children: adopted 12 (the "Rainbow Tribe"), 1954–1965.*

Joined Jones Family Band, St. Louis (1919); became a member of "Dixie Steppers" (1920); appeared in shows, Shuffle Along *and* Chocolate Dandies

Josephine Baker

(1921–25); moved to Paris, France (1925); appeared in Revue Nègre *and at the Folies-Bergère (1926); opened club Chez Joséphine in Paris (1926); "married" Giuseppe (Pepito) Abatino ("Count di Abatino," 1927); went on world tour (1928–29); starred at Casino de Paris (1930–33); starred in Offenbach's* La Créole *(1934); starred in Ziegfeld Follies, New York (1936); became French citizen (1937); fled Paris (1940); worked for French Resistance (1940–44); appeared in Carnegie Hall, New York (1973).*

"If I'm going to be a success, I must be scandalous," Josephine Baker declared, "I must amuse people." And she was and did both of those things. Flamboyant and uninhibited, egocentric and exploitive, she "just wiggled her fanny," wrote one biographer, "and all the French fell in love with her." At age 19, she became a music-hall sensation in Paris when she appeared wearing nothing but a string of bananas, dancing the Charleston. Reviled as a reversion to African primitivism and admired for her natural, earthy demeanor, Baker achieved the notoriety she craved. Uneducated and unsophisticated, she often misused her money and power; she loved children and animals, performing, and her adopted country, France, and hated all forms of racial and religious intolerance and being alone.

Born in a St. Louis ghetto and brought up in filth and poverty, Josephine Baker sought security and stability throughout her life. The lonely, neglected child and the accomplished performer created fantasy worlds to compensate for a less than perfect reality. Josephine's father had abandoned the family. Largely ignored by her mother and stepfather, Josephine learned from her mother Carrie how to survive and to rely on herself. Rebellious and fiercely independent, she found school too restrictive, too regimented for her restless nature. At age eight, Josephine was sent to do housework for a Mrs. Keiser with whom she also lived. Treated like chattel, she slept with the family dog in a box in the cellar. When her employer punished her by plunging her hand in boiling water, Josephine left.

Carrie worked in a laundry to support her family, three girls, a boy, and her husband, Arthur Martin, whose mental instability prevented him from working. At age 13, Josephine was street-smart and able to earn a living on her own; she worked as a waitress in the Old Chauffeur's Club where the best jazz musicians in St. Louis played to well-dressed crowds. Josephine's goals were set—to be on stage, to be glamorous. In 1919, she married Willie Wells, a foundry worker. A few months later, Willie left after Josephine hit him with a bottle when he attacked her. Josephine returned to the Club where she joined the three-member Jones Family Band. Performing on street corners and collecting donations, she was noticed by the manager of the Booker T. Washington Theater who hired the band. In addition to singing and dancing with the band, she joined the chorus line, the Dixie Steppers. But one had to be different to rise to the top, and Josephine had a talent for being noticed. Placed at the end of the chorus line, she kicked out of step, "shaking and shimmying. . . adding a dash of eroticism with a series of bumps and grinds." In no time, she was a solo performer. Ambitious and determined, Josephine left with the Jones Family Band on a tour of the South as part of the Theatre Owners' Booking Association, a vaudeville chain which played only to black audiences. Life on the T.O.B.A. (called "Tough on Black Asses" by the performers) circuit was grueling and often degrading in segregated America.

At the end of the tour the Jones band stayed in New Orleans, but Josephine moved on to Chicago with the Dixie Steppers, then to Philadelphia. Lonely and rootless, she met and married William Howard Baker, a Pullman porter. His family disapproved of her, an underage chorus girl who was darker than the Bakers. This second marriage, at age 15, could not stifle Josephine's need for recognition. She auditioned for Broadway's all-black musical, *Shuffle Along*, but was not hired because of her age. Undeterred, she left her husband and traveled to New York. Her perseverance paid off, and she was signed on with the road company of the show. Baker was darker than the other chorus girls "who drew a vicious color line between themselves and Josephine," calling her "Monkey." Josephine occupied the comic spot, at the end of the chorus line, and her natural talent as a comedienne bloomed. The other chorus girls resented being upstaged, but audiences loved her crazy antics. Noble Sissle and Eubie Blake, the writer-composer duo responsible for *Shuffle Along*, recruited Josephine for their new show, *Chocolate Dandies*. When she crossed her eyes, stuck her rear-end in the air, and shimmied and shook, audiences roared and applauded. Josephine Baker had found a niche, a home, and love and approval.

On tour with *Shuffle Along* in the East and Midwest, Baker earned the astronomical sum of $125 a week. Her success continued after she joined the cast of *Chocolate Dandies* in New York. Her routines included a part in blackface and as a vamp in a sexy white satin dress. When the show closed in May 1925, Baker found work at the Plantation Club in New York which catered to cafe society and where, wrote her biographer, she was "expected to make the customers happy in ways other than singing and dancing." Well paid and popular, Baker wanted more; she wanted to sing like ***Ethel Waters**. It was time to move on, and the opportunity came when she met **Caroline Dudley** who was hiring a cast for an all-black vaudeville show in Paris.

In collaboration with André Daven of the Champs-Élysées Theatre, Dudley recruited 30 black entertainers for the proposed *Revue Nègre*. When the Plantation Club offered her $300 a week to stay, Baker hesitated, but Dudley tripled that offer, and Baker accepted. Money, opportunity, and French racial attitudes all influenced her decision. Dudley and the troupe, including ❧ **Evelyn Anderson**, sailed from New York on September 15, 1925. Baker was fully aware of the momentous step she had made: "When the Statue of Liberty disappeared over the horizon," she later recalled, "I knew I was free." The rootless waif from the St. Louis ghetto would shortly be dubbed the Black Venus and achieve international fame. Baker was impressed with the absence of segregation in Paris and with the popularity of the many American black musicians who played in clubs centered in the Montmartre area. She soon became friends with Bricktop [***Ada "Bricktop" Smith**, 1894–1984], a black American woman who owned a club where Baker met many American expatriates such as the black poet Langston Hughes, then a waiter at the club, and Cole Porter, who had written "Miss Otis Regrets" for Bricktop.

La Revue Nègre opened after a massive publicity campaign. Paris was plastered with posters by the artist Paul Colin which featured Baker and a blatant caricature of two black men. The show opened on October 2, 1925, and Josephine caused a sensation; against the backdrop of a Mississippi levee, wrote her biographer, she entered "walking on all fours, bottom up, head down, dressed in rags, a tattered shirt and cutoff pants," her hair slicked down with grease which "shown like a bowl of caviar." She then rose and danced a spirited Charleston to "Yes Sir, That's My Baby." Some spectators whistled (the French version of booing), fearing that "a new barbarian invasion was swooping down on Paris." But nothing prepared the onlookers for the final number as Baker, wearing only a pink feather between her thighs and rings of feathers around her neck and ankles, was carried on stage by a large black dancer, Joe Alex, and began undulating, wrote one critic, in a kind of "primitive mating dance." Next day almost all the newspapers reviewed the show. Most were favorable, but Baker even welcomed the accusations of "primitivism"—her "*danse sauvage*," she told a reporter, "represents slavery, discrimination, and liberation." "*La Revue Nègre* proved to the French that black is beautiful," ***Janet Flanner** wrote in *The New Yorker* magazine.

❧ **Anderson, Evelyn** (1907–1994)

African-American dancer. Born in 1907; died of pneumonia on October 29, 1994, in Philadelphia, Pennsylvania.

The last surviving member of *La Revue Nègre*, Evelyn Anderson returned to America after the group disbanded in 1926 but continued to visit Europe often. In 1941, she was detained by the Nazis and held for three years, first in a Dutch internment camp, then in a German convent. Eventually, she was released as part of a prisoner-exchange program with the United States.

Paris is the dance, and I am the dancer.

—**Josephine Baker**

Baker loved Paris and easily adapted to her new environment. Paul Colin, now one of her lovers, introduced her to French manners, French fashion, and the sights of Paris. Her habits of eating spaghetti with her fingers and wearing overalls in public became taboo as Baker wanted to be accepted by the refined Parisians. Through acquaintance with Bricktop, Baker became a part of the permissive, free-spending Montmartre coterie who frequented the local "dives, cafés, dance-halls, and bordellos." The show closed on November 19, then began a tour of Berlin and Moscow. Baker was apprehensive about leaving; in Paris, money and celebrity were assured, and rich men willingly paid for her company and favors. Baker knew she had power, and used it with little discrimination, but feared encountering American-type prejudice in these foreign cities. Before departing for Berlin, Paul Derval of the Folies-Bergère approached Baker to appear in his next review and agreed to pay her $5,400 a month. Knowing she would have to abandon Dudley and *La Revue Nègre* and that the show would fold, she signed a contract, then went to Berlin without telling Derval. A third career option came from the famous German film director Max Reinhardt, who wanted her to attend his acting school.

Berlin appealed to Josephine; it satisfied her craving for action.

Baker's dealings with Dudley and Derval were typical of her business relations during her entire career. With her name in lights and her popularity at its height, the "Black Pearl" became a commercial commodity. Josephine Baker dolls, cocktails, and "hair goo" all bore her name. But celebrity and money did not bring her what she most coveted—social acceptance in Parisian high society. As a showgirl, she could never attain her goal. Moreover, she was practically illiterate, spoke ungrammatical English and French, and her lack of education made her "a stranger to the world of education and culture that surrounded her." Sadly, Baker never understood the depth of the chasm separating her world from that of the French *haute monde*.

Baker's star status did attract wealthy admirers who lavished gifts on her in exchange for sex, but an expensive apartment, cars, and jewels did not bring respectability. And love seemed to elude her, until she met a gigolo, Giusseppe ("Pepito") Abatino, at a club she frequented in Paris. Suave and handsome, Pepito flattered her, doted on her, and set out to "make her a lady." Their liaison lasted for nine years. Singing and dancing lessons, French lessons, proper etiquette, and learning to converse helped ease Baker's social insecurities. As her manager, Pepito showed his genius for organization and business; with backing from one of Josephine's former lovers, he acquired a cabaret where Baker could sing. Chez Joséphine opened in December 1926 and was an immediate success.

Her increasing confidence is evident in the first, and best, of her four autobiographies, coauthored by Marcel Sauvage. Written before she considered herself a legend, it had only a vague relationship with fact, revealing her propensity to fantasize ("I don't lie. I improve on life," she once said). To marry "an average man" and have children and pets was her stated goal. But this desire for a home and family was forever overruled by her need to perform, to live in the spotlight. By the end of the second season at the Folies, Baker's wiggles and bumps and grinds were no longer *à la mode*. And racial incidents intruded on her newfound freedom; American tourists objected to having a "nigger woman" present in the classy hotels and restaurants they patronized in Paris. Uncertainty about her career and her need for love and respectability made her consider marrying Pepito on whom she could depend, and who loved her. However, she was still married to Willie Baker, which didn't prevent the "couple" from announcing to the press that they had wed in June 1927. Josephine and Pepito, the self-styled "Count di Abatino," or the "no-account count" as Bricktop called him, gave out varying stories of the wedding. The press was skeptical, but *The Amsterdam News* (a black New York newspaper) accepted the marriage as genuine. A 16-carat diamond ring failed to convince a dubious public, and the pretense was soon dropped.

Opposite page

Michel Gyarmathy's poster for Josephine Baker's appearance at the Folies Bergère.

Josephine's popularity waned, and Pepito sought a new medium for her talents. A short film, *The Siren of the Tropics*, failed, however, to capture Baker's stage presence. She wept when she saw it. To recoup her image (she had also been booed at a benefit performance), Pepito organized a tour of 25 countries in Europe and South America in 1928–29. Racial epithets and noisy demonstrations marred appearances in several European cities; cries of "Congo savage" and "Go back to Africa" were hurled at a startled Josephine. In marked contrast, she received wild acclaim in Latin America. With Pepito's coaching and her rejuvenated celebrity, Baker became more "urbane, softer, more subdued." Unfortunately her attitude towards her manager-lover changed too. She began to treat him as an employee and no longer bothered to hide her one-night stands from him. In 1930, Pepito obtained a contract for Baker to star in a revue at the Casino de Paris, a higher class music-hall than the Folies-Bergère. Baker was thrilled for she finally got to sing.

Vincent Scotto wrote a song especially for her, "J'ai deux amours," which became her theme song. ("I have two loves/ my country and Paris/ by them always/ my heart is ravished.") In a review of the show, Janet Flanner noted that, "On that lovely [feral] visage lies now a sad look, not of captivity, but of dawning intelligence." Baker had been domesticated and not only on stage. She put down roots in Le Vésinet, 45 minutes outside Paris, where she bought a 30-room mansion; she lived there for 18 years. None of the residents objected to her presence, and she became intimately involved in the community, especially the local orphanage.

After starring in an Offenbach operetta and another film, *Zou-Zou*, Baker undertook a tour of the United States in 1935. Pepito arranged for her to appear in New York in the *Ziegfeld Follies* of 1936, but Baker was furious to find she had only secondary billing. And she was bitter about the critical reviews she received in contrast to the raves showered on ***Fanny Brice** and Bob Hope. A stinging reminder of being "home" was realized when she was permitted to stay at the Hotel St. Moritz but was not to be seen in the lobby or using the guests' elevators. Even American blacks chastised her for supporting Italy's invasion of Ethiopia; Baker admired Mussolini and castigated the ruler of Ethiopia, Haile Selassie, whom blacks idolized, as "an enemy of the people." In a rage, she blamed Pepito for all her problems and dismissed him; he returned to France and died of cancer a few months later. Baker remained in New York and opened a nightclub, Chez Josephine, with only marginal success. While in the States, she obtained a divorce from Willie Baker and visited her family. She returned to France to appear in another revue at the Folies-Bergère, and to open a new club, Le Frontenac.

In 1937, Josephine met Jean Lion, a handsome, blond multimillionaire, who regarded her as a "plaything," but eventually decided to marry Baker against his family's wishes. Jean wanted a docile wife who would further his career in politics and whose world would revolve around him. Josephine, however, lacked the necessary social refinement to fit into his social circle, and her behavior shocked and embarrassed Jean in public. They had nothing in common, and the marriage ended in divorce in 1942. But Baker always had her career and the love of the audience. She continued to perform; she shared the stage with Maurice Chevalier at the Casino de Paris, and, in 1939, they entertained French troops as war fever engulfed Europe. And as a licensed pilot, Baker flew supplies to vital areas for the Red Cross.

As the Germans approached Paris in June 1940, Baker fled south to her 50-room château, Les Milandes in central France, but this ardent French patriot, and citizen, had no intention of abandoning her country. Through her acquaintance with Jacques Abtey of the French military secret police, Baker became an official member of a French Resistance group with ties to General Charles de Gaulle. Her prewar connections with Italian and German embassies made her a valuable resource, and, as an entertainer, her presence at embassy parties would not arouse suspicion. She recorded information obtained at diplomatic gatherings in invisible ink on her sheet music and passed it on to Abtey. From Marseille, Lisbon, and Morocco, Baker and Abtey collected valuable intelligence at considerable risk to their personal safety. In 1941, Baker gave birth to a stillborn child in Casablanca, Morocco. Critically ill, she underwent several operations, convalescing at the luxurious palace of the pasha of Marrakesh who had befriended her. After American

forces landed in North Africa in November 1942, Baker was approached by the Red Cross to entertain troops at an interracial canteen. This led to a grueling tour of army camps which took her across North Africa to the Middle East, and eventually to Italy. She also raised funds and produced propaganda for de Gaulle's Free French Forces and was made a member of the Ladies Air Auxiliary. For her work, she was awarded the Legion of Honor and the Medal of the Resistance after the war.

Her war experiences made her long for stability, for a family. Les Milandes, in the Dordogne region of France, would provide the setting for her new life. Baker was determined to adopt children, but for this she needed a husband. In June 1947, she married her fourth husband, Jo Bouillon, an orchestra leader she had met on a tour of army camps in liberated European countries. Les Milandes would be transformed into a tourist complex, a money-making business. To raise funds for this venture, Baker sold her house in Le Vésinet and her apartment in Paris, returned to the Folies-Bergère, and went on tour. While in the United States, she persuaded her mother, her sister Margaret and her husband, and brother Richard to move to France. World War II and tours in America had profoundly affected Josephine and had given her a mission, a cause: "I'm going to dedicate my life to helping my people," she declared. Racism must be abolished and replaced with the brotherhood of man. In the U.S., major hotels refused to admit her and restaurants refused her service. Traveling in the South, incognito under the name Mrs. Brown, she became the victim of Jim Crow laws. Determined to smash racial barriers, Baker was the first black allowed to register at a first-class hotel in Miami and the first to perform for a non-segregated audience in that city. On the tour, she insisted that blacks be hired as musicians and stagehands for her shows. In all major cities, she defied color barriers, and was soundly criticized by blacks and whites for her verbal attacks on America and praise of French racial attitudes. Called a Communist (she admitted she did not know what one was) and threatened by the Ku Klux Klan, she refused to be silenced. Baker never fully grasped the import of these attacks on her, even when some of her engagements were canceled. But nothing deterred her from crusading for brotherhood, even when it adversely affected her career.

In September 1952, Baker took her tour to Argentina where her political naiveté created a furor in the United States. She openly admired Juan Peron and his late wife ***Eva Peron**; through Juan Peron, she became involved in Argentine politics with disastrous results. As a dictator of a fascist state, he used Baker in his propaganda war against the U.S., showering her with gifts, money, and flattery. Praising Peron and referring to Argentina as an "enlightened democracy" and America as a "barbarous land living in a false, Nazi-style democracy," she was denounced in her native land. In response to a threat by the U.S. Immigration Service to bar her from re-entering the States, Baker declared she would consider it an honor to be barred. Refusing at first to see the abject poverty of the masses in Argentina, she eventually grew disillusioned with the regime as she visited hospitals and poor areas. But she never retracted her statements about America.

Her campaign for racial harmony was carried to extremes at times. She wanted to turn her château of Les Milandes and the village of that name into a kind of sovereign State of World Brotherhood where Baker would reign as queen over her "subjects." A flag and fake postage stamps were adopted as symbols of statehood. However, the glitz and gaudiness of her tourist attractions appalled her more conservative, wealthy, castle-owning neighbors. Nevertheless, Josephine was determined to prove that racial harmony was possible, even if only within the confines of her "state." She and Jo Bouillon adopted children of various races and religions, eventually 12 in all—Josephine's "Rainbow Tribe" of ten boys and two girls. Early on, the tourist complex made money, but expenses soon exceeded revenue. Baker continued to perform on stage and go on tour, often for more than six months a year. Though she had her family, she also needed the devotion of an audience. She had become a legend, but her need to dominate alienated her family and destroyed her marriage.

In August 1963, Baker was deeply in debt, but she flew to the United States to participate in the historic March on Washington where Martin Luther King, Jr., addressed the crowd. Josephine told a nephew that she didn't think King's remarks were strong enough: "I could have done it better," she said. Baker desperately wanted to be a part of the civil-rights movement, on her own terms and in a leadership position, but her reputation of being volatile made people wary. When she tried to organize a benefit concert, she had trouble getting people to work for her—Baker had a habit of not paying her bills. Though the concert was a huge success, Baker was often rude to her fans while her manager went unpaid. So did the French government to whom she owed about $200,000. Other French creditors threatened to have her property seized and sold at auction. Rather than economize, Baker made plans

Columbia Records publicity poster.

to turn Les Milandes into an International Brotherhood College. This never materialized, and the architects went unpaid. Despite her appeals for money to the Empress of Iran, King Hassan II of Morocco, Fidel Castro of Cuba and funds from a TV special hosted by **Brigitte Bardot** and other French notables, her debts increased.

When Les Milandes was sold at auction in 1969, Josephine Baker was 62 years old, homeless, and broke, with 12 children. Exhausted and desperate, she was rescued by Princess Grace of Monaco [***Grace Kelly**] who arranged for her to be the guest star at a ball in Monaco. Further, the princess convinced the Red Cross to give Baker a down payment on a villa near Monte Carlo. More than charity or sympathy, Baker needed an adoring audience. An offer to appear in Carnegie Hall in New York in June 1973 proved to be one of the highlights of her long career. A month later, after giving a concert in Copenhagen, she suffered a heart attack and stroke. Refusing to rest, a week later she was working 12-hour days. A pilgrimage to Lourdes and another tour in the U.S. seemed to revitalize her, but she often rambled incoherently and suffered memory lapses. On returning to France, she starred in a revue based on her life. From Monte Carlo, she took the show to Paris in April 1975. It was a hit, and her friends gave a gala in her honor, celebrating 50 years in show business. Two nights later, Baker suffered a cerebral hemorrhage and died in a coma on April 14, 1975.

"She died of joy," said a friend. And the joy she had given generations of Parisians was repaid the next day at her funeral where over 20,000 people and a 21-gun salute paid her tribute. A second, private funeral was held in Monaco; Princess Grace paid for the burial. A fitting end, wrote Josephine Baker's biographer, for "the ragamuffin from St. Louis, who dreamed of castles and kings."

LaVern Baker

SOURCES:

Haney, Lynn. *Naked at the Feast: A Biography of Josephine Baker.* NY: Dodd, Mead, 1981.

Rose, Phyllis. *Jazz Cleopatra: Josephine Baker in Her Time.* NY: Doubleday, 1989.

SUGGESTED READING:

Baker, Jean-Claude. *Josephine: The Hungry Heart.* NY: Random House, 1993.

Baker, Josephine, and Jo Bouillon. *Josephine.* Trans by Mariana Fitzpatrick. NY: Harper & Row, 1977.

Hammond, Bryan. *Josephine Baker.* With theatrical biography by Patrick O'Connor. London: Jonathan Cape, 1988.

Papich, Stephen. *Remembering Josephine: A Biography of Josephine Baker.* NY: Bobbs-Merrill, 1976.

Jeanne A. Ojala, Professor of History, University of Utah, Salt Lake City, Utah

Baker, Kate (1861–1953).

See Franklin, Miles for sidebar.

Baker, Laurie (1976—).

See Team USA: Women's Ice Hockey at Nagano.

Baker, LaVern (1929–1997)

African-American singer. *Name variations: The Countess, Little Miss Sharecropper, Bea Baker. Born Delores Williams in Chicago, Illinois, on November 11, 1929; died in New York City on March 10. 1997.*

Selected albums: LaVern Baker *(includes "Tweedlee Dee" and "Jim Dandy," 1955);* LaVern Baker Sings Bessie Smith *(includes "Gimmie a Pigfoot" and "Preaching Blues," 1959);* Soul on Fire: Best of LaVern Baker *(1991);* Live in Hollywood *(1992).*

Selected singles: "Tweedlee Dee" (1954), "Bop Ting-a-Ling" (1955), "Play It Fair" (1955), "Jim Dandy" and "Jim Dandy Got Married" (1957), "I Cried a Tear" (1958), "Voodoo Voodoo," "Fee Fi Fo Fum," "Humpty Dumpty Heart," "I Can't Love You Enough," "I Waited Too Long," "See See Rider."

With 20 pop hits between 1955 and 1966, LaVern Baker was considered one of rock and roll's finest singers. Like many black singing artists, she got her start singing in church. By the time she was a teenager, she was performing in Chicago clubs, including the Club DeLisa, where she was billed as Little Miss Sharecropper (a name she also recorded under for RCA and National Records). Later, while engaged at Detroit's Flame

Show Bar, Baker did a recording, her second, for Columbia under the name Bea Baker. Following her signing with manager Al Green, she made her debut as LaVern Baker in 1953 with "Soul on Fire" backed by "How can you Love a Man Like This?" on Atlantic, a small independent label that would eventually rival the major studios. Her breakthrough recording came in October of the following year with the novelty song "Tweedle Dee," and Baker became one of Atlantic's first performers to crossover to the pop charts.

The year 1954, however, was also the year "cover" records made their debut. Once white studios discovered that rock and roll was lucrative, they took an interest. When a song was successful by a black artist, a white artist on a major record label "covered" the song by recording a similar version. (The most horrifying example of this practice might be Pat Boone's cover for Little Richard's "Tutti Frutti.") When Baker's version of "Tweedlee Dee" reached number 14 on the charts, ***Georgia Gibbs** was hired to rerecord the song, and Gibbs' version reached number 2.

The momentum of Baker's career was constantly stalled by white cover artists who rerecorded her songs into bigger hits. When Baker came out with the hits "Jim Dandy" and "Jim Dandy Got Married" in 1957, Gibbs also covered "Tra La La," the flipside of "Jim Dandy." While Gibb's version of "Tra La La" reached number 24, Baker's only reached 94. Frustrated, Baker contacted Michigan State Representative Charles Diggs, Jr., urging him to revise the Copyright Act of 1909, making verbatim copying of a song arrangement illegal, but she was unsuccessful. Baker didn't mind having her songs covered, she said, but she did mind the fact that they were copied note for note without any thought of compensation. The bluesy "I Cried a Tear" (1958) was her only Top Ten pop record.

In 1965, Baker left Atlantic for Decca's Brunswick label. In the late 1960s, she began to tour military bases overseas, becoming the entertainment director at the Subic Military Base in the Philippines. After a self-imposed exile of 20 years, she returned to the United States in the late 1980s and continued to do live-performance work; she also recorded "Saved" and "Leaving It up to You" with Ben E. King for the film *Shag*, and "Slow Rolling Mama" for the film *Dick Tracy*. She was inducted into the Rock & Roll Hall of Fame in 1991. In 1995, suffering from diabetes, LaVern Baker was forced to have both legs amputated below the knee. She died two years later, in 1997, at age 67.

Baker, Mary Ann (1834–1905)

Australian bush ranger. *Born Mary Ann Brigg near Berrico, in the upper Gloucester River valley, Australia, in 1834; died on April 12, 1905; only daughter and one of two children of James (a convict shepherd assigned to the Australian Agricultural Company) and Charlotte Brigg; married Edmond Baker, in 1848; met and traveled with Fred Ward, later known as Captain Thunderbolt, with whom she had at least three children; possibly married John Burrows after 1866, and had more children.*

The true story of Australian bush ranger and outlaw Mary Ann Baker lies somewhere outside of published accounts. She was the daughter of James, a convict shepherd assigned to the Australian Agricultural Company, and Charlotte, an Aboriginal woman who reportedly saved James' life by fighting off an attack from "wild Blacks." The two joined forces and parented Mary Ann and her brother before they married in 1848, the same year that Mary Ann wed Edmond Baker, who may have been another Company shepherd.

Not long after her marriage, Mary Ann met Fred Ward (later known as Captain Thunderbolt), who was employed as a stockman but gained his reputation by driving horses to Aberbaldie and on to the Gwydir. Arrested for horse theft in 1856 and sentenced to prison, he made an escape with the help of an Aboriginal woman who was probably Mary Ann Baker. During the 1860s, Baker and Ward traveled together as outlaws in the bush in northern New South Wales and had several children. By some accounts, Baker hunted and provided food for the family, and to this end she developed her own brand of cattle rustling. Dressed as a man and riding astride, she brandished a butcher's knife fastened onto a long stick; she would separate her prey out of the herd, cut the tendon near a hind hoof to bring it down, and then kill it. Thus the family diet was rich in meat, with the addition of some wild yams and waddle gum.

In 1866, Baker and her children were captured by the police, who describe her as "a very smart woman" who could read and write. Her children were evidently taken away to be cared for by others, and Thunderbolt was shot by police in 1872. Details of Mary Ann Baker's later life are unknown. She may have returned to her father's home for some time, married John Burrows, a station hand, and raised yet another large family. She died in 1905, at age 70.

SOURCES:

Radi, Heather, ed. *200 Australian Women.* NSW, Australia: Women's Redress Press, 1988.

Barbara Morgan,
Melrose, Massachusetts

Baker, Nina Brown (1888–1957)

American author of biographies for children. *Born Nina Brown on December 31, 1888, in Galena, Kansas; died on September 1, 1957, in Brooklyn Heights, New York; daughter of Frank and Belle (Warren) Brown; educated at University of Colorado (teaching certificate, 1911); married Sidney J. Baker, in 1915; children: Berenice and Nina.*

Though her teaching career was brief, Nina Brown Baker's interest in educating children never faltered. Focusing on historical figures and world leaders, she wrote a set of biographies for children which were praised above her fiction.

Born on New Year's Eve in 1888, Baker was raised and schooled in Galena, Kansas, and lived with her parents until she entered the University of Colorado at age 20. College was a burden for her; she stayed only long enough to earn her teacher's certificate in 1911. Employed in Galena for one year, Baker then traveled to Alison, Colorado, to run a rural school. Anticipating adventure, she was overwhelmed to find the school on the town's only street, with just two other buildings—a general store and a blacksmith shop. The young teacher boarded in a guest house, where she had to chop her own wood and do other routine and unfamiliar chores. On the first day of classes, she was helped onto a horse and had to ride six miles to school. She had to walk home, however, leading the horse. No one had taught her how to remount.

Finding Colorado too rugged, Baker returned to Kansas City to attend business school. There, she took office jobs, explored city life, and met businessman Sydney J. Baker, whom she married in 1915. Over the years, the couple had two daughters and lived in Omaha, St. Louis, and Chicago, before moving to Brooklyn Heights in 1938.

Writing had always been of interest to Baker. At age 19, when a short story had been accepted by *Good Housekeeping* for $25 and the magazine encouraged further submissions, a career seemed promising. But Baker was cowed by the rejection of her second story and stopped writing. No longer working after her marriage, she resumed her writing and produced several successful pieces, which led to the 1931 mystery for girls *The Secret of Hallam House*. Over the next decade, inspired by her own young daughters, Baker produced six more such books before turning, in 1940, to biographies for young people. For six months, she researched the life of South American militarist and president Simón Bolívar; then in quick, tight drafts, she produced *He Wouldn't Be King* (1941) and earned her greatest praise yet. At last finding a niche, she produced more than a dozen similar works on famous men such as Benito Juarez, Peter the Great, Sun Yat-Sen, Christopher Columbus, and Amerigo Vespucci. By the time Baker died at her Brooklyn Heights home on September 1, 1957, she had written more than 25 books and, though out of the classroom, had been a force in the education of the young.

SOURCES:

Commire, Anne, ed. *Something About the Author.* Vol. 15. Detroit: Gale Research, 1979.

The New York Times (obituary). September 3, 1957, p. 27.

"Nina Brown Baker," in *Current Biography.* NY: H.W. Wilson, 1947, pp. 31–32.

Crista Martin, freelance writer, Boston, Massachusetts

Baker, Nora (1914–1944).

See Khan, Noor Inayat.

Baker, S. Josephine (1873–1945)

American physician who became a major figure in public health reform and helped save infants of poor and immigrant women in the tenements of New York City. *Name variations: Sara Josephine Baker. Born on November 15, 1873, in Poughkeepsie, New York; died of cancer on February 22, 1945, at New York Hospital; daughter of Orlando D.M. Baker (a lawyer) and Jenny Harwood (Brown) Baker; attended public school in Poughkeepsie; graduated Women's Medical College, New York Infirmary, M.D., 1898; graduated Bellevue Medical College (New York University), Doctor of Public Health, 1917; lived with Florence Laighton; never married; no children.*

Moved from Poughkeepsie to New York City to attend medical school (1894); after a one-year internship in Boston, opened private practice in New York (1901); began work with health department (1902); appointed assistant to Commissioner of Health (1907); appointed director of the Bureau of Child Hygiene of the New York Department of Health (1908–23); founded American Child Hygiene Association (1908); founded Children's Welfare Federation (1911); lectured on child hygiene at Columbia and New York universities; became consultant to the U.S. Public Health Service Children's Bureau; served as an infant welfare activist throughout her life.

Selected publications: Fighting For Life *(an autobiography, 1939);* Healthy Mothers *(1920);* Healthy Children *(1920);* Healthy Babies *(1920);* The Growing Child *(1923);* Child Hygiene *(1925).*

In the early 1900s, when Sara Josephine Baker began her medical work in the slums of New York City, babies died at the rate of 1,500 a week during hot summer weather; one-third of all deaths in the city were of children under five years of age. During World War I, according to Baker, it was "six times safer to be a soldier in the trenches of France than to be born a baby in the United States." In her autobiography, *Fighting for Life,* the physician who became a leader and a reformer in the field of child health describes the experiences that led her to realize how many such deaths were unnecessary, the result primarily of ignorance, neglect of basic cleanliness, and general urban despair. During her career, she would save the lives of thousands of babies.

Born in Poughkeepsie, New York, on November 15, 1873, the child who was to become known as the physician S. Josephine Baker was the daughter of Orlando D.M. Baker, a lawyer, and **Jenny Harwood Brown**, who was in the first class to graduate from Vassar College. Baker's maternal grandmother was **Arvilla Danforth Brown**, descended from a prominent Boston family involved in the founding of Harvard College.

In the small city of Poughkeepsie, Baker grew up among the conventional traditions of a moderately wealthy family. In *Fighting for Life*, her memories are of a happy childhood shared with a brother and two sisters, one of whom died at a young age, and parents who were involved in their community and closely associated with Vassar activities. Students from the college were often guests in the Baker home, and once, when Josephine was ill, the Amherst College Glee Club came to her house to sing for her.

Until age 16, Josephine, who always went by her middle name, assumed that she would attend Vassar. When the unexpected death of her father and brother left an inheritance too small to support her, her mother, and her sister who was in poor health, she decided to bypass the possibility of attending Vassar on scholarship. Instead, she chose to use $5,000 of the family inheritance to support herself while going to medical school.

In an era when few women became physicians and women in medicine were not held in high regard, Baker welcomed the challenges of her chosen field. As she wrote later, "I am thoroughly convinced that obstacles to be overcome and disapproval to be lived down are strong motive forces." After taking a year to study for the New York Regents Exam, which was required for medical school entry, she enrolled at the Women's Medical College at New York Infirmary in 1894, when she was 21. Headed by *__Emily Blackwell__, M.D., sister of *__Elizabeth Blackwell__, who had been the first woman medical graduate educated in the United States, Baker's chosen school was known for its high standards. She graduated in 1898, one year before the school merged with Cornell University Medical School and became coeducational.

S. Josephine Baker

In the summers during her medical school years, Baker worked as a laboratory technician at a sanitarium in a town not far from Poughkeepsie, where she had spent her childhood summers. At medical school, she became friends with her classmate **Florence Laighton**, with whom she was to work and live for the rest of her life. After graduation, both went to Boston, where they did one-year internships at New England Hospital for Women and Children, one of the few institutions where women were accepted as interns. It was during this period that Baker became aware of the problems of poverty-stricken women living in the Boston slums, a foretelling of her later work in New York City.

In 1900, Baker and Laighton returned to New York and opened a general medical practice together. On the excuse that it would be needed for house calls, Baker bought her first automobile, a Prescott steamer, but the car also proved to be a joyous adventure for the two young women. In 1901, because the practice was not generating much money, Baker applied to the New York City Department of Health for the job of a medical inspector. With the recommendation of a lawyer acquaintance, she was hired to inspect school children for contagious diseases by what was then a highly corrupt city government at Tammany Hall.

In 1902, a new commissioner began the political cleanup and reorganization of the city's health department. Baker was offered a more secure position, at first as a summer job, in which she searched out sick babies in the area of New York City known as Hell's Kitchen. Spending a part of each day visiting families and examining babies from tenement to tenement, Baker eventually realized that many of the medical inspectors who preceded her had lied about visits they didn't actually make. Shocked and frustrated by the high death rate among her infants and the seeming impossibility of doing anything about it, she gained some understanding of the corruption not only in the Tammany Hall administration but throughout the ranks of the city government.

The force behind New York's public health campaign against infant mortality was S. Josephine Baker.

—Richard Meckel, 1990

In 1907, Baker saw her opportunity to make changes after she was given the title of assistant to the commissioner of health. In *Fighting for Life*, she relates her duty as a self-described troubleshooter, particularly in tracking down and arresting "Typhoid Mary" (***Mary Mallon**), a woman who became notorious as a typhoid carrier and the source of a number of outbreaks of the disease in New York. While this success gained Baker some notoriety in the New York newspapers, she remained primarily interested in child health and in attempts to reduce and prevent infant death.

In the summer of 1908, Baker held the title of chief of the Division of Child Hygiene when she conducted a successful demonstration of ways to reduce infant death rates. She employed city school nurses, available for the summer season, to visit all newborns in the district with the highest infant mortality. By summer's end, she was able to show a record of 1,200 fewer infant deaths in the district than the previous year. The success assured her financial and political support for her new division, which Baker continued to head from 1908 to 1923. By the time she retired, the goal the doctor had set for herself—that all the country's 48 states would have set up divisions of Child Hygiene—had been achieved.

Under Baker's direction, New York's division initiated many activities. It set up Baby Health Stations as support centers for helping immigrant mothers to care for their infants, combining the distribution of free or low-cost milk with the education of the women about healthy ways to feed, clothe, and care for their babies. In response to the problem of "the girl child of the poor forced by poverty to take over the care of the next youngest child because the mother is working," as she describes in *Fighting for Life*, Baker instituted Little Mothers' Leagues, where the young girls were taught lessons in care they could take back to their working mothers. Baker made sure that midwives were registered and taught to apply eye drops to prevent eye infections in newborns, and also developed a baby dress pattern, later picked up and sold by McCall's patterns, for lightweight clothing that simplified the dressing of newborns and avoided the tight swaddling traditional among many immigrant mothers. The innovation was considered so beneficial that Metropolitan Life Insurance Company ordered 200,000 of the patterns to distribute to its policyholders.

In another dramatically successful experiment, Baker tackled the problem of the high death rates among the orphaned, premature, and abandoned infants assigned to foundling hospitals. Though well taken care of in a hygienic setting, the babies were dying, nevertheless, at rates of about 50%. Baker began placing the foundlings in foster homes. Under the supervision of the Bureau of Child Hygiene, poor tenement mothers, experienced in raising healthy families, were paid ten dollars per month for the babies' care. Within four years, the death rates among these high-risk cases had dropped to 30%.

In 1911, Baker's division sponsored an infant welfare exhibition that demonstrated baby bathing, maternal hygiene, home sanitation, infant clothing, and other hygiene measures, which became the model for similar events held in other cities. The idea of "educated motherhood" was also spread through the sponsoring of Baby Weeks throughout the country. Popular magazines began to feature articles on mothering, and, in 1922, *Ladies' Home Journal* contracted with Baker to do a monthly advice column on baby and child care. The activities of the Division of Child Hygiene were not always met with approval by the medical community in New York City. When the institution was criticized for reducing the business of doctors through such programs as school physicals, Baker responded that the complaints were a great compliment to her division's success.

Outside of her medical work, Baker also became active in women's suffrage. She belonged to Heterodoxy, a New York club made up of women from various social and economic movements, including ***Fannie Hurst** and ***Mabel Dodge Luhan**, who held luncheon meetings to hear lectures on topics of current significance. Although not an outspoken leader on the issue of suffrage, Baker participated in the Fifth Avenue suffrage parades and was seen by some as a radical, to the degree that she was blacklisted by the Daughters of the American Revolution. She became the first woman lecturer at the Bellevue Medical College-New York University.

In 1917, Baker received a Doctor of Public Health degree from Bellevue Medical College. Her thesis, on school ventilation and the transmission of respiratory diseases, led the following year to the adoption of practices to prevent the spread of influenza among school children.

In 1923, Baker followed her retirement, at age 50, from the Division of Child Hygiene with lecture tours around the country on topics of child care and continued to write her column for the *Ladies' Home Journal*. She wrote books on child care in 1923 and 1925, before taking up her autobiography, published in 1939, where she reviewed her successes along with those areas of effort where she had achieved less success, particularly in child labor. Baker felt an urgent need for more stringent child labor laws to protect the health of older children; she was also deeply concerned about the continued high infant mortality in the U.S. compared to other countries. In 1934, she made a three-month trip to the Soviet Union, where she was impressed with the health of children she saw but also noted the regimentation and lack of spirit among the population. Attracted to what she called "state medicine" in the ideal, she had serious second thoughts about some of the negative aspects of its implementation.

Josephine Baker lived for many years in Belle Meade, New Jersey. By the time she died of cancer at age 71, in 1945, her ideas on child care and prevention of illness in children had become commonplace among the uneducated poor as well as the educated middle class.

SOURCES:

Baker, S. Josephine. *Fighting for Life*. NY: Macmillan, 1939 (reprinted by NY: Arno Press, 1974).

Duffy, John. *A History of Public Health In New York City*. NY: Russell Sage Foundation, 1974.

Meckel, Richard A. *Save The Babies*. Baltimore, MD: Johns Hopkins University Press, 1990.

Lois A. Monteiro,
Professor of Medical Science and
Associate Dean, Brown University
School of Medicine, Providence, Rhode Island

Baker, Sara Josephine (1873–1945).

See Baker, S. Josephine.

Balabanoff, Angelica (1878–1965)

One-time associate of Benito Mussolini and V.I. Lenin, first secretary of the Communist International, and prominent figure in the European socialist movement, 1902–1921. *Name variations: (Russian) Angelika Balabanova. Pronunciation: Bal-a-BON-off. Born Anzhelika Balabanova in 1878 in Chernigov, Russia; died in Rome, Italy, on November 25, 1965; daughter of Isaak Balabanov (a wealthy merchant and landowner); tutored at home until age 11; attended Princess Obolenskaia Institute in Kharkov, 1889–95, and New University of Brussels, 1897–99 (claimed to have received doctorate); audited classes at universities of Leipzig, Berlin, and Rome, 1899–1902; never married; no children.*

Joined Italian Socialist Party (1902); served as propagandist among Italian women working in Switzerland (1903–07); served as member, Executive Committee of Italian Socialist Party in Switzerland (1904–07); was co-editor of Su, Compagne! *(1904–06); served as member of Executive Committee of Italian Socialist Party (1912–17); was co-editor,* Avanti! *(1912–13, 1928); named Italian representative to International Socialist Bureau (c. 1912–14); co-founded the Zimmerwald Movement (1915–17); served as secretary of International Socialist Commission (1915–19); returned to Russia (June 1917), and shortly thereafter joined Bolshevik Party; was Bolshevik propagandist and agent in Sweden and Switzerland (July 1917-November 1918); served as secretary of Communist International (1919–20); served as commissar of foreign affairs for Ukraine (1919–20); left Russia (December 1921) and expelled from Russian Communist Party (1924); involved in various anti-communist and anti-fascist movements in Vienna (1922–26), Paris (1926–36), and New York (1936–46); returned to Italy (1946); participated in formation of the Italian Social Democratic Party (1947), and was a member of its Executive Committee.*

Angelica Balabanoff

Selected publications: My Life as a Rebel *(New York, 1938, different versions in German, 1927, and Italian, 1946); (translated by Isotta Cesari)* Impressions of Lenin *(Ann Arbor, 1964);* Iz lichnykh vospominanii tsimmervaldtsa *(From the Personal Memoirs of a Zimmerwaldist, Moscow, 1925);* Il traditore: Benito Mussolini and his "Conquest" of Power *(New York, 1942–43);* Tears *(poetry, New York, 1943); plus numerous articles and pamphlets. (Almost all of this work is autobiographical; it is also the major source of information about Balabanoff's life. It should be borne in mind that she was writing many years after the events and often for very different audiences. As a result, her recollections are not always as consistent, candid, or complete as a biographer would desire.)*

On the evening of March 6, 1919, Angelica Balabanoff attended the closing rally of the First Congress of the Communist International held in the Bolshoi Theater in Moscow. As she translated the "optimistic speeches" of the foreign delegates, saw the "overwhelming enthusiasm of the workers" in the audience, and listened to the "revolutionary songs of defiance and victory," it appeared that "the ties of international brotherhood had been renewed" after the long and calamitous First World War. As she later wrote in her autobiography, "It was one of the few moments in my life when it seemed that I had not lived in vain." Not only had a new organization, the Communist International or Comintern, been created to unite proletarian parties throughout the world, but Balabanoff, in recognition of her high standing in the European socialist movement, had been chosen to be the first secretary of its Executive Committee. For many years she had been a member of the Executive Committee of the Italian Socialist Party and co-editor of its newspaper *Avanti!* During the war, she had been cofounder of the Zimmerwald Movement, which united European socialists opposed to the war, and she was still the secretary of the International Socialist Commission.

Balabanoff's euphoria was tempered by a degree of skepticism, however. She was aware that only one of the 35 delegates who attended the congress had a legitimate mandate from his national organization, and that all of the others were prisoners of war or foreign residents of Moscow who had been induced to represent national organizations under false pretenses. It had been obvious at the congress that the Russian communists—G.E. Zinoviev and V.I. Lenin, in particular—were controlling the proceedings and acting primarily to further the interests of the new Soviet state. She also realized that her appointment as secretary "had a definite political significance" in that her reputation among socialists throughout Europe added legitimacy to the new body. Balabanoff had reason to be concerned. She soon found herself isolated from the real work of the Comintern, and her complaints about its dubious operations were ignored. By the time the Second Congress met in 1920, she had been removed from office. Disillusioned, she left Soviet Russia in December 1921, was expelled from the party in 1924, and spent the rest of her long life fighting for the cause of socialism against the threats of Italian fascism and Russian communism.

Angelica Balabanoff's origins were not those usually associated with a leading member of either the Italian Socialist Party or the Communist International. She was born to a life of privilege in Chernigov, a provincial town in the Ukrainian part of Imperial Russia, in 1878. Her father Isaak Balabanov was a wealthy Jewish merchant who could well afford to staff his 22-room house with a host of servants. Surrounded by a beautiful garden and orchards, her home had far more in common with Turgenev's "nest of gentlefolk" than with Marx's industrial slums. Angelica, the last of 16 children seven of whom died young, grew up speaking French and German with her siblings, parents, and governesses rather than either Russian or Ukrainian. Unlike many of her generation and class, she showed no early awareness of 19th-century Russian radicalism. Her apolitical parents sheltered their youngest daughter from potentially harmful outside influences, kept her from having childhood playmates, and hired carefully screened home tutors to impart the social graces of dancing, music, and embroidery rather than the "dangerous" liberal arts. When she was finally allowed to go to school at the age of 11, it was not to an academic gymnasium but to a fashionable girls' boarding school in Kharkov. In part because of this privileged and sheltered existence, Balabanoff experienced none of the anti-Semitism which caused other Russian Jews to seek revolutionary solutions for society's problems.

Angelica remembered very little of her father who died when she was ten. Her mother, "who ruled my life and who for me personified all despotism," was another matter. She was determined that her daughter would be the "crown of the family" and that her upbringing should prepare her solely for marriage to a wealthy man. Balabanoff later claimed that this created an "unbridgeable abyss" and was the source of her own revolutionary temperament. "Mother's treatment of the 'free' servants in our household always aroused my indignation," she wrote in her autobiography.

> My first realization of inequity and injustice grew out of these experiences in my early childhood. I saw that there were those who commanded and those who obeyed, and probably because of my own rebellion against my mother . . . I instinctively sided with the latter. Why, I asked myself, should mother be able to rise when she pleased, while the servants had to rise at an early hour to carry out her orders? After she raged at them for some mistake, I would implore

> them not to endure such treatment. . . . I received my first glimpse of actual poverty and misery when I became old enough to accompany mother on her visits to the poorhouse. . . . I was allowed to distribute the gifts we had brought—aprons, dresses, linen, etc.—in the manner of Lady Bountiful.

As a result of these experiences, Balabanoff developed, in the words of **Marie Mullaney**, "a tremendous burden of guilt over her privileged lifestyle and a gnawing sense of duty toward the unfortunate." She had no idea, however, how she could fulfil that duty. Her education at Princess Obolenskaia's Institute in Kharkov, which she finished in 1895 at age 17, had prepared her only for marriage and the life of a "fine lady." Russian universities were closed to her, as they were to most women in the 19th century and, thus, so were most professions. One alternative, which attracted numerous middle-class Russian women, was to enroll in European universities. Without her mother's knowledge, Balabanoff started to use her linguistic skills to tutor some of these women in German or French before they left Chernigov. In time, she saw study abroad as a way she too could escape her mother's "despotism." Her decision caused "storms and hysterics" in a family that believed "a university was no place for a girl, especially for a girl who did not have to make her living." Ultimately, she prevailed though only after renouncing her family inheritance and leaving with her mother's curse upon her. "But," as she later wrote, "I was happier than I had ever been in all my life."

> Freedom is much more precious to women than it is to men because women go through such a tremendous struggle before they are free in their own minds.
>
> **—Angelica Balabanoff (1918)**

Balabanoff chose to go to the New University of Brussels which she had first heard about from one of the students she had tutored. Its reputation as a bohemian and radical institution attracted many students from Eastern Europe interested in its innovative approaches to the social sciences. For two years, she lived alone in a poorly furnished one-room apartment. Much of what she heard in the classroom and in student discussions explained the injustices she had seen in Chernigov. As she later recalled, "I began to get my first insight into economic theory, the mechanics of capitalism, and the history and meaning of the revolutionary labour movement." She was particularly impressed with the writing of George Plekhanov, "the father of Russian Marxism," whom she met in Brussels. She found in him "a philosophy of method that gave continuity and logic to the processes of history and which endowed my own ethical aspirations, as well as the revolutionary movement itself, with the force and dignity of an historical imperative." While she did not join Plekhanov's Russian Social Democratic Labor Party (RSDRP) at the time, as is often claimed, she nevertheless considered herself a Marxist. As a result of this education, Balabanoff also considered herself to be a Doctor of Philosophy—an honor not substantiated by the university's records.

In 1899, after two years in Brussels, Balabanoff decided to sample more traditional and conservative German education by attending lectures first at the University of Leipzig and then at the University of Berlin. More valuable than the courses, which she found tedious and authoritarian, was the opportunity to meet the leaders of the German Social Democratic Party (SPD)—the largest and most respected socialist party in Europe. In 1901, she moved to Italy where she completed her education at the University of Rome. She was captivated by Antonio Labriola's emotional vision of socialism. As Mullaney has noted, he gave "intellectual justification for the moral fervor that had always been at the core of her radicalism." She also took to heart Labriola's dictum that a socialist intellectual should strive to be a teacher not a leader of the oppressed. Under his influence, she joined the Italian Socialist Party (PSI) in 1902.

Balabanoff had heard from Labriola about the terrible plight of young Italian immigrant women employed in textile factories in Switzerland. Not only were they poorly paid and often unable to communicate in the German-speaking part of the country, but they also were exploited by the Catholic Church which ran the convent hostels where they were forced to live, and they were ignored by the male-dominated Swiss trade unions. She went to St. Gallen, the center of the textile industry in 1903, and offered to work without pay for the Italian Socialist Party in Switzerland (PSIS). Her own needs, then as always, were modest, and she managed to meet them by giving language lessons in her spare time and by using a meager allowance which she received from an older brother in Russia. With the help of the PSIS, she set up an office where she offered advice to the Italian workers and helped them stand up for their rights. Much to her surprise, she found that she had a talent for public speaking. She was fluent in Italian, German, and French, and she knew how to keep her message simple and to gauge the temper of her largely female audiences. The fact that she was an educated woman, but one who lived an unadorned worker's life and knew local problems from first-hand experience, added to her appeal.

In 1904, she was asked to join the Executive Committee of the PSIS, and at its suggestion moved to Lugano to edit a weekly newspaper, *Su, Compagne!*, aimed at female workers in both Switzerland and Italy. In it, she publicized instances of abuse, attacked the oppression of the church and employers, and sought to get women to discuss their own problems. Balabanoff stressed that she was not promoting feminism, that women workers shared many of the same problems as their male counterparts, and that salvation lay in a common fight for socialism. She sought to promote proletarian unity and class consciousness, not female issues and gender consciousness.

While in Switzerland, Balabanoff also came into frequent contact with Russian Social Democrats living in emigration. She met many of the leaders of the RSDRP—Lenin, Julius Martov, Leon Trotsky—and on occasion translated their Russian speeches into Italian, French, German, and even English. In 1907, she was delegated by a group of Russian university students studying abroad to represent them in a non-voting capacity at the Fifth Party Congress in London. Because of linguistic abilities and perceived impartiality, she was also asked to transmit funds from the German Social Democrats to the RSDRP and, when this proved insufficient to pay for the congress, to help convince a wealthy American soap manufacturer, Joseph Fels, to extend the party a loan.

Balabanoff never felt comfortable with the constant factional bickering that characterized Russian Social Democracy in emigration or with the theoretical disputes that absorbed the meetings of the RSDRP. It was therefore with some relief that she returned to Italy in 1908 where her adoptive party put less stress on theoretical matters and appreciated her talents as a propagandist and agitator. She spent the next few years wandering the Italian countryside trying to attract unorganized workers to join trade unions and the socialist party. Once again, her sincerity, her ethical fervor, and her emotional interpretation of socialism made her a highly successful propagandist. In 1912, she was elected to the Executive Committee of the Italian Socialist Party and asked to help edit *Avanti!*, one of the largest and most influential socialist papers in Europe. Her co-editor was Benito Mussolini who ten years later became the head of the Fascist government in Italy and was responsible for the suppression of the PSI.

Balabanoff first met Mussolini in 1904 when he attended one of her lectures in Lausanne. She was struck by his impoverished appearance and militant demeanor. After listening to his complaints, she undertook to give direction to his militancy by completing his political education. She lent him books, helped him earn some money by translating a German socialist tract into Italian, and gave him introductions to other Italian socialists. Always a forceful personality and a fiery orator, his rise in the party was even more rapid than hers. In 1912, he agreed to edit *Avanti!* only if his one-time mentor became his co-editor and assistant. For the next eight months, she carried out many of the disagreeable editorial chores which Mussolini preferred to avoid.

As the First World War approached, an increasing amount of Balabanoff's time was spent serving as the link between the PSI and the Second or Socialist International that united socialist parties throughout Europe. She attended three congresses of the International as well as several associated conferences of socialist women. She also served as her party's representative on the International Socialist Bureau where she came to know almost all of the leaders of European socialism. The most pressing problem facing the International was the war clouds hanging over Europe caused by the colonial and military rivalries of the great powers. The International repeatedly passed resolutions calling on socialist deputies to vote against war credits and for workers to use strikes to paralyze any moves toward war. Balabanoff was shocked, therefore, that when war broke out in August 1914 these pious resolutions were forgotten as socialist politicians and workers alike were swept up in the tide of nationalism which rolled over the belligerent countries of Europe. The Italian Socialist Party was one of the few to hold true to the principles of the International. Even among the Italian socialists, however, war had its supporters. One of them was Benito Mussolini, who up to 1914 had been a militant pacifist but reversed his position when French bribes made it worth his while to do so. Balabanoff denounced her former colleague and fled to neutral Switzerland where she became one of the leaders in the fight against the war.

During the course of the next two years, she played an instrumental role in the four conferences of antiwar socialists held in Switzerland:

the International Conference of Socialist Women in March 1915, the International Conference of Socialist Youth in April 1915, the Zimmerwald Conference in September 1915, and the Kiental Conference in April 1916. In each instance, she helped to organize the meetings and used her linguistic abilities to translate the ensuing debates. In recognition of her services, she was named the secretary of the International Socialist Commission created by the Zimmerwald Conference to take over the duties of the moribund International Socialist Bureau, and she edited its multilingual *Bulletin*. These pacifist efforts were, however, plagued by internal discord. Lenin and a few Bolshevik supporters sought more radical solutions than Balabanoff and the centrist majority were willing to accept. All agreed that the war was imperialist in nature, that it had to be opposed by all available means, and that a peace based on no annexations was essential. The Zimmerwald Left, headed by Lenin, wanted, in addition, the condemnation of the socialist leaders of the Second International who had proven impotent in the face of war, the creation of a new and revolutionary Third International, and implementation of steps to turn the world war into a world civil war. Balabanoff, who admired Lenin as a person, could not understand his intransigence and his obsession with splitting the socialist movement.

These differences were temporarily forgotten when revolution broke out in Russia and toppled the tsar in February 1917. Like Lenin, Balabanoff returned to her native land in a German railway car after an absence of 20 years. Since the continued success of the revolution offered the best opportunity to bring the protracted war to an end, she joined the Bolshevik Party in the summer of 1917. After only five weeks in Petrograd, she was sent to represent Bolshevik interests in Stockholm where she was to remain until October 1918. Lenin wanted to exploit her excellent contacts with European socialist leaders and her position as secretary of the International Socialist Commission to influence European opinion and to keep him informed about events beyond Russia's borders. After the October Revolution brought the Bolsheviks to power, Balabanoff was further charged with distributing money to radical groups in Europe and with purchasing much-needed supplies for the new regime. In October 1918, she switched her base of operations to Switzerland which Lenin felt was more strategically located for the spread of revolution. The Swiss, who feared precisely this, expelled her after less than a month in their country.

When she returned to Russia in December 1918, Balabanoff was given the unusual position of commissar for foreign affairs of the Ukrainian Socialist Republic. Since Ukraine had no formal relations with other countries, she spent most of her time touring the war-torn countryside making propaganda speeches and learning something about her native land. Much to her surprise, she was summoned back to Moscow in early March 1919 to attend the First Congress of the Third or Communist International—a new body that was to replace the discredited Socialist International. Balabanoff viewed its creation with mixed emotions. She had given much of her life to the old International, she stubbornly refused to turn over the records of the Zimmerwald Movement, and in good conscience she could not represent the Italian Socialist Party as Lenin requested. It was soon evident that others had fewer scruples and that virtually none of the 35 delegates had close ties with the countries and parties they purported to represent. These were technicalities that meant little in this emotional setting. Even she was carried away when a long-delayed Austrian delegate rushed into the hall and announced that revolution was rapidly spreading in Central Europe. She also acquiesced to party discipline when Lenin insisted that she become the first secretary of the new Comintern.

Whether Balabanoff recognized it or not, she had been chosen as a front or a figurehead, as a person whose excellent reputation in the socialist world would add credence to the fraudulent creation in Moscow. She soon found that Zinoviev, the president of the Comintern, was calling the shots from Petrograd while she was left with little to do in Moscow. She refused to accept the bourgeois perquisites and trappings of high office which seemed to satisfy many of her revolutionary colleagues. After awhile, she went back to Ukraine to resume her propaganda activities with the equally meaningless title of commissar for foreign affairs. In vain, she protested the growing use of Red terror against members of other revolutionary parties. Zinoviev, who she subsequently considered "the most despicable individual I have ever met" other than Mussolini, grew tired of her moral complaints about his organizational machinations. He sought to get her out of his curly hair by suggesting that she enter a sanatorium for a rest or lead a propaganda train to distant Turkestan. The final straw came when the Second Congress of the Comintern, called in the summer of 1920 virtually without her knowledge, adopted organizational rules that required the splitting of foreign socialist parties and ensured that the resulting communist splinters would remain firmly under the control of the Russian Communist Party.

Disillusioned, Balabanoff went to Lenin and suggested that since "Russia does not need people like me," she should be allowed to leave the country once again. He offered a variety of diplomatic posts, including ambassador to Italy, but only if she would assist in the splitting of the Italian Socialist Party. Various positions in women's organizations, such as secretary of the International Women's Secretariat, were dangled before her, but Balabanoff felt her talents and interests lay elsewhere. Other jobs, all of them more honorific than real, were also proposed and rejected.

In December 1921, she left Soviet Russia never to return. For the next four years, she lived in Vienna, once again giving language lessons and staying in small, poorly furnished apartments. When she expressed her disapproval of Soviet actions in 1924, she was stripped of her party membership. In 1926, Balabanoff moved to Paris where she participated in the activities of the Italian Socialist Party now in exile and for a while resumed her work as editor of *Avanti!* When not attacking her former protege, Benito Mussolini, for the actions of his Fascist government in Italy, she was busy writing poetry and working on her memoirs. In 1936, she left for the United States where for the next decade she worked with Italian-Americans and warned against the twin evils of fascism and communism. The end of the Second World War allowed her to return to Italy which she always considered to be her true homeland. She participated in the formation of the Italian Social Democratic Party and at age 70 resumed her activities as a wandering propagandist. She died in 1965, disillusioned with the materialism and lack of class consciousness of the Italian proletariat.

Balabanoff's values and skills were those of a 19th-century romantic idealist. She believed strongly in the innate goodness of the working classes and in her own duty to serve them in any way she could. Her sincerity, her commitment to ethical values, and her selflessness stand out in a 20th-century socialist movement often dominated by power-seeking cynics all too willing to partake in the material benefits of political office. In part because of her temperament and approach, Balabanoff's "life as a rebel" was also a life of disillusionment: disillusionment with the reaction of European socialist leaders to the outbreak of the First World War, with the actions of Russian communists in their exercise of revolutionary power, with workers everywhere when they at last had a chance to share in Europe's post-1945 prosperity. Her skills were those of a linguist, a propagandist, and a competent administrator. She was never a theoretician, she did not have the instincts of a politician, and she perhaps lacked the self-confidence needed to be a leader. Of slight build, she always remained a simple and unassuming person. Her extensive public life was also her private life. Balabanoff never married. Rumors of an early affair with Mussolini, and even that she had a child by him, are unsubstantiated by either factual evidence or common sense.

SOURCES:

Balabanoff, Angelica. *My Life as a Rebel.* NY: Harper & Brothers, 1938 (unless otherwise noted, all quotations are taken from this source).

———. *Impressions of Lenin.* Translated from the Italian by Isotta Cesari. Ann Arbor: University of Michigan Press, 1964.

Mullaney, Marie Marmo. *Revolutionary Women: Gender and the Socialist Revolutionary Role.* NY: Praeger, 1983.

SUGGESTED READING:

Eshelman, Nancy G. "Forging a Socialist Women's Movement: Angelica Balabanoff in Switzerland," in *The Italian Immigrant Woman in North America.* Edited by Betty Boyd Caroli, R.F. Harney, and Lydio F. Tomasi. Toronto: Multicultural Historical Society of Ontario, 1978.

Florence, Ronald. *Marx's Daughters: Eleanor Marx, Rosa Luxemburg, Angelica Balabanoff.* NY: Dial Press, 1975.

Slaughter, Jane. "Humanism versus Feminism in the Socialist Movement: The Life of Angelica Balabanoff," in *European Women on the Left.* Edited by Jane Slaughter and Robert Kern. Westport, CT: Greenwood Press, 1981.

R.C. Elwood, Professor of History, Carleton University, Ottawa, Canada, and author of *Inessa Armand: Revolutionary and Feminist*

Balas, Iolanda (1936—)

Rumanian high jumper. *Born in Rumania on December 12, 1936.*

Won the Olympic gold medal in the high jump (Rome, 1960, Tokyo, 1964); won the European championship (1958, 1962); claimed the world high-jump record 14 times (1956–61); had 140 consecutive victories (1956–1967).

Women were not allowed to compete in the high jump at the Olympic Games until Amsterdam in 1928. The first gold in this event was awarded to Canada's **Ethel Catherwood**, known as Saskatoon Lily, who faced the bar smiling, then leapt 5'2½". When the comely

See sidebar on the following page

Catherwood was asked if she would now pursue a career in Hollywood, she answered, "I'd rather gulp poison."

Iolanda Balas' career was presaged by **Phyllis Green** of Great Britain, who, on July 11, 1925, became the first woman to clear 5' in the high jump. Thirty-three years later, on October 18, 1958, in Bucharest, Hungary, Balas became the first woman to clear 6'. (Records continued to topple: ***Sara Simeoni** of Italy came in at 6'7" in 1978; ***Ulrike Meyfarth** at 6'7½" in 1984. When U.S. jumper ◄❖ **Louise Ritter** took on Bulgaria's ◄❖ **Stefka Kostadinova** at the 1988 Seoul Olympics, Kostadinova held the world record at 6'10½". With the bar at 6'8", both jumped and missed three times, causing a jump off. The 30-year-old Ritter was the first American to win the event since ***Mildred McDaniel** in 1956.)

But no one—man or woman—dominated the sport like Iolanda Balas of Rumania. She won the first of her 16 Rumanian titles in 1951 with a novice leap of 4'10¼". After placing 5th in the Melbourne Olympics in 1956, she jumped an Olympic record-setting 6'0¾" in Rome in 1960.

❖► **Catherwood, Ethel** (1910–1987)

Canadian track and field champion. *Name variations: Saskatoon Lily. Born on May 2, 1910; died on September 18, 1987; grew up in Saskatoon, Saskatchewan, Canada.*

In the 1928 Amsterdam Olympics, 18-year-old Ethel Catherwood from Saskatoon, Canada, won the gold medal in the high jump. When she returned home triumphant, *The New York Times* proclaimed her new Olympic and World Record by enthusing, she was "the prettiest girl of all the girl athletes." The government of Saskatchewan granted Catherwood a trust fund of $3,000, with the stipulation that the money not be used for training in track and field; rather, it was to be set aside for her piano studies.

❖► **Ritter, Louise** (1958—)

American high jumper. *Born on February 18, 1958. Won the Olympic gold medal in the high jump at Seoul in 1988.*

❖► **Kostadinova, Stefka** (1965—)

Bulgarian high-jumper. *Born on March 25, 1965. Won the Olympic silver medal in the high jump at Seoul in 1988.*

❖► **Gusenbauer, Ilona** (1947—)

Austrian high jumper. *Born on September 16, 1947. Won the Olympic bronze medal in the high jump at Munich in 1972.*

She would set 14 world records in the next ten and a half years. In 1961, Balas leapt 6'3¼", a record that would not be touched for a decade until ◄❖ **Ilona Gusenbauer** of Austria made her mark. In 1964, in the Tokyo Olympics, Balas took another gold while raising the Olympic record to 6'2¾". From December 1956 to June 1967, using a modified version of the scissors, Iolanda Balas won 140 consecutive events.

Balbilla (fl. 130 CE)

Greco-Roman poet who accompanied Emperor Hadrian and Empress Sabina to the province of Egypt where several poems of hers were inscribed on the foot of the Colossus of Memnon in Thebes. *Name variations: Iulia Balbilla; Julia Balbilla. Pronunciation: Bal-BILL-ah. Born around 100 CE; date of death unknown; daughter of C. Iulius Antiochus Epiphanes and* ***Claudia Balbilla;*** *granddaughter of Tiberius Claudius Balbillus, prefect of Egypt under the Emperor Nero, and of Antiochus IV, king of Commagene. Visited Egypt as part of the imperial entourage, 130 CE.*

We know Iulia Balbilla from the three or possibly four poems of hers that survive as inscriptions on the right foot of the Colossus of Memnon in the scared city of Thebes in Upper Egypt. They commemorate a pilgrimage she made there with Hadrian and ***Sabina** on November 20, 130 CE. Of the 39 mostly Greek verse inscriptions on the Colossus, Balbilla's poems are significant for their literary and historical erudition.

Balbilla was descended from several generations of powerful and educated courtiers close to the ruling circles of the Roman Empire. In one poem she names her two famous grandfathers, Antiochus IV, king of Commagene, on her father's side and T. Claudius Balbillus on her mother's. Her father's family was among the Macedonian inheritors of Alexander the Great's conquests. They had ruled the small client-state of Commagene on the Euphrates river southeast of the Taurus mountains in modern Turkey probably from 162 BCE until the Emperor Tiberius annexed it in 17 CE. The Emperor Caligula (Gaius) restored the kingdom in 38 to Balbilla's grandfather Antiochus IV as did Emperor Claudius again in 41. It is likely that this family was partly resident at Rome and familiar with the households of several emperors.

Balbilla's maternal grandfather Tiberius Claudius Balbillus, whom she calls "the Wise," was prefect of Egypt under the Emperor Nero from 55 to 59 CE. This Balbillus was therefore not of senatorial rank but of the second-highest, equestrian, rank. According to the Roman writer Seneca the Younger, Balbillus was a learned man "accomplished in every rare genre of literature."

When his granddaughter Balbilla traveled to Egypt with the Emperor Hadrian half a century later, it was predictable that the imperial company would visit the Colossus of Memnon. The Greeks and Romans believed the Colossus represented the hero Memnon, son of Tithonus (the brother of Priam, king of Troy) and Eos, goddess of the dawn. Achilles killed Memnon in the Trojan war. In actuality, the Colossus honored the Egyptian Pharaoh Amenhotep III. It was a tourist attraction in the Roman period because of the musical sounds it sometimes made in the early hours of the morning, when Memnon was said to be speaking to his mother. Most of the inscriptions on the Colossus, including Balbilla's, refer to these sounds.

It is clear from her poems that Balbilla is aware of a native, Egyptian tradition of the Colossus. But in keeping with a subject matter appropriate to imperial taste, she naturally writes from the Greek mythological perspective. Her poems use a highly literary Greek in which the Aeolic dialect—the dialect of the archaic Greek poet ***Sappho**—predominates. One poem has been seen as apologizing for the carving of the inscription itself. Balbilla contrasts her own and her grandfathers' piety to the "godless barbarian Cambyses," the Persian conqueror of Egypt who defaced the Colossus and was later punished with death. She is clearly proud of the religious scruples of her family but does not fail to commemorate the piety of Hadrian and Sabina as well. Interestingly, she is not the only woman poet to have inscribed her poetry on the Colossus in ancient times: one **Caecilia Trebulla** of unknown date and provenance also left her poems there.

We have no details of Balbilla's personal life, but we can safely hazard that she was a Roman citizen of at least equestrian rank and that, like every Greek or Roman aristocrat, she owned slaves and derived an income from landed wealth.

Balbilla's very existence—as a woman of royal Macedonian descent who belonged to the circle of one of the most cultivated Roman emperors, and who wrote memorable Greek poetry in Egypt in respectful awareness of native traditions—indicates something about the inclusiveness of Roman imperial culture in its time.

SOURCES:

Franz, L. *Corpus Inscriptionum Graecorum*. Vol. III, nos. 4725, 4727, 4729, 4730, 4731. Berlin, 1853.

SUGGESTED READING:

Bernand, André and Étienne. *Les Inscriptions greques et latines du Colosse de Memnon*. Cairo: Institut Franceais D'Archéologie Orientale, 1960.

Alexander Ingle, Research Associate,
Institute for the Classical Tradition, Boston University

Balch, Emily Greene (1867–1961)

Second American woman to receive the Nobel Peace Prize, whose name is synonymous with the Women's International League for Peace and Freedom, an organization she helped direct in its formative years. *Born Emily Greene Balch on January 8, 1867, in Jamaica Plain, Massachusetts; died on January 9, 1961, at Cambridge, Massachusetts; daughter of Francis Vergnies Balch (an attorney) and Ellen (Nelly) Maria (Noyes) Balch (a former school teacher); never married; no children.*

Selected writings: Our Slavic Fellow Citizens *(Charities Publication Committee, 1910);* Approaches to the Great Settlement *(B.W. Huebsch, 1918);* Occupied Haiti *(The Writers Publishing Company, 1927, reprinted, Garland, 1972);* The Miracle of Living *(Island Press, 1941);* Vignettes in Prose *(Women's International League for Peace and Freedom, 1952).*

Although it was only in 1946 (when she received the Nobel Peace Prize) that Emily Greene Balch became known throughout the world, she had long been revered within the peace movement. Indeed, her name—like that of her close friend ***Jane Addams**—was held synonymous with the Women's International League for Peace and Freedom, the leading women's peace organization in the world. In the process, Balch had helped spearhead what had never been attempted before, the effort of women acting together as women to end global conflict. She once said, "Lovers of our own lands, we are citizens of the world, conscious partakers in the sacrament of all human life or more truly of all sentient life."

Stemming from colonial Yankee ancestry, Emily Greene Balch was born on January 8, 1867, in Jamaica Plain (now part of Boston), Massachusetts. Her father Frank Vergnies Balch was a prosperous lawyer concentrating on estates and corporate interests. A compassionate and cultured man, Frank had enlisted as a private in the Civil War and had served as secretary to the reformist Senator Charles Sumner (Rep.-Massachusetts). Her mother **Nelly Noyes Balch** had taught in the pioneering community of Mattoon, Illinois, before marriage. Cousins by

Emily Greene Balch

blood, the Balches raised their six children in the tradition of liberal Unitarianism. Emily later wrote of her upbringing:

> The whole atmosphere was permeated by what you might call Neo-Puritanism without its rigors, narrowness or introspection, but colored and controlled through and through by complete acceptance of the rule of conscience and by a warm and generous sense of the call to service.

Always a stellar student, Balch led her classes at the school of Miss Catherine Innis Ireland, a female academy in Boston. In 1886, Balch entered Bryn Mawr College, where she concentrated in the humanities: the classics, philosophy, and modern languages. Earning her A.B. in 1889 as a member of the charter class, she was the first recipient of the Bryn Mawr European fellowship, the highest honor the college bestowed. As her interests had turned to "the social question," Balch first spent a year under the tutelage of Bryn Mawr sociologist Franklin H. Giddings. In 1890, she traveled to France, where her research was directed by Professor Emile Levasseur. In 1893, the American Economic Association published her findings under the title *Public Assistance of the Poor in France*, a work long recognized as a pioneer sociological study.

Upon returning to the United States in 1891, Balch launched her first career: social work. She immediately apprenticed herself to Charles W. Birtwell, general secretary of the Boston Children's Aid Society. Within several years, she had composed a manual on treatment of juvenile offenders. In December 1892, Balch helped launch Denison House, a settlement house in Boston, which she directed for a year and which led to her crusade for the alleviation of sweatshops. In 1894, she joined the Federal Labor Union, part of the American Federation of Labor, and attended one state labor meeting as a representative of the Cigar Makers Union.

Concluding, however, that she preferred college teaching to social work, she decided in 1893 to embark on her second career. Thanks to her father's financial support, she undertook a series of brief academic programs, often under the direction of an extremely distinguished faculty. The year 1893 saw her at the Harvard Annex, now Radcliffe College. In 1895, she worked at the University of Chicago with sociologist Albion Small. The academic year 1895–96 was spent at the University of Berlin, where she was taught by such renowned professors as Gustav Schmoller, Georg Simmel, and Adolph Wagner.

In 1896, Balch began her academic career at Wellesley College. Advancing slowly up the academic ladder, she received a five-year appointment in 1913 as professor and chair of the department of economics and sociology. Though as a teacher she was absent-minded and disorganized, sometimes forgetting to return exams or tell a class she would be out of town, she attracted students by her intense moral involvement with her subject matter. She taught Wellesley's first course in sociology as well as courses in immigration, the theory of consumption, and the economic roles of women. Her course in socialism used Karl Marx's *Capital* as its text.

Her pedagogy was soon known for its innovation. For example, she personally escorted her pupils to reform schools, prisons, and institutions for "paupers and the feeble-minded." In one course, she had her students design "social maps" of Boston's North End. Soon parents began protesting that their daughters were being asked to investigate brothels.

While at Wellesley, she was almost a quintessential progressive. In 1903, she was a founder and president of the Boston Women's Trade Union League, an organization promoting the unionization of female laborers. In 1913, she helped draft a minimum-wage bill for Massachusetts (which the legislature failed to enact) and aided in organizing the state's first Conference of Charities. She served on the Municipal Board of Trustees in charge of delinquent and neglected children of Boston (1897–98), the Massachusetts State Commission on Industrial Education (1908–09), the Progressive Party's committee on immigration (1912), the Massachusetts commission on immigration (1913–14), and the Boston City Planning Board (1914–17).

In 1906, Balch declared herself a socialist. Three years later, with her Wellesley faculty colleague ***Vida Scudder**, she organized a socialist conference in Boston. Her views, however, were always similar to those of the British Fabians. Balch never accepted Marx's theories of surplus value, the class struggle, and the economic interpretation of history. Writes her biographer, Mercedes M. Randall:

> The existing competitive system seemed to her to be so bad that she hated to appear to acquiesce in it. A system in which production was shaped not with the purpose of making what was needed and making it beautiful and good of its kind, but with the purpose of making a profit, appeared to her a basic topsy-turvydom which had widespread vicious results.

Finding Slavic immigration to the U.S. a significant and neglected research topic, Balch visited ethnic communities as far distant as Texas and Colorado. She spent the summer of 1904 in the mining villages of Pennsylvania; in the winter, she boarded in bohemian tenements on New York's Upper East Side. In 1905, she spent much of the year in Austria-Hungary, researching at her own expense. Treating such groups as Bohemians, Moravians, and Ruthenians all separately, she delved into place of origin, the various types of immigrant, and degrees of success in the New World. The result: her *magnum opus*, a pioneering work entitled *Our Slavic Fellow Citizens* (1910). The book was unique, combining statistics on population, taxes, and wages with such cultural material as Bohemian nursery rhymes and the odyssey of a Ruthenian poet in Canada. The study refuted many stereotypes: that the steamship companies, not the immigrants themselves, were responsible for the exodus from Europe; that the immigrants were drawn from Europe's lowest classes; and that the national character of the Slavs retarded their political and cultural development.

No life known to me has been so consistently and almost exclusively devoted to the cause of peace and with such pervasive good judgment and effect.

—William Ernest Hocking, speaking of Emily Greene Balch

World War I marked Balch's third career and the one by which she will be remembered: peace activist. Although a pacifist since the Spanish-American War, Balch was particularly jolted by the Great War: "When the World War broke out in 1914 my reaction to it was largely a sense of tragic interruption of what seemed to me the real business of our times—the realization of a more satisfactory economic order."

In January 1915, the Women's Peace Party was formed, with the world-famous settlement worker Jane Addams elected president. Balch became active in the Boston and Wellesley branch, and, once she received a sabbatical, in ◂❖ **Crystal Eastman**'s more radical New York City branch. Balch was one of the 42 American delegates to the International Congress of Women, which convened on April 28 at The Hague. Here she met with women from belligerent and neutral nations alike, who collectively offered a unique plan to end the conflict: the neutral countries should establish machinery for continuous mediation, not even waiting for the belligerents to stop fighting. Other resolutions called for the repudiation of all annexations, democratic parliaments for all peoples, compulsory arbitration, equal rights for women, a permanent international court, and liberty of commerce. Along with Jane Addams and bacteriologist ***Alice Hamilton**, Balch co-edited the greater part of the proceedings. Its title: *Women at the Hague* (1915).

❖▸ **Eastman, Crystal** (1881–1928)

American suffragist and pacifist. *Born June 25, 1881, in the village of Canandaigua, New York; died in 1928; daughter of ministers; sister of Max Eastman, who was editor of* The Masses *and* The Liberator.

Crystal Eastman, whose mother was the first woman to be ordained in the Congregational church in New York, was one of the founders of the American Civil Liberties Union (ACLU). In the summers, she and her brother Max Eastman frequently joined in the workings and gatherings of the Provincetown Players.

One of the Congress' six envoys chosen to secure international backing for its plan, Balch first visited the rulers of neutral Scandinavian countries. She then journeyed to Russia, where she was able to see Sergei Sazanov. (The Russian foreign minister failed to tell the group that he had already entered into secret agreements with Britain and France over Constantinople and the Straits.) In July, Balch conferred with British Foreign Minister Sir Edward Grey, U.S. Secretary of State Robert Lansing, and U.S. President Woodrow Wilson.

Balch's efforts ended in failure, for which she always blamed Wilson. On August 19, 1915, the president had assured Balch that he would offer U.S. mediation if the opportunity arose. But Wilson privately feared that Balch's solution would fail, costing the U.S. any possible influence among the belligerents. Six days later, Lansing bluntly told her that any conference of continuous mediation was impractical. Furthermore, the secretary was scandalized at the idea of proposing terms. Yet Balch's efforts were not entirely in vain, for the war aims of the pacifists had a profound effect on Wilson.

In the spring of 1916, Balch was one of 12 members of Henry Ford's unofficial Stockholm Neutral Conference for Continuous Mediation. On August 9, 1916, she would personally meet with President Wilson over the Stockholm plan. She also made two studies for the Stockholm group's Committee on Constructive Peace: one proposed a rehabilitation fund, to be endowed by neutral powers; the other recommended an international administration of colonies that resembled the League of Nations mandate system.

Remaining on leave from Wellesley, Balch returned to the U.S. in July 1916. Before and during U.S. belligerency, she participated in many peace groups, including the Collegiate Anti-Militarism League and the Fellowship of Reconciliation. She was particularly active in the

American Neutral Conference Committee, which in February 1917 became the Emergency Peace Federation (EPF). That May, the EPF reorganized as the People's Council of America for Peace and Democracy, a more radical association. The People's Council not only sought a Wilsonian peace but denounced war profiteering, urged adequate wages for labor, and expressed sympathy with the upheaval in Russia. Once the U.S. entered the conflict, Balch promoted the cause of civil liberties and the cause of conscientious objectors. In March 1918, in cooperation with the American Union against Militarism, she edited *Approaches to the Great Settlement*, a collection of peace proposals.

Pendleton, Ellen Fitz (1864–1936)

American educator. *Born Ellen Fitz Pendleton in Westerly, Rhode Island, on August 7, 1864; died in 1936; daughter of Enoch Burrows and Mary Ette (Chapman) Pendleton; received an A.B., 1886, and A.M., 1891, from Wellesley; studied at Newnham College, Cambridge, 1889–90; awarded Litt.D., Brown University, 1911; LL.D., Mount Holyoke, 1912, and Smith, 1925; never married; no children.*

From 1886 to 1888, Ellen Pendleton tutored in mathematics at Wellesley College; she was an instructor from 1888 to 1897, secretary from 1897 to 1901, dean and associate professor of mathematics from 1901 to 1911, and president of Wellesley from 1911 until her death in 1936.

In May 1918, the trustees of Wellesley College, by a two-vote margin, terminated her professorship. Some colleagues issued a statement ending in the words: "Even when differing from her in opinion or action we have respected her essential fair-mindedness, her courageous and conscientious regard for truth. We feel we have had in our midst a person of rare distinction and nobility." Yet, lacking any bitterness, Balch ignored the promptings of radical editor Oswald Garrison Villard and refused to appeal on the grounds of academic freedom. She said:

> Much as I grieved that the well-known liberality of Wellesley College should have been over-strained by me, I could not be surprised, when after much discussion and much friendly advocacy of my reappointment, the Trustees decided against it.

As Balch wrote Wellesley president **Ellen F. Pendleton**, who had supported her cause, "The way of war is not the way of Christianity. I find it impossible to reconcile war with the truths of Jesus' teaching." Commented one angry colleague, "If the trustees persist in a policy like this, they will fill Wellesley College with a faculty of nonentities." About this time, she stopped calling herself a socialist, for the war had made her skeptical of all government power.

Towards the end of 1918, Balch joined the editorial staff of Villard's weekly magazine *The Nation*, contributing in particular to its international relations section. In May 1919, she attended the second International Congress of Women, held this time in Zurich. The Congress condemned the Versailles Treaty, then established itself as a permanent organization under the name of Women's International League for Peace and Freedom (WILPF). It elected Jane Addams its international president and established its headquarters in Geneva. For the 52-year-old Balch, the formation of the WILPF marked a crucial turning point. She served as secretary-treasurer, setting up the Geneva offices and establishing guidelines for the new organization.

Balch hoped that the new group would "mobilize the moral force of the women of the world against war, cruelty, and aggression." She said in 1920, "Reason and love and freedom in human relations—this is all our program." Yet as it always posited that all changes in the economic order should be nonviolent, the new body was too radical for the world's right, too tame for the world's left. It remained very much a middle-class organization.

In dealing with issues of world peace, Balch was fundamentally a pragmatist, favoring piecemeal reform over sweeping change. Intensely involved in the new League of Nations, Balch criticized the coercive provisions of its covenant and possessed no illusions concerning its ability to solve major conflicts. She sought to enlarge its membership, democratize its structure, and ensure that it recognized the rights of minorities. She was especially delighted when, in 1921, the League admitted Albania, a nation experiencing invasion by both Serbs and Italians. Similarly, she was gratified by the League's protection of Armenian, Syrian, and Greek refugees deported from Asia Minor. She was particularly concerned with the League's specialized agencies, those dealing with such matters as the opium trade, white slavery, international aviation, and disarmament. No utopian, she said in 1921, "The League, if it is to be a reality at all, must necessarily mirror the existing balance of power, but while it mirrors it, it modifies it. And modifies it for the better."

In December 1922, Balch, experiencing bad health, resigned her post. Throughout the interwar period, she resided much of the time in the U.S. while—at one time or other—holding all the influential offices of the U.S. and international WILPF. Included were a brief second term as international secretary, this time without pay (1934–35); president of the American section (1931); and honorary international president (1937). She sponsored summer schools on peace education, helped develop WILPF branches in some 50 countries, and in general acted as the WILPF's minister without portfolio. Although the WILPF housed many pacifists within it, both she and Jane Addams used their influence to keep the body from being restricted to pacifists alone.

Biographer Randall describes Balch at the height of her influence:

> In appearance throughout her sixties and indeed through her seventies, Emily was still tall, unstooped, angular, with a fragility that denied her wiry tenacity. Her step was sprightly "tip-toeing along" as when she was a girl. Her gaze was calm, direct, her grey-blue eyes keen, observant, quizzical, kindly. She had the impersonal air, the gracious aloofness, the dignity of a woman immersed in great affairs.

In February 1926, along with five other Americans, Balch investigated conditions in Haiti, which had been occupied by U.S. marines since 1915. The resulting study, *Occupied Haiti* (1927), was basically her product. Finding the situation highly explosive, the report called on the U.S. to maintain such social services as roads, schools, and bridges while removing its troops. Haiti's government, it said, must be turned back over to the Haitians. In 1927, she personally presented the task force's findings to President Calvin Coolidge. Three years later, President Herbert Hoover adopted policies similar to those recommended by the WILPF group.

Despite her endorsement of the 1928 Kellogg-Briand Pact to outlaw war, she believed that Germany should be allowed to rearm until other nations gave up their own weapons. When Japan attacked Mukden in September 1931, she called for an international administration of Manchuria that would insure treaty rights for all nations. The area, she said, needed a body of paid experts resembling the city-manager system of some American cities. Relying on her training in economics, she sought developmental loans at a low interest rate. Calling for an arms embargo on both China and Japan, she said, "fighting is not the solution . . . and to furnish arms to those we want to help is not truly to help them."

In 1936, however, Balch opposed the U.S. neutrality acts, saying they did not distinguish between aggressor and victim. Noninterference, she said, simply handed the initiative to the "unscrupulous and violent," encouraged international blackmail, and fostered "a greedy and cowardly isolationist nationalism." Between 1936 and 1939, she recommended nonmilitary international sanctions against aggressors, a reformed League of Nations, arbitration procedures, and a world economic conference.

During the Spanish Civil War, she sought mediation, outlining a scheme wherein a moderate Republican government would have ten years to plan in such sensitive areas as religion, education, and land reform. When in 1937 Japan invaded China, Balch called for a ban on raw materials and loans to Japan, saying, "We must not mind irritating the bully." In a small pamphlet, "Refugees as Assets" (1939), she appealed to the U.S. to open its gates to those seeking asylum from Nazi Germany.

When World War II broke out, she had some reservations about the practicality of her old remedy. She wrote in October 1939:

> Of course, I long for mediation by a conference of neutrals . . . but I fear that such a conference could effect little actual accomplishment till the situation has matured one way or another. Yet in the period before that occurs they might be affecting the situation psychologically and getting seminal ideas into the minds of the peoples in a way that would be profoundly important.

Within the powerful American section of the WILPF, she called for unity between pacifists and non-pacifists, based on the common aims of civil liberties, aid to conscientious objectors, and keeping the nation out of war. Once Japan attacked Pearl Harbor, she claimed that fighting was the only option and contributed to community war funds. She did attack the policy of unconditional surrender for unnecessarily prolonging the war and sought to alleviate the plight of interred Japanese-Americans.

In 1946, at age 79, Balch was awarded the Nobel Peace Prize. Sharing the $17,000 prize with John R. Mott of the World Student Christian Movement, she donated most of the money to peace work, declaring, "This honor is not for me—it is for my organization." In that same year, she called for a women's peace party that would cooperate across national lines.

During the Cold War, she claimed that any war against communism, even if fought successfully, would leave conditions that would make more drastic oppression and collectivism inevitable. She lauded the specialized agencies of the United Nations and showed more faith in the U.N. General Assembly than in the Security Council. She retained her mistrust of government as such, saying that the sovereign state was:

> a clumsy irregularly developed instrument for joint action excessively colored by considerations of power and prestige, in some directions meddling excessively with matters that ought to be left to the individual or to non-governmental agencies or to non-governmental regulation, and again neglecting to control what needs governmental direction.

Balch found no reason to believe that a world state, even a federal one, would be run differently than a national one. She found the abolition of armed forces far too utopian a goal and placed much hope in ad hoc international agencies, run independently of participating governments and addressing themselves to such matters as agriculture, underdeveloped areas, airways, nuclear energy, the high seas, strategic bases, and polar regions. She sought the internationalization of major waterways, including Panama, Suez, the Dardanelles, and the Rhine and Danube rivers. In 1948, she endorsed the Marshall Plan but a year later opposed the formation of the North Atlantic Treaty Alliance. In 1955, while calling President Dwight D. Eisenhower a man of peace, she opposed American efforts to rearm Western Europe and Japan and said that Taiwan should be internationalized. From 1924 until her death, she lived in Jamaica Plain, Wellesley, and Cambridge, Massachusetts. On January 9, 1961, Emily Greene Balch died of pneumonia.

SOURCES:

Randall, Mercedes M. *Improper Bostonian: Emily Greene Balch.* Twayne, 1964.

———, ed. *Beyond Nationalism: The Social Thought of Emily Greene Balch.* Twayne, 1972.

SUGGESTED READING:

Addams, Jane, Emily Greene Balch, and Alice Hamilton. *Women at the Hague: The International Congress of Women and Its Results.* Macmillan, 1915 (reprinted, Garland, 1972).

Balch, Emily Greene. *Our Slavic Fellow Citizens.* Charities Publication Committee, 1910.

———. *Approaches to the Great Settlement.* B.W. Huebsch, 1918.

———. *Occupied Haiti.* Writers Publishing, 1927 (reprinted, Garland, 1972).

———. *The Miracle of Living.* Island Press, 1941.

———. *Vignettes in Prose.* Women's International League for Peace and Freedom, 1952.

Bussey, Gertrude, and Margaret Tims. *Women's International League for Peace and Freedom, 1915–1965: Record of Fifty Years' Work.* Allen and Unwin, 1965.

Chatfield, Charles. *For Peace and Justice: Peace in America, 1914–1941.* University of Tennessee Press, 1971.

Marchard, C. Roland. *The American Peace Movement and Social Reform, 1898–1918.* Princeton University Press, 1972.

Wittner, Lawrence. *Rebels Against the War: The American Peace Movement, 1941–1960.* Columbia University Press, 1969.

Justus D. Doenecke, Professor of History, New College of the University of South Florida, Sarasota, Florida

Baldechild, Baldhild, or Baldhilda

(c. 630–c. 680).

See Balthild.

Baldwin, Faith (1893–1978)

Popular American novelist from the 1920s to the 1940s. *Born in New Rochelle, New York, on October 1, 1893; died in Norwalk, Connecticut, on March 18, 1978; daughter of Stephen C. Baldwin (a well-known trial lawyer) and Edith Hervey (Finch) Baldwin; educated in Brooklyn, in private schools, and in Dresden, Germany, 1914–16; married Hugh H. Cuthrell, in 1920 (died 1953); children: two boys, Hugh and Stephen, and two girls, Hervey and Ann.*

A notable writer of light fiction, Faith Baldwin grew up in Brooklyn, New York, and Dresden, Germany, but spent her later years on a farm in Connecticut. Known as a "circulating library" novelist because of her popularity, she began her literary career as a poet, publishing her first work in 1911. She was the author of over 60 novels; one book of poetry, *Signposts* (1924); children's books; and numerous short stories, serials, and articles for popular magazines. Among her novels are *Mavis of Green Hill* (1921), *Alimony* (1928), *Office Wife* (1930), *Week-end Marriage* (1932), *Medical Center* (1940), *Washington, D.C.* (1943), *You Can't Escape* (1943), *Woman on Her Way* (1946), *Golden Shoestring* (1949), *Whole Armor* (1951), *The Juniper Tree* (1952), and *American Family* (1935) which details her family history. Baldwin, who had once longed to be an actress, also wrote for the screen; her film credits include: *The Moon's Our Home* (1936), *Men Are Such Fools* (1937), *Apartment for Peggy* (1950), and *Queen for a Day* (1951).

Baldwin, Maria Louise

(1856–1922)

American educator and first black woman to hold the post of master in a school in New England. *Name variations: Mollie. Born in Cambridge, Massachusetts, on September 13, 1856; died in Boston, Massachu-*

setts, on January 9, 1922; oldest of two daughters and a son of Peter L. (a letter carrier) and Mary E. Baldwin; attended Sargent Primary School and Allston Grammar School in Cambridge, Massachusetts; graduated from Cambridge High School, 1874; graduated from Cambridge training school for teachers.

During the oppressive age in American history when black women held few positions of authority, Maria Louise Baldwin became the only black woman to hold the position of master of a public school in New England, and perhaps the only one in the nation to have charge of a primarily white faculty and student body. A respected figure to generations of students and parents, Baldwin was a leading social and intellectual figure in the progressive community of Cambridge, Massachusetts.

Born into a modest family in Cambridge, Baldwin was educated through college in the Cambridge schools. Before beginning her 40-year association with Cambridge's Agassiz School—named for the great scientist Louis Agassiz—she taught in Chestertown, Maryland, for two years. After teaching every grade from first to the seventh at Agassiz, in 1889 Baldwin was appointed principal. Unsure of her ability, she struck a deal with the Board of Education that, if the new post did not work out, she would be allowed to return to the classroom.

In 1916, Baldwin participated in the expansion of the school to include higher grades, and at that time was made master of the institution's 12 teachers and 500 students. Remaining a student herself, she continued to take courses at nearby Harvard University, as well as other colleges. She was active in several organizations of black women and was a popular lecturer across the country. An extensive reader, Baldwin had a large personal library, which she shared with weekly reading classes in her home on Prospect Street. In 1897, she had become the first woman to deliver the Washington's Birthday address to the Brooklyn Institute, and chose for her subject "The Life and Services of the late Harriet Beecher Stowe."

On January 9, 1922, while making a speech at the Copley Plaza hotel in Boston, Baldwin collapsed and died suddenly of the heart disease that had plagued her later years. Her body lay in state in Boston for two days so that friends and students could pay their respects. The Agassiz school established a scholarship in her honor and named the school auditorium Baldwin Hall. The class of 1922—the last class she taught—presented the school with a tablet in her memory, while the Cambridge *Chronicle* paid tribute to her life noting, "She has left to all whose lives touched hers the memory of a rare and radiant nature, the keynote of whose character was service."

SUGGESTED READING:

Brawley, Benjamin G. *Negro Builders and Heroes.* Chapel Hill: University of North Carolina Press, 1937.

Lerner, Gerda, ed. *Black Women in White America.* NY: Pantheon Books, 1972.

Barbara Morgan,
Melrose, Massachusetts

Baldwin, Ruth Ann (fl. 1915–1921)

American screenwriter and director. *Flourished from 1915 to 1921.*

Filmography: (as writer) The Black Box *(1915); (as director)* Arrangement With Fate *(1915),* The Double Deal In The Park *(1915), (co-director)* End of the Rainbow *(1916),* Recoiling Vengeance *(1916),* The Retribution *(1916),* Black Mantilla *(1917),* The Butterfly *(1917),* Is Money All? *(1917),* It Makes a Difference *(1917),* The Rented Man *(1917),* A Soldier of the Legion *(1917),* The Storm Women *(1917),* Three Women of France *(1917),* Twixt Love and Desire *(1917),* When Liz Lets Loose *(1917),* A Wife on Trial *(1917),* The Woman Who Could Not Pay *(1917),* The Mother's Call *(1918),* Broken Commandments *(1919),* The Devil's Ripple *(1920),* The Marriage of William Ashe *(1921),* Puppets of Fate *(1921).*

Little personal data can be found on Ruth Ann Baldwin, who was certainly one of the pioneers of the motion-picture industry. Having established a career as a journalist and publicist, Baldwin was hired by Universal in 1915 to write a serial called *The Black Box* for Herbert Rawlinson and **Anna Little**, popular matinee idols of the day. Serials were to the silent era what episodic dramas or soaps are to modern television audiences; seen in sequence each Saturday afternoon, the melodramatic tales often ended in a cliff-hanger.

Besides *The Black Box*, Baldwin directed and wrote another successful serial called *The Double Deal in the Park*. After co-directing the feature film *End of the Rainbow*, she became a full-time director. Her first major success came in 1916 with the release of *Retribution* that starred ***Cleo Madison**. Also under contract with Universal, Madison was a popular actress turned director.

Baldwin spent much of her career working for Universal. However, she directed two pictures for rival Metro, *Broken Commandments*, 1919, and *Puppets of Fate*, one of two pictures she directed in 1921. Though an article in *Photoplay* magazine called Baldwin "one of the most capable of the Universal staff," her career after 1921 seems to have ended as abruptly as it began, and any personal information still must be unearthed.

SOURCES:

Slide, Anthony. *Early Women Directors: Their Role in the Development of the Silent Cinema.* NY: A.S. Barnes, 1977.

Smith, Sharon. *Women Who Make Movies.* NY: Hopkinson and Blake, 1975.

Deborah Jones, Studio City, California

Balfour, Betty (1903–1979)

English actress. *Born in London, England, on March 27, 1903; died in 1979.*

One of Britain's more popular stars of the silent screen, Betty Balfour made her debut at 17 in *Nothing Else Matters* and rose to popularity with the title role in *Squibs* the following year. She was a huge audience draw throughout the 1920s, starring mostly in comedies that were produced by her own company. With the arrival of sound, she turned to supporting roles. Her films include *Mary Find the Gold* (1921), *Squibs Wins the Calcutta Sweeps* (1922), *Mord Em'ly* (*Me and My Girl*, 1922), *Wee MacGregor's Sweetheart* (1922), *Squibs' Honeymoon* (1923), *Squibs MP* (1923), *Love Life and Laughter* (1923), *Reveille* (1924), *A Sister of Six* (1924), *Satan's Sister* (1925), *Somebody's Darling* (1925), *Monte Carlo* (1925), *Blinkeyes* (1926), *La Petite Bonne du Palance* (1926), *Sea Urchin* (1926), *The Little People* (1926), *Croquette* (1927), *Le Diable au Coeur* (*The Little Devil May Care*, 1927), *Die sieben Töchter der Frau Gyrukovics* (1927), *The Vagabond Queen* (1929), *Bright Eyes* (1929), *Raise the Roof*, (1930), *Paddy the Next Best Thing* (1933), *Evergreen* (1934), *My Old Dutch* (1934), *Eliza Comes to Stay* (1936), *29 Acacia Avenue* (*The Facts of Love*, 1945).

Balfour, Frances (1858–1931)

English writer and suffragist. *Name variations: Lady Frances Balfour. Born in 1858; died in 1931; tenth of twelve children of the duchess of Argyll and the 8th duke of Argyll; sister of Blanche Balfour; sister-in-law of* ****Constance Lytton*** *(1869–1923) and Betty Balfour; married E.J.A. Balfour (brother of philosopher and statesman Arthur J. Balfour), in 1879.*

Frances Balfour was born in 1858, one of 12 children of the duke and duchess of Argyll. As a small child, Frances suffered from a hip-joint disease; throughout her life, she was in constant pain and walked with a limp. In 1879, to the displeasure of her Liberal family, she married Eustace Balfour who came from a well-known Tory family. His uncle was Lord Salisbury, a Conservative party leader and three-time prime minister; his brother was Arthur Balfour, another successful Tory politician who would be prime minister from 1902 to 1905. Though Eustace did not take an active role in politics, he and Frances constantly clashed ideologically. Frances, a devout Liberal, was a loyal supporter of William Gladstone. Their diverging views caused a rift in the marriage, and though they did not divorce, they spent less and less time together. An alcoholic, Eustace died in 1911.

In 1887, with **Marie Corbett** and **Eva Maclaren**, Frances Balfour had formed the Liberal Women's Suffrage Society; she became, notes Britain's *Dictionary of National Biography*, a "mistress of invective in the cause of women's suffrage." She and her sister-in-law **Betty Balfour** tried hard to persuade Arthur Balfour to support women's suffrage in the House of Commons. Though Arthur was supportive philosophically, he was unwilling to fight for the cause.

A fervent supporter of the Church of Scotland, Lady Frances Balfour organized the rebuilding of London's Crown Court Church; she penned several memoirs and reminiscences.

SUGGESTED READING:

Balfour, Blanche. *Family Homespun.* London: John Murray, 1940.

Balfour, Frances. *Me Obliviscaris* (autobiography). London: Hodder and Stoughton, 1930.

Balin, Mireille (1911–1968)

French actress. *Born in Monte Carlo on July 20, 1911; died in 1968.*

Mireille Balin parlayed her modeling career to become an international star of French films throughout the 1930s. Opposite Fyodor Chaliapin, she played Dulcinea in G.W. Pabst's *Don Quixote* and first played the femme fatale, opposite Jean Gabin, in *Pépé le Moko* in 1937 (a part later played by ***Hedy Lamarr** opposite Charles Boyer in the American remake, *Algiers*). Balin retired in 1947, two years after the liberation of France. Her other films include *Vive la Classe* (1932), *Le Sexe faible* (1933), *Marie des Angoisses* (1935), *Jeunes Filles de Paris* (1936), *Naples au Baiser de Feu* (*The Kiss of Fire*, 1937), *Le Vénus de l'Or* (1938), *Menaces* (1940), *Macao l'Enfer du Jeu* (1940), *Dernier Atout* (1942), *Malaria* (1943), and *La Dernière Chevauchée* (1947).

Balkama (fl. 10 c. BCE).

See Sheba, queen of.

Balkanska, Mimi (b. 1902)

Bulgarian soprano. *Born in Ruse, Bulgaria, on June 23, 1902; founded the Cooperative Theater in 1922; Bulgaria's most popular operetta star who appeared throughout Europe as well as in Turkey, Israel, and the former Yugoslavia.*

A star, impresario, and pioneer in Bulgarian operetta, Mimi Balkanska played over 300 roles in her 45-year career. After World War I, she appeared in Vienna, Budapest, and Berlin. In 1922, she founded the Cooperative Theater in Sofia, where she worked until 1938 when she moved to the Odeon Operetta Theater. In 1942, Balkanska became director of the Khudojestven Operetta Theater, taking a role in every production she directed. When the theater came under state control, she remained director until the end of her career. Much beloved in Bulgaria where she was a pacesetter in the arts, she retired in 1968.

John Haag, Athens, Georgia

Balkis (fl. 10 c. BCE).

See Sheba, queen of.

Ball, Frances (1794–1861)

Irish pioneer in the field of middle-class female education and founder of the Loreto Institute, which at the time of her death had 37 houses throughout the world. *Name variations: Mother Teresa, Mother Teresa Ball, Mother Frances Mary Theresa, Mother Ball, Mrs. Ball. Born Frances Ball in early January 1794 in Dublin, Ireland; died in Dalkey, near Dublin, on May 19, 1861; daughter of John Ball (a merchant) and Mabel (Bennett) Ball; educated at the Convent of the Institute of the Blessed Virgin Mary, York; never married; no children.*

Professed as a nun of the Institute of the Blessed Virgin Mary (BVM) at York (1816); established the first house of the Irish Institute of the BVM, known as the Loreto Institute, at Rathfarnham (1821).

On August 23, 1841, a ship left the quays in Dublin on the first stage of the long and hazardous voyage to India. On board were a number of nuns, charged with the task of establishing the first foundation of their Loreto Institute outside Ireland. The sisters' trepidation at the prospect of the journey and the challenge which faced them in a strange country was heightened by the knowledge that they were unlikely ever to return to their homeland. Hardly less moved was their mother superior and the founder of their congregation, Mother Frances (Teresa) Ball, who watched their departure from the shore. This was one of the very rare occasions on which Ball, normally an impassive and somewhat severe figure, was recorded as displaying emotion, and for that reason it made an unforgettable impression on those who witnessed it. As William Hutch, her first biographer, recorded the event:

> On a tower within the enclosure of the newly established Convent [at Dalkey] . . . was stationed Rev Mother Ball, woe-stricken . . . pale, motionless, mute, in the intensity of her sorrow; and her eyes were never once removed from the receding sails of the out-bound vessel, until they firstly vanished from her sight, leaving her no hope of ever meeting her children again, until she should clasp them to her bosom in that land where there is parting nevermore.

The foundation of an Irish Loreto convent and school in India initiated a new phase in the mission of Mother Ball, who in the course of the previous two decades had established a network of schools throughout Ireland for the education of Catholic middle-class girls. In doing so, she drew on a family tradition of piety and public service. Her mother **Mabel (Bennett) Ball** was described by S.T. Coleridge as "a modest, retiring Christian lady, full of good works and of religious care for her family"; her father John Ball was a prosperous Dublin silk merchant and a convert to Catholicism.

By the closing decades of the 18th century, the legal and political disabilities to which Catholics had previously been subject had begun to disappear, and, as a wealthy man, John Ball was in a position to provide his four daughters with the best education currently available. However, the options available to middle-class Catholic girls were still very restricted; in fact, Frances, like her elder sisters, Anna Maria and Isabella, was sent to school at an English convent, that of the Institute of the Blessed Virgin Mary at Micklegate Bar in York. In 1803, Frances arrived in York and stayed there for five years. She was a clever and serious-minded student, gifted, according to Hutch, "with talents of a high order . . . a clear, sound judgement . . . a retentive memory, and much quickness of apprehension," together with "remarkable application to study." When Frances was 14, however, John Ball died, and Mabel decided that Frances should finish her education and return to live with her in Dublin. Her life there, conventional and pleasant as it was, may well have seemed frivolous in contrast to what she had witnessed of convent life, but she did find a sympathetic friend in a local priest, Dr. John Murray, who encouraged her involvement in charitable effort and guided her in matters of faith and spirituality. Nevertheless, she shared her family's expectation that she would follow the normal path of marriage and motherhood and, according to her own account, had absolutely no attraction towards the religious life at this time.

At age 18, however, Frances was galvanized by a dramatic spiritual awakening. Drawing on her own version of events, William Hutch maintains that the awakening occurred during a ball and was sufficiently vivid to prompt her to an immediate and irrevocable decision, to "devote herself entirely to the service of God" by becoming a nun. For the present, however, she kept the experience a secret from her family and friends, confiding only in Murray. His advice was that she should take no decisive step for three years; in the meantime, she should "wait and pray" in order to test the reality of her vocation.

Privately, however, Murray already had in mind a role which would utilize Ball's remarkable strength of character and her capacity for leadership. Acutely conscious of the part which women could play in the promotion of Catholic belief and practice, Murray, who was soon to become archbishop of Dublin, had a particular interest in female education. He had already been instrumental in the establishment of a new religious congregation, the Sisters of Charity, which was primarily concerned with the education of the poor, but no comparable facility existed for middle-class Catholic girls. Murray now proposed to Frances that she should establish and lead a sisterhood, which would have as its mission the creation of a system of middle-class female education. Her first response was to protest her unworthiness, but she eventually acceded to his request and prepared to embark on her task. Although her family was at first shocked by her desire to become a nun, they did ultimately approve her decision, and, on June 11, 1814, she re-entered the Bar convent at York, this time as a novice rather than as a pupil. As Sister Mary Teresa, she carried out the various duties of a novice, and, in September 1816, having completed her training, she took her final vows as a nun.

Although both she and Murray were anxious that she should return to Ireland as quickly as possible in order to begin her mission there, the shortage of other candidates for the proposed sisterhood made this impossible, and Frances stayed on in York for another five years, during which she taught in the Institute's school, gaining useful experience for her future career. Nevertheless, the period was one of discouragement and depression for her, despite Murray's continued support. In 1819, however, two Irish girls arrived at York for training and, in the following year, were professed as Sisters **Baptist** and **Ignatia**. Meanwhile, Murray had bought a handsome but decrepit mansion at Rathfarnham, just outside Dublin, as a future convent and school, and, on August 10, 1821, Ball, together with the two other sisters, left York to return to Dublin, arriving at the port of Dun Laoghaire to find a huge crowd gathered to greet King George IV. The contrast between the welcome provided for the king, and the virtually unnoticed arrival of the small party of nuns, prompted Hutch to declare that "in truth the cheers should have gone forth, and the banners should have waved . . . on that August morning . . . not for the Fourth of the

Frances Ball

Georges, but for Mother [Frances] Ball and her devoted companions, who in visiting Ireland brought priceless blessings in their train."

In the short term, however, the sisters did not even have a permanent home. Their house was still unfit for occupation, and for over a year Ball and her fellow nuns stayed in temporary lodgings. On November 4, 1822, they were finally able to move into their new convent at Rathfarnham, but problems remained. The renovation of the building was not yet complete, and their first months there were dogged by disaster, including a storm which badly damaged the house and grounds, and illness among both the sisters and their pupils.

However, the number of pupils and of applicants for admission to the religious life soon began to show an increase: in 1823, the nuns were able to open a poor school in Rathfarnham, in addition to their fee-paying establishment, and, by 1825, the congregation itself had nine members, although lack of money continued to be a problem. The school had accommodation for only 40 pupils, and the shortfall between the income from their fees and the costs of running the establishment had to be made up by the dowries customarily brought with them by new entrants to the community. By 1833, with 80 people living in the house, it was apparent that expansion was necessary, and Archbishop Murray, when Ball sought his advice, suggested that rather than simply build a new wing to the existing premises, she should open a second foundation elsewhere. Shortly afterwards, therefore, a new foundation and school were opened in Navan in County Meath. At the same time, Ball set up a new fee-paying day school at Harcourt Street in Dublin, the first such establishment to be run by a religious order in the city. Overcoming some initial difficulties, the school moved in 1841 to new premises on St. Stephen's Green and, within a short time, became one of the leading Catholic girls' schools in the country.

As a schoolgirl in York, Ball had been profoundly impressed by the splendor of the Minster, and she retained a firm belief in the spiritual power of architecture, asserting that when her pupils "have a fine church to pray in, their minds will be impressed with reverence for the great Being who dwells in the tabernacle." In 1838, work began on the building of a new church at the Rathfarnham convent, and she commissioned the celebrated English architect Augustus Pugin to design the interior and the Irish sculptor John Hogan to carve the high altar. However, she herself had a major part in the planning of the new building, and, according to Hutch, the church was "entirely the conception of Mrs Ball herself. She possessed a most accurate knowledge of the principles of architecture . . . and used to prepare her own plans with an accuracy of detail which would reflect credit on many professional men."

The building of the chapel fulfilled one of Ball's dearest wishes. Nevertheless, according to her own account, she was haunted by foreboding: "an inward voice was ever whispering in doleful prophecy, 'You will have the church, but sore trials will follow.'" According to Ball, this misfortune took the form of a number of deaths in the sisterhood, with seven members dying, all of tuberculosis, between 1836 and January 1840. Concern about the incidence of illness in the house confirmed Mother Ball in her wish to acquire what she called "a bathing lodge," where pupils and nuns might retire for rest or convalescence. After some research, she found a suitable site in the small fishing village of Dalkey, established a community there and set about the building of a new convent, reputedly drawing up the plans for it herself.

Meanwhile, after deliberation, she had agreed to the request of a ladies' committee in Calcutta that she send some sisters to run a convent school there. On August 23, 1841, 11 nuns left for India, where they started schools for both European and for poor Indian children, as well as an orphanage. Over the next two years, 14 more nuns were sent out, and ultimately three more convents were founded. These were followed by other overseas projects in Mauritius and Gibraltar (1845), Canada (1847), and Manchester and Cadiz (1851). New houses were also opened at home, and, by 1852, Rathfarnham and its six dependent convents in Ireland housed 126 nuns and 193 boarders, while the "select day-schools for young ladies" had 208 pupils and the free schools 503.

These successes, however, were countered by a number of disappointments. In 1852, Ball lost a valuable supporter and advisor when her old friend Archbishop Murray died. Two years later, on Ascension Day, 1854, the Clontarf convent was destroyed by fire. According to Hutch, Mother Ball showed her customary stoicism and unwavering faith. "She was stunned for a moment; but quickly recovering her self-possession, she said with incredible calmness, 'The Lord gave it, the Lord hath taken it away, and blessed for ever be the name of the Lord.'" Rebuilding began almost immediately, and, by Ascension Day of the following year, the sisters were able to return to Clontarf.

Most serious, however, was the growing unrest and dissension within the community at Stephen's Green, whose members apparently resented Ball's authority. They found a supporter for their case in Murray's successor, Archbishop Paul Cullen, and the dispute dragged on for a number of years, ending only when Mother Ball appealed over the head of the archbishop to the pope, who responded by ordering the dissident sisters back to obedience. Ball declared her joy at being able to "receive them back again to a mother's bosom," but she had been deeply hurt by what she regarded as a betrayal by those whom she had nurtured, and in fact relations between the Green and the mother house continued to be strained until after her death. The sensitivity of the whole affair can be deduced from the fact that Ball's 19th-century biographers made absolutely no mention of the quarrel: on the contrary, in Hutch's words, "the history of the Loreto House, Stephen's Green, since the day of its foundation, may be epitomised in two words—uninterrupted success."

By now 65 years old, Ball was as active as ever in the direction of her various foundations: as she told a colleague, "I am stronger now than 38 years ago. I enjoy more vigour and am more ready to found, when called upon." However, on October 17, 1860, she was hurrying through the corridors of Rathfarnham after a typically busy day when she fell, injuring her hip. Her condition soon worsened, although she survived for another seven months, in increasingly severe pain. In May 1861, aware that she was dying, she insisted on being moved to her "little paradise" at Dalkey, arriving there on Ascension Thursday. According to Hutch, "From the moment that Mrs Ball entered the room assigned to her at Dalkey, she abandoned all hope of ever leaving it alive, and began to make her immediate preparation for the great passage to eternity." A week later, on May 19, Pentecost Sunday, she died peacefully, in the presence of four of her nuns, and was buried a few days later at Rathfarnham.

At the time of her death, Ball had established 37 houses of her Order throughout the world. Enterprise on this scale clearly demanded not just piety, but also outstanding intelligence, toughness, and the ability to command. As Hutch described it, "Mrs Ball was born to rule," possessing "a clear, penetrating mind, solidity of judgement, discernment of character, prudence, forbearance, and a firmness of will which nothing could shake when she believed that what she had resolved upon was right." Her most immediately apparent traits were dignity and reserve, qualities which, according to her, were sometimes "misunderstood, and not infrequently led to a disesteem of her worth." According to those who knew her best, this formidable exterior concealed great thoughtfulness and compassion for those in spiritual or physical distress, but "by many," it was reported, she "was thought stiff and stand off," even "somewhat stern and unamiable," and her autocratic character may have created difficulties in dealing both with subordinates and with high-ranking clergy. Nevertheless, in her determination to fulfil what she believed to be God's will, she insisted on absolute obedience to her dictates. "No military commander," Hutch declared, "had ever drilled his troops into more perfect discipline than she had established among her nuns at Rathfarnham. . . . 'This regularity in our actions,' Ball would say to them, 'is like symmetry in a building, which adds to its beauty as well as to its strength.'"

In some instances, probably in relation to the quarrel with the St. Stephen's Green community, Hutch clearly felt that she had been too autocratic. As he suggests in a rare criticism, in her "zeal for the enforcement of obedience . . . she carried her views of authority too far. . . . In a word, she wished Rathfarnham Abbey to be the centre around which all her other convents should revolve." Such assertiveness was bound to be unpopular in a hierarchical and patriarchal church, but it is characteristic of Ball that, having decided that centralization was an essential part of her strategy, she should persist in it against the opposition even of her own archbishop. To the end of her life, indeed, she displayed her determination to ensure the unity, and thus safeguard the future and the effectiveness of her congregation. In this, as in all her work, the motivating force was her deep and unwavering religious faith. According to Hutch, "God's glory was the principle which shaped and guided her every action. This same spirit she laboured . . . to infuse into the hearts of her children. 'No effort,' she would often say to them, 'should be lost, when there is question of the salvation of souls.'"

While Ball certainly hoped that her legacy would be primarily a spiritual one, her work also had practical implications for the place of women in Irish society. While her pupils included poor children, her schools were principally intended for the daughters of the Irish Catholic middle class and were the first to address the educational needs of this category on a widespread basis. Initially designed to produce godly and virtuous wives and mothers, they adapted impressively to the economic, social, and cultural changes of the later decades of the 19th century, not least in the area of women's rights, and were among the first establishments in which Catholic girls could prepare for state examinations and could study for university degrees. If Ball did not foresee this development, it is likely that she would have approved it. As Hutch recorded, she taught her pupils "to aim at *perfection* in everything, and to be content with nothing less. . . . She frequently repeated to them this favourite maxim of hers: 'whatever is done for God should be well done.'" In this, as in all her precepts, she demanded of herself no less than she did of others.

SOURCES:

Coleridge, Henry James. *The Life of Mother Frances Mary Teresa Ball.* Dublin and London: M.H. Gill & Son, 1881.

Forristal, Desmond. *The First Loreto Sister.* Dublin: Dominican Publications, 1994.

Hutch, William. *Mrs. Ball: A Biography.* Dublin and London: James Duffy and Sons, 1879.

MacDonald, Mother Evangeline. *Joyful Mother of Children.* Dublin: 1961.

SUGGESTED READING:

Clear, Caitriona. *Nuns in Nineteenth-Century Ireland.* Gill & Macmillan, Dublin: 1987.

———. "The limits of female autonomy: nuns in nineteenth-century Ireland," in Maria Luddy and Cliona Murphy, eds. *Women Surviving.* Dublin: Poolbeg Press, 1990, pp. 15–50.

Fahey, Tony. "Nuns in the Catholic church in Ireland in the nineteenth century," in *Girls don't do honours.* Edited by Mary Cullen. Dublin: 1987, pp. 7–30.

COLLECTIONS:

Archives of Loreto Convent, Rathfarnham, Dublin.

Rosemary Raughter,
freelance writer in women's history, Dublin, Ireland

Ball, Lucille (1911–1989)

American actress, star of the television show "I Love Lucy," and co-founder and president of Desilu Productions, which revolutionized television production in America and the world. *Name variations: Lucy. Born Lucille Ball on August 6, 1911, in Jamestown in western New York State; died following heart surgery at Cedars-Sinai Medical Center in Los Angeles, California, on April 26, 1989; daughter of Henry Ball (an electrician) and Desirée ("DeDe") Hunt (a saleswoman); attended public school to ninth grade; married Desi Arnaz, on November 30, 1940 (divorced 1961); married Gary Morton, on November 19, 1961; children: (first marriage) Lucie Arnaz (an actress), and Desi Arnaz, Jr.*

Awards: countless honors, including Emmys for best comedienne (1952 and 1967); induction into the Television Academy Hall of Fame (1984); and Kennedy Center Honors for Lifetime Achievement (1986).

Father died when she was three (1914); lived with her step-grandmother from the ages of seven to eleven; attended Robert Minton-John Murray Anderson School of Drama for six weeks (1926); a tragic shooting accident which maimed and eventually killed a neighboring boy led to a lawsuit that cost the family its home (1927); moved back and forth between Jamestown and New York City, where she supported herself modeling for Bergdorf Goodman and Hattie Carnegie and still photographers (1926–28); went to Hollywood for a six-week stint as a Goldwyn Girl, appearing in Roman Scandal, *starring Eddie Cantor (1933); made more than 60 films, including* Stage Door, The Big Street, DuBarry Was a Lady, *and* The Fuller Brush Girl *for a variety of studios (1933–50), and starred in the CBS-radio show "My Favorite Husband" (1948–50); played the wacky, star-struck housewife Lucy Ricardo as star of the ground-breaking and wildly successful "I Love Lucy" and its spin-off "The Lucy-Desi Comedy Hour" (1951–60) with her then-husband Desi Arnaz, with whom she founded Desilu Productions; starred in the Broadway Musical* Wildcat *(1960–61); starred in three "Lucy" tv-series (1962–74); president of Desilu Productions (1962–67); starred in the film* Mame *(1974) and the tv-movie "Stone Pillow" (1985), and the short-lived series "Life with Lucy" (1986).*

One Saturday afternoon in the early 1920s, a tall slim girl, about 14 years old, with large blue eyes and chestnut hair, sat in the darkness of a vaudeville theater in Jamestown, New York. Exactly who had brought her she could never remember, all she knew was the effect the performer Julius Tannen had on the people around her. A dour figure in a business suit, he stood in the glare of a single light bulb, and, by changing his stance and his accent, he transformed himself from put-upon husband to immigrant woman, from captain of industry to bellboy, uniting through the marvel of his talent the audience of bankers and society matrons and lathe-turners and midwives and moving them from laughter to tears. Lucille Ball felt the waves of emotion crashing around her and vowed that she too would be on the vaudeville stage.

She must have appreciated his ability to evoke a range of emotions as much as she valued the way Tannen lifted people from their daily lives, because almost from infancy she was forced to struggle under trying circumstances and to suppress her own complaints. Her father, an electrician named Henry Ball, died of typhoid when she was three, shortly before the birth of her brother Fred. Her mother Desirée Hunt Ball married Edward Peterson, a factory worker, in

1918, and followed him to Detroit, leaving Ball in Jamestown with Peterson's mother. The dour woman forced Lucille to wash dishes by candlelight and to go to bed on summer evenings at six. Mirrors were completely forbidden, so that about the time she was eight, Lucille was amazed when she caught sight of her face reflected in a trolley window and realized that she was able to entertain herself by making bizarre expressions with her extraordinarily mobile mug.

After Ball was reunited with her mother and the Hunt family in Celoron outside Jamestown, a young boy was fatally injured in a shooting accident on their property. In 1928, Ball's family lost its home in a resulting lawsuit. Forced to leave Celoron, bitterly unhappy in the family's cramped apartment in Jamestown, and something of a scandal to the town because of her romantic involvement with a local hoodlum, Ball was granted her wish—to go to New York to prepare for a career on stage at the Robert Minton-John Murray Anderson School of Drama. "All I learned in drama school was how to be frightened," Ball recalled.

Intimidated by the school's star pupil, ***Bette Davis**, and so homesick and terrified that

Lucille Ball

she could barely speak or move in class, she was invited to leave after six weeks. Until she was 20, Ball moved between Jamestown—where she was the first girl to bob her hair, wear galoshes in the "Flapper" style, and appear publicly in slacks (which she had styled from men's pajamas ordered from a catalog)—and New York City, where she tried to get work as a showgirl with Flo Ziegfeld and Earl Carroll. Flat-chested and shy, she was fired from every company and was close to starving in Manhattan when someone told her that her flat chest would be an advantage as a model. She worked for designer ***Hattie Carnegie**, as well as Bergdorf Goodman and other fashion establishments, and gave up her dream of show business, except for one day in October 1930 when she skipped work to watch ***Clara Bow** make *No Limit* on the city's streets. Carnegie fired her but finally took her back because of Ball's resemblance to ***Constance Bennett**, the most popular film star of the era and an important Carnegie customer.

A chance meeting with an agent led to Ball's being hired to appear in the Eddie Cantor movie *Roman Scandals* as a Goldwyn Girl in 1933. Happy to leave the summer heat of Manhattan, where she was modeling fur and woolen coats, she expected to return from Hollywood in six weeks. Instead, she stayed for 56 years. "My stick-to-itness came out here. Suddenly I was in show business. It interested me because I was learning, and because I was learning, I never complained. Whatever they asked, I did. I did one line, two lines, with animals, in mud packs, seltzer in the face. Eddie Cantor noticed it first. he'd say, 'Give it to that girl, she doesn't mind.'" In Hollywood, she developed a confident façade that she could not effect in New York City, but, because she did not have the sculpted glamorous face of the 1930s, she was not seen as a beauty, and she struggled for parts. Put under contract at the beginning of the talkie era and on the brink of the Technicolor age, it seemed meaningless when she was singled out by a prominent director of the silent era, Edward Sedgwick. Sedgwick, who worked with Buster Keaton, saw her on the Goldwyn lot telling a story with the exaggerated expressions and melodramatic gestures that ***Mabel Normand** struggled to achieve. Although he was then regarded as a has-been, he walked up and said, "Young lady, if you play your cards right, you can be the greatest comedienne in America." Thinking Sedgwick was trying to pick her up, she turned away. The money in films was so good in those Depression days that she was able to reunite her family and support them in Hollywood.

She moved to RKO where she appeared in bit parts, notably in *Top Hat* and *Follow the Fleet,* with ***Ginger Rogers** and Fred Astaire, and came under the protection of studio head Pandro Berman. After she got rave notices in a play *Hey Diddle Diddle,* directed by ❧ **Anne Nichols,** author of the play *Abie's Irish Rose,* Ball made her third lead in the film adaptation of the ***Edna Ferber**-George Kaufman play *Stage Door,* starring Rogers and ***Katharine Hepburn.** It was a story of struggling young actresses in a theatrical rooming house. According to Hepburn, the director Gregory LaCava made up the story as he went along, basing it on scraps of conversation he heard as he eavesdropped on the set. LaCava saw Ball as a girl who dressed well but didn't have the talent or the focus to make it in show business, and he cast her as the one character who chucked her failing career to go home to a nice husband and children in Seattle. As Ball's character departs, Rogers tells Hepburn: "She'll have a photo album of kids and all we'll have is scrapbooks." *Stage Door* was a critical success, but of the star-packed film that included ***Ann Miller, *Eve Arden and Gail Patrick,** who later became a producer of the CBS-TV series "Perry Mason," the one who won an Academy Award was **Andrea Leeds.**

Although Ball was making several pictures a year for RKO and seemed to be earning her $3,500 salary, the studio began to survey audiences and learned that few people could identify her name or face. She was not selling tickets. Trying to build her up, in 1940 RKO put her in *Dance, Girl, Dance* (written by ***Tess Slesinger** and directed by ***Dorothy Arzner**), an adaptation of the Broadway musical *Too Many Girls*, that had been produced and directed by George Abbott. On the day she and ***Maureen O'Hara** completed their fight scene in the film, Ball walked into the RKO commissary where Abbott introduced her to Desi Arnaz, a Cuban band leader who had a featured role in the musical and was making his film debut. She and Arnaz, six years her junior, began a tempestuous courtship on the set, which ended when they married on November 30, 1940, at the Byram River Beagle Country Club in Greenwich, Connecticut. Desi's film career soon sputtered, and he entered the army to serve in World War II. The marriage foundered, and they divorced, for less than one day, in 1944.

In 1943, Ball had moved to MGM where mogul Louis B. Mayer gave her a star build-up that included a significant change of hair color. "When she arrived at MGM, her hair was medium brown," the studio's hair stylist Sydney Guilaroff recalled. "I would not say that it was dull, but it was not interesting. I thought there were enough successful blondes, why not a redhead?" The dyes turned Ball's hair green, however, and colorists worked hours before her hair became a color that was relatively human in shade. Ball's first MGM film, the 1943 *DuBarry Was a Lady* with Gene Kelly and Red Skelton was a hit, but her films soon fell off at the box office, and she was considered a talented supporting player. Over the years, she worked with the Three Stooges, The Marx Brothers, Edgar Bergen, and Harold Lloyd but no one recognized her gift for physical comedy, not even Ball herself who was committed to being a glamorous movie star. The comic gifts of such females as ***Carole Lombard** and ***Rosalind Russell** were recognized, but Ball lacked their verbal timing and witty edge. ***Zazu Pitts**, ***Nancy Walker**, who was then a teen performer, and the great ***Fanny Brice** were popular, but unlike them, Lucy was pretty and on the track for stardom. Buster Keaton tried without success to tell Mayer that Ball was a comic genius, but Mayer could not conceive of this in an attractive woman. Keaton and Sedgwick, who were now both personal friends of Ball's, slowly overcame her objections and trained her in pratfalls, timing, and the transmission and reception of custard pies.

Ball's film career seemed to have bottomed out when the two landed her a contract with the comedy unit of Columbia where she made several knock-about physical comedies, notably *The Fuller Brush Girl*, where the persona of Lucy Ricardo seems ready to emerge. Meanwhile, she was on CBS-radio in 1948–50, playing a scatterbrained housewife in "My Favorite Husband."

Her personal life was in shambles in the late 1940s. Unable to land a role in films, Desi Arnaz went on the road with his band, and the two were seldom together. Despite a series of miscarriages, Ball, who loved her husband desperately, was determined that they would have children together. When she made the 1950 *Fancy Pants* with Bob Hope, she persuaded the comedian to make Desi musical director of his radio show to keep him in Hollywood. Then, when CBS wanted to transfer "My Favorite Husband" to television, Ball insisted that her husband be her costar. Arnaz saw the financial and star potential in television, but Ball was dubious, because film studios blackballed performers who appeared on the medium, unless they were promoting movies. Ball insisted that their show, "I Love Lucy," be filmed in Hollywood, rather than done live in New York. In the fevered negotiations that followed, Ball and Arnaz ended up owning the show and being responsible for its production. CBS executives felt that the couple would be defeated by the challenges, particularly filming for television, and that network executives would find a way to minimize the role of Arnaz, whom they abhorred for his accent and Latin origins. "Who would believe a Cuban band-leader married to a red-blooded American girl?" one asked, incredulous.

Nichols, Anne (1891–1966)

American playwright. *Born in 1891; died in a nursing home in Englewood Cliffs, New Jersey, on September 15, 1966, after a long illness; married actor Henry Duffy (divorced); children: one son.*

Anne Nichols wrote *Abie's Irish Rose*, a theatrical phenomenon that ran from 1922 to 1927. Despite everything the critics threw at the stage, it was the longest running play up to that point in the history of Broadway. Wrote Robert Benchley: "'Abie's Irish Rose' is the kind of play in which a Jewish boy, wanting to marry an Irish girl named Rosemary Murphy, tells his orthodox father that her name is Rosie Murphesky, and the wedding proceeds." As the play continued to fill the house night after night, year after year, Benchley took its success personally, refreshing the blurbs in his weekly theatrical column in *Life*:

> June 22, 1922: ***Abie's Irish Rose***—Among the season's worst.
>
> August 2, 1923: ***Abie's Irish Rose***—A very sore point with this department. Please don't ask us about it. . . .
>
> May 7, 1925: ***Abie's Irish Rose***—If this runs until May 22 it will have broken the record held by "Lightnin'" for length of run. We are as nervous as a witch.
>
> May 28, 1925: ***Abie's Irish Rose***—Now let's just make this fourth year the biggest and best of all.

Nichols also wrote, but with less success, *The Gilded Cage* (1920), *Love Dreams* (1921) and, with **Adelaide Matthews**, *Just Married* (1921).

> The lady was a democrat with a small-d.
>
> —Frank Gorey

Remembering the cinematographer Karl Freund from her days at MGM, Ball, who was awaiting the birth of her first child, Lucie Arnaz, asked that Freund be hired for "I Love Lucy." Intrigued by the challenge, Freund developed a lighting system that made it possible to film the show on three television cameras before a live audience, which was another of Ball's requirements. Also essential to her were her radio writers Jess Oppenheimer, **Marilyn Pugh**, and Bob Carroll, Jr. Although the network and Phillip Morris, its sponsor, did not like the first show, the American public embraced it the Monday night it was broadcast on October 15, 1951. They loved Lucy Ricardo, a home-bound housewife who was determined to thwart her Cuban band-leader husband and trick her way into show business. "I never found a place of my own, never became truly confident until, in the Lucy character I began to create something that was truly mine," she said. "The potential was there. Lucy released it." Soon 14 million Americans, one in nine, were watching the show. Desilu produced such shows as Eve Arden's "Our Miss Brooks" and "The Whirlybirds" and leased facilities to shows starring Danny Thomas and ***Loretta Young**.

Her life was full and pressured. She gave birth to her son Desi, Jr., on January 19, 1953, the same night "Little Ricky" was born on television. The show drew more viewers than the presidential inauguration of Dwight D. Eisenhower on the following day. Within the month, she won her first Emmy, along with one for the

Lucille Ball and Desi Arnaz in "I Love Lucy."

show and signed an $8 million contract with her sponsor Phillip Morris. Positioned as one of the richest women in America, she then became the target of the House Un-American Activities Committee (HUAC), which was conducting a witch hunt on people suspected of being Communists. That she was one of America's most visible and successful capitalists was in no way proof against this. Ball, who had seen several of her friends ruined by HUAC, was certain she and the show would be destroyed. She went before the committee and explained that her grandfather, a socialist who was devoted to the memory of Eugene V. Debs, had asked her to register to vote as a Communist during the Depression, but she was only humoring him and had not voted at all. "In those days," she told the committee with dangerous candor, "that was not a big terrible thing to do. It was almost as terrible to be a Republican." She was the greatest star the committee had ever interrogated, and its members decided to believe her. Although it allowed a cloud to remain over other performers like Larry Parks and ***Judy Holliday**, at Arnaz's insistence a HUAC representative announced that Lucy was no Communist. "The only red thing about this girl is her hair, and even that we're not sure of," Arnaz told reporters, and earned the distinction of making the deadly HUAC something of a joke.

The always stormy Ball-Arnaz marriage collapsed under the pressures of her fame and his business pressures and increasing dependence on alcohol. They divorced in 1961. Hoping to make a new life in New York, Ball starred in the Broadway musical *Wildcat*, which opened December 16, 1960. Her health broke under the strain of the divorce and the physical demands of the show, including singing for which she had no talent or training. She dropped out and, soon after, married Gary Morton, a comedian ten years her junior. Desilu, which produced the show, had to refund $165,000 in ticket sales. Ball returned to Beverly Hills, where she and her "I Love Lucy" co-star ❧▸ **Vivian Vance** began filming "The Lucy Show," which soon made the top ten in the fall of 1962. A few months later, Ball bought out Arnaz's interest in Desilu for $3 million and became company president. Although she relished being a star, she objected whenever anyone said she was powerful. Never happy as an executive, Ball delegated the running of the studio and concentrated on production of her own show. By the mid-1960s, the trend in television was for action-adventure, one-hour films in color and away from the half-hour, black-and-white comedies that had made Desilu's reputation. The studio struggled to find its way, and, against the wishes of her most trusted advisors, Ball approved production of two expensive, innovative shows—"Mission Impossible" and "Star Trek." "Mission" was an early success, but "Star Trek" lagged in the ratings for several seasons, until it became a cult favorite in syndication. "If it had not been for her, 'Mission Impossible' and certainly 'Star Trek' would never have gotten on the air," said Ed Holly, a company officer, "neither of those

❧▸ **Vance, Vivian** (1911–1979)

American actress. *Born in Cherryville, Kansas, in 1911; died of cancer on August 17, 1979, in Belvedere, California; daughter of Robert A. and Mae (Ragan) Jones; attended public schools in Independence, Kansas; grew up outside of Albuquerque, New Mexico; married Philip Ober (an actor), in 1941 (divorced 1959); married John Dodds (a literary agent and publishing executive), in 1961.*

From 1951 to 1959, Vivian Vance played Ethel Mertz, wife of Fred, on "I Love Lucy." But in 1945, six years before she was cast in the show, Vance had had a nervous breakdown while on the road in *The Voice of the Turtle*. "One day I was up and around, the next I was lying in bed in my hotel room, my hands shaking helplessly, in a state of violent nausea, weeping hysterically from causes I didn't know," she told Bart Andrews, author of *The "I Love Lucy" Book*. "A few nights before, on stage, a piece of business called for me to pick up an ashtray. I began to do it and found I couldn't move. The brain ordered, but the arm declined. It was one of the most sickening moments I have ever gone through." For two years, she did not work, until she met a woman psychiatrist who changed her life. In gratitude to Dr. **Eleanor Steele**, Vance established the Vivian Vance Fund at the Philadelphia Psychoanalytic Institute in 1946. She was also once chair of the Connecticut Mental Health Association. For the last few years of series work with ***Lucille Ball**, Vance commuted from her 125-year-old colonial home in Stamford, Connecticut. Though she was persuaded by her publishing executive husband to write her autobiography and actually did so, she changed her mind about publication and shoved the manuscript into a drawer. Vance, who was given an Emmy in 1953 and a Genii Award in 1964, was featured on Broadway opposite Ed Wynn in *Hooray for What*, 1937, and worked with Danny Kaye and ***Eve Arden** in *Let's Face It*, 1941. Her movies include *The Secret Fury* (with ***Claudette Colbert**, 1950), *The Blue Veil* (1951), and *The Great Race* (1965).

SUGGESTED READING:

Castelluccio, Frank, and Alvin Walker. *The Other Side of Ethel Mertz: The Life Story of Vivian Vance*. Manchester, CT: Knowledge, Ideas & Trends, 1998.

shows would ever have been made." In 1967, Ball sold Desilu to Paramount for $17 million. As majority stockholder, her personal share was $10 million.

Ball continued to do "Lucy" shows until 1974, when she made the film *Mame*, a personal disappointment and critical disaster. She emerged from semi-retirement in 1985 to play a homeless woman in the TV-movie "Stone Pillow," which her fans rejected. Her last series, "Life with Lucy," was yanked from the air because of poor ratings. An admitted workaholic and perfectionist, Ball was wretchedly unhappy when she was not before the cameras, and, aside from backgammon and word games, she was unable to fill her days. She was stunned the night of the Academy Awards in April 1989 when she and Bob Hope got a screaming, roaring, standing ovation from crowds within and outside the auditorium. A few weeks later, she was rushed to Cedars-Sinai Medical Center in Los Angeles where she underwent six-and-a-half-hour emergency heart surgery. In the days that followed, when she learned her fans were besieging the hospital with 5,000 cards a day and phoning to learn of her condition, she realized that she was beloved as ever. On the eve of going home from the hospital, around dawn on April 26, 1989, her aorta burst, and she died. Lucy Ricardo, Ball's great contribution to American entertainment, goes on forever.

SOURCES:

Andrews, Bart. *The "I Love Lucy" Book.* NY: Doubleday, 1985.

Bochu, Jim. *Lucy in the Afternoon.* NY: William Morrow, 1990.

Brady, Kathleen. *Lucille: The Life of Lucille Ball.* NY: Hyperion, 1994.

Harris, Eleanor. *The Real Story of Lucille Ball.* NY: Farrar, Straus and Young, 1954.

COLLECTIONS:

Correspondence and clippings at University of Southern California and University of California at Los Angeles; San Diego State University; Margaret Herrick Library of the Academy of Motion Picture Arts and Sciences, Beverly Hills; New York Public Library at Lincoln Center; and the Fenton Historical Society, Jamestown, N.Y., 1989.

RELATED MEDIA:

Hollywood: The Golden Years. BBC Television Productions in Association with RKO Pictures, 1987.

"I Love Lucy." The Voyager Co., 1991.

Lucy and Desi: A Home Movie. Arluck Entertainment, 1993.

Kathleen Brady, author of *Lucille: The Life of Lucille Ball* and of *Ida Tarbell: Portrait of a Muckraker* (University of Pittsburgh Press)

Ball, Mother Teresa (1794–1861).

See Ball, Frances.

Ballard, Florence (1943–1976).

See Supremes, The.

Ballard, Martha Moore (1735–1812)

American midwife and diarist. *Born Martha Moore in Oxford, Massachusetts, in 1735; died in Augusta, Maine, in June 1812; daughter of Dorothy and Elijah Moore; great-aunt of Clarissa Harlowe Barton, also known as* ****Clara Barton****; educated at home; married Ephraim Ballard (d. 1821), in 1754; children: nine, Lucy (b. 1756); Triphene; Jonathan; Dorothy (d. 1769); Martha; Cyrus; Hannah (b. 1769); Dorothy "Dolly" (b. 1773); Ephraim (b. 1779).*

Martha Moore Ballard's hand-bound, linen-covered diaries, covering 1785 to 1812, reveal in minute detail the often harsh life of 18th-century New England settlers. Though the journals had previously appeared as part of Charles Nash's 1904 history of Augusta, Maine, historian **Laurel Thatcher Ulrich** unearthed more of Ballard's story when she rescued the journals from a vault at the Maine State Library, where they had resided since 1930. For her efforts, Ulrich was awarded the Pulitzer Prize in 1990.

Martha Moore was born in Oxford, Massachusetts, in 1735. While her mother was illiterate and used a mark for her signature, Martha benefitted from the schooling of an uncle and brother, both college graduates—Yale and Harvard, respectively. Though women were generally uneducated at that time, Martha would learn the fundamentals well enough to maintain a diary and keep track of family finances. In addition, several physicians within the Moore family passed their learning down to Martha, who knew how to make poultices, emulsions, treatments for cold, cough, dysentery and frostbite, as well as other general remedies.

Martha's early history is known only through her later reflections or from town records. She married Ephraim Ballard in 1754. Over the next 23 years, the Ballards had a farm near Oxford, where they raised eight children. From 1767 to 1770, there was a diphtheria outbreak in Oxford (12% of the town's population of 144 died); in 1769, Martha lost three of her children to the epidemic within ten days.

In October of 1777, the Ballards moved to Hallowell, Maine, a newly settled region along the Kennebec River (land later owned by the city of Augusta). Ephraim assumed operation of the mill, as well as some farm land, and the Ballards settled in a sparsely populated area just above the town. Martha, who had likely assisted birthings in Oxford, delivered her first baby in July of 1778, beginning a vocation which was to become the overriding theme in a diary she would not begin for another eight years. The ninth and last Ballard child was born in 1779.

In January of 1785, Martha Ballard set down her first entry in her diary. It was common for families to keep either a daybook, which detailed daily events and finances, or an almanac, which helped plot weather patterns and crops for farmers. Martha Ballard combined the two forms. Entries rarely exceeded several sentences and encapsulated the movements of the family and community. Ballard captured the drama of life in the new settlement by simply recounting her work. She often traversed the Kennebec, a large, swift river which in bitter winters froze solid. Deaths, births, and illnesses were all subjects of casual mention, which—over the almost three decades of Ballard's diary—build a story.

Hallowell's young population grew quickly. Keeping tabs in her diary, Ballard performed 816 deliveries between 1785 and 1812 and tended to the general health needs of the community. Her records were businesslike, rarely mentioning personal news, with the exception of family events, such as birthdays. When she was not midwifing, Ballard was busy with the family farm. Life was strenuous, not entertaining. Entry by entry, the diary can look monotonous. As a whole, and as a history, it becomes powerful.

Ballard was 77 years old when she attended her last delivery on April 26, 1812. Following her death that June, Martha Ballard's diary was passed down through the family until its donation, more than 100 years later, to the Maine State Library.

SOURCES:

Buck, Claire, ed. *The Bloomsbury Guide to Women's Literature*. NY: Prentice Hall, 1992.

Ulrich, Laurel Thatcher. *A Midwife's Tale: The Life of Martha Moore Ballard, Based on Her Diary, 1785–1812*. NY: Knopf, 1990.

———. "Martha's Diary and Mine," in *Journal of Women's History*. Volume 4, no. 2. Fall, 1992, pp. 157–160.

RELATED MEDIA:

"A Midwife's Tale" on "American Experience," first aired on PBS, January 1998.

Crista Martin, freelance writer,
Boston, Massachusetts

Ballinger, Margaret (1894–1980)

South African politician and a founding member of the Liberal Party. *Born Violet Margaret Livingstone Hodgson in Scotland in 1894; died in 1980; at age ten, immigrated to South Africa with her parents; educated in Port Elizabeth, Wellington; University College of Rhodes, B.A.; Somerville College, Oxford, England, 1914; married William Ballinger.*

For 22 years, Margaret Ballinger battled apartheid from her seat in the African National Congress (ANC). Born in Scotland, she immigrated to South Africa with her parents at the age of ten. She was a history lecturer at Witwatersrand University (in Johannesburg) before meeting her husband William Ballinger, a Scottish trade unionist who had emigrated in 1928. After their marriage in the 1930s, they collaborated on a major study of the protectorates: Bechuanaland (now Botswana), Basutoland (now Lesotho), and Swaziland.

In 1937, Ballinger was drafted to run for one of four seats designated for nonwhite voters under the 1936 Representation of the Natives Act. Winning the Eastern Cape seat, she was reelected five times before her seat was eventually abolished by the Bantu Self-Government Act, which ended representation of Africans in the House and Senate.

Within the Congress, Ballinger was a founding member of the Liberal Party in 1953, and its first national chair. Affirming the "dignity of every human being, his right to develop, and his right to participate in political activities," she attacked racial discrimination and crusaded against apartheid. In addition to her political activities, she founded a home for crippled African children. The home was eventually closed by the Group Areas Act of 1950, which designated established segregated areas in which all Africans and other nonwhites were obliged to live. She was also instrumental in establishing scholarships for African students. At the end of her political career, Ballinger lectured briefly at the Australian Institute of International affairs, then began work on a major historical analysis, *From Union to Apartheid: a Trek to Isolation*, published in 1968.

Barbara Morgan,
Melrose, Massachusetts

Balliol, Ada (fl. 1256)

Scottish royal. *Name variations: Baliol; Ada de Baliol. Born before 1256; daughter of John Balliol (d. 1269) and* ****Devorgilla*** *(d. 1290); sister of John Balliol (1249–1315), king of Scots (r. 1292–1296); married William Lindsay of Lambarton; children:* ***Christina de Lindsay****.*

Balliol, Cecily (d. before 1273)

Scottish royal. *Name variations: Cecilia Balliol or Baliol; Cecily de Burgh. Died before 1273; daughter of John Balliol (d. 1269) and ****Devorgilla*** *(d. 1290); sister of ****Ada Balliol*** *(fl. 1256), ****Margaret Balliol*** *(c. 1255–?), and John Balliol (1249–1315), king of Scots (r. 1292–1296); married John de Burgh; children:* ***Devorgilla de Burgh*** *(1255–1284, who married Robert, 1st baron FitzWalter);* ***Hawise de Burgh*** *(who married Robert de Grelley);* ***Marjorie de Burgh*** *(a nun at Chicksands Priory).*

Balliol, Devorgilla (d. 1290).
See Devorgilla.

Balliol, Eleanor (fl. 1230)

Scottish royal. *Name variations: Eleanor Percy. Flourished around 1230; daughter of Ingelram Balliol; married William Percy (d. 1245); children: Henry Percy (d. 1272, who married ****Eleanor de Warrenne****).*

Balliol, Eleanor (c. 1255–?).
See Balliol, Margaret.

Balliol, Isabel (fl. 1281).
See Isabel de Warrenne.

Balliol, Margaret (c. 1255–?)

Scottish royal. *Name variations: Alianora or Eleanor; Mary. Born around 1255; death date unknown; daughter of ****Devorgilla*** *(d. 1290) and John Balliol; sister of John Balliol (c. 1250–1313), king of the Scots (r. 1292–1296); married John Comnyn; children: John "Red" Comyn.*

Balliol, Margaret (fl. 1300s)

Scottish royal. *Name variations: Margherita of Taranto or Tarento. Flourished in the 1300s; daughter of Philipp or Philip of Tarento (d. 1332), prince of Tarent, and ****Catherine of Tarento****; married Edward Balliol (c. 1314–1363), king of the Scots (r. 1332–1338); married Francisco II del Balzo, duke of Andria.*

On September 24, 1332, at Scone, Edward Balliol, husband of Margaret Balliol, was crowned king of the Scots by the English, but he fled three months later. Restored to the throne in 1333, he fled again the following year, then was restored once more in 1335. This time, Edward lasted three years before he bolted in 1338. He finally renounced all claims to the throne of Scotland in 1356.

Ballon, Ellen (1898–1969)

Canadian pianist who made many pioneering records of Villa-Lobos' work and introduced it to the concert stage. *Born in Montreal in 1898 of Russian immigrant parents; died in Montreal on December 21, 1969. Gave world premiere of Heitor Villa-Lobos' First Piano Concerto under his baton in Rio de Janeiro in 1946.*

A child prodigy, Ellen Ballon was six when she won the director's prize at the McGill Conservatory. At an early age, she earned praises from such pianistic greats as Josef Hofmann, Artur Rubinstein and ***Adele aus der Ohe.** In 1910, Ballon made her New York concerto debut. In 1912, President William Howard Taft invited her to perform at the White House; she performed there again in 1934 for President Franklin D. Roosevelt and in 1954 for President Dwight D. Eisenhower. A major European tour in 1927 won Ballon great critical acclaim. Living and performing in Great Britain and the European Continent in the 1930s, she returned to Canada at the end of that decade and settled in Montreal. Ballon was a warm friend of the Brazilian composer Heitor Villa-Lobos, from whom she commissioned his First Piano Concerto, and she gave the work its world premiere under the composer's baton in Rio de Janeiro in 1946. She also made a number of pioneering recordings of Villa-Lobos' piano compositions. Enthusiastic about the possibilities of disseminating classical music on a mass basis, Ballon made some of the earliest long-playing recordings (released on the Decca/ London label), and appeared on the CBC French-language television series "Heure du concert." In the 1950s, she initiated and sponsored a series of lectures by noted musical personalities including Gian-Carlo Menotti, Deems Taylor, and ***Lotte Lehmann.**

John Haag, Athens, Georgia

Ballou, Esther Williamson (1915–1973)

American composer, teacher, and pianist. *Born in 1915; died in 1973; studied with Luening, Wagenaar, and Riegger; taught at American University.*

Esther Ballou, the first woman composer to have a work premiered at the White House, seemed destined for a brilliant career, when, in 1943, she was crippled by arthritis, a condition she would endure for the next ten years of her life. Finally recovered, she joined the faculty of American University, where she composed and orchestrated *Beguine for two pianos* (1958), performed by the National Symphony Orchestra. She composed as well *A Babe is Born* (1959), and, for orchestra and band: *In memoriam* (1952), *Prelude and allegro for string orchestra and piano* (1952), *Oboe concertino* (1953), *Adagio for bassoon and string orchestra* (1962), *Early American Portrait* (1962), *Concerto for piano and orchestra* (1965), *Concerto for solo guitar and chamber orchestra* (1966), *Konzertstück* (1970), and *Intermezzo for orchestra*.

Baltechildis (c. 630–c. 680).
See Balthild.

Balthild (c. 630–c. 680)

Queen of the Franks who helped enact laws to improve the conditions of slaves' lives and to prevent Christians from being sold into slavery. *Name variations: Balthildis, Bathildis, Bathilde, Baltechildis, Baldechild, Baldhilda, Baldhild. Born around 630* CE *in England; died around 680 at the convent of Chelles, France; married Clovis II (634–657), king of Neustria and Burgundy (r. 639–657), king of the Franks (r. 639–657), in 649; children: Childeric II (650–675), king of Austrasia (r. 656–675), king of the Franks (r. 673–675); Chlothaire or Lothair III (654–673), king of Neustria and Burgundy (r. 657–673); Thierry or Theoderic III (d. 691), king of Neustria and Burgundy (r. 673/75–691), king of the Franks (r. 687–691).*

Balthild was an influential queen of the Franks. Little is known about her birth or childhood, except that she was born in England to Christian Anglo-Saxon parents. As a young woman, she was kidnapped and sold as a slave in Gaul, around the year 641, and was purchased by the mayor (ruler) of Neustria, located in modern-day northeastern France. Apparently the mayor wished to marry Balthild, who managed to deter his interest by dressing in rags and hiding herself from him until he forgot about her. Several years later, on a visit to the palace of Neustria, the Frankish king Clovis II became infatuated with Balthild and, despite her slave status, married her in 648.

Unlike many early medieval queens, Balthild was not a passive queen-consort. Clovis left to her the considerable duties of managing the royal court and also controlling all charitable funds. She gave birth to three sons, all of whom were to become rulers: Lothair III, Childeric, and Theoderic. Balthild's early life as a slave gave her an empathy for the powerless which was unusual in a queen, and she worked for the improvement of the lives of the less fortunate. Among other legislation, the queen helped enact laws to ameliorate the conditions of slaves' lives, and to prevent Christians from being sold into slavery. She also helped the poor by decreasing the heavy tax burden under which they suffered.

When Clovis died in 657, Balthild became regent for the minority of her son Lothair. During these years, she attempted to realize the ambitious goal of unifying the kingdom of the Franks. Due to opposition from powerful landowners, however, this goal remained unaccomplished at the end of her regency (indeed, the kingdom would not be united for several centuries to come).

When Lothair came of age around 665, Balthild, her active political life behind her, retired to the convent at Chelles which she had founded with her own wealth. The monastery of Saint Peter at Corbie, destined to become an important center of learning, also owed its existence to Balthild's deep piety and her willingness to use her money to expand the Church's influence. At Chelles, the Frankish queen was said to have refused acceptance of any honors or privileges as its founder; instead, she worked at menial jobs with the other nuns. She died there about age 50.

Laura York, Anza, California

Balthildis (c. 630–c. 680).
See Balthild.

Baltimore, Lady (d. 1630).
See Arundel, Anne.

Balzac, Madame (1801–1882).
See Hanska, Éveline, Countess.

Bampton, Rose (1909—)

American soprano and mezzo-soprano, well known on radio and in recordings. *Born in Lakewood, Ohio, on November 28, 1909; daughter of an English father and a German pianist mother; married Wilfrid Pelletier (a conductor), in 1937; trained at the Curtis Institute of Music, Philadelphia, Pennsylvania, where she studied with Horatio Connell and Queena Mario; also studied with Martha Graham,* ***Elena Gerhardt****, and* ****Lotte Lehmann****.*

Made debut as Siebel in Faust *at Chautauqua (1929); made Metropolitan opera debut as Laura in* La Gioconda *(1932); sang with the New York City*

Opera; retired in 1950, then taught at the Manhattan School, North Carolina School of the Arts, Drake University, and the Juilliard School.

Born in Lakewood, Ohio, near Cleveland, on November 28, 1909, Rose Bampton was the daughter of an English father and German mother. Since both parents were music lovers (her mother was an accomplished pianist), it is not surprising that Bampton began to study music after the family moved to Buffalo, New York. Her first teacher, Seth Clark, suggested she attend the Curtis Institute in Philadelphia where she studied with Horatio Connell and **Queena Mario**. Judged too tall for opera roles at Curtis, she did not receive much training in this area.

Her first success was at the Chautauqua Opera House in 1929 where she sang Siebel in *Faust*. This, in turn, brought her to the Philadelphia Opera Company, where she remained for three years, singing some concerts with the Philadelphia Orchestra under the direction of Leopold Stokowski. At first, Bampton appeared to be a coloratura soprano, but she also sang contralto in some concerts. Finally, at an audition at the Metropolitan Opera, Bampton's voice was diagnosed as a soprano. On her 23rd birthday, November 28, 1932, she made her debut at the Met as Laura in *La Gioconda*; 68 other appearances would follow. While there, she met conductor Wilfrid Pelletier whom she married in 1937, and his coaching proved invaluable in her career. During this period, she also worked with dancer ***Martha Graham** who influenced her stage performance. Bampton successfully toured Europe in 1937–38 and South Africa in 1939.

Rose Bampton

Bampton's large voice easily filled spacious halls like the Metropolitan and Covent Garden where she performed such roles as Aïda, Leonora in *Il Trovatore*, and Donna Anna in *Don Giovanni*. She was chosen by Arturo Toscanini for his broadcasts of *Fidelio* on NBC in 1944, later released on recordings. From these records, it is possible to judge Bampton's musicianship but not the size of her voice. She adhered to the composer's original concept of the music while displaying ample feeling and temperament. From 1945 to 1949, she was the leading soprano at the Teatro Colón in Buenos Aires, Argentina, and at the Opera in Rio de Janeiro, Brazil, in 1948. An intelligent musician who adapted easily to different musical styles, Bampton was increasingly well known after World War II, and she performed extensively on the radio, in the theater, and in recital. As a teacher, she passed on her broad-based knowledge to a future generation of musicians.

John Haag, Athens, Georgia

Banda (1898–1919).

See Zelle, Margaretha Gertrud (Mata Hari) for sidebar on MacLeod, Juana-Luisa.

Bandaranaike, Sirimavo (1916—)

Sri Lankan politician and the first woman prime minister in the world, who led her country through a stressful period of national growth and raised Sri Lanka to a respectable position in the community of Asian nations. *Name variations: Sirimavo Ratwatte Dias Bandaranaike. Born Sirimavo Ratwatte (or Ratevatte) in Ratnapura, Balangoda, in southern Ceylon (now Sri Lanka), on April 17, 1916; daughter of Barnes Ratwatte and Rosemund (Mahawalatenne) Ratwatte; educated at Ferguson High School, Ratnapura, and St. Bridget's Convent, Colombo; married Solomon West Ridgeway Dias Bandaranaike, in October 1940; children: one son, Anura (b. 1949); two* *daughters, Sunethra Rupasinghe, and* ***Chandrika Kumaratunga*** *(elected president of Sri Lanka in 1994).*

When her husband became prime minister, Bandaranaike was active in Ceylon's main political women's organization, the Lanka Mahila Samiti; after his assassination (1959), she succeeded him as leader of the Sri Lanka Freedom Party (SLFP), then as prime minister (1960–65 and 1970–77).

Born into a family of wealthy and aristocratic landowners in the Ceylonese countryside, Sirimavo Ratwatte grew up a serious, retiring girl who considered herself the heir to a great civilization built on the rational and humane qualities of Buddhism. In the world of international Asian politics, she was to become a popular advocate for national interests and a capable, determined leader of her people.

Ceylon, later called Sri Lanka, is a green tropical island that was a British Crown Colony from 1802 to 1948. British rule ended when Ceylon achieved the dominion status, and the government passed into the hands of the Ceylonese gentry who were Western-educated and oriented. Sirimavo's birthplace was Ratnapura, the capital city of the rural province of Sabaragamuwa. She was one of six children in a family whose members had held high offices under the ancient line of Sinhalese kings. Her maternal grandfather was a Kandyan chieftain, her father a member of the Ceylonese senate, and some of her relatives held high positions in local government service. Sirimavo was close to her father, Barnes Ratwatte, a benevolent administrator who often sided with the interests of the common man. In her youth, she took a keen interest in the conversations of her relatives which related to politics and business.

Sirimavo attended the Ratnapura Convent for her early education. Like many couples of means in developing countries, Sirimavo's parents wanted their daughter to receive a sound secondary education at a Western-style boarding school. At age eight, she was sent off for her formal schooling to the prestigious Ferguson High School in Colombo. Later, one of her teachers would recall the young boarding student as meticulous, orderly, careful, and with a tendency at times to brood.

At home, Sirimavo learned domestic work with her sister as they assisted their mother and the servants in the kitchen. As the eldest child, she took her family responsibilities seriously, helping to care for the younger children and also joining in when they were called upon to help serve guests. By age 18, she was a robust and radiant girl according to the Kandyan standards of feminine beauty and charm. Yet despite the tendencies of youth, Sirimavo was never preoccupied with fashion: "I wore the Kandyan saree in its traditional form with a few pieces of jewellery my mother had made for me: a necklace, a few bracelets and earring. . . . I have always been conventional-minded in dress and fashion for fashion's sake has never meant anything to me."

Sirimavo Bandaranaike

More interesting to Sirimavo at the time was a dynamic new venture in social service which was being introduced to the young people of the area by the district medical officer of Balangoda. She joined the Social Service League, participated in fund-raising projects, and was appointed the group's treasurer, a post she held until early 1940, the year she married.

Her husband Solomon West Ridgeway Dias (S.W.R.D.) Bandaranaike (informally known as Banda) was a highly educated aristocrat, who had already formed a politico-cultural group with clearly defined views that would become his own political party. He was a facile writer who had a reputation as an orator with a golden tongue, and he had already established himself as a chief advocate of the common man. His wife shared his values, and the couple moved to the capital at Colombo, where Sirimavo's husband bought a villa in 1946. They had two daughters and a son.

In 1941, Sirimavo joined the Lanka Mahila Samiti, the primary women's movement organization in Ceylon, which strove to improve the conditions of rural women in the island country. One of the organization's goals was to launch a massive food production effort to meet the shortages that became acute during World War II. As secretary of the western province group of Samiti, Bandaranaike worked with experts and *goiyas* (farmers) to introduce new methods of growing crops that increased paddy yields by more than 150 fold. She did not agree with the commonly held assessment that the peasants made no efforts on their own. Practical and elemental in her ideas and approach, she once remarked, "I came to know at first-hand the agony as well as the ecstasy of the farmer." Family planning and political rights for women were also among the causes she supported.

As a dedicated Buddhist, she visited the sacred city of Anuradhapura several times. Bandaranaike climbed to the peak of Sri Pada, the mountain that had tantalized her as a child when she gazed upon it daily on her way to and from the kindergarten school she attended in Ratnapura. She visited the ancient temple of Mahiyangana, the traditional site of Buddha's first visit to Ceylon, made shortly after his Enlightenment.

I walk the Middle Way in my political career as much as I try my utmost to emulate the tenets of [Buddha's] Middle Path in my personal life.

—Sirimavo Bandaranaike

In 1950, S.W.R.D. Bandaranaike founded the nationalist Sri Lankan Freedom Party (SLFP). In 1956, his party took power over the United Nationalist Party (UNP), which had ruled Ceylon since the country gained independence in 1948. He became prime minister, a post he held until September 1959, when he was assassinated by a Buddhist monk who opposed his support of Western medicine over traditional herbal remedies. Sirimavo entered the world of active politics after her husband's death to rally support for the Sri Lanka Freedom Party. Although opponents called her a political novice, Bandaranaike held that as the wife of a great leader she'd had 20 years of political education before her husband's death.

In the 1960 election campaign, she played tape-recordings of her husband's speeches and made speeches of her own across the country. Her visible emotion was turned against her by opponents who dubbed her "the weeping widow." In May, she was unanimously appointed president of her party. In the July election of that year—receiving the support of many of the small parties on both the right and the left—she won the election with an absolute majority in Parliament. As the seventh prime minister of Ceylon, she became the first woman prime minister in the world. Bandaranaike also held the position of external affairs minister from 1960–65 and remained a member of the Senate until 1965.

From a contemporary perspective, her talents seem the very ones her country needed during the critical years of the 1950s and 1960s, a period of deep unrest that involved a rising tide of nationalism and the collision of traditional Buddhist interests with the Christian values and education that had gained dominance under colonial rule. Her husband's failure to fulfill his political promise to bring the Buddhists back into power had been one of the factors contributing to his assassination. Now in office, his wife wanted to reinstate Buddhism at the center of the national culture while weakening the Western influences that had led to a Westernized, and alienated, elite.

As the new leader of the Sri Lanka Freedom Party, Bandaranaike pressed hard to satisfy some of the Buddhists' demands. She reminded the people that the "Buddha Dharma" (Buddhism) was "one of our chief contributions towards world civilization," and in 1960 her government took over the country's Christian-run schools. These schools had been at the forefront of the development of education on the island and were considered to be the best in Ceylon; the move effectively weakened the role of the Christian churches, and particularly the Roman Catholics, at a time when the Christian minority comprised an economic and political elite in the country. As Bandaranaike explained, "We were committed to a constructive, socialistic policy—of equal opportunities for all." The popularity of this action was evident after the UNP came to power in 1965 and extended Buddhist influence one step further by replacing the Christian Sunday as a public holiday with the Buddhist "poya" day.

Bandaranaike regarded the policy of required English for government officials and proceedings as unnatural, and so introduced a new language policy. She asked, "Was not the whole idea of independence incomplete so long as an exclusive knowledge of the English language was more or less the only passport to the Public Service?" From 1960, her government passed laws enacting the progressive substitution of Sinhalese for English in court proceedings. This act remained inoperative because regulations necessary to make its provisions effective were not promulgated. Nevertheless, she stressed the desire to incorporate the broad masses of the people into the effective life of the polity. She remarked:

> We have tried to eliminate the wide gap which existed between the Government and the governed, between the elite and the masses. . . . By giving the due and rightful place to the Sinhala language as the Official Language of the country we have made it possible for those voiceless nations who spoke only that language, to play an effective part in the affairs of the country. As long as English reigned, their freedom was limited.

Her moves to restore Sinhalese over English were strongly opposed by the country's Tamil-speaking minority.

From 1961, Bandaranaike's government faced a series of strikes organized by leftist trade unions. Urban workers, beset by inflation and high taxes, created a wave of labor disputes; when a strike immobilized the transport system, the prime minister disclosed that the strike was politically motivated and nationalized the Ceylon Transport Board, but she was eventually forced to concede to the strikers' demands. In foreign affairs, her government established a delicate balance between Eastern and Western interests. In general, her government was more sympathetic to the Communist world than any previous Ceylonese government. The friendly ties with China which had existed since 1953 were strengthened, and in order to accommodate various communist groups she broke relations with Israel, but she did not let her pro-Chinese orientation allow her to damage relations with India and the Soviet Union. She also maintained Ceylon's tea exports to Britain and its reliance on the World Bank. At the conferences of non-aligned nations held in Belgrade in 1961 and in Cairo in 1964, she forcefully demanded the immediate suspension of atomic and hydrogen bomb testing. It was the policy of Bandaranaike's government to seek friendship with the African peoples and to condemn South Africa's policy of apartheid; she also appointed the first woman ambassador to Ghana. The primary purpose of her non-alignment policy was to obtain acceptance in the community of nations of her own proposal to make the Indian Ocean a peace zone. In 1962, her country's well established position of positive neutralism enabled her to initiate peace moves over the Sino-Indian border dispute.

Though in 1965 Bandaranaike lost the next elections to the UNP, she remained leader of the opposition and was reelected prime minister in 1970. Her victorious return to office on May 27, 1970, was seen as a justification of the decision made six years before to forge a permanent alliance between the nation's leftists and Sri Lankan Freedom Party; her reelection opened the way to a new round of reforms intended to change the fundamental structure of Ceylonese government. In that year, the SLFP came together with the Communist Party and the Trotskyite Samaj Party to form a "United Front" coalition government. In 1972, Bandaranaike led this government in promulgating a new constitution to remove various alien British elements from the country's institutions. The English name of Ceylon was changed in favor of the Sinhala name of Sri Lanka, and the upper house of the National Assembly, the Senate, was abolished, along with a number of other institutions borrowed from the British political system. Followers of Buddhism and Sinhala were also given special constitutional status in the new government, although the state was to remain secular under the constitution, which stated that it was the duty of the state "to protect and foster Buddhism" while assuring all religions the rights of protection. From 1970, the transition from the post-colonial society of Ceylon, still deeply influenced by the British ways, to the fully independent, authentically Sinhalese society of Sri Lanka based on 2,000-year-old traditions, seemed almost complete.

In 1975, the country's nationalistic movement took an economic turn when the government seized tea, coconut and rubber estates, owned mostly by foreign individuals or British corporations, as Bandaranaike strove for an equitable distribution of land. Legislation was proposed to put a ceiling on the individual and family holdings of agricultural land in order to guarantee its equitable distribution among land-poor peasants who had no other means of livelihood. One of Bandaranaike's main aims was to remove the great weight of rural indebtedness that afflicted a large portion of the peasant population.

After her return to power in 1970, one of Bandaranaike's most constructive achievements was the settlement, on a permanent and amicable basis, of the vexing question of persons of Indian origin in Sri Lanka. She signed an agreement with *Indira Gandhi, prime minister of India, in which some people were asked to repatriate to India while others were allowed to stay in Sri Lanka, resolving all future questions regarding their status.

Critics argued that Bandaranaike allowed too much power to pass into the hands of members of her family during her years as prime minister. In 1970, at least eight of her relatives were elected to Parliament, all as members of the SLFP. After the coalition victory, the prime minister's daughter **Sunethra Rupasinghe** became increasingly important as her mother's political secretary, and Bandaranaike's son Anura became leader of the SLFP Youth League. (Daughter **Chandrika Kumaratunga** would be elected president of Sri Lanka in 1994.) Other relatives who attained powerful positions included the governor-general William Gopallawa, who was commander of the army from 1962 to 1966.

One flaw in her exercise of power was her failure to enlist the support of the country's Tamil minority, who comprised about 11% of the Ceylonese population and who were steadily being forced into positions of second-class citizenship. As early as 1961, the Federalist Party, dominated by the Tamils, demonstrated their resolve to retain their ethnic identity through civil disobedience, by establishing their own postal service and issuing stamps in violation of the postal laws. The government proscribed the Federalists, thereby heightening tensions between the ethnic and religious groups of Sri Lanka. Under Bandaranaike, the government remained indifferent to the legitimate Tamil claims, while the rebel movement gained strength among Tamil youths. In the early 1970s, they began to rebel, at first by launching occasional amateurish attacks against government installations or personnel. By the 1980s, these rebels, now called "tigers," were organized into trained and well-equipped armies of liberation with the northern Jaffna peninsula as their geographical stronghold.

At the polls, in 1977, Bandaranaike and her party suffered a humiliating defeat. In 1980, a Presidential Commission under President J.R. Jayewardene of the United National Party found the Bandaranaike guilty of abuse of power in office. She was denounced and stripped of her civic rights for seven years.

Opposite page

Nina Bang

Bandaranaike had begun her administration with clear goals to open up the society of her own country and to destroy the privileged position of the Western-educated elite. It is likely that even her political enemies would agree that she was a person of stout heart, firm will, and rare energy. In her political world, she was dedicated to democratic, socialist, and non-aligned policies. As the first female prime minister, she helped to raise the status of the women throughout the world, and in Asia she helped to make the island nation of Sri Lanka a respected power.

SOURCES:

Seneviratne, Maureen. *Sirimavo Bandaranaike: The World's First Woman Prime Minister.* Colombo: Hansa Publishers, 1975.

SUGGESTED READING:

Ceylon Today. Colombo: The Ceylon Government Information Department. Vols. 1971–1972.

Nyrop, Richard F., et al. *Area Handbook for Ceylon.* 1971.

Santosh C. Saha, formerly Assistant Professor of History, Cuttington University, Liberia

Bandler, Faith (1918—)

Australian author and Aboriginal activist. *Born Ida Lessing Faith Mussing on September 27, 1918, in Tumbulgum, Murwillumbah, New South Wales; daughter of Ida and Wacvie Mussingkon (a Pacific Islander whose name was anglicized to Peter Mussing); educated at Murwillumbah public schools and Cleveland Street Night School; married Hans Bandler, in 1952; children: one daughter.*

Selected works: Wacvie *(1977); (with Len Fox)* Marani in Australia *(1980);* Welon, My Brother *(1984); (with Fox)* The Time Was Right *(1984);* Turning the Tide *(1988).*

Beginning with her father's emigration from the Hebrides Islands in a slave trade, the life of author and Aboriginal activist Faith Bandler highlights a number of parallels between the African-American and Australian Aboriginal civil-rights movements. Brought to New South Wales in 1882 to work the cane fields, Wacvie Mussingkon's tribal name was changed to the more Anglican Peter Mussing. When his daughter was born, she too was given an acceptably English name.

Faith Mussing attended public school in Tumbulgum, Murwillumbah, until she left day school, at age 15, to become a dressmaker's assistant. Her work as a cook helped supplement the family income further, and she also attended night school to complete her studies. During the Second World War, she served three years in the Women's Land Army, after which she joined a regional dance troupe. The Youth Festival of World Culture drew her to Berlin with the troupe in 1951. During her stay, she was invited to visit Bulgaria; when she returned to Australia, she was accused of having communist sympathies or involvement and her passport was seized. Heretofore uninvolved in politics, Faith's ire was sparked when she was not allowed to defend herself; unwittingly, the government had incited an activist for Aboriginal rights.

Heated debates over civil rights were already taking place, and during these days the civil-rights movement was born. Newly married to Hans Bandler, Faith helped found the Aboriginal-Australian Fellowship (AAF) with ***Pearl Gibbs**. The Federal Council for Advancement of Aborigines was also developed, and Bandler worked heavily in both groups. Concerned with general advancement, social and political rights, the groups forced a national referendum in 1967, in which Aborigines won equal treatment under the law. Its work done, the AAF was disbanded in 1969. For her activism, Bandler was offered the Medal of the Order of the British Empire in 1976. Denying English claim to her country, she refused the award. The Australian equivalent, the Medal of Order of Australia, was proffered in 1984, and she accepted.

Wacvie, the life story of Bandler's father, was her first literary endeavor. Published in 1977, it was followed with another family biography in 1984, *Welon, My Brother*. Partnering with Len Fox, Bandler also wrote several histories of Aboriginal culture and history. She is considered a primary force in the successful assertion of Aboriginal rights.

Crista Martin, freelance writer,
Boston, Massachusetts

Bang, Nina (1866–1928)

Danish historian who, as minister of education, was the first woman in the world to hold a cabinet post. *Born Nina Henriette Wendeline Ellinger in Copenhagen, Denmark, in 1866; died in 1928; daughter of Heinrich August David Ellinger and Charlotte Ida Friedericke Preuss; attended school in Elsinore and received private instruction for matriculation in history at University of Copenhagen, granted Ph.D., 1895; married Gustav Bang (a historian), in 1895.*

Nina Ellinger was born in Copenhagen but, at age four, moved with her family to Elsinore. This translocation to the shore of the Sound separating Denmark from Sweden may have inspired her later interest in exploration of the Sound Tariffs and their significance for trade and social conditions. Bang attended school in

Elsinore and received private instruction for matriculation as a student of history at the University of Copenhagen, where she received her Ph.D. in 1895. Focusing her studies on the history of trade in the 1500s, she became especially knowledgeable about accounts of the Sound Tariffs collected from ships trading in the Baltic.

Danish waterways gave the only access in and out of the Baltic Sea. Where the Sound is narrowest, the Danes had erected a number of castles as elaborate tollbooths on one of Europe's busiest channels. For 428 years, ships had to pay Sound dues (a toll) and dip their flag as they passed the Elsinore castle. Much to the chagrin of neighboring countries, whenever Denmark needed revenue, it raised the tolls. This practice eventually resulted in the Danish phase of the Thirty Years' War which cost Denmark enormously. By the Peace of Bromsbero (August 25, 1645), Sweden was given important territory on its side of the Sound, effectively ending Denmark's exclusive control of the straits and its status as a major European power. As a Marxist historian, Bang used the tariff accounts as a means to illuminate both material and spiritual social conditions. Her findings, which she published in a two-volume work, offered new and valuable insights into the history of English, Dutch, and Scandinavian trade.

Both she and her husband Gustav Bang, also a historian, became the first academicians to join the Social Democratic Party in 1895. Gustav, considered the first Danish politician to have had a thorough knowledge of Marxism, analyzed Danish society and its developmental trends from a Marxist point of view and wrote weekly articles in *Social-Demokraten* (the Social-Democratic newspaper), treating current as well as theoretical concerns. From 1898, Nina Bang, too, worked for *Social-Demokraten* as a writer of articles on foreign politics and political and economical issues. She turned a critical eye on corporate accounts and shares and frequently divulged practices of speculation favoring capitalists. From 1903 until her death in 1928, she would be a member of her party's executive board.

As a council member for the city of Copenhagen from 1913 to 1918, Nina Bang dealt with a wide variety of social and economic cases and issues. She established and maintained contact with leading socialists both in Denmark and abroad, and she attended numerous international conferences. At the peace conference in Stockholm held during World War I, she stood in for the Danish prime minister. Bang became a member of Parliament in 1918 and was reelected in 1920 and 1924. At the formation of Denmark's first social-democratic government in April of 1924, she was appointed minister of education, the first woman cabinet member in the world.

Bang brought to the post extensive insights into matters of state and finance, a strong personal engagement, a great capacity for work, and a keen eye for details. Her chief concern was promotion of stronger local rule with greater responsibility for schools and improved education for teachers.

Although Bang was one of the first established female political activists, she was not an active feminist; she considered women's social and legal issues part of general political issues and part of the general battle for democratic progress. As a woman and a strong, authoritative politician, Nina Bang became a favorite object of right-wing criticism and an easy target for cartoonists. She was, however, greatly esteemed by her party.

SOURCES:

Gyldendal og Politikens Danmarkshistorie. Vol. 12. Ed. Olaf Olsen. Copenhagen: Nordisk Forlag A/S, 1990.

Petersen, Kai A. *Danmarkshistoriens Hvornaar Skete Det.* Copenhagen: Politikens Forlag, 1985.

Inga Wiehl, Yakima Valley Community College, Yakima, Washington

Ban Hui-ji (c. 45–c. 120 CE).

See Ban Zhao.

Ban Jieyu (c. 48–c. 6 BCE).

See Ban Zhao for sidebar.

Bankes, Lady Mary (d. 1661).

See Siege Warfare and Women for sidebar.

Bankhead, Tallulah (1902–1968)

American actress who eschewed formal training, built a career on the stage, and dipped into films, but eventually eclipsed her own career with the force of her public personality. *Name variations: (childhood nickname) Dutch; (adult nicknames) Tallu, Lulas,* Die Donner *(the thunder). Pronunciation: Tuh-LOO-luh BANK-hed. Born Tallulah Brockman Bankhead on January 31, 1902, in Huntsville, Alabama; died of pneumonia in St. Luke's Hospital, New York City, New York, on December 12, 1968; buried in Rock Hall, Maryland; daughter of William "Will" Brockman (a lawyer, U.S. congressional delegate, and speaker of the house) and Adelaide "Ada" Eugenia (Sledge) Bankhead; attended Convent of the Sacred Heart, Manhattanville, New York; Mary Baldwin Seminary, Staunton, Virginia; Convent of the Visitation, Washington, D.C.; Holy Cross Academy, Dunbar, Virginia;*

Tallulah Bankhead

and Fairmont Seminary, Washington, D.C.; married John Emery (an actor), on August 31, 1937 (divorced, June 13, 1941); no children.

Won Picture Play Magazine*'s "Screen Opportunity" contest and went to New York (1917); had walk-on in silent film* When Men Betray *(1918); moved into Algonquin Hotel (1918); had walk-on in* The Squab Farm *(1918); appeared in* The Dancers *in England (1923); returned to U.S. for Paramount Pictures contract (1931); appeared in* The Little Foxes *(1939); purchased "Windows" (1943); named radio's "Woman of the Year" (1951); hosted ABC's "All-Star*

Revue" on television (1952); appeared for last time on Broadway in The Milk Train Doesn't Stop Here Anymore *(1964); filmed* Die! Die! Darling! *in England (1964); appeared on* Batman *(1967).*

Stage roles: Gladys Sinclair in The Squab Farm *(1918); Penelope Penn in* 39 East *(1919); Phyllis Nolan in* Everyday *(1921); Maxine/ Tawara in* The Dancers *(1923); Mary Clay in* Forsaking All Others *(1933); Sadie Thompson in* Rain *(1935); Cleopatra in* Antony and Cleopatra *(1937); Regina Giddens in* The Little Foxes *(1939); Lily Sabina in* The Skin of our Teeth *(1942); Amanda Prynne in* Private Lives *(1944, 1948); Blanche DuBois in* A Streetcar Named Desire *(1956); title role in* Midgie Purvis *(1961); Mrs. Goforth in* The Milk Train Doesn't Stop Here Anymore *(1964).*

Film roles: Nell in Who Loved Him Best? *(Mutual Film Corporation, 1918); Alice Edwardes in* When Men Betray *(Graphic Film Corporation, 1918); Nancy Courtney in* Tarnished Lady *(Paramount, 1931); Pauline Sturm in* The Devil and the Deep *(Paramount, 1932); Carol Morgan in* Faithless *(Metro-Goldwyn-Mayer, 1932); Constance Porter in* Lifeboat *(20th Century-Fox, 1944); The Czarina in* A Royal Scandal *(20th Century-Fox, 1945); Mrs. Trefoile in* Die! Die! My Darling! *(Hammer Films/ Columbia, 1965).*

Radio series: Mistress of Ceremonies, "The Big Show" (NBC, 1950–1952). Television: Mistress of Ceremonies, "All Star Revue" (NBC, 1952–1953); "The Milton Berle Show" (NBC), "The Jack Paar Show" (NBC), "The Tonight Show" (NBC), "Batman" (ABC), "The Merv Griffin Show" (all 1953–68).

Buckets of cold water would eventually stop a tantrum but not always. The spectacle of the young girl thrashing on the floor in rage often resulted in a soaking at the hands of her paternal grandmother, called "Mamma," who wearied of her namesake's unladylike behavior. Mamma did her best to instill the values of proper Southern womanhood in her granddaughters, and the family hoped that age would bring the girl self-control; instead, Tallulah Bankhead turned this type of dramatic exhibition into her personal trademark.

Tallulah Brockman Bankhead was born on January 31, 1902, second daughter of William and **Ada Bankhead**. Just two weeks later, Ada Bankhead died. Consequently, Tallulah and her sister **Eugenia**, who was one year and one week older, lost their father, as he distanced himself in order to come to terms with his grief. Henceforth, the sisters shared celebrations on Eugenia's birthday.

The Bankhead sisters lived with their paternal grandparents in Jasper, Alabama, but also spent portions of their childhood with their aunt **Marie Bankhead Owen** in Montgomery, Alabama, and in Washington, D.C., because of the political demands on both their grandfather, U.S. Senator "Captain John" Hollis Bankhead, and later their father who was elected to the U.S. Congress in 1917. When not living with them, William Bankhead visited the girls often; he also spoiled them. After five years, when John Bankhead insisted that his son take more responsibility for the girls, Will returned to live with them in his parents' home and became the most important person in Tallulah's life. Perhaps to cheer him, Tallulah became a mimic and something of a performer. When Will cuddled Eugenia and talked of his departed wife, Tallulah turned cartwheels to regain the spotlight.

At age 10, along with her sister, Tallulah entered boarding school. Enrolling in the same grade throughout their lives due to Eugenia's frailty, they originally attended the Catholic Convent of the Sacred Heart in Manhattanville, New York, where Tallulah's temper soon had them in trouble. The next year, the girls attended the Mary Baldwin Seminary in Staunton, Virginia. Tallulah's outrageous behavior caused their dismissal before Thanksgiving, and the Bankhead sisters moved to their third boarding school, the Convent of the Visitation, at about the same time that their father remarried. Tallulah's disruptive behavior continued. The family attempted to reign her in by sending Eugenia off to a different school, but Tallulah grew listless until her sister rejoined her at the Holy Cross Academy at Dunbar. The following year, the sisters attended Fairmont Seminary in Washington D.C. to prepare for their Congressional society debuts; neither girl graduated.

At age 15, Bankhead began entering movie-magazine contests. When the *Picture-Play Magazine* Opportunity Contest announced its 12 finalists, the list included Tallulah, winner of a trip to New York to begin a theatrical career. Reluctantly, her grandfather agreed to finance her trip as long as her aunt, **Louise Bankhead Lund**, acted as chaperon.

Despite her connections, Tallulah faced the usual problems of a beginning actor; she lacked formal training, had no experience, and spent her days visiting talent agents. She also had to overcome her aunt's lack of enthusiasm. The two shared an apartment before moving into the famed Algonquin Hotel in February 1918. The Algonquin housed the Round Table or Vicious

Circle, a large number of actors, producers, and writers, including Robert Benchley and *Dorothy Parker. Aunt Louise had naively selected the heart of the theatrical district for her niece's new home.

Finally, Bankhead wrangled a bit part on Broadway as Gladys Sinclair in *The Squab Farm* in March 1918. Soon after, she appeared in a silent film, *When Men Betray*. Although her career seemed to quickly stall, her restless energy and beauty earned her attention from other Algonquin residents. Aunt Louise stood as the only impediment to her social life; finally in the summer of 1919, when she became unable to stand Tallulah's moods, Aunt Louise left her charge and joined the Red Cross in Paris. Aunt Marie took her place, but eventually Tallulah was on her own.

Though Bankhead made another silent film, she disliked the medium and longed to appear on stage. To avoid being called home, she stretched her pennies until she owned only one dress and ate by "tasting" people's dishes while flitting in and out of conversations in the Algonquin dining room. Soon, she was cast in her first speaking role on Broadway as Penelope Penn in ***Rachel Crother**'s *39 East*. She tackled the role by mimicking the previous star, **Constance Binney**, and evidence of her tendency towards disruption appeared. Bankhead refused to place a hat, a visual cue for another actor, in its appointed place.

Bankhead was developing her off-stage persona as well. Utilizing her Southern flair, she ingratiated herself to the Algonquinites, though she did not become one of the Circle. She patterned her personality after the flapper that she had portrayed in Crother's *Nice People* in 1921 ("flappers" were young women who flaunted the bounds of conventional demeanor). Bankhead talked nonstop, dated extensively, spent money she didn't have on gifts, flung insults wildly, sniffed cocaine, and had a propensity for turning cartwheels *sans* undergarments at parties. Eventually, drinking joined smoking as part of her repertoire. By 1922, Bankhead had appeared in several Crothers plays, including one written for her titled *Everyday*, but stardom eluded her. When a British love interest, bisexual Baron Napier Alington or "Naps," returned to England, Tallulah considered taking her career overseas.

Fortuitously, English theater promoter Charles Cochran telegraphed from England about a part. Though he wired again telling her the part had been cast, Bankhead arranged passage anyway and feigned ignorance of the second wire. In London, she checked into the Ritz on borrowed funds and convinced Cochran to hire her and pay the previously engaged actress as well. In 1923, Tallulah Bankhead burst onto the London theater scene in *The Dancers* and developed a dedicated audience, dubbed the "Gallery Girls" by the critics, who cheered fanatically on her entrances and exits. Bankhead made it a point to learn their names and seek their opinions.

When she moved into singing teacher **Olga Lynn**'s well-appointed house at Naps' suggestion, Bankhead escalated her hold on London society. Oggie's home reinforced her grandmother's teachings about lady-like behavior, but Tallulah chose to ignore many of the rules. Though she concealed her behavior from her father by not sending home clippings, she continued to receive visitors naked, served cocktails from her bath, quipped outrageously, held weekly bacchanals, and generally defied social conventions for the sake of publicity. Meanwhile, her stage career continued unabated through *Conchita*, *This Marriage*, and *The Creaking Chair*, all 1924. Savings allowed Bankhead to purchase a green Talbot automobile, but her limited sense of navigation led her to hire cabs to lead her. When her acquaintances found this amusing, Bankhead continued the practice and began to develop an increasing air of helplessness.

> I hate to go to bed, I hate to get up, and I hate to be alone.
>
> —Tallulah Bankhead

Although she apparently enjoyed her new life in England, Tallulah longed for better parts. She appeared in Noel Coward's *Fallen Angels* (1925), followed by *The Green Hat* (1925) and *The Scotch Mist* (1926). Leasing a home, she began creating a household of servant-friends: a dresser, a butler, a cook, and a personal secretary. Their duties ranged from opening cigarette tins to listening to her into the wee hours.

In 1926, Bankhead shifted away from glamorous roles and signed on for the role of the waitress, Amy, in *They Knew What They Wanted*. Though her performance amazed the critics, her gallery disliked it, and Tallulah sorely missed their adoration. In 1927, the British public voted Bankhead one of the nation's ten "most remarkable" women in *The Sphere* magazine poll. Having proven her ability, she returned to gallery-pleasing roles, playing a chorus girl in *The Gold Diggers* (1926), a cabaret dancer in *The Garden of Eden* (1927), and various parts in thrillers like *Blackmail* (1928), *Mud and Treacle* (1928), and *Her Cardboard Lover* (1928). Theatergoers began to complain about the antics of her fans, but Tallulah reveled in their attention.

On the personal side, Bankhead's intention of marrying Naps was thwarted when he married someone else in 1928. Her sister Eugenia appeared in a tiny role in London before running off with another of Tallulah's beaus. Tallulah then shared her house with Count Anthony de Bosdari and they planned to marry, then called it off in May 1929. In 1930, she took on a last dramatic role in another attempt to demonstrate her ability, but *The Lady of the Camellias* proved beyond her scope. That fall, Bankhead signed a lucrative contract with Paramount Pictures and returned to America.

Greeted by her father and stepmother at dockside, Tallulah moved directly into a suite at the Elysee Hotel off Park Avenue in New York. After a whirl of interviews, she plunged into movie production for *The Tarnished Lady*. One scene introduced her to the clubs of Harlem, and Tallulah began to visit there regularly to buy cocaine, listen to jazz, and observe the uninhibited nightclub scene. As she settled back into New York, her circle of friends expanded to include aviator **Louisa Carpenter**, torch singer ***Libby Holman**, and singer ***Billie Holiday**. Paramount Pictures intended Tallulah to become a film star in the mode of Garbo or Dietrich and placed her in films suited to those stars. Bankhead did not fit, however, and they flopped.

Paramount then moved her to Hollywood where she rented a furnished mansion and spent money rashly despite the economic problems of the nation. When the Depression caused Paramount to cut salaries in 1932, Tallulah suffered a double whammy: the federal government ordered her to pay $15,000 in back taxes just as her extended family turned to her for financial assistance. Her sixth film with Paramount, *The Devil and the Deep* (1932), brought a small amount of success, and the company loaned her to Metro-Goldwyn-Mayer. Showing an uncanny sense for bad timing, Bankhead granted an interview to *Motion Picture* magazine in which she expressed her desire for a man. The "I-Want-a-Man-Story" scandalized an industry which had been trying to counteract perceptions of low morals in the film community. Although her MGM movie, *Faithless*, finally gave her a non-Dietrich vehicle, the uproar over the article undercut it. With her contract completed, Tallulah returned to New York.

Dipping into her savings, Bankhead financed a stage production of *Forsaking All Others*. Although she chose her producer and actors well, she ran the show as loosely as she ran her household. While on the road, the play attracted an audience similar to England's fans, but it did not appeal to the average Broadway theatergoer. To further complicate matters, it opened on Broadway on the same day in 1933 that Franklin D. Roosevelt closed the banks in an effort to stabilize the failing financial system. Before the show shuttered after 14 weeks, Bankhead had lost $40,000. She jumped into another play, *Jezebel*, but suffered severe abdominal pain and spent nine weeks in the hospital, while actors rehearsed at her bedside. Numb with codeine, she returned to the play briefly before being readmitted to the hospital for a hysterectomy in November. While friends assumed she had suffered from cancer, a sheepish Tallulah never corrected their belief. She had apparently contracted gonorrhea. Depressed, she developed a dependence on opiates during her recuperation and spent the last of her savings on medical bills.

In 1934, Bankhead opened in *Dark Victory* on Broadway to horrible reviews and, ill with a head infection, bowed out and was replaced by ***Bette Davis**. Although, in her next engagement, Tallulah's portrayal of prostitute Sadie Thompson in *Rain* pleased the tour audiences, once again she failed to garner good reviews on Broadway. Her inability to generate a following in Times Square began to be noticed.

While vacationing on Langdon Island in 1937, the bi-sexual Bankhead met actor John Emery. A few days later, she announced their engagement. With her father ascending to the post of speaker of the house in Congress, it seemed appropriate, and Bankhead believed she was in love. A small family wedding took place at her father's house in Jasper on August 31, 1937, and the couple settled into her suite at the Gotham Hotel. Though the two envisioned an acting partnership and undertook *Antony and Cleopatra* as their first project, the hoped-for pairing failed to materialize. Tallulah's drinking began to cause problems, as did John's already heavy habit.

In 1939, Bankhead landed one of her most successful roles, Regina Giddens in ***Lillian Hellman**'s *The Little Foxes*. When the play opened in New York, she gave a magnificent performance and received rave reviews and a best-actress citation from *Variety*. As the long New York run came to an end and the company prepared to tour, her marriage began to unwind, and both parties turned to extramarital affairs.

While on tour in 1940, Bankhead received word that her father had lapsed into a coma; he died before she could reach him. A month later, she learned that Naps died in the Battle of Britain. When the tour ended in 1941, John requested a divorce to marry actress ***Tamara Geva**; Tallulah agreed but, to avoid any indication that another party influenced their break-up, she exacted a promise that he would not marry for one year. Emery married Geva exactly one year after the final divorce decree.

Meanwhile, Bankhead took the role of Sabina in *The Skin of Our Teeth*. During the production, her reputation as a petulant, troublesome actress was enhanced. She refused to take direction, stormed out of rehearsals, stole lines, and divided the cast. Nonetheless, she was cited Best Actress of 1942 by the New York drama critics. She also bought her house in Bedford Village, New York, and dubbed it "Windows." Bankhead moved her unconventional household and her ever-changing group of "caddies" (her term for a retinue of young, often gay, men who were willing to put up with her whims) into the house. Increasingly, she relied upon them to keep her company and care for her. The household witnessed unusual levels of drinking, drug use, constant entertaining, exotic pets, and Tallulah's unceasing devotion to her afternoon "soapies." Those who left Windows usually did so out of self-preservation; Bankhead gave freely of all she had but exacted an exhausting toll.

During these years, she increasingly relied upon barbiturates, codeine, cocaine, and alcohol. Although she entertained constantly, her visitors slowly declined in number; too often the evenings ended with the hostess passed out. In an effort to raise funds, she returned to films, giving an award-winning performance, her best on screen, in Alfred Hitchcock's *Lifeboat*. The New York Screen Critics awarded her Best Actress of the Year for 1944. The critical success led to her next role as ***Catherine the Great** of Russia in *A Royal Scandal* (1945), but the film did not make her popular with audiences as she had hoped. Wrote biographer Lee Israel: "She was, in all regards, simply too big for the medium."

From the move Lifeboat, *starring Tallulah Bankhead and John Hodiak.*

In 1947, Bankhead returned to Broadway and bombed in *The Eagle Has Two Heads*, before opening in Coward's *Private Lives* in October 1948. After its Broadway stint, the show went on tour, but Bankhead's behavior was becoming more erratic and costly. At one stop, Marblehead, Massachusetts, her nightly party got out of hand. When the police arrived at the door, she greeted them naked and drunk. Her stint in jail was brief, but she was directed out of town. That fall, while testing for the movie of *The Glass Menagerie*, she greeted director Irving Rapper at the door of her dressing room in nothing but a hat. Nevertheless, the part looked to be hers until she drank a fifth of whatever and staggered onto the set spouting curses and demands. Jack Warner, head of Warner Bros., instructed the director to test the next actress. Bankhead began to disrupt the touring production of *Private Lives* on stage as well. She numbed herself with booze, marijuana, and opiates, turned lines into lewd suggestions, played tricks on actors on stage, and mugged for the audience. The rest of the cast avoided her as much as possible. Although the production deteriorated, the audiences were delighted.

The National Broadcasting Company hired her to be mistress of ceremonies for radio's "The Big Show" which premiered in November 1950. Tallulah felt uneasy with the lack of a defined character role and hassled the show's writers before it opened, but her personality made it work. Her stylized persona, supplied with customized material, filled the gaps between the parade of name performers who sang, joked, or played music over the air waves. Despite a London kickoff for the second season, however, the show's appeal faded as listeners wearied of her style.

Increasingly, Bankhead would often call friends the day after and apologize for any public embarrassment she might have caused them. As members of her household and friends continued to drift away, Bankhead sold her country home and purchased a townhouse in New York. She then took on the role of Blanche in *A Streetcar Named Desire* and attempted to subvert her usual self-caricature. Unfortunately, her audience refused to take her seriously when the play toured Florida, but Bankhead worked hard to erase personal traits from her portrayal of Blanche, tacitly demanding the audiences accept Blanche as Blanche and not as Tallulah playing Blanche. She had a relatively successful opening at New York's City Center in February 1956.

The effort seemed too much; she reverted to being Tallulah on stage in her next production, *The Ziegfeld Follies* (1956), and in those that followed. The abuse of her body, and particularly her lifelong chain-smoking, began to affect her ability to perform; her contracts now stipulated a 20-minute break between each of her film scenes so she could catch her breath. She began to stumble and have accidents: breaking ribs, burning her hand with a cigarette, and bruising arms and legs. She refused to wear glasses except to read, and the brittleness of age combined with the pills and alcohol to make her more fragile. Her latest live-in companion feared leaving her alone in the town house—she had once fallen asleep while smoking and set her dog on fire—and her dependence upon opiates caused psychotic episodes.

When Bankhead received the manuscript for *Midgie Purvis* (1961), she went into training; she had a private nurse regulate her substance use, and she ate regularly to prepare for the title role. During rehearsal, there were script changes from night to night and generally the play did not find its mark; the critics gave mixed reviews. Despite her preparations, Tallulah had to face her increasing need for actual assistance in daily living. She sold her town house and bought a condominium to avoid stairs; her emphysema eventually required her to use an oxygen tank, but she could not stop smoking, though she tried repeatedly. As her household and circle of friends diminished, her reliance on her "caddies" increased. She stayed home more and more, filling her waking hours with discussions about politics, the occult, and medical oddities.

She turned down a role opposite Bette Davis in *What Ever Happened to Baby Jane?*, but she accepted Tennessee William's offer to play Flora Goforth in a revision of *The Milk Train Doesn't Stop Here Anymore* in 1964. Again she prepared by reigning in her habits, but she didn't blossom into health like she had in the past. Throughout her life, Bankhead had been able to learn her lines by listening to them twice, now she had trouble remembering them at all. The show closed after five performances on Broadway.

That same year, Bankhead traveled to England to make her last film. Avoiding the press, she put everything into the job, but due to her history of poor health, she arranged for Columbia to hold her $50,000 salary as a guarantee that she would finish the movie. She drank vitamin cocktails and diverted her usual excesses into gambling on horses and playing poker. Though she vigorously objected to the changing of the film's name during shooting, because she hated her trademark "dahling" by that time, it went to theaters as *Die! Die! My Darling!* in 1965.

In December 1968, Bankhead contracted the Asian flu. When she did not respond to treatment, her doctor suggested hospitalization. After several days, she asked to see her sister, but by the time Eugenia arrived, pneumonia had set in and Tallulah lapsed into a coma. The only intelligible words she uttered before dying on December 12, 1968, were "codeine-bourbon." When her friends arranged her burial, they dressed her in one of her favorite cigarette-burned, red silk wrappers and slipped her father's rabbit's foot into the casket.

SOURCES:

Bankhead, Tallulah. *Tallulah: My Autobiography.* NY: Harper, 1952.

Brian, Denis. *Tallulah, Darling: A Biography of Tallulah Bankhead.* NY: Macmillan, 1972.

Carrier, Jeffrey L. *Tallulah Bankhead: A Bio-Bibliography.* Bio-Bibliographies in the Performing Arts series, Number 21. Westport CT: Greenwood Press, 1991.

Israel, Lee. *Miss Tallulah Bankhead.* NY: Putnam, 1972.

SUGGESTED READING:

Campbell, Sandy. *B: Twenty-nine Letters from Coconut Grove.* Verona, Italy: Martino Mardersteig of Stamperia Valdonega, 1974 (a series of letters by one of Bankhead's houseguests while on tour).

Gill, Brendan. *Tallulah.* NY: Holt, 1972 (photobiography).

Rawls, Eugenia. *Tallulah: A Memory.* Birmingham, AL: Board of Trustees of the University of Alabama, 1979 (personal account by a lifelong friend).

Tunney, Kieran. *Tallulah: Darling of the Gods: An Intimate Portrait.* NY: Dutton, 1973.

RELATED MEDIA:

Baxt, George. *The Tallulah Bankhead Murder Case.* NY: International Polygonics, 1987.

Lang, Tony, and Bruce Coyle. *Tallulah Tonight,* one-woman show, starring **Helen Gallagher**, produced at the American Place Theatre, 1988.

Portrait of Tallulah Bankhead by Augustus John. National Gallery, Washington, D.C., 1929.

Siegel, Arthur. *Tallulah: Libretto* (23-page typescript), New York Public Library Reserve Library, 1983.

Siegel, Arthur, and Helen Gallagher. *Tallulah* (recording), Painted Smiles, 1991.

COLLECTIONS:

Bankhead Family papers, State of Alabama Department of History and Archives, Huntsville, Alabama; Theater Collection, Library of Performing Arts, Lincoln Center, New York City, New York; Eugenia Rawls and Donald Seawell Theater Collection, Southern History Collection, University of North Carolina, Chapel Hill, North Carolina; Eugenia Rawls Papers, Denver Public Library, Denver, Colorado; and Fred Allen Papers, Boston Public Library, Boston, Massachusetts.

Oral history interview taped in Phoenix in 1964, resides in the Lewis Audiovisual Research Institute and Teaching Archive, Tucson, Arizona.

Laura Anne Wimberley,
Department of History,
Texas A&M University, College
Station, Texas

Banks, Mrs. G. Linnaeus (1821–1887).

See Banks, Isabella.

Banks, Isabella (1821–1887)

British author known as the "Lancashire" novelist for her portrayals of Manchester and Lancashire life. *Name variations: (pseudonyms) Isabella Varley; Mrs. G. Linnaeus Banks. Born Isabella Varley on March 25, 1821, in Manchester, England; died on May 5, 1887, in Dalston, England; daughter of James and Amelia (Daniels) Varley; educated at Miss Hannah Spray's Ladies' Day School and Rev. John Wheeldon's academy; married George Linnaeus Banks (poet and journalist), in 1846; children: Agnes, Esther, George, and five children who died in infancy.*

Selected works: Ivy Leaves: A Collection of Poems *(1844);* God's Providence House *(1865); (with G. Linnaeus Banks)* Daisies in the Grass *(1865);* The Manchester Man *(1876);* Caleb Booth's Clerk *(1878);* Wooers and Winners *(1880);* Geoffrey Oliphant's Folly *(1886);* The Bridge of Beauty *(1894).*

On March 25, 1821, Isabella Varley was born in a house on Oldham Street in Manchester, England, into a family of chemists who had an artistic bent. When Isabella's father, also an amateur painter, was unable to make a living with his experimental work, he turned the ground floor of the house into an apothecary and millinery. James and **Amelia Varley** often took their four children to local dramatic productions, and Amelia's sister, **Jane Daniels**, who lived with them, told the children stories and histories of their family and the rapidly booming town of Manchester.

Isabella attended schools local to Oldham Street, including Miss Hannah Spray's Ladies' Day School where, at age ten, she unravelled the mystery of tatting lace. When she showed an early proficiency for sewing and design, Isabella's father sold her lace caps, the newest ladies' fashion, in his store.

When Isabella was 12, the family moved to the Manchester suburb of Cheetham. There, she finished her schooling under the tutelage of a local cleric and, at age 17, established the School for Young Ladies. For nine years, until her marriage in 1846 to George Linnaeus Banks, she operated the small school and wrote poetry. Her verse appeared in local publications (the first, at age 16, was the poem "A Dying Girl to Her Mother") before the 1844 release of her collection *Ivy Leaves.*

Vilma Banky

By 1947, George's work as a journalist, speaker, and poet led the couple elsewhere, and Isabella's writing receded to the background. The family, expanding ultimately to three children, though five others were born and died, moved often. In Harrogate, Isabella took advantage of the Mechanics' Institute, an educational center. Membership allowed individuals to attend discussions and use the library. On more than one occasion, Isabella was invited to lecture.

Her one constant through the relocations was needlework. For 45 years, Banks created and published a design monthly. It was not until 1863, when George began to lose his battle with alcoholism, that Isabella turned to writing as a means to support her children. In 1865, the author known as Mrs. G. Linnaeus Banks published her first novel, *God's Providence House.* More than 50 others were to follow in the next 25 years.

Work became Banks' compulsion. Her letters reflect the constant pressure of being the lone breadwinner. Battling cancer, George used alcohol more than ever to assuage the pain, and he frequently threatened suicide. Meanwhile, Isabella's health, fragile since childhood, suffered. During one period of recuperation, she wrote what would become her most famous work, *The Manchester Man*, which initially appeared in serial fashion in the magazine *Cassell's.* Not published in book form until 1876, the work relied heavily on her knowledge of Manchester. The stories her Aunt Jane had told her filled Banks' with an image of working-class neighborhoods she had never visited. Two more books, *Caleb Booth's Clerk* (1878) and *Wooers and Winners* (1880), sealed her reputation as the "Lancashire novelist."

On May 3, 1881, George Banks succumbed to cancer, and Isabella stayed on in their suburban London home with an unmarried daughter. Though she frequently staved off attacks of bronchitis, Isabella grew weaker and died at her home on May 5, 1887, at age 66. *The Manchester Man* remains a widely read depiction of the industrial revolution in Manchester.

SOURCES:

Banks, Mrs. G. Linnaeus. *The Manchester Man.* London: Victor Gollancz, 1970.

Burney, E.L. *Mrs. G. Linnaeus Banks.* Didsbury, Manchester: E.J. Morten, 1969.

Schlueter, Paul, and Jane Schlueter. *An Encyclopedia of British Women Writers.* NY: Garland, 1988.

Todd, Janet, ed. *British Women Writers.* NY: Continuum, 1989.

Crista Martin, freelance writer,
Boston, Massachusetts

Banks, Sarah Sophia (1744–1818)

British naturalist. *Born in 1744, probably at Revesby Abbey, Lincolnshire; died in 1818 in London, England; daughter of Sarah (Bate) Banks and William Banks; sister of botanist Joseph Banks (1743–1820).*

Though not a scientist, Sarah Sophia Banks earned her reputation by assisting her brother, botanist Joseph Banks, with whom she lived. When Joseph married in 1779, his wife joined the household, and the three evidently lived quite harmoniously together until the end of their lives. Said to be somewhat eccentric in appearance and personality, Banks possessed a sharp, inquiring mind. She discussed scientific questions with her brother, and many of her interpretations and ideas found their way into his writings. She also transcribed much of his work; one of her more tedious assignments was copying the entire manuscript of his Newfoundland voyage journal, published in 1766.

Barbara Morgan,
Melrose, Massachusetts

Banky, Vilma (1898–1992)

Austro-Hungarian actress. *Born Vilma Lonchit in Nagyrodog, near Budapest, Hungary, on January 9, 1898; died in 1992; daughter of a prominent politician; married Rod La Rocque (1898–1969, a film star), in 1927.*

Born in Budapest in 1898, Vilma Banky made her stage debut in Vienna; she then made films in Austria and Hungary starting in 1920. In 1925, photos in an Austrian shop window of the 5'6" blue-eyed blonde caught the eye of Samuel Goldwyn who was on holiday in Europe; he tracked Banky down and brought her to Hollywood. Promoted as "The Hungarian Rhapsody," she played the female lead opposite Rudolph Valentino in *The Eagle* (1925) and *Son of the Sheik* (1926). She also teamed with Ronald Colman for *The Dark Angel*. Her last film *The Rebel* was made in Germany in 1932, but she ostensibly retired with the advent of sound. At the time, the silent-screen star, popular throughout the 1930s, spoke little English.

Banky's marriage to film star Rod La Rocque, a well-staged 1927 affair by Hollywood standards, lasted until his death in 1969. Throughout the 1940s, she was the women's golf champion at the Wilshire Country Club. Her other films include *Im letzen Augenblick* (1920), *Galathea* (1921), *Das Auge des Toten* (1922), *Schattenkinder des Glücks* (1922), *Hotel Potemkin* (1924), *Das Verbotene Land* (1924), *Das Bildnis* (1924), and *Das schöne Abenateuer* (*The Lady from Paris*, 1924), *The Winning of Barbara Worth* (1926), *Night of Love* (1927), *The Magic Flame* (1927), *The Awakening* (1928), *Two Lovers* (1928), *Innocent*, and the talkies *This is Heaven* (1929) and *A Lady to Love* (1930).

Banning, Margaret Culkin (1891–1982)

American author. *Born Margaret Culkin in Buffalo, Minnesota, on March 18, 1891; died on January 4, 1982, in Tryon, North Carolina; daughter of William Edgar Culkin and Hannah Alice (Young) Culkin; graduated Vassar College. B.A., 1912; certificate from Chicago School of Civics and Philanthropy, 1913; research fellow of the Russell Sage Foundation; married Archibald Tanner Banning, in 1914; children: two daughters and two sons.*

Margaret Culkin Banning wrote over 40 books and 400 short stories. Her works, consisting chiefly of light fiction, were widely read. Her novels, which often dealt with social issues, included *Too Young to Marry* (1938), *Clever Sister* (1947), *Give Us Our Years* (1949), *Fallen Away* (1951), and *The Vine and the Olive*. Among her nonfictional writings are *Women for Defense* (1942), *Letters from England* (1943), and, with **Mabel Louise Culkin**, *Conduct Yourself Accordingly* (1944) and *Salud: A South American Journal*.

Margaret Culkin Banning

Banti, Anna (1895–1985).

See Longhi, Lucia Lopresti.

Banus, Maria (1914—)

Rumanian poet. *Born in Bucharest, Rumania, in 1914; studied law and philology.*

Known as the grande dame of Rumanian poetry, Maria Banus had her first work published when she was 14. Throughout the 1930s, she was active in anti-fascist movements, and during World War II she worked for the Resistance in Rumania. Though she was named an official "Stalinist poet" following the war and the occupation of Rumania, Banus was soon disenchanted with the Soviet regime and returned to her own voice; her writing varies from what has been called "impetuous and spontaneous" to poems of great precision and tenderness. Banus was also a translator of poetry from the German, Russian, Spanish, Turkish, and French, including the poems of Goethe, Pushkin, Neruda, Hikmet, and Rimbaud. Her works include *The Girl's Country* (1937), *Joy* (1947), *I Am Speaking to You, America!* (1955), *Metamorphosis* (1963), and *Anyone and Something* (1972). *Demon in Brackets* was translated into English by Dan Dutescu and published by Dufour (1994).

Ban Zhao (c. 45–c. 120 CE)

Poet, historian, and writer whose classic work, **Lessons for Women,** ***made her the most noted Chinese woman of letters prior to the 20th century.*** *Pronunciation: Bahn Jao, rhymes with "cow." Name varia-*

tions: Pan Chao; also known in the Chinese literary world by the alternate name Ban Hui-ji and by the title Cao Dagu. Ban Zhao was born sometime between 45 and 51 CE; died sometime between 114 and 120 CE; daughter of Ban Biao (3–54 CE, a noted scholar and administrator of the powerful Chinese Ban family which included a number of famous literary figures), and a highly educated mother whose name is unknown; both her great-aunt and her mother were also literary figures; received a broad education with noted tutors and established a reputation as a poet and woman of letters; sister of Ban Gu and Ban Chao (Pan Ch'ao, 32–102 CE, a famous Chinese traveler and military official in the northern frontiers); married Cao Shishu; children: several sons.

When her brother Ban Gu died before finishing a noted dynastic history, that of the Han dynasty (the Han Shu), Ban Zhao finished the work and made a major contribution to the study of Chinese history; she was also a tutor to the Empress Deng (fl. 105 CE–121 CE) and a noted court memorialist and is most famous for her classic work the Lessons for Women *which became the standard treatise prescribing the rules for the behavior of women within the Chinese family for almost 2,000 years; in addition, she wrote many volumes of poetry as well as a wide range of literary miscellany such as epitaphs and memorials, all recognized models within the world of Chinese traditional letters, and became the model for subsequent generations of Chinese female intellectuals well into the modern era.*

Ban Zhao was born in China at a time of historic reforms. The old feudal system which had been controlled by powerful landed families was being replaced by the imperial system which was governed from the court, increasingly dominated by the Confucian system of values. This was a time of sweeping changes, and Ban Zhao was a full participant in defining them. In particular, her views of the proper place of women in Confucian society were to be central to the Chinese gender system well into the late 19th century.

The complex Chinese political system, within which Ban Zhao was to become a noted figure, had undergone several significant modifications prior to the Han dynasty (206 BCE–220 CE) in which she lived. Prior to the 3rd century BCE, the territory now organized as modern China had been controlled by a series of warring feudal states. In this system, political and military power largely coincided, while great families—sometimes ruling as monarchs, other times as a collection of like-minded local powers—dominated. The short-lived Qin dynasty (221–206 BCE) had united these states under a totalitarian central government. While the megalomaniacal Qin rulers had begun the long process of unifying both the Chinese state and Chinese culture, they proved too heavy-handed, extracting a terrible price from the Chinese people for the advantages of a centralized government. In 206 BCE, they were replaced by the Han dynasty. The first several generations of Han rulers proved capable men who were both great warriors and wise administrators. They evolved a system which recognized the need for unity as well as the need for strong local families who would resist a too-dominant central government.

The primary internal political problem facing the Han was how to incorporate the great families into the central government so as to avoid a resurgence of feudalism in which those families might simply carve out local kingdoms at the expense of the imperial throne. The final solution to this dilemma was not fully formed for many centuries, but the process began in the Han era, and Ban Zhao and her family were important figures in its evolution.

The ultimate solution to the central problem of Chinese politics was to be Confucianism. Named after Confucius (551–479 BCE), a noted Chinese thinker of the pre-Qin era, the system became the central ethos of the Chinese people for almost 2,000 years, finally collapsing only in the early 20th century. In some respects, the Confucian value system continues to be an important aspect of such contemporary Chinese states as the Peoples' Republic of China, Taiwan, Hong Kong, and Singapore, as well as being influential in Japan, Korea, and Vietnam.

The Confucian value system proceeds from a simple analogy: the central model for Chinese society should be a well-ordered family. The emperor was the all-powerful father within the system, and other relationships were based upon the other roles within the family, such as that between husband and wife, elder brothers and younger brothers, and so on. Within the orderly Confucian world, everybody has a place, and the rules for their behavior toward each other are quite clear.

As a political system, the Confucian world was equally hierarchical and orderly. The emperor appointed court officials and local administrators from among men who were learned in the study of the Confucian classic books, a collection of works said to be written by Confucius, and noted commentaries upon those works. The great merit of the system was that it ultimately provided a degree of social mobility which attracted the energies of capable Chinese for well over 1,000 years, ensuring that nearly all such people would support the system, both guaranteeing its stability and constantly refreshing it with new talent. The system proved an irresistible attraction to all those who had the leisure for study, including the sons of the great families. This was, then, the check on feudalism: ambitious leaders could rise within the system and usually had no need to carve out kingdoms or mini-empires of their own.

The system naturally gave great importance to the world of scholarship. It was mastery over the Confucian learning which bought advancement and power, and it was the content of those books which became the value structure of Chinese students well into the 20th century. Ban Zhao's family was present in several generations at the courts of the Han as the Confucian system was founded. Her father Ban Biao (3–54 CE) traced his lineage back well into the time of Confucius himself. Biao was a noted scholar, as well as an administrator. His family possessed classic works which had been given to them earlier, and this learning was an important part of their family tradition.

Ban Zhao's father passed his love of learning on to his twin sons, her brothers Ban Gu and Ban Chao. Ban Zhao was given a broad education in both the Confucian learning and in the other great tradition of Chinese thought, Daoism, which emphasizes the place of man not within society, as does Confucianism, but within nature. Daoism thus became the philosophy which animated Chinese artists and poets. Ban Zhao's grasp over both these traditions ensured that she would understand all of the important ideas of her age, and that she could contribute to further developing those ideas.

Ban Zhao was also fortunate that she lived at the beginnings of the Confucian tradition rather than after it had become more rigidly codified. Ultimately, the place of Chinese women was to become distinctly inferior to that of Chinese men, and later generations of Chinese women rarely had the opportunity to secure such a broad education as did Ban Zhao. In this regard, her age still reflected some of the usages of feudalism. In the feudal age, Chinese women had often been powerful political actors and sometimes rulers in their own right. But the Confucians felt that within the family there could be but one head, and that head was the father-husband.

But in Ban Zhao's time women were educated and their talents highly regarded, even in the increasingly rarified world of Chinese letters. Her great-aunt **Ban Jieyu** was a particularly noted literary figure, and her mother was also said to be highly educated. It was thus quite natural that Ban Zhao, like her father and brothers, should become a familiar figure at the court of the Han emperors.

In the long history of Chinese literature from the days of the ancient odes down to modern times the place occupied by women has been small. . . . The one woman, however, who unquestionably belongs in the foremost rank of Chinese learning is Ban Zhao Cao Dagu of the court of the Eastern Han emperor He (89-95 CE).

—**Nancy Lee Swann**

Like many Chinese women, Ban Zhao married young, at age 14, but she was to be a widow for the greater portion of her life. Her husband Cao Shishu died fairly early in their marriage and little is known of him, nor of their several sons. In later eras, Confucians would force widows into virtual seclusion, but Ban Zhao lived an active and public life at successive Han courts. The period during which she was to be most powerful was that of her maturity.

Her twin brother Ban Gu became the historian of the Han court. This was a very powerful office as Confucians believed that the history of humankind revealed Heaven's judgments as to both good and bad behavior. Historians, with their ability to assign "praise and blame," became the primary arbiters of the Confucian tradition. But the Chinese court was always a dangerous place, characterized by bitter if polite struggles between ambitious men and women and their powerful families. Gu sided with a losing clique and died in prison. At his death, he had been writing the history of the earlier Han

Ban Jieyu (c. 48–c. 6 BCE)

Chinese poet and royal concubine to Emperor Cheng of the Han dynasty. *Born around 48 BCE; died around 6 BCE; great-aunt of **Ban Zhao**.*

Once a royal concubine to Emperor Cheng of the Han dynasty, Ban Jieyu lost favor and was relegated to serving the dowager empress. Ban Jieyu's indignation informed her poetry, including "Resentful Song," which was inscribed on a round fan.

reigns, an important task. The court summoned his sister, Ban Zhao, to finish the work. The work to which she contributed, the *Han Shu* (History of the Han), is said to be the second most noted of the many dynastic histories of China. While her exact contributions to the work have been obscured by time and by the later Confucian disregard for women (her brother is said to be the official editor by later Confucian historians), some scholars have given her the credit as primary author.

Ban Zhao was not only China's most famous female historian, she was also a noted poet. While her poetry filled many volumes, not much of it has survived. But those existing works show her clear mastery of the difficult written Confucian language, and her ability to manipulate the complex styles of the classic literary form. One poem, "The Needle and Thread," translated by her biographer **Nancy Lee Swann,** reveals both her poetic ability and her unique perceptions as a Chinese woman:

> Strong spirit of Pure Steel from autumn's metal cast.
> Incarnate body of power, slight and subtle, straight and sharp!
> To pierce, then to enter gradually in, that is your nature.
> Things far apart all strung into one, that is your task.
> Only your ordered footprints, you wonderful needle and thread, attest the quantity, the variety, the universality of your work. . . .
> All, all together these are your memorials.
> They are found in the village home, they ascend into the stately hall.

While many of her works are indistinguishable from those of noted Chinese male poets, this poem must have been a favorite of the myriad generations of Chinese women who worked diligently at the household tasks of sewing, repairing, and embroidering the very beautiful textiles of classical China. These fabrics have only recently been recognized as true works of art and mounted for exhibition in major museums.

The apogee of Ban Zhao's influence at court came in the reign of the Empress ***Deng**, who both recognized Ban Zhao as her tutor and consulted with her on court matters. While we cannot be sure, it is probable that Ban Zhao's most famous work, the *Lessons for Women*, was written at about this time. One of the central domestic problems of the Confucian family was how to create an orderly home life. This was not an easy task, as the Chinese family sometimes included several wives and concubines, and women were increasingly forced into an isolated existence. The Confucian world had a pressing need for clear hierarchies and for easily learned rules of behavior, and it fell to Ban Zhao to codify the proper deportment of women. In the strictures of the *Lessons for Women*, in part a moral handbook and in part a book of etiquette, Ban Zhao counsels women to accept a subordinate role within the family. In Swann's translation, Ban Zhao states: "It can be said that the Way of respect and acquiescence is woman's most important principle of conduct." In addition, Ban Zhao rules that widows must not remarry; throughout, the *Lessons for Women* condones a rigid double standard which gives men markedly superior status in the marriage relationship.

Previous generations of Western women did not find Ban Zhao's code for Chinese women objectionable but often praised it as the first such work detailing the proper behavior of women in general. If we are to appreciate the true import of Ban Zhao's attitude toward the relationship between the genders we must understand the world in which she lived. She and her family had devoted themselves for generations to the creation and support of the Confucian world-view. The Ban family measured their notions of gender relations against the violent feudal age from which China had only recently emerged. In Ban Zhao's view, nothing was more important to Chinese women than social stability and political order. She, like Chinese women for a millennium, accepted the idea that the family was the model of all of society, and that a proper family had to be hierarchically ordered with one indisputable head: the husband.

In the Confucian view, woman's security is achieved by creating an orderly environment in which the Confucian scholar-administrator (or peasant) can do his demanding work. The wife creates a haven from which the man can sally forth to do battle with the stubborn rice fields or the clique-ridden court. In return, the husband should provide for the material needs of the family, and for its orderly progress as the daughters themselves make good marriages into other well-off families and the sons receive the education necessary to guarantee them and their own families further advancement in the Confucian world of letters.

Ban Zhao did include one lesson in her work for women which was to be largely ignored by later Confucian generations. She insisted that women, too, should receive a good education. In so doing, she perhaps hoped that education would serve to provide a channel of escape for other women, as it had for her.

Ban Zhao used her power at the Han court to see her sons advanced and secured the power of the Ban family for generations; her daughter-in-law was to edit later editions of her works. Ban Zhao died around 120 CE, at over 70 years of age. During a long lifetime, she had written more than 16 volumes of literary works, few of which survive today. But her reputation as Confucian China's foremost woman of letters has endured for almost 2,000 years.

SOURCES:

Chu, T'ung-tsu. *Han Social Structure.* Seattle: University of Washington Press, 1972.

Loewe, Michael. *Crisis and Conflict in Han China.* London: George Allen & Unwin, 1974.

Swann, Nancy Lee. *Pan Chao: Foremost Woman Scholar of China.* NY: Russell & Russell, 1932.

SUGGESTED READING:

Loewe, Michael. *Everyday Life in Early Imperial China during the Han Period, 202 BC–AD 220.* NY: Dorset Press, 1968.

Watson, Burton, ed. *Courtier and Commoner in Ancient China: Selections from the History of the Former Han by Pan Ku.* NY: Columbia University Press, 1974.

Jeffrey G. Barlow,
Professor in the Department of Social Studies,
Pacific University, Forest Grove, Oregon

Bar, countess of.

See Philippa de Dreux (d. 1240).
See Margaret (d. 1275).
See Eleanor Plantagenet (1264–1297).
See Marie of France (1344–1404).

Bar, duchess of.

See Isabelle of Lorraine (1410–1453).
See Jeanne de Laval (d. 1498).
See Catherine of Bourbon (c. 1555–1604).
See Elizabeth-Charlotte (1676–1744).

Bara, Theda (1885–1955)

American silent-film star whose performances popularized "the vamp" and introduced the term into the English language. *Name variations: Theodosia Goodman, Theodosia de Coppet. Born Theodosia de Coppet Goodman on July 20, 1885, in Cincinnati, Ohio; died of cancer on April 7, 1955, in Los Angeles, California; eldest daughter of Bernard (a tailor) and Pauline Louise (de Coppet) Goodman (a hair products representative and housewife); graduated from Walnut Hills High School, 1903; attended University of Cincinnati, 1903–05; moved to New York City with family about 1905; married Charles J. Brabin (a film director), in 1921.*

As Theodosia de Coppet, appeared on Broadway in The Devil *(1908); appeared in the film* The Stain *(1908); signed with Fox film studios (1914) and was given new personal background and name, Theda Bara; starred in* A Fool There Was *(1915) and 39 other Fox "vamp" films through 1919; also appeared in* The Two Orphans *(1915) and* Romeo and Juliet *(1916); appeared in play* The Blue Flame *(1920); attempted film comeback in* The Unchastened Woman *(1925) and* Madame Mystery *(1926); retired in 1926.*

From Theda Bara's first Fox film released in 1915 until Bela Lugosi's film portrayal of Count Dracula in 1931, the popular meaning of the word vampire was synonymous with a Bara-like person. Bara's famous characters, called vampires or vamps, were women who seduced men, especially married ones, purely for the challenge. A vamp held her lover until he was broken, then she callously discarded him. The term "to vamp" came to mean "to seduce."

Bara was born Theodosia Goodman on July 20, 1885, the eldest of three children. Her father Bernard, son of a Jewish family from Poland, was a tailor. Her mother Pauline Louise de Coppet had been born in Switzerland to French parents and was in the hair-products business before her marriage to Goodman. Theodosia graduated from Cincinnati's Walnut Hills High School in 1903 and attended the University of Cincinnati for two years. Apparently, she was already interested in acting and encouraged by her family. About 1905, the entire family moved to New York City.

Bara's early career is obscure, though she worked for a while under the name Theodosia de Coppet. In 1908, she appeared in a Broadway play titled *The Devil* but was no great success on stage. She also performed in a film called *The Stain* as an extra. In 1914, film producer William Fox offered her the female lead in *A Fool There Was*, a film based on a play inspired by Rudyard Kipling's poem "The Vampire." The plot involved a seductive woman's schemes to trap and ruin a prosperous married man. The 29-year-old Theodosia accepted. In connection with her new acting role, Theodosia Goodman became Theda Bara. Despite press releases to the contrary, the name was actually taken from the middle name of her maternal grandfather. Apparently, her family approved; they legally changed the family name to Bara in 1917.

The box office success of *A Fool There Was* ensured that both the movie and Bara's character became prototypes for other films of a woman destroying a man. The most famous line, "Kiss me, my fool," made Bara an institution. "Her silent comment cut through the rubble of

Theda Bara

Victorian sentiment like a stiletto," wrote **Marjorie Rosen** in *Popcorn Venus*, "and an enthralled America parroted her." When she began her career with Fox, she was paid $150 a week; as her popularity increased so did her salary. Eventually, she earned $4,000 a week.

In addition to fame as the silent screen's first successful vamp, Theda Bara was also the first star whose off-screen character was created entirely by a publicity campaign. To preserve the mystery and danger of the on-screen character, studio press agents fabricated an exotic background for Bara. Fan magazines regaled readers with the story of her exotic birth in the Sahara Desert, perhaps under the shadow of the Sphinx. Her father was variously reported as French, Italian, or Arabic, and her mother as Egyptian, Arabic or French. Her name was said to be an Oriental anagram. "Theda Bara" scrambled could read "death of Arab."

Though the facts of her background were available, the public and the media preferred the exotic story. In September 1915, the popular magazine *Photoplay* chose to "disbelieve those stupid people who insist that Theda Bara's right name is Theodosia Goodman and that she is by, of, and from Cincinnati." Yet *Photoplay* also carried articles that proclaimed her "a gentle, slightly melancholy, even timid creature" who regarded "love as a bit of a myth" and a "career of high license . . . something too shocking to contemplate."

Bara was surprised that the public could or did not distinguish between her screen characters and her real life, yet the life she lived for public view was designed to perpetuate the mystery. She was kept from all but the most carefully staged public appearances and interviews. Publicity photos caught her glaring into the camera, talons intact, with her darkly kohled eyes. Her contract reportedly banned her from using public transportation or going out without a heavy veil. It also forbade her to marry. She became known as "The Wickedest Woman in the World" and was the subject of immense speculation by fans and reporters alike.

From 1914 to 1919, Theda Bara starred in some 40 films featuring the vamp character, including *The Serpent*, *The Vixen, The She-Devil*, and *Purgatory's Ivory Angel*, but only *The Serpent* survives. Her portrayal of ***Cleopatra** in a 1917 movie was banned in some places. Trying to avoid typecasting, she appeared in *The Two Orphans* (1915) and as Juliet in *Romeo and Juliet* (1916), but audiences would not allow her to break the mold. Just as ***Mary Pickford** was expected to play the adolescent, Bara was expected to play the vamp.

From 1910 to 1920, she became one of the most popular stars of the decade, due in part to the extreme contrast between her immoral characters and the virtuous women wronged by them. America was at the threshold of great change, still influenced by the restrictive Victorian era but moving toward the flamboyant Roaring Twenties. Early films pandered to audience expectations of a clear definition between good and evil. Simplistic portrayals in both plot and character maintained the social roles and limitations for both women and men.

Prior to Bara's vamp, women had generally been portrayed in film as good and vulnerable, as hard workers in lowly jobs or as faithful wives. Bara's roles were not kind to women. The vamp appeared in scanty clothes and heavy makeup; her express purpose was to ruin men. It was "the vengeance of women on men," explained Bara. "The woman vampire is loved but does not love in return; she exploits men for their money and their sex, and, when they are exhausted of both, abandons them."

> [People] refuse to believe that I, in real life, am not as I am in my screen life.
>
> **—Theda Bara**

Both shocked and thrilled, people flocked to the movies. Men relished the characters. Some women wrote angry letters or defaced movie posters, but others imitated the characters' costumes, makeup, and seductive ways. Reviewers and commentators publicly examined women's essential nature, particularly discussing distinctions between good women and evil women, depending on the nature of their sexuality. "In no way did her creation resemble a woman—unless one wants to give credence to full hips and bare nipples protruding from serpentine bras," writes Rosen. "Yet she was not, in 1915, a figure of ridicule. On the contrary, she was *sex*, blatant and overt and so far removed from reality that she could not possibly be a threat to audiences newly probing their own sexuality."

So popular was Bara's vamp that the image was unashamedly copied by new stars and even established ones, ***Betty Blythe**, ***Vilma Banky**, ***Nita Naldi**, **Valeska Suratt**, **Louise Glaum**, **Lya de Putti**, and ***Pola Negri**. As audiences grew more sophisticated in the aftermath of World War I, however, viewers had trouble believing that a vamp destroyed men simply for the fun of it. The character became too simplistic and was often the subject of satire.

By 1919, Theda Bara's popularity had waned, and, when her contract with Fox ended, she left to appear on stage. Though she announced that she wanted to be "a symbol of purity" and "spread happiness," Bara returned to the vamp character in *The Blue Flame* which was produced on Broadway in March 1920. The play was greeted by critics with derision. The audience, however, liked Bara, and the play did well financially on tour. Still, the vamp of early films was no longer in vogue. In the Roaring '20s, stars imitated Bara's wicked-woman concept but developed more depth for the characters.

In 1921, Theda Bara married one of her directors, Charles J. Brabin. She tried a film comeback in *The Unchastened Woman* (1925) and *Madame Mystery* (1926), then retired from films. Having been careful with her earnings, Bara lived comfortably after her retirement. She and Brabin had one of Hollywood's successful marriages. They lived in Beverly Hills, entertained frequently, and Bara became known for her gourmet meals. Her mother lived near her and the family connections remained strong. As she aged, Bara was described as short, bosomy, and slightly plump. She died of cancer on April 7, 1955, after a two-month hospitalization in Los Angeles.

Theda Bara had added a new word to the English language and a new dimension to women's acting roles, for as one television-era writer put it, "Without Theda Bara, there might never have been *Dynasty*'s Joan Collins." She "bridged the gap between sexual austerity and sexual flamboyance," writes Rosen. "And in so doing, she managed a permanent disservice to women. Before Freud's theories of behavior had become popularized, she cast that ominous shadow, the vagina with teeth. She sucked the blood from her lovers; she deprived them of their self-respect. For her they groveled. And while by the mid-twenties her vamp aroused ridicule, was she not the mother of the *femmes fatales*?" It might be interesting to note that the height of Bara's popularity coincided with the height of the women's suffrage movement. While Bara bared her fangs, women were picketing the White House for the vote.

SOURCES:

Blum, Daniel. *A Pictorial History of the Silent Screen.* London: Spring Books, 1962.

Higashi, Sumiko. *Virgins, Vamps, and Flappers: The American Silent Movie Heroine.* Monographs in Women's Studies. St. Albans, VT: Eden Press Women's Publications, 1978.

Jacobs, Lewis. *The Rise of the American Film: A Critical History.* NY: Teachers College Press of Columbia University, 1968.

Newsweek (obituary). April 18, 1955, p. 71.

Notable American Women: The Modern Period. Edited by Barbara Sicherman and Carol Hurd Green. Cambridge, MA: Belknap Press of Harvard University Press, 1980.

Rosen, Marjorie. *Popcorn Venus.* NY: Coward, McCann, 1973.

Siegel, Scott, and Barbara Siegel. *The Encyclopedia of Hollywood: An A-to-Z of the Heroes, Heroines, and History of American Film.* NY: Facts on File, 1990.

Time (obituary). April 18, 1955, p. 104.

SUGGESTED READING:

Doane, Mary Ann. *Femmes fatales: Feminism, Film Theory, and Psychoanalysis.* NY: Routledge, 1991.

Drew, William M. *Speaking of Silents: First Ladies of the Screen.* Vestal, NY: Vestal Press, 1989.

Everson, William K. *American Silent Film.* NY: Oxford University Press, 1978.

Mast, Gerald. *A Short History of the Movies.* 4th ed. NY: Macmillan, 1986.

Schickel, Richard. *The Stars.* NY: Dial Press, 1962.

Trent, Paul, and Richard Lawton. *The Image Makers: Sixty Years of Hollywood Glamour.* NY: McGraw-Hill, 1972.

Turner, Mary M. *Forgotten Leading Ladies of the American Theatre: Lives of Eight Female Players, Playwrights, Directors, Managers, and Activists of the Eighteenth, Nineteenth, and Early Twentieth Centuries.* Jefferson, NC: McFarland, 1990.

Women and Film. Janet Todd, editor. NY: Holmes & Meier, 1988.

COLLECTIONS:

Photographs, portfolios, scrapbooks, press books, reviews, and manuscript notes in the Theda Bara Collection in the Billy Rose Theatre Collection, and in the Robinson Locke Scrapbooks, both in the New York Public Library; clipping file in the Harvard Theatre Collection.

Margaret L. Meggs, writer of articles and short stories about women's lives, and teacher of women's studies in college and continuing education courses

Barakat, Hidiya (1898–1969).

See Hidaya Afifi in entry titled "Egyptian Feminists."

Baranovskaya, Vera (c. 1870–1935)

Russian actress. *Name variations: Baranovskaia. Born in Russia around 1870; died in 1935; studied with Constantin Stanislavski.*

A favorite of Constantin Stanislavski, Vera Baranovskaya was a leading lady of the Moscow Art Theater when she was chosen to play the lead in Vsevolod Pudovkin's classic movie *The Mother* in 1926. One of the great montage sequences of the film includes a mourning Baranovskaya holding vigil over her husband's corpse as water drips slowly into the bucket that rests beside her. That performance, which one critic maintains imbues the film with emotional lyricism, as well as her role in Pudovkin's *The End of St. Petersburg* the following year, led to international recognition. In 1929, Baranovskaya left Russia to further her acting career in Czechoslovakia, Germany, and France, only to retire four years later. Her films include *The Thief* (1916), *The Burden of Fate* (1917), *The Wolves* (1925), *Ruts* (1928), *Such is Life* (1929), *Poison Gas* (1929), *Monsieur*

Albert (1932), and *Les Aventures du Roi Pausole* (1933).

Baranowska, Tekla Badarzewski

(1834–1861).

See Badarzewski-Baranowska, Tekla.

Barat, Madeleine Sophie

(1779–1865)

French saint and founder of the Sacred Heart Society. *Born in Joigny, France, on December 12, 1779; died in Paris, France, on May 25, 1865; daughter of Jacques (a vinegrower) and Marie-Madeleine (Fouffé) Barat; educated at home by her brother Louis, a priest; accompanied him to Paris in 1880 to continue her education.*

According to biographer C.E. Maguire, Madeleine Sophie Barat wanted nothing more than to lead a cloistered religious life in prayer, or perhaps teach poor children. Instead, she became the founder of the "Madames of the Sacred Heart," a religious congregation known in Europe and America primarily for its education of young ladies of wealth and position. During her lifetime, Madeleine Barat devoted herself to expanding the schools, which numbered 86 at the time of her death in 1865. Her religious calling led her across Europe, as she guided the phenomenal growth of her congregation.

The daughter of a Burgundy vinegrower, Barat was educated by her brother Louis, a priest. In 1800, she accompanied her brother to Paris to continue her education, and there she met Joseph Varin D'Ainville, who persuaded her to fulfill her service to God by instilling Christian principles in the children of postrevolutionary society. In 1802, with four other women, Barat established the first Society of the Sacred Heart in Amiens, where she became superior general and head of the school for girls. Under her direction, the school flourished over the next two years, with a broad curriculum including Bible and church history, French, ancient and modern literature, mythology, music, drawing, domestic economy, mathematics and science. According to Maguire, the ultimate aim of the school was "the glory of the heart of Jesus Christ." The motto of the society later became "One Heart and one mind in the Heart of Jesus." In accordance, Maguire tells us, the nuns set out "not to produce learned ladies, though they sometimes did, but to train Christian mothers . . . women capable of bringing up their sons as well as their daughters, so that Frenchmen might again some day see their lives as God-centered."

In 1804, Barat established a second house of the Society of the Sacred Heart in Grenoble, where she met ***Rose Philippine Duchesne**, who would later introduce the congregation into the United States. (The first American convent was in St. Charles, Missouri.) After leaving Amiens, Mother Barat spent the next 60 years traveling across Europe establishing and visiting her schools, journeys often made at the expense of her frail health. Although she had little chance to teach after leaving Amiens, she remained interested in the intellectual training of her teachers and in the shaping of the society's constitutions, adopted in 1815, to unify the various branches and to guard against the influence of the court circles from which many of the students came. She also was active in resisting a number of efforts to change the constitutions, one of which, in 1839, attempted to bring the Sacred Heart more in line with the Jesuits. (Leo XII had formally approved the society on December 26, 1826.)

During the last years of her life, Barat lived in Paris and devoted much of her remaining energy to improving the studies of her nuns and pupils. In 1855, she had an interesting correspondence with **Constance Bonaparte**, the daughter of Lucien and ***Alexandrine Bonaparte**, about the education of two of her nieces. In one letter Barat warns Bonaparte to "fortify her nieces against 'the glamor of the grandeur and wealth which will be offered them.'"

Mother Barat died on May 25, 1865. Her body was first taken to Conflans, but, when her nuns were driven out of France, it was removed to Jette, Belgium, where it was enshrined. She was beatified in 1908 and canonized in 1925. By the late 20th century, Societies of the Sacred Heart were found in almost every country, with educational programs based on theology and ranging from elementary to university studies.

SOURCES:

Maguire, C.E., Mother. *Saint Madeleine Sophie Barat.* NY: Sheed and Ward, 1960.

Barbara Morgan, Melrose, Massachusetts

Baratotti, Galerana (1604–1652).

See Tarabotti, Arcangela.

Barbara (fl. 3rd c.)

Christian martyr and saint. *Lived and suffered martyrdom in the city of Nicomedia in Bithynia, Asia Minor;*

Saint Barbara

died around 235 CE; the place of her martyrdom is variously given as Heliopolis, as a town of Tuscany, and as Nicomedia, Bithynia; daughter of Dioscorus.

To prevent his daughter Barbara from being disturbed in her studies, Dioscorus built a tower, surrounded by marvelous gardens. There, she spent her youth while receiving philosophers, orators, and poets dispatched by Dioscorus to instruct her in the meaning of all things. Without her father's knowledge, Barbara became converted to Christianity by a follower of Origen and secretly baptized. She threw out her statues of the "false gods," traced the sign of the cross over walls, resolved to remain a virgin, and dedicated herself to God. When Dioscorus threatened to kill his blaspheming daughter, Barbara fled to the mountains, but she was captured and handed over to Martianus, the Roman governor of Bithynia, to be dealt with by the law.

When Martianus failed in his attempts to make Barbara repudiate Christianity, Dioscorus asked for the honor of cutting off his daughter's head in punishment. Scarcely had the deed been done when, according to legend, Dioscorus was struck by lightning. St. Barbara became the patron saint of storms and artillery. At one time, her image was frequently placed on arsenals and powder magazines, and the powder room of a French warship is still called *Sainte-Barbe*. In Raphael's *Sistine Madonna*, she is depicted on the left of the Virgin Mary. The feast day of Saint Barbara is December 4.

Barbara of Braganza (1711–1758).

See Maria Barbara of Braganza.

Barbara of Brandenburg (1422–1481)

Marquesa of Mantua. *Name variations: Barbara Gonzaga. Born in 1422; died in 1481; daughter of John III the Alchemist, margrave of Brandenburg, and *__Barbara of Saxe-Wittenberg__ (c. 1405–1465); sister of *__Dorothea of Brandenburg__ (1430–1495), queen of Norway, Denmark, and Sweden; married Louis also known as Ludovico Gonzaga (1412–1478), 2nd marquis of Mantua (r. 1444–1478); children: Federico (1441–1484), 3rd marquis of Mantua (r. 1478–1484); Francesco (1444–1483, a cardinal); Gianfrancesco (1446–1496), lord of Rodigo; __Susanna Gonzaga__ (1447–1461); *__Dorotea Gonzaga__ (1449–1462); Rodolfo (1451–1495); *__Cecilia Gonzaga__ (1451–1472); *__Barbara Gonzaga__ (1455–1505); Louis also known as Ludovico (1460–1511, bishop of Mantua); *__Paola Gonzaga__ (1463–1497).*

Barbara of Byzantium (d. 1125)

Grand princess of Kiev. *Name variations: Barbara Comnena. Died on February 28, 1125; married Svyatopolk also known as Sviatopolk II, prince of Kiev (r. 1093–1113), around 1103; children: possibly *__Zbyslawa__ (d. 1110).*

Barbara of Cilli (fl. 1390–1410)

Queen of Hungary and Bohemia. *Name variations: Borbala Cillei; Barbara Cilli. Flourished from 1390 to 1410; daughter of Count William of Cilli; second wife of Zygmunt also known as Sigismund I of Luxemburg, king of Hungary and Bohemia (r. 1387–1437), Holy Roman emperor (r. 1410–1437); children: *__Elizabeth of Luxemburg__ (1409–1442, who married Albert II, king of Hungary). Sigismund I's first wife was *__Maria of Hungary__ (1371–1395).*

Barbara of Poland (1478–1534)

Duchess of Saxony. *Born on July 15, 1478; died on February 15, 1534; daughter of Casimir IV Jagiellon (or Kazimierz), grand duke of Lithuania (r. 1440–1492), king of Poland (r. 1446–1492), and *__Elizabeth of Hungary__ (c. 1430–1505); married George the Bearded (1471–1539), duke of Saxony (r. 1500–1539), on November 21, 1496; children: *__Christine of Saxony__ (1505–1549); *__Magdalene of Saxony__ (1507–1534).*

Barbara of Saxe-Wittenberg (c. 1405–1465)

Margravine of Brandenburg. *Born around 1405; died on October 10, 1465; daughter of Rudolf III, duke of Saxe-Wittenberg; married John III the Alchemist (b. 1406), margrave of Brandenburg, in 1412; children: *__Dorothea of Brandenburg__ (1430–1495); *__Barbara of Brandenburg__ (1422–1481).*

Barbara Radziwell (1520–1551).

See Sforza, Bona for sidebar.

Barbara Zapolya (fl. 1500)

Queen of Poland. *Name variations: Barbara Zápolya of Hungary; Szapolyai. Flourished in 1500; sister of John or Jan Zapolya, king of Hungary (r. 1526–1540); first wife of Sigismund I the Elder, king of Poland (r. 1506–1548); children: *__Hedwig of Poland__ (1513–1573, who married Joachim II, elector of Brandenburg). Sigismund's second wife was *__Bona Sforza__ (1493–1557).*

Barbarina, La (1721–1799).

See Campanini, Barbara.

Barbauld, Anna Letitia (1743–1825)

English author. *Born Anna Laetitia Aikin in Kibworth-Harcourt, Leicestershire, England, on June 20,*

1743; died on March 9, 1825; daughter of John Aikin (a Unitarian minister and schoolmaster, who taught her Latin and Greek); sister of English physician John Aikin; aunt of Lucy Aikin; married Reverend Rochemont Barbauld, in 1774 (died 1808).

Anna Letitia Barbauld

During her early education which was directed by the Reverend John Aikin, her Unitarian minister father, Anna Barbauld is said to have displayed unusual talent as a child. In 1758, the family moved to Warrington, where her father was a theological tutor in an academy. Fifteen years later, in 1773, Anna's first volume, *Poems*, appeared and ran through four editions in a year; she also co-authored, with her brother Dr. John Aikin, a volume of *Miscellaneous Pieces in Prose*. In 1774, she married Rochemont Barbauld, a member of a French Protestant family settled in England, who had been educated in the academy at Warrington, and was minister of a Presbyterian church at Palgrave, in Suffolk. That year, the couple founded a boys' boarding school there; her *Hymns in Prose and Early Lessons* was written for their pupils. During the next ten years, Barbauld also wrote the devotional works *Early Lessons for Children* and *Devotional Pieces*.

In 1785, she left England for the Continent with her husband, who was in poor health. On their return about two years later, he was appointed to a church at Hampstead. In 1802, they moved to Stoke Newington, where Barbauld became well known in London literary circles. In 1792, she and her brother initiated a series of prose sketches entitled *Evenings at Home* (1792–95). During her long life (she lived to be 82), Barbauld wrote the life of Samuel Richardson, edited Mark Akenside's *Pleasures of the Imagination* and William Collins' *Odes*, and a collection of the *British Novelists* with memoirs and criticisms. Her writings were distinguished by their pure moral tone, simplicity, and sincerity, and her books for children were considered among the best of their class. Her last work was an ode, "Eighteen Hundred and Eleven," which gave a pessimistic view of Britain and its future.

A collected edition of her works, with memoir, was published by her niece, ***Lucy Aikin**, in two volumes (1825). See also A.L. le Breton's *Memoir of Mrs Barbauld* (1874), G.A. Ellis' *Life and Letters of Mrs. A.L. Barbauld* (1874), and Lady Thackeray Ritchie's *A Book of Sibyls* (1883).

Barberina, La (1721–1799).

See Campanini, Barbara.

Barbi, Alice (1862–1948)

Italian mezzo-soprano, lieder singer, and close friend of Johannes Brahms. *Born on June 1, 1862, in Modena, Italy; died in Rome, Italy, on September 4, 1948; married second husband Pietro della Torretta (Italian ambassador to Great Britain); retired early after a brilliant concert career.*

Alice Barbi is largely remembered for having been "the last love of Johannes Brahms"—a platonic friendship that brightened the final years of the lonely bachelor composer. Described by Max Graf, who often heard her perform in Vienna in the late 1880s and early 1890s, as "a dark Italian beauty with dreamy black eyes," Barbi grew up in her native city of Modena where she first studied violin, an instrument she thoroughly mastered. During these years, she received a solid training in musical theory and learned several foreign languages.

Deciding not to become an instrumentalist, Barbi studied voice and quickly reached a high level of professionalism. Her concert debut as a singer took place in Milan in 1882, which was soon followed by a highly successful appearance in Rome. Before long, she was known throughout Italy, enjoying star status as a concert performer in a country where virtually all singers based their careers on singing opera. Barbi, however, recognized that her strength lay in song recitals and never performed in opera. Early in her career, she decided to specialize in the lieder repertoire, her programs regularly consisted of the songs of Schubert, Schumann, and Brahms. Many decades later, Max Graf would describe her art in the most glowing terms: "The combination of Italian sense of melody, southern beauty, true musical form and deep expression flowing from the soul was never more perfect than in this singer."

By 1884, Alice Barbi was appearing in Great Britain, where she drew large crowds at London's Popular Concerts series. Within a few years, she was performing in Russia, Germany and Austria. At her first concert in Vienna in 1888, she was a virtually unknown foreign artist, and her audience was limited to 50 individuals, several of them influential critics whose tickets were supplied gratis by the concert management. The powerful impression Barbi made on her select audience led to a second concert, which was sold out and brought rave reviews in the Viennese press. All of her subsequent appearances in Vienna would prove artistic and popular triumphs.

Soon after her initial success in the Austrian capital, Barbi met Johannes Brahms. Captivated by her poise, rich contralto voice, and radiant beauty, the bearded, portly composer soon was observed regularly escorting her to restaurants and other places of interest. On one occasion, Brahms took Barbi to an establishment that featured a "Schrammel" ensemble that performed popular Viennese music. After playing several traditional Viennese pieces, the group struck up an American popular tune of the day, "Ta-ra-ra-boom-de-ay." As the "boom" was sounded it was customary to strike the table with one's walking stick or thump it with one's beer stein. One observer of the evening recalled that Brahms, buoyed up in the company of Alice Barbi, could be seen exuberantly rapping his umbrella on the table, "a little boy with a gray beard." Those who knew the details of Brahms' life history of unrequited loves suggested that Barbi, "his last love," perhaps served to remind him of another great singer with whom he had been in love in his youth, **Hermine Spiese**.

In her early 30s, Barbi decided to marry and end her fabulously successful concert career. Shortly before her farewell recital in Vienna, on December 21, 1893, Johannes Brahms appeared unannounced at her dressing room door, astonishing Barbi by requesting that in place of the scheduled accompanist he wished to accompany her at the piano. On that emotion-laden evening, a favored audience not only heard the most beautiful of Brahms' lieder sung by a great artist but also superbly performed on the keyboard by the composer himself.

Barbi was deeply moved by the death of her friend Johannes Brahms in 1897 and was among the most enthusiastic supporters of the committee that collected funds to erect a monument in his honor in his adopted city of Vienna. Although retired from active concertizing, she remained passionately interested in music and the arts, and her elegant home in Rome became a major center of cultural activities. Barbi wrote poetry during these years, some of which was set to music by the composer Antonio Bazzini. She also composed some small-scale works and edited a collection of ancient Italian airs. No doubt relishing her reputation as a brilliant singer of a great epoch of music, she was for many decades a major celebrity in the highest strata of European diplomacy and the arts, having chosen as her second husband Pietro della Torretta, the Italian ambassador to Great Britain. Alice Barbi died at age 86 in Rome on September 4, 1948.

SOURCES:

Chiti, Patricia Adkins. *Donne in Musica.* Rome: Bulzoni Editore, 1982.

Graf, Max. *Legend of a Musical City.* NY: Philosophical Library, 1945.

Hanslick, Eduard. "Ein Monument für Brahms," in *Neue Freie Presse* [Vienna]. April 4, 1898.

Huschke, Konrad. "Johannes Brahms' letzte Liebe" in *Leipziger Neueste Nachrichten.* November 10, 1931.

Kutsch, K.J., and Leo Riemens. *Grosses Sängerlexikon.* 2 vols. Berne and Stuttgart: Francke Verlag, 1987.

Pulver, Jeffrey. "Brahms's Contemporary Singers," in *Monthly Musical Record.* Vol. 64, no. 754. February 1934, pp. 35–36.

John Haag, Associate Professor,
University of Georgia, Athens, Georgia

Barbieri, Fedora (1919—)

Italian mezzo-soprano. *Born in Trieste, Italy, on June 4, 1919; daughter of Rafaele and Ida Barbieri (both shopkeepers); studied with Luigi Toffolo and Giulia Tess; married Luigi Barlozzetti (an impresario), in 1943; children: two sons, Franco (b. 1944) and Ugo (b. 1955).*

Debuted in Florence as Fidelma in Matrimonio segreto *(1940); made debut as Meg Page in* Falstaff *at Teatro alla Scala (1942); after 1946, was a regular performer at Teatro alla Scala; made Metropolitan Opera debut as Eboli in Verdi's* Don Carlos *(1950); appeared often at the Met (1950–68); also debuted at Covent Garden (1950).*

The "meaty" voice of the mezzo-soprano has been often missing on opera stages in the late 20th century, but Fedora Barbieri, born in Trieste, Italy, on June 4, 1919, possessed such a voice. After training with Luigi Toffolo and **Giulia Tess**, Barbieri debuted in Florence in 1940. Following her marriage to Luigi Barlozzetti, the director of Florence's Maggio Musicale, her career prospered. With her magnificent vocal style, she soon appeared on the stages of Teatro alla Scala (1942), the Metropolitan Opera (1950–68) and Covent Garden (1950). On Rudolf Bing's opening night at the Met, she debuted as Eboli in *Don Carlos*. She often sang

Fedora Barbieri

Adalgisa in *Norma* with *Maria Callas in the starring role, and Mario Del Monaco was frequently her partner in *Carmen*. Barbieri made few commercial recordings, and these performances are somewhat marred.

John Haag, Athens, Georgia

Barbosa, Pilar (1898–1997)

Puerto Rican historian and first woman to teach at the University of Puerto Rico. *Born Pilar Barbosa de Rosario on July 4, 1897, in San Juan, Puerto Rico; died at a hospital near her home in San Juan on January 22, 1997; daughter of José Celso Barbosa (founder of the Puerto Rican statehood movement); her mother died when she was quite young; University of Puerto Rico, B.Ed., 1924; M.A., Clark University, Worcester, Massachusetts, 1925; married José Ezequiel Rosario (an economics professor), in 1927 (died 1963); no children.*

Taught at the University of Puerto Rico (1926–1967); established and headed the history and social sciences department at the university, the first woman to head a department there (1927); collaborated with Dr. Antonio S. Pedreira on a series of articles on the history of Puerto Rico (1937); was president and founder of La Obra de José Celso Barbosa y Alcalá, Inc.; received first of four first prizes from the Puerto Rican Institute of Literature for her book on

Puerto Rican autonomism from 1887–97; founded the Historical Society of Puerto Rico with Angel Roberto Diaz and Victor M. Gerena (1967); retired from the university (1967); received the Golden Book Award for 50 years service to Puerto Rican education (1967); recognized by the University of Puerto Rico as Professor Emeritus (1975); given the U.S. Outstanding Leadership Award by President Ronald Reagan and the National Institute of Education during a White House Ceremony in the Rose Garden (1984); received honorary doctorate from the University of Puerto Rico (1992); appointed Official Historian of Puerto Rico (1993); honored with a plaque for lifetime achievement by the House of Representatives of Puerto Rico (March 1997); installation of an oil painting in the gallery of Outstanding Women under the auspices of the Senate of Puerto Rico (March 1999).

Charismatic, influential and intelligent, Pilar Barbosa de Rosario was revered on the island of Puerto Rico. When she died in January 1997, Governor Pedro Rossello proclaimed a three-day mourning period throughout the nation, and six members of the Legislature stood as an honor guard around her coffin. "She leaves a void difficult to fill," said Luis González Vales, president of Puerto Rico Academy of History. "She taught her students to respect differing opinions, the importance of ducumentation and a commitment to history."

Her father José Celso Barbosa was the founder of the Puerto Rican statehood movement, a precursor of the New Progressive Party. Over the years, Pilar Barbosa insisted that the party of statehood embrace the task of social justice, but she was primarily a teacher, the first woman to join the faculty at the University of Puerto Rico. During her tenure (1926–67), she was responsible for establishing the departments of history and social studies; she also became such a noted authority on Puerto Rico's past that, in 1993, she was named the nation's official historian. Her home was like "an intellectual watering hole," recalled Gonzalo Cordova, a fellow teacher. "You didn't come to drink, but for the conversation." Students, politicians, and officials from the government sought her advice and companionship. When she died at age 99, Barbosa was "the mother confessor to generations of Puerto Rican politicians, scholars and intellectuals," wrote a journalist for The New York Times News Service, "widely regarded as the conscience of the ruling New Progressive Party."

SOURCES:

"Pilar Barbosa, 99, Puerto Rican Political Mentor, Dies," in *The New York Times*. January 24, 1997, p. A15.

San Juan Star. January 23 and January 31, 1997.

Washington Post (obit). January 25, 1997.

Pilar Barbosa

Barca, Frances Calderón de la (1804–1882).

See Calderón de la Barca, Frances.

Barca-Theodosia (fl. 800s)

Byzantine empress. *Flourished in the 800s; married Leo V Gnuni, the Armenian, Byzantine emperor (r. 813–820).*

Barcelo, Gertrudis (c. 1820–1852)

Entrepreneur and monte dealer in Santa Fe, New Mexico. *Name variations: La Tules (diminutive of Gertrudis); Doña Gertrudis (doña or don were titles bestowed on families or individuals of highest social standing); Señora Doña Gertrudis Barcelo. Born around 1820, possibly in Valencia County, New Mexico; death date unknown, but buried in Santa Fe, New*

Mexico, on January 17, 1852; one of two daughters and three children of Juan Ignacio and Dolores Herrero (Barcelo); married Manuel Antonio Sisneros, on June 20, 1823; children: Jose Pedro (b. 1823) and Miguel Antonio (b. 1825).

There is much conjecture in historical accounts of the life and times of Gertrudis Barcelo and little to document events of her childhood. Church records reveal the names of her mother, father, sister, and brother, and further record her marriage to Manuel Antonio Sisneros at Tome, on June 20, 1823. The couple settled in Santa Fe, where Gertrudis put her intelligence to work, learning to play the Spanish-American card game of monte well enough to become an expert at dealing. She saved enough from her winnings to establish her own gambling house and saloon of repute, or disrepute, depending on the point of view of any given account.

Barcelo's establishment was a cut above the frontier gambling parlor found in the boom towns of America. Her *sala*—with carpeted floors, candlelit chandeliers, and music, often provided by her husband—attracted the city's elite. Europeans, Americans, and Mexicans frequented the monte table; even women were drawn, writes **Grace Ray**, to the "glittering goddess of chance, often costing them their rings, brooches, and even their rebosas with golden fringe."

There are descriptions of Barcelo as a sultry, green-eyed beauty, clad in fashionable silk or satin, who sported several gold chains around her neck and rings on every finger. She has also been described, however, in less glowing terms. Wrote one contemporary: "Her face bore unmistakably the impress of her fearful calling, being scarred and seamed and rendered unwomanly by those painful lines which unbridled passions and midnight watching never fail to stamp upon the countenance of their votary." Another account speaks simply of her "false teeth and false hair."

Accusations of prostitution surfaced, particularly among the more puritan in spirit, who had difficulty enough with gambling, drinking, and smoking. The rumor of impropriety may also have been perpetuated by writers from the East, who were unfamiliar with the Hispanic culture of the day. Whatever the case, there seems to be no solid proof that Barcelo bestowed any sexual favors. She was sometimes privy to military intrigues though, as well as political and business schemes.

Barcelo amassed a relative fortune and lived well, with a corral of mules, a carriage, and at least three houses in Santa Fe. When attending fiestas in surrounding villages, she was said to have traveled with her leather-covered money chests, which were so heavy it took four men to carry each. By some accounts, she provided assistance to the poor and to the church, but she did not seem to be known for her philanthropy.

Toward the end of her life, widowed, she evidently wearied of monte. Indulging instead in "sweet chocolate drinks and iced cakes," she grew quite overweight. Although the date of her death is unknown, Barcelo's expensive funeral was held in Santa Fe on January 17, 1852. It is reported that at her death she was worth somewhere in the vicinity of $10,000, a great sum for her day. Evidently, her will included every last member of her family except her two sons, causing historians to speculate that they may have predeceased their successful mother.

SOURCES:

Ray, Grace Ernestine. *Wily Women of the West.* San Antonio, TX: Naylor, 1972.

Barbara Morgan, Melrose, Massachusetts

Barcelona, countess of.

See Maria de las Mercedes (b. 1910).

Barcitotti, Galerana (1604–1652).

See Tarabotti, Arcangela.

Barclay, Florence Louisa (1862–1921)

English author of popular romances, including* The Rosary, *which has gone through more than 20 editions. *Name variations: (pseudonym) Brandon Roy. Born Florence Louisa Charlesworth on December 2, 1862, in Limpsfield, Surrey, England; died on March 10, 1921; daughter of Reverend Samuel Charlesworth; niece of* **Maria Charlesworth** *(a children's author); sister of Maud Ballington Booth (1865–1948); married Reverend Charles W. Barclay, in 1881; children: six daughters and two sons.*

Selected works: The Wheels of Time *(1908);* The Rosary *(1910);* The Following of the Star *(1911);* The White Ladies of Worcester *(1917).*

The middle of three sisters, Florence Charlesworth was born in her father's rectory in 1862. Seven years later, Reverend Samuel Charlesworth moved his family to the London parish where Florence was raised and schooled. During an 1879 visit to Belstead, she was introduced to Reverend Charles Barclay, whom she married two years later. Florence was 19 when she moved to Barclay's vicarage in Hertford,

Hertfordshire. On the couple's honeymoon in Palestine, they believed themselves to have been led to the true mouth of Jacob's Well, and the spiritual discovery provided Barclay fodder for a lecture tour to the United States with her sister ***Maud Ballington Booth.**

Daily life was filled with children—the Barclays had eight—and church business such as Bible readings. Generally believed to be psychic, Barclay was said to "charm birds" from the trees and find lost things. For a nine-month period in 1905, she became bedridden after a bike ride was said to have overtaxed her heart. Already a published author, Barclay's first book had been published in 1891, under the pseudonym Brandon Roy. Now, during her convalescence, she wrote *The Wheels of Time*, the first of her romances, published in 1908, and *The Rosary*, published in 1910. *The Rosary*, which sold 150,000 copies in its first year, was only mildly more successful than *The Following of the Star* published in 1911. Another book *The Mistress of Shenstone* (1910) was filmed with **Pauline Frederick** (1883–1938). Over the next decade, Barclay produced a book a year, even in 1912, when she suffered a cerebral hemorrhage from a blow to the head. Amazingly, a second blow by an oar, suffered while boating, was credited with curing her.

Florence Barclay died on March 10, 1921, at age 58, under anesthetic preparatory to surgery. At the time of her death, *The Rosary* had sold more than one million copies. A biography, *The Life of Florence L. Barclay: By One of Her Daughters*, was published soon after.

Crista Martin, freelance writer, Boston, Massachusetts

Bard, Anne Elizabeth Campbell (1908–1958).

See MacDonald, Betty.

Bard, Mary (b. 1904).

See MacDonald, Betty for sidebar.

Bardi, Contessina de.

See Medici, Contessina de.

Baret, Jeanne (1740–?)

French adventurer and research assistant who became the first woman to circumnavigate the world. *Name variations: Jeanne Barret, Jeanne Mercadier. Born into modest circumstances in Bourgogne, France, in 1740; date of death unknown, but she was still alive in 1795; married a soldier named Antoine Barnier (or Antoine Du Bernat).*

Worked in Paris as a servant for the botanist Philibert Commerson and hired on as a male valet for the expedition led by Louis-Antoine de Bougainville (1764); was of great help to Commerson in his botanical research; several newly discovered plants were named for her; returned to France after Commerson's death (1773).

On September 6, 1764, a young woman calling herself Jeanne Baret was hired as a servant by the noted botanist Philibert Commerson. With her move from the provinces to Paris to seek her fortune, Baret enters the pages of history. Unfortunately, much of the documentary record relating to her is spotty and at times confusing. The reliability of her name is questionable; it is sometimes spelled Jeanne Barret, and in her last will and testament she asserted that her real name was in fact Jeanne Mercadier. The precise nature of the relationship between Baret and Commerson also remains obscure, and it is unclear whether she was simply his servant or actually his mistress. Regardless, we know the link between these two individuals from very different social strata involved a mutual respect for one another as they worked together in botanical projects that were intellectually—and sometimes physically—demanding.

One of the most remarkable voyages of discovery during the 18th century's age of science and exploration was the circumnavigation of the earth led by the French navigator Louis Antoine de Bougainville (1729–1811) in the years 1766–1769. Philibert Commerson was the botanist of this expedition, which set sail on December 14, 1766, with the frigate *La Boudeuse* and the transport *L'Étoile*. In the will that Commerson wrote prior to his departure, he left Jeanne Baret an annual pension of 100 livres and ownership of the furniture in his Paris apartment. What Commerson may not have known at the time he boarded *La Boudeuse* was that the male valet named Bonnefoy who also boarded the frigate for the great adventure was none other than his servant Jeanne Baret. Under the excellent leadership of Captain Bougainville, over the next months the expedition visited several ports on the east coast of South America and survived the treacherous currents of the Straits of Magellan to enter the Pacific Ocean. During this time, "Bonnefoy" assisted Commerson in his botanical field trips, discovering a number of valuable specimens and assisting in their preservation and cataloguing.

Baret's deception, if Commerson was in fact being deceived, ended in Tahiti, where she was recognized by local women as one of their own sex. Deeply disturbed by the presence of a woman on his vessel, Captain Bougainville interrogated Commerson, who denied all knowledge of what had been taking place. When Bougainville interrogated Jeanne Baret, she displayed great self-confidence, admitting in an emotional scene that she had desired to participate in a great adventure, and did not in fact regret what she had done. Bougainville, impressed by her courage and strong personality, pardoned Baret and insisted that her identity be kept a secret for the duration of the voyage. For the remainder of the expedition, she continued to work assiduously, collecting and categorizing a large range of botanical specimens. Despite her lack of formal education, Commerson saw in her a valuable scientific collaborator whose energy and knowledge added greatly to the integrity of his data.

The Bougainville expedition returned to France in March 1769. Of a crew of more than 200, only seven had died. Due in large part to the work of Commerson and Baret, a sizeable body of new botanical data was discovered, including the South American climbing plant *Bougainvillea*, named for the captain. Paying homage to Baret, Philibert Commerson named both a genera (*Baretia*) and a species of plant (*Bonna fidia*) in her honor.

After Commerson died in 1773 during an expedition to the island of Madagascar, Jeanne Baret married a soldier named Antoine Barnier and inherited the pension stipulated years before in Commerson's will. By this time, Baret had achieved the status of a celebrity as the first woman to circumnavigate the globe. Showing the admiration and gratitude of the crown, King Louis XV granted her an annual pension of 200 livres. Bougainville's favorable description of her participation in his expedition, published in his 1771 account of the voyage, served to further enhance her reputation. After the death of her husband, Jeanne Baret lived in Chatillon-les-Dombes. Her name disappears from the documentary record after 1795 when she filed a will; she possibly died soon after. Her continuing fondness for her benefactor Philibert Commerson was evidenced by this last will and testament, which instructed that her property be distributed among his heirs.

SOURCES:

Boissel, Thierry. *Bougainville, ou, L'Homme de l'univers.* Paris: O. Orban, 1991.

Bougainville, Louis-Antoine de. *A Voyage Round the World.* Translated by John Reinhold Forster. NY: Da Capo Press, 1967.

Craig, Robert D. *Historical Dictionary of Polynesia.* Metuchen, NJ: Scarecrow Press, 1993.

D'Amat, Roman. "Baret (Jeanne)," in M. Prevost and Roman D'Amat, eds., *Dictionnaire de Biographie Francaise.* Vol. 5, cols. 448–449.

Wilson, Derek. *The Circumnavigators.* NY: M. Evans, 1989.

John Haag, Associate Professor,
University of Georgia, Athens, Georgia

Barker, Cicely Mary (1895–1973)

British artist, author and illustrator of children's books who was best known for her "Flower Fairies" series. *Born in Waddon, Croydon, Surrey, England, on June 28, 1895; died in Worthing, Sussex, England, on February 16, 1973; daughter of Walter (a seed merchant and woodcarver) and Mary Eleanor Oswald Barker; sister Dorothy (b. 1893); attended Croyden School of Art.*

Selected writings—except as noted, all for children, all self-illustrated, all originally published by Blackie & Son: Flower Fairies of the Spring *(verse, 1923);* Flower Fairies of the Summer *(verse, 1925);* Flower Fairies of the Autumn, with the Nuts and Berries They Bring *(verse, 1926);* The Book of Flower Fairies *(verse, 1927); (editor)* Old Rhymes for All Times *(1928);* A Flower Fairy Alphabet *(1934); (editor)* A Little Book of Old Rhymes *(1936);* The Lord of the Rushie River *(fiction, 1938);* Fairies of the Trees *(verse, 1940);* When Spring Came in at the Window *(one-act play; music by Olive Linnell, 1942);* Flower Fairies of the Garden *(verse, 1944);* Groundsel and Necklaces *(fiction, 1946);* Flower Fairies of the Wayside *(verse, 1948);* Lively Stories *(5 vols., 1954–55);* Flower Fairy Picture Book *(verse, 1955);* Lively Numbers *(3 vols., 1960–62);* Lovely Words *(2 vols., 1961–62);* The Sand, the Sea, and the Sun *(1970).*

Illustrator: (With Beatrice A. Waldram) The "Guardian Angel" Series of Birthday Cards *(S.P.C.K., 1923);* Beautiful Bible Pictures *(Blackie & Sons, 1932);* The Little Picture Hymn Book *(Blackie & Son, 1933); Dorothy O. Barker,* He Leadeth Me: A Book of Bible Stories *(Blackie & Son, 1936);* The Flower Fairies Address Book. *Also illustrator of* Laugh and Learn *by Jennett Humphreys and* The Children's Book of Hymns.

Cicely Mary Barker, the frail daughter of a talented woodcarver, began painting in childhood and found a talent she would continue developing for the rest of her life. Best known for her "Flower Fairies" series of self-illustrated children's books, her paintings were exclusively of children, who were more often than not surrounded by flowers. Influenced heavily by ***Kate Greenaway**, Barker once said of her work, "I

Cicely Mary Barker on left with her mother and sister Dorothy.

have always tried to paint instinctively in a way that comes naturally to me, without any real thought or attention to artistic theories."

Suffering with childhood epilepsy, Barker spent long periods in bed and was tutored at home. Her only formal education came from a correspondence course in drawing and evening classes at the Croyden School of Art. At age 15, she sold a set of painted postcards to the printer-publisher Raphael Tuck, beginning her commercial career, and a year later she won second prize in a poster contest run by the Croydon Art Society. Soon after, she was elected to life membership in the Society, becoming their youngest member. Barker served as vice-president from 1961 to 1972 and remained their longest serving member until her death.

In 1912, her beloved father died unexpectedly at age 43. To sustain the family, her sister **Dorothy Barker** opened a school in their home. In 1924, the family moved to 23 The Waldrons in Croydon; their home continued to house Dorothy's kindergarten, while Cicely set up a studio in the garden shed. Cicely adored being surrounded by children and often borrowed a student from the school to use as a model. Despite early rejections for her first book *Flower Fairies*, she had continued to submit it to publishers; it was finally printed when she was 29 by Blackie & Son, who would continue to publish the numerous works to follow. During her career, Barker also produced portraits and church murals. One of her paintings, "The Darling of the World is Come," was purchased by Queen Mary. She also designed a church window in memory of her sister, for St. Edmund's Church in Pitlake, where her father had played the organ and carved the pulpit.

Barker maintained that her greatest influence was the Pre-Raphaelites and their fascination with the simplicity, romance and pageantry of the Middle Ages. She especially liked "the early painting of [John Everett] Millais and, though he is later, the wonderful things of [Edward] Burne-Jones." Completely devoted to her work, she even carried a pencil and sketchbook

The flower fairies of Cicely Mary Barker.

on holidays in order to rapidly sketch interesting children. Her private life revolved around family, religion, and a select group of friends, including artist *__Margaret Tarrant__. Barker made generous contributions to many—the deprived young, the Girl Guides, the Girls Diocesan Association—and each Christmas she painted a picture for the Girls Friendly Society.

In 1954, when Dorothy, who had taken over household chores to free Cicely for her art, died of a heart attack, Barker stopped painting and took over the care of her elderly mother. Six years later, when her mother died at age 91, Barker resumed her work, completing a stained-glass window for the church of St. Edmund's Pitlake in honor of her sister. During her later years, the artist was forced to move to smaller quarters in Storrington, but she retained a studio until failing health and eyesight made her rely on others for care. Cicely Mary Barker died at Worthy Hospital in Croydon, on February 16, 1973, the 50th anniversary of the first publication of her internationally famous "Flower Fairies" series.

SOURCES:

"Centenary of Cicely Mary Barker, the Artist who Created the Flower Fairies," in *This England.* Vol. 24, no. 4. Winter 1995, pp. 35–37.

Commire, Anne. *Something about the Author.* Volume 49. Detroit, MI: Gale Research.

Dalby, Richard. *The Golden Age of Children's Books.* NY: Gallery Books, 1991.

Barbara Morgan, Melrose, Massachusetts

Barker, Kate "Ma" (1872–1935).

See Barker, Ma.

Barker, Ma (1872–1935)

***Notorious outlaw of the 1930s.** Name variations: Arizona Donnie Clark; Kate "Ma" Barker. Born Arizona Donnie Clark, near Springfield, Missouri, in 1872; died in Oklawaha, Florida, on January 16, 1935; married George Barker, around 1892; children: Herman, Lloyd, Dock, and Fred.*

With an outlaw mentality rivaling that of Jesse James, Dillinger, or Baby Face Nelson, a dumpy, middle-aged woman, with a motherly face, masterminded holdups in the Missouri-Oklahoma area for 12 years, terrorizing businessmen and bankers, and prompting F.B.I. director J. Edgar Hoover to call her a "mean, vicious beast of prey. . . a she-wolf." Arizona Donnie Clark, or "Ma" Barker, as she was more commonly known, rose to head one of the last notorious outlaw bands in the country and died in a fierce shootout with Federal agents on January 16, 1935.

The first comparatively uneventful years of Barker's life were spent in the Ozark mountains. At age 20, she married a farm laborer, George Barker, and lived as a model Presbyterian wife and mother of four boys—Herman, Lloyd, Dock, and Fred. This idyllic family picture faded when, as teenagers, the boys started harassing neighbors and robbing local merchants. Staunchly defending them, Barker did whatever she could to keep them away from the police and out of court.

By 1915, Barker and her troubled family were living in a two-room shack, where she set up a "cooling off" service for convicts or crooks on the run. They had only to show up at her door, and she would provide food, shelter, and "how-to" advice on criminal activities. One of the first graduates of her program, an outlaw called Al Spencer, paid his debt to Ma by holding up a passenger train and seizing more than $20,000 in cash and bonds. From then on, throughout the 1920s, Barker acted as the brains behind countless robberies and bank raids for a percentage, keeping herself in funds and out of jail.

Barker left her husband, and lived from town to town with a succession of lovers, planning robberies, kidnappings, and murders for the now notorious Barker Gang (also known as the Holden-Keating Gang). Keeping tight rein over her "boys," she became bolder, visiting target banks herself under the guise of opening "a modest account with the money left me by my dear husband." These visits were opportunities to case banks for the location of the safe and the placement of security.

After a final million-dollar bank raid at Concordia, Kansas, and the kidnapping of the president of the Commercial State Bank of Minneapolis, Barker took to the hideout at Lake Weir in Florida with her son Fred in tow, while the F.B.I. was busy rallying forces and planning their January 16 assault. There are conflicting reports on the details of the final confrontation, but, during a reportedly six-hour siege, the cottage was attacked by machine guns, rifles, and tear gas. Ma Barker was found in an upstairs room, beside her son, with three bullet wounds and a .300 gas-operated automatic rifle still "hot in her hands." According to another report, more than $10,000 in large denomination bills was found in her pocketbook.

Barbara Morgan, Melrose, Massachusetts

Barker, Mary Anne (1831–1911)

British Commonwealth writer, known primarily for early histories of colonial New Zealand. *Name variations: Lady Mary Anne Barker; Lady Broome. Born Mary Anne Stewart in 1831 in Spanish Town, Jamaica; died on March 6, 1911, in London, England; daughter of W.G. Stewart (a Jamaican Island secretary); educated in England; married Captain George Barker, around 1852 (died 1861); married Frederick Napier Broome, on June 21, 1865 (died 1896); children: (first marriage) John Stewart (b. 1853) and Walter George (b. 1857); (second marriage) Hopton Napier (1866–1866), Guy Saville (b. 1870), and Louis Egerton (b. 1875).*

Selected works: Station Life in New Zealand *(1870);* Travelling About Over Old and New Ground *(1871);* A Christmas Cake in Four Quarters *(1872);* Station Amusements in New Zealand *(1873);* First Lessons in the Principles of Cookery *(1874);* A Year's Housekeeping in South Africa *(1877);* Letters to Guy *(1885);* Colonial Memories *(1904).*

Lady Mary Anne Barker was born in 1831 in Spanish Town, Jamaica, the daughter of W.G. Stewart who held a British colonial government post there. At age two, she was put on board a ship and sent to England, where she was schooled for the next 20 years. Around 1852, she married British Royal Artillery officer George Barker. With her two sons, Barker remained in England while her husband was posted first in the Crimea, then in India, where he and his company withstood the Indian mutiny of 1857. For his efforts, George was knighted in 1859. The following year, Lady Barker accompanied him on his next deployment to Bengal. When Sir George died of illness in 1861, she returned to England and lived with her family and sons for the next several years.

Ma Barker

In 1865, 34-year-old Lady Barker married a 23-year-old New Zealand sheep farmer, Frederick Napier Broome, at Prees, Shropshire, England, retaining her title and first husband's name. Within months, Broome convinced his new wife to return with him to New Zealand, arguing that the largely rough-settled island would present an adventure for them. While Barker's two young sons remained in school in England, the couple set sail, arriving in New Zealand that October.

In February of 1866, Broome and Lady Barker teamed up with another man to purchase a Canterbury sheep run. The next month, the couple welcomed their first (Lady Barker's third) son, Hopton Napier, but the boy lived less than two months. In the beginning, his death was one of few adversities Lady Barker experienced. She enjoyed the rough country and, with Broome, adopted a stimulating routine. Not much of a businessman, Broome left most matters to his partner; instead, as a poet, he spent mornings writing and afternoons hunting and trekking the land. He encouraged his wife along a similar path, and Lady Barker began writing detailed letters home, after which she enjoyed outdoor exercise and the activities of farm life.

They lived this way for almost two years, before a snowstorm in late 1867 killed 4,000 of the station's 7,000 sheep. The economic loss was devastating, and the couple quickly sold out their portion of the sheep run to their partner. When Lady Barker and Broome returned to England early in 1868, they were reunited with her sons, and both took up journalism to support the family.

In 1870, the letters Lady Barker had penned to her family were collected and published as *Station Life in New Zealand.* For the next decade, she authored 15 books on colonial life, children's stories, and homemaking and cooking. The 1874 publication of *First Lessons in the Principles of Cookery* earned her an appointment as superintendent for the National Training School for Cookery in London. She and Broome became parents of two more sons.

Beginning in 1875, Broome became involved in colonial governance. Once more, Lady Barker accompanied her husband to his assignments in the British colonies and captured the essence of their experiences in her books. They traveled to Natal in South Africa, and Mauritius, an independent island in the Indian Ocean. In 1882, Broome was named governor of Western Australia where they lived for eight years. For his service to the government, Broome was knighted in 1884, after which Lady Barker changed her name to Lady Broome. In 1891, they were assigned to Trinidad and lived there for five years. It was to be the last outpost. In 1896, on the death of her husband, Barker returned to England and petitioned the Australian government for a pension. It was granted, and the sum kept her comfortably for her remaining 15 years in Eaton Terrace, London. Her book *Colonial Memories*, published in 1904, summed up her traveling experiences.

Though she documented colonial life in a number of British-held territories, Barker's New Zealand experiences have earned her the most lasting reputation. She is considered a literary legend and trailblazer in that country, where her books continue to be reprinted and admired.

SOURCES:

Blain, Virginia, Pat Clements, and Isobel Grundy, eds. *The Feminist Companion to Literature in English.* New Haven, CT: Yale University Press, 1990.

Buck, Claire, ed. *The Bloomsbury Guide to Women's Literature.* NY: Prentice Hall, 1992.

The Dictionary of New Zealand Biography, Volume I. Wellington, NZ: Allen and Unwin, 1990.

McLauchlan, Gordon, ed. *The Illustrated Encyclopedia of New Zealand.* Auckland: David Bateman: 1986.

Sinclair, Keith, ed. *Oxford Illustrated History of New Zealand.* Auckland: Oxford University Press, 1990.

Crista Martin, freelance writer, Boston, Massachusetts

Barking, abbess of.

See Segrave, Anne (fl. 1300s).
See Ethelburga (d. 676?).

Barkova, Ánna Aleksandrovna (1901–1976)

Russian writer whose revolutionary poetry resulted in her 20-year imprisonment. *Name variations: Ánna Aleksándrovna Barkóva; (pseudonym) Kalika perekhozhaia (Wandering Cripple or Wandering Beggar-Bard). Born Anna Aleksandrovna Barkova on July 16, 1901, in Ivanovo-Voznesensk, Russia; died on April 29, 1976, in Moscow; educated at a public school (gymnasium); never married; no children.*

Selected works: Woman *(1922); (play)* Natas'ia Kostër *(Natas'ia Bonfire, 1923).*

Though short-lived, the years immediately following the Russian Revolution saw some of the nation's most intense, emancipated poetry; poetry praised for its individuality. This was precisely the characteristic that earned many Russian authors, including Anna Aleksandrovna Barkova, decades of imprisonment and exile. For more than 20 years, one of Russia's most promising female poets was stifled by political censorship. After *glasnost* in 1989, her country rediscovered her poetry, though Barkóva had been dead for more than a decade.

Anna Barkova was born in 1901 into a working-class family. Little is known of her childhood, outside of poetic descriptions of deep unhappiness. When Barkova was very young, her mother died. Though her father was a heavy drinker, his position as watchman at a local gymnasium allowed her to attend school, a rare opportunity for one of her social status. Finding shelter in books, Barkova began writing as a teenager. Though the Bolshevik Revolution halted her schooling, she believed so strongly in the movement that she regarded its effect on her education irrelevant.

Seeking a writer's community, Barkova joined the "Circle of Genuine Proletarian Poets," as Lenin had dubbed them. Publishing her first poems in their newspaper *Workers' Land*, she also worked as a reporter using the pseudonym Kalika perekhozhaia (Wandering Cripple, or

Wandering Beggar-Bard). She caught the attention of Lenin's commissioner of education, Anatoli Lunarcharski, who, promising to advance her poetry, invited her to Moscow in 1922 and offered her work as his secretary. Later that year, her first volume of collected poems, entitled *Woman*, appeared. A play followed in 1923, along with more illustrious patronage. **Marie Ulyanova**, Lenin's sister, helped Barkova find work at *Pravda*, the country's largest newspaper, and encouraged her to write a second volume. But politics were to intercede.

Ulyanova, Marie (fl. 1880–1930s)
Russian revolutionary. *Name variations: Mariia Ul'lanova, Ulianova. Flourished from 1880 through the 1930s; daughter of Ilya Ulyanov (a school administrator) and Maria Alexandrovna (Blank) Ulyanova; sister of V.I. Lenin (1870–1924, whose real name was Vladimir Ulyanov); sister of Alexander Ulyanov who was arrested for plotting the assassination of Tsar Alexander III and was executed in 1887.*

In Barkova's lifetime, no other collection of her work appeared. Lenin's death and Stalin's assumption of power left writers in peril. On December 26, 1934, Barkova was arrested for her writings. Released in 1939, Barkova was exiled to Kaluga for the duration of World War II. Imprisoned again in 1947, she was not released until Nikita Khrushchev's general amnesty in January 1956. Freedom, however, lasted only a year. Convicted of mailing manuscripts with content "dangerous to society," she was returned to prison for another eight years.

Released for the last time in 1965, Barkova was forbidden to publish. Granted a meager pension by the USSR Writers' Union, she lived in Moscow, "rehabilitated," from 1967 until her death of cancer in 1976. Among her papers a lifetime's worth of writing was recovered, though friends believe some of her work was confiscated or destroyed. Newly published Barkova works include political pieces, love poems dedicated to women, and diatribes against the advancement of old age.

Crista Martin, freelance writer,
Boston, Massachusetts

Barlow, Jane (c. 1857–1917)

Irish poet, critic, and chronicler of peasant life. *Born Jane Barlow in Clontarf, County Dublin, Ireland, around 1857; died on April 17, 1917, in Bray, Ireland; daughter of Reverend James William Barlow (a vice provost of Trinity College, Dublin) and Mary Louisa Barlow; educated at home; never married; no children. Awarded honorary degree from Trinity College.*

Selected works: Bogland Studies *(1892);* Irish Idylls *(1892);* Kerrigan's Quality *(1893);* Maureen's Fairing *(1895);* Strangers at Lisconnel *(1895);* Ghost-Bereft *(1901);* By Beach and Bogland *(1905);* Flaws *(1911);* In Mio's Path *(1917).*

Jane Barlow, who was praised for her "admirable sketches of peasant-life in Ireland," spent her entire life in the environs about which she wrote. The daughter of a scholar and vice provost of Trinity College, she was educated at home with such success that she was awarded an honorary degree from Trinity College in 1904; the conferring of this degree upon a woman was rare, as the institution did not formally accept women.

Barlow was deeply invested in Ireland's past and future. Sympathies for the nationalist cause of Home Rule led to Barlow's first publications, though anonymous, in *Dublin Magazine*. Her first book, *Bogland Studies*, was published in 1892 by Thomas William Rolleston, who also gave W.B. Yeats his first appearance in print. Encouraged, she went on to produce some dozen or so volumes during her 20-year writing career.

Despite her somewhat frail constitution, Barlow loved to take long hikes through the Dublin and Wicklow mountains. She is said to have died of an illness brought on by a particularly harsh winter. Her work, much of it in verse form, was not in the bold realistic style of many Irish writers of her day but delighted readers by capturing not only the peasant dialect, but "the working of the rural mind and the emotions of the heart, fully and sympathetically understood." Her last sketch, "Rescues," appeared in the *Saturday Review* just ten days before her death in 1917 at age 60.

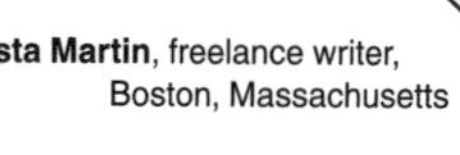

SOURCES:

Madden-Simpson, Janet. *Woman's Part.* Dublin: Arlen House, 1984.

McCarthy, Justin. *Irish Literature, Vol 1.* Chicago, IL: DeBower-Elliott, 1904.

Crista Martin, freelance writer,
Boston, Massachusetts

Barlow, Lucy (c. 1630–1658).
See Walter, Lucy.

Barnacle, Nora Joseph (1884–1951).
See Joyce, Nora.

Barnard, A.M. (1832–1888).
See Alcott, Louisa May.

Barnard, Lady Anne (1750–1825).
See Lindsay, Lady Anne.

Barnard, Kate (1875–1930)

Political reformer and first woman voted into statewide elective office in the U.S. *Born Catherine Ann Barnard in Geneva, Nebraska, on May 23, 1875; died in Oklahoma City, Oklahoma, on February 23, 1930; daughter of John (a lawyer and surveyor) and Rachel (Shiell) Barnard (who died in 1877); attended St. Joseph's Parochial School in Oklahoma City and Oklahoma City Business College; never married; no children.*

Born on May 23, 1875, Kate Barnard would spend much of her life working for Oklahoma's poor and dispossessed, many of them children. Her own childhood was marked with difficulties. When she was only 18 months old, her mother Rachel died, and her father was forced to leave Kate with relatives off and on throughout her youth. At 16, she rejoined him to help homestead 160 acres of land in the newly opened Oklahoma Territory, only to be isolated for months at a time while he was away on surveying trips. A lonely teenager, she often dreamed of accomplishing some "bold and heroic" deed to win her father's love and approval.

In 1892, the two moved to Oklahoma City, where, after graduating from high school, Barnard taught for a few years in rural schools. Restless and disillusioned with teaching, she decided to train as a stenographer. A job as a clerk for the Democratic Party in the Oklahoma territorial legislature provided her first taste of politics and made her some valuable friends and contacts. In 1904, she was chosen to serve as secretary and hostess for the Oklahoma Territory's pavilion at the Louisiana Purchase Exposition, held in St. Louis. In the slums of St. Louis, she witnessed the poverty that accompanied industrialization and urbanization, and vowed to help the less fortunate in Oklahoma avoid a similar fate. Returning home, she wrote a series of articles for the *Daily Oklahoman,* detailing the deplorable working conditions and child-labor abuses she had seen and warning Oklahoma City about its own developing slum districts. Her efforts yielded an outpouring of donations of clothing and food and resulted in her appointment as matron of the newly established Provident Association of Oklahoma City.

In that position, she directed relief to hundreds of poor families and saw to it that their children attended school. Realizing the limits of charity and the need for, in her own words, "justice and the chance to do an honest day's work for a fair wage," she organized Oklahoma City's unemployed into the Federal Labor Union and secured its association with the American Federation of Labor. In 1906, as part of the "Shawnee Convention" (a coalition of farm and labor representatives who met to devise a common platform for the upcoming state constitutional convention), she was instrumental in pushing through planks on compulsory education, child labor abolition, inspections of mines, and an eight-hour work day. The union leaders also wanted to include a suffrage plank, although state Democrats did not support it. For her part, Barnard had no interest in the suffrage issue, possibly because of her father's opposition to women securing the vote.

Barnard's vigorous campaigning helped elect a Democratic majority for the constitutional convention, which met in the fall of 1906. They not only adopted her planks unanimously but established the state Department of Charities and Corrections to oversee the state welfare programs. Barnard addressed the conference in a speech against child labor, among other things, that was later described as "one of the notable events of that historic body."

Leaving her post at the Provident Association, she ignored her father's disapproval of her growing political involvement and decided to run for commissioner of the newly formed charities and corrections department. She launched into another vigorous campaign, utilizing her great personal appeal and eloquent, impassioned speaking ability. One newspaper reporter would later declare, "this 'little ninety-six pound bunch of nerves' held more political power in the state of Oklahoma than any man in either party." She defeated her Republican opponent by over 35,000 votes, making her, at 32, the first woman ever elected to statewide post by an all-male electorate. Now, as the country swept into the Progressive Era, Kate Barnard was in a position to help Oklahoma lead the way.

For seven years, serving two terms, she was an active, successful reformer. Using what she termed a "Scientific Statecraft" approach, she brought to Oklahoma national experts on social welfare issues—child labor, juvenile delinquency, mental health, and prison reform—to speak to the public and the legislature, and even to help draft reform bills. With public and legislative sympathy aroused, Barnard then lent her voice to the battle for legislation. Under her method, child-labor laws and compulsory education were strengthened and progressive labor legislation was passed. She was also instrumental in improving care of mental patients, providing juvenile offenders a better chance for reform, and securing pension benefits for laborers' widows. In addition, she worked for homeless children and for safety laws and inspections in mines and factories.

In the summer of 1909, her unannounced inspection of the Kansas State Prison in Lansing, where Oklahoma convicts were housed on "contract" because their home state had no prison, turned up deplorable conditions and numerous cases of mistreatment. Prisoners were overworked and subjected to inhumane punishments. Barnard's scathing report, and the resulting uproar, inspired Oklahoma to build its own penitentiary, and the state of Kansas to make some needed prison reforms.

In 1911, during her second term, Barnard launched an investigation into widespread fraud in the state court-administered system of guardianship for orphaned Indian minors. Turning up one guardian who had over 50 children in his custody, though he didn't know where any of them were, Barnard uncovered a system which, under the Oklahoma probate court system, was overrun with graft and corruption. The minors were regularly cheated out of their inheritance of land, which was often rich in natural resources.

Knowing she could only do so much on her own, Barnard added attorney J.H. Stolper to her staff, and, within a year, they had recovered close to $1 million for 1,361 defrauded children. But her investigations often implicated the influential as well as the common crooks, and as the probes continued the politicians decided to stop Barnard by first going after Stolper. After forcing him out on a trumped-up charge of wrongdoing, they contrived a political blackmail scheme that ultimately resulted in Barnard losing her budget and staff. Exhausted and demoralized, she did not run for reelection in 1914.

Barnard raised her own money and borrowed from friends to continue battling Indian guardianship fraud by drawing national attention with articles in major city newspapers, including *The New York Times*. But her impassioned plea on the floor of the Oklahoma

Kate Barnard

Senate—the first by a woman—fell on deaf ears. After a letter to President Woodrow Wilson in 1916, asking him to help her cause by reinstating federal jurisdiction over the Indians, she disappeared from sight, finally giving in to what she regarded as "the hypocrisy, deceit, selfishness, and intrigue of modern politics." Her remaining years were spent battling depression, allergies, and a debilitating skin disease, probably psoriasis. She died of heart failure on February 23, 1930, three months short of her 55th birthday.

Although 1,400 gathered for her funeral, and all seven of Oklahoma's former governors served as honorary pallbearers, Kate Barnard was all but forgotten in Oklahoma. Two histories of the state failed to mention her name and her grave remained unmarked until 1982. At that time, a group dedicated a small stone which read, "Intrepid pioneer leader for social ethics in Oklahoma."

SOURCES:

McHenry, Robert, ed. *Famous American Women*. NY: Dover, 1983.

Peavy, Linda, and Ursula Smith. *Women Who Changed Things*. NY: Scribner, 1983.

Truman, Margaret. *Women of Courage*. NY: William Morrow, 1976.

Barbara Morgan, Melrose, Massachusetts

Barnard, Marjorie (1897–1987)

Australian author who, with Flora Eldershaw, wrote more than 20 books under the joint pseudonym M. Barnard Eldershaw. *Name variations: (joint pseudonym with Flora Eldershaw) M. Barnard Eldershaw. Born Marjorie Faith Barnard on August 16, 1897, in Sydney, Australia; died in 1987 in Sydney, Australia; daughter of Ethel Frances (Ashford) and Oswald Holmes Barnard; educated at University of Sydney; never married; no children.*

Selected works—as M. Barnard Eldershaw: A House is Built *(1929);* Green Memory *(1931);* The Glasshouse *(1936);* Plaque with Laurel *(1937);* Tomorrow and Tomorrow *(1947).*

Selected works as Marjorie Barnard: The Ivory Gate *(1920);* Macquarie's World *(1942);* The Persimmon Tree and Other Stories *(1943);* Sydney: The Story of a City *(1956);* Australia's First Architect: Francis Greenway *(1961);* A History of Australia *(1962);* Miles Franklin *(1967).*

Publishing under the joint pseudonym M. Barnard Eldershaw, the writing team of Marjorie Barnard and **Flora Eldershaw** evolved into a well-oiled Australian literary machine. The shy Barnard contributed the majority of the books' text, while Eldershaw cultivated publishers and readers, acquiring an audience who would remain loyal to the pair even when they did not publish together.

The only surviving child of Ethel Frances and Oswald Holmes Barnard, Marjorie Faith Barnard was born and raised in Sydney, where her Oswald's theories of a proper girl's upbringing determined many aspects of her life. Barnard was not permitted to study the alphabet until age seven; she then learned it so quickly that she had to belie her proficiency for fear of displeasing him. Educated by a governess and at Sydney's Cambridge School of Girls' High School, Barnard then entered the University of Sydney. At first, Oswald was opposed to higher education but permitted it on condition that she live at home.

Upon graduation in 1918, Barnard was offered a fully paid scholarship to Oxford University, but her father, who controlled her by controlling her purse strings, refused his permission. Still living at home, she took a post as librarian at the Sydney Technical College in 1920, where she stayed for 12 years. In her hours away from the library, Barnard and Flora Eldershaw, whom she had met at university, began to work together. Barnard was an excellent writer but lacked the spirit to sell her work, while Eldershaw, though a skilled author, excelled more at publicity and public speaking. Together, they developed stories, outlined and assigned portions to be written, and exchanged work for mutual editing.

Though they were voluminous correspondents, the private Barnard burned all her letters. Only occasionally did they sit down together, and it was generally understood that Barnard would perform most of the final writing. The partners made no effort to conceal their identities and viewed the pseudonym M. Barnard Eldershaw as a simplified expression of, and explanation for, their cooperative efforts. Both refused to disclose which portions in any given book were their individual work. "Collaborators should not publicly claim their contributions to a shared book," remarked Barnard. "It is not fair to the book."

Eldershaw, Flora (1897–1956)

Australian author who wrote literary criticism on her own as well as fiction with Marjorie Barnard under the pseudonym M. Barnard Eldershaw. *Name variations: (joint pseudonym with Marjorie Barnard) M. Barnard Eldershaw. Born Flora Sydney Patricia Eldershaw in Sydney, Australia, in 1897; died on September 20, 1956; daughter of Henry and Margaret Eldershaw; educated at Wagga Wagga; graduated from Sydney University, 1918; never married but romantically linked with Frank Dolby Davison; no children.*

As Flora Eldershaw, works include: Contemporary Australian Women Writers *(1931);* The Peaceful Army *(1938, 1988).*

Flora Eldershaw was born in Sydney, Australia, in 1897, the daughter of Henry and **Margaret Eldershaw**, and raised on the family sheep station in Riverina. Though weak in health since childhood, Flora enrolled at Sydney University as a teenager where she met ***Marjorie Barnard**. The two would remain close friends throughout their lives. Following graduation in 1918, Eldershaw worked at Presbyterian Ladies' College in Croydon, then in the departments of Reconstruction and Labour and National Service, but she and Barnard aspired to literary careers. Combining their talents and personalities into the writing persona M. Barnard Eldershaw, the partners became hugely successful. Where Barnard was the stronger writer, Eldershaw often edited and created the storyline. She also shepherded works to publication, a process that Barnard abhorred. When a British editor lost one of their manuscripts, Eldershaw wrote to Barnard, "Don't worry, I'll be nasty to them." Barnard, in turn, wrote another friend: "She can be very competently nasty too, bless her heart." Though Eldershaw published some solo literary criticism, she preferred public lecturing. Flora Eldershaw died in 1956, at age 59.

Crista Martin, Boston, Massachusetts

Finally in 1932, when their presence in the literary community was on the ascendance, Barnard solicited her mother Ethel's assistance to help free her of full-time employment. Ethel successfully pleaded with Oswald to grant their daughter an allowance to support her writing. While Barnard continued to live at home, she and Flora occasionally departed Sydney for a month of side-by-side collaboration. More regularly, their work was confined to a weekend, or to a few hours in a flat they rented together; the room was strictly for writing or entertaining, and neither ever made it a residence.

In 1933, with two successful M. Barnard Eldershaw books behind her, Barnard made her first trip out of Australia, on a ship bound for England. The trip sparked a passion for sea travel and the idea for a third book. Barnard continued living with her parents until Oswald's death in 1940 and Ethel's in 1949. Left with the house and a small sum of money, Barnard was an independent woman for the first time. Having resumed library work in 1942, she again retired in 1950 to write full time.

Though she wrote fiction, Barnard's greater passion was the history of Australia, particularly Sydney. The 1941 book *Macquarie's World*, begun as a Barnard-Eldershaw project, was published under Barnard's name alone. In a sense, this work freed the partners. Though works under their joint authorship were still in demand, each woman felt the liberty, and assurance of positive reception, to pursue her own projects.

Her health long fragile, Flora Eldershaw died in 1956 at the age of 59. The loss of her alter ego weakened Barnard's writing, as did her increasingly failing eyesight. She continued to publish history and literary reviews into the 1960s, but her pen fell almost silent during the following two decades. She died in 1987, having spent more then two thirds of her life in the Sydney home built by her father. Her manuscripts are located at the Mitchell Library in Sydney.

SOURCES:

Rorabacher, Louise E. *Marjorie Barnard and M. Barnard Eldershaw.* NY: Twayne, 1973.

Wilde, William H., Joy Horton and Barry Andrews, ed. *Oxford Companion to Australian Literature.* Melbourne: Oxford University Press, 1994.

Crista Martin, freelance writer, Boston, Massachusetts

Barnes, Catharine (1851–1913).

See Ward, Catharine Barnes.

Barnes, Djuna (1892–1982)

American journalist, novelist, poet, and playwright whose work, though critically neglected for almost 40 years, has greatly influenced 20th-century writing. *Name variations: (pseudonym) Lydia Steptoe. Pronunciation: JOO-na BARNS. Born Djalma Barnes Chappell on January 12, 1892, in Cornwall-on-Hudson, New York; died in New York, New York, on June 18, 1982; daughter of Elizabeth Chappell and Henry Budington (later Wald Barnes); educated at home; studied painting at the Pratt Institute and at the Art Students' League in New York City, 1915–16; married Courtenay Lemon, in 1917 (divorced 1919); lived with Thelma Wood, 1920–31.*

Left home for Greenwich Village (1912); started publishing short stories (1913); published her first book, The Book of Repulsive Women *(1915); moved to Paris and lived with Thelma Wood (1920); published* Ladies Almanack *(1928); published* Nightwood *(1936); returned to New York (1939); published* The Antiphon *(1958); served as trustee, Dag Hammarskjöld Foundation, beginning 1961; given National Endowment for the Arts senior fellowship (1981); offered membership by National Institute of Arts and Letters.*

Selected writings: The Book of Repulsive Women: 8 Rhythms and 5 Drawings *(Bruno Chap Books, 1915);* Ryder *(novel, Liveright, 1928);* Nightwood *(Faber, 1936);* The Antiphon *(verse play, Farrar, Straus, 1958). Contributed to* Vanity Fair, New Republic, The New Yorker *and other publications, sometimes under the name of Lydia Steptoe.*

Despite the fact that her most important novel *Nightwood* never enjoyed popular acclaim and her most important play *The Antiphon* has never been produced in English, Djuna Barnes' influence on 20th-century writing is indisputable. Her work radically departs from realism and conventional narrative structures to embrace a dense symbolism, and she is considered one of the leaders of the modernist movement, along with James Joyce, T.S. Eliot, and Ezra Pound. Equally important to the feminist reader, though, is Barnes' focus on women's sexuality, on social circles dominated by women, and on same-sex attraction between women.

Djuna Barnes had an unconventional childhood. Her father, born Henry Budington, was unusually versatile, even in inventing names. When his father Henry Budington, Sr., and mother **Zadel Barnes** divorced around 1879, he dropped the Budington, adopted Barnes, and dubbed himself Wald. Thus, in 1888, it was Wald Barnes who traveled with his mother

See sidebar on the following page

Barnes, Zadel

Feminist writer. *Name variations: Zadel Budington. Married Henry Budington (divorced around 1879); children: Henry Budington, Jr. (known as Ward Barnes).*

Zadel Barnes published stories and poems under her maiden name in major magazines during the 1870s and 1880s. A fervent feminist, she also wrote novels with feminist themes.

Zadel to England; the following year, he met **Elizabeth Chappell**, a violinist from Rutland studying at England's Academy of Music, and returned with her to the United States.

Although the couple never legally married, Wald and Elizabeth lived together and had five children: Thurn, Djuna (their only girl born June 12, 1892), Zendon, Saxon, and Shangar. The family lived in a house built by Wald on an estate owned by his uncle in Cornwall-on-Hudson, a summer spot frequented by bohemians. Wald had attained the land through the intervention of his mother, who, having divorced her second husband, had come to live with him.

Wald's children inherited his habit for name changing; apparently, Djuna's name was Djalma until one of her brothers mispronounced it; then she became Djuna. Wald would go on to have two more children—a boy and a girl—with his second wife, whom he married when Djuna was older.

Since the family agreed that public schools did not educate their students well, Zadel—who was an accomplished feminist writer and journalist—educated Djuna. In addition to learning to read and write with her grandmother, Djuna learned from her father, who was an amateur in many of the art forms that he loved. He composed operas, wrote librettos, did watercolors, and played the piano better than any other instrument, Djuna later claimed, since she thought Wald could not play any other instrument well. The Barnes believed in educating and exposing their children to as much culture as possible. Djuna learned to play the French horn, the violin and the banjo, and did a bit of acting with the encouragement of her relatives. In this rich, cultural environment, Djuna began writing poems and short plays for the family to perform. She lived in Cornwall-on-Hudson until age 16.

There were enormous tensions in the household, however. The strong-minded Zadel and her daughter-in-law Elizabeth did not get on well. Further, Wald, who made almost a cult out of sex, had numerous mistresses. When he became involved with **Marguerite Amelia d'Alvarez**, a singer of some renown, he brought Alvarez and Alvarez's children to live with the rest of his family at Cornwall-on-Hudson. Note Gillian Hanscombe and Virginia L. Smyers in *Writing for Their Lives*: "Djuna's childhood was so traumatic that it haunted her for the rest of her life; it is even thought by some that she was raped—on her father's instructions and with her mother's collusion—by a farmhand when she was fourteen or fifteen. Scenes of rape, incest, sodomy and bestiality occur frequently in her work, which—taken as a whole—often creates a twisted nightmare world where sex and sexual identity lie at the centre."

Andrew Field, in *Djuna: The Life and Times of Djuna Barnes*, writes that having two women and refusing to send his children to school almost resulted in Wald's arrest and imprisonment, but he got away with both out of sheer bravado. On the one hand, the accusation of bigamy could not legally stick since Wald and Elizabeth were not married; on the other hand, the accusation of neglecting his children's education did not succeed because Wald confronted and routed the school authorities who denounced him, successfully arguing that the schools offered limited education to his children.

Around 1908, the situation at home proved more and more difficult. Elizabeth finally left Wald and moved with her children to a farm in Huntington, Long Island. After a few years of assisting her mother with the farm, Djuna moved to New York around 1912, where she started writing to help sustain her mother, her brothers, and her ailing grandmother. Writing short articles for New York City's newspapers and magazines, she soon became a regular contributor on such subjects as "How It Feels to be Forcibly Fed." (Barnes underwent forcible feeding herself to give the reader a sense of what England's militant suffragists were enduring.) After renting a small apartment in the Bronx, she matriculated in 1915–16 at the Pratt Institute and the Art Students League in New York, then took a steady job as writer for *The Brooklyn Daily Eagle*; she also freelanced for *The World* and *The New York Press*.

As a writer and illustrator, Barnes found enough work to sustain herself financially and afford her time to write and draw. She also became part of the feminist and lesbian circles flourishing in Greenwich Village before the first World War and befriended influential women:

Djuna Barnes

Heap, Jane. See Anderson, Margaret for sidebar.

Freytag-Loringhoven, Elsa von. See Abbott, Berenice for sidebar.

Jane Heap, the Baroness Elsa von Freytag-Loringhoven, *Mina Loy, *Margaret Anderson, *Mabel Dodge Luhan, *Edna St. Vincent Millay, and *Peggy Guggenheim. Barnes was intensely maternal; those she coddled included Heap and Anderson. Wrote Anderson:

> You two poor things, she would say in her warm laughing voice. You're both crazy of course, God help you. I suppose I can stand it if you can, but someone ought to look out for you. She looked out for us by bringing in the first strawberries of spring and the last oysters of winter, but to the more important luxuries of the soul she turned an unhearing ear. Djuna would never talk, she would never allow herself to be talked to. She said it was because she was reserved about herself.

Barnes focused on these circles in her first work, *The Book of Repulsive Women* (1915), an underground Village hit which Guido Bruno published as a small pamphlet in New York. Between 1915 and 1920, she established herself as a writer of the avant-garde. She also began acting, joining with Eugene O'Neill and his Provincetown Players. She soon found, however, that her talents were more suited to playwriting. Her one-acts, *Three from the Earth*, *Kurzy of the Sea*, and *An Irish Triangle*, were produced in the 1919–20 season.

> If genius is perfection wrought out of anguish and pain and intellectual flagellation, then Djuna Barnes' novel *Nightwood* is a book of genius.
>
> **—Rose C. Feld**

During her years with the group, Djuna fell in love with poet **Mary Pyne**, wife of poet Harry Kemp, and nursed her until Mary's death of tuberculosis in 1915. She also became involved and lived with Courtenay Lemon, whose intellect attracted her long enough to have supposedly married him in 1917 (though no record of this marriage has been found). By 1920, Barnes was sailing alone to Paris, where American dollars went farther, to join the vibrant expatriate American community, led by such influential American modernists as ***Gertrude Stein** and T.S. Eliot. While staying at the Hotel Angleterre on rue Jacob, Barnes became acquainted with the latest modernist trends and a number of women writers and artists in the international circles that merged in Paris, including **Thelma Wood**, an American sculptor from Michigan. Wood and Barnes became lovers and lived together from 1920 until 1931. "They were by all accounts, a striking pair," write Hanscombe and Smyers, "both tall, imperious, striding down the boulevards arm in arm, feet moving in time, tossing their heads and their capes."

A Book, a compilation of journalism, poetry, drama and drawings, came out in 1923, the first of three works Barnes wrote during the 1920-31 period. Of more relevance to Barnes' writing career are *Ryder* (1928), which uses a mock-Elizabethan style to chronicle the Barnes' family history, and *Ladies Almanack*, which was published in 1928. *Ladies Almanack* centers on the lesbian circles Barnes frequented, especially that surrounding ***Natalie Clifford Barney**. According to Field, *Ladies Almanack* was published privately, and "Miss Barnes herself and others sold it on the streets of Paris." *Ryder* and the humorous *Ladies Almanack* show the arresting visual imagination, the highly elaborate literary techniques, and the almost total rejection of naturalism that would characterize *Nightwood*. With the proceeds from *Ryder*, which was a bestseller in America, Barnes bought the apartment she and Wood had been leasing at 9 rue St. Romain.

When Barnes' tempestuous relationship with Wood ended in 1931, she left Paris and started to write a novel called *Bow Down*, concentrating on her relationship with Wood. In her wanderings, she spent short periods of time with Peggy Guggenheim in England, with Charles Henri Ford traveling through Vienna and Munich, and in Tangiers, where she stayed with Ford and Paul and **Jane Bowles.**

The publication of *Nightwood* in 1936 marks an important transition in Barnes' life, for it established her—among writers of the younger generation, if not among the critics—as a major writer of the modernist movement. According to **Sheri Benstock** in *Women of the Left Bank*, *Nightwood* "was to become a cult guide to the homosexual underground night world of Paris that Barnes shared with her lover." The novel was endorsed by T.S. Eliot—who wrote an introduction for it—and appeared in New York in 1937. Though American critics seemed more interested in figuring out why Eliot backed Barnes' novel rather than in the merits of the novel itself, *Nightwood* was soon elevated to cult status by established writers; it became "required reading" for those who aspired. James Joyce and Ezra Pound, both admirers of Barnes' work, also championed the novel.

The publication of *Nightwood* changed Barnes' life. An aggressively private person, she did not give interviews and made few efforts to cultivate friendships. From here on, though she was always desperately short of cash, friends and famous strangers helped her survive financially. Samuel Beckett, for instance, who admired her work, gave her a percentage of his royalties from *Waiting for Godot*, while Peggy Guggenheim also helped.

After a short stay in Tangiers, Barnes moved to New York and lived with her mother in Greenwich Village, until her mother's death in 1945; she then took a one-room apartment at 5 Patchin Place in the Village. Though she traveled to Europe on occasion, Barnes spent most of her time alone in her apartment writing and painting, living on less than $20 a month for food, and sometimes unsuccessfully battling alcoholism. Health problems arose with her eyes, teeth, breathing, and she lived on little because of failing royalties; only the kindness of friends kept her afloat.

Djuna Barnes' most important play, *The Antiphon*, which was about her family, was published in 1958. Originally, it had received a mixed response from Barnes' friends and collaborators—and little enthusiasm—because of a disastrous reading in 1956 by an amateur theatrical group, the Poets' Theatre Company. However, Edwin Muir and Dag Hammarskjöld translated *The Antiphon* into Swedish. When it premiered at the Royal Theatre, Stockholm, in 1961, the Swedish public, though a little puzzled, liked the play, and critics gave it a number of positive reviews. *The Antiphon* has never been produced in English.

After the publication of *The Antiphon*, Barnes did little writing; instead, she concentrated on her painting. In 1972, she sold her papers to the McKeldin Library at the University of Maryland and in 1981 received a National Endowment for the Arts grant, which barely helped her financial situation. When Natalie Barney wrote and asked how she was living, Barnes replied: "I live in complete isolation. I have no door-bell, and at one time had no telephone. I have bars at the window, and a police-lock on the front door . . . and all this not from any additional ferocity to my nature, but merely as means to enduring. Living? no, enduring yes." Djuna Barnes lived at Patchin Place in Greenwich Village until she died an angry recluse, age 90, on June 18, 1982. "Life is painful, nasty & short," she had said, "in my case it has only been painful and nasty."

SOURCES:

Benstock, Shari. *Women of the Left Bank: Paris, 1900–1940.* Austin, TX: University of Texas Press, 1986.

Field, Andrew. *Djuna: The Life and Times of Djuna Barnes.* NY: Putnam, 1983.

Wood, Thelma (b. 1901)

American artist and sculptor. *Born in St. Louis, Missouri, in 1901.*

Born well to do, Thelma Wood arrived in Paris in 1920, aged 19. She was the great love of Djuna Barnes' life. From 1920 to 1931, they lived together, in a volatile way, at 173 Blvd St. Germain and at 9 rue St. Romain, in the heart of the Left Bank. Despite Barnes' protestations, Thelma took other lovers. She also drank heavily. When the ten-year relationship ended, Barnes never again lived with anyone.

Hanscombe, Gillian, and Virginia L. Smyers. *Writing for Their Lives: The Modernist Woman, 1910–1940.* London: The Women's Press, 1987.

Herring, Phillip. *The Life and Work of Djuna Barnes.* NY: Viking, 1995.

Le Blanc, Ondine E. "Djuna Barnes," in *Gay and Lesbian Literature.* Detroit, MI: St. James Press, 1994, pp. 27–28.

Scott, James. *Djuna Barnes.* Boston, MA: Twayne Publishers, 1976.

Wiloch, Thomas. "Djuna Barnes," in *Contemporary Authors, New Revision Series.* Vol. 16. Detroit, MI: Gale Research Company, 1981, pp. 29–32.

SUGGESTED READING:

Carpenter, Humphrey. *Geniuses Together: American Writers in Paris in the 1920s.* Boston, MA: Houghton Mifflin, 1988.

O'Neal, Hank. *"Life is painful, nasty & short—in my case it has only been painful and nasty": Djuna Barnes, 1978–1981: an informal memoir.* NY: Paragon House, 1990.

Carlos U. Decena, freelance writer, Philadelphia, Pennsylvania

Barnes, Juliana (c. 1388–?).

See Berners, Juliana.

Barnes, Margaret Ayer (1886–1967)

American novelist and playwright, who won the 1931 Pulitzer Prize for* Years of Grace.** *Born Margaret Ayer on April 8, 1886, in Chicago, Illinois; died on October 25, 1967, in Cambridge, Massachusetts; daughter of Janet and Benjamin F. Ayer (general counsel to Illinois Central Railroad); sister of* ***Janet Ayer Fairbank *(a novelist); educated at University School for Girls, Chicago, 1904, and Bryn Mawr College, 1907; married Cecil Barnes (lawyer), on May 21, 1910; children: three sons, Cecil Jr. (b. 1912), Edward Larrabbee (b. 1915) and Benjamin Ayer (b. 1919).*

Selected works: (play) The Age of Innocence *(1928); (play)* Jenny *(1929); (play)* Dishonored Lady *(1930);* Years of Grace *(1930);* Westward Passage

(1931); Within This Present *(1933);* Edna His Wife *(1935);* Wisdom's Gate *(1938).*

While touring French cathedral towns in 1925, Margaret Barnes suffered broken ribs, vertebrae, and a fractured skull when her car met another car head-on. Consigned to bed, first in the American Hospital in Paris, then home in Chicago, and desperate for entertainment, Barnes laid a notepad on her chest, took pen in hand, and scribbled stories. The jottings not only saw her through her recuperation, they launched her writing career.

Raised in a wealthy Chicago community, Barnes bucked tradition in 1904 when she chose Bryn Mawr College over finishing school and a proper debut. She was a Bryn Mawr leader, popular, outspoken and intelligent. Back in Chicago after graduation, she was an active alumnae through her 1910 marriage to Cecil Barnes and the birth of their three sons. In 1920, she accepted the post of alumnae director, determined to make learning available at all economic levels. Barnes spearheaded the Working Women's Institute at Bryn Mawr which provided scholarships for women, particularly those who took industrial positions during World War I, only to lose them when the soldiers returned home. The program was so successful that it became a model for other institutes around the country.

Barnes retired from the board in 1923 and returned to the normal family routine: summers in Mt. Desert, Maine, winters performing with a small community theater group. Since childhood, she had maintained a friendship with playwright Edward Sheldon, who urged her to continue writing after the 1925 auto accident. Reunited with Sheldon in New York City during a follow-up operation, Barnes showed him her stories. With his help, the *Pictorial Review* accepted one for publication. By 1928, all the pieces she had written during her rehabilitation had found their way into magazines.

Sheldon, suffering from disabling arthritis and failing eyesight, was doing little of his own writing and remained eager to champion Barnes' career. When she expressed an interest in dramatizing ***Edith Wharton**'s *The Age of Innocence*, he offered her advice and encouragement. Actress ***Katharine Cornell** accepted the leading role, and the play was a hit. Sheldon became her writing partner for the plays *Jenny* (1929) and *Dishonored Lady* (1930), the latter again starring Cornell. When a movie production company bought the movie rights, then rejected the Barnes-Sheldon screenplay but used uncredited portions of it anyway, the authors received $500,000 to settle a subsequent plagiarism suit.

While none of her novels inspired the critical acclaim of her Pulitzer-Prize winning *Years of Grace*, Barnes continued to write while living in Chicago, attempting to "re-create in written words the conclusions I had drawn from life itself." Predominant among her subjects were the social history of the upper-class Midwest, and the need, regardless of financial or social status, for women to have a "vocation" to broaden the scope of their daily lives.

All three of Margaret's sons attended their father's alma mater, Harvard University. When her husband Cecil grew ill in the 1940s, Barnes stopped writing and cared for him until his death in 1949. Following her death in 1967, her manuscripts were donated to the Harvard and New York Public libraries.

SUGGESTED READING:

Taylor, Jr., Lloyd C. *Margaret Ayer Barnes.* NY: Twayne, 1974.

RELATED MEDIA:

Dishonored Lady, film starring ***Hedy Lamarr**, produced by United Artists, 1947.

Crista Martin, freelance writer, Boston, Massachusetts

Barnes, Mary Downing

(1850–1898)

American educator and first teacher in the United States to use the Pestalozzian or "source" method in teaching history. *Born Mary Downing Sheldon in Oswego, New York, on September 15, 1850; died in 1898; daughter of educator Edward Austin Sheldon (1823–1892), who founded the Oswego State Normal School; studied at Oswego State Normal School, University of Michigan, and in Cambridge and Zurich; married Earl Barnes, in 1885.*

The daughter of an educator, Mary Barnes followed in her father's footsteps. Edward Austin Sheldon founded the Oswego State Normal School in New York and for years was the leader of the Pestalozzian influence in American education. Barnes studied her father's theories and would later apply them in her classrooms as a teacher of history. After attending her father's institution and the University of Michigan, Barnes took a position at Wellesley College, where she began experimenting in 1876 with what she called her "source" method for teaching history. Instead of using the standard textbook and rote method, her attempt was to encourage students to study various source material, weigh the evidence therein, and come to their own conclusions based on critical thought. To that end, she utilized prepared lists of source material to be read and discussed in class meetings. In 1882, she returned to Oswego Normal School to teach history, Latin, Greek, and Botany.

Mary married former student Earl Barnes, 11 years her junior, and the couple moved to California in 1891, where he headed the education department at newly founded Stanford University and employed his wife's theories. A short time later, she joined the history department at Stanford and, in 1892, published *Studies in American History: Teachers' Manual*, in which Barnes set forth her theories.

Barnes, Pancho (1901–1975)

First woman stunt pilot in motion pictures and first woman to fly from Los Angeles to Mexico City. *Born Florence Lowe in Pasadena, California, in 1901; died in Boron, California, in 1975; daughter of a wealthy Pasadena family that suffered reverses in the 1929 Depression.*

At a time when few women were piloting planes, Pancho Barnes was executing dips and rolls in Howard Hughes' 1929 movie *Hell's Angels*. "The plot isn't much but the aerial photography is sensational," wrote Jay Nash and Stanley Ross in their *Motion Picture Guide*. During the filming, three other pilots were killed, and Howard Hughes was pulled from wreckage with a crushed cheekbone. That same year, Barnes flew in the first Women's Air Derby, where, after securing first place in the second stage of the race, she damaged her plane and was forced to withdraw.

In a career marked by record-breaking, Barnes set a new women's speed record of 196.19 miles per hour, and she became the first woman to fly from Los Angeles, California, to Mexico City, Mexico. The trip was a sightseeing jaunt made in several stages with her mechanic aboard. In 1931, Barnes helped launch a transcontinental race for women, which, with more than 50 planes competing, likely included the majority of women pilots in the country. A few years later, she was part of a flying group that supplied emergency disaster assistance. In one demonstration, they reportedly dropped a crate of eggs from an altitude of 7,000 feet, without breaking a single shell.

In 1933, Barnes purchased an 80-acre ranch abutting Edwards Air Force Base in the Mojave desert, which she later turned into a resort facility. Twenty years later, she brought a $300,000 suit against the commanding officer of the base, Brigadier General J.S. Holtoner, charging that he had threatened to bomb her ranch in order to carry out government plans of enlarging the base by acquiring her property.

Barnett, Ida B. or Ida Wells (1862–1931).

See Wells-Barnett, Ida.

Barney, Alice Pike (1857–1931).

See Barney, Natalie Clifford for sidebar.

Barney, Maginel Wright (1881–1966).

See Wright, Maginel.

Barney, Natalie Clifford (1876–1972)

American-born expatriate author, translator, and foremother of feminist literature, who created an international literary salon in Paris and an Academy of Women to cultivate women writers. *Born Natalie Clifford in Dayton, Ohio, on October 31, 1876; died at age 95 at Hotel Meurice in Paris, France, on February 3, 1972; daughter of Alice Pike Barney (an accomplished painter and arts patron) and Albert Clifford Barney (an industrialist, president of the Barney Railroad Car Foundry); sister of Laura Barney (b. 1879); learned French as a child from her great aunt Louisa and French governess; studied for 18 months at Les Ruches boarding school in Fontainebleau while her mother studied painting in Paris; before her teen years, became completely bilingual; completed formal education at Miss Ely's School in New York; had a German-speaking governess, and spent seven months in Germany during a European tour, where she took lessons in fencing, dancing, and violin; studied French verse and Greek under tutelage of Charles Brun; no formal schooling after that, but learned from numerous intellectuals and writers who frequented her salon, beginning in 1909; never married; had a 50-year relationship with Romaine Brooks.*

Spent first ten years in the country outside Cincinnati, Ohio; family moved to Washington, D.C., and summered in Bar Harbor, Maine, with occasional trips to Europe, including Scandinavia and Russia; lived with parents in Europe (1883); returned to Paris with sister and mother, who studied painting with Whistler among other artists (1887); portrait painted as The Little Page *by mother's teacher Carolus-Duran (1887); lived in Paris on and off for the next 14 years; conducted love affair with famous courtesan Liane de*

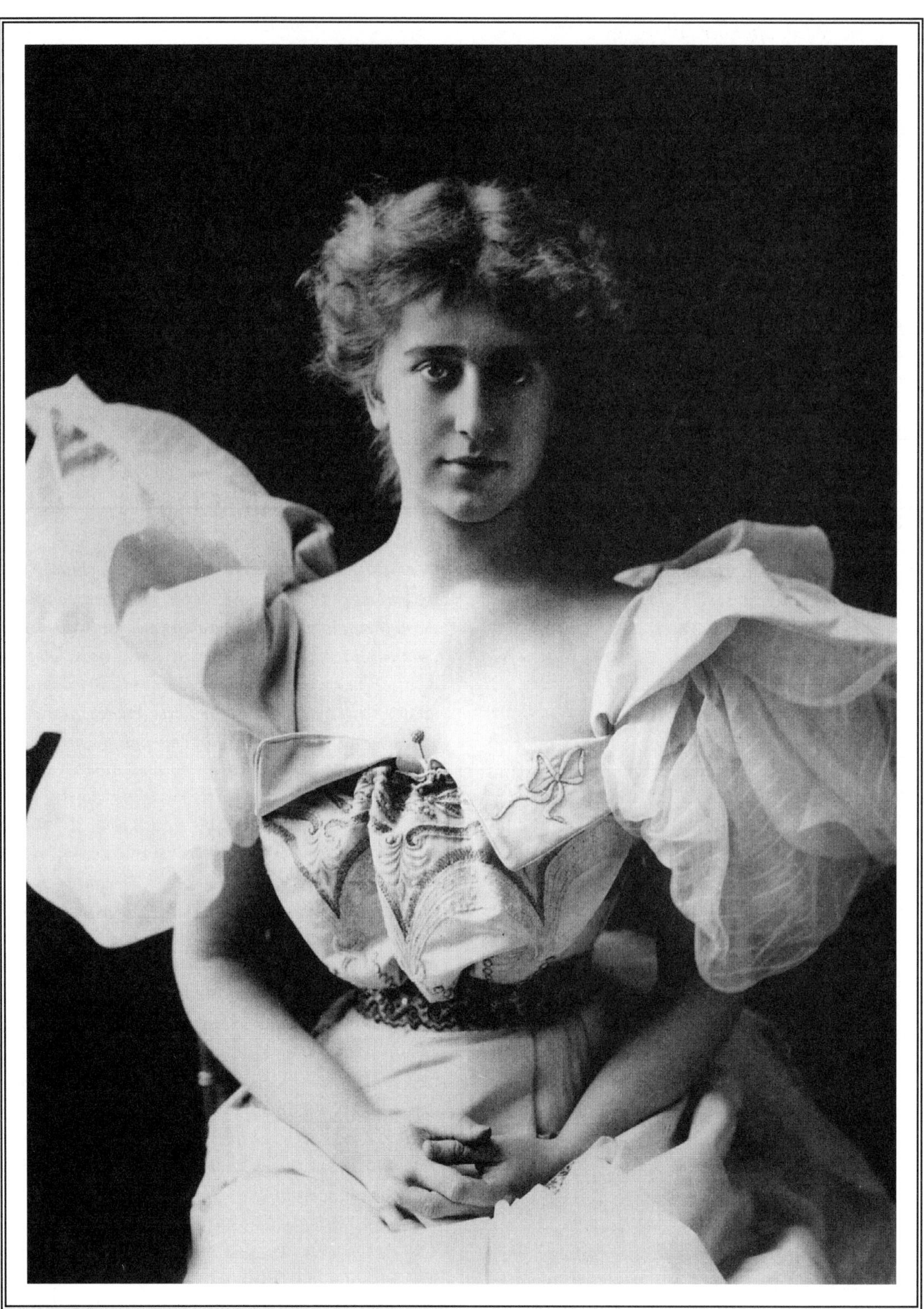

Natalie Clifford Barney

Pougy, starting around 1899, the first of many; reputation for her liaisons with women may have become public when de Pougy published barely disguised autobiographical novel, Idyl saphique *(Sapphic Idyll), featuring a young American girl modeled on Barney, the first of many appearances of her character in fiction (1901); engaged briefly to Lord Alfred-Douglas, Oscar Wilde's former lover (1900); also briefly engaged to William Morrow; met and began affair with Anglo-American writer and poet, Renée Vivien (1900); with Vivien, tried to establish a neo-Sapphic colony on the Greek island of Lesbos for women* *poets, but failed; after her father's death (1902), became independently wealthy with inheritance of $2.5 million and moved permanently to Paris; wrote six of her 14 books during liaison with Vivien; met painter Romaine Brooks sometime before WWI and started longterm liaison; moved to 20 rue Jacob in Faubourg St. Germain and launched her salon for leading writers and intellectuals of the day (1909); met influential but reclusive writer and critic Remy de Gourmont (1910), who published Brooks-Barney correspondence with Barney's approval in* Mercure de France *(1912–13), establishing Barney as a literary figure; remained in Paris and ran her salon during World War I; had affair with* **Dolly Wilde** *(1920s); launched Académie des Femmes (Academy of Women) to celebrate and support women writers (1927); moved to Florence with Romaine Brooks during World War II (1939); revived salon in Paris after the war and ran it until 1968; in her 80s, began 14-year liaison with* ***Janine Lahovary*** *(1958); broke with Brooks and left 20 rue Jacob because of structural problems and legal battle with landlord (1968).*

Selected publications: Quelques portraits-sonnets de femmes *(Ollendorf, 1900);* Cinq petits dialogues grecs *(LaPlume, 1901); (Anon.)* The Woman Who Lives with Me *(privately published, probably 1904);* Actes et entr'actes *(Sansot, 1910);* Eparpillements *(Sansot, 1910); (Anon.)* Je me souviens *(Sansot, 1910);* Poems & poemes: autres alliances *(Paris: Emile Paul, 1920);* Pensées d'une Amazone *(Emile Paul, 1920);* Aventures de l'ésprit *(Emile Paul, 1929; published in English as* Adventures of the Mind, *New York University Press, 1992);* The One Who Is Legion, A.D.'s After-Life *(London: Eric Partridge, 1930);* Nouvelles pensées de l'Amazone *(Mercure de France, 1939); (edited with an introduction by Barney)* In Memory of Dorothy Irene Wilde *(Dijon: Darantiere, 1951); (foreword) Gertrude Stein's* As Fine as Melanctha *(New Haven: Yale University Press, 1954);* Souvenirs indiscrets *(Flammarion, 1960);* Traits et portraits *(Mercure de France, 1963).*

At the end of the 19th century, as an American expatriate, Natalie Clifford Barney chose Paris as her permanent home, a city that would grant her artistic and sexual freedom. In this unfettered atmosphere, she cultivated personal and literary relationships for over 60 years, until she died at age 95. Barney was a charismatic and candid public figure who lived, loved, and wrote as a lesbian and provided a showcase for writers through her international literary salon. She envisioned a Sapphic community on Lesbos to bring women writers together, and created a real Paris Lesbos to inspire and support women's creativity. "So long as I live, the love of Beauty will be my guide," she wrote in her unpublished autobiography:

> [I] have to find or found a milieu that fits my aspirations: a society composed of all those who seek to focus and improve their lives through an art that can give them pure presence. They are the only people with whom I can get along, and communicate and finally express myself openly among free spirits.

Some commentators claim that her life was secondary to her literary work, but for Barney life and work were inherently connected: "Your life is your most beautiful poem; you are your own immortal masterpiece," she wrote in *Actes et entr'actes* (1910). She created her life as an aesthetic and sensual experience. Her own literary output—14 volumes, primarily written in French—ran the gamut: drama, poetry, epigrams, Gothic fiction, portraits of contemporaries, and autobiography. She enjoyed lifelong friendships and amassed correspondence of over 40,000 letters. Natalie Barney wrote about art, life, love, and literature. Her work reflected women's shared experiences.

The life Natalie Barney ultimately created for herself in France was quite unlike the world of her parents. She was born on October 31, 1876, in Dayton, Ohio; her sister **Laura** followed three years later. Their father Albert Clifford Barney was an industrialist who inherited a railroad fortune. Their mother **Alice Pike Barney** was an heiress who became a well-known portrait painter and arts patron. Natalie's maternal grandfather Samuel Pike was a successful entrepreneur of Dutch-Jewish heritage who built an opera house for Cincinnati and replaced the costly structure when it was destroyed by fire.

See sidebar on the following page

French language and culture were part of Natalie's life almost from the start: her grandmother's sister **Louise Miller Este**, who was born in Louisiana, always spoke French and served French cuisine at her dinner parties in Baltimore; she admired Natalie's French which was spoken without an accent. The sisters' French governess insisted on reading Jules Verne in French, which honed Barney's linguistic skills. Surrounded by animals, the girls grew up in a pastoral setting on the outskirts of Cincinnati; summers were spent in Bar Harbor, Maine, where Alice Barney built and fitted out several houses. When the family moved to Washington, D.C., in 1886 and Alice's portrait-painting commissions grew, Natalie became one of her frequently painted subjects. Her mother's other subjects, the beautiful, socially prominent women of the city, were a

Barney, Alice Pike (1857–1931)

America portrait artist. *Born Alice Pike in 1857; died in Hollywood, California, in 1931; daughter of Samuel Pike (an entrepreneur of Dutch-Jewish heritage who built an opera house for Cincinnati); married Albert Clifford Barney (an industrialist, president of the Barney Railroad Car Foundry); studied in Paris with James McNeill Whistler; married, at age 52, 22-year-old Christian Dominick Hemmick, around 1909; children: (first marriage) *****Natalie Clifford Barney*** *(1876–1972) and* ***Laura Barney*** *(b. 1879).*

An heiress in her own right, Alice Pike Barney arrived in Washington D.C., in 1889, in the company of her first husband Albert Barney, and pronounced the city devoid of culture. As an activist-bohemian, Alice set out to change the town and escape the conservatism of her husband; thus, she built a separate townhouse in Sheridan Circle. (Albert Barney died before it was completed.) Called Studio House, it hosted diverse endeavors, including theatrical productions written by Alice, the presentation of Bahaism and its leader Mirza Abul Fazl, and evenings devoted to exotic dance, which introduced *__Ruth St. Denis__ to the Washington scene. But Alice Barney was a serious artist and devoted her mornings to portraiture, the results of which are still being exhibited in Paris, New York, and Boston. Following her death in 1931, her daughters Laura and Natalie Clifford Barney donated the house to the Smithsonian Institution, and it is now sporadically opened to visitors. In 1985, the Smithsonian sponsored the exhibit *Alice Pike Barney: Pastel Portraits from Studio House.*

source of fascination to the young Natalie, who would rub their hands and ankles to soothe their nerves as they posed.

> Being other than normal is a perilous advantage.
>
> —**Natalie Barney**

From the outset, Albert Barney and his wife and daughters lived in different worlds. Though he essentially ignored them, he was intent on avoiding a public scandal that could shame the family. Thus, Albert dallied with a mistress which, for the times, was customary and acceptable in his essentially conservative bourgeois society. He also drank heavily. Committed to this unhappy marriage, Alice Pike Barney took the girls to Europe intermittently during their childhood, where she pursued art instruction with painters like James McNeill Whistler. Albert preferred London, a man's world in Natalie's estimation; she wrote that England was a place "where nothing is provided for women, not even men." She preferred Paris, "where men take second place."

In the climate of the 1890s, Alice Barney could live independently if she didn't cause a scandal. The Barney girls were educated in an upper-class manner: following instruction at home with their governess, they attended Les Ruches, an exclusive boarding school outside Fontainebleau, to learn French poetry, composition, cursive writing, drawing, singing, deportment, dancing, and horseback riding. Natalie's formal education ended at 18 with a stint at Miss Ely's School in New York.

From 1894 until his death in 1902, Albert Barney pressed Natalie to marry a man of her own social class. She returned to Washington for her debut and made the social rounds, but traveling abroad with her mother helped her avoid this traditional route, as well as her father's snobbery and authority. To placate her father, she became engaged to William Morrow (named Freddy Manners-Sutton in her memoir). Author **Karla Jay** suggests that Barney's later engagement to such an undesirable suitor as Lord Alfred-Douglas, former lover of Oscar Wilde, was to mock the institution of marriage. **Sheri Benstock** agrees, suggesting that Natalie came to view marriage as an institution that legalized the victimization of women and children, supported the whims of male sexual desire, and enforced social conformity. By 1899, Barney had had several lesbian affairs.

A friend and confidante in Washington, the diplomat Jules Cambon, suggested she learn French prosody (she could only write blank verse), and he introduced her to Professor Charles Brun. Barney's ostensible reasons for wanting to live in France included improving her French and her knowledge of French poetry, and to learn Greek so she could translate Greek poetry. By studying Greek, she would enter man's domain: generally, women of the time were excluded from studying classical Greek, which normally occurred in the confines of the university.

The relaxed moral atmosphere of Paris, in contrast to America's puritanism or England's rigidity, was another attraction for expatriate writers and artists at the turn of the century. "Paris has always seemed to me the only city in which one can express oneself as one pleases," wrote Barney. "In France, thought, food, and love have remained a matter of personal taste and one's own business." Lesbian eroticism was part of Parisian culture by the 1890s, so the resurrection of *__Sappho__ as a woman's poet whose writing celebrated female love and friendship was important in this era.

As a young woman, Barney lived independently in Paris. When Alice gave Natalie money to have her portrait painted by Whistler, Barney spent the money on presents for various ladies instead. Her first love was the most famous Belle Epoque demimondaine, ▸ **Liane de Pougy**. Barney's plan was to marry her suitor, Freddy Manners-Sutton, in order to raise the necessary funds to support Liane, saving her from a life as one of the *dégrafées* (the unbuttoned) or *grande horizontals*; Freddy agreed to this unusual strategy but later broke off the engagement.

This was the start of a pattern in Barney's life: she would rescue her lovers from their circumstances. **Karla Jay** observes that Barney saw herself as a page, or a knight in training, choosing unsuitable or incompatible lovers; the women had to appear more innocent or helpless than they were. In pursuit of de Pougy, Barney donned a page's costume to call on her and pay poetic tribute. But de Pougy liked the advantages of her life and, after their affair, married a prince. Barney saw herself as the one who loved, then moved on to other adventures.

Many of her lovers admired Barney's sharp blue eyes and wavy golden hair and her seductive personality. Her biographers Jean Chalon and George Wickes refer to her as a female Don Juan, but Jay notes that she attracted both men and women well into her 80s, when her appearance became more dowdy and her hair was no longer golden. Barney's charisma remained. Throughout her life, she preferred separate quarters; living in close proximity, she observed in *Souvenirs indiscrets*, was the quickest way to destroy affection.

By 1900, Barney had written her first volume of poetry, *Quelque portraits-sonnets de femmes* (*Some Portrait-Sonnets of Women*), which featured portraits painted by Alice Pike Barney, including some of her daughter's lovers. Biographers disagree as to whether Alice then realized the relationships of her subjects to her daughter, but an outraged Albert Barney bought all available copies of the book as well as the typesetting plates and destroyed them; in 1899, he had caught Natalie reading a long love letter from Liane. A newspaper headline in Washington denounced her book as libertine. In 1901, Barney told her mother that she was "naturally unnatural." Throughout Barney's long life, her lesbianism was never a cause for shame. She was proudly unconventional and supremely self-confident. Her father's death at 52 in 1902, alone in Monte Carlo, enabled her to be financially independent; eventually, her family inheritance would amount to $3.5 million.

The next year, Liane de Pougy's popular novel, *Idyl saphique* (*Sapphic Idyll*), based on her liaison with Natalie, featured the pseudonymous Florence Temple-Bradford (Flossie) to protect Barney's true identity. However, her biogra-

▸ Pougy, Liane de (1866–c. 1940)

Famed French courtesan. *Name variations: Princess Ghika. Born Anne de Chassaigne around 1866; died after 1936; daughter of an army officer; educated at the Sacred Heart in Rennes; married a naval officer at age 19 (divorced soon after); married Prince Georges Ghika of Moldavia (a penniless Rumanian aristocrat and nephew of the queen of Greece).*

Liane de Pougy was one of the most important *grande horizontals* of the Belle Epoque, sharing her fame with ***Emilienne d'Alençon** and ***La Belle Otero**. Of "Les Grandes Trois," de Pougy was undoubtedly the star. She had beauty, style, poise, and class, not to mention her skill at the guitar and piano.

Born into a bourgeois family, Liane was educated at the Sacred Heart in Rennes, married a naval officer when she was 19, and soon asked for a divorce. Her new husband responded by firing two bullets into her thigh where they lodged permanently. Writes ***Cornelia Otis Skinner** in *Elegant Wits and Grand Horizontals*: "In later years Liane was fond of telling the story and would wind up, 'If anyone doubts me, he can feel the bullets.'"

De Pougy began to support herself by offering piano and English instruction. It is not known when she gave up the teaching profession for other offers, but she was first seen riding with the Marquis MacMahon in an open landau. On her invitation, the Prince of Wales (future Edward VII) caught her debut at the Folies Bergère where she was a showgirl. "Overnight," writes Skinner, "Liane de Pougy became a celebrity if never a very good actress." Her admirers included Pierre de Nolhac, curator of the Versailles museum, Henri Meilhac, a book writer for operettas, Jean Lorrain, a columnist, and poets Catulle Mendès, and Robert de Montesquiou.

Once after being abandoned by a lover, Liane attempted suicide with poison but only induced vomiting "which cleared her system" writes Skinner, "and she emerged frail and lovelier than ever." In her mid-30s, she entered a Dominican convent in Lausanne, Switzerland, as a postulant, taking the name Mary Magdalene of the Penitence. After one year, she left the convent, married, moved to a country cottage, and lived 27 years with her impoverished husband Prince Ghika of Moldavia. Following his death, Liane, at age 70, reentered the convent and once again became Mary Magdalene of the Penitence, tending to the needs of "abnormal" children. Eighty small volumes written by de Pougy, which contain her memoirs, reside at the Bibliothèque Nationale.

pher George Wickes maintains that this bestseller made her private life public. Barney inspired numerous fictional representations. A seductive American, "Miss Flossie," appears briefly in ***Colette**'s novel *Claudine s'en va* in 1903, when she must have known Natalie only by reputation. ***Djuna Barnes** would feature her as Evangeline Musset in *The Ladies Almanack*, which Natalie's Academy of Women would help finance; and ***Radclyffe Hall**'s lesbian novel banned in England, *The Well of Loneliness*, would feature Valerie Seymour, a character also based on Barney.

When she was 20, Natalie met poet ❧▸ **Renée Vivien**. Fleeing an unpleasant family life, Vivien had also settled in Paris and dedicated herself to writing poetry in French. Her themes, influenced by the Symbolists, were solitude and death. Barney was deeply attracted to Vivien's poetic spirit and became her lover and muse. Under Natalie's influence and despite her melancholy, Renée expanded her themes to include joy. They studied French verse and classical Greek together in order to translate the poetry of Sappho into French. Both women wrote prolifically when they were together, and Jay observes that they "daringly created a new approach to gender, sex and sexual preference" during an era when this was discussed "apologetically." According to Benstock, what made them scandalous was that they were women writing about their own sexuality.

Their differing concepts of fidelity strained their relationship, however; Natalie's interpretation with reference to Sappho was that infidelity should strengthen relationships. At first, Vivien responded with intense jealousy to Barney's numerous affairs, until she herself became involved with the **Baroness de Nuylen de Nyevelt**, who seemed to exert great power over her. Natalie suggested to Renée that they go to Lesbos to establish a school of poetry, following in Sappho's footsteps of centuries before. They went but the experiment failed. Years later, Barney would recreate it as the Académie des Femmes (Academy of Women) in Paris. Renée Vivien broke with Natalie and, after a short life of alcohol and little food, died in 1909, probably of anorexia.

According to Jay, three of Barney's books come under the direct influence of Renée Vivien: *Actes et entr'actes* (1910), a series of Romantic formal verse dramas; *Cinq petits dialogues greques*; and *Je me souviens*, a prose poem reflecting on their relationship after its first rupture. In *Memoirs indiscrets*, written in 1960 after the death of another of her friends, Barney wrote that silence was the worst indiscretion; Renée Vivien's papers had been sealed in the National Library in Paris, and her poetry had become obscure. Barney suggests that it's better to be *indiscreet* and keep works in the public eye to celebrate their existence.

Not only was Natalie Barney completely bilingual, she chose French as her literary expression; her principal audience was French. Her classical French was a traditional style from an earlier era. Used by her literary influences, including Baudelaire, Verlaine, and Mallarmé, it gave her work powerful associations, suggests Benstock. She loved French authors and the French language; Jay suggests that Barney hoped one day to be considered one of their own. To reach an international audience, French, as the language of diplomacy, had far-reaching influence.

From a house in Neuilly, in 1909, Natalie moved to 20 rue Jacob, in the Faubourg St. Germain on the Left Bank, where she would remain for more than 60 years. One entered her 300-year-old home through an interior courtyard hidden from the street by a wall. A pavilion was illuminated by blue-green light that was filtered through the windows. Outside, there was a garden and a small doric temple from the First Empire or the Restoration, which Barney named the Temple de l'Amitié (Temple of Friendship). Her home had an aura of general disarray and neglect, but the traditional feast for 20 to 100 salon attendees was first-rate—sandwiches, cakes, tarts, tea, and whiskey later on, though Barney did not drink.

Natalie was a rebel from the start; a salon run by an American ran counter to French etiquette. Salons had been the domain of French nobility. The trial, conviction, and subsequent vindication of the accused Jewish officer Dreyfus, at the turn of the century, had divided the country and even families. Barney's arrival as a wealthy outsider was timely; society needed a neutral outsider. She flaunted her pro-Jewish position, however. "The wild girl from Cincinnati" broke through any barriers and launched her own salon.

Over the years, almost every important intellectual in Europe visited the salon; once established, its ambiance did not change, but the visitors and the program varied. Fridays became the day when Natalie, dressed in a *haute couture* tea gown, would receive her guests and serve them a sumptuous feast, conversation, and introductions to the newest writers and their works. Her theatricals, produced for friends, featured such performers as Colette and **Mata Hari**. The guest list of literati and intellectuals who were regulars at her salon reads like a who's who: Paul Valéry (whose work she translated for an American audience), Auguste Rodin, André Gide, ***Gertrude Stein**, Virgil Thomson, Sinclair Lewis, Pierre Louys (a writer of erotica who served as her mentor), Ford Maddox Ford, James Joyce, Ernest Hemingway, Gabriele D'Annunzio, T.S. Eliot, **Dolly Wilde**, **Elizabeth de Gramont**, Ezra Pound, Djuna Barnes, ***Janet Flanner**, Rainer Maria Rilke, Romaine Brooks, Jean Cocteau, plus publishers, critics, diplomats and scholars (and much later, newer faces such as Truman Capote, Ned Rorem, and Givenchy).

The salon was by invitation; guests invited other guests who could make a contribution. There were poetry readings, recitations, or music. Projects were hatched, such as "Bel Esprit," a funding scheme to sell stock in writers, subsidizing those in need so they could devote themselves to writing. Sinclair Lewis and Barney discussed launching a bilingual magazine, "How to Live by Those Who Have," but the title was as far as it got. **Madame Gaston Bergery**, another American expatriate, remarked: "Natalie gave you a feast of reason, a seasoning of wit, and a

Mata Hari. *See Zelle, Margaretha Gertrud.*

Vivien, Renée (1877–1909)

Anglo-French poet and supporter of the cult of Sappho. *Name variations: Renee; (real name) Pauline Tarn. Born Pauline Mary Tarn in Paddington, England, in 1877; died at age 32 of self-induced starvation in 1909; buried at Passy; daughter of a Michigan heiress and John Tarn, an English gentleman from Kent.*

After wandering in the East, English-born Renée Vivien settled permanently in Paris where she translated the ancient poetry of ***Sappho** and other women of Lesbos, published as *Les Kitharèdes* (1904). Vivien produced collections of her own French verse entitled *Cendres et poussières* (*Cinders and Dust*, 1902), *Evocations* (1903), and *Les Flambeaux éteints* (*Extinguished Torches*, 1907). She also novelized her turbulent relationship with ***Natalie Clifford Barney** in *Une Femme m'apparut* (*A Woman Appeared to Me*, 1904). Twelve volumes of her poetry, *Poésies complètes*, was published from 1901–10 and reprinted in two volumes in 1934.

In 1900, an early love, **Violet Shilleto**, fell ill, and Vivien broke a promise to visit. When Shilleto died soon after, Vivien was inconsolable, spending hours at her graveside. Other romantic losses followed, including Barney. By 1909, Vivien was living alone in Paris, obsessively dieting and exercising, drinking to excess, while suffering from Basedow's disease (a thyroid imbalance). Choking while attempting to eat, she came down with pneumonia, converted to Catholicism, and died soon after.

Vivien's letters and unpublished manuscripts were given to the Bibliothèque Nationale to be opened in the year 2000. "Her genius—for genius she had—is the more extraordinary as she wrote in a language not her own," wrote Salomon Reinach. Notes **Jeannette H. Foster** in *Sex Variant Women in Literature* (Naiad, 1985): "All the critics who grant her this superlative poetic quality agree that she has received nothing approaching her due recognition because of the lesbian element in her work. In view of the small number of persons in any generation who are tolerant of such love, it may be that she will never receive it."

SUGGESTED READING:

Jay, Karla. ***The Amazon and the Page: Natalie Clifford Barney and Renée Vivien.*** Indiana University Press, 1988.

Le Dantec, Y. ***Renée Vivien: femme damnée, femme sauvée,*** 1930.

Gramont, Elizabeth de (fl. 1875–1935)

French memoirist. *Name variations: Duchesse de Clermont-Tonnerre, Duchesse de Gramont. Born around 1875; died after 1935; daughter of duc de Gramont; married the Duc de Clermont-Tonnerre; children: Béatrix Clermont-Tonnerre.*

Elizabeth de Gramont's *Mémoires* in four volumes were published in Paris by Grasset between the years 1928 and 1935. The first volume, *Au temps des équipages* (translated as *Pomp and Circumstance* when it was published in London by J. Cape in 1931), was a cause celebre on its release in 1928. While most French memoirs penned by 18th- and 19th-century aristocrats pined the loss of the good old days, Elizabeth de Gramont's reflections did quite the opposite. "She looks backward with a shrug rather than a sigh," writes ***Janet Flanner** in *Paris was Yesterday* (Viking, 1972). "Avoiding ideas and offering in their place facts, her pen describes late nineteenth- and early twentieth century faubourg French society—voyaging duchesses who sent no postal cards but whose secretaries cabled, to a limited list of friends, 'The duchess is now [a]cross the Rocky Mountains'." In 1927, Elizabeth and her husband, the duke of Clermont-Tonnerre, were successfully sued by their daughter Béatrix for support. Disapproving of her lifestyle, they were withholding funds.

flow of words." Virgil Thomson recalled that Barney and Gertrude Stein would exchange literary guests to make things more interesting for everyone. Natalie served as a catalyst: "She was one of those people who was always trying to bring people together," remarked Truman Capote. Intelligent, charming, and witty, Barney was unshockable, and her salon was a truly international mix of unlikely callers.

Soon after she established her literary salon, Barney wrote *Eparpillement* (*Scatterings*) in 1910. She spoke in epigrams, and these pithy pensées are her best writing, according to Wickes, along with her memoirs. He noted that she was remarkable for her "swift repartee and accuracy of her aim." Some reflect Oscar Wilde-like wit: "Forever is too long," or, "I have perhaps gotten more out of life than it actually possesses." There is social commentary: "He had the three badges of nonentity: a receding chin, the Legion of Honor, and a wedding ring." And feminism: "Marriage? Maternity? The child also limits the woman and then abandons her."

Friendship was precious to Barney. "I am very lazy," she wrote, "once I confer friendship, I never take it back." Friendship is a theme in two of her works, *Pensées d'une amazone* (*Thoughts of an Amazon*, 1920) and *Nouvelles pensées de l'amazone* (*More Thoughts of the Amazon*, 1939). Her affairs, writes Jay, "led to, expressed, or consummated a friendship: They were not goals, but the means." Barney, however, never found a woman partner who shared her ideal of multiple relationships without jealousy, aside from Dolly Wilde, witty niece of Oscar, who was in Barney's life during the 1920s and the 1930s.

Perhaps Barney's greatest conquest was Remy de Gourmont, an influential man of letters. By the time she met Gourmont in 1910, he was a recluse because of his battle with lupus. Barney courted him, visited him, sent him flowers, and coaxed him out of his house for drives, boat trips, and even appearances in public at her masked ball and her salon. Gourmont knew her sexual orientation but fell in love with her emotionally and sensually, writing a series of letters based on their conversations which were published with her approval in *Mercure de France*. *Lettres a l'Amazone* appeared biweekly in 1912–13 and was published in book form in 1914.

The public became interested and curious to learn more about this Amazon, so named because of the riding habit (*en amazone* in French) she wore for her rides in the Bois before visiting Gourmont. In the next two years, the intensity of her friendship waned, and she saw him more infrequently. When Gourmont died in 1915, some criticized her for causing his decline and death, as some had blamed her for causing Vivien's. After his death, the public read her own views on love, friendship, morality, chastity, religion, and war in *Pensées d'une amazone*, in the form of observations and epigrams. As the Amazon, she became a literary figure, and her salon had its glory days between the world wars. Later, it would continue as a shadow of its former self until 1968.

Along with her mother and sister, Natalie was a staunch pacifist. War was associated with male aggression. She was urged to return to America as World War I approached, but France was her home. She stayed, held antiwar rallys at her Temple of Friendship, ignored the war, and did not volunteer to work in the Red Cross like so many of her friends.

In 1927, between the wars, Natalie Barney launched the Académie des femmes (Academy of Women) as a modern Sapphic circle, an environment where women writers could share their work and find support; she might have been responding to the Académie Française, whose members were exclusively men of letters. French women writers were introduced to their American and English counterparts. French members included Colette, Rachilde (***Marguerite Vallette**), **Aurel**, **Nadine Wong**, Elizabeth de Gramont, and **Lucie Delarue-Mardrus**, while America, England, and Australia were represented by Djuna Barnes, ***Mina Loy**, Gertrude Stein, and ***Anna Wickham**. Romaine Brooks was also included as an aspiring writer of memoirs. During a special program, Gertrude Stein's writings were set to music by Virgil Thomson, and there were readings from her work, including Barney's translation of excerpts from *The Making of Americans*. Funds were raised for the publication of Djuna Barnes' *The Ladies Almanack*.

Natalie Barney and the painter Romaine Brooks spent more than 50 years together; exactly when they met is unclear, but it appears to be before World War I at a gathering of bohemian women. Both American and both from privileged backgrounds, they traveled together, danced, and swam. Barney wrote poems for Brooks that addressed her intellect, Brooks designed jewelry for Barney and painted her portrait. According to Brooks' biographer, **Meryle Secrest**, their relationship represented the love and acceptance that Romaine had never received from her mother.

Brooks had great expectations from friends and suffered disappointments; Barney demanded little and maintained her friendships. According to Secrest, Romaine wanted to "possess and be possessed." As in her other relationships, Romaine as Natalie's partner was essentially monogamous, which led to problems as Natalie formed other liaisons concurrently. Brooks painted many in their circle, though she excluded her serious rivals for Barney's affection. The couple collaborated on a book whose theme is androgyny, *The One Who is Legion, or A.D.'s After-Life,* privately printed in English in London in 1930.

Barney's 14-year relationship (for seven, a secret) with a younger woman, **Janine Lahovary**, was the beginning of the end for Brooks and Barney. Natalie was in her 80s, and she had a liberating effect on this wife of the former Rumanian ambassador who only lived for her family. Lahovary met Barney by chance in Nice during the late 1950s. Intelligent and interested in psychoanalysis, Lahovary could provide practical help and compassionate companionship to Natalie. But Barney was the only love of Romaine Brooks' life, according to Secrest, and her jealousy precipitated a final separation. Barney's final appeal to Brooks—"My Angel is, as ever, first in my thoughts and deepest in my heart"—was returned to the sender unopened.

To her biographers, Natalie Clifford Barney's anti-Semitism expressed during World War II is especially troubling and contradictory, given her Jewish ancestry. In her early works, she is open about her background and proud of her family's achievements. In her afterward for *A Perilous Advantage*, **Anna Livia** observes that in Barney's unpublished *Memoirs of a European-American*, a book of wartime reminiscences and commentary, there is a changing perspective on the war. During World War II, Barney and Brooks sought refuge in Italy, outside Florence. Interviewed after the Allied victory in Italy, Barney claimed that they were "artists who knew too little about politics to take any part in them." She had saved Jewish musicians in Italy by giving them her cabin on board a New York-bound ship, yet her friends were interned in concentration camps, and she wrote lightly of "wars of extermination."

Livia believes that Barney's loyalty to Mussolini and the Axis during the war years was confused with the notion that "tradition, artistic expression and personal freedom must prevail over the communist threat." From their villa outside Florence, Brooks and Barney observed Germans in retreat blowing up the famous Florentine bridges. Livia speculates that Barney's change in attitude in her memoirs—by their end, she is proudly pro-American and a pacifist—occurred when the Germans, "champions of Art, History, and Tradition, are systematically destroying irreplaceable objects of beauty."

After losing her 20 rue Jacob address in the courts to her landlord, ostensibly because of structural problems, Barney moved to the Hotel Meurice. After a heart attack and pneumonia, Natalie Clifford Barney died on February 2, 1972. Her longtime maid, **Berthe Cleyrergue**, noted that her Friday funeral was "Mademoiselle's last Friday." Barney was buried in the Cimitiere de Passy at Trocadero, an old cemetery, circa 1900, that is filled with her old friends.

SOURCES:

Barney, Natalie Clifford. *Adventures of the Mind.* Translated by John Spalding Gatton. NY: New York University Press, 1992.

Benstock, Sheri. *Women of the Left Bank.* Austin: University of Texas Press, 1986.

Chalon, Jean. *Portrait of a Seductress.* NY: Crown Books, 1979.

Grindea, Miron, ed. "Amazon of Letters: a World Tribute to Natalie Clifford Barney," in *Adam International Review.* Vol. 29, no. 299, 1962.

Jay, Karla. *The Amazon and the Page: Natalie Clifford Barney and Renée Vivien.* Bloomington: Indiana University Press, 1988.

Livia, Anna, ed. and trans. *A Perilous Adventure; The Best of Natalie Clifford Barney.* Norwich, CT: New Victoria Publishers, 1992.

Secrest, Meryle. *Between Me and Life: A Biography of Romaine Brooks.* Garden City, NY: Doubleday, 1974.

Wickes, George. *The Amazon of Letters: The Life and Loves of Natalie Barney.* NY: Putnam, 1976.

———, ed. "A Natalie Barney Garland," in *The Paris Review.* Spring 1975, pp. 86–134.

SUGGESTED READING:

Barnes, Djuna. *Ladies Almanack.* NY: Harper & Row, 1972.

Colette. *Claudine s'en va.* Paris: Ollendorf, 1903.

———. *Le Pur et l'impur.* Paris: Ferenczi, 1941.

Gramont, Elizabeth de [Duchesse de Clermont-Tonnerre]. *Mémoires.* 4 vols. Paris: Grasset, 1928–35. Vol. 1 (1928): *Au temps des équipages.* Trans. as *Pomp and Circumstance.* London: J. Cape & H. Smith, 1931.

———. *Years of Plenty.* London: J. Cape & H. Smith, 1931.

Gourmont, Remy de. *Lettres a l'Amazone.* Paris: Cres, 1914 (also published as *Letters to the Amazon.* London: Chatto & Windus, 1931).

———. *Lettres intime a l'Amazone.* Paris: La Centaine, 1926.

Grindea, Miron, ed. *Selected Writings.* London: Adam Books, 1963.

Hall, Radclyffe. *The Well of Loneliness.* NY: Covici-Friede, 1928.

Harris, Bertha. "The More Profound Nationality of Their Lesbianism: Lesbian Society in Paris in the 1920s" in *Amazon Expedition: A Lesbian-Feminist Anthology.* Ed. by Phyllis Birlby, *et al.* NY: Time Changes Press, 1973, pp. 77–88.

Pougy, Liane de. *Mes Cahiers bleus.* Paris: Plon, 1977.

Vivien, Renée. *A Woman Appeared to Me.* Trans. by Jeannette H. Foster. Reno, NV: Naiad Press, 1976.

COLLECTIONS:

Some letters and other manuscript materials are in the Beinecke Rare Book and Manuscript Library, Yale University.

Chapon, Francois, Nicole Prevot, and Richard Sieburth, comps. *Autour de Natalie Barney* (1976). Catalogue of Barney's papers, mostly letters written to her, in the Fonds Litteraire Jacques Doucet in Paris.

Laurie Norris, freelance writer, New York, New York

Barns, Cornelia Baxter

(1888–1941)

American magazine illustrator and political activist. *Name variations: Cornelia Barns Garbett. Born Cornelia Baxter Barns in Philadelphia, Pennsylvania, in 1888; died in 1941; daughter of Charles Barns (an impresario); studied art at the Philadelphia Academy of Fine Arts; married Arthur Selwyn Garbett (a music critic); children: son, Charles (b. 1915).*

Began contributing drawings to radical magazine The Masses *(1914); moved to California (1917); continued to draw and also worked as a journalist; one of the few women illustrators to appear in the Socialist press.*

Born in Philadelphia in 1888, Cornelia Baxter Barns was the daughter of theatrical impresario Charles Barns and grew up in a lively, artistically stimulating environment. She studied art at the Philadelphia Academy of Fine Arts and was twice awarded the school's traveling scholarship. After graduation, she began working as an illustrator. Drawn to the more exciting artistic milieu of New York City, she arrived there around 1911.

Barns married the music critic Arthur Selwyn Garbett and gave birth to a son Charles in 1915. Once in New York, she quickly became active in avant-garde art and politics, serving as director of the Art Worker's Club for Women. By 1914, she was contributing illustrations to *The Masses*, the leading Socialist magazine in the United States. In 1915, several of Barns' works were exhibited at the Salon of American Humorists, an exhibition held at the Folsom Gallery. Though her health was delicate, Barns was an active member of the Socialist Party.

Barns was one of the few women to play a significant role in *The Masses*, a fact indicative of the overwhelmingly male-dominated leadership in Socialist politics in the United States, a leadership which often played down or virtually ignored the feminist agenda of the day. Virtually all of the articles on women's issues appearing in *The Masses* were written by men. Her cartoons, which appeared in the publication until its suppression by the government in 1917, avoided portentous statements of universal social analysis, depicting instead average working people living their normal, often difficult, lives. Barns often wielded a gentle and witty pen; in her March 1914 cartoon of an anti-suffrage meeting of males, "United We Stand!," there is considerable wit but little bitterness in her depiction of several foolish men still unwilling to grant women the right to vote.

Stricken with tuberculosis, in 1917 Barns moved with her family to California to find a healthier climate. Committed to radical ideals of political and social change, she continued to contribute to such journals as *Liberator*, *New Masses*, *Suffragist*, and *Woman Voter.* In 1921, she served briefly as both associate editor and art director of *Birth Control Review.* Determined to remain in touch with the radical New York scene, she maintained a lively correspondence with old friends and was visited by a number of them, including Max Eastman and Mike Gold. For many years, Barns published a daily editorial vignette, "My City Oakland," which appeared in the *Oakland Post Enquirer.* She died in 1941.

SOURCES:

Barns, Cornelia. "Twelve-Thirty" [cartoon], in *The Masses.* Vol. 6. January 1915, p. 15.

Churchill, Allen. *The Improper Bohemians: A Recreation of Greenwich Village in its Heyday.* NY: E.P. Dutton, 1959.

City Life Illustrated, 1890–1940. Exhibition catalogue, Delaware Art Museum, 1980.

Mason, Tim. "Cornelia Barns Garbett." California Art Research, Carmel, unpublished research report.

Zurier, Rebecca. *Art for the Masses: A Radical Magazine and Its Graphics, 1911–1917.* Philadelphia, PA: Temple University Press, 1988.

John Haag, Associate Professor, University of Georgia, Athens, Georgia

Baron, Devorah (1887–1956)

Israeli novelist who wrote about life as a Jew in Russia. *Name variations: Deborah Baron. Born in 1887 in Uzda, Russia; died in 1956 in Israel; daughter of a Russian rabbi; married Joseph Aharonovitz (a magazine editor).*

Selected works: (stories) Sipurim *(1927); (episodes)* Parshiyot *(1968);* The Thorny Patch *(1969); also translated Flaubert's* Madame Bovary.

In predominantly Christian Russia, small villages and encampments of Jews, centered around a rabbi or synagogue, grew into self-sufficient communities called shtetls. As the daughter of one such rabbi, Devorah Baron was intimately familiar with the people and movements of shtetls. Following her emigration from Russia to Palestine in 1911, she began publishing stories of shtetl life in the journal *Ha-Po'el ha Za'ir* (The Young Worker), edited by her soon-to-be-husband Joseph Aharonovitz. She also managed a literary supplement for *Ha-Po'el* but, in the four years following World War I, had to continue the work from Egypt as an exile. When she returned to Palestine, shtetl life in Eastern Europe had largely disappeared, but Baron kept the communities alive in three volumes of fiction. The latter two, *Parshiyot* and *The Thorny Patch*, were written from her bed, where she was confined for her last 20 years.

Crista Martin, freelance writer, Boston, Massachusetts

Baroni, Adriana Basile (c. 1590–c. 1640).

See Basile, Adriana.

Baroni, Leonora (1611–1670)

Italian singer. *Born in 1611; died in 1670; daughter of Adriana Basile (an Italian singer) and Mutio Baroni; sister of Caterina Baroni (1620–?).*

Leonora Baroni, daughter of famed Italian singer ***Adriana Basile**, followed in her mother's footsteps, becoming a famous singer in Italy and France. She was often accompanied by her mother on the theorbo while her sister **Caterina Baroni** played the harp. When John Milton heard Baroni's magnificent voice, he was so moved that he composed three Latin epigrams for her; in one of them, the poet compared her to Tasso's Leonora, "for the mad love of whom, he walked raging in the world."

Baronova, Irina (b. 1919).

See Toumanova, Tamara for sidebar.

Barr, Amelia Huddleston (1831–1919)

British-American author of American historical fiction. *Name variations: Amelia Edith Barr. Born Amelia Faith Huddleston on March 29, 1831, in Ulverston, Lancashire, England; died on March 10, 1919, in New York; daughter of Mary Singleton and William Henry Huddleston (a Methodist minister); sporadically educated at home and in private schools; married Robert Barr (1826–1867), on July 11, 1850, in Kendal, England; children: thirteen, including four who died at birth, and Mary (b. 1851), Eliza (called Lilly, b. 1853), Edith (b. 1854), Calvin (b. 1857), Alice (b. 1859), Ethel (b. 1861), Alexander (b. 1863), Archibald (b. 1864), and Andrew (b. 1867).*

Selected works: Jan Vedder's Wife *(1885);* Remember the Alamo *(1888);* Friend Olivia *(1889);* All the Days of My Life *(1913).*

In 1867, widowed in Texas with no money and three daughters, Amelia Barr moved to New York, where she hoped to support her family by writing. A compulsive writer, working until she made herself ill, Barr produced more than 80 books in 40 years of writing, including five novels in 1892 alone.

Born in England in 1831, Amelia Huddleston Barr was one of several children of Mary and William Henry Huddleston, a Methodist minister. The Huddlestons moved often to parsonages throughout Lancashire, and the family was left poorer after a friend absconded with their small inheritance. Though the children attended school only when funding allowed, Amelia loved to read and started writing stories and poetry as a young girl.

With her father's retirement due to illness, Amelia decided to become a teacher to bolster the family income, studying first with a family friend. Through the sponsorship of another minister, she attended a school in Glasgow, Scotland, which taught the Stowe method for educating poor children. There, she met Robert Barr, a Scottish merchant, and married in July of 1850. Robert's mother objected to the marriage because Amelia brought only debts as her dowry. A fear of financial debt was to haunt Amelia throughout her life, both because she often had so little money, and because she worked so hard to earn it.

Robert Barr was a successful entrepreneur, but overzealous dealings soon bankrupted him, and his reputation was ruined in Glasgow. Thus, in August of 1853, three years after their marriage, Robert, Amelia, and two daughters left England covertly (to evade Robert's mother and his business enemies) and sailed for New York. Barr felt confident. In her dreams, she'd had premonitions which assured her that the move was a positive step.

It was not long, however, before their arrival in America was marked by misfortune. Aboard the steamer, Robert had met and become partners with a like-minded businessman from Chicago. By year's end, the Barrs were settled in the North Side of the city, in a house large enough for a school. Three years later, because of more business reversals, the Barrs were forced to move. They went south to Memphis, Tennessee, taking with them the coffin of their small daughter Edith, who had lived only eight months. Six months later, the Barrs were fleeing Memphis and a cholera epidemic.

They sailed to Texas on a slave transport ship, eventually settling in Austin. Good fortune followed with the birth of their first son Calvin, and Robert's job as comptroller for the Texas legislature. By 1861, two more Barr daughters were born, but the political climate had changed. As North and South took up arms against each other, Texas faced the decision of remaining with the Union, joining the rising Confederacy, or returning to its former independence. For fear of entanglement in political affairs, Robert resigned his position in the legislature and turned to accounting. His meager list of clients were scarcely enough to keep his burgeoning family fed. In all, Amelia gave birth to thirteen children, six of whom died in infancy.

With the Emancipation Proclamation of 1864, the Union reasserted its hold on Texas. In 1866, the Barrs moved to Galveston, hoping to find work. A few months later, yellow-fever struck. From April to September of 1867, as the epidemic raged throughout Texas, Barr's husband and four sons died, while Amelia and her three daughters, though near death, survived.

Stunned and weak from her illness, Amelia spent a year trying to forge a life in Texas. Friends helped her establish a boarding house, but the venture failed. Carrying a letter of introduction from a friend, she headed northeast and found work as a music teacher for the sons of a publisher in Ridgewood, New Jersey. The post lasted 18 months, until her young students went to college, at which time she moved her daughters to New York City.

"I was nearly 39 years old," Barr wrote in her autobiography, "when I . . . began a life so different from the lives I had lived in Glasgow, Chicago, Austin and Galveston, that I might have been born again for it." She launched her writing career with an account of the unrest she witnessed in Texas (the distant state was a mystery and curiosity in the Northeast). She became a regular contributor to Henry Ward Beecher's *Christian Union* and spent hours doing research at New York's Astor Library.

Publisher Henry Holt recommended that Barr take on historical fiction. Writing eight to ten hours a day, often until she became seriously ill (including a six-month bout with "inflammation of the brain" in 1880–81), Barr was financially rewarded for her efforts. She also received critical acclaim with the 1885 publication of *Jan Vedder's Wife*. Her exhausting pace continued. "My right thumb was almost useless, . . . and the outside of the little finger was so sensitive that I wrapped it in cotton wool to prevent it feeling the movement on the paper." A typewriter enabled Barr to write even faster, the most famous result of which was the 1888 *Remember the Alamo*.

At last financially secure, Barr established a home, Cherry Croft, in Cornwall-on-Hudson and occasional summered in Europe. Her later years were spent at Richmond Hill, where she lived quietly, surrounded by friends, still devoting most of her time to her writing. When a 1909 fall down the stairs caused paralysis in her right arm, she learned to write with her left hand. In 1911, she wrote her autobiography, *All the Days of My Life*, in just two months. It was published in 1913, six years before she died.

Barr, who did not start writing until she had reached the age of 53, wrote no fewer than 80 novels. The last one completed in June 1918, was entitled *The Paper Cap* and was based on labor troubles in her native England. She was best in historical tales that dealt with religious persecution, and in scenes of Scotland, the north of England, and Dutch New York. "I say gratefully, yes, joyfully," she once wrote, "they were all good days, for always God has been what He promised me—'Sufficient!'"

SUGGESTED READING:

Barr, Amelia. *All the Days of My Life: An Autobiography.* NY: D. Appleton, 1913.

Crista Martin, freelance writer, Boston, Massachusetts

Barr, Margaret Scolari (1901–1987)

Italian-born American art historian and teacher. *Born Margaret Scolari in 1901 in Rome; died in New York City on December 30, 1987; daughter of Virgilio Scolari (an antiques dealer) and Mary Fitzmaurice Scolari; studied at the University of Rome, 1919–22; married Alfred Barr, in 1930; children: daughter, Victoria (also a painter).*

Came to the United States (1925); taught at Vassar College (1925–29); collaborated with husband, the founding director of the Museum of Modern Art (1930–81); active with the Emergency Rescue Committee during World War II; taught art history at the Spence School (1943–80).

Margaret Scolari Barr was a distinguished art historian who played a significant role in saving the lives of endangered artists in Nazi-occupied Europe in the early 1940s. She was born in Rome in 1901, the daughter of Virgilio Scolari, an Italian antiques dealer, and Mary Fitzmaurice, known as an ebullient Irishwoman. Educated at the University of Rome, she came to the United States in 1925, where she received a master's degree in art history at Vassar College, a university at which she also taught. In September 1929, she moved to New York City and was present at the inaugural exhibition of the Museum of Modern Art.

At the museum's opening, she met the young, enthusiastic Alfred Barr, who was the new institution's director. Instantly drawn to each other, they married in Paris in 1930. A day after the wedding, too busy with his work to take time off for a honeymoon, Barr began scouring Paris for paintings for a forthcoming exhibition of the works of Corot and Daumier. Because of Margaret Scolari Barr's linguistic skills and mastery of the history of Western art, she found herself "drafted" to act as his translator, secretary, and indispensable associate. They worked in this fashion throughout the 1930s as they traveled to Europe virtually every summer to beg and borrow paintings for the following year's exhibitions.

Intensely aware of the destructive nature of Nazism and Fascism, Margaret Barr was actively involved in the work of the Emergency Rescue Committee, operating in France in 1940 and 1941, which brought to the United States a number of artists whose lives were threatened for racial or political reasons in Nazi-occupied Europe. These included Max Ernst, Piet Mondrian, Jacques Lipchitz, Yves Tanguy, and André Masson. Europe's loss was America's gain, and the New York art scene was greatly enriched and stimulated through the presence of these and other European emigrés throughout the 1940s. In 1943, with travel to Europe impossible, Barr began teaching at New York's Spence School, a position she would hold until her retirement in 1980. She was known for her ability to connect students to the beauty and power of art. In her introductory art lecture at Spence, she once ended with: "Now plan to enjoy yourselves. As Poussin, the great French painter of the 17th century, remarked, '*Le fin de l'art est la délectation*' (The goal of art is delight)." As Michael Brenson noted in his *New York Times* obituary after her death in New York on December 30, 1987, "The diversity of Mrs. Barr's talents and the force of her personality made her a presence in the New York art world for half a century."

SOURCES:

Barr, Margaret Scolari. "Our Campaigns," in *The New Criterion*. Summer, 1987.

Brenson, Michael. "Margaret Scolari Barr, a Teacher and Art Historian, Is Dead at 86," in *The New York Times Biographical Service*. December 1987, p. 1394.

John Haag, Associate Professor, University of Georgia, Athens, Georgia

Barra (c. 590–640/41).

See Zaynab bint Jahsh.

Barraine, Elsa (1910—)

French composer, considered one of the most gifted since *Lili Boulanger. *Born Jacqueline Elsa Barraine in Paris on February 10, 1910; studied at the Paris Conservatory with Paul Dukas for composition and Jean Gallon for harmony.*

In 1929, Elsa Barraine won the coveted Prix de Rome for her *La vierge guerriere*. From 1936 to 1939, she was Chef du Chant for the RTF (Radio Télevision Français), and, during World War II, she was with the Front National des Musiciens. In 1953, Barraine was appointed professor of musical analysis at the Paris Conservatory. She composed three symphonies, a comic opera, and several pieces for chorus; her fame was built around several compositions known for their evocation of tension and tragedy.

John Haag, Athens, Georgia

Barre, Margot de la (d. 1390).

See French "Witches" (14th–16th centuries).

Barreno, Maria Isabel (b. 1939).

See Three Marias, The.

Barrett, Elizabeth (1806–1861).

See Browning, Elizabeth Barrett.

Barrett, Janie Porter (1865–1948)

African-American welfare worker and founder of one of the first rehabilitation centers for black female delinquents. *Born Janie Porter on August 9, 1865, in Athens, Georgia; died in Hampton, Virginia, on August 27, 1948; graduated from Hampton Institute in*

Hampton, Virginia, in 1884; married Harris Barrett, in October 1889; children: four.

After growing up in the cultured home of the white family for whom her mother worked, Janie Porter graduated from Hampton Institute in 1884 and accepted the first of several teaching positions that would occupy the next five years. In 1889, she married Harris Barrett and opened a small day-care school in her home in Hampton, Virginia. Growing rapidly, the school was formally organized as the Locust Street Social Settlement in October 1890, the nation's first such settlement for blacks. Barrett's organization offered a variety of activities, including clubs, recreation, and training in home management. With support from Hampton Institute, at which she had taught and where her husband served as cashier and bookkeeper, funds were raised to keep the settlement going.

In 1908, Barrett founded and became president of the Virginia State Federation of Colored Women's Clubs, through which she worked to raise money to begin a residential industrial school for black female juvenile delinquents who were being committed to asylums and jails in alarming numbers. In 1915, on a 147-acre farm called Peaks Turnout, the Virginia Industrial School for Colored Girls opened. The 28 girls in residence had the benefit of a program which stressed self-reliance and self-discipline. With advice and help from prominent social workers and the Russell Sage Foundation (a leader in the area of social welfare reform), the girls received individual attention and guidance. A program of academic and vocational training was added later.

In 1915, Barrett was widowed and moved to the school as superintendent. Overseeing every aspect of the program, she personally conducted the parole system by which selected girls were placed in foster homes, given jobs, and supported with follow-up services. In 1920, with an enrollment of about 100, the school became state-run, with supervision shared by the women's club federation. The Virginia Industrial School was rated by the Russell Sage Foundation as one of the five best programs of its kind in the country. Barrett's greatest joy was to see her girls released into society, employed, married, and raising caring families of their own; for Barrett, this was the true measure of rehabilitation.

Barrett's efforts did not go unnoticed. In 1929, she received the William E. Harmon Award for Distinguished Achievement among Negroes, and in 1930 was a participant in the White House Conference on Child Health and Protection. Retired in 1940, Barrett lived in Hampton until her death in 1948. In 1950, the school was renamed the Janie Porter Barrett School for Girls. Another of Barrett's dreams was realized when the school was racially integrated and expanded to include boys.

Barbara Morgan, Melrose, Massachusetts

Barrett, Kate Waller (1857–1925)

Social worker and administrator of the National Florence Crittenton Mission for unwed mothers. *Born Kate Harwood Waller in Falmouth, Virginia, on January 24, 1857; died in Alexandria, Virginia, on February 23, 1925; attended Arlington Institute for Girls, in Alexandria; Florence Nightingale Training School and St. Thomas' Hospital, London, England; Women's Medical College of Georgia, M.D., 1892; married Rev. Robert S. Barrett, in July 1876; children: seven.*

Kate Barrett's interest in the plight of prostitutes and unwed mothers is said to have begun when a young girl holding her baby appeared on the doorstep of the rectory where Barrett lived with her husband, an Episcopal minister. Engaging the young woman in conversation, Barrett was surprised to discover that her background was remarkably like her own. This recognition of commonality galvanized Barrett; she decided to do what she could to help this "outcast class," as they were known in her day.

After attending training courses in social work and receiving a medical degree from the Women's Medical College of Georgia, Barrett contacted Charles N. Crittenton, a businessman turned evangelist, who had opened four homes for "fallen women" in California, naming them for his deceased daughter Florence. In 1893, with $5,000 from Crittenton, Barrett opened a fifth in the chain of Florence Crittenton homes for unwed mothers in Atlanta.

The following year, Barrett moved to Washington, D.C., where she aided in the foundation of the National Florence Crittenton Mission. As vice president and general superintendent, she took charge of the nationwide chain, now numbering 50 semi-autonomous homes. In addition to visiting the homes and establishing a training course for workers, Barrett started a magazine and published a book, *Some Practical Suggestions on the Conduct of a Rescue Home* (1903). Following Charles Crittenton's death in 1909, Barrett succeeded to the presidency of the organization but retained her former duties. Gradually, the homes began to move away from their evangelical approach to a more practical program of training in mothering skills and vocational guidance.

Meanwhile, Barrett became a much sought-after expert in her field. In 1909, she was invited to the White House Conference for the Care of Dependent Children and, in 1914, was a special representative of the Labor Department on a commission investigating the treatment of women deported from the country on moral grounds. She was also active in the National Council of Women, the Virginia Equal Suffrage League, and the National Women's Auxiliary of the American Legion.

Barbara Morgan, Melrose, Massachusetts

Barrientos, Maria (1884–1946)

Spanish soprano who, as a child prodigy, appeared in the world's great opera houses. *Born in Barcelona, Spain, on March 10, 1884; died in Ciboure, Basses Pyrénées on August 8, 1946.*

When Maria Barrientos was 12, she wrote a symphony at the Barcelona Conservatory and conducted it when she graduated that same year. In 1896, few women conducted the world's almost all male orchestras, but Barrientos was determined to make her mark. She took singing lessons until she was not quite 15 and debuted at the Teatro de Novidades in Barcelona. In 1903, she sang in Covent Garden and a year later at La Scala; she was not yet 20. Barrientos appeared in many of the world's opera houses before finally debuting at the Metropolitan Opera in 1916. She recorded frequently and one set of records was made with Manuel de Falla at the piano.

John Haag, Athens, Georgia

Barringer, Emily Dunning (1876–1961)

Surgeon, gynecologist, former president of American Medical Women's Association, and pioneer in opening the field of medicine to women. *Born Emily Dunning in Scarsdale, New York, on September 27, 1876; died in New Milford, Connecticut, on April 8, 1961; attended Cornell University, B.S., 1896; Cornell Medical School, M.D., 1901; married Benjamin Stockwell Barringer, in 1904: children: Benjamin Lang, Emily Velona.*

Emily Dunning graduated second in her class from Cornell Medical School and won first place in competitions for positions at both Mount Sinai and Gouverneur Hospital in New York City. She was denied both appointments, however, because the year was 1901, and she was a woman.

Emily Dunning Barringer

In 1903, learning of Dunning's plight, reform mayor Seth Low vowed that if a woman qualified for a place at Gouverneur Hospital, he would ratify her placement. She took the examination again, won fourth place, and began a two-year internship and residency at Gouverneur Hospital as the first woman ambulance surgeon in New York City. Although some male medical interns in the city petitioned against her appointment, her first emergency call in a horse-drawn ambulance was cheered. When her route included the lower East Side, one paper called her "the beautiful girl on the Bowery run."

Dunning married fellow surgeon Benjamin Stockwell Barringer in 1904, and, a year later, became a member of the Gouverneur Hospital staff; again, she was the first woman to serve in such a position in a New York hospital. During a distinguished career that spanned 50 years, Barringer was president of the Women's Medical Association of New York City, and she was a fellow of the College of Surgeons and the New York Academy of Medicine. She also worked tirelessly for the passage of progressive medical legislation, including the right for women medical doctors to receive commissions in the military.

Barbara Morgan, Melrose, Massachusetts

Barrington, Margaret (1896–1982)

Irish writer of short stories. *Born in Malin, County Donegal, Ireland, in 1896; died in West Cork, Ireland, in 1982; attended Trinity College, Dublin; married Liam O'Flaherty, her second husband.*

Known for numerous short stories and a novel, *My Cousin Justin* (1939), Margaret Barrington also worked in England during the '30s, writing a woman's page for the *Tribune*. A selection of her short stories, *David's Daughter, Tamar*, was published shortly after her death in 1982. Somewhat of a political activist, Barrington helped refugees from Nazi Germany and supported the Republicans in the Spanish Civil War. She returned to Ireland in the 1940s, where she lived in obscurity until her death.

Barriscale, Bessie (1884–1965)

***American actress.** Born Elizabeth Barry Scale in Hoboken, New Jersey, on September 30, 1884; died in 1965; married Howard Hickman (a director and actor).*

Bessie Barriscale began her career on stage. Jesse Lasky brought her to Hollywood with his Famous Players Company and, once there, she starred in DeMille films as well as those directed by Thomas Ince, typically romantic melodramas, during her prominent years of 1914–1920. She then established her own film company. Her films include *Eileen of Erin* (1913), *Rose of the Rancho* (1914), *The Cup of Life* (1915), *The Golden Claw* (1915), *The Painted Soul* (1915), *Honor's Altar* (1916), *The Sorrows of Love* (1916), *The Payment* (1916), *Plain Jane* (1916), *The Hater of Men* (1917), *Borrowed Plumage* (1917), *Wooden Shoes* (*Dutch Shoes*, 1917), *Madam Who* (1918), *Blindfolded* (1918), *Patriotism* (1918), *The White Lie* (1918), *Her Purchase Price* (1919), *The Notorious Mrs. Sands* (1920), *Life's Twist* (1920), *The Broken Gate* (1920), *The Breaking Point* (1921), *Show Folks* (1928), *Secrets* (1933), *Beloved* (1934), and *The Man Who Reclaimed His Head* (1935).

Bessie Barriscale

Barrow, Nita (1916–1995)

***Dame of St. Andrew, Grand Commander of Saint Michael and Saint George, who was the first female governor-general of Barbados.** Name variations: Dame Nita Barrow. Born Ruth Nita Barrow on November 15, 1916, in Barbados; died on December 19, 1995, in Barbados; daughter of Bishop Reginald Barrow (an Anglican priest and political martyr); sister of Errol Barrow (who led Barbados to political independence); attended St. Michael's Girls School, 1928; attended Columbia University, New York City; University of Toronto, Canada; Edinburgh University, Scotland.*

Held nursing and public health posts in Barbados and Jamaica (1940–56); was matron of the University Hospital in Jamaica (1954); served as principal nursing officer, Jamaica (1956–62); was nursing adviser, Pan American Health Organization (1967–71); worked as associate director, Christian Medical Commission of World Council of Churches, Geneva (1971–75); served as director, Christian Medical Commission of World Council of Churches, Geneva (1975–80); served as health consultant, World Health Organization (1981–86); was permanent representative of Barbados to United Nations (1986–90); served as governor-general of Barbados (1990–95). Also served as president of the World YWCA (1973–83); president of the International Council for Adult Education (1982); president of the World Council of Churches (1983); member of the Commonwealth Group of Eminent Persons on South Africa (1986).

Nita Barrow was born into a family bound by a tradition of civic activism: her father was Bishop Reginald Barrow whose outspoken criticism of the social inequities of his time led to his being persecuted by political and ecclesiastical powers in Barbados and abroad; her maternal uncle was Dr. Charles Duncan O'Neal, a champion of the underprivileged and disenfranchised in Barbados during the 1930s; and her cousin Hugh Springer was her immediate predecessor as governor-general. Barrow's own commitment to service was based on her profound love of people. At a time when nursing was one of the few employment alternatives available to women, she distinguished herself in public health and the training and administration of nurses in the Caribbean. She gave encouragement to women by attaining prominent positions both in Barbados and abroad, and was the first black woman to ever become president of the World Council of Churches.

A Woman's life can really be a succession of lives, each revolving around some emotionally compelling situation or challenge, and each marked off by some intense experience.

—**Nita Barrow**

On June 6, 1990, Dame Nita became Barbados' first female governor-general. As a diplomat, she was highly respected internationally for her community service, her work in the women's movement, and her involvement in the struggle against apartheid. In her role as governor-general, she impacted all walks of life and took pride in her country. In spite of international acclaim, she never lost touch with the common people and was greatly loved by Barbadians. Each Christmas, Barrow spent time visiting the almshouses and the home for the infirm and took particular delight and interest in children. "Any one who has ever asked Nita for the telephone number or address of one of her friends soon looks on in amazement at the address book which she produces," wrote Francis Blackman. The thick, leather-bound volume, held together by an elastic band, was "Nita's link with the world." As one journalist put it: she was a woman "for all people and the people's governor-general." On December 19, 1995, Dame Nita Barrow died after suffering a massive stroke while attending the annual Christmas Gala of the Royal Barbados Gazetted Officers.

SOURCES:

The Barbados Advocate. December 1995.

Blackman, Francis. *Dame Nita: Caribbean Woman,* World Citizen, 1995.

Nation. December 1995.

Walters, Ena. *A History of Nursing in Barbados.* Barbados: Caribbean Graphic Production, 1995.

Joan Francis, Professor of History and coordinator of Women Studies at Atlantic Union College, South Lancaster, Massachusetts

Nita Barrow

Barrows, Isabel Hayes (1845–1913)

American editor, ophthalmology surgeon, and penologist. *Name variations: Katharine I. Barrows. Born Katharine Isabel Hayes in Iras, Vermont, on April 16, 1845; died in Croton-on-Hudson, New York, in 1913; attended Woman's Medical College of the New York Infirmary for Women and Children, 1868; studied ophthalmology in Vienna, Austria, 1869; married Samuel June Barrows (an author and eventually Unitarian minister), in 1865.*

In 1865, Isabel Hayes became the wife of Samuel Barrows, an author and stenographic secretary to Secretary of State William H. Seward. When Samuel became ill in 1868, Isabel replaced him, becoming the first women to be employed by the U.S. Department of State in Washington, D.C. That same year, she studied medicine in New York City, graduating with an M.D. degree. After further study in Vienna, she returned to America to open a private medical practice while teaching at Howard University in Washington, and, for 20 years, she edited the *Proceedings of the National Conference of Charities and Correction.* Barrows was honored for her notable service as secretary to the National Prison Association.

Barrows, Katherine I. (1845–1913).

See Barrows, Isabel Hayes.

Barry, Ann Street (1734–1801)

Irish actress. *Name variations: Mrs. Spranger Barry, Mrs. Barry, Ann Crawford, Ann Dancer. Born in Bath, England, in 1734; died on November 29, 1801; married an actor named Dancer; married Spranger Barry (an Irish actor), in 1768 (died 1777); married a Mr. Crawford, in 1778.*

While very young, Ann Barry married an actor named Dancer, and she first appeared on the stage about 1756 under the name Ann Dancer. In 1768, she married Spranger Barry, considered one of the greatest actors of his time and rival of David Garrick. One year after his death in 1777, she married a Mr. Crawford. Ann Barry, not to be confused with actress ***Elizabeth Barry**, was considered the equal of ***Peg Woffington** and ***Susannah Cibber** in tragedy and to have surpassed both in comedy. When she died on November 29, 1801, she was buried near her second husband Spranger Barry in the cloisters of Westminster Abbey.

Barry, Elizabeth (1658–1713)

English actress, one of the most famous of her time. *Name variations: Mrs. Barry. Born in 1658; died on November 7, 1713; children: a child with Lord Rochester and a second with Sir George Etheredge.*

One of the most famous tragic actresses of her time, Elizabeth Barry also created over 100 roles in comedy, including Lady Brute in *The Provoked Wife*. Though details of Barry's early life are sketchy, it is known that she was so unsuccessful on stage initially that she was fired more than once. Then, her former lover, the Earl of Rochester, placed a monetary wager that in a short time, with his coaching, he could turn her into a first-rate actress. Barry was worth the wager. Her 1673 performance as Isabella, queen of Hungary, in the earl of Orrery's *Mustapha*, was said to have caused Charles II and the duke and duchess of York (James II and ***Anne Hyde**) so much delight that the duchess took lessons in English from her. So impressed was the duchess that when she became queen she loaned Barry her coronation robes in which Barry then appeared as ***Elizabeth II** in Banks' *Earl of Essex*. Barry was particularly successful in the plays of Thomas Otway. Thomas Betterton claimed that her acting gave "success to plays that would disgust the most patient reader," while John Dryden pronounced her "always excellent." Colley Cibber maintained that it was on Barry's behalf that benefits—which up to that time had only been given for authors—were first established for actors by command of James II. Barry had one child by Lord Rochester and a second by Sir George Etheredge, both children were provided for by their fathers. Mrs. Barry retired from the stage in 1709, four years before her death on November 7, 1713, and burial at Acton. It was Elizabeth Barry, not ***Ann Street Barry**, who was known as "the great Mrs. Barry."

Barry, Iris (1895–1969)

English-American author and museum official. *Born in Birmingham, England, in 1895; died in 1969; educated in England and at the Ursuline Convent, Verviers, Belgium.*

From 1925 to 1930, Iris Barry was a movie critic for *The Spectator* and movie editor for London's *Daily Mail*. Shortly thereafter, she settled in the United States. From 1932 to 1935, she was librarian of the Museum of Modern Art in New York City and, from 1935 to 1950, was curator, then director, of its motion-picture collection. Barry was known as an authoritative critic and historian of the motion picture; her writings on the subject include *Let's Go to the Pictures* (1926), D. W. Griffith: American *Film Master* (1940), and a widely distributed series of pamphlets comprised of the program notes for exhibitions of motion pictures arranged by the Museum of Modern Art (1935–50). A founding member of the London Film Society (1925), Barry was elected president of the International Federation of Film Archives (1946) and awarded the Chevalier of the French Legion of Honor (1949). She retired in 1950.

Barry, James (c. 1795–1865).

See Stuart, Miranda.

Barry, Jeanne Bécu, Comtesse du (1743–1793).

See du Barry, Jeanne Bécu, Comtesse.

Barry, Leonora M. (1849–1930)

American labor organizer, temperance leader, and popular public speaker. *Name variations: Mrs. Barry-Lake, Mother Lake, Leonora Marie Lake. Born Leonora Marie Kearney in Kearney, County Cork, Ireland, on August 13, 1849; died in Minooka, Illinois, on July 15, 1930; only child of John and Honor Granger (Brown) Kearney; received public school education and private instruction; married William E.*

Barry, on November 30, 1871 (died 1881); married Obadiah Read Lake, on April 17, 1890 (died 1923); children: (first marriage) Marion Frances (b. 1873), William Standish (b. 1875), Charles Joseph (b. 1880).

Born in Ireland, Leonora Barry immigrated to America with her parents in 1852. Her father, a farmer, brought his family to Pierrepont, a rural town in upstate New York. There, Barry attended local schools and took an extra year of private study, receiving a teaching certificate at the age of 16. She taught in a nearby rural school for several years until her marriage to William E. Barry, a fellow Irish immigrant, who was a painter and itinerant musician. With their three children, the couple lived in several towns across upstate New York and western Massachusetts. While living in Amsterdam, New York, in 1881, Leonora Barry lost her husband and her only daughter when the two died within four months of each other.

At first, 32-year-old Barry took in sewing to support her two young sons, but the work proved too erratic, the eyestrain too great. She then took a job in one of Amsterdam's knitwear factories, that city's leading industry. As an unskilled hosiery maker, the young widow was soon overwhelmed by the harsh working conditions and low wages. Like many workers, Barry turned to the trade union movement as a way to alleviate some of the hardships. In 1884, she joined a local assembly of the Knights of Labor. Founded in 1869, the Knights were at their membership peak during the mid-1880s when Barry joined their ranks. She soon moved into positions of leadership, first on the local level when she became president of her local, the Victory assembly which was made up of 1,500 female knitwear workers. In 1885, she became president of District Assembly 65, which represented 52 locals with a total membership of over 9,000. By 1886, Barry was working as an national organizer for the Knights and was constantly on the road for the next three years.

In 1889, Barry retired from organizing and the following year married Obadiah Read Lake, a St. Louis printer. No longer forced to work to support herself, she now used her "tall commanding figure" and warm voice on behalf of the temperance cause as well as the fight for women's suffrage. She did not, however, immediately leave the trade union movement behind. In 1893, she spoke before the World's Representative Congress of Women at Chicago's Columbian Exposition on "The Dignity of Labor." Barry was active in both the Woman's Christian Temperance League and the Catholic Total Abstinence Union of America. Sometimes referred to as "Mother Lake," she was much in demand as a speaker for the Redpath and Slayton agencies and on the Chautauqua circuit until shortly before her death. Leonora Barry died of cancer of the mouth in Minooka, Illinois, a month before her 81st birthday.

SOURCES:

Levine, Susan. *Labor's True Woman: Carpet Weavers, Industrialization, and Labor Reform in the Gilded Age.* Philadelphia, PA: Temple University Press, 1984.

Kathleen Banks Nutter, Department of History, University of Massachusetts at Amherst

Barry, Madame du (1743–1793).

See du Barry, Jeanne Bécu, Comtesse.

Barry, Mrs. (1658–1713).

See Barry, Elizabeth.

Barry, Mrs. (1734–1801).

See Barry, Ann Street.

Barry, Mrs. Spranger (1734–1801).

See Barry, Ann Street.

Barry-Lake, Mrs. (1849–1930).

See Barry, Leonora M.

Barrymore, Diana (1921–1960)

***American actress.** Born Diana Strange Blythe on March 3, 1921; committed suicide in New York City on January 25, 1960; daughter of Blanche Oelrichs Thomas Barrymore Tweed (who, as poet and playwright, used the pseudonym Michael Strange) and John Barrymore; attended Garrison Forest boarding school; married Bramwell Fletcher (divorced); married John Howard (a tennis player); married Bob Wilcox.*

Diana Barrymore was born Diana Strange Blythe (the actual name of the Barrymore family) in March 1921. Her father was John Barrymore, a matinee idol; her mother was poet, playwright ***Michael Strange**, who "wore jackets in the style of Alfred de Musset," writes Vin Packer, "open-collar shirts, and a man's soft fedora; she wore wide-cuffed, rough leather riding gloves and carried a man's walking stick." Michael Strange had been married before to Leonard Thomas of Newport, Rhode Island, and had two sons. Shortly after Diana's birth, her parents parted, and Diana would not meet her father again until she was 14. Hers was a lonely existence; her mother remarried and the rebellious Diana was packed off to boarding school, the first of 16 she would attend.

At age 16, she began to study at the American Academy of Dramatic Arts in New York and took on the part of what she later called the "irrepressible madcap daughter of madcap Jack Barrymore and gifted, unpredictable Michael Strange," plunging headlong into café society. In 1938, columnist Cholly Knickerbocker dubbed her "Debutante of the Year." When Diana signed for a season of summer stock at the Ogunquit Playhouse in 1939, its publicity director saw a chance for national publicity; that July, decked out in a bathing suit, she was on the cover of *Life* magazine.

When Diana made her Broadway debut as Caroline Bronson in *Romantic Mr. Dickens*, Brooks Atkinson gave her a glowing review. Then came a Hollywood contract and the alcoholism to which many of the Barrymores fell prey. She began drinking in L.A., became brash and quarrelsome, and made few friends. On the night *Eagle Squadron*, her first movie previewed, her father died of acute alcoholism. In despair, she married actor Bramwell Fletcher, 18 years her senior. Five pictures later, when Diana was 23, Hollywood was through with her, and she returned to New York. The following year, in 1944, she and her husband opened in the Theatre Guild production of *Rebecca*.

But the downward spiral continued. In 1946, with her half-brother dead from pills and whiskey, her marriage in shambles, and her name a magnet for bad publicity—one story had her appearing on an NBC comedy show with a hangover—she swallowed 30 sleeping pills. Her stomach was pumped and she recovered. Barrymore then began a second marriage to tennis player John Howard which lasted six months. A break came when she was offered "The Diana Barrymore Show" by CBS, for which she was to play hostess to guest celebrities. On the night of the telecast, she arrived drunk, and the network hastily replaced her with **Faye Emerson**. She married again, went through the trust funds, couldn't find work, took a job in vaudeville (once following a juggling act), then turned to her Aunt ***Ethel Barrymore** for a loan. After numerous fresh starts and many affairs, Barrymore made one last comeback following another suicide attempt in April 1955. With the help of Gerold Frank, she wrote her autobiography. *Too Much, Too Soon* was a bestseller in 1957 and made into a film by Warner Bros., starring ***Dorothy Malone**. But the $150,000 in profits went fast. After some stage success on the road with *Cat on a Hot Tin Roof*, she became obsessed with Tennessee Williams whom she was determined to marry. Diana Barrymore's maid found her dead of suicide on January 25, 1960. She was 38.

SOURCES:

Alpert, Hollis. *The Barrymores.* NY: Dial Press, 1964.

Packer, Vin [Marijane Meaker]. *Sudden Endings.* NY: Doubleday, 1964.

Barrymore, Ethel (1879–1959)

Actress known as the First Lady of the American Theater and the last of the "fabulous" Barrymores. *Born Ethel Mae Blyth in Philadelphia, Pennsylvania, on August 15, 1879; died on June 18, 1959; daughter of actors Georgiana Drew (1854–1893) and Maurice Barrymore (whose actual name was Herbert Blyth); educated in Philadelphia at the Convent of Notre Dame; sister of American actors John and Lionel Barrymore; granddaughter of Louisa Lane Drew; aunt of actress* ***Diana Barrymore;*** *grandaunt of actress* ***Drew Barrymore*** *(granddaughter of John Barrymore); married Russell Griswold Colt, on March 24, 1909 (separated 1920, divorced 1923); children: Samuel (b. 1910), Ethel Barrymore Colt (b. 1912), and John (b. 1913).*

Films: The Nightingale *(1914);* The Final Judgement *(1915);* The Kiss of Hate *(1916);* The Awakening of Helen Ritchie *(1917);* The White Raven *(1917);* The Call of Her People *(1917);* The Lifted Veil *(1917);* Life's Whirlpool *(1917);* The Eternal Mother *(1917);* An American Widow *(1917);* Our Mrs. McChesney *(1918);* The Divorcée *(1919);* Rasputin and the Empress *(1933);* None But the Lonely Heart *(1944);* The Spiral Staircase *(1946);* The Farmer's Daughter *(1947);* Moss Rose *(1947);* Night Song *(1947);* The Paradine Case *(1948);* Moonrise *(1948);* Portrait of Jennie *(1949);* The Great Sinner *(1949);* That Midnight Kiss *(1949);* The Red Danube *(1949);* Pinky *(1949);* Kind Lady *(1951);* The Secret of Convict Lake *(1951);* It's a Big Country *(1952);* Deadline USA *(1952);* Just For You *(1952);* The Story of Three Loves *(1953);* Main Street to Broadway *(1953);* Young at Heart *(1955);* Johnny Trouble *(1957).*

One evening in June 1959 at the Broadway performance of ***Lorraine Hansbury**'s *A Raisin in the Sun*, the audience was told that the curtain would go up late that night. At precisely eight o'clock, the house lights dimmed to half for five minutes in silent tribute to the woman for whom the theater had been built and named 31 years before. Ethel Barrymore, the actress with the flashing eyes, had died early that morning, at 80 years of age, and her passing marked the end of the American theater's "royal family."

Ethel Barrymore

Like many royal families, the Barrymores—Ethel and her two brothers, Lionel and John—could claim an impeccable family tree. Their maternal grandfather was John Drew (1827–1862), the leading tragedian of the 19th-century American stage and a beloved Shakespearean actor. Their maternal grandmother was ***Louisa Lane Drew**, who had been an even more formidable presence on the stage than her husband, and who was said to be the only fellow thespian of whom Edwin Booth was afraid. Born in England, Louisa had first appeared on the stage at the tender age of 12 months ("I played a crying baby," she would drily remark), moved to Philadelphia, married John Drew, and eventually managed that city's most famous theater of the time, The Arch. She was known in the theater world as "The Duchess," and no one with hopes for a future on the stage got on her bad side.

John and Louisa Drew's children went on the stage almost as soon as they could talk. ◄ **Georgiana Drew** became the favorite comedienne of discerning Gilded Age audiences; her brother Sidney was a noted comedian, and her second brother John (1853–1927) was eventually dubbed "the First Gentleman of the American stage." To complete the picture, Georgiana married a dashing young Englishman just making a name for himself in American theater. Herbert Maurice Blyth (sometimes spelled Blythe) had been born in India of Anglo-Indian parents, proper civil servants during the British Raj. Horrified that their son had plans to become an actor, they begged him to at least change his name before taking to the boards. Grabbing the nearest book, Herbert put his finger on the first character name he came to and pronounced himself thenceforth Maurice Barrymore. He arrived in America in 1874, secured his first stage role the following year, and shortly afterward married Georgiana Drew.

Ethel, the second of Maurice and Georgiana's three children, was a year younger than her brother Lionel and two years older than John. The children enjoyed an unusually stable childhood given the peripatetic profession of their parents. While Georgiana and Maurice were frequently on tour, the children's grandmother, Louisa, ran the large, comfortable home on Philadelphia's North 12th Street. "Mummumm," as her grandchildren called her, conducted her charges to their classes at local Catholic convent schools, mediated their disputes, and entertained them with stories of the theater. Then there were visits from Uncle Jack or Uncle Sidney, on their way to or from engagements, and houseguests from the best society of Philadelphia, New York, and Boston brought

► Drew, Georgiana Emma (1854–1893)

American actress. *Name variations: Georgiana Emma Drew Barrymore, Georgie. Born in Philadelphia, Pennsylvania, on July 11, 1854; died in Santa Barbara, California, on July 2, 1893; daughter of John Drew and* ****Louisa Lane Drew*** *(both actors); younger sister of actor John Drew, Jr.; married Maurice Barrymore (1847–1905, an actor), in December 1876; children: Lionel (b. April 28, 1878–1954),* ****Ethel Barrymore*** *(1879–1959), and John Barrymore (b. February 15, 1882–1942).*

Allowed backstage during her parents' Friday night performances, Georgiana Drew was stagestruck. The 15-year-old actress who was to excel in comedy made her theatrical debut in the 1872 production of *The Ladies' Battle* at her mother's Arch Street Theatre in Philadelphia; she was so successful that she was allowed to quit school and join the company. Three years later, along with her brother John Drew, Jr., Georgie joined Augustin Daly's repertory company at the Fifth Avenue Theatre in New York City. There, she met Maurice Barrymore whom she married on New Year's Eve, 1876. When her husband began working with ***Helena Modjeska** rumors began to circulate. Initially, Georgie was jealous, but, when the tales proved false, she and Modjeska grew to be close friends. Modjeska influenced Georgie's conversion to Catholicism and her rebaptizing of all her children from Episcopalian to Catholic.

For years, while performing in her husband's formidable shadows, Georgie Drew raised her children. But when his career wavered, hers took off. Known for her wit, she once sent a lengthy telegram while on tour to Charles Frohman, begging for new costumes; when his telegrammed reply was a terse "No," she just as tersely telegrammed, "Oh." Her comedic talents were shown to best advantage in *The Senator* which opened in January 1890. That same winter, she caught a terrible cold which would not loosen its grip. Despite a racking cough, she stayed in the show for almost two years until she was forced to leave the cast in December of 1891 because of tuberculosis. The following year, still ill, she had to cancel another season in San Francisco. She made her stage farewell in New York in February 1893, then journeyed to Santa Barbara, accompanied by her daughter Ethel, seeking a drier climate in which to convalesce. When a doctor in Santa Barbara examined her and asked who was going to care for her, she replied, "My little girl." The 36-year-old Georgie Barrymore and her 13-year-old daughter Ethel enjoyed some happy times before Georgie died there a few months later, on July 2, 1893. Alone, Ethel Barrymore transported her mother's coffin back to New York by train.

SOURCES:

Alpert, Hollis. *The Barrymores.* NY: Dial Press, 1964.

home for long weekends by Georgiana and Maurice. There were trips to England and the Continent when their parents were engaged to play the West End. Born into the aristocracy of American theater, Ethel and her brothers never knew the rough-and-tumble side of the stage world.

Summers were spent at a camp on Staten Island, where 11-year-old Ethel made her acting debut in a homegrown production of Dumas' *The Lady of the Camellias*, with her brothers in the supporting cast. They charged a penny admission to sit in a barn on the camp property which they had converted to a theater. Preparing for her death scene, Ethel practiced a tubercular cough to such effect that a camp supervisor feared she had a bone stuck in her throat. The mimicry, however, may have been learned at home. Her 34-year-old mother Georgie would die of consumption in Santa Barbara two years later.

Although Ethel wanted to be a concert pianist, and Lionel and John aspired to be artists, it seemed inevitable that they would all go on the stage. Acting was the family business and had been providing it with a good living for two generations. At 15, Ethel's first professional appearance in New York City, in 1894, was in a scene with her Uncle Jack in a production of Sheridan's *A School for Scandal* in which he was then starring. Ethel also played opposite the English actor Sir Henry Irving in England in 1898, appearing in the popular plays *The Bells* and *Peter the Great.*

"Nobody in our family ever taught me anything about acting, except by absorption," Ethel wrote many years later, and she absorbed from some of the best talent in the profession, her own family. The hallmark of the Barrymore style was its naturalness; never, as she put it, "let anyone see the wheels going around." The roles she would find most challenging during her long career were those in which she played "normal" people, with whom the audience could readily identify. She would become known for these finely turned, exquisite character roles.

Despite her name and family connections, Barrymore didn't have an easy task when she began visiting agents and casting people as an 18-year-old. There were walk-ons and small parts, and she appeared several more times with her Uncle Jack before audiences in New York and Philadelphia, but it wasn't until 1900 that she was given her first leading role by the most famous impresario of the time, Charles Frohman. She had appeared in minor roles in several of Frohman's productions, and, when he bought the rights to a frothy romantic comedy called *Captain Jinks of the Horse Marines*, he cast Ethel in the lead over the playwright's objections. The show opened at Philadelphia's venerable Walnut Street Theater in late 1900 to a packed house, eager to see how the newest Barrymore would handle her first leading role.

Her entrance as the curtain rose was not auspicious. She was to appear at the top of a ship's gangplank, carrying a small dog, then descend to the stage while burbling winsomely about how good it was to be back in America after such a long time in England. But stagefright got the better of her, and her voice refused to travel as far as the footlights. Encouragement from the audience was immediate: "Speak up, Ethel! You Drews is all good actors!" urged one patron. "We love your grandmother, Ethel, and we love you, too!" shouted another. The show went on, but the next morning's notices were less than encouraging. Barrymore would remember many years later, word for word, the review that stated, "If the young woman who played Madame Trentoni had possessed beauty, charm, or talent, the play might have been a success."

> There are certain sounds that seem to me characteristically American. One of them is the soughing wind in the pine forests. Another is the voice of Ethel Barrymore.
>
> **—Alexander Woollcott**

Despite the poor reception in Philadelphia, Frohman decided to open the show at his Garrick Theater in New York early in 1901. Barrymore, stung by her ordeal, dreaded opening night on Broadway. "I had for the first time the terrible sense of responsibility which ever since has made every first night a kind of little dying," she remembered in her autobiography. This time, however, her Madame Trentoni was a triumph. Barrymore recalled walking to the theater one afternoon, after the show had been running for some weeks: "As we approached the theater, the lights in front of the house looked different to me. . . . I glanced up again and suddenly stood frozen to the spot. ETHEL BARRYMORE was up there in lights."

Among the admirers waiting backstage on opening night was her father Maurice, who presented her with a rose, kissed her on the cheek, and complemented her on her performance. It was a particularly poignant moment for Ethel, for her father had not been well and had not appeared on stage in many months. Later that year, after behaving erratically for some time, Maurice was declared legally insane, the result of syphilis contracted shortly after he had arrived in New York as a young man. The family had little choice but to commit him to an asylum, and it was Ethel's painful duty to sign the commitment papers. He would remain institutionalized for the rest of his life.

Captain Jinks ran for months. Ethel installed herself at the swank Sherry-Netherland Hotel on Fifth Avenue and eventually went on a national tour with the show, reaching an even larger audience. Although not every production in which she appeared over the next several years would be as successful, her place in the Barrymore royal lineage was now firmly validated. Her leading roles in *A Doll's House* by the Norwegian dramatist Henrik Ibsen in 1905, and *Alice-Sit-by-the-Fire* by Scottish dramatist James M. Barrie in 1906, established her as one of the foremost actresses in the American theater. Her portrayal of Lady Helen Haddon—a lower-class woman who enters high society by marriage, only to be destroyed by it—in ***Zoe Akin**'s *Déclassé* was another of her successes in the early 1900s. It prompted then fledgling theater critic for *Vanity Fair* ***Dorothy Parker** (not yet the jaundiced, biting reviewer of her *New Yorker* days) to state precociously: "If, during my theater-going lifetime, there has been one other performance so perfect as the one Ethel Barrymore gives, I can only say I had the hideous misfortune to miss it." Parker would be a consistently loyal fan of the Barrymores in years to come, though Ethel would have nothing to do with the infamous Round Table at the Algonquin Hotel.

Another admirer was Russell Colt, the son of a millionaire inventor, who was a frequent backstage visitor and escort. In 1909, Ethel married him and set up house at the sprawling estate in nearby Mamaroneck, New York, given to them as a wedding present by Russell's father. While Russell commuted to Wall Street every morning, Ethel retired from the stage to give birth to three children between 1910 and 1913: Samuel, ❧▸ **Ethel Barrymore Colt**, and John. Russell's success on Wall Street, however, was less than spectacular, and it would be some time before he would come into his inheritance; by the end of the decade, it was apparent that his interests lay more with other women than with providing for his family. In 1920, the couple separated (they would divorce in 1923) and Ethel, with three youngsters to raise, went back to work.

The same drama in which she had first appeared as an 11-year-old on Staten Island, *The Lady of the Camellias*, would reintroduce her to Broadway. The play opened in a new adaptation in 1918, telling Dumas *fils*' story in flashback, and opening and closing with the title character's moving deathbed scene. So effective was Barrymore's dying six nights a week that New York's bright young theatergoers could be seen rushing to the production crying, "Let's go and see her die!" In 1919, Ethel, Lionel, and John were prominent in the historic actor's strike against the unfair practices of theater owners and managers. Appearing at benefit performances and public rallies, the Barrymores were instrumental in the success of the strike, which forced theater managers and agents to recognize the unionization of the profession under Actors Equity.

While Lionel and John were as busy as their sister on stage, they had been spending increasing amounts of time over a garage on West 61st Street, which contained the offices and studios of Metro Pictures. Metro was one of many hastily formed companies in New York exploiting the potential of the new medium of film. The two brothers publicly extolled the dramatic possibilities of film acting but privately told Ethel that it was the money that was the main attraction. Anxious to legitimize their product as more than a sideshow novelty, the early film companies were willing to pay large sums to established actors. With three children to raise, Barrymore admitted it was the "dough" that brought her to All Star Pictures, which offered her $15,000 to appear in her first film, *The Nightingale*, in 1914. Much of the film was shot on the streets of New York, although Barrymore, playing a poor street singer, refused to shoot outside a mansion on Madison Avenue which happened to be the home of Mrs. Whitney Reid, a long-time family friend. She was horrified that Mrs. Reid might emerge to find her begging for pennies on the front steps. A two-year contract with Metro Pictures followed, at $60,000 a year, for which she shot five films between 1915 and 1917, all of them well received. *The New York Times* critic particularly liked her performance in a Klondike adventure film, *The White Raven*, calling her "lovely to look upon, and never more so than in the sketchy costume of the dance hall" and noting that she "has adapted her fine skill as an actress to the new medium."

Barrymore, whose heart remained on the stage, seemed almost embarrassed by the substantial sums she was paid for her film work and defensively told a newspaper reporter that "it doesn't matter how much we earn, it all goes . . . and gracious knows where it disappears." In later years, she would publicly acknowledge only one of these early Metro films, an adaptation of ***Margaret Deland**'s *The Awakening of Helena Richie.* The rest, she said, were too horrible to remember. She was dismissive of "talkies" when they first appeared in 1927. "People don't want their ears insulted," she said, although Winston Churchill, an early admirer, described her voice as "soft, alluring, persuasive, magnetic." Barrymore agreed to do a voice test for Paramount but refused the contract they offered, as she did all film offers between 1919 and 1933. "I am lost without my audience," she wrote.

Indeed, she was never to forsake her audience for the rest of her professional life. She played Juliet in *Romeo and Juliet* in 1922, and Ophelia in *Hamlet* and Portia in *The Merchant of Venice* in 1925. In December 1928, she opened the Ethel Barrymore Theater in New York City, appearing in *The Kingdom of God.* Other plays in which she starred included *School for Scandal* by Sheridan (1931), *The Twelve-Pound Look* by Barrie (1934), and *The Corn Is Green* by the British playwright Emlyn Williams (1942). Throughout the 1930s and '40s, the name Barrymore became synonymous with acting. Certain public figures were said to have a "Barrymore voice," and, after having delivered a particularly rousing speech, were said to have "done a Barrymore." Ethel Barrymore's professionalism and sang-froid on the stage became legendary among her fellow actors. Her co-star in *The Corn is Green* remembered one performance when he became aware that she had forgotten her next line. Before the audience noticed, Barrymore—still in character—merely said to him, "Don't move," went to the stage-left door, peered out to where the prompter was standing, then returned to her chair. "I thought there was someone at the door," she said. Unperturbed, she carried on with the scene, equipped with the forgotten line.

Despite her disdain for film work, Barrymore was enticed by a $90,000 offer from MGM's head of production, Irving Thalberg, to appear with her two brothers in 1933's *Rasputin and the Empress*, the story of the mad monk's rise and fall in pre-revolutionary Russia. It was the first time in over 35 years that the three Barrymores appeared ensemble, and everyone worried that the shoot might be fraught with clashing sibling egos and merciless scene-stealing. Thalberg was convinced that casting the three Barrymores in the same film would be box-office gold ("something like a circus with three white whales," Lionel remarked), and Ethel duly appeared on the set laden with fake jewels and a heavy gown as Empress ***Alexandra Feodorovna**, to swoon before Rasputin (Lionel) and watch in horror his murder by Prince Chegodieff (John).

There were, to be sure, the expected rivalries among the three. Typical of them was the argument between John and Lionel as to how much of the camera frame each would get in a particular scene, as they were interrupted by Ethel, in full regalia, who reminded them loudly, "You two can argue about the camera all you want, but I still have a voice, you know."

The real problem, however, was exactly that—Ethel's voice; and it became apparent in the first scene she played. By her own choice, she had been absent from films since 1919 and, unlike her brothers, had no experience in playing to a microphone. At the end of the scene, in which even Barrymore admitted she had been "moaning, flailing my arms, and touching curtains all over the set," Lionel approached her.

Colt, Ethel Barrymore (1912–1977)

American actress and singer. *Born in April 1912; died on May 22, 1977; daughter of Ethel Barrymore (an actress) and Russell Griswold Colt; attended the Notre Dame convent school outside Philadelphia; attended private school in Verona, Italy; married Romeo Miglietta (a petroleum executive); children: John Drew Miglietta (an actor).*

Often asked what kind of mother ***Ethel Barrymore** had been, Ethel Barrymore Colt once replied, "Her relations with us were extraordinary in spite of the fact that we were put under the care of governesses and were sent to boarding schools because she was away a good deal of the time. We would see her, after babyhood, at the Ritz in Boston, in Chicago at Christmas, Atlantic City in Easter. We weren't over-mothered by any means. She was a goddess to us. She was wonderful and warm, but let's face it, she did not change our pants."

Ethel Colt, known as Sister in the family, made her professional debut at 18 in a supporting role opposite her mother in *Scarlet Sister Mary* (1930). Her 16-year-old brother Jack Colt was also in the cast. Ethel also appeared in *Scandals, George White's Scandals, Under Glass, Laura Garnett, L'Aiglon, London Assurance, Orchids Preferred, Whiteoaks, Come of Age, Curtains Up!, Take It from the Top*, and *A Madrigal of Shakespeare.* In 1971, she appeared in the featured role of Christine Crane in Stephen Sondheim's long-running *Follies*. She also gave recitals, toured with her one-woman show, and made guest appearances with several opera companies, including the New York City Opera.

"Ethel," he gently asked, "what the hell are you doing?"

"I haven't the faintest idea," she confessed, at which point the Barrymore professionalism came to the fore as Lionel and John gave her a few lessons in moderating her voice for the microphone. All went well from then on, even though Ethel insisted on so many retakes during the shoot that, instead of "Empress of the Russians," the crew dubbed her "Empress of the Rushes." Barrymore never saw the finished film until 25 years later, on television. "I thought it was pretty good," she remarked, "but what those two boys were up to, I'll never know. Wasn't Lionel naughty?" She would go on to appear in 22 films during the next 45 years and win the Oscar for Best Supporting Actress in 1945 for her performance as Cary Grant's mother, Ma Mott, in the screen adaptation of Richard Llewellyn's *None But The Lonely Heart.*

Like her brothers, Barrymore had trouble with alcohol. Early in life, she had turned to the bottle for consolation. In her late 30s, however, unlike John, Ethel went teetotal. "No one in my family should drink," she once said, "because

From the movie None But the Lonely Heart, *starring Ethel Barrymore and Cary Grant.*

it's poison to us." Rumors persisted throughout her life, however, that she was last seen reeling across a stage. Her non-drinking was especially amazing in the light of constant money and IRS problems that plagued her throughout the 1930s. When ***Adela Rogers St. Johns** asked how she handled these difficulties, Barrymore replied: "I suppose the greatest thing in the world is loving people, wanting to destroy the sin and not the sinner. And not to forget when life knocks you to your knees, which it always does and always will—well, that's the best position in which to pray, isn't it? On your knees."

Barrymore continued working until heart disease forced her to slow down and eventually retire in 1958. Through it all, she managed to raise her three children to adulthood—"the most important thing in my life," she said. All three would dabble in theater and film but ultimately abandon them for other pursuits. Ethel outlived both her brothers; John died in 1942, Lionel in 1954.

As for men in Ethel's life, her daughter claims that her mother's existence after the divorce was almost nunlike. Barrymore once told a close friend, "It's not the church affiliation that prevents me from marrying again. The plain truth of the matter is that I've never met the man I would want to be married to." She had many close friends, among them Mrs. Jacques Gordon (who because her first name was Ruth, was often confused with the actress ***Ruth Gordon**), Ethel's intimate for over 20 years, as well as ***Evelyn Walsh McLean**, ***Eleanor "Cissie" Patterson**, and ***Alice Roosevelt Longworth**.

During her final illness, many of Hollywood's stars, who had been just entering the business when Barrymore was at her peak, came to her Beverly Hills home to pay their respects like so many courtiers attending their dying queen. One of them, ***Katharine Hepburn**, brought Barrymore fresh flowers nearly every day. At 80 years of age, and despite her illness, "she was beautiful to look at," Hepburn recalls. "Wonderful hair, exquisite skin, not much makeup, and eyes that, well, scared the death out of you."

At three o'clock in the morning, on June 18, 1959, Ethel Barrymore died, ending a career that stretched from the red plush and gaslights of Gay Nineties music halls to television drama. "All of us work hard in the theater," ***Helen Hayes** said at a memorial service on Broadway, "but none of us can ever give it the luster that she did." Ethel Barrymore is still honored today for setting the tone and style of American acting, long before Stanislavski's Method or other rigorous training programs were developed to keep hidden "the wheels going around." "She lifted the standards of American acting," remarked author ***Cornelia Otis Skinner**, "and gave all who knew her an impetus to live on her level."

SOURCES:

Alpert, Hollis. *The Barrymores.* NY: Dial Press, 1964.

Barrymore, Ethel. *Memories: An Autobiography.* NY: Harper Brothers, 1955.

Kotsilibas-Davis, James. *The Barrymores: The Royal Family in Hollywood.* NY: Crown Publishers, 1981.

Peters, Margot. *The House of Barrymore.* NY: Alfred E. Knopf, 1990.

Norman Powers, writer and producer,
Chelsea Lane Productions, New York, New York

Barrymore, Georgiana Drew

(1854–1893).

See Barrymore, Ethel for sidebar on Georgiana Drew

Barskaya, Margarita A. (d. 1938)

Soviet actress, scenarist, and filmmaker. *Name variations: Barskaia. Date of birth unknown; died in 1938 in a Soviet gulag; married Petr Chardynin (a director). Filmography as a director:* Torn Boots *(1936) and* Father and Son *(1937).*

Margarita Barskaya gained her reputation as an actress in pre-revolutionary Russia. Along with her husband, director Petr Chardynin, the two had successful careers that managed to span the chaotic days during and after the Bolshevik takeover. Barskaya's major contribution came as one of the pioneers in children's films. In 1930, she opened the Laboratory for Children's Cinema and eventually directed the enormously successful *Torn Boots.* A landmark in Soviet film history, *Torn Boots* was the first realistic movie geared toward a young audience.

In 1937, Barskaya directed *Father and Son.* The film concerned the relationship between the overseer of a major factory and his 13-year-old son. Though a good Bolshevik, the overseer finds himself so busy with work and party activities, he ignores the boy who falls in with a rough crowd. When the father renounces his own behavior, he and his son are happily reunited. To Barskaya's escalating horror, authorities were outraged, and Soviet censors considered the film to be unsuitable for public exhibition. One reviewer called it a "slander against Soviet reality." Even the film studio, Soyuzdetfilm, was attacked for allowing the film to be made.

Barskaya was arrested and sent to a concentration camp where she died in 1938.

SOURCES:

Kenez, Peter. *Cinema and Soviet Society 1917–1953.* Melbourne: Cambridge University Press, 1992.

Deborah Jones, Studio City, California

Barstow, Mrs. Montagu (1865–1947).

See Orczy, Baroness.

Bartet, Jeanne Julia (1854–1941)

French actress. *Born Jeanne Julia Regnault in Paris, France, in 1854; died in 1941; trained at the Conservatoire.*

In 1872, Jeanne Julia Bartet began a successful career at the Vaudeville. Seven years later, she was engaged at the Comédie Française, of which she became a *sociétaire* (shareholder) in 1880. For many years, Bartet played leading parts both in tragedy and comedy; her elegance and grand style made her supreme among the younger actresses on the French stage. Her talents were also displayed for a season in London in 1908.

Bartholomew, Ann Sheppard (1811–1891)

English composer, pianist, organist, and teacher. *Born Ann Mounsey in London on April 17, 1811; died in London, England, on June 24, 1891; member of the Royal Society of Musicians.*

In 1817, Ann Bartholomew studied under Logier, who then recommended that she study with the eminent German composer Louis Spohr. The latter was so impressed by her musical abilities that he subsequently printed one of her harmonizations of a melody in his autobiography. After further study with Samuel Wesley and Thomas Attwood, Bartholomew became an organist in 1828; appointed to the same position at St. Vedast's in 1837, she remained for 50 years. She wrote many pieces for organ and piano as well as over 100 songs, an oratorio, and a cantata. Bartholomew gave regular concerts of sacred classical music and introduced a number of Felix Mendelssohn's new organ compositions to the public. She became an associate of the Philharmonic Society in 1834 and in 1839 became a member of the Royal Society of Musicians.

Bartlett, Caroline (1858–1935).

See Crane, Caroline Bartlett.

Bartlett, Ethel (1896–1978)

English pianist. *Born in Epping Forest, England, on June 6, 1896; died in Los Angeles, California, on April 17, 1978; studied with Tobias Matthay and Artur Schnabel; married Rae Robertson (1893–1956, a pianist with whom she frequently performed).*

With her husband Rae Robertson, Ethel Bartlett founded a duo-piano team that had become famous in the United Kingdom by the 1930s; the two also made annual tours in Europe and the United States. Bartlett and her husband gave the first performance in 1931 of Sir Arthur Bax's duo-piano sonata. Benjamin Britten's compositions *Scottish Ballad, Introduction and Rondo alla Burlesca*, and *Mazurka elegiac* were all dedicated to the Bartlett-Robertson team. In 1944, they commissioned a duo-piano concerto from Béla Bartok, which he did not live to compose.

Bartok, Ditta Pasztory (1902–1982)

Hungarian pianist and wife of Béla Bartok who made several recordings of his work. *Born Ditta Pasztory in 1902; died in Budapest on November 21, 1982; married Béla Bartok (the composer). Escaped the Nazis (1940).*

In 1923, Ditta Pasztory married the great Hungarian composer Béla Bartok; she was his second wife. On many occasions, she performed with him in public in Europe and the United States, where they arrived as exiles from Fascism in October 1940. They made a number of recordings of his compositions, including the *Sonata for Two Pianos and Percussion* and selections from *Mikrokosmos*. Béla Bartok wrote his *Concerto for Two Pianos* for himself and his wife to perform, and they gave its premiere on January 21, 1943, with the New York Philharmonic-Symphony Orchestra, Fritz Reiner conducting. On occasion, Ditta Bartok also performed works other than those of her husband, including Mozart concertos. Her optimism was crucial in maintaining her husband's morale during the years of privation and illness that preceded his death in 1945. After Bartok's passing, she returned to Hungary and died in Budapest on November 21, 1982.

John Haag, Athens, Georgia

Bartolini-Badelli, Giustina

Third wife of Jérôme Bonaparte. *Name variations: Giustina Pecori. Born Giustina Pecori-Suárez Grimal-*

di; married Jérôme Bonaparte (1784–1860), brother of Napoleon I, in a religious ceremony, in 1840, and later in a civil ceremony, in 1853.

The widow of an Italian noble, Marchesa Giustina Bartolini-Badelli married Jérôme Bonaparte after bailing him out of debt. In return, Jérôme was unfaithful and squandered her money.

Barton, Clara (1821–1912)

American founder of the American Red Cross, nicknamed the "Angel of the Battlefield," whose impromptu relief work in the Civil War made her a national heroine. *Born Clarissa Harlowe Barton in North Oxford, Massachusetts, on December 25, 1821; died in Glen Echo, Maryland, on April 12, 1912; youngest of five children of Captain Stephen (a farmer) and Sarah (Stone) Barton; never married; no children.*

Began teaching school (1839); departed for Liberal Institute, Clinton, New York (1850); began work at U.S. Patent Office (1854); began volunteer Civil War relief work (1861); participated in Andersonville memorial work with Dorance Atwater (1865); recuperated in Corsica after nervous collapse (1869); worked in the Franco-Prussian War; met with Princess Louise of Baden and with Bismarck (1870); campaigned for American participation in the Geneva Convention and International Red Cross (1878-82); led relief expedition to Cuba during the Spanish-American War (1898); ousted from Red Cross leadership (1904).

Clara Barton's name became familiar to millions of Americans during the Civil War, a byword for nurture and care to wounded soldiers. Her work in founding and running the American Red Cross kept her reputation alive in the later 19th century and into the 20th. But like her American contemporary ***Dorothea Dix** and her British contemporary ***Florence Nightingale,** Barton was a tough, strong-willed, politically shrewd woman with an authoritarian bent, who thrived on combat—the literal combat of battle and the interpersonal combat of politics—in which she was an expert.

Barton was born at North Oxford, Massachusetts, in 1821, youngest of five children and ten years younger than her nearest sibling. Her father was a prosperous local farmer, and her older brothers established themselves as cotton-mill owners, flourishing in the early days of the American industrial revolution. As a child, Clara was shy and withdrawn, but she showed a streak of courage in learning to ride horses and was an excellent and daring rider throughout her life. For nearly two years, from ages 11 to 13, she nursed an injured brother, learning many of the skills which would serve her. She distinguished herself at school and at the age of 18 became a teacher, first in village schools and then in a school she established for the poor children whose parents worked in her family's mills.

Restless and dissatisfied after ten years of hard work teaching, Barton went to an experimental college, the Liberal Institute, at Clinton, New York, in 1850, and continued her education there. But career opportunities for women remained limited, and at the end of her studies she was back in schoolteaching, this time in Hightstown and Bordentown, New Jersey. She founded one of the first free schools in New Jersey, showing great determination in raising the funds and winning local support for the scheme, but once it was well-established she faced the mortification of having a man placed over her as administrator. She lost her voice and had a brief nervous collapse, a condition that would recur at moments of stress in later life, but decided to leave the school and seek work in Washington, D.C.

During her 20s and 30s, Clara Barton received several offers of marriage but turned them all down. One suitor made a fortune as a "forty niner" in the California gold rush and sent her $10,000 from his strike, but she still declined to become his wife. Instead, she went to work at the United States Patent Office in D.C., as a copyist, and there made such a good impression on her superiors as a methodical and precise worker that she survived a government attempt to purge all women from the office. By the time the Civil War began in 1861, she had befriended Senators Charles Sumner and Henry Wilson of Massachusetts, and they became influential patrons in her subsequent work.

Her father Captain Stephen Barton was a veteran of the Indian wars and had fought at the Battle of the Thames where Tecumseh died; from her youth, he had instructed her on military affairs and told her stories of soldiering. When Massachusetts soldiers began flooding into Washington, Barton responded by going to meet them, nursing the sick and those suffering from sunstroke, writing appeals to New England newspapers, and becoming a go-between for the men and their families. Soon her reputation spread throughout Massachusetts, then New Jersey—her former homes—and families sent supplies to her, confident that she would pass them on to their intended recipients. She recognized many of the men as former pupils from her classrooms.

In the summer of 1861, Barton watched the tattered survivors of the first Battle of Bull Run straggling back into Washington and took several of the wounded into her lodgings to nurse them. Finding the army underequipped in doctors, nurses, and medical supplies, she responded by appealing through press and political contacts for more medical supplies and persuaded the authorities in Washington to let her go to the front lines where medical help to the newly wounded was most needed. She arrived at Cedar Mountain two days after the battle with a wagonload of dressings and medicines, just when the field hospital's supplies were exhausted. In August 1862, she traveled to the scene of the second Battle of Bull Run with three railroad cars full of supplies and four other women who had heard of her work and volunteered to join in. There she worked for three days without pausing, feeding soldiers and dressing wounds, directing the loading of wounded men onto railway wagons for transportation back to hospitals in Washington. After two hours' sleep in a waterlogged tent where she was unable to lie down properly—"prevented by the certain conviction that if I did the water would flow into my ears"—she was back at work. She stayed until the last possible moment. As the rearmost train finally carried her and a final group of wounded men away, she watched a troop of Confederate cavalry swarming over the hill where she had been at work a few minutes before.

By good luck, she arrived with wagonloads of aid for another army column just as it became involved in the Battle of Antietam. Her wagons were bringing up the rear of a long slow convoy, but when it camped she got up in the middle of the night and persuaded her teamsters to drive through the woods and get ahead of the other supplies. She again brought medicine, chloroform, and bandages to the field hospitals when they were most desperately needed. While she was giving a wounded soldier a drink, holding him up with her right arm, a bullet from the fierce fighting passed through her loose sleeve and killed the man outright. She had another close escape at the Battle of Fredericksburg that winter:

> An officer stepped to my side to assist me over the debris at the end of the bridge. While our hands were raised in the act of stepping down, a piece of an exploding shell hissed through between us, just below our arms, carrying away a portion of both the skirts of his coat and my dress. . . . I passed on alone to the hospital. In less than a half-hour he was brought to me—dead.

News of her work continued to spread, and press reports began to refer to her as the "Angel of the Battlefield." Troops would pause to cheer her when she appeared at army camps, and a brass band played her ashore when she moved to the Carolina theater of operations in 1863, while officers greeted her as "the Florence Nightingale of America."

She was present at the assault on Fort Wagner, again being able to arrive just before a major engagement because of her influential friends in high places who notified her of where she might find herself most needed. But now, midway through the war, improvements in official organization of relief meant that her services were less imperative. Officials of the U.S. Sanitary Commission began to rebuff her offers of help, medical officers commandeered her new tents, and influential army men encouraged her to return to Washington. For a while, she sank into a profound depression, and diary entries even suggest that she considered suicide. But with the aid of Senator Henry Wilson, who remained devoted to Barton and her work, she had her military passes for access to war zones restored and went to work with Ulysses Grant's army at the Battle of the Wilderness. Her principal work there was in preparing hot food and drink for wounded men and for the overworked surgeons, and in comforting the wounded and dying. She often wrote letters for men unable to write, read to them, and tried to maintain the morale of those still in action. The medical remedies were still primitive, and Barton joined the doctors in sedating amputation cases with whisky when chloroform supplies were exhausted.

At the siege of Richmond, she was reunited with her brother Stephen. Before the war, he had founded a town, Bartonville, in North Carolina, and refused to leave his property when the war began. Union soldiers imprisoned him, suspecting him of treason, but Clara interceded on his behalf with General Benjamin Butler, had him released, and nursed him for several weeks. He was, however, too ill to recover, and died just as the war was coming to an end.

Throughout the war, Barton had been bombarded with letters from families whose sons and husbands were missing. With the fighting ended, she now decided to devote herself to discovering what had happened to those who were missing in action. At first, she worked at her own expense but then received a letter of authorization and an allowance from President Abraham Lincoln just before his death. In a new office in Annapolis, she received tens of thousands of requests and obtained the authorization of President Andrew Johnson to print up lists of all the missing men at the Government Printing Of-

Clara Barton

fice. Lists circulated throughout the country, and, in hundreds of cases, men reappeared from Confederate prison camps or else told of how men on the lists had in fact died. She went with a War Department expedition to Andersonville, Georgia, scene of the notorious Confederate prison camp in which more than 10,000 Union prisoners had died, and there helped former prisoner Dorence Atwater, who had kept secret records of the fatalities, to mark graves.

Barton and Atwater disliked Captain James Moore, the head of the War Department expedition, and a complicated, bitter feud with the department culminated in Atwater's court-martial and imprisonment. For a while, Barton was *persona non grata* in army circles. But her star began to rise again when, in 1866, Congress acknowledged her selfless service to the Union cause, and her personal costs throughout the war, by granting her $15,000. That year, she also began touring the country on the lecture circuit, describing her adventures at the battlefronts and meeting thousands of bereaved families who had heard of her work from their menfolk during the war. Barton had befriended ***Susan B. Anthony** and ***Lucy Stone**, who tried to persuade her to speak also on behalf of women's suffrage. Though she was sympathetic to the cause, Barton did not relish the life of a traveling lecturer and suddenly broke down in the middle of one talk in Portland, Maine.

When [Clara] Barton wrote that her work had been accomplished 'against fearful odds,' she did not refer solely to the difficulties of pursuing a career in the male-dominated Victorian world. She was speaking of the many battles waged internally.

—Elizabeth Brown Pryor

On her doctor's advice, Barton went abroad for a rest cure and settled in Corsica. While there, she learned of the founding of the Red Cross and discovered that the United States was not among the 222 nations which had signed the Geneva Convention. The Red Cross was the creation of Jean Henri Dunant, a Swiss philanthropist who had witnessed the Battle of Solferino in 1859 and ministered to the wounded of both sides. His book about the horrors of the battle and the need for nursing care, and his lobbying efforts, eventuated in the founding of the Red Cross movement in 1863 and the international endorsement of its aims at Geneva in 1864. Barton undertook to campaign for American adherence to the Convention, but, before she could return to America, the Franco-Prussian war broke out. She volunteered to aid Swiss Red Cross workers and, with a new friend, **Antoinette Margot**, made her way to the front lines. With the help of the Grand Duchess ***Louise of Baden** (1838–1923), who had heard of Barton and now befriended her, Clara again worked with wounded men and, at Strassburg, with large numbers of wounded women. Americans began to send aid to the refugees of the war, but, because America had not signed the Geneva Convention, their contributions could not be administered by the well-run central agency the Red Cross had established.

Clara Barton went through the same cycle she had experienced during the American Civil War. She was alert, tireless, and capable in the midst of the Franco-Prussian war zone, but succumbed to depression and ill health as soon as she left the scene. She now endured several years of illness, first in Britain, until 1873, then back in America. Only in 1878 did she resume her active life, campaigning in Washington, D.C., for American involvement in the Red Cross, of which the Swiss leaders had appointed her official American representative. That year, she also wrote and published a pamphlet, "The Red Cross of the Geneva Convention: What It Is," which she distributed free of charge to congressional delegates, senators, governors, and other influential Americans, explaining the organization's humanitarian aims and urging American participation. The section on international law she drafted with particular care, in order that political fears of breaching the Monroe Doctrine (the original objection to American entry) might be quieted. Many of her original political allies had now retired or died, but, from her vast acquaintance and through her reputation and persuasive skills, she was able to create new alliances. After failing to make headway with President Rutherford Hayes, she tried again with President James Garfield, whom she had met on the battlefields years before. She also ran a vigorous publicity campaign from her home in Dansville, New York. Garfield was assassinated but his successor, Chester Arthur, was amenable to her plan and, with his encouragement, the Senate confirmed American participation in the Convention in 1882.

For the next 23 years, Clara Barton led the American Red Cross; at first, her vivid personality and reputation proved to be assets in its growth. Eventually, however, her inability to work with committees and a tendency to work *ad hoc* rather than in collaboration with colleagues led to difficulties for the organization. As her most recent biographer **Elizabeth Pryor** observes: "In her eyes she was the best candidate for every job. . . . Never did she learn to take criticism, and under its yoke she felt either persecution or smug superiority. . . . Sometimes she inspired great loyalty; always she demanded it." At Barton's suggestion, the American Red Cross emphasized from the outset that it would aid not only in wartime but also in times of peace when citizens were faced with natural disasters. As a result, the organization was soon in action bringing relief to the victims of a Michigan forest fire, then helping flood victims in Cincinnati in 1884. When Barton, now aged 62, learned of tornados and flooding in Evansville, Indiana, she chartered a boat and loaded it with emergency supplies. Describing the scene later, she wrote:

> Good assistants, both men and women, were taken on board; the Red Cross flag was hoisted and as night was setting in, after a day of intense cold—amid surging waters and crashing ice, the floating wrecks of towns and villages, great uprooted giants of the forest plunging madly to the sea, the suddenly unhoused people wandering about the river-banks, or huddled in strange houses with fireless hearths—the clear-toned bell and shrill whistle of the *Josh V. Throop* announced to the generous inhabitants of a noble city that from the wharves of Evansville was putting out the first Red Cross relief boat that ever floated on American waters.

Barton went on innumerable relief expeditions in the following years, including visits to two more theaters of war (Turkey in 1896 and Cuba during the Spanish-American War of 1898) and put in a six-week stint following a devastating hurricane at Galveston, Texas, in 1900, when she was approaching her 80th birthday.

Her international stature made Barton a useful diplomat, and she represented the American government at four international conferences: in Geneva (1884), Carlsruhe (1887), Vienna (1897), and St. Petersburg (1902)—at the first of these, she was the only woman present and was lionized by the other delegates for her work in bringing America into the Convention. Indeed, she was the first woman diplomat in American history. The presence of royalty at the conferences encouraged a measure of vanity, and Barton dressed lavishly, often wearing the many decorations she had garnered in her long working life. Her national and international prominence made her feminist friends more eager than ever to enlist her services: Barton was one of few pro-suffrage women who could pack a conference hall with veterans of the Grand Army of the Republic. But although she was dedicated to the women's cause, she always declined to mix its affairs with those of the Red Cross, or to gather an audience under false pretenses.

By the early 20th century, many of Barton's own recruits were chafing at her methods. Contributions were often sent to her, rather than to the Red Cross, and the organization had no disciplined accounting system. Congress reincorporated the Red Cross in 1900 and in 1903 established an investigating committee to ensure proper use of funds. The investigation terminated without issuing a report, but Barton—incensed at what she took to be a challenge to her good faith and under pressure from a hostile press campaign—resigned from the leadership in 1904. When she died in 1912, aged 91, she had been a national institution for almost half a century, universally admired but far from being universally loved, especially by those who had worked too closely with her in her later years. She remains, nevertheless, one of the inspiring figures of 19th-century American history and a pioneer in the development of first aid and attentive care to war and disaster victims.

SOURCES:

Barton, William E. *The Life of Clara Barton: Founder of the American Red Cross.* 2 vols. Boston, MA: Houghton Mifflin, 1922.

Dulles, Foster Rhea. *The American Red Cross: A History.* NY: Harper, 1950.

Gilbo, Patrick. *The American Red Cross: The First Century.* NY: Harper and Row, 1981.

Pryor, Elizabeth Brown. *Clara Barton: Professional Angel.* Philadelphia: University of Pennsylvania Press, 1987.

Ross, Ishbel. *Angel of the Battlefield: The Life of Clara Barton.* NY: Harper, 1956.

Patrick Allitt, Professor of History, Emory University, Atlanta, Georgia

Barton, Elizabeth (c. 1506–1534)

English zealot. *Name variations: The maid of Kent, Nun of Kent, or Holy Maid of Kent. Born, according to her statement, in 1506 at Aldington, Kent; executed at Tyburn on April 20, 1534.*

Elizabeth Barton was a servant in the house of Thomas Cobb, caretaker of an estate near Aldington owned by William Warham, the archbishop of Canterbury. At age 19, she suffered an illness which resulted in "religious hysteria." While convalescing, Barton lapsed into trances that lasted for days; her ravings were of such "marvellous holiness in rebuke of sin and vice," including rebukes of those in power, that the locals believed her to be divinely inspired. Cobb reported the matter to Richard Masters, the parish priest, who in turn informed Archbishop Warham. When Elizabeth Barton recovered and found herself the object of veneration, she continued to feign trances and divulge prophecies, or so she would soon state in a coerced "confession."

In 1526, as Barton's fame grew, Warham instructed the prior of Christ Church, Canterbury, to send two monks to examine her. One of these, Edward Bocking, pronounced her sincere and gained her admission the following year as a Benedictine nun to St. Sepulchre's convent, Canterbury. With Bocking's instruction, Barton's prophecies became even more remarkable. The 20-year-old attracted many followers, who believed her to be, as she asserted, in direct communication with the Virgin Mary.

Though Barton was uneducated, her rantings were directed towards political concerns; a widespread sensation was caused by her declaration that should Henry VIII persist in his intention of divorcing ***Catherine of Aragon**, he "should no longer be king of this realm . . . and should die a villain's death." Even such men as the bishop of Rochester and Sir Thomas More corresponded with Barton. On Henry's return from France in 1532, he passed through Canterbury and is said to have allowed the nun to confront him in an attempt to frighten him into abandoning his marriage. After the Act in Restraint of Appeals granted sovereignty to the English Church court and Henry's divorce was allowed in May 1533, Barton's utterances became increasingly treasonable. She was brought before Thomas Cranmer (who had succeeded as archbishop upon Warham's death) to be examined, and she confessed. On September 25, Bocking and another monk were arrested; in November, Richard Masters and others were implicated. The maid and her fellow accomplices were examined before the Star Chamber and ordered to be publicly displayed at St. Paul's Cross, where they each read a confession. In January 1534, by a bill of attainder, they were condemned to death and executed at Tyburn on April 20. While some have held that Elizabeth Barton's confession was derived by force and therefore is valueless, the evidence of her deception is usually considered conclusive.

Barton, Emma (1872–1938)

***British photographer.** Name variations: Mrs. G.A. Barton. Born Emma Rayson in Birmingham, England, in 1872; died at Isle of Wight, England, in 1938; daughter of a railway porter; married George Albert Barton; children: three daughters, two sons.*

Highly regarded for her portraits and allegorical studies, Emma Barton probably became interested in photography in the 1890s while taking pictures of her children. Most of her work was done in and around her own house in Birmingham, England. Barton began exhibiting in approximately 1901 and was represented in competitions and exhibitions in Britain, Europe, and the United States. Her work was also published in a number of magazines. Her well-known photograph *The Awakening* received a medal at the 1903 Royal Photographic Society exhibition, and it appeared in the British section of the Louisiana Purchase Exposition held in St. Louis, Missouri, in 1904. In 1929, Barton took up residence on the Isle of Wight, where she died nine years later, in 1938.

Barbara Morgan, Melrose, Massachusetts

Barton, Fanny or Frances (1737–1815).

See Abington, Frances.

Barton, Mrs. G.A. (1872–1938).

See Barton, Emma.

Barton, Pam (1917–1943)

***English golfer.** Born Pamela Barton in London, England, on March 4, 1917; died in a plane crash in England on November 14, 1943.*

Twice runner-up for the British Women's Championship (1934, 1935), Pam Barton finally took the top spot in 1936, and again in 1939. In October 1936, she became "the Girl Wonder of British Golf" when she also won the USGA Women's Championship, defeating ***Maureen Orcutt** (Mrs. J.D. Crews) in the final round at the Canoe Brook Country Club in New Jersey. Following in the footsteps of ***Dorothy Campbell Hurd**, an American who held both titles in 1909, Barton was the first English woman to hold English and American titles in the same year. During World War II, Pam Barton enlisted in the Women's Auxiliary Air Force and was killed in a plane crash while on duty.

Bartosova, Marie (1882–1967).

See Majerová, Marie.

Barykova, Anna Pavlovna (1839–1893)

***Russian poet of the Revolutionary period.** Name variations: Barýkova. Born Anna Pavlovna Kamenskaia in St. Petersburg, Russia, on December 22, 1839; died at*

Pam Barton

Rostov on Don, Russia, on May 31, 1893; daughter of Maria Kamenskaia (a writer); granddaughter of Fyodor Tolstoi (an artist); educated at Ekaterininskii Institute; married twice; children: four.

Selected writings: My Muse *(1878);* Tale of How Tsar Akhreian Went to Complain to God *(1883);* A Votary of Aesthetics *(1884).*

Politics have often deeply marked both the rise and suppression of Russian women writers. The career of poet and satirist Anna Pavlovna Barykova was no exception, as it represented the populist, revolutionary spirit of the 1870s and 1880s. Raised in an artistic family, Barykova had both her grandfather, artist Fyodor Tolstoi, and her mother, writer **Maria Kamenskaia,** as creative examples. Such heritage gave her the advantage of education, though mediocre, at a state boarding school in Moscow, and at St. Petersburg's Ekaterininskii Institute, as well as at home. Barykova learned several languages and began writing poetry as a teenager. Employed as a translator for Lev Tolstoy's publishing company called Intermediary, she was almost 40 years old when her first volume of poetry was released. *My Muse* (1878) was publicly followed by *A Votary of Aesthetics* (1884). The two volumes were separated by Barykova's satiric portrait of Alexander III, *Tale of How Tsar Akhreian Went to Complain to God*, published anonymously in 1883. Like many of her peers, she was imprisoned briefly for her political beliefs. Barykova died at age 53, as her writing career was on the ascendance.

Crista Martin, freelance writer, Boston, Massachusetts

Basch, Anamarija (b. 1893)

Yugoslav-Jewish activist in the Belgian resistance and nurse in the Spanish Civil War. *Born in Felz Sentivan, Yugoslavia, in 1893; died after 1945; married Andreas Basch (an engineer); children: son, Jan (b. 1921).*

Active in radical politics, fled Yugoslavia with husband after it became increasingly repressive (early 1930s); settled in Belgium, then went to Spain (1936) to lend support to the embattled Republican government; returned to Belgium after defeat of the Spanish Republic (1939); during World War II, active in the Belgian resistance movement; her husband captured by the Gestapo and killed; survived and moved with son to Hungary after World War II.

From her earliest years in Felz Sentivan, Yugoslavia, Anamarija Basch exhibited a strong commitment to social justice. She joined the Communist movement and was active in various organizations that rendered assistance to poor workers, including adult education courses and consumer cooperatives. Anamarija's political involvement deepened after marrying the engineer Andreas Basch (born in 1890 in Subotica), who was already a seasoned Marxist revolutionary. The birth of their son Jan in 1921 further motivated the couple to work for what they considered a more just world.

In 1929, Yugoslavia became a royal dictatorship and a policy of repression of radicals, already underway for some years, greatly intensified. Andreas was unable to find steady work because of his Communist activism, and in the early 1930s the family felt compelled to move to Belgium. Here, they both found work; Anamarija was a nurse in a large hospital. Alarmed by the proximity of Nazi Germany to Belgium, Andreas became an active member of the Belgian Communist Party. Though busy with her nursing work and young son, Anamarija nonetheless remained politically active. The relatively secure world of the Basch family was shattered in the summer of 1936 when the revolt of Francisco Franco and his Fascist forces in Spain acted as a warning signal for Marxists, democrats, and Jews.

Among the foreigners who came to Spain—not for fame or fortune but to halt Fascism in its tracks—were individuals like the Basch family who had already lost their homelands to dictatorship. Only the arrival of volunteers, men and women alike, to serve in the International Brigades saved the unstable Republic from collapsing. In October 1936, the Basches departed Belgium for a Spain embroiled in a bloody civil war. Andreas was chosen as commandant of the International Brigade barracks at Albacete, and, later in the war, he taught topography at the Pozorubio officers' school. Anamarija became a nurse at the International Brigade hospital in Valencia and later moved closer to the front at the field hospital of the 15th Army Corps. Still in his mid-teens, son Jan, who had recently begun working in Belgium as an electrician, volunteered to serve in the Eleventh Brigade of the Internationals, becoming one of the youngest (some believe *the* youngest) of the international volunteers; later, he served in an artillery unit named for the Rumanian revolutionary ***Ana Pauker**. Jan Basch fought in many of the most savage battles of the war, including the struggle for Madrid's University City and the battles of Jarama, Guadalajara and Huesca.

Miraculously, the Basch family was still alive in October 1938, when the Spanish Republic decided to disband the International Brigades in a desperate measure to pressure the Franco rebels to cut their ties to Hitler and Mussolini, who had been sending vast amounts of men and materiél since the start of the conflict. This gamble of the dying Republic failed; by early 1939, the war was lost, and Franco's Fascist forces had won. The Basch family returned to Belgium, deeply disappointed but proud of their participation. As Communists, they believed they had been in the vanguard of the struggle against the greatest evil of their age, unaware that Stalin's Soviet Union, despite its considerable achievements, had by the late 1930s been transformed into a vast terror-based prison camp.

By the spring of 1940, memories of the Spanish conflict rapidly became ancient history, as Nazi Germany invaded Belgium and Jewish refugees like Anamarija Basch and her family became the objects of repression. By 1941, both Jews and Communists were being rounded up and thrown into concentration camps prior to their deaths. Andreas, now an active member of the Belgian resistance, was arrested by the Gestapo and shipped to a concentration camp where he was murdered. Anamarija and her son Jan were also active members of the resistance but were able to elude the Gestapo net. After the war, they left Belgium for Hungary rather than Yugoslavia. As pro-Soviet Communists, they disapproved of the anti-Stalinist regime of Marshal Tito, preferring to live in a nation that was uncritically loyal to the Soviet Union.

SOURCES:

Lustiger, Arno. *Schalom Libertad! Juden im spanischen Bürgerkrieg*. Frankfurt am Main: Athenäum Verlag GmbH, 1989.

John Haag, Associate Professor, University of Georgia, Athens, Georgia

Bascom, Florence (1862–1945)

American geologist who was the first woman in America to earn a Ph.D. in geology and the first woman awarded a Ph.D. in any discipline by Johns Hopkins University. *Born Florence Bascom on July 14, 1862, in Williamstown, Massachusetts; died in Northampton, Massachusetts, on June 18, 1945, of a cerebral hemorrhage; daughter of John (a philosopher and president of the University of Wisconsin) and Emma Curtiss (a schoolteacher); University of Wisconsin, B.A., B.L., 1882, B.S., 1884, M.S., 1887; Johns Hopkins University, Ph.D., 1893.*

Instructor and associate professor at Ohio State University (1893–95); reader at Bryn Mawr College (1895–1903), associate professor (1903–06), professor (1906–28), professor emeritus (1928–45); geologist, U.S. Geological Survey, publishing major folios (1896–1938); second woman appointed a fellow (1894) and first woman elected an officer (1924) of the Geological Society of America; associate editor for American Geologist *(1896–1905); sabbatical to Germany (1906); honored at special luncheon in her honor by Geological Society of America (1937).*

Selected writings: Bascom, "The Structures, Origin, and Nomenclature of the Acid Volcanic Rocks of South Mountain," Journal of Geology *1 (1893): pp. 813–832; "The Ancient Volcanic Rocks of South Mountain, Pennsylvania,"* U.S. Geological Survey Bulletin *no. 136 (1896); "The Relation of the Streams in the Neighborhood of Philadelphia to the Bryn Mawr Gravel,"* American Geologist *19 (1897): pp. 50–57; "Aporhyolite of South Mountain, Pennsylvania,"* Bulletin of the Geological Society of America *8 (1897): pp. 393–396; "Piedmont District of Pennsylvania,"* Bulletin of the Geological Society of America *16 (1905): pp. 289–328; with Victor Goldschmidt, "Anhydrite Twin from Aussee,"* American Journal of Science *24 (1907): pp. 487–490; with W.B. Clark, N.H. Darton, H.B. Kümmel, R.D. Salisbury, B.L. Miller, and G.N. Knapp, "Description of the Philadelphia District,"* U.S. Geological Survey Atlas, *Folio 162, 1909; with N.H. Darton, H.B. Kümmel, W.B. Clark, B.L. Miller, and R.D. Salisbury, "Description of the Trenton Quadrangle,"* U.S. Geological Survey Atlas, *Folio 167, 1909; "The Petrographic Province of Neponset Valley, Massachusetts,"* Journal of the Academy of Natural Sciences of Philadelphia *2 (1912): pp. 15, 129–161; with B.L. Miller, "Description of the Elkton and Wilmington Quadrangles,"* U.S. Geological Survey Atlas, *Folio 211, 1920; "The Use of the Two-Circle Contact Goniometer in Teaching Crystallography,"* American Mineralogist *5 (1920): pp. 45–50; "The University in 1874–1887,"* Wisconsin Magazine of History *8 (March 1925): pp. 300–301, 308; "Fifty Years of Progress in Petrography and Petrology: 1876–1926,"* The Johns Hopkins University Studies in Geology *no. 8 (1927): pp. 33–82; with G.W. Stose, "Description of the Fairfield and Gettysburg Quadrangles,"* U.S. Geological Survey Atlas, *Folio 225, 1929; with E.T. Wherry, G.W. Stose, and A.I. Jonas, "Geology and Mineral Resources of the Quakertown-Doylestown District,"* U.S. Geological Survey Bulletin, *no. 828, 1931; with G.W. Stose, "Description of the Coatesville and West Chester Quadrangles,"* U.S. Geological Survey Atlas, *Folio 223, 1932; with G.W. Stose, "Geology and Mineral Resources of the Honeybrook and Phoenixville Quadrangles, Pennsylvania,"* U.S. Geological Survey Bulletin, *no. 891, 1938.*

Florence Bascom was born on July 14, 1862—at a time when the Civil War was splitting the country—at Williamstown, Massachusetts, the youngest of three surviving children. Descended from hardy 17th-century New England Calvinists (Miles Standish was a maternal ancestor), she grew up in an intellectual home. Her father John was a professor of oratory and rhetoric at Williams College as well as a powerful pulpit speaker, and her mother Emma Curtiss (John's second wife) had been a teacher. Emma was a graduate of Almira Hart Lincoln Phelps' Patapsco Institute; in accordance with Phelps' view that science could strengthen domestic life, she had a strong science background, especially in botany. A charter member and officer of the Association for the Advancement of Women, Emma believed that the mother needed outside interests and activities to "broaden her knowledge, deepen her sympathies and enlarge her mental vision." Raised by his mother and older sisters, Florence's father once said, "I owe much to women." During his student days at Williams, he had taken numerous science courses. A seminary graduate, he liberally attempted to reconcile science and Christianity in his classroom.

Florence grew up in a college town that endorsed puritanical principles. Interested in temperance and suffrage (***Susan B. Anthony**'s birthplace was nearby), Florence's parents influenced her. A highly intelligent, serious child, she studiously finished her schoolwork and played with her companionable dog. At home, she participated in discussions about politics and contemporary issues. During the Jacksonian era when she matured, science was popular. John Bascom, who struggled with nervous depression, relied on his children to relieve his melancholy. He took them on trips to nearby mountains to exercise, promoting natural science to help them develop "definiteness of aim." They explored the land around their large, two-story gabled home on the banks of the Hoosac (now Hoosic) River and took temperature readings of the thermal spring which traversed the property. The Bascom house contained observatory and laboratory equipment which both parents used to encourage scientific interests.

When Florence was 12, her father accepted the position as president of the University of Wisconsin in Madison so that he could teach philoso-

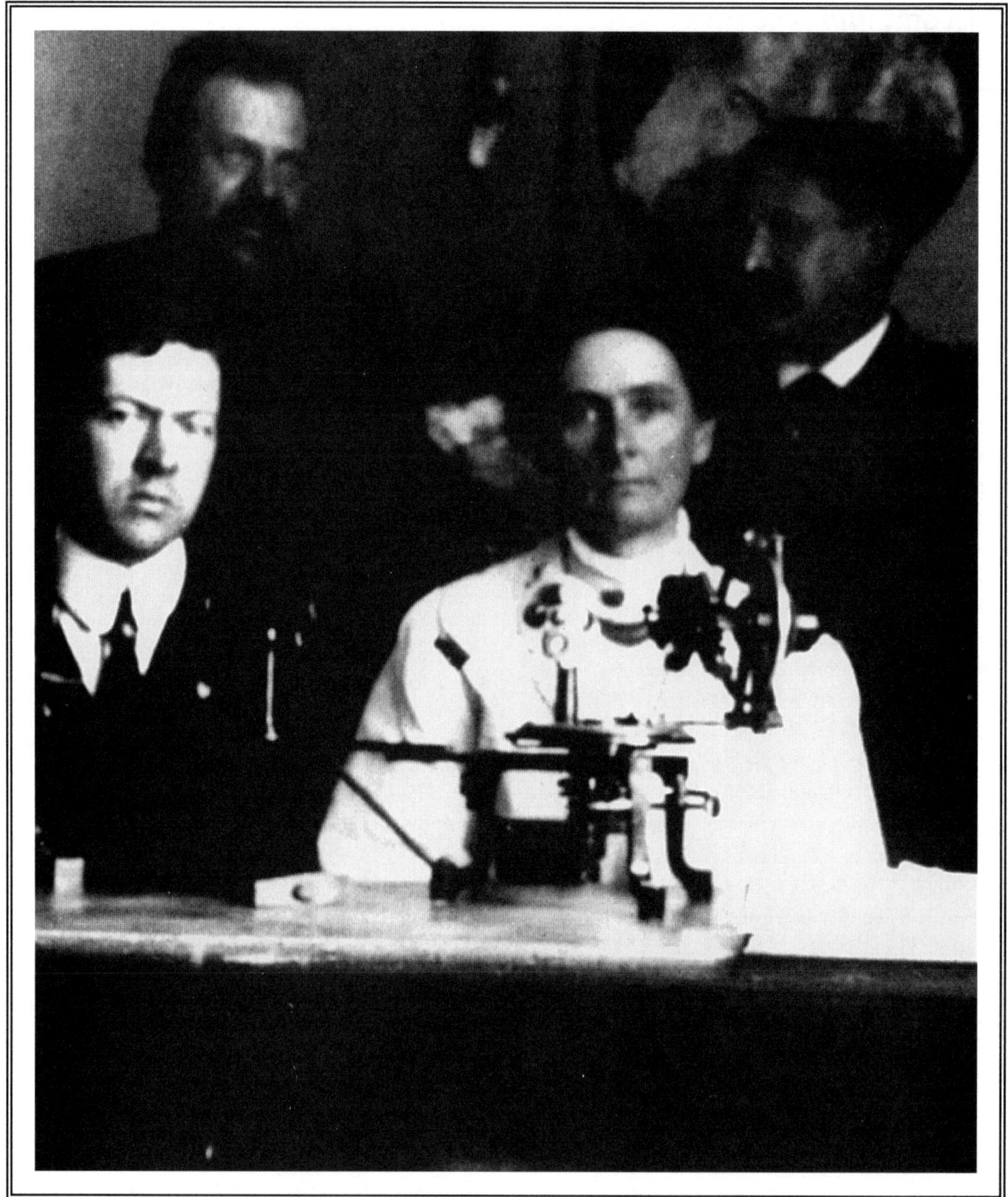

Florence Bascom

phy and ethics. Though Florence did not want to move, she was convinced by a friend that Madison had an impressive marble capitol building like the one in Washington, D.C. Eager to see the lavish capital, Florence was disappointed when her family arrived in late summer to discover that 19th-century Madison was small and drab. Her father was also disillusioned; the students were mediocre and poorly prepared compared to the students at Williams, and the president's house was the only building on University Hill.

Florence attended Madison High School, where she graduated in 1877 with high grades at age 16. At graduation, dressed in a white muslin and silk dress decorated with rosebuds and lace, she read an essay on water. The *Tri-Weekly Journal* commented, "Miss Florence lisped quite prettily, thus adding a charm to the interest of her delivery, which was otherwise expressive and by no means monotonous."

Bascom shared an especially close relationship with her father, with whom she often rode or drove to the family house at Lake Mendota. She was aware of his efforts to liberalize Wisconsin's curriculum, secure more research opportunities for faculty, and guarantee equal education for women. During the autumn of 1877, she enrolled as a freshman at the university. With her sister Jean, she joined the Kappa Kappa Gamma sorority and attended literary meetings at Ladies Hall.

Coeducation was then in its early stages at Wisconsin; women still had separate lecture buildings and could only use the library on specific days. To balance this segregation, John Bascom expanded traditional curricula. Florence pursued the new modern-classical curriculum with classes in German, French, and English literature. She considered academics at Wisconsin to be deficient, however, so her father continued to add to her schooling at home.

Although she had access to many influential professors, she regretted that they did not specialize in research and that there were no graduate students in her classes to inspire academic excellence. She also criticized professors who recited directly from textbooks, adding nothing in the way of fresh insights: "There was only too little general or collateral reading and no manifestation, I should say, of the spirit of research." Studiously acquiring a broad education, Bascom received her A.B. and B.L. degrees at the 1882 commencement.

That autumn, she traveled by train to Hampton, Virginia, to teach in a school for both African and Native Americans that one of her father's friends had founded. After one year, besieged by letters from her mother telling her how to prevent tuberculosis, of which one of her sisters died, Bascom returned to Madison for graduate studies in science. Intrigued, she focused on geology, a choice motivated by several factors. Usually, women were the last to be seated in lectures, but geology professors arranged their students alphabetically, not by gender, which had sparked her interest in science during her junior year. Sitting up front, she became absorbed in the lectures. She was also influenced by a visit with her father to Mammoth Cave in Kentucky. On a drive with her father and family friend Dr. Edward Orton, geologist at Ohio State University and member of the Ohio State Geological Survey, she became aware that landscapes had unseen geological formations. Bascom desired to learn more about the manner in which landscapes were formed.

> The selection of work in which one delights, and a diligent adherence to it, are [the] main ingredients of success.
>
> **—Florence Bascom**

She studied geology with some of the best scholars in the country. Thomas Chamberlin directed the state geological survey, while Professor Roland D. Irving, an authority on Lake Superior, inspired Bascom to remark, "He was a rare teacher and a great geologist." Charles R. Van Hise, a leading structural geologist, was only five years older than his pupil. Van Hise had been a former student of John Bascom and quickly became Florence's scholarly hero. When she received a B.S. in 1884, her professors encouraged her to continue her studies.

While Bascom was a student, Chamberlin completed and published the state geological survey and became director of the division of glacial geology in the U.S. Geological Survey. Aware of such career opportunities, Bascom chose to specialize in petrography (dealing with the description and classification of rocks) and structural geology. She worked closely with Van Hise on her master's thesis while he finished his doctorate. While Irving supervised both of their work, Van Hise taught Bascom to subordinate detail in order to understand regional patterns and acquire results. Her thesis, "The Sheet Gabbros of Lake Superior," contributed to the men's more comprehensive studies. She completed her M.S. in geology in 1887.

In that year, her father resigned as university president. His tenure, often referred to as the university's golden age because of his reforms, ended because he disagreed with the university's regents who resisted his changes. Worried about perceptions of his integrity, he publicly stated that the regents were not interested in education. Returning to Williamstown with her family, Bascom taught Greek and physical geography at a local high school but wanted more challenging work. When her less-ambitious brother returned penniless from a western excursion, she decided to become financially independent.

From 1889 to 1891, Bascom taught geology and chemistry at Rockford College in Illinois, decisively planning to make geology her life work. Her father wrote her: "You are not likely to find any path but that of work. I hope you will be able to make work an immediate joy." She realized that to become a professional geologist she needed to acquire advanced education and technical knowledge. Her Wisconsin professors urged her to apply to the Johns Hopkins University, then the premiere graduate school in America. Bascom's father, concerned about her choice of field and university, told her, "I do not quite understand why you elect a study you can hardly hope to make a specialty in instruction," but promised to support her.

She submitted her application in September 1890. Johns Hopkins did not accept women but made an exception for Bascom to attend lectures because she would be unable to receive equal instruction in petrography anywhere else. She could attend the university, paying only laboratory fees not tuition, because she was not considered a formal candidate for graduation. This discriminatory policy modeled conservative German colleges where faculty refused to consider women as equal scholars.

Johns Hopkins focused on research as the main goal of higher education. Bascom had access to scholars such as crystallographer George Huntington Williams, who had learned microscopical petrography in Heinrick Rosenbusch's Heidelberg laboratory. He introduced petrography methods in which thin rock sections were cut and examined under the polarized light of a microscope. Bascom learned this technique and registered for seminars in inorganic geology and paleontology. Because she was a woman, she had to sit behind a screen in the corner of lecture rooms to shield her from male students.

Bascom's family helped her survive the hostile environment at Johns Hopkins. Her father advised her to be patient and tolerant and "to win what you fairly can, no more." When she complained of male students and faculty staring at her, John told his geologically inclined daughter, "you better put a stone or two in your pockets to throw at those 'heads that are thrust out of windows.'" Bascom admitted that her academic work was not as rigorous as she had imagined it might be. Her mother, worried that the strain might cause her to be exhausted and ill, urged her to "indulge yourself a little and not be such a hard taskmaster over your body."

Florence studied with Williams, analyzing the terrain of the Maryland and Pennsylvania Piedmont. Wearing long skirts and gaiters and carrying a knapsack packed with a geologic hammer, compass, magnifying glass, and notebook, she joined Williams, faculty, and students on fieldwork near Baltimore in the summer of 1892. Enduring the hard work, she hammered rocks while shouldering the stares and curses of curious onlookers. Sometimes, when she went into the field alone, farmers threateningly called her a trespasser and enraged bulls chased her.

Returning to the laboratory and studying collected samples under the microscope, she prepared her dissertation, "A Contribution to the Geology of South Mountain, Pennsylvania." Bascom revealed that the Precambrian rocks of South Mountain were actually formed from ancient lava flows not sediments, a concept which according to the *Baltimore American* "changed the opinion of two generations of geologists." She introduced the term aporhyolite into geological jargon to explain how volcanics undergo extreme metamorphosis.

Her fieldwork was so useful that her professors incorporated her reports in the Maryland Geological Survey and recommended that she become a doctoral candidate because she had "ability, energy and enthusiasm that could be expected of any man." In the fall, she formally applied for a Ph.D. which was approved secretly because of the excellence of her scholarship. The trustees emphasized that her Ph.D. was special, not a precedent. University President Daniel Coit Gilman called her to his office in January 1893 to tell her the news. Bascom's Ph.D. was not only the first awarded a woman at Johns Hopkins, but also the first geology Ph.D. earned by a woman in America. Her new alma mater did not officially admit women until 1907 nor award another female doctorate until 1911.

Nationally, newspapers reported her Ph.D. The *Milwaukee Journal* described her as being of medium height, "a pronounced blonde" who was "completely engrossed in her studies." A

Baltimore Sunday News column said, "She is quiet and self-possessed, a woman who is reserved, of few words and apparently possessed of great determination." When commencement occurred on June 13, 1893, Bascom, a woman who was said to shun notoriety, was traveling by train west to Ohio State University ready to begin to work with Edward Orton. Although she had many discouraging experiences at Johns Hopkins, she gained a great love of research.

Though Bascom decided not to marry, she said she preferred the conversation of men and remarked, "women indulge in small talk." Her father fulfilled her need for affection: "He was all that I needed, association with him gratified all I wanted or needed so far as men were concerned." John Bascom encouraged his daughter to remain unattached, reassuring her that "one thing is as fixed as the stars and far more comfortable than the stars, and that is your love."

In 1895, Bryn Mawr College, which actively recruited intellectual professors to influence the all-female student body, sought Bascom because of her prestige as a research scientist. Founded by the men of Johns Hopkins, the school was overseen by trustees looking for professors who could inspire students with independent and original research. Orton tried to persuade her to teach at Wellesley, while her father suggested Vassar or Mount Holyoke. But Bascom considered Bryn Mawr's offer attractive, given the college's focus on research, though it paid a smaller salary.

Soon after she began teaching, however, Bascom discovered that college administrators were not interested in establishing a geology department. James Rhoads, the president who had hired her and who believed in a strong science curricula, had died and been replaced by ***Martha Carey Thomas** who did not want to spend money on a field she did not think would appeal to many female students. When Bascom first arrived, other departments occupied the main floors of the science building, but she was resourceful in utilizing the laboratory space and supplies she was issued. She began teaching a single geology class. Planning a research-oriented department, she established a geological library with mineral specimens and laboratory equipment, including a petrographic microscope.

Held on the fourth floor of Dalton Hall, Bascom's lectures attracted students. So many students took geology that she proposed an undergraduate major, and by 1903 she hired a second geology faculty member. Having advanced from a reader in geology to full professor by 1906 despite obvious obstacles, she created a graduate program that gained prominence internationally. Hers was the first geology department at a women's college.

Attempting to provide her students the best education possible, she lectured and assigned laboratory and surveying fieldwork. Students learned about historical geology and were taught how to interpret geological maps, take observations, solve problems, and report on geological papers. They accompanied Bascom on trips to Precambrian crystalline formations and Pleistocene and Cretaceous fossils and rocks near the campus, collecting and recording specimens in journals. Students listened to eminent geologists who were invited by Bascom to lecture.

In 1906, she took a year sabbatical to Heidelberg, Germany, where she learned techniques of crystal measurement and how to observe optical characteristics of minerals from Victor Goldschmidt and Rosenbusch. On her return, she introduced optical crystallography methods to American scientists and showed them how to use a two-circle contact goniometer that she had developed to teach crystallography. Bascom also studied paleontology and stratigraphy to complement her work in petrography and structural geology.

An opinionated woman who carefully made observations, upheld high scientific standards, and was committed to her teaching and research, Bascom constantly battled the outspoken and domineering Martha Thomas. Thomas claimed that although Bryn Mawr wanted broader intellectual opportunities for women, she considered geology an inappropriate course. When Thomas demoted the course to a science elective, Bascom resigned, and her students protested. The college's trustees reinstated the major to insure that she stayed. Despite lack of adequate administrative support, space, money, and staff, Bascom continued to build a research reputation.

Through the 1930s, Bascom trained the most important female geologists in the world. Unassuming, she was addressed as Miss Bascom, never Dr. Bascom, by her students and wore a white shirtwaist, skirt, and black robe as required to teach her classes. She insisted on wearing a leather jacket, split skirt, and sturdy shoes on field trips or when riding her bicycle or horse, and Thomas criticized her for this, demanding that she conform to more ladylike attire. Irritated at protocol—such as Thomas requiring her to stay on campus for commencement when she wanted to utilize the time in the field—Bascom refused to comply. She also demanded raises and promotions despite Thomas' blustering and satisfactorily served on a committee to reduce Thomas' presidential powers.

Bascom's scientific impact can be assessed by her students' contributions. She stimulated students such as **Maria Luisa Crawford** who noted, "she was an uncompromising and challenging teacher." **Dorothy Wyckoff** recalled, "She expected of her students clear and honest thinking, not by precept so much as by example." Bascom recognized talented students committed to geology and supported their endeavors, nurturing their talents and training them to research in a mentor-apprentice friendship; she gave her favorite graduate students polished gems mounted in necklaces. Throughout her life, her advice was sought to shape geological careers for women. She hoped her students would become her colleagues and regretted when talented female geologists were "lost to the sciences by marriage." Several students she trained in geological methods became leaders in the profession. One student, **Ida Helen Ogilvie** (1874–1963), earned a Ph.D. from Columbia and was the first woman to teach graduate courses in geology at a major coeducational university.

Extending her geological work outside the classroom, Bascom collaborated with the federal government when she accepted an 1896 appointment to the U.S. Geological Survey, the first woman credentialed for that work. Employment with the government gave her access to laboratory equipment, books, civil-service status, and colleagues unavailable at Bryn Mawr. During her summer vacations, she went into the field, walking, riding her horse, or driving a buggy in the mountains, to gather rocks, take notes, and map crystalline formations of the Mid-Atlantic Piedmont region. A familiar sight in the countryside, she worked long, uncomfortable hours from dawn to dark in the field then drafted maps at night. She surveyed her assigned territory from New Jersey to Virginia, expecting her students to toil diligently in the field beside her. Bascom then analyzed the thin mineral slivers on microscope slides in winter and recorded her results and conclusions. Of her rigorous routine, Bascom wrote, "This is *the life*, to plunge into the wholesome isolation of the field, to return to the stimulating association of Bryn Mawr, to observe and in part to clear up geologic phenomena, to return to the exposition and interpretation of geologic phenomena."

Her reports are considered her most important geological contribution, and her research results were published as seven major United States Geological Survey Folios from 1909 to 1938 that are the basis for geological work in that region. Because of her work, geological maps for every square mile of public domain were prepared. These survey maps indicate areas feasible for economic development and provide scientific insight to the North American continent's physical history.

Bascom eagerly corresponded with her father about her fieldwork, claiming, "The fascination of any search after truth lies not in the attainment, which at best is found to be very relative, but in the pursuit, where all the powers of the mind and character are brought into play and are absorbed in the task." She told him that she found a "joy that is beyond expression in 'sounding the abyss of science' and the secrets of the infinite mind." When her father died in 1911, she lost her intellectual confidante and best friend. While Bascom mourned, her lectures were reserved. She arranged for her father's autobiography to be published posthumously.

Traveling around the world for professional meetings, she attended an International Geological Congress in Moscow, where she rode in the tsar's carriage. She published approximately 40 articles on petrology, geomorphology, and the history of geology. Because Bascom insisted on using her first initial instead of her name, there were occasionally problems such as the hotel which, assuming she was a man, assigned her male roommates at a convention. She enjoyed conversing with peers at professional meetings and being active in the male-dominated Geological Society of America. In 1894, she was the second woman selected as a fellow of the Society (not the first woman fellow as some biographical sketches mistakenly indicate) and the first woman elected an officer in 1924. She held offices in the American Association for the Advancement of Sciences and American Association of University Professors and participated in numerous geological groups and honoraries. Her name was starred in the first edition of *American Men of Science* to indicate that she was a prominent geologist. From 1896 to 1905, she acted as associate editor for *American Geologist.*

Disciplined in all aspects of her life, Bascom exercised her blue roan mare, Fantasy, and her colt, Starlight, daily. She protected wildlife, rescuing trapped animals and rebuking policemen who left their horses exposed to cold weather. If she found an injured animal, it took priority over fieldwork. Marion Edwards Park, Bryn

Mawr president after Thomas, commented that Bascom was the most generous person she knew.

Bascom worked so hard that her health gradually failed, and she retired to her house near Williamstown, Massachusetts, in 1928. Freed from collegiate protocol, she had her hair bobbed at a local barber shop. She filled her home with antiques and books, picked berries, and roamed the countryside she had explored with her father as a child. Bascom read voraciously and drove around town, her dogs always in the backseat. Becoming more eccentric as she aged, she never cooked, but, remembering her mother's dietary influence, ate heartily at nearby farms. When she hosted friends, she heated up canned soup and served fruit.

In later life, she continued her survey work, writing folios and quibbling with other geologists about the interpretation of data, but she became easily fatigued and suffered memory loss. When she was defrauded of $20,000 of stocks, she decided not to return to Washington, D.C., retiring from the survey in 1938. Impoverished, she commented, "I now live modestly though comfortably. . . . It is good discipline to be poor." Bryn Mawr arranged for her to have a special room for research, but she decided after two years that she was aging too much to work. She requested that her graduate students continue her work and methodology, but often these disciples did not follow exactly in her footsteps. She was angered when two of her students, **Anna Jonas** and **Eleanora Bliss**, controversially challenged and modified her interpretations about the age of Wissakickon schist.

Unable to live at Topping alone, Bascom moved in with her sister Jean at their family home on the Williams campus. She wrote a former student that her mind and money were both disappearing quickly. A family friend, **Grace Sutherland**, cared for the women and drove Florence to Topping because she talked so much about it, but the now senile Bascom did not recognize her home, asking only, "Should I know this place?"

Florence Bascom suffered a cerebral hemorrhage and died on June 18, 1945, at Northampton, Massachusetts. She was buried in the Bascom plot at Williams College Cemetery. Eight years earlier, at a special luncheon in her honor at the 50th anniversary meeting of the Geological Society of America, Bascom stressed that she disapproved of segregating scientists by gender. Gazing around the table, she realized that she had trained the majority of the eminent women present.

SOURCES:

Aldrich, Michele L. "Women in Geology," in Gabriele Kass-Simon and Patricia Farnes, eds. *Women of Science: Righting the Record.* Bloomington: Indiana University Press, 1990, pp. 42–71.

American Mineralogist, March-April 1946, memorial issue with bibliography.

Arnold, Lois Barber. *Four Lives in Science: Women's Education in the Nineteenth Century.* NY: Schocken Books, 1984.

Smith, Isabel Fothergill. *The Stone Lady: A Memoir of Florence Bascom.* Bryn Mawr: Bryn Mawr College, 1981.

SUGGESTED READING:

Bascom, John. *Things Learned by Living.* NY: Putnam, 1913.

Fairchild, Herman LeRoy. *The Geological Society of America, 1888–1930.* NY: The Geological Society of America, 1932.

Meigs, Cornelia. *What Makes a College? A History of Bryn Mawr.* NY: Macmillan, 1956.

Rossiter, Margaret W. *Women Scientists in America: Struggles and Strategies to 1940.* Baltimore: The Johns Hopkins University Press, 1982.

COLLECTIONS:

Biographical file, transcripts, alumni records, and Bascom's father's papers are located at the University of Wisconsin Archives, Madison, Wisconsin.

Correspondence, history of geology department, and departmental reports in Florence Bascom Papers and Faculty Minutes, both in the Bryn Mawr College Archives, Bryn Mawr, Pennsylvania. The college's geology department also has some of Bascom's papers, including her fieldwork notebooks.

Correspondence, newspaper clippings, her parents' items, her government survey certificate, and photographs are in the Florence Bascom Papers at the Smith College Library, Northampton, Massachusetts.

Information about Bascom's admission to Johns Hopkins University and her Ph.D. in Special Collections, Eisenhower Library, the John Hopkins University, Baltimore, Maryland.

Elizabeth D. Schafer, Ph.D.,
freelance writer in the
history of technology and science,
Loachapoka, Alabama

Bashemath

Biblical woman. *Name variations: Mahalath. Daughter of Ishamel; married Esau, the last of his three wives; children: son Reuel, founder of the four tribes of Edomites.*

Bashemath (fl. 900 BCE)

Biblical woman. *Daughter of Solomon; married Ahimaaz (one of his officers).*

Bashkirtseff, Marie (1859–1884)

Rising young painter and daughter of wealthy Russian expatriates in Paris in the 1880s who, before her early

Marie Bashkirtseff

death, produced one of the most notable diaries of the 19th century.

Name variations: (Russian form) Maria Konstantinovna Bashkirtseva; (childhood nickname) Moussia. Pronunciation: Bash-KEERT-sev, Bash-KEERT-seva, MOO-sya. Born Marie Bashkirtseff probably on January 24, 1859 (some authorities place her birth as early as November 1858), at her family's estate at Gavronzi outside Kiev, Ukraine, Russia; died in Paris, France, on October 31, 1884; daughter of Konstantin Bashkirtseff (a Russian noble and landowner) and Marie (Babanina) Bashkirtseff; taught by private tutors; trained in art at the Academy Julian (or Julien) in Paris, 1877–84; never married; no children.

Her parents separated (1862); left Russia, along with mother and members of her mother's family (1870); began diary and had love affair at a distance with Lord Hamilton (1873); began to paint (1875); settled in Paris (1877); had her first painting accepted at the Paris Salon (1880); diagnosed with tuberculosis and met Bastien-Lepage (1882); corresponded with Guy de Maupassant; diary published posthumously (1887).

Selected paintings: The Académie Julian *(Hermitage, St. Petersburg, 1880);* Jean and Jacques *(Newberry Library, Chicago, 1883);* The Meeting *(Musée d'Orsay, Paris, 1884).*

Marie Bashkirtseff died tragically at the youthful age of 24. At the time of her death, she had already enjoyed considerable success as a painter, but her artistic achievements were destined to be overshadowed by the voluminous and revealing diary that she left behind. Covering the last ten years of her life, the journal was soon published, albeit in a shortened and expurgated form by Marie's mother. A sensation at the time, the diary has fascinated readers, including many accomplished women, since it first appeared.

Starting in the 18th century, wealthy families of the Russian nobility spent much of their lives in Western Europe. Settling in resorts like Nice and the great cities, notably Paris, they were a colorful presence on the social scene. Thus, the Bashkirtseffs were part of one of the great waves of aristocratic travelers of the time. The Paris in which they finally settled in the late 1870s stood as the artistic center of the Western world. It was predictable, therefore, that the lively and intellectually gifted daughter of the family should become fascinated with the art world of the French capital and begin to paint seriously. The principal surprise in the situation was the depth of talent and the strength of commitment that she displayed.

In this era, Paris offered female artists a unique degree of freedom to receive training and to exhibit their achievements. Nonetheless, even here, women pursuing an artistic career found themselves facing artificial constraints until long after Bashkirtseff's death. They were not admitted to major schools such as the École des Beaux-Arts until 1896, and they were not permitted to enter important competitions such as the Prix de Rome until 1903. Bashkirtseff expressed her bitterness at the limits placed upon her as a female both in her diary and in her attraction to the emerging feminist movement in France.

Marie Bashkirtseff was born at her noble family's estate of Gavronzi near the city of Kiev, capital of the Ukraine and one of the great urban centers of the Russian Empire. Her birthday is January 24, 1859, although, in the Russian calendar of the time, her birth was recorded as occurring on January 12. Some authorities place her birth as early as November 1858. Her father, the son of a Russian general, was a wastrel and a libertine. At the urging of her family, Marie's mother left him when the girl was only two. Following the death of her own mother, Madame Bashkirtseff left Russia in 1870 to travel in Central and Western Europe. She soon settled in Nice, where Marie grew up. The family was wealthy but not socially distinguished by the standards of the aristocratic Russian community; the marital separation of the Bashkirtseffs detracted further from the family's status.

Her mother, along with other relatives who were part of the family household in Nice, indulged Marie with governesses, lavish clothes, and tutors. Her youthful beauty, obvious intelligence, and flowing energy seemed to confirm a fortuneteller's prophecy to her mother: "Your son will be ordinary, but your daughter will be a star." As if to give credence to this prediction, the young girl proved to be both a talented linguist and a promising musician.

At age 14, Marie started her diary. According to **Dorothy Langley Moore**, it was here that she initiated the practice of claiming to be younger than her actual years. Throughout her life, Bashkirtseff amplified her accomplishments by exaggerating her youthfulness. The first entries were made in early 1873, beginning a literary effort that eventually filled 84 volumes. These ranged from small notebooks to large, bound tomes. In previous years, she had kept a brief diary, but it consisted of short notes, and she apparently destroyed this earlier record of her thoughts when she began her larger effort. Bashkirtseff wrote mainly in French, but she used her knowledge of Russian, English, and Italian in making some of the entries.

Marie may have been impelled to start recording her innermost thoughts by her wild infatuation with the young Duke of Hamilton. She never met the young Scottish noble whom she gazed on from a distance during his stay in Nice. Moreover, Hamilton's constant companion was a lovely Italian woman known to be his mistress. Nonetheless, she asked God to "give me the Duke of Hamilton and I shall love him and make him happy!" Bashkirtseff's desire to attract Hamilton by being "surrounded with glory and triumph" led her to embark on a program of self-improvement. Indulged as usual by her family, she employed tutors to enhance her education. When one tutor failed to make the course of studying sufficiently demanding, Marie replaced her.

As her teenage years continued, Bashkirtseff had a series of infatuations with young men from the Italian nobility. When laryngitis, possibly an early hint of the tuberculosis that led to her early death, forced her to give up singing, she turned her formidable energies to drawing and painting. Her indulgent relatives immediately claimed to see her obvious talent, but Marie showed a cold and practical understanding of what she considered her meager artistic accomplishments. "I have decided to settle in Paris where I shall study," she wrote in September 1877. She expected, naively, to start making her mark as an artist within two years.

The strikingly beautiful Russian aristocrat enrolled at a prominent Parisian art school run by Rodolphe Julian, and, in October 1877, she joined the group of other young women—most of them also foreigners—studying there. Within a week, the proprietor told Marie's mother that he no longer thought her art studies were "just the whim of a spoiled child." "She has a strong will and is very gifted," he admitted. The 18-year-old Bashkirtseff reciprocated by throwing herself into her classes in drawing and painting. As usual, she stressed her youth, claiming to be only 16. Her fellow students responded with skepticism. Ironically, Bashkirtseff now caught a glance of her earlier love idol, the Duke of Hamilton, on a Parisian street. The young man she had admired from a distance had now grown stout. Bashkirtseff expelled him from her mind, while lamenting the time she had wasted in her infatuation.

The bohemianism of the art student's world gave Bashkirtseff scope to express some of her innermost desires. In 1875, she had written can-

A Meeting, *1884. Painting by Marie Bashkirtseff.*

didly in a diary entry about her admiration for her body: "I often stay for an hour in contemplation instead of bathing, and I only leave the mirror with difficulty." Now, she enthusiastically removed her clothes for her fellow female art students. As one of them remarked, Marie Bashkirtseff, ostensibly to discuss the aesthetic qualities of her form, "would freely take off her clothes and show us her body, just like a model."

The young woman's diaries have left a vivid picture of her ambitions and the frustrations she encountered as a female art student. She chafed at being barred from the École des Beaux-Arts, and she was outraged at her inability to go unaccompanied to visit the Louvre. "I know that I should become somebody; but with skirts—what can one do?" she wrote. In December 1880, she began to visit the militant feminist ***Hubertine Auclert** and her circle. In the early 1880s, Marie wrote under a pen name for *La Citoyenne*, a feminist and socialist journal.

In 1880, at Julian's urging, Bashkirtseff submitted a painting to the Salon, the prestigious annual art exhibition in Paris. Little more than 20 years old, she found her artistic ambitions confirmed when her large picture of a woman reading, with a bunch of violets at her side, was accepted by the Salon. At the same time, her doctor had begun treating her frequently for throat ailments. If Bashkirtseff suspected she was in danger, she never told her relatives nor did she note her concern in her diary. One biographer, Vincent Cronin, has suggested that Marie's frantic energy and hunger for new experiences reflected a quiet concern about her health. He notes that two of the young Russian's great-aunts suffered from "consumption," the term then used for the lung disease we know as tuberculosis. By the close of the year of her first great success in the art world, Bashkirtseff's body was showing alarming signs of serious illness. Pain developed below her left ear, and she was beginning to go deaf. A round of visits to medical specialists followed. The diagnosis was, indeed, consumption.

At the urging of her mother and aunt, Bashkirtseff returned to the family home near Kiev in 1881 for a round of church visits and prayer. During her stay, she became aware that the disease had spread from one lung to infect the other. In a second visit the following year, her mother hoped to promote a marriage between Marie and an eligible member of the local nobility. The plan produced no result, and Bashkirtseff returned to Paris in 1882 committed to resuming her career as an artist.

She hoped submissions to the Salon in 1883 would bring her more professional recognition, but one picture was virtually ignored, and she received praise only for a small work she herself disliked. In these years, she began to turn her hopes toward a literary career. Since the age of 14, she had kept the voluminous diary, and she now approached a number of noted French authors for encouragement. The first, Alexander Dumas, the younger, rebuffed her, but in 1884 Marie did begin an extended correspondence with Guy de Maupassant.

With barely six months to live, Bashkirtseff adopted the pseudonym of "Miss Hastings" and told the young French author that she wished to become "the confidante of your beautiful mind." She did not wish to see him face to face, but she informed him that "I am charming." Maupassant received piles of fan mail from female admirers, and he tried unsuccessfully to fend her off. Her response included a satirical sketch of how she thought he looked. This initiated a mutually flirtatious correspondence that Marie finally broke off. In the end, she found the young writer cruel and manipulating in his responses to her, and she rejected his continuing efforts to meet her face to face. Vincent Cronin has suggested that Marie was lucky her flirtation with de Maupassant did not reach a level of intimacy. He was psychologically dominated by his mother, and his relations with prostitutes had infected him with syphilis.

> Now here is a girl, the story of whose life as told by herself may be called the drama of a woman's soul.
>
> —Mathilde Blind, on Marie Bashkirtseff

During the last stages of her life, Bashkirtseff developed a close tie to the prominent painter Jules Bastien-Lepage. Although she had admired his work for several years, she met him only in 1882. Soon after they were introduced, she visited Bastien's studio during his absence. In a typically romantic gesture, she removed a small blob of his paint and took it home as if to draw inspiration from this fragment of his work. The two had intense discussions about their work, but, in time, the relationship cooled. An important barrier for Bashkirtseff was Bastien's unimpressive physical stature. She also began to ponder the views of critics who were not impressed with his work. "He's not glorious enough," she wrote. "If he were really an artist-god, like Wagner, it would be different." Ironically, those same critics that were not impressed with his work discounted one of her most accomplished works—the street scene with six ragged boys entitled *The Meeting*—suggesting that, if not actually the work of Bastien-Lepage, at least it had been done with his assistance. *The Meeting* was hailed in the Parisian press, despite the innuendo, and led to the sale of several of her other works.

The final months of Bashkirtseff's life were marked by a flurry of artistic success and a shared experience of illness with Bastien. Now approaching the last stages of tuberculosis, she found that he was suffering from what the doctors first diagnosed as rheumatism. Eventually, she learned that he faced imminent death from cancer of the stomach. Bashkirtseff put aside her earlier reservations about Bastien's physical limitations such as his short stature. Feeling close to him as a fellow artist and a cherished soul mate, she devoted much of her energies to nursing him. Her own failing health pushed her to paint in every spare moment in order to leave as much of an artistic legacy as possible. In a memorable diary entry, she railed against dying without leaving something memorable: "To die like a dog, like a hundred thousand women whose names are scarcely engraved upon their tombstones."

In the final weeks of her life, the two spent hours sitting side by side, barely able to speak to each other. Marie Bashkirtseff died on October 31, 1884. She had continued to make entries in her diary until 11 days before her death. Her last words to her mother were: "Life was so beautiful after all." Bastien's own life ended a little more than a month later.

Marie Bashkirtseff left detailed instructions for her family to follow in preserving her memory. These included the erection of a large funeral chapel, an annual memorial service with performances by noted musicians, the commissioning of a full-size statue of herself, and a prize to be awarded in her name to young painters.

The young artist also left a substantial collection of paintings and drawings, the product of seven years of energetic activity. Her best-known works are portraits and street scenes, and critics most frequently define her as a "genre painter," an artist who concentrated on undramatic scenes from everyday life. For example, *The Meeting* and *Jean and Jacques* show boys on the streets of Paris. The greatest influence on Bashkirtseff was the Realist School of mid-19th century French painting as represented by Gustave Courbet. Thus, *The Meeting*, in showing the six young boys gathered in front of a wooden fence, was painted in almost photographic realism. In short order, the brilliance of the Impressionists was to make paintings like hers appear both superficial and overly sentimental.

Although her painting did not leave a lasting mark, Marie Bashkirtseff's writing won her an important place in the world of 19th-century letters. In 1887, her mother followed the dead young woman's wishes in publishing the huge pile of exercise books in which Marie had compiled her diary. The bereaved mother apparently both transcribed the diary and bowdlerized the work to remove the unflattering picture it presented of Marie's personality and to delete frank passages about her sexual longings. Nonetheless, it remained a remarkable psychological portrait of a girl passing to young womanhood, and retained notable elements of frankness and self-analysis. Its picture of the bohemian art world, the wealthy family milieu in which Bashkirtseff grew up, and her dramatically brief life appealed to readers on both sides of the Atlantic.

Some readers and critics found this account of Bashkirtseff's ambitions, flirtations, and infatuations notable because of its arrogance and egotism. Shortly after the book's publication, one particularly incensed critic responded to it by declaring, "What a horrid little pig she was!" More recently, Doris Langley Moore has described Marie as a "brilliant little barbarian."

The most influential response to the book came in 1889 from the distinguished British politician William Gladstone. He noted the unattractive features of Marie's account of herself: "Mlle Bashkirtseff attracts and repels alternatively, and perhaps repels as much as she attracts." Nonetheless, he was struck by her "phenomenal personality," and the book's "commanding singularity as a psychological study." By the turn of the century, the book was attracting even wider attention. The popularity of Bashkirtseff's writing eventually evoked a satirical response: in 1911, the Canadian humorist Stephen Leacock wrote *Sorrows of a Super Soul: or, The Memoirs of Marie Mushenough*. The city of Nice chose to commemorate the young artist and writer in a more conventional manner, naming a street "Rue Bashkirtseff" and building a fountain in her honor.

Interest in Bashkirtseff has remained strong. In 1966, Moore called Bashkirtseff "the most candid of diarists," fascinating as "an egocentric personality." In their introduction to the 1985 edition of the diary, **Roszika Parker** and **Griselda Pollock** saw the novelty and significance of the book in the following way: "Never before had a woman so urgently proclaimed her ambition to excel, her hunger for public fame." They stressed the constraints she suffered as a female artist, and her role in militant socialist and feminist circles in Paris in the early 1880s.

Over the years, notable women including ***Paula Modersohn-Becker**, ***Anaïs Nin**, and ***Simone de Beauvoir** have expressed their interest in the diary and its author. Modersohn-Becker admired and hoped to emulate the young Russian's accomplishments, explaining passionately, "I say as she does; if only I can become something." In 1905, the rising young German painter studied at the Academy Julian where Bashkirtseff had begun her artistic career almost 30 years earlier. Anaïs Nin was inspired to compose her famous diary by Bashkirtseff's example. As **Deidre Bair**, Nin's biographer, puts it, in all likelihood "Marie's journal first gave [Nin] the idea that she, too, should write for posterity and, therefore, eventual publication."

Most notably Simone de Beauvoir used Marie Bashkirtseff's diary as a major source for *The Second Sex*, her study of women's psychology and social conditioning. First, she found the young Russian's writing an important illustration of the narcissistic thinking and behavior society imposes on females. Beauvoir cited diary passages in which Bashkirtseff repeatedly expressed her need to be admired by others, her sense of constantly being on a stage where she would be highly regarded by a surrounding audience. But Beauvoir was equally interested in how Bashkirtseff, once committed to her life as an artist, expressed outrage and struggled against the social and professional restrictions placed upon her by her identity as a woman.

SOURCES:

Bair, Deidre. *Anaïs Nin: A Biography.* NY: Putnam, 1995.

Beauvoir, Simone de. *The Second Sex.* Translated and edited by H.M. Parshley. NY: Knopf, 1971.

Cronin, Vincent. *Four Women in Pursuit of an Ideal.* London: Collins, 1965.

The Journal of Marie Bashkirtseff. Translated by ***Mathilde Blind**. Introduction by Roszika Parker and Griselda Pollock. London: Virago Press, 1985.

The Letters and Journals of Paula Modersohn-Becker. Translated and annotated by J. Diane Radycki. Metuchen, NJ: Scarecrow Press, 1980.

Moore, Doris Langley. *Marie & the Duke of H.: The Daydream Love Affair of Marie Bashkirtseff.* Philadelphia, PA: J.B. Lippincott, 1966.

Sutherland, Anne, and Linda Nochlin. *Women Artists 1550–1950.* NY: Knopf, 1976.

SUGGESTED READING:

Baynes, D.J. [Dormer Creston, pseud.] *The Life of Marie Bashkirtseff.* London: Eyre & Spottiswoode, 1943.

Cosnier, Colette. *Marie Bashkirtseff: Un portrait san retouches.* Paris: Pierre Horay, 1985.

Cravens, Gwyneth. "Past Present," in *The Nation.* December 10, 1990.

Dunaway, Philip, and Mel Evans, eds. *A Treasury of the World's Great Diaries.* Garden City, NY: Doubleday, 1957.

Greer, Germaine. *The Obstacle Race.* NY: Farrar, Straus, and Giroux, 1979.

Kernberger, Phyllis Howard, and Katherine Kernberger, trans. *I Am the Most Interesting Book of All: The Diary of Marie Bashkirtseff,* Volume One. San Francisco, CA: Chronicle Books, 1997.

Lerner, Michael. *Maupassant.* London: George Allen & Unwin, 1975.

Parker, Roszika, and Griselda Pollock. *Old Mistresses: Women, Art and Ideology.* NY: Pantheon, 1982.

Neil Heyman, Professor of History, San Diego State University, San Diego, California

Bashkirtseva, Maria Konstantinovna (1859–1884).

See Bashkirtseff, Marie.

Basile, Adriana (c. 1590–c. 1640)

Italian singer. *Name variations: Adreana, Adriana Basile Baroni. Born Adriana Basile in Posillip near Naples around 1590 (some sources cite c. 1580); died in Rome around 1640; sister of* ***Vittoria and Margherita Basile*** *(d. 1636?); married Mutio Baroni; children: three, including daughters Leonora (1611–1670) and* ***Caterina Baroni*** *(1620–?) who were also singers and performed with their mother at their salon in Rome. Basile, who performed in Mantua, Naples, and Rome, was awarded a barony for her singing.*

Adriana Basile came from a musical family: her brother Lelio was a composer, and her sisters, **Margherita** and **Vittoria**, were singers. One brother, Giovanni Battista, was a poet. Basile began singing in the Mantuan court around 1610. Within a few months, Monteverdi declared her more gifted than the Medici singer ***Francesca Caccini**. Duke Vincenzo Gonzaga awarded Basile a barony for her singing, and the duke's son Ferdinando bestowed further honors upon her. In 1621, she performed Alessandro Guarini's *Licori, ouvero L' incanto d'amore* in Mantua. Between 1618 and 1623, she also performed in Venice, Rome, and Modena. Released from Mantuan service in 1626, she continued to perform in Naples and Rome. We know that Monteverdi recommended that Basile and her sisters write solos for a dramatic entertainment, so she may have been a composer as well as a singer. Her sister Margherita was also a singer at Mantua and became the principal singer at the court in the 1620s and 1630s. The talent passed on to the following generation, and ***Leonora**

Baroni (1611–1670), Basile's daughter, became a famous singer in Italy and France.

John Haag,
Athens, Georgia

Basilissa, Saint (fl. 54–68).

See joint entry under Anastasia and Basilissa.

Basilissa, Saint (d. 780)

Benedictine abbess of Horren near Trier. *Name variations: Basilissa of Horren. Died in 780. Her feast day is on December 5th.*

Basilissa of Horren (d. 780).

See Basilissa, Saint.

Basilissa of Rome (fl. 54–68).

See joint entry under Anastasia and Basilissa.

Basine (fl. 428)

Frankish queen. *Flourished around 428; married Clodion, chief of the Franks (r. 428–447).*

Basine (fl. 465)

Merovingian queen of the Salian Franks. *Flourished in 465; married Childeric I (436–481), king of the Salian Franks (r. 457–481), in 463; children: Clovis I (465–511), king of the Salian Franks (r. 481–511), who married St.* ****Clotilda*** *(470–545).*

Basinger, Barbara (d. 1497).

See Fugger, Barbara Baesinger.

Basquette, Lina (1907–1995)

American actress. *Born Lena Baskette on April 19, 1907, in San Mateo, California; died at her home in Wheeling, West Virginia, of lymphoma on September 30, 1995; daughter of Gladys Basquette Belcher and stepdaughter of Ernest Belcher (a dance instructor); half-sister of actress-dancer Marge Champion; married Sam Warner (the movie producer), in 1925 (died 1927); married J. Peverell Marley (a cinematographer); also married to Jack Dempsey's trainer and Nelson Eddy (the actor), and three others; children: (first marriage) Lita; one son from another marriage.*

Filmography: "Lena Baskette Featurettes"; Shoes *(1916);* The Gates of Doom *(1917);* The Weaker Vessel *(1919);* Penrod *(1922);* Ranger of the North *(1927);* Serenade *(1927);* The Noose *(1928);* Wheel of Chance *(1928);* Celebrity *(1928);* Show Folks *(1928); Frank Capra's* The Younger Generation *(1929); Cecil B. De Mille's last silent,* The Godless Girl *(1929);* Come Across *(1929);* The Dude Wrangler *(1930);* Hard Hombre *(1931);* The Arizona Terror *(1931);* Goldie *(1931);* Morals for Women *(1931);* Hello Trouble *(1932);* The Midnight Lady *(1932);* Phantom Express *(1932);* The Final Hour *(1936);* Ebb Tide *(1937);* The Buccaneer *(1938);* Four Men and a Prayer *(1938);* A Night for Crime *(1943); and* Paradise Park *(1991).*

Once dubbed the "Screen Tragedy Girl," Lina Basquette led a personal life that was as traumatic as the lives of her silent-movie personas. A raven-haired child ballerina when she began her career, Basquette endured the demands of a legendary stage mother, six marriages, a vicious custody battle, two suicide attempts, and a rape before settling into a second career as the owner of one of the finest Great Dane kennels in the country.

Basquette began performing at the 1915 San Francisco World Fair, where she was featured as "Baby Ballerina" for the Victor Talking Machine Company exhibition. At nine, she signed a contract with Universal to star in a series of shorts, "Lina Baskette Featurettes," and other silents at $50 a week. Following her father's death in 1916, her mother Gladys married dance director Ernest Belcher (their daughter, dancer **Marge Champion**, is Lina's half-sister). The Belchers wangled a part for 16-year-old Lina in the *Ziegfeld Follies of 1923*, with billing as "America's Prima Ballerina," and changed her name from Baskette to Basquette. Turning down an offer from ***Anna Pavlova** to make Lina her protégé, Gladys Belcher preferred work that made money.

Though she retired in 1925 to marry Sam Warner, of Warner Bros. fame, Basquette would return to film after his death. Together, they had a daughter Lita, and when Warner died in 1927 Basquette became entangled in a legal battle with the Warners over custody; she also unwittingly signed away most of her inheritance. During this difficult period, she made what was her last silent and perhaps her most acclaimed film, *The Godless Girl* (1929), for Cecil B. de Mille, in which she played a teenager who becomes an atheist. In 1930, Lita was awarded to the Warners, and Basquette made her first suicide attempt.

Another marriage to Jack Dempsey's trainer and a messy affair with Dempsey resulted in a second suicide attempt. At this time, Basquette was working in westerns and "B" movies like *Morals for Women* (1931), *Midnight Lady* (1932), *The Final Hour* (1936) and *Four Men and a Prayer* (1938). From 1937 to 1939, she toured the world in several plays, including

Black Limelight and *Idiot's Delight*. In 1943, after five more marriages, she filed a rape and assault charge against a 22-year-old Army private, who was found guilty and sentenced to 20 years in prison. Basquette finally settled into a more peaceful existence as owner of Honey Hollow Kennels in Pennsylvania, where she raised prize-winning Great Danes.

SOURCES:

Lamparski, Richard. *Whatever Became of. . . ?* (4th Series). NY: Crown, 1973.

Barbara Morgan,
Melrose, Massachusetts

Bass, Mary Elizabeth (1876–1956)

American physician, teacher, and chronicler of the history of women physicians in America. *Born in Carley, Mississippi, in 1876; died in 1956; second of eight children of Issac Esau and Mary Eliza (Wilkes) Bass; graduated Woman's Medical College of Pennsylvania, M.D., 1904.*

After a long, distinguished career as a pioneering woman physician and medical professor at Tulane University, Mary Elizabeth Bass made perhaps her greatest contribution by chronicling the history of women physicians in America. Her collection of thousands of documents, including over 290 monographs and 1,400 pictures and clippings, comprises the Elizabeth Bass Collection at Tulane University.

Bass was inspired to study medicine after teaching school in Mississippi and Texas during her 20s. Turned away from medical schools in the south because she was a woman, she and her sister attended the Woman's Medical College of Pennsylvania. After graduating in 1904, they moved to New Orleans and set up a private practice but were barred from practicing in the hospitals and clinics in New Orleans because of gender. In 1908, Bass and her sister joined five other woman physicians to found the New Orleans Hospital for Women and Children (later named the Sara Mayo Hospital). Three years later, Bass became one of the first two women appointed to an unpaid faculty position at Tulane University's School of Medicine; she was later promoted to the rank of instructor of clinical medicine.

Bass lobbied for women's rights as a member of the Equal Rights Association of New Orleans. When Tulane began accepting women medical students in 1914, she was always available to offer encouragement and friendship to her women students. She became a full professor in 1920 and remained active in national and local medical associations, including the Orleans Parish Medical Society, the Southern Medical Association, and the Medical Women's National Association. In connection with her collection of historical documents, Bass wrote a column from 1946 through 1956 called, "These Were the First," for the *Journal of the American Women's Medical Association*. The articles chronicled the careers of early women physicians.

In 1949, Bass retired to Mississippi to care for her ailing mother. The medical community honored her in 1953 with the ***Elizabeth Blackwell** Centennial Medal Award. Following her death in 1956, Tulane School of Medicine set up a fund in Bass' name to provide student loans to women pursuing the study of medicine.

COLLECTIONS:

Bass' papers are in the Elizabeth Bass Collection on Women in Medicine of Tulane University's Matas Medical Library, and at the Sophia Smith Collection of Smith College.

Barbara Morgan,
Melrose, Massachusetts

Basseporte, Magdalene (?–c. 1780).

See Carriera, Rosalba for sidebar.

Basset, Florence Knoll (b. 1917).

See Knoll, Florence.

Basset, Mary Roper (fl. 1544–1572)

English writer and translator. *Born before 1544 in England; died in England in 1572; daughter of Margaret (More) and William Roper (both Protestant scholars); married Stephen Clarke (died); married James Basset.*

Mary Roper Basset was the granddaughter of the great humanist scholar Sir Thomas More and the daughter of ***Margaret More Roper** (1505–1544), arguably one of the best-educated women in 16th-century Europe. In accordance with her lineage, Basset grew up surrounded by humanist writers and philosophers and received an excellent classical education. Married twice, first to Stephen Clarke and then to James Basset, she continued her studies despite the daily responsibilities of a middle-class wife. Basset contributed to the growth of English humanism through her translations into English of significant humanist works. Among her translations were *Treatise on the Passion* (1557), written in Latin by her grandfather Thomas More, and a translation into English from her mother's Latin edition of Eusebius' history of the church.

Laura York,
Anza, California

Bassett, Ann (1878–1956)

Supposed outlaw and cattle rustler of the American frontier. *Name variations: Queen Ann, Ann Bassett Willis. Born in Brown's Park, Colorado, in 1878; died in Leeds, Utah, on May 9, 1956; daughter and one of four children of Herbert (a rancher and horse exporter) and May Elizabeth (Chamberlain) Bass; attended school at Craig Colorado; St. Mary's of the Wasatch in Salt Lake City; Miss Potter's School for Girls in Boston; married H.H. "Hi" Bernard, in 1904 (divorced 1911); married Frank Willis, in 1920.*

Ann Bassett was raised on a ranch in Brown's Hole, Colorado, a lawless western settlement that at the turn of the century was said to have given refuge to fugitives, rustlers, and outlaws such as Butch Cassidy. Known as a fearless horsewoman (she may have been the first cowgirl in America to wear a divided skirt so she could ride in a man's saddle), Bassett was also the product of a Boston finishing school, making her a curious blend of gunslinger and refined gentlewoman.

From an early age, she had no patience with ranchers who let their cattle wander off the public grazing lands onto the homesteads of Brown's Hole. Later, when the large cattle companies threatened to buy out the town and "squeeze out the settlers," Bassett took steps to rally the residents and defend what she considered "her own personal fief." Although her tactics included cutting off her property as a common watering place and ringing the entrance to Brown's Hole with bands of sheep so the cattle would not cross, it is questionable whether she really "headed a band of outlaws," as legend would have it. Up until her death at age 78, she remained a controversial figure. Although she always denied that she or any of her friends were rustlers, the *Desert Magazine* in 1949 reported: "She left her mark as one woman who could not be intimidated, held her ground against ruthless antagonists . . . almost single-handed she defied and defeated some of the biggest barons of the cattle industry at their own tough game."

In 1911, Bassett was involved in a lengthy court case when her foreman was accused of stealing and butchering a heifer. After receiving a favorable verdict, she eventually moved to California with her second husband. They later had homes in Arizona, Colorado, and Utah.

SOURCES:

Ray, Grace Ernestine. *Wily Women of the West.* San Antonio, TX, Naylor, 1972.

Barbara Morgan,
Melrose, Massachusetts

Bassi, Laura (1711–1778)

Italian anatomist, natural philosopher, and professor of physics at the University of Bologna. *Born Laura Maria Caterina Bassi in Bologna, Italy, in 1711; died in 1778; awarded Ph.D. from University of Bologna, 1731 or 1732; married Dr. Giuseppe Veratti (a physician and professor), in 1738; children: 12.*

Renowned as a scholar, Laura Bassi held a public disputation on philosophy, at age 21, and received, among many honors, a doctor's degree from the University of Bologna, where she continued studies, lectured, and was eventually appointed to the chair of physics. She married a physician and fellow professor, Dr. Giuseppe Veratti, in 1738 and had 12 children.

Bassi published two Latin dissertations but was noted more for teaching than research. Acquainted with classical, French, and Italian literature, she held membership in a number of literary societies and corresponded with many eminent European intellectuals, including Voltaire, for whom she secured membership in the Accademia. She was known as a deeply religious woman of "good character" and gave generously to the poor. A medal in her honor was coined by the Senate of Bologna.

Bastidas, Micaela (1745–1781)

Peruvian revolutionary leader of the great Inca revolt of 1780–1783. *Born Micaela Bastidas Puyucahua, a pure-blooded Spaniard, in Pampamarca, Cuzco, Peru, in 1745; captured, found guilty of complicity in the rebellion, and executed, May 18, 1781; married José Gabriel Condorcanqui, Túpac Amarú II, in 1760; children: three sons, Hipólito, Fernando, Mariano.*

In November 1780, a revolt of Peruvian Indians led by José Gabriel Condorcanqui, Túpac Amarú II, broke out against Spanish rule as the rebels fought for the removal of burdensome taxes that had reduced many of the local population to abject poverty; it is possible that the rebels were also fighting for independence from Spain. Condorcanqui was a financially well-off *mestizo* descended from both Inca nobles and Spanish conquistadors. Outraged by the cruel and exploitive treatment of his people, he discarded his attire of a Spanish noble and dressed himself in the traditional headdress, loincloth, and cape of his Inca ancestors. His 1780 revolt would quickly engulf the greater part of southern Peru and eventually spread to the Aymara provinces of Upper Peru.

Women played significant roles in the rebellion. Given important posts on virtually all levels of the uprising, they distinguished themselves on many occasions. Micaela Bastidas, the wife of Condorcanqui, is known as the most impressive of these women. Born of pure Spanish blood in 1745 in Pampamarca, Cuzco, she married Condorcanqui on May 25, 1760, when she was 15 and he 22 years of age. A prosperous merchant, he became increasingly bitter when it became clear that the indigenous population of Peru faced increasing impoverishment and humiliation due to the high level of taxation imposed upon them. Although of pure Spanish descent, Bastidas clearly shared her husband's beliefs.

The revolt began in early November 1780 with the arrest, trial, and execution of a hated local Spanish official. From the start of the uprising, Condorcanqui entrusted Bastidas with crucial political and military responsibilities. While he engaged in battle, she worked as commandant of the secretariat located in the rebel stronghold of San Felipe de Tungasuca. Working long hours to coordinate the rebellion, she answered numerous requests from villagers for safe conduct passes, food and supplies. Surviving documents reveal that local officials addressed her as *Señora Gobernadora*, a title of great authority. Her status as the wife of the rebel chieftain gave her a control which the solicitor general of Cuzco, Pablo de Figueroa, described as allowing her to command "with more authority and rigor than her husband."

From the start of the revolt, Bastidas recognized the necessity of winning the hearts and minds of the people. In order to retain areas under nominal rebel control, she warned local governors of the penalties for desertion and issued numerous directives forbidding banditry, thus making it clear that the rebellion could not be used to further degrade and exploit the Indians, but must instead mark the start of a new era of humane treatment of them. The remarkable absence of banditry in the first phase of the Túpac Amarú uprising is a reflection of her forceful presence in the affected areas. Bastidas understood the link between the political and military aspects of the revolt, in which it was crucial to retain the loyalties of both Indian and non-Indian communities.

By early 1781, the revolt was weakening, and soon Bastidas and her husband were prisoners of the Spanish colonial authorities. She and **Tomasa Titu Condemayta**, another woman who had played a leading role in the uprising, were accused of the capital crime of *lesa majestad*, or treason against the Crown. Both women were found guilty. "Because of the decorum of their sex," they were to be garroted, or strangled with an iron collar containing a screw, rather than hanged in public.

The execution took place in Cuzco's *Plaza Mayor* on May 18, 1781. Dressed in the habit of the Order of Mercy, Micaela Bastidas was forced to witness the hanging of her son Hipólito. Then she was bound hand and foot and dragged under the gallows to the garrote. She refused to allow her tongue to be cut out, and, since her neck was too small for the screw to take her life, the executioner placed a lasso around her neck and pulled it tight, striking her on the breast and stomach area until she expired. Tomasa was strangled in the same fashion.

After the deaths of the women, José Gabriel Condorcanqui had his tongue cut out and was executed in a horrifying fashion; failing to be torn apart by four horses, he was spared more suffering by decapitation. The heads and extremities of Micaela Bastidas and Tomasa, as well as those of the men of the Túpac Amarú family, were placed on pikes and displayed in the important public places of five major provinces of Peru as a warning to others contemplating rebellion. (Later, another woman leader of the rebellion, **Cecilia Escalera Túpac Amarú**, would be stripped naked to the waist, mounted on a burro, and driven through the streets while she was lashed 200 times; she would die in prison in April 1783.) Though the uprising failed, the rebellion led by Túpac Amarú and Micaela Bastidas marked the beginning of the end of Spanish colonial rule in Peru.

SOURCES:

Alisky, Marvin. *Historical Dictionary of Peru.* Metuchen, NJ: Scarecrow Press, 1979.

"Bastidas, Micaela," in Carlos Milla Batres, ed., *Diccionario historico y biografico del Peru.* Vol. 1. Lima: Editorial Milla Batres, S.A., 1986, p. 415.

Campbell, Leon G. "Women and the Great Rebellion in Peru, 1780–1783," in *The Americas.* Vol 42, no. 2. October 1985, pp. 163–196.

Fisher, Lillian Estelle. *The Last Inca Revolt, 1780–1783.* Norman, OK: University of Oklahoma Press, 1966.

Lewin, Boleslao. *La Rebelión de Tupac Amaru y los origenes de la emancipación americana.* Buenos Aires: Hachette, 1957.

Lynch, John. "The Origins of Spanish American Independence," in Leslie Bethell, ed. *The Cambridge History of Latin America, vol. III: From Independence to c. 1870.* Cambridge: Cambridge University Press, 1986, pp. 3–50.

John Haag, Associate Professor,
University of Georgia, Athens, Georgia

Bat (r. 267–272).

See Zenobia.

Batchelor, Joy (1914—)

English film animator. *Born May 12, 1914, in London, England; married John Halas (b. April 16, 1912), in Budapest. With Halas, Batchelor formed their own animation studio (1940).*

Selected filmography: "Train Trouble" and "Carnival in the Clothes Cupboard" (commercials, 1940); The Pocket Cartoon *(1941);* Dustbin Parade *(1942);* Digging for Victory *(1942);* Abu *(series, 1943);* Modern Guide to Health *(1946);* Old Wives' Tales *(1946);* Charley *(series, 1948);* First Line of Defense *(1949);* As Old As the Hills *(1950);* Magic Canvas *(1951);* Poet and Painter *(series, 1951);* Submarine Control *(1951);* The Figurehead *(1952);* The Owl and the Pussycat *(1953);* The Moving Spirit *(1953);* Power to Fly *(1954);* Animal Farm *(1954);* Speed the Plough *(1955);* The History of Cinema *(1956);* The Candlemaker *(1956);* To Your Health *(1956);* The World of Little Ig *(1956);* All Lit Up *(1957);* The Christmas Visitor *(1958);* The Cultured Ape *(1959);* The Insolent Matador *(1959);* Piping Hot *(1959);* For Better for Worse *(1959); "Popeye" (first series for American television, c. 1958). Animated series for TV "The Addams Family," "The Jackson Five," and "The Osmonds" (1970s).*

Shorts directed by Batchelor alone: Classic Fairy Tales *(1966);* Colombo Plan *(1967);* The Commonwealth *(1967);* Bolly *(1968);* The Five *(1970);* Wet Dot *(1970);* Contact *(1973);* The Ass and the Stick *(1974);* Carry on Milkmaids *(1974).*

In the late 1930s, Joy Batchelor was working on a color cartoon called *Music Man*, when John Halas, a Hungarian émigré who had studied animation with George Pal, joined the team. Batchelor and Halas married, became business partners, and, as the team of Halas and Batchelor, were the most prolific and successful animators in British history.

Their company was originally formed in 1940 as an independent subsidiary of the J. Walter Thompson Advertising Agency, headquartered in London. During WWII, the agency wanted to develop in-house talent to make animated propaganda films. Following the war, the company intended that the animators stay on to animate in-house commercials. Though Halas and Batchelor's first two efforts, "Train Trouble" and "Carnival in the Clothes Cupboard," were soap commercials, most of the films they made between 1941 and 1945 were for the war effort. One of the first, *Digging for Victory*, encouraged the British citizenry to save scrap metal. Though the subject of the film was less than glamorous, it brought Halas and Batchelor together with composer Matyas Seiber who would eventually compose over 250 scores for the team. Also produced by the British war department was a string of propaganda films called the "Abu" series. Aimed at Arab audiences in the Middle East, Halas and Batchelor created Abu, a young Arab boy, who sought to dissuade his compatriots from following the Axis powers. Hitler, in particular, was portrayed looming and snake-like.

After the war, Halas and Batchelor made instructional and public-relations films. On behalf of Britain's newly elected Socialist government, Sir Stafford Cripps commissioned a film series to help the British understand the new government's intentions. The team introduced a character named Charley, a man-in-the-street cartoon character who voiced popular objections to the new legislation but, once won over, accepted the new ideas enthusiastically.

Eventually, Halas and Batchelor embarked on films that were more personally satisfying. *Magic Canvas* (1948) was an abstract, avant-garde film set to a musical score, a dramatic departure from anything they had done in the past. In the early 1950s, Halas and Batchelor took on their most ambitious project, adapting George Orwell's classic novel *Animal Farm*. Taking nearly three years to complete, *Animal Farm* was the first full-length animated feature to come out of Great Britain, and it brought them international fame.

In the late '50s, the team continued to make industrial or commercial projects for companies like British Petroleum but they also had become well-known in the United States. This led to the first American television series, the popular "Popeye" which ran for at least two decades in syndication. In the 1970s, the couple worked on several cartoon series for children produced by Hanna-Barbera, most notably "The Addams Family," "The Jackson Five" and "The Osmonds."

SOURCES:

Hoffer, Thomas. *Animation: A Reference Guide*. Westport, CT: Greenwood Press, 1981.

Manvell, Roger. *The Story of Halas and Batchelor: Animation Studio 1940–1980*. NY: Visual Communication Books, 1980.

Deborah Jones, Studio City, California

Bateman, Hester (1709–1794)

English silversmith. *Born Hester Needham in 1709; died in 1794; married John Bateman; children: five.*

Without the benefit of a formal education, Hester Bateman, who is now regarded as one of the 18th century's greatest silversmiths, probably learned her craft from her husband John, who worked in silver and gold. Following his death in 1761, she took over the family business and registered her own hallmark, "H.B." For a number of years, with her two sons and an apprentice, she worked for other silversmiths, but her shop eventually won acclaim for its own beautiful domestic silver, especially tea and coffee pots, spoons, and other tableware. She also produced some church and presentation pieces, known for their refined—almost austere—lines and decoration. When Bateman retired in 1790, the business continued for years in the hands of her widowed daughter-in-law, Anne, and one of her five children, Peter.

Bateman, Kate (1842–1917)

American actress. *Name variations: Mrs. George Crowe. Born Kate Josephine Bateman in Baltimore, Maryland, on October 7, 1842; died in 1917; second child of H.L. Bateman (a theatrical manager) and Frances Bateman (an actress and playwright); sister of* ****Ellen Bateman*** *(also a child actor who retired from the stage in 1856 and later married Claude Greppo); married George Crowe, in October 1866.*

Born into a theatrical family and hailed as a child prodigy, Kate Bateman toddled onto the stage at age three, appearing with her father and sister Ellen in *Babes in the Woods*. While still a child, she toured with her sister, showcasing an unusual talent in such classics as *Richard III*, as well as other dramas. The pair also toured in England, where they found even greater success. Back home in 1956, they retired from the stage. Ellen subsequently married, while Kate went on to study acting.

Kate returned to the stage in 1860 in the title role of *Evangeline*, a play, written by her mother **Frances Bateman**, based on the Longfellow poem. But it was her performance two years later as Julie in *The Hunchback* that raised her to star status. This was followed by successful portrayals of Lady Gay Spanker in *London Assurance* and Lady Teazel in *The School for Scandal*, among others. Although Bateman was consistently praised for her integrity and charm, her ability was often called into question, causing one critic to comment, "In some parts (*Juliet* and *Lady Macbeth*, for instance) she seemed utterly at sea."

The year 1860 also saw Bateman in England playing what would become her signature role, the "Jewess" Leah, who was deserted by her Christian lover, in *Leah, the Forsaken*. One critic wrote of her performance: "Its merits are strength, impetuosity and pathos. Its profound defect is its lack of emotional abandon." That year, during the autumn season in London, Bateman played Leah in 211 successive performances. With her career firmly established, she then visited all of the principal British provincial cities, performing her favorite roles in repertory. In the winter of 1866, another London tour was cut short by illness.

Kate Bateman

In October 1866, Bateman, still recuperating, was married to Dr. George Crowe, son of British author and longtime editor of the London *Daily News* Eyre Evans Crowe. After a year off to fully regain her health, she returned to the stage in yet another tour as Leah. In later years, she appeared with Henry Irving in *Macbeth* and played the title role in Tennyson's *Queen Mary*. In 1892, she established a school of acting in London, where she taught for many years.

Bateman, Mary (1768–1809)

British murderer known as the Yorkshire Witch. *Born Mary Harker in Aisenby, Yorkshire, England, in 1768;*

executed on March 20, 1809; daughter of James Harker (a farmer); married John Bateman, around 1792; children: one.

Mary Bateman, the notorious Yorkshire Witch, found her victims among the uneducated and naive villagers of 18th-century England, who were at once awed and terrified by her reported supernatural powers. Her life of crime began at age five with the theft of a pair of shoes. Later, in a bizarre twist on the woman as witch theme, Bateman employed phony witchcraft schemes to extort large sums of money from her victims, leaving them penniless and too frightened of evil retributions to report her to the authorities. Her crime spree finally ended in 1806, when a sinister plot involving poisoning resulted in the death of a young woman. In a sensational trial, Bateman was found guilty of murder and sentenced to hang. But Mary Bateman plied her trade right up until her trip to the gallows, swindling fellow prisoners with lies about releases and stays of execution. Following the execution, her body was displayed in order to raise money for charity. Evidently, thousands filed by for a look and some even paid for strips of her skin, cut off and sold as charms to ward off evil spirits.

Barbara Morgan,
Melrose, Massachusetts

Bates, Daisy Lee (1914—)

Civil-rights activist, journalist, publisher, president of Arkansas NAACP, leader in the move to desegregate public schools in Little Rock, Arkansas, and mentor for the "Little Rock Nine" throughout their tumultuous years at Central High School. *Name variations: Daisy Gatson Bates, Mrs. L.C. Bates. Born Daisy Lee Gatson on November 11, 1914, in Huttig, Arkansas (she relates that her date of birth is listed as 1920 on her driver's license, which has caused a number of errors about her age to appear in print); father worked in local lumber mill; adopted by Orlee and Susan Smith as an infant; attended public schools in Huttig and Memphis; attended Shorter College and Philander Smith College, both in Little Rock; married L(ucius) C(hristopher) Bates, in 1941 (died, August 1980).*

As a teenager, moved to Memphis and graduated from high school there (1934); married, moved to Little Rock and, with husband, founded Arkansas State Press; *first edition published (May 9, 1941); elected Arkansas state president of NAACP branches (1952); led in effort to integrate all grades of Little Rock public schools, including NAACP lawsuit in federal court challenging the "gradual" plan of the all-white school board (1956); spokeswoman, counselor, "surrogate mother" for the "Little Rock Nine" students chosen to pioneer the integration of Central High (1957); initiated NAACP "emergency high school" with teachers from nearby colleges when the nine students were denied enrollment (September 1957); worked successfully with NAACP lawyers to reverse Governor Faubus' segregation orders (September 1957); became target for segregationists (1957–59); arrested and fined for resisting city ordinance requiring disclosure of names of NAACP members and contributors to city council; U.S. Supreme Court reversed conviction in* Bates v. Little Rock *(1960);* State Press *bankrupted by advertisers boycott (Oct. 30, 1959); moved to New York to write memoirs and continue civil-rights activism (1960); enlisted by Kennedy Administration to work in voter registration project, Democratic National Committee; named director of Mitchelville, Arkansas, Office of Economic Opportunity during Johnson Administration (1964); worked with O.E.O. officials and others in community revitalization project in Mitchelville; made headlines during Nixon administration, protesting Nixon's cancellation of O.E.O. programs; active in many community organizations (1970s on).*

Awards and honors: co-winner, along with "Little Rock Nine" students, of Springarn Medal, NAACP (1958); recipient of honorary degrees from Lincoln University (1959), Philander Smith College and Washington University (1984), and University of Arkansas; Harriet Tubman Award; Diamond Cross of Malta from Cotillion Society; Mary Church Terrell Award from Delta Sigma Theta; Sojourner Truth Award; Robert S. Abbot Award; named "one of the top nine news personalities" (1957) by Associated Press; "outstanding citizen of the year" by National Council of Negro Women (1957); named among the top 100 most influential people in the state of Arkansas by Arkansas Gazette *(1984); awarded the Senate Gavel from the Massachusetts State Senate; journalism scholarship established in her name at University of Arkansas; American Book Award from Before Columbus Foundation (1988), for* The Long Shadow of Little Rock. *Has received more than 210 different awards.*

As a leader of the African-American community during the so-called "Battle of Little Rock" in 1957, Daisy Bates faced constant danger from white supremacists trying to thwart school desegregation. The numerous attempts on her life included the use of dynamite, firebombs, and bullets directed at her home. Her courage never wavered, and progress toward integration of the schools and the attainment of full civil rights for the black community, continued.

Daisy Bates was born Daisy Lee Gatson in the small town of Huttig, Arkansas, on November 11, 1914. Huttig, which she describes in her memoir *The Long Shadow of Little Rock*, is located on the red clay soil of southeastern Arkansas on the Louisiana border, 60 miles west of the Mississippi River. During her childhood, the commercial center consisted of the post office, a general store-grocery, an ice cream parlor, and a movie house. The neat, white-painted houses of "White Town" were separated from the drab, red "shotgun shacks" of "Negra Town" by the unpaved Main Street. Other streets were not only unpaved, they were often unnamed. Daisy calls Huttig a "sawmill plantation" because the lumbermill owned most of the town. Her "Daddy" Orlee Smith, a lumber grader, worked for the mill, as did nearly every other paid worker in Huttig. Of course, the schools were segregated then. White children went to a "spacious school with a big lawn," while the African-American children attended a two-room school, using hand-me-down books and an inadequate pot-bellied stove for heat. Daisy recalls the many flowers of Huttig—roses, zinnias, lilacs, Indian paintbrush—as a pleasant memory of her youth.

Bates did not become acutely aware of racism until she was seven years old. Then, on an errand to the meat market, the butcher called her "nigger" and made her wait until white customers behind her had all been served. He then filled her order for center-cut chops with a handful of fat. The pain and humiliation of this moment were compounded for Daisy when, at age eight, a playmate told her that she was adopted. Asking about her natural parents, Bates learned of the rape and murder of her natural mother, apparently by three white men. Following that tragedy, her natural father had placed her in the care of his close friends Orlee and Susan Smith, and left the area. Her mother's brutal fate, and the humiliation suffered by all blacks in the "Jim Crow" South, haunted Daisy for the rest of her childhood. She broke her friendship with white playmates, she explains in her memoir, and had neither a good word nor kind look for any white person for years after.

Her adoptive parents, the Smiths, were gentle people who treated Daisy with kindness, yet discipline. A rude comment made to an adult or a game of marbles played "for keeps" against her mother's command would earn Bates a spanking or time "standing in the corner." Concerned about the change in Daisy's disposition, her frustration and anger toward all whites, Daisy's adoptive parents sent her to visit family friends in the Northern states and Canada. There she met white people who were different from those she knew back home in Arkansas. Slowly, as she related to *Ebony* magazine's Lerone Bennett, "the hate and the hurt dissolved."

In her memoir, Bates recalls that when she was about 20 years old, as her father lay dying of cancer, among his last words were an admonition not to hate. "Don't hate white people just because they're white. If you hate, make it count for something. Hate the humiliations we are living under . . . hate the discrimination . . . the insults . . . and try to do something about it, or your hate won't spell a thing." She calls this her moment of "rebirth."

In 1941, while living in Memphis (where she had attended high school), Daisy Gatson married L.C. Bates and moved to Little Rock. L.C. had majored in journalism at Wilberforce College in Ohio, but the Great Depression had cost him his job writing for the *Kansas City Call* (Missouri). Together they decided to start a newspaper, merging the practical with the ideal: to earn a living and to crusade for civil rights. Leasing a clattering press that had been printing a church paper, the couple founded the weekly *Arkansas State Press*, the only black publication with a certified permit in the entire state. In order to learn the skills needed to manage a newspaper, Daisy attended Little Rock's Shorter College for courses in public relations and business administration. Within a few months of its founding, the *State Press*' circulation grew to 10,000, and reached 22,000 at its peak. Its demise in 1959 left a gap that was to go unfilled for over two decades.

The Bateses quickly filled the *State Press* with stories of interest to the black community. As Calvin Smith writes in the Arkansas chapter of *The Black Press in the South, 1865–1979,* the *State Press* supported the policies of the Roosevelt and Truman administrations and explained the relevance of those policies to Arkansas blacks. It also covered national stories like that of the Montgomery (Alabama) Bus Boycott of 1955–56 (led by Martin Luther King, among others), and pressed for an end to racial discrimination in Arkansas. During the Second World War, the paper editorialized against segregation in the armed services, and for better treatment for black soldiers. In 1946, the paper pushed hard to end what it called the "police brutality" inflicted mainly on Little Rock's African-American population. This campaign peaked in 1942 when a white officer killed a black soldier from nearby Camp Robinson. Daisy Bates' description of the incident in the *State Press* included the following headline, "CITY PATROLMAN SHOOTS NEGRO SOLDIER," along with the subhead, "Body Riddled While Lying on Ground." The ramifications of this story foreshadowed the eventual demise of the paper 17 years later. The story angered whites and store owners, who feared that the "bad publicity" might harm their businesses. Advertisers withdrew their contracts and the *State Press* nearly folded.

In 1946, Daisy and L.C. Bates were arrested for "contempt of court," which stemmed from a controversial news story written by Daisy. That article questioned the fairness of the procedures and judicial instructions to the jury in a trial of three strikers arrested on a picket line. The judge of that case, incensed by the account, sentenced the couple to ten days in prison and a $100 fine. The Arkansas State Supreme Court ordered their release from jail, and later overturned the conviction on first amendment grounds (freedom of the press).

When the war ended in 1945, the return of black soldiers brought an escalation of racial tensions. Having fought for their country and having enjoyed more freedom in other parts of the world, black veterans grew determined to improve conditions at home. The National Association for the Advancement of Colored People (NAACP) was in the forefront of such efforts. Daisy Bates had joined the NAACP, and in 1952 she was elected president of the Arkansas Conference of NAACP branches, a position she held for several years.

Bates' civil-rights activism culminated with her work to desegregate the Little Rock public schools. This episode in her career began in 1954, shortly after the U.S. Supreme Court ruled that laws requiring separation of the races in public facilities violated the "equal protection clause" of the 14th Amendment. Through her NAACP activities and via newspaper editorials, Bates pushed for immediate compliance with the high-court ruling. When the school board announced a "gradual" plan for integration, commencing with grades 10 through 12 in 1957 and moving to lower grades in later years, Bates appealed to Superintendent of Schools Virgil Blossom to immediately enroll African-American children in all grades. Turned down, the NAACP filed a lawsuit in federal district court on behalf of the school children. The court ruled that the gradual integration plan was an adequate step forward towards compliance with federal law, meaning that integration of lower grades would have to wait. Bates then began working with Superintendent Blossom to identify certain black students to begin attending Central High School in 1957. Nine students were selected, the "cream of the crop" from the segregated black schools, including ❧ **Minnijean Brown** and ❧ **Elizabeth Eckford.** They were scheduled to begin their classes on September 3, the day after Labor Day.

The "crisis" started late in the evening on September 2. Watching television, Bates heard Governor Orval Faubus warn that "blood would run in the streets" if black children attempted to enter Central High, and that he was declaring the high school to be "off limits" to them. Further, he surrounded the school with troops of the Arkansas National Guard, to "maintain order."

Bates, by now an experienced and recognized leader in the black community, took charge. She dealt with the press, politicians, and school officials. She met with the families to plan strategy; she counselled each of the students; and she prodded the authorities to carry out their duties. Her name was frequently in the news, and she became a symbol of hope and courage for other black Americans. The reason that Central High was integrated, *Ebony* was later to report, was "because Daisy Bates willed it." For example, when the nine students attempted to enter Central for the first time, on the morning of September 4, 1957, they were escorted through the mob by a group of local ministers, both white and black. Daisy Bates had arranged that, and not without difficulty, in order to provide the nine with some protection and encouragement. (The simple act of supporting the nine students took courage on the part of the ministers as well, and some paid a high price for it. Rev. Dunbar Ogden, for example, was forced to resign as pastor of the Central Presbyterian Church; his son, who also walked with the children that day, committed suicide after much harassment from angry segregationists.) The ministerial escort proved to no avail; the guardsmen (on orders of the governor) refused to let the black students pass through their ranks.

The presence of the National Guard, as well as the threatening segregationist mob outside the school, made it obvious that the crisis was at an impasse. While she worked the legal channels (with other NAACP officials) trying to open the school, Bates made arrangements for the ❧ "Little Rock Nine" to continue their lessons elsewhere. Employing professors from nearby black colleges as stand-in high school teachers, she received permission to hold lessons in a room at Little Rock's Philander Smith College.

❧ ***Little Rock Nine****, included* ***Carlotta Walls LaNier*** *who graduated from Michigan State University (b. 1943);* ***Melba Patillo Beals****, an author and former journalist for* People *and NBC, who wrote a memoir about Little Rock,* Warriors Don't Cry *(b. 1942);* Terrence Roberts *(b. 1942);* ***Gloria Ray Karlmark*** *who went to a northern college and retired in Holland (b. 1942);* ***Thelma Mothershed-Wair*** *who taught in East St. Louis (b. 1941);* Ernest Green *(b. 1942);* Jefferson Thomas *(b. 1942);* ****Elizabeth Eckford****, and* ****Minnijean Brown.***

Brown, Minnijean (1942—)

One of the Little Rock Nine. *Name variations: Minnie Jean; Jean Brown Trickey. Born Minnie Jean Brown in 1942; oldest of four children of Imogene Brown (a nurse) and Bob Brown (a landscaper); attended Southern Illinois University; married Ray Trickey (a zoologist), in 1967 (divorced 1987); children: six, including Spirit Trickey (b. 1980); Leila Trickey (b. 1982).*

"I figured, 'I'm a nice person. Once they get to know me, they'll see I'm okay.'" At least that was the thinking of Minnijean Brown as she dressed for her first day at Little Rock's Central High that September day in 1957. It would take 21 more days before Minnijean and the other members of the Little Rock Nine made it up the school's front steps. "Until then, I hadn't experienced hatred," Brown told *People Weekly* in September 1997.

Brown had been attending all-black Horace Mann High School when the school board, in an attempt to integrate Little Rock's public schools, passed out applications to those interested in transferring to Central. For Brown, it meant a chance to attend a school closer to home—one with newer textbooks and a better percentage of college-bound students. It also meant a chance to join the fight for equality.

But entering the high school turned out to be the easy part; staying there was almost impossible. Like the others, Brown was called names, harassed, kicked, pushed, and threatened on a daily basis. When she finally talked back, six months into the school year, she was expelled. For the next few years, says Brown, she was filled with "anger and sadness," convinced that she had let everybody down.

Her parents sent her to a private school in New York where she lived with friends. Though homesick, she flourished and went on to journalism school at Southern Illinois University. Married during the Vietnam war in 1967, she and her husband Ray Trickey moved to northern Ontario, Canada, so that he could avoid the draft. As of 1997, Brown was a social worker and antiracism consultant in Ottawa. "I would like young people to know about the Little Rock Nine to know that everyone can be heroic," she told an interviewer. "We were just teenagers and friends."

In September 1997, on the 40th anniversary of the school-house confrontation, President Bill Clinton led the Little Rock Nine up the steps of Central High and held open the door as they walked through. Brown was overwhelmed. "It was pretty strong symbolism," she said.

SOURCES:

Hunt, Terence. "This Time, Blacks Are Welcomed at the Door," in *The* [New London] *Day.* September 26, 1997."

Right of Passage," in *People Weekly.* September 29, 1997, pp. 166–170.

Eckford, Elizabeth (1942—)

One of the Little Rock Nine. *Born in Little Rock, Arkansas, in 1942; served in the army as a journalist; married with two sons.*

In 1957, backed by a court order imposing integration, Elizabeth Eckford and eight other black students were allowed to attend the all-white Central High School in Little Rock, Arkansas, a defining moment in the civil-rights battle. However, when 15-year-old Eckford—dressed in dark glasses, crinoline skirt and bobby socks—tried to enter the school alone, she was met by a menacing crowd, shouting, "Lynch her! Drag her over to that tree," and blocked from admittance by Arkansas National Guard bayonets, called out by Governor Orval Faubus. With the help of two white friends, Eckford escaped onto a city bus, her clothes so wet with spit that she had to wring them out when she arrived home. The episode did not play well on national television that evening.

Three weeks later, when President Dwight D. Eisenhower ordered the 101st Airborne paratroopers to escort the students into Central High School, Eckford returned reluctantly. "Somewhere along the line, very soon it became an obligation," she said. "I realized that what we were doing was not for ourselves." Often asked to speak at schools, Eckford once replied: "I have encountered people who just don't understand the emotional cost that entails." Years after the incident, one woman, who had hounded Eckford that first day with taunts, called to apologize.

Soon, NAACP attorneys Wiley Branton and Thurgood Marshall obtained an injunction against the actions of Governor Faubus and the National Guard, and, on September 23rd, the "Nine" entered Central High for the first time. They were unable to stay for the entire school day, however. When the mob outside continued to threaten violence, the police decided to slip them out through a service entrance at the rear of the school and take them home. The mob was too large, the police believed, to be controlled.

Rumors were spread that day that segregationists would seek vigilante "justice" against Daisy Bates and other African-Americans in Little Rock. At the Bates' home, friends and visiting reporters stood watch, well armed. No one slept. Around 11 PM, a police officer stopped by to inform them that a large motorcade of segregationists, armed with guns and dynamite, had just been stopped several blocks from the Bates' residence.

If Daisy Bates would find an honest job and go to work, and if the U.S. Supreme Court would keep its cottonpicking hands off the Little Rock School Board's affairs, we could open the Little Rock schools!

—Governor Orval Faubus of Arkansas

The crisis in Little Rock received national attention from the mainstream press. Portraying it as a clash between federal and state authority, as well as a question of basic civil rights, *The New York Times* carried photos of mob harassment of African-Americans. The nation also learned that reporters from *Life* magazine were beaten, then arrested for causing a disturbance. Columnists wondered in print when the president would take action. On September 24, *The New York Times* carried a story about Daisy Bates entitled "Fighter for Integration," along with a photograph. The column explained that her life was being constantly threatened and that the nine students would not go back to Central High "until the President assured their safety."

President Dwight Eisenhower signed a proclamation authorizing the use of federal troops to ensure compliance with the court-ordered integration, and after nightfall on Tuesday, September 24, 1,100 officers and men of the 101st Airborne Division arrived in Little Rock. Late that evening, Bates was notified that the nine students should ready themselves for school the next morning. Because the families disconnected their telephones at midnight to block harassment calls, Daisy had to visit each personally; she finished this task at 3:00 AM. Early the next morning, the nine students were met at the Bates' home by a convoy of troopers and driven to the school. A cordon of troops around the school made sure they got in safely.

Other students received the nine fairly cordially at first, but the honeymoon was short. Constant pressure by segregationists pushed the conflict into the classroom. Eventually, each of the nine was assigned a trooper as a bodyguard during school hours.

Segregationist whites in Little Rock blamed "agitators" for the social upheaval of integration and identified the NAACP as the foremost of these "agitators." Governor Faubus signed legislation banning any NAACP member from holding a position of employment with the state government, which included high school teaching. At the municipal level, the Little Rock city council passed an ordinance requiring groups such as the NAACP to disclose the names of all members and contributors. Reasoning that public disclosure of members' names might jeopardize their safety, NAACP president Daisy Bates refused to comply with this law, leading to her arrest on October 31, 1957. Convicted and fined, her appeal eventually reached the U.S. Supreme Court. In 1960, the Court found the ordinance to be an unconstitutional infringement upon personal liberty. Since then, the case of *Bates* v. *Little Rock* has been frequently cited by the court in deciding cases where a balance must be drawn between the regulatory power of government and the freedom of the individual.

Throughout that first year, Daisy Bates acted as mentor and "surrogate mother" for the Little Rock Nine. The students gathered frequently at her home for meals, parties, and just to talk. (The documentary series "Eyes on the Prize" includes footage from a Thanksgiving celebration for the Little Rock Nine held at the Bates' home.) The nine students—pioneers of integration in their own right—looked to Bates for leadership and encouragement. The dual public-private roles she played—of public leader and champion for civil rights and justice, on the one hand, and of private, behind-the-scenes counselor and supporter on the other—distinguish Bates from other famous civil-rights activists.

Upon completion of their traumatic first year at Central High, the courage of the Little Rock Nine was recognized by the NAACP. But when they were invited to attend that organization's 49th Annual convention to receive the Springarn Medal, they refused to accept it because Daisy Bates had not been included as recipient. The committee reconvened and agreed that Bates should join the Little Rock Nine in receiving the Springarn Medal for "their pioneer role in upholding the basic ideals of American democracy in the face of continuing harassment and constant threats of bodily injury."

Prior to the start of the "Battle of Little Rock," Daisy and L.C. enjoyed considerable financial success from their newspaper business. They were able to build a modern, $30,000 home and hire a housekeeper (who is visible in numerous press photos taken in the Bates' home). From a material perspective, the couple had much to lose. The *State Press* continued the crusade for justice, but the controversy surrounding school integration proved its undoing. Advertisers boycotted the paper, either out of opposition or because they were intimidated into doing so by the segregationist Capital Citizens Council. Many feared that their own businesses would be boycotted if they continued to support the *State Press*. Further, as Langston Hughes explains in *Fight For Freedom: The Story of the NAACP*, paper carriers for the *State Press* were frequently attacked and beaten, and their papers stolen. The white-owned bank terminated the paper's lease on the building where the presses were located, and city taxes were raised on the Bates' home. The paper lost $10,000 worth of advertising in 1958 (at a time when the price of a chocolate bar was a nickel.) The *Arkansas State Press* published its final issue on October 29, 1959.

Ernest Green, the first African-American graduate of Central High School, received his diploma in May 1958, but the story doesn't end there. That summer, Governor Faubus signed new segregation laws giving him the power to close down Little Rock's high schools entirely, to prevent integration, and that is what he did. During the 1958–59 school year, the *Arkansas Gazette* reported on February 4, 1959, 643 of 2,915 white high school students and 442 of 750 African-American students did not attend school. The other students either transferred to different public-school districts, or went to private schools. Bates continued her efforts to overcome numerous obstacles to integration, and, by September 1959, the schools were open once again, with a few African-American students desegregating them.

By May of 1960, all of the original Little Rock Nine had completed their secondary schooling, and Bates shifted gears. She moved to New York and began writing her memoirs of the affair. Following the election of John F. Kennedy as president, she accepted a position working with the Democratic National Committee registering voters. Eventually, she carried this work to Arkansas, where many black citizens had never before been permitted to vote. On August 28, 1963, she joined other civil-rights leaders in the famous March on Washington for Jobs and Freedom, to urge passage of the Civil Rights Act (passed in 1964). She told the mixed crowd of 250,000, then the largest demonstration ever held in Washington, "The women of this country . . . will sit-in and we will kneel-in and we will lie-in if necessary until every Negro in America can vote." In early January 1967, Bates ran for a seat on the national board of directors of the NAACP. She opposed the more conservative "traditionalists" who preferred less conflictual civil-rights progress, even if that meant moving ahead more slowly. Daisy Bates was the only member of the "Young Turk" faction who was elected to the board.

After Lyndon Johnson became president, Bates worked for the federal Office of Economic Opportunity (OEO), becoming the director of its Mitchelville Office. In this capacity, she worked to improve the living standards of the Arkansas poor. She was centrally involved in the Mitchelville Community Revitalization Project where she and other officials focused on health care, sanitation, water quality, and education in this predominantly black town. She again made headlines during the Nixon Administration when she protested Richard Nixon's decision to cut OEO funds. In 1985, five years after the death of her husband, Bates again began publishing the *Arkansas State Press*, which was purchased by a former employee in 1991.

SOURCES:

Arkansas Gazette. *Crisis in the South: The Little Rock Story.* Little Rock, 1959.

"Bates, Daisy," in *Encyclopedia of Black America.* Edited by W. Augustus Low and Virgil A. Clift. NY: Da Capo Press, 1981.

Bates, Daisy. *The Long Shadow of Little Rock.* NY: McKay, 1962 (reprint, with a new foreword, Little Rock: University of Arkansas Press, 1986).

"Bates, Daisy Lee," in *Contemporary Authors.* Vol. 127. Edited by Susan M. Trosky. Detroit, MI: Gale Research, 1989.

Bennett, Lerone, Jr. "First Lady of Little Rock," in *Ebony.* Vol. XIII, no. 11. September 1958, pp. 17–24.

Blossom, Virgil T. *It Has Happened Here.* NY: Harper, 1959.

"Catfish: 'Down Home Delicacy Becomes Big Business," in *Ebony.* Vol. XXIII, no. 12. October 1968, pp. 140–146.

Huckaby, Elizabeth. *Crisis at Central High School: Little Rock, 1957–1958.* Baton Rouge: Louisiana State University Press, 1980.

Hughes, Langston. *Fight for Freedom: The Story of the NAACP.* NY: W.W. Norton, 1962.

The New York Times. September 8, 23–30, 1957; January 20, 1959; August 14–15, 1959; November 4, 1962; August 29, 1963; November 2, 1966; January 4, 1967; August 29, 1980.

Robinson, Wilhelmena S. "Bates, Daisy Gatson," in *International Library of Negro Life and History.* Vol. II. Edited by Charles H. Wesley. NY: Publisher's Company, 1967.

Smith, Calvin. "Arkansas," in *The Black Press in the South, 1865–1979.* Edited by Henry Lewis Suggs. Westport, CT: Greenwood Press, 1983.

"Whatever Happened to the Little Rock 9?" in *Ebony.* Vol. XXVII, no. 4. February 1972, pp. 136–138.

Williams, Juan. *Eyes on the Prize: America's Civil Rights Years, 1954–1965.* NY: Penguin Books, 1987.

COLLECTIONS:

The Daisy Bates Papers, State Historical Society of Wisconsin, Archives Division, Madison, Wisconsin.

RELATED MEDIA:

"A Matter of Justice" (Program Two) of "Eyes On The Prize: The American Civil Rights Struggle, 1954–1965," television documentary series funded by the Corporation for Public Broadcasting, Blackside, 1986.

Michael D. Cary, Chair, Department of History and Political Science, Seton Hill College, Greensburg, Pennsylvania

Bates, Daisy May (1859–1951)

First anthropologist to carry out a detailed study of Australian Aboriginal culture. *Born Daisy May O'Dwyer on October 16, 1859, at Ballychrine, County Tipperary, Ireland (for years, she had given her birth date as 1863); died on April 18, 1951, at Prospect, near Adelaide, South Australia; only daughter of Marguarette (Hunt) and James Edward O'Dwyer; educated privately; married Edwin Henry Murrant (said to have been "Breaker" Morant), on March 13, 1884, at Charters Towers (no record of a divorce exists); married Jack Bates (a cattle rancher), on February 17, 1885; children: one child, Arnold (b. 1886).*

First settlement founded in Australia at Sidney Cove (1788); Bates arrived in Australia (January 1883); carried out first study of Aboriginal conditions (1899); Commonwealth of Australia founded (1901); appointed "traveling protector" of Aborigines in Western Australia (1910); established residence at Ooldea (1919). Selected publications: The Passing of the Aborigines *(1938); numerous articles in Australian and British newspapers.*

Aborigines, the native peoples of Australia, are today widely recognized as constituting one of the oldest and most culturally complex societies on earth. Present understanding of their customs, traditions, kinship structures and religious practices is the result of many detailed anthropological studies. These studies have their origin at the beginning of the 20th century in the work of a few dedicated individuals who set themselves the task of comprehending Aboriginal society. Foremost among these early pioneers was a quite remarkable woman, Daisy May Bates.

Bates was born on October 16, 1859, in the heart of rural Ireland at Ballychrine, County Tipperary. Her father James was a prominent local landowner whose estates enabled him to live a comfortable life as a country gentleman. Nothing of substance has been recorded about his character except that he seems to have taken little interest in his duties as a husband and father. When his wife Marguarette died giving birth to Daisy, James promptly sent his only daughter to live with her maternal grandmother.

This arrangement lasted until 1871 when, following the death of her grandmother, Daisy was sent to live in the household of Sir Francis Outram in London, England. Outram, an old family friend, was a civil servant who had recently retired from service in India. Generously, he assumed full responsibility for Daisy's education and provided her with private tutors. This assured that she received a solid, if not particularly extensive, grounding in a range of basic mathematical, linguistic, and artistic skills. More important, perhaps, Sir Francis liked to travel and was often accompanied by Daisy on his extensive trips throughout Europe. Thus, from an early age, she was exposed to a wide variety of cultures and ways of life.

When Bates was 23, she was diagnosed as suffering from pulmonary tuberculosis. In order to safeguard the health of her lungs, she was advised to leave England, with its unpredictable climate, and spend some time in a location where the weather was drier and warmer. Displaying a remarkable spirit of adventure, Bates chose to make the long sea voyage to Australia where she arrived, in January 1883, at Townsville, in the state of Queensland. There, she was given accommodation by a friend of Sir Francis, the Reverend George Stanton.

Stanton, appointed the first Anglican bishop of North Queensland in 1878, was widely recognized for his broad intellectual interests (he read extensively in science and philosophy as well as theology) and was a well-known pacifist. As bishop, Stanton had made a point of traveling widely throughout the Australian outback, and this experience had enabled him to reach an intimate understanding of the needs and conditions of the native Aboriginal population. It was thanks to his influence that Bates first became interested in the Aboriginal people of Australia.

Bates was a governess on "Fanny Downs" station when she married Edwin Henry Murrant on March 13, 1884, at Charters Towers, Queensland. In their 1979 book *In Search of Breaker Morant*, **Margaret Carnegie** and Frank Shields claim that her husband was Harry Harbord "Breaker" Morant. Morant, who had a reputation as a breaker of horses, would be condemned to death in a show trial over guerrilla warfare during the Boer Wars in Africa.

Their marriage soon ended when Murrant was arrested on a charge of larceny, but no record of a divorce exists. For one thing, there would not have been time. In February 1885, Daisy married a cattle rancher named Jack Bates at Nowra, New

South Wales; in the following year, the couple had a son whom they named Arnold. Daisy and her son spent the next few years following Jack as he herded cattle throughout Western Queensland. Little is known about this period in Daisy's life or about her relationship with her husband and child. It may be assumed, however, that their days together were not particularly happy; several years later, in 1894, she left Jack and returned alone to England. Her son was left in the care of her husband's family.

On arrival in London, Daisy Bates was fortunate to secure a job with a literary periodical, the *Review of Reviews*. For the next five years, she managed to sustain a precarious existence as an apprentice journalist. Although Bates wrote nothing of note during this period, her experience provided investigative and research skills which later proved valuable in her richly detailed anthropological accounts of Aboriginal life.

In 1899, disturbing rumors began to circulate among the British public concerning the living conditions of the Aboriginal population of northern and western Australia. At this time, practically nothing was known in England about the social and economic circumstances of the Aborigines. Bates, whom it appears had already made up her mind to return to Australia, took this opportunity to approach the London *Times* offering to investigate these rumors with the view to publishing her findings in the newspaper.

When Bates arrived in Australia, she traveled over 800 miles to a remote mission run by Trappist monks at Beagle Bay (in the very north of the country). For the next eight months, she carried out extensive investigations into the status of Aborigines in the surrounding area which were subsequently documented in a series of articles in the *Times*. Bates concluded that the native population was not being actively ill-treated either by government authorities or local European settlers. Nevertheless, she recommended that a great deal could and should be done to improve their living standards.

Early in 1901, Bates rejoined her husband and son at Roebuck Plains, an isolated cattle station situated east of Broome, Western Australia. It is not clear whether she wished to effect a reconciliation. If so, she was not successful. In the short time that they were together, Daisy only grew more estranged from her family. This was partly due to what they perceived as her increasingly eccentric behavior. For example, they found her manner of dress odd. Bates later described her costume as comprising habitually of "a neat white blouse, stiff collar and ribbon tie, a dark skirt and coat." While such attire would not be unusual in normal contexts, it must be recalled that Bates was living in the Australian outback where temperatures regularly reached 120 degrees fahrenheit.

> Living in the most arid bush, surrounded by the most primitive people, [Daisy May Bates] found a revelation, a version of the true nature of things, that was far clearer to her than the normal life we know.
>
> **—Alan Moorehead**

A more frequent cause of comment, however, was her growing absorption in the language and traditions of Aboriginal society. At a time when the great majority of white Australians had no interest in native culture, Bates embarked on the first systematic study of Aboriginal kinship affiliations and customs. She managed to gain the confidence of many Aborigines and their tribal elders and was accorded the rare privilege of being allowed to attend their most important ceremonies and rituals (many of which Aboriginal women were not allowed to attend). Bates was helped in these researches by her natural facility for languages; she later claimed in her autobiography that she eventually came to understand no fewer than 120 different Aboriginal dialects.

After Jack died in 1902, Daisy spent a short period with her son Arnold, herding cattle and tending to the details of her husband's estate. Soon afterwards, however, for reasons that remain obscure, she decided to separate once again from her 16-year-old son. Apart from a few brief meetings later in life, mother and son were estranged.

Two years later, in 1904, her work among the Aborigines was formally recognized by the government of Western Australia. Bates was granted funds to carry out a detailed study of the Bibbulmun tribe who resided on the Maamba reserve in the southwest corner of the state. For the next four years, Bates studied and recorded the language, religious practices, kinship structures and tribal myths of the Bibbulmun. In 1905, she contributed an important paper to the *Victoria Geographical Journal* in which she presented the first comparative study of the marriage customs between the Aborigines in Western Australia and those in other parts of the country.

Just as important as the substance of her research on the Aborigines was the manner in which she conducted her investigations. Bates anticipated modern anthropological practice by sharing the living conditions of the individuals who formed the object of her study. Indeed, for many years, the only home she knew was a tiny six-foot tent often located in the most harsh and inhospitable environment.

Bates' stature as one of the leading living authorities on Aboriginal society received further confirmation in 1910. In that year, the first full-scale scientific expedition arrived from England to carry out a detailed study of the Aboriginal population in the hinterland of Western Australia. Thanks to her reputation, Bates was invited by the leader of this expedition, the distinguished Cambridge anthropologist A.R. Radcliffe-Brown, to join the team in an advisory capacity. When the state authorities were informed of this arrangement, they formalized Bates' position by appointing her their "travelling protector." In effect, Bates was given a special commission to report on the social and economic situation among the Aborigines. She would later claim that Brown ignored her advice and confiscated her working manuscript; her allegations served to win generous support from **Georgina King**.

Daisy May Bates

Bates' principal concern became the condition of elderly and sick natives. (She had a lifelong belief that the young and the healthy were quite capable of fending for themselves.) She was particularly appalled at the physical circumstances which were leading to high mortality rates at two isolation hospitals on the islands of Bernier and Dorré, both located off the coast of Western Australia. These two hospitals (for male and female Aborigines respectively) had been established by the state government in 1904. As Bates pointed out in her subsequent report, the major cause of misery for the inmates lay in the fact that no attempt had been made to respect their tribal and kin affiliations. The unnatural juxtaposition, in the hospitals, of natives from different tribes and kin groups was extremely distressing for individuals whose existences had been intimately structured around such affiliations from birth. It was at this time that, in recognition for her work on their behalf, the Aborigines bestowed on Bates a special mark of their affection. From then on, wherever she went, Daisy was known among the natives as the *Kabbarli* (a name with a deep emotional resonance meaning "grandmother").

In 1912, Bates submitted what was perhaps her most important report to the Western Australia government. Despite her genuine concern for the plight of the Aboriginal peoples, Bates was convinced that what she called this "last remnant of palaeolithic man" was "physically uncivilisable" and was "inevitably doomed to perish." In these circumstances, she saw it as the moral duty of the authorities to "make their passing easier." This was to be achieved, she believed, by the establishment of reservations in remote parts of the country where the native peoples could be protected from the worst ravages of civilization and would be subject to the "highest and best traditions" of British rule. These recommendations were subsequently accepted in part by the state government who established a series of "Aboriginal Protection Boards" whose duties and functions broadly followed Bates' recommendations.

Her work has generated enormous controversy over the years. There are those who feel, despite her self-sacrifice and good intentions, that she took a pessimistic and patronizing view of the Aborigines and held up development of effective welfare programs. "Against that view can be set the tremendous affection for her among the tribes," noted an editor in the *Oxford Companion to Australian Literature*.

Shortly after she submitted this report, Bates established a new residence at Eucla, near the border with Southern Australia, among the Mirning tribe. It was there, in 1914, that the state government of South Australia asked Bates to take on the same duties as she had previously fulfilled in Western Australia and act as "protector" for its Aboriginal population. Although she accepted her new role, Bates was aware that the South Australia government would be unable to provide her with any funds for her work. Undaunted, she decided to sell what remained of her property (a small piece of land near Perth, Western Australia, on which she had hoped to build a retirement home) in order to supply the Mirning with food, clothing, and medical supplies. When eventually this money ran out, Bates turned to her journalistic skills and provided, for a modest fee, a variety of British and Australian newspapers with, what she termed, "my scientific gleanings of general interest."

Early in 1918, Bates became seriously ill and moved to Adelaide (the capital of South Australia). When she recovered, the authorities asked her to take charge of a convalescent home which had recently been established to aid soldiers wounded in the First World War. Bates applied herself to this new task with her usual enthusiasm. Yet, as she later wrote in her autobiography, she felt unnaturally constrained and out of place in the confines of the modern city. She yearned to return to the outback, and, at the end of 1919, Bates resigned her post and once again set out to live among her beloved Aborigines.

She traveled to Ooldea, a small town situated northwest of Adelaide on the trans-Australia railroad, where she was to remain in poverty for the next 16 years. This settlement had been encouraged by the railroad authorities in large part thanks to its abundant local water supply. Ooldea was, however, also an Aboriginal religious site where the native peoples of the region had traditionally performed their most important initiation ceremonies. By the time Bates arrived, the railroad had largely displaced the Aborigines from the pursuit of their customary ancestral practices. Nevertheless, not only did considerable numbers of natives continue to inhabit the surrounding area but they did so in the most appalling social and economic conditions. Bates immediately set to work to do what she could to alleviate this distress.

Because passenger trains often stopped at Ooldea to take on water, increasing numbers of the general public began to be aware of her work. As a result, she established a small, albeit well-deserved, reputation as a defender of Aboriginal rights. In 1920, she was appointed a justice of the peace for the Ooldea district (one of only two women at the time appointed to such a position). Later the same year, when the Prince of Wales (the heir to the British throne) was conducting a cross-country tour of Australia, he insisted that Bates take him on a personal inspection of local Aboriginal sites. The prince's visit was in fact only the first of three such calls by members of the British Royal family in the succeeding years. As a reward for all her efforts, Bates was honored in 1934 by being created a Commander of the British Empire, an event which she acknowledged as "the full reward of my life's services."

In 1935, she returned to Adelaide where she began to serialize her life story in a local newspaper. These columns (originally published under the title "My Natives and I") were collected together three years later with the help of ***Ernestine Hill** and formed the basis of Bates' autobiography, *The Passing of the Aborigines*. The following year, 1936, Bates was awarded a small stipend by the federal Australian government in order that she might prepare her personal papers for deposit at the Commonwealth National Library in Canberra. She was nearing 80 and in failing health. Remarkably, she refused all offers by friends to spend her remaining years in the comfort and security of their homes. Instead, she preferred to complete her work in the type of environment that she had known and loved all her life, in a tiny tent at Pyap by the banks of the Murray River.

By 1945, the austerity of these conditions became too much even for Bates; she was forced to retire, for the last time, to the town of Prospect near Adelaide where she entered an old people's home. Even then, she continued to maintain an active correspondence with anthropologists around the world and to sustain her deep interest in a wide range of Aboriginal problems. It was at this home in Prospect that Daisy May Bates passed away on April 18, 1951.

SOURCES:

Bates, D M. *The Passing of the Aborigines*. London: Murray, 1941.

Hill, Ernestine. *Kabbarli: A Personal Memoir of Daisy Bates*. Sydney: University Press, 1973.

Needham, R. *Remarks and Inventions*. London: Murray, 1974.

Radi, Heather, ed. *200 Australian Women: A Redress Anthology*. Broadway, NSW: Women's Redress Press, 1988.

Royal Anthropological Institute. *Man*. June 1975.

Salter, E. *Daisy Bates*. Sydney: Temple Press, 1971.

SUGGESTED READING:

Abbie, A.A. *The Original Australians.* London: Frederick Miller, 1969.

Bates, Daisy. *The Native Tribes of Western Australia.* Edited by Isobel White. 1985.

Greenwood, G. *Australia: A Social and Political History.* Sydney: Angus and Roberts, 1955.

Salter, Elizabeth. *Daisy Bates: The Great White Queen of the Never Never.* 1971.

RELATED MEDIA:

An opera *The Young Kabbarli* written by Lady **Maie Casey** (music by **Margaret Sutherland**) was performed in 1972.

The Sydney Dance Company staged Barry Moreland's dance-drama, *Daisy Bates,* in 1982.

Dave Baxter, Department of Philosophy, Wilfrid Laurier University, Waterloo, Ontario, Canada

Bates, Katherine Lee (1859–1929)

Professor and head of the English department at Wellesley College for 34 years and author of "America the Beautiful." *Born on August 12, 1859, at Falmouth, Massachusetts; died on March 28, 1929, at Wellesley, Massachusetts; daughter of William Bates (a Congregational minister) and Cornelia Frances (Lee) Bates; attended a village school in Falmouth, Wellesley High School (then Needham High School), Newton High School; attended Wellesley College and Oxford University; lived with Katharine Coman (Wellesley professor of economics); never married; no children.*

Awards: Phi Beta Kappa, Boston Authors Club; honorary degrees Middlebury, Oberlin, Wellesley Colleges.

Childhood spent in seaport town of Falmouth; moved with widowed mother and three siblings to Wellesley Hills (then Grantville), Massachusetts; entered Wellesley College (1876); elected class poet and permanent president of class of 1880; taught Latin, algebra, and English at Natick High School; taught Latin, Greek, and geometry at Dana Hall, a preparatory school for Wellesley; joined English department at Wellesley (1886); spent time at Oxford to prepare for her M.A. (1890–91); appointed professor and permanent head of Wellesley English department (1891); published children's stories, poetry, scholarly work, and, most enduringly, the lyrics for "America the Beautiful"; named director of International Institute for Girls in Spain; gathered outstanding group of women scholars in Wellesley English department; designated professor emeritus (1925).

Selected publications: America the Beautiful and Other Poems *(Thomas Y. Crowell, 1911);* Yellow Clover, a Book of Remembrance, *(E.P. Dutton, 1922);* Selected Poems *(Houghton Mifflin, 1930);* English Religious Drama *(Macmillan, 1893);* American Literature *(Macmillan, 1897);* Sigurd our Golden Collie and Other Comrades of the Road *(E.P. Dutton, 1919);* Rose and Thorn *(Congregational Sunday-School and Publishing Society, 1889);* Spanish Highways and Byways *(Macmillan, 1900). Also edited numerous English and American classics.*

In the summer of 1893, a young New England scholar, recently appointed head of the English department at Wellesley College, made her first journey west, noting along the way the white towers of the World's Columbian Exhibition, the fertile prairies stretching beyond Chicago, and the heat of western Kansas. The traveler's destination was Colorado Springs where she had been engaged to lecture on English religious drama at Colorado College. She found on the summer faculty there the noted realist novelist Hamlin Garland as well as the scholar-politician Woodrow Wilson whom she was long to admire.

It was not, however, her colleagues who were to make that summer memorable for Katherine Lee Bates. It was her decision to join a prairie wagon ascent of Pike's Peak. Since early childhood Bates had expressed herself in verse. Now as she reached the top of the great mountain and gazed at the dramatic panorama spread about her, words flashed into her mind. "O Beautiful for Spacious Skies, for Amber waves of grain. For Purple Mountains Majesties. . . ."

Imaginative reporters would later describe the moment in hyperbole, even fantasy. Bates, so one journalist declared, was a woman athlete who, winning a walking contest up Pike's Peak, in the excitement of her triumph promptly composed the entire text of "America the Beautiful." **Dorothy Burgess**, Bates' niece and biographer, tells the truer tale. The poet, though inspired on the mountain top, reworked her poem for some time, finally publishing it on the Fourth of July, 1895, in *The Congregationalist.*

The poem grew in popularity over the years. Many would-be critics offered suggestions for "improvement." A number of musical settings were composed, but the melody of Samuel Ward's "Materna" was most widely adopted. "America the Beautiful" became in time the official song of the Federation of Women's Clubs. Numerous efforts to have it replace the more warlike "Star Spangled Banner" as the nation's official anthem have failed. Bates herself believed that the on-going appeal of "America the Beautiful" was "clearly due to the fact that Americans are at heart idealists, with a fundamental faith in human brotherhood."

Katherine Bates came naturally by her own brand of patriotic idealism, as well as by her de-

Katherine Lee Bates

votion to poetry and scholarship. Her paternal grandfather, the son of a Revolutionary War soldier, had been an ordained minister and president of Middlebury College. Her father William, also a minister, graduated from Middlebury College and Andover Theological Seminary. Her mother **Cornelia Bates,** whose father was a manufacturer who loved Shakespeare enough to re-read and annotate the Bard's plays, graduated from Mount Holyoke Female Seminary. William and Cornelia were eager to educate their sons and daughters.

The most academically gifted of the four children turned out to be "Katie," the youngest, born at Falmouth in 1859, just a month before her father's early death. The little girl's diaries very soon showed both her lively, critical mind and the quick wit for which she was later to be noted. "Women," the young Bates wrote, "are vixens or old maids or ladies. The worst is an old maid. The vixen next worse. A ladie perfect. . . . Men think they are more important than women. . . . Women . . . are high spirited as a general thing and I am happy to say have become impatient under the restraint men put upon them. So the great question of women's rights has arisen. I like women better than men. I like fat women better than lean." Women's right to a rigorous education was to be the cardinal theme of Bates' life. She seems never to have felt a compulsion to be lean.

Cornelia Bates, widowed and impoverished, was obliged to send her sons into the business world without the education she had enjoyed. The entire family seems to have struggled together to afford their youngest her opportunity. A move from the friendly little seaport town of Falmouth to Grantville, now Wellesley Hills, Massachusetts, brought Katie to Needham, later Wellesley High School, from which she graduated in a class of two in 1874. She was already publishing poems and stories in the *Newton Journal*, and an ever wider world was opening. With another family move, she was able to spend two more high school years preparing herself for college. That college was, of course, to be the nearby and newly founded Wellesley.

In 1875, the year of Wellesley's founding, higher education for women was still hotly debated. Women could not physically withstand intellectual activity, some still argued. Higher education would make them unfit for marriage and motherhood. Scorn of "bluestockings" and feminists was, in fact, wide spread. Horace Greeley, liberal New York editor, he of "Go West, young man" fame, opined that there was nothing wrong with suffragist agitators which a bouncing baby would not cure. Despite opposition and ridicule, Oberlin College had, in 1837, admitted women and in 1848 granted them A.B. degrees. Hillsdale and Antioch Colleges had soon followed. The Civil War had hastened women's entry into fields hitherto closed to them, and colleges had struggled to meet their needs.

Education for women in the 19th century took several forms. Some schools, both private and state-funded, were, like pioneering Oberlin, co-educational. Some were coordinate colleges such as Harvard and Radcliffe, Brown and Pembroke, sharing faculties but with separate administrations and financing. Wellesley, like its "sisters" Bryn Mawr, Vassar, Smith, and Mount Holyoke, from the beginning admitted only women.

Henry Durant, Wellesley founder and benefactor, was passionately devoted to his project. Son of a small-town lawyer, Durant had made a fortune in the legal profession in Boston but had never been accepted by the Boston elite. His flamboyant and highly effective way with juries seems to have alienated his fellow barristers. Durant was cast in a non-traditional mold. At the death of a dearly loved only son, he was converted to a religious pietism which set him still farther apart from Back Bay Unitarianism. Though continuing his successful business ventures, he left the practice of law which he now considered ungodly and became a Christian evangelist. With his wife **Pauline Durant,** he set about establishing Wellesley College.

The original Wellesley statutes stated that "The College was founded for the glory of God and the service of the Lord Jesus Christ, in and by the education and the culture of women. It is required that every Trustee, Teacher and Officer, shall be a member of an Evangelical Church, and that the study of the Holy Scriptures shall be pursued by every student throughout the entire college course under the direction of the Faculty."

Students entered a world of restrictions unimaginable to later generations. In four undergraduate years, a Wellesley woman might never, except for vacation periods, be allowed out-of-doors after seven o'clock at night except to view the night-blooming cereus. But there were rich compensations. Henry Durant was no ascetic. In 1873, he deeded to Wellesley some 300 picturesque acres of hills and woodland fronting on Lake Waban. There he personally superintended every detail of the design and building of College Hall which was to be a place of Beauty. Students were furnished with luxuries so marked that Cornelia Bates, despite her joy at the opportunities Wellesley offered, worried that such surroundings might not be suitable for her modestly raised daughter. Cornelia overcame her qualms, however. Older brother Arthur provided $250, and, in the autumn of 1876, 17-year-old Katherine Lee Bates became a student in the institution to which, with brief intermissions, she was to devote the rest of her life.

With his strong belief in female abilities, Henry Durant hired only women teachers, recruiting his faculty from as far away as Michigan and Wisconsin. Faculty and students lived together in College Hall, the former watching over not only the academic progress but the manners, morals, and posture of their charges. In that setting, *in loco parentis* was no idle term.

Bates, who graduated in 1890 as poet and permanent president of her 43-member class, had published in the *Atlantic* a poem which drew the praise of the venerable Henry Wadsworth Longfellow. Though she would pattern her verse after 19th-century American poets, she did not pattern her life on her noted mentor. Longfellow, graduating from Bowdoin College, had been offered a professorship at his Alma Mater in return for spending a year of study in Europe. Resolved to lead a life in literature, the young man refused the offer.

Bates herself seems at first to have struggled to choose between writing and pedagogy, but pedagogy was for her the winner. For several years, she led the not-too-demanding life of teacher at Natick High School and Dana Hall. Then in 1886, she yielded to Wellesley's lure. In 1890, she went abroad to travel and to study at Oxford University. On her return, she was granted an M.A. and appointed professor and head of the English department.

The study of English literature was not required for graduation, but the courses soon became popular with students. Under Bates, the English department, with its distinguished faculty, was to become Wellesley's largest and most important department. American literature was added to the curriculum and, in the early 20th century, the study of composition. Despite her distinction, Bates received only a meager salary. College teachers were, as a group, ill paid. To add to her income, she made time for her loved "scribbling." The first of her children's books, *Rose and Thorn* (1889), attracted an enthusiastic readership, and she continued to write both fiction and poetry for children.

According to her own informal listing, she published eight books of poetry for adult readers, among them the privately printed *Yellow Clover, a Book of Remembrance*, an unusual sonnet sequence honoring her longtime colleague and friend **Katharine Coman**, a Wellesley professor of economics. For her most popular poem, the lyrics of "America the Beautiful," Bates received no payment except that which had been made by the original publisher. More financially rewarding were her numerous editions of English and American classics—Thomas Heywood's *A Woman Killed with Kindness* and *The Fair Maid of the West*, and works by Coleridge, Shakespeare, Ruskin, Hawthorne, and others. Her lively *English Religious Drama* was in use as a textbook for decades and is currently available in facsimile form.

Bates wrote poetry reviews for Boston and New York papers, inevitably expressing her own critical standards. Poetry without rime was for her deprived of one of its great beauties. She deplored "the small change of cleverness" and did not "care for jazz-like innovations in metre nor showy extravagances." "The Imagists," she wrote, "have done well to call poetry back again to the eyes and ears and call it away from books. But they have done ill in trying to *confine* poetry to the world of sense, denying the world of spirit." A popular but totally different kind of writing surfaced in 1919 in Bates' *Sigurd Our Golden Collie and Other Comrades of the Road* which won the praise of the noted collie fancier and author Albert Payson Terhune.

Bates' religious views seem to have been private. "I have no sympathy with materialistic Unitarianism," she wrote. She believed in God, in Christ as divine, and in the gospel of Love, but she was much troubled by the highly pietistic atmosphere of early Wellesley and was willing to continue her teaching only when assured that she would not be required to join an Evangelical Church. Never joining any church, she attended a variety of services, including those of the Church of England and the Catholic Church when she visited Spain.

Bates had a particular fondness for Spain. She was a director of the International Institute for Girls in Spain and lectured there frequently. Essentially conservative, according to her biographer, she seemed not greatly interested in many of the social reforms of her time other than that of education for women. She did, however, join the Consumers' League and the American Association for Labor Legislation. She helped her colleague, ***Vida Scudder**, formulate plans for the College Settlement Association.

In the fall of 1907, Bates returned from a year spent in England, Spain, Palestine, and Egypt and settled in her new home, Scarab, a comfortable brown-shingled house where she would live with her mother, her sister Jeanie, and her long-time friend Katharine Coman. She was once again abroad, this time visiting Spain and Denmark, when, on March 7, 1914, a fire leveled College Hall. She returned to Wellesley to help with reconstruction and new growth.

Bates retired from active teaching in 1925 and died in 1929. Death came quietly while a friend read to her John Greenleaf Whittier's "At Last," a return to the older American poetry she had always loved. The 20th century would see a growth in higher education for women beyond the dreams of its early proponents. By 1993, 55% of the students in American colleges and universities would be women. Katherine Lee Bates was a dedicated member of a generation which helped to make such an expansion possible.

SOURCES:

Burgess, Dorothy. *Dream and Deed: The Story of Katherine Lee Bates*. Norman, OK: University of Oklahoma Press, 1952.

Converse, Florence. *Wellesley College: A Chronicle of the Years 1875–1938*. Wellesley, MA: Hathaway House Bookshop, 1939.

Hackett, Alice Payne. *Wellesley: Part of the American Story.* NY: Dutton, 1949.

Hart, James D., ed. *Oxford Companion to American Literature.* NY: Oxford University Press, 1965.

Horowitz, Helen Lefkowitz. *Alma Mater.* NY: Knopf, 1984.

James, Edward T., ed. *Notable American Women.* Cambridge, MA: Harvard University Press, 1971.

Newcomer, Mabel. *A Century of Higher Education for American Women.* NY: Harper and Brothers, 1959.

SUGGESTED READING:

Bates, Katherine Lee, and Katharine Coman, eds. *English History as Told by English Poets,* facsimile 1902 edition. NY: Irvington.

———. *The English Religious Drama,* reprint of 1893 edition. Temecula, CA: American Reprint Service, 1985.

———. *O Beautiful for Spacious Skies.* San Francisco, CA: Chronicle Books, 1994.

Becquer, Gustavo. *Romantic Legends of Spain.* Edited by Cornelia F. Bates and Katherine Lee Bates. Reproduction of 1909 edition. Salem, NH: Ayer.

COLLECTIONS:

The Bates Papers, Wellesley College, Wellesley, Massachusetts.

Margery Evernden, free-lance writer and Professor Emerita, English Department, University of Pittsburgh, Pennsylvania

Bates, Mrs. L.C. (b. 1914).

See Bates, Daisy Lee.

Bates, Ruby (1913–1976)

Key American participant in the notorious Scottsboro case. *Name variations: Ruby Schut. Born in Huntsville, Alabama, in 1913; died in Yakima, Washington, on October 27, 1976; had two brothers; married Elmer Schut.*

Perhaps more than any other single event in the 1930s, the Scottsboro case of Alabama made clear to the American public the full extent of racial injustice in those Southern states whose legal and social systems were based on de jure segregation. Two white women, **Victoria Price** and Ruby Bates, accused nine "black boys" ranging in age from 13 to 21 of raping both of them while the "boys" were traveling as hoboes in March 1931 on the Chattanooga-to-Huntsville freight train. Tried without adequate legal counsel, all nine were convicted of rape on the basis of shaky testimony by Price and Bates. The Scottsboro case became a national controversy, as independent liberals, the American Communist Party, and the National Association for the Advancement of Colored People (NAACP) regarded the convictions as an outrageous miscarriage of justice. The sentencing exacerbated the issue, when all but one received death sentences.

Behind the scenes, the defenders of the Scottsboro boys were often at odds. Their legal defense was in the hands of a Communist-affiliated organization, the International Labor Defense, which viewed the case not simply as a question of justice for nine individuals but as a symbol of racial and class injustice in a capitalist society. The NAACP suspected that the Communists were more interested in the defendants' propaganda value as "victims of the system," than their fate as individuals. Applying mass pressure to the Alabama political and judicial system, individual liberals and radicals as well as their organizations bombarded officials, including the governor, with telegrams, postcards and letters demanding justice, including a retrial of all the defendants.

Ruby Bates, in a move that blew up the case, then changed her testimony. Her motives for the dramatic change were apparently mixed. She was annoyed because the other witness, Victoria Price, had pushed her out of the limelight. But the element of conscience was also present, for as she wrote in a letter to a boyfriend, "i wish those negroes are not burnt on account of me." Whatever her reasons, it took considerable courage for her to change her testimony in a racially-charged case in the deep South of the 1930s. Bates found herself vilified, being accused by many of the local elites that she had been bribed by the defense team, which as far as they were concerned was comprised mostly of Jewish Communists who had no right to be in the South. After her testimony, Ruby was taken from the courtroom and hidden by several National Guardsmen.

Recognizing Bates' publicity value, the leftist defenders of the Scottsboro boys took her on a tour of New York and Washington, D.C. At New York's St. Nicholas Arena, she spoke as a poor white woman before a crowd of over 5,000, saying that her initial false story of rape had been the result of having been "excited and frightened by the ruling class of white people." Back in Alabama, hostility toward Bates increased. The Huntsville *Times* noted with sarcasm that she had become "Harlem's darling" and called on the state attorney general to institute perjury proceedings against the "former Huntsville gutter snipe."

After a brief period as a speaker for the International Labor Defense, she vanished into obscurity despite continuing attempts by the Alabama attorney general's office to depict her as a clever liar who had been rewarded by the Communists with a luxurious New York penthouse for "going red." For a while, she worked in a spinning factory in upstate New York.

As for the Scottsboro boys, their attorneys agreed to an unusual plea bargain in 1937 whereby four of them were released while the other five remained in prison. The last of them was not to be released until 1950. Ruby Bates, who had married and taken her husband's name of Schut, died in Yakima, Washington, on October 27, 1976. Two days before her death, Clarence Norris, a resident of New York City and the last of the nine defendants known to be still alive, received a full pardon from the state of Alabama.

SOURCES:

Carter, Dan T. *Scottsboro: A Tragedy of the American South.* Rev. ed. Baton Rouge: Louisiana State University Press, 1979.

Goodman, James E. *Stories of Scottsboro.* NY: Pantheon Books, 1994.

Herndon, Angelo. *The Scottsboro Boys: Four Freed! Five To Go!* NY: Workers Library Publishers, 1937.

Kelley, Robin D.G. "Scottsboro Case," in Mari Jo Buhle, Paul Buhle and Dan Georgakas, eds., *Encyclopedia of the American Left.* NY: Garland, 1990, pp. 684–686.

Norris, Clarence. *The Last of the Scottsboro Boys: An Autobiography.* NY: Putnam, 1979.

"Ruby Schut, 63, Is Dead; Said She Was Involved In 'Scottsboro Boys' Case," in *The New York Times Biographical Service.* October 1976, p. 1477.

Terkel, Studs. *Hard Times: An Oral History of the Great Depression.* NY: Discus Books, 1971.

John Haag, Associate Professor,
University of Georgia, Athens, Georgia

Bateson, Mary (1865–1906)

British specialist in medieval sociology. *Born in 1865; died in 1906; daughter of William Henry Bateson (1812–1881); sister of biologist William Bateson (1861–1926, a pioneer in the study of genetics); attended Newnham College, Cambridge (1887); became a member of the Council at Newnham College.*

A specialist in medieval sociology, Mary Bateson was a lecturer at Newnham College from 1888 until her death in 1906. Influenced by Mandell Creighton, she focused on monastic history, publishing *The Register of Crabhouse Nunnery* in 1889. Bateson then turned to municipal history, editing *Records of the Borough of Leicester* (3 vols., 1899–1905), *The Charters of the Borough of Cambridge* (1901), *The Cambridge Gild Records* (1903), and *Grace Book B* (2 vols. 1903–05). In addition to editing many works for antiquarian societies, Bateson was also a Warburton lecturer at Manchester University. An ardent suffragist, she died in 1906.

Bathiat, Arlette-Léonie (1898–1992).

See Arletty.

Bathilde (c. 630–c. 680).

See Balthild.

Bathildis (c. 630–c. 680).

See Balthild.

Bathildis of Schaumburg-Lippe (1873–1962)

Princess of Waldeck and Pyrmont. *Born Bathildis Mary Leopoldine Anne Augusta on May 21, 1873; died on April 6, 1962; married Frederick, prince of Waldeck and Pyrmont; children:* ****Helen of Waldeck and Pyrmont*** *(1899–1948).*

Bathory, Elizabeth (1560–1614)

Hungarian countess, influential landowner, and mass-murderer, who tortured and killed perhaps 650 women, thereby becoming one of the horrific legends of Europe. *Name variations: Countess Erzsébet Báthory, "The Blood Countess," "Tigress of Csejthe." Born in 1560 into a Hungarian noble family at Castle Ecsed, Transylvania; convicted for murder and imprisoned in Cachtice Castle where she died in 1614; daughter of George and* ***Anna Bathory****; married Count Ferencz Nadasdy; children: one out-of-wedlock (name unknown) and four by marriage, Anna, Ursula, Katherina, and Paul.*

The world into which Elizabeth Bathory was born in 1560 was riven by political turbulence and war. The lands known today as Rumania, Hungary, Bulgaria, Serbia, and Croatia were a battleground between the warlords of Eastern Europe and the Ottoman Empire. Vast armies ravaged the military frontier of Transylvania as Christian king and Muslim sultan vengefully played the various Balkan princes as pawns in a dirty diplomatic game. Plague visited the land with its skeletal grip, and human life was cheap.

Elizabeth's land of Hungary had fallen into a marked state of decline. King Louis II (Lajos II) and nearly all his government and nobility had been massacred by the Ottoman Turks at the battle of Mohacs in 1526. The capital, Budapest, and most of the country, thereafter fell under the Ottoman sway. Feudal lords reasserted local power over those Hungarian areas which had not been conquered and reigned as they willed. The rulers of Transylvania maintained a tenuous independence by siding with the Christian Holy Roman emperor or the Muslim sultan of the Turks as the fortunes of life and war dictated.

The family of Elizabeth Bathory was prominent in the grand events of these times. One of her earliest recorded ancestors, named Wenzelin, had come from German Swabia in the 11th century and had entered the service of King Stephen I the Great of Hungary. By the 14th century, the Bathorys, as the descendants of Wenzelin had become known, were the possessors of tremendous estates and had divided into two familial lines: the Ecsed and Somlyo branches.

Elizabeth was a product of both lines, for her father George was an Ecsed while her mother Anna was a Somlyo. The Bathory family coat-of-arms consisted of three wolf's teeth below a crown encircled by a dragon biting its tail. The Bathorys were rumored to be related to that most infamous personage of the 15th century, Vlad Tepes III of Wallachia, known as Vlad the Impaler, or Dracula.

Elizabeth was born in 1560 at Ecsed Castle where she passed her earliest years. Despite the fact that her family included one cardinal and bishops of the church, judges, governors, sheriffs, two princes of Transylvania, and one king of Poland, her relatives in general hardly can be reckoned to have been a wholesome influence during her childhood. In the words of historian Raymond McNally:

> The constant intermarriage among the few Hungarian noble families evidently caused the blood to run a bit thin. One of Elizabeth's uncles was reputedly addicted to rituals and worship in honor of Satan, her aunt Klara . . . enjoyed torturing servants, and Elizabeth's brother, Stephan, was a drunkard and a lecher. Many members of Elizabeth's family complained in their private letters of symptoms which showed signs of evident epilepsy, madness, and other psychological disturbances.

It was said that Elizabeth herself had epilepsy, though in those days the word epilepsy was used to describe many mental and physical illnesses, and in her youth showed a predilection for torturing animals. She dressed in the clothes of men and played manly games. An intelligent child, Elizabeth was fortunate to be tutored, so that, in time, she would become a highly educated young woman versed in Hungarian, German, and Latin. In those days, an education was a rare commodity even among nobles.

In 1571, at age 11, she was affianced to Count Ferencz Nadasdy who was himself only 16. Ferencz's father Thomas had won the title of Prince Palatine and thereby was empowered to act in Hungary as a viceroy or special governor on behalf of the Holy Roman emperor. This, indeed, was an alliance between two very powerful and wealthy Hungarian families who, additionally, happened to be Protestant in a time of religious reformation, when Catholics and Protestants were engaged in political and even military struggles against each other.

Her betrothal notwithstanding, Elizabeth indulged in amorous games with local peasant boys: by age 14, she was with child. Alarmed by the probability of a scandal, her mother whisked Elizabeth away to a distant Transylvanian castle where the baby, a daughter, was born. A woman who agreed to take care of the unwanted baby was endowed with money and exiled to Wallachia for the duration of Elizabeth's lifetime.

Several months later, in 1575, Countess Elizabeth and Count Ferencz were married at Veranno Castle in one of the most impressive and splashy high-society weddings of the century. Maximilian II Habsburg (the Holy Roman emperor), and other distinguished luminaries attended. Despite the fame of the Nadasdys, Elizabeth insisted on keeping her own name, because the Bathorys were of a more notable and ancient lineage. Ferencz, however, was a rising star. In the words of author Gabriel Ronay, over the next years:

> He became the youngest general to command the border fortress defences of southwest Hungary, and gained the high title of Master of the Emperor's Horse. In 1600 Count Nadasdy was appointed the commander-in-chief of Christian forces in Transdanubia, making him the most powerful person in the country.

Between 1575 and 1603, Ferencz conducted war against the Turks, visiting his wife only occasionally during lapses in the fighting. In the beginning, Elizabeth stayed at the Nadasdy seat at Sarvar Castle where she superintended the household and "disciplined" the servants in increasingly creative ways. Elizabeth beat her serving girls with a cudgel, stuck needles into various parts of their anatomies, and threw young women into the snow naked and had water poured on them until they froze to death. This latter act of barbarity was immortalized by Hungarian artist István Csok, who in the 19th century painted a scene of Elizabeth Bathory seated before several female victims, laughing, as accomplices doused her victims with water. The painting resides in the Hungarian State Archives.

The young couple had no children during the first ten years of marriage. Then, in 1585, Anna was born, followed by two more daughters, Ursula and Katherina, over the next several

Elizabeth Bathory

years. Finally, a son, named Paul, was born to Ferencz and Elizabeth in 1598. According to author William Seabrook, who quotes from one surviving letter written by Elizabeth to Ferencz, Elizabeth had turned to witchcraft in order to induce fertility.

Certainly, the companions with which she had surrounded herself by the late 1500s suggest an unusual preoccupation with the black arts. Among her select coterie was a man, reputedly a sorcerer called Janos Ujvary or, simply, Ficzko ("lad"), three alleged witches with the names of

Helena Jo, **Dorothea Szentes**, and **Anna Darvulia**, and two others known as **Erzsi Majorova** and **Katarina Beneczky**. This small list, however, is by no means exhaustive, for there were other partners in crime who did not appear in court when Elizabeth was placed on trial in 1611.

By all contemporary accounts, Elizabeth, despite her growing depravity, was an exceptionally beautiful woman. The original likeness of her seems to have been "rediscovered" by Dr. Raymond T. McNally during his research at the small town museum at Cachtice in modern-day Slovakia. This "realistic" portrait, which bears the caption "The Tigress of Csejthe," apparently served as the model for a more idealized copy which once hung in Castle Zay-Ugrocz and which reposes today in the Hungarian State Museum in Budapest.

The "idealized" portrait, which appeared in the book *Elizabeth Bathory: The Blood Countess* (Eng. translation of title) by German author R.A. von Elsberg in 1904, represents the standard depiction of Elizabeth Bathory. Like the enigmatic Mona Lisa, the portrait may evoke a different visual interpretation from each viewer. R.E.L. Masters and Edward Lea, authors of *Sex Crimes in History*, noted Elizabeth's:

> astonishingly white flesh, almost translucent, through which one could see clearly the delicate blue veins beneath; long shimmering silken hair, black as the plumage of a raven; sensual, scarlet lips; great dark eyes capable of a doelike tenderness, but sometimes igniting into savage anger, and at other times glazing over with the abandoned somnolence of intense sexual passion.

Elizabeth was proud of her pronounced beauty and whiled away hours preparing herself for the coming day. As the years wore on, she became decidedly narcissistic, and woe to the poor handmaiden who failed to please her mistresses' tastes during these morning ablutions, for the unfortunate victim would be stripped and tortured by Elizabeth and her companions.

Elizabeth Bathory wished to remain young and beautiful not only for those brief interludes when her husband returned from the wars but in order to please her growing list of lovers. According to local witnesses, during the early years of her marriage Elizabeth eloped with a mysterious stranger dressed in black with milk-white skin and sharp teeth. Eventually, Elizabeth returned to her husband without the stranger. Gabriel Ronay recorded that in addition to several affairs, Elizabeth was wont to indulge in "sexual horseplay" with one of her manservants, openly, in front of her castle staff.

Meanwhile, Elizabeth's litany of horror knew no natural bounds. Her victims were universally female who were preferably fair-haired, fair-skinned, large-bosomed, and under the age of 18. Girl servants were beaten until they became unrecognizable lumps of congealed flesh, bone, and blood on the stone floor. Molten wax, knives, branding irons, rods and rope were employed in the most gruesome fashion. Paper doused in oil was ignited between the toes and thighs of young women. At least one victim was smeared with honey, tied to a tree, and abandoned to the mercy of forest insects and other interested scavengers. Several were forced to eat their own flesh and those of other victims. Elizabeth herself, when ill, frequently bit and ripped out pieces of the faces and breasts of attendants who displeased her. Whenever her imagination flagged, her cohorts stepped forward to play out fantasies of their own.

During one beating, Elizabeth was spattered by the blood of her victim. While wiping off the blood, she noted that her skin appeared more smooth, more youthful. Subsequently, the belief that blood could renew her youth and beauty became an obsession which led her into even more heinous crimes. New devices of torture were created. For example, an iron cage with spikes fixed inward was hung from a ceiling. Elizabeth and friends would poke and burn a young woman trapped inside who would struggle in torment. The spikes inside the cage caused severe lacerations and consequent bleeding. Positioned underneath, Elizabeth drank and washed in the blood as it rained down. Conversely, the red source of life was caught in a trough and transported to her bath which she began to take, as a ritual, at four o'clock in the morning.

Another device, called an Iron Maiden, was her *tour de force*. An Iron Maiden was shaped like a coffin with a sculpted face while spikes lined the interior at carefully selected points. Elizabeth's particular model, which had been especially made for her by a German clockmaker, came replete with blonde hair. In this instance, a victim would be placed inside, the door closed (as slowly as Elizabeth desired), and the ensuing river of blood would be collected in a basin, heated, then poured into her bath.

When Elizabeth's husband Ferencz Nadasdy fell ill in 1603 and finally died in January 1604 at age 47, Elizabeth was free to expel from her household the mother-in-law whom she had hated. With her children fully grown, Elizabeth was also free to step up the pace of her activity. As the toll of victims mounted, however, rumors of devilish happenings began to spread. Convenienced with several ancestral holdings, including the impressive castles of Ecsed, Sarvar, Cachtice, and Beckov as well as a townhouse in Vienna, Elizabeth was able to shift her operations and set up torture chambers at will. Her special companions helped establish a far-ranging network of individuals, who, for money and favor, found fresh victims for the countess of blood. The usual come-on, as these procurers ranged about the towns and countryside, was that Countess Bathory was seeking servants and attendants. To impoverished people consigned to the backward hamlets of Transylvania, this offer for their daughters seemed an attractive prospect.

Emboldened by her success in acquiring and in disposing of large numbers of human beings and desperate to combat the effects of aging, Elizabeth began to take chance after chance. Well into her 40s, she found, to her dismay, that neither bathing in blood nor practicing the black arts could turn back the hands of time. Her crony, Darvulia, convinced her mistress that what she now needed was blue blood, from the daughters of the aristocracy.

Her indiscretion and willingness to torture and kill members of the nobility proved her undoing, for the aristocracy had a voice in the high affairs of state. Much of Elizabeth's survival had been due to the fact that her previous victims had been from the peasantry who had no say in government. Peasant claims, and even complaints from minor officials of the church against the powerful Bathorys, would hardly have been countenanced in a court of law. In fact, such claims had gone forward to no avail.

Finally, in 1610, King Matthias II of Hungary, brother of the Holy Roman emperor, ordered the current Prince Palatine, Count George Thurzo, to establish a court of inquiry into the allegations against Elizabeth Bathory. Because Matthias was Roman Catholic while the Bathorys and Count Thurzo were Protestant, the situation was sensitive. Further, Thurzo was Elizabeth's neighbor and had to play carefully with Elizabeth's cousin, Prince Gabor Bathory of Transylvania. Matthias probably acted because stories that had reached him had assumed monstrous and essentially unavoidable proportions. There may have been an additional consideration, however, one based on solid economics. Matthias owed Elizabeth Bathory a considerable sum of money, a sum which, if she were found guilty, would be forfeit to the crown.

As the court sat in the city of Bratislava and collated critical information from hundreds of witnesses throughout autumn, Thurzo became convinced of what he almost certainly must have suspected and even already known, that there was indeed considerable evidence against Elizabeth. Leading a party to her castle residence at Cachtice on the evening of December 29, 1610, in order to place her under house arrest, he began to uncover definite facts. Three of her recent victims and a special torture chamber were found inside.

> When the blood drops were washed off her face, her skin appeared more beautiful; whiter and more transparent on the spots where the blood had been. Elizabeth, therefore, formed the resolve to bathe her face and her entire body in human blood, so as to enhance her beauty.
>
> **—Michael Wagener (1796)**

Thurzo moved quickly in order to keep the scandal as tightly under wraps as possible so as to minimize damage to the illustrious Bathory name. Further, he worked with determination to prevent the confiscation of Bathory lands by the king, an endeavor for which he expected to be rewarded by the appreciative family. The speedy show trials set in the town of Bycta on the 2nd and 7th of January 1611 produced a number of witnesses, including four of Elizabeth's principal companions who had been captured with her during Thurzo's raid. Elizabeth herself was not present at the trials but was kept under guard at Cachtice Castle. At these hearings, Helena Jo, Ficzko, Dorothea Szentes and Katarina Beneczky testified with almost incredible honesty, hoping thereby to alleviate their sentences. (Darvulia already had died a natural death.) Testimonies of witchcraft, torture, vampirism, and even cannibalism surfaced, but only the charge of multiple murder officially was entered into the court proceedings.

The accused admitted to a varied number of killings from 37 to 51, but these confessions clearly were on the low side, for no one had been with Elizabeth at all of her infamous torture chambers. Moreover, the Blood Countess had conducted pathological homicide throughout her life and before finding her special friends. One witness, simply described as "the maid Zusanna," claimed to have knowledge of a ledger in Elizabeth's own handwriting listing the death of 650 women.

If the pronouncement of "guilty" was a foregone conclusion, the severity of sentencing was not. In those days a member of the aristocracy convicted of a capital offense was entitled to decapitation, a form of punishment considered more refined than hanging which was reserved for common criminals. Despite their frank confessions, Helena Jo and Dorothea Szentes had their fingers torn out with fiery pincers, then were burned alive. Ficzko was beheaded, his body drained of blood, then thrown into a fire. Katarina escaped the death sentence, but later in the month another of Elizabeth's accomplices, Ersi Majorova, was apprehended and executed.

Under the circumstances, Thurzo secured for Elizabeth an astounding sentence of clemency: henceforth, she was to be imprisoned for life. Workmen soon arrived at Cachtice Castle and walled the Blood Countess into one room, leaving only enough holes for ventilation and one small opening so that food could be passed to her. Next, four gibbets were erected at the four corners of the castle to symbolize that justice had been done. Count Thurzo then secreted the records of the judicial proceedings away to his own castle where they remained until discovered by a cleric, Father Laszlo Turoczy, in the 1720s.

Elizabeth remained confined as an unhappy prisoner protesting her innocence for three-and-a-half years. Finally, on August 21, 1614, one of her guards peered through a hole of her chamber and saw her lying face down on the floor. Countess Elizabeth Bathory had died at the age of 54. She was interred hastily and without ceremony in the crypt of the church in Cachtice village; however, after many local complaints, the body was soon removed to the Bathory family seat at Ecsed. A contemporary Hungarian historian, István Krapinski, recorded that she had died "suddenly and without crucifix and without light."

SOURCES:

Baring-Gould, Sabine. *The Book of Werewolves: Being an Account of a Terrible Superstition.* NY: Causeway Books, 1973.

Bunson, Matthew. *The Vampire Encyclopedia.* Crown Publishers, 1993.

Frayling, Christopher. *Vampyres: Lord Byron to Count Dracula.* London: Faber and Faber, 1991.

Glut, Donald F. *True Vampires of History.* An official publication of HC Publishers, 1971.

McNally, Raymond. *Dracula was a Woman: In Search of the Blood Countess of Transylvania.* London: Robert Hale, 1984.

———, and Radu Florescu. *In Search of Dracula: a True History of Dracula and Vampire Legends.* NY: Galahad Books, 1972.

Ronay, Gabriel. *The Truth about Dracula.* NY: Stein and Day, 1973.

Seabrook, William. "World Champion Lady Vampire of all Time," in *Witchcraft: its Power in the World Today.* NY: Harcourt, Brace, 1940.

Volta, Ornella. *The Vampire.* London: Tandem Books, 1962.

David L. Bullock, Ph.D., author of *Allenby's War: the Palestine-Arabian Campaigns, 1916–1918* (London: Blandford Press, 1988)

Bathory, Countess Erzsébet (1560–1614).

See Bathory, Elizabeth.

Bathsheba (fl. 1010–975 BCE)

Biblical woman. *Name variations: Bethsabee. Pronunciation: BATH-shee-BAH. Married Uriah, the Hittite (killed); fourth (some sources say second) wife of King David (r. 1010–970 BCE); children: four sons, including Solomon (born around 985 BCE; died around 925 BCE).*

In the Bible, Bathsheba was the wife of Uriah the Hittite, a soldier in King David's army. The greatest Israelite king in the Old Testament, David unified Israel and Judah, vanquished the Philistines, outwitted all rivals, and established a strong kingdom centered at Jerusalem. While he was pacing back and forth on his roof one night, David witnessed Bathsheba bathing. Infatuated with her beauty, he sent for her, slept with her, and she became pregnant. He then appointed Bathsheba's husband Uriah to an exposed position in his armies, which were fighting against the Ammonites, and, as he had intended, Uriah was killed in the fray. After Bathsheba had mourned him, David married her, and she gave birth to a son. Though David was then seized with remorse for his misdeed, it was too late; his prayers and fasting could not keep their son from dying. Bathsheba gave birth to four more sons, the first of whom was Solomon, who ultimately succeeded David on the throne of Israel. Bathsheba is generally described as a woman who possessed a highly cultivated mind and vast knowledge; her son Solomon owed much of his wisdom and reputation to her, as well as a great part of the practical philosophy embodied in his Proverbs. Third and last king of the united 12 tribes of Israel, Solomon ruled during the kingdom's golden age, engaged in trade, international relations, and building projects (including the first Hebrew temple) and reputedly wrote large sections of three Biblical books.

SOURCES:

Bible (Books of 1 Samuel, 2 Samuel, 1 Kings, 1 Chronicles).

Bath Zabbai (r. 267–272).

See Zenobia.

Batson, Flora (1864–1906)

African-American concert singer known as the "Double-Voiced Queen of Song" because of her range from baritone to high soprano. *Born in Washington, D.C., on April 16, 1864; died in Philadelphia, Pennsylvania, on December 1, 1906; raised by her mother, Mary A. Batson, after her father died of Civil War wounds; educated and studied music in Providence, Rhode Island; married James G. Bergen (her manager), on December 13, 1887 (died around 1896); married Gerard Millar.*

Flora Batson—declared "Queen of Song" and "probably the greatest ballad singer in the world"—was raised by her mother in Providence, Rhode Island, following her father's death when she was three. After attending school and studying music, she began singing in church and local concerts in Providence and Boston. Early in her career, she performed temperance work for two years. Her rendition of "Six Feet of Earth Make Us All One Size," repeated for 90 successive performances in New York City's Masonic Temple, is said to have moved audiences to tears.

Batson joined the Bergen Star Concert Company in 1885 and, under the management of James G. Bergen, won international fame. Bergen, a white promoter of black talent, hailed Batson as his greatest discovery, and the couple later married. After her first major appearance in Steinway Hall in New York City on December 8, 1885, followed by her debut in Philadelphia, Batson's big break came when the company's leading soprano was unable to perform in a tour of the South. Batson stepped in and was so impressive that she soon took over as the company's prima donna.

Remarkable for its unusual range, Batson's voice, "showed a compass of three octaves," wrote one critic, "from the purest, clear-cut soprano, sweet and full, to the rich, round notes of the baritone register." Including operatic arias as well as ballads in her repertoire, her appeal was universal, even cutting across color barriers. At a concert in Philadelphia in 1887, Batson was declared "Queen of Song" and was presented with a crown of jewels to mark the occasion. At a subsequent concert in New York City, she was presented with a diamond crown and necklace. Devoted fans in Providence provided matching diamond earrings.

Her numerous worldwide tours were highlighted by appearances before England's Queen ***Victoria**, Pope Leo XIII, and Queen ***Liliuokalani** of Hawaii. She also gave concerts in Fiji, India, China and Japan. After the death of her husband, she toured Africa and Australia with basso Gerard Millar, whom she later married. He also became her manager and wrote the biography, *Life, Travels, and Works of Miss Flora Batson, Deceased Queen of Song*, which was published after her death. As her popularity waned, Batson joined touring companies and sang in vaudeville. Later in her career, she preferred church concerts and charity performances. Her last concert at a Philadelphia church was before a standing-room only crowd.

SUGGESTED READING:

Cuney Hare, Maud. *Negro Musicians and Their Music.* 1936. Reprinted. Washington, D.C.: Associated Publishers, 1974.

Millar, Gerard. *Life, Travels, and Works of Miss Flora Batson, Deceased Queen of Song.* T.M.R.M. Company, 190?. Held by the Library of Congress, the Music Collection of the Boston Public Library, and Brown University.

Barbara Morgan,
Melrose, Massachusetts

Batten, Jean Gardner (1909–1982)

New Zealander who became world famous for her aviation exploits. *Born Jean Gardner Batten on September 15, 1909, in Rotorua, New Zealand; died on November 22, 1982, in Majorca, Spain; daughter of* ***Ellen Blackmore Batten*** *(an artist) and Frederick Harold Batten (a dental surgeon); attended secondary school in Auckland, New Zealand, where she demonstrated considerable talent as a pianist and artist.*

Earned a private pilot's license (1930) and a commercial license (1932) in London; undertook a series of solo flights setting world records (1930s); set women's record on solo flight from England to India (1933); became first woman to fly from England to Australia (1934) and from Australia to England (1935); became first woman to fly across the South Atlantic Ocean from Africa to South America (1935); made the first direct flight to Auckland, New Zealand, from England, setting world record (1936) and from Australia to England with a record solo time (1937); won the U.S. Challenge Trophy (1934, 1935, 1936); won the U.S. Harmon Trophy (1935, 1936, 1937); won the Johnston Memorial Air Navigation Trophy (1935) and the Segrave Trophy (1936); awarded officer of the Brazilian Order of the Southern Cross (1935); named Commander of the British Empire (1936); given the chevalier of the French Legion of Honor (1936). Jean Batten archive established at the

Royal Air Force Museum (1972) and British Airways christened an airliner the "Jean Batten" (1981).

As the Gypsy Moth flew over the shark-infested Timor Sea on the 2,200 mile crossing from Sydney to Darwin, the engine coughed, sputtered, and died. In the eerie silence, the Moth began to glide toward the water while the pilot searched calmly through the toolchest for a hatchet. Like many small planes of the day, Jean Batten's carried no life rafts. If the plane crashed, its wing would have to be hacked off to serve as a raft. She opened and closed the throttle one last time—no response. At the last minute, a great throbbing roar shattered the silence as the engine came to life. Coaxing the plane up to 6,000 feet, Batten flew the next three hours to Kupang, on her way back to England. The first woman to make the round trip between England to Australia. Wrote Michael Ramsden:

> The full significance of Jean Batten's achievements is almost impossible to grasp today, sitting in a jet, listening to stereo and trying not to eat too much. Imagine flying alone for almost six days in a wood and fabric aeroplane with one engine, no navigation-aids and only the most primitive servicing facilities, and all the time just one piston-beat away from death by shark or wild animal.

Jean Gardner Batten was born in Rotorua, New Zealand, on September 15, 1909, the year Louis Blériot made the first crossing of the English channel by air. Her girlhood was filled with excitement. Fascinated by the thermal springs around Rotorua, she and her two brothers would wait for the blasts of steam to jet upward while visiting with the Maori women who washed their clothes in the heated water. She learned to swim when she was four and soon took up basketball and tennis. Sometimes with her mother Ellen Blackmore Batten, she rode horseback on a milk-white mare; with her father Frederick, she sailed on his yacht. After he left for the front when World War I broke out in 1914, her interest in geography grew as his letters opened vistas of distant places. At ten, the flying exploits of Ross and Keith Smith caught her imagination. Her father, seeing his daughter excel at art and the piano, was certain she would

Jean Gardner Batten

be a musician, but he was overlooking her love for speed.

Batten grew up in the golden age of aviation. The 19th century began with the railroad and ended with the automobile. The 20th-century's hallmark would be the airplane. The first planes were flimsy, unstable machines barely able to lift off the ground, but by the late 1920s air transport had become quite reliable. Flying was presented as another skill, like driving a car, that anyone could learn, and in a sense this was true; instrumentation was so rudimentary that pilots often navigated by landmarks, landing speeds were low, and people often survived crashes. Batten's childhood fascination mirrored the public's infatuation with flight.

By the time Batten was 19, women had taken up flying, though it was considered a male profession. In 1928, Charles Kingsford Smith and Charles Ulm flew from America to Australia; the following year, Batten made her first flight, with Kingsford Smith, an experience she never forgot. "Cruising about high above the Blue Mountains I . . . felt completely at home in the air and decided that here indeed was my element."

Batten's announcement that she intended to fly met with paternal opposition. But her father's disapproval and the expense of flying lessons did not deter her; she offered to sell her piano to pay for lessons. Understanding her daughter's passion, Ellen Batten decided to accompany her to England where it would be easier to take flying lessons. They departed early in 1929 and saw the Temples of Ceylon, the Red Sea, Arabia, Vesuvius, and Gibraltar en route. Not long after reaching London, Jean appeared at the London Aeroplane Club at Stag Lane to begin flying lessons, earning her "A" license in 1930. Already dreaming of a flight from England to Australia, she went back to New Zealand to drum up funding. When this failed, Batten returned to London to earn her commercial or "B" license in 1932, which she hoped would open more doors. She studied navigation, attended lectures, and worked with mechanics. Money soon ran out, however, and she began to frequent pawn shops.

Though a logical step for aviation, her dream of linking New Zealand to England by air seemed impractical at the time. A friend agreed to lease her a Gypsy Moth in exchange for 50% of any profits made on long distance flights. But on a night flight, the plane threw a rod, and, though Batten landed safely, the event left her financially undone. Wrote Batten:

> By the time all the damage was repaired and paid for I had nothing but debts to carry on with. . . . So I took my courage in both hands and went to see Lord Wakefield. I knew that he was interested in long-distance flights, and also that he was rich and generous. I was most intimidated when I found myself in his presence. . . . I explained my idea of linking up his country and my own, England and New Zealand, or at any rate, to start with, Australia. He gazed at me for sometime in silence. At last he said: "Very well. But you must use my own products. I manufacture Castrol, you know."

In April 1934, Batten bought another Gypsy Moth for the England to Australia crossing. After she made it to India, a major engine failure forced her to cancel her plans. In her second attempt, she flew to Rome but couldn't find the airport. Batten nearly lost her life landing in the first vacant spot she found—a wireless station full of antennas. Fortunately none of the wires sliced the Moth, and she escaped safely.

> In flying I found the combination of the two things which meant everything to me: the intoxicating drug of speed and freedom to roam the earth.
>
> —**Jean Batten**

On May 8, 1934, Batten set out for Australia a third time in a five-year-old Gypsy Moth with a cruising speed of 80 mph. Flying in an open cockpit, she used a compass, landmarks, and a map to chart her course. She made frequent stops to refuel and often had to hand pump gasoline from the auxiliary tanks to the main tanks in order to stay airborne. Exposed to the elements, she endured extreme cold over the English Channel, dust storms over the Syrian desert, and monsoons over Southeast Asia. When the tiny plane was engulfed by a storm in Rangoon, she nearly had to turn back:

> The rain thundered down on to the wings of my aeroplane like millions of tiny pellets, and visibility was so bad that the wing-tips were not visible and the coastline was completely blotted out. It was like flying from day into night, and in the semi-darkness the luminous instruments glowed an eerie green from the dashboard. Very soon the open cockpit was almost flooded and my tropical flying-suit wet through.

On May 23, 1934, Batten landed in Darwin, 14 days, 22 hours, and 30 minutes after leaving London, setting a new women's record, and beating ***Amy Johnson**'s time on the same flight by four days. Ecstatic Australians mobbed Batten. When she returned to New Zealand, the reception was also astonishing. She was welcomed by the prime minister, honored by the Maoris with a feast in Rotorua, and entertained at receptions and banquets. Using every opportunity to campaign for routine flights between New Zealand, Australia, and England, she spent the next year in New Zealand and Australia lecturing, writing articles, advertising products, and giving passenger flights, all to earn money. Now a public figure, she was shocked when news of a possible engagement made the headlines, but Batten easily came to terms with her fame.

In April 1935, she returned to England in her overhauled Gypsy Moth, a trip which included the temporary engine failure over the Timor Sea. The close call left her nervous during the next 18 days of the flight, but she finally landed safely at Croydon where she was greeted with tremendous enthusiasm by enormous crowds, the first woman to make the round trip between England and Australia. No sooner had Batten arrived than she began to arrange new flights. With the money earned during the previous year, she purchased a closed-cabin Percival Gull, planning to fly from West Africa to Brazil. Only Amy Johnson's husband, Jim Mollison, had made this solo flight across the South Atlantic, and Batten hoped to best his time of 17 hours, 40 minutes.

For the next six months, she filled out forms, applied for visas, and arranged for fuel along the route. She left London for Casablanca on November 11, 1935, and reached the city in 9¾ nonstop hours—a new record. Next she flew 1,600 miles to Thies, navigating across wild, barren country, over which her superb navigational skills stood her in good stead. She arrived in Thies to find that her fuel supplies, now in Dakar, had to be trucked in. When the Gull was finally fueled up, the plane was so overloaded that she had to jettison water drums, the tool kit, and spare engine parts, but Batten refused to part with two evening dresses. Always fashionably attired, she wore an immaculate white jumpsuit in the air; then, shortly after landing, she would appear elegantly dressed in a silk gown, a sure guarantee of front-page photos. Her trip from Thies to Cape San Roque on the Brazil coast was 1,907 miles, with no radio for navigational assistance. Her compass needle began to swing wildly when she crossed the equator, but she pressed on. Despite primitive navigational tools, she arrived within a half mile of her destination. She landed at Port Natal 13½ hours after leaving Africa, breaking Jim Mollison's record by almost 4½ hours.

Jean Batten was now an international superstar met everywhere by cheering crowds. Receptions, lunches, and dinners were held in her honor. In 1935, she was awarded the Brazilian Order of the Southern Cross; the following year, she became a Commander of the Order of the British Empire and a chevalier of the Legion of Honor in France. In 1936, she invited her mother, an ardent supporter of her pursuits, to take a flying holiday with her in Europe. The press went wild when mother and daughter toured the Continent together, and the pair were feted wherever they landed.

But Batten's long-distance flying career had not yet ended. In October 1936, she set out to fly from England to New Zealand, with brief refueling stops. Within eight days, she was touching down in Sydney, Australia, the fastest time ever. The Australians were waiting for her:

> As I circled the city, I saw the great harbour bridge and all the roof-tops black with waving people. I landed at Mascot Aerodrome escorted by aeroplanes of the Royal Aero Club of New South Wales. . . . I shall never forget the full throated roar of welcome that greeted me from thousands of people as I taxied up to the reception dais.

With another 1,330 miles to go to New Zealand, across the treacherous Tasman Sea with its freezing Antarctic gales, Batten asked that no one imperil their lives searching should her plane disappear.

On October 16, 1936, she took off for New Zealand in a time when weather reports were unreliable, especially as few ships sailed the Tasman Sea. Soon caught between foaming waves and raging storm clouds, she fought the wind to keep the Gull on course in sheets of rain. Never sighting land, she flew nine hours, certain she was off course, until New Plymouth came into view. With an almost uncanny navigational ability, an hour later, she reached Auckland where her father and a crowd of thousands awaited her. England and New Zealand had been linked by air for the first time, in 11 days.

In the mid-1930s, Batten turned her hand to writing, authoring *Solo Flight* (1934) and *My Life* (1938), later republished as *Alone in the Sky*. With the advent of World War II, she made one last flight in September 1939. Batten was in neutral Sweden with a "well known count" when she asked the German government for permission to fly her own plane across what was now enemy territory. Respect for the aviator was so great that the guns were silent while she flew over the Third Reich to England. The golden age of aviation ended with this flight. The era of solo pilots in tiny planes was over, and from this point forward huge planes with complex navigation systems would be flown by a crew carrying many passengers.

When the Germans began bombing London, Batten's first instinct was to volunteer for combat. But women were denied this role in Western Europe, although many would distinguish themselves as combat pilots in the Soviet Union. Because the British government did not want to risk losing such a famous personage on a mere cargo mission, Batten was relegated to making speeches and selling war bonds. She never flew again.

But during and after World War II, she remained a well-known figure. She was a beautiful woman who turned down at least five marriage proposals; her name was linked to several men. When asked about her romantic involvements, however, Batten always replied, "My only love is aeroplanes." One of her friends, **Mary Anna Ireland**, said of the flyer, "Jean disliked men. That's not to say she loved women, because she didn't. She was a loner." Batten's closest attachment remained her mother who nursed her daughter's ambition at the expense of her own marriage. After her mother's divorce, the two women lived in Jamaica and then on Tenerife in the Canary Islands. They settled into comfortable exile, joining British clubs, frequenting English libraries, and attending Anglican services. When Ellen Batten died in 1966, Jean buried her mother in the Anglican cemetery at Puerto de la Cruz on Tenerife. Increasingly, she became a recluse, taking long swims in the harbor or long walks through town. A familiar figure, Batten was Garbo-like, with her face hidden by a large, floppy-brimmed hat.

She lived in a small, bare studio apartment on Tenerife with no photographs or displays of her many trophies and medals. The only memento visible was a small silver model of her Percival Gull that graced the top of the television. This simple lifestyle was not due lack of funds—she would never touch her pension funds and had plenty of money for charity—but to preference. Personal contacts were few, though she had friends like Alan and **Nollie Birch**, a retired British couple, who were neighbors.

At the end of her life, Batten would fly solo once more. Alan Birch described her sudden departure:

> One morning we opened our door and found a shopping bag hanging from the knob. It was full of magazines and things. We knew it was from Jean. But she wasn't there. Later we found out that she'd sold her flat to some Germans and simply left. She never said good-bye. We were a bit hurt; but she was always a private person.

Batten hired a taxi and went to the airport, taking a plane to Majorca off the Spanish coast. On November 8, 1982, she sent a note to her accountant about charitable donations she wished to make; it was her last communication. Five years later, Tim McGirk from the London *Times* set out on a three-month journey to locate Batten. Eventually, he ended up in Majorca. McGirk learned that she and her mother had flown there in the 1930s to visit the monastery of Valldemosa where Chopin had once stayed; Batten had been enchanted by the village surrounding the monastery. High up on the mountain, the village overlooked the Mediterranean stretched out far below, a familiar view for someone who had flown many miles. Batten had often spoken of returning to the place. On November 22, 1982, 14 days after her last communication, she died in the village high above the blue sea. Several million tourists visit the island each year, and to local officials Jean Batten was just another visitor. When police failed to locate any next of kin, she was buried in a pauper's grave, which would remain unidentified until 1987. Like Amy Johnson and ***Amelia Earhart**, Jean Batten had simply vanished from the earth.

SOURCES:

"Batten grave mystery," in *Sunday Times* [London]. October 4, 1987, p. 22.

"Batten: Jumping Jean's Latest Hop Chalks Up Some New Marks," in *Newsweek*. Vol. 6, no. 21, November 23, 1935, p. 32.

Batten, Jean. *My Life*. London: G.G. Harrap, 1938 (republished as *Alone in the Sky*, Shrewsbury, England: Airlife Publishing, 1979).

———. *Solo Flight*. Sydney: Jackson & O'Sullivan, 1934.

Boase, Wendy. "'Try Again Jean': Jean Batten" in *The Sky's the Limit*. NY: Macmillan, 1979, pp. 157–176.

"Flying Down to Rio," in *Time*. Vol. 26, no. 22, November 25, 1935, p. 57.

Henshaw, Barbara. "Plane spotter got it wrong," in *Sunday Times* [London]. February 15, 1987, p. 31.

Lauwick, Hervé. "Jean Batten, The Girl Napoleon," in *Heroines of the Sky*. Translated by James Cleugh. London: Frederick Muller, 1960, pp. 186–201.

Lomax, Judy. "Jean Batten: Daughter of the Sky," in *Women of the Air*. NY: Dodd, Mead, 1987, pp. 108–118.

McGirk, Tim. "The Vanishing Aviator," in *Sunday Times Magazine* [London]. February 1, 1987, pp. 20–24, 27.

"Miss Jean Batten: Daughter of the Skies," in *The Times* [London]. September 29, 1987, p. 18.

Peace, David. "Memento of a missing heroine," in *Sunday Times* [London]. February 8, 1987, p. 28.

"Record Flight: Jean Batten Lays London-Melbourne Course," in *Newsweek*. Vol. 3, no. 22, June 2, 1934, p. 22.

Karin Loewen Haag, freelance writer, Athens, Georgia

Battenberg, Princess of (1857–1944).

See Queen Victoria for sidebar on Princess Beatrice.

Bauchens, Anne (1881–1967)

American motion-picture editor. *Born in Saint Louis, Missouri, on February 2, 1881; died on May 7, 1967, in Woodland Hills, California, at the Motion Picture Country Hospital; never married; no children.*

Filmography: The Squaw Man *(1918);* Till I Come Back to You *(1918);* Don't Change Your Husband *(1919);* For Better or Worse *(1919);* Male and Female *(1919);* We Can't Have Everything *(1919);* Something to Think About *(1920);* Why Change Your Wife *(1920);* The Affairs of Anatol *(1921);* Fool's Paradise *(1921);* Forbidden Fruit *(1921);* Manslaughter *(1922);* Saturday Night *(1922);* Adam's Rib *(1923);* The Ten Commandments *(1923);* Feet of Clay *(1924);* Triumph *(1924);* The Golden Bed *(1925);* The Road to Yesterday *(1925);* The King of Kings *(1927);* Chicago *(1928);* Craig's Wife *(1928);* Dynamite *(1929);* The Godless Girl *(1929);* Ned McCobb's Daughter *(1929);* Noisy Neighbors *(1929);* Lord Byron of Broadway *(1930);* Madam Satan *(1930);* This Mad World *(1930);* The Great Meadow *(1931);* Guilty Hands *(1931);* The Squaw Man *(1931);* Beast of the City *(1932);* The Sign of the Cross *(1932);* The Wet Parade *(1932);* Cradle Song *(1933);* This Day and Age *(1933);* Cleopatra *(1934);* Four Frightened People *(1934);* Menace *(1934);* One Later Hour *(1934);* The Crusades *(1935);* The Plainsman *(1937);* This Way Please *(1937);* The Buccaneer *(1938);* Bulldog Drummond in Africa *(1938);* Hunted Men *(1938);* Sons of Legion *(1938);* Television Spy *(1939);* Union Pacific *(1939);* Northwest Mounted Police *(1940);* Women without Names *(1940);* Commandos Strike at Dawn *(1942);* Mrs. Wiggs of the Cabbage Patch *(1942);* Reap the Wild Wind *(1942);* The Story of Dr. Wassell *(1944);* Tomorrow, the World! *(1944);* Love Letters *(1945);* Unconquered *(1947);* Samson and Delilah *(1952);* The Greatest Show on Earth *(1952);* The Ten Commandments *(1956).*

Anne Bauchens' 40-year career in the motion-picture industry began with the dream of becoming an actress. Soon after the turn of the century, she left her native St. Louis, where she had worked as a telephone switchboard operator for the *St. Louis Post-Dispatch*, and headed for New York and the Broadway stage.

Though her acting career never materialized, in 1912 she was hired as secretary to then-playwright William C. DeMille. The position eventually led her to Hollywood and a meeting with DeMille's brother, Cecil B. DeMille, at that time a nascent film director. At one of their first encounters, Bauchens, who had become an assistant editor, said to the young auteur: "Some day I'm going to cut your pictures." According to his autobiography, DeMille replied, "No one will ever cut one of my pictures but me." Two months later, Bauchens was an assistant editor on DeMille's 1919 film *We Can't Have Everything*. From that day until the 1956 remake of *The Ten Commandments*, Bauchens edited every DeMille film. That she edited both versions of DeMille's *Ten Commandments* is unusual, perhaps the only time a director-editor team has collaborated on the same movie project filmed decades apart.

Nicknamed "Trojan Annie" by her Paramount colleagues because she handled so much work, Bauchens was also known as the only one who could say *no* to DeMille. "In every contract I sign to produce a picture one essential clause is that Anne Bauchens will be its editor," wrote DeMille. "That is not sentiment . . . she is still the best film editor I know." Bauchens returned the respect, claiming that DeMille told a story "better than anyone else." Bauchens was a technician's technician. Before becoming an editor, she had created the job of script supervisor, a position that combines secretarial skills with a knowledge of the editing room. During shooting, the script supervisor makes complicated script notations to guide the editor as the film is assembled.

Bauchens considerable contributions to DeMille's work did not go unrecognized. In a September 8, 1935, *The New York Times* review of DeMille's film, *The Crusades*, the critic wrote: "The picture is worth seeing a second time to study the technical skill of Anne Bauchens." Devoted to her work, she never married and, according to a 1957 interview with the *Christian Science Monitor*, lived with a housekeeper, "a wonderful woman who lives with me and takes care of my every need."

Bauchens was nominated for best editing Academy Awards for *Cleopatra* (1934), *The Greatest Show On Earth* (1952), and *The Ten Commandments* (1956) and received the Oscar for *Northwest Mounted Police* (1940). She was also the first recipient of the Life Achievement Award given by her colleagues, the American Cinema Editors (ACE). Anne Bauchens died on May 7, 1967, in the Motion Picture Country Hospital, a retirement home for members of the film industry, in Woodland Hills, California, a community just outside Hollywood.

SOURCES:

Hayne, Donald, ed. *The Autobiography of Cecil B. DeMille.* Englewood Cliffs, NJ: Prentice-Hall, 1959.

DeMille, William. *Hollywood Saga.* NY: Dutton, 1939.

Sammis, Constance Sharp, "Film Editor Indefatigable," in *Christian Science Monitor.* February 11, 1957.

Variety Obituaries. Volume 6, 1964–1968. NY: Garland, 1988.

Deborah Jones, Studio City, California

Bauer, Helene (1871–1942)

Austrian journalist and educator, who was wife and collaborator of Social Democratic leader Otto Bauer. *Born Helene Gumplowicz in Cracow, Russian Poland, on March 13, 1871; died in Berkeley, California, on November 20, 1942; daughter of Ludwig Gumplowicz; studied in Vienna and Zurich; received doctorate in 1905; married Max Landau, in 1895; married Otto Bauer (1881–1938), in 1914; children: (first marriage) Wanda Lanzer, Zbigniew Landau.*

Active in the Polish Social Democratic movement in early years; worked as an editor and journalist in Vienna for Social Democratic Party; also taught evening courses at the Workers' University; fled Austria (1934) for Czechoslovakia; moved to Paris (1938), Stockholm (1939), and U.S. (1941).

Married to Otto Bauer, the leader of the Austrian Social Democratic Party, Helene Bauer was a significant Marxist personality in her own right, with an impressive career in both the Polish and Austrian working-class movements. She was born Helene Gumplowicz into a Jewish home in Cracow, Russian Poland, on March 13, 1871. Her father Ludwig Gumplowicz owned a bookstore, and Helene was raised in a home atmosphere filled with ideas and lively discussions. From her earliest years, she sympathized with the downtrodden workers and peasants; in her teens, she became an ardent Marxist. After her marriage to Max Landau in 1895, she quickly had two children, Wanda and Zbigniew. Determined to make her mark in the Socialist movement, she studied political science in Zurich and Vienna, receiving a doctorate in 1905. By the time of her divorce from Landau in 1911, she had established a successful life for herself in Vienna as a journalist and adult-education teacher. In 1914, she married Otto Bauer (1881–1938), one of the most impressive of the younger leaders of the Austrian Social Democratic Party (SPÖ).

In 1919, the city of Vienna came under the control of the Social Democratic Party, and almost immediately an ambitious program of municipal building and social legislation was put on track. By the mid-1920s, "Red Vienna" had come into existence, with an impressive record of social improvement based on public housing and welfare programs. In 1918, when Otto replaced Victor Adler as undisputed leader of the SPÖ, both husband and wife were at the very heart of Red Vienna. Helene's responsibilities were considerable, including the job of editor-in-chief of *Der Kampf*, the party's ideological journal. Although Bauer customarily functioned in her editorial role, occasionally she was motivated to write an article in the journal, as when she strongly criticized the reactionary corporate state ideals of University of Vienna professor Othmar Spann. Strongly committed to the concept of adult education, she taught a highly rated course on statistics for many years at the party's "Workers' University" (Arbeiterhochschule). Bauer, concerned about the low percentage of university students sympathetic to the ideals of Socialism, played a key role in founding an important Marxist student organization, the Socialist Working Group for Economics and Politics (Sozialistische Arbeitsgemeinschaft für Wirtschaft und Politik).

The Nazi takeover of Germany in 1933 quickly led to a creeping fascist seizure of control in Austria. At first, the erosion of Socialist power took place in a piecemeal fashion, but in February 1934 violence erupted; within a few days, an authoritarian state had been set up in Austria, and Red Vienna had become only a memory. Otto and Helene Bauer fled Vienna as refugees and spent the next four years in Brünn/Brno, Czechoslovakia. Functioning as Otto Bauer's executive assistant, she shared with him the disappointments and occasional elation of running an underground organization in an increasingly dictatorial Austria. She dealt stoically not only with the depressing political atmosphere of exile, but also with the fact that her husband was in love with **Hilde Marmorek**, one of the courageous party members who regularly traveled as a courier between Brünn and Vienna. By early 1938, Nazi pressure on the Czechoslovak government made the situation of the Austrian Socialist exiles in Brünn untenable, and the Bauers moved to Paris. Soon after settling in Paris, Otto Bauer died of a heart attack on July 4, 1938.

Despite her husband's death and her increasing years, Helene Bauer remained active in SPÖ affairs, continuing her editorial work and contributing ideas at countless meetings. But Bauer's commitment to socialist ideals was strongly tempered by a realistic view of the power of Nazi Germany and the dangers of being a Jewish Marxist in a France increasingly threatened by its aggressive neighbor. In the spring of 1939, Helene Bauer and her daughter Wanda moved to Stockholm, where a small but well-organized group of Social Democratic exiles had established themselves. But after the Nazi attack on Poland in September 1939, even Sweden was no longer safe. In 1941, Bauer was fortunate enough to immigrate to the United States on an emergency visa. She settled in California and continued to be actively involved in the often convoluted political debates and personal intrigues that have traditionally constituted exile politics. During the last months of her life she was a member of the Social Democratic faction led by Karl Heinz. Anticipating a return to Vienna after the defeat of Nazism, Helene Bauer died in Berkeley, California, on November 20, 1942.

SOURCES:

Biographical file, "Biografisches Lexikon der österreichischen Frau," Institut für Wissenschaft und Kunst, Vienna.

Ellenbogen, Wilhelm. *Menschen und Prinzipien: Erinnerungen, Urteile und Reflexionen eines kritischen Sozialdemokraten.* Vienna: Hermann Böhlau Verlag, 1981.

Gruber, Helmut. *Red Vienna: Experiment in Working-Class Culture 1919–1934.* Oxford: Oxford University Press, 1991.

Röder, Werner and Herbert A. Strauss, eds. *Biographisches Handbuch der deutschsprachigen Emigration nach 1933.* 4 vols. Munich: K.G. Saur, 1980, vol. 1, pp. 38–39.

Simon, Joseph T. *Augenzeuge: Erinnerungen eines österreichischen Sozialisten: Eine sehr persönliche Zeitgeschichte.* Vienna: Verlag der Wiener Volksbuchhandlung, 1979.

Stimmer, Kurt. *Die Arbeiter von Wien: Ein sozialdemokratischer Stadtführer.* Vienna: Verlag Jugend und Volk, 1988.

Winkler, Ernst. "Otto Bauer," in Norbert Leser, ed. *Werk und Widerhall: Grosse Gestalten des österreichischen Sozialismus.* Vienna: Verlag der Wiener Volksbuchhandlung, 1964, pp. 59–75.

John Haag, Associate Professor, University of Georgia, Athens, Georgia

Bauer, Karoline (1807–1877)

German actress. *Name variations: Countess Montgomery. Born in Heidelberg on March 29, 1807; died in Zurich, Switzerland, on October 18, 1877; morganatic wife of Prince Leopold of Coburg (later king Leopold I of Belgium), 1829, under name Countess Montgomery; married Count Ladislas de Broel-Plater of Poland, in 1844.*

Famous for her talents in both comedy and tragedy, Karoline Bauer was a noted German actress. After an early retirement, she returned to the stage when her morganatic husband Prince Leopold of Coburg became King Leopold I of the Belgians in 1831. (A morganatic marriage is one between a man of the nobility and a woman of lower rank wherein the woman contractually agrees that she and her future children will relinquish rights to the rank and possessions of her husband.) In 1844, Bauer retired once again when she married a Polish count. In her *Posthumous Memoirs*, she tendered a stinging attack on Leopold and Baron Stockmar.

Bauer, Marion (1887–1955)

American composer, teacher, and co-founder of the American Music Guild. *Born Marion Eugenie in Walla Walla, Washington, on August 15, 1887; died in South Hadley, Massachusetts, on August 9, 1955.*

Marion Bauer studied in Portland, Oregon, before going to Berlin and Paris where she studied with ***Nadia Boulanger** as well as others. On returning from Europe, she taught at New York University, becoming an associate professor in 1930. In 1940, she was appointed to the faculty of the Juilliard School where she served until 1944. Bauer, an enthusiastic proponent of American music, had co-founded the American Music Guild in 1921. Throughout her career, she continued to compose, writing over 30 pieces, and her music remained impressionist, perhaps an influence of her studies in Paris. Bauer also wrote regularly for music journals, establishing herself as a writer in her field.

John Haag, Athens, Georgia

Bauer, Marlene (b. 1934).

See Hagge, Marlene Bauer.

Baugh, Laura (1955—)

American golfer, once the youngest U.S. Women's Amateur champion in history. *Born May 31, 1955, in Gainesville, Florida; married Bobby Cole (a PGA Tour professional golfer), in 1980 (divorced 1985; remarried 1988; separated); children: Chelsea (d. 1982); Eric James; Haley; Robby; Michael; Evita (b. April 1995); Jamie Lee.*

Became the youngest U.S. Women's Amateur golf champion in history (13 days younger than ***Beatrix Hoyt*** *when she won in 1896); winner of many tournaments who received numerous commercial endorsements.*

Coached by her father who had been a member of the University of Florida golf team, Laura Baugh began playing golf at age two. At seven, she won the so-called National Peewee championships, then went on to win the Juniors four times. When her parents divorced, she moved to California with her mother, where she continued to compete. Though young, Baugh had the power of an adult and could drive the ball straight down the fairway for 215 yards or more. Following her 1971 win of the U.S. Girls Amateur, the 16-year-old decided to try for the Women's Amateur as well. Despite hands that were cracked and bleeding, Baugh hit over 1,000 practice balls in her determination to win, and her efforts paid off in victory.

In 1973, in order to support herself, Baugh was forced to turn pro as soon as she reached the age requirement. In the first eight events, she won $19,656 and was named Rookie Golfer of the Year. Wilson golf equipment, Ford Motor cars, Suzuki motorcycles, Rolex watches, Colgate, and two golf resorts all paid Laura Baugh to advertise their products. Her many fans were called "Laura's Legions," and she became known as golf's Golden Girl.

But the Golden Girl spent years battling an addiction to alcohol as her marriage disintegrated. In 1996, drinking almost killed her; a maid found her unconscious in a hotel room in California. "They jump started my heart on the way to the hospital," said Baugh. Alcohol destroys platelets. Normally, platelet counts are in the 140–400 range. In May 1996, six weeks after her near-death experience in that hotel room, Baugh's platelet count went down to 40 within a few hours. "The doctor told me I could die. They gave me a couple of platelet transfusions, but they didn't take for four days. I bled from my eyes, my fingernails, my ears." Later that week, Baugh checked into the Betty Ford Center. "Alcoholism slapped me around like I was an infant. It was only when I could admit to not being in control that I could, with God's help, become strong enough to stay sober." In 1998, Baugh competed in 16 tournaments.

SOURCES:

Kornheiser, Tony. "Laura Baugh Attracts Attention, Not Victory," in *The New York Times Biographical Service.* August 1977, pp. 1052–1053.

Kulkin, Mary-Ellen. *Her Way: Biographies of Women for Young People.* Chicago: American Library Association, 1976.

"Last Call," in *People Weekly.* November 16, 1998.

Karin L. Haag, Athens, Georgia

Baum, Marianne (1912–1942)

German-Jewish anti-Nazi activist and leading member of the Herbert Baum resistance circle. *Born Marianne Cohn in Saarburg, Saar Province, on December 9, 1912; arrested on May 22, 1942; sentenced to death by a special Nazi tribunal on July 16, 1942, and executed at Berlin's Plötzensee prison on August 18, 1942; married Herbert Baum (1912–1942).*

Member of the German-Jewish youth organization, then joined the Communist Youth League of Germany (1931); along with husband Herbert Baum, helped organize anti-Nazi resistance cells that undertook many acts of defiance and sabotage against Nazi rule in Berlin (starting 1933); worked as a slave laborer (1940–42); involved in the fire-bombing of the Anti-Soviet Exhibition in Berlin (May 18, 1942).

Recent historical research into the Holocaust era has led to the discovery that many Jews resisted their Nazi and Fascist oppressors both before and during World War II. While the majority of Jews in Germany believed that efforts to overthrow the Hitler regime could not amount to much, a small but determined band of Jewish activists, mostly on the political Left, worked alongside their non-Jewish comrades to fight the Nazi dictatorship through illegal underground activities. Probably the best-organized and most effective of the Jewish resistance groups within Nazi Germany was the Berlin organization led by the Communist activist Herbert Baum. Herbert grew up in Berlin in a lower-middle-class Jewish family, and was active in Jewish youth groups and the *Rote Falken*, the youth organization of the Social Democratic Party. In one of the Jewish groups, the Deutsch-Jüdische Jugendgemeinschaft (German-Jewish Youth Community), he first met Marianne Cohn around 1928.

Born in Saarburg on December 9, 1912, when that city was part of Germany, Marianne grew up in Alsace in the years after that former German province had been returned to France in 1918. After her family moved to Berlin in the 1920s, she became actively involved in Jewish youth activities, moving toward the political Left along with her husband in the early 1930s.

The rapid growth of Nazi power in both the German parliament and the streets radicalized many young Germans. The often weak response of the Social Democrats to the threat of Hitlerism brought despair to Jews and others who had felt secure under a German democracy that was now crumbling. In the early 1930s, a small minority of Jewish activists like Herbert Baum and Marianne Cohn became convinced that the only alternative to Nazism was to be found on the extreme Left, in Communism. Lacking knowledge of events in the Soviet Union under the increasingly harsh dictatorship of Joseph

Stalin, many Germans became members of the Communist Party of Germany (KPD). Marianne Cohn moved in this direction in 1931 along with her future husband, when both became members of the Kommunistischer Jugendverband Deutschlands (KJVD), the Communist Youth League of Germany. In an organization that outlawed all manifestations of anti-Semitism, the emphasis was on preparation for the ideological and political struggles on the horizon.

By the time the Nazis came to power in the early months of 1933, Marianne and Herbert were Communist activists, engaging in such important tasks as distributing the KPD newspaper *Die Rote Fahne* (*The Red Flag*), which had been banned by the Nazis but soon appeared again throughout Germany as an illegal underground organ. By the time they were married, the Baums were seasoned in underground work. Starting in 1936–37, they began systematically building an illegal resistance organization. With a few exceptions, the members of their circle were young Jewish women and men who had been members of the Bund Deutsch-Jüdischer Jugend (Union of German-Jewish Youth), a strongly anti-Nazi Jewish youth group. United by the goal of opposing Fascism and by participating in the worldwide struggle against its spread, the Baum circle included Jews and non-Jews, Communists and non-Communists. Marianne Baum played a major role in the organization and was invariably present when members came to the Baum apartment on Berlin's Stralauer Strasse for secret strategy meetings. As a convinced Marxist revolutionary, she organized and taught revolutionary doctrine to the most youthful members of their group. In 1939, she strongly supported her husband when he made the perilous decision to establish ties between their organization and another Communist group in Berlin, the cells led by Robert Uhrig. Despite the immense risks their group took, for more than five years it continued to grow and engage in significant anti-Nazi activities. With about 35 members whose average age was 22, the Baum Group included members of the Jewish youth organizations that the Nazis had banned in 1938.

By 1940, both Herbert and Marianne Baum had been ordered to work at the Siemens Electrical Motor Factory, he as an electrician, she on the assembly line. Working under terrible conditions as slave laborers, both maintained their revolutionary fervor and infused their fellow workers with hope for the day when Germany and the world would be free of fascist terror and racism.

In late June 1941, Adolf Hitler launched a massive attack on the Soviet Union, aiming to conquer and enslave a great mass of Slavs who could then be mercilessly exploited. Other "subhuman" groups in the East were slated for "special treatment"—death through starvation in labor camps, extermination on the scene, or annihilation in special facilities like Treblinka and Auschwitz. Though Marianne and Herbert Baum received only fragmentary data on these developments, it was clear to them and other German Jews, who by the summer of 1941 were living the lives of slave laborers, that ominous developments were rapidly escalating. In her apartment, Marianne helped write and prepare for distribution the anti-Nazi flyer "An die deutsche Hausfrau" (To the German Housewife) which pointed out the increasing misery to which German families were subjected because of the war against the Soviet Union. To directly undermine the Nazi war effort, the Baum Group distributed *Der Ausweg* (*The Way Out*).

By mid-1941, the distribution of flyers and scratching of graffiti on walls were no longer felt to be a sufficiently militant response to Nazi oppression of Germany's remaining Jews. By early 1942, the underground cell organized by Herbert and Marianne Baum included as active members the Jewish couple Martin and **Sala Kochmann** (d. 1942). A number of non-Jewish women were also recruited for the dangerous underground work, including the office workers **Irene Walter** and **Suzanne Wesse**, who was of French background. They procured forged papers to assist members of the Baum organization to escape from Berlin to carry on their work elsewhere, probably in France. To pay for these activities, membership dues were first assessed. When this did not suffice, risky expropriations of the few well-to-do Jewish homes still remaining empty in Berlin were carried out in early May 1942. These "X" actions, as they were called, were undertaken by Herbert Baum, Heinz Birnbaum, and a non-Jewish member, Werner Steinbrink. The expropriated property, which included oil paintings, were sold and 1,500 Reichsmarks were gained for the group's treasury. The funds were used to pay for propaganda materials (paints, paper, etc.), the acquisition of forged Aryan documents, and the purchase of food.

The most daring, heroic and, as it turned out, tragic act of the Baum resistance circle was their attempt to destroy Propaganda Minister Joseph Goebbels' anti-Soviet propaganda display, sarcastically entitled "The Soviet Paradise," in Berlin's Lustgarten. Inaugurated by Goebbels himself with great pomp in early May

1942, the purpose of the anti-Communist exhibition was to stir up racist sentiments of the Berlin populace, raise their morale at a time when the war on the Eastern front had become bloody and indecisive, and depict the Soviet regime as a diabolical Judeo-Bolshevik plot against Western civilization. As both Jews and Marxists, Marianne, Herbert, and the members of their circle were deeply offended by an exhibition that painted the Soviet Union as a Jewish conspiracy against Western civilization.

After debating the wisdom of carrying out a destructive action against the Goebbels exhibit, all members of the Baum group agreed. Though all wished to participate directly, for security's sake only a small number would actually execute the plot. Initially scheduled for Sunday, May 17, the large number of visitors present that day brought about a postponement. The following evening, May 18, 1942, Herbert and Marianne Baum, Hans Joachim, Sala Kochmann. Gerd Meyer, Suzanne Wesse and Irene Walter went to the exhibit. With incendiary materials earlier procured by Werner Steinbrink, who worked in a chemical facility, flames engulfed the exhibit, and the group escaped without mishap. Unfortunately, the fire brigade arrived quickly and only part of the exhibit was destroyed. Under Goebbels' thumb, the Nazi press did not report the damage, but Berliners circulated the fact that "The Soviet Paradise" exhibition had suffered considerably at the hands of unknown saboteurs.

Elated, Marianne Baum and the other members of the Baum group began discussing their next anti-Nazi action. Their hopes were crushed with the arrest of Marianne and Herbert and three others on May 22. In the next few days, virtually all members of the group were arrested by the Gestapo. After the war, several authors argued that the Baum circle had been infiltrated by a Gestapo agent. This may well have been the case, but it is also important to note that the youthful, and often recklessly enthusiastic, members of this circle did not observe strict rules of conspiracy and sometimes made unguarded anti-Nazi statements in public. After the initial arrests of the group in May 1942, a few remaining members were able to elude the Gestapo for varying periods of time. Eventually, all but a handful were caught. Two active members of the group, Richard and **Charlotte Holtzer**, were never captured and survived the war hiding in Hungary.

In their fashion, the Nazi interrogators attempted to discover all they could about the Baum group. Beaten to a pulp, Herbert Baum was taken to the Siemens plant, where he worked, and asked to identify his accomplices. He never betrayed any of them. On June 11, 1942, the Gestapo informed the prosecutor's office that on that day Herbert Baum had "committed suicide." Though documentation is lacking, witnesses claimed that Baum died as a result of the horrible tortures to which he was subjected. The system of National Socialist "justice" dispatched the other men and women of the Baum circle by execution or eventual death in Nazi camps.

Marianne Baum was sentenced to death by a special Nazi tribunal on July 16, 1942, and executed at Berlin's Plötzensee prison on August 18, 1942. The other women members of the Baum group who died at the hands of the Nazis were Sala Kochmann, **Hanni Meyer** (died 1943), Suzanne Wesse, Irene Walter, **Hella Hirsch**, **Alice Hirsch**, **Edith Fraenkel** (died 1943 in Auschwitz), **Hilde Jadamowitz** (1916–1942), **Marianne Joachim** (1921–1943), **Lotte Rotholz** (1923–c. 1943) and **Hilde Löwy**. Members of the Baum group died believing that the evil of Nazism could, and would, be wiped from the face of the earth, to be replaced by a new world based on human decency and a common morality. That such a world has not emerged does not diminish the value of their belief, or sacrifice.

SOURCES:

Elling, Hanna. *Frauen im deutschen Widerstand 1933–45*. 3rd rev. ed. Frankfurt am Main: Röderberg-Verlag, 1981.

Erpel, Simone. "Struggle and Survival: Jewish Women in the Anti-Fascist Resistance in Germany," in *Leo Baeck Institute, Year Book XXXVIII*. London: Secker & Warburg, 1992, pp. 397–414.

Eschwege, Helmut. "Resistance of German Jews Against the Nazi Regime," in *Leo Baeck Institute, Year Book XV*. London: Secker & Warburg, 1970, pp. 143–180.

Juden im Widerstand. Chug Chaluzi—Gemeinschaft für Frieden und Aufbau—Gruppe Herbert Baum: Drei Gruppen zwischen Überlebenskampf und politischer Aktion, Berlin 1939–1945. Berlin: Informationsstelle "Jugend unterm Hakenkreuz" e.V., 1993.

Kraushaar, Luise. *Berliner Kommunisten im Kampf gegen den Faschismus 1936 bis 1942: Robert Uhrig und Genossen*. Berlin: Dietz Verlag, 1981.

———. *Deutsche Widerstandskämpfer 1933–1945: Biographien und Briefe*. 2 vols. Berlin: Dietz Verlag, 1970.

Kwiet, Konrad, and Helmut Eschwege. *Selbstbehauptung und Widerstand 1933–1945: Deutsche Juden im Kampf um Existenz und Menschenwürde*. Hamburg: Hans Christians Verlag, 1984.

Löhken, Wilfried, and Werner Vathke, eds. *Juden im Widerstand: Drei Gruppen zwischen Überlebenskampf und politischer Aktion Berlin 1939–1945: Sonderausgabe für die Ausstellung*. Berlin: Edition Hentrich, 1993.

Marrus, Michael R. "Jewish Resistance to the Holocaust," in *Journal of Contemporary History.* Vol. 30, no. 1. January 1995, pp. 83–110.

Pikarski, Margot. *Sie bleiben unvergessen: Widerstandsgruppe Herbert Baum. Herausgegeben vom Zentralrat der FDJ.* Berlin: Verlag Junge Welt, 1968.

Schilde, Kurt. "Herbert-Baum-Gruppe," in Wolfgang Benz and Walter H. Pehle, eds., *Lexikon des deutschen Widerstandes.* 2nd rev. ed. Frankfurt am Main: S. Fischer Verlag GmbH, 1994, pp. 225–227.

Steinbach, Peter, and Johannes Tuchel, ed. *Lexikon des Widerstandes 1933–1945.* Munich: Verlag C.H. Beck, 1994.

Suhl, Yuri, ed. *They Fought Back: The Story of the Jewish Resistance in Nazi Europe.* NY: Crown, 1967.

RELATED MEDIA:

Flammen, GDR motion picture, 1967, directed by Konrad Weiss.

John Haag, Associate Professor,
University of Georgia, Athens, Georgia

Baum, Marie (1874–1964)

German-Jewish pioneer of social-work theory and practice, and one of the first German women to receive a doctoral degree in social work. *Born in Germany on March 23, 1874; died in Heidelberg, Germany, on August 8, 1964.*

A descendent of Felix Mendelssohn through her mother's family, Marie Baum was born into an assimilated German-Jewish family on March 23, 1874. A lifelong Lutheran, she thought of herself as a loyal German and dedicated her life to the cause of social reform among her country's poor and neglected. With an acute political sense as well as a strong social conscience, Baum entered politics when the regime of Imperial Germany collapsed in November 1918. Elected as a Reichstag deputy on the German Democratic party ticket in 1919, she represented Schleswig-Holstein and Lübeck from January 1919 through February 1921, when a less liberal spirit swept through her middle-class constituency.

Marie Baum believed that social reforms could significantly improve the lives of millions of poor people in Germany, particularly women and children who suffered most from the catastrophes of war, moral collapse, unemployment and inflation. An innovative thinker in the field of social work, she combined theory with practice, beginning with a job as a factory inspector in 1902. By the 1920s, she had achieved a national reputation in her field, and in 1928 was appointed to a lectureship at the University of Heidelberg. The Nazi takeover of January-March 1933 resulted in the anti-Semitic "Law for the Restoration of the Professional Civil Service" of April 1933 which cost Baum her Heidelberg teaching position on July 28 of that year. Although she was interrogated by the Gestapo, who also maintained surveillance over her daily doings, she refused to be cowed by these measures, spending much of her time instead assisting those individuals who were persecuted by the regime for racial or political reasons. On trips to Great Britain and Switzerland in the late 1930s, she read avidly in the uncensored press about Nazi atrocities she had heard about in Germany only as rumors. In July 1939, she published for her closest friends a private printing of her autobiography, *Rückblick auf mein Leben (Looking Back at My Life).* Refusing to leave Germany despite the clear danger presented by her Jewish ancestry, she was one of a handful of Germans of Jewish origin to survive the war without deportation to a concentration or extermination camp. A November 1941 police search of her home cost her part of her library and her correspondence and research files, but it did not break her spirit. After surviving the Holocaust, Marie Baum lived almost two decades following the defeat of the Third Reich and enjoyed the resumption of her teaching duties at the University of Heidelberg in 1947. In 1950, she saw the publication of her autobiography in a commercial edition. Baum reached her elder years amidst an admiring circle of colleagues, students and friends. She died in Heidelberg on August 8, 1964.

SOURCES:

Otto, Hans-Uwe, and Heinz Sünker, eds. *Soziale Arbeit und Faschismus.* Frankfurt am Main: Suhrkamp Verlag, 1989.

Schumacher, Martin ed. *M.d.R. Die Reichstagsabgeordneten der Weimarer Republik in der Zeit des Nationalsozialismus: Politische Verfolgung, Emigration und Ausbürgerung 1933–1945.* Düsseldorf: Droste Verlag, 1991.

Walk, Joseph. *Kurzbiographien zur Geschichte der Juden 1918–1945.* Munich: K.G. Saur, 1988.

John Haag, Athens, Georgia

Baum, Vicki (1888–1960)

***German-born writer, who was known particularly for her novel* Grand Hotel.** *Born Victoria Baum on January 24, 1888, in Vienna, Austria; died in Hollywood, California, on August 29, 1960; daughter of Mathilde Donat and Hermann Baum; married Max Prels, in 1906 (divorced, c. 1912); married Richard Lert (a conductor), July 17, 1916; children: (second marriage) two sons, Wolfgang and Peter.*

After publishing numerous short stories, wrote Der Weg *(*The Way, *1925); signed a contract with Ullstein Publishers and began writing for the mass market (1926); published novel* stud. chem. Helene

Willfüer *(*Chemistry Student Helene Willfüer*) to great success (1928); published most famous book* Menschen im Hotel *(*Grand Hotel, *1930); fled to U.S. with family because of growing anti-Semitism in Nazi Germany (1931); published* Liebe und Tod auf Bali *(*Tale of Bali, *1937); published* Hotel Shanghai *(1939); switched to writing exclusively in English (1940) and wrote novel* The Ship and the Shore *(1941); published* Marion Alive *(1942); published* The Weeping Wood *about a Brazilian rubber plantation (1943), followed by* Hotel Berlin '43 *(1944),* Mortgage on Life *(1946), and* Headless Angel *(1948); attempted to write more complex plots, producing* The Mustard Seed *(1953), followed by* Written on Water *(1956), and* Theme for Ballet *(1958), her last novel.*

Selected writings: Frühe Schatten: Das Ende einer Kindheit *(Berlin: Reiss, 1914);* Der Eingang zur Bühne *(Berlin: Ullstein, 1920, published in English as* Once in Vienna, *London: Bles, 1943);* Schlosstheater *(Berlin: Deutsche Verlags-Anstalt, 1921);* Die Tänze der Ina Raffay: Ein Leben *(Berlin: Ullstein, 1921);* Die andern Tage *(Stuttgart: Deutsche Verlags-Anstalt, 1922);* Bubenreise: Eine Erzählung für junge Menschen *(Berlin: Ullstein, 1923);* Die Welt ohne Sünde: Roman einer Minute *(Stuttgart: Deutsche Verlags-Anstalt, 1923);* Ulle, der Zwerg *(Stuttgart: Deutsche Verlags-Anstalt, 1923);* Der Weg *(Berlin: Deutsche Verlags-Anstalt, 1925);* Miniaturen *(Berlin: Weltgeist-Bücher, 1926);* Tanzpause *(Stuttgart: Fleischhauer & Spohn, 1926);* Feme: Bussfahrt einer verirrten Jugend *(Berlin: Ullstein, 1927, published in America as* Secret Sentence, *Garden City, NY: Doubleday, Doran, 1932);* Hell in Frauensee *(Berlin: Ullstein, 1927, published in English as* Martin's Summer, *NY: Cosmopolitan, 1931);* stud. chem. Helene Willfüer *(Berlin: Ullstein, 1928, published in English as* Helene, *London: Bles, 1932);* Halloh, wer fängt Flip und Flap? Oder *(Berlin: Arcadia, 1929);* Menschen im Hotel: Ein Kolportageroman mit Hintergründen *(Berlin: Ullstein, 1929, published in English as* Grand Hotel, *London: Bles, 1930; NY: Doubleday, 1931);* Zwischenfall in Lohwinckel *(Berlin: Ullstein, 1930, published in London as* Results of an Accident, *Bles, 1930, and in America as* And Life Goes On, *NY: Doubleday, 1931);* Pariser Platz 13 *(Vienna & Berlin: Marton, 1930);* Das Leben ohne Geheimnis *(Berlin: Ullstein, 1932, published in English as* Falling Star, *London: Bles, 1934);* Das grosse Einmaleins *(Amsterdam: Querido, 1935, published in America as* Men Never Know, *NY: Doubleday, 1935, and in Germany as* Rendez-vous in Paris, *Cologne: Kiepenheuer & Witsch, 1951);* Die Karriere der Doris Hart *(Amsterdam: Querido, 1936, published in English as* Sing, Sister, Sing, *London: Bles, 1936);* Liebe und Tod auf Bali *(Amsterdam: Querido, 1937, nonfiction published in English as* Tale of Bali, *London: Bles, 1937);* Der grosse Ausverkauf *(Amsterdam: Querido, 1937, published in London as* Central Stories, *Bles, 1940);* Hotel Shanghai *(Amsterdam: Querido, 1939, published in America as* Shanghai '37, *NY: Doubleday, 1939, and in London as* Nanking Road, *Bles, 1939);* Die grosse Pause *(Stockholm: Bermann-Fischer, 1941, published in London as* Grand Opera, *Bles, 1940);* The Christmas Carp *(NY: Doubleday, 1941);* The Ship and the Shore *(NY: Doubleday, 1941);* Marion Alive *(NY: Doubleday, 1942);* The Weeping Wood *(NY: Doubleday, 1943);* Hotel Berlin '43 *(NY: Doubleday, 1945);* Mortgage on Life *(NY: Doubleday, 1946);* Headless Angel *(Doubleday, 1948);* Danger from Deer *(Doubleday, 1951);* The Mustard Seed *(Doubleday, 1951);* Written on Water *(Doubleday, 1956);* Theme for Ballet *(Doubleday, 1958);* It Was All Quite Different: The Memoirs of Vicki Baum *(NY: Funk & Wagnalls, 1964).*

Vicki Baum, the author of *Grand Hotel*, was a popular writer by design. Her works were carefully crafted for the mass audience, first in Germany, then America. Her career is all the more remarkable because she was a bestselling

Vicki Baum

author in German before writing in English. When Baum began writing in the 1920s, mass distribution, intense advertising, and promotional campaigns were in their infancy. But she quickly adapted to these techniques, opening new opportunities for those who followed.

Vicki Baum was born into a middle-class, assimilated Jewish Viennese family on January 24, 1888. Her childhood was difficult. Her father Hermann was a tyrannical figure, while her mother Mathilde suffered from manic depression and was eventually institutionalized. Mathilde had some influence on her daughter, however, insisting that she plan for a career at an early age, an unusual notion for the late 19th-century. At age eight, Vicki began studying the harp, attending the Vienna Conservatory from 1904 until 1910. Musically talented, she performed with leading Viennese orchestras as a teenager. Fascinated by words as well as musical expression throughout her childhood and adolescence, Baum wrote short stories, a passion which eventually dominated her life.

> I thought, lived, talked, felt the same as most people did. . . . I had shared their experiences, and their memories were mine, too. . . . For once they found in my books what even the most choosy reader likes best, whether he knows it or not: self-identification.
>
> **—Vicki Baum**

In 1906, 18-year-old Baum married Max Prels, possibly in an attempt to escape her father. For the duration of this brief first marriage, she wrote several short stories, put her husband's name on them, and sold them to a German magazine. Divorcing Prels, Baum left Vienna in 1912 to take a position in Germany with the Darmstadt municipal orchestra where she also taught at the musical conservatory. Two years later, her first novel appeared, *Frühe Schatten* (*Early Shadows*), but it had little impact on readers. While in Darmstadt, she fell in love with Richard Lert, who conducted the symphony orchestra. Married on July 17, 1916, the newlyweds soon moved to Kiel where Lert had obtained another position. Two sons, Wolfgang and Peter, were born soon after. Since Lert's earning ability was precarious at best, Baum decided to contribute to the family finances by writing.

Baum longed to be appreciated as a serious writer. From 1923 to 1925, she worked diligently, perfecting her craft, then entered and won a literary contest judged by Thomas Mann. When it did not bring the critical attention she craved, Baum sought commercial success. In 1926, she accepted a fulltime position with Ullstein, joining the publisher's literary factory. Ullstein's was one of the first publishers to develop what has become the norm in book marketing. Books were created for mass consumption, widely advertised, and sold to a broad audience. Ullstein did not wait for critics to sell their books; instead, the publisher created a climate which sold its products. The turning point in Baum's career came with the serialization of *stud. chem. Helene Willfüer* (*Chemistry Student Helene Willfüer*) which appeared in 1928 in Ullstein's weekly magazine.

In *stud. chem. Helene Willfüer*, Baum portrays a woman who not only seeks personal happiness but a career in a male-dominated field, a subject fairly new to readers. By the 1920s, women's role had undergone major changes. During World War I, many women worked in factories, assuming male jobs to help the war effort. Corsets, long skirts, and petticoats had been exchanged for loose tunics, short skirts, and pants. Society idolized sports heroines while women aviators dominated the media as well. An increasing number of women attended universities, and they demanded new opportunities.

In the novel, Helene Willfüer is a chemistry student who falls in love and becomes pregnant. At first, she decides to have an abortion, but her plan is thwarted when a police raid closes the "clinic." Desperate, Helene puts her fate in the hands of the baby's father Rainer, who feels a double suicide is the best way to end the shame brought on by the pregnancy. He kills himself, but Helene does not. Determined to triumph over social pressure, she finishes her doctorate, bears a son, and achieves professional success. But Helene feels her life is empty and eventually marries and abandons her career. Though the book's ending was traditional, Baum's novel was revolutionary. Issues like abortion, single parenthood, suicide, and women's careers were rarely dealt with, especially in the popular press. It was a huge success.

In 1930, Vicki Baum's book *Menschen im Hotel* (*Grand Hotel*) was published. A huge advertising campaign preceded the novel's release and a serialized version of *Grand Hotel* ran in the *Berliner Illustrirte*. Baum produced a stage version of the book which premiered in Berlin in January 1930 and eventually played throughout the world, including a 444-night run on Broadway with ***Eugenie Leontovitch** (***Greta Garbo** would replace Leontovitch part in the film version). Writes **Lynda J. King:**

> With *Menschen im Hotel* Baum was responsible for a new sub-genre of the novel; the hotel novel, in which the hotel functions as a central location where unrelated individuals of all classes and social groups come together and interact. At the end, they go their separate ways, and new guests arrive. As clichéd as this formula seems today after countless imitations in novels and films, Baum's version was fresh and new in 1929. . . . Baum's Grand Hotel represents modern society in which isolated and alienated individuals come together, interact, and part again without changing or affecting the social structure itself. The characters have little control over the events which take place in the hotel and which affect their lives. . . . Baum did not intend to provide readers with solutions or models for changing the social ills she depicted in *Menschen im Hotel*. Instead she combined melodrama, sensationalism, and an undercurrent of pessimism with a sophisticated style built on fast action, shifting perspectives, and visual imagery to create a complex literary product.

With the publication of *Grand Hotel*, Vicki Baum was no longer a minor author. Her newly won fame was not without consequences, however; critics refused to accept her as a serious writer, and many attacked her portrayal of Helene Willfüer. Increasingly, Baum felt threatened. Since she was Jewish, the growth of Nazi power made her highly vulnerable. Her depictions of German women did not coincide with Hitler's notion of a Germany where women cooked and cleaned, attended church, and bore Aryan children. In 1932, she decided to immigrate to the United States.

Baum was familiar with America. In April 1931, she had participated in Doubleday's massive promotional campaign for *Grand Hotel* and had also negotiated contracts for future novels and screenplays. Though initially settled in New York, Baum felt opportunities for future screenplays were to be found on the West Coast, so the family moved to Hollywood, where she signed a longterm contract with MGM. She would also work for Paramount, Republic, Universal, RKO, 20th Century-Fox, and Warner Bros. Although most writers find it impossible to establish themselves in a foreign country, Baum flourished in America. Along with Garbo, ***Joan Crawford,** Wallace Beery, and John and Lionel Barrymore had starred in the 1932 film version of *Grand Hotel*, an MGM blockbuster that had won an Academy Award for Best Picture of the Year and had inaugurated the genre of multistar films; thus, Baum started her screenwriting career with impressive credentials. (The movie was remade as *Weekend at the Waldorf* in 1945, starring ***Ginger Rogers**, ***Lana Turner**, and Walter Pidgeon. In 1959, A West German production using the original title *Menschen im Hotel*, starred ***Michele Morgan, Sonja Ziemann,** and O.W. Fischer.)

When her novel, *Tale of Bali* (*Liebe und Tod auf Bali*), was published in 1937, Baum went on tour to promote it, as well as her other works. An entertaining speaker, she was soon a hit on the ladies' luncheon circuit. In consequence, sales of her books soared. Kenneth McCormick, her editor at Doubleday, recalled one day in the life of a touring author:

> She was a wow. She was selling *Grand Hotel*. . . . By this time she was a roaring hit. I remember when she got to Minneapolis. She'd begun to get bored with the routine and overenthusiastic ladies and chicken and peas and the speech she gave and everything. But she was a good sport, and she did it. Afterward the ladies came crowding up and said, "You're so wonderful!" Finally there was a little lady standing there who said, "Miss Baum, my son writes stories." Vicki said, "Oh, isn't that nice." Then she thought, "Maybe I'd better find out who . . ." and she said, "What is your name?" The lady said, "My name is Hemingway." Vicki said, "Are you *Ernest* Hemingway's mother?" . . . Mrs. Hemingway turned to the women and said, "You see, Miss Baum has heard of my son."

For several years, Baum continued to write in German, though her works were translated into English as well as several other languages. When the Nazis banned her books in Germany, she ceased writing in her native tongue. By the early 1940s, all her works appeared in English. Wrote McCormick: "She overcame some terrible handicaps—the war, being Jewish and being in Germany, and being a mother with two small children." Baum became fluent enough in English to write *The Ship and the Shore* in 1941. When translations of her earlier books like *stud. chem. Helene Willfüer* did not sell well in America, she switched to her successful *Grand Hotel* plot: *Hotel Shanghai* (1939), *Marion Alive* (1942) and *Hotel Berlin '43* (1944) all used the literary device she had created. But she tired of the genre, so, in 1943, she wrote a different kind of novel. *The Weeping Wood*, a story about rubber plantations in Brazil, resulted and received generally good reviews.

Vicki Baum's books provided a substantial income, allowing the family to settle comfortably in California. Her husband Richard Lert became conductor of the Pasadena Symphony, a position he held for many years. Sons Wolfgang

From the movie Grand Hotel, *based on the novel by Vicki Baum.*

and Peter quickly adjusted to the West Coast way of life. Jeanette Lowe described the household: "It . . . [is] a menage which runs like clockwork, meals for the week planned Saturday morning, and served on the dot; a time for swimming, practicing, writing, and studying." After several years of moving from apartment to apartment and house to house, the couple built a contemporary home high on a hillside. A library filled with books, a terrace overlooking the hillside, and the grand piano in the living room blended the old world with the new. Their home was a refuge for family and friends, a place where Viennese pastries and California wine were often served to guests on the terrace. As increasing numbers of impoverished Central European refugees arrived in California, Baum was generous with her financial and moral support.

With the passage of time, Vicki Baum grew increasingly tired of being, as she noted, "the woman who wrote *Grand Hotel*." She felt intense advertising and promotional campaigns degraded her work. She decided to write a work of "good literature" and possibly publish it under a pseudonym so as to escape the straight jacket in which she had been placed. In 1953, *The Mustard Seed* appeared. It is the story of a faith healer named Giano Benedetto who has come to Los Angeles from a remote mountain region in Italy. Benedetto attempts to rehabilitate his brother who suffers from mental problems. A simple man, Benedetto becomes an overnight sensation in California and soon is giving advice to people overwhelmed by modern life. Unwittingly, Benedetto becomes involved in a murder, though eventually his innocence is proven. Impotence, anxiety, homosexuality, drug addiction, and alcoholism are only a few of the topics Baum took on in the novel. Some have noted that "Giano and Vicki Baum seem to long for escape," perhaps a commentary on Baum's growing disgust with commercial writing. *Written on Water* (1956), *Theme for Ballet* (1958), and *It Was All Quite Different: The Memoirs of Vicki Baum* (1964) were her final works. None of them followed the formulas which had made her such a popular writer.

Continuing a process which began with the invention of the printing press, writing has increasingly reflected mass culture. The debate continues whether literature can reflect popular taste. Yet the public is interested in reading novels which deal with the questions of everyday life in a modern technological society. Baum sensed this, and she successfully wrote about women's liberation, abortion, drug use, and isolation in terms millions could understand. But she was torn between being a "literary writer" and a "people's writer," a dilemma she never resolved. Vicki Baum described herself as "a first-rate second-rate author."

SOURCES:

Atkinson, J. Brooks. "The Play: Grand Hotel," in *The New York Times*. November 14, 1930.

Baum, Vicki. "I Discover America," in *Good Housekeeping*. Vol. 94, no. 7. July 1932, pp. 30–31, 196–199.

Bell, Robert F. "Depicting the Host Country: Vicki Baum's *The Mustard Seed*," in *Kulturelle Wechselbeziehungen im Exil—Exile Across Cultures*. Edited by Helmut F. Pfanner. Bonn: Bouvier Verlag Herbert Grundmann, 1986, pp. 139–150.

Heilbut, Anthony. *Exiled in Paradise: German Refugee Artists and Intellectuals in America from the 1930s to the Present*. Boston: Beacon Press, 1983.

King, Lynda J. *Best-Sellers By Design: Vicki Baum and the House of Ullstein*. Detroit: Wayne State University Press, 1988.

———. "The Image of Fame: Vicki Baum in Weimar Germany," in *The German Quarterly*. Vol 58, no. 3. Summer 1985, pp. 375–393.

———. "The Woman Question and Politics in Austrian Interwar Literature," in *German Studies Review*. Vol. vi, no. 1. February 1983, pp. 75–100.

Lowe, Jeanette. "Translation from the German," in *Arts and Decoration*. Vol. 41, no. 5, September 1934, pp. 27–29.

"Miss Vicki Baum, Author of 'Grand Hotel,'" in *The Times* [London]. August 31, 1960, p. 12.

Riess, Curt. *Das war ein Leben!* Munich and Vienna: Langen Müller, 1988.

Spalek, John M., Joseph Strelka, and Sandra H. Hawrylchak. *Deutsche Exilliteratur Seit 1933. 1 Kalifornien*. Munich: Francke Verlag, 1976.

"Villain Rubber," in *The Commonweal*. Vol. 39, no. 9. December 17, 1943, pp. 233–234.

Walter, Hans-Albert. *Deutsche Exilliteratur 1933–1950. Internierung, Flucht und Lebensbedingungen im Zweiten Weltkrieg*. Stuttgart: J.B. Metzlersche Verlagsbuchhandlung, 1988.

Wolf, Ralph F. "The Hand of Esso," in *The New Republic*. Vol. 110, no. 6. February 7, 1944, p. 188.

Ziegfield, Richard. "Baum, Vicki," in *Contemporary Authors*. Vol. 93–96. Detroit, MI: Gale Research, pp. 38–41.

Karin Loewen Haag,
freelance writer, Athens, Georgia

Baumann, Edith (1909–1973)

German political activist and one of relatively few women among the political leadership of the German Democratic Republic. *Name variations: Edith Honecker. Born August 1, 1909, in Berlin, Germany; died on April 7, 1973; daughter of a bricklayer; received secondary education; became first wife of Erich Honecker, 1947; children: one daughter,* ***Erika Honecker*** *(a lawyer).*

Worked as an activist in Social Democratic youth movement (1925–31); worked for Socialist Workers Party (1931–33); arrested and sentenced to three years' imprisonment (1933); joined Social Democratic Party (1945) and the Socialist Unity Party (1946); served as professional youth movement administrator and deputy chair of Free German Youth (1946–49); member of Central Committee of Socialist Unity Party (1946–73).

Edith Baumann was one of the few women to reach a high position in the political life of the German Democratic Republic (GDR). Her social origins, which were purely working class, gave her superb credentials for her later career in what was declared "the first workers' and peasants' state in German history."

She was born in Berlin on August 1, 1909. Baumann's parents experienced the poverty and insecurity of working-class life in the years after World War I and the Great Depression that began in 1929. Despite her intelligence, Baumann was prevented by poverty from attending a university; instead, she had to take a low-paying job as a typist. In her teens and early 20s, she was active in the Social Democratic youth movement. During the depth of the depression—when Nazi stormtroopers ruled the streets of virtually all German cities—she joined the numerically small, but ideologically vigorous, Socialist Workers Party, which promised to fight Fascism more effectively than the bureaucratically paralyzed Social Democrats or the Stalinized Communists.

The imposition of Adolf Hitler's Third Reich in 1933 led to the rapid collapse of the organized German working class. Even militant and idealistic groups like the Socialist Workers Party, of which Baumann was a member, were no match for the brutal terror tactics of Nazi brownshirts, or the more systematic regime of terror that followed, led by the SS and implemented through the horrors of concentration camps. Baumann's unit was destroyed, and she was sentenced to three years' imprisonment, serving until her release in 1936. For the rest of the Nazi era, she remained politically quiescent, although her Marxist sympathies were never crushed. As the defeat of Nazi Germany in 1945 brought about a revival of political life, convinced anti-Fascists like Baumann strode into the immense vacuum left by the end of Fascism. At first, she joined the revived Social Democratic Party, seeking the militancy that was lacking in the last years of German democracy in the early 1930s. In 1946, convinced that only the unity of the working class would bring about socialism in Germany, she accepted the Soviet-dictated merger of Communist and Social Democratic Parties into a Socialist Unity Party of Germany.

In the years after 1946, Baumann emerged as one of the few women to occupy a significant political post in the Soviet Occupation Zone of Germany. From 1946 until her death, she held high positions with the Freie Deutsche Jugend (FDJ; "Free German Youth"), the state-controlled youth organization of the GDR. Energetic and politically reliable, she rose to the position of deputy chair of the FDJ. While working for the FDJ, she met Erich Honecker, an ambitious administrator with a spotless record as an anti-Fascist who had spent ten years in a Nazi prison. Honecker was Baumann's superior in the FDJ, which led to personal intimacy as well as political compatibility. They were married in 1947, but the marriage soon crumbled when he began an affair with **Margot Feist**. Edith and Erich Honecker had one child, a daughter Erika, who became a lawyer.

By 1953, Baumann's marriage had ended, her energies were again concentrated almost exclusively on politics, and she had advanced to various posts in the Central Committee of the Socialist Unity Party. She also served uninterruptedly from 1949 to her death as a delegate to the Volkskammer ("People's Chamber"), the legislature of the GDR. She represented women's interests in the Socialist Unity Party (SED) Central Committee for a number of years and held high posts in the municipal administration of East Berlin for the last two decades of her life. Edith Baumann died on April 7, 1973.

SOURCES:

Drechsler, Hanno. *Die Sozialistische Arbeiterpartei Deutschlands (SAPD):* Ein *Beitrag zur Geschichte der deutschen Arbeiterbewegung am Ende der Weimarer Republik*. Hanover: SOAK-Verlag, 1983.

Gast, Gabriele. *Die politische Rolle der Frau in der DDR.* Düsseldorf: Bertelsmann Universitätsverlag, 1973.

Herbst, Andreas, Winfried Ranke and Jürgen Winkler. *So funktionierte die DDR.* 3 vols. Reinbek bei Hamburg: Rowohlt Taschenbuch Verlag GmbH, 1994.

Honecker, Erich. *From My Life.* Oxford: Pergamon Press, 1981.

Wyden, Peter. *Wall: The Inside Story of Divided Berlin.* NY: Simon and Schuster, 1989.

John Haag, Associate Professor,
University of Georgia, Athens, Georgia

Bäumer, Gertrud (1873–1954)

German feminist, politician, and writer whose views on marriage and motherhood contributed to the rightward direction of German feminism in the years from 1910 through the 1930s. *Name variations: Baumer. Pronunciation: BOY-mer. Born September 12, 1873, in Hohenlimburg in the German state of Westphalia; died on March 24, 1954, in Bethel, Germany; daughter of a teacher-theologian; attended University of Berlin, receiving a Ph.D., 1904; lived with Helen Lange.*

Taught schools in Magdeburg and other German cities (1892–97); went to Berlin to study at the University of Berlin (1898); became full-time secretary to Helene Lange (1899); elected to the steering committee for the League of German Women's Associations (1900); became an editor for the journal Die Hilfe *(1912); served as president of the League of German*

Women's Associations (1910–19); served in the National Women's Service (1915–18); served as member of the National Assembly of Germany (1919) and member of the German Reichstag (1919–33); worked as a high official in the German Ministry of the Interior (1920–33); edited the journal Die Frau *(1921–44); deprived of Reichstag and Ministry of Interior positions by new Nazi government (1933).*

Selected works: Die Frau im neueren Lebensraum *(Berlin: F. A. Herbig, 1931);* Die Frau in Volkswirtschaft und Staatsleben der Gegenwart *(Stuttgart: Deutsche Verlags-Anstalt, 1914); (with Helene Lange),* Handbuch der Friedensbewegung *(Berlin: W. Moeser, 1901–06);* Lebensweg durch eine Zeitenwende *(Tübingen: Wunderlich Verlag, 1933).*

Faced with an authoritarian state and a militaristic, male-dominated society, German feminists of the late 19th and early 20th centuries tended to ally themselves with the political Left in their country. Such was the case with ***Lily Braun**, whose political allegiance lay with the Marxist Social Democratic party, and ***Anita Augspurg** and ***Lida Heymann**, who combined feminism with pacifism. The most notable exception to this trend was Gertrud Bäumer, the most politically active of all the leaders of the German women's movement, who declared that the natural and honorable role for women in German society was as housewives and mothers. Under her leadership and guidance, the main women's organization in Germany, the League of German Women's Associations, moved steadily rightward during the years leading up to the National Socialist (Nazi) accession to power in that country.

Trained as a schoolteacher, Bäumer grew up in a family which had strong ties to the German Evangelical church. Her father was a teacher and a theologian. The family was sympathetic with the "Christian Socialism" of the minister and politician Adolf Stoecker, who hoped to woo the German workers away from allegiance to the Marxist Party in Germany and make them into strong supporters of the German monarchy. In her memoirs, Bäumer remembered her father fondly, praising his "feisty intellectual energy and realistic, but joyful, view of life." His death in 1883, before she reached her teenage years, was a personal blow to her and a financial blow to the family; after that, they lived in the house of her mother's parents.

While serving as an elementary and high school teacher for six years, Bäumer became interested in politics through her work as a member of the executive committee of the General German Women Teachers' Association. Her curiosity about politics was further piqued when she moved to Berlin in 1898 to study at the University of Berlin. There she renewed an acquaintance with ***Helene Lange** (the two had met the year before), a feminist who had campaigned for the admission of women into German universities. In 1899, Bäumer became Lange's private secretary. The two remained close throughout their lives.

In 1910, only six years after she became one of the first women in Germany to earn a Ph.D., Bäumer gained national prominence when she was elected president of the League of German Women's Associations. Her election was the result of maneuvers by Lange, who had worked to oust the existing president, **Marie Stritt**, because she regarded Stritt as being too radical. Bäumer would serve as president for nine years, although she would exert a major influence on the organization for more than 20 years through her editorship of *Die Frau*, a journal founded by Lange.

> I firmly opposed doctrinaire ideas which tried to force masculine types of freedom onto women and tried to force women to live as men do.
>
> —Gertrud Bäumer

Only 36 years old when she was elected, Bäumer represented a conservative trend in German feminism. Her intellectual mentor was Friedrich Naumann, a political writer who was influential in the rightward drift of German liberalism before World War I. As an editor, beginning in 1912, of Naumann's journal *Die Hilfe*, she argued not only that the women's movement should support the aims of the German nation, particularly its aggressive foreign policy, but that it should also work to minimize social and class conflict.

Before Bäumer became president of the League of German Women's Associations, earlier leaders of the organization had adopted a platform which promised a campaign against the section of the German Civil Code which banned abortion. Bäumer pledged to ignore such provisions in the League's platform, and she encouraged others to do the same. Not only was the foetus a living creature, she wrote, but attempts to legalize abortion would destroy the "mother instinct" of German women. Legalizing abortion, she declared, would contribute to the physical and moral degeneration of the German people, culminating in efforts to glorify the "free sex life."

Bäumer encouraged religiously oriented women's groups, such as Evangelical women's organizations, to join the League. She insisted that they did not have to subscribe to all League programs. It has been argued that her encouragement of the Evangelical movement was a calculated step to counterbalance the influence of more "radical" feminists such as ***Helene Stoecker**, whose New Morality sought for women the same sexual freedom accorded to men.

Bäumer did insist that all publications of Stoecker's League of Motherhood Protection and Sexual Reform be banned from League meetings. Yet Bäumer's religious faith—grounded in her belief that she was a pilgrim attempting to understand the mysteries of God—was integral to her feminism. Of the more than 20 books she wrote—including medieval histories and studies of poets such as R.M. Rilke, Dante, and Goethe—many were religious in nature.

Bäumer criticized other German women leaders for seeking a "formal equality" of women with men. Their "old goal of equal rights," she declared, was simply seeking "the freedom to live as men do." The "outmoded and superficial feminism" of the radical feminists, she declared, represented the "oldest kind of liberal thinking" and ignored the "importance of what women could do for society, and could give to society" through their two special niches: marriage and motherhood. For women, the heart of sexuality was fulfillment of the "soul," culminating in motherhood; whereas for men, it was sensual enjoyment.

Through marriage and motherhood, women might bring their distinct talents and "special nature" to bear on the social life and politics of the nation. Women who devoted themselves to the family were "in some ways truer to the ideas of the women's movement than those who entered traditional male enclaves." Outside of the League, Bäumer promoted her ideas through work in the Advisory Committee for Child Welfare and Protection.

Politically, Bäumer aligned herself with the Progressive Peoples Party, formed in 1910 by the union of three smaller liberal parties. Early in her career, she argued that if women participated in the political system, they risked being partly responsible for "men's politics." By the time the Progressive People's Party had been formed, she had changed her mind; she agreed to join the party only if the words "and women" were added to most of the pledges in the party's platform.

During World War I, Bäumer and the women's leaders whom she regarded as "radicals" found common ground in the Women's National Service, which Bäumer co-sponsored. Working with local German state governments, the Service helped organize the food supply, encouraged women to apply for jobs which were available because of military mobilization, made clothing for soldiers at the front, and organized soup kitchens. The Service also looked after the families of soldiers, including orphaned children.

The idea of a Women's National Service had originally been floated by the more "radical" feminists as a way to demonstrate that women could support the war effort as zealously as men who were actually in combat; the goal was to prove women's fitness for the right to vote. In contrast, Bäumer—who acknowledged that the Service would "not have been possible without the prior work done by the German women's movement"—praised the Service as a signal that women placed the "interest of the Fatherland" above all else. It was a theme Bäumer would continue to advance to the end of her life, arguing that the goal of the women's movement should be to advance "national consciousness"—in the words of Naumann, to "make the masses into a true people."

When the Women's International League for Peace and Freedom met in Geneva in 1915 in order to discuss ways to try to negotiate an end to World War I, Bäumer refused to attend. After the Geneva meeting, participants visited the warring nations, attempting to persuade government leaders to agree to negotiations. Bäumer criticized the trip, opposing it as a step to "weaken Germany" by disarming the Germans "in a world filled with weapons." At the end of the war, she also criticized the Treaty of Versailles, which Germany was forced to sign, as a document which "rides roughshod over German blood."

In 1917, Bäumer was named the head of the new Social Pedagogical Institute in Hamburg, one of a series of well-paying jobs she would hold. Within two years, her interests focused once again on politics, and she returned to Berlin, where she lived most of her adult life. In 1919, after the last German monarch had fled the country, she resigned as head of the League in order to run for the National Assembly, which would write the constitution for the Weimar Republic, Germany's first democracy. Bäumer wrote that "my love of the Fatherland" was a "dark, driving, insistent stream." Disturbed that Germans "came out of World War I as an intellectually rootless, confused people, who trusted no one," she saw her decision to enter national politics as a patriotic, rather than a feminist, gesture.

Bäumer was elected to the main parliamentary body for the Republic, the Reichstag, as a deputy for the new German Democratic Party. She served in that position until the Nazi seizure of power in 1933. She also worked as a high advisor in the German Ministry of the Interior. When Germany was admitted to the League of Nations in the mid-1920s, she became a member of the first German delegation to the League. She was, in the words of one author, "not only a very persuasive" politician but also one of the most "politically savvy of German women leaders" at the time. One author even called her the "only bourgeois woman of any consequence in Weimar Germany."

As National Socialism became stronger in Germany, Bäumer remained distant from the Nazi party, although she did threaten, in 1927, to leave the German Democratic Party because, she said, "Jewish liberals" were exerting too much influence within the party. Following the Nazi accession to power, she was removed from both her Reichstag and Ministry of the Interior positions.

She hoped to demonstrate to the new Nazi government that the women's movement was not hostile to it. When the Nazi government attempted to force the women's movement into the Nazi Women's Front, Bäumer favored the move, although it would have required expelling all Jewish members. She argued that the Nazi-sponsored Front would be an "organization that is only spiritually different" from the women's movement. She also declared that women should join in the *Gleichschaltung*, or Nazi-led "coordination" of German society to Nazi aims and ideas. Rejecting her advice, the leadership of the League of German Women's Associations chose to disband the organization.

Although she said that she was investigated by the Gestapo, and that Heimrich Himmler signed and then withdrew an arrest warrant for her, Bäumer was allowed to retain her editorship of *Die Frau*, which continued publishing through World War II. During the 1930s, she wrote books in which Christian mysticism was mixed with historical topics such as the Middle Ages, as well as studies of literary figures. *Die Frau* seldom commented on politics. She later said that she was trying, through her writings, to offer a "positive alternative" to Nazism. A friend recalled her saying, however, that Nazism was "correct in essence" but had an "impossibly improper way of dealing with people."

Although many German magazines were forced, by rationing, to suspend publication during the wartime years, the Nazi government provided Bäumer with up to 80% of her paper request for *Die Frau*. At the end of World War II, the American and British military governments in occupied Germany regarded her with suspicion. Viewed as a possible Nazi sympathizer, she was denied permission to resume publication of *Die Frau*, and some of her books were banned.

The ban was lifted in the early years of the Cold War, when the Soviet Union was seen as a greater threat than possible Nazi sympathizers. Bäumer attempted to return to politics, founding a conservative Christian Socialist Union with ***Marie Baum**. Deteriorating mental and physical health intervened, however, preventing her from re-entering the political arena before her death in 1954.

Of all the German feminists of her time, Bäumer was the most politically active and probably the most politically influential. She used that influence to promote the idea that German women's greatest contributions to their society would come through their roles as wives and mothers—and to try to convince others that this should be the only true goal of feminism in Germany.

SOURCES:

Bäumer, Gertrud. *Lebensweg durch eine Zeitenwende.* Tübingen: Wunderlich Verlag, 1933.

Evans, Richard J. *Comrades and Sisters: Feminism, Socialism, and Pacifism in Europe, 1870-1945.* Sussex: Wheatsheaf Books, 1987.

———. *The Feminist Movement in Germany, 1894-1933.* Beverly Hills: SAGE Publications, 1976.

Koepcke, Cordula. *Frauenbewegung Zwischen den Jahren 1800 und 2000.* Heroldsberg bei Nürenberg: Glock and Lutz, 1979.

SUGGESTED READING:

Evans, Richard J. *The Feminists: Women's Emancipation Movements in America and Australasia, 1840-1920.* London: Croom Helm, 1977.

Kirkpatrick, Clifford. *Germany: Its Women and Family Life.* Indianapolis: Bobbs-Merrill, 1938.

Stephenson, Jill. *Women in Nazi Germany.* London: Croom Helm, 1975.

COLLECTIONS:

Portions of the correspondence of Gertrud Bäumer are contained in the Deutsches Zentralarchiv, Potsdam, Germany; the Bundesarchiv, Koblenz, Germany; the Archiv des Bundes Deutscher Frauenvereine, Berlin, Germany; and the Helene Lange Archiv, Berlin, Germany.

Niles R. Holt, Professor of History, Illinois State University, Normal-Bloomington, Illinois

Baumgartner, Ann (b. 1923).

See Davis, Dorothy Hilliard for sidebar.

Bavaria, duchess of.

See Judith of Fiuli (fl. 910–925).
See Judith of Bavaria (c. 925–987).
See Gisela of Burgundy (d. 1006).
See Agnes of Poitou (1024–1077).
See Judith of Flanders (1032–1094).
See Wolfida of Saxony (c. 1075–1126).
See Ludmilla of Bohemia (fl. 1100s).
See Gertrude of Saxony (1115–1143).
See Agnes of Looss (fl. 1150–1175).
See Matilda of England (1156–1189).
See Agnes of Saxony (fl. 1200s).
See Matilda of Habsburg (1251–1304).
See Beatrice of Silesia (fl. 1300s).
See Visconti, Thaddaea (d.1381).
See Elizabeth of Sicily (d. 1349).
See Catherine of Gorizia (fl. late 1300s).
See Visconti, Elizabeth (fl. late 1300s).
See Blanche (c. 1392–1409).
See Margaret (1395–1447).
See Margaret of Cleves (fl. early 1400s).
See Anna of Brunswick (fl. 1400s).
See Cunegunde (1465–1520).
See Anna of Brunswick (1528–1590).
See Maria Sophia Amalia (1841–1925).
See Amalie of Saxe-Coburg-Gotha (1848–1894).

Bavaria, electress of.

See Maria Anna of Bavaria (1610–1665).
See Henrietta of Savoy (c. 1630–?).
See Maria Antonia (1669–1692).
See Cunigunde Sobieska (fl. 1690s).
See Caroline of Baden (1776–1841).
See Maria Leopoldina (1776–1848).
See Ludovica (1808–1892).

Bavaria, queen of.

See Caroline of Baden (1776–1841).
See Theresa of Saxony (1792–1854).
See Ludovica (1808–1892).
See Maria of Prussia (1825–1889).
See Maria Teresa of Este (1849–1919).

Bavent, Madeleine (fl. 1642).

See "French Witches" (14th–16th centuries).

Baxter, Anne (1923–1985)

***American film actress, best known for her work in the title role of* All About Eve.** *Born in Michigan City, Indiana, on May 7, 1923; suffered a stroke in New York City on December 4 and died on December 12, 1985; daughter of Kenneth Stuart and* **Catherine Wright Baxter** *(daughter of architect Frank Lloyd Wright); attended private schools in New York City; studied acting with Maria Ouspenskaya; married John Hodiak, in 1946 (divorced 1953); married Randolph Galt, in 1960 (divorced 1968); children: (first marriage) Katrina (b. 1951); (second marriage) Melissa (b. 1961), Maginal (b. 1963).*

Filmography: Twenty-Mule Team *(1940);* The Great Profile *(1940);* Charley's Aunt *(1941);* Swamp Water *(1941);* The Magnificent Ambersons *(1942);* The Pied Piper *(1942);* Crash Dive *(1943);* Five Graves to Cairo *(1943);* The North Star *(*Armored Attack, *1943);* The Sullivans *(1944);* The Eve of St. Mark *(1944);* Guest in the House *(1944);* Sunday Dinner for a Soldier *(1944);* A Royal Scandal *(1945);* Smoky *(1946);* Angel on My Shoulder *(1946);* The Razor's Edge *(1946); (off-screen narrator)* Mother Wore Tights *(1947);* Blaze of Noon *(1947);* Homecoming *(1948);* The Walls of Jericho *(1948);* The Luck of the Irish *(1948);* Yellow Sky *(1949);* You're My Everything *(1949);* A Ticket to Tomahawk *(1950);* All About Eve *(1950);* Follow the Sun *(1951);* The Outcasts of Poker Flat *(1952);* My Wife's Best Friend *(1952);* O. Henry's Full House *(1952);* I Confess *(1952);* The Blue Gardenia *(1953);* Carnival Story *(1954);* Bedevilled *(1955);* One Desire *(1955);* The Spoilers *(1956);* The Come-on *(1956);* The Ten Commandments *(1956);* Three Violent People *(1957);* Chase a Crooked Shadow *(UK, 1958);* Summer of the Seventeenth Doll *(*Season of Passion, *Australia-UK, 1959);* Cimarron *(1960);* Mix Me a Person *(U.K., 1962);* Walk on the Wild Side *(1962);* The Family Jewels *(cameo, 1965);* Las Siete Magnificas *(*The Tall Women, *Sp.-It.-Aus., 1966);* The Busy Body *(1967);* Fool's Parade *(1971);* The Late Liz *(1971);* Little Mo *(originally for television) (1978);* Jane Austen in Manhattan *(1980).*

Although Anne Baxter worked with some of Hollywood's finest directors, received one Academy Award, and was nominated for another, she was destined to be known as a skilled, rather than great, actress. But Baxter outlasted many of her contemporaries, performing in film, as well as stage and television, for four decades.

The granddaughter of architect Frank Lloyd Wright, Baxter made an auspicious Broadway debut at age 13 in *Seen but Not Heard*, which won her praise as a "cute kidlet" and an invitation to study with the famed actress-teacher ***Maria Ouspenskaya**. After a few undistinguished juvenile stage roles, in 1940 Baxter began a seven-year relationship with 20th Century-Fox. For almost a decade, she was often loaned out to other studios or substituted in roles originally planned for someone else.

Baxter reached the high point of her career early, at 23, with her 1946 portrayal of Sophie MacDonald in *The Razor's Edge* for which she won an Academy Award for Best Supporting Actress. Despite the honors, reviews were mixed. Whereas Howard Barnes in the *New York Herald Tribune* wrote, "The tragic Sophie, drowning her unendurable grief in Paris bistros, is beautifully realized in Anne Baxter's sensitive portrayal," *The New York Times*' Bosley Crowther felt otherwise. Audiences, however, made up their own minds, and the film was a huge box-office hit. Still, despite the film's popularity and Baxter's Oscar, she was only offered an offstage narration from her home studio in 1947, before being loaned to Paramount for the lackluster *Blaze of Noon.*

Baxter's second outstanding role—for which she replaced a pregnant ***Jeanne Crain**—was in the 1950 biting show-business satire *All About Eve*. Baxter played a scheming young actress out to usurp the career and life of actress Margo Channing, portrayed by ***Bette Davis.** Though Baxter captured another Oscar nomination for her performance of Eve, the award went

From the movie All About Eve, *starring Celeste Holm and Anne Baxter.*

to *Judy Holliday for her comic portrayal in *Born Yesterday*. Four subsequent films rounded out Baxter's stay at Fox.

Looking for better opportunities, Baxter began freelancing in 1953 with *I Confess* for Warner Bros. Director Alfred Hitchcock had wanted *Anita Bjork for the feminine lead and was outspoken in his displeasure with Baxter, calling her an "awkward substitution." Undaunted, Baxter returned from location in Quebec and immediately recaptured the attention of the Hollywood press by smoking a Havana cigar at a Hollywood restaurant. For the remainder of the '50s, she jumped from studio to studio, and in 1957 attempted a return to the stage in *The Square Root of Wonderful*, which won lukewarm reviews and closed after 45 performances. In 1958, she made an extensive number of television appearances, including "Playhouse 90," and "TV Theatre." She likened the medium to an entertainment smorgasbord remarking, "it dishes out twice-baked beans with caviar."

Baxter's personal life included a marriage to actor John Hodiak in 1946, by whom she had a daughter Katrina in 1951. Divorced in 1953, she married former Air Force pilot Randolph Galt in 1960 and promptly left Hollywood for a 37,000-acre cattle ranch 180 miles north of Sydney, in the isolated Australian outback. The four year odyssey, including the birth of daughters Melissa and Maginal, was chronicled in her critically acclaimed autobiography *Intermission: A True Story.* In 1963, Baxter returned to California saying, "It's an unpardonable thing to leave LA." Following her divorce from Galt in 1968, she commented, "I gave up my career because I was very much in love. My husband didn't want me to give it up. I think he was wiser than I was."

Baxter's roles in the '60s included more television credits, like "Batman" and "Marcus Welby, M.D." In 1969, she was nominated for an Emmy Award for "The Bobbie Currier Story," an episode from the series "The Name of the Game." In 1971, she took over for **Lauren Bacall** as Margo Channing in the Broadway production of *Applause*, based on her film *All About Eve*; this time, however, she played the role Bette Davis had played in the 1950 movie. In 1983, Baxter replaced the ailing Davis in the television series "Hotel," staying with the show until her death from a stroke in 1985.

Perhaps Baxter's own assessment of her career helps explain why she was fated to remain in the trenches without reaching the glittering heights in Hollywood: "I'm an actress—not a personality. It's more successful to be a personality. But can you use it in every role? I don't spill over into everything I do; I do what I do from inside someone else's skin."

SOURCES:

Baxter, Anne. *Intermission: A True Story.* NY: Putnam, 1976.

Parish, James Robert. *The Fox Girls.* NY: Arlington House, 1974.

Barbara Morgan,
Melrose, Massachusetts

Bay, Mrs. Charles Ulrick (1900–1962).

See Bay, Josephine.

Bay, Josephine Perfect (1900–1962)

American financier and the first woman to head a member firm of the New York Stock Exchange. *Name variations: Mrs. Charles Ulrick Bay. Born Josephine Holt Perfect in Anamosa, Iowa, on August 10, 1900; died in New York, New York, on August 6, 1962; daughter of Otis Lincoln and Tirzah (Holt) Perfect; sister of* ***Tirzah Perfect*** *(Mrs. Frederick W. Dunn); graduated from Brooklyn Heights Seminary, in 1916; attended Colorado College at Colorado Springs, Colorado, 1918–19; married Charles Ulrick Bay (a Wall Street financier), in 1942 (died 1955); married C. Michael Paul, in January 1959; children: (adopted) Christopher Bay, Synnova Bay, Frederick Bay.*

Josephine Bay, the first woman ever elected to the presidency and chair of a member firm of the New York Stock Exchange, was ahead of her time. As early as 1957, she was advocating equality of the sexes on the corporate level. Her words of four decades ago remain relevant. "Today's women have a new and deeper responsibility than ever before in our history—to carry their share of leadership along with men of equal ability. . . . What a tragedy it would be if we were to maintain the old superstitions which wall out capable executives merely because they are women!"

Bay, who grew up in Brooklyn, showed an early interest in business. After a year at Colorado College, she returned home to become active in a number of civic groups, including the Brooklyn Junior League; she took over their debt-ridden bookstore and sold it in short order, a deal that not only paid off the League's debts but allowed for a continued share in the bookstore's profit. She and her sister Tirzah also operated a lucrative Christmas-card business for a number of years.

At age 42, Josephine married Charles Ulrick Bay, then a senior partner in the firm of A.M.

Kidder, one of the oldest and wealthiest brokerage houses in Wall Street. He immediately began to tutor her in all of his business enterprises, inviting her to join him at business meetings and using her as a sounding board. "Time and time again he would discuss a business problem with me," she recalled, "urging me to take the opposite viewpoint to help clarify his thinking."

In 1946, Bay accompanied her husband to Norway, where he served as ambassador until 1953. In addition to working on NATO projects in the war-torn country, the couple adopted three Norwegian orphans. In 1950, she became president of the Charles Ulrick and Josephine Bay Foundation, through which the pair made numerous charitable gifts and grants, including scholarships to Norwegian students for study in America, and a medical fund for research and prevention of cerebral palsy among Norwegian children. Their humanitarian efforts were honored in 1957, when Josephine accepted the Commander's Cross of the St. Olav's order—one of Norway's highest decorations.

When Charles Bay took ill in 1955, Josephine succeeded him as a director of the American Export Lines (a passenger and shipping firm) and in the fall of 1956 was elected chair of the executive committee. Knowing fully his plans for Export, she embarked on a business strategy to see his ideas to fruition. Boosting profits, she won a reputation as a savvy businesswoman in her own right.

Following her husband's death, Bay became a limited partner in A.M. Kidder. On December 1, 1956, she was elected unanimously to the presidency and chair of the board of the prestigious firm. From 1959 to 1960, she also served as chair of the board of American Export Lines. Convinced that she was part of a wave of the future, Bay hoped her position would encourage women to become active investment owners, while encouraging men to stop regarding their wives "as just sweet and naïve things to be provided for but not to be told anything about their business."

Until her death in August 1962, Bay remained head of Kidder. She was succeeded by her second husband, C. Michael Paul, who remained in the post until the brokerage firm went out of business in June 1963.

SOURCES:

Candee, Marjorie Dent. *Current Biography.* NY: H.W. Wilson, 1957.

McHenry, Robert, ed. *Famous American Women.* NY: Dober, 1983.

Barbara Morgan,
Melrose, Massachusetts

Bayes, Nora (1880–1928)

American singer and actress. *Born Dora (also cited as Leonora or Eleanor) Goldberg in Milwaukee, Wisconsin (various sources also cite Los Angeles and Chicago as birth places), in 1880; died in New York City on March 19, 1928; married Jack Norwood, in 1908, one of five husbands.*

Nora Bayes

Once billed as "The Greatest Single Woman Singing Comedienne in the World," Nora Bayes made her vaudeville debut in Chicago in 1899 and appeared on Broadway for the first time two years later in *The Rogers Brothers in Washington.* She gained recognition in 1902, with her rendition of Harry von Tilzer's song "Down Where the Wurzburger Flows," which she performed at the Orpheum Theatre in Brooklyn, New York. Bayes toured in variety shows and musicals in Europe from 1904 to 1907, then returned to appear in the first edition of the *Ziegfeld Follies* (1907). In 1908, she married and teamed with Jack Norworth (together billed as "Nora Bayes, Assisted and Admired by Jack Norworth").

As a fixture in Broadway and London musicals, Bayes introduced and popularized many songs, including "Has Anyone Here Seen Kelly?," "Take Me Out to the Ball Game," "Japanese Sandman," and George M. Cohan's rousing World War I song, "Over There." Her theme song, "Shine on Harvest Moon," was written by Norwood and introduced in the *Ziegfeld Follies of 1908.* In 1919, she inaugurated the Nora Bayes Roof at the 44th Street Theatre, with a performance in the musical *Ladies First.* She later appeared in *Her Family Tree* (1920), *Snapshots of 1921,* and *Queen o'Hearts* (1922). Small in stature and large of voice, Bayes was considered a master at delivering a song, particularly in her gestures and facial expressions. The actress died on March 19, 1928.

Barbara Morgan,
Melrose, Massachusetts.

Bayley, Mrs. John Oliver (1919–1999).

See Murdoch, Iris.

Baylis, Lilian (1874–1937)

Manager of the Old Vic and Sadler's Wells Theaters who helped found the companies which became Britain's Royal National Theatre, English National Opera, and the Royal Ballet. *Name variations: The Lady. Pronunciation: BAY-lis. Born Lilian Mary Baylis on May 9, 1874, in Marylebone, London, England; died in Stockwell, London, on November 25, 1937; daughter of Edward William (Newton) Baylis and Elizabeth (Liebe) Cons Baylis; attended private school and St. Augustine's, Kilburn; never married; no children.*

Awards: honorary Master of Arts, University of Oxford (1924); Companion of Honor (1929); honorary Doctor of Laws, University of Birmingham (1934).

Performed as a child with her parents' concert group; went to South Africa and toured with her family (1890); taught music in Johannesburg (1892–97); returned to England (1897), and became assistant to Emma Cons, manager of the Old Vic Theater; succeeded Cons as manager (1912); extended the work of theater during and after the First World War to include seasons of Shakespeare and opera; acquired Sadler's Wells Theater (1926), which became the home of permanent opera and ballet companies (1930s). Publications: contributed regularly to Old Vic *(later* Old Vic and Sadler's Wells*)* Magazine *(1919–37); with Cicely Hamilton, wrote* The Old Vic *(Jonathan Cape, 1926); wrote preface to Kate Neatby's* Ninette de Valois and the Vic-Wells Ballet *(British Continental Press, 1934).*

Lilian Baylis' family had a strong musical background: her father Newton Baylis was a baritone and her mother **Liebe Cons** was a contralto. Her mother's Anglo-German family had a great influence on the young Lilian, especially her aunt and godmother, **Emma Cons**. Baylis was the eldest of five children. Though her education was patchy, she and the others were taught to sing, dance, and play an instrument. She was taught the violin by J.T. Carrodus, composer, violinist and one of the leading teachers of the day. By the age of nine, Lilian was appearing in her parents' concert group which performed in a range of venues throughout England. In her father's absence, Baylis took over the management of the group, later called the Gipsy Revellers, and eventually managed it full-time. In 1890, they were signed by a South African impresario and, between 1890–97, Baylis and her family undertook several arduous tours of South African towns and villages, traversing the country in carts and wagons. In later life, Baylis remembered these tours with great affection. In 1892, she settled in Johannesburg and taught music. The following year, she became engaged to a gold prospector, Jack Webster, but this was broken off three years later. In 1897, following a serious illness, she returned to England at the invitation of her Aunt Emma, a move that determined the rest of her career.

***Beatrice Webb** once described Emma Cons as "one of the most saintly as well as one of the most far-sighted of Victorian women philanthropists," Born in 1838, Cons was a close friend of ***Octavia Hill** and shared her interest in art and philanthropy. Emma Cons became an illustrator and was commissioned by John Ruskin to restore manuscripts in his collection. She subsequently set up a watch-engraving business, employing women, which only collapsed because of opposition from men in the trade. Cons and Hill became involved in the management of slum property, and, in the 1870s, Cons went to work for the South London Dwellings Company. There she witnessed at first hand the violence, crime, and alcoholism which afflicted so many families in the area. In 1879, Cons enlisted the support of wealthy benefactors and turned the Royal Victoria Theater near Waterloo Station into the Royal Victoria Coffee and Music Hall (nicknamed the Old Vic) to provide "wholesome and cheerful recreation for the working classes of London." Though the theater had been famous for melodrama and pantomime, its audiences had an unsavory reputation for drunkenness and fighting before Cons took it over. Under her management, the theater's activities included temperance nights, variety shows, lectures, meetings, and concerts.

When Lilian Baylis arrived back in England, she fully intend to return to her teaching in Johannesburg but found her aunt overworked and was persuaded to become her assistant. Her experience organizing concerts in South Africa was an advantage, and Baylis soon made her presence felt at the Old Vic. Variety was still the main attraction, but, after the appointment of Charles Corri as music director in 1899, there were more symphony concerts and operas on the programs. Baylis was hamstrung by the Old Vic's performing license which discriminated between variety and stage plays. Operas could only be performed in excerpts, accompanied by explanatory *tableaux vivants*, but despite these restrictions they had become very popular. *Tannhaüser* was performed in 1904 and *Lohengrin* two years later; by 1906, the average attendance at operas was 1,600 to 2,000.

When Emma Cons died in 1912, Baylis succeeded her as manager of the Old Vic. Obtaining a theater license, Lilian dropped variety and the ballad and symphony concerts and put on more opera performances. Tentative steps were also taken towards more regular drama performances, particularly Shakespeare. The first combined season of Shakespeare and opera took place in 1914–15, just after the outbreak of the First World War. Baylis ignored the prevalent anti-German hysteria, and German operas like *Lohengrin* continued to be performed. But it was in drama that the war years proved a watershed. Baylis was discriminating in her choice of drama producers, beginning with Matheson Lang and then Ben Greet who stayed at the Vic until 1918. Greet persuaded ***Sybil Thorndike** to join the company, and, in April 1915, Greet and Baylis staged the first Shakespeare Birthday Festival which became an Old Vic tradition. This was followed by the Tercentenary Festival in 1916. Initially, Shakespeare was unpopular with audiences, but Baylis persisted and the plays were appreciated by more thoughtful audiences for whom the Old Vic was virtually the only source of serious drama during the war.

After the war, Baylis faced increasing difficulties with the London County Council about the physical state of the theater, and she had to find £30,000 for urgent alterations and repairs. This was given in a single donation by Sir George Dance. The improved physical amenities reflected a change in the audience which attracted a wider range of support after World War I. In 1925, the *Sunday Times* described the Old Vic audience as "members of a great family sharing a common inheritance." To Harcourt Williams, drama director at the Vic from 1929 to 1933, they were not "masses" but teachers, intellectuals, and typists. "They want intelligent, well thought out, careful performances of good plays in a genuine theatre not given over to the slickness of showmanship." Baylis took a particular interest in organizing children's performances, a cause close to her aunt's heart. She never felt comfortable with wealthy patrons, feeling that they exuded too much of the social exclusiveness of grander theaters like Covent Garden.

In building a sense of community among the Old Vic's audiences, Baylis had a shrewd appreciation of the value of ritual, and the seasons were sprinkled with ceremonies, events, and entertainments: the first and last night speeches, the Christmas and Twelfth Night parties, the annual performance of the Old Vic students, the Shakespeare Birthday Matinee, the Costume

Lilian Baylis

Ball, the performance of *The Lily of Killarney* on St. Patrick's night. There were also her famous curtain speeches in which she harangued, cajoled, and exhorted the audience by turns, usually about money and attendances. The *Old Vic Magazine*, started in 1919, was another valued medium. In her "Manager's Foreword," Baylis not only spurred her "loyal and faithful audience" and staff to greater effort on behalf of the Vic but gave them the latest news about forthcoming programs and events, as well as retirements, engagements, marriages, and births among the staff and the artists.

In a radio broadcast of the early 1920s, Baylis set out her vision of the theatre as the need for working men and women "to see beyond the four walls of their offices, workshops and homes, into a world of awe and wonder." The theater was "the most important and accessible and the most easily understood branch of art for the man and woman in the street." The writer Hugh Walpole thought that this accessibility was Baylis' greatest achievement. "She made it very easy and simple for an onlooker to feel that he is sharing in a creative art . . . [and] she has taken away a great many of the difficulties and artificialities that were ruining the English theater." By the 1920s, the Old Vic was being described as England's national theatre, a project which had been put forward sporadically since the 18th century by people as diverse as David Garrick, Henry Irving, and G.B. Shaw. Baylis acknowledged that it was a national theatre in all but name, and, although she never received any public subsidy in her lifetime, she would have resisted any official interference resulting from such subsidies.

All art is a bond between rich and poor; it allows of no class distinctions.

—**Lilian Baylis**

Shakespeare and opera were the cornerstones of the Old Vic's repertory. The Shakespearean productions were deliberately simple in appearance and style, a reaction to the more elaborate school of Irving and his contemporaries. Audiences at the Vic liked a direct, rhythmic style in verse-speaking which did not sound stilted or artificial. William Poel, whose Elizabethan Stage Circle had a huge influence on the Vic's approach, had worked for Emma Cons in the early 1880s, and Baylis herself had attended performances of his company. There was also more respect for the text, and, from 1916 on, the uncut *Hamlet* was regularly performed. There were revivals of rarities such as *Titus Andronicus, Henry VI,* and *Troilus and Cressida.* Shakespeare seasons in London's West End commercial theater were generally a failure without star names, but the provinces, especially the north of England, were more welcoming, and the company toured there nearly every year.

Other classical dramatists, British and foreign, were also part of the drama repertory. During the first wartime seasons, there were plays by Oliver Goldsmith, Richard Brinsley Sheridan, and Edward Bulwer-Lytton, also the morality play *Everyman* which was performed during Lent and was a personal favorite of Baylis' (who rarely sat through an entire Shakespeare play). The Vic also attracted audiences with novelties such as *The Trojan Women* (with Sybil Thorndike as Hecuba), Ibsen's *Peer Gynt*, and Goethe's *Faust.* The first Chekhov production, *The Cherry Orchard,* was in 1933. Baylis was more dubious about Christopher Marlowe's *Edward II* which she deemed "unsuitable," and about Restoration comedy because of its bawdiness. It was years before she allowed William Congreve's *Love for Love* to be performed and then only because it would be good box office.

Baylis' relationship with her drama directors could be difficult. Robert Atkins, who worked at the Vic from 1920 to 1925, directed all but one of Shakespeare's plays and made Waterloo a mecca for young actors who wanted experience in the classical repertory, among them John Gielgud and ***Flora Robson**. Atkins was increasingly irked by what he considered to be Baylis' meddling, while she disapproved of his heavy drinking and womanizing. After his departure, Baylis remarked that, though he'd been impossible to work with, he was a fine director to whom the Vic owed a great debt. Harcourt Williams, director at the Vic from 1929 to 1933, wrote perceptively and affectionately about Baylis, and what it was like to work for her. She rarely praised his work, which he recognized as her method of avoiding demands and importunities. But when his production of *The Merchant of Venice* attracted press criticism and he wanted to resign, Baylis accused him of being a coward for giving up simply because of a few notices. Tyrone Guthrie, the last major director who worked for Baylis, was described by her as "one of the elect"; she supported Guthrie when his productions provoked opposition from some of the Old Vic governors and from more vociferous traditionalists in the audience. Guthrie's feelings were more mixed at the time and, in his 1960 autobiography, ungenerously dismissive of her.

It was clear by the early 1920s that the Vic was not large enough to accommodate drama and opera which had also expanded after WWI. Clive Carey and Lawrence Collingwood were appointed to the opera staff in 1919 and over the next three years three major Mozart operas were produced, despite the fact that the chorus was part-time and rehearsal periods severely limited. In 1924, Baylis took an interest in the run-down Sadler's Wells Theater in Islington, north London. Like the Vic, Sadler's Wells had a great theatrical history and was situated in a working-class area. An appeal was launched, and the money to purchase it was obtained by the end of 1925. After many delays, the refurbished theater was opened in January 1931, but, during its first years, it caused Baylis major financial headaches. The orchestra had increased and there was a full-time chorus which could now rehearse with the orchestra, but they were both expensive. It also took time for the new theater to find an audience which preferred opera and ballet to Shakespeare and serious drama. In 1935, Sadler's Wells became the permanent home of the opera and ballet companies, while drama remained at the Vic.

The expansion of the repertory at Sadler's Wells between 1931 and 1937 established the opera company's reputation. Fifty operas were produced, among them important productions of neglected Russian works, more Verdi operas, new English operas, and, in 1937, Baylis' cherished dream of Wagner's *Meistersinger*. The 1936–37 season, just before Baylis' death, was the first financially successful season at Sadler's Wells.

There had been many skeptics in 1926 when ***Ninette de Valois** first approached Baylis about establishing a ballet company at the Old Vic, but Baylis was impressed by de Valois' practicality and experience and contracted her and her dancers to work in operas and to teach movement to the drama students. When Sadler's Wells opened, the Vic-Wells Ballet, as it became known, quickly found a devoted audience. To Baylis' relief, it also had wealthy supporters in organizations like the Camargo Society (backed by John Maynard Keynes) and the Sadler's Wells Society which sponsored new designs and scores by distinguished artists and composers. *Job*, choreographed by de Valois to music by Vaughan Williams, was a critical and financial success in 1931 and over the next six years the ballet company increased from eight to thirty-two dancers, had two resident choreographers, de Valois and Frederick Ashton, resident conductor Constant Lambert, and a school of 40 students. De Valois' policy was to create an English ballet company based on the Russian classics and on new choreography, principally by Ashton, who was to become one of the finest choreographers of the century and the creator of a recognizably English style of ballet. In 1936–37, with Baylis' permission, the Vic-Wells dancers appeared several times on the fledgling BBC television service in which she was much interested, though she considered the initial results unimpressive. Baylis and de Valois had an excellent working relationship, perhaps because they had many temperamental similarities. De Valois appreciated Baylis' down-to-earth reality, strength of purpose and "guts" which she demanded of herself and others in the face of adversity. She was also tolerant of Baylis' eccentricities. Others found Baylis difficult and abrupt, particularly at first meetings. They were disconcerted by her custom of conducting business from the stage box, startling actors and directors with comments as they rehearsed. Baylis disliked sycophancy and, as actors discovered, refused to bolster their egos with praise, uttering forthright comments which on occasion could be wounding. She was also scathing when they left the Vic to earn higher salaries. She liked working with men but some men found it difficult to overcome their prejudices when working with her. She was also accused of being prudish about sex, but de Valois found that, in practice, Baylis was "far too human to patronize or condemn."

Baylis seldom went to concerts, art galleries, or the cinema and maintained that she was ignorant about the arts, but colleagues and staff found that she had a good ear for music, appreciated a good voice, and had generally sound instincts about acting and choreography. The issue which caused constant conflict in the running of the companies was money. She was accused of being stingy and penny-pinching. Her celebrated prayer, "Dear God, please send me good actors and cheap," became notorious, but those who worked closely with her knew what an ever-constant anxiety money was. Every penny was saved for her companies, not for herself. She refused to let Harcourt Williams see the box-office returns in case this had an undesirable influence on his work. However, Baylis always paid the salaries she promised and offered the security of an eight-month contract which was rare at the time. To de Valois, Baylis was not mean, she simply thought about money "as a peasant thinks about it—safer in the stocking than in the bank." Baylis often panicked over money, de Valois observed, because she was rarely without financial worry.

In the last decade of her life, Baylis' achievements were recognized. She had already received an honorary M.A. from Oxford in 1924, only the second woman to have been so honored. In 1929, she was made a Companion of Honor by the government and in 1934 was awarded an honorary doctorate of laws by Birmingham University. She regarded these awards as honors for her companies rather than for herself but recognition came for the companies too. In May 1937, the last year of her life, the British Council invited the Vic-Wells Ballet to represent English theatre at the Paris International Exhibition. A month later, the drama company was invited to perform *Hamlet* at Elsinore in Denmark.

Baylis was sustained all her life by a deep Christian faith. She was a lay associate of the Society of Divine Compassion, a neo-Franciscan order within the Church of England whose founder, Father Andrew, was her closest friend and adviser until her death. Baylis went on annual retreats and had a long association with the

St. Giles Leper Home founded by the Society. She had an intense belief in the value of prayer which was the subject of many jokes in her companies. She told Russell Thorndike that she never made any decision until she had asked God what was best, even on such minor matters as a request for a rise in salary.

When Lilian Baylis died suddenly in November 1937, there were fears that the companies at the Old Vic and Sadler's Wells would not survive without her. But this ignored Baylis' achievement in securing over the years the talents of gifted collaborators who put the companies on a sound artistic footing. The ballet company moved to Covent Garden in 1946, with its touring company retaining a base at Sadler's Wells. Both companies received a royal charter in 1956 and became the Royal Ballet. The opera company changed its name in 1968 to the English National Opera and remained at Sadler's Wells until 1974 when it moved to the London Coliseum. The drama company remained at the Old Vic, apart from a wartime hiatus, and, in 1963, the Old Vic became the home of the new National Theatre Company until it moved in 1976 to its custom-built premises not far from the Old Vic. There was regret that none of the three new auditoria were named after Baylis.

SOURCES:

Booth, John. *The Old Vic: A Century of Theatrical History, 1816–1916.* London: Stead's Publishing House, 1917.

Dent, Edward J. *A Theatre for Everybody: The Story of the Old Vic and Sadler's Wells.* London: T.V. Boardman, 1945.

Fagg, Edwin. *The Old "Old" Vic or from Barrymore to Baylis.* London: Vic-Wells Association, 1936.

Guthrie, Tyrone. *A Life in the Theater.* London: Hamish Hamilton, 1960.

Hamilton, Cicely and Lilian Baylis. *The Old Vic.* London: Jonathan Cape, 1926.

Old Vic and Sadler's Wells Magazine, 1919–37.

Thorndike, Russell and ***Sybil Thorndike**. *Lilian Baylis.* London: Chapman and Hall, 1938.

Valois, Ninette de. *Come Dance With Me.* London: Hamish Hamilton, 1957.

Williams, Harcourt. *Four Years at the Old Vic, 1929–1933.* London: Putnam, 1935.

———. *Vic-Wells: The Work of Lilian Baylis.* London: Cobden-Sanderson, 1938.

SUGGESTED READING:

Findlater, Richard. *Lilian Baylis.* London: Allen Lane, 1975.

COLLECTIONS:

Correspondence and memorabilia at the Theater Museum, Covent Garden, London.

Deirdre McMahon, Dublin, Ireland,
Assistant Editor, *Dance Theatre Journal* (London),
and author of *Republicans and Imperialists*
(Yale University Press, 1984)

Bayly, Ada Ellen (1857–1903)

British popular novelist, author of seventeen books, all with a religious theme. *Name variations: Edna Lyall. Born on March 25, 1857, in Brighton, Sussex, England; died on February 8, 1903, in Eastbourne, England; daughter of Mary (Winter) Bayly and Robert Bayly (a lawyer); educated at home and at boarding school in Brighton; never married; no children.*

Ada Ellen Bayly became a celebrity only reluctantly. Her books, strongly religious in view and tone, inspired intense admiration and curiosity in Britain. They were the work of a fragile woman, who was too sickly to attend school. In 1858, the year after her birth, her father died. Three years later, her mother died. At the time, Bayly's two elder sisters and one brother had long since been dispatched to boarding school and were old enough to be independent. Ada passed into the care of an uncle.

She was just 22 when her first book *Won by Waiting* was published under the pseudonym Edna Lyall. Popularity arrived with the 1882 release of another Lyall tome, *Donovan*, about an agnostic who returns to his faith. The book won a recommendation by Prime Minster William Gladstone and also caught the attention of Charles Bradlaugh, a radical free-thinker. As readers clamored for word of the author's true identity, several writers claimed the work but were disproved. Then the rumor spread that the author of these popular books was insane and institutionalized. Only then did Bayly publicly announce her identity. In 1887, she defended herself in *Autobiography of a Slander*, personifying gossip, allowing it to report on its travels and the damages it inflicted. The notoriety, however, continued to promote sales; in 1898, *Hope the Hermit* amazed the literary community by selling 9,000 copies on its first day.

Throughout her life, Bayly lived in her sisters' homes, each of whom had married clerics (her brother Robert Burges Bayly also took up the ministry). She traveled occasionally, including a trip to Italy in 1898, while women's suffrage and charitable work occupied her time away from the desk. The autobiographical *The Burges Letters* and *The Hinderers*, both 1902, were Bayly's final published works. Ada Bayly died of heart failure at age 46 in 1903; she was interred at Brosbury, Herefordshire.

SUGGESTED READING:

Escreet, J.M. *The Life of Edna Lyall,* 1904.

Payne, Reverend George A. *Edna Lyall.* London: John Heywood, 1903.

Crista Martin, freelance writer,
Boston, Massachusetts

Bayne, Beverly (1894–1982)

American silent-screen star, best known for her films with Francis X. Bushman. *Born Beverly Pearl Bain in Minneapolis, Minnesota, in 1894; died on August 12, 1982, in Scottsdale, Arizona; married Francis X. Bushman, in 1918 (divorced 1924); married Charles T. Hvass, in 1937 (died 1953); children: (first marriage) son Richard.*

Major films: The Loan Shark *(1912);* Under Royal Patronage *(1914);* One Wonderful Night *(1914);* The Diplomat Service *(1916);* Romeo and Juliet *(1916);* The Great Secret *(1917);* Social Quicksands *(1918);* Graustark *(1925);* Seven Keys to Baldpate *(1935).*

In the early 1900s, when the nascent motion-picture industry was centered in Chicago, Beverly Pearl Bain was a freshman at Chicago's Hyde Park High School. Intrigued with the glamour of the new medium, she and a friend visited Essanay Studios, where Bain's dark beauty caught the eye of a director who offered her a role in *The Loan Shark*. Young and naive, Bain asked for a salary of $25 a week, a fortune compared to her weekly allowance of 25 cents. In less than a year, she was making $350 and had adopted a more sophisticated spelling, Bayne, of her last name.

Of the 500 movies Bayne made before her retirement, many of which were one- and two-reelers, by far the most successful were the "love team" films with Francis X. Bushman, beginning with *Under Royal Patronage* in 1914. The first film version of *Romeo and Juliet*, in 1916, catapulted the pair to superstardom. They commanded outrageous salaries and even formed their own production company, Quality Pictures. In 1917, they orchestrated a $15,000 deal to co-star in the serial *The Great Secret* for Metro Pictures, then headed by Louis B. Mayer.

The pair married in 1918, but because wedding bells were known to sound the death knell for romantic actors in those days, the marriage was kept a secret from the public. They had a son Richard, and the relationship ended in a bitter divorce in 1924. Bushman would die in 1966, to be followed a year later by the death of their son. In 1937, Bayne married manufacturer Charles Hvass.

After her divorce from Bushman, Bayne continued to make movies, but never again achieved star status. She had some success on the vaudeville circuit during the '20s, and in 1927 starred in the stage production of *The Road to Rome*, followed by the plays *Once in a Lifetime* (1931), *As Husbands Go* (1932), and *The Shining Hour* (1934). In 1935, she made her last movie, *Seven Keys to Baldpate*, with Gene Raymond. During the '30s, Bayne worked in radio and wrote some magazine articles on beauty and diet. In the 1940s, she appeared in the Chicago company of *Claudia* and returned to Broadway in the short-lived play *Loco* (1946). Following the death of her second husband in 1953, Bayne and her son moved to Scottsdale, Arizona, which she called "The West's most Western Town."

Beverly Bayne

Barbara Morgan,
Melrose, Massachusetts

Baynes, Pauline (1922—)

English illustrator, known for illustrating the works of C.S. Lewis and J.R.R. Tolkien. *Born on September 9, 1922, in Brighton, England; daughter of Frederick William Wilberforce (a Commissioner in the Indian Civil Service) and Jessie Harriet Maude (Cunningham) Baynes; attended Farnham School of art, 1937; Slade*

School of Art, 1939–40; married Fritz Otto Gasch (a garden contractor), on March 25, 1961.

Writings (all self-illustrated): Victoria and the Golden Bird *(1947);* How Dog Began *(1986);* Good King Wenceslas *(1987).*

Illustrator: Victoria Stevenson, Clover Magic *(1944); V. Stevenson,* The Magic Footstool *(1946); J.R.R. Tolkien,* Farmer Giles of Ham *(1949); V. Stevenson,* The Magic Broom *(1950); C.S. Lewis,* The Lion, the Witch, and the Wardrobe *(1950); C.S. Lewis,* Prince Caspian *(1951); C.S. Lewis,* The Voyage of the "Dawn Treader" *(1952); Marjorie Phillips,* Annabel and Bryony *(1953); C.S. Lewis,* The Silver Chair *(1953); C.S. Lewis,* The Horse and His Boy *(1954); Rhoda Power,* From the Fury Northmen *(1957); Dorothy Ensor,* The Adventures of Hakim Tai *(1960); Mary C. Borer,* Don Quixote *(1960); Edmund Spenser,* Saint George and the Dragon *(1961); Lynette Muir,* The Unicorn Window *(1961); Alison Uttley,* The Little Knife That Did All the Work *(1962); J.R.R. Tolkien,* The Adventures of Tom Bombadil *(1962); Hans Christian Andersen,* Andersen's Fairy Tales *(1963); Iona Opie and Peter Opie, editors,* The Puffin Book of Nursery Rhymes *(1964); A. Uttley,* Recipes from an Old Farmhouse *(1966); J.R.R. Tolkien,* Smith of Wootton Major *(1967); Jennifer Westwood,* Medieval Tales *(1967); Rumer Godden,* The Dragon of Oq *(1981); Mary Norton,* The Borrowers Avenged *(1982); R. Godden,* Four Dolls *(1983); Peter Dickinson,* The Iron Lion *(1983); Rudyard Kipling,* How the Whale Got His Throat *(1983); Anna Sewell,* Black Beauty *(1984); Ursula Moray Williams,* The Further Adventures of Gobbolino and the Little Wooden Horse *(1984); Cecil Frances Alexander,* All Things Bright and Beautiful *(1986); George Macbeth,* Daniel *(1986); Beatrix Potter,* Country Tales *(1987); B. Potter,* Wag-by-Wall *(1987); J.R.R. Tolkien,* Bilbo's Last Song; Praise Be to God.

Pauline Baynes

Although born in England, Pauline Baynes spent the first five years of her life in a remote jungle in India, where her father was stationed in the Indian Civil Service. When her mother Jessie became ill, Pauline and her older sister Angela were sent back to England and placed in Farnborough Convent while their mother recuperated in a nursing home. Accustomed to having things largely her own way, Baynes found the discipline and enormity of the institution overwhelming. She was constantly being punished for one thing or another: "I remember being made to kneel down in the long gallery in disgrace, and the whole school filed past." The experience, she believes, made her suspicious and belligerent.

After two years at Farnborough, Baynes lived in a variety of hotels and guest houses with her mother and sister, until taking up residence in a proper and strict Victorian boarding school in Camberley, Surrey, where she stayed until she was 15. Again Baynes had difficulty conforming to the rules of conduct and was asked to leave twice for various infractions. "I was always rebelling against any sort of authority and particularly resented older girls telling me what to do." she said. "I must have been very tiresome, difficult, and nonconformist."

Influenced by her sister who attended art school before her, Baynes began to draw at an early age. Art quickly became an obsession, a way for her to excel in school. In 1937, she persuaded her mother to let her enter Farnham Art School instead of taking her certificate examinations. At Farnham, Baynes did not enjoy the disciplines of perspective and life drawing but found a teacher, **Ann Heywood**, who encouraged her to explore her leanings toward design and decorative art. Baynes also mastered art appreciation at Farnham, albeit in a relatively unique way. "The bedrooms at the school were named after different English painters: Watts, Millais, Romney, and so on. In time I slept in most of the rooms, and got to know the pictures."

With the outbreak of World War II, Baynes joined her sister Angela at the Slade School, which had been evacuated to Oxford. As a special concession, she was allowed to work alongside her sister, who was finishing a diploma course. During the 1940s, they both did voluntary war work, which included caring for baby evacuees. They later worked full time for the British army's Camouflage Development and Training Centre, making demonstration models. A colleague at the time, the eccentric printer Perry Powell, engaged Baynes in illustrating books he wanted to publish in paperback, based on the popular Puffin collection. Her first illustrations for the series were for *Question Mark*, about a little boy who was constantly asking questions.

Bayne's career took off as a result of her correspondence with Harry Price, author of *The Most Haunted House in Britain.* Aware of his keen interest in all psychic phenomena, Baynes decorated a letter to him with a ghost hanging on a nail. Price showed the letter to Frank Whittaker, the editor of *Country Life*, which led to a commission to illustrate **Victoria Stevenson**'s *Clover Magic*, Baynes' first "proper" book in hardback.

Her first work for J.R.R. Tolkien, *Farmer Giles of Ham*, resulted in a friendship with the author and his wife, as well as subsequent assignments, including the cover for *The Lord of the Rings*. Although Baynes' reputation was made on illustrations for C.S. Lewis, most of them were done during a short period at the beginning of her career. She met the author on only two occasions, one of which she recorded in her diary in matter-of-fact fashion: "Had lunch with C.S. Lewis. Came home. Made rock cakes." She remembers that he only criticized two things during their association. "I drew someone rowing the wrong way and he very gently asked if I could possibly turn him around; his other request was that I pretty the children up a little."

Baynes has received numerous awards for her work, and her extraordinary output of illustrations has included a number of unusual assignments. One of her favorites was ***Alison Uttley**'s *Recipes from an Old Farmhouse*, which involved the challenge of piecing together ideas from torn-up paper on which the recipes and notes had been submitted to her. For the *National Gallery's Children's Book*, she produced an illustration of Michelangelo's ceiling of the Sistine Chapel. Her most unique commission was a design for the world's largest crewel embroidery for Plymouth Congregational Church in Minneapolis. Although Baynes refers to it as a "little design," she was amazed at the resultant embroidery, which people came from all over the country to see.

In 1961, after years of contented living alone, Baynes met and married Fritz Gasch, a garden contractor. She described him as the best thing that ever happened to her, bringing to her life companionship and love she had never known. After his death, she continued her daily routine, walking her dogs Bertha and Mighty after breakfast, then settling down to work throughout the day. Baynes believes she has led a charmed life. "My sister was indeed a beacon that I could follow, and my husband the light of my life; they are both dead, alas, but the slow-burning candle that is my obsession with illustrating still glows hopefully on."

Barbara Morgan,
Melrose, Massachusetts

Bazán, Emilia Pardo (1851–1921).

See Pardo Bazan, Emilia.

Bazus, Florence de or Leslie de (1836–1914).

See Leslie, Miriam Folline Squier.

Beach, Amy Cheney (1867–1944)

Composer, pianist, and the first American woman to overcome gender bias in music, who attained an international reputation as a composer of large-scale classical music. *Name variations: Mrs. H.H.A. Beach, Amy Marcy Cheney. Pronunciation: Chain-ee. Born Amy Marcy Cheney on September 5, 1867, in Henniker, New Hampshire; died of heart failure in her New York apartment on December 27, 1944; only child of Charles Abbott Cheney (a paper manufacturer and importer) and Clara Imogene (Marcy) Cheney (a singer and pianist); at age six, began studying piano with her mother; attended a Boston private school; studied piano with Ernst Perabo, 1876–82, and Carl Baermann, starting 1880; studied harmony with Junius W. Hill, 1881–82; taught herself orchestration and fugue, translating treatises by Berlioz and François-Auguste Gevaert; awarded honorary Master of Arts from University of New Hampshire, June 18, 1928; married Dr. Henry Harris Aubrey Beach (d. June 28, 1910, a prominent Boston physician and lecturer), on December 2, 1885; children: none.*

Family moved to Chelsea, a suburb of Boston (1871), then Boston (1875); made Boston debut as pianist (October 24, 1883); debuted with Boston Sym-

Amy Cheney Beach

phony (March 28, 1885); began publishing compositions (1885); presented Mass in E-Flat, op. 5, first mass composed by an American woman, performed by Boston's Handel and Haydn Society (February 7, 1892); premiered Eilende Wolken, *op. 18, with New York Symphony Society (December 2–3, 1892); premiered* Festival Jubilate, *op. 17, for the dedication of the Woman's Building at Chicago's Columbian Exposition (May 1, 1893); performed first piano recital devoted to her own compositions, Wellesley College (May 7, 1894); composed* Gaelic Symphony, *op. 32, first symphony by an American woman, presented by Boston Symphony Orchestra (October 30, 1896); premiered Piano Concerto in C-Sharp minor, op. 45 (April 6–7, 1900); premiered Piano Quintet in F-Sharp minor, op. 67 (February 27, 1908); baptized at Emmanuel Church, Boston (November 4, 1910), confirmed (April 2, 1911); lived in Europe (September 5, 1911-September 1914); began to spend winters touring and summers at Hillsboro, New Hampshire, and Centerville, Cape Cod, Massachusetts; began composing at the MacDowell Colony, Peterborough, New Hampshire (summer, 1921); began affiliation with the League of American Pen Women (1921); named first president of the Society of American Women Composers (1924); toured Europe (November 1926–July 1927 and December 1928–May 1929); made permanent winter home in New York City (1930); finished only opera,* Cabildo, *op. 149 (1932); elected first vice president of the Edward MacDowell Association (January 1934); performed at the White House (April 23, 1934 and April 17, 1936); visited London (May–June 1936); premiered Piano Trio, op. 150, in New York (January 15, 1939); honored at a dinner in New York's Town Hall Club (May 8, 1940); made an honorary member of the Town Hall Alumni Association of New York (December 29, 1943). Her 75th birthday anniversary was recognized by The Phillips Memorial Gallery of Washington, D.C. which presented two concerts of her music (November 27–28, 1942); a bust of Beach, sculptured by Bashka Paeff, was donated to the Phillips Gallery, Washington (1942).*

Selected discography: The American Romantic *(Alan Feinberg, piano, Argo, 1990);* Carolyn Heafner Sings American Songs *(Carolyn Heafner, soprano, Dixie Ross Neill, piano, Composers Recordings, 1981);* Chamber Works for Piano and Orchestra, *op. 45;* Piano Quintet in F-Sharp Minor, *op. 67 (**Mary Louise Boehm**, piano, Westphalian Symphony Orchestra, Siegfried Landau, conductor, Vox Turnabout, 1991);* Grand Mass in E-Flat major *(Michael May, conductor, Elaine Bunse, soprano, Barbara Schramm, mezzo-soprano, Paul Rogers, tenor, Leonard Jay Gould, baritone, Daniel Beckwith, organist, Newport Classic, 1989);* The Piano Music of Mrs. H.H.A. Beach *(**Virginia Erskin**, piano, Genesis, 1975); Sonata in A Minor for Piano and Violin, op. 34, in* Recorded Anthology of American Music *(Joseph Silverstein, violin, Gilbert Kalish, piano, New World Records, 1977);* Symphony in E Minor (Gaelic), *in* Music in America *(Royal Philharmonic Orchestra, Karl Krueger, conductor, Musical Heritage, 1968);* The Toledo Trio Paints Three New England Portraits *(Piano Trio in A minor, op. 150, Musical Heritage Society, 1988); "When I Have Sung My Songs," in* Recorded Anthology of American Music*; "The Year's at the Spring" (Emma Eames, soprano, 1976).*

Historically, few women composers have been able to tear down existing gender obstacles to achieve success. Even a cursory glance at Western musical history reveals that works by women are largely absent. For the most part, their compositions have remained outside the standard music-history textbook and concert repertoire. Remarkably, almost everything in Amy Cheney Beach's life seemed to work in her favor, allowing her to overcome gender discrimination with her incredible talents and emerge as an eminent international composer of classical music.

Born on September 5, 1867, in Henniker, New Hampshire, Amy Marcy Cheney was the only child of **Clara Marcy Cheney** and paper manufacturer Charles Abbott Cheney. Her parents, both scions of distinguished New England pioneers, enjoyed considerable wealth and high social position. Amy's ancestors were among the original settlers of Woodstock, Connecticut; she was also a direct descendant of William Learned Marcy, who was governor of New York, secretary of war, and secretary of state, and General Henry Dearborn, secretary of war and later U.S. minister to Portugal. Many of Amy's maternal relatives were musical: her mother was a fine amateur singer and pianist, her grandfather played the clarinet, and her aunt and grandmother sang.

Extraordinarily precocious, Amy Cheney possessed exceptional musical ability, including absolute pitch. Reputedly, by age one, she had memorized 40 tunes and sang them flawlessly. "If anyone sang a song to her with a slightly different rhythm or melody than . . . when she first heard it," wrote **Janet Nichols**, "she complained that it was being sung incorrectly." Before reaching two, she improvised and sang alto lines against her mother's soprano melodies. By age four, she composed and played her first piano pieces and, after one hearing, played church hymns by ear in perfect four-part harmony. Beach associated colors with major keys: C was white, F-sharp black, E yellow, G red, A green, A-flat blue, D-flat violet or purple and E-flat pink. Before long Amy required a wider range of colors. Realizing that music had a powerful influence over her child's moods (lively music gave Amy joy, sad music made her cry), Clara Cheney came up with a creative form of punishment for mischievous behavior. She disciplined her daughter by playing Louis Moreau Gottschalk's lugubrious *Last Hope* on the family piano.

In 1871, when Amy was still four, the family moved to Chelsea, Massachusetts, a suburb of Boston; at age six, she began to receive formal instruction on the piano from her mother three times a week. The following year, she started performing at a few small church musicales and private soirees: her repertoire consisted of Beethoven's Sonatas, op. 47, nos. 1 and 2, Chopin's Waltz in E-flat, op. 18, and a variety of piano transcriptions written by the great European masters. Often after being called back on stage for encores, the seven-year-old would amaze her listeners by playing one of her own compositions, such as *Mama's Waltz.*

In 1875, the Cheneys moved to Boston, a hub of cultural activity and a well-established breeding ground for music in the worshipped German tradition. In a short time, the family became involved with a social circle that included prominent Harvard faculty members, writers, musicians, artists, and patrons. Several of these pillars of Boston society became Amy's sponsors, including the famous poet Henry Wadsworth Longfellow, who was so delighted by "Miss Amy's" musical genius that he spoke openly of her brilliance and invited the prodigy to play at his home. At 14, after one such visit, Amy thrilled Longfellow by setting his poem "The Rainy Day" to music. In 1883, Oliver Ditson issued the song, and it became her first published composition.

Aware of Amy's unique talent, several of Boston's distinguished musicians recommended that she follow the example of many 19th-century American composers and continue her musical education in Europe. Nevertheless, the Cheneys enrolled their only child in a local private school and asked three Boston masters to teach her music: Ernst Perabo and Carl Baermann, once a pupil of Franz Liszt, were selected to teach Beach piano, while, for one year, Junius W. Hill was chosen to instruct her in harmony and counterpoint. For the most part, Beach was self-taught. She learned counterpoint by transcribing Bach's piano pieces from memory, then studying her mistakes. She learned orchestration by paying close attention at concerts; once home, she transcribed the piece from memory, along with the instrumentation, then compared her work with the written score. She also studied, in the original French, Hector Berlioz's *Treatise on Instrumentation.*

If you feel deeply and know how to express what you feel, you make others feel.

—Amy Cheney Beach

On October 24, 1883, just after her 16th birthday, Beach made her formal public debut as a pianist, performing in A.P. Peck's Anniversary Concert at the Boston Music Hall. Her program included Ignaz Moscheles' G-minor Concerto with orchestra and the Rondo in E-Flat by Chopin as part of a larger variety concert which presented performances by both a leading Boston violinist and a vocal quartet. All 11 newspaper reviews agreed, however, that the most important event of the evening was the debut of Amy Cheney.

On March 28, 1885, she debuted with the Boston Symphony Orchestra, performing Chopin's F-minor Concerto, op. 21, with Wilhelm Gericke conducting. Recognizing that Amy's talent deserved special attention, Gericke invited the young pianist to attend future rehearsals of the Boston Symphony in order to closely examine the art of orchestration and musical composition. She then journeyed to New York for her debut with the New York Philharmonic. During rehearsal, conductor Theodore Thomas slowed the tempo of Felix Mendelssohn's Piano Concerto in G Minor, anxious to make the piano section more manageable for the young pianist. "After the orchestra played the opening measures alone," wrote Nichols, "seventeen-year-old Amy launched into her first entrance at a lively clip, forcing the conductor to rev up the orchestra to match her speed."

Sometime during the early 1880s, when Amy injured a finger, Clara had taken her to visit the prominent surgeon, Dr. Henry H.A. Beach, an instructor at Harvard Medical School. Widowed in 1880, the doctor had attended some of Amy's concerts and admired her work. An amateur musician, he had a deep appreciation for the fine arts; he loved to play the piano, sing, read, paint, write poetry, and collect art. The friendship between patient and doctor blossomed, and it soon became apparent that Amy Marcy Cheney and Dr. H.H.A. Beach, who was 24 years her senior, were very much in love. At a student recital on January 16, 1885, the doctor had displayed his affection by performing "Jeune fille et jeune fleur," op. 1, no. 3, Amy's newly composed love song.

On December 2, after turning 18, Amy Cheney married the 43-year-old physician, and, since it was only proper for all proper married Bostonian women, she insisted on using her married name, Mrs. H.H.A. Beach, professionally. Henry Beach had a strong influence over his young wife. It was Henry who encouraged her to limit her performances and donate her fees to charity. It was Henry who discouraged her desire for formal study, fearing it might hamper her originality. And it was Henry who strongly urged her to turn her skills to composition. Henry and Clara were untiring supporters of Amy's work. They were, wrote Beach, "the kindest, most helpful, and most merciless critics I ever had. How often they would make me work over a phrase—over and over and over!—until the flow of the melody and the harmonization sounded right! The result was that I had two critics before facing a professional critic."

The year of their marriage was also the year that Arthur P. Schmidt of Boston began to publish her compositions. Since Henry and Arthur were close friends, the publication of Beach's work was given special attention. His company, committed to cultivating an American school of composition, had offices in New York and Leipzig, as well as in Boston, and remained Beach's only publisher until 1914.

On February 7, 1892, the Handel and Haydn Society of Boston proudly presented the first mass composed by an American woman. Mrs. H.H.A. Beach's first large work, the Mass in E-flat, op. 5, was conducted by Carl Zerrahn at the Boston Music Hall. The Mass, which had taken three years to complete, was well received by both the critics and the public. In New York, reviewers also praised the work, and the New York audience gave the composer a standing ovation. When the contralto soloist for the Mass asked Beach to write her a "grand dramatic aria," the composer responded with her usual speed and on December 2 and 3, 1892, Walter Damrosch led the New York Symphony Society in the premiere of *Eilende Wolken*, op. 18. The composition, a recitative and aria for voice and orchestra based on the words of Schiller, depicted ***Mary Stuart, Queen of Scots'** emotions after being released from prison. It was the first time that the New York Symphony Society had presented the work of a woman composer.

Beach was then commissioned to write a work for the dedication of the Woman's Building of the Columbian Exposition to be held in Chicago on May 1, 1893. Two other women—***Ingeborg von Bronsart** of Weimar and **Frances Ellicott** of England—were invited to submit compositions for this occasion. Bronsart and Ellicott composed orchestral works while Beach wrote *Festival Jubilate*, op. 17, for orchestra and a mixed chorus of 300 voices. In spite of poor acoustics, the performance of *Festival Jubilate*, conducted by Theodore Thomas, was a huge success, and the event gave Beach's music new international exposure. According to W. Waugh Lauder, correspondent for the *Musical Courier*, the work "made a deep and satisfying impression, and gave an official seal to woman's capability in music." Lauder's remark was an obvious attempt to undermine late 19th-century theories that supposedly "proved" women's creative inferiority.

Although Beach had achieved much success with her previous compositions, the premiere of her *Gaelic Symphony*, op. 32, despite mixed reviews, firmly established her as a major American composer. On October 30, 1896, the work was performed by the Boston Symphony Orchestra under Emil Paur. According to Percy Scholes in the *Oxford Companion to Music*, Beach was not only the first American woman to compose a symphony, but the first American composer "to write a symphony of importance." It was astounding that a largely self-taught composer could produce such a technical masterpiece. Her 14 years spent studying orchestration and musical composition with the Boston Symphony Orchestra had clearly paid off.

On April 6, 1900, appearing as soloist with the Boston Symphony Orchestra at Boston's Music Hall, Beach premiered her Piano Concerto in C-Sharp minor, op. 45, which was dedicated to the Venezuelan pianist ***Teresa Carreño**. For the first time, the majority of Boston's critics disliked Beach's work. In the *Boston Journal*, Philip Hale angrily wrote that "the concerto was a disappointment in nearly every way" and went on to suggest that Beach's ambition far outweighed her musical knowledge. Beach was later vindicated when German critics praised the concerto.

Beach's seemingly charmed life suffered a downward shift in 1910 and 1911. On April 25, 1910, while making a house call, Henry Beach fell down a steep flight of stairs and was badly injured. He died on June 28, at age 66. Following his funeral, Beach, along with her mother, sought refuge at her Cape Cod cottage in Centerville. In quiet seclusion, she found new comfort in meditation and reading. Upon her return to Boston that autumn, she renewed her faith and, on November 4, was baptized at a private service in Boston's Emmanuel Episcopalian Church. Prior to her husband's death, Beach had been religious, but she had not chosen to affiliate with any particular church. Eighteen months after Henry's death, Beach's mother Clara died on February 18, 1911. Clara Cheney had long been her daughter's closest friend. Devastated, Beach turned to her newly found faith for spiritual strength. On April 2, 1911, she was confirmed at the Emmanuel Episcopalian Church.

On September 5, 1911, after closing her home on Boston's Commonwealth Avenue, Beach left for Europe, first to recuperate and then to concertize and establish herself as an international composer and pianist. Before she sailed, she told an interviewer: "Since I am a very bad sailor, I have never quite summoned the requisite courage until this year to attempt a voyage across the ocean. Indeed I had almost concluded that until the journey could be made by some other way—perhaps by a flying machine—I should have to forego the pleasure of travel in Europe." In a letter written to Arthur Schmidt on November 30, 1912, she observed that successful European concerts would enhance her reputation back in the United States: "Even a limited number of European performances will help at home you know." When Amy Beach arrived in Europe, she was already known as an eminent American composer. Many leading musicians had introduced several of her compositions to European audiences. The Violin Sonata, op. 34, had been performed by Carreño in Berlin in 1899 and by Sigmund Beel in London in 1901; throughout 1894, ***Lillian Russell** had performed the song "Ecstasy," op. 19, no. 2, in London; during 1904, ***Emma Eames** had included the composer's most popular song, "The Year's at the Spring," op. 44, no. 1, in her European concerts; and for several years, **Marcella Craft**, an old friend of Amy's who sang with the Munich opera, had presented a number of Beach's songs in her European recitals.

Beginning in the autumn of 1912, Beach appeared as piano soloist and accompanist, presenting her Piano Concerto, op. 45, *Gaelic Symphony*, op. 32, Sonata for Violin and Piano, op. 34, Piano Quintet, op. 67, and piano pieces and songs in a number of German cities. The reviews were favorable, and she was warmly received. Dr. Ferdinand Pfohl, one of Germany's foremost music critics, praised Beach's ability to compose large-scale classical music and observed that "one need only mention the name of Amy Beach in order to refute the foolish prejudices concerning women composers." Her brief journey to Europe lasted three years.

In the fall of 1914, shortly before the outbreak of World War I, Beach arrived in Boston triumphant. By attaining a distinguished musical reputation in Europe, she had firmly established her concert career in the United States and was scheduled to perform 30 recitals during the upcoming concert season. Her songs and piano music were especially popular, and American musical organizations, professional women's clubs, and colleagues viewed her as a musical hero. For the next four years, Beach concertized extensively throughout the U.S., performing her works in major cities, including Boston, Kansas City, Portland, Detroit, New York, Los Angeles, San Francisco, Salt Lake City, Pittsburgh, Chicago, Philadelphia, and San Diego. Distinguished orchestras such as the Philadelphia Orchestra, Chicago Symphony, Boston Symphony, St. Louis Symphony, and the Minneapolis Symphony Orchestra performed the *Gaelic Symphony*, op. 32, and the Piano Concerto, op. 45.

In the years following 1918, Beach gave fewer large concert-hall appearances. Surrounded by friends and supporters, she now became more active in professional organizations and often performed small intimate recitals on their behalf, including the League of American Pen Women, the MacDowell Colony, the National Federation of Musical Clubs, and the Music Teachers National Association. She had become wealthy from the sales of her sheet music, most especially her songs. Aware of the singularity of her good fortune among women musicians, Beach helped found the Society of American Women Composers in 1924 and was the group's first president.

Since her husband's death, Beach had rented her Commonwealth Avenue home in Boston to physicians and never returned there to live. She spent her winters mostly on tour, while part of her summer was spent at the home of **Jessie Parker** in Hillsboro, New Hampshire. Drawn to the Parker family because of their "serious, scholarly nature," Beach loved to sit in their kitchen and visit over coffee. Throughout her life, her cottage in Centerville, Cape Cod, purchased entirely with proceeds received from her famous song "Ecstasy," remained her main summer residence. Beginning in 1921, Beach also took time each summer to compose at the MacDowell Colony in Peterborough, New Hampshire. Established by ***Marian MacDowell** in 1908, the Colony was a natural haven where artists worked in peaceful bliss, faraway from the routines of everyday living.

Beach often traveled abroad. On November 20, 1926, she sailed on the S.S. *Martha Washington* for "a complete rest from musical work," traveling to Greece, Italy, France, and Belgium, sightseeing and attending concerts. On July 12, 1927, she returned to America. Feeling rejuvenated, Beach once again began to concentrate on her composing and concertizing, before another five-month trip to Europe on December 11, 1928. In Rome, she composed her String Quartet, op. 89, and appeared in concerts at the American Academy and the American embassy.

In 1930, at age 63, Amy Beach decided to make New York City her winter residence. Up until October 1942, she resided at the American Women's Association Clubhouse. After that, she rented an apartment at New York's Barclay Hotel. During the summer, she continued to return to Hillsboro, Centerville, and the MacDowell Colony because life in the New England woods "was her greatest joy." Captivated by nature from childhood, the musician chose to do her composing outdoors when weather permitted. During the summer of 1921, she had composed two of her most popular pieces at MacDowell: *The Hermit Thrush at Eve*, op. 92, no.

1, and *The Hermit Thrush at Dawn*, op. 92, no. 2. The pieces were based on transcriptions of bird song that Beach collected from the hermit thrush who sang outside her studio. She was also fascinated with folk music. Approximately 30 of her compositions were inspired by Irish, Scottish, Balkan, African-American, or Native American melodies. In 1922, a Native American woman had sent the composer a well-known Omaha dance tune. Overjoyed by the kind gift, Beach based her piano composition, *From Blackbird Hills*, op. 83, on the tribal dance.

From 1931 to 1944, Beach's choral works gained widespread popularity throughout the northeast. Her own church, St. Bartholomew's Episcopal, regularly performed several of her choral compositions. Beach's sacred works, in particular the *Canticle of the Sun*, op. 123, remain in America's church repertory. When **Ruth Shaffner** resigned as soprano soloist at St. Bartholomew's after many years of service, Beach gifted her with a brief trip to London. The two sailed from New York on May 8, 1936, visiting many English gardens and estates. Beach was scheduled to return to Europe on March 2, 1938, but a fire aboard her ship before embarkation postponed the sailing indefinitely. She never traveled to Europe again.

By the late 1930s, it became apparent to Beach and her friends that some of her former admirers were beginning to lose interest in her music. Many critics and musicians considered her work to be hopelessly out of vogue because it avoided modern avant-garde compositional styles such as Impressionism and atonality. Like the New England composers of her youth, she wrote in a late Romantic style. Her music, often described as Lisztian, relied on a natural gift for melody and contained a hefty amount of chromaticism, modulation, and emotional intensity. Terse notes in Beach's diary indicate that she was also bothered by some of the music written by her contemporaries. For instance, on more than one occasion she describes the orchestral music of Copland and Stravinsky as being "horrid."

During the last 14 years of her life, Beach composed a considerable amount of music, though only two works—her first and only opera *Cabildo*, op. 149 (1932), and the Piano Trio, op. 150 (1939)—are considered especially noteworthy. Both were written during her summers at the MacDowell Colony. "I can't compose in New York," confessed Beach. "I have too many friends and there are too many good concerts." The Piano Trio premiered on January 15, 1939, at the MacDowell Club in New York. But the opera *Cabildo*, based on Pierre Lafitte's escape from Cabildo prison in New Orleans during the War of 1812, only brought her frustration. On August 24, 1940, Hugh Hodgson, head of the music department at the University of Georgia, visited Beach and discussed the possibility of premiering the opera at the university, but continued postponements and World War II intervened before its premiere in 1945, a year after her death.

In 1942, Amy Beach's 75th birthday year, a bust of Beach, sculptured by Bashka Paeff of Cambridge, was donated to the Phillips Gallery (now the Phillips Collection) in Washington. In addition, many retrospective concerts of her works were given in her honor. Though Beach's health did not allow her to attend any of the festivities, she was extremely moved by the warm tributes. Two years later, on December 27, 1944, America's first distinguished woman composer died of heart failure in her New York City apartment.

Amy Cheney Beach's career was one of incredible musical achievement. In an era when women had barely won the right to vote, she found a way to successfully overcome gender discrimination in music and attain international recognition as an eminent composer. What she did was nothing short of amazing. "Not only was it unheard of for a woman to compose music for orchestra," wrote Janet Nichols; "it was unacceptable for them to acquire any hands-on experience by playing orchestral instruments. Most young ladies played the piano a little, and a few played harp or guitar. The violin was out, since a woman's pretty face was distorted when she pressed her chin into the instrument. A woman clutching a cello between her knees was considered scandalous. A young lady blowing into a wind instrument or beating a drum was simply vulgar." Beach's success broke ground for future generations of women composers, and her music contributed greatly to America's rich musical heritage.

SOURCES:

Ammer, Christine. *Unsung: A History of Women in American Music.* Westport, CT: Greenwood Press, 1980.

Block, Adrienne Fried. "Why Amy Beach Succeeded as a Composer: The Early Years," in *Current Musicology.* Vol. 36, 1983, pp. 41–59.

Jenkins, Walter S. *The Remarkable Mrs. Beach.* Warren, MI: Harmonie Park Press, 1994.

Wilson, Arthur. "A Conservation on Musical Conditions in America," in *The Musician.* Vol. 17, no. 1. January 1912.

Wise Brown, Jeanell. *Amy Beach and her Chamber Music.* Metuchen, NJ: Scarecrow Press, 1994.

SUGGESTED READING:

Block, Adrienne Fried. "Amy Beach's Music on Native American Themes," in *American Music*. Vol. 8, no. 2, 1990, pp. 141–166.

Tuthill, Burnet C. "Mrs. H.H.A. Beach," in *Musical Quarterly*. July 1940, pp. 297–310.

Upton, George P. *Women in Music*. Chicago, IL: A.C. McClurg, 1886.

COLLECTIONS:

Scrapbooks, diaries, personal correspondence, manuscript scores, and memorabilia in Amy Beach Collection, Special Collections Department, University Library, University of New Hampshire, Durham, New Hampshire, and Fuller Library Collection of Hillsboro, New Hampshire, both on permanent loan to University of New Hampshire; Amy Beach clipping file, New York Public Library, collection of magazine articles, correspondence between Beach and B.C. Tuthill, and newspaper reviews; Arthur P. Schmidt Collection, Library of Congress, Washington, D.C. (all business correspondence between The Arthur P. Schmidt Company, publisher, and Amy Beach 1898–1944); Crawford Collection, Library of Congress, Washington, D.C. (letters and memorabilia collected and donated by Rebekah Crawford).

Cheryl Gillard, musicologist and freelance writer, Ottawa, Canada

Sylvia Beach

Beach, Mrs. H.H.A. (1867–1944).

See Beach, Amy Cheney.

Beach, Sylvia (1887–1962)

American bookshop owner and publisher who was at the center of the American and English literary colony in Paris during the 1920s. *Name variations: changed her first name to Sylvia in 1901. Born Nancy Woodbridge Beach in Baltimore, Maryland, on March 14, 1887; died in Paris, France, on October 5, 1962; second daughter of Sylvester Woodbridge Beach (an American Presbyterian minister) and Eleanor (Orbison) Beach (who was born in a missionary family in India); educated mainly at home; never married; companion of Adrienne Monnier; no children.*

In the 1920s and 1930s, Sylvia Beach owned and ran Shakespeare and Company, a Paris bookshop. The shop became the community center for "lost generation" intellectuals from Britain and America, including James Joyce, Ezra Pound, Ernest Hemingway, John Dos Passos, Stephen Spender, ***Djuna Barnes**, ***Kay Boyle**, ***Natalie Barney**, ***Mina Loy**, ***Margaret Anderson**, and ***Gertrude Stein**, as well as for prominent French writers like Paul Valéry, André Gide, and Paul Claudel. When the vogue for literary exile had passed, Sylvia Beach stayed in France and endured the Second World War under the Nazi occupation.

She was born in Baltimore, christened Nancy, and moved as a child to Bridgeton, New Jersey, where her father Sylvester Woodbridge Beach, D.D., served as Presbyterian minister. Nancy (who changed her name to Sylvia as a teenager) was the second of three sisters, each of whom learned to be independent and grew up to have a career of her own. The youngest, ➧ **Cyprian**, became a French film star during the First World War. Sylvia first went to France in 1902 when her father became minister of an American church in Paris, and she lived there from ages 15 to 17. Next the family took up residence in Princeton, New Jersey, where the Reverend Beach had Princeton president and future U.S. president Woodrow Wilson as a member of his congregation at the First Presbyterian Church. As the girls grew up, their parents were increasingly estranged, and, from 1914 onwards, mother and daughters lived almost all the time in Europe: first Spain and then France. They were in Paris during World War I, and Sylvia, despite a childhood of neurasthenic headaches, uncertainty about her future, and dilettantism, volunteered for an arduous job as a farm worker in Touraine. The 12-hour work days appeared to make her healthier and soon afterwards she found her long sought vocation.

One of her closest French friends was **Adrienne Monnier**, who owned a bookshop on the Rue de l'Odéon called the Maison des Amis des Livres, on the west bank of the River Seine. After meeting Monnier, who became her lifelong companion, Beach decided not to return to America, despite her mother's pleading, but to stay on permanently in Europe. At the end of the war, however, she spent six months away from Paris after volunteering

Beach, Cyprian (1893–1951)

Younger sister of Sylvia Beach. Born on April 23, 1893, in New Jersey; died of cancer of the bladder on July 26, 1951; studied music with Jean Alexis Perier; lived with ***Helen Eddy****.*

While living in Paris at the Palais Royale with her sister Sylvia, Cyprian Beach studied opera and, unbeknownst to her parents, secretly pursued a film career. She knew early success when she portrayed Belle-Mirette in the French serial *Judex*, directed by Louis Feuillade. But when mother **Eleanor Beach**'s marriage and health took a turn for the worse, it was Cyprian who sacrificed her fledgling career and returned home to Princeton to help out.

Monnier, Adrienne (c. 1892–1955)

French bookseller, writer, and publisher who discovered and aided new writers. *Born around 1892 (she was five years older than Sylvia Beach); daughter of Clovis Monnier; committed suicide in France on June 19, 1955, a victim of Mènière's syndrome (aural disturbances of the inner ear); elder sister of* ***Marie Monnier****; companion of Sylvia Beach.*

In 1915, with money awarded her father Clovis for injuries sustained in a railway accident, Adrienne Monnier founded Maison des Amis Livres (The House of the Friends of Books), where she sold works of significant new French writers and lived above her shop. Before this, she had read palms, taught school, and worked as a secretary. Monnier's bookshop was a French literary center, frequented by the likes of André Gide, Jean Schlumberger, Paul Valéry, Jean-Paul Fargue, Erik Satie, Valéry Larbaud, and Jules Romain. Books were sold or rented and readings were held in the back parlor where Mme Monnier was forever hostess. She was also responsible for the French language publication of *Ulysses* and the costly, short-lived magazine *Le Navire d'Argent*.

In 1917, Adrienne Monnier met ***Sylvia Beach**. Two years later, when Beach opened her own bookshop, Monnier and Beach became friends, especially after the death of Monnier's business partner **Suzanne Bonnière** that same year. In 1921, Beach moved her bookstore directly across the street from Monnier's on the Rue de l'Odéon. "The immediate compatibility of these two extraordinary women shopkeepers, opposite numbers in what became a cultural Franco-English language stream flowing down their street, visibly added to its picturesque quality," wrote ***Janet Flanner** in *Paris was Yesterday*.

> Adrienne was mildly spectacular. Buxom as a handsome abbess, she was a placidly eccentric neighborhood figure in a costume she had invented for herself and permanently adopted. It consisted of a full long gray skirt and a sleeveless velveteen waistcoat worn over a white blouse. . . . [She] looked like some character actress from the Théâtre de l'Odéon at the head of their street, who had strolled out from a dress rehearsal in full stage costume.

Soon, Beach moved in with Monnier, and they lived together until 1937. That year, Monnier became involved with the photographer ***Gisèle Freund**, and Beach began to live above her own shop. Monnier and Beach remained lifelong companions, however, and, after Monnier took an overdose of sleeping tablets in 1955 (for nine months, she had complained of maddening noises), Beach wrote: "My loves were Adrienne Monnier and James Joyce and Shakespeare and Company."

Sylvia Beach and Adrienne Monnier had an enormous impact on the cognoscenti of literary Paris. Following his first visit to Paris in 1923, Archibald MacLeish wrote:

> Turning up from St. Germain to go home past the bottom of the gardens to the Boulevard St. Michel one kept Shakespeare and Company to starboard and Adrienne Monnier's Amis des Livres to port, and felt, as one rose with the tide toward the theatre, that one had passed the gates of dream. . . . It was enough for a confused young lawyer in a grand and vivid time to look from one side to the other and say to himself, as the cold came up from the river, Gide was here on Thursday and on Monday Joyce was there.

SUGGESTED READING:

Monnier, Adrienne. *The Very Rich Hours of Adrienne Monnier.* Translated by Richard McDougall. Bison Books, 1996.

with her sister ◀❦ **Holly** to join a Red Cross mission to Serbia. Sylvia worked as a translator and secretary and found the domineering ways of the Red Cross' male leaders a stimulus to her interest in feminism. Serbia was shattered from years of war and famine, and Beach's experiences there intensified her conviction that war could never be justified, a view she retained until the Second World War forced her to see the legitimacy of forceful resistance to Nazism.

My mother in Princeton got a cable from me, saying simply: 'Opening bookshop in Paris. Please send money,' and she sent me all her savings.

—**Sylvia Beach**

From Adrienne Monnier, Beach learned the book business and realized, as the exile community swelled after the war, that an English-language bookstore in Paris might be economically viable. With Monnier's encouragement and with a $3,000 check from her mother back in the States, Beach set up shop just around the corner from the Maison des Amis, in 1919, in a building that had previously been a laundry. It doubled as a lending library and setting for public readings, and in the early days Beach slept in a room behind the store to save money. Even so, the shop required further transfusions of cash from her mother and from sister Holly to stay afloat, and always carried the air of a hobby-project as much as a hard-headed business proposition. "Fitting people with books is about as difficult as fitting them with shoes," wrote Beach in her memoirs, and she always took a close personal interest in the lives and tastes of regular customers. To add to the club-like atmosphere, she usually kept the shop open from nine in the morning until midnight.

***Janet Flanner**, who wrote Paris articles for *The New Yorker* (founded 1925) and was a close friend, noted that Beach was as "thin as a schoolgirl," and "dressed like one, in a juvenile short skirt and jacket over a white blouse with a big white turndown collar, like one of Colette's young heroines, and a big colored bowknot at the throat." With the help of influential literary friends, her shop quickly prospered, bringing in American and British exiles as well as French literary stars. Certain American writers, particularly Edgar Allan Poe and Walt Whitman, enjoyed a great vogue in France at that time, and the presence of an English language bookstore and literary circle attracted other French authors. In 1926, Beach mounted a Whitman exhibition, backed by a gigantic stars-and-stripes banner left over from Paris' welcome to the American doughboys in 1917. André Gide was one of many writers experimenting with homosexually explicit writing, and he treated Whitman as a homoerotic antecedent. Despite her Presbyterian upbringing, Beach was uncensorious and did not object. Besides, it is fairly certain that she and Monnier were lovers: they spent most weekends together at Monnier's parents' house in the countryside near Chartres cathedral and went away to an old farmhouse in the Savoyan alps every summer.

Beach was a gifted writer in her own right but self-effacing: she preferred the reflected glory of her friends to a spotlight of her own. Paris had many attractions for American writers after the First World War. Many often felt a sense of intellectual inferiority to Europe and regarded London and Paris as the centers of the intellectual world. A favorable exchange rate meant that a writer with a small dollar income could live much better in Paris than at home. Prohibition, in effect from 1919, dismayed hard-drinking novelists like Hemingway, as did the morally censorious and politically repressive atmosphere which followed the war. Paris, by contrast, offered an open and tolerant mood. Gertrude Stein, writer, art patron, and friend of Picasso, Braque and Matisse, who had already been living in Paris for 15 years, was among Beach's new customers. With her inseparable companion ❦▶ **Alice B. Toklas**, Stein often spent time at the shop discussing literature with Sylvia Beach and meeting other exiles. One young American, Stephen Vincent Benet, who was then an aspiring novelist, admired Stein but was afraid to visit her alone, so Beach chaperoned him to Stein's salon. She also befriended Man Ray, the avant-garde photographer, and he made portraits of many of her regular customers, in addition to photographing life at Shakespeare and Company. (Photographer ***Gisèle Freund** also documented the bookstore.) Surviving photographs show groups of literary

❦▶ **Beach, Holly** (b. 1884)

Older sister of Sylvia Beach. *Name variations: Holly Beach Dennis. Born Mary Hollingsworth Morris Beach on June 17, 1884, in New Jersey; eldest daughter of Sylvester Woodbridge Beach (an American Presbyterian minister) and Eleanor (Orbison) Beach; married Frederic James Dennis (d. 1945), on January 21, 1929.*

lights standing before an array of their own portraits, with short, modest Sylvia Beach standing beside them. One features Hemingway with a theatrical-seeming bandage around his head after an accident with a skylight, being smiled upon by Sylvia.

Among Beach's closest literary friends was James Joyce, the Irish novelist. She was his most enthusiastic supporter as he wrote *Ulysses*, and he reveled in her friendship, often coming to Shakespeare and Company and reading long passages to her aloud. Sections of this revolutionary stream-of-consciousness novel had already appeared in little magazines at the end of the teens and the start of the 1920s, but under Beach's guidance Joyce finally gathered his massive manuscript together for publication. She appealed to all the English and American visitors to her shop to help finance the work since its unconventional style and (for the time) very sexually explicit passages led conventional publishers to fear prosecution for obscenity. While assistants took care of Shakespeare and Company, she then found typesetters in Dijon to assemble the work, who were handicapped by lack of an English speaker among their entire crew. Not surprisingly, in view of this language barrier and in view of the book's 730-page length, with literally tens of thousands of invented words, there were a huge number of typographical errors, repetitions, and omissions. Even so, Joyce was so excited when he saw the proof sheets that he promptly wrote another 90,000 words, which had to be painstakingly (and expensively) inserted into the text. After months of work, the first copies arrived in February 1922, just in time for Joyce's 40th birthday.

British and American censors both labeled *Ulysses* obscene and seized copies as they entered their countries but enough copies sold in Europe to make Joyce comfortably well-to-do after years of privation. Until then, he had been a shameless scrounger, hitting up everyone he knew for loans which he never repaid and sometimes even taking money from the till at Shakespeare and Company, leaving little IOUs for Sylvia. Now he began to spend money on himself, his family, and friends with reckless abandon. "Joyce's tips were famous," she wrote. "The waiters, the boy who fetched him a taxi, all those who served him, must have retired with a fortune." With Joyce, she was always forgiving, convinced that he was a genius who must be indulged and exempted from the normal rules of conduct. She enjoyed his annual birthday parties, which were also anniversaries of *Ulysses*, and liked to hear him, half-drunk, singing Irish songs while accompanying himself at the piano. She was indignant when pirate publishers, in Europe and America, began reprinting unauthorized versions of Joyce's books, and all the more indignant by the 1930s when she began to discover translations in other languages, all made without his consent. He in turn was annoyed when Sylvia Beach left Paris for her annual vacations in the mountains. He wanted her nearby at all times and bombarded her with plaintive letters and telegrams, urging her to cut short her holidays and come back to Shakespeare and Company. She remained firm but tolerant and even forgave him when he declined to offer her any of the $45,000 he was given for *Ulysses* once it was cleared for unexpurgated publication in America by Random House.

In addition to seeing *Ulysses* into print, Beach helped promote the many little magazines which her friends started in the 1920s, including Ford Madox Ford's *Transatlantic Review*, Ernest Walsh's *The Quarter*, and Arthur Moss' *Gargoyle*, which introduced the work of Hemingway, Ezra Pound, and T.S. Eliot to both French and American audiences. Eugene Jolas' little magazine *transition* was a platform for the early publication of James Joyce's "Work in Progress," the book which, on its completion, became *Finnegan's Wake*. Meanwhile Adrienne Monnier was promoting a parallel group of French literary magazines from her own store nearby.

In the 1930s, the decade of the Great Depression, many of the American authors in Paris went home but Sylvia Beach was resolved to stay. "I missed them," she wrote, "and I missed the fun of discovery and the little reviews and the little publishing houses. It had been pleasanter emerging from a war than going toward another one." But she was consoled by the continued presence of Joyce and Hemingway, and by the arrival of Henry Miller, ***Anais Nin**, ***Katherine Anne Porter**, Thomas Wolfe, and other literary newcomers. The shop itself, first mentioned in the American press in the early 1920s when it had the flavor of a risqué and bohemian setting, was a famous stop for all American visitors to Paris by 1935. Even so, the Depression cut deeply into the profits of what had always been a shaky business. Bankruptcy was imminent in 1936, prompting André Gide to gather a group of prominent French admirers to underwrite a loan. Their way of doing it was to pay 200 francs each to join a club whose members met at the shop once each month to listen to a public reading of an unpublished work by a

Toklas, Alice B.. *See Stein, Gertrude for sidebar.*

Sylvia Beach in front of Shakespeare and Company.

prominent member. Gide led the way, followed by Paul Valéry and André Maurois. Among the English supporters of the bail-out were T.S. Eliot, *Bryher, Stephen Spender, and even Hemingway, who hated reading aloud but made an exception for his old friend. Their collective help to their longtime friend, publisher, and patron enabled her to survive the crisis.

The onset of World War II led to a much greater exodus of Americans than the onset of the Great Depression, and the American embassy urged Sylvia Beach to leave too, offering to make all the arrangements for her. She declined the offer and was still working in her shop when the German army swept into Paris in June 1940. As other entertainments became scarce, books became more attractive than ever, and Beach now had a large, albeit mainly French, clientele. She risked persecution by hiring as her assistant **Françoise Bernheim**, a Jewish student who had been expelled from the Sorbonne because of her race. For the next two years, America was a neutral power in the war, but, after the Japanese attack on Pearl Harbor in December 1941, Germany and the U.S. declared war on each other. Beach now saw the writing on the wall. Rather than letting her stock be seized, as a German army officer threatened, she hid as much of it as she could manage, then abandoned the shop. For a while, she was permitted to stay in Paris, so long as she agreed to register each week as an enemy alien. But in August 1942, she was arrested and taken off to an internment camp at Vittel in Eastern France, where she passed the time in a converted hospital with dozens of other American and British women internees. She kept busy as unofficial postmistress and assistant to a group of nursing nuns. Released after six months, Beach returned to Paris, where she was allowed to live out the rest of the occupation quietly, though she was in touch with the literary members of the French Resistance.

American, French, and British soldiers liberated Paris in August 1944, and the next day her old friend Hemingway returned. Beach was now 58 years old and a celebrity. *Life* magazine ran a story about her years in occupied France and about the dramatic "rescue" of her books when she hosted a party for her literary friends in the apartment where they had been stored. Despite the urging of T.S. Eliot, Louis Aragon, Paul Valéry, and other old friends, she said she was now too old and frail to restart the business. But as ever she stayed in Paris with Adrienne Monnier, now helping the Red Cross and the American library, translating modern French literature into English, and befriending a new literary generation, including the rising star of French feminism, ***Simone de Beauvoir**, and the African-American novelist Richard Wright.

In 1956, Beach published her memories of Joyce. Three years later, she issued a book of her own memoirs, *Shakespeare and Company*, a lively conversational account of the shop during the interwar years. She had a large collection of James Joyce's first editions, manuscripts and memorabilia, and as Joyce's reputation continued to grow—though he had died in 1940—Beach was approached by dozens of Joyce scholars for access to her collection. The greatest sorrow of her last years was the death of Adrienne Monnier in 1955, who committed suicide prompted by delusions of continuous deafening noise, a side effect from Mènière's syndrome (aural disturbances of the inner ear). For Sylvia, writes Noel Fitch, "personal happiness went with the death of Adrienne, who for thirty-eight years had been a sister, lover, mother, and mentor." Beach herself died, widely admired and honored for her life's work, in 1962, and after a Paris funeral, her ashes were sent for burial in Princeton.

SOURCES:

Beach, Sylvia. *Shakespeare and Company.* NY: Harcourt Brace, 1959.

Ellman, Richard. *James Joyce.* NY: Oxford University Press, 1982.

Fitch, Noel Riley. *Sylvia Beach and the Lost Generation.* NY: Norton, 1983.

Hemingway, Ernest. *A Moveable Feast.* NY: Scribner, 1964.

COLLECTIONS:

Sylvia Beach Papers, Princeton University Library, Princeton, New Jersey; James Joyce Collection, State University of New York, Buffalo, Lockwood Memorial Library.

Patrick Allitt, Professor of History, Emory University, Atlanta, Georgia

Beale, Dorothea (1831–1906)

Reforming head teacher who helped revolutionize education for middle-class girls in England. *Pronunciation: BEEL. Born Dorothea Beale on March 21, 1831, in London, England; died in Cheltenham in 1906; daughter of Dorothea Margaret (Complin) Beale and Miles Beale; taught at home by governesses; attended boarding school and a finishing school; enrolled as a student at Queens College, London, 1849; never married; no children.*

Awards: Officier d'Academie (1889); Societé des Professeurs de Langues Vivantes (1890); Tutor Durham University (1896); corresponding member of the National Education Association of the United States (1898); on advisory board of the University of London (1901); Freedom of the borough of Cheltenham (1901); Honorary LL.D, Edinburgh University (1902).

Student and tutor at Queens (1849–57); named head teacher at Casterton (1857); served as head teacher at Cheltenham Girls School (1858–1906); gave evidence to the Taunton Commission (1865); was joint founder of Association for Headmistresses (1874); sat on Bryce Commission (1894); elected president of Association for Headmistresses (1895).

Selected publications: The Student's Textbook of English and General History, Self-examination, *and* Work and Prayer in Girls' Schools.

Dorothea Beale was born at a time when educational provision for middle-class English girls was of poor quality. Most were taught at home by governesses, a few went to boarding schools. When they reached adolescence, girls were sent to finishing schools to complete their education. At the end of this expensive schooling, they were able to play a few tunes on the piano, to sing, to dance the Minuet, to draw a simple sketch, to sew a delicate sampler and sometimes speak a little French. These accomplishments helped them fulfil the Victorian ideal of a perfect woman: a decorative, poised, and often empty headed, companion to their future husband. Dorothea Beale was one of a number of women who sought to change this model of education.

Dorothea Beale

Dorothea Beale was born in London in 1831. She was the fourth of eleven children of Dorothea Margaret Beale, a lady of Huguenot descent, and Miles Beale, a doctor interested in educational issues. Dorothea Beale grew up in an intellectually charged atmosphere, but her formal education was meager. Like most girls of her time, Beale wasted precious years on trivial preoccupations. Educated by a rapid succession of inadequate governesses, she and her sisters were taught very little. Beale wrote in her autobiography: "My mother advertised and hundreds of answers were sent. She began by eliminating all those in which bad spelling occurred. . . . I can remember only one really clever and competent teacher."

When Dorothea Beale was sent to a boarding school in Essex, it offered no better education than the multitude of governesses. Subjects were ingested parrot fashion without understanding. In an attempt to encourage a superficial polish and sophistication, the girls were expected to communicate in French at all times. This, according to Beale, was a foolish idea "because our thinking power was hindered from developing by intercourse with one another, because we were required to speak in a tongue in which we could indeed talk, but in which conversation was impossible; and the language we spoke was one peculiar to English boarding-schools."

At the age of 13, Beale was removed from school because of poor health. For the next three years, she shared lessons in classics with her brothers and was given access to the London Institution and Crosby Hall libraries. She read and read. She then taught herself mathematics, geometry, and algebra. "I borrowed a Euclid . . . and read the first six books, carefully working through the whole of the fifth, as I did not know what was usually done."

In 1848, Beale's parents sent her to a finishing school on the Champs Élysées in Paris which enjoyed a favorable scholarly reputation. Unfortunately, the French system of education was little different from the English. After years of independent learning, Beale was crushed by the mechanical teaching methods, the narrow curriculum, and the repressive school regime. "Imagine our disgust at being required to . . . learn even lists of prepositions by heart. . . . I felt oppressed with the routine life; I, who had been able to moon, grub, alone for hours . . . was now put into a cage and had to walk round and round like a squirrel. I felt thought was killed." Fortunately for Beale, the 1848 French revolution interrupted her Parisian education. Concerned about the increasing level of violence, her parents demanded she return to England. Back home, she taught her younger sisters and superintended her brothers' Latin. It was the beginning of a long teaching career.

Less than a year later, at age 18, Dorothea Beale enrolled as a student at Queens College which had recently opened to upgrade the academic qualifications of governesses and practicing teachers. She soon became one of its star pupils. At the end of her studies, she was awarded certificates in mathematics, English, French, German, geography, and Latin. More important, in the middle of her studies, she was offered a job, the first teaching post held by a woman at Queens. For seven years, Beale instructed at Queens. She began teaching mathematics, then became Latin tutor and lastly head teacher of the school attached to the college. She enjoyed teaching and had a strong sense of her own destiny. A profoundly religious Christian, she believed that she had been called by God to the teaching profession. Despite this, Beale resigned from the college because women were given little or no responsibility.

After leaving Queens, she was appointed to a post at the Clergy Daughters' School in Casterton, a small village in Westmoreland in the north of England. It was an unwise decision. At Casterton, she was thrust into taking charge of an isolated school in the middle of the bleak English countryside. When she took up the post on January 6, 1857, the school's reputation was poor. A combination of inadequate diet and bad air had affected the physical health of the pupils. Typhoid, scrofula, scarlet fever and consumption were common. The school's educational health was equally impoverished. Since it was understaffed, Beale was expected to teach arithmetic, history, geography, English grammar and literature, French, German, Italian, Latin and Scripture. Objecting, she demanded a reduced timetable, believing that no one, however intelligent and assiduous, could prepare ten curriculum subjects with appropriate care. Discipline was equally problematic. It was maintained by punishment, rewards were few. Once again, Beale criticized the regime at Casterton. Discipline, she believed, was maintained by rewarding good behavior and hard work. Such ideas were considered too innovative and radical for the conservative-minded establishment at Casterton. In 1857, less than a year at her post, she received a letter of dismissal:

> On your last interview with the Committee you implied an intention of resigning in case certain alterations should not be made by the Committee.
>
> The Committee are of opinion that under the circumstances it would be better that your connection with the school should cease after Christmas next, they paying you a quarter's salary in advance.

This was a humiliating experience for the previously successful Dorothea Beale. She returned home discouraged and disappointed. Luckily, she did not need to teach for a living; her parents were sufficiently prosperous to support her. Beale, however, did not waste her time. She taught part-time at a school in Barnes, near London, and wrote two books, *The Student's Textbook of English and General History*, an overview of world history, and *Self-Examination*, a book which rested on a theme of duty towards God and one's neighbor.

When the post of principal became vacant at Cheltenham Ladies' College, Dorothea Beale applied. In 1858, aged 27, she was appointed. Cheltenham Ladies' College had opened four years previously as a day school. By the time Beale arrived, attendance had dropped significantly. Rebuilding the college was to be her life's work. Little by little, Beale transformed the school into one of the most prestigious in England. Gradually, mathematics, science, Latin and Greek made their way into her prospectus. New teaching methods were adopted. Textbooks were discouraged in case they were memorized by the students without understanding. One of her many gifts was to inspire teachers to make their students think. At a speech to the Social Science Congress in 1865, Beale outlined her educational principles:

> I think that the education of girls has too often been made showy, rather than real or useful; that accomplishments have been made the main thing, because these would . . . enable a girl to shine and attract, while those branches of study especially calculated to form the judgement, to cultivate the understanding, and to discipline the character have been neglected.

Convinced that sport was wasteful of educational time, Beale discouraged it, but under pressure from staff and parents she bought a large field and built hockey pitches and tennis courts. Field hockey, played from about 1890 at Cheltenham, was a sport that Beale found hard to understand; she was said to have remarked, "The children will hurt themselves if they all run about after one ball. Get some more balls at once." Competitive team sport was anathema to Beale so she refused to allow Cheltenham pupils to play other schools. Dorothea Beale disapproved of competition in any form. Prize days, the mark of the English educational system, were never held because she disapproved of contests in which the success of one person involved the failure of others.

Beale changed Cheltenham Ladies' College in other ways. Unlike many English schools, there were no uniforms: girls were free to dress as they wished. Discipline was imposed by unusual methods. Silence was strictly enforced throughout the school. From the moment pupils entered the building—during lessons, in the corridor, at meal times—an awesome silence descended. High academic standards were also expected. Written work was marked with a "G" by the side if it was good, or comments such as "a penny a line" or "words, words, words" if it was found to be unsatisfactory. Each week, marks were read out and commented upon in front of the entire class as an incentive to work hard.

Miss Buss and Miss Beale
Cupid's darts do not feel
How different from us
Miss Beale and Miss Buss

—Anon.

At first, Dorothea Beale encountered the same prejudices and resistance she had found at Casterton. Both the parents and governors disapproved of her innovative approach. "My dear lady, if my daughters were going to be bankers, it would be very well to teach arithmetic as you do, but there is no need" said one father, who then yanked his daughters out of the school. Beale also failed to attract new pupils. A year after her appointment, only 65 pupils remained. Slowly, but systematically, she was able to persuade parents that her educational philosophy was appropriate for middle-class girls. By 1880, she was inviolable. Numbers had increased to 500, new buildings were erected, and parental support was secured, all of which put the school, and Dorothea Beale, in a strong position.

Cheltenham Ladies' College never was—and Dorothea Beale never meant it to be—a school which favored social equality. It remained highly exclusive. High fees and selection procedures debarred the majority of girls in Cheltenham. Only the daughters of "independent gentlemen" or professionals were accepted. Cheltenham Ladies' College refused to admit any girl who was in a "lower" class of society. Daughters of tradespeople were refused admittance even when they could afford the fees. Nevertheless, Cheltenham Ladies' College provided inspiration to others. It proved that girls could reach and maintain high educational standards.

Although Beale supported women's suffrage, she believed that women should play a subordinate role. She argued that "the habits of obedience to duty, of self restraint . . . the humility which a thoughtful and comprehensive study of the great works in literature and science tends to produce, these we would specially cultivate in a woman, that she may wear the true woman's ornament of a meek and quiet spirit." At first, she advocated separate examinations for girls and boys. But experience changed her mind, and her girls were entered for the Cambridge exams and the London Matriculation alongside boys. Regardless of disagreements, Beale worked well with other women educationalists. On December 22, 1874, she chaired a group of nine head mistresses formed to exchange educational ideas and act as a pressure group. This became the influential Association for Head Mistresses.

Dorothea Beale's educational influence extended beyond that of Cheltenham Ladies' College. Three different institutions—all called St. Hilda's after her favorite saint ***Hilda of Whitby**—were founded with Beale's financial and practical support. The first, St. Hilda's College Cheltenham, was opened in 1885 to train secondary teachers. Students remained at St. Hilda's for four years, studying for the Oxford University exams and practicing their theory at the school. In 1893, a new house was bought near Oxford which became St. Hilda's College, part of the university. The third St. Hilda's was built in Shoreditch, East London, to educate working-class women.

In recognition of her contribution to women's education, the government sought her advice. In 1864, the Schools' Enquiry Commission, called the Taunton Commission after its leader Lord Taunton, was set up to examine the state of the nation's endowed schools. Dorothea Beale welcomed the commission, gave evidence to it and edited the 20-volume assistant commissioner's reports. When it released its findings in 1869, the commission presented a pessimistic picture of education for girls: "We find, as a rule, a very small amount of professional skill, an inferior set of schoolbooks, a vast deal of dry, uninteresting task work, rules put into the memory with no explanation of their principles, no system of examination worthy of the name." When another Royal Commission, the Bryce Commission, was established in 1894, Beale was one of the first women to be appointed to such a body. The recommendations of the Bryce Commission, embodied in the 1902 Education Act, transformed secondary education in England.

In the latter part of her life, Dorothea Beale received a number of prestigious awards for her remarkable achievements. In 1889 in Paris, she was made Officier d'Academie; in 1890, she was elected to the Societé des Professeurs de Langues Vivantes; in 1896, Durham University made her Tutor; in 1898, she was corresponding member of the National Education Association of the United States; in 1901, she was placed on the advisory board of the University of London and given freedom of the borough of Cheltenham; in 1902, she received an honorary LL.D from Edinburgh University.

Given the contributions made by Dorothea Beale to educational reform, it is not surprising that she remained single. Career and husband were incompatible for women in 19th-century England so Beale declined her many offers of marriage. Cheltenham Ladies' College, she said, was her true spouse. When she died, aged 75, in 1906, the school was one of the most famous in England. By this time, the genteel, ill-educated governess was a thing of the past. In its place stood an academic profession in which female teachers enjoyed an enhanced social status and were ready to provide a challenging education for girls—a process begun by the indefatigable Dorothea Beale.

SOURCES:

Bryant, Margaret. *The Unexpected Revolution.* London: University of London Institute of Education, 1979.

Hunt, Felicity, ed. *Lessons for Life.* London: Basil Blackwell, 1987.

Kamm, Josephine. *How Different From Us: A Biography of Miss Buss and Miss Beale.* London, 1958

Raikes, Elizabeth. *Dorothea Beale of Cheltenham.* London: Archibald Constable, 1909.

Steadman, F. Cecily. *In the Days of Miss Beale.* Edited by J. Burrow. London, 1931.

Paula Bartley, University of Wolverhampton, Dudley, United Kingdom, author and joint editor of "Women in History" series, Cambridge, University Press

Beale, Mary (1632–1699)

English portrait painter and miniaturist whose works have often been confused with those of Sir Peter Lely and other noted painters. *Born Mary Cradock in Suffolk, England, in 1632; died in 1699 (some sources cite 1697); daughter of a minister and amateur artist; married Charles Beale; children: two sons, including Charles Beale (an artist).*

The daughter of a minister and amateur painter, Mary Beale was born in Suffolk, England, in 1632. It is believed her first art lessons were given by her father's friend Robert Walker, who was a painter of Thomas Cromwell. Beale also studied with Thomas Flatman, a lawyer, poet, and miniaturist. Although it is not known whether she was actually a student of Sir Peter Lely, he did allow her to copy from his personal art collection, one of the largest in London at the time.

After her marriage to cloth manufacturer Charles Beale, she began her professional apprenticeship. While her husband managed the household, which included two infant sons, and the mechanics of her career by preparing her canvases and mixing her colors, she established herself as an independent artist, working out of a studio in Covent Garden. Her portraits in pastels, watercolor, and oils were much in demand, and many of the city's most prominent people sat for her. Beale also gained popularity for her portraits of children. Her husband's diaries, which extensively catalogued her work, indicate that she was prolific and earned a substantial income.

As described by **Nancy Heller**, Beale posed her subjects in the standard style of the day: "half-length seated figures" sat "against dark backgrounds, their eyes fixed on the viewer." But she was highly praised for her use of color, as is apparent in **Germaine Greer**'s description of a Beale self-portrait: "The colours are warm and harmonious, the skin tones fresh without being voluptuous." As a companion piece, Beale produced a portrait of her husband, which Greer describes as "remarkable in the sense of domestic sensuality that it conveys."

In 1665, just before the Great Plague, the Beales left London, returning in 1670 to a house on Pall Mall. Beale's career flourished until around 1680, when Lely's death and changing styles caused her popularity to dwindle. During this late period, she did numerous copies of Lely's work, as well as her own, which may have ultimately caused the confusion surrounding her original paintings.

Beale taught both of her sons to paint portraits. Her son Charles had a successful career as an artist, while her eldest son became a doctor. Another of her students, **Sarah Curtis**, also became a noted portraitist.

Mary Beale,
Self-Portrait,
1666.

SOURCES:

Greer, Germaine. *The Obstacle Race.* NY: Farrar, Straus, 1979.

Heller, Nancy G. *Women Artists.* NY: Abbeville, 1987.

Barbara Morgan,
Melrose, Massachusetts

Opposite page

Jessie Tarbox Beals

Beals, Jessie Tarbox (1870–1942)

Canadian-born photographer and America's first female press photographer, known also for her portraits, architectural documentation, landscapes, and gardens. *Born Jessie Richmond Tarbox, in Hamilton, Ontario, Canada, on December 23, 1870; died in New York, New York, on May 31, 1942; daughter and youngest of four children of John Nathaniel (a machinist and inventor) and Marie Antoinette (Bassett) Tarbox; attended Collegiate Institute of Ontario; married Alfred T. Beals, in 1897 (divorced); children: one daughter, Nanette (b. 1911).*

A primitive camera catapulted Jessie Tarbox Beals from the life of a New England schoolmarm to a pioneering career as the first woman news photographer. For three decades after her groundbreaking photographs appeared in the *Buffalo Inquirer* and the *Courier* in 1903, she won national acclaim, receiving more exposure than any other female photographer of her era.

Born in 1870 in Hamilton, Ontario, Canada, Jessie had an idyllic childhood which came to an abrupt end when her father John lost his fortune and started drinking. In the end, he finally left home. Her mother Marie supported the four children by gradually selling the family treasures. Forced to earn her own living, Beals was 16 when she took a teaching position in a remote country school near Williamsburg, Massachusetts, where she had settled with her mother.

Obtaining a small, tin-box camera for selling magazine subscriptions, Beals began taking portraits of her students, as well the schoolhouse and its surroundings. She read voraciously about photography to improve the quality of her pictures and saved up two-weeks' salary ($12) to buy a folding Kodak camera with roll film. During a summer vacation, she converted a closet into a dark room, established Williamsburg's first photography studio on her front porch, and made more money than she had during the entire school year. The following summer, she set up her camera near a picnic spot favored by students from Smith College. Charging a dollar for four prints, she had no problem getting the young coeds to pose.

In 1893, when her brother moved his business to nearby Greenfield, she accompanied him and met Alfred T. Beals, a machinist and graduate of Amherst College, whom she married. In 1900, bored by teaching, which she called "genteel, sheltered, monotonous and moneyless work having neither heights nor depths," Beals taught her husband the basics of photography, then persuaded him to take to the road with her. As itinerant photographers, they set out with a few personal necessities, two bicycles, and a tent which served as a dark room. Their first train stop was the fairground at Brattleboro, Vermont, where they secured lodging at a local boarding house. Beals then went about finding editors to purchase her photographs of the fair. Two newspapers were interested: the *Windham County Reformer* and the *Phoenix*. The next day, she became the first woman in America to have news photos published and credited in the press. For the rest of the fall, Beals biked around town, recruiting customers and taking pictures, while Alfred developed glass-plate negatives and made prints; this division of labor would define their roles for the remainder of their partnership.

"Patchin Place, Greenwich Village, N.Y.C.," 1916. Photo by Jessie Tarbox Beals.

With the close of the fair, they spent nearly a year taking pictures in Florida until funds ran out, then settled in upstate New York. There, a pregnant Jessie decided to slow down, and Alfred took a job. On March 6, 1902, Beals gave birth to a daughter, but the infant died 12 hours later. When she was well enough to work again, Beals landed a job as a staff newspaper photographer in Buffalo, which began the physically grueling, sometimes dangerous, tasks that would establish her credentials. She covered daily life in the city and special assignments, including a devastating fire in the City of Rochester. Her first scoop was the sensational inquest into the murder of Edwin L. Burdick. Because spectators were not allowed in the courtroom, Beals climbed a bookcase in an adjoining room and shot photos through the door's transom. "Hide the camera, boys, and help me down," she said to a congregation of reporters below, and the pictures were snapped up for the front page of the *New York American and Journal*. Beals brought an artistic quality to her work, unusual in newspaper pictures of the day, and won high marks over the 18 months that she was in Buffalo.

Next she and Alfred set their sights on the 1904 World's Fair in St. Louis, an opportunity she regarded as a steppingstone toward establishing a studio on New York's Fifth Avenue. Arriving in St. Louis without an official press card, she managed to wheedle a pre-Exposition permit, which prohibited sale of any photographs taken before the fair's opening. Ignoring the rules, she sold one of her first pictures—of the Patagonian Giants of South America—to the local newspapers and for national syndication. Overnight, Jessie Beals became a fully accredited press photographer when a St. Louis newspaper claimed she carried "the first permit to be issued to a woman authorizing the taking of photographs on the World's Fair Grounds." Lugging 30 pounds of equipment, Beals photographed exhibits and numerous celebrity visitors, including President Theodore Roosevelt. She often put herself at risk for the perfect shot. When officials refused to let her ascend in a hot-air balloon during the fair's International Balloon Race, Beals managed to sidestep the ban. The *Philadelphia Public Ledger* of January 26, 1921, reported: "Just as one of the balloons was being set free, the huge crowd was thunderstruck to see a woman, a camera slung over her shoulder, grip the top of a basket and pull herself aboard. The balloon was off, and with it, the intrepid woman photographer." From her rising perch, Beals took a prizewinning bird's-eye view of the fair.

Though some of Beals' success was due to Alfred's speed in the dark room, he began to resent life on the move. In 1905, they compromised by settling in New York's Greenwich Village arts community. Beals' ability to hustle got business off the ground. There she took on any assignments, from sessions with famous New York personalities to portraits of pet cats for wealthy society matrons. She framed child portraits with verse that she composed; she advertised Tuesday as half-price day for children's portraits. During April 1906, Beals joined 32 women photographers in an exhibition sponsored by the Camera Club of Hartford, Connecticut, one of the few times she participated in a group show. She shot a number of documentation projects around New York, including a haunting series on children of the slums. She also traveled a great deal, taking assignments from Maine to Minnesota. When home, she enjoyed café society, while Alfred fretted about money and was uneasy with her friends and her bohemian ways.

The marriage became unbearable. By 1907, it was little more than a business arrangement, and Beals, nearing 40, longed for a child. In 1910, she had an affair and became pregnant. **Nanette Tarbox Beals** was born on June 8, 1911. Alfred accepted the child, and the couple continued the pretense of a normal domestic life. But when Nanette was six, she came down with infantile rheumatoid arthritis and was cared for in the charity ward of St. Luke's Hospital for several months. The days of stress finally put an end to the marriage. Although Beals had desperately wanted a child, her hours with her daughter were limited by her need to make a living and her tendency to spend. Nanette passed most of her time at boarding school or with friends.

Beals opened a small shop in Greenwich Village where she sold her photographs as well as paintings and prints made by friends. She shared an apartment in a $13-a-month tenement and joined the Liberal Club, whose qualifications for membership included "intellectual interests and radical ideas, while a bohemian temperament was a desirable secondary qualification."

By 1920, Beals had established herself in a huge new studio, formerly the workshop of Louis Comfort Tiffany. Having blazed a trail for women photographers, she was now faced with competition in the field. But she persevered, still taking a wide variety of assignments and hiring out as a speaker among women's groups. With topics like "Celebrities I Have Photographed," and "What One Sees Through the Eye of the Camera," she attracted large audiences. She also gained a reputation as a poet and joined the League of American Pen Women. In 1928, a friend published a book of Beals' poems, *Songs of a Wanderer*.

As Beals grew older and less willing to chase fire engines, she began photographing gardens of the wealthy for major gardening magazines. In 1928, with 17-year-old Nanette in tow, she moved to California in hopes of finding work. Nanette describes the strange experience of living with her mother for the first time: "My mother was forty-one years older than I and she knew nothing about being a mother. I, on the other hand, really didn't know how to give and take of home life."

Business was good until the Wall Street crash ended Beals' lavish California lifestyle. She moved back East, first to Chicago, where an anticipated lucrative assignment didn't pan out, and then to New York. The last six years of her life were spent in a basement apartment on West 11th Street, where she lived and worked, shooting pictures into her late 60s. In 1936, she won four Grand Awards in the yard-and-garden photographic competition run by the *New York Herald Tribune*.

In the end, ill health claimed all of Beals' money. She died of hardening of the arteries, at age 71, in the charity ward of Bellevue Hospital and was buried in the narrow strip between the graves of her parents in Williamsburg, Massachusetts. The eclectic collection of Jessie Beals' stunning photographs—her life's work—all but disappeared from public view following her death.

SOURCES:

Alland, Alexander, Sr. *Jessie Tarbox Beals: First Woman News Photographer.* NY: Camera-Graphic Press, 1978.

Rosenblum, Naomi. *A History of Women Photographers.* NY: Abbeville Press, 1994.

Weatherford, Doris. *American Women's History.* NY: Prentice Hall, 1994.

Barbara Morgan, Melrose, Massachusetts

Bean, Ann (1899–1962).

See Adler, Polly.

Bear-Crawford, Annette (1853–1899)

Australian feminist. *Born Annette Ellen Bear in East Melbourne, Australia, in 1853: died in London, England, on June 7, 1899; eldest of eight children of Annette Eliza (Williams) Bear and John Pinney Bear (a stock and station agent); attended Cheltenham Ladies' College, Gloucestershire, England; married William Crawford, in 1894.*

Born in East Melbourne, Australia, into a household that valued education even for young ladies, Annette Bear-Crawford attended college and trained in social work in England, where she became acquainted with the women's movement and was active in the National Vigilance Committee. In 1890, after the death of her father, she rejoined her mother in Melbourne, becoming a leader in Melbourne's women's movement, which was struggling to get the vote. Noted for her organizational and speaking skills, Bear-Crawford set out to strengthen and unite existing suffrage societies. With the support of the Woman's Christian Temperance Union, she formed the Victorian Women's Suffrage League and, in 1894, was instrumental in the founding of the United Council for Women's Suffrance, serving as its first president. In spite of lobbying and petitioning, the council proved unable to persuade the legislature to pass a suffrage bill.

In 1894, upon her marriage to William Crawford, Annette assumed the hyphenate Bear-Crawford. She then set out to educate other women for public work, training them in public speaking and encouraging them to run for school boards, sign on as police matrons, or become administrators for the Infant Life Protection Act (1890). She was one of the first members of the Society for Prevention of Cruelty to Children and the Victorian Vigilance Society. Bear-Crawford also worked to secure legislation to raise the age of consent to 16 and to improve conditions in factories and mental asylums. In 1897, she organized the successful Queen's Willing Shilling fund to found Queen Victoria Hospital for Women, but would not live to see the facility opened.

Described by ***Beatrice Webb** as a "gentle-tempered intelligent woman who keeps me company in the dowdiness of her dress," Bear-Crawford traveled to England in November 1898 to attend the Women's International Conference. She died of pneumonia on June 7, 1899, while in London.

Beard, Mary Ritter (1876–1958)

Historian and feminist activist who wrote extensively on the worldwide history of women and on American culture. *Born Mary Ritter on August 5, 1876, in Indianapolis, Indiana; died in Phoenix, Arizona, on August 14, 1958; daughter of Narcissa (Lockwood) Ritter (an erstwhile teacher) and Eli Foster Ritter (a banker); graduated A.B. DePauw University, 1897; postgraduate work, Columbia University, 1902–04; married Charles Austin Beard (a historian), on March 8, 1900; children:* ***Miriam Beard*** *(a historian); William (a historian).*

Joined staff of the National Women's Trade Union League; became editor, The Woman Voter *(1910–12); joined staff of the Wage Earners' Suffrage League; joined staff of the Congressional Union (later the National Woman's Party, 1913–17); independent writer.*

Selected publications: (with Charles A. Beard) American Citizenship *(Macmillan, 1914);* Woman's Work in Municipalities *(Appleton, 1915);* A Short History of the American Labor Movement *(Harcourt, 1920); (with C.A. Beard)* A History of the United States *(Macmillan, 1921); (with C.A. Beard)* The Rise of American Civilization *(Macmillan, 1927);* On Understanding Women *(Longmans, 1931); (editor)* America Through Women's Eyes *(Macmillan, 1933); (editor, with Martha B. Bruère)* Laughing Their Way: Women's Humor in America *(Macmillan, 1934); (with C.A. Beard)* The Making of American Civilization *(Macmillan, 1937); (with C.A. Beard)* America in Midpassage *(Macmillan, 1939); (with C.A. Beard)* The American Spirit: A Study of the Idea of Civilization in the United States *(Macmillan, 1942); (with C.A. Beard)* A Basic History of the United States *(Doubleday Doran, 1944);* Woman as Force in History: A Study in Traditions and Realities *(Macmillan, 1946);* The Force of Women in Japanese History *(Public Affairs Press, 1953);* The Making of Charles A. Beard *(Exposition, 1955).*

The career of Mary Ritter Beard contains many paradoxes. The foremost historian of women of her generation, she possessed only the bachelor of arts, turned down all honorary degrees, and never held an academic post. Though a prolific and respected author, her works—in the words of biographer **Nancy F. Cott**—"were loose-joined, oddly organized, her prose florid, her references sometimes obscure." While ever pointing to the accomplishments of women from Cleopatra to Madame Curie, Beard often bitterly fought ideological battles with members of the one group most likely to be her natural constituency: those of the feminist movement.

Similarly, she conducted a worldwide crusade for women's studies as an autonomous discipline but refused to separate the cause of women from other major social forces. "Everything is related to everything else," she wrote in 1931. It was essential to see "the interplay of government, politics, economics, modes of living and working, schools of thought, religion, power, class, society and family, the arts and ambition, and the biological and cultural aspects of sex."

Mary Ritter was born on August 5, 1876, in Indianapolis, the third of six children of **Narcissa Lockwood Ritter** and Eli Foster Ritter. Her mother, who came from one of central Indiana's most prominent families, had been a teacher. Her father was a lawyer who had served as a colonel in the Civil War. The family heritage included Methodism, temperance, and the Republican Party. Mary grew up in middle-class comfort in a suburban part of the city. At age 16, she enrolled at DePauw University in Asbury, Indiana, where she began her study of political science, languages, and literature. Graduating in 1897, she taught high school German in Indiana for a year, then in 1900 married the budding social scientist Charles A. Beard, also a DePauw graduate.

Mary Ritter Beard

Like Charles, Mary was strongly influenced by the reform currents of the 1890s. Immediately after their marriage, the couple traveled to England, where the Beards immersed themselves in various reforms. Living in Manchester, Mary helped to found an extension division of Ruskin Hall, a school for workers based in Oxford. Here she saw firsthand what she called the "ghastly deprivation" of urban working-class life. She plunged into the woman suffrage movement, where she worked closely with such militants as ***Emmeline Pankhurst**. Returning to New York in 1902, the Beards enrolled at Columbia University. Mary began a graduate program in sociology that only lasted two years. For the rest of her life, she was strongly critical of higher education, saying in 1946 that "the value of learning lies not in sheer erudition, if there at all." Rather it lay in social transformation. Increasingly attracted to what was then called the New History, she believed that the study of the past had one fundamental purpose: to reform the present and thereby change the course of the future.

> In the Republic of Letters no American woman holds higher place than Mary Ritter Beard.
>
> —***Newsweek*, March 18, 1946**

By 1910, Mary Beard was active in labor and suffrage organizations. Among them were the Equality League for Self-Supporting Women, a suffrage group, and the National Women's Trade Union League (NWTUL). She became secretary of the NWTUL's legislative committee and was briefly treasurer of the association. With her husband, she defended the McNamara brothers, who were accused of dynamiting the leading newspaper in Los Angeles, and, after the famous Triangle Shirt Waist fire of 1911, she crusaded for strong factory legislation. In 1910–12, she edited *The Woman Voter*, published by ***Carrie Chapman Catt**'s Woman Suffrage Party of New York. She was also vice-chair of the party's Manhattan branch.

In 1912, Beard concentrated her activities on the Wage-Earners' Suffrage League, the party's adjunct for working women. Working women, she claimed in 1912, needed a public voice in dealing with a host of problems: "the white slave traffic, mothers' pensions, unemployment, education, child labor, war, the tariff and all else that affects the cost of living, pure food and water, city planning, parks and playgrounds, employers' liability, transportation and the policing of cities." Not only did Beard write, organize, and raise funds in the suffrage cause; she canvassed from door to door, particularly in tenement districts.

In 1913, Beard broke with the Woman's Suffrage Party, which she found far too moderate. She rallied behind ***Alice Paul**'s Congressional Union (CU), a group that embodied the more extreme wing of the suffrage movement. CU repudiated the traditional strategy of a state-to-state approach in favor of a national constitutional amendment. Also in 1913, Beard successfully, and against opposition, insisted that black women be included in a major suffrage parade in Washington, D.C. A year later, she testified before a House committee examining women's suffrage. In 1915, she resigned from CU's executive committee, finding that her modest income, family demands, and scholarly research prevented her from taking a more active role. Yet she remained active in its New York State organization. In 1917, Beard led a New York delegation to the capital to protest against the imprisonment of suffragists arrested for picketing.

After 1917, Beard's support for CU (then called the National Woman's Party [NWP]) lapsed. Biographer Cott suspects that Beard's withdrawal was rooted in her abhorrence of certain NWP tactics, such as its public burning of the speeches of President Woodrow Wilson. Beard always opposed Paul's crusade for an Equal Rights Amendment. In 1933, in addressing Paul's organization, Beard queried: "Do we want to be preachers, bankers, Babbitts, merely for the sake of equality with men? Do we want to be labor racketeers?" Far better, she believed, for CU feminists to work at creating a more humane society than settling for an equal share in an exploitative one.

Often writing from the Beard farmhouse in New Milford, Connecticut, Mary Beard's reputation as an author was first made in the field of labor. Her *Woman's Work in Municipalities* (1915) was a lengthy essay in the muckraking tradition. Her *Short History of the American Labor Movement* (1920) was a pro-labor account written for a working-class audience.

Mary served as co-author with Charles on a number of projects. Their high school textbook *American Citizenship* (1914), written at her instigation, consciously sought to bring women into the study of the body politic. So too did such general accounts as *A History of the United States* (1921) and *The Making of American Civilization* (1937).

All this time, the couple was undertaking more creative efforts. Their *Rise of American Civilization* (1927) was a truly magisterial effort, offering an analytical narrative that began in colonial times and was carried down to the "normalcy" of the 1920s. Written with what historian Carl Becker called "verve and swift facility," it possessed an influence unmatched by any such synthesis before or since. Charles claimed that, outside of the political narrative, the book was genuinely Mary's, though (as with all their joint efforts) Charles received the limelight—and the occasional attack. A sequel, *America in Midpassage* (1939), covered the '30s, while a fourth volume—*The American Spirit* (1942)—explored various facets of American culture through extensive quotation. *The Basic History of the United States* (1944) was one of their most popular works, one that Charles called "our last will and testament to the American people."

Mary's first love, however, was the topic with which her name was often synonymous: the history of women. She edited two anthologies: *America Through Women's Eyes* (1933) and *Laughing Their Way: Women's Humor in America*, written with **Martha B. Bruère** (1934). In the former work, Beard wrote:

> If there is in all history any primordial force, that force is woman—continuer, protector, preserver of life, instinctive, active, thoughtful, ever bringing thought back from sterile speculation to the center of life and work.

In the same preface, however, she stressed women's collaboration with men from colonial to contemporary times.

Of far greater importance was *On Understanding Woman* (1931). In some ways, the book was an advanced intellectual and social history of the entire Western tradition, with hundreds of references to women included. She began her account in primitive times, then moved successively through the Golden Age of Greece, Imperial Rome, the early and medieval church, the Reformation, the Renaissance, the Enlightenment, and the reform movements of the 19th century. All through history, she said, women had participated in almost "everything that went on in the world":

> They have shared in the burdens and privileges of their respective classes, have joined in wars, have owned and managed vast estates, have insisted on dominance in disputes among ruling families, have displayed the lusts of men, have served the temples, and have been deified as gods.... There was no great historical contest in politics in which they did not appear somewhere. There was no religious cult which they did not affect. There were no exercises in intellectualism which they did not practice.

In the Middle Ages alone, she noted, women served as theologians and saints. They headed convents and schools, worked in crafts, labored in the fields, suffered as witches, died as heretics, and even produced military leaders, such as Joan of Arc.

In all her writings on women, Beard brought a unique point of view. Insisting that women's contributions were central to human society, she drew a direct connection between women's primary responsibility for the care of life and their potential for enacting major social change. At a congress held in 1933 by the National Council of Women in the United States, an umbrella group representing some five million women, Beard drafted a manifesto. She consciously sought to differentiate her "second women's movement" from "the first women's movement," one whose aims were embodied in Declaration of Sentiments drafted by ***Elizabeth Cady Stanton** and formulated at the famous Seneca Falls meeting of 1848. Beard's statement read:

> We believe that every person, to whatever sex, race or nationality she or he may belong, is entitled to security of life, work, the reward of labor, health, and education; to protection against war and crime, and to opportunity for self-expression. Yet, even in parts of the world where feminism has made its largest gains, these fundamentals of security and the good life are sadly lacking. Hence it is against social systems, not men, that we launch our second woman's movement. We enter now a social-planning era following the harsh experiment with *laissez faire* and national aggressions, with a World War, and its horrible aftermath in the economic collapse. All civilization is at stake and the condition of society cannot be ignored.

Beard continually fought what she saw as the "deadening" views of some feminists, who saw the record of women in the past as either a blank or the story of defeat. At best, it was a tale of masculine tyranny and female subjection. Such a view, Beard believed, had unwittingly contributed to the false belief that history had been made by men alone and that masculine labors had created civilization. This perspective she found dangerous, for once women accepted such an interpretation of their heritage, their collective strength was undermined.

Beard also opposed a juxtaposition of "women of achievement," who were active in business and the professions, and mere "homemakers" who—in some eyes—failed to achieve their fullest potential. Over the long span of history, she wrote in 1946, the woman of the home had been a force for "lifting thought to new creative levels."

Nor would Beard accept the view that women were fundamentally noble, men fundamentally corrupt. From at least 1930, when she wrote an article "Women and the War Habit" for *Woman's Journal*, she denied that "women as such react differently from men on the issue of right by might." "History," she continued, "is in fact a shocking discovery of the share women have had in brawls, revenge, the raising of troops and their ruthless sacrifice, aggression and spoilation."

Biographer **Ann J. Lane** notes that Beard made three distinct claims about women. First, Beard found women indistinguishable from men, both in such positive traits as wisdom and such negative ones as cruelty. Second, Beard saw women as the creators of life itself, sustaining it through agriculture and launching civilization through the creation of art and beauty. Indeed, all the essentials of life—food, clothing, shelter, medicine, the arts—were launched by the women of primitive times. Moreover, Beard maintained that, in the future, women will "be assuming chief responsibility for the continuance and care of life." Third, Beard said that women were different from men, developing skills of domesticity while men advanced industry and commerce. While Lane claims that Beard was correct in affirming the centrality of women in history, she asserts that Beard was less successful in creating a theoretical model that could reconcile these apparently contradictory perspectives.

In 1934, Beard drafted a 50-page syllabus for a women's studies program, published by the American Association of University Women. Its title: "A Changing Political Economy As It Affects Women." A truly equal education, she wrote, did not simply extend male education to females. "Man's education of himself and of his women understudies has become so rigid, so scholastic," she wrote in the preface, "that to parallel it with the same woman's education of herself would count for very little. . . . But if equal education could now be undertaken, not merely with a view to discovering how far this is both a man's and a woman's world, both sexes might better comprehend how their destinies are bound together and why."

When the Hungarian-born feminist and pacifist ***Rosika Schwimmer** sought to create an archive focusing on woman suffrage and peace activity, Beard widened its scope to include women in all walks of life. Between the years 1935 to 1940, Beard was able to establish an office in New York's Rockefeller Center for a World Center for Women's Archives. The project failed, due to factional disputes, lack of funds, and the absence of an institutional base. Furthermore, the advent of World War II diverted much attention from the new project. Beard's materials, however, served as the matrix for such major archives as the Sophia Smith Collection at Smith College and the Schlesinger Library at Radcliffe College.

As World War II approached, both Beards were vigorously anti-fascist but staunchly opposed to U.S. intervention. In late June 1939, three months before war broke out in Europe, Mary said that the U.S. should base its foreign policy on "quite decent barter with other countries, exchanging directly what we have to excess for what we need." "Thundering at dictators," she maintained, was counter-productive. "Going into the present war or trying to help Europe solve its own continuous messes," she asserted in February 1940, "will be to jeopardize our economy and civilization." The isolationism of the Beards was unpopular, particularly in the very intellectual circles that had once lionized them. Early in 1944, when the U.S. had been at war for over two years, the feminist historian wrote a friend: "The name 'Beard' is anathema in many many quarters, I assure you, whether Charles or Mary is prefixed to it."

After the war ended, Charles was bitterly attacked by much of the historical establishment, for he had accused President Franklin D. Roosevelt of deliberately attempting to maneuver the U.S. into the global conflict. Mary strongly defended Charles after he died in 1948, writing impassioned letters against what she considered the "vultures" who defamed his name. Like her husband, Mary destroyed all her correspondence before she died, something that biographers Cott and Lane suspect was rooted in the bitterness of the recent war.

During this time, Beard continually sought to rectify stereotypes concerning women. In 1942, at the request of the *Encyclopedia Britannica*, she offered a 42-page critique of its contents. In response, the editors added some biographies of notable women, but otherwise acted little on her many suggestions.

Beard's magnum opus was published in 1946, when she was 70. *Woman as Force in History* was the culmination of her many years of study. Adding several fresh examples to her 1931 work, she reiterated her claim that women "played a great role in directing human events as thought and action." Again as in 1931, her discussion was wide-ranging, encompassing women philosophers of Greece, mystics of Medieval Europe, and hostesses of 18th-century French salons. Once more, she challenged the claim that historically females had been subservient. She particularly sought to counter the attention given to William Blackstone's *Commentaries on the Laws of England* (1756). The prominent British jurist, she maintained, bore the principle responsibility for the "dogma of women's complete subjection to men," doing so by focusing on the legal status of women in the common law. Beard, to the contrary, stressed other legal sources that gave the woman more protection, among them equity, legislation, and custom.

In 1954, she published a work on the role of women in the history of Japan, taking the story from the days of the Sun Goddess to those of the American occupation. Featured were various empresses, influential ladies at court, and women in the arts. Until 1955, Beard lived as a widow in New Milford. While visiting Arizona, she fell ill and remained there. Mary Ritter Beard spent her last years in Phoenix, where on August 14, 1958, she died of kidney failure.

SOURCES:

Cott, Nancy F., ed. *A Woman Making History: Mary Ritter Beard through Her Letters*. New Haven, CT: Yale University Press, 1991.

Lane, Ann J. *Mary Ritter Beard: A Sourcebook*. NY: Schocken, 1977.

SUGGESTED READING:

Carroll, Bernice A. "Mary Beard's *Woman as Force in History*: A Critique," in *Massachusetts Review*. Winter-Spring 1972, pp. 125–143.

Degler, Carl. "*Woman as Force in History* by Mary Beard," in *Daedalus*. Vol. 103. Winter 1974, pp. 67–73.

Turoff, Barbara Kivel. "Mary Beard: Feminist Educator," in *Antioch Review*. Vol. 37, fall 1979, pp. 277–292.

COLLECTIONS:

Material on Mary Beard can be found in the DePauw University Library, the Radcliffe College Library, and the Sophia Smith Collection at Smith College.

Justus D. Doenecke, Professor of History, New College of the University of South Florida, Sarasota, Florida

Bearden, Bessye (1888–1943)

African-American political and civic worker, known particularly for her work with the Democratic Party.

Born Bessye Jeanne Banks in Goldsboro, North Carolina, in October 1888; died on September 16, 1943, in New York, New York; daughter of George T. and Clara (Carrie Ocott) Banks; attended Hartshorn Memorial College in Richmond, Virginia; graduated from Virginia Normal Industrial Institute in Petersburg, Virginia; post-graduate work at the University of Western Pennsylvania, Pittsburgh; studied journalism at Columbia University, New York, New York; married Richard Howard Bearden; children: son Romare (b. 1914, who became an artist).

Bessye Bearden settled in Harlem with her husband and young son shortly after World War I. Active in the political, civic, and social activities in her community and nationwide, she was appointed to the New York City Board of Education in 1922, where she was elected chair of the 12th District, becoming the first black woman member of the board. Bearden subsequently wrote a society column for the *Chicago Defender*, a weekly African-American newspaper. In 1935, she was named deputy collector in internal revenue for the Third New York Collection District, the first African-American appointed to that position. She later worked in tax processing and as an auditor.

In the 1930s, Bearden became active in Democratic Party politics as founder and president of the Colored Women's Democratic League in New York. In 1937, she was elected delegate to the First Judicial District Convention, where she was involved in congressional campaigns and rallies to reelect President Franklin Roosevelt. Bearden was also aligned with the National Council of Negro Women, of which ***Mary McLeod Bethune** was the national president. Bearden served as well in the advisory committee of the Emergency Relief Bureau, working for economic justice for blacks in New York City. She chaired the New York State Committee to Abolish the Poll Tax and was on the executive board of the New York Urban League.

On the community level, Bearden served on numerous boards, including the Citizens Welfare Council, the Harlem Community Council, the NAACP, and the Utopia Neighborhood Club. She received a number of honors for her devoted service, including medals from the Citizens' Welfare Council and Veterans of Foreign Wars. After a long illness, Bessye Bearden died on September 16, 1943.

Beath, Betty (1932—)

Australian composer who wrote chamber, choral, and instrumental music as well as music for the theater.

Name variations: Elizabeth Margaret Beath Cox. Born Elizabeth Margaret Eardley on November 19, 1932, in the Gooburrum district near Bundaberg, Queensland; oldest of five daughters of Edith Mary and Maurice Wilmot Eardley (a cane farmer); married John Beath (a patrol officer), in 1953; married David Cox (a writer and artist), in 1970; children: (first marriage) two. Awarded the University of Queensland Music Scholarship to study at the Sydney Conservatorium of Music (1950).

Realizing that her daughter was talented and resources in the district were limited, **Edith Eardley** felt study in a distant town with a respected teacher was her daughter's only alternative. Thus, Betty Eardley (Beath) was sent away at age three to study piano with **Lorna Pollard**. Beath would later recall that her early training called for a pink ribbon on her right wrist, a blue on her left. These ribbons corresponded with treble notes in pink on the score and bass notes in blue. Her family then moved to Brisbane so that Beath could live at home and study music. While in school, she regularly presented recital programs on the Australian Broadcasting Commission's Young Australia Program.

In 1950, she began studying at the Sydney Conservatorium of Music with the composer Frank Hutchens. Her marriage in 1953 interrupted her studies, and she did not return to full-time musical activity until her two children were older. She and her husband John Beath, a patrol officer, went to Papua and the tiny island of Abau where she was the only white woman.

In 1970, she met and married David Cox, a writer and artist, who encouraged his new wife to pursue her composing interests. In 1972, they collaborated on a 40-minute opera for children titled

The Strange Adventures of Marco Polo. Other commissions followed as Beath literally began her career in middle age. The couple created another opera *The Raja Who Married an Angel*, which was also quite popular. A volume of poems by **Carmen Bernos de Gasztold**, *The Beasts' Choir*, handed to Beath as she was leaving a dinner party, provided the inspiration for her next work, *Songs from the Beasts' Choir*. Roman Gales premiered this work at Carnegie Hall. In 1984, Beath developed a program about women composers which came to be a regular feature on Australian radio about the works of women.

John Haag, Athens, Georgia

Beatrice (1242–1275).

See Eleanor of Provence for sidebar.

Beatrice, Countess of Edessa.

See Agnes of Courtenay for sidebar.

Beatrice, Dona (c. 1684–1706)

Congolese religious leader, who formed her own sect, called Antonianism, and preached national unity. *Name variations: Kimpa Vita, Saint Anthony. Born Kimpa Vita around 1684 in the Belgian Congo (subsequently Zaire, now Republic of Congo); died at the stake in 1706; children: one son.*

Dona Beatrice rose to power in central Africa's Belgian Congo, during a period in the 17th century when the area, reduced to a Portuguese conquest, was ravaged by clan rivalry and famine. With the King Pedro IV's inability to unify the kingdom's chieftains and retake the capitol of São Salvador which had been destroyed and deserted, Beatrice established herself as a religious leader and savior of her people.

The 20-year-old Dona Beatrice claimed that, while ill, she had had a vision of Portuguese-born Saint Anthony, who appeared to her as a black man and instructed her to save the Congo through a new nationalistic religion. Beatrice then built a church and established the Antonian sect, a synthesis of European and African culture. Called Antonianism, the new religion celebrated black culture, professed that Christ had been born in the Congo, and permitted polygamy. For two years, she preached her dogma throughout the country, attracting many followers and threatening the power of the Portuguese missionaries and the Catholic Church. Hailed as a minor queen and credited with performing resurrections and other miracles, her appearances in São Salvador drew such crowds that they stimulated a period of economic growth.

But at a time when her power seemed unassailable, Beatrice brought about her own demise. She fell in love with her "Guardian Angel" in the sect, a man named Barro, by whom she became pregnant. Beatrice fled with Barro, leaving her disciples to believe she had gone to visit God and would return. When she was found with her lover and infant by the king's men, she was quickly brought to trial and sentenced to death. In July 1706, both Beatrice and Barro were burned at the stake. By some accounts, the child was killed with her. Others claim the boy was spared and baptized Jerome.

Barbara Morgan,
Melrose, Massachusetts

Beatrice, Princess (1857–1944).

See Queen Victoria for sidebar.

Beatrice d'Este.

See Este, Beatrice d'.

Beatrice of Anjou (d. 1275)

Titular empress of Constantinople. *Name variations: Beatrix. Died in 1275; daughter of* ****Beatrice of Provence*** *(d. 1267) and Charles I of Anjou (brother of Louis IX, king of France), king of Sicily (r. 1266–1282) and Naples (r. 1268–1285); married Philipp de Courtenay, titular emperor of Constantinople, on October 15, 1273; children:* ****Catherine de Courtenay*** *(d. 1307).*

Beatrice of Battenberg (1857–1944).

See Queen Victoria for sidebar.

Beatrice of Beja (1430–1506)

Duchess of Beja and Viseu. *Name variations: Beatriz. Born in 1430; died on September 30, 1506, in Beja; daughter of* ****Isabella of Braganza*** *(1402–1465) and Joao or John of Portugal, grand master of Santiago; married Fernando also known as Ferdinand, duke of Beja and Viseu, on March 16, 1452; children: Joao, duke of Beja and Viseu (1456–1483);* ****Eleanor of Portugal*** *(1458–1525);* ****Isabella of Braganza*** *(1459–1521); Diego (1460–1484), duke of Beja and Viseu; Duarte (b. 1462, died young); Diniz or Denis (b. 1464, died young); Simiao (b. 1467, died young); Caterina (1467, died young); Alfonso (b. 1468, died young); Emmanuel or Emanuel also known as Manuel I the Fortunate (1469–1521), king of Portugal (r. 1495–1521).*

Beatrice of Beja's son Manuel ascended the throne of Portugal in 1495. Her descendants reigned in that country until Manuel II abdicated in 1910.

Beatrice of Brandenburg

(1360–1414)

Duchess of Austria. *Name variations: Beatrix of Zollern. Born in 1360 in Nurnberg; died on June 10, 1414, in Perchtoldsdorf, Lower Austria; second wife of Albrecht also known as Albert III (c. 1349–1395), duke of Austria (r. 1365–1395); children: Albert IV (1377–1404), duke of Austria.*

Beatrice of Burgundy (d. 1310).

See Beatrix de Bourgogne.

Beatrice of Canossa (c. 1020–1076).

See Matilda of Tuscany for sidebar on Beatrice of Lorraine.

Beatrice of Castile (d. 1179).

See Berengaria of Navarre for sidebar on Sancha of Castile and Leon.

Beatrice of Castile and Leon

(1242–1303)

Queen of Portugal. *Name variations: Beatriz; Beatriz de Guillén. Born in 1242; died on October 27, 1303; illegitimate daughter of Alphonso X, king of Castile and Leon (r. 1252–1284), and* ****Mayor Guillen de Guzman*** *(d. 1262); married Alphonso III (1215–1279), king of Portugal (r. 1248–1279), in 1253 or 1254; children:* ****Branca*** *(1259–1321); Fernando (1260–1262); Affonso (1263–1321); Sancha (b. February 2, 1264–1302); Maria (b. November 21, 1264–1304); Vicente (1268–1271); Diniz or Denis the Farmer (1261–1325), king of Portugal (r. 1279–1325); Costanza (b. before November 23, 1271). Alphonso's first wife was* ****Matilda de Dammartin*** *(d. 1258).*

Beatrice of Castile and Leon (1293–1359).

See Maria de Molina for sidebar.

Beatrice of Cenci (1577–1599)

Noblewoman of Rome. *Name variations: Beatrice Cenci; "the Beautiful Parricide." Born in 1577 (some sources cite 1583); executed on September 11, 1599; daughter of Francesco Cenci (1549–1598) and his first wife whose name is unknown.*

In 16th-century Rome, Beatrice Cenci was the youngest of 12 children of Francesco Cenci and his first wife. Following his second marriage, Francesco, a Roman noble of enormous wealth, began to treat the children of his first marriage, including Beatrice, reprehensibly. It was even rumored that he had hired bandits to murder two of his sons on their return from Spain.

Beatrice of Cenci

One medieval source states that as Beatrice matured, her father was attracted to her beauty: "The beauty of Beatrice inspired him with the horrible and incestuous desire to possess her person; and with mingled lust and hate he persecuted her from day to day, until circumstances enabled him to consummate his brutality." On September 9, 1598, Beatrice's friend Olimpio Calvetti and a hired assassin drove a large nail into Francesco's brain while he lay sleeping.

Differing scenarios have been painted by historians to explain the events prior to Francesco's murder. In Italian historian Lodovico Muratori's version of the events, Beatrice sought the help of relatives and Pope Clement VII but received no assistance. Therefore, in the company of her brother Giacomo and her stepmother, she planned the murder of her father. Other historians maintain that Beatrice was indeed innocent and cite her date of birth as 1583 instead of 1577, claiming she was only 16 at the time of her father's death.

Italian historian Bestolotti had far more sympathy for the father. Bestolotti maintains that Francesco, though profligate, was not a monster, and that Beatrice was not a 16-year-old girl at the time of the killing, but a 21-year-old, who was far from beautiful and had an illegitimate son. He further asserts that the sweet and mournful countenance of Beatrice painted by Guido, one of the treasures of the Barberini Palace in Rome, could not have been painted from life, as Guido did not paint in Rome until nine years after her death.

When the crime was discovered, Beatrice and Giacomo were tortured; Giacomo confessed, but Beatrice continued to declare her innocence. Despite efforts to obtain a pardon from the pope, all three were condemned and beheaded on September 11, 1599. The tragedy has inspired a number of literary works, including *The Cenci* by Percy Bysshe Shelley and a novel by Francesco Guerrazzi.

Beatrice of Falkenburg (c. 1253–1277).

See Falkenstein, Beatrice von.

Beatrice of Kent (d. after 1280)

English abbess and author. *Died after 1280 at Lacock Abbey, Wiltshire, England; never married; no children.*

Few facts are known about the life of Abbess Beatrice of Kent. She entered the convent at Lacock Abbey in Wiltshire sometime after its founding in 1239. At that time, the abbess of Lacock was Countess **Ela of Salisbury**, the abbey's founder. Beatrice rose in the abbey's hierarchy to be elected abbess upon Ela's retirement in 1257. After Ela's death in 1261, Beatrice composed a biography of the countess, although no copies are extant. Despite the heavy responsibilities of governing a large and wealthy establishment like Lacock Abbey, Beatrice found time to write poetry and other works. She retired from her position around 1269.

Laura York, Anza, California

Beatrice of Lorraine (c. 1020–1076).

See Matilda of Tuscany for sidebar.

Beatrice of Modena (1750–1829).

See Maria Beatrice of Modena.

Beatrice of Naples (1457–1508)

Queen of Hungary. *Born in 1457; died on September 23, 1508, in Ischia; daughter of* ****Isabel de Clermont*** *(d. 1465) and Ferdinand also known as Ferrante I (1423–1494), king of Naples (r. 1458–1494); married Matthias Corvinus, king of Hungary (r. 1458–1490), in 1476; married Vladislas also known as Ladislas II of Bohemia, king of Bohemia (r. 1471–1516) and Hungary (r. 1490–1516), in 1490 (divorced, 1500). Ladislas' first wife was* ****Anne de Foix.***

Beatrice of Nazareth (c. 1200–1268)

Belgian nun, mystic, philosopher, and prioress at Notre-Dame-de-Nazareth who experienced visions of God and described the nature of mystical experience. *Name variations: Beatrijs; Beatrice of Tirlemont. Born between 1200 and 1205; died in 1268 at Nazareth priory in Brabant; daughter of Bartholoméus (also mentioned as Bartholomaeus, Bartholomew, Barthélémy) de Vleeschouwer of Tirlemont (merchant and lay brother) and Gertrudis; had one brother and two sisters, Christina (Christine) and Sybilla (Sibylle); educated at the school of the Beguines at Léau, at Bloemendaal (Florival) Convent, and at Rameia (La Ramée); never married; no children.*

Selected works: The Seven Modes of Sacred Love; On the Intensive Use of Time; On the Threefold Exercise of Spiritual Affections; On the Two Cells Which She Constructed in Her Heart; On the Five Mirrors of Her Own Heart; On the Spiritual Convent; On the Fruitful Garden of Her Own Heart; On Her Aspirations to Achieve Self-Knowledge; On a Certain Rule of Spiritual Life Which She Kept for Some Time; *and two prayers,* Oh, Righteous Lord, *and* Oh, Most Righteous and Almighty God.

Beatrice of Nazareth was a Flemish holy woman and writer who was born into a wealthy, devout family: her father Bartholoméus was a lay brother who established three of the convents to which Beatrice would belong; her mother Gertrudis was noted for piety and charity. Beatrice, a shy and frail child, was so religious that she had memorized the Book of Psalms (commonly a first reader) by the age of five.

When Gertrudis died, Bartholoméus sent seven-year-old Beatrice to be educated at the school of the Beguines in Léau where she received a rudimentary education in the liberal arts trivium—grammar, rhetoric, and dialectic—and extensive religious education. Beatrice seems to have been an apt pupil, as revealed in her later writings. She completed the trivium program at the Bloemendaal convent and also completed the quadrivium, comprised of music, geometry, arithmetic and astronomy.

By 1215, Beatrice's health was so poor that Bloemendaal almost denied her application to become a novice. She was determined, however, and strictly observed the rules which required, among other penances, self-starvation and sleeping on thorns. Though the severe asceticism of the Cistercian tradition made her extremely ill, she would drag herself to class or ask support of another girl rather than "let any of her time pass without the viaticum of knowledge." Of her own volition, she would rise in the middle of the night to sing the Holy Office. Incredibly devoted, Beatrice stood out in a society that regularly encouraged extreme displays of devotion.

When she was 16, Beatrice took the vows of a Cistercian nun and was sent to the convent in

Rameia, where she learned calligraphy and manuscript illumination, talents which would serve to provide copies of liturgical materials for the establishment of new religious communities. She also had her first vision at Rameia in 1217 and met *Ida of Nivelles**, an older novice who acted as her spiritual guide. Such deep personal friendships were part of the Cistercian tradition, and Beatrice shared many throughout her life. Her friendship with Ida was so close that Beatrice would be made ill by Ida's death in 1232.

Upon her return to Bloemendaal, Beatrice suffered a great depression. The *Book of Her Own Life*, which is based closely on her diary of religious experience, records many visions which occurred during worship or religious meditation. These were usually abstract visions, of symbols or powers without context, such as the blood from Christ's wounds cleansing her soul. Other sensations, particularly voices and touch, often complemented the visual simplicity. In one early vision, Beatrice was embraced by Christ and accepted as his bride: "Let us make a pact, let us make an alliance, that we may not be separated from each other, but that we may be truly unified together." Although she recognized the significance of this vision, she lived in fear that she would be inadequate to the task, unable to serve Christ properly.

But on September 14, 1225, shortly after she and the other nuns of Bloemendaal had left for the convent at Maagdendaal, she experienced another vision during communion: the embrace of Christ and the assurance of God that she was chosen by him and that she would not yearn for death because of suffering, but only because of her yearning for heaven. As a result of this, her fears were dispelled. Her next years were marked by the remembered pleasure of this vision.

In February 1234, a vision of the Trinity revealed to Beatrice the mysteries of divine and human life. Experiencing the operation of divine justice, she learned that the Father is the creator, the Son provides wisdom, and life continues by virtue of the Holy Spirit. After this vision, she was ill for a year, caused, she wrote, by God taking over her will.

In May 1236, along with her sisters, her brother, and her father, all of whom had been with her for most of her life, Beatrice formed the Cistercian house called Notre-Dame-de-Nazareth in Brabant to which she was elected prioress. She remained at Nazareth for over 30 years, earning widespread recognition for her deep piety and spiritual advice to others. Beatrice believed she had a special message from God to share with others, and wrote an autobiographical record of her spiritual growth and acceptance of God's love, published as *The Seven Ways of Loving*. In this highly emotional book, written in Flemish and later translated into Latin, Beatrice describes her visions and gives her interpretations of them, while revealing her thorough knowledge of contemporary theology. *The Seven Ways* describes the levels of ascent, the many stages before the soul can find union with God. At the sixth stage, the soul surrenders to love in peace and comes to know God. At the seventh stage, the soul cries out for God's love, wishing an end to the earthly existence that now seems like a prison. Writes Beatrice:

> Love has drawn her and guided her, has taught her Her ways; the soul has followed Love faithfully, in great toils and countless works, in noble aspirations and violent desires, in great patience and great impatience, in suffering and in happiness, in numerous torments, in quest and supplication, loss and possession, in ascent and in suspense, in pursual and in embrace, in anguish and cares, in distress and in troubles; in immense trust and in doubt, in love and in affliction, she is ready to endure everything. In death or in life, she wishes to devote herself to Love; in her heart she endures endless sufferings and it is for Love alone that she wishes to reach her Fatherland.

Considered a spiritual authority, Beatrice of Nazareth was consulted by people from all classes on a range of religious questions. She died at the convent in 1268.

SOURCES:

Brunn, Emilie, and Georgette Epiney-Burgard. *Women Mystics in Medieval Europe.* NY: Paragon House, 1989.

McDonnell, Ernst W. *The Beguines and Beghards in Medieval Culture.* NY: Octagon, 1969.

Waithe, Mary Ellen, ed. *A History of Women Philosophers, Vol. 2.* Boston, MA: Martinus Nijhoff, 1987.

Catherine Hundleby, M.A. Philosophy, University of Guelph, Guelph, Ontario, Canada

Beatrice of Portugal (c. 1347–1381)

Countess of Albuquerque. *Born around 1347; died on July 5, 1381, in Ledesma; probably the daughter of* ****Inez de Castro*** *(c. 1320–1355) and Pedro also known as Peter I, king of Portugal (r. 1357–1367); married Sancho (b. 1373), count of Albuquerque, in 1373; children: Fernando or Ferdinand, count of Albuquerque (b. 1373);* ****Eleanor of Albuquerque*** *(1374–1435).*

Beatrice of Portugal (1372–after 1409)

Queen of Castile and Leon. *Name variations: Beatrix, Beatriz, Brites. Born in February 1372 (some sources cite 1373) at Coimbra, Portugal; died after 1409 in*

*Madrigal, Portugal; daughter of Fernando also known as Ferdinand I the Handsome, king of Portugal (r. 1367–1383), and *****Leonora Telles*** *(c. 1350–1386); married Edward, duke of York, in July 1381 (annulled 1382); became second wife of Juan also known as John I, king of Castile and Leon (r. 1379–1390), on April 30, 1383; children: none. John of Castile's first wife was *****Eleanor of Aragon*** *(1358–1382).*

Beatrice's unfortunate story begins with her illegitimate birth to Ferdinand I, king of Portugal, and ***Leonora Telles**, his mistress. When it became clear that he would have no sons, Ferdinand had Beatrice officially legitimized and named his heir. He negotiated many betrothals for her but changing national power prevented each from being finalized. Eventually, Ferdinand was forced by the more powerful King Henry II of Castile to sign a marriage agreement between Beatrice and John, the son of the Castilian king. This agreement was a triumph for Henry II, who looked forward to adding Portugal to his Castilian domains when Beatrice succeeded her father. However, Henry predeceased Ferdinand, and his son became King John I of Castile.

At age 12, Beatrice married John of Castile in 1383, the same year her father died. Beatrice's mother Leonora Telles attempted to establish herself as regent for Beatrice, but the marriage agreement between Beatrice and her husband gave the Portuguese crown to King John, and there was little Leonora could do to prevent John of Castile from ruling Portugal. Wishing to remain independent of Castile, the Portuguese people strongly resented this virtual *coup d'état* by the Castilians; consequently, they refused to support Beatrice as their queen because accepting her rule meant accepting the rule of her Castilian husband. Instead, they denied the validity of her claim to the throne and supported the much weaker claims of an illegitimate half-brother of King Ferdinand, who accepted their support and was crowned as King John I of Portugal. In 1386, Beatrice's mother Leonora died. With Portugal already lost, Beatrice's husband no longer wanted or needed the Portuguese alliance. In 1387, he had their marriage annulled, then married into the English royal house. Beatrice returned to Portugal where she died some years later.

Laura York, Anza, California

Beatrice of Portugal (d. 1439)

Countess of Arundel. *Died on October 23, 1439, in Bordeaux, France; interred at Collegiate Church, Arundel; illegitimate daughter of Inez Perez and João I also known as John I (1385–1433), king of Portugal (r. 1385–1433); married Thomas Fitzalan, 12th earl of Arundel, on November 26, 1405; married John Holland, duke of Huntington, on January 20, 1432.*

Beatrice of Portugal (1504–1538)

Duchess of Savoy. *Name variations: Beatriz; Maria Beatriz, countess d'Asti. Born on December 31, 1504, in Lisbon; died on January 8, 1538, in Nice; daughter of Manuel I the Fortunate (1469–1521), king of Portugal (r. 1495–1521), and *****Maria of Castile*** *(1482–1517); married Carlo also known as Charles III (d. 1552), duke of Savoy (r. 1504–1553), on September 29, 1520; children: Emmanuel Philibert (1528–1580), 10th duke of Savoy (r. 1553–1580).*

Beatrice of Provence (d. 1267).

See Eleanor of Provence for sidebar.

Beatrice of Rethel (fl. 1150s)

Queen of Sicily. *Flourished around 1150s; married Roger II, king of Sicily (r. 1103–1154), duke of Apulia (r. 1128–1154); children: Roger of Apulia; William I the Bad, king of Sicily (r. 1154–1166); *****Constance of Sicily*** *(1154–1198).*

Beatrice of Sardinia (1792–1840).

See Maria Beatrice of Sardinia.

Beatrice of Savoy, countess of Provence (d. 1268).

See Eleanor of Provence for sidebar.

Beatrice of Savoy, queen of Naples and Sicily.

See Constance of Sicily for sidebar.

Beatrice of Saxe-Coburg (1857–1944).

See Queen Victoria for sidebar.

Beatrice of Saxe-Coburg (1884–1966).

See Marie of Rumania for sidebar.

Beatrice of Silesia (fl. 1300s)

Holy Roman empress. *Name variations: Beatrix of Glogau. Flourished in the 1300s; first wife of Louis III, duke of Bavaria (r. 1294–1347), also known as Ludwig IV of Bavaria or Louis IV, Holy Roman emperor (r. 1314–1347); children: *****Matilda of Bavaria;*** *Louis V (1315–1361), margrave of Brandenburg (r. 1347–1361, who married *****Margaret Maultasch****); Stephen II, duke of Bavaria (r. 1363–1375). Louis IV's second wife was *****Margaret of Holland*** *(d. 1356).*

Beatrice of Swabia (1198–1235)

Queen of Castile and Leon. *Name variations: Beatrice Hohenstaufen; Beatrice von Hohenstaufen. Born in 1198; died in Toro, Castile and Leon, Spain, on August 11, 1235; daughter of Philip of Swabia (1176–1208), Holy Roman emperor (r. 1198–1208), and* ****Irene Angela of Byzantium*** *(d. 1208); sister of* ****Marie of Swabia*** *(c. 1201–1235); granddaughter of* ****Beatrice of Upper Burgundy*** *(1145–1184); became first wife of Otto IV of Brunswick (c. 1175–1218), earl of York, count of Ponthieu, duke of Bavaria, king of the Romans (r. 1198–1209), and Holy Roman emperor (r. 1209–1215), on July 2, 1212; became first wife of Fernando also known as Saint Ferdinand or Ferdinand III (1199–1252), king of Castile (r. 1217–1252) and Leon (r. 1230–1252), on November 30, 1219; children: Alphonso X (c. 1226–1284), king of Castile and Leon (r. 1252–1284); Fadrique (d. 1277); Enrique also known as Henry (d. 1304); Felipe, archbishop of Seville; Leonor (died young); Berenguela (a nun); Sancho (1233–1261), archbishop of Toledo and Seville; Manuel of Castile (1234–1283); Maria (1235–1235). Otto's second wife was* ****Mary of Brabant*** *(c. 1191–c. 1260). Ferdinand's second wife was* ****Joanna of Ponthieu*** *(d. 1279).*

Beatrice of Tirlemont (c. 1200–1268).

See Beatrice of Nazareth.

Beatrice of Tuscany (c. 1020–1076).

See Matilda of Tuscany for sidebar on Beatrice of Lorraine.

Beatrice of Upper Burgundy (1145–1184)

Holy Roman empress and queen of Germany and Italy. *Name variations: Beatrice of Burgundy; Beatrix of Burgundy. Born in 1145; died on November 15, 1184; daughter of Rainald also known as Renaud III, count of Burgundy and Macon, and* ***Agatha of Lorraine****; married Frederick I Barbarossa (1123–1190), Holy Roman emperor (r. 1152–1190), on June 10, 1156; children: Henry VI (c. 1165–1197), Holy Roman emperor (r. 1190–1197); Frederick (d. 1191), duke of Swabia; Otto, count Palatine; Philip of Swabia (c. 1176–1208), Holy Roman emperor (r. 1198–1208). Frederick Barbarossa's first wife was* ****Adelaide of Vohburg****.*

Beatrice of Vermandois (880–931)

Queen of France. *Name variations: Beatrice de Vermandois. Born in 880; died in 931; daughter of Hubert I, count of Senlis; married Robert I (c. 865–923), king of France (r. 922–923), around 893 or 895; children:* ****Emma of Burgundy*** *(d. 935); Hugh the Great also known as Hugh the White (c. 895–956), count of Paris and duke of Burgundy; Adela (who married Herbert II, count of Vermandois).*

Beatrice of Wittelsbach (1344–1359)

Swedish royal. *Name variations: Beatrix Wittelsbach. Born in 1344; died on December 25, 1359; daughter of Louis IV the Bavarian, Holy Roman emperor, and possibly* ****Margaret of Holland*** *(d. 1356); married Erik XII (c. 1339–1359), co-regent of Sweden (r. 1356–1359), in December 1355; children: two sons.*

Beatrice Plantagenet (1242–1275).

See Eleanor of Provence for sidebar on Beatrice.

Beatrice Portinari (c. 1265–1290)

Florentine woman who is said to have inspired Dante. *Born around 1265 or 1266; died on June 9, 1290; daughter of Folco Portinari (a Florentine noble); married Simone di Geri de Bardi (or Pardi).*

Some say Beatrice Portinari was the heroine and inspiration of Dante's *La Vita Nuova* (The New Life), of his *Divine Comedy*, and of his life. When he was a boy in 1274, Dante Alighieri first met the nine-year-old Beatrice at the house of her father. "Already nine times after my birth the heaven of light had returned as it were to the same point," wrote the poet, "when there appeared to my eyes the glorious lady of my mind. Her dress on that day was of a most noble color, a subdued and goodly crimson, girdled and adorned in such sort as best suited her tender age. At that moment I saw most truly that the spirit of life which hath its dwelling in the secretest chamber of the heart began to tremble so violently that the least pulses of my body shook therewith."

In the *La Vita Nuova*, Dante narrates the story of his passion from its beginnings to within a year after Beatrice's death. He saw Beatrice only once or twice, but it is likely that his worship was stronger for the remoteness of its subject. The last chapter of the *La Vita Nuova* relates Dante's inspiration after her death:

> It was given me to behold a wonderful vision, wherein I saw things which determined me to say nothing further of this blessed one until such time as I could discourse more worthily concerning her. And to this end I labor all I can, as she in truth knoweth. Therefore if it be His pleasure through

> whom is the life of all things that my life continue with me a few years, it is my hope that I shall yet write concerning her what hath not before been written of any woman. After the which may it seem good until Him that my spirit should go hence to behold the glory of its lady, to wit, of that blessed Beatrice who, now gloriously gazes on the countenance of Him who is the master of grace.

Beatrice's identity and her allegorical significance in the *Divine Comedy* (*Divina Commedia*) has been the subject of extensive literature. "In Beatrice, Dante created one of Western culture's most perfect pictures of idealized womanhood," writes Mervin and Prunhuber, "a theme cherished by the troubadours of courtly love and the Romantic poets. And yet he probably never met the little girl or the young woman he glimpsed in the streets. She may have existed only in his imagination. No one knows."

If the theory is true that Beatrice was indeed the daughter of the Florentine noble, Folco Portinari, she was a married woman, and the mother of a family, who apparently perished without ever knowing her effect on the young poet. The death of her father in 1289 is said to have hastened her own. On June 9, 1290, at age 24, Beatrice Portinari died. For 13 years, her mortal love had guided Dante; her immortal spirit would purify his later life, reveal to him the mysteries of Paradise, and inspire his *Divine Comedy*.

SOURCES:

Mervin, Sabrina, and Carol Prunhuber. *Women: Around the World and Through the Ages.* Wilmington, DE: Atomium Books, 1990.

Beatrijs.

Variant of Beatrice.

Beatrix.

Variant of Beatrice.

Beatrix, queen of the Netherlands

(1938—).

See Wilhelmina for sidebar.

Beatrix da Silva (1424–1490)

Spanish saint. *Born in 1424; died in 1490.*

Beatrix da Silva was said to be so beautiful that she had to escape the Spanish court to ward off admirers. In 1484, she founded the order of the Conceptionists, in honor of the Virgin Mary. At first, the order followed the Cistercian rule before adopting that of St. Francis of Assisi in 1511.

Beatrix de Bourgogne (1257–1310)

Duchess of Bourbon. *Name variations: Beatrice of Burgundy, Beatrice of Bourbon; Béatrix. Born in 1257; died on October 1, 1310, at Château-Murat; daughter of Jean de Bourgogne also known as John of Burgundy and Agnes de Dampierre (1237–1287); married Robert of France (1256–1317), count of Clermont, in 1271 or 1278; children: Louis I the Grand (1270–1342), count of Clermont.*

Born into the noble houses of Burgundy and Bourbon, Beatrix de Bourgogne received an excellent education. She was betrothed early and married Robert of France, son of the count of Clermont. As her parents had no surviving sons, Beatrix—their eldest daughter—was named their heir. When her mother, ***Agnes de Dampierre**, died in 1287, Beatrix inherited the duchy of Bourbon (located in modern-day central France). She ruled as duchess for 23 years, until her death in 1310.

Laura York, Anza, California

Beatrix of Burgundy (1145–1184).

See Beatrice of Upper Burgundy.

Beatrix of Falkenburg (c. 1253–1277).

See Falkenstein, Beatrice von.

Beatrix of Glogau (fl. 1300s).

See Beatrice of Silesia.

Beatrix of Modena-Este (1750–1829).

See Maria Beatrice of Modena.

Beatriz.

Variant of Beatrice.

Beatriz of Spain (b. 1909)

Spanish princess. *Name variations: Beatrix; the Infanta. Born Beatriz Isabel Frederica Alfonsa on June 22, 1909, in La Granja, San Ildefonso, Segovia; daughter of* ***Ena** *(1887–1969) and Alphonso XIII (1886–1941), king of Spain (r. 1886–1931); married Alessandro Torlonia, prince of Civitella-Cesi, on January 14, 1935; children:* ***Sandra Vittoria Torlonia** *(b. 1936, who married Clemente, count Lequio di Assaba); Marco Alfonso (b. 1937), prince Civitella-Cesi; Marino Riccardo (b. 1939);* ***Olimpia Emanuela Torlonia*** *(b. 1943, who married Paul-Annik Weiller).*

Beatty, Bessie (1886–1947)

American journalist, author, and radio commentator. *Born on January 27, 1886, in Los Angeles, California; died on April 6, 1947; eldest of five children of Thomas Edward and Jane Mary (Boxwell) Beatty; attended Occidental College in Los Angeles; married William Sauter (an actor), August 15, 1926.*

Bessie Beatty achieved her childhood aspirations by the time she was 18: in 1904, she took a job while in college, writing for the Los Angeles *Herald*. Within three years, she was the *Herald*'s drama editor and chief editor of the women's page. She then moved into a cabin in Nevada while researching a story on its gold-mining district. In 1907, her first book was published as a series of sketches called *Who's Who in Nevada*.

From 1907 to 1917, Beatty was a reporter for the San Francisco *Bulletin*, then under the editorship of Fremont Older who, according to ***Ishbel Ross** in her history of American newswomen, fostered Beatty's interest in "radical thought and social reform." During Beatty's association with the *Bulletin*, she wrote a broad range of articles, from the Progressive movement in Washington to life in Alaska. In 1917, she initiated a series called "Around the World in Wartime," which took her to Japan, China, and finally to Russia, where she spent eight months observing the Revolution first hand. Her 1918 book, *The Red Heart of Russia*, summarized her experiences and observations. She would later write and lecture extensively on Russia and find Americans hard-pressed to understand the ramifications of the political and economic revolutions she had witnessed.

On her return to the U.S., Beatty edited *McCall's* magazine for three years before restlessness led her back to Russia as a correspondent for *Good Housekeeping* and Hearst's *International* magazine. With articles intended to be non-political and non-controversial, she interviewed Lenin and Trotsky, as well as ordinary Russian workers emerging from revolution and famine. She then visited Turkey to study women under the new regime. Back in the States, she wrote short stories and articles for a variety of magazines before taking on another newspaper assignment in 1924, a series on the new Labour government in England.

After her marriage to the distinguished actor William Sauter in 1926, Beatty had a brief experience writing for films, which led to a collaboration with Jack Black on a play called *Saltchunk Mary*. In 1933, she moved into a new field, directing the National Label Council in an educational program to instruct the public in the buying of labeled clothes; this work segued into her own public-relations bureau, which took on publicity primarily for social organizations, including the Museum of Costume Art and The Neighborhood Playhouse School of Theatre. Beatty also directed publicity for the women's division of the New York State Democratic Committee during the 1932 and 1936 campaigns. During World War II, she toured England, collecting material for articles on aspects of the war there, which she later sold to the *Christian Science Monitor*.

Beatty's multifaceted career culminated in a 45-minute morning radio program on New York's WOR. Beginning in September 1940, she combined chat about current events, books, plays, and personal experiences with the informal endorsement of products from her sponsors. A final segment of the show included guest interviews with various celebrities, including actors, writers, and political figures. Assisting on the show were an announcer and Beatty's husband Bill, who was drafted after a couple of successful casual appearances. Presented in an informal style to an audience whose intelligence, she believed, was often underrated, the program was an unqualified success, receiving the highest ratings of any program of its kind in 1942. It was also cited for its efforts to encourage listeners to assist in the war effort. The following year, Beatty received the annual radio award of the Women's International Exposition of Arts and Industries. Perhaps most indicative of her success was the overwhelming response to her recommendations for shows or restaurants, and her requests for charitable donations or civilian participation.

Barbara Morgan, Melrose, Massachusetts

Beatty, Josephine (1895–1984).

See Hunter, Alberta.

Beauchamp, Anne (1426–1492)

Countess of Warwick. *Name variations: Lady Anne de Beauchamp. Born in September 1426 in Caversham; died on September 20, 1492; daughter of Richard Beauchamp (1381–1439), 5th earl of Warwick, and* ****Isabel Despenser*** *(1400–1439); married Richard Neville the Kingmaker (1428–1471), 16th earl of Warwick (r. 1449–1471), in 1434; children:* ****Isabel Neville*** *(1451–1476);* ****Anne of Warwick*** *(1456–1485, married King Richard III).*

Beauchamp, Catherine (c. 1313–?).

See Mortimer, Catherine.

Beauchamp, Eleanor (1408–1468)

Duchess of Somerset. *Born in 1408; died on March 6, 1468, in London, England; daughter of Richard Beauchamp, 5th earl of Warwick, and* ****Elizabeth Berkeley****; married Thomas Roos, 9th baron Ros; married Edmund Beaufort, 1st duke of Somerset, before 1436; children: (second marriage) Henry Beaufort (1436–1464), 2nd duke of Somerset; Edmund Beaufort (1438–1471), 3rd duke of Somerset; John Beaufort (d. 1471);* ****Margaret Beaufort*** *(d. 1474);* ****Eleanor Beaufort*** *(d. 1501); Elizabeth Beaufort (d. before 1492, who married Henry Lewes); Anne Beaufort (who married William Paston);* ***Joan Beaufort*** *(d. after 1492, who married Robert Howth, Lord of Howth, and Richard Fry); and two others.*

Beauchamp, Elizabeth (fl. 1420)

Countess of Ormonde. *Name variations: Elizabeth Butler. Flourished around 1420; daughter of William Beauchamp, Lord Abergavenny; married James Butler (known as The White Earl), 4th earl of Ormonde; children: James Butler (c. 1390–1452), 5th earl of Ormonde; John Butler, 6th earl of Ormonde; Thomas Butler (c. 1424–1515), 7th earl of Ormonde.*

Beauchamp, Elizabeth (d. c. 1480).

See Beaufort, Joan (c. 1379–1440) for sidebar.

Beauchamp, Elizabeth, Baroness Abergavenny.

See Beaufort, Joan (c. 1379–1440) for sidebar.

Beauchamp, Isabel (fl. 1285)

Countess of Winchester. *Name variations: Isabel Despenser; Isabel Chaworth. Flourished around 1285; daughter of William Beauchamp, 1st earl of Warwick, and* ***Maud Fitzjohn****; married Patrick Chaworth; married Hugh Despenser, Sr. (c. 1262–1326), earl of Winchester (executed, October 1326); children: (first marriage)* ****Maud Chaworth*** *(1282–c. 1322); (second marriage) Hugh Despenser, Jr. (c. 1285–1326);* ***Isabel Despenser*** *(who married John Hastings, 2nd baron Hastings).*

Beauchamp, Isabel (1400–1439).
See Despenser, Isabel.

Beauchamp, Kathleen (1888–1923).
See Mansfield, Katherine.

Beauchamp, Margaret (d. 1482).
See Beaufort, Margaret for sidebar.

Beauchamp, Philippa (fl. 1368–1378).
See Stafford, Philippa.

Beaufort, duchess of.
See Estrées, Gabrielle d' (1573–1599).

Beaufort, Eleanor (d. 1501)

***Countess of Ormonde.** Pronunciation: BOE-fort. Died on August 16, 1501; daughter of Edmund Beaufort, 1st duke of Somerset, and *__Eleanor Beauchamp__ (1408–1468); married James Butler, 5th earl of Ormonde, in April 1458; married Robert Spencer; children: (second marriage) __Margaret Spencer__ (b. 1471).*

Beaufort, Joan (c. 1379–1440)

***Countess of Westmoreland who was instrumental in the creation of the Beaufort political faction in 15th-century England.** Name variations: Joanna Neville. Pronunciation: BOE-fort. Born illegitimate at Beaufort Castle, Anjou, France, around 1379; died at Howden, Humberside, England, on November 13, 1440, and buried in Lincoln Cathedral; daughter of John of Gaunt (1340–1399), duke of Lancaster, and Catherine Swynford (c. 1350–1403); half-sister of Henry IV, king of England (r. 1399–1413); grandmother of kings Edward IV and Richard III; married Sir Robert Ferrers, 2nd baron Ferrers of Wemme, in 1392 (died); married Sir Ralph Neville of Raby (created 1st earl of Westmoreland by Richard II, 1397), in 1396 (died 1425); children: (first marriage) ➧ __Elizabeth Ferrers__ (1392–1434); ➧ __Mary Ferrers__ (d. 1457); (second marriage) *__Catherine Neville__ (c. 1397–1483); Richard (1400–1460), earl of Salisbury; William (d. 1463), lord of Fauconberg and earl of Kent; George (d. 1469), lord of Latimer (who married ➧ __Elizabeth Beauchamp__); Edward (d. 1476), lord of Abergavenny; Robert (d. 1457), bishop of Durham; Cuthbert; Henry; Thomas; ➧ __Eleanor Neville__ (c. 1413–1472), countess of Northumberland; ➧ __Anne Neville__ (d. 1480), duchess of Buckingham; Jane also known as Joan Neville (who became a nun); Cecily Neville (1415–1495), duchess of York.*

Joan betrothed to Sir Robert Ferrers (1386); legitimation of the Beaufort children by Papal Bull (1396), and by royal writ and act of parliament (1397); Henry Bolingbroke banished by Richard II (1398); death of John of Gaunt (1399); Lancastrian inheritance forfeited (1399); abdication of Richard II (1399); Henry Bolingbroke crowned Henry IV (1399); legitimacy of Beauforts confirmed again by Henry IV (1407); death of Henry IV (1413); Joan patron of poet Thomas Hoc-

➧ **Ferrers, Elizabeth** (1392–1434)

***Lady Greystoke.** Name variations: Lady of Wem or Wemme. Born in 1392 (some sources cite 1394); died in 1434; interred at Black Friars', York; daughter of Robert Ferrers, 2nd baron Ferrers of Wemme, and *__Joan Beaufort__ (c. 1379–1440); married John Greystoke, 6th Lord Greystoke, around October 28, 1407; children: Ralph Greystoke, Lord Greystoke.*

➧ **Ferrers, Mary** (d. 1457)

***English noblewoman.** Name variations: Lady of Oversley. Born before 1394; died on January 25, 1457; daughter of Robert Ferrers, 2nd baron Ferrers of Wemme, and *__Joan Beaufort__ (c. 1379–1440); married Ralph Neville (son of the 1st earl of Westmoreland); children: John Neville of Oversley.*

➧ **Beauchamp, Elizabeth** (d. c. 1480)

*Died around 1480; daughter of Richard Beauchamp, 5th earl of Warwick, and *__Elizabeth Berkeley__ (daughter of Thomas, Viscount L'Isle); married George Neville (d. 1469), 1st baron Latimer; children: Henry Neville.*

➧ **Neville, Eleanor** (c. 1413–1472)

***Countess of Northumberland.** Name variations: Eleanor Neville. Born around 1413; died in 1472; daughter of *__Joan Beaufort__ (1379–1440) and Sir Ralph Neville of Raby; married Richard Despenser, Lord Despenser; married Henry Percy, 2nd earl of Northumberland, in 1414; children: Henry Percy (b. 1421), earl of Northumberland; Thomas Percy (b. 1422), 1st lord Egremont; Katherine Percy (who married Edmund Grey, 1st earl of Kent).*

➧ **Neville, Anne** (d. 1480)

***Duchess of Buckingham.** Died in 1480; daughter of *__Joan Beaufort__ (1379–1440) and Sir Ralph Neville of Raby, 1st earl of Westmoreland; married Humphrey Stafford (1402–1460), 1st duke of Buckingham, 1st earl of Stafford; married Walter Blount, 1st baron Mountjoy; children: (first marriage) Humphrey Stafford (d. 1455), 7th earl of Stafford; Henry Stafford (d. 1471), who married *__Margaret Beaufort__ (1443–1509); twins William and George Stafford; Edward Stafford; John Stafford, 9th earl of Wiltshire (r. 1469–1473); *__Anne Stafford__ (d. 1472); __Joan Stafford__ (who married Sir William Knyvet); *__Catherine Stafford__ (d. 1476).*

cleve (1421); death of Henry V (1422); Joan awarded custody of Richard, duke of York (1423); death of Ralph Neville, earl of Westmoreland (1425); Ralph, 2nd earl of Westmoreland contested inheritance (1429); Cecily married Richard, duke of York (1429); Joan founded Chantry in the name of her mother, Catherine Swynford, at Lincoln Cathedral (1437).

In February 1396, the cathedral town of Lincoln stood fast against the icy winds of winter. Occasionally, a heavily clad figure moved quickly through the narrow streets. The stones of the great cathedral stood silent and grey, and the water in Lincoln's main well, cold and frozen. This bleak winter scene was relieved when an army of horsesoldiers descended upon the town, colorfully clad in the livery of John of Gaunt, the duke of Lancaster. In his 56th year, the wealthiest and most powerful magnate in England had come to Lincoln to marry his third wife ◂❧ **Catherine Swynford.**

The daughter of a Hainault knight, Catherine Swynford had long been a familiar figure at the English court. For the last 20 years, she had also been John of Gaunt's mistress, and in 1381 was publicly attacked for their relationship in Parliament. Upon the death of John of Gaunt's first wife ◂❧ **Blanche of Lancaster** in 1369, Catherine Swynford had become foster mother to his three children. Throughout his second marriage to ◂❧ **Constance of Castile,** Catherine lived in the duke's household and gave birth to four children, among them the youngest, Joan. The offspring of John of Gaunt and Catherine Swynford took the surname of Beaufort, from the French estate of John of Gaunt.

The Beaufort children enjoyed equal status with the children of John of Gaunt's first marriage. When, a few days before the marriage of their parents in 1396, John of Gaunt's eldest son Henry Bolingbroke (later Henry IV) was admitted to the fraternity of Lincoln Cathedral, so were Joan and her brother John. Among those also present were Geoffrey Chaucer and his wife.

The marriage of John of Gaunt and Catherine Swynford immediately transformed the social position of the Beaufort children. A papal bull, dated 1396, legitimized the offspring of the union, and King Richard II and Parliament soon followed suit in 1397. The marriage was not, however, universally popular. As the French chronicler Froissart noted:

❧▸ **Swynford, Catherine** (c. 1350–1403)

Duchess of Lancaster. *Name variations: Katherine Rouet; Catherine de Ruet or Catherine de Roet; Katherine Swynford. Born around 1350; died on May 10, 1403; interred at Lincoln Cathedral; daughter of Sir Payne Roelt (a knight from Hainault, France, who arrived in England with the train of Edward III's queen* ****Philippa of Hainault****); married Sir Hugh Swynford of Lincolnshire (d. 1372), around 1367; was mistress, as of 1388, before becoming third wife of John of Gaunt, duke of Lancaster, on January 13, 1396; children: (first marriage) Thomas (c. 1368–1433, a friend and companion of Henry IV and supposed murderer of Richard II); Blanche Swynford (b. around 1370); (second marriage) four, all of whom were born before the marriage but were declared legitimate in 1396 and 1397: John Beaufort (c. 1373–1410), earl of Somerset; Henry (1375–1447); Cardinal Beaufort (b. around 1375); Thomas (c. 1377–1426), earl of Dorset and chancellor of England;* ****Joan Beaufort*** *(c. 1379–1440). Catherine Swynford's children took the name Beaufort from one of her husband's castles in Anjou.*

❧▸ **Blanche of Lancaster** (1341–1369)

Duchess of Lancaster. *Born in 1341; died on September 12, 1369, at Bolingbroke Castle, Lincolnshire, England; daughter of Henry of Lancaster (c. 1299–1361), 1st duke of Lancaster, and* ****Isabel Beaumont*** *(d. 1368); married John of Gaunt, duke of Lancaster (1340–1399), in 1359; children:* ****Philippa of Lancaster*** *(c. 1359–1415, who married John I, king of Portugal); John (1362–1365);* ****Elizabeth of Lancaster*** *(1364–1425, who married John Holland, duke of Exeter); Edward (1365–1368); John (1366, died young); Henry Bolingbroke (1367–1413), later Henry IV, king of England (r. 1399–1413); Isabel (c. 1368, died young).*

❧▸ **Constance of Castile** (1354–1394)

Spanish noblewoman and duchess of Lancaster. *Name variations: Constanza. Born in Castrojeriz, Castile, in 1354; died at Leicester Castle, Leicestershire, England, on March 24, 1394; daughter of Peter the Cruel, king of Castile and Leon (r. 1350–1369), and* ****Marie de Padilla*** *(1335–1365); became second wife of John of Gaunt, duke of Lancaster, on September 21, 1371; children:* ****Catherine of Lancaster*** *(1372–1418, who married Henry III, king of Castile); John (1374–1375).*

> Out of love for his children the Duke of Lancaster married their mother Madame Catherine [Swynford], which caused much astonishment in France and England, for she was of humble birth. . . . When news of this marriage reached the great ladies of England . . . and other ladies with royal blood in their veins, they . . . said "The Duke of Lancaster has quite disgraced himself by marrying his concubine."

By the time of her parents' marriage, Joan Beaufort was already a young widow of 18 and engaged to become the second wife of Sir Ralph Neville of Raby. Though not a great beauty by contemporary standards, Joan Beaufort has often been described as a handsome woman. Few details of her early life survive, save the fact that her parents saw to it that she was well educated. Her intellectual gifts were clearly evident from an early age, and, unlike most women of her class and generation, Joan Beaufort was fully literate. It must also have been during this period that Joan acquired her political acumen, which assisted that of her famous father.

As with most marriages of noblewomen, the marriage of Joan Beaufort had important political overtones. Sir Ralph Neville, although a politically marginal figure, was nevertheless a magnate of considerable wealth. The location of the Neville estates in the north magnified his significance in the eyes of Joan's father, for John of Gaunt saw the match as a means of checking the growing influence of the Percy family in the north. Thus, the marriage of Joan and Ralph secured an alliance with a family of growing importance, who could be relied upon to support Lancastrian interests in the politically sensitive counties of northern England. The factional intricacies of Joan's marriage were not lost on the young bride. Throughout her life, she demonstrated an unfailing instinct for the medieval game of strategic matchmaking.

In 1397, the so-called Merciless Parliament was held in London. The Parliament, which had charged five of Richard II's closest advisors with treason, presented an overt challenge to royal authority. Joan and her husband supported the king against the Lords Appellant, who had been chosen to try the case. Among them were Joan's half-brother, Henry Bolingbroke, the heir of John of Gaunt. When the Lords Appellant upheld the charge of treason, four of Richard II's councillors were executed, while the fifth, Michael de la Pole, Richard II's infamous chancellor, escaped to France. Joan and her husband were rewarded by Richard for their timely support; Sir Ralph Neville was elevated as the first earl of Westmoreland.

Henry Bolingbroke, however, was banished from England. A year later, in 1399, the death of his father John of Gaunt provoked a crisis of national proportions. Upon John's death, Richard II seized the vast Lancastrian domain. The seizure deprived Henry Bolingbroke of his inheritance and proved to be a turning point in Joan's support for Richard II. While Richard II was away on expedition in Ireland, Bolingbroke returned to England to reclaim his inheritance as Henry IV. Most of the English nobility rallied to his side, and what had begun as a bid to restore the Lancastrian patrimony soon snowballed into a movement to depose the unpopular Richard.

The dethronement of Richard II in 1399 would not have occurred had it not been for the support of the Beaufort family. As a result, the grateful Henry IV made significant grants of offices and lands to Joan and her husband. But it was in the last years of Henry IV's reign that the substantial successes of the Beauforts took on the spectacular proportions that made the family such a pivotal factor during the 15th century.

Between 1412 and 1436, Joan engineered the most successful series of child marriages in English history. Her daughters systematically married the heirs of Mowbray (1412), Percy (1414), Stafford (1422), and York (1429). Richard, the eldest of Joan's sons, was betrothed to ***Alice Montacute**, daughter and heir of the duke of Salisbury, while her youngest son William wed Joan, heir to Lord Fauconberg. In 1424, Joan arranged the union of her third son George with ⚜▸ **Elizabeth Beauchamp**, the earl of Warwick's stepdaughter.

By 1429, most of the leading families of England were related to the Beauforts by marriage. These included all the families who had opposed the deposition of Richard II. The marriages engineered by Joan thus served to bind the leading families of the realm to the Lancastrian crown, while simultaneously keeping the connection separate from the royal line of succession. This mas-

⚜▸ **Beauchamp, Elizabeth**

*Baroness Abergavenny. Daughter of *Isabel Despenser (1400–1439) and Richard Beauchamp, earl of Worcester; stepdaughter of Richard Beauchamp, the 5th earl of Warwick; married Edward Neville, 1st baron Abergavenny (r. 1438–1476); children: Richard Neville; George Neville (d. 1492), 4th lord Abergavenny. Edward Neville's second wife was *Catherine Howard (d. after 1478).*

terful network of alliances also underlined the Beauforts' position as the most powerful family in England, excluding the royal family.

The leading role of the Beauforts in the life of the nation was naturally reflected in the honors accorded them. In 1423, for instance, Henry VI granted Joan and her husband custody of young Richard of York, heir to the vast Yorkist legacy. After the death of Joan's husband Ralph Neville in 1425, Henry VI again confirmed the "grant to Joan, Countess of Westmoreland, by advice of the council, and on her petition . . . (that she have) the custody of Richard, Duke of York, as executrix of Ralph, Earl of Westmoreland, her late husband." Joan and Richard of York were thereafter familiar figures at the court of Henry IV, where they lived for several years. In another act of the Privy council, provision for their support by the crown was made.

In widowhood, Joan Beaufort proved herself to be as astute as in marriage. Not only did she collect the royal allowance allocated for the support of York, she also took a further 300 marks a year from Richard's estates in Dorset and Suffolk. But the marriage of her daughter ***Cecily Neville** to Richard of York in 1429 was perhaps her greatest accomplishment. For it united the royal families of York and Lancaster through marital bonds with the Beauforts. The match was to result in the birth of two kings, Edward IV and Richard III.

With the death of Ralph Neville of Westmoreland, leadership of the Beaufort family passed more overtly into the hands of Joan. But her husband's death also created several problems. Chief among these was a new, potentially dangerous split within the family, resulting from Joan's determination to endow her own children at the expense of the children of her husband's first marriage. When her stepson Ralph, 2nd earl of Westmoreland, came of age in 1429, he quickly asserted his right to challenge Joan and her son Richard, earl of Salisbury, for the bulk of the Westmoreland inheritance. By 1430, the quarrel had developed into a private civil war, and a royal council was forced to intervene. In August, Westmoreland and Joan were both forced to pay a bond of £2,000 each, in order to guarantee the peace. The private feud between Joan and Westmoreland, however, erupted again four years later. Westmoreland again complained bitterly that he had been deprived of his rights, and again the two parties were placed under bond.

In that same year, a will of Joan's husband, dated 1400, came to light in the monastery of Durham. This will pre-dated that of 1404, which had deprived the elder branch of the inheritance. Pressed by Westmoreland to open the will and read it publicly, the prior of Durham sent his attorney to report its discovery to Joan in London. After the prior delivered the will to her, it disappeared without a trace.

While the ins-and-outs of noble politics took up much of Joan's life, she still found time for less robust activities. Her love of letters was evident in later life, and she sponsored several writers. The poet Thomas Hoccleve, for instance, dedicated his collection of poems entitled *Complaint* to "my lady of Westmoreland" by her "humble servant . . . T. Hoccleve." As well, Joan endowed several religious houses and founded a chantry in the name of her mother, Catherine Swynford, at Lincoln Cathedral. Such patronage followed a pattern set by Blanche of Lancaster, John of Gaunt's first wife, who had patronized the chronicler Froissart, as well as John himself, who had endowed Corpus Christi College at Cambridge.

Joan Beaufort died on November 13, 1440, and was buried in Lincoln Cathedral. Her death helped to hasten a settlement between Westmoreland and Joan's eldest son, Richard, earl of Salisbury. In 1443, Westmoreland formally acknowledged Salisbury's right to the Westmoreland estates in Yorkshire, Cumberland, Essex, Westmoreland, and York. In return, Salisbury abandoned his claims to all remaining property.

In many ways Joan Beaufort proved an exemplar model of the noble medieval wife. She was adept at estate management and the running of a large household, and she gave birth to 15 children, fulfilling perhaps the greatest contemporary criteria of the successful aristocratic spouse. She also demonstrated an ability to exploit profitable wardships and to defend herself, both on the battlefield and in the councils of state.

In the management of her children on the medieval marriage market, Joan proved herself to be nothing short of brilliant. The marriages of the Beaufort children have no parallel in English history, and it was through Joan that the Beaufort family found itself at the center of a political and economic web that dominated the history of England during the 15th century. But the matchmaking skills of Joan Beaufort did more than simply aggrandize the Beaufort family. The alliances which she forged, in the wake of the dethronement of Richard II, stabilized the crown and the country, at a time when the external pressure of the Hundred Years' War was having a telling effect on the economic and political life of the realm.

SOURCES:

Froissart, Jean. *The Chronicles of England, France and Spain.* NY: E.P. Dutton, 1961.

Jacob, Ernest Fraser. *The Fifteenth Century, 1399–1485.* Oxford: Clarendon Press, 1961.

Johnson, P.A. *Duke Richard of York, 1411–1460.* Oxford: Clarendon Press, 1988.

McFarlane, K.G. *England in the Fifteenth Century.* London: Hambleton Press, 1981.

Rosenthal, Joel T. *Nobles and the Noble Life, 1295–1500.* London: George Allen, Unwin, 1976.

SUGGESTED READING:

Armitage-Smith, Sydney. *John of Gaunt.* London: Archibald Constable, 1904.

H.A. Stewart, M.A., University of Guelph, Guelph, Ontario, Canada

Beaufort, Joan (c. 1410–1445)

Queen of Scotland and wife of James I who attempted after his murder to become regent of Scotland. *Name variations: Jane Beaufort; Queen Joan; Jane or Johanna. Pronunciation: BOE-fort. Born in England around 1410; died in Dunbar Castle, Lothian, Scotland, on July 15, 1445, and buried in the church of the Carthusian Monastery in Perth; daughter of Margaret Holland (1385–1429) and John Beaufort, earl of Somerset; married James I (1394–1437), king of Scotland (r. 1406–1437), in February 1424; married Sir James Stewart of Lorne, in July 1439; children: (first marriage) Margaret of Scotland (1424–1445); Isabel Stewart (d. 1494); Jean Stewart (d. 1486);* ***Eleanor Stewart*** *(d. 1496); (twins) Alexander (1430–1430) and James II (1430–1460), king of Scotland (r. 1437–1460)); Mary Stewart (d. 1465), countess of Buchan;* ***Annabella Stewart*** *(d. after 1471); (second marriage) James; John Stewart, 1st earl of Atholl (c. 1440–1512); Andrew.*

Treaty of London signed (December 1423); crowned queen of Scotland (May 21, 1424); nobility swore fealty (1428); gave birth to twin sons (October 16, 1430); nobility swore fealty (1435); marriage of Princess Margaret to the French dauphin (June 1436); regicide of James I (February 20–21, 1437); Joan Beaufort arrested and imprisoned (August 3, 1439); the Appoyntement Agreement ratified (September 4, 1439); marriage of Isabel to Francis I, duke of Brittany; marriage of Mary to Wolfaert count of Grandpre (1444); siege of Dunbar Castle (1444).

During his long captivity in England, James I of Scotland gazed out his window in the castle tower, spied a strolling maiden, and fell in love. Inspired by Chaucer's translation of a French allegory, James wrote a long love poem, *The Kingis Quair* (The King's Book), which included the lines:

> And therewith cast I down my eye again,
> Where as I saw, walking under the tower,
> Full secretly knew coming her to play,
> The fairest or the freshest young flower
> That ever I saw . . . before the hour,
> For which sudden surprise, non assert
> The blood of all my body to my heart.

While the courtship of Joan Beaufort was a rare affair of the heart, it is improbable that it occurred in the romantic fashion described in *The Kingis Quair*. Rather, the marriage was largely the formulation of the Beaufort family who, barred from the English succession by the 1407 charter of Henry IV, nonetheless sought to enhance their prestige through a union with the Stewart dynasty. Indeed, the English commissioners sent to Scotland were given secret instructions on the subject of marriage. If the Scots raised the question of an English bride for their king, the commissioners were told to proceed with negotiations. However, if the Scots did not raise the issue, the commissioners were instructed not to allude to it "since Englishwomen, at least noble ones, are not wont to offer themselves in marriage to men of other parts." The proposed marriage was the subject of intricate negotiation, for the bridegroom had been a prisoner of the English since 1406. In the Treaty of London, it was agreed that James would be released in return for a ransom of £40,000 and a seven-year truce. A remission of 10,000 marks was made as Joan's dowry.

Stewart, Eleanor (1427–1496)

Archduchess of Austria. *Name variations: Eleanor Stuart. Born on October 26, 1427; died in 1496 (some sources cite November 20, 1480); daughter of James I (1394–1437), king of Scotland (r. 1406–1437), and* ****Joan Beaufort*** *(c. 1410–1445); married Sigismund von Tirol, archduke of Austria, on February 12, 1449.*

Stewart, Annabella (d. after 1471)

Countess of Huntly. *Name variations: Annabella Stuart. Died after 1471; daughter of James I (1394–1437), king of Scotland (r. 1406–1437), and* ****Joan Beaufort*** *(c. 1410–1445); married Louis, count of Geneva, on December 14, 1447 (divorced 1458); married George Gordon, 2nd earl of Huntly, before March 10, 1459 (divorced 1471); children: (second marriage)* ***Isabella Gordon*** *(who married William Hay, 3rd earl of Erroll); Janet Gordon; Elizabeth Gordon; Margaret Gordon; Agnes Gordon; Alexander, earl of Huntly.*

The daughter of John Beaufort, earl of Somerset, and ◂ Margaret Holland, Joan grew to womanhood in the bosom of the Beaufort clan, undoubtedly the most successful English family of the 15th century. Like many Beaufort women, she possessed both political acumen and beauty. Her quasi-royal genealogy distinguished her as a rare prize on the medieval marriage market, and even George Buchanan, the patriotic Scottish scholar, was to note that she was "the loveliest woman of her time, of whom [James] was passionately enamoured." The marriage took place at the church of St. Mary Overy in Southwark. Afterward the bride's uncle, Henry Beaufort, Bishop of Winchester, gave a wedding feast at his nearby palace. Among the wedding gifts were silver and gold plate and several rich tapestries, one of which depicted the life of Hercules.

In April 1424, the newlyweds crossed the border into Scotland. James, determined to restore order to his kingdom after 18 years of regency government, vowed that "if God grant me life, though it be but the life of a dog, there shall be no place in my realm where the key shall not keep the castle and the brackenbush the cow." The triumphal progress of Joan and James took them to Edinburgh. The couple "came on Care-Sunday in Lent to Edinburgh," wrote John Leslie, "where a great concourse of people were assembled all eager to gaze on Joan, who was accounted the most beautiful woman of the day." After 18 years of captivity, their king had finally returned, and he had brought with him a bride worthy to be their queen. Even if, as some grumbled, she was English.

The coronation took place on May 21 at Scone, the ancient coronation site of Scottish monarchs. Both the king and queen were crowned in a ceremony presided over by the bishop of St. Andrews and the earl of Fife, who exercised his hereditary right to place James upon the throne. But the new king was faced with the formidable task of restoring the prestige of the crown and its finances. Scotland was an impoverished country, as described by Aeneas Sylvius Piccolomini, the future Pope Pius II, after a visit in 1435:

> In this country I saw the poor, who almost in a state of nakedness begged at church doors, depart with joy in their faces on receiving stones as alms. This stone [coal], whether by reason of sulphurous or some other matter which it contains, is burned instead of wood, of which the country is destitute.

The firmness with which James I governed his unruly kingdom contrasted sharply with his immediate predecessors. He embarked on a far-reaching program of social and legislative reform: provision was made for the maintenance of law and order, new taxes were raised, and the power of the nobility was curbed. Aware of the danger of his actions, in 1428 and 1435 James demanded that the nobility swear oaths of fealty to Joan. Toward the end of his reign, James went so far as to obtain written assurance of the fidelity of Parliament to his wife. Indeed, throughout his rule, James I displayed unwavering confidence in Joan Beaufort's ability to govern and indicated that he wished her to be appointed regent in the event of his death.

A few weeks before Christmas, 1424, Joan gave birth to her first child. The king was present at the birth and the child was christened ***Margaret (of Scotland)**. The young princess, however, was debarred from the succession, out of fear that she might be seized and married by the rival claimants to the throne, the Albany Stewarts.

In an effort to enforce the rule of law, in the summer of 1428 James summoned 40 chiefs of the Gaelic clans to his Parliament at Inverness. As each appeared, they were seized by men-at-arms. Three of the company were hung and the rest released on promises of good behavior. Such clemency was wasted on Alexander, Lord of the Isles. When the king left Inverness, Alexander returned and burned the burgh to the ground. James led an army into Lochaber and defeated Alexander in battle. On August 27, 1429, Alexander of the Isles appeared before the high altar of Holyrood Abbey in the garb of a penitent. While on his knees, he presented his sword, hilt forward, to the king. Joan pleaded for mercy, and Alexander was saved from her husband's wrath.

▸ **Holland, Margaret** (1385–1429)

Countess of Somerset. *Name variations: Lady Somerset. Born in 1385; died on December 30, 1429 (some sources cite 1439) at St. Saviours Abbey, Bermondsey, London; buried at Canterbury Cathedral, Kent, England; daughter of Thomas Holland, 2nd earl of Kent, and* ***Alice Fitzalan*** *(1352–1416); married John Beaufort, earl of Somerset (1373–1410, son of John of Gaunt and* ***Catherine Swynford***), *on September 28, 1397; married Thomas, duke of Clarence, in 1411 or 1412; children: (first marriage) Henry, earl of Somerset (1401–1418); John Beaufort, duke of Somerset (1404–1444); Thomas, earl of Perche (1405–1432); Edmund, duke of Somerset (1406–1455);* ***Margaret Beaufort***, *Countess of Devon (c. 1407);* ***Joan Beaufort*** *(c. 1410–1445).*

Joan played an active part in government and often restrained her husband's fiery temper. In another instance, during a stormy session in the council chamber, one noble struck another. James ordered the culprit to lay his hands on the table, then, handing his sword to the victim, requested that he strike off the hands of the offender. In horror, Joan begged that the offender be spared, and the king relented.

On October 16, 1430, Joan gave birth to twin sons at Holyrood. The anonymous writer of the *Book of Pluscarden* informs us that in Edinburgh:

> Seeing that they were born in the monastery of Holyrood, bonfires were lighted, flagons of wine were free to all and victuals publicly to all comers, with the sweetest harmony of all kinds of musical instruments all night long proclaiming the praise and glory of God for all his gifts and benefits.

The eldest of the two boys was christened Alexander, the youngest James (the future James II). With the queen in attendance, the two infants were baptized and knighted in a ceremony attended by members of the nobility. Alexander did not survive infancy, but James, known as "the Fiery Face" due to a birth mark on the left side of his face, survived and was named duke of Rothesay and heir to the throne. Thus, in the sixth year of her marriage, Joan had fulfilled the primary function of a medieval queen: she had secured the succession by providing Scotland with an heir.

In 1435, negotiations with France began for the marriage of Princess Margaret. Involved in every aspect of the talks, Joan took great care to see that her daughter's interests were protected. As with most royal marriages, political considerations soon overshadowed the proceedings. The French were anxious to secure the military assistance of the Scots against their mutual enemy, Henry VI, the king of England. As Aeneas Sylvius noted, "Nothing pleases the Scots more than abuse of the English."

At length, the alliance between Scotland and France was agreed upon, and the king and queen consented to the marriage of their daughter, age 11, to the 13-year-old French dauphin. Joan made several stipulations as to the treatment of her daughter: Margaret was to live at court and be under the supervision of ***Marie of Anjou**, the queen of France, who agreed to "treat her as her own child and teach her the bearing and manners that would be expected of her in France." But the French fleet, sent to collect the bride, ran into an autumnal gale before reaching the safe port of Dumbarton. Upon learning of the torturous crossing, Joan insisted that Margaret wait until spring before setting sail for France. In March, a farewell banquet was held for Margaret, and Joan wept openly throughout the evening.

At the 11th hour, King Henry VI of England dispatched a herald to warn the king and queen that if they insisted on sending their daughter to France "she should be taken, with all her company, by Englishmen lying on the sea biding her coming." This threat of piracy and kidnapping did not deter James nor his wife, although it must have brought back painful memories of James' own abduction on the high seas, when as a boy of 12 he was kidnapped while enroute to the French court for safekeeping. The threat angered James enough to launch an attack on England, and it would seem surprising if Joan had not agreed.

James I's predominance in domestic affairs had been largely achieved through legislative reforms which were difficult for the nobility to counteract. By undertaking the siege of Roxburgh in August 1436, James broke the spell cast by his abstinence from the use of force. The siege was an inglorious failure. The nobility of Scotland, arrayed for war, sensed their own power and were no longer daunted by their king. It was to Roxburgh that Joan would hasten in the summer of 1436 to warn her husband of a plot against him.

Opposition to James was not merely based on class interests. It was based upon a deeply rooted ideal of leadership, which argued that the removal of a monarch was justified if he imperiled the common good of the realm. This would have been a theory alien to the absolutist England of Joan's childhood. But in Scotland such an idea had its origins in Celtic notions of leadership and authority which pre-dated the feudal monarchy of Scotland. James knew the risks he ran in implementing his reformist policies, and there was an element of fatalism in the oath he uttered at the beginning of his reign: "If God grant me life."

After a long voyage north, as the king was relaxing in Perth, he sat in his wife's chamber amusing Joan and her ladies-in-waiting with the tale of another ominous warning given to him by a Highland woman. Scottish history is full of such portents and just as full of those who have failed to heed them. Hearing the clatter of armed men in the hallway, James, who was unarmed, immediately grasped the situation. He ripped up the floorboards which covered a drain that led to the courtyard and sought to escape. Unfortunately, a few days previously he had ordered it to be stopped up so that his tennis balls would not fall in. There was barely enough room for him to hide.

When the assailants, including the earl of Atholl, Sir Robert Stewart, and Robert Graham, entered the room and demanded to know the king's whereabouts, Joan pleaded ignorance, and, after a brief search, the party left the room. They had not been gone long, however, when they remembered the drain and returned to pound on the door. Legend has it that, **Katherine Douglas**, one of Joan's ladies-in-waiting, put her arm through the u-shaped loop that held the door bolt in an attempt to give James time to escape. When the intruders forced open the door, they broke her arm. For her deed, she is remembered as "Kate-Bar-Lass."

In a desperate bid to save her husband's life, Joan attempted to shield her husband as he was dragged from the drain. He was killed, and she was severely injured. Joan's marriage to James I had been a happy one, and the king's conjugal fidelity was exceptional for a Stewart monarch. The murderers did not enjoy the fruits of their regicide for long. If Joan could be merciful in dealing with the likes of Alexander of the Isles, the wrath she meted out at the death of her beloved husband was gruesome indeed. Though the tortured executions of the conspirators were motivated by the queen's desire for revenge, they also served a more politic purpose. They deterred members of the nobility from wavering in their support of her.

In the aftermath of the assassination, the custody of James II was vital, and one of Joan's first acts was to hasten to Edinburgh and secure the possession of her son. Recognized by Parliament as the custodian of the new king, she was granted an allowance of 4,000 marks a year for his maintenance. While James I would have wished his wife to rule Scotland as regent, this was not to be. Too many powerful factions lurked offstage. A triumvirate was convened to rule the kingdom, composed of the Earl of Douglas as lieutenant-general, Bishop Cameron as chancellor, and the queen.

In the rough and tumble of regency politics, two families were to emerge who would dominate the struggle for power throughout much of the minority of James II. The first were the Crichtons, led by Sir William Crichton, a trusted former servant of James I, sheriff of Edinburgh and keeper of Edinburgh Castle. Second were the Livingtons, represented by Sir Alexander Livington of Callendar, keeper of Stirling Castle.

Within two years of the death of James I, Crichton managed to deny the queen access to her son. Joan sought the support of the earl of Douglas, but he refused to move against Crichton. Crichton seems to have been motivated by equal measures of self-interest and a genuine, if misguided, fear that the queen's English connections posed a threat.

Joan's response was to kidnap her own son. Announcing her intention of making a pilgrimage to the White Kirk in Lothian, she smuggled James II through the Edinburgh Castle gates in her luggage. The ship which she boarded sailed west instead of east, traveling up the Firth of Forth to her residence at Stirling Castle. There, Joan allied herself with Sir Alexander Livington, who offered to besiege Edinburgh Castle. He too sought the assistance of Douglas, but the latter refused. At length, Crichton and Livington made peace, recognizing that Douglas wished his two rivals to destroy each other.

The death of the Earl of Douglas, in 1439, left a power vacuum in the realm. This was partially filled by William Crichton, who supplanted Bishop Cameron as chancellor. Joan, in an attempt to strengthen her position and assume the powers of regent, married Sir James Stewart, known as the Black Knight of Lorne. This manoeuvre for the regency was forestalled, however, when Joan and her new husband were arrested by Alexander Livington, whose actions were motivated by a desire to protect his family's influence. The drastic step of imprisoning Joan underlined the weakness of her political position and caused much popular dissatisfaction.

On September 4, 1439, Joan's release was negotiated by Parliament, but the conditions of her release, set out in the Appoyntement Agreement, were extremely favorable to Livington. He was absolved of treason for seizing the queen, and instead Parliament declared that he was motivated by "great truth and loyalty." Joan agreed to forgive the "grief and displeasance" caused by the incident. Livington was awarded the custody of James II, and Joan was forced to entrust Livington with the 4,000 mark annuity for James' support. The Appoyntement Agreement ended any practical possibility of Joan becoming a dominant political figure during the minority of her son. As the years passed, a constant tug-of-war continued between the Livingtons, the Crichtons, and the Douglases for control of the government.

The years 1442 and 1444 saw Joan negotiate the successful marriages of her daughters

Isabel Stewart and Mary Stewart to important members of the European nobility. The marriage of her daughter Jean Stewart to the earl of Angus was not as successfully arranged. The government opposed such a union and favored a European marriage, but Joan resisted their wishes. From Dunbar Castle, Joan and her husband, as well as the earl of Angus and Adam Hepburn of Hailes, continued to defy the wishes of the government. The castle was laid to siege, and it was during the siege that Joan died on July 15, 1445. She was buried beside James I in Perth.

An alien in a strange land, Joan Beaufort adapted well to her role as queen of Scotland. As the wife of James I, she gave birth to eight children and exercised considerable influence upon royal policy. Upon his death, in 1437, Joan showed herself to be strong and resolute, seizing her son and hanging the assassins. If she failed in her bid to enforce her husband's wish that she rule as regent, it was largely due to her nationality and gender. Not one example of a long-serving female regent exists in the history of medieval Scotland. And during a period when the sword so often overawed the law, the reason can be easily discerned.

SOURCES:

Buchanan, George. *The History of Scotland.* Glasgow: Blackie, Fullarton, 1827.

Cook, E. Thornton. *Their Majesties of Scotland.* London: John Murray, 1928.

Harris, G.L. *Cardinal Beaufort.* Oxford: Clarendon Press, 1988.

McGladdery, Christine. *James II.* Edinburgh: John Donald Publishers, 1990.

Shirley, John. *The Life and Death of King James the First.* Edinburgh: Maitland Club, 1887.

SUGGESTED READING:

Balfour-Melville, E.W.M. *James I, King of Scots.* London: Methuen, 1936.

Hugh A. Stewart, M.A., University of Guelph, Guelph, Ontario, Canada

Stewart, Isabel (d. 1494)

Duchess of Brittany. *Name variations: Isabella, duchess de Bretagne; Isabel Stuart. Died in 1494; daughter of James I (1394–1437), king of Scotland (r. 1406–1437), and* ****Joan Beaufort*** *(c. 1410–1445); married Francis duc de Bretagne also known as Francis I, duke of Brittany, on October 30, 1442; children:* ****Marguerite de Foix*** *(fl. 1456–1477); Marie of Dreux (who married John, viscount de Rohan).*

Stewart, Mary (d. 1465)

Countess of Buchan. *Name variations: Mary Stuart. Died on March 20, 1465; interred at Sandenburg-ter-Veere, Zeeland; daughter of James I (1394–1437), king of Scotland (r. 1406–1437), and* ****Joan Beaufort*** *(c. 1410–1445); married Wolfaert van Borselen, count of Grandpre, in 1444; children: two sons.*

Stewart, Jean (d. 1486)

Name variations: Jean Stuart; Joan Stewart or Stuart; Joan "the Dumb Lady." Died after October 16, 1486; daughter of James I (1394–1437), king of Scotland (r. 1406–1437), and ****Joan Beaufort*** *(c. 1410–1445); married James Douglas, 3rd earl of Angus, on October 18, 1440; married James Douglas, 1st earl of Morton, before May 15, 1459; children: (second marriage) John Douglas, earl of Morton; Janet Douglas; James Douglas; Elizabeth Douglas. Jean Stewart was born a deaf mute.*

Beaufort, Margaret (c. 1407–?)

Countess of Devon. *Pronunciation: BOE-fort. Name variations: Margaret Courtenay. Born around 1407; daughter of John Beaufort, marquess of Somerset (son of John of Gaunt and* ****Catherine Swynford****) and* ****Margaret Holland*** *(1385–1429); sister of* ****Joan Beaufort*** *(c. 1410–1445); married Thomas Courtenay (1414–1458), 5th earl of Devon; children: Thomas (b. 1432), 6th earl of Devon (executed in 1461); John (c. 1435–1471), 7th earl of Devon; Henry Courtenay (executed in 1466);* ***Joan Courtenay*** *(who married Sir Roger Clifford);* ***Elizabeth Courtenay*** *(who married Sir Hugh Conway).*

Beaufort, Margaret (d. 1474)

English noblewoman. *Pronunciation: BOE-fort. Died in 1474; daughter of Edmund Beaufort, 1st duke of Somerset, and* ****Eleanor Beauchamp*** *(1408–1468); cousin and sister-in-law of* ****Margaret Beaufort*** *(1443–1509); married Humphrey Stafford (d. 1455), 7th earl of Stafford, before 1454; married Richard Darell; children: (first marriage) Henry Stafford, 2nd duke of Buckingham, and one other; (second marriage) one.*

Beaufort, Margaret (1443–1509)

Countess of Richmond and Derby who might have tried to claim the throne of England but instead secured that position for her son, Henry VII, and all the Tudor line. *Name variations: Lady Margaret; Margaret of Lancaster. Pronunciation: BOE-fort. Born Margaret Beaufort on May 31, 1443 (some sources cite 1441, but 1443 is documented), at Bletso in Bedfordshire; died in Abbot's house at Westminster on June 29, 1509; daughter of John Beaufort (c. 1404–1444), 1st duke of Somerset, and Margaret Beauchamp (d. 1482); be-*

trothed to John de la Pole, 1st duke of Suffolk, 1450 (dissolved, 1453); married Edmund Tudor (d. 1456), earl of Richmond, in 1455; married Henry Stafford (d. 1471), in 1458; married Thomas Stanley (d. 1504), earl of Derby, in 1472; children: (first marriage) Henry (b. January 28, 1457), later Henry VII, king of England (r. 1485–1509).

Involved in political conflicts of Wars of Roses (1459–71 and 1483–87); declared femme sole *(1485); took vow of chastity (1499), though last husband was still living; founded divinity professorships at Oxford and Cambridge (1502), Cambridge preachership (1503), Christ's College (1505), and licensed St. John's College (1508) which was founded in her memory (1511); translated* De Imitatione Christi *from French to English (1504) and* Mirror of Gold for the Sinful Soul *(1506).*

Margaret Beaufort

Almost from the day of her birth, Margaret Beaufort was caught in the midst of political struggle. Her grandfather John Beaufort, earl of Somerset, was half-brother to Henry IV, in a direct line from Edward III, and so was vaguely a part of the royal succession. Though John Beaufort was the oldest of several illegitimate children of John of Gaunt, duke of Lancaster, and ***Catherine Swynford**, the Beaufort family had been legitimated by the pope in 1397. Many in the aristocracy, however, were willing to challenge their status. Margaret's father, also John Beaufort, was an honored duke and military commander, despite his belonging to a "bastard line" up until 1443. In that year, just after his only daughter's birth, he led a major expedition to France. He bungled the mission, lost vital ground in the Hundred Years' War between France and England, and returned in disgrace. Banished from the court, with his property confiscated, John Beaufort died, possibly by his own hand, before Margaret was two years old.

Margaret was left in the care of her twice-widowed mother ⇒ **Margaret Beauchamp**. The young Margaret lived at Bletso, where she was born, and was raised with great care in the company of the children of her mother's first marriage. Her childhood, brief as it was, appears to have been a happy one. Later in life, Margaret would use her influence to benefit her half-siblings, the St. Johns. Needlepoint was a favorite pastime throughout her life; some of her work exists to this day, most notably a small tapestry of the St. John coat-of-arms. Margaret learned to read and write in English and in French. Her education, while certainly out of the reach of most women of the era, was not unusual for the heiress of a high noble. Her fondness for devotional literature was evident throughout her life.

Margaret Beaufort was too important an heiress to be left without an official protector for long, and King Henry VI named William de la Pole, earl of Suffolk, as her guardian. This wardship gave Suffolk the control of her estate and the arrangements for her marriage. He betrothed her at age seven to his son, John, no doubt aware of her potential connection to the throne. Henry VI had other plans for the young bride, however, and sought to dissolve her marriage to John de la Pole and transfer her wardship to his own half-brothers, Jasper and Edmund Tudor. To do this, he needed the girl's consent, and she was told to make her decision. According to legend, Margaret, not yet ten years old, prayed to St. Nicolas, "the patron and helper of all true maydens," and had a vision informing her to choose Edmund Tudor, the earl of Richmond.

Margaret married Edmund in 1455, and the couple moved to Pembrokeshire in the south of Wales. Their time together was brief, however, for Edmund was called away before a year was out to defend the house of Lancaster. Two of the family lines descending from Edward III, the Yorks and the Lancasters, were struggling for dominance of the English Crown. This conflict was to eventually be called the "Wars of the Roses" because the red rose was one emblem of the house of Lancaster and the white rose belonged to the house of York. Margaret and Edmund Tudor were both of the Lancaster line, and their marriage was significant. If Henry VI had no surviving children, their offspring stood to inherit the crown. For that reason, the couple consummated the marriage immediately, in spite of Margaret's youth. Edmund was captured in 1456 while on a campaign against the Yorks. Though he was eventually released, he died of plague in that year.

At 13, Margaret was pregnant, widowed, and far from her family. She went to live with her brother-in-law and former guardian, Jasper Tudor, at Pembroke castle. It was there that she gave birth to her only son on January 28, 1457.

According to legend, the name "Owen" was suggested to her, but she chose the name "Henry" because it was "the name of kings." Due to her age and some difficulty in delivery, Margaret never conceived again. She had a strong bond with her son, however, and for the rest of her life his safety and success were her main concerns.

In March 1457, Jasper Tudor and Margaret traveled to see the duke of Buckingham to discuss her possible marriage to his second son, Henry Stafford. She was still an important heiress, more so since the birth of her son, but her personal involvement in these marriage arrangements suggest she wanted some control over her future. Permission for this marriage was required from the church because Henry Stafford was Margaret's second cousin; the two were married on January 3, 1458. This match, which was to last 14 years, seems to have been an affectionate and stable union.

Henry Stafford had been initially a supporter of the Lancasters. After Edward IV was crowned in 1461, however, Stafford offered his loyalty to the new, Yorkist, king. This won for him and Margaret a pardon, preserving her estate and title. Still, Margaret had little cause to rejoice. Her son, the young Henry Tudor, was considered a potential threat, and Edward granted wardship of the five-year old boy to a loyal commander named William Herbert. Henry received an appropriate education and much care in this household, but Margaret did not stop working from afar on her son's behalf. She and her husband had already successfully preserved and improved her own estates when she approached several influential nobles to discuss her son's future land and titles. These were dangerous moves in light of the delicate political balance, and her actions may have aroused the suspicions of King Edward.

It was nine years before Margaret Beaufort was reunited with her son. In 1471, a rebellion against Edward IV had returned power temporarily to Henry VI. During this restoration of the Lancasters, Margaret and her husband managed to finally visit young Henry Tudor. Yorkist forces eventually prevailed against the Lancaster rebellion, however, and Edward regained the throne; this time, Henry VI and his son did not survive. With the main line of the Lancasters extinguished, Henry Tudor was the only immediate threat to Edward's claim to the English Crown. For this reason, Margaret's son was in more danger than ever before. Margaret reluctantly agreed with Jasper, her brother-in-law, that Henry would only be safe outside the country; she saw the two of them leave from the port of Tenby for France in September 1471. Her loneliness was magnified when, a few weeks later, Henry Stafford died of illnesses associated with wounds received in the recent rebellion.

With her son safely out of England, Margaret was forced to concentrate on her own well-being. In June 1472, less than a year after Henry Stafford's death, Margaret married Thomas Lord Stanley, the earl of Derby and a trusted minister of Edward IV. Stanley gained the extensive territory of Margaret's vast estates, and she gained protection and influence at the Yorkist court. She was also able to keep up correspondence with her exiled son while maneuvering to restore him to royal favor. Though Margaret wanted to settle portions of her estates and those of her mother on Henry as the earl of Richmond, his status as an exiled Lancaster meant that she needed the king's permission to do so. She had limited success in this endeavor. There was even some talk of marrying Henry Tudor to ***Elizabeth of York** (1466–1503), the oldest daughter of Edward IV. Such a match would have undoubtedly come with conditions, for the reigning king would never have consented to a union that could threaten his power. The potential problems must have occurred to Margaret at the time, for in 1482 she advised her son to be wary of any marriage offers from the royal family.

In 1483, Edward IV died, leaving two young sons under the protection of Richard, duke of Gloucester. Richard proclaimed that the boys were illegitimate, had himself crowned Richard III, king of England, and placed the two boys under arrest in the Tower of London. His actions split the house of York, giving Margaret new hopes for bringing her son home from France. But the new king kept her under close scrutiny, and she had to be extremely careful. In

Beauchamp, Margaret (d. 1482)

Countess of Somerset. *Died on August 8, 1482; daughter of John Beauchamp, 3rd baron Beauchamp of Bletso, and Edith Stourton; married Oliver St. John; married John Beaufort, earl of Somerset, in 1439; married Lionel Welles, 6th baron Welles; children: (first marriage) Edith St. John (who married Geoffrey Pole, grandfather of the archbishop of Canterbury); Oliver St. John (Lord St. John); John St. John; (second marriage)* ****Margaret Beaufort*** *(1443–1509); (third marriage) John Welles, 1st viscount Welles (d. 1499).*

Margaret Beaufort

an effort to gauge the extent of their loyalty, Richard commanded Thomas and Margaret to take part in his coronation ceremony. Margaret Beaufort carried Queen ***Anne of Warwick**'s train in the procession and served afterwards as a hostess at the banquet. In spite of this show of obedience, Margaret was soon ready to challenge Richard's authority by supporting a plot to rescue the sons of Edward from the Tower. However, the attempt to storm the Tower failed, and the young princes were never seen again. Thus, a new strategy to defeat Richard was formulated, this one designed to put Henry Tudor on the throne.

The idea of marrying Henry to Elizabeth of York was resurrected, and Margaret carried on a secret communication with ***Elizabeth Woodville** (1437–1492), widow of Edward IV. The messenger was Margaret's physician; he could visit both noble ladies without suspicion. When the former queen agreed to the match, the young couple vowed betrothal to each other despite the distance that separated them. As all of this was being arranged, a rebellion against Richard III was led by the duke of Buckingham, who had written to Henry Tudor in late 1483, inviting him to take part. Sadly, on the designated day, Buckingham's rebels were easily defeated, and Henry's small fleet was turned away from the coast of Dorset. Henry returned once more to France, and Buckingham was beheaded. When Margaret's involvement in the plan was discovered, she was charged with conspiracy and treason against the king. Her life was spared only because King Richard hoped to maintain the loyalty of Thomas Stanley, who had not taken part in the conspiracy. Margaret was forced to forfeit her title and lands and remain without household servants or loyal friends in some "secret place," probably one of Stanley's estates. The lands that would have been preserved for Henry Tudor were dispersed among nobles loyal to Richard, while Stanley maintained the rights over his wife's former holdings.

In spite of his apparent obedience to the king, Stanley allowed Margaret to keep up communication with her son. She still believed that a marriage between a York and a Lancaster, specifically Elizabeth and Henry, was the only way to bring stability to the English throne. With a small group of trusted confidants, she planned Henry's victorious return to England. The proposed union bought the support of Yorkists who distrusted Richard. In early August 1485, Henry led an army across the channel and landed in the south of Wales, close to his childhood home. On the battlefield at Bosworth, it was reportedly the last-minute defection of Thomas Stanley from the side of Richard to that of Henry Tudor that guaranteed success. Richard III was killed, and the crown was given to Henry.

Margaret Beaufort enjoyed the company of her son, the new king, for almost a month at her manor before they set out for London to arrange the coronation. It is said to have been an emotional reunion, taking place after almost 15 years of danger and struggle. Margaret's life up to this point had been one of extreme reversals of fortune and uncertainty. It is no wonder the woman was something of a pessimist: sources say she wept at her son's coronation as Henry VII out of joy but also with a sense of foreboding and fear. Involved now in much of court ceremony, Margaret sat at Henry's side during the coronation of his bride Elizabeth and was in charge of their wedding arrangements.

Much has been made of the fact that Margaret never seriously pressed her own claim to the throne, something which is usually attributed to her love for her son. She was a practical and determined woman, though, with a clear understanding of the politics of her time. How else could she have played the game so shrewdly? More recent historians believe that Margaret understood that her own reign would have been controversial and not well supported. As the beloved mother of a king and the agent of a Yorkist-Lancaster marriage, however, she enjoyed a great deal more influence and control than she would have as a queen. It is likely that her ambitions never extended to the entire kingdom. Nevertheless, her role during her son's reign was not limited to ceremony, nor did she gracefully retire after the coronation of Henry VII. She regained her title and estates and was granted *femme sole* status by royal proclamation, allowing her full and independent use of her property. She received temporary custody of the young earl of Warwick, who was a potential threat to the Tudor king. She designated a panel of learned men to oversee justice in her territories, and undertook a number of land-improvement measures. During this period, Margaret made careful plans for all of her land and even pursued the acquisition of some distant ancestral lands in France. She meant to leave a sizable legacy for her descendants.

From the time of the marriage of the new king and queen, Margaret was in charge of the royal household. She composed the Ordinances as to what preparation was to be made against the deliverance of a queen and also for the christening of the child of which she shall be delivered, which spelled out everything from the arrangement of the furniture to how the beds should be made. She saw to the care of her first grandchild, Arthur, born in 1486. Elizabeth had taken ill soon after Arthur's birth, and Margaret's help was sorely needed. Most of the time, Margaret lived at Collyweston, keeping in touch with her son through frequent letters, gifts, and occasional visits. She often accompanied the royal couple in their travels, and it is said that Henry had great respect for his mother's diplomatic skill.

As much as the king relied on his mother's advice in the early years of his reign, he soon began to enjoy the confidence and security of his own rule. Not unlike his mother in character, Henry proved to be a shrewd and distrustful monarch. That he asserted his own authority as a king seems to have been no loss to Margaret, as their letters reveal a constant and mutual respect. Their only well-known disagreement concerned the palace at Woking, one of Margaret's favorite houses. Henry decided in 1503 that he wanted that house for his own use; Margaret fought him and only maintained the right to use the palace occasionally at a fixed rent. She must have had sore feelings over the settlement, because she managed to regain Woking soon after her son's death in 1509.

All Englonde for her dethe had cause of wepynge.

—**John Fisher, Bishop of Rochester**

Margaret's influence in her territory was reflected in the work she had done on her residence at Collyweston between 1499 and 1501. After her palace-like manor was enlarged to accommodate the reception of important visitors, she had a series of smaller buildings added to the estate, including a council house with adjoining chambers and a prison. She was approached on a regular basis by "suitors," people from the area who wanted judicial matters settled in her court. Henry, the king, also delegated authority to his mother's council as a way of taking some of the burden from his own council. Margaret's unique position made her a precedent for women holding the office of justice of the peace.

Margaret Beaufort's lasting impact on the country is most evident in the work she did with universities and charities. Her intimate friendship with her confessor, John Fisher, was likely to have made her sympathetic to the needs of Cambridge and other institutions of learning. Be that as it may, Margaret's personal affinity for religious knowledge and guidance were well known. It is said she rose at five o'clock every morning to begin her prayers. She spent a good deal of her time in prayer, alone or with her companions, and she frequently wore hair shirts to ensure her own humility. Margaret is often portrayed in a nun's habit, reflecting her piety and simple life. She met Fisher in 1494 and five years later took a vow of chastity with the permission of her husband. She and Sir Stanley were maintaining separate households by this time and each concentrated on their own concerns. Stanley died in 1504.

Margaret had already long been active in acts of charity: one of her houses was inhabited by 12 poor men and women. She cared for the sick with her own hands and saw to the decent burial of those in her lands that could not afford it. She meant to financially support a number of monastic houses, but Fisher convinced her that active learning was more important than seclusion. Her first contribution towards the great universities was the foundation, in 1502, of an endowed lectureship in theology at both Cambridge and Oxford. Two years later, she founded a preachership at Cambridge. Like the previous lectureships, the purpose of this position was to allow learned men to go out and reach as many people as possible.

In 1505, Margaret went on to found a new college at Cambridge, Christ's College, where she had private rooms reserved for her own use above the master's lodge. It was while working in these rooms that Lady Margaret, according to legend, leaned out of a window to remind an instructor to be gentle with a student he was correcting. Traces of Margaret's authority exist elsewhere in the statutes of the college. She appointed Fisher to the position of Visitor for his lifetime and bequeathed to him the use of her rooms. She reserved for herself the right to appoint the master and fellows. She also saw to the details of the health and cleanliness of the students there, assigning a nurse and providing laundry facilities.

While involved with the continued improvement of Christ's College, Margaret spent time translating devotional literature from French into English. In 1504, she completed translation of the fourth book of *De Imitatione Christi*. She regretted that she had never learned Latin, for without it she could not read the original first three books of this work, or many other great religious manuals. Two years later, she translated *Mirror of gold for the sinful soul*. Margaret also acted as patron of William Caxton and of Wynkyn de Worde, both of whom composed, translated, and printed many books at her special request. Caxton dedicated his *Blanchardine and Eglantine* to her, and de Worde referred to her as "the most excellent princess my lady the king's grandame" in his dedications.

By 1508, Margaret Beaufort had already shown a great deal of interest in the dilapidated hospital of St. John. She wanted to transform it into another college, and made provisions for it in her will. It was to be her last great endowment. At age 65, suffering greatly from arthritis, she set about getting her affairs in order. Sadly, she did not expect to outlive her son. Henry VII fell ill early in 1509 and died in April. Margaret's grief was intense, and she went into isolation to pray. By this time, she had outlived three husbands and her only child. The young Henry VIII, Margaret's sole surviving grandson, was never as dear to her as her son had been. Lady Margaret appeared at her son's funeral and at her grandson's coronation, but after that took to bed at the abbot's lodge at Westminster. She died on June 29, 1509, and was buried at Westminster Abbey in the same chapel as her son Henry VII and his Queen Elizabeth, who had died in 1503.

John Fisher, Margaret's longtime friend and confidant, immortalized her in more ways than one. He wrote a eulogy, *The mornynge remembraunce had at the month mynde of the noble prynces margarete countesse of Rychemonde and Darby*, in which he praised her life of caring and constant activity. He recounted stories to illustrate Margaret's dignity and piety, claiming, "she was bounteous and lyberall to every persone of her knowledge or aquayntance." He also worked hard to see her plans for St. John's College realized, as the young king Henry VIII was trying to seize her estates for his own use. Backed with papal authority, however, Fisher saw St. John's College founded and made the school a memorial to the life of Lady Margaret. It is a fitting tribute for Margaret Beaufort, one of the noblest figures of the era.

SOURCES:

Fisher, John. "Mornynge remembraunce," in *The English Works of John Fisher, Bishop of Rochester.* John E.B. Mayor, ed. London: Oxford University Press, 1876 (reprinted, 1935).

Jones, Michael, and Malcolm G. Underwood. *The King's Mother: Lady Margaret Beaufort, Countess of Richmond and Derby.* Cambridge, England: Cambridge University Press, 1992.

Routh, E.M.G. *Lady Margaret: A Memoir.* London: Oxford University Press, 1924.

Simon, Linda. *Of Virtue Rare: Margaret Beaufort, Matriarch of the House of Tudor.* Boston, MA: Houghton Mifflin, 1982.

SUGGESTED READING:

Cooper, C.H. *Memoir of Margaret, Countess of Richmond and Derby.* 1874.

Pollard, A.J. *The Wars of the Roses.* London: Macmillan Education, 1988.

Tytler, Sarah. *Tudor Queens and Princesses.* London: James Nisbet, 1896.

Nancy L. Locklin, Ph.D. candidate, Emory University, Atlanta, Georgia

Beauharnais, Eugénie Hortense de or Hortense de (1783–1837).

See Hortense de Beauharnais.

Beauharnais, Josephine de (1763–1814).

See Josephine, Empress.

Beauharnais, Josephine de (1807–1876).

See Josephine Beauharnais.

Beauharnais, Stephanie de (1789–1860).

See Stephanie de Beauharnais.

Beaujeu, Anne de (c. 1460–1622).

See Anne de Beaujeu.

Beaumont, Alice (fl. 1318).

See Comyn, Alice.

Beaumont, Amicia (fl. 1208).

See Montfort, Amicia.

Beaumont, countess of.

See Jeanne of Valois (c. 1304–?).
See Blanche of France (1328–1392).

Beaumont, Eleanor (c. 1318–1372).

See Eleanor Plantagenet.

Beaumont, Ermengarde (d. 1234).

See Ermengarde of Beaumont.

Beaumont, Hawise (d. 1197)

Countess of Gloucester. *Died in 1197; daughter of Robert Beaumont (1104–1167), 2nd earl of Leicester, and* ***Amicia de Waer****; married William Fitzrobert (d. 1183), 2nd earl of Gloucester, in 1119; children:* ****Amicia Fitzrobert*** *(d. 1225); Mabel Fitzrobert;* ****Avisa of Gloucester*** *(c. 1167–1217).*

Beaumont, Isabel (d. 1368)

Duchess of Lancaster. *Name variations: Isabel de Beaumont; Isabel of Lancaster. Died in 1368; daughter of Henry Beaumont, 1st baron Beaumont, and* ***Alice Comyn****; married Henry of Grosmont (c. 1299–1361), 1st duke of Lancaster, around 1334; children:* ***Maud Plantagenet*** *(1335–1362);* ****Blanche of Lancaster*** *(1341–1369).*

Beauvoir, Simone de (1908–1986)

French novelist, memoir writer, essayist, pioneer of modern feminism, and intellectual companion of French philosopher Jean-Paul Sartre for 51 years. *Name variations: nickname le Castor (the Beaver). Born Simone Lucie Ernestine Marie Bertrand de Beauvoir in Paris, France, on January 9, 1908; died in Paris on April 14, 1986; daughter of Georges Bertrand de Beauvoir and Françoise Brasseur; degrees from the Sorbonne and École Normale Superièure, 1929; never married; no children.*

Met Jean-Paul Sartre (1929); death of Elizabeth Le Coin (1929); taught in lycées (1931–43); published L'Invitée *(August 1943); published* The Blood of Others *(September 1945); published Vol. I of* The Second Sex *(October 1949); published first volume of memoirs (September 1958); met Sylvie Le Bon (later her adopted daughter, November 1960); served as president of "Choisir" (To Choose, June 1972); served as president of the League of Women's Rights (January 1974); death of Jean-Paul Sartre (April 15, 1980).*

"I was not a child, I was me," Simone de Beauvoir wrote in the first volume of her memoirs, and she remained a fiercely independent "me" all her life. A member of the French intellectual elite, de Beauvoir has been characterized as opinionated, self-centered, inelegant, indomitable, humorless, and bisexual. She viewed marriage, motherhood, and "bourgeois" values with disdain and "detested all animals." To her, literature was more important than life, and her goal was to become a famous writer, thereby achieving an earthly immortality.

Born into a well-to-do bourgeois family in the Montparnasse area of Paris, Simone recalled that her parents were ever "present, but not too close" to her and her younger sister **Hélène** ("Poupette"). Her stage-struck father made a satisfactory living as a lawyer; a non-believer, he married a convent-educated, devout Catholic girl from a wealthy provincial banking family. Even as a child, Simone was aware of the contrasting lifestyles of men and women. Her father had a profession and an active life outside of the family, while her mother's world was limited to the "drudgery" of household chores. However, Beauvoir recalled that she was loved and catered to, spoiled and flattered for her unique qualities, "a gay little girl" who flew into "fits of rage" over minor annoyances. Georges and Françoise de Beauvoir encouraged the natural talents of their daughters—Simone loved books and writing, and Hélène was artistic. Summers spent at the country estates of various Beauvoir relatives introduced Simone to the beauty of nature and the rejuvenating effects of long walks and of solitude.

At age five, she was enrolled in a private Catholic girls' school, Cours Désir, in Paris. For the first time in her life, Simone experienced a separate existence, a separate identity, life outside her narrow family environment. By the age of seven, she had written two short stories and begun to "teach" her sister and her dolls. Beauvoir had decided on the future course of her life from which she never deviated: she would be a teacher and a writer. If she resented being classed and treated as a child, she never regretted being a girl since "the boys I knew were in no way remarkable." Being a female and surrounded by girls of her own "superior class," as she described it, Simone was a self-satisfied child. But no human relationships prepared her for the deep friendship she developed with her classmate, **Elizabeth Le Coin** ("Zaza"), at age 10. Simone and Zaza established a close intellectual bond. Cynical, intelligent, and more mature than Simone, Zaza became her idol. Void of girlish frivolities, they curiously refrained from affectionate displays, addressing one another using the formal *vous.* Zaza died in 1929, and for the rest of her life Simone tried, unsuccessfully, to immortalize her dear friend in her fiction.

The "gay little girl," who had been so obedient and wanted to please adults, grew into an unattractive and rebellious adolescent. Dressed in drab, ill-fitting, cast-off clothes from her cousins, Beauvoir delighted in reading forbidden books and retreating into sullen silences or expressing unorthodox opinions on literature and politics to annoy her parents. And at age 14, she lost her faith in God. The formerly pious believer who thought of becoming a nun decided that "He no longer intervened in my life and I concluded . . . that He had ceased to exist for me." Simone later admitted this left a void in her life, a "silence," and an obsessive fear of death. For two years, she kept her secret until she told her sister who admitted that she, too, no longer believed.

A brilliant student, Beauvoir received her *baccalauréat* degree from the Cours Désir at age 17. Her father's neglect of his legal profession had reduced the family to "genteel poverty," and he bluntly informed Simone that she could not expect a dowry so probably would remain unmarried. But this plain, dowdy young woman had already made up her mind to become a teacher and a "famous" writer. "I always looked upon marriage with disfavour," she wrote, motherhood was a form of "servitude," and babies "a great nuisance." Her goal was to earn a doctorate in philosophy, a seemingly unrealistic aspiration for a woman in France in the 1920s. Since her mother refused to allow her to attend the Sorbonne, afraid she would lose her faith, Beauvoir enrolled at first in the Institut Catholique and Institut Sainte-Marie.

At age 21, she had earned a degree from the Sorbonne (the *license-ès-lettres*) and the prestigious *agrégation* in philosophy from the elite École Normale Superièure, the youngest *agregée de philosophie* in France. Beauvoir was respect-

Simone de Beauvoir

ed by her fellow students and for the first time in her life she developed solid friendships with male students who treated her as an intellectual equal. The independent, professional life she had sought was now a reality, but she still hoped to find someone to love. Socially timid, and a virgin, Beauvoir valued the platonic friendship of intellectuals such as Maurice Merleau-Ponty and René Maheu who gave her the nickname Castor (Beaver). A life of books and study was soon embellished with "real life" experiences. A female friend took Simone in hand and convinced her to improve her appearance; certainly intelligence and femininity were not antithetical. Her education had not changed her into a man but had determined her to fulfill "my destiny as a woman."

I flattered myself that I combined 'a woman's heart and a man's brain'... I considered myself to be unique—the One and Only.

—Simone de Beauvoir

Beauvoir longed to meet the ideal man: "The day when a man would dominate me by his intelligence, his culture and his authority, I will be in love." She met this man, a fellow student at the École Normale, in 1929: Jean-Paul Sartre had won first place in their degree exams (she placed second, 1/50 of a point behind him). "For a man to be my equal, he had to be a little bit superior to me," she noted, and Sartre met her criterion. A philosopher and future founder of Existentialism, Sartre was 5'2" tall, had a squint, only 10% vision in one eye, and an insatiable sexual appetite. But Beauvoir had found her "superior" companion, and they remained inseparable until he died 51 years later. The nucleus of the Beauvoir-Sartre "Family" had been launched. Sartre was candid about his sexual promiscuity and continued to see his present mistress. Beauvoir accepted his self-styled polygamy as she did all of his faults and failings. Never the Great Lovers, as the press depicted them, they always lived in separate residences and referred to each other as *vous*, not as a concession to societal convention but from choice. Sartre was a vital, essential part of her life. Scorning marriage, this unusual couple agreed to a two-year contract, pledging absolute honesty in their relations, accepting the equality of the partnership, and allowing "contingent" (supplementary) love affairs.

Beauvoir did not completely subordinate her life to Sartre's, but editing his writing and attending to his every need precluded her working on her own literary career. Despite Sartre being, and remaining, emotionally adolescent, he and Simone were amazingly alike. Neither had an interest in world affairs; self-interest dominated their lives, and theories and abstractions rather than action and involvement characterized their lives until middle age. Beauvoir could have been assigned to teach in a lycée, but she was hesitant to leave Paris. However, when Sartre left to teach in Le Havre, she took a position in Marseille. Alone for the first time in her life, she realized that she needed "to make her own life, to make herself." Thus began her itinerant, peripatetic life, moving from one furnished hotel room to another, feeling no desire for a "home." Hers would be a life of the mind, not the confining, smothering conventionality of middle-class materialism which restricted one's independence. She enjoyed her freedom, but she needed to write which "would justify my existence . . . [and] I would serve humanity." Her literary efforts were meager, however, and she did not attempt to publish them.

In 1932, Simone moved to a lycée in Rouen, closer to Sartre and to Paris. Soon she longed to escape the stifling bourgeois atmosphere of the town and school, to be in Paris, and to write. The future appeared unpromising; Sartre had gone to Berlin to study, teaching was a "constraint . . . a role imposed on her," and she was a failure as a writer. Oblivious to the threat of fascism in Europe, the worldwide depression, and war in China, her novels, like herself, ignored the outside world. Based solely on her own limited experiences and circle of friends, her novels lacked depth and engaging plots. Beauvoir admired writers like Hemingway and Dos Passos who had lived, had acted, but self-absorption restricted her view of the world and human diversity. Thus, her characters and plots were often flat and unconvincing. Literature was more important than life, Beauvoir believed, and a paucity of experience is evident in her prose.

Simone's primary concerns revolved around her floundering career as a novelist and Sartre's continuous involvement with a succession of women. Their lives became still more complicated after Sartre returned to Le Havre from Berlin—the couple was replaced by a "trio." Sartre had volunteered to take part in a medical experiment conducted by a physician friend. After taking mescaline, he suffered from nightmares, hallucinations, and visions; unable to devote herself to nursing him, Simone persuaded a former student, **Olga Kosakievicz**, to care for him. Beauvoir had befriended Olga whom she and Sartre regarded as an "authentic" person, one "incapable of any dishonesty and reacting only through emotion." Not surprisingly, the emotionally immature Sartre fell in love with this indolent, dependent young woman. She became Sartre's lover and the first addition to their reinvented Family, a permanent member until Sartre's death. Olga served as the model for one of Simone's characters in *L'Invitée* (*She Came to Stay*, 1943), a common feature of Beauvoir's novels in which, according to **Margaret Crosland**, "she invented very little."

When Simone was assigned to a lycée in Paris in 1936, she again chose to live in a cheap furnished hotel room; Olga moved to Paris, to the same hotel. Shortly, Olga's sister **Wanda** joined them and became Sartre's mistress after he began teaching in Paris the following year. These "contingent" affairs never interfered with the annual holidays Beauvoir and Sartre had shared from the beginning of their relationship. But in 1938, Sartre informed Simone that he could not accompany her on her usual marathon walking tour because his numerous love-sexual affairs required all his attention. However, their mutual friend, Jacques-Laurent Bost, joined Simone; she seduced him and their liaison provided the love interest in *L'Invitée*. Beauvoir attracted both men and women; Olga had loved her before becoming Sartre's mistress, and in 1938 and 1939, two more former students made their way to Simone's hotel room to consummate their affections. **Bianca Bienenfeld** claims, in her own book, that Beauvoir encouraged her to have sex with Sartre, a "three-cornered love affair." The Family was enlarged again with the arrival of **Nathalie Sorokine** who became Simone's lover. Without feeling the need to justify her sex life, Beauvoir stated in a 1982 interview, "every woman is a bit . . . homosexual. Quite simply, because women are more desirable than men."

All these complex relationships were interrupted when Sartre and Bost were mobilized as the French prepared for war with Nazi Germany. Beauvoir did nothing to help the war effort, but she shouldered the responsibility for supporting their extended Family and sending Sartre whatever he needed in the way of books and writing materials. While the French army waited for the German assault, Sartre concentrated on his writing which Simone continued to edit and comment on. Their daily letters reflect their slender interests—themselves and their Family. Simone was absorbed in dealing with her bisexuality and her femininity, "the way I am of my sex and not of it." In a journal, kept during the war years, she wrote, "I feel I'm a complete woman. I'd like to know what sort of woman." Her noted study of women, *The Second Sex*, deals with these issues. In May 1940, the Germans invaded France; Beauvoir fled Paris on June 10, but returned to the German-occupied city on the 28th. "I was bored," she explained. Paris was her home, and she could not function, or create, deprived of its vitality. She resumed teaching and her daily routine of writing in the Left Bank cafés Le Dôme and Le Flore. Sartre had been taken prisoner on June 21 but was released the following March. Neither he nor Beauvoir would ever comment on his release. Had he made a deal with his German captors?

Beauvoir and Sartre not only survived the Occupation unscathed, but their careers flourished. Simone tried to discourage Sartre from getting involved with the French Resistance movement. In fact, Sartre's comedic attempt to form his own resistance group, "Socialism and Liberty," failed because no one trusted him. He was brilliant but naive and immature, and his group folded after only a few months. Beauvoir was relieved. She and Sartre did contribute articles to Albert Camus' underground paper *Combat*, but were not actively involved with his Resistance activities. In 1942, Simone suddenly found herself without an income. She was dismissed from her teaching position, charged with corrupting a minor by Sorokine's mother. She was now free to devote herself to writing, and the publication of *L'Invitée* finally brought the fame she had craved. This novel about women is not a feminist tract, but it appealed to women more than men which delighted the author. A year later, *Pyrrhus and Cineas* appeared, a series of essays on human relationships and endeavors, personal responsibility, and the non-existence of God. Simone enjoyed her long-awaited celebrity and gained further recognition with the publication of *The Blood of Others* in 1945 and *All Men are Mortal* in 1946.

Beauvoir had come to realize one must live before one could write, and her life during the Occupation was richer and more varied than ever before. To supplement her income, she wrote historical sketches for the Vichy government-owned radio and was severely criticized for associating with this collaborationist government. During the war years, Simone became increasingly aware that "there was a feminine condition," that women lived as "relative beings." In *L'Invitée*, she wrote that women must be "authentic": "You must be a person, you must choose your own existence, you alone are responsible for it." Simone de Beauvoir had done just that; financially independent, sexually liberated, and living a self-prescribed lifestyle, she considered herself an "authentic" woman. Before the war ended, Beauvoir and Sartre established and edited an influential journal, *Les Temps Modernes* (*Modern Times*), a vehicle for disseminating existentialist and eventually feminist thought.

On a lecture tour of the United States in 1947, Beauvoir began to consider writing a book on women. She viewed the U.S. as a male-dominated society and American women as "dependent and relative." The genesis of *The Second Sex* is seen in her question, "Why is woman the *Other*?" Her previous self-absorption, her search for the meaning of her own womanhood, slowly expanded into looking at the feminine condition in general. While in America, Beauvoir experienced her first passionate love affair with the American writer Nelson Algren. It confused and delighted her, but she refused to marry and live with him in Chicago. Paris, Sartre, her Family, her work, her contempt for the institution of marriage and her fear of becoming "dependent and relative" outweighed her love for Algren. With the publication of Volume I of *The Second Sex* two years later, Simone began a lifelong involvement with feminist issues. Over 200,000 copies of the book sold in a week. French men generally reacted negatively, and the Catholic Church banned the book. Undeterred, the second volume which began, "One is not born, but rather becomes a woman," caused an even greater sensation.

Intellectually tied to Sartre, Beauvoir led an independent life of her own—a public persona and a new "contingent" affair with Claude Lanzmann—but she never repudiated their contract. Her investigation on how one becomes a woman, how *she* became a woman, is the theme of her four volumes of memoirs, the first published in 1958, the last in 1972. Happy and involved with outside interests, she finally acquired an apartment, a home, and traveled to the U.S. several times, also to China, Cuba, Brazil, and almost all the states of Europe. Internationally recognized, Beauvoir received the prestigious Goncourt Prize for *The Mandarins* in 1954. And rather late in life, she and Sartre developed an interest in politics; they were openly antipathetic to the government of Charles de Gaulle and in favor of Algerian independence, unpopular sentiments in France in the 1950s. Consequently, she and Sartre received death threats which caused them only momentary concern. Women's issues now occupied her thoughts. Birth control and abortion (both illegal in France) were essential, she maintained, for women to achieve true liberation. She signed the Manifesto of the 343, declaring her solidarity with women who had had abortions (she never had one). As president of Choisir (To Choose), she promoted contraception, and as president of the League of Women's Rights, she worked to end sex discrimination in France. She and Sartre were involved in writing for and editing left-wing newspapers and the journal they founded in 1944.

But sharing a happy old age with Sartre, as she had envisioned, eluded her. Excessive drinking and dependence on stimulants had undermined his health. He was going blind and becoming immobile and incontinent. However, his propensity for adolescent love affairs continued unabated. Amazingly, Simone accepted his promiscuous behavior and ardently defended his philosophical works with honesty and determination. But when he adopted one of his mistresses in 1965 without consulting her, Simone was not pleased. During their annual summer holiday in Rome, she began to tape their conversations and to keep a journal chronicling Sartre's physical deterioration. These provided the material for her published tribute to him after his death. Beauvoir was only vaguely aware that an intellectual gulf was separating her from her companion. Always fearful of growing old, or growing up, Sartre revised or recanted some of his earlier philosophical ideas, trying to appeal to a more youthful audience. Existentialism and "Castor" were relegated to his past. Such cruel comments wounded her, though she still lived an active, satisfying life of her own. Involved with feminist groups and revitalizing love affairs with younger men, she, too, was in touch with the younger generation. In 1960, a former student, **Sylvie Le Bon**, contacted Beauvoir in Paris. They became close friends, and Simone eventually adopted her.

Sartre died on April 15, 1980, and Beauvoir mourned her partner of 51 years. The publication of *Adieux—Farewell to Sartre* in 1981 provided the necessary catharsis for her to resume a "single" life. Two years later, she published Sartre's letters but refused to include her own which she said were "nobody's business." Beauvoir had not published a novel since *The Woman Destroyed* in 1968, a banal reiteration of the theme of women having to make their own lives. However, her four volumes of memoirs had been well-received and enhanced her literary reputation. She was gratified to see the election of a Socialist president of France in 1981 and accepted the post of honorary chair of the Commission on

Women and Culture offered by President François Mitterand. By the mid-1980s, Beauvoir's health deteriorated due to drinking, and in March 1986 she underwent surgery for liver damage. She died on April 14, 1986, just eight hours short of the sixth anniversary of Sartre's death, and from the same ailments. Simone was buried next to Sartre in the cemetery of Montparnasse, the district of Paris where she was born, raised, and lived most of her life.

In *The Second Sex*, Beauvoir asks how women can attain full humanity. Her own life provided the model—she lived as a Woman, not as an "Other." She knew from the time she was a child "with the mind of a man" that she wanted to be an intellectual, a famous writer who "would burn like a flame in millions of hearts." Unconventional, aloof, obstinate, and determined, Simone de Beauvoir achieved all her goals and inspired other women in the quest for their humanity.

SOURCES:

Bair, Deirdre. *Simone de Beauvoir: A Biography.* NY: Summit Books, 1990.

Crosland, Margaret. *Simone de Beauvoir: The Woman and Her Work.* London: Heinemann, 1992.

Winegarten, Renée. *Simone de Beauvoir: A Critical View.* Oxford: Berg Publishers, 1988.

SUGGESTED READING:

Asher, Carole. *Simone de Beauvoir: A Life of Freedom.* Boston, MA: Beacon Press, 1981.

Evans, Mary. *Simone de Beauvoir: A Feminist Mandarin.* London: Tavistock, 1985.

Francis, Claude, and Fernande Gontier. *Simone de Beauvoir.* NY: St. Martin's Press, 1987.

Jeanne A. Ojala, Professor of History, University of Utah, Salt Lake City, Utah

Beaux, Cecilia (1855–1942)

American artist who was acclaimed, during America's Gilded Age, as the greatest living "woman artist" and, in the 1920s and 1930s, as one of the 12 most influential women in America. *Name variations: (nicknames) Leilie and Bo. Pronunciation: Boe. Born Eliza Cecilia Beaux on May 1, 1855, in Philadelphia, Pennsylvania; died of coronary thrombosis at Gloucester, Massachusetts, on September 17, 1942; daughter of Jean Adolphe Beaux (a silk manufacturer) and Cecilia Kent (Leavitt) Beaux (grandmother of historian* ****Catherine Drinker Bowen****); educated by homestudy until age 14, then attended Miss Lyman's School for Girls in Philadelphia two years; trained as a painter in Catherine Ann Drinker's studio, at Adolf Van der Whelan's art school and privately for two years with William Sartain; later on in adult life, studied in Paris at the Académie Julien, 1888–89; granted honorary LL.D., University of Pennsylvania, 1908; granted honorary M.A., Yale University, 1912; never married; no children.*

Brought up by grandmother and two aunts in Philadelphia; studied painting in teens with William Sartain; awarded Mary Smith Prize from the Pennsylvania Academy of Fine Arts for painting Les Derniers Jours d'Enfance *which was exhibited in Paris in the official government sponsored Salon (1885); won three more annual Mary Smith awards for the best painting by a resident woman artist (1887–89); went abroad for further study, to Paris, Italy, and England (1888–89); the next few years spent working in her Philadelphia studio brought numerous honors; taught at the Pennsylvania Academy of the Fine Arts (1895–1915); moved studio to New York City (1900); built Green Alley, her famous summer home in Gloucester (1905); commissioned to do three portraits of the Allied World War I leaders at the Paris Peace Conference (1919); broke hip in France (1924), which thereafter curtailed her mobility and painting career; published an autobiography,* Background With Figures *(1930).*

Medals, prizes and honors: Mary Smith Prize, Pennsylvania Academy of the Fine Arts (1885, 1887, 1891, and 1892); Philadelphia Art Club, gold medal (1893); Member Society of American Artists (1893); Dodge Prize, National Academy of Design (1893); Associé Société Nationale des Beaux Arts (1896); bronze (1896) and gold (1899) medals, Carnegie Institute, Pittsburgh; Pennsylvania Academy of the Fine Arts gold medal of honor (1898) and Temple gold medal (1900); gold medal, Paris Exposition (1900); gold medal, Pan American Exposition, Buffalo (1901); First Corcoran Prize, Society of American Artists (1902); member National Academy (1903); gold medal, Universal Exposition, St. Louis (1904); Saltus gold medal, National Academy (1913); medal of honor, Panama Pacific Exposition (1915); gold medal, Art Institute of Chicago (1921); invited to paint self-portrait for Uffizi Gallery at Florence, Italy (1924); gold medal, Academy of Arts and Letters (1926); gold medal, Chi Omega (1933).

Lithograph: The Brighton Cats *(published 1874). Paintings:* Les Derniers Jours d'Enfance *(private collection of Henry S. Drinker, Merion, Pennsylvania, 1883);* Little Girl *(****[Fanny Travis Cochran]****, Pennsylvania Academy of the Fine Arts, 1887);* William R. Darwin *(family collection, 1889);* Rev. Matthew B. Grier *(1891–92);* **Cynthia Sherwood** *(1892);* Mrs. Stetson *(1893);* Sita and Sarita *(original, Luxembourg Palace Gallery in Paris, replica Corcoran Art Gallery, Washington, D.C., 1893–94);* ***Ernesta Drinker** with

Cecilia Beaux

Nurse *(private collection of Henry S. Drinker, Merion, Pa., 1894);* The Dreamer *(Butler Art Institute, Youngstown, Ohio, 1894);* Self Portrait No. 3 *(Pennsylvania Academy of the Fine Arts, 1894);* Reverend William H. Furness *(Unitarian Church, Philadelphia, Pa., 1885);* New England Woman *(Pennsylvania Academy of the Fine Arts, 1895);* **Mrs. Alexander Biddle** *(family collection, 1897);* Mr. and Mrs. Anson Phelps Stokes *(Metropolitan Museum of Art, 1898);* The Dancing Lesson *or* Dorothea and Francesca *(Art Institute of Chicago, 1899–1900);* **Mrs. Alexander Sedgwick** and **Christina** *(Berkshire Museum, Pitts-*

field, Mass., 1900–01); **Bertha Vaughan** *(Radcliffe College, Cambridge, Mass., 1901);* **Mrs. Theodore Roosevelt** with her daughter **Ethel** *(Ethel Roosevelt family, 1901);* Man with the Cat *([Dr. Henry S. Drinker], National Collection of Fine Arts, Smithsonian Institution, 1902);* After the Meeting *(Toledo Art Museum, 1914);* A Girl in White: Ernesta *(Metropolitan Museum of Art, New York, 1914);* Cardinal Mercier *(1919);* Admiral Sir David Beatty, Lord Beatty *(1919);* Georges Clemenceau *(National Museum of American Art, Washington, D.C., 1920);* Self-Portrait No. 4 *(Uffizi Gallery, Florence, Italy, 1925);* **Mrs. Marcel Kahler** *(1925–26);* Dressing Dolls *(private collection of Henry S. Drinker, Merion, Pa., 1928).*

Although artist John Singer Sargent (1856–1925) ended his career painting murals, in the late 1880s he was the most sought after portrait painter in England and the United States. However, a Philadelphia woman, who was born the year before Sargent, enjoyed a longer career and one that was entirely devoted to portraiture. Sargent's contemporary female rival was the remarkable and gifted artist Cecilia Beaux. While analyzing a display of both their paintings, noted art critic Bernard Berenson was overheard commenting that Sargent had signed his best paintings "Cecilia Beaux." It was, of course, an ironic way of flattering Beaux, a lesser-known female artist, whose technique and style of painting were similar to Sargent's but the quality of whose work Berenson quite boldly judged as being superior. Despite her uncommon ability to earn a comfortable living for herself from painting commissions alone and the dozens of prizes and gold medals that Beaux received during her lifetime, her portraits were, nevertheless, ignored by art critics for the next 40 years.

Jean Adolph Beaux, a French Huguenot silk manufacturer, emigrated from Avignon in southern France around 1850 to start a business in Philadelphia. He soon met and married Cecilia Kent Leavitt who belonged to a culturally refined, socially well-connected New York textile family—the John Wheeler Leavitts. Unfortunately, his wife's family had recently lost most of their wealth. The couple had three daughters, but the death in infancy of the oldest was followed by that of the wife 12 days after the youngest was born. Left alone with their grief-stricken father whose own business was then failing, infant Cecilia and two-year old ❧ **Ernesta** were sent to live with their maternal grandmother, an industrious and frugal Connecticut woman of Puritan descent. Being unable to care for his family as he wished, Jean Beaux returned to France at some point, visiting so rarely that when he did, his two daughters regarded him as a "foreigner" with peculiar manners. Nevertheless, the Leavitt family brought up the girls to be as proud of their French ancestry as of their English descent.

The extended family with whom Cecilia Beaux lived for the next 45 years moved from New York after Grandfather Leavitt's death to West Philadelphia to be near other relatives and friends. Also living in her grandmother's home were her two aunts, **Eliza** and **Emily Leavitt.** After Aunt Emily's marriage to William Foster Biddle, he too joined Grandmother Leavitt's household. "Leilie," as Cecilia Beaux was called at home to distinguish her from her late mother, was sheltered inside this predominantly female family circle and educated through home study until she was 14. Their stubborn Puritan and Quaker values were instilled in her early. She later recalled instructing one of her china dolls, whom she imagined were married women, to embrace grandmother's passion for completing whatever tasks she started.

The Leavitt's refined and intellectual lifestyle had lasting influence on the future artist. For example, as an adult she recalled all the piano playing and group singing of hymns as well as classical music. Grandmother Leavitt read great literature and poetry aloud. Aunt Eliza, a watercolorist, always carried her sketchbook wherever she went and thus provided a role model for Cecilia who soon developed keen powers of observation and a natural flair for drawing. Her artistic aunt also lovingly brushed and braided her niece's thick, straight, long brown hair and sewed the blue-eyed, pug-nosed girl's wardrobe. Her aunts tutored her in French and math, taught her how to write compositions, and encouraged her to keep a diary. Cecilia loved the stories she wrote down as her aunt dictated them, as well as the feel of holding the pen. Cecilia and Ernesta were taught to recite the Calvinist Shorter Catechism and Bible verses. The family included the little girls in visits to public art galleries and private collections, giving them their first exposure

❧ **Drinker, Ernesta**

Born Aimeé Ernesta Beaux around 1853; daughter of Jean Adolphe Beaux (a silk manufacturer) and Cecilia Kent (Leavitt) Beaux; sister of ***Cecilia Beaux;*** *married Henry Sturgis Drinker (brother of* ***Catherine Ann Drinker*** *and president of Lehigh University).*

After the Meeting, *1914. Painting by Cecilia Beaux.*

to things European. In 1869, they decided to send their 14-year-old to Miss Lyman's School for Girls on South Broad Street, an exclusive, ungraded, "finishing" school, for two winters. Thus, by the time Beaux started school, she was already immersed in high culture.

Going to school with other girls further broadened Beaux's horizon. For the first time, she was outside the family, seeing new, diverse characters. She described school as spectacle: "a drama of unforgettable vividness." Having completed her general education at 16, she prepared to support herself until she chose to marry.

The family decided to let her have her way, to study drawing. The one male figure in her immediate family, William Biddle, assumed a key role in directing and financing his niece's preparation from this point on and chose traditional methods to protect her from the sort of eccentric art students who attended Thomas Eakins' classes at the Pennsylvania Academy. He decided that Beaux would begin by taking lessons from his cousin, **Catherine Ann Drinker**, at a studio on Independence Square. After spending about a year at Drinker's studio, and now 17, Beaux continued at Adolf Van der Whelan's Art School. The Dutch Realist painter taught her linear and aerial perspective and how to draw shadows and light by practicing with plaster shapes. Then she studied skull bones to learn the skeletal structure of the head, something that later would affect her portraiture. When Whelan turned the school over to Catherine Drinker, she in turn gave Cecilia Beaux her own position as drawing teacher at Miss Sanford's School. At this time, Beaux also started to give private drawing lessons herself. While she thus started to make some of her own money, she still never dreamed of someday becoming a great "artist."

As her professional career took off, Beaux's uncle decided to provide further opportunities. He arranged to take her to a lithography studio where she was shown how to carve the stone used for the lithographic process. The lithographer gave her fossils as models to inversely carve into the stones, which were eventually processed into a government geological volume. From these attempts to master the art of lithography, she quickly learned to handle volume through meticulous shading. When her lithograph of an actress' head was accepted for a magazine advertisement, she already had several career choices. Beaux published another charming lithograph of the heads of two sleepy cats in 1874.

Next, she enrolled in a short course on painting china. Although she later scorned the technique of over-glaze painting as an "ignoble art," she became an overnight success at painting portraits of children on plates, which were done by mail-order from photos. Because she immediately received so many orders—mothers of friends purchased these plates from as far away as California—Beaux realized that there was nothing mothers in those days wouldn't do to get portraits of their children.

Drinker, Catherine Ann (1841–1922)

***American painter.** Name variations: Kate; Katherine Ann Janvier. Born Catherine Ann Drinker in 1841; died in 1922; daughter of Sandwith Drinker (a sea captain in the East India trade) and Susan Drinker; aunt of historian Catherine Drinker Bowen; studied art at the Maryland Institute with Dutch painter Adolf van der Whelan, and with Thomas Eakins at the Pennsylvania Academy; married Thomas Allibone Janvier, in 1878.*

The first woman permitted to teach at the Pennsylvania Academy, Catherine Ann Drinker was a traditional painter who was fond of historical and Biblical subjects. She was the daughter of Susan and Sandwith Drinker, a sea captain, and spent her childhood in Hong Kong. Following Sandwith Drinker's death in Macao in 1857, the Drinker family boarded the ship *Storm King* to return to Baltimore. It is said that during the voyage home, when the captain was discovered to have depleted the rum kegs, Catherine Ann, trained by her father, took over the navigation.

In 1857, after Susan Drinker's death, Catherine took over her mother's girls' school and the support of her sister, grandmother, and her brother Henry Sturgis Drinker. After a term studying art at the Maryland Institute, she moved the family to Pennsylvania and began to study under Adolf van der Whelan, then Thomas Eakins at the Pennsylvania Academy. In 1880, Catherine was awarded the academy's Mary Smith Prize for her painting *The Guitar Player*. That same year, she published her book *Practical Ceramics for Students*.

"Kate Drinker's clothes were all wrong," wrote her niece ***Catherine Drinker Bowen** in *Family Portrait* (Little, Brown, 1970). "No matter how styles changed, Kate remained one lap behind. When women wore plain sailor hats, hers had flowers; if their stockings were beige, hers stayed black." At age 37, Drinker married Thomas Janvier, and together the couple traveled throughout the world. Much of their time was spent in Provence, France, where Drinker earned recognition for her English translations of romantic novels of Provençale.

Amid all this commercial artistry, Beaux carried on an active social life, which included many male friends and prospective suitors. Her family, however, never pushed her into marrying any of them, and she became increasingly dedicated to her career. When she started to study for two more years at a higher level with William Sartain, a New York artist who came to Philadelphia to give private classes, she turned a very sharp corner, she recalled in her autobiography, "into a new world which was to be continuously mine." Sartain had studied in Munich; consequently, he introduced her to the style of that Realistic school of painting that used a dark palette. Conquering Sartain's ideal of merging exact likeness with individual personality required Beaux's utmost perception and understanding; but, by making this ideal her own, she transformed herself forever from being merely an expert draftswoman into a genuine "artist," in the most eloquent sense of the term.

After Sartain's classes ended, Beaux rented a spacious studio of her own in downtown Philadelphia. For several years, she worked there independently, free from family distractions and housework, concentrating for several hours a day. Finally she was inspired to try a large canvass. This time her family supported her effort by lending furniture and a carpet for the background, and, more important, by enabling her sister Ernesta and son to be the sitters. In 1885, when the painting, entitled *Les Derniers Jours d'Enfance* (*The Last Days of Childhood*), was entered in an exhibition at the Pennsylvania Academy of the Fine Arts, it won the Mary Smith Award for the best painting by a resident woman artist. The following year, a friend took the canvass to Paris and successfully entered it in the Salon of 1887. It was the first of over 200 oil portraits Beaux was to complete either of relatives or as commissions.

Ah, yes, I see! Some Sargents. The ordinary ones are signed John Sargent, the best are signed Cecilia Beaux.

—Bernard Berenson

In the 1880s and '90s, during the so-called "Gilded Age," when America's industrial aristocracy splurged on lavish architecture, fashions, and portraits of their family as evidence of their new wealth and power, American artists went abroad to complete their study. Although well established and already in her 30s, Beaux decided to make the first of many voyages to Paris to study for two winters at the Académie Julien, copying paintings of the Old Masters at the Louvre. Once there, she admired Rubens, Memling, and Mabuse; of them, she later wrote, "These men were not reformers. Theirs was the earnest desire toward perfection. Not to break down, but to build." This opinion thereafter personified her own philosophy of art.

Back in Philadelphia from 1895 to 1915, Beaux taught Drawing and Painting from the Head at the Pennsylvania Academy, commuting from New York where she had moved after her grandmother's death in 1892 led to complete dispersal of the Leavitt family. The Paris Salon of 1896 included six more of her portraits, which she went to see exhibited. She visited the leader of the Impressionist movement, Claude Monet (whose work she admired but thought lesser artists ought not copy) at his country home, Giverny, and was elected to membership in the Société des Beaux Arts. She was acclaimed as the greatest living "woman painter," a category she ridiculed in her lectures by saying that that would be flattering when the category of "man painter" also existed.

By now she had become such an international celebrity as a society painter that she became independent enough to be artistically selective. In fact, she has been quoted as saying, "It doesn't pay to paint everybody." She did paint first lady of the United States, Mrs. Theodore Roosevelt (***Edith**) and her daughter **Ethel** in the Red Room of the White House, and lunched beside the president at his vacation home. She also knew her famous contemporaries in the international world of art: Thomas Eakins, John Singer Sargent, ***Mary Cassatt**, and Childe Hassam. In 1905, Beaux designed and built a summer home, Green Alley, in Gloucester, Massachusetts, where every summer and fall she painted in her studio as well as entertained renowned intellectuals, family members, and close friends. Visitors described her as a handsome, witty, outspoken, romantic woman who liked male companionship but whose spirit would not be conquered; one who was gifted with originality and hated imitation but also showed determination, worked tirelessly standing at her easel, and slowly struggled with her canvasses to depict the spirituality of her artistic vision.

In 1919, Cecilia Beaux was thrilled to be chosen by the U.S. War Portraits Commission to do three portraits of Allied leaders who had cooperated to win the First World War. These were destined to be hung in the National Museum of American Art at the Smithsonian Institution in Washington, D.C. The city of San Francisco paid Beaux $25,000 for portraits from life of: (1) the British Admiral Sir David Beatty, who had played a significant role in the Battle of Jutland on May 31 and June 1, 1916; (2) Désiré Joseph, Cardinal Mercier of Belgium, a scholar who became an advocate for his invaded neutral country and (3) "The Tiger" Georges Clemenceau, a physician, journalist, and novelist who had been reappointed as premier of France in 1917. Beaux watched from the gallery and sketched as Clemenceau read the text of the treaty to the French National Assembly before its ratification, and this was how she painted him in 1920.

The War Portraits Project was the capstone to her fabulous career and life. In 1923, she was named one of America's greatest living women by the League of Women Voters. The following summer, while in Paris, Beaux broke her hip, but she refused recommended surgery so that it never healed properly. Forever afterward walking on crutches and with the onset of bursitis, arthritis, and cataracts, her productivity was slowed. As she became more nostalgic in her advanced years, her last significant painting, done in 1928, was of herself as a child dressing her dolls. With restricted mobility, she redirected most of her energy toward writing her autobiography, *Background with Figures* (1930). The next year, *Good Housekeeping* magazine awarded her the distinction of being one of America's 12 most influential women. First lady ***Eleanor Roosevelt** pinned Chi Omega Sorority's National Achievement Gold Medal on her in 1933. Beaux was honored as "the American woman who had made the greatest contribution to the culture of the world." Then in 1935–36, when she was 80, the American Academy of Arts and Letters, New York City, exhibited the largest solo show of her work (62 items) held in her lifetime. Beaux died September 17, 1942, at age 87, at Green Alley and was buried in West Laurel Hill Cemetery, Bala Cynwyd, Pennsylvania, not far from the family home.

For about 40 years thereafter, Cecilia Beaux was neglected as an artist. The American Renaissance of the Gilded Age of expansion and power had been replaced following World War I by the economically austere times of the Great Depression, both in the U.S. and Europe. Moreover, advances in camera technology and affordability led to the replacement of portraiture by photography. Even within painting, the popularity of Realism had been superseded by that of Impressionism, a movement that had little effect on Beaux's society portraits—where a flattering likeness was what customers expected—although it more greatly affected her experimental works portraying members of her family. And Impressionism, in turn, was eclipsed by Cubism and Abstract Expressionism, styles so unconducive to portraiture that patronage shifted elsewhere. Despite the variety and spontaneity within her work, Beaux's devotion to the academic tradition and to portraiture alone never wavered. As Frank H. Goodyear, Jr., noted, "Her art was more like a person than anything else."

SOURCES:

Barnard, Susan B. "Cecilia Beaux rediscovered: an annotated bibliography with introductory essay," in *Bulletin of Bibliography.* Vol. 45. March 1988, pp. 3–7.

Beaux, Cecilia. *Background with Figures.* NY: Houghton Mifflin, 1930.

———. *Cecilia Beaux and the Art of Portraiture.* Philadelphia, PA: Pennsylvania Academy of the Fine Arts, 1974.

Bowen, Catherine Drinker. *Family Portrait.* Boston, MA: Little, Brown, 1970.

"Cecilia Beaux" (obituary). *The New York Times.* September 18, 1942, p. 21.

Cortissoz, Royal. *A Catalogue of an Exhibition of Paintings by Cecilia Beaux.* NY: American Academy of Arts and Letters, 1935.

Drinker, Henry S. *The Paintings and Drawings of Cecilia Beaux.* Philadelphia, PA: The Pennsylvania Academy of the Fine Arts, 1955.

Goodyear, Frank H., Jr. and Elizabeth Bailey. *Cecilia Beaux: Portrait of an Artist.* Philadelphia, PA: Pennsylvania Academy of the Fine Arts, 1974.

Oakley, Thornton. *Cecilia Beaux.* Philadelphia, PA: Howard Biddle Printing, 1943.

Platt Frederick. "The War Portraits," in *Antiques.* Vol. 126, 1984, pp. 142-53.

Tappert, Tara Leigh. *Cecilia Beaux and the Art of Portraiture.* Washington: Smithsonian Institution, 1995.

SUGGESTED READING:

Drinker, Henry S. *History of the Drinker Family.* Merion, PA: private printing, 1961.

Hill, Frederick D. "Cecilia Beaux, the Grande Dame of American Portraiture," in *Antiques.* January 1974, pp. 160–68.

McKibbon, David. *Sargent's Boston.* Boston, MA: Museum of Fine Arts, 1956.

Morris, Harrison S. *Confessions in Art.* NY: Sears Publishing, 1930.

The Pennsylvania Academy of the Fine Arts. *The One Hundred and Fiftieth Anniversary Exhibition.* Philadelphia, PA: 1955.

Tappert, Tara Leigh. "Cecilia Beaux: A Career as a Portraitist," in *Women's Studies.* Vol. 14, no. 4, 1988, pp. 389-411.

Weinberg, H. Barbara, Doreen Bolgar, and David Park Curry. *American Impressionism and Realism: The Painting of Modern Life, 1885–1915.* NY: Metropolitan Museum of Art, 1994.

Whipple, Barbara. "The Eloquence of Cecilia Beaux," in *American Artist.* Vol. 38, September 1974, pp. 41–51, 80–85.

COLLECTIONS:

The Cecilia Beaux Papers and the Carnegie Institute Papers at the Archives of American Art, Smithsonian Institution; the Catherine Drinker Bowen Papers in the Manuscript Division of the Library of Congress; and the George Dudley Seymour Papers in Manuscripts and Archives at the Yale University Library, New Haven, Connecticut.

June K. Burton, author, editor, and historian emeritus, Akron, Ohio

Beavers, Louise (1902–1962)

African-American film actress of the 1930s and '40s. *Born in Cincinnati, Ohio, on March 8, 1902; died of a heart attack in Los Angeles, California, on October 26, 1962; graduated from Pasadena High School, June 1920; married LeRoy Moore.*

Filmography: Uncle Tom's Cabin *(1927);* Wall Street *(1929);* Golddiggers of Broadway *(1929);* Glad Rag Doll *(1929);* Barnum Was Right *(1929);* Coquette *(1929);* Nix on Dames *(1929);* Our Blushing Brides *(1930);* Back Pay *(1930);* She Couldn't Say No *(1930);* Wide Open *(1930);* Safety in Numbers *(1930);* Up for Murder *(1930);* Party Husband *(1930);* Reckless Living *(1930);* Sundown Trail *(1930);* Annabelle's Affairs *(1930);* Six Cylinder Love *(1930);* Good Sport *(1930);* Girls about Town *(1930);* Freaks *(1932);* Ladies of the Big House *(1932);* Old Man Minick *(1932);* Unashamed *(1932);* It's Rough to Be Famous *(1932);* Night World *(1932);* What Price Hollywood? *(1932);* Street of Women *(1932);* We Humans *(1932);* The Expert *(1932);* Wild Girl *(1932);* Jubilo *(1932);* Young America *(1932);* Divorce in the Family *(1932);* Too Busy to Work *(1932);* Girl Missing *(1933);* What Price Innocence? *(1933);* Her Bodyguard *(1933);* Bombshell *(1933);* Her Splendid Folly *(1933);* Notorious but Nice *(1933);* She Done Him Wrong *(1933);* Pick Up *(1933);* A Shriek in the Night *(1933);* I'm No Angel *(1933);* Imitation of Life *(1934);* I've Got Your Number *(1934);* Beside *(1934);* The Merry Frinks *(1934);* Cheaters *(1934);* Glamour *(1934);* I Believe in You

From the movie Imitation of Life, *1934, starring Louise Beavers.*

(1934); I Give My Love *(1934);* Merry Wives of Reno *(1934);* A Modern Hero *(1934);* Registered Nurse *(1934);* Hat, Coat and Glove *(1934);* Dr. Monica *(1934);* West of the Pecos *(1934);* Annapolis Farewell *(1935);* Bullets or Ballots *(1936);* General Spanky *(1936);* Wives Never Know *(1936);* Rainbow on the River *(1936);* The Last Gangster *(1937);* Make Way for Tomorrow *(1937);* Wings Over Honolulu *(1937);* Love in a Bungalow *(1937);* Scandal Street *(1938);* The Headleys at Home *(1938);* Life Goes On *(1938);* Brother Rad *(1938);* Reckless Living *(1938);* Peck's Bad Boy with the Circus *(1939);* Made for Each Other *(1939);* The Lady from Kentucky *(1939);* Reform School *(1939);* Parole Fixer *(1940);* Women Without Names *(1940);* I Want a Divorce *(1940);* No Time for Comedy *(1940);* Virginia *(1941);* Sign of the Wolf *(1941);* Belle Starr *(1941);* Shadow of the Thin Man *(1941);* The Vanishing Virginian *(1942);* Reap the Wild Wind *(1942);* Holiday Inn *(1942);* The Big Street *(1942);* Seventeen Sweethearts *(1942);* Tennessee Johnson *(1942);* There's Something about a Soldier *(1943);* Good Morning Judge *(1943);* DuBarry Was a Lady *(1943);* All by Myself *(1943);* Top Man *(1943);* Jack London *(1944);* Dixie Jamboree *(1944);* South of Dixie *(1944);* Follow the Boys *(1944);* Barbary Coast Gents *(1944);* Delightfully Dangerous *(1945);* Young Widow *(1946);* Banjo *(1947);* Mr. Blandings Builds His Dream House *(1948);* For the Love of Mary *(1948);* Good Sam *(1948);* Tell It to the Judge *(1949);* My Blue Heaven *(1949);* Girls School *(1950);* The Jackie Robinson Story *(1950);* Colorado Sundown *(1952);* I Dream of Jeannie *(1952);* Never Wave at a Wac *(1953);* Goodbye My Lady *(1956);* You Can't Run Away from It *(1956);* Teenage Rebel *(1956);* Tammy and the Bachelor *(1957);* The Goddess *(1958);* All the Fine Young Cannibals *(1960);* The Facts of Life *(1961).*

After performing the song "Pal of My Cradle Days" in an amateur contest at the Philharmonic Auditorium, Louise Beavers received a call from Central Casting in Hollywood. The first of her 125 film roles came in the silent version of *Uncle Tom's Cabin* for Universal Studios. In a day when bigotry and gender bias in the movie business circumscribed the roles available to black women, Beavers played stereotypical characters, prompting critic Donald Bogle to call her "the ever-enduring, resourceful mammy goddess."

Only occasionally was Beavers provided the opportunity to eschew the part of maid or white-child's "mammy" to display the broad range of her talent. Her role as the black mother of ***Fredi Washington** in the ***Claudette Colbert** film *Imitation of Life* received accolades from critic Jimmie Fidler, who singled her out as best performer of 1935. Another role as a mother, in *The Jackie Robinson Story*, allowed Beavers one more crack at breaking out of the mold.

In the early 1950s, she replaced ***Hattie McDaniel** on the radio and television series "Beulah" with great success, and, in 1954, she renewed a friendship with ***Mae West** to perform at the Congo Room in Las Vegas (the two had worked together in the film *Bombshell* in 1930). A member of the board of the Screen Actors Guild, Beavers often spoke to high school students and at community events. Louise Beavers was inducted into the Black Filmmakers Hall of Fame in 1957.

Barbara Morgan,
Melrose, Massachusetts

Becher, Eliza (1791–1872).

See O'Neill, Eliza.

Becher, Lilly (1901–1976)

German Communist author and publicist. *Name variations; Lilly Korpus. Born Lilly Korpus in Nuremberg, Germany, on January 27, 1901; died in East Berlin in 1976; daughter of a naval officer; her mother was the stepdaughter of Albert Ballin; married Johannes R. Becher.*

Joined Communist Party of Germany (KPD, 1919); did editorial work on Communist newspapers and journals in Berlin; appointed to high leadership positions within KPD (1924–25); fled to France (1933); worked with Willi Münzenberg in Paris to produce the first documentation of Nazi anti-Semitism, Der gelbe Fleck; *fled France for Soviet Union (1935), where she broadcast for Radio Moscow; returned to Germany (1945); editor-in-chief of* Neue Berliner Illustrierte; *was founding member of Democratic Women's League; chair of German-Soviet Friendship Society.*

Looking only at Lilly Becher's early years, spent at the very heart of the German establishment, it would be difficult to predict that her entire adult life would be dedicated to the Communist movement. She was born Lilly Korpus in Nuremberg on January 27, 1901, to a father who was one of the few officers of Jewish origin to serve in the German Navy and a mother who was an adopted daughter of Albert Ballin. Ballin, the Jewish director of the Hamburg-America Line, was an intimate advisor of Kaiser Wilhelm II; an ardent German patriot, Ballin committed suicide in November 1918 when he heard the news of his country's defeat in World War I. Like many of her generation, Becher was radicalized by the immense suffering of the war. In 1919, she joined the fledgling Communist Party of Germany (KPD). After the murder of its founders Karl Liebknecht and ***Rosa Luxemburg**, the KPD was open to talented, energetic young men and women, and Becher soon found a place for herself in Berlin as an editor of the party newspaper *Die rote Fahne* (The Red Flag).

During the 1920s and early 1930s, she became a well-known personality in KPD literary and propaganda circles, serving as founder and editor-in-chief of the party's periodical targeting women, *Die Arbeiterin* (The Woman Worker). She revealed considerable talent as the innovative editor of the *Arbeiter-Illustrierte-Zeitung*, which blended Marxist propaganda and entertaining stories with the use of eye-catching graphics. During these years, she worked with Willi Münzenberg, known as the resourceful propaganda czar of the KPD. Because of Becher's organizational skills, she held a number of significant KPD leadership positions, including political head of the Berlin-Brandenburg district in 1924–1925. She also published several short stories and novels, using her maiden name Lilly Korpus. By the end of the 1920s, her first marriage, to a Communist functionary, had ended in failure.

Realizing that her name had been placed high on Nazi arrest lists as a "dangerous Bolshevik," Becher fled to Paris within days of the Nazi seizure of power in 1933. She continued working with Münzenberg, and it was the brilliant work of the "Münzenberg firm" of talented writers and propagandists like Lilly Becher that played a significant role in alerting the world to the menace of a Nazified Germany. Becher's most important work during her years in Paris was the book *Der gelbe Fleck* (The Yellow Spot), the first systematic exposé of the anti-Semitic policies of Nazi Germany. (Although published without an author's name on the title page, *Der gelbe Fleck* was indeed written by Becher.) In 1935, she was called to Moscow where she continued her propaganda work and married the former expressionist poet Johannes R. Becher (1891–1958). In the Soviet capital, she worked as a translator and editor for the respected literary journal *Internationale Literatur—Deutsche Blätter*. An adroit cultural politician, Johannes Becher was able to survive the Stalinist terror and save his wife from the gulag. During World War II, the Bechers lived in Moscow, writing anti-Nazi propaganda which they broadcast to Nazi Germany and to the German soldiers on Soviet soil via Radio Moscow.

After the defeat of Nazi Germany in the spring of 1945, the Bechers returned to the Soviet Occupation Zone of Berlin. As honored members of the anti-Fascist ruling elite, they both joined the Socialist Unity Party (SED) when it was created in 1946. After the creation of the German Democratic Republic (GDR) in 1949, Johannes rapidly moved up the bureaucratic ladder of SED-dominated cultural life, eventually becoming minister of culture. Lilly returned to journalism, becoming editor-in-chief of the *Neue Berliner Illustrierte*. She also became active in organizational work, helping to found and run the Democratic Women's League and serving as chair of the German-Soviet Friendship Society. After her husband's death in 1958, Lilly Becher was appointed director of the special archive for his papers established as part of the German Academy of the Arts in East Berlin. After a long career of loyalty to the Stalinized German Communist movement, in 1961 Lilly Becher was awarded the Silver Medal for Service of the GDR. On the occasion of her 65th birthday in 1966, the SED leadership sent her a letter of congratulations. Honored in her final years as a "party veteran," but largely unknown to the younger generation of the GDR, Lilly Becher died in East Berlin in 1976.

SOURCES:

Der gelbe Fleck: Die Ausrottung von 500,000 Juden. Vorwort von Lion Feuchtwanger. Paris: Éditions du Carrefour, 1936.

Frey, Gerhard, ed. *Prominente ohne Maske DDR.* Munich: FZ-Verlag, 1991.

Hein, Christoph M. *Der "Bund proletarisch-revolutionärer Schriftsteller Deutschlands": Biographie eines kulturpolitischen Experiments in der Weimarer Republik.* Münster and Hamburg: Lit Verlag, 1991.

Müller, Reinhard, ed. *Die Säuberung. Moskau 1936: Stenogramm einer geschlossenen Parteiversammlung.* Reinbek bei Hamburg: Rowohlt Taschenbuch Verlag GmbH, 1991.

Pütter, Conrad. *Rundfunk gegen das "Dritte Reich": Deutschsprachige Rundfunkaktivitäten im Exil 1933–1945.* Ein Handbuch. Munich: K.G. Saur, 1986.

Weber, Hermann. *Die Wandlung des deutschen Kommunismus: Die Stalinisiuerung der KPD in der Weimarer Republik.* 2 vols. Frankfurt am Main: Europäische Verlagsanstalt, 1969.

John Haag, Associate Professor,
University of Georgia, Athens, Georgia

Becker, Christiane (1778–1797)

German actress. *Born Christiane Luise Amalie Neumann at Krossen in Neumark, Germany, on December 15, 1778; died at Weimar on September 17, 1797; daughter of Johann Christian Neumann (a well-*

known German actor); married Heinrich Becker (a German actor).

A famous German actress, Christiane Becker performed in both comedy and tragedy. She was admired by Goethe who, after her death at a young age, wrote of her in the elegy "Euphrosine."

Becker, Elizabeth (1903–1989).

See Becker-Pinkston, Elizabeth.

Becker, Lydia Ernestine

(1827–1890)

English botanist and women's rights advocate. *Born in 1827; caught diphtheria and died at the health resort of Aix-les-Bains in 1890; eldest of 15 children of Hannibal Becker (owner of a chemical works in Manchester) and Mary (Duncuft) Becker; educated at home; never married; no children.*

In a lifetime devoted to women's rights, botanist Lydia Becker established the Manchester Ladies Literary Society, in 1865, as a forum for the study of scientific subjects among women. In 1867, she co-founded and became secretary of the Manchester Women's Suffrage Committee, which became the National Society for Women's Suffrage later that year. Becker edited the *Women's Suffrage Journal* from 1870 to 1890, as well as other pamphlets on women's suffrage. She also served on the Manchester School Board from 1870.

Becker, Marie Alexander

(1877–194?)

Belgian housewife and mass poisoner. *Born Marie Alexander in 1877 in Belgium; date of death lost during the German occupation of Belgium in World War II; married to a cabinetmaker.*

Marie Alexander Becker

The 53-year-old Marie Becker of Liège, Belgium, was said to be a quiet, law-abiding housewife until she was captivated in 1932 by the advances of Lambert Beyer, a man she met while shopping. Becker then embarked on a passionate affair that led her to poison her cabinetmaker husband with digitalis. Soon bored with Beyer, she dispatched him in the same manner. To obtain money for subsequent romances with a series of gigolos, Becker began poisoning elderly women patrons of her new dressmaking shop, stealing what she could. After each murder, ten in all, she reportedly attended the funeral of her victim, dressed in black and making a dramatic show of her grief and sorrow. Finally caught through an informant, Becker was said to have gloated over her crimes. She was found guilty and sentenced to life in prison where she eventually died in obscurity while Germany occupied Belgium during World War II.

Becker, May Lamberton

(1873–1958)

American critic and journalist who edited a column titled "Reader's Guide" for 40 years. *Born May Lamberton in New York, New York, on August 26, 1873; died on April 27, 1958; daughter of Emma (Packard) Lamberton and Ellis Tinkham Lamberton; educated at her mother's private school and Jersey City High School; married Gustav Louis Becker (a musician), in 1894 (divorced 1911); children: Beatrice Becker Warde.*

Selected works: (editor) "Reader's Guide" (1915–55); A Reader's Guide Book *(1924);* Adventures in Reading *(1927);* Books as Windows *(1929);* First Adventures in Reading *(1936);* Choosing Books for Children *(1937);* Introducing Charles Dickens *(1940).*

Born in New York City, May Lamberton was raised in Jersey City, New Jersey, where her mother Emma ran a small private school for girls. (Her father Ellis died when she was 12.) Becker enjoyed learning so much that, when she advanced to public high school, "the teachers were so amazed to find somebody who enjoyed study that they shoved me on with speed and glory." She graduated at age 16, and, though a teacher offered to pay her tuition, she turned down Barnard College. Becker worked as a newspaper theater critic, writing columns that were popular because, like her readers, she had never formally studied drama. Following her marriage in 1894 to pianist and composer Gustav Becker, she began lecturing to women's groups, first on music and later on literature. The Beckers had one child and divorced in 1911.

May Lamberton Becker was invited to begin a literary reference column in 1915 and thus launched the "Reader's Guide" at the New York *Evening Post*. The column, which answered inquiries from readers who were seeking books on specific topics, moved to the *Saturday Review of Literature* in 1924, and to the *Herald Tribune* in 1933, where it ran until Becker retired on May 1, 1955. For many years, Becker lived in New York City, as she said, "at the home of my Siamese cats" and summered with her daughter in London, writing the "Reader's Guide" from a rooftop garden. May Lamberton Becker died on April 27, 1958.

Crista Martin, freelance writer,
Boston, Massachusetts

Becker-Modersohn, Paula (1876–1907).

See Modersohn-Becker, Paula.

Becker-Pinkston, Elizabeth (1903–1989)

American Olympic diver. *Name variations: Elizabeth Becker; Elizabeth Pinkston; Elizabeth Pinkston-Becker; Betty Becker Pinkston Campbell. Born Elizabeth Becker on March 6, 1903; died of heart failure in Detroit, Michigan, on April 6, 1989; married Clarence Pinkston (1900–1961, an American diver); married once more.*

The first woman to win two Olympic diving titles, Betty Becker won gold medals off the springboard at Paris in 1924 (as Elizabeth Becker) and off the platform at Amsterdam in 1928 (as Elizabeth Pinkston). She also won a silver medal in platform diving in Paris. During the 1928 Games, Elizabeth was coached by her new husband, Olympic diving champion Clarence Pinkston, who won a gold, a silver and two bronze medals in the 1920 and 1924 Olympics.

Beckman-Shcherbina, Elena (1881–1951)

Russian pianist. *Born in 1881; died in 1951; studied under Konstantin Igumnov.*

A student of Konstantin Igumnov (1873–1948), Elena Beckman-Shcherbina was trained in the Russian School of virtuoso pianism. She was a highly respected artist who left behind an impressive recorded legacy of music by Anton Rubinstein, Sergei Rachmaninoff, and Alexander Scriabin. She knew Scriabin personally and frequently played his own music for him.

Beckwith, Martha Warren (1871–1959)

American folklorist, ethnographer, teacher and author. *Born in Wellesley Heights, Massachusetts, on January 19, 1871; died at age 88 in Berkeley, California, on January 28, 1959, and buried in Makawao cemetery, Maui; youngest child of George Ely and Harriet Winslowe (Goodale) Beckwith (both schoolteachers); grandniece of* ****Lucy Goodale Thurston;*** *graduated from Mt. Holyoke College, 1893; obtained M.A. in anthropology, Columbia University, 1906.*

A close childhood friend of naturalist ***Annie Alexander**, Martha Beckwith grew up on Maui, surrounded by her cousins, especially the Alexanders and Baldwins. After graduating from Mt. Holyoke in Massachusetts, she returned to Hawaii to teach at Punahou School for two years. She then taught at Mt. Holyoke, Smith, and Vassar for the next ten years, before studying anthropology under Frank Boaz at Columbia. She returned to teaching at Vassar in 1920, retiring in 1938.

Beckwith's books are firsthand accounts of the folklore and ethnography of Hawaiians, Jamaicans, Native Americans, and the Portuguese residents of Goa. They include: *The Hawaiian Romance of Laieikawai* (1919); *Folklore in America* (1931); *Hawaiian Mythology* (1940); and *The Kumulipo* (1951), which was dedicated "to the memory of Annie M. Alexander, lifelong friend and comrade from early days in Hawaii."

SOURCES:

Petersen, Barbara Bennett, ed. *Notable Women of Hawaii.* Honolulu: University of Hawaii Press, 1984.

Bécu, Marie Jeanne (1743–1793).

See Du Barry, Jeanne Bécu.

Beddingfield, Ann (1742–1763)

English murderer. *Born in England in 1742; burned at the stake on April 8, 1763, in Rushmore, England; married John Beddingfield.*

Ann Beddingfield was a young newlywed with a well-to-do husband John and a large manor house on a farm estate in Suffolk when she seduced one of the servants, a 19-year-old named Richard Ringe. In the throes of their less-than-discreet affair, Beddingfield implored Ringe to murder her husband, promising him half the master's estate. Although the couple dropped subtle hints of their plan to other servants throughout a three-month period, authorities were not informed.

In March 1763, Ringe strangled John Beddingfield while he slept and then hastened to the room of his paramour to report on his success. Bursting into her darkened room, he whispered, "I have done for him." Ann replied, "Then I am easy." Unfortunately, he was unaware that Ann Beddingfield was in bed with a servant girl who was being using as a bedwarmer, following a common practice of the day. When none of the servants, including the servant girl, made their suspicions known to the coroner, the coroner's jury determined that John Beddingfield had died of natural causes, probably strangling himself in the bed sheets.

As soon as she received her monthly pay, however, the servant girl rushed to the authorities. The lovers, by now estranged, were arrested and placed on trial in April 1763. Filled with guilt, Ringe not only confessed but lectured the assembled crowd on "the snares and pitfalls of wicked women." Ann Beddingfield steadfastly insisted she had nothing to do with the murder. Both were convicted and sentenced to death. Though Ringe was hanged, Ann Beddingfield was burned alive at the stake on April 8, 1763, a form of punishment then reserved for unfaithful and murderous wives.

Bedell, Harriet M. (1875–1969)

Protestant Episcopal deacon, known as the "white sister" of the Florida Seminole Indians. *Born in Grand Island, New York, on March 19, 1875; died in Davenport, Florida, in 1969; daughter and one of three children of Horace Ira and Louisa Sophia (Oberist) Bedell; graduated, State Normal School, Buffalo, in 1894.*

A devoutly religious, adventurous young woman, Harriet Bedell left her teaching position in Buffalo, New York, to train as a mission teacher through the Protestant Episcopal Church. She would spend the remainder of her life as a missionary in service of the Cheyenne Indians of northwestern Oklahoma, the Alaskan Indians in the remote Alaskan Arctic Circle, and the Mikasuki Seminole Indians of Florida. Known affectionately as "White sister" to the Seminoles, Bedell tended to the medical and educational needs of Indian children, as well as to the practical and spiritual concerns of Indian communities struggling to assimilate. She traveled miles on horseback in Oklahoma, drove a dog team across isolated Alaskan terrain, and encountered snake- and alligator-infested waters in the swamps of the Florida Everglades, to tend to the sick and needy and sow her credo: "The needs of a hungry soul can best be met in a sound body." Moving to Davenport, Florida, in 1960, she continued her work with church and civic groups well into her 80s, even after losing her world-renowned Glade Cross Mission House and most of her personal possessions to Hurricane Donna.

SOURCES:

Hartley, William and Ellen Hartley. *A Woman Set Apart: The Remarkable Life of Harriet Bedell.* NY: Dodd, Mead, 1963.

Bedford, countess of.

See Philippa of Hainault for sidebar on Isabella (1332–1382).

See Russell, Lucy (c. 1581–1627).

Bedford, duchess of.

See Anne Valois (c. 1405–1432).

See Woodville, Elizabeth for sidebar on Jacquetta of Luxemburg (c. 1416–1472).

See Woodville, Katherine (c. 1442–1512).

Bedford, Sybille (1911—)

Anglo-German journalist, novelist and biographer. *Born Sybille Von Schoenebeck in Brandenburg, Germany, on March 16, 1911; daughter of Elizabeth Bernard and Maximilian Von Schoenebeck; educated at village and private schools in Germany, Italy, England and France; married Walter Bedford, in 1935.*

Selected works: A Legacy *(1956);* Faces of Justice *(1961);* Favourite of the Gods *(1963);* A Compass Error *(1968);* Biography of Aldous Huxley *(1973–74);* Jigsaw: An Unsentimental Education *(1989).*

Details of Sybille Bedford's life have been revealed largely through her semi-autobiographical fiction. She was born in Brandenburg, Germany, to Elizabeth and Maximilian Von Schoenebeck on the eve of World War I. As Germany met with defeat, her parents separated. Sybille remained in Baden with her father while attending village schools, but she often traveled in Europe on holiday with her mother. At age 19, living alone in England while her mother was in drug rehabilitation in Italy, Bedford wrote her first novel *A Legacy* in 1930 (it would be published more than two decades later, in 1956). She was also introduced to Aldous Huxley, a writer who inspired her, and found stability staying in the London home of family friends. There, she undertook a study of the legal system, later securing work as a law reporter.

In the 1950s, she returned to novels and, over the next 20 years, produced six books, including the two-volume set on Huxley, commissioned by his family. Sybille Bedford spent more than a decade working on her autobiographical *Jigsaw: An Unsentimental Education*, which appeared in 1989.

Crista Martin,
Boston, Massachusetts

Bedott, Widow (1811–1852).

See Whitcher, Frances Miriam Berry.

Beeby, Doris (1894–1948)

Australian union organizer. *Born Doris Isabel Beeby on July 30, 1894; died on October 17, 1948; one of four children of Helena Maria (West) and Sir George Stephenson Beeby (a labor politician and judge); attended Church of England Grammar School for Girls, Sydney, Australia; attended University of Sydney as an unmatriculated arts student.*

Australian-born Doris Beeby began her career in 1920 as an associate to her father following his appointment as a judge of the New South Wales Industrial Court of Arbitration and president of the Board of Trade. Her duties included assisting the inquiry into a reduction of working hours—from 48 to 44—for the iron and building trades. She continued with her father after his appointment to the Commonwealth Arbitration Court in 1926, where he supported practices geared to raising productivity and linking wage levels to increased profitability.

In 1939, Beeby was in London, where she joined the Spanish Relief Movement which offered aid to refugees from Spain's Civil War, as well as to those from Great Britain's Communist Party. Returning to Sidney, she joined the Australian Communist Party and worked as an organizer for the Sheetmetal Workers' Union. Her work focused on improving working conditions and pay equity for the many women hired during wartime. To better understand her constituency, Beeby took a job in the factory. She resigned as an organizer after the war, when the number of women in the union fell off.

Through the United Associations of Women, Beeby supported the Women for Canberra Movement and the Australian Women's Charter, which attempted to address the needs of women in the postwar social order and to mobilize a political force to insure that those needs were part of reconstruction efforts. The Charter, though widely supported, eventually fell victim to the Cold War, which divided support and destroyed the movement. Beeby also wrote for the *Tribune* and the *Australian Women's Digest*, the monthly publication of the United Associations of Women. After a lifetime commitment to better conditions for laborers, Beeby died on October 17, 1948, following a long battle with cancer.

Beech, Olive Ann (1903–1993)

American aviation pioneer and co-founder and chief executive officer of Beech Aircraft Corporation. *Name variations: O.A. Beech. Born Olive Anne Mellor in Waverly, Kansas, on September 25, 1903; died on July 6, 1993, in Wichita, Kansas; daughter of Frank B. (a carpenter and building contractor) and Suzannah (Miller) Mellor; attended public school in Paola, Kansas, and American Secretarial and Business College, Wichita; also attended night school; married Walter H. Beech, on February 24, 1930; children: Suzanne Mellor Beech and Mary Lynn Beech.*

Began work in aviation as secretary-bookkeeper (mid-1920s); became knowledgeable in various aspects of aviation (1930s); co-founded Beech Aircraft Company (1932); because of husband's poor health during World War II, ran Beech Aircraft during a time of rapid expansion; became president and chair of the company after husband's death (1950); elected Woman of the Year by the Women's National Aeronautical Association of the U.S. (1951); under her leadership, Beech Aircraft became a leading manufacturer of private aircraft, also winning major missile and space contracts; retired from presidency (1968); sold company (1980).

From a $20-a-week job as a bookkeeper, Olive Ann Beech rose to become chief executive officer of the multimillion dollar Beech Aircraft Corporation. Founded with her husband, the company was a leading Midwest producer of light commercial aircraft and military training planes, which supplied 90% of the planes used for training American bombardiers and navigators during World War II.

Born in 1903, Beech grew up in a Kansas farming community. After finishing public school, she attended a business college and improved her stenographic and bookkeeping skills. She worked several years as a bookkeeper for a manufacturing firm, then in 1925 she began working as a secretary-bookkeeper for the Travel Air Manufacturing Company, a struggling firm producing airplanes for business and sport purposes, founded that year by aviation pioneer Walter H. Beech. Dedicated and conscientious, she was soon promoted to the post of office manager and secretary to Walter Beech. But Olive had never been near a plane. During the first few weeks, she had to have the chief engineer prepare a breakdown drawing of a plane, with all the parts marked, because she couldn't tell an empennage from a cowling. "I used this drawing for many years when teaching new employees the nomenclature of aircraft," she told the *Christian Science Monitor* in 1951.

As the only woman of the company's 12 employees, Beech quickly caught the eye of her charming, but somewhat difficult, bachelor boss. On her first day, he warned her not to bother the married men, and she countered by letting him know that she would not be bothering him either. In 1930, shortly after the company merged with Curtiss-Wright, they married. Walter's work (he was now an executive officer of the new firm) took him to New York City, during which time Olive was not active in the business. Two years later, the couple returned to Wichita because Walter missed the hands-on construction of aircraft.

In 1932, they founded the Beech Aircraft Company (later Corporation), announcing that the purpose of their new firm would be to "make the best airplanes in the world." Olive served as secretary-treasurer, then director. From the fledgling company came the two airplanes that would provide its foundation for years to come: the classic Model 17 single-engine Staggerwing biplane and the Model 18 Twin. Olive Beech played an important role in winning the 1936 Bendix Transcontinental Speed Dash, convincing her husband that a victory would be more impressive if their Model 17 was flown by women. As a result, **Louise Thaden** and **Blanche Noyes** flew a Beechcraft to victory in America's most famous cross-country race and set a new transcontinental speed record for women.

By the late 1930s, the company had landed enough defense contracts to qualify as a critical war industry. By 1938, their sales exceeded $1 million, and the company dominated the market of private-owner and commercial planes in the 285 to 459 horsepower class. By 1940, they had military orders worth $22 million. That same year, when Beech was pregnant with her second daughter, Walter was stricken with encephalitis from which he would never fully recover. While her husband lay in a coma, Olive Beech took over running the company from her own bed in the maternity section of the hospital. She oversaw negotiations for a $23 million loan and $50 million in revolving credit from 36 banks to finance the continuing production of planes to meet mounting orders. In the spring of 1941, the company began producing its Beechcraft Model 18, which served throughout the war as a bomber trainer and as a short-haul airship. She also dealt with the numerous management problems of sudden expansion, including recruiting, training workers, and finding subcontractors for parts. Under her guidance, sales reached a wartime peak of $122 million in 1945. By the end of the war, the company had produced 7,400 Beechcrafts, plus spare parts. At its peak production, the firm employed 15,000 workers.

Olive Ann Beech

The postwar years were often difficult, as the number of workers dropped to 2,600 in 1949. Beech Aircraft was highly adaptive, however, and turned into a diversified manufacturing enterprise that produced corn harvesters, cotton pickers, washing machines, and such humble but popular consumer items as pie plates. The death of Walter Beech in November 1950 did not disrupt the company's future since Olive Ann Beech had been de facto chief executive officer (CEO) of Beech Aircraft for many years. She now held the titles of president, board chair, and CEO. The Korean War brought large orders from the Pentagon, but Beech knew that defense orders alone would not guarantee her firm's long-term financial health.

Surrounding herself with "people who like to find ways to do things, not tell me why they can't be done," she guided Beech Aircraft toward industrial prominence through planned policies of expansion and diversification, and by early entry into the nation's space program. In December 1955, Beech Aircraft announced the first flight of its Model 73 jet trainer, a craft designed to train pilots in the operation of turbojet aircraft. Other plane designs in the following decades indicated that the spirit of innovation remained alive and strong in the company.

For much of her career, Olive Beech was also a mother and homemaker who found time to serve a variety of other interests. She was active as a philanthropist, patron of the arts, and supporter of youth. Beech earned respect from her peers in aviation and business as the recipient of awards and appointments to high-ranking positions, including the Board of Directors of the U.S. Chamber of Commerce. In 1943, she was chosen by *The New York Times* as one of America's 12 most distinguished women. In 1951, she was chosen as "woman of the year" by the Women's National Aeronautical Association. She was twice named by *Fortune* magazine as one of the top ten businesswomen in the United States. As a highly respected industrialist, she was appointed to national boards by presidents Eisenhower, Johnson, and Nixon. In 1968, Beech turned over the presidency of Beech Aircraft to her nephew Frank E. Hedrick but retained the post of chair. In the final years of her control, the payroll was more than 10,000 and annual sales were over $900 million. In 1980, Beech Aircraft was purchased by Raytheon Company, and Beech was elected to the parent company's board and executive committee.

Opposite page

Catharine Beecher

Olive Ann Beech was honored in 1980 with the "Sands of Time" Kitty Hawk Civilian Award, conferred at the Wright Brothers Banquet of the Los Angeles Chamber of Commerce. That month, she also received the Wright Brothers Memorial Trophy "in recognition of significant public service of enduring value to aviation in the United States." In July 1980, she was inducted into the Aviation Hall of Fame, joining her late husband who was so honored in 1977. Olive and Walter Beech became only the second couple to be enshrined in the Aviation Hall of Fame, the other being Charles and ***Anne Lindbergh**. In 1982, Olive Beech became chair emeritus of Beech Aircraft and retired from the board of Raytheon. She died on July 6, 1993, at the age of 89.

SOURCES:

Bird, Caroline. *Enterprising Women*. NY: W.W. Norton, 1976.

Candee, Marjorie Dent, ed. *Current Biography 1956*. NY: H.W. Wilson, 1956.

Chronicle of Aviation. Liberty, MO: JL International, 1992.

McDaniel, William H. *Beech: A Quarter Century of Aeronautical Achievement*. Wichita, KS: The McCormick-Armstrong, 1947.

"Olive A. Beech, 89, Retired Head of Beech Aviation," in *The New York Times Biographical Service*. July 1993, p. 933.

John Haag, Associate Professor of History, University of Georgia, Athens, Georgia

Beecher, Catharine (1800–1878)

American educator and writer who campaigned for women to assume the role of redeemers of their society through values learned in their domestic duties as mothers and wives. *Born Catharine Esther Beecher on September 6, 1800, in East Hampton, Long Island; died on May 12, 1878, in Elmira, New York; daughter of the Reverend Lyman and* ***Roxana (Foote) Beecher****; sister of Harriet Beecher Stowe; attended a private school in Litchfield, Connecticut; no other formal education; never married; no children.*

Moved with Beecher family to Litchfield, Connecticut (1810); became woman of the house after the death of her mother (1816); taught school in New London (1820); death of fiancé Alexander Metcalf Fisher (1822); opened Hartford Female Seminary (1823); moved to Cincinnati, where she established the Western Female Institute (1831); took part in a published exchange with Angelina Grimké over abolitionism and the duties of American women (1837); toured the West, establishing female teaching academies (1837–47); founded the National Popular Education Association, later known as the American Woman's Educational Association (1847); taught briefly in Massachusetts and Connecticut; wrote on domestic science and critiqued the direction of American feminism up to the time of her death.

Selected publications: The Elements of Mental and Moral Philosophy, Founded on Experience, Reason, and the Bible *(1831);* Letters on the Difficulties of Religion *(1836);* A Treatise on Domestic Economy *(1841);* The Duty of American Women to Their Country *(1845);* The Domestic Receipt Book *(1846);* Common Sense Applies to Religion *(1857);* The American Woman's Home *(1869).*

In 1822, Catharine Beecher's four-month engagement to Alexander Metcalf Fisher, a professor of mathematics at Yale known for his winsome personality and brilliant scholarship, ended with his death in a shipwreck at sea. The loss became the defining event in the life of the light-hearted and delicately pretty young woman. Beecher had been raised as the dutiful daughter of an evangelical Presbyterian minister and was personally filled with the Calvinist beliefs of predestination and unmerited grace. As a bereaved fiancée, Beecher felt the burden of a theological concern beyond the weight of ordinary grief, knowing that Fisher had not demonstrated the conversion experience essential to Calvinism. The fear of how Fisher's soul might spend eternity was to cause her to reject her previous life as vain and worldly, and to pursue a lifelong crusade of reform activities related to the education of women.

Born in East Hampton, Long Island, Catharine Beecher was the oldest of four daughters of the eight surviving children born to her mother Roxana. Her father, the Reverend Lyman Beecher, was active in the temperance and other reform movements and became famous for his dedication to defending Calvinism against the varied intellectual challenges of the day. Her sister ***Harriet Beecher Stowe** would grow up to write *Uncle Tom's Cabin.* By 1810, the ever-growing family had moved to Litchfield, Connecticut, a lively community of culture and advanced social thought. With the death of her mother when Catharine was 16, she was put in charge of the household for about a year, until her father's remarriage to **Harriet Porter**. At that time, the young Catharine wrote a deferential letter of welcome to her new stepmother, who would give birth to three more Beecher sons and one more daughter.

Catharine's formal education was limited to a brief period of attendance at a private girls' school in Litchfield; her most significant learning came from her reading and from life in the Beecher household, where ideas about literature, religion, and reform were constantly under discussion. Before she met Fisher, Beecher had been a school teacher in New London, Connecticut. In the year following his death, she began to define a new calling for herself as the leader of a crusade to encourage women in the exercise of their moral stewardship, and in 1823 she founded the Hartford Female Seminary. While her outward personality grew more somber, the inner pilgrimage which she had begun (and which she would explore over the years in her writings) would eventually result in her rejection of Calvinism's creed. Although she continued to attend her father's church during his lifetime, after his death she and her sister Harriet both joined the Episcopal Church.

There seems to be no very extensive sphere of usefulness for a single woman but that which can be found in the limits of a school room.

—Catharine Beecher

In 1831, Beecher followed her family to Cincinnati, where she founded the Western Female Institute; it was one of several educational institutions where she was to work preparing women to be teachers in the American West. The same year, she also wrote her first published treatise, *The Elements of Mental and Moral Philosophy, Founded on Experience, Reason, and the Bible*, which she had privately printed. The work was an exercise in "Scottish commonsense" philosophy, in which human nature learns, via reasoning and study of the Biblical scriptures, to develop the moral sense the author saw as common to all humanity. In language both sober and metaphysical, Beecher explored the idea of the harmony established when natural order contained a moral order which provided the best guide to a proper social order. The point of view was essentially a socially conservative one. Its assertion of a social system which provided moral guidance grounded in God was a message of reform against the behavior of those who ignored the "voice" of their own innate moral reason.

During the 1830s, Beecher wrote several volumes on the practical application of religion to daily life and also took up the issue of abolition, on which she stated her views in *An Essay on Slavery and Abolitionism With Reference to the Duty of American Females*, published in 1837. The issue of abolition, growing crucial in her time, provides a good example of the way in which Beecher's conservative outlook often isolated her from the major developments in the history of American reform. Believing that good manners were essential even in social agitation and debate, she held that all Christian women were abolitionists by definition but urged gradual rather than immediate emancipation. In her view, meekness and tact were desirable in any criticism of the slaveholders. In the heat of reform, women must not lose their innate qualities of moral goodness and superiority. Although slavery was acknowledged as evil, the means to attack it must be predicated on expediency.

The South Carolina-born abolitionist ***Angelina Grimké** wrote a rejection of Beecher's position, using the language of Garrisonian absolutism. In her *Letters to Catharine E. Beecher in Reply to an Essay on Slavery and Abolitionism*, Grimké denounced slaveholders as evil and nonslave holders as guilty of sin for doing nothing to stop the evil institution. There were many differences between these two thinkers, but the prevailing distinction may have been that Grimké was "born a lady" and expressed herself as a liberated person, while Beecher's more modest background inclined her to strive for respectability by urging self-improvement for herself and other women.

In 1837, Beecher's Cincinnati school was closed. She spent the next decade touring the American West, setting up a number of female teaching academies, while writing the books that were to insure her fame and historical reputation. In 1841, she published *A Treatise on Domestic Economy*, followed by *The Duty of American Women to Their Country* (1845) and *The Domestic Receipt Book* (1846). In all these works, she promoted the merits of a thrifty household supervised by a wise and loving wife acting in the role of domestic engineer, a perspective that underlines the nature of her dispute with other feminists and feminism: she remained a genteel critic of slavery and was a foe of the franchise for women, believing that women's true role as redeemers rested in their domestic duties as mothers and wives.

Beecher's books sold well; nearly a quarter-century after they first appeared, she revised and rewrote them, with the help of Stowe, for publication as *The American Woman's Home* in 1869. Although her message did not please feminists like ***Elizabeth Cady Stanton** and ***Susan B. Anthony**, Beecher manifested a presence and an influence in her day, based on the division (pointed up by her position) between autonomous and domestic expressions of feminism in American history.

Autonomous feminism recognized the equality of the sexes in regard to the right of citizenship, as well as in the marketplace and in general social life. In contrast, domestic feminism derived from both the conjugal family and the social stresses that were a part of economic growth. In the cultural veneration of the modern family and the home, women placed family and home life first and then extended these domestic values to civil society, the state, and the world.

Beecher was among the champions of domestic equality, who believed that women had special civilizing qualities needed by family, home, and state. Her domestic feminism took the form of outrage over how far the actual life experiences of women differed from her ideal, and it offered a set of principles around which society could consolidate. Her ideal was a well-ordered self-sufficiency, expressed through means that included furniture, architecture, and human relationships. The home was viewed as the natural place for women and the basic building block of a good society; it stood for certainties and completion that could unite personal and national goals.

Catharine Beecher, like others in her family, sought to establish the cultural dominance of these ideas in 19th-century America by rescuing the nation from a secular and self-indulgent existence. Her particular contribution was a vision of the manner in which the female might shape the home, and thus the nation, into a kinder as well as more efficient organization. In that endeavor, Beecher saw the need for female sacrifice, as opposed to the franchise for women. In the course of her long and productive life, her philosophy of domestic feminism changed tactics, eventually linking antebellum moral reform to the Victorian science of society, while continuing to allow women to express the superiority of their domestic virtues.

Unfortunately for her historical reputation, many women embraced other expressions of feminism, in particular the right to vote. Even so, the legacy of Catharine Beecher is complex: though she wanted careers for women, she did not agitate for rights for women; she was a capable educator, shrewd and hard-working, with a strong mind and will, but she was never willing to struggle for the liberation of women. Rebellious spirit and a style grounded in libertarian idealism were not for her; she strove instead for women's self-improvement. Nevertheless, she was a vital part of 19th-century reform and the larger story of American feminism.

In the 1850s, in a gesture that expressed both 19th-century sentimental values and a desire for private grief, Beecher visited the family home of Alexander Fisher, where she sat by the fire and burned all the letters exchanged by the ill-fated couple. She taught for brief periods in Massachusetts and Connecticut and lived throughout her life with various members of her family. When she died, in 1878, she was in Elmira, New York, at the home of her half-brother Thomas. Of the institutions she established, only the Milwaukee Normal Institute remains, though under a different name.

SOURCES:

Rugoff, Milton. *The Beechers, An American Family in the Nineteenth Century.* NY: Harper & Row, 1981.

Sklar, Kathryn K. *Catharine Beecher: A Study in American Domesticity.* New Haven, CT: Yale University Press, 1973.

SUGGESTED READING:

Boyston, Jeanne. *The Limits of Sisterhood: The Beecher Sisters on Women's Rights and Woman's Sphere.* Chapel Hill: University of North Carolina Press, 1988.

Caskey, Marie. *Chariot of Fire: Religion and the Beecher Family.* New Haven, CT: Yale University Press, 1977.

French, Earle A., ed. *Portraits of a Nineteenth Century Family.* Hartford, CT: Stowe-Day Foundation, 1976.

Pickens, Donald K. "Domestic Feminism and the Structure of American History," in *Contemporary Philosophy.* Vol. 12. November–December 1989, pp. 14–22.

COLLECTIONS:

The Schlesinger Library at Radcliffe College has a large collection of Catharine Beecher's letters.

Donald K. Pickens, Professor of History, University of North Texas, Denton, Texas

Beecher, Isabella (1822–1907).

See Stowe, Harriet Beecher for sidebar on Hooker, Isabella Beecher.

Beere, Thekla (1901–1991)

Irish civil servant, first female head of an Irish government department, and first chair of the Commission on the Status of Women. *Name variations: T.J. Beere. Pronunciation: THEK-lah. Born Thekla June Beere on June 20, 1901, in Streete, County Westmeath, Ireland; died on February 19, 1991, in Dublin, Ireland; daughter of Rev. Francis John Armstrong Beere (Church of Ireland cleric) and Lucie M. (Potterton) Beere; educated at home; attended Alexandra School and College, 1916–19; Trinity College, University of Dublin, 1919–23; prizes in political economy, criminal and constitutional law, jurisprudence and international law; graduated 1923 with senior modera-*

torship in legal and political science and degree of Bachelor of Laws (LL.B.); never married; no children.

Joined Irish civil service (1924); awarded Rockefeller Fellowship for study in the U.S. (1925–27); returned to Irish civil service, department of Industry of Commerce (1927); served as senior staff officer, Statistics Branch (1927–41); co-founded (1931) and later became president of An Óige (Irish Youth Hostel Association); served as superintending officer and principal officer, transport and marine division, Department of Industry and Commerce (1941–53); worked as secretary (1949–55) and president (1971–74) of Statistical and Social Inquiry Society of Ireland; served as assistant secretary, Department of Industry and Commerce (1953–59); served as secretary, Department of Transport and Power (1959–66); awarded LL.D, University of Dublin (1960); served as member of the Council of Alexandra College (1962–86); named a member of the Public Service Organisation Review Group (Devlin Committee, 1966–69); served as first chair of the Government Commission on the Status of Women (1970–75); appointed governor of Irish Times Trust (1974); named Irish delegate to World Population Conference, Bucharest, Rumania (1974); governor of the Rotunda Hospital; president of the Irish Film Society.

Selected publications: "The Language Revivals of Finland, Norway and Wales," in JSSISI (Journal of the Statistical and Social Inquiry Society of Ireland, *vol. 14, 1929–30); "Cinema Statistics in Saorstát Eireann," in* JSSISI *(vol. 15, 1935–36); "Schemes for the Rehabilitation of Youth in Certain Countries, with Special Reference to Labour Service," in* JSSISI *(vol. 16, 1938–39); Commission on the Status of Women: Report to the Minister of Finance (Dublin 1972); "Commission on the Status of Women: Progress Report,"* Administration *(vol. 23, 1975); "International Women's Year: (1) Equality,"* Alexandra Guild Magazine *(vol. CXLIX, June 1975).*

The publication of the Report of the Commission on the Status of Women in December 1972 was a landmark for women's rights in Ireland and provided a blueprint for effective action over the next decade and beyond. As chair of the commission, Thekla Beere, who supervised the report's publication, was in her own career an inspiration and an example to Irishwomen seeking to eliminate the political, legal, social and economic barriers restricting their advancement in Irish public life.

Her father, the Reverend Francis John Armstrong Beere, was a Church of Ireland cleric who moved around the country to different parishes. Because of childhood illness, Thekla had no formal education but was taught by her mother **Lucie Beere** who had wanted to study medicine and was determined that her daughter would have the educational opportunities she missed. Thanks to her mother's teaching, by the time Thekla Beere went to Alexandra School at 15, she was well up to the academic standard. Her parents had little money, and she made her way through school and university by scholarships. When she went to Trinity College Dublin in 1919, she remained at Alexandra as a housemistress, and she retained close links with her old school for the rest of her life.

Beere was the only woman in the Trinity law school. When she graduated in 1923, despite a distinguished university career, she found it difficult to get a job as opportunities for women were limited. She was interested in public administration, and on the advice of one of her Trinity teachers she joined the Irish civil service. This was an unusual step for several reasons. Only two years had passed since Irish independence, and Trinity College was widely regarded as a pro-British bastion in Ireland and thus unsympathetic to the new Irish state; it was far more common for Trinity graduates to enter the British civil service than the Irish. Beere was also a Protestant, a member of the Church of Ireland at a time when a narrow Catholic ethos was making itself felt in many areas of Irish life. Last, but by no means least, she was a woman, and women—whatever their education and attainments—were still expected to confine themselves to marriage, family, and the home. These were formidable obstacles, but Beere's ability surmounted them. "I used to think that things could be weighted against me," she recalled, "because I was a woman, and a Protestant at that—but it just wasn't so. In fact, I got ahead a bit faster than normal."

In 1925, she was awarded a Laura Spellman Rockefeller fellowship and spent two years studying and working in institutions across America and Canada, including Columbia University, the Brookings Institute, and the University of California at Berkeley. She was also briefly involved in the campaign to reprieve Sacco and Vanzetti—an Irish colleague later noted Beere's great hatred of injustice. After her return from America, she rejoined the Statistics Branch of the Department of Industry and Commerce. The pay was meager; as a single woman, she was paid less than married men although she had a widowed mother to support. She augmented her earnings by teaching evening classes at Trinity and by writing for the Dublin Chamber of Commerce journal.

In the 1930s, Beere became a member of the Statistical and Social Inquiry Society of Ireland and published three important papers in their journal. The first, on language revival movements in Finland, Norway, and Wales, had some pertinent conclusions for the Irish government's intensive efforts to revive the Irish language. Her second paper, on the importance of the cinema in Ireland, resulted from her own love of films. Her third paper, on youth rehabilitation schemes, also reflected a personal interest: she was a founder member in 1931 of An Óige, the Irish Youth Hostel Association, and was involved with it for the rest of her life.

When the government changed in 1932 and Eamon de Valera's Fianna Fail Party took office, the Department of Industry and Commerce became the most dynamic government department under its new minister Sean Lemass. Beere had expected to be promoted to more traditional women's areas like health and social welfare, but in 1941 she was promoted to the transport and marine division of Industry and Commerce. This division was of vital importance in the middle of the Second World War, as Ireland was neutral and suffering from a critical shortage of shipping for essential imports. After the war, there were further major developments in marine policy in which Beere was closely involved. She helped to draft the 1946 Harbours Act from a complicated mass of existing statutes, the legislation for the 1948 International Convention on Safety at Sea, and the 1955 Mercantile Marine Act. There were also major developments in land transport with the 1944 Transport Act which created Coras Iompair Eireann (CIE), the national train and bus company. In 1953, Beere was appointed assistant secretary at Industry and Commerce and assumed responsibility for the department's labor division which sponsored important legislation in the 1955 Factories Act and the 1958 Offices Premises Act. She also headed the Irish delegation at meetings of the International Labour Office (ILO) at Geneva.

In 1959, when Prime Minister Lemass (Beere's former minister at Industry and Commerce) created a separate department of Transport and Power, she was appointed secretary, marking the first time such a senior government position had been held by a woman. The department was responsible for such key semi-state bodies as CIE, Irish Shipping, the Electricity Supply Board, Aer Lingus, Aer Rianta (Irish Airports Authority), Bord Failte (Tourist Board), and Bord na Mona (Turf Development Board)—organizations which were pivotal to the Irish economy. At Beere's suggestion, her minister Erskine Childers had regular meetings with the administrators of these bodies which helped to establish good relations with the department and to resolve problems when they arose. Beere was respected for her energy, toughness and independence. Dr. C.S. Andrews, chair of CIE, praised her "directness and honesty of purpose, coupled with clarity of vision. . . . [S]he had no hesitation in expressing her views, however unpalatable, to the heads of state companies and to the Minister."

> If women are to succeed in the field of their choice, they should arm themselves with the qualifications and skills to seize their new opportunities.
>
> —Thekla Beere

In 1966, Beere retired from the public service but was almost immediately appointed a member of the Public Service Organisation Review Group, or Devlin Committee as it became known. The Committee's Report in 1969 was a major, and controversial, study of Irish public-service performance. The report concluded that civil servants were too immersed in day-to-day business to formulate policy properly. It also recommended better promotion opportunities for staff, to be based on merit rather than seniority. Although these proposals met with considerable resistance within the civil service, the report had a long-term influence on its future development.

In March 1970, the Irish government appointed Beere chair of the Commission on the Status of Women. The Commission's terms of reference were "to examine and report on the status of women in Irish society, [and] to make recommendations on the steps necessary to ensure the participation of women on equal terms and conditions with men in the political, social, cultural and economic life of the country." The Commission issued an interim report on equal pay in August 1971 which recommended: implementation of equal pay, the end of gender and marriage discrimination in public-service pay scales, and the end of the marriage bar which had forced women to resign employment on marriage. These were issues about which Beere, after her long career in the Irish public service, felt strongly.

Issued in December 1972, the Commission's complete report was acclaimed for its clear, succinct proposals. In Chapter 2, the most discussed of the report, the Commission analyzed the underlying factors restricting women's participation in Irish life, chief of which were the stereotyped role assigned to women and the inculcation of attitudes in both boys and girls in their formative years that there were definite and separate roles for the sexes: "It is from this cultural mould that formal discrimination arises and it is only by the removal of such traditional attitudes that women can hope to achieve complete self-fulfillment and equal participation in all aspects of the life of the community." The Commission's recommendations covered eight areas: employment; social welfare; taxation; the law; politics and public life; education and cultural affairs; and women and the home, which included such issues as household management, family planning and marriage counselling.

During a debate in the Irish senate on the report, the Irish prime minister, Liam Cosgrave, affirmed the government's commitment to end existing discrimination against women, although the following year he voted against his own government's plans to liberalize family-planning legislation. Despite this setback, the report's recommendations were gradually implemented, and in 1975, International Women's Year, Beere wrote a progress report on what had been achieved since the report's publication.

On equal pay, the Anti-Discrimination (Pay) Act 1974 provided for full equal pay by December 31, 1975; on employment, the government was preparing legislation against sex discrimination; and the marriage bar was removed from public service employment in 1973. Provisions for maternity leave were also instituted in the public service. In social welfare, the more blatant discriminatory measures against women in pensions and benefits were removed, particularly for widows and deserted wives. In the area of law, where women suffered particular disabilities, long awaited reforms were initiated in family law and in jury service for women. In the conclusion of her progress report, Beere wrote that she was "greatly encouraged" by the change of attitudes displayed in government departments, while recognizing that in other spheres much had still to be achieved.

Beere resigned from the Commission in 1975 as she felt that a new face was needed for the next stage of its work. Such was the esteem with which she was regarded that in 1976, following the sudden resignation of the President of Ireland, Cearbhall O Dalaigh, the Commission wanted to recommend her as a candidate for the presidency. Though nothing came of this proposal, she lived to see the election of Ireland's first woman president, ***Mary Robinson**, who was also an alumna of the Trinity Law School.

In her last years, Beere remained active in her many interests. She died in February 1991. Her funeral was attended by President Mary Robinson who praised her pioneering contribution to equality issues.

SOURCES:

Andrews, C.S. *Man of No Property.* Dublin, Ireland: Mercier, 1982.

Irish Times. February 23, 1991, p. 20.

O'Rourke, Frances. "Dr. Thekla Beere: A Profile," in *Administration.* Volume 23, 1975.

M.H.S. [Honor Stuart]. "Thekla Beere," in *Alexandra College and Guild Magazine.* Vol. CLXV, December 1992.

Deirdre McMahon, Assistant Editor, *Dance Theatre Journal* (London), Dublin, Ireland

Beeton, Isabella Mary (1836–1865)

***English authority on cooking and domestic science, best known for her popular book* Household Management.** *Name variations: Mrs. Beeton. Born Isabella Mary Mayson in Cheapside, London, England, in 1836; died in England in 1865; eldest daughter of Benjamin (a soft-goods merchant) and Elizabeth Mayson; married Sam Beeton, in 1856; children: four sons, two of whom died in childhood.*

So popular were her writings on domestic science among her Victorian audience, Isabella Mary Beeton may well be considered the **Martha Stewart** of her day. Beeton was also a talented pianist and accomplished linguist. Stricken with puerperal fever—a disease contracted in childbirth before the advent of modern antiseptics—she would die two months short of her 29th birthday, at the height of her career.

Born in Cheapside, London, England, in 1836, Beeton was the eldest daughter of Benjamin and Elizabeth Mayson. Isabella grew up in an enormous family of 21, most of the children were born during her mother's second marriage to Henry Dorling, a widower who arrived with four children of his own. Although cooking was not considered a suitable pursuit for a proper Victorian young lady, Isabella could not help but occasionally find herself in the kitchen, given the size of her family. After her marriage in 1856 to publisher Sam Beeton, she began writing articles for her husband's newest undertaking, *The Englishwoman's Domestic Magazine.* Aimed at the young, middle-class Victorian woman, the new publication boasted the first "agony column," which offered advice on the pressing social problems of the day. After the loss of her first two children, one to croup at three months and another to scarlet fever at the age of three, Isabella became more involved in the magazine and found solace

Isabella Mary Beeton

in work. She tried out all of the recipes sent to the magazine and experimented with her own; she traveled to Paris for fashion plates and illustrations and consulted experts for advice on financial and health matters.

Beeton's lavishly illustrated book *Household Management* was four years in preparation. It became a reference "Bible" for homemakers, containing information, as well as recipes, on nutrition, budgeting, and every aspect of kitchen management, down to a discussion of appropriate footwear: "Do not go about slipshod. Provide yourself with good, well-fitting boots. You will find them less fatiguing in a warm kitchen than loose, untidy slippers." Eventually the *Dictionary of Cookery* was extracted from the main volume and became a bestseller.

Beeton reveled in the birth of two more sons in 1863 and 1865. After her second son was born, however, she contracted the fever that would take her life, but not before she had encouraged an entire generation of Victorian women to regard household management as an art.

SOURCES:

Blake, John. "The Remarkable Mrs. Beeton," in *This England*. Autumn 1986.

Barbara Morgan,
Melrose, Massachusetts

Beeton, Mrs. (1836–1865).

See Beeton, Isabella Mary.

Begga (d. 698).

See Gertrude of Nivelles for sidebar.

Begga of Egremont (fl. 7th c.)

Norwegian saint. *Name variations: Beggha. Born in Ireland in the 7th century.*

Daughter of a king of Ireland, Begga of Egremont was betrothed to the king of Norway, but she was determined to remain a virgin and fled on the eve of her wedding. She received the veil from St. Aidan and founded a convent at Copeland. For many centuries, Begga was venerated in northwest England as well as in Norway. Her feast day is October 31.

Beggha.

Variant of Begga.

Beggue of Austrasia (613–698).

See Gertrude of Nivelles for sidebar on Begga.

Begtrup, Bodil (b. 1903)

Delegate to the United Nations and crusader for women's rights who was Denmark's first female ambassador. *Born Bodil Gertrud Andreasen in Nyborg, Denmark, on November 12, 1903; daughter of Judge Christian A. and Carla Sigrid (Locher) Andreasen; attended secondary school in Aalborg, Jutland; graduated from University of Copenhagen, Master of Economics, 1929; married Erik Begtrup, in February 1929 (divorced 1936); married L.B. Bolt-Jorgensen, in 1948 (deceased); children: (first marriage) one child and several stepchildren.*

Served as Envoy Extraordinary and Minister Plenipotentiary, Reykjavik (1949); served as ambassador (1955); was head of department, Ministry for Foreign Affairs (1956); served as Permanent Representative of Denmark to the Council of Europe, Strasbourg (1956); served as ambassador, Berne (1959–68); served as ambassador to Lisbon (1968–December 1973); was head of the Danish delegation to the World Population Conference, Bucharest (1974).

Bodil Begtrup

Awarded honorary Doctor of Law, Smith College (1949); was a member of the Executive Committee of the National Council of Women (1929), vice-chair (1931), chair (1946–49); was a member of the joint Council of the Maternity Welfare Service (1939–59); was a member of the Danish delegation to the 19th Assembly of the League of Nations (1938); was a member of the Danish delegation to the General Assembly of the UN (1946–52); served as chair of the UN Commission on the Improvement of the Social Status of Women (1947 and 1948–49); was a member of the Council of the "Norden" Association (1956); granted Order of the Falcon of Ireland, First Class.

With a large number of artists, writers, and musicians in her family, it was assumed that Bodil Andreasen (Begtrup) would follow the same path. But the Chinese philosopher Ku Hung Ming's book on the religion of citizenship inspired her to serve her fellow Danes, especially women. "I found there was much work to be done in Denmark," she recalled, "and applied myself as earnestly and intelligently as I could." Choosing to study economics at the University of Copenhagen, she was also active in student affairs and won a scholarship for study in Geneva.

After her marriage in 1929 to Erik Begtrup, a physician, her continuing work was combined with the new responsibilities of a family of stepchildren, as well as a child of her own. As a member of the Danish National Council of Women, she became vice-chair of the board (1931) and president (1946). In 1938, Begtrup was a member of her country's delegation to the League of Nations Assembly at Geneva; a year later, she was appointed to the Council for Maternal Health as well as to the chair of the Commission for Children's Health. Also beginning in 1939, Begtrup served as one of three Danish film censors. In this capacity, she worked to ban American gangster movies and, during the war years, prevented the showing of hundreds of German movies. She later became chief Danish Film censor and was a member of the Danish Board for Cultural Films and the film committee of the International Women's Organization.

In 1946, she was a representative to the First United Nations Assembly in London. In April of that year, she traveled to the United States to attend meetings of the United Nations Subcommission on the Status of Women—a unit subordinate to the U.N. Commission on Human Rights headed by *Eleanor Roosevelt—where she was quickly elected chair.

Charged with examination of the political, civil, and economic status of women, with special regard for discrimination and limitation because of sex, the eight-women subcommission prepared a detailed document in two weeks, covering four major points: political rights; rights in the family and civil rights; rights on the labor market; and the right to education. The plan was first referred to the Commission on Human Rights, whose membership included nine men along with Eleanor Roosevelt. The document was admonished as too ambitious and, despite Begtrup's defense, the final version that went to the Economic and Social Council was cut to a few paragraphs. The Council was more generous, elevating the subcommission to commission status and praising them for "the first step they have achieved in raising their status to that of men." But it was to be a long battle, with Begtrup remarking when asked about progress on implementation of the goals, "See me in a thousand years." Her estimate was not unfounded. It would take nearly 30 years for the commission to materialize as the Conference of the International Year of the Woman, in 1975.

In the meantime, Begtrup went on to serve as Denmark's first female ambassador. Appointed in 1955, she served at the foreign office in Copenhagen (1956–59). Foreign posts included Switzerland (1959–68) and Portugal (1968–73). In 1974, she participated in the World Population Conference in Bucharest, Rumania. Modest of her many achievements, Begtrup was known to shun the honors frequently bestowed upon her throughout her long and distinguished career.

SOURCES:

Danish Journal: Women in Denmark, Ministry of Foreign Affairs of Denmark, 1980.

Rothe, Ann. *Current Biography.* NY: H.W. Wilson, 1946.

Who's Who, 1982. West Sussex, England: European Association of Directory Publishers, 1982.

Barbara Morgan,
Melrose, Massachusetts

Behn, Aphra (1640?–1689)

English Restoration dramatist and novelist, usually acclaimed as the first English woman to make her living as a writer. *Name variations: Afra, Aphara, Ayfara; (pseudonym) Astrea. Pronunciations: Ben or Ban. Possibly born in Wye, Surrey, or Canterbury, Kent, around 1640; died in 1689 and is buried in Westminster Abbey; daughter of John and Amy Johnson, or Amis; married a city merchant of Dutch background named Behn, around 1658 (widowed by 1666); no known children.*

Plays: The Forced Marriage; The Amorous Prince; The Dutch Lover; The Town Fop; Abdelazer; or, The Moor's Revenge; The Debauchée; The Rover; The Counterfeit Bridegroom; Sir Patient Fancy; The Feigned Courtesans; The Young King; The Revenge; The Second Part of the Rover; The False Count; The Roundheads; Like Father, Like Son; The City Heiress; The Lucky Chance; The Emperor of the Moon; The Widow Ranter; The Younger Brother.

Poems, novels and translations: Poems upon Several Occasions; Oroonoko, or, The Royal Slave: A True History; Love-Letters Between a Noble-Man and his Sister; *(trans.)* La Montre, or, The Lover's Watch; *(trans.)* The History of Oracles and the Cheats of the Royal Priests; *(trans.)* A Discovery of New Worlds; *(trans.)* Agnes de Castro; *(trans.)* Lycidas: Or, The Lover in Fashion; The Lucky Mistake; The Lady's Looking-Glass, to dress herself by; The Histories and Novels of the Late Ingenious Mrs. Behn: In One Volume . . . Together with The Life and Memoirs of Mrs. Behn, Histories, Novels, and Translations, written by the most ingenious Mrs. Behn; the second volume.

Aphra Behn wrote during the time of the English Restoration, the period immediately following the return of the Stuart monarchy to the throne in 1660. Restoration London was a lively place and playwriting the center of literary activity. Aphra Behn was exactly the kind of entrepreneurial young woman to have delighted in and, sometimes, profited from this new spirit of adventure in England. She had lived an exotic adolescence in the West Indies and had returned to London, at about age 18, to amuse the new king, Charles II, and his court with her wit. She married, was widowed, sent to Antwerp as a spy during the Dutch wars, then returned to London to earn her living writing for the newly restored theater.

Appropriately, perhaps, the details of Behn's birth and childhood are mysterious. She may have been born in Wye, Surrey, or Canterbury, Kent. Parish registers, her own comments later in life, and suggestive statements by her friends and acquaintances all link her birth to at least three conflicting locations. We are not even sure whether her family was well-born. Some evidence connects her to the local family of Lord Willoughby, and she seems to have been introduced at court through some upper-class connections, as Sir Thomas Killigrew, groom of the bedchamber to Charles II, evidently knew her mother. On the other hand, notations in a manuscript written by one of her younger contemporaries, ***Anne Finch**, Countess of Winchelsea (1661–1720), imply that Behn's father was a barber and that she thus was more likely to have been born into a lower class. Generally—given the extent of Behn's evident education and her social sophistication, neither of which could have been easily acquired by a young woman from the lower classes in late 17th-century England—scholars have concluded that Behn's family must have been from the upper-middle class and fairly well off.

What *is* known is that sometime during Behn's adolescence, her father was appointed to the post of lieutenant-general of Surinam in the British West Indies, and the family left England, traveling with him to this exotic and decidedly non-British post. Behn's father died at sea, but the family settled in Surinam, in what Behn later described as the best house in the colony, a residence called "St. John's Hill." The young Aphra seems to have delighted in the tropical life she encountered there. Years later, she wrote a novel, *Oroonoko*, about it, describing with evident pleasure the animals of that colony. There were "marmosets," she recalled, "a sort of monkey . . . of a marvellous and delicate shape . . . [with] face and hands like a human creature; and cousheries, a little beast in the form and fashion of a lion, as big as a kitten . . . little parakeats, great parrots, macaws, and a thousand other birds and beasts of surprising forms, shapes and colours."

In Surinam, Behn began writing verse, read historical romances of the kind she would later write herself, and perhaps even composed her first play. She traveled the area, fell in love, kept a journal, and made the acquaintance of slavery. This last seems to have had the greatest effect on her. (The subtitle of *Oroonoko* is *The Royal Slave.*) Her observations on slavery are acute. In her later writings, she records in great detail the operations of the slave trade, noting in particular its most immoral practices, always in ironic juxtaposition with the professed teachings of the Christian tradition. In reference to Surinam, she notes sarcastically that the English colonists did not enslave the local Indian inhabitants, preferring to import Africans as slaves, because the English both feared the Indians, who vastly outnumbered them, and depended on them for their agricultural and hunting skills and for supplies for trading. As one scholar, **Angeline Goreau**, points out, Behn was insightful for her period in seeing slavery as purely a matter of power, rather than as an example of the "natural" superiority of one race over another.

The details of Behn's return to London are not clear. Perhaps her mother simply decided to go back; perhaps the family's return had something to do with the English resignation of Surinam to the Dutch. In either case, Behn apparently married shortly after returning to London but was evidently widowed quite early, as her husband's name does not appear in subsequent records of her life. Tradition has it that he was a Dutch merchant, possibly because state correspondence of 1666 shows that Aphra Behn acted as a spy in Antwerp during the Second Dutch War.

The extraordinary nature of Behn's employment in the context of spying should be stressed. "Public employments in the field and court are usually denied to women," wrote **Bathsua Makin**, one of Behn's female contemporaries. And indeed, there were no other women employed in any capacity (other than as servants) at the court of Charles II. Behn herself noted this episode in her life as "unusual" in one of her later poems:

> By the . . . King's Commands
> I left these Shades, to visit Foreign Lands;
> Employed in public toils of State Affairs,
> Unusual with my Sex, or to my Years.

We do not know what she actually did in Antwerp, but we do have records of her correspondence with English government officials indicating that not only was she not paid what was owed her for her services, but the ingratitude was compounded when that same government briefly imprisoned her for debt on her return.

It may be that it was the need to support herself that drove Behn to the writing of plays. The London stage was more receptive to women than it had ever been; for example, actresses rather than young boys were at last being permitted to play the female roles. Moreover, much of London's social life revolved around the theater, which had been closed during the years of republican rule; thus, its reopening, in 1660 with the Stuart restoration, had been a long-anticipated event. The audience had changed considerably since the early 1600s when plays had last been performed, and the new audience wanted variety, wit, social satire, and material more contemporary in characters and setting than Shakespeare and his fellow dramatists had supplied for the earlier era. New plays followed each other in quick succession, and playwrights were encouraged by the success of innovation to try their hands at comedy, tragedy, satire, whatever would sell. Initial runs were short, and there were only two theaters regularly producing plays; thus new plays were much in demand. It was the perfect moment for an innovative, industrious, and resourceful writer, and Aphra Behn was apparently just that kind of playwright.

Makin, Bathsua (1608–1675)

***English educator.** Name variations: Basua. Born Bathsua Pell around 1608; died around 1675; daughter of a Sussex rector; sister of John Pell (1610–1685), an eminent mathematician.*

Bathsua Makin was a tutor for the daughters of Charles I, including ***Elizabeth Stuart** (1635–1650), instructing them in Greek, Latin, Hebrew, French, Italian, and Spanish; she also taught them mathematics. After the death of Elizabeth in 1650, Makin returned to the private sector as governess until she established a school of her own in London. In 1646, she met and became a friend of ***Anna Maria van Schurmann**, and the two kept up a lively correspondence. Blending her ideas and that of Schurmann's, Makin published an anonymous polemic, in 1673, entitled, *An Essay to Revive the Antient Education of Gentlewomen in Religion, Manners, Arts and Tongues*. The opening preface disingenuously begins with "I am a man myself, that would not suggest anything prejudicial to our sex," then goes on to show that if women's education were improved, men would reap the benefits.

SOURCES:

Goreau, Angeline. *The Whole Duty of a Woman: Female Writers in Seventeenth-Century England*. NY: Dial Press, 1984.

According to her contemporaries, Behn seems to have written quickly and easily. "Her muse was never subject to bringing forth with pain, for she always writ with the greatest ease in the world, and that in the midst of company, and discourse of other matters," wrote one of her friends (and later literary executor), Charles Gildon. She probably gained entrance to the theater through either Killigrew, who had established one of the theaters, or through other well-connected friends, most likely the Howard family, whom she had known from childhood.

In either case, she learned her craft quickly. Her first recorded performance was the play *The Forced Marriage; or, the Jealous Bridegroom* (in 1670), which ran for six nights, a good run for that time and especially for a first play. Its popularity must have been particularly welcome for Behn; at this time, a playwright's royalties were the receipts of the box office for the third day's performance. Restoration audiences were notorious for their short attention spans and their demanding requirements for entertainment. Frequently plays did not reach that third-day performance, and thus their authors went unpaid.

Although Behn's plays as a whole seem to have been successful in supplying an adequate income for their author, it is also clear from her earliest plays that Behn had interests other than income. In the "Epistle to the Reader" from her third play, *The Dutch Lover*, Behn directly confronts what must have been one topic of gossip of the day, the writing of plays by women. Setting aside lesser, and to her mind possibly marginal, arguments against women writers, Behn goes directly to the point: plays are not the place for the narrow "learning" of men, what today we would call pedantry: "Waving the examination why women having equal education with men, were not as capable of knowledge, of whatsoever sort as well as they: I'll only say as I have touched before, that plays have no great room for that which is men's great advantage over women, that is learning," she asserts. She then goes on to prove her point: "We all well know that the immortal Shakespeare's plays . . . have better pleased the world than Jonson's works . . . and for our modern [dramatists] . . . I dare to say I know of none that write at such a formidable rate, but that a woman may hope to reach their greatest heights." Plays, she thus vigorously asserted, were for entertainment, not scholarly quibbling over "musty rules," and as such were as "intelligible and as practible by a

Aphra Behn

woman." Behn thus quickly gained a reputation for such vigor and directness and almost immediately became a member of the group of dramatists and critics who were to dominate the London stage during these years.

Behn was also, evidently, a threatening competitor and thus attracted her share of satirical attacks, most of which used references to her sex as part of the satire. Yet she also formed some secure and influential friendships. The Earl of Rochester, the leading actress ***Elizabeth Barry**, the writers John Dryden, Thomas Otway, and Edward Ravenscroft were all supporters throughout her life. Moreover, the fact that she regularly contributed verses or commentary to collections appended to the writings of others also suggests that she was very much at the center of the production of and discussion about Restoration drama.

During these years, she also had a rather unhappy love affair with a cold, bisexual lawyer named John Hoyle. This certainly seems out of keeping with the recorded character and personality of Aphra Behn. According to the memoir (by an allegedly intimate friend) that was appended to the 1696 collection of her *Histories and Novels*, Behn was:

> of a generous and open temper, something passionate, very serviceable to her friends in all that was in her power, and could sooner forgive an injury than do one. She had wit, honor, good humor, and judgment. She was a mistress of all the pleasing arts of conversation, but used 'em not to any but those who loved . . . plain dealing. She was a woman of sense, and by consequence a lover of pleasure.

Nevertheless, the attachment to Hoyle continued almost to the end of her life, and he is alleged to have been the author of the verses on her tombstone in Westminster Abbey.

The rest of Behn's life was spent writing for the theater. Her play *The Rover; or, The Banish't Cavaliers* was her most popular, both in her lifetime and subsequently, and she wrote a sequel to it late in her career. At some point, she also began writing novels and doing translations of French romances into English. Her most popular novel, *Oroonoko*, depends on those early years in Surinam. As the first treatment of black slavery in English literature, it has remained in print to the present day.

Not only did Behn achieve success as an author, she did it without apologizing for, or, at the other extreme, trading on her oddity as a woman writer. Throughout her life, she met criticism head on. Nine of her plays call attention to her sex, and three have what we might describe as feminist prefaces. As **Katharine Rogers**, one of her modern biographers, notes: not the least of Behn's contributions to literary history is the fact that she successfully demonstrated that a woman could indeed succeed as an author.

> I value Fame as much as if I had been born a Hero.
>
> **—Aphra Behn, Preface to "The Lucky Chance"**

Nevertheless, Aphra Behn did die in poverty. Her impoverished circumstances, however, were more a consequence of the demise of the theater than of a lessening in her talent and determination. In 1685, when Charles II died, the theater was operating in severely reduced circumstances, and many of Behn's friends had either died or were suffering financial reversals similar to hers. Indeed, at the end of her own life, Behn borrowed money, a debt which she could ill afford, to help a dying friend. If she died in poverty, however, she did not die in obscurity. Burial in Westminster Abbey has traditionally been the highest tribute that England pays to her literary figures. Aphra Behn lies in the Abbey, near to the greatest of her male contemporaries, John Dryden.

SOURCES:

Behn, Aphra. *Oroonoko, The Rover and Other Works.* Edited by Janet Todd. London: Penguin Books, 1992.

Cameron, William J. *New Light on Aphra Behn.* Auckland, NZ: University of Auckland Press, 1961.

Gildon, Charles. "An Account of the Life of the Incomparable Mrs. Behn." Prefixed to *The Younger Brother.* London: Printed for J. Harris & Sold by R. Baldwin, 1696.

Goreau, Angeline. *Reconstructing Aphra: A Social Biography of Aphra Behn.* NY: Dial Press, 1980.

Hutner, Heidi, ed. *Rereading Aphra Behn: History, Theory, and Criticism.* Charlottesville: University Press of Virginia, 1993.

"The Life and Memoirs of Mrs. Behn, written by One of the Fair Sex." Prefixed to *The Histories and Novels of the Late Ingenious Mrs. Behn: In One Volume . . .* London: Printed for S. Briscoe, 1696.

Rogers, Katharine. "Aphra Behn," in *Dictionary of Literary Biography 80: British Dramatists, 1660–1800.* NY: Bruccoli, Clark, Layman, 1993.

Woodcock, George. *The Incomparable Aphra.* London: Bordman, 1948.

SUGGESTED READING:

Brown, Laura. "The Romance of Empire: Oroonoko and the Trade in Slaves," in *The New Eighteenth Century.* Edited by Felicity Nussbaum and Laura Brown. NY: Methuen, 1987.

Cotton, Nancy. *Women Playwrights in England, c. 1363–1750.* Lewisburg: Bucknell University Press, 1980.

Duffy, Maureen. *The Passionate Shepherdess: Aphra Behn.* London: Cape, 1977.

Gosse, Edmund. "Behn, Afra, Aphra, Aphara, or Ayfara," in *Dictionary of National Biography.* London, 1885.

Mendelson, Sara Heller. *The Mental World of Stuart Women: Three Studies.* Brighton: Harvester, 1987.

O'Donnell, Mary Ann. *Aphra Behn: An Annotated Bibliography of Primary and Secondary Sources.* NY: Garland, 1986.

Pearson, Jacqueline. *The Prostituted Muse: Images of Women and Women Dramatists, 1642–1737.* London: Harvester, 1988.

Spencer, Jane. *The Rise of the Woman Novelist: From Aphra Behn to Jane Austen.* Oxford: Blackwell, 1986.

Todd, Janet. *The Sign of Angellica: Women, Writing and Fiction 1660–1800.* London: Virago, 1989.

———. *The Secret Life of Aphra Behn.* New Brunswick, NJ: Rutgers University Press, 1998.

———, ed. *The Collected Works of Aphra Behn.* 7 vols. Columbus, OH: Ohio State University, 1992–96.

COLLECTIONS:

Summers, Montague, ed. *The Works of Aphra Behn.* 6 vols. London, 1915.

Todd, Janet, ed. *The Complete Works of Aphra Behn.* Vol. 1. Columbus: Ohio State University Press, 1992.

Ann Hurley, Assistant Professor, Skidmore College, Saratoga Springs, New York

Behrens, Hildegard (1937—)

German soprano. *Born in Oldenburg, Germany, on February 9, 1937; law degree from the University of Freiburg; studied voice with* ***Ines Leuwen*** *at the Freiburg Music Academy.*

Debuted in Freiburg (1971) as the Countess in Le nozze di Figaro; *appeared at the Deutsche Oper am Rhein in Düsseldorf; performed several roles in Berg's* Wozzeck; *debuted at Covent Garden and the Metropolitan Opera (1976); appeared as Salome in Salzburg (1977); sang Brünnhilde at Bayreuth (1983).*

A Wagnerian soprano, Hildegard Behrens earned this title in 1977 when she performed as Salome in Salzburg under the direction of Herbert von Karajan. However, she also appeared in such non-Wagnerian roles as Elektra in Mozart's *Idomeneo*, Elena in Janácek's *The Makropoulous Case*, and the Empress in Richard Strauss' *Die Frau ohne Schatten.* An intelligent singer with a law degree from the University of Freiburg, Behrens carefully researched all her characters, and her acting abilities were said to be as great as her singing talent. Her top notes distinguished her voice which was powerful and stunning, but with the passage of time parts of her voice showed the effects of the inevitable strain of performing large roles. Though an excellent actress, Behrens sometimes lacked stamina, causing audiences to fear she might run out of voice. She made numerous recordings and will be particularly remembered for her performances as Salome and Elektra.

John Haag, Athens, Georgia

Beinhorn, Elly (1907—)

German aviator and author who is known as "Germany's Amelia Earhart." *Name variations: Elly Beinhorn-Rosemeyer. Born Elly Beinhorn on May 30, 1907, in Hanover, Germany; married Bernd Rosemeyer (a racing driver), in 1936 (died in a racing accident in 1938).*

Made a number of dramatic flights, including one to Africa (1931), a Round-the-World Flight (1931–32), for which she was awarded the Hindenburg Cup, a Round-Africa Flight (1933), and a Western Hemisphere Flight (1934–35); as a prolific author, published a number of articles and books; was one of the few women in Nazi Germany to have a widely reported career.

Selected writings: "Der Flug in das Paradies" in Rhein-Mainsche Wirtschaftszeitung *(March 18, 1932); "Weltflug und Zukunftspläne," in* General-Anzeiger, Stettin *(July 30, 1932); "Meine kulturellen Aufgaben" in* Deutsche Zeitung *(April 23, 1933); "Südwest von deutschem Geist erfüllt," in* Der Tag *(Berlin, June 25, 1933); "Warum ich fliege," in* Der Tag *(Berlin, April 6, 1933);* 180 Studen über Afrika *(Berlin: Scherl Verlag, 1933);* Flying Girl *(introduction by Richard Halliburton, translated by Winifred Ray, NY: Henry Holt, 1935);* Grünspecht wird ein Flieger: Werdegang eines Flugschülers *(Leipzig: Breitkopf & Härtel, 1935);* Mein Mann, der Rennfahrer: Der Lebensweg Bernd Rosemeyers *(Berlin: Deutscher Verlag, 1938);* 180 Studen über Afrika: Mein Flug zu den Deutschen in unseren ehemaligen Kolonien *(Dresden: Neuer Buchverlag, 1937 [*Deutsche in aller Welt, *3]);* Ich fliege um die Welt *(Berlin: Ullstein Verlag, 1952);* So waren diese Flieger *(Herford: Koehler Verlag, 1966).*

The years 1927 to 1935 were a time of extraordinary activity in aviation, and women played a significant role during this period in pushing forward the frontiers of air travel. Although American, British, and French pilots tended to dominate the scene and steal newspaper headlines, women of other nationalities also played active roles in the often dangerous world of pioneer aviation. One of the boldest flyers in this lesser-known group was German aviator Elly

Beinhorn. Born in the city of Hanover on May 30, 1907, Beinhorn exhibited an interest in travel and adventure from an early age. After several years of practice in gliders and training planes, by 1930 she secured sufficient financial backing to organize her first major flight. Part of a scientific expedition, this trip began in Berlin in 1931, during the cold and gloomy month of January. Beinhorn's flight received widespread coverage in the German press. At a time when rapidly growing unemployment and the explosive expansion of the Nazi Party had brought many average Germans to the edge of despair, the story of a courageous Elly Beinhorn brought a note of optimism. To many Germans, Elly Beinhorn was their beleaguered nation's Amelia Earhart.

With thousands of miles of desolate terrain to provide few opportunities for surviving an emergency landing, Beinhorn's Africa expedition had the near-legendary city of Timbuktoo as its destination. She reached the city with relatively few problems and returned to Berlin in April 1931, now a veritable national heroine. The American explorer Richard Halliburton, whom she would meet on a later flight, described Beinhorn as "the most celebrated, the most admired, and the most beloved young woman in Germany." Immediately after her return, Beinhorn began to plan for a Round-the-World Flight, which began in December 1931. Once again her luck held, and she completed the flight pretty much according to schedule, flying through the Balkans and Asia Minor, across the Indian subcontinent, stopping to visit Mt. Everest, and then on to Australia. Arriving by ship in Balboa, the Panama Canal Zone, she resumed her epic flight with a grand tour of South America. In June 1932, Beinhorn was awarded the Aviation Cross of Peru in a ceremony in Lima. A little over a week later, she successfully flew over the Andes from Santiago, Chile, to Mendoza, Argentina. On her return to Germany, she was enthusiastically greeted by both press and public.

Beinhorn's next adventure in the air took her to Africa in 1933, the year Adolf Hitler and his Nazi movement seized power in Germany. More than ever before, the German press reported her exploits with almost daily updates on a trip that eventually covered 28,000 kilometers (17,402 miles). Beinhorn, whose own political sympathies were dyed-in-the-wool conservative and nationalistic, had little difficulty accepting the new mood of German manifest destiny evident in the statements of the National Socialist regime. After returning from her second African trip in the summer of 1933, a number of articles written by her appeared in *Der Tag* and other Rightist newspapers sympathetic to the new Hitler government. Among the subjects she treated in her journalism was a favorite theme of German nationalists, namely the survival of the "German spirit" in former colonies like southwest Africa (now Namibia), a fact that presumably strengthened Berlin's continuing demands for a return of these territories.

Despite occasional journalistic work on political themes, Beinhorn remained primarily a courageous aviator. She departed on her last major trip in 1934, a tour of the United States and Latin America. Although her flying skills were as impressive as ever, on this occasion local enthusiasm had waned markedly, in part because some perceived her to be a symbol of the new dictatorial regime in Germany.

Her flying career essentially over, she updated her memoirs (first published in 1932), which had gone through eight printings in Germany by 1939 (her memoirs appeared in English-language editions in London and New York in 1935). In 1935, she published a book for children, *Grünspecht wird ein Flieger*, which tells of the adventures of an apprentice aviator. In 1936, she married the race-car driver Bernd Rosemeyer, who was to die in a racing accident two years later. Beinhorn celebrated his short, adventurous life in a best-selling biography that appeared in the year of his death. Like ***Leni Riefenstahl** and ***Margret Boveri**, Elly Beinhorn was among the few women to have a significant career in Nazi Germany. This is likely due in part to the fact that her career began before 1933 and to the emphasis placed on Germany's resuming a leading role in world aviation by the Nazis. In this light, it is not surprising that Beinhorn's account of her 1933 trip to Africa was published in 1939 as a book assigned to soldiers for their recreational reading. Surviving the 1945 bombing of Germany, Beinhorn went on to write more books and to serve as a link with a more innocent and hopeful Germany, one that had already been essentially destroyed by the time she ended her flying career in the mid-1930s.

SOURCES:

Beinhorn-Rosemeyer, Elly. *Berlin—Kapstadt—Berlin. Meine 28,000-km-Flug nach Afrika.* Berlin: Siegismund Verlag, 1939 [*Deutsche Soldatenbücherei*, C/1].

May, Charles Paul. *Women in Aeronautics.* NY: Nelson, 1962.

John Haag, Associate Professor, University of Georgia, Athens, Georgia

Bejarano, Esther (1924—)

German-Jewish Holocaust survivor, who built a successful career as a singer of folk and political songs after World War II. *Born Esther Loewy (or Löwy) in Saarlouis, Saar Territory (then French-controlled Germany), on December 15, 1924; daughter of Rudolf and Margarethe Loewy; sister of* ***Ruth Loewy****, who was killed by German security forces after being expelled from Switzerland; married Nissim Bejarano.*

Born in Saarlouis, Saar Territory, on December 15, 1924, Esther Loewy grew up in materially modest but emotionally secure circumstances. Her father Rudolf Loewy taught at the school maintained by the local Jewish community. By early 1935, when the French-administered Saar Territory was returned to Germany as a result of a plebiscite administered by the League of Nations, it was clear that the future of the Loewy family was in question. By the end of 1935, the Nuremberg Laws had turned them into second-class citizens stripped of virtually all civil liberties. In November 1938, the local synagogue was destroyed, the sisters could no longer go to school, and the family was placed at the mercy of the local Nazi storm troopers.

The indignities continued, including the obligatory wearing of the Star of David on articles of clothing (September 1941), and culminated in the deportation of her parents to the Kaiserwald concentration camp near Riga, where they were killed. Her sister Ruth was able to find temporary safety in Switzerland, but Swiss immigration police eventually deported her back to Germany, where she was shot at the border. Esther was sent to Auschwitz on April 20, 1943, the 54th birthday of Adolf Hitler. In Auschwitz, with a background in music, Esther was assigned to play the accordion in the orchestra of the women's camp. Conducted by Viennese-born ***Alma Rosé**, the orchestra quite literally played for its life. As long as the camp's commandants were pleased with their musical renditions, the orchestra members could avoid the gas chambers, which were visible from Esther's barracks. The camp was liberated by Soviet soldiers in January 1945. Surrounded by her liberators and fellow prisoners, Esther played her accordion while a picture of Adolf Hitler was consumed on a bonfire.

Unable to continue living in the country that had destroyed her family, Esther emigrated to Israel, where she married Nissim Bejarano and attempted to create a new life. This was only partially successful. After more than two decades in Israel, she and Nissim decided to confront their past and return to Germany. Esther Bejarano did not find it easy to become part of German life. Germany had few Jews, and many Germans of the older generation, even if they were not Nazi sympathizers, simply wanted to forget the past and enjoy their new, hard-won prosperity. During the first years after her return, she had nightmares of black boots kicking her; she would awaken with a scream and a piercing headache would remain after the recollection of terror.

Supported by her husband and encouraged by both her German and Jewish friends, Bejarano fought the demons of her past with music. Having saved her life during her years in Auschwitz, music was now the balm for her soul. She became an acclaimed performer at music festivals dedicated to German-Jewish reconciliation. At these festivals, she met and performed with musical stars like Harry Belafonte, ***Miriam Makeba** and **Maria Farandouri** whose strongly felt political views paralleled her own. One of her close artistic collaborators, Günther Schwarberg, also became a close personal friend. Ironically, during the years Bejarano and her family had been persecuted by the Nazis, Schwarberg was a young man serving in Hitler's armed forces. Schwarberg and other of her German friends would always be deeply moved when she sang the song of the doomed Vilna Ghetto partisans of World War II, *Zog nit keynmol az du geyst dem letstn veg* ("Oh, never say that you have reached the very end").

Bejarano remained active in the Auschwitz Committee which she had helped found and considered it her duty to speak about her Holocaust experiences in public, particularly to a new generation of German schoolchildren. As painful as it often was, in the mid-1990s Esther Bejarano not only continued to perform but also to speak out against the growing threat of neo-Nazism and racism in a united Germany.

SOURCES:

Schwarberg, Günther. "Mir lebn ejbig: Zum 70. Geburtstag der jüdischen Sängerin Esther Bejarano," *Neues Deutschland.* December 15, 1994, p. 12.

John Haag, Associate Professor, University of Georgia, Athens, Georgia

Bejart, Geneviève (c. 1622–1775).

See Bejart, Madeleine and Armande for sidebar.

Bejart, Madeleine and Armande

French actresses, belonging to a 17th-century theatrical family, who originated roles in the plays of Molière.

Bejart, Madeleine (1618–1672). Name variations: Béjart. Born Madeleine Bejart in 1618; died on February 17, 1672; daughter of Joseph (an official in the Chief Bureau of Forests and Waterways) and Marie (Hervé) Bejart.

Bejart, Armande (c. 1642–1700). *Name variations: Mlle Menou, "Miss Puss." Born Armande Grésinde Claire Elizabeth Bejart in 1642 or 1643; died in 1700; possibly daughter of Madeleine Bejart and the Count of Modène; married Molière (the dramatist), in 1662 (died 1673); married Isaac-François Guérin d'Estriché (an actor), in 1677; children: (with Molière) daughter Ésprit-Madeleine (b. 1666), and two sons (both of whom died in infancy).*

The Bejart family, including Madeleine, Armande, Joseph, Louis, and **Geneviève**, all acted in the plays of Molière (pseudonym of Jean Baptiste Poqueline) and were members of his troupe, performing in Paris and in the provinces.

Madeleine Bejart headed up a traveling company, which included her siblings Geneviève, Joseph, and Louis, before meeting Molière and forming the Illustre Théâtre in June 1643. By some accounts, it was Molière's love for Madeleine that inspired him to become involved in the theatre. Securing for herself contract rights to select the roles she wished to play, Madeleine acted in the troupe and also managed its finances until her death in 1672. Her most famous roles, some of which were created especially for her by Molière, were Marotte in *The Affected Young Ladies* (1659), Lisette in *The School for Husbands* (1661), and Dorine in *Tartuffe* (1664).

Some sources claim that Armande was the sister and not the daughter of Madeleine Béjart, though the reported dates of birth do not bear this out. Armande may have been Madeleine's child with the aristocratic Count of Modène, but it was also scandalously rumored that Molière was Armande's father. Molière married Armande when she was 19 and he was 40. Theirs was reportedly an unhappy union; it is said that Molière was passionately jealous while Armande was a great flirt. Their first son, born in 1664, did not live. After the birth of a daughter in 1666, the pair separated only to see each other at performances until their reconciliation in 1671. A second son, born in 1672, also did not survive. Said to be a charming actress and the best interpreter of Molière's plays, Armande was at her finest as Celimène in *Le Misanthrope* and was deemed outstanding as Angélique in *The Imaginary Invalid.*

Bejart, Geneviève (c. 1622–1775)

French actress. *Name variations: Geneviève Hervé. Born around 1622; died in 1775; daughter of Joseph (an official in the Chief Bureau of Forests and Waterways) and Marie (Hervé) Bejart. Geneviève performed under her mother's maiden name of Hervé.*

After Molière's death, Armande merged the troupe with the failing Theatre du Marais, to form the Troupe du Roi. The new group floundered somewhat until 1679, when it absorbed the company of the Hotel de Bourgogne, in Paris, securing at the same time the services of the great tragedienne ***Marie Champmeslé**. The combined troupe became the renowned Comédie Française. Armande married the actor Isaac-François Guérin d'Estriché in 1677. In 1694, she retired from the stage, six years before her death.

SOURCES:

Bulgakov, Mikhail. *The Life of Monsieur de Molière.* Translated from the Russian by Mirra Ginsburg. NY: Funk & Wagnalls, 1970.

Mander, Gertrud. *Molière.* NY: Frederick Ungar, 1973.

Walker, Hallan. *Molière.* Boston, MA: Twayne, 1971.

Barbara Morgan, Melrose, Massachusetts

Bekker, Elizabeth (1738–1804).

See Deken, Aagje for sidebar.

Beland, Lucy (1871–1941)

American drug peddler. *Name variations: Mrs. Lucy Beland; Ma Beland. Born in Texas in 1871; died in Texas in 1941; married J.H. Beland (deceased); children: six.*

With a *modus operandi* paralleling the notorious ***Ma Barker**, Lucy Beland used her children to commit crimes, turning them into drug addicts and prostitutes in an illegal drug wholesaling operation that peaked in the late 1930s. Beland's early married life in Grandview, Texas, reportedly gave no indication of what was to come. In 1908, she convinced her husband, an engineer for a cotton-oil mill, to move to Fort Worth. In order to acquire more of the good things in life she was determined to have, she then emptied the couple's bank account. After her husband left her, she moved to Fort Worth's red-light district, sent her daughters out on the streets, and began dealing in heroine and morphine, instructing her sons to peddle drugs throughout Texas.

Beland became the major wholesaler of illegal drugs in the Southwest. She grew rich and powerful, especially after the passage of the Harrison Narcotics Act of 1914, when drugs became scarce. Although she bribed Texas officials to overlook her operations, the Federal Bureau of Narcotics kept her under close scrutiny. Four of her children became addicts. In 1931, her daughter Willie was caught and jailed; her son Charlie met the same fate in 1935. One daughter eventually died of an overdose which had been smuggled into her prison cell by her mother. In 1937, Beland was trapped while making a drug deal with an undercover agent. Because of her advanced age, she was given only a two-year sentence. Beland died in 1941, two years after her release.

Barbara Morgan, Melrose, Massachusetts

Belestiche or Belistiche (fl. 268–264 BCE).

See Bilistiche.

Belfrage, Sally (1936–1994)

American journalist and memoirist whose first book,* A Room in Moscow, *brought her instant fame. *Born Sally Mary Caroline Belfrage in Hollywood, California, on October 4, 1936; died in London on March 14, 1994; daughter of Cedric Belfrage and Molly Castle; studied in New York City and at the London School of Economics; married Bernard Pomerance, in 1965; children: Eve and Moby.*

Selected writings: A Room in Moscow *(London: André Deutsch, 1958);* Flowers of Emptiness: Reflections on an Ashram *(NY: Dial Press, 1981);* Living With War: A Belfast Year *(NY: Viking Press, 1987);* Freedom Summer *(with a Foreword by Robert P. Moses, Charlottesville: University Press of Virginia, 1990);* Un-American Activities: A Memoir of the Fifties *(NY: HarperCollins, 1994).*

Sally Belfrage was born in Hollywood, California, on March 14, 1936, to British parents who were distinctly un-American in their attitudes. Her father Cedric was born into a well-to-do physician's family; sent to Cambridge University, he arrived there along with his manservant and a "meager" allowance of two pounds a week. By the time Sally was born, both of her parents had established themselves as successful journalists. Cedric Belfrage's transformation into an intellectual iconoclast was well underway, and by the 1940s he was proudly calling himself an "independent radical." In 1948, he founded a spirited left-wing journal, *The National Guardian.* Sally's mother **Molly Castle**, who was less interested in politics, was known to have more than her quota of British eccentricities. Largely because of her father's leftist politics, Sally felt herself an outsider while growing up in California and New York City, where she attended the Bronx High School of Science and Hunter College. Above all else, she wanted to be accepted as an "All American Girl," a difficult task given her family's politics. Her Jewish fiancé's mother was fiercely determined to protect her son from the dire threat of "a *shiksa* Red spy's daughter," and broke up his relationship with Belfrage.

The most traumatic event of these years for Belfrage was her father's 1955 departure from the United States after ***Elizabeth Bentley** accused him of having been involved in Communist espionage. Belfrage went to England with her father and enrolled at the London School of Economics. Encouraged by her father and intrigued in her own right, she traveled to Moscow in 1957 as a member of the United States delegation to the World Youth Festival. Defying a Washington ban on travel to the People's Republic of China, Belfrage also traveled there to see for herself what the McCarthyites believed she should not examine firsthand. On her return from Peking to Moscow, she decided to remain in Moscow for five months and took a job at the Foreign Languages Publishing House. There, she rented a room of her own—a unique achievement for a foreigner, let alone a Soviet citizen—and met the British spy Donald Maclean.

The book Belfrage wrote about her experiences in the Soviet Union, *A Room in Moscow*, became a worldwide bestseller. The reviewer for the respected *Manchester Guardian* praised it as "a unique, outrageous, lively and intelligent account of a winter in Moscow spent among a group of Muscovite bohemians." The American celebrity machine, then still in its infancy, took a fancy to the spunky young woman barely out of her teens. Mike Wallace interviewed her for network television, ***Dorothy Parker** gave a party in her honor, and ***Eleanor Roosevelt** graciously chatted with her. Theodore White gave her book his blessing, calling it "a gem of perceptive reporting."

Following Eleanor Roosevelt's suggestion that she go to the Middle East to gather material for another book, Belfrage spent a year in Egypt, Israel, Jordan and Syria. Her notebooks filled up, and she contracted a sham marriage with Sari Nashashibi, the son of a distinguished Palestinian family, in order to help him acquire American citizenship. But her time spent in the region never led to a book, as Belfrage decided she was too emotionally conflicted to achieve any reportorial distance on the Middle East's countless conflicts. After her return to the United States, the FBI decided that she was a chip off the Belfrage block. Regarding her as a potential "security risk," the agency began to assemble a file on Belfrage that over two decades grew to several hundreds of pages.

The rise of the civil-rights movement in the American South contained the elements of extreme conflict and basic human questions that attracted Belfrage as both a reporter and private citizen. She spent the summer of 1963 in Mississippi as a volunteer with Stokely Carmichael's voter registration campaign. Despite the considerable risks involved, she probed every aspect of the racism that had distorted the lives of both blacks and whites in the Deep South since the end of the Civil War. The result of her stay was the book *Freedom Summer*, which received high critical praise upon publication. Writing in the *New York Review of Books*, noted Southern writer Walker Percy described the work as "a low-keyed and all the more effective treatment of the gritty routine of running a Freedom library, of the Negroes, the daily procession of small harassments, the obscene phone calls, the cars that try to run you down in the street, and finally the registration drive and a week-end in the Greenwood jail." The book has become a classic and was reprinted in 1990.

Belfrage married writer Bernard Pomerance in 1965 and became mother to a son and a daughter. The family moved to London, Pomerance achieved success with his play *The Elephant Man*, but the marriage broke down. She began the 1980s immersing herself in the ways of the followers of Guru Bhagwan Shree Rajneesh, joining two of her friends at his ashram in Poona, India. The insightful and often extremely humorous book that resulted was the 1981 volume *Flowers of Emptiness*. The review in *Newsweek* described the book as "an utterly absorbing odyssey."

Much more serious was her investigation of the violence in Northern Ireland. Belfrage spent many months interviewing participants in the sectarian hatreds of the poverty-stricken neighborhoods of Belfast; eventually, she reached the sad conclusion that it would prove difficult to end the conflict because many individuals and groups had vested interests in keeping intact the existing system of injustice and violence. When her book appeared in print in 1987 as *Living With War: A Belfast Year* (British title, *The Crack*), many reviewers declared it one of the best studies yet of the tragic conflict in Ulster.

Belfrage had friends and admirers all over the world and was known for her courage, sense of humor, and lack of snobbery. An active participant in the women's movement in the United Kingdom, she was one of a group of close friends who supported ***Jill Tweedie** during her final illness. Days after Tweedie's death in December 1993, Belfrage learned that she had terminal cancer. By this time, she had completed the manuscript of her last book, the autobiographical *Un-American Activities: A Memoir of the Fifties*. Sally Belfrage spent the last weeks of her life going over the galley proofs of what **Nora Sayre** called her "fascinating and irresistible" memoir of life in the conformist years of the Cold War and Senator Joseph McCarthy. The reviews of *Un-American Activities* were enthusiastic, with Victor Navasky leading the pack: "Sally Belfrage's beautiful memoir is heartrending, hilarious, and as roller-coasterish as the decade she has forever captured." It was a review Belfrage did not live to see. She died in London on March 14, 1994. Many years before, her friend Orson Welles affectionately captured her essence, calling Belfrage "a good old-fashioned international nuisance."

SOURCES:

Fowler, Glenn. "Cedric Belfrage, 85, Target of Communist Inquiry," in *The New York Times Biographical Service*. June 1990, p. 596.

Pace, Eric. "Sally Belfrage Dies; Writer Specializing in Memoirs Was 57," in *The New York Times Biographical Service*. March 1994, p. 396.

"Sally Belfrage," in *The Times* [London]. March 16, 1994, p. 21.

John Haag, Associate Professor, University of Georgia, Athens, Georgia

Bel Geddes, Barbara (1922—)

***American actress, who originated the part of Maggie the Cat in Tennessee Williams'* Cat on a Hot Tin Roof.**

Born in New York City on October 31, 1922; daughter of Norman Bel Geddes (a stage designer, producer, and theater architect) and Helen Belle (Sneider) Bel Geddes; graduated from Buxton Country School, Putney School, and Andebrook School in Tarrytown, New York; married Carl Schreuer (an engineer), in January 1944 (divorced 1951); married Windsor Lewis (a producer and director); children: (first marriage) a daughter; (second marriage) a daughter.

Filmography: The Long Night *(1947);* I Remember Mama *(1948);* Blood on the Moon *(1948);* Caught *(1949);* Panic in the Streets *(1950);* Fourteen Hours *(1951);* Vertigo *(1958);* The Five Pennies *(1959);* Five Branded Women *(1959);* By Love Possessed *(1961);* Summertree *(1971);* The Todd Killings *(1971).*

In July 1940, after apprenticing in summer stock, an 18-year-old Barbara Bel Geddes made her debut as a walk-on in Moliére's *School for Scandal* at the Clinton Playhouse in Clinton, Connecticut. She made her New York debut at the Windsor Theatre on February 11, 1941, playing Dottie Coburn, the ingenue, in *Out of the Frying Pan*. Four years later, she was given the New York Drama Critics Award for her performance as Genevra Langdon in *Deep Are the Roots*.

One year after her movie debut in *The Long Night* in 1947, Bel Geddes was nominated for best supporting actress for her role in the film *I Remember Mama*. But her movie career stalled in the 1950s, along with hundreds of others, when she was made to appear before the House Un-American Activities Committee hearings. The actress turned to live television, appearing in dramas for "Studio One," "Schlitz Playhouse," and "Alfred Hitchcock Presents."

One of Bel Geddes' more successful Broadway performances was as Patty O'Neill in F. Hugh Herbert's *The Moon is Blue* (1951). "Mr. Herbert ought to regard her as a treasure," wrote Brooks Atkinson. "Everyone else inevitably does." She then created the part of Maggie the Cat, opening in Tennessee Williams' *Cat on a Hot Tin Roof* at the Morosco on March 24, 1955. In 1961, she triumphed in **Jean Kerr**'s comedy, *Mary, Mary*, at the Helen Hayes Theater.

Though Bel Geddes was sidelined with cancer from 1971 to 1973, she returned to the stage in February of 1973 playing Katy Cooper in *Finishing Touches*. From 1978 to 1990, she played the role of Miss Ellie Ewing on the hit television series "Dallas" (she was forced to take a leave of absence in 1984 because of a heart operation).

Belgians, queen of the.

See Carlota (1840–1927) for sidebar on Louise d'Orleans (1812–1850).

See Maria Henrietta of Austria (1836–1902).

See Astrid of Sweden (1905–1935).

See Baels, Liliane (b. 1916).

See Paola (b. 1937).

Belgioso, Cristina (1808–1871)

***Italian revolutionary and author.** Name variations: Countess of Belgioso; Principess di Belgioso, Belgioioso, or Belgiojoso; Cristina Trivulzio. Born in Milan, Italy, on June 28, 1808; died in 1871; daughter of Gerolamo Trivulzio (d. 1812, a distinguished figure at the court of Napoleon's viceroy) and **Vittoria Trivulzio**; married Prince Emilio Barbiano di Belgioso d'Este, on September 24, 1824; children: **Marie Barbiano, countess of Belgioso** (b. 1838, who married Marchese Ludovico Trotti).*

Before the Italian Revolution of 1848, Cristina Belgioso worked in Paris writing propaganda pamphlets and articles advocating political justice and constitutional democracy for her Italian homeland, which was struggling to rid itself of French and Austrian occupation and papal oppressors. On behalf of Italian nationalism, she founded the *Gazetta Italiana* (1843) and also contributed articles for the *Constitutionnel*, and the *Revue des deux mondes*. Distinguished by a wraith-like appearance, with huge dark eyes and a pale, gaunt face, Belgioso held a famous salon in France from 1835 to 1843, befriending Honoré de Balzac, Heinrich Heine, Franz Liszt, and Alfred de Musset. In the midst of her political activity, she also produced the four-volume study, *Essai sur la formation du dogme Catholique*.

In the late 1840s, she returned to Naples. Belgioso financed and organized a legion of volunteers and led them into Milan to participate in the attempt to drive Austrian troops from northern Italy. When the revolution was defeated, she spent years in exile. Even after she was severely injured in an assassination attempt, she continued to campaign for Italian unification, forming several short-lived newspapers to plead the cause. In 1855, she was allowed to return to Milan. Her later works included, *Souvenirs d'Exil* (1850), *Histoire de la Maison de Savoie* (1860), and *Réflexions sur l'État Actuel de l'Italie et sur son Avenir* (1869). Belgioso died in 1871, just one year after Italy was finally unified under a single government.

SUGGESTED READING:

Brombert, Beth Archer. *Cristina: Portraits of a Princess*. NY: Alfred A. Knopf, 1977.

Barbara Morgan,
Melrose, Massachusetts

Belgium, countess of.

See Johanna of Flanders (c. 1200–1244).
See Margaret of Flanders (1202–1280).

Belgium, queen of.

See Belgians, queen of the.

Cristina Belgioso

Belishova, Liri (1923—)

***Albanian politician and World War II partisan leader.** Born in the village of Belishova in 1923; educated in Tirana; married Nako Spiru.*

Fought against German and Italian occupying forces (1941–44); wounded and lost an eye; served as president of People's Youth (1946–47); purged and exiled until 1948; politically rehabilitated (1948); and elected to Central Committee of Albanian Communist Party (ACP); elected to Central Committee and Politburo of ACP; named secretary of ACP secretariat.

Europe's poorest nation Albania did not declare its independence from the Ottoman Empire until 1912. Remaining impoverished and isolated until World War II, Albania underwent a radical transformation in the early 1940s when a new spirit of fierce national pride emerged. This nationalistic movement was led largely by a small but determined group of Communist revolutionaries, who built a reputation as tough guerrilla fighters, and Albanian patriots combating the Italian and German occupying armies.

Liri Belishova was among the few women in Albania's leadership elite in the 1940s. Born in a village named Belishova, she graduated before World War II with a degree from the Tirana Girls Pedagogical Institute. Already an ardent Communist before the war, she joined the partisan movement soon after its creation in 1941. She fought with a partisan unit throughout the bitter and bloody war, losing one of her eyes. In 1945, she married Nako Spiru, an important Communist functionary who was a member of both the Central Committee and the more powerful Politburo. Starting in 1944, Belishova was a member of the Albanian Antifascist Youth organization, and, in 1946, she was leader of the Albanian delegation to the Third Congress of Yugoslav Youth held in Zagreb. She also traveled to Moscow for a Soviet Physical Culture Festival. During these years, Belishova was president of People's Youth, the Communist-controlled national youth organization.

The suicide of her husband in 1947 marked an abrupt end to her political career. Belishova lost her jobs and was unceremoniously transferred to the city of Berat as a schoolteacher. In 1948, after the Titoist elements were drastically purged from the Albanian Communist movement, she was rehabilitated and elected to both the Central Committee and the Politburo of the party. In 1954, she was elevated to the important post of secretary of the party secretariat.

John Haag, Athens, Georgia

Bell, Acton (1820–1849).

See Brontë, Anne.

Bell, Currer (1816–1855).

See Brontë, Charlotte.

Bell, Ellis (1818–1848).

See Brontë, Emily.

Bell, Gertrude (1868–1926)

British intelligence agent and advisor, author, archaeologist and world traveler. *Born Gertrude Margaret Lowthian Bell on July 14, 1868, at Washington Hall in County Durham, northeast England; died on July 12, 1926, in Baghdad, Iraq; eldest of two children of Sir Hugh (an iron and steel industrialist) and Mary Bell; granddaughter of Sir Isaac Lowthian Bell; graduate of Oxford University; never married; no children.*

Became a distinguished scholar, poet, author, historian, archaeologist, linguist, explorer, and mountaineer, and is best known for her role in the Middle East as an intelligence advisor for the British government; traveled into interior of Arabia (1913); appointed to military intelligence staff, then as political secretary at Baghdad (1917); helped mold postwar administration of Mesopotamia, siding with forces bringing Faisal to throne of Iraq (1921).

Selected writings: Safah Nameh—Persian Pictures *(1894);* Poems from the Divan of Hafiz *(1897);* The Desert and the Sown *(1907); (with Sir William Ramsay)* The Thousand and One Churches *(1909);* The Monasteries of Tur Abdin *(1910);* Amurath to Amurath *(1911); (archaeological work)* The Palace and Mosque of Ukhaidir *(1914).*

Gertrude Bell was one of the most remarkable figures of her time. She had entered the world stage long before her publication *The Desert and the Sown* attained the bestseller list in the United States in 1907. To her fellow travelers, including the legendary Lawrence of Arabia, she remained a source of inspiration. Once, during the Arab revolt against the Ottoman Empire in World War I, Lawrence asked the Bedouin Auda abu Tayi, who was probably Arabia's greatest warrior, to divert to a portion of the Syrian desert which "Gertrude Bell and other storied travelers" had crossed. And yet, there was little in Bell's background to suggest she would carve such a redoubtable career in the East, even though at the earliest age there was much evidence that her life would be no ordinary one.

Born on July 14, 1868, at Washington Hall in County Durham, northeast England, Gertrude Margaret Lowthian Bell was fortunate to have been born into a wealthy family: her paternal grandfather, Sir Lowthian Bell, had made a fortune in the iron and steel industry, while her father, Sir Hugh Bell, had successfully continued the family business.

Gertrude was the older of two children born to Hugh and Mary Bell. Her mother died shortly after giving birth to Gertrude's younger brother, Maurice. Left without a mother at the age of three, Gertrude was raised by family governesses. Then, when she was eight, her father remarried, this time to **Florence Olliffe**, daughter of the Irish doctor Sir Joseph Olliffe. A devoted attachment soon formed between the new Lady Bell and the children. Although Gertrude played with dolls and tended her flowers and garden, she displayed an unusually adventurous energy around the family estate and often got her younger brother into difficulties. She also displayed a fondness for her new half-siblings,

Gertrude Bell

Hugo, Elsa, and Molly who were added to the family from 1878–81.

In the words of **Sarah Graham-Brown,** Bell was fortunate "not merely because she was born into a socially privileged class, but because her parents recognized the talents of their physically restless and intellectually gifted child." Consequently, at age 15, she was sent to Queen's College, London, in order to complete her secondary education. Although Bell displayed little talent or interest in sewing, cooking, music, religion, or spelling, she made outstanding marks in history. Thanks to this proclivity, she was accepted to Lady Margaret Hall in Oxford before turning 18. A fellow student, **Janet Hogarth**, described the teenaged Bell in her early days at Oxford for biographer **Elizabeth Burgoyne**:

> She was only seventeen, half child, half woman, rather untidy, with auburn hair, greenish eyes, a brilliant complexion, a curiously long and pointed nose, and a most confiding assurance of being welcome in our society. Obstacles had a trick of melting away when she encountered them, there were so few that she could not take in her stride. She could swim, she could fence, she could row, she could play tennis and hockey, she could keep pace with modern literature and was full of talk about modern authors, most of whom were her childhood friends. Yet she could, and did, put in seven hours a day of solid reading.

In 1888, Bell received a "First" Honors in Modern History. Before leaving Oxford, she had already gone on vacation to Germany but at matriculation was free to begin her far-flung travels. That year, she was invited to stay with her aunt, whose husband was serving as British minister in Bucharest, Rumania. There, she met two men who would figure prominently in her life: Valentine Chirol (later "Sir"), who would be a lifelong friend, and the future Lord Hardinge of Penshurst, who, in 1916, while serving as viceroy of India, would be responsible for sending her to Iraq. From Rumania, she traveled to Constantinople, capital of the aging Ottoman Empire, where she began to fall in love with the exotic mysteries of the East.

After returning to England, she next went to the Middle East in 1892, after her uncle, Sir Frank Lascelles, received a diplomatic posting in Teheran, Persia. While in Persia, she experienced her first broken heart when she fell in love with a junior civil servant, Henry Cadogan. Unfortunately, her parents refused to consent to a marriage devoid of obvious prospects, and Cadogan died suddenly within months of the ill-fated courtship. These events plunged Bell into a profound emotional abyss.

From 1893 to 1897, she returned to England and variously traveled throughout Europe before going to live again with her aunt and uncle who had been transferred to the British Embassy in Berlin. Bell had already studied Arabic and Persian (Farsi), and during these years had published her first two books, *Safah Nameh—Persian Pictures* (1894) and *Poems from the Divan of Hafiz* (1897), which she had translated from Farsi into English.

While in Germany, Bell tried her hand at mountaineering, and she suffered another emotional blow when her aunt died. Then, in 1899, she journeyed once more to her increasingly beloved East when she received permission to join the entourage of a family contact, Dr. Fritz Rosen, who was then the German consul in Jerusalem. Bell recommenced learning Arabic and, from 1899–1900, began her first excursions into the desert from Jerusalem, excursions which included Petra, Deraa, Palmyra, Beirut, Damascus, and other locations in Syria and Palestine which were at that time under the banner of the Ottoman Empire. Historian H.V.F. Winstone has commented that her photographs, sketches and notes, while "chiefly of Islamic and Crusader buildings and historical sites," also revealed German engineering accomplishments along the Hejaz railway between Damascus and Medina, and that this information later would be valuable to British military, cartographical, and intelligence specialists. As she prepared to return to Britain, she wrote her father an exuberant letter which ended with the words: "I shall be back here before long! One does not keep away from the East when one has got into it this far."

True enough, from 1901 to 1902, Bell returned home, then proceeded to Switzerland where she earned a name for herself with the Alpine Club. Her climbing adventures, which included a side excursion to Mount Carmel in Syria, won her the accolade of British Colonel E.L. Strutt who would contribute the following passage in the *Alpine Journal* shortly after her death in 1926:

> Everything that she undertook, physical or mental, was accomplished so superlatively well, that it would indeed have been strange if she had not shone on a mountain as she did in the hunting-field or in the desert. Her strength, incredible in that slim frame, her endurance, above all her courage, were so great that even to this day her guide and companion Ulrich Fuhrer—and there could be few more competent judges—speaks with an admiration of her that amounts to veneration.

Gertrude Bell lost little enough time after climbing before once more taking to the road—this time an around-the-world tour which took her through India, Burma, Java, China, and the United States with her traveling companion Hugo Furse. En route, she made a determined effort to learn Hindustani and Japanese. After returning to England in July 1903, she went on to Berlin with her father and passed much of 1904 in Switzerland and in studies at the Bibliothèque Nationale in Paris.

The first five months of 1905 were spent in the Middle East where she visited castles, churches, and other archaeological ruins in Syria, Palestine, Lebanon, and Asia Minor. Bell passed the balance of 1905 and 1906 between London, studying in Paris, and writing at the family estate, Rounton Grange, near Northallerton, in North Riding, Yorkshire. The year 1905, in fact, was a pivotal time in her life; thenceforward, the Middle East would increasingly dominate.

From Rounton Grange, she wrote *The Desert and the Sown* (published 1907) and, during the next years, collaborated with Sir William Ramsay on the book *The Thousand and One Churches* (1909), and authored other books on Middle Eastern subjects: *The Monasteries of Tur Abdin* (1910), *Amurath to Amurath* (1911), and *The Palace and Mosque of Ukhaidir* (1914). While writing these works, Bell found the time to travel extensively throughout Asia Minor in 1907, visit Italy in 1910, and spend the first half of 1911 in Syria, where she crossed the desert to Mesopotamia and had her first meeting with the not-yet-famous T.E. Lawrence, who was participating in archaeological digs. Prophetically, Bell had written home that Lawrence "is going to make a traveler."

Ironically, for a woman who had to her credit so many singular accomplishments, Gertrude Bell not only refused to join the growing women's suffrage movement in Britain, but in 1908 had joined the Women's Anti-Suffrage League alongside such redoubtables as Lord Cromer and Lord Curzon. Author Graham-Brown has suggested that precisely because of her accomplishments, Bell may not have been sympathetic to "the constraints under which most British women laboured." Further, Graham-Brown has pointed out that Gertrude Bell's mentors had been men, from her father, to whom she wrote extensive letters, to Dr. David G. Hogarth, who would champion her entry into the Arab Bureau in 1915, to Sir Percy Cox, who became high commissioner in Iraq in 1922. Certainly, she felt most content in the companionship of men, although she did not suffer fools of either gender lightly. According to Graham-Brown, Bell's attitude was "one of considerable self-confidence." She believed "that she was the equal, intellectually, of most of the men she knew."

By 1912, Bell's travels had given her a critical insight into the increasing turmoil in the Middle East. One of her letters presaged the dissolution of the Ottoman Empire: "I should not be surprised if we were to see, in the course of the next ten years, the break-up of the empire in Asia also, the rise first of Arab autonomies, then of Armenian perhaps." In the case of the Arabs, at least, she was completely correct. By the end of 1913, Bell set out once more for the Middle East. She was driven not only by her consuming passion for the people and archaeology of the region, but by the need to escape England and find relief from her own emotional anguish, for she had fallen in love with a married man. The man in question was Captain Charles Doughty Wylie (nephew of the famed desert explorer Charles Doughty), who would be killed at Gallipoli in 1915. Because of the need in Edwardian times to keep such matters circumspect, few details of the relationship have survived.

> His first and most inspired find was Gertrude Bell, for a woman with an ability to speak Arabic, the resourcefulness to survive long spells in the desert, and a keen understanding of archaeology and ancient architecture to justify her travels, was at that time almost too good an intelligence prospect to be true.
>
> —H.V.F. Winstone

Bell's 1913–14 adventure took her into Haïl (Hayil), in the Arabian Peninsula, and into the camp of Ibn Rashid, who was destined to be one of the key players in any Arab revolt against the Ottoman Empire. The diaries of Colonel Alfred Chevalier Parker reveal that Bell was in no little danger, for the Ottoman administration was not happy with the prospects of a suspected British agent taking up even temporary residence in northcentral Arabia. Ibn Rashid, in fact, kept her as a house prisoner until her release was negotiated. On the way home, in May 1914, she stopped in Constantinople and visited the British ambassador, Sir Louis Mallet. The information she acquired in Haïl would become of national value when World War I began, scarcely three months after her trip, for Britain soon found herself grouped with France and Russia against Germany, Austria-Hungary, and the Ottoman

Empire. The journey was the most rigorous of her life, and, in appreciation for her achievement, the Royal Geographic Society presented her with a gold medal.

When the European nations went to war in August, Gertrude Bell was at Rounton Grange. Almost immediately, she began a speaking tour on behalf of the British war effort, then spent the balance of 1914 and January through October of the following year engaged first in hospital duties, then as staff for the office of Missing and Wounded located in London as well as in Boulogne, France.

In November, her unique skills were finally called on by Dr. David Hogarth of the Royal Geographic Society, who was assembling a team of Middle-Eastern experts and explorers in Cairo. This group, known as the Arab Bureau, was, in the words of author Edward Said, "bound together by contradictory notions, and personal similarities: great individuality, sympathy and intuitive identification with the Orient, a jealously preserved sense of personal mission."

While in Egypt, Bell met with Hogarth and the young man she earlier had correctly assessed as a rising star in Middle-Eastern affairs, T.E. Lawrence. The British were negotiating with Hussein ibn Ali, Sherif, Amir of Mecca, and Keeper of the Holy Cities, who was sounding out the possibility of military aid should he promote an Arab rising against Ottoman Turkish imperial rule. The British, for their part, had much to gain politically, for Hussein's position within the Islamic world would be an effective counter-weight to the Turkish caliph's call to Holy War against the allied powers of Britain, France and Russia.

While in Egypt, Bell lived at the Grand Continental Hotel in Cairo. Her initial work with the Arab Bureau, who as a band were sometimes known as the *Instrusives*, involved cataloging the sheiks and tribes with which she had become familiar over the years and storing the information in the intelligence files. In the meantime, the impetus for a British-backed Arab Revolt had grown, yet the intelligence departments in Egypt and India were at odds over spheres of responsibility in the Middle East. Consequently, in January 1916, Bell was transferred to Delhi, India, for a short tour as a liaison agent between the departments, and came to advise none other than the viceroy, Lord Hardinge, who happened to be an old and friendly professional acquaintance. From India, Bell was transferred to the Intelligence branch of the General Headquarters staff of General Sir Percy Lake in Basrah, Mesopotamia. In addition to acting as intelligence advisor, she continued in her role as a liaison agent with the Arab Bureau in Cairo.

Next, in 1916, she was transferred onto the staff of the chief political officer, Sir Percy Cox. Over the next ten years, Bell and Cox would form a warm and mutually supporting professional relationship, while advising General Headquarters in Mesopotamia—known after the war as Iraq—as well as diplomatic and political representatives of the British government. Her work during 1916–18 was published in the Bureau's intelligence circular, the *Arab Bulletin*, and covered such topics as "The Basis of Government in Turkish Arabia," "The Situation in Haïl," and a profile on the future leader of Saudi Arabia, Ibn-Saud. Sir Kinahan Cornwallis said of these reports:

> She wrote them as an official for official purposes, but officialdom could never spoil the freshness and vividness of her style or the terseness of her descriptions. Throughout them all can be seen the breadth of her knowledge and her sympathy and understanding for the people whom she loved so well.

When Baghdad fell to the advancing British troops in formerly Turkish-administered Mesopotamia in March 1917, Bell moved with Cox to the British Residency buildings where she would work to the end of her life. The times were as exciting as they were unsettling. British General Sir Edmund Allenby opened an offensive against the Turks from Palestine in September 1918 and succeeded over the next weeks in driving them from the war. On November 1, the crumbling Ottoman Empire signed an Armistice with Britain and the stage was set for a major restructuring of the Middle East.

As oriental secretary, Bell would ably assist Cox in his post as British high commissioner in the troubling times ahead and exerted disproportionate influence which made itself felt beyond Baghdad and Cairo to London and even Paris, where the Treaty of Versailles was being hammered out at the end of the world war to end all wars. By August 1920, Britain received from the League of Nations a mandate to administer the territory of Mesopotamia, which stretched from Mosul in the north to the Persian Gulf.

The British helped sponsor elections in which the son of the Sherif [Hussein] of Mecca, the Amir Faisal [I], was named king of Iraq, an Iraq which with the passage of time was to become an independent state. Bell had been vociferous in her support of Faisal and continued to back him in the years ahead. She worked for Cox until May 1923 and then for Sir Henry Dobbs who succeeded him as high commissioner in Baghdad. From 1923, Bell split her labors between official work as oriental secretary, and the new museum she had helped found in Baghdad which housed the antiquities of Iraq.

The new Iraq was far from tranquil: some of the tribes were rebellious, there were continuing border disputes with Ibn Saud to the south and with the Turks to the north, and there was serious religious disaffection between the Sunni and Shi`a sects of Islam. By June 1926, however, several encouraging events had transpired. An Iraqi parliament had been formed, and the boundary disputes had been settled. Gertrude Bell attended the ceremonious state banquet held by King Faisal on June 25, 1926, to celebrate the signing of the boundary treaty with the Turks, but it would be the last official function she would attend.

Syrian writer Amin Rihani provided a portrait of Gertrude Bell in her sunset years:

> Her figure is quite English—tall and lank; her face is aristocratic—rather long and sharp; and her silver hair is not inharmonious with the persistent pink in her delicate complexion. . . . She keeps the reins of conversation in her own hand. She speaks Arabic almost without an accent, often mixing it with her English and emphasising it with a dogmatic though graceful gesture. Her energy and agility amazed me.

And yet, it was an energy that was failing. Bell had become increasingly ill over the years with various local maladies, and her chief reason for not wishing to visit England in 1926 was her fear the doctors might not let her return to Iraq. Tellingly, one of her English friends commented with great sadness that she looked "like a leaf that could be blown away by a breath." On July 11, she went to sleep and passed away in the early morning hours of the following day, one day shy of her 58th birthday.

Gertrude Bell was given a military funeral. In attendance were all the key British and Iraqi officials who could be assembled on such short notice. In memoriam, King Faisal ordered the principal wing of the Museum of Iraq, where she had served as honorary director of antiquities, to be named for her, and later, friends established a bronze monument with bust and inscription inside the museum. Condolences arrived for her family from the four corners of the globe.

Sir Henry Dobbs published the official notification of her death wherein he commented: "At last her body, always frail, was broken by the energy of her soul." Her stepmother, Lady Bell, provided a final capstone for one whose life had encapsulated so much achievement in its brief 58 years: "But let us not mourn, those who are left, even those who were nearest her, that the end came to her so swiftly and so soon. Life would inexorably have led her down the slope—Death stayed her at the summit."

SOURCES:

Bell, Gertrude. Introduction by Sir Kinahan Cornwallis. *The Arab War.* Privately printed, England: The Golden Cockerel Press, 1940.

———. Introduction by Sarah Graham-Brown. *The Desert and the Sown.* Boston, MA: Beacon Press, 1985.

Bell, Lady [Florence Bell], selected and edited by. *The Letters of Gertrude Bell.* 2 vols. NY: Boni and Liveright, 1927.

Burgoyne, Elizabeth. *Gertrude Bell: From Her Personal Papers, 1889–1914 and 1914–1926.* 2 vols. London: Ernest Benn, 1958.

Lawrence, T.E. *Revolt in the Desert.* London: Jonathan Cape, 1927.

Osband, Linda, ed. *Famous Travelers to the Holy Land.* London: Prion, 1989.

Richmond, Lady, ed. *The Letters of Gertrude Bell.* London: Penguin Books, 1953.

Said, Edward. *Orientalism.* NY: Pantheon Books, 1978.

Winstone, H.V.F., ed. *The Diaries of Parker Pasha.* London: Quartet Books, 1983,

———. *Gertrude Bell.* London: Jonathan Cape, 1978.

———. *The Illicit Adventure.* London: Jonathan Cape, 1982.

SUGGESTED READING:

Kamm, Josephine. *Gertrude Bell: Daughter of the Desert.* Vanguard, 1956.

Wallach, Janet. *Desert Queen: The Extraordinary Life of Gertrude Bell.* Doubleday, 1996.

David L. Bullock, Ph.D., author of *Allenby's War: the Palestine-Arabian Campaigns, 1916–1918* (London: Blandford Press, 1988)

Bell, Jocelyn (b. 1943).

See Burnell, Jocelyn Bell.

Bell, Laura (1829–1894)

Irish missionary and courtesan who worked with Prime Minister William Gladstone to aid London prostitutes. *Born in 1829 in Antrim, Ireland; died in 1894 in England; married Augustus Frederick Thistlethwayte, in 1852.*

Calling herself "a sinner saved by grace through faith in the Lamb of God," London's pre-eminent courtesan spent her declining years as a social missionary, working to save London's prostitutes and preaching with a zeal and eloquence that drew large crowds. Laura Bell, the daughter of the respectable bailiff to the Mar-

Laura Bell

quis of Hertford, worked in a Belfast shop before becoming one of Dublin's most fashionable courtesans. In 1850, she moved to London where she was known as the "Queen of London Whoredom," turning heads wherever she went. In 1852, she married the eccentric Augustus Thistlethwayte, who, in spite of his reputation as an officer and a gentlemen, had the unusual habit of summoning his servants by firing a pistol at the ceiling. Around the time the marriage reportedly began to unravel, Bell is said to have been suddenly swept away with religious fervor. She gained respectability as an evangelical preacher, who, through her work with Prime Minister William Gladstone, aided London prostitutes. Bell continued her charitable deeds until her death in 1894.

Bell, Marie (1900–1985)

French actress. *Born Marie-Jeanne Bellon-Downey, on December 23, 1900, in Bégles, France; died in 1985; studied drama at the Paris Conservatory.*

After making her debut as a dancer in England at age 13, Marie Bell turned to an acting career. In 1924, she began a string of supporting roles in French silent films and became a member of the Comédie Française in 1928. With the advent of sound, Bell moved up to film leads. In her two most successful films, she played a dual role in Jacques Feyder's *Le Grand Jeu* in 1934 and a rich, middle-aged widow in Julien Duvivier's *Un Carnet de Bal* (*Life Dances On*) in 1937. For her work in the French Resistance during World War II, Bell was awarded the Legion of Honor by Charles de Gaulle. Her other films include *Paris* (1924), *La Valse de l'Adieu* (1926), Madame Récamier (1928), *Figaro* (1929), *La Nuit est à nous (The Night is Ours,* 1930), *L'Homme qui assassina* (1930), *La Fédora* (1934), *Polichè* (1934), *La Garçonne* (1936), *Pantins d'Amour* (1937), *Lègion d'Honneur* (1938), *La Charrette fantôme (The Phantom Carriage,* 1939), *Ceux du Ciel* (1940), *Vie privée* (1942), *Le Colonel Chabert* (1943), *La Bonne Soupe (Careless Love,* 1964), *Vaghe Stelle dell'Orsa (Sandra,* 1965), *Hotel Paradiso* (1966), and *Les Volets clos* (1973).

Bell, Marilyn (1937—)

Canadian swimmer and first person to swim nonstop across Lake Ontario. *Born in Toronto, Ontario, Canada, on October 19, 1937; eldest daughter of Sydney Thomas (an accounting clerk) and Grace (Phillips) Bell; attended St. Mary's School, Toronto, and Loretta College School, Toronto.*

On September 9, 1954, at 11:59 PM, a freckled, 119-pound teenager touched breakwater and was hauled ashore after a record 24 hour, 59 minute swim across the black, icy waters of Lake Ontario. Canadian Marilyn Bell had begun the marathon at 11 PM the previous evening, competing against American ***Florence Chadwick** and Canadian **Winnie Roach Leuszler**. (The Canadians were swimming in defiance of the Canadian National Exhibition [C.N.E.] rules that only sanctioned Americans for the competition.) At 4:30 in the morning, Chadwick and Leuszler had been hauled out of the water, ill and exhausted. Battling 12-foot waves and blood-sucking lampreys, Bell was barely hanging on, swimming with her arms only, her legs dead weight. After rubbing herself with liniment sent out to her by an escort boat, she struggled on. Food (predigested cereal, corn syrup and lemon juice) was passed to her each hour; notes of encouragement scribbled on a blackboard were held high for her to see. By afternoon, when it seemed she couldn't go on, one of her friends swam beside her for a few minutes. By evening, Bell was merely treading water. Although her father wanted to take her out of the water, her coach prodded her on, calling "fifteen minutes more." The C.N.E., relaxing its rules, now offered a $10,000 prize, while an anonymous Air Force officer added another $6,000 incentive. When Bell finally made it to shore and into a waiting ambulance, she had become a national celebrity. She later said she had made the swim "for the honor of Canada."

Marilyn Bell was born in Toronto, Ontario, Canada, on October 19, 1937, the eldest daughter of Sydney Thomas Bell, an accounting clerk, and Grace Phillips Bell. Due to her father's job transfers, Marilyn spent her childhood on the move, often living in hotel rooms when the family could not find housing. Taught to swim by her dad when she was four, she began to take the sport seriously at the Oakwood Swimming Pool in Toronto, where she won her first medal for swimming a mile in 40 minutes. The following year, at age 12, she began training with championship coach Gus Ryder. Around this time, Bell also became interested in instructing children partially paralyzed by polio, and by the time she was 14, in addition to training, she was employed as a children's swimming coach at the Club. Ryder entered her in her first marathon in July 1954. To everyone's surprise, she finished seventh in the 26-mile swim.

Five days after her spectacular conquest of Lake Ontario in 1954, Bell was "near collapse," reported the Washington *Post and Times Herald*, not so much from the swim but from the resulting furor and public appearances. After stints on radio and television shows in Canada, she flew to New York to guest on Ed Sullivan's "Toast of the Town." Gifts totalling $50,000 poured in, and, though she turned down an offer from Hollywood in order to complete her education, she did agree to star in a documentary film about her historic swim.

The next summer, the Toronto *Telegram* offered Bell $15,000 to swim the English Channel. Accepting the challenge, she made the crossing in 14 hours, 36 minutes, becoming the youngest swimmer ever to accomplish the feat. Hailed by Mayor Nathan Phillips as the "sweetheart of all Canada," she was also named "Woman of the Year," for the second year in a row, by the women editors of the Canadian Press.

On March 26, 1956, to honor Bell's Lake Ontario swim, a plaque engraved with her image as she stroked through the water was mounted on a building near the spot where she had touched shore. It was dedicated by Premier Leslie M. Frost with the Ontario Legislature in attendance. Described as a gentle, caring woman, Bell continued her education and her work with children.

SOURCES:

Candee, Marjorie Dent, ed. *Current Biography 1956*. NY: H.W. Wilson, 1956.

Spires, Randi. "Our Marilyn: Miss. . . or Myth? Kamikazi Hearts," in *Canadian Woman Studies/ Les Cahiers de la Femme*. Summer 1988.

Barbara Morgan,
Melrose, Massachusetts

Bell, Vanessa (1879–1961)

English painter and central member of the Bloomsbury group. *Name variations: Vanessa Stephen, 1879–1906; Vanessa Bell 1906–1961. Born Vanessa Stephen at 22 Hyde Park Gate in London, England, on May 30, 1879; died on April 7, 1961; daughter of Sir Leslie Stephen (an author and editor) and Julia (Jackson) Stephen (widow at age 24 of Herbert Duckworth); sister of Virginia Woolf; given private painting lessons, mainly at home, but also studied at Royal Academy and Slade School of Art, London; married Clive Bell, in 1906; children: (with Bell) two sons, Julian (1908–1937) and Quentin (b. 1910); (with Duncan Grant) one daughter, Angelica Garnett (b. 1918, a writer).*

Selected paintings: **Lady Robert Cecil** *(1905);* Saxon Sydney Turner *(c. 1908);* Iceland Poppies *(1909);* Lytton Strachey *(Anthony d'Offay Gallery, London, 1911);* The Bathers in a Landscape *(Victoria and Albert Museum, 1911);* Studland Beach *(Tate Gallery, 1912);* Landscape with Haystack, Asheham *(Anthony d'Offay Gallery, London, 1912);* Nursery Tea *(1912);* Adam and Eve *(Anthony d'Offay Gallery, London, 1913);* A Conversation *(Courtauld Institute Galleries, London, 1913–16);* Abstract *(Anthony d'Offay Gallery, London, c. 1914);* **Mrs. Mary Hutchinson** *(Tate Gallery, 1914);* Iris Tree *(1915);* Self-Portrait *(Yale Center for British Art, c. 1915);* The Madonna Lily *(Anthony d'Offay Gallery, London, 1915);* The Tub *(Tate Gallery, 1918);* Quentin Bell *(1919);* Interior with a Table, San Tropez *(Tate Gallery, 1921);* The Open Door, Charleston *(Bolton Museum and Art Gallery, 1926);* Portrait of Aldous Huxley *(c. 1929–30);* Roger Fry *(King's College, Cambridge, 1933);* Interior with Housemaid *(Williamson Art Gallery, Birkenhead, 1939);* Poppies and Hollyhocks *(Anthony d'Offay Gallery, London, c. 1941);* Self-Portrait *(1958);* **Henrietta Garnett** *(Royal West of England Academy, Bristol, 1959). Paintings are signed VB, Vanessa Bell, or unsigned.*

Vanessa Bell was one of the central figures in the Bloomsbury group, an English literary and artistic coterie which, in the early decades of the 20th century, challenged the conventions and morality of the Victorian era in which they had been raised. A painter, she lived at the center of an influential circle of friends, of whom the most famous was her younger sister, the novelist ***Virginia Woolf**. Bell was, says her biographer **Frances Spalding**, "composed of paradoxes: a prey to vagueness, she could be unusually sharp; chilling formality went hand in hand with a quick sensitivity; she upheld the controlling power of reason yet was a victim of her emotions and intuitions and was led to subterfuges that de-

Vanessa Bell

nied honesty." In her personal life, she appeared immune to moral convention. Bloomsbury historians, including her children, continue to debate whether her unusual personal life was an exhilarating example of individual liberty or a baleful case of self-denial and deception.

Her father was Sir Leslie Stephen, a formidable Victorian patriarch, famous for his agnosticism, and the editor of the *Dictionary of National Biography*. They lived in solid upper-middle-class comfort in Kensington but Vanessa, Virginia, and their two brothers, Thoby and Adrian, suffered a succession of domestic disasters as children. Their mother **Julia Stephen**, who had previously been married to Herbert Duckworth, died unexpectedly in 1895 when Vanessa was 16. A half-sister, **Stella Duckworth**, took over their upbringing, but she too died two years later, aged only 28, of peritonitis. To make matters worse, Vanessa and her sister Virginia had to endure as teenagers the unwanted sexual advances and abuses of their half-brother George Duckworth. Despite these difficulties, Vanessa was already studying doggedly to become an artist, learning from her father's example to work with diligence and single-minded concentration. She studied drawing from a fellow of the Royal Academy, Arthur Cope, took lessons from John Singer Sargent, and then won a competitive exam to enter the Royal Academy schools to study painting technique. She worked on drawing nude models three days each week and disliked being taken from her art work to attend the society functions which her family and class required. As Virginia wrote: "Underneath the necklaces and the enamel butterflies was one passionate desire—for paint and turpentine, for turpentine and paint."

When Vanessa was 25, in 1904, their father also died. He had encouraged his daughters to read widely, and they were far more rigorously educated than most young women of their social class. But they were denied the chance of going to college and had to enjoy it vicariously through their brothers instead, each of whom went to Cambridge. From Cambridge, Vanessa's brothers brought home a succession of fascinating and intellectually gifted friends, many of whom belonged to the elite "Apostles" club. Among these visitors, who in turn were fascinated by the beauty and intelligence of the Stephen sisters, were Lytton Strachey, John Maynard Keynes, Duncan Grant, and Clive Bell, all of whom were to become famous in their own right in later life.

Vanessa and Virginia, determined to live a more independent life after their father's death, moved with their brothers from Kensington to a big house in Gordon Square, Bloomsbury (the area of London around the British Museum), which was then unfashionable for people of their class and carried a hint of bohemianism. They were anything but starving artists, however, having inherited plenty of money, and they took the attendance of servants for granted. Vanessa was the more practical sister (Virginia had already suffered her first bout of mental illness), and she arranged all the buying and selling. The Thursday night salons they held there (around which the mythic ideal of "Bloomsbury" developed) were modeled on the Cambridge Apostles' meetings, often with one of the family members or friends giving a talk or a reading from a work in progress. They prided themselves on their absolute commitment to honesty and truth, and swore to obliterate what seemed to them the insincerity and hypocrisy of the Victorians, their parents. Others in the circle, which met in various forms well into the 1920s and 1930s, were E.M. Forster, Roger Fry, Desmond McCarthy, and Leonard Woolf (who later married Virginia). The two sisters were lifelong friends but felt competitive with one another. Vanessa Bell was older, stronger, healthier, more practical, and had children, all of which stimulated Virginia's envy, while Vanessa always thought of herself as being overshadowed by her sister's literary genius.

Clive Bell, an art critic, fell in love with Vanessa and twice proposed to her, but she turned him down. He proposed a third time just after her oldest brother's death in 1906; this time, she accepted, even though, according to the rest of the family and friends, he was unworthy of her. Henry James, the American novelist who lived in England and knew the family, wrote that Clive was a "quite dreadful-looking little stoop-shouldered, long-haired, third-rate" man. But for a time, she seemed fully content. Virginia described her sister, seen walking with Clive. "She had a gauze streamer, red as blood flying over her shoulder, a purple scarf, a shooting cap, tweed skirt, and great brown boots. Then her hair swept across her forehead, and she was tawny and jubilant and lusty as a young God." After their marriage, the couple took over the Gordon Square house while Virginia and Adrian, the surviving brother, moved to Fitzroy Square nearby.

The marriage began with enthusiasm and mutual rapture but became unconventional and unstable. Soon after the birth of their son Julian in 1908, Clive Bell began a flirtation with his sister-in-law Virginia (even though she had also written of him very disparagingly) and later had sexual affairs with many other women. Between 1911 and 1913, Vanessa Bell was in love with the art critic Roger Fry, whose 1910 exhibition in the Grafton Gallery had helped bring European post-Impressionist artists to popular notice in Britain. This affair began when Vanessa and Clive went with Fry to Constantinople and rural Turkey. She was taken ill and only discovered later that she had been pregnant and then suffered a miscarriage. (Her second son Quentin, born only a month earlier, had been left with a

Iceland Poppies, *1909. Painting by Vanessa Bell.*

nurse back in England.) Fry resourcefully found local remedies and supervised a hasty return to Britain. At the same time, he realized that the two of them had fallen in love. Later she wrote that with Fry, "I realized what an absolutely enthralling companion had come into one's life. Our feelings jumped together at each new sight; for the first time there was someone who could convey his feelings and show that he understood mine." But they disagreed on matters of art. Fry was a better promoter and critic than creative artist, and, being 13 years older than she, sometimes seemed to her more like a father figure than a lover. After two stormy years, she broke off their relationship when she felt it had become a "dead, drab affair," causing him years of anguish and forlorn hope that they might revive it. She did remain his friend and admired him to the end of his life: Virginia Woolf later wrote his biography.

In 1914, and for most of her life afterwards, Bell began to live with another artist, Duncan Grant, even though he was a homosexual and had a series of passionate relationships with other men throughout their lives together. He was six years younger than her and almost 20 years the junior of Roger Fry. Most of Bell's close friends then, and later, were homosexuals, and she seemed to relish their company. In 1914, in a letter to economist John Maynard Keynes, himself bisexual and one of Grant's lovers (Keynes would later marry ***Lydia Lopokova**), Bell showed how far she had thrown off the repressive conventions of her father's era. "Did you have a pleasant afternoon buggering one or more of the young men we left for you? It must have been delicious. I imagine you . . . with your bare limbs intertwined with him and all the ecstatic preliminaries." With Grant, despite his preference for men, she did have sex occasionally, with the result that they had a child, Angelica, in 1918. Spalding describes Vanessa Bell as "voraciously maternal" in her devotion to her children, but Grant was certainly not voraciously paternal; he and Clive Bell were both willing to go along with the convenient fiction that Clive was Angelica's father.

But the real shared love of Vanessa and Duncan was painting. Clive Bell and Roger Fry were both aestheticians who loved to discuss art and theorize about it, whereas she and Grant preferred actually to create it, and unlike many men of his generation he enthusiastically encouraged her to carry on improving her technique. As **Germaine Greer** observed in her history of women artists, *The Obstacle Race*, many male artists were indifferent to the work of their female contemporaries and offered no encouragement. Even in the Bloomsbury circle there was a case in point, ***Dora Carrington**, who in early life had been an enthusiastic and talented painter. The total indifference to her art shown by Lytton Strachey, whom Carrington loved, discouraged her to the point of abandoning it altogether.

Bell's own paintings often relied on the use of blocks of color. Spalding observes that:

> Vanessa Bell disliked story-telling in art; she shared the Bloomsbury belief that art only achieves unity and completeness if it is detached; she selected her subjects for the reflections, shapes, colours, patterns, lines and spatial relationships that they presented.

A popular post-Impressionist, she did not win a prominent place in English art-history, and her work is valued as much because it illustrates the characters and settings of the Bloomsbury Group as for its intrinsic merits.

In 1916, she began to rent a farmhouse named Charleston in the south English county of Sussex, so that Grant and his lover David "Bunny" Garnett could work there as farm laborers instead of being drafted to fight in the First World War. She later bought the house and lived there for the rest of her life. Though Grant moved in with her permanently, his male friends also came to stay for long periods, while Vanessa's husband Clive Bell, fully aware of the complex emotional affairs of the house and still on friendly terms with his wife, also stayed sometimes for months at a time and brought his women friends along. As **Janet Malcolm** writes: "What could be a better riposte to Victorian hypocrisy and dreariness than a husband who brought his mistresses around for amused inspection and a lover who was gay? By any standard the Bell-Grant household was the strange one, and in the 1920s there were still plenty of people who could find it excitingly scandalous."

> Her commitment to art never wavered: it runs like a rod of steel through her life, an unbending central core of conviction.
>
> **—Frances Spalding**

In the 1920s, Bloomsbury became a well-known feature of English intellectual and artistic life. Duncan Grant had his first solo exhibition of paintings in 1920, and Vanessa Bell had hers two years later, when she was 43. Her former lover, Roger Fry, gave the exhibition a favorable press review, but artists she was not personally attached to were also enthusiastic. From then on, she was able to get commissions for portraits and mural decorations and to make a decent income from painting. Her brother-in-law, Leonard Woolf, ran the Hogarth Press, and Bell was a regular cover designer and illustrator for its novels and poetry, including the first editions of Virginia Woolf's novels. Grant and Bell began to spend part of most years at a French farmhouse, La Bergere, in Provence, and they befriended many of the prominent European artists of the era, Picasso, Derain, and Matisse, after the breach of the war years.

In 1932, Bell's lifelong friend Lytton Strachey, who had become famous with his books *Eminent Victorians* and *Queen Victoria*, both masterpieces of anti-Victorian debunking, died of cancer. Two years later, her old lover and longtime friend Roger Fry also died. Much worse was to follow. In 1937, her oldest son Julian, who had volunteered to fight with the Republican side in the Spanish Civil War, was killed at the Battle of Brunete. And in 1941, suffering from recurring "voices" and fits of derangement, her sister Virginia Woolf committed suicide by drowning. This succession of tragedies cast a severe shadow over the rest of Vanessa Bell's life. But she was extremely resilient. She had painted a group portrait of the Bloomsbury Group in the 1920s, using her common method of putting each of the figures in a distinctive pose but leaving the faces blank. In the 1940s, she returned to the theme and did another group portrait, this time with the faces fully formed, and showing hung paintings of the group's dead members (Strachey, Fry, and Virginia Woolf) on the walls behind those who were still living.

The incestuous quality of friendships and relationships among the Bloomsbury clique was never shown more vividly than when Bell's daughter Angelica, fathered by Duncan Grant, became the wife of her father's former boyfriend David Garnett, who was now a minor novelist. **Angelica Garnett**'s much later memoir *Deceived by Kindness* (1984) knocked a good deal of bloom off the Bloomsbury rose. It gave a withering account of her mother's complicated emotional life, arguing that Vanessa Bell had masochistically degraded herself in living with Grant, whose succession of homosexual lovers continued into old age. "Self-denigration and timidity became a habit," wrote Angelica, "expressed outwardly in drab, unstylish clothes, a shrinking from society, and the constant reiteration that Duncan's work was so infinitely better than her own." In later years, Bell routinely declined social invitations and, as she aged, became reluctant to meet anyone new, while remaining loyal to her oldest friends.

Bell and Grant spent most of the Second World War years back at the Sussex farm. Her younger son Quentin, who had also become a painter, suffered from tuberculosis and was declared unfit for military service so he passed the duration of the war working as a laborer on the nearby farm of Maynard Keynes. The life of rural painting, varied by trips to France and sometimes Italy, resumed after the war. Vanessa Bell realized that the Bloomsbury Group was becoming a historical phenomenon and soon became impatient with interview requests from the aspiring biographers of Keynes, Strachey, Fry, and her sister Virginia. Unable to drive, she found it difficult to travel and went less and less frequently to London. She died in 1961, greatly mourned by her surviving friends and relatives. As her biographer Spalding wrote, it was she who had kept the Group together. "Her hospitality is one reason why the disparate individuals who composed Bloomsbury continued to meet, to retain a group identity long after the circumstances that had helped shape their homogeneity had vanished."

SOURCES:

Bell, Quentin. *Bloomsbury.* London: Weidenfeld and Nicolson, 1968.

Edel, Leon. *Bloomsbury: A House of Lions.* NY: Avon, 1979.

Greer, Germaine. *The Obstacle Race.* London: Secker and Warburg, 1986.

Malcolm, Janet. "A House of One's Own," in *The New Yorker.* June 5, 1995, pp. 58–79.

Marler, Regina, ed. *Selected Letters of Vanessa Bell.* NY: Pantheon, 1993.

Spalding, Frances. *Vanessa Bell.* NY: Harcourt Brace, 1985.

SUGGESTED READING:

Bell, Vanessa, edited by Lia Giachero. *Sketches in Pen and Ink: A Bloomsbury Notebook.* London: Hogarth Press, 1998.

COLLECTIONS:

University of Sussex Library; British Library Manuscript Department; Tate Gallery Archives.

Patrick Allitt, Professor of History, Emory University, Atlanta, Georgia

Bellamy, George Anne (1730–1788).

See Woffington, Peg for sidebar.

Bellamy, Madge (1899–1990)

American film actress of the 1920s. *Born Margaret Philpott in 1899 (some sources cite 1902) in Hillsboro, Texas; died on January 24, 1990, in Upland, California; daughter of William Bledsoe (an English professor and football coach at Texas A&M) and Anne "Annie" Margaret (Derden) Philpott; attended St. Mary's Hall, a junior college affiliated with Vassar; married Logan Metcalf, in 1928 (divorced).*

Filmography: The Riddle: Woman *(1920);* The Cup of Life *(1921);* Passing Thru *(1921);* Blind Hearts *(1921);* Love Never Dies *(1921);* The Call of the North *(1921);* Hail the Woman *(1921);* Lorna Doone *(1922);* The Hottentot *(1922);* Garrison's Finish *(1923);* Are You a Failure? *(1923);* Soul of the Beast *(1923);* Do It Now *(1924);* No More Women *(1924);*

Madge Bellamy

The White Sin *(1924);* Love's Whirlpool *(1924);* His Forgotten Wife *(1924);* The Fire Patrol *(1924);* The Iron Horse *(1924);* On the Stroke of Three *(1924);* Love and Glory *(1924);* A Fool and His Money *(1925);* The Dancer *(1925);* The Parasite *(1925);* The Reckless Sex *(1925);* Secrets of the Night *(1925);* Wings of Youth *(1925);* The Man in Blue *(1925);* Lightnin' *(1925);* Havoc *(1925);* Thunder Mountain *(1925);* Lazybones *(1925);* The Golden Strain *(1925);* The Dixie Merchant *(1926);* Sandy *(1926);* Black Paradise *(1926);* Summer Bachelors *(1926);* Bertha, The Sewing Machine Girl *(1926);* Ankles Preferred *(1927);*

The Telephone Girl *(1927);* Colleen *(1927);* Very Confidential *(1927);* Silk Legs *(1927);* Soft Living *(1928);* The Play Girl *(1928);* Mother Knows Best *(1928);* Fugitives *(1929);* Tonight at Twelve *(1929);* White Zombie *(1932);* Gigolettes of Paris *(1933);* Riot Squad *(1933);* Gordon of Ghost City *(a serial in 12 chapters, 1933);* Charlie Chan in London *(1934);* The Great Hotel Murder *(1935);* The Daring Young Man *(1935);* Under Your Spell *(1936);* Northwest Trail *(1945).*

One of the few silent stars who arrived in Hollywood by way of Broadway, Madge Bellamy was among the most highly regarded and highest paid actresses of that era. Hailed by *Motion Picture Classic* in 1921 as "the most sensitive face on the screen," this leading comedic talent of the '20s was also known for her disputes with studio bosses. In 1928, Bellamy walked out of her Fox contract, virtually ending her career. On the publication of her 1989 autobiography *A Darling of the Twenties*, Kevin Brownlow noted that it was Bellamy's attempt to "confront the strange and willful personality that was hers . . . sixty years ago."

Madge Bellamy was born Margaret Philpott in Texas in 1899. Her father was an English professor at Texas A&M, before he embarked on a series of business ventures; her mother was a talented pianist, who guided her daughter's career from her earliest performance at age nine in a touring company of *Aida*. Although Bellamy's first appearance on Broadway was as a chorus girl in *The Love Mill*, she was singled out with a nod from one critic: "Good dancing by Margaret Philpott." She also caught the attention of theatre owner Daniel Frohman, who suggested a name change to the more melodious Bellamy, and recommended her for the touring company of *Pollyanna*. Bellamy had stage roles in *Dear Brutus* and *Peg O' My Heart*, and played **Geraldine Farrar**'s daughter in the movie *The Riddle: Woman*, before winning a screen test for the Thomas Ince Studio and moving to Hollywood with her mother.

***Janis, Elsie**. See Draper, Ruth for sidebar.*

For her first movie under contract, Bellamy did her own hair and makeup and supplied her own costumes, which were sewn by her mother. From the start, she would write in her autobiography, she was disturbed by the way she was treated. "It is very hard for a girl brought up in the South, as I had been, . . . to be told to stand up while they looked her over like a horse."

In 1922, Bellamy won the prize part in *Lorna Doone*, directed by France's Maurice Tourneur. Publicity for the movie included a U.S. tour which began in the Harding White House, where Bellamy gave make-up tips to first lady ***Florence Harding** and posed with General John J. Pershing. Upon her return to Hollywood, she was passed over for the role in Eugene O'Neill's *Anna Christie*, the first of many serious dramatic roles she would lose. Although she was publicized as a serious actress, Bellamy bemoaned the fact that she did comedies for most of her career. "Tragediennes are supposed to suffer," she once said, "and so I suffer—in comedies."

Bellamy was lent out to other studios on many occasions, once to MGM, where Irving Thalberg had chosen her to star in *Ben Hur*. She thanked him but turned it down, saying, "It will just be a lot of horses." By her own admission, she was full of herself in those days, arguing with most of her directors, employing one as a target for her shoe. Once when Louis B. Mayer offered her a film, she turned him down, because Mayer did not stand when she walked into the room.

Bellamy had no problem finding suitors, even with her mother in tow. She mingled with celebrities, such as Paul Whiteman, Howard Hughes, Jack Dempsey, and Bennett Cerf, and received numerous marriage proposals from tycoons, directors, and leading men. Although there were always men in her life, Bellamy had difficulty establishing an enduring relationship. Her one marriage, to stockbroker Logan Metcalf, lasted only six days.

In 1928, Bellamy signed a four-year contract with Fox and made her first talkie, *Mother Knows Best* by ***Edna Ferber**, based on the life of the vaudevillian **Elsie Janis**. This was her finest role, allowing Bellamy to demonstrate her versatility with impressions of Harry Lauder, ***Anna Held**, and Al Jolson. She received raves from the critics, who were at the same time enthusiastic about her future in sound.

Soon after her triumph, however, Bellamy quit Fox over a dispute. Instead, she made a film for Universal for half her salary. With the stock market crash of 1929, work dried up, and, due to her mother's less than savvy business sense, Bellamy soon faced financial ruin. Her last notable film was the horror classic *White Zombie*, in which she played a young bride who falls under the spell of a mad plantation owner portrayed by Bela Lugosi. During the 1930s, she concentrated more on stage roles, playing a number of parts in new plays, including *Intermission* and *Holiday Lady*. She also made live appearances on a tour of the great motion-picture theaters in the East, doing impersonations for which she wrote her own scripts. It was a grueling schedule, with six shows a day.

Bellamy's four-year off-and-on affair with lumber tycoon Stan Murphy, which began in 1937, ended with Murphy marrying another woman. Feeling betrayed and distraught, Bellamy fired three shots at him as he was leaving the Commonwealth Club in San Francisco. Although the assault charge brought against her was eventually dismissed, the negative publicity surrounding the incident negated any chance for a comeback. Her final movie, the forgettable *Northwest Trails*, was made in 1945, when she was just past 40.

Following her retirement, Bellamy lived briefly in New Mexico, then moved to Ontario, California, where she cared for her mother during a final illness. The real-estate boom of the 1980s brought her much needed money from a property holding, ending what she referred to as her abject poverty. In her final years, she devoted time to political activism, including the causes of civil rights and feminism. In addition to her autobiography, she wrote two novels, a play, and a number of short stories, none of which were published. Madge Bellamy lived past her 90th birthday and died on January 24, 1990.

SOURCES:

Bellamy, Madge. *A Darling of the Twenties.* NY: Vestal Press, 1989.

Drew, William M. *Speaking of Silents: First Ladies of the Screen.* Vestal, NY: Vestal Press, 1989.

Barbara Morgan, Melrose, Massachusetts

Bellanca, Dorothy (1894–1946)

Latvian-American labor leader and political activist. *Born Dorothy Jacobs on August 10, 1894, in Zemel, Latvia; died in New York City on August 16, 1946; youngest of four daughters born to Harry (a tailor) and Bernice Edith (Levinson) Jacobs; attended Baltimore public schools until age 13; married August Bellanca (an Amalgamated Clothing Workers of America [ACWA] organizer), in August 1918; children: none.*

Garment worker and organizer for the ACWA; member of the ACWA executive board and vice-president (1934–46); appointed to several state and federal commissions (1930s); founder of the American Labor Party (ALP, 1936); state vice-chair of the ALP (1940, 1944).

Born in Latvia in 1894, six-year-old Dorothy Jacobs arrived in the United States with her family. By age 13, she was working ten hours a day in a Baltimore mens' overcoat factory, making buttonholes for three dollars a week. According to historian Herbert Gutman, "The experience left her with misshapen index fingers and a lifelong commitment to organized labor." By 1909, Bellanca had helped form Local 170 of the United Garment Workers of America (UGWA). The UGWA was a craft-based union which primarily represented the interests of native-born male garment workers. Young immigrant women such as Bellanca felt their concerns were not being met by the UGWA, and in 1914 she led her local into the recently organized Amalgamated Clothing Workers of America (ACWA). From its beginnings, the ACWA was a more radical, industrial-based union and much more suited to the politics of Dorothy Bellanca.

Bellanca soon rose to prominence in the ACWA, based in part on her organizing abilities. She was active in the 1915 Chicago strike as well as in New York and Philadelphia in 1917. Elected to the ACWA executive board in 1916, Bellanca became the union's first full-time woman organizer a year later. Although she resigned from the executive board in 1918 when she married fellow ACWA organizer August Bellanca, Dorothy Bellanca remained active in the union the rest of her life. She was head of the ACWA Women's Bureau from 1924 to 1926 and participated in several strikes. During a 1933 strike in Rochester, New York, the editor of the ACWA newspaper wrote: "Dorothy is loved by the strikers, admired by the neighbors around the factory, and feared by the police." Bellanca also put a great emphasis on building strong locals, especially in rural areas where small, non-union shops employed young women at very low wages.

Her commitment to industrial unionism was still evident in 1937 when she became a member of the Committee for Industrial Organization's (CIO) Textile Workers' Organizing Committee. Bellanca was also actively involved with the Women's Trade Union League and the Consumers' League of New York. She was appointed to several New York City and State commissions and, in 1938, named to a maternal and child-welfare national advisory committee by U.S. Secretary of Labor **Frances Perkins**. During World War II, Bellanca served on two committees focused on issues regarding the employment of women.

During the 1930s, Bellanca's labor radicalism had spilled over into electoral politics. She supported the candidacy of Fiorello LaGuardia for mayor of New York City in 1933, and, three years later, she founded the American Labor Party (ALP). In 1938, Bellanca was the ALP Party's unsuccessful candidate for the U.S. Congressional seat representing New York's Eighth District. She was, however, twice elected vice-chair of the state ALP in 1940 and 1944. She died in New York City, shortly after her 52 birthday.

COLLECTIONS:

Dorothy J. Bellanca Papers, Catherwood Library, Cornell University.

Kathleen Banks Nutter,
Department of History,
University of Massachusetts at Amherst

Belleville, Jeanne de (fl. 1343).

See Jeanne de Belleville.

Belleville-Oury, Anna Caroline de (1808–1880)

Pianist of French descent, known for her chamber music performances with her husband. *Born Anna Caroline de Belleville in Landshut, Germany, on June 24, 1808; died in Munich, Germany, on July 22, 1880; daughter of the director of the Bavarian Court Opera; married Antonio James Oury (the violinist), in 1831.*

Though Anna Caroline de Belleville-Oury's family was French, she spent most of her life in Germany where her father was director of the Bavarian Court Opera in Munich. She studied with Czerny in Vienna for four years, making her debut in that city. After well-received tours of European musical centers during which she was compared to Clara Wieck (later ***Clara Schumann**), Belleville-Oury settled in London. Married in 1831 to the violinist Antonio James Oury, she and her husband toured Europe and Russia as a highly successful chamber-music team. She was the composer of many piano works, over 180 of which found their way into print. Anna Caroline de Belleville-Oury died in Munich on July 22, 1880.

Bellincioni, Gemma (1864–1950)

Italian soprano. *Born on August 18, 1864, in Monza, Italy; died in Naples on April 23–24, 1950; daughter of Cesare Bellincioni (a buffo bass) and Carlotta Savoldini (a contralto); studied with her father and her husband as well as Luigia Ponti dell'Armi and Giovanni Corsi; married Roberto Stagno (a tenor).*

Made debut in Dell'Orefice's Il segreto della duchessa *(1879); sang in Spain and Portugal and appeared in Rome (1885); sang at Teatro alla Scala (1886); first Italian Salome under Strauss' baton in Turin (1906); continued to appear occasionally in The Netherlands in the 1920s.*

Gemma Bellincioni and her husband Roberto Stagno performed many operas together. Bellincioni continued a tradition begun by her parents Cesare Bellincioni, a bass, and **Carlotta Savoldini**, a contralto. Hers was a life of music after her birth in Monza, Italy, on August 18, 1864. Her father was her first teacher. She continued to study with her husband Roberto Stagno, a tenor, whom she met in 1886. After her first performance of *Cavalleria rusticana*, Bellincioni was in demand all over the world. Idolized in Italy, she won acclaim in opera houses throughout Europe. She made several early recordings which are of exceptional interest to collectors. In 1903, she made four titles for the Gramophone and Typewriter Company and, in 1905, a further ten for Pathé. At the time, Bellincioni had been singing for 24 years. Her singing was characterized by a strong vibrato and extensive use of the chest register. She had a fine technique, strong sense of drama, and wide range of vocal color. Fortunately, her performances were captured on the gramophone, because her interpretation of the aria from *Cavalleria rusticana* is considered a model for subsequent interpreters of the role of Santuzza.

SUGGESTED READING:

Bellincioni, Gemma. *Io e il palcoscenico* (autobiography). Milan, 1920.

John Haag, Athens, Georgia

Belloc-Lowndes, Marie (1868–1947)

British author who wrote novels, short stories, plays and memoirs, 69 volumes in all. *Name variations: Mrs. Belloc Lowndes, Marie Belloc, Philip Curtin, Elizabeth Rayner. Born Marie Adelaide Belloc in London, England, on August 5, 1868; died in Eversley Cross, Hampshire, England, on November 14, 1947; daughter of Elizabeth (Bessie) Rayner (Parkes) (a writer and feminist) and Louis S. Belloc (a lawyer); sister of Hilaire Belloc (a writer); educated at home; married Frederick S.A. Lowndes (a journalist) on January 9, 1896; children: one son, Charles (b. 1898) and two daughters, Susan and Elizabeth.*

Selected works: The Heart of Penelope *(1904);* Barbara Rebell *(1905);* The Pulse of Life *(1907);* The Lodger *(1913);* The End of Her Honeymoon *(1914);* I, Too, Have Lived in Arcadia *(1941);* Where Love and Friendship Dwelt *(1943);* Merry Wives of Westminster *(1946).*

As the child of a French father and a British mother, Marie Belloc loved France and England, and spoke the languages of both countries fluently. The Bellocs lived in La Celle St. Cloud,

France, until Louis Belloc's death in 1872; after which mother and daughter spent equal time in Britain. Marie was educated at home and read constantly, while the literary connections of her mother, writer and feminist ✥ **Bessie Parkes**, introduced her to such women as George Eliot (***Mary Anne Evans**) and ***Elizabeth Barrett Browning**. Traveling unaccompanied, Marie went out on her own in her 20s, working as a journalist in England and France for the *Pall Mall Gazette*.

On January 9, 1896, Marie married Frederick S.A. Lowndes, and the couple settled in Westminster, at No. 9 Barton Street, where they raised their three children. Frederick, an editor for the *Times*, worked from three in the afternoon to three in the morning, while Marie rose at five to write for several hours. In the afternoon and evening, Belloc-Lowndes received guests and dined out with England's elite. Among her friends were Henry James, Oscar Wilde, H.G. Wells, Graham Greene, and Prime Minister Herbert Henry Asquith. She wrote letters and diaries of the day's events: "Yesterday I went to the Titanic enquiry," she noted, or, "I hear the King has stopped away from Goodwood because of the Morocco affair." Most commonly her writings began: "Lunched with . . ." or, "I had a most interesting talk with. . . ." Her attentions were drawn to the extraordinary or unusual stories of life, a focus reflected in her more than 40 novels which often dealt with a catastrophic event (such as murder) but was more concerned with the characters' reactions to it.

Through two world wars, Belloc-Lowndes tracked the effects on the country and her own family, with her son Charles enlisted in the armed forces for both wars. Whereas the first war had inspired a sense of victorious nationalism, the second was marked more by the threat of foreign invasion and bombing; this influenced many, including Belloc-Lowndes, to move from their homes in the cities. Having always believed No. 9 Barton Street to be haunted, Belloc-Lowndes wrote to her daughter on their departure, "It will have more ghosts now—my ghost certainly."

After 30 years at the *Times*, Frederick Lowndes retired in 1938; Marie's letters and diaries reflect her pleasure at his more regular company. In March of 1940, he fell suddenly ill and died within days. To a friend, she wrote, "I shall always be very, very glad I was with him, and alone, when he died. . . . We were very united." Belloc-Lowndes never had a permanent residence after Barton Street but instead rented houses or, as during the air raids in the summer of 1940, lived with or near one of her daughters. Following World War II, she remarked to her daughter **Elizabeth Lowndes**, "I feel, sometimes, as if I had lived a thousand years. So great are the changes since I married 50 years ago." Marie Belloc Lowndes, a bestselling author in England and abroad, grew ill in August of 1947 and died on November 14. She was at her daughter's home in Hampshire.

✥ ***Parkes, Bessie.*** *See Evans, Mary Anne for sidebar.*

SOURCES:

Lowndes, Susan, ed. *Diaries and Letters of Marie Belloc Lowndes*. London: Chatto and Windus, 1971.

Todd, Janet, ed. *British Women Writers*. NY: Continuum, 1989.

Crista Martin, freelance writer, Boston, Massachusetts

Bellon, Denise (b. 1902)

French photographer. *Born Denise Hulmann in Paris, France, in 1902; married Jacques Bellon (divorced early 1930s); married Armand Labin (deceased); children: (first marriage) Yannick (a film director) and Loleh (an actress and writer); (second marriage) Jérôme.*

Denise Bellon was working for a psychology degree at the Sorbonne, when she abandoned her studies to marry and have a family. Following her divorce, around 1930, she took up photography, establishing herself through the group agencies Studio Zuber and Alliance-Photo. Widely published in art magazines, Bellon became interested in the surrealistic art movement and photographed all the group's exhibitions in Paris, while making portraits of notable artists of the movement including Marcel Duchamp, Joan Miró, and Salvador Dalí. A commission by Paris-Match also took her to French Africa. Bellon later married Armand Labin and settled in Lyons, where she had a third child. After her husband's death in 1956, she returned to Paris.

Belmont, Alva Smith (1853–1933)

American social reformer and socialite. *Name variations: Mrs. O.H.P. Belmont; Mrs. Oliver Belmont; Mrs. William K. Vanderbilt; Alva E. Belmont; Alva Murray Smith. Born Alva Erskine (or Ertskin) Smith on January 17, 1853, in Mobile, Alabama; died on January 26, 1933, in Paris, France; educated in France; married William Kissam Vanderbilt I (1849–1920), in 1875 (divorced 1895); married Oliver Hazard Perry Belmont (d. 1908), in January 1896; children: (first marriage)* ****Consuelo Vanderbilt*** *(1877–1964), duchess of Marlborough; William Kissam Vanderbilt II (1878–1944); Harold Stirling Vanderbilt (1884–1970).*

Born into southern aristocracy in 1853, Alva Smith Belmont was educated in France, where the family had moved after the Civil War devastated the American South. They later returned to New York, where Belmont made her society debut and, in April 1875, married William K. Vanderbilt, grandson of Cornelius. Despite their vast wealth, the Vanderbilts were excluded from the cream of New York Society, then dominated by the Astor and McAllister families. Craving acceptance, the new Mrs. Vanderbilt set out to make her mark, commissioning Richard M. Hunt to build a family mansion on Fifth Avenue. She followed with houses on Long Island and in Newport, the latter "cottage" reportedly costing $9 million with furnishings. She also lit up the social calendar of 1883 with the most extravagant entertainment ever seen in New York—a masquerade ball for 1,200 guests.

Alva Smith Belmont

After securing her place in the coveted "Four Hundred," New York's most elite of the elite, Alva then stunned her new society friends by charging her rich husband with adultery and filing for a divorce. The ensuing scandal was reinforced by gossip regarding her own involvement with Oliver Hazard Perry Belmont, the son of a prominent banker, who was a few years her junior. A year after her divorce, she married Belmont in a civil ceremony, her only recourse at the time. Following his death eight years later, Alva Belmont found a new direction for her life.

Focusing energy on the cause of women's rights, in 1909 she lent her support to the striking garment workers, organizing meetings and encouraging wealthy friends to boycott non-union dress manufacturers. With personal visits to jails, she provided bail for a number of union strikers, an act that initially met with skepticism coming from such an unlikely source. That same year, she paid for the Fifth Avenue offices of the National American Woman Suffrage Association and subsequently financed a speaking tour by English suffragist ***Christabel Pankhurst**. Belmont co-authored a feminist operetta, *Melinda and Her Sisters*, and staged it at the exclusive Waldorf-Astoria Hotel in 1916. Starring ***Marie Dressler**, the production brought in $8,000. With the women's vote finally secured, Belmont, who authored the slogan "Pray to God. She will help you," was elected president of the National Woman's Party, a post she held from 1921 to the end of her life.

Alva Belmont spent her later years in France, continuing to represent American women's interests at international conferences. She renewed an interest in architecture which had first surfaced with the building of the Vanderbilt mansions, and in the 1930s and '40s she became a noted architectural designer, restoring a 15th-century castle, among other projects. In honor of her achievements, she was one of the first women ever elected to the American Institute of Architects. Alva Smith Belmont died in Paris on January 26, 1933, a few days after her 80th birthday.

Barbara Morgan,
Melrose, Massachusetts

Belmont, Mrs. August (1879–1979).

See Belmont, Eleanor Robson.

Belmont, Eleanor Robson (1879–1979)

Actress and philanthropist, known as "the woman who single-handedly saved the Metropolitan Opera."

Name variations: Mrs. August Belmont. Born Eleanor Elise Robson on December 13, 1879, in Wigan, Lancashire, England; died on October 26, 1979, in New York, New York; daughter of Charles Robson (a musician and conductor) and Madge Carr-Cook (an actress); attended St. Peter's Academy on Staten Island, New York; married August Belmont, Jr., February 26, 1910, in New York City (died, 1924).

In 1910, Eleanor Belmont gave up a successful acting career to marry wealthy widower August Belmont, Jr. Throughout a second career as a philanthropist, her extraordinary efforts on behalf of numerous organizations, most notably the American Red Cross and the Metropolitan Opera, were unparalleled. At the time, it was said that she probably helped raise more money than any other woman in America.

Belmont was born Eleanor Robson in Wigan, England, the third generation of a well-known theatrical family. Her father died when she was very young, and her mother later married actor Augustus Cook and moved with him to the United States, placing Belmont in a convent on Staten Island while she toured with the

Daniel Frawley Stock Company of San Francisco. (Known as ❧ **Madge Carr-Cook**, Eleanor's mother would best be remembered for her performance in the title role in *Mrs. Wiggins of the Cabbage Patch.*) As a shy 17-year-old, Belmont rejoined her mother and stepfather and found herself performing bit parts with the company for $15 a week. (Later, she claimed to have been hired not because anyone thought she could act, but so her mother could keep an eye on her.) When the company's ingénue quit the company, Belmont was pressed into more serious roles. She was not only beautiful—blonde, with large blue eyes—but a quick study. According to her mother, Eleanor didn't learn lines, she absorbed them, mastering 13 different roles in as many days.

At 21, she made her Broadway debut, playing Bonita Canby, the lead in Augustus Thomas' *Arizona*. In 1904, she appeared in *Merely Mary Ann*, written at her suggestion by Israel Zangwill from his own short story. After a successful run in New York, she appeared in the equally well-received London tour. Her performance particularly enthralled young playwright George Bernard Shaw, who called her a "Joan of Arc" and, in spite of his notorious reputation as a misogynist, sent her a glowing letter, one of many to follow. "I take no interest in mere females; but I love all artists," he wrote. "They belong to me in the most sacred way; and you are an artist." His platonic crush on Belmont endured for many years, and he created the play *Major Barbara* as a vehicle for her, though her producer at the time would not release her from her contract to accept the role.

During the height of her theatrical career, Eleanor was persistently pursued by August Belmont, Jr., a wealthy widower with three sons. While August busied himself with building the New York subway system, his real passion was for breeding and racing horses. He became somewhat of a stage-door Johnny, showering Eleanor with flowers and adoring notes. Although he was 27 years her senior, and her decision to marry him may have been more practical than passionate, the two wed in January 1910. Just weeks before the nuptials, in her final stage performance as the character Glad in *The Dawn of a Tomorrow*, she delivered a prophetic curtain line: "I'm going to be took care of now."

Belmont fit easily into her newly acquired role as wife to a very rich man, writing: "A private railroad car is not an acquired taste. One takes to it immediately." In addition to enjoying the high life (including a party at which Harry Houdini performed one of his famous escapes), Eleanor Belmont threw her enormous energy and creative talents into fund-raising. One of her first philanthropic creations was the Working Girls' Vacation Association, a fund to help young working women get out of the city for a week or so each year. She also founded the Society for the Prevention of Useless Spending to confront the problem of a growing number of overlapping fund-raising appeals. The society served as a planning agency, which studied areas of need and convinced wealthy donors to allocate their gifts in a manner that allowed more people to get a portion of the pie.

During the First World War, Belmont turned her attention to the American Red Cross. In the first three months of the war, she made 45 speeches in ten states in an appeal to raise money. In the fall of 1917, she made a dangerous trip across the Atlantic to visit the European troops, carrying with her a letter of introduction to General John Pershing, commander of the U.S. forces, from Theodore Roosevelt. In accordance with the gender parlance of the day, the letter outlined her mission and pinpointed her special abilities: "She has a man's understanding, a woman's sympathy, and a sense of honor and gift of expression such as are possessed by very few either among men or women." Belmont made a number of other tours on behalf of the Red Cross before the end of the war and also established a children's unit of the Red Cross in New York. In 1919, she was elected to membership in the Red Cross' governing body. Indeed, she would continue to be active in Red Cross activities throughout her life, receiving medals honoring her work in 1934 and 1939.

❧ Carr-Cook, Madge (1856–1933).

English actress. *Born in Yorks, England, on June 28, 1856; died on September 20, 1933; sister of T. Morton Powell (a theatrical manager); married Charles Robson; married* ***Augustus Cook*** *(an actor); children: (first marriage)* ****Eleanor Robson Belmont*** *(1879–1979).*

Madge Carr-Cook made her stage debut at age three, appearing as Fleance in *MacBeth*. Following many tours within England, she moved to the U.S. in 1887, joining the Lyceum stock company under Daniel Frohman's management. Carr-Cook had her first taste of fame when she opened as Elvira Wiggs in *Mrs. Wiggs of the Cabbage Patch*. First produced in Louisville, Kentucky, in October 1903, the ***Alice Hegan Rice** play opened at the Savoy Theatre in New York in September 1904. Carr-Cook retired from the stage following her daughter **Eleanor Robson**'s marriage to August Belmont in 1910.

Widowed in 1924, at age 45, Belmont, with her snow white hair and elegant demeanor, settled comfortably into the role of *grande dame*. She auctioned off her husband's stable of 113 thoroughbred horses and sold a mansion on Madison Avenue, as well as the couple's Newport "cottage." She would make her home in a large apartment on Fifth Avenue and maintain a summer cottage in Maine until the late 1950s. During the Depression, she was chair of the Women's Division of the Emergency Unemployment Relief Commission for New York City. She also founded the Adopt-a-Family Committee to care for white-collar workers who needed short-term relief. Her artistic talents were again put to work; in 1924, she collaborated with **Harriet Ford**, adapting Ford's novel *In the Next Room* into a successful play.

Belmont's fund-raising skills were perhaps best utilized in her work for the Metropolitan Opera, which was on the brink of closing its doors after the Great Crash of 1929. Appointed to the then all-male board of directors in 1933, Belmont described her first meeting as something akin to opening night in the theatre. Her ap-

Eleanor Robson Belmont

proach to saving the Met was creatively geared to creating a new generation of youthful and middle-class opera-goers. Enduring criticism that she was "cheapening" the opera, she instituted Saturday afternoon radio broadcasts from the Metropolitan stage and ran a "What the Opera Means to Me" contest, with a weekend in New York and tickets to a performance as the prize. She established group discounts for children and students. When the Met's front curtain had to be replaced, Belmont had the old curtain cleaned, cut, and sewn into souvenir bookmarks and eyeglass cases by a network of volunteers. The sales of the Gold Curtain Souvenirs brought in $11,000.

In 1935, Belmont organized the Metropolitan Opera Guild, which provided members with special perks, like early ticket purchase, discounts for various performances, and subscriptions to an opera newsletter. Most attractive to many members was the privilege of attending opera rehearsal. During its first year, 2,000 people became guild members, with numbers climbing each year to reach 60,000. In 1957, over and above ticket sales to members, the Guild raised $2 million for the Metropolitan Opera Association.

During World War II, Belmont headed up the Guild's wartime activities, which included distributing opera tickets to service personnel. She also assumed the presidency of the Motion Picture Research Council, an organization formed to raise the standards of American films, and became a member of the advisory board of the National Broadcasting Company.

Eleanor Belmont remained active well into her 70s and 80s, giving small lunches and keeping a full-time secretary busy with correspondence. In 1949, she made a final visit to G.B. Shaw at his home in England. Whenever possible, she continued to attend the opera, although she had to be lifted from a wheelchair to her special chaise in her box. Awards and honors collected until the end of her days included a lifetime appointment as founder and president emeritus of the Opera Guild. Belmont received a distinguished service medal from the Theodore Roosevelt Association and was awarded honorary degrees from Yale and Columbia Universities. On the occasion of her 90th birthday, when she was reported to be in ill health, *The New York Times* prepared a full-page obituary. It did not appear until nearly 10 years later, when Eleanor Robson Belmont died in her sleep just shy of her 100th birthday.

SOURCES:

Birmingham, Stephen. *The Grandes Dames.* NY: Simon and Schuster, 1982.

Current Biography. NY: H.W. Wilson, 1944.

Barbara Morgan, Melrose, Massachusetts

Belmont, Mrs. O.H.P. (1853–1933).

See Belmont, Alva Smith.

Beloff, Nora (1919–1997)

English author, journalist and first woman correspondent in Britain. *Born in London, England, on January 24, 1919; died on February 12, 1997; third of five children of Simon and Marie (Spivak) Beloff; sister of* ****Anne Beloff-Chain*** *(1921–1991) and Max Beloff; granted B.A., Lady Margaret Hall, Oxford, 1940; married Clifford Makins (sports editor for the* Observer*), on March 7, 1977 (died 1990); children: none.*

Selected writings: The General Says No *(1963);* Transit of Britain *(1973);* Freedom under Foot: The Battle over the Closed Shop in British Journalism *(1976);* No Travel Like Russian Travel *(1979, published as* Inside the Soviet Empire: The Myth, the Reality, *1980); and* Tito's Flawed Legacy.

Always curious, even as a child, about what was really going on in the world, Nora Beloff gravitated to journalism. "Obviously, the right choice," she wrote. "I had the necessary qualifications: inexhaustible stamina, insatiable curiosity and a thick skin." Beloff began her career in the British Foreign Office, joined Reuters News Agency in 1946, and wrote for *The Economist* in Paris. In 1948, she began as an editorial leader writer for the British *Observer* and lived on assignment in Washington and Moscow for the national weekly during the 1950s; by 1964, she was Britain's first female political correspondent in most of the major capital cities of the world, holding that position until 1976. She left the *Observer* in 1978 over a disagreement with a new editor and began to freelance, exploring the Soviet Union and the former Yugoslavia. She was eventually arrested in Russia and expelled from Yugoslavia.

Outspoken and unpopular on Fleet Street, Beloff's authoritarian manner was often compared to that of American journalist ***Dorothy Thompson**. One of only a handful of British female journalists during her time, Beloff claims she had an advantage, "Men behave much better to us than to each other." Later in her career, when she had established her reputation and discovered that she had more to say than would fit into newspaper format, Beloff authored several books, including one on the Soviet Union. Presented as a travelogue account of her experience and observations as a correspondent, it was praised for its feisty style and honest observations.

Barbara Morgan, Melrose, Massachusetts

Beloff-Chain, Anne (1921–1991)

British biochemist internationally recognized for her work on the metabolism of carbohydrates and hormonal aspects of diabetes. *Name variations: Anne Beloff Chain. Born in London, England, on June 26, 1921; died in London on December 2, 1991; one of five children of Simon and Marie (Spivak) Beloff; sister of* ****Nora Beloff*** *(1919–1997) and Max Beloff; educated as a chemist at Oxford University and University College London; married Ernst Boris Chain (1906–1979, Nobel Prize winner for his work on penicillin), in 1948; children: two sons. Taught at Imperial College, London (1964–86); taught at the University of Buckingham (1986–91).*

Although the worldwide reputation of her husband, noted Nobel Prize winner Sir Ernst Chain, sometimes overshadowed her scientific accomplishments, Anne Beloff-Chain was a highly respected scientist in her own right who was confident that her research could hold its own in the highly competitive world of modern biochemical research. Beloff-Chain was born in London on June 26, 1921, into a family of Russian-Jewish origins that had the highest respect for learning and scholarship. The youngest of five gifted children who would all go on to distinguished careers, Anne was expected to excel academically. She earned a D.Phil. at Oxford, then quickly picked up a first-class honors degree from University College London.

In the early 1940s, she met Ernst Boris Chain, a brilliant young Jewish refugee from Nazi Germany, whose laboratory was close to the one in which she carried out her first research work. In 1946, she went to Harvard University for an extended period of research; upon her return two years later, she married Chain. From 1948 through 1964, they worked together on a number of joint projects at the Department of Biochemistry of the Instituto Superiore di Sanita. Beloff-Chain's numerous publications in major journals dealt with the intermediary metabolism of carbohydrates and the mechanism of action of insulin and hormonal control in relation to diabetes and obesity. One of her major achievements was the discovery of a new insulin secretagogue hormone beta-cell tropin present at abnormal levels in the blood of the obese. This hormone enabled researchers to establish a key link between diabetes and obesity.

In 1964, Anne and her husband returned to London, where she taught biochemistry at Imperial College, finally receiving a personal chair in 1983. Her retirement from Imperial College did not end her scientific work, and she was able to persuade the Clore Foundation to fund the establishment of a new Department of Biochemistry at the University of Buckingham, which she headed and staffed with members of her Imperial College team. Here she worked until the end of her productive life. When Anne Beloff-Chain died in London on December 2, 1991, she was survived by a solid body of scientific work, two sons who were productive scientists, and a large number of colleagues and friends who would miss her dedication and contributions.

SOURCES:

"Anne Beloff-Chain," *The Times* [London], December 17, 1991, p. 16.

John Haag, Associate Professor, University of Georgia

Belote, Melissa (1956—)

American swimmer. *Born in Springfield, Virginia, on October 16 (some sources cite the 10th), 1956; daughter of Florence and Ernest Belote.*

Won Olympic gold medals in the 100-meter backstroke, the 400-meter medley relay, and the 200-meter backstroke in the Munich Olympics (1972).

"When Melissa came to me, she came with an airline ticket to Munich," remarked Belote's coach Ed Solotar. Though no one could be certain the young girl was of Olympic caliber, many like Solotar could not overlook her determination. Melissa Belote was the second-born of Florence and Ernest Belote's three daughters. Like many other American suburban families, the Belotes belonged to a community pool where their daughters learned to swim. When Melissa's friends on the swim team began waving flashy blue, first-place ribbons under her nose, she wanted to join in. Thus, in 1964, at age eight, she joined the Tigersharks at the Springfield Swim Club where Dick Donahue was her first coach. Belote swam freestyle, butterfly, backstroke, and relay and was soon amassing her own blue ribbons.

In 1966, ten-year-old Belote joined the Starlit Aquatic Club under the coaching of Ed Solotar. Since his team trained year round, her schedule revolved around swimming: up at five, she practiced from six to seven and again after school. By age 11, she had learned to put forth a burst of speed in the last 15 meters to overcome the competition, and her sights were set on becoming an Olympic athlete. At 12, Belote entered her first national swim meet, competing in the backstroke to avoid the red-rimmed, teary eyes from hours in chlorinated water. But winning was not as easy at the national level as it had been at local meets. In swimming, as in most competitive sports, athletes often struggle against one particular competitor. **Susie Atwood** of California was Belote's backstroking nemesis. Try as she would, a frustrated Belote could never wrench first place from Atwood. Said Ernest Belote to his petulant daughter: "When you finally beat Susie Atwood, she will never beat you again." His words proved prophetic.

During her first year of national competition, Belote won the 200-meter individual medley, the 100-meter backstroke, and the relay. At the Amateur Athletic Union (AAU) Junior Olympic meet in Washington, D.C., she set national records in the 50-yard backstroke with a time of 19.8 and in the 100-yard backstroke with a time of 1:05.3. Winning the 100-yard freestyle as well, she qualified for the National Junior Olympics. In San Diego, California, Belote set a record for her age group in the 100-meter backstroke with a time of 1:13.8. But at the 1969 Nationals in Louisville, Kentucky, Belote did not do well, nor did she have a good showing at the National AAU short course championship in Cincinnati or at the Los Angeles National AAU Long Course championship. She then placed eighth in the 100-yard backstroke at the 1971 National Short Course in Pullman, Washington. Politics intervened when friction developed between the management of the Swim Club and Belote's Solotar. Refusing to take sides, Belote swam unattached for awhile, eventually signing with the Solotar Swim Team.

In June 1972, Belote entered the Santa Clara Invitational determined to jettison the pressure of earlier losses. Something worked. She won the 200-meter backstroke and finally beat Susie Atwood. A month later at the Eastern Championships, Belote won the 100- and 200-meter backstroke. Taking charge of her sport, she set six records in the 100- and 200-meter backstroke, the 400-meter individual medley, the 400-meter freestyle, the 200-meter individual medley, and the 800-meter freestyle. By early August, she was off to Chicago for the Olympic trials, where she finished first in the 100- and 200-meter.

Soon Belote was training with Sherm Chavoor, the Olympic team coach, at the University of Tennessee. On September 2, 1972, at Munich, Belote won a gold in the 100-meter backstroke with a new Olympic record of 1:05:78. During the 400-meter medley relay, Belote led off with the backstroke, giving teammates ❧▸ **Catherine Carr** (breaststroke), **Deena Deardurff** (butterfly), and ❧▸ **Sandy Neilson** (freestyle) a lead the Americans never lost; the team set another Olympic record of 4:20.75 and a world time as well. Belote took the 200-meter backstroke with new world and Olympic records of 2:19.19 for her third gold. Though the 1972 Munich Olympics were an unqualified success for the American swim team, they were a horror for the other athletes. Arab terrorists held the Israeli wrestling team hostage, killing several athletes, in one of the most abhorrent terrorist offenses in history.

After 1972, the East Germans increasingly dominated women's swimming. In the fall of 1973, no other team came close to their showing in the World Swimming Championship in Belgrade, Yugoslavia. East Germany's success was not attributable to drugs but rather to their new swimsuits. For years, women had been required to wear a swimsuit with a quarter-panel skirt in front, a holdover from the days when women wore swimming dresses. AAU rules specified that all American swimmers must wear this quarter-panel skirt. It was just enough material to drag on American swimmers while their East German opponents utilized the skin-tight "Belgrade" suit to gain the precious fractions of a second needed to win races. After Belote and several other swimmers campaigned for the newer suit, the quarter-panel swim skirt went the way of bustles and corsets as women ushered in a new era of swimming fashion designed for performance not someone else's idea of propriety.

Karin Loewen Haag,
Athens, Georgia

❧▸ Carr, Catherine (1954—)

American swimmer. *Born on May 27, 1954.*

In the Munich Olympics, 1972, Catherine Carr won gold medals in the 100-meter breaststroke and the 4x100-meter relay.

❧▸ Neilson, Sandy (1956—)

American swimmer. *Born Sandra Neilson on March 20, 1956.*

In Munich, Germany, in 1972, Sandy Neilson won Olympic gold medals in the 100-meter freestyle, the 4x100-meter freestyle relay, and the 4x100-meter medley relay.

Belousova or Belovsova, Ludmila

(b. 1936).

See Protopopov, Ludmila.

Beltran, Lola (c. 1931–1996)

Mexican singer. *Name variations: Lola la Grande (Lola the Great). Born around 1931 (Beltran made a point of not discussing her age); died of a stroke in Mexico City on March 24, 1996; children: daughter Maria Elena Leal.*

The soulful Lola Beltran, whose emotional Spanish renditions of mariachi ballads entertained Latin Americans for 50 years, was "one of the greatest woman singers in the high-octane pop-ranchera style," wrote Michael Erlewine. She sang of pain, heartache, loneliness, and loss; she sang of life's perpetual melancholy. In 1994, novelist Carlos Fuentes noted: "Passion and desire, joy and risk, tenderness and the cry for existence are the wings of this dove that is the voice of our lady Lola Beltran. I have spent my life living and writing and loving and traveling with the voice of Lola Beltran close to me, on records, over the airwaves, but above all in the soundtrack of memory."

SOURCES:

Erlewine, Michael. *All Music Guide.* San Francisco: Miller Freeman, 1992.

Beltrano, Aniella (1613–1649).

See Rosa, Anella de.

Bemberg, Maria Luisa (1922–1995)

Argentine director and screenwriter. *Born in Argentina on April 14, 1922; died of stomach cancer in Buenos Aires, Argentina, on May 7, 1995; daughter of influential German immigrants in Argentina; married in 1942 (divorced 1952); children: four.*

Selected filmography: (documentaries) El mundo del mujeres *(*The World of Women, *1972),* Juguetes *(*Toys, *1974); (screenplays)* Crónica de una señora *(*Story of a Lady, *1972),* Triángulo de cuatro *(*Triangle of Four *(1972); (produced and directed)* Momentos *(Moments, 1981); (directed)* Camila *(1984),* Miss Mary *(1986),* Yo, la peor de todas *(*I, Worst of All, *1991),* De eso no se habla *(*I don't want to talk about it, *with Marcello Mastroianni, 1993).*

Before the opening frame of Maria Luisa Bemberg's 1993 film *De eso no se habla*, there is an inscription that reads, "This tale is dedicated to all people who have the courage to be different in order to be themselves." The modest message would also apply to Bemberg.

Born in 1922 to a family of Argentine aristocrats, Bemberg grew up surrounded by servants and was educated privately by a governess on her family's vast *estancia*. But privilege came with strict limitations for women of that era. Though dutifully married by age 20, and eventually a mother of four, Bemberg never fit in as a society matron. Always outspoken, she claimed her rebellious, creative nature drove her to filmmaking. The films she produced, as she told writer Caleb Bach in an interview for *Américas*, "propose images of women that are vertical, autonomous, independent, thoughtful, courageous and spunky."

In the late 1960s, after having been deeply influenced by writer ***Simone de Beauvoir**, Bemberg and a few women formed their own feminist group. For her part, Bemberg was working with ideas that would change the nature of films from the macho melodramas of the past to women-driven films with modern themes. But this was a dangerous time for outspoken women. For years, any effort to buck the patriarchal system was effectively suppressed by the military regime that followed the Argentine dictator Juan Peron.

Bemberg, however, was determined to speak her truth. With her own money, she financed and made two documentaries, *El mundo del mujeres* and *Juguetes*. The latter was a groundbreaking film which argued that traditional toys reinforce stereotypes: shove a fire truck into the hand of a little boy and he'll want to be a fireman; insist that a girl play only with dolls and she'll become a housewife or a nurse.

In 1972, Bemberg wrote her first feature-length screenplay, *Crónica de una señora*, which revolved around a wealthy but dissatisfied housewife, a story Bemberg admitted was autobiographical. Directed by Raul de la Torre, the film not only provoked great controversy but was hugely successful. Bemberg's next film, *Triangulo de cuatro*, concerned a man who has to choose between his independent mistress and his traditional wife. Also a great success, the film brought Bemberg her first award as a screenwriter. Though the film was well directed by Fernando Ayla, Bemberg was never fully satisfied with a male director's interpretation of her female characters, and she decided to go behind the camera herself.

In 1981, at age 59, Bemberg wrote, produced, and directed *Momentos*, a film about a love affair gone sour between a married couple that, at its core, explored the idea of role reversal. Bemberg felt the movie marked "the beginning of a long-lasting complicity between the female audience of Argentina and the first successful grandmother filmmaker in the country."

The success of *Momentos*, along with the election of a more liberal political regime, allowed Bemberg to resurrect a previously censored screenplay about a homemaker who goes on a protest strike. She had written *Senora de nadie* in 1972 and was apprehensive about its reception from working-class women. But when the film was previewed at a film festival in Sicily, a group of women "dressed in black, with weather-beaten faces, very cross . . . said '*Grazie in il nome di donne di Catania*' (Thank you in the name of the women of Catania)." Their response proved to Bemberg that women from all social ranks and of all ages have a great sense of solidarity.

Bemberg then earned an Oscar nomination in the Best Foreign Film category for her 1984 film *Camila* which was based on the true story of **Camila O'Gorman**, a rebellious 19th-century aristocrat who eloped with her priest, Father Ladislao Gutierrez. Because the couple had the misfortune of falling in love during a particular-

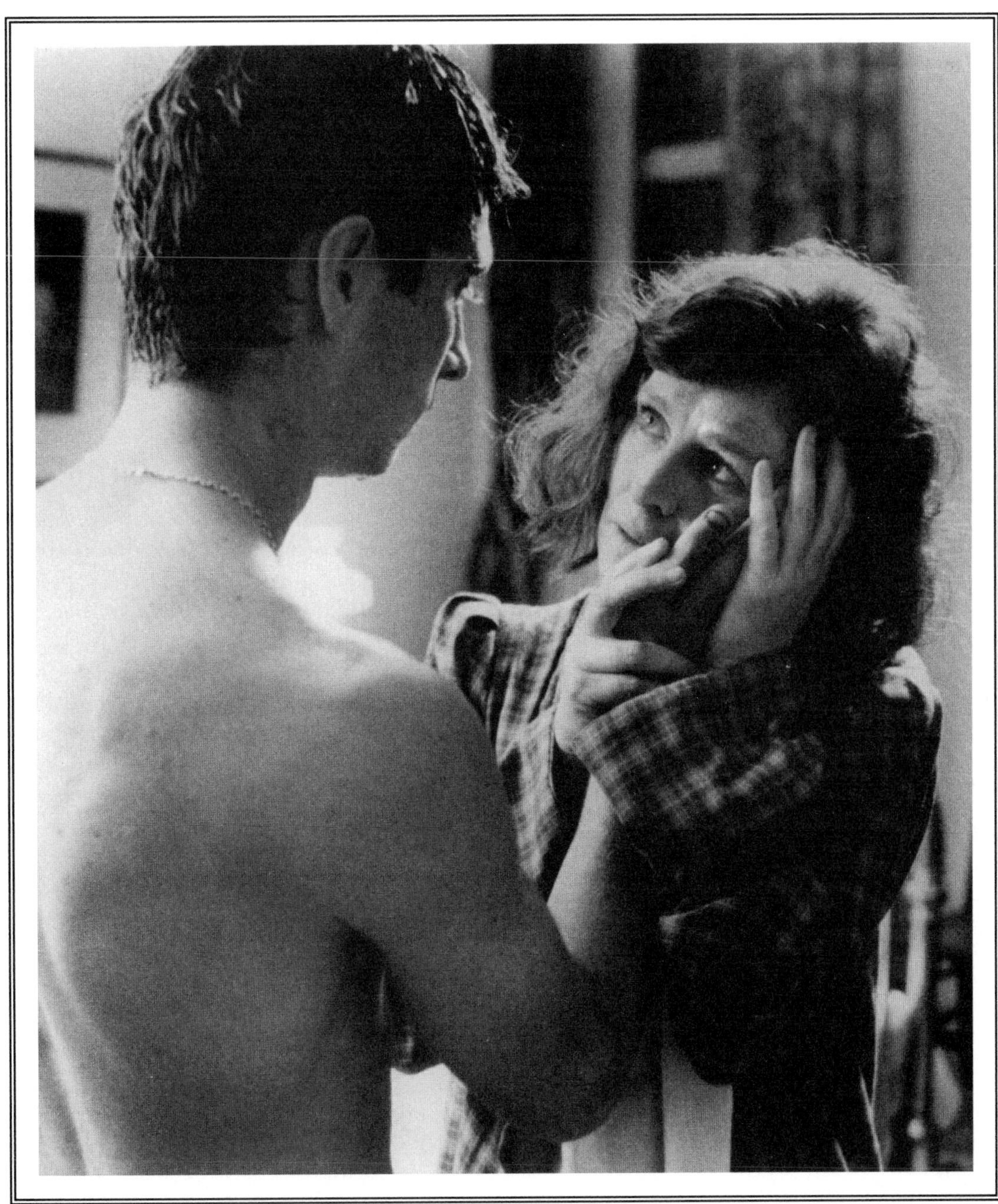

From the movie Miss Mary, *starring Julie Christie, directed by Maria Luisa Bemberg.*

ly repressive regime, they were caught and executed. With the Oscar nomination and the success of *Camila* came the recognition from the international film community that Maria Luisa Bemberg was a major talent.

Because *Camila* was such a success both artistically and financially, Bemberg was able to attract the internationally known star **Julie Christie** for the title roll of her next film. *Miss Mary* tells of a lonely English governess who is brought to Argentina to care for the children of an philandering *estanciero*. Bemberg links the personal family drama and, in particular, the patriarchal subjugation of women, with the social unrest about to explode just beyond the gates of the perfectly manicured estate.

Her next project, set in the 17th century and entitled *Yo, la peor de todas*, portrays the life of legendary poet ***Juana Inés de la Cruz**, a Mexican nun who was eventually destroyed by the fanaticism of the Inquisition.

In May 1993, Bemberg completed what was to be her final and perhaps most controversial film. *De eso no se habla*, with Marcello Mastroianni. In the movie, the aristocratic woman Leonor, upon discovering that her only child Carlotta is a dwarf, refuses to talk about or even acknowledge her daughter's difference. Instead, she sets out to make sure that her daughter becomes the most accomplished child in the village. That the daughter ages but remains forever childlike because of her condition is a metaphor for Bemberg's own privileged but sequestered upbringing. Though Carlotta eventually marries an older worldly gentleman, and thus moves from her mother's care to the care of her husband, she never becomes "herself" until an eye-opening experience changes her life. Like Bemberg, who rebelled against her family and husband's wishes when she entered the work place, Carlotta steals away in the night to see the forbidden—a seedy traveling circus. Because "the forbidden" in Bemberg's own life was certainly the movies, the final scene of *De eso no se habla* is made more poignant with its autobiographical facets when Carlotta, riding a white horse, leads the circus parade as they leave the home of her childhood forever. As Bemberg said, she had found the courage to be different in order to be herself.

Bemberg was 71 when she completed *De eso no se habla*. By then, notes *Time*, she had become "one of Latin America's foremost female film directors." She died of stomach cancer in Buenos Aires in May 1995.

SOURCES:

Bach, Caleb. "Maria Luisa Bemberg Tells The Untold," in *Americas*. March–April 1994, pp. 20–27.

Brunette, Peter. "Political subtext in a fairy tale from a feminist," in *The New York Times*. September 25, 1994. Sec. 2, p. 14.

Jaehne, Karen. "I Don't Want to Talk About It," in *Film Quarterly*. Winter 94–95, pp. 52–55.

Quart, Barbara Koenig. *Women Directors: The Emergence of a New Cinema*. NY: Praeger, 1988.

Time [obituary]. May 22, 1995, p. 27.

Deborah Jones, Studio City, California

Bemis, Polly (1853–1933).

See Nathoy, Lalu.

Benario, Olga (1908–1942)

German-Jewish Communist and revolutionary activist, who was committed to social justice and fought against the Nazis. *Pronunciation: Beh-NAIR-ee-YO. Name variations: Olga Benario Prestes, Olga Benario-Prestes. Born Olga Benario in Munich, Germany, on February 12, 1908; gassed along with other German women political prisoners at Bernburg Hospital in early February 1942; daughter of Leo Benario (a wealthy Social Democratic attorney) and Eugenie Guttmann Benario (a socialite); received extensive leadership training ranging from Marxist theory to skydiving in USSR; married Luis Carlos Prestes (unofficially); children: one daughter* ***Anita Leocádia Prestes*** *(b. November 1936).*

Joined the Young Communist League in Munich and became one of the most promising young women in the German Communist movement (1923); after engineering the rescue of Otto Braun in Berlin, fled with him to the Soviet Union (1928); traveled to France, Belgium, and England on Communist Youth International mission (1931); assigned by the Comintern to go to Brazil with Brazilian revolutionary leader Luis Carlos Prestes to lead a revolutionary upheaval which failed (November 1935); captured with Prestes by the fascist regime of Getulio Vargas and held until shipped, seven months pregnant, to Nazi Germany, where she gave birth to her daughter in prison (1936).

At the time of her murder in a Nazi concentration camp a few days short of her 34th birthday, Olga Benario had squeezed considerable exhilaration, joy, and suffering into her brief life. She had been born into the safe middle-class environment of a prosperous assimilated Jewish family during the final years of Europe's pre-1914 "golden age of security," but defiantly rejected the cultural and political norms of her family and class in favor of becoming a militant Communist revolutionary. While living and dying for a political ideology that would eventually be discredited, Benario demonstrated a passionate commitment to social justice.

Born on February 12, 1908, in the Bavarian city of Munich, Olga Benario was deeply influenced by her father Leo, a wealthy and successful lawyer who had a powerful sense of social justice and was a member of the moderate reformist Social Democratic Party. Leo Benario used his legal expertise to assist workers who wished to bring claims against their employers, and never turned down a case because the worker could not afford to pay. It was through him that Olga Benario first learned about the depths of social injustice. Reading her father's files, she was introduced to the inequities of a chaotic and unstable German social order in the years following World War I. Although Olga's political and social views became more radical than those of her father, she always recognized his essential decency and deep concern for the downtrodden.

Her relationship with her mother, on the other hand, was tense and one of increasingly mutual rejection. **Eugenie Guttmann Benario** was interested in little more than the elegant social events her husband's position made possible, and her superficial aspirations were regarded by her daughter as unacceptable in a time of social upheaval and vast suffering by the majority of Germany's people. Although the Benario family, who lived in an elegant home on the Karlplatz, was physically safe from the violence that raged in Munich in 1919 when a short-lived Soviet Republic ruled Bavaria, their young daughter was already determined to play a role in creating a better society than the one passed on to her.

Her hometown of Munich meanwhile became notorious as the center of a new radical-Rightist movement, the National Socialist German Workers Party led by an Austrian-born demagogue named Adolf Hitler. In the summer of 1923, a few months before Hitler made an unsuccessful bid to seize power (through a gangland-style event known as the Beer-Hall Putsch of November 9, 1923), Olga was only 15 when she joined an underground Communist youth squad in order to act against the growing danger of fascism. Headquartered in Munich's artists' colony of Schwabing, the group specialized in putting up illegal revolutionary posters around town, and its members were suspicious at first of the girl who had grown up, unlike them, in an atmosphere of affluence. But Benario soon proved to be fearless and resourceful. Quick-witted on the street, where the police might show up at any instant, she also displayed extraordinary intellectual depth, having mastered many of the theoretical tomes of Marxism before she was out of her teens. Her presence gave the group new energy and goals.

Olga Benario

In 1924, while working at a fashionable Munich bookshop, 18-year-old Olga Benario met the first great love of her life, Otto Braun (1901–1974). Seven years older, Braun already enjoyed a considerable reputation in Munich as a political radical and "lady's man." Olga expected him to be disheveled, bearded, and generally unkempt; instead, she was introduced to a handsome, vital 23-year-old Marxist activist, with hair parted meticulously and dressed in stylish creased trousers and brushed suede boots. While his most bohemian feature was probably his pipe, he had already chalked up impressive revolutionary credentials. Five years earlier, in the spring of 1919, Otto had still been in his teens when the fledgling Bavarian Communist Party relegated him the task of halting a convoy of German government troops moving toward Munich to crush the shaky Bavarian Soviet Republic that had just been proclaimed. Although superior force eventually crushed this Bolshevik experiment on German soil, Braun led the action that prolonged the life of the Munich Soviet for several additional weeks. His imprisonment for this action was the first of several political incarcerations, and, since those dramatic days, he had grown more skilled as a military theorist. By the time he met Benario, he was part of the secret apparatus of the German Communist Party (KPD) and was probably carrying out intelligence assignments for the Soviet authorities.

Soon lovers, Otto guided Olga's reading, acquainting her with the great works of military history and strategy. At party cell meetings, the stunningly beautiful young woman with the soft blue eyes now began to insist that her comrades also take up such works systematically, in preparation for the day when the fight to the death against fascism began.

Olga Benario eventually decided to move to Berlin, a metropolis with a large and militant Communist movement, and Braun convinced his superiors that he, too, could better serve KPD interests in the larger city. The couple rented a tiny room in the impoverished working-class district of Neukölln and carried out their clandestine party missions under the names issued on their false documents, as "Arthur Behrendt," a traveling merchant, and his wife, "Frieda Wolf Behrendt." The young lovers rarely had much time to themselves, as the party demanded their ever greater dedication to the task of preparing for the German working-class revolution. When they were together, Braun brought up the idea of marriage, but Benario rejected it. Fiercely opposed to the idea of becoming another person's property, she argued that their love was perfect as it was, and that the institution of marriage might destroy their relationship.

Early in 1926, Benario was barely 18 when she was made secretary of Agitation and Propaganda for the Communist Youth League of the city of Berlin. She spent her time organizing groups of young militants to hang posters, picket factories, and distribute pamphlets, and her strategies of protest were often ingenious. On one occasion, she organized dozens of couples to pose as lovers in the heart of Berlin, standing on street corners, window-shopping, and pausing outside bars and ice-cream parlors, until a loud whistle signaled for them to fill the street and chant as a group, while hammer-and-sickle banners and red flags were unfurled in the windows of adjacent shops and office buildings. By the time police arrived, a powerful demonstration of Communist protest had been mounted.

But such successes also made Benario a prime target for the Berlin political police. In early October 1926, she was arrested, at the same time Otto was arrested in another part of Berlin. Two months later, in early December, she was suddenly released from Moabit Prison, but Otto's release did not follow, and it became clear that the government planned a large-scale crackdown on the KPD. When state prosecutors prepared a charge against Braun of high treason, Benario began to organize for his rescue. Moabit Prison, where he was being held, was no ordinary jail, but a virtual fortress occupying an entire block in the heart of Berlin. In the early spring of 1928, when Otto's trial was imminent, it was decided that the rescue attempt would have to be made at one of his pre-trial hearings, during the few moments when he was being transferred from the waiting room to the main trial chamber.

On April 11, 1928, precisely at 9 AM, an armed squad made up of Benario and five of her most trusted comrades burst into the room where Braun was about to be interrogated. Olga pressed a pistol into the neck of a guard and demanded release of the prisoner, and an instant later seven Communists were speeding away in a van toward the safety of "Red Neukölln." The Berlin press had a field day with headlines, and a profoundly embarrassed government quickly offered a reward of 5,000 Marks for information leading to the capture of Otto Braun, Olga Benario, and their co-conspirators. Their photographs were plastered everywhere and even shown in movie theaters before the film presentation, but proletarian solidarity held firm and the police received no significant leads. The long-range prospects for the couple to remain at large in Germany were dim, however, and in June 1928 they traveled secretly to the Soviet Union.

In Moscow, Benario took the code name "Olga Sinek" and began to work for the Communist Youth International (CYI), a branch of the Communist International (Comintern). After speaking to countless groups of workers and young people throughout the Soviet Union for some months, she was elected to the Central Committee of the CYI and became busier than ever, attending meetings as well as learning English, French, and Russian. Ever more militant in her Communist beliefs, she helped to create the organizational framework for a CYI military branch, and she pressured her superiors to send her to a Red Army camp near the Caspian Sea where she learned the fundamentals of light and heavy weapons. She also passed a basic equestrian course. As her paramilitary activities kept her away from Otto, and he grew increasingly possessive, their relationship began to deteriorate rapidly and ended in 1931. Late that year, Benario went to France, using the name "Eva Kruger," on an important CYI mission; Otto went to China, where he spent most of the decade of the 1930s involved in intelligence activities or acting as a military advisor to Mao Zedong during the legendary Long March of the Chinese Red Army when the Chinese Communist movement was in a critical phase of development.

In Paris, Olga Benario helped to mediate between feuding French Communist youth factions, while her revolutionary passions also drew her into various street demonstrations, leading to several arrests before she was finally deported to Belgium. Belgian Communists enabled her to travel to London, where she participated in the growing protests against unemployment and fascism, and was arrested by British authorities. Finally, she returned to Moscow and discovered that in her absence she had been elected to the presidium of the Communist Youth International. One offshoot of this promotion was her selection for training in piloting and parachuting at the Zhukovski Academy, and while attending this course she first heard from a fellow student about a remarkable military episode that had recently taken place in Brazil.

A full century after having freed itself from Portugal in the 1820s, Brazil remained a profoundly backward nation, with its economy controlled largely by foreign capital and the great majority of its people living in hopeless poverty under near-feudal conditions. Politics was a corrupt game played by a small and selfish elite, while middle-class intellectuals whiled away their days in cafés lamenting the lack of change. In 1924, this dispiriting picture had altered radically when a military revolt broke out against Brazil's inept, corrupt president. While most of the revolutionary forces were soon suppressed, a small unit had survived and was carrying on increasingly successful guerrilla activities in the almost impenetrable jungles of the Brazilian interior.

At the head of these forces was Luis Carlos Prestes, born into a wealthy family of high social standing with a long military tradition. Intelligent, handsome and an instinctive leader, Prestes had advanced rapidly in his chosen branch of army engineering. Although not a political sophisticate, he was a fierce nationalist and deeply resented Brazil's continual humiliation and exploitation by foreign economic interests, aided and abetted by a greedy and corrupt oligarchy of merchants and landowners. Through his charismatic leadership, he was able to commit his entire battalion to the mutiny in July 1924, and for three years afterward his "Prestes Column" survived in the brutal and merciless jungle and avoided capture by government forces. In March 1927, when the last unit of Prestes' forces surrendered their weapons to Bolivian authorities, their epic long march had covered the incredible distance of almost 25,000 miles on foot. Prestes had escaped to Bolivia and spent the next few years wandering in Latin America. He remained a strong nationalist, and while his program called for major social reforms in Brazil, he was not a Marxist, or even a Socialist in any but the vaguest of terms.

In 1930, Prestes first met with Arthur Ewert (1890–1959), a German-born Comintern representative who had been active in Communist Party affairs in Germany, Great Britain, Canada, the U.S., China and various parts of Latin America. Ewert made an intriguing offer to Prestes: come to the Soviet Union and witness the building of a new Socialist society. When and if he was sufficiently impressed by what he saw, Prestes could then work with the Soviets to help bring about a Communist revolution in Brazil. Prestes accepted Ewert's offer and arrived in Moscow in November 1931, bringing along members of his family: his mother **Leocádia**, and his four unmarried sisters, **Clotilde**, **Heloísa**, **Lúcia**, and **Lígia**.

Picking up the optimistic spirit of the first of many Soviet Five Year Plans, Prestes took a job as an engineer for the Central Inspectorate of Civil Construction. Leocádia struggled with the task of keeping herself and her daughters alive, since Luis had refused the special privileges offered to him as a visiting technician, preferring that he and his family accept the same difficult standard of life as the average Soviet family. The extreme cold of the Russian winter was a great trial for the five Prestes women, but through luck and discovered skills they survived and learned to respect the ordinary people of a country that seemed to have little else but immense suffering as the core of its historical experience.

Prestes first heard about "Olga Sinek" from ***Elena Stasova**, a revered Old Bolshevik and associate of Lenin, who told him about a young German woman who was making meteoric progress as a leader of the Communist Youth International. The two did not meet until November 1934, when Benario was assigned to Prestes as his bodyguard. That summer the die had been cast, when the Comintern secretary, Dmitri Manuilski, decided that Brazil was ripe for revolution and assigned several of his best agents, including Luis Carlos Prestes, Olga Benario, **Elise Ewert** and her husband Arthur, to launch an upheaval in that strategically vital nation. On December 29, 1934, Luis and Olga departed from Moscow for Paris, their mission to travel to Brazil as a middle-class married couple via an indirect route (avoiding Germany, where Benario was well-known to the Gestapo). Prestes' assumed identity was "Pedro Fernandez," a Spaniard, while Olga remained Olga Sinek, a Soviet citizen. Concerned about the poor quality of their false passports, Benario and Prestes went first to Brussels where they felt threatened by police agents. Eventually an official at the Portuguese consulate in Rouen, France, who held liberal opinions even though his government was reactionary, helped them to attain genuine new passports which presented them as António and Maria Bergner Vilar, a wealthy couple from Lisbon. By this time Prestes had fallen deeply in love with Olga. Although they were never to legally wed, she fully reciprocated his love, and the couple lived as man and wife and honeymooned happily in New York, where their passports picked up an additional patina of authenticity in the form of valid U.S. entry and exit visa stamps.

By mid-April 1935, Prestes and Benario had arrived in Brazil, and flew in a four-engine hydroplane to the city of Florianópolis, where the pilot of their postal airliner made an unauthorized landing to let them off, on the excuse that it would facilitate Olga's reaching her relatives in the state of northern Paraná. The airport had no customs officials, and from there they went by taxi to Curitiba, and then on to Sao Paulo. From Sao Paulo, they traveled to Rio de Janeiro and rented a house not far from the exclusive Ipanema beach district where the Ewerts were already located. Along with the Ewerts, whose false names were "Harry Berger" and "Machla Lenczycki," the team included Victor Allen Barron, an American Communist well-versed in radio transmission, several veteran Brazilian Communists, the journalist Astrojildo Pereira, the pharmacist Otávio Brandao, and Rodolfo Ghioldi, an Argentine Communist leader who was a member of the Comintern's executive committee.

In 1935, Brazil was ruled by Getulio Vargas, who had seized power in 1930 and instituted a number of genuine reforms, but was now moving rapidly toward a permanent form of dictatorship at least superficially resembling the European fascist regimes of Hitler and Mussolini. One ominous aspect of the Vargas dictatorship was its increasing reliance on a secret political police, led by the police chief of Rio de Janeiro, Filinto Müller, a lawyer and army captain whose top officials were often of German ancestry. Müller was ruthless in his war against "un-Brazilian activities" and tireless in enhancing the effectiveness of his repressive machinery. Some of his animosity toward Luis Carlos Prestes may have been due to the fact that he had served briefly in the Prestes Column, had deserted with a substantial portion of its funds, and had been publicly denounced by Prestes as a coward and deserter. Müller customarily shared ideas and data with Gestapo officials resident in Brazil as part of a joint struggle against "Jewish-Bolshevik subversion."

Despite the combination of populist demagoguery by Vargas and harsh repression by Müller, a grassroots democratic movement was alive and growing in Brazil in the mid-1930s. Much of the effort for profound social reforms centered in the National Liberation Alliance (ANL), a coalition of various groups ranging from Communists to liberals and socially conscious Catholics that was compatible with the anti-fascist Popular Front ideology then espoused by the Comintern. Founded in March 1935 as the first significant political movement to emerge in Brazil since the revolution of 1930, the ANL had a broad popular agenda and clearly posed a threat to Vargas and his allies. The president, frightened by its democratic potential, banned it on June 11, 1935. Liberals and moderates then abandoned the ANL, which went underground and became almost exclusively led by the Communists. During this period, Prestes, Benario, the Ewerts and their group met often to discuss strategy. Olga and Elise Ewert, code-named "Sabo," strolled on nearby Ipanema beach and attended theaters and cinemas. Luis was more cautious and, on one occasion, was almost recognized by a former comrade of the Prestes Column now reinstated in the army. Whenever Luis went out, he was accompanied by Olga, who carried an automatic weapon. While the revolutionaries took precautions in Rio de Janeiro to avoid being snared by Müller's agents, Moscow apparently preferred to taunt the Vargas regime. The August 25, 1935, issue of *Pravda* announced that Prestes had been elected a full member of the executive committee of the Comintern, and while the newspaper mentioned that Prestes was in Moscow, the announcement doubtless served as a red flag, heightening desire of the Brazilian regime to snare the revolutionary if he should be found on his native soil.

In late November 1935, a series of spontaneous military revolts in the cities of Natal and Recife attempted to spark a national revolution aimed at toppling Vargas and installing a government based on the ANL reform agenda. Both insurrections were poorly led and bloodily suppressed, shattering the ANL and creating a crisis in Rio for the Ewert-Prestes group. One last hope remained for a successful revolutionary spark: the cadets of the Army Aviation School in Rio de Janeiro. Relying on his near-mythical reputation as the Brazilian people's "Cavalier of Hope," Prestes had made secret appeals and won over virtually all of these young and impressionable apprentice aviators, many of whom were like himself, from wealthy and socially prominent families. But on November 26, 1935, Prestes' call for the cadets to revolt was heeded by only a handful, and, after 11 hours of bloody fighting and heavy losses among the youths, this revolt was also snuffed out. Vargas could now brand all attempts at social change in Brazil the work of "Bolsheviks," foreign-born or foreign-trained, and on December 20, 1935, few Brazilians protested when he proclaimed a state of martial law.

Police and secret agents swarmed throughout Rio and its suburbs, and Prestes now knew that Müller and his agents would never rest until he and Benario were captured. On December 26, 1935, time ran out for the Ewerts. Olga was on her way to their home with some of Prestes' notes on the political situation, when she turned the corner in time to witness Arthur Ewert being shoved into a van and Elise being dragged off to another vehicle. Realizing that Prestes was in great danger, Olga returned home and fled with him from their house just before police arrived and ransacked it for documents.

The couple found temporary refuge in the city's Copacabana area, while the Ewerts were subjected to tortures by Brazilian and German Nazi police interrogators on loan to Müller's staff. Elise Ewert was raped by dozens of soldiers while her husband was forced to watch, then was placed in a coffin and spuriously buried alive, but neither revealed anything to the police. When police chief Müller held press conferences to announce what had been discovered about the activities of Arthur and Elise Ewert, the information actually came from detailed intelligence reports supplied to Müller by the Gestapo, British Intelligence, and the U.S. State Department, all of whom supported the implacable crusade of the Vargas regime against Brazilian revolutionary elements.

Olga and Luis managed to rent a modest house in the Meyer section of Rio, where they lived for several months while preparing for an eventual escape. In this time, several more members of their group were captured and tortured, including the radio operator Victor Barron, whose "suicide" occurred under suspicious circumstances. Rodolfo Ghioldi was arrested and only "moderately" mistreated, but cracked under the pressure and revealed the fact, unknown to the police, that Prestes was in Brazil with a foreign-born wife named Olga. In the predawn hours of March 5, 1936, in torrential rain, their house was surrounded by fifty soldiers and three police. When they broke in, Benario pushed in front of Prestes, shouting "Don't shoot, he's unarmed!" an instinctive gesture that may have saved him from gunfire. At police headquarters, he was ushered into a tiny elevator, and as the gate slammed shut, the two looked at each other for the last time.

Although Olga attempted to maintain her identity as Maria Bergner Vilar, the fiction evaporated when a detailed letter from the Brazilian ambassador in Berlin, who was on the friendliest possible terms with the German Gestapo, provided Müller with a detailed biography of the mystery woman revealed to be "Olga Benario, . . . an Israelite [and] . . . Communist agent of the Third International known for her great intelligence and courage." In prison, Olga soon joined her fellow inmates in the singing of revolutionary songs to maintain group morale. Many of her fellow prisoners were women who had hoped to create a political and social democracy in Brazil through the ALN program. One of Olga's most important accomplishments was the calming effect she had on Elise, whose mental balance had been seriously weakened by her time under torture, and whose husband Arthur had literally lost his mind.

Hoping that she might be imprisoned in Brazil or even deported to a non-fascist nation, Benario, who was pregnant, found her worst fear realized in September 1936, when she and Elise Ewert were deported to Nazi Germany. Many contemporary observers regarded the deportation of Benario as President Vargas' "gift to Hitler" and most saw it for what it was: a death sentence. Luis Prestes, too popular in his country to be martyred, received a sentence of 30 years imprisonment.

On November 27, 1936, one year to the day after the collapse of the frustrated Brazilian revolution, Benario's child was born in the Berlin Women's Prison, a girl named **Anita Leocádia Prestes** after ***Anita Garibaldi**, wife of the great Italian liberator. The new mother was informed by the prison matron that she could keep her infant as long as she was able to breastfeed. Radicals and liberals, outraged by this circumstance, attempted a worldwide campaign to free mother and daughter. Particularly vocal was the proud new grandmother, Leocádia, who traveled to Europe to mobilize public opinion on behalf of Olga and Anita. But the Nazis were determined to destroy the Communist Jew and separated her from her daughter on January 21, 1938. In a letter to Luis, she revealed this, along with the day of their capture, as among the darkest days of her life.

The infant Anita eventually reached the arms of Leocádia. Olga and Elise were meanwhile transported to the infamous Ravensbrück concentration camp, where Ewert, broken in body and spirit, died in the autumn of 1939. At Ravensbrück, Olga Benario would continue to display courage, maintaining the spirit of defiance that kept her, and many of her compatriots, within the circle of humanity despite countless attempts by her captors to strip her of every vestige of dignity.

In February 1942, sensing the end was near, Olga Benario penned a farewell letter to her family, on the eve of her transport to Bernburg Hospital, where she died, gassed by the SS, with a group of anti-fascist activist women. Luis was released from prison in 1945, when he learned about Olga's death at the hands of the Nazis. A genuine rebel to the end, he broke with the Brazilian Communist Party in the 1980s and lived in Rio de Janeiro until his death in March 1990. Leocádia died in 1943, having rescued her granddaughter who lived to become a university professor in Rio. Arthur Ewert, released from prison in 1947 and sent to East Germany, died in 1959 without regaining his sanity.

The life of Olga Benario, and its passionate commitment to social justice is meanwhile honored in the streets named after her in seven cities of the former German Democratic Republic, as well as 91 schools, factories and workers' brigades found in the same formerly Communist state. In Riberao Preto, a city in Brazil, a street bears her name.

SOURCES:

Amado, Jorge. *O Cavaleiro da Esperanca: Vida de Luis Carlos Prestes.* Rio de Janeiro: Colecao Novos Horizontes, 1956.

Braun, Otto. *A Comintern Agent in China 1932–39.* Stanford, CA: Stanford University Press, 1982.

Dulles, John W.F. *Anarchists and Communists in Brazil, 1900–1935.* Austin: University of Texas Press, 1973.

———. *Brazilian Communism, 1935–1945: Repression during World Upheaval.* Austin: University of Texas Press, 1983.

Hermlin, Stephan. *Die erste Reihe.* Dortmund, 1975.

Hornstein, David P. *Arthur Ewert: A Life for the Comintern.* Lanham, MD: University Press of America, 1993.

Langbein, Hermann. *. . . nicht wie die Schafe zur Schlachtbank: Widerstand in den nationalsozialistischen Konzentrationslagern 1938–1945.* Frankfurt am Main: Fischer Taschenbuch Verlag, 1980.

"Luis Carlos Prestes, 92, Brazilian Communist," in *The New York Times Biographical Service.* March 1990, p. 232.

Macaulay, Neill. *The Prestes Column: Revolution in Brazil.* NY: New Viewpoints, 1974.

Morais, Fernando. *Olga.* Translated by Ellen Watson. London: Peter Halban Publishers, 1990.

Müller, Charlotte. *Die Klempnerkolonne in Ravensbrück: Erinnerungen des Häftlings Nr. 10787.* Berlin, 1983.

Schiese, Rudolf. *Olga Benario Prestes 1908–1942.*

Werner, Ruth. *Olga Benario.* Berlin, 1977.

John Haag, Associate Professor,
University of Georgia, Athens, Georgia

Benchley, Belle (1882–1973)

American director of the San Diego Zoo from 1927 to 1953. *Born Belle Jennings on August 28, 1882, near Larned, Kansas; died on December 17, 1973; eldest daughter and one of eight children of Fred Merrick Jennings and Ida Belle (Orrell) Jennings; educated at Roosevelt School (in the Jennings home); attended Russ High School; graduated from San Diego Teachers College, 1902; married William L. Benchley, on June 25, 1906 (divorced 1924); children: son Edward Jennings.*

Nothing in the first 40 years of Belle Benchley's life hinted at a career as director of the San Diego Zoo. Born in Kansas, she grew up in Point Loma, California, where the family moved when she was four. Wandering the hills and beaches of the Point with her eight younger brothers and sisters, she developed a healthy respect for animals and learned to identify birds, shells, and flowers, but these experiences were nothing out of the ordinary. Following graduation from San Diego Teachers College, she taught school on the Pala Indian Reservation for three years, before her marriage to William Benchley in 1906. While raising her son Edward, she served two consecutive terms on the Fullerton, California, Board of Education.

In 1924, Belle and William divorced, leaving her with a teenage son to support. She returned to San Diego and took a bookkeeping

Belle Benchley

course. After working part time in the County Assessor's office, Benchley accepted a position as temporary bookkeeper in the Zoological Garden of San Diego in 1925. About an hour into her new job, a call came in from a man who wanted to settle a bet with a friend. "How long is the tail of a hippopotamus?" he asked, and Benchley realized her work was to exceed the conventional duties of a bookkeeper. His was the first of many telephone queries that challenged Benchley's curiosity and sent her in search of information. Her duties also included overseeing the care and feeding of some 800 animals, checking that visitors paid their dime admission fee, raising money for payroll, soliciting grocers for food for animal feed, and speaking to civic groups about the zoo. This involved adapting to incredibly long hours and a variety of unusual problems. Later, when asked what a zoo director does, Benchley would answer, "whatever the day brings forth."

After trying out several new directors and finding them lacking (including Frank Buck of "bring 'em back alive" fame), the zoo's founder, Dr. Harry Wedgeforth, decided to take a risk and appoint Benchley, only in her second year, head of the San Diego Zoo, with the title executive secretary. (More recent heads have been named "director," a title that eluded Benchley until after her retirement, when her letterhead title read "director emeritus.") Throughout her career, Benchley remained dedicated to carrying out Wedgeforth's plans for the zoo, though she often did battle with him. Until his death in 1941, she referred to him as "Dr. Harry," while he called her "girl," or, as the years progressed, "old girl."

Benchley soon found that she had a talent, hitherto unsuspected, for dealing with animals. In her book *My Life in a Man-Made Jungle*, published in 1940 after some 13 years on the job, she described herself as housekeeper, dietitian, consulting physician, and homemaker to an adopted family of animals. Benchley made it her business to learn each animal's likes, dislikes, and eccentricities and discovered that they were as complex and temperamental as human beings.

The acquisition of two gorillas, the largest in captivity, put the San Diego Zoo on the map. Benchley, who had obtained Mbongo and Ngagi at great expense, fell in love with her charges, stopping by each day to proffer them treats with hopes that they would become the largest in the world. Her grandmotherly relationship with the apes attracted a good deal of publicity for the zoo and is documented in her book *My Friends, the Apes*. When Mbongo died suddenly in 1942, Benchley wrote, "Never has the death of any animal in the San Diego Zoo created so much personal feeling of sorrow or regret as that of Mbongo."

But her respect and affection for the gorillas extended to all animals; she would not tolerate poor treatment of any under her care. Benchley drove through the zoo each day to check up on things. She also championed the trend toward the natural habitat, where animals could be displayed without undo confinement; the San Diego climate was ideal for this type of environmental exhibit. In an effort to protect the lives of animals taken from their natural habitat or bred within the Zoo, Benchley also consulted scientists in the design of exhibits that could include family groups. Although she envisioned that her animals led full and contented lives in the zoo setting, she was criticized by those who believed—as many still do—that certain species suffer when removed from their natural habitat.

During Benchley's initial days as director, she encountered some who resented the idea of a woman zoo director, but through the years she became affectionately known as the "Zoo Lady." Benchley gained notoriety through her speaking engagements (in 1939 alone, she gave some 150 lectures) and through radio broadcasts, appearances in newsreels, and articles she contributed to *Nature Magazine*, *Westways*, *Recreation*, and *Zoonooz* (the publication of the Zoological Society of San Diego). Her lively, anecdotal books also brought her public attention.

A year into her tenure, Benchley instituted the school-bus program, utilizing the zoo's buses to pick up children, bring them to the facility for an educational tour, and return them to their school. In 1985, the education programs benefitted over 150,000 students. She served as a mentor to many of her young staff members, or "pups," as she called them, some of whom stayed at the zoo for years and rose to important positions. Also instrumental in recruiting women as zoo keepers, Benchley hired numbers of them during the war when the male working pool was reduced. Zoo attendance climbed under Benchley's leadership. By the summer of 1951, yearly attendance exceeded one million visitors.

Benchley's retirement in 1953 was marked by Belle Benchley Day on December 10. At a farewell civic dinner attended by over 800 guests, she received countless tributes and the gift of a trip around the world. In 1963, she returned to the zoo for the dedication of Belle Benchley Plaza. Subsequent awards included the city's Outstanding Citizens Award, presented by the mayor of San Diego on September 5, 1969. The citation accompanying the award called her the first woman in the world to manage a zoo and cited her for making the San Diego Zoo "the greatest in the world." Belle Benchley died on December 17, 1973. The plaque on her gravestone bears the outline of a gorilla.

SOURCES:

Block, Maxine, ed. *Current Biography 1940*. NY: H.W. Wilson, 1940.

Hahn, Emily. *Eve and the Apes*. NY: Weidenfeld & Nicolson, 1988.

Norwood, Vera. *Made From This Earth.* Chapel Hill, NC: University of North Carolina Press, 1992.

Williams, Betty Jo F. "Belle Benchley and Me," a paper delivered to The Wednesday Club, 1986.

Barbara Morgan,
Melrose, Massachusetts

Bendish, Bridget (c. 1650–1726).

See Cromwell, Bridget for sidebar.

Bene, Adriana Gabrieli del (c. 1755–1799)

Italian soprano who originated roles in two of Mozart's immortal operas. *Born Adriana Gabrieli La Ferraresi around 1755 in Ferrara, Italy; died in 1799 in Venice; studied with Antonio Sacchini at the Conservatorio dei Mendicanti in Venice; married Luigi del Bene, in 1783.*

Sang in London (1785–86), at the Teatro alla Scala (1787); in Vienna (1788–91); premiered in Mozart's Cosi fan tutte *(1790); sang in Warsaw (1792–93).*

Adriana Gabrieli del Bene was brought up at an institution for illegitimate girls in Venice, where she and her peers were given an outstanding musical education by the finest masters in Italy. Antonio Sacchini, the composer, was one of del Bene's teachers. Her career, however, did not begin until after she was almost 30 when she eloped with Luigi del Bene. In 1785, she performed at the King's Theater in London and was given leading roles. Although reviews for these first performances were mixed, her reputation was such that the Burgtheater in Vienna engaged del Bene as their prima donna. Audiences and critics were astounded by the extraordinary range of her voice, although Emperor Joseph II was not a fan. In Vienna, she became the mistress of Lorenzo Da Ponte, the librettist of the Burgtheater. In 1789, she took the part of Susanna in *Le nozze di Figaro* (*Marriage of Figaro*), singing two new arias Mozart composed for her. He also wrote arias for her as Fiordiligi in *Cosi fan tutte*. After she left Vienna in 1791, she no longer sang in leading opera houses, but, because Mozart wrote compositions expressly for her in two immortal operas, Gabrieli del Bene's place in the history of opera is secure.

John Haag, Athens, Georgia

Benedict, Ruth (1887–1948)

American anthropologist whose research on Native Americans, as well as contemporary Europeans and Asians, made her a leading member of the culture and personality school of anthropology. *Name variations: (pseudonym) Anne Singleton. Born Ruth Fulton in Shenango Valley, New York, on June 5, 1887; died in New York City, on September 17, 1948; daughter of Beatrice (Shattuck) Fulton and Frederick Fulton; sister of* **Margery Fulton** *(b. 1889); attended Norwich Public School, 1895–1900; attended St. Margaret's Academy, 1901–05; A.B. Vassar College, 1909; M.A., New School for Social Research, 1921; Ph.D., Columbia University, 1923; married Stanley Rossiter Benedict, on June 18, 1914 (separated 1931); children: none.*

Father Frederick Fulton died (March 1889); traveled to Europe (1909); worked for the Charity Organization Society, Buffalo, New York (1911); taught at the Westlake School for Girls, Los Angeles, California (1911–12); taught at the Orton School for Girls, Pasadena, California (1912–14); completed biography of Mary Wollstonecraft (1917); enrolled at New School for Social Research, New York (1919); enrolled at Columbia University (1921); undertook field work on the Serrano Indians (1922); lectured at Columbia University (1923–26); undertook field research on the Pueblo Indians (1924); separated from Stanley Benedict (1931); was editor of the Journal of American Folklore *(1924–39); was assistant professor Columbia University (1931); death of Stanley Benedict (1936); served as member of the National Research Council (1941–43); death of Franz Boas (1942); employed by the Office of War Information (1943–46); served as leader of the Columbia University Contemporary Cultures Project (1946–48); elected president of the American Anthropological Association (1947); diagnosed with a heart condition (1947); appointed full professor at Columbia University (1948).*

Selected publications: Patterns of Culture *(Boston: Houghton Mifflin, 1934);* Zuni Mythology *(NY: Columbia University Press, 1935); "Religion," in* General Anthropology *(Franz Boas, ed. Boston: D.C. Heath, 1938);* Race: Science and Politics *(NY: Modern Age, 1940);* The Chrysanthemum and the Sword: Patterns of Japanese Culture *(Boston: Houghton Mifflin, 1946);* Thai Culture and Behavior *(Data Papers No. 4, Southeast Asia Program. Ithaca, NY: Cornell University, 1952).*

Ruth Benedict was born June 5, 1887, on a farm in the Shenango Valley of upper New York State. Her mother **Beatrice Shattuck Fulton** was a graduate of Vassar College, and her father Frederick Fulton was a doctor of medicine. In January 1889, Ruth's only sister Margery was born. The siblings were a study in contrast. While Margery was sociable and talkative, Ruth proved to be studious and shy. Her shyness was

belatedly explained in 1895, when it was discovered that Ruth was partially deaf.

When Frederick Fulton died of a mysterious illness in March 1889, the loss had a profound impact on Ruth Benedict. Years later, she could still recall his last days:

> My memories have to do . . . with a worn face illuminated with the translucence of illness and very beautiful. . . . The power that such faces had over me I never associated with my father till the day I took my mother to the Boston Museum to see my favorite of all such faces, El Greco's Fray Hortensio Paravicino. . . . Finally she turned to me and said, "It is your father. It is your father just before he died. There are no pictures of him as he looked then, but now you know what he looked like."

In 1892, the family moved to Norwich, New York, where Benedict's mother taught school. Beatrice Fulton was extraordinarily independent for a woman of her day. From Norwich, Beatrice moved her family to St. Joseph, Missouri, Owatonna, Minnesota, and finally, Buffalo, New York, pursuing her career as a teacher and librarian. Every summer, the family returned to the farm in the Shenango Valley.

In Buffalo, Beatrice enrolled her daughters in the prestigious St. Margaret's Academy. Both sisters excelled academically. In 1905, they enrolled at Vassar College, where Ruth studied English literature, indulging a long held passion, and made Phi Beta Kappa. Throughout her life, she wrote fiction and poetry, eventually publishing under various pen names, including Anne Singleton. Upon graduation in 1909, Ruth traveled to Europe with friends, while her sister married Robert Freeman, a minister.

Upon her return, Benedict briefly worked for the Charity Organization Society in Buffalo. In 1911, she moved to California to join Margery and her husband. There Ruth taught at the Westlake School for Girls and the Orton School for Girls. In California, Benedict confronted the limitations imposed upon women in early 20th-century America. In 1912, she wrote: "So much of the trouble is because I am a woman. To me it seems a very terrible thing to be a woman. There is one crown which is perhaps worth it all—a great love, a quiet home, and children."

In 1913, she fell in love with Stanley Benedict, a biochemist and brother of a Vassar friend. Seeking emotional and intellectual fulfillment through marriage, on June 18, 1914, she wed. The couple moved to Long Island, New York, where Stanley began a distinguished career at Cornell Medical College. Meanwhile, Ruth busied herself with providing a home for her husband. During World War I, however, she learned that she was unable to bear children. It was a crushing blow, which swept away the illusion of marital bliss. Over the years, the couple would grow apart, eventually separating in 1931. Neither would ever remarry, and, upon his death in 1936, Stanley Benedict would will his entire estate to his estranged wife.

In the early years of her marriage, Benedict became increasingly interested in feminism. In order to fill the void, she set out to write the biographies of ***Margaret Fuller**, ***Olive Schreiner**, and ***Mary Wollstonecraft**. Only the Wollstonecraft biography was ever finished. The book was as much an exploration of Wollstonecraft's struggle to find intellectual and spiritual fulfillment, as it was of Ruth Benedict's own efforts. Completed in 1917, the Wollstonecraft manuscript was rejected by a succession of publishers. Still searching for a creative outlet, in the fall of 1919, Benedict enrolled at the New School for Social Research. As ***Margaret Mead** noted:

> During the whole decade beginning in 1911, when she had successively tried social work and teaching and then put so much hope into her marriage to Stanley, her desperate need was to find herself—to commit herself to a way of life that had meaning for her and that drew on all her talents. . . . The decisive turning point in her life came in 1919, when she went to the New School for Social Research.

There, Benedict discovered the young discipline of anthropology, through the courses of Alexander Goldenweiser and ***Elsie Clews Parsons**. Her initial attraction to the field paralleled her interest in Wollstonecraft. Why, she asked, did contemporary culture push women to the peripheries of society? Benedict's interest in feminism led to a broader examination of the factors which marginalized people, occupational groups, or classes within culture.

Parsons convinced the 34-year-old Benedict to enroll in the doctoral program under Franz Boas at Columbia University. As head of the anthropology department, Boas was responsible for admitting dozens of female graduate students—more than could be found in other campus anthropology departments. While at Columbia, Benedict met Margaret Mead. What began as a teacher-student relationship, soon blossomed into a lifelong friendship. As Benedict's first graduate student, Mead occupied a special place in her life, and upon Benedict's death she became her literary executor.

Franz Boas rejected the theories of scholars, such as G. Elliot Smith and W.J. Perry, who argued that a single wellspring existed for the world's cultures. He was equally opposed to the German school, represented by Fritz Graebner, W. Koppers and others, who stressed the diffusion of cultural traits and values from a small pool of ancient civilizations. Instead, Boas advocated a comparative approach, which emphasized the diversity of cultural attributes and the effect of cross-fertilization of various cultures.

Ruth Benedict's 1923 dissertation, "The Concept of the Guardian Spirit in North America," revealed the depth of Boas' influence. She challenged Emile Durkheim's assertion that the source of religious values are imbedded in social structures. Instead, Benedict sought the origin of religious attitudes in the presence or absence of associated spiritual concepts, and an appraisal of the impact of such ideas upon different Native American tribes. She also contrasted magic and religion, based upon the motivational, valuative, and attitudinal discrepancies of the devotee and the spiritual leader.

> Her life illustrates an important intersection of women's history and the history of a social science.
>
> —**Judith Modell**

Benedict's thesis came to the attention of Edward Sapir, then at the University of Ottawa. The talented linguist wrote to her: "I put it in with such papers as Goldenweiser's 'Totemism' (1910) and Waterman's 'Exploratory Element in American Mythology' (1914) except that it impresses me as being decidedly more inspiring than either of these." Benedict and Sapir developed a strong bond, based on professional interests and a mutual love of poetry. They encouraged each other in attempts to publish their verse. By 1928, both had completed manuscripts of their collected works. The failure of either Benedict or Sapir to attract a publisher, however, led Benedict to devote her energy to anthropology.

Her early career moved slowly. From 1923 onward, she was a lecturer at Columbia University. In 1925, she was appointed editor of the *Journal of American Folklore*. It was not until 1931 that she was rewarded with the post of assistant professor in the department of anthropology—without tenure. In 1937, she was promoted to associate professor, but her gender always held her back. As Mead noted, when the question of a full professorship arose, "the faculty . . . felt that the addition of a woman to their ranks . . . would lower their standing in the academic community."

Opposite page

Ruth Benedict

Aside from her initial field work with the Serrano Indians in 1922, Benedict's early research was conducted primarily with printed sources. In 1924, however, she undertook field work with the Zuni Pueblos, and in 1927 a project was begun among the Pima Indians. Ruth Benedict was acutely aware that these cultures were vanishing rapidly; one of her great contributions was the recording of their ceremonies and myths. Due to her deafness, however, she was unable to learn their languages, which makes her field research all the more remarkable.

While working with the Pima in 1927, Benedict was struck by the extraordinary difference between Pueblo and Plains Indian culture. She employed Friedrich Nietzsche's schema of Apollonian and Dionysian to describe the contrast. Benedict argued that the Zuni Pueblos were a somber and moderate culture and should therefore be classified as Apollonian. The Pima Indians, on the other hand, represented a more expressive, emotional, ecstatically spiritual culture, which fell into the category of Dionysian.

These psychological portraits have been strongly criticized over the years, on the grounds that they are stereotypical and abstract. Although many have argued that Benedict's theoretical framework was too rigid and her evidence too general, colleagues such as Boas and Mead were quick to defend her. Benedict, they argued, did not advocate cultural types based on psychological or biological determinates. Rather, she sought to uncover the cultural development of a community, often using extreme case studies to highlight the traits which make a culture unique.

While Benedict worked with the Pima, Boas was completing a textbook entitled *General Anthropology* and asked her to contribute a chapter on religion. As in her earlier work, Benedict distinguished magic and religion mainly in terms of the differing values between the worshipper and the practitioner.

During the spring of 1932, Ruth Benedict decided to write her first book. Her efforts resulted in the pioneering study *Patterns of Culture* in which she rejected the piecemeal classification and dissection of customs and cultural values. Edward Sapir shared her view. In 1928, after reading her dissertation, he had suggested an approach which became the foundation of Benedict's theory of Configurationalism. Sapir wrote:

> A logical sequel . . . is another paper on the historical development of the guardian spirit in a particular area, the idea being to show how the particular elements crystallized into the characteristic pattern. This "how" would involve consideration of some of the more general patterns of the area or tribe and should perhaps show, unless you balk at psychology under all circumstances, how the crystallization could form a suitable frame of adequate individual expression.

Configurationalism, Benedict's most important theoretical contribution, approached cultures holistically. She attempted to identify the fundamental traits of each culture. Thus, she applied to groups the psychological concepts generally applied to individuals. While individuals within a culture might possess different strengths and weaknesses, cultures value ideal types, and therefore she argued, encourage conformity. Benedict believed that those who best approximated the ideals of their culture were also the ones who were the most well adjusted. In her theory of cultural relativism, she pointed out that the same trait that might label a person an outcast in one culture might make them a saint in another.

Patterns of Culture demonstrated that culture was individualized on a grand scale. The character of culture, Benedict argued, is formed by a multigenerational process of selection and rejection, of adaptation and incompatibility, and of elaboration or contraction. The nature of the personality of a culture, and choices faced by it, in turn help to shape individual members.

Although Franz Boas had retired in 1936 after falling seriously ill, Ruth Benedict was not appointed associate professor until 1937, when it became necessary for her to become acting head of the department. Ralph Linton was eventually appointed head of the anthropology department.

The rise of anti-Semitism and racial distinctions in Europe and the United States brought Benedict into conflict with members of the Columbia faculty. Many accused her of being a Communist, but she was fearless in her defense of free speech. In 1939, she took a sabbatical from Columbia and penned a thin volume entitled *Race: Science and Politics*, in which she coined the term "racism." Although an early advocate of cultural relativism, Benedict developed the concept of synergy, which argued that any culture which is detrimental to the advancement of humanity was liable to be judged as such. She refuted the claims of racial superiority and analyzed the motivation of racial propagandists. The book created a storm of controversy, especially with those scientists who were backing master-race theories espoused by Hitler and Germany. In the foreword to the 1945 edition, Benedict wrote:

> In race attitudes the behavior of the employer, the union member, the neighbor on our block, the waiter in the restaurant, the customer in the grocery store add up to the only total there is or can be.... For the dominant race cannot have freedom for themselves unless they grant it without regard to race or color. As Booker T. Washington once said, "To keep a man in the ditch, you have to stay there with him."

Race: Science and Politics became a bestseller, and an important means of furthering the comparative approach to cultural analysis. Benedict's writing did not flinch from pointing out flaws in contemporary society. *Race: Science and Politics* led to the publication of a Public Affairs pamphlet, "The Races of Mankind," and an animated-short film, *Brotherhood of Man*.

With the involvement of the United States in World War II, Ruth Benedict joined the National Research Council. In 1943, she was invited to work for the Office of War Information. There, Benedict produced cultural studies of Rumania, Germany, Holland, Belgium, Thailand, and Japan. Her work was an important departure, for it attempted to study complex cultures through interviews with foreign nationals living in the United States.

Her study of Japan resulted in *The Chrysanthemum and the Sword*. As with her other books, *The Chrysanthemum and the Sword* became a bestseller, portraying a country governed by complex social obligations, which made up the fabric of Japanese society. It is not known whether General Douglas MacArthur read the book, but his Japanese postwar occupation policy bore a striking resemblance to Benedict's ideas. In one of the more prescient passages of *The Chrysanthemum and the Sword*, she wrote: "Japan, if she does not include militarization in her budget, can, if she will, provide for her own prosperity before many years, and she could make herself indispensable in the commerce of the East."

Ruth Benedict returned to Columbia University in 1946. In the wake of her work on Japan, the Office of Naval Research allocated a grant to establish a program of research into contemporary cultures. The most ambitious research program of its time, it involved dozens of anthropologists, and Benedict became its head. In 1947, she was elected president of the American Anthropological Association. A year later, she was finally appointed full professor at Columbia University.

For several years, Ruth Benedict had been plagued by headaches and dizziness. In 1947, she was diagnosed with a heart condition. Two days after returning from a trip to Europe, she suffered a coronary thrombosis, and she died on September 17, 1948.

Ruth Benedict was one of the leading figures in the culture and personality school, which dominated anthropology during the 1930s and the 1940s. Her legacy is the continued emphasis on the comparative approach to culture, and values and themes which give cultures their distinct personalities. Her most important work, *Patterns of Culture*, was responsible for popularizing the concept of culture, hitherto a technical term known only to specialists. The theory of Configurationalism has become a useful tool for all anthropologists. *Patterns of Culture*, translated into a dozen languages, remains one of the best introductory anthropology texts available. *Race: Science and Politics* demonstrated Benedict's social consciousness at a pivotal juncture in American history. The book sought to influence public opinion and foster social tolerance. Today no university library collection is complete without a copy. The same may be said of other works, such as the immensely popular *The Chrysanthemum and the Sword*.

Ruth Benedict was one of the first women in the United States to attain prominence as a social scientist. Her work, during and after the Second World War, initiated the study of contemporary culture from an innovative perspective. The techniques she developed are still in use among academic and governmental institutions the world over. Benedict was a shy woman and found lecturing a chore, especially given her poor hearing. Nevertheless, she had a lasting impact on her students, many of whom went on to become leading anthropologists. Following the death of Franz Boas in 1942, Ruth Benedict became the undisputed master of American anthropology.

SOURCES:

Barnouw, Victor. "Ruth Benedict," in *American Scholar.* Vol. 49. Washington, DC: United Chapters of Phi Beta Kappa, 1980, pp. 504–509.

Fleming, Donald. "Benedict, Ruth Fulton," in *Notable American Women 1607–1950.* Edward T. James, ed. Cambridge, MA: Belknap Press, 1971.

Mead, Margaret. *An Anthropologist At Work: Writings of Ruth Benedict.* NY: Atherton Press, 1966.

———. *Ruth Benedict.* NY: Columbia University Press, 1974.

———. "Ruth Benedict," in *Totems and Teachers.* Sydel Silverman, ed. NY: Columbia University Press, 1984.

Modell, Judith. "Ruth Fulton Benedict," in *Women Anthropologists.* Edited by Ute Gacs, Aisha Khan, Jerrie McIntyre, and Ruth Weinberg. NY: Greenwood Press, 1988.

SUGGESTED READING:

Modell, Judith. *Ruth Benedict: Patterns of a Life.* Philadelphia, PA: University of Pennsylvania, 1983.

Hugh A. Stewart, M.A., University of Guelph, Guelph, Ontario, Canada

Benedicta, Mother (1825–1862).

See Riepp, Mother Benedicta.

Benedicta, Sister (1891–1942).

See Stein, Edith.

Benedictsson, Victoria (1850–1888).

See Key, Ellen for sidebar.

Benedikte (1944—)

***Danish princess.** Name variations: Benedikte Oldenburg. Born Benedikte Astrid Ingeborg Ingrid on April 29, 1944, in Amalienborg Palace, Copenhagen, Denmark; daughter of ***Ingrid of Sweden** (1910—) and Frederick IX, king of Denmark (r. 1947–1972); sister of ***Margrethe II**, queen of Denmark (b. 1940), and ***Anne-Marie Oldenburg** (b. 1946); married Richard, 6th prince of Sayen-Wittgenstein-Berleburg, on February 3, 1968; children: Gustav (b. 1969); **Alexandra of Sayn-Wittgenstein** (b. 1970); **Nathalie of Sayn-Wittgenstein** (b. 1975).*

Benett, Etheldred (1776–1845)

***English geologist.** Born in 1776; died on January 11, 1845; second daughter of Thomas Benett, of Pyt House near Tisbury.*

One of the earliest of English women geologists, Etheldred Benett was born at Pyt House, near Tisbury. She later resided at Norton House, near Warminster, in Wiltshire, and for more than 25 years devoted herself to collecting and studying the fossils of her native county. She contributed "A Catalogue of the Organic Remains of the County of Wilts" to Sir R.C. Hoare's *County History*. A limited number of copies of this work were printed as a separate volume (1831) and privately distributed.

Bengelsdorf, Rosalind (1916–1979).

See Browne, Rosalind Bengelsdorf.

Bengerd of Portugal (1194–1221).

See Berengaria.

Benham, Gertrude (fl. 1909)

British mountain climber and the first woman to climb Mount Kilimanjaro.

Little is known about the publicity-shy Gertrude Benham, who spent more than 30 years walking the world. Her journey included 17 visits to Switzerland, a walk across South America from Valparaiso to Buenos Aires in 1908, and a walk across Africa from west to east in 1913. She traveled to every part of the British Empire, except Tristan da Cunha and some small islands, and climbed more than 300 peaks of 10,000 feet or over. In 1909, Benham was the first woman to conquer the 19,700-foot Kilimanjaro. During her estimated seven trips around the world, she is said to have carried a Bible, copies of *Lorna Doone* and Kipling's *Kim*, a pocket Shakespeare, and her knitting.

Benincasa, Caterina or Catherine di (1347–1380).

See Catherine of Siena.

Benincasa, Ursula (1547–1618)

***Italian religious.** Born in 1547; died in 1618.*

Ursula Benincasa founded the Oblate Sisters of the Immaculate Conception of the Blessed Virgin Mary in 1583. Members of the order were known as Theatines, or Theatine nuns.

Benizelos, Philothey (fl. 1650)

***Greek abbess.** Flourished 1650 in Greece; never married; no children.*

Very few facts are known about the life of Philothey Benizelos. An abbess who founded a convent school around 1650 which became a popular refuge for local women, she seems to have come into conflict with local authorities over her management of the abbey's lands, and was forced to take arms against the rebellious peasants who were tenants on her properties. Eventually sentenced to prison, Benizelos was apparently murdered soon afterwards.

Benjamin, Hilde (1902–1989)

***German Communist lawyer and much-feared judge, known as "Red Hilde" in the German Democratic Republic (GDR), where she served as minister of justice from 1953 through 1967.** Born Hilde Lange in Bernburg an der Saale on February 5, 1902; died in East Berlin on April 18, 1989; daughter of a sales director of a department store; married Georg Benjamin (1895–1942, a physician); children: son Michael (b. 1932).*

Joined German Communist Party (1926); became a lawyer (1928); forbidden to practice law (1933); joined German Central Judicial Authority (1946); served as vice president of GDR Supreme Tribunal (1949–53); served as minister of justice (1953–67); notorious for presiding over 1950s political show trials; member of Socialist Unity Party central committee (1954–81).

Selected writings: Vorschläge zum neuen deutschen Familienrecht *(Berlin: Deutscher Frauen-Verlag, 1949); (with others)* Grundriss des Strafrechtsverfahrens der Deutschen Demokratischen Republik *(Berlin: Deutscher Zentralverlag, 1953);* Die Hauptaufgaben der Justiz bei der Durchführung des neuen Kurses *(Berlin: VEB Deutscher Zentralverlag, 1953);* Karl Liebknecht, zum Wesen und zu Erscheinungen der Klassenjustiz *(Potsdam-Babelsberg: Akademie für Staats- und Rechtswissenschaft der DDR, Informationszentrum Staat und Recht, Abt. Publikationen, 1976);* Zur Geschichte der Rechtspflege der DDR 1945–1949 *(Berlin: Staatsverlag der Deutschen Demokratischen Republik, 1976);* Georg Benjamin: Eine Biographie *(Leipzig: S. Hirzel Verlag, 1977);* Zur Geschichte der Rechtspflege der DDR 1949–1961 *(Berlin: Staatsverlag der Deutschen Demokratischen Republik, 1980).*

Although the German Democratic Republic (GDR) never saw the full extent of political terror experienced in the Soviet Union under Stalin in the 1930s and several of the satellite "people's democracies" in the late 1940s and early 1950s, its legal system was a highly politicized one designed to ruthlessly eliminate political and ideological deviations. The individual most responsible for this hard-line conception of Socialist justice was the militant Communist lawyer Hilde Benjamin, known to most GDR citizens as simply *die rote Hilde* (Red Hilde), or even *roter Fallbeil* (Red Guillotine). With graying hair, held by a severe knot at the neck, and a wrinkled, often swollen face, this physically unremarkable woman inspired fear in her German populace.

She was born Hilde Lange in the industrial town of Bernburg an der Saale on February 5, 1902, into a solidly middle-class family of four children. Her father was a successful manager, her mother conventionally conservative and religious. Intellectually independent from an early age, Hilde was the family rebel. She declared herself to be an atheist in her early teens and put up a strong argument against being confirmed in the Lutheran faith. A brilliant student, extremely well-read, Hilde was a loner who graduated with honors from high school in 1920. Deciding upon a career in the law, she studied at the universities of Berlin, Hamburg, and Heidelberg. While in Berlin, she joined the Social Democratic student organization, but, showing her critical temperament, she quickly began to criticize the timidity of the parent party, which she saw as a complacent, reformist body that would be unable to create a classless society or meet the challenges of the newly emergent Fascist movements led by violently anti-Marxist demagogues like Benito Mussolini and Adolf Hitler. Increasingly disillusioned with establishment Socialism, Hilde found herself attracted to the rhetoric and ideals of the German Communist Party, which advocated world revolution under the leadership of Soviet Russia.

Following graduation from the University of Berlin in 1924, she became first a junior barrister (*Referendar*), then an assessor, and finally a full attorney in 1928. The social privation and misery that she witnessed in Berlin convinced her that only a radical transformation of society could eliminate injustice. Virtually all of her law practice was devoted to defending the economic rights of unemployed or injured workers, or fighting for the right of women to enjoy full reproductive freedom. In the course of her fight for social change, she met and married an idealistic physician, Dr. Georg Benjamin (1895–1942). Born into a wealthy and gifted Jewish family that included the noted critic Walter Benjamin, Georg practiced medicine in Wedding, one of Berlin's largest working-class districts, where he tirelessly dispensed medical assistance free of charge in most instances. He too was drawn to the revolutionary program of the German Communist Party. For the next five years, both Georg and Hilde Benjamin became well-known and much respected among the poor and unemployed workers of "Red Wedding," a virtual fortress of revolutionary sentiments within the heart of the German capital.

Unrelenting in her legal work for what she regarded as poor and virtually powerless workers and their families, Hilde Benjamin had little time for private life. Convinced that only the triumph of Communism in Germany could end misery, exploitation, and war, she and her husband spent long hours being of assistance to the workers of Wedding. The rise of Nazism in Berlin in the late 1920s alerted both Benjamins to the danger from the political Right. The physical danger posed by brownshirted storm troopers in Berlin's streets only strengthened their resolve. In her modest law office, Hilde worked long hours assisting working men and women neglected by the law, people unable to receive pensions or compensation for work-related injuries. She was active in efforts to repeal the law making abortion illegal, and fought for full economic and social rights for women. Privately, these years were marked by both tragedy and joy. In 1931, her infant son died a few days after his birth, a loss that was devastating to both parents who had long desired a child. Long-sought family happiness finally arrived on December 27, 1932, when Hilde gave birth to another son, named Michael.

Less than five weeks after Michael's birth, on January 30, 1933, the Benjamins' world began to collapse. Adolf Hitler was appointed chancellor of Germany as the result of a deal between his Nazi Party and a coalition of desperate and gullible conservatives. Radicals like the Benjamins were high on the enemies lists of local Nazi cells. Known throughout Wedding as militant Communists and heroes of the working-class men and women of the unemployment-racked district, their lives were now at risk. Georg Benjamin was fired from his job as a school physician, and in April 1933 he was taken away from his family to Racked, one of the first Nazi concentration camps. Here he was mistreated both physically and psychologically by storm troopers intent on getting even with a "Bolshevik Jew" known throughout Berlin from hate-filled Nazi propaganda literature. When he was released in December 1933, his health had been shattered and his license to practice medicine was taken from him, though his revolutionary faith was intact. Hilde was hated as much as her husband, having achieved notoriety several years previously when she served as one of the defense attorneys of Ali Höhler, the man accused of murdering Horst Wessel, a Nazi student and pimp who became "immortal" for having written the words of the Nazi anthem. Within weeks of the Nazi seizure of power, she was stripped of her license to practice law.

Hilde Benjamin relied on other anti-Nazis for assistance during the first years of Nazi rule, always fearing arrest but refusing to leave Germany because she believed the Nazi regime might still be overthrown by a revived working class. She eventually found employment at the Soviet Embassy in Berlin, where she advised the trade division on legal matters. Her emotional energies were divided between raising her only child Michael and trying to secure information on the condition of her husband, who would never see his son grown. Georg Benjamin was rearrested in May 1936 as a result of his continuing involvement in anti-Nazi underground activities. His October 1936 sentence was six years' imprisonment at the Brandenburg penitentiary. With the signing of the Hitler-Stalin pact of August 1939, Hilde Benjamin's services were no longer required at the Soviet trade delegation, and life became even more precarious. Occasionally, she received word through the anti-Nazi underground of Georg's stubborn determination to survive his term of imprisonment. Though his sentence was served in May 1942, the administration of Brandenburg concluded that after six years in a National Socialist correctional facility Georg Benjamin remained at heart an ardent revolutionary. As a Jew and Communist, his continued survival in Nazi Germany was "not desired." He was transferred to infamous Mauthausen concentration camp near Linz, Austria. After several months of ghastly mistreatment, he was murdered at Mauthausen on August 26, 1942. A shaken Hilde Benjamin carried on, protecting her son from air raids while she endured the war jobs she had no choice but to accept.

The collapse of Nazi Germany in the spring of 1945 opened up a new world for Benjamin. As the widow of a militant Communist humanitarian and as a certified anti-Nazi in her own right, she, and her son, qualified for the moral and material benefits accruing to "Victims of Fascism." Benjamin was energized by the forced fusion of Social Democratic and Communist parties in 1946, and she was a charter member of the resulting Socialist Unity Party. Her legal career was revived, and she now worked with enthusiasm as district attorney of Berlin-Lichterfelde, serving in this post from 1945 through 1947. Her political reliability propelled her into an important job in the Central Justice Administration of the Soviet Occupation Zone, which she held until 1949. With the creation of the German Democratic Republic (GDR) in October 1949, she became a vice president of the new state's Supreme Court.

A personal tragedy of the postwar years was the insistence of her party superiors that her son Michael be sent to the Soviet Union for his education. Although she was a strong supporter of Stalin and the Soviet system, Benjamin had hoped to keep her son with her in Germany. Party loyalty overcame personal feelings, however, and Michael was educated in Leningrad; he returned to the GDR in 1956. Weeks after the workers' uprising of June 17, 1953, was suppressed, Hilde Benjamin was appointed GDR minister of justice. Universally regarded as a hard-liner, she inspired fear in both anti-Communists and reformers within the Socialist Unity Party (SED). She remained in this position until July 1967, strengthening her reputation as an uncompromising

Communist of classic Bolshevik attitudes. To this class warrior whose life had been shattered by the Nazis, dissent was tantamount to treason. Meanwhile, on the other side of the Berlin Wall, Benjamin became a Cold War caricature; in the words of one imaginative journalist, she was quite simply "the world's worst woman." The lost human potential of an intelligent idealist whose beliefs had been twisted by a cruel century did not find its way into these portrayals.

In the age of uncompromising cruelty that claimed her husband, Benjamin had survived by becoming cold and ideologically hard as steel. A geriatric marvel in the 1970s and into the 1980s, she enjoyed the status of being a "party veteran" of German Communism. It is possible that she did not notice that the foundations of her German Democratic Republic had been built on sand, and that most of her Communist state's population had grown tired of old slogans appropriate to the world of the 1920s and '30s rather than the 1980s. With her death on April 18, 1989, Hilde Benjamin was spared the pain of watching all she had lived for collapse in a few weeks' time.

SOURCES:

Buch, Günther. *Namen und Daten wichtiger Personen der DDR.* Berlin and Bonn: Verlag J.H.W. Dietz Nachf. GmbH, 1979.

Gast, Gabriele. *Die politische Rolle der Frau in der DDR.* Düsseldorf: Bertelsmann Universitätsverlag, 1973.

Herff, Jeffrey. "East German Communists and the Jewish Question: The Case of Paul Merker," in *Journal of Contemporary History.* Vol. 29, no. 4. October 1994, pp. 627–661.

König, Stefan. *Vom Dienst am Recht: Rechtsanwälte als Strafverteidiger im Nationalsozialismus.* Berlin and NY: Walter de Gruyter, 1987.

Kraushaar, Luise. *Deutsche Widerstandskämpfer 1933–1945: Biographien und Briefe.* 2 vols. Berlin: Dietz Verlag, 1970.

Muhlen, Norbert. "The World's Worst Woman," in *Saturday Evening Post.* Vol. 228, no. 1. July 2, 1955, pp. 25, 74–76.

Ostler, Fritz. *Die deutschen Rechtsanwälte 1871–1971.* 2nd revised ed. Essen: Deutscher Anwaltsverlag, 1982.

"Register," in *Der Spiegel.* Vol. 43, no. 17. April 24, 1989, p. 260.

SBZ von A bis Z: Ein Taschen und Nachschlagebuch über die Sowjetische Besatzungszone Deutschlands. Herausgegeben vom Bundesministerium für gesamtdeutsche Fragen. 10th rev. ed. Bonn: Deutscher Bundes-Verlag, 1966.

Shaw, Gisela. "East German 'Rechtsanwälte' and German Unification," in *German Life* and *Letters.* Vol. 47, no. 2. April 1994, pp. 211–231.

Sprengel, Rita. *Der rote Faden: Lebenserinnerungen. Ostpreussen, Weimarer Republik, Ravensbrück, DDR, Die Wende.* Berlin: Edition Hentrich, 1994.

John Haag, Associate Professor,
University of Georgia, Athens, Georgia

Bennett, Barbara (1906–1958).

See Bennett, Joan for sidebar.

Bennett, Belle Harris (1852–1922)

American church worker. *Born Isabel Harris Bennett on December 3, 1852, in Whitehall, near Richmond, Kentucky; died on July 20, 1922, in Richmond, Kentucky; educated privately in Kentucky and Ohio.*

Belle Bennett began a long career in church work as a Sunday-school teacher for the Southern Methodist Church. In 1889, she undertook a plan to establish a training school similar to the one founded in Chicago by **Lucy R. Meyer** for the Northern Methodist Church. With the approval of the Southern Methodist Woman's Board of Foreign Missions, Bennett initiated a strenuous fund-raising drive, and a large gift from Dr. Nathan Scarritt of Kansas City, Missouri, made possible the Scarritt Bible and Training School, which was dedicated in Kansas City in September 1892 (it was later moved to Nashville, Tennessee, and renamed Scarritt College for Christian Workers). Bennett went on to raise over $130,000 for the project. In 1897, she opened the Sue Bennett Memorial School in London, Kentucky, in honor of her older sister.

Named to the central committee of the Woman's Parsonage and Home Mission Society in 1892, Bennett later became the society's president. In 1898, as president of the newly organized Woman's Board of Home Missions, Bennett helped establish more than 40 "Wesley Community Houses" for whites and "Bethlehem Houses" for blacks throughout the segregated South. In 1910, she became president of the unified Woman's Mission Council, a post she held until her death. Responsible for both home and foreign mission work, she helped establish a woman's college in Rio de Janeiro (later named for her) as well as the Woman's Christian Medical College in Shanghai. She also campaigned to gain admission of women to full lay status in the Southern Methodist Church. In 1919, with admission finally granted, Bennett became the first woman elected a delegate to the church's General Conference. She died on July 20, 1922, before the conference convened.

Barbara Morgan,
Melrose, Massachusetts

Bennett, Constance (1904–1965)

American actress and star of the original **Topper** ***series.*** *Born in New York, New York, on October 22, 1904; died of cerebral hemorrhage in Fort Dix, New*

*Jersey, on July 24, 1965; daughter of actor Richard Bennett and actress *Adrienne Morrison; sister of actresses *Barbara Bennett (1902–1958) and *Joan Bennett (1910–1990); married Chester Moorehead, in 1921 (annulled); married Philip Plant, in 1925 (divorced 1929); married Henri Falaise (the Marquis de la Coudraye), in 1931 (divorced 1940); married Gilbert Roland, in 1941 (divorced 1944?); married John Coulter, in 1946; children: (second marriage) Peter Bennett; (fourth marriage) Lorinda and Christina Consuelo ("Gyl").*

Filmography: The Valley of Decision *(bit, 1916);* Reckless Youth *(1922);* Evidence *(1922);* What's Wrong With the Women? *(1922);* Cytherea *(1924);* Into the Net *(1924);* The Goose Hangs High *(1925);* Code of the West *(1925);* My Wife and I *(1925);* My Son *(1925);* The Goose Woman *(1925);* Sally, Irene and Mary *(1925);* Wandering Fires *(1925);* The Pinch Hitter *(1925);* Married? *(1926);* This Thing Called Love *(1929);* Rich People *(1930);* Son of the Gods *(1930);* Common Clay *(1930);* Three Faces East *(1930);* Sin Takes a Holiday *(1930);* The Easiest Way *(1931);* Born to Love *(1931);* The Common Law *(1931);* Bought *(1931);* Lady With a Past *(1932);* What Price Hollywood *(1932);* Two Against the World *(1932);* Rockabye *(1932);* Our Betters *(1933);* Bed of Roses *(1933);* After Tonight *(1933);* Moulin Rouge *(1934);* The Affairs of Cellini *(1934);* Outcast Lady *(1934);* After Office Hours *(1935);* Everything Is Thunder *(UK, 1936);* Ladies in Love *(1936);* Topper *(1937);* Merrily We Live *(1938);* Service De Luxe *(1938);* Topper Takes a Trip *(1939);* Tail Spin *(1939);* Submarine Zone (Escape to Glory, *1941);* Law of the Tropics *(1941);* Two-Faced Woman *(1941);* Wild Bill Hickock Rides *(1942);* Sin Town *(1942);* Madame Spy *(1942);* Paris Underground *(1945);* Centennial Summer *(1946);* The Unsuspected *(1947);* Smart Woman Angel on the Amazon *(1948);* As Young As You Feel *(1951);* It Should Happen to You *(1954);* Madame X *(1966).*

Constance Bennett

Known as lively and headstrong, Constance Bennett, the eldest of the Bennett sisters, waltzed from her glittering debutante ball into marriage at 16, followed by a quick annulment. Her first major screen role in *Cytherea* (1924) led to a number of roles in the silents, but a second marriage to steamship and railroad heir Philip Plant diverted her to Europe and the swinging international set.

After the birth of her son Peter and a divorce from Plant in 1929, she returned to the States and established herself as a leading lady in her first talkie, a fast-moving comedy titled *This Thing Called Love.* Lending her husky voice to both sophisticated comedies and melodramatic tear-jerkers, Bennett is especially remembered for her role as the heroine of *Topper* (1937), with Cary Grant. She repeated her success with the 1939 sequel, *Topper Takes a Trip.*

Bennett made her stage debut around the time of her divorce from third husband Henri Falaise in 1940, touring in Noel Coward's comedy *Easy Virtue.* Other stage performances would follow, as well as two additional marriages, one to screen actor Gilbert Roland (with whom she had two children), and another to Air Force Colonel John Coulter, perhaps her happiest. In addition to performing, Bennett also tried her hand at business with a cosmetics line and "fashion frocks," for which she designed dresses. After Bennett's long absence from the screen, her final movie *Madame X,* made in 1964, was released after her sudden death from a brain hemorrhage in 1965.

Barbara Morgan,
Melrose, Massachusetts

Bennett, Enid (1895–1969)

Australian actress. *Born on July 15, 1895, in York, West Australia; died in 1969; sister of actress* ***Marjorie Bennett*** *(1896?–1982); married Fred Niblo (a director).*

Enid Bennett was touring with an Australian stage troupe when she arrived in the United States during World War I. Discovered for the screen by Thomas Ince, Bennett starred as Maid Marion opposite Douglas Fairbanks, Sr., in Allan Dwan's *Robin Hood* (1922); she also appeared in *The Sea Hawk* with Milton Sills (1924). Her other films include *The Battle of Gettysburg* (1914), *Princess of the Dark* (1917), *Happiness* (1917), *The Girl Glory* (1917), *The Mother Instinct* (1917), *Naughty, Naughty!* (1917), *The Marriage Ring* (1918), *The Biggest Show on Earth* (1918), *The Vamp* (1918), *Fuss and Feathers* (1918), *Happy though Married* (1919), *The Haunted Bedroom* (1919), *Stepping Out* (1919), *Hairpins* (1920), *Her Husband's Friend* (1920), *Silk Hosiery* (1920), *Keeping Up with Lizzie* (1921), *The Bootlegger's Daughter* (1922), *The Courtship of Miles Standish* (1923), *The Fool's Awakening* (1924), *The Red Lily* (1924), *A Woman's Heart* (1926), *The Wrong Mr. Wright* (1927), *Waterloo Bridge* (1931), *Intermezzo* (1939), and *Strike Up the Band* (1940). Bennett retired from the screen soon after her marriage to director Fred Niblo. She accompanied her husband to Italy in 1926, assisting him on the filming of *Ben-Hur*.

Bennett, Gwendolyn B. (1902–1981).

See Women of the Harlem Renaissance.

Bennett, Joan (1910–1990)

American actress, and popular leading lady of the 1930s and 1940s. *Born in Palisades, New Jersey, on February 27, 1910; died of cardiac arrest at her home in Scarsdale, New York, on December 7, 1990; daughter of actor Richard Bennett and actress (Mabel) Adrienne Morrison; sister of screen actresses Constance Bennett (1904–1965) and* ❧ **Barbara Bennett** *(1906–1958); married John Fox, on September 15, 1926 (divorced, August 1928); married Gene Markey, in 1932 (divorced 1937); married Walter Wanger, in 1940 (divorced 1965); married David Wilde, in 1978; children: (first marriage) Adrienne Ralston ("Ditty," b. 1928); (second marriage) Melinda ("Mims," b. 1934); (third marriage) Stephanie (b. 1943) and Shelley (b. 1948).*

Filmography: The Valley of Decision *(bit, 1916);* The Eternal City *(bit, 1923);* Power *(1928);* Bulldog Drummond *(1929);* Three Live Ghosts *(1929);* Disraeli *(1929);* The Mississippi Gambler *(1929);* Puttin' on the Ritz *(1930);* Crazy That Way *(1930);* Moby Dick *(1930);* Maybe It's Love *(1930);* Scotland Yard *(1930);* Doctor's Wives *(1931);* Many a Slip *(1931);* Hush Money *(1931);* She Wanted a Millionaire *(1932);* Careless Lady *(1932);* The Trial of Vivienne Ware *(1932);* Week-Ends Only *(1932);* Wild Girl *(1932);* Me and My Gal *(1932);* Arizona to Broadway *(1933); (as Amy)* Little Women *(1933);* The Pursuit of Happiness *(1934);* The Man Who Reclaimed His Head *(1935);* Private Worlds *(1935);* Mississippi *(1935);* Two for Tonight *(1935);* She Couldn't Take It *(1935);* The Man Who Broke the Bank at Monte Carlo *(1935);* 13 Hours by Air *(1936);* Big Brown Eyes *(1936);* Two in a Crowd *(1936);* Wedding Present *(1936);* Vogues of 1938 *(1937);* I Met My Love Again *(1938);* The Texans *(1938);* Artists and Models Abroad *(1938);* Trade Winds *(1938); (as Queen Maria Theresa)* The Man in the Iron Mask *(1939);* The Housekeeper's Daughter *(1939);* Green Hell *(1940);* The House Across the Bay *(1940);* The Man I Married *(1940);* The Son of Monte Cristo *(1940);* Man Hunt *(1941);* She Knew All the Answers *(1941);* Wild Geese Calling *(1941);* Confirm or Deny *(1941);* Twin Beds *(1942);* The Wife Takes a Flyer *(1942);* Girl Trouble *(1942);* Margin for Error *(1943);* The Woman in the Window *(1944);* Nob Hill *(1945);* Scarlet Street *(1946);* Colonel Effingham's Raid *(1946);* The Macomber Affair *(1947);* The Woman on the Beach *(1947);* Secret Beyond the Door *(1948);* Hollow Triumph *(The Scar, 1948);* The Reckless Moment *(1949);* Father of the Bride *(1950);* For Heaven's Sake *(1950);* Father's Little Dividend *(1951);* The Guy Who Came Back *(1951);* Highway Dragnet *(1954);* We're No Angels *(1955);* There's Always Tomorrow *(1956);* Navy Wife *(1956);* Desire in the Dust *(1960);* House of Dark Shadows *(1970);* Gidget Gets Married *(TV-movie, 1972),* The Eyes of Charles Sand *(TV-movie, 1972);* Inn of the Damned *(unreleased, 1974);* Suspiria *(It., 1977).*

Enid Bennett

❧ See sidebar on the following page

One of the most popular leading ladies of the 1930s and 1940s, Joan Bennett was the youngest daughter of stage idol Richard Bennett and actress ❧ **Adrienne Morrison**. Growing up in the famous theatrical family was not always easy. Bennett was alternately awed and terrified by her father (like living with a "tidal wave"), who parted with her mother in a very public divorce when Bennett was 13. Also intimidated by her beautiful

❧ See sidebar on the following page

Bennett, Barbara (1906–1958)

American actress. *Name variations: Mrs. Morton Downey. Born on August 13, 1906; died in Montreal, Canada, on August 9, 1958; daughter of actor Richard Bennett and actress* ****Adrienne Morrison****; sister of screen actresses* ****Constance Bennett*** *(1904–1965) and* ****Joan Bennett*** *(1910–1990); married Morton Downey (a singer), on January 28, 1929 (divorced 1941); married Addison Randall, in 1941 (died 1945); married Laurent Surprenant, in 1954; children: (first marriage) Michael (adopted), Sean, Lorelle Ann, Anthony, Kevin.*

Filmography: Syncopation *(1929);* Mother's Boy *(1929);* Love among the Millionaires *(1930).*

Described by her sister Joan as the quiet, least ambitious of the three Bennett sisters, Barbara Bennett began her brief theatrical career as a dancer, touring with renowned exhibition dancer Maurice Mouve. Leaving him just before their New York debut, she went on to dance in a few Broadway musicals and an occasional movie. She met tenor Morton Downey making the film *Syncopation*, and the couple married three weeks later. They settled on a 49-acre farm in Connecticut and raised five children. As Downey's career separated him more and more from family life, Bennett felt increasingly alone and started drinking. In a bitter divorce in 1941, Downey won custody of the children, which devastated her.

Weeks after her divorce was final, she married Addison Randall, who was killed on a movie set in 1945. For the remainder of her life, Bennett would battle depression and alcoholism. She married Canadian journalist Laurent Surprenant in 1954 "only," she said, "out of loneliness," and spent the last four years of her life in Montreal. She died there in 1958, age 52.

Morrison, Adrienne (1889–1940)

American actress, literary agent, and mother of the Bennett sisters. *Born Mabel Adrienne Morrison in New York on March 1, 1889; died on November 20, 1940; married Richard Bennett (an actor), on November 8, 1903; married Eric Pinker; children: (first marriage) actresses* ****Constance*** *(1904–1965),* ****Barbara*** *(1906–1958), and* ****Joan Bennett*** *(1910–1990).*

Following her marriage to famed actor Richard Bennett, Adrienne Morrison married Eric Pinker and became his business partner; he was subsequently jailed for embezzlement.

Opposite page

From the movie Moby Dick, *starring Joan Bennett and John Barrymore.*

and successful older sisters, she decided on a career in interior decorating but side-stepped into a teenage marriage, a baby, and a divorce.

In 1928, finding herself on her own and needing to make a living, Bennett was offered the ingenue role opposite her father in the play *Jarnegan*. A successful debut was followed with a few minor film roles and a screen contract with United Artists, before her first major screen role in *Bulldog Drummond*, opposite Ronald Colman. The filming proved a daunting experience, with frequent lectures from director Richard Jones on her inadequacies, and unfavorable comparisons to her sister ***Constance Bennett** from Sam Goldwyn. Bennett emerged with her ego barely intact, and only made one other film for United Artists before being released from her contract. She then began to freelance, appearing in *Disraeli* for Warner Bros.

Many consider Bennett's early films, including her acclaimed portrayal of Amy in *Little Women* (her own favorite), merely a prelude to the films she made after her 1940 marriage to Walter Wanger, and his subsequent supervision of her career. Two of her most acclaimed performances would come in films directed by Fritz Lang: *The Woman in the Window* (1944) and *Scarlet Street* (1945). She would also work for Jean Renoir in *The Woman on the Beach* (1947).

Bennett attributes a simple change of hair color—for the 1939 film *Trade Winds*—as the real turning point in her career. After a decade of playing "insipid blonde ingenues," she was now in a dark wig, with eyes at half-mast and voice lowered an octave, "I positively smoldered all over the South Sea," said Bennett. The results were so positive that she kept the new color, which many believed made her resemble ***Hedy Lamarr**. Whatever the cause for her appeal, she was convinced the new image was the only reason she was considered for the coveted role of Scarlett O'Hara in *Gone With the Wind*. The part went to English actress ***Vivien Leigh**.

As good as Bennett was in her "vamp" roles, she was also remembered for her performances in light comedy, notably as the mother in *Father of the Bride* and *Father's Little Dividend*, co-starring with **Elizabeth Taylor** and Spencer Tracy. Probably at her best portraying sensual, greedy, ambitious women, she nonetheless received critical acclaim for her role as the desperate mother under the threat of a blackmailer in *The Reckless Moment*.

Bennett's personal life was filled with men, many of whom she wed. Her first marriage to would-be film producer John Fox came when she was 16 and saw the birth of a daughter, Adrienne. Her second union, with Gene Markey in 1932, brought a second daughter, Melinda, and what Bennett called "probably the warmest and most amicable parting in Hollywood history." But her marriage to Walter Wanger was more complex. As much as he may have been responsible for putting her career into high gear, Bennett suggests he was also responsible for ending it. In a highly publicized incident in 1951, after the marriage had begun to unravel, Wanger was arrested and jailed for several months after shooting and wounding Bennett's agent Jennings Lang in a jealous rage. Bennett believed the scandal and resulting publicity destroyed her career, evidenced by her 65 films made before the incident and five in the decade that followed. In Bennett's opinion, the responsibility for the crime fell to her, as is so often the case when a man's crime is justified, and thus legitimatized, by the woman who "drove him to it." "Suddenly I was the villain of the piece," writes Bennett, "the apex of a triangle that had driven my husband to a shocking act of violence. I might just as well have pulled the trigger myself. The movie business was still bound by an inviolable code of behavior." In fact, Hollywood producers rallied around Wanger and, though critical of his behavior, "stuck by him and protected him within their exalted circle." Partially because of their two daughters, Stephanie and Shelley, Bennett did not divorce Wanger until 1965. Her fourth and final marriage to movie and drama critic David Wilde came in 1978.

Bennett appeared in several stage productions during the '50s and '60s, including *Janus*, *The Pleasure of His Company*, and *Never Too Late*. From 1966 to 1971, she appeared in the Gothic television soap opera "Dark Shadows," which provided the most taxing working conditions of her career. After 13 weeks of 10-hour days, she feared she'd have to take a "rest cure," but five years later she had made her peace with what she termed her "electronic stock company." Her later years also included an autobiography, *The Bennett Playbill*, published in 1970. (A beauty book, titled *How To Be Attractive*, had been written in 1943.) Joan Bennett died in 1990.

SUGGESTED READING:

Bennett, Joan, and Lois Kibbee. *The Bennett Playbill*. NY: Holt, Rinehart and Winston, 1970.

Barbara Morgan,
Melrose, Massachusetts

Bennett, Louie (1870–1956)

Irish trade unionist. *Born Louie Guillemine Bennett in Dublin, Ireland, in 1870; died in Dublin in 1956; daughter of James Cavendish Bennett (an auctioneer); privately educated in London; never married; no children.*

Founded the Irish Women's Suffrage Federation and the Irish Women's Reform League (1910); founded the Irish Women's International League (1914); reorganized the Irish Women Workers' Union (IWWU, 1916); served as IWWU vice-president (1917); served as IWWU general secretary (1919–55); elected first

woman president, Irish Trades Union Congress (1932). Publications: two romantic novels.

Though Louie Bennett was born in Dublin, Ireland, in 1870, she was educated in London and Bonn, Germany. By 1910, when the 40-year-old Bennett returned to the land of her birth, she was "in search of a crusade." At first, she became involved with the fight for women's suffrage as well as for world peace. However, in 1916, when she joined the struggle to improve labor conditions for the working women of Ireland, Bennett found the crusade to which she would dedicate the rest of her life.

Established in 1911, the Irish Women Workers' Union (IWWU) fell apart after the bloody Irish Easter Rising in the spring of 1916, when Irish rebels took on the British. British reaction to the Rising was swift and at times brutal. Because the fledgling women's union had allied itself with the cause of Irish independence, it suffered the loss of several key leaders—one executed, six imprisoned. By the end of 1916, Louie Bennett stepped forward, offering to reorganize the IWWU with a less nationalistic sentiment. While she was hardly unsympathetic to the fight for Irish independence, Bennett's ardent pacifism separated her from some of the more radical nationalists. Even more important, Bennett felt strongly that women's trade unionism would advance further and faster if it were not so strongly connected to Irish nationalism.

In the first year after Bennett's appearance, the IWWU did indeed grow. In 1917, the organization represented 2,300 women workers in a variety of trades—textiles, printing, laundries, and boxmaking. By 1918, the IWWU had added another 3,000 women to its ranks. Its credibility was further established through affiliation with the Dublin Trades' Council and with the Irish Trades Union Congress. This tremendous growth during World War I was due in part to the increased number of women in the industrial sector as well as to Bennett's cautious approach, one which emphasized conciliation rather than conflict. However, by 1920, as Great Britain accelerated its anti-Irish policies, Louie Bennett put her caution aside.

In 1920, Bennett went to America to help publicize British brutalities against the Irish, specifically the use of British police forces known as the Black and Tans. Once in New York, the 50-year-old woman was told she should replace her old-fashioned hat for a new, more fashionable model, "a pink feathered creation." When remembering this episode years later, Bennett remarked that "a woman in public life could afford to be neither dowdy or eccentric, so I took the hat home with me to Ireland." Ever the diplomat, Bennett was not above shaping both her argument and her image to suit the audience she wished to reach. Following her trip to the United States, she secured a five-minute appointment with British Prime Minister David Lloyd George. Still sporting the pink hat, Bennett delivered the same message to Lloyd George that she had brought to America: "take the Black and Tans out of Ireland." Peace, of a sort, came more than a year later with the partitioning of Ireland. However, by then, Bennett was once again focused on the issue of trade unionism for women, a task made even harder by the severe postwar economic depression.

During the 1920s, the IWWU was faced by rising unemployment and wage cuts for those still working. For women, already marginally employed at low wages, bad working conditions were made worse. At the same time, the IWWU was beset with political disputes, both internally and with the male-dominated Irish Trades Union Congress. In 1929 and again in 1930, Bennett threatened to resign her post as IWWU general secretary if internal staff problems were not resolved. Bennett was especially concerned about the association some IWWU leaders, such as ***Helena Molony**, had with the Communist Party. At the 1929 IWWU annual convention, Bennett declared: "Communist affiliations are undesirable." A resolution to that effect passed 40 to 15, and Bennett was thus persuaded to stay on. The following year, she again threatened to resign but instead took a leave of absence while the IWWU staff reorganized itself. The widespread opinion—even among those IWWU leaders who disagreed with her—was that Louie Bennett was what kept the IWWU together. More important, her primary goal was the same as the goal of those who differed from her politically: the increased organization of Irish women workers as a way to improve their conditions of labor.

In recognition of her dedication to the labor cause, the Irish Trades Union Congress nominated Bennett for president of that organization in 1932. Upon election, she became the first woman to hold that office. However, debate at the time centered more on her class origins than her gender. One labor newspaper claimed, "the degradation of the labour movement was completed when it elected as President a person from outside the ranks of the working class." For Bennett, the issue of most importance was the cause of working women. During her term as president of the Congress and beyond, she championed the rights of women workers. As the Great Depression deepened during the 1930s, women were increasingly seen as a threat to the already limited employment opportunities for men. Nonetheless, in 1935, Bennett spoke out for "equal pay for equal work" for women and demanded that the Congress recognize "equal rights . . . for all citizens."

By the end of the 1930s, the now almost 70-year-old Bennett began to show the strains of constant struggle. Ill-health forced her to ask for another leave of absence at the end of 1938 which stretched into 1939. However, as the Irish economy revived somewhat with the coming of World War II, Bennett stayed on as IWWU general secretary. She saw the union through the crisis of war and postwar economic adjustment. In 1949, the IWWU had grown to represent almost 7,000 women workers including nurses, printers, laundresses, and boxmakers. Now almost 80, Bennett turned much of the day-to-day operations of the IWWU over to the staff. Even so, as general secretary, she continued to work on those issues she saw as critical for working women in the postwar era: emigration, equal pay, and factory conditions.

In April of 1956, Louie Bennett wrote what was to be her last letter to the membership of the IWWU. Forty years earlier, she had put aside her interest in world peace to devote herself to the interests of Irish women workers. Now, in her last public statement, she urged a new generation of working-class women to think in more global terms. Bennett asked them "to consider what they can do to help forward this great job of world cooperation." Seven months later, on November 25, 1956, Louie Bennett died at the age of 86.

SOURCES:

Jones, Mary. *These Obstreperous Lassies: A History of the Irish Women Workers' Union.* Dublin: Gill and MacMillan, 1988.

COLLECTIONS:

Papers of the Irish Women Workers' Union, IWWU Archives, Dublin.

Kathleen Banks Nutter, Department of History, University of Massachusetts at Amherst

Bennett, Louise Simone (1919—)

Jamaican poet, actress, folklorist, singer and radio personality who pioneered poetry written and read in Jamaican dialect. *Name variations: Miss Lou. Born in Kingston, Jamaica, on September 7, 1919; only child of Kerene (Robinson) Bennett and Augustus Cornelius Bennett (a baker); educated at St. Simon's College, Friends College and the Royal Academy of Dramatic Art; married Eric "Chalk Talk" Coverly, in 1954.*

Selected works: Verses in Jamaican Dialect *(1942);* Jamaican Humour in Dialect *(1943);* M's Lulu Sez: A Collection of Dialect Poems *(1949);* Jamaican Folk Songs *(recording, 1954);* Laugh With Louise *(1961);* Jamaica Labrish *(1966);* Honourable Miss Lou *(recording, 1981);* Selected Poems *(1982).*

Only in recent decades has Louise Simone Bennett's work been categorized in literary circles as poetry. For more than 25 years, her often spoken, humorous, dialect rhymes and musings were termed performance art or comedy. The Jamaican Creole dialect, in which Bennett most often worked, was not appreciated until the late 1950s, delaying her recognition as one of Jamaica's most popular poets.

> I have found a medium through which I can pretend to be laughing.
>
> —**Louise Simone Bennett**

Raised in Kingston, Bennett was the daughter of a well-to-do baker whose fortunes and mental health declined when a batch of bread caused food poisoning among his customers. He died when his daughter was seven years old. Bennett credits her mother Kerene's customers with educating her about Jamaican life; Kerene made a living as a dressmaker. Educated at Kingston elementary and high school, Bennett began writing poetry in childhood. She quickly moved from conventional poetry, in proper English and on traditional subjects such as nature, to stories of the city and its people, finding humor in even the most serious subjects. "On a Tramcar" was Bennett's first dialect poem, in which she tells the other passengers, "Pread out yuhself, one dress-oman a come."

Bennett performed her poetry at outdoor theaters and was occasionally published, but the Jamaican literary community was difficult to penetrate. She would later note, "I have been set apart by other creative writers a long time ago because of the language I speak and work in." Her acting talent earned her a 1945 scholarship to the Royal Academy of Dramatic Art in London when she was 26 years old. Returning home in the late 1940s, Bennett was still greeted coolly by the literary community. She returned to London in 1950 for a radio show, then moved to New York in 1953 to work in the American theater. With Eric Coverly, an early supporter of her career, Bennett coproduced the folk musical *Day in Jamaica.* In 1954, she and Coverly married.

When the couple returned home in 1955, respect for Jamaican dialect was increasing. As a drama specialist on the Jamaican Social Welfare Commission, Bennett was selected an artistic envoy and traveled the country performing and teaching. Audiences grew with her frequent publications, radio shows, and commentary until, at folk festival readings, she began to draw crowds of 60,000. Jamaican affection for Miss Lou, as Bennett is popularly known, is perhaps comparable to a line from her poem "Colonisation in Reverse": "I feel like me heart gwine burs'."

SUGGESTED READING:

Bennett, Louise. *Jamaica Labrish.* Jamaica: Sangster's Book Stores, 1966.

Scott, Dennis. "Bennett on Bennett," in *Caribbean Quarterly.* March–June 1968, pp. 97–101.

Crista Martin, freelance writer, Boston, Massachusetts

Benoist, Marie (1768–1826)

French painter. *Name variations: Comtesse Benoist. Born Marie Guillemine (or Guilhelmine) Lerouix de*

Portrait of a Negress, *1800, by Marie Benoist.*

*la Ville in 1768 in Paris, France; died in 1826 in Paris, France; daughter of an administrative official; student of Elisabeth Vigée-Lebrun, *Adelaide Labille-Guiard, and Jacques Louis David; married Pierre Vincent Benoist, in 1793.*

Selected paintings: Innocence between Virtue and Vice *(1790);* The Farewell of Psyche; Portrait of a Negress *(1800).*

Encouraged by her father, Marie Benoist was only about 13 or 14 when she began studying painting with ***Elisabeth Vigée-Lebrun**, who influenced her early pastel portraits. While Vigée-Lebrun's studio was under reconstruction, Benoist was placed under the tutelage of the great Neoclassical painter Jacques Louis David, despite the king's decree that forbade young women artists to be trained at the Louvre. David's influence moved Benoist into the more linear and brilliant history paintings and formal portraits, exhibited at the Salon of 1791, that would dominate the rest of her career.

In 1793, she married royalist Pierre Vincent Benoist, whose anti-Revolutionary activities occasionally threatened their lives and prevented Benoist from exhibiting in the Salon of 1793. In 1800, she painted her best-known work *Portrait of a Negress*, which is said to have been inspired by the 1794 decree abolishing slavery. This painting established her reputation and was later acquired by Louis XVIII.

Around 1804, Benoist was officially commissioned to paint Napoleon's portrait for the Palais de Justice at Ghent, for which she received a gold medal. She also received an annual stipend from the government for producing official portraits of the emperor's family. Toward the end of her career, she began painting the sentimental scenes of family life that were becoming popular with the middle class. There is speculation that she may have begun a studio for women around this time, but details of this venture are unknown. At the height of her fame, Benoist was forced to stop participating in public exhibitions when her husband was appointed to a position in the Restoration government. She died in Paris in 1826.

Barbara Morgan,
Melrose, Massachusetts

Benoit, Joan (b. 1957).

See Samuelson, Joan Benoit.

Benson, Mildred (b. 1905)

American author, pilot, and journalist who, under the name Carolyn Keene, effectively created the character of "Nancy Drew." *Name variations: Mildred Augustine; Mildred Wirt Benson; Mildred A. Wirt; Ann Wirt; (pseudonyms) Frank Bell, Joan Clark, Don Palmer, Dorothy West; (collective pseudonyms) Julia K. Duncan, Alice B. Emerson, Frances K. Judd, Carolyn Keene, Helen Louise Thorndyke. Born Mildred Augustine in Ladora, Iowa, on July 10, 1905; daughter of J.L. (a doctor) and Lillian (Mattison) Augustine; University of Iowa, A.B., 1925, M.A., 1927; married Asa Alvin Wirt (d. 1947, affiliated with the Associated Press); married George A. Benson (d. 1959, editor of the* Toledo *[Ohio]* Times*), in 1950; children: (first marriage) Margaret Wirt.*

Selected works: (under collective pseudonym Alice B. Emerson) "Ruth Fielding" series (eight titles); (under Mildred A. Wirt) "Ruth Darrow Flying Stories" (four titles); (under collective pseudonym Carolyn Keene) "Nancy Drew Mystery Stories," including The Secret of the Old Clock *(1930),* The Hidden Staircase *(1930),* The Bungalow Mystery *(1930),* The Mystery at Lilac Inn *(1930),* The Secret at Shadow Ranch *(1930),* The Secret of Red Gate Farm *(1931),* The Clue in the Diary *(1932),* The Clue of the Broken Locket *(1934),* The Message in the Hollow Oak *(1935),* The Mystery of the Ivory Charm *(1936),* The Whispering Statue *(1937),* The Haunted Bridge *(1937),* The Clue of the Tapping Heels *(1939),* The Mystery of the Brass Bound Trunk *(1940),* The Mystery at the Moss-Covered Mansion *(1941),* The Quest of the Missing Map *(1942),* The Clue in the Jewel Box *(1943),* The Secret in the Old Attic *(1944),* The Clue in the Crumbling Wall *(1945),* The Mystery of the Tolling Bell *(1946),* The Clue in the Old Album *(1947),* The Ghost of Blackwood Hall *(1948),* The Clue of the Velvet Mask *(1953); (under collective pseudonym Julia K. Duncan) "Doris Force Mystery Series" (two titles); (under Ann Wirt) "Madge Sterling" series (three titles); (under collective pseudonym Frances K. Judd) "Kay Tracey Mystery Stories" (12 titles); (under Mildred A. Wirt) "Mildred A. Wirt Mystery Stories" (seven titles); (under pseudonym Joan Clark) "Penny Nichols Mystery Stories" (four titles); (under collective pseudonym Carolyn Keene) "Dana Girls Mystery Series" (12 titles); (under Mildred A. Wirt) "Trailer Stories for Girls" (four titles); (under pseudonym Dorothy West) "Dot and Dash" series (five titles); (under Mildred A. Wirt) "Penny Parker Mystery Stories" (17 titles), "Brownie Scout" series (six titles), and "Dan Carter" series (six titles); (under pseudonym Don Palmer) "Boy Scout Explorers" series (three titles).*

Between the years 1927 and 1959, author Mildred Benson, using her own name and a variety of pseudonyms, wrote over 100 series books for the Stratemeyer Syndicate, a writing house that produced juvenile fiction, including the popular "Tom Swift," "Bobbsey Twins," and "Hardy Boys" series. Her most popular creation, the girl sleuth Nancy Drew, has endured for over 70 years of printed life and has entertained more than three generations of young girls. Between 1938–1939, several of the Nancy Drew stories were even made into feature films, starring ***Bonita Granville**. Benson was as spunky and daring as her intrepid heroine. Well into her 80s, she piloted her own plane and, in her 90s, continued holding down a job at *The Blade* in Toledo, Ohio, writing a weekly column called "On the Go."

The daughter of a surgeon and a homemaker, Mildred Benson was born and raised in the small town of Ladora, Iowa. In 1925, after distinguishing herself as the first woman to receive a Master's degree from the University of Iowa's journalism school, she left for New York City to become a writer. While making the rounds in the city, she met Edward Stratemeyer, who put her credentials on file. Benson eventually returned to

Mildred Benson

Iowa where she dabbled in journalism, wrote some children's books, and married newsman Asa Wirt.

In 1929, she received a call from Stratemeyer, offering her an opportunity to work on the Syndicate's established "Ruth Fielding" series. When her work proved more than satisfactory, Stratemeyer tapped her for his new "Nancy Drew" mystery series, which he viewed as the counterpart to his successful "Hardy Boys" mysteries. After receiving a brief plot and character outline for the first book, *The Secret of the Old Clock*, Benson crafted a smart, adventurous heroine, one she hoped would break the stereotypical mold. "Women had little opportunity in those days," she says. "Nancy came along when women were ready for a change." As it turned out, Stratemeyer thought the first manuscript was "too flip," but the publishers loved it, and Benson was signed for two more books. Her contract was standard for the Syndicate at the time, paying a flat fee of $125 per manuscript, with no royalties, and demanding that she not use the Syndicate pseudonym for any of her own books.

For years Benson, under the name Carolyn Keene, produced a new 200-page Nancy Drew story every six weeks or so, writing 22 of the next 29 books in the series, and frequently drawing on her own experiences for inspiration. "Even though she says she's not Nancy Drew," says Indiana writer Geoffrey S. Lapin, who in the 1960s tracked down Benson as the writer of the series, "the similarities are striking. Millie flew a plane until a couple of years ago; Nancy flew a plane. Millie is an avid golfer; one whole Nancy Drew book is devoted to golf. Millie went on archeological digs; Nancy also was an explorer."

In addition to Nancy Drew, Benson also worked on several other Stratemeyer projects, including the "Doris Force," "Kay Tracy," and "Dana Girls" series. She also published volumes under her own name, or variations of her own name, including the "Ruth Darrow Flying Stories."

After the death of her first husband, with whom she had a daughter, Margaret, Benson married George A. Benson, editor of Ohio's *Toledo Times*. Following his death in 1959, she put her fiction career behind her and embraced the newspaper business, covering everything from court trials to sports. In the late 1960s, when she was approached by an editor to start another series for young people, she was initially tempted. "Plots began to percolate," she said. "Then fog settled over my typewriter. The teenagers for whom I wrote lived in a world far removed from drugs, abortion, divorce and racial class. Regretfully, I turned down the offer. Any character I might create would never be attuned to today's social problems."

The Nancy Drew series continued after Benson left the Syndicate and has sold more than 80 million copies since its inception. Of late, the fictional girl detective has become the subject of scholarly studies and dissertations, and Benson has been hailed as a trailblazing feminist author. In 1993, the University of Iowa, Benson's alma mater, hosted a conference at which the topics under discussion included "Stereotypical Racial and Ethnic Images in Nancy Drew" and "Lesbian Code in Nancy Drew Mystery Stories." Benson simply rolls her eyes at all the hullabaloo, denying that there were any hidden motives in her work. "I never tried to influence anybody," she snaps. "I just tried to write a fast-moving story. I've heard all the different theories. They're a waste of time."

SOURCES:

Halliwell, Leslie. *The Filmgoer's Companion*. 4th ed. NY: Hill and Wang, 1974.

Olendorf, Donna. *Something about the Author*, Vol. 65. Detroit, MI: Gale Research.

Plummer, William, and John T. Slania. "Her Own Woman," in *People*. December 21, 1998.

Barbara Morgan,
Melrose, Massachusetts

Benson, Sally (1900–1972)

***American writer, best remembered for her "Junior Miss" stories that began in* The New Yorker.** *Name variations: (pseudonym) Esther Evarts. Born Sara Mahala Redway Smith on September 3, 1900, in St. Louis, Missouri; died on July 19, 1972, in Woodland Hills, California; daughter of Alonzo Redway (a cotton broker) and Anna (Prophater) Smith; attended Mary Institute, St. Louis, Missouri; Horace Mann High School, New York, New York; married Reynolds Benson, on January 25, 1919 (divorced); children: one daughter, Barbara.*

Selected writings: People Are Fascinating *(short stories, 1936);* Emily *(short stories, 1938, published in England as* Love Thy Neighbour, *1939);* Stories of the Gods and Heroes *(1940, reprinted, 1979);* Junior Miss *(short stories, 1941, reprinted, 1968);* Meet Me in St. Louis *(1942);* Women and Children First *(short stories, 1943, reprinted 1946).*

Screenplays: Shadow of a Doubt *(Universal, 1943);* Experiment Perilous *(RKO, 1944);* National Velvet *(M-G-M, 1944);* Anna and the King of Siam *(20th Century-Fox, 1946);* Come to the Stable *(20th*

Century-Fox, 1949); Conspirator *(M-G-M, 1950);* No Man of Her Own *(Paramount, 1950);* The Belle of New York *(M-G-M, 1952);* The Farmer Takes a Wife *(20th Century-Fox, 1953);* The Adventures of Huckleberry Finn *(M-G-M, 1960);* Bus Stop *(20th Century-Fox, 1961);* Summer Magic *(Walt Disney, 1962);* Viva Las Vegas *(M-G-M, 1963);* Signpost to Murder *(M-G-M, 1963);* The Singing Nun *(M-G-M, 1966). Plays: (With Walter Kent)* Seventeen *(1954);* The Young and Beautiful *(1956).*

Although Sally Benson is best remembered as the creator of Judy Graves, the teenage heroine of *Junior Miss*, her work covered a broad spectrum, including short stories, novels, newspaper features, film reviews, plays, screenplays, and movie and television adaptations.

Benson married soon out of high school, had a daughter, and later divorced. She started writing as an interviewer for the New York *Morning Telegraph*, doing a piece a week on various celebrities. From there, she reviewed movies for a pulp-paper house, producing some 32 reviews a month in addition to some interviews. Her segue to the prestigious *New Yorker* was dramatic in its simplicity: Benson sent off her very first short story and it came back with a check and a request for more. So buoyed was she by her good fortune that she did not write another piece for a year, until she ran out of money. "My style fits here and it wouldn't most places," said Benson about her association with *The New Yorker*. "Every once in a while editors of some of the national magazines have asked for stuff, but what they really want are healthy, clean-limbed, hearty young people on a raft, and that isn't for me." In *American Women Writers*, **Mary Anne Ferguson** discusses Benson's sharp edge, describing her stories as "'slices of life' in which characters, through stream-of-consciousness or dialogue, reveal foolish pretenses; swift narration and irony preclude sentimentality but sometimes result in cruel revelations."

Sally Benson

Benson's first books were collections of her *New Yorker* stories. *People are Fascinating*, published in 1936, contains "The Overcoat" and "Suite 2049," two O. Henry prize stories for 1935. In 1941, she was astonished by the success of the "Junior Miss" collection. Benson had not intended to write more than one or two stories, but was convinced by Harold Ross, then editor of *The New Yorker*, that she'd be a fool to drop them. She was further amazed by plans to turn the stories into movies or plays, feeling that they lacked the kind of plot and continuity that movie and play producers wanted. The adaptations, however, proved extremely successful. After the stage play in 1941, the first radio show, "Junior Miss," starring ***Shirley Temple (Black)**, premiered on CBS in 1942. It led to a second radio version, which ran from 1948 to 1954, and a television movie, starring **Carol Lynley**, Don Ameche, and ***Joan Bennett**, in 1957.

Published in 1942, Benson's novel *Meet Me in St. Louis* was based on her own childhood memories as well as diaries her older sister had kept at the time of the World's Fair in St. Louis at the turn of the century. Sold to Hollywood, the book was transformed into a popular musical film starring ***Judy Garland**.

Benson's two plays were both adaptations. The musical *Seventeen*, written with Walter Kent, was adapted from the popular novel by Booth Tarkington, about a 17-year-old boy who falls in love for the first time. *The Young and Beautiful* was based on F. Scott Fitzgerald's "Josephine" stories. Of Benson's numerous film scripts, several have become classics, including *National Velvet*, which starred **Elizabeth Taylor** and Mickey Rooney, and *Come to the Stable*, which won ***Loretta Young** and ***Celeste Holm**

Oscar nominations. For her screenplay *Anna and the King of Siam*, Benson was nominated for an Academy Award in 1946.

In a widely publicized 1965 case, Benson testified that her California doctor had given her injections of codeine over an 18-month period that resulted in a drug dependency. She brought the case to the attention of the narcotics bureau, which led to an investigation and indictment for a narcotics violation. After the ordeal, the 68-year-old Benson unexpectedly found it easy to cure herself of the drug dependency and resumed a busy writing schedule. She died on July 19, 1972, at the age of 71.

Barbara Morgan,
Melrose, Massachusetts

Benson, Stella (1892–1933)

Modernist English novelist, poet, and travel writer who actively campaigned for women's rights before and during World War I and in Hong Kong during the early 1930s. *Name variations: Stella Benson O'-Gorman Anderson. Born Stella Benson on January 6, 1892, in Shropshire, England; died on December 6,*

From the movie Junior Miss, *starring Mona Freeman and Peggy Ann Garner, based on the writings of Sally Benson.*

1933, in Hongay in the Chinese province of Tongking (now Vietnam), of pneumonia and heart failure; buried on the Ile de Charbon near Baie d'Along; daughter of Caroline Essex (Cholmondeley) and Ralph Beaumont Benson, both landed gentry; educated at home; married Shaemus (James) O'Gorman Anderson (a Chinese government customs official), on September 29, 1921; children: none.

Awards: French Vie Heureuse Prize (1932) for Tobit Transplanted *(published in U.S. as* The Far-Away Bride*) and the A.C. Benson silver medal for service to literature (1932).*

Began lifelong practice of writing diary (1901); wrote I Pose *(1915), a feminist satire about the suffrage movement; wrote novels, poems, and short stories, mixing fantasy and satire; traveled alone, often ill but self-supporting, to Berkeley, California (1918–19), to China and India (1920–21); traveled to the U.S. with husband; moved to China with husband, settling in Mengtsz (1922–25), then Shanghai, followed by Lung Ching Tsun (1925–27), Nanning (1929–30), Hong Kong (1930–31), and Pakhoi (1931–33).*

Selected writings: I Pose *(1915);* This Is the End *(1917); (poems)* Twenty *(1918);* Living Alone *(1919);* Kwan-Yin *(1922);* The Poor Man *(1922);* Pipers and a Dancer *(1924); (self-illustrated essays)* The Little World *(1925);* The Awakening: A Fantasy *(1925);* Goodbye, Stranger *(1926); (self-illustrated essays)* Worlds within Worlds *(1928);* The Man Who Missed the Bus: A Story *(1928);* The Far-Away Bride *(1930, republished as* Tobit Transplanted, *1931);* Hope Against Hope and Other Stories *(1932);* Christmas Formula and Other Stories *(1931); (with Count Nicolas de Toulouse Lautrec de Savine, K.M.)* Pull Devil, Pull Baker *(1933);* Mundos: An Unfinished Novel *(1935);* Poems *(1935);* Collected Short Stories *(1936).*

Stella Benson came of age during the woman's suffrage movement in early 20th-century England. In 1910, forced by severe illness to spend 18 months convalescing in a sanatorium, Benson, aged 18, devoted her time to reading and reflecting on the feminist ideas and arguments which were then drawing considerable attention in the popular intellectual and political press; she determined to strike out on her own.

It is difficult to imagine a less likely candidate for feminine independence than Stella Benson. At that time, it was usual for girls of her upper-class status to remain in their parents' keep, reared as Edwardian ladies, supported at home until marriage. Moreover, Benson was a frail child, beset by serious respiratory illnesses, often bedridden for months. Judged too sick to attend school, she had been tutored at home by governesses. Nevertheless, in 1913, against her mother's objections, 21-year-old Stella Benson left her home in Shropshire for an independent life in London, where she took up a series of jobs to support herself, producing novels which eventually brought her fame as a modernist writer and launching her own "private Stellarian Suffrage Campaign" of argument and persuasion.

By the spring of 1913, the suffrage movement had turned confrontational. In her thinking about the struggle for the vote for women, Benson shifted away from support for the moderate, constitutional methods of protest espoused by ***Millicent Fawcett**'s National Union of Suffrage Societies to explore the more militant policies of ***Emmeline Pankhurst**'s Women's Social and Political Union. Benson's reconsideration was influenced by the admired suicide of the militant suffragist ***Emily Wilding Davison**, who had flung herself in front of the king's horse at the Derby. Davison's suicidal act became a defining event in Benson's first novel, *I Pose* (1915), narrated from a feminist point of view. Through wit, irony, and understatement, *I Pose* deftly underscores limited potential identities, or "poses," for women. Her woman hero can conceive of but two roles for self-creation: she may either submit to love in marriage with a charming man who does not honor her autonomy, or she may fight as a militant suffragist, indeed, deliberately killing herself while causing an explosion in a church in an effort to expose an anti-woman collaboration between business and the Anglican Church. The critic R. Meredith Bedell asserts: "Benson's recurring concern is the isolation of the individual in the modern world. And her vision is broad enough, her compassion great enough, to include both sexes in her sympathy." *I Pose* punctures pretensions, satirizing commercialized art, institutionalized religion, and organized causes, including even the suffrage movement, which prompted ***Rebecca West**, a suffragist herself, to write in 1915: "How superbly you've done the snake that was the soul of the suffrage movement. How lucky you are to have written the only novel of genius about the Suffrage."

Born on January 6, 1892, in Lutwyche Hall in Shropshire, England, Stella Benson was the third child of four and the second daughter of Caroline Essex Cholmondeley and Ralph Beaumont Benson. The Cholmondeleys belonged to the acknowledged ruling elite of England, whereas the Bensons had gathered their fortune more recently in the 18th century by managing slaves in the West Indies, a taint that haunted Stella Benson's serious-minded, disciplinarian father.

Lutwyche Hall, an Elizabethan mansion, cold in winter, had been the Benson family residence for over 100 years. It was an unhealthy environment in which to raise children with fragile health. Stella's sister, two years her senior, fell ill and died when Stella was seven. Although the family had regular quarters at Lutwyche and in London on Norfolk Square, there were many visits to other parts of England and to northern France in search of climate and conditions which would improve Stella's health. Stella had frequent, painful, debilitating, life-threatening bouts of bronchitis, pleurisy, and sinus infection. Of her health, she eventually wrote: "I insist on ignoring the whole condition. Since I can't cure it, I won't be patched up. If I must die, I'll die as alive as I can."

Even as a child, Stella Benson was a gifted writer, artist, and musician. In 1901, aged nine, she began her lifelong habit of writing a diary; it is housed in its remarkable, sparkling entirety at University Library in Cambridge, England, and is quoted extensively in a biography of Benson authored by **Joy Grant**. In 1905, one of Benson's poems won an award for extreme merit in *St. Nicholas Magazine*, a high-minded periodical for children. In 1910, she traveled to Freiburg, Germany, to study music and to learn German and French. Her health broke down after one month, whereupon she was sent to Arosa in Switzerland for a year and a half of recuperation and a series of sinus operations which left her permanently deaf in one ear. In Arosa, Stella Benson adopted a feminist position and decided that she would live independently, although before doing so, she took a cruise to Jamaica with her mother, using the time to start writing her first novel, *I Pose*.

In 1913, aged 21, Stella Benson moved to the Hoxton section of London, a cockney working-class neighborhood marked by its poverty and violence. Illness returned her home. When she later reentered London, she again strove to be financially independent, finding work with the Charity Organization Society. In addition, she went into partnership with a crippled woman making paper bags; she also taught basket-weaving. During the first part of World War I, Benson was a secretary for the Women Writers' Suffrage Union and then for the United Suffragists. Her second novel, *This Is the End*, was published in 1917. In it, she privileges fantasy. Factuality and marriage punctuate the prosaic, negative denouement of her "suffragetty" woman hero. Her volume of poetry, *Twenty*, appeared in 1918. As part of the war effort, Benson volunteered to raise vegetables on a farm in Cornwall, missing 48 out of 112 days of work because of illness.

Advised by her physicians to leave England, Benson sailed for New York in 1918. She traveled alone, supporting herself when she ran out of money by working on a farm in Colorado. By December, she arrived in Berkeley, California, where she worked and partied beyond her strength, falling ill with pleurisy which hospitalized her for several weeks. While in California, she supported herself with an assortment of jobs: collecting bills, selling boys' books, giving French lessons, teaching writing at the University of California, and working as a reader for the University of California Press. She co-initiated a poetry club and wrote *Living Alone* (1919), a novel about a woman who prefers living without liaisons with men. In 1920, weary and heartbroken by a disappointing relationship, she bolted San Francisco for Hong Kong, where she arrived despite a bloody bout of influenza in Japan along the way. Physicians, as they often did, feared tuberculosis.

> Of one thing I am certain—when we have the vote, men will see what a small gift it was, and future generations will ask why it was grudged so bitterly.
>
> **—The suffragist in *I Pose* by Stella Benson**

In Hong Kong, she taught at a boys' school; in Peking, she was an x-ray technician. While in China, she met her future husband Shaemus (James) O'Gorman Anderson, an official in the Imperialist Chinese Maritime Customs Service, a department of Chinese government staffed by foreigners. Anderson dramatically rescued Benson and her companions from entrapment by Chinese warring factions on the Yangtze River. After continuing her round-the-world travels to India, then home to England, Stella Benson married on September 29, 1921, becoming Mrs. James C. O'-Gorman Anderson in private life. Before returning to China, the O'Gorman Andersons drove a car across the United States. Her novel, *The Poor Man* (1922), satirized aspects of American culture, outraging her friends in California.

Thereafter, Stella Benson lived according to her husband's postings in various outposts of China, an isolation sometimes relieved by travel to California and England. Her loneliness engendered self-criticism and uncertainty. She was intensely alienated by social life among missionaries, whom she came to despise, and bureaucrats, both British and French, none of whom offered the intellectual companionship she sought. Animals, particularly dogs, filled her heart. The O'Gorman Andersons lived in Mengtsz between 1922 and 1925, then Shanghai briefly before settling in Lung Ching Tsun, an extremely cold and remote region near Siberia, where Benson sympathized with the exiled White Russian community. She wrote religiously in her diary and carried on a lively correspondence with friends around the world—with **Bertha Pope**, **Laura Hutton**, and Sydney Schiff, for instance, as well as with members of her family and with some of the major women writers of her day, ***Winifred Holtby**, ***Storm Jameson**, ***Naomi Mitchison**, and ***Virginia Woolf**, among others. Benson wrote articles and books: *Pipers and a Dancer* (1924), a novel about a lover-like relationship between two women, continues to focus on the problem of women isolated in ill-fitting feminine roles; *The Little World* (1925) is a collection of travel essays illustrated by Benson; *Goodbye, Stranger* (1926) is a novel which uses fantasy to explore crucial problems of identity and isolation.

Returning from an unhappy two-year leave in Europe and England (1927–29), Benson wrote her husband: "I insist on being a writer first and a wife second: a man artist would insist and I insist." In the last stages of writing *Tobit Transplanted* (1931), she joined her husband in Nanning in southern China; six months later, they escaped amid bombs just before the city was razed by warring Chinese armies. In Hong Kong, Benson organized a campaign against selling young Chinese girls into government brothels, a form of sexual slavery condoned by the silence of British officialdom. She felt snubbed and unappreciated by the British community. While her reputation in the world at large was increasing, booksellers in Hong Kong were reluctant to order her books because there was no interest in them. Her collection of short stories, *Pull Devil, Pull Baker* (1932), attacked the British colonial experience.

In 1932, Stella Benson was awarded the prestigious French Vie Heureuse Prize for *Tobit Transplanted* and the A.C. Benson silver medal for "services to literature." Her writing was generating more money. On a trip to England, she bought a house in London, hoping to return permanently with her husband.

Tobit Transplanted, published as *The Far-Away Bride* in the United States, was Stella Benson's most widely read and acclaimed novel. She had always been recognized by a small following as a significant voice, a writer's writer. With *Tobit Transplanted*, her writing became popular; the book was chosen to represent England in an International P.E.N. Club competition for the best novel written in the last two years.

In *Tobit Transplanted*, Benson converts the story of Tobit in the Apocrypha into a description of Russian exiles in China—demystifying Biblical occurrences and psychologically rationalizing its characters. Her characters recognize their existential isolation. Her heroine Tanya yearns for unsullied integrity, for separation from men and mating; she meditates:

> Containers of uneasy blood, that's all we are. Big and little, male and female, two-legged, four-legged, six-legged, winged and creeping, wise and foolish, we slide and stride and wiggle about the earth until something called death lets the blood out, to be soaked into the ground, to be dried into the air, to form again other containers. . . . Why should there be any of this merging between one skin-full of blood and bones and another? Why can't we get used to the loneliness of having separate blood? Pitchers may go to the same well, be dipped, and come home full, clinking handles, tinkling together—but always separate—each with its dreadful integrity complete—its inviolate solitary storm of contents. Not till the pitcher is spilled is there a merging—a cold, loveless merging into thirsty space.

Nevertheless, unlike many of Benson's former fictional characters, those in *Tobit Transplanted* grow and change, choosing fragile connection through pity for the vulnerability of others. Virginia Woolf wrote to Benson praising *Tobit*:

> [Y]ou are getting to the bare bones of things, and I love the bareness, the whiteness, the hardness of your bones. But I don't think that when you say you are dealing with what is common you mean what is cheap, nasty, commonplace, trivial, silly, affected. Not at all, I should say what you have done in *Tobit* is precisely the opposite—You've eaten away the soft mash and laid bare the bone. And I admit I envy you.

Benson joined her husband in Pakhoi, China, in 1932. On December 6, 1933, while on holiday attempting to restore her health, Stella Benson, aged 41, died of heart failure caused by pneumonia. Her unfinished novel *Mundos* and a volume of poetry were published posthumously in 1935. Until a revival in the 1980s, her literary reputation languished, along with critical attention to her works.

SOURCES:

Bedell, R. Meredith. *Stella Benson*. Boston, MA: Twayne, 1983.

Benson, Stella. *I Pose*. London: Macmillan, 1915.
———. *The Far-Away Bride*. (*Tobit Transplanted* in England.) NY: Harper & Brothers, 1930.
Grant, Joy. *Stella Benson: A Biography*. London: Macmillan, 1987.
Roberts, Richard Ellis. *Portrait of Stella Benson*. London: Macmillan, 1939.

SUGGESTED READING:

Eastman, Kitti Carriker. "Stella Benson," in *Dictionary of Literary Biography*. Vol. 36. Detroit, MI: Gale Research, 1985.
Woolf, Virginia. *The Letters of Virginia Woolf*. Vols. 3, 4, 5. Edited by Nigel Nicholson and Joanne Trautmann. NY: Harcourt Brace Jovanovich, 1979.

COLLECTIONS:

The Diary of Stella Benson 1902–1933. University Library, Cambridge, England.

Collections of Stella Benson correspondence: The Manuscript Room, The British Library, London, England; Humanities Research Center, Austin, Texas; Harvard University Library, Cambridge, Massachusetts; Berg Collection and Research Libraries, New York Public Library; Mills College, Oakland, California; Library of Congress, Washington, D.C.

Jill Benton, Professor of English and World Literature, Pitzer College, Claremont, California

Bentivoglio, Ippolita.

See Sforza, Ippolita.

Bentivoglio, Lucrezia (d. 1516/18).

See Este, Lucrezia d'.

Bentley, Catherine (fl. 1635)

English-Flemish nun who translated and had published a life of St. Clare of Assisi. *Name variations: Sister Magdalene Augustine. Flourished around 1635; daughter of English parents; never married; no children.*

Little is known about Catherine Bentley's life. Born of English parents, she entered the order of Poor Clares in Douai (Flanders) and took the name Sister Magdalene Augustine. The Poor Clares (known as Minoresses in England) was an ascetic order of women dedicated, as its name suggests, to poverty, simplicity, and charity. Bentley was well educated by the nuns of her order and showed an aptitude for languages which led her to complete several translations of devotional works. Among these were a life of St. ***Clare of Assisi**, founder of the Poor Clares, which was published in 1635 and dedicated to the English queen ***Henrietta Maria**.

Bentley, Elizabeth Turrill (1908–1963)

American anti-Communist witness during the McCarthy era in the United States. *Born in New Milford, Connecticut, in 1908; died in New Haven, Connecticut, on December 3, 1963; graduated from Vassar College, 1930; master's degree from Columbia University, 1933.*

Joined Communist Party (1935) while a student at Columbia University; served as secretary to Jacob Golos, head of a Soviet espionage network; later claimed that as a Soviet spy courier she had uncovered a vast network of treason in Washington, D.C. (1930s–45); played an important role in anti-Communist investigations and prosecutions during early years of the Cold War; described by media as the "Red Spy Queen," her testimony was significant in bringing about the convictions of Ethel and Julius Rosenberg and William Remington.

By alleging in 1948 that she had proof of treasonous activities of high officials in the United States government, Elizabeth Bentley helped set the tone of American political life during the first phase of the Cold War. A number of rising political figures, including Joseph R. McCarthy and Richard M. Nixon, built their political careers on an aggressive variety of anti-Communism. They benefitted from the national hysteria triggered by the testimony of Bentley and others who declared that the United States was under attack from a vast number of spies, traitors and saboteurs. For several years, Bentley and other ex-Communists, including Whittaker Chambers, upset and fascinated millions of Americans.

Elizabeth Turrill Bentley was born in 1908 in New Milford, Connecticut, into a middle-class Republican family. In 1930, she graduated from Vassar College and went on to receive a master's degree in foreign languages from Columbia University in 1933. While studying in Italy at the University of Florence, Bentley saw the impact of the Fascist regime on the lives of ordinary Italians and was revolted by incontrovertible evidence of repression. Upon her return to the United States in 1935, she joined a Communist cell at Columbia University, where she continued to take courses.

Bentley claimed that she became an underground Communist agent in 1938, being assigned by her party superiors to work for Jacob Golos, a Russian-born American citizen who was an agent of the Soviet secret police, the NKVD. Using a travel agency known as World Tourists as a front, Golos headed an espionage ring that collected industrial and strategic data of potential value to the Soviet Union. Elizabeth Bentley began working as a courier for the spy network headed by Golos; she also became his lover. She made biweekly trips to Washington, D.C., where her main contact was an economist with the Farm Security Administration, and carried rolls of exposed but undeveloped film back to New York. After Golos' death in November 1943, Bentley continued her espionage chores and worked for several handlers, including the first secretary of the Soviet embassy. For a while, she also worked for a second spy network headed by an economist at the War Production Board. On her own, she collected information of possible strategic importance to the Soviets, gathering most of the data from acquaintances in New York City.

In August 1945, Bentley walked into the FBI field office in New Haven, Connecticut, and told the special agents that she had worked for a Soviet spy ring for a half-dozen years and had decided to break with Communism. Apparently, Bentley did not make a strong impression, for it was 11 weeks before the New York field office of the FBI held a follow-up interview. This was a time when the first chill winds of the Cold War began to blow and a new mood of fear permeated American public life. In September 1945, Igor Gouzenko, a cipher clerk in the Soviet embassy in Ottawa, Canada, defected and told the Royal Canadian Mounted Police that for a number of years he had been part of a network gathering intelligence on the American atomic-bomb project. The public began to regard spy stories as normal newspaper fare as World War II started to fade into history.

Alerted by the Gouzenko revelations, the FBI tracked down Elizabeth Bentley and interviewed her on November 7, 1945. In great detail, she told the story of her life and her work as a courier for the Soviets and provided the FBI with the names of 14 individuals she claimed were Soviet spies. Of these, six had served with the Office of Strategic Services (OSS), predecessor of the Central Intelligence Agency (CIA). One of them, she asserted, had been OSS general counsel and was a former law partner of the OSS director William J. "Wild Bill" Donovan. Among the remainder, who were in one way or another connected with the Treasury Department, the most prominent, Bentley asserted, was Harry Dexter White, a close advisor of Treasury Secretary Henry Morgenthau. These accusations were dramatic enough, but in subsequent interviews Bentley kept increasing the number of people whom she accused of being Soviet espionage agents: the number went from an initial 43 to more than 100 by the time she became known to the public in 1948 as a result of her appearance before the House Committee on Un-American Activities (HUAC). In 1947—before Cold War hysteria had totally taken over American public life—Elizabeth Bentley's sweeping allegations seemed so outlandish that an attempt to convene a grand jury, to indict the Treasury Department employees named by her as spies, failed. A year later, however, the psychological climate of the country would change dramatically, and many Americans would be receptive to her accounts of massive subversion in Washington.

In July 1948, Bentley's story of widespread treason in Washington came to the attention of the American public in a series of sensationalistic articles published in the conservative *New York World-Telegram*. To add spice to the story, she was described as a "Red Spy Queen." Politicians eager for publicity sensed that her information, although rejected by a grand jury a year earlier, now appeared more credible in the light of world tensions. A few weeks later, in August 1948, Bentley became a national celebrity by testifying before congressional committees, repeating the accusations that she had made to the FBI almost three years earlier. By now, most Americans regarded the Soviet Union as an international adversary of the United States in places like Germany, where the Berlin airlift was taking place, and in Greece, where a Communist-led insurrection had plunged that country into a bloody civil war. In Czechoslovakia, the Communists had overthrown a democratic government in February 1948, and in China the Communist forces led by Mao Zedong were rapidly gaining the upper hand over American-backed Nationalist forces. Frightened by sensationalistic press and magazine stories, many Americans were expecting a Third World War to break out at any time. The atmosphere inside the country was charged, and conservative Republicans in Congress were determined to end the New Deal and discredit Democrat Harry Truman, who had succeeded to the presidency upon the death of Franklin D. Roosevelt in April 1945. Truman's initial response to Bentley's charges was to describe the hearings at which she testified as a "red herring" designed to distract attention from the fact that the Republican-controlled Congress had not been able to bring runaway inflation under control.

The small group of Americans brave enough to risk their careers to defend the full spectrum of civil liberties guaranteed in the constitution noted that Bentley's congressional testimony was entirely uncorroborated and lacking in documentary evidence. Even FBI director J. Edgar Hoover worried that she was too volatile to be a credible witness in court. Some of the intelligence information she claimed had been passed to the Soviets by her spy ring, such as armament and aircraft production statistics, appeared to be of strategic value, but other data, such as a project to make synthetic rubber out of garbage, sounded far-fetched if not bizarre in the extreme. Although significant discrepancies were found in her testimony, Elizabeth Bentley became a key witness for the government as it prosecuted a number of individuals alleged to have been Communists or Soviet intelligence agents. Needless to say, in return for her cooperation with the FBI and government prosecutors, she escaped indictment for her own espionage activities.

None of the United States government employees whom Bentley claimed had given her information for transmission to the Soviet Union were ever convicted of espionage, but by 1949 she was regarded by government prosecutors as an important part of their strategy to convict the leaders of the Communist Party on charges of conspiring to overthrow the United States government by force and violence. In 1951, she published her autobiography *Out of Bondage* which received respectful, rather than enthusiastic, reviews. Some critics, including Joseph Alsop, failed to be convinced by Bentley, detecting in the book "a smell of phoniness" at least in part because it had been written "in the prose of True Confessions." Some were suspicious, noting that half the book consisted of long stretches of dialogue purporting to reproduce conversations ten and fifteen years old.

Despite the less than unanimous praise for her autobiography, Bentley continued to figure as a major star of the anti-Communist universe of the early 1950s. As a national celebrity, she lectured throughout the country on the dangers of espionage and world Marxism. Though she had never met either of them, Bentley figured as a key government witness in the 1951 espionage trial of Julius and ***Ethel Rosenberg**. Both of the Rosenbergs were sentenced to death. Despite worldwide protests against the severity of the sentence, including an appeal for clemency from Pope Pius XII, husband and wife were executed in the electric chair on June 19, 1953.

In the trial of William Remington, Elizabeth Bentley had one final dramatic role to play. Remington, a government official, had received scant mention in her tales of spying in Washington, but he had dared to sue her for libel, and won his case, receiving $9,000 in damages. Although he had appeared before grand juries in 1947 and 1950, Remington was not indicted in either instance, and it appeared that he would be able to resume his career, having also been cleared by the government loyalty review board. But the government was as much interested in rehabilitating the reputation of Bentley, whose effectiveness as an anti-Communist witness was fading, as it was determined to convict Remington on perjury charges. In Remington's 1953 trial, Bentley's testimony was instrumental in convicting him, though it was revealed during her testimony that, six days before, she had signed a contract with her publisher for another anti-Communist book which would contain charges against Remington that could only be safely published if he were indicted and convicted. Despite the questionable nature of much of the evidence presented at the trial, Remington was found guilty of perjury. He was sent to Lewisburg prison, where soon after his admission he was beaten to death by several prisoners who claimed to be anti-Communist zealots.

The Remington trial marked the end of Elizabeth Bentley's career as a Cold War celebrity. In 1954, the excesses of Senator Joseph McCarthy led to his censure by his Senatorial colleagues led, in part, by ***Margaret Chase Smith**. Slowly, the atmosphere of hysteria that had engulfed the United States for nearly a decade began to weaken if not disappear. The public had heard enough of red scares and spy stories; they strongly desired the demise of an intellectual reign of terror that had cost at least 50,000 men and women their jobs because their opinions were deemed "un-American" by ex-Communist informers, politicians, and J. Edgar Hoover. Few Americans were now interested in hearing what Bentley had already said on eight occasions before Congressional committees or in the testimony she had given in four trials. By the late 1950s, few could remember her name, and she had to support herself not as a Cold War lecturer but as a teacher. Drifting into obscurity, Bentley taught at schools in Grand Coteau, Louisiana, and Hartford, Connecticut. During the last five years of her life, she was an English teacher at the Long Lane School for Girls, a state correctional institution in Middletown, Connecticut. Described by many who encountered her as unstable and unhappy, Elizabeth Bentley attempted to find solace in religion, announcing in 1950 that she had embraced the Roman Catholic faith. In the last years of her life, however, she regularly attended the Holy Trinity Protestant Episcopal Church in Middletown.

Leaving no immediate survivors when she died at age 55 in New Haven, Connecticut, on December 3, 1963, Elizabeth Bentley vanished into obscurity. She had appeared on the American scene at a time when political life was permeated by a malignant spirit of fear and paranoia. Her personal motives are often difficult to separate from those of a society sometimes timid in its commitment to democratic ideals.

SOURCES:

Bentley, Elizabeth. *Out of Bondage: The Story of Elizabeth Bentley.* NY: Devin-Adair, 1951.

Cook, Fred J. "The Remington Tragedy: A Study of Injustice," in *The Nation.* Vol. 185, no. 22. December 28, 1957, pp. 485–500.

Donner, Frank J. *The Un-Americans.* NY: Ballantine Books, 1961.

"Elizabeth Bentley Is Dead at 55; Soviet Spy Later Aided U.S.," in *The New York Times.* December 4, 1963, p. 47.

Fariello, Griffin. *Red Scare: Memories of the American Inquisition. An Oral History.* NY: W.W. Norton, 1995.

Gentry, Curt. *J. Edgar Hoover: The Man and the Secrets.* NY: W.W. Norton, 1991.

Goodman, Walter. *The Committee.* NY: Farrar, Straus and Giroux, 1968.

Navasky, Victor S. *Naming Names.* NY: Penguin Books, 1981.

Packer, Herbert L. *Ex-Communist Witnesses: Four Studies in Fact Finding.* Stanford, CA: Stanford University Press, 1962.

Schneir, Walter and Miriam Schneir. *Invitation to an Inquest.* NY: Pantheon Books, 1983.

Steinberg, Peter L. *The Great "Red Menace": United States Prosecution of American Communists, 1947–1952.* Westport, CT: Greenwood Press, 1984.

Theoharis, Athan G. and John Stuart Cox. *The Boss: J. Edgar Hoover and the Great American Inquisition.* Philadelphia, PA: Temple University Press, 1988.

John Haag, Associate Professor,
University of Georgia, Athens, Georgia

Bentley, Gladys (1907–1960)

African-American pianist and blues singer. *Born in Philadelphia, Pennsylvania, in 1907; died in 1960.*

As one of the most notorious and successful lesbian entertainers of the 1920s and '30s, Gladys Bentley performed in top hat and white tuxedo at swank New York nightclubs. Darling of gays, Harlem-hopping royalty, and the demimonde, she invented scandalous lyrics to the tunes of the day. Bentley's headlining days were over with the arrival of the repressive McCarthy era which robbed the nation of much of its greatest talent.

Gladys Bentley

Bentley, Helen Delich (1923—)

American maritime reporter and U.S. Congressional Representative from January 3, 1985, to January 3, 1995. *Born in Ruth, Nevada, on November 28, 1923; one of two daughters and six children of Michael (a miner) and Mary (Kovich) Ivanesvich; attended the University of Nevada and George Washington University; granted B.A. from the University of Missouri School of Journalism, 1944; married William Roy Bentley, on June 7, 1959.*

In 1952, before women had grappled their way into most of the male-dominated professions, Helen Bentley was patrolling docks around the world as the maritime editor of the Baltimore *Sun*, a position that would win her national prominence as an expert on the maritime industry and, in 1969, an appointment by President Richard Nixon as chair of the Federal Maritime Commission. Later, as a member of Congress, Bentley would continue her efforts as a passionate advocate of a more powerful American merchant marine.

Bentley grew up in Ely, Nevada, one of six children of Yugoslavian immigrants. When she was eight, her father died of the mining disease, silicosis, throwing the family into financial turmoil. Helen went to work at age 12 and worked throughout high school and college. Despite her hours spent earning a living, she participated in many extracurricular activities in White Pine High School and served on the *Ely Record* as a part-time reporter. Charles Russell, editor of the *Record* and later governor of Nevada, encouraged Bentley to go into journalism and to join the Republican Party.

Graduating as valedictorian in 1941, she entered the University of Nevada with two scholarships. In the fall of 1942, Bentley transferred to the University of Missouri after spending her summer vacation working on the campaign of senator James G. Scrugham. In 1943, she was a secretary in Scrugham's senate office in Washington, while attending George Washington University evenings. In October, she was back at Missouri, finishing her degree and holding down three jobs, including one as a stringer for United Press (U.P.).

Receiving her journalism degree in September 1944—after three years rather than four—she continued with U.P. then worked briefly as telegraph editor of the Lewiston (Idaho) *Tribune*. In June 1945, she began her long association with the Baltimore *Sun*, as a reporter specializing in labor matters. Two years later, Bentley became the first woman to cover an American Federation of Labor convention. In 1948, the city editor offered her a new territory: "Go down and take a look at the port; we've had nobody there since before the war."

Bentley educated herself in the problems of the nation's shipping, interviewing everyone from dockhands to government officials. Her hard-hitting coverage conveyed both her love of the sea and her concern for the declining U.S. merchant fleet. In 1952, she was promoted to maritime editor, and her "Around the Waterfront" column was syndicated in 15 newspapers. Bentley's confrontational style brought her scoops of national and international importance, often paving the way for legislative action, but this was not without its price. One column on union featherbedding, the practice of requiring an employer to hire unnecessary employees, brought a suit against her and the *Sun* for $26 million in damages.

Beginning in 1950, Bentley wrote and produced a weekly television show, *The Port that Built a City and State*, for a Baltimore station. The show was so well received that she was called upon to produce similar shows on the ports of the Delaware Valley. Known for her ability to juggle a variety of activities at once, including her marriage in 1959 to schoolteacher Roy Bentley, she also worked as a consultant for the American Association of Port Authorities and did freelance writing and film producing.

Helen Delich Bentley

As chair of the maritime commission, Helen Bentley was outspoken in her concern for the general state of U.S. shipping. She bemoaned the decaying condition of the merchant fleet and the fact that the United States had slipped from first place among maritime nations. "The shipowners are not going to be able to continue operating these tubs once the Vietnam War dies down," she remarked. "Military leases are supporting them now, but if nothing is done, we'll be totally in the hands of foreign shipping powers."

In 1975, Bentley retired to the private sector, working as an executive with a shipping company and writing a column for *World Port Magazine* before returning to politics. Her unsuccessful challenges to longtime incumbent Clarence Long as a Republican candidate for the House of Representatives in 1980 and 1982 were followed by her eventual victory over him in 1984. Bentley served four consecutive congressional terms, during which she was a member of the Committee on Merchant Marine and Fisheries and the Committee on Public Works and Transportation. During the 101st Congress, she was on the Budget Committee and the Select Committee on Aging. Successful in achieving federal support for the dredging and improvement of Baltimore harbor, Bentley also supported legislation to protect America's jobs and industry against foreign competition.

SOURCES:

Moritz, Charles, ed. *Current Biography 1971.* NY: H.W. Wilson, 1972.

Office of the Historian. *Women in Congress, 1917–1990.* Commission on the Bicentenary of the U.S. House of Representatives, 1991.

Barbara Morgan,
Melrose, Massachusetts

Bentley, Phyllis (1894–1977)

English author who wrote regional novels of life in West Riding. *Born Phyllis Eleanor Bentley in Halifax, Yorkshire, England, on November 19, 1894; died in Halifax in June 1977; daughter of Eleanor (Kettlewell) Bentley and Joseph Edwin Bentley (a cloth manufacturer); educated at Cheltenham Ladies' College, B.A., 1914; never married; no children.*

Selected works: (self-published) The World's Bane *(1918);* Environment *(1922);* The Infamous Bertha *(1922);* The Spinner of the Years *(1928);* The Partnership *(1928);* Trio *(1930);* Inheritance *(1932);* A Modern Tragedy *(1934);* Sleep in Peace *(1938);* Take Courage *(1940);* Manhold *(1941);* Rise of Henry Morcar *(1947);* Some Observations on the Art of Narrative *(1947);* Life Story *(1948);* Quorum *(1951);* "O Dreams, O Destinations": An Autobiography *(1962);* Tales of West Riding *(1974).*

In the West Riding region of England, textile manufacturing was prosperous, popular work, and Joseph Edwin Bentley supported his four children, first as a junior partner, later as an owner, of a mill. The Bentley family was, according to its only daughter Phyllis, "Essentially proper, essentially respectable, essentially middle class." By the time Bentley was four, her ten-year-old brother Frank had taught her to read, spell, count, and tell time. A sickly child, highly susceptible to infections, she attended small private schools in Huddersfield and Halifax when she was well.

At Halifax High School for Girls, where Bentley was "plain and unpopular, a coward and not good at games," she met **Barbara Clark (Callow)**. As they became friends, Callow inspired in Bentley a confidence her family had not and "turned me back," wrote Bentley, "from the neurotic abyss to which I was tending." In 1910, at age 15, Bentley entered Cheltenham Ladies' College, graduating in December 1914.

Thinking it would allow her time to write, Bentley took a high school teaching job, but her students drove her to abandon the idea within her first semester, and she returned to her parents' home to write full time. In 1918, during World War I, she landed a job at the Ministry of Munitions. That same year, a book of short stories was accepted for publication on the condition that Bentley cover the printing costs. Her brother Norman paid for 750 copies. But Bentley's independence lasted only as long as the war. "Suddenly it became the duty of all women to clear out . . . and leave the jobs open for the returning men."

Back in Halifax, she wrote and did volunteer work for three years until she became a cataloguer. At the Library of Halifax, the Municipal Library in Sowerby Bridge, and at the large Bradford Library and Literary Society, Bentley instituted the Dewey Decimal system and catalogued almost 80,000 books. "I loved this work," she wrote, "and the classifying of so many diverse books, which necessitates a slight knowledge of them all, or at least an understanding of their subject, was I think very profitable for me." All the while, she wrote and submitted her second manuscript, *Environment*, for publication. When the manuscript was rejected, Bentley was discouraged. "What are you writing?" her mother had once asked. "Rubbish? You couldn't write a [good] book . . . to save your life." Bentley persisted. In 1922, *Environment* and *The Infamous Bertha* were published to modest sales.

Despite her early failure as a teacher, Bentley began to lecture effectively on the regional novel, an area in which she was considered a new talent. But she remained the child in her parents' home until Joseph Bentley died in 1926, and Bentley took over the household. Regular earnings brought in by novels and book reviews sustained Bentley and her mother through the Depression, and the family business, nearly ruined by the 1929 stock-market crash, was also buoyed by her financial support. When her greatest success, *Inheritance*, was published in 1932, Bentley's reputation as a West Riding novelist was made secure. *Inheritance* would see 29 editions.

Success, especially in the United States, gave Bentley a certain comfort. America "unkinked many of my complexes," she wrote. "I became quite a conversationalist, laughing and talking, no longer huddled in the corner but expanding in the center of the room. . . . Inferiority complexes unmottled themselves at record speed." During World War II, again wishing to contribute to Britain's efforts, she worked for the Ministry of Information, beginning in March 1942. The most rewarding part of her service was the two years living in London alone and the surprising pleasure of returning to Halifax. "It is lovely to be home again. Yorkshire is life, even in the rain. . . . My material is here and I belong to the West Riding." Then she added, "But of course as a person I am miserable." Once again, she had returned to her mother's home; once again, her independent life had ceased. Portraits of her parents, "though not their circumstances," wrote Bentley, may be found in her novel *Carr* (1929).

Barbara Clark Callow, an accomplished scientist and author, remained a close friend and correspondent, and her daughter Sylvia, born in 1927, was Bentley's godchild. When Bentley could, she visited Callow, though Callow did not venture to Halifax because Bentley's mother held her in disdain. Callow, who went increasingly deaf until she was found to have an inoperable brain tumor, died on September 10, 1948. Six months later, Bentley's mother died. Having been her mother's primary companion and caretaker, Bentley had given up regular writing.

The years after were a "period of great personal happiness" for Bentley: she wrote, lectured widely, and expanded her friendships to include author **Joan Ingilby** and illustrator **Marie Hartley**. Bentley continued to reap renown for her regional works, though she was never sure of her talent. "I wished simply to write a great novel giving a superb picture of life as it really is," she wrote in her 1962 autobiography. "That I did not succeed is obvious. I was not endowed with the necessary genius." She remained in her Halifax childhood home until her death.

SUGGESTED READING:

Bentley, Phyllis. *"O Dreams, O Destinations": An Autobiography.* London: Victor Gollancz, 1963.

Crista Martin, freelance writer, Boston, Massachusetts

Bentos, Annita (c. 1821–1849).

See Garibaldi, Anita.

Bentzen, Th. (1840–1907).

See Blanc, Marie Thérèse.

Ben Zvi, Rachel Yanait (1886–1979)

First lady of Israel who co-founded the Shomer, her country's first defense force. *Born Rachel Yanait in Russia in 1886; died in 1979; married Itzhak Ben Zvi (president of Israel).*

Born in Russia in 1886, Rachel Yanait Ben Zvi co-founded the Poalei Zion movement there in 1906. Two years later, she came to Eretz Israel where she established a Hebrew high school and the country's first socialist journal entitled *Ahdut*; she was also often a delegate to World Zionist Congresses. Her partner in her work, Itzhak Ben Zvi, became her husband and Israel's second president (1952), making her first lady from 1952 to 1963. Both were active in founding the Shomer, Israel's first defense force. After World War II, Rachel Ben Zvi was known as an educator of both female agricultural workers and youth. Her autobiography *Coming Home* was published in English in the U.S. (1964) by Herzl Press, based on her Hebrew text, *Anu Olim* (1959). She also wrote *Before Golda*, the biography of ***Manya Shochat**, who created the first collective in Eretz Israel in 1907. The book was published in Jerusalem in 1976 and reprinted by Biblio Press in 1989.

Beranger, Clara (1886–1956)

American screenwriter and director. *Born in Baltimore, Maryland, in 1886; died in 1956; attended Goucher College; married William De Mille, in 1928 (her second marriage).*

Screenplays: Tale of Two Cities *(1917);* Exit the Vamp *(1921);* The Gilded Lily *(1921);* A Heart to Let *(1921);* Miss Lulu Bett *(1921);* Sheltered Daughters *(1921);* The Wonderful Thing *(1921);* Bought and Paid For *(1922);* Clarence *(1922);* Her Husband's Trademark *(1922);* Nice People *(1922);* Grumpy *(1923);* The Marriage Maker *(1923);* Only 38 *(1923);* The World's Applause *(1923);* The Bedroom Window *(1924);* Don't Call It Love *(1924);* The Fast Set *(1924);* Icebound *(1924);* Locked Doors *(1925);* Lost Wife *(1925);* Men and Women *(1925);* New Brooms *(1925);* Don Juan's Three Nights *(1926);* Almost Human *(1926);* The Forbidden Woman *(1926);* The Little Adventuress *(1927);* Craig's Wife *(1928);* The Idle Rich *(1929);* This Mad World *(1930);* His Double Life *(1933);* Social Register *(1934).*

A screenwriter for three decades, Clara Beranger arrived in Hollywood after having worked as a successful New York City journalist. Early in her West Coast career, she freelanced, writing scenarios, as early screenplays were called, for silent-film companies like Vitagraph and Edison. When "talkies" became the rage, Beranger wrote primarily for MGM and Pathé.

Beranger also collaborated with director-producer William De Mille, brother of the legendary director Cecil B. De Mille, on many films, and William became her second husband in 1928. The couple continued to work together into the '30s, living in New York City and Playa del Rey, a beach community outside Los Angeles. Unlike many writers of her generation, Beranger detested the idea of working on a studio lot, preferring an office in her home.

During her long career, she often gave interviews on the art of screenwriting and lectured on screenwriting at the University of Southern California, following her retirement. In 1950, she authored *Writing for the Screen*, long considered a classic on the subject. Some of the battles waged by screenwriters, that Beranger touched on, continue to be waged. "It was the custom for producers," wrote Beranger, "to put a number of writers on the job . . . without any of the writers knowing others were working on the same story." The producer "did not seem to realize that every story, like every other work of art, has a style and voice of its own." Though Beranger was one of many successful screenwriters who came of age during Hollywood's early years, she was one of the few who believed in screenwriting's potential as an art form.

SOURCES:

Beranger, Clara. *Writing for the Screen*. NY: Little, Brown, 1950.

McCreadie, Marsha.*The Women Who Write the Movies: From Frances Marion to Nora Ephron*. NY: Birchlane Press, 1994.

Smith, Frederick James. "Money Doesn't Make The Film," in *Photoplay*. September 1924, p. 54.

Deborah Jones, Studio City, California

Berber, Anita (1899–1928)

German dancer who epitomized the decadent spirit of the Berlin cabaret scene of the Weimar Republic.

Born into a respectable middle-class family in Leipzig in 1899 (some sources state 1898); died of tuberculosis and drug addiction in 1928; daughter of Felix Berber (a concertmaster of the Leipzig Gewandhaus Orchestra).

Anita Berber was born in 1899 into an artistic family in Leipzig. Her father Felix Berber was a highly respected violin virtuoso who served as concertmaster of the renowned Leipzig Gewandhaus Orchestra and founded his own string quartet. Growing up in comfortable and highly respectable middle-class circumstances, Anita studied ballet and showed great promise as a dancer from an early age, but the political and cultural ferment of Berlin cut short her formal training, drawing her to the city in 1918 like a moth to the flame.

When the collapse of the German Imperial regime in November 1918 resulted in an almost immediate relaxation of stage and film censorship, nudity and explicit sexuality quickly appeared in countless presentations. Some of these were attempts to make significant artistic statements, but many were sensationalistic, prurient, and designed to cash in on republican Germany's newly achieved artistic freedom. Energetic and enthusiastic, Berber quickly became a celebrity, first appearing in a Rudolf Nelson revue, dancing the Shimmy dressed in a dinner jacket. Soon, she gravitated toward *Nacktballet*, instantly becoming a superstar. Emotionally unprepared for stardom, Berber found herself moving in the German capital's fastest, most decadent circles. For many observers, it was difficult to tell where her skills as a dancer ended and her notoriety began.

In chalk-white makeup and generally in the nude, Berber's uninhibited dancing at such night spots as the White Mouse attracted both Berliners and foreign tourists drawn to the open city. Berber became known as the "Queen of the Bohemians" and enjoyed a reputation for promiscuity that was prodigious even by contemporary standards. At the height of her fame, sensation-seekers from around the world flocked to the White Mouse on the Behrenstrasse, where Berber offered her strangely fascinating "Dances of Horror, Lust and Ecstasy." She went on to perform in nightclubs in Hamburg, Vienna, and Budapest. Often seen in the company of shady characters from the fringes of "polite" society, she attended boxing matches or the immensely popular fad of the day, the Six-Day Bicycle Races at the Sportpalast.

In the last years of Anita Berber's brief life, she sought oblivion through cocaine, morphine, and alcohol. Henry, her American-born lover during these final years, remained faithful to her, despite her wasted physical state and the appearance of tuberculosis that made her death inevitable. After wandering aimlessly through Europe, she ended up ill and penniless in Baghdad. Berber's Berlin theater friends took up a collection to bring her home to die. Henry appeared late at her funeral, having remembered at the last minute to buy a bouquet of white roses for his Anita. At the time of her death, Berber was 29.

SOURCES:

Fischer, Lothar. *Tanz zwischen Rausch und Tod: Anita Berber 1918–1929 in Berlin*. 2nd ed., Berlin: Haude und Spener Verlag, 1988.

Friedrich, Otto. *Before the Deluge: A Portrait of Berlin in the 1920s.* NY: Avon Books, 1973.

Gill, Anton. *A Dance between Flames: Berlin Between the Wars.* NY: Carroll & Graf, 1994.

"Körperspiegel der Geschichte," *Der Spiegel.* Vol. 47, no. 17, April 26, 1993, p. 224.

PEM (Paul Erich Marcus). *Heimweh nach dem Kurfürstendamm.* Berlin: Lothar Blanvalet Verlag, 1952.

Senelick, Laurence. "Nudity," in Martin Banham, ed., *The Cambridge Guide to Theatre.* Cambridge: Cambridge University Press, 1995, pp. 802–803.

Spoto, Donald. *Lenya: A Life.* Boston, MA: Little, Brown, 1989.

"Tanzrevolutionär Praunheim," *Der Spiegel.* Vol. 39, no. 7. February 11, 1985, p. 175.

Vollmer-Heitmann, Hanna. *Wir sind von Kopf bis Fuss auf Liebe eingestellt: Die zwanziger Jahre.* Hamburg: Kabel Verlag, 1993.

"Von Praunheims Kino des Lasters," *Der Spiegel. Vol. 42, no. 11. March 14, 1988, p. 259.*

RELATED MEDIA:

Anita—Tänze des Lasters, West German film, directed by **Rosa von Praunheim**, 1988.

John Haag, Associate Professor,
University of Georgia, Athens, Georgia

Berberova, Nina (1901–1993)

***Russian-born writer whose life as an exile was vividly portrayed in her autobiography,* The Italics Are Mine.** *Name variations: Berbérova. Born Nina Nikolaevna Berberova in St. Petersburg, Russia, on August 8, 1901; died in Philadelphia, Pennsylvania, on September 26, 1993; daughter of Nikolai and Natalia (Karaulova) Berberova; lived with the poet Vladislav Khodasevich for over a decade, starting in 1922; married Nikolai Makeyev (divorced); married George Kochevitsky, in 1954 (divorced 1983).*

Grew up in the last years of pre-Bolshevik Russian literary and artistic culture; left Russia (1922) after Communist takeover, living mostly in Paris (1920s–1930s); existed in near-poverty, at the same time writing novels that remained unpublished in France; survived World War II hiding in French countryside; immigrated to U.S. (1950); had a successful academic career at Yale and Princeton Universities (1958–71); returned to visit Russia (1989); became famous in English-speaking countries in later years.

Although it was not until the last decade of her life that Nina Berberova became a literary superstar, books and words were at the center of her existence from infancy on. Born into an upper-middle-class family that was passionately involved in the arts, by the age of ten she had confidently chosen the writing of poetry as her adult career. Both of Nina's parents were active participants in the intellectual life of St. Petersburg; her father Nikolai was a civil servant of Armenian ancestry, while her mother **Natalia Karaulova Berberova** was descended from an old Russian noble family. One of these ancestors was a slothful landowner of 400 pounds who served as the model for Oblomov, the famous character described by Ivan Goncharov in his classic novel depicting the decline of Russia's aristocracy. Characterizing her youthful decision to embark on a literary career, Berberova described the power she felt as a child:

> Verses gushed out of me. I choked in them, I couldn't stop. I wrote them at the rate of two or three a day and read them to myself, to Dasha, to Mademoiselle, to my parents, to their friends, to whoever was there. This rigorous sense of vocation has never left me.

Life was pleasant for Berberova until 1917, when the Bolshevik revolution signalled the end of the leisurely existence enjoyed by Russia's intelligentsia. Civil war, foreign blockade, and a terrible famine seemed to only make more intense the struggles of the nation's artists. Berberova's manuscripts were passed from hand to hand, and the noted poet Nikolai Gumilev encouraged her to carry on writing despite the obstacles. Nina continued to dream of success as a writer, but the acquiring of skills for survival took up most of her energy: "I had not been taught anything useful; I did not know how to sew felt boots, to comb out lice from children's heads, to bake a pie out of potato peels." She did not abandon her quest to become a renowned writer, however, and somehow managed to pursue her studies at Rostov University. But the specter of Bolshevik cultural repression made her leave Soviet Russia in 1922; Nina Berberova never saw her parents again—they died of cold and hunger in 1943.

Berberova had by now fallen in love with a fellow writer, the brilliant but unstable poet Vladislav Khodasevich, and for the next few years this inseparable pair traveled throughout Europe as members of Maxim Gorky's household. In 1925, Berberova and Khodasevich settled in Paris where her income as a book, theater and film reviewer, and occasional contributor of critical essays and short fiction to the exile newspaper *Poslednye Novosti* often barely enabled her to pay their room and board.

Life with Khodasevich was often emotionally trying, and by the early 1930s Berberova had left him, eventually marrying the journalist Nikolai Makeyev. During the 1930s, she wrote novels and biographies, including a study of the composer Tchaikovsky that included a frank discussion of his homosexuality. By the late 1930s, despite the need to earn a living through her routine journalistic work, she had been able to publish three novels and a series of novellas based on the countless tragedies and rare triumphs of emigré life. Berberova's sharply etched evocations of the lives of Russian exiles in the Paris suburb of Billancourt, where thousands of them carried on precarious existences as workers in the Renault automobile factory, have taken their place as classic achievements of modern Russian literature.

During these years, Berberova's personal life was complex and multifaceted. Although separated from Khodasevich, she remained on good terms with him and spent years nursing him through what proved to be a terminal illness. The years of World War II were full of fear and suffering, with many of her friends dying. Poverty was never far from Berberova's door, when she and her husband hid from the Germans by living in the French countryside. The end of the war in 1945 seemed to bring fresh energies to Berberova, who continued to write novels and other pieces as well as remaining active as a working journalist. She played a key role in the establishment of the first new Russian newspaper in Paris in many years, *Russkaya mysl.* Her reports of the trial of Viktor Kravchenko, author of *I Chose Freedom* and a sharp critic of the Soviet system of terror, began the slow process of informing French public opinion about the existence of the gulag system in the Soviet Union.

By 1950, Nina Berberova had decided that the time had come for a major change in her life. She divorced her husband and set out for the United States. Arriving in New York virtually penniless and speaking almost no English, she exhibited a courage verging on recklessness. For almost a decade, she worked at many different jobs, only occasionally being able to publish in a Russian-language journal. Once more gaining in confidence as a writer, she published a novella in 1958. That same year, she joined the editorial board of the emigré journal *Mosty*. Her 1954 marriage to the musician George Kochevitsky, although it ended in divorce in 1983, helped provide almost three decades of relative stability in her private life.

In September 1958, Berberova became a member of the Slavic Department at Yale University. Her friends almost immediately noticed signs of a profound intellectual rejuvenation, not only in the classroom but in her writings. Among the signs of this new creativity were experimental works of free verse, well-argued critical articles, and translations of T.S. Eliot into Russian. In 1963, Berberova joined the Princeton University Slavic Department, remaining there until her retirement in 1971. It was during her Princeton years that she published her autobiography, *The Italics Are Mine* (1969). This richly textured, highly opinionated memoir first brought Berberova's life and personality to the attention of the English-speaking world. The doomed world of Old Russia and the tragedies of emigré life in Paris in the 1920s and 1930s were now recreated on the pages of a brilliantly written autobiography. Reviews were enthusiastic, and the process of turning Nina Berberova into a literary superstar, the last survivor of the great tradition in Russian literature, now began to gather momentum.

Berberova's retirement from teaching in 1971 signalled the start of the most intense productivity of her writing career. During the next years, she wrote several important books, including a biography of ***Moura Budberg**, a collection of poetry, and a history of Russian Freemasonry in the 20th century. Advancing years served to intensify rather than slacken her intellectual energies, and she thoroughly enjoyed writing, preparing her older works for the press, and entertaining a steady stream of visitors. Continuing to live in university housing at Princeton, she was a familiar figure at the faculty club and library. She enjoyed travels to Europe, continued to drive her car well into her 80s, and bought a computer which she thoroughly mastered.

A high point of her final years was doubtless her 1989 trip to the Soviet Union. Accepting an invitation by the Soviet Writers' Union, her appearances were little short of triumphal. Returning to Russia after an absence of 67 years, she packed every auditorium in Leningrad and Moscow where she read from her works and answered questions from the audience. Now ranked with the greats of Russian literature, some critics began to compare her writings with the works of Chekhov and Turgenev. After decades of neglect and poverty, Berberova clearly enjoyed her belated fame and affluence. Her autobiography had sold well in the United States, but in France in the 1980s her books were explosive bestsellers. By the time of her death, Berberova's books were available in translations in 22 languages. France made her a Chevalier dans l'Ordre des Arts et des Lettres in 1989, while Yale University awarded her an honorary doctorate in 1992. Despite her advancing years, Berberova continued to plan for the future, moving to Philadelphia in 1990 and purchasing a condominium in a building designed by I.M. Pei that provided a striking view of the Delaware River and Society Hill. It was here that she fell in March 1993, suffering a cerebral hemorrhage. After a brief hospitalization, Nina Berberova was moved to a nursing home where she died on September 26, 1993. Thus ended a remarkable life, full of work and achievement (and disappointments as well) which had begun in the radically different milieu of tsarist Russia. In her final years, the world came to fully appreciate the life and work of a remarkable woman whose willpower to prevail over adversity had been more than matched by her artistic talent.

SOURCES:

Barker, Murl G. "In Memoriam Nina Nikolaevna Berberova 1901–1993," in *Slavic and East European Journal.* Vol. 38. No. 3. Fall, 1994, pp. 553–556.

Barker, Murl. "Nina Berberova on Surviving," in *Selecta: Journal of the Pacific Northwest Council on Foreign Languages.* Vol. 11, 1990, pp. 69–72.

Berberova, Nina. *Histoire de la Baronne Boudberg: Biographie.* Translated by Michel Nigueux. Paris: Actes Sud, 1991.

———. *The Italics Are Mine.* Translated by Philippe Radley. Rev. ed. NY: Alfred A. Knopf, 1992.

———. *The Tattered Cloak and Other Novels.* Translated by Marian Schwartz. NY: Alfred A. Knopf, 1991.

———. *The Ladies from St. Petersburg.* Translated by Marian Schwartz. NY: New Directions, 1998.

Bethea, David M. *Khodasevich: His Life and Art.* Princeton, NJ: Princeton University Press, 1983.

Buck, Joan Juliet. "Nina Berberova," in *The New Yorker.* Vol. 69, no. 35. October 25, 1993, pp. 94–95.

Collins, Glenn. "Nina Berberova, 92, Poet, Novelist and Professor," *The New York Times Biographical Service,* September 1993, p. 1339.

Collins, Louise Mooney, and Lorna Mpho Mabunda, eds. *The Annual Obituary 1993.* Detroit, MI: St. James Press, 1994.

Kakutani, Michiko. "An Émigré in Paris Willing to Start Afresh," in *The New York Times.* April 14, 1992, p. B2.

Raeff, Marc. *Russia Abroad: A Cultural History of the Russian Emigration, 1919–1939.* Oxford: Oxford University Press, 1990.

Rose, Phyllis, ed. *The Norton Book of Women's Lives.* NY: W.W. Norton, 1993.

Tucker, Martin, ed. *Literary Exile in the Twentieth Century: An Analysis and Biographical Dictionary.* NY: Greenwood Press, 1991.

John Haag, Associate Professor, University of Georgia, Athens, Georgia

Berengare.

Variant of Berengaria.

Berengaria (1194–1221)

Queen of Denmark. *Name variations: Berengaria Henriques, Enriques or Enriquez; Berengaria of Portugal; Bengerd of Portugal; (Span.) Berenguela. Pronunciation: Ber-en-GAR-ee-uh. Born in 1194; died on March 27, 1221, in Ringsted, Denmark; daughter of Sancho I, king of Portugal (r. 1185–1211 or 1212), and* ****Douce of Aragon*** *(1160–1198), queen of Portugal; became second wife of Valdemar also known as Waldemar II the Victorious, king of Denmark (r. 1202–1241), in 1213; children:* ****Sophia of Denmark*** *(1217–1248); and three kings of Denmark—Eric IV Ploughpenny (1216–1250), king of Denmark (r. 1241–1250); Abel (r. 1250–1252); and Christopher I (r. 1252–1259). Waldemar II's first wife was* ****Dagmar of Bohemia*** *(d. 1212).*

Berengaria of Castile (1180–1246)

Queen of Leon. *Name variations: Berengeria, Berengare; (Spanish) Berenguela. Pronunciation: Ber-en-GAR-ee-uh. Born in 1180 in Castile; died on November 8, 1246, in Castile; daughter of Alphonso VIII, king of Castile and León (d. 1214), and Eleanor of Castile (1162–1214, daughter of* ****Eleanor of Aquitaine****); sister of* ****Blanche of Castile*** *(1188-1252) and* ****Urraca of Castile*** *(1186–1220); married Conrad II, duke of Swabia, in 1188 (annulled); became second wife of Alphonso IX (1171–1230), king of León, in 1197 (annulled in 1204); children: (second marriage) Ferdinand III (St. Ferdinand, 1199–1252), king of Castile (r. 1217–1252) and Leon (r. 1230–1252);* ****Berengaria of Castile*** *(b. around 1199, who married John I de Brienne);* ***Constanza of Castile*** *(1200–1242); Leonor (1202–1202); Alfonse de Castilla (c. 1204–1272).*

Berengaria was born a princess of Castile (in modern central Spain), the eldest daughter of Alphonso VIII and his queen **Eleanor of Castile.** In 1197, Berengaria was married to Alphonso IX, king of León (in southcentral modern Spain), and eventually gave birth to three daughters and two sons. Her first born, Ferdinand, was a pious child who would later become King Ferdinand III of León-Castile and be proclaimed a saint after his death. Ironically, this future saint was born of a marriage which was annulled as unlawful several years later by the pope, on the grounds of consanguinity.

Eleanor of Castile. *See Blanche of Castile (1188–1252) for sidebar.*

After the annulment, Berengaria seems to have returned to Castile. In 1214, her father died, and her young brother Henry (I) succeeded to the throne. Berengaria acted as regent for Henry, who died in 1217. Because he left no heirs, Berengaria then inherited the kingdom, but, instead of ruling, she abdicated in favor of her son, Ferdinand III. In 1230, her former husband Alphonso XI died, and she aided her son in inheriting his throne. Ferdinand reigned over the combined kingdoms of León-Castile until 1252. Berengaria continued to advise her son on matters of state until her death in 1246.

Laura York, Anza, California

Berengaria of Castile (b. around 1199)

Empress of Constantinople. Name variations: Infanta of Castile. Born around 1199; death date unknown; daughter of ***Berengaria of Castile** *(1180–1246) and Alphonso IX, king of León; married John I de Brienne, king of Jerusalem (r. 1210–1225), emperor of Constantinople (r. 1228–1237), in 1224; children: Alfons d'Acre, count of Eu; Jean de Brienne (d. 1296); Louis de Brienne; possibly* ***Marie de Brienne****.*

Berengaria of Navarre (c. 1163–c. 1230)

Berengaria of Navarre

Spanish princess who reigned as queen of England with Richard the Lionheart, although she never set foot on English soil. *Name variations: Berengare, Berengeria. Pronunciation: Ber-en-GAR-ee-uh. Born in Pamplona, in the kingdom of Navarre, about 1163 (some sources cite 1165); died after 1230 in l'Epau Abbey near Le Mans, France; daughter of Sancho VI the Wise, king of Navarre (r. 1150–1194), and Sancha of Castile and Leon (d. 1179); daughter-in-law of Eleanor of Aquitaine; married Richard I the Lionheart, king of England (r. 1189–1199), on May 12, 1191, in Cyprus; no children.*

Although she was born a princess and was eventually crowned queen of England and Cyprus, Berengaria of Navarre's story has been almost completely obscured by the fame surrounding her husband and his family. Her life and subsequent anonymity exemplify the fate of many medieval princesses, who, as political pawns, were often forced to play a secondary role to the men to whom they were related.

Berengaria was the eldest daughter of King Sancho VI (called the Wise) of Navarre and Queen **Sancha of Castile and Leon**. During the 12th century, Navarre was a small kingdom situated in the Pyrenees mountains, between France and the larger kingdoms of Castile and Aragon on the Spanish peninsula. Although lacking in size, Navarre was a politically important kingdom because of its strategic location, and thus the leaders of other European countries were often eager to ally themselves with its royal house.

Though both of Berengaria's parents were of Spanish descent, the culture she grew up in was more French than Spanish. Navarre, by virtue of its proximity to France, had adopted many of the Provençal tastes and fashions of southern France. In her father's castles, the princess grew up speaking *langue d'oc*, the French dialect spoken in the southern regions of France (although she knew Spanish as well). The chroniclers unfortunately do not describe Berengaria to us very clearly; we know she had dark hair and dark eyes and was said to be "beauteous" and "fair," but these were adjectives applied to most royal daughters. She was educated in the accomplishments considered vital to daughters of the upper classes—reading and writing, poetry, playing an instrument, singing, and fine needlecraft. She was thus a part of what has been called the 12th-century renaissance, a time of increased production of poetry and music, and also a part of the age of the troubadours and the "courts of love," from which the concepts of chivalry were developed. Similar to other medieval princesses, it was expected that Berengaria would eventually marry a prince from a foreign country and become that country's queen-consort; her brother, Sancho

(VII), the Strong, would inherit their father's crown under the rules of primogeniture.

Betrothals in the 12th century among royal houses were usually made when the bride- and groom-to-be were small children. Betrothal was not, as in the 20th century, a private promise to wed but a binding legal contract signed by the parents of the betrothed. The bride's dowry (monetary payments and land grants to be made by the bride's parents to her new family) and her dower (usually lands or estates to be given to her by her husband's family upon marriage) were the most important part of the betrothal contract. Although royal marriages were arranged early, Berengaria was not formally betrothed to anyone until she was almost 30. It is not clear from the records why her father refused to marry her until such a late age; it was probably not for lack of offers, although perhaps Sancho and Sancha were hoping to gain a major political alliance from their eldest daughter and so refused bridegrooms of small, unimportant kingdoms.

The details of Berengaria's betrothal to and subsequent, though much delayed, marriage to King Richard I the Lionheart of England have often been romanticized by chroniclers and later historians. The facts are much less clear than these storytellers have made them seem, for we have no actual evidence of Berengaria's feelings toward Richard or his own toward her at any time during their years together. They met in 1177 at a tournament given by Berengaria's brother Sancho in Pamplona. At the time, Richard was 20 years old, a young English prince already in rebellion against his father, King Henry II. Richard had been betrothed as a boy to the Princess ***Alais of France** (b. 1160) and was still engaged to her when he met Berengaria, but his constant fighting with his father and Alais' rumored affair with King Henry II prevented his wedding to Alais from taking place.

Richard, whose parents were both French-born, had been raised by his mother, ***Eleanor of Aquitaine**, in the same Provençal culture Berengaria knew. This probably accounts in part for Richard's affection for members of the royal house of Navarre; he was a close friend to Prince Sancho the Strong, for both were great warriors and poets, and he often visited Pamplona during his younger years. Yet Richard was also politically astute in choosing his friendships, for he was duke of Aquitaine (a province which included most of southern France) and he could see that a political alliance with Navarre through marriage could only help his power struggles, both against his rebellious vassals and his father.

Sancha of Castile and Leon (d. 1179)

Queen of Navarre. *Name variations: sometimes referred to as Beatrice or Beatrice of Castile. Died on August 5, 1179 (some sources cite 1177); daughter of Alphonso VII, king of Castile and Leon (r. 1126–1157), and* ****Berengaria of Provence*** *(1108–1149); married Sancho VI the Wise or el Sabio (d. 1194), king of Navarre (r. 1150–1194); children: Sancho VII (b. after 1170), king of Navarre (r. 1194–1234);* ****Berengaria of Navarre*** *(1163–1230);* ****Blanche of Navarre*** *(d. 1229, who married Theobald III, count of Champagne); Costanza (died young); Fernando (d. 1207); Ramiro (d. 1228), bishop of Pamplona.*

Richard's previous betrothal to Alais of France was an obstacle to Berengaria's marriage that must have seemed impossible to overcome. His relationship to King Philip II Augustus of France was constantly fluctuating, from allies to enemies; thus at times Richard's wedding to Philip's half-sister Alais seemed imminent, only to be delayed again when the constant intrigues of the English and French royal houses shifted alliances between King Henry II, his sons, and King Philip. But after meeting Berengaria in 1177, Richard realized that he might do well to marry into the House of Navarre, although his legal bond to Alais prevented him acting on this idea.

This stalemate might have lasted indefinitely if it were not for the death of King Henry II in July 1189. In the meantime, Berengaria had remained in Navarre; although the chroniclers do not tell us how she occupied her time, it is unlikely that other possible bridegrooms were considered after Richard expressed interest. (This would have been especially true after 1183, when Richard's older brother Henry, heir to the throne, died of a fever, and Richard became the new heir). But with his father's death, Richard, now king of England, believed himself free to marry whomever he chose. Thus, a few months after his coronation, he sent his mother Eleanor to Navarre to negotiate a marriage contract while he journeyed to Naples, Italy, to meet with Philip of France; the two were preparing to accompany each other on a Third Crusade to the Holy Land. In his absence, Eleanor was to act as Richard's regent.

Sancho readily agreed to the marriage contract and gave Richard two strategically located castles, St.-Jean-Pied-de-Port and Roquebrune, as Berengaria's dowry; Berengaria was granted extensive estates in the county of Maine (in modern-day northwestern France) as her dower. Eleanor, by now in her late 60s, traveled with

Berengaria (who was about 27 years old) to Naples, arriving in the later part of 1190. In bringing his prospective bride to Italy, Richard placed himself in a politically dangerous situation. The Princess Alais was being kept a virtual prisoner in the castle of Rouen, in Richard's Aquitainian lands; her brother would not accept her back in France because she was betrothed to Richard, yet Richard would neither marry her nor let her out of Rouen. Richard thus had to find a way to break off the marriage contract to Alais without completely alienating the powerful king of France, with whom he had to work closely if the Crusade were to be a success.

While Richard pondered this dilemma and completed preparations for the army's departure, Eleanor and Berengaria left Naples to spend the winter in the small town of Brindisi, where they remained until the spring of 1191. In the meantime, Richard went to Sicily, where he found a solution to his conjugal problems. His sister, Queen ◂ **Joanna of Sicily**, had been recently widowed by William II of Sicily; William's nephew Tancred had then seized the throne and imprisoned Joanna, and Richard came to Sicily to demand his sister's freedom (which his great army and fierce reputation easily secured). While there, Tancred informed Richard that his supposed ally, King Philip, was secretly plotting against him.

When Richard subsequently met with Philip in Messina, he demanded the end of his betrothal to Alais. The reasons he gave were Philip's recent betrayal and the Princess Alais' affair with his father Henry II. Thus confronted, Philip had little choice but to formally break the betrothal contract and free Richard to marry Berengaria. Only one obstacle remained in preventing the princess of Navarre's wedding: it was the period of Lent, when no weddings could be performed. Since all preparations for the crusade were completed, Richard and Berengaria decided to depart for the Holy Land and hold off their wedding until they reached their destination.

Because Berengaria was as yet unmarried, etiquette prevented her from sailing on Richard's ship. Instead, she took another vessel from Messina, in the company of the widowed Sicilian queen, Richard's sister Joanna, and their commodious baggage. The two women, who were almost the same age, quickly became close friends and remained so for life; a contemporary chronicler of the crusade, Piers of Langtoft, wrote of Berengaria that "Queen Joanna held her dear/ They lived as doves in a cage."

Sailing from Messina to Acre, to which they were bound, usually took about three weeks, but it was six adventurous weeks before the royal ladies and Richard reached Acre's shores. A terrifying storm drove many of the ships bearing towards Acre off course, while others were lost at sea (including that carrying the chancellor of England). Richard's ship was spared, but it took days of searching the harbors of the islands of Crete, Rhodes, and Cyprus, before he knew for sure the fate of all the lost vessels.

One of the missing vessels was that carrying Berengaria and Joanna; after some time, the ship was discovered, intact, off the coast of the island of Cyprus. Driven off course, its captain had sought shelter in the island's harbor of Famagusta, but the crew and the royal ladies were kept from coming ashore by the Lord of Cyprus, Isaac Comneni. The Greek Isaac distrusted Westerners, especially Crusaders, and brought soldiers to the shores of Cyprus as a warning to the ship not to attempt a landing. So for days

▸ Joanna of Sicily (1165–1199)

Queen of Sicily. *Name variations: Joan or Johanna of Sicily; Joanna of England. Born in Angers in 1165; died in childbirth in 1199; third daughter of Henry II, king of England, and* ****Eleanor of Aquitaine****; sister of Richard the Lionheart, king of England, and* ****Matilda of England****, among others; married William II (d. 1189), king of Sicily (whose mother was* ****Margaret of Navarre****), in 1177; married Raymond VI (d. 1222), count of Toulouse, in 1196.*

After the death of her husband William II of Sicily in 1189, Joanna accompanied her brother Richard the Lionheart and ***Berengaria of Navarre** to the Holy Land. The sisters-in-law became lasting friends. Richard proved his skill and ruthlessness in successive battles against Saladin, notably in a victory at Arsuf, despite being outnumbered three to one. Although rudimentary rules of war had been worked out among Christian princes in the preceding centuries, none of them applied to the "infidel" Muslims, and Richard showed his mercilessness by massacring the Saracen prisoners taken during the battle of Acre. The fighting in the Holy Land was punctuated by periodic negotiations, but the crusaders' demand for the entire Holy Land was far more than Saladin was willing to yield. At one point, Richard even suggested that in return for Jerusalem he would arrange for a marriage between Joanna and Saladin's brother Saphadin; the plan was scotched, however, when Joanna indignantly refused, unless Saphadin would convert to Christianity (which, of course, he would not). Upon returning to Europe, Joanna married Raymond VI of Toulouse.

Berengaria was kept almost a prisoner by Isaac; the ship was too damaged by the storm to set sail, yet it could not be brought into the harbor.

When Richard discovered the ship holding his future bride and his beloved sister anchored off the island and learned of their treatment at Isaac's hands, he did not hesitate in making war on Isaac and the Cypriots. His army soon conquered the entire island and took Isaac and his daughter captive. Richard presented Isaac's daughter to Berengaria as her own prisoner; it is recorded that Berengaria did not punish the young girl for her father's actions but rather set about educating her. The princess kept the girl (whose name is not recorded) at her side as an attendant throughout the crusade.

After the conquest of Cyprus, Richard and Berengaria decided to celebrate their marriage on the island, in the capital city of Limassol. A three-day festival preceded the wedding, which took place on May 12, 1191. At this long-awaited event, the princess of Navarre wore a white dress banded by jeweled ribbons at her neck and waist; over this was a brocaded mantle (cape) and a white veil covered her hair. Berengaria's coronation as both queen of England and queen of Cyprus immediately followed the wedding. At last, she was a queen, a position she had been promised for over 14 years, yet one she would only hold for eight. But Berengaria had little time to enjoy her new-found status, for soon after the festivities ended, the army set sail again for Acre.

The chroniclers do not give us much information about Berengaria during the rest of the crusade, only that she saw very little of her new husband, who was constantly occupied with directing the army's efforts. The Christian army remained in the Holy Land from June 1191 to September 1192, until it was all but completely destroyed in the fruitless attempt to conquer the Muslim army of Saladin. Leading what remained of the army, Richard set out for home. (Because of illness, Philip had abandoned the crusade in 1191, soon after the battle of Acre.) Once again Berengaria and Joanna of Sicily boarded a ship, again without Richard, who, fearing his many enemies, had decided to disguise himself and take another ship back to his domains.

The two royal women journeyed safely to Naples and then went on to Rome, presumably to wait for Richard. But many weeks later they learned that Richard had been discovered and captured by his enemy, King Leopold of Austria, who was holding him hostage. For fear of Leopold and the Holy Roman Emperor Henry VI, both of whom declared Richard the Lionheart their mortal enemy, Berengaria decided to remain in Rome under the pope's protection. After six months of waiting for news of her husband's whereabouts, she begged the pope to send her under guard to her husband's lands in Aquitaine; the pope agreed and she was brought safely to Marseilles. There the king of Aragon provided safe transport for the young English queen, along with the widowed queen of Sicily, to the town of Poitou in Aquitaine, where they arrived about the middle of 1193. It was another year before Richard was ransomed and returned safely to England, in April 1194.

At this time, it became clear that Richard and Berengaria had become estranged. He did not bring her to England during his stay there after his return, nor did he visit her when he was in Aquitaine on the Continent. The reasons for this rupture are unknown; historians have suggested that Richard knew Berengaria was barren, for there had not even been a rumor of a pregnancy since her marriage, and thus avoided her, but the couple had almost never been together since May 1191, so this conclusion seems unlikely. Others have suggested that Richard was in love with another woman or that he might have been homosexual, but these theories have not been proven or disproven.

Thus, Berengaria settled down into a somewhat ambiguous position. She was Richard's wife, yet rarely saw him; she was queen of England but rivaled another woman for the title: Richard's mother, Eleanor of Aquitaine. Despite the fact that her own husband was deceased and the new king had a wife, Eleanor continued to hold the responsibilities, privileges, and title of queen of England; she still signed documents and letters with her accustomed signature, *Alienor Dei Gracia Regine Anglorum* (Eleanor, by the Grace of God Queen of England), and acted as the true ruler of England while Richard was absent (which was most of his reign). Thus, Berengaria was denied a role in the administration of the kingdom, a privilege which most queens enjoyed. Yet she seems to have possessed at least the outward respect due to her as a crowned queen, and there is no evidence that she was unhappy with her circumstances. As historian **Amy Kelly** writes in *Eleanor of Aquitaine and the Four Kings*, "Though apparently on fair terms with Eleanor, who had certainly usurped her function, [Berengaria] seems to have kept mainly to her own dower properties in Maine, but without establishing a court for herself or Richard."

After about a year of living in Maine, the princess of Navarre was reconciled with her husband. This was in the spring of 1195, when Richard, only 38 years old, fell suddenly and violently ill. Despairing of his life, he vowed that if he recovered he would repent of his sins and never forsake his wife again. He did recover and sent for Berengaria to meet him in Poitiers later that year. Though they remained together for a couple of years, the beginning of 1199 found Berengaria back on her estates in Maine, while Richard continued the provincial wars he was waging against his rebellious vassals.

She lived to a great age, and died beloved by all and full of honour, [the] only English queen who never saw England.

—Elizabeth Villiers

Berengaria was still in Maine in April 1199, spending her time in the administration of her estates and in reading, embroidery, and music, when she received word that Richard had been killed while besieging the castle of Château-Chalus. How the newly widowed queen felt is uncertain, for we have no letters or descriptions of her state of mind during her initial mourning period. Several days after Richard's death, word came that her beloved friend and longtime companion Joanna of Sicily (who had remarried) had died in childbirth. A week or so later, Berengaria heard that her only sister ***Blanche of Navarre** (d. 1229) had also died giving birth to a son.

It is perhaps not surprising given the sorrows she bore that Berengaria, only 36 years old, chose at this time to retire to a life of seclusion in the old city of Le Mans in the county of Maine. But she did not pass her time idly. Instead, she set to work founding a new abbey and convent, called L'Epau Abbey, at Le Mans, using her dower income to support its construction as well as to give generously to charitable works. She was rarely seen outside the city after 1199, although several times she sent messages and letters to King John (Richard's brother, who had succeeded him), asking for payment of the annuity which she had a right to as the king's widow. John was unable or unwilling to help her settle her accounts, and it wasn't until his son succeeded as Henry III that Berengaria was able to force the crown, with the help of the pope, to give her her due.

The widowed queen became renowned throughout France and England for her charitable nature during her years in retirement. The abbey's construction was finally completed in 1230. At that time, Berengaria moved into the convent at L'Epau, where she lived as a nun, although she did not take a nun's vows. The queen of England who never saw England died at her stately abbey several years later and was buried in the abbey church in a magnificent tomb. This tomb, which can still be seen today at the abbey, bears a beautiful carved effigy of Berengaria as she had appeared on her wedding day, 40 years earlier.

SOURCES:

Hewitt, Mary E. "Berengaria of Navarre," in *Lives of Some Famous Women of All Ages.* NY: Birdsey-Somers, 1912.

Kelly, Amy. *Eleanor of Aquitaine and the Four Kings.* Cambridge, MA: Harvard University Press, 1950.

Villiers, Elizabeth. "The Queen Who Never Saw England," in *Love Stories of English Queens.* Philadelphia, PA: David McKay, 1918.

SUGGESTED READING:

Bridge, Antony. *Richard the Lionheart.* London: Grafton Books, 1989.

Hallam, Elizabeth, ed. *The Plantagenet Chronicles.* NY: Weidenfeld and Nicholson, 1986.

Labarge, Margaret Wade. *Women in Medieval Life.* London: Hamish Hamilton, 1986.

Laura York, freelance writer in women's history and medieval history, Anza, California

Berengaria of Provence (1108–1149)

Queen of Castile. *Name variations: Berengeria, Berengare; (Spanish) Berenguela of Barcelona. Born in 1108; died on February 3, 1149, in Valencia; daughter of Raymond Berengar I, count of Provence, also known as Ramón Berenguer IV, conde de Barcelona (r. 1131–1162), and* ***Douce I****, countess of Provence; married second husband Alphonso VII (1105–1157), king of León and Castile (r. 1126–1157), in 1128; children: Sancho III (b. 1134), king of Castile (r. 1157–1158);* ****Constance of Castile*** *(d. 1160, who married Louis VII, king of France); Garcia (died young);* ****Sancha of Castile and Leon*** *(d. 1179, who married Sancha VI, king of Navarre); Ferdinand II (1137–1188), king of Leon. Following Berengaria's death, Alphonso married* ****Ryksa of Poland*** *(d. 1185); he also had a daughter,* ****Urraca of Castile*** *(d. 1179), with* ***Gontrada Perez****.*

Berengeria.

Variant of Berengaria.

Berenguela.

Spanish variant of Berengaria.

Berenice (c. 35 BCE–?)

Jewish princess who was the mother of Herod Agrippa I. *Name variations: Bernice. Pronunciation: Ber-e-NEE-kay. Born into the Herodian family around 35 BCE; death date unknown; daughter of Salome (sister*

of Herod the Great) and Costobar (executed about 25 BCE after he was probably found guilty of plotting with the Parthians against Herod's life); married Aristobulus (a son of Herod the Great) around 15 BCE; married Theudion (brother of Herod's wife Doris, who was also the mother of Antipater); children: (first marriage) three sons, Aristobulus (who married ***Jotape****, daughter of the king of Emesa), Herod (became king of Chalcis), and Agrippa (born c. 10 BCE and became Herod Agrippa I, king of Judea); and two daughters, Herodias (who would take as her second husband, Herod Antipas, the son of Herod the Great by Malthace, another of his ten wives), and Mariamne II.*

When Berenice was born about 35 BCE, the eastern Mediterranean was in a state of confusion. Rome was in the process of consolidating its control of the region, largely through the transformation of one-time client states (subordinate, but independent allies) into provinces directly ruled by Roman military administrators. In addition, by the time of Berenice's birth, the Roman Republic had been devastated by a series of civil wars for about a century. These conflicts had given rise to ambitious war-lords seeking control of the resources of the East as a means to dominate the Roman state. In fact, some, like Marc Antony, came to base their political ambitions almost exclusively on the control of the eastern Mediterranean, meaning that they were ever willing to meddle in the domestic politics of eastern states. This put eastern rulers in a quandary: even those who desired good relations with the Roman state found it next to impossible not to get involved in partisan Roman politics, for the feuding Romans themselves would not tolerate neutrality in their civil wars. Thus, especially since the consequences of backing a Roman loser were invariably dire, it is no wonder that eastern authorities felt insecure in their power during the last century of the Roman Republic, or that they collectively tended to paranoia—a state of mind which lingered even after Rome's condition had settled. Rome's civil wars did not end until 31 BCE, when the forces of Octavian (later to be honored with the new name, Augustus) finally overthrew Marc Antony and ***Cleopatra VII** of Egypt, giving Octavian uncontested mastery over the entire Mediterranean basin. What followed over the next generation was the slow metamorphosis of the Roman Republic into the Roman Empire.

As if this were not enough to disquiet Judea, foreign affairs fueled the fires of uncertainty even more. Embroiling a frontier which had long been volatile, in the 50s BCE the Roman dynast Crassus had invaded the Parthian Empire to the east of Rome's sphere of influence. This effort cost Crassus his life. Thereafter, the rivalry between the two states quickened and in one escalation of the conflict (41–38 BCE), the Parthians struck westward through Asia as far as the Palestinian coast. Hoping to seize the initiative along their frontier with Rome, the Parthians then attempted to reconstruct the political infrastructure of western Asia by establishing candidates favorable to their interests in positions of authority within strategically situated states, Judea among them. In Judea, Parthian interests were aided by intense political rivalries within the long-established Hasmonian royal house that had existed previous to their arrival.

In fact, the political fortunes of the Hasmonians had been shaky for over a generation before the Parthian invasion. Although that house had ruled over Judea and other nearby territories since the 160s BCE, by the middle of the 1st century BCE the combination of increasing Roman pressure and the declining competence of the Hasmonian kings had led to Judea's political and religious fragmentation. Amid the intrigues of the period, non-Hasmonians amassed increasing political influence. One such figure was Herod (later to be dubbed "the Great"), an Edomite whose father had been granted Roman citizenship in 47 BCE. After Rome had pushed the Parthians back from the Mediterranean coast, it enthroned Herod (37 BCE), as king of Judea.

Herod's elevation precipitated a crisis of its own. Herod was not a Hasmonian, and, although he was a Jew by faith, his ancestry on both sides was Arab. Because the Hasmonians had been the first Jewish rulers of an autonomous Judea for a very long time, they remained popular among the inhabitants of Judea and dynastic loyalty to their house remained strong. Since the autonomy of Judea and Jerusalem's Temple were sources of great pride to the kingdom's Jews, so too was the family which had won that freedom. Herod's elevation (coming as it did with Roman backing, without any consideration for local feeling), therefore, did not get off to a smooth start.

In part to overcome the fact that he, a non-Hasmonian, was about to unseat Antigonus, the last of that family to hold power, Herod took as his second wife (he was polygamous and had some ten wives overall, although not all at the same time), **Mariamne the Hasmonian**, a Hasmonian princess and the niece of Antigonus. Herod's marriage to Mariamne by no means made him universally popular, but it did begin to

See sidebar on the following page

legitimize his ambitions in the minds of many. If he could quickly father sons by Mariamne and openly establish one as his political heir, thus merging his line with the Hasmonian legacy, he had the potential of winning over more local supporters. Regardless, life was never to be simple for Herod: his marriage to Mariamne may have been popular with the masses, but it offended many of his oldest and closest supporters—among them, his sister ◆ **Salome**, and those who stood behind **Doris**, his first wife. (Doris gave birth to Herod's first son Antipater, a fact which would complicate subsequent affairs at Herod's court.) These supporters had little to gain through Mariamne's epiphany and had much personal influence to lose by her coming. Factional rivalries ran rampant in the unsettled atmosphere of Herod's Jerusalem. As they did so, Mariamne gave birth to three sons, two of whom, Alexander and Aristobulus, lived to reach maturity. These sons posed a challenge to their older half-brother Antipater, the son of Doris. At about the same time that Alexander and Aristobulus were born, Herod's sister Salome, married to Costobar, gave birth to Berenice.

The atmosphere of Herod's court became even more highly charged as Herod obviously became infatuated by Mariamne, whom he soon established as his favorite wife. However, with Doris and Salome eager to blacken Mariamne's name, rumor (who knows how true) began to circulate that Mariamne was unfaithful to Herod. Around 29 BCE, convinced of her adultery, Herod had her put to death. He quickly rued Mariamne's loss, both because of his private passion and because of her Hasmonian connections. As a result, Salome's and Doris' victory was but a Pyrrhic one, for, although Mariamne was removed from the scene, Herod began more and more openly to favor Alexander (his older son by Mariamne) over Antipater (his first-born son by Doris) as his successor. Herod realized the potential of marriage diplomacy in securing Alexander's status as his political heir. At the appropriate moments, Herod carefully chose wives for his sons. Alexander's marriage to **Glaphyra**, the daughter of Archelaus, the king of Cappadocia, established the credentials of Herod's emerging heir in the international arena.

In an effort to shore up factional rivalries at court—and especially to unite those who stood behind Doris and Salome with those closely allied with the Hasmonian legacy—Herod married Doris' son Antipater to a daughter of Antigonus (the Hasmonian whom Herod had replaced as Judea's king), and he married Aristobulus (Mariamne's son and Alexander's younger brother) to Salome's daughter Berenice. Though Herod was hoping to realize a consolidation of factional interests in the expectation that rivalries at court could be extinguished, his hope would be in vain, for Antipater and his friends never ceased plotting against the interests of Mariamne's sons.

Berenice married Aristobulus in about 15 BCE. This union produced five children: three sons (Herod, Aristobulus, and Agrippa) and two daughters (***Herodias** and **Mariamne II**). Of these five children, Herod would one day become the king of Chalcis, Aristobulus would marry **Jotape**, the daughter of the king of Emesa, and Agrippa (under several titles) would rule several lands, most notably Judea, as King Herod Agrippa I. Of Berenice's daughters, Herodias would take as her second husband Herod Antipas (the son of Herod the Great by **Malthace**, another of his ten wives), who, as a tetrarch, would long rule both Galilee and Perea.

◆ **Mariamne the Hasmonian** (c. 60–c. 29 BCE)

Wife of Herod the Great. Name variations: Mariamme the Hasmonaean. Born around 60 BCE; executed around 29 BCE; daughter of Alexandra (d. 27 BCE) and Alexander (d. 49 BCE); granddaughter of Hyrcanus II; became second wife of Herod the Great, 37 BCE; children: Alexander and Aristobulus (both born around 35 BCE); grandchildren: Herod of Chalcis and Herod Agrippa I.

Mariamne's prominence as Herod's favorite wife was bitterly opposed by Herod's first wife **Doris** and his sister **Salome**, whose partisans took every opportunity to blacken Mariamne's name. Ironically, Herod's very obsession with Mariamne ultimately led to her downfall, for it was not long before rumors began to circulate that Mariamne was unfaithful to her husband. By 29 BCE, Herod became convinced of Mariamne's infidelity with the tragic consequence that he had her executed for adultery.

◆ **Salome** (fl. 65–20 BCE)

Flourished around 65 to 20 BCE; daughter of Antipater (an Idumaean) and ***Cyprus*** *(an Arab); sister of Herod the Great (73–4 BCE); established friend of Caesar Augustus' wife ****Livia****; married Costobar; children: Berenice (c. 35 BCE–?).*

When Salome's nephew Herod Antipas married ***Herodias** and fathered a daughter, he named her Salome, in honor of his aunt. The younger Salome would become the ***Jezebel** of the New Testament.

Berenice's marriage to Aristobulus seemed happy until court intrigue and Herod's paranoia once again precipitated a political crisis. Maintaining as close a relationship with Rome as possible, Herod carefully cultivated Augustus (who at the time was consolidating his control over Rome's political establishment, much as Herod was attempting to do in Judea) and his family. In the process, Herod frequently used members of his immediate household—especially his son Alexander and sister Salome—as political liaisons with Rome. Alexander's employment in this capacity was particularly reasonable, since it had come to be expected by most that he would succeed to his father's authority. However, Alexander was unfortunate enough to become too popular both in Rome and among his own people, especially those who served in the army. Suspicious by nature particularly of those close to himself, Herod came to wonder whether the rising popularity of Alexander might lead to Alexander's premature elevation, and thus to his own premature disposal. As Herod stewed, Alexander helped himself not at all by preening in his preeminent status and by engaging in political intrigue, if not directly against Herod at least against the interests of his potential rivals for Herod's legacy. Alexander's primary rival was Antipater, but he also kept a close eye on his half-brother Aristobulus, Berenice's husband, lest any threat arise from that quarter.

Learning of Herod's fears, Antipater revitalized his own political aspirations. Antipater took advantage of Herod's debilitating paranoia by spreading rumors of Alexander's eagerness to unseat Herod (rumors which may not have been completely unfounded), and by cleverly making it appear as if every one of Alexander's public responsibilities would only precipitate Alexander's elevation. By 7 BCE, Herod was at the breaking point; in that year, he formally accused Alexander of treachery. Nervous about disposing the heir whom Rome had come to count upon, Herod had Alexander tried before a Roman-dominated tribunal, on the slimmest of evidence. Nevertheless, Alexander was convicted (over the objection of the presiding Roman judge), and he was executed. In the fallout of this scandal, Herod also put Berenice's husband Aristobulus to death since Antipater had effectively implicated Aristobulus in his brother's "crimes."

Antipater was thus established as Herod's successor, until a short time later the moody Herod began to long again for an heir from among the line of Mariamne. As a result, Herod took steps to insure that the young children of Alexander and Aristobulus were carefully raised at court, where he at least once openly acknowledged them to a gathering of his friends. At that time, Herod lamented the fate of their fathers, prayed that no such fortune would come their way, and further besought his grandchildren to remember how he had cared for them so that, some day, they might repay him for his concern. Such a display, coupled with the emerging groundwork for their future political marriages, sent a clear message to Antipater that his status as Herod's heir was by no means secure.

> Agrippa I won the friendship of Antonia . . . for his mother [Berenice] ranked high among Antonia's friends and had asked Antonia to promote Agrippa's concern.
>
> —**Josephus, *Jewish Antiquities*, 13.143**

Alexander's wife Glaphyra was returned to her homeland after her husband's execution. Berenice, however, remained prominent in Judea after the death of Aristobulus. Part of the reason for Berenice's continuing distinction lay in the close friendships she and her mother had established with the women of the Roman imperial family: Salome was an intimate of Augustus' wife ***Livia** (mother of Tiberius and Drusus) while Berenice ranked high in the esteem of ***Antonia Minor**, the wife of Livia's younger son Drusus. So close was Berenice to Antonia that when her son Agrippa was about six and thus old enough to leave his mother's care, he was sent by Berenice to Rome both to be educated and well positioned to eventually pursue an important future. In Rome, Agrippa was welcomed by Antonia who treated him virtually as one of her own, and he grew up as a close friend of Antonia's famous sons Germanicus and Claudius. Although Antonia's son Germanicus died before he could personally occupy the Roman throne, Antonia's grandson Caligula succeeded Tiberius as the emperor of Rome, while Antonia's other son Claudius followed Caligula in that capacity. Thus, Agrippa was raised as the intimate of his generation's most important up-and-coming figures. It is little wonder that Agrippa would one day be placed on the throne of Judea by his Roman patrons.

While her young son Agrippa was occupied in Rome, Berenice remained in Judea where, at her cousin Antipater's connivance, she was married to Theudion, the brother of Herod's wife Doris (and thus the uncle of Antipater). Antipater obviously arranged this marriage so as to strengthen his own position at court and to try to head off any possibility that one of Berenice's sons by Aristobulus might take precedence over himself in the line of succession. For a time, Antipater appeared to have succeeded in his efforts to be clearly indicated as Herod's heir. However, Antipater's attempt to seize control of Judean politics, as Herod declined, backfired, for shortly before the latter's death in 4 BCE, Herod executed Antipater. Even as his own death loomed, Herod would not cede an iota of royal authority to anyone, no matter how close. (Herod's extermination of his sons sparked Augustus—who knew something about Jewish dietary laws—to quip that, all things considered, he would much rather have been Herod's pig than his son.)

After the death of Herod, we hear nothing else of Berenice, nor do we know when she died. It is probable, however, that her marriage to Theudion did not long survive the deaths of Antipater and Herod. That union had the potential of hindering the advancement of her children by Aristobulus, which, as a savvy survivor of the bloody Herodian court, she would surely have known.

SOURCES:

The Jewish War. Harmondsworth: Penguin, 1959.

Josephus. *Jewish Antiquities.* Vols 8 & 9. Loeb Classical Library. Cambridge: Harvard University Press, 1963, 1965.

SUGGESTED READING:

Avi-Yonah, Michael, ed. *The World History of the Jewish People: The Herodian Period.* New Brunswick, NJ: Rutgers University Press, 1975.

Schürer, Emil. *The History Of The Jewish People in the Age of Jesus Christ.* Vol. 1. Edinburgh: T&T Clark, 1973.

William Greenwalt, Associate Professor of Classical History, Santa Clara University, Santa Clara, California

Berenice (28 CE–after 80 CE)

Jewish princess and supporter of Rome against Judea during the period of the Jewish revolt, who lived in Rome with Titus, until popular opinion forced him to reject her before his accession as emperor. *Name variations: Julia Berenice; Bernice. Pronunciation: Ber-e-NEE-kay. Born in 28 CE; died after 80 CE; eldest daughter of Herod Agrippa I and Cypros (both grandchildren of Herod the Great); married Marcus Julius Alexander (scion of one of Alexandria's [in Egypt] most prominent Jewish families), in 41; married her uncle King Herod of Chalcis, in 46 (died, 48); lived with her brother Agrippa II, who was Herod's successor, until 53; married Polemon, the priest-king of Olba in Anatolian Cilicia; became intimate with Titus (the Roman general and future emperor) during the period of his Jewish conquests (67–70).*

The eldest daughter of Herod Agrippa I and **Cypros** (both grandchildren of Judea's one-time king, Herod the Great), Berenice was born in 28 CE. At the time of her birth, the entire eastern Mediterranean, including the many lands which had once been autonomously ruled by her ancestors, was beginning to chafe as a result of the Roman envelopment of previously independent states and the birth of the Roman Empire out of the deceased Roman Republic.

Berenice's family, the Herodians, had long been important players in the politics of Palestine and, since the time of Herod the Great, had occasionally known royal status in and around Judea. In 47 BCE, the Romans recognized the local significance of the Herodians when Julius Caesar himself granted the family Roman citizenship. As a result, many Herodians (with Berenice following suit) went by their Roman nomenclature: thus, officially Berenice was known as "Julia Berenice." By the time that Berenice was a young girl, however, her family had lost Judea (along with Sumaria and Idumaea) when it was annexed by the Romans in 6 CE as a province under the authority of a procurator. This action was taken by Rome in the name of administrative efficiency, for none of the Herodians then of age was deemed (probably correctly) competent to control the many contentious factions then constituting the local population. This extension of direct Roman rule backfired both because the procurators of the new province (including Pontius Pilate, 26–36 CE) lacked the tact to deal with the peculiar religious atmosphere of Palestine, and because the increased Roman presence stimulated a zealous religious nationalism within the new "Roman" subjects. Messianic tendencies blossomed (particularly within those Jews who longed for a restoration of regional autonomy), even as the plethora of local splinter groups inhibited unified action against Rome. Nevertheless, the Roman Emperor Caligula's decision in 39 to erect a statue of himself within Jerusalem's sacred Temple would have sparked a widespread,

Cypros (fl. 28 CE)
Name variations: Cyprus. Granddaughter of Herod the Great (73–4 BCE); married Herod Agrippa I; children: ****Berenice*** *(28 CE–after 80 CE) and Agrippa II. Cypros' name was a synonym for Aphrodite, the Greek goddess of love.*

unanimous Jewish rebellion had not an assassin's sword struck Caligula down in 41 before his order could be carried out.

Although Caligula's assassination helped to defuse an explosive situation, emotions continued to run high enough for Caligula's successor Claudius to temporarily rethink the wisdom of the direct Roman rule of Judea. As a result, in 41 Claudius presented Judea to Berenice's father, Agrippa I, whom Claudius had known since their respective youths when Agrippa came to Rome to live and be educated with Claudius' family. (Since 37, Agrippa I had served as the tetrarch of the Palestinian territories once ruled by his uncle, Philip. Thus, in 41 Claudius merely added one more realm to the authority previously entrusted to Agrippa I.) About the same time, Berenice married Marcus Julius Alexander, the nephew of the famous Jewish intellectual Philo and a member of one of the most prominent Jewish families in Egyptian Alexandria. Theirs was a political marriage of great importance for Jews everywhere, because it linked the interests of the two wealthiest and most influential Jewish communities in the world of the 1st century CE.

In 44, Berenice's father Agrippa I died, and Claudius, fearing the development of a significant regional confederation of Jews at a time when messianic rumblings threatened an armed conflict with Rome, returned Judea to the rule of procurators. We do not know how the marriage of Berenice and Marcus Julius Alexander ended, but two years after her father's death Berenice took as her second husband her paternal uncle Herod, King of Chalcis (a region in modern Syria). Because of the connections of the Herodian family, in addition to the kingship of Chalcis, Berenice's new husband inherited the official charge of Jerusalem's Temple with the right to appoint its High Priests—a right which would also fall to his nephew (Berenice's brother) Agrippa II when he ascended the throne of Chalcis. Despite their age difference, Berenice gave Herod two sons, and she remained with him until his death in 48. As the mother of boys who might one day rule Chalcis, Berenice stayed put after Herod's death. But their accession was not to be. In 50, the Emperor Claudius took matters into his own hands by appointing Agrippa II, Berenice's brother, as king of Chalcis.

When Agrippa was reunited with his sister Berenice, she was only 22 years old. A stunning beauty and a woman of enviable charm (both perhaps inherited from her mother Cypros), Berenice thus rejoined her brother when she was in her physical prime and an established woman of the world. Agrippa II proved incapable of resisting temptation, and within a short time he and his sister began an incestuous relationship. Brother-sister love was not unknown in the East during the Hellenistic period, especially when such relationships tended to consolidate dynastic interests; it was, however, anathema among traditional Jews. But Agrippa II and Berenice were among those of the Jewish aristocracy who had been sufficiently influenced by foreign customs so as to consider certain attitudes and practices acceptable from a "cosmopolitan" perspective. As long as he and his sister ruled over the mostly Gentile population of Chalcis, his unofficial union with Berenice raised eyebrows but little more. However, this changed significantly when in 53 Claudius added the lands once associated with the tetrarchies of Philip and Agrippa I, as well as Abilene and Arcene, to Agrippa II's realm, for in these regions lived a much larger Jewish population, intolerant of sibling incest. As a result—so as to mitigate the political fallout of their relationship—in 53 Berenice officially married her third husband, Polemon, the priest-king of Olba in Cilicia (southern Anatolia). The marriage did not last long, though, and Berenice was soon back in the arms of her brother.

Berenice remained with him for about a decade, active in the political and religious affairs of the region. Both she and Agrippa II utilized his authority over the Jerusalem Temple to engage in affairs technically beyond the run of his political writ. Among the interesting anecdotes associated with this period was the appearance of the Christian missionary St. Paul before Berenice and Agrippa II (both of whom kept a close eye on potentially destabilizing religious movements) as a prisoner at Caesarea. When Paul was brought before them, they are said to have remarked, "This man . . . is doing nothing deserving of death or imprisonment." Whatever the pair might have thought about Paul, his own Roman citizenship protected him from their justice and interference.

Throughout this period, Agrippa II and Berenice were among those liberal Jews who wished to act as liaisons between the Roman Empire and their less worldly Jewish contemporaries, especially as the rift between Rome and the various religious factions of Jerusalem widened. Indeed, such efforts were welcomed in Rome, where Claudius' successor Nero (who assumed the Roman throne in 54), eventually added to the regions already under Agrippa II's and Berenice's rule.

Nevertheless, however effective was the diplomacy of the Jewish aristocracy in the short-term, by the 60s CE terrorism and small-scale guerrilla conflicts routinely upset the peace in and around Jerusalem. Eventually, what began as scattered and uncoordinated acts of violence coalesced into a mass desire to drive Rome, and those like Agrippa II and Berenice who willingly acknowledged Roman rule, entirely from the region. Despite diplomatic attempts by both Berenice and Agrippa II to forestall an open rebellion against Rome, the Jewish revolt took place in 66. With open war, both Agrippa and Berenice declared for Rome and Vespasian, Rome's initial general, against the insurgents. This willingness to back Rome openly may have been influenced by Berenice's previous connection with the family of Tiberius Julius Alexander, brother to Berenice's first husband Marcus and an early supporter of Rome in general and Vespasian in particular.

On the next day Agrippa and [Berenice] arriving in full state entered the audience hall accompanied by high ranking officers and notable citizens. On the order of Festus, [St.] Paul was brought in. . . . "This man," said [Agrippa and Berenice], "is doing nothing deserving of death or imprisonment."

—*Acts* 25.23; 26.31

The importance of maintaining good relations with Vespasian and his faction increased dramatically two years later, when in 68 the irresponsible Emperor Nero lost the confidence of Rome's armies throughout the empire and was forced to commit suicide. Because Nero had no credibility and no heir, his death threw the imperial throne up for grabs and civil war erupted among several frontier generals, including Vespasian. Thereafter, Vespasian left Judea to successfully pursue his imperial ambition. Left behind in Judea to crush the Jewish insurgency was Titus, Vespasian's eldest of two sons. Titus would accomplish his mission with the sack of Jerusalem in 70, but before he did so he would meet—and be bedazzled by—Berenice.

Titus' victory was to have a tremendous impact upon Jewish history, for his destruction and looting of Jerusalem's Temple and his stationing of a Roman legion in Jerusalem under an imperial legate (a step up from the status of procurator) helped to inaugurate the age in which synagogues replaced the Temple as the focus of Judaism. The joint victories of Titus and his father Vespasian also had a tremendous impact on Berenice, because Titus' passion for her opened the possibility that she might one day become the spouse of the man who stood to inherit the greatest power known to the world of the 1st century CE. But before Titus could become Rome's emperor a couple of significant obstacles had to be overcome. First, Berenice was a Jew, however liberal and Romanized, and her people had just engaged Rome in a bloody war. Second, the Roman people retained vivid memories of eastern beauties enthralling Roman commanders (*e.g.* ***Cleopatra VII** and Marc Antony) and were extremely suspicious that traditional Roman institutions and virtues would be "corrupted" by the accession of an oriental empress. The delicacy of the situation prevented Titus from immediately inviting Berenice to Rome, where he stayed active helping to consolidate his father's political mastery.

By 75, however, Titus thought that things had progressed to the point where it was safe to beckon Berenice (with Agrippa II in tow) to Rome. There, he openly established Berenice as his mistress, although he did not tempt fate by trying to marry her. The years between 75 and 79 seem to have been idyllic ones as far as Titus was concerned, and we can only surmise that Berenice enjoyed both Titus' intimacy and her proximity to the corridors of Roman political power. What Agrippa II thought about the situation is unknown, but we can guess that these developments did not please him at all. The idylls ended abruptly for Titus and Berenice in 79 when Vespasian died and Titus became Rome's emperor. Though somewhat willing to tolerate Titus' infatuation with Berenice when he was but heir apparent, the people of Rome would not extend their courtesy once Titus emerged fully from his father's shadow. As a result of a Roman bias he could neither eradicate nor ignore, Titus reluctantly dismissed Berenice from his bed, his life, and almost certainly from Rome. What happened to Berenice thereafter is unknown. Whether she returned again to Agrippa II, whose eastern prominence lingered into the late 90s, is not recorded, nor is her date of death.

SOURCES:

Acts of the Apostle. xxv, xxvi.

The Jewish War. Harmondsworth: Penguin, 1959.

Josephus. *Jewish Antiquities.* Vol. 9. Loeb Classical Library. Cambridge, MA: Harvard University Press, 1965.

Seutonius. *The Twelve Caesars* ("Life of Titus"). Harmondsworth: Penguin, 1957.

SUGGESTED READING:

Avi-Yonah, Michael, ed. *The World History of the Jewish People: The Herodian Period.* New Brunswick, NJ: Rutgers University Press, 1975.

Schürer, Emil. *The History Of The Jewish People in the Age of Jesus Christ.* Edinburgh: T&T Clark, 1973.

William Greenwalt,
Associate Professor of Classical History,
Santa Clara University, Santa Clara, California

Berenice I (c. 345 BCE–c. 275 BCE)

Macedonian-born queen of Egypt, whose children ruled as kings, queens, and the consorts of tyrants in Cyrene, Epirus, Macedonia, Thrace, Anatolia, Sicily, and Egypt. *Pronunciation: Ber-e-NEE-kay. Born in Macedonia around 345 BCE; died around 275 BCE; probably the daughter of Lagus (a Macedonian aristocrat) and Antigone (the niece of Antipater, who was well-connected in Macedonian circles); married a Macedonian named Philip (widowed); married half-brother Ptolemy I Soter (d. 283); children: (first marriage) Magas (who eventually became the king of Cyrene) and several daughters, including Antigone (who married Pyrrhus, the king of Epirus) and Theoxena (who married Agathocles, the tyrant of Syracuse); (second marriage) Arsinoe II Philadelphus (c. 316–270 BCE); Ptolemy II Philadelphus (r. 285–247 BCE).*

Berenice was born about 345 BCE. Her father was probably a Macedonian aristocrat named Lagus, although some have argued that his name was really Magas (in either case, the name has to be reconstructed from a source in a poor state of preservation). Her mother **Antigone** was the daughter of a Cassander and the niece of the Antipater who was the most important living Macedonian between the death of Alexander the Great in 323 and Antipater's own demise in 319. We know nothing of Berenice until her first marriage to another Macedonian noble named Philip, by whom Berenice had at least one son, Magas (who later would serve as the Ptolemaic ruler of Cyrene [northern Libya]), and two daughters, **Antigone** (whom Pyrrhus of Epirus would one day woo out of respect for Berenice) and ⚜▸ **Theoxena** (who for a time would be a wife of the Syracusan tyrant Agathocles). Each of these children would play prominent roles in the administration and diplomacy of Ptolemaic Egypt, where his or her utility depended upon the status not of their deceased father but of Berenice.

We do not know how her first husband died, but Berenice was a widow in 322 when Antipater arranged the marriage of his daughter ⚜▸ **Eurydice** to Ptolemy I, whose power base was in Egypt. This union was part of the attempt by Antipater, whose power base was in Macedonia, to stave off a debilitating round of civil wars in the wake of Alexander the Great's death. The sudden loss of Alexander—who was without a competent, legitimate heir when he died—threatened to set Macedonian against Macedonian until a new order could arise. In an effort to maintain harmony within Alexander's empire, Antipater arranged for the marriages of his several daughters to the most promising of his younger military and political peers, including the marriage between Eurydice and Ptolemy I, hoping thereby to weave an alliance which could protect the unity of the Macedonian empire until a competent member of Alexander's house availed himself. As luck would have it, Antipater's efforts to stymie civil war and maintain the unity of Alexander's legacy failed, but not before Eurydice and Ptolemy I wed.

In the train accompanying Eurydice traveled Berenice, who would thereafter live her life not in her native Macedonia but in Egypt at the court of Ptolemy I, likely her half-brother. How soon after Berenice's arrival in Egypt (the new capital of which, Alexandria, was then under construction) she came to Ptolemy's attention, no one can say. However, if the two were half-siblings, as seems probable, there is a good chance that their reunion occurred almost at once upon Berenice's arrival. It is too melodramatic to believe that Ptolemy fell for Berenice at once or insulted Eurydice by immediately courting one of her maids-in-waiting. It is clear, though, that not too many years had passed before Berenice became a major figure at the Ptolemaic court. What attracted Ptolemy I to Berenice can only be surmised, but it is clear that she possessed both a charismatic personality as well as a formidable intellect. So strong and attractive was her character that not only was Ptolemy enthralled by her, but so too was Pyrrhus who would one day rule Epirus. When as a young prince Pyrrhus paid a visit to the Ptolemaic court seeking political contacts, he

⚜▸ Theoxena (fl. 315 BCE)

Flourished around 315 BCE; daughter of ***Berenice I*** *(c. 345 BCE–c. 275 BCE) and a Macedonian noble named Philip; married Agathocles (the tyrant of Syracuse).*

⚜▸ Eurydice (fl. 321 BCE)

Macedonian aristocrat and third wife of Ptolemy I. *Name variations: Eurydice I. Flourished around 321 BCE; daughter of Antipater (a Macedonian aristocrat who died in 319 BCE); sister of Phila and* ****Nicaea****; married Ptolemy I Soter, king of Egypt, around 321 BCE; children: several, including Ptolemy Ceraunus (or Keraunos, d. 279 BCE); daughter* ****Ptolemais*** *(c. 315–?); and daughter* ****Lysandra****.*

The first wife of Ptolemy I Soter, Eurydice was replaced by **Berenice I** (c. 345–c. 275 BCE), then driven out of Egypt by the year 290 BCE.

was so impressed by Berenice's intelligence and influence that he sought to tie himself to Ptolemaic interests through a marriage to Antigone, Berenice's daughter by her first husband. Clearly, if Berenice's status in the eyes of Ptolemy I had not been absolutely secure, such a tie would have not sufficed to satisfy Pyrrhus' ambitions. Ptolemy formally took Berenice as his second wife around 318 BCE. Not long thereafter, Berenice had a daughter (c. 316), ***Arsinoe II Philadelphus**. A second daughter, **Philotera** (who never married and about whom little is known), followed, as eventually did a son, Ptolemy II in 308.

[Berenice] had the greatest influence of Ptolemy's wives and surpassed the others in character and intellectual power.

—**Plutarch, *Life of Pyrrhus*, 4**

In 310 BCE, Alexander the Great's house became extinct. Nevertheless, it was four years before any of Alexander's one-time generals dared to claim the title of king. The first Macedonian not of Alexander's dynasty to claim the royal title was Antigonus I (in 306), the most dominant warlord in Asia. Nevertheless, Antigonus' self-elevation was considered by all to be a risky declaration and was only attempted after he had won a major military victory against some Macedonian rivals. One of Antigonus' enemies at the time was Ptolemy, who feared that Antigonus might eventually be able to attract enough loyalty among the dispersed Macedonians to accomplish the dream of reuniting Alexander's empire under his personal authority. To counter the potential propaganda value of Antigonus' assumption of the royal title, Ptolemy and others who would be Antigonus' peers—not his inferiors—proclaimed themselves to be "kings." What Berenice thought about Ptolemy's elevation is not attested, but it seems evident that she enthusiastically supported her husband's decision, for within a few years of his accession (in about 300) Berenice fully endorsed the marriage of their daughter Arsinoe II to Lysimachus, the new king of Thrace and Anatolia. This new alliance was intended to stabilize the international situation and preserve for both parties their respective spheres of influence.

Although no source credits Berenice with an active role in the administration of Ptolemaic Egypt, Ptolemy's continuing affection for her and the increasing importance of her children in the public affairs of that state indicates that she retained influence over her husband out of the public's eye. Clearly Pyrrhus thought her important enough to court, as did Lysimachus and Agathocles of Syracuse, all of whom married her daughters. Two other indications of her importance manifested themselves: Ptolemy's selection of Magas, Berenice's son by Philip, as his man in Cyrene and, even more important, Ptolemy II's elevation to the Egyptian throne over the claims of Eurydice's son Ptolemy Ceraunus.

The affection between Ptolemy I and Berenice, which would be immortalized in the 17th idyll of the famous poet Theocritus, was so lasting that it was to eventually drive Eurydice out of Egypt around 290. When Eurydice left Egypt for Miletus on the Anatolian coast is unknown, but she certainly did not do so until it became clear to her that her son by Ptolemy was to be displaced as Ptolemy I's heir by his younger half-sibling, Berenice's child, Ptolemy II. This decision had been made at latest by 285, when Ptolemy I publicly raised Ptolemy II to the position of joint-king, from which status Berenice's son became Egypt's sole ruler when his father died two years later.

After Berenice's death (c. 275), she continued to enchant the citizens of Alexandria, an enchantment which was directly exploited by her son Ptolemy II. Playing on the popularity of his parents, and hoping to anchor the legitimacy of his dynasty through a manipulation of religiosity not uncommon in his era, Ptolemy II posthumously deified both Ptolemy I and Berenice as "savior gods" whose continuing beneficence would secure the peace of Egypt and the fortunes of its new royal house. In no way would such a step have been taken if the pair so honored had not been considered popular benefactors while still alive. Not only did Berenice, thus linked with Ptolemy, continue to receive traditional offerings of incense and the associated animal sacrifices as long as her dynasty ruled Egypt, but she also was singularly honored by the Alexandrians in her own temple, where her memory was merged into the persona of the goddess Aphrodite (not an inappropriate association, considering Ptolemy's longstanding affection for her). Associated in this manner with the divine, Berenice received all the trappings given to goddesses, perhaps the most impressive of which was her statue molded of ivory and gold which was publicly displayed at appropriate moments. Clearly, Berenice became a well-known model for the subsequent behavior of Ptolemaic queens. Equally as manifest, Berenice's appropriate handling of her royal responsibilities helped to forge a climate in Egypt which allowed the continuing participation of royal women in the politics of the realm to a degree tolerated nowhere else in the Hellenistic world.

SOURCES:

Pausanias, *Guide to Greece.* Vols. 1 & 2. Penguin, 1971.
Plutarch, *The Age of Alexander.* Penguin, 1983.

SUGGESTED READING:

Green, Peter, *Alexander to Actium.* University of California, 1990.
Macurdy, Grace H., *Hellenistic Queens.* Johns Hopkins, 1932.

William Greenwalt,
Associate Professor of Classical History,
Santa Clara University, Santa Clara, California

Berenice II of Cyrene (c. 273–221 BCE)

Co-ruler of Egypt with her second husband Ptolemy III, then her son Ptolemy IV, until he had her murdered. *Name variations: Berenice of Cyrene. Pronunciation: Ber-e-NEE-kay. Born around 273 BCE; died around 221 BCE; daughter of Magas, the ruler of Cyrene (and stepson of Ptolemy IV of Egypt) and Apama (a daughter of the Seleucid king Antiochus I); betrothed to Ptolemy III, Euergetes, of Egypt; married Demetrius (half-brother of the Macedonian king Antigonus I); married Ptolemy III (died, 222 BCE); children: (second marriage) five, including Ptolemy IV, Magas, Alexander, an unnamed son, and a daughter, Arsinoe III (who married her brother Ptolemy IV and shared his throne).*

Born in 273 BCE, Berenice represents several unsuccessful attempts by the Macedonian dynasties of the early Hellenistic period to forge diplomatic relations among themselves by virtue of marriage alliances. Her father Magas was the son of ***Berenice I** of Egypt by her first husband, a Macedonian named Philip. Magas owed his position in Cyrene (now coastal Libya), which he was expected to rule as a dependent of Egypt, to Berenice I's influence over her second husband Ptolemy I and their son Ptolemy II, who was Magas' half-brother. Her mother ❧ **Apama,** however, was a Seleucid princess, the daughter of Antiochus I and thus the sister of Antiochus II.

Though Magas owed his position in Cyrene to his Alexandrian kin, when the First Syrian War erupted between his half-brother Ptolemy II and Apama's father Antiochus I (274–271), Magas rebelled against Ptolemy and Egypt. This gambit succeeded so that at war's end Magas was recognized officially as Cyrene's king, although nominally he remained under the suzerainty of Ptolemy. A near-autonomous Cyrene under Magas was tolerated because, either at the same time as Magas' assumption of the royal title or shortly thereafter, Ptolemy II betrothed his heir, Ptolemy III, to Magas' daughter, Berenice; thus, Ptolemy II expected Cyrene to be returned to Egypt through marriage, negating any need for him to consider alternative means of securing Cyrene.

However, when Magas died (c. 255?), the Seleucid sympathies of his wife Apama and the general sentiment of the people of Cyrene opposed an Egyptian marriage for Berenice. As a result, Apama arranged for Berenice to be married to a Macedonian prince named Demetrius (nicknamed "the Fair," for he was very handsome). Although Berenice and Demetrius' marriage was arranged against the interests of Egypt, Demetrius was not without some Ptolemaic blood; his mother was ❧ **Ptolemais,** a daughter of Ptolemy I by his first wife ❧ **Eurydice.** This made Demetrius the second cousin of Berenice.

❧ ***Eurydice*** *(fl. 321 BCE). See Berenice I for sidebar.*

Demetrius was chosen not so much because he had Ptolemaic ties as because he was also the half-brother (sharing the same father) of Antigonus I, who had firmly established himself as the king of Macedonia. Demetrius worked closely with Antigonus who himself had allied with the Seleucids against Ptolemy II's ambition to control the sea lanes of the eastern Mediterranean. As a result, it was hoped that Demetrius could sustain the autonomy of Cyrene. Such was the dream, but the dream turned into a nightmare for Berenice when, not long after her marriage, she caught Demetrius in bed with her own mother. Taking a bitter revenge, Berenice had Demetrius murdered in her mother's arms, while Berenice remained in a forechamber until the deed was done. Apama escaped execution, for it was Berenice's intention that her mother should live with her horror and shame, but from that time on Berenice wielded authority in Cyrene.

❧ **Apama** (c. 290 BCE–?)

Seleucid princess. *Name variations: Apame. Born around 290 BCE; daughter of Antiochus I and ****Stratonice I*** *(c. 319–254 BCE); sister of Antiochus II, ****Stratonice*** *II (c. 285–228 BCE); married Magas; children:* ***Berenice II of Cyrene*** *(c. 273–221 BCE).*

❧ **Ptolemais** (c. 315 BCE–?)

*Daughter of Ptolemy I and ****Eurydice;*** *cousin of Magas and Ptolemy II; married Demetrius Poliorcetes ("the City Besieger"); children: Demetrius the Fair (who married* ***Berenice II of Cyrene*** *(c. 273–221 BCE).*

Several years later, Berenice completed her revenge when she arranged for the second time to be married to Ptolemy III, heir to the Egyptian throne. The union was accomplished in 247, and, much to Apama's dislike, Cyrene returned to the Ptolemaic fold. Within a year of Berenice's arrival at the Alexandrian court, Ptolemy III had both succeeded his father and begun to put pressure on his brother-in-law, Antiochus II of Syria, to live up to his obligations as the husband of Ptolemy III's sister, ***Berenice Syra**. Antiochus married Berenice Syra in an effort to join the interests of the Seleucids with those of the Ptolemies, but Antiochus soon grew tired of his Ptolemaic wife and abandoned her and his son by her, in order to return to his first wife, **Laodice I**, and their two sons. This rejection of Berenice Syra humiliated her and dishonored her family. After months of cajoling by Ptolemy III, it so appeared that Antiochus might accede to his demands until Laodice had him poisoned. A nasty dynastic spat followed, with Laodice determined that neither Berenice Syra nor Berenice Syra's son live to threaten the royal inheritance of Laodice's two boys.

When Ptolemy learned of the death of Antiochus II, he knew that his sister and nephew, virtually alone in an alien land, were in danger. Because he was fond of his sister, and because he didn't want the murderous Seleucids to seize Berenice Syra's enormous dowry, Ptolemy III mobilized an army and rushed to his sister's defense. Although he came too late to save either Berenice Syra or her son, he did ravage the Seleucid countryside and start another war (the Third Syrian War) to avenge their fates.

Although Berenice II and Ptolemy III would make evident their affection for one another throughout their marriage, Berenice II had no assurances that Ptolemy III would return from his Syrian war. Yet, far from opposing his effort, she sent him on his way with a much publicized dedication of a lock of her hair to the goddess Aphrodite at a temple in Alexandria. This episode would later by glorified in the poetry of Callimachus and, much later, in that of the Roman Catullus. When Ptolemy returned unscathed from his war, laden with booty and religious icons which had been removed from Egypt centuries earlier (the return of which procured for him the epitaph "Euergetes," meaning "the Doer-of-Good Deeds"), he had a star in the firmament named "The Lock of Berenice."

Unlike many of their family, Ptolemy III and Berenice II seemed to have been faithful to one another. At least, theirs was not a scandal-ridden court, and they were always on the closest of terms in public. Ptolemy shared power and titles with Berenice (she, too, was hailed "Euergetes"), and the two ruled jointly as virtual co-rulers until Ptolemy III's death in 222. By all accounts, Berenice II and her husband were relatively decent monarchs who strove to reign competently. Although accountable, Berenice and her husband did not deny themselves the pleasures of life, and Berenice is known to have loved exotic perfumes. Lavish in their public displays, the two sponsored much religious building through their generally serene reign.

However near idyllic the rule of Ptolemy and Berenice might have been, it was not without its sorrows. In 237, they lost a young daughter, another Berenice, for whom they staged an opulent funeral which was long remembered. More important for the future of Egypt, their excessive spending necessitated a debasement of the coinage in 225, a sign that, for all of their good intentions, they were not the best of financial managers.

Berenice and Ptolemy produced at least five other children: Ptolemy IV, Magas, Alexander, an unnamed son, and a daughter, ***Arsinoe III** (who would marry Ptolemy IV and share his throne)—not all of whom inherited their parents' more responsible qualities. In particular, Ptolemy IV grew up to be little better than a pampered hedonist.

For about a year after Ptolemy III's death, Berenice shared royal authority with her oldest son Ptolemy IV. As it became increasingly clear that regal authority was corrupting Ptolemy IV, Berenice began to waver in her support for his continuation as king. Unfortunately, as a faction began to develop around Ptolemy's brother, Magas, the new king reacted viciously. First, Ptolemy IV removed his potential rival by scalding him to death, and then he exterminated several other members of the ruling house, including his mother Berenice whom he murdered before the end of 221. Though responsible for Berenice II's execution, Ptolemy IV, perhaps at the prompting of his new sister-wife Arsinoe III, appointed a special priestess to oversee the establishment of an official cult in his mother's honor only a few years after her death.

SOURCES:

Athenaeus. *The Deipnosophists*. Vol. 8. Translated by C.B. Gulick. Loeb Classical Library. Cambridge: Harvard University Press, 1941.

Justin. *Epitome of the Philippic History of Pompeius Trogus*. Translated by J.C. Yardley. Atlanta: Scholars Press, 1994.

Polybius. *The Rise of the Roman Empire.* Translated by F.W. Walbank. Penguin, 1979.

SUGGESTED READING:

Green, Peter. *Alexander to Actium.* University of California, 1990.

Macurdy, Grace. *Hellenistic Queens.* Johns Hopkins University, 1932.

William Greenwalt,
Associate Professor of Classical History,
Santa Clara University, Santa Clara, California

Berenice III (c. 115–80 BCE).

See Cleopatra Berenice III.

Berenice IV (fl. 79–55 BCE)

Egyptian queen who was murdered by her father Ptolemy XII Auletes. *Pronunciation: Ber-e-NEE-kay. Born after 79 BCE; died in 55 BCE; reigned between 58 and 55; eldest child of Ptolemy XII Theos (or Auletes) and Cleopatra V Tryphaeana; older sister of the famous Cleopatra VII; briefly married to a man nicknamed Cybiosactes (fishmonger) by the Alexandrians; briefly married to Archelaus; no children.*

Berenice IV's father was Ptolemy XII Theos Philopater Philadelphus Neos Dionysus (meaning the Father-loving, Sister-loving God, the new Dionysus), although he was known around Alexandria as Nothos (the Bastard) and even more commonly as Auletes (the Flute-player). Her mother was ***Cleopatra V Tryphaeana** (meaning, the extremely sumptuous). Ptolemy and Cleopatra were apparently full siblings, but incestuous unions had long been common at the Ptolemaic court by the time of their marriage in 80 BCE. Although the year of Berenice's birth is unknown, it may have been as late as 75, for Ptolemy XII (hereafter, Auletes) was only 15 in 80, while Cleopatra V seems to have been even younger. Even by Ptolemaic standards, Auletes and Cleopatra were young at the time of their union, but their marriage was mandated by a crisis which significantly threatened the continuation of the Ptolemaic dynasty and Egypt's very independence.

Egypt at this time was very vulnerable to a takeover by the Roman Republic which, for the past 75 years, had been swallowing up autonomous states throughout the eastern Mediterranean and turning them into provinces from which a lucrative tax income had been harvested. The first Hellenistic kingdom to fall directly under Roman rule had been Macedonia (in 148), but several other states both great and small had since succumbed. Ironically, what had kept Egypt free of direct Roman rule as late as 80 was the general willingness of the later Ptolemies to be recognized as clients of the Roman Republic, thus surrendering at least some autonomy in the arena of foreign affairs in return for a minimum of Roman interference in Egypt's domestic affairs.

In addition to the Roman threat, Egypt had recently faced a debilitating intra-dynastic feud and the libertine lifestyle of Auletes' father, Ptolemy IX. Deposed in 107 in favor of his younger brother, Ptolemy X, Ptolemy IX returned to power in 87 and ruled until his death in 80. Since he fathered no legitimate heir by either of his two official sister-wives, when Ptolemy IX died his daughter ***Cleopatra Berenice III**—a popular figure whose association with the reigns of both Ptolemy IX and Ptolemy X had helped to mollify otherwise indifferent subjects to their rule—occupied the throne. Though Cleopatra Berenice III was among the most popular of the later Ptolemies, tradition mandated that a male consort from her family should share her royal authority. Thus, she married Ptolemy XI, a son of her first husband, who was the last living, legitimate, male of the Ptolemaic royal house. Seventeen days into his marriage with Cleopatra Berenice, Ptolemy XI had her murdered. This carnage enraged the citizens of Alexandria, who as one rose up in rebellion. When the dust settled shortly thereafter, Ptolemy XI had been lynched.

> When Berenice IV had been enthroned, [the Alexandrians] sent to Syria for a husband worthy of her. There arrived in Egypt a certain Cybiosactes (a purported member of the Seleucid family) whom the queen had strangled within a few days because she could not bear his uncouth vulgarity.
>
> —Strabo, ***The Geography,*** **17, 796**

The double murders of Cleopatra Berenice III and Ptolemy XI led to a dynastic crisis, necessitating the accession of the young Auletes, who was a manifestly illegitimate son of Ptolemy IX by an unnamed concubine. (Hence, the Alexandrians nicknamed him "Nothos.") Seeking legitimacy in ostentatious titles and as many connections with his royal predecessors as possible, Auletes wed his sister Cleopatra V, another illegitimate offspring of Ptolemy IX, probably by the same mother as Auletes. Although the citizens of Alexandria acknowledged Auletes as Egypt's monarch out of necessity, few liked him and his hold on the throne was always tenuous. Contributing to Auletes' unpopularity was his ancestry, his notoriously spendthrift and hedonistic lifestyle, and his identity as a devoted musician in an age when musicians ranked with thieves and prostitutes insofar as social status was concerned. Auletes' preferred instrument was a flute-like reed which he insisted on playing in public, thus demeaning in the eyes of his subjects the office for which his already dubious ancestry had barely made him eligible.

By the mid-60s, Auletes' antics had begun to wear thin in Alexandria, at a particularly inopportune time. The Roman Pompey spent the years between 66 and 62 in the East where he defeated Mithradates of Pontus for the last time, extended Rome's sphere of influence throughout Anatolia, besieged Jerusalem, and turned the once independent Seleucid Empire into the Roman province of Syria. With the threat of annexation and with his popularity at home at an all-time low, Auletes realized that his continuation as Egypt's king would mandate Rome's official recognition of his royal status, a recognition which had never been officially granted. In 59, Auletes finally accomplished his desire, but only after a huge bribe had been paid to Julius Caesar (then a Roman consul) to sponsor the necessary legislation. So angered were some of Caesar's political rivals when news of this deal began to circulate that in the next year Cato (one of the most tenacious of the anti-Caesarians), seeking to penalize Auletes for enriching Caesar, saw a bill passed which annexed the one-time Ptolemaic possession of Cyprus to the Roman province of Cilicia.

This latter action was a serious blow to Auletes in Egypt, for, returning home with Rome's recognition in hand, Auletes was forced to collect the money owed to Caesar by force from his subjects. In 58, the Alexandrians violently opposed Auletes' tactics and expelled him from Egypt when he would not, as a condition of any revenue collection, demand that Rome either return Cyprus or lose Egypt's "friendship." Auletes secretly fled to Rome, where, in order to finance an extravagant lifestyle and raise enough cash for the additional bribes it would take to get him restored, he borrowed huge amounts of money from a banker-partisan of Pompey's named Rabirius Postumus.

Meanwhile in Egypt, Aulete's wife Cleopatra was probably dead and Berenice IV assumed the throne she would hold until her own demise three years later. When Berenice learned of her father's whereabouts and his intention to reclaim the throne, she inaugurated a power struggle by sending an embassy to Rome to present her grievances and initiate a defense of her royal accession. When this delegation arrived, Auletes provoked a scandal by assassinating some of its members and bribing others. After news of this activity reached the Roman Senate, a cry arose for a formal investigation until Auletes, picking his targets carefully, managed to derail the effort by bribing important members of that house. But when rumors of bribe-taking Senators circulated, popular outrage followed, especially after a statue of Jupiter was struck by lightening, which many interpreted as a sign that the gods did not look favorably upon such corruption. Frustrated that his bribery was producing no tangible results, in 57 Auletes left Rome for Ephesus where he took sanctuary in that city's famous temple of Artemis while attempting to make contact with Gabinius (the Roman governor of Syria and another partisan of Pompey's) so as to financially induce that commander, far from the eyes of Roman peers, into action.

In Egypt, the Alexandrian court did everything it could to fortify Berenice's position, including engaging in a frantic search to find her a husband whose ties could make it much more difficult for Auletes to realize his restoration. The initial choice as Berenice's spouse was a less-than-promising Seleucid cousin of Auletes' who had once unsuccessfully made his way to Rome (in 75) to put forward a weak claim to Egypt's throne. When he died before marriage arrangements could be made, another Seleucid (Philip, the son of the king whom the Romans had deposed so as to transform Syria into a province) was pursued, but Gabinius, not anxious to see Berenice's cause strengthened while Auletes still had so much money to spend, forbade the match as against Rome's interests.

In 56, with Gabinius poised to intervene on Auletes' behalf, a husband of Seleucid ancestry was finally procured for Berenice. This man, who is known today only by the nickname Cybiosactes (the Fish-monger) given to him by the Alexandrians, was apparently so unspeakably vulgar that after only a few days of marriage Berenice had him strangled. Expecting Gabinius to lead an invasion, Berenice's backers quickly arranged a second marriage for their queen. This man, named Archelaus, claimed to be the son of Mithradates of Pontus who had been Rome's greatest antagonist in the East. However, in reality, this Archelaus bore the name of his father, the elder Archelaus, who had been one of Mithradates' generals. Although Archelaus senior had in his day made his peace with Rome, his son leapt at the chance to seek Egyptian power through Berenice. In a breathtaking bit of double dealing, as Gabinius accepted Auletes' coin so as to invade Egypt, he also accepted Archelaus' bribe to allow the latter to make his way to Berenice's side. Undoubtedly, Gabinius did so knowing full well that the powerful army at his own disposal was more than a match for any possible Egyptian resistance.

By this time, Auletes' flagrant efforts had won over not only Gabinius, but also Pompey, to whom the exiled king once more appealed. Traveling to Rome where Pompey was able to cow the Senate into submission, Auletes was once again hailed as Egypt's legitimate king in Rome's eyes, while most of Berenice's embassy (still in the city) were ruthlessly eliminated at the demand of the vindictive Auletes. To enforce Rome's decision, in 55 Gabinius invaded Egypt where he easily overcame local opposition. Archelaus was either killed defending the fortress at Pelusium or murdered at Auletes' command. As soon as Auletes returned to Egypt, he had his daughter Berenice murdered. So too did Auletes, now deeply in debt, see to the execution of Berenice's supporters, especially the wealthy ones, whose property he immediately made his own. Back on the Egyptian throne, Auletes was nevertheless little more than a Roman puppet during the last four years of his life. Firmly established at his side as his "finance minister" was Rabirius Postumus, the Roman banker to whom Auletes' owed great sums. Thus, the riches of Egypt were pumped directly through Roman banks into the coffers of Rome's most powerful politicians.

SOURCES:

Dio Cassius. *Roman History.* Vol. 3. Translated by E. Cary. Loeb Classical Library. Cambridge: Harvard University Press, 1914.

Strabo. *The Geography.* Vol. 8. Translated by H.L. Jones. Loeb Classical Library. Cambridge: Harvard University Press, 1932.

SUGGESTED READING:

Green, Peter. *Alexander to Actium.* University of California, 1990.

Macurdy, Grace. *Hellenistic Queens.* Baltimore, MD: Johns Hopkins, 1932.

William Greenwalt,
Associate Professor of Classical History,
Santa Clara University, Santa Clara, California

Berenice Syra (c. 280–246 BCE)

Queen of the Seleucid Empire whose arrival at Antioch stimulated a dynastic rivalry which led to the murder of her son and, soon after, her own bravely faced execution. *Pronunciation: Ber-e-NEE-kay SEER-a. Born around 280 BCE; murdered in 246 BCE; daughter of Ptolemy II Philadelphus and Arsinoe I of Egypt (fl. 280 BCE); married Antiochus II, king of the Seleucid Empire, in 252 BCE; children: one son.*

Berenice Syra's parents were Ptolemy II, the king of Egypt, and ***Arsinoe I**, a daughter of Lysimachus, the king of Thrace and Anatolia. She was named after her paternal grandmother ***Berenice I**, whose memory was revered in Alexandria at the time of Berenice Syra's birth. Exactly when Berenice was born is unknown, but it must have been no later than 280, for in the next year Ptolemy's sister ***Arsinoe II Philadelphus** made her way back to Egypt where she would become Ptolemy's second wife. For whatever reason, soon after the return of Arsinoe II, Ptolemy II exiled Arsinoe I to Coptos in upper Egypt. (An ancient source claims that Arsinoe I plotted against her husband, but it is more likely that the rising status of Arsinoe II at court forced Ptolemy's move.)

Although Arsinoe I went into exile, her children remained with their father and stepmother in Alexandria, where they clearly retained their standing (Berenice's full brother, Ptolemy III, for example, succeeded his father as king of Egypt). We do not know what relationship Berenice maintained with her stepmother, but there is no indication of ill will, and Ptolemy II appears to have doted on his daughter. After Berenice's marriage and move to the Seleucid capital, her father would provide her with bottled water from the Nile River, so that she would never have to drink water from any other source. Whatever else might have been behind this gesture (it has been guessed that Nile water was thought beneficial to Berenice's fertility), it displays a personal concern of a father for a daughter not always demonstrated in royal circles.

In the 270s, Berenice's father Ptolemy II launched an aggressive naval policy to gain control for Egypt of the main maritime trade routes of the eastern Mediterranean and the Black Sea. For this policy to succeed, Egypt needed to control many of the strategic ports along the Anatolian, Syrian, and Palestinian coasts also coveted by the Seleucids. The resulting rivalry led to the "First Syrian War" (274–271) in which Egypt attained most of its essential objectives. This success, however, came at about the same time that Antigonus I secured the throne of Macedonia for his dynasty. As Ptolemy II pressed forward with a policy adversely affecting the concerns of Antigonid Europe as well as those of

Seleucid Asia, an alliance based upon mutual self-interest naturally formed between his adversaries. Ptolemaic fortunes began to wane somewhat in the 260s, as a number of Ptolemaic allies in southern Greece (including especially Athens) suffered defeat in the Chremonidean War (268–262) at the hands of the Macedonians. Soon after this victory, Antiochus I died (261), leaving his son, Antiochus II, as the sole ruler of the Seleucid Empire. We know little about Berenice until her marriage to Antiochus II Theos (meaning, the god). Reportedly an alcoholic and certainly something of a "ladies" man, Antiochus II nevertheless inaugurated the "Second Syrian War" (259–253), an ambitious and largely successful assault upon the Asian components of Ptolemy's maritime empire. Losing large hunks of the Anatolian coast (Antiochus won the name "Theos" for his liberation of Miletus), by 253 an aging Ptolemy II wanted a firm peace to be forged with a dynastic alliance between his house and that of the Seleucids.

Learning that men had been sent to kill her, Berenice barricaded herself at Daphina, and when it was reported to the cities of Asia that she was under siege there with her little boy, they all sent help to her.

—**Justin, *Epitome of the Philippic History of Pompeius Trogus*, trans. J.C. Yardley**

The key to the new peace was to be the never-married Berenice, who came to be called "Syra" as a testimony to the role she would soon play in Syria. Why Berenice had never wed before this time will never be known, but most Ptolemaic princesses were married no later than their late teens (some even before reaching puberty). Berenice may not have been physically attractive (this might explain why Antiochus II quickly abandoned her), but that would not much have diminished her desirability to a prospective son-in-law of the Egyptian king, Ptolemy. Perhaps Berenice stood too high in her father's esteem for him to consider allowing her to leave his court except under the most pressing of circumstances. Speculation aside, when she traveled to Syria to marry Antiochus II (252), she was so extravagantly dowered that many referred to her as Phernephorus (the Dower-bringer). Above and beyond the territory won by Antiochus II, Ptolemy surrendered to Berenice (not legally to Antiochus, for a dowry was the property of a wife until she passed it on to legitimate children) the revenues of the part of Palestine which Egypt continued to control even after the Second Syrian War.

A provision of the treaty which brought Berenice to Antiochus II forced him to divorce his first wife ***Laodice I** (who was also his half-sister), by whom he had already fathered two potential heirs, so as to establish Berenice as the sole legitimate queen of the Seleucid realm. This was not to Laodice's liking, both because she seems to have been fond of Antiochus and because her rejection in favor of Berenice had the effect of dispossessing her sons. Regardless, Laodice departed Antioch for Ephesus so as to make room at the Seleucid capital for Berenice.

Within a year, Berenice had produced a son by Antiochus II, in whose person was the promise of a lasting peace between the Ptolemies and the Seleucids. Nevertheless, only a few months after the birth of this child, Antiochus abandoned Berenice and Antioch for Laodice and Ephesus. For the next five years, Berenice remained in Antioch, raising her son and hoping for the return of her husband. Indeed, she had every reason to anticipate this return, as her father Ptolemy II applied increasing diplomatic pressure on Antiochus II to live up to the promises which had brought Berenice to his bed. While Berenice and Egypt were too important to humiliate, Antiochus remained too fond of Laodice to return to Antioch and thus did little for years but procrastinate.

Although Ptolemy II never effected a reconciliation between Antiochus and Berenice, his death in January 246 brought the more energetic Ptolemy III, Berenice's brother, to Egypt's throne. Unwilling to tolerate a continuation of Berenice's degradation, Ptolemy III upped the ante so that by August of 246, it began to appear as if Antiochus might cave in to Egyptian demands. Refusing to accept the total rejection of her and her sons which would result if Antiochus II returned to Berenice, Laodice had Antiochus II poisoned and her older son, Seleucus, proclaimed king. In order to save the Seleucid throne for her sons, Laodice bribed the appropriate officials in Antioch and orchestrated first the arrest and imprisonment of Berenice and her young son in a suburb of Antioch, and then the kidnapping and murder of Berenice's son.

Before Berenice learned of her child's fate, however, she frantically confronted the chief magistrate of Antioch, who was in Laodice's employ. Receiving no satisfaction from that quarter, and beginning to understand that he was more a part of the problem (perhaps because she had been made aware of a substitute look-alike for her son, produced so as to assuage the suspicions of those listening to Berenice's pleas for his return), the frenzied Berenice publicly struck and killed the obstructionist official. Then she threw herself—alone, amid a sea of dynastic enemies—as a suppliant before the assembled crowd, desperately appealing for the life of her son. Most present were not aware of the child's murder but soon began to pity the woman who was so obviously distraught not for herself, but for the life of her missing son. Ironically, the wave of sympathy which began to build for Berenice not only in Antioch but also throughout the Seleucid cities of Asia would insure her own execution.

Hoping to save his sister, a newly married Ptolemy III left his bride ***Berenice II of Cyrene** to organize an army and rush to Antioch. By the time he arrived, however, Berenice Syra too was dead. A curious postscript to her life involved a few of her female attendants and eventually her brother, who for a while maintained the fiction that Berenice lived, so as to publish letters which permitted Ptolemy III to seize the lands and resources of Berenice's dowry without having to fight for them. The murder of Berenice Syra enraged her brother Ptolemy III, who as a result began the "Third Syrian War" (246–241) in which he vindictively ravaged much Seleucid territory and carried off much booty. Among the wealth that Ptolemy brought back to Egypt were religious icons which had been removed from Egypt about 300 years earlier by the Persian king Cambyses. For the return of these relics, Ptolemy III received the name Euergetes (the Doer of good things) by grateful subjects.

Although Berenice's son never sat on the Seleucid throne nor established a lasting peace between the Ptolemaic and Seleucid Empires, her unselfish bravery in the face of insurmountable odds made her a model which at least several women of her family would subsequently come to emulate.

SOURCES:

Athenaeus. *The Deipnosophists.* Vol. 1. Translated by C. Gulick. Loeb Classical Library. Cambridge: Harvard University Press, 1927.

Justin. *Epitome of the Philippic History of Pompeius Trogus.* Translated by J.C. Yardley. Atlanta, GA: Scholars Press, 1994.

Polyaenus. *Stratagems of War.* Vol. 2. Translated by P. Krentz and E.L. Wheeler. Chicago, IL: Ares Press, 1994.

SUGGESTED READING:

Green, Peter. *Alexander to Actium.* University of California, 1990.

Macurdy, Grace. *Hellenistic Queens.* Johns Hopkins, 1932.

William Greenwalt,
Associate Professor of Classical History,
Santa Clara University, Santa Clara, California

Berenson, Mary (1864–1944)

American art expert who married Renaissance art scholar Bernard Berenson. *Name variations: (pseudonym) Mary Logan. Born Mary Smith in 1864 in Philadelphia, Pennsylvania; died in Italy in 1944; daughter and one of three children of Hannah (Whitall) Smith (1832–1911) and Robert Smith (a preacher); sister of Alys Smith Russell (first wife of Bertrand Russell); attended Smith College, Northampton, Massachusetts and Harvard Annex (later Radcliffe College), Cambridge, Massachusetts; married Frank Costelloe (a London barrister) on September 3, 1885, in England (died, 1899); married Bernard Berenson, on December 29, 1900, in Italy; children: (first marriage) two daughters, Ray Costelloe and Karin Costelloe (who married Adrian Stephen, brother of* ****Virginia Woolf****).*

Mary Berenson

Mary Berenson's 50-year union with renowned art scholar Bernard Berenson was a tumultuous one, played out on the culturally refined stage of the turn-of-the-century art world. Their villa, I Tatti, northeast of Florence, was visited by some of the most celebrated personalities of the period, including ***Edith Wharton, *Gertrude Stein, Gabriele D'Annunzio**, John Maynard Keynes, and ***Isabella Gardner**. An invaluable partner to her husband, both in his business ventures and as the editor of almost all his writings, Mary Berenson also became an art expert in her own right.

The daughter of wealthy Quaker parents, Mary was married with two small children when she met and fell in love with the charismatic Bernard Berenson, who embodied the culture and brilliance she found lacking in her husband Frank Costelloe, a London barrister whom she had met while attending Harvard Annex (later Radcliffe College). Though she had already separated from Costelloe in 1892, he would not agree to divorce and demanded custody of their daughters so he could supervise their Catholic education. Undaunted, Mary followed Bernard to Florence, ignoring the ensuing scandal and

Smith, Hannah (Whitall). See Thomas, M. Carey for sidebar.

the outrage of her mother **Hannah (Whitall) Smith**. The early years of the affair were troubled by Berenson's conflict over her family responsibilities, especially her children, whom she loved dearly but could not tolerate having underfoot. (She would begin to take a real interest in the girls when they were in their teens.) After Costelloe's death in 1899, Mary and Bernard married, and, having spent years living in separate residences, set up housekeeping at I Tatti. The children were placed under the guardianship of Mary Berenson's mother.

By this time, Berenson had established her own reputation as an art critic with the publication of her *Guide to the Italian Pictures at Hampton Court* (1894) and various other magazine articles and reviews. As Costelloe had objected to her using his name, she had written under the name Mary Logan. Bernard's successful book *Venetian Painters of the Renaissance* had also been favorably received, leading to a renewed acquaintance with art collector Isabella Gardner, who requested Bernard's help in assembling pictures for her Boston palace, Fenway Court. The resulting 30-year partnership with Gardner, as well as with the London-based Duveen Brothers, was highly profitable and made possible the extravagant lifestyle the Berensons enjoyed.

Between their business ventures, travel, and writing, the Berensons found time to torture one another with flirtations and love affairs. Before their marriage, Mary had dallied with the sculptor and artisan Hermann Obrist, and had flirted mildly with Bertrand Russell, who was engaged to her sister **Alys** at the time. Beginning in 1906, Mary had an ongoing relationship with Geoffrey Scott, the handsome and somewhat neurotic nephew of C.P. Scott, editor of the *Manchester Guardian*. Bernard, in what seemed to be a retaliatory move, fell passionately in love with ***Belle da Costa Greene**, librarian to Pierpont Morgan, whom he had met in New York. She was but one of many women he would be involved with over the years.

With a variety of notable business associations and a steady stream of visitors to I Tatti, Mary Berenson was personally acquainted with a number of the more colorful personalities of her day, as is revealed in her letters and diary entries. In a letter to her family dated November 7, 1907, she recounts the visit of theatrical designer, producer, and director Gordon Craig (son of actress ***Ellen Terry**), who arrived for dinner in an inappropriate open shirt and sandals and expounded on his offbeat ideas for the theatre: "He says the only thing is to banish actors and especially actresses from the boards, and substitute cubes of various sizes, which move by machinery and are lighted in various complicated ways." Author Edith Wharton, despite a poor first impression, eventually became a close friend. Berenson wrote her family: "She *is* heavy-handed, but when you like her it becomes rather endearing. I think she is a very good friend to her friends."

In 1918, when Bernard became involved with Baroness **Gabrielle La Caze**, a French art collector and traveler, Mary lapsed into a depression (mood swings were inherited from her father's side of the family and also plagued her sister Alys and daughter Karin) and succumbed to a succession of painful illnesses that, though some have speculated were psychosomatic, were also due to persistent and debilitating cystitis.

During the 1920s, the couple experienced new conflicts over money. Mary was bitter over Bernard's arrangement to leave his fortune to Harvard University, instead of his heirs, and increasingly felt that she should receive a proportion of Bernard's earnings in return for her work for him. Bernard adamantly disapproved of the way she handled money and was especially critical of the expensive gifts she showered upon her children and grandchildren.

By 1927, Berenson found entertaining tedious and left more and more of the hostessing to **Nicky (Elizabeth) Mariano**, who had been hired as the couple's librarian. (Mariano would also enter into a love relationship with Bernard.) But traveling still intrigued Berenson and, buoyed by her trip with Bernard to Egypt in 1921 to study what was to them a new and fascinating art, they undertook visits to the more remote areas of Turkey, Palestine, Syria, and North Africa. Berenson took great pleasure in writing of her experiences and chronicled her travels in Palestine and Syria in her one and only book, *A Modern Pilgrimage*, which would be published in 1933.

By 1931, the American stock-market crash had taken its toll, and the Berensons were forced to drastically cut their lavish expenditures. During that year, Mary's health deteriorated and she underwent an operation to try to end her nagging cystitis. Following surgery, a fever nearly killed her. Never fully recovered, she became largely invalided by 1935. Her relationship with Bernard mellowed somewhat during this period, and three winters with her new great-grandson in residence provided some relief.

In the turbulent days leading up to World War II, the Berensons decided to remain in Italy. In 1940, though it became difficult for the Berensons to get news of family outside Italy, Berenson was shattered to learn from the Red Cross that her daughter Ray had died of heart failure during an unexpected operation. When Germany took over Italy in 1943, Bernard, now very much in danger as a Jew, fled the villa, accompanied by Nicky Mariano, for the home of a friend in Florence. Mary, too ill to be moved, remained at I Tatti under the care of Mariano's sister. In February 1944, suffering almost constant pain, she wrote to Mariano, giving her permission to marry Bernard after her death. She added that she was glad Bernard could not see her in such pain and weakness. "I love to think how in spite of all our failings and so-called infidelities we have always stuck together and stuck to Italy," she wrote, "and when I am able to think at all I think of him with tender affection."

Following Mary Berenson's death in the spring of 1944, she was laid to rest in a little chapel just outside I Tatti. Bernard, who lived on into his 90s, enjoyed a remarkably productive period, publishing three volumes of diaries, books on aesthetics, art history, travel, and autobiography. Nicky Mariano remained his adoring companion but declined his marriage proposal. Upon Bernard's death in 1959, the villa went to Harvard University, which expanded the property and established the Harvard University Center for Renaissance Studies and an extensive library on the site.

SUGGESTED READING:

Strachey, Barbara, and Jayne Samuels, eds. *Mary Berenson: A Self-Portrait from Her Diaries and Letters.* NY: W.W. Norton, 1983.

Barbara Morgan,
Melrose, Massachusetts

Russell, Alys Smith (1866–1951)

American wife of Bertrand Russell. *Name variations: (nickname) Lurella or Loo. Born Alys Pearsall Smith in 1866 in Philadelphia, Pennsylvania; died in 1951; daughter and one of three children of Hannah (Whitall) and Robert Smith (a preacher); sister of* ****Mary Berenson;*** *graduated from Bryn Mawr; married Bertrand Russell (pacifist, philosopher and author), in December 1894 (divorced 1921).*

Alys Smith, the beautiful younger sister of Mary Smith Berenson, captured the romantic attentions of Bertrand Russell when he was but 17 and a frequent visitor to the Smith home. However, the Russells disapproved of her (perhaps due to the age difference; she was five years his senior), and when the couple became engaged four years later they sent Bertrand off to Paris for three months in hopes of cooling his ardor. In Paris, he met Alys' sister Mary, who admired his intelligence and found him excellent company. The two became fast friends.

Alys and Bertrand wed in 1894, but the marriage was troubled almost from the start. Although Alys adored "Bertie," unlike Mary she could not abide the intellectual conversations he thrived on and found his smoking deplorable. One of Mary's letters, dated August 26, 1898, provides a glimpse into the couple's failing relationship: "Bertie says that he has resigned himself to being always bored after he is about 30. 'At home, even?' Alys asked. 'Especially at home' Bertie answered remorselessly."

By 1902, Bertrand admitted to having fallen out of love, and the marriage ended, though the two stayed together for the next nine years with increasing misery on both sides. Alys, who would continue to love Bertrand her entire life, suffered a nervous breakdown and bouts of depression (as did other members of the Smith family). She also became so reportedly critical and self-righteous that even her sister found her unbearable. In 1911, Bertrand had an affair with another woman and did not return to Alys afterward, but the couple did not divorce until 1921, when Bertrand forced the issue in order to marry ***Dora Black (Russell)**, who was pregnant. At this time, Alys was serving a year-long appointment as a housemother at Bryn Mawr, her alma mater. Alys saw Bertrand only once after 1911, a few months before her death in 1951.

Berenson, Senda (1868–1954)

Jewish-American basketball innovator and physical educator who modified and wrote the rules for women's basketball which remained in use until the 1960s. *Born Senda Valvrojenski in Biturmansk (or Butrimonys), Lithuania, on March 19, 1868; died on February 16, 1954; daughter of Julie and Albert Valvrojenski; sister of Bernard Berenson (noted art collector); married Hebert Vaughn Abbott (an English professor at Smith College), on June 15, 1911.*

Senda Berenson, sister of noted art collector Bernard Berenson, was born Senda Valvrojenski in Lithuania in 1868 (her father changed the family name to Berenson when they arrived in America in 1875). Though frail as a child, in 1890 the 22-year-old Senda enrolled in the Boston Normal School of Gymnastics, a women's teachers' college, where she studied with **Amy Morris Homans** and ***Mary Hemenway.** It was an age that saw the standardization of sports, with the development of rules and extensive organization. Often excluded from golf courses, tennis courts, and other athletic arenas, women met the challenge by developing their own clubs and associations.

Senda Berenson

When Berenson left school in 1892, she began teaching physical education at Smith College, where she was to lead that department of the all-female university for 19 years. In an effort to offset the long, tedious hours of repetitive gymnastic work, she organized the first basketball match between her first-year and second-year classes on March 23, 1893. Though men were not allowed to view what were regarded as the potentially embarrassing exertions demanded by the game, lines formed outside the gym one hour before start time. Wearing their team's colors, the supporters of each class sat on opposite sides of the gym. Because cheering was not then included in the "present scheme of womanliness," the audience took to singing songs with brio. Soon after the game, Berenson and her students modified basketball inventor James Naismith's original rules, which had been proposed in nearby Springfield, Massachusetts, in 1891. "To eliminate roughness and to minimize the danger of overexertion," wrote Allen Guttmann in *Women's Sports*, Berenson's new rules included a court divided into three zones which kept players from crossing the dividing lines. Players were not allowed to steal the ball from other players. They could not hold the ball for more than three seconds or dribble more than three times. In 1899, Senda Berenson established the first official rules for girls' basketball, a sport which would become increasingly popular. The work of Berenson and her colleagues—**Lucille Eaton Hill** at Wellesley, **Clara Baer** at Newcomb College, ***Martha Carey Thomas** and ***Constance Applebee** at Bryn Mawr—refuted the contentions of England's Henry Maudsley and America's Edward Clarke who warned that physical exercise during puberty would expend a girl's fixed supply of energy. Berenson maintained that as "all fields of labor and all professions are opening their doors," a woman "needs more than ever the physical strength to meet" such demands.

For 12 years, Berenson chaired the American Association for the Advancement of Physical Education (AAAPE) Committee on Basketball for Girls. Her book, *Line Basket Ball for Women*, was the first published work on women's basketball and included her philosophy about the sport as well as her assertions regarding its positive psychological and physiological effects. In 1911, Berenson married a professor at Smith, Hebert Vaughn Abbott. Shortly thereafter, she became director of physical education at the Mary A. Burnham School in Northampton, Massachusetts, where she would remain until her retirement in 1921. In this position, Berenson introduced fencing and folk dancing and brought remedial gymnastics to students with special needs. Following her retirement, Berenson traveled and in 1929 moved to California, where she lived until her death in 1954. Senda Berenson was inducted into the Naismith Memorial Hall of Fame and the International Women's Sports Hall of Fame in 1984.

SOURCES:

Guttmann, Allen. *Women's Sports: A History.* NY: Columbia University Press, 1991.

Woolum, Janet. *Outstanding Women Athletes: Who They Are and How They Influenced Sports in America.* Phoenix, AZ: Oryx Press, 1992.

Karin L. Haag, Athens, Georgia

Beretrude (d. 620)

Queen of Neustria and the Franks. *Name variations: Bérétrude; Berthetrude; Bertrude. Died in 620 (some sources cite 610); married Chlothar also known as Clotaire or Lothair II (584–629), king of Neustria (r. 584–629), king of the Franks (r. 613–629); children: Dagobert I (c. 606–639), king of Austrasia (r. 623–628), king of the Franks (r. 629–639); Caribert or Charibert II (606–632), king of Aquitaine (r. 629–632).*

Berg, Gertrude (1899–1966)

American actress, producer, and author, who was famous for the hit radio and television series "The Goldbergs." *Born Gertrude Edelstein on October 3, 1899, in New York City; died on September 14, 1966, in New York City; only child of Jacob and Diana Netta (Goldstein) Edelstein; attended Wadleigh High School, New York City; Columbia University, extension courses in playwriting; married Lewis Berg, December 1, 1918; children: Harriet and Cherney Robert.*

Selected writings: "Effie and Laura" (radio drama, 1927); "The Rise of the Goldbergs" (radio series, 1929–31, book version, 1931); "The Goldbergs" (radio series, 1931–34, 1936–50, television series, 1949–59); "House of Glass" (radio drama, 1935); Make a Wish *(film, released 1937); "Kate Hopkins" (radio drama, 1941–42);* Me and Molly *(play, produced 1948); (film, with N. Richard Nash)* Molly *(1950);* The Molly Goldberg Cookbook *(1955); (with C. Berg)* Molly and Me *(1961).*

Gertrude Berg made a career playing the loquacious and lovable Jewish housewife Molly Goldberg, who, with her family of five and some 200 other characters over the years, captured the hearts of Americans for three decades. Beginning on November 29, 1929, with the premiere radio broadcast of "The Rise of the Goldbergs" (shortened to "The Goldbergs" in 1931), Berg wrote, acted in, and produced over 5,000 radio scripts featuring her fictitious family from the Bronx. Second only to "Amos and Andy" in popularity and longevity, the radio classic "The Goldbergs" eventually swept the entertainment media, spinning off as books, a play, a television series, and a movie.

A second generation American, Berg grew up in New York and attended the city's public schools. In 1918, she gave up extension courses in playwriting to marry an engineering student, Lewis Berg. The couple spent a few years in Louisiana, where Lewis worked as a mechanical engineer for sugar refineries, before moving back to New York, where Berg produced her first short-lived radio series, "Effie and Laura," about two worldly employees of a five-and-dime. Two years later, Berg presented her script for the Goldbergs to the powers at NBC, reading it aloud to ensure the liveliness of the characters and the accuracy of the Yiddish intonation. Enthralled with the script, NBC management urged Goldberg to play the part of Molly.

The Goldberg family—including Molly and Jake, their teenage children Rosalie and Sammy, and the comical Uncle David—met with instant success. Four weeks into broadcasting, when Berg came down with a sore throat and a substitute played Molly, the radio station received 11,000 protests. By 1931, the show, sponsored by a soap company, was aired five times a week. Berg worked nine-hour days in order to prepare the five 121/2-minute scripts, which were constructed toward a Friday climax to leave listeners eager to tune in on Monday.

Berg's characters were drawn from her childhood and extensive research into Yiddish culture. From the characteristic opening "Yoo-

Gertrude Berg

hoo! Mrs. Bloo-oom!" yelled up the airshaft to her neighbor, Molly lovingly schmoozed, meddled, and plotted through the domestically driven story lines. Berg's humor, derived from Yiddish dialect and garbled syntax ("If it's nobody, I'll call back."), was never cruel or patronizing. Often the characters expressed Berg's own philosophy, while the Goldberg children, Rosalie and Sammy, provided the point of view of first-generation Americans, trying, without much success, to separate their parents from their old-world ways.

Many of the neighborhood characters Berg created were played by amateur actors in their real-life roles, such as clerks, delivery boys, and elevator operators. "The Goldbergs" was also one of the first programs to eschew sound "effects" in favor of the real thing, like running water and frying bacon. If sounds were too complicated to be produced in the studio, then the broadcast was made from an outside location. Realism was occasionally carried a step further, incorporating events from the actors' own lives into episodes. When Sammy was called to duty in World War II, the episode was broadcast from Pennsylvania Station, where both the actor's departure for duty and the troop train he boarded were genuine.

During the brief periods when the show was off the air, Berg kept busy. In 1935, she created another series, "The House of Glass," based on memories of her summer vacations at a Catskill's resort hotel owned by her father. Although it enjoyed a moderate success, the show was not nearly as popular as "The Goldbergs." She also created scripts for "Kate Hopkins," a serial about a visiting nurse. In 1948, Berg starred in her own play *Me and Molly*, produced at the Belasco Theatre in New York. Critic Brooks Atkinson of *The New York Times* was lavish in his praise: "Mrs. Berg is a real human being who believes in the people she writes about. . . . The result is a leisurely, intimate, cheerful portrait of interesting people and the humor is kind-hearted." He went on to praise her integrity "amid the gag traps of Broadway."

Launched in 1949, the television version of "The Goldbergs" quickly drew some 13 million viewers. Shortly after winning an Emmy in 1950 for her television work, Berg appeared in the movie *Molly*, co-authored with N. Richard Nash. Capturing audiences from many different ethnic and religious groups, "The Goldbergs" was often cited as promoting intercultural and interfaith understanding. The show received awards from the National Conference of Christians and Jews, Veterans of Foreign Wars, American Heritage Foundation, and B'nai B'rith, among others. In 1950, the Girls Clubs of America cited Berg as the Radio and TV Mother of the Year.

After performing in summer stock during the mid '50s, in 1959 Berg returned to Broadway in Leonard Spigelgass' long-running play *A Majority of One*, in which she portrayed Mrs. Jacoby, a Jewish widow who lost a son in World War II. Berg received critical acclaim and won a Tony for her performance. In 1963, she starred in *Dear Me, the Sky is Falling*.

In addition to her books, *The Rise of the Goldbergs* (1931) and *The Molly Goldberg Cookbook* (1955), Berg wrote her memoirs, *Molly and Me*, with her son Cherney in 1961. Her real family, including daughter Harriet, appeared to be as solid as the Goldbergs. When her character Molly referred to "a home, full of hearts and faces dat's yours and you is deirs" as the most important thing in life, perhaps she spoke for Gertrude Berg.

SOURCES:

Mainiero, Lina, ed. *American Women Writers: A Critical Reference Guide from Colonial Times to the Present.* NY: Frederick Ungar, 1979.

McHenry, Robert. *Famous American Women.* NY: Dover, 1983.

Moritz, Charles, ed. *Current Biography 1960.* NY: H.W. Wilson, 1960.

Barbara Morgan,
Melrose, Massachusetts

Berg, Helene (1906—)

German Communist activist and political leader in the German Democratic Republic. *Name variations: Lene Ring. Born in Mannheim, Germany, on April 4, 1906; attended Lenin School in Moscow, 1931–1932.*

Trained to be a dressmaker; became politically active (1921); joined Communist Party of Germany (1927); involved in underground activities in Germany (1933–35); immigrated to Soviet Union (1935); returned to Germany (1946); active in propaganda and ideological work for Socialist Unity Party (SED); director of Institute for Social Sciences, Berlin (1951–58); candidate and member of Central Committee of SED (1958–89); active in political life of GDR until collapse of Communist rule (1989).

Exhibiting remarkable powers of physical stamina and political longevity, Helene Berg was one of the very few women to play a significant role in the leadership of the German Democratic Republic (GDR). She could boast of a true proletariat background, having been born in

Mannheim on April 4, 1906, into a poor family. Her education ended with the completion of primary school, and she then began to work as a dressmaker. In 1921, 15-year-old Berg joined the Socialist Worker's Youth League, beginning a life of intense political involvement that would last until the end of the 1980s. Dissatisfied with the reformist attitudes of the Social Democrats, she joined a Communist youth organization in 1924 and completed her conversion to revolutionary Marxism in 1927 by joining the Communist Party of Germany (KPD). Deemed a promising Communist activist by the KPD leadership, Berg was sent to Moscow, where she studied revolutionary ideology, strategy and tactics at the Lenin School from 1929 to 1931. Her good marks in Moscow led to further advancement on her return to Germany, and she was promoted to a position as a staff member of the KPD Central Committee.

The Nazi seizure of power in 1933 resulted in a catastrophe for German Communism, with the leadership thrown into concentration camps or fleeing into exile. Like most lower-rank party members, Helene Berg remained in Germany to pick up the pieces of a failed policy. For two years, she engaged in dangerous underground work, until in 1935 she was given permission to move to the Soviet Union. Berg arrived just in time for the bloody Stalinist purges, which decapitated the German Communist movement in Soviet exile. Though Berg escaped the gulag, many of her colleagues were arrested and disappeared forever in the terror.

Nazi Germany's attack on the Soviet Union in June 1941 created new tasks for German Communists like Helene Berg in exile there. Most of her energy was spent as a teacher in schools for German prisoners of war. Using the name Lene Ring, she attempted to reeducate soldiers whose basic ideals had been those of Adolf Hitler's racist regime. For several years, she taught anti-Fascist courses at the Comintern school at Kusharenkovo. Returning to Germany in 1946 after the defeat of Nazism, Berg joined the Communist-dominated Socialist Unity Party (SED). With her experience from years of work as a teacher and propagandist, she was assigned to propaganda work in the province of Saxony-Anhalt, a post she held from 1946 to 1951. In 1951, Berg became director of the Institute for Social Sciences, a division of the Central Committee of the SED. This job brought her in close touch with the ruling elite of the GDR, virtually all of whom were Stalinists and hard-liners. Berg was also granted the title of professor—a remarkable advancement for an individual whose formal education had ended with primary school.

One of the very few women in a high political post in the GDR, Berg became a candidate member of the SED Central Committee in 1954, advancing to full membership in 1958, a post she would hold until the collapse of Communist rule in the fall of 1989. As a completely reliable SED member, and one able to spot ideological deviations, she held the important position of the party's representative in Prague for the international Communist journal *Problems of Peace and Socialism.* Displaying remarkable physical energy and intellectual alertness, Berg served from 1978 to 1989 as a consultant in the SED Central Committee division concentrating on international relations. She lived long enough to witness the collapse of her ideals and the regime that claimed to embody them.

SOURCES:

Berg, Lene. *Die nationale Frage in Deutschland unter besonderer Berücksichtigung des gegenwärtigen Kampfes um die Einheit.* Leipzig and Jena: Urania-Verlag, 1954.

Buch, Günther. *Namen und Daten wichtiger Personen der DDR.* Berlin and Bonn: Verlag J.H.W. Dietz Nachf. GmbH, 1979.

Bundesministerium für gesamtdeutsche Fragen, Bonn. *SBZ von A-Z, Ein Taschen und Nachschlagebuch über die Sowjetische Besatzungszone Deutschlands.* 10th rev. ed. Bonn: Deutscher Bundes-Verlag, 1966.

Gast, Gabriele. *Die politische Rolle der Frau in der DDR.* Düsseldorf: Bertelsmann Universitätssverlag, 1973.

Herbst, Andreas, Winfried Ranke and Jürgen Winkler. *So funktionierte die DDR.* 3 vols. Reinbek bei Hamburg: Rowohlt Universitätsverlag, 1994.

John Haag, Associate Professor,
University of Georgia, Athens, Georgia

Berg, Patty (1918—)

Foremost American women's golfer and first president of the LPGA, who was responsible for making professional golf a sport in which women could not only compete but support themselves. *Born Patricia Jane Berg on February 13, 1918, in Minneapolis, Minnesota; third daughter of Theresa D. (Kennedy) and Herman Berg (a grain broker); never married; no children.*

Named Associated Press Woman Athlete of the Year (1938); won over 60 professional golf tournaments (1941 to 1962); won three Vare Trophies for the lowest average score (1953, 1955, and 1956); received the Bob Jones Award in recognition of her "sportsmanship" (1963); given the Ben Hogan Award for playing despite a handicap (1975); received the Herb Graffis Award for contributions to golf as recreation (1981).

Patty Berg's athletic career began on the football field where she played halfback on the neighborhood boys' team, the Minneapolis 50th Street Tigers, until she switched to quarterback. The team was composed of serious and talented players, including Bud Wilkinson, the future football coach, who lived down the street. Berg also loved hockey, baseball, track, and speedskating and, at 15, would win the Minnesota speedskating title in the girls' junior division. Herman and Theresa Berg were not as enthusiastic about their daughter's stint on the football team as they were about her other sports. Patty rarely bothered to change out of schoolclothes, and more than one good skirt was ruined in the rough-and-tumble game. Her mother didn't mind the physical aspect of football; it was the skirt mending that irked her.

Berg's sporting life expanded when she was 13. Her father, a wealthy grain broker, loved golf and bought Patty's younger brother a golf membership at the country club. "Where's mine?" asked Berg. Her father, who reasoned that golf might be a dandy alternative to football, secured her a membership with the proviso that she

Patty Berg

practice daily. Patty started playing with a makeshift set of clubs—three old brassies, three irons, and a putter. In the beginning, it took the young golfer 112 strokes to get around an 18-hole course, but she improved rapidly. With the help of her father, who was also her chief instructor, in 1935 Berg won the Minnesota state championship, a feat she would repeat in 1936 and 1938. She also reached the match play finals of the U.S. Women's National Amateur Tournament in 1935. Only 17, she found herself battling ***Glenna Collett Vare,** the famous golfer for whom the Vare Trophy is named. Noted *Time*:

> Reporters were amazed by Patty's earnestness, her freckles, her costume of a boy's sweatshirt and the assurance with which, though she weighs only 110 and is just over 5 ft., she consistently drove 200 yards. Patty Berg amazed them further by beating five opponents in a row. In the final, she played Mrs. Vare. The match appeared to be over when "Glenna" was 4 up with six holes left to play. Patty won two of the next three. Mrs. Vare won only by sinking a hard putt on the 34th green.

Patty Berg, 1940s.

Berg was determined, playing with a power that astonished many. By now a score of 70 on an 18-hole course was routine. Her powerful 200-yard drive was astounding. It didn't seem possible that the petite Patty could slam a ball that far with such accuracy. Few knew, however, that after the give-and-take of the football field, the golf course was pretty tame. After Berg's 1935 match with Vare, she became a sports celebrity compared with great golfers like Bobby Jones. It would "only be a matter of time," declared one sportswriter, "before the 17-year-old would prove herself the foremost woman golfer in the United States." Wrote William Steedman in the *Seattle Times*:

> The new star is a kid of eighteen named Patty Berg who has as many freckles as a plover's egg, and, so they tell us, as many golf-shots as she has freckles. We'll have to see how she does for the next couple of seasons before we can hail her as another Alex, or Glenna, or Virginia. But, in view of what she has done, and what the Eastern critics say about her, she'll do as a guess for future preeminence until a better guess comes along.

Although Berg didn't know it, she would be instrumental in creating a very different sport during her career. Until this time women's golf was played by amateurs. Although ***Helen Wills Moody** had made tennis a popular sport as a professional in the late 1920s and early 1930s, golf had remained a secondary game. Berg's potential to transform the sport was immediately recognized. "Her miraculous saves in the 1935 national kicked up the attendance figures to fully 15,000 for the week," wrote Bernard Swanson in *The American Golfer*, "and, for the first time really poured money into the women's coffers in the United States Golf Association." The public adored the little redhead who performed feats women were thought incapable of accomplishing.

Pressure on the links was intense, for Berg was under enormous public scrutiny at a young age. But, having been the only girl on a boys' football team, she was used to being the underdog and adapted quickly to her new status. For the first year, she wore the same sweater and hat in tournaments because they "brought her luck." She always lined her clubs, thirteen irons and five woods, against the wall of her room, ready for the next big match. As she grew more self-assured, she discarded some of these habits and began showing up in slacks or a skirt, frequently with a beret perched on her head. An earnest player who kept a strict schedule and was often in bed by 8:30 in the evening, she had brains and she had perseverance. "When that kid gets to the green, she expects to hole every putt," said former national champion **Helen Hicks**. "When she misses one of ten feet, she is provoked. And, when she misses, she practices putting until the turf cries out for mercy. You can't go far wrong that way."

Berg's parents were deeply involved with their daughter's career. Her mother, who had been lame since childhood, could not follow her daughter around the course, but she was at each match and watched intently from her chair even when the young athlete was no more than speck in the far distance. Her father stayed close at hand. When things went poorly for his daughter, he began to whittle furiously on a piece of wood. Her parents' support meant a great deal to the young player who continued to amass honors. In 1936 and 1938, she represented the U.S. in the Curtis Cup matches against women from Great Britain. In 1937, she lost to **Estelle Page** in the final round of the U.S. Women's Amateur title, but the following year she defeated Page. "As bonny Mrs. Page ran over to the new champion and plopped a kiss on her cheek," reported *Time*, "the gallery of 3,000 yelled themselves hoarse for the temperamental little red-head, the darling of all golf galleries, who had just climaxed one of the best seasons any woman golfer has ever had—her tenth victory in 13 tournaments. But the new champion would rather be an All-American football star."

In 1938–39, many changes occurred in Berg's life. She became a business student at the University of Minnesota, though she continued to play despite the demands of a college career. Her 1939 season was cut short, however, by an appendectomy which required several weeks of recovery. A more serious blow followed a few months later when her mother died. Theresa Berg had been Patty's constant companion and major support. Her presence reassured the young player. Berg decided she must keep playing, however, and, after a temporary absence from the game, she entered several tournaments in 1940. From 1934 to 1940, Berg competed in 28 amateur tournaments, winning every notable local, state, and amateur title. She had become a force to be reckoned with.

In the summer of 1940, Berg announced she was turning professional. At that time only a handful of women were golf pros, including Helen Hicks, ***Opal Hill**, **Helen Dettweiler**, **Helene MacDonald**, and ***Babe Didrikson Zaharias**. Now a junior in college, Berg decided to work for the Wilson Sporting Goods Company while completing her studies. Her salary was $5,000 a year, a considerable sum at the time, plus a commission on "Patty Berg" golf clubs. With her fresh-faced good looks, her steely determination, and celebrity status, she was an ideal company representative. But relinquishing her amateur status was not an easy decision in 1940; there were only half a dozen U.S. tournaments open to women golf pros. Of these, only three offered a combined purse of $500. "Henceforth, the onetime national champion, who has been accustomed to winning five out of every six tournaments she entered," noted *Time*, "must confine her competitive golf to the half-dozen U.S. tournaments open to women pros." But Berg had decided to gamble on the growth of women's golf, a decision she would never regret.

Off to a good start, she won her first professional title, the Women's Western Open, in

Hicks, Helen (1911–1974)

***American golfer.** Name variations: Helen Hicks Harb. Born Helen B. Hicks in Cedarhurst, New York, on February 11, 1911; died on December 16, 1974; married. Member of the Curtis Cup team (1932).*

In 1931, at age 20, the long-hitting Helen Hicks reached her peak, winning the U.S. Women's Amateur championship by defeating ***Glenna Collett Vare**; that same year, Hicks won the Women's Metropolitan (she would repeat that win in 1933). Though she made the finals in the 1933 nationals, she lost to **Virginia Van Wie**. In the spring of 1934, Hicks signed with Wilson Sporting Goods and became the first U.S. Women's Amateur champion to turn pro.

Page, Estelle Lawson (b. 1907)

***American golfer.** Name variations: Estelle Lawson, Mrs. E.L. Page. Born Estelle Lawson on March 22, 1907, in East Orange, New Jersey; married; lived in Chapel Hill, North Carolina.*

Estelle Page took the 1937 USGA Amateur, defeating ***Patty Berg**; she was also a runner-up in 1938 and a semifinalist in 1941 and 1947. A member of the Curtis Cup team in 1938 and 1948, Page won many nationals championships, including the North and South in 1933, 1936, 1940, 1941, 1946, 1947, and 1949. At one time, she held the world record score of 66 in medal-play competition.

Dettweiler, Helen

American golfer.

Along with ***Patty Berg**, ***Babe Zaharias**, ***Betty Jameson**, **Betty Hicks**, and **Betty Mims**, Helen Dettweiler helped form the LPGA. In 1958, she won the LPGA Teacher of the Year Award.

1941. But, on December 8, the day after the bombing of Pearl Harbor, Berg was severely injured in an automobile accident in Texas, and her knee was shattered. Set badly, it had to be rebroken and reset three times. Throughout the ordeal, Berg remained determined to return to golf. After a year and a half of diligent exercise, she began to play again, though she would always walk with a limp. In 1943, during World War II, she signed up for Marine Corps duty; for the next two years, she was assigned to play exhibition golf matches to raise funds for war-service agencies. She also recruited for the Corps and became a poised public speaker. In 1946, Berg returned to professional golf, winning the first National Open. Amazingly, the pinnacle of her career was still to come.

Power is the theme of [Berg's] golf, but it isn't everything. She has brains and perseverance.

—Literary Digest

Organizing women's professional golf became her passion. Considered a pastime for the rich, golf had always been deemed an acceptable sport for women. No one, however, gave any thought to women supporting themselves by playing the game. After World War II, replaced by returning soldiers, women poured out of the factories they had either worked in or managed during the long conflict and settled back into unpaid work at home. This pattern served quite well in the sports world as well, or so many thought. Berg disagreed. She was being paid $7,500 a year by Wilson Sporting Goods, but purses for tournaments were pathetic. In women's golf, $500 was considered an enormous sum. The game would not progress, she felt, until more professional tournaments with larger purses existed. Babe Didrikson Zaharias' manager, Fred Corcoran, agreed with Berg. He brought Zaharias, Berg, and ***Betty Jameson** together to form the nucleus of a new organization, the Ladies Professional Golf Association (LPGA) in 1948, and Berg served as the LPGA's first president until 1952. Wilson Sporting Goods was also instrumental in supporting the new organization. Berg particularly enjoyed working with Zaharias, a rival on the course. The two women were opposites—Zaharias was flamboyant while Berg was earnest—but they appreciated each other and enjoyed promoting the sport together until Zaharias' untimely death in 1956.

In the 1950s, Patty Berg demonstrated the potential of professional golf for women. She won nine of her fifteen major championships from 1948 to 1962. Shooting a score of 64 at the Richmond (California) Open, she set a women's professional record which lasted for a dozen years. Berg also showed that women could make money as professional golfers. Through her efforts as a Wilson spokeswomen and a founding member of the LPGA, the sport was becoming more popular. Tournaments with larger purses were sprouting up throughout the United States. In the mid-1950s, Berg was the leading money winner on the LPGA tour. In 1954, at a time when $10,000 purchased a home, she won $16,011; in 1955, she won $16,497; and in 1956, $16,272. She was the first professional golfer to win over $100,000, and her total earnings would be well over $200,000 in her golfing lifetime.

Berg continued to win tournament after tournament. In 1953, she won the Glenna Vare Trophy for the lowest playing average in LPGA-sponsored events with a 75. She repeated this feat in 1955 with an average of 74.47 and in 1956 with a 74.57. She also won *Golf Digest*'s performance average award which assesses a player's performance relative to other players in official events. In 1955, her score was .894, in 1956, .882, and in 1957, .830. Although her career was at its peak in the '50s, Berg did not lose her competitive edge. She won LPGA victories in the early 1960s, and, in 1975, she qualified for the ***Dinah Shore** Open. After battling cancer in 1971, Berg was back out on the links, continuing to compete on the women's professional tour until 1981.

Patty Berg made so many outstanding contributions to golf that honors naturally followed. In 1959, she received the Richardson Award from the Golf Writers Association of America (GWAA). The U.S. Gold Association gave her the Bob Jones Award in recognition of her "sportsmanship" in 1963. The Joe Graffis Award followed in 1975, awarded by the National Golf Foundation (NGF) for her contributions to golf education. In 1981, she received the Herb Graffis Award for contributions to golf as recreation. Because she walked with a limp after her accident in 1941, her courage was also recognized. The GWAA gave her the Ben Hogan Award in 1975 for playing despite her impairment. She was the first woman to receive the Humanitarian Sports Award in 1976 from the United Cerebral Palsy Foundation. In 1978, the LPGA established the Patty Berg Award in honor of its first president. She was also named as one of golf's five most influential women in the July 1982 *Golf Digest*. This short list included ***Betsy Rawls**, ***JoAnne Carner**, **Helen Lengfeld**, and **Peggy Kirk Bell**. The Smithsonian also honored the golfer, installing Berg as a "champion of American sport."

When she left professional golf in 1981, Berg continued to perform as "Golf's Goodwill Ambassador." She probably introduced more women to the sport than any other player, traveling to thousands of clinics to teach and put on exhibitions. It was not unusual for Berg to travel 60,000 miles a year for this purpose. She was well known in Japan, Europe, Australia, and New Zealand, in fact in any country where golf was played. She also co-authored several books on the sport: *Golf* (1943) with Otis Dypwick, *Golf Illustrated* (1950) with Mark Cox, and *Inside Golf for Women* (1977) with Marsh Schiewe.

Through her victories on the links and her relentless promotion, Patty Berg became the first lady of golf. She was a trailblazer in American sports. Although she excelled as an amateur, she was one of the first to realize that women must play as professionals if they are to improve their status in sport. From 1941 to 1962, she won 60 professional golf tournaments, earning substantial amounts of money. Today, professional women golfers are a normal part of the sports world thanks, in part, to Patty Berg's unrelenting efforts as well as her tremendous gifts as a golfer.

SOURCES:

"America's Interesting People," in *American Magazine.* Vol. 122, no. 3. September 1936, p. 85.

Block, Maxine, ed. *Current Biography 1940.* NY: H.W. Wilson, 1940, pp. 75–77.

Kupelian, Vartan. "Sarazen, Berg to be Honored at Patrick Tournament," in *Detroit News and Free Press.* July 24, 1994, section E, p. 11.

"Pat for Patty Jane," in *Literary Digest.* Vol. 121, no. 10. March 7, 1936, p. 40.

"Patty," in *Time.* Vol 27, no. 10. March 9, 1936, p. 27.

"Patty's Day," in *Time.* Vol. 32, no. 14. October 3, 1938, pp. 53–54.

"Patty Goes Pro," in *Time.* Vol 36, no. 3. July 15, 1940, p. 34.

"They Said It," in *Sports Illustrated.* Vol. 73, no. 9. August 27, 1990, p. 8.

Karin Loewen Haag, freelance writer, Athens, Georgia

Berganza, Teresa (1934—)

Spanish mezzo-soprano. *Born on March 16, 1934, in Madrid, Spain; studied with* ***Lola Rodriguez Aragon****; married Felix Lavilla (a composer).*

Won a singing prize in Madrid (1954); debuted at Aix-en-Provence Festival (1957), as Dorabella in Cosi fan tutte*; debuted at Piccola Scala and Glyndebourne (1958); made American debut in Dallas (1958); debuted at Covent Garden (1960); made debut at Metropolitan Opera (1967).*

Teresa Berganza

Teresa Berganza specialized in early Italian opera, singing roles by Monteverdi, Purcell, and Handel although she later became known for her roles by Mozart and Rossini. Especially noted as an interpreter of Rossini, she frequently performed as Rosina in *Il barbiere di Siviglia* (*Barber of Seville*) and as Cinderella. Her voice, sweet and light, was said to blend perfectly with the orchestra. A lively actress, she was effective in evoking the tragic and heroic aspects of Mozart, as well as the comic. Berganza made several recordings which demonstrate the deftness of her coloratura.

John Haag, Athens, Georgia

Berger, Erna (1900–1990)

German soprano. *Born on October 19, 1900, in Cossebaude, near Dresden; died on June 14, 1990, in Essen; studied with Hertha Boeckel and Melitza Hirzel in Dresden.*

Debuted in Dresden (1925), and in Berlin and Bayreuth (1930–33); made debut at Covent Garden (1935) and the Metropolitan Opera (1949); retired from opera (1955); continued to concertize until 1964; taught at the Hamburg Musikhochschule (1959 on); awarded the German Service Cross (1953, 1976);

made an honorary member of the Berlin Academy of Arts (1980).

Born near Dresden on October 19, 1900, Erna Berger was working as a stenographer in a local bank when her father, a railroad engineer, decided to move the family to the interior of Paraguay. For a short while, the Berger family lived in a tent, but Erna was sent to study voice and piano in Montevideo. The family returned to Germany by ship in 1924, and during this trip she gave the ship's concert which was an immense success. Many passengers felt the young singer should study further, so on her return to Dresden Berger began taking lessons with **Hertha Boeckel** and **Melitza Hirzel**. She auditioned for the Dresden Opera in 1925 and instead of winning a scholarship, she was given small roles, making her debut as the First Boy in Mozart's *Die Zauberflöte* (*The Magic Flute*). Erna Berger was a member of the Dresden Opera from 1926 to 1934.

In 1929, Toscanini asked her to sing the role of the Shepherd in *Tannhäuser* at Bayreuth. Her career continued to flourish with engagements in Berlin and London. Beginning in 1930, she appeared in Berlin which became her operatic home, singing with the Berlin Städtische Oper and the Berlin Staatsoper until 1953. After the end of World War II, Berger was one of the first German singers to perform in London and New York. She made her debut at the Metropolitan Opera in 1949 where she performed until 1953. Making extensive concert tours between 1946 and 1953, Berger toured North and South America, Australia, Africa, and Japan. A lieder singer of first rank as well as an operatic performer, Berger's voice was regarded as pure and ageless, described by one as a "coloratura like diamonds strung on a silver thread." After her retirement from the opera stage in 1955, she continued to concertize until 1964. Erna Berger remained active in the musical life of Essen until her death at age 90.

John Haag, Athens, Georgia

Erna Berger

Berger, Nicole (1934–1967)

***French actress.** Born in 1934; died in 1967.*

A leading lady of the French cinema whose career was cut short by her death at 33, Nicole Berger starred with ***Edwige Feuillère** in an intelligent adaptation of ***Colette**'s novella *Le blé en herbe* (*Game of Love* or *The Ripening Seed*, 1954). The Roman Catholic Church condemned the movie as "immoral and obscene," and it was subsequently prohibited in Nice and Chicago, factors likely contributing to its success. Berger's other films include *Juliette* (1952), *Le Premier Mai* (1957), *Love is My Profession* (1958), *Les Dragueurs* (also known as *The Young Have No Morals* or *The Chasers*) with Charles Aznavour and ***Anouk Aimée** (1959), and *Tirez sur le pianiste* (*Shoot the Piano Player*, 1962).

Berghaus, Ruth (1927–1996)

***German theater and opera director known throughout Europe for her innovative and often controversial productions.** Born in Dresden, Germany, on July 2, 1927; died of cancer on January 25, 1996, in Berlin, Germany; married Paul Dessau (a composer), in 1954 (died 1979).*

Ruth Berghaus, one of postwar Germany's most innovative stage directors, was born in Dresden on July 2, 1927. She began her career as a dancer, studying at the famous Palucca School in her native city from 1947 to 1950. During this time, she became a member of the Socialist

Unity Party and chose to remain in the German Democratic Republic (GDR) at a time when many artists and intellectuals made the decision to flee to West Germany. Her theater career began in 1964, when she was chosen as a choreographer by the prestigious Berliner Ensemble, the internationally acclaimed theater group formed by Bertolt Brecht and *Helene Weigel. The quality of her work resulted in her appointment as director (*intendantin*) of the Berliner Ensemble in 1971, a post she held until 1977.

In 1954, she had married Paul Dessau, a noted composer who was 30 years her senior, and Berghaus began directing his operas. In the 1960s, she had staged operas for East Berlin's Deutsche Staatsoper that astonished audience members who had grown accustomed to artistically unadventurous costumes and sets. Many of her opera productions displayed a strongly ideological character, emphasizing the Marxist concept of permanent class struggle. The most discussed Berghaus production from this period was Rossini's *Barber of Seville*, which remained in the repertory of the Deutsche Staatsoper for more than two decades. Berghaus' production began with a stage filled by an enormous female nude, and the character of Rosina made her first appearance peeping out of a nipple. In 1980, her fame brought a new challenge to Berghaus, when she began working at the Frankfurt Opera as one of a team of guest directors which included Alfred Kirchner, Christof Nel, and Hans Neuenfels.

Ruth Berghaus' presentations in Frankfurt were often as ideologically controversial as they were artistically stimulating. Her 1981 *The Abduction from the Seraglio* elicited a mixed reception, much of it an attempt to pin down ideological fine points. The physical and psychological confinement of the harem was represented by the empty, white box-like set, which at critical moments in the opera heaved and rolled. One of the points made by Berghaus in this production was the notion that women as well as men should enjoy freedom of choice in their personal lives. Among the most intellectually challenging and provocative of Berghaus' stagings were the music dramas of Richard Wagner. Presented in 1985–87, her *Ring* presented to audiences an astonishing sequence of images, breathtaking in their originality and as stimulating to some music- and theater-lovers as they were outrageously offensive and subversive to other, more conservative, devotees of the arts. Instead of Nibelungs, she presented grotesque mask-like objects. The undisputed objective of much of her Wagnerian staging was to debunk, demythologize and deconstruct the traditions that still clung to the ethos and legacy of Richard Wagner. The audacious images conjured up by Ruth Berghaus have been praised by many critics, who argue that they often strike home "at some deep subconscious level," and for those individuals willing to exercise their imaginations "the rewards can be great."

The gestures that Berghaus taught actors under her direction are equally innovative. The choreography of these gestures represented a conscious break with the last vestiges of naturalism still found in German and Austrian opera houses as late as the 1970s. Audience response was mixed, but more positive than might be expected. A highly original use of stage props was often made by Berghaus in her various mature theatrical and opera productions. In Wagner's *Die Walküre*, Fricka is represented by a chair, neatly symbolizing both authority and domesticity, but at the same time evoking the element of the absurd. Though often highly original, the ideas of Berghaus derived inspiration from well-established theatrical traditions including the work of Brecht and Samuel Beckett and the Theater of the Absurd. In her production of Wagner's *Siegfried*, the Wanderer and Alberich sat comically side by side clasping their knees like Beckett's pair of tramps waiting for Godot. The affinity of the Wanderer and Siegfried were brilliantly underlined by one mouthing the words of the other.

With the controversial and even troubling nature of her presentations, Ruth Berghaus was firmly established as a major innovative force in European theatrical life by the 1980s. She delighted some theatergoers, puzzled others, infuriated a small but vocal minority, and perhaps forced many to rethink some of their most cherished traditions. In a 1989 interview, she noted, "I don't think I can have a direct impact on daily life, but I want at least to give motivation." Berghaus was not afraid to put herself on the line for her productions. When *Teresa Stratas fell ill on the opening night of Berghaus' production of Alban Berg's *Lulu* and could not sing the title role, Berghaus, at 60, acted the part herself while another soprano sang offstage. Referring to her life in a Germany shattered by Fascism (her home city of Dresden was destroyed in a notorious incendiary air raid in February 1945) and her choice to live on the "other" side of the Berlin Wall in the German Democratic Republic, Berghaus provided a key to understanding her life's work in a 1989 interview: "I consider wanting to forget a crime, because it encourages the spread of things that prevent our liberation as human beings. I, for one, would like to pass on the things that mark our way to the truth."

SOURCES:

Bertisch, Klaus. *Ruth Berghaus: Regie im Theater.* Edited by Claudia Balk. Frankfurt am Main: S. Fischer Taschenbuch Verlag, 1990.

Buch, Günther. *Namen und Daten wichtiger Personen der DDR.* Berlin and Bonn: Verlag J.H.W. Dietz GmbH, 1979.

Millington, Barry. "The Ring according to Berghaus," in *The Musical Times.* Vol. 128, no. 1735. September 1987, pp. 491–492.

Neef, Sigrid. "Producers in the Spotlight: Ruth Berghaus," in *Prisma.* No. 1, 1989, pp. 16–21.

———. *Das Theater der Ruth Berghaus.* Berlin and Frankfurt am Main: Henschelverlag/ S. Fischer Verlag, 1989.

"Ruth Berghaus" (obit), in *The Times.* February 6, 1996, p. 21.

"Ruth Berghaus und Heiner Müller im Gespräch," in *Sinn und Form: Beiträge zur Literatur.* Vol. 41, no. 1. January–February 1989, pp. 114–131.

John Haag, Associate Professor,
University of Georgia, Athens, Georgia

Bergman, Ingrid (1915–1982)

Swedish actress who was one of the most beloved, condemned, and beloved-again stars in the history of the silver screen. *Born Ingrid Bergman on August 29, 1915, in Stockholm, Sweden; died on August 29, 1982; daughter of Justus Samuel Bergman and German-born Friedel (Adler) Bergman; married Petter Lindstrom (a dentist), on July 10, 1937; married Roberto Rossellini (an Italian director); married Lars Schmidt, in 1958; children: (first marriage) Friedel* ◆ ***Pia Lindstrom*** *(b. 1938); (second marriage) Robertino (b. February 2, 1950), and (twin girls) Isabella Fiorella Elettra Giovanna (**Isabella Rossellini**) and **Isotta** Ingrid Freida Giuliana (b. June 18, 1952).*

Filmography: Munkbrogreven (The Count from the Monk's Bridge, *Sweden, 1934);* Branningar (Ocean Breakers *or* The Surf, *Sw., 1935);* Swedenhielms (The Family Swedenhielms, *Sw., 1935);* Valborgsmassoafton (Walpurgis Night, *Sw., 1935);* Pa Solsidan (On the Sunny Side, *Sw., 1936);* Intermezzo *(Sw., 1936);* Die Vier Gesellen (The Four Companions, *German, 1938);* Dollar *(Sw., 1938);* En Kvinnas Ansikte (A Woman's Face *(Sw., 1938);* En Enda Natta (Only One Night, *Sw., 1938);* Juninatten (A Night in June, *Sw., 1940);* Intermezzo: A Love Story *(U.S., 1939);* Adam Had Four Sons *(U.S., 1941);* Rage in Heaven *(U.S., 1941);* Dr. Jekyll and Mr. Hyde *(U.S., 1941);* Casablanca *(U.S., 1943); (2-reel doc.)* Swedes in America *(U.S., Office of War Information, 1943);* For Whom the Bell Tolls *(U.S., 1943);* Gaslight *(U.S., 1944);* Spellbound *(U.S., 1945);* Saratoga Trunk *(U.S., 1945);* The Bells of St. Mary's *(U.S., 1945);* Notorious *(U.S., 1946);* Arch of Triumph *(U.S., 1948);* Joan of Arc *(U.S., 1948);* Under Capricorn *(U.K., 1949);* Stromboli *(Italy, 1949);* Europa '51 (The Greatest Love, *It., 1952);* Siamo Donne (We the Women, *It., 1953);* Viaggio in Italia (Journey to Italy, *It., 1953);* Giovanna d'Arco al Rogo (Joan at the Stake, *It., 1954);* Angst (Fear, *Ger.-It., 1954);* Elena et les Hommes (Paris Does Strange Things, *Fr.-It., 1956);* Anastasia *(U.S., 1956);* Indiscreet *(U.K.-U.S., 1958);* The Inn of the Sixth Happiness *(U.K.-U.S., 1958);* Goodbye Again (Aimez-vous Brahms?, *U.S.-Fr., 1961);* Der Besuch (The Visit, *Ger.-Fr.-It.-U.S., 1964);* The Yellow Rolls-Royce *(U.K., 1964);* Stimulantia *(Sw., 1967);* Cactus Flower *(U.S., 1969); (from a novel by **Rachel Maddux**)* A Walk in the Spring Rain *(U.S., 1970);* From the Mixed-Up Files of Mrs. Basil E. Frankweiler *(U.S., 1973);* Murder on the Orient Express *(U.K.-U.S., 1974);* A Matter of Time *(U.S.-It., 1976);* Herbstsonate (Autumn Sonata, *Ger.-Nor.-U.K., 1978).*

Theater: Liliom *with Burgess Meredith (1940);* Anna Christie *(Santa Barbara, 1941);* Joan at the Stake *(directed by Roberto Rossellini, opened at the Teatro San Carlo in Naples, December 1952);* Tea and Sympathy *(opened in Paris at Théâtre de Paris, December 2, 1956);* Hedda Gabler *(opened at Théâtre Montparnasse, Paris, December 10, 1962);* A Month in the Country *(opened in Guildford, England, 1965); Eugene O'Neill's* More Stately Mansions *(opened at the Broadhurst on Broadway, 1967);* Captain Brassbound's Conversion *(opened in London, 1971, New York, 1972); W. Somerset Maugham's* The Constant Wife *(opened in London and New York, 1975); (with *Wendy Hiller)* Waters of the Moon *(opened at the Haymarket, London, 1979).*

Television: Henry James' "The Turn of the Screw" (NBC, 1959); "Twenty-four Hours in a Woman's Life" (CBS, 1961); (with Michael Redgrave, Trevor Howard, and Ralph Richardson) "Hedda Gabler" (BBC and CBS, 1963); (one-character play) Jean Cocteau's "The Human Voice" (ABC, 1966); "A Woman Called Golda," Paramount, 1982.

Ingrid Bergman was not only breathtakingly beautiful, she was forthright, unaffected, and de-

◆ **Lindstrom, Pia (1938—)**

American newscaster in New York City. *Born Friedel Pia Lindstrom on September 20, 1938; daughter of Ingrid Bergman and Petter Lindstrom (a dentist); married Joseph Daly, in December 1971; children: Justin (b. 1973).*

Ingrid Bergman

mure. She was Sister Benedict, Joan of Arc, and the virginal Maria. She was every man's fantasy of the perfect mate, every woman's fantasy of the perfect friend. And when she fell from grace, she was metaphysically tarred, feathered, run out of town, and condemned on the floor of the United States Senate.

Born on August 29, 1915, in Stockholm, Sweden, Bergman was just turning three when her mother died of a liver ailment. Her debonair father Justus Bergman (second youngest of 12 siblings) owned a successful photography shop at No. 3 Strandvägen, an elegant boulevard in Stockholm, where the Bergmans lived in a large apartment on the top two floors. Ingrid, an only child (her mother had lost two children in earlier pregnancies), was reared by Justus and Ellen, his 49-year-old single sister with a heart condition, who moved into the household. Ellen Bergman was a suspicious Lutheran who sought out sin. In summer, Ingrid stayed with her maternal grandparents, the Adlers, who were also devout, and many other aunts in Hamburg, Germany.

During a childhood defined by rigidity, Ingrid had one oasis: her father. Affectionate by nature, Justus doted on his only daughter. His artist's sensibility contrasted with the family's severity: he was a painter who loved music and hoped that his daughter would be an opera singer. Ingrid took piano lessons and delighted in playacting for him. Growing up on Strandvägen, she watched from her window as theatergoers arrived for evening performances at Sweden's greatest theater, the Royal Dramatic, a few yards away. The Röda Kvarn (Red Mill), a film palace, was also near. Ingrid was 11 when her father took her to her first stage presentation. Spellbound by the acting, she announced at intermission, "That's what I'm going to do."

In those early years, Bergman attended a prestigious girls' school in Stockholm, the Palmgrenska Samskolan. She was not a particularly good student, and her shyness warded off any potential popularity. At nine, she was joyous when a governess, 18-year-old **Greta Danielsson**, arrived. Also musically inclined, Greta became a close friend to Ingrid, while a romance blossomed between Greta and Justus, who was then 53. Though they wanted to marry, Aunt Ellen threatened to leave, and the family's propriety won out. Greta was driven from the house.

Soon after, when Ingrid was 12, Justus was diagnosed with cancer. With Greta by his side, he journeyed to Bavaria for a cure but returned a gaunt, dying man. Greta was still not allowed in the house until a maternal aunt arrived from Hamburg for a brief stay. Aunt Mutti (German for mother), who became an anchor for Ingrid, was a formidable, no-nonsense woman, and she saw to it that Greta was allowed to stay at Justus' bedside. "I remember my Father turned his head to look at Greta," recalled Bergman, "and then he turned his head to look at me, and I smiled at him. And that was the end."

For the next six months, Ingrid continued to live under the stern eye of Aunt Ellen until one night in the darkened apartment Ellen cried out for help. As her heart gave out, Ellen died in the young girl's arms. A traumatized Ingrid moved in with her Uncle Otto. Though more animated, Otto and his family were also devoutly Lutheran, lived on a tight budget, and began to depend on Ingrid's inheritance for support. While Aunt Hulda slept on a portable bed in the hallway, two girls shared one room, three boys another. Ingrid, treated as the rich relative, had a room to herself.

Now entering her teens, while living with this passel of cousins, she would retreat to her room, play different roles, and fantasize her future as the next Sarah Bernhardt. Still awkward in school, she came alive when asked to read or perform. "At school, Ingrid's shyness was so intense," wrote biographer Alan Burgess, "that occasionally it became a nervous affliction, an allergy for which her doctor could find no explanation. Her fingers swelled up and she couldn't bend them. Her lips and eyelids swelled too. . . . Drama school ended all her illnesses, and most of her inhibitions."

In late 1931, Ingrid was 16 when Greta took her to the Svensk Filmindustri studios outside Stockholm to apply for a job as an extra. Elated by her first walk-on, Bergman decided to audition for the Royal Dramatic Theatre, but the competition was keen: 75 would-be's were vying for eight slots. Bergman hired a drama coach and took private gymnastics; then came the day of the tryout. Wrote Bergman: "A run and a leap into the air, and there I am in the middle of the stage with that big gay laugh that's supposed to stop them dead in their tracks. I pause, and get out my first line. Then I take a quick glance down over the footlights at they jury. And I can't believe it! They are not paying the slightest attention to me." Even so, she was accepted.

Now grown to her full height, 5'9'', the 18-year-old Bergman began dating Dr. Petter Aron Lindstrom, a young dentist, whom she had met on a blind date. Petter had obtained the only medical dentistry degree in Stockholm, spent a summer north of the Arctic Circle working on teeth of Laplanders in a tuberculosis sanatarium, and served as an associate professor at the Dental College of Karolinska Institute. He was a champion boxer, champion skier, generous, caring, in love with the theater, and 26. He was also a solicitous advisor, a take-charge kind of fellow. While Ingrid pursued her career, Petter began to handle the mundanities of everyday living. In July 1936, they exchanged engagement rings in Hamburg, among her mother's relatives, the Adlers, who were greeting all with "Heil Hitler" and advised Petter to drop the Aron from his name because it sounded Jewish. Aunt Mutti was now living with a man high up in the Nazi party who was selling uniforms to the SS. To Petter's alarm, Ingrid, who was and would remain naively apolitical, "heiled" along with the crowd. They were married the following July in Petter's hometown of Stöde, Sweden.

Bergman snagged her first film role in the comedy *The Count of the Monk's Bridge* (1934). Blessed with an abundance of self-confidence, she was soon showing Sweden's greatest comedienne **Tollie Zellman**, who had a scene wrapping fish, just how to wrap fish. "And who's this?" Zellman asked the director. "A young girl who's just started," he replied. "Oh, she starts well, doesn't she," quipped Zellman. Offered a film contract, Bergman left drama school after only one year. From then on, unschooled in technique, she had to rely on instincts.

Her second film *Ocean Breakers*—considered one of Sweden's best films of 1935—was entered in the Venice Film Festival. That same year, Bergman starred opposite her idol, reigning star Gösta Ekman in *The Family Swedenhielms*. She made six films in quick succession before the public caught up with her. The defining movie was *Intermezzo*, again with Ekman, the story of a world-famous violinist, married with family, who falls in love with a beautiful young pianist. The haunting soundtrack gave the film enormous power. "It wasn't just a *pilsnerfilm* [beer movie]," Bergman would later comment. "It was so well written that you felt pity for everybody." Along with *Autumn Sonata* and *Casablanca*, *Intermezzo* was one of the films, claimed Bergman, that made her career. When it opened on November 16, 1936, the Stockholm *Daily* reported that the audience sat stunned at movie's end. Amazingly, while playing the part of a potential homewrecker, Bergman conveyed screen innocence. Writes biographer Laurence Leamer, "For her audience, she sanctified behavior that the moral dictates of her time considered slightly sordid or improper. It was a role she would play again and again."

On the home front, Petter adored his wife and handled the household, money matters, and any unpleasantries in her career. She would later reflect: "Men make women helpless by deciding and telling them what to do. Men in my life taught me to be dependent, beginning with my father, and after that Uncle Otto, who didn't want me to become an actress, and then Petter, even before our engagement—not that it was Petter's fault. I was the one who asked him for advice and help in those early days." Throughout her life, Bergman would attract mentors, male and female, strong people who would gravitate to her seeming helplessness and come to her aid.

> I am a *flyttfågel* [bird of passage]. I have always, ever since I was a little girl, looked for something new, new.
>
> **—Ingrid Bergman**

Fluent in German, Bergman was enticed by the promise of playing ***Charlotte Corday** and signed a three-picture deal with the German studio UFA in 1938. As a now-pregnant Bergman entered Berlin, Hitler marched into Austria, but she continued to be unaware of global politics. Precedent had been set by other Swedish actresses who had gone the German route to international careers, including ***Signe Hasso**, ***Sarah Leander**, and ***Kristina Söderbaum** (who would star in the notorious *Jew Süss*, an anti-Semitic remake of a pro-Jewish English movie). After completing her first German film, a non-political comedy *The Four Companions*, Bergman returned home to give birth to Friedel Pia Lindstrom, known as Pia, on September 20, 1938. Ingrid was not comfortable with motherhood, and, though the movie on Corday had been canceled, she planned to return to Berlin for her second movie. But it was 1939, and Petter warned her that if she returned to Berlin it would be the end of their marriage; he then cast about for roles in America.

Deterred from returning to Germany, Bergman would forever credit ***Kay Brown**, the New York story editor for David Selznick, for her American career. Brown viewed the Swedish production of *Intermezzo* and alerted her boss. "I reported on Intermezzo to David as story material," said Brown, "but I did not go overboard about it. But I went *madly* overboard about the girl. I thought she was the beginning and end of all things wonderful." Selznick decided to remake *Intermezzo*, starring Bergman and Leslie

Howard, and Ingrid arrived in New York on the *Queen Mary* on April 20, 1939.

Despite a production code demand that "the 'girl's punishment' will have to be made a little heavier," *Intermezzo* began filming. At first, Selznick wanted Bergman to change her name, feeling that Americans would never learn to pronounce "Ingrid"; it was too Germanic. He also wanted to repair her teeth and pluck her eyebrows. To his credit, Selznick changed his mind, and when the makeup people stalked with powder and puff, he warded them off. They would film her as *au natural* as lighting would allow. Selznick, a genius at producing and promoting, wisely knew not to thrust another "foreign star" on a sated public as *his* discovery; rather, he had Bergman keep a low profile, thinking it best to have Americans discover her for themselves.

Oblivious to the frigid reception from the Hollywood elite who deemed her an overgrown peasant, Bergman threw herself into the work routine: hours with her piano coach and hours with her English coach **Ruth Roberts**, sister of George Seaton. Bergman would insist that her good friend Roberts be written into each contract for future productions. Her other close friend was Selznick's wife, ***Irene Selznick**. Though Bergman found David Selznick demanding, she respected him highly and, as she did with Petter, sought his advice on most everything.

At filming's end, Bergman returned to Sweden while Selznick's publicity machine began to smooth over her ties to Germany. When ***Louella Parsons** wrote that Ingrid had had a relationship with a high Nazi official, Bergman wired a denial. *Intermezzo* opened in October 1939. Though critics were lukewarm about the film, they issued hosannas to Bergman, calling her wholesome, natural, and incandescent. In January 1940, she returned to Hollywood, this time with Pia; Petter remained behind. While Selznick hunted for her next property, she successfully opened on Broadway in Ferenc Molnar's *Liliom* with Burgess Meredith.

Bergman hated being idle. With Selznick still looking for material, she was loaned out to Columbia for *Adam Had Four Sons*, though she wasn't taken with the script. Finishing *Adam* on the evening of December 11, 1940, she began filming *Rage in Heaven* the following morning, this time on loan out to MGM. She was then slotted to be cast as the "good" woman in MGM's *Dr. Jekyll and Mr. Hyde*, starring Spencer Tracy, while ***Lana Turner** played the trollop. But Bergman convinced director Victor Fleming to switch the parts. Meanwhile, Selznick had his eye on the role of Maria in Ernest Hemingway's bestseller *For Whom the Bell Tolls*, purchased by Paramount. ***Martha Gellhorn**, who had just married Hemingway, had shared an ocean crossing with Bergman and been struck by the "woman with the baby on her back." While Hemingway and Selznick pushed for Bergman, Paramount settled on Norwegian ballerina ***Vera Zorina**. Petter arrived to take up medicine at the University of Rochester in upstate New York; the couple had now lived apart for almost half their marriage.

During the filming of *Jekyll and Hyde*, Bergman became involved with both Fleming and Tracy. "Ingrid told me often that she couldn't work well unless she was in love with either the leading man or the director," recalled Petter. Wrote Leamer: "She knew that when she made love to a man as the cameras rolled, she would give a better performance if she were making love to him offscreen as well. It was not a question of morality. Nor was it a matter of profound romantic love, a fact that it would take several men a good while to understand." It was not love that Ingrid craved, that made her feel alive, maintains Leamer, it was a good part.

She moved to Rochester to live with her husband and daughter but was restless and rarely stayed long. When Hal Wallis called from Warner Bros. with a movie called *Casablanca*, Bergman signed, script unseen, since the film was only partially written. The writers Julius and Philip Epstein had "winged it" in the story conference with Selznick. Unlike most Hollywood films, each scene in *Casablanca* was shot in story sequence, mostly because no one knew the ending throughout the filming. Bergman repeatedly asked director Michael Curtiz who she was in love with: Humphrey Bogart or Paul Henreid. Curtiz would reply, "We don't know yet, play in between."

Before returning to Rochester, Bergman learned that Paramount was unhappy with Zorina in *For Whom the Bell Tolls*, now being filmed by director Sam Wood in northern California's Sierra Nevada mountains. Bergman was secretly tested, given the role, and swept to the location, where she immediately fell in love with Gary Cooper. Determined to work together again, Cooper and Bergman would sign on for ***Edna Ferber**'s bestseller *Saratoga Trunk*. Theirs was a two-picture romance. "In my whole life I never had a woman so much in love with me as Ingrid was," said Gary Cooper. "The day after the picture ended I couldn't get her on the phone."

Meanwhile, *Casablanca* had opened and received six Academy Award nominations, including Best Film. When *For Whom the Bell Tolls* opened in August 1943, Bergman was on the cover of *Time* magazine and nominated for Best Actress. Petter moved West and took up a surgical internship at Stanford University Hospital in San Francisco.

Bergman was at the top of the heap. Loaned out again to MGM for *Gaslight*, starring Charles Boyer, she was nominated for and won the 1944 Academy Award for Best Actress. That same year, Petter began his neurosurgical residence at Los Angeles County Hospital, and the Lindstroms bought their first home in Benedict Canyon. The family was finally together, but as soon as Bergman had a chance to settle in, she was off selling bonds around the country or doing a radio show in New York. In quick order, she filmed Hitchcock's *Spellbound*, with Gregory Peck, and *Bells of St. Mary's*, with Bing Crosby. She then spent a day or two at home in Benedict Canyon before signing on for a European USO tour and embarking on June 13, 1945. While on tour, she had affairs with musician

From the movie Casablanca, *starring Ingrid Bergman and Humphrey Bogart.*

From the movie For Whom the Bell Tolls.

Larry Adler and war photographer Bob Capa, affairs she would continue on her return to L.A., though Adler noted that theirs was more talk than passion. "I felt guilty for not being satisfied with all I had," wrote Bergman. "Again and again I repeated to myself how fortunate I was, a faithful husband who loved me and did everything he could for me, a good child, a beautiful home. I had health and money and success in my work, but still I was in a constant struggle inside, looking for something I couldn't put my fingers on. Petter understood my restlessness, maybe better than I did. We had long talks about our lives, and I felt a great relief in leaning on him and letting him make the decisions."

Following the filming of Hitchcock's *Notorious* with Cary Grant, Bergman broke free of her Selznick contract and began work on her first independent production, Erich Maria Remarque's *Arch of Triumph*, with Charles Boyer. Outwardly placid, she was inwardly tense. She began to smoke heavily in addition to being a serious drinker. Pia, now seven, began to ask why her mother wasn't home more.

Since childhood, Bergman had wanted to play the role of Joan of Arc, a part Selznick had long promised. Offered Maxwell Anderson's *Joan of Lorraine* for Broadway, she opened in New York on November 18, 1946. The play was a sizeable hit, and she received over 21 awards. Planning began in earnest for the movie, with Victor Fleming directing and Walter Wanger producing. As a partner in the production, Bergman began filming *Joan of Arc* on September 17, 1948; she also began an affair with Fleming. Though the partners lavished attention to detail on the film, the script by Anderson was weak.

In 1946, Bergman attended a movie house on 49th Street in New York to see Roberto Rossellini's *Open City*, starring ***Anna Magnani**. Unlike *Casablanca*, this was a cold, hard look at war and the Nazi occupation. Bergman was bowled over by the direction. A few months later, she saw the same name on a tiny movie-house marquee on Broadway; she went in alone and watched a movie entitled *Paisan*; again, she was riveted to her seat. By this time, Bergman was growing concerned about her career, as her first two yet-to-be-released movies away from the Selznick stable looked like possible failures. Tired of doing the same kind of film and ready to shake things up, she sent a letter to the Italian director. Rossellini responded, asking if she'd be interested in collaborating on a film to be shot in Stromboli. Since actors are rarely consulted on a script before the script is written, Bergman was intrigued. Rossellini did not mention that he had originally intended the film for the woman he was living with, Anna Magnani.

Arch of Triumph opened and confirmed Bergman's worst fears. For the first time in her career, the critics were dismissive, and the film was Hollywood's biggest monetary loser to date. *Joan of Arc* then opened to a publicity blitz—the cover of *Life*, an eight-story figure of Bergman astride her mount in Times Square—but the reviews were mixed, and it was another commercial disaster. "I have to get out of Hollywood," said Bergman to all who would listen. Rossellini symbolized a higher form of art and a chance to prove her talent once again. "Probably, subconsciously, he offered a way out from both my problems: my marriage and my life in Hollywood," wrote Bergman. "But it wasn't clear to me at that time." Rossellini arrived from Italy having eluded Magnani by announcing he was going out to walk the dog. He stayed in the Lindstrom guest house.

Ingrid Bergman left for Italy to film on March 9, 1949—and took everything with her. The photographers had a feast as she wended her way to Stromboli, holding hands with Rossellini as they drove through the Italian countryside; that same repast was sent over the wires of the Associated Press. She wrote Petter and asked for a divorce, saying she had fallen in love with Roberto, she had fallen in love with Italy. As the couple sped south, a tidal wave of negative publicity was forming. It would reach all distant shores.

Stromboli began filming under the auspices of RKO and Howard Hughes, but there still was no script, and, rather than collaborate as he had promised, Rossellini was parceling out dialogue at a meager rate, page by page, while Bergman and a group of amateurs eagerly waited. Stromboli was a remote island off the coast of Italy with a 3,000-foot volcano, one of the most active in the world, at its center. There were no telephones; there was no electricity. The lovers were unaware of the volcano erupting in the world's press, but boats began to enter Stromboli's harbor, bobbing with journalists.

In Hollywood, industry regulars were alarmed. Walter Wanger knew that any new money to be reaped from *Joan of Arc* was about to fly out the window. Production code director Joseph Breen warned Bergman by telegram to deny the rumors that she had left husband and child for a married man, or lose her career. Meanwhile, Petter pleaded with his wife just to meet, to talk over the divorce, and he demanded that she be the one to break the news to Pia. But the woman who wanted her freedom and avoided unpleasantness at all cost was now with a man who was domineering and jealous; Roberto threatened to shoot himself if she met with Petter.

Sometime in late May, Bergman learned that she was pregnant. On August 6, the news was announced in an Italian paper. Three days later, when Hollywood gossip columnist ***Hedda Hopper** arrived in Rome, Bergman denied her pregnancy, knowing full well that, when the truth came out, Hopper would look gullible and Bergman would have made a powerful enemy. It was Hopper's rival, ***Louella Parsons**, who broke the story in December, bumping the news of the development of the hydrogen bomb off the front page.

On January 3, 1950, Roberto was issued an Austrian annulment of his first marriage. On February 2, Ingrid gave birth to a boy Robertino, and her Mexican divorce was granted the following week. Because of laws in Rome, the baby was registered at City Hall: "Father, Roberto Rossellini; mother unknown." Theater owners of America took a strong moral stand, declaring that they would ban *Stromboli* if it did not make money in its first few days. In Indianapolis, an owner of a group of theaters called for a boycott of Bergman films; a legislator called for the Maryland Assembly to condemn *Stromboli.* On March 14, Senator Edwin C. Johnson from Colorado stood on the Senate floor and denounced the Swedish actress, calling her "one of the most powerful women on earth today—I regret to say, a powerful influence for evil." He then proposed a bill demanding the "licensing of actresses, producers and films by a division of the Department of Commerce." Just over two months later, Bergman and Rossellini were married on May 24, 1950.

On its release, *Stromboli* was Bergman's third consecutive commercial disaster. Though it received awards in Europe, American critics judged it banal. Rossellini railed against the American version which hinted at a happy ending. While he was off filming or spearfishing, Bergman grew restless, but Rossellini adamantly refused to allow her to work for any other director. In the fall of 1951, she began shooting his *Europa '51*. The American critics sniped once again, though *Europa '51* would become a favorite of young European filmmakers.

On November 10, 1950, nine days after an American divorce was granted, 12-year-old Pia Lindstrom arrived at the Federal Court in Los Angeles and became an American citizen; she also changed her name to Jenny Ann. Petter would not allow her to visit her mother in Italy for fear that she would be kidnapped by Rossellini. Bergman filed suit for visitation. In another court, Pia repudiated any need for her mother and said she preferred to stay with her father. Petter and Pia moved to Pittsburgh, and he remarried three years later. On June 18, 1952, Bergman gave birth to twin girls, Isabella and Isotta. But Rossellini was not husband material. Remarked actress ***Giulietta Masina**, "He was a man who was born to be alone."

That same summer, Rossellini directed Bergman in one of five segments of *We, the Women*, followed by *Journey to Italy. Journey* was another disappointment until rediscovered by filmmakers in 1958. *Fear*, made in Germany with her new husband, was also a financial flop. Finally, Rossellini allowed her to make a picture without him, loaning her out to his friend, an aging Jean Renoir, for *Elena et les Hommes* (*Paris Does Strange Things*) in 1956. It was her first hit in years.

Then Kay Brown, who was now working as an agent for ICM, rang up with a new movie for 20th Century-Fox. ***Anastasia** concerned the daughter of Nicholas and ***Alexandra** who was thought to have escaped the Russian death squad. Before casting Bergman, Fox took a poll of theater owners to make sure there might be an audience. Despite a lukewarm response, producer Darryl F. Zanuck and director Anatole Litvak insisted on her. When she told Rossellini that she was going to England to make a picture, he reacted in his usual way, said Bergman, "he threatened to drive the Ferrari into a tree." Though, in the past, his threats had frightened her, she was determined to do *Anastasia*. "I just didn't believe his suicide threat anymore."

Anastasia was Bergman's American rebirth. Though Ed Sullivan took a poll of viewers as to whether or not the American public was ready for her return, and the reviews were mixed, Bergman arrived in New York on January 19, 1957, to be feted by the New York Film Critic's for her performance. She was also nominated for and won an Academy Award for Best Actress, which Cary Grant accepted on her behalf on March 27.

That same year, Bergman met theatrical producer Lars Schmidt and was the hit of Paris in *Tea and Sympathy*. Though her career was once more on the ascendance, the same was not true for Roberto. As she stood on stage, reaping the cheers of the Parisian audience, he stood in the wings, furious. "They were standing up and screaming, standing up and applauding, and the 'bravos' never stopped." said Bergman, "Then I took my solo bow in the center of the stage, and as I bent over I turned my head and I looked at Roberto. Our eyes met. We looked straight at each other. I knew then my marriage was over."

While filming in India, Roberto made his own headlines on May 17, 1957, embroiled in a relationship with an upper-class married woman in India who also became pregnant. It was Bergman who smoothed things over with Prime Minister Nehru to allow Roberto to return to India and finish filming. She separated from her husband on November 7, 1957, and the marriage would be annulled in June 1958. More headlines followed when 19-year-old Pia met with her mother in July 1957 for the first time in years.

Bergman went on to shoot *Indiscreet* with Cary Grant in 1957, and portrayed the life of ***Gladys Aylward** in *Inn of the 6th Happiness* in 1958. She also married Lars Schmidt on December 21 of that year. He soon took over all her financial affairs, and they lived at Choisel, an hour outside of Paris. This marriage became one of convenience, and Bergman turned her attention to her career. On television, she appeared in Henry James' "The Turn of the Screw" (NBC, 1959), winning an Emmy for Best Dramatic Performance; she followed with "Hedda Gabler" in 1960. For film, she shot *The Visit*, *The Yellow Rolls Royce*, and **Françoise Sagan**'s *Aimez-vous Brahms?* In 1974, *Murder on the Orient Express* earned her an Academy Award for Best Supporting Actress.

On June 15, 1974, Bergman underwent a biopsy for a lump in her left breast. The tumor was malignant, and her left breast was removed. On Friday June 3, 1977, Roberto Rossellini died; the following day, Lars' mistress gave birth to a boy. Throughout, Bergman kept working. During the 1977 filming of Ingmar Bergman's *Autumn Sonata*, co-starring ***Liv Ullmann**, for which Bergman was nominated for her fifth Academy Award, she discovered another lump under her arm which necessitated the removal of her right breast.

In 1982, because she had never worked with heavy makeup, Bergman was reluctant at first to take on the role of ***Golda Meir** in the four-hour television miniseries "A Woman Called Golda" to be shot in Israel. Bergman demanded a screentest to be sure she could carry it off. By the time she had finished mental preparation for the role, however, little makeup was needed, though padding was necessary. Bergman was rapidly losing weight due to her illness and the effects of ongoing chemotherapy, and she had to overcome more than casting against type. Writes Leamer:

> Ingrid had to play Golda as a fortyish mother and as a nearly eighty-year-old grandmother dying of leukemia. That would have been challenge enough, but she had to play the role with a right arm that had become grotesquely swollen. When her right breast was removed, the lymph glands had been affected, and now large amounts of body fluid flowed into her arm. When she was not being filmed, she rested her arm on a telescoping stand that she called "the gun." At night she slept with her arm strapped above her head.

On August 29, 1982, after quietly observing her 67th birthday with a small circle of friends, Ingrid Bergman died sometime in the night. Her daughter Pia accepted a posthumous Emmy for her mother's work on *Golda*.

SOURCES:

Bergman, Ingrid, with Alan Burgess. *Ingrid Bergman: My Story.* NY: Delacorte, 1980.

Leamer, Laurence. *As Time Goes By: The Life of Ingrid Bergman.* NY: Harper & Row, 1986.

SUGGESTED READING:

Spoto, Donald. *Notorious: The Life of Ingrid Bergman.* NY: HarperCollins, 1997.

Bergman, Marilyn (1929—)

***American lyricist and songwriter whose collaboration with husband Alan produced lyrics for such films as* The Way We Were, Tootsie, *and* Yentl.** *Born Marilyn Keith on November 10, 1929, in New York, New York; daughter of Albert A. Katz (in the clothing business); graduated from High School of Music and Art in New York, 1945, and New York University; married Alan Bergman, on February 9, 1958; children: one daughter, Julie (b. 1960).*

Films include: Any Wednesday *(lyr., 1966);* Stop the World—I Want to Get Off *(add. material, 1966);* The Thomas Crown Affair *(lyr., 1968);* Gaily, Gaily *(song, 1969);* The Happy Ending *(song, 1969);* John and Mary *(song, 1969);* Doctors' Wives *(lyr., 1970);* Pieces of Dreams *(lyr., 1970);* The African Elephant *(lyr., 1970);* Le Mans *(lyr., 1970);* Sometimes a Great Notion *(lyr., 1970);* The Life and Times of Judge Roy Bean *(song, 1972);* Molly and Lawless John *(lyr., 1972);* Forty Carats *(lyr., 1973);* Breezy *(lyr., 1973);* The Way We Were *(lyr., 1973);* 99 and 44/100% Dead *(lyr., 1974);* Ode to Billy Joe *(lyr., 1975);* From Noon to Three *(lyr., 1976);* Harry and Walter Go to New York *(lyr., 1976);* A Star Is Born *(lyr., 1976);* The One and Only *(lyr., 1978);* Same Time Next Year *(lyr., 1978);* And Justice for All *(lyr., 1979);* The Promise *(lyr., 1979);* Starting Over *(lyr., 1979);* A Change of Seasons *(lyr., 1980);* Back Roads *(lyr., 1981);* Author! Author! *(lyr., 1982);* Best Friends *(score, 1982);* Tootsie *(lyr., 1982);* Yes, Giorgio *(lyr., 1982);* The Man Who Loved Women *(lyr., 1983);* Never Say Never Again *(lyr., 1983);* Yentl *(lyr., 1983);* Micki & Maude *(song, 1984);* Shy People *(song, 1987);* Big *(song, 1988);* The January Man *(lyr., 1988);* Major League *(lyr., 1989);* Shirley Valentine *(lyr., 1989);* Welcome Home *(song, 1989).*

In musical circles, Marilyn Bergman and her husband Alan are an anomaly. Whereas most song-writing partnerships produce words and music, the Bergmans collaborate primarily on lyrics. One of the most important wife-husband lyric-writing teams in the history of American popular music, the couple have been awarded Oscars, Emmys, and several Golden Globe Awards.

Born Marilyn Keith on November 10, 1929, Marilyn Bergman grew up in Brooklyn, New York, with dreams of becoming a concert pianist; she studied with private teachers and graduated from New York's High School of Music and Art, a school for gifted teens. For a brief period, she was a pre-med student at New York University before switching to English (creative writing) and psychology. A broken shoulder changed everything. While recuperating in California in the early 1950s at her parents' home, she was encouraged by a friend, lyricist Bob Russell, to fill the downtime writing songs. Her first effort was recorded by ***Peggy Lee**.

In 1953, Marilyn was introduced to Alan Bergman, who was writing special material for "Shower of Stars" and other primetime television shows. Soon, they were writing lyrics together. Their romance blossomed on a business trip to New York to consult with composer-publisher Frank Loesser. "It was the best thing Loesser ever did," Marilyn once commented, "maybe even better than *Guys and Dolls*." Success came in 1957 when they wrote the lyrics to a West Indian folk tune. Released by Norman Luboff as "Yellow Bird," it was later recorded by Arthur Lyman and Roger Williams, and has become a standard in the U.S. and abroad. One year later, the collaborators married.

By 1960, the year of their daughter Julie's birth, the Bergmans were working with various composers and tailoring their songs for individual performers and movies. Their first collaboration with composer Lew Spence produced "Nice and Easy" for Frank Sinatra and the title song to the film *The Marriage-Go-Round*, sung by Tony Bennett on the soundtrack. Again with Spence, they wrote "I Never Left Your Arms," "Sleep Warm," and "That Face" for a Fred Astaire television special.

The Bergmans made their Broadway debut with lyrics for the Sammy Fain short-lived musical *Something More*. Work in Hollywood was magical in comparison. The theme song "The Windmills of Your Mind," for *The Thomas Crown Affair* (1968), initiated a productive collaboration with Michel Legrand, who would become one of Hollywood's leading composers. "Windmills" went on to win an Oscar and a Golden Globe. Later collaborations with Legrand would yield the songs for the movie *Yentl* (1983), with the soundtrack under the direction of **Barbra Streisand** going platinum in 1985. The Bergmans and Legrand also won Oscars in 1984 for the overall score of *Yentl*, as well as its two lead songs, "The Way He Makes Me Feel" and "Papa Can You Hear Me?" "Incredible things happen," Legrand once said. "Their words say exactly what my music says—always."

Known for blending their poetry with the varying styles of their collaborators, the Bergmans display a rare versatility. Their long list of collaborating composers includes Henry Mancini and Maurice Jarre. With John Williams, they wrote "If We Were in Love" for Luciano Pavarotti's screen debut in *Yes, Giorgio* (1982). With composer Marvin Hamlisch, the Bergmans captured another Oscar, two Grammys, and a Golden Globe for the title song of *The Way We Were* (1973), which became Streisand's first gold single. They also worked with Hamlisch on "The Last Time I Felt Like This," for the movie *Same Time, Next Year* (1978), a song that became a hit duet for Johnny Mathis and **Jane Olivor**.

The Bergmans wrote theme songs for several hit television shows, including "Maude," "Good Times," and "The Sandy Duncan Show," all three in collaboration with Dave Grusin. In 1974, they won two Emmys for the score of *Queen of the Stardust Ballroom*, written with Billy Goldenburg. The score was later rewritten into a Broadway musical starring **Dorothy Loudon**. In 1976, they received Emmys for their songs for *Sybil*, with music by Leonard Rosenman.

The Bergmans write lyrics only after the music has been composed, explaining, "The composer needs the freedom to write the strongest possible melody to be a leitmotif for the spine of the score." If they are writing for a movie, they view the film in its entirety first, then work on isolated sequences. They describe themselves as "two potters passing the clay back and forth. At the end of the song, we rarely know who wrote what." The lyricists make their home in Los Angeles and are politically active in a number of liberal causes. In 1980, "A Tribute to Alan and Marilyn Bergman" was held at the Los Angeles Music Center and raised $150,000 for the American Civil Liberties Union.

Marilyn Bergman served on the board of directors of the American Society of Composers,

Authors and Publishers (ASCAP) starting in 1985; she was elected president in 1994 and re-elected for another two-year term in 1996.

Barbara Morgan, Melrose, Massachusetts

Bergmann, Gretel (b. 1914).

See Lambert, Margaret Bergmann.

Bergmann-Pohl, Sabine (1946—)

German political figure and last head of state of the German Democratic Republic. *Born Sabine Schulz on April 20, 1946, in Eisenach, Thuringia; trained as a physician, specialist in respiratory diseases; married twice.*

The last head of state of the German Democratic Republic (GDR), as it prepared for its merger with the German Federal Republic in 1990, was a woman who had been virtually unknown a year before even to expert observers of GDR political life. Born Sabine Schulz in Eisenach, Thuringia, on April 20, 1946, Sabine Bergmann-Pohl followed in her father's footsteps to study of medicine. By the late 1970s, she was practicing as a respiratory specialist in East Berlin, advancing to become director of that city's respiratory clinics. A practicing Lutheran, in 1981 she joined the Christian Democratic Union (CDU), a satellite political party controlled by the ruling Socialist Unity Party. Relatively little known to the public, she earned a reputation for competence in her medical area as well as in the field of social welfare.

The collapse of the Communist dictatorship in the fall of 1989 radically transformed GDR political life. An independent CDU now emerged and Sabine Bergmann-Pohl (the names derive from her two marriages) now became a major political figure in a society starved of free political expression for almost 60 years. In the March 1990 elections to the *Volkskammer* ("People's Chamber"), she made a strong showing, coming in second to the new prime minister, Lothar de Maziere. A month later, she was elected president of the *Volkskammer*. In effect, this made Bergmann-Pohl head of state of the German Democratic Republic, the only democratically elected one in its 40-year history. If only for a period of a few months, she would now serve as the first female head of state in modern German history. In June 1990, a half-century after the Holocaust, she and **Rita Süssmuth**, the president of the Bundestag of the Federal Republic of Germany, made an emotion-laden visit to Israel in which they both spoke of the need for reconciliation between the German and Jewish people.

After unification of the two German states was achieved in October 1990, Bergmann-Pohl entered the Bundestag, joining Federal Chancellor Helmut Kohl's cabinet as minister without portfolio. Although she was elected on the CDU list in December 1990 as a deputy from Berlin, some observers were surprised when she did not receive a post in Kohl's reshuffled cabinet, viewing it as a snub to the population of the former GDR. The post she *did* receive was a lesser one as state secretary in the Federal Ministry of Health. In 1991, Sabine Bergmann-Pohl published her memoirs, *Departure without Tears: A Look Back at the Year of Unity.*

SUGGESTED READING:

Bergmann-Pohl, Sabine. *Abschied ohne Tränen: Rückblick auf das Jahr der Einheit.* Berlin: Ullstein Verlag, 1991.

John Haag, Associate Professor, University of Georgia, Athens, Georgia

Bergner, Elisabeth (1897–1986)

Austrian-born actress of stage and screen who charmed and fascinated audiences in Europe for over 50 years with her androgynous persona and dramatic versatility. *Born Elisabeth (Ella) Ettel on August 22, 1897, in Drohobycz, Austrian Galicia (now Drogobych, Ukraine); died in London, England, on May 12, 1986; daughter of a merchant; family soon moved to Vienna with her and an older sister Lola and a younger brother Friedrich; married Paul Czinner (a producer-director), in 1933 (died 1972).*

Made stage debut in Innsbruck (1915); performed in Zurich (1916–18); after some time in Vienna, where she was a member of the Austrian Communist Party and served as liaison between its leadership and the imprisoned Béla Kun, moved to Berlin (1922), and became a star in the role of Rosalinde in Shakespeare's As You Like It; *played in her first motion picture,* Der Evangelimann; *began collaboration with Paul Czinner (1924); made more films and performed in plays of Shakespeare (*Merchant of Venice*), G.B. Shaw and W. Somerset Maugham; befriended German actor Hans Otto (1928), who was murdered by the Nazis (1933); wrote the screenplay for her film* The Dreaming Mouth *(1932); remained in England after moving there in late 1932; had successes on stage and screen; was a sensation as Gemma Jones in Margaret Kennedy's* Escape Me Never; *assisted émigrés with money and advice; with husband, came to U.S. (1940) under a cloud that took years to dissipate; had much less success in America than Britain, collaborating with*

Elisabeth Bergner

Bertolt Brecht and involved in exile politics (Council for a Democratic Germany); toured Germany and Israel (1949–50); returned to England (October 1950); gave performances in Berlin and Vienna (1954); elected member of Arts Academy of Berlin (1956); performed on stage and television in Germany, UK (1950s–1970s); performed last stage role but continued to make television films (1973); retrospective exhibitions in Berlin (1987) and Vienna (1993).

Filmography: Der Evangelimann *(Ger., 1923);* Nju (Husbands or Lovers, *Ger., 1924);* Der Geiger von Florenz (Impetuous Youth Liebe, *Ger., 1926);* Donna Juana *(Ger., 1927),* Köulein Luise *(Queen Louise, Ger., 1927);* Fräulein Else *(Miss Else, Ger., 1929);* Ariane (The Loves of Ariane, *1931);* Derträumende Mund (Dreaming Lips, *Ger., 1932);* Catherine the Great *(U.K., 1934);* Escape Me Never *(U.K., 1935);* As You Like It *(U.K., 1936);* Dreaming Lips *(U.K., 1937);* Stolen Life *(U.K., 1939);* Paris Calling *(U.S., 1942);* Die Glückliche Jahre der Thorwalds *(Ger., 1962);* Strogoff (Courier to the Czar, *Ger., 1968);* Cry of the Banshee *(U.K., 1970); (cameo)* Der Fussgänger (The Pedestrian, *Ger., 1974);* Der Pfingstausflug *(Ger., 1978);* Feine Gesellschaft *(Ger., 1982).*

From 1923 to 1933, "die Bergner" ruled the German stage and screen, but her career was indelibly marked by the upheavals of the 20th century, especially Nazism. She was born Elisabeth (Ella) Ettel on August 22, 1897, in Drohobycz, Austrian Galicia (modern-day Drogobych, Ukraine), into a Jewish family that had assimilated German language and culture. Soon after her birth her father, a merchant, changed the family name to the more Germanic-sounding Bergner. The family moved to Vienna when Elisabeth was a small child. She grew up in the Leopoldstadt, the Austrian capital's predominantly Jewish district. In 1907, Elisabeth, her sister Theodora (Lola) and her brother Friedrich began tutoring with Jacob Levy Moreno (1889–1974), the well-known founder of group psychology and psychodrama who became a lifelong friend.

The little girl showed a great interest in acting and in 1911 was enrolled at a private acting school. In 1912, she began attending classes at the Academy for Music and Performing Art. One of her teachers, Stefan Hock (1877–1947), instilled a deep respect for the great German classics. Bergner always remained close to him, assisting him financially when he arrived in London as an impoverished refugee in the 1930s. At the beginning of her acting career, her friends included the young writer Albert Ehrenstein and the artist Oskar Kokoschka. In October 1915, her first professional stage appearance took place in Innsbruck, and by December of that year she had appeared in the role of Nora in Ibsen's *A Doll's House*. An offer from the Municipal Theater of Zurich, Switzerland, followed.

During World War I, Zurich was a center of intellectual and political ferment, and many new ideas emerged out of its atmosphere of intense cultural experimentation and political nonconformity. The vivacious young actress counted the leaders of the Dada movement as friends as well as ***Else Lasker-Schüler**, Yvan and **Claire Goll**, Franz Werfel, Frank Wedekind, Wilhelm Lehmbruck and Alexander Moissi. Alfred Reucker, director of the Zurich theater, presented a brilliant *Hamlet* in which Bergner was Ophelia and Alexander Moissi played Hamlet. Moissi, a celebrated Albanian-born actor, fell fervently in love with Bergner, but she ignored his overtures.

Bergner was involved with the expressionist sculptor Wilhelm Lehmbruck (1881–1919), for whom she had modeled. The gifted but unbalanced Lehmbruck, who gave her the name "Marja," was convinced that Bergner's purity could save him from catastrophe. Infected with venereal disease through contact with a prostitute, he implored her to make love with him, casting her in the role of Ottegebe, the virginal maiden who cures the sick knight of his affliction in Gerhart Hauptmann's play *Der arme Heinrich*. Unwilling to make this sacrifice, Elisabeth deepened her relationship with Albert Ehrenstein and soon moved to Berlin and Vienna to accept major roles. In Vienna, she received a desperate telegraph from Lehmbruck: "Marja, if you want to rescue me, come back!" She did not answer. Two days later, she read in the papers that Lehmbruck committed suicide in Berlin on March 25, 1919. Beside herself with grief and guilt, Bergner sought help from the psychologist Alfred Adler and over a period of time overcame this crisis. In the fall of 1919, she performed brilliantly in several of Frank Wedekind's plays exploring female sexuality, including *Earth Spirit* and *Pandora's Box* (***Louise Brooks** would play the lead in the movie).

The period between the two world wars was unstable and chaotic in Central Europe. Austria had shrunk almost overnight from a great multinational state to a tiny landlocked republic unable to feed itself and at the mercy of its hostile neighbors. While the Habsburg monarchy was dissolved, revolution had swept away tsarist rule in the Russian Empire. Although Bergner's knowledge of Marxist ideology was sketchy at best, she sympathized with the poor and oppressed, desiring a world free of war and exploitation. Her decision to join the militant Austrian Communist Party was typical of youth of the period. She became involved in the Hungarian revolution led by Béla Kun in 1919, serving as a courier between Austrian Communist leaders and Kun for several months. This period represented the height of Bergner's political involvement, though throughout her life she remained sympathetic to the persecuted and oppressed.

Bergner suffered several periods of depression at the beginning of her career. In June 1918, she spent time in a sanitarium because of ex-

From the movie Catherine the Great, *starring Elisabeth Bergner and Flora Robson.*

haustion. After seeking Adler's help over Lehmbruck's suicide in 1919, she received psychiatric treatment the following April and May at the Steinhof facility near Vienna. She resumed her acting career, appearing in the role of August Strindberg's *Miss Julie* at Vienna's Burgtheater. In 1921, she impressed Munich critics with her performance in the local premiere of Hugo von Hofmannsthal's *Der Schwierige*. That same year, she also made a guest appearance in Berlin with Conrad Veidt and Alexander Granach. Encouraged by these successes, Bergner moved permanently to Berlin in 1922 where she had a starring role in Arnolt Bronnen's expressionistic play *Vatermord* and performed at Max Reinhardt's Deutsches Theater as well.

With her disheveled chestnut-red locks, the huge dark pensive eyes and the touchingly tiny shoulders, which always appear to be held up in anxious anticipation, [Bergner] has the charm of a helpless and extremely disquieting small girl.

—Tilly Wedekind

Stardom came in 1923 when Bergner appeared as Rosalinde in Shakespeare's *As You Like It*. Directed by Victor Baranowsky, this production at Berlin's Lessing Theater made Elisabeth Bergner the toast of Berlin. An overnight sensation in her mid-20s, she was now a theater personality equal to ***Tilla Durieux**. The celebrated actor Fritz Kortner declared that "all of Berlin is in love with her" while the journalist Kurt Tucholsky wrote in *Die Weltbühne*: "Bergner! Bergner! acclaimed the gallery. And we who were present nodded our heads and wished her nothing but the best. Praying that God preserves her as she is, so young, so beautiful, so gracious. And that she never is involved with films." Tucholsky's concern that Bergner's gift might be wasted in films did not prevent her from accepting a small role that same year in *Der Evangelimann*, a silent film based on the opera by Wilhelm Kienzl.

By 1924, Bergner was established enough that George Bernard Shaw insisted Max Reinhardt give her the starring role in his play *St. Joan*. That same year, she began a crucial collaboration with Paul Czinner (1890–1972), appearing in a film directed by him, *Nju, A Tragicomedy of Daily Life*. From 1924 until 1938, Czinner would be responsible for the screenplays and direction of all her motion pictures, though she would not marry him until 1933. Bergner's financial independence now enabled her to purchase a house in the exclusive Dahlem section of Berlin. Berlin was a heady place in the 1920s, and the popular actress threw herself enthusiastically into its stimulating cultural milieu.

Elisabeth Bergner's appearance was novel, provocative, and disturbing. Slight, with bent shoulders, she was, in the words of Sir John Gielgud, "an eager, mischievous, elfin figure with pathos beneath her childish charm." Her film roles in the 1920s emphasized her youthful appearance. In his analysis of Bergner's starring role in the 1926 film *The Violinist of Florence*, film historian Siegfried Kracauer argued that by dressing in boy's clothing and appearing to be "half lad, half girl," she created an androgynous character who was immensely appealing to millions of Germans. In her later film roles, including *Miss Else* (1929) and *The Loves of Ariane* (1931), Bergner would evolve into a child-woman, fragile, complex and enigmatic. Under the inspired direction of Max Reinhardt, her talents flourished in portrayals of Shakespearean heroines. She played 560 consecutive performances of Rosalind, her favorite role, in *As You Like It*, breaking all records for Shakespearean runs in the German capital. Wearing a tiny, cone-shaped hunter's hat, a velvet cape draped across a shoulder in a cavalier fashion, and boldly swinging a sword, Bergner projected youthful bravado night after night to thousands of theatergoers enchanted by this girl disguised as a boy.

In 1924, Bergner began her film career with Czinner's movie *Nju*. He used the intimate setting, dim lighting, and subtle gestures of the *Kammerspiele*, a form of theater that brought out the best in the actress. In *The Violinist of Florence*, Elisabeth Bergner held her violin so delicately that she conjured up a magical moment, while gliding across the drawing room as in a dream. By the late 1920s, she was a superstar in the German entertainment world. Her theater appearances were invariably sold out, and her films were box-office successes. In July 1927, she traveled to Spain, appearing in the film *Doña Juana*. The last years of the decade were particularly productive for her. In 1928–29, she starred in her most successful silent film, *Miss Else*. Stardom brought new friendships. In 1928, she became acquainted with the splendid actor Hans Otto (1900–1933), a committed artist, active Communist, and a passionate anti-Nazi. Bergner's involvement with Otto deepened her political consciousness as she became increasingly aware of the Fascist danger in Germany. While filming *Miss Else*, she met the actor Paul Morgan, who was also Jewish and concerned about the growing threat of anti-Semitism. Otto and Morgan would both be killed by the Nazis. In November 1929, Bergner appeared in a German version of Eugene O'Neill's *Strange Interlude*, ensuring that O'Neill's plays would be a staple of the German-language theater.

The New York stock market crash in October 1929 had profound economic and political consequences in Europe. Political violence followed massive unemployment. In September 1930, Adolf Hitler's National Socialists won an overwhelming victory transforming the German Reichstag, a parliament that had become incapable of governing. As democracy died in Germany and Central Europe, Jewish artists like Elisabeth Bergner were suddenly at risk. She and Czinner found it prudent to work in the English-speaking world, preparing for political catastrophe in Germany. Her first sound film, *Ariane*, produced in 1930–31, also appeared in an English-language version entitled *The Loves of Ariane*. By 1932, Nazi storm troopers routinely beat their political foes to death. Jewish artists like Bergner were warned by their "Aryan" colleagues to leave Germany. In late 1932, her costar Werner Krauss told her, "Elisabeth, Elisabeth, what I have to tell you makes me gag: They no longer want you to remain here." On November 11, 1932, she and Krauss appeared together in a benefit performance of Gerhart Hauptmann's *The Flight of Gabriel Schilling*, one of her last performances in Berlin.

Even before Adolf Hitler was appointed chancellor of Germany on January 30, 1933, Czinner and Bergner had fled to London and were married there on January 9. Although her knowledge of English was adequate, Bergner worked to perfect her mastery of the language, signing up for lessons with the noted language teacher **Florence "Flossie" Freedman**. Her reputation as well as her husband's contacts opened doors, and, by late November 1933, Bergner appeared in the starring role of Gemma Jones in *Escape Me Never*, a play by the novelist ***Margaret Kennedy**. On the first night at the Opera House in Manchester, Bergner was so nervous that the director had to push her onto the stage for her first entrance. But all went well, and *Escape Me Never* was an unqualified success when it reached London. Almost overnight, she became the darling of the British; no foreign-born actress except ***Sarah Bernhardt** had been so popular. Bergner took *Escape Me Never* to New York in 1935 where it was highly acclaimed. A successful film version the same year resulted in a nomination for an Academy Award.

Success abroad did not negate grim news from home. In late November 1933, her close friend Hans Otto was tortured and thrown to his death from the Berlin police station as a warning to all intellectuals and "reds" who opposed the Third Reich. Fearing for friends and family, she sent money to help them escape. As a successful actress, her income gave her ample resources to aid those in need. The film version of Shakespeare's *As You Like It*, starring Bergner and Laurence Olivier, premiered in New York in November 1936. Both actors received excellent reviews. Alexander Woolcott asserted that Bergner was "probably the ablest actress living today," and some critics suggested that she would soon challenge ***Greta Garbo**. In 1936 in London, Bergner appeared in James M. Barrie's *The Boy David*. Although the play was not critically well received, it delighted its playwright, the famous author of *Peter Pan*. The aging Barrie became infatuated with the beautiful actress and left her $10,000 in his will for "the best performance ever given in any play of mine."

In 1937, Elisabeth Bergner completed a British remake of her German hit *Dreaming Lips*. In July 1938 as war loomed, she and Czinner became British citizens. That same year, she appeared in *Stolen Life*, her first film not directed by her husband. Her appearance as St. Joan at the Malvern Festival in 1938 caused an awkward moment for the actress. She cut the famous "Bells" speech in the play without realizing that George Bernard Shaw was in the audience that afternoon. An infuriated Shaw threw the book at her after the performance, but she gave him back as good as she got.

Bergner's mother and sister escaped the Nazis' clutches, arriving in London before Germany attacked Poland on September 1, 1939. In 1940, Bergner starred in *49th Parallel*, a film about six survivors of a Nazi submarine who try to escape from Canada to a still-neutral United States. With excellent acting by Leslie Howard, Raymond Massey, Laurence Olivier, Eric Portman, and Anton Walbrook, *49th Parallel* was one of the best Allied propaganda films of World War II. Bergner played Anna, an unsophisticated German-speaking Hutterite girl living on a farm near Winnipeg. She learned Hutterite customs and dialect living at one of their colonies located at Elie, Manitoba, 30 miles west of Winnipeg. During a lull in the shooting, Bergner lit a cigarette and took a few puffs before an irate Hutterite woman snatched the offending item from her lips. Hutterite women did not smoke. Although the *49th Parallel* conveyed a powerful anti-Nazi message, Bergner did not complete her role. Instead, she defected to the United States with no forewarning. Director John Powell saved the film, which went on to become a commercial success, by replacing Bergner with the talented British actress **Glynis Johns**. Bergner can still be seen in the long shots, which were retained in the final version of the film, released in the United States under the title *The Invaders*.

When the British public learned of Bergner's defection, they were outraged. The discovery that she had sewn jewelry into her clothing made them angrier still. Standing alone against the Nazi threat, the British did not take kindly to an act they regarded as cowardice. Few among them, however, could have known the panic which had enveloped Bergner and her husband. As Jews, they knew only too well the fate which awaited them if Nazi armies successfully crossed the Channel. Before the U.S. entered the war in 1941, the Nazi invasion was a very real possibility. The Czinners fled not because they had lost faith in Britain's will to fight, but because of pure terror, an intelligent analysis in light of what was learned later of the fate of six million Jews.

In America, Bergner was faced with beginning anew for the third time. Her husband immediately began working in Hollywood, but roles were difficult for her to procure. It was not until the final months of 1941 that she received a starring role in an anti-Nazi film called *Paris Calling*. A lugubrious and unconvincing motion picture, *Paris Calling* was Bergner's only appearance on the American screen. She returned to the stage, touring in *Escape Me Never*, and scored a major Broadway success in *The Two Mrs. Carrolls*, a thriller which was performed more than 300 times in 1943–44. This triumph earned her the Delia Austrian Medal of the Drama League of New York. As the tide of war changed in favor of the Allies in 1943, Bergner deepened her contacts with leftist exile circles. She and her husband provided funding for the famous German exile playwright Bertolt Brecht who crafted a modern version of John Webster's 17th-century play *The Duchess of Malfi*. There were many difficulties in this project, including the firing of one of the initial collaborators and his replacement by the poet W.H. Auden. By the time the play finally premiered in October 1946, it had become essentially a Brecht-Bergner collaboration. Unfortunately, the critics were savage in their reception of the play. Bergner continued to be involved in émigré political life, appearing as a signer of the declaration of principles of the Council for a Democratic Germany. This document cautioned against a policy of harsh punishment based on the notion of collective guilt and called for thoroughgoing social reforms in Germany.

The postwar years were difficult for Bergner and her husband. No longer young, she was cast infrequently. Her appearance in *The Cup of Trembling*, a study of alcoholism, in 1948 was one of the few times she appeared on stage after the war. Cold War tensions and McCarthyism in the late 1940s forced Bergner to consider leaving the United States. A religious crisis led her to become a Christian Scientist in 1949. In November of that same year, she toured Israel and Germany. In October 1950, the Czinners returned to London. Her defection, however, was not easily forgiven by older Britains while the younger generation had simply never heard of this aging actress with a German accent. Doggedly, she worked at reestablishing her reputation, and, by 1954, she was professionally and emotionally ready to return to the German stage. In March 1954, she appeared in a German production of Terence Rattigan's *The Deep Blue Sea* in West Berlin. Highly acclaimed by critics and audiences alike, she reestablished herself as one of the leading actresses in German theater. By October 1954, she was "back home," appearing in a guest role at Vienna's Theater in der Josefstadt.

From this point forward, Bergner received many major roles in Germany, Austria, and Britain. By the 1960s, the British had forgiven her, and she appeared in starring roles in a number of distinguished television films. Honors also came in profusion, including the Friedrich Schiller Prize of the City of Mannheim in

Johns, Glynis (1923—)

English actress. *Born on October 5, 1923, in Durban, South Africa; daughter of Mervyn Johns (an actor) and Alys Steele.*

In 1935, 12-year-old Glynis Johns made her London stage debut; three years later, she appeared in her first film, *South Riding*. The lady with the gravel-voice and a flair for comedy won a Tony award for her performance in Stephen Sondheim's Broadway musical *A Little Night Music*. She was also nominated for an Oscar as Best Supporting Actress in *The Sundowners* (1960). Her films include *Around the World in 80 Days* (1956), *All Mine to Give* (1958), *Shake Hands with the Devil* (1959), *The Cabinet of Caligari* (1962), *Papa's Delicate Condition* (1962), *Mary Poppins* (1964), *Under Milkwood* (1971), and *Zell and Me* (1988). When her father remarried in 1976, her stepmother was actress **Diana Churchill** (b. 1913).

1962—the first time an actress had been awarded that coveted distinction. In 1973, Bergner appeared on stage for the last time, in London's Greenwich Theater in a production of Istvan Örkeny's *Catsplay*, though she continued to work in films for almost another decade. Her memoirs, written entirely by herself and subtitled *Elisabeth Bergner's disorderly memories*, appeared in Germany in 1978, receiving positive reviews. In 1980, her native Austria awarded her the "Cross of Merit for Science and Art." The Eleonora Duse Prize and a 1983 Berlin Film Festival retrospective dedicated to actors and actresses exiled by the Nazi regime followed. Ill with cancer in 1985, she visited East Berlin to receive honorary membership in the Deutsches Theater and the Hans Otto Medal of the German Democratic Republic, named for her friend. In April 1985, she gave a moving account of her life on an Austrian radio interview.

Full of years and honors, the 88-year-old Elisabeth Bergner died in her London home, 42 Eaton Square, on May 12, 1986. Hers had been a long life, rich in achievements and upheaval. Said her friend Sir John Gielgud: She was "an amazingly original and enigmatic personality of enormous fascination; I am very proud to have known her and to have counted myself among her friends."

SOURCES:

Belach, Helga, ed. *Elisabeth Bergner*. Berlin: Stiftung Deutsche Kinemathek, 1983.

Belloc, Mrs. Lowndes. "A New Queen of the Stage," in *New York Herald-Tribune* magazine section. November 25, 1934, pp. 14–15.

Bergner, Elisabeth. *Bewundert viel und viel gescholten . . . Elisabeth Bergners unordentliche Erinnerungen*. Munich: C. Bertelsmann Verlag, 1978.

Bolbecher, Siglinde, and Konstantin Kaiser. . . . *Unsere schwarze Rose Elisabeth Bergner*. Vienna: Historisches Museum der Stadt Wien, 1993.

Danischewsky, Monja. *White Russian—Red Face*. London: Gollancz, 1966.

Eisner, Lotte H. *The Haunted Screen: Expressionism in the German Cinema and the Influence of Max Reinhardt*. Berkeley: University of California Press, 1969.

"Elisabeth Bergner, Heroine of the German Theater Who Fled Nazism," in *The Times* [London]. May 13, 1986, p. 14.

"Elisabeth Bergner, an Actress in Plays and Films, Dies at 85 [sic]," in *The New York Times Biographical Service*. May 1986, p. 627.

Eloesser, Arthur. *Elisabeth Bergner*. Berlin: Williams, 1927.

"Ernest Betts on the New Films. Garbo's Biggest Rival is Bergner," in *Sunday Express* [London]. April 4, 1935.

Feld, Hans. "Jews in the Development of the German Film Industry—Notes from the Recollections of a Berlin Film Critic," in *Leo Baeck Institute Year Book XVII*. London: Secker & Warburg, 1982, pp. 337–365.

Gielgud, Sir John. "Elisabeth Bergner," in *The Times* [London]. May 19, 1986, p. 14.

Gough-Yates, Kevin. "Jews and Exiles in British Cinema," in *Leo Baeck Institute Year Book XXXVII*. London: Secker & Warburg, 1992, pp. 517–541.

Heilbut, Anthony. *Exiled in Paradise: German Refugee Artists and Intellectuals in America from the 1930s to the Present*. Boston, MA: Beacon Press, 1983.

Kracauer, Siegfried. *From Caligari to Hitler: A Psychological History of the German Film*. Princeton, NJ: Princeton University Press, 1947.

Lyon, James K. *Bertolt Brecht in America*. Princeton, NJ: Princeton University Press, 1980.

Petro, Patrice. *Joyless Streets: Women and Melodramatic Representation in Weimar Germany*. Princeton, NJ: Princeton University Press, 1989.

Riess, Curt. *Das Gab's nur Einmal: Das Buch der schönsten Filme unseres Lebens*. 2nd ed. Hamburg: Verlag der Sternbücher, 1952.

Völker, Klaus. *Elisabeth Bergner: Das Leben einer Schauspielerin*. Berlin: Edition Hentrich, 1990.

Wünsche, Dagmar. *Elisabeth Bergner: Dokumente ihres Lebens/ Ausstellungsverzeichnis*. Berlin: Akademie der Künste, 1990.

Zuckmayer, Carl. *A Part of Myself*. Translated by Richard and **Clara Winston**. NY: Carroll & Graf, 1984.

John Haag, Associate Professor,
University of Georgia, Athens, Georgia

Bergroth, Kersti (b. 1886)

Finnish dramatist, novelist, and critic. *Born in Karelia, Finland, in 1886.*

Best known for her rustic comedies portraying life in Karelia, Kersti Bergroth also wrote five novels, including *Kiirashnli* (1922) and *Balaisuntemme* (1955), and a series of books for young girls. During the 1920s and the 1930s, she was the editor of two Finnish avant-garde literary magazines which had a great influence on cultural life. Although she lived in Rome for a prolonged period, she continued to contribute anecdotes and stories to Finnish papers.

Berkeley, Elizabeth (fl. 1390–1410)

English royal. *Name variations: Elizabeth Beauchamp. Flourished between 1390 and 1410; daughter of Thomas Berkeley, viscount L'Isle, and Margaret Warren; married Richard Beauchamp, 5th earl of Warwick; children: Margaret Beauchamp (who married John Talbot, earl of Shrewsbury);* ****Eleanor Beauchamp*** *(1408–1468);* ****Elizabeth Beauchamp*** *(d. 1480).*

Berkeley, Elizabeth (fl. 1408–1417).

See Fitzalan, Elizabeth.

Berlioz, Madame (1800–1854).

See Smithson, Harriet Constance.

Bernadette of Lourdes (1844–1879)

French nun and saint. *Name variations: Bernadette Soubirous. Born Bernadette Soubirous in Lourdes in the French Pyrenees on January 7, 1844; died in 1879; daughter of François and Louise (Casterot) Soubirous.*

Born into a poor family, Bernadette Soubirous was placed into domestic service from the age of 12 to 14, until she returned home to prepare for her first Communion. On February 11, 1858, at age 14, she claimed that the Virgin Mary appeared in the crevasse of a rock on the bank of the Gave as she was collecting firewood with her sister and a friend. From then until July 16th, the Virgin reappeared 18 times; it was said she imparted miraculous powers of healing to the waters of a spring near a grotto and entered into conversations with the young girl: "I promise to make you happy, if not in this world, at least in the next," was imparted on February 18 and "I am the Immaculate Conception" on March 25.

The visions were declared authentic by the Roman Catholic Church, and the Lourdes grotto became a shrine for pilgrims. In 1866, Bernadette joined the Sisters of Charity, a group of women bound by annual vows to religious and charitable work, at Nevers, France, and nursed the wounded in the Franco-Prussian war (1870–71). In 1877, she became a nun. Bernadette was beatified in 1925 and canonized in 1933. Her feast day is on April 16.

The Song of Bernadette, a film based on the novel of the same name by Franz Werfel, starred ***Jennifer Jones** (who won an Academy Award for Best Actress in the role) and ***Anne Revere**. Produced by 20th Century-Fox in 1943, the film was a major box-office success and was nominated for Best Movie of the Year.

Bernadotte, Mother (1905–1935).

See Mathews, Ann Teresa.

Bernadotte, Astrid (1905–1935).

See Astrid of Sweden.

Bernadotte, Bridget (b. 1937).

See Birgitta of Sweden.

Bernadotte, Christina (b. 1943).

See Christina Bernadotte.

Bernadotte, Desiree (b. 1938).

See Desiree Bernadotte.

Bernadotte, Ingeborg (1878–1958).

See Ingeborg of Denmark.

Bernadotte, Louise (1851–1926).
See Louise of Sweden.

Bernadotte, Madeleine (b. 1982).
See Madeleine Bernadotte.

Bernadotte, Margaret (b. 1934).
See Margaret Bernadotte.

Bernadotte, Margaretha (1899–1977).
See Margaretha of Sweden.

Bernadotte, Martha (1901–1954).
See Martha of Sweden.

Bernadotte, Victoria (b. 1977).
See Victoria Bernadotte.

Bernár, Nina Annenkova (1859/64–1933).
See Annenkova-Bernár, Nina.

Bernard, Catherine (1662–1712)

French novelist. *Born in 1662 in Rouen, France; died in 1712 in Paris; never married; no children.*

A well-educated, probably wealthy woman, Catherine Bernard moved to Paris at age 17. She made her way into the elite of Parisian society, where her imaginative stories found a receptive, intellectual audience. Bernard supported herself well through her writing, probably from commissions from well-to-do literary patrons. She never married but dedicated herself to producing plays, novels, short stories, and fairy tales, a genre much in vogue at the time. All of her works centered on the theme of love, both happy and tragic. Among her more popular works were *The Misfortunes of Love* (1687) and *Ines of Cordoba* (1696). Although her works were often realistic in their portrayal of love relationships in her society, Bernard sometimes interwove her fairy tales into a novel's central plot. Catherine Bernard died about age 50.

Laura York, Anza, California

Bernard, Jessie (1903–1996)

American sociologist. *Born Jessie Ravitch in Minneapolis, Minnesota, in 1903; daughter of Rumanian-Jewish parents who were immigrant shopkeepers; died in Washington on October 6, 1996; attended the University of Minnesota; awarded Ph.D. from Washington University, 1935; married Luther Lee Bernard (died 1951); children: three.*

At the advent of the feminist movement in 1963, Jessie Bernard was a 60-year-old widowed professor at Penn State, one year away from retirement. Over the next 16 years, she published a list of books that earned her a reputation as the foremost scholar of the women's movement. *Academic Women* (1964), a work exploring the marginal position of women in academic life, was derived from her own experiences. She followed that with *The Sex Game* (1968), *The Future of Marriage* (1972), *The Future of Motherhood* (1974), *Women, Wives, Mothers* (1975), and *The Female World* (1980). Bernard had lived a conventional life, marrying her childhood sweetheart Luther Lee Bernard, relocating from town to town while following his career. Though the couple co-authored *Sociology and the Study of International Relations* (1934) and *Origins of American Sociology* (1943), Jessie Bernard was in her 40s, her children grown, before she began earnestly seeking her own academic career, moving to Pennsylvania State University in 1949. In 1978, Bernard also wrote the autobiographical *Self Portrait of a Family.*

Bernardino, Minerva (1907–1998)

Dominican Republic feminist who was a major player in the founding of the UN Commission on the Status of Women. *Born in Seibo, the Dominican Republic, in 1907; died on August 29, 1998, in the Dominican Republic, age 91; daughter of Alvaro and Altagracia Bernardino.*

Awards: honored as the "Woman of the Americas" and awarded the Pan American Union's Bolivar and San Martin medal (1948); granted the Hispanic Heritage Award for excellence in education.

A pioneer among Latin American feminists, Minerva Bernardino was the predominant force in founding the United Nations Commission on the Status of Women. In 1997, Secretary General Kofi Annan noted that the commission was "to an important extent" Bernardino's "creation."

Granddaughter of a provincial governor and eldest child in a family of four girls and three boys, Minerva Bernardino was born in Seibo, in the Dominican Republic. She came from an unconventional family, receptive to the notion of women's rights. "My mother was very progressive," she once told **Ann Foster** of the *Christian Science Monitor*, "and I was reared in an atmosphere that was, at that time, most unusual in my country." Her father evidently shared her mother's views. When Bernardino complained of the social strictures on women and travel, he replied, "Go out if you like, travel if you want, and let criticize who will."

Orphaned at 15, Bernardino, along with her eldest brother, became the chief support of her sib-

Opposite page

Publicity for the movie The Song of Bernadette, *based on the life of Bernadette of Lourdes.*

Minerva Bernardino

lings. "We both believed in equality from the beginning," she told Foster, "and were determined that he should go in for law, that my sister should do as she also wished, and become a doctor, and that I should enter public life." While earning a bachelor of science degree, she pursued a career in the civil service, eventually becoming head of the file office of the Dominican Republic's Department of Development and Communications in 1926, chief of a section of the Department of Agriculture in 1928, and chief of the statistics section of the Department of Education from 1931 to 1933. By 1929, she was also a leader in Acción Feminista Dominica, a women's rights organization credited for successfully leading the battle to insert suffrage and civil rights for Dominican women into the amended Constitution of 1942.

In 1933, Bernardino was appointed Dominican delegate to the Inter-American Commission of Women to be held in Montevideo, the first such body formed to advance the rights of women. The group, sponsored by the Organization of American States, was to convene every five years. By 1938, when the commission met at Lima, Bernardino was its rapporteur. In autumn 1939, when **Ana Rosa de Martinez Guerrero** of Argentina was elected chair, Bernardino was chosen vice chair.

During World War II, in November 1943, Bernardino effectively presented a resolution urging the women of Chile and Argentina to press their governments to "sever diplomatic relations with aggressor nations" (Germany, Italy, and Japan). But siding with the Allies was unpopular with the government of Argentina. When Martinez Guerrero's Argentine organization, the Junta de la Victoria, comprised of 50,000 women, raised funds for the Allies, it was disbanded, and the Argentine government replaced Martinez Guerrero as a delegate to the Inter-American Commission with **Angelina Fuselli**. On November 3, 1943, Bernardino was elected chair to fill the vacancy; she held that office for the next six years.

In 1945, Bernardino was one of only four women seated at the Inter-American Conference on Problems of War and Peace which convened at Chapultepec, Mexico, and the only woman with the power to vote. The Act of Chapultepec pledged joint action by all American republics against aggression directed at any member nation.

That same year, Bernardino attended the founding conference for the United Nations in San Francisco and was one of only four women to sign the United Nations Charter. It was Bernardino, along with ***Bodil Begtrup** of Denmark and ***Berta Lutz** of Brazil, who demanded the document contain the phrase "to ensure respect for human rights and fundamental freedoms without discrimination against race, sex, condition, or creed." In 1946, Bernardino teamed with ***Eleanor Roosevelt** and three other delegates to the first United Nations General Assembly—**Jean McKenzie** of New Zealand, **Evdokia Uralova** of the Soviet Union, and ***Ellen Wilkinson** of Great Britain—to write an "Open Letter to the Women of the World," urging them to take a more active role in politics and government.

In January 1950, Bernardino was appointed her country's Minister Plenipotentiary to the United Nations, a post that put her only one step below Dominican ambassadors throughout the world. Even so, she opposed the dictatorship of Rafael Trujillo and, at one point, went into self-imposed exile to draw attention to her views.

"Bernardino spoke up for women in the aftermath of World War II," said **Kristen Timothy,** deputy director of the UN Division for the Advancement of Women, "understanding that [postwar] life for women would never be the same." The Minerva Bernardino Foundation in Santo Domingo was formed to continue her mission, to highlight the contributions of women to society, and to "train female leaders for the coming millenium."

SOURCES:

Crossette, Barbara. "Minerva Bernardino, 91, Dominican Feminist," in *The New York Times*. September 4, 1998.

Rothe, Anna, ed. *Current Biography*. NY: H.W. Wilson, 1950.

Bernauer, Agnes (d. 1435)

Bavarian who was condemned for witchcraft. *Birth date unknown; drowned in 1435; daughter of an Augsburg baker; secretly married Albert (1401–1460, son of Ernest, duke of Bavaria-Munich), about 1432.*

Agnes Bernauer, daughter of an Augsburg baker, secretly married Albert, son of Ernest, the duke of Bavaria-Munich, around 1432. Ignorant of this fact, the duke urged his son to marry and reproached him for his relationship with Agnes. Albert then declared Bernauer was his lawful wife. While Albert was away, Bernauer was seized by order of her father-in-law and condemned to death for witchcraft. On October 12, 1435, she was drowned in the Danube near Straubing, where her remains were buried by Albert. Her story, which lived long in the memory of the people, afforded material for several German dramas. Adolf Böttger, Friedrich Hebbel, and Otto Ludwig have each written works entitled *Agnes Bernauer*.

Bernays, Marie (1883–1939)

German Jewish social worker. *Born in Munich, Germany, in 1883; died in a monastery in 1939.*

Active member of the Deutsche Volkspartei; founded a school of social work in Mannheim (1919), serving as its director (1919–32); after the Nazi takeover, converted to Roman Catholicism.

From the mid-19th century until the Nazi takeover in 1933, Germany's Jewish population participated actively not only in the intellectual and cultural life of the country but also in its politics. While many were drawn to the Social Democratic and liberal parties because of their strong rejection of anti-Semitism, a smaller number of Jews were members of the major parties on the Right. A new conservative party that emerged after the German defeat of 1918 was the *Deutsche Volkspartei* (DVP), the German People's Party. Founded by the rising political star Gustav Stresemann, the DVP was strongly nationalistic but rejected anti-Semitism. During World War I, Stresemann had briefly appeared to be making concessions to the growing mood of anti-Semitism when he backed the idea of a census of Jews in the armed forces, a measure meant to "expose" Jewish lack of patriotic zeal. But when it became clear by the end of the war that the willingness of German Jews to die for the Fatherland was as strong as Germans of other faiths (12,000 Jews gave their lives in combat), Stresemann's new party strongly condemned anti-Semitic innuendos.

Among the Jewish members of the DVP was Marie Bernays, an exceptional personality during the brief flowering of German democracy known as the Weimar Republic. Bernays was born into a family that had converted to Protestantism and emphasized German cultural ideals. Her father taught the history of literature at the University of Munich. She chose a career in social work and together with **Elisabeth Altmann-Gottheimer** founded the School of Women's Social Work in Mannheim, serving as its director from 1919 to 1932. As a participant in the public life of the new German democracy that emerged after the defeat of November 1918, Bernays enjoyed sufficient status in her profession to be placed on the national list of the German People's Party in the Reichstag elections of 1920. Although she did not win a seat, her political reputation was enhanced by her spirited campaign. She did win a seat in the *Landtag* (Provincial Assembly) in 1921, serving until 1925.

Unafraid of controversy, Marie Bernays often appeared at debates to argue her conservative point of view. She was determined to open up dialogues with spokespersons of even the most radical viewpoints, and in April 1919 she organized a series of "sociological discussion evenings" with Eugen Leviné, a then-notorious revolutionary and one of the leaders of the short-lived Soviet Republic of Bavaria. Believing that in the long run the forces of reason and compromise would prevail over prejudice and violence, Bernays wrote countless articles and pamphlets on various contemporary themes, including the role of women in a democracy, the raising of children, and the best methods of implementing social welfare in a complex industrial society. Distressed both by the rightward drift of the DVP and the rise of Nazism, she entered a convent in 1933 and converted from Protestantism to the Roman Catholic faith. To the Nazis, Marie Bernays remained a Jew. Were it not for her death in 1939 of natural causes, we can speculate as to the unlikelihood that she would have survived the Holocaust.

John Haag, Associate Professor,
University of Georgia, Athens, Georgia

Berners, Juliana (c. 1388–?)

English writer on hawking and hunting. *Name variations: Julyans or Julians Barnes or Bernes. Born around 1388; either the daughter of Sir James Berners, who was beheaded in 1388, or the wife of the holder of the manor of Julians Barnes near St. Albans.*

Considered one of earliest published women writing in Britain, Juliana Berners was possibly the daughter of Sir James Berners who was beheaded in 1388 or possibly the wife of Julians Barnes. Though not much is known of her life, as a noblewoman she was probably brought up at court and certainly possessed a love of hawking, hunting, and fishing, as well as a passion for field sports. The only documentary evidence regarding her is the statement at the end of her treatise on hunting contained in the *Boke of St. Albans*, "Explicit Dam Julyans Barnes in her boke of huntyng."

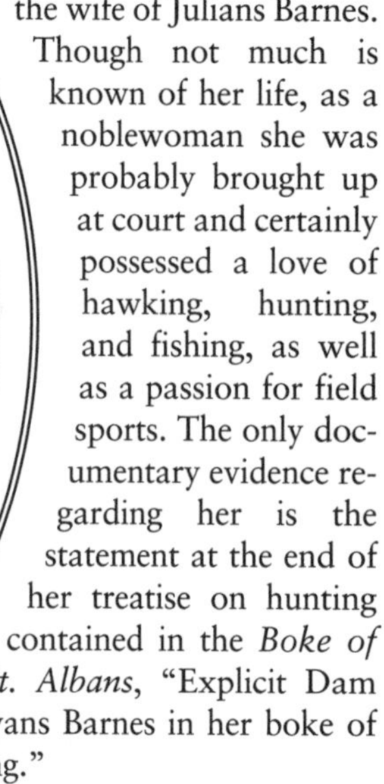
Juliana Berners

The first and rarest edition of the *Boke of St. Albans*, which has no title page, was printed in 1486 by an unknown St. Albans schoolmaster. Wynkyn de Worde's edition ten years later, also without a title page, begins: "This present boke shewyth the manere of hawkynge and huntynge: and also of diuysynge of Cote armours. It shewyth also a good matere belongynge to horses: wyth other comendable treatyses. And ferdermore of the blasynge of armys: as hereafter it maye appere." Adorned by three woodcuts, this edition included a "Treatyse of fysshynge wyth an Angle" not contained in the St. Albans' edition. Worde also changed her name to "dame Julyans Bernes."

J. Haslewood, who published a facsimile of that of Wynkyn de Worde (London, 1811), with biographical and bibliographical sections, closely examined Worde's claim that Berners was the earliest woman author in the English language. Haslewood asserted that the book was the work of multiple authors and attributed little to her, except part of the treatise on hawking and the section on hunting. It is expressly stated at the end of the "Blasynge of Armys" that the section was "translatyd and compylyt," and it is likely that the other treatises are translations, probably from the French. An older form of the treatise on fishing was edited in 1883 by T. Satchell from a manuscript in possession of A. Denison. This treatise probably dates from about 1450 and formed the foundation of that section in the book of 1496. Only three perfect copies of the first edition are known to exist. A facsimile, entitled *The Book of St. Albans*, with an introduction by William Blades, appeared in 1881. During the 16th century, the work, edited by Gervase Markham in 1595 as *The Gentleman's Academie*, was extremely popular and often reprinted. The theory that Berners had been prioress of Sopwell nunnery, Hertfordshire, near St. Albans is thought to be false. There is a gap, however, in the records of the priory of Sopwell between 1430 and 1480.

Bernhard, Ruth (b. 1905)

German-born photographer, known for nudes, still lifes and portraits, as well as advertising and fashion work. *Born in Berlin, Germany, on October 14, 1905; daughter of Lucien Bernhard (graphic and typeface designer); parents divorced when she was an infant and she was raised by school teachers Helene and Katarina Lotz; attended boarding school, Academy of Fine Arts, Berlin, 1927; became U.S. citizen, 1935.*

Following her parents' divorce, Ruth Bernhard was put into the care of sisters **Helene** and **Katarina Lotz** when she was an infant, so that her father could pursue his blossoming career in advertising. As teachers, the two sisters provided Bernhard with an environment in which her natural curiosity flourished. "They took her on nature walks, to the meadows, to the seashore," writes **Charlotte Painter**; "they indulged her enjoyment in collecting things, as if they knew she had eyes that especially needed to linger upon objects, as if they understood then what she had realized fully only in maturity: that her enjoyment of life began with her eyes." At 11, Bernhard was placed in boarding school and later attended the Academy of Fine Arts in Berlin.

Emigrating from Germany in 1927 to join her father in New York City, Bernhard landed her first job with *Delineator* magazine (work she found impersonal) but was fired for being "unenthusiastic." Using her severance pay to buy photographic equipment, she began to freelance in fashion and advertising, working for friends of her father's and picking up contracts with *The New York Times* and *Advertising Art*, as well Macy's and Sloane's department stores. In 1934, she became the photographer for *Machine Age*, a publication of the Museum of Modern Art.

By her own admission, Bernhard did not take her work seriously until a chance meeting with Edward Weston in 1935. She was so impressed with his work that she moved to Santa

Monica, California, with plans to study with him. Finding that he had moved to Carmel, she took up her freelance career in Los Angeles.

Primarily photographing still lifes and female nudes, Bernhard had a fascination with shells that led to a collaboration with conchologist **Jean Schwengel** during the 1940s. In 1953, she moved to San Francisco, where she lived and worked out of a small Victorian house.

"A powerful feeling would come over her," writes Painter, "telling her that she must capture the image that had caught her imagination. Often she would work for days to align the photograph with the spirit of that original impulse. It might be a seashell or a crushed teapot, a doll's head or a nude, but, whatever the subject, the image would come fully into her mind first, before it could appear on film and paper."

Bernard published two portfolios of prints, *The Gift of the Commonplace* and *The Eternal Body*, as well as a monograph of her work *Collecting Light*. She has been exhibited in various galleries, and in 1971, received the ***Dorothea Lange** award at the Oakland Museum, in Oakland, California. Bernhard remained open to experience throughout her life. She celebrated her 80th birthday by climbing Mount Fuji in Japan.

SOURCES:

Painter, Charlotte. *Gifts of Age*. San Francisco, CA: Chronicle Books.

Rosenblum, Naomi. *A History of Women Photographers*. NY: Abbeville Press, 1994.

Barbara Morgan,
Melrose, Massachusetts

Bernhardt, Sarah (1844–1923)

French actress, generally considered her country's greatest, whose ego, extravagance, eccentricities, numerous affairs, immense talent, magnetism, energy, will, and courage made her one of the most famous women of her time. *Name variations: The, or, La Divine Sarah. Pronunciation: (Fr.) Bare-NAHR; (Eng.) BEARN-hart. Born (Sarah-Marie-?) Henriette-Rosine Bernard, or Bernardt, or Bernhardt, probably on October 22 or 23, 1844 (born between 1841 and 1845, with 1844 the preferred choice) in Paris; adopted the name Sarah Bernhardt in her early teens; died in Paris of uremia on March 26, 1923; buried in Père-Lachaise Cemetery; daughter of Judith ("Youle") Van Hard (a.k.a. Julie Bernard, or Bernardt, or Bernhardt, a Dutch-Jewish courtesan) and an unknown French father; educated at Grand-Champs convent school (Versailles) and the Paris Conservatoire (1860–62); married Ambroise-Aristide (a.k.a. Jacques) Damala, 1882–89; children: (with Prince Henri de Ligne) son, Maurice Bernhardt (b. 1864).*

Appeared at the Comédie-Française (1862–63), but contract was canceled for misbehavior; became well-known at the Odéon (1866–72), where she ran a hospital during the Franco-Prussian War (1870–71); returned and starred at the Comédie (1872–80); left the Comédie to strike out on her own after sensational appearances in London (1879); initiated the first of nine tours in North America (1880–81), followed by numerous European tours and nearly annual seasons in London established an immense international reputation; leased and produced and acted at the Porte Saint-Martin theater (1883–93), the Théâtre de la Renaissance (1893–98), and the Théâtre de la Nation, renamed the Théâtre Sarah-Bernhardt (1899–1923); made gigantic world tour to Europe, the Americas, Hawaii, Australia, New Zealand, and Dakar, Africa (1891–93); honored by a "Day of Glorification" gala (1896); made last grand tour of Europe (1908–09); offered a National Tribute by the English (1912); awarded the Legion of Honor (1914); right leg amputated (1915); made last American tour (1916–18); returned to the Paris stage after a six-year absence (1920); gave her last performance, in Turin, Italy (1922).

Most notable roles, date of debut: Zacherie in Racine's Athalie *(1867); Anna Damby in Dumas* père's Kean *(1868); Zanetto in Coppée's* Le Passant *(1869); Queen Maria in Hugo's* Ruy Blas *(1872); Voltaire's* Zaïre *(1874); Racine's* Phèdre *(1874); Doña Sol in Hugo's* Hernani *(1877); Scribe and Legouvé's* Adrienne Lecouvreur *(1880); Gilberte in Meilhac and Halévy's* Froufrou *(1880); Marguerite Gautier in Dumas* fils' La Dame aux Camélias *(1880); Sardou's* Fédora *(1882),* Théodora *(1884), and Floria Tosca in* La Tosca *(1887); Barbier's* Jeanne d'Arc *(1890); Sardou's* Cléopatre *(1890) and* Gismonda *(1894); Melissinde in Rostand's* La Princesse lointaine *(1895); de Musset's* Lorenzaccio *(1896); Photine in Rostand's* La Samaritaine *(1897); Shakespeare-Schwon-Morand's* Hamlet *(1899); Duc de Reichstadt in Rostand's* L'Aiglon *(1900); Zoraya in Sardou's* La Sorcière *(1903); Pelléas in Maeterlinck's* Pelléas et Melisande *(1905); Moreau's* Le Procès de Jeanne d'Arc *(1909);* La Reine Elisabeth *and* La Dame aux Camélias *(silent films, 1911); Strasbourg in Morand's* Les Cathédrales *(1915);* Athalie *(Racine, 1920); Verneuil's* Daniel *(1920).*

Except for Britain's Queen ***Victoria** (1819–1901), who reigned over a quarter of the world's population, French actress Sarah Bernhardt was the best-known woman in the world at the turn of the 20th century. She was probably the first "superstar," a word invented two years after she died and not commonly used until the late-1960s. The massive publicity that made her superstar status possible was disseminated by the linotype machine, the rotary printing press, and the telegraph, telephone, radio, phonograph, and motion-picture camera. Save for the earlier telegraph, all these inventions appeared during her career. Her personality was ideally fitted to exploit this historic opportunity, for she craved attention, loved to be talked about, and was driven by a boundless ambition for fame. She had an unerring instinct for publicity—an actress who was forever "on stage"—but her behavior also provided fodder for a legion of critics who snidely damned her as "Sarah Barnum," after the notorious American showman P.T. Barnum. Still, even they would usually admit that she was truly a great actress, one of the greatest who ever lived. Floods of publicity she had, but also an ocean of talent.

Bernhardt was not a conventionally beautiful woman, even in her physical prime. A fellow actress wrote, "One could no more have said that this face was pretty than affirm it was ugly." Her hair was a frizzy, golden-red mop. Her liquid eyes, one of the most compelling features of a face capable of a great range of expressions, were wide-set and seemed to change color with her moods, green when angry, dark blue when content. She had a strong nose, fairly thin lips over beautiful white teeth, and a firm, laterally creased chin. Of barely average height, she was exceedingly slim and small-busted, thus contradicting the current ideal, which favored plumpness, an ideal her example did much to change. It was her magnificent carriage and fluid grace of movement which redeemed any bodily defects. She seemed to float about effortlessly and especially liked to present a spiral effect by wearing clinging gowns that masked the thinness of her limbs while enhancing their graceful movement. The vision of her making an entrance down a staircase seldom failed to evoke ecstatic oohs and aahs.

A final feature, perhaps the most commented upon, was her voice. Writers struggled to put its qualities into words. Usually they described it as "golden," but "silvery" was closer to the mark. It lacked the power generated by her great predecessor ***Rachel** (1821–1858), making her less suited to some of the classical roles. But it was sparklingly clear, penetrating enough to be readily audible, and infinitely charming, even bewitching. Needless to say, her pronunciation and articulation were flawless, honed in her youth by the venerable exercises taught at the Paris Conservatoire.

Bernhardt was nearly 30 before she became a star, an unusually long delay for an actress in those days. Much about her origins is unclear. She was the eldest of three daughters born to **Julia Van Hard** (variously known as Julie or "Youle" Bernard or Bernardt or Bernhardt), a Jewish Dutch girl of uncertain ancestry from Haarlem or Amsterdam, who, with her sister Rosine, set off looking for adventure and ended up in Paris pregnant with Sarah. Undaunted, Julia would become one of the most prominent courtesans in town, the paid mistress of a string of wealthy, influential men. Sarah's father was probably either an aristocratic naval officer, Paul Morel, or (more likely) a law student, Edouard Bernhardt, who became a notable Le Havre attorney but died fairly young in 1857. She was probably born between 1841 and 1845, with 1844 the preferred choice; the certificate disappeared when the Hôtel de Ville was burned during the Paris Commune (1871).

Sarah, who was at first called Rosine after her aunt, was an inconvenience, so Julie left her to be raised by friends or relatives, finally depositing her at Grand-Champs, a Catholic boarding school in Versailles. During all these years, Julie or Aunt Rosine would stop by occasionally on their travels with or between lovers and promise to come and get her, but they seldom kept their word. Sarah—high-strung, temperamental, imaginative, and frequently ill—grew up desperately wanting love and attention and devised ways of getting it through headstrong behavior.

At Grand-Champs, she became entranced with Catholic ritual, found a caring soul in the Mother Superior, **Sainte-Sophie**, and resolved to become a nun. One of Julie's patrons, the Duc de Morny, the most powerful man in France save for his half-brother Emperor Napoleon III, ended the discussion by suggesting, perhaps seriously, that the already theatrical girl really belonged at the Conservatoire, the state training school for the stage. That very evening, she later wrote, she witnessed her first play at France's most prestigious theater, the Comédie-Française, as a guest of Morny and the novelist and playwright Alexandre Dumas *père*. Enthralled, she watched the great red curtain go up: "It was as though the curtain of my future life was being raised."

Sarah's qualities may have impressed the admission jury at the Conservatoire, but it is likely that Morny's influence turned the trick. And a word from him helped again when she graduated (1862) after two years of rigorous training, for the Comédie signed her despite her having

Sarah Bernhardt

Sarah Bernhardt

won only second prizes. Barely seven months after an unremarkable debut (August 11, 1862), she was fired. A formidable senior actress, **Madame Nathalie**, had shoved Sarah's youngest sister, **Régine**, against a pillar backstage for stepping on her train. Sarah, enraged, had slapped Mme Nathalie's face and then refused all appeals to apologize.

Determined to establish her independence, Sarah resisted family pressure to marry a rich, elderly suitor. But she still needed Julie's connections, which got her a position for a year at the fashionable Théâtre du Gymnase (1863–64). Bernhardt alleged that she left because she disliked a scheduled role. She apparently went to Spain and Belgium for awhile, but until August 1866, when she began at the Odéon, her exact movements are obscure. What is certain is that on December 22, 1864, she gave birth to a son, Maurice, whose father was a young Belgian aristocrat, Henri, Prince de Ligne. For him to marry an actress was out of the question: at that time, they were only a little more "respectable" than courtesans since they were mostly poorly paid and thus expected to be supported by wealthy patrons in return for their "favors." Sarah lavished on her son Maurice all the love she had wanted from her mother; for the rest of her life, she backed his runaway spending without complaint, even when it meant selling her personal possessions.

It was at the Théâtre de l'Odéon (1866–72), France's second theater, that she finally became a star. She had sought out Camille Doucet, minister of fine arts and friend of Morny. After she promised to behave herself, he introduced her to Félix Duquesnel, the Odéon's associate director. Overcome by her charm, Duquesnel persuaded his skeptical chief, Charles de Chilly, and the contract was hers. She soon began drawing notice in plays by ***George Sand**, who befriended her, became the toast of the Latin Quarter students while appearing in Dumas *père's Kean*, and had all Paris raving about her performance as a young male minstrel in François Coppée's one-act poetic reverie *Le Passant* (January 14, 1869). When the Franco-Prussian War (1870–71) closed the theaters, Sarah quelled murmurings about her German name and ancestry by espousing a fervent patriotism (to which she remained true for life) and converting the Odéon into a military hospital with herself as head nurse during the siege of Paris. On stage again by October 1871, she saw her star status sealed when Victor Hugo chose her to play the queen in a revival of his *Ruy Blas* and knelt to kiss her hand after her sensational debut (February 19, 1872).

Swallowing the company's pride, the Comédie's director, Emile Perrin, now induced her to break her Odéon contract. Although she was a junior member of the staid temple of French drama and hence often obliged to accept secondary roles or plays ill-suited to her, she became for the public the Comédie's brightest light, blazing in Hugo's *Hernani* (November 21, 1877) and Racine's *Phèdre* (December 21, 1874), that supreme test for French dramatic actresses, which became one of her staples.

Her off-stage life, meanwhile, sated the press with stories of her many lovers, extravagant spending, eccentricities, tantrums, forays (quite respectable) into painting and sculpture, and escapades. (Perrin, to his shock and outrage, looked up one day during the Exposition of 1878 to behold his top box-office draw sailing out of Paris with two men in a balloon.) Her notoriety preceded her across the Channel and prepared the way for the June 2–July 12, 1879, London engagement of the Comédie. It was the turning point of her career. The English public could not get enough of Sarah. Despite Perrin's heated objections, she even gave lucrative private performances, which a formidable American impresario, Edward Jarrett, booked for her. The London triumph opened her eyes to the possibility of striking out on her own. On April 18, 1880, she finally resigned from the Comédie—which sued her and won a queenly 100,000 francs. She now embarked on an unprecedented career of acting and management in her own theater in Paris and making nearly annual tours abroad with her own company, beginning with a return to London, trips to Brussels, Copenhagen, and the French provinces, and an extensive tour in the U.S. and Canada organized by Jarrett (October 15, 1880–May 4, 1881).

In Paris, she performed exclusively at a succession of theaters she leased: the Porte Saint-Martin (1883–93), the Renaissance (1893–98), and the 1,700-seat theater at the Place du Châtelet, modestly renamed the "Théâtre Sarah-Bernhardt" (1899–1923). She supervised every facet of their operation and acted, produced, and directed, doing it all with high professional skill. Being a woman in unaccustomed roles bothered her not a whit. As for the tours, she loved them, even if sometimes (especially in America) she had to perform in arenas or tents; besides, they were highly profitable and helped cover the occasional huge losses of failed Paris productions. These tours were veritable royal progresses. Her troupe with props and vast wardrobe usually traveled by special train with a private car for the star and her current leading man. She made nine tours in the United States between October 1880 and November 1918, sometimes with side tours in Canada and Latin America; the last four were billed as "farewell" tours. Interspersed were short and long tours in Europe and vacations of a few weeks at her island estate off the coast of Brittany. An ability (like Napoleon's) to fall asleep instantly and wake fully refreshed in half an hour helped her sustain this unrelenting activity to the end of her life.

And so did will power. "You ask me my theory of life? It is represented by the word *will.*" Early in life, she adopted a motto, "*Quand même*" ("No matter what"), even though ill health often plagued her. On October 9, 1905, she injured her right knee and greatly aggravated it in a performance of *La Tosca* in Rio de Janeiro, when a stagehand forgot to put a pad on the floor to cushion her suicide leap at the end. Until February 22, 1915, when the leg was amputated, she acted despite acute pain. The amputation did not deter her. She adapted roles so she could stand supported or sit and was skillful enough to make audiences forget her handicap. Off stage, she was carried about in a sedan chair.

Given her background, Bernhardt grew up with little concern for the sexual conventions of Victorian society and roundly ignored them. She had a score of lovers which legend, abetted by former intimate friend **Marie Colombier**'s sensationally scabrous *Mémoires de Sarah Barnum* (1883), multiplied beyond measure. Unlike her mother's, her liaisons, mainly with men in the theater and literary worlds, were for emotional and sexual satisfaction (rather than money) which apparently she never fully found. Still, most of her ex-lovers remained her friends. Her sole marriage was a disaster. Jacques Damala, 12 years her junior, was a strikingly handsome Greek soldier, diplomat, Don Juan, and morphine addict. They married in London on April 4, 1882. She (if few others) thought he had acting talent and even bought him a theater to appease his jealousy and conceit. He soon walked out, she obtained a separation in 1883, and he died of drug abuse in 1889. Bernhardt kept a bust of him in her home and would not speak ill of him. Later (1910–13), she again discovered supposed talent in another smashingly handsome adventurer, Lou Tellegen, but did not marry him. After two American tours, he left her for silent-film stardom and married the opera diva ***Geraldine Farrar**.

Bernhardt worked to the end. She suffered a short uremic coma while rehearsing Sacha Guitry's *Un Sujet de roman* in December 1922 and never again appeared on stage. On March 15, 1923, while filming Guitry's *La Voyante* at her exotic Paris mansion, she collapsed in another attack of uremia, which finally killed her on March 26. A vast throng escorted her to burial at Père-Lachaise. Her stone states simply, as if no more were needed: SARAH BERNHARDT.

Bernhardt did not lack detractors among theater critics, notably George Bernard Shaw, who much preferred her Italian rival ***Eleanora Duse** (1859–1924). Many, suspicious of huge commercial success and scorning the veritable cult surrounding her, charged that her flagrant self-promotion prostituted her art for applause and money. (Anti-Semitism also raised its head; she met it by proudly and simply affirming that she was "a Roman Catholic and a member of the great Jewish race.") It is true she had a keen sense of what the public liked and gave it to them without worrying overmuch if it qualified as high art. At the same time, she never descended to the merely cheap or vulgar. Certainly she was not infallible in choosing plays or judging her ability to succeed in them. She was ready to try new works and methods but also was a shrewd manager, ready to trot out old warhorses to pay the bills piled up by flops. In short, "art for art's sake" was not what she lived for; staging a first-class production, giving the audience a memorable serving of "la Divine Sarah" and (usually) a good cry—and making a ton of money at it—was.

As for Bernhardt's place in theater history, she epitomized the spirit of romanticism and more than anyone else infused it into the playing of French classical roles. Her Phèdre was a real woman torn by lust and guilt, not the noble, sexless demi-goddess enshrined by two centuries of tradition. As the pope of French critics, Francisque Sarcey, sensed upon her return to the Comédie in 1872, the event was "serious and violently revolutionary: it is the wolf in the fold." At the same time, her classical training enabled her later, as a critic wrote, to "elevate the most worthless melodrama to the height of tragic grandeur." Her style thus blended the Comédie with the much freer Boulevard theater.

A long debate over whether her method was emotionalist or anti-emotionalist was fueled by contradictions between her statements favoring the former and her highly polished technique. She made intense efforts to become the characters she portrayed and wrote in *L'Art du théâtre*, "When the average audience is moved to tears by an actor's suffering, the actor will know that he has achieved his artistic goals." On the other hand, she knew all the tricks. An actress (**May Agate**) testified that "she could simulate tears and conduct a conversation about something else." When a young pupil complained she could not perform a scene in a certain way because she didn't "feel" it that way, Madame Sarah replied firmly, "If you're going to be an actress, you've got to be able to do it that way or any other way." At her death, a critic offered an apt synthesis: "Though intoxicated, she remains lucid in her intoxication."

Bernhardt's repertoire was vast—over 130 roles, most of them leads; she memorized them in four or five concentrated readings and thereafter almost never forgot a line. She studied them thoroughly and worked hard to avoid mere stereotypical interpretation. While her range of characters was broad, her repertorial range was mostly classical and romantic French; she had no feel for the new "realistic" school of Ibsen, Strindberg, Chekhov, and Shaw, with their "problem" plays and neurotic, sex-starved, middle-class heroines—"that northern stuff" ("*des norderies*"), as she called it. She had striking successes in young male (*travesti*) roles. Traditional in the French theater but a novelty for her English-speaking audiences, they were also a means to disguise her aging, which she dreaded and denied. She argued that roles like Hamlet or Napoleon's son (*L' Aiglon*) portray youths of 20 with the minds of men of 40; hence, unlike the older actors usually assigned, "the woman more readily looks the part and yet has the maturity of mind to grasp it."

It was above all in romantic melodrama portraying women in love that Bernhardt excelled. Victorien Sardou supplied her with a string of highly popular vehicles. Her most-performed role, however, was as **Marguerite Gautier**, a courtesan redeemed by love but heroically giving up her lover before dying of consumption, in Dumas *fils' La Dame aux Camélias* (oddly known to English-speaking audiences as "Camille"). Bernhardt projected a "chaste sensuality" which Victorian audiences found irresistible. They also wanted tears, and she could bring them up as nobody before or since, with death scenes her specialty. The critic Jules Lemaître noted that she broke new acting ground in two respects: the use of her entire body, and her display of femininity. She exuded sex and portrayed it unmistakably, challenging repressive Victorian conventions. But she never crossed the line into cheapness or obscenity: more important to her even than passion was beauty—which stamped her as a true romantic. It must be added, however, that an element of titillation also entered her audiences' experience, for everyone knew that almost always her stage lover was playing that role offstage too.

Finally, Bernhardt made the grand tour *de rigueur* well into the 20th century for anyone wishing to be a great star. The device was "invented" by ***Adelaide Ristori** (1822–1906) with her American tours, but Bernhardt revealed its potential to produce deluges of money and fame. Remarkably, she performed abroad only in French yet drew huge crowds; audiences received a translation or a plot summary as at an opera. Despite the often circus-like atmosphere of the tours, she took the business seriously. When responding to a great formal celebration offered her in 1896, she said, "I have planted the dramatic literature of France in foreign hearts. That is my proudest achievement." And she continued to do and to believe so. Even though the French government decorated her (finally) in 1914, neither it nor the French people ever fully appreciated how very much she had done to win renewed respect for France and French culture abroad in the wake of the defeat of 1870–71, and most especially to help prepare the people of England and the United States to come to suffering France's aid during the First World War (1914–18).

> There are five kinds of actresses: bad actresses, fair actresses, good actresses, great actresses—and then there is Sarah Bernhardt.
>
> —**Mark Twain, c. 1912**

Sarah Bernhardt was an endless entertainer and a fount of contradictions, as vain, demanding, and all-around "impossible" as the most stereotypical great star, yet also a generous, sensitive woman who kept a host of friends for life. Perhaps her most impressive quality, aside from sheer magnetism, was her courageous will—in surmounting childhood neglect; in following the call of her talent despite early failures and devastating attacks of stage fright throughout her life; in fighting through pain and disability in order to perform as contracted and at the level expected of her; and, most strikingly, in defying the myriad conventions of her time enforcing the helplessness of women in order to make herself a truly independent woman "no matter what."

Gautier, Marguerite. *See Plessis, Alphonsine.*

SOURCES:

Aston, Elaine. *Sarah Bernhardt: A French Actress on the English Stage*. Oxford: Berg, 1989.

Bernhardt, Sarah. *My Double Life: Memoirs of Sarah Bernhardt*. London: William Heinemann, 1907.

Castelot, André. *Ensorcelant Sarah Bernhardt*. Paris: Librairie Académique Perrin, 1961.

Gold, Arthur, and Robert Fizdale. *The Divine Sarah: A Life of Sarah Bernhardt*. NY: Alfred A. Knopf, 1991.

Richardson, Joanna. *Sarah Bernhardt*. London: M. Reinhardt, 1959.

———. *Sarah Bernhardt and Her World*. NY: Putnam, 1977.

Salmon, Eric, ed. *Bernhardt and the Theater of Her Time*. Westport, CT: Greenwood Press, 1984.

Skinner, Cornelia Otis. *Madame Sarah*. Boston, MA: Houghton Mifflin, 1966.

Taranow, Gerda. *Sarah Bernhardt: The Art Within the Legend.* Princeton, NJ: Princeton University Press, 1972.

SUGGESTED READING:

Agate, May. *Madame Sarah.* NY: Benjamin Blom, 1945, 1969.

Baring, Maurice. *Sarah Bernhardt.* NY: D. Appleton-Century, 1934.

Bernhardt, Lysiane. *Sarah Bernhardt: My Grandmother.* Translation. NY: Hurst & Blackett, 1945.

Bernhardt, Sarah. *The Art of the Theater.* Translated by H.J. Stenning. London: Geoffrey Bles, 1924.

——— and Sandy Lesberg. *The Memoirs of Sarah Bernhardt.* NY: Beekman House, 1977.

Berton, Thérèse. *Sarah Bernhardt as I Knew Her: Memoirs of Mme. Pierre Berton as Told to Basil Woon.* London: Hurst & Blackett, 1923.

Emboden, William. *Sarah Bernhardt.* London: Macmillan, 1974.

Hahn, Reynaldo. *Sarah Bernhardt.* Translation. London: Elkins, Matthews & Marrot, 1932.

Jullian, Philippe. *Sarah Bernhardt.* Paris: Editions Ballard, 1977.

Kobler, John. "Bernhardt in America," in *American Heritage.* Vol. 40, no. 5, 1989, pp. 52–65.

Rostand, Maurice. *Sarah Bernhardt.* Paris: Calmann-Lévy, 1950.

Verneuil, Louis. *The Fabulous Life of Sarah Bernhardt.* Translated by Ernest Boyd. NY: Harper & Brothers, 1942, 1972.

COLLECTIONS:

In Paris: Bibliothèque de l'Arsenal, Bibliothèque de la Comédie-Française, Bibliothèque Nationale, the Cinémathèque Française, and the Phonothèque Nationale. In New York: The New York Public Library of the Performing Arts.

RELATED MEDIA:

"The Incredible Sarah," produced by Helen M. Strauss for Reader's Digest Films, 1976, starring **Glenda Jackson**, directed by Richard Fleischer.

"Sarah Bernhardt," Films for the Humanities and Sciences (FFH), No. PI–1840.

David S. Newhall, Professor of History, Centre College, Danville, Kentucky

Bernice.

Variant of Berenice.

Bernstein, Aline (1882–1955)

American scenic designer and writer. *Born Hazel Frankau on December 22, 1882, in New York, New York; died on September 7, 1955, in New York, New York; first of two daughters of Joseph (an actor) and Rebecca (Goldsmith) Frankau; attended New York School for Applied Design; married Theodore Bernstein, in November 1902; children: Theo (1904–1949) and Edla (b. 1906).*

Selected set designs: The Little Clay Cart *(1924);* The Miracle *(1924);* The Dybbuk *(1925);* Grand Street Follies *(several editions from 1923);* Ned McCobb's Daughter *(1926);* Reunion in Vienna *(1931);* Alison's House *(1931);* Animal Kingdom *(1932);* We the People *(1933);* The Children's Hour *(1934);* She *(movie, 1935);* The Last Days of Pompeii *(movie, 1935);* Days to Come *(1936);* The Seagull *(1937);* The Little Foxes *(1939);* The Male Animal *(1940);* The Spellbound Child *(ballet, 1946);* Regina *(opera, 1949).*

Selected writings: (short stories) Three Blue Suits *(1933); (novel)* The Journey Down *(1938);* An Actor's Daughter *(1941); (juvenile)* The Martha Washington Doll Book *(1945); (novel)* Miss Conden *(1947); (published posthumously)* Masterpieces of Women's Costume of the Eighteenth and Nineteenth Centuries *(1959).*

Aline Bernstein may be remembered more for her love affair with author Thomas Wolfe than for her work as a theatrical designer and writer, perhaps because of the enormous impact she had on Wolfe's short writing career. However, as much as Bernstein's personal life was consuming, her work remained a sustaining force. "It was as worker that this woman was supreme," wrote Wolfe. "The true religion of her soul, the thing that saved her . . . was the religion of her work. It . . . took her out of herself, united her life to a nobler image which was external to her and superior to the vanities of the self."

Bernstein's early childhood in New York revolved around her father Joseph Frankau's acting career. Aline, along with her mother Rebecca and younger sister Ethel, alternately toured with him and lived in a boarding house for actors run by her aunt. Family life was cut short with the death of her mother when Aline was 11, and the death of her father five years later. Bernstein wandered from relative to relative, eking out a living by designing and selling greeting cards door-to-door, and by creating hats and dresses with her sister Ethel. As a teenager, Bernstein considered becoming an actress before deciding on a career as a painter. She studied at the School of Applied Design and later with Robert Henri, the leading proponent of the new urban realism, dubbed the "Ashcan School" in the 1930s. A gifted artist and master teacher, Henri nurtured Bernstein's talents and she thrived under his instruction.

In 1902, Aline married Theo Bernstein, a handsome young clerk on Wall Street, whose moderate personality provided balance to her less temperate nature. Bernstein rejoiced in her first pregnancy, without the inhibition common at the time. "I look magnificent," she proclaimed to friends, placing their hands on her

Aline Bernstein

swollen stomach so they could feel the baby move. Theo, Jr. (Teddy), born in 1904, suffered serious heart problems as a child and would die of a massive heart attack when he was only 45. A second child, Edla, was born in 1906 and would later recall feeling distanced from her mother as a youngster: "Mother was principally involved with her own life. She was only really happy when she was working. . . . It wasn't just something she did to fill out her life . . . it *was* her life." Edla credited Bernstein's sister Ethel, who lived with them during her childhood, for providing a steady home life.

After Edla's birth, Bernstein returned to her art studies with Henri, also rejoining his Tuesday night gatherings of artists, writers, and political activists—a salon of sorts—where she formed lifetime friendships with ***Emma Goldman**, George Bellows (with whom she was also purported to have had an affair), Man Ray, and Stuart Davis. Bernstein's reputation for attracting friends was beginning to grow; indeed, it would become almost legendary. Wolfe, who later imbued his character Esther Jack with the same charisma, described it as not merely sexual, but a "richness" of spirit: "People wanted to be near her; she gave them a feeling of confidence, joy and vitality which they did not have in themselves."

Through her sister Ethel, Bernstein found her way into the theater. As a volunteer at the Henry Street Settlement House on the Lower East Side, Ethel enlisted Bernstein to help with the girls' dramatic club, led by **Rita Morgenthau** and **Irene** and **Alice Lewisohn**. Bernstein created costumes for the club's performances, then gradually moved on to props and sets. By 1913, the club had raised enough money to build a permanent theater—the Neighborhood Playhouse—which was the first theater in New York to design and make its own scenery, costumes and props. Bernstein would later say that the profession of "scene designer" began at the Playhouse. Critic John Gassner agreed, and further credited their experimental productions as "revealing resources of taste and style still largely absent in the uptown theatres."

During these early years, Bernstein scrambled to learn more about stagecraft and to incorporate her art training into design for the theater. She picked up a great deal from collaborations with established designers like Robert Edmond Jones, with whom she worked on an early Playhouse production of a 14th-century miracle play, building his extravagantly designed costumes on a shoestring budget. She was accepted into the Saturday morning workshop run by Norman Bel Geddes, who was already receiving wide acclaim for both his sets and costumes. In 1922, Bernstein was invited to work with the celebrated designer Lee Simonson on the elaborate production of Shaw's *Back to*

Methuselah. As difficult and volatile as Simonson was, they became friends and collaborated often on a variety of Theatre Guild productions.

Bernstein remained with the Neighborhood Playhouse through its dissolution in 1927, achieving notice with her designs for *The Little Clay Cart* and *The Grand Street Follies* (both in 1924). During the 1920s, Playhouse productions occasionally moved uptown for limited runs, where more people saw Bernstein's work, and producers began to seek her out. In 1925, she executed her most famous designs for the Theatre Guild's first U.S. production of *The Dybbuk*, by Shloyme Zanvi Rappoport (S. Ansky). Critic Brooks Atkinson compared her sets to "a Rembrandt canvas." Her designs for *Ned McCobb's Daughter*, rendered for the Theatre Guild in 1926, continue to appear in contemporary anthologies of stage design.

As a recognized designer, in 1924 Bernstein applied for membership into Local 829, the Brotherhood of Painters, Decorators and Paperhangers, of the American Federation of Labor. Although there was annoyance over the union's refusal to distinguish artist from mechanic, the union was demanding such rights for designers as full program credit, pay for extra work, and permanent ownership of their original designs. It was also enforcing restrictions on what a nonunion designer might do in the theatre, making work for outsiders scarce. Bernstein was turned down for two years; she was finally admitted as the first woman member in 1926. The set designers eventually formed their own arm of the union, the United Scenic Artists.

During the 1920s and '30s, Bernstein also worked as the resident designer for ***Eva Le Gallienne**'s Civic Repertory Theatre, during which time she designed costumes and scenery for five ***Lillian Hellman** plays, including *The Children's Hour* (1934), which introduced the new playwright to the American theatre and broached the then daring subject of lesbianism, and *The Little Foxes* (1939). Bernstein also designed the costumes for her first movie, *She*, starring her good friend ***Helen Gahagan Douglas**. "Her clothes for me were simply superb," said Douglas. "They were almost breathtakingly creative, and yet absolutely perfect technically—but then, that was Aline's genius." Bernstein worked on a second movie, *The Last Days of Pompeii*, but her respect for the movie industry was largely limited to its technology.

Bernstein first met Thomas Wolfe in 1925 while on a shipboard return from Europe, where she had done some architectural research for *The Dybbuk*. Coincidentally, Wolfe's play *Welcome to Our City* was being considered by the Neighborhood Playhouse, and Bernstein had carried a copy of the manuscript overseas to Alice Lewisohn. Despite a 20-year difference in their ages—Bernstein the elder at 44—their attraction was overwhelming, and the love affair that followed lasted until Wolfe's untimely death in 1938. Although the relationship was torturous for Bernstein and left her suicidal, she brought what little order there was to Wolfe's life, and his genius flourished. Ironically, the waning years of the affair also unleashed Bernstein's own writing ability. Her analyst suggested that she express her feelings on paper, and writing became a new creative outlet. She produced a number of published and extremely well-received works, beginning with *Three Blue Suits*. Her later novel, *The Journey Down*, was deemed "breathtaking" by one reviewer. Poet ***May Sarton** provided one of Bernstein's most gratifying reviews: "I was up all night reading your book," she wrote. "It is a beautiful piece of work, with the intensity, texture and peculiar sustained excitement of a poem."

The relationship between Bernstein and Wolfe is documented through the character of Esther Jack in Wolfe's *The Web and the Rock* (1939) and *You Can't Go Home Again* (1940), and in Bernstein's own short stories and novels. Biographer **Carole Klein** recounts Theo Bernstein's reaction to her affair and credits him with a near saint-like compassion: "He never wavered in his devotion and his profound conviction that Aline was a uniquely precious person—with a nature so rare and so much larger than other people's that she required extraordinary sustenance."

In 1937, Bernstein concentrated on plans for a costume museum. After initial consultations with Lee Simonson and Irene Lewisohn, she leased a loft on 46th Street and devoted every spare moment to the new project, collecting clothing from friends, antique stores, and people throughout the world. She equipped her museum with a library of books on period apparel and on paintings and sculptures of the time, so that broad spectrums of culture could be viewed. In 1939, Bernstein was able to expand the museum with the gift of a suite of rooms in Rockefeller Center and a sizable monetary contribution from Nelson Rockefeller. In 1944, the museum found a permanent home by merging with the Metropolitan Museum of Art.

During the 1940s, Bernstein taught costume design and was a production consultant at Vassar College, which she considered one of the richest experiences of her life. Throughout her career,

Bernstein also took on a number of young designers as assistants, including Russell Wright, Sointu Syrjala, and *Irene Sharaff. She continued to design; her later work included the biographical study of *Harriet Beecher Stowe called *Harriet*, starring *Helen Hayes and directed by Elia Kazan. Bernstein also designed the ballet *The Spellbound Child*, a fantasy with music by Maurice Ravel. In 1949, while still recovering from the death of her son Teddy, Bernstein threw herself into designs for *Regina*, a musical of *The Little Foxes*, with music by Marc Blitzstein, for which she won the *Antoinette Perry ("Tony") Award.

In 1950, at age 70, Bernstein worked on *The Happy Time* for Richard Rogers and Oscar Hammerstein, who threw an elaborate birthday party for her backstage at a Broadway theatre. In spite of the infirmities of her age and the progressive deafness she had endured since 1922, she did four productions during the 1950–51 season, including Arthur Miller's adaptation of Ibsen's *An Enemy of the People*. In 1953, she was asked to help stage and costume *The World of Sholem Aleichem*, which critics praised as a sensitive recollection of the old days on the Lower East Side of New York City.

Bernstein suffered a stroke in 1953, which was less severe than the one Theo experienced a year earlier but debilitating nonetheless. Although she continued to see occasional visitors, most of her prolonged illness was spent alone with Theo, in the care of her sister Ethel and **Peggy Murphy**, Bernstein's housekeeper for many years. Although she could no longer walk, and he could not talk, the bond between wife and husband apparently tightened. Aline Bernstein died on December 7, 1955. Her funeral was described by Murphy as "a grand party," which Bernstein no doubt would have appreciated. Theo lived on with Ethel until his death in 1958.

SOURCES:

Boardman, Gerald. *The Oxford Companion to American Theatre*. NY: Oxford University Press, 1984.

Klein, Carole. *Aline*. NY: Harper & Row, 1979.

SUGGESTED READING:

Wolfe, Thomas. *Look Homeward Angel*. NY: Scribner, 1929.

———. *Of Time and the River*. NY: Scribner, 1935.

———. *The Web and the Rock*. NY: Harper and Brothers, 1939.

———. *You Can't Go Home Again*. NY: Harper and Brothers, 1940.

Barbara Morgan,
Melrose, Massachusetts

Bernstein, Theresa Ferber (b. 1903).

See Nevelson, Louise for sidebar.

Berry, Agnes (c. 1405–1479).

See Paston, Agnes.

Berry, duchess.

See Margaret of Savoy (1523–1574).
See Marie Louise (1695–1719).
See Caroline of Naples (1798–1870).

Berry, Martha McChesney (1866–1942)

American educator regarded as one of the most outstanding women in Georgia's history. *Born Martha McChesney Berry on October 7, 1866, near Rome, Georgia; died on February 27, 1942, in Atlanta, Georgia; second daughter and one of eight children of Thomas (a cotton dealer) and Frances (Rhea) Berry; educated by private tutors; attended Edgewood Finishing School, Baltimore, 1882.*

Martha McChesney Berry was a soft-spoken Southern belle, born into wealth and privilege, who devoted her life to educating poor Southern mountain children. At the time of her death in 1942, Berry's Schools—established in 1902 in a crudely constructed log cabin—were housed in 125 buildings on 35,000 acres of land in the mountains of northwestern Georgia. Of the 1,300 students enrolled, most did not pay tuition but earned their education instead by working for the institution.

Born in 1866, Martha McChesney Berry grew up on a cotton plantation, Oak Hill, near Rome, Georgia, on the edge of the highest Appalachian belt, where her early contacts with the impoverished highlanders of the area came through her father Thomas. As a volunteer in the Georgia infantry during the Civil War, he had enlisted large numbers of the mountaineers for his company. After the war, as he stoically rebuilt a successful cotton business with loans from wealthy business friends, he continued to help the men who had served him and then returned to lives of poverty. He often took young Martha with a him on Sunday trips into the mountains to dispense supplies or offer advice. In a gesture characteristic of what would be her life's work, she once gave her best coat to a mountain child who was shivering in the cold.

As was the custom of the day, the Berry children were tutored at home by their governess, **Ida McCullough**, while **"Aunt Marth" Freeman**, a black woman, managed the household chores and kept the children in line. To prepare her for a place in southern aristocracy,

Martha McChesney Berry

Berry was sent, at 16, to an exclusive finishing school in Baltimore, which she hated. Among the big-city girls, she felt self-conscious about her country clothes and manners. Before the end of her first year, her father suffered a stroke and she was called home, where she helped with the family business and became her father's companion. Captain Berry provided his daughter with the lessons in charity that would shape her future. "If you simply hand things to somebody you destroy his pride," he told her, "and when you do that you destroy him." He believed in charity that afforded an opportunity to work. When he died a few years later, she inherited a substantial tract of land, as well as his abiding concern for the mountain people.

Berry's career began on a Sunday afternoon while reading in the log cabin her father had built on the property as a playhouse. Suddenly aware of three grimy, wide-eyed mountain boys standing outside, staring in, Berry invited them in and entertained them with Bible stories and refreshments. On succeeding Sundays, more children arrived, sometimes dragging along other family members. Soon, the congregation was overflowing the cabin, and Berry held sessions in an abandoned wooden church at Possum Trot, which she encouraged her students to fix up by holding work parties. Soon, she began to utilize other abandoned church buildings, enlisting the help of her sister and some friends from town to assist in conducting classes. Concluding that Sunday school was not enough to satisfy the curiosity of her students, she used the land she had inherited to build a small day school. Before long, four such day schools were in operation. But Berry's work cost her a fiancé, who did not envision a wife with interests outside the home.

After initial success with the day schools, Berry planned a year-round, live-in educational experience designed to prepare mountain boys for life experiences. In January 1902, she opened the first Boys' Industrial School, a crude log building outfitted with castoffs from Oak Hill's attic and items she procured from neighbors. Aware of her own lack of training as a teacher, Berry hired **Elizabeth Brewster**, an impressive graduate of Leland Stanford University who had a particular interest in educating the underprivileged. The two women, over objections from Berry's family, took up residence in the dormitory of the new school.

In a pioneering work-study program, Berry's first dozen or so students contributed two hours of work a day in addition to their studies, which kept the school operating and provided what Berry considered valuable vocational training. The boys planted gardens and raised livestock, often bringing the animals with them when they came to school. In 1909, Berry opened a school for girls, which she hoped, among other things, might provide suitable wives for her male graduates. (Reportedly, Berry was so pleased when a marriage occurred between her students that she personally gave the bride away.) The schools offered high school-age students scholastic as well as vocational, agricultural, and domestic training, in a religious but nondenominational setting. Berry was said to hold her students to high levels of performance and discipline, reflecting both the demands of the mountain parents and her own. By 1912, the state of Georgia had opened 11 schools using Berry's model; other states soon followed.

As the schools flourished, surviving fire and flood, Berry soon had more applicants than space. Forced to solicit more support from outside, she was undaunted in her attempts to raise money, though early efforts in the East yielded little. "I will go anywhere and talk to anyone," she said. She once took afternoon tea with a potential donor but generated only pleasant conversation. Around one o'clock the following morning, she was urgently called back to his house, and he handed her $10,000, her largest contribution to date. The patron wanted to be sure, he said, that the school was important enough for Berry to come out after midnight.

Berry also pursued philanthropist Andrew Carnegie tenaciously but proved unable to enlist his support until she presented herself at his residence in New York. Their meeting took place while he posed for a portrait and produced nothing more than a long endowment application form. After she returned the completed document, Carnegie offered $50,000, with the condition that Berry raise a matching $50,000 from other sources. Berry went to work raising funds, but a few weeks later had only collected $7,000. She then received a call from Carnegie, inviting her to tea, where she met ***Margaret Olivia Sage**, widow of the American financier Russell Sage, who was also soliciting Carnegie for a contribution to a foundation she was establishing. In a move approaching blackmail, Carnegie explained to Sage the terms of his contribution to Berry and added: "Wouldn't you like to help Miss Berry, as you want me to help you with that Foundation you're setting up?" Sage contributed $25,000.

> She . . . is a dreamer, whose visions were born in human sympathy and given substance by the magical touch of faith; an educator who trains equally the heart and the hand, the spirit and the head.
>
> **—On citation awarding Martha Berry the Theodore Roosevelt Medal of Distinguished Service**

In addition to using her charm and eloquence to raise money, Berry entertained philanthropists during carefully orchestrated on-campus visits; indeed, she was known for her skill in dramatizing her achievements. Perhaps her greatest conquest was Henry Ford, who was so captivated by what Berry described as "a home-grown meal, a home-cooked dinner and a home-spun school" that he became a frequent visitor. During the 1920s, Ford donated a collection of Gothic-style buildings worth four million dollars. In 1926, Berry College was established, and later a Model Practice School was added. The campus became a self-sustaining city, with a mill, orchards, goat and cattle herds, a bakery, and an automobile shop where Ford puttered during his visits while his wife took in the more domestic activities in the girls' wing.

A woman of indomitable faith, Berry took the first harbingers of the Depression lightly.

Gradually, however, her pledges dried up, and checks bounced with regularity, even while the self-supporting campus of the school flourished. Berry offered some of her vacant acreage for campsites to house some of the increasing legions of homeless, who labored for the school in exchange for food and shelter. Now in her 60s, she worked alongside her students to cope with the extra load, as did her staff. The school kept hundreds of people alive through the Depression years, although institutional finances continued to dwindle. At one point, had not an eccentric benefactor written a generous check to keep it going, the school would have closed.

Over the years, Berry's schools won national attention. President Theodore Roosevelt paid a visit, and a quote from the speech he gave that day, "Be a lifter, not a leaner," became the school's slogan. Berry was showered with awards and citations, becoming the first woman regent of Georgia's university system and the first woman member of the state's planning board. She received numerous honorary degrees and in 1925 was named one of America's 50 greatest women by journalist ***Ida Tarbell**. That year, she was also awarded the Theodore Roosevelt Memorial Medal for Distinguished Service. At the White House award ceremony, presided over by President Calvin Coolidge, Berry brought five of her recent graduates. When newspaper reporters expressed surprise at this, she retorted: "Who deserves the honor more?" In 1934, Berry was received at the Court of St. James by England's King George V and Queen ***Mary of Teck**. In 1939, when she was 73, Berry was awarded a gold medal from the National Institute of Social Sciences. Previous recipients of the award included Madame ***Marie Curie**, Chief Justice Charles Evan Hughes, and presidents William Taft, Calvin Coolidge, and Herbert Hoover.

Berry still fretted over her schools. Hospitalized in October 1941 with cancer, she called her new board chair, John Sibley, telling him that, more than death, she feared well-meaning people who might change Berry, making it into just another school. "It's different," she told Sibley, "and it must remain so."

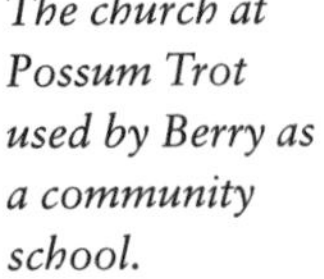

The church at Possum Trot used by Berry as a community school.

Martha Berry died on February 26, 1942, the same day that Atlanta experienced its first complete blackout of World War II. Amid great fanfare, she was laid to rest on the campus of her school. Although the next to last of Berry's Schools, Berry Academy, a preparatory school for young men, closed its doors in 1983, Berry College still stands as a living monument to its founder, with the world's largest college campus and an enrollment of over 1,600 students. Fostering a self-help attitude, Berry College provides financial assistance through an extensive work program, whereby full-time students are assured an opportunity for on-campus employment. In addition to campus buildings erected in the early 1900s of Gothic, Georgian and Early American design, Oak Hill, the Ford Buildings, the Roosevelt Cabin, and the Possum Trot church and schoolhouse are preserved landmarks. Every fall, a homecoming is held for relatives and friends of families who lived near Possum Trot when the area was a farming community. Preserved also is the Berry motto: "Not to be ministered unto, but to minister."

SOURCES:

Block, Maxine, ed. *Current Biography 1940.* NY: H.W. Wilson, 1940.

Flemming, Alice. *Great Women Teachers.* Philadelphia, PA: Lippincott, 1965.

James, Edward T., ed. *Notable American Women 1607–1950.* Cambridge, MA: Belknap Press of Harvard University Press, 1971.

Kane, Harnett T., with Henry Inez. *Miracle in the Mountains.* NY: Doubleday, 1956.

Myers, Elisabeth P. *Angel of Appalachia: Martha Berry.* NY: Julian Messner, 1968.

Barbara Morgan,
Melrose, Massachusetts

Berry, Mary (1763–1852)

English writer. *Born in Yorkshire, England, in 1763; died in 1852.*

After the death of her mother in 1763, Mary Berry and her younger sister Agnes, who would become her lifelong companion, were raised by their grandmother until 1770, when they moved to Chiswick. Mary began writing a journal in 1783, while on a European tour with her father. The *Journals*, which were published after her death in 1865, span 70 years, from the 18th century to the time of Thackeray.

In 1788, Mary and Agnes became friends of Horace Walpole. He called the sisters his "twin wives" and reportedly made a proposal of marriage to Mary, which she turned down. (She was briefly engaged to General O'Hara, governor of Malta, in 1794). Walpole persuaded the women to move into Little Strawberry Hill (Clivenden) in 1791 and introduced them into literary society. When he died in 1797, Mary edited nine volumes of his works (1798–1825), as well as the *Letters of* ****Mme Deffand*** to Walpole and to Voltaire.

Mary Berry

Mary Berry did not become a professional writer until after her father's death in 1817. Her major work was *Social Life of England and France, from Charles II to 1830*, although she also produced a biography of Lady ***Rachel Russell** (1636–1723), and a play, *Fashionable Friends*. Intelligent and personable, Berry was included in fashionable literary circles until her death at the age of 90.

Barbara Morgan,
Melrose, Massachusetts

Berry, Miriam (1811–1852).

See Whitcher, Frances Miriam Berry.

Berta.

Spanish variant of Bertha.

Bertha (719–783)

Queen of the Franks. *Name variations: Bertrada, Berthrada; Berthe au grand pied; Bertrada II of Laon. Born in 719; died at Choisy on July 12, 783; daughter of Heribert also known as Caribert, count of Laon; married Pepin III the Short (715–768), mayor of Neustria (r. 741), king of the Franks (r. 747–768), in 741; children: Charles also known as Charlemagne (c. 742–814, who ruled as king of the Franks for 46 years and as Holy Roman emperor for 13 years);* ****Irmentrude*** *(d. 820); Carloman also known as Karlman (c. 751–771);* ****Gisela*** *(c. 753–807).*

The mother of Charlemagne was called *Berthe au grand pied* (Bertha with the large foot), because one foot was greater than the other. Without doubt, her son Charlemagne—Carolus Magnus, Charles the Great, Karl der Grosse—was one of the great figures of medieval Europe.

His reign was viewed as a "Golden Age," and he was regarded as one of the Nine Worthies, along with Abraham and Julius Caesar.

In 751, when Bertha's son was only about nine, Pope Stephen II deposed Childeric, king of the Franks, thus ending the Merovingian line, and anointed her husband Pepin the Short as king. When Pepin died in 768, following Frankish custom he was succeeded by his two sons, Charlemagne and Carloman, who became joint kings.

Of Bertha, her daughter Gisela, and her sons' life little is known. Even Einhard, Charlemagne's biographer, who had lived through the reign and began to compose his *Life of Charlemagne* (*Vita Caroli*) some 15 years after Charlemagne's death, lamented: "It would be foolish for me to write about Charlemagne's birth and childhood . . . for nothing is set down in writing about this and nobody can be found still alive who claims to have any personal knowledge of these matters."

Bertha has been celebrated with poems and legends for many centuries. Some romances have made Bertha the daughter of an emperor of Constantinople; others trace her descent from Flore, the king of Hungary, and the queen **Blanche-Fleur**. One of these rhymed romances, by a French minstrel named Adenès le Roi, was written in the second half of the 13th century from popular legends reaching back to the 8th century. As to Bertha's descendants, Charlemagne married ***Himiltrude**, then ***Desiderata**, the daughter of Desiderius, king of the Lombards, but the marriage was repudiated; he then married ***Hildegarde of Swabia** in 771, and the couple gave birth to Charles, Pepin (king of Italy), Louis the Pious (emperor of the Romans), and others. Following Hildegarde's death in 783, Charlemagne married ***Fastrada** and, later, ***Luitgard**.

SOURCES:

Bullough, D. *The Age of Charlemagne*. 2nd ed. Paul Elek, 1973.

Duckett, E.S. *Carolingian Portraits: A Study in the Ninth Century*. University of Michigan Press, 1962.

Einhard and Notker the Stammerer. *Two Lives of Charlemagne*. Translated by L. Thorpe. Penguin (reprint), 1969.

Tierney B. and S. Painter. *Western Europe in the Middle Ages, 300–1475. 4th ed. Knopf, 1983.*

Bertha (779–after 823)

Frankish princess. *Born in 779; died after 823; daughter of ****Hildegarde of Swabia*** *(c. 757–783) and Charles I also known as Charlemagne (742–814), king of the Franks (r. 768–814), Holy Roman emperor (r. 800–814); associated with Angilbert, the abbott of St. Riquier; children: (with Angilbert) Nithard (b. around 800, the historian); Hartnid.*

Bertha-Eudocia the Frank (fl. 900s)

Byzantine empress. *Flourished in the 900s; died young; first wife of Romanos or Romanus II, Byzantine emperor (r. 959–963); no children. Romanus II's second wife was ****Theophano*** *(c. 940–?).*

Bertha-Irene of Sulzbach (d. 1161)

Byzantine queen. *Name variations: Bertha of Sulzbach; Irene of Sulzbach. Born Bertha of Sulzbach; birth date unknown; died in 1161; daughter of Berengar II, count of Sulzbach; sister of ****Gertrude of Sulzbach*** *(d. 1146); sister-in-law of Conrad III (1093–1152), Holy Roman emperor (r. 1138–1152); became first wife of Manuel I Comnenus, emperor of Byzantium (r. 1143–1180), in 1146; children: two daughters.*

Bertha-Irene of Sulzbach was the daughter of the count of Sulzbach, and sister-in-law of the Holy Roman emperor Conrad III, who arranged her betrothal to Manuel Comnenus, emperor of Byzantium. The marriage was celebrated at Constantinople in 1146. The new empress, who changed her christened name of Bertha to Irene, a name more familiar to the Greeks, became a devoted wife, and by the simplicity of her manner contrasted favorably with most Byzantine queens of the age. Manuel, however, cared little for his first wife, who gave him two daughters, and he had numerous affairs. After Bertha-Irene's death in 1161, he married ***Marie of Antioch** (fl. 1180–1183), who mothered his only legitimate son Alexius II Comnenus (1168?–1183), emperor of Byzantium.

Bertha of Avenay (fl. 6th c.)

Frankish saint. *Died at end of the 6th century; married Gumbert (also canonized as a saint).*

Bertha of Avenay and her husband Gumbert were related to the kings of the Franks. After Gumbert was martyred in Ireland where he had gone as a missionary, Bertha founded a convent near Avenay in Champagne and became its abbess. She was killed there by her nephews who objected to the generous gifts she had bestowed on the church. Bertha's feast day is on May 1.

Bertha of Avenay (c. 830–c. 852)

Abbess of Avenay. *Born around 830; died after 852; daughter of ****Irmengard*** *(c. 800–851) and Lothair also* *known as Lothar I (795–855), Holy Roman emperor (r. 840–855).*

Bertha of Blangy (d. 725)

French saint. *Possibly born in Artois; died around 725; married a noble; children: several.*

Following the death of her husband, a noble of the Merovingian court, Bertha founded the abbey of Blangy, where she went into seclusion with her two daughters. Eventually, she resigned as abbess and spent the rest of her life in enclosure, living in a cell beside the abbey church. The room had a window that looked on the altar and was opened each day to allow her to assist at mass and speak to the community. One of Bertha's daughters succeeded her as abbess. Her feast day is July 4.

Bertha of Brittany (d. 1163)

Duchess of Brittany. *Name variations: Bertha Fergaunt. Birth date unknown; died in 1163; daughter of Conan III, duke of Brittany, and Matilda (illegitimate daughter of King Henry I of England); married Odo of Porhoet, duke of Brittany; married Alan III, 1st earl of Richmond; children: Conan IV, duke of Brittany.*

Bertha of Burgundy (964–1024).

See Matilda of Flanders for sidebar.

Bertha of Burgundy (d. 1097)

Queen of Castile and Leon. *Died in 1097; daughter of William I, count of Burgundy, and* ***Etienette de Longwy****; became third wife of Alphonso VI (c. 1030–1109), king of Leon (r. 1065–1070, 1072–1109) and Castile (r. 1072–1109), in 1093.*

Bertha of Chartres (d. 1084)

Countess of Brittany. *Died in 1084; daughter of Odo II, count of Blois, and possibly Emelia; married Alan III, count of Brittany; married Hugo IV, count of Maine, in 1046; children: (first marriage) Conan II, duke of Brittany; ****Hawise of Brittany*** *(d. 1072).*

Bertha of Holland (1055–1094)

Queen of France. *Name variations: Bertrada. Born in 1055; died in 1094 (some sources cite 1093); daughter of Florent I, count of Holland; stepdaughter of Robert the Frisian; became first wife of Philip I the Fair (1052–1108), king of France (r. 1060–1108), in 1072 (divorced 1092); children: Louis VI (c. 1081–1137), king of France (r. 1108–1137); ****Constance of France*** *(fl. 1100s, who married Bohemund of Taranto, prince of Antioch).*

Bertha of Kent (c. 565–c. 616)

Queen of Kent and religious founder. *Born around 565 in Paris; died around 616 in Kent, England; daughter of Cherebert also known as Caribert or Charibert I, king of Paris (r. 561–567), and possibly ****Ingoberge*** *(519–589); great-granddaughter of ****Clotilda*** *(470–545); married St. Ethelbert (Aethelbert), king of Kent (r. c. 560–616), before 589; children: Aethelbald also known as Eadbald, king of Kent (r. 616–640); Ethelberga of Northumbria (d. 647), later queen of Northumbria; great-grandmother of ****Elflaed****, abbess of Whitby (fl. 640–713).*

Bertha was an influential queen of Kent, in southeastern England. Born into the royal Merovingian house of France, she was brought up as a Christian and married King Ethelbert of Kent before 589. As queen of Kent, she brought Merovingian Christian culture to southeast England. Her marriage treaty stipulated that she have free exercise in her religion, and she was active in promoting Christianity in her realm; her husband was the first English king to convert to the new faith, in large part due to her influence. In 597, Bertha also convinced him to receive Augustine, legate of Pope Gregory the Great, along with 40 monks, an event which led to the conversion of all of Kent. Together, Bertha and Ethelbert founded Canterbury Church, still one of England's most important religious establishments. Bertha had at least two children, Eadbald and ***Ethelberga of Northumbria**. Eadbald, who succeeded Ethelbert as king of Kent, reverted to paganism after his parents' deaths, but by that time Christian beliefs were already too strongly founded in southeast England for the kingdom as a whole to revert. Bertha's daughter Ethelberga, who remained a Christian, married King Edwin of Northumbria. King Ethelbert died in 616 after a long reign; it is believed that Bertha died soon after.

Laura York, Anza, California

Bertha of Marbais (d. 1247)

Saint. *Name variations: Bertha de Marbais. Died in 1247; related to ****Johanna of Flanders*** *(d. 1244).*

Bertha of Marbais was a nun at the abbey of Aywières, then abbess of the abbey of Marquette. Her feast day is celebrated on July 18.

Bertha of Savoy (1051–1087)

Holy Roman empress. *Born on September 21, 1051; died on December 27, 1087, in Mainz, Germany; daughter of Otto, count of Savoy, and* ***Adelaide of Turin;*** *married Henry IV (1050–1106), king of Germany and Holy Roman emperor (r. 1056–1106), in 1066; children: Conrad (d. 1101), king of Germany (r. 1087) and Holy Roman emperor (r. 1093–1101); Henry V (1081–1125), king of Germany and Holy Roman emperor (r. 1106–1125); Agnes of Germany (1074–1143).*

Wife of the Salian emperor Henry IV of Germany, Bertha of Savoy had three children: Conrad, king of Germany (1087) and Italy (1093) who died in 1101; Henry who married ***Matilda of England** (1102–1167) in 1114, and was crowned Henry V, king of Germany, in 1106, and ***Agnes of Germany**, who married Frederick, duke of Swabia. Bertha was with her husband Henry in 1076, when, threatened with excommunication, he made his famous midwinter dash across the Alps to meet with ***Matilda of Tuscany** and Pope Gregory VII at Canossa (*see Matilda of Tuscany entry for more information on the "incident at Canossa"*). Her husband's last years were also marred by the rebellion of their sons. Following Bertha's death, Henry married ***Adelaide of Kiev**.

Bertha of Sulzbach (d. 1161).

See Bertha-Irene of Sulzbach.

Bertha of Swabia (fl. 900s).

See Adelaide of Burgundy for sidebar.

Bertha of Toulouse (fl. late 700s)

Queen of Italy. *Flourished in the late 700s; married Pippin also known as Pepin I (773–810), king of Italy (r. 781–810), in 795; children: Bernard (c. 799–818), king of Italy (r. 810–818); and five daughters (names unknown).*

Berthe.

Variant of Bertha.

Berthgyth (fl. 8th c.)

English nun and letter writer. *Born in England in the 8th century; died in Thuringia (modern Germany); daughter of Cynehild (a scholar and teacher); never married; no children.*

During the 8th century, Berthgyth was born and raised in England. When her mother **Cynehild**, a highly educated woman who shared her learning with her daughter, traveled to Thuringia (in modern-day Germany) to teach and help convert the native population to Christianity at the request of St. Boniface, she brought young Berthgyth with her while leaving her other children in England. Berthgyth remained in Thuringia for the rest of her life, deeply involved in St. Boniface's missionary work even after Boniface's death in 754 and her mother's death some years later. Berthgyth's life has been preserved through three letters she wrote to her brother Balthard, in England. The letters, written in highly refined Latin and containing some original Latin verse, express her feelings of isolation and sorrow after Cynehild's death and ask Balthard to visit. They were well preserved, probably due to the author's connection with the revered St. Boniface and their own literary value.

Laura York, Anza, California

Berthrada (d. 783).

See Bertha.

Bertie, Catharine (1519–1580)

Duchess of Suffolk. *Name variations: Katherine or Catherine Willoughby; Dowager of Suffolk. Born on March 22, 1519 (some sources cite 1520, but her baptism was on March 26, 1519, in Parham, Suffolk); died on September 19, 1580; interred at Spilsby, Lincolnshire; only child of William Willoughby, 8th baron Willoughby of Eresby, and* ***Mary de Salinas;*** *married Charles Brandon (1484–1545), duke of Suffolk (r. 1514–1545), on September 7, 1534 or 1536; married Richard Bertie (1516–1582), M.P., in 1553; children: (first marriage) Henry Brandon (b. 1535), 2nd duke of Suffolk; Charles Brandon (b. 1537), 3rd duke of Suffolk; (second marriage) Peregrine Bertie (b. 1555), Lord Willoughby of Eresby.*

Catharine Bertie, duchess of Suffolk, was a fervent advocate for the Reformation. Her husband Charles Brandon was also married to ***Anne Browne** (d. 1511), ***Margaret Neville** (b. 1466), and ***Mary Tudor** (1496–1533).

Bertille (d. 705/713)

French saint. *Born into a landowning family near Soissons, France; died between 705 and 713.*

Bertille became a nun at the abbey of Jouarre which followed the strict rule of St. Columbanus. A few miles away, the tiny convent of Chelles was built by Queen **Chrodegilde**. In

658, it was enlarged by Queen *Balthild who then brought Bertille from Jouarre to be its director. When Balthild was driven from the throne around 665, she spent the last 14 years of her life under the rule and guidance of Bertille, who was abbess at Chelles for 46 years. Her feast day is on November 5.

Bertin, Louise Angélique (1805–1877)

French poet and composer. *Born in 1805; died in 1877.*

Louise Angélique Bertin was a painter, poet, and musician. She wrote the operas *Guy Mannering* (Opera Comique, 1827), *Fausto* (Italiens, 1831), *La Esméralda*, text by Victor Hugo (Grand Opera, 1836), and *Le Loup-garou*. According to Halévy, she had "an abundance of ideas and often revealed a rare power of expression." Her volume of poems, entitled *Les Glanes* (1842) was honored by the French Academy.

Bertini, Francesca (1888–1985)

Italian actress. *Born Elena Seracini Vitiello in Florence, Italy, on April 11, 1888; died in 1985; daughter of a stage actress; married Paul Cartier (a Swiss count), in 1921.*

A dark, fiery Neapolitan, Francesca Bertini made her film debut in *La Dea del Mare* in 1907. Her first Italian success was in *Il Trovatore* in 1910; her first international success was in the 1915 realist film *Assunta Spina*, directed by Gustavo Serena. Italy's first screen diva, Bertini was prominent in the early period of Italian cinema, influencing fashion the world over. Though she reputedly had signed a million-dollar contract with Fox in 1920, she retired from film when she married Count Paul Cartier in 1921 but returned sporadically, most notably appearing with a host of international stars in Bernardo Bertolucci's film *1900* in 1976. Her autobiography *Il Resto non conta* was published in 1969, and Giancalo Mignozzi's film *The Last Diva*, which documented her career, was released in 1983.

Her films include *La Dea del Mare* (1907), *Il Trovatore* (1910), *Ernani* (1911), *Giulietta e Romeo* (*Romeo and Juliet*, 1911), *Tristano e Isota* (*Tristan and Isolde*, 1911), *Francesca da Rimini* (1911), *Re Lear* (*King Lear*, 1911), *Lorenzo il Magnifico* (1911), *Il Mercante di Venezia* (1912), *La Rosa di Tebe* (1912), *Idillio tragico* (1912), *La Gloria* (1913), *Terra promessa* (1913), *La Madre* (1913), *Salome* (1913), *Eroismo d'Amore* (1914), *Assunta Spina* (1915), *La Signora dalle Camelie* (*Camille*, 1915), *La Perla del Cinema* (1916), *Fedora* (1916), *Odette* (1916), *Andreina* (1917), *La Tosca* (1918), *Frou-Frou* (1918), *Anima allegra* (1918), *La Donna nuda* (1918), *La Contesa Sarah* (1919), *Spiritismo* (1919), *Beatrice* (1919), *Anima selvaggia* (1920), *Marion* (1921), *La Giovinezza del Diavolo* (1921), *Conseulita* (1922), *Monte Carlo* (1928), *Odette* (1928), *Possession* (1929), *Dora* (1943), *A Sud Niente di Nuovo* (1956), *Novecento* (*1900*, 1976).

Francesca Bertini in Assunta Spina, *1915.*

Bertrada.

See Bertha (d. 783).

Bertrada of Evreux (fl. 1170s)

Countess of Chester. *Name variations: Bertrade d'Evreux. Flourished in the 1100s; daughter of Simon, count of Evreux, and* ***Amice de Beaumont****; married Hugh de Kevilioc, 3rd earl of Chester; children: Ranulf de Blondville, 4th earl of Chester (c. 1172–1232, who was the second husband of* ****Constance of Brittany*** *[1161–1201]);* ****Maude of Chester*** *(1171–1233); Hawise, countess of Lincoln; Adeliz de Keveliock; Agnes, Lady of Chartley.*

Bertrada of Montfort (d. after 1117)

Queen of France. *Name variations: Bertrada de Montfort; Bertha; countess of Anjou. Birth date unknown; died after 1117; married Fulk IV the Rude, count of Anjou, in 1089 (annulled before 1093); be-*

*came second wife of Philip I the Fair (1052–1108), king of France (r. 1060–1108), in 1092 or 1095; children: (first marriage) Fulk V the Younger, count of Anjou and king of Jerusalem; (second marriage) Philip; *Cecilia of France (who married Tancred, prince of Antioch). Philip I was also married to *Bertha of Holland (1055–1094).*

Following the death of her second husband Philip I, king of France, in 1108, Bertrada of Montfort entered the convent and became a nun.

Beruriah (fl. 2nd c.)

Woman of the Talmud renowned for her learning and valor. *Lived in the 2nd century, during the revolt of Bar Kochba (132–135 CE); daughter of Rabbi Hanina ben Teradion; married Rabbi Meir.*

Beruriah is known as the only woman of Talmudic literature whose views were seriously considered by scholars. Living during the revolt of Bar Kochba (132–135 CE), the Jews' final attempt to liberate themselves from Roman rule, she was a teacher in the academy, a highly unusual position for a woman. In her own time and thereafter, Beruriah was legendary, and the phrase "Rightly did Beruriah say . . ." precedes stories that tell of her wisdom and righteousness.

Beruriah's husband Rabbi Meir, perhaps due to his wife's great talents, maintained a more tolerant attitude toward women's participation in studies than other Rabbis, allowing their attendance at his lectures. Eruvim 53b tells us that Beruriah expressed her own view as to the rabbinic attitude toward her sex by subtly confronting the prejudice against women:

> Rabbi Jose the Galilean was once on a journey when he met Beruriah.
> "By what road," he asked her, "do we go to Lydda?"
> "Foolish Galilean," she replied, "did not the sages say this: 'Engage not in much talk with women?' You should have asked: 'By which to Lydda?'"

The most famous story about Beruriah concerns the sudden deaths of her two sons on the Sabbath. In order to avoid disturbing her husband's Sabbath peace, she withholds this news in a gesture which has been seen as illustrative of her role as a good wife and of her realization that her emotional strength surpassed that of her husband. Following Havdalah, the ceremony which marks the Sabbath's close, she tells her husband (*Midrash Proverbs 30, 10*):

> Some time ago I was entrusted by a friend with some jewels for safekeeping and now he wants them back. Shall I return them?
> Of course, answered Rabbi Meir, the jewels must be returned.
> Beruriah then took him to where their dead sons were lying. When he collapsed and cried, she gently reminded him: "Did you not say we must return to the owner the precious jewels he entrusted to us? The Lord has given the Lord has taken away. Blessed be the name of the Lord."

The legend of Beruriah's tragic death maintains that Rabbi Meir, in order to test his wife and prove that the prejudices against women were not without basis, secretly arranged for one of his pupils to seduce her. Beruriah, feeling herself tempted by the pupil, realizes her weakness and kills herself. Following the death of his wife, it is said that Rabbi Meir fled to Babylonia, brokenhearted.

SOURCES:

Henry, Sondra, and Emily Taitz. *Written Out of History: Our Jewish Foremothers.* NY: Biblio Press, 1990.

Bervoets, Marguerite (1914–1944)

Belgian resistance leader, teacher, and poet. *Born in La Louviere, Belgium, in 1914; executed in August 1944; studied literature and philosophy in Brussels and taught at the École Normale in Tournai.*

Active in underground activities from the start of the Nazi occupation of her country; produced an illegal newspaper in her home and also was involved in procuring weapons and recruiting new members for the underground; captured (1942); deported to Germany (1943); after captivity in many prisons and concentration camps, sentenced to death (March 1944), a sentence that was carried out in August of that year.

Marguerite Bervoets was a sensitive, cultured woman who harbored intense patriotic feelings about her native Belgium, a country that suffered severely from German invasions in both World Wars. Her intellectual curiosity drew her to study not only literature and philosophy, but also law, art history and music. On the eve of World War II, in 1937, she began teaching at the École Normale in Tournai; this way of life was interrupted, however, with the German invasion of the lowlands in May 1940.

Political repression and a tightening noose around the Jewish community in Belgium characterized the Nazi occupation. The response of young patriotic intellectuals like Bervoets, who found the behavior of the German occupiers morally intolerable, was to engage in underground work, including armed struggle. She joined the Tournai branch of the resistance organization "Légion Belge" and was instrumental in linking this unit with similar ones in Charleroi, Mons and Lille. She eventually procured weapons and recruited new members of the underground; she also used her home as a storage center for the local resistance cells and to print a clandestine newspaper, *La Déliverance*. By 1942, Bervoets was active in Northern France, protecting and supporting Allied parachutists involved in various intelligence missions.

Bervoets' luck ran out on August 8, 1942, when she was arrested while taking photographs at the Chievres-Brugelette airport. First imprisoned and interrogated at Mons prison, she was deported to Germany in June 1943, where she spent time in prisons in Essen and Cologne, as well as at the Mesum concentration camp. Transferred to Leer prison, she was sentenced to death on March 22, 1944. As the machinery of the Nazi punitive system broke down in the last year of the regime's life, she was once more moved to other prisons in Osnabrück, Bremen, Brunswick, and Wolfenbüttel. At Wolfenbüttel, Bervoets was executed by decapitation on August 9, 1944.

Before her arrest, she had written a friend:

> I assign to you the task of alleviating my mother's pain in the event of my death. Tell her that I died so that the sky over Belgium can be purified and that all who come after me can live in freedom, which is what I would have wished for myself, and that despite everything that has happened I regret nothing.

John Haag, Athens, Georgia

Berwick, Mary (1825–1864).

See Procter, Adelaide.

Besant, Annie (1847–1933)

British journalist, social reformer, Theosophist, and political leader who played an active role in the British trade union and Indian nationalist movements. *Name variations: Annie Wood; (pseudonym) Ajax. Pronunciation: BEZ-ant. Born Annie Wood on October 1, 1847, in London, England; died on September 20, 1933, in Madras, India; daughter of William Burton Persse (an insurance underwriter) and Emily (Morris) Wood; graduated from London University, B.Sc. 1880; married Frank Besant, on December 21, 1867; children: Arthur Digby (b. January 16, 1869) and Mabel Emily (b. August 28, 1870); (wards) Krishnamurti and Nityananda Naryaniah.*

Lived with and was educated by Ellen Marryat (1855–63); published short stories in Family Herald *(beginning in 1870); joined National Secular Society and began writing regular columns and articles under pseudonym Ajax for the* National Reformer; *convicted under obscenity laws for disseminating birth-control information (1877); entered London University; founded and edited* Our Corner *and* Link; *joined Fabian Society (1885); participated in Bloody Sunday riot and began to organize trade unions; elected to London School Board (1889); joined Theosophical Society and repudiated atheism and earlier stance on birth control (1890); assumed leadership of main Theosophical Society faction and moved to India (1893); established schools and lectured on need for social reform and Indian self-autonomy; founded and edited* Commonweal *and* New India; *elected president of Indian National Congress in 1917.*

Publications: On the Deity of Jesus of Nazareth *(1872);* Auguste Comte: His Philosophy, His Religion and His Sociology *(1875);* The Gospel of Atheism *(1877);* Law of Population *(1878);* England, India and Afghanistan *(1879);* Autobiographical Sketches *(1885);* Why I Am a Socialist *(1886);* Modern Socialism *(1886);* Why I Do Not Believe in God *(1887);* My Path to Atheism *(1889);* Why I Became a Theosophist *(1889);* Reincarnation *(1892);* Seven Principles of Man *(1892);* An Autobiography *(1893);* Death and After *(1893);* Building of the Kosmos *(1894);* In the Outer Court *(1895);* Karma *(1895);* The Self and its Sheaths *(1895);* Path of Discipleship *(1896);* Man and his Bodies *(1896);* Four Great Religions *(1897);* The Ancient Wisdom *(1897);* Three Paths to Union with God *(1897);* Revolution of Life and Form *(1898);* Dharma *(1899);* The Story of the Great War *(1899);* Avâtares *(1900);* Ancient Ideals in Modern Life *(1901);* Esoteric Christianity *(1901);* Thought Power *(1901);* The Religious Problem in India *(1902);* Pedigree of Man *(1903);* A Study in Consciousness *(1904);* Theosophy and the New Psychology *(1904);* Hints on the Bhagavad Gita *(1905);* Wisdom of the Upanishats *(1906);* H.P. Blavatsky and the Masters of Wisdom *(1907);* Wake Up India *(1913);* Man: Whence, How and Whither *(1913);* How India Wrought for Freedom *(1915); (co-authored with C.W. Leadbeater)* Occult Chemistry *(1919); (co-authored with Leadbeater)* Thoughtforms *(1919);* The Future of Indian Politics *(1922);* The Coming of the World Teacher *(1925);* India, Bond or Free *(1926);* Indian Ideals *(1930);* India a Nation *(1930).*

Few women to emerge from Victorian Britain aroused as much hatred, outrage, and

Annie Besant

public disapproval as Annie Besant. In a career spanning more than 60 years, she used her role as an influential journalist, political activist, and social reformer to challenge and reform existing attitudes about birth control, religion, the plight of industrial laborers and the growth of Indian nationalism. Her many controversial and contradictory campaigns, which alienated friend and foe alike, had a dramatic and lasting impact on British and Indian political and social development in the late 19th and early 20th centuries.

Born in October 1847 into a middle-class Irish family living in London, Annie was the second of three children of William Burton Persse Wood and **Emily Morris Wood.** When Annie was five, her father, a sometime scholar and dilettante, died from an infection caught while attending the autopsy of a tuberculosis victim. Within a few months, Annie's younger brother Alfred also contracted a fatal illness and soon followed his father to the grave. Although William Wood had made a comfortable living as an insurance underwriter, he left no money behind to care for his grieving family. Faced with the prospect of poverty, Emily and her children left their comfortable home in the fashionable London suburb of St. John's Wood and went to live with relatives in nearby Clapham.

Two years later, Emily moved her family to Harrow where she opened a boarding house catering to pupils of the nearby elite public school. This not only allowed Emily to provide for her family, it also enabled her to buy a quality education for her remaining son Henry, so that he could fulfill his father's dying wish and enter the legal profession. Annie's education, on the other hand, was left to **Ellen Marryat**, a wealthy and philanthropic evangelical Christian, who taught a select group of underprivileged pupils at her home in Dorset. For the next eight years, Besant was to remain in Marryat's charge, returning home only for occasional brief holidays. While in Dorset, she received a very unorthodox education for a Victorian girl. Instead of learning to sew and keep house, Besant acquired the same academic education—with particular emphasis on religious instruction, writing ability, and foreign language skills—as her male peers within the Marryat household. This early grounding in religion and education sparked the beginning of a religious odyssey and search for wisdom that were to occupy her for the rest of her life.

By 1863, Besant had absorbed all that her teacher had to offer and was sent home to Harrow where she spent the next three years continuing her own education by reading widely. Her religious awakening also continued in this period and led her closer to Catholicism, which she had first encountered on the Continent with Ellen Marryat the previous year. During Easter of 1866, Besant began writing a history of the Holy Week as recounted in the Gospels. What began as an act of religious devotion soon ended in intense religious doubt as she uncovered numerous discrepancies in the stories of the Resurrection as recorded in the four Gospels.

In the midst of all this, Frank Besant, a young teacher and cleric, began courting Annie with her mother's encouragement. His proposal apparently caught the 18-year-old offguard and before she knew it she found herself engaged. Although thrilled by her daughter's engagement, Emily refused to allow a public announcement until the following year on the grounds that Annie was still too young. In the meantime, Besant was sent to Switzerland in the summer of 1866 for a last brief *wanderjahr* before her marriage. While in Switzerland, she met and befriended William Roberts, a radical lawyer involved in the growing British trade-union movement. Under his tutelage, she began learning about the horrors of factory work and the plight of the urban poor.

Besant returned to England in the fall and began preparing for her impending nuptials. Her marriage, which finally took place in late December of 1867, was a disaster from the beginning. Like most Victorian women, she had led a sheltered life and had little knowledge of sex. As a result, her wedding night came as a horrible shock from which she recovered only with great difficulty. Her growing unhappiness was compounded when Frank secured a teaching post at Cheltenham College the following month. Bored and depressed by her new surroundings, Besant retreated into books and the start of what was soon to become a prolific writing career.

Her first literary attempt was a hagiography of little-known saints. While the manuscript made the rounds of various publishers before eventually disappearing, Besant also began work on a series of short stories which were accepted for publication in the *Family Herald*. Her delight at receiving payment for her work was soon crushed when Frank, exercising a husband's rights over his wife's property, appropriated the check. Although she persevered and soon added religious pamphlets to her repertoire, Besant's budding literary career was almost snuffed out by her husband's disapproval and the birth of her two children, Arthur Digby and Mabel, in quick succession.

As she was recovering from Mabel's birth in August of 1870, Besant learned that a dishonest solicitor had bilked her mother of her savings. The following spring, Annie Besant collapsed after nursing both of her children through bouts of whooping cough. When the 24-year-old emerged from her sickbed, she was a changed woman and began railing against the injustice of a God who allowed the weak and innocent to suffer. Although her new attitude further weakened her already tenuous marriage, she accompanied Frank when he gave up his teaching post and accepted a position as vicar of a small village in Lincolnshire. Soon after her arrival in the village of Sibsey, Besant realized that she had made a dreadful mistake. Finding that the charity work traditionally expected of a vicar's wife did little to alleviate her sense of isolation, she quickly slipped back into depression. When Frank, already overbearing and highly critical, turned physically abusive in the summer of 1872, Besant fled to her mother.

While in London, she met and befriended Reverend Charles Voysey, a leading Dissenter and renegade cleric. Her relationship with Voysey soon led Besant into contact with other Dissenters and Freethinkers, including the influential publisher Charles Scott. Encouraged to continue her exploration of her own religious doubts, Besant cast off the trappings of Christianity and embraced Theism. When she returned to Sibsey later that fall in an attempt at reconciliation with Frank, Besant found that her new religious beliefs and subsequent publication of a theist pamphlet, entitled *On the Deity of Jesus of Nazareth*, had embarrassed her husband and raised an impenetrable barrier between them.

This unhappy situation was finally resolved the following spring when Frank issued an ultimatum after Besant took the children to visit her mother and brother in Southsea. Finding his demand for her immediate return and total conformity to all Church doctrine and practices more than she could bear, Besant initiated proceedings to formally end their marriage. To her dismay, she discovered that divorce was a very complicated matter for Victorian women. Not only were women denied the right to act on their own behalf in legal matters, they had to prove that they were the victims of adultery, cruelty, or desertion in order to qualify for a divorce. Although she found herself unable to prove that Frank was guilty of cruelty, Besant was able to get him to agree to a legal separation in late October of 1873; she was to retain custody of Mabel and was to receive a quarter of Frank's income as child support. Her visitation rights for Digby, who was to remain in his father's care, were limited to one month per year.

Although finally free of her unhappy marriage, Annie Besant faced new and equally daunting problems. Victorian society was not kind to divorced women and Besant, who had compounded matters by espousing non-traditional religious beliefs, found herself a social outcast with very little income on which to support herself and her daughter. To stave off the indignity of poverty, Besant was eventually forced to take a temporary position as a governess. Although she had finally made enough money by the end of 1874 to rent and furnish her own home, her happiness at this prospect was tempered by news that her mother had become fatally ill. In the months leading up to Emily's death, Besant found refuge in the British Museum reading room where she conducted research for a new series of religious pamphlets which her friend Scott had commissioned.

While Besant was grateful for the work, she found that her writing was insufficient to occupy either her time or intellect. In an effort to unearth kindred spirits and alleviate her own loneliness, she joined the Liberal Social Union and quickly developed a taste for lecturing after speaking out at several meetings. By the time she made her formal debut on the lucrative lecture circuit in late August 1874, Besant's ongoing religious doubts had transformed her into an atheist and led her to join the National Secular Society. The success of her first public lecture brought her to the attention of the Society's president and founder, Charles Bradlaugh, who subsequently offered her a steady job as a writer and assistant editor of the *National Reformer*. From the beginning, her weekly articles (which mocked opponents of Freethought, advocated social reform, women's suffrage and called for an end to imperialism around the world) appeared under the pseudonym Ajax to spare Scott, for whom she also still wrote, a potentially embarrassing connection to the often controversial *National Reformer* and its parent organization.

Besant's efforts at anonymity did not, however, last. At her second appearance, which dealt with the plight of women and their demand for suffrage, her identity as Ajax was revealed. Although this fact was suppressed in the many reviews of her lecture, Scott was forced to publish Besant's next piece anonymously lest he risk permanent damage to his business prospects. Their working relationship received another serious jolt in the summer of 1878 when a member of the audience interrupted one of Besant's lectures to accuse her of supporting promiscuity and free love. While nothing could have been further from the truth, Besant's decision not to defend herself publicly damaged her reputation and caused her estranged husband to attempt to regain custody of Mabel. His efforts were only foiled through Bradlaugh's timely intervention and repeated threats of legal action.

In the meantime, Besant rose rapidly within the National Secular Society due to her eloquence and the vehemence of her attacks on the society's opponents. A scant year after joining the organization, she had become vice president and had emerged as one of its more vocal and influential members. In the spring of 1876, Besant moved into a house in St. John's Wood and began circulating the so-called "monster petition," demanding an end to parliamentary grants to the royal family. After presenting the petition to Parliament, which chose to ignore it, Besant began writing more and more articles in the *National Reformer* calling for widespread political and social reform.

Her growing public radicalism led Besant into deep trouble. When Charles Watts, a Bristol book merchant, was indicted under Victorian Britain's obscenity laws for publishing Charles Knowlton's *Fruits of Philosophy*, which both described and promoted various methods of birth control, Besant reviewed the book and insisted that it was defensible on medical grounds. Desperate to avoid a jail sentence, Watts pled guilty, much to Besant's disgust. Convinced that Watts' plea was a victory for censorship, in early 1877 Besant and Bradlaugh decided to challenge the basis of the Obscene Publications Act. In order to provoke a test case, they established the Freethought Publishing Company and brought out a new version of *Fruits of Philosophy*. Within weeks, both had been arrested and began defending themselves in a highly publicized trial which aroused enormous public interest due to both the subject matter and Besant's own spirited testimony. Despite an eloquent defense, both defendants were found guilty and sentenced to a fine and six months imprisonment. Freed on appeal, Besant began to publicly advocate the use of birth control. Her ideas were presented in the *Law of Population* which was first serialized in the *National Reformer* and then issued separately as an enormously popular pamphlet.

By August of 1877, Besant found herself in enormous demand on the lecture circuit due to the trial's publicity. As her influence grew, along with the size of her audience, she began to speak more often about peace, anti-imperialism, and the need for social justice. In January of the following year, the Court of Errors, after finally hearing their appeal, dismissed the case against both Besant and Bradlaugh on a technicality. Unfortunately, her good fortune ended here. Frank, incensed at his estranged wife's actions and association of his family name with atheism and birth control, formally sued to regain custody of Mabel. When Besant's brother declined to appear in court on her behalf, as he had done during her earlier legal battles with Frank, Bradlaugh offered to take over. His decision to use the custody hearings as a new forum in which to advocate Freethought ideology proved to be disastrous and caused Besant to lose her case. Subsequent appeals for Mabel's return and a new bid for a divorce also failed and led to increasingly restrictive visitation rights which Besant eventually decided to forego entirely in the hope that her children would seek her out on their own when they legally came of age.

Infuriated by these setbacks, she vowed to overcome the system and earn a law degree so that she might be better prepared for any future legal battles. To this end, she matriculated at London University in 1879, a scant year after the institution opened its doors to women. In order to pass the entrance exam required of all new students, Besant had turned to a fellow Freethinker, Edward Bibbins Aveling, to tutor her in science. As a result of these sessions, Besant abandoned law in favor of biology and earned a first-class degree the following year despite massive resistance and prejudice from within the male-dominated university community. Determined to pass on what she had learned, Besant began teaching courses of her own in the National Secular Society's Hall of Science.

> Society is to be reformed by a slow process of evolution, not by revolution and bloodshed.
>
> **—Annie Besant**

Although busy with teaching duties and her own studies, Besant still found time to lecture and write in support of social and political reform. At an open meeting in early February of 1880, she formally called for an end to primogeniture, advocated state seizure of land not in use for cultivation, and demanded immediate reform of the tax code in an effort to improve the plight of urban and rural laborers. The popularity of this platform led Besant to create the Land League, with help from both Aveling and Bradlaugh, and paved the way for the latter's first successful campaign for election to Parliament. As an atheist, however, many felt that Bradlaugh's oath of allegiance to the Crown, something required of all MPs, was meaningless. When his opponents seized upon the issue and used it to deprive him of his seat, Besant began campaigning tirelessly on Bradlaugh's behalf. These efforts were to occupy the bulk of her time for the next four years.

With Bradlaugh diverted by the effort to take up his parliamentary duties, the National

Secular Society began to fall into disarray. When Aveling joined socialists, a group which Bradlaugh had long opposed, and began a long-term romantic attachment with *__Eleanor Marx-Aveling__, he was expelled from the Society in disgrace. Deprived of her two mentors and colleagues, Besant began evolving her own political philosophy. Her ideas first appeared in 1884 in a series of *Autobiographical Sketches* which she published in her own newly founded journal entitled *Our Corner*. The next phase of Besant's political evolution came when she met and befriended George Bernard Shaw after he began submitting pieces for publication in *Our Corner*. Shaw soon led Besant to embrace socialism and supported her June 1884 application for membership in the newly founded Fabian Society, a group of intellectuals who called for the gradual reform of British society by freeing land and capital from individual ownership.

By March of 1885, Besant had been elected to the Fabian's executive committee and began leading many of the Society's subsequent reform campaigns. This growing public commitment to socialism finally estranged her from Bradlaugh and led to her 1887 resignation as co-editor of the *National Reformer*. Freed of her editing responsibilities, she turned her full attention to the plight of the working class. When a series of increasingly militant demonstrations by unemployed workers in the fall of 1888 resulted in mass arrests, Besant led the Fabians in arranging bail, organizing jail visits, and speaking out in support of the arrested workers. In the aftermath of the Bloody Sunday riots, which subsequently erupted in mid-November after the government tried to ban a planned mass meeting in Trafalgar Square, Besant's efforts on behalf of workers increased. Along with the journalist W.T. Stead, she created the Law and Liberty League and founded a new journal, *Link*, both of which were dedicated to reform efforts aimed at improving the lot of Britain's working classes.

Besant's continued exposés on factory conditions in *Our Corner, Link*, and the *National Reformer* triggered a strike later that year by women working in the match industry. After helping the women to unionize and win concessions from their employers, Besant was elected secretary of the union and was sent as one of its delegates to the International Trades Union Congress. Her successful intervention on behalf of the matchworkers led to appeals for her help from other groups, causing Besant to soon become a potent and influential force in the labor movement. Her increasing militancy and political activism did not end there. In late October of 1889, she was elected to the London School Board as the representative for Tower Hamlets. Within a few weeks, Besant had acquired a seat on all of the board's influential committees and began using her position to force firms receiving school-board contracts to abide by union rules and pay workers according to union mandated-wage scales. Flushed with success, she allowed both *Link* and *Our Corner* to fold and began devoting more and more of her time to the board's educational reform efforts.

In the midst of this frenzy of activity, Besant, to the consternation and disappointment of her reformist friends and colleagues, suddenly abandoned atheism and returned to religion. As she herself was later to describe, her atheism had been based on an unsuccessful search for a rationale behind the suffering which was plainly evident in the world around her. After reading *__Helena Blavatsky__'s *The Secret Doctrine* in early 1890, Besant felt that she had finally found her answers and eagerly joined Madame Blavatsky's mystical Theosophical Society. Despite having read reports that the Society's occult activities in India were fraudulent, Besant found its combination of mysticism, reincarnation, karma, and spiritual evolution very hard to resist. Encouraged by her new mentor to retract her ideas about birth control and family planning, both of which interfered with the process of reincarnation that was central to the Theosophical movement, Besant began buying up all the existing copies of her very successful *The Law of Population* and had the printing plates destroyed. Not content with this, within months she had taken over as editor of *Lucifer*, the society's journal, and began using its pages to complete her ideological reversal and advocate celibacy.

Shocked and horrified by these events, both Shaw and Bradlaugh sprung into action and tried to talk Besant out of her growing commitment to Theosophy. Her response was to resign from the Fabian Society and gradually disengage herself from many other commitments. When Bradlaugh became ill and had to step down as head of National Secular Society in February of 1890, Besant fully expected to take his place. To her dismay the Society's rank and file, disturbed by her socialism and Theosophical attachments, chose another candidate instead. Upset and humiliated, she resigned two weeks later and began devoting all her time to lecturing, traveling, and writing on behalf of the Theosophical movement.

As she was preparing to leave for the United States on a lecture tour the following year, Besant was surprised and delighted by the sudden return of her children, who having come of age, were anxious to reestablish contact and judge their mother for themselves. When the news of their actions finally reached Frank, he became infuriated and permanently severed all ties with both children. With her home life still in flux, Besant finally left for a highly successful lecture tour of the U.S. in early April of 1891. She returned home the following month to the news that Blavatsky had died and named Besant as her successor and leader of the Indo-European faction of the Theosophical Society. Blavatsky's partner and co-founder, Colonel Henry Olcott, began encouraging Besant to immigrate to India so that she could help manage the Society's headquarters in Madras. As a result, she declined to seek reelection to the school board the following year and began concentrating instead on fund-raising efforts to help support the movement and her impending emigration.

Besant finally left for India in the fall of 1893. On arrival, she embarked on a lecture tour and began learning Sanskrit to enhance her Theosophical studies. Within a year, however, the Theosophical Society was enveloped in a bitter and widely reported feud which erupted after the leader of the American faction, W.Q. Judge, attempted to take control of the entire movement. The failure of his attempted coup eventually prompted Judge and his followers to split off and form their own rival splinter group. Although Olcott remained nominally in charge as president, Judge's defection effectively transferred de facto control over the parent organization to Besant.

In the aftermath of the movement's leadership crisis, Besant concentrated her efforts on lecturing, writing books supporting Theosophy, advocating Indian Home Rule and promoting education. Drawing on her experience as a member of the London School Board, she founded Hindu Central College as a school for boys in 1898. Other schools followed and eventually led her back to the center of controversy. Shortly after her arrival in India, Besant met Charles Leadbeater, a notorious spiritualist and Theosophist of dubious repute. Although Blavatsky had never liked or trusted him, Besant began rapidly promoting Leadbeater within the organization and collaborated with him on several books linking science and mysticism. When Leadbeater, who had joined in her educational efforts, was subsequently brought up on charges that he was a pederast and had been teaching students to masturbate, Besant outraged parents and her fellow Theosophists by defending him.

Despite the damage to her reputation caused by continued association with Leadbeater, she was formally elected president of the Theosophical Society after Olcott's death in February of 1907. Now 60, Besant celebrated with a barnstorming tour of Australia that did much to revive the flagging organization's reputation. This was not, however, to last very long. In 1909, Leadbeater found two Indian boys and presented one of them, Krishnamurti Naryaniah, to Besant as the movement's Avatar, or future world teacher, who was to lead humanity in its evolution to a higher spiritual stage. After obtaining legal guardianship over the two boys in the spring of 1911, Besant took them to England to be educated. On her return to India later that fall, she resumed her lecturing career and, in addition to touching upon her now familiar themes of Indian home rule, the need for education and the pernicious effects of child marriage, Besant also began telling her audiences about the coming of the world teacher. Hearing that his son was being deified, Krishnamurti's father sued to regain custody of his children. When Besant lost the case in an Indian court, she appealed to the Privy Council in London and was eventually granted permanent custody in 1914.

As she fought her custody battles in the courts, Besant's preoccupation with mysticism temporarily declined, leaving her free to concentrate on Indian politics instead. In 1913, her anti-imperialism, already more than three decades old, took a new turn when she joined the Indian National Congress and began accusing England of looting Indian wealth, stifling its industry, and promoting racial discrimination in the name of imperial rule. In an effort to spread her message, Besant launched a new journal, *Commonweal*, and set off on yet another lecture tour across the Indian sub-continent. When the First World War broke out in 1914, she used the pages of the *New India*, a defunct newspaper which she had acquired the previous year, to call for Indian participation in the war effort. Her support for the war, however, came with a price. Unlike some Indian nationalists, Besant refused to cease her agitation for Indian home rule during the war years. These efforts, which eventually led to the 1916 creation of the Home Rule League, simultaneously made Besant a villain to the British and a hero to Indians. Her activities were eventually considered so dangerous and subversive by the British government that it ordered her interned for three months in 1917. On her release, Besant's popularity in India rose to new heights and led to her election as president of the Indian National Congress.

Within a few months, however, Besant's newly created image among Indian nationalists was tarnished by her growing public opposition to Mohandas Gandhi's passive resistance campaign. Although she professed great personal admiration for Gandhi and his efforts, Besant remained convinced that passive resistance would only end in bloodshed. In the aftermath of the Armritsar massacre of 1919, which saw British troops open fire on trapped Indian protestors, Besant felt that her opposition had been entirely justified and was surprised to find that the color of her skin had suddenly discredited her in the newly radicalized movement. Although she lost her bid for reelection to the presidency of the Indian National Congress in 1920, Besant refused to retreat from politics and concentrated instead on efforts to get Indian nationalists to draft and present their own constitution to the British Parliament for ratification. When Parliament rejected the proposed constitution in 1925, Besant finally retired from politics and resumed her emphasis on Theosophy.

Although well into her late 70s, Besant resumed a punishing schedule on behalf of the Theosophical Society. Back in India in time for her 80th birthday, she was horrified to find that Krishnamurti, her adopted son and the Society's supposed messiah, had begun to question his commitment to Theosophy and had gradually begun to withdraw from the movement. When Krishnamurti formally and publicly repudiated Theosophy in 1929, Besant threw herself into a desperate attempt at damage control, a task which occupied her until her death on September 20, 1933.

While the complex and contradictory nature of her life and work defy easy description, there can be no doubt as to Annie Besant's ability to influence, shock, and reform the world around her. As a journalist, social reformer, union organizer, and political activist, she broke free of the many restrictions placed on Victorian women and left an indelible imprint on British and Indian society that remains unmatched to this day.

SOURCES:

Dinnage, Rosemary. *Annie Besant.* Hammondsworth: Penguin Books, 1986.

Longford, Elizabeth. *Eminent Victorian Women.* NY: Alfred A. Knopf, 1981.

Nethercot, Arthur. *The First Five Lives of Annie Besant.* Chicago: University of Chicago Press, 1960.

——. *The Last Four Lives of Annie Besant.* London: Rupert Hart-Davis, 1963.

Taylor, Anne. *Annie Besant.* Oxford: Oxford University Press, 1992.

West, Geoffrey. *Annie Besant.* NY: Viking Press, 1928.

SUGGESTED READING:

Chandrasekhar, S. *"A Dirty, Filthy Book."* Los Angeles: University of California Press, 1981.

Chaudhuri, Nupur, and Margaret Strobel, eds. *Western Women and Imperialism.* Bloomington: Indiana University Press, 1992.

Kumar, Raj. *Annie Besant's Rise to Power in Indian Politics 1914–1917.* New Delhi: Concept Publishing, 1981.

Lewis, Jane. *Women in England 1870–1950: Sexual Divisions and Social Change.* Bloomington: Indiana University Press, 1984.

Manvell, Roger. *The Trial of Annie Besant and Charles Bradlaugh.* NY: Horizon Press, 1976.

COLLECTIONS:

Correspondence, papers and manuscripts located in Theosophical Society Archives, Adyar, Madras, India and London, England; the National Secular Society Archives, London, England; British Library, London, England; Churchill College, Cambridge University, Cambridge, England; the Fabian Society Papers in Nuffield College, Oxford University, Oxford, England; the privately owned Bradlaugh Bonner papers; and the transcript of *Besant* v. *Wood,* Public Record Office, London, England.

Kenneth J. Orosz,
Ph.D. Candidate in European History
at Binghamton University, Binghamton, New York

Beskow, Elsa (1874–1953)

Swedish author and illustrator of children's books. *Born Elsa Maartman on February 11, 1874, in Stockholm, Sweden; died in 1953; daughter and one of six children of Bernt (a businessman) and Augusta (Fahlstedt) Maartman; attended Stockholm Technical School (now National College of Art, Craft, and Design); married Fredrik Natanael Beskow (a minister and headmaster), in 1892 or 1897; children: six sons.*

Selected writings—all children's books; all self-illustrated: Tant Grroen, Tant Brun, och Tant Gredelin *(1924, published in America as* Aunt Green, Aunt Brown, and Aunt Lavender, *1928);* Pelle's New Suit *(translated from the Swedish by M. Woodburn, 1929);* Aunt Brown's Birthday *(1930);* The Tale of the Wee Little Old Woman *(translated from the Swedish by Marion Woodburn, 1930);* Peter's Voyage *(translated from the Swedish by Rita Scherman, 1931);* Buddy's Adventures in the Blueberry Patch *(translated from the Swedish by Siri Andrews, 1931);* The Adventures of Peter and Lotta *(1931);* Elf Children of the Woods *(translated from the Swedish by Zita Beskow, 1932).*

Elsa Beskow said that her future was planned at the age of seven, when she made up her mind to "write and draw fairy-tale books." Between the years 1897 and 1952, she wrote and illustrated thirty-three books and eight collections of fairy tales. Through the years, her books have sold over three million copies in Sweden and have been translated into many languages. Beskow's stories have been praised for their insight into a child's perspective and for the accuracy and fine detail of their illustrations. Mary Oervig in *Top of the News* commented, "It is clearly seen how deeply Elsa Beskow understood children and with what genuine simplicity she talked to them."

Beskow's recollections of her own childhood, with summers spent at an idyllic lake-side country estate, among her "happy flock" of brothers and sisters, might have been torn from a page in one of her books. At an early age, she developed a passion for drawing and painting, as well as an enthusiasm for reading and making up fairy tales. By the age of 15, she was off to study at the Technical School in Sweden. Four years later, she abandoned her education when she became engaged to a young artist and theologian, and took a job as a technical teacher. By the time she married, Beskow had completed a series of painting books for children and her first storybook *The Wee Little Old Woman*, published in 1892. She produced books from that time on, using her husband as an advisor, and her six sons as models and critics.

During her 50-year career, Beskow won a number of awards, including the Swedish Library Association, Nils Holgersson Plaque, in 1952. After her death in 1953, the Elsa Beskow Award for best Swedish picture book illustrator was established in her honor. The first recipient of the plaque was ***Tove Jansson** in 1958.

Barbara Morgan, Melrose, Massachusetts.

Besnyö, Eva (1910—)

Hungarian-Dutch photographer, specializing in documentation. *Name variations: Besnyo. Born in Budapest, Hungary, in 1910; children: (with Wim Brusse) two.*

After training with established Budapest photographer Jozsef Pécsi, Eva Besnyö began her career in Berlin, shooting for magazines and industry. A liaison with Dutch photographer John Fernhout led her to Amsterdam, where she joined the Dutch Photographers' Society and worked commercially in architecture, portraits, and fashion, while also doing large mural work. In 1937, she helped organize the exhibition *Foto 37* at the Stedelijk Museum.

Of Jewish background, Besnyö was forced underground after the German takeover of the Netherlands. Following the liberation, an affair with graphic designer Wim Brusse, with whom she had two children, kept her out of circulation until 1968, when she separated from Brusse and went back to work. From 1970 to 1976, she was associated with the activist feminist group Dolle Mina. Exhibitions of Besnyö's early works were held in London (*Modern Spirit in Photography*, 1932) and at the Van Lier Gallery in Amsterdam (1933). In 1982, a retrospective of her work was exhibited at the Historisch Museum in Amsterdam.

Bess of Hardwick (1518–1608).

See Talbot, Elizabeth.

Bessborough, countess of (1761–1821).

See Lamb, Caroline for sidebar on Spencer, Henrietta Frances.

Betham-Edwards, Matilda (1836–1919)

British novelist and travel writer. *Born Matilda Barbara Betham-Edwards at Westerfield, Suffolk, England, on March 4, 1836; died at Hastings, Sussex, England, on January 4, 1919; daughter of Edward Edwards (a East Anglian farmer); niece of* ***Matilda Betham*** *(1776–1852, a poet and diarist); cousin of Amelia Blanford Edwards (an author and Egyptologist); educated at home and at a village school; never married, no children.*

Selected works: The White House by the Sea *(1857);* A Winter with the Swallows *(1866);* Through Spain to the Sahara *(1867);* Forestalled *(1880);* Love and Marriage *(1884);* Reminiscences *(1898);* Mid-Victorian Memories *(1919).*

"I suppose every one of us goes down to the grave with some wrankling regret, some unsatisfied wish," Matilda Betham-Edwards wrote in her autobiography *Reminiscences* (1898). "Mine will be a hankering after the Rule of Three." The three r's of formal schooling—reading, writing, and arithmetic—were considered unnecessary for girls, and Betham-Edwards and her two sisters were taught at home by their mother when chores for the family farm were done. For books and magazines, Betham-Edwards turned to the local Mechanics Institution, supplementing the oft-read family library of classics. She attended a small village school from age ten to twelve, during the slow farming seasons. When her mother died in 1848, an uncle recommended that she attend the Peckham School, which his daughter ***Amelia Blanford Edwards** attended. The young girls became friends and lifelong correspondents, often confusing the literary community with their similar names. For six months at Peckham, Betham-Edwards traded service as a governess for her tuition until she was called home to help with the farm. She also penned *The White House by the Sea* when she was a teenager. Published when she was 21, *The White House* was reprinted for 40 years, though she was only paid in copies.

Betham-Edwards left home to make her living as an author and journalist, covering French topics for the *Daily News*. With longtime friend ***Barbara Bodichon**, founder of England's first women's university Girton College, she traveled through Europe wrote guides of their experience. It was Bodichon who provided Betham-Edwards with an introduction to George Eliot (***Mary Anne Evans**). Eliot invited select intellectuals to her home for roundtable discussion. While Betham-Edwards never had a friendship with Eliot, "Thenceforward I was invited to the famous Sunday afternoon at the Priory." Famous friends also included Frederic Harrison and Henry James, whose correspondences and anecdotes Betham-Edwards shared in her *Mid-Victorian Memories* (1919).

Betham-Edwards was frail in her final years. As a houseguest, she provided her hosts an advance list of needs, including cotton, unlavendered sheets, one glass of Chablis at lunch, and absolutely no noise from her bedding hour to the time she arose. A herd of noisy cows opposite a friend's house once provided cause for concern. Though her body failed, Betham-Edwards' mind remained tuned to writing. In March of 1918, she wrote a friend: "Haven't been out of the house for months this year. Once out and then slipped down on wet cobblestones. . . . Quite well now and just finishing a set of fire-eating short stories." Matilda Betham-Edwards suffered a stroke on December 8, 1918, and died at home in January, just prior to publication of her *Mid-Victorian Memories*.

SUGGESTED READING:

Betham-Edwards, Matilda. *Mid-Victorian Memories*. London: John Murray, 1919.

———. *Reminiscences*. London: George Redway, 1898.

Crista Martin, freelance writer, Boston, Massachusetts

Bethell, Mary Ursula (1874–1945)

New Zealand naturalist poet. *Name variations: (pseudonym) Evelyn Hayes; Ursula Bethell. Born Mary Ursula Bethell in England on October 6, 1874; died in Christchurch, New Zealand, on January 15, 1945; daughter of Isabel Anne Bethell and Richard Bethell (both sheep farmers); educated at Christchurch Girls High School, a Swiss finishing school, and Oxford; longtime companion of Effie Pollen; no children.*

Selected works: From a Garden in the Antipodes *(1925);* Time and Place *(1936);* Day and Night: Poems 1924–1935 *(1939);* Collected Poems *(1950).*

Born in England in 1874, Mary Ursula Bethell moved with her family to Canterbury, New Zealand, as a young girl. There her father raised sheep, and she attended primary and high school. After an interval at finishing school in Switzerland, she returned to New Zealand, settling in Christchurch in 1892 where she performed charity work. Three years later, she set sail for Europe once more: the study of painting took her to Geneva, the study of music to Dresden, and work with the "Grey Ladies," a religious society dedicated to poor children, to London. By 1919, Bethell was back in New Zealand. In the Cashmere Hills of Christchurch, she retired from volunteering and lived for more than a decade with companion **Effie Pollen**. "From her I have had love, tenderness and understanding for 30 years," wrote Bethell.

In November of 1934, Pollen died after a brief illness. Yearly, on or near the anniversary of her death, Bethell wrote a memorial poem: "Today I trimmed my lonely dwelling place with flowers;/ . . . I see you, darling,/ Dispose, deft-handed, your bright bunches in that happy house of ours." On their hill in Christchurch, Bethell lived alone for another decade, until her death in January of 1945.

Ursula Bethell conceived most of her poetry in the garden overlooking the valley, and the view was often reflected in her lines. Originally, she only shared her work with correspondents. After a friend showed her writing to a publisher in England, Bethell would only permit publication under the pseudonym Evelyn Hayes or under a reference to a former publication ("by the author of *Time and Place*"). Though her identity was eventually revealed, it was not acknowledged in print until her collected poems appeared posthumously in 1950. Though Bethell is celebrated in New Zealand, wrote one critic, she is "not enough read elsewhere."

SUGGESTED READING:

Bethell, Mary Ursula. *Collected Poems*. Christchurch, New Zealand: The Caxton Press, 1950.

Crista Martin, freelance writer, Boston, Massachusetts

Bethoc (fl. 1000)

Heiress of Scone. *Name variations: Beatrice or Beatrix, heiress of Scone. Flourished around the year 1000;*

daughter of Malcolm II, king of Scots; married Grimus also known as Crinan (d. 1045), mormaer of Atholl and abbot of Dunkeld, around 1000; children: Duncan I (c. 1001–1040), king of Scots (r. 1034–1040); Maldred Dunkeld (d. after 1045), and a daughter (name unknown, who had a son Moddan).

Bethsabee (fl. 1010–975 BCE).

See Bathsheba.

Bethune, Louise Blanchard

(1856–1913)

American architect and first woman elected to the American Institute of Architects. *Born Jennie Louise Blanchard on July 21, 1856, in Waterloo, New York; died on December 18, 1913, in Buffalo, New York; graduated from Buffalo High School, 1874; married Robert Bethune (an architect), in December 1881.*

At the time Louise Bethune was apprenticing with a Buffalo architect, it was argued that women were unsuited to the demanding profession of architecture, but Bethune paid little heed. Following her graduation from high school, she traveled and taught school before abandoning her plans to attend Cornell University in favor of a position as a draftsperson in the architectural office of Richard A. Waite. In 1881, at age 25, she opened her own architectural office in partnership with Robert Bethune, whom she later married.

Louise Bethune worked on a broad range of structures, including stores, factories, chapels, banks, schools, houses, and apartment buildings. Notable among the 18 schools she designed in Western New York was the Lockport Union High School, a characteristic Romanesque revival edifice made of brick and sandstone. More unusual in style was Buffalo's 225-room Hotel Lafayette, which she completed in 1904, in the French Renaissance style. The Cottier & Daniels music store, another of Bethune's designs, was one of the country's first buildings with a steel-frame construction and poured concrete slabs to resist fire.

During her 30-year career, Bethune joined a number of architectural societies. In 1885, she became a member of the Western Association of Architects, of which she served a term as vice president. In 1888, she was the first woman elected to the American Institute of Architects, and became their first woman fellow the following year.

By the early 1890s, Bethune was the best-known woman practicing architecture in the country. She was also outspoken in her feminist views, refusing to enter the Woman's Building competition held at the World's Columbian Exposition of 1892, because the winner was not awarded a honorarium equivalent to that awarded to male architects at the fair. As to the popular practice of limiting women architects to the designing of homes, Bethune countered that it was the worst paid work an architect did; therefore, to make it a special branch for women was "quite out of the question." She believed that women had to be willing to get their hands dirty, pointing out that those who overlook the "brick-and-mortar-rubber-boot-and-ladder-climbing period of investigative education remain at the tracing stage of draftsmanship." Bethune's final years were spent in semiretirement. She died in Buffalo, on December 18, 1913.

Louise Blanchard Bethune

SOURCES:

Torre, Susan, ed. *Women in American Architecture.* NY: Whitney Library of Design, 1977.

Barbara Morgan,
Melrose, Massachusetts

Bethune, Mary McLeod

(1875–1955)

One of America's most outstanding educators, as well as a major advocate of racial equality and civil rights. *Pronunciation: Beth-OON. Born Mary McLeod on July 10, 1875, near Mayesville, South Carolina; died on May 18, 1955, in Daytona Beach, Florida; 15th child of Samuel McLeod (a farmer) and Patsy McIntosh; educated at Trinity Presbyterian Mission School for Negroes near Mayesville, South Carolina; Scotia Seminary, Concord, North Carolina; Moody Bible Institute, Chicago, Illinois; married Albertus Bethune, in 1898; children: one son, Albert (b. 1899).*

On the afternoon of July 10, 1974, a crowd of over 20,000 gathered to witness the mayor of Washington, D.C., dedicate a monument in the city's Lincoln Park, the first statue in the capital to honor either an African-American or a woman. There was no doubt, however, that the individual it commemorated richly deserved the distinction: Mary Bethune was one of America's most outstanding educators and principled advocate of racial equality and civil rights.

She was born exactly 99 years earlier on a small farm near the town of Mayesville, South Carolina. Her parents, Samuel and Patsy McLeod (along with the elder of her 16 brothers and sisters), were ex-slaves who had gained their freedom following the victory of Northern forces in the Civil War. The cotton farm which they had managed to acquire in the early 1870s was only about 35 acres in extent which, for such a large family, meant a constant struggle to maintain a subsistence income. As a result, all the children grew up spending much of their time helping in various tasks around the farm. The senior McLeods were both strong Methodists and constantly emphasized to their children the importance of moral standards and the virtues of hard work.

In these economic circumstances, the children had little hope of any kind of formal, substantive education. Mary, however, was unique. From an early age, her parents recognized that

Mary McLeod Bethune

she was a particularly bright and inquisitive child. As such, they went to great lengths and made considerable sacrifices (both of themselves as well as their other children) to ensure that Bethune received a genuine education. Even so, she was almost 11 years old before her parents managed to save enough money to send her to the recently opened Trinity Presbyterian Mission School for Negroes. The school was located in Mayesville about five miles from their farm, a distance Bethune had to walk twice daily.

During Mary's three years at Trinity, her scholastic and intellectual talents blossomed, and she caught the attention of **Emma Wilson**, an energetic teacher who later went on to found the African-American Mission School. Determined that Bethune continue her education, Wilson contacted **Mary Chrissman**, a wealthy Quaker schoolteacher originally from Denver, Colorado, and persuaded her to act as Mary's financial patron. Chrissman provided sufficient funds for a scholarship to Scotia Seminary in Concord, North Carolina. Noted for its austere religious atmosphere, Scotia Seminary also provided a sound secondary education in a variety of artistic and domestic subjects. In the six years she spent there, Mary excelled in music and public speaking. She graduated in 1894.

Deeply influenced by her own Methodist background as well as the religious instruction received at Scotia, Bethune wished to serve as a missionary in Africa. To this end, she entered the interdenominational Moody Bible Institute in Chicago. After one year of study and graduation, she applied to the Missionary Society for a placement overseas. In what she later referred to as the "biggest disappointment of her life," she was told that the Society considered her too young for such a situation. Moreover, Bethune was also informed that, as a black, she could not be placed in any position of authority as a missionary.

Instead, she traveled to Augusta, Georgia, where she secured a position as teacher at ***Lucy Laney**'s Haines Institute, founded by Laney and Bethune's close friend Emma Wilson. While there, Bethune became convinced that education was the most powerful tool African-American women could employ to improve their socioeconomic and political positions. Bethune left the Institute to take up a more senior and demanding teaching position at the Kendall Institute located in Sumter, South Carolina.

During this period, she had met Albertus Bethune then an employee at a Presbyterian parsonage. The couple were married in May 1898 and, in the following year, their son Albert, an only child, was born. Mary and Albertus were never particularly close, and their marriage was not happy. Shortly after the birth of their son, Albertus was offered a minor teaching position in Savannah, Georgia, and, when they moved, Bethune was forced to give up her job at the Kendall Institute. She soon decided that, if faced with a choice between her marriage or her career, the latter would take precedence. After only a few weeks in Savannah, she accepted a job at a missionary school in Palatka, Florida. With her young infant in arms, Bethune left her husband (although they remained legally married until Albertus' death in 1918) and set out to face her next challenge.

Bethune did not stay long at the missionary school. In 1900, she established her own presbyterian parochial school in Palatka. From the beginning, this school was plagued with financial difficulties and, despite all her efforts (including taking a part-time job selling life insurance), it was soon forced to close. A similar fate awaited another independent school she founded two years later. In 1904, Bethune visited Daytona Beach, Florida, where she was deeply distressed by the plight of children of African-American railroad workers. Desperately poor, these children had little or no opportunity to gain even the rudiments of a basic education. Bethune was determined to make another attempt to build a school that would address itself to their needs. By October of the same year, she founded what was eventually to become one of the most important and significant educational establishments in the American South, the Daytona Normal and Industrial Institute for Girls.

As always, Bethune was faced by a lack of resources (she would later describe her total assets at this time as "a dollar and a half, and faith in God"). It is not surprising then that the Daytona Institute consisted of a rented cabin which was so small that initial enrollment had to be restricted to just five pupils (aged eight to twelve) as well as her own son. Bethune was determined, however, that this school would not go the way of her other efforts and fail through financial difficulties. She put her pupils to work part-time on an adjoining farm and, in this manner, was able to maintain a cash income and establish a regular, if often barely sufficient, source of food. While these measures were adequate to ensure the short-term durability of the school, Bethune realized that long-term survival would depend on its ability to grow and expand. To this end, she embarked on an ambitious and aggressive program of fund raising.

Bethune, who had always had a talent for music, organized her pupils into a choir which raised money by giving concerts throughout Florida. She then began a series of lecture tours in order to explain the educational principles upon which the Daytona Institute was founded. These concerts and tours were initially supported by local black churches (particularly the Mount Bethal Baptist Church under the guidance of Pastor A.L. James) but quickly drew the attention of the white community as well. In 1905, a Ladies' Advisory Board, consisting of socially prominent and well-off members of the Daytona district, was formed to suggest methods of raising funds. This board was subsequently able to attract a number of wealthy patrons, including John D. Rockefeller of Standard Oil and James N. Gamble, chair of the Proctor and Gamble Manufacturing Company. Moreover, beyond material benefits, this board demonstrated to Bethune the possibilities inherent in genuine interracial cooperation. In her own words, it became a "crossroads of culture and human relations."

Although she was larger than life, her philosophy, her goals were all realistic.

—**Walter Washington**

Within two years, Bethune and her colleagues had raised enough money to purchase land and build new facilities while enrollment at the school expanded to some 250 pupils (which now included boys). Bethune added depth to the curriculum by introducing a wide variety of new courses. In addition, she was one of the first in the area to organize summer schools. She also strongly encouraged her pupils to participate in outreach programs and community projects in the vicinity. Although not all members of the community were happy with Bethune's success (she was, for instance, occasionally threatened by members of the Ku Klux Klan), the school prospered.

Bethune was flexible in her approach to new problems; thus, when fresh needs arose, she was able to respond in a practical fashion. In 1911, she was one of the prime movers in organizing what became known as the McLeod Hospital. This institution, the first of its kind in the South, was founded when white-owned-and-managed hospitals refused to provide training facilities for African-American physicians and nurses.

Bethune did not, however, confine herself to the field of education. During World War I, she was elected president of the Florida Federation of Colored Women's Clubs and directed the membership to support various types of war work. Similarly, she acted as a lecturer for the Red Cross and became co-founder of the Circle of Negro War Relief for New York City.

Her interests continued to expand in the postwar years. In 1920, she encouraged the Florida clubwomen to found a home for delinquent girls in Ocala which provided support and training until such time as they could re-enter the community. At the same time, she served on the executive board of the Southeastern Association of Colored Women and as vice-president of the Commission on Interracial Cooperation. Bethune was a founder and executive member of the National Association of Wage Earners and of the International Council of Women of the Darker Races of the World.

Perhaps Bethune's greatest educational triumph came in 1923 by which time the Daytona Institute had over 300 pupils and a staff of 25. Its burgeoning reputation made it possible to organize a merger with the Cookman Institute, a co-educational college located in Jacksonville, Florida. Cookman was a Methodist college which, over the previous 50 years, had managed to create its own distinguished name. This merger effectively relieved Bethune of any further worries since her partners were able to provide needed technical services and further financial assistance. Within a few years, the newly named Bethune-Cookman College had become one of the leading junior colleges in the United States. It was for this achievement that Bethune would be awarded the prestigious Spingarn Medal for educational services in 1935 (the second African-American woman to receive this award).

Between 1924 and 1928, Bethune served two terms as president of the National Association of Colored Women (NACW) which at that time was the most important secular organization for black women. Under her guidance, the NACW attempted to forge an activist role for black women in international affairs. Bethune sought, she said, to "make this national body of colored women a significant link between the peoples of color throughout the world." Her role in the NACW was complemented in 1935 when she founded the National Council of Negro Women (NCNW) for which she served as president for 14 years. The NCNW acted as an umbrella organization coordinating the activities of a wide variety of African-American women's groups, pressuring the national political system for reforms in the areas of public housing, social security, welfare, and anti-discrimination legislation.

By the mid-1930s, Bethune's increasingly prominent public role brought her into contact with *Eleanor Roosevelt, who was also deeply interested in interracial issues and the problems of youth. The two women soon became close, and it was thanks to this friendship that Bethune gained access to the president. Franklin D. Roosevelt's most important initiative in these years was a social and economic program that was known as the New Deal. From 1936, Bethune served as the director of Minority Affairs in the New Deal's National Youth Administration, an organization set up in the previous year to assist young people. In 1939, she became director of the Division of Negro Affairs, at that time the most important appointment an African-American woman had ever held in U.S. government service. Bethune's job was to coordinate other black members of Roosevelt's administration. This, in turn, led to the formation of the Federal Council on Negro Affairs which produced a series of recommendations on civil liberties. These were distributed widely and had the effect of producing more black appointments in government as well as more federal intervention in racial issues.

In 1941, Bethune was a vocal supporter of A. Philip Randolph's March on Washington Movement which led to a presidential order banning racial discrimination in the federal government and in all defense industries. Moreover, following America's entry into World War II in December of the same year, Bethune was appointed a special assistant to the secretary of war and was responsible for the selection of the first females for officer-training schools. Thanks to Bethune's insistence, a fixed portion of the available places were formally reserved for African-American women. Finally, through her participation in the National Youth Administration programs and the Women's Interest Section of the War Department's Bureau of Public Relations, she was able to promote the employment of black youth and women in national defense plants from which they had previously been excluded.

Inevitably, the punishing schedule which Bethune set for herself began to have a serious effect on her health. For many years, she had suffered from chronic asthma which increasingly restricted her ability to travel. Following a particularly severe attack in 1942, Bethune formally relinquished the presidency of her beloved Bethune-Cookman College.

At the end of 1945, she represented the National Association for the Advancement of Colored People's (NAACP) at the conference in San Francisco to write the inaugural charter for the United Nations. This conference was overshadowed by the death of President Roosevelt, and Bethune's attendance was interrupted when she was asked to speak at the memorial service in Washington, D.C., as representative of all of America's minority groups. At the end of the service, Eleanor Roosevelt presented Bethune with her late husband's cane as a mark of the respect and esteem in which he had held her.

On the occasion of her 75th birthday in 1950, Mary McLeod Bethune finally left public life and retired to her small home on the Bethune-Cookman campus. Even then, she maintained a strong interest in African-American affairs, establishing a black holiday resort (at Bethune-Volusia beach in Florida) and by creating the philanthropic Bethune Foundation. In January 1952, she was asked by the government to journey to Liberia in Africa as U.S. delegate at the inauguration of President William Tubman.

During her last years, Bethune's public service was rewarded by a number of official honors from various sources: the Thomas Jefferson Award (from the United States), the Medal of Honor and Merit (Haiti) and the Star of Africa (Liberia). These honors were overshadowed, however, by the U.S. Senate's McCarthy Commission which, without any evidence, smeared Bethune as a communist subversive. As a result, local authorities in Englewood, New Jersey, denied her the right to speak at a conference on civil rights. Shortly afterwards, on May 18, 1955, Bethune died of a heart attack.

Perhaps the best summation of the principles that guided Mary Bethune's life is that found in her own words written shortly before her death and which are carved on the pedestal of her monument in Washington, D.C. She wrote: "I leave you love, I leave you hope. I leave you the challenge of developing confidence in one another. I leave you a thirst for education. I leave you respect for the use of power. I leave you faith. I leave you racial dignity."

SOURCES:

Finkelstein, Louis. *Thirteen Americans: Their Spiritual Autobiographies.* NY: Harper, 1953.

Holt, Rackham. *Mary McLeod Bethune.* Garden City, NY: Doubleday, 1964.

Lerner, Gerda. *Black Women in White America.* NY: Random House, 1973.

Peare, Catherine Owen. *Mary McLeod Bethune.* NY: Vanguard, 1951.

Sterne, Emma Gelders. *Mary McLeod Bethune.* NY: Alfred A. Knopf, 1957.

SUGGESTED READING:

Deutrich, Mabel, and Virginia Purdy. *Clio was a Woman: Studies in the History of American Women.* Washington, D.C.: Howard University Press, 1980.

Smith, Elaine. *Notable American Women: The Modern Period.* Cambridge, MA: Harvard University Press, 1980.

COLLECTIONS:

The most significant collections of Mary Bethune's papers are held at the Bethune Foundation, Bethune-Cookman College; Armistad Research Center, New Orleans; the National Archives for Black Women's History, Washington, D.C.

Dave Baxter, Department of Philosophy, Wilfrid Laurier University, Waterloo, Ontario, Canada

Betkin, Elisabeth (fl. 1476).

See Scepens, Elizabeth.

Betterton, Mrs. (d. 1712).

See Bracegirdle, Anne for sidebar on Saunderson, Mary.

Bettignies, Louise de (d. 1918).

See de Bettignies, Louise.

Bettina (1785–1859).

See Arnim, Bettine von.

Bettis, Valerie (1919—)

American dancer and choreographer. *Born Valerie Elizabeth Bettis in Houston, Texas, on December 20, 1919; one of two children of Royal Holt and Valerie Elizabeth (McCarthy) Bettis; attended the University of Texas; studied dance with Rowena Smith and Tina Flade in Houston, and with Hanya Holm in New York; married Bernardo Segall (a Brazilian concert pianist and composer), in 1943 (divorced); married Arthur A. Schmidt.*

Born in Houston, Texas, in 1919, Valerie Bettis began her dancing lessons at age ten, three years before the death of her father. After a year of college, she left for New York to study under ***Hanya Holm** in whose *Trend* she made her professional debut in 1937. The following year, Bettis joined the Hanya Holm company, where she remained for two years. Her first major solo was in *The Desperate Heart* in 1943. In 1944, Bettis founded her own group, presenting, among others, *As I Lay Dying* and *Domino Furioso*. Three years later, she choreographed *Virginia Sampler* for the Ballet Russe de Monte Carlo, and in 1948 she enjoyed a huge success on Broadway as Tiger Lily in the musical *Inside U.S.A.* Bettis choreographed for television in the 1940s before turning to film; in Hollywood, she worked on two ***Rita Hayworth** vehicles for Columbia Pictures in 1951: *Affair in Trinidad* and *Salomé*. Bettis also choreographed and appeared in the off-Broadway and London productions of *Ulysses in Nighttown* in 1958. She founded her own dance studio in New York in 1963 and also taught at the Perry-Mansfield School at Connecticut College.

Pauline Betz

Betz, Pauline (1919—)

American tennis champion. *Name variations: Bobbie Betz, Pauline Betz Addie. Born Pauline May Betz in Dayton, Ohio, on August 6, 1919; daughter of a tennis-playing mother who taught physical education; grew up in Los Angeles; bought 12 tennis lessons with Dick Skeen; studied economics at Rollins College in Florida, graduated, 1943; won a graduate scholarship to Columbia University; married Bob Addie (a sportswriter for the* Washington Post*); children: five.*

Known as a baseline player, Pauline Betz' first major win was the U.S. singles title in 1942 over ***Louise Brough**. She took the title once more from Brough in 1943 and in 1944 beat out ***Margaret Osborne**. On V-J Day in 1945, Betz lost in the U.S. singles finals to **Sarah Palfrey**, during what was considered one of the best matches ever played at Forest Hills. Betz reclaimed the U.S. crown in 1946, routing **Pat Todd**.

But the women stars of the 1940s were little known; their names had been lost under the blanket of news coverage during World War II. After a bomb landed in Centre Court and abolished 1,200 seats in 1940, Wimbledon was suspended for the first half of the decade; repairs were not fully completed until 1949. France's famed Roland Garros was used as a holding pen by the Germans for death-camp deportees.

Betz was one of many athletes whose international careers were dormant during the war years. Shortly before leaving for Wimbledon in 1946, she was seated on a train next to a soldier and enjoyed his questions concerning her upcoming match. When they parted at the station, he said, "Well, good luck, Getz." Betz, who was called Getz for years by friends, placed first at Wimbledon, beating Brough in the finals 6–2, 6–4. In 1947, both Pauline Betz and Sarah Palfrey turned pro and took their games on tour. Betz then taught tennis well into her 60s in Bethesda, Maryland.

Beurton, Ruth (b. 1907).

See Kuczinski, Ruth.

Bevan, Mrs. Aneurin (1904–1988).

See Lee, Jennie.

Bevier, Isabel (1860–1942)

American educator and reformer in the study of home economics. *Born near Plymouth, Ohio, on November 14, 1860; died in Urbana, Illinois, on March 17, 1942; the youngest of nine children; attended Plymouth High School and Wooster Preparatory School, Wooster, Ohio; graduated Wooster College, 1885, M.A., 1888; attended Case School of Applied Science, 1888–89; Harvard, 1891; Wesleyan, 1894; Western Reserve, Cleveland, Ohio; Massachusetts Institute of Technology, Cambridge, Massachusetts.*

Selected writings: (with Susannah Usher) Food and Nutrition *(1906); (with Usher)* The Home Economics Movement *(1906, later enlarged into* Home Economics in Education, *1924);* The House: Its Plan, Decoration and Care *(1907).*

A vital force in educational reform, Isabel Bevier brought the subject of home economics into the realm of scientific study on the university level. In a talk she gave to the alumnae of Glendale College in February 1911, she referred to home economics as "a sane and safe program for meeting some of the demands of this industrial age."

After her graduation from Wooster College in 1885, Bevier worked as a high school principal in Shelby, Ohio, for two years and taught Latin for a year before receiving her master's degree. She took a professorship at Pennsylvania College for Women in Pittsburgh where she taught science courses for nine years. During summers, she took advanced courses in agricultural chemistry and calorimetry at Harvard and Wesleyan. Bevier also did field studies on nutrition in Pittsburgh and Hampton, Virginia, in 1898; her findings were later published in bulletins of the U.S. Department of Agriculture.

In 1900, she was appointed head of the new home-economics department at the University of Illinois (Urbana), which she quickly renamed the department of "household science." Determined to make the course one of scientific instruction rather than domestic training, she demanded the same high entrance and academic standards as the other departments within the university. On campus, she established one of the first home-economics laboratories, in which she tested her theories, and in 1915 she took over the home-economics section of the university extension program. Over the years, she gradually won respect for the department, although her blunt manner was not always appreciated. During her tenure, 630 students graduated from the department.

From 1910 to 1915, Bevier served as the second president of the American Home Economics Association. During World War I, she served briefly in Washington, D.C., as an advisor on food conservation. She also chaired the home-economics department of the University of California at Los Angeles from 1921 to 1923, and lectured at the University of Arizona for a semester, before returning to Illinois as professor of home economics. In addition to her books, Bevier wrote numerous articles, bulletins, and circulars during her career. She is also credited with the idea of using a thermometer in the cooking of meat. In 1928, the home-economics building at the University of Illinois was named in her honor. She retired in 1930, at age 70, and died in Urbana, Illinois, on March 17, 1942.

Barbara Morgan,
Melrose, Massachusetts

Beyer, Helga (1920–1942)

German-Jewish member of the anti-Nazi resistance. *Born in Breslau (now Wroclaw, Poland) on May 4, 1920; murdered at the Bernburg hospital near Dessau in February 1942; daughter of Adolf Beyer (a Jewish businessman) and Else Beyer (who was not Jewish); sister of Ursel Beyer (b. 1918).*

Joined an anti-Nazi resistance cell (1933); became a member of the German-Jewish youth group Kameraden, resisting Fascism under the sign of the Weisse Möwe (White Gull); for more than three years, worked as a courier in a resistance cell organized by a group of Communist Oppositionists in Breslau; arrested (January 28, 1938), convicted of "preparation for high treason," and sentenced to three and one half years imprisonment; though sentence was scheduled to end August 1941, was moved to the women's concentration camp, Ravensbrück; taken to Bernburg near Dessau and killed as part of a group of other female "undesirables" (February 1942).

Helga Beyer was an idealistic German youth of mixed Jewish-Christian parentage whose principled opposition to Nazism led her inexorably into a life of resistance to the Nazi regime. Born in Breslau (now Wroclaw, Poland) on May 4, 1920, Helga, along with her older sister ◂ **Ursel**, grew up in secure middle-class circumstances. Her father Adolf Beyer was from an assimilated Jewish family, and both he and his older brother Georg, who became a journalist and associate editor of the *Rheinische Zeitung* in Cologne, were deeply committed to the ideals of democracy and were members of the Social Democratic Party. Helga's mother Else, who died while Helga and Ursel were young, was not Jewish (neither was the woman who became Helga's stepmother in 1934). Although her father was not religious in an Orthodox Jewish fashion, neither did he deny his heritage, and he raised his daughters in the Jewish faith. With the Nazi seizure of power in Germany, Adolf Beyer and his daughters would defiantly remain Jewish, as much out of political and moral conviction as out of any traditional religious faith.

In 1930, when she was ten, Helga Beyer joined a youth group, the Deutsch-Jüdischer Wanderbund (DJW). Strongly influenced by the romantic and idealistic notions of the German youth movement, the DJW saw itself as "above the fray" of political corruption and compromise. The organization's main goal was to mold physically strong, morally pure human beings through fellowship, hikes and trips. In the next several years, Helga was active in Jewish youth organizations in Breslau, so that by early 1933, when the Nazis came to power in Germany, she had established a number of strong friendships. Out of these personal ties—and her growing conviction that the evil of Nazism had to be resisted in a practical as well as idealistic fashion—her commitment to fighting the Hitler regime developed.

▸ **Beyer, Ursel** (b. 1918)

Name variations: Ursula. Born in Breslau on April 12, 1918; daughter of Adolf Beyer (a Jewish businessman) and Else Beyer (who was not Jewish); sister of Helga Beyer.

Both Helga and her sister Ursel were strongly attracted to the Socialist Workers Party. This was a faction of Marxists deeply suspicious of the Stalinized German Communist Party (whose "line" was dictated by Moscow) and disillusioned with the official policies of the Social Democratic Party. Despite their extreme youth, both sisters were interested in other ideological stirrings on the Left, particularly those emanating from a small group of anti-Stalinist Communists, the "oppositionist" KPO. Convinced that the Soviet Union had become a bureaucratized dictatorship that did not represent the needs of the working class, these remarkably astute young women were drawn to the numerically tiny but ideologically persuasive revolutionaries of the Communist Party "opposition" group.

By 1934, when she was only 14, Helga was actively involved in KPO underground activities. In addition to meeting in cells to discuss revolutionary ideology and strategy, her work included risky assignments like crossing over the German-Czech frontier as a courier to retrieve information from the KPO groups operating in a still-democratic Czechoslovakia. Increasingly aware of this "treasonous" activity, the Gestapo benefitted from relentless intelligence efforts with the arrest of 35 members of the Breslau KPO organization between October 1937 and April 1938. Helga Beyer and her sister Ursel were seized on January 28, 1938. Though her sister Ursel was acquitted and able to immigrate to the U.S., Helga was sentenced to three and one-half years in December 1938. Helga's aunt Emma had also immigrated to Palestine in 1936, but other family members were not so fortunate. Her aunt Paula was killed in Auschwitz, and her aunt **Klara Junker**, who managed to survive the war years, fell victim to the chaos created during the exodus of Germans from Breslau when that city was captured by Soviet troops and annexed by Poland.

Held in several prisons during the first part of her sentence, Helga Beyer expected to be released when her term was served. However, as a Communist, even if not of the Stalinist variety, she was regarded as particularly dangerous. The defiant commitment to Judaism of this "racially" half-Jewish woman further marked her for "special treatment." Instead of being released at the conclusion of her term in 1941, she was transferred to Ravensbrück, the notorious women's concentration camp for political prisoners. Helga Beyer did not survive Ravensbrück. Sometime in February 1942, she was murdered at the Bernburg hospital near Dessau. In March 1942, her aunt Klara in Breslau received a small package from the camp. It contained an urn with her niece's ashes. Several weeks before, Klara had received a form letter informing her that Helga Beyer had died "of pneumonia."

SOURCES:

Bergmann, Theodor. *"Gegen den Strom": Die Geschichte der Kommunistischen-Partei-Opposition.* Hamburg: VSA-Verlag, 1987.

Dertinger, Antje. *Weisse Möwe, gelber Stern: Das kurze Leben der Helga Beyer.* Berlin and Bonn: Verlag J.H.W. Dietz Nachf., 1987.

Drechsler, Hanno. *Die Sozialistische Arbeiterpartei Deutschlands (SAPD): Ein Beitrag zur Geschichte der deutschen Arbeiterbewegung am Ende der Weimarer Republik.* Hanover: SOAK-Verlag, 1983.

Erpel, Simone. "Struggle and Survival: Jewish Women in the Anti-Fascist Resistance in Germany," in *Leo Baeck Institute, Year Book XXXVII.* London: Secker & Warburg, 1992, pp. 397–414.

Merson, Allan. *Communist Resistance in Nazi Germany.* London: Lawrence and Wishart, 1985.

John Haag, Associate Professor, University of Georgia, Athens, Georgia

Bhutto, Benazir (1953—)

Pakistani political leader and prime minister. *Born in Karachi, West Pakistan, on June 21, 1953; daughter of Zulfikar Ali Bhutto and Nusrat Bhutto (b. 1929); attended convent schools in Pakistan, Radcliffe College, Harvard University, Lady Margaret Hall, Oxford University; married Asif Ali Zardari; children: three, including son Bilawal (b. 1988) and daughter Asifa.*

Placed under house arrest (1977–84); along with her mother, leader in exile of Pakistan People's Party; returned to Pakistan (1986) to lead Movement for the Restoration of Democracy; appointed prime minister (1988), becoming the first woman to head a modern Muslim state; removed from office on charges of corruption (1990); served second term as prime minister (1993–96).

The first woman to become head of government of a modern Muslim state, Benazir Bhutto was born in Karachi, West Pakistan, on June 21, 1953. She was the firstborn of ***Nusrat Bhutto** and her husband Zulfikar Ali Bhutto whose family was among the leading landowners of the Larkana district of Sind province in southeastern Pakistan. Zulfikar was often away building a political career that rapidly propelled him from diplomatic posts to the presidency. Strongly influenced by both parents, Benazir was first educated at home by an English governess, then sent off to attend several elite Roman Catholic convent schools, one of which was located in a breathtaking setting in the foothills of the Himalayas.

In 1969, at age 16, Benazir Bhutto enrolled at Radcliffe College in Cambridge, Massachusetts, taking classes in comparative government. Although her mother had spent several weeks getting her settled in, her new life contrasted sharply with the extraordinary privileges she had taken for granted in Pakistan. In the United States, it was a shock for her to have to walk to classes, after having been taken to and from school in a chauffeur-driven car in Pakistan. In addition to having to "walk and walk and walk," Benazir had to learn to live in bitterly cold weather and eat without being served by a staff of servants. She exchanged her saris for blue jeans and—despite her fears of being deported—marched in a number of anti-Vietnam War demonstrations. She also made a number of critical observations of American life, noting how little respect children showed their parents. Arriving in the U.S. during the anti-authoritarian 1960s, she was horrified at what she perceived as students' utter lack of respect for their teachers, evidenced by their putting legs up on chairs and smoking in class.

Back home in Pakistan, her father Zulfikar was emerging in the 1960s as the country's leading voice of opposition to an increasingly repressive series of military rulers. After resigning his post of foreign minister, in 1967 he formed a new political party, the Pakistan People's Party (PPP), which promised the nation's impoverished masses "Bread, Clothing, Shelter." The Bhutto house at 70 Clifton Road in Karachi soon became a bustling headquarters of the new party, and before her departure for the United States Benazir had experienced her first introduction to political life by helping to sign up new PPP members. Political and economic chaos helped the new party gain strength; in the national elections of December 1970, it picked up 72 out of 138 National Assembly seats.

The loss of East Pakistan, which became the independent nation of Bangladesh in 1971, totally discredited the old regime. In the last days of that year, Zulfikar Ali Bhutto took over as president of a crises-ridden nation. Although still a student in the U.S., Benazir followed events at home with great interest, often having to explain the situation to American friends whose knowledge of the intricacies of Pakistani politics was slight to nonexistent. Benazir's father was clearly grooming his brilliant daughter for the future when, during her 1972 summer vacation trip home, she accompanied him on a summit trip to India for a series of meetings with ***Indira Gandhi**. After completing her studies in

Benazir Bhutto

America, Benazir Bhutto enrolled at Lady Margaret Hall, Oxford University, for advanced study of economics and political philosophy. Graduating with honors in 1976, she was urged by her father to remain for another year to take a foreign-service course. During this period, she was elected to a three-month term as president of the Oxford Union, the first foreign woman to be accorded this considerable honor.

In the summer of 1977, Bhutto flew home to find Pakistan in turmoil. The PPP had won a recent parliamentary election, but the opposition parties charged that the election had been rigged. Riots ensued, and soon the country was paralyzed, a situation that provided the army chief of staff with a pretext to arrest Zulfikar Bhutto and other politicians. Soon after, he was taken into custody, old political grudges surfaced and Zulfikar was charged with conspiracy to murder the father of a former political ally who had become a PPP adversary. Benazir spoke out vigorously to protest her father's incarceration. Within weeks of his arrest, she too paid the price for political dissent and was held under house arrest until early in 1978. In March of that year, her father was sentenced to death. Because of her protests against the sentence, Benazir was arrested again in October 1978 for her "objectionable speeches." Despite worldwide protests, Zulfikar Ali Bhutto was hanged in April 1979. Benazir remained under custody, was not permitted to attend his burial at the family estate in Larkana, and was only released some two months after his execution. Still regarded by the regime as a dangerous political foe, Benazir was again arrested in October 1979 on charges of holding an unauthorized meeting, creating alarm, and bringing the armed forces into disrepute. She remained in custody until early April 1980. After several more arrests, she was finally released in January 1984 in order to receive medical attention for a serious middle-ear and mastoid infection.

In exile in London, Benazir and her mother Nusrat organized the Pakistani opposition. A family tragedy that likely had political origins was the mysterious death in France of her younger brother Shahwanaz in July 1985. Pakistani exiles suspected he was poisoned because of his militant opposition to the Karachi regime. When Benazir accompanied his body back for burial next to his father at the family estate, the funeral procession turned into a major political protest. Once more, Benazir was placed under house arrest but was permitted to leave the country after several months.

Benazir Bhutto and her mother returned to Pakistan permanently in 1986. Together, they co-chaired a renewed PPP. Nusrat arranged a marriage for Benazir with Asif Ali Zardari, member of a prominent landowning clan, in 1987, assuring her daughter that love would come later. The government hoped to use Benazir's forthcoming pregnancy against her and the PPP by scheduling national elections for the due date of her baby. Her firstborn, a boy named Bilawal, arrived five weeks early, however, giving Benazir a month to regain her strength before the election campaign. "The baby outmaneuvered them all," said Bhutto. To further weaken her party's chances, the government instituted national identity cards for voters, eligibility for which the government controlled. Despite these obstacles, the PPP won a narrow victory in the November 1988 elections. After years of imprisonment and family sacrifices, Benazir Bhutto became prime minister of Pakistan. Her mother Nusrat was appointed senior minister.

Benazir Bhutto's term of office was relatively brief, controversial, and turmoil-ridden. Civil liberties were restored and some steps were made to address the grinding poverty of the great majority of the nation's people. But civil disorder became common in the streets of the cities, and the military never trusted Benazir. Furthermore, a growing Islamic fundamentalist movement viewed the secular-oriented PPP with growing suspicion. In August 1990, the president removed Benazir Bhutto as prime minister, charging her with corruption and nepotism. Several months later, her husband, called by some "Mr. Ten Percent" for his eagerness to profit from some business transactions, was arrested and charged with participation in a kidnapping. Although the PPP did poorly in the elections of October 1990, both Benazir and Nusrat Bhutto remained in the National Assembly as leaders of the opposition, where they continued to speak out vigorously. In November 1992, Benazir Bhutto led a large protest march in Islamabad, charging the government with electoral fraud and other crimes. Though she was banned from the capital, her PPP remained the only hope for a better life for millions of Pakistanis. Basing much of her political strength in her native Sind province, at the end of the year she led a "long march" through the country, speaking to large and enthusiastic crowds.

In October 1993, a rejuvenated PPP won a plurality in the elections to the National Assembly, and heading a fragile coalition government Benazir Bhutto once again became prime minister of Pakistan. This time, however, there was considerably less euphoria about what she and her party could do for Pakistan in the short-term. The country remained mired in poverty, corruption, and crime. A huge foreign debt crippled hopes for economic expansion, while at the same time the nation's immensely wealthy and powerful feudal landlords paid virtually no taxes (not a single individual in the history of Pakistan had ever been prosecuted for tax evasion). With one of the highest birth rates in the world, Pakistan in the mid-1990s had a literacy rate no higher than 25%, an average per capita income of $400, and an educational situation in which most children never attended a school. In her second term as prime minister, Bhutto had to face bitter facts, virtually abandoning an ambitious agenda for social reform. With her acceptance of the economic austerity program dictated by the International Monetary Fund, spending for social programs had to be drastically curtailed and the economy remained stagnant at best. Women, while theoretically moving toward equal status with men, remained second-class citizens. In November 1996, Bhutto's government was again dismissed by political rivals who accused her of corruption; in reality, Pakistan's enormous foreign debt may have been the main cause. "The debt servicing is breaking our backs—debt that I didn't incur," Bhutto told *Time* magazine in September 1996. "But as Prime Minister, I have to pay it back." Whatever the specific outcome of her political efforts, Bhutto's achievements thus far have pointed the way for others to emulate.

SOURCES:

Bhutto, Benazir. *Daughter of Destiny: An Autobiography.* NY: Simon and Schuster, 1989.

———. *Pakistan: The Gathering Storm.* New Delhi: Vikas Publishing House, 1983.

———. *The Way Out: Interviews, Impressions, Statements, and Messages.* Karachi: Mahmood Publications, 1988.

"Bhutto, Benazir," *1986 Current Biography Yearbook.* NY: H.W. Wilson, pp. 39–42.

John Haag, Associate Professor, University of Georgia, Athens, Georgia

Bhutto, Nusrat (1929—)

First lady of Pakistan and head of the Pakistan People's Party who was imprisoned from 1977 to 1980. *Name variations: Begum Nusrat Bhutto (Begum refers to a Muslim princess or woman of high rank). Born Nusrat Isphahani in Bombay, India, on March 23, 1929; daughter of Mirza Mohamed Isphahani and Fatima Sultana Isphahani; married Zulfikar Ali Bhutto, in 1951; children: two daughters, including Benazir Bhutto (b. 1953), and two sons, including Shahwanaz (d. 1985).*

Captain in Women's National Guard (1947–48); First Lady of Pakistan (1971–77); served as chair, Pakistan Red Crescent Society (1974–77; elected to National Assembly (1977); imprisoned (1977–80); served as chair, Pakistan People's Party, and leading member of Movement for the Restoration of Democracy; member, National Assembly (1988—).

Born in Bombay, India, in 1929 into a wealthy mercantile family of Iranian background, Nusrat Isphahani grew up in a world of privilege and leisure. In 1951, she became the second wife of Zulfikar Ali Bhutto, whose family wealth was based on their long-established ownership of large estates in the Sind district of West Pakistan, making the Bhutto clan a leading political force in that region of the country. In the first years of their marriage, which saw the birth of two sons and two daughters, the couple lived in semi-feudal opulence on the Bhutto estate of Al-Murtaza near the town of Larkana.

Zulfikar Bhutto, who had been politically inactive as a university lecturer, made a rapid political ascent after the creation of a military dictatorship in 1958 by General Ayub Khan. Zulfikar went from United Nations delegate to commerce minister, energy minister, head of the United Nations delegation, and finally minister of foreign affairs. Nusrat usually accompanied her husband on his many trips abroad while their children were cared for by an English governess and an extensive household staff. Though Nusrat was a Shi'ite Muslim and Zulfikar was from the Sunni branch, they had few if any differences in religion. Indeed, they agreed that their children would attend Roman Catholic convent schools; the schools did not require conversion to Christianity for admission. They agreed as well that their children should receive a Western college education. (Zulfikar Bhutto had graduated from Oxford and the University of California, Berkeley.)

In 1969, Nusrat Bhutto accompanied her eldest child, 16-year-old daughter ***Benazir Bhutto**, to the United States to supervise her enrollment at Radcliffe College, the women's undergraduate branch of Harvard University. After remaining for several weeks in Cambridge, Massachusetts, Nusrat left, pleased that Benazir was in good hands with John Kenneth Galbraith and **Catherine Atwater Galbraith**, old friends who would act as Benazir's "parents in residence."

The next few years saw major changes in Pakistan, where a corrupt government was swept out of office in December 1971 as a result of the loss of East Pakistan, which became the Republic of Bangladesh. As the nation yearned for reforms, Zulfikar Bhutto, who had several years earlier founded a reformist Pakistan People's Party (PPP), became president of the country on December 20. He became prime minister in August 1973.

Many reforms were instituted during Zulfikar Bhutto's term of office, including land reforms, electrification efforts and minimum-wage legislation. To signal a change in attitude toward the rights of and opportunities for women, the civil service and police force were opened to them for the first time. Dramatizing these moves toward female emancipation, Nusrat headed the Pakistani delegation to the International Conference on Women held in Mexico City. In 1977, she was elected to the National Assembly, but in July of that year Zulfikar's government fell due to riots and political chaos. The new rulers charged him with the murder of a fellow politician's father and placed him under house arrest; he was hanged in April 1979. With her husband's death, Nusrat became head of the PPP, although in reality the power had largely passed to her daughter Benazir. Soon, Nusrat was also arrested and was imprisoned at the central jail in Karachi. Although she was released in 1980, there were indications that her health had been permanently impaired as a result of her incarceration. Fortunately, a malignancy on one of her lungs responded to medical treatment in Germany in 1982.

As the Pakistani government became more dictatorial throughout the 1980s, Nusrat and Benazir Bhutto increased the pressure of the PPP on the regime. In July 1986, she and her daughter were elected co-chairs of the party. Nusrat also persuaded Benazir to enter into an arranged marriage in July 1987 with a man she considered a suitable candidate, Asif Zardari; mother assured daughter that, unlike in the West, love would come after the marriage.

When the dictator General Zia was killed in a mysterious plane crash, the way was opened for major political changes, and in 1988 Benazir Bhutto became prime minister of Pakistan. Few were surprised when Nusrat Bhutto was appointed senior minister, a post that made it possible for Benazir to await the delivery of her second child (a daughter, in January 1990) while her mother retained a firm family grip on power.

In August 1990, the president dismissed Benazir, charging corruption and nepotism. The entire Bhutto clan was accused of having misused its power to enrich itself. Many in the impoverished nation took the charges seriously, even if detailed proof was lacking. Though Benazir served a second term as prime minister from 1993 to 1996, she was once again dismissed with charges of corruption. For Benazir and Nusrat Bhutto, a particularly dismaying aspect of losing power was the reversion to certain aspects of traditional Islamic law which subjugated women.

Nusrat Bhutto

SOURCES:

Bhutto, Benazir. *Daughter of Destiny: An Autobiography.* NY: Simon and Schuster, 1989.

John Haag, Associate Professor, University of Georgia, Athens, Georgia

Bianca.

Variant of Blanche.

Bianca de Medici (1548–1587).

See Cappello, Bianca.

Bianca Maria Sforza (1472–1510).

See Sforza, Bianca Maria.

Bianca Maria Visconti (1423–1470).

See Visconti, Bianca Maria.

Bianca of Navarre.

See Blanche of Navarre.

Bianca of Sicily (1385–1441).

See Blanche of Navarre.

Bianco, Margery Williams (1881–1944)

***English novelist, translator, and author of books for children, including* The Velveteen Rabbit.** *Name variations: wrote under Margery Williams, Margery Williams Bianco, and Margery Bianco. Born Margery Williams on July 22, 1881, in London, England; died on September 4, 1944, in New York, New York; youngest of two daughters of Robert (a barrister, distinguished classical scholar, and journalist) and Florence (Harper) Williams; limited formal education: attended the Convent School in Sharon Hill, Pennsylvania, for two years; married Francesco Bianco (a dealer in rare books and manuscripts), in 1904; children: son Cecco; Pamela Bianco (artist and illustrator of children's books).*

Selected writings: The Late Returning *(1902);* The Price of Youth *(1904);* The Bar *(1906);* Paris *(1910);* The Thing in the Woods *(1913);* The Velveteen Rabbit *(1922);* The Little Wooden Doll *(1925);* Poor Cecco *(1925);* The Apple Tree *(1926);* The Adventures of Andy *(1927);* The Skin Horse *(1927);* All About Pets *(1929);* The Candlestick *(1929);* The House That Grew Smaller *(1931);* A Street of Little Shops *(1932);* The Hurdy-Gurdy Man *(1933);* The Good Friends *(1934);* More About Animals *(1934); (with J.C. Bowman)* Green Grows the Garden *(1936);* Tales from a Finnish Tupa *(1936);* Winterbound *(1936);* Rufus the Fox *(1937);* Other People's Houses *(1939); (with G. Loeffler)* Franzi and Gizi *(1941);* Bright Morning *(1942);* The Five-and-a-half Club *(1942);* Penny and the White Horse *(1942);* Forward Commandos! *(1944);* Herbert's Zoo *(1949);* The New Five-and-a-half Club *(1951).*

Although Margery Bianco wrote successfully in many genres, she is best remembered for her children's classic *The Velveteen Rabbit*, which, written in 1922, still finds its way into children's hearts. This fantasy of a stuffed toy that is transformed into a live bunny through the power of love, was, according to Bianco, an "accident" and became the inspiration for many toy stories that followed. Bianco, who respected children, believed that literature nourished the imagination. "It is through imagination that a child makes his most significant contacts with the world about him," she said, "that he learns tolerance, pity, understanding and the love for all created things."

Bianco's early years in London were influenced by her father's philosophy that children should be taught to read at a young age but should not attend school until age ten. Her favorite books from her father's library included the three volumes of Wood's *Natural History*, which contributed to her early study of animals that is reflected in so much of her work. Childhood reading also included Hans Christian Andersen, to whom she was later compared. Following her father's death when she was seven, the family moved to New York, then to a farm in Pennsylvania. Bianco's limited formal education—day school in Philadelphia and two happy years at the Convent School in Sharon Hill—seemed quite enough to set her career in motion. Her first book, *The Late Returning*, an adult novel written when she was 17, was published in England in 1902. A second and third novel followed, as did her marriage to Francesco Bianco, a graduate of the University of Turin and also a lover of books. After the birth of their son in 1905 and a daughter in 1906, the Biancos lived in Paris and London until 1914, when World War I took them to Turin, where Francesco served in the Italian army. In 1919, they returned to London.

Most of Bianco's stories were written after her own children were beginning to grow up. Following *The Velveteen Rabbit*, she produced *The Little Wooden Doll* (1925), illustrated with her daughter ➧ **Pamela Bianco**'s early drawings. *Poor Cecco*, populated once again by family toys, was written the same year. Bianco's relationships with the family toys was not limited to her stories. She once wrote her daughter, assuring her that the Tubbies—Pamela's cherished playthings—were well and happy in her absence. "As a matter of fact," she wrote, ". . . Jensin's mother telephoned to ask if they couldn't stay over Wednesday, so as to go to a picnic, which she had arranged—with dancing afterwards, and I felt sure you wouldn't mind."

The broad range of Bianco's work included an autobiographical story, *Bright Morning* (1942), based on her childhood in London with her older sister. Her books about gardening and animals were also created from her own experiences. Two works, *Winterbound* (1936) and *Other People's Houses* (1939), which Bianco called "experiments," were considered precursors of the young adult novel and were heralded as stories of everyday life, a welcome alternative to the sentimental stories usually provided for young women at the time. It tells the story of the four Ellis children, who spend a hard winter alone in a Connecticut farmhouse where they overcome a number of potential disasters. Critics praised Bianco's skill with characterization, citing that even the most minor of characters was carefully and richly defined.

Bianco, Pamela (1906—)

Artist and writer for children. *Born on December 31, 1906, in London, England; daughter of Francesco Giuseppe (a bibliographer and poet) and *Margery (Williams) Bianco (a writer); attended private schools in France, England, and Italy; married Robert Schlick, in 1930 (divorced 1955); married Georg Theodor Hartmann (an artist), on July 25, 1955 (died 1976); children: (first marriage) son, Lorenzo Bianco.*

Selected writings—self-illustrated children's books: The Starlit Journey *(1933);* Beginning with A *(1947);* Playtime in Cherry Street *(1948);* Joy and the Christmas Angel *(1949);* Paradise Square *(1950);* Little Houses Far Away *(1951);* The Look-Inside Easter Egg *(1952);* The Doll in the Window *(1953);* The Valentine Party *(1954);* Toy Rose *(1957).*

Illustrator: Flora: A Book of Drawings by Pamela Bianco with Illustrative Poems by Walter de la Mare *(1920); Margery Williams Bianco's* The Little Wooden Doll *(1925); (poems by Glenway Wescott)* Natives of Rock *(1925); Margery Bianco's* The Skin Horse *(1927); (poems by William Blake)* The Land of Dreams *(1928); Oscar Wilde's* The Birthday of the Infanta *(1929); Juliana Ewing's* Three Christmas Trees *(1930); Hans Christian Andersen's* The Little Mermaid *(1935); John Symond's* Away to the Moon *(1956).*

Although she was born in London, Pamela Bianco's first memories are of Paris; her family moved there when she was four. She first became aware of pictures and books while watching her mother at work. When the family went to live in Turin, Italy, where her father was stationed during World War I, Pamela began writing poems and stories, which she sometimes made into small books with illustrations, mostly of children, Madonnas, cherubs, and angels. Though as a child she also enjoyed embroidery, sewing, and lace-making, she recalls drawing every day, first in pencil, then in pen-and-ink and watercolors.

Bianco was only 11 when her extraordinary drawings were exhibited at the Circolo degli Artisti in Turin. The following year, they were shown at Leicester Galleries in London where some of the drawings inspired Walter de la Mare to write poems which were later published with Bianco's drawings in the book *Flora* (1920). In 1922, when Bianco received an invitation to exhibit at the Anderson Galleries in New York, she came to America and made the country her home. Many solo exhibitions followed in San Francisco, Boston, Chicago, and numerous galleries in New York. After receiving a Guggenheim Fellowship in 1930 to paint abroad, she returned to Europe, specifically Florence, Italy, and wrote *The Starlit Journey* (1933), the first book she both authored and illustrated.

Bianco found inspiration in many things, from music and stars, to little girls in white-lace party dresses. Her approach to writing was similar to her approach to painting, beginning with an idea that rolled around inside her head until it crystallized into a plot. "The plot is then worked out in its entirety," wrote Bianco, "and all the problems therein solved. Only then does the actual writing take place. When writing for children I try to keep the words and sentences as simple as possible, while at the same time striving to give a particular rhythm to the paragraphs."

Most of Bianco's books originate in her imagination, though *Two, Paradise Square*, about her childhood with her brother Cecco, and *Little Houses Far Away*, based on a train ride through the Alps, came from actual experience. Bianco's works are held by the Museum of Modern Art and Hirshhorn Museum.

As a frequent contributor to *Horn Book* magazine, Bianco was also known for the quality of her criticism, to which she brought a vast knowledge of literature, impeccable standards, and a gift of insight into human nature. Her uncanny ability to almost crawl inside a child's mind made her an invaluable literary critic.

Margery Bianco died in 1944, after a three-day illness. In 1951, Valenti Angelo, to whom Bianco was a friend and mentor, summarized the author's contribution in his tribute "A Living Friendship," which appeared in the book *Writing and Criticism: A Book for Margery Bianco*: "No person who has left to the world of literature for children such wisdom and sympathy and love of Nature will ever die. Her work should not go unnoticed in time to come. There is a great need for her kind of writing today, for her work is reaching for some lost dignity in life, and in reaching helps to bring it back."

Barbara Morgan,
Melrose, Massachusetts

Bibesco, Elizabeth (1897–1945).

See Asquith, Margot for sidebar.

Bibesco, Marthe Lucie (1887–1973)

Rumanian novelist and essayist. *Name variations: Princess Bibesco; (pseudonym) Lucile Decaux. Born*

Marthe Lucile Lohovary on January 28, 1887, in Rumania; died in Paris on November 29, 1973; daughter of Jean Lohovary (a minister for foreign affairs and president of the Senate) and Princess ***Smaranda "Emma" (Mavrocordato) Lohovary*** *(a collateral descendant of the Prince Mavrocordato); educated in France; married Prince George Bibesco (grandson of the Prince of Wallachia, now Rumania), in 1902.*

Selected writings—novels: Catherine-Paris *(1928),* The Green Parrot *(1929),* Balloons *(1929),* Worlds Apart *(1935),* Katia *(1939). Non-fiction: (travel memoir)* The Eight Paradises *(1923),* Isvor: The Country of Willows *(1924),* Royal Portraits *(1928),* Egyptian Day *(1930),* Some Royalties and a Prime Minister *(1930),* Lord Thomson of Cardington *(1932),* Crusade for the Anemone: Letters From the Holy Land *(1932),* Alexander of Asia *(1935),* A Daughter of Napoleon *(1937),* Flowers: Tulips, Hyacinths, Narcissi *(1940).*

Marthe Lucie Bibesco produced her first travel book at 18. During her career, she wrote numerous books under her own name and six historical novels under the pseudonym Lucile Decaux (only one of which, *Katia*, was translated into English). Authorship of these books was not acknowledged until *Katia* was made into a film. Bibesco wrote in French, although her books were translated into various European languages. Her love of gardening resulted in a book about spring flowers in 1940.

Born in Rumania, Bibesco lived most of her life in France. At 16, she married her cousin, Prince George Bibesco, and endured a devastating wedding night. From then on, the beautiful and cosmopolitan socialite spent most of her time away from her husband, dividing her time between Paris, a summer home at Posada in the Carpathians, and her husband's ancestral Palace of Mogosoëa in Rumania.

Highly praised for her novels and travel books by critics such as Anatole France and Marcel Proust, she was best known in England and America for her reminiscences of titled and diplomatic circles. Princess Bibesco had a long string of admirers—relationships that were romantic and intellectual rather than physical—that included a king of Spain, a crown prince of Germany, a British prime minister, and a premier of France. One critic called her interest in royalty "that of a commoner" and added, "Unlike most aristocratic authors, Princesse Bibesco writes well." When she died in Paris in 1973, she was essentially destitute. Marthe Bibesco is survived by 65 volumes of her manuscript diaries.

SUGGESTED READING:

Sutherland, Christine. *Enchantress: Marthe Bibesco and Her World.* NY: Farrar, Straus, 1996.

Barbara Morgan,
Melrose, Massachusetts

Bibesco, Princess (1887–1973).

See Bibesco, Marthe Lucie.

Bibesco, Princess (1897–1945).

See Asquith, Margot for sidebar on Bibesco, Elizabeth.

Bibiana (d. 363)

Roman martyr. *Name variations: Vivian. Birth date unknown; died in Rome in 363 CE; daughter of Flavian (formerly prefect of Rome) and Dafrosa.*

Death came to Bibiana and her parents during the Christian-baiting reign of Roman emperor Julian the Apostate (355–363). Her father Flavian, who had been prefect of Rome, was branded on the forehead a slave and exiled to Aquae Taurinae in Tuscany where he died of starvation; her mother **Dafrosa** was beheaded. Apronianus tied Bibiana to a pillar, and she was beaten with leaded cords until she died. Her feast day is December 2.

Bickerdyke, Mary Ann (1817–1901)

American nurse and Sanitary Commission agent in the Civil War, whose strength, tireless devotion, and care for the wounded "boys in blue" earned her the respect and friendship of generals. *Name variations: Mary Anne Ball Bickerdyke or Byckerdyke; Mother Bickerdyke; "Calico Colonel." Born Mary Ann Ball on July 19, 1817, in Knox County, Ohio; died in Bunker Hill, Kansas, on November 8, 1901; buried in Galesburg, Illinois; daughter of Hiram Ball (a farmer and businessman) and Anne (Cassady) Ball; may have attended Oberlin College around 1833 (the evidence is vague as some biographers claim that Bickerdyke received only the most "rudimentary" education); married Robert Bickerdyke (a widower, housepainter, and musician), on April 27, 1847 (died 1859); children: John Ball (b. 1849), James Rodgers (1850–1904), Hiram Ball (1854–1909), and Martha M. (1858–1860).*

Family moved to Galesburg, Illinois (1858); volunteered as a "nurse" in the Civil War (1861–65); worked with the Chicago Home for the Friendless (1866–67); operated a boarding house for veterans in Salina, Kansas (1867–69); worked for the Protestant Board of City Missions in New York City (1870–74); helped Kansas locust plague victims (1874); worked at the U.S. Mint in San Francisco, California (1876–87); granted a pension from Congress (1886); returned to Kansas (1887). A monument was erected to her memory in Galesburg, Illinois (1903).

Perhaps the most common story told about Mary Ann Bickerdyke (whether it is apocryphal is difficult to ascertain) begins on a June morning in 1863, around 11 o'clock, when Bickerdyke visited a ward of the Gayoso Hospital in Memphis, Tennessee. She discovered that the assistant surgeon had been on a drunken spree the night before, causing him to sleep late, and had neglected to make out the special diet list for his ward. As a result, his badly wounded patients had no breakfast and were faint with hunger. Confronting the negligent surgeon, Bickerdyke reprimanded him in harsh terms. According to numerous sources, the doctor laughed off her scolding and asked what the problem was. "Matter enough, you miserable scoundrel!" she is reported to have responded, "Here these men, any one of them worth a thousand of you, are suffered to starve and die, because you want to be off upon a drunk! Pull off your shoulder-straps, for you shall not stay in the army a week longer." Three days later, the doctor was discharged. Outraged, he went to headquarters and asked to be reinstated, presenting his case to Major General William T. Sherman, who was then in command. After listening to the surgeon's account, Sherman asked who had secured the discharge. The doctor replied, "That woman, that Mrs. Bickerdyke." "Oh!" said Sherman, "well, if it was her, I can do nothing for you. She ranks me." Throughout the Civil War, the hard-working Bickerdyke earned the admiration of several generals who were known to defer to her judgment on issues related to military hospitals.

Mary Ann Bickerdyke

Mary Ann Bickerdyke's Civil War years are well documented, but not much is known about her early years. Born in Knox County, Ohio, in 1817, she was the second daughter of Anne Cassady and Hiram Ball. When Bickerdyke was 17 months old, her mother died and her father sent her to live with her grandparents on a farm in Richland County, Ohio. Upon the death of her grandparents, Bickerdyke went to live with an uncle until 1833 when she moved to Oberlin, Ohio. Unfortunately, records do not survive which would reveal how she spent her youthful days.

The information about Bickerdyke becomes even murkier after 1833. According to her 1896 biographer and personal acquaintance, **Julia A. Houghton Chase**, a 16-year-old Bickerdyke went to Oberlin, Ohio, to attend school and paid for her education by working as a domestic. Subsequent biographers have been unable to verify that she attended Oberlin, and Chase acknowledges, perhaps in an attempt to explain Bickerdyke's absence from official records, that she left the college six weeks before graduation.

Chase's biography contains another "story" which conflicts with other available information but has also become a part of Mother Bickerdyke lore. The biographer records that Bickerdyke moved to Cincinnati, shortly after her stay in Oberlin, and trained as a nurse under Dr. Reuben Dimond Mussey during an 1837 cholera epidemic. Training programs for nurses, however, did not become established until years later. Furthermore, the epidemic in question seems to have been the 1849 outbreak and not 1837 as reported by Chase. It is known that Bickerdyke moved to Hamilton County, near Cincinnati, around 1837 and again stayed with her uncle's family. At this point in her life, it is possible that she studied "botanic" medicine, which stressed the use of native herbs.

On April 27, 1847, in Cincinnati, Ohio, Mary Ann Ball married Robert Bickerdyke, a widower with several children. Mary Bickerdyke's first child was born in 1849 and lived only a few minutes. Over the next eight years, Bickerdyke gave birth to three more children: two sons who lived to middle age and one daughter who died when only two years old. The Bickerdykes did not prosper in Cincinnati, and, in 1858, they moved to Galesburg, Illinois. Robert suffered from poor health, and it was hoped that the change in climate and a "good" physician could help. A few months after the move, however, he died suddenly at the age of 54. Mary, a widow with three children to support, earned her living as a housekeeper and a botanic doctor. The skills needed for both jobs would serve her well when she volunteered to nurse the Union soldiers in the Civil War.

> Men of the Army of Cumberland, or of the Tennessee, knew her; they remember that old sun-bonnet and the old white mule she rode, and when she rode into our camp or came into the dreaded field hospital, how the shouts went up, "Hurrah for Mother Bickerdyke!"
>
> —**Dr. Benjamin Woodward**

Shortly after the war started, Dr. Benjamin Woodward, a young Galesburg doctor who joined the army after the fall of Fort Sumter, wrote a plea for supplies to Reverend Edward Beecher of the Brick Congregational Church. When the reverend read the letter to members of his congregation, they were deeply moved by the doctor's words and immediately raised $500. Bickerdyke, inspired by love for her country (feelings shared by many of the women who became Civil War nurses), volunteered to take the supplies to Fort Defiance in Cairo, Illinois. Leaving her two sons with friends and neighbors, she arrived in Cairo on the morning of June 9, 1861.

There, she found the conditions of the sick much worse than Woodward's letters had indicated. Three tents, standing apart from the others in the camp, comprised the hospital. When Woodward escorted Bickerdyke through the tents, she saw one or two soldiers on cots and the rest lying on straw covered with filthy blankets or coats. There was excrement mixed with the mud on the floor, flies buzzing around patients, and patients lying in their own vomit. Before distributing any of her supplies, including a rather lavish dinner, Bickerdyke insisted on cleaning up the tents and soldiers. After the scrubbing was accomplished and the meal eaten, one young soldier called out to the departing Bickerdyke, "Good night, Mother." By the end of the summer, the title *Mother* became fixed, and all the young men of Fort Defiance addressed her accordingly.

Thus began Bickerdyke's sojourn which would last until the end of the war. She was present at 19 battles and, at several, tended the wounded on the field as well as in the hospitals. She directed the management of diet kitchens and had a knack for rounding up supplies when others could not. Her insistence on the importance of cleanliness and her determination to minimize waste led her to introduce, then manage, army laundries. As she fought for the best possible care for the ailing, Bickerdyke earned a reputation as a "terror," especially when confronted with incompetent doctors or officers. The soldiers in the ranks, however, adored her.

Bickerdyke remained in Cairo for about nine months, during which time she was instrumental in moving wounded and sick soldiers from the hospital tents into the new military hospital building. For some reason, the surgeon in charge of the hospital complained to Brigadier General Ulysses S. Grant, who took over command at Cairo in the fall of 1861, that he wanted nurses from the Army Nurse Corps, which was then being organized by ***Dorothea Dix** in Washington, D.C., and that he wanted to get rid of Mother Bickerdyke. Grant turned down the surgeon's request and appointed Bickerdyke the matron of the new hospital. Though she had no official connection, one of her duties included accepting and distributing the supplies sent from the recently established U.S. Sanitary Commission. Relying on private donations, the commission's main job was to keep military hospitals supplied.

When Grant and his troops left Cairo, Bickerdyke accompanied them. She was present at the battle of Fort Donelson, cared for the wounded in the field in makeshift sheds, and carted supplies from the Sanitary Commission's supply boat to the fields. After Shiloh, Bickerdyke was appointed a Sanitary Commission field agent and paid $50 a month, until this time she had been working for the army with no official appointment, rank, or authority. She used her salary to settle her sons in a boardinghouse near Chicago.

The Sanitary Commission recognized Bickerdyke's growing fame and, after several attempts, two Commission managers, ***Jane Hoge** and ***Mary A. Livermore**, finally convinced her to participate in a speaking tour to raise funds and supplies for the soldiers. Bickerdyke preferred caring for the soldiers to fundraising and was often quite abrupt to her audiences when appealing for funds. In Milwaukee, Wisconsin, her "thank-you" to the Chamber of Commerce for their contribution sounded less than sincere. "I am much obliged to you gentlemen for the kind things you have said," she began. "I am glad you are going to give twelve hundred dollars a month for the poor fellows in the hospitals; for it's no more than you ought to do, and it isn't half as much as the soldiers in the hospital have given you." She then went on to compare the Chamber of Commerce's monetary contribution to the limbs and lives of the soldiers in the field.

After her tour, in early 1863, she arrived at the Gayoso military hospital in Memphis, Tennessee, and prepared to take charge of it. But it was not long before she again moved on. Bickerdyke joined up with Grant's army as it besieged Vicksburg. September 1863 found her traveling with Sherman and his soldiers on their way to Chattanooga. When the troops arrived at their destination in November, Bickerdyke immediately set up her field hospital, using tents and old storehouses. She was often the only woman present at the battles and in the hospitals, but this never seemed to faze her. She worked in adverse conditions near Chattanooga. Mud and freezing rain made it difficult to care for the wounded, but somehow she managed to find food, prepare warm drinks, and comfort the sufferers. As the new year, 1864, dawned, Bickerdyke was joined by ***Eliza Porter**, and the two women worked together for the next nine months at Chattanooga and Huntsville, Alabama. They then accompanied Sherman on his march from the mountains through Georgia to the sea, their task made more difficult by the lack of supplies.

On May 23, 1865, General Sherman's army completed its "Victory March" into Washington, D.C., to join the Grand Review of Union forces. Bickerdyke was given a place of honor in the victory parade, but, characteristically, she also set up a latrine and refreshment center for those convalescents who insisted on marching down Pennsylvania Avenue. On the day the last Illinois volunteer received a discharge, she resigned as a Sanitary Commission agent and returned to Illinois and her sons.

Bickerdyke's work in the Civil War and her impatience with the oft-present government or military "red tape" earned her a reputation that she was not always comfortable with. Her contemporaries and her biographers have characterized Bickerdyke as "brusque," possessing "turbulent energy," a "demon," "at war with the army," "stern and vindictive" toward negligence, "a woman rough, uncultivated, even ignorant, but a diamond in the rough." It has been suggested that she tried to refute these impressions with the stories, perhaps not always true, she told her early biographers. Bickerdyke's behavior and physical appearance directly contrasted with the popular notions of "true womanhood" then prevalent among the 19th-century middle class, and this may explain, in part, the unflattering assessments and characterizations.

Bickerdyke continued to work on behalf of the veterans of the Civil War. For the remainder of her life, she acted, intermittently, as a pension attorney and made several trips to Washington, D.C., to secure pensions for army nurses and veterans. Immediately after the war, she assisted at Chicago's Home for the Friendless, a home for indigent women and children, though she did not stay in Chicago long. She decided to follow the numerous ex-soldiers moving west to Kansas who were taking advantage of the government's project to settle unemployed veterans.

With financial support from the Kansas Pacific Railroad Company, she opened a boardinghouse-hotel in Salina. The town of Salina, Kansas, lay on the Santa Fe route and several trains and wagon trains passed through it daily. Bickerdyke's hotel became a popular stopover for railroad passengers and served as a social center for relocated veterans. Despite the setting and the customers, she was unable to make her boardinghouse a financial success, and, within two years, the railroad company foreclosed on her mortgage. Upset by the turn her fortunes had taken, Bickerdyke chose not to remain in Kansas and moved to New York. With the help of ***Mary Jane Safford**, a friend and co-worker at Cairo, Bickerdyke secured a position as a missionary for the Protestant Board of City Missions of New York City in 1870.

In 1874, Bickerdyke's sons, James and Hiram, asked their mother to come back to Kansas and manage their farm, which was located near Great Bend. Since Kansas seemed to be "on the high road to prosperity," Bickerdyke returned to the state. Not long after, Kansas was decimated by a plague of locusts. Bickerdyke, not one to sit idly by if others needed help, quickly became involved in finding relief for the destitute. She sent an appeal to the people of Illinois who responded with "twenty car-loads of goods and a large sum of money." She not only traveled east many times to obtain aid for the devastated Kansas counties, but she also oversaw the distribution of many of the supplies. When the strenuous work of aiding the locust-plague victims drew to a close, Bickerdyke was exhausted and in poor health.

In 1876, at the urging of friends, Bickerdyke moved to California, where she allowed herself a brief period of rest and relaxation. In need of remunerative employment, she applied for a position in the U.S. mint in San Francisco. Two wartime friends, General Logan, now a senator from Illinois, and General Miller, a senator from California, endorsed her application and secured the appointment. She remained at the mint until 1887. While in California, Bickerdyke continued to work on behalf of the Union soldiers. In her role of pension agent, she made several trips across the country as the representative of veterans seeking pensions. She also helped to organize the California branch of the Woman's Relief Corps, an auxiliary of the Grand Army of the Republic. In 1886, Congress gave her a pension of $25 a month.

Returning to Kansas in 1887, Bickerdyke lived with her son James in Salina and Bunker Hill. Although she was sickly in her last years, she was still able to write letters and articles about issues she was interested in, such as temperance. On November 8, 1901, at the age of 84, Mary Ann Bickerdyke died at the home of her son in Bunker Hill. Her sons brought her back to Galesburg, Illinois, and buried her next to her husband and daughter. Two years later, a monument, which portrays Bickerdyke cradling a wounded soldier, was erected in her memory.

SOURCES:

Brockett, Linus Pierpont and Mary C. Vaughan. *Woman's Work in the Civil War.* Philadelphia, PA: Zeigler, McCurdy, 1867.

Chase, Julia A. Houghton. *Mary A. Bickerdyke, "Mother."* Lawrence, KA: Journal Publishing House, 1896.

James, Edward T., ed. *Notable American Women, 1607–1950: A Biographical Dictionary.* Vol. 1. Cambridge, MA: Belknap Press, 1971.

Litvin, Martin. *The Young Mary, 1817–1861.* Galesburg, IL: Log City Books, 1977.

Robbins, Peggy. "General Grant's 'Calico Colonel,'" in *American History Illustrated.* Vol. 14, April 1979, pp. 4–6, 43–48.

SUGGESTED READING:

Baker, Nina Brown. *Cyclone in Calico: The Story of Mary Ann Bickerdyke.* Boston, MA: Little, Brown, 1952.

Henshaw, Sarah Edwards. *Our Branch and Its Tributaries.* Chicago, IL: Alfred L. Sewell, 1868.

Hoge, Mrs. A.H. [Jane]. *The Boys in Blue.* Chicago, IL: E.B. Treat, 1867.

COLLECTIONS:

Correspondence, papers, newspaper clippings, and other printed matter located at the Library of Congress, Manuscript Division, Washington, D.C.

Gayle Veronica Fischer,
historian and author of several articles on dress reform movements in the United States

Bickerdyke, Mother (1817–1901).

See Bickerdyke, Mary Ann.

Bid'a (856–915)

Arab composer who sang for Caliph al-Mutamid and became enormously wealthy. *Born in 856* CE*; died in 915; studied under Oraib.*

Bid'a was the most famous pupil of ***Oraib**, an Arabian singer born in Baghdad. When Oraib was offered 100,000 dinars for Bid'a, she asked Bid'a if she wished to be sold. Bid'a's answer that she wished to stay with Oraib prompted the mistress to grant the pupil's freedom. While accompanying Oraib, Bid'a sang with her and composed many of her own songs. Her fame reached its pinnacle after her performance at the circumcision festival of Prince al-Mutazz. Caliph al-Mutamid (r. 870–892) prized her singing and composition highly, and her stature was such that when she died Caliph al-Mutamid's son led the prayers at her funeral.

John Haag, Athens, Georgia

Bielenberg, Christabel (1911—)

English writer. *Born Christabel Burton in Totteridge, England, of Irish ancestry; married Peter Bielenberg (a lawyer), on September 29, 1934; children: John (b. 1935), Nicky (b. 1936), Christopher (b. 1942).*

In 1932, while Christabel Bielenberg was studying to become an opera singer in Hamburg, she met her husband Peter, a law student, and they applied for a marriage license two years later. But when Christabel traded in her British passport, the German Embassy official remarked casually, "You've not made a very good swap I'm afraid."

The Bielenbergs were concerned about the country's unrest and the rise of Hitler. Settling in Hamburg, they enjoyed the friendship of liberals and intellectuals, including their best friends Adam and **Clarita von Trott zu Solz,** and Helmut Moltke. In 1939, naively thinking that the German generals were near revolt and that a political battle to oppose Hitler was still possible, the Bielenbergs moved to Berlin. Over the next

12 years, as they witnessed the cruelties of the Reich and desperately tried to enlist Allied support to start a revolution from within, they became tangentially involved in the failed plot to assassinate Hitler on July 20, 1944. When Peter was arrested, Christabel did all she could to secure his release.

Christabel Bielenberg chronicled her story in *The Past Is Myself* (1968), reprinted as *Christabel* (1984); it was adapted for "Masterpiece Theatre" in 1989. At the time of the book's reissue, ***Doris Lessing** wrote in *The Guardian* that the book, published 16 years earlier, had "lost nothing of its value." The Bielenbergs managed to survive the war intact and eventually moved to Ireland.

Christabel Bielenberg

Biermann, Aenne (1898–1933)

German photographer, specializing in still lifes, portraits, and montages. *Name variations: changed name to Aenne or Anne when she began to take photographs. Born Anna Sibilla Sternefeld in Goch am Niederrhein, Germany, in 1898; died in Gera, Germany, in 1933; married Herbert Biermann, in 1920; children: Helga and Gershon (Gerd).*

Aenne Biermann did not begin her photographic career until well after her marriage and the birth of her two children. She started taking pictures of her family after they moved to Gera, a culturally progressive center in Germany. In 1927, she collaborated with geologist Rudolf Hundt, photographing minerals, and then expanded her work to include close-up plant studies. Between 1929 and 1932, she produced approximately 3,000 negatives, from which 400 prints have survived. With solo exhibitions at Kunstkabinett, Munich (1928) and Kunstverein, Gera (1930), Biermann was also represented in several important group exhibitions, including *Film und Foto* (Stuttgart, 1929) and *Die neue Fotografie* (Basel, 1930). In 1949, a special section was devoted to her work in the group exhibition *Des Foto* (Stadthalle, Gera, 1949). Her photographs were published by the German art historian and photographer Franz Roh in *60 Fotos*.

Bigot de Morogues, Marie (1786–1820)

Alsatian pianist. *Born in Colmar, Alsace, on March 3, 1786; died in Paris, France, on September 16, 1820.*

This remarkable pianist who was respected by both Haydn and Beethoven was born in Colmar, Alsace, on March 3, 1786. After hearing her play, Haydn said admiringly, "My dear child, that music is not mine; it is yours." Beethoven was believed to have said to her, "That is not exactly the reading I should have given, but go on. If it is not quite myself, it is something better." In 1814, Marie Bigot de Morogues reputedly played Beethoven's *Appassionata* Sonata at sight from the manuscript. An 1807 letter to her from Beethoven strongly suggests that the great composer was in love with her, even though she was already married.

Bigottini, Emilie (1784–1858)

Italian ballerina. *Born in 1784; died in April 1858; daughter of an Italian actor who toured the provinces; sister of Louise Bigottini, who became* ***Mme Milon****, wife of the dancer Milon; children: four.*

First public appearance in Pygmalion *staged by Milon (1799); debuted in Gardel's* Psyché *(1800); danced the title roll in* Nina, ou la folle par amour *(November 23, 1813), the title role in* Clari, ou la Promesse

Emilie Bigottini

de Mariage *(1820), and Suzanne in* Le Page inconstant; *also appeared in Aumer's* Alfred le Grand, Cendrillon, *and* Aline, Reine de Golconde.

In a world of intrigue, Emilie Bigottini was known as generous. In a world of beauty, Bigottini was plain. But the public found her an appealing ballerina. In 1801, she was a 17-year-old debutante; three years later, she was dancing solo. By 1812, she was *premiere danseuse*, starring in many new ballets: eleven by Gardel and three by Milon. But her strength was not in technique, it was in acting, which was only discovered when **Milon** staged the story-ballet *Nina, ou la folle par amour* on November 23, 1813, leaving the audience red eyed. The emotional life Bigottini brought to the role of Nina was even more powerful when the audience suspected that her tears might be over the recent death at the Battle of Bautzen of her lover, Général Géraud-Christophe-Michel Duroc, the duke de Frioul, who was a friend of Napoleon and the father of two of her children (another child was conceived with the Comte de Fuentes). In 1820, she followed Nina with the title role in *Clari, ou la Promesse de Mariage*. Before retirement, she performed ten additional roles and acted in a farewell benefit (December 18, 1823) opposite Mlle Mars (***Ann Françoise Mars**), who was contributing her time away from the Comédie-Française.

Bijns, Anna (1493/94–1575)

Flemish religious poet. *Name variations: Byns; Sappho of Brabant. Born in 1493 or 1494 in Antwerp (Netherlands); died on April 10, 1575, probably in Antwerp; never married; no children.*

Known as the Brabantine Sappho, Anna Bijns was one of many women whose religious writings found a receptive audience in the 16th century, though she was one of the few who was not a nun to achieve success. Bijns, who did not marry but chose to live with relatives her entire life, was a schoolteacher with a strong devotion to the Catholic Church, which was threatened with a serious decline as Protestant ideas spread through Western Europe. Along with teaching, Bijns wrote poetry, often lamenting the attacks made on Catholicism and making her own attacks on the leaders and ideas of the Protestant movement. She also composed some poetry on secular themes. In the 1530s, Bijns founded her own school, but this did not keep her from her literary endeavors. She eventually published three collections of her verses on religious themes. Anna Bijns died about age 82.

Laura York, Anza, California

Bilchilde (d. 675)

Queen of Austrasia and the Franks. *Name variations: Bilichild; Blitilde. Died in 675; daughter of Hymnegilde also known as* ****Himnechildis****, regent of Austrasia (r. 662–675), and Sigebert or Sigibert III (630–656), king of Austrasia (r. 634–656); married Childeric II (656–675), king of Austrasia (r. 656–675), king of the Franks (r. 673–675), in 668; sister of St. Dagobert; children: Chilperic II (670–721), king of Neustria (r. 715–721).*

Bilhah

Biblical woman. *Name variations: Bala. Handmaid of* ****Rachel*** *who was Jacob's wife; children: sons Dan and Naphtali.*

Bilistiche (fl. 268–264 BCE)

Winner of two Olympic chariot races and mistress of Ptolemy II, king of Egypt. *Name variations: Belestiche, Belistiche, Blistiche. Pronunciation: Bee-lee-STEE-kay. Birth date unknown; various sources list her birthplace as Argos, the coast of Macedonia, or in an unspecified "barbarian" region; died before 246 BCE in Canopus (modern-day Maadie); daughter of an otherwise unknown Philo; one of the mistresses of Ptolemy II, king of Egypt.*

Owner of winning four-colt chariot at the Olympic games (268 BCE) and of the victorious two-colt chariot in the games (264 BCE); was processional basket-bearer in Alexandria (251–250 BCE); was deified after her death and worshipped as "Aphrodite Bilistiche."

Following the premature death of Alexander the Great in 323 BCE, his vast empire was divided among his Macedonian generals. Ptolemy I "Soter" founded the Greek dynasty that was to rule Egypt until the suicide of ***Cleopatra VII** in 30 BCE. He and his son Ptolemy II (308–246) laid the foundations of a dazzling new center of Greek culture in their capital, Alexandria. The most famous monuments of their reigns were the "Museum," an institution for scholarly research at state expense; the enormous royal library, comprising perhaps 700,000 volumes at its destruction; and the towering lighthouse on the island of Pharos, one of the Seven Wonders of the ancient world. By the reign of the younger Ptolemy, the Greek court in Egypt had become a haven for poets and artists from the older centers of Greek culture.

The official cultivation of the traditional Hellenic arts was not the only innovation of the Alexandrine court, however. The population of the Ptolemaic domain was overwhelmingly Egyptian, mindful heirs of a cultural tradition thousands of years old, and the influence of certain native habits and viewpoints was sure to affect the outlook of the minority newcomers to some degree. Evidence of such influence is strongest in the religious and political aspects of the regime. Ptolemy II introduced a system of dynastic cult in order to firmly establish his primacy in the land. To the rest of the Greek world, one of the most repugnant aspects of this policy was the marriage of Ptolemy II to his sister ***Arsinoe II** between 279 and 274 (whence his epithet Philadelphus, "sister-lover"). As a further affront to more traditional sensibilities, the ruling brother and sister were also worshipped as "The Sibling Gods." It is not certain, however, to what extent the marriage went beyond political expediency. The modern historian Edwyn Bevan suggests that at the death of Arsinoe in 258, Ptolemy may have only "sincerely mourned the loss of her strong directing intelligence. For the rest, he had many mistresses to amuse him." Indeed, Athenaeus, a Graeco-Egyptian author writing some four centuries after the reign, finds occasion to list a fair number of the more famous of them.

For us moderns, it is Bilistiche, the mistress whom Athenaeus records as, "of high repute, deriving her ancestry from the Atreidae" (the family of Agamemnon and Menelaus of Trojan War fame) who is both the most interesting and best known, despite the paucity of information available on her career and personality. Her name occurs incidentally in a number of later Greek authors besides Athenaeus (including Clement of Alexandria, Pausanius, and Plutarch), and in a couple of papyrus fragments discovered in Egypt only within the last couple of centuries. In addition to their variations on the spelling of her name, these authors are not in agreement over her origin and ethnicity. "Bilistiche" is an odd name, as it does not "sound" Greek. Thus the claim that she was not only of Greek, but also royal, ancestry might be seen as an effort to dignify her humble beginnings in order to maintain the glory of her paramour; such an opinion is probably behind Plutarch's bitter contention that she was a barbarian. Modern scholarly consensus as represented by Alan Cameron, however, maintains that the name is purely Macedonian, and Pausanius' assertion that she came from "the seaboard of Macedonia" may thus be as close to the truth of her origins as we can get.

And, by God, Bilistiche—was she not a barbarian wench bought in the market-place, whom now the Alexandrians worship in temples and sanctuaries, having been consecrated by the love of the king "Bilistiche, Goddess of Love"?

—Plutarch

We know nothing about how Bilistiche first came to Ptolemy II's attention, but by 268 BCE, the year that we first hear of her activities, she must have been already very close to the king's heart. In July or August of that year, she won her first Olympic victory in the four-colt chariot race, a feat which does not necessarily indicate athletic prowess, but the fact that she had access to the large sums of money required to sponsor such an event. Indeed, there is absolutely no evidence that Bilistiche or any other woman actually drove a team into victory at the Olympic games. Yet women were not exempted from second-party sponsorship of teams and charioteers, a practice which became common at the Olympics because of the great expense of the equestrian events. In fact, before Bilistiche, we have on record the names of another female victor in the four-colt event, ***Cynisca**, and a female victor in the two-colt event, ◆ **Euryleonis**; soon after Bilistiche, another female, ***Berenice II of Cyrene** (c. 273–221 BCE), is recorded as a victor in the four-colt event. The fact that all three of these other women came from royal stock (the first two were members of the Spartan royal family, the latter was a Ptolemaic queen) may suggest that Bilistiche was employing her wealth in this way in order to assert her regal pretensions. On the other hand, the note that she enjoyed another win at the next festival in 264 (this time in the newly introduced two-colt chariot event) could indicate a genuine enthusiasm for the track. H.A. Harris says that victors in the equestrian races were entitled to erect monuments which might represent horses, chariot, charioteer, and even the owner, but none connected with Bilistiche survive.

Euryleonis
(fl. 368 BCE). Spartan princess and horse breeder. Victor in the two-colt event in the 103rd Olympiad, 368 BCE.

Fresh information on minor antique personalities rarely surfaces, but recently an interesting literary footnote relating to Bilistiche's role as royal hetaira and Olympic victor has been opened by Alan Cameron. Ptolemy II's court attracted the talents of many Greek poets; indeed, the school known as "Alexandrian," famed for its extreme elegance, polish, and learning, had its beginnings during the reigns of the first two Ptolemies. Among the duties of the court poets would fall the composition of celebratory epigrams or elegies on the occasion of athletic victories. Bilistiche's chariot win would have been a prime opportunity for a poet to flatter the courtesan and king, and it is hard to imagine that no one took it. In fact, we do have the title of a poem "On Bilistiche" by a contemporary called Sotades, but its contents are unknown. Cameron's contribution is in the domain of interpretation. A four-line poem which he ascribes to Posidippus had been traditionally viewed as one of a ribald genre which exploit, in the delicate words of A.S.F. Gow, "the equation between amatory and equestrian exercises." Cameron points out several features of the poem which indicate the real (rather than the figurative) victory of a woman rider, marking Bilistiche as the likely subject. If this interpretation is correct, the brief poem neatly memorializes the courtesan in two of the passions for which she was famous, and in a risqué mode typical of the elegant society in which she moved.

Bilistiche's interesting role in the religious life of the city is the last aspect of her career into which we have any insight, and it is founded on only two notices. The less informative of the two is based on a papyrus fragment which indicates that she was chosen *kanephoros*, or ritual basket-bearer in the sacred procession of a religious festival, in 251 or 250 BCE. **Sarah B. Pomeroy** suggests that Bilistiche must have been at least 30 years old at this point, which is well beyond the age of virginity, a usual requisite for the *kanephoroi* in other Greek states. This is likely another honor due at least in part to her privilege as a royal mistress. As the courtesan of a god, however, her religious distinction was to be increased much further. Not only was Bilistiche appointed to an eponymous priesthood (i.e. the presiding role in the administration of her *own* cult) during her lifetime, but after her death she was worshipped in a number of Alexandrian temples and shrines as "Bilistiche-Aphrodite," apparently an incarnation of the traditional Greek goddess of love in the idealized person of the beloved courtesan. This was certainly a mark of the especial esteem in which Ptolemy held his favorite, but it also indicates the process of consolidation by which the king was attempting to bring both religious and political activity in the state under his human and divine sovereignty. It is interesting to note that one of his other mistresses, while not idealized as the divinity of sexual love *per se*, was chosen as the model for statues depicting the divinity "Philadelphia," or the incestuous marriage bond of the king and queen; the very notion shows just how far the strands of personal and private, family and romantic, love were enmeshed in his rule.

Bilistiche's ancient testimonials bear witness not only to her prowess as a lover, but also to her standing as a woman willing to take advantage of the new freedoms open to her sex in the Hellenistic monarchies. Despite our lack of information about her personality, her Olympic triumphs, and her literary persona, even the papyrus fragments that note two loans from her personal coffers in 239–38 hint at an individual will at work in the history. Nothing of her tomb on the promontory of Rhacotis or of her shrines has survived, and until relatively recently scholarship has focused little attention on a woman who in her lifetime was associated with one of the most powerful men in the world. The work of scholars like Cameron and Pomeroy has done something to salvage a shadow of her contemporary grandness; in our day, she will be remembered as more than simply a member of a large harem.

SOURCES:

Athenaeus. *The Deinosophists: Books XIII–XIV. 653b.* Edited and translated by Charles Burton Gulick. Cambridge: Harvard University Press, 1993, pp. 113 and 217.

Bevan, Edwyn. *The House of Ptolemy: A History of Egypt under the Ptolemaic Dynasty.* London: Methuen, 1927 (reprinted, Chicago: Ares Publishers, 1968).

Cameron, Alan. *Callimachus and his Critics.* Chapter IX.2. Princeton: Princeton University Press, 1995.

Clement of Alexandria. "The Exhortation to the Greeks" in *Clement of Alexandria.* Edited and translated by G.W. Butterworth. London: William Heinemann, 1939, pp. 107–109.

Harris, Harold Arthur. *Sport in Greece and Rome.* Ithaca: Cornell University Press, 1972.

Pausanias. *Description of Greece.* Volume II: Books III-V. Edited and translated by W.H.S. Jones and H.A. Ormerod. London: William Heinemann, 1960. p. 425.

Plutarch. *Dialogue sur L'Amour (Eroticos).* Edited with a French translation by Robert Flaceliere. Paris: Société d'Édition *Les Belles Lettres,* 1953, p. 58–59.

Pomeroy, Sarah B. *Women in Hellenistic Egypt: from Alexander to Cleopatra.* NY: Schocken Books, 1984.

SUGGESTED READING:

Harris, H.A. *Greek Athletes and Athletics.* Bloomington: Indiana University Press, 1966.

Peter H. O'Brien, Boston University, Boston, Massachusetts

Bilkas or Bilkis (fl. 10th c. BCE).

See Sheba, Queen of.

Billington, Elizabeth

(c. 1765/68–1818)

English soprano in the late 18th century whose fame was so extraordinary that the term "a Billington" became synonymous with "a great singer." *Born Elizabeth Weichsell or Weichsel in London, England, between 1765 and 1768; died in Venice on August 25, 1818; daughter of Carl Weichsell (a German-born oboist and clarinet player); her mother was a well-known singer and pupil of Johann Christian Bach; married James Billington, in 1783 (died around 1795); married Fellissent or Felican.*

So enormous was Elizabeth Billington's reputation as a singer that for a time "a Billington" was a popular term for any great singer. Hers was a musical family. Her mother was a singer who studied with Johann Christian Bach, her father was an oboist and clarinet player, her brother played the violin, and Elizabeth played the piano as a child. Before she was 12, she composed two sets of piano sonatas and at 14 sang at a concert in Oxford. In 1783, she married James Billington, a singing teacher and double-bass player. After her marriage, the Billingtons left for Dublin where they performed at the Crow Street Theater. Billington was later engaged for a season at Covent Garden at £1,000, a large sum for the day, where she sang Rosetta in Arne's *Love in a Village* and had great success. She began to work with Mortellari to improve her technique, even traveling to Paris to study with Sacchini. After six years of singing opera, ballad opera, oratorios, and concerts in

London and the provinces, Billington's voice was technically mature.

In 1794, Billington, her husband, and brother went to Naples where she gained international renown and performed as the heroine of a new opera, ◄ *Inez di Castro*, written for her by F. Bianchi. Her husband died not long after, but she and her brother soon set out on a triumphal tour of Italy's great opera houses. In Italy, she married a second time in 1799, but this marriage did not last, perhaps because she was ill treated, and she left her husband in 1801. When she returned to England the same year, Billington was in such demand that she sang at two theaters, Covent Garden and Drury Lane, on alternate nights. Her brother usually conducted the orchestra as she felt this ensured proper accompaniment of her cadenzas. Haydn described this serious and hardworking singer as "a great genius" and wrote "Arianna abbandonata" for her. Her voice had a wide range and her intonation was very accurate. Crowds converged to hear her sing until 1810 when ill health forced her to abandon her profession. In 1817, her second husband returned to London, and Billington decided to follow him back to Venice in the following year. She died shortly thereafter, on August 25, 1818, some said due to foul play. Though her death remains obscure, her fame as a great singer does not. A friend of ***Emma Hamilton**'s, Elizabeth Billington was also much admired by the Prince of Wales, and Joshua Reynolds painted her as St. ***Cecilia**.

►
Inez di Castro. *See Castro, Inez de.*

Teresa Billington-Greig

SUGGESTED READING:

Earl of Mount-Edgcumbe. *Musical Reminiscences.* London, 1825.

John Haag, Athens, Georgia

Billington-Greig, Teresa (1877–1964)

English suffragist. *Born Teresa Billington in 1877 in Lancashire, England; died in 1964; attended Blackburn Convent and Manchester University extension classes; married F.L. Greig, in 1907, with both partners taking their combined surnames.*

Selected writings: Towards Women's Liberty *(1906);* The Militant Suffrage Movement *(1911);* Women and the Machine *(1913).*

The daughter of an English shipping clerk, Teresa Billington-Greig was employed as a teacher when she began working for the equal-pay movement in 1904. She was a national organizer for, and member of, the Women's Social and Political Union from 1903 until 1907, when she left to found the Women's Freedom League with ***Charlotte Despard** and ***Edith How-Martyn**. In addition to organizing large propaganda campaigns, Billington-Greig wrote for *The Vote.* Although she endured two imprisonments for her political activities, after 1911 she was critical of extremist tactics. She worked independently in her later years, fading from public prominence after World War I.

Bin, Queen (d. 1895).

See Min, Queen.

Bing, Ilse (1899–1998)

German photojournalist. *Born in Frankfurt, Germany, in 1899; died in New York City on March 17, 1998; attended University of Frankfurt; married Konrad Wolff, in 1937.*

Raised in an affluent family, Ilse Bing received early training in music and art, and pursued a degree in the history of art at the University of Frankfurt. In 1928, she began photographing architecture to illustrate her doctoral thesis on German architect Friedrich Gilly. Much to her family's disappointment, she abandoned her studies in 1930 and moved to Paris to photograph full time. Although she was primarily a photojournalist, she worked from time to time in advertising.

After Bing achieved some success in French publications, the author Hendrik William Van Loon, who was living in New York City, introduced her work in the United States. In 1932, she was included in the exhibition *Modern European Photography: Twenty Photographers.* While visiting New York in 1936, she was offered a position with *Life* magazine, which she turned down. The following year, her work appeared in an exhibition at the Museum of Modern Art, *Photography, 1839–1937.*

In 1937, Bing married the pianist and musicologist Konrad Wolff with whom she relocated to New York with the advent of World War II. She continued to work until 1959, after which she was virtually forgotten until 1976 when her photographs appeared in two New York exhibitions: one at the Museum of Modern Art and another at the Witkin Gallery. Bing died in March 1998, age 98, two weeks before another retrospective of her work was to be held at the Edwynn Houk Gallery on Fifth Avenue in New York City.

Barbara Morgan,
Melrose, Massachusetts

Bingay, Roberta Gibb.

See Samuelson, Joan Benoit for sidebar.

Bingham, Amelia (1869–1927)

American actress-manager. *Born Amelia Smiley on March 20, 1869, in Hicksville, Ohio; died on September 1, 1927, in New York, New York; attended Ohio Wesleyan College; married Lloyd Bingham (a manager of a traveling professional theater company).*

Theater: The Struggle of Life *(1892);* The Power of Gold *(1892);* A Man Among Men *(1892);* The Mummy *(1896);* His Excellency, the Governor *(1899);* Hearts Are Trumps *(1900);* The Climbers *(actress-manager, 1901);* Lady Margaret *(actress-manager, 1902);* The Modern Magdalen *(actress-manager, 1902);* The Frisky Mrs. Johnson *(actress-manager, 1903);* The Lilac Room *(actress-manager, 1907);* Great Moments from Great Plays *(1909);* The New Henrietta *(1913);* The Pearl of Great Price *(1926).*

Pursuing the theater against the wishes of her deeply religious family, Amelia Smiley was induced to leave Ohio Wesleyan College by Lloyd Bingham, the manager of a traveling theater company, who saw her in an amateur production and thought she had talent. After touring the West Coast with the McKee Rankin Company, she headed to New York in 1892 to appear in a series of melodramas, including *The Struggle for Life*, *The Power of Gold*, and *A Man Among Men*. Now married to Bingham, she won her first important role in *The Mummy*, opposite Robert Hilliard (1896). Subsequent performances established her popularity and in 1897, after winning a newspaper popularity poll over such stars as ***Lillian Russell**, ***Fanny Davenport**, ***Ada Rehan**, and ***Maude Adams**, she went to work for Charles Frohman and played leading roles under his management for four years.

In late 1900, Bingham decided to become an actress-manager in the manner of England's ***Laura Keene**. She leased the Bijou Theatre, assembled a company, and successfully produced Clyde Fitch's *The Climbers*, in which she played Mrs. Sterling. Historical accounts vary as to the success of her subsequent ventures, *Lady Margaret* and *The Modern Magdalen*, both produced in 1902. By some accounts, her 1903 production of *The Frisky Mrs. Johnson* enjoyed a modest run only because of publicity surrounding her battle with a critic who panned the production. Disputes with the playwrights as well as another critic embroiled her 1907 production of *The Lilac Room* which closed in its first week.

Bingham went on to play in different stock companies and in 1909 toured Great Britain in *Big Moments from Great Plays*. From 1913 through 1916, she performed in *The New Henrietta* with Douglas Fairbanks and William H. Crane. Following the death of her husband in 1915, Bingham retired from the stage but returned in 1925 to appear in *Trelawney of the Wells*. The following year, she gave her last performance in *The Pearl of Great Price*. Amelia Bingham died in New York City, on September 1, 1927, having distinguished herself as the first American actress to succeed at both producing and performing.

Bingham, Anne Willing (1764–1801)

American socialite, known for her 18th-century Philadelphia salon. *Born Anne Willing on August 1, 1764, in Philadelphia, Pennsylvania; died on May 11, 1801, in St. George's, Bermuda; married William Bingham (a merchant, banker, member of the Continental congress, also U.S. senator, 1795–1801), in 1780.*

Anne Willing Bingham, a wealthy Philadelphia socialite and wife of banker and politician William Bingham, made her mark with the establishment of an 18th-century salon, patterned on those she had encountered in France during an extended European tour from 1783 to 1786. Known for her beauty, wit, and lavish entertaining style, Bingham attracted Philadelphia's literary and political personalities, as well as distinguished for-

Anne Willing Bingham

eign guests. With the new federal government centered in Philadelphia, her salon became the acknowledged "Republican Court," attracting Federalist leaders, including George Washington. Bingham died in St. George's, Bermuda, in 1801, while convalescing from an illness.

Barbara Morgan,
Melrose, Massachusetts

Bingham, Henrietta (1901–1968).

See Carrington, Dora for sidebar.

Bingham, Millicent Todd (1880–1968)

American geographer, conservationist, author, and educator. *Born Millicent Todd on February 5, 1880, in Washington, D.C.; died on December 1, 1968; daughter of David Peck (an astronomer specializing in the study of eclipses) and Mabel (Loomis) Todd (a writer and lecturer); attended Mrs. Stearns' School in Amherst, Massachusetts, and Miss Hersey's School, Boston, Massachusetts; awarded B.A. from Vassar College, Poughkeepsie, New York, 1902; M.A. in geography, Radcliffe College, Cambridge, Massachusetts, 1917; Ph.D. in geography, Harvard University, Cambridge, 1923; married Walter Van Dyke Bingham (a psychologist), on December 4, 1920 (died 1952).*

Selected writings: (biography) Life of Mary E. Stearns *(1909); (biography of maternal grandfather)* Elben Jenks Loomis *(1913);* Peru, Land of Contrasts *(1914); (with Raoul Blanchard)* The Geography of France *(1919);* La Floride du sud-est et la ville de Miami *(1932); (editor)* Letters of Emily Dickinson *(1931);* Mabel Loomis Todd: Her Contribution to the Town of Amherst *(1935); (editor with Mabel Loomis Todd)* Bolts of Melody *(1945);* Beyond Psychology *(1953); (editor)* Emily Dickinson: A Revelation *(1954);* Emily Dickinson's Home: Letters of Edward Dickinson and his Family, with Documentation and Comment *(1955).*

As the first woman to receive a doctorate in geology and geography from Harvard and a leading expert on ***Emily Dickinson**, Millicent Todd Bingham distinguished herself in the fields of both geography and literature. She devoted several decades to editing many of Dickinson's unpublished letters and poems, and, as a legacy of her lifelong concern with conservation, in 1960 Bingham presented the Todd Wildlife Sanctuary on Hog Island, Maine, to the National Audubon Society as a perpetual preserve.

Bingham's early interest in geography was encouraged by her father, an astronomy professor at Amherst College. As a young woman, she accompanied him on astronomical expeditions to exotic locales throughout the world, including Peru, Chile, and Russia. After receiving her degree in biology at Vassar College, where she was elected to Phi Beta Kappa and named commencement speaker, she taught French at Vassar and Wellesley colleges while pursuing postgraduate studies at the University of Grenoble and the University of Paris. In 1918, after receiving her M.A. degree in geography from Radcliffe, she worked for the U.S. Army Education Corps, lecturing American soldiers on the geography of France. Bingham completed her education at Harvard, receiving her Ph.D. in 1923. From 1928 to 1929, she lectured on geography at Columbia University and Sarah Lawrence College. In 1920, she married Walter Van Dyke Bingham, a psychologist. Throughout the marriage, she took an active interest in his work; after his death in 1953, Bingham would write the book *Beyond Psychology* in her husband's memory.

Bingham's mother ◆ **Mabel Loomis Todd** had collaborated with Thomas Wentworth Higginson in preparing the first editions of Dickinson's poems (published in 1890, 1891, 1896) and subsequently inherited a Chinese camphorwood chest filled with Dickinson's unpublished manuscripts. Mabel Todd had been preparing them for publication when a controversy with the Dickinson family interrupted the project. As a joint undertaking, mother and daughter began working anew on an enlarged edition of the 1894 *Letters of Emily Dickinson*, which they saw published in 1931. Then, as they began preparing the unpublished poems, Mabel Todd died in 1932, leaving her daughter Millicent to fulfill the promise she had made to "set the record straight." Bingham realized that she had reached what she called a "point of no return" and abandoned her geographical studies to complete the Dickinson project.

She faced a number of challenges in preparing Dickinson's unpublished poetry (*Bolts of Melody*, 1945), not the least of which were the variations in handwriting that appeared in the manuscript. Bingham discussed the problem of Dickinson's handwriting in the introduction of the book and also in an article for the *New England Quarterly* (June 1949) titled "Emily Dickinson's Handwriting: A Master Key."

For her publication of the Dickinson family letters, Bingham decided to prepare a reconstructed overview showing Amherst as it had been in Dickinson's day. She traveled extensively to collect materials, using newspaper accounts and court records to supplement the material in the letters. The resulting *Emily Dickinson's Home: Letters of Edward Dickinson and his Family, with Documentation and Comment* was published in 1955. Some additional letters from Dickinson to her father's best friend, Otis Phillips Lord, were published in 1954 (*Emily Dickinson—A Revelation*), and the remaining fragmented material from the chest appeared in a *New England Quarterly* article, "Prose Fragments" (September 1955), bringing the project to a close. Bingham subsequently presented the manuscripts to Amherst College, including the daguerreotype that is the only known likeness of Emily Dickinson as an adult.

The Hog Island property off the coast of Maine was also part of Bingham's inheritance from her mother, who had hoped to protect the land from loggers. In 1935, the island was renamed the Todd Wildlife Sanctuary and in 1936 the Audubon Society, of which Bingham was a longtime member, set up a nature camp on the site to provide instruction on the principles of conservation. In 1960, when Bingham donated the land permanently to the Audubon Society, it was estimated that 6,000 visitors had attended the two-week course.

Until her death in 1968, Millicent Bingham was concerned about the destruction of the bountiful natural resources in the United States. The warning she issued early in the 1960s still echoes in the pleas of conservationists: "Man can now be ranked with earthquakes and tidal waves as a geological agent of destruction," she wrote, "one potentially even more powerful now that the atom is at his disposal. The people in the country must realize what is happening, for the hour is late."

Barbara Morgan,
Melrose, Massachusetts

◆ ***Todd, Mabel Loomis**. See Dickinson, Emily for sidebar.*

Bingham, Sybil Moseley (1792–1848).

See Kaahumanu for sidebar.

Bingley, Blanche (b. 1864).

See Hillyard, Blanche Bingley.

Binh, Nguyen Thi (1920–1992).

See Nguyen Thi Dinh.

Binkiene, Sofija (1902–1984)

Lithuanian rescuer of Jews during World War II, honored as one of the Righteous by Yad Vashem, Jerusalem. *Born in 1902; died in 1984; married Kazys Binkiene (a writer); children: four, including Lilianne.*

Married to Kazys Binkiene, a well-known writer, Sofija Binkiene was the mother of four children. She had little contact with Jews prior to the Nazi occupation of Lithuania, which began in the early summer of 1941. Yet, almost from the first days of Nazi rule, she determined to do as much as possible to assist Jews fleeing from the Kovno ghetto. Scores of Jews of all ages spent varying periods of time in the Binkiene home, despite the danger this presented Binkiene's entire family. Even after her husband died of a heart ailment in 1942, Binkiene continued to assist Jews, though little food was available and the danger of discovery by the German security forces was great. In 1944, when the remnants of the Kovno ghetto were liquidated by the Nazis, Binkiene roved the streets nearby in the hope of bringing a few more Jewish stragglers to the relative safety of her home.

In testimony deposited after the war at the Yad Vashem Archives in Jerusalem, **Gita**

Hillern, Wilhelmine von (1836–1916).
German novelist. Born in Munich, Germany, on March 11, 1836; daughter of Charlotte Birch-Pfeiffer and C.A. Birch; married Baron von Hillern, in 1857 (died 1882).

German novelist Wilhelmine von Hillern began her career as an actress but retired from the stage upon her marriage in 1857. After 1889, she lived in Oberammergau and won fame as a novelist. Her most popular works are *Ein Arzt der Seele* (1869, 4th ed. 1886), and *Die Geier-Wally* (1883), which was dramatized and translated into English as *The* Vulture Maiden *(1876).*

Yudelevitz, one of the Jews rescued by Sofija Binkiene, recounted her life as a 12-year-old in 1941 when she was first rescued from certain death by **Jadwiga Muzaliene**, a friendly Lithuanian woman who in turn brought her to Binkiene's home, which quickly became known as a place of refuge. Here, the frightened Gita was comforted and warmly welcomed. Introduced to the family, Gita soon was in possession of an "Aryan" identification card that made it possible for her to go out on errands. During the summer, Gita accompanied the Binkiene family to their home on the Dangiene river. After the war, Gita Yudelevitz was reunited with her parents, who were among the few Lithuanian Jews who had been able to flee to the forest and survive the Holocaust.

After 1945, Sofija Binkiene worked for the children's service of the Lithuanian Radio. She also wrote a book about Lithuanians who had saved Jewish lives during the three years of Nazi occupation. Highly respected in what remained of the Jewish community of Lithuania, she was ostracized as the "Queen of the Jews" by some of her fellow Lithuanians who had—despite everything the Holocaust had revealed about the insanity of hatred—retained their anti-Semitic prejudices.

SOURCES:

Binkiene, Sofija. *Ir be ginklo kariai.* Vilnius: Mintis, 1967.

Paldiel, Mordecai. "Binkiene, Sofija," in *Encyclopedia of the Holocaust.* Vol. 1, p. 217.

———. *The Path of the Righteous: Gentile Rescuers of Jews During the Holocaust.* Hoboken, NJ: KTAV Publishing House, 1993.

John Haag, Associate Professor,
University of Georgia, Athens, Georgia

bint Jahsh, Zaynab (c. 590–640).

See Zaynab bint Jahsh.

Birch-Pfeiffer, Charlotte (1800–1868)

German playwright and actress. *Born Charlotte Karoline Pfeiffer in Stuttgart, Germany, on June 23, 1800; died in Berlin on August 24, 1868; daughter of an estate agent named Pfeiffer; married Christian A. Birch (historian), in 1825; children:* ***Wilhelmine von Hillern*** *(a writer).*

Selected works: Das Pfefferrösel *(1833);* Gesammelte Dramatische Werke *(Collected Dramatic Works in 23 volumes, 1863–1880).*

Charlotte Birch-Pfeiffer's entire adult life was spent working for the theater, beginning with her debut on stage in Munich at age 18. In her early career, she toured Europe, appearing as the lead in tragic roles. Though she had married the historian Christian Birch of Copenhagen in 1825, she continued to act. From 1837 to 1843, the family settled in Zurich where, for six years, Birch-Pfeiffer managed the Zurich theater. In 1844, she accepted an engagement at the royal theatre in Berlin; she remained there until her death on August 24, 1868.

Birch-Pfeiffer's popular novels and tales, *Gesammelte Novellen und Erzählungen,* were collected in three volumes (1863–1865). Her intimate knowledge of stage structure and technique prepared her for the successful dramatization of many of these novels, which were often visibly adapted from novels or short stories by recognized authors such as Charles Dickens, ***Charlotte Brontë**, Victor Hugo, ***George Sand,** and George Eliot (***Mary Anne Evans**). Her 70 plays, adapted and original, fill 23 volumes, *Gesammelte dramatische Werke* (1863–1880). Though short on critical success, her plays were popular well into the 20th century.

Crista Martin, freelance writer,
Boston, Massachusetts

Bird, Isabella (1831–1904).

See Bishop, Isabella Bird.

Biret, Idil (1941—)

Turkish pianist who revived many neglected piano works which came to be included in the classical piano repertoire. *Born in Ankara, Turkey, in 1941; studied in Paris with Alfred Cortot and in Germany with Wilhelm Kempff.*

Born in Ankara, Turkey, Idil Biret studied in Paris with Alfred Cortot and in Germany with Wilhelm Kempff. Her 1952 Paris debut was a great success. A virtuoso artist interested in often-neglected music, she made the first recording of Liszt's transcription of the Berlioz *Symphonie fantastique*. Her recordings of Ravel's *Gaspard de la nuit* and Alban Berg's Piano Sonata reveal a strong technique and intellect. The French composer dedicated his piano sonata to her.

Birgitta.

Variant of Bridget.

Birgitta of Sweden (1937—)

Swedish royal and princess of Hohenzollern. *Name variations: Bridget Bernadotte. Born Birgitta Ingeborg on January 19, 1937, at Haga Palace, Stockholm, Sweden; daughter of Gustavus Adolphus (1906–1947), duke of Westerbotten, and* ****Sybilla of Saxe-Coburg-Gotha*** *(1908–1972); sister of Carl XVI Gustavus, king of Sweden; married Johann Georg, prince of Hohenzollern, on May 25 or 30, 1961; children: Carl Christian (b. 1962); Desiree Margaretha (b. 1963); Hubertus Gustaf (b. 1966).*

Birgitta of Vadstena (1303–1373).

See Bridget of Sweden.

Birmingham Four.

See Davis, Angela for a sidebar on Addie Mae Collins, Denise McNair, Carol Robertson, and Cynthia Wesley.

Birney, Alice McLellan (1858–1907)

American founder and first president of the National Congress of Mothers, which later became the Parent-Teacher Association (PTA). *Born Alice McLellan Birney in Marietta, Georgia, on October 19, 1858; died in Chevy Chase, Maryland, on December 20, 1907; attended Mt. Holyoke Seminary, South Hadley, Massachusetts, for one year (1875).*

In 1897, Alice McLellan Birney, a former child-welfare worker, was a founding member and the first president of the National Congress of Mothers, which convened in Washington, D.C. According to Birney, the goal of the organization was to unite the forces of home, school, and community in recognizing "the supreme importance of the child." Within two years, the organization had grown in membership to 50,000. Ill health forced Birney to resign her post in 1902, but she went on to write *Childhood*, a book on child rearing. A year after her death in 1908, her organization was renamed the Parent-Teacher Association.

Bishop, Ann Rivière (1810–1884)

English singer. *Name variations: Madame Anna Bishop, Ann Reviere Bishop. Born in London, England, in 1810; died in New York, on March 18, 1884; married Sir Henry Rowley Bishop (an English musician, composer), in 1831 (died, April 30, 1855); married a Mr. Schultz, in 1858.*

An English singer in oratorio and opera known as Madame Anna Bishop, she made her debut on the concert stage in 1837, and retired in 1883. Her voice was a high soprano.

Bishop, Bernice Pauahi (1831–1884)

Hawaiian high chiefess and philanthropist whose will established the Kamehameha Schools. *Name variations: Her name "Pauahi" (meaning fire-finished). Born Bernice Paki on December 19, 1831, in Honolulu, Hawaii; died in Honolulu on October 16, 1884; only daughter of Abner (adviser to King Kamehameha III, judge of the Supreme Court, acting governor of Oahu, privy councilor, member of the House of Nobles, and chamberlain) and* ***Konia Paki****; by tradition, was taken as an infant to live with high chiefess and co-ruler Kinau from 1832–1839; after Kinau gave birth to a daughter, Bernice was returned to her parents at their request; attended Chiefs' Children's School (known as Royal School after 1846); married Charles Reed Bishop (1822–1915), on June 4, 1850.*

Bernice Pauahi Bishop was born into distinguished lineage. As tradition dictated, she spent her early childhood with the high chiefess ***Kinau** until the birth of Kinau's own daughter, **Victoria Kamamalu**. In exchange, Bishop's parents Abner and **Konia Paki** were given the future Queen ***Liliuokalani** to raise. Bishop was returned to her parents, then in 1839 entered Chiefs' Children's School which had been established by the American missionary couple Amos and **Juliette Cooke**. From the age of eight to eighteen, Bishop boarded there, forming a daughterly bond with Cooke. By the age of 16, she was so proficient in literature and music that she was excused from her studies to teach piano and singing to the other students. At the school, she met Charles Bishop, a customs collector who had come to Hawaii in 1846. The couple married in 1850. Initially Bernice's parents opposed the match because they had hoped their daughter would marry royalty, but they eventually came around, and, with time, built a home for the couple called Haleakala.

While Charles prospered as a partner in Hawaii's first bank, the couple became increasingly civic minded. Bernice was active in church and charitable organizations and became a social leader in Honolulu. A frequent hostess to visiting international dignitaries, she served as a link between Hawaiian and American communities. So high was her status in the community that just before King Kamehameha V died he asked her to take the throne, which she refused. In 1875, the Bishops made a tour of the U.S. and Europe, and while in London Bishop was presented to Queen ***Victoria**.

Bernice Bishop died of cancer in 1884 at age 52. By that time, she had inherited some 353,000 acres, which represented approximately 11% of Hawaii's entire land mass. Her will established a perpetual charitable trust, the income of which would go toward the formation and maintenance of two schools for children of Hawaiian ancestry; one for boys and one for girls. Under the trusteeship of her husband, the boys' school opened in 1887, with the school for girls following in 1894. In 1889, Charles Bishop used his own funds to establish the Bernice Pauahi Bishop Museum in Honolulu. Dedicated to Hawaiian and Polynesian ethnology and to the display and preservation of Hawaiian artifacts, the museum is internationally renowned.

SOURCES:

Petersen, Barbara Bennett, ed. *Notable Women of Hawaii.* Honolulu: University of Hawaii Press, 1984.

Barbara Morgan,
Melrose, Massachusetts

Bishop, Elizabeth (1911–1979)

American poet, generally regarded as one of the finest and most influential in the 20th century. *Born on February 8, 1911, in Worcester, Massachusetts; died in Boston on October 6, 1979; daughter of William Thomas (an executive with J.W. Bishop Company) and Gertrude Bulmer Bishop; attended public schools in Nova Scotia and Massachusetts; entered Walnut Hill boarding school in Natick (near Boston) at 16; granted A.B. in English Literature from Vassar College, 1934; lived with Lota de Macedo Soares for 15 years; never married; no children.*

Spent a short time in early childhood with her maternal grandparents in Nova Scotia, after her father's untimely death and her mother's subsequent breakdown; lived with her paternal grandparents (Worcester) and then an aunt (Boston) from the age of six until she went away to school; began writing, mostly short fiction, while at Vassar; met Marianne Moore (1934); first trip abroad, to Paris (1935); moved to Florida (late 1930s); lived in Key West until after the end of WW II; lived in Mexico for nine months (1943); began a friendship with Pablo Neruda; met Randall Jarrell (1946) who introduced her to Robert Lowell, one of her lifelong friends (1947); set off on a trip around South America and the Straits of Magellan (1951); while visiting Rio de Janeiro, suffered a violent allergic reaction to cashew fruit and was forced to curtail her journey; remained in Brazil for the next 15 years, sharing a house near Petropolis with a Brazilian friend, Lota de Macedo Soares; returned to the U.S. (1966); taught for two terms at the University of Washington in Seattle; lived intermittently in Brazil and the U.S. for a number of years; taught at Harvard University as poet in residence until mandatory retirement (1977); taught one term at New York University (Fall 1977); continued to write poetry until her death.

Books and awards: Houghton Mifflin Poetry Award (1945); North & South *(1946); Guggenheim Fellowship (1947); Consultant in Poetry, Library of Congress (1949–50); American Academy of Arts and Letters Award (1951); First Lucy Martin Donnelly Fellowship, Bryn Mawr College (1951); Shelley Memorial Award (1952); Life Membership, National Institute of Arts and Letters (1954);* Poems: North & South—A Cold Spring *(1955);* Partisan Review *Fellowship (1956); Pulitzer Prize for Poetry (1956);* The Diary of "Helena Morley" *(1957); Amy Lowell Traveling Fellowship (1957); Chapelbrook Fellowship (1962);* Brazil *(1962); Fellowship of the Academy of American Poets Award (1964);* Questions of Travel *(1965); Rockefeller Foundation Grant (1966–67);* Selected Poems *(London, 1967);* The Ballad of the Burglar of Babylon *(1968); LL.D., Smith College (1968);* The Complete Poems *(1969); Merrill Foundation Award (1969);* The Complete Poems *(London, 1970); National Book Award (1970); Order of Rio Branco, Brazil (1970);* An Anthology of Twentieth-Century Brazilian Poetry *(1972); LL.D., Rutgers University (1972); LL.D., Brown University (1972);* Poem *(1973); Harriet Monroe Award (1974); St. Botolph Club Arts Award (1975); Books Abroad/ Neustadt International Prize for Literature (1976); Membership, American Academy of Arts and Letters (1976);* Geography III *(1976); National Book Critics Circle Poetry Award (1976); LL.D., Adelphi University (1977); LL.D., Brandeis University (1978); Guggenheim Fellowship (1978); LL.D., Dalhousie University (1979); LL.D., Princeton University (1979);* The Complete Poems: 1927–1979 *(1979, 1983);* The Collected Prose *(1984).*

In his memorial tribute to Elizabeth Bishop, offered at the American Academy of Arts and Letters in December 1979, the poet Richard

Wilbur reflected upon the search for ultimate answers recorded in her poetry: "In and out of her poetry, she lamented her want of a comprehensive philosophy, yet I cannot be sorry that so honest a nature as hers refused to force itself into a system, and I question whether system is the only way to go deep into things." Over the course of her professional career, which spanned more than 40 years and included poetry, fiction, memoir and translation, Bishop worked *to go deep into things*; her poetry is an especially compelling record of her efforts. Many of the poems reflect upon loss and exile or describe the experience of traveling from one location to another in search of a place to feel at home: each motif had its basis in Bishop's lived experience.

The first years of Bishop's life were "marked by losses," as Robert Giroux explains in his introduction to *The Collected Prose*. Bishop's father died when she was eight months old; her mother **Gertrude Bulmer Bishop** was permanently traumatized by his death. Gertrude became incurably insane when Bishop was five, in a process of degeneration and collapse that Bishop detailed in her story, "In the Village," written many years later. Bishop and her mother never saw each other again after the events chronicled in this story, although Gertrude lived for another 20 years.

Elizabeth Bishop lived with her mother's parents in Great Village, Nova Scotia, until she was six, when she was suddenly and (as she saw it) inexplicably taken away to live with her father's parents in Worcester, Massachusetts. Even in a life filled with journeys, this brief sojourn in Bishop's childhood stands out. Losing Great Village, the final catastrophe in a series of related events, convinced her that favorite places, like beloved people, could simply vanish from one's life. She recounted some of the events of this period in a memoir called "The Country Mouse," which recalls "a dismal time" made hideous by grief, loneliness, asthma, eczema, boredom, and a claustrophobic sense of self-consciousness: "I had been brought back unconsulted and against my wishes to the house my father had been born in, to be saved from a life of poverty and provincialism, bare feet, suet puddings, unsanitary

school slates, perhaps even from the inverted *r*'s of my mother's family."

Bishop's response to unsettling circumstances in childhood was to follow her imagination into places that did not change. An interview Bishop gave in middle age (*Shenandoah*, Winter 1966) recalled those years. "I was crazy about fairy tales—Andersen, Grimm, and so on. Like Jean-Paul Sartre (as he explains it in *Les Mots*) I also read all kinds of things I didn't really understand. I tried almost anything." Bishop stayed only nine months in Worcester before she was moved again, to live with her Aunt Maude in Boston, putting an end to her wandering for awhile. She grew up in Boston and visited her maternal relatives every summer until she was 13. In 1927, Bishop was enrolled at Walnut Hill boarding school, and in 1930 she entered Vassar College.

Her years in college, which she shared with ***Mary McCarthy**, ***Muriel Rukeyser**, and other writers who went on to find their own fame, served as Bishop's professional apprenticeship. While at Vassar, she wrote for *The Vassar Review*, helped to start *The Conspirito*, a rival magazine, and contributed to the review formed when the two magazines were combined. And it was while still a student at Vassar that Bishop met ***Marianne Moore**, whose poems she admired. They met in March 1934, in front of the third-floor reading room of the New York Public Library. (They hit it off at once, discovering that they shared a number of interests besides literature. Two weeks after their first meeting, they went to the circus, and an early letter from Bishop offers Moore a chance to examine a new book on tattooing.) Bishop's relative anonymity within the American poetic tradition can be traced in part to her friendship with Moore, an important bond for both women but one sometimes misrepresented as the relationship between a mentor and her young follower. This connection and some superficial similarities in their work—particularly in the precision with which each renders the details of the physical world—led some readers to think of Bishop's work as simply "more of the same." Bishop and Moore were amused but sometimes irritated by this identification; their correspondence reveals that each saw the other as friend and colleague, rather than as teacher or disciple.

Bishop made the first of many important journeys in her adult life when she went abroad in 1935. She spent time in Belgium, France, Brittany, and Paris; then in 1936, she traveled to England, North Africa, and Spain. After a brief sojourn in Florida, she returned to Great Britain and the Continent. She settled in Key West, Florida, in 1939. This period of travel was a productive one for Bishop's writing. By 1941, she had enough poems, some of which had already been published in *Poetry*, *Partisan Review*, and other magazines, to fill a small volume. But her first book, *North & South*, (which received Houghton Mifflin's poetry prize) did not come out until 1946, after another period of travel abroad, to Europe, Africa, and Mexico. *North & South* introduces favorite points of reference for Bishop—images, settings, and shifts in perspective—that explore the difficulty of various kinds of travel, real and imaginary. The speaker in such a poem hopes to find a message that is "comprehensive, consoling" like the small red sun in the seascape described in "Large Bad Picture."

Praise and recognition followed the publication of her first book. In 1947, Bishop was awarded a Guggenheim fellowship, and, in 1949, she moved to Washington, D.C., to begin work as consultant in poetry at the Library of Congress. While there, she occasionally visited Ezra Pound, a patient at St. Elizabeth's Hospital. "Visits to St. Elizabeth's," written and published that year, is one response to those visits. Constructed on the lines of "The House That Jack Built," the poem is both sad and comical in its description of Pound, the man who "lies in the house of Bedlam." Bishop did not enjoy her year in Washington; when her duties came to an end, she decided to use her recent literary prizes to fund a sailing trip around South America. She embarked in November 1951, stopping to visit friends in Rio de Janeiro on her way to the Straits of Magellan. An allergic reaction to cashew fruit was so severe that she had to be hospitalized in Rio. Once she recovered, she decided to remain; for the first time in a number of years, Bishop felt herself to be *at home*. She and her friend **Lota de Macedo Soares** spent the next 15 years together, living and working and entertaining in an apartment in Rio and a house in the mountains. Macedo Soares was able to help Bishop curtail her drinking habits, which had affected her physical and mental health for some years, but Bishop's recurrent asthma continued to demoralize her. Finding medication with better than temporary palliative effects was an ongoing concern.

Bishop brought out her next collection, *Poems: North & South—A Cold Spring*, in 1955. It received the Pulitzer Prize the following year. For approximately the next decade, most of Bishop's attention went toward learning Portuguese, reading the literature of Brazil, and translating works by Brazilian writers for publication in the United States. She translated *Minha Vida de Menina* (*My Life as a Little Girl*); a classic in Brazil, the book was the diary of "Helena Morley," a girl who grew up in a mining town in the 1890s. During the same period, Bishop wrote a book on Brazil, edited and published by *Life* World Library. Her work was considerably altered by the editors, who identified themselves as co-authors, and she found the finished product less than satisfactory. She tended to downplay her involvement with the project in later years. Bishop's primary interest during this decade was translating Brazilian poetry. Some of her best and best-known work in translation was of poetry by Carlos Drummond de Andrade, then one of Brazil's most important living poets. She included her translations in *The Complete Poems* (1969), and in *An Anthology of Twentieth-Century Brazilian Poetry* (1972), which she co-edited with Emanuel Brasil.

Bishop's work on Portuguese language and literature did not preempt her own poetry altogether, but her pace in writing was, as ever, careful and slow. She wrote about 20 finished poems about her life in Brazil. Most appeared first in *Questions of Travel* and were also included in later collections. The title poem in this book speculates on the value and significance of travel, wondering whether it signals "lack of imagination." The restless traveler cannot decide where home lies or what value her travels actually have: "Think of the long trip home. / Should we have stayed at home and thought of here?" The book also includes poems from "Elsewhere," most of which look back to her childhood in Great Village. Bishop's time in Brazil fostered an important development in her poetry; many of the poems written during and after these years show her (or someone like her) revisiting the past, in hopes of transforming old losses.

Such transformations are difficult to achieve and nearly impossible to sustain, according to the perspective in "One Art," a late poem on the speaker's efforts to think of loss as a voluntary exercise within a larger discipline. She explains that if one starts small, with keys, hours, "places and names, and where it was you meant to travel," it is possible to progress to larger, more important losses, like favorite houses, whole continents, even a beloved person—"the joking voice, a gesture / I love. . . ." This poem had its source in her companion Macedo Soares' death by suicide in 1967, probably the most devastating loss of Bishop's adult life.

For the next several years, Bishop traveled between the house she was renovating in Brazil and the United States, where she taught a number of college and university courses in poetry. She received the 1969 National Book Award for *The Complete Poems*, but Bishop's professional career was clearly far from over. *Geography III* was published in 1976 and contains some of her finest work, including "In the Waiting Room," "Crusoe in England," and "The Moose." "In the Waiting Room" is an account of yet another collision with old suffering. No other poem brings the poet and the speaker together so explicitly; the "I" in the dentist's waiting room who endured a brief but terrifying moment of panic was "an Elizabeth."

> Whatever the landscape had of meaning appears to have been abandoned.
>
> **—Elizabeth Bishop, from "Cape Breton"**

Bishop settled in Boston in 1974, where she lived, off and on, until her death in 1979. She shared the last years of her life with **Alice Methfessel**, her friend since 1971, who became her literary executor. These years, which she spent teaching at Harvard or traveling to Maine and other favorite spots, were the most settled since those she had spent in Brazil. *The Complete Poems: 1927–1979* includes poems that Bishop wrote between 1976 and her death, as well as her translations from Portuguese, some juvenilia, and a few brief occasional poems. *The Collected Prose*, published in 1984, includes short fiction and memoirs and spans her whole career.

The whole of Bishop's *oeuvre* takes up less than a foot of bookshelf space, but every well-crafted piece of her work is original and alive, animated by Bishop's lifelong interest in the external world of landscapes and artifacts and the multiple inner worlds of human experience. In many ways, Bishop represents the individual talent as T.S. Eliot describes it in "Tradition and the Individual Talent." She separates "the [woman] who suffers" from "the mind which creates." Bishop's poetry typically offers a translation of emotion rather than direct access to emotion. She allows the reader only guarded access to her most intimate experiences and feelings. Yet the overall impression she creates is of a person who values and believes in connection, her modesty and reserve notwithstanding, and despite many disappointments.

SOURCES:

Bishop, Elizabeth. *The Collected Prose.* NY: Farrar, Straus and Giroux, 1984.

Brown, Ashley. "An Interview with Elizabeth Bishop," in *Shenandoah.* Vol. 17. Winter 1966, pp. 3–19.
Kalstone, David. *Becoming a Poet.* NY: Farrar, Straus and Giroux, 1989.
MacMahon, Candace W. *Elizabeth Bishop: A Bibliography, 1927–1979.* Charlottesville: University Press of Virginia, 1980.
Stevenson, Anne. *Elizabeth Bishop.* NY: Twayne Publishers, 1966.
Wilbur, Richard. "Elizabeth Bishop," in *Ploughshares.* Vol. 6, no. 2, 1980, pp. 10–14.

SUGGESTED READING:

Giroux, Robert, ed. *One Art: Letters of Elizabeth Bishop.* NY: Farrar, Straus, 1994.
Goldensohn, Lorrie. *Elizabeth Bishop: The Biography of a Poetry.* NY: Columbia University Press, 1992.
Millier, Brett C. *Elizabeth Bishop: Life and the Memory of It.* Berkeley, CA: University of California Press, 1993.
Parker, Robert Dale. *The Unbeliever: The Poetry of Elizabeth Bishop.* Urbana, IL: University of Illinois Press, 1988.
Schwartz, Lloyd and Sybil P. Estess. *Elizabeth Bishop and Her Art.* Ann Arbor, MI: University of Michigan Press, 1983.

COLLECTIONS:

Correspondence and other papers located at Houghton Library, Harvard University; The Rosenbach Museum and Library, Philadelphia; Vassar College Library, Poughkeepsie; Olin Libraries Special Collections of the Washington University Libraries, St. Louis.

Mary M. Lacey,
Assistant Visiting Professor of English and Humanities, Earlham College, Richmond, Indiana

Hazel Bishop

Bishop, Hazel (1906–1998)

American chemist and cosmetics manufacturer. *Born Hazel Gladys Bishop on August 17, 1906, in Hoboken, New Jersey; died on December 5, 1998; only daughter and one of two children of Henry (an entrepreneur and pioneer motion-picture exhibitor) and Mabel (Billington) Bishop; graduated from the Bergen School for Girls in Jersey City, New Jersey; B.A. from Barnard College, 1929; graduate study at Columbia University.*

During the 1950s, any American woman who wore make-up probably owned at least one tube of Hazel Bishop "Lasting Lipstick." What she may not have known was that it took 309 experiments and two years of testing to produce the revolutionary product, most of it done in the home kitchen of a research chemist who had once dreamed of becoming a doctor.

Hazel Gladys Bishop, daughter of a New Jersey entrepreneur, completed a pre-med course at Barnard College in 1929 and was forced by the Depression to shift her graduate studies at Columbia University to the night-school program. Working days as a chemical technician in the New York State Psychiatric Hospital, in 1935 Bishop became the research assistant to Dr. A. Benson Cannon, a leading dermatologist. During World War II, she was a senior organic chemist for Standard Oil, where she concentrated on studies of aviation fuels which eventually led to the development of special gasoline for bomber planes. In 1945, she continued petroleum research with the Socony Vacuum Oil Company.

All the while, Bishop spent evenings at home developing and testing a formula for a "no-smear" lipstick. After years of perfecting the product, she introduced it at a Barnard College Club fashion show in 1949. The following year, she formed Hazel Bishop, Inc., to manufacture the lipstick and launch the product with an unprecedented $1,410,000 advertising campaign. Its success was overwhelming, with copycat "non-smear" products appearing almost daily. In August 1951, *Consumer Reports* published the results of a test on 31 lipsticks: "The claims of Hazel Bishop to indelibility are not without foundation. But of course no lipstick is permanent.... The fact is, nevertheless, that the new long-staying lipsticks do color the lips for a considerably longer time than the standard versions." Bishop remained president of the company until resigning in November 1951 over a dispute with majority stockholders. When a pending lawsuit was settled in 1954, the company had annual sales in excess of $10 million. However, as agreed in the settlement, Bishop sold her remaining stock and severed all connection with the firm.

After a stint as a consultant to the National Association of Leather Glove Manufacturers, where she developed a cleaner for washing leather gloves, Bishop founded H.B. Laboratories to conduct research into consumer-oriented chemical products. This company produced another leather-cleaning product, in addition to a number of other personal-care and cosmetic items. Among several subsidiary companies formed to manufacture new products was Perfemme, Inc., which in 1957, introduced a solid perfume concentrate in lipstick size.

Bishop believed that women brought insight and first-hand knowledge to cosmetology that men could never match. Declaring her desire to make cosmetics "an integral part of a woman's total wardrobe rather than as a manifestation of vanity," she viewed cosmetics as serious business. During the 1950s, she was elected to the New York Academy of Sciences and named a fellow of the American Institute of Chemists and a member of the Society of Cosmetic Chemists. She was also a member of the Society of Women Engineers and of the national board of the Women's Medical College of Pennsylvania. In 1957, she received the first "Women of Courage" award of the Assembly of Brooklyn Jewish Women's Organizations, cited for "her courageous endeavors as a woman leader in industry, business and civic affairs."

Bishop's later career took her out of cosmetic research. In 1962, she became a registered agent for the brokerage firm of Bache and Company, had some success on Wall Street, and worked as a financial analyst. In 1978, she was appointed head of the cosmetics and marketing program at the Fashion Institute of Technology and was the first to occupy the Revlon chair at that institution.

Barbara Morgan,
Melrose, Massachusetts

Bishop, Isabel (1902–1988)

American artist of genre scenes who is known particularly for paintings of working women and men of New York City's Union Square. *Born Isabel Bishop on March 3, 1902, in Cincinnati, Ohio; died in February 1988 in Riverdale, New York; youngest of five children of Dr. J. Remsen (an educator) and Anna Bartram (Newbold) Bishop; attended Easton High School, Detroit, Michigan; John Wicker's Art School, Detroit, 1917; New York School of Applied Design for Women, 1918; Art Students League of New York, 1922–24; married Harold George Wolff, on August 9, 1934 (died, February 21, 1962); children: one son, Remsen Wolff (b. April 6, 1940).*

Selected paintings: Self-Portrait *(Wichita Art Museum, 1927);* Virgil and Dante in Union Square *(Delaware Art Museum, Wilmington, 1932);* Nude *(Whitney Museum of American Art, New York, 1934);* Two Girls *(The Metropolitan Museum of Art, New York, 1935);* Young Woman's Head *(The Butler Institute of American Art, Youngstown, Ohio, 1937);* Lunch Hour *(private collection, 1939);* Ice Cream Cones *(Museum of Fine Arts, Boston, 1942);* Subway Scene *(Whitney Museum of American Art, 1958);* Soda Fountain with Passerby *(Virginia Museum of Fine Arts, Richmond, 1960);* Five Women Walking No. 2 *(Wichita State University Art Museum, Wichita, Kansas, 1969);* High School Students No. 2 *(Midtown Galleries, New York, 1973);* Student's Entrance to Union Square *(Midtown Galleries, 1980);* Self-Portrait *(private collection, 1986).*

For 50 years each workday morning, Isabel Bishop left her home in the wealthy Riverdale section of the Bronx to catch the early train to Manhattan; at Grand Central Station, she transferred to the subway for the final trip to her studio, located atop an old office building in the then shabby business district of Union Square. Tall, thin, and immaculately dressed, with her hair pulled back to reveal a sculptured profile, Bishop was an elegant, dignified presence. Arriving at her studio before nine, she donned a paint-streaked lab coat and began the day's work. Her method was deliberate and painstaking, involving countless preliminary sketches and etchings, limiting her output to only a few paintings a year. Despite her success, Bishop often admitted to feelings of self-doubt. A quote from Henry James' short story of an artist, *The Middle Years*, hung in her studio. "We work in the dark. We do what we can—we give what we have. Our doubt is our passion, and our passion our task. The rest is the madness of art."

Isabel Bishop was the youngest in a family of four other children (two sets of twins). Her father was an educator, and her mother **Anna Bishop** was an unpublished writer who taught herself Italian with hopes of producing a new English translation of Dante's *Inferno*. What Bishop remembered most about her mother, who gave birth to Bishop late in life, was her maternal indifference. "I wanted to be special," Bishop said. "I always wanted more than I got." A 13-year age gap between Bishop and the youngest twins also set her apart. Only her father took a particular interest in her, often inveigling her to take his side against the rest of the family, which did little to bring her closer to her mother and siblings.

When Bishop was still an infant, the family moved to Detroit, where her father taught and later worked in secondary-school administration. She remembers living in an area of Detroit which bordered a working-class neighborhood. Although she was not allowed to play with the workers' children, she was drawn to the warmth of their community, which may, at least in part, explain her later fascination with the community of New York's Union Square. The working women of the Depression and the students who came to dominate the Square in the 1980s would be the subject of most of her paintings.

At age 12, Bishop began Saturday morning classes at the John Wicker Art School. "It was a

Isabel Bishop

shock to walk into class and find a great fat nude woman posing," she recalled. "The theory was that it was best to learn to draw from life." After graduating from high school at 15, she left home and enrolled at the New York School of Design for Women, intending to fulfill her mother's wish that she achieve independence by becoming an illustrator. The disciplinary exercises in drawing that she learned there would strongly affect her later method of painting, but the stimulating ambiance of the revived modern art movement drove the idea of a commercial art career from her mind. She accepted a monthly stipend from a wealthy relative and, in 1920, enrolled in the Art Students League.

With her first teacher Max Weber, Bishop explored cubism and futurism, but Weber's arrogance and relentless criticism of her work in front of the other students was devastating. A better match was found with Kenneth Hayes Miller, who had been part of the Armory Show of 1913 that had introduced the American art world to the modernists. Although Miller was interested in modern art, he had not completely severed his classical ties. "Instead of imitating a current trend," Bishop explained, "he taught us to dig something of our own out of the old masters." Miller's defined ideas about classic form and commonplace contemporary content had a profound impact on Bishop, but the most important thing she learned from him was that art demanded passionate commitment. Among Miller's students at the time was Reginald Marsh, with whom Bishop would have a lifetime friendship, and to whom she would often be compared. Another mentor at the League was the satiric painter of New York café life, Guy Pène du Bois, who also became a friend and ultimately encouraged Bishop's independent growth as an artist. "I was influenced spiritually by Dub," she told a friend, "more by his point of view than by his painting, which is very beautiful and underrated now."

Still leaning on her generous relative for support, in 1926 Bishop made the decision to leave the League and rent her first studio on West 14th Street in Union Square. Setting up her home next to her work space, she was prolific in her attempt to incorporate the powerful influences of Miller into a style uniquely her own. This was a lonely, wrenching transition for Bishop, made more difficult by the end of a love affair, after which she attempted suicide on three separate occasions. In an interview for *People* magazine in 1975, she described jumping into the Hudson River: "But my body just wouldn't die. It began to swim."

The work of this period appears to reveal little of the emotional turmoil she was experiencing. Bishop experimented with still life, which she did not pursue. Her drawings and etchings show a preoccupation with figures in motion, especially a series related to the simple action of taking off and putting on clothing. Union Square began to emerge as a subject: the park wall, the statuary, and the idle men in sitting, standing, and leaning positions. After a series of drawings of herself—executed, she says "because I was there"—she produced the beautiful *Self-Portrait* of 1927, the first of a series of self-portraits which would culminate with the ruthlessly honest portrait completed shortly before her death. These masterpieces, as well as her female nudes, are considered by some as unique among American women painters, reminiscent more of Europeans like ***Käthe Kollwitz** and ***Paula Modersohn-Becker**. Of her nudes, who are usually engaged in some awkward activity, Willem de Kooning reportedly said, "That woman's nudes are the best damn nudes ever."

Another important early work, *Dante and Virgil in Union Square*, painted for her father when she was only 30, demonstrated her further attempt to assimilate the classic qualities of the Renaissance artists she so much admired. Utilizing the structural devices of Michelangelo and Rubens, the painting is a precursor of later works in which she would use the same composition to portray her fascination with movement. A series of Walking Pictures, done over a period from 1960 to 1980, are examples of this "ballet of everyday life," as Bishop called it. She once told **Grace Glueck** in an interview: "I keep trying to find some way of getting motion into my figures—motion you can feel in your nervous system."

In 1934, Bishop married Harold George Wolff, an intriguing and brilliant young doctor, and moved to his Riverdale home. Although Wolff was described by colleagues as "a formidably authoritarian and rigid personality," Bishop did not hint at these domineering traits in any discussion of her marriage but insisted that her husband was passionately interested in the arts and had a liberated attitude toward her work. Even after the birth of their son Remsen (1940), Bishop reported that Wolff insisted she immediately return to her routine. "We left the house together every morning; he went on to his work and I went to my studio. There was never any question about it." After 28 years of marriage, Wolff died of a cerebral hemorrhage in February 1962. Her son Remsen, after an apparently difficult adolescence, went on to become a photographer.

By 1940, Bishop was under contract with Midtown Galleries, where she had her first solo show; she would exhibit there throughout her career. Also by this time, she had been part of a number of important group exhibitions and had collected the first of many awards received during her lifetime. In 1935, her oil *Two Girls* had been purchased by the Metropolitan Museum of Art, bringing her national attention. The painting, as well as many of the paired female figures to follow, was praised for its "body language" and "a marked responsiveness to specifically feminine situations." That same year, Bishop was appointed as instructor at the Art Students League. In 1938, she was commissioned by the U.S. Treasury Department to execute a mural for a post office in New Lexington, Ohio, one of her few large-scale works.

Following her exhibition at the New York World's Fair in 1940, and the award of first prize in a show at the American Society of Graphic Artists, honors showered Bishop, including her election as an Associate of the National Academy of Design in New York. In 1946, she was the first woman to be elected an officer of the National Institute of Arts and Letters since its founding in 1898. In 1974, the Whitney Museum mounted a retrospective, and in 1987 she received the Gold Medal for Painting of the American Academy and Institute of Arts and Letters.

Bishop's numerous sketches, drawings, etchings, and aquatints, which served as studies for proposed paintings, were often praised as masterpieces in their own right, a fact that bothered Bishop, who thought of them merely as preliminary steps. The semitransparent, luminous quality she achieved in her paintings was obtained through careful, painstaking preparation of the canvas. The procedure included prepping the masonite panel with as many as eight coats of gesso, and painting a ground of random horizontal gray stripes made up of gelatin, powdered charcoal, and white lead, creating almost a vibrating surface upon which the drawing was added. Color, overlaid, was used tentatively, with a limited palette.

Fragment of Two Girls, *painting by Isabel Bishop. The Metropolitan Museum of Art, Arthur A. Hearn Fund, 1936 (36.27).*

One of Bishop's most interesting projects was a commission during World War II to make a series of pen-and-ink drawings for a proposed new edition of ***Jane Austen**'s *Pride and Prejudice*. She labored on the project for a year, working with models and giving utmost attention to the period costumes. Due to a shortage of funds, the publication was postponed, though Bishop's 31 illustrations were shown, along with several new paintings, at a Midtown Galleries exhibition in 1955. In 1976, they appeared in the new edition of *Pride and Prejudice*, published by E.P. Dutton. In an Afterward to the book, Bishop discussed the effectiveness of Austen's selectivity, the manner in which she limited and controlled what the reader was told and what they wanted to be told. Bishop found much in this literary technique for the visual artist to learn.

Bishop was forced to give up her beloved Union Square studio after a stroke in 1984. During the remaining four years of her life, she worked in a studio in her Riverdale home. Her funeral following her death in February 1988 was marked by a ceremony as quiet and dignified as the lady herself, with a service at her own Christ Church in Riverdale attended by her family, neighbors, and members of the Manhattan art world. She was eulogized only by her priest, who included passages from her favorite poet Gerard Manley Hopkins. Although Isabel Bishop was respected both inside and outside the art community during her lifetime, her importance has diminished over the years, perhaps due in part to the overwhelming dominance of abstract art in the United States which began in the 1950s.

SOURCES:

Current Biography 1977. NY: H.W. Wilson, 1977.
Lunde, Karl. *Isabel Bishop*. NY: Harry N. Abrams, 1975.
Yglesias, Helen. *Isabel Bishop*. NY: Rizzoli International, 1989.

SUGGESTED READING:

Mendelowitz, Daniel M. *A History of American Art*. NY: Holt, Rinehart and Winston, 1970.
Reich, Sheldon. *Isabel Bishop*. Tucson: The University of Arizona Museum of Art, 1974.

Barbara Morgan,
Melrose, Massachusetts

Bishop, Isabella (1831–1904)

Travel writer, explorer, and one of the first women to be made a fellow of the Royal Geographical Society, London, England. *Name variations: Isabella Bird, Isabella Bird Bishop, Isabella Lucy Bishop, Isa, IB. Born Isabella Lucy Bird on October 15, 1831, in Boroughbridge, Yorkshire, England; died on October 7, 1904, in a nursing home in Edinburgh, Scotland; daughter of Reverend Edward (a barrister turned cleric) and Dora (Lawson) Bird; received no formal schooling but was given a broad education by her parents and continued to teach herself; married John Bishop (a physician), on March 8, 1881; no children.*

Isabella Bishop

After many years of illness, including a spinal tumor, traveled to Canada and North America on advice of her doctor (1854); as a result, traveled throughout her life and published many authoritative works on what she observed; major trips include Australia and New Zealand (1872), returning via the Sandwich Isles (now Hawaii) and the U.S. (1873), Japan (1878), Malaya (1879), Kashmir and Ladakh in northern India, and Tibet (1889), Persia (now Iran, 1890), Kurdistan (area of Middle East inhabited by Kurds which today includes parts of Turkey, Iran and Iraq, 1891), Japan, Korea, and China (1894–96), and Morocco (1901).

Selected publications: The Englishwoman in America *(John Murray, London, 1856);* Six Months in the Sandwich Islands *(John Murray, London, 1875);* A Lady's Life in the Rocky Mountains *(John Murray, London, 1879);* Unbeaten Tracks in Japan *(John Murray, London, 1880);* The Golden Chersonese and the Way Thither *(John Murray, London, 1883);* Journeys in Persia and Kurdistan *(John Murray, London, 1891);* Among the Tibetans *(Religious Tract Society, London, 1894);* Korea and Her Neighbours *(John Murray, London, 1898);* The Yangtze Valley and Beyond *(John Murray, London, 1899);* Chinese Pictures *(a book of photographs, Cassell, London, 1900).*

In 1873, a small, soft-spoken Englishwoman, who had been a semi-invalid for most of her life, woke up inside her tent on the edge of the active volcano of Mauna Loa, in what was then called the Sandwich Isles (Hawaii). "The phrase, 'sleeping on the brink of a volcano,' was literally true," she wrote:

> for I fell asleep, and fear I might have been prosaic enough to sleep all night, had it not been for the fleas which had come up in the camping blankets. . . . Creeping over the sleeping forms . . . I crept cautiously into the crevasse in which the snow-water was then hard frozen, and out upon the projecting

> ledge. The four hours in which we had previously watched the volcano had passed like one; but the lonely hours which followed might have been two minutes or a year, for time was obliterated.

This was only one of the early adventures of the respectable, religious, and, in many ways, typical Victorian Englishwoman. But travel was to prove her to be somewhat unconventional. The pleasure Isabella Bishop found in wandering drove her to extraordinary feats of endurance. Though she was always a sharp and critical observer of religion in all its forms, her deep interest in everything she saw was stronger than her Victorian sensibilities, and she took everything in her stride, from nakedness to opium smoking. She was also a gifted writer and her books are particularly important because it was the cultures of native peoples that she sought out on her travels, not Western-style comforts. However trying the circumstances, be it a vermin-infested inn or a howling snowstorm, nothing could detract from her enjoyment of the experience as a whole. It is this spirit of sheer pleasure and curiosity in the world around her, conveyed in the best of her writing, that is most inspiring about Isabella Bishop.

> There never was anybody who had adventures so well as Miss Bird.
>
> —*Spectator* (1879)

Isabella Lucy Bird was born on October 15, 1831, the eldest child of Edward, a zealous minister, and **Dora Bird**, a minister's daughter. Because Isabella was not a strong child and suffered frequently from ill-health, doctors recommended she have as much fresh air as possible, so for many years she rode with her father around his parishes, while he taught her the names of the wildlife and quizzed her on everything they saw. The family was respectable, devout, and upper-middle class, and her kin included many bishops and missionaries. She was also related to William Wilberforce, the campaigner against slavery. Biographer **Anna Stoddart** notes that several of Isabella's aunts refused sugar in their tea "as a sacred protest against slave-grown products." She had just one sister, **Henrietta**, known as Hennie, to whom she was devoted. Over the years, as Edward Bird moved from parish to parish, the family had many homes. Both daughters grew up with a strong sense of duty and became involved in parish work, Isabella taking Sunday school classes and instructing the choir. She was a very bright child, who enjoyed serious adult texts from an early age.

When she was 18, Isabella had an operation to remove a tumor from her spine, and she remained weak and in pain. Despite regular family holidays in the Scottish Highlands where her health improved a little, she nevertheless remained a semi-invalid. Finally, Bishop's doctor recommended that she take a long sea voyage, and, in 1854, with £100 from her father, she set off for North America in the company of relatives returning to Canada.

The freedom, independence, and stimulation of travel proved the cure for Isabella, who relished every moment of the journey which lasted several months. Even in the most unlikely situations, her pleasure is evident from her writing. On a train to Chicago, she found herself crammed in among a colorful collection of characters, including "prairie-men" complete with decorated boots, spurs, earrings, and pistols. Bishop noted their handsomeness and commented: "Dullness fled from their presence; they could tell stories, whistle melodies, and sing comic songs without weariness or cessation: fortunate were those near enough to be enlivened by their drolleries during the tedium of a night detention."

In England, encouraged by her friends, Isabella wrote up her travels and showed the work to John Murray, who was to become her friend and publisher for life. The book, *An Englishwoman in America*, was proof of Bishop's gift for writing and sold well. At age 26, the young author put some of her profits towards providing deep-sea fishing boats and tweed-making equipment in an area of great poverty in the West Highlands of Scotland. When her health began to suffer in 1857, doctors again urged her to travel, and she set off for North America for a second time, though little is known of that trip.

Shortly after her return, her father died. With her mother and sister, Isabella moved to Edinburgh where her mother's death soon followed. The two sisters then lived together both in Edinburgh and on the Scottish island of Null. Once again, Bishop devoted her time to charitable causes and in particular the plight of the Highlanders. She made several trips to America as part of a Highland resettlement project, but her health remained poor. Although she took holidays in New York and in the Mediterranean, she still felt no better. Nevertheless, at age 40, Isabella undertook a more demanding trip to Australia and New Zealand.

The journey started out badly because she did not like either country, and at first her health grew worse. She wrote to her sister that she hated the bluebottles, the heat, the dust, and the "colonial ladies afflicted with hysteria." But once on the ship home via California she began to feel better. While helping to nurse a passenger's critically ill son, Bishop was urged to disembark with them when the ship reached Honolulu in the Sandwich Isles. Enchanted by the islands' beauty and the generous hospitality of the people, Isabella was to stay six months.

It was in the Sandwich Isles that she learned to ride again. The problems with her back had made riding sidesaddle impossible, but here both men and women rode astride. This was made possible by a very respectable Hawaiian riding dress—special breeches that were hidden by the folds of a skirt when the wearer was not on horseback—and she was to take great offense when it was later suggested in *The Times* that she wore "masculine habiliments" when riding in the same style of clothing in the United States.

Bishop explored the island on horseback and climbed to the crater of the active volcano, Kilauea, at a height of 4,000 feet. She also took a perilous trip around the northeast coast of the island and then climbed to the summit of Mauna Loa at just under 14,000 feet, with a Mr. Green. Despite her lack of experience on such expeditions, Bishop proved to have extraordinary determination and physical strength. She also had a robust digestive system, which her husband was later to compare with that of an ostrich.

From the Sandwich Isles, Bishop headed to California and the Rocky Mountains around Denver, Colorado, where consumptives often went to seek a cure. As the American West was still being settled, the countryside was wild and sparsely populated. She rode up to Estes Park, a remote valley among the highest mountains of northern Colorado, where she stayed on the cattle ranch of a Welshman called Griff Evans.

It was while she was here that she came across a character whom many consider to have been the great, though most unlikely, romance of her life—James Nugent. Otherwise known as "Rocky Mountain Jim," he was a famous scout and drunken desperado with only one eye—the other, he claimed, he had lost in a fight with a bear. But he was also well-read, intelligent, and chivalrous.

Nugent offered to guide Bishop and two young men up Long's Peak, the 14,700-foot mountain that overlooks the park. It was a dangerous scramble to the top, but she wrote of her achievement: "It was something at last to stand upon the storm-rent crown of this lonely sentinel of the Rocky range, on one of the mightiest of the vertebrae of the backbone of the North American continent." She would probably not have made it with a less determined or devoted guide than Nugent. "I had various falls, and once hung by my frock, which caught on a rock, and 'Jim' severed it with a hunting-knife, upon which I fell into a crevice full of soft snow."

Some weeks later, Bishop set off on a pony called Birdie to explore the region further. She visited Denver and Colorado Springs and wandered through the mountains, often following only the barest of tracks. Returning to Denver, she discovered that a banking crisis had left her temporarily without funds, so she returned to Estes Park where Griff Evans owed her money.

It was during this stay that Nugent declared his feelings towards her. In a letter to her sister, Bishop wrote, "He is a man who any woman might love, but who no sane woman would marry." Though she admitted to Henrietta that she felt deeply for him, she knew she could not trust her happiness to him because of whiskey. It was not without regret that she finally left Estes Park and Jim Nugent, and she continued to write to him until he was killed, shot in a quarrel with Griff Evans. Though there were many versions of this incident, none has proved conclusive.

When she returned to Edinburgh, Bishop edited the contents of her letters to her sister and wrote *Six Months in the Sandwich Isles*. Her adventures in the Rocky Mountains were serialized in a magazine and would be published in book form in 1879. She also became involved in a project to build a shelter and coffee house for Edinburgh cab drivers. But gradually her health began to decline, and once again travel was prescribed.

Her next trip was to Japan. This time she undertook a much more systematic and thorough study of the country than she had done on previous occasions. The area of Japan that interested her most was the island of Yezo (now Hokkaido) and its native inhabitants, the Ainu. It is believed that few Europeans had visited this island before Bishop, and the Ainu culture remained almost untouched by Western influence. Although the Ainu were looked down upon by the Japanese, Isabella was moved by the dignity of the people, and she stayed in an Ainu home where she received great hospitality. "Little acts of courtesy were constantly being performed; but I really appreciated nothing more than the quiet way in which they went on with their ordinary lives." It was her book of this trip, *Unbeat-*

en Tracks in Japan, that established Bishop as a serious geographer and anthropologist. In a letter to John Murray, she noted that the book's reputation "vindicated a woman's right to do what she can do well."

From Japan, she traveled to Hong Kong, China, and the Malay States. Her book on this area, *The Golden Chersonese and the* Way *Thither,* includes a detailed and gruesome account of a prison she visited in Canton and also tells of her colorful experiences in the Malay States, which were part of the British Empire at that time. Bishop visited many of the British administrators of the different states, known as Residents.

The Resident she most admired was the diligent and original Mr. Low, in the state of Perak, who was away when she appeared, half-drenched, at his door. It seems that the elephant she'd been riding took a shower. The servants made her comfortable and later announced that dinner was served. Isabella, who had been looking forward to some solitude, was annoyed to see the table set for three, until she learned that her dinner companions were two apes and a retriever who was tied to her chair. "What a grotesque dinner party! What a delightful one! My 'next of kin' were so reasonably silent; they required no conversational efforts."

From The Golden Chersonese, *Bishop's book about her trip to the Malay Peninsula in 1878.*

Bishop returned home in 1879, only to be grief-stricken by the death of her sister Hennie, of typhoid, the following year. Though Bishop continued to write to friends about her later travels, her letters never again conveyed the pleasure or delight in all she did and saw that she captured in the letters to her sister. Some months later, Dr. John Bishop, who had looked after both Hennie and Isabella, and had proposed marriage to Isabella on several previous occasions, asked for her hand once more. This time she accepted. At the age of 50, Isabella was married, but she was still in mourning for her sister and insisted on wearing black. The couple settled in Edinburgh, but Isabella found married life difficult at first and continued to miss Hennie. It was not until John Bishop caught a serious skin disease from one of his patients that she realized her feelings for him. Though ill herself, she nursed him devotedly until he died, in 1886.

Isabella planned her next trip to Asia as a tour of medical missions—a movement that John had supported. She also took a three-month nursing course in London. Three years after her husband's death, in 1889, Bishop was 58 when she founded a mission hospital in Srinigar, in Kashmir, northern India, in his memory. Then, fleeing the English who came up to the cooler hills for the summer season, she took off for Leh, the capital of Ladakh, an area of northern India that is more Tibetan in its culture and climate. She rode on a wild Arab steed with an escort who was later arrested in Leh for murder.

She also teamed up with a member of the Moravian Mission to explore the area further to the north. At heights of 18,000 feet everyone except Bishop suffered from altitude sickness—even the horses, which had to be exchanged for yaks. It was a terrifying journey and Bishop nearly died crossing a furious river, escaping with just a few broken ribs. But she had no doubts that their exertions had been worthwhile and enjoyed in particular a visit to the remote Buddhist monastery at Deskyid. The book that resulted from this trip, *Among the Tibetans*, was not published by John Murray but by the Religious Tract Society. Though a valuable account of the area and its people, it is generally accepted as the least appealing of her works.

While in India, Bishop met a Major Sawyer from the Intelligence Branch of the Indian Army who was about to leave for a geographical and military mission of southwestern Persia—an area that was recognized to be key to the control of power in Central Asia by both Britain and its rival force in the region, Russia. It was also an area that greatly interested Isabella, but she had been told it was far too dangerous for her to travel there alone. She managed to persuade Sawyer to allow her to accompany him as far as Tehran.

It proved an arduous journey. It was midwinter and they faced gales and snowstorms, and once Isabella literally froze to her saddle. She had also gained the reputation for being a doctor, and wherever they stopped a crowd of sick people gathered to be cured. With only her nursing training and a basic medicine chest, there was little she could do although she tried. "Nothing is more painful," she wrote, "than to be obliged to say that one cannot do anything for them."

From Tehran, Bishop went south to Isfahan, where she again joined up with Sawyer to explore the area of Luristan. Although they made good traveling companions in many ways, Isabella was to disagree strongly with Sawyer on his rude treatment of the native peoples. It was spring and the countryside was wild and beautiful but the tribes of the region were at war, and on several occasions the party was fired upon. Once again, Bishop found herself acting as doctor to the crowds who queued up outside her tent. She was also called upon by Sawyer to help with his surveying of the area, when his regular assistant became ill.

For the last part of her journey, to Trebizond, Isabella traveled alone, riding on a large, fiery Persian stallion called Boy. Since the route she had chosen was particularly long and dangerous, she had found it difficult at first to get men and mules for her party. She enjoyed the trip greatly. On her first encounters with the Kurds, she found them a spirited and hospitable people, but she was to revise this opinion towards the end of her journey when she witnessed their persecution of Syrian and Armenian Christians.

Isabella now had no real home to return to, and felt restless in both Scotland and London. She wrote articles on the situation of the Syrian and Armenian Christians, and was invited to address a government committee on "The Armenian Question." She also wrote *Journeys in Persia and Kurdistan* and gave many talks.

Bishop was a member of the Royal Scottish Geographical Society, so in 1883, when London's Royal Geographical Society admitted members of other societies to its ranks, it found itself with women members for the first time. When many of the male members, horrified at the new situation, wanted women excluded, the issue became one of public debate. Bishop refused to become involved in the matter. "She did not have enough faith in or sympathy *for* the great majority of womankind" to be any sort of suffragist, suggests biographer **Pat Barr**, although Bishop did write to a friend: "The proposed act is a dastardly injustice to women." In the end, it was decided that women such as Bishop, who were already members, should remain members, but that no new women should be admitted.

In 1894, at age 63, Bishop set off for Yokohama, in Japan. Her plan this time was to report on the work of missions in Korea and China. She also took photography equipment with her—a skill she had recently learned. From Japan, she went to Seoul in Korea, where she hired a sampan for a journey up the River Itan to the Diamond Mountains in the east. From the boat, Bishop took meticulous records of all she saw, even concocting an on-board dark room for developing her pictures. When the party could progress no further by boat, they took to ponies which carried them into the Diamond Mountains. Here she visited several Buddhist monasteries—some calm retreats, others bustling with activity. She then took a steamer around the Korean coast to Chemulpo, only to discover that the country was at war, being fought over for control by China and Japan in what was to be known as the Sino-Japanese War of 1894–95.

Forced to leave the country immediately, Bishop spent the next six months in China and Russia, then returned to Korea to find the country still at war. She became intrigued by the political situation and on several occasions met the Korean king Kojong (Yi T'ae Wang) and Queen ***Min**. Once the king entrusted her with a top secret message for the Foreign Office in London, which Bishop asked her publisher to deliver.

Bishop went on to travel around China, and stayed briefly in Japan to recuperate from an illness. But learning that Korea was in fresh tumult, she returned there to discover that the Korean queen, who had been the power behind the throne, had been murdered by the Japanese. Bishop explored Korea further and found the country fascinating, but she was horrified by the terrible poverty and the devastation of the war.

In 1896, she went to Shanghai, in China. Though Shanghai was a bustling, cosmopolitan, Westernized port of little interest to her, it was also at the mouth of the 3,433 mile-long Yangtze

River, which she was to use as a route for exploring inland China. She traveled the first 1,000 miles up river by steamer and continued by native boat. The journey involved the boat being hauled up over rapids that even Bishop had to admit, "fully warrant the worst descriptions which have been given them."

As the boat made its way further and further inland, Isabella found herself increasingly fascinated with the countryside around her. When the river turned away from the route she had chosen to the West, she left it to travel by road. She was carried in an open chair and was much more visible and exposed to any xenophobia among the people. Although she wore Chinese dress, her hat was Japanese which, though practical, served to provoke the Chinese. Entering one city, she was surrounded by a furious mob, yelling "Foreign devil" and "Child-Eater." Her bearers barely managed to force their way into an inn, but the mob surged forward. Just as they were about to set fire to the room she was hiding in, troops arrived to break up the riot.

Despite this incident, Bishop was determined to continue on her way. In the city of Paoning Fu, she was impressed with the work of the Chinese Inland Mission, whose members followed the local customs of dress and etiquette and did not believe in Western cultural superiority. Here, too, she financed the setting up of a hospital in the name of her sister Henrietta. Continuing further west, nearer to the Tibetan border, she could not resist the opportunity to go on into the mountains. This involved crossing a gruelling mountain pass at 12,000 feet, but she loved the wonderful position of the city of Somo beyond, and the charm of its people.

Back in England, Bishop worked hard at her books, first *Korea and Her Neighbours,* then *The Yangtze Valley and Beyond.* She also gave many talks. Again, she tried to make herself a home in several different places, in both England and Scotland, but was happy in none of them. She began to plan another trip to China, but her doctors would not allow her to go. Instead she went to Morocco. On a huge black charger, which required a ladder for her to mount and dismount, she headed for the Atlas mountains where she visited the Berbers. In Marrakesh, she met the young sultan of Morocco, and must have made quite an impression on him, for "When I wished the Sultan long life and happiness at parting, he said that he hoped when his hair was as white as mine, he might have as much energy as I have. So I am not quite shelved yet!"

In 1902, Bishop took seriously ill and went to Edinburgh, where she was to move from nursing home to nursing home for the following two years. Stoddart wrote that she remained "cheerful and uncomplaining" and received many visitors. Isabella Bishop died on October 7, 1904. In London, her bags were still packed for the trip she had planned to China.

SOURCES:

Barr, Pat. *A Curious Life for a Lady: The Story of Isabella Bird.* London: John Murray, 1970.

Havely, Cicely Palser. *This Grand Beyond: The Travels of Isabella Bird Bishop.* London: Century Publishing, 1984.

Middleton, Dorothy. "Isabella Bird" in *Victorian Lady Travellers.* London: Routledge & Kegan Paul, 1965.

Stoddart, Anna. *The Life of Isabella Bird (Mrs Bishop).* London: John Murray, 1906.

The works of Isabella Bishop.

COLLECTIONS:

Original letters held by John Murray, Publisher.

Francesca Baines, freelance writer, London, England

Bisland, Elizabeth (b. 1863).

See Seaman, Elizabeth Cochrane for sidebar.

Bissell, Emily (1861–1948)

American welfare worker and founder of Christmas Seals. *Born Emily Perkins Bissell on May 31, 1861, in Wilmington, Delaware; died on March 8, 1948, in Wilmington; first daughter and second of four children of Champion Aristarcus Bissell (a banker and real estate investor) and Josephine (Wales) Bissell; educated in the Wilmington schools and at Miss Charlier's in New York City.*

Emily Bissell's name will forever be associated with the first Christmas Seals, though she was active in a number of charities in her hometown of Wilmington, Delaware, for her entire life. Organizer of the first chapter of the American Red Cross for Delaware, she also created the first public playground and the first free kindergarten in Wilmington.

The concept of selling a Christmas stamp to raise funds to battle tuberculosis was the idea of a postal clerk in Denmark. Remarkably successful from the onset, the idea was publicized in the U.S. by Danish-born journalist Jacob Rils. After reading an article by Rils, Bissell designed her own seal surrounded by a wreath and the words "Merry Christmas." Borrowing money to have 50,000 stamps printed, she launched her own campaign, which netted $3,000. In 1907, she persuaded the American Red Cross to mount a nationwide strategy to sell the stamps. Subsequently, the National Tuberculosis Association took over their creation and sale. For her contribution on behalf of those stricken with tuberculosis, in 1942 Bissell was the first lay person to be awarded the Trudeau Medal of the National Tuberculosis Association. She was further honored in 1980 with the issuance of a U.S. stamp bearing her likeness.

Barbara Morgan,
Melrose, Massachusetts

Bjelke-Petersen, Marie (1874–1969)

Danish-Australian novelist. *Born Marie Bjelke-Petersen at Jagtvejen, near Copenhagen, Denmark, on December 23, 1874; died at Lindisfarne, Hobart, Tasmania, on October 11, 1969; only daughter of Georg Peter and Caroline Vilhellmine (Hansen) Bjelke-Petersen; attended schools in Denmark, Germany, and London.*

Selecting writings: The Mysterious Stranger *(1913);* Before an Eastern Court *(1914);* Muffled Drums *(1914);* The Captive Singer *(1917);* The Immortal Flame *(c. 1919);* Dusk *(1921);* Jewelled Nights *(1924);* The Moon Minstrel *(1927);* Monsoon Music *(1930);* The Rainbow Late *(1932);* The Silver Knight *(1934);* Jungle Night *(1937).*

Marie Bjelke-Petersen's childhood, a reflection of her father's Spartan ideals, included instruction in the Bible, Greek mythology, and gymnastics. When the family immigrated to Tasmania (off the southeastern coast of Australia) in 1891, her brother Hans opened a Physical Culture School in Hobart, the capital city. Bjelke-Petersen was an instructor there and in the Hobart schools, until illness forced her to abandon her teaching career, and she took up writing.

After a number of her stories were published in Sydney papers, Bjelke-Petersen published three romantic religious sketches beginning with *The Mysterious Stranger* in 1913. Praised as a classic, it was translated into Arabic and reissued by London's Religious Tract Society in 1934. Her first novel *The Captive Singer*, written when she was 42, was set in Tasmania's Marakoopa Caves and was inspired by a guide who sang there. The book enjoyed immense popularity, selling 100,000 copies in English and 40,000 in Danish. Eight more sentimental novels followed, each containing an evangelical theme.

Bjelke-Petersen gained greater popularity in the U.S. and England than in Australia, although she did attract young women fans wherever she traveled. Critics praised her the authenticity of characters and the credibility of her plots, but some were less enthusiastic about her love scenes, with a writer for the *Australasian* suggesting that she should "exercise a little restraint over both her imagination and her vocabulary." Her passion for accuracy led her to travel into remote areas for firsthand information. In the 1920s, she was the first woman to go underground with working miners at Queenstown. Her 1924 book *Jewelled Nights* takes place on the Savage River osmium fields, with its settings and vernacular developed from on-site visits.

In 1935, Bjelke-Petersen received a King's Jubilee Medal for literature, and she was helpful in establishing the Tasmanian Fellowship of Australian Writers. In addition to her novels, she enjoyed painting (the career her father would have chosen for her). She also wrote verses, some of which she set to music. Marie Bjelke-Petersen died in 1969, well into her 90s.

Barbara Morgan,
Melrose, Massachusetts

Björk, Anita (1923–)

***Swedish actress who starred in the film version of Strindberg's* Miss Julie.** *Name variations: Bjork. Born April 25, 1923, in Tällberg, Sweden; attended Royal Dramatic Theatre School, Stockholm.*

Filmography: The Road to Heaven *(1942);* No Way Back *(1947);* Woman Without a Face *(1947);* The Realm of Men *(1949);* The Quartet That Split Up *(1950);* Miss Julie *(1951);* Secrets of Women *(1952);* Night People *(US, 1954);* Die Hexe *(1954);* Song of the Scarlet Flower *(1956);* Married Life/Of Love and Lust *(1957);* Guest at One's Own Home *(1957);* Lady in Black *(1958);* The Phantom Carriage *(1958);* Model in Red *(1958);* Good Friends and Faithful Neighbors *(1960);* Lady in White *(1962);* Square of Violence *(US/Yugo., 1963);* Loving Couples *(1964);* Adalen 31 *(1969).*

Regarded as one of Sweden's leading actors of stage and screen, Anita Björk made her film debut at the age of 19, in Alf Sjöberg's *The Road to Heaven*. Her appearance in the title role of another Sjöberg film, an adaptation of August Strindberg's *Miss Julie*, established her as a star, with critics calling her powerful performance the best in screen history. The movie also won acclaim for the director. Björk subsequently appeared in several Ingmar Bergman films including *Secrets of Women* (1952), and in Nunnally Johnson's *Night People* (1954), an American film shot in Germany. In her later years, she appeared at the Royal Dramatic Theatre in Stockholm and on Swedish television.

Barbara Morgan,
Melrose, Massachusetts

Blaché, Alice Guy (1875–1968).

See Guy-Blaché, Alice.

Blachford, Theodosia (1745–1817)

Irish reformer. *Born Theodosia Tighe in 1745; died in 1817; married Reverend William Blachford, in 1770 (died 1773).*

Theodosia Blachford was present at the inaugural meeting of the Friends of the Female Orphan House in 1790. In 1802, she founded the House of Refuge on Baggot Street. Prominent in the Methodist movement in Ireland, Blachford also authored a number of tracts.

Black, Clementina (1854–1922)

English trade unionist and writer. *Born in Brighton, England, in 1854; died at her home in Brighton in 1922; daughter of David Black (a solicitor) and Maria (Patten) Black (a successful portrait painter); never married; no children.*

Selected writings: A Sussex Idyll *(1877); (novel)* An Agitator *(1895); (novel)* The Princess Desirée *(1896); (novel)* The Pursuit of Camilla *(1899);* Sweated Industry and the Minimum Wage *(1907); (novel)* Caroline *(1908);* Makers of Our Clothes: a Case for Trade Boards *(1909); (novel)* The Linleys of Bath *(1911);* Married Women's Work *(1915).*

Clementina Black was born in Brighton, England, in 1854. Her father David Black was Brighton's Town Clerk, but when Clementina was small he became seriously ill and lost the use of both his legs. In 1875, her mother Maria Black died from a rupture caused by lifting her invalid husband. After a number of years spent caring for her invalid father and seven younger brothers, Clementina Black arrived in London to teach and write. She was immediately concerned with the issues of work and wages for women and in 1886, befriended by ***Eleanor Marx**, became secretary of the Women's Protective and Provident League. She also created a Consumers' League, supported the London Match Girls' Strike in 1888, and initiated the Equal Pay resolution at the Trade Union Congress that same year.

Resigning from the League, Black joined the new Women's Trade Union Association and took up the cause against sweatshop labor. In 1894, she became a founding member of the Women's Industrial Council of which she would later serve as president. She was also vice-president of the National Anti-Sweating League. Later in her career, Black became a member of the National Union of Women's Suffrage Society and editor of the *Common Cause*. In 1906, she initiated the suffrage petition. Though much of Black's writing was in support of labor rights, she also authored five novels.

Black, Dora (1894–1986).

See Russell, Dora.

Black, Martha Louise (1866–1957)

Canadian politician and writer. *Born Martha Louise Munger in 1866 in Chicago, Illinois; died in 1957; attended St. Mary's College, Notre Dame, Indiana; married William Purdy, in 1887 (died); married George Black, in 1904; children: (first marriage) three.*

Martha Black's well-known autobiography *My Seventy Years* documents her transformation from ordinary wife and mother to mining pioneer and politician. Born in Chicago in 1866, Black married William Purdy at the age of 21 and had three children. She separated from her husband in 1898 and took her children to the Yukon, where she joined the Klondike Gold Rush, working a claim and managing a sawmill. After her husband's death, she married George Black, who became commissioner of the Yukon in 1912.

During World War I, Black took on war work in London but returned to Canada, where her husband George served twice as a member of Parliament (1921–35 and 1940–49). During her husband's long illness, Black was elected to represent the Yukon from 1935 to 1940, only the second woman after ***Agnes Macphail** to serve as an MP. In 1936, she published the book *Yukon Wild Flowers*.

SUGGESTED READING:

Black, M.L. *My Seventy Years: as told to Elizabeth Bailey.* Price, 1938.

Black, Shirley Temple (1928—)

American child movie star whose famous dimples saved 20th Century-Fox from bankruptcy and who later went on to a diplomatic career. *Born Shirley Temple on April 23, 1928, in Santa Monica, California; daughter of George Francis and Gertrude Amelia (Krieger) Temple; trained at* **Ethel Meglin** *Studios and with private tutors; attended Westlake School for Girls; married John Agar (an actor), on September 19, 1945 (divorced 1950); married Charles Alden Black, on December 16, 1950; children: (first marriage) Linda Susan; (second marriage) Charles Alden, Jr., and Lori Alden.*

Shirley Temple Black

Awards: Dame, Order of Knights of Malta; Life Achievement Award of the American Center of Films for Children; miniature "Oscar" and full-sized "Oscar," Academy of Motion Picture Arts and Sciences; honorary degrees from Santa Clara University, Lehigh University, College of Notre Dame.

Began work for Educational Films Corp. (1932); appeared in short films; appeared in first full-length film Red-Haired Alibi *for Tower Productions (1932); signed contract with Fox Films (1934); appeared and starred in over 30 feature films (1934–49); named number one box-office attraction in U.S. (1935–38);*

contracted with Selznick International (1943–50); narrated and appeared in television series "Shirley Temple's Storybook" (1958–61); entered Republican politics, campaigning for Richard Nixon (1960); ran for Congress (1967); appointed representative to 24th General Assembly of the United Nations (1969–70); served as ambassador to Ghana (1974–76); served as U.S. chief of protocol (1976–77); was officer and founding member of American Academy of Diplomacy (1981); appointed first Honorary Foreign Service Officer of the U.S. (1981); served as ambassador to Czechoslovakia (1989). Publications: Child Star: An Autobiography *(NY: McGraw-Hill, 1988), and a variety of magazine articles.*

Filmography: The Red-Haired Alibi *(1932);* To the Last Man *(1933);* Out All Night *(1933);* Carolina *(1934);* Mandalay *(1934);* Stand Up and Cheer *(1934);* Now I'll Tell *(1934);* Change of Heart *(1934);* Little Miss Marker *(1934);* Baby Take a Bow *(1934);* Now and Forever *(1934);* Bright Eyes *(1934);* The Little Colonel *(1935);* Our Little Girl *(1935);* Curly Top *(1935);* The Littlest Rebel *(1935);* Captain January *(1936);* Poor Little Rich Girl *(1936);* Dimples *(1936);* Stowaway *(1936);* Wee Willie Winkie *(1937);* Heidi *(1937);* Rebecca of Sunnybrook Farm *(1938);* Little Miss Broadway *(1938);* Just Around the Corner *(1938);* The Little Princess *(1939);* Susannah of the Mounties *(1939);* The Blue Bird *(1940);* Young People *(1940);* Kathleen *(1941);* Miss Annie Rooney *(1942);* Since You Went Away *(1944);* I'll Be Seeing You *(1945);* Kiss and Tell *(1945);* Honeymoon *(1947);* The Bachelor and the Bobby-Soxer *(1947);* That Hagen Girl *(1947);* Fort Apache *(1948);* Mr. Belvedere Goes to College *(1949);* Adventure in Baltimore *(1949);* The Story of Seabiscuit *(1949);* A Kiss for Corliss *(1949).*

In the midst of the Great Depression, Shirley Temple was credited with bringing escape and cheer to audiences across America. "It is a splendid thing," declared President Franklin D. Roosevelt, "that for just fifteen cents an American can go to a movie and look at the smiling face of a baby and forget his troubles." Fifty years later, in 1987, Secretary of State George P. Shultz ap-

From the movie The Littlest Rebel, *starring Temple and Bill "Bojangles" Robinson, MGM, 1935.*

pointed the first Honorary Foreign Service Officer of the United States. The honoree was a poised, 59-year-old woman, a longtime public figure, with the name of Shirley Temple Black.

Shirley Temple was born on April 23, 1928, in Santa Monica, California, a picturesque seaside town and site of several fledgling motion-picture studios. Shirley's parents were George Francis Temple, a cheerful, extroverted bank manager, and **Gertrude Krieger Temple**, a romantic but determined woman. The Temples, people of modest means, already had two sons—George, Jr. and Jack—when, at age 34, Gertrude resolved to produce a daughter and a talented one. Believing strongly in prenatal influences, she listened to classical music on the radio during her pregnancy, read good books aloud, attended romantic films, and took walks to enjoy natural beauty. She also practiced self-discipline so that her child might have the same trait.

When Shirley was three years old, Gertrude enrolled her in Mrs. Meglin's Dance Studio where Shirley and other toddlers were taught to balance books on their heads, fall gracefully, and perform a wide variety of dance steps, from simple tap and soft-shoe fundamentals to the Charleston, rhumba, and tango, even a bit of ballet. The Meglin method involved unending repetition, but Shirley, with her excellent coordination and sense of rhythm, accepted and enjoyed the routine.

Directors from Educational Films Corporation spotted the little girl among the Famous Meglin Kiddies and offered her a screen test. In January 1932, three-year-old Shirley appeared in the first of a series of Baby Burlesks, one- and two-reel spoofs of major productions. The films have been called "exploitative," "sexy," even at times physically dangerous to the child actors involved.

Gertrude Temple was by now bent upon a major career in motion pictures for her charismatic daughter. She herself designed and made Shirley's costumes, arranged her curls, drilled her nightly on her lines, spent long hours daily at the studio watching over her and admonishing "Sparkle, Shirley, sparkle," whenever the little girl was before the cameras.

It was the era of child stars. The juvenile galaxy included Jackie Cooper, Jackie Coogan, whose bitter legal battle with his parents inspired better protection for the young actors who came after him, ***Deanna Durbin**, the treasure of Universal Pictures, ***Jane Withers**, ***Judy Garland**, Mickey Rooney, Bobby Breen, ***Bonita Granville**, Freddie Bartholomew and, in the '40s, **Elizabeth Taylor**, ***Margaret O'Brien**, ***Peggy Ann Garner** and ***Natalie Wood**. In box-office appeal, Shirley Temple would top them all.

Biographer **Anne Edwards** lists 57 films in which, between 1932 and 1949, Shirley appeared. The earliest of these were the shorts which continued to be produced by Educational Films. In 1934, Fox Films, near bankruptcy, offered her a contract. A studio official was later to declare that without Shirley Temple there would have been no 20th Century-Fox.

Black's first big hit was *Stand Up and Cheer* with James Dunn. Having memorized the script, she innocently corrected the routine of her dancing partner. Dunn was amused, and the unexpected take was left in the final film.

> Like everyone else in America I loved Shirley Temple in those days when a depression-haunted world forgot the drab dreariness for a few hours in a neighborhood movie house, especially when a tiny, golden-haired girl named Shirley Temple was on the screen.
>
> **—Ronald Reagan**

Shirley appeared for Fox and later for Selznick International, who loaned her to other studios, with a host of major adult stars, including the great black dancer Bill "Bojangles" Robinson who was to become a lifelong friend. Her starring films included *Bright Eyes*, *Little Miss Marker*, *The Little Colonel*, *Curly Top*, *The Littlest Rebel*, *Captain January*, *Poor Little Rich Girl*, *Wee Willie Winkie*, *Heidi*, *Rebecca of Sunnybrook Farm*, *Little Miss Broadway*, *The Little Princess*, *Susannah of the Mounties*, and others. For four years, from 1934 to 1938, Shirley Temple was the greatest box-office attraction in the industry, surpassed only by Bing Crosby, who was the top attraction for five years during the 1940s. At the height of her career, her films annually brought into her studios more than six million dollars.

The life of "America's Princess" was rich with privileges and adulation. Her parents purchased a handsome home in Brentwood Heights with an adjacent badminton court, swimming pool, stable, and a playhouse sizable enough to become a honeymoon cottage. Her doll collection was one of the largest in the world.

Fox constructed a luxurious studio playhouse. By now there were said to be four million members of Shirley Temple Clubs. Little girls all over America adopted Shirley Temple curls, Shirley Temple clothes, Shirley Temple items of all kinds. She was inundated with gifts, 135,000 for her eighth birthday alone. Heads of state received and visited her. The president of Chile, a loyal fan, sent her the specially tailored uniform of an admiral of the Chilean navy.

This fairy tale success came at a price. Child actors were not well protected legally. Working hours could be long, sometimes six days a week, with no pay for rehearsals. Black's contacts with other children were strictly limited by her mother, partially to protect her from germs. She was not allowed to make friends with the children who acted with her. One studio observer at Shirley's eighth birthday party saw her as a lonely child, resembling the role she played in *Poor Little Rich Girl.* When she left the security of home or studio for travel or public appearances, thousands of demanding fans crowded round her, some attempting to tear off parts of her clothing for souvenirs. Her parents feared kidnapping.

Graham Greene, the English novelist and critic, wrote a scathing review in which he claimed that "infancy with Shirley is a disguise," that she had in fact become "a fancy little piece" with "a well developed rump" and "dimpled depravity." There were even rumors that she was an adult midget with a child of her own. In her teens, she was not spared the proverbial Hollywood sexual propositions. Always, there were the internecine rivalries and scandals of studio life.

As much as possible, the Temples shielded their daughter. Despite moments of mischief, Shirley seems not to have rebelled either against her directors or her loving but unendingly demanding mother. Many years later, when in 1985 the American Academy of Arts and Sciences awarded her an Oscar, she said, "This is really for my mother, Gertrude Temple, and this evening a tribute for her."

Even Gertrude could not avoid one inexorable problem. Increasingly, as her daughter matured, there were serious casting difficulties. Shirley could no longer play the part of a dimpled innocent. *Just Around the Corner*, 1938, did not prosper at the box office. Though *The Little Princess*, based on the children's classic written by ***Frances Hodgson Burnett** and released in 1939, was successful, *Susannah of the Mounties*, also released in 1939, was unwisely chosen by Darryl Zanuck, Black's longtime producer. *The Blue Bird*, 1940, was a box-office failure, and Shirley's career at 20th Century-Fox was ended. Signed by Selznick International who loaned her to a number of other studios, she made 11 more films, returning to Fox for *Mr. Belvedere Goes to College* with Clifton Webb. Her last films, *A Kiss for Corliss* and *The Story of Seabiscuit*, were panned by reviewers. The glowing child star had not made the transition to successful adult actress.

Well before her final pictures, Black's life had taken a fresh turn. Perhaps a nascent wish to escape her mother's domination helped impel her to marriage on September 19, 1945, the first of her graduating class at Westlake School for Girls to wear a wedding ring. Her husband was John Agar, the handsome older brother of one of her Westlake classmates. A daughter Susan was born on January 30, 1948. Neither of the two young people was ready for marriage, especially one between a husband with a career still to make and a teenaged wife who was already world-renowned. After many difficulties, Shirley filed for divorce. Agar would go on to a minor career in film and chose never to criticize his wife publicly.

With the divorce pending, Shirley flew to Hawaii where she met and fell in love with Charles Alden Black, son of the wealthy and socially prominent president of the Pacific Gas and Electric Company. Educated at Stanford and Harvard, Charles had been a naval officer in World War II and had received the Silver Star and a presidential citation for bravery. Though he declared that he had never seen a Shirley Temple film, this did not prevent his following Shirley back to California. The two were quietly married at the Del Monte home of the elder Blacks 11 days after Shirley's divorce from Agar became final.

When Black's contract with Selznick International ended and an audition for the Broadway role of Tinker Bell in *Peter Pan* went badly, she announced that she would not act again. The Korean War was now underway. Lieutenant Commander Black, recalled to active duty, was stationed in Washington, D.C., and Charles Alden, Jr. was born on April 28, 1952, in Bethesda Naval Hospital. The Blacks were soon caught up in Washington social life and for the first time Shirley heard extended talk of politics and world affairs, topics which had long interested her husband. Charles was a Republican. The Temples, though not politically active, had also been Republican. Shirley emerged as a determined fiscal conservative but a moderate on social issues. (After *Roe* v. *Wade*, she would be pro-choice on abortion.) Her first public announcement on a political issue was a defense of General Douglas

MacArthur whom President Harry Truman removed from his command in Korea.

She took another step into the public arena by joining John F. Kennedy, Frank Sinatra, and *Grace Kelly in raising funds for the National Multiple Sclerosis Society. Good at fund-raising, Black was eager to help fight the disease which had recently stricken her brother George. In the election of 1952, she campaigned for Dwight D. Eisenhower.

With the end of the Korean War, the Blacks returned to California where daughter Lori Alden was born on April 9, 1954, at Santa Monica Hospital. The family soon moved to the San Francisco area when Charles became head of business administration for Stanford Research Institute in Menlo Park. As a suburban housewife, Shirley decorated their new redwood ranch house in Japanese modern, cared for her children, and continued charity work, for the Multiple Sclerosis Society and for the Sierra Club.

Biographer Edwards speculates that the woman who had worked since babyhood was bored, perhaps also haunted by guilt at having

Shirley Temple, c. 1934.

disappointed her mother by leaving her career when it was at a low ebb. In 1958, responding to one of numerous television offers, she appeared as narrator and occasional actress in "Shirley Temple's Storybook" for NBC. The TV series was well received, and *Shirley Temple's Storybook*, *Shirley Temple's Fairyland*, and *Shirley Temple's Stories That Never Grow Old*, published by Random House, sold over 100,000 copies each. Shirley Temple dolls, dresses, coloring books and other items sold well, with Shirley controlling the licensing rights for all these products. A projected TV series about a crusading woman social worker did not fare so well, and the series was never completed.

The new Black home, a handsome English Tudor house in affluent Woodside, south of San Francisco, continued to shelter a disciplined and close-knit family, but Shirley's interests were still broadening. In 1963, she traveled with her husband to Russia on behalf of the International Federation of Multiple Sclerosis Societies. The quest to bring home help for MS patients, including her brother, was unsuccessful. Nikita Khrushchev, who had greeted Shirley when he visited San Francisco in 1969, was no longer premier and refused to see her. Russian treatment for MS, she learned from a noted neurologist, was of a type already practiced in the United States.

Black now turned directly to politics. Encouraged by the examples of Hollywood actors Ronald Reagan and George Murphy, she decided in 1967 to seek the Republican nomination for Congress from California's 11th District. Her husband was her manager, and her children also took part in the campaign. Black favored increasing tuition at state universities so that students might "value their education." She labeled President Lyndon Johnson's Great Society "a great flop" and blamed him for "a lack of leadership" in preventing the Watts riots. She upheld the war in Vietnam, believing that "the Communists of North Vietnam" must be defeated. Her lengthy speeches were written by her husband. Perhaps the Blacks underestimated the need for professional help in running a political campaign. The candidate's name recognition was great but may not have helped her win serious voter consideration. She was soundly defeated at the polls.

Undaunted, she threw herself into the campaign to nominate Richard Nixon for president. In the months before the Republican Convention of 1968, she raised over a million dollars, delivering more than 200 speeches in 22 states. After the Convention, she decided to go overseas to organize American voters living abroad, as well as to set up further branches of the Federation of Multiple Sclerosis Societies. Arriving in Czechoslovakia, she was caught in the Soviet invasion of that country but escaped unharmed. Within a few days, she returned to Europe on behalf of the Republican National Committee.

In August 1969, President Nixon named her a member of the U.S. delegation to the 24th Assembly of the United Nations. She was by now a director of a number of corporations, including the Bank of America, Fireman's Fund Insurance Company, BANCAL Tri-State Corporation, and the Delmonte Corporation. Pursuing a long time interest in medicine, she was also a member of the California Advisory Hospital Council.

In 1972, Black was appointed special assistant to the chair of the American Council on Environmental Control—another long-held interest. Later, she became a representative to the UN Conference on Human Environment in Stockholm and a delegate to the treaty on environment, USSR-USA Joint Committee. The next year, after recovery from breast cancer, she became a member of the U.S. Committee for UNESCO. Disney Productions elected her a director in 1974.

That same year, President Gerald R. Ford appointed her to what she later called "the best job" she had ever had, the ambassadorship to the African nation of Ghana. Despite threats from a local terrorist group, Ghana, with its strong matriarchal tradition, welcomed a woman ambassador, and Black became deeply interested in the problems of Africa. An unfortunate political embroglio in which she urged a visit to Ghana by Secretary of State Henry Kissinger, a visit which would have seriously embarrassed the regime of General Ignatius Kutu Acheampong, may have led to her recall. President Ford offered her instead the position of U.S. chief of protocol.

The office was by no means an honorary one. Black, with her excellent memory, was immediately busied introducing and arranging the activities of foreign dignitaries. Her most challenging task was arranging details of the inauguration of President Jimmy Carter. A Democratic victory ended what were perhaps her hopes for a career in national politics, but she was not yet done with public life. In 1981, she became a member of the U.S. Delegation on African Refugees and member of the UN Association for the United States. She was appointed to the board of directors of the National Wildlife Federation, became a founding member of the American Academy of Diplomacy, and acted as co-chair of the Ambassadorial seminars.

It was in recognition of such work that Secretary Shultz, in 1987, designated her Honorary Foreign Service Officer, the first in the nation's history. The citation read: "In recognition of your distinguished contributions to the diplomacy of the country you have so ably represented at home and abroad, and with grateful appreciation for your willingness to share your experience, insights and wisdom in the training of virtually every first-time ambassador appointed since January 1981. Truly it can be said that you have had an excellent effect on your country's interests abroad."

In 1989, President George Bush appointed Black U.S. ambassador to Czechoslovakia. There, where she had once been in peril, she witnessed Czechoslovakia's "velvet revolution," its peaceful transition from Communism back to Western-style democracy. Charles Black has said of his wife, "I think she's one of the most unusual women who ever lived. Her whole life has been spent in various types of public service, either by entertaining people or by serving them."

SOURCES:

Black, Shirley Temple. *Child Star.* NY: McGraw-Hill, 1988.

Cadden, Vivian. "Return to Prague," in *McCall's.* Vol. 117, April 1990, p. 60.

David, Lester and Irene. *The Shirley Temple Story.* NY: Putnam, 1983.

Edwards, Anne. *Shirley Temple: American Princess.* NY: William Morrow, 1988.

Yorkshire, Heidi. "Shirley Temple Black Sets the Record Straight," in *McCall's.* Vol. 116, March 1989, p. 88.

SUGGESTED READING:

Smith, Patrick R. *Shirley Temple Dolls and Collectibles.* Paducah, KY: Collector Books, 1977.

Windeler, Robert. *The Films of Shirley Temple.* Secaucus, NJ: Citadel Press, 1978.

Zierold, Norman J. *The Child Stars.* NY: Coward-McCann, 1965.

COLLECTIONS:

A variety of repositories including: Academy of Motion Picture Arts and Sciences, Los Angeles, California; Government Documents Library, Seely G. Mudd Library, Yale University, New Haven, Connecticut; 20th Century-Fox Archives, University of Wisconsin, Madison, Wisconsin; United States Mission to the United Nations, New York; Warner Bros., Universal Studios and RKO Studios Film Archives, University of Southern California, Los Angeles, California.

Margery Evernden, Professor Emerita, English Department, University of Pittsburgh, and freelance writer

Black, Winifred Sweet (1863–1936)

American journalist whose versatile reporting helped build William Randolph Hearst's newspaper empire.

Name variations: Winifred Black Bonfils; (pseudonym) Annie Laurie. Born Winifred Sweet on October 14, 1863, in Chilton, Wisconsin; died on May 25, 1936, in San Francisco, California; daughter and fourth of five children of Benjamin Jeffrey (an attorney) and Lovisa Loveland (Denslow) Sweet; attended private schools in Chicago and Lake Forest, Illinois, and Northampton, Massachusetts; married Orlow Black, in June 1892 (divorced 1897); married Charles A. Bonfils (separated, 1909); children: (first marriage) one son (died in a childhood drowning accident); (second marriage) one daughter; one son (who died in childhood).

The life of turn-of-the-century journalist Winifred Sweet Black, who wrote under the pen name "Annie Laurie," was as colorful as her exposés. During the era that ushered in yellow journalism, Black made her mark in the daredevil style of Nellie Bly (***Elizabeth Seaman**), often risking her life, or engaging in elaborate stunts, to get a scoop. Though her stories—filled with anecdotes, flowery descriptions, heart-wrenching quotes, and repetitious phrases—would be considered "soft" by later standards, in a career that spanned 50 years she helped build a newspaper empire for William Randolph Hearst and proved to be one of the most versatile journalists of her time.

With her good looks and lively spirit, Black started out in the theatre, playing bits and secondary roles for the Black Crook touring company. She had grown up on a farm in the Chicago area but fell in love with San Francisco on a family trip west in 1890. Ready to try her hand at journalism, she charmed herself into a job with the *San Francisco Examiner.* Her first assignment, a local flower show, proved a humbling experience. Black submitted her story, waited with great anticipation to see it in print, and was dismayed to find it rewritten: "I could see at a glance that the two or three opening paragraphs told everything that was important about the flower show—where it was, who was giving it, who offered the prizes, who won them—and I had never given a thought to one of these good plain facts."

Black next went to work on her first exposé, addressing the questionable treatment of women in the city hospital's emergency room. In an elaborate stunt, Black dressed herself in threadbare clothes and fainted in front of a carriage. After being prodded with a club by the police, she was placed on the hard, wooden floor of a horse-drawn carriage for the trip to the hospital. There, she was subjected to lewd remarks by the attendants and released after treatment with an emetic of mustard and hot water. When her sensational narrative hit the street 36 hours later, it not only established Black as a journalist but resulted in the dismissal of some hospital personnel and the establishment of a regular ambulance service.

The undercover story soon became a Hearst trademark, with Black engaged in a series of fascinating assignments, covering the lepers on the Hawaiian island of Molokai, polygamy among the Mormons in Utah, and an investigation of the juvenile court system in Chicago. She became the first woman to report a prize fight and the second to interview a president. The first was ***Anne Royall**, in the 1830s, who reputedly cornered John Quincy Adams as he was swimming naked in the Potomac and sat on his clothes until he gave her an interview. In 1892, Black cornered Benjamin Harrison on his campaign train, after she had been smuggled on board by Governor Henry Markham of California and hidden under a dining-car table which was covered by a larger-than-usual white table cloth. When the president entered and sat down, she popped out with pen and pad.

Winifred Sweet Black

Black became known for her emotional approach to reporting, perhaps best demonstrated in her articles about children or the downtrodden. A 1935 story, concerning a little girl who runs away from home, falls asleep on the road, and is run over, ends with Black's heart-tugging plea to her readers not to grieve for the child: "Even if she did not find the Lake of Swans or the Road to Camelot, she had the grace and the understanding to look for them and that is something in itself, isn't it?"

Black often borrowed freely from Lewis Carroll, one of her favorite authors. The people about whom she sometimes reported had "sentimental chins" or "grinned in fiendish triumph." She was frequently playful with words, often picking out a particular sound or expression and sprinkling it through a piece. "Tut, tut," was a favorite, as well as the colorful "oof," such as in "Oof, what a relief!" Finally, it has been said that she had a particular talent for overkill, as evidenced in the epitaph "Woman's suffrage is a failure. A dead failure."

In 1895, Hearst took Black east with him to launch the *New York Journal*, but she disliked the city and left after two years to join the lively *Denver Post*. She continued to write for Hearst, however, and through him got her most important assignments, including the September 1900 tidal wave that struck Galveston, Texas. Disguised as a boy, Black slipped through police lines to become the first reporter to file an eyewitness account of the disaster that took 7,000 lives. While covering the tragedy, she opened a temporary hospital in the city and administered relief funds collected through the Hearst papers.

On April 16, 1906, in response to a one-word telegram from Hearst that said simply "Go," Black left Denver to cover the earthquake-ravaged city of San Francisco. The following year, she covered the trial of playboy Harry K. Thaw, who was charged with the 1906 murder of architect Sanford White but was acquitted with an insanity verdict. In the course of the trial, Black—along with a battalion of female feature writers including ***Dorothy Dix**, **Nixola Greeley-Smith**, and **Ada Patterson**—created such gushing sympathy for Thaw's wife and star witness ***Evelyn Nesbit** that Irvin S. Cobb of the *World* coined the epithet "sob sister" in his column. (Cobb, a talented wordsmith, also popularized the terms "innocent bystander" and "stuffed shirt.") Unfortunately, "sob sister" became widely used to describe all women reporters, and, much to Black's chagrin, she was called "the first and greatest sob sister of them all."

Winifred Black's personal life was marked by two unhappy marriages. Her first marriage to *Examiner* colleague Orlow Black lasted five years and produced a son who died in a childhood swimming accident. In 1901, she had married Charles Alden Bonfils, brother of the co-publisher of the *Denver Post*. They had two children, a son, who also died in childhood, and a daughter. Although Black remained married to Bonfils until her death, they were often separated by work, but more often by choice.

Black covered World War I and the Versailles peace conference in Europe for the *Denver Post*. Writing under the byline Winifred Black, she changed her style to accommodate the unlimited space she was allotted for her feature articles. Although her work at the *Post* is thought to provide an interesting anecdotal history of the time, some assert that the writing style lacks the drama of her work for Hearst. Black would also turn out two commercially published books: *Dope: The Story of the Living Dead* (1928), based on her anti-narcotic campaigns, and *The Little Boy Who Lived on the Hill*, about her eldest son's drowning. She would compile two books of reprints of her columns, and a privately-printed volume on the life of Hearst's mother ***Phoebe Apperson Hearst**, done at Hearst's request after his mother's death in 1919. The Hearst historians were less than gracious about the biography, labeling it "inaccurate" and "the work of a sob sister in a hurry."

Regardless of her travels, Black remained devoted to San Francisco. Often using her column in the *Examiner* to mobilize public support, she saved the street-corner flower stands and stopped demolition of the Palace of Fine Arts (built for the Exposition of 1915). In one of her more ambitious undertakings, she raised funds for the "Little Jim" ward at Children's hospital; the ward was dedicated to a sickly child born in the city's prison hospital who was turned away from Children's Hospital because he was incurable. Black's Christmas edition of the Examiner raised $10,000 toward the project. Jim was the first patient on the new wing.

Nearly blind and confined to bed with diabetes, she continued to work well into her '70s, dictating some nine articles a week for Hearst, whom she called "The Chief." Upon her death in 1936, the mayor of San Francisco ordered her body to lie in state at City Hall. Thousands filed past in tribute, while the *Examiner* carried stories about her on the front page for three days.

In her final interview, for *Time* magazine, Black expressed her love of the newspaper business and respect for her colleagues. "I'm proud of being, in a very humble way, a member of the good old newspaper gang—the kindest-hearted, quickest-witted, clearest-eyed, most courageous assemblage of people I have ever had the honor and the good fortune to know."

SOURCES:

Belford, Barbara. *Brilliant Bylines.* NY: Columbia University Press, 1986.

McHenry, Robert. *Famous American Women.* NY: Dover, 1983.

Read, Phyllis J. and Bernard L. Witlieb, ed. *The Book of Women's Firsts.* NY: Random House, 1992.

Barbara Morgan, Melrose, Massachusetts

Black Agnes (1312–1369).

See Dunbar, Agnes.

Black Dahlia, The (1925–1947).

See Short, Elizabeth.

Black Mary (c. 1832–1914).

See Fields, Mary.

Black Meg (1202–1280).

See Margaret of Flanders.

Blackburn, Helen (1842–1903)

Irish suffragist. *Born in Knightstown, Valentia Island, Co. Kerry, Ireland, on May 25, 1842; died in London, England, on January 11, 1903; buried in Brompton cemetery; daughter of a civil engineer who was manager of the Knight of Kerry's slate quarries on the island.*

Selected writings: Handbook for Women engaged in Social and Political Work *(1881);* The Condition of Working Women *(with Jessie Boucherett, 1896);* Women's Suffrage: a Record of the Movement in the British Isles *(1902);* Women under the Factory Acts *(1903).*

Still in her teens, Helen Blackburn moved from Ireland to London in 1859. She began her work on behalf of women's suffrage in 1874, serving as secretary for the National Society of Women's Suffrage until 1895. Giving up activist work to care for her ailing father who had been in a riding accident (he died three years later), she became editor of the *Englishwoman's Review* (1881–90) and secretary of the West of England Suffrage Society. Blackburn's interests expanded to include women in industry, and in 1885 she organized an exhibition of women's industries in Bristol. She later founded the Freedom of Labour Defence, which was active in protecting the earning capability and personal liberties of women. Among her writings is a classic history, *Women's Suffrage: A Record of the Movement in the British Isles* (1902), as well as several books on women in industry.

Blackburn, Molly (c. 1931–1985)

South African civil-rights activist. *Born around 1931; died in an automobile accident on December 28, 1985, near Port Elizabeth, South Africa.*

One of South Africa's leading white anti-apartheid advocates, Molly Blackburn became a social and political activist in 1960 when she joined the Black Sash, a women's civil-rights group that provided legal and economic aid to blacks and their organizations. A member of South Africa's official opposition party, the Progressive Federals, she joined the Cape Provincial Council in 1975. Blackburn was instrumental in arranging medical and legal assistance for the victims of South Africa's violent unrest, and through the years was arrested on a number of occasions for attending illegal gatherings or entering black townships without the necessary permit. She was one of the first whites arrested after President Pieter W. Botha's crackdown of dissidents in July 1985, which gave the country's security forces unlimited powers to search, seize, and arrest. Blackburn was arrested while attending a memorial service for Matthew Goniwe, a black civic leader and active member of the anti-apartheid movement. Of 15,000 mourners, she was the only one arrested and charged with attending an illegal meeting.

Calling the arrest "pure harassment," Blackburn was taken into custody shortly before she was supposed to meet with officials of a Ford Foundation fact-finding committee that included former United States Secretary of State Cyrus Vance and former Secretary of Defense Robert McNamara. She was later released on $50,000 bond.

On December 28, 1985, Molly Blackburn died in an automobile accident near her home, Port Elizabeth. Brian Bishop, a civil-rights attorney riding with her, was also killed when their car collided head-on with another vehicle as they were returning from the black township of Humansdorp, where they had been interviewing blacks arrested by security police. At her funeral, she was eulogized by Reverend Allan Boesak, president of the World Alliance of Reformed

Churches, who praised her continuing efforts in opposing white domination of South Africa. "There are precious few white people in the country who have been able to do what Molly Blackburn has done. . . . [She] brings us together and anticipates what this country can and should be. She was a true daughter of Africa."

Barbara Morgan, Melrose, Massachusetts

Blackwell, Alice Stone (1857–1950).

See Stone, Lucy for sidebar.

Blackwell, Antoinette Brown (1825–1921).

See Brown Blackwell, Antoinette.

Blackwell, Elizabeth (1821–1910)

First woman doctor of modern times, who worked to expand professional medical opportunities for women and to provide quality medical care for poor women and children. *Born on February 3, 1821, in Counterslip, England, near Bristol; died on May 31, 1910, in Hastings, England; daughter of Samuel (a sugar refiner and reform activist) and Hannah Lane Blackwell; sister of Emily Blackwell; sister-in-law of Lucy Stone (who married Henry Browne Blackwell) and* ****Antoinette Brown Blackwell*** *(who married Samuel Blackwell); aunt of* ◆ ***Alice Stone Blackwell;*** *tutored at home by governesses; attended Geneva College (M.D. 1849); additional medical study at La Maternité, Paris, and St. Bartholomew's Hospital, London; children: Katharine Barry (b. 1847; adopted 1854).*

Emigrated from England to New York with her family (1832); moved to Cincinnati, Ohio (1838); after stints as a teacher in Ohio, Kentucky, and North Carolina, entered medical school at Geneva College in New York (1847); graduated (1849) at the top of her class, thus becoming the first woman doctor of modern times; because of prejudices against women doctors in U.S., continued her medical training in Paris and London; contracted ophthalmia, resulting in the loss of an eye; opened dispensary for poor women and children in New York City (1853); during Civil War, provided nurses for Union army; founded Women's Medical College of New York Infirmary (1868); moved to England and worked for repeal of the Contagious Diseases Acts and for dissemination of sanitary knowledge (1869).

Selected publications on medical topics: Counsel to Parents on the Moral Education of Their Children *(1880);* Wrong and Right Methods of Dealing with Social Evil *(1883);* The Human Element in Sex *(1884); (autobiography)* Pioneer Work in Opening the Medical Profession to Women *(1895);* Essays in Medical Sociology *(1899).*

In 1847, when the medical faculty at Geneva College received a request for admission from a woman, they were dumbfounded. Throughout the United States, the study and practice of medicine was exclusively a male preserve. If women were involved in medicine at all, it was as midwives or as completely disreputable abortionists. Although the Geneva professors opposed the admission, they decided to circumvent the highly charged issue by consigning the admissions decision to the medical students themselves, confident that the all-male student body would never countenance a woman as a fellow student. Much to everyone's surprise, however, the medical students voted unanimously to admit the female applicant. Their decision was a joke—they never expected a woman actually to attend the school or, if she did, to complete the course of study. But for Elizabeth Blackwell, admission to Geneva College was a completely serious undertaking; it marked the initial step on her journey to becoming the first woman doctor of modern times, a renowned figure in the U.S. and Europe, and an inspiration to the many female doctors who followed in her pioneering path.

Elizabeth Blackwell was born on February 3, 1821, in the small town of Counterslip, England, just outside the bustling port city of Bristol. She was the third of nine children of Samuel Blackwell, the owner of a sugar refinery, and **Hannah Lane Blackwell**, a wealthy merchant's daughter. Elizabeth Blackwell's parents had met as Sunday School teachers, and the Blackwell family was firmly committed to its non-conformist Congregational faith. Samuel Blackwell was also actively involved in various reform movements of his time in England, including electoral reform, temperance, school reform and, surprisingly for someone whose business depended in large measure on the produce of plantation slave labor, abolition of slavery. He was also unusual in his commitment to providing the same education for boys and girls. Thus all the Blackwell children, including Elizabeth and her sisters, studied Latin, mathematics, metaphysics, and astronomy under the direction of a succession of tutors. The girls also pursued more traditionally feminine subjects such as French, music, painting, and embroidery.

◆ **Blackwell, Alice Stone**. See Stone, Lucy for sidebar.

In 1832, shortly after the Blackwell sugar refinery burned to the ground, the family decided to immigrate to the United States. Samuel

Elizabeth Blackwell

Blackwell's plan was to promote the use of beet sugar to undermine the slave-based plantation economy of cane sugar. Accompanied by three of Samuel's unmarried sisters and the children's governess, the Blackwell family settled first in New York City and then across the Hudson River in Jersey City. The Blackwells continued their involvement in reform activities. They became close friends of the radical abolitionist, William Lloyd Garrison, and even sheltered an abolitionist minister in their home after a rioting mob attacked his church. The sugar business failed to thrive in the East, however, and in 1838 Samuel Blackwell, believing that greater opportunities awaited along the expanding Western frontier, moved his family to Cincinnati.

For Samuel Blackwell, unfortunately, Cincinnati marked the end rather than a new beginning. He died shortly after the family arrived in Ohio. His wife and children, although vaguely aware of his business difficulties, were startled to realize after Samuel's death that only $20 in assets remained to sustain the family. The two oldest sons, Samuel and Henry, quickly went out to work, while Elizabeth and her older sisters **Anna** and **Marian**, opened a boarding school for girls. As their brothers' careers prospered, the Blackwell sisters were able to close their school in 1842, apparently much to their relief. Despite her dislike for teaching, Elizabeth accepted a post at a girls' district school in Henderson, Kentucky. Surprisingly, given her family's long history of anti-slavery activism, this marked the first time Blackwell had viewed slavery firsthand. Deeply disturbed by what she saw and by her inability to change it, and feeling isolated and alone, Blackwell soon returned to Cincinnati.

A thriving intellectual life existed in Cincinnati in the 1840s, and the Blackwells were an integral part of that milieu. Although Elizabeth Blackwell had been baptized an Episcopalian in 1838, she was soon attracted to Unitarianism. Through William Ellery Channing, a Unitarian minister with connections to New England intellectual circles, Blackwell and her siblings were introduced to transcendentalism. The Blackwells also became close friends of the Beecher family, including ***Catharine Beecher** and ***Harriet Beecher Stowe**, the future author of the famous anti-slavery novel, *Uncle Tom's Cabin.* Despite such stimulating companionship, Blackwell felt that she was devoting too much time to a frivolous social life. "I must have something to engross my thoughts," she wrote, "some object in life which will fill this vacuum and prevent this sad wearing away of the heart."

A female friend dying of cancer suggested one possible avenue—Blackwell should study medicine and devote herself to serving women patients. "Had I been treated by a lady doctor," stated the friend, "my worst sufferings would have been spared me." Initially, however, Blackwell recoiled from the suggestion because she "hated everything connected with the body, and could not bear the sight of a medical book." Soon, however, she came to regard the idea of opening the medical profession to women as much more than a career; it was to be another aspect of the reforming activities so important to Blackwell and her family. She later wrote, "The idea of winning a doctor's degree gradually assumed the aspect of a great moral struggle, and the moral fight possessed an immense attraction for me." She never completely overcame her initial disinclination towards the actual practice of medicine. Throughout her long career, she was always drawn more to the social and moral ramifications of medical knowledge than to its more mundane practical applications.

Blackwell realized, however, that she would need further education in science and classical languages, as well as money to finance her medical education, in order to undertake her great crusade. In 1845, she moved to North Carolina to teach music at a school run by the Reverend John Dickson who, not coincidentally, was also a doctor. Within a year, Blackwell went to work and studied with Dickson's brother, Samuel, one of the foremost physicians in the country. Thus prepared intellectually and financially, Blackwell tried to gain admittance to a medical school. Even in Philadelphia, a Quaker city traditionally responsive to expanding women's sphere and also the center of the American medical profession, Blackwell was unceremoniously rejected. Many medical schools, engaged in fierce competition for fee-paying students, were apparently afraid that if they admitted women the men, who must necessarily form the bulk of the student body, would be scared away. Some sympathetic physicians suggested to Blackwell that her only hope lay in traveling to Paris and attending medical lectures there disguised as a man.

In October of 1847, however, Blackwell received the fateful acceptance letter from Geneva College. The students and faculty were not the only ones who viewed Blackwell's ambitions as a joke. According to Blackwell, the citizens of the small town of Geneva, New York, believed that she was either a "bad" woman or insane, and shunned her accordingly. However, her quiet demeanor and serious devotion to her studies soon won over most detractors. "The notice I attract is a matter of perfect indifference," she wrote her mother. "I sit quietly in this large assemblage of young men, and they might be women or mummies for aught I care." During the summer of 1848, Blackwell acquired some practical medical experience through her work at an almshouse in Philadelphia. Her stint in the women's syphilitic ward aroused a lifelong interest in the problems wrought by venereal disease and the white-slave trade. Blackwell's medical school thesis on typhus also grew out of her experiences in Philadelphia, where she ministered to Irish immigrants stricken with the disease.

In January 1849, Blackwell graduated from medical school at the top of her class. Her brother Henry, who attended the commencement exercises, reported that the president of the school had stated in his valedictory that "by her ladylike and dignified deportment [Blackwell] had proved that the strongest intellect and nerve, and the most untiring perseverance were compatible with the softest attributes of feminine delicacy and grace, to all which the students manifested, by decided attempts at applause, their entire concurrence." (Henry would soon marry ***Lucy Stone**).

Despite her academic success, Blackwell realized that she needed additional hands-on training to be able to actually practice in her chosen profession. Like most medical schools at that time, Geneva College required only that its students study under a physician prior to admission and then follow two courses of lectures of 16 weeks each for its graduates to qualify for practice. Blackwell realized that she could not acquire the necessary experience in the tightly closed medical world of the U.S. and thus resolved to complete her training in Europe.

Although fêted in London, where she was introduced to leading medical men and permitted to observe operations, Blackwell had a more difficult time being admitted to hospitals in Paris, where she hoped to follow physicians on their daily rounds. Eventually, she went to work at La Maternité, one of the largest maternity hospitals in the world and an important training center for midwives. Despite the hard work and the fact that she was treated as an aide rather than a degreed physician, Blackwell described the experience as "invaluable. It enabled me later to enter upon practice with a confidence in one important branch of medicine that no other period of study afforded." While treating an infant with ophthalmia, however, Blackwell contracted the disease herself. Though her doctors were able to prevent the complete loss of her vision, her left eye eventually had to be removed.

Despite this tremendous physical and emotional setback, Blackwell persevered in her medical training. Returning to London, she studied at St. Bartholomew's Hospital, where she was cheered by her fellow students at the first lecture she attended. She also came to know ***Barbara Bodichon** and ◂❖ **Bessie Rayner Parkes**, proponents of expanding educational and professional opportunities for women, and ***Florence Nightingale**, soon to become famous for her nursing work in the Crimean War. Buoyed by her professional successes in London and sustained by a burgeoning network of friends, Blackwell seriously considered remaining in England to pursue her career. She decided, however, that both the expense of opening a medical practice in Britain and the prejudices faced by a woman doctor there would be greater than in the United States. She wrote to her mother that it was in America that, "Women will first be recognized as the equal half of humanity." Blackwell accordingly returned home in the summer of 1851.

***Parkes, Bessie Rayner**. See Evans, Mary Anne for sidebar.* ❖▸

Things might be better for women on the American side of the Atlantic, but Blackwell found it difficult to carve out a niche for herself in the medical profession in New York, where she had decided to settle. She wrote to her younger sister ***Emily**, who was also contemplating a career in medicine, "A blank wall of social and professional antagonism faces the woman physician that forms a situation of singular and painful loneliness, leaving her without support, respect or professional counsel." To raise money, Blackwell presented a series of lectures on physical education for girls. These talks brought her some patients, notably women from prominent Quaker families in the city. Blackwell, however, also wanted to help less fortunate women. Because no dispensary would accept her services, she opened her own dispensary in 1853. Its goal was to allow poor women the opportunity to consult a physician of their own sex. Blackwell also seized the opportunity to implement and disseminate among her impoverished patients information on sanitation that she had absorbed from Nightingale. Establishing herself as an accepted physician was an uphill battle, however. On a few occasions, when a sick woman died, an angry mob stormed the building, shouting that the lady doctor was murdering her patients.

The dispensary flourished nonetheless, and Blackwell was soon assisted in her practice by two other female physicians: ***Marie Zakrzewska**, a Polish immigrant whom Blackwell had assisted in enrolling in the medical school at Western Reserve University in Cleveland and who later founded the New England Hospital for Women and Children in Boston, and Blackwell's sister Emily, another graduate of Western Reserve. On May 12, 1857, the dispensary was rechristened as the New York Infirmary for Women and Children. Over the next 90 years, it served more than one million patients.

In 1858, Blackwell returned briefly to England. She enrolled herself on the medical register there, becoming the first woman to do so. She also gave a series of lectures in London on women in the medical profession. One young woman in the audience, ***Elizabeth Garrett (Anderson)**, was so inspired by Blackwell's speech that she resolved to pursue a career in medicine herself, and became the first female doctor in Britain.

When the Civil War broke out in the United States, Blackwell assisted the Union army in recruiting nurses. The government was initially reluctant to employ female nurses, despite the desperate need for medical personnel, because the common perception was that all nurses were drunks or prostitutes. Blackwell served as chair of the registration committee for The Women's Central Relief Association, whose chief function was to supply nurses for the army. She vetted many of the candidates herself, to ensure that they would not contribute to the already low reputation of female nurses, and also gave a series of lectures to the novice nurses.

After the war, Blackwell was able to fulfill one of her long-standing ambitions—to found a medical school of the first rank for women. Although women's medical schools had been established as early as 1848 in Boston and 1850 in Philadelphia, and other medical schools had begun accepting women as well as men students, Blackwell was concerned that women studying at these institutions would receive inadequate training and thus impugn the status of all women in the medical profession. In 1868, the Women's Medical College of the New York Infirmary opened its doors. The school, which enjoyed access to clinical facilities at several major New York hospitals, boasted a rigorous curriculum with three years of required study and an emphasis on sanitation in medicine. Blackwell herself was professor of hygiene at the new school. In 1899, Cornell University absorbed the Women's Medical College into its own medical school.

Unlike Marie Zakrzewska and Emily Blackwell, Elizabeth remained unfulfilled by the practice of medicine. She wrote to Zakrzewska, "I am different from you in not being a natural doctor; so, naturally, I do not confine myself to practice. I am never without some patients, but my thought, and active interest, is chiefly given to some of those moral ends, for which I took up the study of medicine." Blackwell had long desired to settle in England to pursue these "moral ends" through broader social reform work, and, in 1869, after she had saved enough money to ensure herself an independent income, Blackwell and **Kitty Barry**, the girl Blackwell had adopted in 1854, departed for England. Increasing friction with Emily over the administration of the Infirmary and Medical School may also have hastened her departure.

In England, Blackwell became involved in a variety of social reform movements. Some of her activities grew out of her experiences in the United States. Beginning in 1874, Blackwell worked with Elizabeth Garrett and ***Sophia Jex-Blake**, another woman doctor, to establish the London School of Medicine for Women, the first women's medical school in Britain. Drawing on her interest in sanitation, Blackwell was a founding member of the National Health Society. Seeking to live up to its motto that "Prevention is Better Than Cure," the organization provided instruction and resources for the improvement of public health.

> For Doctrix Blackwell—that's the way
> To dub in rightful gender—
> In her profession, ever may
> Prosperity attend her!
>
> —*Punch* **Magazine**

Blackwell also used her fame as the first female physician to voice her opinion on some of the more controversial social issues of the day. Backed by her experiences at the Philadelphia almshouse some 20 years earlier, she participated in the debate on sexual morality, claiming that the sexual double standard—which allowed men to engage in premarital and extramarital sex while demanding that women remain chaste before marriage—was harmful to society, leading to prostitution and venereal disease. In her book *Counsel to Parents on the Moral Education of Their Children*, she argued for a single sexual standard but also urged the importance of chastity for both men and women. Blackwell also opposed Britain's Contagious Diseases Acts which required registration and periodic medical examinations of prostitutes—but not their male customers—to prevent the spread of venereal disease. In 1881, she founded the Moral Reform Union to oppose the legislation and to provide information about sexual morality to the public. In the early 1880s, she also became involved with the Social Purity Alliance which condemned social vice and urged men to abandon their sinful ways. Her ideas on sexual morality led Blackwell to reject artificial birth control, fearing that it would lead to immorality and harm women's health. Instead, she argued that women should control the timing of sexual relations and that couples should exercise self-control in sexual matters.

Blackwell's evolving social philosophy led her away from mainstream developments in medicine. In the 1880s and 1890s, she became involved with various religious groups. In a speech presented to the Christo-Theosophical Society and later published as *Christianity in Medicine*, Blackwell argued, much like *__Mary Baker Eddy__ and the Christian Scientists, that disease originated in sin. Based on this anti-materialist view of medicine, Blackwell opposed vaccination. Her acquisition of two dogs in the late 1880s led to her involvement with the anti-vivisection movement. She came to believe that vivisection resulted in over-reliance on surgery in medicine, and she came to see operative medicine as mutilation rather than a means to cure disease.

During her first decade in England, Blackwell moved frequently and spent a good deal of time traveling on the Continent. In 1879, however, she and her adopted daughter Kitty finally settled in Hastings, a seaside resort on the southern coast of England. Eventually Blackwell's sisters Anna and Marian also moved to the town. Though Blackwell had cut back on public activities after 1895 owing to ill health, she did make one final visit to the United States in 1906—her first trip back to America since her departure in 1869. In 1907, Blackwell fell while on vacation in Scotland and suffered a head injury that permanently impaired her mental faculties. She died in Hastings on May 31, 1910, and was buried in Scotland.

SOURCES:

Blackwell, Elizabeth. *Pioneer Work in Opening the Medical Profession to Women.* London: Longmans, Green, 1895.

Ross, Ishbel. *Child of Destiny.* NY: Harper & Brothers, 1949.

Sahli, Nancy Ann. *Elizabeth Blackwell, M.D. (1821–1910).* Ph.D. diss., University of Pennsylvania, 1974.

SUGGESTED READING:

Bell, Enid Moberly. *Storming the Citadel: The Rise of the Woman Doctor.* London: Constable, 1953.

Bonner, Thomas. *To the Ends of the Earth.* Cambridge, MA: Harvard University Press, 1992.

Hays, Elinor Rice. *Those Extraordinary Blackwells.* NY: Harcourt, Brace & World, 1967.

Lovejoy, Esther Pohl. *Women Doctors of the World.* NY: Macmillan, 1957.

COLLECTIONS:

Blackwell Family Papers at the Schlesinger Library, Radcliffe College, Cambridge, Massachusetts, and The Library of Congress, Washington, D.C.

Mary A. Procida, University of Pennsylvania, Philadelphia, Pennsylvania

Blackwell, Emily (1826–1910)

American pioneer in opening the medical profession to women, who served as physician to generations of poor women and children and facilitated other women's entry into medicine through her work as dean and professor at the Women's Medical College in New York. *Born on October 8, 1826, in Bristol, England; died in September 1910 in York Cliffs, Maine; daughter of Samuel Blackwell (a sugar refiner and reform activist) and Hannah Lane Blackwell; sister of Elizabeth Blackwell; sister-in-law of ****Lucy Stone*** *(who married Henry Browne Blackwell) and ****Antoinette Brown Blackwell*** *(who married Samuel Blackwell); aunt of* ***Alice Stone Blackwell****; tutored at home by governesses; attended Rush Medical College, 1852; Western Reserve University (M.D., 1854); children:* ***Anna*** *(b. 1871; adopted).*

As *__Elizabeth Blackwell__, the first female doctor of modern times, lay ill with ophthalmia in a Paris hospital, apparently facing the imminent loss of her vision, her younger sister, Emily Blackwell, yearning for a career in medicine herself, wrote, "Ah, I fear if E[lizabeth] be prevented from her work I shall never be able to fill her place, but I will try." In history, as in life, Emily has often been overshadowed by her pioneering elder sibling. Yet, in her lifelong work as a practicing physician and leading figure in promoting medical education for women, Emily Blackwell played a significant role in securing women's place in the medical profession.

The sixth child of Hannah Lane Blackwell and Samuel Blackwell, a sugar refiner and reform activist, Emily Blackwell was born on October 8, 1826, in Bristol, England, into a family fiercely committed to its non-conformist religion and equally devoted to such causes as abolition, temperance, and education reform. Blackwell immigrated with her family to the United States in 1832, where they settled in New York City for six years, and then in Cincinnati, Ohio. Because of her parents' liberal views, Blackwell and her sisters were educated privately in the same subjects as their brothers, an unusual privilege in an age when girls usually studied music and embroidery rather than astronomy and mathematics.

Perhaps inspired by the accolades accorded her sister Elizabeth (and equally, perhaps, discouraged by her experiences as a teacher, then the only "acceptable" career for women), Emily Blackwell also decided to pursue a career in medicine. Though several medical schools for women had been established in the United States, Blackwell felt that the training they offered was inferior to that of the better-established all-male schools. She applied to 11 medical schools—including Geneva College, her sister's alma mater—and was rejected by all of them. Elizabeth introduced Emily to Horace Greeley, the reform-minded editor for whose paper their elder sister **Anna** served as correspondent in France, and he secured permission for Emily to spend the summer of 1852 observing medical rounds at Bellevue Hospital. In the fall of that year, Blackwell was accepted at Rush College in Chicago. However, Rush refused to readmit Blackwell for her second and final year of training after being censured by the Illinois Medical Society for their acceptance of a female medical student. Blackwell, therefore, finished her medical training at Western Reserve University in Cleveland, graduating in 1854. She then went to Europe to augment her clinical experience, studying in Edinburgh with Sir James Simpson, a pioneer in the use of chloroform in childbirth, and in Paris, London, Berlin, and Dresden. From abroad, she shared with her sister Elizabeth, who was establishing her medical practice in New York City, the latest developments in medical statistics and medical apparatus.

Blackwell returned to New York in 1856, where she joined Elizabeth in her dispensary practice serving poor women and children in the city. In 1858, the sisters' dispensary was chartered as the New York Infirmary for Women and Children. Emily Blackwell devoted all of her time to the infirmary practice, serving as administrator as well as physician, and never developed a private practice of her own. In 1868, Elizabeth Blackwell founded a medical school for women affiliated with the Infirmary. After her older sister's departure for Europe in 1869, Emily Blackwell took over administration of the Women's Medical College, as well, serving as dean and professor of obstetrics and gynecology. In 1871, Blackwell was elected to the New York County Medical Society.

Emily Blackwell never married, but she maintained a close personal relationship with her colleague and companion, Dr. **Elizabeth Cushier**. She also adopted a daughter, Anna. After Blackwell's retirement from medical practice and administrative duties in 1900, she and Cushier traveled to Europe where they visited Elizabeth Blackwell. Emily Blackwell died on September 7, 1910, in York Cliffs, Maine, at her summer residence.

Mary Procida, University of Pennsylvania, Philadelphia, Pennsylvania

Blackwell, Lucy Stone (1818–1893).

See Stone, Lucy.

Blackwood, Hariot (fl. 1845–1891).

See Blackwood, Helen Selina for sidebar.

Blackwood, Helen Selina (1807–1867)

Helen Selina Blackwood

British-Irish poet. *Name variations: Lady Dufferin, Countess of Dufferin, Countess of Gifford; Helen Selina Dufferin, Helen Selina Sheridan; author under pseudonym Impulsia Gushington. Born Helen Selina Sheridan in 1807; died on June 13, 1867, at Dufferin Lodge, Highgate, Middlesex, England; interred at Friern Barnet, Middlesex; daughter of Thomas Sheridan (a colonial treasurer) and Caroline Henrietta (Callander) Sheridan (a novelist); granddaughter of Richard Brinsley Sheridan and *__Elizabeth Linley__ (1754–1792); sister of Caroline Norton (1808–1877) and Jane Georgina Sheridan (d. 1884); married Price Blackwood (a naval officer), 4th baron Dufferin, in 1825; married on his deathbed George Hay, earl of Gifford, on October 13, 1862; children: (first marriage) Frederick Temple Hamilton-Temple-Blackwood, 1st marquis of Dufferin and Ava (1826–1902, a British diplomat who married* ⊱ ***Hariot Blackwood****).*

See sidebar on the following page ⊱

Blackwood, Hariot (fl. 1845–1891)

Irish reformer and author. *Name variations: Lady Dufferin; Marchioness of Dufferin and Ava, Hariot Hamilton. Born Hariot Rowan Hamilton around 1845; died after 1891; daughter of Captain A. Rowan Hamilton, of Killyleagh Castle, Down; married Frederick Temple Hamilton-Temple-Blackwood, 1st marquis of Dufferin and Ava (1826–1902, a British diplomat); children: three daughters and four sons, including Terence (b. 1866).*

Helen Blackwood's son, Lord Dufferin, became one of the most admired public servants of his time. Known for his diplomacy, he held the posts of under-secretary for India (1864–66) and under-secretary for war (1866), successively; he was chancellor of the duchy of Lancaster, outside the cabinet (1868–72). In 1862, he married Hariot Hamilton of Killyleagh Castle, Down, and his viceroyalty was also memorable for his wife's work. When he was appointed governor-general, she accompanied him to Canada (1872–79) where his abilities were brilliantly displayed in dealing with the problems of the newly united provinces of the Canadian Dominion. She also accompanied him on his other posts. In 1879, he accepted the appointment of ambassador to Russia and was transferred to Constantinople as ambassador to Turkey in 1881. From October 1882 to May 1883, Lord Dufferin was in Egypt as British commissioner. In 1884, he was appointed viceroy of India; his viceroyalty was a period of substantial progress.

While in India, Lady Dufferin started the Countess of Dufferin's Fund in Support of the National Association for Supplying Female Medical Aid to the Women of India, which provided better medical treatment for native women. Eventually, the Fund would provide Zenana wards and hospitals, such as the Dufferin Maternity Hospital in Agra and the Dufferin Hospital for Women in Agpur. The fund also set money aside for Indian nurse training, as well as for training women doctors. Rudyard Kipling's "The Song of the Women" was dedicated to Lady Dufferin. Interested in photography, Lady Dufferin compiled an album, "My First Efforts in Photography, India, 1886," which is now held at the Public Record Office of Northern Ireland. She also recorded her experiences in her books *Our Viceregal Life in India* (1889) and *My Canadian Journal* (1891).

Sheridan, Caroline Henrietta Callander. *See Norton, Caroline for sidebar.*

Helen Selina Blackwood was the oldest of "the beautiful Sheridan sisters," one of three unusually accomplished siblings, the other two being the ***Jane Georgina Sheridan**, duchess of Somerset, and ***Caroline Norton**. Helen was the daughter of Thomas and **Caroline Henrietta Callander Sheridan** and granddaughter of Richard Brinsley Sheridan, the dramatist and politician. When Helen was six, the family relocated to the Cape of Good Hope, South Africa. Her father died four years later, and her mother returned with her daughters to England, where they lived at Hampton Court. The 18-year-old Helen's marriage to Price Blackwood in 1825 went against his parents' wishes. The Irish Blackwoods were of old Scottish stock, tracing their descent back to the 14th century. John Blackwood of Bangor, the ancestor of the Irish line, made a fortune and acquired landed property in county Down, and his great-grandson Robert was created a baronet in 1763. Sir Robert's son married the heiress of the Hamiltons, earls of Clanbrassil and viscounts of Clandeboye ("clan of yellow Hugh"), and thus brought into the family a large property in the borough of Killyleagh and barony of Dufferin, County Down.

Because of the enmity caused by the marriage, the couple lived for two years in Florence, Italy, where their son Frederick Temple Hamilton-Temple-Blackwood, first marquis of Dufferin and Ava, was born on June 21, 1826. Eventually, Lady Dufferin's intelligence, talent, and beauty won over her Blackwood relatives. In 1839, her husband succeeded to the title and estates; the family then lived in Italy, England, and Clandeboye, County Down.

Two years later, in 1841, when Lady Dufferin's husband died of an accidental overdose of morphine, her son came under her influence, and she left a lasting mark on his development. In 1863, they journeyed down the Nile, and her recollections were recorded in her *Lispings from Low Latitudes, or Extracts from the Journal of the Honorable Impulsia Gushington,* a satire on high life in the 19th century. She wrote in the preface that the work "was intended to serve an earnest purpose in lightening the tedium and depression of long sickness in the person of a beloved friend." A year earlier, she had married George Hay, earl of Gifford, 14 years her junior, on his deathbed; it is believed that the two had been close, but she refused his entreaties for marriage until he suffered lethal injuries in an accident and was brought to her house to be nursed.

Helen Selina Blackwood lived until 1867 and is commemorated by the "Helen's Tower" put up by her son in her honor at Clandeboye (the Irish seat of the Blackwoods) in 1861, and adorned with epigraphical verses written by Tennyson, Browning and others. Edited by her son, Lady Dufferin's songs and lyrics were collected into one volume (1895). Recited by thousands of Irish school children, "The Bay of Dublin," "Katey's Letter," "Terence's Farewell," and "Irish Emigrant's Lament" were the best known.

Her comedy *Finesse, or a Busy Day in Messina* was played by Buckstone and Wigan at the Haymarket, London, in 1863, but she never attended nor acknowledged authorship.

Blagg, Mary Adela (1858–1944)

British astronomer. *Born in Cheadle, North Staffordshire, England, in 1858; died in Cheadle in 1944: daughter of Charles Blagg (a lawyer); educated at private boarding school, London.*

Mary Adela Blagg was an entirely self-taught astronomer. After a private-school education and a variety of community activities, including the care of Belgian children during World War I, Blagg was led by an innate curiosity to take up the study of mathematics. Borrowing her brother's school books, she learned all she could about the subject, becoming competent enough to understand basic astronomy.

Following her attendance at a lecture by astronomer J.A. Hardcastle, Blagg decided to pursue independent astronomical studies. With Hardcastle's encouragement, she became involved in the process of standardizing lunar nomenclature, which first necessitated clarifying some of the inconsistencies in the use of names to describe lunar formations. As part of a committee formed in 1907, Blagg was appointed to collate the names given to lunar formations on existing maps of the moon. After her preliminary list was published in 1913 (*Collected List of Lunar Formations Named or Lettered in the Maps of Nelson, Schmidt, and Madler*), she was appointed to the Lunar Commission of the newly founded International Astronomical Union. She then served on the subcommittee that prepared the definitive list of lunar names that subsequently became the standard authority (*Named Lunar Formations*).

At the same time, Blagg became involved in the study of variable stars with astronomer H.H. Turner. On a volunteer basis, she helped analyze raw data from a manuscript of Joseph Baxendell's original observations. The resulting series of 10 papers appeared in the *Monthly Record* (1912–1918). Credited with nearly all of the editing of the work, Blagg was cited by Turner for the "patience and care" with which she undertook her efforts.

Although Blagg had amateur status and functioned mainly under the direction of others, she utilized unusual skill and imagination in approaching the tedious problems of her work. Her contribution to astronomy was recognized in 1915, when she was elected to the Royal Astronomical Society. Upon her death in 1944, the Lunar Committee named a small lunar crater in her honor.

Barbara Morgan,
Melrose, Massachusetts

Blagoeva, Stella Dimitrova (1887–1954)

Bulgarian Communist revolutionary and diplomat. *Name variations: Stela. Born in 1887; died in Moscow on February 16, 1954; daughter of Dimitur Blagoev (a revolutionary leader) and Vela Blagoeva (a teacher); studied music, history and philology and became a high school teacher.*

Joined Socialist Party (1915) and Communist Party (1919); removed from teaching post after failure of Communist uprising (September 1923); fled to Soviet Union (1926); worked in the Communist International (Comintern) until its dissolution (1943); returned to Bulgaria (1945); served as vice-president of Bulgarian Pan-Slav Committee (1946–49); served as Bulgarian ambassador to the Soviet Union (1949–54).

Stella Blagoeva followed in the footsteps of her father Dimitur Blagoev (1856–1924), a near-legendary revolutionary figure in the history of modern Bulgaria. Blagoev spent his youth fighting the Turkish occupiers of his country and in 1883, while studying in Russia, founded one of the first Social Democratic groups in that country. Stella's mother **Vela Blagoeva** (1858–1921) was an equally remarkable figure, a teacher and gifted novelist who shared the dangers and triumphs of her professional revolutionary husband. Born in 1887, Stella Blagoeva grew up in a world of ideas, strongly held beliefs and, often, crushed hopes. Interested in the arts as well as politics, she studied music in Prague, then studied philology and history at the University of Sofia. She began teaching in a high school, becoming politically active by joining the Tesniak (Socialist) Party. In 1919, after the Bolshevik revolution, she followed the lead of her parents and joined the nascent Communist Party of Bulgaria.

Both politically and ideologically, the Bulgarian Communists felt themselves strongly linked to the struggling Russian Soviet Republic, and in September 1923 they made an ill-advised attempt to seize power in an armed insurrection. When this failed, the conservative forces carried out a bloody and thorough White Terror to root out all traces of Marxist revolutionary spirit in the country. Both of Blagoeva's parents died before the full weight of the repressions made itself felt in all aspects of Bulgarian public life. Blagoeva lost her teaching job and in 1925 was arrested by the political police. Upon her release in 1926, she went to the Soviet Union, where many among the Bulgarian Communist leadership had fled after the disastrous failure of their 1923 attempt to emulate the Bolshevik revolution.

Rapidly rising in the bureaucracy of professional revolutionaries, Stella Blagoeva remained in the Soviet Union for almost the next two decades. Of proven loyalty to Joseph Stalin, she benefitted from the purges of the Communist International (Comintern), moving into positions of responsibility vacated by those deemed wavering in their loyalty to the Kremlin. By the 1930s, she had advanced to the important post of director of the cadre section of the Latin-language countries, which included not only France, Spain and Italy but also all of Latin America. When Stalin dissolved the Comintern as a wartime concession to his allies, Blagoeva was named to the foreign bureau of the Bulgarian Communist Party, and also joined the presidium of the Pan-Slav Committee in Moscow. The Pan-Slav Committee was part of Stalin's strategy to win over non-Communists in Eastern Europe on the basis of their shared culture and language with Russians and other Slavic members of the Soviet Union. Extremely visible to the public in her work at the Pan-Slav Committee, Blagoeva had advanced to the presidency of the organization by the end of World War II.

Returning to Bulgaria after the defeat of Nazi Germany, she became the most visible woman political leader in the newly created People's Republic of Bulgaria. She served as vice-president of the Bulgarian Pan-Slav Committee from 1946 through 1949, when the Soviets abruptly terminated their cultural offensive based on shared Slavic ties. At the 1948 congress of the Bulgarian Communist Party, Blagoeva remained the most prominent woman in the nation's political life and was elected an alternate member of the ruling central committee. Skillfully surviving the pitfalls of Balkan Communist politics, she would become a full member of the central committee in 1950. In 1949, she reached the summit of her political career with her appointment as Bulgaria's ambassador to the Soviet Union. As one of the few female diplomats of ambassadorial rank in the immediate post-1945 era, Stella Blagoeva proved herself equal to the task of survival in the last years of an increasingly paranoid Joseph Stalin. She outlived Stalin by less than a year, dying in Moscow while still in her ambassadorial post on February 16, 1954.

SOURCES:

Bell, John D. *The Bulgarian Communist Party from Blagoev to Zhivkov.* Stanford, CA: Hoover Institution Press, 1986.

Blagoeva, Stella. *Dimitrov: A Biography.* NY: International Publishers, 1934.

Bulgarian Academy of Science. *Information Bulgaria: A Short Encyclopaedia of the People's Republic of Bulgaria.* Oxford: Pergamon Press, 1985.

Held, Joseph. *Dictionary of East European History Since 1945.* Westport, CT: Greenwood Press, 1994.

Lazitch, Branko and Milorad M. Drachkovitch. *Biographical Dictionary of the Comintern.* New, revised and expanded edition. Stanford, CA: Hoover Institution Press, 1986.

"Mrs. Stela Blagoeva," in *The New York Times.* February 17, 1954, p. 31.

Rothschild, Joseph. *The Communist Party of Bulgaria: Origins and Development 1883–1936.* NY: Columbia University Press, 1959.

John Haag, Associate Professor,
University of Georgia, Athens, Georgia

Blahetka, Marie Leopoldine (1811–1887)

Austrian pianist, darling of the Viennese concert stage in the 1820s. *Born in Guntramsdorf, Austria, on November 15, 1811; died in Boulogne, France, on January 12, 1887.*

A child prodigy who studied with Moscheles and Friedrich Kalkbrenner, Marie Leopoldine Blahetka was the idol of Vienna in the 1820s. Chopin met her in 1829 and was impressed by her art, describing her as being "young, pretty and a pianist." She was also a prolific composer; a *Konzertstück* for Piano and Orchestra, Op. 25 became her best-known composition. Residing in France starting in 1840, she died in Boulogne on January 12, 1887.

Blahoski, Alana (b. 1974).

See Team USA: Women's Ice Hockey at Nagano.

Blaine, Vivian (1921–1995)

***American actress, best known for her role in* Guys and Dolls.** *Born Vivian Stapleton on November 21, 1921, in Newark, New Jersey; died on December 9, 1995, in New York, New York; daughter of Lionel P. and Wilhelmina (Tepley) Stapleton; attended Southside High School, Newark, New Jersey; American Academy of Dramatic Arts; married Manuel George Frank (divorced); married Milton Rackmil, in 1959 (divorced 1961); married Stuart Clark.*

Filmography: Through Different Eyes *(1942);* It Happened in Flatbush *(1942);* Girl Trouble *(1942);* He

Hired the Boss *(1943);* Jitterbugs *(1943);* Greenwich Village *(1944);* Something for the Boys *(1944);* Nob Hill *(1945);* State Fair *(1945);* Doll Face *(1945);* If I'm Lucky *(1946);* Three Little Girls in Blue *(1946);* Skirts Ahoy! *(1952); (cameo)* Main Street to Broadway *(1955);* Guys and Dolls *(1955);* Public Pigeon No. 1 *(1957); (cameo)* Richard *(1972);* The Dark *(1979);* I'm Going to Be Famous *(1981);* Parasite *(1982).*

Vivian Blaine is best remembered for her portrayal of Miss Adelaide, the long-suffering chorus girl and perpetual fiancée of gambler Nathan Detroit in the Frank Loesser musical *Guys and Dolls.* She began performing on the vaudeville stage at the age of three. Her early career also included a nightclub act as well as tours in a variety of shows, including the musicals *One Touch of Venus, Light Up the Sky,* and *Born Yesterday.*

In 1942, Blaine made her film debut in *Through Different Eyes,* and she appeared in a number of musicals and light films during the '40s. Most notable was her portrayal of Emily Edwards in the first version of Rogers and Hammerstein's *State Fair* in 1945. Five years later, the plum role of Adelaide in the 1950 stage production of *Guys and Dolls* was absolutely golden for Blaine. In addition to introducing several plucky musical numbers like "A Bushel and a Peck" and "Take Back Your Mink," Blaine stopped the show each night with her rendition of "Adelaide's Lament," in which she complained of a variety of cold symptoms—a cough, la grippe, the post-nasal drip—brought on by her never-ending betrothal. In addition to a long Broadway run, Blaine played in the successful London production, and appeared in the 1955 movie version with Frank Sinatra, Marlon Brando, and **Jean Simmons.** She later starred on Broadway in *Say Darling* (1958) and *Enter Laughing* (1963), and made numerous television appearances.

Blaine was married three times. Her first husband was a talent representative, Manuel George Frank. After their divorce, she married former president of Universal Pictures, Milton Rackmil. Her third husband was Stuart Clark. Vivian Blaine died on December 9, 1995, at Beth Israel Hospital in New York City.

Barbara Morgan,
Melrose, Massachusetts

Blair, Betsy (1923–)

***American actress who won an Oscar for her role in* Marty.** *Born Betsy Boger on December 11, 1923, in New York City; married Gene Kelly, 1947 (divorced, 1957); married Karel Reisz, in 1963 (divorced 1969); married a third time to a physician.*

Filmography: The Guilt of Janet Ames *(1947);* A Double Life *(1948);* Another Part of the Forest *(1948);* The Snake Pit *(1948);* Mystery Street *(1950);* Kind Lady *(1951);* Marty *(1955);* Calle Mayor/ The Lovemaker *(Sp., 1956)* Il Grido/ The Outcry *(It., 1957);* The Halliday Brand *(1957);* I Delfini/ The Dauphins *(It., 1960);* Senilita *(It., 1961);* All Night Long *(UK, 1962);* Mazel Tov ou le Mariage/ Marry Me! Marry Me! *(Fr., 1968);* A Delicate Balance *(1973);* Descente Aux Enfers *(1986);* Betrayed *(1988).*

Following a stage career, Betsy Blair made her first film in 1947 and subsequently went on to win acclaim for playing drab and unhappy women. Although she was usually a supporting player, her lead role in the 1955 film *Marty* won an Oscar and the Cannes Festival Award, both for Best Actress. Her later work was done in Europe, notably Bardem's *The Lovemaker* and Antonioni's *The Outcry.* Blair made few appearances during her marriage to director **Karel Reisz** in 1963. After their divorce, she married a third time and settled in London.

Barbara Morgan,
Melrose, Massachusetts

Blair, Bonnie (1964—)

American speedskater and first American woman in any sport to win gold medals in consecutive Winter Olympics. *Born Bonnie Blair in Cornwall, New York, on March 18, 1964; youngest of six children of Charles (a civil engineer) and Eleanor Blair (a real-estate agent); first coached by Cathy Priestner Faminow; married Dave Cruikshank (a speedskater), on June 23, 1996.*

First American woman in any sport to win gold medals in consecutive Winter Olympics; first American speedskater to win gold medals in more than one Olympics; most decorated American Winter Olympian of all time, winning five gold medals and one bronze in three Olympics. Won the Olympic gold medal in the 500 meters and the bronze in 1,000 meters at Calgary (1988); won Olympic gold medals in the 100, 500, and 1,000 meters at Albertville (1992); won gold medals in the 500 and 1,000 at Lillehammer (1994).

Seven years after the birth of her last child, Eleanor Blair was surprised to find herself pregnant again at age 46. On March 18, 1964, Charlie Blair dropped his near-term wife off at a hospital, then continued on with three of his children who were competing in a skating meet

Bonnie Blair

that he was officiating; news of "another skater in the family" was announced over the loud speaker. That day, Bonnie Blair became the sixth and youngest child in a family of competitive skaters. Four of her siblings would hold speed-skating titles.

When Bonnie was still an infant, Charlie, who called the new baby "missy" because the pregnancy was a mistake, took a new job and moved the family to Champaign, Illinois, then considered a mecca for speedskating. On her first trip to the rink, at the age of three, Bonnie teetered around the ice in the smallest pair of figure skates her mother could find, inside of which she was still wearing baby shoes. A year later, she entered her first competition. By age six, she was winning against girls three and four years older; by age seven, she competed in the Illinois State championships. By the end of her career, Bonnie Blair was considered the best female speedskater ever produced by the United States. Utilizing technique and mental strength to compensate for her small size (5'5" and 125 pounds), she was hailed as the best technician in the world over the sprint distance (500 and 1,000 meters)—man or woman.

Bonnie Blair's training began in earnest in 1979, when **Cathy Priestner** Faminow, a Canadian silver medalist in the 1976 Olympics, moved to Champaign to coach speedskating. Faminow was the first to work with Blair on her technique, and she cleared the way for the young skater to use the University of Illinois rink for early morning practices. Late in 1979, Blair competed in her first Olympic-style race. Though her time qualified her for the U.S. Olympic trials, she missed making the 1980 speedskating team by a narrow margin. During 1980 and 1981, Blair trained while attending Champaign's Centennial High School, where she also participated in track and gymnastics. Recounting these early years, she credits a happy and supportive home life for her positive attitude. "There were very few times that I was angry or mad," she told a reporter, "and it's this outlook that I brought with me to sports. . . . If I put in the physical work and my competitor does the same kind of training, but doesn't have the strong positive mental outlook that I do, then she's going to be beaten."

Up to this point, Blair was competing for the most part in pack skating, in which several skaters race each other on 110-meter ovals. To increase her chances for the 1984 Olympics, Faminow urged Blair to travel to Europe, where she could practice on an Olympic-size rink and compete in the Olympic style: against the clock with just two skaters on the track at once. Though Blair was eager to go, she lacked financial backing. Unable to obtain funds from the U.S. Speed Skating Federation for training abroad or from her parents who had already retired, Blair set about raising the money herself. With the help of Champaign's police department, who held a series of bake sales and raffles on her behalf, and a private donation by a friend of her brother's, she was on her way. She finished high school by correspondence course while competing in Europe.

Qualifying for the 1984 U.S. Olympic team, Blair finished 8th in the 500 meters at the Winter Games in Sarajevo. She admits to being in "total awe" of the East German skaters, ***Karin Kania-Enke**, ***Christa Rothenburger-Luding**, ***Andrea Mitscherlich Schöne**, and ***Gabi Schönbrunn Zange**, who dominated the event that year. Now working with speedskating coach Mike Crowe, who had a training facility in Butte, Montana, Blair improved her times and refined her technique. During the mid- and late 1980s, she lived in Butte with her boyfriend Dick Silk, also a speedskater, and his parents. With Silk's encouragement, Blair concentrated on stabilizing her sometimes haphazard training schedule, which expanded to include a grueling cross-training regimen of skating, weight-training, running, roller skating, and bicycling. In 1986, she gave up pack skating after winning the world championship in short-track skating, which features an 111-meter track and requires specially constructed skates. Crediting pack skating for teaching her how to get off with a quick lead and avoid collisions, Blair now turned her full attention to Olympic-style skating.

> I don't think winning means anything in particular. It's the satisfaction you get from knowing you did your best.
>
> **—Bonnie Blair**

During the 500 meters in the 1986 World Sprint championships, a chance to break the East German lock on international speedskating came within sight when Blair tied for second place with East German Christa Rothenburger-Luding, the 1984 gold medalist in the event. With success in reach, Blair doubled her training efforts. During the 1986–87 season, she broke the world record by skating 500 meters in 39.43 seconds. A week later, she turned in an unofficial time of 39.28. Though her one 500-meter loss to East Germany's Karin Kania-Enke cost her the World Sprint championship, the World Cup championship was hers.

Blair entered the 1988 Winter Olympics in Calgary, Canada, under terrific pressure. At a World Cup event there one year before, she had lost the 500 meters to Rothenburger-Luding, who had also set a new world record with a time of 39.39. Blair was nervous on race day. Fearing she might upset an already jittery stomach, she ate only a peanut-butter-and-jelly sandwich for lunch. The heat was turned up when Rothenburger-Luding skated two pairs before Blair and clocked in at 39.12 seconds, breaking her own record. With uproarious lung support from friends and relatives in the stands, Bonnie not only won the 500 meters, but beat Rothenburger-Luding by two-hundredths of a second, the length of a skating blade, setting a new world record of 39.10. She also turned in one of her best starts ever, flashing over the first 100 meters in 10.55. "My first turn wasn't as good as I would have liked, but the rest of the race was perfect," Blair said later. By winning the gold medal along with a bronze in the 1,000 meters, she was America's only double-medal winner in the Calgary Games and was nominated by her teammates to carry the American flag in the closing ceremonies. Her conviviality and unabashed tears as she stood on the victory podium endeared her to an American public. She returned home to such a flurry of endorsement offers that she had to hire an agent to manage this new aspect of her career. Finances would no longer be a problem.

Following a move back to Butte, where she enrolled at Montana Technical University, Blair took a brief rest from skating. In 1989, attempting a crossover into another sport, she took up

Blair trained with the backing of the Champaign Police Benevolent Association.

bicycle racing. After qualifying for the U.S. cycling team, she gave it up, returning to full-time speedskating training in the summer of 1991. Blair struggled throughout that year, placing only 5th overall in the world championships. When asked, she responded that she just didn't feel comfortable on her skates.

With a new coach, Peter Mueller, she prepared for the 1992 Winter Olympics in Albertville, France, and her old nemesis Christa Rothenburger-Luding. A new threat, **Ye Qiaobo** of China, was also in the field. With the usual contingency of family and friends in the bleachers, now known as The Blair Bunch, Blair took the 100 meters and overcame poor track conditions to knock off the 500 meters with a time of 40.33 seconds. She dedicated her 500-meter medal to her father, who had died in 1989. Blair also took the 1,000 meters, squeaking out two-hundredths of a second ahead of Ye, to become the first American woman to win three gold medals in a Winter Olympics. (In 1992, Russia's **Lyubov Egorova** [1967—] won three golds and two silvers in cross-country events, becoming the most successful woman athlete in a single winter game.) At the 1994 Winter Olympics in Lillehammer, Norway, Blair again dominated her sport, becoming the first American to win the same event in three consecutive Winter Games. She took two more gold medals, in the 500 and 1,000.

Aside from her remarkable achievements, Blair seems to have a great zest for life. Self-described as always happy, she is incredibly well-liked, and her well-scrubbed looks and neon smile make her a natural in front of a camera. Her image has graced items from cereal boxes to a postage stamp in the small Caribbean nation of Saint Vincent and the Grenadines. Away from the fierce competition of her sport and the glare of public attention, Blair relaxes with the romance novels of **Danielle Steele**, follows the soap operas, and plays golf.

In addition to her Olympic victories in 1994, Blair won the overall gold medal in the World Sprint Championships and was named the Associated Press 1994 Female Athlete of the Year. As her remarkable skating career came to a close, she received the 1994 Babe Zaharias Female Amateur Athlete Award in November. That December, Bonnie Blair was named *Sports Illustrated*'s Sportswoman of the Year. She even graced millions of breakfast tables, beaming from the front of Wheaties boxes.

Ye Qiaobo

Chinese speedskater. *Won an Olympic silver medal in the 500 and 1,000 meter (1991).*

Ye Qiaobo was expected to challenge **Bonnie Blair** in Calgary's 1988 Olympic games, but she was packed up and sent home when she tested positive for steroids. Banned from international competition for the next 15 months, Ye was reviled in the Chinese press: she had brought disgrace, they said, to her family and to her homeland. Though Ye maintained she was only following the orders of the team doctor, no one listened. When team officials finally admitted that the doctor—not the speedskater—was responsible, Ye prepared once more for the 1992 Olympics in Albertville while watching video tapes of Blair's technique.

Ye was off to a slow start in the 500 meter in Albertville but picked up some time on the backstretch. Though she claimed that Russia's **Elena Tiouchniakova** obstructed her on a crossover, the judges ruled that it had not affected the outcome. Even so, Ye had a strong finish, coming in at 40.51. Ten minutes later, Bonnie Blair took to the ice and finished .18 in front of Ye. Blair took the gold, but Ye had won China's first winter medal in the Olympic games. In the 1,000 meters, Ye came in .02 seconds behind Blair for her second silver.

SOURCES:

Brand, David. "Bonnie the Blur," in *Time.* March 7, 1988, p. 69.

Current Biography. NY: H.W. Wilson. 1962.

Friedman, Jack. "A Racer's Edge: Speed in the Family," in *People Weekly.* February 15, 1988, pp. 34–35

The [New London] Day, January 11, 1995, Section C, pp. 1 and 5.

Barbara Morgan,
Melrose, Massachusetts

Blake, Lillie Devereux (1833–1913)

American suffragist, reformer, and writer. *Born Elizabeth Johnson Devereux in Raleigh, North Carolina, on August 12, 1833; died in Englewood, New Jersey, on December 30, 1913; daughter of George P. (a wealthy southerner of Irish descent) and Sarah Elizabeth (Johnson) Devereux (of New York and New England families); educated at private schools in New Haven, Connecticut; married Frank G. Quay Umsted (a Philadelphia lawyer), in June 1855 (died, May 1859); married Grenfill Blake (a New York merchant), in 1866 (died 1896); children: (first marriage) two.*

When her husband Frank Umsted died of an apparent suicide in May 1859, leaving her with little money and two small children to support, Lillie Devereux turned her attention to writing and completed several successful novels. In 1866, she married Grenfill Blake, a New York merchant.

Aligned with the women's suffrage movement, Lillie Blake delivered many addresses on the subject throughout the country. She also spoke on education and was an active promoter in the founding of Barnard College. As president of the New York State Woman's Suffrage Association from 1879–90, she was largely instrumental in securing a law permitting woman's suffrage in school elections, a law providing for matrons in police stations (passed in 1891), and a law requiring storekeepers to provide seats for saleswomen. Blake's writings include *Southwold* (1859), *Rockford* (1863), *Fettered for Life, or Lord and Master* (1874), and *A Daring Experiment* (1892). In 1883, she delivered a series of lectures in reply to the Lenten discourses on "the calling of a Christian Woman" by Reverend Morgan Dix, D.D.; these attracted much attention and were published under the title *Woman's Place Today*. When Blake failed in an attempt to succeed ***Susan B. Anthony** as president of the National Woman Suffrage Association in 1900, losing to ***Carrie Chapman Catt**, she formed her own National Legislative League. Illness forced her to withdraw from activism in 1905.

Blake, Louisa Aldrich (1865–1925).

See Aldrich-Blake, Louisa.

Blake, Sophia Jex (1840–1912).

See Jex-Blake, Sophia.

Blamire, Susanna (1747–1794)

English writer, known as the Muse of Cumberland for her regional songs and poetry. *Born Susanna Blamire at Cardew Hall, near Dalston, in Cumberland, England, on January 12, 1747; died in Carlisle, England, on April 5, 1794; daughter of Isabella (Simpson) and William Blamire (a yeoman); educated at village schools; never married; no children.*

Selected works: Poetical Works *(1842).*

In 1754, when **Isabella Blamire**'s death left her husband William with four children to care for, he sent daughters Susanna and Sarah to live with their maternal aunt, a Mrs. Simpson of Thackwood. Educated in the village schools of Raughton Head, Susanna Blamire began writing poetry and songs at a young age; her earliest effort, "Written in a Churchyard, on seeing a number of cattle grazing," was in imitation of Gray's "Elegy." Following the 1767 marriage of her sister Sarah to Colonel Graham of Gartmore, Susanna began to visit them in London, Ireland, and Scotland, but mostly she lived an uneventful life in Raughton Head among the farmers of the neighborhood. "An Epistle to her friends at Gartmore" gives a playful description of the mundane simplicity of her days.

A correspondence with Lord Osulton, the fourth earl of Tankerville, took on romantic tones, but Blamire's family rank probably precluded marriage. Instead, she remained single, and when Sarah's husband died in 1773, she became her sister's constant companion. Her best friend was **Catharine Gilpin** of Scaleby Castle. The two women spent the winters together in Carlisle, writing verse. Though she wrote poetry throughout her life, Blamire was known only for her songs, the most popular of which was "The Nabob." Called the Muse of Cumberland, she was often recognized in public and asked to play the guitar and sing.

Affected by rheumatism at an early age, Blamire remained optimistic, but she often referred to illness in her writings:

> When wearisome sickness has taught me to languish
> For Health, and the blessings it bears on its wing;
> Let me hope (ah! how soon would it lessen my anguish)
> That to-morrow will ease and serenity bring.

On April 5, 1794, Susanna Blamire died at age 47 and was buried at Raughton Head. Her poems, which were not collected during her lifetime, were first published in 1842 by Henry Lonsdale as *The Poetical Works of Miss Susanna Blamire, the Muse of Cumberland,* with a memoir by Patrick Maxwell. Some of her songs rank among the best of northcountry lyrics. "And ye shall walk in silk attire" and "What ails this heart o' mine," are well known, and were included in Johnson's *Scots' Musical Museum.*

SUGGESTED READING:

Maxwell, Patrick. "Preface and Memoir," in *Poetical Works of Miss Susanna Blamire.* Edinburgh: John Menzies, 1842.

Crista Martin, freelance writer,
Boston, Massachusetts

Blanc, Marie-Thérèse (1840–1907)

Prolific French novelist and literary critic, primarily of American and English authors, who devoted much of her work to popularizing the history and attainments of the American women's movement for her French readers. *Name variations: Blanc usually appears under her pseudonym (derived from her mother's maiden name), variously given as Th. Bentzon, Th. Bentzen, or Thérèse or Théodore Bentzon; yet she is sometimes referred to by contemporaries as Thérèse* *de Solms or, simply, as Mme Blanc. Pronunciation: BLÃ; BEN-tzen. Born Marie-Thérèse de Solms on September 21, 1840, in Seine-Port, France; died in Paris in 1907; daughter of the German count of Solms and Olympe de Bentzon (the Danish daughter of Major-General Adrien Benjamin de Bentzon, one-time governor of the Danish Antilles); educated at home by an English governess; married M. Blanc (a French banker), in 1856 (divorced 1859).*

Blanc's literary output spanned the years 1868–1907, during which she published 51 books and 116 articles—mostly literary criticism for the Revue des Deux Mondes, *a prestigious French literary journal—and translated or wrote prefaces to 16 American or English literary works. Two of her novels and one nonfictional book were lauded by the French Academy.*

Selected publications: Un divorce *(1871);* Un remords *(acclaimed by the French Academy, 1878);* Tony *(acclaimed by the French Academy, 1884);* The Condition of Woman in the United States: A Traveller's Notes *(English translation of* Notes de Voyages: Les Américaines chez elles *by Abby Langdon Alger, Boston: Roberts Brothers, 1895, also acclaimed by the French Academy);* Choses et Gens d'Amérique *(Paris: Calmann Lévy, 1898);* Notes de Voyages: Nouvelle France et Nouvelle-Angleterre *(Paris: Calmann Lévy, 1899);* Femmes d'Amérique *(Paris: Armand Colin, 1900);* Questions américaines *(Paris: Hachette, 1901);* En France et en Amérique *(1909, posthumously).*

The 19th-century American literary critic Theodore Stanton praised Marie-Thérèse Blanc for her "broad understanding of America and Americans, things so exceedingly rare among her fellow countrymen and women." Indeed, in spite of her formidable general output of novels and significant writings on the women's movement, she is most remembered for introducing her French readers to America and American literature. Yet Blanc's provincial and genteel upbringing hardly hinted at her future career and interests.

Marie-Thérèse Blanc was born in the picturesque village of Seine-Port, in the department Seine et Oise, on September 21, 1840. On both sides of the family, her background was aristocratic and cosmopolitan, a circumstance that was to have a marked impact on her outlook on life. Danish Major-General Adrien Benjamin de Bentzon (1777–1827), Blanc's maternal grandfather, not only frequented the literary circles of Copenhagen, having obtained a first prize for work at the university there, but met leading Europeans such as Metternich, Talleyrand, and Hardenberg in the course of his diplomatic career. Bentzon's first wife—whom he divorced—was **Magdalen Astor**, daughter of John Jacob and ***Sarah Todd Astor**; he apparently met his second wife, Blanc's grandmother, **Henriette Franciska Coppy** (1781–1858), in the West Indies. While the general clearly left a strong intellectual legacy, he died before Blanc's birth. She herself viewed her grandmother's second husband, the Marquis de Vitry, as her real grandfather. The dashing—and spendthrift—Vitry was an ex-officer of the royal bodyguard during the Restoration period and a typical representative of the old regime. Blanc's mother, Olympe de Bentzon, married twice. Her first husband, Blanc's father, was the count of Solms, a proud German-Alsatian aristocrat who traced his lineage back to the era of Charlemagne and numbered many counts and princes of the Holy Roman Empire among his ancestors. It was to him that Blanc attributed her inherited "German" qualities of idealism, enthusiasm, and sentimentality.

Blanc's formative years were spent in aristocratic provincial society, surrounded by devoted servants and caring nurses. She passed much of her childhood in the Orléanais country home of her financially straitened grandparents, and sometimes spent her summers in Touraine, her winters in Paris, along with her parents. The rather conservative traditions of her grandparents, who, as Blanc later put it, kept her "a century behind in many things," were to exert a considerable influence. Young Marie-Thérèse was educated at home, along with her brother, by their mother and a well-read English governess, one Miss Robertson, who passed on to Blanc a love for English literature, particularly the Romantics. Soon reading the Waverley novels and Washington Irving, she excelled in composition and rhetoric and was already writing at an early age; her proud father even carried around her copybooks to show friends and acquaintances. While Blanc described her education as one "by fits and starts without diplomas at the end, with much reading and dreaming, with meditation in the country and with some travel, especially a never-to-be-forgotten sojourn in Germany," she did consider these formative experiences crucial in awakening her poetic imagination.

At age 16, Blanc's father forced her to marry one M. Blanc, a banker. The Blancs had one son, later an academician and member emeritus of the French Geographical Society. There is some speculation that the match was designed to buttress the family's faltering finances. Such arranged marriages between a successful bourgeois and the daughter of an impoverished—but prestigious—noble house were not uncommon, and the practice was long known in France as an exercise in *redorer le blason* ("regilding the coat-of-arms"). Under the circumstances, the marriage was not a happy one and ended in divorce, after only three years. Subsequently, Blanc's husband disappeared to Haiti under mysterious circumstances related to obscure financial dealings. This separation, and the final "melting away of what fortune I had," caused her to turn to writing as a means of gaining her livelihood.

Meanwhile, Blanc's mother had divorced her first husband and remarried, this time to a French aristocrat, the Count d'Aure. The noble house of Aure had issued from the family of the counts of Comminges, who traced their ancestry back to the medieval dukes of Aquitaine and Gascony. Blanc's new father was equerry to Emperor Napoleon III and commander of the Saumur Cavalry School, in her own words "a superior man in every respect." Aure was later to prove crucial in introducing his stepdaughter to the brilliant Parisian world of literary salons and aristocratic society, as well as to the female novelist and champion of the women's cause, ***George Sand**, whom Blanc much admired.

The hour of the woman has chimed; it is time to solicit the opinion of woman on all matters. May God watch over her, that her opinion be a reasonable one, and not add another false note to the general cacophony.

—**Marie-Thérèse Blanc**

After her own divorce, Blanc moved in with her mother—to whom she was very close—leaving the rustic provincial setting of her childhood for the glitter of the metropolis. Here she remained until her mother's death in 1887, after which she kept a residence in Paris and at a family property in Ferté-sous-Jouarre. The Count and Countess d'Aure had their town-house on the *rue de l'Université*, in the highly fashionable quarter of St. Germain, and **Olympe d'Aure** held her own literary salon. To an independent-minded, cosmopolitan, and talented young woman like Blanc, it seemed a new world of opportunity beckoned.

France in 1859 had regained the international prestige it had lost with the defeat of Napoleon I. Commerce and industry were booming, and French engineers were putting the last touches to the Suez Canal. Napoleon III, the great Napoleon's nephew, had brought France out of isolation and victoriously participated in the Crimean War (1854–56). Hosting the peace conference in Paris not only stirred French nationalism to new heights, but spotlighted the grandeur of Baron Haussmann's vast urban renewal. The prefect of the Seine had transformed the metropolis from a medieval maze of narrow streets into a modern city of elegant boulevards and imposing squares. Such was the atmosphere of the capital Blanc made her new professional home.

Blanc began her writing career around 1862, as a newspaper journalist. While she did publish a few short pieces in the *Revue Moderne*, in 1868 and 1869, it was not until late 1869 that she was given a chance at publication in a truly well-known literary magazine. She herself dates her actual literary debut to that year, for it was then that the nephew of François-Edouard Bertin, editor of the *Journal des Débats*, commissioned her to write a story for that periodical. She wrote the piece during a trip to Goslar, Germany—where she often spent her vacations with relatives and friends—and submitted it immediately after the outbreak of the Franco-Prussian War (1870). Subsequently, her friend and greatest formal literary influence, Caro, professor of philosophy at the Sorbonne, called François Buloz's attention to her new story. Buloz, editor of the prestigious and internationally known literary periodical *Revue des Deux Mondes*, was favorably enough impressed to commission a novelette for publication in the review. It appeared in January of 1872.

Blanc's debut with the *Revue des Deux Mondes* was to mark the beginning of a long and fruitful writing career, during which she published at least one novel or monograph every year, not to mention the scores of articles and a good dozen translations or prefaces over a 40-year period. Her work appeared in both French and American periodicals, among them the *Revue Bleue*, *Revue Moderne*, *Century Magazine*, *The Forum*, and the *North American Review*, a prestigious Boston literary and historical quarterly. Her book publishers included the renowned Parisian houses of Hachette, Armand Colin, and Calmann Lévy. A few of her novels appeared in serialized form in the *Revue des Deux Mondes*, while some articles were subsequently issued under one cover, as essay collections.

Her novels aside, the bulk of Blanc's work—in strictly quantitative terms—was devoted to literary criticism. While she did write a few pieces on Continental European authors, such as her own compatriot George Sand, or the Russian Turgenev, most of her criticism was devoted to contemporary Anglo-American literature. At least one modern author, P. Leguay, has considered her less of a critic than a popularizer. However that may be, the self-avowed Americanophile did introduce her readers to writers such as Bret Harte, Thomas Aldrich (with whom she enjoyed a 25-year friendship), ***Sarah Orne Jewett**, Edward Bellamy, ***Frances Hodgson Burnett**, Walt Whitman, Artemus Ward, Henry James, George Cable, Richard Stoddard, Sidney Lanier, Hamlin Garland, Booker T. Washington, and Mark Twain—of whom she was very critical, apparently stimulating his antipathy for France. It also seems Blanc exercised a substantial influence on Henry James, whom she met first in France, in 1876, when he visited her at the ancestral Solms home in the provinces, and later in London in 1891 and 1899. While it is impossible to establish the exact nature of their personal relationship, it seems fairly clear that Blanc herself, along with her work, inspired many characters in James' writings. The influence is especially marked during his Parisian period, and evident in *The Ambassadors*. British authors reviewed by Blanc include Sir Henry Haggard, Rudyard Kipling, George Eliot (***Mary Anne Evans**), and Robert Stevenson, whom she particularly admired.

Blanc's work was her life, and she labored incessantly for the recognition of her talent both as an individual, and particularly as a woman, in a French society still far from achieving any semblance of equal opportunity. Her literary output reflected Blanc's socialization as a well-bred, cosmopolitan and aspiring young woman, thrown upon her own means after a failed marriage, in an environment where single women necessarily struggled hard to attain professional success. Many of her novels and short stories dealt with the place of women in society and the relationship between the sexes, and specific themes seem to reveal strong autobiographical characteristics; e.g. *Une vie manquée*, which evoked the theme of forced marriage, or *Un divorce*, doubtless inspired by her mother's and her own experience. In one novelette, *Emancipée*, the heroine is a young and ambitious Frenchwoman aspiring to become a physician in a hostile, male-dominated academic and social environment. The plot revolves around a classic dilemma: the young woman is forced to choose between her career and her lover, and the resulting emotional anguish of the parties involved is a vivid evocation of the social tensions caused by changing gender roles. The resolution of the conflict is a significant comment on Blanc's own moderate position vis-à-vis the women's movement. While the heroine does finally choose her lover over a medical career—the traditional choice—she leaves no doubt that she has chosen of *her own free will*.

The women's movement in France was making headway during Blanc's lifetime, but progress was slow and in many ways incomplete, if compared with the success of women across the Atlantic. In the year of her birth, Etienne Cabet, a major promoter of the feminist cause, had called for equal access to education and the professions—but not political rights—in his *Voyage en Icarie*. In 1843, the more militant ***Flora Tristan** published *L'Union ouvrière*, a socialist manifesto which demanded the equality of the sexes and emancipation of women, full political rights, the right to work, and the right to education; but the radical nature of her position placed her far ahead of her time. The second half of the 19th century brought with it jobs and prosperity created by the accelerating industrial revolution, and women entered the labor market in ever greater numbers. While during the 1870s women primarily worked for equal rights in private salons with an increasingly political bent, the 1880s and 1890s witnessed the proliferation of feminist periodicals, women's associations and congresses. The program was there, but its realization took time, and real gains came slowly, mainly in the realm of access to higher education. During Blanc's adulthood, the first woman graduated with a B.A. (1861), earned an M.D. (1875), and was granted a Ph.D. in the sciences (1888). It was not until seven years after her death that the first woman obtained a Ph.D. in Blanc's own field, letters. In the domain of civil rights, progress was even slower, for a married working woman could not freely dispose of her own wages until 1907. So progress was perhaps moderate, but nonetheless real, given the 19th century's point of departure—Napoleon's *Code Civil* with its paternalistic legislation for women.

Blanc was very much interested in keeping her readers abreast of developments in the women's movement, particularly on an international scale and in those countries where progress appeared greater than in France, namely Britain and the United States, though she also wrote about the plight of women in Russia. True to her early journalistic training, Blanc always traveled to the countries in question, to see for herself and to interview local authorities, while never neglecting serious research into contemporary printed sources. When necessary, she quoted relevant passages in official government publications or local newspapers.

In 1893–94, and again in 1897, Blanc—who must rank as the premier 19th-century French student of the American woman—traveled to the United States, observing women of all classes and races, both urban and rural, in the East, South and Midwest. Keeping a diary proved an invaluable aid in writing up her experiences. In 1897, she was accompanied by Ferdinand Brunetière, famous critic, Sorbonne lecturer in literature, and editor of the *Revue des Deux Mondes*. She intended to popularize American women's history in general, and the attainments of the women's movement, in particular, for her French sisters. Blanc summed up her prize-winning *Les Américaines chez elles* as "a woman's notes about everything that relates to the condition of women." She wanted, "quite simply, . . . to take note of some of the great progress that interests the whole world. It has been accomplished, without much ado, by a group of women I have admired while at work, and whom I have considered worthy to serve as models for all other women." Thus, she examined the co-educational system, also visiting the blossoming women's colleges; commented on the position of women on the labor market and in the professions; and looked up the main women's clubs, both the literary and more politically oriented. She also researched the impact of women on public welfare and philanthropy, finally inquiring into the state of the suffrage movement. Her travels throughout the country took her from New York to New Orleans, from Boston to Galesburg, Illinois. In the nation's capital, she even attended sessions of both houses of Congress. The list of men and women she met and interviewed reads like a roll-call of 19th-century American philanthropists and feminists, including prominent figures such as ⇾ **Jeannette Gilder**, ***Kate Field**, ***Ednah Dow Cheney**, ***Julia Ward Howe**, and ***Ellen Gates Starr**.

Yet her overall enthusiasm did not prevent Blanc from being critical of what she saw, and some aspects of American feminism were too strong for the moderate Frenchwoman's palate. Here her traditionalist childhood and youth left their mark. While American women were more liberated than the French, and Blanc admired them for their educational and professional opportunities, some women, she felt, were forgetting their domestic duties and neglecting their feminine *persona* while scrambling for the attainment of more ambitious goals. Why, she asked, should homemaking or a woman's personal appearance suffer in the struggle? In the end, Blanc did not consider the time ripe for full political participation. Better to let the men do battle in the sordid arena of politics and leave the high moral ground to women—a decidedly 19th-century attitude. Women, she argued, were by nature better suited to quietly promote reform from behind the scenes, and the record of achievement in women's philanthropy testified to the success of such a strategy. On balance—at least compared to the "more radical" English—the American women's movement had been spared the excesses of the "real feminist party" and been tempered by the wisdom of its leaders. As to the impact of her own efforts at keeping Frenchwomen informed of such developments abroad, Blanc believed they had contributed "not a little to advance in France the moderate and rational side of the woman cause." Indeed, the acclaimed *Les Américaines chez elles* was something of a bestseller in its day, running through five editions.

In 1899, Blanc traveled to London for the second quinquennial meeting of the International Council of Women, which she attended, reporting back to her French readers in a lengthy article. Again, her aim was popularization, for her piece is nothing less than an introduction to the history of the council, including a country-by-country report of the state of the women's movement and a survey of the papers delivered at the conference. Clearly, she was most interested in developments in self-help, social welfare, civil rights, working conditions, and the role of women in the international peace and disarmament movement.

Blanc died in Paris at age 67. Her last article was published posthumously by the American *Century Magazine* in 1908 and introduced her American readers to the French Academy—the arbiter of language and literature that had crowned her work, though membership for a woman in that male bastion of letters was impossible. A year later, Hachette issued her last book, the comparative work *En France et en Amérique*.

Blanc's reception by contemporaries and moderns has been largely mixed. Theodore Stanton, writing in 1898 in the *North American Review*, termed her "perhaps the most distinguished of living French female writers." Mario Bertaux, who, in his preface to *The Condition of Woman in the United States*, called her both a realist and an idealist, noted that she was quite popular in America and Britain. Angelo de Gubernatis, in the *Dictionnaire international des écrivains du monde latin* (1905), stressed her "great talent," pointing out that she would have been admitted to the French Academy, had that august body accepted women into its midst. On the other hand, a hostile reviewer of *The Condition of Woman*, in the New York weekly *The*

Nation (1895) accused her of "slap-dash" journalism and prejudice, though omitting to cite any concrete examples. Nor is the brief article devoted to Blanc in the standard French national biography (1949) any more flattering. Its author, archivist P. Leguay, doubted whether she really understood the American authors she wrote so much about. He concluded that "Neither her books of literary criticism, nor her numerous novels, reveal a truly strong personality, only a terrible facility at writing." Recent scholarly appraisals have tended towards a more positive view, so that Joan West in 1987 qualified Blanc's interpretation of American literature and society in general as "authoritative," while this contributor demonstrated her methodical research into, and balanced perception of the American woman, in particular. An unequivocal testimony to her continued influence in social history—if not literature—is the listing of *Les Américaines chez elles* as a major 19th-century source on American women in Pierre Grimal's manual on global women's history.

SOURCES:

Bibliographie de la littérature française, 1800–1930. Ed. by Hugo P. Thieme. Paris: E. Droz, 1933.

Blanc, Marie-Thérèse. "Autobiographical Notes." Collated by Theodore Stanton. *North American Review,* May 1898.

———. *Notes de Voyages: Les Américaines chez elles.* 5th ed. Paris: Calmann Lévy 1896.

Dansk Biografisk Leksikon. 3rd ed. Copenhagen: Gyldendal, 1979–84.

Dictionnaire de Biographie Française. Edited by M. Prevost and Roman D'Amat. Paris: Letouzey et Ané, 1949.

Dictionnaire de la noblesse. Ed. by François Aubert de la Chenaye-Desbois. (1863–1876) Paris: Berger-Levrault, 1980.

Dictionnaire biographique, comprenant la liste et les biographies des notabilités des départements: Seine-et-Marne. Paris: Flammarion, 1893.

Grimal, Pierre, ed. *Histoire Mondiale de la Femme.* 4 Vols. Paris: Nouvelle Libraire de France, 1965.

Gubernatis, Angelo de. *Dictionnaire international des écrivains du monde latin.* Rome: chez l'auteur, 1905.

Neues allgemeines deutsches Adels-Lexikon (1859–1870). Edited by Ernst Heinrich Kneschke. Leipzig: Verlag Degener, 1930.

Perrot, J. "Un-Amour-de-James (James, Henry and Bentzon, Mme. Th.)" *Revue de Littérature Comparée.* Vol LVII, no. 3, 1983, pp. 275–93.

SUGGESTED READING:

Chew, William L. III. "Marie-Thérèse Blanc in America: A Fin de Siècle Perspective of the American Woman," in *Re-Discoveries of America.* Edited by Johan Callens. Brussels: VUBPress, 1993, pp. 17–61.

Fliche, Mme. Paul. *Mme. Th. Bentzon.* Paris: P. Lethielleux, 1934.

West, Joan M. "America and American Literature in the Essays of Th. Bentzon: Creating the Image of an Independent Cultural Identity," in *History of European Ideas* (Great Britain). Vol VIII, no. 4–5, 1987, pp. 521–35.

William L. Chew III,
Professor of History, Vesalius College,
Vrije Universiteit Brussel, Brussels, Belgium

Gilder, Jeannette Leonard (1849–1916)

American journalist. *Born Jeannette Leonard Gilder on October 3, 1849, in Flushing, New York; died in 1916; daughter of Reverend Gilder (a minister and Union Army chaplain).*

After her father died of smallpox while serving as a chaplain with the Union Army during the Civil War, 15-year-old Jeannette Gilder found a job to support the family. Following a stint at the *Newark Morning Register*, she moved to New York and became literary editor of the *New York Herald.* Gilder and her brother Joseph then co-founded (1881) the weekly literary magazine the *Critic*, which she edited for 25 years (1881–1906). She was also the author of *The Autobiography of a Tomboy* (1901) and *The Tomboy at Work* (1904). Wrote Gilder: "Tomboy was the accepted name for such girls as I was, and there was no use in arguing the case. After all, it made little difference. I did not care what they called me, so long as they let me alone."

Blanca.

Variant of Blanche.

Blanca de Navarre.

See Blanche of Navarre.

Blanca Maria (1423–1470).

See Visconti, Bianca Maria.

Blancard, Jacqueline (1909—)

French pianist, highly regarded for her performances of Debussy and Schumann. *Born in Paris, France, in 1909; studied at the Paris Conservatory.*

Jacqueline Blancard first studied at the Paris Conservatory, winning a medal there in 1923. Later, she worked with the renowned Isidor Philipp and won a first prize in his class in 1926. Blancard continued her training with Alfred Cortot, mastering both the standard German repertoire and the modern French school. She was highly regarded as a Schumann specialist and made the first recording of Debussy's *etudes*. In 1938, she became the first pianist to make a recording of Maurice Ravel's Concerto for the Left Hand. Her 1948 New York debut, in which she performed three Mozart concertos, was a highly acclaimed event. At the end of her life, she lived in Geneva.

Blanchard, Madeleine Sophie (1778–1819)

French pioneer balloonist, appointed to the honorary post of Chief of Air Services by Napoleon. *Born Marie-Madeleine-Sophie Armand on March 25, 1778, in Trois-Canons, France; died in a balloon accident in Paris on July 6, 1819, the first woman to die in an aviation accident; daughter of Madame Armand; married Jean-Pierre Blanchard (1753–1809, a famous balloonist), in 1796.*

Madeleine Sophie Armand was born in the village of Trois-Canons near La Rochelle, France, on March 25, 1778. A chance encounter between her mother and the pioneer balloonist Jean-Pierre Blanchard at an inn almost two decades before her birth sowed the seeds that would yield a life of adventure and danger. Captivated by Madame Armand, Jean-Pierre told her that if she ever had a daughter he would return to her village and marry the girl, whom he was certain would be beautiful and charming.

Madeleine Sophie Blanchard

True to his word, he returned and in 1796 married Madeleine Sophie, immediately making her his partner in his ballooning adventures.

One of the first balloonists, Jean-Pierre Blanchard made the earliest airborne crossing of the English Channel in January 1785. Combining an entrepreneurial spirit with a flair for the dramatic, he found his wife more than willing to share both the dangers and thrills of his flights. Over the ensuing years, vast crowds paid good money to be temporarily distracted from the revolutionary turmoil of the times and see the Blanchards defy the law of gravity. Realizing that ordinary balloon ascensions would not attract a paying crowd, the couple developed a thrilling act that included dangerous acrobatics on a net that hung from their balloon gondola. The Blanchards became a sensation throughout Europe, appearing at fairs and other public events in all the large cities and towns of France, England, and the states of Germany. After close to 60 such ascensions together, in February 1808 Jean-Pierre became ill after a flight in the Netherlands and probably suffered a stroke. He died on March 7, 1809.

Her husband's death did not discourage Madeleine Sophie Blanchard from continuing flying a balloon. The adulation of the crowds was not easily given up, and she also was close to bankruptcy, as her husband had been less successful on the ground with his money. A solo flyer, she was the first woman to fly alone under a variety of circumstances. On June 24, 1810, as part of the celebrations commemorating the marriage of Emperor Napoleon I to ***Marie Louise of Austria**, Blanchard made what was called a thrilling ascent at the festive display given by the Imperial Guard for the illustrious newlyweds. Her appearance was the high point of the event. Appointed to the honorary post of chief of Air Services by Napoleon, she toured Europe and France as an ambassador and flew in balloons at State festivals.

Blanchard made ballooning look glamorous and carefree, when it was in fact an exhausting and dangerous activity. She took great risks: while crossing over the alps at 9,000 feet, she almost froze and her nose bled profusely, but her skill and luck saw her through. At Nantes in 1817, she mistook a flooded field for a grassy meadow and, upon landing, almost drowned.

Though balloons had now been in existence for more than a generation, the novelty of air travel, and the chance to see a brave and beautiful woman defy nature, continued to draw enthusiastic crowds in the peaceful years after the fall of the Napoleonic Empire. But one such public display would prove fatal for Blanchard. The Tivoli fairground, a park within Paris that had been opened years before by ***Marie Antoinette**, now served as a site of mass amusement for the emerging middle classes. On Sundays, Tivoli was frequented by as many as 15,000 women, men, and children who enjoyed theatrical shows, dancing, and gambling on slot machines. The leading attraction at Tivoli on July 6, 1819, was Madeleine Sophie Blanchard, who promised to make an "exceptional ascent" in which her balloon would let off "fireworks and a crown of Bengal Lights" while airborne. On this, her 67th ascent, the balloon rose with a wire trailing behind it carrying the crown of fireworks. At a height of 300 meters, the fireworks went off in a spectacular display. Immensely pleased, the crowd expected Blanchard to land, but to their horror the gondola and the balloon exploded in a fireball and plummeted. The fireworks had ignited the hydrogen she was using as a propellant. Blanchard's balloon crashed on the roof of a house at the corner of the rue de Provence, near the rue Chauchat, at a spot that can still be identified. A vast throng, virtually "*tout Paris*" (all of Paris), turned out for her funeral to pay homage to her skill and courage. Fully aware of the great risks of her unconventional profession, Blanchard helped to open the new and exhilarating world of aviation.

SUGGESTED READING:

Coutil, Léon. *Jean-Pierre Blanchard,* physicien-aéronaute. *Évreux: Imprimerie C. Hérissey, 1911.*

John Haag, Associate Professor,
University of Georgia, Athens, Georgia

Blanchard, Theresa Weld (1893–1978)

American and six-time winner of the women's figure-skating championship. *Name variations: under Theresa Weld won first and second U.S. figure-skating titles (1914 and 1920); all others under Blanchard; also infrequently indexed as Weld-Blanchard. Born Theresa Weld in 1893; died on March 12, 1978; daughter of A. Winsor Weld; married Charles Blanchard, in 1920.*

First American ladies' figure-skating champion (won the title six times); while skating with Nathaniel W. Niles, won nine gold medals in the U.S. pairs competitions; influential in the U.S. Figure Skating Association for many years, helping to build the sport.

Theresa Weld Blanchard was America's first figure-skating celebrity. During her tenure in the 1910s and 1920s, women's figure skating focused almost entirely on cutting figures on the ice; the only jump was a toe hop. Blanchard changed the sport by performing daring loops and jumps, though she was penalized with lower scores by some judges for being "too unladylike."

Theresa Weld was born in 1893, the daughter of A. Winsor Weld who was devoted to figure skating. It was Winsor who harnessed her pony for the oft-repeated three-mile drive to the Skating Club of Boston when she began practicing at age 12. A member of the club's board, he encouraged the international mode which was a freer, more fluid style than the stiff manner in which Americans then skated.

In 1914, Theresa won the first ladies' championship at New Haven, Connecticut; she went on to win the singles' title every year from 1920 to 1924. She also took a bronze medal in the 1920 Olympics held in Antwerp, Belgium (**Magda Julin-Mauroy** of Sweden won the gold). Following her marriage to Charles Blanchard in 1920, the media referred to Theresa as "Mrs. Figure Skater, U.S.A." Starting in 1924, while skating pairs with Nathaniel W. Niles, she won nine gold medals in U.S. pairs competitions.

In 1921, Winsor Weld became the U.S. Figure Skating Association's first president. Theresa became editor of the association's magazine *Skating* in 1923, a post at which she would remain for 50 years. She often served as an official at the Olympics as well.

Karin L. Haag,
Athens, Georgia

Blanche (c. 1392–1409)

Duchess of Bavaria. *Name variations: Blanche Plantagenet. Born around April 1392 in Peterborough Castle, Cambridgeshire, England; died on May 22, 1409; daughter of Henry IV, king of England, and* ****Mary de Bohun*** *(1369–1394); married Louis, duke of Bavaria, on July 6, 1402; children: one.*

Blanche Capet (c. 1247–1302).

See Blanche of Artois.

Blanche Capet (c. 1260–?).

See Margaret of Provence for sidebar.

Blanche of Artois (c. 1247–1302)

Queen of Navarre and countess of Lancaster. *Name variations: Blanche Capet; duchess of Lancaster. Born around 1247; died on May 2, 1302, in Paris, France;*

*interred at Minoresses Convent, Aldgate, London; daughter of Robert I (1216–1250), count of Artois, and *****Maude of Brabant*** *(1224–1288); married Henry I the Fat, king of Navarre (r. 1270–1274), also known as Henry III of Champagne, in 1269; married Edmund the Crouchback (1245–1296), 1st earl of Lancaster (r. 1267–1296), before February 3, 1276; children: (first marriage) *****Joan I of Navarre*** *(1273–1305), queen of Navarre; (second marriage) Thomas (1276–1322), 2nd earl of Lancaster; Henry (1281–1345), 3rd earl of Lancaster; John (c. 1286–c. 1327 or 1337), lord of Beaufort; Mary Plantagenet (died young).*

Blanche of Boulogne (1326–1360)

Countess of Auvergne. *Name variations: sometimes referred to as Jeanne of Boulogne or Joan of Boulogne. Born on May 8, 1326; died on September 29, 1360, at Château d'Argilly; daughter of Robert of Auvergne; married Philip Capet (d. 1346, son of Eudes IV of Burgundy), on September 26, 1338; became second wife of John II (1319–1364), king of France (r. 1350–1364), on February 19, 1350; children: (first marriage) *****Jeanne of Burgundy*** *(1344–1360); Marguerite (b. 1345, died young); Philip of Rouvres (b. 1346), count of Artois. King John II's first wife was *****Bona of Bohemia*** *(1315–1349).*

Blanche of Bourbon (c. 1338–1361)

Queen of Castile and León. *Name variations: Bianca; Blanche of Castile. Born in France around 1338 or 1339; died at Medina Sidonia, Spain, in 1361; daughter of Pierre also known as Peter I, duke of Bourbon, and *****Isabelle of Savoy*** *(d. 1383); married Pedro el Cruel also known as Peter I the Cruel (1334–1369), king of Castile and Leon (r. 1350–1369), on June 3, 1353.*

During her marriage to Peter the Cruel of Castile, Blanche of Bourbon was unjustly accused of infidelity and imprisoned; her death in 1361 has been ascribed to poisoning. Blanche's tragic fate, similar to that of ***Margaret of Burgundy** (1290–1315), has frequently been documented in verse. Peter the Cruel also secretly married ***Marie de Padilla** (1335–1365) in 1353.

Beatrice of Provence *(d. 1267). See Eleanor of Provence for sidebar.*

Blanche of Bourbon (1868–1949)

Grand duchess of Tuscany. *Name variations: Blanka of Bourbon-Castile. Born on September 7, 1868, in Graz; died on October 25, 1949, in Viareggio; daughter of *****Margaret of Parma*** *(1847–1893) and Charles, duke of Madrid; married Leopold Salvator, grand duke of Tuscany (1863–1931), on October 24, 1889; children: five daughters and five sons, including* ***Margaretha*** *(1881–1986, known as Meg);* ***Maria Dolores*** *(1891–1974);* ***Maria Immaculata*** *(1892–1971); Rainer Karl (1895–1930); Leopold (1897–1958);* ***Maria Antonia*** *(1899–1977); Franz Joseph (1905–1975); Charles Pius Salvator (1909–1953).*

Blanche of Burgundy (1288–1348)

Countess of Savoy. *Name variations: Blanche de Bourgogne. Born in 1288; died on July 28, 1348, in Dijon; daughter of *****Agnes Capet*** *(1260–1327) and Robert II (b. 1248), duke of Burgundy; married Edward the Liberal, count of Savoy, on October 18, 1307.*

Blanche of Burgundy (1296–1326).

See Mahaut, Countess of Artois, for sidebar.

Blanche of Castile (1188–1252)

Queen of France and actual ruler for 14 years during the reign of her son, Saint Louis IX. *Name variations: Blanca of Castille. Born on March 4, 1188, in Valencia, Castile (some sources cite 1187); died on November 27, 1252, in an abbey near Melun, France; third daughter of Alphonso VIII (b. 1155), king of Castile (r. 1158–1214), and Eleanor of Castile (1162–1214); sister of Urraca of Castile, queen of Portugal (1186–1220), Berengaria of Castile (1180–1246), and* ***Eleanor of Castile*** *(1202–1244); privately educated; married Louis VIII (1187–1226), king of France (r. 1223–1226), on May 23, 1200, in Normandy; children: (twelve, five of whom lived to adulthood) Louis IX (1214–1270), king of France (r. 1226–1270); Robert I (1216–1250), count of Artois; Alphonse (1220–1271), count of Poitiers and Toulouse; *****Blessed Isabelle*** *(1225–1270); Charles of Anjou (1226–1285), king of Sicily (r. 1266–1282), king of Naples (r. 1268–1285), who married* ***Beatrice of Provence.***

Became queen of France (1223); Louis VIII died (1226); named regent for son, Louis IX (1226–34); rebellion of the French nobles (1226–30); made regent again (1248–52).

Following her birth in 1188, Blanca, or Blanche, as the French would call her, spent a happy childhood in Valencia, Castile, as the third daughter of King **Alphonso VIII** and Queen **Eleanor of Castile** (1162–1214). This Spanish kingdom was known at the time for its sunny climate, high culture, and colorful troubadours. But lurking beneath the superficial gaiety was the constant threat from Saracens, Muslims from North Africa who then occupied parts of Spain.

By the year 1200, when Blanche was 12 years old, her oldest sister, ***Berengaria of Castile** (1180–1246), was already queen of Leon, and there was talk of an engagement for ***Urraca of Castile** (1186–1220), the middle sister. Excitement ran high, as their maternal grandmother, the legendary ***Eleanor of Aquitaine** was en route with her entourage for a visit. This former queen of France and, later, of England was coming to select from among her granddaughters a wife for the future king of France. All assumed that Urraca would be the chosen bride to become the pawn, as royal children often were in those days, in a proposed truce between the English and French kings.

The aging queen Eleanor hoped to end the territorial struggles between her son, King John of England, and King Philip II Augustus of France. Perhaps a marriage between her granddaughter, a niece of King John, and Philip's oldest son, Louis, would help bring peace. What a surprise when several weeks later the senior Eleanor and her French advisors chose Blanche over her sister Urraca. After becoming acquainted with the two girls, Eleanor had evidently found in 12-year-old Blanche the making of a wise and strong royal consort. Grandmother and granddaughter made their way over the Pyrenees in the spring of 1200.

Upon reaching Bordeaux, the 80-year-old Eleanor was exhausted and sent Blanche on in the care of an archbishop to Normandy. There the treaty of peace was signed between Blanche's uncle, King John of England, and her future father-in-law, King Philip Augustus. The following day, Blanche and the future king **Louis VIII** were married in Normandy.

After the wedding, the couple proceeded to Paris, where they would live as companions and fellow students for four years until beginning life as husband and wife. Chronicles of the time report that Blanche and Louis had almost immediately become best of friends and that the marriage was extremely happy. It produced 12 children, including the future Saint Louis IX.

At this time, the early 1200s, France consisted of scattered royal domains centered about Paris and the Ile de France. Many of the greatest French territories, such as Burgundy and Provence, were virtually independent entities ruled by feudal lords who fought among each other, ruled their people autocratically, and were only nominally loyal to the king. Under the prevailing feudal system, the great lords took oaths of fealty to the king and were expected to give him financial and military support. How strictly these obligations were actually observed depended greatly on the relative strengths of nobles and kings. Philip, determined to expand the royal domain, succeeded through strategic marriages and military prowess to rein in many of the nobles and to expel the English from French territory. France was moving toward a more centralized government. After Blanche's husband became King Louis VIII, he too would lead military expeditions to expand royal power and territory; but it would not be until the reign of

Eleanor of Castile (1202–1244)

Queen of Aragon. Name variations: Leonor. Born in 1202; died in Burgos, Castile and Leon, Spain, in 1244; daughter of Alphonso VIII, king of Castile, and ***Eleanor of Castile** *(1162–1214); became first wife of James I (1208–1276), king of Aragon (r. 1213–1276), also known as Jaime the Conqueror of Aragon, on February 6, 1221 (divorced, 1229); children: Alfonso of Aragon, infante (d. 1260, who married* **Constance de Marsan***). James I's second wife was* ***Iolande of Hungary** *(1215–1251).*

Eleanor of Castile (1162–1214)

Queen of Castile. Name variations: Eleanor of England; Eleanor Plantagenet. Born on October 13, 1162 (some sources cite 1156), in Domfront, Normandy, France; died on October 31, 1214, in Burgos, Castile and Leon, Spain; interred at Abbey of Las Huelgas, Burgos, Castile; daughter of ***Eleanor of Aquitaine** *(1122–1202) and Henry II, king of England (r. 1154–1189); married Alfonso or Alphonso VIII (1155–1214), king of Castile (r. 1158–1214, also known as Alphonso III), in September 1170; children: Sancho (1181–1181);* ***Berengaria of Castile** *(1180–1246, who married Alphonso IX, king of Leon); Sancha (1182–1184);* ***Urraca of Castile** *(1186–1220, who married Alphonso II of Portugal); Enrique also known as Henry I (1204–1217), king of Castile (r. 1214–1217);* ***Blanche of Castile** *(1188–1252, who married Louis VIII of France); Mafalda of Castile (c. 1190–1204); Fernando (1189–1211);* ***Eleanor of Castile** *(1202–1244, first wife of James I, king of Aragon); Constanza of Castile (c. 1204–1243, who became abbess of Las Huelgas); Henry (died young); Constance (died young).*

The second daughter of ***Eleanor of Aquitaine**, Eleanor of Castile married Alphonso VIII, king of Castile, in 1177. When the pope wanted to annul the marriage, Alphonso refused because of his affection for his wife; he also built Las Huelgas Convent in Burgos for her. Widowed in 1214, Eleanor died a few days later. She is buried at Las Huelgas.

Blanche's son Louis IX that the king in Paris could truly be called "king of France."

While the indomitable Philip was still king and Blanche's husband Louis was heir to the throne, the barons of England rose up against the excesses of King John whose diabolical cruelties had led the barons to try to end his reign of terror. Forced to sign the Magna Carta in 1215, King John had no intention of abiding by this charter which would limit his power. Finally, in desperation, the English nobles offered the throne of England to Louis and Blanche. As a granddaughter of England's late great King Henry II, Blanche was descended in a direct line from William the Conqueror. She, with her husband, could be the instrument of peace—but only after a military invasion. Landing with his army in England, Louis was enthusiastically greeted, but wily John now played his last card. He died, leaving his nine-year-old son Henry (III), Blanche's first cousin, among Louis' rivals for the English throne. Unhappy with the thought of a child-king and a regency, the English nobles again asked Louis to be their king.

Blanche of Castile

Once more, Louis heeded the call, invaded England, but suffered adversities and needed more support. His father, King Philip, completely unsympathetic with the scheme, refused aid. Then Blanche, a loyal wife and would-be queen of England, revealed the determination that would characterize her future career. She begged Philip for men and money to put his son on the throne of England. Again, Philip refused. In the end, however, the formidable King Philip Augustus, pacifier of great magnates of France, gave in to his daughter-in-law, for she had threatened to pawn her own child, his grandchild, in order to raise the funds.

Blanche then rode about France gathering troops and raising additional money to assemble a fleet which she personally organized. When the fleet sailed for Dover but was driven back by a great storm, Louis had no choice but to obey the call to a peace settlement arranged by little Henry's mother, Queen ***Isabella of Angoulême**. Meanwhile, the pope, who had been asked to intercede, favored Henry; Louis' support fell away, and he agreed to withdraw his claim in exchange for a large sum of money.

Six years later, in 1223, King Philip died and Blanche's husband became King Louis VIII. His three-year reign was spent campaigning in order to maintain and expand the royal domains. After a long and exhausting siege in the intense heat of the summer of 1226, Louis became ill on his way back to Paris. Meanwhile, Blanche and their 12-year-old son, young Louis, had set out to meet him halfway. King Louis died before the longed-for reunion could take place. Observers reported that on hearing the news, Blanche, "mad with grief," tried to kill herself. Before dying, the king had named her regent during the minority of their young son Louis.

Blanche rallied from her grief, and, within a mere three weeks, she had arranged Louis IX's coronation. Though she knew that many of the great nobles, restive under the powerful Philip and his son, would waste no time taking advantage of a child and his mother, she was well-prepared for the awesome task ahead. Her husband had shared with her the problems of maintaining and expanding territories and power against continual enemies, the English, and even the church. From now on, the French realm would depend on Blanche's vigilance and sagacity. She would determine when to win support through marriage alliances, negotiations, gifts of land, castles, and titles—or when to threaten with force. Usually, the threat of force proved sufficient, and, according to one biographer, she never shed blood to prove her point.

Medieval chroniclers tell us that both Blanche's demeanor and appearance commanded respect. She is described as beautiful and even "magnificent," elegantly robed and truly regal. Standing side-by-side, she and her slim, blond, handsome son were evidently an impressive sight. Her personality, however, remains difficult to assess because—as in the case of most strong, assertive leaders—admirers and enemies present conflicting pictures. Her opponents saw her as cold, imperious, cunning, tenacious; her supporters saw her as warm, sympathetic, caring. Always, she was pious. As a devout and practicing Christian, she trained her children, particularly Louis, to try to avoid sin, protect their souls, and pray frequently. Louis is said to have adhered to these teachings throughout his personal and public life. Years later, he often related: "Madame used to say to me that if I were sick unto death, and could not be cured save by acting in such-wise that I should sin mortally, she would let me die rather than I should anger my Creator to my damnation."

She was perhaps the outstanding woman of the thirteenth century.

—**Margaret Wade Labarge**

After the coronation, Blanche was quick to gain an ally. To strengthen the allegiance of strategically located Flanders, she freed, reinstated, and reimbursed a high-ranking Flemish leader who had been imprisoned by Philip, leaving Flanders indebted to the French crown. But for those she could not win over, she used other devices. Within a few months of the coronation, many of France's most powerful nobles revolted and formed an alliance to undo the centralizing efforts of Philip and Louis VIII. During the next five years, Blanche would have to deal with constant outbreaks and conspiracies. When Louis IX was 13 years old, she thwarted a plot to ambush and kidnap him by raising the people of Paris to protect him. She enlisted this "people's army" who swarmed out of Paris to the nearby castle where he and his inadequate guard were trapped. The people surrounded their king and escorted him back to Paris.

In another instance, Blanche led an army to persuade certain rebel leaders to switch sides. Among those who did so was Theobald of Champagne, a significant noble and troubadour. In the tradition of medieval troubadours, he composed and sang songs of love and praise to his "lady," Queen Blanche. Although it was well-known that these flowery expressions of devotion were an accepted part of the tradition, Blanche's enemies spread scurrilous rumors. Angry with Theobald's desertion and Blanche's success, they accused the two of having more than a lady-and-vassal relationship. When the accusation was denied, they asserted that she should not be ruler because she was a "foreigner." (She had now lived in France for 26 years.) Detractors often called her "virago," and no doubt to her enemies the epithet was well-deserved.

Gender, too, was said to be an issue. Her enemies asserted that: "Queen Blanche ought not to govern so great a thing as the Kingdom of France, and it did not pertain to a woman to do such a thing." In medieval Europe, appointing a queen mother as regent for her minor son was not unheard of; but the regent usually was amenable to her councilors. Blanche, on the other hand, was ruler-in-fact, not purely in name, and at times she even organized and led military expeditions.

Finally, in 1230, she broke the back of the nobles' rebellion. Together, Blanche and the 16-year-old Louis IX led the royal army to the scene of a campaign to request negotiations with the enemy. So reluctant were the rebel lords to fight their anointed king that they asked him to withdraw from the site. When he refused, one by one the rebels capitulated and the coalition disintegrated. Now, Blanche could concentrate on administering the kingdom, but she could never relax her vigilance. Her informants throughout the realm acted as ears and eyes for news of incipient plots on the part of the nobility. She did not fear her more lowly subjects for she had won over the common people who loved their young king.

Blanche trained Louis to be firm when he was sure of his position but to be sympathetic with the weak and the poor. The piety she preached was not an empty facade of faith and ritual. Through her example, Louis became a champion of the poor, the lowly, and the oppressed. Stories abound, whether true or apocryphal, of Blanche ordering trees to be cut for firewood to warm freezing soldiers, and of Louis personally feeding beggars in the palace courtyard and inviting the poor to his dining hall. Blanche taught him as well only to use the sword as a last recourse. In the traumatic first years of his kingship, Louis learned that trading benefits, bestowing gifts, negotiating, and forming peaceful alliances could solve most of the conflicts.

By 1234, Louis was 20 years old and of age to rule on his own. Officially, the regency ended. In fact, however, Blanche continued at her son's side as a virtual co-ruler. She remained as a member of Louis' council and sometimes represented the crown as a secret negotiator. In certain crises, she was informed of the danger first, afterward explaining the situation to King Louis. A letter to Blanche eight years after Louis' marriage is addressed to "queen of the French" and her "serene Highness." It seems that Blanche was still thought of as "the queen" for years after 13-year-old ***Margaret of Provence** married Louis in 1234.

This marriage helped strengthen ties between Provence and the French throne. Louis is said to have been devoted to his young queen and continued to be so throughout his life. However, he never allowed her to play a political role. (Still, later in life, Margaret would show that like her mother-in-law she, too, was strong and determined, despite the years of living in Blanche's shadow.)

Contemporaries describe strained relations between the two queens. Apparently, Blanche tried to keep the young lovers apart during the day—ostensibly to keep Louis' attention on affairs of state. In one of their favorite castles, the young couple's separate rooms were joined by a spiral staircase which they climbed as frequently as possible. They ordered the servants to give a warning knock on the door whenever Blanche appeared. Louis had the authority to dismiss Blanche both as counselor and councilor but evidently chose not to do so.

Historians believe that by 1244, when she was 56 years old, Blanche was tempted to retire from political life. France was enjoying relative peace, education and culture were flourishing, and new abbeys arose. Thanks in part to Blanche's economies, money was available for building cathedrals in that great age of Gothic architecture. Work on Notre Dame continued and in 1243 construction began on that glory of French art: Sainte-Chapelle.

Blanche must also have felt reassured that her religious teachings had formed strong roots in her son. Considering all of these auspicious conditions, she may have felt that she was no longer needed. She could not have imagined that another trying regency, to last six years, yet lay before her. Undoubtedly pleased that Louis was in truth a "most Christian king," she was nevertheless shocked when he announced in 1244 that he was going on crusade to rescue Jerusalem from Muslim control. In this age, the highest form of Christian devotion was believed to be risking, and even giving, one's life to redeem the Holy Land from non-Christians. The accepted explanation for Louis' decision relates that in 1244 he became gravely ill of dysentery and was near death. Miraculously, he recovered and promised God that in gratitude he would lead a crusade to save Jerusalem. Blanche and other advisors tried to dissuade him, protesting that France needed his leadership. His mother reminded the 30-year-old Louis: "Remember the virtue it is, and pleasing to God, to heed your mother and agree with her judgments." In spite of the maternal plea, he stood firm.

Plans for the great enterprise proceeded; but not until four years later did the crusaders actually leave France. Recruiting men, outfitting ships, and raising money were formidable tasks. The government reduced its expenses and raised new revenues from the clergy and from cities and towns. Amid these preparations, just before leaving, Louis turned his thoughts to a domestic concern. In 1247, he issued orders to set up a royal system of investigators who would travel throughout the kingdom listening to people's grievances. He was especially concerned about reports of abuses and injustices at the hands of his own administrators. High and low, rich and poor, Christian and Jew, serf and free subjects of all conditions were to be questioned about unjust treatment. Blanche's biographer, **Regine Pernoud**, notes the queen-mother's influence, especially in the inclusion of Jewish subjects, as Blanche was known to defend Jews against persecution and to respect their faith.

While Queen Margaret accompanied her husband on crusade, Blanche, aged 60, along with her council of three clerics and two of Louis' brothers, was once again left in charge of the French government. As Louis left Paris, Blanche is said to have fainted, after crying: "Alas, my fine son. I will never see you again in this mortal life." Her prediction would prove true.

For the crusaders, the enterprise was a disaster, particularly for the many thousands who died of disease or in battle. Other thousands were imprisoned and tortured. King Louis was captured, well-treated, and ransomed. At that point, most French, including Blanche, assumed he would return home. But her pleas were in vain, for he refused to leave while so many of his men were still held captive. Moreover, the crusading remnants were still in Egypt, a long way from their goal of Jerusalem.

Louis was free to continue his campaign only because of his mother's leadership, but she was now tired and disheartened. She was not, as she had hoped, destined to retire quietly to her favorite Cistercian abbey and live out her remaining years in peace. Once more she was responsible for raising more funds and more men from an unenthusiastic populous.

In 1251, with Louis still abroad, she faced two especially difficult crises. A peasants' crusade had formed in the countryside, at first with Blanche's blessing. These would-be crusaders marched en masse to Paris where they became an ugly mob attacking Jews and clergy, creating riots and general mayhem. The queen ordered them to disperse, force was used, and some of the peasants were killed before the movement finally died.

A few months later, Blanche personally dealt with another crisis involving peasants. The serfs of nearby church lands under the jurisdiction of Notre Dame Cathedral revolted against additional taxes levied by the cathedral. The serfs claimed the taxes to be excessive and illegal. When their leaders were imprisoned and starved, Blanche intervened, asking for an inquest and the serfs' release. The church, angry at the queen's interference in what it considered a purely church affair, threw the wives and children of the leaders into extremely hot, tiny cells in which some died. This time, enraged by the inhumane treatment, Blanche led a body of troops to the cathedral where they found the door locked. She demanded and received the key, marched to the dungeon door, personally (according to one version but disputed by others) cudgeled it open, and released the prisoners.

Ordering an investigation, Blanche demanded that the peasants be liberated from their serfdom, as she had in the past liberated many serfs. But the bishops brought suit against her for acting outside her jurisdiction. Exhausted from administering her son's domain for a second time and anxious to know the court's decision, Blanche entered the Cistercian abbey which she had founded 16 years earlier. She asked to be made a nun, was clothed in the habit, and lay down to die. According to witnesses, she had lost the power of speech, but as she died, she began to intone a prayer. She "gave up her soul little by little, muttering between her teeth the rest of the prayer." Queen Blanche was buried in Maubuisson Abbey on November 29, 1252, at age 64. A chronicler wrote: "At her death the common people sorrowed much, for she had ever a care that they be not fleeced by the rich, and did well defend the right."

King Louis was still in the East trying unsuccessfully to rescue the Holy Land. In fact, he never made it to Jerusalem. Word of his mother's death did not reach him until the following summer. Eyewitnesses reported that on hearing the news, he "burst into tears" and went into seclusion for two days, saying that he "loved his mother above all mortal creatures."

The king began preparations to return home, but not until 1254, after many additional trials and tribulations, did Louis finally reach France. He had been absent for six years. Altogether, during 14 of his first 26 years on the throne, his mother had actually ruled for him. Louis IX lived for 13 more years, dying from illness on yet another disastrous crusade after invading Tunis in mid-summer of 1270.

Between crusades, Louis became known as a just but firm king and, above all, as a peacemaker. The Peace of Paris in 1259, involving disputed lands in France, brought 34 years of peace between England and France. Beloved as a wise arbitrator, Louis is described by his biographer Jean Richard as the "greatest peacemaker that the 13th century had known." To praise the peace-making of the crusading Louis may sound ironic. However, for the 13th century, reducing armed conflict within Europe alone was an unusual and major triumph. Queen Blanche's spirit and teachings lived on with her son who, in 1297, was proclaimed a saint by Pope Boniface VIII.

SOURCES:

Kelly, Amy. *Eleanor of Aquitaine and the Four Kings.* Cambridge, MA: Harvard University Press, 1950.

Labarge, Margaret Wade. *Saint Louis: Louis IX, Most Christian King of France.* Boston, MA: Little, Brown, 1968.

Pernoud, Regine. *Blanche of Castille.* Translated by Henry Noel. London: Collins, 1975.

Richard, Jean. *Saint Louis: Crusader King of France.* Translated by Jean Burrell. Cambridge, England: Cambridge University Press, 1992.

Emily Gilbert Gleason,
freelance writer in history, Sylvania, Ohio

Blanche of France (1253–1321)

French royal. *Name variations: Blanche Capet. Born in 1253 in Jaffa; died in 1321 in Paris, France; daughter of* ****Margaret of Provence*** *(1221–1295) and Saint Louis also known as Louis IX (1214–1270), king of France (r. 1226–1270); sister of Philip III the Bold (1245–1285), king of France (r. 1270–1285); married Ferdinand de la Cerda of Castile and Leon (son of Alphonso X), on October 30, 1268; children: Alphonso de la Cerda (c. 1270–1327); Ferdinand de la Cerda (b. 1272).*

Blanche of France (c. 1266–1305)

French princess. *Name variations: Blanca. Born around 1266 (some sources cite a much later date); died on March 19, 1305, in Vienna; daughter of* ****Isabella of Aragon*** *(1243–1271) and Philip III the Bold (1245–1285), king of France (r. 1270–1285); first wife of Rudolph or Rudolf III (1281–1307), king of Bohemia and Poland (r. 1306–1307).*

Blanche of France (1328–1392)

Duchess of Orléans and countess of Beaumont. *Name variations: Duchess of Orleans. Born in 1328; died in 1392; daughter of* ****Joan of Evreux*** *(d. 1370) and Charles IV the Fair (1294–1328), king of France (r. 1322–1328); married Philippe also known as Philip (1336–1375), count of Beaumont and Valois, duke of Orléans (brother of John II, king of France).*

Blanche of Lancaster (1341–1369).

See Beaufort, Joan (c. 1379–1440) for sidebar.

Blanche of Namur (d. 1363)

Queen of Sweden and Norway. *Name variations: Blanca of Namur; Blanka of Namur. Died in 1363; daughter of John, count of Namur; married Magnus II Eriksson or Erikson (1316–1374), king of Sweden (r. 1319–1356, 1359–1365), king of Norway as Magnus VII (r. 1319–1350), in 1335; children: Erik XII (c. 1339–1359), king of Sweden (r. 1356–1359); Haakon VI (c. 1339–1380), king of Norway (r. 1355–1380); and three daughters (names unknown).*

In 1335, Magnus II Eriksson, king of Norway and Sweden, married Blanche of Namur, and, by 1340, they had two sons. Erik (XII), the elder, would be king of Sweden; the younger son, Haakon (VI), would become king of Norway. The boys' governess in the early years, and Blanche's lady-in-waiting, was ***Bridget of Sweden**. As the brothers grew to manhood and ascended their thrones, relations between Magnus Eriksson and his sons were marked by turbulence, jealousy, and aggression. In 1362, when Erik died, Haakon was named as his brother's successor in Sweden; he was to rule jointly with his father. The two kings then entered into a war with their powerful neighbor Waldemar IV of Denmark over rights to Skaane. During this war, Magnus and Haakon enlisted the aid of the Hanseatic League, a powerful alliance of German cities with trading interests in northern Europe. Shortly thereafter, in 1363, Magnus and Haakon arrived at an agreement with Waldemar.

The friendship was cemented by the marriage of the 23-year-old Haakon with Waldemar's 10-year-old daughter **Margaret (I)** (1353–1412), who would be one of Scandinavia's greatest monarchs, reigning from 1387 to 1412.

Blanche of Naples (d. 1310)

Queen of Sicily and Aragon. *Died in 1310; daughter of Charles II, duke of Anjou (r. 1285–1290), king of Naples (r. 1285–1309), and* ****Marie of Hungary*** *(d. 1323); sister of* ****Lenore of Sicily*** *(1289–1341); married Jaime also known as James II, king of Sicily and Aragon (r. 1291–1327); children: Alphonso IV the Benign (1299–1336), king of Aragon (r. 1327–1336);* ****Constance of Aragon*** *(d. 1327, who married Juan Manuel "el Scritor" of Castile);* ****Maria of Aragon*** *(who married Peter, regent of Castile).*

Blanche of Navarre (d. 1158)

Queen of Castile. *Name variations: Blanche Jimeno. Born after 1133; died on August 11 or 12, 1158; daughter of Garcia IV, king of Navarre (r. 1134–1150), and* ****Marguerite de l'Aigle*** *(d. 1141); married Sancho III (1134–1158), king of Castile (r. 1157–1158), on January 30, 1151; children: Alphonso VIII (b. 1155), king of Castile (r. 1158–1214).*

Blanche of Navarre (d. 1229)

Countess of Champagne. *Born after 1177; died in childbirth in 1229; daughter of Sancho VI the Wise, king of Navarre (r. 1194–1234), and* ****Sancha of Castile and Leon*** *(d. 1179); only sister of* ****Berengaria of Navarre*** *(c. 1163–c. 1230); married Thibaut also known as Theobald III, count of Champagne, on July 1, 1199; children: Teobaldo or Theobald I (1201–1253), king of Navarre (r. 1234–1253, also known as Theobald IV of Champagne).*

Blanche of Navarre (fl. 1239)

Duchess of Brittany. *Flourished around 1239; daughter of Theobald I, king of Navarre (r. 1234–1253), and probably* ****Agnes of Beaujeu*** *(d. 1231); married John I the Red, duke of Brittany; children: John II (1239–1305), duke of Brittany (r. 1286–1305).*

Blanche of Navarre (1331–1398)

Queen of France. *Name variations: (Spanish) Blanca de Navarra. Born in 1331 (some sources cite 1330); died in 1398; daughter of Philip III, king of Navarre (r. 1328–1349), and* ****Joan II of Navarre*** *(1309–1349), queen of Navarre (r. 1328–1349); married Philip VI of Valois (1293–1350), king of France (r. 1328–1350), in 1349; children: Jeanne (who married John of Aragon, duke of Gironda).*

Following his marriage to ***Jeanne of Burgundy** who died in 1348, King Philip VI of France married Blanche of Navarre in 1349; he died the following year. When Blanche died in 1398, she left behind a valuable collection of manuscripts.

Blanche of Navarre (1385–1441)

Queen of Navarre and Sicily. *Name variations: Bianca of Navarre, Bianca of Sicily, Blanche of Sicily; (Spanish) Blanca de Navarre, Doña Blanca. Born in 1385 (some sources cite 1386 or 1391) in Navarre; died on April 3, 1441, in Santa Maria de Nieva, Aragon; daughter of Charles III, king of Navarre, and Eleanor Trastamara (d. 1415); married Martin I the Younger (d. 1410), king of Sicily (r. 1390–1409), in 1404; married John II (1398–1479), king of Sicily and Aragon (r. 1458–1479), on January 18, 1419, or 1420; children: (second marriage) Carlos also known as Charles (1421–1461), prince of Viana; Juana of Aragon (1423–1425);* ****Eleanor of Navarre*** *(1425–1479);* ****Blanche of Navarre*** *(1424–1464, queen of Castile, who married Henry also known as Enrique IV). King Martin's 1st wife was* ****Maria of Sicily*** *(d. 1402).*

Blanche was the eldest daughter of **Eleanor Trastamara** and Charles III, king of Navarre, a small kingdom in the Pyrenees. At age 19, she married Martin I the Younger, king of Sicily. When he died only six years later in 1410, without heirs, Blanche inherited the throne of Sicily. The succession of a woman to a throne in medieval times often signaled both a series of rebellions by the kingdom's feudal barons and the appearance of pretenders to the throne; Blanche's succession was no different. In every region of Sicily, powerful landholders reasserted ancient rights to land and income which were supposedly the king's property; their refusal to support the crown forced Queen Blanche to borrow money from private sources. In addition, the Grand Justiciar of Sicily attempted to seize the throne for himself.

Eleanor Trastamara *(d. 1415). See Joanna of Navarre for sidebar.*

Without much popular support or the money to raise an army to defend herself, Blanche's power quickly slipped away. Realizing she had little chance of political survival, she assembled a committee of nobles to choose the new king, Ferdinand I of Castile. In 1412, when he declared himself king of Sicily, Blanche returned to her homeland of Navarre. She married King John II of Aragon in 1419 and subsequently gave birth to three children. Six years later, Blanche succeeded her father Charles III of Navarre as queen. She died about age 56.

Laura York,
Anza, California

Blanche of Navarre (1424–1462).

See Eleanor of Navarre for sidebar.

Blanche of Rossi (d. 1237)

Italian noblewoman and soldier. *Born in Rossi, Italy; died in 1237 in Ezzelino, Italy; married Battista of Padua.*

Blanche of Rossi was a participant in the Italian war between two powerful political factions, the Ghibellines and the Guelfs. The wife of Battista of Padua, she fought alongside her husband to protect the town of Ezzelino in 1237. Battista was killed in the battle and the town's defenses collapsed. Apparently, the leader of the conquering army demanded that the townspeople turn Blanche over to him, but Blanche chose suicide over such dishonor.

Blanche of Savoy (c. 1337–?)

Milanese noblewoman. *Name variations: Bianca of Savoy. Born Blanche Mary in Savoy around 1337; daughter of Aymon, count of Savoy; sister of Amadeus VI, count of Savoy; married Galeazzo II Visconti, lord of Milan (r. 1354–1378), in August of 1350; children: Gian Galeazzo Visconti, lord of Milan (r. 1378–1402), duke of Milan (r. 1396–1402); ****Violet Visconti*** *(c. 1353–1386).*

Blanche of Sicily (1385–1441).

See Blanche of Navarre.

Blanche of Valois (c. 1316–?)

Holy Roman empress. *Born around 1316; daughter of ****Mahaut de Chatillon*** *(d. 1358) and Charles I, count of Valois (1270–1325, son of Philip III, king of France); half-sister of Philip VI of Valois (1293–1350), king of France (r. 1328–1350), and ****Jeanne of Valois*** *(c. 1294–1342); first wife of Charles IV Luxemburg (1316–1378), Holy Roman emperor (r. 1347–1378).*

Wencelas Charles of Bohemia and Luxemburg, who would become Holy Roman emperor Charles IV, met his first wife Blanche of Valois at the court of her cousin Charles IV, king of France. A fresco of the couple can be found in the castle of Karlstein, near Prague. Emperor Charles also married ***Anna of Schweidnitz** and ***Elizabeth of Pomerania** (mother of Sigismund, king of Hungary and Bohemia).

Blanchfield, Florence (1884–1971)

American nurse and the first woman to receive a regular commission in the U.S. Army. *Born Florence Aby Blanchfield on April 1, 1884, in Front Royal, Virginia; died on May 12, 1971, in Washington, D.C.; daughter and one of eight children of Joseph Plunkett (a stone mason) and Mary Louvenia (Anderson) Blanchfield (a nurse); attended business college in Pittsburgh; University of California; Columbia University; graduated from South Side Training School for Nurses, Pittsburgh, Pennsylvania, 1906; additional training at Johns Hopkins Hospital.*

Florence Blanchfield's work may have been influenced by her mother **Mary Blanchfield**, a nurse who came from a long line of doctors. Indeed, all of the Blanchfield daughters went into nursing, although Florence alone combined her nursing with an exceptional military career.

After completing her education, Florence Blanchfield held a succession of civilian nursing positions before enlisting in the Army Nurse Corps in 1917. She spent World War I on the bloody battlefields of France, working under regular army officers who knew little about medicine. Returning to civilian life briefly after the war, she then rejoined the Army Nurse Corps and served over the next 15 years in various posts in the U.S., China, and the Philippines. In 1935, she was on the surgeon general's staff in Washington; in 1942, when World War II broke out, she was assigned as assistant to Colonel ❧▸ **Julia Flikke**, superintendent of the Army Nurse Corps. A year later, Blanchfield succeeded Flikke as colonel and superintendent, but at the time of her promotion her rank was only a formality which did not carry with it the pay or benefits of full rank. In addition to the responsibilities she was about to undertake, she became involved in an effort to secure full rank for all army nurses.

During World War II, Blanchfield supervised some 60,000 nurses on fronts from Australia to Alaska. Men with her rank, by comparison, often commanded no more than 500. In 1945, the army awarded her the Distinguished Service Medal for "devotion to duty." Although her case for full rank was won on a temporary basis in 1944, it was not until 1947—with congresswoman *Frances Payne Bolton in her corner—that the Army-Navy Nurse Act was passed, granting nurses full status. General Dwight D. Eisenhower awarded Blanchard the first regular commission ever given to a woman in the United States Army.

Following her retirement, Blanchfield recorded the history she had witnessed, producing two books: *The Army Nurse Corps in World War II* (1948) and *Organized Nursing and the Army in Three Wars* (1950). In 1951, she was honored by the International Red Cross, with the Florence Nightingale Medal. She died in Washington, D.C., on May 12, 1971. Seven years later, the United States Army hospital in Fort Campbell, Kentucky, was named after her.

SUGGESTED READING:

Aynes, Edith A. *From Nightingale to Eagle: An Army Nurse's History.* Englewood Cliffs, NJ: Prentice-Hall, 1973.

COLLECTIONS:

The Blanchfield papers located in the Col. Florence A. Blanchfield Collection, in the Nursing Archives at Boston University's Mugar Library.

Barbara Morgan,
Melrose, Massachusetts

Flikke, Julia Otteson (b. 1879?)

American superintendent of Army Nurse Corps. *Born around 1879 in Viroqua, Wisconsin; married.*

Married and soon widowed, Julia Flikke joined the Army Nurse Corps during World War I and was stationed with the American Expeditionary Force (A.E.F.) in France. She then served a year in China and a year in the Philippines. From 1925 to 1937, Flikke was stationed at the Walter Reed Hospital in Washington, D.C., then was assigned to the office of the surgeon general with the rank of captain. When Major ***Julia C. Stimson** retired as superintendent of the Army Nurse Corps, Flikke replaced her and was offered the rank of major. In March 1942, she was promoted to colonel.

Bland, Dorothea (1761–1816).

See Jordan, Dora.

Bland, Edith (1858–1924).

See Nesbit, Edith.

Bland, Lillian (1878–1971)

British aviator and first woman in the British Isles, possibly in the world, to design, build, and fly her own plane. *Born in Kent, England, in 1878; died in 1971.*

Lillian Bland established a reputation as a press photographer and sportswriter before undertaking the construction of a bi-plane glider. Spurred on by the achievements of the Wright brothers, she successfully flew her plane, the *Mayfly*, in 1910, after modifying it with the addition of an engine. Bland was reportedly diverted from her aviation career by her father's offer of a car, which developed into a position running a motor agency. She subsequently married and took up residence in Vancouver. At age 93, Bland is said to have told the *Belfast Telegraph* that the only excitement left to her was gambling.

Bland, Maria Theresa (1769–1838)

English soprano. *Name variations: Maria Romanzini. Born in London, England, in 1769; died in London on January 15, 1838; daughter of Italian Jews named Romanzini; studied with Dibdin; married George Bland (an actor), in 1790; children: Charles (a tenor) and James (1798–1861, a buffo bass).*

Maria Theresa Bland first sang in London at the Hughes' Riding School in 1773. She made her debut at Drury Lane in 1786. A member of the Drury Lane Company from 1789 to 1824, she excelled in the operas of Storace and Arnold; she also sang at the Haymarket and Vauxhall. In 1824, suffering from depression, she abandoned her career.

Blandina (d. 177 CE)

Christian martyr and saint. *Tortured in the amphitheater at Lyons in 177 CE.*

Blandina was a female slave who, during the persecution of the Christians, was brought into the amphitheater at Lyons in 177 to be put to death. Along with Biblis, Pothinus, Maturus, Sanctus, Ponticus, Attalus, and other martyrs, she was hung by her arms to a post; then animals were let into the arena. The crowd waited in happy anticipation for all the martyrs to be devoured. Amazingly, however, the animals did not touch Blandina, nor did they savage Ponticus. Both were saved for the last day of the spectacle and subjected to even more horrors. That day, wrote Eusebius, Blandina "never ceased exhorting her young companion, who died with courage. As for her, after having been flogged, mutilated, and burned, she was wrapped in a net and exposed to a bull, which played with her, tossing her into the air; then, finally, they finished her off with a sword. The pagans swore that never had they seen a woman suffer with such courage." Blandina's feast day is on June 2.

Blandy, Mary (1719–1752)

English murderer who was convicted and hanged for poisoning her father. *Born at Henley-on-Thames, England, in 1719; convicted of murder and hanged at Oxford, England, in 1752; only daughter of Francis Blandy (a lawyer).*

Mary Blandy was the well-born daughter of an esteemed lawyer, Francis Blandy. Her downfall began with her engagement to Captain William Henry Cranstoun (the titled son of a Scottish peer) who was already married and the father of two children. Upon discovering Cranstoun's deception, Blandy's father renounced the betrothal and sent the deceiver scurrying back to Scotland. From there, Cranstoun reportedly sent Mary Blandy some powders, instructing her to lace her father's food and drink in order to soften him up. As Blandy did so, she was seen by the servants who turned her in after her father succumbed to the poison and died. Blandy was subsequently arrested and tried. In spite of her best efforts in her own defense, she was sentenced to death and hung in 1752. It is said that upon hearing of his lover's arrest, Cranstoun fled to France and joined a Catholic monastery where he later died.

Barbara Morgan, Melrose, Massachusetts

Blane, Sally (1910–1997).

See Young, Loretta for sidebar.

Blankers-Koen, Fanny (1918—)

Dutch athlete and greatest woman track-and-field star of her generation, who won four Olympic gold medals in 1948, set 13 world records, and won 58 Dutch titles. *Name variations: Fanny Koen. Pronunciation: BLANK-ers COON. Born Francina Elsje Koen outside the village of Baarn near the Queen's castle of Soestdyk, the Netherlands, on April 26, 1918; only girl in a family of five born to farmers; married Jan Blankers (an athlete and coach), in August 1940; children: son Jan (b. 1941) and daughter Fanny (b. 1946).*

At age five, moved with family to Hoofddorp; won every sprinting event in Holland as well as two competitions in Germany; participated in the 1936 Olympics, tied for 6th place in the high jump; took third place at the European women's championships in Vienna, running the 100-meter dash in 12 seconds flat (1938); married Jan Blankers and moved to Amsterdam (1940); won the 80-meter hurdles in the European championships in Oslo (1946); won four gold medals at the Olympic games in London, the 100-meter race in 11.9 seconds, the 200-meter race in 24.4, the 80-meter hurdles in 11.2 and the 4x100-meter relay while anchoring the Dutch women's team (1948); competed at Berne, Switzerland, sweeping all five first places in the women's pentathlon and collecting an unheard of 4,185 points (1951); made a final, unsuccessful Olympic appearance (1952).

The greatest woman track-and-field star of her generation, perhaps of the century, was born on a 62-acre dairy, rye, and potato farm. Her farmer father, however, proved no less soil-bound than his daughter would grow up to be. He gave up farming and went into the transportation business by the time Fanny Koen was five years old. With that change in occupation, the family moved to the village of Hoofddorp, in the windmill country, nine miles south of Amsterdam.

The Koens were a physically active family. Fanny's parents swam, skated, jumped, and played tennis as a matter of course. Thus, they were not particularly surprised when their only daughter did the same. Fanny jumped and ran; she also rang doorbells and swiped apples with impunity because she was faster than anyone in the village, including her four brothers, two older and two younger. "I know you can outrun anybody in Hoofddorp," a frustrated neighbor would yell, "but if I ever catch you, I'll wring your neck!" At age six, she joined the local gymnastics club and soon competed with the boys in swimming, skating, and sprinting. Blankers-Koen became an excellent swimmer.

One summer day in 1935, when she was 16 and had finished school, Fanny was suddenly aware as she helped her mother with housekeeping chores that the work would be insufficient to fill her days and expend her energy. That instant, she made up her mind to become an Olympic champion. But she had to choose between two sports: swimming or track and field. Diving and swimming had been the traditional Olympic events for women since making their first appearance in the Olympic games in 1912. In 1928, women had been privileged to compete among themselves in a special series of track-and-field events, and, in the 1932 Games, ***Babe Didrikson [Zaharias]** had won two Olympic gold medals. Didrikson's success may have influenced the thinking of Fanny's swimming coach who encouraged her to choose track and field. Holland already had first-rate swimmers, he explained. Fanny agreed and subsequently joined the Amsterdam Dames' Athletic Club where she went twice a week to compete with the best Holland had to offer.

That August of 1935, she competed in the women's 200-meter track event in Groningen and gave a lackluster performance. Possibly her prerace jitters, which would leave her with clammy hands before all subsequent events and on the verge of a nervous collapse prior to some, got the better of her; at any rate, in her next race, the 800-meter run against Holland's long-distance woman champion, **Ans Kellenaers**, Fanny had enough time to overcome a slow start and outrun the favorite. It was a significant event not only because she won the race, but because her future coach and husband-to-be, Jan Blankers was watching. Like any good coach, he was cheering his protégé Kellenaers, he said, "and I never doubted she'd win, either. Fanny's forte was jumping; the ADA people themselves told me she wasn't any good at running. Well, her style was truly terrible, and she dragged her feet the first six hundred meters, but just when Ans was beginning to lose her wind, Fanny came up like a shot and won the race. 'That girl will make a fine sprinter,' I said to myself."

Fanny Blankers-Koen

Due to a permanently damaged Achilles tendon, Jan Blankers had been forced to give up his own athletic career, but his expertise in track and field was well known, and he devoted his spare time from a job in the Amsterdam police force to coaching young men and women athletes, among them Kellenaers. When Jan was asked to coach the Dutch track-and-field team for the Berlin Olympics in the summer of 1936, he asked Fanny to join the team. Neither pupil nor teacher, however, had quite enough time to develop the sprinter in Fanny. She competed in the high jump event, jumping only 5'1", not even approaching her Amsterdam record. The Games also cast a shadow over Europe which Fanny recalled later. "I remember seeing [Hitler] in 1936 getting into a jeep with all his soldiers and their rifles and riding around the Berlin Stadium, waving and saluting. It made me feel afraid."

Back home, Jan Blankers persuaded Fanny to leave the Amsterdam Dames and let him take over her coaching. Having seen her potential as a runner, he wanted to mold her without interference from Fanny's club, which insisted she should jump, not run. Jan therefore created a new club to promote Fanny's talents as well as those of five other young women he persuaded to sign up. He named his creation "Sagitta," the Latin word for arrow. Under his watchful eye, Fanny streamlined her style. "Every Tuesday and Thursday, rain or shine, she made the eighteen-mile round trip from Hoofddorp on her bicycle," said Jan. Within a year, the tall, somewhat awkward village girl had won every sprinting event in Holland and two competitions in Germany. In 1938, she came in third at the European women's championships in Vienna with a time of 12.0 in the 100 meters. Then Jan added broad jumping to Fanny's regimen of high jumps and sprints, gradually starting her on hurdles.

By then five years had passed, five years of working closely together and forging a trusting, loyal teacher-student relationship, from which had grown the mutual respect and affection which transformed it into marriage. Although he was 14 years older, the coach fell in love with his protégé. Fanny and Jan celebrated their union in August of 1940 and moved into a four-room apartment at 158 Haarlemmermeer Straat, in Amsterdam, ten minutes from the Olympia track. She remained a pupil and an athlete in training, and continued to do so as the mother of little Jantje, who was born within a year. Blankers-Koen would arrive at the track pushing her baby carriage and, if necessary, would nurse her infant son before and after performances in athletic events. Nor would the birth of Jantje's little sister Fanneke in 1946 present a hardship in the development of Fanny's career; she became a familiar sight in Amsterdam pushing a baby carriage at top speed. If she couldn't train on the track, she'd train while running errands, the children in tow. Motherhood was a minor obstacle; far more hurdles had been put up by the upheaval of World War II and the discontinuance of the 1940 and 1944 Olympics. Remembering those years, Blankers-Koen recounted, "People were being taken away, and friends of mine in the underground were shot and people were hungry and were in the streets begging for food. We could get some potatoes and a little milk, very thin milk, not nice from the cow."

From a competitive standpoint, everything was against Fanny Blankers-Koen at the end of the war. Having won all the championships worth having in the Netherlands, she was barred from further competition. In sheer desperation, she once entered a men's race and came in fourth in the 100-meter dash with a time of 11.5 seconds. Finally in 1946, seven months after giving birth to little Fanneke, she could compete in the European championships in Oslo. Fanny won the 80-meter hurdles and brought the Dutch relay team to victory. It was an impressive performance, but her days of glory were yet to come.

After 12 long years—during which athletes throughout the world saw their Olympic potential waning as no amount of training could stave off the effects of advancing age—the Summer Olympic Games of 1948 were to be held in London. By then Blankers-Koen was the holder of six world records—100 meters, 80-meter hurdles, high jump, long jump, and two relays. She was also 30 years old and a frequent topic of sports columns. The British press deemed her too old to win the sprints and usually referred to her as a "housewife too old to run." No one took her attempts seriously, adhering to the concept that once a woman married and had children, her abilities disappeared. "I got very many bad letters," said Fanny, "people writing that I must stay home with my children and that I should not be allowed to run on a track." The negative publicity did little to buoy Fanny's spirits as she and Jan boarded a plane for London. She could not shake the memory of her failure at the 1936 Olympics. Not only would she miss her children, she also wondered if the competition would be worth the drubbing she was taking at the hands of the press which would only get worse when she faltered.

It rained on Monday, August 2, making the muddy track less than desirable for the 100 meter. Just before the event, Jan taunted her with, "Don't forget, Fanny, you are too old." Blankers-Koen stilled the skeptic voices by winning the 100-meter race at 11.9, equaling the Olympic record and coming in more than three yards ahead of **Dorothy Manley** and ***Shirley Strickland**. The Dutch housewife had won her first Olympic gold medal, but she had three gruelling events ahead of her.

Next came the 80-meter hurdles, which were especially trying because Fanny was pitted against the British favorite, 19-year-old ballet dancer **Maureen Gardner**. At the starting gun, Fanny allowed her mind to wander, and Gardner went flying by; little by little, Blankers-Koen closed in. At the fifth hurdle, the two competitors were neck-and-neck when Fanny stumbled. "I was going so fast that I went too close to the hurdle, hit it, and lost my balance," recalled Fanny. "What happened after that is just a blurred memory. It was a grim struggle in which my hurdling style just went to pieces." Rushing forward, she caught up with Gardner, and at the last moment lurched across the finish line. She, Gardner, and Shirley Strickland had broken the tape almost simultaneously. As the judges processed the results of the photo finish, the crowd waited quietly. Then the band struck up England's "God Save the King." Blankers-Koen, who assumed it was being played in honor of her British competitor's first place finish, was puzzled when her name went up in the first place slot. The British anthem had not been played to honor Gardner; it was in honor of King George VI and Queen ***Elizabeth (Bowes-Lyon)** who had made a sudden appearance in their viewing box. Fanny Blankers-Koen had crossed the finish line a hair's breath in front of Gardner, thus winning an uncomfortably close race in 11.2 seconds, .2 slower than she had run the same race back in Amsterdam. Now she had won a second gold medal.

Suddenly, Fanny Blankers-Koen was the athlete of the hour. For the first time in Olympic history, a woman was receiving more attention than any of the male athletes. Her confidence wavered as international attention focused on her. Prior to the semifinals of the 200-meters, she felt so much stress that she told her husband she wanted to withdraw. Jan's encouragement proved futile until he reminded her of the considerations she owed her parents and their children. Reluctantly, the obliging daughter and the proud mother agreed to run. She won the heat by six yards—setting an Olympic record of 24.3 seconds—and took the final by seven yards, the largest margin ever recorded in the women's 200 meters. When she broke the tape, she was 15 meters ahead of her nearest competitor. The crowd went wild over "Flying Fanny." Blankers-Koen had established herself as the outstanding woman athlete of her time. She had outdone even Babe Didrikson, who at the 1932 Olympics had taken gold in the javelin and hurdles. To her three medals, Fanny added a fourth as anchor of the Dutch women's team in the 4x100-meter relay. When she took the baton for the final leg, her team was in fourth place, five meters behind the leader, but Fanny was able to catch the front runner, **Joyce King**, just before the finish line. Fanny Blankers-Koen had won four of the nine women's track-and-field events. Only Jesse Owens, who had won three personal titles and shared the victory of his winning relay team in the Games of 1936, shared that record.

Back in Amsterdam, Blankers-Koen was received with more enthusiasm than Churchill or

Manley, Dorothy (1927—)

***English runner.** Name variations: Dorothy Gladys Hall. Born Dorothy Gladys Manley on April 29, 1927, in London, England; married.*

Dorothy Manley first trained as a high jumper until her coach **Sandy Duncan** turned her into a sprinter. Manley was Essex County 100 yards champion for 1947, 1948, and 1949, and won the 100-meters silver medal in the 1948 London Olympics.

Gardner, Maureen (1928–1974)

***English runner.** Born Maureen Angela Gardner in Oxford, England, on November 12, 1928; died in September 1974; married Geoffrey Dyson (an Olympic coach).*

Once a ballet dancer, Maureen Gardner turned to athletics as a means of regaining her health after a serious illness in 1947. In her first major competition, she won the National 100 meters. Within three years, she had broken the British 80-meter hurdles record, first at Chadwick in the National championships, then later in Paris, Luxemburg, and Motspur Park all within one week. In the London Olympics in 1948, Gardner also took the silver medal in the 80-meter hurdles.

King, Joyce (1921—)

***Australian runner.** Born on September 1, 1921.*

Joyce King won a silver in the 1948 London Olympics in the 4x100 meter relay.

Eisenhower at war's end. While onlookers cheered, she and her family were brought from the railroad station in an open coach, drawn by four magnificent white horses, to the town hall and an awaiting lord mayor. All along the road, the Dutch saluted her, hanging out windows, sitting atop lamp posts and streetcar roofs. But her attitude towards her own accomplishments were a good deal more earthbound than her stride. Dressed in her blue Dutch Olympic uniform, she was overwhelmed by the public outpouring of affection. "All I've done is run fast," she told the lord mayor. "I don't quite see why people should make so much fuss about that." Her neighbors gave her a new bicycle, "so she won't have to run so much," and a group of villagers arrived with a basket of eggs—a generous present and a measure of their admiration at a time when people were accorded only one egg per person every other week. "Everyone had been listening on the radio," noted Blankers-Koen. "I couldn't help thinking how different these streets were from just a few years before. This was the first celebration in my country since the war. Maybe I cried just a little."

All I've done is run fast. I don't quite see why people should make so much fuss about that.

—Fanny Blankers-Koen

She explained this boisterous welcome from the stalwart, sensible Hollanders in terms of her "commonness." "They like to see a busy *huisvrouw* [hausfrau or housewife] like myself do something on her own and do it well. Jan and I and the two children are just an ordinary family. People applaud me because I do my training and winning between washing dishes and darning socks." The British cartoonist who had depicted Fanny with Dutch cap and wooden shoes, dashing off to the races, admonishing her children not to put their thumbs in the dikes while she was away, had suggested as much. At 5'9" and 140 pounds, Blankers-Koen ranked among the best, and her physical prowess equalled or exceeded her predecessors. But Fanny was a devoted housewife. Being a wife and mother was as integral to her life as running and training. Unlike the pre-World War II image of aggressive or masculine women athletes that had been painted on the collective consciousness by the press, she had already married, had children, and darned socks, and for that she was cheered and applauded as a vision for the everyday woman, an inspiration to all who saw in her one of their own. In short, she was not threatening. As Jill Tweedie wrote on the same subject many years later in England's *The Guardian*:

> To wholly admire . . . female athletes one must appreciate them visually and to do that means readjusting . . . preconceived notions of feminine beauty and worth. What is the Western stereotype at the moment? A sleek, smooth, soft and curving body with not a muscle or tendon in sight, a body that gives only intimations of sexual pleasure, a pliant body willing to pose its limbs as will best please a man, a submissive body that could not defend itself in dark corners on dark nights. A body, in other words, there to be done unto and never to do.

For Fanny, invitations to athletic meets came from everywhere and filled the next four years. She continued to win national and international honors, notably the women's pentathlon at Berne, Switzerland, in 1951. With five European gold medals, Blankers-Koen held more European championships than anyone until 1986 when ***Irena Kirszenstein-Szewinska**, the Polish athlete, duplicated that feat.

The 1952 Olympic Games in Helsinki proved a great disappointment for the Dutch star and a sad anticlimax to a marvelous career. Blankers-Koen had contracted a blood infection from blisters that required medication. Although her doctor insisted that she cut back on her schedule, she was determined to forge ahead. But the medicine made her dizzy, and she was not performing well. In the 80-meter finals, she hit two hurdles and dropped out; her former rival Shirley Strickland not only took the Olympic title but the world record in that event. Blankers-Koen then failed to qualify in the 100 meter, and the relay team finished last in the 4x100. Fanny left the Games to recuperate, finally hanging up her running shoes in 1955 at the age of 37. For a time, she tried coaching but found it did not agree with her. During the 1968 Olympics, she served as manager of the Dutch team.

The concept of mixing career and motherhood was new when Blankers-Koen triumphed in the 1948 Olympics. Even decades later, the concept remains controversial. When she was in her 60s, the track star defended her decisions: "I was a good mother. I had no time for much besides my house chores and training, and when I went shopping it was only to buy food for the family and never to buy dresses." Her son Jan, who grew up to teach geography in an Amsterdam college, was proud of his mother, though he admitted his childhood was not always easy but not for the reasons one would assume. "I remember when I was growing up, there were always so many people greeting my mother on the street that I was embarrassed. I'd walk five paces behind her."

The Blankers family lived the most ordinary of lives. Macaroni was a favorite food; bridge was a favorite game; and ice cream a favorite treat. Yet, Fanny Blankers-Koen was remarkable. She was the first woman track-and-field athlete in history to have a statue erected in her honor, which still stands in Amsterdam. During her career, she won 58 Dutch national titles, set 13 World records, and won five European championships as well as four Olympic gold medals. No woman in track history, from any nation, has won as many national titles. "I still walk about five paces behind her," her son once said of his 60-year-old mother. "That's because she walks so fast. Mother still goes everywhere in a hurry."

SOURCES:

Berkow, Ira. "Fanny Blankers-Koen: Olympian Ahead of her Time," in *The New York Times Biographical Service*. October 1982, p. 1276.

"Famous Dutch Legs Win Again," in *Life*. September 10, 1951, pp. 129–132.

Hauser, Ernest O. "Look at That Girl Go," in *Saturday Evening Post*. Vol. 221, no. 3. January 16, 1949, pp. 24–25.

Hendershott, Jon. *Track's Greatest Women*. Los Altos, CA: Tafnews Press, 1987.

Lardner, John. "Strong Cigars and Lovely Women," in *Newsweek*. Vol. 33, no. 23. June 6, 1949, p. 75.

Life. August 23, 1948 (photos).

Newsweek. August 16, 1948, p. 70.

Schaap, Richard. *An Illustrated History of the Olympics*. NY: Alfred A. Knopf, 1963.

Inga Wiehl, Yakima Valley Community College, Yakima, Washington

Blatch, Harriot Stanton (1856–1940).

See Stanton, Elizabeth Cady for sidebar.

Blaugdone, Barbara (c. 1609–1705)

English Quaker and author. *Born around 1609 in England; died in 1705 in England; never married; no children.*

Barbara Blaugdone was an active participant in the early period of the Quaker movement in England. In its founding years, Quakerism included the almost equal participation of women members in preaching and prophesizing, and Blaugdone, like many other women, was drawn to Quakerism for the opportunities it presented. After her conversion at middle age, she began traveling extensively around England and Ireland to promote the new ideas of the Society of Friends. Her writings reveal the freedoms she enjoyed, as well as the hardships and dangers a lone female minister faced, especially as Quaker ideas grew in popularity and English authorities began to crack down on its heretical leaders. After she retired from active preaching, she composed an autobiography entitled *An Account of the Travels, Sufferings, and Persecutions of Barbara Blaugdone*, which was published in 1691.

Laura York, Anza, California

Blavatsky, Helena (1831–1891)

Russian spiritual leader, author, mystic, and a founder of the Theosophical Society. *Name variations: Madame Blavatsky or simply HPB. Born Helena (Elena or Helen) Petrovna Gan on July 31, 1831, in Ekaterinoslav, Russia; died of flu complications on May 8, 1891, in London, England; daughter of Captain (later Colonel) Peter Alekseevich Gan (1798–1873, a career military officer) and Elena Andreevna (Fadeeva) Gan (1814–1842, an author who wrote novels as "Zinaida R-va"); sister of writer* ***Vera Zhelikhovskaya*** *(1835–1896); married Nikifor Vasileevich Blavatsky, in 1849; children: one child, Nikolai, who died a few years after his birth around 1862.*

Helena Petrovna Blavatsky, termed both a charlatan and a great thinker, occasionally at the same time, was an exceptionally complicated figure who inspires deep reactions to this day. Charismatic and compelling, yet often belligerent and coarse, she established an international organization that preached a Universal brotherhood of all peoples based on Western and Eastern philosophies. At the same time, much of her fame was and is based on the numerous psychic illusions and tricks that she and her followers experienced—phenomena she almost certainly staged herself. One of her most notable achievements was the introduction, albeit in a slightly altered form, of Eastern philosophies to Western audiences.

Helena's parents, Captain Peter Alekseevich Gan and **Elena Andreevna Gan**, were married in 1830 in Ekaterinoslav, Russia (now Dnepropetrovsk, Ukraine). Helena, their first child, was born on the night of July 30–31, 1831, an auspicious beginning, since Russian folklore has it that those born on that night are endowed with the power to control spirits. The Gans also had a son Sasha, who died in 1833 shortly after his birth, a second daughter Vera, born in 1835, and another son Leonid, born in June 1840.

See sidebar on the following page

The maternal side of Blavatsky's family descended from the Dolgorukovs, an influential family of the Russian nobility—her grandmother was a princess—and Helena had a very privileged childhood. She received instruction in many subjects and learned to speak several lan-

Gan, Elena Andreevna (1814–1842)

Russian author. *Name variations: Helena Gan; (pseudonym) Zinaida R-va or Zenaida R-va. Born Helena Andreevna Fadeeva in 1814; died in June 1842; daughter of* ***Elena Fadeeva*** *(1788–1860, a botanist with international connections); married Captain (later Colonel) Peter Alekseevich Gan (1798–1873, a career military officer), in 1830; children:* ****Helena Blavatsky*** *(1831–1891), son Sasha (who died in infancy, 1833),* ***Vera Zhelikhovskaya*** *(1835–1896, a writer), Leonid (b. June 1840).*

One of the Russian Romantics, Elena Gan wrote novels which probed the lot of the intellectual outsider. Her writings include *Utballa* (1838), *Dzhellaledin* (1843), originally published as *The Moslem* in 1838, *Teofaniia Abbadzhio* (1841), and *A Vain Gift*. The later books hint of a "developing social pathos and a movement towards realism cut short by her premature death," wrote Claire Buck in *The Bloomsbury Guide to Women's Literature*.

guages. She also had an unusually liberal access to books and journals and absorbed considerable quantities of information on a wide range of topics, including science, philosophy, and the occult.

Blavatsky also traveled a great deal during her childhood as her father was often transferred about Russia as part of his military service. After living in a series of provincial towns in the early 1830s, the family was eventually relocated in 1836 to the capital St. Petersburg. When Peter was shortly transferred once again, this time his family did not follow him; they moved instead to Astrakhan province with Blavatsky's grandparents. The Gans' later travels included Poltava and Odessa.

When Helena was approximately five years old, her mother began writing novels, a career she pursued under the name "Zinaida R-va," as Russian women often wrote for publication under pseudonyms. Elena Gan's promising career was short-lived, however, as she died only five years later, in June 1842. Blavatsky and her siblings moved in with their maternal grandparents in Saratov.

According to her family's later reminiscences, Helena's connections with inexplicable occurrences began early. As a child and young adult, she apparently experienced hallucinatory visions and occasionally wrote messages in handwriting other than her own. She was also reportedly able to move objects without touching them—a phenomenon known as telekinesis.

In July 1849, at the age of 17, she married 40-year-old Nikifor Blavatsky, a highly placed state official who was later made the vice-governor of Erevan Province. The marriage lasted only a few months, however, when she abruptly left him and, after several months visiting relatives, Russia as well.

The chronology of the 20 years of Blavatsky's life after the disintegration of her marriage are difficult to untangle. In later years, she tended to embroider her past as she saw fit. According to her version, one accepted by most of her followers, in the 1850s Blavatsky traveled to the Americas and the West Indies, as well as Tibet and India, where she made her first contact with a Brotherhood of Mahatmas (learned sages). She also reportedly wandered among the native tribes of the Russian Caucasus for a time in the early 1860s. She later maintained that she spent the years 1867 to 1871 traveling about the Orient and Europe, at which time she professed to have fought alongside Italian leader Guiseppe Garibaldi in the 1867 Battle of Mentana.

While her wanderings might not have been quite as wide-ranging as she later claimed—she most probably did not make it to either the Americas or India, nor is it likely that she was at the Battle of Mentana—she did spend most of the 1850s traveling extensively throughout Europe, as well as Turkey and Egypt. Although her exact activities are impossible to determine, she probably served for a time as a lady's companion to raise money, and at one point she became involved with Hungarian opera singer Arkadi Metrovich, with whom she toured Europe. She also maintained her interest in the occult, and while in Paris in 1858 she met Daniel Home, a famed American medium.

It is accepted that in late 1858 Blavatsky returned to Pskov, Russia, to spend time with her recently widowed sister Vera. Although she later claimed to have left again almost immediately, it seems likely that she remained in Russia for most of the following decade. While there, she was briefly reunited with her husband Nikifor, although the marriage was as disastrous as ever. She also apparently became involved with Nikolai Meyendorff, a Russian devotee of Spiritualism, which is the belief that the spirits of the dead can be contacted through mediums and seances.

In late 1861 or early 1862, Helena gave birth to a son, Nikolai. She claimed Meyendorff was the father, a fact he denied, claiming in turn that Helena was still involved with Metrovich and that he was the father. In any event, Niko-

Helena Blavatsky

lai's life was a short one; having been born with an unidentified deformity, he died in 1867. Following his death, Helena stayed in Russia for several more years. She spent time with various family members, including her cousin Sergei Witte, the future finance minister under Tsar Nicholas II.

The disparate versions of Blavatsky's life begin to reconverge with the summer of 1871, when she and Arkadi Metrovich set sail for Cairo on the S.S. *Eumonia*. Disaster struck on July 4, when the ship's powder magazine exploded, killing virtually all of the ship's 400 passengers. Blavatsky was among the 17 who were saved, although Metrovich was not as fortunate. Blavatsky continued on to Cairo alone, where she stayed briefly, setting up a society to study Spiritualism. She soon abandoned that endeavor and toured Europe for several more months.

For our own part, we regard [Helena Blavatsky] neither as the mouthpiece of hidden seers, nor as a mere vulgar adventuress; we think that she has achieved a title to permanent remembrance as one of the most accomplished, ingenious, and interesting impostors in history.

—Richard Hodgson

In July 1873, Blavatsky left Europe and immigrated to the United States, where she settled in New York City. While in the U.S., she dabbled further in the Spiritualist movement, which had recently gained a large American following, investigating psychic phenomena, attending lectures, and becoming acquainted with other devotees. It was while investigating the site of a reported Spiritualist phenomenon in 1874 that she met Henry Steel Olcott (1832–1907), a lawyer and journalist as well as a follower of the Spiritualist movement. They began working together, writing and translating articles on Spiritualism and related subjects. Their working collaboration was to continue for most of the rest of Blavatsky's life.

Blavatsky soon began to turn away from orthodox Spiritualism when she revealed that she was communicating telepathically with an organization of learned men living in Egypt, the Brotherhood of Luxor, who were serving as her spiritual mentors. She convinced Olcott of the presence of the Brotherhood and helped turn him away from conventional Spiritualism as well. On September 8, 1875, they, along with an American named William Judge, established the Theosophical Society which was based on the teaching she was receiving from the Brotherhood. The date of the Society's inauguration, November 17, 1875, was later used as the organization's official founding date.

The teachings of the Society, termed theosophy, were a blend of Buddhism, Hinduism, and the occult. Opened to those of any nationality, race, or religious faith, the Society's aims were no less than the discovery and teaching of the truths that govern the Universe. Theosophists believe that all religions have the same goal, the pursuit of truth, and the Society's motto is "there is no religion higher than truth."

At the time of the Society's founding, Blavatsky was working on her first major literary work, *Isis Unveiled*, which was published in September 1877. In keeping with the tenets of theosophy, the book was an attempt to uncover the eternal truth in the workings of science and theology, themes she would more fully explore in her later work, *The Secret Doctrine*.

In the spring of 1878, Blavatsky became the first Russian woman to be naturalized in the United States, only to move to India with Olcott in December of that year. Shortly after their arrival, they began publishing a journal, the *Theosophist*, on oriental arts and philosophy as well as theosophical matters. Together they traveled around India and Ceylon (now Sri Lanka) for several years, conducting seances, meeting with spiritual leaders and establishing branches of the Society across the region. Blavatsky and Olcott strove to work among both the Indian population and the British citizenry who were there as part of the Raj. The fact that they worked and socialized with the Indian people was highly unusual and controversial, and Blavatsky made well-known her dislike of the English tendency to remain isolated from the native population.

Blavatsky's fame was based not only on her inclusive theosophist ideology, however, but also on the miraculous events that she often seemed to precipitate. Letters from her spiritual guides, the India-based Brotherhood of the Mahatmas who had displaced the Egyptian Luxor Brotherhood, fell into recipients' laps from the ceiling; invisible bells chimed in her presence; and everyday objects appeared in unusual places as symbolic messages from the Brotherhood to their followers. On December 19, 1882, Olcott and Blavatsky established the headquarters of the Theosophical Society in Adyar, just outside of

Bombay, where it remains to this day. This international Society quickly spawned independent branches in countries around the world, including the U.S., England, India, and Australia.

Blavatsky's time in India was not an unblemished success, however. She was diagnosed with Bright's Disease, a painful kidney ailment that was to plague her for years, and she was professionally denounced by Swami Dayananda Saravasti, an Indian reform advocate whom she and Olcott had wanted very much as an associate. There were also charges that one of the letters written by the most prolific corresponding Brother, Koot Hoomi, was in fact plagiarized from a lecture published in the British journal *Banner of Light*. Nevertheless, in the early 1880s, Blavatsky and the Society developed an international following numbering in the thousands.

Blavatsky returned to Europe in February 1884, staying first in France, then in Germany. Around this time, one of her former disciples, **Emma Coulomb**, began claiming publicly that Blavatsky and the Society were a fraud and that the events Blavatsky claimed were the work of the Mahatmas were in fact staged by Blavatsky herself, with Coulomb's help. Coulomb was promptly dismissed from the Society for her accusations. However, her claims came to the attention of the newly established Society for Psychical Research (SPR), formed specifically for the study of alleged psychic phenomena, and, in May 1884, the SPR launched an investigation into the Society's activities.

While somewhat contemptuous of the Society in general and Olcott in particular, the SPR's preliminary report dismissed the fraud charges. However, subsequent findings, released in December 1885 as the so-called "Hodgson Report" determined that the Society had in fact been engaged in fraudulent practices. Furthermore, the report's author, Richard Hodgson, hypothesized that Blavatsky was a Russian spy, an allegation that had haunted her throughout her time in India. The claim was a specious one and only undermined the report's credibility on the fraud charges. (In 1986, the SPR partially retracted Hodgson's findings.)

Despite its spotty conclusions, the Hodgson Report served to erode the Theosophical Society's waning credibility, and Society membership, already declining, continued to fall. Furthermore, Blavatsky's personal history was beginning to emerge. During her years as a spiritual leader, she had either ignored much of her past, including her marriage and the birth of her son, or blatantly falsified it. The disclosures caused Blavatsky's personal credibility to dissolve along with that of the Society. After a brief, and ultimately final, visit to India in late 1884, Blavatsky traveled about Europe from 1885 to 1887, staying eventually in Würzburg, Germany, and Ostend, Belgium. She was in the initial phases of writing what was to become *The Secret Doctrine*, and she remained comparatively out of the public eye for several years.

It was during the mid-1880s that her relationship with Olcott, always somewhat rocky, began to seriously unravel. She officially severed connections between the Indian-based Society, which was led by Olcott, and the branch in London, which she could better control from her new base in Europe. In May 1887, Blavatsky moved to London and became a permanent resident of England. Despite ongoing accusations of wrongdoing and occasional falls from public favor, both the Society and Blavatsky retained a substantial following. She accepted in her London home a steady stream of visitors who were seeking spiritual guidance, among them the poet William Butler Yeats, the future Mahatma and Indian leader Mohandas Gandhi, and the socialist and reformer ***Annie Besant**. That year, Blavatsky again sought to ensure that the power in the Society would remain focused on her. She personally established a new London branch, called the Blavatsky Lodge of the Theosophical Society, in direct competition to the already existing branch run by former disciple Alfred Sinnett. She also began publishing a new journal, *Lucifer*, to compete with *The Theosophist*.

In the summer of 1888, Blavatsky consolidated her control of the Society still further by creating a so-called Esoteric Section within the Lodge. The Section was to have 12 hand-picked members who would receive personal instruction from Blavatsky. Olcott's power in European theosophical circles was by now virtually nonexistent, and he chose to focus his proselytizing efforts in India, where he remained for close to 20 years until his death in 1907.

It was in London that Blavatsky finished *The Secret Doctrine*, her most wide-ranging and influential book. The two-volume work was published in October 1888. *The Secret Doctrine* continued Blavatsky's efforts to explore and explain the universal truth, and stated as part of that truth that all existing spirit and matter form an omnipresent reality, that there exists a universal evolutionary cycle of change, and that all human souls form part of a great oversoul. Blavatsky also published two minor works in

1889: *The Voice of Silence*, a prose poem that was meant to serve as a daily spiritual guide, and *The Key to Theosophy*, a short accessible collection of the teachings found in *Isis Unveiled* and *The Secret Doctrine*.

Much of the last few years of Blavatsky's life were spent grooming the newly converted Annie Besant to replace Blavatsky as the Society's leader after her death. During these years, Besant gradually became Blavatsky's only confidante, particularly after Blavatsky's relations with Olcott had turned to virtual enmity. In September 1889, Besant was made the editor of *Lucifer*, and, in January 1890, she became the head of the Blavatsky Lodge. Besant had become so integral to the Society that in the summer of 1890 her home was made not only the Society's headquarters but also Blavatsky's residence.

One of Blavatsky's last efforts was the establishment in August 1890 of a Home for Working Women with funds donated anonymously to the Society. However, she was growing weaker, losing ground to the numerous ailments that had plagued her throughout her life, including edema, Bright's Disease, and rheumatism, which were compounded by years of overwork. In early May 1891, she caught influenza, which she was unable to shake. She died a few days later, on May 8, 1891, at age 59. To this day, members of the Theosophical Society commemorate Blavatsky and her life's work on White Lotus Day, the anniversary of her death.

SOURCES:

Blavatsky, H.P. *H.P. Blavatsky Collected Writings.* 14 vols. Compiled by Boris de Zirkoff. Wheaton, IL: The Theosophical Publishing House, 1950–91.

Carlson, Maria. *No Religion Higher than Truth.* Princeton, NJ: Princeton University Press, 1993.

Cranston, Sylvia. *HPB: The Extraordinary Life and Influence of Helena Blavatsky, Founder of the Modern Theosophical Movement.* NY: Putnam, 1993.

Harris, Ian, et al. *Contemporary Religions: A World Guide.* The High, Harlow, Essex: Longman Group UK, 1992.

Meade, Marion. *Madame Blavatsky: The Woman Behind the Myth.* NY: Putnam, 1980.

Murphet, Charles. *When Daylight Comes: A Biography of Helena Petrovna Blavatsky.* Wheaton, IL: The Theosophical Publishing House, 1975.

Nicholson, Shirley. "Theosophical Society," in *Encyclopedia of Religion.* NY: Macmillan, 1987, pp. 464–65.

SUGGESTED READING:

It is important to note that works on Blavatsky tend to be either obsequious or unrelentingly harsh. The following were written by Blavatsky's contemporaries:

Coulomb, Emma. *Some Account of My Intercourse with Madame Blavatsky.* London: Elliot Stock, 1885.

Olcott, Henry Steel. *Old Diary Leaves.* NY: Putnam, 1895.

Sinnett, Alfred. *Incidents in the Life of H.P. Blavatsky.* NY: Ayer, 1976 (originally published 1886).

OTHER SECONDARY WORKS:

Endersby, Victor A. *The Hall of Magic Mirrors.* NY: Carlton Press, 1969.

Kingsland, William. *The Real H.P. Blavatsky: A Study in Theosophy and a Memoir of a Great Soul.* London: John M. Watkins, 1928.

Symonds, John. *Madame Blavatsky: Medium and Magician.* London: Odhams Press, 1959.

THE HODGSON REPORT CONTROVERSY WAS PLAYED OUT IN THE FOLLOWING:

Society for Psychical Research, "Report of the Committee Appointed to Investigate Phenomena Connected with the Theosophical Society," in *Proceedings of the Society for Phychical Research.* No. 3. December 1885.

Harrison, Vernon. "J'Accuse: An Examination of the Hodgson Report of 1885," in *Journal of the Society for Phychical Research.* Vol. 53. April 1986.

Susan Brazier, freelance writer, Ottawa, Ontario, Canada

Blazejowski, Blaze (b. 1957).

See Blazejowski, Carol.

Blazejowski, Carol (1957—)

American basketball player and first woman to be awarded the Margaret Wade Trophy (1978). *Name variations: Blaze Blazejowski. Born Carol Blazejowski in Cranford, New Jersey, in 1957; attended Montclair State University.*

"One of the best," said fellow teammate ***Nancy Lieberman-Cline** of 5'10" Blaze Blazejowski, who played for Montclair State College in Upper Montclair, New Jersey. During her college career, the three-time All-American Blazejowski amassed 3,199 points, won the first **Margaret Wade** Trophy in 1978, and set a record of 52 points in a single game at Madison Square Garden on March 6, 1977, before a crowd of 12,000. "Talk about being in the zone, that was the epitome," recalled Blazejowski. "In the first half, I was terrible. Early in the second half, I got a quick fourth foul. We were losing and my coach said: 'I can't pull you, just take jump shots. Don't drive to the basket.' I never missed after that."

Blazejowski was a member of the silver-medal winning U.S. team at the World University Games in Bulgaria in 1977 but missed out on the 1980 Summer Olympics in Moscow because of President Jimmy Carter's Russian boycott. Instead, she signed with the New Jersey Jems in 1981 but played for only one season; the league went bankrupt. In 1984, she joined the New York Club of the Women's American Basketball Association. A decade later, in 1994, Blazejowski was inducted into the Basketball Hall of Fame and later into the New Jersey Sports Hall of Fame.

In 1991, Blazejowski became director of the Women's Basketball Development for National Basketball Association (NBA) Properties. Her efforts to build a women's professional basketball league proved fruitful, for in 1997 she was named vice president and general manager for the newly formed New York Liberty of the WNBA.

Bleibtreu, Hedwig (1868–1958)

Austrian actress who had a long and distinguished career as one of the greatest tragediennes in German-speaking Central Europe. *Born in Linz, Austria, on December 23, 1868; died in Pötzleinsdorf, a suburb of Vienna, on January 25, 1958; daughter of Sigmund Bleibtreu (1819–1894, an actor) and Amalie (Hirsch) Bleibtreu (1835–1917, an actress); sister of actress* ***Maximiliane Bleibtreu*** *(1870–1923); married Alexander Rompler, in 1900; married Max Paulsen, in 1911.*

Began career in Vienna (1892); became member of Vienna's Burgtheater (1893); began acting in motion pictures (1923); acted in the Salzburg Festivals (1920s–1930s); received countless awards including the Burgtheater Ring (1930).

One of Austria's greatest actresses, Hedwig Bleibtreu was born on December 23, 1868, in Linz, Austria, into the most prominent acting dynasty of late 19th-century Central Europe. Her father Sigmund Bleibtreu (1819–1894) was a man of many talents, whose career included years as a military officer, painter, and playwright as well as a highly respected actor. Immensely popular with the audiences of the day, in 1882 he received the honor of acting in the Hofburg, the imperial palace of the Habsburg dynasty. For many years, he was the acclaimed artistic director of the Josefstadt Theater. Hedwig's mother **Amalie Bleibtreu** (1835–1917) was also a distinguished actress, much beloved for decades by Viennese theatergoers under the stage name of "Hybl." Hedwig's sister Maximiliane also established a strong reputation on the stages of Graz and Vienna, and was best known as a "master of masks."

Hedwig Bleibtreu studied acting at the Vienna Conservatory, completing her training in 1884. After making her stage debut in Augsburg, Germany, she returned in 1887 to her native Austria, starring at the theater in Brunn, Moravia. The next several years were busy ones as her reputation as a young star rapidly grew,

Carol Blazejowski

and she appeared on the stage in Berlin, Kassel, and other German and Austrian cities. By 1893, she was performing on the stage of Vienna's Burgtheater, the pinnacle of theatrical life in German-speaking Central Europe, and her association with that theater would last almost half a century. In the early years of her career, Bleibtreu played sentimental and youthful heroic roles. In later decades, she excelled in the roles of mothers and mature women in drawing-room comedies. By 1906, when she received the signal honor of imperial recognition as a *Hofschauspielerin*, she dominated the great Goethe and Schiller roles of Klärchen, Joan of Arc, Elisabeth (in both "Maria Stuart" and "Don Carlos"), and Iphigenie. She also excelled in portraying several Shakespearean roles, including that of Ophelia. Over the many decades that she performed at the Burgtheater, she took on approximately 200 roles.

Bleibtreu survived the many catastrophes that befell her native Austria during World Wars I and II: inflation, dictatorship, and the emigration or death of colleagues who were Jewish or anti-Nazi. As one of the pillars of the Viennese stage for several generations, she received numerous honors and awards, including honorary citizenship of Vienna, the Emperor Franz Joseph Golden Cross of Achievement, the Goethe Medal for Art and Science, and—very important in a title-conscious culture—the designation "Professor." At the very end of her career, Bleibtreu's image was immortalized for future generations in the motion picture *The Third Man.* After one of the most extraordinary careers in the history of the German-language stage, Hedwig Bleibtreu died in Pötzleinsdorf, a suburb of Vienna, on January 25, 1958.

SOURCES:

Doublier, Gerda. "Hedwig Bleibtreu," in *Neue Österreichische Biographie.* Vol. 16, pp. 132–139.

———. *Hedwig Bleibtreu: Ein Beitrag zur Geschichte des Burgtheaters.* Vienna: Gerold, 1933.

——— and Walter Zeleny. *Hedwig Bleibtreu: Wesen und Welt einer grossen Burgschauspielerin, zu deren 80. Geburtstag am 23. Dezember 1948.* Vienna: Donau-Verlag, 1948.

Friedmann, Mitzi. *Hedwig Bleibtreu: Das Portrait einer Schauspielerin.* Vienna: Augartenverlag Stephan Szabo, 1933.

John Haag, Associate Professor,
University of Georgia, Athens, Georgia

Bleibtrey, Ethelda M. (1902–1978)

American swimmer and Olympic gold medalist. *Born in Waterford, New York, on February 27, 1902; died in May 1978; lived in New York City; married; children: a daughter who was also a swimmer.*

Won Olympic gold medals in 100-meter freestyle, 300-meter freestyle, and the 4x100 freestyle relay in Antwerp (1920); won the U.S. national championship in the 100 yards (1921).

Ethelda Bleibtrey won three gold medals in the three swimming events allowed to women in the 1920 Olympics held in Antwerp, Belgium. The first American woman to win a gold medal in her sport, she took the 100- and 300-meter freestyle, and with teammates ➧ **Margaret Woodbridge**, ➧ **Frances Schroth**, and ➧ **Irene Guest** won a team gold in the 4x100 relay at a time of 5:11.6. All three of Bleibtrey's winning times were world records. A year later, she won the U.S. national championship in the 100 yards with a time of 1:03.4 (without the benefit of starting blocks and modern turns), a record that would hold for 11 years. On a public beach, her fame, as well as her thin, one-piece tank suit, drew crowds.

Previously, however, Bleibtrey had been barred from swimming in the Hudson River in her hometown of Waterford, New York, because of what she called her "perfectly respectable bathing suit." The irony was not lost on her when she was asked "to exhibit in the same town after I had become well-known, at which time I wore a silk racing suit which was acceptable all over the world but not in Waterford, New York, unless the rest of the world liked it too." She retired undefeated in 1922 and wrote articles on swimming for *Liberty*, *McCall's*, and *New York World.*

Bleschamps, Madame de (1778–1855).

See Bonaparte, Alexandrine.

Blessington, countess of (1789–1849).

See Blessington, Marguerite.

Blessington, Marguerite, Countess of (1789–1849)

Irish author who published a number of popular novels of fashionable life and for many years presided over the most brilliant salon in London. *Name variations: Marguerite Gardiner; Marguerite Power; Lady Blessington; Margaret, Sally. Born Marguerite Power on September 1, 1789, at Knockbrit, near Clonmel, County Tipperary, Ireland; died in Paris, France, on June 4, 1849; daughter of Edward (or Edmund) Power (a landowner, magistrate and newspaper editor) and Ellen (Sheehy) Power; educated at home and for a short period at boarding school; married Captain Maurice St. Leger Farmer, in 1804 (died 1817); married Charles John Gardiner, 1st earl of Blessington, in 1817 (died 1829); no children.*

Published first book (1822), and in same year embarked with husband on a lengthy European tour, visiting Italy and France; following husband's death (1829), returned to London in reduced financial circumstances; for many years, supported herself and her partner, Count d'Orsay, by her writing, while entertaining the leading figures in the arts and politics at her home, Gore House in Kensington; endured acute financial difficulties (mid-1840s); fled to Paris to escape debtors (1849), dying there shortly afterwards.

Selected writings: The Magic Lantern, or Sketches of Scenes in the Metropolis *(1822);* Grace Cassidy, or the Repealers *(1833);* Conversations with Lord Byron *(1834);* The Two Friends *(1835);* Flowers of Loveliness *and* Confessions of an Elderly Gentleman *(1836);* The Victims of Society *(1837);* Gems of Beauty *and* Confessions of an Elderly Lady *(1838);* The Governess, Desultory Thoughts and Reflections *and* The Idler in Italy, *Vols I and II (1839);* The Idler in Italy, *vol III, and* The Belle of a Season *(1840);* The Idler in France *(1841);* Lottery of Life and Other Tales *(1842);* Strathern *(1843);* The Memoirs of a Femme de Chambre *and* Lionel Deerhurst *(1846);* Marmaduke Herbert *(1847).*

However melodramatic the plots of Lady Blessington's novels, few could have been more unlikely than the story of her own life. Born in poverty and obscurity in the Irish countryside, she was a plain child who became a dazzling beauty. Married against her will at 14 to a vicious husband, whom she left after just a few months, she went on to marry into the aristocracy and to become London's most celebrated hostess. Despite her scandalous reputation, her wit, intelligence and generosity made her the confidante of many of the most eminent men of her day, and her close friends included the poet Lord, George Gordon Byron, the novelist Charles Dickens, and the future prime minister, Benjamin Disraeli. Renowned for the extravagance of her lifestyle, she was also an indefatigable worker, who supported herself and her establishment by a constant stream of literary works, which included novels, travel books, and memoirs, as well as journalism. Nevertheless, it is clear that the disruption and unhappiness of her early years left an indelible mark on her, in her unconventional private life, in her improvidence and compulsive generosity, and in her need for admiration and attention. Ultimately, she was to find herself bankrupt and ignored by many of those whom she had regarded as her friends. Even in that final disaster, however, she retained the courage, optimism, and sense of style which had enabled her to make her first, unlikely escape, to reshape her identity, and to shine for so many years as "the gorgeous Lady Blessington."

Marguerite Power was born in 1789, at Knockbrit, near the town of Clonmel in County Tipperary, one of several children of Edward Power, an impoverished landowner, and **Ellen Sheehy Power**. A gentle and ineffectual woman, Ellen Power was too weak, according to Blessington's biographer, J. Fitzgerald Molloy, "to influence her husband or avert his ruin" or, indeed, to have much impact on the life of her gifted and strong-willed daughter. Edward Power was an extremely handsome man, with a reputation as a dandy, known as "Beau Power" or "Shiver the frills" to his neighbors. His character was considerably less attractive than his appearance. Described by **Frances Gerard** as "hasty in temper, extravagant in habits, fond of play, horses, wine and revelry, inattentive to business, improvident in expenditure," Power's career was punctuated by increasingly desperate efforts to recoup his financial losses. Although born a Catholic, he converted to Protestantism, almost certainly in the hope of improving his fortunes, and for a time served as a magistrate. Political and agrarian unrest was currently rife in the countryside, and Power became notorious for his brutal treatment of suspected law-breakers; on one occasion, indeed, he was actually tried for murder but was acquitted. He subsequently became editor of a local newspaper, the *Clonmel Gazette*, but this, in common with all of his schemes, was unsuccessful. Meanwhile, his family suffered financially as a result of these successive failures, and emotionally as a result of his ill-temper, although his daughter was to inherit both his extravagance and his expansive personality.

As the only plain child in an outstandingly handsome family, the young Marguerite asserted herself by her precocious intelligence and by her storytelling skills. Her education was apparently rudimentary, although she did spend a short period at a boarding school. However, her stay there was marred by humiliating delays in the payment of her fees, and her education was cut short when her father found the expense of a daughter's education insupportable. She re-

Woodbridge, Margaret (b. 1902)
American swimmer. Born in 1902.

In the 1920 Antwerp Olympics, Margaret Woodbridge was awarded a silver medal in the 300-meter freestyle and a gold in the 4x100-meter freestyle relay.

Schroth, Frances (b. 1893)
American swimmer. Born April 11, 1893.

In 1920, in Antwerp, Belgium, Frances Schroth took bronze medals in the 300-meter freestyle and 100-meter freestyle and a gold in the 4x100-meter freestyle relay.

Guest, Irene (1900–1979)
American swimmer. Born on July 22, 1900; died in 1979.

Irene Guest won the silver medal in the 100-meter freestyle and a gold in the 4x100 freestyle relay in the Antwerp Olympic games of 1920.

Marguerite, Countess of Blessington

turned home to yet another financial crisis, and her father, by now deeply in debt, saw in her a new opportunity to recoup his own fortunes. Her childhood plainness had disappeared, and, as an extremely beautiful girl, she had already attracted the admiration of a number of officers at the nearby army garrison.

In 1804, when she was just 14, Marguerite received an offer of marriage from one of these officers. Captain Maurice St. Leger Farmer's reputation was generally admitted to be appalling, and Marguerite herself was strongly opposed to the match, but her father forced her to accept, or according to some accounts, actually sold her to Farmer. According to Blessington's own version of events, her husband quickly proved himself to be a sadist, prone to periodic fits of insanity and to "ungovernable outbursts of passion," who locked her in her room while he was away, and was physically violent towards her. After just three months, Marguerite fled to the safety of her parents' home.

The marriage was clearly at an end; a formal separation was arranged, and shortly afterwards Farmer was forced to leave the army in disgrace. Subsequently, he joined the East India Company and went abroad, leaving Marguerite to make the best of, what was for a woman, an extremely difficult situation. Unable to remarry, traumatized by her experiences, she received little sympathy from her family: her father's financial circumstances were as unstable as ever, and her parents regarded her as an impediment to their other daughters' chances of finding suitable marriage partners. At some point, she left Tipperary and by 1809 was living in Dublin. From there, she moved on to London, where she became the mistress of Charles Gardiner, first earl of Blessington. Immensely rich, with estates in Ireland, a town house in London, and an income of £30,000 a year, Gardiner was also extravagantly generous. Having reportedly paid £10,000 to her previous lover, he now lavished gifts on Marguerite. More unusually, he was willing to marry her, and in 1817 this became possible, when Farmer suddenly died as the result of a fall from a window during a drinking bout. A few months later, on February 16, 1818, Marguerite became the countess of Blessington. The combination of her husband's wealth and her own beauty, charm, and intelligence quickly established her as one of London's leading hostesses, with an eclectic guest-list, which included politicians such as Lords Castlereagh and Palmerston, actors such as John Kemble and Charles Mathews, and the artist, Sir Thomas Lawrence, an old acquaintance, who in 1809 had painted the first portrait of the young Marguerite.

In 1822, the Blessingtons left England, with the intention of making an extended tour of France and Italy, and taking with them an entourage which included Marguerite's sister, **Mary Ann Power**, and Count Alfred d'Orsay, a handsome and aristocratic dilettante, and a well-known figure in London society. Arriving at Genoa, Lady Blessington eagerly anticipated her meeting with the most celebrated English poet of the day. Lord Byron was presently living in the city, having been forced to leave England following the breakdown of his marriage, but the scandalous rumors about him merely enhanced his glamorous image in the eyes of his devotees, among them Marguerite, who confided her excitement to her diary. "Am I indeed in the same town with Byron? And tomorrow I may perhaps behold him!!!!! I never felt before the same impatient longing to see anyone known only to me by his works. I hope," she added, on a more prosaic note, "he may not be fat . . . for a fat poet is an anomaly, in my opinion." In common with most of the contemporary literary public, the countess identified the man with his work; having met him, she professed herself disappointed by his failure to meet her "preconceived notion of the melancholy poet," finding him "witty, sarcastic and lively enough" to have written *Don Juan*, but finding little trace in him of his romantic hero, Childe Harold. No prude herself, she was startled by "the perfect *abandon* with which he converses to recent acquaintances, on subjects which even friends would think too delicate for discussion," and she continued throughout their acquaintance to be confused by his apparent inconsistency. As she complained, "the day after he has awakened the deepest interest, his manner of scoffing at himself and others destroys it, and one feels as if one had been duped into a sympathy, only to be laughed at." However, she conceded that "there is something so striking in his whole appearance, that could not be mistaken for an ordinary person," and she was quickly won over by his attentions to her, and by his behavior to others: the local people, she noted, "seem all to know his face, and to like him; and many recount their affairs, as if they were sure of his sympathy."

Byron for his part enjoyed the company of "Miladi," whose conversation was both witty and stimulating, and whom he considered "very pretty." However, he did not fall in love with her. As he reassured his mistress **Countess Guiccioli**, who was wary of this suspected rival, "what little communication I had with this new Goddess of Discord was literally literary." Besides, he went on, he had reached his "years of discretion and would much rather fall into the sea than in love any day of the week." Perhaps, too, he suspected that beneath the "flippancy" which he deplored in Marguerite, was a shrewdness which detected the insecurity underlying his pose of the haughty noble. As she remarked, with the perspicacity of one whose own social status was decidedly precarious, "she had never met anyone with so decided a taste for aristocracy," a vanity which "resembles more the pride of a parvenu than the calm dignity of an ancient aristocrat." Similarly astute was her comment that "Byron is a person who, without reflection, would form engagements which when condemned by his friends and advisers, he would gladly get out of . . . without reflecting on the humiliation such desertion must inflict."

However, entertaining her company, Byron might well have found such perception uncomfortable. Nevertheless, the Blessingtons' departure for Rome in May 1823 was an emotional occasion for all concerned. According to Marguerite, Byron, who was shortly to leave for Greece, "had a conviction that he should never return," and "yielding to this presentiment, made scarcely an effort to check the tears that flowed plentifully down his cheeks." However, this account of their parting, from Lady Blessington's *Journal of Conversations with Lord Byron* (1834) may have owed more to hindsight than to accuracy—Byron did, indeed, die in Greece in the following year, but his friend, John Cam Hobhouse, on reading this version of events, felt that such behavior was entirely uncharacteristic of him. In general, Byron's biographers have regarded the *Conversations* as an essential source on the poet's character, but one which has to be approached with some caution, since Marguerite tended to present the facts in the light most favorable to herself.

Guiccioli, Teresa (c. 1801–1873)

Italian noblewoman. *Name variations: Countess Guiccioli. Pronunciation: GWEE-cho-lee. Born Teresa Gamba in Italy around 1801; died in Rome on March 26, 1873; daughter of Count Gamba; married Count Guiccioli, around 1817; married Marquis de Boissy, in 1851.*

An Italian woman, best known for her relationship with Lord Byron, Teresa Gamba married Count Guiccioli when she was 16 and met Byron a few months later. After about a year, the count objected to her liaison with Byron, and Teresa returned to her father's house. From then until Byron's death in 1824, however, she maintained her relations with him. Following his death, she is said to have returned to her husband. In 1851, she married the Marquis de Boissy and in 1868 published, in French, *My Recollections of Lord Byron.*

> Friends are the thermometers by which we may judge the temperatures of our fortunes.
>
> —**Lady Blessington**

Arriving in Rome, the Blessingtons set up house at the Palazzo Nigroni, and a visit to their salon became an essential part of every English traveler's visit to the city. D'Orsay was by now an established member of their household and, during their stay in Rome, married Lady **Harriet Gardiner**, Lord Blessington's 15-year-old daughter by his first marriage. The marriage was purely one of convenience and unsurprisingly, given the gulf of age and experience between the two partners, lasted only a few months. Throughout this period, the d'Orsays lived under the Blessingtons' roof, and this arrangement continued after the breakdown of the marriage, despite continuing gossip about the count's relationship with Lady Blessington.

In 1829, the whole party moved on to Paris, where they intended to stay for some time, and where they established themselves in their customary splendor. Lord Blessington rented Marshal Ney's magnificent town house and fitted it up in the most luxurious style: as Marguerite wrote to a friend, "a queen could desire nothing better." Shortly afterwards, however, Lord Blessington, then aged 46, died suddenly of an apoplexy, leaving his affairs in utter confusion. He had no heir, his only legitimate son having died a few years previously, and, as a result of his extravagant way of life, his annual income had declined from £30,000 in 1818 to £23,000 at the time of his death. Marguerite's own income was now just £2,000 per annum, which, while adequate to support her, was far too little to fund the lifestyle to which she had become accustomed. Moreover, Lord Blessington had left behind him a tangle of debts and litigation, which was to harry her for the rest of her life.

Lady Blessington stayed on in Paris during the Revolution of 1830, returning to England in the following year, in company with d'Orsay. She quickly resumed her position at the center of London's literary and political worlds: "Everybody goes to Lady Blessington," noted Hayden in his diary. Her guests, who included the most notable figures in the worlds of politics and the arts, were drawn not just by the lavishness of the entertainment offered, but also by their hostess' personality. Now in her 40s, she remained as charming and as attractive as ever: one of her contemporaries noted her beauty and vivacity, "a voice merry and sad by turns, but always musical, and manners of the most unpretending elegance . . . one of the most lovely and fascinating women I have ever seen." However, others were less generous: the diarist Charles Greville, for instance, complained about the standard of conversation, and blamed this on the hostess, whom he described as "vulgar, ignorant and commonplace," her talk "never enriched by a particle of knowledge, or enlivened by a ray of genius or imagination." Respectable society, too, was outraged by her scandalous private life. In about 1836, she set up house openly with d'Orsay, and while the couple entertained the most brilliant and cultivated men in London at Gore House in Kensington, few women would risk entering such an irregular establishment.

Financial responsibility for the maintenance of Gore House, the lavish hospitality, and d'Orsay's personal expenses rested entirely on Lady Blessington's literary efforts. In 1822, she had published her first work, *The Magic Lantern*, and in the same year, *Sketches and Fragments*. Now, with her income from her husband's estate much diminished, authorship became a financial necessity rather than an amusing pastime, and over 15 years, she produced 18 books, many of them multi-volume novels. While some of these, such as her first novel, *Grace Cassidy* (1833) had an Irish background, most were set in fashionable London society, many of the characters supposedly being based on celebrated individuals. As the *Edinburgh Review* remarked, her literary works "are strongly characterised by the social phenomena of the times. . . . The characters that move and breathe throughout them are the actual persons of the great world, and the reflections with which they abound belong to the philosophy of one who has well examined the existing manners." Her own eventful life was reflected in a number of her works: many of her heroines, for instance, were the victims of tyrannical or cruel men. She also published accounts of her travels, in *The Idler in Italy* (1839–40) and *The Idler in France* (1841), and of her friendship with Lord Byron, in *Conversations* (1834). Although financial necessity dictated that she write with an eye to popularity rather than literary excellence, the *Review* did note some development in her work over the course of her career, observing that "in her writing there has been a marked and progressive improvement, as if by the self-study that belongs to application, powers previously unknown to herself had been gradually developed."

For a time, her novels, with their dramatic incident and vivid description, were extremely popular, particularly with subscribers to the new circulating libraries, and brought her a substantial annual income of between £2,000 and £3,000. These earnings, however, were not sufficient to meet the expenses which she and d'Orsay were incurring, and their debts mounted steadily: in 1841, the count's liabilities totalled £107,000, and, in order to escape his creditors, he was for a time forced to confine himself to Gore House. Lady Blessington herself lost a considerable amount of money when the publisher of a society periodical with which she was associated died insolvent, and her literary earnings declined as her books began to go out of fashion. Her troubles were intensified in 1845 by the outbreak of the Great Famine in Ireland, which seriously diminished her income from her husband's estates there. The couple's financial difficulties were now acute. Dogged by creditors' demands and haunted by the fear of imprisonment for debt, they were now little better than prisoners in their own house.

Finally, in April 1849, under immediate threat of arrest, d'Orsay fled to Paris, taking only his valet and one portmanteau, to be followed a few days later by Marguerite. In the following month, Gore House and all its contents, including Lawrence's early portrait of her, was put up for sale. The affair attracted enormous public interest: 20,000 curious sightseers visited the house over the three viewing days, and the auction itself lasted 13 days. It was attended by many of Lady Blessington's former guests, who now clamored to bid for her belongings, with little apparent feeling for the woman whose hospitality they had enjoyed on so many occasions. According to the countess' French manservant who was present, and who wrote her a report on the event, the only person to show any emotion was the novelist William Makepeace Thackeray, who, he observed, had tears in his eyes as he watched the dispersal of so much magnificence.

The sale of Gore House and its contents fetched a total of £13,000, and, after settlement of the creditors' demands, a balance of £11 was paid to Lady Blessington. Characteristically, and at the age of 60, she regarded the ending of one disastrous chapter in her life as freeing her to begin another, and immediately began planning the recovery of her fortunes. She and d'Orsay established themselves in an apartment off the Champs Élysees, and she hoped to benefit from the fact that Prince Louis Napoleon, who during his exile in England had been among her guests, was now head of the French government. She was to be disappointed in this: the prince-president proved unhelpful, although, as Blessington did not hesitate to remind him, his own situation in a volatile political climate was hardly more secure than her own. Meeting him by chance in the street, she parried his enquiry as to whether she was intending to stay long in Paris with the retort, "I don't know—are you?"

For Lady Blessington, however, there was to be no new chance. Just two months after her arrival in Paris, on June 4, 1849, she died very suddenly in her apartment. D'Orsay, who survived her for three years, was ostentatiously grief-stricken and turned his energies to designing a monument for erection over her grave at St. Germain, where he himself also intended to be buried. The grandiose memorial bore little relation to the woman whom it commemorated, but the inscription on it, composed by her friend, the novelist Walter Savage Landor, comes closer to capturing her essential spirit. "Underneath lies all that could be interred of a once beautiful woman. Her own genius she cultivated with zeal, in others she fostered its growth with equal assiduity. The benefits she conferred she could conceal, but not her talents. Elegant in her hospitality to strangers, she was charitable to all." In its honesty and generosity, it is a fitting tribute to a courageous and life-enhancing personality, whose gift was for life itself rather than for literature.

SOURCES:

Blackburne, E. Owens. *Illustrious Irishwomen.* London: Tinsley Brothers, 1877.

Gerard, Frances A. *Some Fair Hibernians.* London: Ward and Downey, 1897.

Marchand, Leslie A. *Byron: A Portrait.* London: John Murray, 1971.

Molloy, J. Fitzgerald. *The Most Gorgeous Lady Blessington.* London, 1896.

Shattock, Joanne, ed. *The Oxford Guide to British Women Writers.* Oxford University Press, 1993.

Todd, Janet, ed. *Dictionary of British Women Writers.* London: Routledge, 1989

SUGGESTED READING:

Adburgham, Alison. *The Silver Fork Novelists.* London: Constable, 1983.

Blessington, Lady. *Conversations of Lord Byron.* Edited by Ernest J. Lovell. Princeton, 1968.

Madden, R.R. *The Literary Life and Correspondence of the Countess of Blessington.* London, 1855.

Sadleir, M. *Blessington Dorsay.* London: Constable, 1933.

Rosemary Raughter, freelance writer in women's history, Dublin, Ireland

Blind, Mathilde (1841–1896)

German-English poet. *Name variations: (pseudonym) Claude Lake. Born Mathilde Cohen in Mannheim, Germany, on March 21, 1841; died in London, England, on November 26, 1896, bequeathing her property to Newnham College, Cambridge; daughter of a banker named Cohen but assumed the name Blind from her stepfather Karl Blind (1826–1907); educated by her mother as well as at schools in England and in Zurich, Switzerland.*

Though the daughter of a banker named Cohen, Mathilde Blind assumed the last name of her stepfather Karl Blind. A political writer, Karl was an ardent supporter of 19th-century movements for the liberty and autonomy of struggling nationalities and one of the leaders of the Baden insurrection in 1848–49. Because of this, the family was compelled to take refuge in England, where Mathilde devoted herself to literature and the higher education of women.

Mathilde's first volume of poems (published in 1867 under the pseudonym Claude Lake) was dedicated to her friend, Italian nationalist Giuseppe Mazzini. A critical essay on the poetical works of Shelley in the *Westminster Review* appeared under her own name in 1870; it was based upon W.M. Rosetti's edition on the poet. In 1872, she wrote an account of the life and writings of Shelley, to serve as an introduction to a selection of his poems in the Tauchnitz edition. She later edited a selection of letters of Lord Byron with an introduction, and a selection of his poems with a memoir.

Blind won fame with her own writings, which included the longer poems: "The Heather on Fire" (1886), an indignant protest against the evictions in the Scottish Highlands; "The Ascent of Man," which traces the progress of man from his primitive condition; and "The Prophecy of St. Oran" (1881), based on a Scottish legend. She wrote biographies of George Eliot (***Mary Anne Evans**, 1883) and ***Madame Roland** (1886), and translated *The Memoirs of *Marie Bashkirtseff* (1890) and D.F. Strauss' *The Old Faith and the New* (1873–74). Her first novel *Tarantella* appeared in 1885.

Her minor poems, many of which are known as strong in feeling and admirable in form, entitled her to a distinguished place among the lyric poets of England. Blind was an ardent advocate of the betterment of the position of woman in society and the state. To this end, she worked and wrote for an improved education and against a one-sided morality for the sexes.

SUGGESTED READING:

A. Symons, ed. *The Poetical Works of Mathilde Blind.*

Bliss, Lillie P. (1864–1931).

See Rockefeller, Abby Aldrich for sidebar.

Bliss, Mary Elizabeth "Betty" (1824–1909).

See Taylor, Margaret Mackall for sidebar.

Bliss, Mildred Barnes (1879–1969)

American art collector, philanthropist and patron of the arts who, with her husband, commissioned and collected works of art for their home, Dumbarton Oaks. *Name variations: Mrs. Robert Woods Bliss. Born Mildred Barnes in New York City in 1879; died in Washington, D.C., on January 17, 1969; daughter of Demas Barnes and Anna Dorinda Blaksley; married Robert Woods Bliss (1875–1962, a diplomat).*

Born to great wealth as heir to a patent-medicine fortune, Mildred Barnes married diplomat Robert Woods Bliss and traveled with him to various postings, including Brussels, Leningrad, Paris, Stockholm and Buenos Aires. Following his retirement from the Foreign Service in 1933, Robert and Mildred Barnes concentrated on transforming their home in the Georgetown section of northwestern Washington D.C., Dumbarton Oaks, into a center of beauty and culture. The land, with a history that traced back to a 1702 grant, was a working farm well into the 19th century. The mansion was a part of American history, having belonged to John C. Calhoun when he was U.S. vice-president in the 1820s. By the time the Blisses purchased the home in 1920, the property had seen better days, but Mildred Bliss immediately set out to transform it. In 1922, she hired landscape gardener ***Beatrix Jones Farrand** (1872–1959) to oversee the task of bringing the grounds and gardens to a state of perfection. A follower of British landscape designer ***Gertrude Jekyll**, Farrand had earned a reputation designing landscapes at Princeton and Yale and, in 1899, had been among the founding members of the American Society of Landscape Architects. Together, Bliss and Farrand worked for 25 years to bring the most appropriate shrubs and trees to the garden of Dumbarton Oaks, agonizing over the correct sites, proportions and colors for every detail.

Enthusiastic, discriminating collectors of art, Mildred Bliss and her husband amassed a collection of pre-Columbian artifacts that has been termed nothing short of dazzling. Their collection of Byzantine objects, particularly coins and jewelry, is a treasure-trove of beauty and history. To make these superb collections useful to scholars, a library was assembled over the decades. In 1940, the Blisses gave Dumbarton Oaks to Harvard University so that the academic world could benefit from the history they had collected. Moving to a smaller house a few blocks away, they nonetheless arrived at the mansion virtually every day to meet with the world's most eminent scholars, who were invited to work at the Byzantine research center that Dumbarton Oaks had become. The collection is particularly strong in coins (with over 11,700 catalogued) and lead seals (13,000), objects of great importance for history and chronology.

The greatest library in the world related to Byzantium—over 90,000 volumes—is housed in the mansion. A fellowship program enables scholars to spend extended periods of time engaging in research at the center.

Functioning as patrons of the arts on a scale worthy of the Medicis, the Blisses made it possible for academic endeavors to thrive in breathtaking surroundings. Neither were other arts neglected. To celebrate their 30th wedding anniversary on April 14, 1938, they commissioned Igor Stravinsky to compose a work for the occasion. The result, his *Dumbarton Oaks Concerto*, had its premiere in the home's Florentine-style music salon. The conductor on this occasion was renowned music pedagogue ***Nadia Boulanger**. During World War II, Dumbarton Oaks achieved a place in world history when it was chosen by President Franklin D. Roosevelt as the site for a conference that led to the formation of the United Nations.

Bliss worked to the end of her long life to add treasures to Dumbarton Oaks. In 1963, after her husband's death, she built a graceful garden library to house what had evolved into a major book collection on landscape architecture. Until her last days, she could be seen there every Wednesday afternoon, entertaining rare book dealers as they displayed their latest discoveries before her discerning eyes. Mildred Barnes Bliss died in her Washington home, several blocks from her beloved Dumbarton Oaks, on January 17, 1969.

SOURCES:

"Mrs. Robert Woods Bliss, 89, Ambassador's Widow, Is Dead," in *The New York Times*. January 19, 1969, p. 73.

Olmert, Michael. "Dumbarton Oaks: stately link from past to the present," *Smithsonian*. Vol. 12, no. 2. May 1981, pp. 92–101.

Whitehill, Walter Muir. *Dumbarton Oaks: The History of a Georgetown House and Garden, 1800–1966*. Cambridge, MA: The Belknap Press of Harvard University Press, 1967.

John Haag, Associate Professor, University of Georgia, Athens, Georgia

Bliss, Mrs. Robert Woods (1879–1969).

See Bliss, Mildred.

Blistiche (fl. 268–264 BCE).

See Bilistiche.

Blitch, Iris Faircloth (1912–1993)

U.S. Representative, Democrat of Georgia, 84th–87th Congresses, January 3, 1955–January 3, 1963. *Born near Vidalia, Georgia, on April 25, 1912; died in San Diego, California, on August 19, 1993; interred in Pinelawn Cemetery, Homerville, Georgia; married Brooks E. Blitch, Jr., in October 1929.*

Iris Faircloth Blitch

Before her first unsuccessful run for the Georgia General Assembly in 1940, Iris Blitch worked with her husband Brooks E. Blitch, Jr., in several business endeavors, including pulpwood production and cattle and hog farming. She won election to the Georgia Senate in 1946 and to the state House of Representatives in 1948 but was defeated for reelection in 1950. She was elected to the state Senate again in 1952, at which time she also served the Democratic Party as secretary of the state executive committee and as a state representative on the National Committee. In 1954, she beat incumbent William M. Wheeler and began a tenure in the House of Representatives that would run four terms.

In March 1956, Blitch, along with 95 other senators and representatives from 11 southern states, signed the "Southern Manifesto," a pledge to work to reverse the 1954 Supreme Court decision outlawing racial segregation in public schools. Her tenure in the House was also marked by efforts to encourage the growth of industry throughout Southern Georgia (and to protect her own district's jute-packing trade), through support of an amendment to the 1930 Tariff Act which made it more difficult for foreign-made jute to enter the country. Blitch did not run for a fifth term due to ill health. In 1964, she left the Democratic Party to support Republican presidential candidate Senator Barry M. Goldwater.

SOURCES:

Office of the Historian. *Women in Congress, 1917–1990.* Commission on the Bicentenary of the U.S. House of Representatives, 1991.

Blixen, Karen (1885–1962).

See Dinesen, Isak.

Blodgett, Katharine Burr

(1898–1979)

American physicist who became the first woman research scientist hired by General Electric laboratories and the first woman to earn a Ph.D. in physics from Cambridge University, best known for her invention of non-reflecting glass. *Pronunciation: BLAH-jet. Born Katharine Burr Blodgett on January 10, 1898, in Schenectady, New York; died on October 12, 1979, in Schenectady; daughter of George Bedington (a patent attorney) and Katharine Buchanan (Burr) Blodgett; graduated Bryn Mawr, A.B., 1917, University of Chicago, M.S., 1918, Cambridge University, Ph.D., 1926; never married; no children.*

Hired by General Electric Research Laboratories, Schenectady, New York (1918); developed color gauge to measure extremely thin films (1933); invented non-reflecting glass (1938); devised smokescreen for Allied military use in World War II; received American Association of University Women's Annual Achievement Award (1945); won the Francis P. Garvan Medal for women in chemistry presented by the American Chemical Society, (1951); starred in the seventh edition of American Men of Science; won the Photographic Society of America Progress Medal; retired from General Electric (1963).

Selected publications: "Irving Langmuir," Journal of Chemical Education *(Vol. 10, 1933, pp. 396–399); "Films Built By Depositing Successive Monomolecular Layers on a Solid Surface,"* Journal of the American Chemical Society *(Vol. 57, June 1935, pp. 1007–1022); with Langmuir, "Built-Up Films of Barium Stearate and Their Optical Properties,"* Physical Review *(Vol. 51, June 1, 1937, pp. 964–982).*

In 1933, Katharine Burr Blodgett was carrying out research at the General Electric laboratories when she made the discovery that was to mark the highlight of her career. Her mentor, Irving Langmuir, had directed her to seek a practical application for his findings that oily substances will spread naturally on the surface of water to form a single molecular layer. By December of that year, Blodgett had experimented unsuccessfully with a number of ideas before she decided to add a sprinkling of talc to the film of oil she was observing on a watery surface, in order to see the resulting motion. She then dipped a metal plate into the solution and watched the talc-covered film coat the plate. As she lifted the plate out of the water, she expected the film to stay in the solution, but the film adhered to the plate; submerging the plate again, she was surprised to see a second film layer added to the first. These layers, only one ten-millionth of an inch thick, were the beginning of what would be known as Blodgett's "built-up films" research and would ultimately find widespread application, benefitting not only high-tech users of optical devices like astronomers and photographers, but every driver of an automobile.

Katharine Burr Blodgett was born on January 10, 1898. Her father George Bedington Blodgett was a patent attorney for General Electric, who had moved his family from Boston to Schenectady, New York, in the 1890s, to be director of the patent department at General Electric's newly opened research facilities there. George Blodgett died several weeks before his daughter was born in the family's Front Street home, leaving his widow Katharine Buchanan Blodgett with a young son and an infant daughter. Believing Schenectady to be too small a town for much opportunity, Mrs. Blodgett moved the family several times, first to New York City, where they lived for three years, and then to France and Germany where she hoped the children would learn languages more easily while they were young. A strong believer in education, she eventually returned to the United States to insure that they also retained their native English vocabulary.

Young Katharine's education was unique for a child of her social class. She did not attend school until she was eight years old, when she was enrolled for one year at the public school in Saranac Lake, New York. Following that, she

Katharine Burr Blodgett

attended the Rayson School, run by three English sisters in New York City. The emphasis there on the proper use of English-speaking patterns helped to form Blodgett's lifelong habit of carefully thinking before she spoke or wrote. The qualities of exactness, clarity, and conciseness in communication were to be crucial to her future work.

Blodgett was encouraged at the Rayson School to pursue a career in science. Her excellent grades in competitive examinations earned her a scholarship to Bryn Mawr, a school she admired for its high academic standards. Entering the college in 1913, Blodgett welcomed the challenge provided by mathematician Dr. ***Charlotte Scott** and physicist Dr. James Barnes. Barnes, in particular guided Blodgett toward her career as a physicist. By her senior year, she had decided that science offered the best economic opportunities for women but found the prospect of a traditional teaching career unchallenging. She preferred the idea of going into research and hoped that rumors of employment shortages caused by World War I, then under way, might open up opportunities for women in laboratories. That Christmas, she made a sentimental journey to Schenectady, seeking information about the father she had never known, and visited the General Electric Research Laboratories.

Guided through the plant by Irving Langmuir, a distinguished physicist and the laboratories' assistant director, the studious 18-year-old received advice about her scientific training and encouragement that there might be a research position available for her there. Langmuir suggested that she broaden her scientific back-

Katharine Blodgett in the G.E. lab.

ground after Bryn Mawr by seeking a master's degree in physics at the University of Chicago.

In 1917, Blodgett moved to Chicago, where she completed her postgraduate academic program within a year. Her thesis focused on chemical activity and problems in gas masks, a timely subject since Allied troops in Europe, confined to a war being fought in the trenches, were suffering from bombardments with gas by the Germans. Since most women of that era were discouraged from studying science at any level, Blodgett's master's degree in physics was a rarity. She was granted a singular opportunity for high-caliber training and fair treatment in the classroom at an institution where male and female students in science were treated as equals.

In the spring of 1918, at age 20, Blodgett became the first woman research scientist hired in the General Electric laboratories. Despite a prevailing bias against female scientists in industry, her scholastic strengths and the wartime shortage of male researchers helped gain her the position, as well as the word put in by her father's former colleagues with the company's administrators. But her career was to be the exception that proved the rule and did not open many doors for other women scientists. Industry at that time generally held the position that the costs incurred in training for high-level positions did not merit the risk of investing in women, who might marry and quit work to raise families. For women in science, it took the backing of a prominent man like Langmuir to pursue research, and most American women who demonstrated a scientific bent found their careers confined to teaching in high schools and women's colleges.

When Blodgett arrived at General Electric, Langmuir was already acknowledged as a premier research scientist. A proponent of pure science, he had received his doctorate from the famous German university at Göttingen and had joined General Electric in 1909. Numerous patents had been filed in his name, including the gas-filled incandescent lamp. Langmuir made Blodgett his assistant; she worked with him on projects that were to culminate in his being awarded the Nobel Prize in chemistry in 1932.

Delving into chemistry and physics, Blodgett spent six years on laboratory problems that included measuring electric currents flowing under restricted conditions, and she collaborated with Langmuir on several papers for technical journals. Blodgett stressed effective communication as the foundation for professional training in science. Her technical writing skills and logical presentation of information earned praise from GE's laboratory director, Dr. William D. Coolidge, for enabling non-scientists to comprehend the material.

Langmuir valued Blodgett's work deeply, calling her a "gifted experimenter" with a "rare combination of theoretical and practical ability." But to qualify for an advanced position, she would have to have a Ph.D. Under his influence, she was able to bypass the stringent admission standards and long waiting list at England's Cambridge University. Arriving in 1924, she studied in the fabled Cavendish Laboratory with some of the world's best physicists, including concentrated study with Nobel Prize winner, Sir Ernest Rutherford. In 1926, Katharine Burr Blodgett became the first woman to earn a Ph.D. in physics from Cambridge.

You keep barking up so many wrong trees in research. . . . I think there is an element of luck if you happen to bark up the right one.

—Katharine Burr Blodgett

Returning to Schenectady and the GE laboratories, Blodgett became a member of Langmuir's core research group and collaborated with him on surface chemistry. Quickly absorbed in her work, she renewed experiments begun before she had departed for Cambridge. Langmuir at first directed Blodgett to focus on problems improving tungsten filaments in electric lamps, and, according to colleague Lawrence A. Hawkins, "She early showed not only exceptional aptitude for experiment and delicate manipulation but also a high degree of originality and sound judgment, so in later years her researches have been largely independent."

One area of Blodgett's research was atomic structure in relation to thin films. When Langmuir asked her to explore the phenomena related to his discovery of how oily substances spread on water surface, she expanded his research technique, depositing oil films, especially fatty and stearic acids, on a solid surface. The research duo at first found no practical purpose for these layers, however, and in 1933 Langmuir set her the task of seeking some application. Blodgett recalled, "You keep barking up so many wrong trees in research. It seems sometimes as if you're going to spend your whole life barking up wrong trees. And I think there is an element of luck if you happen to bark up the right one. This time I eventually happened to bark up one that held what I was looking for."

In 1933, success arrived finally through her work to uncover the properties of oil film layers, leading eventually to the discovery that the films could be laid down in great numbers. As the acid transferred from the solution to the solid, she also found that films varying in both thickness and color could be created. The plate holding such films reflected rainbow colors like an oily spot in a mud puddle. In pursuit of a practical use for this discovery, Blodgett created a standardized color gauge that could measure the depth of such films to within one micro-inch. According to Blodgett, "Anyone who wishes to measure the thickness of a film which is only a few millionths of an inch thick can compare the color of his film with the series of colors in the gauge." The instrument was simple and accurate, and more affordable than the expensive optical instruments previously used for such measurements.

With Langmuir, Blodgett first publicized her method of depositing successive monomolecular layers of stearic acid on glass in the February 1935 *Journal of the American Chemical Society*. In June of that year, another article by Blodgett in the same journal, "Films Built By Depositing Successive Monomolecular Layers on a Solid Surface," acknowledged her mentor's influence on her research techniques, as she noted her collaboration with Langmuir, followed by independent research while he was away in the Orient. "The writer is indebted to Dr. Langmuir for urging her to develop further the method described in the previous paper," she wrote, "and for contributing many important suggestions which have been included in this paper." A final paper in the series, "Built-Up Films of Barium Stearate and Their Optical Properties," was completed with Langmuir upon his return and published in the June 1, 1937, *Physical Review*.

In December 1938, General Electric announced that Blodgett was the inventor of non-reflecting glass, a development that grew out of her efforts to refine her technique of depositing films on solids. When her minutely thin oil films were layered onto a pane of glass, she found that the panes did not reflect light, a discovery that was to usher in an era of specially created optical devices, including windshields, telescopes, periscopes, and camera lenses. In her research, Blodgett had applied a coating of 44 layers of one-molecule-thick transparent liquid soap to glass to reduce surface reflections, producing a total thickness of only four millionths of an inch, or one-fourth the length of an average white light wave. The glass meanwhile appeared invisible, because the soap film reflection neutralized the reflection, and the two sets of light waves canceled each other out. The soap allowed 99% of the light to pass through the glass, and no light was reflected.

Two days after GE's announcement, two physicists at the Massachusetts Institute of Technology, C. Hawley Cartwright and Arthur F. Turner, stated that they had made non-reflecting glass by evaporating calcium fluoride in a vacuum and applying it to glass. Both Blodgett's product and theirs were marred by the delicacy of the films, which were easily rubbed off the underlying glass. It was left to other scientists to develop means for making the coatings more durable, and manufacturers of lenses and optical equipment have advanced well beyond her original fundamental research. In the beginning, however, it was due to the overwhelming support and publicity given to her achievement by GE that the discovery found so many immediate applications.

The outbreak of World War II shifted Blodgett's focus at General Electric to military needs. Part of her research was to devise an improved generator to produce smokescreens for obscuring ground movements of troops from enemy forces, work which has been credited in *Science Illustrated* with saving thousands of lives during the Allied invasions of France and Italy. She also was assigned the problem of creating better methods for de-icing the wings of airplanes.

After the war, in 1947, her research for the Army Signal Corps reunited her with the study of thin films for the purpose of designing an instrument to measure humidity in the upper atmosphere. Blodgett's model, carried aloft in weather balloons, proved to be insufficiently sensitive at high altitudes. She was then vital in recruiting Vincent J. Schaefer, who had participated in early weather modification experiments, to join Langmuir's staff. Schaefer, with the assistance of Blodgett and others, invented the technique to create artificial rain by dropping dry ice pellets into clouds from airplanes. According to the April 9, 1951, issue of *Chemical and Engineering News*, Blodgett also aided in the construction of a high-resistance electrical material, formed by heating lead glass in hydrogen to produce thin, low-conductivity surface films that remain stable at high voltages.

The research on thin films gained Blodgett international recognition. She was named a fellow of the American Physical Society and a member of the Optical Society of America, and received honorary doctorates from many colleges, including Brown University and Russell Sage. On March 29, 1945, she was one of the first recipients of the Annual Achievement Award of American Association of University Women, one of the highest honors available to a female scholar. In April 1951, she was honored by the American Chemical Society with the Francis P. Garvan Medal for women in chemistry for her work in surface chemistry. The only scientist honored by Boston's First Assembly of American Women of Achievement, she also presented two James Mapes Dodge Lectures at the Franklin Institute, was starred in the seventh edition of *American Men of Science*, won the Photographic Society of America Progress Medal, and was honored in her hometown of Schenectady for her many accomplishments with the celebration of Katharine Blodgett Day.

In addition to her scholarly research and writing, Blodgett penned a biographical sketch of Langmuir which provided readers with insights into his family and home life as well as her own professional interaction with her mentor. She frequently visited the Langmuir family when they entertained in their home at Christmas and at their camp at Lake George. According to Blodgett, Langmuir's "praise is discerning and wholly without personal bias," and the "laboratory worker who wins from him just the two words, 'Very fine,' had won a compliment greatly to be prized." An admirer of the discipline he brought to the laboratory, Blodgett admitted that Langmuir was "stern toward workers whose mental processes are vague and whose theories are badly thought out" because "he has never tolerated stodginess in his own mental faculties." He had enthusiasm only for researchers whose intelligence he respected, especially Blodgett, and could act icily toward everyone else. Like Langmuir, Blodgett found little time for people or concerns not oriented toward research. Despite her ground-breaking technological innovations, she resisted the modernization of her own laboratory furnishings. According to one colleague, "In all her career as a research scientist Dr. Blodgett has used a battered old table and scarred wooden stool, with which she refused to part when her laboratory was moved into a new glass and steel building."

Soon after returning from Cambridge, Blodgett bought a brick house in downtown Schenectady at 18 North Church Street, near the house where she was born. A mere five feet tall, she was described as "a modest, plump, pleasant-faced woman with an uptilted nose and merry eyes." She enjoyed stargazing and nature, and owned land two hours from her home, near the Langmuirs at Lake George, where she could unwind from the pressures of the laboratory. Her leisure hours were spent digging into the rich earth of her garden, playing bridge with friends, shopping for antiques, attending the Presbyterian church, and participating in civic affairs as treasurer of the Travelers Aid Society. What she relished most, however, was her research work and interaction with colleagues, and she served eagerly as president of the General Electric employees' club.

After retirement from General Electric in 1963, Blodgett enjoyed carrying out horticultural experiments. Gardening continued to be her favorite form of relaxation, except at those times she admitted to being "thrown into a shrieking panic in meeting face to face a common garter snake."

Katharine Blodgett died at home on October 12, 1979, at age 81. In the 1980s, two of her papers on what has become widely known as the Langmuir-Blodgett film were still important enough to be cited an average of 100 times each. Her written work about methods in chemistry and biophysics remain useful to contemporary researchers, who quote her techniques and research philosophies. The vitality of Katharine Burr Blodgett's techniques have transcended time.

SOURCES:

Barlow, W.A. *Special Issue on Langmuir-Blodgett Films.* Lausanne: Elsevier Sequoia, 1980.

"Blodgett, Katharine Burr," in *Current Biography.* NY: H.W. Wilson, 1952.

"Katharine Burr Blodgett," in *Physics Today.* Vol. 33. March 1980, p. 107.

Yost, Edna. *American Women of Science.* Philadelphia, PA: J.B. Lippincott, 1955.

SUGGESTED READING:

Hawkins, Lawrence A. *Adventure into the Unknown: The First Fifty Years of the General Electric Research Laboratory.* NY: William Morrow, 1950.

Rossiter, Margaret W. *Women Scientists in America: Struggles and Strategies to 1940.* Baltimore, MD: The Johns Hopkins University Press, 1982.

Wise, George. *Willis R. Whitney, General Electric, and the Origins of U.S. Industrial Research.* NY: Columbia University Press, 1985.

———. "A New Role for Professional Scientists in Industry: Industrial Research at General Electric, 1900–1916," in *Technology and Culture.* Vol. 21. 1980, pp. 408–429.

COLLECTIONS:

Irving Langmuir Collection, Library of Congress, Washington, D.C.

Blodgett's and Langmuir's personnel files, manuscripts, laboratory notebooks, and research notes, as well as other archival materials, are available at the General Electric Research and Development Center, Schenectady, New York.

Elizabeth D. Schafer, Ph.D., Freelance writer in History of Technology and Science, Loachapoka, Alabama

Blois, countess of.

See Adelaide (fl. 860s).

See Maud of Normandy (d. 1107).

See Adela of Blois (1062–c. 1137).

See Adele of Champagne for sidebar on Maud Carinthia (c. 1105–1160).

See Eleanor of Aquitaine for sidebar on Alice (1150–c. 1197).

See Marguerite (r. 1218–1230).

See Marie de Chatillon (r. 1230–1241).

See Jeanne de Chatillon (d. 1292).

See Jeanne de Penthièvre (c. 1320–1384).

See Françoise-Marie de Bourbon (1677–1749).

Blom, Gertrude Duby (1901–1993).

See Duby-Blom, Gertrude.

Blomfield, Dorothy (1858–1932)

British poet and hymn writer, best known for her oft-sung wedding hymn, "O Perfect Love." *Born Dorothy Frances Blomfield in London, England, in October 1858; died in London, England, 1932; eldest of five children of Frederick G. Blomfield (an Anglican minister); sister of Katherine, Isabella, and Daisy Blomfield; granddaughter of the Rt. Rev. C.J. Blomfield (a distinguished bishop of London); married Gerald Gurney (an Anglican minister), in 1897.*

To this day, a tradition in many old-fashioned English weddings is the singing of a century-old hymn "O Perfect Love," written by the poet Dorothy Blomfield for her sister's wedding in 1883. The words were set to the music of J.B. Dykes' hymn "Strength and Stay," a particular favorite of the bride-to-be who, nonetheless, considered the words inappropriate for a wedding and challenged her sister to write new ones. Blomfield reputedly created the verse in less than 15 minutes, saying later that she felt God had helped her write it. The hymn gained popularity in 1889, when Queen ***Victoria**'s granddaughter ***Princess Louise** chose it for her wedding to the Duke of Fife. Ironically, the princess loved the words, but not the tune, and had new music for it composed by Joseph Barnby, a Yorkshire composer. It is to his tune that the hymn is sung today.

Blomfield also produced several volumes of quotable verse, including the popular poem "God's Garden." At age 40, after years of caring for her aging parents, she married an Anglican minister, Gerald Gurney, son of poet and hymn writer Rev. Archer Thompson Gurney (1820–1887). In 1919, the couple stunned their family and friends when, after 22 years in service to the Church of England, they converted to Catholicism. Their later years, spent in London, were somewhat of a struggle. Blomfield died there at the age of 74, having never received a penny in royalty for her famous hymn, although it was widely used throughout the world.

SOURCES:

Appleyard, Simon. "'O Perfect Love,'" in *This England.* Summer 1990.

Barbara Morgan,
Melrose, Massachusetts

Blond, Elizabeth Le (1861–1934).

See Le Blond, Elizabeth.

Blondell, Joan (1906–1979)

American actress. *Born on August 30, 1906, in New York, New York; died of leukemia on December 25, 1979, in Santa Monica, California; daughter and one of three children of Eddie (a stage comedian, one of the original Katzenjammer Kids) and Kathryn (Cain) Blondell (a vaudeville performer); sister of* **Gloria Blondell**, *who also appeared in film and television; attended Venice (California) Grammar School, Erasmus High School, Brooklyn, New York, and Santa Monica High School, California; married George Scott Barnes, in 1933 (divorced 1935); married Dick Powell, in 1936 (divorced 1945); married Mike Todd, in 1947 (divorced 1950): children: (first marriage) Norman Scott Barnes (b. 1934); (second marriage)* **Ellen Powell** *(b. 1938).*

Filmography: The Office Wife *(1930);* Sinners' Holiday *(1930);* Illicit *(1931);* Millie *(1931);* My Past *(1931);* God's Gift to Women *(1931);* Other Men's Women *(1931);* Public Enemy *(1931);* Big Business Girl *(1931);* Night Nurse *(1931);* The Reckless Hour *(1931);* Blonde Crazy *(1931);* The Greeks Had a Word for Them *(1931);* Union Depot *(1932);* The Crowd Roars *(1932);* The Famous Ferguson Case *(1932);* Make Me a Star *(1932);* Miss Pinkerton *(1932);* Big City Blues *(1932);* Three on a Match *(1932);* Central Park *(1932);* Lawyer Man *(1932);* Broadway Fad *(1933);* Blondie Johnson *(1933);* Gold Diggers of 1933 *(1933);* Goodbye Again *(1933);* Footlight Parade *(1933);* Havana Widows *(1933);* Convention City *(1933);* I've Got Your Number *(1934);* He Was Her Man *(1934);* Smarty *(1934);* Dames *(1934);* The Kansas City Princess *(1934);* Traveling Saleslady *(1935);* Broadway Gondolier *(1935);* We're in the Money *(1935);* Miss Pacific Fleet *(1935);* Colleen *(1936);* Sons O'Guns *(1936);* Bullets or Ballots *(1936);* Stage Struck *(1936);* Three Men on a Horse *(1936);* Perfect Specimen *(1937);* Back in Circulation *(1937);* The King and the Chorus Girl *(1937);* There's Always a Woman *(1938);* The Amazing Mr. Williams

Joan Blondell

(1939); East Side of Heaven (1939); Good Girls Go to Paris (1939); Kid from Kokomo (1939); Off the Record (1939); I Want a Divorce (1940); Two Girls on Broadway (1940); Lady for a Night (1941); The Nurse's Secret (1941); Model Wife (1941); Three Girls About Town (1941); Topper Returns (1941); Cry Havoc (1943); A Tree Grows in Brooklyn (1945); Don Juan Quilligan (1945); Adventure (1945); Christmas Eve (1947); The Corpse Came C.O.D. (1947); Nightmare Alley (1947); Without Honor (1949); For Heaven's Sake (1950); The Blue Veil (1951); The Opposite Sex (1956); Desk Set (1957); Lizzie (1957); This Could Be the Night (1957); Will Success Spoil Rock Hunter? (1957); Angel Baby (1961); Sunday in New York (1964); Advance to the Rear (1964); The Cincinnati Kid (1964); Paradise Road (1965); Ride Beyond Vengeance (1966); Waterhole No. 3 (1967); Kona Coast (1968); Stay Away, Joe (1968); Big Daddy (1969); Support Your Local Gunfighter (1971); Won Ton Ton, The Dog Who Saved Hollywood (1976); Opening Night (1978); Grease (1978); The Champ (1979); The Glove (1979); The Woman Inside (1981).

Spanning seven decades, Joan Blondell's career included stage, film, radio, and television. It began when she joined her parents' vaudeville act, "Ed Blondell and Company," at the tender age of three and debuted in Sydney, Australia. The act toured Europe and China before returning to the U.S. when Blondell was five. Joined by her brother and sister in turn, she was part of the act for 15 years, traveling back and forth across the country, and attending school sporadically or, as she put it, "only when the Gerry Society demanded it." At 17, while doing stock with a company in Dallas, Texas, she won a Miss Dallas beauty contest and a prize of $2,000. With the advent of movies, the Blondells were struggling to obtain bookings, and the prize money helped Joan bring the family to New York. She continued to support them, working at odd jobs during the day and acting without pay at night at the Provincetown Theatre in Greenwich Village. It was her hope to get the act on the road again, but it wasn't to be. Blondell finally landed a small part in a Broadway production of *Tarnished*, which was followed by roles in *The Trial of Mary Dugan* and the *Ziegfeld Follies*. In 1929, she was cast in George Kelly's *Maggie the Magnificent*, playing the sassy, gum-chewing wife of a bootlegger portrayed by a then-unknown James Cagney. Blondell and Cagney were so good that they won a line or two from the critics and were cast together again in the stage melodrama, *Penny Arcade*. Al Jolson took an option on the movie rights to *Penny Arcade* and subsequently sold them to Warner Bros. with the suggestion that they use Blondell and Cagney in their original roles. Although Warner Bros. brought them both to Hollywood, the pair was regarded as inexperienced and were cast in much smaller roles. The movie was released in 1930 under the title *Sinners' Holiday*.

Warners was impressed with Blondell, however, and awarded her a five-year contract which jump-started her film career. Typically playing the cynical, wisecracking blonde with a heart of gold, she became the studio workhorse, making some 20 films between 1931 and 1933. "They'd even pan me going to the ladies' room," she joked. Looking back on these early years, Blondell wished she had fought more with the front office for better roles, but she was grateful at the time—during the depth of the Depression—to be able to support her family. Two films of this period stand out: *Public Enemy*, in which she played a gangster's moll, and *Gold Diggers of 1933*, in which she offered a unique, non-singing rendition of "Remember My Forgotten Man."

Of her roles in more than 80 movies, her favorite also proved the most memorable, the part of Aunt Sissy in the 1945 *A Tree Grows in Brooklyn*. Later, in 1951, Blondell received an Academy Award nomination as Best Supporting Actress for her performance in *The Blue Veil*. During the '50s, she left the movies for a period of about five years to concentrate on stage and television. During that time, she toured in productions of *Come Back, Little Sheba*, *The Time of the Cuckoo*, *Call Me Madame*, and *Dark at the Top of the Stairs*. Of her small role in a 1957 production of *The Rope Dancers*, critic Brooks Atkinson wrote, "It's small, but it's gold." Blondell was also seen in numerous television roles; most notable among them was her portrayal of the earthy barmaid in the series "Here Comes the Bride," for which she won two Emmy Award nominations.

Blondell's private life was beset by failed marriages. Her first, to cinematographer George Scott Barnes (his third marriage), produced a son, Norman Scott. (Blondell worked until the seventh month of her pregnancy. "They kept shooting me higher and higher," she recalled, "and finally shot me standing behind furniture.") She met Dick Powell while shooting *Gold Diggers of 1933*, divorced Barnes in 1935, and married Powell in 1936. After their daughter Ellen was born in 1938, the Powells both left Warner Bros. in hopes of finding better parts elsewhere. The best Blondell could land was the role of Powell's wife in Paramount's *I Want a Divorce*, which offered only a few small comic scenes but led to a successful radio series of the same name. Between the radio work and entertaining for the USO, Blondell did not return to film until 1943. Around that time, she caught the eye of Broadway producer Mike Todd, while her husband Dick Powell fell head over heels for ***June Allyson**, a young dancer cast with him in *Meet the People* (1944). Blondell and Powell went their separate ways in 1945. Less than three weeks after the divorce, Powell married Allyson. Todd and Blondell carried on a tempestuous courtship and finally married in 1947.

While Blondell continued to make movies, Todd moved his headquarters to California. The couple later moved to an estate in New York where they enjoyed a lavish, if short-lived, lifestyle, financed with a hefty loan from Blondell and income from her stage work. By the time they divorced in 1950, Todd was on the brink of bankruptcy, and Blondell was out some $80,000. Mike Todd went on to a notorious union with actress **Elizabeth Taylor** and was killed in a plane crash in 1958. Late in life, Blondell had mellow recollections of the men in her life. "Each was totally different," she said,

"If you could take a part of each one of them and put them into one man you'd have a helluva husband." She never married again, although she reportedly hated living alone.

During the '60s and '70s, Blondell was reduced to second-rate movie roles. In 1965, however, the National Board of Review, in a belated gesture to her long career, voted her the year's best supporting actress for her minor role in *The Cincinnati Kid*. At the end of her career, Blondell became discouraged by the quality of scripts that were sent her way, calling them "pointless, rotten and unnecessary." She always retained a down-to-earth outlook on Hollywood and never took herself too seriously. Admitting that she was never terribly comfortable being on display, she spent the last years of her life living in New York City pursuing interests she felt she had finally earned the right to enjoy, including completing a non-biographical novel, *Center Door Fancy*, published in 1972. Joan Blondell died of leukemia in 1979.

Barbara Morgan,
Melrose, Massachusetts

Bloody Mary (1516–1558).

See Mary I.

Bloom, Ursula (1893–1984)

British author of historical and romance novels totaling 564 volumes. *Name variations: (pseudonyms) Deborah Mann, Sheila Burns, Mary Essex, Rachel Harvey, Sara Sloane, Lozania Prole (joint). Born Ursula Bloom in Chelmsford, England, in December 1893; died in Nether Wallop, Hampshire, England, on October 29, 1984; daughter of Mary and J. Harvey Bloom; educated at home; married Arthur Denham-Cooke, in November 1916 (died 1918); married Charles Gower Robinson, in November 1925; children: (first marriage) one son, Pip Denham-Cooke (b. November 1917).*

Selected works: The Great Beginning *(1924); (autobiography)* Life Is No Fairy Tale *(1976).*

"This is a true story—my own. Much has happened to me—a clergyman's daughter, brought up in one of the loveliest parts of England, near Stratford-on-Avon. Personally I am rather glad that it cannot happen again," wrote Ursula Bloom, who was two years old when her family settled in Whitchurch, a village of 120 people, where her father was granted a parish. The post was probationary, as J. Harvey Bloom had just come off a two-year suspension for extramarital affairs. His stipend was small, but the Blooms had servants and nannies "for appearances." To supplement his income, he wrote fiction, and both he and his wife **Mary Bloom** substituted at Trinity College in Stratford. Ursula's education fell to her mother. She learned to read by age three and played violin at orchestra level but was taught no math or geography. For amusement, she wrote stories. "Tiger" was published in 1900, thanks to neighbor ***Marie Corelli**, but, wrote Bloom, "unfortunately my parents butted in" and edited all the personality out.

Bloom's father walked a straight path until she was nine. Then, on errands with him, she was often left sitting outside on the stoop of a strange woman's house. Afraid to hurt her mother, Bloom was silent and guilt-ridden until she began to experience chronic high fevers at ages 14 and 15; during one fever, she revealed her father's indiscretions. On doctor's orders that Ursula be removed from the source of her great distress, Mary Bloom left her husband. Though the couple never divorced, her father continued his affairs without censure from the church.

In Stratford, Ursula became the head of the household when Mary Bloom, ill from surgery for breast cancer, was bedridden. Since her father gave them only a small sum, Bloom took a job as a cinema pianist and played two shows a day, up to four hours per show. Brother Joscelyn, away at school, was called home to work in a local bank. With the advent of World War I, Joscelyn enlisted, and Ursula and Mary moved to Walton. When Mary's cancer spread, Bloom took odd piano-playing jobs and cared for her mother full time. "Too frequently," she remembered, "I had to fill up with just bread, and, believe me, you get a bit sick of it." As a contrast to her poverty, army captain Arthur Denham-Cooke courted Bloom with elegant dinners and car rides. In May 1916, he proposed, and she enjoyed the thought that her burdens might ease. "I told him that I was not in love, in the accepted sense," Bloom said. But she was "deeply fond of him, and would do anything that I could to make him happy."

In fact, both Denham-Cooke's wealth and life were tightly controlled by his mother, who refused to attend the November wedding. Within months, Bloom learned that her husband was an alcoholic whose career was in jeopardy. The day after Bloom's mother died, Denham-Cooke was demoted and transferred to Holland. Only his family's influence gained his return to England in time for his son Pip's November 1917 birth. Though Bloom convinced her husband to enter a treatment program, he resumed drinking the day of his release and was eventually discharged from the army. Weak from years of abuse, his body had no resistance to the Spanish Flu which took his life during the epidemic of 1918.

Though Bloom had written throughout her marriage, she had always burned her work because her husband had disapproved. In the months following his death, however, she won a publishing contract and lived off earnings as a crime reporter for the *Empire News*, in Harlow, outside London. Her first novel was published in 1924. "Thank God that the love of writing is such a strong driving force, which has helped me round many a corner in a difficult life," she wrote in her 1976 autobiography *Life is No Fairy Tale*. Bloom sometimes worked 16 hours a day, producing an average of ten books a year until 1976. In addition, she designed needlework patterns, at one craft show displaying 150 pieces.

In 1925, she met and married Charles Gower Robinson, a naval officer. Deeply in love, she followed her "Robbie" to his base ports, including three years in Portsmouth. When Bloom developed migraine headaches for which all treatments were ineffective, Robinson retired from the navy and took a job in the Foreign Office in London, hoping to ease her strain. Their London home was destroyed in the bombings of World War II and rebuilt when they returned to the city. After years of illness, Bloom consented to surgery on her trigeminal nerve. Her headaches were cured but she had permanent facial paralysis and scarring. She ceased publishing with her 1976 autobiography and died eight years later in Hampshire, England.

SOURCES:

Bloom, Ursula. *Life Is No Fairy Tale*. London: Robert Hale, 1976.

May, Hal, ed. *Contemporary Authors*. Vol. 114. Detroit, MI: Gale Research, 1985.

Nasso, Christine, ed. *Contemporary Authors*. Vol. 25–28. Detroit, MI: Gale Research, 1977.

Crista Martin, freelance writer, Boston, Massachusetts

Bloomer, Amelia Jenks (1818–1894)

American feminist and temperance crusader best known for her advocacy of dress reform. *Pronunciation: BLOOM-er. Born Amelia Jenks on May 27, 1818, in Homer, Cortland County, New York; died on December 30, 1894, in Council Bluffs, Iowa; daughter of Augustus Jenks (a clothier) and Lucy Jenks; received no formal education; married Dexter C. Bloomer, in 1840; children: none.*

Selected writings: editor and publisher of The Lily *(1849–55) and numerous articles in feminist and temperance journals.*

One morning in 1850, the citizens of Seneca Falls, New York, were astounded to see two young women walking down the main street in a new, rather strange costume. ***Elizabeth Cady Stanton** and her cousin ❧▸ **Elizabeth Smith Miller** were wearing what quickly became known as a "Bloomer" dress, a name derived from the woman who had done more in the popular imagination to promote the cause of female dress reform than anyone else—Amelia Jenks Bloomer.

Amelia Jenks was born on May 27, 1818, in the small hamlet of Homer, situated in Cortland County, New York. Her father Augustus (or Ananias) was a successful clothier who was later killed during the battle of Gettysburg when serving as an officer in the Union army. Little is known of **Lucy Jenks**, Amelia's mother, except for the fact that she was a deeply religious woman who attempted to raise Amelia and her siblings in accordance with Biblical precepts. Both parents were strong supporters of the then powerful and influential temperance movement, taking an active part in the campaign to limit and control the consumption of alcohol.

Bloomer's education was restricted to a few terms at the local district school in Homer. She was, however, a bright and enquiring student who was encouraged by her parents to spend much of her spare time reading a broad variety of subjects. When Amelia was 17, her academic abilities were recognized, and she was employed to teach several terms at the school. In 1837, Amelia and her family moved to Waterloo, New York, where she became governess to the three small children of a prominent local businessman. Waterloo was a larger and more cosmopolitan community than Homer, and Bloomer, well-liked and popular, expanded her circle of friends.

One such, Dexter C. Bloomer, was a young man only a few years older than Amelia. Though he was an aspiring law student, Dexter took a greater interest in local and state politics. He was also part-owner and editor of a small, but successful, local newspaper, the *Seneca County Courier*, in the nearby town of Seneca Falls. The young couple fell in love and, after a brief engagement, were married in April 1840. By this time, Amelia was already beginning to develop her own ideas about the proper role of women in society. Accordingly, with Dexter's support, she requested that the word "obey" not be included as part of her wedding vows. Bloomer also took this occasion to reinforce what had now become her own strong pro-temperance beliefs by refusing to consume any alcohol at the wedding reception.

Indeed, at that time, the temperance cause was Bloomer's most urgent social concern. Shortly after her marriage, two founders of the Great Washingtonian Temperance Reformation visited Seneca Falls and stayed with the Bloomers. Subsequently, Amelia founded a local chapter of the society. Thanks to her infectious enthusiasm, the branch soon had well over 500 members. Shortly after, she began contributing a series of short articles, under the pseudonym Gloriana, for the national temperance journal, *The Water Bucket*. At the same time, Bloomer began to write a series of (unsigned) commentaries for the *Seneca County Courier* on a variety of social, moral, and political issues.

In 1847, Elizabeth Stanton and ***Lucretia Mott**, two of the leading advocates of women's rights, arrived in Seneca Falls to organize the first public meeting in the U.S. on female emancipation. According to their announcement placed in the *Seneca County Courier*, they aimed to discuss "the social, civil and religious conditions and rights of women." Toward the end of the meeting, Stanton called for a show of hands in support of a woman's right to vote. This was an extremely radical proposal for the time and, although it was eventually passed by a narrow majority, had the effect of splitting and dividing the delegates present. Much to Stanton's annoyance, Amelia Bloomer, who had attended the convention simply in a role of spectator, refused to sign the "Declaration of Sentiments," a statement of intent which included the call for female suffrage.

Although Bloomer had serious reservations about Stanton's strategy, she had no doubts about the need for female emancipation. The Bloomers took an important step towards advancing the cause of women's rights in 1849 following Dexter's appointment as postmaster of Seneca Falls. In accepting this political assignment (which necessitated relinquishing his position as newspaper proprietor), he insisted that his wife be appointed assistant postmaster. Amelia Bloomer thus became the first woman to hold such a position in the United States. She was later to describe her experience as a practical demonstration of a "woman's right to fill any place for which she had a capacity."

Bloomer's principal concern during this period, however, remained the temperance movement. Shortly after assuming her duties as postmaster, she became a founding member of the nationally based Ladies Temperance Society and was elected to the governing council. When this council subsequently decided that the society required a journal to propagate and promote its views, they turned to its one member who already had substantial journalistic experience. On the first of January 1849, Bloomer edited and published the first edition of *The Lily*, then a monthly publication, six pages long and the first of its kind produced by a woman in North America.

The initial editions of *The Lily* were solely devoted to exhorting its principally female audience to back prohibition and advising it on how to withstand the effects of spousal drunkenness. From the beginning of 1850, however, the focus of the journal underwent a significant alteration. This was connoted on the front page of the publication which began to carry the new, more all-embracing masthead, "Devoted to the Interests of Women." What this meant in practical terms was the adoption of a broader range of issues concerning women. From then on, articles on such topics as education, unjust marriage laws, and female suffrage (often written by such leading reformers as Stanton) made a regular appearance in the pages of *The Lily*. The result was dramatic. From an initial subscriber's list of be-

Miller, Elizabeth Smith (1822–1911)

American reformer. *Name variations: Lizzie or Libby Miller. Born Elizabeth Smith in Hampton, New York, on September 20, 1822; died in 1911; daughter of Gerrit Smith (a prominent politician); cousin of Elizabeth Cady Stanton; married Charles Dudley Miller (a well-known New York lawyer), in 1850.*

In 1851, Libby Miller, after her Grand Tour of Europe honeymoon and years of feeling constrained in the long skirts of the day while attending her garden, came up with an outfit that would allow her to prune and dig unfettered. Fashioned after women she had seen in sanatoria in Switzerland who were recuperating from the effects of tight-lacing and lack of exercise, it was described by her as a "short dress" with a skirt that stopped "some four inches below the knee" under which she wore "Turkish trousers to the ankle." Her cousin ***Elizabeth Cady Stanton** was delighted and took quickly to the idea, while ***Amelia Jenks Bloomer** began advocating the attire in a women's reform paper called the *Lily*. Because of Bloomer's fervent backing, the Turkish trousers became known as Bloomers. Elizabeth Miller also wrote a bestselling cookbook, *In the Kitchen*, which was published in 1875.

tween 200 and 300 in late 1849, circulation of the journal would rise to over 4,000 (for an expanded bi-monthly edition) by 1853.

The reasons for this dramatic rise in circulation were two-fold. First, the militant stance which the journal now adopted on questions of women's rights and social reform accurately reflected the increasingly combative attitude assumed by the nation's leading feminists. Secondly, and more significantly, *The Lily* had also begun to advocate a revolution in women's style of dress.

Throughout the 1840s, there was an increasing realization among women that their "fashionable" clothes were both awkward and unhealthy. Current norms dictated that the "well-dressed" woman wear a costume that was comprised of at least half a dozen cumbersome skirts and petticoats that, because of their length, frequently became coated in dust and mud. Moreover, the tightly laced stays and rigid bodice which accompanied this costume served to restrict breathing (causing shortness of breath and abdominal pains) and was responsible for needless complications in pregnancy and childbirth. The restricting

Amelia Jenks Bloomer

garments could even stunt the normal physical development of a young woman.

In addition, the question of women's fashion had broader implications. During the late 1840s, English feminist ➽ **Helene Marie Weber** argued that, regardless of any other social and legal reforms in their status, women would not be considered equal with men unless they were permitted to dress in the same manner. A broadly similar view came to be held in the U.S. by Stanton and another leading advocate of women's rights, ***Susan B. Anthony.** The problem was to find a form of dress that would combine greater comfort and practicality without relinquishing current middle-class norms of respectability and constraint.

A solution was thought to have been found in 1850 by Stanton's cousin, Elizabeth Smith Miller, during a visit to a sanatorium in Switzerland. It was there that Miller observed some of the staff wearing an imitation of the clothing then customarily worn by Turkish women. This costume constituted a three-quarter length tunic, belted at the waist, over a knee-length skirt and was completed by a pair of ankle-length baggy pantaloons (or trousers). Although a comparable attire had first made an appearance in North America on the New York stage in 1849 (courtesy of the English actress, ***Fanny Kemble**), its first public display was by Stanton and Miller on the streets of Seneca Falls the following year. When Stanton's son asked that she not wear the outfit when she visited him at school, she replied: "Suppose you and I were taking a long walk in the fields and I had on three long petticoats. Then suppose a bull should take after us, why you with your arms and legs free, could run like a shot, but I, alas, should fall a victim to my graceful flowing drapery. . . . Why do you wish me to wear what is uncomfortable, inconvenient, and many times dangerous . . . [because] you do not like to have me laughed at[?]"

Amelia herself enthusiastically adopted the new style and, shortly afterwards, wrote an editorial in *The Lily* strongly endorsing its adoption by all women. In response to a patronizing editorial by a conservative gentleman who had purchased the *Courier* and was suggesting tongue-in-cheek that women should, indeed, wear Turkish pantaloons, she replied: "Had we broached this subject, the cry would have been raised on all sides, 'She wants to wear pantaloons,' and a pretty hornet's nest we should have got into. But now that our cautious editor of *The Courier* recommends it, we suppose that there will be no harm in our doing so. Small waists and whale-bones can be dispensed with, and we shall be allowed breathing-room; and our forms shall be what nature made them. We are so thankful that men are beginning to undo some of the mischief they have done us." She was then deluged by letters, from all over the U.S., from women asking for more details and a pattern in order that they could make the new "Turkish" or "American" costume, as Amelia initially called it, for themselves. These names were not to last for long. Despite the fact that Amelia was neither the first woman to publicly wear the costume nor its inventor, the national press in both North America and Europe quickly nicknamed it the "Bloomer" costume. It was not long before all female advocates of equal rights became popularly known, and diminished, by such nicknames as "Bloomerettes" or, more simply, "Bloomers."

➽ Weber, Helene Marie (b. 1824)

European feminist. *Name variations: Hélène Marie Weber. Born in 1824.*

Europe's Helene Marie Weber was known to plow her land during the day and write through the night on behalf of women's rights, specifically the right to retain property, to study in universities, to become ministers and priests, and to vote and engage in politics. She was also known for her attire: a black coat and pantaloons. For dress up, she would wear a dark-blue dress coat with gilt buttons, an elegant waistcoat and trousers. "Those who suppose that women can be the political, social, pecuniary, religious equal of man without conforming to his dress, are deceiving themselves," wrote Weber, who advocated androgyny. "While the superiority of the male dress for all purposes of business and recreation is conceded, it is absurd to argue that we should not avail ourselves of its advantages."

> I had no idea . . . that my action would create an excitement throughout the civilized world.
>
> **—Amelia Jenks Bloomer**

Broadly speaking, two different groups of women adopted the Bloomer style. On the one hand, women such as farm workers and pioneers found the freedom and comfort of the new fashion conducive to the requirements of life on the frontier. On the other hand, a smaller group of radical feminists (who came to call themselves the "ultras") viewed this breakthrough simply in terms of its symbolic significance for women's liberation.

The eager response of both these groups was in sharp contrast to many leading newspapers who interpreted the adoption of this (vaguely) male form of dress as a fundamental threat to the structure of existing society. The *New York Herald*, for example, editorialized that any woman who adopted the Bloomer costume should either be sent to prison or, preferably, to an asylum. Similarly, the dress outraged many members of the clergy who publicly denounced it as "devilish." These condemnations did not, however, prevent several enterprising entrepreneurs from tapping into the widespread public curiosity surrounding this phenomenon. Before long, several theatrical productions and operettas appeared dealing with "Bloomerism," along with specially commissioned waltzes and polkas, even a range of china figurines.

Like many other fashions, the craze for the Bloomer outfit was shortlived, and, by the end of 1852, it had largely run its course. A few feminist stalwarts, such as Stanton, persisted, but she too abandoned it in 1854 when she realized that increasing public ridicule was taking away from the more serious demands of the women's movement. "Like a captive set free from his ball and chain," wrote Stanton, "I was always ready for a brisk walk through sleet and snow and rain, to climb a mountain, jump over a fence, work in the garden, and was fit for any necessary locomotion. What a sense of liberty I felt with no skirts to hold or brush, ready at any moment to climb a hill-top to see the sun go down." Because of her special association, Amelia felt an obligation to continue wearing the costume, and she only finally abandoned it 1857. She later wrote, echoing Stanton, that "the dress was but an incident, and we were not willing to sacrifice greater questions to it." Despite this apparent failure, however, within the next few decades a variant of the Bloomer costume had become accepted gym uniform for all American women.

By 1853, the costume had made Amelia the most publicized lecturer in the United States and, indeed, a figure of worldwide fame. Later that same year, Dexter and Amelia's contract with the post office in Seneca Falls came to an end, and the couple moved to Mt. Vernon, Ohio. Dexter then became part-owner and editor of a pro-temperance newspaper, the *Western Home Visitor*. Although Bloomer continued to write and produce *The Lily*, she also served as assistant editor of her husband's publication and contributed many articles on the topics of temperance and women's rights. Moreover, despite the determined resistance of their male employees, the Bloomers attempted to give concrete expression to their belief in women's emancipation and insisted on hiring female printers and typesetters.

Twelve months later, Dexter sold his interest in the *Western Home Visitor*, and the couple migrated west to Council Bluffs, Iowa, then a small frontier settlement. This move represented the fulfillment of one of Amelia's deepest desires, to become a pioneer. Unfortunately, it also meant the end of her involvement in *The Lily*, as Council Bluffs was too far from the railroad to make mailing the newspaper a practicable proposition (the paper was sold and continued to be published in Richmond, Indiana, for three more years). This did not, however, mark the end of Bloomer's reforming activities. In 1856, she was asked to address the House of Representatives of the Nebraska legislature where she spoke in favor of a bill, then before the assembly, granting women's suffrage. Although this bill subsequently lost in the state senate, subsequent legislation allowing women to hold and own property was passed largely thanks to Bloomer's influence. Later, she sought to establish a small women's cooperative in Council Bluffs that aimed to relieve women of the daily burden of household chores through an equitable division of day-care responsibilities, cooking, and the sharing of various labor-saving devices. Unfortunately, insufficient funds were available for this experiment in social reform to proceed.

The outbreak of the Civil War in 1861 found Bloomer a strong supporter of the Northern cause. Like other women reformers of the time, she was an uncompromising opponent of slavery. She organized the women of Council Bluffs to supply warm clothing and hospital supplies to the federal troops. Her efforts were so successful that, at the end of the war, General Ulysses S. Grant, commander of the Northern armies and future president of the United States, made a special request to meet Bloomer to thank her for the example she had given others.

Although the Bloomers never had children of their own, they adopted the young son and daughter of friends who had died during the war. Amelia continued to lecture despite these extra responsibilities and, in 1867, made what was to be the first of several journeys to New York to attend the inaugural meeting of the Women's Suffrage Association. Bloomer was still one of the most popular feminist reformers in the country, and this standing was reflected by the association's choice of her as vice-president. Three years later, she further solidified her standing as one of the nation's great feminists by becoming president of the Women Suffrage Society of Iowa.

In his later years, Dexter was instrumental in developing the public-school system in Council Bluffs, and Amelia became the leading advocate of hiring female teachers. Her main concerns always remained, however, temperance and women's suffrage. Although she did not live to see the fruition of the former cause, she was overjoyed when, in 1869, the territory of Wyoming became the first jurisdiction in the U.S. to grant women the vote (to be followed shortly after by similar measures in Utah and Colorado). Amelia Bloomer spent her last years in quiet retirement in Council Bluffs where she died on December 30, 1894, at the age of 76.

SOURCES:

Anthony, Susan B., Elizabeth Cady Stanton, and Ida Husted Harper. *History of Woman Suffrage.* Vols. 1–3. Fowler and Wells, 1881 (reprint, NY: Arno, 1969).

Bloomer, Dexter C. *The Life and Writings of Amelia Bloomer.* Boston, MA: 1895 (reprinted by Schocken).

Gattey, Charles Neilson. *The Bloomer Girls.* London: Femina Books, 1967.

SUGGESTED READING:

Newton, Stella Mary. *Health, Art, and Reason.* London: 1974.

Riegal, R. *American Feminists.* Kansas: University of Kansas Press, 1963.

Stanton, Elizabeth C. *Eighty Years and More.* NY: 1898.

Dave Baxter, Department of Philosophy, Wilfrid Laurier University, Waterloo, Ontario, Canada

Bloomfield-Zeisler, Fannie (1863–1927).

See Zeisler, Fannie Bloomfield.

Bloor, Ella Reeve (1862–1951)

American labor organizer, suffragist, journalist, and Communist Party leader, who devoted over 50 years of her life seeking justice for the working class. *Name variations: Ella Reeve Ware, Ella Reeve Cohen, Mother Bloor. Pronunciation: Bloor rhymes with more. Born Ella Reeve on July 8, 1862, on Staten Island, New York; died in a nursing home in Richlandtown, Pennsylvania, on August 10, 1951; daughter of Harriet Amanda (Disbrow) Reeve and Charles Reeve (owner of a drug store); attended public school in Bridgeton, N.J., and the Ivy Hall Seminary before being taught at home by her mother; later attended the University of Pennsylvania; married Lucien Ware, in 1881 (divorced 1896); married Louis Cohen, in 1897 (divorced 1902); married Andrew Omholt, in 1930; assumed the surname of her companion Richard Bloor while on a trip to Chicago and was thereafter known by that name; children: (first marriage) Pauline (1882–1886), Charles (1883–1886), Grace (b. 1885), Helen (b. 1887), Harold (1889–1935), Hamilton (b. 1892); (second marriage) Richard (b. 1898) and Carl (b. 1900).*

While giving birth to six children in ten years, she also became active in the suffrage and temperance movements and joined the Knights of Labor and the Ethical Culture Society (1880s); joined the Social Democracy of America (1897); joined the Socialist Labor Party (1900), then the Socialist Party (SP, 1902); ran for secretary of state in Connecticut on the SP ticket (1908); elected SP state organizer for Ohio (1910); worked with Elizabeth Gurley Flynn for the Workers Defense Union (WDU, 1917–19); joined the newly formed Communist Labor Party and appointed national organizer for the Eastern Division (1919); was organizer for the International Labor Defense Council (ILD, 1920s); appointed organizer for the United Farmers League (1931); elected to the U.S. Communist Party (CPUSA) Central Executive Committee (1932–48); named delegate to the Women's International Congress Against War and Fascism, held in Paris (1934); appointed chair of the Pennsylvania CP and ran for Congress on the CP ticket (1940); made 80th Birthday Tour, part of the CPUSA "Win the War Against Fascism" campaign (1942); arrested 36 times.

Selected publications: Three Little Lovers of Nature *(1895);* Talks About Authors and Their Works *(1899);* We Are Many *(1940); and numerous articles.*

In 1937, *Life* magazine referred to Ella Reeve Bloor as "the grand old lady of the U.S. Communist Party." Known the world over by the affectionate name of Mother Bloor, she was a living symbol of the American Communist movement for three decades, and a rabble-rouser who stirred up many an audience with her fiery oratory. At the same time, Bloor's personal correspondence reveals a loving, if frequently absent, mother and a faithful friend who served as an inspiration to many. She joined the Communist Party in 1919, at age 57, because she felt it was the organization most capable of furthering the cause of working men and women. Party membership for Bloor was a means to the ultimate end—freedom and justice for the American worker.

Ella Reeve Bloor was born July 8, 1862, on Staten Island, New York, the oldest of ten children. Both her mother **Harriet Disbrow Reeve** and her father Charles could trace their families back to the original settlers of Connecticut. Charles Reeve was a druggist, moving his family to

Ella Reeve Bloor

Bridgeton, New Jersey, where he owned a drug store. The Reeve family was a prosperous one, and Bloor's childhood was comfortable. After several years of public school, Bloor briefly attended the Ivy Hall Seminary. She later remembered hating school and left at the age of 14 to be taught at home by her mother. During this period, she was an avid reader of the novels of such authors as George Eliot (***Mary Anne Evans**) and Charles Dickens and the essays of Ralph Waldo Emerson. She was also active in the Presbyterian Church, often joining the minister on visits to the poor.

As Bloor increasingly came to question the social conditions of her day, she grew close to her paternal great-uncle, Dan Ware. Her parents, especially her father, disapproved of their daughter's nascent radicalism. In Dan Ware, a former abolitionist and supporter of the Greenbackers, Bloor found a supportive and influential role model. He introduced the young woman to the work of the agnostic Robert Ingersoll and of Charles Darwin as well as to the teachings of the Unitarian Church. Bloor was 17 when her mother died. Until her father remarried two years later, she took care of her younger siblings and the house. Bloor did not take kindly to the new Mrs. Reeve, supposedly one of the richest women in Bridgeton. Shortly after her father's remarriage, 19-year-old Bloor married Dan Ware's son, Lucien.

Lucien Ware was a court stenographer and the young couple lived in various New Jersey towns wherever he could find work. In just under three years, Bloor gave birth to three children. Soon after the third birth, the older two children suddenly died within hours of each other, victims of spinal meningitis. There would be three more babies born to Ella and Lucien Ware in the next seven years. Still, the shock of losing two children on the same day was a tragedy which haunted Bloor the rest of her life. Eventually, the Wares settled in Woodbury, New Jersey. It was there, while tied to the house caring for four small children and feeling "well on the way to becoming just a household drudge," that Bloor decided to act. She joined the fight for women's suffrage and wrote articles for local newspapers demanding the vote. By the mid-1880s, Bloor was the president of the Woodbury branch of the Women's Christian Temperance Union (WCTU) and a member of the Prohibition Party. She was also a member of a "mixed local" of the Knights of Labor.

Thousands of women similar to Bloor in education and upbringing joined the suffrage and temperance campaigns in the 1880s. Her affiliation with the Knights of Labor, however, was less typical. Bloor would later write that it was the influence of ***Frances Willard**, president of the WCTU and a member of the Knights of Labor, which caused Bloor to join her first union. While Bloor would be interested in women's rights and the cause of temperance throughout her public life, it was the labor movement to which she dedicated her life. By the early 1890s, she traveled frequently to nearby Philadelphia, taking botany and biology courses at the University of Pennsylvania. She also joined the Ethical Culture Society of Philadelphia and through that group, first became exposed to Marxism. Bloor organized women weavers in the Philadelphia suburb of Kensington and came to believe that organization was the only hope for the working class.

Throughout this period, she and her husband grew increasingly apart. Around 1895, torn by feelings for her husband, worry over the needs of her children, and a burning desire to become even more active in labor organizing, Bloor suffered a nervous breakdown and was incapacitated for two months. Much like other women, such as ***Jane Addams** and ***Charlotte Perkins Gilman**, Bloor emerged from her breakdown determined to make a difference. By 1896, now divorced from Lucien Ware, she moved to New York City, her four children in tow. There she met the socialist Eugene Debs, joined his newly formed Social Democratic Party, and organized railroad workers in Brooklyn. In 1897, Bloor married Louis Cohen, a Fels Naphtha soap salesman and fellow socialist, with whom she would have two more children. This marriage would end five years later.

> It has been a joy and privilege to carry the torch of socialism.
>
> —Ella Reeve Bloor

During the early years of the 20th century, the American socialist movement was frequently divided by theoretical disputes. Bloor's brand of socialism was a practical one, less driven by theory than by her concern for the working class. By 1900, disillusioned with the "utopian" nature of the Social Democrats, Bloor joined the Socialist Labor Party (SLP), then led by Daniel DeLeon, and worked as an organizer for the SLP's union, the Socialist Trade and Labor Alliance. Within two years, factional disputes within the SLP drove Bloor back into the arms of Eugene Debs and his renamed Socialist Party (SP) of America. Now separated from Louis Cohen, Bloor was appointed state organizer for the SP in Pennsylvania and Delaware in 1902, working primarily with miners in the Wilkes-Barre area.

Around this time, for the sake of her children, she established a home in the utopian, single-tax community in Arden, Delaware. There, the children were looked after by other residents while Bloor traveled from state to state on behalf of the Socialist Party. During the years 1905 to 1908, Bloor worked on and off in Connecticut where she was particularly active in the fight for child-labor legislation. She wrote several moving pieces for local newspapers and national periodicals such as *Wiltshire's* and *Pearson's* on the horrible conditions children faced in factories and mines. In 1908, she ran for Connecticut secretary of state on the Socialist Party ticket. Although she was unsuccessful in her bid, Bloor was elected SP state organizer that same year.

In 1906, still known as Ella Cohen, Bloor traveled to Chicago at the request of her friend and fellow socialist, Upton Sinclair. His recently published novel, *The Jungle*, was causing a public outcry over the deplorable conditions found in the nation's meatpacking industry. In response, President Theodore Roosevelt established a commission to investigate. Unable to go to Chicago to gather more evidence, Sinclair asked Bloor to go in his place. However, Sinclair felt it would be improper and possibly unsafe for the 44-year-old mother of six to travel alone. Ella Cohen went to Chicago in the company of the young Welsh immigrant, Richard Bloor; they posed as man and wife. She then wrote articles using Bloor's name about the conditions the couple found in the Chicago slaughterhouses. While the two soon parted company, the name stuck. She would be known as Ella Reeve Bloor for the next 45 years.

Ella Bloor spent several years organizing for the Socialist Party and for numerous unions. In 1910, she was elected Ohio state organizer for the SP and worked with coal miners in that state and in West Virginia. During this period, she came to be known as Mother Bloor. Just over 50, her blond hair now streaked with grey, the petite grandmother worked the coal fields alongside another famous "Mother," ***Mary Harris Jones**. True to her beginnings, Bloor took time out from labor organizing to participate in the 1913 Ohio women's suffrage referendum campaign. Shortly before Christmas, 1913, she traveled to Calumet, Michigan, to work with the striking copper miners. In one of the most dramatic passages of her autobiography, Bloor recalled the suffocation death of 73 children attending the miners' union Christmas party. The union would eventually claim that it was the local deputies, at the request of the mining company, who yelled "Fire!" into the crowded hall where the party was held. In the panic to escape down a narrow stairwell from a fire which was not there, several children fell and were trapped. "They laid out the little bodies in a row on the platform beneath the Christmas tree," Bloor later wrote. "Afterwards I saw the marks of the children's nails in the plaster, where they had scratched to get free, as they suffocated." Bloor left this massacre only to witness another. In April 1914, she was in Ludlow, Colorado, working with the striking miners. On April 20, 13 children and a pregnant woman were burned to death after the state militia set fire to the strikers' tent colony. As a mother who had lost children of her own, the violent death of so many children, children who in her mind were the innocent victims of capitalist repression, represented to Bloor the dire need of workers to organize.

When the United States entered World War I in 1917, Bloor was living in New York City, working as a national organizer for the United Cloth Hat and Cap Makers Union. As a member of the left-wing of the Socialist Party which viewed the conflict as an act of imperialism, Bloor actively campaigned against the war. Although she avoided arrest under the Sedition Act, as field organizer for the Workers Defense Union, she spoke across the country on behalf of those arrested for their antiwar activities. One bright spot of hope for Bloor and for many of her friends was the Russian Revolution in 1917. For Bloor, "It brought new courage and inspiration to all who made the workers' cause their own. It brought what had seemed a distant, shining ideal into the realm of practical, living reality."

In 1919, disappointed in the Socialist Party's stance on the war, Bloor was one of several who participated in the formation of the American Communist Party. For the next 30 years, she worked tirelessly for the party, organizing across the country. Bloor faced arrest numerous times for speaking, especially during the 1920s and the height of anti-radical reaction in the United States. On January 2, 1920, she narrowly missed arrest in Worcester, Massachusetts. On that one day, thousands of Communists, Socialists, and radical labor organizers were arrested as part of the Palmer raids, directed by then U.S. Attorney General A. Mitchell Palmer. Hundreds would be imprisoned or deported. Bloor spent most of 1920 speaking on behalf of the political prisoners and was eventually arrested during a protest at the federal prison in Leavenworth, Kansas.

After a trip to the Soviet Union in 1921 as a trade union delegate to the first Red International of Labor Unions, Bloor spent the next several years organizing in the western United States. In 1925, in order to raise funds for the newly established Communist Party newspaper, the *Daily Worker*, the 63-year-old woman hitchhiked alone from California to Massachusetts. Two years later, Bloor hitchhiked across the country again, raising funds for the Sacco and Vanzetti defense fund. Sacco and Vanzetti, two Italian immigrant anarchists, had been charged and convicted of murdering a payroll guard during a Massachusetts robbery. Their case interested many American radicals who felt the government was more concerned about Sacco and Vanzetti's politics than their possible involvement in a hold up. Bloor arrived in Boston in time to join the massive demonstrations protesting the execution of the two men and was arrested twice in one day for inciting to riot.

Throughout the 1920s, Bloor continued her efforts among American workers. She helped organize textile workers in Lawrence, Massachusetts, and Passaic, New Jersey. She went on a speaking tour to raise funds for women textile workers on strike in Gastonia, North Carolina. Working for the National Miners Union, Bloor organized coal miners in Pennsylvania, Kentucky, and Indiana. During this period, she tried to avoid the factional disputes within the Communist Party. Her devotion was to the workers, and she saw the party as the most expedient way of achieving justice for the working class. Theoretical disputes were of little interest to her. Nonetheless, when summoned to Moscow in 1929 by Joseph Stalin, Bloor went. She successfully defended herself against charges that she was part of an American faction disobeying the orders of the Comintern, the international ruling body of the Communist Party. Unlike several other comrades, Bloor was not expelled from the party. However, perhaps as a form of banishment, she was sent to North Dakota where she spent the next two years organizing American farmers.

Even before the stock market crash of 1929, agriculture had suffered greatly in America. Bad weather, poor harvests, and an unstable market meant farmers were already in a precarious financial state when the Great Depression began. Although Bloor had spent 30 years organizing industrial workers, she instinctively knew how to reach many of the farmers throughout the Dakotas and Montana. As an organizer for the United Farmers' League, Bloor was active in the Farmers' Holiday movement. By refusing to produce food stuffs, they hoped that the nation would recognize the vital role small farmers played in the American economy.

The Communist Party apparently appreciated Bloor's work with the farmers, for in 1932 she was elected to the Central Executive Committee, the party's highest ruling body. More good fortune came to Bloor during her stint in the American West. In 1930, she met and married Andrew Omholt, a North Dakota farmer and Communist more than 20 years her junior and a foot taller than the petite Bloor. The two came east in 1933 where Bloor took part in the Ambridge, Pennsylvania, steel strike, one of the most violent labor actions during the Great Depression. In 1934, Bloor was arrested for the 36th and final time in Loup City, Nebraska, where she spoke on behalf of striking women chicken pluckers. While out on bail, she traveled to Paris for the Women's International Congress Against War and Fascism.

The following year was a difficult one for Bloor. After all appeals were exhausted, she spent 30 days in an Omaha, Nebraska, jail for her part in the Loup City strike. Also in 1935, Bloor suffered the loss of her oldest son and fellow Communist, Hal Ware. She devoted an entire chapter of her 1940 autobiography to her son, detailing his work for the party as agricultural expert. Yet again, Bloor rallied and spent the summer of 1936 campaigning for Communist Party candidates across the country, accompanied by Omholt and two of her granddaughters. In 1937, after traveling to the Soviet Union as an honored guest of the 20th Anniversary of the October Revolution celebration, Bloor "retired" in her 75th year. The occasion of her birthday that year became a "colossal festival and mass celebration" sponsored by the Communist Party on Staten Island, New York. Thereafter, Mother Bloor birthday celebrations became an annual Communist Party event.

Also in 1937, an American unit fighting the fascists in Spain named itself the Mother Bloor brigade. Although supposedly in retirement on the Pennsylvania apple farm where she and her husband now lived, Bloor would continue her public life, representing her party in the fight against fascism. While she had been an avowed pacifist during World War I, Bloor, like many others, felt quite differently about the second World War. Communism was ideologically opposed to fascism and the American Communist Party put its full weight behind sustaining the war effort. As part of her 80th birthday tour in the summer of 1942, Bloor and fellow CP leader **Anita Whitney**, who was celebrating her 75th birthday, made 23 appearances in 20 days. After a brief rest, Bloor continued the tour alone and made another 21 appearances in a month. Speaking on the party's "Win the War Against Fascism" theme, her goal was to particularly attract women to party membership. Their numbers did increase during this period.

In the years after World War II, the U.S. government once again reacted against radical movements. The Taft-Hartley Act, the Smith Act, and the McCarthy hearings all took their toll on the American Communist Party. Perhaps because of her age, Bloor was never indicted nor was she called to testify as so many of her comrades were. By 1948, the FBI which had followed her movements for almost 30 years noted that her "mind wanders" and in 1949 canceled her security index card due to "mental decrepitude."

Ella Reeve Bloor died in a nursing home in Richlandtown, Pennsylvania, on August 10, 1951. She was 89 years old. The woman known as Mother Bloor to countless workers was remembered fondly in death. In the *Daily Worker*, ***Elizabeth Gurley Flynn** wrote, "Her life was devoted to fighting against capitalism and all its foul deeds." On the afternoon of August 14th, Bloor's body lay in state in New York City's St. Nicholas Arena. Seven thousand mourners passed by the open casket and another 3,000 attended the funeral service that night. The next day, she was buried in the same Camden, New Jersey, cemetery as the poet, Walt Whitman. The service ended with the reading of one of Bloor's favorite works by Whitman, "The Magic Trumpeter": "War, suffering gone/ The rank earth purged/ nothing but joy left!"

SOURCES:

Barton, Anne. *Mother Bloor: The Spirit of '76.* NY: Workers Library Publishers, 1937.

Bloor, Ella Reeve. *We Are Many.* NY: International Publishers, 1940.

Flynn, Elizabeth Gurley. *Daughters of America: Ella Reeve Bloor and Anita Whitney.* NY: Workers Library Publishers, 1942.

SUGGESTED READING:

Buhle, Mari Jo. *Women and American Socialism, 1870–1920.* Urbana, IL: University of Illinois Press, 1981.

Draper, Theodore. *American Communism and Soviet Russia: The Formative Period.* NY: Vintage Books, 1960.

COLLECTIONS:

Correspondence, papers, and memorabilia located in the Sophia Smith Collection, Smith College, Northampton, Massachusetts.

Kathleen Banks Nutter,
Department of History,
University of Massachusetts,
Amherst, Massachusetts

Blount, Elizabeth (c. 1502–c. 1540).

See Six Wives of Henry VIII for sidebar.

Blount, Martha (1690–1762)

English literary executor. *Born near Reading, England, on June 15, 1690; died in Berkeley Row, Hanover Square, London, 1762; educated at Hammersmith and in Paris.*

Martha Blount was an intimate friend of Alexander Pope, who dedicated his *Epistle on Women* (1735) to her. In his will, Pope left Blount £1,000, many books, and all his household goods; he also made her residuary legatee.

Blow, Susan Elizabeth (1843–1916)

American educator who opened the first public kindergarten in the U.S. at the Des Peres School in St. Louis, Missouri. *Born Susan Elizabeth Blow on June 7, 1843, in Carondelet (now St. Louis), Missouri; died on March 26, 1916, in New York, New York; daughter of a prosperous entrepreneur and later congressional representative; educated by tutors and at a private school in New York.*

Susan Blow studied the revolutionary teaching methods of Friedrich Froebel while in Germany as part of a European tour, and later furthered her studies with **Maria Kraus-Boelté** in New York. With permission from the superintendent of the St. Louis schools, who was also a devotee of the German idealist philosophy, Blow opened the first public kindergarten in America at the Des Peres School in 1873. The next year, she established a training school for kindergarten teachers. By 1880, with Blow acting as an unofficial and unpaid supervisor, kindergartens were part of every public school in the city, and the St. Louis system became the model as the movement spread across the country.

Blow's adherence to Froebel's doctrines did not allow for much flexibility, but younger teachers nonetheless began to experiment with new techniques in the 1880s. Suffering from deteriorating health, Blow eventually began to lose control of the schools. In 1889, she moved east, lectured on Froebelian theory, and wrote on kindergarten practice. In an excerpt from her article "Letters to a Mother on the Philosophy of Froebel," written in 1900, Blow addresses what she viewed as the susceptibility of children to corruption: "Many are injured by all kinds of ugly and tawdry playthings, and by badly drawn and crudely colored picture.... [W]e forget that all true beauty implies strength and simplicity and we warp the taste of children by the excessive luxury of our homes." From 1905 to 1909, Susan Blow was a lecturer at Columbia University Teacher's College. She died in New York on March 26, 1916.

Barbara Morgan,
Melrose, Massachusetts

Blum, Arlene (1945—)

American mountaineer, author, and chemist. *Born in 1945; raised in Chicago, Illinois; daughter of a physician and a violinist; graduated from Reed College, Portland, Oregon, and University of California, Berkeley; children: one daughter.*

Organized and led the first all-women's expedition to the summit of Mount Denali, Alaska (1970); organized and led the first all-female expedition to the summit of Annapurna I in the Himalayas (1978); hiked entire length of the Great Himalaya Range; did scientific research that led to the ban of a carcinogenic chemical from use in American clothing; taught at Stanford University, Wellesley College, and University of California, Berkeley; awarded Gold Medal from the Society of Women Geographers.

Born at the end of World War II, Arlene Blum was raised in Chicago by grandparents after her parents' divorce. In high school, she earned high marks in advanced science and math classes, and attended Reed College with a desire to be a chemist. "I knew 'girls weren't supposed to be chemists,'" she later said, "And it's always sort of nice to do things you're not supposed to do." This outlook would drive her to some of her greatest achievements.

Blum began climbing mountains in college, later combining this avocation with her career as a chemist. After participating in expeditions to Mexico and the Andes, she applied to join an expedition to Afghanistan but was denied because she was a woman. It was believed then that women could not handle the highest elevations and would adversely affect the morale of all-male teams. After again being excluded from an expedition going to Alaska's Mount Denali, she organized her own all-women's team. In July 1970, they made history when they stood at summit. In 1976, she was part of the American bicentennial ascent of Mount Everest.

In 1978, Blum again proved women had the stamina to succeed in this sport when she led an all-female assault on the hazardous Annapurna I, the tenth-highest mountain in the world. The American Women's Himalayan Expedition

Arlene Blum

raised the $80,000 needed in part by selling t-shirts bearing the slogan, "A Woman's Place Is On Top . . . Annapurna." Two of the team's climbers reached the summit along with two Sherpas, but tragically, two other team members died on the mountainside. Blum wrote a book about the experience that detailed logistical problems, personality conflicts among the team, and her own struggles with the demands of leadership. The book was re-published in 1998 on the 20th anniversary of the feat.

In addition to her notable accomplishments in chemistry and her teaching experience, Blum has led and participated in dozens of climbs and treks after Annapurna, sometimes accompanied by her daughter. She has contributed articles and photographs to such distinguished publications as *National Geographic.* She also presented motivational lectures and leadership training seminars across the United States and Nepal.

SOURCES:

Blum, Arlene. *Annapurna: A Woman's Place.* San Francisco, CA: Sierra Club Books, 1980.

Johnson, Anne Janette. *Great Women In Sports.* Detroit, MI: Visible Ink, 1998, p. 45.

Jacquie Maurice,
Calgary, Alberta, Canada

Blumental, Felicja (1918—)

Polish pianist and champion of the music of Polish composer Karol Szymanowski. *Born in Warsaw on December 28, 1918; studied at the Warsaw Conservatory.*

Felicja Blumental studied at the Warsaw Conservatory, making her debut in 1938. After an adventurous escape from Nazi-occupied Poland in 1942, she launched a successful career in the 1940s in Brazil. The great Brazilian composer Heitor Villa-Lobos dedicated his *Fifth Piano Concerto* to her, and Blumental gave its world premiere in 1956 with the London Philharmonic Orchestra. An enthusiastic believer in reviving old and little-known piano works, she made well-received recordings of a number of neglected concertos by Ries, Clementi and others. Felicja Blumental championed the music of the Polish composer Karol Szymanowski and recorded his *Symphonie* concertante, Op. 60. The modernist Polish composer Krysztof Penderecki composed his *Partita* for Harpsichord and Orchestra for her.

John Haag,
Athens, Georgia

Blunt, Anne (1837–1917).

See Lovelace, Ada Byron for sidebar.

Blunt, Katharine (1876–1954)

American educator and first woman president of Connecticut College. *Born in Philadelphia, Pennsylvania, on May 28, 1876; died on July 29, 1954; daughter of Stanhope English (an army officer and author of technical articles) and Fanny (Smyth) Blunt; attended "The Elms" and Miss Porter's school in Springfield, Massachusetts; received B.A. from Vassar College; attended Massachusetts Institute of Technology; received Ph.D. in organic chemistry from University of Chicago.*

Selected writings: (in collaboration with Florence Powdermaker) Food and the War *(1918); (with Ruth Cowan)* Ultra-Violet Light and Vitamin D in Nutrition *(1930); many articles on food chemistry for technical journals.*

Katharine Blunt, the third president (and first woman president) of Connecticut College, was a dynamic and driving force in the institution's formative years. In a college publication called *Chapters in the History of Connecticut College,* she is called "a woman of judgment, of social instinct, of snap and vigor; sometimes imperious, sometimes flashing fire . . . a woman able to do a man's work with the encouragement a man needs, or without it." As a female college president in 1929, she was no doubt well served by her feisty nature.

A Phi Beta Kappa graduate from Vassar College, Blunt went on to receive a Ph.D. in organic chemistry from the University of Chicago. Beginning her teaching career at Pratt Institute in Brooklyn, New York, in 1913, she was then appointed to the home-economics faculty at the University of Chicago, where she remained until 1925. Blunt became chair of the department and raised the study of home economics to the graduate level, providing high quality, specialized study. During World War I, she worked for the Federal government as an expert on nutrition, writing leaflets on food conservation. In 1918, Blunt collaborated with **Florence Powdermaker** on a series of lesson plans for colleges called *Food and the War,* which was published by the U.S. Food Administration. During this time, she also became active in the American Home Economics Association, serving as president of the Illinois chapter, as national vice president, and as national president from 1924 to 1926.

When Blunt was appointed president of Connecticut College in 1929, it was the only college in the state offering a four-year course for women. As the first woman and only the third president of the young institution, she built up the college's faculty and increased financial resources. Blunt is credited with the construction of 18 building from 1929 through 1942, during which time she kept a constantly escalating budget in check. She increased research revenue and upgraded faculty salaries and benefits. She expanded the curriculum, helped develop and finance more scholarships, provided campus accommodations for resident students, and instituted apprenticeships in public affairs, economics, home economics, and business.

Blunt was also responsible for a number of innovative summer institutes, beginning in 1941, with the Latin American Institute. Organized at the request of Nelson Rockefeller (then coordinator of Inter-American Affairs), the institute examined Latin American trade relations, economics, and politics. A secretarial school also met for a six-week session that summer, and in 1942 the college held an eight-week summer "War Session" for the training of secretaries, chemists, accountants, statisticians, and nursery-school teachers. In addition to the summer institutes, Blunt encouraged college-sponsored lectures, conferences and concerts. The Institute of Women's Professional Relations, established in 1929 as a informational clearinghouse for business and professional women, was also headquartered at the college.

In 1943, Blunt retired, age 67, but was called back two years later when the succeeding president, Dr. **Dorothy Schaffter,** returned to nonacademic work. Blunt served until June 1946, when she retired for a second time. In addition to an honorary LL.D. from Connecticut College, she was awarded honorary degrees from Wesleyan University, Mount Holyoke College, and the University of Chicago. Blunt believed that women could shape the world around them and that they should be encouraged to participate in every field open to them. In the *Journal of the Association of American University Women,* she directed teachers to provide their students with the "contacts with life which vitalize the theory and destroy 'ivory tower isolation'." Katharine Blunt died on July 29, 1954.

Barbara Morgan,
Melrose, Massachusetts

Katharine Blunt

Bly, Nellie (1864–1922).

See Seaman, Elizabeth Cochrane.

Blyth, Ann (1928—)

***American actress and singer, nominated for an Oscar for her performance in* Mildred Pierce.** *Born Ann Marie Blyth in Mt. Kisco, New York, on August 16, 1928; attended St. Stephen's and St. Patrick's schools and the New York Professional Children's School; studied voice and spent three years as a soprano with the San Carlo Opera Company; married James McNulty (a doctor, and brother of singer-comedian Dennis Day), on June 27, 1953; children: five.*

Filmography: Chip Off the Old Block *(1944);* The Merry Monahans *(1944);* Babes on Swing Street *(1944);* Bowery to Broadway *(1944);* Mildred Pierce *(1945);* Swell Guy *(1947);* Brute Force *(1947);* Killer McCoy *(1947);* A Woman's Vengeance *(1948);* Another Part of the Forest *(1948);* Mr. Peabody and the Mermaid *(1948);* Red Canyon *(1949);* Top o' the Morning *(1949);* Free for All *(1949);* Our Very Own *(1950);* The Great Caruso *(1951);* Katie Did It *(1951);* Thunder on the Hill *(1951);* The Golden Horde *(1951);* The House in the Square *(1951);* I'll Never Forget You *(1951);* Sally and Saint Anne *(1952);* One Minute to Zero *(1952);* The World in His Arms *(1952);* All the Brothers Were Valiant *(1953);* Rose Marie *(1954);* The Student Prince *(1954);* The King's Thief *(1955);* Kismet *(1955);* Slander *(1957);* The Buster Keaton Story *(1957);* The Helen Morgan Story *(1957).*

Ann Blyth

Actress Ann Blyth, who is often remembered for her dazzling smile and soprano voice in the 1950's musicals *The Student Prince* and *Kismet*, was also a fine dramatic actress. For an early film role as ***Joan Crawford**'s vindictive daughter in *Mildred Pierce* (1945), a role that is sometimes overlooked in light of her later work, Blyth was nominated for an Oscar as best supporting actress. Another dramatic effort in ***Lillian Hellman**'s *Another Part of the Forest* (1948) is indicative of her impressive range.

The product of a broken home, Blyth was brought up by her mother on New York City's East Side and knew at an early age that she wanted to be an actress. She began her career on the radio at the age of five and, while still a schoolgirl, sang with the San Carlo Opera Company. In 1941, at only 13, she played the daughter in Lillian Hellman's *Watch on the Rhine*, which caught the attention of a Universal Pictures' talent scout. Blyth made her film debut in *Chip off the Old Block* (1944), opposite Donald O'Connor, followed by a few other forgettable teenage parts. After her success in *Mildred Pierce*, performed while on loan to Warner Bros., Blyth was scheduled for another dramatic role in *Her Kind of Man* (1946), when she fractured her back in a tobogganing accident. After seven months in a steel brace, she returned to wonderful notices for her portrayal of the amoral young Regina Hubbard in *Another Part of the Forest* (1948). Although she seemed destined for a career as a dramatic actress, she opted instead for more conventional ingenue roles.

In the 1950s, Blyth starred opposite Mario Lanza in *The Great Caruso* (1951) and ***Claudette Colbert** in *Thunder on the Hill* (1951). She was also featured in a few adventure films, as well as three operettas: *Rose Marie* (1954), *The Student Prince* (1954), and *Kismet* (1955), all of which made use of her trained singing voice. Her last films were a pair of screen biographies in 1957, *The Buster Keaton Story* (with Donald O'Connor) and *The* ***Helen Morgan** *Story*. She then retired to a family life that included her husband James McNulty and five children, although she continued to venture forth for an occasional appearance in a summer-stock musical or television commercial.

Barbara Morgan,
Melrose, Massachusetts

Blythe, Betty (1893–1972)

American leading lady of the silent era. *Born Elizabeth Blythe Slaughter in Los Angeles, California, on September 1, 1893; died in 1972; niece of writer Samuel G. Blythe; educated in a convent and at the University of Southern California; married Paul Scardon, in 1924 (died 1954).*

Filmography: His Own People *(1918);* Over the Top *(1918);* A Game with Fate *(1918);* Fighting Destiny *(1919);* The Man Who Won *(1919);* Undercurrent *(1919);* The Third Generation *(1920);* The Silver Horde *(1920);* Nomads of the North *(1920);* Queen of Sheba *(1921);* The Truant Husband *(1921);* His Wife's Husband *(1922);* How Women Love *(1922);* The Darling of the Rich *(1923);* Chu Chin Chow *(1923);* Sinner or Saint *(1923);* The Breath of Scandal *(1924);* She *(Britain, 1925);* Snowbound *(1927);* The Girl from Gay Paree *(1927);* Sisters of Eve *(1928);* Stolen Love *(1928);* Tom Brown of Culver *(1932);* Pilgrimage *(1933);* Only Yesterday *(1933);* Ever Since Eve *(1934);* The Scarlet Letter *(1934);* The Gorgeous Hussy *(1936);* Conquest *(1937);* Honky Tonk *(1941);* Where Are Your Children? *(1944);* Docks of New York *(1945);* Madonna of the Desert *(1948); (cameo)* My Fair Lady *(1964).*

Silent film buffs remember Betty Blythe for her title role in the 1921 hit *The Queen of* ***Sheba***, in which she wore nothing above the waist but delicate, strategically placed chains. This was the role and costume she never tired of talking about, often recounting her screen test for the part, during which she tripped over the elaborate train on the gown.

After her father, a Los Angeles lawyer, died when she was two, Blythe and her two sisters were raised by their mother. Though Blythe was more interested in baseball than boys or theatrics, her mother encouraged a stage career and provided voice lessons. As a teenager, Blythe traveled to Europe with a theatrical company, playing in *The Peacock Princess*. Her mother died soon after her return, leaving her on her own. In 1915, she landed a role on Broadway in *High Jinks*, and the following year went on the road with the hit *So Long Letty*. After the tour, she suffered a dry spell until she accompanied a friend to an interview at the Vitagraph Company in Brooklyn, where the director W.P.S. Earl and his star Earl Williams spotted her in the reception room and hired her on the spot.

Her best roles were in the late teens and 1920s, although her voice training allowed her to move into talkies with ease. Among her most important films in addition to *Sheba*, were *She* (1917), which was later remade as a talkie with ***Helen Gahagan Douglas**, and *Chu-Chin-Chow* (1925). Blythe worked steadily through the 1930s but in smaller roles for second-rate pictures. She was last seen in a bit part in *My Fair Lady* (1964).

Throughout her career, Blythe earned most of her income by teaching acting and diction out of the large home in Hollywood that she shared with her husband of 34 years, Paul Scardon. She also occasionally appeared in road company productions, including *The Man Who Came to*

Dinner (1940) and *Wallflower* (1944). In 1967, over a decade after her husband's death, Blythe moved to the Motion Picture Country home in Woodland Hills, California, where she lived in a cottage once occupied by the late Gareth Hughes who costarred with her in two movies. She lived out her final years regaling oldtimers with stories of her heyday in Hollywood.

Barbara Morgan,
Melrose, Massachusetts

Blyton, Enid (1897–1968)

Prolific English writer of children's stories who has been consistently popular with young readers for over 50 years but whose writing has been frequently condemned by librarians, teachers, and literary critics.

Name variations: Mary Pollock. Born Enid Mary Blyton on August 11, 1897, in East Dulwich, London; died on November 28, 1968 in Hampstead, London; eldest child and only daughter of Thomas Carey Blyton, Jr. (worker in a wholesale clothing business) and Theresa Mary (Harrison) Blyton; attended St. Christopher's School for Girls, Beckenham, 1907–15, and Ipswich High School, 1916–18; married Major Hugh Alexander Pollock, on August 28, 1924 (divorced 1943); married Kenneth Darrell Waters, on October 20, 1943 (died, September 15, 1967); children: (first marriage) Gillian Mary (b. July 15, 1931); Imogen Mary (b. October 27, 1935).

Father left home (1910); Enid left home (1916); three poems accepted by Nash's Magazine *(1916–18); taught at Bickley Park School (Jan.–Dec. 1919); hired as nursery governess (January 1920–April 1924); collaborated with artist friend, Phyllis Chase (1921); wrote* Child Whispers *(1922); wrote* Teachers' World *(1923); began to edit* Sunny Stories *(1926); became interested in People's Dispensary for Sick Animals (1933); turned* Sunny Stories *into a weekly (1937); wrote last entry to* Teachers' World *(Nov. 14, 1945); met Harmsen van der Beek (1949); withdrew from editing* Sunny Stories *and started fortnightly* Enid Blyton Magazine *(1953); had first performance of* Noddy in Toyland *(December 1954); published last edition of* Enid Blyton Magazine *(September 9, 1959).*

Selected writings: well over 400 publications, not counting numerous articles and stories in periodicals, including (fantasy) Adventures of the Wishing Chair, *(1937); (holiday adventure)* The Secret Island *(1938),* Five on a Treasure Island, *(1942),* The Island of Adventure *(1944),* The Rockingdown Mystery *(1949); (detective fiction)* The Mystery of the Burnt Cottage *(1943),* The Secret Seven, *(1949); (circus stories)* Mr. Galliano's Circus *(1938); (family stories)* The Children of Cherry Tree Farm (1940); (school stories) *Naughtiest Girl in the School* (1940), *The Twins at St. Clare's* (1941), *First Term at Mallory Towers* (1946); (nursery stories) *Mary Muse and the Dolls' House* (1942), *Little Noddy Goes to Toyland*, (1949).

In writing about Enid Blyton one is drawn into seemingly incredible statistics. It has been claimed that she negotiated personally with over 40 publishers and that she could stipulate a first printing of 25,000 copies even during the paper shortage of World War II. She is said to have written at the rate of 10,000 words a day and, according to the *Oxford Guide to British Writers*, "could complete a full-length children's book between Monday and Friday of the same week." Over 700 titles have been published bearing her name, and she has been translated into more than 126 languages and dialects. Ten years after her death, English language sales of her books had topped 200 million copies and were still increasing at the rate of 5 million books a year. Many of her stories are still read avidly by children the world over, and, since 1990, 792 of her books and their derivatives have been in print using virtually every well-known British publisher. Who was this woman who, even in her lifetime, was referred to on more than one occasion as "a phenomenon?"

Enid Blyton lived all her life in and around London, though both her parents came from Sheffield, an industrial town in Yorkshire. At the time of his marriage, Enid's father Thomas Carey Blyton was a salesperson with a cutlery firm, but he came from an intellectually minded family and his varied hobbies included astronomy, nature, languages, music, painting, photography, and collecting books. Enid's mother Theresa was dark and pretty, but she had little sympathy with her husband's many interests and was engrossed in being a highly efficient housewife. This disparity was to cause friction later in their marriage, but at first all went well. The Blytons moved to London shortly after their wedding in 1896, and on August 11 of the following year Enid Mary was born. She was followed two years later by Hanly and three years after by Carey. Enid had been born in a small apartment over a shop, but by 1902 Thomas' situation had improved. He was working in the wholesale clothing business, and the family was living in a solidly middle-class house with a garden in which the children could play.

From the beginning, Thomas seems to have felt a special bond with his daughter. He

Enid Blyton

claimed to have saved her life by nursing her through the night when she was dangerously ill with whooping cough when only three months old. In her early years, Thomas helped Enid tend her own little patch of garden, gave her the run of the library, quoted poetry, told her stories, and took her for country walks while teaching her all he knew about the things they saw. When she was six, he began to teach her the piano, for it was his ambition that his daughter should become a concert pianist.

In contrast, Theresa favored her sons. She felt that, as a girl, Enid should be content to help her in the house, and Theresa resented the way in which Thomas encouraged their daughter's other interests. Perhaps, too, Theresa was jealous of the warm relationship which existed between father and daughter, for she was a stern disciplinarian and found it hard to show affection even to her more tractable sons. It also has to be admitted that Enid had a fiery temper and could not tolerate her mother's domineering manner because she, too, wished to dominate.

Enid's first school was a small nursery class near home, run by two unmarried sisters. Although she always had difficulty with math,

Enid was a ready pupil, and, in 1907, she went to St. Christopher's School for Girls, Beckenham. The Blytons had been steadily growing more antagonistic towards one another, and a move into an even larger house did nothing to ease the tension. The sounds of Thomas playing the piano in the evenings which had so often lulled the children to sleep were exchanged for the sounds of quarrelling and the name of another woman. But, following the conventions of the time, nothing was said to Enid or her brothers. Finally, shortly before Enid's 13th birthday, Thomas left home. He gave no explanation to the daughter whose companion he had been for so long, and Theresa, intent upon keeping up appearances before the neighbors, failed to give Enid the support she so badly needed; the children were instructed to say that their father was "away on a visit." Then, the family, minus Thomas, soon moved yet again. Thus, at a highly vulnerable age, Enid suffered rejection by the person she loved most, her father, and was taught by her mother to deal with the hurt by ignoring it. This lesson was to have repercussions throughout her life.

Outwardly Enid's school life was completely untouched by this domestic trauma. Even her best friend, **Mary Attenborough**, had no idea Thomas Blyton had left home. After becoming the first girl in the school to adopt the new fashion of shoulder-length hair rather than the conventional long plait, Enid's nickname among boarders was "the hairless daygirl." As a senior girl, helped by Mary and a small group of other friends, she organized end-of-term entertainments for the entire school which consisted of singing, dancing, and short sketches. Blyton was academically gifted, good at games (she became tennis champion and captain of the lacrosse team) and, despite a penchant for practical jokes, was sufficiently popular with both girls and staff to be made Head Girl towards the end of her time there. In company with many other girls before and since, she and two of her closest friends wrote a small magazine for awhile and, when apart, wrote to each other in code.

Although living with another woman, Thomas never lost touch with his family. His financial position was now such that he could afford to house them in an expensive residential area of Beckenham, pay the children's school fees and all household expenses. He still insisted on Enid doing her daily hour of piano practice and, in time, began to visit occasionally and to take her on outings. However, their former father-daughter intimacy had been lost forever.

Before Thomas left the family home, Enid had learned to shut out the sounds of discord downstairs by telling herself stories as she fell asleep. In the new house, she once again shut out her unhappiness, spending more and more time locked in her own room away from the unwelcome company of her mother and brothers and retreating into a fantasy world of stories and poetry. Encouraged by winning a poetry competition in Arthur Mee's *Children's Magazine*, she began to send off many articles, stories and poems to other periodicals but, apart from one poem accepted by *Nash's Magazine*, they were for many years rejected.

Her other method of dealing with the uncongeniality of her home was to stay away as much as possible. The Blytons had strong connections with the Baptist denomination (Enid's brother Carey was the third generation to hold the name of William Carey, the man who had helped to found the Baptist Missionary Society), and all three children had attended Sunday School at Elm Road Baptist Church. Here Mary Attenborough's father was superintendent, and her unmarried aunt, **Mabel Attenborough**, was teacher of the older girls' class. Mabel lived with her parents and was always glad to welcome Mary and Enid to her home. As time went by, Enid began to turn to Mabel for the sympathy, understanding, and encouragement which she had never received from her mother. When the Blytons moved yet again, this time to a smaller house, Enid spent more time than ever with Mabel.

Enid's life was to change completely in 1916. In accordance with her father's wishes, she was already enrolled as a student at the Guildhall School of Music in London for the autumn term, but before this she went on holiday to a farm in Suffolk run by George and **Emily Hunt**, friends of Mabel Attenborough. There, Blyton enjoyed helping with the animals, joking with the young officers billeted at the farm (for it was war time), and making friends with Ida and Marjory, the Hunts' daughters. **Ida Hunt** was a kindergarten teacher, and, when on Sunday she went to Woodbridge Congregational Church Sunday School, Enid accompanied her. Ida was surprised how well the children responded to Enid, while Enid was surprised by how much she enjoyed it.

Before the holiday was over, Blyton had decided not to take up her place at the Guildhall but rather to train as a teacher by taking the same National Froebel Union course that Ida had taken at Ipswich High School, about ten miles away from the Hunts' farm. Blyton received her father's permission over the telephone but for some reason seems not to have told her mother. What is more, she never again returned home. Theresa Blyton felt obliged to resort to lies once more in order to save face in front of neighbors. This time, she spread it about that Enid had joined the Women's Land Army. As **Barbara Stoney** writes in *Enid Blyton, a Biography*:

> Such subterfuge may be difficult to understand in these days of emancipated women and reformed divorce laws, but in the narrow, suburban circles in which Theresa moved, not only was a wife living apart from her husband treated with suspicion but an unmarried daughter leaving home and not communicating with her family was even more suspect. No "nice" girl would consider such a step unless she had "something to hide."

During her time at Ipswich, Blyton shared lodgings with Ida and spent the holidays with the Hunts or with Mabel and her parents. She enjoyed her training and was an excellent student. In her testimonial, Miss Gale, the head mistress, called Enid "one of the best students we have had for some years." By January 1919, Blyton was teaching at Bickley Park School, Kent, but, at the end of the year, she left to become nursery governess to the four sons of Mabel's relations: Horace and **Gertrude Thompson** who lived in Surbiton, Surrey. Here she remained for four years, teaching not only the four boys, but also several other local children. All holidays were now spent at the Attenboroughs'.

It was during Blyton's time in Surbiton that her father died of a heart attack, aged only 50. She must have been grief-stricken, for the two were still in contact, but she never spoke of his death and did not attend the funeral. Slight contact with her brother Hanly was resumed, but Carey was in the Air Force, and Enid continued to ignore the existence of her mother.

Blyton submitted entries for publication with little success until, in 1920, she met up with an old school friend, illustrator **Phyllis Chase,** and they decided to do some work together. It was at this point that Blyton's literary fortunes began to improve, although it is important to note that not all the entries she submitted at this time were collaborations. However, the first story Blyton had published in *Teachers' World* on February 15, 1922, was illustrated by Chase, as well as the small book of verse, *Child Whispers*. The book was an instant success, and the story in *Teachers' World* marked the beginning of an association between that periodical and Blyton which lasted until 1945. Between 1923 and 1927, she wrote a column, "From my Window" and, from 1927 to 1929, a "Letter to Children" which was then expanded to a whole "Children's Page." She also began, in 1926, to edit and later write *Sunny Stories*.

Probably because of her teaching background and her early association with *Teachers' World*, many of Enid Blyton's first publications were of an educational nature. Between 1923 and 1936, she wrote plays (sometimes in collaboration with the composer Alec Rowley), as well as school readers and nature books; she also retold well-known folk stories and edited teaching manuals and books of information. Even as late as 1939, she published three books of plays for school performance. Though these were interspersed with occasional works of original fiction, it was not until the publication of *Adventures of the Wishing Chair* in 1937 that these began to predominate.

During her teens and early 20s, Blyton had little opportunity to meet young men of her own age and took little romantic interest with those she did meet. When she finally fell in love, it was with a man older and more experienced. Major Hugh Alexander Pollock was an editor at Newnes, the publishers. He was about ten years her senior, had fought with the Royal Scots Fusiliers, and had been awarded the D.S.O. in 1919. Though he was already married, his wife had left him during the war, and Hugh obtained his divorce at Easter, 1924, the same time Blyton left her post at Surbiton. About a year after meeting, they were married on August 28, 1924, and moved into a top-floor apartment in Chelsea. Early in 1926, the couple relocated to a new house in Beckenham. Enid called it Elfin Cottage.

> Her critics accused [Blyton] of using a limited and unchallenging vocabulary, of sexual stereotyping, of racism, and of middle-class bias. It had little effect on her popularity or her sales.
>
> —Joanne Shattock

Her life soon fell into a comfortable pattern. She and Hugh tended the garden, though the heavy work was done by Barker, a jobbing gardener. While Hugh was at work, Enid wrote, for there was a maid to attend to household tasks as befitted a middle-class couple of the period. Sometimes she visited publishers or Mabel who lived nearby, but the evenings were devoted to Hugh. She bought her first domestic pet (a dog) and mastered both the typewriter and driving a car. When, in 1929, the Pollocks heard that a new arterial road was to be built near Elfin Cottage, they moved to a 16th-century thatched cottage at Bourne End in Buckinghamshire.

Life at Bourne End was rather different from that at Beckenham. Both Enid and Hugh became involved in the social life of the surrounding area, playing tennis and bridge, being entertained and entertaining in return. In October 1930, they went on a cruise to Madiera and the Canary Islands; on their return, Enid, who had found it difficult to conceive and had now been married six years, learned that she was pregnant. The much longed for baby, a girl named Gillian Mary, arrived on July 15, 1931. Like many a new mother, Blyton seems to have had prenatal fantasies that she would be able to look after the baby and still have time for all her other activities. When she found that this was not so, she employed a young girl to help her, and soon Betty was virtually in sole charge of Gillian while Enid continued to write and socialize as before.

It was while they were living at Old Thatch that Hugh began to be afflicted with a mental illness. He, like Enid and so many others at this time, had tried to deal with life's unpleasantnesses by refusing to talk about them. But when great responsibilities at work (including, significantly, helping to publish Winston Churchill's World War I memoirs) were coupled with frequent social commitments at home, he began to break down under the strain and turned to drink in an attempt to cope. During 1933 and 1934, he took a series of holidays to try to "get away from it all."

On October 27, 1935, following a miscarriage the previous year, Enid gave birth to a second daughter, Imogen Mary. The nurse employed to look after mother and new child, **Dorothy Gertrude Richards**, was (with gaps) to remain Enid's lifelong friend. This was the more surprising as Blyton was not an easy employer, demanding exceptionally hard work from her staff and often dismissing them on a whim, although this again was not particularly unusual for the period. Richards was a convert to Roman Catholicism, and Blyton toyed with the idea of converting likewise, but decided against it because she felt it would be "too constricting."

Hugh's mental state seems to have been more stable for awhile until, worrying about the deteriorating situation in Europe, he once again began secretly drinking in an attempt to shut out a problem which was beyond his control. A serious bout of pneumonia in early summer, 1938, revealed his secret. For a while his life was in danger, but the crisis passed and the whole family went on holiday to the seaside.

They returned, not to Old Thatch, but to Green Hedges, a larger house in Beaconsfield, a Buckinghamshire town about 25 miles from London. Although the Pollocks had been looking for another home for some time, it was chosen by Enid and Dorothy, without consulting Hugh. None of this seems to have impinged upon Blyton's writing, apart from providing her with material for her *Teachers' World* column. Even the naming of Green Hedges was turned into a competition.

For the next 25 years, Enid Blyton's literary output was prodigious. Gradually original fiction took over from her other writing. In 1938, she published the first of her circus books, *Mr. Galliano's Circus*, and also the first of her full-length adventure stories, *The Secret Island*. Both initially appeared in serial form in *Sunny Stories*. The year 1942 saw the first of the 21 "Famous Five" books about four children and a dog. The "Adventure" books started in 1944 with *The Island of Adventure*, and the "Secret Seven" series began in 1949. All these books catered for children of about the same age, but the "Barney" books, also started in 1949, seemed aimed at an older audience. Though her books have been criticized for their "unreality," Bob Mullan argues that they appeal to children because they are grounded in their imaginative play where an adult concept of "reality" has no place.

Blyton also wrote school stories. Her first series, started in 1940 with the *Naughtiest Girl in the School*, was set in a co-educational school. This is unusual for the genre, but as, once again, it was first serialized in *Sunny Stories*, it was probably aimed at both boys and girls. A series about an all-girls' school, St. Clare's, commenced the following year, while six books about "Malory Towers" immediately followed from 1946 to 1951.

Blyton was engaged, too, in writing for younger children. During the Second World War, she produced a highly successful set of tiny books making use of magazine offcuts which, in more affluent times, had been thrown away. And, in 1949, the character for whom Enid Blyton came to be best known first made its appearance. The earliest "Noddy" books were a collaboration between Enid and a Dutch illustrator, Harmsen van der Beek. Some people have claimed that it was he, rather than she, who was responsible for the books' popularity. The drawings were so distinctive that when van der Beek died in 1953 others were able to continue the series virtually unnoticed. Commercially, Noddy was a great success. As well as stories, Blyton wrote a Christmas play, Noddy in *Toyland* and, as Barbara Stoney says, "there were 'Noddy' toys and games of every description, toothbrushes, soap, stationery, chocolate, clothing, cutlery, pottery and furnishings." Noddy also had his own record and a British television series.

Though Blyton is best remembered for her stories, she raised thousands of pounds for charity during her life, both giving time and money and encouraging children to support worthy causes in her weekly publications. She was particularly involved with the People's Dispensary for Sick Animals, the Shaftesbury Society Babies' Home at Beaconsfield, the Sunshine Homes for Blind Babies, and a center for spastic children at Chelsea. She was always aware of the responsibilities which her popularity with children laid upon her and, despite the criticisms which her books received even during her lifetime, sincerely felt that she provided her readers with a positive moral framework upon which to base their lives.

Although it did not appear to affect her writing and the more pressing affairs of wartime kept it out of the newspapers, there was great upheaval in the Pollock's domestic life in the early 1940s. When Hugh's wartime commitments kept him away from home for long periods, both began to form other romantic attachments and the situation culminated in divorce in 1943. On October 20, Blyton married a London surgeon, Kenneth Darrell Waters, and six days later Hugh married a colleague, **Ida Crowe**. Blyton's handling of her children at this time seems surprising in view of her own experience 30 years earlier. Neither was told of the breakup until a few days before the wedding, and Hugh was never allowed any further contact with his daughters.

Blyton seems to have been very happy with her second husband who was profoundly deaf, despite the fact that he had an uncertain temper and was not always easy to live with. However, he was proud of his wife's successes and protective of her interests. For many years, Enid had managed all her business affairs, but in 1950, at Kenneth's instigation, a company was formed, Darrell Waters Limited, to relieve her of some of the burden. Even so, she did not approve of all of its transactions and still insisted on dealing with her publishers personally over new manuscripts. In order to relax, Blyton added golf to her other hobbies. Gillian and Imogen adopted Kenneth's surname and went to boarding school and university. Gillian married in 1957 and Imogen ten years later. Sadly, at the end of her life, Enid's brain failed her. After suffering for several years from what Imogen called "pre-senile dementia," Blyton died in a Hampstead Nursing Home on November 28, 1968.

SOURCES:

Blyton, Enid. *The Story of My Life.* London: Pitkins, 1952.

Mullan, Bob. *The Enid Blyton Story.* London: Boxtree, 1987.

Ray, Sheila. *The Blyton Phenomenon.* London: Andre Deutsch, 1982.

Smallwood, Imogen. *A Childhood at Green Hedges.* London: Methuen, 1989.

Barbara Evans, Research Associate in Women's Studies at Nene College, Northampton, England

Boadicea (26/30–60 CE).

See Boudica.

Boardman, Eleanor (1898–1991)

American actress. *Born in Philadelphia, Pennsylvania, on August 19, 1898; died in Santa Barbara, California, in 1991; attended Academy of Fine Arts, Philadelphia; married film director King Vidor, in 1926 (divorced); married film director Harry d'Abbadie d'Arrast; children: (first marriage) two daughters.*

Films include: The Stranger's Banquet *(1922);* Gimme *(1923);* Souls for Sale *(1923);* Vanity Fair *(1923);* Three Wise Fools *(1923);* The Day of Faith *(1923);* Wine of Youth *(1924);* Sinners in Silk *(1924);* The Turmoil *(1924);* The Silent Accuser *(1924);* So This Is Marriage *(1924);* The Wife of the Centaur *(1924);* The Way of a Girl *(1925);* Proud Flesh *(1925);* Exchange of Wives *(1925);* The Only Thing *(1925);* The Circle *(1925);* Memory Lane *(1926);* The Auction Block *(1926);* Bardelys the Magnificent *(1926);* Tell It to the Marines *(1926);* The Crowd *(1928);* Diamond Handcuffs *(1928);* She Goes to War *(1929);* Mamba *(1930);* Redemption *(1930);* The Great Meadow *(1931);* The Flood *(1931);* Women Love Once *(1931);* The Squaw Man *(1931);* The Phantom President *(1932);* The Big Chance *(1933).*

Eleanor Boardman

Clad in black-and-white stripes against a field of daisies, 16-year-old Eleanor Boardman gained national attention as the Kodak girl on publicity posters for Eastman Kodak. A few years later, she left her home in Philadelphia for New York, thinking more of a career as a costume or set designer than as an actress. Her elegant beauty, however, did not escape several producers who suggested a screen test. In 1922, against the wishes of her strict, religious family, she signed a contract with the Goldwyn Company, soon to become Metro-Goldwyn-Mayer. Although she made films for other studios, she remained under contract with MGM until 1932, playing in comedies as well as romantic dramas.

Praised for her naturalness in front of the camera, Boardman is best remembered for her leading role in *The Crowd* (1928), a realistic study of life in an American city, directed by King Vidor, to whom she was married. The film was revolutionary at the time because of its realistic presentation and its down-to-earth story of a young married couple trying to raise their status without breeding or education. Boardman's portrayal, praised by *The New York Times* critic Mordaunt Hall as "a wonderful combination of charm and sympathy," captivated audiences a second time in 1981 when the movie was revived for a London Film Festival.

Despite her screen success, Boardman's association with Louis B. Mayer was difficult, as was her marriage to Vidor, which ended in divorce and a bitter custody battle over their two daughters. Disillusioned, Boardman left for Europe in 1933, where she made her last screen appearance in *The Three-Cornered Hat*. After a second marriage to director Harry d'Abbadie d'Arrast, Boardman divided her time between Europe and the United States. For a few years in the 1950s, she wrote a column on Paris for the Hearst International News Service. Following the death of d'Arrast in 1968, Boardman reunited with Vidor, who was a frequent visitor to her house during her last years in Montecito, California.

Barbara Morgan,
Melrose, Massachusetts

Boardman, Mabel (1860–1946)

American Red Cross leader. *Born Mabel Thorp Boardman in Cleveland, Ohio, on October 12, 1860; died in Washington, D.C., on March 17, 1946; daughter of William Jarvis and Florence (Sheffield) Boardman: attended private schools in Cleveland, New York, and Europe.*

Called "the administrative genius" of the American Red Cross, Mabel Boardman is credited with transforming the turn-of-the-century, 300-member society into a thriving institution, with 29 million junior and senior members. Her 44 years of service, spent primarily behind the scenes as head of the Volunteer Special Services, was marked by an early struggle to break from the authoritarian leadership of ***Clara Barton**, who founded the American Red Cross in 1881.

A Victorian debutante who might otherwise have been destined for a circumscribed life, Boardman had an energy and drive that quickly marked her for public service. In 1900, when the Red Cross received a federal charter, Boardman's socially prominent name was placed on the organization's board of incorporators without her knowledge. Taking her inclusion quite seriously, she secured a seat on the executive committee and began to travel, studying the work of the organization in the United States and overseas. These early trips would later be compiled into a book, *Under the Red Cross Flag at Home and Abroad*, published in 1915. Boardman began to agitate for change, and, though Barton resisted stepping down, Boardman used her political clout to obtain Barton's resignation in 1904. Under a new charter, and reincorporation by Act of Congress in 1905, President Theodore Roosevelt appointed William Howard Taft to head the organization. Boardman retained executive power by resuming the seat on the executive committee from which pro-Barton forces had earlier suspended her.

Catering to the bias of her day, Boardman insisted that men occupy the more conspicuous positions in the organization. She preferred working behind the scenes to develop support for the Red Cross among the socially prominent. Her efforts netted a large endowment fund, established branches across the country, and fostered cooperation with groups like the American Nursing Association. Unlike Barton before her, Boardman stayed away from work in disaster areas, remaining at her administrative post in Washington. In 1913, she raised $800,000 in public subscriptions which, together with an appropriation from Congress, made it possible to begin construction of a new headquarters. Completed in 1917, the white-marble building, dubbed the Marble Palace, was located near Washington's Potomac Park.

Boardman's early work with the Red Cross was widely recognized. In 1909, she was decorated by the king of Sweden and the Italian government. She subsequently received the French Medal of Merit, 1st Class, and the Légion d'Honneur, as well as recognition from Japan, Belgium, Portugal, Serbia, and Chile. She received honorary degrees from Yale, Western Reserve, and Smith College, and represented the Red Cross at international conferences held throughout the world.

But, as the war in Europe began to drain Red Cross resources, there was a move to reorganize the administration. By 1917, the executive committee was replaced with a Red Cross War Council. Boardman was not reappointed to the reconvened executive committee in 1919 and was left with little to do. In September 1920, she was selected by President Woodrow Wilson to serve as the first woman member of the Board of Commissioners of the District of Columbia. Through her new post, Boardman became a well-recognized figure in Washington. Imposingly tall, with graying hair and wearing pearls in the manner of a grand lady, she was said to have resembled England's Dowager Queen ***Mary of Teck**.

In 1921, Boardman returned to the Red Cross, serving as a central committee member and national secretary. When professionals took over the leadership of the Red Cross social services, Boardman became director of Volunteer Services, organizing the activities of the Staff Assistance Corps, the Home Service Corps, the Motor and Canteen Corps, and the "Gray Ladies," among others. In 1938, upon the death of national chair Admiral Cary Grayson, Boardman was urged to succeed to his position. She declined.

When Boardman retired as director of Volunteer Services in 1940, there were over 2.7 million volunteers. She continued on the central committee and as national secretary, directing major relief problems during World War II until her retirement on December 14, 1944. At a testimonial luncheon, she received the first Distinguished Service Medal ever awarded by the Red Cross. The citation referred to her as "inspirer, leader, and practical idealist."

Barbara Morgan,
Melrose, Massachusetts

Bobolina (1771–1825).

See Bouboulina, Laskarina.

Bocanegra, Gertrudis (1765–1817)

Mexican freedom fighter. *Born in Pátzcuaro, Mexico, in 1765; died by execution in Pátzcuaro in 1817; married Lazo de la Vega (a soldier for the Spanish royalists); children: a son and daughters.*

Gertrudis Bocanegra was a philanthropist, who founded schools for Indian children in Mexico, before the War of Independence in 1810 transformed her into a patriot and martyr. When Mexican nationalists rose up against the Spanish government, Bocanegra, her husband Lazo de la Vega, who had been a soldier for the Spanish royalists, and her ten-year-old son aligned with a group of insurgents. She carried important messages between the rebel groups and organized an underground army of women, which eventually included her daughters, to join in the fighting, considerably aiding the attack on the city of Valladolid. With her husband and son already killed in battle, Bocanegra was captured in Pátzcuaro while gathering military information and attempting to win royalist soldiers over to the insurgent cause. Imprisoned with her daughters, the 52-year-old Bocanegra was later tried and sentenced to death. She was executed in 1817.

Bocchi, Dorotea (fl. 1390–1430)

Italian teacher of medicine. *Name variations: Dorotea Bucca; daughter of a professor of medicine.*

Dorotea Bocchi was appointed professor of medicine at the University of Bologna in 1390, succeeding her father, who was an educator and physician. She continued in that capacity for 40 years.

Bocher, Joan (d. 1550)

Anabaptist martyr. *Name variations: Boucher or Butcher; Joan of Kent. Executed in 1550.*

Joan Bocher, a friend of ***Anne Askew**, maintained that Christ did not "take flesh of the virgin." After being interrogated by Thomas Cranmer, archbishop of Canterbury, she was imprisoned and later burned at Smithfield. Cranmer followed her to the stake six years later.

Bochkareva, Maria (b. 1889).

See Botchkareva, Maria.

Bodard, Mag (c. 1927—)

***Italian-French film producer responsible for the acclaimed* Umbrellas of Cherbourg.** *Name variations: Margherita Perato. Born Margherita Perato in Turin, Italy, around 1927; attended Institution Mainterion in Paris, France; married Lucian Bodard (divorced after 25 years).*

Selected filmography: Umbrellas of Cherbourg *(1964);* Le Bonheur *(1965);* Les Demoiselles de Rochefort *(1965);* Benjamin Ou Les Memoirs D'un *(1966);* La Chinoise *(1967);* Mouchette *(1967);* Le Viol *(1967);* Peau d'Ane *(1970).*

Margherita Perato, who would be known as Mag, was born in Turin, in northern Italy, the daughter of winegrowers. At age five, she and two younger siblings went to live with their aunt and French-born uncle in Paris, where her parents thought the educational opportunities were

From the movie Umbrellas of Cherbourg, *starring Catherine Deneuve, produced by Mag Bodard.*

better. Mag attended the Institution Mainterion during the school year, returning to Italy for the summer months.

She was studying interior decorating at a private atelier when she met journalist Lucian Bodard. After their marriage, work often kept them apart; at the advent of World War II, Lucian was in England while Mag was in Paris, working as a designer. In an interview for *The New Yorker* in 1969, Mag Bodard was asked if she worked for the underground during the Occupation. "I did what was normal in my circle," she replied, "hid people who had to be hidden, passed letters that had to be passed."

Lucian Bodard worked for Agence France-Presse following the war. Because he had been born in China to a family of diplomats, he and Mag were sent to Southeast Asia where he was a correspondent for *France-Soir*. During the couples' stay in Vietnam, from 1948–55, Mag Bodard wrote articles about everyday life in Saigon for *France-Soir* as well as for *Elle*. Around the time of the siege at Dien Bien Phu, the turning point for the French in Vietnam, the articles were collected and published under the title *C'est Aussi Comme Ca* (*It's Also Like That*) to great success.

Upon returning to France, Bodard had a brief but unsuccessful excursion into television. Convinced that she was "in a new world now" and "it would be easier to reach the new world through pictures rather than words," she set out to make movies. In 1962, French director Jonathan Demy showed Bodard the script he had written for *Les Parapluies de Cherbourg* (*The Umbrellas of Cherbourg*). By then, Bodard had formed her own film company called Parc Film; under this banner, she managed to co-finance Demy's project with the help of America's 20th Century-Fox, Germany's Beta (a film distribution company), and France's Cinema Center (a collective of French producers). Overwhelmingly successful, the film won the top prize at the Cannes Film Festival in 1964. In the U.S., not only was the movie a huge commercial success, but *Umbrellas* was also nominated for an Academy Award in the Best Foreign Film category. Oddly, Bodard's native Italy was one of the few countries worldwide where the film failed.

Her next movie, *Le Bonheur* (*Happiness*), was one of Bodard's favorite projects. Directed by ***Agnes Varda**, the work won a special jury prize at the Berlin Film Festival in 1965. "This film was very, very important," Bodard told an interviewer for *The New Yorker*. "It was a film made by a woman and it is exactly what goes on inside the head of every woman, except that she doesn't know it." *Le Bonheur* was one of several motion pictures produced by Bodard that were considered part of the cadre of the French "New Wave" movement. The films of this era dealt with the changing morals in relationships between men and women.

Following *Le Bonheur*, Bodard worked with several of the top French directors and produced films like Jean-Luc Godard's *La Chinoise* (*The Chinese Girl*), Robert Bresson's *Mouchette*, and Jacques Doniol-Valcroze's *Le Viol* (*A Question of Rape*). During this period, Bodard produced around 20 films. Mag Bodard was one of the few independent women producers of her day, as well as one of the most prolific.

SOURCES:

Bergan, Ronald, and Robyn Karney, ed. *The Holt Foreign Film Guide*. NY: Henry Holt, 1988.

"Talk of the Town: Producer," in *The New Yorker*. January 4, 1969, p. 25–27.

Deborah Jones,
Studio City, California

Bodichon, Barbara (1827–1891)

English feminist and educator who founded Portman Hall. *Name variations: Barbara Leigh-Smith or Barbara Leigh Smith. Born Barbara Leigh-Smith at Watlington, Norfolk, England, on April 8, 1827; died at Robertsbridge, Sussex, on June 11, 1891; illegitimate daughter of Benjamin Leigh Smith (1783–1860; long an M.P. for Norwich) and Ann Longden (a milliner's apprentice); sister of* ***Anne Leigh Smith****; first cousin of* ****Florence Nightingale****; attended Bedford College for Women, London, enrolling in 1849; married Dr. Eugéne Bodichon (an eminent French physician), in 1857.*

Born in 1827 into a radical 19th-century family that believed in women's equality, Barbara Bodichon early showed a strength of character and benevolence that would later win her a prominent place among philanthropists and social workers. Her mother **Anne Longden** was a 17-year-old milliner; her father was Benjamin Leigh Smith, a 40-year-old MP. The couple did not marry, and the illegitimate birth caused a scandal. Even so, Anne remained Benjamin's common-law wife until she died of tuberculosis when Barbara was seven years old.

In 1852, after matriculating at Bedford College for women, she opened Portman Hall School in Paddington, with her friend **Elizabeth Whitehead**. In 1857, she married an eminent French physician, Eugene Bodichon. Although she wintered for many years in Algiers, Bodichon continued to lead movements she had initiated on behalf of Englishwomen. In 1869, she published a *Brief Summary in Plain Language of the Laws of England Concerning Women*, which helped advance the passage of the Married Women's Property Act. In 1866, with ***Emily Davies**, Bodichon promoted the extension of university education to women; the first small experiment at Benslow House, Hitchen, developed into Girton College, to which Bodichon gave liberally of her time and money.

In addition to her public interests, she found time for friends and painting, studying under William H. Hunt. Her watercolors, exhibited at the Salon and elsewhere, showed originality and talent, and were admired by the French landscape painters Corot and Charles Daubigny. Bodichon's London salon included many of the literary and artistic celebrities of her day; she was a close friend of ***Mary Anne Evans** (George Eliot), and, according to Bodichon, the first to recognize the authorship of *Adam Bede.* The title character in Eliot's 1863 novel *Romola* is said to be based on Bodichon. She also helped finance the *Englishwomen's Journal* and wrote *Women and Work* (1857), *Reasons for the Enfranchisement of Women* (1866), and *Objections to the Enfranchisement of Women Considered* (1866). At the time of her death, Bodichon left £10,000 to Girton College.

SUGGESTED READING:

Burton, H. *Barbara Bodichon.*

Herstein, S.R. *A Mid-Victorian Feminist: Barbara Leigh Smith Bodichon.*

Bodil of Norway (fl. 1000s)

***Queen of Denmark.** Flourished in the year 1000; married Erik Ejegod or Erik Egode, king of Denmark (r. 1095–1103); children: Knud or Canute Lavard (who married **Ingeborg of Russia**).*

Bodley, Rachel (1831–1888)

***American chemist and botanist.** Born in Cincinnati, Ohio, on December 7, 1831; died of a heart attack, at age 56, in Philadelphia, Pennsylvania, in 1888; daughter and third of five children of Anthony (a carpenter) and Rebecca (Talbott) Bodley (an educator); attended private school in Cincinnati; graduated from Wesleyan Female College, Cincinnati, 1849; graduated from Polytechnic College, Philadelphia, Pennsylvania, 1860.*

Credited with helping to raise the profile of women in science, Rachel Bodley attended a private school run by her mother **Rebecca Talbott Bodley** before enrolling at Wesleyan Female College. After completing advanced studies in the natural sciences, Rachel embarked on her teaching career at the Cincinnati Female Seminary, in 1862. Three years later, she was named first chair of chemistry at Female Medical College (later Woman's Medical College). She became dean of the school and was elected school director in Philadelphia's 29th School District. In 1883, she was one of the first women appointed to the State Board of Public Charities.

Barbara Bodichon

Throughout her teaching career, Bodley classified and mounted an extensive collection of plants. In 1881, she conducted a statistical survey concerning the careers of graduates of the Woman's Medical College. Her study, one of the first relative to women and the professions, was published in the pamphlet, *The College Story.* Several of her lectures were also published.

Bodley held membership in a number of scientific societies, including the Academy of Natural Science of Philadelphia (1971), the New York Academy of Sciences (1876), the American Chemical Society (1876), and Philadelphia's Franklin Institute (1880). Woman's Medical College awarded her an honorary M.D. in 1879.

Barbara Morgan,
Melrose, Massachusetts

Bog, Harriet (b. 1922).

See Holter, Harriet.

Bogan, Ann.

See Marvelettes.

Bogan, Louise (1897–1970)

***Poet and** New Yorker **critic who was one of America's most influential women of letters.** Born on August 11, 1897, in Livermore Falls, Maine, a small mill town; died at her home in Washington Heights, New York, on February 4, 1970, of coronary occlusion; daughter of Daniel Joseph Bogan (a clerk and superintendent of*

Louise Bogan

a paper mill) and Mary "May" Helen Murphy (Shields) Bogan; married Curt Alexander (a German-born captain in the army), on September 4, 1916 (died 1920); married Raymond Holden (a writer), on July 10, 1925 (legally separated, 1934); children: one daughter, Maidie Alexander (b. October 19, 1917).

Selected writings: Body of this Death *(Robert M. McBride, 1923);* Dark Summer *(Scribner, 1929);* The Sleeping Fury *(Scribner, 1937); (collection)* Poems and New Poems *(Scribner, 1941);* Achievement in American Poetry: 1900–1950 *(Regnery, 1951);* Collected Poems, 1923–1953 *(Noonday Press, 1954);* Selected Criticism: Poetry and Prose *(Noonday Press, 1955); (co-compiled with William Jay Smith, anthology of poetry for children)* The Golden Journey *(Reilly & Lee, 1965);* The Blue Estuaries: Poems, 1923–1968 *(Farrar, Straus, 1968); (posthumously; a collection of journals and unpublished materials)* Journey Around My Room *(1980). Frequent contributor to the* Partisan Review, Saturday Review of Literature, The New Yorker, Times Literary Supplement, *and* Poetry: A Magazine of Verse.

Louise Bogan was reticent when speaking about her early years. She was born on August 11, 1897, in the small mill town of Livermore Falls, near Lewiston, Maine, where her father Daniel Bogan worked in a paper mill for the International Paper Company. Though Irish Catholic, the family lived in a mill-owned house in the Protestant section. Her mother **May Bogan** hated the mill, the smell, the town, and its provinciality.

When Louise was four, the family moved to another mill town in Milton, New Hampshire. For the next two years, they lived in the Hotel Milton where Louise shared a room with her mother, while her father shared a room with her older brother. Liberated from her stifling life in Livermore Falls, May Bogan socialized on the veranda of the guest hotel and began a life of intrigue. Still a young child, Louise was aware of whisperings, odd looks, and clandestine meetings, the ill-concealed evidence of her mother's many trysts.

As May took lovers—admirers as she called them—she would bring Louise along on her assignations and leave her waiting out in the hall. On more than one occasion, her mother vanished for a few weeks, only to return repentant and docile. Scenes between her parents could be violent. A rebellious May would spew epithets at Daniel until he rejoined with threats. "[May] had a hunger for experience that was never appeased," wrote **Elizabeth Frank** in *Louise Bogan: A Portrait*, "a jealousy for the prerogatives of independence enjoyed at that time only by men." Louise loved her mother deeply and felt protective toward her. "I never truly feared her," said Bogan. "Her tenderness was the other side of her terror." Nevertheless, Bogan maintained that she became "the semblance of a girl, in which some desires and illusions had been early assassinated: shot dead."

When Louise was seven, the family moved once more, this time to Ballardvale, Massachusetts, a mill town near Andover, where her father and brother began working at a bottling plant. For the first time, they moved into a house of their own on Chester Street, followed by a move to Oak Street, then to Tewksbury Street. Homebound with a bout of scarlet fever, Louise learned to read from a book titled *Heart of Oak*: "Its contents were as delicious as food. They *were* food; they were the beginning of a new life." She soon learned she could ward off the yelling between her parents behind the sturdy wall of a book. In Ballardvale, her mother formed another circle of friends and conspirators. When they visited, Louise was told to stay in the living room, where the child listened to the low voices emanating from the kitchen. While her mother made amatory forays into Lowell or Boston, from which she would again return contrite, Louise was left with a Mrs. Parsons. In the absence of other supports, Louise relied on her books, her brother's, and those of her mother's which included a generous helping of ***Celia Thaxter**. Louise's older brother Charlie, whom she adored, was crippled by the domestic situation. He lived at home, occasionally smashing furniture, until he joined the service.

In July 1906, nine-year-old Louise was packed off to her mother's old school, Mount Saint Mary Academy in Manchester, New Hampshire, while her mother went on a 12-month junket cross country to California, along with a friend and another admirer. A grade ahead in school, though she was not one of the nun's favorites, Bogan ended the year in the top ranks. But, among more well-off classmates who had visiting mothers, she was a lonely outcast. "The social world was to her, from its beginnings, composed of malice, gossip, insult, cliques, cruelty, pettiness, and preferment," writes Frank. Boarding school, Bogan observed, was "about the best place in the world to make bitter enemies as well as close friends."

Because she had skipped a grade, Bogan was kept out of school from 1908–09. When the family moved to a railroad apartment in the Roxbury section of Boston in 1909, she continued to sleep with her mother, while her father and brother shared another bedroom. Now 12, Bogan was determined to be a famous opera singer; but, by the time she entered seventh grade in Boston, she had begun to write. Her mother sent her to Girls' Latin School, a public high school for gifted students. For the next five years, Bogan was extended one of the best college-prep educations available; her days were filled with Latin, Greek, French, along with literary societies and debating societies. "I began to write verse from about fourteen on," said Bogan. "The life-saving process then began."

She patterned her early work after that of William Morris, the Rosettis, and Swinburne, and she devoured back issues of *Poetry* magazine at the Boston Public Library. By the time she was 18, Bogan had a "thick pile of manuscript, in a drawer in the dining room" and had "learned every essential" of her trade. Her poems appeared in the school paper, *The Jabberwock*, and she was designated Class Poet. Her only setback was her Irish ancestry, reported a schoolmate, writer ***Martha Foley**. At that time, the Irish were widespread victims of discrimination, and the headmaster warned May Bogan that "no Irish girl could be the editor of the school magazine." In 1912, Bogan's first poem was printed in the *Boston Evening Transcript*.

In autumn 1915, Bogan entered Boston University and continued her immersion in books. Entranced with Arthur Symons' treatise on the Symbolist movement in poetry, she also read Walter Pater, Max Stirner, Aubrey Beardsley, ***Amy Lowell**, ***Louise Imogen Guiney**, Compton Mackenzie, ***Alice Meynell**, and everything written by Alice's daughter ***Viola Meynell**. Bogan next turned to lyric poetry, devouring the works of ***Christina Rossetti**, ***Sara Teasdale**, ***Lizette Woodworth Reese**, and Meynell and Guiney. These were followed by her readings of ***Edna St. Vincent Millay**, and ***Elinor Wylie**. In her own work, Bogan borrowed from the Imagists, but only techniques of interest to her.

Though she won a scholarship to Radcliffe for the fall of 1916, Bogan fell in love and instead married Curt Alexander, a German-born captain in the army, on September 4, 1916. She was 19; he was 28. They moved to Bleecker Street in New York's Greenwich Village. In April of the following year, with the entrance of the U.S. in World War I, Curt was sent to Panama. Four months pregnant and perpetually ill, Louise followed on a troop ship that May. In the heat and humidity of Panama, marital disillusionment arrived along with their daughter Mathilde (later rechristened Maidie) who was born on October 19, 1917. Seven months later, Bogan returned home to mother. A few weeks before the October 1918 Armistice of World War I, her beloved brother Charlie, age 33, was killed at Haumont Wood in France. In later years, Bogan was to speak of him rarely.

On her husband's return, the couple reunited and lived at an army base in Portland, Maine. He was then stationed in Fort Dix, New Jersey, from which Bogan would take the ferry to Manhattan to see friends in Greenwich Village. In the summer of 1919, she left her demanding husband, entrusted Maidie to her parents, and rented an apartment on New York's West Ninth Street. After Curt Alexander died of a gastric ulcer the following year, Bogan received widow's benefits, though she was, and would always be, strapped for cash. She took a job as a clerk at Brentano's bookstore and quickly became a Village bohemian, surrounded by the likes of Malcolm Cowley, Paul Rosenfeld, ***Lola Ridge**, ***Mina Loy**, John Reed, ***Louise Bryant**, and

Conrad Aiken. She visited her parents and daughter every few weeks.

Around 1921, Bogan became friends with Edmund Wilson and had five poems accepted for ***Harriet Monroe**'s *Poetry* magazine. By the end of the year, she was being published by *The New Republic*, *Vanity Fair*, *Voices*, *The Liberator*, *The Literary Review of the New York Evening Post*, and a "little" magazine, *The Measure*. The work of William Butler Yeats became a measuring stick for her own work. Frank notes that under the tutelage of Ridgely Torrence, literary editor of *The New Republic*, Bogan began fusing "delicate feminine perceptiveness with the roughness and vitality of Yeats' common speech." Meanwhile she made money gluing book pockets into books at the New York Public Library, St. Mark's Place branch, seated next to aspiring poet ***Marianne Moore**. Wrote Bogan:

> This was the winter before I went to Vienna, and I was in a dazed state of mind, and Marianne, as well as everyone else, came through to me rather foggily. But I remember very well, working with her in the winter afternoons, upstairs in that library with its general atmosphere of staleness and city dinginess. Her hair was then a beautiful shade of red; she wore it in a thick braid. She was continually comparing the small objects with which we worked—mucilage brushes and ink and stamping rubbers—to oddly analogous objects; and she smiled often and seemed happy. . . . She had no idea that I wrote poetry, and always treated me kindly, but rather like some assistant more or less invisible to her (as indeed I probably was, being, at that time, more or less invisible to myself, as well).

Bogan was experiencing one of her many longterm bouts of depression. "I must get well," she wrote:

> Walk on strong legs, leap the hurdles of sense,
> Reason again, come back to my old patchwork
> logic . . .
> I must feel again who had given feeling over,
> Challenge laughter, take tears, play the piano,
> Form judgments, blame a crude world for disaster.

Though she began analysis, the depression would not abate. In 1922, Bogan sailed to Paris, then traveled to Zurich, and settled in Vienna "to stop writing like magazines," and get back to "hard, painfully produced poems that sounded like myself." But her emotional distress was great and she wrote little, except for the poem "Stanza." Throughout her life, she could not force the writing of poems, they had to arrive unbidden. On her return to America in October, the poems began to come: "My Voice Not Being Proud," "The Romantic," "The Frightened Man," "Men Loved Wholly Beyond Wisdom," "The Changed Woman," and "Fifteenth Farewell." Her first book of poems *Body of this Death* was published in 1923. Though most critics treated the poetry with respect, they found the poems too obscure. "She was a linguistic pragmatist," wrote Frank, "who believed that words could mean what they said; the problem was for the writer to have something to say. . . . In her view, the farther the art of language detached itself from the actuality of experience while remaining alive to its ungraspable and anarchic magnitude, the more richly that art justified its claim to approximate and even displace experience."

In 1924, Bogan began to live with the still-technically-married writer Raymond Holden, with whom she had a turbulent relationship, and eventually brought her daughter Maidie into the household. Before he dissipated his inheritance, the well-off Holden supported them both. Socially, her time with Holden was enjoyable and loaded with bootleg gin. Her retinue of friends had grown to include ***Léonie Adams**, ***Genevieve Taggard**, Rolfe Humphries, ***Margaret Mead**, ***Ruth Benedict**, Scudder Middleton, and Robert Wolf. Now 27 and feeling "very minor" as a poet, Bogan began to write criticism in 1924, at the insistence of her friend Edmund Wilson. Her career as a critic was inaugurated in *The New Republic* with a review of D.H. Lawrence's *Birds, Beasts and Flowers*.

On July 10, 1925, Holden and Bogan were married. Three years later, in the summer of 1928, they bought a run-down farmhouse in Hillsdale, New York, where they renovated, wallpapered, scraped floors, and put in a heating system. "Louise loved the house," wrote Frank, "and the hard work. While Raymond put in windows, she planted a bulb garden and contemplated writing a book about common and beautiful flowers." She grew bucolic and wrote prolifically, more content than she had been in years. "How happy I feel!" she wrote Edmund Wilson. "How easy art really is!" Her next book of poems *Dark Summer* appeared in a handsome edition by Scribner in 1929. Yvor Winters, among others, lauded the book. That Christmas, the family returned from visiting Raymond's mother to find the house burning down. All her manuscripts were lost—poems, stories, notebooks, letters, as well as books and photographs.

Having invested the greater portion of his money in the stock market, Raymond lost most of it in the October crash, and the couple could not rebuild. A week later, they returned to New

York City. Holden took a job as managing editor at *The New Yorker*, while Bogan continued with her poetry and reviews for *The New Republic* and *Poetry*. But her depression returned throughout 1930, resulting in what she called "creative despair." She took long streetcar rides through the city, drank too much, and was envious of other women writers. She was certain that Holden was having affairs, certain of his inevitable betrayal; in his 1935 autobiographical novel *Chance has a Whip*, Holden blamed her strong jealous streak for their problems. Presented with the John Reed Memorial Prize from *Poetry* magazine, Bogan told ***Harriet Monroe:** "the hazards of self-exposure seem to outweigh the rewards." She set out to break down her creative method and start over.

In March 1931, after fiction editor ***Katherine S. White** convinced publisher Harold Ross to print serious poetry in *The New Yorker*, Bogan was asked to write a poetry review, a job she would continue for the next 38 years. She could not, however, shake the depression and so entered the Neurological Institute as a volunteer patient, where, she later said, she was "taken apart, like a watch." Her distress was focused on Raymond whom she accused of clandestine trysts. Reluctantly, Bogan returned to their apartment with a slight rise in self-confidence but hardly cured. Finding it hard to write, she did manage to compose profiles for *The New Yorker* on ***Gertrude Vanderbilt Whitney** (which was rejected) and ***Willa Cather**, as well as five stories.

In August 1932, she wrote in her journal: "The continuous turmoil in a disastrous childhood makes one so tired that 'Rest' becomes the word forever said by the self to the self. The incidents are so vivid and so terrible that to remember them is inadequate: they must be forgotten." Or, possibly explored. At this time, she wrote the reverie "Journey Around My Room." Longing to be alone, she applied for and received a Guggenheim fellowship. To begin a year of travel abroad, she sailed on April 1, 1933, to Italy. Soon homesick, she worried about Raymond's faithfulness. She returned to New York in August with little writing.

Upon arrival, her worst fears proved true. Despite a surfeit of epistolary protestations, Raymond had been living with a woman in her absence. Her pride made it impossible for her to forgive or divorce him, and the depression returned in full force. That November, Bogan entered the New York Hospital in White Plains, where, for five months, she worked to ease her demands for perfection. Released at the end of April 1934, she recorded one doctor's prognosis in her journal: "She will never get entirely better. She has too many things to contend with—but she'll be able to do her work." That July, she filed for a legal separation.

> I have written down my experience in the closest detail. But the rough and vulgar facts are not there.
>
> —Louise Bogan

For the time being, the fog had lifted. Bogan had regained her sense of humor, as evidenced in the title of her poem "Lines Written in a Moment of Such Clarity as Verges on Megalomania." She entered into a pleasing fling with 26-year-old poet Theodore Roethke. By the spring of 1936, theirs had settled into friendship. In an article published in the *Michigan Quarterly Review* called "The Poetry of Louise Bryant," Roethke proved prophetic: "Her poems create their own reality, and demand not just attention, but the emotional and spiritual response of the whole man. Such a poet will never be popular, but can and should be a true model for the young. And the best work will stay in the language as long as the language survives."

In the spring of 1937, Bogan published *The Sleeping Fury*. It was to be her last important work. Wrote Frank:

> The possibility, often said to be feared by people who are both creative and neurotic, that psychiatric treatment would cure their neurosis but in the process kill their creativity, may well have been, for Louise Bogan, uncannily close to the truth. With the publication of *The Sleeping Fury*, her most productive days as a poet were over. She did not immediately stop writing poetry, and the high standard of her work did not lapse, but her career as a critic began increasingly to feed on the energies that had hitherto gone into waiting for poems and nurturing them when they arrived.

In 1941, her first collected edition *Poems and New Poems* was published and well received. Marianne Moore, writing for *The Nation*, called Bogan's poetry "compactness compacted. She uses a kind of forged rhetoric that nevertheless seems inevitable." But another poem did not come to Bogan until 1948. Seven years, in her words, of "being uninvited by the Muse."

For all the praise Bogan received from the likes of W.H. Auden and Edmund Wilson, the women garnering the most recognition were Léonie Adams and ***Laura Riding**. Though Bogan saw herself as slighted by the academic and literary worlds, she did not contribute in efforts to become better known. With precarious finances and a strong belief that interest in poetry was on the wane, she left her longtime editor John Hall Wheelock at Scribner, the house which had published most of her works; as a result, all her books were soon out of print. Despite having been abandoned by his writer, Wheelock put her name in nomination before the National Institute of Arts and Letters in 1951 and the Academy of American Poets in 1954 (she was elected to membership in 1969). Bogan did not find another publisher that would handle her poetry until Noonday Press published *Collected Poems: 1923–1953* in 1954.

Nonetheless, recognition was forthcoming. She was asked to become a fellow in American Letters of the Library of Congress, 1944, and a consultant in poetry, 1945–46. From 1949 to 1960, she taught poetry at many colleges and universities, including New York University, the University of Arkansas, University of Washington, Brandeis University, as well as at the 92nd Street YMHA in Manhattan. She spent many summers at the MacDowell Colony where she added three new friends: **Elizabeth Mayer**, English professor **Ruth Limmer**, and ***May Sarton** who wrote of their first meeting in *A World of Light: Portraits and Celebration*. Becoming somewhat of a mentor, Bogan once advised Sarton: "You keep the Hell out of your work."

In 1964, while teaching at Brandeis in Boston, possibly too close to her New England roots, the old malaise swept in. Bogan tried to shake it, went on medication, and eventually returned to New York; by mid-September 1965, she had once again entered the New York Hospital in White Plains. Plagued by anger and mourning for many losses, she reluctantly underwent shock therapy. In spring 1966, she came out of the hospital low on energy and still weepy, especially in the mornings. In 1967, she was awarded $10,000 from the National Endowment for the Arts for her lifetime's work. The following year, her last book of poetry *The Blue Estuaries: Poems, 1923–1968* was published, prompting William Meredith in *The New York Times Book Review* to recognize her "career of stubborn, individual excellence," pronouncing Louise Bogan "one of the best women poets alive." But, in her early 70s, Bogan remained emotionally distraught. In September 1969, she left her job of 38 years with *The New Yorker*. Three months later, on February 4, 1970, she was found dead in her apartment of coronary occlusion.

Bogan had once told Sarton: "I have been *forced* to learn to wait, to be patient, to wait for the wheel to turn. . . . I have *been forced* to find a way of loving my destiny; of not opposing it too much with my will. . . . I have *been forced* 'to forgive life' in order to get through existence at all."

SOURCES:

Frank, Elizabeth. *Louise Bogan: A Portrait.* NY: Alfred A. Knopf, 1985.

SUGGESTED READING:

Limmer, Ruth, ed. *What the Woman Lived: Selected Letters of Louise Bogan, 1920–1970.* 1973.

———. *Journey Around My Room.* 1980.

Bogan, Lucille (1897–1948)

African-American blues singer. *Name variations: recorded under the name Bessie Jackson. Born Lucille Anderson in Amory, Mississippi, on April 1, 1897; died in Los Angeles, California, on August 10, 1948; married Nazareth Bogan; reportedly married James Spencer; children: (first marriage) two.*

Although there are inconsistencies regarding the life of Lucille Bogan, one constant remains: she was one of the greatest blueswomen of all time. Big-voiced and provocative, Bogan, who often recorded under the name Bessie Jackson, sang down-and-gritty blues songs dealing with sex, violence, dope, and life in the underworld.

Born in Mississippi on April 1, 1897, Bogan moved to Birmingham, Alabama, at an early age, where she was raised and first started singing. Some reports link her with Birmingham's black underground, an industrial environment that lent itself to the blues. In 1927, she moved to Chicago, recording for Paramount and Brunswick between 1928 and 1930. Her "Alley Boogie" with pianist Charles Avery was noteworthy, as was "They Ain't Walking No More" (later remade with its uncensored title "Tricks Ain't Walking No More") which lamented the economic downside of prostitution during the Depression.

During the 1930s, Bogan put forth in these songs a tough-woman image in the style of ***Bessie Smith**, ***Ma Rainey**, and ***Victoria Spivey**, whose songs also celebrated what was then considered anti-social behavior. Bogan broached the subject of lesbianism with "Women Won't Need No Men" (1927) and "B.D. [bull dyke] Woman's Blues" (1935). Even by contemporary standards, her uncensored version of "Shave 'Em Dry" stands alone for overwhelming shock value (she also made a tamer recording of the same song).

After 1935 when she stopped performing, Bogan may have returned to Birmingham and managed a group called Bogan's Birmingham Busters. Sources differ on the facts of her 1948 death. One says she was killed by an automobile, another that she died at home of coronary sclerosis. She is buried at Lincoln Memorial Park Cemetery, in Los Angeles.

Barbara Morgan,
Melrose, Massachusetts

Boggs, Lindy (1916—)

U.S. Representative, Democrat of Louisiana, 93rd–101st Congresses. *Name variations: (nickname) Rolindy, for her father Roland, which later became Lindy. Born Corinne Morrison Claiborne at Brunswick Plantation, Louisiana, on March 13, 1916; daughter of Roland and* ***Corinne (Morrison) Claiborne****; graduated from Sophie Newcomb College of Tulane University, 1935; married Thomas Hale Boggs (U.S. Congressional representative and majority leader), on January 22, 1938 (died, March 1973); children: Barbara Boggs Sigmund (mayor of Princeton, New Jersey, from 1984 until her death in 1990); Thomas Hale Boggs (Washington lawyer and lobbyist); Corinne "Cokie" Roberts (b. 1944, National Public Radio and ABC-TV correspondent who married Steve Roberts).*

In 1990, citing "family considerations," Lindy Boggs shocked Capitol Hill by announcing that she would not seek reelection to Congress, ending a 17-year legislative career. Although it was a difficult decision for Boggs—who had succeeded her husband Hale in March 1973, five months after his small plane vanished over Alaska during a campaign trip—she left to spend time with her daughter Barbara, who was critically ill with cancer.

Raised on two plantations in Pointe Coupee Parish, Louisiana, Lindy Boggs graduated from Tulane University and taught history before marrying Hale Boggs, whose political career included 14 terms as representative and a stint as majority leader of the House. Beginning in 1948, she ran her husband's campaigns, managed his Capitol Hill office, and headed a number of other organizations, including the Women's National Democratic Club, the Democratic Wives' Forum, and the Congressional Club. She chaired the committees for both John Kennedy's and Lyndon Johnson's inaugural balls. Her election to Congress in 1973 meant a changing role for Boggs: "I went from being president of everything to being a mere member of Congress," she quipped.

Lindy Boggs

Raising her three children while commuting between Washington and New Orleans, Boggs juggled work, motherhood, and her husband's drinking problem. She also had to cope with the enmity of many Louisiana constituents because of the family's support of the civil-rights movement; a cross was once burned in their yard. Her daughter **Cokie Roberts**, news correspondent for ABC-TV, recalled: "She was always there, but she was always working. We thought she was the most beautiful woman alive." It wasn't until Boggs became a widow that she thought much about feminism, when it proved difficult for her to get credit to purchase her own condominium in her husband's absence.

Boggs had a reputation for tenacity and Southern charm; one colleague remarked, "You could get diabetes standing next to Lindy—she's that sweet." Her legislative interests were wide-ranging, including equal opportunity for women and minorities, housing-policy issues, technological development, and Mississippi River transportation. Boggs took the greatest pride in helping to establish the Select Committee on Children, Youth and Families, which assesses the conditions of the nation's families and children. In 1976, she became the first woman to preside over a national political convention when she served as chair of the Democratic National Convention. That year, Boggs also worked to expand awareness of American history and served as chair of the Joint Committee on Bicentennial Arrangements. She chaired the Commission on the Bicentenary of the U.S. House of Representatives for three terms and was a member of the Commission on the Bicentennial of the U.S. Constitution.

Boggs' daughter **Barbara Boggs Sigmund** lost an eye to cancer in 1982. Before Sigmund's death in 1990, when Boggs was preparing to retire, Barbara thought it would be difficult for her mother to find another job that would match her talents and vitality, calling Boggs "a 40-year-old-woman trapped in a 74-year-old-body." Lindy approached retirement more philosophically. "Of course I will miss it and my friends. But I don't think I will be lonely. I always said that being a Congresswoman was an interruption of my regular life." In 1997, Lindy Boggs was appointed U.S. ambassador to the Vatican.

SOURCES:

Office of the Historian. *Women in Congress, 1917–1990.* Commission on the Bicentenary of the U.S. House of Representatives, 1991.

People Weekly, April 13, 1990.

SUGGESTED READING:

Boggs, Lindy, and Katherine Hatch. *Washington Through a Purple Veil: Memoirs of a Southern Woman.* NY: Harcourt, Brace, 1994.

Roberts, Cokie. *We Are Our Mothers' Daughters.* NY: William Morrow, 1998.

Barbara Morgan,
Melrose, Massachusetts

Boginskaya, Svetlana (1973—)

Belarus gymnast. *Name variations: Svetlana Boguinskaia. Born on February 9, 1973, in Belarus, in the Soviet Union.*

While competing for Russia in Seoul, Korea, in 1988, gymnast Svetlana Boginskaya, won a bronze medal in the all-around individual, a silver medal in the floor exercises, a team gold in the all-around, and a gold medal in the horse vault. Throughout the competition, she toted Jack, a stuffed puppy, under one arm and a book under the other. In 1991, with her balletic grace, Boginskaya was named world all-around champion, then lost her title to **Kim Zmeskal**, in a highly touted rivalry, in 1992.

With the dissolution of the Soviet Union, Boginskaya competed for the Unified Team in Barcelona, Spain, in 1992, winning team gold in the all-around. In 1996, she participated in the Atlanta Olympics representing Belarus but failed to medal.

Boguinskaia, Svetlana (b. 1973).

See Boginskaya, Svetlana.

Bohemia, duchess of.

See Hemma of Bohemia (c. 930–c. 1005).

Bohemia, queen of.

See Libussa (c. 680–738).
See Drahomira of Bohemia (d. after 932).
See Adelaide of Hungary (d. 1062).
See Cunigunde of Hohenstaufen (fl. 1215–1230).
See Constance of Hungary (d. 1240).
See Margaret of Babenberg (fl. 1252).
See Cunigunde of Hungary (d. 1285).
See Judith (1271–1297).
See Ryksa of Poland (1288–1335).
See Elizabeth of Poland (fl. 1298–1305).
See Elizabeth of Bohemia (1292–1339).
See Maria of Hungary (1371–1395).
See Sophia of Bavaria (fl. 1390s–1400s).
See Barbara of Cilli (fl. 1390–1410).
See Foix, Anne de (fl. 1400s).
See Madeleine (c. 1425–1486).
See Maria Anna of Bavaria (1574–1616).
See Elizabeth of Bohemia (1596–1662).
See Gonzaga, Eleonora I (1598–1655).
See Maria Anna of Spain (1606–1646).
See Gonzaga, Eleonora II (1628–1686).
See Maria Leopoldine (1632–1649).

Bohemia, regent of.

See Ludmila (859–921).

Böhl von Faber, Cecilia (1796–1877)

Spanish novelist. *Name variations: Cecilia Böhl de Faber or Bohl de Faber, Madame de Arrom; Bohl; (pseudonym) Fernán Caballero. Born Cecilia Francisca Josefa Böhl von Faber in Morgues, Switzerland, on December 25, 1796 (some sources cite 1797); died in Seville, Spain, on April 7, 1877; educated in Germany.*

Selected writings: Mouette *(Sp:* La Gaviota; *Eng:* The Sea-Gull*).*

Considered the creator of the modern novel in Spanish literature, Cecilia Böhl von Faber was 52 years old when her first novel *Mouette* (*The Sea-Gull*) was published. The book, written in French under the name Fernán Caballero, brought its author immediate fame. Linking romanticism and the regional movements, she was considered Spain's most renowned novelist of the 19th century until the Revolution of 1868 and the advent of realism. A strict Roman Catholic with a conservative streak that informed her work, Böhl von Faber also wrote *A Summer Season at Bornos, Elia, Sola* (written in German and published anonymously in 1840), *Lágrimas* (*Tears*, 1850), *Clemencia* (1852), *Poor Dolores, Lucas Garcia, Un servilón y un liberalito* (*A Groveller and a Little Liberal*, 1855), *La Familia Albareda* (*The Family of Alvareda*, 1880). Her first collection of Spanish poems and popular stories were published as *Cuentos y Poesías Populares Andaluces* (Andalusian Popular Tales and Poems, 1859–77). A number of her short stories are collected under the titles *Cuadros de Costumbres* (*Tales of Customs*, 1862) and *Relaciones* (1857).

Böhlau, Helene (1859–1940)

German author. *Name variations: Bohlau or Boehlau. Born Helene Böhlau in Weimar, Germany, on November 22, 1859; died in Widdersberg, Germany, on March 28, 1940; daughter of Therese and Hermann Böhlau (a publisher); educated privately; married Friedrich Helwig Arnd, in 1886; children: one son.*

Selected works: Rathsmädelgeschichten *(Stories of Councilors' Daughters, 1888);* Der Rangierbahnhof *(The Railway Junction, 1896);* Das Recht der Mutter *(The Right of the Mother, 1896);* Halbtier! *(Half-animal!, 1899).*

Born on November 22, 1859, in Weimar, Germany, Helen Böhlau was the daughter of Hermann and **Therese Böhlau**. Her parents' wealth allowed for frequent travel as well as a private tutor for her because she was too sickly to attend school. Though her father disapproved of women working as writers, his publishing house launched Böhlau's first book, a collection of novellas, in 1882. Known for its humorous look at life in the Weimar region, Böhlau's fiction met with early success, though her popularity would wane with time.

Böhlau met and fell in love with Friedrich Helwig Arnd, a Russian Jew who was already married. When Arnd's wife refused a divorce, Böhlau and Arnd traveled to Turkey in 1886 where Arnd converted to Islam, which permitted divorce without a wife's consent. Taking the name Omar al Raschid Bey, he then married Böhlau, and the couple lived in Turkey with their one son until Arnd's death in 1911. Soon after, Böhlau returned to Germany and lived in Munich, visiting Turkey annually for vacations. During World War I, her son renounced his Turkish citizenship to join the German army; by World War II, he was a doctor in the Nazi Party. Though she was not an open supporter of the Nazi Party, throughout the 1930s, Böhlau actively denied her husband's Judaism. She died, at age 80, in 1940, seven months after Hitler's invasion of Poland.

Crista Martin,
Boston, Massachusetts

Bohley, Bärbel (1945—)

German political activist, known as the "Mother of the Revolution" in the closing months of 1989 in the German Democratic Republic (GDR). *Born in Berlin, Germany, on May 24, 1945.*

Active as a leading member of the East German opposition, arrested and imprisoned on several occasions (1980s); appraised by the Stasi (secret police) in her file as the "mother of the underground"; instrumental in the founding of the New Forum organization which focused the grievances of the population against the Communist regime of Erich Honecker

Bärbel Bohley

(September 1989); believing that a radically reformed GDR could survive as an independent state, opposed German unification; though her organization New Forum played a major role in transforming East Germany (1989), it virtually disappeared in the first free elections (March 1990); withdrew from politics with the achievement of German unity, only rarely making critical statements about the situation in the states of the former GDR.

Born in Berlin on May 24, 1945, only a few weeks after Germany's defeat in World War II, Bärbel Bohley grew up to be an artist, but she could never escape the burdens and responsibilities history had placed on her country. Bohley lived in the Communist eastern part of Germany, which was founded as a Soviet satellite state in October 1949, calling itself the German Democratic Republic (GDR). Life was difficult in the poorer, totalitarian German state, and after 1961 the raising of the Berlin Wall made it virtually impossible for people to leave the GDR, even on vacation. For intellectuals like Bohley, however, there were compensations for living in the east. If one chose not to challenge the regime, there was job security, cradle-to-grave health care, heavily subsidized cultural events, and inexpensive vacations. Beyond the economic benefits, by the 1970s a clear sense of national pride and identity had emerged, particularly because of GDR triumphs in Olympic sports.

Yet for all of the achievements that made the GDR the most prosperous Communist nation, by the late 1970s a sense of national malaise had begun to emerge. Economically, the system was stagnating and production increases were minuscule at best. Within the regime, dissident voices were raised against the monopoly of power exercised by the Socialist Unity Party (SED). Non-Marxist dissidents found their spiritual and moral home within the Lutheran church, and strongly criticized the abuses of power that inevitably appeared in a rigidly totalitarian society like the GDR. The appearance of a third group of dissidents, in which women played a major role, took place in the early 1980s.

The immediate grievance for a small group of women (approximately 150), led by the ceramic artist Bärbel Bohley, was the conscription law of 1982, which included a provision making women liable for military service. Calling themselves "Women for Peace," Bohley and her group were determined to launch a strong protest against the militarization of GDR society. Although numerically insignificant, they were almost immediately perceived as a threat to the system by the omnipresent secret police, the *Stasi*. On October 16, 1983, Bohley and 30 other women, all dressed in black, marched to East Berlin's main post office on the Alexanderplatz to mail to high government officials their declarations of intent refusing to perform any required military service. The security forces arrested five women; Bohley and **Ulrike Poppe**, another leader of the peace activists, barely escaped detention.

Bohley's luck ran out in December 1983, and she began serving a two-month prison term for having had contacts with a peace activist of the West German Greens. (The Green Party promoted ecology, non-violence, grassroots democracy, and social responsibility.) Refusing to be intimidated, she continued to work with activists on the political left who felt that the "real existing Socialism" of the Erich Honecker regime was a perversion of socialist ideals. Although the number of activists in her circle was small, the Stasi agents who kept a close eye on her activities assessed her to be a dangerous individual, personally incorruptible and therefore a threat to the SED dictatorship. One Stasi report prophetically characterized Bohley as the "mother of the underground." Engaged in a relentless nonviolent attack on the regime, she emphasized that the government, a self-proclaimed "peoples' democracy," had completely lost touch with its own people. In January 1988, the GDR dissidents used the occasion of the 69th anniversary of the murders of Karl Liebknecht and ***Rosa Luxemburg** to organize a public protest. Once more, Bohley was arrested in the aftermath of this embarrassment to the regime. Realizing the wisdom of not turning her into a martyr, the Stasi allowed her to leave the GDR for several months in the summer and fall of 1988, during which she spent time in West Germany and the United Kingdom.

The events of 1989 were as unexpected for Bohley as they were for everyone else in the country. Like most GDR dissidents, she was well aware of her country's injustices but had no timetable for a drastic transformation. After her return from the West, she was soon aware that major changes were in the offing. In the Soviet Union, the Gorbachev reform movement offered promise of genuine democratization, and the fresh winds from Moscow, as well as from neighboring Poland and Hungary, were shaking the moribund Honecker dictatorship to its foundations. Thousands of East Germans fled to the West via Czechoslovakia and Hungary that summer, and by September 1989 dissident elements were encouraged to take a bold stand for basic changes despite the obvious risks involved in speaking out openly.

On September 11, Bohley and Ulrike Poppe founded the New Forum; their aim was not to directly challenge the regime, but rather to open its eyes to the need for immediate and fundamental reforms through a serious dialogue with all dissident elements. The next few weeks were tense as the police attempted to frighten dissidents into mute submission. A mass movement quickly emerged, however, and over 200,000 angry yet hopeful women and men of all ages and backgrounds signed the New Forum manifesto calling for dialogue and change. Within a month's time, Honecker had been pushed out of office by desperate SED "reformers." On November 9, the Berlin Wall was opened up; within hours, thousands of Germans from east and west crossed freely in both directions for the first time in more than 28 years.

The next months witnessed dramatic changes in the GDR, many of which were viewed less than enthusiastically by Bohley. She was hailed throughout Germany and in the world press as the "mother of the revolution," a label that annoyed her. From the start of her fame, she felt that her ideas and ideals had been largely misunderstood. The goal of her courageous opposition had never been the destruction of the GDR, but rather its salvation through reform. A democratic socialist, her visits to the West had convinced her that individualistic capitalism could also create major social evils. The goal of New Forum had been to start the process that would bring about a truly democratic socialist society. Thus, Bohley reacted to the opening of the Berlin Wall with little enthusiasm, knowing how powerful the wealthy consumer society of West Germany was, and how easily it could swallow up the weak, as yet unreformed, GDR.

In the first democratic elections ever to take place in the GDR, held in March 1990, New Forum participated as a movement rather than as a conventional political party. The Forum was allied with two other reform groups, "Democracy Now" and the "Peace and Human Rights Initiative"; the three campaigned as "Alliance 90." Despite the combined effort, they won only a disappointing 2.9% of the vote. Although New Forum could boast a membership of 150,000 in January 1990 and was even able to publish its own weekly newspaper *Die Andere* ("The Other One"), the organization was too vague in its aims to compete against the Western-style parties that now dominated GDR politics in the brief period of East German democracy.

Bärbel Bohley decided not to participate in the political life of united Germany, which she regarded as an unfortunate historical evolution. She withdrew back into private life, attempting to live again as an artist rather than a political celebrity; this was not always possible, however, and she did occasionally grant interviews. In 1992, she lamented the "swallowing up" of the GDR and the former GDR citizens who "retreated into lethargy" after reunification. In 1993, she sharply attacked Manfred Stolpe, premier of the state of Brandenburg who was accused of being a pre-1989 collaborator with the Stasi. Exhibiting some of the passionate spontaneity that characterized her life of the 1980s, Bohley accused Stolpe of having "rightly become a symbol of repression." Bärbel Bohley regarded truth and justice above personal advancement.

SOURCES:

Bond, Martyn. *A Tale of Two Germanys.* Wilmington, DE: Atomium Books, 1990.

Fulbrook, Mary. *Anatomy of a Dictatorship: Inside the GDR 1949–1989.* NY: Oxford University Press, 1995.

Heydt, Barbara von. *Candles Behind the Wall: Heroes of the Peaceful Revolution that Shattered Communism.* Grand Rapids, MI: Eerdmans, 1993.

Kinzer, Stephen. "Dannenwalde Journal: A Portrait of the Informer (as People's Champion)," in *The New York Times.* April 15, 1993, p. A4.

———. "One More Wall to Smash: Arrogance in the West," in *The New York Times.* August 12, 1992, p. A4.

Lucas, Michael and Adrienne Edgar. "Germany After the Wall: Interviews," in *World Policy Journal.* Vol. 7, no. 1. Winter 1989–90, pp. 189–198.

McElvoy, Anne. "Freedom's unlikely fighter," in *The Times* [London]. November 6, 1989, p. 21.

Osmond, Jonathan. *German Reunification: A Reference Guide and Commentary.* Harlow, Essex, UK: Longman Current Affairs, 1992.

Philipsen, Dirk. *We Were the People: Voices From East Germany's Revolutionary Autumn of 1989.* Durham, NC: Duke University Press, 1993.

Schmemann, Serge. "East German Movement Overtaken by Followers," in *The New York Times.* October 16, 1989, p. A6.

Torpey, John C. *Intellectuals, Socialism, and Dissent: The East German Opposition and Its Legacy.* Minneapolis, MN: University of Minnesota Press, 1995.

John Haag, Associate Professor,
University of Georgia, Athens, Georgia

Bohm-Schuch, Clara (1879–1936)

German Social Democrat and anti-Nazi activist. *Born on December 5, 1879, in Stechow, Westhavelland; died as a result of mistreatment on May 6, 1936.*

Worked as a salaried retail employee; active member of the Social Democratic Party of Germany; active in humanitarian educational work; served in the

German Reichstag (1919–33); protested Nazi atrocities (1933).

Selected writings: Die Kinder im Weltkriege *(Berlin-Karlshorst: A. Baumeister/Verlag der "Internationalen Correspondenz," 1916);* Willst Du mich hören? Weckruf an unsere Mädel *(Berlin: Arbeiterjugend-Verlag, 1928); (editor)* Die Vorgeschichte des Weltkrieges *(vols. X-XI, Berlin: Deutsche Verlagsgesellschaft für Politik und Geschichte, 1930).*

From the late 1870s to the creation of the Nazi dictatorship in 1933, the German Social Democratic Party fought for economic democracy and basic social reforms, including improved working conditions, old age pensions, and the abolition of child labor. The party also championed the rights of women, including suffrage and reproductive freedom. Among the many German women attracted to the ideals of Social Democracy was Clara Bohm-Schuch. Born on December 5, 1879, in Stechow, Westhavelland, she grew up in poverty. Unable to afford higher education, she found work as a salesperson. After some years as a reliable and enthusiastic Social Democrat, Bohm-Schuch advanced through the ranks of the party's women's organizations and was chosen to represent a Berlin district in the German Reichstag. She served with considerable distinction from January 1919 through early 1933, when the Nazis seized power.

Although the Nazi regime did not officially ban the Social Democratic Party until June 1933, their reign of terror began immediately after Adolf Hitler's appointment as chancellor on January 30 of that year. Particularly in the larger cities of Germany, where the Left had its greatest support, Social Democrats and Communists found themselves at the mercy of Nazi storm troopers who burst into their homes to brutalize them and their families. One of Clara Bohm-Schuch's friends and political comrades, Berlin Social Democratic city council member **Marie Jankowski** was attacked in March 1933. Exhibiting great courage and a considerable degree of political naiveté, Bohm-Schuch wrote a strong letter of protest to Hermann Göring, president of the Reichstag and one of the leading Nazis.

The Nazis of her native Berlin never forgave Bohm-Schuch for her bold protest. In August 1933, after a search of her home, she was arrested. Although she was incarcerated for only two weeks, first in the Alexanderplatz police station and then in the Barnimstrasse women's prison, the harsh interrogations shattered her already fragile health. Adding to the psychological stress of her arrest and imprisonment, she remained under surveillance for an indefinite period. Her health broken, Clara Bohm-Schuch died of a stroke in Berlin on May 6, 1936. Her funeral, held at the Baumschulenweg cemetery, provided her friends and sympathizers an opportunity for a silent protest against Nazism.

SOURCES:

Archiv der sozialen Demokratie, Bonn. Nachlass M. Schwarz.

Institut für Zeitgeschichte, Munich. Folder ED 106/35.

Juchacz, Marie. *Sie lebten für eine bessere Welt: Lebendbilder führender Frauen des 19. und 20. Jahrhunderts.* Hanover: J.H.W. Dietz Verlag, 1971.

Leo Baeck Institute, New York. Wiener Library collection of newspaper clippings on Nazis and Women 1933–1939, AR 7187, microfilm reels 95 and 109.

Milton, Sybil. "Deutsche und deutsch-jüdische Frauen als Verfolgte des NS-Staates," in *Dachauer Hefte.* Vol. 3, no. 3. November 1987, pp. 3–20.

Schumacher, Martin and Katharina Lubbe, eds. *M.d.R. Die Reichstagsabgeordneten der Weimarer Republik in der Zeit des Nationalsozialismus: Politische Verfolgung, Emigration und Ausbürgerung 1933–1945: Eine biographische Dokumentation.* Düsseldorf: Droste Verlag, 1991.

Wickert, Christl. *Unsere Erwählten: Sozialdemokratische Frauen im Deutschen Reichstag und im Preussischen Landtag 1919 bis 1933.* 2 vols. Göttingen: SOVEC Verlag, 1986.

John Haag, Associate Professor,
University of Georgia, Athens, Georgia

Bohun, Alianore (d. 1313)

Countess of Hereford and Essex. *Died on February 20, 1313; interred at Walden Abbey; daughter of* ****Eleanor de Braose*** *(fl. 1250s) and Humphrey Bohun (d. 1265), 6th earl of Hereford and Essex; married Robert de Ferrers, earl of Derby, on June 26, 1269; children: John (b. 1271), baron Ferrers of Chartley;* ***Alianore de Ferrers*** *(who married Robert, 1st baron FitzWalter).*

Bohun, Eleanor (fl. 1327–1340)

Countess of Ormonde. *Name variations: Eleanor Butler; Eleanor Dagworth. Flourished between 1327 and 1340; daughter of Humphrey Bohun, 4th earl of Hereford, 3rd of Essex, and* ****Elizabeth Plantagenet*** *(1282–1316); married James Butler (c. 1305–1338), 1st earl of Ormonde, in 1327; married Thomas Dagworth, Lord Dagworth; children: (first marriage) James Butler (1330–1382), 2nd earl of Ormonde.*

Bohun, Eleanor (1366–1399)

Duchess of Gloucester. *Name variations: Eleanor de Bohun. Born in 1366; died on October 2, 1399; buried in Westminster Abbey, London; daughter of Humphrey Bohun, 7th earl of Hereford, Essex, and Northampton,* *and *Joan Fitzalan (d. 1419); married Thomas of Woodstock, 1st duke of Gloucester (r. 1356–1397), in 1374; children: Humphrey (c. 1382–1399); *Anne Plantagenet (1383–1438); *Joan (1384–1400); *Isabel (1386–1402); Philippa (c. 1389–1399).*

Following the murder of her husband Thomas of Woodstock, Eleanor Bohun entered the convent. She appears in Shakespeare's *Richard II.*

Bohun, Elizabeth (1264–1297).

See Eleanor of Castile (1241–1290) for sidebar on Elizabeth Plantagenet.

Bohun, Elizabeth (d. 1385).

See Fitzalan, Elizabeth.

Bohun, Joan (fl. 1325).

See Fitzalan, Joan.

Bohun, Joan (d. 1419).

See Fitzalan, Joan.

Bohun, Margaret (fl. 1330).

See Courtenay, Margaret.

Bohun, Mary (1369–1394).

See Mary de Bohun.

Bohun, Maud (fl. 1240s)

***Countess of Pembroke.** Name variations: Maud de Bohun. Daughter of ***Maud of Lusignan** (d. 1241) and Humphrey Bohun (1200–1275), 2nd earl of Hereford, 1st of Essex (r. 1220–1275), and constable of England (some sources cite him as 6th earl of Hereford and Essex); married Anselme Marshall (d. 1245), 6th earl of Pembroke (some sources cite 9th earl of Pembroke); married Roger de Quincy, 2nd earl of Winchester, after 1245.*

Bohun, Maud (fl. 1275)

***Countess of Hereford and Essex.** Name variations: Maud de Fiennes; Maud de Bohun. Flourished in 1275; died before 1298; interred at Walden; daughter of Enguerrand II de Fiennes (d. 1270) and a daughter of Jacques de Condé; married Humphrey Bohun, 3rd earl of Hereford, 2nd of Essex (some sources cite 7th earl of Hereford and Essex), in 1275; children: Humphrey Bohun (1276–1321), 4th earl of Hereford, 3rd of Essex.*

Bohuszewiczowna, Maria (1865–1887)

***Polish revolutionary leader and a key member of the generation of "Socialist martyrs" whose organization was destroyed by the tsarist-occupation authorities.** Born into a family of impoverished nobles on January 4, 1865, in Cepercach near Slutsk, Poland; died in Russia en route to her designated place of exile in Siberia in 1887; trained to be a teacher.*

Despite the bloody suppression of two uprisings against Russian rule in 1830–31 and 1863–64, Polish nationalists in the closing decades of the 19th century continued to dream of a successful national upheaval that would restore the independence of their nation. By the 1880s, the rise of an industrial working class added an additional potential for revolution to the complex social and political situation. In October 1882, 17-year-old Maria Bohuszewiczowna was among the founding members of a small but determined group of Marxist revolutionaries who formed the first modern revolutionary party in Warsaw. An idealist from an impoverished *szlachta* (high nobility) family that included a long line of patriots and recklessly brave revolutionaries, Bohuszewiczowna was particularly proud of being the grandniece of the celebrated patriotic leader Tadeusz Kosciuszko.

Showing a natural talent for the dangerous and conspiratorial nature of their party's work, she became a member of the organization's welfare section, named "Red Cross." Her task was to render assistance to the families of imprisoned members. In this work, she used a number of names, including "Regina," "Wanda," and "Weneda." Because of her reputation for reliability and fearlessness, within a few months she became director of the entire "Red Cross" operation.

The idealism and courage of the party's "proletariat" members was no match for the tsarist police in Warsaw. By the summer of 1884, the leader of the party, Stanislaw Krusinski, had been arrested, and other members of the group were on the run. As one of the few senior party activists still at liberty, Bohuszewiczowna took over the leadership of the organization in August 1884. At this time, she also became a member of the central committee of the entire "proletariat" organism.

Eluding the police, Bohuszewiczowna kept the organization intact as best she could, attempting to strengthen the shattered party with a fresh type of organizational structure. She also wrote a new statute for the organization. These efforts proved largely futile in the face of the immense power of the tsarist police who were determined to crush another Polish insurrectionary movement in the bud. Bohuszewiczowna was arrested on September 30, 1885, and placed in detention in the infamous "Tenth Pavillion," the section of the Warsaw Citadel reserved for political prisoners. During more than a year of relentless interrogations by the Russian police officials, she showed great courage. Sentenced to banishment in Siberia, she left Warsaw in police custody on May 12, 1887. She died several weeks later of physical exhaustion en route to Siberia. Sacrificed as a martyr in the cause of her nation's freedom at age 22, Maria Bohuszewiczowna was a leading member of the first generation of Poland's "Socialist martyrs." Almost immediately after their deaths, the lives of these idealistic young men and women took on a mythical aura and served as powerful inspiration for Poland's next generation of dreamers, conspirators, and revolutionaries.

SOURCES:

"Bohuszewiczowna, Maria," in *Wielka Encyklopedia Powszechna PWN.* Vol. 2. Warsaw: Panstwowe Wydawnictwo Naukowe, 1963, p. 40.

Dziewanowski, Marian Kamil. *The Communist Party of Poland: An Outline of History.* Cambridge, MA: Harvard University Press, 1959.

Haustein, Ulrich. "Sozialismus und nationale Frage in Polen: Die Entwicklung der sozialistischen Bewegung in Kongresspolen von 1875 bis 1900 unter besonderer Berücksichtigung der Polnischen Sozialistischen Partei (PPS)" Unpublished Ph.D. dissertation, University of Mainz, 1965.

Strobel, Georg W. *Quellen zur Geschichte der Kommunismus in Polen 1878–1918: Programme und Statuten.* Cologne: Verlag Wissenschaft und Politik, 1968.

John Haag, Associate Professor,
University of Georgia, Athens, Georgia

Boiardi, Helen (1905–1995)

Italian-American businesswoman who founded Chef Boyardee with her husband Hector Boiardi. *Born in 1905; died in Shaker Heights, Ohio, in July 1995; married Hector Boiardi (1898–1985); children: son, Mario.*

By any criterion, the careers of hardworking Italian-Americans Helen and Hector Boiardi make for an American success story. They arrived in the United States as impoverished immigrants, full of hope and ambition. Hector had learned about cooking as an apprentice in an Italian hotel at age 11, while Helen, as an Italian woman raised in a traditional culture, had learned cooking at an early age. In America, they quickly saw that many Americans who had been raised on English, Irish, and German food were delighted by Italian cooking once introduced to it. By the mid-1920s, the Boiardis were running a successful Italian restaurant in the financial district of Cleveland, Ohio.

Their menu was so popular that many patrons asked for pasta, sauce and cheese to take home, and the growing popularity of their takeout food prompted the couple to go into the packaged-food business in 1928, calling the new company Chef Boiardi. When it soon became obvious that many customers—even some of the company's dealers—were having difficulty pronouncing the name Boiardi, Hector and Helen put sales above family pride and changed the company name to the phonetic "Chef Boyardee." The name change, along with the introduction of the picture of a smiling Italian chef on the label, greatly enhanced sales.

By the late 1930s, the Chef Boyardee label could be seen in grocery stores from coast to coast as Americans enjoyed Italian food at home when many could not afford to eat out. In 1946, the Boiardis sold the company to American Home Food Products, a subsidiary of American Home Products. Hector Boiardi served as a consultant to American Home Foods until 1978 and died in 1985. Helen Boardi advised her husband informally but with vigor, and spent the final decades of her life involved in community and family affairs. After her death in July 1995, Chef Boyardee Italian foods remained in the marketplace.

SOURCES:

Di Stasi, Lawrence. "The Face that Made Spaghetti Famous," in Lawrence Di Stasi, ed. *Dream Streets: The Big Book of Italian-American Culture.* NY: Harper & Row, 1989, pp. 72–73.

"Hector Boiardi, 87, Is Dead; Founder of Chef Boy-ardee," in *The New York Times Biographical Service.* June 1985, p. 729.

"Helen J. Boiardi, 90; Started Line of Pasta," in *The New York Times Biographical Service.* July 1995, p. 967.

John Haag, Associate Professor,
University of Georgia, Athens, Georgia

Boissevain, Inez M. (1886–1916)

American suffrage leader and lawyer. *Born Inez Milholland on August 6, 1886; died in Los Angeles, California, on November 25, 1916; graduated from Vassar College, 1909; attended law school at New York University; married Eugene Boissevain (a Dutch electrical engineer), in 1913.*

Inez Milholland Boissevain graduated in 1909 from Vassar College where she was prominent in athletics and championed radical social ideas. During a vacation, she went to England, joined suffragist ***Emmeline Pankhurst**'s forces, and was arrested in a demonstration. In 1912, she entered the Law School of New York University, a year before her marriage to Eugene Boissevain, a Dutch electrical engineer. During the next three years, Boissevain's enthusiasm and ability as a speaker and organizer made her invaluable to the Woman's Party, and there was deep regret upon her early death, at age 30, in Los Angeles, California, where she had been overtaken by illness during a speaking tour.

Boissevain, Mia (1878–1959).
See joint entry with Manus, Rosa.

Boivin, Marie Anne (1773–1847)

French midwife. *Born Marie Anne Victoire Gillain in Montreuil, France, in 1773; died in 1847 (some sources cite 1841); educated by nuns; married in 1797.*

Marie Anne Boivin spent three years in the study of anatomy. Widowed with a baby daughter and no fortune, she undertook the study of midwifery at La Maternité Hospital, as an assistant to ***Marie Lachapelle**. In 1801, Boivin was appointed chief superintendent of the institution, and at her suggestion a special school of accouchement was added. An order of civil merit was conferred upon Boivin, and she received the degree of M.D. Published in 1824, her *Mémorial de l'art des accouchements* went through many editions.

Bok, Mary Louise Curtis (1876–1970).
See Zimbalist, Mary Louise Curtis.

Boland, Mary (1880–1965)

American actress. *Born in Philadelphia, Pennsylvania, on January 28, 1880; died in June 1965; daughter of W.A. Boland (an actor from Detroit); mother unknown; attended Sacred Heart Convent school in Detroit, Michigan.*

Films include: The Edge of the Abyss *(1915);* The Price of Happiness *(1916);* The Stepping Stone *(1916);* Mountain Dew *(1917);* The Prodigal Wife *(1918);* The Perfect Lover *(1919);* His Temporary Wife *(1920);* Secrets of a Secretary *(1931);* The Night of June 13th *(1932);* Evenings for Sale *(1932);* Trouble in Paradise *(1932);* If I had a Million *(1932);* Mama Loves Papa *(1933);* Three-Cornered Moon *(1933);* The Solitaire Man *(1933);* Four Frightened People *(1934);* Six of a Kind *(1934);* Melody in Spring *(1934);* Stingaree *(1934);* Here Comes the Groom *(1934);* Down to Their Last Yacht *(1934);* The Pursuit of Happiness *(1934);* Ruggles of Red Gap *(1935);* People Will Talk *(1935);* The Big Broadcast of 1936 *(1935);* Two for Tonight *(1935);* Early to Bed *(1936);* A Son Comes Home *(1936);* Wives Never Know *(1936);* College Holiday *(1936);* Marry the Girl *(1937);* Danger—Love at Work *(1937);* There Goes the Groom *(1937);* Artists and Models Abroad *(1938);* Little Tough Guys in Society *(1938);* The Magnificent Fraud *(1939);* The Women *(1939);* Night Work *(1939);* He Married His Wife *(1940);* New Moon *(1940);* Pride and Prejudice *(1940);* In Our Time *(1944);* Nothing but Trouble *(1945);* Julia Misbehaves *(1948);* Guilty Bystander *(1950).*

Mary Boland

Following in her actor-father's footsteps, Mary Boland made her debut in Detroit in 1901, as Eleanor Burnham in *A Social Highwayman*, and played in various stock companies while still a teenager. Her Broadway debut came in 1905, as Dorothy Nelson in *Strongheart*. Although she started as a tragedienne, she eventually made her mark in comedy. Boland was at her best portraying madcap, scatterbrained wives and mothers on stage in the 1920s and in films during the 1930s. Her portrayals of the stepmother in *Clarence* (1919) and the flighty matron in *The Vinegar Tree* (1930) were two such successful stage roles. Between theater and films, Boland's career spanned five decades. One of her most memorable film roles was opposite Charlie Ruggles in *Ruggles of Red Gap*, in 1935. She last appeared on the New York stage as the domineering mother in the 1954 production of *Lullaby*.

Bolduc, Marie (1894–1941)

***French-Canadian singer and musician who was Canada's first great* chansonniére.** *Name variations: La Bolduc; Mary Travers. Born Marie or Mary-Rose-Anne Travers in Newport, Gaspésie, Quebec, Canada, on June 4, 1894; died in Montreal, Quebec, Canada, on February 20, 1941; married Édouard Bolduc (a plumber), in 1914.*

Left home, age 13, to earn a living in Montreal (1907); multitalented as a musician, began to perform professionally (1927); composed more than 80 songs and made many recordings (1930s).

In 1994, Canada issued a postage stamp to commemorate the centenary of the birth of La Bolduc, one of the great *chansonniérs* of the French language. Marie Travers was born on June 4, 1894, in the town of Newport in the Gaspé region to parents of French-Canadian and Irish origins. At age 13, she left her large family to support herself in Montreal as a maid. In August 1914, she married Édouard Bolduc, a plumber, and the couple soon began to raise a large family. In her spare time, Marie Bolduc revealed that she was an excellent musician, equally adept at playing an accordion, harmonica, violin, and the Jew's harp.

In the mid-1920s, the Bolducs found themselves in economic crisis due to the temporary incapacitation of Édouard. To make ends meet, Marie began to accompany the famous French-Canadian singer Ovila Légaré on his recordings. Her reputation grew, and soon she was performing as a *violoneuse* at the Veillées du bon vieux temps concerts at the Monument National Theater in Montreal. In 1927, she was asked by the concert manager Conrad Gauthier to sing in public. After an extraordinarily successful debut, he asked her to compose some songs. Although she had had little formal education and was technically only semi-literate, La Bolduc, as her fans now called her, possessed great intuitive insights into the emotional lives of people like herself and her family and friends; over the next dozen years, she wrote songs that addressed the hopes, joys, fears, and tragedies of ordinary working people. Some of her first recordings, "La Cuisiniére" and "La Servante," became instant hits, selling 12,000 copies, an unprecedented accomplishment in Quebec.

Bolduc's songs were often sharp-edged in their criticism of economic exploitation and defended the rights of working women in simple words grounded in the experience of real life. The contemporary distress of economic depression often was reflected in such songs as "Le Commerçant des rues," "L'Enfant volé," "Les Cinq Jumelles," "Les Colons canadiens," "La Grocerie du coin," "Les Agents d'assurance," "Les Conducteurs de chars." Of an optimistic nature, La Bolduc's songs were sharply satirical but avoided spite. She enjoyed meeting her many fans throughout Quebec and parts of Ontario and New Brunswick, as well as the French-speaking towns of New England, and performed before audiences in rural parish halls or on spacious concert stages in Montreal. After her tours, she would return to her east-end Montreal home to resume a life as wife and mother of a large family.

Her fans enjoyed knowing that La Bolduc had not been spoiled by her success. Even the poorest among them could reasonably expect that her concert tours would eventually bring her to their impoverished and isolated Quebec communities. Highly popular among working-class and rural folk during the Depression, Bolduc's singing was often sneered at by Quebec's educational and economic elite, who saw her as a "vulgar" and "common" entertainer of the masses. Determined to maintain the ideals of high culture, the programming executives of Radio-Canada adamantly refused to broadcast her recordings. Bolduc, amused by such class snobbery and puritanism, found them proper subjects for her song lyrics. Reflecting the struggles and dreams of the poor farmers of Quebec and the unemployed of the Montreal tenements, her songs were rooted in the musical traditions of her native region of Gaspésie. La Bolduc's *turluttes* (mouth music) were derived from her Irish origins, while her unsophisticated, but rich, poetry came from the popular language of French Canada.

In 1938, Marie Bolduc was diagnosed with cancer. After her death in Montreal on February 20, 1941, her influence continued to grow. Her recordings remained in print, inspiring numerous singers and composers of a younger generation. Now universally acknowledged to be Canada's first *chansonniére*, La Bolduc has taken on legendary status. Marius Barbeau spoke admiringly of her songs, with their "reckless verve and unique twist of the tongue in the manner of the singers of the true soil."

SOURCES:

Benoit, Réal. *La Bolduc*. Montreal: Les Éditions de l'Homme, 1959.

Day, Pierre. *Une histoire de la Bolduc.* Montreal: VLB éditeur, 1991.

Laframboise, Philippe. "Bolduc," in Helmut Kallmann, Gilles Potvin and Kenneth Winters, eds., *Encyclopedia of Music in Canada.* 2nd ed. Toronto: University of Toronto Press, 1992, pp. 137–138.

———. *La Bolduc: Soixante-douze chansons populaires.* Montreal: VLB éditeur, 1992.

Lonergan, David. *La Bolduc: La vie de Mary Travers.* Bic: Isaac-Dion éditeur, 1992.

Thério, Adrien. "On revient á la Bolduc," in *Lettres québécoises.* No. 67, Autumn 1992, p. 48.

John Haag, Associate Professor, University of Georgia, Athens, Georgia

Bolena, Anna (1507–1536).

See Boleyn, Anne.

Boleyn, Anne (c. 1507–1536)

English queen who precipitated the English Reformation and gave birth to England's most famous queen, Elizabeth I. *Name variations: Nan Bullen; Anne of the Thousand Days. Pronunciation: BOE-lin. Born 1507 (some sources cite 1501) somewhere in England; executed May 19, 1536, in London; daughter of Thomas Boleyn, earl of Wiltshire (diplomat and courtier) and Elizabeth Howard (daughter of the earl of Surrey); educated at royal courts in the Netherlands and France; married Henry VIII, king of England, on January 25, 1533; children: Elizabeth (1533–1603, later Elizabeth I, queen of England); Henry Tudor, duke of Cornwall (1534–1534), and an unnamed baby (1536–1536).*

Appointed lady-in-waiting to Catherine of Aragon (1526); beloved by Henry VIII (1527); became Henry's mistress (1532); crowned queen of England (1533); miscarried male child (January 1536); accused of adultery and treason (May 1536).

On Thursday, May 19, at eight o'clock in the morning, Anne Boleyn entered the courtyard of the Tower of London. Dressed in a robe of black damask covered by an ermine mantle of white, she was escorted by the Tower's Constable Sir William Kingston, followed by four ladies-in-waiting. As was customary in 16th-century executions, she addressed the large crowd from the scaffold with a short and simple speech. Explaining that she had come to die, rather than preach, Anne Boleyn prayed for the king, who she described as a "good, gentle and sovereign lord." She then removed the ermine headdress and tucked her long flowing hair into a small linen cap. Blindfolded, she knelt down repeating the words, "To Jesus Christ I commend my soul; Lord Jesu, receive my soul." With a stroke of the sword her words were silenced forever. The woman who had captured the heart of a king, ushered in a religious Reformation, and been crowned queen of England was dead. Her fall was as spectacular as her rise to power.

The date of Anne Boleyn's birth was never recorded and has remained a matter of debate among historians. Most place it around 1501 while others prefer the later date of 1507. What *is* certain is that she was one of three children born to Thomas Boleyn and ❧▸ **Elizabeth Howard**, daughter of the earl of Surrey. Although the Boleyn family had rather humble beginnings as small tenant farmers, by the mid-15th century Sir Geoffrey Boleyn was lord mayor of London. He also acquired prosperous lands and manors in Norfolk and Kent. Additional manors were obtained when Anne's grandfather married one of the richest heiresses in England. Anne's own father had steadily risen to a prominent place at the royal courts of Henry VII and Henry VIII and, in the spring of 1512, Thomas Boleyn was sent as an envoy to the Netherlands. His six-year-old daughter soon followed.

Anne Boleyn spent two years at the court of ***Margaret (of Austria)**, archduchess of Austria, regent of the Netherlands. Here she resided with young girls from the royal families of Europe, three of whom became the future queens of France, Denmark, and Hungary. In the royal nursery at the court of Malines, Anne was taught to speak French as well as the traditional accoutrements of any well-bred young woman. Hence she was taught to sing, to play musical instruments, such as the lute and the clavichord, to dress stylishly, and to be a good conversationalist.

Anne's peaceful sojourn was interrupted when Henry VIII's sister ***Mary Tudor** married King Louis XII of France in August 1514. Since the Boleyn family accompanied the wedding party to France, Anne's presence was also re-

❧▸ Howard, Elizabeth (?–1538)

Countess of Wiltshire. *Birth date unknown; died on April 3, 1538, at Barnard Castle, Durham, England; buried at Lambeth Church, London; daughter of Thomas Howard (1473–1554), 2nd duke of Norfolk, and* ****Elizabeth Tylney*** *(d. 1497); married Thomas Boleyn, earl of Wiltshire, before 1507; children: George Boleyn, 2nd viscount Rochford (d. 1536);* ****Mary Boleyn*** *(d. 1543);* ****Anne Boleyn*** *(c. 1507–1536); Thomas and Henry (both died young).*

Anne Boleyn

quired. By November 1514, she was residing at the French court with the king's daughter *Renée of France. When Louis died in January 1515, Anne remained in France to attend Queen *Claude of France, the wife of the new king, Francis I.

Anne Boleyn spent seven years on the Continent. During these formative years, she became thoroughly fluent in the French language, as well as immersed in French culture. For the rest of her life, she retained a taste for Franco-Flemish music and French fashion. She was also introduced to ideas for religious reform. Francis I's sister, ***Margaret of Angoulême** (1492–1549), queen of Navarre, wrote both secular and religious literature that focused on a more personal, mystical faith based on readings from Scripture. Although she never advocated schism from the Roman Catholic Church, Margaret of Angoulême's ideas were believed to be heretical by several French theologians. It is evident that Anne's own religious beliefs were inspired by these early reforming ideals. In later years, she debated and discussed theological issues with Henry VIII as well as supporting the belief that Scriptures should be read in the vernacular.

Anne's early years in France and the Netherlands also exposed her to strong female role models. Both Margaret of Austria and ***Louise of Savoy**, Francis I's mother, ruled as regents for two of the most powerful monarchs of 16th-century Europe. In a society that barred the majority of women from exercising any kind of public authority, these women provided Anne with examples of intelligent and influential female power. Finally, Anne grew up in the company of royal children. Historian **Retha Warnicke** has concluded that this "served to heighten her sense of her personal worth and to strengthen her determination to elevate her status and lineage."

In 1521, Anne returned to England. Her father, whose star was steadily rising at the court of Henry VIII, was busily arranging marriage alliances for his children. Anne's sister ⚜▸ **Mary** was married to William Carey the year before, and it was clear that Thomas Boleyn desired a favorable alliance for his other daughter. Negotiations for her marriage to the son and heir of Sir Piers Butler, earl of Ormond, began even before Anne had returned to England. While the negotiations were in progress, Anne was placed as a maid of honor in the household of Henry VIII's sister, Mary Tudor, the former queen of France.

By 1523, the negotiations had broken off. For Anne, this was a welcome relief, as she had already formed a romantic attachment to Lord Henry Percy, heir to the earldom of Northumberland. Unfortunately, their love affair was discovered by the king's chief minister, Cardinal Wolsey, who forced Percy to give up the relationship. Although the status of the Boleyn family was rising, Percy was a member of one of the richest and most influential noble families in England. Neither the king nor the cardinal would ever allow the heir of Northumberland to marry below his station. Hence a year later, in 1524, Henry Percy was married to Lady **Mary Talbot**. From all accounts, the marriage proved to be an unhappy one.

Anne's reaction to the loss of her betrothed is unrecorded. In any event, it was a lesson in power politics that she never forgot. Marriage alliances among noble families had little to do with affection or choice; instead, satisfying the requirements of parents and the crown were the determining factors. Her disgrace is evident for there are no records of her actions or whereabouts between 1524 and 1527.

During those three years, however, one important development arose which was to change her life forever. Henry VIII was becoming increasingly concerned that he would have no male heir to succeed him. In 1509, shortly after acceding to the throne, Henry married his brother Arthur's widow, ⚜▸ **Catherine of Aragon**. For the next 16 years, he waited for an heir. Although Catherine was often pregnant and gave birth to several children, only one child, Mary (later ***Mary I**), born in 1516, had survived. Like most other 16th-century parents, Henry believed that this failure to beget a male heir was a sign of God's punishment. In order to placate an angry God, Henry went on pilgrimages and prayed several times a day. After 1518, he began to respond to the Protestant reformer, Martin Luther. In 1521, he wrote a treatise refuting Luther's beliefs that instantly became a hot seller. As a reward for his efforts, Henry VIII was named "Defender of the Faith" by Pope Leo X.

◂⚜ ***Catherine of Aragon**. See Six Wives of Henry VIII.*

In spite of these efforts, by 1525 Henry concluded that Catherine was no longer able to bear children. His anxiety over the future of England escalated. The following year, he finally made up his mind that his marriage to Catherine must be dissolved. Although previous historians have argued that it was the king's love for Anne Boleyn that drove him to seek a divorce, recent research has concluded that Henry arrived at the decision to terminate his marriage alone. More signifi-

⚜▸ **Boleyn, Mary** (d. 1543)

Sister of Anne Boleyn. *Name variations: Mary Carey; Mary Stafford. Died on July 19, 1543; daughter of Thomas Boleyn, earl of Wiltshire, and* ****Elizabeth Howard;*** *married William Carey (gentleman of the privvy), on January 31, 1521; married William Stafford; children: (first marriage) Henry Carey (c. 1524–1596), 1st baron Hunsdon;* ****Catherine Carey*** *(1529–1569, who was chief lady of the bedchamber).*

cantly, he was determined to end his marriage before he had even met Anne Boleyn.

Henry's decision was a matter of conscience. He truly believed that his inability to beget a male heir was a result of God's anger. The justification was found in the Old Testament commandment that a man must not marry his brother's widow. In 1501, Catherine of Aragon had married Henry's brother Arthur. One year later, Arthur was dead. Although Catherine swore that the marriage had never been consummated, Henry was convinced that by ignoring the commandment, God was preventing them from producing a male heir. As Defender of the Faith, Henry also believed that his theological expertise would not be challenged. By 1527, however, all of his attention was soon focused on a young lady who had just returned to court.

In December 1526, Anne Boleyn had secured an appointment as one of Queen Catherine's ladies-in-waiting. Six months later, she met Henry VIII. The 36-year-old king was tall, fair-haired, graceful and athletic. He was a well-educated, deeply religious man who composed music and hunted vigorously. He also fell deeply in love with this woman, who was 16 years his junior. The object of his affections was not a beauty by contemporary standards. Instead of the customary blond hair and blue-eyes, 20-year-old Anne Boleyn had lustrous, thick dark brown hair, black eyes and an elegant, long neck. Her allure was due more to her charm and self-confidence than her personal appearance. She was a graceful and elegant dancer, a good conversationalist, and a skilful singer and musician. As Warnicke has concluded, she was an "intelligent, quick-witted noblewoman" whose "energy and vitality made her the center of attention in any social gathering." Although later inimical writers described her as having a sixth finger on her left hand, this has never been confirmed. After meeting her, the king was even more convinced that his first marriage must come to an end.

In May 1527, secret proceedings were held in which Henry was called to defend himself on the charge of having cohabited with his deceased brother's wife. This began what became known as "the King's Great Matter." In June, Henry informed Queen Catherine that he wanted a divorce, and by July he was determined to marry Anne Boleyn. Although the customary solution to a king's amorous affection for a young woman was to make her his mistress, Anne Boleyn declined this role. She was in love with the king but was determined not to become his concubine. Consequently, for the next five years, she sustained Henry's passion by denying him full sexual relations. The extent of his desire is evident in several love letters he wrote to her during the summer and autumn of 1528 when they were separated during an outbreak of the sweating sickness. Written in his own hand, the letters declare his undying love for her.

By the early months of 1529, Henry was becoming increasingly anxious to have his marriage annulled. In May, the papal legate Cardinal Campeggio convened a tribunal to dissolve the marriage. Catherine of Aragon soon learned of the proceedings and requested that her case be heard in Rome. She also repeated that her marriage to Arthur had not been consummated. For the king, this was an unfortunate admission, as his entire case was built around the Biblical injunction against marrying his brother's wife. If Catherine's marriage to Prince Arthur had never been consummated, as she claimed, Henry's justification for the divorce was nullified. In addition, the situation was complicated by 16th-century politics. Catherine of Aragon's nephew was the Holy Roman Emperor, Charles V. Two years earlier, Charles' Imperial troops had sacked the city of Rome and kidnapped Pope Clement VII. Consequently, Clement was unwilling to slander the emperor's aunt by granting Henry's request for a divorce.

For Henry, the matter was not running as smoothly as he had hoped. In July, the proceedings of the tribunal were stayed and a decision was never given. While much of his anger was directed towards Campeggio and the pope, the bulk of the king's wrath fell upon Cardinal Wolsey. The cardinal's fall was swift. In October 1529, he was commanded to hand over the great seal thus signifying his dismissal as lord chancellor of England. Shortly after, his goods and property were seized and a year later he was dead.

Contemporaries blamed Anne for Wolsey's fall, although it was the cardinal's failure to secure a quick divorce for the king that led to his demise. Wolsey's fall from grace was noted by the king's new minister, Thomas Cromwell, who recognized that the king's desire for a divorce would not prevent him from turning his back on loyal servants. It was not only unwise, but politically dangerous, to disappoint King Henry.

After 1529, the king was forced to look for new methods to obtain the divorce. Led by Cromwell, steps were taken to divert power away from the papacy and into the king's hands; the English Reformation had begun. In 1531, Henry VIII was declared Supreme Head of the

Church of England. A year later, the clergy surrendered their legal autonomy to the king; all future clerical legislation required royal assent. It was also evident, from the summer of 1531, that Queen Catherine was no longer the king's consort. Until that summer, Henry had taken care to treat his wife cordially, allowing her to accompany him to state functions and religious festivities. By August 1531, however, Catherine of Aragon was banished from court and the king's presence. Anne Boleyn's star, in the meantime, was steadily rising. She was given separate apartments close to the king and now appeared openly at his side on formal occasions. Henry showered her with gifts of clothing, furs, jewelry and books as well as giving members of her family land and minor government offices.

Unfortunately, Catherine's banishment did nothing to improve public opinion of Anne. She was very unpopular and was openly referred to as the "King's whore." Nonetheless, she went from one triumph to another. In September 1532, she was created Lady Marquess of Pembroke and was given lands and manors in Wales and Middlesex. More significantly, in October, Anne accompanied the king to Calais where they visited Francis I. It was also sometime during this visit that Anne and Henry finally became lovers. By December, she was pregnant and on January 25, 1533, they were secretly married. From this point on, events moved rapidly.

In April, the English Parliament approved the Appeals statute, which prohibited appeals of marriage and divorce cases to Rome and allowed the king's marital dispute to be settled in England. After Parliament was prorogued, the king publicly announced his marriage to Anne Boleyn and, in early May, Thomas Cranmer, the new archbishop of Canterbury, decreed that the king's marriage to Catherine of Aragon was invalid. Catherine was asked to give up the title of queen, although she refused. In July, Pope Clement condemned the king's marriage to Anne. By this point, however, his condemnation was meaningless. Anne Boleyn had already been crowned queen of England.

Henry VIII and Anne Boleyn

For Anne, this was surely the greatest day of her life. On May 29, 50 barges, decorated with colorful banners, streamers, and flags escorted her from Greenwich along the Thames River to the Tower of London. Here, she was greeted by the king who escorted her into the Tower where they spent the next two nights together. On June 1, Anne made her triumphal entry into London. Carried on a litter of gold and white, the new queen was dressed in a crimson gown encrusted with precious stones. Her long hair hung down, and she carried flowers in her hand. Along the route, the long procession of nobles and attendants was greeted by various forms of entertainment and elaborate pageants.

For I never had better opinion in woman, than I had in [Anne Boleyn] . . . next unto your Grace, I was most bound unto her of all creatures living.

—Thomas Cranmer, Archbishop of Canterbury

The event was significant both for its pageantry and its symbolism. It not only allowed Henry VIII to introduce his new queen officially, but also to display the wealth and prestige of the crown to his subjects. It was also hoped that the celebrations would convince the public that his new wife was here to stay. On Sunday, June 1, at eight o'clock in the morning in Westminster Hall, Anne Boleyn was anointed and crowned queen of England by the archbishop of Canterbury. She had reached the pinnacle of her life. As queen, she was able to exercise great social and political influence. As Warnicke concludes, she also "set a high moral and charitable standard" for the court and country. She instructed her ladies-in-waiting to sew clothes for the poor, and she provided stipends for poor university students. But most important for Anne, she was five months pregnant with the king's long-hoped-for male heir.

Elaborate preparations were made for the royal delivery but both Anne and Henry were disappointed when she gave birth to a girl, ***Elizabeth (I)**, on September 7, 1533. Nonetheless, Henry was still confident that Anne would bear an heir. He commanded his eldest daughter Mary to give up the title of princess of Wales, and shortly thereafter she was declared illegitimate. In the early months of 1534, Anne was again pregnant, and the king was once more hopeful for a male heir. In late June, however, their hopes were dashed when she miscarried. From this point on, Henry's feelings for his wife began to dissipate, and by September it was widely rumored that he had taken a mistress. Neither of these events alleviated Anne's unpopularity among the English populace. She was still viewed by many as an adulterer who had destroyed the king's first marriage. The extent of his subjects' continuing dislike of her led Henry to pass a statute making it treasonable to criticize the new queen.

In spite of these trials, Anne remained optimistic about her future, especially when she found herself pregnant once more in autumn 1535. Unfortunately, her confidence was shattered when she prematurely delivered a stillborn male child in January 1536. This event led to her tragic downfall. Recent research has concluded that not only was the child premature, but it was also deformed. In the 16th century, it was believed that witches gave birth to deformed children due to their excessive lust and tendency to engage in illicit and deviant sexual acts. When Henry decided to cast off his second wife, it was precisely those charges that were used to convict her. Henry's commitment to Anne had already begun to wane even before her miscarriage. His eyes were soon attracted to a new member of Anne's household, ***Jane Seymour**. By mid-March 1536, Henry made his commitment to Jane public. From this point on, Anne's fate was sealed and few people at court remained loyal to her.

On April 30, five men, one of whom was her brother, were arrested on charges of having committed adultery with the king's wife. Shortly thereafter, Anne herself was charged with inciting these five men, through the use of witchcraft, to have sexual relations with her. In addition, she was accused of afflicting the king with bodily harm and of plotting his death. Anne's public unpopularity contributed to widespread acceptance of the charges against her, though none of them could be substantiated. Her only true crime was having failed to provide a male heir. Even Henry began to assert that she had "bewitched" him. Although she confronted him with three-year-old Elizabeth in her arms and proclaimed her innocence, the king was intractable.

On May 2, she was taken by barge to the Tower of London where she was housed in the same quarters in which she had awaited her triumphant coronation just three years before. During her imprisonment, she was closely watched. Observers noted that she wept often and, just as often, had fits of hysterical laughter, an understandable emotional state, considering that she had recently recovered from a miscarriage, then been repudiated and imprisoned by the man she loved.

Anne Boleyn's trial took place on May 15, 1536. She confronted her 26 male judges in a calm and composed manner. Although she denied all the charges, they declared her guilty. Her uncle, the duke of Norfolk, sentenced her to death, with discretion given to the king as to whether she would be burned or beheaded. Two days later, Henry divorced her. On the same day, the four men, including her brother, who had been accused of being her lovers, were executed on Tower Hill. On May 18, when Anne was told that she was to be beheaded, she commented, "I have heard say the executioner was very good, and I have a little neck." Then, she put her hands around her neck and laughed. The following morning, she was executed in front of a large crowd. Twenty-four hours later, Henry VIII was formally betrothed to Jane Seymour whom he married on May 30, 1536. (*See also* Six Wives of Henry VIII.)

SOURCES:

Fraser, Antonia. *The Wives of Henry VIII.* Harmondsworth: Penguin, 1992.

Ives, E.W. *Anne Boleyn.* Oxford: Basil Blackwell, 1986.

Warnicke, Retha. *The Rise and Fall of Anne Boleyn.* Cambridge: Cambridge University Press, 1989.

From the movie Anne of the Thousand Days, *starring Genevieve Bujold and Richard Burton.*

SUGGESTED READING:

Scarisbrick, J.J. *Henry VIII.* Berkeley, CA: University of California Press, 1968.

RELATED MEDIA:

Anne of the Thousand Days (146 min.), starring Richard Burton and **Genevieve Bujold**, directed by Charles Jarrott, 1969.

The Life of King Henry VIII by William Shakespeare.

Private Life of Henry VIII (97 min.), starring Charles Laughton, ***Merle Oberon** as Anne Boleyn, ***Elsa Lanchester**, **Wendy Barrie**, **Binnie Barnes**, produced by United Artists, 1933.

Six-part BBC series (9 hrs.), "Six Wives of Henry VIII," starring **Annette Crosbie** as Catherine of Aragon, **Dorothy Tutin** as Anne Boleyn, **Ann Stallybrass** as Jane Seymour, **Elvi Hale** as Anne of Cleves, **Angela Pleasance** as Catherine Howard, and **Rosalie Crutchley** as Catherine Parr, with Keith Mitchell as Henry VIII.

Margaret McIntyre, Trent University, Peterborough, Ontario, Canada

Boleyn, Mary (d. 1543).

See Boleyn, Anne for sidebar.

Bollmann, Minna (1876–1935)

German Social Democratic Reichstag and Landtag deputy who ardently represented her working-class constituents throughout the troubled history of the Weimar Republic. *Born Minna Zacharias on January 31, 1876, in Halberstadt, Saxony, Germany; committed suicide in Halberstadt on December 9, 1935; married; children: Otto Bollmann (d. 1951).*

A politically militant working-class woman, Minna Zacharias Bollmann gave much of her life to political struggle. Born into poverty in Halberstadt in the Harz mountain district of Saxony on January 31, 1876, she was drawn from her earliest years to the egalitarian ideals of the Social Democratic movement. By the time the German monarchy collapsed in November 1918, and women received the right to vote and sit in representative assemblies, she was well known to her fellow socialists, and the party leadership selected her to run for the Reichstag in January 1919. Winning the seat to represent the Magdeburg-Anhalt electoral district, she served until June 1920. Bollmann then ran successfully on the Social Democratic ticket for a seat in the Prussian Landtag (Provincial Assembly), serving from 1921 until 1933.

The onset of the Nazi dictatorship in 1933 led to the outlawing of the Social Democratic movement in Germany, and Bollmann lost her seat in the Prussian Landtag along with all of the other deputies. She made no attempts to accommodate to the new regime, and the people of Halberstadt knew that alongside the radical changes that were taking place in Germany Bollmann remained at heart a Social Democrat and a believer in human decency. Under the Nazis, daily life became difficult for Bollmann and countless other German anti-Fascists. To survive, she was employed in a working-class tavern. Her political past continued to provide excuses for Nazi harassment: her home was searched, and she was interrogated on several occasions by Gestapo agents. Her son Otto, who was also a committed Social Democrat, took increasingly great risks as a member of the local cell of the party. Memories of past terrors, and fears of a Germany in the grip of the Nazis, led Bollmann increasingly to despair, and she committed suicide on December 9, 1935. On January 21, 1936, Otto Bollmann was arrested as an anti-Nazi activist. First sentenced to 18 months in a penitentiary, at the end of his term he was transferred to the Sachsenhausen concentration camp. Although he survived the Nazi regime, his health was permanently impaired. He died in 1951, a delayed consequence of the years of brutal treatment by his Nazi captors.

SOURCES:

Archiv der sozialen Demokratie, Bonn. Biographical file on Minna Bollmann.

Schumacher, Martin. *M.d.R. Die Reichstagsabgeordneten der Weimarer Republik in der Zeit des Nationalsozialismus: Politische Verfolgung, Emigration und Ausbürgerung 1933–1945: Eine biographische Dokumentation.* Düsseldorf: Droste Verlag, 1991.

Wickert, Christl. *Unsere Erwählten: Sozialdemokratische Frauen im Deutschen Reichstag und im Preussischen Landtag 1919 bis 1933.* 2 vols. Göttingen: SOVEC Verlag, 1986.

John Haag, Associate Professor, University of Georgia, Athens, Georgia

Bol Poel, Martha (1877–1956)

Belgian feminist. *Name variations: Baroness Bol Poel. Born Martha De Kerchove de Deuterghem in Ghent, Belgium, in 1877; died in 1956; daughter of a distinguished Ghent family; attended Kerchove Institute, founded by her grandfather; studied painting at Académie Julien, Paris, France, 1895; married Bol Poel (an industrialist and politician), in 1898.*

Born Martha De Kerchove de Deuterghem in Ghent, Belgium, in 1877, Baroness Martha Bol Poel came from a distinguished Ghent family; her grandfather founded the Kerchove Institute where she matriculated. In one of her earliest acts of social reform, Bol Poel established a maternity center at her husband's metal works at La Louvrière, the first of its kind. During the

German occupation of Belgium in World War I, she organized a secret correspondence service which led to her imprisonment. While incarcerated, she became seriously ill and was exchanged for another prisoner in 1917, whereupon she went into exile in Switzerland.

Bol Poel resurfaced in the 1920s as a leading figure in the Belgian women's movement, serving as president of the National Council of Women in 1934 and of the International Council of Women from 1935 to 1940. After another German invasion of Belgium in 1940, she again became active in the underground. Following World War II, she resumed her activities with the International Council of Women.

Barbara Morgan,
Melrose, Massachusetts

Bolton, Frances Payne (1885–1977)

U.S. congressional representative, Republican of Ohio, 76th–90th Congresses, February 27, 1940–January 3, 1969. Born Frances Payne Bingham in Cleveland, Ohio, on March 29, 1885; died in Lyndhurst, Ohio, on March 9, 1977; fourth of five children of Charles William and Mary Perry (Payne) Bingham; attended Hathaway-Brown School in Cleveland, Ohio; attended the Dieudonne Bornel, Oise, France, and Miss Spence's School for Girls in New York City; married Chester Castle Bolton (U.S. congressional representative, 1929–1937, and January 3, 1939–October 29, 1939), on September 14, 1907; children: Charles Bingham, Kenyon Castle, and Oliver Payne Bolton.

Frances Bolton's life was distinguished by her philanthropic work and an extraordinary 28-year political career. Like many early female congressional representatives, she began her career with the decision to run for the seat left vacant by the death of her husband.

Growing up in an extremely wealthy Ohio family, Frances Payne Bingham first became involved in the city's visiting nurses' program as a member of a debutante club in Cleveland, and a lifelong interest in nursing and public health was to follow. In 1907, she married Chester Bolton, a lawyer who had made his own fortune in steel. She devoted much of the next ten years to raising her three sons.

The couple moved to Washington in 1917, the same year that Bolton gained access to a sizable trust fund established in her name by her uncle Oliver Hazard Payne, a founder of Standard Oil. In addition to working with various nursing groups to support World War I efforts, Bolton established the Payne Fund, through which she made philanthropic donations. In 1923, she gave $1.5 million to endow a nursing school at Cleveland's Western Reserve University. She also financed a log-cabin nursery center in Kentucky and provided support for studies on the social value of radio and movies in education, children's literature, and parapsychology. Serving as vice president of the American Social Hygiene Association, she actively supported state and congressional appropriations for the control of venereal diseases.

Bolton had little to do with politics until 1928, when her husband was elected to the House of Representatives, and she became involved with political life in the capital. When Chester failed to win reelection in 1936, the couple moved back to Cleveland where she served as vice chair of the Republican national program committee and as a member of the Republican Central Committee of Ohio. Her husband regained his House seat in 1938 but died in Octo-

Frances Payne Bolton

ber 1939, leaving a vacancy in his district. With the encouragement of the Ohio Republicans, Bolton decided to run for his seat. She won the election with a greater vote than her husband had ever enjoyed, becoming the first congresswoman to be elected from Ohio.

Bolton entered Congress as an isolationist and a critic of Roosevelt's New Deal. She voted against the Lend-Lease program to aid Britain and the Soviet Union before U.S. entrance into World War II. In September 1941, she gained national attention by opposing the conscription policies of the selective service bill. In an impassioned speech, she warned, "I cannot help see in it more danger than defense, more dictatorship than democracy." Once the United States entered the war, Bolton strongly supported the military effort.

During her second term, Bolton took a seat on the Committee on Foreign Affairs, a post she would hold throughout her congressional career. In March 1942, she voted for the creation of the Women's Auxiliary Army Corps and authored the Bolton Act of 1943, which created the U.S. Cadet Nurse Corps. In 1944, Bolton toured military hospitals in England and France, becoming the first member of Congress to visit a war theater. After the war, she continued her travels as a member of the Foreign Affairs Committee and in 1947 headed up a tour of the Middle East, the Soviet Union, and Poland, to become the first woman to lead a congressional mission. In 1949, she was appointed to the advisory committee of the Foreign Service Institute.

Due to reapportionment of various Ohio Districts in 1952, Bolton's youngest son, Oliver Payne Bolton, was elected Representative from the 11th District, marking the only time a mother and son have served in Congress concurrently. The 1950s also saw Bolton's appointment as a U.S. delegate to the United Nations General Assembly. By 1960, she was the longest serving woman sitting in the House of Representatives and a ranking Republican on Foreign Affairs. Among countless honors and awards, she received the ***Adelaide Nutting** award of the National League of Nursing Education. She was the first American woman, and the second woman internationally, to receive the William Freeman Snow award. When Frances Bolton finally lost her bid for reelection in 1968, she returned to Lyndhurst, Ohio, where she resided until her death on March 9, 1977.

SOURCES:

Candee, Marjorie Dent, ed. *Current Biography 1954.* NY: H.W. Wilson, 1954.

Office of the Historian. *Women in Congress, 1917–1990.* Commission on the Bicentenary of the U.S. House of Representatives, 1991.

SUGGESTED READING:

Loth, David. *A Long Way Forward: The Biography of Congresswoman Frances P. Bolton.* NY: Longmans, Green, 1957.

Barbara Morgan,
Melrose, Massachusetts

Bolton-Holifield, Ruthie (1967—)

African-American basketball player who was named the 1991 USA Basketball Female Player of the Year.

Name variations: Ruthie Bolton. Born Alice Ruth Bolton on May 27, 1967, in Lucedale, Mississippi; one of 20 children of Reverend Linwood and Leola Bolton; Attended McClain High School in McClain, Massachusetts; graduated from Auburn University with a degree in Exercise Physiology, 1990; married Mark Holifield, in 1991.

During her 1986–90 sojourn at Auburn University, Ruthie Bolton-Holifield, a 5'9" guard, was selected to the 1988 and 1989 Southeastern Conference (SEC) All-Academic Teams; was chosen for the 1989 ALL-SEC second team; won three SEC championships; was named to the 1988 and 1989 NCAA Mideast Region All-Tournament Teams and the 1988 NCAA Final Four All-Tournament Team; made four NCAA Tournament appearances and advanced to the NCAA championship game twice (1989 and 1990); and was named the 1991 USA Basketball Female Player of the Year. Bolton-Holifield was a member of many USA Basketball teams, winning a team gold medal with the World University team in 1991, the team bronze with the World Championship team and a team gold with the Goodwill team, both 1994.

At a time when an after-college career for women basketball players in the U.S. was nonexistent, Bolton-Holifield continued playing overseas. Her initial professional season was with Visby in Sweden (1989–90). She then became the first American woman to play in Hungary when she took on guard duty with the Tungstrum (1991–92). From 1992 to 1995, she played for Erreti Faenz in Italy, then signed with the Galatsaray in Turkey for the 1996–97 season. In 1995–96, Bolton-Holifield was a member of the USA Basketball Women's National Team that toured the world, culminating in a 1996 team gold medal at the Olympics in Atlanta. In January 22, 1997, she signed with the Women's National Basketball Association (WNBA) to play for the Sacramento Monarchs. In the WNBA's inaugural year, Bolton-Holifield had a spectacular season, scoring 34 points in two games, averaging 19.4 (PPG) points per game, along with 5.8 rebounds, and 2.6 assists. She was named to the 1997 All-WNBA First Team.

Ruthie Bolton-Holifield

Bombal, María Luisa (1910–1980)

Chilean author who wrote early Latin American feminist fiction in the style of magical realism. *Born María Luisa Bombal in Viña del Mar, Chile, on June 8, 1910; died in Chile, on May 6, 1980; educated at French boarding schools; graduated from the Sorbonne, 1931; married Count Raphael de Saint-Phalle (a financier), around 1945; no children.*

Selected works: La ultima niebla *(The Final Mist, 1935);* La amortajada *(The Shrouded Woman, 1938);* El Canciller *(The Foreign Minister, 1946).*

At age 12, María Luisa Bombal left her native Chile for France, where she lived and studied literature and philosophy until her graduation from the Sorbonne in 1931. Returning briefly to Chile, Bombal received an invitation to Buenos Aires, home of then unknown poet Pablo Neruda. Bombal's *La ultima niebla* (*The Final Mist*) was written at Neruda's kitchen table. She then moved to Argentina to work on scripts for the film company Sonofilm, and the eventual sale of the movie rights to her second novel, *La amortajada* (*The Shrouded Woman*), made her financially comfortable.

During a domestic dispute in 1940, Bombal shot and severely wounded her lover, political activist and anti-Communist Eulogio Sánchez Errazuriz. Jailed until his recovery was assured, she was then banished from Chile and settled in New York. There she found an active film community and met the French-born financier Count Raphael de Saint-Phalle, whom she married around 1945. The 1946 release of *El Canciller* (*The Foreign Minister*) was her last publication, as she grew progressively more dependent on alcohol. Three years after the death of her husband in 1970, Bombal returned to Chile. She died in her sleep on May 6, 1980, following a brief illness. She was 69.

Crista Martin,
Boston, Massachusetts

Bombeck, Erma (1927–1996)

American humor columnist and author. *Born Erma Louise Fiste on February 21, 1927, in Dayton, Ohio; died on April 22, 1996, in San Francisco, California; daughter and only child of Cassius (a laborer for the city of Dayton) and Erma (Haines) Fiste; attended Patterson Vocation High School, Dayton; awarded B.A. from University of Dayton, 1949; married William L. Bombeck, on August 13, 1949; children: Betsy, Matthew, and Andrew.*

Selected writings: At Wit's End *(1967);* Just Wait Till You Have Children of Your Own! *(1971);* I Lost Everything in the Post-Natal Depression *(1973);* The Grass Is Always Greener over the Septic Tank *(1976);* If Life Is a Bowl of Cherries, What Am I Doing in the Pits? *(1978);* Aunt Erma's Cope Book *(1979);* Motherhood: The Second Oldest Profession *(1984);* Family Ties That Bind . . . and Gag! *(1978);* I Want to Grow Hair, I Want to Grow Up, I Want to Go to Boise *(1989);* When You Look Like Your Passport Photo It's Time to Go Home *(1991);* A Marriage Made in Heaven—or, Too Tired for an Affair *(1993);* All I Know About Animal Behavior I Learned in Loehmann's Dressing Room *(1995).*

With her syndicated column "At Wit's End," a string of best-selling books, and 11 years as a correspondent on ABC's "Good Morning America," Erma Bombeck was known for almost 30 years as America's wisecracking champion of the suburban housewife. Focusing her wry wit and self-deprecating humor on the events of everyday life, from housework ("My second favorite household chore is ironing. My first being hitting my head on the top bunk bed until I faint."), to vacations ("Jet lag can damage your biological clock and cause you to give birth at age 53"), Bombeck credited her success to identification. "A housewife reads my column and says, 'But that's happened to ME! I know just what she's talking about!'"

Bombeck, who always retained her Midwestern unpretentiousness, said her life story could be told in 15 minutes tops. From the eighth grade on, she was writing humor columns for her school paper and devouring books by humorists James Thurber, Robert Benchley, H. Allen Smith, and Max Schulman. In 1944, fresh out of high school, she worked as a copy girl at the *Dayton Journal-Herald* but left after a year to attend college. Four years later, she returned to the *Journal-Herald* where she was relegated to writing obituaries and radio listings before landing a feature spot on the women's page. Bombeck described her first housekeeping column to a *Newsday* reporter as "sort of a sick Heloise." "I told people to clean their johns, lock them up, and send the kids to the gas station at the corner." In 1949, she married William Bombeck (who left sportswriting to become a public-school administrator) and, after the birth of her first child in 1953, quit her job to become a full-time housewife and mother.

Ten years and two more children later, she needed to know whether she could do something more than get stains out of bibs. "I was 37," she recalled, "too old for a paper route, too young for social security, and too tired for an affair." On a typewriter that was propped on the edge of a bed, she began writing a humor column for a local weekly, the *Kettering-Oakwood Times*. A year later, in 1965, she was once again hired by the *Dayton Journal-Herald* to produce two columns a week. Within a year, she was syndicated and, by the 1990s, was carried in over 600 papers. The bedroom workspace gave way to an office in a nine-room ranch house in a suburb of Phoenix, Arizona, where the Bombecks moved in 1971. Even with the increasing work demands, Bombeck's family always came first. "I can't be gone more than two days," she once quipped, "because that's all the underwear we have." As the years went by and the nest emptied, Bombeck took up the subjects of grown children, working women, retirement, and aging.

In 1967, she published her first book, a compilation of her columns entitled *At Wit's End*. Her second effort, *Just Wait Till You Have Children of Your Own*, was written in collaboration with cartoonist Bil Keane in 1971 and chronicled the traumas of living with an adolescent. A series of bestsellers followed at regular intervals. **Pamela Marsh** reviewed her 1973 book, *I Lost Everything in the Post-Natal Depression*, for the *Christian Science Monitor*. "This is no Class A Number 1 out-of-control housewife we have here," she wrote, "but a deliberate comic who doesn't place a foot or a word wrong without deliberate intent." Bombeck turned serious in 1989, with a book of interviews with children surviving cancer entitled *I Want to Grow Hair, I Want to Grow Up, I Want to Go to Boise*, which received the American Cancer Society's 1990 Medal of Honor.

Erma Bombeck held strong opinions on politics and world affairs but kept them out of her columns. "I stick close to home," she told Herbert Mitgang of *The New York Times Book Review* in 1978. "I'm still exploiting my children, husband and family life. I know what my domain is." She campaigned for two years for passage of the Equal Rights Amendment (ERA), though she thought the movement ignored housewives. She sometimes broached serious issues in her books. In *I Lost Everything in the Post-Natal Depression*, she decried the violence children witness on the six o'clock television news. "My children in their short span on earth have seen Watts in flames, mothers with clubs and rocks protesting schools, college students slain by national guardsmen, mass slaughter in California, and political conventions that defy anything they have seen on a movie screen. . . . I challenge you to protect a generation from violence that has seen the horrors of Kent, Dallas, and Attica."

Erma Bombeck

Bombeck was beset with medical problems, beginning at the age of 20 with polycystic kidney disease, a hereditary disorder that slowly forms tissue-destroying cysts. (Her father, who died of a heart attack when she was nine, may have also had the disease, as do her two sons.) In 1992, she was diagnosed with breast cancer and underwent a mastectomy. About a year later, her kidneys began to fail. She went on a waiting list for a new kidney while undergoing dialysis four times a day at her home. After losing a kidney in 1995, Bombeck was urged by friends to use her clout to skip to the top of the transplant list, but she preferred to wait her turn. Abhorring pity, she resisted sharing her health problems with her millions of fans. "What a crummy exit," she told *People* magazine in 1994, "to have someone say, 'Yeah, I remember, she had cancer and kidney disease.' I want people to remember 29 years of work and a line of books in the library to give 'em a laugh."

Erma Bombeck died on April 22, 1996, of complications following her awaited transplant.

SOURCES:

The [New London] *Day.* April 23, 1996.

Green, Carol Hurd, and Mary Grimley Mason, eds. *American Women Writers.* NY: Continuum, 1994.

McHenry, Robert, ed. *Famous American Women.* NY: Dover, 1983.

Moritz, Charles, ed. *Current Biography 1979.* NY: H.W. Wilson, 1979.

"Speaker of the House," in *People.* May 5, 1996, p. 226.

SUGGESTED READING:

Forever Erma. Kansas City: Andrews and McMeel, 1996.

Barbara Morgan,
Melrose, Massachusetts

Anne of Lusignan. *See Louise of Savoy for sidebar.*

Bona.

Variant of Bonna.

Bona of Bohemia (1315–1349)

Bohemian princess. *Name variations: Bonne of Luxemburg; Judith de Luxembourg or Judith of Luxemburg. Born in 1315; died of the plague in 1349; daughter of* ****Elizabeth of Bohemia*** *(1292–1339) and John I of Luxemburg also known as John of Bohemia, king of Bohemia (r. 1310–1346); sister of Charles IV Luxemburg, Holy Roman emperor (r. 1347–1378), and John Henry, margrave of Moravia (d. 1375); became first wife of John II the Good (1319–1364), king of France (r. 1350–1364), on July 28, 1332; children: Charles V the Wise (1338–1380), king of France (r. 1364–1380, who married* ****Jeanne de Bourbon****);* ****Jane of France*** *(1343–1373);* ****Marie of France*** *(1344–1404); Agnes (1345–1349); Margaret (1347–1352);* ****Isabelle of France*** *(1349–1372); Philip the Bold (1342–1404), duke of Burgundy (who married* ****Margaret of Flanders*** *[1350–1405]); John of Berri; Louis I (1339–1384), duke of Anjou. King John II's second wife was* ****Blanche of Boulogne*** *(1326–1360).*

Bona of Pisa (c. 1156–1207)

Italian saint. *Name variations: Bonna of Pisa. Born in Pisa about 1156; died on May 29, 1207; buried in the church of San Martino in Pisa.*

Bona of Pisa grew up in the charge of her mother after her father died when she was quite young. It was reported that throughout her childhood she was blessed with visions and that she determined to go on pilgrimage to Jerusalem as soon as she was able. Returning from Jerusalem, she met a hermit who encouraged her to undertake the task of converting the Saracens, but the Saracens had her imprisoned. Despite this, upon her release Bona continued her pilgrimages to sacred places, including Santiago de Compostela and the tomb of St. Peter in Rome. In an Apostolic Letter of March 2, 1962, Pope John XXIII declared her patron saint of flight attendants because of her frequent travels. Her feast day is May 29.

Bona of Savoy (c. 1450–c. 1505)

Duchess of Milan. *Name variations: Bona di Savoia; Bona Sforza. Born around 1450 in Savoy; died around 1505 in Italy; daughter of Louis, duke of Savoy, and* ***Anne of Lusignan****; sister of* ****Charlotte of Savoy*** *(c. 1442–1483), queen of France; married Galeazzo Maria Sforza (1444–1476), 5th duke of Milan (r. 1466–1476); children: Gian Galeazzo Sforza (1469–1494), 6th duke of Milan (r. 1476–1479); Ermes (1470–after 1502);* ****Bianca Maria Sforza*** *(1472–1510), Holy Roman empress; and* ****Anna Sforza*** *(1473–1497); (stepchildren) Carlo (b. 1461);* ****Caterina Sforza*** *(c. 1462–1509);* ***Chiara Sforza*** *(b. around 1464); and Alessandro.*

Born into the ducal house of Savoy, Bona of Savoy was betrothed to Galeazzo Maria Sforza, son of the duke of Milan, as part of a political alliance between the two families. By then, Galeazzo had sired four illegitimate children with ***Lucrezia Landriani**: one of whom was ***Caterina Sforza**. Bona married Galeazzo and moved to the Milanese court in 1468, two years after he succeeded as duke. Known to be a loving mother to her son Gian Galeazzo and daughters Bianca Maria and Anna, Bona was said to have loved her stepchildren as well.

She had been married for eight years when Galeazzo was brutally murdered in 1476 by political foes. Their young son Gian Galeazzo succeeded as duke, and Bona was named regent of Milan. Her few years of governing were moderately successful, given the chaotic and warlike condition of Italian politics at the time. In 1480, she met and fell in love with Antonio Tassino, who was beneath her socially, and the Milanese people disapproved of their relationship. Maintaining the connection eventually cost Bona much of the support of the Milanese which she had previously enjoyed. This rift between the duchess-regent and her subjects was exploited by the Italian noble Ludovic Sforza, "Il Moro," who used it to his advantage when he usurped Bona's position and declared himself duke of Milan in 1480. Forced to retire to France, Bona returned to Italy after some years to seek support for her reinstatement as duchess. Bona of Savoy died around 1505.

Laura York,
Anza, California

Bonaparte, Alexandrine Jouberthon (1778–1855)

Second wife of Lucien Bonaparte. *Name variations: Madame de Bleschamps. Born Alexandrine Bleschamps in 1778; died in 1855; daughter of a lawyer; daughter-in-law of* ****Letizia Bonaparte*** *(1750–1836); sister-in-law of Napoleon I, emperor of France (r. 1804–1815); married Jean-François-Hippolyte Jouberthon, around 1797 (died); became second wife of Lucien Bonaparte, in May 1803 (he was first married to* ****Christine (Boyer) Bonaparte*** *[1773–1800]); children: (first marriage) two; (second marriage) Charles or Carlo, prince of Canino; Laetitia; Jeanne; Paul; Lucien; Pierre; Antoine; Marie; Constance; and one who died in infancy.*

A beautiful, eccentric redhead, Alexandrine was, by some accounts, still married to her banker husband when she met and fell in love with Lucien Bonaparte. Pregnant with Lucien's son, she was secretly married the day after she gave birth. Napoleon, who had planned a royal marriage for his brother Lucien, demanded that he denounce Alexandrine, but Lucien refused and took her to live in Rome. Lucien was subsequently offered several crowns on the condition that he divorce Alexandrine, but the marriage endured and produced ten children.

Bonaparte, Carlotta (1780–1825).

See Bonaparte, Pauline.

Bonaparte, Carolina (1782–1839)

Queen of Naples. *Name variations: Caroline Murat; Countess Lipona, Countess of Lipona. Born Maria Annunciata or Maria-Nunziata Caroline at Ajaccio, Corsica, on March 25, 1782; died of stomach cancer in Florence, Italy, on May 18, 1839; daughter of* ****Letizia Bonaparte*** *(1750–1836) and Carlo Bonaparte (a Corsican lawyer); youngest sister of Napoleon I, emperor of France (r. 1804–1815); married Joachim Murat, king of Naples, in 1800 (died); married Francesco Macdonald; children: (first marriage) Napoléon Murat;* ***Laetitia Murat****; Lucien Murat;* ***Louise Murat.***

As ambitious as her brother Napoleon, Carolina became queen of Naples in 1808. Her infidelities were frequent during her marriage to Joachim Murat, but the couple shared a strong bond of upward aspirations. She encouraged him to betray Napoleon in 1814, which led ultimately to Murat's defeat and execution in 1815. Caroline renamed herself the Countess of Lipona and took refuge with her children in Trieste. A year after her husband's death, she secretly married Francesco Macdonald, a soldier formerly in Napoleon's service. Like so many of the Bonapartes, Caroline died of stomach cancer, in 1839.

Carolina Bonaparte

Bonaparte, Christine (1773–1800)

First wife of Lucien Bonaparte. *Name variations: Christine-Eléonore; Catherine Boyer. Born Christine Boyer in 1773; died in childbirth in 1800; daughter of Pierre-André and Rosalie (Fabre) Boyer; became first wife of Lucien Bonaparte (1775–1840), on May 4, 1794; daughter-in-law of* ****Letizia Bonaparte*** *(1750–1836); sister-in-law of Napoleon I, emperor of France (r. 1804–1815); children: Charlotte Bonaparte; Christine Bonaparte; and two who died in infancy.*

Lucien Bonaparte married Christine Boyer, the illiterate sister of an innkeeper with whom Lucien had lodged. Because the marriage was in haste, without the consent of the Bonaparte family, ***Letizia Bonaparte** felt betrayed upon hearing the news, but eventually accepted her daughter-in-law in order to foster peace in the family. Lucien's brother Napoleon was bitterly opposed to the union, however, calling the marriage "idiotic." Christine died in childbirth in 1800.

Bonaparte, Elisa (1777–1820)

Grand duchess of Tuscany, princess of Piombino, and ruler of Lucca. *Name variations: changed name from Marie Anna to Elisa after marriage; Elisa Lucca; Elisa Bacciochi, Marie Anna Bonaparte; Contessa di Compignano. Born Marie Anna at Ajaccio, Corsica, on January 3, 1777; died near Trieste on August 7, 1820; daughter of Letizia Bonaparte (1750–1836) and Carlo Bonaparte (a Corsican lawyer); eldest sister of Napoleon I, emperor of France (r. 1804–1815); married Felice Pasquale Bacciochi, on May 1, 1797; children: Jérôme; Frederic; Napoléon; Elisa Baccioci.*

Of the two Maria Anna Bonapartes born to Carlo and ***Letizia Bonaparte**, one died and the other became known as Elisa. Described as "sour-faced and evil-tempered" and disliked by her brother Napoleon, Elisa was made princess of Lucca where she became a successful and respected sovereign. In 1806, she became princess of Piombino and in 1809 grand duchess of Tuscany. Intellectual and ambitious, she was known to surround herself with interesting, intelligent people. She had a number of affairs, including one with violinist Paganini, whom she appointed court musician. Her final years were spent at Trieste, where she was a patron of the arts and theater.

Bonaparte, Elizabeth Patterson (1785–1879)

American socialite who married into the family Bonaparte. *Name variations: Betsy Patterson; Elizabeth Patterson; Elizabeth Bonaparte-Patterson; Madame Patterson. Born Elizabeth Patterson in Baltimore, Maryland, on February 6, 1785; died in Baltimore, Maryland, on April 4, 1879; daughter of William Patterson (president of Baltimore's largest bank); daughter-in-law of* ****Letizia Bonaparte*** *(1750–1836); sister-in-law of Napoleon I, emperor of France (r. 1804–1815); married Jérôme Bonaparte (1784–1860), king of Westphalia, in Baltimore, on December 24, 1803 (divorced 1813); children: one son, Jerome ("Bo," b. July 7, 1805), from whom the American Bonapartes descended.*

The belle of Baltimore, Elizabeth Patterson met 19-year-old Jérôme Bonaparte, the younger brother of Napoleon, on his visit to the United States in 1803. Although he was underage and forbidden to marry without his mother's consent, he proposed to Elizabeth through the Spanish ambassador, and the two married within a month of their meeting. Despite orders to return home without his wife, Jérôme set sail with Elizabeth. When they reached Lisbon, however, she was not permitted to land. Traveling on to England, she gave birth to a son on July 7, 1805. Napoleon granted Elizabeth an annual pension of $12,000 and arranged for a nullification of the marriage in October 1806, despite protests from the pope. Napoleon then formed an alliance with Germany's Westphalia, the following year, by marrying his younger brother Jérôme off to Princess ***Catherine of Wurttemberg**.

Eventually returning to Baltimore, Elizabeth was granted a divorce by the Maryland legislature in 1813, but she refused to drop the name Bonaparte. In 1815, following Napoleon's defeat at Waterloo, Elizabeth returned to Europe, where she was admired for her wit and beauty, and courted by many important men of the day, including Arthur Wellesley, Duke of Wellington. Though she was reunited with the Bonaparte family, and her son was finally declared legitimate, she saw Jérôme only once again, in an art gallery. Elizabeth returned to Baltimore in 1861, where she lived in obscurity until her death in 1879. She reportedly left over one million dollars to her two grandsons.

Bonaparte, Hortense de Beauharnais (1783–1837).

See Hortense de Beauharnais.

Bonaparte, Josephine (1763–1814).

See Josephine.

Bonaparte, Julie Clary (1771–1845)

Queen of Spain and wife of Joseph Bonaparte. *Name variations: Marie Julie; Julie Clary. Born Julie Clary in 1771; died in 1845; daughter of François Clary (a prosperous merchant of Marseille); older sister of* ****Désirée*** *(1777–1860, later queen of Sweden, who became a love interest of Napoleon I); daughter-in-law of* ****Letizia Bonaparte*** *(1750–1836); sister-in-law of Napoleon I, emperor of France (r. 1804–1815); married Joseph Bonaparte, on August 1, 1794, in Cuges, France; children: Zénaide Bonaparte; Charlotte Bonaparte.*

Short and plain in appearance, Julie Clary was known as sweet natured and loving. She was also exceedingly rich; her marriage to Joseph Bonaparte helped established the Bonaparte fortune and made her a favorite with her mother-in-law Letizia. Julie lived apart from her husband more often than not, and some have speculated that this was the reason the union endured. In 1815, Joseph fled to America, leaving her in Italy. Reunited in 1844, Julie spent the last year of her life with him.

SOURCES:

Decaux, Alain. *Napoleon's Mother.* London: The Cresset Press, 1962.

Stirling, Monica. *Madame Letizia: A Portrait of Napoleon's Mother.* NY: Harper & Brothers, 1961,

Bonaparte, Letizia (1750–1836)

Corsican mother of Napoleon I. *Name variations: Marie-Letizia Bonaparte or Buonaparte; Letitia or Lætitia; Letizia Ramolino; known as Madame Mère. Born Maria Lætitia or Letizia Ramolino at Ajaccio, Corsica, on August 24, 1750; died in Rome on February 2, 1836; daughter of Jean-Jérôme (a town official) and Angèle-Maria Ramolino; married Carlo Bonaparte, on June 2, 1764; children: twelve, of whom eight survived, including Joseph (Giuseppe, 1768–1844); Napoleon (Napoleone, 1769–1821), emperor of France (r. 1804–1815); Lucien (Lucciano, 1775–1840); Elisa (Maria-Anna, 1777–1820); Louis (Luigi, 1778–1846); Pauline (Maria-Paola, 1780–1825); Carolina (Maria-Annunziata, 1782–1839); Jérôme (Girolamo, 1784–1860).*

Letizia Bonaparte was the mother of three kings, a queen, two princesses, and Napoleon I during a century of tumultuous European history, from the reign of King Louis XV to the year prior to Queen ***Victoria**'s ascension to the throne of England. Born into obscurity, married at 13, and widowed at 34 with eight children, Letizia became the center of her remarkable, eccentric family, binding them to their Corsican roots and struggling to maintain peace and unity among their ranks. Her pride in Napoleon was tempered with constant fear for his safety and foreboding that his meteoric rise to power would be followed by an equally sensational fall from grace.

Little is known of her early childhood. Like most of her countrywomen, Letizia had little schooling and was barely literate. Her father died when she was six, and her mother quickly remarried a handsome captain in a Swiss regiment named Franz Fesch. Around the time of the birth of her half-brother Joseph, who would later become her economic and spiritual advisor, plans were under way for the 13-year-old town beauty to marry. The chosen groom was a charming, self-indulgent, 18-year-old law student named Carlo Bonaparte, described in colorful terms by one biographer as "a foppish ne'er-do-well who attitudinized all day and fornicated all night." A marriage contract was signed on June 2, 1764.

Letizia's devotion to Carlo would endure his philandering and his passion for risky business enterprises that compromised the family fortune. Early on, he aligned himself with the Corsican patriot Pasquale Paoli to fight for Corsica's independence, often with Letizia by his side. After the French Conquest in 1769, he became loyal to France and later represented Corsica at the Court of Louis XVI. Detractors have argued that his greatest contribution to his marriage was to see that his children were educated at public expense.

For 20 years, Letizia devoted herself to childbearing, with intermittent medical complications. Puerperal adynamo-ataxia caused two years of constant fevers accompanied by a loss of feeling down the right side of her body. Initially pregnant at 14, she lost her first two babies, a son and a daughter. These tragedies cut deeply, especially in a country where a woman's worth was measured by the number of children, especially sons, she produced for her husband. Letizia faced her losses stoically, considering her youth, and found solace in religion. In 1768, she gave birth to Joseph, the first child to survive infancy. Her second son Napoleon, born nine days before her 19th birthday, was described as a puny baby, but none the worse for his mother's perilous journeys on horseback over the Corsican battlefields during her pregnancy.

By 1778, Letizia had given birth to three more children: Lucien, ***Elisa**, and Louis. As she approached 30, she had her tenth child, ***Pauline**, and 15 months later, her eleventh, ***Carolina**. The household was filled with children, a number of relatives, and a nurse. Letizia's memoirs describe a large room set aside for the children to play in on rainy days, where they could be wild, noisy, and even write on walls without interference. The boys were taught to horseback ride from an early age, and Letizia encouraged them to be adventuresome but to face failure stoically. In the manner of the day, she also provided the discipline, counteracting the indulgent nature of her husband and mother-in-law.

Letizia's greatest distress was likely over family finances. Historians only recently unearthed information that Carlo, in his never-ending search for ready cash, actually sued the Ramolinos—his wife's family—for a portion of Letizia's dowry that had not been entirely paid over. His lawsuit, seemingly a dismal display of greed and insensitivity, resulted in an order by

Letizia Bonaparte

the Royal Courts of Ajaccio demanding that the Ramolino trustee sell off the family's remaining possessions, mostly furniture, to pay the back debt. Although, according to custom, Letizia was not consulted in this matter and remained silent, it undoubtedly put a tremendous strain on her household.

Her last child Jérôme was born ten days after her husband left Corsica for consultation on a prolonged illness (probably stomach cancer, which afflicted many of the Bonapartes). She would not see Carlo again. Only 39, he died just after New Years', 1785, leaving Letizia with eight children to support, five of them still under ten years of age. Though her eldest son Joseph hurried home to manage the family property, it was 15-year-old Napoleon, the only child trained for a profession, who would determine the family's future.

Amid growing political chaos in Corsica, the family faced economic struggle. Although still beautiful and pursued by a number of admiring men, Letizia remained single-minded in her devotion to her family. Napoleon, now a young lieutenant, was of great comfort to her, often taking leave of his regiment to visit, as well as providing her with money. In 1793, when the Bonapartes were labeled *personae non gratae* by the Nationalists, Letizia fled with her family to France, where she lived in poverty and exile, a humiliating experience that was to leave a lasting impression. While she suffered in economic despair, Napoleon was on the brink of greatness. After a successful defense of Toulon, he was made brigadier general and given command of the Army of Italy. By age 30, he was the ruler of France.

When Napoleon became emperor in 1804, he not only bestowed wealth upon his family, but elevated them to positions of authority, for which they had little aptitude. Given to greed, sexual escapades, and internal squabbling, the Bonapartes have been described as "a peculiarly unpleasant set of people." Napoleon himself lamented: "I do not believe that any man in the world is more unfortunate in his family than I am." Given his Corsican loyalties, however, in 1905 he made Elisa princess of Piombino, a position for which she, as an exception, seemed well suited. In the months that followed, Joseph was named king of Naples; Louis, king of Holland; and Jérôme (now married to his second wife, Princess ***Catherine of Wurttemberg**), king of Westphalia.

Now bearing the weighty title *Madame la Mére de l'Empereur* and charged as Protectress of the Hospital Sisters and of the Sisters of Charity throughout the empire, Letizia impressed the courts of Europe with her grace and dignity. Doubting the future, she wisely invested her new found wealth and turned her attention to the formidable job of unifying her unruly family. There were a host of unfortunate marriages to keep her eyes on, not the least of which was Napoleon's own disastrous union with ***Joséphine de Beauharnais**, whose inability to produce a male heir led to a heart-wrenching divorce and brought on another daughter-in-law, ***Marie Louise of Austria** (1791–1847). Lucien's hotly contested second marriage to ***Alexandrine** in 1803, had caused a rift between him and Napoleon that would take Letizia 20 years to resolve. There were Pauline's numerous amours and Louis' illnesses, in addition to political intrigues and quibbling over a successor, which, before Marie Louise settled the problem with a son in 1811, resulted in yet another unlikely union between Napoleon's brother Louis and Joséphine de Beauharnais' daughter by her first marriage, ***Hortense de Beauharnais**.

With the logistics of her family, it is not surprising that the happiest times of Letizia's life were reportedly during her months at Elba, where she joined Napoleon in his first exile. For the first time in years, she was able to provide companionship and moral support for her offspring in an atmosphere relatively free of worry. Such was not to last, however, as Napoleon made his way back to Paris for his final 100 days. One last family dinner before the debacle at Waterloo was attended by all of Letizia's children with the exception of Louis. The poignant goodbye between Napoleon and Letizia was described by the actor Talma, an old family friend, in his memoirs. "Oh what a beautiful and tragic scene was I a witness. What a spectacle, this separation of Madame Mère and her son! Although it forced no outward sign of emotion from the Emperor, yet the expression of his fine features, and his attitude and unspoken thoughts were eloquent." This was one of only six occasions on which Letizia openly wept.

> Who knows whether all these kings won't some day come to me begging for bread?
>
> **—Letizia Bonaparte**

In 1818, Letizia purchased a 17th-century palace in Italy for her own retirement. Except for visits from children and grandchildren, her life was pious and introspective, as she waited despairingly for word of Napoleon, who was now exiled at St. Helena. Numerous appeals regarding the fate of her son went unanswered. After news of his death reached her on July 22, 1821, she surrounded herself with a "museum of memories," including the campbed Napoleon used on his campaigns, as well as numerous portraits and busts of her children. Her all-consuming grief was to be further deepened by the untimely deaths of Elisa and Pauline, as well as several of her grandchildren. Six months before her own death at 87, nearly blind but remarkably clear-minded, she dictated her memoirs—a brief six pages—in which she admonished her children for succumbing to "grandeurs and flattery at Court," and said of her own final years, "My life came to an end with the downfall of the Emperor. From that moment, I gave up everything for ever."

Letizia Bonaparte died in Rome on February 2, 1836, and was buried in an obscure spot in the convent church of the Sisters of the Cross and Passion, at Corneto. She left 1,700,000 francs to be divided among her children, although her estate was probably worth at least double that amount. By some accounts, in a codicil to her will, she left her heart to the town of Ajaccio. Her brother, who died in 1839, provided money for a mortuary chapel there, which was finally built by Napoleon III. Letizia Bonaparte's body was moved to Ajaccio in 1851 and into the Imperial Chapel in 1860.

SOURCES:

Decaux, Alain. *Napoleon's Mother.* London: The Cresset Press, 1961.

Seward, Desmond. *Napoleon's Family.* NY: Viking, 1986.

Stacton, David. *The Bonapartes.* NY: Simon and Schuster, 1966.

Stirling, Monica. *Madame Letizia: A Portrait of Napoleon's Mother.* NY: Harper & Brothers, 1961.

Barbara Morgan,
Melrose, Massachusetts

Bonaparte, Maria-Letizia (1750–1836).

See Bonaparte, Letizia.

Bonaparte, Maria-Nunziata Caroline (1782–1839).

See Bonaparte, Carolina.

Bonaparte, Maria-Paoletta or Marie Pauline (1780–1825).

See Bonaparte, Pauline.

Bonaparte, Marie (1882–1962)

Princess of Greece. *Born on July 2, 1882; died in 1962; daughter of Prince Roland Bonaparte (1858–1924) and* ***Marie Blanc*** *(1859–1882); married Prince George of Greece (son of George I of Greece and ****Olga Constantinovna****), on December 12, 1907; children: Peter Oldenburg (b. 1908, an anthropologist); Eugénie Oldenburg (b. 1910, who married Dominique Rainer, Prince Radziwill, and Raymond, duke of Castel).*

Bonaparte, Marie Julie (1771–1845).

See Bonaparte, Julie Clary.

Bonaparte, Pauline (1780–1825)

Princess Borghese and duchess of Guastalla. *Name variations: Marie Pauline; Maria-Paoletta. Born Carlotta Bonaparte in Ajaccio, Corsica, on October 20, 1780; died in Florence, Italy, on June 9, 1825; daughter of ****Letizia Bonaparte*** *(1750–1836) and Carlo Bonaparte (a Corsican lawyer); younger sister of Napoleon I, emperor of France (r. 1804–1815); married Charles Victor-Emmanuel Leclerc, in 1797 (died); married Prince Camillo Borghese, on August 28, 1803; children: (first marriage) one son, Napoléon Dermide.*

Pauline was Napoleon's youngest and favorite sister. Known for her beauty and promiscuity (Canova's statue of her as Venus is famous), she married General C.V.E. Leclerc, a staff officer of Napoleon in 1797. Following his death from yellow fever, she married Prince Camillo Borghese, only to tire of him and return to Paris, where her appearance and behavior (she was said to dress oddly and frequent fortune-tellers) caused somewhat of a scandal. She received the title of duchess of Guastalla in 1806, but her shabby treatment of Napoleon's second wife, ***Marie Louise of Austria,** led to her removal from court in 1810. Pauline retired to Elba in 1814 with her mother and was legally separated from her second husband in 1816. She died of stomach cancer, as did many of the Bonapartes, in 1825, after being reconciled with her husband for the last few months of her life.

Pauline Bonaparte

Bonaparte-Patterson, Elizabeth (1785–1879).

See Bonaparte, Elizabeth Patterson.

Bona Sforza.

See Sforza, Bona (b. 1493).

Bonaventuri, Bianca (1548–1587).

See Cappello, Bianca.

Bond, Carrie Jacobs (1862–1946)

American composer. *Name variations: Jacobs-Bond. Born Carrie Jacobs in Janesville, Wisconsin, on Au-*

gust 11, 1862; died in Hollywood, California, on December 28, 1946; married E.J. Smith, in December 1880 (divorced 1888); married Dr. Frank L. Bond, in June 1889 (died 1895).

Born in Janesville, Wisconsin, on August 11, 1862, Carrie Jacobs Bond wrote songs for years before she saw the publication of "Is My Dolly Dead?" and "Mother's Cradle Song," in 1894. The next year, following the death of her second husband, she moved to Chicago, where she ran a boarding house and gave recitals and concerts in private homes to supplement her income. Steadily gaining an audience for her songs, in 1901, Bond published *Seven Songs as Unpretentious as the Wild Rose*, which included two favorites "I Love You Truly" and "Just a-Wearyin' for You." With the money from the songbook, she opened a shop where she sold sheet music which she both designed and printed. By 1910, Bond had played at the White House for Theodore RooseveltRoosevelt, Theodore and had performed at recitals in New York and in England, where she appeared with the young Enrico Caruso. She then published "The End of a Perfect Day," which became her most popular song, selling over five million print copies, as well as piano rolls and recordings that went uncounted.

Bond moved to Hollywood and continued to write some 400 songs (170 of which were published), all in the sentimental style that characterized much of 19th-century music. However, World War I brought social change and new musical tastes, and by the late 1920s her style of song was passé. In 1927, she published a memoir, *The Roads of Melody*, followed by a collection of thoughts and verses called *The End of the Road* in 1940. She died on December 28, 1946.

Barbara Morgan,
Melrose, Massachusetts

Bondar, Roberta (b. 1945).

See Astronauts: Women in Space.

Bondfield, Margaret (1873–1953)

Trade union organizer, advocate of child welfare improvement, lecturer, and first woman member of a British Cabinet. *Name variations: Maggie; (pseudonym) Grace Dare. Born Margaret Grace Bondfield on March 17, 1873, in Furnham, Somerset, England; died in Sanderstead, Surrey, on June 16, 1953; daughter of William (foreman of a lace-making factory) and Ann (Taylor) Bondfield; attended elementary school until 14; never married; no children.*

Apprenticed to a drapery store; joined the National Union of Shop Assistants, Warehousemen and Clerks and became one of its full-time officials (1898), a post she held until 1908; also acted on behalf of the Women's Trade Union League, the National Federation of Women Workers, and the Women's Co-operative Guild; became chief woman officer of the National Union of General and Municipal Workers (1920), a post occupied until 1938 but with secondments when she was a Member of Parliament; served as MP for Northampton (1923–24); served as junior minister in the Labour Government (1924); elected MP for Wallsend (1926–31); served as minister of labour in the Labour Government (1929–31); was British Information Services lecturer in U.S. (1941–42).

Publications: articles and pamphlets on industrial questions; Why Labour Fights *(British Information Services, 1941);* A Life's Work *(Hutchinson 1949).*

Carrie Jacobs Bond

On June 15, 1929, the weekly journal *The Economist*, in an appraisal of the newly formed government of Ramsay MacDonald, commented: "The Ministry of Labour is given to Miss Margaret Bondfield whose record and abilities have fittingly earned her the distinction of being the first woman to reach Cabinet rank." Five years earlier, in January 1924, Margaret—or, as she was often known to friends and colleagues, Maggie—Bondfield had created a precedent as the first woman to reach ministerial office, when she had been appointed to a minor post in the government. These two appointments, which were widely, and usually favorably, commented on at the time, marked an advance in the political status of women in a period when in many countries women's right to vote was still disputed or had been a matter of recent and often reluctant recognition.

Margaret Bondfield, the tenth of a family of eleven children (seven boys, four girls), was born in Furnham, a village near the small market town of Chard, in Somerset. Her father, who had been born in 1814, had been active in radical causes, especially in the 1840s, when the agi-

Margaret Bondfield

tation for the "People's Charter"—a program of political reform—had been at its height. He was able to support his large family both from his wages as the overseer of a small lace-making factory and from the food he grew in the field attached to his cottage. Margaret's father had been a lay preacher, as had other of her forebears, and she always kept to the religious principles in which she had been raised. In particular, she believed that Christianity was a social gospel; as she wrote in her autobiography:

> Christianity is not merely a spiritual and mystical and personal religion, but is quite definitely a social scheme—and what is more a scheme for the proper and just management of the whole world. It is only to the degree in which we love our neighbour that we can know anything of the love of God. The personal life of a Christian has to be also a social life.

As a trade union leader and Labour Party politician, she sought to apply her faith in an everyday context, and she believed that the foundations of the labor movement should be built on ethical values drawn from the precepts of Christianity.

Bondfield's education was of the elementary sort provided for children of her background. By the age of 13, having acquired knowledge of reading, writing and arithmetic, the main subjects at her school (and most others that were run by the local authorities), she was paid three shillings a week to teach younger children. This she did for about a year and was then apprenticed to the drapery trade in Brighton, where a brother and sister also lived. The first shop at which she worked was a family business with an extensive postal trade to India.

When the proprietor of this establishment retired, she was taken on in the outfitting department of a larger shop. Bondfield quickly realized that behind the genteel exterior of such premises was considerable squalor. Most assistants in the larger businesses were expected to "live in"; their quarters were usually cramped and spartan. Petty regulations, enforced by fines, operated in these dormitories, which could be stifling in summer and icy in winter. Usually, the assistant's possessions had to be kept in a box under her bed. Facilities for cooking food or taking a bath were often nonexistent. In addition, shopowners regarded such accommodation, which increased their authority over those required to occupy it, as part of the employees' payment. Cash wages were therefore very small; after 15 years' experience, Margaret Bondfield was paid less than an unskilled male worker and was expected to work some 65 hours each week (most shops were open six days a week, usually until late in the evening). Very few belonged to the small local associations of shop assistants or to the National Union of Shop Assistants, Warehousemen and Clerks which had been formed in 1891.

After five years in Brighton, Bondfield moved to London where a brother, an active trade unionist, also lived. Soon after finding a post, she began to get involved in organizations that sought to improve social and economic conditions. She joined the shop assistants' union and the Social Democratic Federation. Since the latter included many followers of Karl Marx who believed in his doctrines of class conflict, something that she could not accept, she eventually moved over to the more moderate socialism of the Independent Labour Party. By the mid-1890s, she was on the executive committee of her trade union which met on Sundays, the only day its members were free. At that time, the union's campaigns were centered on three issues: an end to the living-in system; the abolition of fines and deductions, which could reduce the assistants' already small salaries; and shorter working hours. Late at night, against her employer's regulations, she would burn a small light while writing letters and articles (under the pen name of Grace Dare) on behalf of the union.

In 1898, the importance of her trade union work was recognized when she was appointed to the full-time post of assistant secretary. Her salary was £2 a week, more than twice what she had been paid as a shop worker. In the next few years, Bondfield helped to double the size of the union membership. She attended and spoke at the annual Trades Union Congress in 1899, when she was the only woman delegate. With Lady *Emily Dilke and ✤▸ Gertrude Tuckwell, she worked on behalf of the Women's Trade Union League, which operated as a pressure group to improve the lot of all working women. In 1906, she became involved with the Women's Labour League, an organization closely associated with the Labour Party. She was active too in the Adult Suffrage Society and campaigned for the franchise to be extended to all adults, as opposed to those who advocated women should receive the vote on the same terms (which involved a property qualification) as men. When another pioneer of shop assistants' trade unionism, *Mary Reid Macarthur, formed the National Federation of Women Workers in 1906, Bondfield gave that body her support also. In 1908, after, in the words of her autobiography, "ten slogging years as officer" and "drained of vitality," she resigned from the shop assistants' union.

By this time, Bondfield had become a well-known figure in trade union and progressive circles. Dressed in a neat and simple way, somewhat below average height and with a pleasant, rounded face, she was an eloquent platform speaker. In 1904, she made what was to be the first of many foreign visits when she attended the International Congress of Women in Berlin. At the invitation of *Elizabeth Glendower Evans, she spent five months in lecturing and touring the United States in 1910; her autobiography records the visit in detail, drawn from a diary kept at the time. In Chicago, she stayed at Hull House and befriended *Jane Addams; in New York on November 1, she had meetings with *Carrie Chapman Catt ("a powerful personality"), *Rose Schneiderman and W.E.B. Du Bois.

Towards the end of 1911, Margaret Bondfield's health broke down, and it was not until well into the following year that she resumed her activities. At the request of *Margaret Llewelyn Davies of the Women's Co-operative Guild, Bondfield took part in a campaign for improved maternity and child welfare facilities. This involved publicizing examples of hardship, lobbying politicians, and encouraging the individual members of the Co-operative Guild, who numbered some 32,000, to work for the campaign at branch level. A collection of letters written by working women about their circumstances, published in 1915 under the editorship of Davies with a preface by *Virginia Woolf as *Maternity: Letters from Working Women*, is still a valuable source for the social historian.

✤▸ Tuckwell, Gertrude (1861–1951)

English trade unionist. *Born Gertrude Mary Tuckwell in Oxford, England, in 1861; died in 1951; daughter of a parson.*

Gertrude Tuckwell was educated at home by her father who was master of New College School. After a seven-year stint teaching in elementary schools in London (1885–93), she became secretary to her aunt, Lady *Emily Dilke (1893). On Lady Dilke's death, Tuckwell was elected president of the Women's Trade Union League (1904–1921). Along with *Mary Reid Macarthur, Adelaide Anderson, and others, Tuckwell led crusades against white lead poisoning and organized the Sweated Goods Exhibition (1906), spurring the Trade Boards Act of 1909. After World War I, Tuckwell's energies turned to social reform, in particular, Macarthur's work on maternity. Gertrude Tuckwell was the first woman justice of the peace for the County of London (1920); founded the maternal Mortality Committee (1927); was president of the Women Sanitary Inspectors and the National Association of Probation Officers; and sat on the Central Committee on Women's Training and Employment. She also published *The State and its Children* (1894), *Women in Industry* (1908), and, with Stephen Gwynn, a biography of Sir Charles Wentworth Dilke (1917).

When World War I broke out, Bondfield was as shocked by the accompanying spirit of militarism as she was by the scale of subsequent casualties. However, rather than opposing the war, her energies were spent in trying to reduce the problems caused on the home front with regard to rising prices, conscription, war widows' pensions and so forth. In common with others in the Independent Labour Party, she welcomed Woodrow Wilson's "Fourteen Points" as the basis of a peace settlement, but the British government refused to issue her a passport to the United States or to The Hague conference of the Women's International League for Peace and Freedom, whose president was her friend Jane Addams.

In common with other progressive figures, Bondfield hoped a new and better order could be shaped once the war ended. She was a delegate to the international conference of socialist parties held in Berne in January and February 1919. In the summer, she was a fraternal delegate to the conference of the American Federation of Labor; again her autobiography includes a diary of her stay in the U.S. where she was able to renew her acquaintanceship with activists such as *Lillian Wald and Rose Schneiderman, who helped to entertain her and accompanied her to meetings ("dear little Rose," Bondfield recorded on one occasion in her diary, "good as always"). Although war had ended in much of Europe in December 1918, there was still turmoil in the Soviet Union (created after the Communist revolution of 1917). To inquire into the situation, a delegation of the British labor movement, including Margaret Bondfield, traveled to Russia in May 1920. In spite of meeting some of the Bolshevik leaders, including V.I. Lenin, and calling for the end of hostilities between the Soviet Union and Poland, she was not converted to the ideas of the new regime. Her view, supported by the other delegates and publicized on their return to England in August, was that military intervention in Russia should end: it was a desire for peace and sympathy with the sufferings of the people that motivated her. Communism as a creed she rejected.

No worker in any Movement ever had a colleague who was more single-minded, generous, and loyal. She is in many ways the type of what all Labour women should be—unflinchingly staunch to her cause, fair to her opponents, radiating good will to all.

—**Margaret Llewelyn Davies**

In 1920, the National Federation of Women Workers amalgamated with the National Union of General and Municipal Workers, and the position of chief woman officer was created. Margaret Bondfield occupied the post until 1938, though many of the duties were carried out by a deputy; it was intended that her efforts on behalf of working women should be in the wider public sphere.

Women over 30 had been brought within the parliamentary franchise in 1918 and were also allowed to stand as candidates for election to the House of Commons. Bondfield had unsuccessfully contested Woolwich for a seat on the London County Council in 1910, but early in 1920 she stood as a parliamentary candidate of the Labour Party in a by-election at Northampton. Although defeated, she continued to nurse the constituency and again represented Labour there in the general election of 1922. Once more, she was unsuccessful, but at her third attempt to win the Northampton seat, in the general election of December 1923, she came top of the poll. Early in 1924, the Labour Party formed a government for the first time. Lacking a parliamentary majority, it survived only nine months, though it was also notable for including, in the junior post of parliamentary secretary to minister of labour, the first woman to hold a ministerial office in Parliament, Margaret Bondfield.

However, in the general election of October 1924, which followed the defeat of the government, she lost her Northampton seat. At the start of the election campaign, she was in North America, as leader of a delegation inquiring into the settlement of children and other migrants to Canada. She was regarded by the Labour Party as someone whose services should be available in the House of Commons and when a by-election was called in Wallsend, a constituency in the northeast of England near Newcastle upon Tyne, the local party was requested to nominate her. In July 1926, she was returned to Parliament and comfortably won the seat again in the general election of 1929.

In 1929, her party, though it had more members than either the Liberals or the Conservatives, was able to form only a minority government. She was made minister of labour, a Cabinet office, and as such recognized by membership of the Privy Council. Margaret Bondfield was the first woman to sit in a British Cabinet and the first to be appointed to the Privy Council. The post was a particularly difficult one, as the level of unemployment, which the Labour Party hoped to lessen on taking office, continued to increase. Like other members of the Cabinet, in the face of several problems, she struggled rather than succeeded. In the economic crisis of August 1931, the government collapsed; in the general election that followed in October, she lost her Wallsend seat.

Her trade union had continued to retain her in the post of chief woman officer, and she nominally resumed its duties. However, the strain of office had affected her health and for a time she suffered from fibrositis. By 1933, Bondfield was well enough to accept an invitation to speak in Chicago at a women's congress on "Economic Security through Government, under Fascism, under Communism and under Democracy." She took the opportunity to travel to Washington to visit ***Frances Perkins**, the secretary of labor in Franklin D. Roosevelt's administration.

At the general election of 1935, Bondfield unsuccessfully attempted to regain the Wallsend seat. However, when members of the Reading Labour Party invited her to become their candidate for the next election, she accepted, withdrawing only during World War II when it was apparent that the election would be delayed. In 1938, at age 65, Bondfield retired from her trade union post, and soon after traveled again to the United States where for about a year she lectured and visited friends. Her familiarity with American audiences led her to spend several months

Beulah Bondi

during the war touring the towns and cities of the U.S. and Canada, under the auspices of British Information Services, where she explained the war as a contest between "the evil spirit of a brutal paganism" and "the Christian way of life." Those who knew her recalled the clear, musical voice, combined with a sincerity of manner, which seldom failed to impress an audience.

After the war, she wrote a substantial volume of memoirs, published in 1949 under the title *A Life's Work*. Her last years were spent in retirement, occasionally entertaining visitors in her cottage garden. Margaret Bondfield died on June 16, 1953, at Sanderstead, Surrey.

SOURCES:

Bondfield, Margaret. *A Life's Work*. London: Hutchinson, 1949.

Collette, Christine. *For Labour and for Women: The Women's Labour League, 1906–18*. Manchester: Manchester University Press, 1989.

Hamilton, Mary Agnes. *Margaret Bondfield*. London: Leonard Parsons, 1924.

SUGGESTED READING:

Middleton, Lucy, ed. *Women in the Labour Movement: The British Experience*. Towata, NJ: Rowman and Littlefield, 1977.

D.E. Martin, Lecturer in History, University of Sheffield, Sheffield, England

Bondi, Beulah (1892–1981)

American actress in great demand as a character actress who appeared in more than 60 feature films. *Born Beulah Bondy on May 3, 1892, in Chicago, Illinois: died of pulmonary complications in Woodland Hills, California, on January 12, 1981; daughter of A.O. (a realtor) and Eva Bondy; attended Convent of the Holy Name of Jesus and Mary, Montreal, Canada, 1907; attended Frances Skinner Academy, 1908; graduated from Hyde Park High School, Chicago, 1909, and Valparaiso University, Valparaiso, Indiana, 1913; studied at Chicago Little Theater during World War II.*

Films include: Street Scene *(1931);* Arrowsmith *(1931);* Rain *(1932);* The Stranger's Return *(1933);* Christopher Bean *(1933);* Finishing School *(1934);* Registered Nurse *(1934);* The Good Fairy *(1935);* The Invisible Ray *(1936);* The Trail of the Lonesome Pine *(1936);* The Moon's Our Home *(1936);* The Gorgeous Hussy *(1936);* Make Way for Tomorrow *(1937);* Maid of Salem *(1937);* The Buccaneer *(1938);* Of Human Hearts *(1938);* Vivacious Lady *(1938);* The Sisters *(1938);* On Borrowed Time *(1939);* The Under-Pup *(1939);* Mr. Smith Goes to Washington *(1939);* Remember the Night *(1940);* Our Town *(1940);* Penny Serenade *(1941);* The Shepherd of the Hills *(1941);* One Foot in Heaven *(1941);* Tonight We Raid Calais *(1943);* Watch on the Rhine *(1943);* Our Hearts Were Young and Gay *(1944);* And Now Tomorrow *(1944);* The Southerner *(1945);* Back to Bataan *(1945);* Sister Kenny *(1946);* It's a Wonderful Life *(1946);* The Sainted Sisters *(1948);* The Snake Pit *(1948);* So Dear to My Heart *(1949);* The Black Book *(1949);* The Life of Riley *(1949);* The Baron of Arizona *(1950);* The Furies *(1950);* Lone Star *(1952);* Latin Lovers *(1953);* Track of the Cat *(1954);* Back From Eternity *(1956);* The Big Fisherman *(1959);* A Summer Place *(1959);* The Wonderful World of the Brothers Grimm *(1962);* Tammy and the Doctor *(1963).*

Known as a superlative actress, Beulah Bondi spent her entire career in supporting character roles. At seven, she made her first stage appearance in a production of *Little Lord Fauntleroy*, then spent 24 years in stock and repertory before her Broadway debut in *One of the Family* (1925). After playing the landlady in the 1929 production of *Street Scene*, she was recruited by Samuel Goldwyn to repeat the role in the film version, made in 1931. With her film career under way, she would return to the stage only four times: in *The Late Christopher Bean* (1932), *Mother Lode* (1934), *Hilda Crane* (1950), and *On Borrowed Time* (1953).

Though Bondi appeared in over 60 feature films, she never signed a long-term contract with a major studio; this allowed her to be selective in the roles she accepted and to demand the pay she felt she deserved. As a result, she commanded some $500 a week as early as the 1930s. Of her numerous roles, each uniquely crafted, she was nominated for Oscars for *Gorgeous Hussy* (1936) and *Of Human Hearts* (1938). Retiring from films in the 1960s (tempted back only once, for the role in *Airport* that won ***Helen Hayes** an Oscar in 1970), Bondi continued to make television appearances through the 1970s.

Bondi never married and was never part of the Hollywood scene, though she made her home in the Hollywood Hills. She traveled extensively, including two round-the-world trips and several to Africa, a country which held a particular fascination for her. She appeared to take both her career and retirement in stride. "I have a very good, full life away from the stage and studio," she said. "I don't rule out working again but I don't have to either for my bank account or my ego. I feel very fulfilled."

Barbara Morgan,
Melrose, Massachusetts

Bonds, Margaret (1913–1972)

African-American composer, pianist, historian, and lecturer was known for her sacred and vocal compositions. *Born Margaret Allison Richardson in Chicago, Illinois, on March 3, 1913; died in Los Angeles, California, on April 26, 1972; daughter of Estella C. Bonds (an organist); graduated from Northwestern University and then studied at Juilliard.*

Margaret Bonds was five years old when she composed her first song. A classically trained musician, she began studying composition and piano with ***Florence B. Price** and William Dawson at Northwestern University, receiving bachelor's and master degrees of music from that institution. After completing her studies, she attended the Juilliard School of Music in New York City where she studied with Robert Starer. Henry Levine, Roy Harris, and Emerson Harper. A brilliant student, Bonds received a Rosenwald fellowship, a National Association of Negro Musicians award, and a Rodman Wanamaker award. In the 1930s, she opened the Allied Arts Academy in Chicago, a school for ballet and music. Bonds became known for her arrangements of spirituals, and ***Leontyne Price** commissioned her for several such recordings. In addition, Bonds composed art songs, popular

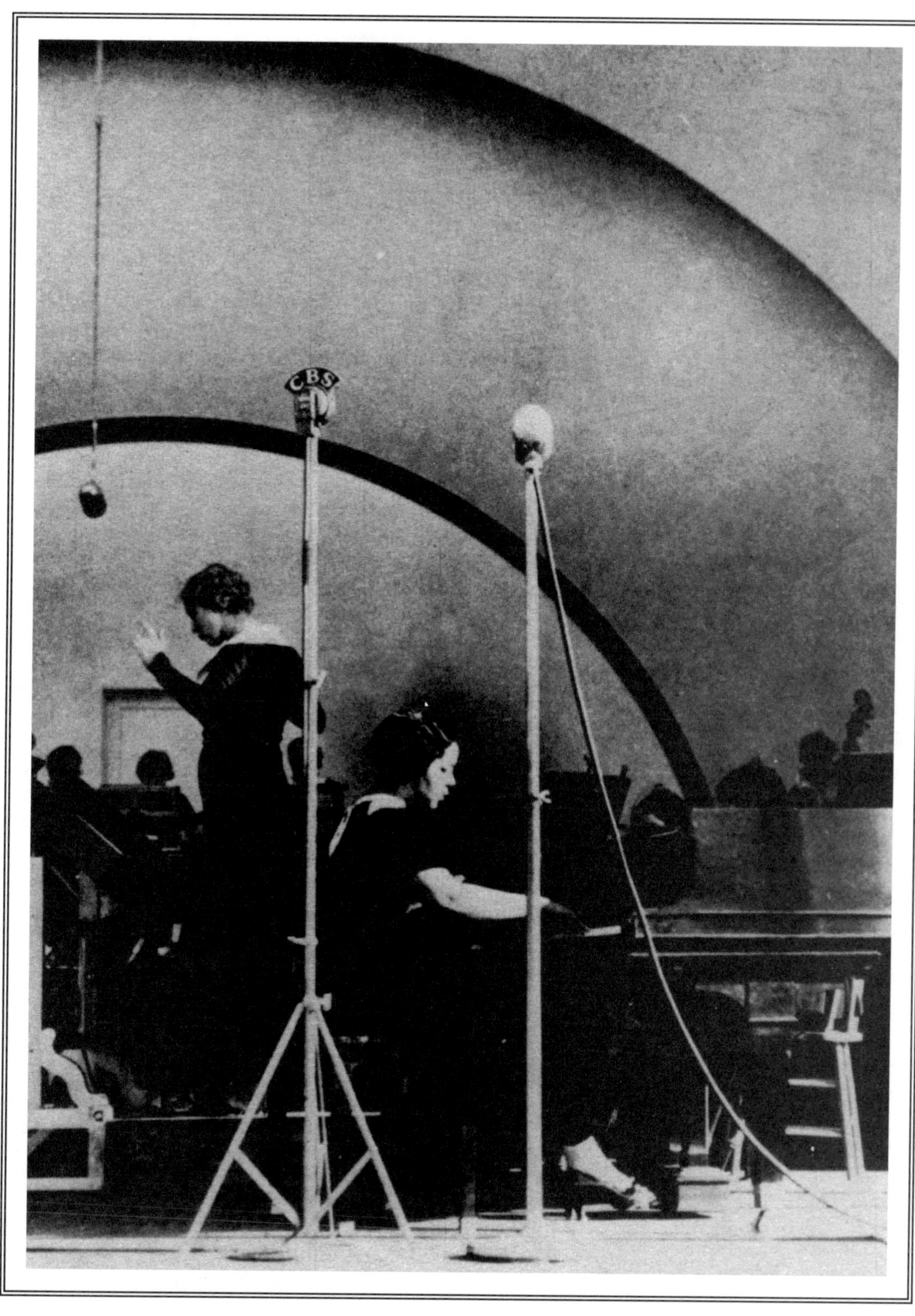

Margaret Bonds

songs, theatrical and orchestral music, as well as piano pieces; she also appeared on radio in New York and Hollywood. Her works for piano featured jazz harmonies, spiritual materials, and social themes. Bonds served as musical director for several music theaters in New York. From 1968 to 1972, she worked with the inner-city Cultural Center in Los Angeles. A singer as well as a composer, in 1933 Bonds became the first black guest soloist to appear with the Chicago Symphony at the Chicago World's Fair. In 1967, she received the Alumni medal, Northwestern University's highest honor granted to alumni who have achieved eminence in their fields.

John Haag,
Athens, Georgia

Bonds, Rosie (c. 1944—)

African-American track star. *Born around 1944; grew up in Riverside, California; attended the Junior College of the University of California at Riverside.*

Set several national records in the hurdles; won the national outdoor hurdles championship (1963, 1964); competed internationally, though her athletic career failed due to lack of financial support; represented U.S. in Tokyo Olympics (1964).

Competitive sports have long had an aristocratic cast. In the 19th century, many with private fortunes were free to spend their hours on the playing field, and for many years this high-born perspective mandated that Olympic athletes remain amateurs who did not sell their skills in the marketplace. This bias was profoundly detrimental for athletes without private means to subsidize their training, many of whom were forced to leave Olympic competition. It had an especially negative effect on many exceptional African-American athletes struggling against poverty. Competing in the mid-1960s, Rosie Bonds was one such athlete who fell victim to the class structure of athletics in the U.S.

Bonds grew up in a black-Mexican ghetto in Riverside, California, although her father earned enough money to purchase the family home. One of her brothers was California's high hurdles champion and the other held the state championship in the long jump; a third was a professional baseball player. In a family of athletes, Bonds' determination to participate in track and field was considered quite normal. In a world where the only whites she ever saw were her schoolteachers, Bond began reading books by Richard Wright and the Black Muslims to gain perspective on racial inequities. She graduated from Polytechnic High School, before attending the Junior College of the University of California at Riverside where she worked with coach Dennis Ikenberry, who encouraged her to train seriously in track and field.

As Bonds' athletic talent soon became apparent, Ikenberry had her competing locally and then nationally. Films of her races from these early days demonstrate a clumsy style and lack of training. During the 80-meter hurdles at the national 1963 AAU outdoor meet in Dayton, Ohio, Bonds stopped each time she ran up to a hurdle before clearing it; yet, despite the lack of style, she beat **Jo Ann Terry**, who had won a gold medal in the 80-meter hurdles at the Pan American Games that year and held the American women's outdoor record in the 70-meter hurdles. Rosie Bonds was the national outdoor hurdles champion in 1963, a feat she repeated the following year, setting a new American record in the 80-meter hurdles of 10.8, equaling the time of **Irina Press** at the Rome Olympics in 1960.

Despite a meteoric rise, Bonds soon stumbled. She was chosen as a member of the U.S. team at the 1963 European meet held in several cities, including Moscow, Warsaw, and Braunschweig, Germany. This competition was held at the height of the Cold War when athletes represented not only themselves but the political system which had trained them. Tension was high in Moscow because of the pressure and disagreements over discipline between athletes and coaches. The Americans lost ten out of ten events, and Bonds was disqualified for false starts in two races. From Moscow, the team went on to Warsaw where things got worse. Again, Bonds made two false starts and was disqualified. When the coaches replaced her with **Tammie Davis** in a race held in Braunschweig, Germany, it was a great humiliation. The European tour did little for Bonds' reputation; in American track circles, she and her teammates were considered undisciplined.

Determined to regain her position, in 1964 Bonds won the national outdoor hurdles championships in Hanford, California, where she set a new American record. In August, she was at the Olympic trials. Five minutes before her race someone stole her track shoes, and Bonds was forced to run in borrowed shoes. Nevertheless, she ran her race in 10.8 seconds, equaling her previous record and coming in ahead of **Cherrie Sherrard** of Oakland, California, and **Leaseneth O'Neal** of Hawaii. Bonds had qualified for the Tokyo Olympics.

Bonds' track career was never easy. Lacking the money to train, she struggled to survive. In the weeks before the Olympics, her attention was split between training and figuring out how to buy clothes for the trip to Tokyo and pay rent while she was away. Bonds finally got a job at a building-trades union three weeks before she left for Tokyo. Once at the Games, she ran the 80-meter hurdles in 10.6 seconds, faster than any other American woman had ever run, but out of the six finalists she ran last.

Bonds made the U.S. team traveling to Europe in 1965 and was determined to show the Russians and the Poles she was a contender. In Moscow, once again she had the fastest time of any American. She ran the 80-meter hurdles in 10.9 seconds, but Soviet Irina Press ran the same race in 10.5 seconds. Bonds finished the race in third place. Coaches of the 1965 U.S. track team were still disgruntled over the 1963 losses; they blamed their members for being undisciplined and still viewed Bonds as a contributor to the fiasco. The night before the team was to leave Moscow for Warsaw, Bonds was not in her room at bed check. Deciding to implement some discipline, the coaches sent her home and Bonds dropped from sight.

Wrote Michael D. Davis: "Rosie was a prime example of an American woman athlete of great natural ability completely isolated from the opportunity to train adequately. . . . If she had kept training, she would probably have been the United States best chance for a gold medal at Mexico City." In the 1968 Mexico City Olympics, no American woman medaled in the hurdle. No American woman had won the gold medal since ***Babe Didrickson Zaharias** in the 1932 Amsterdam Olympics.

SOURCES:

Davis, Michael D. *Black American Women in Olympic Track and Field.* Jefferson, NC: McFarland, 1992.

Karin Loewen Haag,
Athens, Georgia

Boneta, Prous.

See Women Prophets and Visionaries in France at the End of the Middle Ages.

Bonfanti, Marietta (1847–1921)

Italian ballerina. *Name variations: Maria and Marie. Born in Italy in 1847; died in New York, New York, on January 25, 1921; studied with Carlo Blasis, and at the ballet school of Teatro all Scala, Milan; married George Hoffmann (an American businessman).*

Marietta Bonfanti made her American debut in *The Black Crook*, often called the first musical comedy, at Niblo's Garden, New York, in 1866. Three years later, she went on tour throughout the U.S. She was prima ballerina of the Milan Italian Grand Opera (1884) and the Metropolitan Opera in New York (1885–86). Following several U.S.-European tours from 1888 to 1894, Bonfanti opened a ballet school in New York. ***Ruth St. Denis** was one of her pupils.

Bonfils, Winifred Black (1863–1936).

See Black, Winifred Sweet.

Bonham-Carter, Violet (1887–1969)

British peer. *Name variations: Lady or Baroness Asquith of Yarnbury. Born Helen Violet Asquith on April 15, 1887, in London, England; died on February 19, 1969; only daughter of Herbert Henry Asquith (1852–1928, later earl of Oxford and Asquith) and* ***Helen Kelsall (Melland) Asquith*** *(died, 1891); stepdaughter of* ****Margot Asquith****; sister of Herbert Asquith (1881–1947) and Raymond Asquith (killed in action in WWI, 1916); stepsister of Elizabeth, Princess Bibesco (1897–1945); grandmother of actress* ***Helena Bonham-Carter*** *(1966—); educated privately at home and in Dresden and Paris; married Sir Maurice Bonham Carter, in 1915 (died 1960); children: Helen Cressida (who married Jasper Ridley); Laura Miranda (who married Joseph Grimond); Mark Raymond; Raymond Henry.*

Violet Bonham-Carter politically supported her father Prime Minister Herbert Henry Asquith (1908–16) and his Liberal causes from 1905–1918, including old-age pensions, limiting the House of Lords veto, and the passage of Home Rule for Ireland. Her father, however, opposed women's suffrage until 1918, drawing the scorn of militant suffragists. A close friend of Winston Churchill, Violet was an ardent opponent of David Lloyd George. She was president of the Women's Liberal Federation (1923–25 and 1939–45) and of the Liberal Party (1945–47). Defeated in elections at Wells (1945) and Colne Valley (1951), she was vice-chair of the United Europe Movement (1947) and president of the Royal Institute of International Affairs (1964–69). Bonham-Carter was also governor of the BBC (1940–46) and the Old Vic (1945), and she was the first woman to give the Romanes lecture at Oxford in 1963. Created a Dame of the British Empire (DBE) in 1953 and created baroness in 1964, she published *Winston Churchill as I Knew Him* in 1965.

Bonheur, Rosa (1822–1899)

French painter, famous for her naturalistic depictions of animals, who was one of the most successful women artists of the 19th century. *Pronunciation: Bau-NUR. Born Marie Rosalie Bonheur on March 16, 1822, in Bordeaux, France; died of complications following pneumonia in By, France, on May 25, 1899; daughter of Raimond Oscar-Marie Bonheur (an artist*

Rosa Bonheur

and teacher) and **Sophie (Marquis) Bonheur;** *sister of Juliette Bonheur (1830–1891); lived with artist Nathalie Micas (d. 1889); lived with American artist Anna Klumpke.*

Exhibited paintings at the Paris Salon for the first time (1841); exhibited The Horse Fair, *her most famous work (1853); awarded the Cross of the Legion of Honor (1865); befriended, and painted a portrait of, "Buffalo Bill" Cody (1889).*

Paintings: Rabbits Nibbling Carrots *(Musée des Beaux Arts, Bordeaux, France, 1840);* Red Oxen of Cantal *(1846);* Ploughing in the Nivernais *or (original version)* Labourages Nivernais *(Musée National du Château de Fontainebleau, Fontainebleau, France, 1849);* The Horse Fair *(The Metropolitan Museum of Art, New York, 1853);* Col. William F. Cody *or* "Buffalo Bill" Cody *(The Buffalo Bill Historical Center, Cody, Wyoming, 1889). Signs work: Rosa Bonheur.*

The history of women's art abounds with instances of talent taking a back seat to the demands of family and children: gifted women renounced their careers to become caretakers. Rosa Bonheur took a different route; by eschewing marriage for the companionship of a woman, she gained a freedom from the domestic expectations placed upon her sex which allowed a total dedication to work and study. These circumstances, rare for a woman in any profession, contributed greatly to her achievement of international success and renown.

Rosa's father Raimond Bonheur had married his former drawing pupil Sophie Marquis in 1821. The mystery surrounding Sophie's true heritage (she was the ward of a wealthy merchant and considerably more cultured and well-connected than her spouse) led Rosa in later years to the unfounded belief that she was of aristocratic descent, a factor she believed to have played a part in her success. Born a year after their marriage, Rosa was the first of their four children and raised in loving, if impecunious circumstances, which eventually forced the family to move to Paris in search of work. Though employed as a drawing teacher, Raimond's great interest was in the creed of St. Simonism, a Utopian-socialist sect which took up much of his time and led him, in 1832, to spend some months in a St. Simonian monastery. Here, an egalitarian code assigned new work roles to each member, so Raimond became a gardener, leaving his family behind in a state of destitution. Despite these early privations, the St. Simonian beliefs in equality and the importance of the artist's role in society became primary influences in Rosa's life.

It was this commitment to equality which led Raimond Bonheur to enroll Rosa in a boys' school to enable her to receive an education generally denied to girls. Unperturbed by her singularity, Rosa demonstrated a fearless and confident nature: "I was generally a leader in all the games, and I did not hesitate to use my fists," she later reported. When the death of **Sophie Bonheur** in 1833 (of "exhaustion") left Raimond with four children to care for, Rosa's formal education was terminated, and she was apprenticed to a dressmaker. Not surprisingly, this occupation failed to suit the boisterous and unruly girl, and her time there was shortlived. Finally, her father succumbed to her wishes to be tutored in painting by him. At home, her training took the traditional route: pencil drawing first, then watercolors, followed by the copying of the Great Masters at the Louvre. By age 14, Rosa was one of the youngest of the many women who, unable to gain access to the art academies, developed their skills with visits to the famous gallery. The other Bonheur children, Auguste, Isidore, and ❧ **Juliette**, followed the same path and eventually worked in the communal family studio.

From an early age, Rosa's primary interest was in the study of animals: her first exhibit at the Paris Salon, in 1840, *Rabbits Nibbling Carrots*, was a simple work, naturalistically depicted. The entire family worked from live observation of the animals they kept in their barn-like studio, and legend has it that one sheep was carried daily down five flights of stairs by Rosa's brother to be let out to graze. In the tradition of painters such as Jean Louis Gericault, Bonheur supplemented her studio training with frequent drawing trips to the abattoir (slaughterhouse). To avoid unwanted attention, she dressed in men's clothing for these visits, perhaps influenced by the dress code of the famous writer ***George Sand**, whom she much admired. Since the wearing of men's clothes in public was an illegal act for a woman at that time, the artist was awarded a formal *Permission de Travestissement* by the police which allowed it "for health reasons." Throughout her life, Bonheur was rarely seen in a skirt, and in later years, as other women remained corsetted and constricted, able only to ride sidesaddle, a contemporary described her garb: "She was just dismounting from her horse and was attired in a sort of masculine costume that was really grotesque. It consisted of a frock-coat, loose gray trousers with understraps, boots with spurs, and a queer hat."

At the Paris Salon of 1845, Bonheur's skills achieved critical recognition for the first time when five of her works were accepted for exhibition and she was awarded a Third Class Medal. The following year, a trip to the Auvergne provided her with the subject matter for *Red Oxen of Cantal*, a painting which was sold to a British buyer for the (then) huge sum of £600. On the basis of these successes, she received a government commission of 3,000 francs to produce a work on the subject of ploughing. The result—*Ploughing in the Nivernais* (or *Labourages Nivernais*)—established her reputation as an animal painter and so laid the foundation for life-

❧ Bonheur, Juliette (1830–1891)

French painter. *Name variations: Madame Peyrol. Born in 1830; died in 1891; daughter of Raimond Oscar-Marie Bonheur (an artist and teacher), and* ***Sophie Marquis Bonheur.***

The younger sister of Rosa Bonheur by eight years, Juliette Bonheur "painted sentimental studies of pet animals," writes **Germaine Greer**, "with a degree of commercial and some academic success."

SOURCES:

Greer, Germaine. *The Obstacle Race.* NY: Farrar, Straus, 1979.

Fragment of Plowing in the Nivernais, *1849, by Rosa Bonheur.*

long financial security. Inspired by a George Sand story, the painting depicts six pairs of oxen being driven in two teams as they plough the rich sienna earth under a clear blue sky. On exhibition, the work inspired great fervor from contemporary critics: "it charts the labor of the earth accomplished like a sacred rite by the peasant, sublime in his inferiority, the secret agent of the mysterious process of nature," gushed Eugène de Montrosier. In the surge of republicanism following the revolution of 1848, during which King Louis Phillippe had fled the country, the intelligentsia was seized with romantic notions of the life of the "noble peasant," and, though some critics noted the poor representation of her human figures, Bonheur's painting provided an apposite image.

In 1849, Raimond Bonheur was given the directorship of the School of Drawing for Young Girls in Paris, a role which was taken over by Rosa on his death only a few months later. For the next decade, in spite of her fame, she continued to teach there, supported by her sister, Juliette. Meanwhile her brother, Isidore, was achieving recognition as a sculptor, and it is thought that Rosa, though skilled, gave up this practice in deference to him.

In spite of her avowed socialist commitment, Bonheur had no difficulty in adapting to the new political milieu brought about when Louis Napoleon (Napoleon III), the nephew of Napoleon Bonaparte, became emperor in 1852. Government commissions continued as her popular representations of realistic bucolic scenes complemented the current mood of the people, especially the growing bourgeoisie which had rejected history and religious paintings for representations they could understand. For many years, with prospective buyers flocking to her studio, Bonheur no longer needed to exhibit at the Paris Salon.

Since 1836, Rosa had spent much of her time with the family of her closest friend, **Nathalie Micas**. In the absence of her own mother, the Micas' had almost adopted her as their second daughter and cared for Bonheur's everyday needs. When Rosa went to live with them following Raimond's death, Nathalie came to play the role typically taken by an artist's wife: keeping house, protecting her from unwanted visitors, and providing emotional support. Nathalie was also a painter, though of disputable talent, who loved to dress in gypsy costume and was given to displays of jealous rage. Despite these foibles, Rosa's devotion to her was evident, and the relationship fulfilled the needs of both women.

Rosa returned to the Paris Salon in 1853 with her masterpiece, *The Horse Fair*. This huge canvas—almost 16 feet wide—attracted legions of viewers, drawn both by its unique size for an animal painting and by the astonishing fact that it was the work of a young woman. The result of two years of painstaking study of equine physiognomy, *The Horse Fair* represents a circle of horses being led around and displayed for sale. "As the powerful horses reel and plunge and their handlers strain to control them in what seems to be a near-stampede," observes **Rosalia Shriver**, "one can almost hear the shouting and snorting and feel the ground shake under the assault of the hooves." Such was the success of the painting that Rosa was declared *hors de concours*, a title bestowed upon artists whose work was outstanding enough to release them from the normal procedure of submitting Salon entries to a jury.

After Bonheur's home town of Bordeaux refused to buy the painting for the bargain price of 12,000 francs on the grounds that it was too expensive for a work by a woman, it was eventually purchased by a Belgian art dealer, Ernest Gambart. Many art historians feel that Gambart subsequently played a large part in ensuring the continued popularity of Bonheur's work. An astute operator within the art market, he had already established a clientele among the industrial merchant class of England and recognized the potential appeal of Bonheur's paintings. *The Horse Fair* was transported to England, amid great advertisement and fanfare, where it was displayed to critical acclaim and taken to Windsor Castle on Queen ***Victoria**'s request, thus ensuring even greater public attention. Eulogies

Fragment of The Horse Fair *by Rosa Bonheur.*

and poems were written on the subject, and the *Sunday Times* of July 29, 1855, wrote, "It is not only a complicated representation of animal life, executed with wondrous force and precision, but it is a grand composition, pervaded by a manly thought, which could hardly be conceived possible in a work executed by a female hand."

The following year, Gambart introduced the painter herself to Britain, providing the opportunity for Rosa to meet with the most famous of contemporary animal painters, Edwin Landseer. He was captivated by the French woman, joking, in spite of his known commitment to bachelorhood, that he would like to become "Sir Edwin Bonheur." Although she remained a great admirer and collector of Landseer's work, Bonheur never subscribed to the romantic and anthropomorphic imagery which was his trademark, preferring instead to capture the movements of animals in a truly natural state. Both Rosa and Nathalie (who accompanied her on all her trips) were enchanted by the mists and heather of the Highlands of Scotland where the unusual breeds of cattle and sheep inspired the artist to make sketches which would provide the basis for the next few years of her work. (They also arranged for the shipping of some of these beasts back to their home in France to be observed at leisure.) Victorian England, with its obsessive and romantic views of animals, provided the main source of revenue for Bonheur in the decade of the 1860s.

> The point of departure must always be a vision of the truth. The eye is the route of the soul, and the pencil or brush must sincerely and naively reproduce what it sees.
>
> **—Rosa Bonheur**

Not content with the British success of *The Horse Fair*, Gambart sent the painting to the U.S. where it arrived in New York in 1857 to begin a three-year tour. He had extended its appeal by selling the rights to lithograph reproductions. "Every copy will be a magnificent specimen of art, forming a parlor ornament unsurpassed in interest by anything ever before issued on this side of the Atlantic," boasted a journal. Newspapers published special editions with the lithograph as a "free gift" and it is believed that *The Horse Fair* became the most universally recognized painting in North America in the mid-19th century.

In 1860, Rosa and Nathalie, seeking a more reclusive existence, moved into the small château at By, on the edge of the forest of Fontainebleau. The social demands of fame had become tiresome, and gossip surrounding their relationship, fuelled by Rosa's eccentric dress and statements like, "The fact is, in the way of males, I like only the bulls I paint," had increased. Fewer and fewer guests were received, and Bonheur worked mainly on foreign commissions, inciting criticism that she had rejected her native France.

In 1865, while working, Rosa was surprised by the entrance of the Empress ***Eugenie**, who had come to bestow the highest award of the state—the Cross of the Legion of Honor—for the first time upon a woman artist. As she became less republican in her later years, Bonheur loved to tell the tale of this visit, evincing an unerring loyalty to the empress and a fascination with the life of the nobility. The patriotic fervor of which she was capable was evidenced during the Franco-Prussian war of 1870 when, dressed in her usual men's clothes, she joined the home guard and practiced drill with a gun. When the other inhabitants of the small village of By rejected invitations to support her, she began an almost solitary mission to withhold the enemy, drafting plans in the event of being captured which included eating her own pets. When the village was taken and officers were billeted in the château, Rosa refused to speak with them and continued a campaign of small rebellious acts.

In a break with the themes of previous decades which had focused on domestic or working animals, Bonheur became more interested in felines in later life. When trips to the zoo provided insufficient material for her work, a pair of lions were shipped to the château at By, enabling continuous observation and adding exoticism to the existing menagerie. The United States and the life of the "wild west" also sparked Rosa's imagination. When Buffalo Bill's "Exposition of the Wild West," arrived in Paris, in 1889, complete with buffalo and famous Western characters like the sharp-shooting ***Annie Oakley**, Bonheur was quick to invite Mr. William Cody to the château. She soon became a frequent visitor to his camp, making sketches of both animals and humans, and producing many paintings on these themes. Her portrait of "Buffalo Bill" Cody, seated on his favorite horse, became a familiar image to most Americans and the prized possession, legend has it, of William Cody who, on hearing that his house was burning down, implored his wife to leave everything but the "Rosa Bonheur."

Nathalie Micas died in June 1889, leaving Rosa to practice her painstakingly naturalistic form of representation in the face of growing criticism from French critics who now preferred the Impressionist painters such as Renoir and Monet. Commissions from abroad remained constant, however, providing a steady source of work and income until her death. This wane in popularity at home was exacerbated by unfounded reports that, not only was she an eccentric lesbian, but she was of Jewish origin, at a time when overt anti-Semitism was in vogue. Happiness came again towards the end of her life when the American artist, **Anna Klumpke**, became her constant companion and sole beneficiary of her will, living with Rosa for the short time until Bonheur died, following a bout of pneumonia, on May 25, 1899.

At the peak of her fame, Rosa Bonheur was known by many as the "Greatest Woman Artist ever," the kind of praise, notes **Germaine Greer**, that diminishes all other women in honoring one. The false praise is "meted out to token women, single individuals whose recognition is taken to absolve the observer from a charge of prejudice and to give him licence to denigrate or ignore all the other women in the same category." In spite of declining popularity in France, Bonheur's works were collected avidly: the studio sale after her death realized over 2 million francs. But modern reappraisal of her work often regards it as being overestimated. Greer believes her success to have been "a nice coincidence of the work with the tastes and preoccupations of the time" though real genius was "revealed in patches." Even so, Bonheur remains one of the most renowned names in the history of women's art.

SOURCES:

Ashton, Dore, and Denise Hare. *Rosa Bonheur—A Life and A Legend.* NY: Viking Press, 1981.

Greer, Germaine. *The Obstacle Race.* NY: Farrar, Straus, 1979.

Lepelle de Bois-Gallais, F. *Memoir of M'mselle Rosa Bonheur.* Translated by James Parry. NY: Williams, Stevens, Williams, 1857.

Shriver, Rosalia. *Rosa Bonheur with a checklist of works in American Collections.* Associated University Presses, 1982.

SUGGESTED READING:

Klumpke, Anna. *Rosa Bonheur: The Artist's (Auto)biography.* Translated by Gretchen van Slyke. Ann Arbor: University of Michigan Press, 1997.

Stanton, Theodore. *Reminiscences of Rosa Bonheur.* NY: Appleton, 1910.

Diane Moody, freelance writer, London, England

Klumpke, Anna Elizabeth (1856–1942)

American painter of portraits and landscapes. *Born Anna Elizabeth Klumpke in 1856; died in 1942; daughter of Dorothea Tolle Klumpke and John Gerard Klumpke (a San Francisco real-estate magnate); attended Académie Julian, 1883–84; studied with Tony Robert-Fleury and Jules Lefebvre in Paris; sister of Augusta Klumpke (1859–1927), Dorothea Klumpke (1861–1942), and* ***Matilda and Julia Klumpke.***

Anna Klumpke had four sisters: ***Augusta Klumpke** was the first woman intern at a Paris hospital and wrote a book on nervous pathology with her husband Joseph Jules Dejerine; ***Dorothea Klumpke** had a doctorate in mathematics from the Sorbonne and became an astronomer. **Julia Klumpke** was a violinist composer; and **Matilda Klumpke** was a pianist. Anna became an artist. The four sisters owed their success to their strong-willed mother, **Dorothea Tolle Klumpke**, who left her prosperous husband with his real-estate holdings back in San Francisco and took her girls to Switzerland where they were privately tutored.

Anna Klumpke, whose work won many prizes, became a companion of her mentor ***Rosa Bonheur** in 1898. After Bonheur's death the following year, Klumpke inherited Bonheur's studio-estate at By and wrote a biography, *Rosa Bonheur, sa vie, son oeuvre* (1908). She also painted portraits of Bonheur and ***Elizabeth Cady Stanton**. In 1940, Anna Klumpke published her autobiography *Memoirs of an Artist.*

SUGGESTED READING:

Klumpke, Anna. *Rosa Bonheur: The Artist's (Auto)biography.* Translated by Gretchen van Slyke. Ann Arbor: University of Michigan Press, 1997.

Bonhoeffer, Emmi (1905–1991)

German anti-Nazi and wife of Klaus Bonhoeffer, member of the anti-Nazi resistance. *Born Emmi Delbrück in Berlin, Germany, in 1905; died in Düsseldorf on March 12, 1991; one of six children of Hans Delbrück (a historian and political publicist) and Lina (Thiersch) Delbrück; married Klaus Bonhoeffer (chief counsel of the German Lufthansa Airline Company and leading civilian member of the military resistance to the Hitler regime), in 1930 (murdered, April 23, 1945); children: three.*

Though occupied raising their children, strongly supported her husband's decision to oppose Nazism, assisting him on countless occasions both morally and practically; husband arrested (October 1944), sentenced to death (February 1945), murdered by the SS (April 23, 1945); barely escaped being killed when her house was destroyed in the last days of the war; moved with her children to Schleswig-Holstein to rebuild their lives (June 1945); was active in activities aiding war refugees, as well as anti-Nazi educational work and various humanitarian efforts.

Born in Berlin in 1905, Emmi Delbrück grew up in the exclusive suburb of Grunewald in an environment of intellectual brilliance and personal tolerance. Her father, the historian and political publicist Hans Delbrück, had cosmopolitan, liberal attitudes that were critical of much of the narrowly militaristic spirit of Kaiser Wilhelm II's Germany. During World War I, Hans Delbrück strongly criticized Pan-German extremists who aimed for a total German victory, arguing that their attitudes would lead the Reich to a terrible catastrophe. Emmi flourished in a family circle that included leading writers and intellectuals. The neighborhood, too, fostered liberality of thought and action. One neighbor was Emmi's uncle, Adolf von Harnack, world-famous as a theologian and the founder of modern critical Biblical exegesis. Unlike some German elite families, the Delbrücks were not anti-Semitic. Among Emmi's closest friends were two Jewish girls, **Brigitte (Tutti) Fischer** and **Suse Lissauer**, who would manage to emigrate from Nazi Germany in the 1930s. When she was a young girl, Emmi's best friends were the four Bonhoeffer children—**Christel**, Klaus, and twins Dietrich and **Sabine**—who were also neighbors. The rich, lifelong relationship between Emmi and the Bonhoeffers was destined to be violently severed because of the tragic nature of modern German history.

In 1930, Emmi married Klaus Bonhoeffer, who had become a lawyer for the German Lufthansa airline. As the family grew and his career prospered, Germany descended into the darkness of the brutal Nazi dictatorship. Both Emmi and Klaus were deeply opposed to the flouting of humanitarian traditions and basic human rights by the Hitler dictatorship, but at first there was little they could do to resist the regime. Emmi, who never saw Adolf Hitler in person, recalled that his voice, which she often heard on the radio, was that of "a man who always screamed." The humanistic family tradition of both the Bonhoeffer and Delbrück families had inoculated them against Nazi racism and intolerance. Defying the anti-Jewish Nazi boycott of April 1, 1933, Klaus' paternal grandmother poked one of the storm troopers in front of a Jewish-owned grocery shop on his shiny boots, insisting, "I'll buy my butter where I have always bought my butter." The Nazi toughs let her through unmolested.

Promoted to corporate counsel for Lufthansa in 1936, Klaus enjoyed significant opportunities to establish contacts both in Germany and abroad with anti-Nazi individuals and groups. Through his brother Dietrich Bonhoeffer, a brilliant young Protestant theologian, Klaus kept abreast of developments within Christian anti-Nazi circles. With the coming of war in 1939, the plans of the anti-Nazi resistance groups within the regime concentrated on an assassination of Hitler and a military coup that would seize the government and end the war. Klaus established contact with the military plotters through his brother-in-law Hans von Dohnanyi and developed links with the Social Democratic opposition groups through Emmi's cousin, Ernst von Harnack.

Fully sharing her husband's detestation of the Nazi regime, Emmi Bonhoeffer was more than aware of the risks of involvement in resistance to Hitler's tyranny. While raising her three children, she supported Klaus in every possible fashion, passing on coded messages as well as funds to finance special activities of the resistance groups. But the strain of the war and the anger induced by the knowledge she shared with her husband and his fellow-conspirators sometimes led to potentially dangerous incidents. On one occasion, while shopping for vegetables in the summer of 1942, Emmi remarked to a neighbor: "Now they are beginning to gas and burn up the Jews in the concentration camps." Her indiscreet comment was overheard by a saleswoman who warned, "Frau Bonhoeffer, if you don't stop spreading such atrocity stories you too will wind up in a concentration camp. All of us heard what you said, and nobody will be able to help you."

On another occasion, some months earlier, she was on a Berlin streetcar when an old Jewish woman, wearing the Star of David, boarded. A worker offered her a seat; whereupon the conductor warned him that offering a seat to a Jew was forbidden by law. To this, the worker replied with an obscenity and got off. At this point, Emmi Bonhoeffer whispered into the ear of the frightened Jewish woman, "Please feel free to sit down," and demonstratively stood next to her until the old woman reached her stop. Fortunately, there were no Gestapo agents on the streetcar. While it was apparent from their attitudes that the passengers sympathized with the elderly Jewish woman rather than the conductor, none dared to speak out. Years of Nazi terror and propaganda had taught them the dangers of helping another human being who was defined by Nazism as "sub-human."

After the failure of the attempt to assassinate Adolf Hitler on July 20, 1944, Klaus Bonhoeffer was arrested in October 1944. Although he was sentenced to death by the Nazi People's Court on February 2, 1945, a friend of Emmi's in the Ministry of Justice intercepted his file. This left both

Klaus and Emmi optimistic that his sentence would never be carried out. They were mistaken. On April 23, 1945, he was executed by SS guards with a shot in the back of his neck.

The same day her husband was murdered, Emmi was nearly killed when a direct hit by an Allied bomb destroyed her house. By the time the war ended two weeks later, Emmi Bonhoeffer had lost her husband Klaus, her brother-in-law Dietrich Bonhoeffer, and her relatives Hans von Dohnanyi, Rüdiger Schleicher, and Ernst von Harnack. She lost as well her brother Justus Delbrück who was arrested by Soviet authorities in May 1945, ostensibly because he had information on the plot against Hitler. Emmi never saw her brother again; he died of illness in a Soviet prison camp in October 1945.

After the war, Emmi Bonhoeffer moved with her children to Schleswig-Holstein to attempt to rebuild her shattered life. She took strength from a letter her husband had written shortly before his death, containing instructions for the moral education of their children. Turning her attention to helping others, she sent food parcels to the Soviet Occupation Zone. In the early 1960s, she became involved in assisting the hundreds of witnesses who came to Germany for the famous Auschwitz trial that convicted a number of war criminals. Determined that the younger generation of Germans be aware of the horrors that had taken place under German rule, she often antagonized those of her generation who wanted to forget, or sweep under the carpet, the crimes of Nazism. In her final years, Emmi Bonhoeffer globalized her concerns for justice by working for Amnesty International.

SOURCES:

Bethge, Eberhard, and Renate Bethge, eds. *Last Letters of Resistance: Farewells from the Bonhoeffer Family.* Philadelphia, PA: Fortress Press, 1986.

Bucholz, Arden. *Hans Delbrück and the German Military Establishment: War Images in Conflict.* Iowa City: University of Iowa Press, 1985.

John, Otto. *Twice Through the Lines: The Autobiography of Otto John.* NY: Harper & Row, 1972.

Meding, Dorothee von. *Mit dem Mut des Herzens: Die Frauen des 20. Juli.* 2nd ed. Berlin: Wolf Jobst Siedler Verlag, 1992.

John Haag, Associate Professor,
University of Georgia, Athens, Georgia

Boninsegna, Celestina (1877–1947)

Italian soprano. *Born on February 26, 1877, in Reggio Emilia, Italy; died on February 14, 1947, in Milan; studied with Mattieli in Reggio Emilia and Virginia Boccabadati in Pesaro.*

Debuted as Norina (1892) at the Teatro Municipale in Reggio Emilia and at the Teatro Piccinini in Bari (1897); made debut at Covent Garden (1904), Teatro alla Scala (1904–05), Metropolitan Opera as Aïda (1906–07), Boston (1909–10), Barcelona (1912), St Petersburg (1913); retired (1923).

Celestina Boninsegna

Celestina Boninsegna is known more for her recordings than for her appearance on the operatic stage. Made for several companies between 1904 and 1919, these splendid transcriptions document the voice of a major artist, yet her career on stage was not especially illustrious. Boninsegna sang the most demanding roles alongside the most famous singers of her era but was never allowed to step into the spotlight. Her stay at most major companies was short. While she blamed jealousy for her undistinguished career, some have cited her acting, rather than her voice, as the cause of her operatic failure. Physique may have also played a role. Boninsegna was tall in an era when large women were discouraged from appearing on stage. She was best suited to middle and late Verdi, specifically the two Leonoras from *Il Trovatore* and *La forza del destino*, and *Aïda*.

The voice on her recordings has been described as unusually attractive, dark and resonant with a spectacular chest register and clear, ringing top. Her range was not especially exceptional, and she sometimes left breaks exposed, though she negotiated difficult passages without forcing. Boninsegna left over 100 recordings which establish her legacy. Thanks to this electronic medium, her voice was handed down to posterity which has judged her more kindly than did her contemporaries.

John Haag,
Athens, Georgia

Bonita, Maria (c. 1908–1938)

Backwoods consort of the famous Brazilian bandit and folk hero Lampião who accompanied her lover on a series of campaigns against government forces in 1930s Brazil and, in so doing, became a legend in her

own right. Name variations: Pretty Mary, Dona Maria, Maria Déia, Maria Déia de Nenem. Pronunciation: Mah-REE-uh Boo-NEE-tuh. Born Maria Déia in the interior of the Brazilian state of Bahia in 1908 or 1909; gunned down in a military ambush at Angicos ranch in the state of Sergipe on July 28, 1938; daughter of José Felipe and Maria de Oliveira Déia; illiterate; married in her teens to José Nenem (a cobbler); children: one girl (three other children, all boys, died in infancy).

Born into primitive circumstances in the most impoverished region of Brazil (c. 1908); spent early years with her family just scraping by; married in her teens to a cobbler, José Nenem, but as the match was loveless, spent more and more time with her parents; made acquaintance of Lampião, whose fame as a bandit in the Brazilian backlands had by that time grown to legendary proportions (early 1931); ran away with Lampião; entered a life of adventure and crime that only ended with both of their deaths in an engagement against the army (1938).

The barren backcountry of northeastern Brazil has regularly given rise to figures of heroic proportions. It could hardly be otherwise. The weather there is the most brutal in the country, with heat so blistering that outsiders can only catch their breath with great difficulty. The air itself is often so dry and dusty that it seems illuminated by the rays of the sun; it is impossible under such circumstances to discern a horizon, and it leaves sand, thorn forest, and mirage to blend together in a swimmingly hot vista in every way reminiscent of Hell. Little wonder that popular imagination in the Northeast often turns to supernatural themes: to animals who speak, to miraculous apparitions of devils and angels who battle with golden swords in the sky, to wild-eyed prophets who make streams run with wine or with blood, and, most commonly, to heroes and heroines who, without any blemish on their own reputations, manage to deliver the poor from the worst sorts of despotism. Every so often real historical personages appeared on the scene in the Northeast who seemed to encapsulate these qualities. Two such figures were the "bandit-king" Lampião, and his female companion, Maria Bonita.

The historical facts behind the appearance of these two are, on the one hand, straightforward enough and, on the other hand, quite obscure. The Sertão, as the Northeast is usually called, was undergoing considerable change at the turn of the present century. Long the most ignored area of Brazil, until the 1890s it was the exclusive preserve of cowpunchers, minor rural bosses, and scrub farmers who only rarely made a go of it.

The fall of the empire in 1889, however, brought with it direct government intervention on several levels. The new republic demanded standardization of weights and measures, and sent new scales and new government tax inspectors into the Sertão, where they were met with great hostility by the *sertanejos*. The latter knew nothing of the metric system but feared, with good reason, that the republic would impose increased taxes and take what little money that they had. Sugar planters and commercial entrepreneurs on the coast gained the cooperation of the new regime in bringing pressure on the *sertanejos* to give up their pre-capitalist ways (and, in effect, become day-laborers and debt *peons*).

But the *sertanejos* would have none of this. Their steadfast loyalty to the old habits—and their religiosity—provided the backdrop for a series of major rebellions in the 1890s and 1900s. On several occasions, most notably at the Bahian town of Canudos, these revolts took on the aspect of a holy war. Government troops came from as far away as Rio de Janeiro and São Paulo. They brought with them modern repeating rifles and artillery pieces of impressive calibers. Still the *sertanejos* refused to give up. The final all-out assault on Canudos in 1896 left the community almost flattened and nearly its entire population dead. But rebellions large and small continued to plague the Northeast for another decade.

In the aftermath of these rebellions, the Sertão was outwardly quiet, reconciled now to the presence of outside government officials and to the republican regime that they represented. Other signs of outside authority, such as state schools and regular stage lines, were grudgingly accepted. Yet, at the periphery of *sertanejo* society, a continued resistance to the government was seen in the activities of armed bands of rebel cowboys, or *cangaceiros*. The most famous leader among these *cangaceiros* was Lampião. His chosen woman was Maria Bonita.

"Pretty Mary" was the first woman to enter the ranks of Lampião's *cangaceiro* band. That women should take an active role in such mobile bands was not, in itself, unusual in the Sertão. Traditionally, female camp-followers accompanied their men onto the range. They prepared their simple meals of beef and cornmeal, washed their neckerchiefs and undershirts, provided solace and companionship after long days of backbreaking labor, and had babies. Maria Bonita did all of these things, but she did something else as well. She carried a rifle.

She was born Maria Déia in 1908 (or perhaps 1909) in the Jeremoabo region of northern Bahia. Her family were dirt-poor ranchers, almost always hungry, and with many mouths to feed. Maria had five brothers and seven sisters. Her parents, José Felipe and Maria de Oliveira Déia, habitually worked on the Malhada de Caiçira ranch, and it was on this poor estate that Maria Bonita grew up. Not much is known of her childhood and youth. We can assume that she got a smattering of religious education, and that she learned something of the usual avocations of *sertanejo* women: leatherworking, cooking, embroidery, and, of course, field work.

Maria married early, as was traditional in the Northeast. Her husband José Nenem was the local cobbler, relatively well-established by *sertanejo* standards, with a house and shop at the nearby village of Santa Brígada. His brother had already married one of Maria's sisters, and he seemed perfectly placed to offer the pretty Mary a good life. In fact, however, their marriage was loveless. José did not diverge from his everyday customs. Maria was high-strung, with a sense of curiosity and adventure about her, and with a desire to see something more of life than just the tall pile of shoes waiting to be mended by her husband. She found herself regularly pulled back to the ranch and to her parents, who understood her ambitions, even if they did not really approve of them. It was on one of these periodic visits to her parents that she met Lampião.

Lampião was born in July 1897 in the interior of Pernambuco state. His given name was Virgulino Ferreira da Silva, and he only took the name Lampião after he began his life of crime. Like Maria Bonita, he spent his earliest years on a ranch, where he became an expert leatherworker and rodeo artist. The two occupations functioned well with each other: young Virgulino could present himself as the perfect horse rider, outfitted with the perfect backlander attire of leather breeches, heavy leggings, colorful bandannas, and a wide-brimmed leather hat, characteristically turned upward at the front and ornately decorated with inlaid crosses, Mogen Davids, and silver coins. Dressed in this manner, Virgulino looked the part of the *cangaceiro*. Soon he added cartridge belts to his costume and made the transition to full-fledged outlaw.

Lampião first made the headlines in 1922, when his armed band, which numbered around 50, sacked the home of the former baroness of Agua Branca in the state of Alagôas. The choice of the baroness was understandable, as it was believed that she had considerable wealth in her home. In addition, her sons controlled the chief political machine in the county and were strong allies of the police officials who enforced the tax laws. Lampião's own father had been killed by such officials. The attack on Agua Branca, therefore, combined several themes dear to the *cangaceiro* that also were understandable to all *sertanejos*: the desire to avenge the dishonoring of one's relative, the need to right wrongs done the poor, and, of course, clear availability of loot.

Lampião was only one *cangaceiro* among many in the band that raided Agua Branca. Soon, however, through the force of his own magnetism, he eclipsed many older members. The tip of his deftly wielded knife convinced younger members to likewise stay in their place. His band became an effective fighting force under his command and on various occasions numbered in the hundreds. His raids took him to every corner of the Sertão, traversing thousands of miles in the process. His face became familiar to the countryfolk throughout the region, and not merely because of his now-legendary exploits against the rich and the authorities. His men frequently distributed their loot to the neediest members of the *sertanejo* community. Lampião gave to poor churches and to the indigent. He spoke as an equal with the most powerful political bosses of the interior and never allowed any one of them to touch him militarily. After a decade in the bush, he could rightfully claim the popular title of "Bandit-King."

When Maria Bonita came into Lampião's life in early 1931, his name was already the stuff of ballads in the Sertão. Almost certainly he had already met her parents; their ranch lay in the Sergipe-Bahia border area through which he often passed. Like most *sertanejos*, they probably feared the legendary outlaw, yet at the same time they respected him as a great man and leader. It was Maria's mother who supposedly told Lampião how much her daughter admired him.

On the day Maria happened to come to the ranch while Lampião was present, the bandit, it is said, fell in love with her at first sight. In appearance, she was a fairly typical *sertaneja*; she was short, a bit stocky, had good teeth, very dark hair and eyes, and cinnamon-brown skin. She was then in her early 20s, as opposed to Lampião's 33 years. Lampião's passion for her was evidently genuine. After a few days, when the *cangaceiro* band departed, he took her with him, with her consent and that of her mother.

Lampião's desire for Maria might initially have been driven by her beauty, but he soon began to respect her for her other qualities. She rode as hard as any of the men. An accomplished seamstress, she often made her own and the bandit's clothes and elaborately decorated such things as hats, bandoliers, and the small packsacks (*bornais*) in which they carried their money, jewels, and personal items. Lampião even managed once to steal a sewing machine for her.

Maria Bonita did not initially carry a gun. Women camp followers were taught by their *cangaceiro* lovers how to shoot, as a matter of self-protection, but normally they were kept apart in battle whenever possible. *Cangaceiros* frowned upon their women straying too far from traditional women's pursuits. But Maria Bonita proved to be an innovator in this respect. Her own spunk, which distinguished her from the beginning, was doubtlessly an element in convincing Lampião to permit her to go about armed. Perhaps the Bandit-King felt so certain of his own authority among his men that he could permit an unusual departure from normal *cangaceiro* practice. In any case, by the mid-1930s, as the fortunes of Lampião's band grew more precarious, Maria Bonita (and, indeed, all of the band's women) was never found far from a rifle. On one occasion, she was wounded with that rifle in her hand.

By this time, Lampião had made the news nationally. His band had killed scores of government agents, soldiers, and police. He had made raids in at least half a dozen states and stolen money from many well-known people. Worst of all, his reputation in the Northeast was that of a Robin Hood, and although none of the lettered classes in that region thought it likely that he could become a political force, many among the poor were far less certain.

In Rio de Janeiro, the president's office had fallen to Getulio Vargas, a hardbitten Gaúcho from the southern state of Rio Grande do Sul, and a man little given to compromise with outlaws. Vargas sent federal monies to bolster the anti-*cangaceiro* campaign. Artillery, machine guns, some airplanes, and, most important, modern military trainers arrived in the state capitals of the Northeast to be used against Lampião and his ilk.

From 1935 on, these measures of the federal government began to pay off. Lampião was necessarily more on the move than ever before. Several costly ambushes by *sertanejos* on the state payroll sapped the strength of the band. So did the frequent desertions. The core group around Lampião and Maria Bonita remained loyal, but they were increasingly anxious, and very, very tired. The story of the couple, and of the *cangaceiro* band they led, began to take on the character of a Greek tragedy, in which the players and the audience all know that doom lies ahead. The government offered amnesty to Lampião's men. Most did not take it.

In early 1938, after some months of relative inactivity, Lampião launched several major raids, pillaging 17 villages in Alagôas before retreating again into Sergipe. At one point he captured a nationally famous jazz combo (rather than mistreat them, he paid them a handsome sum to play for him and Maria Bonita). These raids were both costly and bloody, and soon the group was again on hard luck. Witnesses reported that its members now wore ragged clothes and were extremely dirty, with hair down to their shoulders and little hope.

On July 28, 1938, Lampião and Maria Bonita, together with a much-reduced band, had come to the Sergipe border region at Angicos, purportedly to make contact with other bands still technically under the chieftain's command. Police informants became aware of their presence immediately. Troops arrived in the middle of the night and stealthily began to encircle the camp. Lampião's dogs put up no ruckus because they had sought shelter from a sudden and tremendous downpour. For the same reason, no sentries had been posted.

It was all over in 20 minutes. The soldiers and police had set up machine guns and rifle stands and opened fire immediately. Surprised for once, Lampião rose from his place by the fire to reach for his weapon and was instantly cut down. Maria had also risen to cock her rifle. After seeing Lampião's bloodied body, several *cangaceiros* began to break and run, and Maria called to them, reminding them of their sworn loyalty to their chief. They all turned, rejoined her, and fought to the end. Maria was shot several times before dying.

After the battle, the jubilant soldiers mutilated the dead. Both Lampião and Maria Bonita were decapitated. Maria's headless corpse was left in a grotesque position, its legs pulled apart and a large stick rammed into the vagina. The heads were removed to the state capital for exhibition (they eventually served for many years as a key attraction at the Nina Rodrigues Museum in Salvador). What was left of the bodies remained at Angicos to be viewed by the curious, and consumed, in the end, by vultures.

The deaths of Lampião and Maria Bonita ended most *cangaceiro* activity in the Northeast. That the *cangaço* should end so violently encouraged the transformation of the pair from rural bandits to permanent features of folklore. Popular modern-day literature commonly focuses on their exploits. And, indeed, their exploits have not ceased: on the cover of one popular pamphlet published in Bahia in the early 1970s, Lampião is shown arriving in Hell, and he is forcefully booting Satan out in order to make that infernal domain his own. Just behind him, never flagging in her loyalty, stands Maria Bonita, rifle in hand.

SOURCES:

Chandler, Billy Jaynes. *The Bandit King: Lampião of Brazil.* College Station, TX: Texas A&M Press, 1978.

Correa de Araujo, Antonio Amaury. *Lampião: As Mulheres e o Cangaço.* São Paulo, 1985.

RELATED MEDIA:

The Black God and the White Devil, Brazilian film by Glauber Rocha.

O Cangaceiro, Brazilian film by Lima Baretto.

Thomas Whigham,
Associate Professor of History,
University of Georgia, Athens, Georgia

Bonna of Pisa (c. 1156–1207).

See Bona of Pisa.

Bonne of Armagnac (d. 1415)

Duchess of Orléans. *Name variations: Bonne d'Armagnac; duchess of Orleans. Died in 1415 (some sources cite 1435); daughter of Bernard VII d'Armagnac and* ***Bonne of Berry;*** *became second wife of Charles Valois (1391–1465), duke of Orléans, in 1410. Charles Valois' first wife was* ****Isabella of Valois*** *(c. 1389–c. 1410); his third was* ****Marie of Cleves*** *(1426–1486).*

Bonne of Artois (d. 1425)

Duchess of Burgundy. *Name variations: Bona or Bonne d'Artois. Died in 1425; second wife of Philip the Good (1396–1467), duke of Burgundy (r. 1419–1467). Philip the Good's first wife was* ****Michelle Valois*** *(1394–1422); his third was* ****Isabella of Portugal*** *(1397–1471).*

Bonne of Luxemburg (1315–1349).

See Bona of Bohemia.

Bonneau, Marie (1629–1696).

See Miramion, Madame de.

Bonner, Antoinette (1892–1920)

Rumanian-born jewel thief. *Born in Rumania in 1892; immigrated to the U.S.; committed suicide in New York, New York, 1920.*

In 1910, after learning all she could about evaluating gems from her father and winning the respect and trust of jewelers throughout the world, Antoinette Bonner was known as the "Queen of Diamonds." She set up an office, drummed up wealthy clients in search of the perfect diamond, and jewelers began to turn their diamonds over to her to sell. With commissions approximating $100,000 a year, the lure of the stones apparently overcame Bonner's good business judgment. In 1914, she disappeared with stones estimated to be worth one million dollars. Tracked down in Paris, Bonner claimed that she was not absconding with the jewels, but that her long sojourn in Paris had been caused by difficult negotiations for their sale. She was released and, after several years, reestablished her reputation.

In 1928, however, Bonner succumbed to temptation once again. She was caught in her office planning a getaway after selling $500,000 worth of rare uncut diamonds entrusted to her by a group of jewelers. When informed of her impending arrest for jewel theft, she reportedly pulled out a bottle of strychnine, downed it in front of the stunned police officers, and fell dead. She was 28 years old.

Barbara Morgan,
Melrose, Massachusetts

Bonner, Catherine Sherwood (1849–1883).

See Bonner, Sherwood.

Bonner, Elena (1923—)

Daughter of high-ranking Soviet officials, victims of Stalin's purges, who became a physician, a civil-rights activist in the Soviet Union, and a spokeswoman and representative for her husband Andrei Sakharov. *Name variations: Luisa (childhood name still used by her family). Pronunciation: Ye-LAY-na BAH-ner. Born on February 15, 1923, in Merv in Soviet Turkestan; daughter of Levon Sarkisovich Kocharov (occupation unknown) and Ruth Grigorievna Bonner (subsequently Communist Party official); stepdaughter of Gevork Sarkisovich Alikhanov (Communist Party official); attended Herzen Teachers Institute, 1940–41, and First Leningrad Medical Institute, 1947–53; married Ivan Vasilyevich Semyonov, in 1950 (separated 1965); married Andrei Sakharov, in*

1971 (died 1989); children (first marriage): Tatyiana (b. 1950), Alexei (b. 1956).

Parents arrested (1937); joined Communist Party youth group (1938); served as nurse in World War II (1941–45) and wounded in action (1941); mother re-arrested (1950); attended medical school (1947–53); mother released from imprisonment (1954); separated from first husband, joined Communist Party (1965); Soviet invasion of Czechoslovakia (1968); met Sakharov (1970); left Communist Party (1972); received medical treatment in Italy, accepted Nobel Prize for Sakharov (1975); Helsinki Accords Watch Group founded (1976); received medical treatment in Italy (1979); accompanied Sakharov into exile (1980); arrested and sentenced to exile in Gorky (1984); medical treatment in Italy and the U.S. (1985–86); Sakharov released from exile (1986); death of Sakharov (1989); collapse of the Soviet Union (1991); established Sakharov memorial library in Moscow (1994).

Publications: Alone Together *(1986);* Mothers and Daughters *(1992).*

Elena Bonner

During the decades following the Russian Revolution of November 1917, a new ruling elite emerged out of the ranks of the victorious Communist Party. In local party organizations, in positions in the central apparatus at Moscow, and in international communist organizations like the Comintern, numerous members of Soviet society with roots in revolutionary circles now found themselves governing officials. Individuals linked to high-ranking Communist leaders like Sergei Kirov, rose and fell with the fortunes of their mentors.

For tens of thousands of such individuals, the transformation of the Soviet Union under Joseph Stalin made their prominence a source of peril. Following the relatively quiet years of the 1920s, Stalin plunged the USSR into a turbulent era. The government directed a rapid and brutal program of forced industrialization. At the same time, the mass of the population, which still consisted of peasants in rural villages, was forced into collective farms. Stalin tightened his grip on the political system, relying increasingly upon the secret police. By the closing years of that decade, members of the upper ranks of the Communist Party were often the victims of the dictator's suspicions. Families whose members had basked in privileges saw many of their members imprisoned, exiled, and murdered. The children of such families had to find a new role in Soviet society.

As such a child of members of the Communist elite and through her adult years, Elena Bonner was a participant, both willing and unwilling, in many of the dramatic events that affected the life of the Soviet Union over a period of six decades. As a witness to the purges of the 1930s, as a member of the armed forces during World War II, and as a leading dissident in the era following the death of dictator Joseph Stalin, she observed and helped to shape the course of her country's history.

Elena Bonner is the daughter of a Russian-Jewish mother, **Ruth Bonner**, and an Armenian father. She has never been forthcoming about the role of her natural father, Levon Kocharov, other than to record occasional meetings with him before and during World War II. But her stepfather, Gevork Alikhanov, was an important figure in the Communist Party. Her mother, who joined the party the year after Elena's birth, likewise rose in the political hierarchy.

The girl's first 14 years saw her family move frequently in response to her parents' shifting political fortunes. Elena was born in Central Asia in 1923, but her mother and stepfather soon returned to Moscow. Conflict between Alikhanov and Gregory Zinoviev, the head of the Comintern, sent the family back to Central Asia. On the other hand, the rising fortunes of Sergei Kirov, a mentor for her parents, gave her family the opportunity to return to the country's great urban centers. They lived in Leningrad and then Moscow from 1926 to 1937.

As a prominent party family—her stepfather was a leading figure in the Comintern, the international organization of Communist parties—Bonner's mother and stepfather enjoyed a special supply of food, dachas in the countryside, and superior educational opportunities for Elena and her younger brother. Elena's playmates were the children of other party leaders, and she had lifelong memories of party figures like Kirov patting her on the head while she was a youngster.

But the signs of gathering danger became evident. In 1934, her stepfather's patron Sergei Kirov was murdered in mysterious circumstances. The event, carried out under Stalin's direction, was the signal for a spreading purge of Soviet society. Tension grew in the privileged circles around her family as it became evident that the purge was spreading to include ranking members of the Communist Party.

As Elena passed into her teenage years—with a love of reading and a growing interest in boys—the fathers of her friends began to disappear. In her parents' apartment building, reserved for the Soviet elite, wax seals appeared on the doors of families that had been arrested the night before by the secret police. "The taking away of people," she later wrote, "became an ordinary, commonplace event."

In May 1937, Bonner returned from taking her school exams one day to find that her stepfather had been arrested at work. Soldiers were in the midst of searching the family apartment. Her stepfather's arrest was followed at the end of the year by the arrest of her mother. Elena and her brother were now what the Soviet writer Ilya Ehrenburg described as the era's "strange orphans." Searching for relatives willing to take them in, the children went to live with their grandmother in Leningrad. The young girl, still in her late teens, worked as a cleaning woman in order to finish her education, and she battled officials of the Komsomol, the Communist Youth organization, when they tried to expel her.

The war years brought another series of dramatic changes to Bonner's life. One childhood comrade after another, including her teenage sweetheart, became a fatal victim of the conflict. She herself was permanently disabled by a bomb blast in 1941 although she continued to see service as a nurse throughout World War II. Her wounds virtually destroyed her sight in one eye and led to a progressive weakening of vision in the other.

Following her wartime service, Elena Bonner was educated as a physician, married and had two children. Her work as a pediatrician included a period of service abroad in Iraq. In 1965, she separated from her first husband. By the close of the 1960s and the early 1970s, she became a leading member in the Soviet dissident community. Her disillusion with the Communist Party, which she had joined in 1965 and left only in 1972, stemmed from a variety of causes. There were events of national weight such as the Soviet invasion of Czechoslovakia in 1968. There were personal traumas like the conviction of her nephew, the Jewish dissident Eduard Kuznetsov, for attempting to hijack an airplane in 1970.

In late 1970, Bonner met Andrei Sakharov at a protest demonstration. The following year, the two were married. She was now linked personally to one of the nation's greatest scientists and by then an internationally renowned critic of Soviet political life. As his professional partner, she took on an increasingly significant role in Soviet life. When Sakharov could not leave the Soviet Union to receive the Nobel Prize awarded him in 1975, she received it in his place. When dissidents formed watch committees to assure that the Helsinki Accords guaranteeing civil rights to the population of signatories like the Soviet Union were honored, she joined as a representative of her family.

Bonner's life, along with that of her husband, took a dramatic turn in 1980. Sakharov, a vocal critic of the Soviet invasion of Afghanistan, was sentenced to exile in Gorky, an industrial city closed to foreigners and located 250 miles east of Moscow. Bonner became his chief spokesperson and link to the outside world. The perils of such a role became evident in 1984 when she was arrested for anti-Soviet activities and, like her husband, put in internal exile in Gorky.

In late 1985, following a hunger strike in which both Bonner and Sakharov participated, she received permission to travel abroad for medical treatment. By then, Bonner's children and her mother were already in the United States, thanks in part to earlier hunger strikes by which the two dissidents had managed to put pressure on the Soviet government. Bonner's health was now seriously endangered: her persistent eye problems were accompanied by a dangerous heart condition. Her stay in the U.S. included multiple bypass surgery in Boston and a trip to the White House. In the end, however, she returned to the Soviet Union. In the book *Alone Together*, which she wrote during her trip abroad, she noted the strains of reentering Soviet life: "It takes incredible will power to force yourself to learn once again how to breathe without air."

By 1986, however, the Soviet Union was in the midst of a growing wave of political reform directed by the new leader of the Communist Party, Mikhail Gorbachev. A crucial event at the close of the year was Gorbachev's sudden decision to free the Sakharovs from their confinement in Gorky. It was a sign to the Soviet Union and the entire world that the process of reform, to which the Sakharovs had contributed, was now moving forward irreversibly. Sakharov went on to play a prominent role in Soviet political life until his death in December 1989.

What is happening now would have seemed like a Christmas fairy tale a few years ago.

—Elena Bonner (1994)

Unlike her late husband, Bonner was present as the Soviet Union collapsed in late 1991. She continued the family tradition both as a spokeswoman for reform and as the custodian of her husband's legacy. In 1992, she warned publicly about the role that the forces of the former Soviet military system were taking in bullying former non-Russian Soviet republics to come back under Russian domination. In 1994, using a financial grant from the U.S. Congress, she inaugurated a library in Sakharov's honor in Moscow. Ironically, the library collection includes documents that the Soviet secret police (KGB) had once seized from Sakharov and now returned to her possession. Bonner took the occasion to announce her plans to open a human-rights museum in honor of Sakharov in Moscow during 1996.

Apart from her role as a political activist, Bonner has become an important contributor to the historical record of her nation's recent past. Her book *Mothers and Daughters*, published in 1992, has as its centerpiece an extraordinary eyewitness account of the Stalinist purges of the late 1930s by the daughter of purge victims. **Andrea Lee**, reviewing the book in *The New York Times*, places it in the same category as *The Diary of Anne Frank* as an example of historical horror seen in personalized form through the eyes of a young girl.

Opposite page

Sherwood Bonner

SOURCES:

Bonner, Elena. *Alone Together.* Translated by Alexander Cook. NY: Alfred A. Knopf, 1986.

———. *Mothers and Daughters.* Translated by Antonina W. Bouis. NY: Alfred A. Knopf, 1992.

———. "Red Army Redux," in *Wall Street Journal.* April 7, 1992.

Boudreau, Richard. "Soviet Dissident Sakharov's Widow Inaugurates Library," in *Los Angeles Times.* May 22, 1994.

Lee, Andrea. "The Adults Were Disappearing," in *The New York Times Book Review.* March 22, 1992.

Tokes, Rudolph L., ed. *Dissent in the USSR: Politics, Ideology, and People.* Baltimore, MD: The Johns Hopkins University Press, 1975.

SUGGESTED READING:

Bouis, Antonina W., and Jean-Claude. "An Evening with the Sakharovs," in *Life.* July 1989.

Goldberg, Paul. *The Final Act: The Dramatic, Revealing Story of the Moscow Helsinki Watch Group.* NY: William Morrow, 1988.

Rubinstein, Joshua. *Soviet Dissidents: Their Struggle for Human Rights.* 2nd ed., revised and expanded. Boston, MA: Beacon Press, 1985.

COLLECTIONS:

Diaries, letters, and secret police files located in Andrei Sakharov Library, Moscow; diaries located in Brandeis University Library, Waltham, Massachusetts.

RELATED MEDIA:

Sakharov (118 min), starring Jason Robards, Jr. and **Glenda Jackson**, directed by Jack Gold, produced by HBO, 1984.

Neil M. Heyman, Professor of History, San Diego State University, San Diego, California

Bonner, Katherine Sherwood (1849–1883).

See Bonner, Sherwood.

Bonner, Mary (1885–1935)

American artist noted for her etchings of the American West. *Born in Bastrop, Louisiana, in 1885; died in San Antonio, Texas, on June 26, 1935.*

Mary Bonner, who would gain international attention for her etchings of the American West, did not begin printmaking until 1922, at age 37. Originally interested in lithography, she was told the technique might be too strenuous, so she journeyed to Paris to study etching with Edouard Leon. Her first exhibition in Europe (1925) was enthusiastically received and won her the Palmes Academique from the French government.

Bonner was hailed as one of the most original interpreters of the American West. Her friezes, described by **Doris Dawdy** as characterized by borders of "rattlesnakes and bats, game roosters and horned frogs," were lauded as "the only absolutely new motif in design since the Italian Renaissance." Her work is displayed at the New York Public Library and the Luxembourg Museum. Several of her friezes were purchased by the French government; others were acquired by the British Museum.

SOURCES:

Dawdy, Doris Ostrander. *Artists of the American West.* Vol. II. Chicago, IL: Swallow Press, 1981.

Bonner, Sherwood (1849–1883)

American 19th-century writer of the "local color" school. *Name variations: Catherine or Katherine Bonner McDowell; (pen names) Clayton Vaughn, Katharine McDowell, Kate McDowell, Anonymous, A Citizen of Holly Springs, and Bohemian. Born Catherine Sherwood Bonner in Holly Springs, Mississippi, on February 26, 1849; died in Holly Springs on July 22, 1883; daughter of Charles (a planter and physician) and Mary (Wilson) Bonner; sister of* ***Ruth Maring Bonner*** *(b. 1851), Samuel Wilson (b. 1854), and* ***Anne Lea Bonner*** *(b. 1858); attended Holly Springs Female Institute; Hamner Hall, in Montgomery, Alabama; Select School for Young Ladies, Holly Springs, Mississippi; married Edward McDowell, on February 14, 1871 (divorced, c. 1881); children:* ***Lilian McDowell*** *(b. December 10, 1871).*

Selected writings: Like unto Like *(1878);* Dialect Tales *(1883);* Suwanee River Tales *(1884);* Gran'mammy: Little Classics of the South, Mississippi *(1927);* The Valcours *(a novella, 1881). Works also include pamphlets and countless periodical contributions.*

Sherwood Bonner's promising literary career, which spanned two decades following the Civil War, was cut short by her untimely death at the age of 34. She is remembered mainly for her short stories and especially for her realistic use of regional dialects and humor. A pioneer in the local-color movement, she is placed in that group of writers which includes George Washington Cable, Thomas Nelson Page, ***Mary Noailles Murfree**, and ***Kate Chopin**, and is important as a forerunner for Southern women writers, such as ***Flannery O'Connor** and ***Eudora Welty**.

Born into Mississippi aristocracy in 1849, Bonner's brief life was tinged with controversy. Her teenage years were marred by the Civil War and the personal losses of her younger sister and mother. At age 22, married and with a child, she shocked her family by abandoning her husband and infant daughter and moving to Boston in 1871 to pursue her dream of becoming a writer.

Bonner's first story had been published in 1864 by Nahum Capen, who helped her get settled in Boston. Capen may have also facilitated her meeting Henry Wadsworth Longfellow, who became a mentor and a friend, though there is evidence that Bonner made her initial contact with the poet through a letter. During a trip to Europe in 1876, she wrote a number of travel articles which were published in the Memphis *Avalanche* and the Boston *Times*. Her short stories also appeared in *Lippincott's*, *Harper's Weekly*, and *Youth's Companion*. Her only novel, *Like Unto Like*, was published in 1878.

Through her "Gran'Mammy" tales, particularly one called "Gran'Mammy's Last Gifts" (1875), considered by Hubert H. McAlexander "one of the strongest genre pieces that Sherwood Bonner was ever to write," she created a literary portrait of a black woman who was an integral part of her Southern white family and may have presented "the first example of black dialect published in a Northern magazine." Also among her regional fiction is a story about a farm girl called "On the Nine-Mile," the result of Bonner's 15-month stay in Illinois (the most productive period in her career), which is told in lower-class dialect. Both her novel *Like Unto Like* and a novella, *The Valcours*, are set in the Reconstruction period after the Civil War and provide insight into the South during this period of enormous social change.

After returning to Holly Springs in 1878 to nurse her father and brother during fatal illnesses with yellow fever, Bonner was struck with breast cancer in 1881 just as her career was gaining momentum. That same year, she divorced her husband but not before raising eyebrows over a liaison with Longfellow. By the time she saw a doctor for the painful lump in her breast, it was diagnosed as cancer in an advanced stage. Bonner continued to work, making a last trip to Boston before returning to Holly Springs, where she wrote until her death on July 22, 1883.

SOURCES:

Mainiero, Lina, ed. *American Women Writers: From Colonial Times to the Present*. NY: Frederick Ungar, 1981.

McAlexander, Hubert Horton. *The Prodigal Daughter: A Biography of Sherwood Bonner*. Baton Rouge, LA: Louisiana State University Press, 1981.

Barbara Morgan,
Melrose, Massachusetts

Bonnevie, Kristine (1872–1948)

Zoologist and first woman professor in Norway. *Born Kristine Elisabeth Heuch Bonnevie in Trondheim, Norway, in 1872; died in 1948; one of nine siblings; sister-in-law of feminist Margarete Bonnevie; awarded doctorate at the University of Oslo (1906); professor of zoology, University of Oslo (1912); director, Institute of Genetics (1916); pursued studies in Zürich, Würzburg, Naples and New York.*

Kristine Bonnevie's research into human genetics included the study of twins, as well as the development and genetics of finger prints. Her comparative research into animal and human malformations led to the adoption of the designation "Bonnevie-Ullrich syndrome" for a certain disease in humans. Known as an inspiring lecturer at both popular and academic levels, Bonnevie played a role in local and national politics as a Freethinking liberal. She took the initiative to establish student canteens and dormitories at the University of Oslo and was a supporter of the program for introducing civil confirmation ceremonies. She was awarded the Order of St. Olav in 1945. Her sister-in-law was the feminist ***Margarete Bonnevie.**

SOURCES:

Aschehoug & Gyldendal's *Store Norske Leksikon*. Oslo: Kunnskapsforlag, 1992.

Lie & Rørslett, eds. *Alma Maters døtre* (Alma Mater's Daughters). Oslo: Pax, 1995.

Elizabeth Rokkan, translator,
formerly Associate Professor, Department of English,
University of Bergen, Norway

Bonnevie, Margarete Ottilie (1884–1970)

Norwegian feminist, humanist, and reforming author. *Born Margarete Ottilie Skattebøl in Hallingdal, East Norway, in 1884; died on March 28, 1970; married Thomas Bonnevie (1879–1960), a judge and brother of Kristine Bonnevie.*

Margarete Ottilie Bonnevie was born in Hallingdal, East Norway, in 1884, to a father who was for a time a member of the Storting (Norwegian parliament). He did not consider that his daughter needed to prepare herself for a university education; fortunately, she was able to study for two years in Paris, and she became a qualified translator. She would finally sit for the university entrance examination and matriculate at the age of 58.

Her bent was for practical solutions to problems, and Bonnevie wrote many articles on literature, politics, and social science, which were published in the leading Oslo newspapers. After bringing up her children, she wrote half-a-dozen books on family policies, nursery schools, part-time work, and equal pay for women. These works included *Patriarkatets siste skanse* (The Last Bastion of Patriarchy, 1948) and *Fra mannssamfunn til menneskesamfunn* (From a Society for Men to a Society for People, 1955). For ten years, from 1936–46, she chaired Norsk Kvinnesaksforening (The Norwegian Association for Women's Rights), founded by ***Gina Krog,** working to keep alive the women's movement at a period when general interest had waned.

Margarete's husband Thomas Bonnevie (1879–1960), brother of ***Kristine Bonnevie,** was a judge who became involved in the public investigation and debate concerning the fall of Norway in 1940. He was also a strong supporter of the Vigeland Sculpture Park in Oslo.

At her death on March 28, 1970, Bonnevie left her books and papers to the University Library in Oslo, to be used by researchers from the newly established field of Women's Studies. As the author of the introduction to this archive wrote in 1977: "Much of the progress enjoyed by women in Norway during the past thirty to forty years has come about, directly and indirectly, thanks to her efforts." In a television interview taped when she was in her 80s, Bonnevie listed her basic values: "freedom and justice, truth, warmth and human sympathy."

SOURCES:

Aschehoug & Gyldendal's *Store Norske Leksikon.* Oslo: Kunnskapsforlaget, 1992.

Ringnes, Haagen, "Margarete Bonnevie," in *Tanker om tvil og tro* (Thoughts on Doubt and Belief). Oslo: Cappelen, 1969.

Støren, Thordis, "Margarete Bonnevie. En kvinneprofil" (Profile of a Woman). With bibliography. Universitetsbiblioteket i Oslo, 1977.

Elizabeth Rokkan, translator,
formerly Associate Professor, Department of English,
University of Bergen, Norway

Bonney, Anne (1700–?).

See joint entry under Read, Mary, and Anne Bonney.

Bonney, Linda (1949—)

Princess of Yugoslavia. *Born Linda Mary Bonney on June 22, 1949, in London, England; daughter of Holbrook Van Dyke Bonney and* ***Joan Evans;*** *became second wife of Tomislav Karadjordjevic of Yugoslavia, on October 16, 1982; children: Princess George (b. 1984); Prince Michael (b. 1985).*

Bonney, Mary Lucinda (1816–1900)

American educator who worked for Native American reform. *Born in Hamilton, New York, on June 8, 1816; died in Hamilton, New York, on July 24, 1900; graduated from Emma Willard's Troy Female Seminary, 1835; married Thomas Rambaut (a minister), in 1888 (died 1890).*

A teacher by profession, Mary Bonney held positions in schools around the country before she and a friend opened the Chestnut Street Female Seminary in Philadelphia, of which she served as principal for 38 years. (In 1883, the school was moved to Ogontz, Pennsylvania, and renamed the Ogontz School for Young Ladies.) Bonney was also active in the missions of her Baptist church, as well as the interdenominational Woman's Union Missionary Society of America for Heathen Lands.

In 1879, Bonney was outraged when she read that Congress proposed to abolish the treaties reserving lands in Indian Territory for certain tribes. Rallying her missionary circles, she mounted a petition campaign calling for the treaties to be honored. In 1880, a petition with 13,000 signatures was presented to President Rutherford B. Hayes and then to Congress. By January 1881, Bonney's group, now calling themselves the Central Indian Committee, submitted a second petition with 50,000 names to the Senate through Senator Henry L. Dawes. The group formally organized later that year as the Indian Treaty-Keeping and Protective Association (eventually the Women's National Indian Association), of which Bonney became president. They presented yet another petition to Senator Dawes, this time bearing 100,000 signatures and outlining a proposal drafted by ***Amelia S. Quinton** for the allotment of tribal lands to individual Native Americans.

In 1883, under Bonney's leadership, the organization devoted itself to missionary work among the Native Americans, offering training in English, religion, and domestic skills. Although Bonney retired from the presidency in 1884, she remained active in Native American reform. The efforts she initiated finally culminated in passage of the Dawes Severalty Act of February 1887, which embodied the allotment principle. Bonney married at the age of 72 and was widowed only two years later. She died in Hamilton, New York, at age 84.

Barbara Morgan,
Melrose, Massachusetts

Bonney, Thérèse (1894–1978)

American photographer and war correspondent. *Born Mabel Thérèse Bonney in Syracuse, New York,* *in 1894: died in Neuilly-sur-Seine, France, in 1978; daughter of Anthony and Addie Bonney; attended University of California; M.S. in romance languages from Harvard University; prepared for Ph.D. at Columbia University, but completed studies at Sorbonne, Paris, with honors.*

Thérèse Bonney originally planned a career as a college professor, but after completing her Ph.D. at the Sorbonne in Paris she set out instead to develop cultural relations between the United States and France. After living in Paris and writing for newspapers and periodicals in England, France, and the U.S., she founded the Bonney Service, the first American illustrated-press service in Europe. Reacting to what she regarded as the static quality of most news photography, her first effort, a behind-the-scenes series of photographs on the Vatican, was published in *Life* magazine in 1938. A year later, the series was published as the book *The Vatican*.

In 1939, Bonney's intended photographs of the Olympic games in Finland turned out to be documentation of the outbreak of the Russo-Finnish War. She returned to France in 1940, where she traveled with the Ninth Army to photograph the Battle of the Meuse and the Battle of Bordeaux. Her war photographs were shown at the Library of Congress in Washington, D.C., and at the Museum of Modern Art in New York City. They were also presented in a traveling exhibit which toured the U.S.

Bonnin, Gertrude Simmons
(1876–1938)

Important activist in early 20th-century Pan-Indian movements, writer of fiction and nonfiction, and the first indigenous woman to receive a Ph.D. *Name variations: Gertrude Simmons; "Zitkala Sa," "Zitkala-Sa," and "Red Bird." Born on February 22, 1876, at the Yankton Agency in Dakota Territory; died on January 26, 1938, in Washington, D.C.; daughter of Ellen Simmons (a Yankton Sioux woman) and a white man named Simmons; married Raymond T. Bonnin (a Yankton man), in 1902; children: Raymond O. Bonnin.*

During the late 19th century and first three decades of the 20th century, most American indigenous tribal people, particularly those in the American West, experienced massive cultural change. With military subjugation of the tribes complete by the turn of the century, civilian missionaries and federal government functionaries continued their relentless campaign to acculturate the tribal people along the lines of "white civilization." The results were, at best, mixed. A small faction of each tribe embraced the "White Man's Way" wholeheartedly, but most accepted the acculturation only partially or even attempted to resist it entirely. Torn between these competing images of the future, most tribal people endured the uncertain stages of accelerated cultural change.

Until recently, American historians have recorded how indigenous males, mostly the so-called "Patriot chiefs," responded to this alteration of worldview and paid scant attention to what indigenous women underwent. Women's historians have remedied this oversight with several key studies of the female side of the story. This new attention has brought to light the life and career of one of the most energetic and forthright woman leaders, Gertrude Simmons Bonnin. Known often by her Yankton Sioux name "Zitkala Sa," Bonnin led a full life as a Pan-Indian activist, writer, lobbyist, and spokesperson. Although she herself was a product of the Euroamerican schooling system, Bonnin resisted much of the assimilationist viewpoint and championed the worth and resiliency of tribal culture. Instrumental in the development of early 20th-century Pan-Indianism through the Society of American Indians and later the National Council of American Indians, Bonnin helped lay the groundwork for the burst of rejuvenated tribalism and militancy after World War II.

By the time Bonnin was born in 1876, her mother's people, the Yankton Sioux, had already given up most of their land, some 11 million acres, and were residing on a 40,000-acre reservation in southeastern Dakota Territory. **Ellen Simmons** watched her daughter grow up in a West that settlers were increasingly attempting to remold in their own image. After the defeat of Custer and his troops further West in that year, indigenous people quickly lost the military advantage. Land speculators and Office of Indian Affairs personnel joined the garrisons in pressuring the tribal peoples into assimilation. Bonnin's family felt the sting of this confrontation as well as the loss of family members to disease. Ellen Simmons, who had also banished her white husband for abusing their son David, taught her young daughter to distrust whites.

According to her later *American Indian Stories*, despite these conditions and the absence of her father, Bonnin had a happy, nearly idyllic childhood under her mother's upbringing. That changed in 1884, when she persuaded her mother to let Quaker missionaries send her to White's

Manual Labor Institute in Wabash, Indiana, where her brother had already spent three years. She was eight years old. Although the missionaries had enlivened her imagination with images of exhilarating cultural transformation, Bonnin encountered much humiliation and maltreatment. Typically, the institute attacked indigenous culture as worthless and sought to shock and shame its charges into rapid acceptance of Euroamerican lifestyle. But Bonnin resisted her teachers' ministrations, and, after three years of terrible homesickness, she returned to South Dakota. There she spent the next four years until she was 15 trying to retrieve her indigenous culture.

The appeal of white book-learning, however, proved irresistible for the Yankton teenager. She resumed her studies at White's Institute, received her diploma after three years, and then, in 1895, over her mother's wishes, enrolled at Earlham, a Quaker-affiliated college, in Richmond, Indiana. There Bonnin bloomed into a superb, contented student. She developed her talents for writing and oratory, as well as discovering multiple musical gifts with the piano, violin, and her voice. In February 1896, she won the college's oratory contest, and then placed second at the statewide contest in Indianapolis, the only female and person of color among the contestants. Her speech was an impassioned plea for whites to treat magnanimously the native peoples they had displaced. Other contestants, however, humiliated her by holding up a sheet with a crude drawing of an indian girl and the word "squaw" inscribed below. Although her own college mates cheered her accomplishment, Bonnin was not able to reconcile her yearning for achievement in the white academic world with her ties to her culture and her mother. She suffered a breakdown and spent six weeks recovering with a nearby family. Once back at college, she continued as a contributor to the school newspaper and an ephemeral student periodical, the *Anpao*. She was determined to retain her pride in her culture and to succeed in the white world. But continuing ailments, stomach complaints and weariness, deflected her plans, and, in 1899, Bonnin left Earlham before receiving a degree.

Uncomfortable with the prospect of heading home, Bonnin hired on as a teacher at the prominent Carlisle Indian School in Pennsylvania. Captain Richard Henry Pratt, the institute's founder and director, snapped up the acculturated Yankton woman immediately. She didn't enjoy the teaching especially, but at Carlisle she made many contacts and expanded her writing career. In January 1900, *The Atlantic Monthly* published her first article, "Impressions of an Indian Childhood," and followed with two more stories in the next two months. Her writings evinced an obvious pride in indigenous culture and her rise within the white world. Captain Pratt, however, who was worried about her attachment to her past, separated her from the Eastern literary circles and sent her West to recruit students for the school. While there, she visited her Yankton family, only to find her mother and brother impoverished and her tribe's limited lands under heavy pressure from land-hungry settlers. Although she went back to Carlisle, Bonnin was quite embittered about the hollow promises of assimilationist doctrine.

Gertrude Simmons Bonnin

Unable to fit back in at Carlisle, Bonnin resigned and headed to the New England Conservatory of Music in Boston in late 1900. There she had a productive and happy stay, playing music and writing more stories. But Captain Pratt wrote a stinging critique of her writings, calling their author a pagan. The wounded woman turned to a kindred spirit, Carlos Montezuma, with whom she had recently fallen in love. Montezuma, a Yavapai, had also taught at Carlisle, but, in 1896, he had left for private practice as a physician in Chicago. Somehow he and Bonnin met, and, by 1901, they were discussing marital plans. Despite their love, however, the twosome were unable to agree on the assimilationist philosophy. Their long letters ring with ideological conflict. That spring, she traveled back to the reservation alone, Montezuma having refused to go along. In August, she gave him back the engagement ring. Soon after that she met and married Raymond Bonnin, a man from her own tribe. The two had a son, also named Raymond, shortly after marriage, and her husband accepted a clerk position on the Uintah reservation in Utah in 1903.

Out among the Utes, Bonnin found a demoralized people bereft of any improvements from Euroamerican culture. Her husband took over his new job with great assiduousness, but until 1905 she could only find temporary voluntary employment, teaching music, basketweaving, and hygiene. In 1906, her mother died and a half-brother defrauded her and her brother out of their allotment. For the rest of the decade, the Bonnins languished at the Fort Duchesne agency in Utah. Downplaying her mixed blood heritage, Bonnin began to assert her indigenous identity even more strongly. At the same time, however, she commenced a lifelong connection with the Mormon church, perhaps because they, too, were targets of cultural persecution by others.

In October 1911, indigenous activists met in Columbus, Ohio, and organized what became the Society of American Indians. This aggressive group of highly educated indigenous leaders were dedicated to self-determination, reform of the federal bureaucracy, and increasingly to the concept of Pan-Indianism. Although some of their goals paralleled those of 19th-century "Friends of the Indians" organizations, the Society of American Indians insisted on indigenous membership and leadership. In 1913, the society held its annual convention in Denver. Bonnin expressed some interest in attending, but her husband decided against it. Over the past three or four years, she had rejuvenated her musical education in Salt Lake City and even re-established her friendship with Carlos Montezuma. Increased tension entered the Bonnins' marriage as Bonnin began to resent having to live with her husband in the desolate West so far from Eastern culture. "I seem to be in a spiritual unrest. I hate this eternal tug of war between being wild or becoming civilized," she wrote. She stayed with Raymond, but she made sure that their son went to a Benedictine boarding school in the East.

In 1914, Bonnin joined the advisory board of the Society of American Indians. Responding to the society's call for expanded community service on the reservations, she reinvigorated her classes for indigenous women on the Ute reservation. At the 1915 annual convention, the society applauded her community center model. Her urge to write returned, and her identification with indigenous culture deepened in her prose and poetry. Soon she was using her Sioux name exclusively again. In 1916, she enlarged her commitment to the Society of American Indians, accepting the role of secretary, a position that entailed a move to Washington, D.C. Bonnin leaped at the chance to return eastward and to be close to the seat of power. Sensing the depth of his wife's strong drive, Raymond Bonnin agreed to the relocation. Tired of rural living, she insisted on residing in the heart of the city. Even throughout Raymond's service as an army lieutenant during World War I, the Bonnins managed to earn enough to keep a respectable city address.

At the Society, Bonnin found males dominating the group, but, through her efforts, more young, energetic indigenous females joined. Most, however, kept their feminist goals separate from or subordinate to the Society's agenda. That was not so much the case with Bonnin. She redirected her writing to matters important to total tribal survival, such as water rights and land holdings. Moreover, she wrote about the efforts of strong female leaders in the past, such as ***Pocahontas** and the Utes' **Chipeta**. Within the organization, however, factions were rising, arguing with each other about the Bureau of Indian Affairs, peyote usage, and the Society's reform platform. Hardly a timid person, Bonnin soon found herself embroiled in these disputes.

Bonnin's old friend Carlos Montezuma was one of the first to dissociate from the Society and criticize those who romanticized the indigenous past at the expense of the present conditions. Guilty of some of this romanticization herself, Bonnin strove to moderate Montezuma's criticism and maintain his friendship. A more acrimonious antagonism arose with **Marie Baldwin**, a Turtle Mountain Chippewa, who was the Society's treasurer. Although both opposed peyote use and shared similar education levels, Bonnin and Baldwin differed in their appraisal of tribal heritage. For the Yankton woman, indigenous self-identity was still viable in the present; for the Chippewa, that identity was a relic of the past. The two also clashed over day-to-day operational matters at Society headquarters. Bonnin moved some of the functions to her own home to avoid what she considered meddling by Baldwin. By 1917, Baldwin departed from the Society, and Bonnin took on the duties of treasurer.

But perhaps the most pointed conflict came over the subject of peyote use. Although many indigenous leaders defended that usage as a traditional religious right, Bonnin linked up with many progressives to denounce the drug. When Congressional Representative Carl Hayden's peyote prohibition bill came up for a hearing in the Senate, she was a key witness on behalf of the measure. She incurred the opposition of ethnologist James Mooney, whose own research had attempted to dispel the image of the mescaloid as dangerous. Opponents tried to discredit Bonnin with false publicity statements, but she had the last laugh, when the committee reported the bill favorably and included her remarks and her essay, "Peyote Causes Race Suicide," in its report.

But, as often happens, one controversy phased into another. With the United States fully in World War I, the Society of American Indians canceled its 1917 meeting. Bonnin pressed to have the patriotism of indigenous peoples recognized. During the hiatus, however, *American Indian Magazine* editor-in-chief Arthur C. Parker tried to elevate the power of the editorial board to supplant the Society. Although the two leaders feared the peyote contingent, they were diverging on other issues such as abolition of the Bureau of Indian Affairs, which her friend Carlos Montezuma was espousing in his magazine, *Wassaja*. When Parker tried to postpone the conference again in 1918, Bonnin outmaneuvered him and managed to have the Society meet in South Dakota. Shortly thereafter, she ousted the Seneca from the editor-in-chief position and thus reached a place of high leadership in the organization. Within the year, however, Bonnin lost her influence and left the Society. She did edit the magazine effectively and contributed some of her own pieces that characteristically depicted the innate nobility of native peoples in romanticized manner. But politically she alienated many members with her anti-peyote stance, her strident calls for dismantling the Bureau of Indian Affairs, and her pro-Sioux loyalties that ostensibly ran counter to the Pan-Indian ideals of the organization, and she failed to use her position to bring more women aboard. Additionally, the Society's overall influence on federal Indian policy seemed to have been diminishing. For example, demands that President Woodrow Wilson allow an indigenous contingent to sit in on the Versailles peace-treaty negotiations backfired miserably. For Bonnin personally, the decade that represented her rise to prominence ended with departure from the Society.

Leaving the Society of American Indians did not constitute a retreat from reform for Bonnin. She shifted her efforts to other avenues. Worn out from the political battles and suffering from some probably psychosomatic symptoms, she still regrouped her energies. She thwarted her husband's suggestions to move back to South Dakota and instead launched into assembling her writings into a book. She had already published in 1901 one collection, *Old Indian Legends*, which she used to interest publishers in a second anthology. In 1921, her second book, *American Indian Stories*, appeared. Whereas, the first book had adopted an idealistic tone of shared cultural coexistence, the second chastised whites for undercutting those possibilities with assaults on the remaining indigenous land base and water resources. In terms of more concrete actions, Bonnin became involved in two allotment disputes on the Yankton reservation. From 1919 to 1921, she squared off with the Bureau of Indian Affairs which was holding hearings about "fictitious" allotments. She aided her brother David in protesting a fraudulent claim on behalf of one **Ellen Bluestone**. Although the Simmons-Bonnin faction lost this appeal, the protest served to reaffirm Bonnin's commitment to indigenous self-determination.

Fresh from that defeat, Bonnin looked to the General Federation of Women's Clubs for new allies. The Federation had become by the 1920s arguably the strongest woman's political force in the country, and many of its members and chapters had a history of supporting indigenous causes. Bonnin offered the Federation's Indian Welfare Committee her services as an investigator and a speaker. In 1922 and 1923, she toured the Midwest and the South, stumping for Indian citizenship. Her first investigative assignment took her to Oklahoma, where, since the turn of the century, mounting corruption had been depriving indigenous people of land and resource ownership. Together with Matthew Sniffen and Charles Faben, Bonnin published their report, "Oklahoma's Poor Rich Indians," in 1924, to dispel the image that the state's indigenous people were living luxuriously on oil profits. Bonnin concentrated on individual cases of poverty and fraudulence. The report caused Congress to open hearings in November 1924. Oil company attorneys and some unsympathetic members of congress succeeded in discrediting the report and censuring its authors. Bonnin stayed away from the hearings, suspicious of a whitewash or at best some half-measure of correction, which her strong empathy for the Oklahoma victims would not brook.

Disappointed with the Oklahoma hearings, Bonnin threw in her lot with John Collier's rising American Indian Defense Association. Collier, a New York lawyer and social worker, had come to Taos, New Mexico, in 1920 and become enchanted with indigenous lifestyle and philosophy, envisioning them as salvation for what he perceived as a bankrupt white culture. He dedicated himself to preserve tribal heritage and devoted his legal talents to defeating such measures as the Bursum Bill, which would have given much Pueblo lands to white squatters. Such courage endeared Collier to Bonnin, and The New Yorker provided her with a renewed berth in the reform movement as a member of the National Advisory Board of the American Indian Defense Association and a circle of performers and intellectuals she craved so strongly.

I am what I am. I owe no apologies to God or men.

—Gertrude Bonnin

By 1926, Bonnin found herself seeking a complete leadership role not just an advisory position. Two years earlier, Congress had passed the Indian Citizenship Act, and Bonnin thought that indigenous peoples should exercise their new power. But the Society of American Indians, to her way of thinking, was defunct. She still, however, embraced the principles of Pan-Indianism. The solution would be to form a new Pan-Indian group. Thus, in 1926, Bonnin started organizing the National Council of American Indians to capitalize on and mobilize what she expected would be an indigenous political power bloc. Her husband filled the secretary-treasurer slot, and the new association moved into the Bliss Building in Washington with the Bureau of Indian Affairs and Collier's group.

Although the National Congress of American Indians obtained John Collier's blessing, the organization had a rough time attracting a solid national following. Probably this was due to Bonnin's insistence on controlling the agenda. Too often the group appeared to be a one-person operation. But Bonnin did petition Congress about the historic grievances indigenous people shared, and her group aided in the defeat of two senators in South Dakota and Oklahoma by getting out the indigenous vote. Much of her efforts concentrated on land issues at the Yankton reservation and the prevention of mining at the sacred Pipestone quarries in Minnesota. The Simmons-Bonnin faction attracted plenty of internal criticism, but Bonnin stood firm. Still she sought a more national audience and arena. Through the organization's newsletter, she kept urging indigenous people to unite and safeguard their rights and heritage. In 1926, she and Raymond traveled around to reservations, over 10,000 miles of driving, and secured information and opinions to place before Congress the following year. At the Senate subcommittee, she testified about Bureau of Indian Affairs incompetence and substandard living conditions on the reservations, initiating a pattern of testimony she would repeat over the next few years.

The persistent infighting back at the Yankton reservation, however, drained off much of Bonnin's energy and entangled her in the very sort of factional intrigue she deplored. In the late 1920s and early 1930s, the Simmons-Bonnin faction lost a few key battles, but ironically they did pick up some support and protection from Commissioner of Indian Affairs C.J. Rhoads. This in turn lead to friction with John Collier. Angling for the Commissioner position in what he expected would be a Democratic administration after the upcoming elections, Collier courted Gertrude and Raymond Bonnin to support his denunciation of the Indian Bureau. But as the Bonnins had just reached a compromise with the Commissioner and the Bureau, they were hesitant to undo that newfound support. In a letter, they lectured Collier about stirring up trouble among indigenous people. Collier, who had perhaps taken the Bonnins for granted, was somewhat stung by this defection. He wrote back that the National Council of American Indians did "not own the Indians of the United States" and that if they did, it would be "a sad situation." Washington newspapers publicized the break. Collier, for his part, devoted most of his energy to securing the commissionership. Bonnin and her husband started making plans to counter Collier's increasing political influence.

John Collier did gain the appointment in the Franklin Roosevelt New Deal government, and together with Congress, he reversed 50 years of Indian policy with the passage of the Wheeler-Howard or Indian Reorganization Act in 1934. Among other measures, the act sought to restore and preserve indigenous peoples' heritage in the form of reconstituted tribes and protected religious and cultural freedom. Collier hailed the act as "Indian Independence Day," but Bonnin feared Collier would be as oppressive as the Bureau of Indian Affairs had been. She and the Bonnin faction geared up to control the process of implementation of the Wheeler-Howard Act on the Yankton reservation. By November 1935, when the administration's proposed tribal constitution came up for a vote, the Bonnins had convinced two out of three Yankton to turn it down. The Bonnins offered up their own version, a more radical one that would have given sizeable power to the tribal council, extended voting rights to all Yanktons (on the reservation or not), and granted membership to all Yankton children. Predictably, Collier did not accept their plan. Wrangling over a suitable compromise continued until 1938, when the commissioner gave up hope of reorganizing the Yankton Sioux. Bonnin won her final battle, although her recalcitrance probably hurt her tribe in this case, depriving it of some of the real advances and benefits of the "Indian New Deal." Collier's visionary policies were not totally coherent nor perfect, but they represented major improvements over the 50 years of ethnocentric blindness so central to the Dawes Act allotment doctrine from 1887 to 1934. But Bonnin allowed her personal opposition to Collier to cloud her understanding of the repercussions of rejecting the Wheeler-Howard act benefits.

On January 26, 1938, Gertrude Bonnin died unexpectedly at Georgetown Hospital in Washington, after a return trip from the Yankton reservation. Memorial services took place at a Mormon church in the northwest quarter of the capital city and burial followed at Arlington National Cemetery. The burial place was certainly appropriate, for although Bonnin maintained her tribal loyalties to the end, she had been a national spokesperson for indigenous rights for the last two decades of her life. Moreover, as one of the most acculturated indigenous women of her generation, she bridged indigenous and Euroamerican cultures more effectively than she herself realized. Although she often felt divided between the two cultures and frustrated in her marriage, Bonnin's life and career represented a composite triumph of spirit and integrity. Cultural and political indigenous militants in later decades would owe much to this proud Yankton Sioux woman who stood up staunchly against the Bureau of Indian Affairs and others who strove to remold native peoples in an image alien to tribal heritage.

SOURCES:

Bonnin, Gertrude. *American Indian Stories.* Glorieta, New Mexico: The Rio Grande Press, 1921.

———. *Old Indian Legends.* Boston, MA: Ginn, 1901.

Welch, Deborah. "Zitkala-Sa: An American Indian Leader, 1876–1938." Ph.D. dissertation, University of Wyoming, 1985.

SUGGESTED READING:

Dippie, Brian. *The Vanishing American: White Attitudes and U.S. Indian Policy.* Lawrence: University Press of Kansas, 1982.

Fisher, Dexter. "Zitkala Sa: The Evolution of a Writer," in *American Indian Quarterly.* Vol. 5. August 1979, pp. 229–238.

Hertzberg, Hazel. *The Search for American Indian Identity: Modern Pan-Indian Movements.* Syracuse, NY: Syracuse University Press, 1971.

Hoxie, Frederick E. *A Final Promise: The Campaign to Assimilate the Indians, 1880–1920.* Lincoln: University of Nebraska Press, 1984.

Iverson, Peter. *Carlos Montezuma and the Changing World of American Indians.* Albuquerque: University of New Mexico Press, 1982.

Johnson, David L. and Raymond Wilson. "Gertrude Simmons Bonnin, 1876–1938: 'Americanize the First Americans,'" in *American Indian Quarterly.* Vol. 12. Winter 1988, pp. 27–40.

Olson, James and Robert Wilson. *The Native American in the Twentieth Century.* Urbana: University of Illinois Press, 1984.

Philp, Kenneth. *John Collier's Crusade for Indian Reform, 1920–1954.* Tucson: University of Arizona Press, 1977.

Prucha, Francis Paul. *American Indian Policy in Crisis: Christian Reformers and the Indian, 1865–1900.* Norman: University of Oklahoma Press, 1976.

Thomas L. Altherr, Professor of History and American Studies at the Metropolitan State College of Denver, Denver, Colorado

Bonstelle, Jessie (1871–1932)

American actress and theater manager. *Born Laura Justine Bonesteele near Greece, New York, on November 18, 1871; died in Detroit, Michigan, on October 14, 1932; married Alexander H. Stuart (an actor), in April 1893.*

Dubbed "Maker of Stars" for her discovery and promotion of talented newcomers to the American theater, Jessie Bonstelle's lifetime in the theater was distinguished by her work as one of the first women theater managers in the country. She was the driving force behind one of the earliest community-based repertory theaters.

Little is known of Bonstelle's childhood. She was trained for the theater by her mother and toured California, around age 11 or 12, playing the deserted wife in the road company of *Bertha, the Beautiful Sewing Machine Girl*, instead of attending school. During a subsequent tour with a small Midwestern company, her name changed from Bonesteele to Bonstelle, either through a typesetting error or because the person preparing the theater marquee ran out of "e's." She continued to tour and in 1900 was asked by the Shubert brothers to organize a stock company for their newly acquired theater in Rochester. The success of that enterprise—in which Bonstelle acted, directed, and managed—led to positions managing stock companies in Buffalo and Detroit. These two companies were eventually merged into a single firm under the direction of Bonstelle, along with Edward D. Stair and Dr. Peter Cornell, the father of ***Katharine Cornell**. One of her great successes during this period was **Marian de Forest**'s dramatization of ***Louisa M. Alcott**'s *Little Women* (1912), featuring ***Alice Brady** in one of her earliest roles. In 1919, Bonstelle directed Katharine Cornell in the London premiere of the play.

Bonstelle's subsequent experiences directing the Municipal Theater in Northampton, Massachusetts (1912–17) and the Opera House in Providence, Rhode Island (1922–24) laid the groundwork for the development of a community-supported professional theater. In 1925, taking over Detroit's Playhouse, she used income from Broadway touring productions to finance special programs in drama and dance for children and adults in the community. By 1928, the theater had emerged as the Detroit Civic Theater. In operation until 1933, it became a model for dozens of civic repertory theaters around the country.

In addition to giving Alice Brady and Katharine Cornell their first exposure, Bonstelle is credited with discovering Jessie Royce Landis, Melvyn Douglas, ***Ann Harding**, William Powell, Ben Lyon, and Frank Morgan. She also employed stage designer **Jo Mielziner** and director Guthrie McClintic early in their careers.

Barbara Morgan,
Melrose, Massachusetts

Boop, Betty (1904–1966).

See Kane, Helen.

Booth, Agnes (1843–1910)

Australian-American actress. *Born Marian Agnes Land Rookes in Sydney, Australia, on October 4, 1843 (some sources cite 1846); died in 1910; married Harry Perry, in 1861 (died 1863); married Junius Brutus Booth, the younger (an actor), in 1867 (died 1883); married John B. Schoeffel (her manager), in 1885.*

Agnes Booth

Born in Sydney, Australia, Agnes Booth joined a dance troupe at 14 and arrived in San Francisco the following year. She would remain in America for the rest of her life. In 1867, she married her second husband Junius Brutus Booth, the younger (elder brother of Edwin and John Wilkes Booth), and joined Edwin Booth's theater company in New York where she played supporting roles to Edwin, as well as Edwin Forrest, E.A. Sothern, and Lawrence Barrett. In 1890, while with Palmer's Company, she played leads at Madison Square Theater in New York. Booth had a home in New York and a home in Manchester-by-the-Sea on the Massachusetts coast.

Booth, Catherine (1829–1890).

Victorian preacher and campaigner against social injustice who, with her husband William Booth, founded the Salvation Army. *Born Catherine (Kate) Mumford on January 17, 1829, in Ashbourne, Derbyshire, England; died on October 4, 1890, in Clacton-on-Sea, Essex; only daughter of John (a coachbuilder) and* ***Sarah (Milward) Mumford****; educated at home and at a private girls' school in Boston, Lincolnshire, 1841–43; married William Booth, on June 16, 1855; children: William Bramwell (b. March 8, 1856); Ballington (b. July 28, 1857); Catherine (b. September 18, 1858);* ❧ ***Emma Moss Booth-Tucker*** *(b. January 8, 1860); Herbert Henry (August 26, 1862); Marian Billups (May 4, 1864); Evangeline Cory Booth (1865–1950); Lucy Milward (April 28, 1867).*

Experienced conversion (June 15, 1846); expelled from Wesleyan Church (c. 1850); became Sunday school teacher in Methodist Reform Church (c. 1850); met William Booth (1851); published first pamphlet, Female Ministry *(January 1860); first spoke from pulpit, Whit Sunday (1860); began to conduct meetings independently (June 1864); settled in London (summer, 1865); passing of Criminal Law Amendment Act (1884); cancer diagnosed (1888).*

When Catherine Booth died in 1890, her body was placed in a coffin with a glass panel and visited by almost 40,000 mourners; 36,000 attended her funeral in London. Had there been room, the number would have swelled, for many had to be turned away from Olympia where the service took place. Since early in the 1860s, Catherine and William Booth had worked tirelessly for the organization which in 1877 became known as the Salvation Army. Affectionately called the "Mother of the Army," Booth helped form its precepts with many of her beliefs and convictions.

She was born Catherine Mumford on January 17, 1829, the only girl in a family of five children. Her earliest memory was of being taken by her mother to see the body of a brother who had just died; she was probably about two years old. Catherine's three elder brothers all died in infancy, and little seems to be known about the youngest child, John, who was born in 1833. Booth's granddaughter, **Catherine Bramwell-Booth**, thinks he went to boarding-school. At 16, he immigrated to America and possibly became an atheist, for shortly before her death Catherine ordered her daughter, ***Evangeline Booth**, "Write to Uncle John. . . . I have tried hard for his soul but he would not yield."

Booth was born into a Christian home. Years earlier, her mother Sarah Milward had been engaged to a man deemed eminently suitable by her family and friends. However, when, on the eve of her wedding, she discovered something about him which she *could* not condone (in keeping with Victorian reticence we are given no details), Sarah immediately broke off her engagement and steadfastly refused to marry him. Later, she met and married John Mumford. In this, she once again displayed her independence of spirit, since her father strongly opposed the match.

Sarah Mumford carried her strong views and religious principles into her marriage. Contrary to middle-class practice at the time, Catherine was not consigned to the care of a nurse or governess but was brought up by her mother and early imbued with her strict moral standards. Booth tells of how, at only four years of age, she was grief-stricken and unable to sleep because she had told a lie. Her mother dealt with the situation by praying with her for Jesus' forgiveness. By the age of five, Catherine was reading the Bible aloud and by the age of twelve had read it from beginning to end eight times.

For many years, Booth was not allowed to mix with other children for fear their lax moral standards might contaminate her. She was 12 before she attended school. Although denied childish companions, she was encouraged to participate in childish activities. She had a large family of dolls and, at times, was allowed to play by herself in the street in front of her house. One story tells of the time she was out bowling her hoop and saw a drunken man being taken to the police-station by a constable, followed by a jeering mob. Booth walked alongside the drunk because she pitied him in his isolation.

John Mumford was a coachbuilder and something of an innovator. He took an active interest in promoting the spread of tramcars as a form of public transport. He also designed and built perambulators, including, in later years, one for his grandchildren that could fold flat for easy transportation. After working hours, he was a Methodist preacher of some power. A strong advocate of temperance, he was also concerned with the politics of the day.

Booth was fond of her father. His interests were wider ranging than those of her mother, and from an early age Catherine was encouraged to discuss topics on equal terms with him and his friends. In 1833 or '34, the family moved to Mumford's home town of Boston in Lincolnshire. It was here that he became caught up in the new temperance movement; his daughter shared his convictions. By age seven, said Booth, she had "washed her hands of strong drink." She became secretary of the junior section of the local temperance society and secretly contributed anonymous articles on the subject to the various magazines to which her father subscribed. She was also a keen attender of missionary meetings—empathizing particularly with black Africans.

As business stresses mounted, John Mumford turned away from religion and, at least for a time, became a heavy drinker. It seems he also had a hasty temper; when his daughter was 12, he had her pet dog shot. Her deep affection for her father made his action all the harder to bear. Years later, she recalled:

> We had a beautiful retriever, named Waterford, which was very much attached to me. It used to lie for hours on the rug outside my door; and if it heard me praying or weeping, it would whine and scratch to be let in, that it might in some way manifest its sympathy and comfort me. Wherever I went the dog would follow me about as my self-constituted protector—in fact, we were inseparable companions. One day, Waterford had accompanied me on a message to my father's house of business. I closed the door, leaving the dog outside, when I happened to strike my foot against something, and cried out with sudden pain. Waterford heard me, and without a moment's hesitation came crashing through the large glass window to my rescue. My father was so vexed at the damage done that he caused the dog to be immediately shot.

Mumford's action may be easier to understand if placed within the context of the period. Kindness to animals was an attitude which was

Booth-Tucker, Emma Moss (1860–1903)

American missionary. *Born Emma Moss Booth in Gateshead, England, on January 8, 1860; died near Dean Lake, Missouri, in 1903; daughter of William and* ****Catherine Booth*** *(1829–1890); married Frederick Booth-Tucker (who also worked for the Salvation Army).*

Emma Moss Booth-Tucker, consul for the Salvation Army, worked in India before working in America from 1896–1903.

Catherine Booth

only just developing. The Royal Society for the Prevention of Cruelty to Animals (RSPCA) was started in 1824, the first of its kind in the world, but it had little effect on the country at large. ***Anna Sewell**'s *Black Beauty* would not be published until 1877, and ***Frances Power Cobbe** would wage a war against vivisection for the last three decades of the 19th century, a battle still far from won.

Catherine Booth was ahead of her time in her extreme sensitivity to the suffering of animals. As a child, she would weep inconsolably at the sight of sheep being goaded as they were driven along the street. In later years, she would remonstrate with donkey-boys at the seaside, leavening her lectures with small gifts of money. She would secretly feed corn to overworked and underfed horses turned out to graze, and on one occasion she almost lost her life by jumping out of a moving carriage in order to prevent a boy from causing further injury to a donkey he was hitting with a heavy-headed hammer.

Perhaps it is not surprising, then, that Booth was never able to feel quite the same about her father after the death of Waterford. For a long time after, she was tortured with mental anguish. Though Catherine did not speak of it, her mother noticed how wan and withdrawn she had become. Biographer Bramwell-Booth speculates that Catherine went through a period of doubting the existence of God. Sarah Mumford decided to send her to a carefully chosen school: the principal was a Chapel friend for whom Sarah had a high regard, and there were reports of some of the girls having had conversion experiences while there.

Though she only attended school for two years, Booth seems to have been an eager student. She particularly enjoyed history and geography but had trouble with arithmetic which, in later years, she said was taught in a "senseless way." She enjoyed mixing with the other girls but found their teasing hard to bear. It seems she had inherited her father's hasty temper. When accused of being "teacher's pet," she would fly into a rage which she afterwards regretted. Perhaps the other pupils' teasing had some justification, for she was incapable of telling a lie and would therefore be called upon by members of staff for the "facts" when any of her classmates were in trouble. By 14, incipient curvature of the spine caused Catherine to leave.

Little was known in Victorian times about the importance of healthy diet, exercise, and fresh air, and many girls embarked upon a life of semi-invalidism for lack of these necessaries. Curvature of the spine was usually treated by strapping a heavy wooden board to the patients back and by many months (even years) of rest—much of it in a recumbent position. Booth spent her period of forced inactivity studying books of theology and church history. She suffered from ill-health throughout her life and came to be a great believer in homeopathic medicine and hydropathy.

In 1844, the Mumfords moved to Brixton, a district of London. Though Booth had always had a fervent awareness of God and attended the Methodist Church with her mother, she had not become a member because she did not consider herself personally converted. So at 16 or 17, she began to consciously strive for a dramatic religious experience. After a period of agonizing and intensive prayer, she felt the assurance of personal salvation that she had been seeking. On the morning of June 15, 1846, she read in her hymn book:

> My God, I am Thine,
> What a comfort divine,
> What a blessing to know that my Jesus is mine.

"The words came to my inmost soul with a force and illumination they had never before possessed," she wrote. "I no longer hoped that I was saved; I was certain of it."

Booth became a member of the Wesleyan Methodist Church in Brixton and joined a Bible class where she was encouraged to pray aloud, something she found initially stressful. By the autumn of 1846, she was ill again—this time with inflammation of the lungs. In May 1847, she paid an extended visit to relations in Brighton in the hope that the sea air would counteract the very real threat of tuberculosis. While there, she kept a diary. In later years, she maintained that it was the only time she was not too enveloped in events to record them.

By the time she returned home, quarrels within the Methodist Church were culminating in a Reform Movement. Members of orthodox Wesleyan Chapels suspected of sympathizing with the Reformers had their tickets of membership withheld, effectively expelling them from the church. One such member was Catherine Booth. Joining Binfield House, a chapel newly opened by the Reformers, she soon became a teacher of the senior girls' class in the Sunday school. Booth was a conscientious leader, preparing her lessons with care and holding lengthy prayer meetings after the rest of the school had dispersed.

It was here that she met the man who was to become her husband and cofounder of the Salvation Army—William Booth. Born in Nottingham, William early became an apprentice pawnbroker on the death of his father. Though brought up in the Church of England, he wandered into a Wesleyan Chapel some time before his 15th birthday, liked what he saw, continued to attend, experienced conversion, and became a member. In 1849, William moved to London, and, in June 1851, joined the Reformers. Catherine, who first met him when he preached at Binfield House, considered his sermon, "One of the best I have heard in this Chapel." They met again at the home of Mr. Rabbits, a wealthy chapel member. After William had been prevailed upon to recite a popular American temperance monologue titled "The Grog-seller's Dream," Catherine championed the cause of total abstinence against some of the less-convinced guests.

It was not unusual at this time for non-Conformist ministers to have their salaries provided by wealthy believers. By April 1852, William had left pawnbroking and was pastor at Binfield House, his salary being paid by Mr. Rabbits. On April 10, William and Catherine separately attended a service in Cowper Street. Catherine was taken ill, and William was asked to escort her home. "Before we reached my home," wrote Catherine, "we both . . . felt as though we had been made for each other." A month later, they were engaged.

She was GOOD . . . she was LOVE . . . she was a WARRIOR.

—William Booth

Between April 1852 and June 1855, many love letters passed between them. Incorporated with her desire that she and William should only act as God directed, Catherine had some decided views about how her fiancé's career should progress. She exhorted him to study and tried to devise ways in which he could fit it into a life already packed with ministering and evangelizing. William became pastor of a Reform Chapel in Spalding, Lincolnshire, but by the beginning of 1854 he had offered himself for ordination with the Methodist New Connexion which Catherine felt combined the best from both the Reformers and the Wesleyans: enthusiasm for salvation linked with a well-structured organization. He merged his duties as assistant pastor in a large London Circuit with highly successful evangelizing trips around the country. On June 16, 1855, the couple were married quietly—with only her father, her aunt, the caretaker, and the presiding minister present.

After a week's honeymoon on the Isle of Wight, the couple moved to the Channel Islands where William was due to lead revival meetings. For the next few years, they traveled about England incessantly though Catherine was frequently ill and frequently pregnant. Their stay in Halifax, Yorkshire, was extended to allow for the birth of William Bramwell on March 8, 1856, and thereafter the baby and his nurse journeyed with them. When the boy was nearly a year old, Sarah offered to look after him, but Catherine preferred to take charge of his upbringing herself. In a letter dated May 15, 1857, Booth wrote: "I know, my darling mother, you could not wage war with his self-will so resolutely as to subdue it. And then my child would be ruined, for he must be taught implicit, uncompromising obedience." Later, however, as both her family and her preaching commitments grew, Catherine relaxed her early scruples, and her children spent time with their grandparents and at home with the servants in her absence.

From 1857 until 1860, the Booths were settled in a Circuit, first at Brighouse where Catherine took an adult Bible class and gave temperance addresses to young people, then at Gateshead. By January 1860, the family had increased to four children and three or four servants, including the nurse. A few weeks before the birth of her fourth child, Booth wrote a pamphlet urging the rights of women to preach. Called *Female Ministry*, it was written in reply to one published by a Reverend Arthur Rees attacking women preachers. It is still used as the basis for Salvation Army teaching on the subject as, for its period, it shows a highly enlightened attitude towards the abilities of women.

It was not until Whitsunday, 1860, however, that Booth exercised the right she had championed. One morning, at a large outdoor meeting led by her husband, Catherine felt moved to give testimony when members of the congregation were invited to speak about their experiences of God. That evening, she gave her first sermon. Her text was "Be ye filled with the Spirit." From then on, she was a sought after preacher, and when William became ill she substituted for him as Circuit superintendent until he was well again.

By Easter 1861, both of the Booths were conducting services in Hartlepool. William returned home, but Catherine remained without the children. Nevertheless, she labored hard to combine her public and private lives. When the children had whooping cough, she supervised the water bandages on their chests and the soaking of their feet in hot water and mustard. She complained to her mother that she found it impossible to find time for both preparing her addresses and making her children's clothes.

When the Methodist Conference once again refused William's request to be a full-time evangelist, he left the New Connexion, with Catherine's complete approval, though it meant that the family had no obvious means of support. Indeed, from this time on, the Booths received their income entirely from collections, donations from wealthy patrons, and their writings. Though forced to live economically, they never seemed to experience poverty. They briefly stayed with Catherine's parents, until they were invited to hold Revivalist meetings in Cornwall where they remained for 18 months. During this time, Catherine began to hold meetings for women only and her fifth child was born.

In February 1863, the Booths moved to Wales. Here they embarked upon an innovation which was to become a commonplace—they hired a secular building in which to hold their meetings. In his book, *The Life of Catherine Booth*, Frederick de Lautour Booth-Tucker explained the advantages of this practice:

> By this course they secured, in the first place, the largest buildings in the town, and could thus reach a greater number of people. Again they were unembarrassed by denominational differences, and were on common ground where all Christians could unite. Finally, they could secure the attendance of the non-church-going masses, toward whom their hearts were increasingly drawn out.

It was in Wales that Catherine met **Mrs. Billups** who was to remain her lifelong friend and correspondent. Their letters afford biographers much insight into Catherine's activities over a number of years.

Until June 1864, the Booths conducted their revivalist meetings jointly, but as soon as Catherine resumed public life, five weeks after the birth of her sixth child, she began to work independently. In February 1865, she came to London, and it was quickly decided that the whole family should settle there. Soon William was working with the poor of the East End, while Catherine worked with the rich of the West End. The money collected from one helped to support the other. Catherine journeyed to holiday resorts with the intention of attracting people who, when at home, would not leave their customary place of worship to hear her. It was while she was traveling between London and various holiday places that her mother became incurably ill. The Mumfords moved to a house near the Booth's London home, where Sarah Mumford would die on December 16, 1869.

By the end of April 1867, William and Catherine had eight children who were all dedicated to God at their births and rigorously trained to follow in their parents' footsteps. They were taught almost entirely at home by governesses as Catherine had a mistrust of schools even deeper than her mother's. She had cause: when Bramwell won a place to the City of London School, some of the boys held his arms and legs and bashed him against a tree "to bang Salvation out of him." Otherwise, it seems that the Booth household was a happy, lively place. There was always plenty of conversation, singing, and laughter. William and Catherine's *Training of Children*, published to give guidance to Salvation Army parents, was based upon their own practices and contains much common sense in an era when many children were treated severely or even cruelly. Nevertheless, Booth could exert what, in a later climate, seems an excessive amount of pressure on her children in order to achieve what she wanted. For example, at the age of seven, Bramwell was urged by his mother to "declare for Christ." When he refused, she made no attempt to hide her bitter disappointment. In later years, Bramwell said, "I can never forget my feelings on seeing the tears fall" through her hands; three months after, he did as she wished. It was the same when he was older. Once, evidently considering becoming a doctor, Bramwell told his mother he found preaching a "burden physical, mental and spiritual." Catherine refused to take any of his misgivings seriously, bombarding him with letters and prayers until eventually he engrossed himself wholeheartedly in the Salvation Army.

It was in 1865 that Booth came in contact with the Midnight Movement, a Christian organization working with prostitutes. In the 1880s, she once again came face to face with prostitution. What horrified her most was the number of children caught up in the trade. Legally the age of consent was only 13, but many girls much younger than this could be found in English brothels and were sold by their parents to be taken to brothels abroad. A small Salvation Army home was set up for girls who wished to leave prostitution, while Bramwell headed a fact-finding mission. The help of ***Josephine Butler**, the well-known campaigner on behalf of exploited women was acquired. When Parliament failed to act, W.T. Stead was persuaded to publish an exposé in his *Pall Mall Gazette*. Booth inaugurated what came to be known as the Purity Crusade: she held meetings and wrote letters to influential people, including the prime minister and Queen ***Victoria.** In only 17 days, between 343,000 and 393,000 signatures were collected on a Petition to the House of Commons. In August 1885, the Criminal Law Amendment Act was passed, raising the age of consent to 16 and giving greater protection to women generally.

At first, the evangelical work in London was run on democratic lines, but, by 1877, it was becoming more autocratic with William as its commander in chief. A few months into the year, a bill advertised it as the "Hallelujah Army." By Christmas, notepaper was headed "The Christian Mission or The Salvation Army." When "The Salvation Army" was first painted at the back of the platform in the Whitechapel Hall, where much of the East End preaching took place, some of the older members disapproved, but soon militaristic terms were introduced to distinguish the varying ranks of the evangelists. By 1878, Catherine was designing a uniform. Before her death, the Salvation Army would spread throughout America, Australia, Europe, India, Canada, Iceland, Argentina, and parts of South Africa.

Throughout her life, Catherine Booth suffered a series of serious illnesses, and she often worked until she was in a state of nervous and physical exhaustion. During 1866 and 1867, she was continually ill with dysentery. From 1873 on, she was the victim of angina, but her death on October 4, 1890, was caused by breast cancer, first diagnosed in 1888. Advised to have an operation, she had refused, though she underwent painful electrical treatment in May 1889. During her illness, William was occupied in setting up Salvation Army night shelters, and their derivative social work. Much of his book, *In Darkest England and the Way Out*, was written in consultation with Catherine as she lay ill. The last months of her life were spent at a rest home for staff officers at Clacton-on-Sea, Essex. By then, she was so revered that a short-hand typist was hidden behind a screen to secretly record what she said.

SOURCES AND SUGGESTED READING:

Booth-Tucker, F., de L. *The Life of Catherine Booth*. London: The Salvation Army, 1893.

Bramwell-Booth, Catherine. *Catherine Booth: The Story of her Loves*. London: Hodder and Stoughton, 1970.

Chappell, Jennie. "Catherine Booth," in *Four Noble Women and their Work*. London: S.W. Partridge.

Barbara Evans, Research Associate in Women's Studies at Nene College, Northampton, England

Booth, Elizabeth.

See Witchcraft Trials in Salem Village.

Booth, Eva Gore (1870–1926).

See Gore-Booth, Eva.

Booth, Evangeline (1865–1950)

Fourth general of the Salvation Army, daughter of its founder, who was noted for her eloquence. *Name variations: known as Eva (1865–1904), then Evangeline (1904–50). Born Eveline Cory Booth on December 25, 1865, in the East End borough of Hackney, England; died in Westchester County, New York, on July 17, 1950; daughter of William and Catherine Booth (founders of the Salvation Army); seventh of eight children, all of whom were involved in Salvation Army work; never married, no children.*

Preached from the age of 15; appointed field commissioner of the Salvation Army (1885–94); made envoy to America (1896); served as head of the Salvation Army in Canada (1896–1904); was head of the Salvation Army in U.S. (1904–34); appointed general of the Salvation Army (1934–39); retired (1939).

Evangeline Booth was a larger than life evangelist and organizer who directed the religious and social work of the American Salvation Army for the first three decades of the 20th century. Suspected at first of being an intrusive agent of British dominance, she soon quieted American Salvationists' fears and became the embodiment of the organization, rising at the age of 69 to world leadership.

Her father William Booth was an English Methodist minister who turned to preaching among the poorest and most degraded population of London. Her mother ***Catherine Booth** was also a charismatic preacher of a more intellectual bent who preached in London's wealthier West End until late in each of her eight pregnancies. Eva, seventh of the eight, was born on Christmas Day of 1865 in the East End borough of Hackney and grew up in a lively, religiously supercharged household. She made her public debut at the age of seven, singing in a strong clear voice to follow one of her father's fiery sermons. She always had a histrionic streak and thrived on public attention. In 1878, when she was 13, her parents renamed their East End mission the Salvation Army. They adopted dark blue uniforms with red trimmings for men and plain dresses with poke bonnets for women, promoted brass band music and a semi-military approach to evangelical revivals, and published a newspaper titled *The War Cry*, all aimed at catching the attention and imagination of poor Londoners. From 1880, William Booth's assistant George Railton, with seven female volunteers, carried the Salvation Army's message to America, and it was soon thriving in both countries. Recruits enjoyed the music, the close family atmosphere, even the sentimental rhetoric in which women were "lassies" and to die was to be "promoted to glory."

As a teenager, Evangeline Booth's first regular work for the Army was selling *The War Cry*; at age 17, she also began preaching. She went to live in the Seven Dials district of the East End and, with a group of other volunteers, spread the gospel, visited sick and poor at home, and gradually converted local residents from an attitude of suspicion to one of gratitude. She preached with particular ardor against prostitution, "white slavery," and the liquor trade, which worsened the degradation of poor workers. At times, disguised as a match-seller or flower-girl, she lived the life of the people she aimed to help and made frequent visits to prisons to read scripture with penitent inmates. At the Salvation Army's Great Western Hall in Marylebone, she preached almost every night, sermons in which brimstone, arm-waving, and sentimentality jostled together, attracting larger audiences as word of her spellbinding oratory spread.

When her preaching and exhortation began to harm the liquor trade, publicans and brewers retaliated by using hired thugs, the "Skeleton Army," to break up her meetings and, they hoped, intimidate her into silence. Undeterred, she persuaded former gang leaders whom she had converted to act as her bodyguards. The 1880s witnessed a series of pitched battles between Salvationists and Skeleton Army soldiers, with the police often declining to intervene. Hurt in some of these attacks, overworked, and constantly moving among diseased people, she became violently ill in 1887, at age 22, and nearly died of scarlet fever. Recovering, she discovered that most of her auburn hair had fallen out. For the rest of her life, she was obliged to wear a wig. Like many notable women of her era, Booth fought a lifelong battle against disabling infirmities and refused to let them slow her down.

William Booth recognized that Eva, his favorite child, was also one of his most gifted. He promoted her to the rank of field general and in the following decade sent her to sort out controversies occasioned by the Salvation Army's unconventional methods. The seaside town of Torquay, for example, passed an ordinance against band music on Sundays; when the Salvation Army's band played anyway, its members were taken to jail. Evangeline went to Torquay and made a series of speeches on behalf of the imprisoned band members while organizing a relief fund for their families. Risking imprisonment, she led more musical parades (she played the harp, banjo, and accordion at Army meetings) and later gave testimony to Parliament which upheld the band's right to perform on Sunday. In 1892, William promoted her again to principal of the Army's International Training Home in Clapton, which prepared volunteers for service in the rapidly growing overseas missions. A master of the Army's military idiom, she declared in one farewell speech to graduates of the Home: "Be an enemy—a fighting enemy of the world, the flesh, and the devil. Be an aggressor; carry the war into the enemy' camp. Be a fighter, a soldier, a man or woman who has the fire of war against sin in blood and bone."

In 1896, Eva went to America to negotiate with her brother Ballington Booth and his wife ***Maud Ballington Booth** who had seceded from the Army and renamed their followers the Volunteers of America rather than follow Father

Evangeline Booth

William's command to return to England. There were already tensions between William and Ballington over the degree of independence from English headquarters the American branch could enjoy. Much of the American press saw the dispute as evidence that Britain, at least a corner of it, still had imperial designs on America, especially as the incident coincided with a foreign policy crisis which caused Anglo-American conflict. Evangeline, labeled a "minion of British despotism" by the local press when she arrived to arbitrate, tried to soothe ruffled feathers all round. Her first public speech in New York's Cooper Union on March 1, 1896, began with angry heckling and hissing from the audience, but by seizing and waving an American flag she silenced and then won round the crowd. She was able in the following months to retain the loyalty of nearly all the American Salvationists, many of whom had threatened to follow Ballington into the Volunteers, and then handed over American leadership to her sister **Emma** and her brother-in-law Frederick Booth-Tucker.

Booth-Tucker, Emma Moss. *See Booth, Catherine for sidebar.*

Eva went next to Canada where she succeeded another brother, Herbert, as national director of the Salvation Army. Two years after her arrival, the Yukon gold rush brought an influx of gold seekers to Canada. She made three visits to the gold country and sent a group of Army evangelists into the lawless camps to rescue them from the clutches of prostitutes and saloon keepers. In 1904, after eight years in Canada, she became commander in the United States where she changed her name to Evangeline and settled in to consolidate the work of her sibling-predecessors. One Salvationist historian, Edward McKinley, gave a harsh, possibly biased, view of her qualities as she arrived for the job:

> Raised as a kind of junior princess in her father's hectic household court, she was allowed—even encouraged—to abandon herself to her strong inherited dramatic impulses. The young woman was placed in positions over thousands, in which she was responsible to no one save God and her father (who usually left her to the Former). Thus it is natural that at age thirty nine Evangeline was imperious and condescending. She was also vain of her appearance, which in fact was pleasantly unexceptional, impetuous, given to emotional flourishes, and something of a poseur.

McKinley is careful to add that she was an exceptionally talented administrator, speaker, and fund raiser. Quickly becoming involved in American politics, she campaigned for prohibition and for women's suffrage, without letting these issues distract her from her primarily religious mission. She set up hostels for homeless people, low-cost workingmen's hotels, soup kitchens to feed the hungry, kindergartens, homes where unmarried mothers could give birth, and an anti-suicide bureau to counsel the despairing. Two years after her arrival, the San Francisco Earthquake caused a housing and food emergency. With her chief assistant George, she organized rapid relief efforts to complement those of other volunteer and government agencies. The Salvation Army provided beds and food for 30,000 refugees, and Evangeline spent two weeks at work in the ruins of the California city, culminating in a mass rally at Golden Gate Park.

William Booth, her father, visited America twice in 1907, once en route to Japan but the second time for a long preaching tour. With him, Evangeline went for dinner at the White House at the invitation of President Theodore Roosevelt. The Army's Founder also opened a session of the Senate with a prayer, but his daughter took most of the important initiatives of the era. She established an annual event, "The Siege," a month dedicated to particularly vigorous work, as the *War Cry* explained, "to destroy every kind of evil work resulting from sin, such as drink, blasphemy, hatred, half-heartedness, shame, hypocrisy, cant, lukewarmness, jealousy, cowardice, fashion, pride, conceit, lies, and other enemies of God and man." The Army's volunteers concentrated on prisons and saloons trying to preach the gospel to the most recalcitrant population. Thanksgiving Day 1909 was also the first national "Boozers' Day," on which volunteers gathered as many drunks as they could find, attracting them with the promise of free food and a parade, whose central feature was a man chained to a ten-foot-high whiskey bottle made of papier maché. Reformed alcoholics preached to the crowd, and Salvation Army workers tried to keep in touch with those inspired to take the pledge.

The Salvation Army was in an anomalous position among American religious groups in the early years of the 20th century, most of which favored either a "social gospel" of aid to the poor and needy, or a strict concentration on gospel preaching. The Salvation Army aimed to do both—it was theologically fundamentalist but at the same time socially oriented. Evangeline Booth would never have said, as did such liberal Protestant contemporaries as Walter Rauschenbusch and Washington Gladden, that the road to salvation lay *through* social progress. For her, the supernatural was paramount and good works merely an instrument to help lead needy people to conversion and the promise of eternal life.

Evangeline's father died in 1912. Two years later, at an international Salvation Army Conference in London, she led the American delegation, riding a horse and wearing a cowboy hat instead of her regulation uniform. The First World War began a few months later, and she at once launched an "Old Linen" campaign, gathering fabric to be sterilized and shipped to Britain for bandages. When America joined the Allied war effort in April 1917, she reminded American Salvationists that their task was to care for suffering people on both sides of the battle-lines and that "there is only one war in which we can glory—that supreme struggle to triumph over sin and strife and death, with purity, peace, and life everlasting." During the war, the American Salvationists operated next to army camps at home and in France, where their freshly baked doughnuts became a symbol of Salvation Army work and an immense source of good will. For the Army's aid to the war effort, President Woodrow Wilson presented her with the Distinguished Service Medal in 1919.

In the postwar years, Booth was gratified by passage of Constitutional amendments which inaugurated Prohibition and votes for women but disappointed by the results of both. Alcoholism did not disappear, and the new legal situation facilitated the rise of organized crime. But Booth thought the price worth paying and believed that drunkenness among the poor was becoming rarer. She twice gave testimony to congressional committees in support of preserving the amendment and refused to accept contributions from sympathizers who opposed Prohibition (George Bernard Shaw had raised the question of the Salvation Army accepting "tainted" money in his 1905 play *Major Barbara*). In 1919, for the first time, she tried to shift the Salvation Army's financing from *ad hoc* local collections to a nationwide coordinated campaign. The Army's good wartime publicity ensured the success of the campaign which soon raised $16 million, three million dollars more than her target figure. The Salvation Army was now a permanent fixture on the American religious landscape, and from its small beginnings it had become a major property-owner. Its rate of growth, however, had slowed.

Prohibition dogged the Salvation Army during the 1920s. The presidential election of 1928 pitted "dry" Republican Herbert Hoover against "wet" Democrat Al Smith, and Evangeline Booth's support of Prohibition was so vocal that she appeared to be endorsing the Republicans, though she swore that it was, for her, a moral issue. Even when Prohibition was abandoned at the start of the New Deal, she remained adamant, declaring: "Long before Prohibition the Salvation Army was the greatest temperance organization in this country and will continue its unalterable opposition to intoxicating liquors." Throughout the 1920s and early 1930s, Evangeline was still eager to appear on stage dressed in rags as a poor Cockney girl with an accordion, playing her former self as "White Angel of the Slums" before turning to the day's preaching.

In elite circles she *was* the Salvation Army.

—Sallie Chesham

The Wall Street Crash of 1929 coincided with a momentous change in the governance of the Salvation Army. Begun by her parents when she was only ten, it was now a worldwide organization and needed a new administrative structure. Imbued with democratic principles from her 30 years' work in North America, Evangeline argued at the High Council of 1929 for a democratic rather than autocratic system of government. She had been at loggerheads with her brother Bramwell, the current general, on this issue since 1920, when he had tried to dislodge her from permanent leadership of the American branch. Like her brother Ballington in the 1896 crisis, she had no wish to leave and pressure from her American supporters led Bramwell to relent. Strong willed, sometimes insecure and self-centered, like nearly all the Booths, she knew how to use her popularity as a weapon to get her way. At the 1929 meeting, she was part of a large majority which favored deposing Bramwell and moving to a democratic method of electing leaders. The reform prevented the Salvation Army from becoming a hereditary monarchy of Booths.

Evangeline was 65 in 1930 when the Salvation Army celebrated its 50th year of work in America. John Philip Sousa, the composer, wrote a "Salvation Army March" for the Army's massed bands and conducted them in the Jubilee parade. Evangeline rode down crowded New York streets in an open car and made a speech in Carnegie Hall on "Women Who Have Made History," then dedicated a new national headquarters building at West 14th Street. "To the American public Evangeline Booth personified the Salvation Army, and as its head she received the tributes paid to the Army," wrote Salvationist historian Herbert Wisbey. "Presidents Theodore Roosevelt, Taft, Wilson, Harding, Coolidge, Hoover, and Franklin Roosevelt each received her and endorsed the work of the Salvation Army."

The worsening Great Depression brought out the best qualities in the Salvation Army once again, and, through the long years of the 1930s, it gave away hundreds of thousands of free meals to the destitute and places to stay for the homeless. In the middle of the crisis, Booth was elected general of the Salvation Army, following the retirement of Bramwell's successor, Edward Higgins. Now 69, she was an internationally famous figure, and on her return to the United States from the High Council of 1934 was given an official welcome by the mayor of New York and a ticker-tape parade.

In England, Evangeline's generalship received mixed reviews. Some of the English Salvationists disliked her showy side; the huge Cadillac she had brought from America which could scarcely fit on London's narrow streets, her American staff, which had become a substitute family, and her liking for dramatic gestures during public preaching events. But as one biographer says, she was popular because she had inherited her father's magnetism. "Upon her, more than upon his other children, had fallen the mantle of his genius for striking fire in men's imaginations, of making them see visions and dream dreams." During the five years of her generalship, she traveled throughout the world, visiting India, Australia, New Zealand, all the European countries, and making frequent trips back to America and Canada. The Salvation Army suffered severe financial setbacks during the Great Depression and lost properties in several countries, but Booth took the view that material losses, though regrettable, could be borne so long as the Army retained its spiritual vitality.

After retiring as general in 1939, she decided to spend her last years in America and sailed through the submarine hazards of the North Atlantic back to New York in the fall of 1939. Booth lived in Westchester County, New York, until her death in 1950, surrounded by Salvation Army friends, still making frequent speeches to the faithful and honored for her life's work, but finding it difficult to let go of the Army's affairs. She was dismayed to see the Salvation Army absorbed into the United Services Organization (USO) during the Second World War rather than carrying out the kind of distinctive work it had achieved during the first war. Evangeline Booth was still riding daily on horseback until she was 81, and made light of the cancer pains which finally "promoted her to glory" at the age of 85.

SOURCES:

Chesham, Sallie. *Born to Battle: The Salvation Army in America.* Chicago, IL: Rand McNally, 1965.

McKinley, Edward. *Marching to Glory.* San Francisco, CA: Harper and Row, 1980.

Troutt, Margaret. *The General Was a Lady: The Story of Evangeline Booth.* Nashville, TN: A.J. Holman, 1980.

Whitwell, Wilson P. *General Evangeline Booth.* NY: Revell, 1935.

Wisbey, Herbert, Jr. *Soldiers Without Swords: A History of the Salvation Army in the United States.* NY: Macmillan, 1955.

SUGGESTED READING:

Booth, Evangeline, and Grace Livingston Hill. *The War Romance of the Salvation Army.* Philadelphia, PA: Lippincott, 1919.

Lavine, Sigmund. *Evangeline Booth, Daughter of Salvation.* NY: Dodd, Mead, 1970.

Ludwig, Charles. *The Lady General.* Grand Rapids, MI: Baker Books, 1962.

Sandall, Robert. *History of the Salvation Army.* 3 vols. NY: Thomas Nelson, 1947–55.

COLLECTIONS:

Salvation Army Archives and Research Center, New York City.

Patrick Allitt, Professor of History, Emory University, Atlanta, Georgia

Booth, Margaret (b. 1898)

American film editor. *Name variations: (nickname) Maggie. Born in Los Angeles, California, in 1898; sister of actor Elmer Booth; graduated from Los Angeles High School.*

Selected films: Husbands and Lovers *(1924);* Why Men Leave Home *(1924);* Fine Clothes *(1925);* Memory Lane *(1926);* The Gay Deceiver *(1926);* Bringing Up Father *(1927);* The Enemy *(1927);* In Old Kentucky *(1927);* Lovers *(1927);* A Lady of Chance *(1928);* The Mysterious Lady *(1928);* Telling the World *(1928);* The Bridge of San Luis Rey *(1929);* Wise Girls *(1929);* The Lady of Scandal *(1930);* A Lady's Morals *(1930);* Redemption *(1930);* The Rogue Song *(1930);* Strictly Unconventional *(1930);* The Cuban Love Song *(1931);* Five and Ten *(1931);* It's a Wise Child (1931); New Moon (1931); Susan Lenox, Her Fall and Rise *(1931);* Smilin' Through *(1932);* The Son-Daughter *(1932);* Strange Interlude *(1932);* Bombshell *(1933);* Dancing Lady *(1933);* Peg o' My Heart *(1933);* Storm at Daybreak *(1933);* The Barretts of Wimpole Street *(1934);* Riptide *(1934);* Reckless *(1935);* Mutiny on the Bounty *(1935);* Camille *(1936);* Romeo and Juliet *(1936);* A Yank at Oxford *(1937);* The Owl and the Pussycat *(1970);* To Find a Man *(1972);* Fat City *(1972);* The Way We Were *(1973);* Funny Lady *(1975);* Sunshine Boys *(1975);* Murder by Death *(1976);* The Goodbye Girl *(1977);* California Suite *(1978);* Chapter Two *(1979);* Annie *(1982).*

Margaret Booth, supervising editor at Metro-Goldwyn-Mayer for three decades, sits high in the ranks of film editors, unsung warriors in the movie industry. From 1937 to 1968, no film left the studio without her imprint. Starting as a "cutter" for D.W. Griffith, Booth led a pioneering career that spanned over 60 years.

Margaret Booth had not planned on becoming a film editor. When her brother Elmer, an actor with D.W. Griffith, was killed in an automobile accident, she had to provide some of the family income. Fresh out of high school, Booth was hired by Griffith to work in the splicing room for ten dollars a week. From there, she moved to L.B. Mayer's Mission Road studio, where she was fortunate enough to be mentored by John Stahl. "He taught me the value of a scene," she recalled. "When a scene drops or doesn't drop, and when it sustains. You have to feel this, intuitively, in your work." Irving Thalberg believed that Booth's eye was good enough to go into directing, but Booth wanted only to be the best film editor ever.

After Thalberg's death, Booth took over as supervising editor of MGM. She was known for being fast and tough, editing such classics as *The Bridge of San Luis Rey*, *The Barretts of Wimpole Street*, *Romeo and Juliet*, and *Camille*. In 1935, she received an Academy Award nomination for her editing of *Mutiny on the Bounty*, losing out to the editor of *Midsummer Night's Dream*. She admitted that when *Mutiny* came out, no one thought much of the film. "Now," said Booth, "everyone hails it as a classic."

With the advent of talkies, she had to learn how to edit sound on her own. Not only did Booth master the process, but she created pioneering methods that others would later follow. In 1963, she was loaned out to work with Ray Stark on the movie *A Boy Ten Feet Tall* which won a prize at the Cannes Film Festival. They worked together again after she left MGM, with Booth overseeing Stark's films: *The Way We Were*, *Funny Lady*, *The Goodbye Girl*, and *Annie*. For the quality of her cumulative work, Booth won an honorary Academy Award in 1977. She was also awarded a Lifetime Achievement Award in 1990 by the American Cinema Editors for her broad contribution to the field.

Barbara Morgan,
Melrose, Massachusetts

Booth, Mary Louise (1831–1889)

American journalist, translator, and editor. *Born in Millville (now Yaphank), a village of Suffolk County, Long Island, New York, on April 19, 1831; died in New York City on March 5, 1889; her father was a school principal at Williamsburg, Long Island; educated at home, the district school, and Long Island academies.*

Mary Louise Booth translated some 40 important French works, including the writings of Pascal and Victor Cousin's *Secret History of the French Court; or Life and Times of* ***Madame de Chevreuse***. In 1859, Booth published her *History of the City of New York*. The first of its kind, the work went through four editions. She also translated Edouard Laboulaye's *Paris in America* (1863), Count Agénor de Gasparin's *Uprising of a Great People: The United States in 1861*, Augustin Cochin's *The Results of Slavery* and *The Results of Emancipation* (both 1863), and Henri Martin's abridgment of his *History of France* (6 vols., 1880). Mary Louise Booth was the first editor of *Harper's Bazaar* from its inception until her death in 1889. During the first ten years of her tenure, the magazine grew to a circulation of 80,000.

Mary Louise Booth

Booth, Maud Ballington (1865–1948)

American reformer and welfare leader who founded Volunteers of America. *Name variations: Mrs. Ballington Booth (upon her marriage to Ballington Booth, she adopted both his names); Maud Charlesworth Booth. Born Maud Elizabeth Charlesworth at Limpsfield, Surrey, England, on September 13, 1865; died in Great Neck, Long Island, on August 26, 1948; daughter of Reverend Samuel Charlesworth and a welfare worker mother; niece of* ***Maria Charlesworth*** *(1819–1880, a children's author); sister of* ****Florence Louisa Barclay*** *(1862–1921); married Ballington Booth (d. 1940, son of William Booth and leader of the Salvation Army in Australia and U.S.), in September 1886; daughter-in-law of Catherine Booth; sister-in-law of* ****Evangeline Booth****; became a naturalized American citizen, 1895.*

Daughter of a cleric, Maud Ballington Booth became interested in the work of the Salvation Army when young and, at age 17, left home and

Maud Ballington Booth

became a companion of *Catherine Booth in organizing a branch of the Salvation Army in Paris. Maud remained there two years, then accompanied a party of Salvationists to Switzerland where, after experiencing setbacks and even imprisonment, she succeeded in establishing a Salvation Army corps. In 1886, she married Ballington Booth (1859–1940), the second son of Catherine and General William Booth, the English religious leaders and founders of the Salvation Army. When she and her husband withdrew from the Salvation Army in 1896, Maud and Ballington founded the Volunteers of America, of which she became president in 1940. She devoted her attention mainly to the Prison League of this organization, doing evangelical work in state and federal prisons, including Sing Sing. Maud was also one of the founders of the Parent-Teachers Association. Her writings include: *Branded* (1897), *After Prison, What?* (1903), and *Relentless Current* (1912), as well as *Twilight Fairy Tales* (1906) and other books for children.

Booth, Shirley (1907–1992)

American actress who won an Academy Award and Tony Award for her portrayal of Lola in Come Back, Little Sheba. *Born Thelma Booth Ford in New York, New York, on August 30, 1907; died on October 16, 1992, in North Chatham, Massachusetts; eldest daughter of Albert J. (an IBM district manager) and Shirley (Wright) Ford; attended Public School 152 in Brooklyn, New York, until age 14; married Edward Gardner, on November 23, 1929 (divorced 1942); married William H. Baker, in 1943 (died 1951).*

Selected stage appearances: made first appearance in Hartford in The Cat and the Canary *(1919); made debut in New York as Nan Winchester in* Hell's Bells *(1925); played Mabel in* Three Men on a Horse *at the Playhouse (1935); Mrs. Loschavio in* Excursion *at the Vanderbilt (1937); Elizabeth Imbrie in* The Philadelphia Story *at the Shubert (1939); Ruth Sherwood in* My Sister Eileen *at the Biltmore (1940–42); Leona Richards in* To-Morrow the World *at the Ethel Barrymore (1943–44); Louhedda Hopsons in* Hollywood Pinafore *at the Alvin (1945); Susan Pengilly in* Land's End *at the Playhouse (1946); Grace Woods in* Goodbye, My Fancy *at the Morosco (for which she won the Antoinette Perry Award, 1948); Abby Quinn in* Love Me Long *at the 48th Street Theater (1949); Lola in* Come Back, Little Sheba *at the Booth (for which she won the Antoinette Perry Award, 1950, and an Academy Award, 1952); Cissy in* A Tree Grows in Brooklyn *at the Alvin (1951); Leona Samish in* The Time of the Cuckoo *at the Empire (for which she won the Antoinette Perry Award, 1952); Lottie Gibson in* By the Beautiful Sea *at the Majestic (1954); Bunny Watson in* Desk Set *at the Broadhurst (1955).*

Filmography: Come Back, Little Sheba *(1952);* Main Street to Broadway *(1953);* About Mrs. Leslie *(1954);* The Matchmaker *(1958);* Hot Spell *(1958). On radio: played Miss Duffy on "Duffy's Tavern." On television: played the title role on the 1961–66 NBC series "Hazel," for which she received an Emmy award.*

Acting may have appealed to Shirley Booth because of a shy, lonely childhood during which she liked to imagine herself as someone else, or perhaps Booth simply succumbed to what she described as the "heady" experience of her first performance at the age of three, singing "In the Good Old Summertime" in a Sunday School show. Regardless of her motivation, she blossomed into one of the finest character actresses of her time, mesmerizing audiences for over five decades on stage, screen, radio, and television.

Booth's earliest formal contact with the theater was through J. Hammond Daly, an actor friend of the family who snagged her a part in a stock production of *Mother Carey's Chickens* when she was 12. After a summer with the com-

Shirley Booth

pany in Hartford, Booth returned to school for only a year before she left home, against her father's wishes, to pursue the theater in New York.

Taking up residence with a friend of her mother's, Booth landed an ingénue's part with the Poli stock company. Assigned to its New Haven unit, she spent a year there, then toured the major cities in the Eastern United States. Her first Broadway role was opposite a very young Humphrey Bogart in *Hell's Bells*, in 1925. For the next ten years, she alternated stock engagements with parts in short-lived Broadway plays. Appearing in nearly 600 stock productions, she had roles in plays as diverse as Oscar Wilde's *Lady Windermere's Fan* and Henrik Ibsen's *The Wild Duck*. Booth recalled her stock days as good training ("You get your cue and you come out acting"), and she felt compelled to continue her stock work even after other opportunities began to come her way. "I was big in stock. I had a reputation and a public. I could afford to hang around New York and take my chances, but I had to go where people believed in me. . . . I had to keep acting, so I could believe in myself."

Her appearance in *Sunday Nights at Nine* (1934) brought her to the attention of George Abbott, who gave Booth the first substantial role of her career, as a good-hearted gangster's moll in the hit comedy *Three Men on a Horse* which ran for two years. After subsequent roles in a couple of flops, she moved to the West Coast to vacation for a year. She returned to New York in 1939 to play the wisecracking photographer Elizabeth Imbrie in the Theater Guild's production of *The Philadelphia Story,* for which she received as many raves from the critics as did the show's star ***Katharine Hepburn.** Booth's next role, as Ruth Sherwood in *My Sister Eileen,* afforded her another two-year run during which she also performed the comedic turn as Miss Duffy in the popular radio program "Duffy's Tavern," which was written and produced by her husband Ed Gardner. She divorced Gardner in 1942 and a year later married William Baker, Jr., a New York investment counselor who died in 1951. Booth also appeared in other top radio variety shows and performed various dramatic roles on "Theater Guild of the Air."

The early 1940s brought the play *To-Morrow the World*, which was successful despite its serious story about a teacher who tries to reeducate a young Nazi, and Booth's first musical comedy, *Hollywood Pinafore* (1945), in which she played a movie columnist named Louhedda Hopsons (based on real-life columnists ***Hedda Hopper** and ***Louella Parsons**). One of her numbers in *Pinafore*, called "Little Miss Butter-up," was George Kaufman's clever take on Gilbert and Sullivan's "Buttercup." New York *Herald Tribune* critic Howard Barnes was delighted with Booth's musical ability: "There are some who knew she could sing like a lark. . . . Those who did not know it will derive tremendous pleasure from her handling of the lovely songs."

For her part as the cynical secretary in *Goodbye, My Fancy* (1948), Booth received the ***Antoinette Perry** Award (Tony) for Best Supporting Actress. She saw enormous success with her role of Lola Delaney, a frowzy middle-aged housewife, in the Theater Guild drama *Come Back, Little Sheba* (1950), for which she won not only the Tony, but also the Drama Critics Circle Award. Drama critic Brooks Atkinson observed, "She has the shuffle, the maddening garrulity and the rasping voice of the slattern, but withal she imparts to the role the warmth, generosity and valor of a loyal and affectionate woman." The show's director Daniel Mann was more succinct: "She doesn't act, she lives on the stage." Booth repeated the role of Lola in the 1952 film version of the play, winning an Academy Award as Best Actress as well as the Best Actress of the Year award from both the National Board of Review and the New York Film Critics. In addition, she was named "the world's best actress" at the sixth International Film Festival at Cannes, France.

In 1951, Booth played the feisty Aunt Cissy in the musical *A Tree Grows in Brooklyn,* prompting the *New York Post* to call her, "one of the wonders of the American stage." For her role as the lonely Leona Samish in *The Time of the Cuckoo* (1952), Booth received her third Tony and the 1953 Delia Austrain Medal of the Drama League of New York (the play was subsequently made into the film *Summertime* with Katharine Hepburn). Booth went on to do another musical *By the Beautiful Sea* (1954) and the comedy *The Desk Set* (1955), for which she received the ***Sarah Siddons** Award in Chicago.

During the 1960s, Booth found a new and loyal following as the lovable know-it-all maid in the NBC television series "Hazel" (1961–66). For her work in the show, she received a total of 28 awards, including the Emmy. Early in her career, Booth had told a reporter, "I want to keep improving, to keep acting and to play many character parts." She did just that, right up to her final Broadway appearance in a 1970 revival of *Hay Fever*.

SOURCES:

Boardman, Gerald. *The Oxford Companion to American Theatre*. NY: Oxford University Press, 1984.

Current Biography 1953. NY: H.W. Wilson, 1953.

Morley, Sheridan. *The Great Stage Stars*. London: Angus and Robertson, 1986.

Barbara Morgan,
Melrose, Massachusetts

Booth-Tucker, Emma Moss (1860–1903).

See Booth, Catherine for sidebar.

Boothe or Boothe-Luce, Clare (1903–1987).

See Luce, Clare Boothe.

Boothroyd, Betty (1929—)

British politician and first female speaker of the House of Commons. *Born Betty Boothroyd in 1929; daughter of union activists; never married.*

Betty Boothroyd, the daughter of union activists, spent the 1940s on tour with a dancing troupe called the Tiller Girls, before entering politics in 1950 as an assistant to several members of Parliament. After a side step to the United States to campaign for John F. Kennedy, she returned to London in 1962 and made a few unsuccessful runs for MP within the Labour Party. She was victorious in 1973 and became deputy speaker in 1987. In 1992, she was elected speaker in a landslide victory.

As the first female speaker in the House of Commons, Boothroyd sacrificed much to the demands of her position but remained a spirited and independent thinker. Refusing to wear the traditional wig when presiding (she conceded to the robe), she ruled over the sometimes unruly House sessions in a style that was a cross between schoolmarm and seducer. During heated debates that often dissolved into name-calling shouting matches, she remained dignified and in charge, with an uncanny ability to know how long to let the antics proceed before making her presence felt. A formidable force when necessary, she has expelled and sanctioned members of the House, regardless of their status. During her speaker tenure, Boothroyd, who never married, resided in a lavish apartment located within the Houses of Parliament.

RELATED MEDIA:

Interview on "60 Minutes," CBS television, July 14, 1996.

Betty Boothroyd

Bora, Katharina von (1499–1550)

Wife of German theologian Martin Luther who, in presiding over the first Protestant parsonage, did much to determine the tone of German Protestant domestic life. *Name variations: Catherine de Bora or Bohra; Katherine von Bora Luther; "Kette" (meaning chain, as in "ball and chain"), a pun on the diminutive "Katya" or "Katie" and often used by her husband. Born Katharina von Bora in January 1499; died in Wittenburg on December 20, 1550; married Martin Luther, on June 13, 1525; children: Hans (b. June 7, 1526); Elizabeth (b. December 10, 1527, and died young);* ***Magdalene Luther*** *(b. May 4, 1529); Martin (b. November 9, 1531); Paul (b. January 29, 1533); and* ***Margareta Luther*** *(known as Lenchen, b. December 17, 1534–1548).*

Katharina von Bora would not be remembered in history, except that she was the wife of the German theologian who led the Protestant Reformation that altered the Western world. Had it not been for the importance of "Kette" in the life of Martin Luther, however, Protestantism might well have evolved into an institution very different than what it is, and for that reason she deserves attention.

The "von" in the name of Katharina von Bora indicates that she belonged to a family of lower nobility. Little is known of her early life except that she was born in January 1499. When she was ten years old, her father remarried, and she was placed in a Cistercian nunnery at Nimschen. At age 16, she took the vows of holy orders, but within a few years she was ready to accept the anti-monastic doctrines of Martin Luther then sweeping through Germany.

On Easter morning, 1523, Katharina joined eight other nuns aided by Leonard Kopp, a trusted follower of Luther, in escaping the convent, hidden in a wagon used to deliver smoked herring. On the following Tuesday, the fugitives arrived at Wittenburg, but their relatives refused to take them in. Since the late-medieval society

Katharina von Bora

they were reentering offered virtually no means of support for single women, their welfare and survival became Luther's responsibility.

Out of Katharina's group, one woman was qualified to obtain a lowly position as a teacher. For all the female refugees being emptied from the monasteries and pouring into Wittenburg, marriage was their only remaining option. Since Katharina, at age 24, was one of the oldest, she was considered the least marriageable. For a year and a half, she boarded in the home of **Argula**

von Grumbach (1492–c. 1563), one of Luther's more forthright female disciples, who then began to urge Luther to marry the former nun.

Luther had good reasons to resist. Beyond the usual reluctance of a 40-year-old bachelor, 16 years older than the proffered bride, the theologian could truthfully point out that he was not a safe person to marry. Having been labeled as a heretic, condemned by the pope, and declared an outlaw by the emperor of the Holy Roman Empire, which encompassed Germany, he was a man with a price on his head, who had ample reason to worry about leaving his bride a widow; he was also living in a country currently being ravaged by the Peasants' War, which lasted from 1524 to 1525. There was no pretense, therefore, that this was to be a romantic love match. When Martin later listed several reasons for getting married, falling in love was not one of them; it was primarily out of his sense of responsibility for provoking the events that had thrust her out of the safety of her monastic world. The event of his marriage, on June 13, 1525, occurred because the minister had come to believe that he could do no other.

Nevertheless, the union was quick to demonstrate its benefits, beginning with the attendance of Martin's now-aged parents at the wedding. A bitterness of 20 years had existed between the father and his eldest son. Old Hans Luther had poured much of the family's hard-earned wealth into educating young Martin, and then had felt angered and betrayed when Martin became a monk and priest. Mollified by the marriage, Old Hans became fully reconciled at the time of the birth of Martin's first son.

As time passed, Martin rationalized his marriage by declaring that it had occurred out of religious conviction. As he often put it, marriage allowed him to thumb his nose at the pope, and make the angels laugh and devils weep as he sealed his testimony of faith with contempt for clerical celibacy. As the marriage of convenience came to reinforce Martin's religious commitment, Katharina's desire to share and reinforce the religious commitment of her husband also grew, and the couple came to genuinely love each other.

Children came promptly. On October 21, 1525, Martin reported Katharina's first pregnancy to a friend by declaring that she was fulfilling the words of Genesis 3:8, "In pain you shall bring forth children!" On June 7, 1526, she gave birth to a boy, named Hans after Martin's father. On December 10, 1527, the couple's first daughter, Elizabeth, was born, but soon died, and was grieved for mightily. Katharina then had four more children, born approximately two years apart: Magdalene, Martin, Paul, and Margareta. Margareta was named for Luther's mother, Paul became a successful physician, and Magdalene, known as Lenchen, was perhaps her father's favorite.

Although Katharina von Bora's view of her married life was not recorded in documents that have survived, the enthusiasm of her husband attests to the feelings of both of them. At the outset, he confided to a friend, "I am not madly in love, but I cherish my wife and would not exchange her for France or Venice." Later he is said to have added that he "would not exchange her for the riches of Croesus."

> [Luther] ruefully confessed that he relied more on Katie than on Christ. "In domestic affairs," said he, "I defer to Katie. Otherwise I am led by the Holy Ghost."
>
> **—Roland Bainton**

Along with their six children, the Luthers adopted eleven more. By all accounts, their home was a happy one. As time passed, Martin came to depend upon his "beloved Katie" and confessed that he relied upon her more than he did Christ. On occasion, he did register frustration with her in his use of his pet nickname, "Kette" (*chain*), but any complaint against her is offset by one famous letter, written to his good friend George Spalatin, who also married an ex-nun named Katharina. Martin exhorted him to take his bride to bed immediately, and wrote, "As you penetrate your Katie, I'll penetrate mine, and we'll be united in Jesus Christ." In a more characteristic sentiment, he wrote, "The first love is drunken. When the intoxication wears off, then comes the real married love." To the bride, he wrote: "My dear, make your husband glad to cross his threshold at night." To the groom, he wrote: "Make your wife sorry to have you leave."

Katharina von Bora was helpmate to a busy and difficult man, the mother in charge of their many children, and the first woman to preside for the public as host in a Protestant clerical household at their home in Wittenburg. As a typical 16th-century woman bearing children during her 20s and 30s, she had pregnancies that were difficult but not dangerous, suffered the usual dizziness, headaches, nausea, toothache, and swelling of the legs. When one or more of the babies cried incessantly, father Martin commented, "This is the sort of thing that has caused the Church fathers to vilify marriage." Looking at his family on one occasion, the frustrated Luther observed, "Christ said we must have become as little children to enter into the kingdom of heaven. Dear God, this is too much. Have we got to become such idiots?"

Katharina von Bora not only raised and tended to the sicknesses of her normal but not always healthy children, but had to give special attention to her overworked, overwrought husband who suffered from a full range of physical ailments, diseases, and eccentricities. Martin's ailments stemmed largely from poor diet and lack of exercise as he overlooked the practical necessities of life while fighting the public battles. But all the past petty irritations of family life melted away when Katharina and Martin Luther knelt at the deathbed of their beloved Lenchen. As the mother backed away, dumb with grief, the father held the dying child in his arms and prayed that God's will be done. The death of Lenchen, at age 14, darkened the remaining three years of his life.

In addition to the care she gave her family, Katharina von Bora became responsible for the many who flocked to Wittenburg as the new followers of their embattled Reformer of the Faith. In a building known as the Black Cloister, where Martin had lived as a monk, she established a hostel for the many hundreds, perhaps even thousands, of visitors and religious refugees requiring food and rest and sometimes medical care. The building had 40 rooms on the ground floor, with smaller cells above them. Katharina supervised the remodeling, then acted as host to the travelers, who came from all over Germany, and from as far away as Hungary and England. Some arrivals were rich and prominent, and some were of noble blood, demanding and scornful of the inferior lodgings. Others were exiles from religious persecution or refugees from the turmoil of Europe's wars. Most were poor and sick, and some came there to die. In accordance with the necessities of a world without commercial hotels, they would often stay for weeks and even months at a time. If their prodigally generous host had had his way, most would have paid nothing for their room and board. It was up to Katharina to be the hard-nosed hostess, demanding payment and evicting the most overbearing of the freeloaders.

Although Martin Luther's greater age made it likely that he would die before her, he derided her desire to accumulate real-estate property, which might help to secure her economic position. He not only preached about the "birds and the lilies of the field" that relied upon the good Lord for their sustenance as described in Matthew 6:26–30, but he considered property to be bondage to place and situation. In fact, the only enduring result of Katharina's plunge into the 16th-century version of real-estate acquisition was to blacken her reputation. To subsequent generations of Lutherans, Katharina von Bora has often been cast as the grubby materialistic counterpart to their spiritual founder of the faith. As Martin Luther was the first to testify, however, he would not have been able to "serve Christ and combat Satan in the appropriate ways" without his wife to help him.

On February 18, 1546, the great religious leader died, and Katharina von Bora's fight to retain their property proved to no avail. When the Schmalkaldic wars, the military conflict waged earlier between Protestant princes and the Roman Catholic Emperor Charles V, broke out again, the Lutheran forces were defeated this time by the emperor, and the widow was forced into exile. After a short time, she was able to return home to Wittenburg, where she found devastation and chaos and was soon forced to leave again. After a second return home, while she was still trying to rebuild from her losses, she was injured in an accident. After three months of intense suffering, Katharina von Bora died on December 20, 1550. Her last words were recorded as "I will stick to Christ as a burr to a top coat."

According to his own testimony, Martin Luther, the instigator of the Reformation, would not have been able to challenge the celibate clerical domination of medieval Christianity were it not for his wife. Their home, writes Reformation scholar, E.G. Rupp, "became a more effective apologetic for marriage of the clergy than any writing and the prototype of a Christian minister's household." In fact, it was Katharina rather than Martin, through her own sense of religious conviction, who broke the traditional medieval concept of Christian ministry as the work of men only. At the head of the newborn Protestantism, the couple lived in contradiction to the monastic model followed for centuries according to the life of the man Jesus, who had repudiated his mother "to be about my business" and never married at all. The Luthers thus became responsible for shaping the family-centered aspect for half of Western Christendom. The alternative family model they created in Christian ministry has dominated Protestant Christianity throughout the world and in some areas, particularly North America, presents a strong challenge to Roman Catholic Christianity almost five centuries later. Martin Luther helped to refocus the Christian religion, with the family unit as its center. But if Luther was the one to proclaim this difference, Katharina von Bora became the first to show how it could work.

SOURCES:

Bainton, Roland H. *Women of the Reformation in Germany and Italy.* Minneapolis MN: Augsburg, 1971.

———. *Here I Stand: A Biography of Martin Luther.* Nashville, TN: Abingdon, 1950.

Boehmer, Heinrich. *The Road to Reformation.* NY: Meridian Books, 1957 (c. 1946).

Marius, Richard. *Luther.* Philadelphia, PA: Lippincott, 1974.

SUGGESTED READING:

Kroker, Ernst. *Katharina von Bora.* Leipzig, 1906.

Thoma, Albrecht. *Katharina von Bora.* Berlin, 1900.

David R. Stevenson, Professor of History, University of Nebraska at Kearney, Nebraska

Borbala.

Variant of Barbara.

Borboni, Paola (1900–1995)

***Italian actress.** Born in 1900; died on April 9, 1995, in a nursing home in Varese, Italy, two days after suffering a stroke; married Bruno Vilar (an actor), in 1972.*

An Italian actress who appeared in hundreds of theatrical productions of distinguished playwrights, including those of Pirandello and Shaw, Paola Borboni was known for her ability to foment controversy throughout her extraordinary 77-year career. Rome's newspaper *Il Messaggero* dubbed her "Paola of the Scandals." In 1925, she bared her breasts on stage, later claiming, "I was neither sensual nor vulgar, I was just young and my bare breast didn't bother anyone." In 1972, she again made headlines when at age 72 she married the 30-year-old actor Bruno Vilar. Six years later, the two were in an automobile accident. Borboni was injured, her young husband killed. Borboni continued to perform until March 1993, shortly before entering a nursing home in the northern city of Varese where she died.

Borden, Lizzie (1860–1927)

***Accused murderer of her father and stepmother in a gruesome case that riveted late 19th-century America; legal scholars and amateur criminologists have been arguing the case and the identity of the "real" murderer ever since.** Name variations: Lizzie. Pronunciation: BOR-den. Born Lizbeth Andrew Borden on July 19, 1860, in Fall River, Massachusetts; died on June 1, 1927, in Fall River; daughter of Andrew and Sarah (Morse) Borden; sister of **Emma Lenora Borden** (b. 1849); attended Fall River public schools; never married; no children.*

On the last morning of their lives, Andrew and Abigail Borden rose early to avoid the worst of an uncomfortably hot New England summer. Temperatures had remained in the 90s for weeks, and, now that August had arrived, humidity had settled over Fall River, Massachusetts, like a damp blanket. Indeed, most of the Borden household had been ill the previous day from, it was said, consuming spoiled meat that had been left too long in the stifling heat. But this morning—August 4, 1892—Andrew and Abigail seemed to have recovered as they sat down to a breakfast of mutton broth, johnnycakes, fruit, and coffee, shared with Andrew's brother-in-law from his first marriage, John Vinnicum Morse, a frequent houseguest. The Bordens' two daughters, Lizbeth and Emma, were absent from table. Lizbeth, or Lizzie, remained upstairs in her bedroom, while Emma was away visiting relatives in a nearby town.

The Bordens were well-known—economically, if not socially—in this prosperous mill town in southeastern Massachusetts. There were, in fact, no less than 126 Bordens listed in the city directory of that year, all descended from one John Borden, who had arrived from England in 1638. Andrew had begun his professional life as an undertaker, but in a series of shrewd investments and partnerships, had steadily built his fortune until, by 1892, he was president or on the boards of several Fall River banks, as well as owner of a yarn mill and a cotton and wool factory. He had married well, taking as his first wife **Sarah Morse**, the daughter of an equally prosperous Fall River family. Sarah gave birth to two daughters, Emma, born in 1849, and Lizzie, born in 1860. Sarah died two years after Lizzie's birth, and in 1864 Andrew had married **Abigail Durfee**.

Abby was known as a genial, easy-going woman, though Fall River gossip maintained that relations between Abby and the two Borden daughters, especially Lizzie, were cool and distant. Lizzie, it had been long noted, always referred to Abby as "Mrs. Borden," and everyone knew about the argument that had broken out in the household when Andrew had loaned Abby's sister and brother-in-law a considerable sum, allowing them to take advantage of a lucrative real-estate deal. The rumor was that Lizzie had complained so loudly at this favoritism that Andrew had been forced to spend an equal sum to purchase land for his two daughters. Lizzie was also said to resent the fact that her father insisted on living "in town"—that is, close to the commercial center of Fall River—rather than on "The Hill," where all the best families had their elegant homes. But Andrew preferred being near his business interests, purchasing a stolid, two-family woodframe house on Second Street, near City Hall, and converting it into a one-family dwelling. By 1892, however, all this was old news and to all outward appearances, Andrew Borden and family lived a quiet, respectable existence. Both Lizzie and Emma were active in several religious and women's charitable organizations, and Lizzie had even, in 1890, taken the traditional grand tour of Europe, although it was the last time she was to venture so far from home.

Despite the outward tranquility of that summer of 1892, Lizzie confessed to a family friend, **Alice Russell**, of being depressed; "as if," Miss Russell was later to paraphrase Lizzie's words, "something is hanging over me that I cannot throw off." Lizzie confided her feelings on the night before the murders of Andrew and Abby, saying she believed the family's sickness the day before had been due to someone trying to poison their milk. When Russell tried to talk her out of this idea, Lizzie said her father had enemies and told of a man who had come to the house just a day or two before and had angrily left after an argument with her father, some of which Lizzie had overheard; it had something to do, she said, with property.

But Andrew knew nothing of Lizzie's feelings that morning of August 4. Having finished breakfast, he embarked on his usual morning business rounds, leaving the house shortly after 8:00. John Vinnicum Morse left soon afterward to visit relatives across town. This left Abby, Lizzie, and the Bordens' maid, **Bridget Sullivan**, alone in the house. Abby went upstairs to make up the guest room in which John Morse was staying, while Bridget—whom Lizzie insisted on calling "Maggie," the name of Sullivan's predecessor—set herself the task of washing the windows, inside and out, affording her the opportunity to observe every room in the house. She would later swear that she saw no one, especially strangers, enter the house. Lizzie came down from her room soon after Sullivan finished the windows. The two women chatted for a few minutes in the kitchen, Lizzie mentioning that Abby had received a note asking her to visit the sickbed of a friend and had left the house—news Lizzie later passed on to her father when she let him into the house around 10:30, the lock on the front door somehow being stuck.

By now, the heat had begun to build. Andrew retired to the parlor on the first floor to lay down, while Bridget Sullivan—still suffering the effects of yesterday's illness—went up to her room on the second floor for a rest. The house was quiet, until shortly after 11:00, when Lizzie's shrill voice called out to her. "Maggie, come quick! Father's dead! Somebody's come in and killed him!"

Andrew's body was found sprawled on the sofa in the parlor, his face and skull horribly slashed, ripped and battered by some sharp instrument, the blood still fresh and glistening on the ghastly wounds. Lizzie was left alone in the house while Sullivan ran for a doctor and to summon Alice Russell. A next door neighbor, **Miss Churchill**, noticed a distraught Lizzie standing on the front porch of the Borden home, and hurried over to see what was the matter. Later, while the little group stood in horror before Andrew's body as the doctor conducted his examination, Lizzie mentioned to Churchill that she thought she had just heard Abby coming in and going up to her room. Before Churchill and Sullivan even reached the top of the stairs, they could see Abby's body lying on the floor of the guestroom just off the landing. Abby, too, had been savagely attacked on the face and head.

All these points would be meticulously reconstructed in the coming days, as the Borden murder case took on a bizarre, sometimes macabre, dimension. The medical examiner who came for the bodies inexplicably performed an autopsy on the dining room table before removing the corpses to the morgue. No less than six Fall River policemen swarmed over the house on the day of the killings, each interviewing Lizzie in turn until, when one of them asked about relations with her mother, Lizzie snapped out, "She is *not* my mother, sir! She is my stepmother! My mother died when I was a child." Lizzie told another policeman that while Andrew was taking his rest in the parlor, she had gone out to the barn to look, oddly, for sinkers she intended to take with her on a fishing trip. But on examining the barn, as the policeman would later tell the court, not only were there no disturbances in the fine layer of dust covering the floor, but it was so unbearably hot in the barn that he doubted anyone could have remained inside it for more than a minute or two. Doctor Bowen, the doctor summoned by Sullivan, mentioned that he had the impression that Lizzie had changed her dress at some point during the time he was in the house. In the days following the murders, Borden was seen burning a dress on which she claimed to have spilled paint and, it being pointed out to her that this might seem suspicious, became extremely upset and asked why no one had warned her. No trace of the note Lizzie claimed Abby had received could be found, nor anyone in town to whom Abby paid a visit that morning. In the cellar of the Borden home, the police discovered a carton containing several axes and one axe-head, broken off from its shank as if by a violent blow; and two Fall River pharmacists reported that Lizzie had dropped by several days before her parents' deaths wanting to buy prussic acid, a deadly poison, claiming she needed it to clean a sealskin coat of hers (neither would sell her any, it being a prescription item only).

Seven days after the gruesome discovery of Andrew's and Abby's bodies, on August 11, 1892, Lizzie was formally charged—although at first only with Andrew's murder. It was not until four months later, when the Grand Jury returned its findings, that Borden was charged with three counts of murder—one each for Abby and Andrew, and one for both of them together. She was bound over for trial, set for June 5, 1893, in nearby New Bedford.

The events leading up to the trial, and the trial itself, were also not without their oddities. At her inquest, before Judge Josiah C. Blaisdell, Borden was allowed to testify in secret and her testimony sealed. It would remain so, not even being made available to the jury at the June trial, at which Lizzie herself did not take the stand, thus depriving the jury of key evidence in their deliberations. Further, Judge Blaisdell refused to excuse himself from sitting on the bench for the ensuing probable cause hearing—even though such recusals were, and still are, customary. At the hearing, Blaisdell allowed the defense the unusual liberty of forcing the prosecution to produce all of its witnesses for cross-examination, thus allowing the defense to gain a clear picture of the prosecution's case long before normal pre-trial discovery. Blaisdell then found probable cause and bound Lizzie over to the Grand Jury.

The legal peculiarities continued. Normally, only the prosecution is allowed to present its evidence to a Grand Jury, since that body's responsibility is merely to determine if enough evidence exists to warrant a trial. The guilt or innocence of the accused is not part of a Grand Jury's deliberations. Nonetheless, the prosecution offered no objection to allowing the defense to present *its* evidence as well—the first and only time such an occurrence has been recorded in all of Massachusetts' legal history. In effect, the entire case was argued, as if in rehearsal, before a body which had no business hearing it. The Grand Jury returned no indictments against Lizzie. But some weeks later, the prosecution asked it to reconvene to rehear testimony from Alice Russell, to whom Lizzie had confessed her apprehensions the night before the murders. Russell had apparently forgotten or omitted something from her earlier testimony, although exactly what that was has been lost from the records. The next day, December 1, 1892, Borden was formally indicted and bound over for trial the following June. Even so, the lead prosecutor for the state, Hosea M. Knowlton, the district attorney for the Southern District, expressed a curious lack of enthusiasm, not to say reluctance, toward the trial. "Personally, I would like very much to get rid of the trial of the case," he wrote to his superior, State Attorney General Arthur Pillsbury, "and I feel that my feelings in that direction may have influenced my better judgment." He did not mention that it was the attorney general's prerogative to try all murder cases in the state, but that Pillsbury had declined to take the Borden case on and handed it off to Knowlton.

In the months leading up to the trial, public opinion was guided by some of the worst excesses of the age of yellow journalism. Reporters from every major newspaper and syndicate in the nation swarmed over Fall River, churning out florid prose declaiming Lizzie's innocence, the evil intentions of the police and prosecutors, the weakness of their case and the nobility with which Borden bore her suffering. Massachusetts society rallied around Lizzie, too, exhorting public officials to reopen the investigation of the murders and discover the real perpetrator who, they no doubt expected, would be from the lower classes. Charitable organizations to which Lizzie had contributed her time, most notably the Women's Christian Temperance Union, staged public meetings and raised money for Borden's defense. By the time June 5 arrived, New Bedford had become a media circus not unlike that surrounding famous trials of the 20th century. It was during these months that the famous rhyme was first heard in the streets and public houses:

> Lizzie Borden took an axe,
> And gave her mother forty whacks.
> And when she saw what she had done,
> She gave her father forty-one.

The trial got off to a sensational start when Hosea Knowlton, making his opening argument to the all-male jury, accidentally bumped against the table containing the exhibits in the case. From a large cloth bag on the table rolled two skulls, those of Abby and Andrew, clearly bearing the signs of the assault upon them. Borden promptly fainted, and the trial had to be halted while she recovered. Court was once again adjourned some days later when one of the jurors fainted as the medical examiner described in some detail how the murderer delivered the fatal blows, first to Abby, who had died up to an hour and a half before Andrew. He went on to describe the autopsies he'd performed in the Borden dining room, carefully delineating how he had removed Abby's and Andrew's stomachs, tied the ends of each, and placed them in sealed jars; and how he had later decapitated both corpses at the morgue after first obtaining Lizzie's consent to having her parents buried headless.

Even the most ardent of Lizzie's supporters must have been dismayed as the prosecution built its case—admittedly circumstantial but damning when considered as a whole. In modern detective parlance, Borden seemed the only one to have had the means (the axes found in the cellar) and the opportunity (no one except Lizzie and Andrew were known to have been on the first floor of the house at the time of Andrew's death as fixed by the medical examiner), although a motive for such a desperate act remained unclear. There was the police testimony about Lizzie's angry response that Abby wasn't her mother; and in the sealed testimony withheld from the jury, Borden hinted at her cool relations with Abby, declining to characterize them as "cordial" but refusing to say anything further. There was Russell's testimony about the dress-burning (it was she who had warned Lizzie about it); the policeman's testimony about the pristine state of the barn, with no evidence anyone had been inside it recently; the pharmacists' statements about the prussic acid; and Bridget Sullivan's testimony that she saw no one enter or leave the house while she was washing the windows, less than an hour before Andrew was slain. Although both Russell and Churchill, the next door neighbor, testified they saw no evidence of blood on Lizzie's clothes that morning, there was Dr. Bowen's statement to the Court that he thought Lizzie had changed her dress at some point during the time in question. The prosecutors also produced **Hannah Reagan**, the matron of the Fall River jail, in whose private quarters Borden had been confined for her inquest, there being no suitable accommodations for a woman elsewhere in the building. Reagan testified that Emma Borden came to visit her sister, and that while Reagan politely stepped into an antechamber during the visit, she said she distinctly heard Lizzie exclaim to her older sister, "You have given me away!"

The defense stressed to the jury Russell's recounting of Lizzie's story of the angry man who had accosted her father; the fact that two burglaries had occurred at the Borden home over the past two years, indicating there must have been others who knew the habits of the family and the inside of the house; and Bridget Sullivan's statement that the kitchen door may have been off the hook at least once during the morning. Two clothes cleaners were produced to testify that prussic acid was, indeed, used to clean sealskin. A number of character witnesses took the stand to testify to Lizzie's position as a sober, useful member of the community. The defense then rested its case. Neither side called Borden to the stand.

After the summations and the bench's instructions, the jury filed out to begin their deliberations. They returned 90 minutes later to pronounce Lizbeth Andrew Borden not guilty of the charges against her.

From that moment to the present, researchers and legal scholars have been arguing about whether or not justice was served that June day in 1893, and amateur sleuths have been pointing a finger at virtually everyone involved in the case as the real murderer. One of the more recent claims, outlined by Arnold Brown in his book *Lizzie Borden: The Legend, The Truth, The Final Chapter* (1991), is that Andrew Borden had an illegitimate son, William, who had been making increasingly strident demands for a property settlement. It was William, Brown claims, who was the man Lizzie heard arguing with her father. Brown asserts that John Vinnicum Morse was the mediator between the two men, and that the real reason for his visit to Andrew that summer was to arrange a meeting between father and son to settle the matter once and for all. Brown speculates that William was let into the house by Morse the night before the murders (accounting for the jammed lock on the front door that frustrated Andrew the next morning); that Lizzie's activities that morning were just as she described; that William confronted Abby in the guest room upstairs and that Abby taunted him for thinking that Andrew would ever settle a cent on him, leading to her murder and, later, Andrew's, since Andrew would have guessed the identity of the killer. Brown even claims that Lizzie discovered William in the house while Sullivan was out getting help, and agreed to take the blame for the killings if William would disappear and never bother the family again—a remarkable act of courage, not to mention faith in the legal system. Brown claims he got his information from a friend of his father-in-law, who was a descendent of William.

And what of Lizzie? She remained in Fall River for the rest of her life, eventually moving from Second Street to a fine house on "The Hill," where she had always wanted to live. Fall River society would have little to do with her, in stark contrast to its support during her ordeal, and Lizzie became somewhat of a recluse, seen only occasionally around Fall River in her handsome carriage driven by a devoted chauffeur. Emma left Lizzie in 1904, for reasons which remain unexplained. The two sisters never saw each other again. Lizzie Borden died in 1927, at the age of 67. She was buried in the family plot, next to Andrew and Abby.

SOURCES:

Brown, Arnold R. *Lizzie Borden: The Legend, the Truth, the Final Chapter.* Nashville, TN: Rutledge Hill Press, 1991.

Kent, David. *Forty Whacks—New Evidence in the Life and Legend of Lizzie Borden.* Emmaus, PA: Yankee Books, 1992.

Sullivan, Robert. *Goodbye Lizzie Borden.* Brattleboro, VT: Stephen Green Press, 1974.

Norman Powers, writer/producer, Chelsea Lane Productions, New York, New York

Bordoni, Faustina (c. 1700–1781)

Italian mezzo-soprano. *Name variations: Faustina Hasse. Born around 1700 in Venice, Italy; died on November 4, 1781, in Venice; married Johann Adolf Hasse (a composer), in 1730; studied with Michelangelo Gasparini.*

Debuted in Venice (1716), Naples (1721), Rome (1722); Munich (1723); debuted in London as Rossane in Handel's Alessandro *(1726); appeared on stages throughout Europe until 1751; appeared in concerts in Dresden until 1763.*

Daughter of a Venetian patrician family, Faustina Bordoni trained under Michelangelo Gasparini and Alessandro and Benedetto Marcello. Age 16 when she appeared in Pollarolo's *Ariodante*, she performed in some 30 operas in Venice as her ability to memorize roles quickly made it possible for her to accept many engagements. Though travel at the time was difficult and time consuming, she maintained a schedule much like modern divas who have the advantage of air travel.

In 1726, Handel brought Bordoni to London where she was a huge success in his opera *Allessandro*. She created many roles for Handel, including Alcestis in *Admeto*, Pulcheria in *Riccardo Primo*, Emira in *Siroe*, and Elisa in *Tolomeo*. Bordoni was known for her intelligence and civility, but the latter was missing during one slug fest with her chief rival, soprano ***Francesca Cuzzoni.** During a performance of Bononcini's *Astianatte* at London's Royal Academy of Music (managed by Handel) in 1727, the two singers came to blows. Fueled by an eager press and rowdy audiences of side-taking partisans, the rivalry between the prima donnas delighted opera lovers and sold plenty of tickets but it also effectively destroyed company cohesiveness. This, along with Bordoni's illness, closed the Royal Academy in 1728, and Bordoni returned to Italy.

Two years later, at age 30, she married Johann Adolph Hasse and moved to Dresden. The couple lived and performed there until 1763 when they moved to Vienna and Venice. A superstar in her era, Bordoni was much beloved throughout Europe. Her portrait by ***Rosalba**

Carriera hangs in the Ca'Rezzonico, Venice. Bordoni was also the subject of an opera by Louis Schubert, *Faustina Hasse* (1879).

John Haag,
Athens, Georgia

Bordoni, Irene (1895–1953)

Corsican-American musical-comedy star. *Born in Corsica in 1895; died in 1953; married E. Ray Goetz.*

Known for her slightly risqué performances in the manner of ***Anna Held**, Irene Bordoni first appeared in New York in *Broadway to Paris* (1912). Her breakthrough came in the 1920 production of *As You Were*, in which her husband E. Ray Goetz cast her in the lead. During her heyday, she introduced some classic musical numbers. In *The French Doll* (1922), she sang "Do It Again," and in *Paris* (1928), she introduced Cole Porter's famous "Let's Do It." She also sang Irving Berlin's "It's a Lovely Day Tomorrow" in *Louisiana Purchase* (1940). During her career, Bordoni performed in vaudeville and straight plays. Her last major appearance was as Bloody Mary in a 1951 touring production of *South Pacific.*

Irene Bordoni

Borg, Dorothy (1901–1993)

American historian of modern East Asia and defender of academic freedom during the McCarthy era. *Born in Elberon, New Jersey, on September 4, 1901; died in New York City in October 1993; daughter of Sidney C. and Madeleine (Beer) Borg; graduated from Wellesley College; graduated Columbia University, A.M., Ph.D.*

Studied in China (1940s); helped defend Owen Lattimore from charges of having "lost" China to the Communists; taught at Harvard and Columbia Universities.

Selected writings: The United States and the Far Eastern Crisis, 1933–1938 *(Cambridge, MA: Harvard University Press, 1965); (editor with Waldo Heinrichs)* Uncertain Years: Chinese-American Relations, 1947–1950 *(NY: Columbia University Press, 1980).*

Dorothy Borg, a distinguished member of the first generation of American scholars of East Asian history, refused to be intimidated by the chill winds of McCarthyism in the early 1950s. Born in 1901 in Elberon, New Jersey, she graduated from Wellesley College and earned master's and doctoral degrees in history at Columbia University. Eager to gather firsthand information about the history of East Asia, she spent several years in Beijing and Shanghai as a staff member of the American Council of the Institute of Pacific Relations.

In 1951, at the height of the Cold War, the normally quiet scholarly world of East Asian studies was rocked by accusations that many of its most respected teachers and researchers were in fact either conscious or unwitting agents of subversion. Sensing that useful publicity could be achieved from accusing professors of not fully supporting hardline Cold War policies in East Asia, unscrupulous politicians like Senators Joseph R. McCarthy and Pat McCarran hurled unsubstantiated charges of treason against many distinguished professors and State Department experts on Chinese and East Asian affairs. A series of dramatic hearings before the newly created Internal Security Subcommittee in 1951 and 1952 led to accusations of "disloyalty" and accused some individuals of behavior that had led to the "loss" of China to the Communists in 1949. The most distinguished of the accused academicians, Professor Owen Lattimore of Johns Hopkins University, was accused by McCarthy of being the "top Russian espionage agent" in the United States.

Although her own academic career was not yet fully established, Dorothy Borg responded with vigor to the mudslinging of McCarthy and other "patriotic" politicians. She put her own research plans on the back burner and strove quietly but with determination to defend Lattimore and other scholars whose reputations were being assassinated. She also worked tirelessly to defend the reputation of the Institute of Pacific Relations, which had been accused of not being sufficiently supportive of hardline Cold War policies, including uncritical backing of the defeated Nationalist Chinese regime.

An efficient scholar and administrator, Borg successfully combined the roles of research, writing and the organizing of academic programs. As a research scholar at Harvard University, she was instrumental in organizing area programs that, starting in the 1960s, trained scholars in both American and East Asian history. From 1966 until her retirement a quarter-century later, Borg was a senior research associate at the East Asian Institute of Columbia University. Here, she became known to several generations of scholars both for her learned lectures and skill at organizing and directing countless academic conferences. A highly regarded diplomatic historian, Borg served as a mentor to generations of scholars for more than four decades, and she published several books which remain useful to both scholars and general readers. Dorothy Borg died in New York City in October 1993.

SOURCES:

Saxon, Wolfgang. "Dorothy Borg, 91, East Asia Scholar At Columbia, Dies," in *The New York Times*. October 28, 1993, p. A13.

Schrecker, Ellen W. *No Ivory Tower: McCarthyism and the Universities*. Oxford: Oxford University Press, 1986.

John Haag, Associate Professor,
University of Georgia, Athens, Georgia

Borgia, Lucrezia (1480–1519)

Duchess of Ferrara, who has been known alternately as a monster, a pawn, a beauty, a loving mother, and a great patron of the arts. *Name variations: Madonna Lucrezia; Lucrece Borgia. Pronunciation: Lu-CRE-jha BOR-jha. Born in Rome on April 18, 1480; died in childbirth in Ferrara, Italy, on June 24, 1519; daughter of Rodrigo Borgia (later named Pope Alexander VI) and Vannozza Cattanei; married Giovanni Sforza, in June 1493 (divorced 1497); married Alfonso di Biselli (Alphonso of Aragon), in 1498 (killed, 1500); married Alfonso I d'Este (1476–1534), 3rd duke of Ferrara and Modena, in November 1501; children: (second marriage) Rodrigo di Biselli (1499–1512); (third marriage) Ercole II (1508–1559), 4th duke of Ferrara and Modena (who married* ****Renée of France****); Cardinal Ippolito II (1509–1572); Alessandro (1514–1516);* ****Eleonora d'Este*** *(1515–1575); Francesco d'Este (1516–1578).*

Few people in history have achieved the level of notoriety that Lucrezia Borgia accumulated during her lifetime and for centuries afterwards. Born into a powerful and dangerous family, Lucrezia survived many scandals and intrigues before she finally made a place for herself at the court of Ferrara. Rumors begun by the rivals and gossips of her era survived well into the 19th century, providing a basis for Victor Hugo's play, *Lucrece Borgia*, and Gaetano Donizetti's opera by the same name. In those fictional accounts, Lucrezia Borgia is represented as a murderer and sexual fiend. Early in the 20th century, however, historians began working out the complicated details of her life. Biographies written in the 1930s and 1940s offer a more sympathetic representation of Lucrezia Borgia.

Cattanei, Vannozza (1442–1518)

Italian noblewoman. *Name variations: Vanozza dei Catanei; Rosa Vanozza. Probably born in Mantua in 1442; died on November 26, 1518; buried in Santa Maria del Populo with the highest honors; mistress of Alexander VI (Rodrigo Borgia) from c. 1468–1482; married Domenico d'Arignano (an officer of the church); married Giorgio san Croce (an Apostolic clerk and Venetian scholar), in 1480 (died 1486); married Carlo Canale (a protégé of the Gonzaga family), in 1486; children: (with Rodrigo Borgia) Cesare (1475–1507); Juan I (1476–1497), 2nd duke of Gandia;* ****Lucrezia Borgia*** *(1480–1519); Geoffredo also known as Joffré (1482–1517); (second marriage) Ottaviano.*

Because of her long and loving relationship with Rodrigo Borgia, Vannozza Cattanei lived in comfort. She saw her children of this union often but did not live with them. Except for short periods, she was married to others and lived a dignified and conventional life away from Rodrigo. During her marriage to Giorgio de Croce (1480–46), she lived in an imposing house in Rome, next to Rodrigo's, in Piazza Pizzo di Merlo. The house, which faced the piazza, was light and sunny, with many rooms, and her beloved garden. When Giorgio died, Vannozza remarried and went to live in Piazza Branca in the Arenula district. A large bequest to the Brotherhood of the Gonfalonieri ensured a splendid funeral when she died in 1518, age 76. "They decided to honor her 'with a proud and splendid monument,' writes **Rachel Erlanger**, 'and to celebrate a yearly mass on the anniversary of her death, as well as other ceremonies 'for the purpose of commending her soul's salvation to God.' For some unknown reason, the monument was never erected, but the masses were sung for over two hundred years, after which the soul of Vannozza was left to fend for itself."

SOURCES:

Erlanger, Rachel. *Lucrezia Borgia: A Biography*. NY: Hawthorn, 1978.

She was born on April 18, 1480, to ❧ **Vannozza Cattanei** and Rodrigo Borgia, who was then an acting cardinal in Rome. Vannozza was the favored mistress of the cardinal, and he used his position to make sure she was well cared for, providing her with a well-to-do husband and a large home on the Piazza Pizzo di Merlo. Vannozza had four children with Rodrigo; besides Lucrezia, there were Cesare, Juan, and Joffré. Like many others born to cardinals and bishops at this time, the children were raised with all the privileges of royalty. Each could look forward to a fairly secure position later in life and had the potential to gain great power. Lucrezia was to be a highly valued marriage partner, and several noble families would have been pleased to align themselves with the powerful Rodrigo Borgia by arranging a marriage with his daughter.

In early childhood, Lucrezia lived with Vannozza at her home. It is not clear how long she stayed with her mother, but at some point Rodrigo Borgia entrusted the care of his daughter to a cousin, ❧ **Adriana Mila**. Adriana saw to Lucrezia's education, probably in a respected local convent. There are no records indicating where

Lucrezia Borgia

or how Lucrezia was educated, but noble girls at this time were usually taught classical literature, music, art, and some philosophy. It is known that Lucrezia could speak Spanish, Greek, Italian, French, and a little Latin. She enjoyed music, loved to dance, and is said to have tried her hand at poetry, though none of it survives. Much of her education was designed to make her a social success and a tribute to any family. Whatever else was said about Lucrezia, nearly all of the chroniclers and correspondents of the day remark on what a lovely and charming woman she was.

By the age of 13, Lucrezia had been betrothed twice. The first marriage contract, in 1491, was to a young Spanish noble named Don Juan de Centelles. The Borgia family had Spanish origins, and Rodrigo was content with finding a match for Lucrezia in that country. For unknown reasons, Rodrigo broke that contract within a year and signed a new one with another Spaniard, Gaspare de Procida, the Count of Aversa. That marriage would have gone on without a hitch were it not for a remarkable development in 1492, the same year Columbus landed in the West Indies. Rodrigo Borgia was elected pope, and all his plans were changed. Though Rodrigo's uncle had been named Pope Calixtus III, and Rodrigo certainly had dreams of grandeur, he had not expected to achieve his glory so early. As Pope Alexander VI, he could make an even better match for his daughter, one of national importance that had the potential to enhance the power of the Borgias. Gaspare was simply ignored, and Lucrezia was married to Giovanni Sforza of Pesaro on June 12, 1493.

Italy at this time was not a single country but a series of related kingdoms and territories. Many of the personal alliances made by Pope Alexander, through Lucrezia or other family members, depended on the ever-changing balance of power. At this juncture, the pope and the regent of Milan were allied with the French king, Charles VIII, against the king of Naples. The Sforza family represented a strong connection with other potential enemies of Naples, and Giovanni Sforza was a good political catch despite his youth.

There is nothing to indicate what Lucrezia thought about her new husband or the politics that gave him to her. For some time before the wedding, Lucrezia had been living with Adriana Mila and **Giulia Farnese**, a new companion to the pope, in the palace of Santa Maria in Portico. It was a splendid place, provided and furnished by Alexander, located near enough to the Vatican so he could spend much of his time with his three favorite women. Giulia was his mistress and Adriana, his cousin, was a confidante and friend. The pope's affection for his daughter is legendary, and they corresponded enthusiastically whenever they had to be separated. This may be one of the reasons that later rumors of incest were started by critics of the Borgia family. Nevertheless, they were a fun-loving group and indulged in festivity when the occasion arose. Lucrezia's wedding was such an occasion, and the merrymaking that took place was the subject of much destructive gossip. Those chroniclers present tell only of excessive feasting, dancing, and parlor games, but none of the perverted activities hinted at by outside sources.

Giovanni stayed with his young wife in Rome for only one month before returning to Pesaro, while Lucrezia, only 13 years old, stayed on with Adriana and Giulia in Portico. The marriage had not been consummated, as is clear in a letter from the pope to Giovanni, offering him the entirety of the dowry money if he would return to Rome and see to this duty. No marriage was legally complete without consummation. Giovanni came to Rome briefly in November and again in January 1494. There are few details

Mila, Adriana (fl. 1469–1502)

Italian noblewoman. *Name variations: Adriana da Mila, Adriana Milo, Adriana Orsini. Probably born in Rome; died after 1502; daughter of Pedro de Mila (a Catalan); second cousin to Rodrigo or Roderigo Borgia; married Ludovico Orsini (died before 1489); children: Orsino Orsini.*

Farnese, Giulia (1474–1518?)

Italian noblewoman. *Name variations: Julia Farnese. Born in 1474; died after 1518; daughter of Pier Luigi Farnese; sister of Alessandro (Alexander) Farnese who later was elected Pope Paul III; married Orsino Orsini, on May 21, 1489; mistress of Alexander VI (Rodrigo or Roderigo Borgia).*

While Cesare and ***Lucrezia Borgia** were living at the Orsini palace with Adriana Mila, "the magnificent and unaffected" 15-year-old Giulia Farnese arrived on the arm of her new husband Orsino Orsini, Adriana's son. Giulia, known as "Giulia Bella," came from an ancient family belonging to the provincial nobility with estates around Lake Bolsena. By November 1493, Giulia was Rodrigo Borgia's favorite mistress. To show his favor, Borgia, who had been elected Pope Alexander VI a year earlier, made Giulia's brother Alessandro a cardinal. (Alessandro Farnese would later be elected Pope Paul III). A portrait of Giulia Farnese by Luca Longhi shows her with the mythical unicorn, a symbol of Chastity.

available about his visits, but, in May of that year, Lucrezia and her two companions left to join Giovanni in Pesaro. They may have left Rome in order to escape an outbreak of the bubonic plague in the city. Once having arrived in Pesaro, the three ladies entertained the local nobility but were not impressed with the town. In several letters to the pope, Lucrezia complained about the limited social occasions out in the province. Adding to her boredom, perhaps, was the fact that her new husband was often absent. Most of the year spent in Pesaro was monotonous, but at one point, there were rumors of Lucrezia suffering a mental breakdown. The pope did not rest until he received a letter directly from Lucrezia saying that she was fine.

She is a most intelligent and lovely, and also exceedingly gracious lady. . . . In short, her character is such that it is impossible to suspect anything "sinister" of her.

—**Ambassador of Ferrara**

Politics would intrude on what was, up to this point, a fairly normal arranged marriage. Pope Alexander's discreet participation in the alliance against Naples had placed him in a difficult position. The Sforza family was not doing well, politically, and the pope now worried that he had made a mistake in linking up with them. Meanwhile, Naples had successfully repelled the French army, and was now a force to be reckoned with. Deciding to cut his connection to Pesaro, Alexander began the process of divorcing his daughter from Giovanni. When Giovanni and Lucrezia returned to Rome in 1495, Alexander requested that his son-in-law agree to an annulment. It is not clear what Lucrezia's feelings for her husband were, though she was certainly respectful to him in public. Some sources say she may have saved his life, however, by convincing one of his grooms to hide in her room and eavesdrop on a conversation between her and an agent of her father's. According to the legend, the conversation made clear that Giovanni would be eliminated if he did not leave on his own, and the groom reported this to Giovanni. Whether or not this actually took place, Giovanni left Rome without warning in 1495.

The pope used his position to decree an annulment of the marriage based on non-consummation; he proclaimed widely that Giovanni was impotent. In response to this insult, Giovanni spread the rumor that Alexander had annulled the marriage because he wanted his daughter "for himself." The suggestion of incest was eagerly picked up by enemies of the pope. In the meantime, Lucrezia had retired briefly to the convent of San Sisto on the Via Appia, and new rumors declared that she was hiding because she had had an affair and was carrying an illegitimate child. A messenger named Pedro Calderon was the alleged lover, and he was reportedly murdered by Lucrezia's brother, Cesare Borgia. There is no mention of what happened to the supposed child.

Alexander's new choice for Lucrezia was Duke Alfonso di Biselli, a favored illegitimate son of the king of Naples. Alfonso was also the brother of ❧ **Sancha of Aragon**, a friend of Lucrezia's and the wife of Lucrezia's brother, Joffré. Lucrezia and Alfonso, both aged 18, took well to each other and were married some time in July 1498. They lived a rather gay life together in Rome, and within a year Lucrezia was pregnant. This was to be, unfortunately, one of many miscarriages. She recovered easily, however, and was pregnant once more when Alfonso was forced by her father and brother to leave Rome. Alexander and Cesare had renewed and strengthened an alliance with France, which was still an enemy of Naples. Cesare was ambitious and hoped to further his political career by pleasing the French crown. To do this, he needed to rid the Borgias of their inconvenient connection to Naples.

Lucrezia was heartbroken, so the story goes, and her father made her acting regent of Spoleto so he would not have to listen to her cry. He may also have hoped that giving her an official duty would make it more difficult for her to defy him and join her husband at Naples. She was also granted Sermoneta and Nepi, and retained as well her position of duchess of Biselli through her husband. As regent, she was entitled to all revenues from the territory, and she governed for several months. When her first child was born on November 1, 1499, she named the boy Rodrigo, after her father. In 1500, she returned to Rome with her new son and was joined there by Alfonso, who came at the pope's invitation. All was well until July 15, when Alfonso, after a friendly dinner with his wife and the pope, was leaving the Vatican. He and his companions were attacked by swordsmen in the street, and Alfonso, badly injured, was saved and brought back to the Vatican. Lucrezia and Alexander were horrified, and a carefully guarded sick room was set up in the pope's apartments.

Assisted by Sancha, Lucrezia took personal care of Alfonso, preparing his food by hand in his room to avoid any chance of a poisoning. One of them was always by his side. Cesare, with his well-known ambitions and willingness to use violence, was the obvious suspect in the attack. It is even said that he visited Alfonso's bedside and remarked: "What is not accomplished at noon may be done at night." Alfonso's tense recovery continued until, on August 18, Lucrezia and Sancha were tricked or forced into leaving his bedside. The young duke was strangled within minutes.

Once more, Lucrezia was sent away by her father to grieve in private. This time, at her own request, she worked as the governor of Nepi for several months. While there, Cesare came to visit in an attempt to right things between them. Lucrezia had always been in awe of her older brother, and they had been fairly close. Rumors had circulated for years, suggesting that the powerful brother and sister were a bit too close. According to some sources, however, Cesare understood what damage his sister suffered because of his political intrigues. Not knowing what reaction to expect from her after the murder of Alfonso, he was accompanied by armed soldiers when he visited her at Nepi. When facing Lucrezia, Cesare may have claimed that Alfonso was likely to have killed him, and that he only protected himself by moving first. Whatever passed between them at Nepi, their relationship was repaired. In later years, Lucrezia would become his greatest advocate, and he protected his sister with ferocity. He visited her often, even if it meant traveling days out of his way; on one occasion, when Lucrezia was suffering from a fever and had refused medical care, Cesare appeared at her bedside and convinced her to let the doctors bleed her.

When it came time to return to Rome, Lucrezia wrote to a trusted servant that she was filled with "misgivings and anxiety." It is said that when she last saw her father she had raged against his inability or unwillingness to protect her husband from Cesare. In truth, Alexander at the time had already started looking for her next husband—someone who would not upset the new alliance with the French. He was not likely to have stood in Cesare's way when the chance to be rid of Alfonso arose. Lucrezia had probably suspected this and accused her father of compliance in the murder. Now, Lucrezia cautiously returned to Rome to make up with her father and await new developments.

In 1501, Pope Alexander wished to travel and oversee some of the fighting in the never-ending territorial struggles. Cesare had recently invaded and confiscated Pesaro, and the pope saw the chance to expand his own territory. He

Sancha of Aragon (1478–1506)

Italian noblewoman. *Name variations: Sanchia of Aragon. Born in Gaeta in 1478; died in Naples in 1586; illegitimate daughter of Alfonso also known as Alphonso II of Aragon (1448–1495), king of Naples (r. 1494–1495), and* ***Trogia Gazzela;*** *niece of Ferrante of Aragon, king of Naples; sister of Duke Alfonso di Biselli (husband of *****Lucrezia Borgia****); betrothed to Joffré Borgia in 1493.*

left Lucrezia, who had been living with her infant son at the Palace of Saint Peter's, in charge of all papal correspondence. It was most unusual for a lay person, especially a woman, to handle such important business. She was to ask the respected Cardinal of Lisbon for guidance in matters of importance.

The next proposed match for Lucrezia was Alfonso d'Este, prince of Ferrara, a 24-year-old, childless widower, who stood to inherit a great dukedom. Though Alfonso was opposed to the marriage, his father, Duke Ercole, reportedly made the arrangements. Neither of them, however, was thrilled to be receiving such an infamous lady into such an old and respected family as the Estes. They sent ambassadors to Rome to meet Lucrezia and send back their opinions. The reports that came back were positive, and negotiations began.

In spite of the clear danger linked with marrying Lucrezia Borgia, Alexander had received many offers of marriage for his recently widowed daughter. So far, her husbands had suffered terrible fates. Alexander, on the other hand, was determined to win over the house of Este. Lucrezia, too, was eager for these arrangements to be finalized. Perhaps she was ready to leave Rome and start anew, hoping that a powerful enough match would remove her from the manipulation of her family. Many sources indicate that Lucrezia was pushing harder than anyone for this marriage to take place.

Among the dowry demands being proposed by Este was that the people of Ferrara be released indefinitely from paying tithes to the church, and that the house of Este be guaranteed control of the duchy of Ferrara. These arrangements would ensure that the territory could not be taken over by the pope once he was a relative. Lucrezia began corresponding with Duke Ercole, promising her help in these matters. When he asked her to use her influence to have several nuns from

Viterbo and Narni transferred to a newly established convent in Ferrara, she saw that it was done; she then offered the nuns as a gift to her new father-in-law. Ercole also expected religious posts for several of his relatives, which he eventually procured. The arrangements were made over the next few months, and the contract was signed. On November 5, 1501, festivities began in Rome. The marriage was performed in the Vatican on December 30, with someone standing in as proxy for Prince Alfonso. Lucrezia would join her husband later in Ferrara.

There was one last scandal before Lucrezia left Rome, and it concerned a party thrown in her honor by Cesare. There were reports of explicit sexual performances given by local prostitutes, with Lucrezia and the pope in the audience. Whether or not this actually happened is a mystery that will never be resolved; there are a number of conflicting stories. Nevertheless, there were many parties given for Lucrezia in the days before she left. Finally, she was prepared to leave with a Ferrarese escort and her own entourage on the morning of January 6, 1502. It had been decided that Rodrigo, Lucrezia's son by the duke of Biselli, would remain in Rome in the care of a relative. Lucrezia would provide for his care and education out of her own money so the Estes family would not have to take him in. Lucrezia said goodbye to her father at the Vatican; she was never to see him again.

Her departure from Rome is considered to be a major turning point in her life. The worst that was said about her after this day was that she spent too long on her hair and general toilet, a habit that held up the entourage as it traveled through Italy to Ferrara. A Ferrarese ambassador complained of her constant need for rest and washing, which delayed them in almost every city along the way. However, Lucrezia was passing through many cities now owned by her brother, and some that she had once governed herself. At each stop, she was welcomed and honored. It is likely that she was more concerned with making a good impression than with keeping to an arranged schedule. The group made progress, however, and on February 1, they met up with ***Isabella d'Este** (1474–1539), the marchesa of Mantua and sister of Alfonso d'Este. Isabella finished the journey by Lucrezia's side, and they approached Ferrara together. Alfonso also rode out some distance to meet his new wife and lead her procession into the city.

The festivities in Ferrara were splendid, designed to impress the new duchess and her followers, as well as the representatives of France who were there to witness the event. During the weeklong carnival, Lucrezia established the nature of her new relationships. Alfonso was attentive and respectful in public and performed his husbandly duties each night with vigor. The pope was happy to receive the report that his daughter and her new partner consummated the match several times on the first night. During the day, however, Alfonso was free to pursue his favorite activities, alternating between military exercises and visits to brothels. Over the next several years, Lucrezia was to experience countless pregnancies, most of them ending in miscarriage.

Isabella and Lucrezia regarded each other as rivals for the position of the most admired woman at court. Their initial letters to each other and to friends are littered with cool, but catty, remarks about hair, dress, and conversation. Isabella and her companions were the primary critics of Lucrezia's habit of sleeping late and spending hours on her appearance. Over time, however, the two women became friendly, if not actually close friends. In later years, they corresponded regularly and with a certain affection. Although it is said that Lucrezia eventually had an affair with Isabella's husband, Francesco Gonzaga, it did not seem to affect the relations between the women. Isabella is widely considered to have been a stronger and more intelligent leader than her husband, the marquis, and it is possible she had little affection for him.

The most heated conflicts Lucrezia encountered in the first few years at Ferrara were with her father-in-law, Ercole. He gave her an allowance and the Castel Vecchio, at which she established her court. However, the money he offered was less than she was used to spending, and when direct arguments failed to get her a raise, she complained to her father. The pope gently convinced the duke to advance Lucrezia more money, but then tried to remain above the fray. Alfonso, perhaps wisely, also avoided getting involved in the issue. Their second conflict concerned the make-up of Lucrezia's court: Spaniards, personal favorites, and relatives. According to legend, their outlandish and wild partying offended the more somber Ferrarese. There were also several locals who had been hired by Ercole to serve Lucrezia; he preferred his own people over the "foreigners" that accompanied his daughter-in-law. Eventually, Ercole simply dismissed the Spanish attendants and ignored Lucrezia's tearful complaints of loneliness.

When Pope Alexander VI died on August 18, 1503, the fortunes of the Borgia clan changed abruptly. The newly elected pope, Julius

II, was a rival of the family, and the king of France decided it was worth more to be in a pope's favor than to look out for alliances that had lost their meaning. Cesare was abandoned to fate, and, in 1504, he was taken out of Italy as a prisoner of Spain. Lucrezia faced potential danger, but the Estes decided to let her be. Within a few months, she had lost her father, seen her brother destroyed, and suffered another of many miscarriages. Her grief briefly overwhelmed her, but her personality and loyalty to her new family may have saved her. For whatever reason, she remained safe, and Ercole even indulged her in her petitions to get Cesare freed. Lucrezia tirelessly wrote to the new pope and to the king of France, hoping to save her brother.

In 1505, Ercole died, and Alfonso became the new duke of Ferrara. Lucrezia gave birth to a son, Alessandro, who died after only two months. Continued territorial skirmishes called Alfonso away from Ferrara to fight for the pope in a war on Milan. In 1506, Lucrezia acted as regent of Ferrara in conjunction with her brother-in-law, Cardinal Ippolito. A military man like his brother, Ippolito also left Ferrara for the war, and Lucrezia governed alone, on and off for the next few years. Between 1509 and 1513, Pope Julius II tried to seize Ferrara, and Alfonso and Ippolito again left Lucrezia in charge. She received praise in her governing abilities. It is said that in 1509 she passed one of the few laws in Ferrara protecting the Jews from persecution. Lucrezia also pawned most of her jewels and gowns to help finance the war, as well as to found a convent and a hospital.

For the last ten years of her life, Lucrezia enjoyed relative stability and content. She was pregnant almost constantly; when Cesare was killed in 1507, the news had been kept from her for almost a month while she suffered from a complicated pregnancy. In 1508, Alfonso returned to Ferrara and was temporarily in control of his territory. On April 4 of that year, Lucrezia gave birth to a son, and they named him Ercole. He would grow up to be the next duke of Ferrara. In 1509, while acting as regent of the city, she had another son, named Ippolito, who became a cardinal like his uncle and namesake. Unfortunately, in 1512, while Ferrara was fighting off the pope's armies, Lucrezia received word that Rodrigo di Biselli, her first-born son, had died of an illness in Rome. In 1514, a third son was born, named Alessandro, who lived only two years. Lucrezia's only daughter, Eleonora, was born in 1515, followed by another son, Francesco, in 1516. Only five of Lucrezia's children outlived her.

In addition to her political and maternal activities, Lucrezia Borgia had also successfully created a cultural center at her court. Alfonso had no care for intellectual pursuits, and Lucrezia happily replaced Duke Ercole as the city's greatest art patron. She enjoyed a close friendship with the poet Ercole Strozzi until his murder in 1508; the convent she founded was near the site of his death. Lucrezia had a more romantic friendship and correspondence with Pietro Bembo, a poet and later a papal secretary. Bembo dedicated his famous work, "Asolani," to Lucrezia in 1505. There are hints of passion in their flowery letters to one another, but it is unclear whether they had the opportunity or inclination for a physical relationship. Lucrezia funded painters and performers across the city and entertained at Vecchio whenever she could. A catalogue of her personal library reveals a preference for religious works and romantic prose, as well as some philosophy.

On June 15, 1519, Lucrezia Borgia collapsed during another difficult pregnancy. After giving birth prematurely to a girl who only lived a few hours, Lucrezia lingered for more than a week, in and out of consciousness. She dictated a letter to Pope Leo X, asking for the highest blessing and forgiveness as she faced death. She seemed comforted when she received word that he had granted it, and she died at the age of 40 on the night of June 24, with Alfonso at her side.

SOURCES:

Bellonci, Maria. *The Life and Times of Lucrezia Borgia.* Italy: Arnoldo Mondadori, 1939. Translation, NY: Harcourt, Brace, 1953.

Chamberlin, E.R. *The Fall of the House of Borgia.* NY: Dial Press, 1974.

Gardner, Edmund. *Dukes and Poets in Ferrara.* NY: E.P. Dutton, 1904.

Gregorovius, Ferdinand. *Lucrezia Borgia: A Chapter from the Morals of the Italian Renaissance.* NY: Phaidon, 1948.

Mallet, Michael. *The Borgias: The Rise and Fall of a Renaissance Dynasty.* NY: Barnes and Noble, 1969.

Shankland, Hugh, trans. *The Prettiest Love Letters in the World: Letters between Lucrezia Borgia and Pietro Bembo, 1503–1519.* London: Collias Harvill, 1987.

RELATED MEDIA:

Donizetti, Gaetano. *Lucrezia Borgia* (sound recording, opera). NY: National Philharmonic Orchestra (Great Britain), 1977.

Hugo, Victor. *Lucrece Borgia: Oeuvres Completes de Victor Hugo.* Paris: Librairie Charpentier et Fasquelle, date unknown.

Nancy L. Locklin, Ph.D. candidate,
Emory University, Atlanta, Georgia

Borgström, Hilda (1871–1953)

Swedish actress. *Name variations: Borgstrom. Born on October 13, 1871, in Stockholm, Sweden; died in*

1953; studied drama and ballet at Stockholm's Royal Dramatic Theater.

Films include: A Summer Tale *(1912);* A Secret Marriage *(1912);* Lady Marion's Summer Flirtation *(1913);* Ingeborg Holm *(*Give Us This Day, *1913);* Do Not Judge *(1914);* Brandsoldaten *(1916);* Fru Kristina *(1917);* Caroline Redivinaa *(1920);* The Phantom Carriage *(*Thy Soul Shall Bear Witness, *1921);* Flight From Paradise *(1924);* The Lady of the Camelias *(1925);* Giftas *(1926);* Adalens Poesi *(1928);* Värmlänningarna *(1932);* The Andersson Family *(1937);* A Woman's Face *(1938);* Bastard *(1940);* A Crime *(1940);* The Fight Goes On *(1941);* Dangerous Roads *(1942);* Flames in the Dark *(1942);* Ride Tonight! *(1942);* Women in Prison *(1943);* I Killed *(1943);* A Day Shall Dawn *(1944);* Appassionata *(1944);* The Invisible Wall *(1944);* The Emperor of Portugal *(1944);* Royal Rabble *(1945);* Mandragora *(1945);* Desire *(1946);* Music in Darkness *(*Night Is My Future, *1948);* Banquet *(1948);* Eva *(1948);* The Girl From the Gallery *(1949).*

Hilda Borgström, one of Sweden's most admired silent-screen actresses, trained for the ballet as a child. Appearing on the stage while still a teenager, she became a leading lady even before her screen debut in 1912. Borgström appeared in the films of Victor Sjöström and other great directors of the silent era. She went on to play supporting roles in countless talkies throughout the 1940s, including an early film directed by Ingmar Bergman.

Bori, Lucrezia (1887–1960)

Spanish soprano. *Born Lucrecia Borja y Gonzales de Riancho on December 4, 1887, in Valencia, Spain; died on May 14, 1960, in New York; daughter of an aristocratic family; educated in a convent; studied with Melchiorre Vidal in Milan and at the Valencia Conservatory.*

Debuted as Micaela in Carmen *in Rome (1908), at Teatro alla Scala (1909), Paris (1910); debuted at the Metropolitan Opera in* Manon Lescaut *(1912), continuing to appear there until 1936; first woman elected to the Metropolitan Opera Board of Directors, a position in which she served from 1935–60.*

Singing was not easy for Lucrezia Bori. At age 28, she had to withdraw from the Met when nodules developed on her vocal cords, and the operation to remove them was unsuccessful. A second procedure was tried in Milan in 1916 which also failed. The surgeon warned her that only long silence could cure her voice. Anxious to continue her career, she followed his advice and did not use her voice for 12 months. A year later, she spoke only in a whisper. During her illness, she regularly visited a shrine of St. Francis, vowing to dedicate her life to charity if her voice was returned. After an absence of five years, she was finally able to return to the stage. "Never during the long dark months when I was not permitted to talk, let alone sing, did I lose faith," she once said. "But it *was* terrible. I felt as must those stricken with sudden blindness, just as the sun of spring flooded the world."

Lucrecia Borja studied in her native Spain before going to Italy. There, she changed the spelling of her name from Borja to Bori to minimize her connection with the sinister Borgias to whom she was, in fact, related. Her success in Italy was immediate. When Bori returned to the Metropolitan Opera in 1921 as Mimi in *La Bohème*, she was a devout Roman Catholic and had dedicated her voice to God. An instant love affair flared between Bori and her American audience; from this point forward, her career would mainly unfold in the U.S. where her beautiful voice and superb acting skills made her a favorite for many years.

When the Depression hit, Bori spent her free time campaigning for funds to save the Met, writing letters and making speeches on behalf of the great opera house. She was the first woman elected to the board of directors and remained on the board until her death. Bori also served as honorary chair of the Metropolitan Opera Guild. Never forgotten in her native Spain, when Bori died thousands lined the streets of Valencia to bid her farewell. Most were grateful for the funds she had raised for the city after devastating floods in 1957. Summing up the city's attitude, one mourner remarked, "It is because of her I have a roof over my head." Those who work at the Metropolitan Opera could say the same.

John Haag,
Athens, Georgia

Boring, Alice Middleton (1883–1955)

American cytologist, geneticist, and zoologist who bridged scientific understanding between East and West. *Born in Philadelphia, Pennsylvania, in 1883; died in Cambridge, Massachusetts, in 1955; one of four children of Edwin (a pharmacist) and Elizabeth (Truman) Boring; graduated Friends' Central School, Philadelphia, 1900; Bryn Mawr College, B.A., 1904, M.A., 1905, Ph.D., 1910; fellow at University of Pennsylvania, 1905–06.*

Lucrezia Bori

Alice Boring's unusual academic career encompassed three scientific fields and two cultures. At Bryn Mawr College, she majored in cytology (the study of the formation, structure, and function of cells) and genetics, working with noted cytology and genetics professors ***Nettie Stevens** and Thomas Hunt Morgan. With Morgan, Boring also co-authored the first of some 36 works. Her studies included a year at the University of Pennsylvania under biologist Edwin Conklin, as well as some time at the University of Würtzburg in Germany. Boring's Ph.D. dissertation investigated the behavior of chromosomes in the formation of spermatozoa in insects.

In 1918, after teaching for eight years in the University of Maine's zoology department, Boring accepted a two-year teaching post as assistant professor of biology at China's Peking Union Medical College. She fell in love with China's culture and people. Returning to the U.S. in 1920, she taught briefly at Wellesley College, only to return to China as soon as a temporary position opened at Peking University (later called Yenching University). Although she asked for only a two-year leave of absence from Wellesley, she soon became so involved in Chinese social and political concerns, that these became the foundation of her life's work. She changed her scientific focus and began the study of China's lizards and amphibians, making contributions to literature in the field. As a teacher, she provided Chinese students with the benefit of her Western point of view. Her broader contribution was a bridge for scientific understanding between East and West.

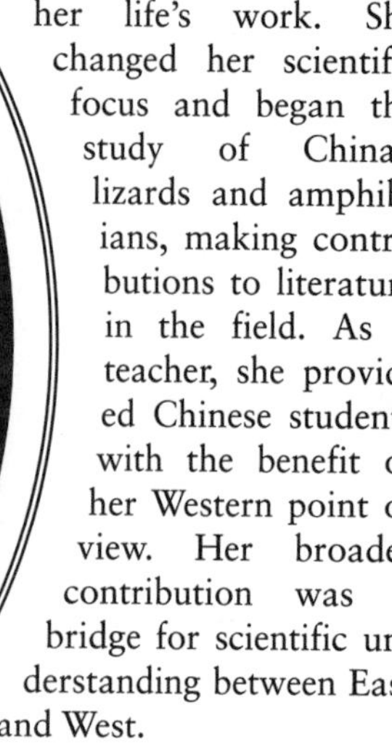

Inge Borkh

During the 1937 Japanese invasion, life at the university became difficult. Mail delivery was curtailed and money became scarce. In 1941, the English and American faculty members of the university were put in a concentration camp in Shantung, during which time Boring's family had no contact with her. In 1943, she was repatriated. In a letter to a friend, written during the voyage back to the United States, Boring wrote that she and her colleagues had survived quite well. "We shall not look like physical wrecks when you see us in New York, even if our clothes may be rather dilapidated."

Upon her return, Boring held positions at Columbia University and Mount Holyoke. In 1946, she returned to Yenching University, which was now in the midst of new conflicts between China's Communists and Nationalists. Boring began to soften toward the Communists' approach, writing to her family in 1949 that she was "surprised to find that in spite of my opposition in the past, I now am full of hope!" Called home in 1950, due to her sister's failing health, Boring settled in Cambridge, Massachusetts, but took a part-time teaching position at Smith College in Northampton. She died of cerebral arteriosclerosis in 1955.

Barbara Morgan,
Melrose, Massachusetts

Borja, Ana de (c. 1640–1706)

Vice-queen of Peru. *Pronunciation: BOR-ha. Born in Spain around 1640; died on September 23, 1706; daughter of the duke of Bejar; third wife of Pedro Fernandez de Castro, Andrade y Portugal, Count of Lemos (1634–1672).*

Third wife of the Count of Lemos, Ana de Borja accompanied her husband from Spain to Peru when he was appointed viceroy of Peru in 1667. In 1668 and 1669, during the absence of the viceroy in Charcas, she was left in charge of the government, a singular event for a woman in Spanish America.

Borkh, Inge (1917—)

Swiss soprano. *Born Ingeborg Simon on May 26, 1917, in Mannheim; married Alexander Welitsch (a singer); studied acting at the Max Reinhardt seminar in Vienna and singing at the Salzburg Mozarteum and in Milan.*

Debuted in Lucerne (1940–41); appeared in Basel (1951); debuted in San Francisco as Verdi's Lady MacBeth (1955); debuted at Metropolitan Opera as Salome (1958); gave first Covent Garden performance (1967).

Inge Borkh shared the operatic stage with such singers as ***Birgit Nilsson**, ***Maria Callas**, ***Renata Tebaldi**, ***Zinka Milanov**, and ***Leontyne Price** in the golden age of dramatic sopranos. Despite this competition, recordings reveal Borkh had a dramatic excellence all her own. Few singers performed both Italian and German roles with equal security. Indeed, Borkh was one of the few German singers who could be mistaken for an Italian, yet she excelled in the German as well. Her complete recording of *Turandot* is an excellent example of her artistry in Italian music. Her crowning achievement was probably as Elektra in Richard Strauss' opera.

John Haag,
Athens, Georgia

Bosboom-Toussaint, Anna (1812–1886)

Dutch novelist. *Name variations: Anna Louisa Toussaint. Born Anna Louisa Geertruida Toussaint at Alkmaar in north Holland on September 16, 1812; died at The Hague on April 13, 1886; daughter of a local chemist named Toussaint; married Johannes Bosboom (1817–1891, a Dutch painter), in 1851.*

Anna Bosboom-Toussaint's father, a local chemist of Huguenot descent, saw that she had a fair education. Early in her career, she developed a taste for historical research, which was perhaps nurtured by a forced indoor life due to ill health. In 1851, she married the Dutch painter Johannes Bosboom, and was known thereafter as Mrs. Bosboom-Toussaint. Her first romance, *Almagro*, appeared in 1837, followed by the *Graaf van Devonshire* (*The Earl of Devonshire*) in 1838, the *Engelschen te Rome* (*The English at Rome*) in 1840, and *Het Huis Lauernesse* (The House of Lauernesse) in 1841, an episode of the Reformation which was translated into many European languages. Founded on some of the most interesting epochs of Dutch history, many of these stories were said to reveal a strong assimilation of facts and situations, combined with Anna's great mastery over her mother tongue. Bosboom-Toussaint devoted the ten years between 1840 and 1850 mainly to further studies, which resulted in the appearance in 1851–54 of *Leycester in Nederland* (3 vols.), *Vrouwen van het Leycestersche Tydperk (Women of Leicester's Epoch,* 3 vols.), and *Gideon Florensz* (3 vols.), a series dealing with Robert Dudley's adventures in the Low Countries. After 1870, she abandoned historical romance for the modern society novel, but her *Delftsche Wonderdokter* (The Necromancer of Delft, 1871, 3 vols.) and *Majoor Frans* (Major Frank, 1875, 3 vols.) did not command the success of her earlier works. *Major Frank* was translated into English in 1885. Her novels were published in a collected edition (1885–1888, 25 vols.).

Boscawen, Fanny (1719–1805)

British diarist, correspondent, and co-founder of the Bluestocking group. *Born Frances Evelyn Glanville on July 23, 1719, in St. Clere, Kent, England; died on February 26, 1805, in London, England; daughter of Frances and William Evelyn Glanville (a politician and sheriff); educated at home; married Edward Boscawen (a naval officer), on December 11, 1742; children: Edward Hugh (1744–1774); Frances (b. 1746); Elizabeth (b. 1747); William (1751–1769); Benjamin (b. 1758).*

By describing political, social and familial scenes in letters to her husband and friends, Fanny Boscawen left a diary of England's military and colonial decline during the 18th century. She was born in St. Clere, Kent, England, on July 23, 1719. Her mother **Frances Glanville,** heir to a considerable family legacy, died during a subsequent childbirth. Taking his wife's surname for status, William Evelyn Glanville remarried in St. Clere, Kent, while Fanny spent most of her youth with relatives.

Through her cousins, 18-year-old Fanny met the 23-year-old naval captain Edward Boscawen in 1738, and the two courted, though they kept the romance secret while he spent the next three years largely at sea. When he made port in May of 1742, they were engaged, then married by year's end. Fanny's navy life began abruptly. While she established their home in London, Ned, as the captain was known, set sail and was away almost continually for 18 months. The long absence was followed by an equal length of shore duty, during which Boscawen's first two children were born. Ned set sail again in the spring of 1746, and Fanny obtained a rented country home. This acquisition required negotiation with her father, who withheld her inheritance to keep his second family in their accustomed manner, but she obtained enough to take the cottage at Beddington. From then on, she kept a home outside London, believing country air to be better for her children's health.

Throughout 1746 and 1747, Ned was at sea frequently, defending Britain's colonial holdings. He was promoted to rear admiral following a financially successful battle in which a huge bounty was taken (after the government took its cut, a ship's crew divided seized loot). All the while, Fanny wrote to her husband, sharing news of politics, friends, as well as her daily activities and those of her children. In May of 1747, the third Boscawen child was born. Six months later, Ned was sent to the West Indies, a mission that lasted until April 1750. When letters could not reach him, Fanny kept journals and shipped them in bundles on navy boats. "I chat with you, my dear love, as if you could answer me," she wrote, "and I will not allow myself to reflect that is not the case." Gaps in her journal occur when his ship was dashed in rough seas or damaged in battles, and when he served shore duty for long stretches and filled his seat in Parliament. In 1751, a fourth child was born, and the admiral began a four-year period ashore.

From 1755 to 1760, however, the Seven Years' War kept him constantly away from home, either at sea, at the Admiralty, or at Parliament, with only short trips to the Hatchlands, a country estate near Guilford to which the family had moved. During that period, the Boscawens' final child was born, and they commissioned the building of a larger Hatchlands. The admiral's efforts at sea made the Boscawens national heroes, and Ned was promoted to general of Marines. Exhaustion from constant work broke his health in September of 1760. Nursing him until his death that January, Fanny Boscawen would live longer as the admiral's widow than as his wife. For a year, she went into seclusion, but she emerged to enliven the Bluestocking group, a roundtable of intellectual women whom she and ***Elizabeth Montagu** gathered. Destined to span roughly two generations, the Bluestocking Circle became one of London's most celebrated societies for female members of the leisured gentry. A "bluestocking philosophy," concerned with literature rather than politics, emerged as a means of what members called "rational entertainment" for women.

Like their father, the Boscawen boys were drawn to the military. William joined up at age 12 and drowned at 17 while swimming in Jamaica. Benjamin was allowed to enlist at age 16 and served a dangerous tour during the American Revolution. Fanny Jr. married naval captain John Leveson-Gower and endured the same long absences and constant worry her mother had known. Boscawen sold the Hatchlands and moved to Colney Hatch in 1773. She visited her daughters and grandchildren frequently, kept correspondence with a number of friends, and welcomed visitors regularly. England was at war for 11 of her final 12 years. She wrote constantly of her own and her family's perspective on the battle—Benjamin's place in Parliament, Leveson-Gower's death in service, the country's decline as the strongest international power. Boscawen died on February 26, 1804, and was buried next to the admiral at Cornwall. Her letters and diaries were bequeathed first to her second cousin, then granddaughter, then great-great-granddaughter who married into the Oglander family. Cecil Aspinall-Oglander edited the papers to create Fanny biographies, *Admiral's Wife* and *Admiral's Widow.*

SOURCES:

Aspinall-Oglander, Cecil. *Admiral's Widow.* London: The Hogarth Press, 1942.

———. *Admiral's Wife.* London: Longman's, Green, 1940.

Buck, Claire, ed. *Bloomsbury Guide to Women's Literature.* NY: Prentice Hall, 1992.

Crista Martin,
Boston, Massachusetts

Boschek, Anna (1874–1957)

Austrian Socialist pioneer who organized strikes, gave countless speeches, and played a major role in building up a strong women's section within the Austrian Social Democratic movement. *Born in Vienna, Austria, on May 14, 1874; died in Vienna on November 19, 1957; third of eight children of a locksmith and a former agricultural laborer; never married; no children.*

Left primary school after four years to help support family; worked at various unskilled factory jobs; attended night school and joined Social Democratic movement (early 1890s); involved in strikes and political agitation; became secretary of the Social Democratic Party (SDP) trade union commission (1894); was a tireless advocate of political organization of Austrian working-class women; was a member of Austrian delegation to International Socialist Women's Conference (1907); was the first woman to serve in SDP Executive Committee (1909); served in various capacities in Austrian Parliament (1919–34); was responsible for several major pieces of social legislation; unable to resume political career after 1945 due to declining health, but remained personally active within Social Democratic circles.

A genuine child of the proletariat, Anna Boschek was born the third of eight children into an impoverished working-class family in Vienna on May 14, 1874. Her parents were barely able to feed, clothe and shelter their growing brood in a time of laissez-faire capitalism. The Social Darwinist theory of the day argued that assisting workers with higher wages would only encourage them to become more dissolute and irresponsible (i.e., to have more children and go deeper into debt). Private charity remained virtually powerless in the face of a rapidly growing industrial work force that was often unemployed and destitute because of the vagaries of the market. Anna's father died when she was nine, and she was forced to work in a factory to help feed the desperate family. With virtually no child-labor legislation on the books, she worked long hours under dangerous conditions for minuscule wages. The more demanding of the many jobs Boschek held over the next few years included working in a galvanizing factory, where the acids scarred her face and hands, and a harmonica-manufacturing plant, where she and other 14-year-old girls worked 11 hours a day producing harmonica parts at unsafe presses.

A growing spirit of solidarity among many of the female factory workers brought ideas of union organization to Anna Boschek. On one occasion, when she working in a knitting mill, she was on the verge of tears because her yarn was defective which meant her wages would be reduced due to a fall in productivity. Another worker helped her by providing practical advice about improving the quality of her production. The coworker left her with an important idea: women workers needed to assist each other, so that "as a result of our sticking together all of us will be able to improve our material circumstances."

Boschek's discovery in 1892 of the educational organization of the Social Democratic

Party (SDP) was of great importance. Formed in 1889, the SDP was grounded in Marxist principles, believing that the future of the industrial world belonged to an educated and militant working class. For Anna Boschek, whose formal education had ended after four years of primary schooling, a new world opened. World literature, philosophy and music were unveiled every Sunday in lectures designed to impart basic culture and knowledge to enthusiastic working men and women. Soon, she was a militant Socialist.

By 1894, Boschek's energy and intelligence had brought her to the attention of the women's branch of the SDP. She was entrusted with the important task of serving as secretary of the party's trade-union commission. The next years were busy; Boschek organized strikes, gave countless speeches, and played a major role—along with ***Adelheid Popp** and **Therese Schlesinger**—in building a strong women's section within the Austrian Social Democratic movement. The forces keeping women subjugated, whether from a patriarchal society or a repressive government, were not easily overcome. At first, few women joined unions. In 1893, of the 31,522 union members in the Austro-Hungarian Monarchy, only 659 were women. Through the tireless agitation of Anna Boschek and her fellow Socialists, these statistics improved dramatically over the next years; by 1905, 28,402 women were registered union members. For years, Boschek traveled throughout the German-speaking industrial districts of the monarchy, speaking to female workers desperate for a better life.

By 1909, her record of achievement found recognition within the leadership of the Austrian Social Democratic Party, which voted her the first woman to serve on its Executive Committee. By 1914, she was also the only woman serving in the leadership boards of several of the leading Austrian trade unions. During World War I, Boschek experienced the countless tragedies of friends and comrades whose sons died at the front. She was also torn by the serious ideological stresses that severed working-class unity. Despite everything, she remained loyal to the Social Democratic ideal, which was Marxist yet democratic, that dominated the political Left in Austria. A positive moment of these traumatic years came in 1918 when women were granted the vote. As a consequence of this major reform, Boschek was one of seven Social Democratic women elected in February 1919 to the Austrian National Assembly, the first women to serve in the national parliament.

In the first years of her parliamentary service, Boschek was determined to bring about major social reforms for the workers of the new Austrian Republic. Despite the terrible poverty that plagued the mini-state that the once proud empire of the Habsburgs had now become, Boschek and the Social Democrats nevertheless effected major legislative reforms, including the eight-hour workday and great improvements in the laws relating to domestic labor and health insurance.

A much respected party veteran in the 1920s, Boschek witnessed the decline and fall of democracy in the Austria of the early 1930s. The bloody suppression of democracy in February 1934 ended the model administration of "Red Vienna" and Anna Boschek's career in public life. Along with the other Social Democratic deputies, she was expelled from parliament and placed on a "watch list." Boschek survived the Nazi occupation of Austria to welcome the return of democracy in the spring of 1945. By now a venerable old lady with failing eyesight, she could no longer be an active participant in the daily tumble of politics but was still to be seen at most meetings. Anna Boschek died in her beloved Vienna on November 19, 1957. In 1959, a new building for female apprentices was dedicated in her honor. Working-class Vienna, particularly its women, owes much to her.

SOURCES:

Biographical file, Arbeitsgemeinschaft "Biografisches Lexikon der österreichischen Frau," Institut für Wissenschaft und Kunst, Vienna.

Gruber, Helmut. *Red Vienna: Experiment in Working-Class Culture 1919–1934.* Oxford: Oxford University Press, 1991.

Hamer, Thomas L. "Beyond Feminism: The Women's Movement in Austrian Social Democracy, 1890–1920" (unpublished Ph.D. dissertation, Ohio State University, 1973).

Lengaur-Losch, Andrea. "Anna Boschek: 'Die liederliche Dirne aus Wien'," in Edith Prost and Bigitta Wiesinger, eds., *"Die Partei hat mich nie enttäuscht . . .": Österreichische Sozialdemokratinnen.* Vienna: Verlag für Gesellschaftskritik, 1989, pp. 44–86.

Österreichisches Institut für Zeitgeschichte, Vienna, Nachlass Alma Motzko, manuscript "Frau und Staatsbürgertum."

Pluskal-Scholz, L. "Anna Boschek," in Norbert Leser, ed., *Werk und Widerhall: Grosse Gestalten des österreichischen Sozialismus.* Vienna: Verlag der Wiener Volksbuchhandlung, 1964, pp. 92–96.

Sporrer, Maria and Herbert Steiner, eds. *Rosa Jochmann, Zeitzeugin.* 3rd ed. Vienna: Europa Verlag, 1987.

Stimmer, Kurt. *Die Arbeiter von Wien: Ein sozialdemokratischer Stadtführer.* Vienna: Verlag Jugend und Volk, 1988.

Weinzierl, Erika. *Emanzipation? Österreichische Frauen im 20. Jahrhundert.* Vienna: Verlag Jugend und Volk, 1975.

John Haag, Associate Professor,
University of Georgia, Athens, Georgia

Bose, Abala (1865–1951)

Indian educator and reformer. *Born Abala Das in 1865; died in 1951; daughter of Durgahohan Das (founder of the Sadharan Brahma Samaj and Brahmamoijee); attended Calcutta University; studied medicine in Madras; married physicist Jagadish Chandra Bose, in 1887.*

When Abala Bose was five, her family was ostracized by their community for advocating the remarriage of widows. Five years later, in 1875, her mother died. Her father Durgahohan Das was a role model in his campaign for higher education for young women; he established the Bethune Collegiate School for Girls, where Abala and her sister Sarla received their education. The sisters went on to become two of the first women to attend Calcutta University, after which Abala studied medicine in Madras. Following her marriage to the renowned physicist Jagadish Chandra Bose in 1887, Abala Bose devoted herself to furthering educational opportunities for women in her country.

During the three decades between 1896 and 1933, Bose traveled to Europe a number of times, visiting schools and bringing the newest educational approaches and methods back to India. Through her appointment as secretary of the Brahmo Balika Shikshalaya (School for Girls), she became an educational innovator, broadening the curriculum to include self-defense and introducing new methods such as the ***Maria Montessori** system. In 1919, she launched the Nari Shiksha Samiti to help spread education to women throughout the country. She later established the Sister ***Nivedita** Adult Education Fund.

But Bose's concerns for the women of India went further than education, and in 1925 she established a home for widows. In 1935, she opened the Women's Industrial Co-operative Home in Calcutta, which later became a relief and rehabilitation center for women from Bangladesh. Abala Bose died in 1951, shortly after establishing the Sadhuna Ashram in Calcutta.

Barbara Morgan,
Melrose, Massachusetts

Bosomworth, Mary (c. 1690–c. 1763).

See Musgrove, Mary.

Bosone, Reva Beck (1895–1983)

U.S. Representative, Democrat of Utah, 81st–82nd Congresses, January 3, 1949–January 3, 1953; first woman U.S. Representative from Utah. *Born Reva Zilpha Beck in American Fork, Utah, on April 2, 1895; died in Vienna, Virginia, on July 21, 1983; only daughter and one of four children of Christian M. and Zilpha (Chipman) Beck; graduated from Westminster Junior College in Salt Lake City, 1917; B.A. from the University of California, Berkeley, 1920; Doctor of Laws degree from the University of Utah, 1930; married Joe P. Bosone, on October 8, 1929 (divorced); children: one daughter, Zilpha Theresa.*

Reva Bosone, the great-granddaughter of Mormon pioneers, was born and educated in Utah and taught high school English and speech for seven years before pursuing studies at Utah College of Law. She married Joe P. Bosone, a lawyer, just one year before receiving her degree in 1930. The couple moved to the mining region of Carbon County, where they opened a private law practice, Bosone and Bosone.

In 1932, Bosone ran for State legislature, conducting a door-to-door campaign with her two-year-old daughter in tow. She was elected to the State House with the "highest vote received by any candidate for any office in the county." Returned to office in 1934, she was elected Democratic floor leader. While a legislator, she worked for passage of a women's and children's wage-and-hour law and a child-labor amendment to the State constitution, which won her commendations from ***Frances Perkins** and ***Eleanor Roosevelt**.

In 1936, Bosone was elected a police and traffic court judge of the Salt Lake City Municipal Court, becoming Utah's first woman judge. Serving successively until 1948, she instituted extraordinarily high traffic fines for convicted drunk drivers, but also took a personal interest in their rehabilitation. During World War II, she chaired the Women's Army Corps Civilian Advisory Committee of the Ninth Service Command and was an official observer at the United Nations' founding conference in San Francisco in 1945. In 1947 and 1948, she served as the first director of the Utah State Board for Education on Alcoholism.

In 1948, Bosone became the first woman from Utah to be elected to the House of Representatives and won a second term in 1950 over Republican National committeewoman and future treasurer of the United States, ***Ivy Baker Priest**. Bosone's political philosophy stressed principle over popularity. During her freshman term, Bosone served on the Committee on Public Lands. Hoping to encourage Native American self-government, she introduced a bill to gradually reduce federal administration of Indian affairs. She also worked to promote land management and reclamation efforts, often taking stands unpopular with her largely conservative state. During her second term, she was appointed to the Committee on House Administration and the Committee on Interior and Insular Affairs.

Bosone lost her bid for a third term in 1952, and again in 1954. She returned to her law practice in Salt Lake City until becoming legal counsel to the Safety and Compensation Subcommittee of the House Committee on Education and Labor in 1957. In 1961, she was appointed the Post Office Department's judicial officer and chair of its contract board of appeals. She served that post until retiring in January 1968. Bosone made her home in Vienna, Virginia, until her death on July 21, 1983.

SOURCES:

Office of the Historian. *Women in Congress, 1917–1990.* Commission on the Bicentenary of the U.S. House of Representatives, 1991.

SUGGESTED READING:

Clopton, Beverly B. *Her Honor, the Judge: The Story of Reva Beck Bosone.* Ames: Iowa State University Press, 1980.

Riva Beck Bosone

Bosse, Harriet (1878–1961)

Norwegian-born Swedish actress, third wife of playwright August Strindberg, who pioneered a modern style of acting in Sweden. *Name variations: Mrs. August Strindberg. Born Harriet Bosse on February 19, 1878, in Christiania (now Oslo), Norway; died on November 2, 1961, in Oslo; one of 13 children of Johann Heinrich Wilhelm Bosse (1836–1896, a publisher and bookseller) and Anne Marie Lehman Bosse (1836–1893); attended the Royal Conservatory of Music in Stockholm, 1894–97; married August Strindberg (1849–1912, the playwright), on May 6, 1901 (divorced 1904); married Gunnar Wingard, in 1908 (divorced 1911); married Edvin Adolphson, in 1927 (divorced 1932); children: (first marriage) daughter* ***Anne Marie Strindberg*** *(b. 1902); (second marriage) a son (b. January 1909).*

Began acting career (1896); had starring role in Strindberg's To Damascus I, *Stockholm (1900); besides performing starring roles in Strindberg's plays, became a leading actress in plays by Maeterlinck, Sudermann, von Hofmannsthal and other major playwrights of the early years of the 20th century; her enduring influence is to be found in the late work of Strindberg, whom she inspired, and in the modern style of acting she pioneered in Sweden.*

Although she was born and died in Oslo, Norway, Harriet Bosse, one of the greatest Scandinavian actresses of modern times, considered herself Swedish rather than Norwegian. Bosse is a major figure in the history of the Swedish stage, but it is her brief marriage to the eminent playwright August Strindberg that continues to fascinate biographers and readers alike. She was born in Christiana (now Oslo), Norway, on February 19, 1878, into the large family (13 siblings, of whom 7 survived childhood) of German-born publisher and bookseller Johann Heinrich Wilhelm Bosse and Danish-born **Anne Marie Lehman Bosse**. Harriet's first love was music, and, because her older sister **Dagmar** had become an opera singer in Stockholm, she too went to that city to study at the Royal Conservatory of Music. This period of intensive study was to be her only formal preparation for the acting career to follow. Another older sister, **Alma,** was an actress in Christiania and it was through her influence that Harriet launched her career. An affair with Alma's actor-husband Johan Fahlstrom led to a permanent break between the sisters; they never saw one another again.

By 1900, the delicate, petite ingenue was appearing on stage at Stockholm's Royal Dramatic Theater, fascinating audiences with her dark hair, almond-shaped eyes and silvery voice. That November, Bosse appeared as the female lead in Strindberg's *To Damascus I*. Although she was at the time romantically involved with the play's leading man, she responded to the pursuits of Strindberg who had fallen in love with her. By the time he met Harriet Bosse, Strindberg had two failed marriages behind him, the first of which had produced four children. His involvement with women led to grief but seemed to stimulate his artistic creativity. His 1877 marriage to **Siri von Essen,** the unhappy spouse of a guards officer, had resulted in his first novel *The Red Room*, which made Strindberg nationally famous. His brief marriage of 1893–95 to the young Austrian journalist **Frida Uhl** brought him to the point of insanity though he expanded his intellectual horizons with experiments in alchemy and the study of theosophy.

Harriet Bosse

After a whirlwind courtship, Harriet Bosse and August Strindberg were married on May 6, 1901. In addition to the 30-year difference in their ages, their personalities were radically dissimilar. The marriage proved an exceptionally disastrous union, and even the birth of a daughter, Anne Marie, on March 25, 1902, did little to calm down their turbulent relationship. Although their personal affairs were chaotic, Strindberg's exhortation to Bosse as an actress—to "Become now for us the actress of the new century"—was taken seriously. Despite her youth, she rapidly matured as an artist. Strindberg was not only infatuated with Bosse, but he had also detected a great talent in her, regarding her as having been "born with all the fresh ideas of the new century." The style of acting she evolved, a subdued intimate realism, anticipated a more modern style of dramatic presentation, exemplified by Constantin Stanislavski and ***Eleonora Duse**. After their marriage ended in divorce in 1904, she remained strongly linked with Strindberg. For a while after the divorce, they remained physically intimate, and Bosse took Anne Marie to see her father on a regular basis. Bosse remained Strindberg's Muse and served as inspiration for themes and motifs in his late works, including the poems "The Golden Eagle" and "The Dutchman." She sent a flower anonymously each day during Strindberg's final illness in 1912.

By 1908, when she married Gunnar Wingard, her co-star from *Romeo and Juliet*, Bosse had become one of the pillars of the Stockholm stage. This second marriage proved more tragic than the first. By 1911, after giving birth to a son in January 1909, she and Wingard were divorced. In October 1912, only a few months after Strindberg's death, Wingard committed suicide.

Despite her personal grief, these were years of professional triumphs, as Bosse added nuances to her already masterful interpretations of not only Strindberg, but the plays of Maurice Maeterlinck, Hermann Sudermann, and Hugo von Hofmannsthal. Although she was aging well and had retained the full range of her acting skills, fewer roles were available to Harriet Bosse in the 1920s. In 1927, she made a third and final attempt at marriage. Her union with Edvin Adolphson, which lasted until 1932, was another mismatch, one which ended with Bosse smashing a mirror over Adolphson's head after he accused her of doing "a confounded injustice" to Strindberg by hiding his letters to her.

By the 1930s, Bosse was playing small roles at Stockholm's Royal Dramatic Theater. Her main concern at this point was to function as the guardian of the Strindberg heritage. This she did by granting interviews to scholars and generally assisting those working in the field of Strindberg studies. Although she had burned her own letters to Strindberg after his death when they were returned to her, his letters to her survived, and she assisted in their publication. After giving her final stage performances in April 1943, Harriet Bosse appeared in several Swedish motion pictures. In one of these, the film *Appassionata*, she played a cameo role opposite the female lead, the young *Viveca Lindfors. When the film was shown on Swedish television in the 1980s, Bosse's superb acting was acknowledged. In her final years, Harriet Bosse returned to her native Oslo, where she died on November 2, 1961. With her death, one of the last representatives of an extraordinarily creative period of European theatrical history passed from the scene.

SOURCES:

"Harriet Bosse is Dead," in *The New York Times*. November 7, 1961, p. 33.

Lagercrantz, Olof. *August Strindberg*. Translated by Anselm Hollo. London: Faber and Faber, 1984.

Meyer, Michael. *Strindberg*. NY: Random House, 1985.

Strindberg, August. *Letters of Strindberg to Harriet Bosse: Love Letters from a Tormented Genius*. Edited and translated by Arvid Paulson. NY: Grosset and Dunlap, 1959.

Waal, Carla. *Harriet Bosse: Strindberg's Muse and Interpreter*. Carbondale: Southern Illinois University Press, 1990.

John Haag, Associate Professor, University of Georgia, Athens, Georgia

Bosshardt, Alida M. (1913—)

Dutch lieutenant colonel in the Salvation Army, known for her work in the Red Light district of Amsterdam. *Born Alida Margaretha Bosshardt in the Netherlands on June 8, 1913; only daughter and one of three children (one brother was adopted).*

Lieutenant colonel Alida Bosshardt, known affectionately in Holland as "the major," has spent the greater part of her career living and working in the section of the Old City of Amsterdam called the *Zeedijk*, home of the notorious Red Light district. In 1948, "with 100 guilders, a flag and a blessing," Bosshardt began dispensing the social and spiritual services of the Salvation Army to the prostitutes, the alcoholics, the drug addicts, the poor and troubled, and the homeless in the area. From one room in the cellar of an old building, she built a thriving *Goodwillcentrum*, comprised of four buildings, with a staff of over 135 social workers, district nurses, and home helpers providing services to the city's needy.

Alida M. Bosshardt

Bosshardt grew up in a poor family with two brothers, Henk and Jan. She didn't attend church or Sunday school until she was 12, when her father became a Roman Catholic and occasionally took her to church with him. Around the same time, her mother began attending the Christian Reformed Church. By her own account, Bosshardt was a difficult child and had trouble in school. "When my teacher told me the school was much nicer on the days when I was at home sick, my parents decided they would look for another school, but I didn't want to go any more." She never went to high school, but later attended college for a degree in social work.

In 1931, 18-year-old Bosshardt attended her first meeting of the Salvation Army, filling in for her brother Jan who was taken ill. She was struck by the Salvationist's simple message, "The God who loves me, also loves you," a message she had not so clearly found in church. As she began attending meetings regularly, a new direction for her life emerged. Bosshardt decided to join the Army but obeyed her parents' wishes that she hold off any commitments for a year. On June 19, 1932, she took the oath to "become a faithful soldier of The Salvation Army" until death; with a uniform and bonnet purchased by her father, she set out for training school in Amstelveen.

Commissioned in 1934, Bosshardt was stationed at the Children's Home, "Zonnehoek," in Amsterdam, where she stayed until after World War II. She was then given an administrative post at the Territorial Headquarters across from the Central station and bordering the city's Red Light district. Walking through the neighborhood, she wondered why the Army was not active in such a depressed area and brought the matter to the attention of her commander. She and some colleagues started street-corner work, singing and "witnessing" every Friday night, until they became part of the scenery. For the next ten years, she ate and slept in the same little room, while offering practical help to the poor, finding beds, food, and shelter when needed.

As more and more of Amsterdam's needy found their way to Bosshardt, who was known for her warm smile and outgoing nature, her center and reputation grew. The press discovered her, followed in turn by radio and television. In 1959, she was surprised and honored with an appearance on the Dutch version of "This is Your Life," which brought her new found notoriety, and, more important to Bosshardt, donations from all over the Netherlands.

In 1960, she was one of three honored guests received by Queen ***Juliana** during a stay at the Royal Palace in Amsterdam. A royal occasion five years later, involving Princess ***Beatrix**, caught the imagination of press and public alike. Intrigued by the Salvation Army, Beatrix asked if she might accompany Bosshardt one evening. With the princess disguised in a wig and thick glasses, the curious twosome made the usual appointed rounds, visiting prostitutes and residents and selling *The War Cry*, the Army's biweekly publication. They were unnoticed until they finished up in a popular neighborhood pub, where a photographer recognized the princess and snapped a picture which appeared on the front page of every newspaper the next day.

The Silver Medal of the City of Amsterdam was among the countless honors and tributes received by Bosshardt through the years. In 1962, she was admitted to The Order of the Founder, the highest Salvation Army Order of Merit. In 1966, she was promoted to lieutenant-colonel and received a knighthood in the Order of Oranje Nassau. On another occasion, Air Holland named one of its fleet of planes the *Major Alida Bosshardt*. Through all, she has remained humble: "I serve the Lord to serve people. He, not me, should be praised."

Bosshardt officially retired in 1978, though her activities continued. She lived on the same canal, in two rooms, on the third floor of a building not far down the street from the center. She still gave lectures, scheduled meetings, kept up an extraordinary correspondence, and sold *The War Cry* in the Red Light district. In an interview given on a visit to Canada in 1990, she expressed concern over the breakdown of the family and the decline in church attendance. Her greatest concern for the Salvation Army is the lack of leadership from women. "From the beginning women were leaders in the Army, but now I think a lot of women are willing to let the men do it. I don't like that."

Bosshardt's practical approach to her years of *Goodwillwerk* is exemplified in one of her favorite Bible stories, from Acts 3, "where the lame man is healed at the gate of the temple. That man was helped in his totality," she explains. "He wasn't begging the next day. He went out and got a job!"

SOURCES:

Duncan, Denis. *Here Is My Hand: The Story of Lieutenant Colonel Alida Bosshardt of the Red Light Area, Amsterdam.* London: Hodder and Stoughton, 1977.

"Women at Work: Lieutenant-Colonel Alida Bosshardt," in *Sally Ann.* April 1991, pp. 6–7.

Barbara Morgan,
Melrose, Massachusetts

Boston, Lucy Maria (1892–1990)

British author of children's books. *Born Lucy Maria Wood in Southport, Lancashire, England, on December 10, 1892; died in Hemingford Grey, Huntingdonshire, England, on May 25, 1990; daughter and one of six children of James (an engineer) and Mary (Garrett) Wood; attended Somerville College, Oxford; married an officer in the Royal Flying Corps, in 1917 (marriage dissolved, 1935); children: one son, Peter.*

Selected writings: The Children of Green Knowe *(illustrated by son Peter Boston, 1954);* Yew Hall *(1954);* Treasure of Green Knowe *(illus. by P. Boston, 1958);* The River at Green Knowe *(illus. by P. Boston, 1959);* A Stranger at Green Knowe *(illus. by P. Boston, 1961);* An Enemy at Green Knowe *(illus. by P. Boston, 1964);* The Castle of Yew *(illus. by Margery*

Lucy Maria Boston

Gill, 1965); The Sea Egg *(illus. by P. Boston, 1967);* The House that Grew *(illus. by Caroline Hemming, 1969);* Strongholds *(1969);* The Horned Man; or, Whom Will You Send to Fetch Her Away? *(play, 1970);* Nothing Said *(illus. by P. Boston, 1971); (nonfiction)* Memory of a House *(1973);* The Fossil Snake *(illus. by P. Boston, 1975);* The Stones of Green Knowe *(illus. by P. Boston, 1976); (nonfiction)* Perverse and Foolish *(1979).*

At age 62, Lucy Boston entered the literary world and, within a short time, distinguished herself in juvenile fiction. Most of her books (many of which were illustrated by her son Peter) were inspired by and set in her 12th-century manor house in Hemingford Grey, which, through extensive renovations, became her work of art.

Raised in a strict evangelical family, Boston recalled her early childhood as "a starvation of everything but hymns and sermons." Her father died when she was six, and several years later her mother's failing health necessitated a family move to the country, where Boston reveled in the wonders of nature and spent her free moments roaming the English countryside. After a year at a Quaker school in Surrey to eliminate her broad Lancashire accent, followed by finishing school in Paris, Boston entered Oxford, where she reportedly broke all the rules before leaving for London to train as a nurse. She served in a French hospital during World War I, then married an English officer and settled in Cheshire, England, where her son Peter was born. When the marriage dissolved in 1935, she left England to study painting in Italy and Austria. Returning to England just before World War II, Boston settled into the old Manor House at Hemingford Grey that she renovated from the ground up over a two-year period. Jasper Rose, author of a monograph on Boston, attributes her emergence as a writer to the house. "In some mysterious way," he writes, "Mrs. Boston's spirit has been nourished, calmed and enlarged by her house, and in a sense all her books commemorate her debt to it."

Most notable among Boston's work is the "Green Knowe" series, which includes *A Stranger at Green Knowe*, winner of the 1961 Carnegie Medal, and *The Children of Green Knowe*, winner of the 1969 Lewis Carroll Shelf Award. The books of the series detail the mysterious, ancient house called Green Knowe and its inhabitants. Rose praises Boston for her subjects—ghosts, giants, escaped gorillas, and witches—and her exploration of real human predicaments, such as what it's like to be blind, to confront evil, or to withhold a secret from a loved one. When asked if there was a conscious difference in her writing for adults and children, Boston answered: "No, there is no difference of approach, style, vocabulary or standard. I could pick out passages from any of the books and you would not be able to tell what age it was aimed at."

Many of Boston's stories were reactions to events in her own life. *The Sea Egg* (1967) was triggered by the gift of a Cornish serpentine egg sent to her by a friend in memory of Kynance Cove, where the two had played as children. The award-winning *A Stranger at Green Knowe* (1961) was inspired by a newspaper photograph of Guy, a gorilla in the London Zoo; through the story, Boston expressed her concern over the zoo's supposition that animals actually prefer captivity to freedom. "The subject to me was a big one," she said. "I had to contain the whole force of my belief that all life, not merely human, must have respect, that a man-centered conception of it was false and crippling, that these other lives are the great riches of ours."

Boston continued to write well into her 80s. Her last book *Perverse and Foolish: A Memoir of Childhood and Youth* was published when she was 87. The author died after a stroke on May 25, 1990.

SUGGESTED READING:

Rose, Jasper. *Lucy Boston*. London: Bodley Head, 1965.

Barbara Morgan,
Melrose, Massachusetts

Boswell, Cathy (1962—)

African-American basketball player who won a team gold medal in the 1984 Olympics. *Born in Joliet, Illinois, on November 10, 1962.*

All-time women's scoring leader at Illinois State University; winner of the Willye White Award in 1979; winner of a team gold medal in basketball for the 1984 Olympics in Los Angeles.

Cathy Boswell brought women's basketball to new heights in the United States. After winning the 1979 ***Willye White** Award as the top female high-school athlete in Illinois, Boswell enrolled at Illinois State University. While there, she was on the Kodak All-Region team and was twice a finalist for the Wade Trophy. In 1983, she was named to the J.C. Penney All American Five. She competed on the Jones Cup team (1980); the U.S.A. Dial Jr. Women's team (1981); the U.S.A. Select team (1982); and the World University team (1983). In 1979 and 1981, she played in the National Festival. One of Illinois State's best athletes, Boswell was all-time leading scorer on its Lady Redbird basketball team with 2,005 points and 1,060 rebounds. Other records include: highest field-goal percentage (.599), most free throws scored (101), most free throws attempted (119), highest free-throw percentage (.848), and most field goals scored (274). As a forward, she was the first woman whose jersey was ever retired at the university. Only Illinois State athlete Doug Collins, the great NBA star, scored more than Boswell. In 1984, Cathy Boswell qualified for the U.S. Olympic basketball team which won the gold medal that year in Los Angeles.

SOURCES:

Page, James A. *Black Olympian Medalists.* Englewood, Colorado: Libraries Unlimited, 1991.

Karin L. Haag,
Athens, Georgia

Boswell, Connee (1907–1976)

American jazz singer who performed with her sisters and whose tenure with the Dorsey Brothers' Band earned her great fame. *Name variations: changed the spelling of her name to Connee when she went solo. Born Connie Boswell in New Orleans, Louisiana, on December 3, 1907; died in New York, New York, on October 11, 1976; married Harold Leedy (her manager), in 1935; crippled at the age of three, Boswell performed in a wheelchair with the Boswell Sisters, a vocal trio.*

Connee Boswell and her sisters—**Helvetia** ("Vet") and **Martha**—grew up in a middle-class home where they listened to blues, spirituals, and opera; they consequently formed a trio called the Boswell Sisters. While Connee played the cello, piano, alto sax, and trombone, Martha played piano, and Vet the violin. All three sisters played in the New Orleans Philharmonic Orchestra before they began to concentrate on close-harmony singing; Connee did the group's vocal arrangements.

Winning local talent shows, the sisters eventually signed with the Dorsey Brothers' Band, secured recording contracts (Brunswick), and headlined radio shows. Connee, who had been crippled by polio in infancy, became increasingly featured because of her sense of timing and rhythmic phrasing. The polio, later aggravated by a fall, had left both legs paralyzed, and she sang from a wheelchair.

In 1935, due to her sisters' marriages, Connee embarked on a solo career, changing the spelling of her name from Connie to Connee. This new phase of her life was marked with difficulty. Producers who had only heard her on radio shows had no idea she was in a wheelchair. Boswell later noted how painful it was to be called in to audition: "As soon as they saw me in

The Boswell Sisters

a wheelchair they'd freeze. . . . But I said to myself, 'Connee, to get ahead, you've got to be better than the next fella. And if you've got a handicap, then you've simply got to be better than that.' So I really started working."

She often appeared on radio, was a frequent guest on "Bing Crosby & Kraft Music Hall," and entertained the troops during World War II. While touring, she used a custom built wheelchair that, when covered by her gown, gave the impression she was standing. Boswell also appeared in several movies, including *Moulin Rouge*, *Artists and Models*, *Transatlantic Merry-Go-Round*, *The Big Broadcast of 1932*, *Syncopation*, and *Kiss the Boys Goodbye*. One of many white musicians who brought black singing style increasingly into the mainstream, Boswell retired from touring in the 1950s but continued to appear as a featured guest on television in the 1960s. In the early 1970s, she was hospitalized with stomach cancer. After a series of operations, she gave her last performance with Benny Goodman at Carnegie Hall (1975). She died the following year.

Botchkareva, Maria (1889–?)

Russian military commander who rose from the peasantry during World War I and organized the most successful women's battalion for the Provisional Government in 1917. *Name variations: Leona Botchkarova, Mariya Bochkareva; nicknamed Yashka. Pronunciation: BOK-car-AVA. Born Maria Leontievna Frolkova in July 1889 in Nikolsko, Russia; date of death is unknown; daughter of Leonti Semenovitch Frolkov (a Novgorod peasant) and Olga Nazarev Frolkova; married Afanasi Botchkarev, in 1905; children: none.*

Ran away from husband (1908); spent time in Yakutsk Prison with her lover, Yakov Buk (1912–14); ran away from Yakutsk and joined Russian army (1914); fought on Russian-German front (1915–17); wounded and won several medals for heroism (1915–17); organized Russian Women's Battalion of Death (1917); disbanded Battalion and imprisoned (1917); left Russia for the U.S. (1918); had audience with President Woodrow Wilson (1918); returned to Russia (1918); removed from active service and faded into obscurity (1918).

Opposite page

(Top) Women soldiers at the Front; (bottom) Maria Botchkareva.

Maria Botchkareva was a stout, semi-literate peasant woman who ran away from an unrequited, prison-camp relationship to join the Russian army during World War I. Wounded several times in combat, she eventually organized an all-women's battalion in an effort to inspire the Russian military and bolster the Provisional Revolutionary Government that replaced the tsar in early 1917. Although they distinguished themselves in combat, Botchkareva's battalion disbanded rather than support the Bolshevik government that took power in late 1917. Botchkareva, after a period of imprisonment, visited the United States and Great Britain in an unsuccessful effort to gain support for rebel elements resisting the Communist regime governing Russia.

Maria Frolkova was born in July 1889 in Nikolsko, Russia. Her father Leonti Semenovitch Frolkov was born into serfdom in the province of Novgorod and served in the Russo-Turkish War in 1877–1878. Maria's mother Olga Nazarev was the daughter of the poorest fisherman in the village of Tcharanda when she met and married Leonti Frolkov. Maria was the third of four daughters born to the poverty stricken Frolkov family. When she was a year old, her father went to Petrograd hoping to improve conditions for his family, but he drank heavily and was abusive and unreliable; they did not hear from him for five years. When Maria was six (1895), he moved the family to Kuskovo, a village beyond Tomsk in Siberia. The destitute family had to beg for food during the train trip. Kuskovo proved to be a poor choice for farming, and Leonti Frolkov had to work in Tomsk. After two years, he moved the family there. Maria, not yet nine, babysat to augment the family's meager income. From age nine to fifteen, she worked in a grocery store for room and board, after her father, in a drunken rage, beat her and threw her into the streets.

During the years Maria worked in the grocery store, many soldiers were stationed in Tomsk because of the Russo-Japanese War. In 1905, she was seduced by Lieutenant Vasili Lazov on a promise of marriage. When his unit was reassigned, he refused to marry her because her class and illiteracy would hinder his advancement in the army. A disillusioned 15-year-old, Maria met Afanasi Botchkarev, a common soldier returning from the front. In a hasty decision, she agreed to marry Botchkarev only to find she had exchanged her father's cruelty for that of her husband. The young couple worked as barge loaders and then took better jobs in a company producing asphalt floors for public buildings. She advanced more rapidly than her husband, and he beat her severely because he resented her larger salary. After two years, Maria ran away to Barnaul which was the home of her married sister. When Afanasi found her, she tried to drown herself in the Ob River. For a time, her husband tried to improve himself but gradually drifted back to his cruel, jealous and petty ways. When he discovered and spent a sum of money she had hoarded, Maria unsuccessfully tried to kill him, then fled to Irkutsk where her sister had relocated. She once more found employment in the asphalt business but illness cost her the job in 1910.

When Maria's sister moved back to Tomsk, Maria took domestic employment in the town of Stretinsk. Upon arriving in there, Maria soon realized, however, that she had been misled and would be employed in a brothel. While contemplating suicide, she met a young man who sympathized with her circumstances. Yakov or Yasha Buk, a 24-year-old butcher's son with a high-school education, took Maria to live with his family. They fell in love, but because of her previous marriage they lived together by civil agreement without the sanction of the church, a common practice in Russia due to the difficulty of obtaining a divorce. For about three years, their life was hard but happy. They opened their own butcher's shop where Maria also produced and sold ice cream. Yasha was something of an adventurer who often helped those fleeing from tsarist authorities. In 1912, he aided a dangerous revolutionary, and he and Maria were arrested. Though beaten for seven days, she did not confess to any crimes, but when Yasha was sentenced to four years of exile in a Yakutsk prison, she convinced the court to permit her to accompany him. To save Yasha from extreme hardship, Maria reluctantly slept with Governor Kraft of Yakutsk. But Yasha changed in prison and became violent. In the late summer of 1914, in a drunken and jealous mood, he tried to murder her. World War I had just begun, and Maria, partly from a desire to escape Yasha and partly inspired by patriotism, fled from Yakutsk to fight for her country.

In November 1914, Botchkareva tried to enlist at the Headquarters of the 25th Reserve Battalion in Tomsk. When she was told that women could not serve in combat, she persisted until the commander telegraphed her request to Tsar Nicholas II (1894–1917), who authorized her enlistment. Because the Russian soldiers called each other by nicknames, she asked to be known as "Yashka" from the earliest days of her training. In early 1915, when her regiment received orders to move to the front, she was assigned to the Second Army headquartered under the command of General Vladimir Gurko at Polotsk. Her unit moved to the trenches and attacked across a field of barbed wire. Only 48 of the 250 men with her came back. She helped to rescue several wounded

men by crawling and dragging them back to the Russian lines. The following day, Maria was wounded in the right leg and had to lay on the battlefield for over four hours. She spent much of the spring of 1915 recovering in a hospital in Kiev. Rejoining her company, she took part in many skirmishes with guns and grenades. On August 15, 1915, she was shot in the hand and forearm by a sniper while rescuing her comrades after a battle that left 10,000 Germans killed. She recuperated with her unit while serving as a medical assistant. In October 1915, she went on a scouting mission that resulted in a grenade and bayonet battle. She bayoneted a German soldier in a skirmish that saw the loss of two-thirds of her fellow soldiers. Late in 1915, she suffered frostbite and was sent to a hospital at Beloye. Botchkareva would not permit an amputation of her right foot and soon recovered enough to again rejoin her company.

Soldiers and Peasants! Remember that only a full, clean sweep of the Germans from our soil can give you the free Russia you long for.

—Maria Botchkareva, 1918

On March 6–7, 1916, Maria was gassed during the Battle of Postovy and her eyes burned for three weeks. During another offensive on March 18, her right leg was shattered by a gunshot, and she lay in pain the entire day before being rescued. She spent three months in Ekaterina Hospital in Moscow before rejoining her regiment at the town of Lutzk. On June 22, a German shell fragment lodged near the end of her spinal column, and she was returned in a paralyzed condition to Moscow. After four months of paralysis and morphine and six months on crutches and in therapy, Botchkareva passed her physical examination. She was promoted to the rank of senior under-officer and returned to combat. A month later, she was in a force captured by the Germans. After eight hours, Botchkareva and other soldiers escaped during a Russian counteroffensive. She made over 100 combat incursions into "no man's land" and was decorated three times, but always maintained that she only received Third Degree Medals because she was a woman.

In February 1917, word came that the tsar had been overthrown, and the soldiers all swore to fight for the Provisional Government. Maria optimistically believed that the February Revolution was against the ill-conceived military policies of the tsar. When the soldiers and government both faltered in their resolve, she pleaded with her fellow soldiers to maintain order and to fight the Germans who were their real enemies. In May, unable to accept the collapsing discipline and defeatism at the front, Botchkareva traveled to Petrograd and secured a meeting with Michael V. Rodzianko, president of the Duma. He took her to meet the soldiers' delegates at the Taurida Palace, and it was there that she proposed the formation of a women's combat battalion to serve as an inspiration in battle to the Russian army. Although surprised by her proposal, Rodzianko and General Aleksi Brusilov, commander-in-chief of the Russian army, were willing to support her idea. On May 15, they took her to meet Minister of War Alexander Kerensky at the Winter Palace. Kerensky agreed to her proposal if she would guarantee the conduct, morality, and reputation of the women. Botchkareva agreed to these stipulations, and they named the new unit the "First Russian Women's Battalion of Death."

On May 21, when Botchkareva joined Kerensky and other speakers at the Mariynski Theater, she spoke with great fervor: 1,500 women applied that evening to join the battalion. The number of volunteers reached 2,000 after the newspapers reported the plan to the public. This number would rapidly decrease once physical examinations, military haircuts, uniforms, rifle training and discipline were confronted by the volunteers. Their uniforms included white epaulets with a red-and-black stripe, while a red-and-black arrowhead insignia was worn on the right arm. One day, when the training center was visited by ***Emmeline Pankhurst**, the English suffragist leader, the two women became friends. During the ensuing weeks, Botchkareva and Pankhurst joined Kerensky for dinner at the Astoria Hotel, and Kerensky asked Maria if her unit would march in a parade to help offset the impact of Bolshevik demonstrations against the Provisional Government. By agreeing, she earned the absolute hatred of the Bolsheviks. When her battalion marched at Mars Field, though generally well-received by the public, it was attacked by the Bolsheviks. Botchkareva was knocked out and some of her troops were wounded.

On June 21, 1917, Maria met with Kerensky and General Lvar G. Kornilov, whose courage and patriotism she greatly admired. Later in the day, her unit went to the St. Isaac Cathedral where her battalion was consecrated and received its battle banners and standard. Botchkareva was given the unprecedented honor of having her name placed on the banner, and she was promoted to the rank of lieutenant.

Maria Botchkareva's Women's Battalion of Death left on June 24 for the front lines, assigned to the 525th Kuriag-Daryinski Regiment in Senki. On July 8, her battalion attacked the Germans during a major Russian offensive. Of the 300 women remaining in her battalion, 40 were wounded or killed, but her soldiers had performed with honor while their poorly disciplined and demoralized male counterparts argued among themselves, retreated, or failed to advance at all. The women held their position against German counter attacks for several hours but were finally forced to retreat when no reinforcements arrived. During the retreat, Botchkareva was knocked unconscious by an exploding shell. Though her hearing and speech were affected, after a few weeks in a Petrograd hospital, she returned to her battalion with the rank of captain. Once again, her battalion went into action and made an excellent account of themselves against the Germans.

On several occasions, Botchkareva tried to convince Kerensky that capital punishment and discipline must replace committee organization in the Russian army if it were to become an effective fighting force. A disillusioned Botchkareva had once bayoneted one of her own soldiers discovered making love to a male soldier during a lull in the combat. In the fall of 1917, news arrived that Kerensky and Kornilov had split over the discipline issue. In November, word arrived at the front that Kerensky had been overthrown and the Bolsheviks had seized Petrograd. Russian soldiers began to riot and accused Botchkareva's battalion of siding with Kornilov and espousing discipline rather than committee governance of the army. Twenty of Maria's soldiers were lynched. For their safety, Botchkareva led her remaining troops into a dense forest and instructed them to disband.

Botchkareva traveled to Petrograd but was arrested by the Bolsheviks when she arrived in the city. She was brought before V.I. Lenin and Leon Trotsky who hoped she would support their revolution. When she argued against their program and a weak peace with Germany, they smiled condescendingly before discharging her and issuing her a passport and train ticket to her home in Tomsk. After staying with her family for a short time, she received a telegram from a "General X" that her services were needed once again. Arriving back in Petrograd on January 18, 1918, she was sent to assess the military situation of rebel General Kornilov against the Bolshevik forces in the Don River region. Disguised as a nun, she reached Kornilov at his headquarters in Novocherkassk but refused to join the rebels after seeing Russians fighting Russians. During her return, she was arrested and witnessed firsthand the atrocities committed by the Bolsheviks. She saw her fellow captives executed, but her fame spared her for official trials in Moscow. She was imprisoned and abused for over a month before being released because of her peasant origins and gender.

As she traveled towards Tomsk, Botchkareva heard of new German offensives and saw the people gradually turning against the Bolshevik Government. She had located 30 of her soldiers, now invalids, in Moscow and took them home with her. After seeing to their safety, she and her sister, **Nadia**, traveled to Vladivostok. Botchkareva had decided to take her message to the world to gain support for democratic Russians fighting both the Bolshevik Government and Germany. With the help of the British Consulate in Vladivostok, Maria, Nadia, and Lieutenant Leonid Filippov, one of her former military aides, left Russia on the American transport ship *Sheridan*, on April 18, 1918.

After arriving in the U.S., Botchkareva held interviews with the press and made impassioned speeches across the country. Looking older than her age, she had strong features and the square, solid build of a Russian peasant. With her military trousers tucked into the high laced-boots and her uniform jacket decorated with her distinguished service medals, she created quite a commotion with the American public. During most of her visit, Botchkareva had as a patron Mrs. J. Borden Harriman (***Florence Harriman**), a leading advocate of women's rights issues. While staying in the Prince George Hotel in New York City, Maria met and began collaborating with author Isaac Don Levine on a book about her life. She also attended a luncheon at the home of former president Theodore Roosevelt who arranged for a serialization of the Botchkareva-Levine book, *Yashka*, in the *Metropolitan Magazine*.

Botchkareva went on to Washington and through Harriman's connections met several dignitaries, including Secretary of State Robert Lansing. Eventually, she was briefly received by President Woodrow Wilson. Lieutenant Filippov reported that Botchkareva knelt on both knees while entreating Wilson to send American forces and equipment to help the democratic forces in Russia.

From the United States, Botchkareva traveled to London, England. Her patrons during her visit were her old friend Emmeline Pankhurst and Lady ***Muriel Paget**. Botchkareva continued to speak to patriotic organizations and to use her connections to gain the ears of public officials. She finally convinced the British War office to send her to Archangel with General F.C. Poole's invasion force in August 1918. After the landing, she was frequently seen at the allied headquarters at Shenkursk. She hoped to either form another women's battalion or to have the British intercede on her behalf with the Provisional Government. Eventually, she received an audience with General William Ironside, who, out of compassion, sent her to General Vladimir Marushevsky of the North Russian army for a military assignment. He was not sympathetic to Botchkareva's requests. On December 27, 1918, he issued an Order of the Day based on the premise that summoning women for military duties, inappropriate for their sex, would be a disgraceful stain on the armies of the Northern Region. This effectively stripped Botchkareva of her uniform and rank.

Following her separation from the military, Maria faded into obscurity. Once hailed as the "Russian Joan of Arc" by Western correspondents and proclaimed as "the greatest woman of the century" by Emmeline Pankhurst, Botchkareva's name disappeared from newspaper accounts. There are no references to her in any official records of the Soviet Union. The circumstances of Maria Botchkareva's death are unknown.

SOURCES:

Botchkareva, Maria. *Yashka: My Life As Peasant, Officer and Exile.* NY: Frederick A. Stokes, 1919.

***Dorr, Rheta Childe**. *Inside the Russian Revolution.* NY: Macmillan, 1917.

Harriman, Florence Jaffray. *From Pinafores to Politics.* NY: Holt, 1923.

Levine, Isaac Don. *Eyewitness to History.* NY: Hawthorne Books, 1973.

SUGGESTED READING:

***Bryant, Louise**. *Six Red Months In Russia.* NY: Arno Press, 1970.

Long, Robert Crozier. *Russian Revolution Aspects.* NY: Dutton, 1919.

Russell, Charles Edward. "Russia's Women Warriors," in *Good Housekeeping.* Vol. 65. October, 1917, pp. 22–23.

Phillip E. Koerper, Professor of History, Jacksonville State University, Jacksonville, Alabama

Botchkarova, Leona (b. 1889).

See Botchkareva, Maria.

Botelho, Adélaïde-Marie-Émilie-Filleul, Souza (1761–1836).

See Souza-Botelho, Adélaïde-Marie-Émilie-Filleul, Marquise of.

Botsford, Anna (1854–1930).

See Comstock, Anna Botsford.

Botta, Anne C.L. (1815–1891)

American poet and essayist. *Name variations: Anne Lynch Botta. Born Anne Charlotte Lynch in Bennington, Vermont, on November 11, 1815; died in New York City on March 23, 1891; graduated with honors from the Albany Female Academy; married Vincenzo Botta (a New York University professor), in 1855.*

Anne C.L. Botta was four when her father died at sea. She grew up in Connecticut before taking a teaching position in Providence, Rhode Island, where she had relocated with her mother. A sculptor of merit, she began her literary career in Providence and moved to New York in 1842. From the time of her marriage at age 40 to Professor Vincenzo Botta to her death, Botta's New York residence was a center for literary and artistic friends and is known as the first important salon in the history of American letters. Among Botta's friends were Edgar Allan Poe, Andrew Greeley, and ***Margaret Fuller**.

Her publications include a collection of poems (1848, with a new edition in 1884), many essays, reviews and criticisms, and a *Handbook of Universal Literature* (1845), which was widely used as a textbook. Botta was influential in promoting the establishment of Barnard College and founded the prize which was awarded every half decade for many years by the French Academy for the best essay on "The Condition of Women."

SUGGESTED READING:

Memoirs of Anne C.L. Botta. Compiled by "Her Friends." 1894.

Botting, Eirene Adeline (1899–1930).

See White, Antonia.

Bottome, Margaret McDonald (1827–1906)

American author and religious organizer. *Born Mary McDonald on December 29, 1827, in New York, New York; died on November 14, 1906, in New York, New York; married Rev. Frank Bottome, in 1850.*

In 1886, Margaret Bottome and nine other women formed a Christian study group called King's Daughters, an outgrowth of Bottome's long-standing practice of giving informal talks on the Bible. In order to expand the organization, each woman in the original group of ten initiated another group of ten, and so on. In 1887, men were admitted to the organization, which was renamed the Order of the King's Daughters and Sons. With Bottome as president, membership increased over the next 20 years to approximately one-half million in the United States and Canada. By that time, the organization had become international.

Bottome also contributed to the Order's magazine, *Silver Cross*, and wrote a column in the *Ladies' Home Journal* for members. Her other published works included *Crumbs from the King's Table*, *A Sunshine Trip: Glimpses of the Orient*, *Death and Life*, *Seven Questions*, *After Easter*, and *The Guest Chamber*. In 1896, Bottome was elected president of the Medical Missionary Society. She died on November 14, 1906.

Bottome, Phyllis (1884–1963)

British novelist and lecturer whose work concentrated on life in post-Imperial Austria and the psychological theories of Alfred Adler. *Born in Rochester, Kent, England, on May 31, 1884; died in Hampstead, England, on August 22, 1963; daughter of William Macdonald Bottome (a cleric) and Margaret Leatham; married A.E. Forbes Dennis, in 1917.*

Grew up in England and U.S.; traveled extensively and published first novel (1905); showed strong interest in psychology throughout writing career, publishing almost fifty novels and two collections of short stories.

Selected publications: Raw Material *(1905);* Broken Music *(1907);* The Dark Tower *(1909);* The Crystal Heart *(1911);* Old Wine *(1920);* Belated Reckoning *(1925);* Windlestraws *(1929);* Wind in His Fists *(1931);* Devil's Due *(1931);* The Advances of Harriet *(1933);* Private Worlds *(1934);* Innocence and Experience *(1935);* Level Crossing *(1936);* The Mortal Storm *(1937);* Alfred Adler: A Biography *(1939);* The Heart of a Child *(1940);* Masks and Faces *(1940);* The Mansion House of Liberty *(1941);* London Pride *(1941); (autobiography)* Search for a Soul *(1947);* Under the Skin *(1950);* Man and Beast *(1953);* Against Whom? *(1954);* Eldorado Jane *(1956);* Walls of Glass *(1958); (autobiography)* The Goal *(1963).*

Phyllis Bottome was born of Anglo-American parentage in Rochester, Kent, England, on May 31, 1884. Her father was an American cleric from New York, and her mother was from a distinguished Yorkshire family. Beginning travel early, over the years Bottome visited, and lived for, extended periods in the U.S., Switzerland, Italy, France and Austria. Her first novel *Raw Material* received positive reviews upon its publication in 1905. Other novels soon followed, and by 1911, when *The Common Chord* appeared, Bottome had become deeply interested in the new psychological theories that were challenging virtually all of European culture's intellectual and moral foundations.

In 1917, she married Captain A.E. Forbes Dennis and, shortly after the end of World War I, accompanied him to Vienna where he had received a diplomatic assignment. Witness to the contrast of past glories and present suffering of post-1918 Vienna, she saw instances of extraordinary human tenacity, tenderness and folly by keeping her novelist's eyes open to the nuances of life. Bottome's literary stature increased significantly as a result of her years in Vienna, and her 1926 novel *Old Wine*, a colorful chronicle of Viennese aristocratic life, generally received high critical marks.

During her stay in Vienna, Bottome met and became a follower of Alfred Adler, one of the most impressive psychologists to have broken with the teachings of Sigmund Freud. Published in 1939, two years after Adler's death, Bottome's biographical study of him was written from the perspective of a fervent disciple; nevertheless, it remains of considerable value with insights into both Adler's character and his method of analysis.

Although her previous novels had attracted a relatively small but loyal band of readers, Bottome had to wait until 1934 to publish an acclaimed bestseller. In that year, *Private Worlds* appeared to superb reviews, a success she repeated in 1937 with *The Mortal Storm*, a passionately anti-Nazi book set in Vienna which made Bottome's name a household word in the English-speaking world. In the years immediately preceding World War II, she made three extensive lecture tours of the United States. Although she would never repeat the popular success of *The Mortal Storm*, she continued writing finely crafted books to the end of her life. During World War II, because of her personal hatred of Fascism as well as her firsthand experience with Adolf Hitler's homeland of Austria, she worked as a lecturer for the British Ministry of Information.

In 1947, Bottome's first volume of autobiography, *Search for a Soul*, sensitively analyzed the first 18 years of her life. In her 1950 work *Under the Skin*, she left the world of Europe behind to study human passions in the West Indies. The 1953 *Man and Beast* dealt with the complex relationships between animals and humans. Other works that appealed to loyal fans throughout the 1950s were *Against Whom?* (1954), *Eldorado Jane* (1956) and *Walls of*

Glass (1958). Bottome completed and published in 1962 a second autobiographical volume, entitled *The Goal*, before her death in Hampstead, England, on August 22, 1963.

SOURCES:

Bottome, Phyllis. *Alfred Adler. A Biography.* NY: Putnam, 1939.

———. *The Goal.* London: Faber and Faber, 1962.

———. *Search for a Soul (Fragment of an Autobiography).* NY: Reynal & Hitchcock, 1948.

"Miss Phyllis Bottome, An Accomplished Novelist," in *The Times* [London]. August 23, 1963, p. 10.

John Haag, Associate Professor, University of Georgia, Athens, Georgia

Bouboulina, Laskarina (1771–1825)

Greek freedom fighter and naval commander whose heroic exploits became the subject of countless folk songs, ballads and plays. *Name variations: Lascarina Bobolina or Boubalina; (nickname) Capitanissa. Born on the island of Spétsai (Spetses) in 1771 (some sources cite 1783); killed in 1825; daughter of a sea captain from the island of Spétsai; twice married, twice widowed; children: six.*

Widowed for the second time soon after the outbreak of the Greek War of Independence (1821), enthusiastically supported the struggle against the Ottoman occupiers of her homeland; paid for the outfitting of four ships as well as an army unit, and personally participated in the naval blockades of Monemvasia and Nauplia; her death (1825) was the result of involvement in a family feud.

Laskarina Bouboulina had to wait until she was an older woman to enter the pages of both Greek and women's history. Born in 1771 on the island of Spétsai, she had been twice married, twice widowed, and the mother of six, by the time the Greeks rose up against their Turkish overlords in April 1821. From the start of the Greek revolt, it was clear that control of the sea would determine the outcome of the war. With virtually all the maritime communities of the Greek archipelago rising up against the Ottoman Empire, the rebels had a fair chance of success. Accustomed for thousands of years to the risks of seafaring, Greek mariners had a tradition as warriors as well as sailors. For centuries, they honed their martial skills by fighting against Barbary pirates and occasional brigands from their own communities. Nearly all Greek captains and sailors volunteered for the war of independence which was a serious blow to the Turks, because the bulk of the sailors in the Turkish sultan's navy were of Greek origin. Not only was this source of recruiting now cut off for the Turkish naval command, but their crews were now largely composed of involuntarily recruited dock workers and peasants, men lacking in both skills and belief in a cause. Although quantitatively overwhelmed by the vessels of the Turkish fleet, the Greek sailors—superbly experienced men of the sea, willing to die for their cause—actually held the upper hand in the epic struggle for Hellenic freedom.

Bouboulina's father was an experienced sea captain and merchant. Like many Greeks, she absorbed from childhood the myriad details of maritime life, and by the time she married had become quite knowledgeable in seafaring matters. Although she was the mother of six children, she had a reputation for being able to drink the most masculine of men under the table. Some of the stories that circulated during her lifetime suggested that she was so physically unattractive that she had to seduce her lovers at pistol point. It is difficult, if not impossible, to separate fact from fiction in such Bouboulina tales that found their way into songs, ballads, and popular plays.

When the war against Turkish rule began in April 1821, Bouboulina's husband owned a fleet of four small vessels. He died soon after the start of the uprising, and she had little time for mourning. Bouboulina actively took over command of her vessels, which now became part of the revolutionary naval forces.

From the start of her command, she displayed tremendous powers of leadership. Assisted by her sons and brothers, she commanded a small fleet that distinguished itself on many occasions, including the naval blockades of Monemvasia and Nauplia, during which many Greek towns were relieved from sieges by the Turks. Brave and also reckless, she sailed her ships to wherever they were most needed. This was true during the siege of Tripolis, to which Bouboulina brought her ships to assist the besieged Greek insurgents. After the fierce battle ended, she was the first of the liberating forces to enter the relieved town, doing so in dramatic fashion on horseback. Indeed, it was not uncommon for her enthusiasm and courage to motivate her to temporarily abandon her flagship and venture ashore on horseback at bloody and decisive land battles. Fortunately, her lieutenants were able to maintain discipline and follow her orders to the letter in her absence. Whether on sea or land, she was universally respected both by her own crews and by Greek soldiers of the liberated territories as their *Capitanissa*, the brave, resolute woman naval commander of the Free Hellenes.

Bouboulina's compassion was as noteworthy as her courage, and, after the town of Tripolis was captured by the Greeks, she determined to save as many lives as possible through political compromise. A skilled diplomatic negotiator, she worked out a deal with the Turkish military commander, Elkas Aga, whereby Greek ecclesiastical leaders were exchanged for the harem of the Turkish vizier and governor of the Peloponnesus, Hourshid Pasha. Given the fanatical, virtually genocidal nature of the Greek-Turkish conflict, Bouboulina's diplomatic approach did not appeal to a large number of Greek and Albanian soldiers who thought that the only good Turk was a dead Turk. Determined to deal with their anger and opposition, she asked that the soldiers assemble to hear her side of the issue. Speaking to them not as a revered *Capitanissa* but as a middle-aged widow and mother, Bouboulina addressed them as "my children" so as to share her personal grief with those assembled. She mentioned that it had been "barely eight days since my son John was killed by the Turks," while remaining vehement that they must seek no revenge and that no harm should come to the Turkish harem women. Allowing the soldiers to take the jewels and coins of the women, Bouboulina forbade them to injure or molest the women in any way, insisting: "Whoever attempts to do so will have first to pass over my dead body." Most of the soldiers obeyed her commands, but a few irreconcilables set fire to the fortress in which the Turkish women were imprisoned. Bouboulina was able to contact the local Greek commanders in time, joining them with sword in hand to protect the harem women, who were soon sent to safety in a chartered vessel to the shores of Asia Minor.

Though the Greek War of Independence was idealized in contemporary writings by Philhellenic poets like Lord Byron, it was in reality characterized by countless instances of savagery on both sides. Most often, however, the terrors of the war were ignored in favor of a poesy of heroic deeds. In their search for heroes, the Philhellenes in Europe and the New World saw virtually every incident as comparable in heroic virtue to the great heroes of classical Greece. The Mainote brigand-rebels became the Modern Spartans, and the Albanian Suliote leader Marco Botsaris was seen by the journalists and poets of the 1820s as the Modern Leonidas. Laskarina Bouboulina became one of the most popular of the heroes to emerge during the first phase of the Greek War of Independence; quickly, she was dubbed the Greek ***Joan of Arc**, or even the Modern ***Artemisia.**

Laskarina Bouboulina

Despite her remarkable exploits, Laskarina Bouboulina had rivals and enemies as well as admirers within the Greek independence movement. In a society that was often passionately self-destructive in its clan loyalties, even within her own family this strong-willed woman often engendered deep personal animosities. In 1825, during a violent argument with a family member over an unresolved vendetta, she was killed by a bullet that may or may not have been intentionally aimed at her. With her death, her legend only grew stronger and more myth-laden. Additional entertainments were written to add to the already large body of hero-worship produced during her lifetime. More than a century after her death, visitors to her house at Spétsai were still able to see traces of her blood on the wall where she had been fatally wounded. In 1930, her portrait appeared on one of the series of commemorative postage stamps issued by Greece to celebrate the centenary of the War of Independence.

SOURCES:

Finlay, George. *History of the Greek Revolution.* 2 vols. Edinburgh and London: W. Blackwood and Sons, 1861.

Howarth, David. *The Greek Adventure: Lord Byron and Other Eccentrics in the War of Independence.* NY: Atheneum, 1976.

St. Clair, William Linn. *That Greece Might Still Be Free: The Philhellenes in the War of Independence*. London: Oxford University Press, 1972.

Tsigakou, Fani-Maria. *The Rediscovery of Greece: Travellers and Painters of the Romantic Era*. New Rochelle, NY: Caratzas Brothers, 1981.

John Haag, Associate Professor,
University of Georgia, Athens, Georgia

Boucher, Joan (d. 1550).

See Bocher, Joan.

Boucherett, Jessie (1825–1905)

English feminist. *Born in Wellingham, Lincolnshire, England, in 1825; died in 1905; educated at Stratford.*

Jessie Boucherett, the daughter of a landowner and High Sheriff, was inspired by the feminist writings of ***Harriet Martineau** and began working for the women's movement as a member of the Langham Place Group. In 1860, she joined ***Barbara Bodichon** and ***Adelaide Ann Procter** to found the Society for Promoting the Employment of Women, which advocated jobs for women in farming, engraving, nursing, and clerical work, as well as special training courses in arithmetic and bookkeeping.

Boucherett was the editor of *The Englishwoman's Review* from 1866 to 1871 and served on the committee to present a petition for women's suffrage to Parliament in 1866. As a Conservative, opposed to protective legislation, she was a founding member of the Freedom of Labour Defense League. Her writings include a collaboration with ***Helen Blackburn** titled *The Condition of Working Women* (1896).

Boucicault, Nina (1867–1950).

See Adams, Maude for sidebar.

Boudica (26/30–60 CE)

Queen of the Iceni tribe who fought to drive the Romans from British soil. *Name variations: Boudicca or Boudicaa; the popular spelling, Boadicea, was derived from an error in an influential Renaissance manuscript. Pronunciation: (roughly) Boodika. Born as a member of the Royal House of the Iceni tribe probably between the years 26 CE to 30 in the modern shires of Norfolk and northern Suffolk, England; died around 62; married King Prasutagus of the Iceni prior to 49 CE; children: two daughters, whose names are unknown.*

Made regent on behalf of her daughters upon the death of Prasutagus (59 or 60 CE); became queen and led revolt against the Roman occupation of Britain (60); won victories at the modern sites of Colchester, London, and St. Albans and ambushed a Roman force in the field before succumbing to the Romans in 60, the same year in which she is believed to have taken her own life.

During the course of the year 60 CE, one woman's leadership challenged the might of Imperial Rome. Yet, few written records exist which could illuminate the dramatic events of that year or the life story of the queen who stood at center stage. Only four documents from the hands of three ancient authors have survived the centuries. Two of these works, the *Annals of Imperial Rome* and the *Agricola* are from the stylus of the Roman historian, Cornelius Tacitus, who recorded the details of Queen Boudica's rebellion 50 years after the fact. Tacitus is considered the primary source concerning Boudica because, having served as Roman senator and consul, he had access to critical archives; above all, Tacitus had spoken at length with his father-in-law, Julius Agricola, who had been in Britain during the famous revolt and who had become governor of that province in 78. Additionally, Greek historian Cassius Dio covered the Boudican revolt in his late 2nd century work, the *History of Rome*. Dio, unfortunately for posterity, seems to have used the earlier writings of Tacitus as his main, although not only, source. Finally, a single sentence reference to Boudica by Suetonius Tranquillus in the *Biographies of the Twelve Caesars* exhausts the extant documentary sources handed down by the ancients. For further detail, 20th-century researchers must rely on archaeological evidence.

Boudica's tribe, the Iceni, inhabited the areas of Norfolk and northern Suffolk (East Anglia) in modern England. The first forerunners of the Iceni seem to have migrated around 500 BCE from the modern-day regions of Belgium and Holland: sailing across the North Sea, they arrived in southeastern England, north of present-day London, and settled alongside the indigenous peoples, bringing with them a knowledge of iron-making. Southeast England was soon subjected to a second invasion after 450 BCE, when warriors from the Marne Valley in Gaul (modern France) arrived with iron and bronze tools of war, tools superior to those which had been seen previously by the local population and which included the light wooden and wicker-work chariot drawn by horses. These groups, which were Celtic, were the ancestors of the Iceni.

Unfortunately for the historian, the Celts maintained an oral tradition and did not commit their culture to the written word. We therefore have to rely on the tracts of foreign chroniclers and to compare these words to what is known from archaeological evidence. The Roman chroniclers, Julius Caesar, the Stoic philosopher Strabo, and Tacitus agreed that the Celts were a war-like people adept at single combat. In the words of the distinguished modern British historian **Antonia Fraser**:

> They also observed that the Celts fought naked, something they were well equipped to do; for this was a robust, well-muscled race who placed much emphasis on physical fitness. Furthermore, the Celts, as perceived by the Classical writers and depicted in Classical sculpture, were not only strong but tall and big-boned, with thick, flowing, fair or reddish hair.

This warrior people, cast in the Homeric mold, sported the image of the horse on its coins and produced swords and shields which were enameled and ornate with decoration. The high quality of artisanship evident among the Iceni also was demonstrated in more peaceful ways: bracelets, brooches, bronze mirrors, and above all heavy and beautiful golden necklaces (such as were worn by Boudica during her speeches to her people) have figured prominently among ar-

Boudica

chaeological finds. Nor was Iceni dress drab: "clothing (like Boudica's cloak) was generally stained and dyed in a variety of hues and stripes, making a kind of early tartan."

In demeanor, the Iceni were bold and fun-loving. Ancient writers have left us the image of a musical people who sang and played clappers and trumpets and who feasted at length. At least on special occasions, wine for the nobility and wheaten beer for the people flowed from large, communal cups which were laced with the spice, cumin. In comparison, Iceni homes were simple and appeared primitive to the Roman eye. The houses of the common people, which were remarkably durable given the vagaries of English weather, were circular with sloping roofs and perhaps averaged 50 feet across, each with a centrally located fireplace. The warrior aristocracy would have lived in larger but similarly shaped dwellings and the palace of King Prasutagus and Queen Boudica would have sported smaller, outlying roundhouses as well. Sadly, while archaeologists project the tribal center of the Iceni and Boudica's palace as probably lying near the modern English town of Thetford, neither has been located conclusively.

In at least two other ways the Iceni, and indeed the wider Celtic world which stretched from the modern countries of Germany across France to Spain and north to Britain, filled Roman chroniclers with curiosity and even disdain. While Roman society was unequivocally male-oriented, Iceni women lived a relatively "freer" life among the tribe. In large part, the role of women may well have been improved by the fact that Celtic society had worshipped goddesses. Roman records acknowledge the presence of Celtic women on the battlefield, and evidence points to the probability that women figured among the Druids, that priestly class of Celtic society which met to carry on religious rites in sacred groves. These Druids, in fact, have the distinction of being one of the only groups the Romans ever persecuted for religious belief: central to the Celtic religion, Boudica's religion, was the human head, which was considered the embodiment of the human soul. Celtic (and Iceni) warriors took the heads of their enemies in

Boudica

battle and embalmed those of the more famous in cedar oil for religious display.

The Romans first had encountered the Iceni during the invasions of the island of Britain by Julius Caesar in the respective years 55 and 54 BCE. These "invasions," in fact, were little more than raids in force launched for the purpose of punishing the Celts in Britain for the support of their tribal brethren on the Continent during the Roman conquest of Gaul. The real invasion occurred in 43 when the Roman emperor Claudius ordered four legions dispatched to Britain. From that year, as the empire's troops marched north and west from their initial base in southeastern Britain, Roman influence spread. The Celtic diplomatic and military response was uneven. In the words of historian Leonard Cottrell: "There was no standard pattern: resistance was piecemeal, loyalties local and personal, never national. There was no 'British nation.'" Between the years 43 and 50, the Iceni, under King Prasutagus, accepted Roman rule, at least temporarily. The Iceni, however, participated in the rebellion which occurred throughout East Anglia and Wales against the Romans in the year 50. The tribes of East Anglia were the first to be put down; the rebels in Wales, however, held out for several years under the charismatic leader Caratacus before surrendering.

Between 51 and 61, the Roman administration of what is today central and southern England (the Trent-Severn river line) encouraged the British to construct and move into cities and to become "civilized" according to the laws and culture of the empire. Unfortunately, Roman moneylenders, with more enterprise than scruple, targeted many of the British chiefs who were willing to attempt to accommodate themselves to the new order. Among these was Prasutagus, whom the empire accepted as an ally and client-king. Prasutagus had married Boudica, a member of the Royal House of the Iceni, shortly before the rebellion of 50, and in the ensuing years had fathered two daughters. Boudica, who seems to have been born somewhere between 26–30, was probably in her 30s. The historian, Cassius Dio, has described the queen as a tall woman with a mass of tawny red hair flowing to her waist who possessed a harsh voice and a fearsome countenance. Before his death in 60, the king placed Boudica in charge of his lands which he willed jointly to his daughters and to the Roman emperor Nero.

By this legacy, Prasutagus hoped to preserve his kingdom intact and to gain protection against the encroachments of the local Roman administration. The fate of the Royal House of the Iceni, however, was served poorly by this gesture. In the words of the Roman historian Tacitus:

> Kingdom and household alike were plundered like prizes of war, the one by Roman officers, the other by Roman slaves. As a beginning, his widow Boudica was flogged and their daughters raped. The Icenian chiefs were deprived of their hereditary estates as if the Romans had been given the whole country. The king's own relatives were treated like slaves.

These brutal acts were obviously intended to symbolize the subjection of the British populace. Simultaneously, three other outrages were being committed by the empire against the Britons. Roman moneylenders already had begun calling in their considerable loans which the British chiefs found impossible to pay. Secondly, Roman colonists were persisting in land appropriations which seemed to the Britons as no more than being turned out of hearth and home. Thirdly, a Roman expeditionary force had marched through northwestern Wales and had put the Isle of Mona (modern Anglesey) under siege. Mona housed the sacred groves of the Druid priests and priestesses and was the religious font of the Celtic peoples.

> Consider how many of you are fighting—and why. Then you will win this battle, or perish. That is what I, a woman, plan to do!—let the men live in slavery if they will.
>
> **—Queen Boudica**

The Iceni, fearing worse to come, revolted and were joined by the Trinovantes as well as other tribes. According to Tacitus, the leadership of the resistance fell to Boudica; when the Britons went to war, gender was not necessarily a barrier: "They hunted down the Roman troops in their scattered posts, stormed the forts, and assaulted the colony itself, which they saw as the center of their servitude; and there was no form of savage cruelty that the angry victors refrained from."

In addition to the random slaughter of Roman colonists carried throughout the countryside, Boudica specifically targeted three of the empire's cities for destruction: Camulodunum (Colchester), Verulamiam (St. Albans), and Londinum (London). According to Cassius Dio, Boudica's speech of war delivered to her assembled forces was full of high drama which portrayed the Romans as a civilized society gone soft while her Britons were a rugged breed filled with courage and honor. There can be little doubt her intent was to hurl the Romans back into the seas from which they had come.

Colchester, which in their improvidence the Romans had failed to fortify, was first to feel her wrath. Some scholars have estimated the tribal host at 120,000; in any event, after a two-day siege in which the defenders made their last stand in the temple of the hated foreign gods, Boudica had no difficulty overwhelming the tiny garrison and city which had been filled with Roman colonists as well as British settlers who had sought to acclimatize themselves to Roman rule.

The Roman response was swift if rash. Collecting some 2,000 infantry and 500 cavalry of the 9th Legion, Petillius Cerealis tried to relieve Colchester by forced marches. Intercepted in an ambush by Boudica's forces, most likely while taking the road through the thick forest, his expedition came to grief. In the words of historian Graham Webster:

> By attacking them while in extended line of march, the Britons gave the enemy little opportunity to move into battle formation. The Roman legionaries were thus cut into isolated groups. Doubtless they sold their lives dearly, and the Britons lost many of their best fighting men that day.

Jubilant, Boudica's tribal masses forged onward and converged almost simultaneously on St. Albans and London. These cities fell as easily as Colchester. Tacitus recorded that the deaths of the Romans and their British allies had reached 70,000 at this point. No prisoners were taken. In the words of Tacitus, the Britons "could not wait to cut throats, hang, burn, and crucify." Subsequently, archaeologists have unearthed the telling layers of soot and ash underlying these modern cities and have been able to confirm the mass destruction.

Even as Boudica's forces grew over-confident, however, what was left of the Roman Empire in Britain was preparing to counter-attack. The governor, Gaius Seutonius Paulinus, had already advanced on London with a small reconnaissance force and had determined that the city had to be abandoned. Before this reconnaissance, he had organized the 14th Legion as well as sections of the 20th. Now he prepared to meet Boudica on a battleground of his own choosing.

Boudica met Suetonius for the final confrontation most likely in the west Midlands in Warwickshire, possibly near the modern locality of Nuneaton and Atherstone. Choosing wisely, Suetonius settled into a defile with a thick copse of woods to his rear, thereby depriving Boudica of her one strength; numerical superiority. Suetonius gambled that as her Britons advanced to the attack, as was their nature, they would be pressed into a bottleneck where Roman martial discipline and qualitative superiority in weaponry could tell to their maximum advantage. Even so, he realized his 10,000 legionaries would be pitted against some tens of thousands.

Before the battle, Boudica addressed her men and those women who chose to fight. Behind her battle masses were arrayed the families of her warriors who had turned out to watch this unparalleled spectacle from the relative comfort of their wagons. In rousing tones, the queen of the Iceni appealed to her people:

> I am fighting as an ordinary person for my lost freedom, my bruised body, and my outraged daughters. . . . Consider how many of you are fighting—and why. Then you will win this battle, or perish. That is what I, a woman, plan to do!—let the men live in slavery if they will.

Surging forward amidst the great fanfare of trumpets, the Britons pressed into the defile. At 40 yards, thousands of Roman javelins or *pila* feathered Boudica's first wave. Then, the second. As the highly trained and uniformly armored legionaries stood their ground, reserve forces moved up and down the formation to relieve those comrades exhausted from the hot press of war. Disordered, the British warriors halted, then received the inevitable Roman countercharge. Bunched in mass and unable to wield their long swords, the Britons fell back. Then, the Roman advance pressed Boudica's troops back against their own wagons where they were slaughtered trying to escape. Tacitus, almost surely with exaggeration, states that 80,000 of the British died in this armageddon. Neither man nor woman nor child was spared.

In the aftermath, the Romans received reinforcements from the empire and set about quelling lingering British resistance. The Britons themselves, not having been able to tend to the harvest during the campaign, now faced a cruel winter and the ugly face of starvation. Boudica, queen of the Iceni, surmising her fate if captured, survived the battle only to die of poison administered by her own hand. Dio Cassius recorded that her people gave her an expensive burial, although the site of her grave remains a mystery. The fate of her daughters is unknown.

In the 1850s, centuries after the Romans had evacuated British shores, Britons surveyed their own empire, which would eventually embrace one-fourth of the world's surface. Ruled by another queen, *Victoria, they hearkened back to the age of Boudica and past glory. One of the leading European artists, Thomas Thorncroft, was commissioned by Prince Albert and the British Government to sculpt a massive statue of Boudica mounted on her war chariot with her daughters. This colossal masterpiece, which stands today near the House of Commons and Big Ben, was not finished until 1902. Inscribed thereon are the immortal words of writer Thomas Cowper: "Regions Caesar never knew/ Thy Posterity shall sway."

SOURCES:

Cottrell, Leonard. *The Roman Invasion of Britain.* NY: Barnes and Noble, 1992.

Fraser, Antonia. *The Warrior Queens.* NY: Alfred A. Knopf, 1989.

Tacitus, Cornelius. *The Agricola and the Germania.* Translation (revised) by S.A. Handford. London: Penguin Books, 1970.

———. *The Annals of Imperial Rome.* Translated by Michael Grant. London: Penguin Books, 1989.

Webster, Graham. *Boudica: the British Revolt against Rome AD 60.* London: B.T. Batsford, 1978, rev. ed., 1993.

SUGGESTED READING:

Matthews, John, and Bob Stewart. *Celtic Battle Heroes.* Poole, Dorset: Firebird Books, 1988.

David L. Bullock, Ph.D., author of *Allenby's War: the Palestine Arabian Campaigns, 1916–1918* (London: Blandford Press, 1988)

Boudicaa or Boudicca (26/30–60 CE).

See Boudica.

Boufflers, Madeleine-Angelique, Duchesse de (1707–1787)

French Salonnière. *Name variations: Madeleine-Angelique de Neufville-Villeroi, duchesse de Luxemburg or Luxembourg; Maréchale de Luxembourg. Born in 1707; died in 1787; married the Duc de Boufflers; married the Maréchal (Marshal) of Luxembourg.*

Her first husband was the Duc de Boufflers; her second, the maréchal (marshal) of Luxembourg. In the latter part of the 18th century, Madeleine-Angelique, duchess de Boufflers, held a salon that was a popular meeting place for the cream of society. She was a patron of Rousseau.

Boufflers, Marie (1706–1747)

Marquise de Boufflers. *Born Marie Françoise Catherine de Beauvais-Craon in 1706; died in 1747; sister of the Maréchale de Mirepoix (a friend of Mme de Pompadour); children: Stanislas-Jean Boufflers, chevalier de (1737–1815, a cavalry officer and writer of light verse).*

Marie Boufflers

A beautiful and witty woman, Marie Boufflers was one of the charmers of her age. She lived in Lorraine, was a friend of Voltaire, and the mistress of King Stanislas Leczszinski, ex-king of Poland.

Boufflers-Rouvrel, Marie Charlotte Hippolyte, Countess de (1724–c. 1800)

French salonnière. *Name variations: Comtesse or Countess Boufflers-Rouvrel; Rouveret. Born in Paris, France, in 1724; died around 1800; married the Comte de Boufflers-Rouvrel (d. 1764).*

Following the death of her husband in 1764, Countess Marie Boufflers-Rouvrel became the reputed mistress of the Prince de Contí and hosted his receptions. A leader in Parisian literary literary circles, she was a friend of J.J. Rousseau, Hume, and Grimm. She is often confused with *Marie Boufflers, mother of author Stanislas-Jean Boufflers and friend of Voltaire. In the year 1775, in the diary of James Boswell, Mme Boufflers-Rouvrel visited Dr. Samuel Johnson in the Temple.

Boughton, Alice (1866–1943)

American photographer specializing in portraits and theatrical work. *Born in Brooklyn, New York, in 1866; died in Bay Shore, New York, in 1943.*

The available facts of Alice Boughton's life and career are few, beyond a number of her exhibitions over the short period from 1902 to 1909. She studied painting in Paris and Rome before becoming an assistant in the studio of ***Gertrude Käsebier**. In 1904, she became an associate of the Photo-Secession (she was later elected a fellow) and was represented in Alfred Stieglitz's initial exhibition of 1905, which included the work of three dozen Secessionists. Boughton's portrait work included children. She also painted and photographed nude figures, sometimes using sand dunes as a setting. In 1907, she exhibited with William B. Dyer and C. Yarnall Abbott. Her work was last published in *Camera Work* (1909). In 1931, she closed her New York City studio and moved to Brookhaven, New York.

Bouhired, Djamila (1937—)

Algerian heroine of the War of National Liberation from France, 1954–1962, known throughout the Middle East as "the Arab Joan of Arc." *Name variations: Djamilah. Born in 1937 to a middle-class Muslim family in Algiers (some sources cite 1935); married Jacques Vergès (her French attorney); children: three, Nadyah (adopted), Maryam, Ilyas.*

It is one of the ironies of modern Algerian history that the greatest heroine of the Algerian War of National Liberation grew up in the 1940s believing herself to be French rather than Arab. Born in 1937 into a middle-class family, Djamila Bouhired was educated in Algiers at a school that inculcated in its students the belief that they were French. Like virtually all of the young Algerians fortunate enough in the 1940s to find themselves in school, and the great majority were not, she was raised with a French cultural consciousness and never learned to read or write in Arabic, the language that she and her family spoke at home. French was the language of instruction in her school, with the "foreign" languages offered being German, Italian, and finally Arabic. In a 1971 interview, she recalled that when she was a schoolgirl her teachers "taught us with the assumption that we were French. Paris was the capital, the mother of us all. The French parliament was our parliament, Vincent Auriol was our president, the French flag was our flag. Algeria? At that time it didn't exist. It was French Algeria. And we carried around our French identity every day in school. It wasn't easy to get rid of that identity; we'd had it all of our lives."

Having lost its empire in India and North America in the 18th century, France began in 1830 to create a new empire centered in North Africa. Although the ports were easily captured, Algerian resistance remained strong. Northern Algeria was not conquered until 1857, and the conquest of the southern part of the country was not completed until 1882. Local rebellions, including a massive one in eastern Algeria in the early 1870s, made it clear that European rule continued to be resented. The tripling of the indigenous population from 1830 to 1914 only worsened the poverty and ignorance of most Algerians. With few exceptions, the role of women remained subordinated to that of men in a traditional system of patriarchy. As late as the 1930s, less than nine percent of Muslim children went to school; only a handful of these were female. The hopes raised by World War II were dashed by the reversion to old colonial patterns by the end of the conflict. A tragic turning point in French-Algerian relations took place in 1945, when Djamila was eight years old. That May, French troops carried out a bloody massacre of the Algerian population when celebrations of the victory over Nazi Germany turned into nationalist demonstrations. Many thousands of Algerians were killed, but few if any significant reforms were initiated by the French colonial regime.

Harsh repressions by the French authorities and lack of a unified strategy among the Algerian nationalist leadership delayed by almost a decade any strong response to the continuing injustices of colonialism, but an armed uprising initiated by the National Liberation Front (FLN) on November 1, 1954, marked the beginning of the Algerian revolution. Although the uprising brought on a rhetorical response about the desirability of political and social reforms from Paris, the essential French reaction consisted of increasingly bloody military reprisals. By September 1955, there were more than 120,000 French soldiers in Algeria, a number that increased to 400,000 by the end of 1956. Although the Algerian rebels had to give up the idea of permanently capturing towns or large tracts of territory, French repression only strengthened the rebels' appeal to the Muslim majority, and by 1956 they had become highly effective at a strategy of urban guerrilla warfare.

The start of the War of National Liberation in late 1954 first resulted in an enthusiastic response from Djamila's brother who in turn recruited her for the nationalist cause. Youthful Algerian nationalists like Djamila became increasingly radicalized by the brutal treatment of FLN prisoners by the French. In one particularly dramatic instance of the escalating French efforts to crush the rebellion in blood, in June 1956 two FLN prisoners, one of whom had been crippled by his severe wounds while fighting the French, were guillotined. The response of the FLN was to announce that for every guillotined member of their organization, 100 French would be killed indiscriminately. The Algiers network led by Saadi Yacef, son of a Casbah baker, of which Djamila was now a member, was told to "kill any European between the ages of 18 and 54. But no women, no children, no old people." Within a week of the June 1956 executions of the two FLN prisoners, Yacef's squads had shot down 49 French civilians at random. The pied noir colonial settlers, assisted by allies in the French armed forces, retaliated with indiscriminate terror of their own, blowing up three Muslim houses, with a death toll of more than 70 including women and children.

By the end of 1956, Saadi Yacef had created a well-organized force of over 1,400 militants in Algiers, most of them young and willing to give their lives for the FLN cause. A key element in Yacef's terrorist strategy would be the use of young, attractive and Westernized Muslim women to plant bombs to spread terror among the European population of Algiers. Djamila Bouhired, who was personally devoted to Saadi Yacef, played a key role in recruiting many of his most selfless female militants. Besides Bouhired, these included **Zohra Drif** and **Samia Lakhdari**. On September 30, 1956, Bouhired, Drif, and Lakhdari attended a meeting with Saadi Yacef in one of his Casbah hideouts. Here they were told that the same afternoon each of them would place a bomb in a selected location in the European quarter of Algiers. When the first response of the young women appeared to be one of disbelief and shock, Yacef reminded them of the horrible mutilations suffered by Muslim children as a result of French bombings. Djamila and the other women took off their veils, tinted their hair, and put on the kind of bright, summery dresses worn by young European girls spending a carefree day at the beach.

As depicted in the 1966 film *The Battle of Algiers* in which Saadi Yacef played himself, each of the women was given a bomb of little more than a kilogram in weight. The bombs, which were timed to go off at one-minute intervals, were concealed in beach bags under bikinis,

Djamila Bouhired

beach towels, and suntan-oil. Two of the three bombs went off, one at a Milk Bar and the other at a popular cafeteria frequented by young couples. Djamila Bouhired's bomb, which she had placed in the hall of the Air France terminus, failed to go off due to a faulty timing mechanism. A number of deaths and severe mutilations resulted from the explosions, and as expected the French response was to ratchet up their violence against the Muslim population. Spontaneous outbursts of hatred between the French and Muslim populations erupted after each bombing, and on one occasion an innocent young Muslim mechanic was lynched by an outraged pied noir mob. Convinced that her activities would hasten the day of Algerian independence, Bouhired continued recruiting young women, some as young as 16, for the FLN cause; she also continued planting bombs herself. More than a decade later, she would recall: "My job was to plant bombs. I carried death with me in my handbag, death in the shape of time bombs."

Intense French efforts succeeded in smashing Saadi Yacef's organization by the end of February 1957. In April of that year, Bouhired was arrested while walking out of the Algiers Casbah. Strolling a few paces behind her, disguised as a woman and carrying a submachine gun under his traditional Muslim clothing, Saadi Yacef responded to Bouhired's arrest by drawing his gun and firing at her. She was only wounded, but it was clear that Yacef's goal had been to kill in order to prevent her from revealing important information about himself and his organization to the French. As soon as she had recovered from her wounds, Bouhired's French captors interrogated her using extreme forms of torture including electrodes attached to her body. Despite the intensity of her suffering, she revealed nothing. She derived strength and inspiration during her ordeal from the knowledge that other young women had chosen to sacrifice their lives for the goal of a free Algeria. One of her comrades, Aminah, had been discovered while on a bomb-placing mission; rather than endure torture, Aminah had taken poison and died. Other young FLN women, including a 19-year-old named Hasibah, had chosen death when the French troops gave her and her two male comrades a choice of emerging from their hideaway in a house or being blown up. All three chose to remain in the house and died in the resulting explosion.

Drawing upon her own courage and a rapidly growing tradition of revolutionary martyrdom by young Algerian women, Djamila Bouhired kept herself from revealing any secrets during 17 days of torture. Before his own capture in late September 1957, Saadi Yacef and his unit made several attempts to rescue her from the Maillot military hospital. Bouhired received a smuggled message concerning a rescue attempt in which she was to deceive the French by claiming to lead them to Yacef, and in which she was to throw herself to the ground while Yacef's forces ambushed her captors. She refused to participate in this action, not wanting "any brothers" to "risk their lives" to liberate her from French captivity. Another attempt to free her was frustrated at the last minute when French paratroopers took her away in a military vehicle just before the arrival of a FLN rescue team.

Few observers doubted the outcome of Djamila Bouhired's trial, which took place before a military court in Algeria in mid-July 1957. The special tribunal had an agenda of crushing the continuing Muslim insurrection and ignored the spirited defense of Bouhired's French attorney, Jacques Vergès. The entire trial was marked by irregularities and regarded by many observers as a travesty of justice. Bouhired and another defendant, **Djamila Bouazza**, were both found guilty and sentenced to die on the guillotine. By this time, however, public opinion—both in France and internationally—had begun to turn against an interminable war that saw ever more torture and other inhumane methods used to crush the efforts of national liberation. Bouazza's age (19) and the obvious courage of both women made a deep impression on public opinion outside of Algeria. French intellectuals took up the cause of Djamila Bouhired with passionate intensity, with her lawyer Jacques Vergès coauthoring an influential pamphlet discussing the merits of her case. Committees pledged to save Bouhired and Bouazza from the guillotine were formed in a number of European countries, and, as her case was discussed in the press, key members of the French government began to recognize the propaganda defeat they would suffer if the women were in fact put to death. In an Arab world awakening to the energies of national rebirth, Djamila Bouhired was celebrated in the media as "the Arab Joan of Arc."

In the last days of 1957, French President René Coty received an impassioned plea from Princess **Laila Ayesha** of Morocco asking that Bouhired's life be spared. The international furor over her fate did not abate, and, in early February 1958, a letter signed by 76 British Labour Party members of Parliament urged President Coty to grant Bouhired a reprieve from the guillotine as well as open an inquiry into the trial that had sentenced her to death. More dramatic and to the point were three days of demonstrations in front of the French embassy in London in February 1958 demanding that Djamila Bouhired not be executed. Bowing to the intense international pressure, on March 13, 1958, the French president commuted to life imprisonment not only the death sentences of Bouazza and Bouhired, but also the death sentence of another young female FLN activist, **Jacqueline Netter Guerrodj**.

Djamila Bouhired was taken to France where she was imprisoned until summer 1962 at the Rheims prison. With the achievement of Algerian independence in 1962, she was released and returned to Algiers. Soon after her return home, she married Jacques Vergès, the French attorney who had defended her with such energy at her trial in July 1957. Bouhired and her husband raised a family, beginning with an adopted daughter, Nadyah, whose father had died in the Algerian revolution. Two children of her own, a daughter Maryam and a son Ilyas, soon followed. Bouhired and her husband, a militant Communist, believed that Algeria's many problems could best be understood from a Marxist perspective. She ran unsuccessfully for a seat in Algeria's first post-independence National Assembly. Along with her husband and another of Yacef's former operatives, Zohra Drif, she published a radical journal, *Révolution africaine*.

The hopeful dreams of the early days of Algerian independence quickly evaporated. In 1963, a purge of Communists and other leftists forced Bouhired and her husband from the staff of *Révolution africaine*. Subsequently, she divorced Vergès and became involved in a business venture selling cosmetics. Bouhired withdrew from the national political scene, concentrating on raising her three children and working in local social improvement projects in her neighborhood in Algiers. As she entered middle-age, Djamila Bouhired became part of the history of not only her own country but the history of women seeking emancipation and equality in the modern Muslim world. The dreams of full equality for women, one of the goals of the Algerian revolution, were not realized as the 20th century came to an end. Massive problems of a stagnant economy and rapid population growth resulted in the growth of Islamic fundamentalism in the 1980s and a virtual civil war in the 1990s. Though the hopes of the Algerian women of Bouhired's generation were not realized after the achievement of independence, the courageous example she set both during and after the revolution may one day guide a new and more fortunate generation of women in Algeria.

SOURCES:

Alleg, Henri, *et al. La Guerre d' Algérie.* 3 vols. Paris: Temps Actuels, 1981.

Amrane, Djamila. "Les combattantes de la guerre d'Algérie," in *Matériaux pour l'Histoire de Notre Temps.* No. 26, 1992, pp. 58–62.

———. *Les femmes algériennes dans la guerre.* Paris: Plon, 1991.

Arnaud, Georges and Jacques Vergès. *Pour Djamila Bouhired.* Paris: "Documents," 1958.

Courriere, Yves. *La Guerre d'Algérie: Les Temps des leopards.* Paris: Fayard, 1969.

Fanon, Frantz. *A Dying Colonialism.* Translated by Haakon Chevalier. NY: Grove Press, 1967.

Fernea, Elizabeth Warnock and Basima Qattan Bezirgan, eds. *Middle Eastern Women Speak.* Austin, TX: University of Texas Press, 1977.

Gacemi, B. "La longue marche des femmes algériennes," in *Confluences Méditeranée.* Vol. 3, 1992, pp. 87–94.

Horne, Alistair. *A Savage War of Peace: Algeria 1954–1962.* Rev. ed. NY: Penguin Books, 1987.

Kraft, Joseph. "I Saw the Algerian Rebels in Action," in *Saturday Evening Post.* Vol. 230, no. 29. January 18, 1958, pp. 30, 89–90.

Perkins, Kenneth J. "Bouhired, Djamila," in John L. Esposito, ed. *The Oxford Encyclopedia of the Modern Islamic World.* 4 vols. New York and Oxford: Oxford University Press, 1995, vol. 1, pp. 230–231.

"Princess Bids Coty Save Doomed Algerian Girl," in *The New York Times.* December 31, 1957, p. 3.

"Reprieve Urged," in *The Times* [London], February 8, 1958, p. 4.

"3 Algerian Women Escape Guillotine," in *The New York Times.* March 14, 1958, p. 6.

Tillion, Germaine. *The Republic of Cousins: Women's Oppression in Mediterranean Society.* London: Al Saqui Books, 1983.

Vidal-Naquet, Pierre. *Face à la raison d'État: Un historien dans la guerre d'Algérie.* Paris: Éditions la Découverte, 1989.

———. *Torture: Cancer of Democracy. France and Algeria 1954–62.* Translated by Barry Richard. Harmondsworth, Middlesex: Penguin Books, 1963.

Violations of Human Rights in Algeria. NY: Arab Information Center, 1960 [Arab Information Center Information Paper No. 11, April 1960].

RELATED MEDIA:

Battle of Algiers (120 min.), produced by Magna-Rizzoli, directed by Gino Pontecorvo, 1967, was nominated for an Oscar for Best Foreign Film.

John Haag, Associate Professor,
University of Georgia, Athens, Georgia

Bouillon, Duchess de (1649–1714).

See Mancini, Marie-Anne.

Boulanger, Lili (1893–1918)

French composer, first woman to win the Premier Grand Prix de Rome for music, whose early death cut short a promising composing career. *Pronunciation: Boo-lawn-jay. Born Juliette Marie Olga Boulanger on August 21, 1893, in Paris, France; died of tuberculosis on March 15, 1918, in Paris; daughter of Ernest Boulanger (the composer) and Raissa or Raïssa (Princess Michetsky or Mychetsky) Boulanger (a vocalist from St. Petersburg); sister of* ****Nadia Boulanger*** *(1887–1979), famous teacher of 20th-century composers.*

The second of her parents' two daughters, Lili Boulanger was born into an extremely talented musical family. Her father Ernest Boulanger, who had won the Prix de Rome for composition, was well known, especially for his operas. Her mother **Raissa Boulanger**, many years younger, had been a pupil of her husband's when he came to St. Petersburg and was determined to marry him. Despite several decades difference in age, the Boulangers had a happy marriage, and the family was close. Nadia, who was six years old when Lili was born, was taken into the room where her mother was holding the newborn and told to swear she would look after her baby sister. She solemnly pledged she would.

Ernest Boulanger died when Lili was three, but life continued to revolve around music. Raissa learned harmony, in order to teach her daughters the rudiments, and both Lili and Nadia read, played, and composed music at early ages. Because Lili's health was poor from birth and she had no regular course of schooling, Nadia and her mother devoted much time and energy to her education; in consequence, Lili was a child prodigy. When she entered the Paris Conservatoire in 1909, she studied composition with Georges Gaussade and Paul Vidal. She found her

Lili and Nadia Boulanger

own musical personality almost at once, proving to be an extremely gifted composer. Hers was "the instinct of genius marked by death," said Marcelle de Manziarly.

Lili composed continuously despite extremely precarious health. Daunted by her younger sister's drive, Nadia devoted her energies to teaching rather than composing, a decision which was to profoundly affect the 20th-century musical world. After only a year at the Paris Conservatoire, Lili won the Prix Lepaulle. In 1912, she entered the Prix de Rome competition. Though not successful at her first attempt in Rome, when no prizes were given, she tried again in 1913 and was admitted to the final round of the Prix de Rome that May, the only woman of the five contestants. Thin and ill but elegantly dressed, Lili—only 19 years old—conducted a performance of her composition *Faust et Hélène*. She won over not only the audience but also the jury. Thirty-one out of thirty-six voting members of the Académie des Beaux-Arts decided she should be the first woman to receive the Premier Grand Prix de Rome in music.

Though she continued to compose, Lili Boulanger's health deteriorated. In 1911, she had written *Nocturne* for flute or violin and piano; in 1912, *Pour les funérailles d'un soldat* had been composed for orchestra; in 1916–17, *Three psalms* for orchestra was composed; and in 1917, she was at work on an unfinished opera. She also wrote a work for soprano, strings, harp, and organ in 1918, the year of her death. In that short life, Lili Boulanger produced a significant body of vocal and instrumental works and had a great impact on the musical world. By instituting a prize in composition, Nadia kept her beloved sister's name alive. A brilliant composer, Lili Boulanger broke new ground for women, before she died at age 24.

SOURCES:

Kendall, Alan. *The Tender Tyrant: Nadia Boulanger, a Life Devoted to Music.* London: MacDonald and Jane's, 1976.

Rosenstiel, Léonie. *Nadia Boulanger: A Life in Music.* NY: W.W. Norton, 1982.

John Haag,
Athens, Georgia

Boulanger, Nadia (1887–1979)

French composer, performer, and first woman to conduct the London Philharmonic, New York Philharmonic, Boston Philharmonic, and Philadelphia orchestras, who was best known as a teacher of music, including among her students Leonard Bernstein, Virgil Thomson, and Aaron Copland, thereby making her one of the most influential musicians of the 20th century. *Pronunciation: Nah-dya Boo-lawn-jay. Born Juliette Nadia Boulanger in Paris, France, on September 16, 1887; died in Paris on October 22, 1979; daughter of Ernest (a composer and professor of voice at the Paris Conservatoire de Musique) and Raissa or Raïssa (Princess Michetsky or Mychetsky) Boulanger (a vocalist from St. Petersburg); sister of Lili Boulanger (1893–1918); attended The Paris Conservatoire de Musique; never married; no children.*

Won the first of many First Place competitions at Paris Conservatoire de Musique at age 11 (1898); began performing career (1903); began studies with Italian pianist and composer Raoul Pugno (1904); collaborated with Pugno on the music for Gabriele d'Annunzio's drama, La Ville morte, *and began lifelong friendship with Igor Stravinsky (1910); abandoned performing in favor of teaching (1920); became teacher of Aaron Copland at Fontainebleau (1921); made concert tour of U.S. and offered teach-*

Nadia Boulanger

ing chair at the Curtis Institute in Philadelphia (1924); accepted position at the École Normale du Musique in Paris, teaching organ, harmony, counterpoint, and the history of music, an unprecedented appointment for a woman; became first woman to conduct the Royal Philharmonic Orchestra in London (1936); repeated the honor with the Boston Symphony Orchestra (1938), and the New York Philharmonic and Philadelphia orchestras (1939); appointed judge of the prestigious Tchaikovsky Competition in Moscow (1966); inducted as a Grand Officer of the Legion of Honor (1977).

In 1921, when the American composer Aaron Copland became one of the first music students of Nadia Boulanger at Fontainebleau, he was so impressed by her teaching that he decided to ask for private lessons. Years later, reflecting on the sexism then rampant in the music field, Copland admitted to taking the step with some trepidation. "No composer ever had a woman teacher. It wasn't Nadia Boulanger I was worried about—it was my reputation!" After three years of study with Boulanger, Copland's appreciation of his teacher never wavered, and over the years he sent her many students from the United States. Virgil Thomson, Leonard Bernstein, and George Gershwin were only a few of the century's brilliant American musicians who made their way to France to study under the internationally known conductor, composer, and teacher known to all her pupils as "Mademoiselle."

Juliette Nadia Boulanger was born on September 16, 1887, her father's birthday, in the ninth arrondissement of Paris. Ernest Boulanger was a well-known figure in the musical world, a talented musician and composer who came from a long line of famous opera singers and actors, and a professor of voice at the prestigious Paris Conservatoire de Musique. Nadia's mother, Raissa Michetsky, or Mychetsky, was a Russian who claimed to be a princess, and may well have been, though the claim has never been substantiated. She had met Ernest Boulanger in St. Petersburg, probably in 1874, when he was directing concerts there. The young Russian vocalist was quite taken with the French professor, who was 43 years her senior, and arranged to become his student. They fell in love and their marriage remained a happy one despite the vast difference in their ages. Nadia was born on Ernest's 72nd birthday, and her sister, Juliette Marie, called ***Lili**, who also became a talented composer and musician, was born five years later.

Raissa Boulanger was a strict disciplinarian whose life revolved around her children and music. By the age of five, Nadia was applying herself rigorously to French music courses, and at eight she began to study organ with Louis Vierne. The following year, she entered the Conservatoire National du Musique to learn the system of music study known as *solfège*; at age 11, she was the youngest entrant in the school's *solfège* competition when she won first place. By the time of her father's death the following year, Nadia's life was immersed in music. At age 14, she was studying with the famous composer Gabriel Fauré and was awarded the conservatory's second prize in harmony. Two years later, in 1903, she won a first prize, as well as firsts in organ, piano accompaniment, fugue, and composition. At 16, she was teaching piano to students who were often her own age. She began to perform professionally, playing before the president of the republic, Émile Loubet, at the Trocadero Palace.

The close relationship of Raissa Boulanger and her two daughters was cemented by the extremely precarious health of Lili. Nadia was devoted to her extremely talented younger sister, who was destined to die at an early age. In 1904, Nadia began to study with the famous pianist Raoul Pugno, who was a friend of the family and spent summer vacations with the Boulangers. He soon began to send her students, including her first American. In 1906, Boulanger and Pugno began to compose and to perform together, and it may have been Pugno who encouraged Nadia to present herself as a candidate for the Concours de Rome. No woman had ever carried off a first prize in this musical competition, and Boulanger made three attempts without ever succeeding. But since women rarely competed at that level, the competition garnered a great deal of publicity for her and heightened her status in the musical world at a young age. Against such odds, the second place that she won was considered a great victory and recognized around the world by women in music.

In that era, the world of classical music was still primarily a male domain. Although some women managed to establish successful concert careers, playing in an orchestra was seldom an option (even at the close of the 20th century there were a dwindling number of orchestras, such as the prestigious Vienna Philharmonic, that remained entirely male); once women did attain acceptance in music's hierarchical ranks, they were paid less than men. In 1913, a book by Otto Ebel listed more than 800 women composers throughout musical history. Subsequently, the achievements of Nadia Boulanger would help to revolutionize the music field.

Although raised a strict Catholic, Boulanger showed a streak of rebelliousness from childhood. At an early age, she preferred to wear the black velvet suits traditionally worn by little boys. As she grew older, her clothing remained masculine, and black was always a favorite color. She traveled around Paris unchaperoned day and night, behavior considered radical for a respectable woman before World War I. In 1910, Boulanger collaborated with Pugno on the music for the drama *La Ville morte*, by Gabriele d'Annunzio, the Italian poet whose works and scandalous escapades were known throughout Europe. Boulanger formed a friendship with the most famous of his mistresses, the Italian actress ***Eleonora Duse**. That same year, she saw *Firebird*, the modern ballet by Igor Stravinsky that was then rocking the musical world, and she gained an introduction to its youthful composer. It was the beginning of their lifelong friendship.

In 1913, Lili was studying under her older sister when she decided to enter the Concours de Rome. Succeeding where Nadia had failed, Lili became the first woman to win the Premier Grand Prix de Rome. That same year, Nadia began a concert tour with Raoul Pugno, going to Berlin and then on to Russia, but during the tour Pugno died suddenly of a pulmonary embolism. He had been her teacher, friend, and probably a love interest, and the unexpected death was a great shock. Even so, Boulanger was forced to continue working because her mother and sister both depended on her for support. Then Lili, who veered from one health crisis to the next, died of tuberculosis in March 1918, before reaching 25. For Nadia, the loss was enormous.

By 1920, the demands of practicing, performing, teaching, and composing were taking their toll on Boulanger's health. Forced to withdraw for a while and recover, she decided to concentrate on teaching and composing rather than performing, and began to take on students in Paris and at nearby Fontainebleau. She became friends with Walter Damrosch, an American musician of first rank, beginning another lifelong friendship that would provide her with many American students and permanently establish her influence in the American music world. Because of her gender, however, years would pass before she was offered a position at the conservatory where her father had taught. Nevertheless, the École Normale du Musique put her in charge of classes in organ, harmony, counterpoint, and the history of music. Her appointment, the first of its kind for a woman, caused a sensation. Her classes were so popular that enrollment soon had to be limited.

In 1924, after she had taught Copland, Boulanger came to the U.S., where she gave a series of 26 concerts which received rave reviews. Thanks to Damrosch, she made many important contacts and was offered a permanent chair of music at the Curtis Institute in Philadelphia, but she returned to Paris because of her mother's failing health. In Paris, America then began to come to her, and the teacher known to everyone as Mademoiselle could now take her pick of the world's most talented students.

Nadia Boulanger was a relentless taskmaster. Weak or mediocre students were ruthlessly weeded out of her teaching schedule, and she demanded total dedication from her students. Remaining open to innovation, she became widely known for her ability to interpret the music of Stravinsky; she was also open to non-classical forms. When the Argentinean Astor Piazzola studied with her, Nadia made clear that she was unimpressed with his composition and playing, until she learned one day that he improvised tangos. Insisting that he demonstrate some of his compositions, she listened to him play with fascination and then told him, "That's your field! Give up symphonic music and dedicate your energies to the tango." Piazzola, who always regarded Boulanger as his second mother, went on to become the king of the tango.

> If there is one person who shaped the course of music from 1920 to 1940, that person has been Nadia Boulanger.
>
> **—Harold Schonberg**

By the mid-1930s, Nadia Boulanger was called the "princess of music." She was known as organizer of the Poulinac and Cercle Interallié concerts, and she was awarded the Grand Prix du Disque for her Renaissance recordings, which made her name a household word. Her career was in full ascendancy. Then, her mother died, on March 19, 1935, four days after the 17th anniversary of the passing of her sister, Lili. For Boulanger, the month of March became a time of mourning. She would withdraw from all except the most essential social events and activities.

In 1936, Nadia Boulanger became the first woman to conduct the Royal Philharmonic Orchestra at Queen's Hall in London. The engagement caused an uproar within the orchestra, and at her first rehearsal the reception she received from the musicians was chilly. She quickly established her authority from the podium, and at the conclusion of her stay she was applauded by musicians and critics alike. In 1938, she won instant respect as the first woman to conduct the Boston Symphony Orchestra, and she repeated her success the following year with both the New York Philharmonic Orchestra, in Carnegie Hall, and the Philadelphia Orchestra. Players and critics bowed alike to the quality of her work. Wrote one critic: "The prejudice against women conductors, which lurks in the bosom of every orchestra player, breaks down instantly when it comes in contact with Mlle. Boulanger's masterful touch."

Over the next 20 years, Boulanger's career went from success to success. In February 1962, at the invitation of Leonard Bernstein, she led the New York Philharmonic in performing Gabriel Fauré's *Requiem*, Virgil Thomson's *A Solemn Music*, and Lili Boulanger's *Psaumes*. In this triumphal last tour of the U.S., she performed with the Cleveland, Chicago, and Boston orchestras and was invited to lunch at the White House with John and ***Jacqueline Kennedy**. In 1966, she was invited to judge the Tchaikovsky Concours in Moscow, and the visit to her mother's homeland also added to her international reputation. In 1967, when Nadia Boulanger was 80, Prince Rainier and Princess Grace of Monaco (***Grace Kelly**) sponsored a celebration in her honor. At the Monte Carlo Opera, she was welcomed by the prince and given a standing ovation; the following day, she was honored with a dinner and awarded the insignia of the Commander of the Legion of Honor.

Despite her advancing age, Boulanger's professional life continued to be busy. In 1975, she taught at the Royal Academy in London and lectured at Cambridge. Early in 1976, although her health by now was failing, she was filmed in her apartment on the rue Ballu; toward the end of the year, she fell seriously ill. On February 9, 1977, she rallied for her induction, as a Grand Officer of the Legion of Honor, bestowed on her by the President of the Republic, M. Giscard d'Estaing. As she continued to grow weaker, students came to visit, often to perform for her; others kept watch outside her door. On September 16, 1979, Leonard Bernstein visited for the last time. Nadia Boulanger succumbed, finally, on October 22, at age 93.

SOURCES:

Kendall, Alan. *The Tender Tyrant, Nadia Boulanger: A Life Devoted to Music.* London: McDonald and Jane's, 1976.

Monsaingeon, Bruno. *Conversations with Nadia Boulanger.* Translated by Robyn Marsack. Boston, MA: Northeastern University Press, 1988.

Page, Tim and Vanessa Weeks Page, eds. *Selected Letters of Virgil Thomson.* NY: Summit Books, 1988.

Rosenstiel, Léonie. *Nadia Boulanger: A Life in Music.* NY: W.W. Norton, 1982.

Spycket, Jérôme. *Nadia Boulanger.* Translated by M.M. Shriver. Stuyvesant, NY: Pendragon Press, 1987.

Thomson, Virgil. *Virgil Thomson: An Autobiography.* NY: E.P. Dutton, 1985.

Zaimont, Judith Lang, Catherine Overhauser and Jane Gottlieb, eds. *The Musical Woman: An International Perspective.* Vol. II, 1984–1985. CT: Greenwood Press, 1987.

Karin Loewen Haag,
freelance writer, Athens, Georgia

Boulaz, Loulou (1912—)

Swiss climber. *Born in Avenches, Switzerland, in 1912. Made first ascent of one of the classic routes on the big cliff, Les Paturages in the Salève; first ascent by women (with* ***Lulu Durand****) of the Southwest Face of the Dent du Géant (1933) and the Dent du Requin (1932); first all-female traverse of the Southwest Face and the Northwest Ridge of the Grands Charmoz (1935), and the Droites (1935); first female ascent (and second ascent by anyone) of the North Face of the Petit Dru with Raymond Lambert (1935); first ascent of the North Face of the Velan and the north shoulder of the Rothorn in the Valais (1941); first female ascents of the North Faces of the Schreckhorn, the Studerhorn, and the Jungfrau in the Bernese Oberland; Montagnes de 'Air, including first ascent of Tour Loulou (1977).*

Born in Avenches, Switzerland, in 1912, Loulou Boulaz went to live in Geneva when she was nine. She loved skiing as a child, and in her 20s she was a member of the Swiss national team (1936–41). In 1936 and 1937, Boulaz was the international champion of France, and in 1937 she came in third in the World Slalom Championships in Chamonix.

She started climbing at age 20. In 1930, the last great Alpine challenges included the North Face of the Matterhorn (the Cervin), the North Face of the Grandes Jorasses, and the North Face of the Eiger. The North Face of the Matterhorn was conquered by Franz and Toni Schmid in 1931. The Grandes Jorasses continued to withstand attacks: a 1928 attempt by the legendary Armand Charlet had failed, a 1931 German team failed, and a few days later two Germans trying the same route were killed; in 1933, two great Italian climbers faltered; in 1934, there was another death and Charlet failed again.

In June 1935, an Italian expedition of six set out that included 23-year-old Loulou Boulaz and experienced mountaineer Robert Lambert; two in the party retreated early, one with a dislocated shoulder. After two days and one night, battled by a storm, they reached the summit by way of the Central Spur, only to find that two Germans had been there two days before. Boulaz, however, had become the first woman to make the ascent.

Loulou Boulaz made four attempts to conquer the North Face of the Eiger (1938, 1942, 1958 and 1962) but never succeeded. In 1982, she told her interviewer, "Four times we tried the Eiger, four times we had to retreat. But, I'm still alive!"

SOURCES:

Birkett, Bill, and Bill Peascod. *Women Climbing: 200 Years of Achievement.* London: A. & C. Black, 1989.

Loulou Boulaz

Bouliar, Marie Geneviève

(1762–1825)

French portraitist. *Name variations: Bouliard. Born in Paris, France, in 1762; died at Château d'Arcy (Saône-et-Lire) in 1825; only daughter of a tailor, though she may have been related to artists with similar names; studied with Joseph Siffred Duplessis (1725–1802).*

Selected works: Self-Portrait *(1792);* Aspasia *(1794);* Portrait of Chevalier Alexandre-Marie Lenoir *(1796);* Portrait of Adélaïde Binart *(*Mme. Alexandre Lenoir*) (1796).*

Little is known about the life and career of Marie Geneviève Bouliar. Although over 40 paintings and drawings are attributed to her through various records, only ten paintings and one drawing have survived. She may have studied with a number of teachers, but her relationship with Joseph Duplessis, the most celebrated portraitist in Paris during the 1770s and 1780s, is the only one documented. He is named as her teacher in the Livrets de Salon of 1796 and 1798. Whereas his influence is evident in her work, Bouliar's portraits are regarded as simpler and freer in style. According to **Anne Sutherland** and

Linda Nochlin in *Women Artists: 1550–1950,* Bouliar was "one of those rare practitioners of the genre able to present another human personality without seeming to impose her own."

Bouliar's first recorded work was a portrait of a young woman which was signed and dated 1785. She initially exhibited at the Salon of 1791 and sent work there until 1817. Her most famous painting *Aspasia* won a Prix d'Encouragement in 1795. Her subject for the portrait, ***Aspasia**, wife of Pericles, and one of the most famous women of 5th-century Athens, is portrayed surrounded with flowers, gazing in a mirror, with her flimsy undergarment falling from her shoulder to expose one breast, an unlikely pose, perhaps, for such a respected woman. The use of classical subjects to advance modern morality was a prevalent practice in France. Sutherland and Nochlin postulate that Bouliar's message is that learning and femininity are not mutually exclusive, thus the painting is a "gentle plea, couched in the most respectable of artistic language, for the equality of women."

SOURCES:

Sutherland, Anne, and Linda Nochlin. *Women Artists: 1550–1950.* NY: Alfred A. Knopf, 1976.

Barbara Morgan,
Melrose, Massachusetts

Boulmerka, Hassiba (1968—)

Algerian runner. *Born on July 10, 1968, in Algeria; grew up in Constantine, 350 miles east of Algiers.*

Won the 800-meter and 1,500 meter races at the African Games (1988); won the world championship in the 1,500 meters (1991 and 1995); won the Olympic gold medal in the 1,500 meters in Barcelona, Spain (1992).

Hassiba Boulmerka started off by winning a foot race. Despite death threats from Islamic fundamentalists for immodestly showing her bare legs, she kept on running, and her parents supported her as she trained four to eight hours a day. In 1988, she won the 800-meter and 1,500-meter races at the African Games. That same year, she represented Algeria at the Olympic Games in Seoul, Korea. For this, she was spat on, stoned, and denounced by religious leaders and had to practice in hiding.

But there were those in her country of Algeria who were ecstatic when she won the gold medal in the 1,500 meters in Barcelona, Spain, in 1992, arriving at the finish line with a time of 3:55.30. In August 1995, Boulmerka won the world championship in the same event. "Her mere decision to run is courageous," said track commentator Craig Masback. At the close of the 20th century, several Muslim countries, including Pakistan and Kuwait, continue to ban women from the Olympics. In Tokyo in 1991, when Boulmerka won the 1,500 meters and became the first female world champion in Algeria's history, she grabbed her hair and howled. "I was screaming for Algeria's pride and Algeria's history," she said. "I screamed finally for every Algerian woman, every Arabic woman." Boulmerka was awarded the Medal of Merit, one of Algeria's highest honors.

Boulogne, countess of.

See Ida of Lorraine (1040–1113).
See Mary of Atholl (d. 1116).
See Sybilla of Anjou (1112–1165).
See Constance Capet (c. 1128–1176).
See Marie of Boulogne (d. 1182).
See Ide d'Alsace (r. 1173–1216).
See Matilda de Dammartin (d. 1258).

Boulton, Agnes (1893–1968)

English-born writer, second wife of Eugene O'Neill, and mother of Oona O'Neill Chaplin. *Name variations: Agnes Boulton O'Neill. Born in London, England, on September 19, 1893; died in Point Pleasant, New Jersey, on November 25, 1968; daughter of Edward W. Boulton (a painter); sister of Margery Boulton; married a man named Burton; married Eugene O'Neill (the playwright), on April 12, 1918 (divorced 1929); married Morris Kaufman (a freelance writer); children: (first marriage) Barbara Burton; (second marriage) Shane Rudraighe O'Neill (b. October 30, 1919);* ****Oona O'Neill Chaplin*** *(b. May 14, 1925).*

Agnes Boulton, along with her three younger sisters, grew up in a progressive and artistic atmosphere fostered by her father, a painter, and her emancipated mother. Born in London where her parents were staying, Boulton grew up in Philadelphia, as well as New Jersey and New York. It is said that playwright Eugene O'Neill was drawn to her because she resembled his early love ***Louise Bryant**. "But where Louise was charged with nervous energy, carried herself proudly and dressed vividly," writes Louis Sheaffer, "Agnes was quiet, softly feminine, and favored subtle colors." The couple met soon after Boulton had arrived in the city as a young widow determined to support herself, her parents, and her two-year-old daughter left behind on a farm she owned in Connecticut. From the age of 17, Boulton had been selling stories to better magazines and pulps, including *Black Cat*, *Cavalier*, the *Evening World*, and had just earned $150 on a novelette. But because neither the farm nor her writing were monetarily sufficient, she was looking for a day job. Soon a denizen of Greenwich Village, she fell in love with and was habitually seen on the arm of young O'Neill. Catholic journalist ***Dorothy Day** was often on the other arm. "I was in love with his work," said Day, "while Agnes was in love with him. She had a great sweetness."

Agnes Boulton wrote of those early years in her book *Part of a Long Story* (Doubleday, 1958). "Overall a fine achievement," writes Sheaffer, "it gives a vivid, persuasive portrait of her onetime husband and recalls with considerable sensitivity a bygone bohemia of Greenwich Village and Provincetown." Boulton also wrote the highly praised *The Road Is Before Us.*

SOURCES:

Sheaffer, Louis. *O'Neill: Son and Playwright.* Boston: Little, Brown, 1969; *O'Neill: Son and Artist.* Little, Brown, 1973.

Bouness, Elisabeth (1862–1911).

See Bré, Ruth.

Boupacha, Djamila (1942—)

Algerian nationalist heroine who was arrested as a terrorist in 1961. *Name variations: Djamilah. Born in Algeria in 1942; married.*

Born into a middle-class Muslim family in 1942, Djamila Boupacha was more French than Algerian in her earliest years. The onset of the Algerian war of independence in November 1954 forced her to choose between cultures; like virtually all Muslim Algerians who had been raised in the French cultural and linguistic tradition, Boupacha joined the National Liberation Front (FLN) which fought a bitter and bloody guerilla war against French military forces. She was convinced that France and the pied noir settlers would never treat the Muslim majority as equals.

In 1961, Boupacha was arrested and accused of having bombed the "Brasserie des Facultés," a café near the University of Algiers. Because she refused to confess to the charges, she suffered a series of tortures including being beaten, kicked and subjected to electric shocks. To make her confess, cigarettes were ground out against her legs and breasts, and she was raped with an empty bottle. When she came to trial,

Djamila Boupacha

Boupacha had as her attorney ***Gisèle Halimi**, a woman determined to fight for justice even in a colonial society under martial law. Largely due to Halimi's legal skills, eloquence and passion for the truth, Boupacha had her case taken through a series of courts in Algeria. Eventually, Boupacha was transferred to France and won release from prison at the time of the amnesty that accompanied the achievement of Algerian independence in 1962.

French public opinion, although long aware of the torture used by French military authorities in Algeria, was nevertheless incensed by the nature of the atrocities committed against Boupacha. The determination of Halimi, which resulted in a book on the case coauthored with ***Simone de Beauvoir**, led to the creation of a Djamila Boupacha Committee in Paris, which received the support of many of the luminaries of French intellectual life, including Simone de Beauvoir, François Mauriac and **Germaine Tillion**. Despite the determination of Halimi to secure justice for her client by exposing the individuals who had tortured her, the French Army refused to cooperate in the investigation, and the magistrates who were attempting to secure justice found themselves faced by a stone wall of official resistance.

As a young radical woman, following the war of independence, Djamila Boupacha could not help but become embroiled in the often chaotic world of post-independence Algerian politics. Always outspoken, she made powerful enemies and on at least one occasion was briefly under arrest. When she married, her close friend Gisèle Halimi was one of the guests of honor.

Although it was discouraging to see how little progress the majority of Algerian women had made since the achievement of independence from France in 1962, Djamila Boupacha continued to speak and write on the subject of women's emancipation in a Muslim society. In this work, she exhibited much of the same courage and energy that had impressed the world in the days she had risked her life as an FLN guerilla, and some observers noted that the obstacles in this new struggle for equality were at least as great as in the war of national liberation several decades earlier.

SOURCES:

Beauvoir, Simone de, and Gisèle Halimi. *Djamila Boupacha: The Story of the Torture of a Young Algerian Girl which Shocked Liberal French Opinion.* Translated by Peter Green. NY: Macmillan, 1962.

Horne, Alistair. *A Savage War of Peace: Algeria 1954–62.* Rev. ed. NY: Penguin Books, 1987.

Vidal-Naquet, Pierre. *Torture: Cancer of Democracy: France and Algeria 1954–62.* Harmondsworth, Middlesex: Penguin Books, 1963.

John Haag, Associate Professor, University of Georgia, Athens, Georgia

Bourbon, Anne Geneviève de, Duchesse de Longueville (1619–1679).

See Longueville, Anne Geneviève de.

Bourbon, duchess of.

See Isabelle of Savoy (d. 1383).
See Agnes of Burgundy (d. 1476).
See Jeanne of Bourbon (1434–1482).
See Marie Louise d'Orleans (1750–1822).

Bourbon, ruler of.

See Agnes de Dampierre (1237–1288).
See Beatrix de Bourgogne (d. 1310).
See Mahaut I (r. 1215–1242).

Bourbon-Parma, duchess of.

See Pia of Sicily (1849–1882).

Bourchier, Anne (c. 1417–1474)

***Duchess of Norfolk.** Name variations: Eleanor Bourchier; Anne Mowbray. Born around 1417; died in 1474; daughter of William Bourchier, count of Eu, and *__Anne Plantagenet__ (1383–1438); married John Mowbray (1415–1461), 3rd duke of Norfolk; children: John Mowbray (b. 1444), 4th duke of Norfolk. Following Anne Bourchier's death in 1474, John Mowbray married *__Catherine Neville__ (c. 1397–1483).*

Bourchier, Anne (1512–1571)

***Countess of Essex.** Name variations: Baroness Bourchier. Born in 1512; died on January 28, 1571 (some sources cite 1570); daughter of Henry Bourchier, 2nd earl of Essex, and __Mary Say__; married William Parr, marquess of Northampton, on February 9, 1526 (annulled in April 1543).*

Bourchier, Eleanor (c. 1417–1474).

See Bourchier, Anne.

Bourchier, Elizabeth (b. 1598).

See Cromwell, Elizabeth.

Bourchier, Joan (fl. 1468).

See Neville, Joan.

Bourdil, Marguerite Taos (1913–1976).

See Amrouche, Marie-Louise.

Bourgeois, Louise (1563–1636)

***French midwife and medical writer.** Born in 1563 near Paris (France); died in 1636 in France; married Martin Boursier (a barber-surgeon); children: three.*

The works of French midwife and writer Louise Bourgeois were accepted and used as the leading texts on gynecology and obstetrics for many years after their publication. Little is known about Bourgeois' childhood except that she was born near Paris into a middle-class family and was trained to earn a living as a lacemaker. She married Martin Boursier as a young woman; a barber-surgeon, Boursier worked in Paris and was also an assistant to Ambroise Pare, head surgeon of the Hôtel Dieu in Paris. From her husband and Pare, Bourgeois learned anatomy and the fundamentals of surgical practice. Finding herself drawn to the field of medicine, she gave up lace-making and was apprenticed to a Parisian midwife. By 1593, Bourgeois had established herself as a talented midwife, gaining a widespread reputation for her skill and learning. In 1601, she reached the apex of the midwife's profession, becoming in that year the royal midwife to the queen, ***Marie de Medici**, while maintaining her own private practice.

Between 1593 and 1609, Bourgeois supervised close to 2,000 births, while acquiring experience and practical training unsurpassed in Europe. She believed it important for her to catalog her knowledge for the use of other women in her profession and so authored three texts on midwifery, gynecology, and obstetrics. The first work was published in three parts, between 1609 and 1626. Entitled *Various Observations on Sterility, Miscarriage, Fertility, Confinements, and Illnesses of Women and Newborn Infants*, this book became a standard text for midwives. With information on almost every aspect of pregnancy and childbirth, from signs of pregnancy to inducing

Louise Bourgeois

labor to choosing a wet nurse, *Observations* was based on Bourgeois' practical experience but included some of the pseudo-scientific medical theories popular in her time.

Her second midwifery work, *True Account of the Birth of the Ladies and Gentlemen, the Children of France*, covering her supervision of the births of Queen Marie's children, was published in 1617, along with the third, a minor treatise entitled *Instructions to My Daughter*. Although she was licensed and trained as a midwife only, Bourgeois' long history of healing led her to compose a fourth book the year before her death, called *A Collection of the Secrets of Louise Bourgeois*. This last work covered the treatment of a wide assortment of diseases unrelated to pregnancy and childbirth and thus infringed on the medical "territory" of university-trained doctors, giving advice on conditions such as the common cold. Louise Bourgeois continued to practice midwifery until her death at about age 73.

SOURCES:

Anderson, Bonnie S., and Judith P. Zinsser. *A History of Their Own: Women in Europe from Prehistory to the Present.* Vol. I. NY: Harper and Row, 1988.

Buck, Claire, ed. *The Bloomsbury Guide to Women's Literature.* NY: Prentice Hall, 1992.

Laura York,
Anza, California

Bourgeois, Louise (1911—)

French-born American sculptor and painter whose recognition as a major artist came late in her career. *Born in Paris, France, on December 25, 1911; daughter of Louis Bourgeois and Josephine (Fauriaux) Bourgeois; sister of Henriette Bourgeois and Pierre Bourgeois; studied mathematics at Lycée Fénelon and the Sorbonne, 1932–35; married Robert Goldwater, in 1938; children: three sons, Michel, Jean-Louis, Alain.*

Worked in the atelier of Fernand Léger, then mostly interested in painting and drawing; first became aware of surrealism (mid-1930s); married and moved to U.S. (1938); concentrated on printmaking, painting and drawing, but also began work in sculpture, developing a highly subjective style of expression; presented first one-person show, New York (1945); remained relatively undiscovered as a major artist until the 1970s; her sculptural depictions of human sexuality and her own emotions and memories were widely praised and analyzed by critics; a retrospective exhibition of her work at New York's Museum of Modern Art was an honor rarely accorded a living artist and signaled her acceptance into the highest echelons of American art celebrities (1982); presented with the National Medal of Arts by President Bill Clinton (1997).

Born in Paris on December 25, 1911, Louise Bourgeois is a sculptor whose reputation as a major artist came late in her career, after many decades of dedication. Her parents, Louis and **Josephine Bourgeois**, were owners of a tapestry restoration business, and by age ten, at her mother's urging, Louise began making drawings that were used for the reconstruction of lost sections of tapestry. Hers was an emotionally turbulent childhood. Her father, a womanizer, carried on an affair with his children's foreign-language tutor, deliberately provocative behavior which caused Louise great suffering. Many decades later, she would recall the resentment, rage, and jealousy she felt as the intermediary in the liaison, drawing on these feelings as a source for her artistic statements. In a 1994 interview, the pain was still palpable: "He abandoned us. He left us stranded." Some of the spiral configurations in her sculptures refer back to this difficult and formative period of her life: "Twisting is very important for me. When I dreamt of getting rid of the mistress, it was by twisting her neck." Twisting also reminded her of the washing of tapestries, one of the essential chores associated with her parents' business.

As a student at the Lycée Fénelon, Bourgeois was fascinated with mathematics. She excelled particularly at geometry, the world of which did not permit the arbitrariness and confusion that were representative of an often unhappy family life. As a student at the Sorbonne, she continued to study mathematics, also investigating major ideas in philosophy. By 1935, however, she knew that she would have to create a career for herself in the art world. For the next several years, she studied at some of the most important art schools in Paris. The strongest impact was made on her by the noted artist Fernand Léger, who aroused her latent interest in sculpture. Even at this early stage of her career, she began to exhibit a notable independence of thought. During these years, her drawings and paintings were strongly influenced by the dominant Parisian school of surrealism.

In 1938, Bourgeois met and married the American art historian Robert Goldwater, who had gone to Paris to complete his doctoral dissertation on the relationships between primitivism and modern art. Bourgeois arrived in New York in October and soon became part of the vibrant local art scene, studying painting at the Art Students League. She produced an impressive range of paintings, drawings and prints, influenced by cubism, which expressed her continuing love of geometry. In 1939, she exhibited for the first time in her adopted home at a group show at the Brooklyn Museum. As a result of the war in Europe, a number of major artists appeared in New York during the next few years and stimulated Bourgeois to explore her own artistic styles and intellectual assumptions. The work of Max Ernst, whom she had already met in Paris, brought her closer to the surrealist school.

By 1940, Bourgeois spent much of her time sculpting, and by the end of that year 17 of her wooden sculptures went on view at a New York gallery. Wood was to be her primary medium for the next several decades, and the pieces she produced were customarily columnar figural abstractions. By the early 1960s, she began experimenting with other materials, including stone, plaster, plastics, marble, rubber latex and bronze. Although she conceded that her compositions had became considerably more complex and varied—a change she would describe as a "change from rigidity to pliability"—Bourgeois explained to interviewers that the medium always remained secondary to the ideas or emotions she hoped to convey. "I am," she said, "completely free from allegiance to material." As her confidence increased, the works often took on a strongly personal character. In some instances, the autobiographical origins of her pieces were unmistakable. In her 1974 "Destruction of the Father," Bourgeois evoked the scene of a man being devoured by his children. Few critics doubted that here the artist was struggling with the demons of her youth and using her art as a form of personal exorcism.

By the late 1960s, Bourgeois was rapidly being recognized as a major artist. Feminists somewhat belatedly designated her as a significant voice of their *Weltanschauung* (world view). Although in some cases her discovery represented a long period of neglect, her new celebrity represented an exciting reassessment of the expressive possibilities of sculpture. In a 1993 interview, Bourgeois asserted, "I am interested in the forbidden!!! All my work is about it." Her retrospective exhibition at New York's Museum of Modern Art, which opened in November 1982, made clear her status as a strong voice in 20th-century art.

SOURCES:

Armstrong, Tom, *et al. 200 Years of American Sculpture*. Boston, MA: D.R. Godine, 1976.

"Bourgeois, Louise," in *Current Biography 1983*. NY: H.W. Wilson, pp. 31–35.

Brenson, Michael. "Louise Bourgeois: A Sculptor Comes Into Her Own," in *The New York Times Biographical Service*. October 1982, pp. 1278–1281.

Heller, Nancy. *Women Artists: An Illustrated History*. NY: Abbeville Press, 1987.

Hughes, Robert. "A Sense of Female Experience," in *Time*. Vol. 129, no. 21. November 22, 1982, p. 116.

Kuspit, Donald. *Bourgeois: An Interview with Louise Bourgeois by Donald Kuspit*. NY: Random House, 1988.

Larson, Kay. "Women by a Woman," in *New York*. Vol. 15, no. 46. November 22, 1982, pp. 74, 76.

Mifflin, Margot. "What Do Artists Dream?," in *Art News*. Vol. 92, no. 8. October 1993, pp. 144–149.

Robins, Corinne. "Louise Bourgeois: Primordial Environments," in *Arts Magazine*. Vol. 50, no. 10. June 1976, pp. 81–83.

Slonim, Jeffrey. "The Horror!," in *Artforum International*. Vol. 32, no. 8. April 1994, pp. 11–12.

Wilkin, Karen. "The Best and the Worst of Louise Bourgeois," in *The New Criterion*. Vol. 12, no. 10. June 1994, pp. 26–31.

John Haag, Associate Professor,
University of Georgia, Athens, Georgia

Bourgeois, Marguerite (1620–1700).

See Bourgeoys, Marguerite.

Bourgeois, Marguerite Taos (1875–1956).

See Mistinguett.

Bourgeoys, Marguerite (1620–1700)

French Catholic founder of the Congrégation de Notre Dame de Montreal who dedicated most of her long life to educating the poor and underprivileged in the pioneer settlement of Ville-Marie, New France, later to become Montreal, Canada. *Name variations: Marguerite Bourgeois; Soeur du Saint-Sacrement. Born on April 17, 1620, at Troyes, Champagne, France; died on January 12, 1700, at Montreal, Canada; daughter of Abraham Bourgeoys and Guillemette (Garnier) Bourgeoys; beatified by the Roman Catholic Church in 1950; canonized in 1982.*

Born into a large and affectionate family in the prosperous French town of Troyes; though not particularly religious, underwent a spiritual experience at age 20 which transformed her life; became dedicated to the service of God and had a particular devotion to the Virgin Mary; well trained in Troyes as an external member of the Congrégation de Notre Dame; refused entry into several established religious orders; was 33 when she accepted the invitation of the governor of Ville-Marie (Montreal) to accompany him to New France (Canada) as a teacher; as the settlement grew, so did the number of her pupils, the size of the community of women which she established and the number of her schools; her ideas about pedagogy, based on those of Pierre Fourier, stressed kindness and encouragement rather than punishment; established the Congrégation de Notre Dame de Montreal, an order of teaching women who were not cloistered nuns but women who served the community by living and working in it.

Not content with her day schools and boarding schools now flourishing inside the confines of Ville-Marie, Marguerite Bourgeoys set out to take education to the native children of Canada. The sisters went by canoe, on horseback, and on foot to isolated settlements far distant from the main settlement, and in 1678 she established a permanent mission school in the Indian village of Montagne. Despite the ever-present danger of capture, torture, and death at the hands of hostile tribes, Bourgeoys justified the activities of her Congrégation, in these first missions specifically aimed at native children, by citing an irrefutable precedent: "The apostles went forth into every quarter of the world to preach Jesus Christ; like them we feel urged to make Him known in every part of this country to which we may be sent."

Marguerite Bourgeoys was born during one of France's most turbulent centuries. The middle-class daughter of Abraham Bourgeoys, candle-maker and employee of the mint in Troyes, she lived in a time which saw France ravaged first by the Thirty Years' War and then by the Civil War called the Fronde, a period in which unprecedented magnificence was created by

Marguerite Bourgeoys

Louis XIV at his court at Versailles and during which bad harvests brought famine, disease, and death to the poor. Marguerite, the 7th of 13 children, was 19 when her mother died and must have assisted her elder sister in caring for the younger members of the family.

A lively and popular girl, fond of pretty clothes and not particularly religious, Bourgeoys refused an invitation to join a group of young women who met regularly for religious instruction at the convent of the Congrégation de Notre Dame. Although the nuns had not initially been forbidden by their rule to leave the convent, their movements were being increasingly restricted, as were those of most female religious orders in 16th-century France. Rather than the sisters leaving the convent, the lay or external women went to them and, as well as lessons in the Catholic faith, the young women were taught the essentials of how to teach, so that they might serve as an "outreach" arm, spreading instruction and education in the community where the sisters could not. According to her memoir, which she wrote almost 60 years later, Bourgeoys keep her distance because she was fond of fine clothes and was afraid of being thought a religious fanatic. However, in 1640 an event occurred which changed her life—an event which mystics frequently refer to as a "conversion experience." Walking in a religious procession, she passed in front of the convent of Notre Dame, where there was a stone statue above the door. "When I looked up and saw it I thought it was very beautiful, and at the same time I found myself so touched and changed that I no longer knew myself. On my return to the house everybody noticed the change, for I had been very light-hearted and well-liked by the other girls."

From this point onward, Bourgeoys was to develop both the mystical and the practical sides of her nature and to devote both aspects to the service of God. Her first step was to enter the external congregation of the sisters of Notre Dame. The sister placed in charge of the group was **Marie Louise de Chomedey de Sainte-Marie**, sister of Paul de Chomedey de Maisonneuve, the recently appointed governor of Ville-Marie, a settlement in New France. Prospective candidates usually had to apply twice before being granted admission, but Marguerite was admitted at once. It was probably felt that such a popular young woman would attract still more members, and this proved to be the case: she lead the group for 12 years and during that time its membership expanded from about 30 to more than 400 young women.

The religious order of which the Congrégation de Notre Dame de Troyes was a part had been established in 1598 by Pierre Fourier and Alix le Clerc, and one of its primary aims was to improve the education, both spiritual and otherwise, of young girls, for its founders were deeply aware of the important role these girls would one day play as mothers of families. Fourier was a great innovator in the area of pedagogy, and his ideas concerning the dedication required of teachers, the need to serve the poor as well as the wealthy, and the necessity of using kindness rather than harsh discipline were to become cornerstones of Bourgeoys' own teaching method.

> "When God in His divine goodness gave New France to the Blessed Virgin . . . , she wished to have the little girls formed as good Christians so that they might later become good mothers. . . . For this she chose poor women without learning, without distinguished bearing, without talent and without money."
>
> **—Marguerite Bourgeoys**

Much as she must have enjoyed her work as an external sister, teaching in people's homes and sharing prayers with the other young women while still living with her own family, Marguerite soon felt the need for a life of even greater religious sacrifice. Her decision to become a nun was probably influenced by the advice of the priest who was the group's spiritual director, Father Antoine de Gendret. It was perhaps Gendret who suggested that she apply to the Carmelite order but, as Bourgeoys records, "the Carmelites refused me, even though I was strongly drawn to them." This rejection is puzzling; at 23, Marguerite was certainly old enough to know her own mind, and her father had agreed to provide her with the necessary dowry. Her most recent biographer, **Patricia Simpson**, suggests that Bourgeoys, with her solidly bourgeoisie background, may not have been socially acceptable to the now fashionable and upper-class order. She tells us that she tried other orders "but did not succeed either"; in these cases, Simpson speculates, the orders may not have met Marguerite's own needs for a strict religious life combined with community service.

Not finding a home in an existing religious order, Bourgeoys began the construction of her own spiritual way; a process that was to continue all her life:

> I gave myself to God in 1640. A few years later, upon the advice of my confessor, I took the vow of chastity and some time later, the vow of poverty. I made both of these vows with all the zeal and all the perfection possible to me, together with the resolution to keep them all my life. I have never had a thought contrary to this.

However, hers was to be a life of work as well as renunciation, and once again, Father Gendret assisted in finding the way:

> M. Gendret . . . told me one day that Our Lord had left three states of women to follow Him and to serve the Church: the role

> of Magdalene was filled by the Carmelites and other recluses; that of Martha, by cloistered religious who serve their neighbour; but the state of the journeying Virgin Mary, which must also be honoured, was not yet filled. Even without veil or wimple, one could be a true religious. This was very acceptable to me because I had compassion on the young women who, for lack of money, could not enter the service of God. I always held to the purpose which we had hoped to realize in Troyes—that there would be a refuge for those girls who had all the qualities but who could not become religious for lack of money.

The model of the "journeying Virgin Mary" was to serve Bourgeoys well, although her first attempt to emulate her in a more regulated way did not yield permanent results.

In the years between 1644 and approximately 1651, Bourgeoys established a residence with two other women in Troyes, in an apartment belonging to a married sister of de Maisonneuve, living lives of devotion and service according to a rule developed by Gendret and another theologian. But the arrangement did not last; one of the women married and the other died. Marguerite returned home in time to care for her dying father, and his death, in October 1651, left her once again searching for the way.

Paul de Chomedey de Maisonneuve passed through Troyes in 1652, taking time to visit his sisters while on a mission to provide settlers and financing for his fledgling settlement of Ville-Marie in New France. He was now 41, 8 years older than Bourgeoys, a devoutly religious man who had embarked on a military career at the age of 13 but had turned from warfare to the even more challenging task of assisting in the conversion of the native people of Canada, then called New France, to Christianity. Ville-Marie, the settlement named after the Virgin Mary, which was to become known as Montreal, had been established ten years earlier.

In 1642, de Maisonneuve himself had carried a heavy cross for the altar to the top of the mountain and joined in the prayers of the settlers that God would grant the conversion of the Indians and that they would come, submissively, to be instructed. But, after a deceptively peaceful first year, the task had proven more difficult than anticipated and while some tribes had been responsive, the Iroquois had staged a series of attacks on the tiny settlement, killing and carrying off women and men to torture and death. The eradication of the mission at Sainte-Marie and the murder of its priests by the Hurons in the autumn of 1649 convinced most of the colonists that the days of New France were numbered unless France sent reinforcements. Even de Maisonneuve seems to have been ready to abandon the faltering experiment, when ***Jeanne Mance**, the devout woman who had been one of the community's first settlers, supplied the money for de Maisonneuve to journey back to France in order to seek settlers and financial support. His efforts were successful, and in 1653 de Maisonneuve was to return with new recruits and with Marguerite Bourgeoys.

Sister Louise had tried to persuade her brother to allow her to accompany him to Montreal with a small group of nuns, but he refused. He was well aware that his tiny and embattled settlement was not yet ready to support a religious community. He did, however, see the need for a teacher. Marguerite, who was then 33 and free of all family obligations, offered to fill that role and de Maisonneuve accepted her. Not a woman guided by impulse, Bourgeoys had sought guidance from God in prayer and had consulted with several religious authorities whose opinions she trusted before committing herself. In a dream the night before meeting de Maisonneuve, Marguerite had seen St. Francis "and another bald man, dressed simply like a priest going into the country, not an intellectual." She immediately recognized de Maisonneuve as the man in her dream. She had also shared with Father Gendret her regret that the new project would mean the end of her cherished ambition to establish a community of lay women, dedicated to the service of the Virgin Mary, in Troyes: "M. Gendret told me that what God had not willed in Troyes, He would perhaps bring to pass in Montreal."

Bourgeoys left Troyes in February 1653 but it was late June of that year before her ship was ready to sail. Along the way, she had recurrent doubts about the wisdom of the path she was taking, doubts which were stilled by prayer and a vision which came shortly before departure: "One morning, when I was fully awake, a tall woman dressed in a robe of white serge, said to me very clearly: 'Go, I will never foresake you.' I knew it was the Blessed Virgin. This gave me great courage and I found nothing difficult, even though I feared illusions." Accompanied by the 108 colonists recruited by de Maisonneuve, 100 of whom survived the journey, the ship had to return to port because it was taking on water, and it sailed again on July 20, the feast of St. Margaret, finally landing at Quebec on September 22, 1653.

Bourgeoys was to dedicate the remaining 47 years of her life to the service of Montreal. She began her service on the ocean voyage, nursing the sick and bringing spiritual counsel to the men so that they became "as gentle as true monks . . . changed like freshly washed linen." However, she may well have experienced momentary hesitation on her first sight of the her new land. After the carefully tended fields, neat villages and temperate climate of her native Champagne, Bourgeoys was transported to a place of towering forests, with winters in which exposed limbs could freeze in minutes, a land in which isolated European settlements were surrounded by warlike natives, eager to capture and kill the unwelcome colonists. She found the settlement at Quebec "so poor it was pitiful," with no more than five or six houses. Refusing an invitation to stay at the Ursuline convent, Bourgeoys started out as she intended to continue, sharing the spartan accommodation of the colonists. As she was later to instruct her community: "When the sisters are travelling and it is necessary to sleep away from home, they ought to choose the homes of the poor where they ought to give very good example and always give some informal instruction." In mid-November, as soon as the sick recruits were well enough to travel, Marguerite went with them to Montreal.

Her first home was in the Governor's House, inside the fort. This was the home for all of the new arrivals who had not yet left to build their own houses; the only other buildings in the settlement were the priests' quarters and the soldiers' barracks. It was to be five years before Bourgeoys would have the school which she longed for; there were, as yet, not enough children to justify a building. In 1653, there were only 14 women and a total of 15 children in the settlement. In her earliest years, Marguerite performed a variety of functions, taking care of the linen and general maintenance in the Governor's House, providing support, advice and spiritual counsel to the families, and caring for the sick, as well as giving private lessons to the children. In 1654, 15 marriages took place and soon the number of children began to grow, although infant mortality was a continuing concern.

Although her fellow immigrants on the ship from France, aware of her spiritual calling, had begun to call Marguerite "sister," she had not joined any formal order, and the vows of chastity and poverty she had taken were personal and private ones. While she considered herself completely dedicated to God, she probably dressed much like any of the other women, not in any formal habit that would proclaim her mission. It is this apparent ambivalence about her status that perhaps explains an incident reported by Sister **Marie Morin** in later years. De Maisonneuve, experiencing spiritual difficulties, which we can only assume were of a sexual nature, consulted a Jesuit priest who advised him to marry. Sister Morin says that he sought Marguerite's advice, but perhaps he may also have been sounding her out as a possible wife. Whatever de Maisonneuve's motives, the response he received from her was that, instead of marrying, he should take a vow of chastity. He followed Marguerite's suggestion, and the two remained friends and allies for another decade, until de Maisonneuve left the settlement for the last time in 1665.

In the meantime, there was much to be done, and de Maisonneuve did not hesitate to delegate significant responsibilities to Marguerite. Soon after her arrival, she was given an escort of 30 men to restore the original cross on the mountaintop which had been overthrown by the Iroquois. While visiting the site, she found the remains of a banner which Sister Louise had given her brother on behalf of the Congrégation de Notre Dame of Troyes, an image of the Virgin surrounded by the message which was a play on words: "*Sainte Mère de Dieu, pure Vierge au coeur royal, gardez-nous une place en votre Montroyal*" ("Holy Mother of God, pure Virgin with a royal heart, keep a place for us in your Montreal"). Bourgeoys viewed her discovery as a confirmation of her mission to the new world. The following year, she was placed in charge of having a chapel built some distance from the fort itself; de Maisonneuve helped to drag the trees, Marguerite repaid the men by doing sewing and mending. The Chapel of Notre-Dame-de-Bon-Secours (Our Lady of Good Help) still stands.

But Bourgeoys' main mission was to teach, and finally, in the spring of 1658, she was able to open her school. De Maisonneuve obtained a stone stable for her, the former property of a cowherd killed by the Indians in 1652. The deed of gift makes clear that the school was to serve the girl children of the settlement, and that there was to be a community of women teachers who would reside there. Still a community of only one, Marguerite oversaw the renovations to the building which included the installation of a chimney for heat, and the digging of an encircling ditch along with the installation of a removable ladder to the loft as rudimentary protection against Indian raids. But within a few months of the school's opening she had to close it temporarily and return to France. Jeanne

Mance needed specialized medical care for a broken arm, and Bourgeoys agreed to accompany her, deciding to use the visit to fulfil a long-cherished dream:

> Five years later I returned to Troyes to bring back some women to help me teach a few girls and boys able to learn. We would live in community as we had planned it and in conformity with what we had planned in France. . . . I promised . . . that we would have bread and soup and that we would work for our living.

Just two months before the voyage, Marguerite had already demonstrated her love for the native people of this new land; she had reluctantly adopted an Iroquois baby, the child of a single mother whom she describes as "somewhat neglectful." The child, the first Iroquois to be baptized, was called **Marie-des-neiges** (Marie of the Snows). Bourgeoys, with typical reserve, records merely that "she died at the age of 6 in our house," but it is clear that she loved her very much, and she kept her name alive by bestowing it on other girls whom she later adopted.

Watercolor of Bourgeoys' 17th-century chapel drawn by Jean-Marie Gaillot, according to archaeological information.

During the six months which she spent in France, most of it in her native city of Troyes, Bourgeoys found four women willing to accompany her back to New France, a group which would, at last, form the nucleus of a community of lay women, dedicated to community service and prayer. The form that the community would take was not yet clearly defined; it was to based on the rule which had been drawn up for the projected house in Troyes, but this group would develop in a very different environment, with its main goal that of educating children, both those of the settlers and of the native peoples.

From the first, Bourgeoys was determined that the community be completely egalitarian; those recruited to teach, like Edmée Chastel, were valued no more highly than **Catherine Crolo**, the "sturdy wench" whose strong arms would produce the bread and take care of the laundry. Edmée renounced her share of the family property before leaving with Marguerite, stating in the legal document which was drawn up that she was going to New France to spend her life "in a congregation of women which is established in the said region on the island of Montreal to care for young French girls and even Indians as far as this is possible." Her father insisted that Edmée sew enough gold pieces into her corset to cover the cost of her return to France, should the spartan life in New France prove too harsh for her; none of the four women who accompanied Bourgeoys to Montreal was ever to return to France.

The new community was essentially established on the ship which sailed for Canada on July 2, 1659; this hardy group of secular women formed the nucleus of the Congrégation de Notre Dame of Montreal. Their primary function was to teach, and in this they were guided by the constitutions of the co-founder of the original Congrégation de Notre Dame, Pierre Fourier. Recognizing that women were best suited to educate other women, he had called upon the sisters to realize that the girls they taught would grow up to perform an essential role as mothers of families:

> Although still small in years, they are not a small or paltry portion of the Church of God even in the present, and in a few years will be capable of great good. For this reason, it is very expedient to see that everything necessary is done for their own well-being and for that of their fathers and mothers, the families they will one day govern, and the state itself.

Marguerite adopted Fourier's ideas, adapting them, as required, to the needs of New France.

The sisters were not to usurp the authority of the family but were rather to work with the parents, using kindness and good example rather than punishment, to lead the children to learning. Punishment was to be administered "very rarely, always with prudence and extreme moderation, it being remembered that one is in the presence of God." The sisters were to find places for the poor as well as the rich in their stable school and, as well as religion, reading and writing, also taught what might be called "life skills," preparing the girls both for the harsh pioneer life and for earning their own living if necessary. Resisting the strict hierarchical divisions of her day, Marguerite stressed the importance and value of honorable work; in order to offer the children a free education, she and the sisters supported themselves by doing needlework and laundry for the still largely male population of settlers. Until the mid-1660s, they probably taught both boys and girls since Montreal's first school for boys did not open until 1668.

By 1662, with the number of pupils growing rapidly, the stable school had become too small, and Bourgeoys acquired two new pieces of property, a house and land for a farm. She used the house to accommodate the *filles du roi*, the young orphan girls sent from France as wives for the settlers. Her colleagues at the school had no wish to take responsibility for these latest raw recruits, but Bourgeoys felt differently: "I went to meet them at the shore, believing that we must open wide the doors of the Blessed Virgin's house to all young women." Settlers seeking new brides came to meet them under Marguerite's roof and were doubtless subject to her close scrutiny. These were harsh times; food was scarce, Indian raids were intense and destructive, and the struggle must have seemed unremitting, yet Bourgeoys was to look back upon these years as the most satisfying of her life. No task was beneath her: as Simpson has observed, "Marguerite had that special kind of inner security that not only set her free from many of the class attitudes of her time, but also enabled her to perform with total unselfconsciousness, services that many people, both now and then, would regard as demeaning, yet she did so without compromising her dignity as a person and as a woman."

A new, more prosperous period for New France was to commence in 1664 when a contingent of French troops arrived at Quebec under General de Tracy in sufficient numbers to deter the Iroquois from further attacks. Their arrival signalled the recall of de Maisonneuve to France after 25 years in Montreal. He retained the title of governor until 1668 but never returned to Canada. On his death in September 1676, he left the biggest portion of his estate to Bourgeoys and her Congrégation. With peace established, Montreal quickly grew in numbers and prosperity. Marguerite, the only one of the early leaders to remain active through the second half of the century, frequently reminded her companions not to be seduced by material comforts and security: "O my dear sisters, let us revive at least among ourselves the true spirit of cordiality and love which formed the glory and beatitude of the first Christians."

The *filles de la Congrégation*, the name by which Bourgeoys and her companions were known, were given approval in 1669 by Bishop François de Laval, the apostolic vicar of New France, and were authorized to teach on the Île de Montreal and all other places in Canada that should request their services. At this time, the sisters' simple clothing of long dress, shawl and bonnet seems to have been approved as a religious habit. In 1670, Bourgeoys crossed the Atlantic once again to obtain confirmation from the king in order to ensure the continuity of her community. The document, given in May 1671, records:

> Not only has she performed the office of school mistress by giving free instruction to the young girls in all occupations that make them capable of earning their livelihood, but, far from being a liability to the country, she has built permanent buildings, cleared land concessions, set up a farm. . . .

On her return to Canada, Bourgeoys brought three of her nieces back from France, two of whom were later to become sisters of the Congrégation and the third was to marry a settler.

While Marguerite agreed to open a boarding school for the daughters of noble and bourgeois families in Montreal in 1676, her main interest was always in the poor and native children. She set up domestic training schools to teach needlework to the poor and sent members of her community to establish mission schools for the native girls, with a permanent school set up in the Indian village of Montagne. Following his visit to the Mountain Mission in 1685, Bishop Laval reported:

> . . . about forty Indian girls are clothed and brought up according to the French way of living. Manual labour forms a good part of their training, while at the same time they are taught the mysteries of the Faith, the hymns and prayers of the Church, not only in their own tongue, but also in ours, so that they may, little by little, become used to our manners and customs.

Despite the approval which the Congrégation had received from Bishop Laval and the French king, Bourgeoys still saw the need for further, more formal recognition. Her group still represented an anomaly within the church of the day: women who took no formal religious vows and who were not confined to a convent but who emulated the "wandering" life of Mary by teaching and spreading the faith. Fearing that change would be imposed after her death, in 1680, at the age of 60, she journeyed to France for the third time, seeking reassurance, only to be snubbed by Bishop Laval and denied permission to recruit any more women. Overwhelmed with responsibilities, the bishop was clearly growing impatient with this independent-minded woman and the issue of recognition remained unresolved. By December 1683, Bourgeoys was ready to step down as superior of the community, but a fire at the mother house in Montreal resulted in the deaths of two of the sisters being considered to succeed her, forcing Marguerite to resume the leadership once again.

The order continued to grow, especially under Bishop Laval's successor, Bishop Saint-Vallier. It was Saint-Vallier who expanded the service provided by the Congrégation from the Montreal area, first to a school on Île d'Orleans and then to one in Quebec City in 1692. Bourgeoys was finally able relinquish her duties as head of the community in 1693, when she was 73 years old, but still her struggles were not over. Like Laval before him, Saint-Vallier attempted to "regularize" the Congrégation, first by trying to bring about a merger with the Ursuline nuns and then by trying to impose a rule of his own design upon the community. Bourgeoys must have assisted her successor, **Sister Barbier**, in resisting these efforts and in continuing the struggle for recognition of their unique form of life and service. Finally, in July 1698, the Congrégation won official recognition as a community of "secular nuns"; Marguerite's new name was "Sister of the Holy Sacrement" and she was able to spend the last two years of her life in prayer and seclusion in the chapel of the mother house.

As **Hélène Bernier** has observed, the manner of Bourgeoys' death represented the same combination of realism and mysticism which had typified her life. In the winter of 1700, a young nun, Sister **Catherine Charly**, was dying. Reliable witnesses were later to testify that Marguerite offered her own life to save the young nun, praying, "O God, why do you not take me instead, I who am useless and good for nought!" Almost immediately Sister Catherine began to recover and Bourgeoys, quite healthy until that time, was taken ill with a heavy fever. Marguerite Bourgeoys died a few days later, on January 12, 1700.

In an era of spiritual and heroic women, Bourgeoys' contemporaries realized the remarkable holiness and dedication of her life. Objects which had touched her body were treasured as holy relics, and her remains were divided between the parish of Ville-Marie, where her body was buried, and the Congrégation, which kept her heart.

While the missionary spirit is one which seems distant and perhaps even misguided to the modern observer, Marguerite Bourgeoys pursued her calling with compassion and sympathy, convinced that she was bringing "the light" of the true religion and the benefits of civilization to the native children. Hers was indeed an exceptional life, not only in terms of her piety, bravery, and dedication to New France but in ways which still have echoes for us today: her advanced views about educational methodology, her insistence that education should be free for all, and her stubborn defense of a mode of life and service which was considered unsuitable for the women of the day. Using the Virgin Mary as her model, she refused the option of the cloistered life: "The Holy Virgin was not cloistered, but she everywhere preserved an internal solitude, and she never refused to be where charity or necessity required help." On her death in 1700, Bourgeoys left 40 sisters to continue her work; by 1961, there were over 6,000 members of her order in 262 communities in Canada, the United States and Japan, teaching some 100,000 pupils. She was made a saint of the Catholic Church in 1982.

SOURCES AND SUGGESTED READING:

Bernier, Hélène. "Bourgeoys, Marguerite," in *Dictionary of Canadian Biography.* Vol. 1. Toronto: University of Toronto Press, pp. 115–119.

Butler, Elizabeth. *The Life of Venerable Marguerite Bourgeoys, Foundress of the Congregation de Notre Dame of Montreal.* NY: P.J. Kennedy, 1932.

Simpson, Patricia. *Marguerite Bourgeoys and Montreal, 1640–1665.* Montreal: McGill-Queen's University Press, 1997.

Dr. Kathy Garay, Assistant Professor of history and women's studies, McMaster University, Hamilton, Canada

Bourgogne, countess or duchess of.

See Burgundy, countess or duchess of.

Bourignon, Antoinette (1616–1680)

Flemish mystic. *Born at Lille, Flanders (now a city in northern France) on January 13, 1616; died at Franeker, Friesland, on October 30, 1680.*

Influenced by religion from a young age, Antoinette Bourignon was convinced that she was the direct recipient of supernatural revelations. She entered a convent at age 20 before taking charge of a hospital in Lille, followed by one in East Friesland. Her work as a reformer took her to France, Holland, England, and Scotland. Bourignon believed that she had been appointed by God to restore the spirit of early Christianity. Teaching that true Christianity consisted of emotional impulses that had a supernatural source, she disregarded all sects and maintained that her religion could not be found in the canons or practice of any church. Known as Bourignianism, her doctrine became widespread among Roman Catholics and Protestants as she drew both dedicated followers and zealous persecutors.

Her following dwindled after her death at Franeker, Friesland, in 1680. In the early 18th century, however, her influence was so prevalent in Scotland that it prompted the condemnation of her doctrines at the Presbyterian general assemblies of 1701, 1709 and 1710. The established Church of Scotland demanded a renunciation of her precepts from every entrant to the ministry at the time of ordination. Her writings, an account of her life and of her visions and opinions, were collected by her disciple, Calvinist minister Pierre Poiret (19 vols., Amsterdam, 1679–1686), who also published her life (2 vols., 1679). At least three of her works have been translated into English: *An Abridgment of the Light of the World* (London, 1786), *A Treatise of Solid Virtue* (1699), and *The Restoration of the Gospel Spirit* (1707).

SUGGESTED READING:

Hauck, *Realencyklopädie.* Leipzig, 1897.

M.E.S. *Étude sur Antoinette Bourignon.* Paris, 1876.

Bourke-White, Margaret

(1904–1971)

Pioneer industrial photographer, photojournalist, war-photographer, and writer, who became an American celebrity in her own right. *Born on June 14, 1904, at Harrison Avenue in the Bronx, New York; died from Parkinson's disease on August 27, 1971, at Stamford Hospital in Connecticut at the age of 67; daughter of Joseph and Minnie (Bourke) White; graduated from Cornell University, 1927; married Everett Chapman, in 1925; married Erskine Caldwell (a writer), in 1939; no children.*

Established a studio in Cleveland, began industrial photography (1927); hired by Fortune *magazine (1929); undertook first visit to Soviet Union (1930);*

Opposite page

Commemorative portrait of Marguerite Bourgeoys by Pierre Le Ber.

had cover photograph on first issue of Life *(1936); photographed the siege of Moscow (1941); torpedoed on troop ship in the Mediterranean (1942); photographed Battle of Monte Cassino (1944); was with troops liberating Buchenwald and other camps (1945); visited India, meetings with Gandhi (1946–48); photographed in Korean War, denied red-baiters' accusations (1952).*

Margaret Bourke-White was one of the pre-eminent photographers of 20th-century America. Brave, resourceful, artful in unsnarling bureaucratic obstacles, she pioneered in several ways: she was the first photographer to capture many industrial operations on film, the first photographer featured by *Fortune* and *Life* magazines, the first to present "photo-essays," and one of the first to show the possibilities of aerial photography. Like many artists of the interwar years, she loved machinery, and one of her best-remembered styles is the romanticized dam, factory, and airplane.

Her mother **Minnie White** was Irish Catholic and her father Joseph, an engineer and inventor, was Jewish. But he had abandoned his family's religion, and Margaret saw little of his side of the family as she grew up. She kept her part-Jewish heritage a closely guarded secret throughout her life. The family were devotees of Ethical Culture, a secular substitute for religion created by Felix Adler in the 1870s, which stressed moral responsibility and self-control. Adler himself married the Whites in 1898, and Margaret was born in 1904, in the Bronx. The family were perfectionists who instilled in their son and two daughters a mixture of fastidiousness and ambition. Joseph White was also an amateur photographer, and from childhood Margaret helped him develop glass-plate negatives in a bathtub full of chemicals.

In 1922, she began to study with Clarence White, a member of the Photo-Secession group and a friend of Alfred Stieglitz. During vacations, she blended her growing interest in photography with her childhood interest in wildlife (she was thinking seriously about becoming a student of snakes—a herpetologist) by working at a summer camp as nature and photography teacher. There she began to make postcards and portraits and was soon running a small tidy business. After her father's death in 1922, a local philanthropist paid Bourke-White's fees to go to the University of Michigan where she showed an increasing skill in photography. Making photographs for the college newspaper helped pay her way through.

She fell in love with a fellow student, Everett Chapman, and married him at the end of her sophomore year. When Chapman graduated and took a job as an engineering professor at Purdue, she left Michigan to go with him but soon found the marriage running into trouble. Her husband would not face up to the demands of his possessive mother nor protect Margaret against her attacks. Chapman himself was moody, and Margaret despaired of their future together. Several times, she underwent a self-induced abortion, fearing that children born to them were destined for an unhappy life; after two years, she left him altogether. She never spoke of him again and kept the marriage as much a secret as she could throughout her life, mentioning it in print for the first time only in her 1963 autobiography.

Bourke-White now went to Cornell University (her sixth college) and graduated. She showed her huge portfolio of photographs to a New York architect who assured her that she had the skill to become a professional; with this encouragement, she set up a studio in Cleveland in 1927. Most of her early work consisted of photographing the houses of wealthy Clevelanders, for the owners or the architects. After a shaky start as a businesswoman, she soon learned her way around, writing in her diary: "[T]he only way to make ninety percent of my wealthy clients appreciate the work is to charge simply unheard of prices." Unlike most women photographers of her era, she was attracted to heavy industry and began to make her reputation photographing blast furnaces for the annual reports of the Otis Steel Corporation. Her father had introduced her to industrial machinery. "I always see machinery through my fathers eyes," wrote Bourke-White. "And so I worship factories." Her work in the Otis factory had to overcome great technical difficulties—the low light, the searing heat and brilliance of molten metal being poured, and the difficulty of access. After months of tireless experimentation and by seizing on every new technical innovation in the fast-developing world of photography, she was finally able to make a high-quality series of prints which so impressed the owner of Otis that he gave her $100 per picture.

Her greatest break came when Henry Luce, editor of *Time*, hired her to work for his new magazine *Fortune* in 1929. Though she was *Fortune*'s first staff photographer, she initially agreed to work only half time, for a salary of $1,000 per month, to preserve her independence. Her photographs dominated the inaugural issue of *Fortune* and appeared in almost every issue of the

Margaret Bourke-White

magazine in its early years. While most photographs used in the magazine were anonymous, Bourke-White's name appeared prominently in the credits. To facilitate her work for Luce, she moved to New York in 1930 and rented a studio in the Chrysler Building. One of the best-known photographs of her was taken by her gifted darkroom technician, Oscar Graubner, with whom she had a long and profitable working relationship. It shows Bourke-White perched on one of the building's stainless steel eagle-shaped gargoyles, 77 stories above Manhattan.

Tolstoy and Gandhi may damn the machine as a devourer of spiritual virtues, as a sort of modern Antichrist, laying waste to the soul of man. But to Miss Bourke-White the machine is a noble and wondrous creation, an object of beauty and grandeur. . . . To Miss Bourke-White the machine is first and foremost an artistic creation.

—Maurice Hindus

Many of her pictures from the 1920s and 1930s were in a style which photography historian James Guimond terms "sooty romanticism," in which the power and magnitude of factories, refineries, and railroad yards were given heroic treatment. Machinery with its sharp angles and clean surfaces also gave photographers the chance to create an abstract effect. This was the favored style of Paul Strand, Charles Sheeler, and Edward Weston in much of their industrial photography, a style which Bourke-White emulated. Her photograph of a concrete dam, on the cover of the first edition of *Life* magazine (1936), is of this type, with its strong shapes overpowering the tiny human figures at the base of the structure. Guimond summarized: "Bourke-White's pictures follow all the conventions of industrial public relations photography—intricate patterns, large machines running themselves, insignificant workers—but she also used a variety of modernist techniques such as exotic camera angles, high contrast lighting, and rhythmic, abstract patterns to make these subject look more grandiose and melodramatic."

Fortune sent her on assignment to Germany in 1930. While there, she persuaded the Soviet Embassy to give her a passport into Russia, at a time when they were very difficult to get. Impressed by her photographs, they admitted her, and she toured the Soviet Union at the height of its first five-year plan, when factories, blast-furnaces and dams were being built from scratch all over the country. She made her excursion the basis of a book, *Eyes on Russia* (1931), for which she provided both text and pictures. Unconcerned with politics, she told colorful anecdotes about the chaotic inefficiency, the lack of shoes, and the optimistic but uneducated people she met. As with her American pictures, industry on a grand scale dominated the Russian photographs—people were added for scale and effect. State bureaucrats in the Soviet government admired them—they fell in with the Soviets' self-conception as heroic modernizers.

In a subsequent trip to Germany and Russia, Bourke-White gradually became more aware of the political implications of her photographic subjects, and like many artists in the 1920s and 1930s moved from a primarily aesthetic to a more politically engaged outlook. She made speeches for left-wing artists' causes and decorated the Soviet consulate in Washington, D.C., but was too closely tied to advertising and business to think about becoming a Communist. Eventually her developing social conscience and her annoyance with the limitations of commercial work made her resolve to give up advertising work altogether, and the instant success of *Life*, on which she played as major a role as she had with *Fortune*, made it possible for her to live up to this resolution. In the early issues of *Life*, she created a new genre which editor-in-chief Henry Luce named the "photo-essay" and which became a staple of picture journalism for the next several decades.

New schemes in the 1930s included her introduction to aerial photography, which she developed on a TWA advertising project but then turned to good effect on a study of the dust bowl, and mural-sized photographs to decorate corporate headquarters. Throughout these years, she was making a large income but spending extravagantly (she had expensive tastes in clothes and loved to make a splash for her growing circle of admirers). As the Great Depression ground on, she was constantly on the brink of bankruptcy. In 1936, Bourke-White toured the south with Erskine Caldwell, a Southern novelist famous for *Tobacco Road* (1932), which had become a stage success on Broadway. Their plan was to write a report on the suffering of Southern sharecroppers. After an uneasy beginning to their tour, they became lovers, and then worked well together, he talking with the sharecroppers and she photographing scenes of rural poverty. Similar scenes and people were also the subject of ***Dorothea Lange**, Arthur Rothstein, and other Farm Security Administration (FSA) pho-

"Lansome, Arkansas" from You Have Seen Their Faces. *Photograph by Margaret Bourke-White*

tographers. But, except for Lange, the mood of Bourke-White's pictures was different from theirs. She emphasized the individuals' faces rather than the desolate landscape they farmed, and was on the lookout for extremes of poverty and deformity rather than representative men and women. She and Caldwell also made up the captions to the pictures rather than quoting the subjects' own words, and did it in a style which seems patronizing and condescending by modern-day standards. Their method made for a highly successful book, however, and when it appeared as *You Have Seen Their Faces*, it sold tens of thousands of copies and completely overshadowed the slightly later James Agee and Walker Evans' *Let Us Now Praise Famous Men* (1941), even though the latter is generally regarded as much the better book.

Bourke-White and Caldwell next traveled to Czechoslovakia, in 1938, in time to witness the Austrian *anschluss*, Hitler's takeover, and the mobilization of German troops at the border of the Czech Sudetenland. They collaborated on another book *North of the Danube* (1939) and then a more general study of the American scene, *Say, Is This the USA?* (1941). After a stormy romance, they were married in 1939 though each of them was temperamental and sometimes overbearing, and the marriage broke up in 1941. For awhile, Bourke-White left *Life* and moved to a daily picture newspaper, *PM*, but her laborious, precise technique was unsuited to the pressure of the everyday deadlines; after six months she was back with *Life* again.

Margaret Bourke-White, 1945.

The Second World War presented Bourke-White with unequalled opportunities, and she seized them eagerly, setting off again for the Soviet Union and persuading the authorities there to relax their prohibition on photographers. She was in Moscow for the first air raids in the fall of 1941, and, rather than descend to the air-raid shelters, she climbed onto her hotel roof to photograph the bombs and the anti-aircraft fire. On this expedition, she was carrying 800 lbs. of equipment and never got it lower than 250 lbs. on later wartime trips even by excluding hundreds of items. She continued to use large format cameras throughout the 1930s, rather than moving over to light-weight, small-format cameras which were then coming into vogue, and still favored elaborate artificial lighting, tripods, and careful contrivance of every picture. In addition, she had a reputation for exposing hundreds of negatives for every one picture finally printed—a cause of scorn among other *Life* photographers, with whom she was not popular.

Many of Bourke-White's large-format cameras were lost in 1942 when she was aboard a troopship torpedoed and sunk by a German submarine in the Mediterranean. She was able to escape and spent a night on an open boat before being picked up and taken ashore. Even on the later wartime trips, her personal luggage alone weighed 55 pounds. In Italy during the Monte Cassino campaign of 1943–44, her gear included seven cameras, thirty lenses, and an immense assortment of flash equipment and spare parts. Of all the army's accredited photographers, she was the most burdened and needed an aide to move from place to place. Nevertheless, the power and skill of her wartime work made the army and the media confident that they had been justified in bending the rules to admit her.

Some of her most haunting and memorable pictures were taken at Buchenwald concentration camp, where she arrived within a day of the liberation in 1945, showing thousands of emaciated corpses, and the listless, disoriented survivors staring blankly through the barbed wire. Bourke-White was repeatedly in the right place at the right time for "scoops," which she managed by tireless politicking with the army command, tactical use of tears, and constant trading on her already high reputation.

She also put her prior experience of aerial photography to good use during the war: she flew several hazardous missions, including a bombing run over German-occupied Tunis in a B-17 Flying Fortress, and dozens of hops in artillery spotter planes. Her aerial photographs of devastated German cities were used by the Strategic Bombing Survey in its effort to determine how effective the bomber campaigns had been. She would carry on her aerial photography work in the Korean War and would be one of the first photographers to appreciate the possibilities of helicopters as stationary flying platforms. A famous close up of the Statue of Liberty's face and crown with each tourist's face visible, taken in the mid-'50s, is one of her best-known helicopter photographs.

By war's end, Bourke-White was well on the way to being a national institution and was featured in dozens of newspaper and magazine stories in her own right. When she went to India to meet Gandhi and to photograph the traumatic period of British imperial withdrawal and the mass migrations of Hindus to India and Muslims to Pakistan (1946–48), she was herself one of the celebrities in the story. Again she arrived at the most dynamic moments. Gandhi was cold to her at first, but later they became friendly and had a long interview together early in the day on which he was assassinated. Having already seen horrific scenes in the war, she was hardened to the sight of Indian massacres in the period of transition, and another famous sequence, featured in *Life*, showed the bloated corpses of Indians killed in sectarian riots being eaten by vultures. Her visits to India culminated in another book, *Half Way to Freedom*, which showed greater political sophistication than her earlier books.

In 1951, Bourke-White, like many artists of her era, suddenly faced the accusation of being a Communist sympathizer. The charge was made by columnist Westbrook Pegler, an ardent McCarthyite, and prompted Bourke-White to issue vigorous denials and to go on a speaking tour to affirm her anti-Communism and her faith in democracy. She was vulnerable to the accusation because of her many visits to the Soviet Union in the 1930s and 1940s and the sympathetic tone of her reporting there—also because of her membership in several Communist "front" organizations. She now asked *Life* to send her to the Korean War, as a way of consolidating her anti-Communist credentials, and there she covered the irregular, guerrilla war going on behind the lines of the main armies.

When she returned, having made another series of memorable pictures for *Life*, she began to discover that movement of her left arm and leg were becoming difficult. After trying to work around this disability for a while, she consulted a doctor who recognized the symptoms of Parkinson's disease. The illness gradually began to affect her more and more seriously. Beyond 1956, Bourke-White was unable to continue her photography work. Volunteering for a surgical method which was then in its early experimental stages, she gained some remission from the symptoms and was well enough to write her autobiography, which was published in 1963. But Parkinsonism could not be halted and progressively the paralysis worsened. Bourke-White lived on until 1971, struggling bravely to overcome the increasing limitations on her mobility, and died only after a serious fall had immobilized her. Margaret Bourke-White's reputation and her influence on photography were immense. Through her entire life, she had shown a singlemindedness and self-reliance that few, if any, of her contemporaries could equal.

SOURCES:

Bourke-White, Margaret. *Portrait of Myself.* NY: Simon and Schuster, 1963.

———. *Dear Fatherland, Rest Quietly.* NY: Simon and Schuster, 1946.

———. *Eyes on Russia.* With a preface by Maurice Hindus. NY: Simon and Schuster, 1931.

Callahan, Sean and Theodore Brown. *The Photographs of Margaret Bourke-White.* NY: Graphic Society Press, 1972.

Goldberg, Vicki. *Margaret Bourke-White: A Biography.* NY: Harper and Row, 1986.

Guimond, James. *American Photography and the American Dream.* Chapel Hill, NC: University of North Carolina Press, 1991.

Moeller, Susan. *Shooting War: Photography and the American Experience of Combat.* NY: Basic Books, 1989.

Patrick Allitt, Professor of History, Emory University, Atlanta, Georgia

Boutet, Anne Françoise Hippolyte (1779–1847).

See Mars, Ann Françoise.

Bouvier, Jacqueline (1929–1994).

See Kennedy, Jacqueline.

Boveri, Margret (1900–1975)

German author who was one of West Germany's best-known journalists. *Born on August 14, 1900, in Würzburg, Germany; died in West Berlin on July 6, 1975; daughter of Theodor Boveri (1862–1915, a highly respected professor at the University of Würzburg) and* ***Marcella (O'Grady) Boveri*** *(1864–1950, an American-born biologist who also pursued a scientific and teaching career well into the seventh decade of her life).*

Studied literature and history into her 30s, starting a career as a journalist (mid-1930s); regarding herself a "German patriot," decided to remain in Nazi Germany, working for non-Nazi newspapers and

journals; traveled in Asia, the Middle East and U.S. (1936–42); worked as a journalist in Portugal and Spain (1942–44); survived the bombing and battle of Berlin (1944–45); became one of the best-known journalists in West Germany (1950s); author of many highly regarded books and articles.

Born in the summer of 1900 in the pleasant university town of Würzburg, Margret Boveri spent her early years in the last part of the "golden epoch" of pre-1914 Europe, an age of incredible luxury and security for the upper class and aristocracy. She came from a family of wealthy, prominent scholars and entrepreneurs, the business side of which created a substantial fortune through their involvement with the Brown-Boveri Company, a major industrial corporation with branches in Germany and Switzerland. The family's intellectual achievements were equally formidable. Margret's father Theodor Boveri was an internationally recognized zoologist and pioneer geneticist who for many years carried out his path-breaking research at the Zoological Station in Naples, Italy. Her mother, born Marcella O'Grady in New England, was a descendant of an old American family; she kept alive her interests in biology while raising a family and in the late 1920s would return to the United States to start a college teaching career.

Without financial worries, the Boveri family employed servants and took long, leisurely trips. Margret's first trip abroad, to Naples, took place in 1901. The following year, she accompanied her family to the U.S.—a country she would visit two more times by 1909. This world would crumble with the advent of World War I and the death of her father. Theodor Boveri became seriously ill in November 1914; his death in October 1915 removed an element of stability from Margaret's life and initiated a long period of uncertainty. Profoundly shaken by Germany's defeat in 1918, she gravitated to the extreme right of the political spectrum, becoming a member of a strongly nationalist youth group, the Deutsch-Nationaler Jugendbund. Untroubled by the need to earn a living and determined to find a career that would provide intellectual stimulation, she became a student of history, German and English at the University of Würzburg. After graduation in 1924, she taught German and English for a year in a secondary school in Würzburg. During this period, Boveri asserted her independence, taking flying lessons, purchasing her own automobile, and having a love affair.

By the late 1920s, she was slipping into a deep depression. Uncertain as to what she should do with her life, she took advantage of family connections in 1927 to secure the position of secretary to Reinhard Dohrn, director of the Zoological Station of Naples where her father had carried on most of his important research projects. She remained emotionally distraught until she met and fell in love with a brilliant African-American scientist, Ernest Everett Just (1883–1941). From the viewpoint of her era's social conventions, Boveri's passionate affair with Just was doomed, but it helped her pull back from self-destruction and cured her of any lingering romantic illusions she might have had about marriage as a life's goal. When her relationship with Just finally terminated in 1931, Boveri had made up her mind to seriously carve out a career for herself.

Starting in October 1929, she lived in Berlin and studied politics at the Deutsche Hochschule für Politik, an institute of advanced studies in political science that attracted a distinguished faculty and eager students from both Germany and abroad. At the Deutsche Hochschule für Politik, unemployed workers took classes alongside representatives of the upper class like Boveri. Determined to end a life of drifting, she also enrolled in the doctoral program in history at the University of Berlin. Boveri's doctoral dissertation, on German foreign policy before 1914, was directed by the internationally noted historian Professor Hermann Oncken. During these years, she engaged in countless political debates with democrats, Socialists, Communists, and Nazis. Starting in September 1930, the Nazi Party became a major political force both in parliament and in the streets; in the minds of many observers, German democracy was now doomed. Boveri used her time during the next few years wisely, working on her dissertation on Sir Edward Grey and pre-1914 British diplomacy, reading a great variety of newspapers and magazines, and discussing the complexities of an international landscape made increasingly unstable by the onset of the world economic depression.

A few months after she was awarded her doctoral degree, Boveri witnessed the Nazi seizure of power in the first months of 1933. She watched the Nazis use a combination of propaganda and terror to destroy the German labor movement and other democratic forces, as well as convince gullible conservatives that National Socialism would be the salvation of the German nation. At the heart of the Nazi victory was middle-class fear of Marxism and disorder, which made it possible to persuade a significant sector of the German middle class to abandon democracy for the promise of a national renaissance based on patriotism and discipline. The price for this "national revolution" was a high one; it meant the creation of a dictatorship in which traditional standards of legality and human rights were scuttled.

Boveri was almost immediately affected by the new regime, as most of her Jewish and leftist friends reasonably believed their lives to be at risk in Adolf Hitler's Germany and thus fled the country as free but penniless refugees for uncertain futures in other countries. Though she had the possibility of fleeing Germany to live with her mother, who some years earlier had returned to her native United States to teach, Boveri did not feel sufficiently threatened by Nazism to leave her homeland for an unknown future abroad. She decided to remain in Berlin, where, despite her slow progress, she still aspired to become a full-time journalist. Although she condemned the Hitler regime bitterly in private and moved in circles that would in time plot against the Nazis at the expense of their lives, Boveri's conservative background trained her to think of the Third Reich as Germany's legitimate government, and to think of herself as a loyal, patriotic subject of the state. Since 1928, Boveri had contributed occasional articles to newspapers such as the prestigious *Frankfurter Zeitung* on various subjects, including current issues of international relations. Impressed by her writings, the editor of the *Berliner Tageblatt,* Paul Scheffer, hired Boveri in July 1934 to write articles on foreign affairs for his newspaper. The *Berliner Tageblatt* had been known for its strongly liberal and anti-Nazi stance before 1933 and was now being kept alive by the Third Reich to give the outside world the impression that the Hitler regime was essentially responsible and peace-loving.

By 1935, Boveri's work had so impressed Scheffer that he delegated her to represent him on a tour of Greece by the leading newspaper editors of Germany. On her return, Margret Boveri was arrested by the Gestapo in late June 1935, and her apartment was thoroughly searched. Under suspicion of having contacts with an underground anti-Nazi organization, the Socialist Workers' Party, she was interrogated at Gestapo headquarters, but was quickly released due to lack of solid evidence. Boveri resumed her work with the *Berliner Tageblatt*, writing feature articles and commentary pieces. By the end of 1935, Adolf Hitler's inner circle had taken note of her thoughtful, moderate articles.

Hitler was as angered by the gender of the author of these non-Nazi commentaries as by their content, and the *Berliner Tageblatt* prudently responded to this instance of Nazi misogyny by labeling Boveri's articles from that point on as authored by "Dr. M. Boveri." Boveri was by this time virtually the only female reporter still working in Nazi Germany. As the *Berliner Tageblatt* struggled to retain at least a degree of independence from the Nazi Party, Paul Scheffer did his best to keep his newspaper from becoming a Nazi propaganda organ. On only one occasion was he unable to prevent the publication of an anti-Semitic article, when he found himself directly ordered by the Ministry of Propaganda and Public Enlightenment to print the piece. Perhaps Scheffer's most extraordinary feat was to retain a Jewish Communist, Rudolf Herrnstadt, as his newspaper's correspondent in Warsaw. Perceptive readers of the *Berliner Tageblatt* could derive knowledge from the carefully crafted articles of Margret Boveri, while taking heart from essays which implied criticism of Hitlerism through critical dissections of Stalin's harshly totalitarian regime.

Boveri's reputation as a clear-eyed observer led Scheffer to send her in 1936 to write a series of articles on the changing geopolitical landscape of the Mediterranean region. After visiting Malta, Egypt and the Sudan, her impressions appeared not only in the *Berliner Tageblatt* but also as a book, *Das Weltgeschehen am Mittelmeer*. Some of Boveri's illusions about maintaining at least a slight degree of professional independence in the Third Reich ended in April 1937, when an increasingly frustrated and pessimistic Paul Scheffer resigned his editorial post. She, too, resigned her position, taking a trip to the British isles to consider her options for the future. An attempt to get a job with the only other non-Nazi paper of distinction in Germany, the *Frankfurter Zeitung*, did not succeed. Discouraged, Boveri sought solace with a trip to a country she loved, Italy. In order to stay at the heart of political events, she then took an editorial job with the Atlantis-Verlag in Berlin. Further contacts with the *Frankfurter Zeitung* in the fall of 1937 resulted in a more positive assessment of her abilities by that newspaper's editors, and in 1938 she was hired by them. Boveri's first assignment, an extended trip to the Near East, resulted in the publication of two travel books, one of which was published in an English-language edition by Oxford University Press in 1939.

On the eve of World War II, in May 1939, she was transferred by the *Frankfurter Zeitung* to Stockholm. During the next months, Sweden and the other Scandinavian nations tried desperately to avoid being involved in war, and her reports from Stockholm provided German readers with perceptive insights into a rapidly evolving diplomatic picture. Because of her proven abilities and knowledge of the English language, Boveri arrived in New York City in October 1940 to serve as the U.S. correspondent of the *Frankfurter Zeitung*. She had traveled across the Soviet Union on the Trans-Siberian Railroad, and now reported on an increasingly anti-Nazi U.S. to a German reading public that had been exposed to Nazi propaganda for more than seven years. Boveri's reports were attempts to retain a spirit of objectivity in reportage without antagonizing Nazi officials who carefully scrutinized every aspect of the *Frankfurter Zeitung*'s output. In her private life, Boveri met with her mother, who taught biology at a college in the Boston area. After agonizing over whether or not she should return to Germany, Boveri decided that despite her distaste for the Nazis at heart she remained a patriotic German, and she would return home when the time came.

In one of the greatest blunders of his career, Adolf Hitler declared war on the U.S. immediately after Pearl Harbor. On the same day, December 9, 1941, Margret Boveri and other high-ranking Germans in the United States were placed under arrest. She was repatriated to Europe in May 1942 and found work as the Lisbon correspondent of the *Frankfurter Zeitung*. Lisbon during World War II was a bustling center for journalists, spies, and adventurers of all stripes. Boveri took advantage of this rich mixture of rumor, fact and fiction, writing colorful articles on American and British politics and culture. The year 1943 was a turning point in the war; Nazi Germany lost the decisive battle of Stalingrad, and radical Nazis like Propaganda Minister Joseph Goebbels decided that "total war" was the only way to save the Third Reich. In keeping with the new course, the *Frankfurter Zeitung* was banned on August 31, 1943. Margret Boveri's expertise was still of use to the regime, however, and she briefly worked as an advisor on American affairs to the German Embassy in Madrid.

Increasingly homesick, Boveri went back to Berlin in March 1944 despite the dangers of returning to a Germany under almost constant air attack. Her home had been destroyed some months earlier in a bombing raid, but she was determined to remain in Berlin to the end. Despite the difficult conditions, Boveri wrote polished articles that appeared regularly in *Das Reich* and the *Kölnische Zeitung*. She also began working again for the Atlantis-Verlag. During the terrifying bombing raids, as Berlin crumbled around her, she consoled herself listening to her prized recordings of Johann Sebastian Bach. Her favorite authors were Goethe, Rilke, H.G. Wells and ***Virginia Woolf**. She sought to learn more about the war by listening to BBC broadcasts, keeping her radio turned very low since listening to enemy broadcasts made one a *Feindhörer* (hostile listener), a grave offense punishable by imprisonment in a concentration camp, or death.

The liberation of Berlin in May 1945 brought out the best in Boveri. Displaying tenacious powers of survival, she went forth each day from her tumbledown dwelling, returning many hours later with scraps of food and drinkable water. Quite fearlessly, she was able to prevent Soviet soldiers from stealing her most precious possession, her bicycle. Protein-starved and quick-witted, she was overjoyed when she had the opportunity to hack chunks of meat from a dead but still warm horse she found in a street. Though she worked as a journalist throughout the Nazi period, Boveri never joined the Nazi Party nor produced outright propaganda. She was able to continue her career, writing for a number of journals including the American-licensed *Kurier* in Berlin; Boveri also was a regular contributor to the respected *Badische Zeitung*, a newspaper published in Freiburg in Breisgau. In 1946, she showed an increasing sense of independence by publishing *Amerika-Fibel*, an analysis of American ideals and attitudes that was not always complimentary. Angered, American occupation officials banned her book for its "lack of respect" for the conquerors. However, as Allied occupation policies liberalized, the book was eventually cleared by the censors, appearing in a new edition in 1948.

Showing the strength to build a career as a respected writer and journalist in the divided Germany of the Cold War decades, Boveri began publishing essays on the current political and cultural scene in the journal *Der Merkur*, starting in 1947. As West Germany rebuilt from the ruins of war, Boveri, increasingly enjoying the fruits of prosperity, rebuilt her life both psychologically and materially. In 1951, she purchased an abandoned Wehrmacht barracks in West Berlin, transforming it over the years into an attractive home where her friends and colleagues met to discuss politics and the arts. Starting in 1956, she began to publish her highly praised multivolume study of treason in the 20th century, which devoted much space to the plotters against the Hitler regime, men and women whom she had in some instances known personally. Boveri never ceased asking herself, "Why did I remain in Nazi Germany?" and her struggle to answer that difficult question influenced much of her work in the closing decades of her life. In her massive historical study of the *Berliner Tageblatt*, published in 1965 under the title *Wir lügen alle* (*We All Lied*), Boveri openly admitted to having been a collaborator with the Nazi regime to the extent that she, and her colleagues, had consciously decided to remain in Germany and had offered their talents to provide the regime with a more decent, humane image. She also raised many questions about the paradoxes of the East-West split that turned post-1945 Germany into two hostile and opposing republics. Up to the day of her death of cancer in West Berlin on July 6, 1975, Margret Boveri served as one of the few voices of conscience in a Germany grown prosperous but often morally complacent in the climate of the Cold War. While she never completely explained all the nuances of the choices she had made during the most evil and destructive epoch in German history, her pursuit of the truth after 1945 helped put her own behavior and that of many of her contemporaries into a more understandable context. Rather than run away from her own past, or that of her often profoundly troubled and perplexing nation, she confronted it head on.

SOURCES:

Boveri, Margret. *Amerika-Fibel für erwachsene Deutsche: Ein Versuch Unverstandenes zu erklären*. Berlin: Minerva-Verlag, 1946. 2nd ed., Freiburg im Breisgau: Badischer Verlag, 1948.

——. *Ein Auto, Wüsten, blau Perlen: Ein Bericht über eine Fahrt durch Vorderasien*. Zurich, Leipzig and Berlin: Atlantis-Verlag, 1939.

——. *Minaret and Pipe-Line: Yesterday and Today in the Near East*. London and NY: Oxford University Press, 1939.

——. *Tage des Überlebens: Berlin 1945*. Munich: R. Piper, 1968.

——. *Treason in the Twentieth Century*. Translated by Jonathan Steinberg. NY: Putnam, 1963[?].

——. *Verzweigungen: Eine Autobiographie*. Edited and with an Afterword by Uwe Johnson. Munich and Zurich: R. Piper & Co. Verlag, 1977.

——. *Das Weltgeschehen am Mittelmeer: Ein Buch über Inseln und Küsten, Politik und Strategie, Völker und Imperien*. Zurich, Leipzig and Berlin: Atlantis-Verlag, 1936.

——. *Wir lügen alle: Eine Hauptstadtzeitung unter Hitler*. Olten: Walter-Verlag, 1965.

Frei, Norbert and Johannes Schmitz. *Journalismus im Dritten Reich*. Munich: Verlag C. H. Beck, 1989.

Heuss, Theodor. *Anton Dohrn: A Life for Science*. With a Contribution by Margret Boveri. Edited by Christianne Groeben, Translated by Liselotte Dieckmann. Berlin: Springer-Verlag, 1991.

Koonz, Claudia. *Mothers in the Fatherland: Women, the Family, and Nazi Politics*. NY: St. Martin's Press, 1987.

Manning, Kenneth R. *Black Apollo of Science: The Life of Ernest Everett Just*. Oxford: Oxford University Press, 1983.

"Register," in *Der Spiegel*. Vol. 29, no. 29. July 14, 1975, p. 108.

John Haag, Associate Professor, University of Georgia, Athens, Georgia

Bow, Clara (1904–1965)

Popular star of the silent screen and early talkies who was the idol of the "flappers" and, as the "'It' Girl," with her spit curls, bee-stung lips, and kewpie-doll eyes, came to epitomize the devil-may-care, flaming youth of the 1920s. *Name variations: The "'It' Girl," The Brooklyn Bonfire, The Red Head, Paramount's Forest Fire, The Blaze from Brooklyn, The Queen of the Flappers, The Personality Kid, The Playgirl of Hollywood, and, by studio staff, simply as The Kid. Born Clara Gordon Bow in the Bay Ridge section of Brooklyn, New York, on July 29, 1904 (and not 1905 as usually given or 1907 as occasionally found); died of a heart attack in Los Angeles, California, on September 27, 1965; daughter of Robert and Sarah Gordon Bow; attended public schools 111 and 98 in Sheepshead Bay, Brooklyn, which she left after 8th grade at age 14; married Rex Bell (né Beldam, an actor), in December 1931; children: Rex Lardlow Beldam, nicknamed "Tony" (b. 1934); George Francis Robert Beldam (b. 1938).*

Won a beauty contest conducted by Shadowland *magazine, received a screen test, and cast in* Beyond the Rainbow *(1922); in Hollywood, signed by Preferred Pictures (1923); moved to Paramount Studios appearing in the silent films (1926); cast in talking films (1928).*

Filmography—silent films: Down to the Sea in Ships *(1922);* Enemies of Women *(1923);* Maytime *(1923);* Daring Years *(1923);* Grit *(1924);* Black Oxen *(1924);* Poisoned Paradise *(1924);* Daughters of Pleasure *(1924);* Wine *(1924);* Empty Hearts *(1924);* This Woman *(1924);* Black Lightning *(1924);* Capital Punishment *(1925);* Helen's Babies *(1925);* The Adventurous Sex *(1925);* My Lady's Lips *(1925);* Parisian Love *(1925);* Eve's Lover *(1925);* Kiss Me Again *(1925);* The Scarlet West *(1925);* The Primrose Path *(1925);* The Plastic Age *(1925);* Keeper of the Bees *(1925);* Free to Love *(1925);* Best Bad Men *(1925);* Lawful Cheaters *(1925);* Ancient Mariner *(1926);* My Lady of Whims *(1926);* Dancing Mothers *(1926);* Shadow of the Law *(1926);* Two Can Play *(1926);* The Runaway *(1926);* Mantrap *(1926);* Kid Boots *(1926);* It *(1927);* Children of Divorce *(1927);* Rough House Rosie *(1927);* Wings *(1927);* Hula *(1927);* Get Your Man *(1927);* Red Hair *(1928);* Ladies of the Mob *(1928);* The Fleet's In *(1928);*

Three Weekends *(1928)*. *Talking films:* The Wild Party *(1929);* Dangerous Curves *(1929);* Saturday Night Kid *(1929);* Paramount On Parade *(1930);* True to the Navy *(1930);* Love Among the Millionaires *(1930);* Her Wedding Night *(1930);* No Limit *(1930);* Kick In *(1931);* Call Her Savage *(1932);* Hoopla *(1933)*.

Clara Bow was born in the Bay Ridge section of Brooklyn, New York, on January 29, 1904, the youngest and only surviving child of Robert and **Sarah Gordon Bow** (two earlier daughters died in infancy). Of mixed English, Scottish, and French descent, Clara Bow came from a poor background and had an unhappy childhood, not hesitating to assert in later years that "nobody wanted me in the first place." In his biography of Bow, David Stenn makes much of her "gothic" upbringing but admits to having drawn most of his data from a three-part series of articles in *Photoplay* magazine based on interviews that she gave to the noted reporter ***Adela Rogers St. John** in 1928; thus, it would be unwise to take uncritically.

What seems to be true was that her father was a ne'er-do-well and that her maternal grandmother, **Sarah Hatton Gordon**, became mentally ill and was committed to the Long Island State Hospital in August 1906 and died not long afterwards. In addition, there seems to be no doubt that for whatever reasons, her family moved about regularly from one Brooklyn tenement to another so that Bow had lived in over a dozen cold-water flats before leaving for Hollywood. On the other hand, the idea that her mother, though she had her mental problems, was actually insane and that she once threatened to kill Clara with a knife seems far-fetched. Her cousin Billy Bow, who lived with the family from time to time, stated that his aunt was suffering from pernicious anemia, and even Clara admitted that her mother did not begin to suffer from "fits" until after she fell down a flight of stairs in 1911.

As a child, Clara was lonely and hypersensitive, covering this with an exterior that eventually evolved into the devil-may-care "jazz baby" persona of her Hollywood years. She was also burdened with a slight stammer that arose in later years whenever she was nervous or under pressure. Leaving school after the eighth grade, she sold french fries from a stand in Coney Island one summer and then secured a job as a sort of receptionist for a doctor. In any case, poverty and deprivation were not to be her lot for long.

In 1921, still only 17 but already an ardent movie fan and devourer of movie magazines such as *Photoplay*, *Shadowland*, and *Motion Picture Classic*, she borrowed two dollars from her father to have some cheap photographs taken of herself and with them entered a beauty contest conducted by *Shadowland*. One of 20 finalists, she was called back for a screen test and won first prize: a trophy, her picture in the January 1922 issue, and an introduction to some casting offices in New York. One of these agencies gave her a small part in a ***Billy Dove** film titled *Beyond the Rainbow* but when it appeared, Bow's part had been cut. Nevertheless, her photograph in *Shadowland* had been seen by a director who, three months later, hired her at $50 per week, to appear as a stowaway in *Down to the Sea in Ships*, an opus filmed in Bedford, Massachusetts. Almost simultaneously, Bow learned that her mother had been taken to a state mental hospital, where she shortly died (January 1923) and that an agent had gotten her a three-month contract with Benjamin P. Schulberg, a former Paramount executive, who had left to head one of the lower-end Hollywood studios, Preferred Pictures. Shortly thereafter, though she was still less than 18 and half his age, Schulberg made her his mistress.

Clara Bow was never to know poverty again. Schulberg elevated his inamorata to major roles, and she quickly began to catch the public's eye. Stardom came almost at once; the heartbreaks were to follow. Bow made 12 pictures in 1923–24, most of them drivel (though *Grit* had been scripted by F. Scott Fitzgerald), and many of them were filmed at other studios to which Schulberg lent her out to build up her value, charging $500 a loan while paying Bow $200 and pocketing the rest. Though there is no question that Schulberg exploited Bow both financially and sexually, it is also true that it was due to his providence that Bow never had to worry about money once her career came to an end. He forced her to invest half her salary (which eventually rose from $1,000 to $5,000 per week), and though she spent everything that came into her hands, thanks to Schulberg, she was never allowed to squander it all.

Schulberg had purchased a popular novel *The Plastic Age* which he thought would make Bow a star, and so it did in 1925. It also made Bow too important to have to knuckle down any longer to Schulberg's demands. *The Plastic Age* starred a handsome new Mexican actor, who was to have a long career under the name Gilbert Roland, and, in short order, he became the first of a long line of lovers of her own choice. Gary Cooper was next; the directors Vic-

Clara Bow

tor Fleming and William Wellman overlapping him, much to his chagrin.

But though Bow was extraordinarily pretty and by no means untalented, she would never have gotten as far as she did had it not been for the remarkable concurrence of her personality and the era that was ready for it. In what was perhaps the first age in history to glorify youth, Clara Bow (together with ***Colleen Moore** and, to a lesser extent, the very young ***Joan Crawford**) was presented in her films as the epitome of what the youth of the day had come to represent, and she was featured as such in no less than 37 pictures in her first five years on the screen. The so-called "Roaring '20s" was the period of cynicism and anomie that followed immediately upon the First World War. It was beyond any doubt, a reaction to the disillusionments of that war and a revolt against the values that had characterized the era that had preceded it. From the new "lost generation" of free-living young men known as "sheikhs" and carefree young women called "flappers," the fashions, fads, and follies of the day quickly spread to other levels of the population. For women, this meant knee-length skirts, flat chests, short haircuts, slathers of make-up and an uninhibited lifestyle (including the swilling of illegal bootleg liquor and abandoned sex in parked cars), that sent the chaperon packing. To cash in on this new world of easy morals and hot jazz, Hollywood needed only to find a model who could set the tone for the day—both to epitomize it and establish and affirm its norms. Clara Bow filled the bill with astonishing success.

For seven years, Clara Bow was the queen of the movies, the embodiment of everything that the flapper supposedly was or wanted to be. Everywhere, young, and not so young, women copied her hair, her kewpie-doll make-up, and her flippant mannerisms. Saucily winking an eye, pursing pouty lips, flashing a dazzling smile, coyly peeking over a raised shoulder were all part of her stock in trade, coupled with a what-the-hell insouciance and a readiness to fly to the dance floor at the first Charleston beat that suggested everything that the postwar "Jazz Age" stood for. There is no question that she was gifted with an extraordinary sense of fun. Yet for all this, Clara Bow was capable of looking more deeply than did her audiences into the character she portrayed, on one occasion saying: "All the time the flapper is laughin' and dancin' there's a feelin' of tragedy underneath. She's unhappy and disillusioned and that's what people sense, that's what makes her different."

The studio publicity mills, the fan magazines, and the Hollywood gossip columnists were at pains to assure audiences that Bow was exactly the same hell-raising hoyden off screen as she was on. Unfortunately, this appears to have been true. Equipped with a Brooklyn accent, a tough-gal demeanor, and a mouthful of wisecracks and four-letter words, Clara Bow became a byword in Hollywood for her numerous affairs and the scandals that clouded the last years of her career. Not all of her escapades actually took place, of course, the studio having a definite stake in perpetuating the notion that Clara Bow the woman and Clara Bow the star were one and the same. Nevertheless, as movie stars began to take themselves more and more seriously, Clara Bow and her public antics were seen as an embarrassment, and, early on, Hollywood hosts and hostesses made it a point to keep her off their guest lists.

To her family, Clara Bow was devoted, clear evidence that her home life could not have been all that wretched. She brought her father to live with her in the modest (and untidy) home on Hollywood Boulevard that she shared with Artie Jacobson; she also financed her father's ill-conceived attempts to establish a business, including a dry-cleaning operation and a restaurant both of which failed, and gradually encouraged all her relatives to join her in sunny California. A petite red-head (5'2", weighing about 110 lbs.), with brown eyes and a dazzling smile, Clara Bow was sincere and unaffected. She tended to be trusting—too much so—and was known for keeping her word. Despite her humble origins and her rapid rise, she never developed a swelled head, was pleasant to everybody high and low, and by all accounts remained extremely likable. Poorly educated, she was by no means unintelligent (she had a B+ average in high school), and after her retirement from the screen did much to educate herself on her own. Sexually, she appears to have been as liberated as anyone else in Hollywood at that time, though she tended to be more open about it and made no secret of either her lovers or one-night stands.

Although Clara Bow's career had begun incredibly early and she was a star before she was 20, the pinnacle of its short span was not reached until she was signed to a new five-year contract by Schulberg, who had left Preferred Pictures to become the Western managing director of production at Paramount Studios, on the eve of the advent of talking films, and had taken Bow with him. Shortly after this, she came to the attention of author ***Elinor Glyn**, who, having shocked America with her shallow but startling novel *Three Weeks* in 1907, fancied herself a lady of letters and convinced Hollywood to do the same. Inventing the term "it" to refer to sex appeal, which she then used as the title of her latest novel, Madame Glyn, as she liked to be called, declared Clara Bow to be the very personification of the ideal. Though "it" was little more than a shrewd device for self-promotion on Glyn's part, when Bow was cast in the silent adaptation of Glyn's novel (1927), the film not only became a huge success but made Bow an international star. Her salary soon soared to $2,700 per week.

It is a myth that the studios rushed into the making of talking films. With some 20,000 movie theaters in the United States, the cost of wiring them for sound was a formidable obstacle, and there was a wide belief that talking pictures, which had been tried before, were only a fad. Thus, for two years, Clara Bow continued to be featured in silent films only. So successful were these, that Paramount—and Schulberg—gradually lost interest in the development of Bow as an actress and instead banked on her continued appeal in her conventional role, placing her in one formula picture after another. The first of these was *Rough House Rosie*, which was filmed early in 1927 and set the tone for the rest: a poor young woman seeks fame and fortune, uses her vivacious charms to hit the top, then, after many adventures and diverse men, realizes that the fellow she left behind is her only true love and returns to his waiting and forgiving arms. From then on, Paramount, realizing that audiences came to see Bow cavort and little else, saw no point in spending money on production values, expensive leading men, or scripts that varied her characters. Over and over, whatever the name given to her in the film (Rosie, Trixie, Lila, Bubbles, Mayme, Lolly, Hula), Bow was simply cast as Bow clowning around. For all this, some of her last silents were not without interest: *Hula* (1927) had a nude scene in it with Bow floating on her back in a pond that made the front pages around the world; *Ladies of the Mob* (1928) was a promising, albeit sole, attempt at a dramatic role; and *Red Hair* (1928) had a sequence in the then new Technicolor process that showed off her hair as advertised in its title. Also, she didn't always play a baddie, and her performance as the wartime ambulance driver Mary Preston in the prestigious *Wings* (a 1927 silent with added sound effects that cost the studio some $2 million to produce) was much appreciated. But it was now becoming clear that Bow was being overworked as well as exploited. She had had her first breakdown after the filming of *Rough House Rosie* and had to enter the Glendale Sanitarium to recover.

Meanwhile, her public continued to adore its "'It' Girl." Her fan mail came in by the train load—33,727 letters in May 1928 alone; 35,339 pieces in June. In August, a van had to be called to her home to haul 250,000 pieces to storage. Hailed in an exhibitor's poll as the top box-office draw of 1928 and 1929, she was mobbed at Grand Central Station on a trip to New York in January 1930. As late as 1932, when after the completion of *Call Her Savage Fox* sent Bow on a tour of Europe, she would attract enormous attention in Paris and, going on to Berlin, receive an autographed copy of *Mein Kampf* from the hands of its author, Adolf Hitler, who was also besmitten.

At last, in 1929, after considerable dithering, Paramount let Bow make her first talkie, ***Dorothy Arzner**'s *The Wild Party*, with young Fredric March as her co-star. Though the need to stand close to the hidden microphones cramped her style, which had always included bouncing all over the set, and her voice initially disappointed her fans, Bow made a successful transition with her popularity undimmed. She never got used to the new talking pictures, however, and always claimed that she hated the medium. The talkies, as they were quickly dubbed, proved disastrous to some silent film stars, either they hadn't the voices to match their looks (John Gilbert), couldn't speak English (Emil Jannings), or spoke with such heavy accents that their voices were better suited to comedy than to serious roles (***Vilma Banky**, ***Pola Negri**). They proved no problem, however, for Bow. After some concerns in her initial talking venture, her sassy Brooklynese turned out to be perfectly suited to the type of role that she played. Nevertheless, Bow took voice lessons and the practice of pear-shaped tones gradually had her speaking "real refined." In time, she added singing to her previous charms, warbling competently in a couple of talkies, if offering no threat to the professional chanteuses of the day.

But Clara Bow had begun to get reckless. While hospitalized with appendicitis, she fell in love with a young intern, Earl Pearson. Unfortunately, Pearson was married. After a brief affair, Bow found herself the subject of a lawsuit, charged with alienation of affections. She wisely settled out of court, reputedly paying Mrs. Pearson some $30,000, but the affair brought her considerable bad publicity and proved to be only the first of a series of scandals that were to rock her career and wreck her precarious health. The Pearson affair was followed by an over-publicized and abruptly canceled marital engagement to cabaret artist Harry Richman, who had once been the piano accompanist for ***Mae West** in her vaudeville days and who had come to Hollywood to make his first, and only, talking picture. Shortly afterwards, in 1930, while filming in Nevada, Bow went gambling with Will Rogers at the Calneva Lodge in Lake Tahoe and, ignorant of the rules, ran up a $13,500 debt that she later refused to pay. Only after more bad publicity did she agree to settle what she owed. Next, when she sued her maid, one **Daisy de Boe** (who called herself Daisy de *Voe*, to avoid confusion with her employer), for embezzling money from her bank account, the latter retaliated with sordid revelations of Bow's private life and numerous lovers—naming Richman, Pearson, Cooper, Lothar Mendez, and a certain young man named Rex Bell. The maid even went so far as to suggest that her own character had become corrupted through association with such a creature, thus explaining her casualness towards the bank account whose access had been entrusted to her by Miss Bow. Finally, the publisher Frederic H. Girnau, after printing Miss De Boe's more salacious anecdotes about Bow in his Hollywood tabloid, *The Coast Reporter*, was jailed for eight years for sending obscene materials—his scandal sheet—through the mails. None of this, however, was a match for the ribald stories, true and untrue, that were passed from mouth to mouth, first in Hollywood and then throughout the country.

Preoccupied by her legal battles (which a more hardened entertainer like Mae West would have had the nerve and savvy to turn to her own advantage), Clara Bow was off the screen for almost two years (1931–32), though afterwards, far from finding herself finished, offers continued to pour in. The producer Earl Carroll wanted her in New York for his *Vanities*, Flo Ziegfeld wanted to create a Broadway show around her, the Shuberts wanted her for a 20-week stage tour at $20,000 per week, and she was being offered as much as $10,000 for an interview or a personal appearance. As far as the movies were concerned, both Metro-Goldwyn-Mayer and Howard Hughes were seeking her services. Nevertheless, the strains of the scandals, the trials and the ugly headlines, proved too much for Bow, who, having inherited the fragility of her mother and her maternal grandmother, now suffered a second nervous breakdown that forced her to abandon work on her latest film, *The Secret Call*, and take refuge in the Glendale sanitarium in May 1931. With appalling callousness, Schulberg chose that same month to announce that Paramount, for which she had made millions, would release her from her contract, due to expire in October. Bow took this fresh blow with dignity and grace and never spoke out against either Schulberg or the studio. Despite the offers still coming in, she was slipping and she knew it. ***Jean Arthur** had stolen one picture from her, and she lost her chance to play a good dramatic role in *City Streets*, a part that went to ***Sylvia Sydney**. Meanwhile, in small town America, the women's clubs, so powerful in those days, were railing against her.

The one bright spot in all this was that just as her career was drawing to an undistinguished close, Bow fell in love with a handsome stunt man and cowboy actor named Rex Bell (né Beldam), the last of a long line of lovers, who, after her release from the sanitarium (which he had convinced her to enter), took her to live on the small ranch he had bought near Searchlight, Nevada. There, in a rough-hewn cabin, he nursed her back to health. Born George F. Beldam in Chicago in 1903, Bell had been brought to Hollywood by his family while still a teenager and had attended Hollywood High School. By all accounts he was a fine "all-American boy," who always wanted to have his own ranch, and who would abandon his hopes of a Hollywood career as soon as he could afford one. After his father died in 1924, he had been left the sole provider for his mother and younger siblings and was driving a truck when he was discovered by a studio. Admitting that he couldn't act, he was nevertheless hired as a stunt man and worked at this for four years. Then, in 1930, he was co-starred with Bow in *True to the Navy*, one of her poorer formula films that was a wretched successor to her recent hits *Dangerous Curves* and *Paramount on Parade*. Her career nearing the rocks and his never having quite taken off, the two seemed to find in each other the "real" person behind the Hollywood facade, and both decided simultaneously to get off the carousel and return to the real world. They were married in Las Vegas in December 1931.

That year, her health apparently recovered, Clara Bow came out of her recent retirement, signing with her old friend Sam Rork to do four pictures for Fox. Even then, however, she waited almost a year before settling on a picture that she felt willing to do. In the name of "keeping faith with her public," she showed courage and considerable integrity in her search for just the right script for her return to the screen but, unfortunately, to little avail. She appeared in two poor films over the next year, *Call Her Savage* (1932) and *Hoopla*. In 1933, while waiting for the release of *Hoopla*, she had said:

> The minute that I see the first sign that my public doesn't want me any longer I'll retire. People tell me I'm crazy to talk about quittin' when I'm only 27. Well, maybe I am. But I want to stop when they still want me. I want to quit at the top—not at the bottom of the scale. I've been criticized because I won't cut my salary. I get $75,000 a picture and

> $25,000 more if the picture grosses over a certain amount. Here's how I feel—the minute that I can't get $75,000 it's because I'm not worth it. And when I'm not worth that much anymore, it's because the public is beginning to tire of me. Then it's time to quit.

Both movies were failures, and Bow, released from her obligation to do the remaining two pictures by Rork's untimely death, calmly accepted the end of her career.

Thereafter, Bow and Bell settled down at Rancho Clarita, as he had named his spread. Now grown to 360,000 acres, its original cabin was replaced by a modern home consisting of a two-storey, 12-room hacienda with a 50-by-30 foot living room, a swimming pool with piped in water, and its own electric generating plant. There Bow eased into the comfortable if unlikely role of middle-class matron. Two children were born to the couple, Rex Lardlow Beldam, nicknamed Tony (1934), and George Francis Robert Beldam (1938). Tony, who looked like his father, made a movie debut in a bit part in a western in 1964 but chose to became a lawyer, taking the name Rex Anthony Bell, and eventually becoming district attorney for Clark County, Nevada. George took after his mother in appearance but steered clear of show business. In between the two boys, Bow lost a baby girl after which her husband encouraged her to go into business as a means of occupying herself. Her venture, "The It Cafe" at the corner of Hollywood Boulevard and Vine Street, was not a success, however, and the family returned to Rancho Clarita. There Bow resumed the role of wife and mother, romping with her sons, whom she adored. Unfortunately, her mental health remained precarious, and she suffered from acute insomnia, as well as from other ailments both real and imagined. Though she was usually rational, she was often severely distraught and never ceased to require considerable medical care.

But Clara Bow was not forgotten during the long years that followed her retirement from the screen. As time went on, a nostalgia developed for the 1920s. The Charleston, which had had a brief vogue in the middle of the decade, was taken as having pervaded the era, the short-lived short skirts were taken as the typical wear, and Clara Bow came to epitomize the flapper to such an extent that the flapper era became forever associated with her name. In the early 1930s, she was obviously the model for the title character in the Betty Boop cartoons. Offers still came in to do films, but she refused them, and, if she ever missed being the "'It' Girl" of the silver screen, she never said so. In 1950, when *Life Magazine* devoted a special issue to commemorate the midpoint of the century, a color photograph of Bow, her age considerately given as 41 (which would have made her enter the movies at 13) was chosen, along with those of Charles Lindbergh, Herbert Hoover, Grover Cleveland, and ➤ **Gilda Gray**, to represent the 1920s.

Bow's marriage to Bell had remained the one solid bedrock of her life. If Clara Bow, so amoral in her early youth, ever had another lover after she married Bell, no one ever knew it. For his part, Bell never seemed to be concerned with what people thought of him for marrying a woman whose name for looseness had once been a by-word in Hollywood. He loved her, saw the best in her, and had the strength of character to forget the rest. Eventually, however, Bell was no longer able to endure his wife's instability and hypochondria, and they separated in 1950. By mutual agreement, he retained custody of the two boys. Thereafter, Bow moved back to Los Angeles, living first in the Los Altos Apartments in the Wilshire district for a year and then in the Gramercy Apartments in the same neighborhood. Rex and her sons visited from time to time. Increasingly reclusive, she finally took a small house in Santa Monica when it became clear that only a private residence would suit her need to be left alone. There, attended by a live-in maid and two dogs, she passed her time swimming, painting, keeping up with current affairs, and maintaining a voluminous correspondence, her income from her trust fund providing for all her needs. She had once taken a speed-reading course and now took up serious books including Gibbon's *Decline and Fall of the Roman Empire* and Shirer's *The Rise and Fall of the Third Reich*. An avid movie-goer, but attending only drive-ins to protect her privacy, Bow adored ***Marilyn Monroe** and was so taken by Marlon

➤ **Gray, Gilda** (1901–1959)

Polish dancer and actress. *Born Marianna Michalska on October 24, 1901, in Krakow, Poland; died in 1959.*

Gilda Gray, who was born in Poland but immigrated to America in 1908 at age seven, starred in a number of silents between 1923 and 1936. She is credited with inventing the dance-craze, the shimmy. Her films include: *Lawful Larceny* (1923), *Aloma of the South Seas* (1926), *Cabaret* (1928), *The Devil Dancer* (1928), *Piccadilly* (U.K., 1929), *Rose Marie* (1936), and *The Great Ziegfeld* (1936).

Brando that she arranged to have him come to her home so she could meet him. She continued to suffer from a nervous condition, however, as well from acute insomnia and was in and out of sanitariums according to how ill she was from one month to the next. In 1955, Bow's father, who had been working for a casino in Las Vegas, retired and returned to California to live with her once again. He died two years later at the age of 84. In time, Rex Bell entered politics, rising to become lieutenant governor of Nevada in 1954. Ever loyal to Bow but making no secret of her condition, he never admitted the actuality of the separation, asserting that his wife lived in Los Angeles because her medical needs could not be satisfied in Nevada. He died of a heart attack in Las Vegas on July 4, 1962, at the age of 58 while running for governor of his home state. Bow was not present at her husband's funeral, but she did attend a second funeral service held at Forest Lawn Cemetery, her first public appearance in 15 years as well as her last. Swathed in black, and accompanied by her sons, she gamely smiled for journalists, who marveled at how little she had changed.

In her last years, Bow continued to be in poor health and until just before her death had been treated for her chronic insomnia in a local sanitarium. For several years, she had maintained her own apartment there and had a private nurse on duty at all times, though she was free to come and go. On September 27, 1965, Clara Bow died in her Hollywood home of a heart attack at the age of 61. An autopsy revealed that she had been suffering from severe heart disease and that this had not been her first seizure, the previous symptoms having been overlooked as part of her chronic hypochondria. She was buried beside her husband in Forest Lawn.

Viewed in the light of present-day medical knowledge, it is not clear that Clara Bow—or, for that matter either her mother or grandmother—was actually mentally disturbed, and it is not at all impossible that all three were simply victims of a glandular or chemical disorder causing acute depression and irrational behavior, a condition now treated with such medications as Prozac. Whatever the exact nature of her illness, however, there is no question that her single marriage was the wisest move she had ever made, and her sons remained the center of her life in the long years that separated her from her days of fame and glory until her death more than 30 years later. Although most of Clara Bow's silent films are now lost (*Mantrap*, *Kid Boots*, *Get Your Man*, and *Red Hair* are among those that survive) and only a very few of her talkies are available on video cassette, her vivacious charm still comes through on the small screen, and her name has not been forgotten. Two biographies appeared of her in due course: *The "It" Girl*, a rather sensational pot-boiler in 1976, by Morella and Epstein, who specialized in unauthorized biographies; and *Clara Bow: Runnin' Wild*, a much more serious tome written in 1988 by David Stenn, who enjoyed the cooperation of her family. Years after Bow's death, Madonna's manager ventured to call his client "the 'It Girl' of the 'eighties," while **Madonna** stated her desire to portray Clara Bow on the screen. But perhaps the best tribute to Clara Bow's memory was the one given her by her film contemporary and fan ***Louise Brooks**, who, after Bow's death, said simply that "Clara Bow *was* the 'twenties."

SOURCES:

Bow, Clara. "My Life Story," as told to Adela Rogers St. Johns in *Photoplay.* February–April, New York, 1931.

Philadelphia Free Library, Theater Collection.

Shipman, David. *The Great Movie Stars: The Golden Years.* Rev. ed. New York, 1979.

Stenn, David. *Clara Bow: Runnin' Wild.* NY: Doubleday, 1988.

SUGGESTED READING:

Morella, Joe, and Edward Epstein. *The "It" Girl: The Incredible Story of Clara Bow.* New York, 1976.

Rosen, Marjorie. *Popcorn Venus.* NY: Coward, 1973.

Robert H. Hewsen, Professor of History, Rowan University, Glassboro, New Jersey

Bowen, Betty (1775–1865).

See Jumel, Eliza Bowen.

Bowen, Catherine Drinker (1897–1973)

American author whose biography,* Yankee from Olympus, *was an immediate critical and popular success. *Born Catherine Shober Drinker on January 1, 1897, in Haverford, Pennsylvania; died on November 1, 1973, in Haverford; youngest of six children of Henry Sturgis (a lawyer and longtime president of Lehigh University) and Aimee Ernesta (Beaux) Drinker; attended St. Timothy's, Catonville, Maryland; Peabody Conservatory of Music, Baltimore, Maryland; Institute of Musical Art, New York; married Ezra Bowen (an economist), in 1919 (divorced 1936); married Thomas McKean Downs (a surgeon); children: (first marriage) Ezra (b. 1921) and Catherine Drinker (b. 1924).*

Selected works: The Story of an Oak Tree *(1924);* A History of Lehigh University *(1924);* Rufus Starbuck's Wife *(1932); (with B. von Meck)* Friends and Fiddlers *(1935);* Beloved Friend: The Story of Tchaikowsky and Nadejda von Meck *(1937);* Free Artist: The Story of Anton and Nicholas Rubinstein *(1939);* Yankee from Olympus: Justice Holmes and His Family *(1944);* John Adams and the American Revolution *(1950);* The Writing of Biography *(1951);* The Biographer Looks for News *(1958);* The Lion and the Throne: The Life and Times of Sir Edward Coke, 1552–1634 *(1959);* Adventures of a Biographer *(1959);* The Nature of the Artist *(1961);* The Historian *(1963);* Francis Bacon: The Temper of a Man *(1963);* Miracle at Philadelphia: The Story of the Constitutional Convention, May to September, 1787 *(1966);* Biography: The Craft and the Calling *(1969);* Family Portrait *(1970);* The Most Dangerous Man in America: Scenes from the Life of Benjamin Franklin *(1974).*

Catherine Drinker Bowen

Catherine Drinker Bowen, who was destined to become a highly respected biographer, devoted much of her early life to the pursuit of music, even bypassing college to play her violin. After a year of musical study in Baltimore, where her first orchestra conductor suggested that she "put her fiddle in the oven and burn it," she went on to obtain a teacher's certificate from the Institute of Musical Art in New York. She eventually abandoned thoughts of a musical career to marry Ezra Bowen, an economist at Lehigh University. Two children followed, a boy and a girl, while Catherine occupied her spare time writing articles on music and other subjects for popular periodicals including *Current History*, *Pictorial Review*, and the *Woman's Home Companion*. After experimenting with a children's book, a local history, a novel, and a book of essays on music and musicians, she eased into what would become her specialty—biography.

In 1936, Bowen divorced and returned to her hometown of Haverford, Pennsylvania, keeping her ex-husband's name for the sake of her children and budding literary career. (In 1939, she would marry Dr. Thomas McKean Downs and be known to her friends as "Mrs. Dr. Downs.") Bowen's first biographies centered on men of music. *Beloved Friends: The Story of Tchaikowsky and* ***Nadejda von Meck*** (1937), based on letters by the composer and his wealthy patron, was highly praised, especially by music critics. It became a Book-of-the-Month Club choice and was translated into several foreign languages. Her second biography, *Free Artist: The Story of Anton and Nicholas Rubinstein*, dealt with the Rubinsteins' relationship to the musical and political worlds of late tsarist Russia. Meticulously researched in museums and libraries in Russia, Germany, and France, as well as through interviews with people who had known the musicians, the book was considered even superior to the well-received *Beloved Friends*.

Bowen found an even more comfortable niche with biographies focusing on the men who shaped American constitutional law, the first of which centered on Chief Justice Oliver Wendell Holmes, Jr. With the avowed intention "to bring Justice Holmes out of legal terms into human terms," Bowen undertook four years of research on the background, family, and career of the Supreme Court justice. The resulting book *Yankee from Olympus: Justice Holmes and His Family* (1944) was an immediate critical and popular success. The book was praised as a lively, readable account of the man, but many objected to its "fictionalized" form. Max Lerner, also an author of a book on Holmes (*The Mind and Faith of Justice Holmes*), remarked, "the semi-fictional form becomes in itself a symbol of the effort, in the literature of recognition, to make things easy that will never be anything but hard."

Bowen too disapproved somewhat of her own literary choices, but went on to say, "without the scenes I have to create, my biographies read like children's notebooks." She next undertook scholarly, though still lively, accounts of John Adams and Sir Edward Coke, with the latter winning a prize from the American Philosophical Society as well as a National Book Award. After a study of Francis Bacon in 1963, her book *Miracle at Philadelphia*, which focused on the interactions and compromises necessary for the adoption of the Constitution, became assigned reading for political-science majors at hundreds of colleges.

In spite of the enormous amount of hours devoted to research and writing, Bowen also found time for both her family and her music. Reportedly, one of her greatest wishes was to play a quartet with Albert Einstein. She occasionally strayed from biography to take up the topic of biographical writing; *Adventures of a Biographer* (1959) and *Biography: The Craft and the Calling* (1968) offer readers insight into her travels, and the ups and downs of the research trail. Bowen's last book was *The Most Dangerous Man in America: Scenes from the Life of Benjamin Franklin*, which was published in 1974, a year after her death. In addition to exploring five periods in his life, the book contains Bowen's personal, and very positive, reflections on the American diplomat, author, and scientist.

SOURCES:

Current Biography 1944. NY: H.W. Wilson, 1944.

Mainiero, Lina, ed. *American Women Writers: A Critical Reference Guide from* Colonial Times to the Present. *NY: Frederick Unger, 1979.*

Barbara Morgan,
Melrose Massachusetts

Bowen, Elizabeth (1899–1973)

Irish novelist and short-story writer of the acclaimed* House in Paris, Death of the Heart, *and* In the Heat of the Day, *whose novels focused on the world of the middle and upper classes and the cracks in their veneer. *Name variations: Mrs. Alan Cameron. Pronunciation: BOH-en. Born Elizabeth Dorothea Cole Bowen in Dublin, Ireland, on June 7, 1899; died on February 22, 1973; buried in the churchyard near grounds of what was once Bowen's Court; only child of Henry Bowen and Florence (Colley) Bowen; married Alan Cameron, on August 4, 1923; no children.*

Selected writings: Encounters *(short stories, 1923);* Ann Lee's *(short stories, 1926);* The Hotel *(Constable, 1926);* The House in Paris *(1935);* The Last September *(1929);* Joining Charles *(short stories, 1929);* The Death of the Heart *(1938);* Seven Winters *(childhood memoirs, Cuala Press, 1942);* Bowen's Court *(a history of the Bowens in County Cork, 1942);* The Demon Lover *(short stories, 1945);* A World of Love *(1955);* In the Heat of the Day *(1959);* A Time in Rome *(1960);* Afterthought *(essays and short stories, 1962);* The Little Girls *(1963);* A Day in the Dark *(collection, 1965);* Eva Trout *(1968).*

Born on June 7, 1899, Elizabeth Bowen spent her early years with her parents at Bowen's Court in what she called, "psychological closeness to one another and under the strong rule of the family myth." The court was built in 1775 and handed down from a long line of Protestant Bowens, but it was never finished for lack of funds. Hardly grand, the house was drafty, damp, and sparsely furnished; though there were two waste closets in the tower, bathrooms would not arrive until 1950 (to the dismay of Bowen's American editor ***Blanche Knopf**, maids brought tin baths to the rooms). Bowen admitted that the house had a Charles Addams quality—"If you want anything, just scream"—but it was filled with life. On the eve of World War II, she would write a history of this family home (*Bowen's Court*, 1942).

Bowen's father, a barrister, was unworldly and introspective; he was also obstinate and rejected the traditional Bowen prescriptions for success: possessions, horses, and upper-class bias. Not interested in being a gentleman farmer like his father, Henry Bowen took pride in accomplishment rather than displays of wealth. **Florence Bowen**, Elizabeth's mother, was a font of ideas and described as rebellious, funny, and vague.

In accordance with Henry's law practice, the family spent half the year at their house in Dublin, where Elizabeth attended dancing school, took walks with her governess, and went to Sunday services at the Protestant St. Stephen's. Bowen was barely aware that she was in the doctrinal minority; she realized only that she went to church once a week while Roman Catholics were called to mass seven days a week, suggesting to her some "incontinence of the soul."

Elizabeth loved her mother, while her mother, having waited nine years to conceive a child, doted on her. "She thought of me constantly," wrote Bowen, "and planned ways in which we could meet and be alone." Florence's gregarious nature could not abide children who "burrowed when they were introduced," so she brought up her daughter to be a social maven, an inveterate partygoer and partygiver who thrived on company. Bowen's opening line in *The Last September* describes the arrival of guests, "About six o'clock, the sound of a motor, collected out of the wide country and narrowed under the trees of the avenue, brought the household out in excitement on to the steps."

When Bowen was five, her father left the bar for the Irish Land Commission, a job which came with enormous pressure. No one noticed anything too unusual until Henry po-

Elizabeth Bowen

litely rose in the middle of a contractual negotiations meeting and tossed all the legal documents out the window. Though the elder Bowens had a happy marriage, wrote biographer **Victoria Glendinning,** they "were accustomed to living together in long phases of happy absence of mind, punctuated by moments of impetuous communication"; thus, Florence was one of the last to know that the pressure was undoing her husband, and Elizabeth pursued, as she later wrote, a "campaign of not noticing."

Once the severity of the situation was realized, the family hastened Henry to England for treatment. On his return, he was still unstable, and, following an episode in which he became violent, checked himself into a mental hospital. Though the strain brought mother and daughter closer, according to Glendinning, it left Bowen with the slight stammer which would remain with her into adulthood, especially when tired. The stammer, however, never interfered with her speaking engagements. In later years, when one member of the British Council queried another on her effectiveness as a lecturer in light of her stammer, the reply was decisive: "She is a *most* successful lecturer with a *most* successful stammer."

At age seven, Bowen moved to England with her mother. Struggling financially, they rented villas along the Kent coast and were tended by a swarm of maternal aunts and cousins. Over the next five years, they were constantly on the move, with Elizabeth's schooling spotty at best since her mother was intent on not "tiring her brain." Florence blamed brain tiring on her husband's difficulties.

What [Elizabeth Bowen] saw was an Eden in the seconds after the apple has been eaten, when Evil was known, immanent and unavoidable but while there was still awareness of what Innocence had been.

—Spencer Curtis Brown

By the time Elizabeth, known as Bitha, turned 12, her father was back at work and began to visit. Though her parents had never been closer, her mother was reluctant to return to Ireland; she also had just been informed that she had cancer. Following an operation, she was warned that she had six months to live. "I have good news," Florence told a sister-in-law; "now I'm going to see what Heaven's like." She died less than two months later at the end of September 1912, and Elizabeth moved in with relatives and sobbed into the night. Writes Glendinning, "One of the words at which her stammer consistently balked her was 'mother.'"

Royde-Smith, Naomi. See *Macaulay, Rose for sidebar.*

Bowen was brought up by a regiment of aunts in Harpenden, surrounded by a slew of cousins. Socially, school was her salvation. Largely unsupervised, she took up cursing and witchcraft with ease. Summers were spent at Bowen's Court with her father, and her childhood has been described as "protracted."

In September 1914, Bowen entered Downe House, a girls' boarding school near Orpington, Kent. Its headmistress **Olive Willis**, formerly of Somerville College, Oxford, had started the school in 1907 with **Alice Carver**, the international hockey player. Though the powerful Willis disdained "silliness," vocal amusement was the school currency. As one graduate remarked about the effects of her education at Downe House, "To this day, the briefest lull at a luncheon or a dinner party is instantly filled by me with remarks of an inanity which startles even my children."

Elizabeth was a voracious reader, exulting in ***E. Nesbit**, ***Baroness Orczy**, George Macdonald, and H. Rider Haggard's *She*. She would later acknowledge Dickens and ***Jane Austen** as major influences. When she began writing and producing revues, she took to walking around without her glasses for vanity's sake. Thus, her writing focused on nearby detail. In later life, while engrossed in talking, Bowen once walked into a hedge, then backed out "like a bus," recalled Stuart Hampshire, and kept on talking. Known as observant, analytical, and empathic, she had a sense of the comic. A year after she graduated in the summer of 1917, her father remarried; fortunately, Bowen liked her stepmother and visits to Bowen Court revolved around seeking invitations to garrison dances. She soon fell in love with a British army lieutenant John Anderson, but the engagement fell through.

Though Bowen had longed for a career as an artist, she began writing stories at age 20. She determined that all writers lived in London, and so sought out a London aunt and moved there. Olive Willis, her boarding-school headmistress, knew author ***Rose Macaulay**, and the connection produced an invitation to tea. The meeting with Macaulay "lit up a confidence I never had," wrote Bowen, and introduced her to **Naomi Royde-Smith**, then editor of the *Saturday Westminster*, in which Bowen saw her first published story. Invited to Macaulay and Royde-Smith's literary gatherings, Bowen met many important writers, including ***Edith Sitwell**, Walter de la Mare, and Aldous Huxley.

In 1923, Bowen's first collection of short stories, *Encounters*, was published. The same year, she married Alan Charles Cameron, a 30-year-old war veteran with two years at Oxford, who was then working as assistant secretary for education for Northamptonshire. "Their marriage," writes Glendinning, "which as the years passed sometimes seemed incomprehensible to the outside world, lasted." Alan doted on Bowen and took good care of her; he also took charge of her wardrobe, for she was not known for her fashion sense. Though in later years Bowen was often absent, she always returned to Alan.

Within the next two years, she wrote two books, a collection of stories titled *Ann Lee's* and her first novel *The Hotel* (which would be published by Constable in 1926). "I was now located," she wrote, "the mistress of a house; and the sensation of *living* anywhere, as apart from paying a succession of visits, was new to me." Having signed with an agent, she was selling stories to magazines in England and the United States. Bowen once described her subject as "human unknowableness. . . . The stories are questions asked: many end with a shrug, a query, or, to the reader, a sort of over-to-you." Her early fiction concerned pent-up characters who, in her words, lived "life with the lid on." Her camera was always panning just off to the side.

In 1925, when Alan was appointed secretary for education at Oxford, the couple moved there and would stay for the next ten years. They soon became friends with John and **Susan Buchan** and Lord David Cecil. During these years, Bowen would produce at least one book a year, including her second novel *The Last September* which was based on the world of Bowen's Court. Her father Henry, again plagued by mental illness, died in 1930, leaving the court to his daughter. Though she continued to live at Oxford, in summer she entertained at Bowen's Court, even though the house was forever a drain on her budget. She could not bear to sell it.

In 1931, Bowen began to review for *The New Statesman* and *The Tatler*. She also published two novels in quick succession, *Friends and Relations* (1931) and *To the North* (1932). In 1933, she fell in love with a man who has gone nameless; he was eight years her junior and engaged to be married. Well into their affair, he did marry, and, though his new wife was aware of Elizabeth, the affair continued. Bowen hung on, "living," she said, "at full height." But she found it hard to separate the fiction from the fact of the relationship. She wrote to him: "One may—I may—easily forget that a relationship with a person isn't a book, created out of, projected by, one's own imagination and will. That it is not, in fact, a one-man show. And that the exacerbations, perils and snags of joint authorship all lie in wait. That is where I went wrong with you." The affair would not end until 1936, when he took a job abroad. The year after, Bowen's *A House in Paris* was published.

The book, which drew on her love affair (there would be others), was her friend ***Virginia Woolf**'s favorite. Though she had previously cautioned Bowen about being too clever, Woolf wrote that in *A House in Paris*, "the cleverness pulls its weight instead of lying to dazzle on the top." Bowen would be a house guest of Leonard and Virginia Woolf just a few weeks before Virginia committed suicide in March 1941. Wrote Bowen:

> The last day I saw her . . . I remember her kneeling on the floor—we were tacking away, mending a torn Spanish curtain in the house—and she sat back on her heels and put her head back in a patch of early spring sun. Then she laughed in this consuming, choking, delightful, hooting way. And *that* is what has remained with me.

Bowen hated the tragic portrayals of Woolf thereafter and longed for a biographer to portray her friend's "capacity for joy."

In 1935, Alan had been appointed secretary to the Central Council of School Broadcasting at the BBC, and they moved to a terrace house in Regent's Park, London, where Bowen, called by **Elizabeth Jenkins**, "the last *salonnière*," became an enthusiastic host. Like Woolf, Bowen began a series of mentorships with young writers, including ***May Sarton**, who describes her in *A World of Light: Portraits and Celebrations*:

> Hers was a handsome face, handsome rather than beautiful, with its bold nose, high cheekbones, and tall forehead; but the coloring was as delicate as the structure was strong—fine red-gold hair pulled straight back into a loose knot at her neck, faint eyebrows over pale-blue eyes. I was struck by her hands, which she used a great deal, often holding one in the air before her with a cigarette in it. They were awkwardly large; the heavy bracelets she wore became them.

Through all this, Alan seems to have been an outsider, but Bowen was loyal and always spoke of him with respect. A good husband, he was much smarter than her dinner-table compatriots gave him credit. Bowen was dependent on him, especially in practical matters; once, as he watched her struggle with Britain's new dialing system, he cracked: "Just watch the *whole great mind* concentrate itself on a mere telephone." It's thought that Alan knowingly suffered her infidelities; some said he may have considered it a small price to pay for such a fascinating wife.

In 1937, Bowen was made a member of the Irish Academy of Letters. The following year, she published one of her most popular books, *The Death of the Heart*. Though she continued to produce short stories, nonfiction, and fiction reviews (as a reviewer she was reputed to be a soft touch), it would be 11 years before her next novel.

In 1939, when Britain took on the Nazi Axis, Alan joined the Home Guard, and Elizabeth became an air-raid warden. "Air raids were much less trying," she said, "if one had something to do." Early in the war, a V-1 bomb touched down across the street from their house in Regent's Park, wrecking every room. In the summer of 1944, the house was hit again; the blast blew out all the windows and brought down the ceilings. Despite the fact that they narrowly escaped alive, Bowen wrote Edmund Wilson that she was enjoying London during the blitz. "Everything is very quiet, the streets are never crowded, and the people one dislikes are out of town."

World War II effectively took the lid off Bowen's life. It brought her in contact with people she would have rarely gotten to know, producing an effect she described as "the thinning of the membrane between the this and the that." The result was *In the Heat of the Day*. Published in 1949, the book has become the classic novel of London during the war years. "I suppose you must know, inside you, what you've done," wrote her old school friend ***Rosamond Lehmann**. "The sustained excitement, the almost hyper-penetration, the pity and terror. It is a great *tragedy*. Oh, and the wild glorious comedy, the pictorial beauty, the unbearable re-creation of war and London and private lives and loves. You do, you really *do*, write about love."

Now recognized as a major novelist, Bowen was named Commander of the British Empire in 1948, and Alan began taking over her business dealings. For the next two years, she made lecture tours outside the country for the British Council and was asked, along with one other woman, Dame ***Florence Hancock**, to join the Royal Commission on Capital Punishment (the commission reported in 1953 in favor of abolition). In 1949, Trinity College, Dublin, awarded Bowen an honorary D.Litt., and, in 1951, Harrap published *The Shelbourne*, her popular history of the Dublin hotel. With all this activity, her writing suffered.

In 1952, she and Alan began to spend more time at Bowen's Court. Alan, who had sustained an eye injury in WWI, was now losing sight in his good eye and had to resign his job at the BBC. He died on August 26th of that year. Bowen would later write her American publisher Alfred Knopf, on the death of her friend Blanche Knopf: "I felt maimed when Alan died—after twenty-nine years together. That is the last thing he would have *wanted* me to feel; so I suppose it has been partly for his sake that I have tried to live my life well since." Alan's pension could not cover Bowen's predilection for picking up the tab for all comers. She worked hard to ease the debt, writing for magazines, especially American magazines that paid well. But, in 1959, she had to sell Bowen's Court to pay off debts, and the buyer demolished the house soon after.

From 1952 until her death, Bowen lived a nomadic existence. She spent a good deal of time in America, where she formed a close friendship with ***Eudora Welty** and lectured at a host of universities. Popular with students, she was writer-in-residence at Vassar as well as the American Academy in Rome and had a fellowship at Bryn Mawr. But Bowen regarded herself as an intuitive writer, not an intellectual, saying, "I am fully intelligent only when I write. I have a certain amount of small-change intelligence, which I carry round with me as, at any rate in a town, one has to carry small money, for the needs of the day, the non-writing day. But it seems to me I seldom purely *think* . . . if I thought more I might write less."

In 1962, she sublet a flat in Oxford. One year later, *The Little Girls* was published, and she bought a small house in Hythe, on the Kent Coast where she had lived years before with her mother. "I suppose I like Hythe out of a back-to-the-wombishness, having been there as a child in the most amusing years of one's childhood—8 to 13. But I can't see what's wrong with the womb if one's happy there, or comparatively happy there."

In 1969, Elizabeth Bowen undertook her autobiography *Pictures and Conversations*. In early 1972, she lost her voice and was diagnosed with cancer of the lungs. She died on the morning of February 22, 1973, and was buried in Farahy churchyard near her husband and her father, just across from the grounds of Bowen Court.

SOURCES:

Bowen, Elizabeth, V.S. Pritchett, and Graham Greene. *Why Do I Write?* London: Percival Marshall, 1948.

Brooke. Joselyn. *Elizabeth Bowen*. London: The British Council, 1952.

Glendinning, Victoria. *Elizabeth Bowen: A Biography.* NY: Alfred A. Knopf, 1978.

Kenney, Edwin J. *Elizabeth Bowen*. Lewisburg, PA: Bucknell University Press, 1975.

Lehmann, Rosamond. *The Swan in the Evening*. London: Collins, 1967.

Sarton, May. *A World of Light: Portraits and Celebrations*. NY: Norton, 1976.

Bowen, Gretta (1880–1981)

Irish artist. *Born in Dublin, Ireland, on January 1, 1880; died on April 8, 1981, at age 102; married*

Matthew Campbell; children: three sons, including George and Arthur Campbell, both painters.

Born in Dublin in 1880, Gretta Bowen was married in her early 20s to Matthew Campbell with whom she moved to Belfast. Upon her husband's death in 1925, left with little money and three sons, she took student boarders into her home in the university district. Bowen's own talent was discovered when she was in her 70s, after she worked with some paint left behind by her sons George and Arthur who had become painters. She agreed to exhibit only under her maiden name, not wanting to ride the coattails of her son George who had already made a name for himself. She exhibited three times in Belfast under the Arts Council of Northern Ireland, and her work was sold to patrons in England, America, France, and Morocco. In 1979, when she was 100 years old, Bowen was invited to contribute to the first international exhibition of naïve art. Her primitive paintings of childhood scenes, combined with her advanced age, inevitably brought comparisons with ***Grandma Moses**, who was 20 years her senior. In 1975, the Arts Council of Northern Ireland commissioned her son George to paint her portrait. Bowen's work is represented in the Ulster Museum.

Bowers, Jess (1900–1973).

See Buffington, Adele.

Bowers, Lally (1917—)

***English actress.** Born Kathleen Bowers on January 21, 1917, in Oldham, Lancashire, England; daughter of Albert Ernest and Kate (Richardson) Bowers; attended Hulme Grammar School, Oldham.*

After working as a secretary, Lally Bowers studied with James Bernard before joining the Shakespeare Memorial Theater, Stratford-on-Avon, working as an understudy and taking small walk-on roles. After additional experience at Manchester Repertory (1936–38) and Sheffield (1938–43), Bowers joined the Old Vic Company. During the 1943 season, her roles included Nora in *A Doll's House* and Viola in *Twelfth Night.* Her first appearance on the London stage was at the Phoenix Theater, on June 7, 1944, as Norrie in *The Last of Summer.*

Lally appeared in repertory and London productions for three decades, winning the Clarence Derwent Award in 1958 for her role as Madame de Montrachet in *Dinner With the Family.* Her single New York appearance was as Mrs. Mercy Croft in *The Killing of Sister George* at the Belasco Theater in October 1966. Bowers' own favorite roles included Candida, Lady Cicely Wayneflete in *Captain Brassbound's Conversion*, Mrs. Millamant in *The Way of the World*, and Maggie Hobson in *Hobson's Choice.*

Barbara Morgan,
Melrose, Massachusetts

Bowles, Camilla Parker (b. 1949).

See Parker-Bowles, Camilla.

Bowles, Caroline (1786–1854).

See Southey, Caroline Anne Bowles.

Bowring, Eva Kelly (1892–1985)

***U.S. Senator, Republican of Nebraska, 83rd Congress, April 16, 1954–November 7, 1954.** Born in Nevada, Missouri, on January 9, 1892; died in Gordon, Nebraska, on January 8, 1985; married, in 1924 (widowed); married Arthur Bowring, in 1928.*

Eva Kelly Bowring

Eva Kelly Bowring came to the U.S. Senate by way of Governor Robert B. Crosby, who appointed her to fill the vacancy caused by the death of Senator Dwight Griswold. She was sworn in on April 26, 1954, and her term, according to Nebraska law, would run until the next general election, when another candidate would be selected to finish out Griswold's term.

Bowring brought with her political experience and a personal understanding of the needs of Nebraska's agricultural constituents. While helping her second husband work his cattle ranch near Merriman, Nebraska, she was active in local Republican politics and in the Nebraska Stockgrowers Association. She later served eight years as vice chair of the Nebraska Republican Central Committee and was director of women's activities for the Nebraska Republican Party.

Her tenure in the Senate included membership on the Committee on Interstate and Foreign Commerce, the Committee on Labor and Public Welfare, and the Committee on Post Office and Civil Service. Bowring's first speech on the Senate floor was to advocate a program of flexible agricultural price supports. She also sponsored legislation providing for flood control works in the Gering Valley of Nebraska and, with senator Hugh A. Butler, introduced a bill for the construction of the Red Willow Dam and Reservoir.

In June 1954, Bowring announced that she would retire from the Senate rather than enter the election for the two-month term to complete Griswold's tenure. She then served on the national advisory council of the National Institutes of Health and on the board of parole of the Department of Justice. She died on January 8, 1985, in Gordon, Nebraska.

SOURCES:

Office of the Historian. *Women in Congress, 1917–1990.* Commission on the Bicentenary of the U.S. House of Representatives, 1991.

SUGGESTED READING:

Donovan, R.G. "Lady from the Sand Hills," in *Independent Woman 33.* June 1954, pp. 204–06.

Barbara Morgan,
Melrose, Massachusetts

Box, Betty (1920—)

British film producer. *Name variations: Betty Rogers. Born on September 25, 1920, in Beckenham, Kent, England; sister of producer Sydney Box; sister-in-law of writer-director* ***Muriel Box;*** *married Peter Rogers (a director-writer), in 1949.*

Filmography—as producer: The Seventh Veil *(1945);* The Years Between *(1946);* Dear Murderer *(1947);* When the Bough Breaks *(1947);* Miranda *(1948);* The Blind Goddess *(1948);* Vote for Huggett *(1948);* Here Come the Huggetts *(1948);* Don't Ever Leave Me *(1949);* The Huggetts Abroad *(1949);* So Long at the Fair *(1950);* The Clouded Yellow *(1950);* Appointment with Venus *(1951);* The Venetian Bird *(1952);* A Day to Remember *(1953);* Doctor in the House *(1954);* Mad About Men *(1954);* Doctor at Sea *(1955);* Checkpoint *(1956);* Iron Petticoat *(1956);* Doctor at Large *(1957);* Campbell's Kingdom *(1958);* A Tale of Two Cities *(1958);* Carve Her Name With Pride *(1958);* The Wind Cannot Read *(1958);* The 39 Steps *(1959);* Conspiracy of Hearts *(1960);* No Love for Johnnie *(1961);* No, My Darling Daughter *(1961);* A Pair of Briefs *(1961);* The Wild and the Willing *(1962);* Doctor in Distress *(1963);* Hot Enough for June *(1964);* High Bright Sun *(1965);* Deadlier Than the Male *(1966);* Doctor in Clover *(1966);* Nobody Runs Forever *(1968);* Some Girls Do *(1969);* Doctor in Trouble *(1970);* Percy *(1970);* The Love Ban *(1972);* Percy's Progress *(1973);* It's Not the Size that Counts *(1974).*

Dubbed "Miss Box Office" by the British press, Betty Box was one of the most prolific and commercially successful producers in the history of British cinema. She was trained as a commercial artist but developed a taste for motion pictures while working as a "tea girl" at Gainsborough Studios. Her brother, producer Sydney Box, was engaged in the financial reorganization of a failing production company called Verity Films. Within a year, Sydney transformed Verity from near bankruptcy to the largest documentary production company in Britain. His wife ***Muriel Box** directed many of the documentaries, and Sydney put his sister Betty, who began with the company in 1940, in charge of several filmmaking units. Betty Box had produced close to 200 British propaganda films by war's end.

When Box returned to Gainsborough Studios after the war, it was as a full-fledged producer with a reputation as a shrewd executive. She launched her first feature film, *The Seventh Veil* (written by her sister-in-law Muriel), in 1945. In 1947, Betty produced *Dear Murderer* with a script co-written by Muriel, Sydney, and Peter Rogers. Though the film proved only a semi-successful adaptation of a play, Peter Rogers had cast his fate with "The Box Team" as Betty, Muriel and Sydney were often called. Betty and Peter were married in 1949.

The following year, Box began what would be her most important professional collaboration. Beginning in 1950, her work with the

From the movie The 39 Steps, *starring* Kenneth More, *produced by* Betty Box.

British director Ralph Thomas yielded more than 20 years of lightweight, skillfully executed, and commercially successful movies. Winning popular success, though not critical recognition, the Box-Thomas team primarily entertained a middle-class English audience that was anxious to forget their everyday cares. Her three decades of filmmaking earned Betty Box, along with Ealing Studios' Michael Balcon, consideration as one of Britain's two dominant early postwar feature producers.

SOURCES:

Barr, Charles. *International Dictionary of Films and Filmmakers: Writers and Production Artists.* Vol 4. Edited by Samantha Cook. Detroit, MI: St. James Press, 1993.

Heck-Rabi, Louise. *Women Filmmakers: A Critical Reception.* London: Scarecrow Press, 1984.

Deborah Jones,
Studio City, California

Box, Muriel (1905–1991)

English writer, director, and producer. *Name variations: Violette Muriel Baker, Lady Gardiner. Born Violette Muriel Baker in Surrey, England, in 1905; died in 1991; attended Holy Cross Convent, Wimbledon, Right Street Polytechnic, Surbiton High School, and*

Pitman's College; married Sydney Box, on May 23, 1935 (divorced 1969); married Sir Gerald Gardiner, a Lord Chancellor, on August 28, 1970; children: (first marriage) Leonora (b. November 5, 1936).

Filmography—as screenwriter: Alibi Inn *(1935);* The Facts of Love *(1945);* The Seventh Veil *(1945);* The Years Between *(1947);* Here Come the Huggetts *(1948);* Holiday Camp *(1948);* The Smugglers *(1948);* The Brothers *(1948);* Dear Murderer *(1948);* Easy Money *(1949);* The Blind Goddess *(1949);* Daybreak *(1949);* The Girl in the Painting *(1949);* Christopher Columbus *(1949);* A Girl in a Million *(1950);* Good Time Girl *(1950);* The Lost People *(1950);* Mr. Lord Says No! *(1952);* Street Corner *(1952);* Both Sides of the Law *(1954);* A Novel Affair *(1957);* The Truth About Women *(1958).*

Filmography—as producer: The Smugglers *(1948);* Dear Murderer *(1948);* The Brothers *(1948);* A Girl in a Million *(1950);* The Truth About Women *(1958).*

Filmography—as director: Mr. Lord Says No *(1952);* Street Corner *(1952);* A Prince For Cynthia *(1953);* Both Sides of the Law *(1954);* The Beachcomber *(1955);* Simon and Laura *(1956);* Cash on Delivery *(1956);* Eyewitness *(1956);* A Novel Affair *(1957);* The Truth About Women *(1958);* This Other Eden *(1959);* Subway in the Sky *(1959);* Too Young To Love *(1960);* The Piper's Time *(1962);* Rattle of a Simple Man *(1964).*

From age ten, when she "took impish delight in bursting into outrageous mime," Muriel Box knew she was destined for a career in show business. At 16, most likely against her parents' wishes, she talked her way into a job as a motion-picture extra. At 17, as a rebellious teenager, she left a not-so-cryptic note to her parents that said, "gone to the devil," then set out to make a name for herself. For the next 40 years, Box wrote, co-wrote, produced, or directed some 70 plays, numerous documentaries, and over three dozen feature films, making her one of the most prolific talents of the British stage and screen.

Her career was launched in 1929 when she started working as a shorthand-typist in the scenario department for British Instructional Films. She learned to write movie scripts on the fly when the paid scenarists, accustomed to writing silent movies, had difficulty writing dialogue. Box was only too happy to offer dialogue suggestions to the delight of grateful writers. For the next few years, her jobs ranged from continuity "girl," to casting assistant, to reading scripts, a position that would later be termed "director of development." The variety of her experience gave Box the opportunity to learn the nascent industry from the ground up.

In 1932, she met and fell in love with Sydney Box, an established journalist who moonlighted as a playwright. Married with two children, Sydney divorced his wife and married Muriel on May 23, 1935, beginning a personal and professional collaboration that would last three decades. Though their first screenplay, *Alibi Inn*, was well received, the Boxes remained tied to the theater; by 1939, the team had written more than 50 one-act plays, several full-length plays, and the librettos for a number of musicals.

With the advent of World War II, Sydney took over a failing production company called Verity Films. From 1939 to 1945, the Boxes wrote, and Muriel directed, documentary films for the British war effort. Sydney's sister ***Betty Box** joined the duo as their producer.

Muriel and Sydney worked exclusively in features following the war. Their first effort, *29 Acacia Avenue*, was passed over by critics as too simplistic or "just entertainment," but it heralded a long line of films made by the couple that were financially and popularly successful. In retrospect, Muriel Box's work has been considered pioneering. In 1952, she made the extremely popular *Street Corner*, a realistic portrayal of women on the police force, one of the first to deal with that subject matter. She followed it with another success in the same genre, *Both Sides of the Law*.

In 1958, Box directed and co-wrote with Sydney her favorite film, *The Truth About Women*. The movie was humorous, openly feminist, and the most expensive she ever directed. Costing £183,000, it was shot in color, had 40 sets, and lavish costumes designed by Cecil Beaton. The film opened to mostly upbeat reviews. In *Films and Filming* (April 1958), reviewer Derek Conrad found it: "excellently acted, beautifully photographed . . . and well directed." Philip Hartung writing in *Commonweal* called the film a "tour de force." Much to Box's dismay, however, *The Truth About Women* did not fare as well at the box office as was hoped.

In 1959, Sydney had a breakdown brought on by stress. Though Muriel continued her work, her husband handed over his part of the business to brother-in-law Peter Rogers. Though the couple was unaware at the time, Sydney's collapse signalled the beginning of the end of their collaboration.

Muriel Box's last feature film, *Rattle of a Simple Man*, concerned an innocent and lonely working-class man who has a chance encounter with an equally lonely, if not so innocent, prostitute. The film was taken to task for treating the subject matter too simplistically. Wrote *Commonweal*'s critic: "Muriel Box has directed her characters well but *Rattle*, in spite of its occasional poignant moments, has to be chalked up as just another fanciful movie." If Box was ultimately disappointed by the way her films were received, it never seemed to deter her.

In 1964, she published her first novel, *The Big Switch*, to glowing reviews. Not long after, the Boxes separated. Sydney relocated to Australia while Muriel co-founded a publishing company, Femina Books, with fellow writers ***Vera Brittain**, ❧▸ **Anona Winn**, and **Anne Edwards**. Box wrote the first book published by the company, a biography of feminist pioneer ***Marie Stopes**. In 1969, she divorced Sydney, and, on August 28, 1970, married Sir Gerald Gardiner, a lord chancellor, thus becoming Lady Gardiner. In 1974, she wrote her autobiography, *Odd Woman Out*. Muriel Box died in 1991.

Though often criticized for making popular, rather than artistic, films, the Boxes dominated the British film industry when it came to mass producing entertaining movies that consistently made a profit. Whereas a man who directed such films might be praised as a "master of entertainment," the few women directors of Box's day were held to a different standard. For her part, Muriel Box was ahead of her time when it came to writing leading roles for women. The number of movies she co-produced, scripted, or directed remained unmatched by any other woman filmmaker at the close of the 20th century.

SOURCES:

Box, Muriel. *Odd Woman Out*. London: Leslie Frewin, 1974.

Heck-Rabi, Louise. *Women Filmmakers: A Critical Reception*. London: Scarecrow Press, 1984.

Deborah Jones,
Studio City, California

Boyce, Neith (1872–1951).

See Glaspell, Susan for sidebar.

Boyd, Ann Carr (b. 1938).

See Carr-Boyd, Ann.

Boyd, Belle (1844–1900)

Confederate patriot and spy who engaged in courier and espionage activities throughout the Civil War, became revered as a symbol of Southern independence and pride, and later wrote her memoirs and gave dramatic readings of her war exploits. *Born on May 9, 1844, in Martinsburg, Virginia; died on June 11, 1900, in Kilbourn (now Wisconsin Dells), Wisconsin; daughter of Benjamin Reed Boyd (a business owner) and Mary Rebecca (Glenn) Boyd; graduated from Mount Washington Female College near Baltimore (a finishing school); married Samuel Wylde Hardinge, on August 25, 1864 (later missing, presumed dead); married John Swainston Hammond, on March 17, 1869 (divorced, November 1, 1884); married Nathaniel Rue High, Jr., on January 9, 1885; children: (first marriage) Grace; (second marriage) Arthur, Byrd, Marie, John.*

Belle Boyd grew up in the Virginia town of Martinsburg, commonly referred to as the "Northern Gateway to the Shenandoah," which was to become the center of activity during the impending Civil War; 112 military engagements would occur in the region. Combined with her family's 130-year loyalty to their homeland, Boyd could hardly have chosen more fitting circumstances to become the celebrated spy and Southern patriot, the "Siren of the Shenandoah."

Maria Isabella Boyd was born on May 9, 1844, the first of eight children, four of whom died in infancy. The Boyds owned a successful business, allowing the family a comfortable life. "I passed my childhood as all happy children usually do," she wrote in her memoirs, "petted and caressed by a father and mother, loving and beloved by my brothers and sisters." From this safe environment grew an impulsive, athletic, and headstrong girl who was a skilled horsewoman to boot.

At age 12, Boyd was sent to Mount Washington Female College outside Baltimore, a finishing school designed as much to educate as to build and polish Southern womanhood. She excelled at her school work and participated in animated political debates with her fellow classmates. Following her graduation in the fall of

❧▸ Winn, Anona

Australian-born radio singer and revue artist.

Trained as a lawyer, Anona Winn found fame as a singer with the help of ***Nellie Melba**. Following World War II, Winn was a popular member of the game-show panel on the BBC's "Twenty Questions."

Belle Boyd

1860, Boyd had her "coming out" in the city of Washington. Chaperoned by her mother **Mary Rebecca Boyd**, Belle experienced the excitement of the big city as only a debutante could. There were lavish parties, visits to the theater, musical performances, and a general rubbing of elbows with important government officials.

While Boyd enjoyed societal perks, serious political events were fomenting. For years the issues of states' rights, political underrepresentation, and slavery had been simmering in the South. The election of antislavery candidate Abraham Lincoln to the office of president in November 1860 brought them to a boil. South Carolina seceded from the Union the following month and, along with Alabama, Mississippi, Georgia, Florida, Texas, and Louisiana, formed the Confederate States of America in February 1861. With hostilities seemingly imminent, Boyd and her mother returned to Martinsburg the following spring, eager to do their part to help the Confederacy. They didn't have long to wait.

As the war heated up, Union Brigadier General Robert Patterson crossed the Potomac River into Virginia and on the 3rd of July, captured Martinsburg. The Union's victory celebration was paired the following day with the observance of Independence Day, July 4. Drunken soldiers brawled among themselves and vandalized the small town. When rumors were circulated that Belle Boyd had decorated her room with rebel flags, an angry mob gathered and forced their way into her home, only to find it void of Confederate paraphernalia. (Boyd's vigilant servant had quickly burned the flags before the mob arrived). Desiring satisfaction, the troops attempted to attach a Union flag to the house. This piqued Boyd's mother; Mary Boyd told the crowd that every member of her household "would die before that flag shall be raised over us." With that, a foul-mouthed soldier insulted her. "I could stand it no longer," wrote Belle; "my indignation was roused beyond control; my blood was literally boiling in my veins; I drew out my pistol and shot him. He was carried away mortally wounded, and soon after expired." Enraged, the mob tried to burn down the house. A Federal officer arrived in time to quell the crowd.

During the forthcoming hearing, it was obvious that Boyd was guilty of the killing; surprisingly, she was acquitted and told she had "done perfectly right." Speculation strongly suggests that this decision was politically based, an attempt to keep other states from seceding from the Union. Convicting and imprisoning (or executing) a 17-year-old Southern girl would have made Belle Boyd a martyr for the Confederate cause. So, as would often happen in her dealings with the Union, she slipped through the cracks.

As a result of the shooting, however, sentries were ordered to watch her home and unwittingly fostered her apprenticeship in espionage. While engaged in banter with the Union sentries, she found that tidbits of useful military information could be extracted. Flattered by her compelling laugh, the soldiers had no idea of her more ambitious intentions. "Belle Boyd was a lively, spirited young lady, full of caprices and a genuine Rebel," wrote one young Union Major William E. Doster. He described her as "tall, with light hair and blue eyes," though her "features were too irregular to be pretty." Boyd's "air of joyous recklessness" is what made her most appealing.

In order to expedite the removal of the Federals from Martinsburg, Boyd began sending covert messages concerning camp talk she had overheard. Her plan worked briefly, until one of her secret dispatches was intercepted. Boyd had made the amateurish mistake of writing the note by hand and not using code or cipher. Though her lack of remorse or repentance infuriated the Union officer overseeing her investigation, yet again she was released.

Later that July, at the battle of Bull Run, the Union line was pushed back to the Potomac River, defeated. It was a major turning point in the war. Boyd took this opportunity to travel to Manassas to visit her father who had enlisted in the Confederate army. During her stay, she worked as a military courier and assisted, among others, General Stonewall Jackson and General Pierre Beauregard with their communications. She had discovered her true calling; the use of her talents to further the Southern war effort.

While staying in the Union-controlled town of Front Royal, she was courted by an eager Union officer, Captain Keily. After being showered with flowers, gifts, and the needed information, she promptly left the man heartbroken. In another incident, Boyd lacked the proper passes to take an out-of-town trip. Feigning helplessness, she convinced a Union lieutenant to escort her; she even had him carry one of her packages. When stopped by authorities, the packages were found to be Confederate dispatches, labeled with the friendly Union officer's name (a deed Boyd had secretly accomplished). Suspicion was turned to the officer, and she was once again released. The unfortunate lieutenant was later court-martialled and dismissed from the service.

In May of 1862, Union forces assembled for an offensive strike in the Shenandoah Valley, while Confederate general Stonewall Jackson marched north toward Front Royal. When he reached the outskirts of town, the occupying Union army was caught off guard. Boyd could see the Confederates in the distance and realized that, if Jackson attacked now, he could take the town. With no thought of herself, she dashed out on foot to inform the Southerners. Sporting a white sun-bonnet and a blue dress covered by a white apron, Boyd made an inviting target. Yet she endured musket and cannon fire from the town, while also braving the Confederate crossfire. The image of a young Southern lady risking death while running to assist her nation was nothing short of heroic. Upon reaching the soldiers and catching her breath, Boyd instructed them to attack the town immediately, and the Confederates, led by Jackson, fought and captured Front Royal. Boyd received a "thank you" letter from Jackson, and all marveled at the bullet holes which peppered her dress but never touched her. Several days later, however, the town was reoccupied by Union forces, hot on the heels of the retreating Jackson. Even so, a legend had been born.

Curiously, the Federals tolerated Boyd's presence in Front Royal, despite her acts against the Union and new-found status as a symbol of Southern pride. Their restraint was made clear when she was caught giving messages to two "Confederate" soldiers. In fact, the men were Union spies who had devised the scheme to entrap her. This time there was no escape; the secretary of war had ordered her into custody, to be delivered to Washington. In July of 1862, Boyd was brought to the Old Capital Prison in Washington, which was used primarily to house inmates guilty (or presumed so) of offenses associated with the war. Though government officials attempted to coerce her to swear allegiance to the Union, she stood her ground. While interned, Boyd's prison experience was mitigated by gifts of food from well-wishers and an accommodating warden who promised "whatever you wish for, ask for it and you shall have it." After a month of confinement, she was released in a prisoner exchange and sent south to Richmond.

> Belle Boyd was a "most dangerous rebel, and a malignant enemy of the Federal Government."
>
> **—Annie Jones, informant**

Boyd's reputation preceded her. When she renewed her acquaintance with Jackson, she "received my commission as Captain and honorary Aide-de-camp." Her position included all the perks of an officer, and her example was to be an inspiration to the troops. But in the spring of 1863, after several months of touring the South, Boyd received a harsh blow. Jackson, her hero and mentor, had died from wounds received in the battle of Chancellorsville. Stunned and confused, she longed for consolation from her family. Support would come at some risk, however, as Martinsburg was again held by the Union. Damning the odds, she headed for home.

On arrival, Boyd learned that her mother was pregnant and in ill health and that her father was home on medical leave from the military. Perhaps to stall until further orders, the Union officers allowed her to care for her parents. Finally, in the late summer of 1863, she was arrested and again sent to Washington. This time, Boyd was kept in the Carroll Prison, not far from her former accommodations. By now the "Rebel" was accustomed to prison life and easily adapted to the routine. Her pluckiness was not the least diminished. While the prison superintendent was in an adjoining room, she bribed a guard for his bayonet and used it to gouge a hole in her cell wall in order to communicate with her neighbor.

After prolonged delays over several months, Boyd was sentenced to "banishment to the South—never to return North again during the war." Upon her departure, contraband consisting of Confederate letters of introduction, "twenty thousand dollars in Confederate notes, five thousand in greenbacks, and nearly one thousand in gold," was discovered hidden in her dress.

Shortly after her release, her father passed away. Because of her "banishment" from Union occupied territory, she was unable to visit her family and fell into a depression lasting several weeks. Still burdened by her father's death but wanting yet again to contribute to the war effort, Boyd decided to act as a courier of Confederate dispatches to the capitals of Europe. However, the vastly superior Union navy had done a thorough job of blockading the Southern ports, strangling the South's trade and making sea voyages hazardous. Ignoring the risks, Boyd traveled to Wilmington, North Carolina, in May of 1864 and boarded the blockade runner, *Greyhound*. Despite precautions, including a night-time departure, the ship was discovered and pursued by a Union warship. The luckless *Greyhound* was then boarded, confiscated, and put in the command of a Union officer, Lieutenant Sam Hardinge. In her autobiography, Boyd admits to an immediate attraction to the handsome and dashing officer, which was soon to be returned. Two days after their meeting, Hardinge proposed marriage. Even though enthralled, Boyd was still on duty. "If he felt all that he professed to feel for me," she wrote, "he might in future be useful to us." She kept the love-struck lieutenant in suspense as he escorted the *Greyhound* to Boston. Once there, in an unusual twist, Boyd agreed to marry the Yankee officer.

Her loyalties were immediately put to a test. While the *Greyhound* was at anchor, its Confederate captain had somehow escaped to shore and eluded capture. Along with several others, Hardinge was charged with having assisted in the escape. His "wife to be" pleaded ignorance when in fact she had helped plan and execute the scheme. Though cleared of complicity, Boyd was in violation of her previous parole agreement, never to return North. Through the intervention of friends and family, she was exiled to Canada with the knowledge that "if I was again caught in the United States, or by the United States authorities, I should be shot." Boyd departed, leaving her fiance to fend for himself.

Not long after her arrival in Canada, Boyd was certain she was being followed by Federal agents. On the advice of friends, she boarded a ship for England. There she met with Hardinge, who had been suddenly dismissed from the navy (why he was not prosecuted is unclear). Following a joyous reunion, they were married in London on August 25, 1864. Shortly thereafter, Hardinge returned to the United States, ostensibly to get acquainted with his new wife's family. Modern historians speculate that he may have been involved in Boyd's espionage work, for he was arrested and jailed. Stories conflict as to his fate: some say he was released and returned to London; others say he drowned at sea or died in prison. In any event, one thing is certain; several months after being arrested, Sam Hardinge disappeared forever without a trace.

Alone, pregnant, and stranded in a foreign country, Boyd wrote and published her memoirs and began an acting career, debuting in the (Manchester) Theatre Royale's rendition of *The Lady of Lyons*. After giving birth to her first child (by Hardinge), she returned to the postwar United States in 1866.

Belle Boyd had lived a lifetime in a short 22 years and was now ready to take a slower pace. She continued her touring theatrical career, often billing herself as "The Rebel Joan of Arc" or "The Cleopatra of the Secession." At the age of 24, she retired to marry businessman John Hammond in March of 1869. The couple had four children and often relocated according to Hammond's business dealings. After 15 years, they divorced, and she married Nathaniel Rue High, Jr., an actor. By necessity, Boyd returned to the stage; this time, she gave dramatic readings of her Civil War exploits entitled "North and South, or, The Perils of a Spy." She died on June 11, 1900, while on tour in Kilbourn (now Wisconsin Dells), Wisconsin.

Though her work was not as strategically oriented as that of other spies because she lacked the anonymity required to obtain such information, Belle Boyd's noteworthy accomplishments were two fold. First, she was able to gain practical, short-range military information from a direct source—the soldier. Second, and probably most significant, she was a symbol of defiance and pride. While originally supporting the Confederate cause, in later years her image would represent the newly rejoined Union. Northerners identified with her staunch patriotism and loyalty and adopted Belle Boyd as a common nationalistic symbol. Ironically, the woman who fought the Union tooth and nail was now its hero.

SOURCES:

Bowman, John S., ed. *The Civil War Almanac.* NY: World Almanac, 1983.

Boyd, Belle. *Belle Boyd in Camp and Prison.* Cranbury, NJ: Thomas Yoseloff, 1968.

Current, Richard N., ed. *Encyclopedia of the Confederacy.* Vol. I. NY: Simon and Schuster, 1993.

Denney, Robert E. *The Civil War Years: A Day-by-Day Chronicle of the Life of a Nation.* NY: Sterling, 1992.

Faust, Patricia L., ed. *Historical Times Illustrated Encyclopedia of the Civil War.* NY: Harper & Row, 1986.

Johnson, Allen, ed. *Dictionary of American Biography.* Vol. I. NY: Scribner, 1964.

Markle, Donald E. *Spies and Spymasters of the Civil War.* NY: Hippocrene Books, 1994.

Scarborough, Ruth. *Belle Boyd; Siren of the South.* Macon, GA: Mercer University Press, 1983.

Sobol, Donald J. *Two Flags Flying.* NY: Platt and Munk, 1960.

Van Doren Stern, Philip. *Secret Missions of the Civil War.* NY: Bonanza Books, 1990.

SUGGESTED READING:

Sigaud, Louis A. *Belle Boyd; Confederate Spy.* Richmond, VA: Dietz, 1944.

Matthew Lee,
Colorado Springs, Colorado

Boyd, Louise Arner (1887–1972)

American explorer and geographer who was the first woman to make a successful flight over the North Pole. *Born on September 16, 1887, in San Rafael, California; died on September 14, 1972; only daughter and one of three children of John Franklin (a mining operator) and Louise Cook (Arner) Boyd; attended Miss Stewart's School, San Rafael; Miss Murison's School, San Francisco.*

Louise Boyd has been described as a woman of paradoxes: a rugged adventurer who sloshed about on ship's deck in oil skins and hip boots and trekked across a mountain of icy rocks, while clinging to accepted expressions of femininity and claiming no use for masculine women. "At sea, I didn't bother with my hands, except to keep them from being frozen," she said. "But I powdered my nose before going on deck no matter how rough the sea was. There is no reason why a woman can't rough it and still remain feminine." The first woman to gain status in polar expedition, Boyd set her own standard.

Boyd grew up the daughter of a mining magnate in an opulent mansion in San Mateo, California, and enjoyed the privileges of wealth, including private schools, riding and shooting lessons, and an extravagant social debut. Clouding her young life, however, were the deaths of all her immediate family. Her invalid brothers were both born with rheumatic hearts and bedridden until their deaths in their teens. By the time Boyd was 32, both her parents had also died, leaving her the sole heir of Boyd Investment Company. As pointed out by **Elizabeth Olds** in *Women of the Four Winds*, freed of family responsibilities and with plenty of money, Boyd could have chosen "anything from a morbid retreat to an unbridled plunge into the reckless self-indulgence and profligacy of the 1920s." Boyd opted for the middle ground of travel, making two relatively conventional European tours with her friend **Sadie Pratt**, the socialite widow of General Conger Pratt.

Louise Arner Boyd

With no apparent motivation other than to indulge a girlhood interest in the Arctic, Boyd planned her first cruise to Iceland, Greenland, and Lapland in 1924. Aboard a small tourist ship, she wrote of her extraordinary experience.

"Far north, hidden behind grim barriers of pack ice, are lands that hold one spellbound. Gigantic imaginary gates . . . seem to guard these lands. The gates swing open, and one enters another world where men are insignificant amid the awesome immensity of lovely mountains, fiords, and glaciers." This trip was a turning point for Boyd and became the impetus for the seven expeditions to the Arctic that were to follow.

Boyd returned to Greenland in 1926 to organize her own expedition. Aboard the chartered Norwegian motorship *Hobby*, she led several friends on what was primarily a hunting expedition to Franz Josef Land (the northernmost land in the Eastern Hemisphere), but which included the beginning of the extensive photography of the Arctic that would ultimately become Boyd's legacy. (Olds describes her pictorial documentation: "every aspect of landscape from distant perspectives to close-up studies of cliffs, glaciers, inlets, ice in every form, animals, plants—an archive that would become of immense usefulness to her country during World War II.") The expedition returned with a number of polar bears; some reports cite as many as 29. Years later, when hunting safaris became less admired, Boyd said the number was exaggerated and denied shooting the animals for anything but food.

When Boyd, while preparing another trip to the Arctic in 1928, learned of the disappearance of polar explorer and Norwegian hero Roald Amundsen, she immediately joined in the search. Donating her ship *Hobby* and other resources to the efforts of the French and Norwegian governments, Louise undertook her own three-month, 10,000-mile search, making extensive photographic records of her journey, including 20,000 feet of motion-picture film and thousands of still photographs. Although Amundsen was never found, Norway acknowledged Boyd's efforts by awarding her the decoration of the Order of St. Olaf, first class, and naming her a Chevalier of the French Legion of Honor.

Louise Boyd made four additional expeditions from Norway aboard the *Veslekari*—in 1931, 1933, 1937, and 1938—and included the regions in and around Franz Josef Land, Spitsbergen, Greenland, Jan Mayen Island, and eastern arctic Canada. She was the first to sail to the inner ends of Ice Fjord, Greenland. The Danish government would name the territory, in the vicinity of the de Geer glacier, Louise A. Boyd Land. During her 1938 expedition, she traveled further north along the Greenland coast than any other American had ever traveled by sea.

Most of Boyd's expeditions were carried out under the auspices of the American Geographical Society, to which she reported her scientific findings. This association enabled Boyd to incorporate an interdisciplinary approach to her geographic studies which added to the scientific integrity of her expeditions. The society also published her books on the Arctic (*The Fiord Region of East Greenland* in 1935 and *Coast of Northeast Greenland* in 1949) as well as articles which appeared in its quarterly *Geographical Review*. (Boyd also wrote a non-Arctic book, *Polish Countrysides*, which was published by the society.) In 1960, to honor her long association with the society, Boyd would be elected to its council, the chief policy-making body, thus becoming the first woman councilor in the association's 108-year history.

In 1941, she was employed as a technical expert for the National Bureau of Standards, and in 1942 and 1943 she worked for the War Department, providing thousands of maps, photographs, and scientific reports on the strategic Arctic areas she had visited. For her contribution, the Department of the Army awarded her its Certificate of Appreciation for outstanding patriotic service.

When at home on her suburban estate, Maple Lawn, with a staff of nine (including a personal maid who accompanied her on her expeditions), Boyd was the grande dame of San Francisco society. Between her expeditions, she maintained a highly visible civic role in the Bay area. For years, she was a member of the board of the San Francisco Symphony, and she served as an officer of the San Francisco Garden Club and the California Botanical Society, among others. Boyd also attended every important social event and was described by society reporters as "strikingly handsome." Always impeccably dressed, with a trademark camellia—from her prize-winning greenhouse—pinned on her shoulder, she once remarked, "I don't feel dressed unless I'm wearing flowers. Even in Greenland I'd find something and wear it with a safety pin."

At age 67, Boyd fulfilled her childhood dream of going to the North Pole. On June 16, 1955, she chartered a plane in Norway and, with an American crew, made a successful flight over and around the North Pole, taking photographs of the area. In an article for *Parade* magazine, she described the moment of encounter: "For directly below us, 9,000 feet down, lay the North Pole. No cloud in the brilliant blue sky hid our view of this glorious field of shining ice. Suddenly I felt we had an invisible passenger—the Almighty." Although this marked her final expedition, she continued to spend four or five months out of the year in travel. In 1967, at age 80, she was honored at the annual Explorers Club Dinner in Manhattan as "one of the world's greatest woman explorers."

Toward the close of her life, Boyd's health deteriorated, and her finances mysteriously evaporated, leaving her in the support of a few generous friends. She died in a nursing home on September 14, 1972, days before her 85th birthday. Her dying wish had been to have her ashes scattered over the polar region in Greenland that had been named in her honor. However, problems and costs connected with reaching the site were insurmountable and the ashes were alternatively scattered in the last polar region Boyd had visited in Alaska, over the ice of the Arctic Ocean.

SOURCES:

Current Biography 1960. NY: H.W. Wilson, 1960.

Olds, Elizabeth. *Women of the Four Winds.* Boston, MA: Houghton Mifflin, 1985.

SUGGESTED READING:

Waldman, Carl, and Alan Wexler. *Who Was Who in World Exploration.* NY: Facts on File, 1992.

Barbara Morgan,
Melrose, Massachusetts

Boyd, Mary (fl. 1487)

Scottish royal. *Name variations: Marion Boyd. Flourished around 1487; daughter of Archibald Boyd of Bonshaw; first wife or paramour of James IV (1473–1513), king of the Scots (r. 1488–1513); children: Alexander Stewart, archbishop of St. Andrews (c. 1487–1513); Catherine Stewart (d. after 1554, who married James Douglas, 3rd earl of Morton).*

Boye, Karin (1900–1941)

Swedish writer who is often considered Sweden's greatest woman poet. *Born in Göteborg on October 26, 1900; walked into the woods on April 23, 1941, and was found dead, apparently a suicide, a few days later; daughter of Carl Fredrik "Fritz" Boye (manager of an insurance business) and Signe (Liljestrand) Boye; attended a private junior school in Göteborg; married Leif Björk (divorced); no children.*

Selected works: Moln *(Clouds, 1922);* Gömda land *(Hidden Lands, 1924);* Härdarna *(The Hearths, 1927);* Astarte *(1931);* Merit vaknar *(Merit Awakes, 1933);* Kris *(Crisis, 1934);* För trädets skull *(For the Tree's Sake, 1935);* För lite *(Too Little, 1936);* Kallocain *(1941); (published posthumously)* De sju dödssynderna *(The Seven Deadly Sins, 1941).*

Widely regarded as Sweden's greatest woman poet, Karin Boye lived a short life marked by the struggle to understand and be worthy of her own personal freedom. In her youth, the conflict between her religious callings and her growing awareness of her sexual preference for women foretold the passions and contradictions with which she would live and ultimately choose to die. With her suicide, at age 40, following the warm reception of her prose masterpiece *Kallocain*, a voice that had spoken to the universal defeats and triumphs of existence was silenced, yet the honesty of her poetry and prose secured for Boye a reputation from which to inform future generations about her most private, as well as life's most public, dilemmas.

She was born at the turn of the century, on October 26, 1900. Originally from Bohemia, Boye's paternal family had produced men who typically engaged in commercial and financial activity in South America and Europe. Her grandfather established a cotton and textile importing business in Göteborg, the place of Karin's birth, and took up Swedish citizenship in 1849. Karin's father Fritz was head of Göteborg's Svea Fire-Life Company; he married one of his employees, **Signe Liljestrand**, 18 years his junior, whose vitality is said to have complemented his retiring, somewhat dour disposition. Karin was the first of their several children.

Extremely well-read in European classical literature, Karin's mother Signe provided her initial education while Fritz Boye remained a distant, relatively insensitive figure in his children's upbringings. His speculative, imaginative mind, however, foreshadowed his daughter's inclinations, as did Signe's interest in spiritualism and oriental religions. At her private junior school in Göteborg, Karin—described as a "round, soft little girl"—made a lasting impression on her first teacher. Boye's biographer **Margit Abenius** writes that in these early years Karin outdistanced her schoolmates, often answering questions posed to her "with a little rhyme or other inventive and well-chosen words."

Fritz Boye suffered from an emotional instability that perhaps contributed to the distance he maintained from his children. In 1909, after his early retirement due to illness, the family moved to Stockholm, and he would later serve as an inspector in the Swedish Private Insurance Supervisory Service. During these years, Karin read Rudyard Kipling, Dumas, Maeterlinck, and H.G. Wells. The poetry of Rabindranath Tagore was evidently an enormous influence, as she sought to immerse herself in Indian mythology. Making serious attempts to learn Sanskrit, she identified strongly with Buddhism and acted the part of

Karin Boye

guru as she and her friend **Signe Myrbäck** sat crosslegged together, practicing the art of breathing. When their ecclesiastical history teacher informed the class of Sweden's small minority of Buddhists, Karin maintained that she was one of them. She began a move from Buddhism toward Christianity in her last two years at school, recording her religious meditations in diaries.

Boye also wrote in her diary about her experiences at Christian summer camps where she is said by biographer David McDuff to have "approached the fairly routine group discussions with extraordinary intensity." Of the close attachments she formed to other girls and women at this time, one would be of great importance until the end of her life. Seven years older than Boye, **Anita Nathorst** was a theology and humanities student at Uppsala University who served as the group mother at the Christian summer camp Boye attended at Fogelstad. Wrote Karin to another friend: "I think I could dare to say all that I think and wonder to Anita and be certain that she would never misunderstand me. And one understands so well what she says. My goodness, it is not everyone of whom one can say that one understands what they mean." A student at Uppsala University by 1920, Boye also became a group mother. McDuff credits Nathorst with helping Boye work through her "revulsion at, and fear of, human suffering." In a letter to her friend **Agnes Fellenius**, the young Boye articulated her growing identification with Christ:

> I fancied I saw the world in a new light—in the sign of the Cross, of representative suffering. God's cross extends through every time and every space. And what else is holy communion but an initiation to the Cross, the new union with God: one initiates oneself in order for His sake to take a part of His eternal suffering—upon oneself, to fight God's fight in the world: it involves great pain.

Boye's struggle over whether to study theology—as was the wish and advice of the rector at her training college—or psychology and teaching was a major crossroad in her life. Unlike the study of theology, which she saw as an act of true self-sacrifice, the pursuit of psychology and teaching was for Boye a powerful act of self-assertion. The decision sparked a crisis that was fueled by Boye's discovery of her sexual desires for women. She would have to deny her sexuality if she pursued a career in the Church, a denial which, she felt, would kill the artist in her. "You see, there has been a hard battle within me," she wrote Fellenius, "and I have stood hesitating between whether to give up my will or to worship my will. Forgive me if I hurt you by writing this. You will quite certainly say that I did the wrong thing—I have chosen the latter." The decision, however, did not immediately resolve Boye's internal conflict. In February of 1921, the 20-year-old found a means to express her turmoil, writing the poems that would comprise her first collection, *Moln* ("Clouds"), and perhaps finding in her art a means of both sacrificing and realizing the self.

She became a student of humanities at Uppsala University, studying Greek (she wanted to read Plato in the original), Nordic languages (she was influenced particularly by the songs of the Edda), and the history of literature (which she found to discourage independent thinking). Becoming known as "Teo" to her fellow female students, she was a subject of much interest and, in McDuff's words, elicited "distant adulation" from those who encountered her. McDuff continues: "She made a striking impression. . . . Though she could not be said to be beautiful in a conventional way, her face had an openness and a sensual prettiness that were given fascination by the sense of intellectual clarity and emotional depth that lay behind them." Nonetheless, Boye had reservations about her appearance which, according to Margit Abenius, "concerned not her face but her figure, which she would have liked to be more supple and masculine. 'It's a pity I'm so ugly,' she told her friend Agnes."

Boye spent a good deal of her time at Uppsala in extra-curricular activities, serving as secretary and later president of the students' union. She had a short love affair with poet Nils Svanberg and participated in activities of the students' "messes" (*matlag*) which served as societies. The society to which Boye and Anita Nathorst belonged was largely involved with discussions of psychoanalysis, and both women were by this time adherents of Freudianism. In her last year of school, Boye joined the peace organization Clarté, of which ***Ellen Key** and ***Selma Lagerlöf** were also members. Her decision to join this idealistic group, with its left-wing, anti-religious orientation, surprised many who knew Boye, including Nathorst. Increasingly looking to Nathorst for support, Boye was prone to episodes of weeping, and her deepening awareness of her sexual orientation is said to have influenced the darker, tragic note developed in her poetry.

Published in 1924, *Gömda land* ("Hidden Lands") was considered by both Boye and the critics a better work than *Moln. Härdarna* ("The Hearths") followed in 1927, with critic Hagar Olsson (who was a close friend of Finland-Swedish poet ***Edith Södergran**) writing in the newspaper *Svenska pressen*:

> One has looked in vain for a sign of renewal within Swedish poetry. . . . [One has said to oneself:] Will there ever be a single lyre in the land of Sweden that is able to create life and tone in this oppressive, twilight-of-the-gods silence? . . . Recently a small, unassuming collection of poetry appeared: *The Hearths*, by Karin Boye. . . . The cover shines with a brilliance that is different from and more enduring than that of fame: the

> brilliance of fire fighting its way through. One reads Karin Boye, and it is with love that one commits it to memory. One thinks: here is one of the first swallows.

Olsson's review was likely responsible for adding Karin Boye's name to the list of major contemporary Swedish poets.

Fritz Boye died of cancer in 1927. The following year, Karin graduated from Uppsala and moved to Stockholm where her involvement with the Clarté movement continued. The two main threads of the movement, whose goal was world peace, centered around social transformation and inner transformation via psychoanalysis. Participating in the administration and organization of the movement, which included some five or six hundred Scandinavian political activists and radical intellectuals, Boye also edited the movement's magazine.

Precisely in *the freedom of the will* does our *unfreedom* lie. Freedom is to act in full accordance with one's nature: thus, true freedom has no choice, only one way to go.

—Karin Boye

She began psychoanalysis with Alfred Tamm, an experience, said some who knew her, which changed Boye in myriad ways. McDuff maintains that without it she likely would not have arrived at marriage. Leif Björk was a left-wing radical with whom Boye shared a common interest in psychoanalysis; their marriage, which probably did not have a strong sexual component, did not last long. "The couple," writes McDuff, "were too estranged from everyday reality, too over-complicated, and their household economy too precarious for this essentially bourgeois 'social form of love'."

Following her divorce from Björk, Boye experienced a severe depression in January 1932 and became suicidal. That month, she moved to Berlin and began analysis with the Freudian Walter Schindler. He worked with Boye for two months, during which he considered her a perplexing patient whose situation was serious. Schindler apparently remarked to a colleague: "This will end badly. Within ten years she will have taken her own life."

She then began analysis with a woman, **Grete Lampl**. In Berlin, Boye and a German-Jewish woman named **Margot Hanel**, 12 years Boye's junior, began a sexual relationship, and Boye became an editor of the Swedish literary magazine *Spektrum*, an avant-garde publication which published the early works of Harry Martinson, Gunnar Ekelöf, Boye, and other Swedish modernists. Though she also worked as a literary translator, Boye made little money, a situation compounded by the expense of psychoanalysis. Despite her precarious financial state, she attended the theater and enjoyed the cafe life of Berlin, moving with a gay crowd. In these years of Nazism, she viewed clashes between extreme left-wing and right-wing sympathizers. Boye is said to have raised her arm in the Hitler salute during an election meeting in the Sportpalast, but it must be remembered that a refusal to do so could have cost her life. McDuff maintains that there is no evidence to suggest that she ever embraced the principles of Nazism.

In addition to her poetry, Boye wrote fiction as both a means to express herself and earn a living. Novels such as *Crisis*, *Astarte*, and *Merit Awakes* have been described as schematic and "less pure" than her poetry; however, by speaking to her day's controversial issues, some of this work was undoubtedly of strong significance to her readership. The documentary novel *Crisis*, which reveals Boye's discovery of her own sexual orientation and the religious crisis of her youth, was written while discussions were taking place in Sweden around 1933 about a liberalization of the laws regarding homosexuality. Considered one of her strongest prose works, *Crisis* contributed to the continuing debate.

In 1934, Boye was back in Sweden where she purchased a small, "functionalistically cold" flat in Stockholm. Desperate from the solitude, she invited Margot Hanel to move from Berlin to be with her. Initially, the arrangement provided Boye with an unprecedented reassurance and calm. Within months, however, the jealous, dependent Hanel was refusing to let Boye see her literary friends, and Boye was retaliating with personal cruelty. As Hanel developed chronic illnesses, her emotional and physical dependence on Boye became total. Boye's novel *Too Little* was written at this time, and in 1935 her fourth poetry volume *För trädets skull* ("For the Tree's Sake") was published to mixed reviews.

The following year, she began teaching at Viggbyholm boarding school. Located near Stockholm, the school had been founded by Per Sundberg, a Christian pacifist seeking to bring together children of differing ethnic backgrounds; the school educated many children who were refugees from Hitler's Germany, as well as many children of divorce and children with developmental difficulties. Boye began by instructing very young students but soon lost control of her charges. She was then relocated to the gymnasium, or grammar school, where she became a beloved teacher. In time, she moved to Viggbyholm, and her relationship with Margot Hanel evidently took on a somewhat different tone. Boye stopped referring to her disparagingly. "It was to Margot Hanel," writes McDuff, "that Karin wrote the epigram 'To You' in July 1937."

> You my despair and my strength,
> you took all the life I owned,
> and because you demanded everything,
> you gave back a thousandfold.

Nonetheless, the problems inherent in their relationship seemed to intensify, with Boye remarking of "events that have made my life into chaos." She wrote in German to the handwriting expert, Dr. Blum: "[Y]our words about resignation hurt me a little. For I am in just such a situation where an absolute self-sacrifice—of joy in my work, of friendship, of artistic creation, of peace, of harmony—is demanded of me, and I find it so hard to make such a sacrifice—at any rate, it cannot happen with joy. Do you really believe that resignation can be the meaning of my life? (A too personal question. . . . The answer can never come from someone else.)"

On a travel scholarship from the Swedish Academy, Boye journeyed to Greece in the summer of 1938, visiting Vienna, Prague, and Istanbul en route. That autumn, she began teaching full time at Viggbyholm; the resulting strain and exhaustion were compounded by her sensitivity to the horror unraveling in Europe which saw the persecution of the Jews and the German invasion of Czechoslovakia. Her inability to write poetry crippled her spirit. Suffering from a painful nerve inflammation in one arm, she left Viggbyholm for a return to Stockholm.

Around this time, she began a more frequent correspondence with Anita Nathorst, her friend for almost 20 years. Still in love with her, Boye traveled to Alingsås, near her own childhood home of Göteborg, to attend to the ailing Anita who had contracted a form of skin cancer that was devouring her body from the outside in. Wrote Boye to a friend: "That not even the times and decline of the West should prevent one from collapsing like a house of cards and burning like a piece of tinder and that when one finally attains something that has lain in one for twenty years, the person concerned is dying of cancer. . . . We agreed that life is macabre in a way that no reforms can ever remove, macabre to its innermost kernel."

While in Alingsås, Boye corresponded with Hanel, to whom she expressed continued loyalty. The stay with Anita was accompanied by a feverish pitch of writing, resulting in a good deal of poetry and what is considered Boye's prose masterpiece, *Kallocain.* This novel, a fierce protest against totalitarianism, takes its title from a truth serum invented by Boye's character Leo Kall, a worker in a state chemical plant. In a World State of the future, reminiscent of the Nazis' Third Reich and Stalin's Soviet Union, Kall seeks to overthrow the nation. In a Europe draped with totalitarianism, enthusiastic reviews met the work's publication in 1940, with one critic calling it, "a thoroughly thought-through, thoroughly felt, one might even say thoroughly suffered work of art." Boye was among the writers and poets invited to the German-occupied Denmark for participation in a "Swedish week," during which she was introduced to the Danish royal family, and the Danish press wrote enthusiastically of her novel. Reinforcing her fame and international reputation, this experience helped insure that she would be remembered as one of Sweden's greatest poets.

Though Boye was still in Alingsås, Anita Nathorst relocated to Malmö in a move that McDuff says was perhaps not entirely motivated by medical necessity. Margot Hanel, despite the geographical separation, remained completely emotionally dependent on Boye. Doubting Nathorst, and experiencing profound ambivalence toward Hanel, Karin Boye could no longer stave off the despair that had accompanied so much of her life. Taking with her only a bottle of sleeping pills, the 40-year-old left the Alingsås house on April 23, 1941, and walked into the winter forest. Some days later, she was found dead of exposure by a passer-by. The two women whom she loved would not long survive her absence. Margot Hanel gassed herself a month after Karin's death, and in August Anita Nathorst succumbed to cancer.

Published posthumously in 1941, the collection of poetry *De sju dödssynderna* (*The Seven Deadly Sins*) is often considered Boye's finest work. The following lines in the poem "Your Voice," translated by McDuff, were written to Anita Nathorst:

> All say it: your time is short, I know.
> I cannot imagine that you will ever go.
> There is no world to live in, where you do not live.
> My mind denies the miracle. But in my heart, belief.

SOURCES:

Boye, Karin. *Complete Poems.* Translated by David McDuff. Great Britain: Bloodaxe Books, 1994.

SUGGESTED READING:

Abenius, Margit. *Drabbad av renhet* (Afflicted by Purity). Stockholm: Bonniers, 1950.

Boyer, Catherine (1773–1800).

See Bonaparte, Christine.

Boyle, Kay (1902–1992)

American expatriate writer and poet, member of the Lost Generation in the 1920s and 1930s, who battled fascism, Nazism, McCarthyism, and the Vietnam War. *Born Katherine Evans Boyle on February 19, 1902, in St. Paul, Minnesota; died on December 27, 1992, in Mill Valley, California; daughter of Katherine Evans and Henry Peterson Boyle; married Richard Brault, on June 24, 1923; married Laurence Vail (a scholar and poet), on April 2, 1931; married Joseph von Franckenstein, on February 20, 1943; children: (with Ernest Walsh) Sharon Walsh; (second marriage) Apple-Johan, Kathe, Clover, Faith Carson, Ian Savin.*

Grew up in France and Switzerland, returning to Cincinnati when World War I broke out; studied violin and then architectural studies at Ohio and Columbia universities; at 18, married and went to France; published Short Stories *in Paris (1929) followed by many other novels, poems, and nonfiction works; received a Guggenheim fellowship (1934); won the O. Henry Memorial Award for short stories "The White Horses of Vienna" (1936) and "Defeat" (1941); returned to U.S. as a celebrity to escape Hitler's armies (1941); published her novel* Avalanche *which became a bestseller (1944) and wrote extensively for magazines like* The New Yorker, Vanity Fair, *and* Harper's Bazaar; *was blacklisted for being too leftist during the McCarthy reign of terror (1950s); her husband, who worked with the State Department, also lost his job, though he was later reinstated; became a professor of English and creative writing at San Francisco State University (1963–79); a member of the Lost Generation of the 1920s, identified with the Beatniks in the 1950s and the Flower Children of the 1960s; was a passionate opponent of the Vietnam War, and antiwar experiences are recounted in* The Underground Woman *(1975).*

Selected works—novels: Plagued by the Nightingale *(Cape and Smith, 1931, reprinted with author's introduction, Virago, 1981);* Year before Last *(H. Smith, 1932);* Gentlemen, I Address You Privately *(Smith & Haas, 1933);* My Next Bride *(Harcourt, 1934, reprinted Virago, 1986);* Death of a Man *(Harcourt, 1936);* Monday Night *(Harcourt, 1938);* The Crazy Hunter: Three Short Novels *(Harcourt, 1940);* Primer for Combat *(Simon & Schuster, 1942);* Avalanche *(Simon & Schuster, 1944);* A Frenchman Must Die *(Simon & Schuster, 1946);* 1939 *(Simon & Schuster, 1948);* His Human Majesty *(Whittlesey House, 1949);* The Seagull on the Step *(Alfred A. Knopf, 1955);* Generation without Farewell *(Alfred A. Knopf, 1960);* The Underground Woman *(Doubleday, 1975).*

Nonfiction: Breaking the Silence: Why a Mother Tells Her Son about the Nazi Era *(Institute of Human Relations Press, American Jewish Committee, 1962);* The Long Walk at San Francisco State and Other Essays *(Capra Press, 1972);* Words that Must Somehow Be Said: Selected Essays of Kay Boyle, 1927–1984 *(North Point Press, 1985).*

Poetry: A Statement *(Modern Editions Press, 1932);* A Glad Day *(New Directions, 1938);* American Citizen: Naturalized in Leadville, Colorado *(Simon & Schuster, 1944);* The Lost Dogs of Phnom Penh *(Two Windows, 1968);* Testament for My Students and Other Poems *(Doubleday, 1970);* A Poem for February First 1975 *(Quercus Press, 1975).*

Short stories: Short Stories *(Paris: Black Sun, 1929);* Wedding Day and Other Stories *(Cape & Smith, 1930, reprinted Books for Libraries Press, 1972);* The First Lover and Other Stories *(Random, 1933);* The White Horses of Vienna and Other Stories *(Harcourt, 1936);* Thirty Stories *(Simon & Schuster, 1946);* The Smoking Mountain: Stories of Post-War Germany *(McGraw, 1951);* Nothing Ever Breaks Except the Heart *(Doubleday, 1966);* Fifty Stories *(Doubleday, 1980);* Life Being the Best and Other Stories *(New Directions, 1988).*

On February 19, 1902, Kay Boyle was born in St. Paul, Minnesota, to **Katherine Evans Boyle** and Henry Peterson Boyle. Financially comfortable, the family traveled constantly. Sometimes they lived in New York, sometimes they resided in France or Switzerland, and sometimes they lived in Philadelphia, where they rented a house in Bryn Mawr owned by the painter John Singer Sargent. When later asked where she grew up, Boyle replied: "It's difficult to say. I was born in St. Paul and lived there for six months. I suppose that's the nearest thing to a home that I've had over here." Boyle's education reflected the family's nomadic life, with her formal studies ending in eighth grade.

Kay Boyle was greatly influenced by her mother and namesake, **Katherine Evans Boyle**. A fervent supporter of Eugene V. Debs, leader of the American Socialist Party, Katherine was a liberated woman. She was a friend of photographer Alfred Stieglitz, and, like him, took this art

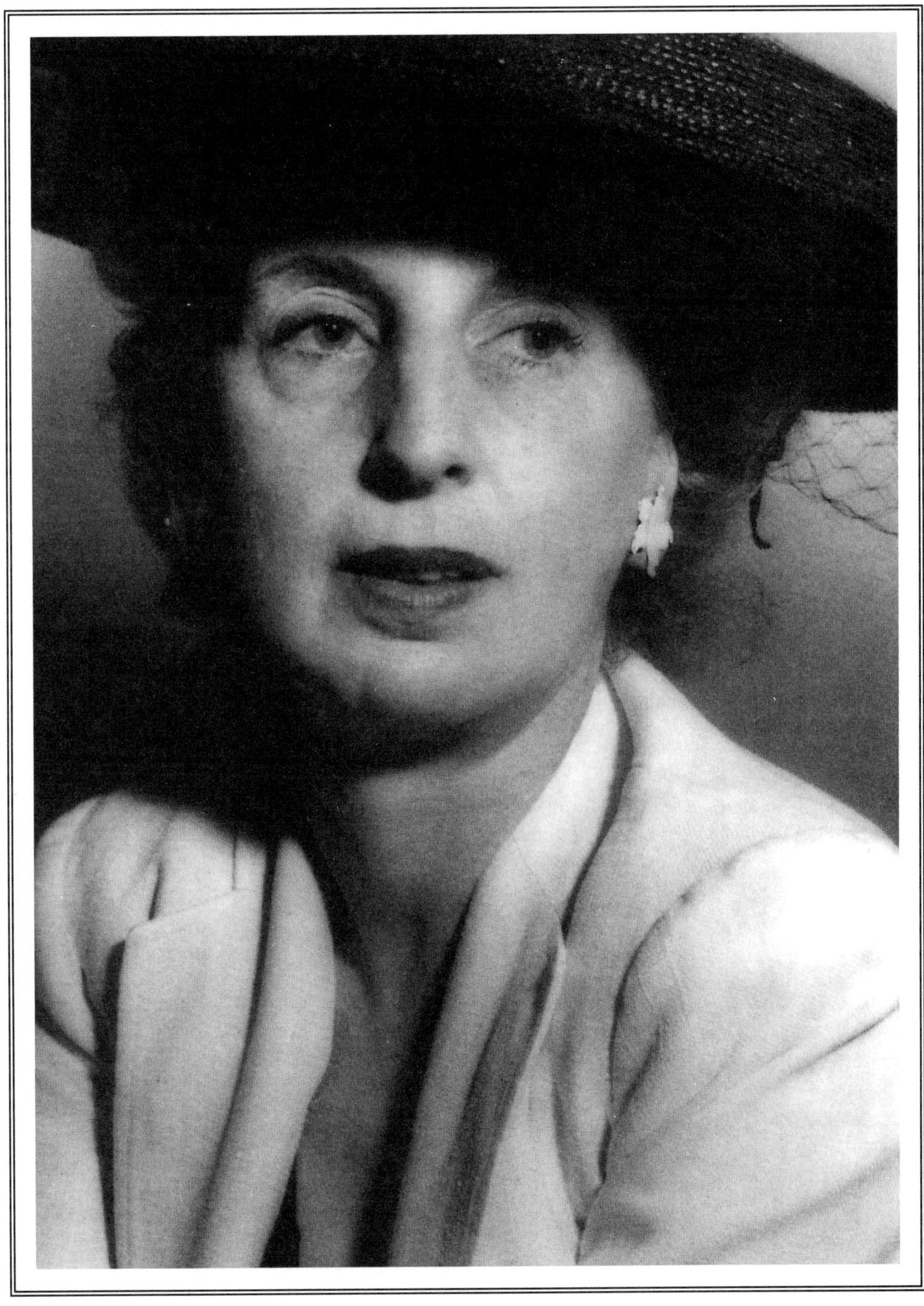

Kay Boyle

form seriously. Katherine's father-in-law deemed photography an inappropriate occupation for a woman of her status. She eventually abandoned this "unwomanly pursuit" when pressure from him, her constant travel, and her growing involvement with her daughters, Janet and Kay, demanded much of her time. Nonetheless, Katherine remained a great advocate of the arts, believing that her daughters' best opportunities to express themselves would come in this area. Music, art, and literature were strongly encouraged in the Boyle household, and, as a child, Kay filled notebooks with stories and poems. When she grew older, she also played the violin. Boyle studied architecture at Ohio and Columbia universities, never forgetting her mother's belief that art could offer a woman an individual identity.

When Kay was 16, her father's business failed, and subsequent economic troubles changed her life. In 1922, she moved to New York City to work at *Broom* magazine in which several of her pieces appeared. At 18, she married Richard Brault, a young French engineer she had met in Cincinnati in June 1922. The following year, they visited Richard's family in northern France. Though they intended to return to the U.S. on an advance Boyle hoped to secure from a publisher, their plans went awry when Richard fought with his family and the publisher's advance failed to materialize. In his book about American writers in Paris in the 1920s, Humphrey Carpenter describes the living conditions faced by the now-stranded couple:

> They set up home in LeHavre on the pittance Richard was being paid for his work there with an electric company. Their apartment was cold and primitive; all the water had to be carried from a pump half a mile up the hill; they shared a stinking outside lavatory; and it took Kay most of the morning to get the coal stove alight so that she could begin to cook.

Under these harsh circumstances, Boyle's health deteriorated, and she contracted tuberculosis. In 1925, Ernest Walsh, a young American poet and editor, asked Boyle to contribute to *This Quarter*, a new avant-garde magazine. When he discovered that she was ill, he cabled her: "Insist that you see my lung specialist in Paris. I will take care of everything. *La vie est belle*. We want you to join us here. Come quickly." Under doctor's care, her health improved, and she soon joined Walsh, known as Michael to his friends, and **Ethel Moorhead**, his co-editor and financial backer, at their villa in Southern France. In the warm sun, Boyle flourished, and her health improved. She soon realized she had fallen in love with Walsh. Pregnant with his child, she confessed the affair to her husband.

Strangely enough, Richard joined his wife and her lover in Southern France, and the two men became friends. When Michael suffered a series of hemorrhages from a previous lung injury, Richard nursed him. Walsh died on October 16, 1926, in Monte Carlo. In March 1927, Kay gave birth to their daughter Sharon. Although she and Richard remained on good terms, their marriage was clearly over. Boyle returned to Paris with Sharon where she joined a communal art colony led by Raymond Duncan, ***Isadora Duncan**'s brother. Garbed in togas and sandals, the group subsisted on goat cheese and yogurt. Boyle spent several years in the commune before becoming disillusioned with Raymond's covert materialism. During this time, she formed a lifelong friendship with playwright Samuel Beckett.

In 1931, Boyle married Laurence Vail, a scholar and poet. During this second marriage, she published a great deal and raised a large family. (She would eventually have six children.) The family led a nomadic life, moving frequently throughout Europe, living in France, Austria, Spain, and England, to take advantage of the best exchange rate as a means of preserving their income. Boyle's reputation as a writer grew steadily, and, in 1934, she was awarded a Guggenheim fellowship for her work. In 1936, she won the O. Henry Memorial Award for her short story, "The White Horses of Vienna." The title alludes to those "relics of pride," the famous Lippizaner horses, which in the story symbolized Europe's disintegration after World War I. Focusing on the relationship between two doctors—one Jewish and the other Nazi—who are drawn together by circumstance, the work is a classic tale of human relationships under difficult circumstances. In 1941, she would win the O. Henry prize a second time for her short story "Defeat."

Boyle was a prolific writer, whose volumes of fiction, poetry, and nonfiction challenged the status quo. Much of her work from this period reflected the increasingly grim political situation on the Continent, recording the collapse of democracy as fascism swept across Western Europe in the years between two World Wars. Many of her stories are about people living in small French villages whose lives are altered by political chaos. Expatriate women and stateless men struggle against circumstances beyond their control. An outspoken critic of Nazism, Boyle's anti-fascism began to cause problems in her second marriage. Determined to help Jewish and leftist refugees flooding France to escape to freedom, she undertook the extremely dangerous job of obtaining false papers for as many as she could. Though Vail grew increasingly concerned with his wife's activities and begged her to stop, Boyle was undaunted.

The outbreak of World War II exacerbated tensions in their marriage. While helping refugees obtain false papers to escape from Europe, Boyle met a Viennese aristocrat Joseph von Franckenstein. Their burgeoning relationship had little in its favor. Joseph was several years younger than Kay whose children were still quite young. The fact that Joseph soon joined the Vail household intensified the situation. The future looked quite grim in the summer of 1941; the Blitzkrieg swept over country after country as Hitler made his bid to establish the Third Reich. Realizing they must leave Europe immediately if they were to get out at all, the entire household, including Joseph, sailed for the United States.

By the time of her arrival, Kay Boyle was already a celebrity in America; her escape from Europe only enhanced her reputation. Contracts and money soon poured in. Featured in *Harper's Bazaar*, she was an elegant figure, more model than writer. Determined to end her second marriage and begin anew, Boyle believed her mission was to warn Americans about the evils of fascism while making as much money as she could. In 1944, her book *Avalanche* made the bestseller list. Her articles appeared regularly in *The New Yorker*, *Vanity Fair*, and *Harper's Bazaar*. Though the excitement of celebrity made the chaos in her personal life easier to bear, she and Vail fought bitterly over her involvement with von Franckenstein and the impact of the relationship on the children. Caught in the middle, the children often sided with their more stable father, rather than with their inconstant mother. As always, passion dominated Kay Boyle's life, and on February 20, 1943, she married Joseph von Franckenstein.

Despite what others characterized as her erratic behavior, Kay Boyle thought her life quite settled. **Joan Mellen** describes Boyle's tendency to omit inconvenient details when summarizing her own life:

> [S]he rose at seven, tended to household duties until eight-thirty, wrote until lunch, rested, might play a game of chess—this a veiled reference to Joseph who loved the game—worked until tea time, had friends to dinner, and went to bed by ten: no mention of the children in that. Kay Boyle was too honest, however, to praise her domestic skills. She could cook, she admitted, "only in a haphazard way."

Boyle was often in love and had numerous affairs. The author William Shirer was one of many who had a lifelong infatuation with her. Her inability to separate her amorous nature from daily life caused chronic chaos for her children and her spouses; she loved them, but they took a backseat to her passions. Her instability was to cause rifts with her children throughout her long life, although they usually forgave their mother's behavior.

In 1943, Joseph applied for espionage work with America's OSS (Office of Strategic Services). In February 1945, he donned a German uniform and parachuted into northern Italy with false papers. Arrested in Milan, he shot his captor on the way to Gestapo headquarters and escaped. Joseph then made his way to Innsbruck where he teamed up with Dr. Karl Gruber and Fritz Molden to create the first liberated zone in Austria. On April 28, 1945, his identity was discovered. Picked up by the Gestapo, Joseph was tortured and sentenced to death on May 1. By this time, Adolf Hitler had committed suicide and the Third Reich was crumbling. Fortunately for Joseph, American soldiers arrived in Innsbruck and his life was spared. When the war ended, Boyle was making a good deal of money in the U.S. with the promise of more to come. Joseph joined the State Department, so the couple shuttled between America and Europe, a familiar pattern which she enjoyed. But this peaceful period was short lived.

> A dangerous radical cleverly disguised as a perfect lady.
>
> **—Kay Boyle, a self-description**

During the war, the Soviets had been critical to military success; the Allies could never have defeated the Nazis without help from the USSR whose people were willing to undergo any sacrifice to save their homeland from Nazi invaders. This alliance ended with the fall of the Third Reich, and the Communists quickly replaced the Germans as enemies. In the U.S, J. Edgar Hoover began collecting information on American Communists while Senator Joseph McCarthy investigated leftist "subversives."

Kay Boyle was not a Communist, but she was an easy target for the likes of Hoover and McCarthy. For them, an eccentric lifestyle was a sure sign of political deviancy. Boyle's FBI file sums up the witch-hunters' mentality that dominated this era: "Regarding Kay Boyle Franckenstein, ——— described her as a temperamental and impulsive woman who was prone to lend her name to causes which allegedly were in the interest of the common man, whether they were or not." While in different times, support of worthless causes would not constitute a crime, during the McCarthy era such support could be very costly. Joseph Franckenstein soon lost his job with the State Department, Kay Boyle was blacklisted, and contracts with magazines like *The New Yorker* dried up.

Joseph, a war hero who had risked his life for his adopted country, and Kay, who had risked her life to combat fascism in Europe long before it was fashionable in the U.S., fought their attackers throughout the 1950s. After several years, Joseph was reinstated in his State Department job, but by this time he was suffering from cancer; he died in 1963. His death made Boyle's life more precarious financially, and, shortly thereafter, she was pleased to receive a professorship at San Francisco State University. This appointment both recognized her contribution to American literature and offered a steady income.

A member of the Lost Generation in the 1920s, Boyle now gravitated toward the Beatniks of the '50s, saying:

> It may be of interest to all of you to point out here that we expatriate writers . . . were not more respected in our time than the beatniks are today. We are looked on with a curious respect now that we are all either dead or approaching the grave. In the twenties we were not considered of much enduring value, of any value at all, by American critics or American editors or American publishers. . . . And now, even at my time of life there are long periods when I feel I am completely with and of the beatniks. The beats, for instance, are appalled by the materialism of contemporary life. . . . I, too, am appalled by this.

San Francisco provided Boyle the opportunity to develop a new identity with the flower children of the 1960s. She lived in a series of apartments in black neighborhoods where she felt at home, and she was immediately drawn to Haight Ashbury with its hippie residents. Unlike most members of her generation, she understood these young people and identified with their desire for a more equal society free from conflict. When her students began protesting against the war in Vietnam, Boyle joined them. She was jailed twice during protests against the war, experiences which are recounted in *The Underground Woman* (1975).

Kay Boyle was involved in many of the 20th century's greatest social struggles; she fought fascism in Europe and racism in the U.S. with equal fervor. Yet, she made one decision seemingly antithetical to her identity as a dedicated radical: Boyle rejected feminism totally, regarding the women's liberation movement as an attempt to segregate men and women. Throughout her life, men remained a central passion she could not live without, and she refused any part in feminism's struggle.

Old age did not temper Boyle. She traveled frequently to Europe, even when it was necessary to borrow money to do so. Her relationship with her family remained both tempestuous and loving, and her health was good except for some occasional pains in her joints. Then, in July 1992, Boyle fell and broke her pelvis. After being admitted to a nursing home, she told her family she was ready to die and stopped eating. But her resolve wavered, and she became more interested in life again, until that December when she again stopped eating. After receiving the Last Sacrament from a priest, she fell into a coma and died on December 27, 1992.

From her youth on the streets of Paris where, as an important member of the Lost Generation, she walked with Ernest Hemingway, ***Gertrude Stein**, and Samuel Beckett, to the 1960s when she marched with America's youth to protest a war half a world away, Kay Boyle led a life marked by personal, social, and political passion. Her fiery spirit and determination to fight injustice provided a small yet steady light on the dark corners of the 20th century.

SOURCES:

Bell, Elizabeth S. *Kay Boyle: A Study of the Short Fiction.* NY: Twayne, 1992.

Carpenter, Humphrey. *Geniuses Together: American Writers in Paris in the 1920s.* Boston, MA: Houghton Mifflin, 1988.

Cohen, Kay. "Oh, Kay!," in *Harper's Bazaar.* No. 3389, April 1994, p. 229.

Ford, Hugh. *Four Lives in Paris.* San Francisco, CA: North Point Press, 1987.

———. *Published in Paris: American and British Writers, Printers, and Publishers in Paris, 1920–1939.* NY: Macmillan, 1975.

Gado, Frank. "Kay Boyle: From the Aesthetics of Exile to the Polemics of Return." Ph.D. dissertation, Duke University, 1968.

Gelder, Robert van. *Writers and Writing.* NY: Scribner, 1946.

Hoefer, Jacqueline. "Boyle, Kay," in *Contemporary Novelists.* 1991, pp. 125–127.

"Kay Boyle," in *The Annual Obituary 1992.* Edited by Louise Mooney. London: St. James Press, 1992.

"Kay Boyle 1903—," in *Short Story Criticism.* Vol. 5, pp. 51–77.

"Kay Boyle, 90, Writer of Novels and Stories, Dies," in *The New York Times Biographical Service.* December 1992, p. 1684.

Loeffelholz, Mary. *Experimental Lives: Women and Literature, 1900–1945.* NY: Twayne, 1992.

Madden, Charles, ed. *Talks with Authors.* Carbondale, IL: Southern Illinois University Press, 1968.

Matuz, Roger, ed. *Contemporary Literary Criticism.* Vol. 58. Detroit, MI: Gale Research, 1990.

Mellen, Joan. *Kay Boyle: Author of Herself.* NY: Farrar, Straus & Giroux, 1994.

Sharp, Roberta. "A Bibliography of Works by and about Kay Boyle," in *Bulletin of Bibliography.* Vol. 35, no. 4. December 1978, pp. 180–189, 191.

Spanier, Sandra Whipple. *Kay Boyle. Artist and Activist.* Carbondale, IL: Southern Illinois University Press, 1986.

———. "Kay Boyle: 'No Past Tense Permitted,'" in *Twentieth Century Literature.* Vol. 34, no. 3, 1988, pp. 245–275.

West, Ray B. Jr. *The Short Story in America.* NY: Gateway Editions, 1956.

Yalom, Marilyn. *Women Writers of the West Coast: Speaking of Their Lives and Careers.* Santa Barbara, CA: Capra Press, 1983.

Karin Loewen Haag,
freelance writer, Athens, Georgia

Bozyk, Reizl (1914–1993)

Yiddish actress. *Name variations: Reizel. Born in Poland in 1914; died at St. Vincent's Hospital in New York on September 30, 1993; married Max Bozyk (a Yiddish actor; died 1970).*

Reizl Bozyk began acting in Poland at the age of five or six, performing first with her parents and then with her future husband Max Bozyk. The couple fled the Nazis in 1939, traveling first to Argentina and in 1941 to New York City. For 30 years, they worked together on New York's Yiddish stage, starring in one play or revue after another, until Max died in Reizl's arms after a performance at New York's Town Hall in 1970. Reizl Bozyk received top billing for more than 60 years. She appeared in hundreds of productions as a comedian, and later as the typical mother-in-law who often stole the show. In 1988, at age 74, she undertook her first English-language role, the matchmaking grandmother in **Joan Micklin Silver**'s "Crossing Delancey."

Brabant, countess of.

See Mary of Brabant (c. 1191–c. 1260).
See Maude of Alsace (1163–c. 1210).

Brabant, duchess of.

See Marie of France (1198–c. 1223).
See Sophia of Thuringia (1224–1284).
See Margaret (1275–1318).
See Adelaide of Burgundy (d. 1273).
See Margaret of Flanders (d. 1285).
See Marie of Evreux (d. 1335).
See Joanna of Brabant (1322–1406).

Brabant, Marie de (c. 1530–c. 1600).

See Marie de Brabant.

Bracciano, duchess of (c. 1642–1722).

See Marie-Anne de la Trémouille, Princess of the Ursins.

Brace, Julia (1806–1884).

See Bridgeman, Laura for sidebar.

Bracegirdle, Anne (1671–1748)

English actress. *Name variations: Mrs. Bracegirdle. Born in 1671; died in London, England, in 1748; buried in the cloisters of Westminster Abbey; mistress and possibly wife of William Congreve.*

Though details of her life are sparse, it is supposed that, as a child, Anne Bracegirdle was placed under the care of actor-playwright Thomas Betterton and his wife, actress **Mary Saunderson** (d. 1712). Anne is thought to have first appeared on stage in 1680 as the page in *The Orphan*'s initial performance at Dorset Garden. In 1688, at the Theater Royal, she played Lucia in Thomas Shadwell's *Squire of Alsatia*; she also played Araminta in *The Old Bachelor* in 1693. Bracegirdle's first appearance in a comedy was as Angelica in William Congreve's *Love for Love* at Lincoln's Inn Fields in 1695.

She created the parts of Belinda in Sir John Vanbrugh's *Provoked Wife* (1697), Almeria in Congreve's *Mourning Bride* (1697), and Millamant in Congreve's *The Way of the World* (1700). Bracegirdle also played the heroines in some of Nicholas Rowe's tragedies, as well as acting in contemporary versions of Shakespeare's plays. Known for her many admirers, in 1692 she was the innocent cause of the killing of actor William Mountfort, who was stabbed to death by one of her jealous suitors. Though Rowe was also devoted to her, her name has been most closely connected with Congreve. Bracegirdle was said to have been his mistress and possibly his wife, but whatever the nature of their relationship, he was at least always her intimate friend, and he is known to have left her a legacy.

In 1705, she followed Thomas Betterton to the Haymarket, where she found a serious com-

Saunderson, Mary (d. 1712)

English actress. *Name variations: Mrs. Betterton, Mrs. Saunderson. Died in 1712 (some sources cite 1711); married Thomas Betterton (1635–1710, an actor), in 1662.*

A member of the Lincoln's Inn company, Mary Saunderson was the first female actor for hire. Until then, all women had been played by men. Her husband Thomas Betterton, considered one of the great actors of the English stage, ran the Dorset Garden Theatre and the Haymarket Theatre, while Saunderson's Lady Macbeth was lauded by actor-dramatist Colley Cibber. After her husband's death, Saunderson was granted a pension by Queen Anne.

petitor in actress *Anne Oldfield (1683–1730), who was then coming into public favor. A celebrated talent competition between Bracegirdle and Oldfield took place in 1707, when each played Mrs. Brittle in Betterton's *Amorous Widow* on successive nights. According to legend, the decision as to who was the better comedy actress was left to the audience. When the vote was given to Oldfield, Bracegirdle retired from the stage in disgust, though she played once more in 1709 at a benefit for Betterton who had lost all his money from speculating.

Anne Bracegirdle had a reputation for goodness, and Lord Halifax was at the top of a long list of contributors who gave her 800 guineas, presented as a tribute to her integrity. Her charity to the poor in Clare Market and around Drury Lane was evident, wrote Colley Cibber, "insomuch that she would not pass that neighbourhood without the thankful acclamations of people of all degrees."

Bracetti, Mariana (1840–c. 1904)

Puerto Rican revolutionary. *Name variations: Braceti; Brazo de Oro (Golden Arm). Born in Añasco, Puerto Rico, in 1840; died around 1904 from aphasia; married second husband Manuel Rojas; married Santiago Labiosa.*

With her second husband Manuel Rojas, Revolutionary leader Mariana Bracetti played an important role in the Puerto Rican insurrection against Spanish rule, known as the "Grito de Lares." The couple belonged to the Lares Revolutionary Board which was founded on February 24, 1868, and Bracetti embroidered the Banner of Lares, a symbol of the First Republic of Puerto Rico. Marianna, who aborted a baby while briefly imprisoned, was released when the Spanish granted amnesty to political prisoners.

Brachvogel, Carry (1864–1942)

German-Jewish novelist and author. *Born in Munich, Germany, on June 16, 1864; died in the Theresienstadt-Terezin concentration camp on November 20, 1942; daughter of Heinrich Hellmann and Zerlina (Karl) Hellmann; married Wolfgang Josef Emil Brachvogel (died 1892); children: son, Heinz (b. 1889).*

Began in 1895 to publish a series of well-received novels; completely assimilated into German culture, made no attempt to leave Germany during the Nazi years; was deported to the Theresienstadt-Terezin concentration camp (July 1942).

Much of modern German culture was created by Germans of Jewish origin who regarded themselves as the champions and guardians of a great spiritual and artistic heritage. Pre-1914 Germany experienced considerably less anti-Semitism than Russia, Austria-Hungary, or France, and German Jews flourished in an environment that granted them civil rights as well as economic and cultural freedom. Restrictions against Jews (for example, in the military and the higher civil service) were of an "informal" nature and many expected that these would soon disappear.

Carry Brachvogel was a German-Jewish woman who took advantage of these freedoms. An author who has been largely forgotten even in Germany, she enjoyed a solid reputation in the "golden era" of pre-1914 middle-class prosperity and optimism. Born as Carry Hellmann into an assimilated and financially comfortable family in Munich on June 16, 1864, she grew up in the Bavarian capital at a time when it was enjoying a reputation as the artistic heart and soul of Germany. An intense rivalry with "soulless" Berlin convinced Munich's intellectuals that theirs was the superior German city, a warm-hearted, vibrant metropolis, tolerant toward personal eccentricity as well as generously supportive of the arts. Intensely proud of being a native of Munich, Carry married the author and editor Wolfgang Brachvogel, a Roman Catholic. Their only child, a son named Heinz, was born in May 1889. Carry's husband died in 1892, and she never married again.

Brachvogel created a series of highly regarded novels, novellas, and essays. Her first novel, *Alltagsmenschen* ("Everyday People"), was published in 1895 by S. Fischer, a publishing firm that would soon change the face of German literature by becoming Thomas Mann's publisher. *Alltagsmenschen* was a well-received study of a woman pushed toward adultery because of the boredom of her marriage. It was followed two years later by a collection of novellas written in a realistic manner; among these, *Der Erntetag* ("Harvest Day") is known as a superb study of Bavarian peasant life. Several other books by Brachvogel would appear in the years before the First World War. By the time she had reached the age of 50, her reputation as a skilled and perceptive writer was assured. She lived through the difficult years of World War I, the inflation that followed, and the Hitler *Putsch* (uprising) that convulsed Munich in November 1923. As was true of many German Jews, she never conceived of being persecuted or harmed in her own country. When the Nazis came to power in 1933,

Brachvogel remained in her native city, convinced that the troubles would pass. Instead, the situation worsened with each passing year. By September 1935, the infamous Nuremburg Laws turned her and other German Jews into second-class citizens.

By the late 1930s, Brachvogel's home offered refuge to her brother Siegmund Hellmann, a professor driven from his academic post by the Nazi terror. The start of World War II in September 1939 effectively cut off the escape for aged Jews like the 75-year-old Carry. Now a stranger in her own land, she and her brother lived from day to day, their hopes fading as Nazi armies surged across Europe. On July 22, 1942, Brachvogel and her brother were deported from Munich to the Theresienstadt-Terezin concentration camp in the occupied Czech Republic. Despite the cultivated image of normality at this camp, conditions were dreadful. Carry Brachvogel died on November 20, 1942, after months of psychological demoralization and physical privation.

In the 1980s, Brachvogel's name began to emerge from almost total obscurity in Germany. The revival of her work did more than signify respect for, and guilt over, a writer's murder by the Nazi regime. What scholars began to discover was a writer of distinction who had articulated in the years before World War I a clear vision of modern women fully exercising their civil and personal rights. Brachvogel's writings entertained another generation with their sharply-etched portraits of great women rulers, strong-willed actresses and artists, tough-as-nails Bavarian peasants, and determined daughters of the urban bourgeoisie who, like herself, shaped productive, successful lives for themselves in an imperfect, often unforgiving world.

SOURCES:

Heuer, Renate. "Carry Brachvogel (1864–1942), Schriftstellerin," in Manfred Treml, Wolf Weigand and Evamaria Brockhoff, eds., *Geschichte und Kultur der Juden in Bayern: Lebensläufe.* Munich: K.G. Saur, 1988, pp. 211–216.

Walk, Joseph. *Kurzbiographien zur Geschichte der Juden 1918–1945: Herausgegeben vom Leo Baeck Institute, Jerusalem.* Munich: K. G. Saur, 1988.

John Haag, Associate Professor,
University of Georgia, Athens, Georgia

Brackett, Leigh (1915–1978)

American author and screenwriter who was dubbed the "Queen of Space Opera" for her contribution to the science-fiction genre. *Name variations: George Sanders, a pseudonym used for the mystery novel* Stranger at Home. *Pronunciation: Lee BRACK-it.*

Leigh Brackett

Born Leigh Douglass Brackett on December 7, 1915, in Los Angeles, California; died on March 18, 1978, at age 63; only child of Margaret (Douglass) Brackett and William Franklin Brackett (a certified public accountant); attended private girls' schools; completed four years of high school in three years and refused a college scholarship; married Edmond Hamilton (a science-fiction writer), on January 1, 1947 (died 1977); no children.

Discovered fantasy-science fiction by reading E.R. Burroughs' The Gods of Mars *"on or about" her eighth year; began writing and submitting novels to editors (1928); sold first story to* Astounding *(1939); published first full-length novel, the mystery* No Good from a Corpse *(1944); collaborated with William Faulkner on screenplay of* The Big Sleep *(1944); won 1963 Silver Spur Award from the Western Writers of America for* Follow the Free Wind, *the only western she wrote; was working on the screenplay for George Lucas'* Star Wars: The Empire Strikes Back *when she died (1978).*

Selected writings: No Good from a Corpse *(NY: Coward-McCann, 1944); (mystery)* Stranger at Home *(NY: Simon and Schuster, 1946);* The Sword of Rhiannon *(NY: Ace Books, 1953);* The Galactic Breed *(NY: Ace Books, 1955);* The Long Tomorrow *(Garden City, NY: Doubleday, 1955);* The Tiger among Us *(Garden City: Doubleday, 1957);* Rio Bravo *(NY: Bantam Books, 1959);* The Nemesis From Terra *(NY: Ace Books, 1961);* Follow the Free Wind *(Garden City, NY: Doubleday, 1963);* People of the Talisman *and* The Secret of Sinharat *(NY: Ace Books, 1964);* The

Coming of the Terrans *(NY: Ace Books, 1967);* The Ginger Star *(NY: Ballantine Books, 1974);* The Best of Planet Stories No. 1 *(NY: Ballantine Books, 1975); (trilogy)* The Book of Skaith *(Garden City, NY: Nelson Doubleday, 1976); (edited by Edmond Hamilton)* The Best of Leigh Brackett *(Garden City, NY: Nelson Doubleday, 1977).*

In 1939, Leigh Brackett was 23 when she sold her first story, "The Martian Quest," to *Astounding*. Most of her tales were published not in book form but in "the Pulps," magazines—like *Astounding, Startling Stories*, and *Planet Stories*—which were the lifeblood of an American subculture of science fiction and fantasy. Through these publications, authors enjoyed a highly interactive relationship with the fans who read their stories, and, largely due to this alliance, science fiction developed throughout the mid-20th century into a specialized genre with particular tenets and traditions. Leigh Brackett was at her most successful and prolific during the height of this literary renaissance, from 1939 to 1974, publishing over 50 stories in more than 13 magazines. She was so much a part of the sci-fi world that Brackett's fans adoringly named her the "Queen of Space Opera," and her work would help shape the genre.

Born in Los Angeles, California, on December 7, 1915, Brackett was the first and only child of **Margaret Douglass Brackett** and William Franklin Brackett, a certified public accountant and amateur writer. When Leigh was not yet three years old, her father died at age 30, a victim of the 1918 flu epidemic. After his death, she and her mother moved to the beach area of Los Angeles, into the home of Brackett's maternal grandparents. Though they did not get along well when Brackett was very young, Brackett's relationship with her grandfather, Archibald Douglass, mellowed into a happy one; he served *in loco parentis*, offered his support by providing a home that she loved, and would later underwrite her budding career until it took off in her mid-20s.

Although she spent most of her childhood at her grandparents' home at the beach, Brackett did a good deal of traveling. During visits with wealthy relatives in San Francisco, she was introduced to the American upper class, which she met with some distaste. Her Great Aunt Sarah took Leigh and Margaret Brackett on trips around much of the country; still, Leigh preferred the beach. "The company of Ladies can become trying," wrote Brackett in *Speaking of Science Fiction*, "especially when one's own feet and hands grow too large and *capable*, and one's skin lacks that transparent pallor. I just never made it in that league. Druther go fishing." If not fishing, Brackett was reading, writing, swimming, or acting, living an active physical life atypical of the women in her family. She would later tell **Juanita Roderick** and Hugh G. Earnhart in a 1975 interview:

> I guess that I was liberated on the day I was born, because my mother was a feminine, helpless little person and all the women of my family were professional ladies with a capital "L." A lady never did anything for herself; somebody always did it for her. They looked down on me a great deal because I was big and husky and active, running up and down the beach, playing with the boys and doing things. Oh, goodness, I got so many lectures. I think I was just the opposite type, that's all, and possibly became even more opposite because I so despised their attitude. I thought it was ridiculous.

In several of her autobiographical accounts, Brackett tells of her first reading of Edgar Rice Burroughs' science-fiction classic *The Gods of Mars*. This was her first encounter, at about age eight, with space. "Suddenly, at one blazing stroke, the veil was rent and I had a glimpse of the cosmos," she later wrote. "I cannot tell you what a tremendous effect that idea of *Mars*, another planet, a strange world, had on my imagination." The impact of *The Gods of Mars* would remain with Brackett her entire life, and she would write many stories set on that planet.

Brackett attended private girls' schools from grammar level to high school, where she was taught by Catholic nuns. An avid reader, she was an erratic student who excelled only when interested in the subject. Her attitude about herself as an autonomous person—equal to all others regardless of gender—was cultivated and strengthened by her teachers. Writes **Rosemarie Arbur** in her essay *Leigh Brackett: No "Long Goodbye" Is Good Enough*: "We may assume that her teachers not only imparted a strict, no-nonsense approach to the proprieties of written English but also stood as role models—dedicated professionals and figures of authority, almost all women." Brackett was 13 when she began to submit, in longhand on lined paper, "heavy problem novels," short stories, and poems to editors. More than ten years would pass before any of her work made it into print.

In school, Brackett was introduced to the study of speech and drama, for which she developed a great passion. With a love of acting, she hung around theaters (taking delight even in sweeping the stage) and sometimes took on roles designed for men which she performed with zeal. At one point, to the horror of her family, she considered acting as a career. Brackett won a scholarship to college, but refused the opportunity for more schooling, eager to explore other avenues of life. A budding novelist, she was hooked on science fiction, later telling Roderick and Earnhart:

> Everyone warned me, "You'll starve to death. It's not a very respectable field, you know. I mean, only nut cases write for it and only nut cases read it.". . . My aunt used to say, "Why don't you write nice stories for the *Ladies' Home Journal*?" I used to say, "I wish I could, because they pay well, but I can't read the *Ladies' Home Journal* and I'm sure that I couldn't write for it."

In 1939, her first published works, "Martian Quest" and "The Treasure of Ptakuth," were bought by John W. Campbell for the magazine *Astounding*, which later became *Analog*. In the late 1930s through the 1950s, *Astounding* was the most popular and interactive of the science-fiction magazines. As its editor, Campbell had great influence in shaping the literature of the genre and fueling its surrounding subculture. Many of Brackett's peers were surprised that he took an interest in her work. Prone to discount stories by women in favor of works by men that had a more "masculine" feel to them, Campbell tended to select material for *Astounding* that portrayed women as helpless and dimwitted, which Leigh Brackett was not about to do.

At that time, science fiction was a male-dominated genre to the extent that both the profession and the content of the stories was more often than not anti-female. Many critical essays disputing the ability of women to contribute to the field of science fiction were published in the 1930s, '40s and '50s. Technology and the future were considered inappropriate topics for women, and nearly all of the heros of science-fiction stories and novels of Brackett's era were male. Undaunted, Brackett considered herself a writer, not a "woman writer" or even "a woman." "I was always me," she wrote, "an individual, free-standing and in the round. . . . I have always refused to be bound by stereotyping, or limited by any other limitations than my own. To me, sex has never been of the slightest importance outside the bedroom."

Brackett's refusal to write stereotypical females limited her access to *Astounding*. She sold only one more story to Campbell, though she generally sent her manuscripts to him first. Most of Brackett's work was published in *Planet Stories*, a popular but not as respected magazine. She also wrote often for *Astonishing Stories*, *Thrilling Wonder Stories*, *Super Science Stories*, *Amazing*, *Strange Stories*, *Comet*, *Tops in Science Fiction*, *Startling Stories*, *Space Stories*, *Fantasy and Science Fiction*, *Venture Science Fiction*, and *Great Science Fiction Magazine*. Her success helped break down the gender bias in the science-fiction field. Though, in concert with the times, most of her protagonists were male—a fact that feminist critics often rue—she created strong women characters within her stories. "Her heroines," wrote critic Tom Milne of her sword and sorcery tales, "never melt, simper, faint or whimper."

> I used to get letters in the letter columns of the old mags when I first began, saying that a woman couldn't write science fiction, and I thought it was just about as sensible as saying that a one-legged man is incapable of playing the violin.
>
> —Leigh Brackett

In addition to her reputation as a prolific, respected science-fiction writer, Brackett established herself as a screenwriter, beginning with her 1946 work for Howard Hawks. Brackett's first full-length novel, the mystery *No Good from a Corpse*, brought her to Hawks' attention. In need of a writer for *The Big Sleep*, he read Brackett's classic hard-boiled prose style in this story of a private detective on the case of a murdered femme fatale and decided she was the "right man for the job." Recalled Brackett in 1972: "Hawks liked my dialogue and called my agent. He was somewhat shaken when he discovered that it was Miss and not Mister Brackett, but he rallied bravely and signed me on anyway, for which I have always been extremely grateful." Brackett collaborated on the project with William Faulkner, both of them working on separate parts of the book in separate offices. Asked to comment on the completed script, Humphrey Bogart criticized Brackett about lines he found too genteel; as it turned out, these lines were Faulkner's contributions. Bogart nicknamed Brackett "Butch" and brought her any dialogue he thought needed to be roughed up. Brackett would write five films for Hawks, three of them Westerns. During her career, she was to write more than 20 screenplays and teleplays, ending with *Star Wars: The Empire Strikes Back* on which she was working at the time of her death.

Brackett made lasting friendships with people in the science-fiction world. Her friends were almost all male, and almost all famous. Ray Bradbury was one of her closest, and the two spent hours reviewing each other's work, playing volleyball at Muscle Beach, and talking endlessly about science fiction. She was also close with Henry Kuttner, a reader for *Astounding*, who became somewhat of a mentor. Kuttner helped perfect her writing style by providing lengthy criticisms of her unpublished work. As her success grew, she met more and more members of the science-fiction community, fans and professionals alike. In 1940, Brackett's agent introduced her to science-fiction writer Edmond Hamilton, whom she married in 1947.

For the first few years of their marriage, the couple lived in Los Angeles and spent much of their time writing. Their free time was spent renovating a dilapidated farmhouse in Kinsman, Ohio. Around 1950, they moved into the farmhouse, visiting California in the summertime. Although they were life partners, they collaborated on only one, unpublished, writing project. Careful to retain their individuality, they did not review each other's work until it reached the last draft, minimizing any influence; but they did sometimes seek advice when stumped. Their writing styles remained entirely different. In 1964, Brackett and Hamilton were co-guests of honor at the World Science Fiction Convention. Brackett edited Hamilton's anthology, *The Best of Edmond Hamilton*, while Hamilton edited *The Best of Leigh Brackett*. Their fondness for each other is reflected in their many interviews.

Unlike much of the science fiction of her day, Brackett's stories centered around her characters and their surroundings rather than around the stories' plots. A one-draft writer, she would begin a story without a written outline, create the setting, and then let the story unfold. Remarks one of her characters in *The Ginger Star*: "The land shapes us. If we were in another place, we would be another people." Watching many of her contemporaries focus on plot, Brackett was well aware that her science fiction was both culturally and stylistically in the avant-garde. The qualities which excluded her from the higher-class pulps made her work extremely valuable as literature.

In stories replete with heroics, Brackett created characters, often cunning and physically strong, who inhabit imaginative, even impossible, settings that take on a super-reality through her narrative. Nowhere is this more evident than in her "Skaith" trilogy, featuring the character of Eric John Stark. Said to have been her favorite character, Stark appears in more than five of her works. He is born to human parents in a mining colony in Mercury's Twilight Belt. Shortly after his birth, his parents are killed in a mining accident and Stark is abandoned on the harsh planet. He is found and fostered by the native "subhuman aboriginals clawing a precarious existence out of the sun-stricken valleys," who call him N'Chaka, the Man-Without-a-Tribe. He lives with them, learning to love and survive, until he is found by ruthless Earthmen who slaughter his foster family out of greed. They cage him and torment him, but he is rescued by Simon Ashton, an ambassador for the Ministry of Planetary Affairs on Earth. Ashton searches Mercury Metals and Mining's records to find N'Chaka's parents and his true name. The Man-Without-A-Tribe becomes Eric John Stark, and his adventures in space begin. Highly intelligent, he possesses finely tuned "animal" senses acquired while living on Mercury, instinctive sympathy for alien races, an almost perfect physique, and a knack for survival. By occupation, Stark is a mercenary, and he uses all of his attributes to investigate, fight, rescue and stay alive. Brackett was writing a fourth book featuring Stark, the ultimate space hero with a touch of sensitivity, when she died.

During her career, Brackett frequently ventured from science fiction to radioplays, teleplays, screenplays, poetry, mystery novels, and a western *Follow the Free Wind*, which won the 1963 Silver Spur Award for the year's best western. She wrote seven mystery novels, including one under the pen name George Sanders. She offered the following words to her successors: "My advice to young women, who might be doubtful about taking up science fiction as a career, is simply this. . . . if you want to write science fiction, write it, and why the hell be doubtful?" Leigh Brackett died in 1978, the year after her husband's death.

SOURCES:

Arbur, Rosemarie. *Brackett, Bradley, McCaffrey: A Primary and Secondary Bibliography.* Boston, MA: G.K. Hall, 1982.

Brackett, Leigh. *The Ginger Star.* NY: Ballantine Books, 1974.

Carr, Terry, ed. *Classic Science Fiction: The First Golden Age.* NY: Harper and Row, 1978.

Del Rey, Lester. *The World of Science Fiction, 1925–1976.* NY: Garland, 1980.

Roderick, Juanita and Hugh G. Earnhard, Interview with Leigh Brackett as part of the Youngstown State University Oral History Program, October 7, 1975.

Staicar, Tom, ed. *The Feminine Eye: Science Fiction and the Women Who Write It.* NY: Frederick Ungar, 1982.

Walker, Paul, ed. *Speaking of Science Fiction.* Oradell, NJ: Luna, 1978.

SUGGESTED READING:

Hamilton, Edmond, ed. *The Best of Leigh Brackett.* Garden City, NY: Nelson Doubleday, 1977.

Mallardi, Bill and Bill Bowers, eds. *The Double Bill Symposium.* Akron, OH: DB Press, 1969.

COLLECTIONS:

Nearly complete American science fiction periodical collections are located at Eastern New Mexico University and Temple University Library.

RELATED MEDIA:

The Big Sleep, screenplay by Leigh Brackett and William Faulkner, Howard Hawks Production, 1944.

Star Wars: The Empire Strikes Back, science-fiction screenplay by Leigh Brackett, George Lucas Film, 1980.

Tanya Carelli,
freelance writer in science fiction and women's history, San Diego, California

Bracquemond, Marie (1840–1916)

French impressionist painter. *Born Marie Quivoron in 1840, at Argenton, Brittany; died in 1916; studied painting with M. Wassor; married Felix Bracquemond (an engraver), in 1869.*

While some of the Impressionists were born into the prosperous society class of France, this was not so in the case of Marie Bracquemond. She was born Marie Quivoron in 1840, at Argenton, Brittany, to poor parents. Her father died shortly after her birth, and her mother remarried; the family then moved about Europe for a dozen years before settling in Etampes, south of Paris. Marie began to study painting with M. Wassor and often spent the summers painting in the countryside. In 1857, she made her first submission to the Salon, a drawing of her mother, her sister, and Wassor. Her confidence at a young age in her emerging talent was borne out by the acceptance of her work by the Salon. Through a friend of the family's, Marie was introduced to Ingres, and she has sometimes been characterized as a "student of Ingres." In fact, her letters indicate that while she admired Ingres' work, she found the man himself distasteful and did not pursue his instruction, nor follow his advice. It was her goal, she wrote, to "work at painting, not to paint some flowers, but to express those feelings that art inspires in me."

While working as a copyist at the Louvre, Marie met Felix Bracquemond, the engraver, whom she married in 1869. By 1877, Marie was beginning to follow the same pattern as many of the other Impressionists, working outdoors and intensifying the colors in her palette. She took part in the 1879 Impressionist exhibition, although the works she exhibited were drawn from her work in design for the Haviland studio. More representative of her style as an artist were the three paintings of hers included in the 1880 Impressionist exhibition, among them *The Woman in White.* This was a portrait of her sister **Louise**, her closest friend and staunchest supporter throughout her life. She also exhibited at the 1886 Impressionist exhibition, perhaps her last concerted effort to advance her career in the face of her husband's growing disapproval.

Her work showed the typical Impressionist fascination with the effect of sunlight on color, evident for example in *Tea Time, The Three Graces,* and *The Woman in White* (all 1880), but she was perhaps uniquely skilled in the exploration of the effects of warm interior light. In *Under the Lamp* (1887), her subtle exploration of the effects of light on objects echoes Vermeer. In 1919, a retrospective exhibition at the Galerie Bernheim Jeune displayed 156 of her works, most of which are no longer on public display anywhere.

The career of Marie Bracquemond is stark evidence of the impact marriage could have on the aspirations of a female artist in the 19th century. Rather than marrying after becoming an established artist, as ***Berthe Morisot** did, she married early in her career, with disastrous results. Felix Bracquemond was himself considered a secondary figure in the Impressionist circle (despite the fact that he opposed their approach to art), and, as his wife, Marie was never considered more than tertiary. Additionally, he relentlessly belittled and criticized her work, until by 1890 Marie virtually ceased to paint. The Impressionist movement thus lost a very talented proponent, though they hardly seemed to notice. She died in 1916. Marie Bracquemond continued to be a largely ignored figure until the late 20th century, and she remains a sad example of a brilliant capacity for artistic expression stifled.

SOURCES:

Bouillon, Jean-Paul, and Elizabeth Kane. "Marie Bracquemond," in *Women's Art Journal.* Vol. 5, no. 2. Fall 1984–Winter 1985, pp. 21–27.

William MacKenzie,
University of Guelph, Guelph, Ontario, Canada

Braddock, Bessie (1899–1970)

Member of British Parliament (1945–1970). *Name variations: E.M. Braddock. Born Elizabeth Margaret Bamber in Liverpool, England, on September 24, 1899; died on November 13, 1970; daughter of Hugh and Mary Bamber; attended public schools in Liverpool until age 15; married John Braddock, in 1972.*

Known among her working-class constituents as "Battling Bessie," Elizabeth Margaret Braddock was a Labour Member of Parliament for 35 years, during which time she was an outspoken champion of social reform. Braddock was born among the Merseyside dockers of Liverpool, England, and received her early lessons in political reform from her parents. Her mother **Mary Bamber** was both national organizer of the National Union of Distributive and Allied Workers and a Labour Party worker; her father Hugh was an active Liverpool Socialist. At age 15, Braddock left school to work as an assistant in the Liverpool Co-operative Society. She was a vocal pacifist during World War I and, during the postwar years, became an active trade unionist and political worker.

In 1930, after a brief flirtation with the Communist Party, Braddock was elected a Labour member of the Liverpool City Council. With her husband, also a member of the council, she launched a campaign to rid the city of its slums. Her search for improved housing was unrelenting. "I don't care whose houses we take," she said "even if they're Lord Derby's or the Earls of Stamford's—when working-class people are living like herrings in a tin" (New York *Herald Tribune*, August 5, 1943). Her determined efforts for the city also resulted in expanded maternity and child-welfare programs, as well as the establishment of several homes for the elderly. In 1955, she became an alderman of the council.

Braddock was elected to Parliament on the Labour ticket in 1945, ending the Tory stronghold in the Exchange division. Her opposition to the Conservatives was immediately apparent, as was her overwhelming loyalty to her constituency. During Braddock's lengthy tenure in the House (until her death in 1970), she negotiated an end to a five-week national dock strike, championed a bill nationalizing the trucking industry, uncovered an illegal arms shipment to the Liverpool docks which resulted in a halt on surplus arms shipments, and exposed mistreatment of prisoners in a Liverpool jail which sparked an inquiry by the secretary of state for the Home Department.

An imposing woman of 200 pounds, Braddock was known for her colorful oratory and unorthodox demonstrations. In 1952, during a fight to ease an unemployment crisis in the textile industry, she was ordered out of the House of Commons and suspended from five sessions for demanding to speak in a debate and refusing to be seated. In 1954, she and one other Member refused to sign a commemorative volume to be presented to Winston Churchill on his 80th birthday, because of his involvement in breaking up a coal strike in Tonypandy, Wales. Perhaps most dramatic was her 1956 protest of the widespread purchase of air pistols by juveniles without licenses. Confiscating two pistols from the Liverpool police, Braddock obtained a license for them and fired them off during a House session. She explained: "You see I have to startle this House before anyone does anything about anything."

In 1955, *Time* magazine called Braddock "salty as [Liverpool's] docks, as fierce as its wind, and biting as its rain." She died on November 13, 1970.

SOURCES:

Current Biography 1957. NY: H.W. Wilson, 1957.

Barbara Morgan,
Melrose, Massachusetts

Braddock, E.M. (1899–1970).

See Braddock, Bessie.

Braddon, Mary Elizabeth (1835–1915)

English novelist and editor. *Name variations: Mrs. M.E. Maxwell; (as an actress) Mary Seyton. Born Mary Elizabeth Braddon on October 4, 1835, in London, England (some sources cite 1837); died on February 4, 1915, in Richmond, Surrey, England; daughter of Henry Braddon (a lawyer and writer) and Fanny (White) Braddon; sister of Sir Edward Braddon, prime minister of Tasmania; married John Maxwell (a London publisher), in 1874; children: seven, including two sons, William B. Maxwell and Gerald Maxwell, who became novelists.*

Selected writings: The Trail of the Serpent; or Three Times Dead *(1861);* Lady Lisle *(1861);* Lady Audley's Secret *(1862);* Aurora Floyd *(1863);* Eleanor's Victory *(1863);* John Marchmont's Legacy *(1863);* Henry Dunbar *(1864);* The Doctor's Wife *(1864);* Birds of Prey *(1867);* Charlotte's Inheritance *(1868);* The Green Curtain *(1911);* Mary *(published posthumously, 1916).*

Born on October 4, 1835, in London, Mary Elizabeth Braddon was four when her parents separated, and she was raised by her mother. Early on, she began writing for magazines in order to supplement the family income. In 1861, after a brief fling on the stage under the name Mary Seyton, she produced her first novel, *The Trail of the Serpent; or Three Times Dead*. That same year, she was praised for an epic poem on Garibaldi, as well as a short novel, *Lady Lisle*. Her most famous novel, *Lady Audley's Secret*, was written in 1862, for *Robin Goodfellow*, a serial owned by London publisher John Maxwell, but was published later in three volumes in the *Sixpenny Magazine*, owned by William Tinsley. Favorably reviewed, it not only established Braddon's reputation as a novelist, but made a fortune for Tinsley, who built a villa called Audley Lodge from the proceeds. The book, one of the first sensation novels of the 1860s, involved bigamy, arson, and murder attempts, subjects hitherto unacceptable in fiction, but made palatable by Braddon's style and treatment. She followed with *Aurora Floyd* (a novel with a strong affinity to *Madame Bovary*) and *Eleanor's Victory*, in which murder was a central theme.

Braddon is credited with introducing an innovation into popular fiction whereby wickedness, traditionally portrayed as ugly, is imbued with grace and beauty. She is also known for inventing a crime mystery surrounded by everyday circumstances, yet devoid of the formulaic "detective novel" mechanism. Her later novels were noted for their artistic form and finish, and her *Mohawk* was considered an excellent study of fashionable life in the time of Pope, Walpole, and Chesterfield.

While Braddon's literary career took off, a love affair with publisher John Maxwell developed. Maxwell was unable to marry because his wife was in an asylum, so the couple lived together, with Braddon bearing a child in 1862. They finally married in 1874, amid great scandal, and had six more children.

In the meantime, Braddon turned out novels in rapid succession, all in the same vein, all achieving instant popularity. By 1899, 57 of her titles were available in cheap editions called yellowbacks. She also published in a variety of popular periodicals of the period, including *Reynolds' Miscellany*, the *London Journal*, and *All the Year Round*. She edited *Belgravia* for ten years beginning in 1876, and the *Belgravia Annual* (1867–1877), both owned by Maxwell.

As Braddon wrote well into her 70s, she became less sensational in her later fiction, refining her artistic form and concentrating more on the psychological aspects of her stories. Her 80th book, *The Green Curtain* (1911), was published when she was 74. Her last novel, *Mary*, was published in 1916, a year after her death.

SOURCES:

Shattock, Joanne. *The Oxford Guide to British Women Writers*. NY: Oxford University Press, 1993.

Braden, Anne (1924–)

American journalist and civil-rights activist. *Born Anne Gamrell McCarty in Louisville, Kentucky, in 1924 into a financially comfortable Southern family; attended Stratford and Randolph-Macon colleges; married Carl Braden (1914–1975, a journalist), in 1948.*

Grew up in Mississippi and Alabama; returned to Louisville (1947); met and married Carl Braden (1948); both involved in labor struggles for the CIO and the Progressive Party; arrested in Mississippi (1951) for protesting execution of a black man; arrested and blacklisted (1954); worked for the Southern Conference Educational Fund (SCEF); opposed witch-hunting tactics of House Un-American Activities Committee (HUAC, 1958); served prison term and helped launch National Committee to Abolish HUAC; made effective use of media to dramatize struggle for civil rights and racial justice; arrested for "sedition" in Kentucky (1967); retired from SCEF (1972); edited The Southern Patriot*; continued political activism after husband's death (1975), creating the Southern Organizing Committee for Economic and Social Justice.*

Born into an affluent white Southern family in Louisville, Kentucky, in 1924, Anne Gamrell McCarty was exposed to a number of influences that reinforced her inborn passion for fairness and justice. The Christian teachings she discovered through the Episcopal Church opened the door to the concept of a good society based on love and compassion, and a number of her professors at Stratford and Randolph-Macon colleges presented her with a historical and philosophical context useful for her intellectual growth. After graduation from college in 1947, she took a job as a reporter in Louisville, where she met and fell in love with Carl Braden, a fellow reporter ten years her senior. From a working-class background, Carl had been strongly influenced by the Socialist ideals of his father and the social gospel beliefs of his Roman Catholic mother. He had intended to prepare for the priesthood but, after a crisis of faith, became a newspaper reporter during the depression. Anne and Carl married in 1948, the same year they left reporting to work full-time for the Congress of Industrial Organizations (CIO), which was attempting to unionize workers in the South. Also in 1948, they worked for the Progressive Party, whose candidate Henry A. Wallace was attempting to move the United States away from Cold War policies.

Despite the decisive defeat of the Progressives in the November 1948 elections, the Bradens remained committed to ending the segregationist system of Jim Crow in the Southern states. As one of a handful of liberal Southern women at the height of the Cold War and McCarthyism, Anne Braden was fearless in opposing injustice. She was jailed in Mississippi in 1951 for leading a delegation of women to the governor's office to protest the execution of Willie McGee, a black man charged with raping a white woman. In 1954, Anne and Carl were both arrested in Louisville, Kentucky, and charged with plotting to incite insurrection. The charge against them was highly questionable. Their real offense in the minds of the segregationist power elite was their purchase of a house in a white neighborhood in order to then sell it to a black family, that of Andrew Wade. To a society that regarded segregation as a way of life, such an action was deemed as profoundly treasonous. The local press blasted them, and they were blacklisted, unable to find employment. State prosecutors confiscated their library as "evidence" of subversive intent. The house in which Andrew Wade and his family lived was virtually destroyed by a bomb blast.

Held on extraordinarily high bail of $40,000, Carl Braden was found guilty of "sedition"; he had served eight months of his fifteen-year sentence when a higher court overturned his conviction. Anne brought the events to national attention with her book about the Wade case, *The Wall Between*. Despite Carl's release, the Southern establishment remained adamantly resistant to change, and neither Anne nor her husband could get jobs at their chosen profession of reporting. The couple became field organizers and writers for an organization dedicated to the cause of racial integration, the Southern Conference Educational Fund (SCEF). The work of this militant organization quickly came to the attention of Senator James Eastland of Mississippi, whose Senate Internal Security Subcommittee labelled SCEF an un-American Communist front.

In 1958, the House Committee on Un-American Activities (HUAC) called both Bradens to testify at hearings in Atlanta. Carl Braden was adamant in defending his constitutional liberties as guaranteed by the First Amendment, telling the committee members: "My beliefs and my associations are none of the business of this committee." As a result of this and other confrontations, the Bradens became convinced that First Amendment liberties of freedom of belief and association, like the developing struggle for black rights, were integral to all other movements for social change. Fighting a regime of blacklisting and intellectual conformity, Anne Braden wrote and circulated a pamphlet, *HUAC: Bulwark of Segregation*, which played a significant role in bringing about the discrediting of this organization.

Trained as reporters, the Bradens used the media expertly to alert the public on issues of injustice and endangered civil liberties. Even though both state and federal officials tried to smear them as "reds," they fought back spiritedly and often with wit and sarcasm. In 1967, they were chosen as executive directors of SCEF. Their interracial agenda continued to infuriate diehard enemies of change, and the same year they were arrested on sedition charges for setting up a community organizing project among poor whites in Appalachia. In 1972, the Bradens retired as SCEF directors but remained active in a training institute for community activists. Much of Anne Braden's energy now went into editing the SCEF newspaper, *The Southern Patriot*.

Prior to Carl Braden's sudden death in 1975, conflicts within SCEF had led to their departure from the organization. Anne continued to crusade for racial harmony and social justice by working for the creation of effective interracial coalitions. Although they were members of a numerically tiny minority, the Southern white radicals, the Bradens refused to be intimidated by the forces of intolerance and privilege. After the heroic phase of the struggle for racial justice in the South had passed, she remained eloquent on behalf of her beliefs. Said Anne Braden in a 1978 interview with the *Louisville Defender*: "Our future and that of our children rides with the fate of the Black struggle for progress, and [we must] join in that struggle as if our very lives depend on it. For, in truth, they do."

SOURCES:

Anne and Carl Braden Papers, Wisconsin Historical Society, Madison.

Braden, Anne. *The Wall Between*. NY: Monthly Review Press, 1958.

Fariello, Griffin. *Red Scare:* Memories of the American Inquisition, an Oral History. *NY: W.W. Norton, 1995.*

John Haag, Associate Professor, University of Georgia, Athens, Georgia

Bradley, Amy Morris (1823–1904)

American educator, Civil War nurse, and administrator. *Born on September 12, 1823, in Vassalboro, Maine; died on January 15, 1904, in Wilmington, North Carolina; fourth daughter and youngest of eight children of Abired (a shoemaker) and Jane (Baxter) Bradley.*

A frail child given to bronchial attacks, Amy Bradley lost her mother when she was six and lived with her older married sisters until the age of 15, when she began a teaching career. Working in the public-school system, Bradley also taught privately to help finance her studies at the academy in East Vassalboro. At 21, she was named principal of a grammar school in Gardiner, Maine. She then moved to higher paying positions in Charlestown and Cambridge, Massachusetts, until severe bronchitis forced her to accept a position in the restorative climate of San José, Costa Rica, where she opened an English School for children of various nationalities. After three successful years, she was called back to New England by her father's illness.

Shortly after the outbreak of the Civil War, Bradley offered to serve the Union effort as a nurse with the Maine volunteers. She began her duty at Alexandria, Virginia, in the regimental hospital tents of the 5th Maine Regiment. Bradley's skill in organizing and outfitting a hospital were quickly noticed, and she was named superintendent of the brigade hospital. She tended to her administrative duties, which included finding people to cook and do laundry, and took a personal interest in her patients, some of them former students. When the hospital was dismantled, Bradley volunteered for the Sanitary Commission and was appointed superintendent of the floating hospital *Ocean Queen*, where she helped care for some 1,000 patients on their way to New York from the battlefields. Bradley's diary reveals her renewed horror at each new arrival of wounded: "I shall never forget my feelings, as, one by one, those mutilated forms were brought in on stretchers, and carefully placed on these comfortable cots. 'What,' said I, 'must I see human beings thus mangled? O, my God, why is it? why is it?'" Bradley subsequently served as superintendent on a number of other transport boats until the end of the Peninsula campaign.

In 1862, she was assigned as matron and administrator of a Soldiers' Home in Washington, D.C. Late that same year, Bradley was transferred to her most challenging assignment, a neglected convalescent camp dubbed "Camp Misery," where she oversaw the needs of some 5,000 soldiers. In addition to supervising housekeeping needs, Bradley helped the men with practical matters, like letter writing and filing paperwork for back pay claims. In 1864, after some time off to recuperate from an illness caused by overwork, she initiated a weekly *Soldiers' Journal*, with profits going to orphans of soldiers who had been at the camp.

After the war, Bradley turned her attention to the educational needs of the ravaged South. Under the auspices of the Soldiers' Memorial Society of Boston and the American Unitarian Association, she opened a school in Wilmington, North Carolina, for poor white children. The project was slow to start, requiring visits to the homes of the poor to distribute clothes and supplies and encourage parents to send their children to school. After three years, she had won the support of the city and had expanded her original classroom of three to a school for seventy-five. With a generous contribution from philanthropist ***Mary Porter Tileston Hemenway** and another from the Peabody Fund, Bradley built additional schools. In 1869, she was named superintendent of the newly restored school system. Three years later, again with Hemenway's help, she opened Tileston Normal School in Wilmington to train local women for teaching positions. Ill health forced Bradley to retire in 1891. She spent her declining years in a cottage that Hemenway provided for her on the grounds of the Tileston School. She died in 1904 and was buried in Wilmington.

SOURCES:

James, Edward T., ed. *Notable American Women 1607–1950.* Cambridge, MA: The Belknap Press of Harvard University Press, 1971.

Moore, Frank. *Women of the War.* Hartford, CT: S.S. Scranton, 1866.

Read, Phyllis J. and Bernard L. Witlieb, ed. *The Book of Women's Firsts.* NY: Random House, 1992.

Barbara Morgan,
Melrose, Massachusetts

Bradley, Lydia Moss (1816–1908)

American philanthropist. *Born on July 31, 1816, in Vevay, Indiana; died on January 16, 1908, in Peoria, Illinois; married Tobias S. Bradley, in May 1837; children: six.*

A native of Indiana, Lydia Moss married Tobias S. Bradley in 1837 and moved with him to Peoria, Illinois, where he amassed a fortune in land and banking. Upon his death in 1867, Bradley was left with the means to pursue the couples' dream of endowing an educational institution in memory of their six children who had all died young. Carefully managing the estate through wise investments, Bradley began her philanthropic activities with gifts to her church and the establishment of a home for elderly women. In 1876, a charter for Bradley Polytechnic Institute was obtained, and three years later the first buildings—Bradley Hall and Horology Hall—were built. Endowing the 28-

acre campus with $2 million, Bradley saw her dream fulfilled before her death in 1908. The academy, which combined academic and practical training, pioneered in the field of domestic science, subsequently adding art and music schools. In 1920, Bradley's school achieved full college status, awarding its first baccalaureate degrees. It became Bradley University in 1946.

Bradshaw, Maria (1801–1862).

See Kean, Ellen for sidebar.

Bradstreet, Anne (1612–1672)

America's first woman poet, who broke into a male-dominated avocation by writing epic and lyric poems, excelling in expression of feeling for life, nature, and love of family. *Pronunciation: BRAD-street. Born Anne Dudley in 1612 in Northamptonshire, England; died on September 16, 1672, in Andover, Massachusetts; daughter of Thomas Dudley (steward for a landlord in England and later governor of Massachusetts) and Dorothy Yorke; married Simon Bradstreet, in 1628; children: Samuel, Dorothy, Sarah, Hannah, Simon, Mercy, Dudley, and John.*

Came to New England with family and parents (1630); wrote first poem (1632); moved to Agawam (Ipswich), Massachusetts (1635); resided in Andover, Massachusetts (early 1640s–72); collected poems published in London by her brother-in-law, Rev. John Woodbridge (1650); wrote last extant poem, "A Weary Pilgrim, now at Rest" (1669); six years after her death, a second edition of her work, with poems added to those of the first edition, was published in Boston (1678).

Anne Bradstreet led the way in proving that women could achieve fulfillment in marriage and family and still pursue their creative intellectual talents. What made Bradstreet's accomplishments all the more remarkable was that she lived in a strict Puritan society, which denied women identity beyond their domestic duties, and that she and her family arrived in America at the beginning of settlement in the wilderness. Anne Bradstreet, however, had advantages not usually afforded members of her sex in either England or America, a sound book learning as well as kinfolk and friends, themselves well educated, who encouraged her literary endeavors.

Bradstreet's father and husband became powerful political figures in the Massachusetts Bay Colony, each serving as governor. Thus Anne considered herself relatively free from pressures of censorship, not that she veered far from established mores or values, but she did emphatically sound the message for equality between men and women and even implied criticism of church and political authority. Although Bradstreet never confronted the establishment head-on, as did ***Anne Hutchinson**, she let it be known that women's voices should be heard.

One of six children and first daughter of Thomas Dudley and **Dorothy Yorke**, Anne was born in Northamptonshire, England. Thomas Dudley, who in his youth did stints as a soldier and a law secretary to an English judge, married into a family of moderate wealth. When Anne was seven years old, Thomas became the steward (manager) for the estates of Theophilus Clinton, the earl of Lincoln, and the Dudley family lived at Tattershall Castle. Anne was brought up in the strict Puritan households of her father and the earl of Lincoln. Taught by tutors, she was allowed to study in a broad field of learning and to read from the tomes of literature, history, and the sciences in the castle library. Bradstreet absorbed Greek, Latin, and Hebrew, and studied the Genevan (Calvinist) version of the Bible. She had a special fondness for Sir Walter Raleigh's *History of the World* and the translated poetry and prose of French Huguenot writer Guillaume Du Bartas; both sources provided inspiration and information for Anne's early poems.

Into Anne's quiet and aristocratic environment appeared 18-year-old Simon Bradstreet, an orphan and fresh graduate of Cambridge University who functioned as her father's assistant from 1621 to 1624. Simon left the Lincoln household to serve as steward to the future **Countess of Warwick**, and the Dudleys moved to nearby Boston [in England], with Anne's father continuing to serve the earl of Lincoln. At Boston, the Dudleys formed close ties among the congregation of Reverend John Cotton, vicar of St. Botolph's Church. One can assume that Simon Bradstreet regularly visited the Dudley home. In 1628, Anne, age 16, wed Simon, nine years her senior.

Countess of Warwick. *Probably wife of Robert Rich, 2nd earl of Warwick, son of Lady* ****Penelope Rich***.

The late 1620s was an uncomfortable time for Thomas Dudley and other Puritans who wished to strip the Anglican Church of its Catholic trappings and to base religious doctrine and practice solely on the Bible. Attracted to the New World, in search of greater economic opportunity and latitude to be unmolested in their religious beliefs, a group of Puritans formed the Massachusetts Bay Company. Dudley and 11 other Puritan members of the company signed the Cambridge Agreement, whereby it was arranged that they could establish the company's government in America. Thus Anne, her husband Simon, and the Dudleys made the journey on the *Arbella* in 1630 and joined in the founding of the Massachusetts Bay Colony. Bradstreet at first considered the pioneering life a liberating experience but soon realized that her new community was to be closely linked to religion. She wrote at the time: "I found a new *world* and new manners, at which my heart rose. After I was convinced it was the way of God, I submitted to it and joined the church of Boston."

The Bradstreets settled at Newton (modern-day Cambridge) in 1631; after four years, they moved to Ipswich and then, about a decade later, went further north on the frontier to Andover, on the Merrimac River, where Anne lived the rest of her life. It is recorded that during the first year at Ipswich, Anne, always of weak physical strength, "fell into a lingering sickness like a consumption, together with a lameness." Earlier in England, she had battled smallpox. Bradstreet had doubts about her religious faith, and she despaired of having children. But finally, in 1634, she gave birth to her first child Samuel. During her despondency, Anne had written her first poem: "Upon a Pit of Sickness" (1632). Like most of her early short poems, this devotional verse, with couplets of alternate eight- and six-syllable lines, had little literary merit. With a sense of futility, she says: "But what's this life, but care and strife?/ since first we came from womb,/ Our strength doth waste, our time doth hast,/ and then we go to th' Tomb."

The major part of Bradstreet's writings before 1650 consisted of two categories: elegies (memorializing dead heroes or heroines) and quaternions (relating to four-part phenomena). In her poems, she leans too much on prose and poems of other authors, without considering her own feelings and experience. Besides imitating the stilted Elizabethan style, with its profusion of alliteration and metaphors drawn from mythology and nature, Bradstreet gleaned information from ancient literature and contemporary historians, such as Raleigh, John Speed (*Historie of Great Britaine*, 1611) and William Camden (*Britannia*, English translation from the Latin in 1610). One of the elegies, "In Honour of that High and Mighty Princess, Queen Elizabeth," posits that women should have a place in worldly affairs along with men. Thus, Bradstreet declares: "Nay Masculines, you have thus tax'd us long,/ But she though dead, will vindicate our wrong./ Let such, as say our Sex is void of Reason,/ Know 'tis a Slander now, but once was Treason." Anne also honored Du Bartas and Sir Philip Sidney, soldier and poet who was killed at the battle of Zutphen in 1586. Two modern commentators, **Pattie Cowell** and **Ann Stanford** note that "there is a little heaven in Anne Bradstreet's elegies. The apotheosis for the three characters she celebrates is not a higher Christian transformation, but fame."

Like the elegies, the quaternions are also in iambic couplets. "The Four Humours in Mans Constitution"—Blood, Choler (yellow bile), Melancholy, and Phlegm (respiratory mucus)—are depicted allegorically as female figures, quarreling with each other as to whom is superior to the others in relation to the body. Melancholy, though a state of mind, claims physical importance. Phlegm (or as Anne spells it, "Flegm") at the end of the poem asks for cooperation, and thus "This loving counsel, pleas'd them all too well/ That flegm was judg'd for kindness to excell." "The Four Elements" again has members of the sisterhood arguing: "The Fire, Air, Earth, and Water did all contest/ Which was the strongest, noblest, and the best."

> Anne Bradstreet . . . reached heights of feeling and controlled expression not attained by an American poetess prior to Emily Dickinson.
>
> —John C. Miller

"The Four Ages of Man" has as its speakers a small boy and three men. Childhood tells of "the sins and dangers I am subjected to"; Youth admits to being "as wild as is the snuffing Ass:/ As vain as froth, or vanity can be." Middle Age contends that "Man at his best is vanity." Old Age expresses a strong sense of values and speaks of his accomplishments, concluding that he shall see "My strong Redeemer, coming in the skies:/ Triumph I shall, o're Sin, o're Death, o're Hell,/ And in that hope, I bid you all farewell." The characters of "The Four Seasons of the Year" correspond to the figures in the "Four Ages."

"The Four Monarchies," also in the quaternion series, was Anne's longest poem, 5,000 lines in iambic rhyming couplets. Largely an adaptation from Sir Walter Raleigh's *History of the World,* the poem covers 15 centuries of ancient history before the birth of Christ, in the context of the Assyrian, Persian, and Roman empires. There is a pattern of degradation and brutality as the monarchies unfold. From a providential view of history, there is hope for a better world with the advent of Christianity. The more Bradstreet progressed in writing this epic poem, the more frustrated she became. Rearing her children and maintaining a house were not conducive to the serious scholarship she sought to attain. Her prologue in "The Four Monarchies" is both apologetic for shortcomings and an assertion of the right of herself and other women to be contributors to literature. She complained that "If what I do prove well, it won't advance,/ They'l say it's stoln, or else was by chance. . . . Men have precedency and still excell. . . . Yet grant some small acknowledgment of ours."

Anne Bradstreet was the first American writer to suggest that the American colonists were mature enough to give advice to the mother country. "A Dialogue between old England and New," finished in early 1643, when Bradstreet learned of the beginning of civil war in England, has two female figures conversing with each other, a mother (England) in ragged royal clothes and her daughter (New England) in neat homespun attire. Old England bemoans the devastation and plunder in her homeland, while the daughter tells her to be cheerful for the future. Bradstreet lets it be known which side she prefers in the war between king and Parliament. The poem concludes: "Farewell dear Mother, Parliament prevail,/ And in a while, you'le tell another tale." When the poem was published in a second edition, with the Parliamentary rule ended and the monarchy restored, Bradstreet substituted "rightest cause" for Parliament. A century later, New Englanders in a revolutionary mood would make the same substitution to justify greater independence from England.

Bradstreet intended that her poems be solely for the enjoyment of family and friends. Her brother-in-law, Reverend John Woodbridge, however, was eager to have them published. Without her knowledge or consent, he took copies of the poems on a visit to England and the collection was published in London in 1650 as *The Tenth Muse Lately sprung up in America.* In the Preface, Woodbridge wrote:

> Had I opportunity but to borrow some of the Author's wit, 'tis possible I might so trim this curious Work with such quaint expressions, as that the Preface might bespake thy further perusall; but I feare 'twil be a shame for a man that can speak so little, to be seene in the title page of this Womans Book, lest by comparing the one with the other, the Reader should passe his sentence, that it is the gift of women, not only to speak most, but to speake best.

For her later poems, Bradstreet turned away from her bookish sources, and wrote from her own feelings and experience. In July 1653, her revered father, whom Anne had always sought to please, died. Anne expressed her grief in the writing of "To the Memory of my dear and ever honoured Father, Thomas Dudley." Other emotional poems followed during the free time that Anne, now in declining health, had in caring for a houseful of children. The poems were in iambic rhyming couplets as her earlier work had been. Bradstreet's love for her children is evident in the poem "In reference to her Children," which begins:

> I had eight birds hatcht in one nest,
> Four Cocks there were, and Hens the rest,
> I nurst them up with pain and care,
> Nor cost, nor labour did I spare,
> Till at the last they felt their wing,
> Mounted the Trees, and learn'd to sing.

The short poems touching family members and events are among the best of Bradstreet's poetry. She likens her husband's love to Christ's love and the bond between herself and her husband as a union in Christ. Thus in "To My Dear and Loving Husband," she says, "If ever two were one, then surely we. . . . Then, while we live, in love let's so persever,/ That when we live no more we may live ever." "A Letter to Her Husband, Absent upon Public Employment" carries the same theme: "Flesh of thy flesh, bone of thy bone,/ I here, thou there, yet both but one."

In "Flesh and the Spirit," like one of her earlier poems "Of the Vanity of all Worldly Creatures" (based on the Old Testament book, *Ecclesiastes*), Bradstreet declares her Christian faith. "Flesh and the Spirit," according to historian Samuel Eliot Morison, was "one of the best expressions in English literature of the conflict described by St. Paul" in *Romans*, chapter eight. Of the two sisters in the poem, Spirit triumphs over Flesh: "If I of Heaven may have my fill,/ Take thou the world, and all that will."

At last Bradstreet found expression for the beauty and joy of the New England landscape. "Contemplations," probably her best poem, consisting of 32 seven-line stanzas, rhyming *ababccc*, and a final stanza of eight lines in rhyming couplets, anticipated the sonnets of the later English romantic poets. The poem, inspired by an October walk through the countryside, meanders in references to the Creation and the Garden of Eden. Like other Puritans (contrary to their modern-day image), Bradstreet had a love for music, and in the "Contemplations," she frequently reflects on the pervasiveness of melody in nature. In one charming passage, she says: "I heard the merry grashopper then sing,/ The black clad Cricket, bear a second part,/ They kept one tune, and plaid on the same string,/ Seeming to glory in their little art."

Anne Bradstreet died in 1672, but no gravestone that marked her final resting place remains in an Andover burial ground. A few months before her death at age 60, she had mourned the passing of the only one of her eight children who did not survive her, **Dorothy**, who had married Reverend Seaborn Cotton. Four years after Bradstreet's death, her husband Simon remarried; he lived to be 94.

In 1678, a second edition of Bradstreet's poems was published in Boston by John Foster: *Several Poems compiled with great variety of Wit and Learning full of Delight.* This work consisted of all the poems of *The Tenth Muse* and those "found amongst her Papers"; a few were from the early period, but most were written after publication of the first edition. Bradstreet also left a small body of prose work and several more poems that were not included in the first two editions. John Harvard Ellis' *Works of Anne Bradstreet's Prose and Verse* (1867) contains for the first time the prose and 19 previously unpublished poems and verse fragments.

Bradstreet's brief spiritual autobiography, as well as "Religious Experiences," "Occasional Meditations" (poem), and "Meditations Divine and Moral" (prose), form the bulk of the new material in the 1867 edition. The "Meditations Divine and Moral," in 77 segments, intended as instruction for her son Samuel, comprise the best collection of aphorisms by an American before the appearance of Benjamin Franklin's *Poor Richard's Almanack*. A sampling of Bradstreet's pithy observations attest to her human understanding: "A ship that bears much sail, and little or no ballast, is easily overset"; "Fire hath its force abated by water not by wind, and anger must be allayed, by cold words and not by blustering threats"; "A sharp appetite and a thorough Concoction, is a signe of an healthful body, so a quick reception and a deliberate cogitation argues a sound mind"; or "Authority without wisdom, is like a heavy axe without an edge, fitter to bruise than polish."

Critics long viewed Anne Bradstreet mainly as a curiosity, a well-educated English gentlewoman on the frontier writing poetry largely of the Elizabethan genre, derivative and imitative of a few other authors. Scholars in the 20th century, however, have shown that her poems were influenced by a great variety of sources and had a creativity that reflected her own individuality. Modern readers have been attracted to Bradstreet's writings because of the superb quality of those poems that reveal the intimate, caring side of the American Puritans. Even the formal poetry has been reassessed as capable work. Bradstreet's celebration of the feminine mystique and advocacy of expansion of women's horizons have contributed to her current appeal. In his introduction to a published selection of her poems, Perry Miller provided a fitting tribute. If Bradstreet's formal poems, said Miller, showed "that a Puritan could combine deep piety with a genial culture, more importantly [the] occasional lyrics, inspired by the native setting or the homely incidents of her daily life [demonstrated] that a Puritan could further combine piety with sexual passion, love of children and good furniture, humor—that a female Puritan, in short, could be both a Puritan and a woman of great charm."

Although adhering to conventional literary style, Anne Bradstreet exhibited a transition from Elizabethan-Renaissance poetry to what would become Romanticist expression. She left a body of work, diverse and touching the human spirit, that stands on its own as literary achievement. She was, as she said of mankind, "made for endless immortality."

SOURCES:

Cowell, Pattie, and Ann Stanford, eds. *Critical Essays on Anne Bradstreet.* Boston, MA: G.K. Hall, 1983.

Morison, Samuel Eliot. Builders of the Bay Colony. *Boston, MA: Houghton Mifflin, 1930.*

Rosenmeier, Rosamond. Anne Bradstreet *Revisited.* Boston, MA: Twayne, 1991.

Stanford, Ann. *Anne Bradstreet, The Worldly Puritan: An Introduction to Her Poetry.* NY: Burt Franklin, 1974.

White, Elizabeth Wade. *Anne Bradstreet: "The Tenth Muse."* NY: Oxford University Press, 1971.

SUGGESTED READING:

Berryman, John. *Homage to Mistress Bradstreet.* NY: Farrar, Straus, 1956.

McElrath, Joseph R., Jr. and Allan P. Robb, eds. *The Complete Works of Anne Bradstreet.* Boston, MA: Twayne, 1981.

Piercy, Josephine K. *Anne Bradstreet.* New Haven, CT: College & University Press, 1965.

RELATED MEDIA:

Cohen, Hennig. *Anne Bradstreet* (43-min. lecture), recording and sound cassette, De Land, FL: Everett-Edwards, 1976.

Harry M. Ward, author of *Colonial America, 1607–1763* (Prentice Hall, 1991) and *The American Revolution, Nationhood Achieved, 1763–1788* (St. Martin's Press, 1995)

Bradwell, Myra (1831–1894)

American founder, publisher, and editor of* Chicago Legal News *who, denied the right to practice law because of her gender, reformed the legal profession, especially laws discriminating against women. *Born Myra Colby on February 12, 1831, in Manchester, Vermont; died of cancer in Chicago, Illinois, on February 14, 1894; daughter of Eben (a farmer) and Abi-*

gail Hurd (Willey) Colby (both descendants of early Boston patriots); attended secondary school, Kenosha, Wisconsin, and Ladies Seminary, Elgin, Illinois; married James Bolesworth Bradwell, on May 18, 1852; children: Myra (1854–1861); Thomas (b. 1856); Bessie Bradwell Helmer (b. 1858); James (b. 1862).

Family moved from Vermont to New York to Illinois; following graduation, taught in schools near Elgin; following marriage, taught in public schools and in a private school run in partnership with husband in Memphis, Tennessee (1853–55); back in Chicago, worked during Civil War with Northwestern Sanitary Commission, with leading role in Sanitary Fairs of 1863, 1865, 1867; read law under husband's tutelage, passed examination, but denied admission to bar on grounds of gender (1869); founder, manager, and editor of Chicago Legal News *(1868–94); proposed many reforms for women's rights, the legal profession, and Chicago which were eventually adopted; appointed representative for Illinois to Centennial Exhibition, Philadelphia (1876); admitted to bar by Illinois Supreme Court on court's own motion (1890); named to Board of Lady Managers, Chicago Columbian Exposition.*

On October 8, 1871, fire raged through the city of Chicago, killing some 250 people and consuming over 17,000 buildings in an area of 3.5 square miles. For Myra Bradwell, as for many others, it was a terrifying night. Her home, her husband's large law library, and the records for her business, the immensely popular and profitable *Chicago Legal News*, were destroyed. Worse, her 13-year-old daughter Bessie was missing. Frantic, Bradwell and her husband James retreated to Lake Michigan, "and there, amid smoke and falling cinders and a heat that was almost stifling," they remained. The next day, her daughter reappeared, together with the *Legal News* subscription book which she had snatched as she fled. With her daughter and her business records restored, Bradwell took the manuscript for the Saturday edition of the *News* by train to Milwaukee, where she had it printed and distributed three days later, on its regular date of publication. Although she appealed to lawyers around the country to contribute books to their destitute colleagues in Chicago, the canny entrepreneur also recommended to legal book publishers that they advertise in her paper because "in no place in the world will there be such a demand for law books as in Chicago during the next few months." Never shy about proposing new legislation, Myra Bradwell made recommendations to establish proof of titles to real estate, and a special session of the legislature passed the Burnt Records Act incorporating her suggestions. Thanks to her shrewdness in having earlier secured through special legislation the right of the *Chicago Legal News* to be used as evidence in court, back issues of the *News* owned by lawyers downstate were of enormous value to prove previously established facts. Myra Bradwell returned to Chicago to rebuild her life and her business, "cheery and indomitable, uttering brave prophecies of future good."

Myra Colby, born on February 12, 1831, was descended on both sides from early participants in the young nation's history. Her mother, **Abigail Willey Colby**, came from a family which had settled in Boston in 1640; two Willeys had fought at Bunker Hill. Her father Eben's maternal ancestry encompassed the well-known Bishop Philander Chase and Salmon P. Chase, chief justice of the U.S. Supreme Court.

Myra was the last child in a family which included three other daughters and a son. Shortly after her birth, the family moved to Portage, New York, where they lived until she was 12. In 1843, they moved further west, to a farm in the township of Schaumberg in Cook County, near present-day Elgin, Illinois. Myra was sent to live with a married sister in Kenosha, Wisconsin, where she attended school. She finished her education at the Elgin Female Seminary, and began teaching, first at the Seminary, and then in local district schools.

Not far from the Colby farm was the Bradwell farm, belonging to English immigrants who had settled on the prairie in 1834 when their son James was 12. James Bradwell had worked his way through Knox College for three years and begun the study of law. The Colbys at first opposed the marriage of their daughter to a poor law student, but the young couple were wed on May 18, 1852.

The Bradwells moved to Memphis, Tennessee, where they established a successful "select" (private) school. Their daughter Myra was born in 1854. The couple moved back to Illinois, where their son Thomas was born in 1856, and their daughter Bessie in 1858. James Bradwell had continued to read law, and in 1855, having been admitted to the bar, he joined his brother-in-law to form the firm of Bradwell and Colby, which attracted a large practice. In 1861, he was elected a judge of Cook County, a position which had jurisdiction in all probate cases. That same year, their daughter Myra died. The following year, another son, James, was born, but died in 1864.

Myra Bradwell had been a childhood friend of the Lovejoys, and the mob murder of abolitionist Elijah Lovejoy in 1837 had inspired her opposition to slavery and injustice. During the Civil War, she tended sick and wounded soldiers and involved herself in the work of the Northwestern Sanitary Commission which raised money for soldiers' aid. Bradwell took part in the Soldiers Fair of 1863, as well as the great Sanitary Fair of 1865 in Bryan Hall. As secretary of the Committee on Arms, Trophies and Curiosities, she was recognized for mounting an "artistic and beautiful exhibition." The *Voice of the Fair* on June 9, 1865, also noted that "in the midst of a melange of questions, which would have frenzied an ordinary person, her courtesy and kindness have maintained an equable glow." Bradwell worked on the Fair of 1867 for the benefit of families of soldiers, and later served as president of the Soldiers Aid Society and for many years on the board of the Soldiers Home. But in her editorial on the assassination of President James Garfield in 1881, she expressed the hope that his martyrdom might help heal a nation which had taken too long to forget the Civil War.

While she was honing her executive abilities in fund-raising, Myra Bradwell was also studying law with her husband, in order to help him in his practice. Although law schools were beginning to offer professional training, it was common throughout the 19th century to "read" law in the office of a man already in practice. In 1869, she passed the qualifying examination with credit, and applied for admission to the Illinois bar. At first, she was refused admission by the Supreme Court of Illinois because of her married status: the ancient principle of "coverture" held that under the law husband and wife were one person, and a woman lawyer would therefore not be entitled to keep her client's confidences to herself. When she argued against the married state being considered any longer a disability, the Court refused admission solely on the grounds that she was a woman. Among the reasons offered were that if the legal profession were open to women, then "every office in this state may be filled by women. . . . [W]omen [would] be made governors and sheriffs." The court also supposed that the "hot strifes of the bar" would "tend to destroy the deference and delicacy with which it is a matter of pride of our ruder sex to treat [women]."

Myra Bradwell took her case to the U.S. Supreme Court, where it was argued in 1871 by Senator Matthew Carpenter of Wisconsin, a constitutional lawyer who supported the rights of women. Finally in 1873, the Supreme Court upheld the lower court, in effect leaving professional requirements to individual states. (Her cousin, Chief Justice Chase, dissented). By then, Illinois had passed a law giving women equal opportunity with men in selecting an occupation, but Myra Bradwell did not reapply. In 1890, the Illinois Supreme Court granted her a license to practice law on its own motion, retroactive to the date of her original application in 1869.

One thing we do claim—that woman has the right to think and act as an individual—believing if the great Father had intended it to be otherwise, he would have placed Eve in a cage and given Adam the key.

—Myra Bradwell

Bradwell had not reapplied because she was already busy with a new career. In September of 1868, she had released a prospectus for a new publication, the *Chicago Legal News*, announcing that a four-page journal devoted to legal information and decisions important to practicing lawyers and entrepreneurs would be issued every Saturday. She also promised to comment freely but fairly on the conduct of judges, members of the bar, officers of courts, and the activities of members of Congress and the state legislature. There was only one significant departure from her plan: so much advertising was bought for the first edition on October 3, 1869, that eight pages were printed instead of four; thereafter, there were never fewer than 12 pages during the next quarter century. A special charter was passed by the state legislature to allow Myra Bradwell to overcome her dependent status as a married woman and to act as publisher, manager, and editor-in-chief of the paper. She edited over 1,300 issues of the *Chicago Legal News*. For at least two decades, according to her biographer **Jane M. Friedman**, it was the most widely circulated legal newspaper in the country. The Bradwells also started the Chicago Legal News Corporation, which printed stationery, legal forms (many of which Myra designed), and briefs. It was the leading firm in Chicago to print cases on appeal.

In the very first issue she made good on her claim that the paper would "battle for improvement in everything directly or indirectly connected with the practice of law." The lead editorial concerned the Cook County courthouse where her husband presided as a judge. Myra Bradwell railed against the "accumulated filth of years" and the "piles of old furniture in the country courtroom." Her detailed plan for constructing a new courthouse was the first of many of her suggestions which were eventually adopted. Appropriately, the motto of the paper was *Lex Vincit*, "Law Conquers."

Other lawyers and journalists predicted the *Legal News* would fail, but it filled an important niche. The paper published the Illinois session laws well before any other edition. Until her final illness, Bradwell personally took a printed copy of the new laws to Springfield for comparison. Beginning in 1877, she published every other year an edition of Hurd's Revised Statutes of Illinois, including the laws of the previous session. As the first legal weekly west of the Alleghenies, the *News* supplied information to a growing community of lawyers who settled the conflicts of eager entrepreneurs who had rushed to the developing territory. It also covered legal news of the whole country. Attracting advertising, the paper grew rapidly and, several times before the fire, had been forced to move to larger quarters.

Myra Bradwell was able to use the burgeoning influence of her paper to push for many reforms in the law. Since women could not vote, the power of the written word was virtually the only way a woman could agitate for change. Often James, who served in the Illinois state legislature for a number of years, helped to pass the bills she drafted or proposed. Bradwell was vitally interested in abolishing laws which discriminated against women. In her third issue, she argued that a married woman should be able to keep her earnings free and clear of her husband's debts. Soon after, she learned the story of a working woman whose wages had been garnisheed by a tavern keeper who had sold her husband liquor. Outraged, Bradwell drafted a bill giving married women the right to their own earnings, and she lobbied in Springfield, together with her husband, ***Elizabeth Cady Stanton**, ***Mary Livermore**, ⚜➤ **Catherine Waite** and Judge Charles Waite, until it passed.

In 1873, James introduced a bill which Bradwell probably had helped compose to make women eligible to hold school offices in the state. She printed in full the minutes of the Illinois House Judiciary Committee opposing the bill and pointed out the errors in their arguments. The bill was enacted, and, within three years, there were 12 women county superintendents of schools in Illinois. Later, she used their example to argue for the right of women to hold other offices. Also in 1873, she urged passage of a law providing for the equal guardianship of children (previously, the fathers had been preferred in child-custody cases). In 1868 and 1870, Myra Bradwell was prevented by her gender from becoming a notary public; in 1875, this legal disability was removed. As early as 1870, she called for women to be allowed to serve as jurors. Whenever women were elected or appointed to a public position, she would note it in an editorial. The last of her proposals for women's rights to become law in Illinois was that women should be paid the same amount as men for the same work.

Bradwell was also active in support of women's suffrage. During the planning for the first suffrage convention held in Chicago in February 1869, she obtained the endorsement of all the judges in Cook County, many members of the bar, and a number of leading ministers. Stanton praised her as "a woman of great force and executive ability." Myra and James lobbied to amend the state constitution to allow women to vote. For a number of years, Bradwell served on the executive committee of the Illinois Woman Suffrage Association formed at the convention.

In spite of her suffrage activity, Bradwell is largely absent from contemporary accounts of the suffrage movement. Friedman ascribes this to disagreements with ***Susan B. Anthony** over how to win the vote. When Anthony and Stanton and their National Woman Suffrage Association opposed the 15th Amendment because it enfranchised blacks and not women, ***Lucy Stone** called for moderates to attend a meeting in Cleveland to form a parallel women's rights organization. Myra and James Bradwell attended the Cleveland convention in November 1869 to form the American Woman Suffrage Association. While the National urged passage of a federal Constitutional Amendment, the American planned to work for woman suffrage in individual states. Myra served as corresponding secretary of the convention, and James was chosen temporary chair. Bradwell's moderate position would have appealed to her male readers, many in a position to influence a suffrage bill, as did her argument that "devoted mothers and wives" would be more effective lobbyists than "the class who term man 'a tyrant.'" Bradwell further alienated Anthony by working for partial suffrage laws, and by allowing Matthew Carpenter to argue her case before the Supreme Court with the explicit reservation that admitting Bradwell to the bar would not imply she had a constitutional right to vote.

Reform of institutions was another of Bradwell's concerns. In one of the first issues of the *Legal News*, she criticized the treatment of prisoners and the mentally ill. She also attacked the Chicago Reform School. Most of the inmates were children who were orphans or abandoned, and they were being forced to work to the point of exhaustion. She exposed these facts in her paper, as well as a letter from the superintendent of schools, claiming she'd misstated the facts. She repeated them, in effect daring him to sue her for libel. Ultimately, her efforts led to the closing of the Chicago Reform School. Bradwell was a charter member of the Illinois Industrial School for Girls. She was appointed in the early 1870s by the governor of Illinois as a delegate to the Prison Reform Congress in St. Louis, where she lobbied hard to ensure that women be allowed to serve as officers, though afterwards she declined to accept a position herself.

She became involved with the issue of arbitrary confinement when her longtime friend ***Mary Todd Lincoln**, the widow of President Abraham Lincoln, was incarcerated in 1875 by her sole surviving son, Robert, after a commitment hearing about which Bradwell had not been informed more than an hour in advance, and at which she was not allowed to testify. Bradwell visited her friend in the asylum and arranged for two other reporters to publish the facts of the case. The resulting publicity led to Mary Lincoln's release.

Bradwell advocated a number of other reforms: to abolish discrimination in taxation between blacks and whites; to install a modern indexing system for the recorder of deeds; in civil cases, to receive a majority verdict or dispense with a jury; to limit the ability of a court of last resort to reverse its decision; to allow the accused to testify in criminal cases; to secure better treatment of witnesses, then often treated worse than the criminal; to abolish whipping as punishment for a crime; to regulate railroads and other large corporations; to permit foreign corporations to loan and invest money in Illinois; to establish intermediate federal appellate courts; and to regulate the height of proposed buildings, one of the first zoning laws.

She also called for many reforms of the legal profession, including specialization of lawyers in large cities; the recommendation that judges should not run for other political offices without first resigning; compulsory retirement and pensions for judges; and the creation of the Chicago Bar Association (formed with her help in 1873), the Illinois Bar Association (she was elected an honorary member at its second annual meeting, although she was not then a member of the bar), and the American Bar Association.

Bradwell worked on behalf of her community as well as on behalf of her fellow citizens. She was appointed by the governor in 1876 as a member of the Illinois Centennial Association, to represent the state in the Centennial Exposition in Philadelphia, and served as treasurer of the Women's Branch of the Association. By 1888, she was lobbying for a World's Fair to be held in Chicago in 1892, to commemorate the 400th anniversary of Christopher Columbus' voyage to the Americas. The governor appointed her to the committee to promote the fair, and she accompanied the commissioner to Washington to petition Congress for appropriations. Potter Palmer, the president of the fair, was convinced that her "charm and diplomacy secured for Chicago the World's Columbian Exposition." She served on the fair's Board of Lady Managers, and as chair of the committee on law reform of its auxiliary congress.

Bradwell was well-traveled for a woman of her day. In 1872, she was elected a vice president of the Illinois Press Association, and often went on its annual excursions throughout the United States. She visited Europe three times, in 1869, in 1881, and finally in 1891, to consult Sir Spencer Wells of London, who confirmed a diagnosis of cancer made in January. In spite of her illness, she was determined to see the fair she had worked so hard to promote. Against the advice of her doctor and friends, she insisted on

Waite, Catherine (1829–1913)

American writer, suffragist, and lawyer. *Born Catherine Van Valkenburg on January 30, 1829, in Dumfries, Ontario, Canada; died of a heart ailment in Park Ridge, Illinois, on November 9, 1913; daughter of Joseph and Margaret (Page) Van Valkenburg; attended Knox College, Galesburg, Illinois; graduated from Oberlin College, 1853; attended Union College of Law (later Northwestern University Law School), 1885; admitted to the bar, June 1886; married Charles B. Waite (a Chicago lawyer), in 1854; children: Lucy, Jessie, Margaret, Joseph, and Charles.*

For four years, Catherine Waite lived with her husband Charles B. Waite in Utah Territory, following his appointment to the Utah Territory Supreme Court by Abraham Lincoln. Upon her return to Chicago, Waite wrote of her experiences in *The Mormon Prophet and His Harem* (1867), protesting the practice of polygamy. Enrolling in law school in 1885, she passed the bar and, for three years, published the *Chicago Law Times*; she also served as president of the International Woman's Bar Association.

SUGGESTED READING:

Notable American Women, 1607–1950. Cambridge; MA: Belknap, 1971.

visiting a hotel near the grounds, from which she went forth in a wheelchair to visit the fair for a couple of hours every day for a week in September 1893. She died on February 14, 1894, three days before her 63rd birthday.

Alice Brady

Myra Bradwell liked to use her life as proof that giving women their rights would not render them unfit wives and mothers. She was extremely close to her grown children, who shared a house with their parents, even after they were married and had children of their own. Both her son and her daughter became lawyers; Bessie Bradwell graduated in 1882 as head of her class from Union College of Law (later Northwestern Law School). After their mother's death, with their father's help, they continued her work: ◂❦ **Bessie Bradwell Helmer** with the newspaper until 1925 and Thomas Bradwell with the printing company. Helmer also continued her mother's work for women's rights as the chair of the American Association of University Women's committee for graduate fellowships.

SOURCES:

Bird, Caroline. *Enterprising Women.* NY: Norton, 1976.

Friedman, Jane M. *America's First Woman Lawyer: The Biography of Myra Bradwell.* Buffalo, NY: Prometheus Books, 1993.

Gale, George W. *American Bar Association Journal.* Vol. 39. December 1953, p. 1080.

Kogan, Herman. "Myra Bradwell, Crusader at Law," in *Chicago History.* Vol. 3, no. 3. Winter 1974–75, pp. 132–140.

Kristie Miller, author of *Ruth Hanna McCormick: A Life in Politics, 1880–1944* (University of New Mexico Press, 1992)

❦▸ Helmer, Bessie Bradwell (1858–1927)

American lawyer and editor. *Born in Chicago, Illinois, on October 20, 1858; died in Battle Creek, Michigan, on January 10, 1927; daughter of* ***Myra (Colby) Bradwell** *(a legal reformer and entrepreneur) and James Bolesworth Bradwell; graduated first in class, Chicago High School, 1876; graduated first in class Union College of Law (later Northwestern University Law School), 1882; married Frank A. Helmer (a lawyer), in 1885.*

Following her mother's death in 1894, Bessie Bradwell Helmer became assistant editor of the *Chicago Legal News.* From 1907 until her death in 1927, Helmer was editor-in-chief and president of the company.

Brady, Alice (1892–1939)

American actress. *Born in New York City on November 2, 1892; died of cancer in 1939; daughter of William A. Brady (noted stage and film producer); studied voice.*

Filmography: As Ye Sow *(1914);* The Boss *(1915);* The Cup of Chance *(1915);* The Lure of Woman *(1915);* The Ballet Girl *(1916);* Tangled Fates *(1916);* Miss Petticoats *(1916);* La Vie de Boheme *(1916);* The Gilded Cage *(1916);* Bought and Paid For *(1916);* A Hungry Heart *(1917);* The Dancer's Peril *(1917);* Darkest Russia *(1917);* Maternity *(1917);* The Divorce Game *(1917);* Betsy Ross *(1917);* The Maid of Belgium *(1917);* Her Silent Sacrifice *(1917);* Woman and Wife *(1918);* The Knife *(1918);* The Spurs of Sybil *(1918);* The Ordeal of Rosetta *(1918);* The Whirlpool *(1918);* The Death Dance *(1918);* The Indestructible Wife *(1919);* Marie Ltd. *(1919);* Redhead *(1919);* His Bridal Night *(1919);* The Fear Market *(1920);* Sinners *(1920);* The New York Idea *(1920);* Out of the Chorus *(1921);* Little Italy *(1921);* The Land of Hope *(1921);* Dawn of the East *(1921);* Hush Money *(1921);* Anna Ascends *(1922);* Missing Millions *(1922);* The Leopardess *(1923);* The Snow Bride *(1923);* When Ladies Meet *(1933);* Broadway to Hollywood *(1933);* Beauty for Sale *(1933);* Stage Mother *(1933);* Should Ladies Behave? *(1933);* The Gay Divorcée *(1934);* Gold Diggers of 1935 *(1935);* Lady Tubbs *(1935);* Metropolitan *(1935);* The Harvester *(1936);* My Man Godfrey *(1936);* Go West Young Man *(1936);* Three Smart Girls *(1937);* Mama Steps Out *(1937);* 100 Men and a Girl *(1937);* In Old Chicago *(1938);* Joy of Living *(1938);* Goodbye Broadway *(1938);* Zenobia *(1939);* Young Mr. Lincoln *(1939).*

Alice Brady made her stage debut at 14. Starting her screen career in 1914, she played romantic leads throughout World War I but reappeared on the New York stage in 1918 and became a Broadway star. When she returned to Hollywood in the early 1930s, she abandoned straight roles for light comedy. Brady was nominated for an Academy Award for Best Supporting Actress in *My Man Godfrey* in 1936 and won Best Supporting Actress for her performance in *In Old Chicago* in 1938. She died soon after shooting a featured role in John Ford's *Young Mr. Lincoln* (1939).

Brady, Mary (1821–1864)

Irish-born Civil War nurse. *Born in Ireland in 1821; died in 1864, in Philadelphia, Pennsylvania; married a lawyer, in 1846; children: five.*

The patriotism of Mary Brady, a volunteer nurse during the Civil War, was particularly noteworthy given that she was not an American. Born in Ireland, she immigrated to America with her husband in 1846. With no relatives in the war, Brady was evidently driven by charitable motives and periodically left her home in Philadelphia, and her five small children, to endure the hardships of the front lines and field hospitals, tending to the sick and wounded.

In July 1862, Brady and a few others began volunteering at the Satterlee Hospital in West Philadelphia, where some 3,000 soldiers were housed in less than ideal quarters. Headed by Brady, the small group organized into a Soldiers' Aid Society with the purpose of visiting hospitals, evaluating needs, and distributing supplies from a central-supply depot. For some months, their activities were limited to daily rounds of Philadelphia-area hospitals. In November, they organized a Thanksgiving dinner for some 1,600 soldiers, soliciting contributions and overseeing preparation and distribution (in covered wagons) of enormous amounts of food.

As news of Brady's work became known, Soldiers' Aid Societies sprung up across the state. More and more donations began to arrive in Philadelphia, entrusted to Brady for distribution. Not content to leave the contributions with unknown agents, Brady set out to personally distribute the supplies to field hospitals in Alexandria. Her journeys took her to some 40 military hospitals in and around Washington, bringing her in contact with 30,000 sick and wounded. At several of the Alexandria hospitals, she was the first woman ever to visit. She went further into the front lines of fighting, at one point on a four-mule wagon, stopping wherever a red flag indicated a sick tent.

Over a two-year period, Brady alternated trips to the front lines with respite at home in Philadelphia, where she became well known for her charitable work. In 1864, after her fifth trip to the front, she arrived home worn out and was diagnosed with a weak heart. Although never again well enough to travel, she continued to administer collections in Philadelphia when she could. Upon her death in May 1864, at age 42, hundreds of soldiers attended her funeral. Others sent tributes expressing appreciation for her work on their behalf.

SOURCES:

Moore, Frank. *Women of the War.* Hartford, CT: S.S. Scranton, 1866.

Braganza, duchess of.

See Isabella of Braganza (1459–1521).
See Catherine of Portugal (1540–1614).
See Anne of Velasquez (1585–1607).
See Luisa de Guzmán (1613–1666).
See Elizabeth Maria of Thurn and Taxis (1860–1881).

Brahe, Sophia (1556–1643)

Danish student of astronomy and chemistry. *Born in Denmark in 1556; died in 1643; one of ten children of Otto and Beate (Bille) Brahe; sister of astronomer Tycho Brahe (1546–1601); married Otto Thott (died 1588); married Erik Lange; children: (first marriage) one.*

Highly educated in classical literature, astrology, and alchemy, Sophia Brahe made her contribution to science as an assistant to her brother, astronomer Tycho Brahe. Sophia assisted with the observations that led to his computation of the lunar eclipse of December 8, 1573, and often visited his well equipped observatory on the island of Hveen.

Brahe was 19 or 20 when she married her first husband and had a child. Following her husband's death in 1588, she managed their property at Ericksholm and became an excellent horticulturist, as well as a student of chemistry and medicine. She subsequently remarried.

As testament to her contribution, Brahe is mentioned in Gassendi's *De Tychonis Brahei Vita* as having great talent and enthusiasm for science: "She has been exposed to the study of mathematics, and as a result not only did she love astronomy but she was especially ready to engage in these exciting astrological studies."

Braithwaite, Lilian (1873–1948)

British actress. *Name variations: Dame Lilian Braithwaite. Born Lilian Florence Braithwaite in 1873 in Ramsgate, England; died in 1948; daughter of a minister; married Gerald Lawrence (an actor); children: daughter, Joyce Carey (b. 1892), also an actress.*

One of the grande dames of the British stage, Lilian Braithwaite gained popularity early in her career playing a succession of suffering heroines, but in later years expanded her reper-

Lilian Braithwaite

toire to become a well-respected actress.

Born in Ramsgate, England, in 1873, the daughter or a minister, Braithwaite grew up to be remarkably beautiful, with classical features, including a wonderfully long nose—slightly broad at the end—that was said to have sent artists into raptures. Though she appeared in amateur theatricals with the Strolling Players and the Oxford University Dramatic Society, her desire to go on the professional stage was met with a storm of family protest. But in 1897, at age 24, she joined the William Haviland and Gerald Lawrence Shakespearean company, making her first professional appearances in minor roles in South Africa. (Married to Gerald Lawrence, Braithwaite had had a daughter Joyce in 1892; the marriage was subsequently dissolved.)

After an appearance at Stratford-upon-Avon in *Pericles* (for which she learned the role of Marina in one day), she made her London debut at Crouch End Opera House as Celia in *As You Like It*, playing opposite ➧ **Julia Neilson**. However, it was her portrayal of Lady Olivia Vernon in the original Haymarket production of *Sweet Nell of Old Drury* (1900) that brought Braithwaite to the attention of playgoers. In 1901, she joined Frank Benson's company at the Comedy Theater to gain more experience in Shakespeare, and she returned to the West End a year later, where her technique and radiant beauty made her a huge box-office draw. Signing with the George Alexander company, she was seen in *The Wilderness*, *Liberty Hall*, *Paolo and Francesca*, *The Importance of Being Earnest*, *Lady Windermere's Fan*, *Old Heidelberg*, and *Mr. Wu*, a 1913 hit which ran for a year. Though Braithwaite could have presumably played the West End successfully for the rest of her career, she occasionally strayed from London to play more challenging roles in the provinces, sacrificing salary to gain experience.

After considerable success as Margaret Fairfield in *A Bill of Divorcement* (1921), Braithwaite took a risk with a different kind of role. She played opposite Noel Coward in his early play *The Vortex* (1924), about a young dope addict and his neurotic mother, who is having an affair with one of his friends. (The part became Braithwaite's when **Kate Cutler** left the cast in a dispute with Coward.) The play, daring in theme for the 1920s, brought Braithwaite status as a serious actress. The production "was shattering," wrote her daughter **Joyce Carey**. "I'd never seen anything like it on the stage in my life and the last act left one literally shaking with excitement. Both my mother and Noel were fantastically good." While playing in the New York production of the play, Braithwaite received such an enormous round of applause at her first entrance that she nearly forgot her lines. Upon her return to London, Braithwaite's role as Mrs. Phelps, the possessive matriarch in *The Silver Cord*, fully entrenched her as an actress to be reckoned with. Four years later, she took on a second role intended for another actress—this time, ***Constance Collier**—in Ivor Novello's comedy *The Truth Game*. Displaying a great talent for delivering the most malicious insults in a honeyed tone, she subsequently played in a series of Novello comedies, including *Symphony in Two Flats*, *Party*, *Fresh Fields*, *Full House*, and *Comedienne*.

Braithwaite was also known for her terrific wit, reminiscent of ***Mrs. Patrick Campbell**, though she was thought to be kinder. According to Eric Johns, Braithwaite frequented the Ivy Restaurant, occupying a favorite table by the door, where anyone entering would have to pass scrutiny, thus becoming fair game for her endearing sarcasm. "At one time Margaretta Scott favoured a cloak and tricorne, looking like a picturesque Dick Turpin character. As she swept past the Braithwaite table on her way to a matinée, Lilian remarked, 'There goes Peggy—off to York!'" Johns also writes that critic James Agate so relished Braithwaite's remarks that he gave her twopence each time he felt she had outdone herself. He relished goading her. "At supper one night he crossed to her table to say, 'I've just seen a very good performance from London's second best actress.' Lilian replied, 'What encouraging praise from London's second best critic.'"

During World War II, Braithwaite worked for the Entertainments National Service Association (ENSA), an organization that provided entertainment for the armed forces. At her office in the Drury Lane Theater, she oversaw arrangements for units to entertain at various hospitals, often arguing with authorities who sought to stop her performers from leaving in times of danger. In the midst of wartime, she took time from ENSA to play Abby Brewster in *Arsenic and Old Lace*. Then 69 years old, the actress made her way to the theater for 1,337 performances, even when the West End was in danger of bomb blasts.

Braithwaite was close to her daughter Joyce, although for a time she tried to discourage her from going into the theater. She finally came around and arranged for her to study with **Kate Rorke** at the Florence Etlinger Dramatic School. Joyce enjoyed some success as an actress, best known for her roles in a number of Coward plays. She also wrote a popular play, *Sweet Aloes* (1934), under the pseudonym Jay Mallory.

Even late in her career, Braithwaite's flair and wit won her the respect of her colleagues old and young. She may be best remembered for the particular dignity she brought to her calling. As

Neilson, Julia Emilie (1868–1957)

English actress and theater manager. *Born in 1868; died in 1957; educated in Wiesbaden and at the Royal Academy of Music; married Fred Terry, in 1891 (died 1933).*

Julia Neilson made her acting debut at the Lyceum Theater in 1888. For the next 12 years, she acted in plays opposite such luminaries as Sir Herbert Beerbohm Tree, Sir John Hare, and Sir George Alexander. In 1891, she married Fred Terry, the brother of actress ***Ellen Terry**. From 1900 to 1930, in collaboration with her husband, Neilson was actor-manager on a series of successful productions, including *Sweet Nell of Old Drury* (1900), *The Scarlet Pimpernel* (1905), and *Henry of Navarre* (1909). She made her last stage appearance in the 1944 presentation of *The Widow of Forty*.

Eric Johns points out, she "became the epitome of the West End stage presentation of a Lady."

SOURCES:

Hartnoll, Phyllis, and Peter Found, eds. *The Concise Oxford Companion to the Theatre.* NY: Oxford University Press, 1992.

Johns, Eric. *Dames of the Theatre.* New Rochelle, NY: Arlington House, 1974.

Barbara Morgan,
Melrose, Massachusetts

Bramley, Jenny Rosenthal (1910—)

American engineer. *Born in 1910; married Arthur Bramley (also an engineer).*

Jenny Rosenthal Bramley has been cited for achievement in spectroscopy, optics, and mathematical techniques and their applications. Her basic research for the invention of the microwave-pumped, high-efficiency lamp was applied to subsequent development of high efficiency lasers. In the 1950s, Bramley headed the mathematics department at Monmouth Junior College, where she and her husband did pioneering work applying electroluminescence to solid state display and storage devices. The patents they obtained on their work were later licensed to IBM. Bramley also invented techniques of coding and decoding pictorial information, which were later used in classified studies. Some of her work on alphanumerics was of interest to the FBI. Her research of the hyperfine structure anomaly was required reading for students doing research in nuclear physics or hyperfine structure.

Branca (c. 1192–1240)

Portuguese princess. *Born around 1192; died on November 17, 1240, at Guadalajara; daughter of *****Douce of Aragon*** *(1160–1198) and Sancho I (1154–1211 or 1212), king of Portugal (r. 1185–1211 or 1212).*

Branca (1259–1321)

Abbess of Lorvano. *Born on February 25, 1259, in Guimaraes; died on April 17, 1321, in Burgos; daughter of *****Beatrice of Castile and Leon*** *(1242–1303) and Alphonso III, king of Portugal (r. 1248–1279).*

Brandegee, Mary Katharine (1844–1920)

American botanist. *Name variations: Katherine Layne. Born Mary Katharine Layne in 1844 in Tennessee; died in 1920 in Berkeley, California; daughter and second of ten children of Marshall and Mary (Morris) Layne; graduated from University of California, San Francisco, M.D., 1878; married Hugh Curran, in 1866 (died 1874); married Townshend Brandegee (a civil engineer), in 1889.*

Shortly after her first husband's death in 1874, Mary Katharine Brandegee entered the University of California to study medicine. After receiving her M.D. in 1878, she took up the study of plants, concentrating on their medicinal value before expanding to a more general approach. Through her mentor, Dr. Hans Herman Behr, she began working at the California Academy of Sciences, where she was curator of botany from 1883 to 1893.

With her second husband, Townshend Brandegee, also an avid plant collector, she established and edited a series of *Bulletins* of the California Academy of Science. The couple also founded *Zoe*, a journal of botanical observations from the western United States, in which Brandegee published most of her works.

According to **Marilyn Ogilvie** in *Women in Science*, Brandegee's plant collections were important in determining range boundaries. "She was especially interested in locating intermediate forms of newly described species, thereby demonstrating that the new 'species' were actually only subspecifically different." Two new species of plants were named for Mary Katharine Brandegee: *Astragalus layneae* and *Mimulus layneae*.

SOURCES:

Ogilvie, Marilyn Bailey. *Women in Science.* Cambridge, MA: MIT Press, 1993.

Brandenburg, electress of.

See Cunegunde (d. 1357).
See Elizabeth of Bavaria-Landshut (1383–1442).
See Margaret of Baden (d. 1457).
See Catherine of Saxony (1421–1476).
See Anne of Saxony (1437–1512).
See Margaret of Saxony (1449–1501).
See Elizabeth of Denmark (1485–1555).
See Magdalene of Saxony (1507–1534).
See Hedwig of Poland (1513–1573).
See Sabine of Brandenburg-Ansbach (1529–1575).
See Catherine of Custrin (1549–1602).
See Elizabeth of Anhalt (1563–1607).
See Anna of Prussia (fl. 1599).
See Louisa Henrietta of Orange (1627–1667).
See Sophie Charlotte of Hanover (1668–1705).

Brandenburg, margravine of.

See Jutta of Saxony (d. around 1267).
See Hedwig of Habsburg (d. 1286).
See Barbara of Saxe-Wittenberg (c. 1405–1465).

Brandon, Anne (d. 1557)

English baroness. *Died in January 1557; daughter of Charles Brandon (1484–1545), 1st duke of Suffolk (r. 1514–1545), and his second wife* ****Anne Browne*** *(his first wife was* ****Mary Tudor*** *[1496–1533]); married Edward Grey (d. 1552), 3rd baron Grey of Powys; married Randle Hansworth.*

Brandon, Eleanor (c. 1520–1547).

See Mary Tudor for sidebar.

Brandon, Frances (1517–1559).

See Grey, Lady Jane for sidebar.

Brandt, Marianne (1842–1921)

Austrian who was one of the early Wagnerian mezzo-sopranos. *Born Marie Bischoff in Vienna, Austria, on September 12, 1842; died in Vienna on July 9, 1921.*

Though Marianne Brandt was Viennese, she first appeared in Berlin in 1868, performing there until 1882. She studied in Vienna with Janda and Zeller and in Baden-Baden with ***Pauline Viardot.** In 1872, Brandt made her Covent Garden debut in *Fidelio.* Two years later, she sang Amneris in the first Berlin performance of *Aïda.* Though she originally refused the part of Waltraute in *Götterdämmerung*, Brandt replaced **Luise Jaide** with short notice at the first Bayreuth Festival in 1876. In 1882, Brandt performed Kundry at the second performance of *Parsifal* at Bayreuth. Throughout the 1870s and 1880s, though she disliked Wagner, Brandt performed his work in Berlin, London, and New York. Her large, well-projected voice made her a perfect choice for these demanding operas. From 1884 to 1888, she appeared at the Metropolitan Opera. Brandt gave the first American performance of Weber's *Euryanthe* in 1887. She retired in 1890.

Marianne Brandt

Brandt, Muriel (1909–1981)

Irish painter. *Born in Belfast in 1909; died in Our Lady's Hospice, Dublin, on June 10, 1981; won a scholarship to the Royal College of Art, London; married Frank Brandt (an artistic adviser); children: one son and two daughters, including* ***Ruth Brandt,*** *also an artist.*

Muriel Brandt's first major commission was a set of panels of Adam and Eve for the Franciscan Church on Merchants' Quay in Dublin. Her portraits include Sir Alfred Chester Beatty, George O'Brien, and a group seating of Michael Mac Liammoir, **Christine Longford,** and Hilton Edwards which hangs in the foyer of the Gate Theater.

Branham, Sara Elizabeth (1888–1962)

American bacteriologist and researcher in the field of public health who conducted pioneering work on meningitis. *Born in 1888 in Oxford, Georgia; died in 1962; attended Wesleyan College, Macon, Georgia; University of Colorado, Ph.D., 1923; M.D., 1934.*

Paralleling the work of ***Hattie Alexander,** Sara Elizabeth Branham is known for her pioneering research on meningitis, a disease that attacks the membrane around the brain and spinal cord. Her success in demonstrating that sulfa drugs inhibit the activity of meningococcal bacteria helped pave the way to successful control of the often fatal disease.

Branham, a native of Georgia, studied biology at Wesleyan College, then taught in Atlanta before becoming an assistant in bacteriology at the University of Colorado, where she earned a Ph.D. in 1923. In the midst of studying for a medical degree, she accepted a position as a bacteriologist with the U.S. Public Health Service (now the National Institute of Health, or NIH) where she would remain for 30 years (with a brief leave in 1934 to complete her M.D.).

While there, she became involved with the meningitis epidemic of 1927. Although a antiserum had been effective in controlling an earlier outbreak, it seemed ineffective against the new strain of bacteria, *Neisseria meningitidis*. Branham's battle against the disease was labor-intensive, due to the fragile nature of the meningococci cultures, which demanded subculturing every other day to keep the strain viable. She was successful in identifying several different strains of meningococci and in proving that the type and virulence of the meningococcus was as important a factor in the spread of the disease as the number of infected people in the population. By 1937, she had found sulfa drugs to be effective in treating the disease. When another epidemic threatened the United States in 1940, a new serum was in place. Sara Branham retired from NIH in 1958, when she was 70. In 1959, she was named Women of the Year by the American Medical Women's Association.

Brannon, Hazel (1914–1994).

See Smith, Hazel Brannon.

Branscombe, Gena (1881–1977)

Canadian-born American composer, conductor, teacher, and pianist, who was especially well known for her choral compositions. *Pronunciation: Branskum. Born Gena Branscombe in Picton near Kingston, Ontario, on November 4, 1881; died in New York City on July 26, 1977; daughter of Henry W. and Sara (Allison) Branscombe; graduated Chicago Musical College; studied with Rudolph Ganz, Felix Borowski, and Engelbert Humperdinck; married John Ferguson Tenney, in 1910; children: Gena, Vivian Allison, Betty, and Beatrice.*

Gena Branscombe began composing at age five and was still actively composing at 92. Her main area of expertise was choral composition. She studied with Felix Borowski, Alexander von Fielitz, Arthur Friedheim, Hans von Schiller, and Rudolph Ganz at the Chicago Musical College before becoming director of Whitman College's piano department. Branscombe also studied with Engelbert Humperdinck (composer of the opera *Hansel und Gretel*) in Berlin during 1909–10. Moving to New York in 1910, she lived and worked in the U.S. for three-quarters of a century but kept her Canadian roots. Her *Quebec Suite* was premiered in 1930 by the Chicago Women's Symphony Orchestra. *Pilgrims of Destiny* won the League of American Pen Women's annual prize in 1928 for the finest work produced by a woman. *Coventry's Choir* (1944), a large choral work with piano accompaniment, typified Branscombe's evocative and richly textured late Romantic style. It was performed throughout the United States, Canada, and Great Britain. Often she used her own texts for her vocal works. In 1933, she founded the Branscombe Chorale of New York, which performed for over 20 years. She was president of the Society of American Women Composers and director of the National Association of American Composers and Conductors.

John Haag,
Athens, Georgia

Brant, Mary (c. 1736–1796).

See Brant, Molly.

Brant, Molly (c. 1736–1796)

Mohawk clan mother whose diplomacy and intelligence-gathering during the American Revolution made her a power broker among both the Iroquois nations and British government officials in Canada. *Name variations: Mary Brant; (in Mohawk) Koñwatsi'tsiaiéñni (meaning "someone lends her a flower"). Pronunciation: Gon-wat-si-jay-en-ni. Born around 1736 in the Mohawk village at Canajoharie near Little Falls, New York; died on April 16, 1796, at Kingston, Ontario, Canada; daughter of Margaret and Peter (Christianized Mohawks of the Six Nations Confederacy); granddaughter of Sagayeeanquarashtow, Iroquois representative to the English court; sister of Joseph Brant (c. 1742–1807); married Sir William Johnson, c. 1759 (his second marriage); children: Peter (b. 1759); Elizabeth (b. 1761); Magdalene (b. 1763); Margaret (b. 1765); George (b. 1767); Mary (b. 1769); Susanna (b. 1771); Anna (b. 1773) and one unnamed baby who died shortly after birth.*

Accompanied Mohawk delegation to Philadelphia to protest fraudulent sales of tribal lands (1754–55); marriage to Superintendent of Indian Affairs for the Northern Colonies placed her in charge of the Johnson household and estate, and, from time to time, the Indian Department itself (1759–74); as Johnson's widow and a powerful clan mother, persuaded her nation to ally with the Crown during the American Revolution (1775–83); credited with saving St. Leger's Loyalist forces besieging Fort Stanwix from surprise attack by an American relief militia (1777); forced from her Mohawk Valley home by invading rebel colonists, spent most of the war at Fort Niagara and on Carleton Island, New York, negotiating the Crown's interests with other displaced Iroquois; at war's end, resettled her family at Cataraqui (Kingston) Canada.

Early one August morning in 1777, the American General Nicholas Herkimer's young Oneida wife opened her front door to find an angry, threatening Mohawk Loyalist on her doorstep. General Herkimer had been observed leading the entire Tryon County, New York, militia off on a secret mission, and "Mistress Molly" Brant of the Six Nations Confederacy demanded to know where he was bound.

While most of the Iroquois nations supported the British cause in the American Revolution, the Oneidas had sided with the rebels, a fact which infuriated the head of the Six Nations Society of Matrons. After all, was it not backcountry colonists, now in rebellion against the Crown, who pillaged Indian lands and murdered innocent villagers? And was it not British officials who had tried to keep the peace and protect Indian rights? Molly's own husband, Sir William Johnson, negotiated the Treaty of Fort Stanwix in 1768, guaranteeing Iroquois sovereignty over their hunting grounds on the Ohio and limiting colonial expansion into Indian country. And now this Oneida traitor dared to defy her. "Where has your husband gone?" Brant repeated menacingly. "And remember, I am a clan mother—do not even think of lying to me!" Shaking with fear, the young woman blurted out what she knew. With that information, Molly Brant succeeded in saving her brother's Iroquois warriors and their British allies from annihilation.

Born in 1736 into the Mohawk nation of the powerful Iroquois Confederacy (Mohawk, Cayuga, Onondaga, Oneida, Seneca, and Tuscarora tribes), Molly Brant probably spent some of her childhood years at Cuyahoga in the Ohio hunting grounds of the Mohawk, for it was there that her younger, equally famous brother, "Chief" Joseph Brant, was born in 1742. Details of her parentage and early life are obscure. Some sources assert that her father Peter (who died when she was a child) was a notable warrior, and that her mother Margaret was a granddaughter or possibly niece of the great Mohawk chief Theyanoguin (also known as King Hendrick). Others state that Molly's parents were of humble origin and that

Molly Brant

Margaret's subsequent marriage to a prosperous mixed-blood, Nickus Brant, elevated her family to prominence within the Mohawk community. Molly's early life at Canajoharie, located in the thriving Mohawk River Valley, may have included some formal education, as in later life she could read and write English fluently—though she preferred to speak Mohawk.

Her political activity seems to have begun in 1754 when she accompanied 12 Mohawk leaders (including King Hendrick) to Philadelphia to complain to Pennsylvania officials about unscrupulous Connecticut land speculators operating in Mohawk territory. Her presence in such a delegation was not unusual. Tribes of the Six Nations Confederacy were not merely matrilineal; Iroquois women customarily exercised considerable economic and political power. They controlled the fields, selected peace chiefs and religious leaders, decided the fate of captives, and commanded—usually through the Clan Mothers' Council—a voice in tribal policy-making. No treaty was considered valid without their assent, and no war could be prosecuted without their permission, for they supplied the food and extra moccasins for war parties. Molly Brant's subsequent influence over restless young warriors during the American Revolution derived not only from her own talents but also from long-standing traditions of matriarchal authority among the Iroquois.

In 1759, Molly Brant became the common-law wife of Sir William Johnson, the most substantial European settler in Mohawk Valley. An

Irish merchant and land developer, Johnson had come to the valley some 20 years earlier to manage his Uncle Peter Warren's North American estates. In time, Johnson's adept handling of his frontier neighbors—Indian and European—elevated him to superintendent of Indian Affairs for His Majesty's Northern Colonies; military successes and valor during the French and Indian War (1756–63) earned him a baronetcy. The famed Covenant Chain of friendship between the Six Nations Confederacy and the British Crown owed much to his honest and affectionate dealings with the Iroquois. The Mohawks especially considered him their trusted friend and patron. Long acquainted with the Brant family, and now a widower with three teenage children, Sir William brought Molly into his home as housekeeper, hostess, and mistress. Although no record can be found of a legal marriage or an Indian ceremony, Brant remained his sole consort until his death in 1774; their eight surviving children bore Sir William's name and were, like their mother, well provided for in his will.

You have great influence with your people, Miss Molly. Your word is law to them.

—Colonel John Butler

Just as Johnson's marriage to a well-connected Mohawk cemented his ties to the Confederacy, Brant likewise used her position to augment her influence among the Iroquois. She supervised a large household of servants, slaves, and children, first at Fort Johnson on the Mohawk River, and then at Johnson Hall, the baronial mansion he built in 1763 near Johnstown, New York. Records reveal that Brant even directed the routine business of the Indian Affairs Department during her husband's frequent absences on business and military matters. She purchased large quantities of trade goods which she distributed to Iroquois sachems, gift-giving being a much-honored practice among Eastern Woodlands tribes. She entertained peace chiefs, governors, and hundreds of important British visitors at Johnson Hall. "When treaties and purchases were about to be made," reported one observer, "she often persuaded the obstinate chiefs into compliance with the proposals." In due course, Molly Brant became the most influential Mohawk matron in the valley.

Joseph Brant (also known as Thayendanegea) clearly benefitted from his older sister's union with Johnson. A promising young warrior at age 16—he fought under Johnson in the successful 1759 campaign against the French at Fort Niagara—Joseph now became Johnson's much-favored protégé. Sir William educated his young brother-in-law at his own expense and personally trained him in the art of diplomacy during vacations from boarding school. Joseph enjoyed all the privileges of a son and, like Molly, found himself utterly charmed by the Irish chieftain of Johnson Hall.

Sir William's untimely death in 1774 left Brant a widow at age 41, but in no way diminished her status among either the Iroquois or British officials. Johnson Hall passed into the hands of her stepson, Sir John Johnson, while Brant established a spacious home for her children and servants on land she inherited near Canajoharie. There she continued to influence decision-making among her clan, little suspecting how completely her family's comfortable existence would be shattered by the coming war.

As revolutionary fervor mounted among the rebel colonists, the Six Nations Confederacy faced its most serious crisis in decades. The Iroquois Confederacy had built and maintained its power in North America by remaining united, and by playing off one enemy against another. The Covenant Chain of friendship with the Crown—based as it was on trade and peaceful co-existence—was one thing; involving themselves in the White Man's internal conflicts, quite another. Even the Mohawks, the most pro-British tribe in the Confederacy, preferred to stay neutral. But Molly Brant and her family were staunch Loyalists. She and Joseph used all their powers of persuasion to swing the Six Nations to the Crown's side. In the end, most of the Mohawks, Onondagas, Cayugas, and Senecas backed the British and chose Joseph Brant as their war leader; most of the Oneidas and Tuscaroras threw in their lot with the Americans. Tragically, this split ultimately proved fatal to the Iroquois people on both sides.

Molly and Sir William's 16-year-old son, Peter Warren Johnson, became a lieutenant in the British army, where he distinguished himself in September of 1775 by capturing the patriot leader, Ethan Allen, at Montreal. Soon Joseph headed to England to negotiate a formal alliance with the Crown, while Molly, at considerable risk to her personal safety, did everything she could to feed, clothe, and arm Loyalist refugees of both races in Mohawk country.

In August of 1777, she rendered her most dramatic service to the Loyalist cause. As British and Iroquois forces led by Matthew St. Leger and Joseph Brant lay siege to Fort Stanwix (Rome,

New York), Molly observed her former neighbor, Nicholas Herkimer, march away from Canajoharie at the head of a sizable rebel militia. Seizing Herkimer's Oneida wife, and threatening her as only a Mohawk clan mother could, Molly pried out of the terrified woman details of Herkimer's plan to attack the Loyalists outside Fort Stanwix. Brant sent Indian runners to her brother, who then arranged a successful ambush of Herkimer's army at Oriskany, New York. More than any other participant, Molly determined the course of military events that month in the region, but she paid dearly for her partisan deed: her home was ransacked and destroyed by revenge-minded rebels, and she and her young children were forced to flee for their lives.

Taking refuge first in Onondaga, the Six Nations capital, and then among her Cayuga relatives, for the next several weeks Brant continued to urge all out war against the Americans. When British General John Burgoyne's disastrous surrender in October caused some of the chiefs to waver, Brant used her standing as Johnson's widow to force their continuing loyalty. In one critical council, when a leading Seneca war chief urged peace, she publicly rebuked him for daring to break the Covenant Chain and desert the ideals of his old friend, Sir William. Her oratory prevailed, and the council of chiefs stuck to their alliance with the British. Johnson's son-in-law, Colonel Daniel Claus, admitted to General Frederick Haldimand (later governor-general of Canada): "One word from her is more taken notice of by the Five Nations than a thousand from any white man."

For nearly two years, Brant lived at Fort Niagara, summoned there by Colonel John Butler, who thought her political activism essential to maintaining the Iroquois alliance. By September of 1779, however, Fort Niagara was bulging with loyalist refugees, and General Haldimand invited her to safer, more comfortable quarters in Montreal. After settling her older children in boarding school there, she hastened back towards Fort Niagara, alarmed by news of British defeats and further rebel depredations in Iroquois country. She got only as far as Carleton Island, New York, a forwarding post in the St. Lawrence River. There she found a large Indian population, angry and resentful over Britain's failure to protect their villages. Officials feared the younger warriors might turn on their British allies. For the remainder of the war she lived at Carleton Island, asserting her authority as head of the Society of Six Nations Matrons. A grateful Commandant Alexander Fraser wrote to Haldimand in 1780: "[The Indians'] uncommon good behaviour is in great measure to be ascribed to Miss Molly Brants influence over them, which is far superior to that of all their Chiefs put together." On a brief visit to her children in Montreal that summer, Brant received the bitterest news of all: her older son, Peter, had died in action four years earlier at Philadelphia. He was just 17.

At war's end (1783), Molly Brant did not know with whom she was angrier: the Americans who had driven her people from their homeland and killed her son, or the British, for handing over all Iroquois lands to the new American government and abandoning their Six Nations allies in the peace agreement. Now she and her brother faced the daunting task of resettling the survivors in Canada. In 1785, Joseph negotiated from the Crown a large land grant on the Grand River in Upper Canada where he set about reconstructing, at least partially, a fractured Iroquois Confederacy. Brantford, Ontario, and the Six Nations Reserve stand as living testimony to his determination to create a new life out of the ashes of war and betrayal. Molly Brant and other Mohawks at Carleton Island chose to accept land across the bay at Cataraqui (soon to be renamed Kingston). In consideration for her services to the Crown, Governor Haldimand awarded her a pension of £100 per year (the highest paid to any Native American) and compensation for some of her wartime losses. The Canadian government built her a comfortable residence, as well as a second dwelling to accommodate Joseph's frequent visits.

When in 1785 Molly returned briefly to her old home in the now-devastated Mohawk Valley, the American government tried to lure her back to the New York frontier permanently. Hoping that she might act as a calming agent among tribes to the west, officials offered financial compensation for her confiscated lands. Contemptuously, she rejected what she saw as a naked bribe. Five of her daughters were now married to Englishmen of distinction, three of them living at Kingston; her surviving son, George, farmed and taught school near Brantford; and the Bay of Quinte Mohawk community still sought her advice and counsel. Canada was to be Brant's home for the rest of her life.

Little is known of her later years, except for an occasional glimpse provided by travelers to Kingston. A devout Anglican, Brant regularly attended St. George's Church where it was reported that she "sat in an honourable place among the English." When Indian delegations arrived to confer with government officials, Lieutenant Governor John Simcoe always invited "Miss Molly" to attend. And in 1795 she gave Simcoe an Indian remedy for his persistent cough, which cured him "in a very short time." Molly Brant died in 1796, aged 60. She was buried in St. George's Church cemetery at Kingston.

A controversial figure because she was both pro-British and pro-Iroquois, Molly Brant strode with authority in both worlds. Tall, high-spirited and resolute, she asserted her will with Indian chiefs and Anglo officials alike. She nearly always wore traditional Mohawk dress, even at Johnson Hall, and spoke and wrote primarily in Mohawk rather than English. Yet, her nearly 20-year association with Sir William Johnson had taught her the wisdom of pragmatic accommodation. She saw to it that her children acquired a white world's education and advantages, for at the end of the 18th century, the old Indian ways that had empowered her were fading away. The strength and unity that once made the Iroquois peoples feared and honored were gone now, eclipsed by Euro-American civilization whose agents evidenced little appreciation for Iroquois custom and culture. Molly Brant was an extraordinary woman by any standard, but she was also the last Mohawk woman to wield such far-reaching influence over individuals and events.

SOURCES:

Graymont, Barbara. "Koñwatsi'tsiaiéñni," in *Dictionary of Canadian Biography.* Vol. 4. Toronto: University of Toronto Press, 1979, pp. 416–419.

Green, Gretchen, "Molly Brant, Catherine Brant and Their Daughters: A Study in Colonial Acculturation," in *Ontario History.* Vol. 81. September 1989, pp. 235–250.

Gundy, H. Pearson. "Molly Brant—Loyalist," in *Ontario History.* Vol. 45, 1953, pp. 97–108.

Hamilton, Milton W. *Sir William Johnson: Colonial American, 1715–1763.* Port Washington, NY: Kennikat Press, 1976.

———. "Sir William Johnson's Wives," in *New York History.* Vol. 38, 1957, pp. 18–28.

SUGGESTED READING:

Flexner, James Thomas. *Lord of the Mohawks: A Biography of Sir William Johnson.* Boston, MA: Little, Brown, 1979.

Kelsay, Isabel Thompson. *Joseph Brant, 1743–1807: Man of Two Worlds.* Syracuse, NY: Syracuse University Press, 1984.

Merritt, Susan E. *Her Story: Women from Canada's Past.* St. Catharines, Ontario: Vanwell Publishing, 1993.

COLLECTIONS:

Brant Manuscripts, Draper Collection, State Historical Society of Wisconsin; Haldimand Papers, National Archives of Canada; and Sullivan, James (ed.). *The Papers of Sir William Johnson.* 14 vols. Albany, NY: State University of New York Press, 1921–1965.

RELATED MEDIA:

"The Broken Chain," made-for-TV biography of Joseph Brant, starring Eric Schweig, Wes Studi, Pierce Brosnan, and **Buffy Sainte-Marie** (1 hr. 40 min.), Turner Pictures, 1993.

Constance B. Rynder, Professor of History, University of Tampa, Tampa, Florida

Karin Branzell

Branzell, Karin (1891–1974)

Swedish singer whose powerful contralto and large, powerful frame made her a perfect Wagnerian figure. *Born Karin Maria Branzell in Stockholm, Sweden, on September 24, 1891; died in Altadena, California, on December 15, 1974; daughter of Anders (a school principal and church organist) and Jenny (Pearson) Branzell; studied under* ***Thekla Hofer*** *in Stockholm; also studied with Louis Bachner, Enrico Rosati, and* ***Anna Schoen-René****; married Fedya Reinshagen (opera stage director), in 1946.*

As a teenager, Karin Branzell was discovered by the then Crown Princess, ***Margaret of Connaught**, while singing a solo with her father's choir in Hjorthagen, a suburb of Stockholm. After studying in Stockholm, Branzell performed with the Stockholm Royal Opera from 1912–18 before going to the Berlin Staatsoper from 1918–23. There she was the Nurse in the Berlin premiere of Strauss' *Die Frau ohne Schatten.* She then went to Vienna to sing Kundry and on to America where she debuted as Fricka in *Die Walküre* at the Metropolitan in 1924. Branzell continued at the Met singing major contralto roles including Amneris and Delilah until 1942. In 1930 and 1931, she performed at Bayreuth. She appeared at Covent Garden under Sir Thomas Beecham in 1935, 1937, and 1938. A singer in the grand manner, Branzell's voluminous, rich voice seemed made for the big Wagnerian roles. She taught singing in New York and California after her retirement from the stage.

John Haag,
Athens, Georgia

Braose, Annora de (d. 1241)

English noblewoman and recluse. *Died in 1241; daughter of William and Maud de Braose (d. 1211); married Hugh de Mortimer (a wealthy baron).*

Annora de Braose was a noblewoman born to William and ***Maud de Braose**, powerful nobles of west England. When she was a young woman, Annora married the wealthy baron Hugh de Mortimer. Some time later, King John confiscated her parents' property for suspected treason, forcing them to flee England. Her father made it to France, but her mother was captured and put in prison, where she died. The lands held by Annora's sister ***Loretta de Braose** were also confiscated.

Annora was also imprisoned for possibly conspiring against the king with her family, though the facts of the case remain obscure. After some time, she was released through the intervention of the papal legate. Several years later, her husband died, leaving her a childless widow.

Probably tired of the world of politics and danger, and without a wish to remarry, Annora sought permission to become a recluse. In medieval times, a recluse had a very specific meaning: she was a woman of exceptional character who received special permission to enclose herself in a one- or two-room suite, never to leave it. The local bishop was obligated to arrange a recluse's support while the recluse spent her days counseling those who came to ask her advice. Annora received the necessary permission and enclosed herself at Iffley about 1231. There, she received annual payments from King Henry III, a great supporter of recluses, until her death ten years later.

Laura York,
Anza, California

Braose, Beatrice de (d. 1383).

See Mortimer, Beatrice.

Braose, Eleanor de (fl. 1250s)

English noblewoman. *Name variations: Eleanor Bohun; Eleanor de Bohun. Interred at Llanthony, Gloucester; daughter of ****Eve de Braose*** *(fl. 1220s) and William de Braose, lord of Abergavenny; married Humphrey Bohun (d. 1265, son of the 6th earl of Hereford and Essex); children: Humphrey Bohun (c. 1248–1298), 3rd earl of Hereford, 2nd of Essex (some sources cite 7th earl of Hereford and Essex); Gilbert Bohun; ****Alianore Bohun*** *(d. 1313). Humphrey Bohun's second wife was ****Joan de Quinci.***

Braose, Eve de (fl. 1220s)

Lady of Abergavenny. *Name variations: Eva Marshal; Eve Marshall. Daughter of William Marshall (b. 1146), 1st earl of Pembroke, and ****Isabel de Clare*** *(c. 1174–1220); married William de Braose, lord of Abergavenny; children: ****Isabel de Braose*** *(d. 1248?); ****Maud Mortimer*** *(c. 1229–1301); ****Eleanor de Braose*** *(fl. 1250s).*

Braose, Gladys de (d. 1251).

See Gladys the Black.

Braose, Isabel de (d. 1248?)

Welsh queen and princess of Gwynedd. *Died before February 1248; daughter of William de Braose and ****Eve de Braose;*** *married David ap Llywelyn of Wales (David II), prince of Gwynedd (1240–1246), Ruler of All Wales (r. 1240–1246), in 1230.*

Braose, Loretta de (d. 1266)

English religious activist. *Name variations: Loretta de Briouze; Loretta of Leicester. Born before 1186; died in 1266 in Hackington, England; daughter of William de Braose and Maud de Braose (d. 1211); sister of Annora de Braose (d. 1241); married Robert Beaumont, earl of Leicester, around 1196 (died 1204); children: none.*

Loretta was an English recluse who also became an important religious activist. She was the sister of ***Annora de Braose**, also a well-known recluse. Loretta was the child of William and *Maud de Braose, English nobles who were caught up in King John's political persecutions in 1204, although they reportedly had been strong supporters of the king. The family was broken up and their lands seized; William fled to France, but Maud was unable to escape, and died in prison. Young Loretta had married Robert Beaumont, earl of Leicester around 1196, but he died eight years later, leaving Loretta with her dower estates as well as a portion of the earl's lands. These were also seized by the king and Loretta fled to France after her father.

Ten years later, Loretta returned to England and was granted her properties again. It is unclear what transpired during the decade she lived on the Continent, but the childless widow, probably about 30 years old now, immediately began preparing to enclose herself for the rest of her life. Perhaps it was the violence and cruelty she had experienced through the persecution of her family that made her desire a life separate from others, isolated from the outside world. Yet even after she finally received all the necessary permissions and entered a cell in the village of Hackington in 1221, Loretta did not simply disappear from sight and spend her days in silent prayer and meditation, as recluses were supposed to do.

She instead became an activist, helping establish the Franciscan order in England and writing to the king himself asking for favors for her ecclesiastical friends. She did not actually leave her cell, but she spent much time counseling those who came to speak with her, and discussing secular matters of politics and the rights of kingship with her relatives and friends. Loretta was highly respected by the local people, and was granted money and other gifts by the king and local nobles. She was in her early eighties when she died.

SOURCES:

LaBarge, Margaret. *A Small Sound of the Trumpet: Women in Medieval Life.* Boston, MA: Beacon Press, 1986.

Laura York,
Anza, California

Braose, Maud de (d. 1211)

Baroness. *Name variations: Maud de St. Walerie; Maud of St. Valery; Lady Bramber. Died of starvation while in prison around 1211 in Windsor, Berkshire, England; married William de Braose, Lord of Bramber (d. around 1212); children: William de Braose (d. 1211, sheriff of Herefordshire who raised a rebellion in Wales against King John); Reginald de Braose, baron de Braose (d. 1221, who married* ***Groecia de Bruere****); **Annora de Braose* (d. 1241); **Loretta de Braose* (d. 1266).*

Braose, Maud de (c. 1229–1301).

See Mortimer, Maud.

Brasova, Natalia or Nathalie (1880–1952).

See Sheremetskaia, Natalia.

Brassey, Anna (1839–1887)

British travel writer who wrote bestselling travel diaries of family sea voyages around the world. *Name variations: Lady Anna or Annie Brassey, Annie B., Baroness Brassey. Born Anna Allnutt in London on October 7, 1839; died at sea in the South Pacific on September 14, 1887; daughter of Elizabeth (Burnett) and John Allnutt; educated at home; married Baron (later Lord) Thomas Brassey (a politician), on October 9, 1860; children: Thomas Allnutt, Mabelle Annie, Muriel Agnes, and Marie Adelaide.*

Selected works: The Flight of the Meteor *(1869);* A Cruise on the Eöthen *(1872);* A Voyage in the "Sunbeam" Our Home on the Ocean for Eleven Months *(1878).*

Only an infant when her mother died, Anna Allnutt moved with her father to her grandfather's home in Clapsham, England. There, she had extensive grounds to play on and a private library from which she read voraciously, teaching herself botany and several languages. Annie, as she was known, later returned with her father to London, where a tutor rounded out her education. Two days after she turned 21, Annie married Baron Thomas Brassey, a railway contractor's son who was at the time financially independent but aimless. Annie guided him toward politics, and he entered Parliament in 1861. Living in Hastings, by age 31 Annie Brassey had given birth to three children and published a novel.

Lord and Lady Brassey (titles they inherited) began their sea journeys in 1872, when Parliament called on Thomas to research the culture, economy, and labor of other nations. The sailing yacht *Eöthen*, fully crewed, was commissioned to sail the Brasseys to North America. What began as Annie's journal-like letters to her father became *A Cruise in the Eöthen*, which was published in 1872 for circulation among family friends. Its great popularity gave rise to travel novels for public readership based on Brassey's circumnavigation of the globe. *A Voyage in the "Sunbeam" Our Home on the Ocean for Eleven Months* (1878) had 19 editions in ten years, including translations in five languages. In all, the family took at least eight sailing trips which lasted a minimum of four (but more commonly six to eight) months. These were not, however, pleasure cruises; Thomas demanded a rigorous sailing schedule and considered his duty before convenience, often to his wife's disappointment and frustration.

Brassey's books contain little about herself, including near silence on her almost constant seasickness and debilitating bouts of neuralgia. Not much is known of her personally, aboard ship or ashore, and details of her life and death were closely guarded. In August 1887, Anna Brassey grew abruptly ill on a voyage to Australia. Her last diary entry before her death at sea on September 14 was made on August 29, 1887. The ship's log only records that she was buried at latitude 15° 50' S, longitude 110° 35' E, 100 miles from Makassar in the South Pacific. Her family finished out their voyage, which took another three months.

SOURCES:

Blain, Virginia, Pat Clements, and Isobel Grundy, eds. *The Feminist Companion to Literature in English*. New Haven, CT: Yale University Press, 1990.

Brothers, Barbara, and Julia Gergits, eds. *Dictionary of Literary Biography*. Vol. 166. Detroit, MI: Gale Research, 1996.

Crista Martin,
Boston, Massachusetts

Brathwaite, Yvonne (b. 1932).

See Burke, Yvonne Brathwaite.

Braun, E. Lucy (1889–1971)

Botanist and conservationist, who was a pioneering ecologist of the early 20th century. *Name variations: Emma Lucy Braun. Born on April 19, 1889, in Cincinnati, Ohio; died on March 5, 1971, in Mt. Washington, Ohio; eldest of two daughters of George Frederick (a school principal) and Emma Moriah (Wright) Braun; sister of* ***Annette Braun*** *(1884–1978), an entomologist and international authority on moths; granted A.B. from University of Cincinnati, 1910; A.M. in geology, 1912; Ph.D. in botany, 1924.*

E. Lucy Braun, a pioneering ecologist of the early 20th century, was born in Cincinnati and grew up in a family of nature lovers. Braun, and her younger sister Annette, often accompanied their parents on nature walks to identify plant wildlife. Their mother, an amateur botanist, kept a collection of dried plant specimens for study. An excellent student throughout her public-school days, Braun progressed quickly through her courses at the University of Cincinnati, earning her Ph.D. in botany before her 25th birthday. She undertook a teaching career at the university in like fashion, rising to associate professor of botany in 1927. Full professorship, however, eluded her until 1946, two years before her retirement.

Braun's early studies and publications centered on the plant life of the Cincinnati region and culminated in the classic book, *Deciduous Forests of Eastern North America* (1950), the most respected of her scholarly works. Her pioneering study in the 1920s and '30s, comparing the current Ohio flora with the flora of 100 years before, was one of the first of its kind in the U.S., and it became a model for comparing changes in particular flora over a period of time. In 1935, Braun became the first woman president of the Ohio Academy of Science. Under the auspices of the Academy, she later established the Ohio Flora Committee (1951) and became its chair.

After her retirement in 1948, Braun continued field research and published several additional major works. An extensive study in 1955 theorized that the plant populations in the Southern Appalachians that had survived glaciation gave rise to other forest communities. The extensive summary of the study ("The Phytogeography of Unglaciated Eastern United States and Its Interpretation") was published in *Botanical Review*. In conjunction with the Ohio Flora Committee, whose goal was to prepare a comprehensive study of the vascular flora of Ohio, Braun produced two authoritative books, *The Woody Plants of Ohio: Trees, Shrubs, and Weedy Climbers, Native, Naturalized, and Escaped; A Contribution Toward the Vascular Flora of Ohio* (1961) and *The Monocotyledoneae: Cat-tails to Orchids* (1967).

Braun and her sister Annette, an entomologist and noted authority on moths, lived together in Mount Washington, near Cincinnati, turning their home into a laboratory and conservatory for studying rare and unusual plants. They were dedicated conservationists whose property included an experimental garden and a nature preserve. Braun established a chapter of the Wild Flower Preservation Society in Cincinnati and edited its national magazine, *Wild Flower*. She particularly championed conservation of wildlife habitats, contributing numerous articles on the subject. The scientific community honored Braun with numerous awards, including the **Mary Soper Pope** Medal for achievement in the field of botany (1952) and a Certificate of Merit from the Botanical Society of America (1956). E. Lucy Braun died at the age of 81; she is buried in Spring Grove, Cincinnati.

SOURCES:

Bailey, Brooke. *The Remarkable Lives of 100 Women Healers & Scientists.* Holbrook, MA: Bob Adams, 1994.

Sicherman, Barbara, and Carol Hurd Green. *Notable American Women: The Modern Period.* Cambridge, MA: The Belknap Press of Harvard University Press, 1980.

Barbara Morgan,
Melrose, Massachusetts

Braun, Eva (1912–1945)

German mistress, and wife for one day, of Adolf Hitler. *Born Eva Anna Paula Braun in Munich, Germany, on February 6, 1912; committed suicide with Hitler on April 30, 1945; daughter of Franziska Katharina (Kranburger) Braun and Fritz Braun; sister of* ***Ilse Braun*** *(b. 1909) and* ***Gretl Braun Fegelein*** *(b. 1915); married Adolf Hitler, on April 29, 1945.*

First met Hitler (1929); became Hitler's mistress (1932); lived in villa in Munich; attempted suicide (May 1935); moved to Hitler's house "Berghof," Obersalzberg (1936); followed Hitler into his Berlin bunker and married him (April 29, 1945); the next day, both committed suicide and their corpses were burned in the bunker's garden.

Eva Braun was unknown to the world until after her death in the final days of the battle of Berlin in April 1945. She was born in Munich, Germany, on February 6, 1912, and grew up in a solidly middle-class family. Her father Fritz Braun (1879–1964) was a tenured civil servant, and her mother **Franziska Kranburger Braun** (1885–1975) also came from solid circumstances as the daughter of a veterinarian. Eva had two sisters, Ilse, who was three years older than she, and Gretl, who was three years younger. Soon after Eva's birth, World War I broke out in August 1914, and Fritz Braun was called to the colors. He served as a lieutenant on the Western front, and was among those fortunate enough to survive the carnage and return home in 1918. Soon after his return, he joined an anti-revolutionary *Freikorps* unit that fought to free Munich from the rule of a short-lived Soviet Republic. In 1919, another war veteran, an obscure Austrian named Adolf Hitler, had just returned to Munich from the front to begin a fateful career in politics.

Uninterested in abstract ideas or ideals, Eva Braun led a happy, untroubled childhood and adolescence, delighting in friendships and the pleasures of youth. She was a good dancer, conscious of her attractive figure, and matured into an attractive young woman who enjoyed flirting with men. Without career ambitions, she accepted the conventional pattern of working an undemanding job so as to live life and "let things take their natural course." By the late 1920s, Munich had become a city dominated by the Nazi Party, a radically racist and nationalist movement led by Adolf Hitler. Braun had certainly heard of Hitler and may even have seen him prior to accepting employment with Heinrich Hoffmann, owner of a photography shop, who had worked for the Nazi Party as its official photographer since 1921. In 1929, Hitler had shown an interest in Hoffmann's daughter **Henriette**, but since she was already involved with another Nazi, the student leader Baldur von Schirach, Hoffmann pointed out to Hitler the pretty young woman he had recently hired. For the next two years, Hitler was seriously involved with another young woman, his niece **Geli Raubal**. The complex relationship between Hitler and Raubal ended in September 1931 with her suicide, an event that has never been adequately explained.

Although Hitler was devastated by Raubal's death, he was soon attracted to Eva Braun. By the time he was appointed chancellor of Germany on January 30, 1933, she had become his mistress. During the next 12 years, throughout the span of the Nazi dictatorship, the relationship between Adolf Hitler and Eva Braun was a state secret. Never once did the German press or radio even hint at the fact that the *führer*, whose only bride was said to be the German Reich, was in fact in a permanent relationship with a conventional young woman of no particular distinction. Hitler, who paid no income taxes and was quite wealthy as a result of the vast sales of his book *Mein Kampf*, bought Braun a villa on Munich's Wasserburgerstrasse (now named Delpstrasse in honor of a victim of the Nazis), as well as a Mercedes and a personal chauffeur. Despite the luxury, Braun was often bored by her cocooned isolation. Hitler, busy consolidating his power, rarely had time to spend with his Bavarian inamorata, and Braun wrote in her diary: "He only needs me for certain purposes." Hitler's views on the role of women were brutally patriarchal, centering around the notion that their role was to keep house, bear children, and please men in all ways possible. As for himself, he noted to his associates that marriage would have been a "terrible burden" for him, and that having a mistress like Eva Braun gave him the freedom to rule Germany as he saw fit. Eva's mother, on the other hand, was sufficiently concerned about her daughter's future to write a letter to Hitler asking what his intentions were regarding Eva; the letter drew no response.

In May 1935, Braun tried to kill herself with sleeping pills. Hitler responded the next year by removing his half-sister **Angela Raubal** from the position of hostess and housekeeper at his mountain retreat, the Berghof, near Berchtesgaden, and Eva Braun became the woman of the house, though her existence remained known to only a handful of powerful people in Germany. With the start of World War II in September 1939, Hitler spent increasingly less time at the Berghof. Eva Braun was never permitted to accompany Hitler to his headquarters near the front. She spent her time watching movies (she and Hitler both loved to watch *Gone With the Wind*), doing calisthenics and skiing. Much of her life remained empty and boring, prompting Hitler's chauffeur to assert after the war that she had been "the unhappiest woman in Germany. She spent most of her life waiting for Hitler."

Eva Braun

Her 33 photo albums, which survived the war and are now in the U.S. National Archives, document the trivial ways in which she filled her days with old Munich friends and the small Berghof circle.

Toward the end of the war, after her sister Gretl had married the ambitious SS General Hermann Fegelein, Heinrich Himmler's liaison officer to Hitler, it was easier for Braun to be seen at more functions at the Berghof since the appearance presented was of two sisters visiting each other. As battlefield disasters became commonplace, however, the opportunities for social events in the Bavarian alps dwindled. The more ominous the situation grew, the more loyal Braun became to Hitler. After Hitler survived an attempted assassination on July 20, 1944, she wrote to him in an emotion-laden letter: "From our first meeting I swore to follow you anywhere—even unto death—I live only for your love."

By early 1945, it was dawning on even the most fanatical Nazis that Germany had lost the war. Although she understood little or nothing of the strategic details of the conflict, Eva Braun knew that to remain with Adolf Hitler would probably mean the end of her life. On April 15, 1945, going against Hitler's stated wishes, Eva Braun accompanied the *führer* to his Berlin bunker for the last time. On April 29, 1945, with Soviet forces only blocks away, Hitler and Braun were married. The next day, they committed suicide, and their bodies were partially burned. Soviet forensic experts took the remains to Moscow, and they were returned to Germany where they were secretly buried. The ashes of Adolf Hitler and Eva Braun were finally disposed of only several decades later. Both of Eva's parents lived into old age, surviving their daughter by decades. Fritz Braun died on January 22, 1964, with his widow Franziska surviving him by more than a decade, dying on January 13, 1975.

SOURCES:

"Eva Braun's Album," in *Life*. Vol. 23, no. 3. July 21, 1947, pp. 48, 53–54.

"Eva's Private Poses," in *Life*. Vol. 23, no. 3. January 20, 1947, pp. 36–37.

Frank, Johannes. *Eva Braun: Ein ungewöhnliches Frauenschicksal in geschichtlich bewegter Zeit*. Preussisch Oldendorf: Verlag K. W. Schütz, 1988.

Grunfeld, Frederic V. "Sunday Afternoons with a Monster," in *Saturday Review of the Arts*. Vol. 1, no. 3. March 3, 1973, pp. 42–46.

Gun, Nerin E. *Eva Braun: Hitler's Mistress*. NY: Meredith, 1968.

"Hitler's Eva Braun . . . From Her Own Albums," in *Look*. Vol. 23, no. 23. November 10, 1959, pp. 85–90.

Honan, William H. "On the Trail of Hitler's Love Letters," in *The New York Times*. March 13, 1993, p. 16.

Infield, Glenn B. *Eva and Adolf*. NY: Grosset, 1974.

Koonz, Claudia. *Mothers in the Fatherland: Women, the Family and Nazi Politics*. NY: St. Martin's Press, 1987.

Melchior, Ib. *Eva*. NY: Dodd, Mead, 1984.

"People," in *Time*. Vol. 97, no. 25. June 21, 1971, p. 34.

"Register," in *Der Spiegel*. Vol. 30, no. 4. January 19, 1976, p. 124.

Speer, Albert. *Inside the Third Reich*. NY: Avon Books, 1971.

Trevor-Roper, H.R. *The Last Days of Hitler*. London: Macmillan, 1947.

———. "The Story Behind the Eva Braun Enigma," in *Look*. Vol. 23, no. 23. November 10, 1959, pp. 92, 94, 96.

COLLECTIONS:

U.S. National Archives, Washington, D.C., Modern Military Records Branch, Eva Braun Photograph Albums.

John Haag, Associate Professor, University of Georgia, Athens, Georgia

Braun, Julie (1883–1971).

See Braun-Vogelstein, Julie.

Braun, Lily (1865–1916)

German feminist who repudiated her origins in the German aristocracy to assert in her 1901 book* Die Frauenfrage *that capitalism laid a basis for the economic oppression of women. *Pronunciation: Brawn. Born on July 1, 1865, in Halberstadt, Germany; died on August 9, 1916, at Zehlendorf; first child of Hans von Kretschman (a captain in the Prussian military) and Jenny von (Gustedt) Kretschman (a descendant of an ancient baronial family); educated by governesses, tutors, and an aunt; married Georg von Gizycki, in 1893 (died 1895); married Heinrich Braun, in 1896; children: (first marriage) one son, Otto.*

Father forced to retire from Prussian military (1889); family moved to an apartment in Berlin, where Braun became acquainted with a wide variety of social and cultural reformers (1890); published correspondence of maternal grandmother Jenny von Gustedt, with the German poet Goethe (1891 and 1893); began publishing, with Minna Cauer, the twice-monthly journal Die Frauenbewegung *(1894); joined the Social Democratic Party (1895); published her major work* Die Frauenfrage *(1901); worked in Helene Stoecker's League for the Protection of Motherhood and Sexual Reform (1906–10); on her death, her husband Heinrich married* ****Julie Braun-Vogelstein.***

Selected writings: Die Frauenfrage, Ihre geschichtliche Entwicklung und ihre wirtschaftliche

Lily Braun

Seite *(Leipzig: Hezel, 1901);* Memoiren einer Sozialistin *(Munich: Albert Langen, 1908–09).*

Feminists and Marxists were seldom common allies in late 19th-century Europe. Most Marxists assumed that women's emancipation would automatically occur as part of a proletarian, or workers', revolution. For them, the revolution was the goal, and it was a wasteful diversion of revolutionary energy to focus on the problems of women. By the same token, most feminists came from upper-class or middle-class families, and they avoided parties that advocated total revolution. Lily Braun was an exception. A German aristocrat, she came to the conclusion that feminism and Marxism were natural allies. In several books and more than 100 articles, many translated from her native German and published in up to four other European languages, she argued that feminists and Marxists battled a common enemy: capitalism. Working in the repressive atmosphere of late 19th-century Germany, she anticipated many issues still debated in feminist circles.

Most of Lily Braun's career was a repudiation of her high birth. Both her parents held noble titles. Her father Hans von Kretschman was a Prussian army officer who would eventually become general of the infantry. The family had lived in the city of Nuremberg since the 1500s and had earned its noble title during the 1700s in recognition of service to various princes of the Holy Roman Empire. Her mother **Jenny von Gustedt Kretschman**'s family was of even older noble lineage, having held baronial titles since the 10th century.

Lily was the eldest of two children, although her sister Maria ("Mascha") was not born until 13 years later. A sickly but independent child, Lily was taught by her mother that though women's virtues included an ability to suffer in silence, women might also dominate and control men. Braun was so afraid of her father, a harsh and authoritarian figure, that she had nightmares about him even after he was dead. She did remember, however, that he could be charming, that he told her about the wonders of plant life during nature walks with him, and that he taught her the ideas of the 19th-century French philosopher Auguste Comte.

What she never forgot was that her father, who spent recklessly on hobbies and financial speculations, had dissipated all of his wife's dowries and an inheritance that Lily was to receive from her mother. He had also used a future inheritance that Lily was expected to receive from her Aunt **Clothilde von Herman**—a wealthy widow of the Baron Ulyss von Herman—to secure a loan for 78,000 marks, a very large sum at the time.

Like most children of the German aristocracy in the 19th century, Braun studied foreign languages—English and French—and reading and writing. Private tutors came to the home to teach history and a smattering of literature, and governesses taught her to draw and to play the piano. She learned to read the writings of the German poet Wolfgang Goethe, including *Faust*, the *Sorrows of Young Werther*, and *Iphigenie*. She also read Wagner, Ibsen, Nietzsche, Shelley, and Browning.

Despite this, her parents considered manners more important for a woman than education and placed emphasis on the ladylike skills of needlepoint, sewing, and cooking. In order to acquire social skills, Braun was sent, at age 15, to a finishing school near her Aunt Clothilde's. There she was introduced to much of the aristocratic and intellectual elite of southern Germany and Austria. Two years later, she returned home, a slender beauty who was a witty conversationalist and full of social graces.

For eight more years, Braun lived at home, helping her mother with the care of her younger sister Mascha and with household duties. She wrote that, in these years, she felt like a "lap dog" which was periodically "rewarded for good behavior." She was also introduced to officers her father brought to the house, to show off his daughter and perhaps help her find suitable marriage material. Braun attracted men, including Gottfried von Pappenheim and Major Moritz von Egidy, a founder of a movement of socially conscious Christianity. One observer described her as having a "narrow and fine aristocratic face" surrounded by short-cut hair which gave a "radiance" to her face. Marriage was a possibility for such a beauty, but Braun showed little interest. She refused to forego activities which potential suitors found unattractive in a woman, such as horseback riding, smoking in public, and showing an interest in intellectual ideas.

Two events in 1889 proved pivotal in her life. The first was the forced resignation from the German army of her father, who had angered the German emperor Wilhelm II. During the emperor's games, Hans von Kretschman and the men under his command had had the temerity to defeat a mock army commanded by the emperor.

The second development was the death of her maternal grandmother **Jenny von Gustedt**. Included in Lily's inheritance were papers, letters, and poems written by, or to, her grandmother, who had lived in the royal court at Weimar and had drawn the attentions of Goethe. Braun chose to edit and publish many of the papers and correspondence. While researching the volumes, published in 1891 and 1893, she was welcomed at the Goethe Archive, treated royally, invited to dinner with the grand duke of Weimar, and even offered a position at the archive. She turned it down, regarding both the scholarly life and marriage as being too sedate for her taste.

Characteristically, Braun kept only a minority of the royalties for herself; the remainder she sent to her family, which was badly in need of money. When the family moved to a Berlin apartment in 1890, Braun was fascinated by the variety of radical causes and reformers in the city, including Russian emigres and religious and social reformers. She had already decided that she did not want to become a "social parasite" like many of her class, whom she accused of participating in charities mainly as a way to keep the poor from flocking to socialism.

One of the organizations she joined during her early years in Berlin was the German Society for Ethical Culture—copied after a similar United States organization. One of the Society's German founders drew her attention. He was Georg von Gizycki, an associate professor of moral philosophy at the University of Berlin. Gizycki was one of the "Socialists of the Chair," the name given to German professors of socialist leanings. Paralyzed from the waist down by a childhood illness, Gizycki nevertheless lived an active life. As editor of the Society's journal *Ethische Kultur*, he furnished a platform for many of Braun's early articles.

When Lily married him in the summer of 1893, she was also marrying the causes he championed, including the emancipation of women and religious skepticism. The marriage, however, alarmed Braun's family, which already had become uncomfortable with Lily's articles expressing sympathy for the working class and crusading for an end to the tradition that each German city sponsor a municipally owned brothel.

In the early 1890s, Braun also became active in the *Frauenwohl* (Association for Women's Welfare), founded by the feminist ***Minna Cauer** (1841–1922). *Frauenwohl* conducted courses in secondary high school subjects and taught trade skills to women who wished to become financially independent. The organization went beyond asking for legal rights for women, campaigning instead for the right to vote, for an end to state sponsored prostitution, and for the addition of an equal-rights amendment to the German constitution. In 1894, Braun and Cauer founded the twice-monthly journal *Die Frauenbewegung* (The Women's Movement). Braun's "calm, alto voice" was often heard at feminist rallies in "clipped, concise" sentences. The years of the 1890s and after were also years of travel (London in 1896 and Paris in 1900), and on these trips she met socialists and feminists such as Leon Blum and George Bernard Shaw.

Gizycki died in 1895. Lily's second marriage, to the socialist Heinrich Braun, created a bit of a scandal. In early 1895, two months after winning custody of his two sons in a heated divorce proceedings with his first wife, Heinrich had married his housekeeper. Lily visited him a short time later to seek financial advice, and the two fell in love. Following rumors that Heinrich and Lily had tried unsuccessfully to convince his new wife to accept a *menage a trois*, Heinrich divorced his second wife and married Lily in 1896.

The marriage completely alienated Braun from her family. Relatives stopped corresponding with her; some returned her letters. Her father, in a heated argument, produced a gun. She was also cut off from the possibility of a future inheritance of Aunt Clothilde. As the years went by, the rift with her family widened. Mascha generously shared her inheritance from Aunt Clothilde with the Brauns. Eventually, Mascha gave them more than 40,000 marks. When she later found herself in financial trouble and asked for the return of the money, however, the Brauns refused, and an ugly court battle followed.

> Women became aware of being oppressed only after their many chores as housewives were taken over by industry, so that the women of the propertied classes . . . came to feel superfluous.
>
> **—Lily Braun**

One thing that alarmed Braun's family was that Heinrich was a full-fledged member of the Social Democratic Party, the Marxist party in Germany. Lily had joined the faction in December 1895. When a party representative had spoken to an Ethical Culture meeting, Lily had been impressed enough to ask for more information. Excited by the prospect of converting such a high-born German to their ranks, the leaders of the party had prövided Braun with royal treatment, including a tour of working-class districts in Berlin. She concluded that the Marxist movement stood for what she believed in: radical liberalism, feminism, concern for the oppressed, and a self-sacrificing idealism. The Brauns were considered a major "catch" for the Social Democratic Party (SPD).

But they were never fully accepted by many party leaders. One reason was the mixed reputation of Heinrich himself, a brilliant scholar. The son of a middle-class Jewish family, he had so impressed his professors when he obtained a doctorate in economics at the University of Berlin that they offered him an academic appointment, which Heinrich refused. An early Marxist, he was a founder, along with SPD leaders Wilhelm Liebknecht and Karl Kautsky, of the journal *Neue Zeit*. He also corresponded with Marx. His aggressive, argumentative nature made enemies, however; he was accused of enjoying making other people look foolish, and his writings were often viewed as overly preachy. He was also accused of being unreliable in financial dealings.

Lily's membership in the party was often criticized by ***Clara Zetkin**, the leader of the women's movement in the SPD. Zetkin's motives were partly personal and partly ideological. Believing that working women should fight against class oppression, and that equal rights for women would come only when class oppression was ended, Zetkin argued that there should be a "clear separation" between the party, which she saw as highly dedicated, and outside groups, which she saw as "dilettante groups in reform." Zetkin also thought that Braun's bearing was more fitting for an aristocratic organization than a proletarian one.

Although Braun would remain in the party until a few years before her death, she was involved in numerous disputes with Zetkin. Zetkin insisted that working women did not need any special legal protection on their jobs; they would be revolutionized by experiencing the same working conditions as their husbands. Lily argued otherwise, noting that the minimum number of working hours for women over 16 in German industry in 1891 was 65 hours. Even pregnant women were required to work such hours. Such conditions, she insisted, led to an increased number of miscarriages and premature births. She demanded that pregnant women be protected from dangerous working conditions, and that furloughs be given both before and after birth, with regular wages during this time. She also wanted women to have a guarantee of a job when they returned to work after pregnancy.

In ideological terms, the dispute between Braun and Zetkin illustrated a basic split that was developing within the SPD. As a Marxist party, the SPD regularly committed itself to work for a proletarian revolution which would completely transform European countries. In the 1890s, however, "a revisionist" movement, led by Eduard Bernstein, argued that the party, rather than waiting for a revolution, should work actively within the German political system to bring about reforms to help the workers. Some revisionists even thought that Marxist goals might be achieved through such change—"evolution instead of revolution."

Like Bernstein, Braun believed that the party should participate in day-to-day politics, fighting for improvements in workers' economic and cultural conditions. She also wanted the party to broaden its base of votes by appealing to many middle class, more moderate, reformers. She believed that progressive elements in the middle class were looking for a political home but that the esoteric language of the party's journals too often turned such people off.

Braun's Marxism was outlined in her major book, *Die Frauenfrage*. The book discussed the historical development of "women's work," beginning in ancient times. The growth of the Industrial Revolution and capitalism, it argued, had a negative effect on women of all classes. Because of the Industrial Revolution, upper-class and middle-class women were free to spend increased time at leisure but lived lives that seemed "empty" and "superfluous"; working-class women were coerced to leave their homes and work in a place "removed from home and family," at degrading, unsafe, and demoralizing factories. Capitalism created a "dependency relationship" for women of all classes, so that "even those with strong personalities" lost their sense of identity.

The book argued that upper-class and middle-class women—though their lives contained less unpleasantness than working-class women—would be the natural leaders of a movement to improve working conditions. "The women who first became aware of the repression and suffering of their sex," she wrote, "were not those likely to be the worst treated, but those who had gained a certain amount of education and understanding of the situation."

Between 1904 and the start of World War I in 1914, Braun emphasized the importance of motherhood for the women's movement. She joined the League for the Protection of Motherhood and Sexual Reform, an organization headed by the feminist ***Helene Stoecker**. In 1906, Braun became vice-chair of the organization. Her main contribution to the platform of the organization was the idea of motherhood insurance—paid leave and stipends for pregnant women. She called motherhood the "epitome" of womanhood; she went so far as to say that a woman without a child was a "second-class woman."

Her emphasis on motherhood continued during World War I. She was openly critical of

German feminists who insisted that women should oppose the war by carrying out a "pregnancy strike." Instead, she suggested that the German government, for eugenic reasons, should "do all in its power" to encourage motherhood. In some ways, she moved politically rightward during the war, as in her staunch defense of proposals to annex to Germany some captured foreign lands. In other ways, she moved leftward. She resigned her membership in the SPD, complaining that it had lost its hostility to capitalism.

When Lily Braun died in 1916—in a way, a merciful death, since it came less than two years before the death in battle of her beloved son Otto—she left behind a legacy of writings which argued that Marxism might become a central theme to unite women of all classes. She insisted that women should demand more than the right to vote; they should also examine all institutions of their society for signs that they contributed to the oppression of women. They could do this even without the important right to vote:

> Of course we women do not have the power to make our convictions speak through the use of the ballot. The government in its paternalism has declared us to be the same as minors, the insane, and criminals. Nevertheless we are able to make our influence felt; with the strength of our convictions and enthusiasm we can prod our brothers, our husbands, and particularly our sons forward rather than let them wallow in timid ignorance.

SOURCES:

Braun, Lily. *Selected Writings on Feminism and Socialism.* Trans. and ed. by Alfred G. Meyer. Bloomington: Indiana University Press, 1984.

———. *Memoiren einer Sozialistin.* Munich: Albert Langen, 1909.

Meyer, Alfred G. *The Feminism and Socialism of Lily Braun.* Bloomington: Indiana University Press, 1985.

SUGGESTED READING:

Evans, Richard J. *The Feminist Movement in Germany, 1894–1933.* London and Beverly Hills: Sage Publications, 1976.

Quataert, Jean J. *Reluctant Feminists in German Social Democracy, 1885–1917.* Princeton, NJ: Princeton University Press, 1979.

COLLECTIONS:

The correspondence of Lily Braun is housed in the archives of the Leo Baeck Institute, New York City.

Niles Holt, Professor of History,
Illinois State University, Normal-Bloomington, Illinois

Braun-Vogelstein, Julie (1883–1971)

German-Jewish art historian and author. *Name variations: Julie Vogelstein Braun. Born Julie Vogelstein in Stettin (now Szczecin, Poland), on January 26, 1883; died in New York City on February 6, 1971; daughter of Heinemann Vogelstein and* ***Rosa (Kobrak) Vogelstein****; sister of Hermann Vogelstein (1870–1942), Theodore Max Vogelstein (1880–1957), and Ludwig Vogelstein (1871–1934); studied art history and Egyptology in Munich and Berlin; received Ph.D., University of Heidelberg, 1919; married Heinrich Braun (a Social Democratic leader); came to U.S. (1936); active in German exile circles.*

Julie Braun-Vogelstein was born in Stettin (now Szczecin, Poland) on January 26, 1883, into a wealthy German-Jewish family that embraced the arts. Her father Heinemann Vogelstein was a rabbi and had earned a doctorate in oriental studies. Her three brothers all went on to successful careers in various fields: Hermann became a respected rabbi while Theodore Max and Ludwig both went into business, substantially increasing the family fortune. Julie early exhibited a strong academic orientation and studied archaeology, art history, history, and philosophy at the universities of Berlin, Munich, Vienna, London, and Paris. Egyptology was among her many interests during this period. Her family's affluence and her own enthusiasm for new experiences made her an indefatigable traveler. After a leisurely period of study, she was finally awarded a doctorate in art history from the University of Heidelberg in 1919.

A turning point occurred in Julie Vogelstein's life when she met and fell in love with the Social Democratic journalist and Marxist propagandist Heinrich Braun (1854–1927). A brilliant but often difficult man, Braun met Julie at a time when his marriage with the feminist writer ***Lily Braun** was in shambles. Despite the great difference in age between the two, an intellectual and physical attraction quickly developed between the radical politician and the aspiring scholar. After Lily Braun's death in 1916, Vogelstein and Braun lived together, finally marrying in 1920.

The great tragedy of Heinrich Braun's life was the battlefield death in 1918 of his son Otto. Born in 1897, Otto Braun was an extraordinary young man who had impressed virtually all who met him with his leadership abilities as well as his decency and compassion. Determined that Otto Braun receive the honor that was his due, Julie Braun-Vogelstein carefully edited his posthumous writings, including his diary, publishing them in 1920. Though anti-Semitic sentiments were strong in postwar Germany, the half-Jewish Otto Braun spoke eloquently from his soldier's grave, and the book became a bestseller and a literary sensation. Throughout the 1920s, the Braun-Vogelstein home in Berlin was a center of the city's cultural and political life. The often bitter conflicts that convulsed the Social Democratic Party during the Weimar Republic were often discussed in Julie and Heinrich's drawing room. After Heinrich Braun died in 1927, Julie maintained her links with artists and politicians, remaining alert for new talents that she might choose to support.

When the Nazis seized power in Germany in 1933, Julie Braun-Vogelstein had options many of her fellow Jews did not have. Because of her family's wealth and international business connections, she could leave Germany at any time without fearing a life of penury abroad. However, regarding herself as a good German, she decided to remain with hopes that the evil of National Socialism would soon be swept aside. When this did not take place, she emigrated from Germany in 1935, first settling in France. In 1936, she moved to the United States where, more fortunate than most of the other exiles from Germany, she soon settled in and was able to lighten the burdens of a number of refugees, enabling them to start new careers or function more effectively as anti-Nazi activists. Among the individuals that Braun-Vogelstein supported and encouraged during their American exile years was the Social Democratic leader Friedrich Stampfer (1874–1957). Likely the most interesting and tragic individual she encountered and encouraged was Adam von Trott zu Solz (1909–1944), a leading anti-Nazi conspirator. A brilliant intellectual who had been a Rhodes Scholar, von Trott despised the Nazis and was able to take effective action to diminish Nazi harassment against Braun-Vogelstein before she left Germany. She strongly admired him, and he stayed at her house in Carmel, California, during his two visits to the U.S. in 1937 and 1939–40 when he unsuccessfully attempted to gain the support of the State Department for his group of anti-Nazi conspirators.

Julie Braun-Vogelstein remained active as a writer and patron of the arts to the end of her long life. Her sweeping interpretation of the artistic heritage of Western civilization, *Art, the Image of the West*, was published to positive reviews in 1952. In her final years, she published her autobiography and was pleased to see new editions of her books on Otto Braun and Heinrich Braun appear in print in a Germany that had survived the terror of Nazism. Julie Braun-Vogelstein died in New York City on February 6, 1971.

SOURCES:

Braun, Otto. *The Diary of Otto Braun, with Selections from his Letters and Poems.* Edited by Julie Vogelstein. Translated by Ella Winter. NY: Alfred A. Knopf, 1924.

——. *Fragment der Zukunft: Aufzeichnungen eines Frühhvollendeten.* Edited by Julie Braun-Vogelstein. Stuttgart: Deutsche Verlags-Anstalt, 1969.

Braun-Vogelstein, Julie. *Art, the Image of the West.* NY: Pantheon Books, 1952.

——. *Heinrich Braun: Ein Leben für den Sozialismus.* Second, revised ed., Stuttgart: Deutsche Verlags-Anstalt, 1967.

——. *Die ionische Säule.* Berlin: Walter de Gruyter, 1921.

——. *Lily Braun: Ein Lebensbild.* Berlin-Grunewald: H. Klemm A.G., 1922.

——. *Was niemals stirbt: Gestalten und Erinnerungen.* Stuttgart: Deutsche Verlagsanstalt, 1966.

"Dr. Julie Braun-Vogelstein Dies; German Party Leader's Widow," in *The New York Times.* February 9, 1971, p. 42.

Klemperer, Klemens von, ed. *A Noble Combat: The Letters of Shiela Grant Duff and Adam von Trott zu Solz 1932–1939.* Oxford: Clarendon Press, 1988.

Meyer, Alfred G. *The Feminism and Socialism of Lily Braun.* Bloomington: Indiana University Press, 1985.

John Haag, Associate Professor, University of Georgia, Athens, Georgia

Braund, Mary (b. 1765).

See Bryant, Mary.

Braunschweig, countess or duchess of.

See Brunswick, countess or duchess of.

Braunschweig-Lüneburg, Elisabeth von (1519–1558)

German ruler and writer. Name variations: Elisabeth of Brunswick-Luneburg. Born in 1519 in Brandenburg (Germany); died in 1558 in Braunschweig-Lüneburg (Germany); daughter of Joachim I, Prince of Brandenburg; married Erich I, duke of Braunschweig-Lüneburg, in 1534 (died 1540); children: one daughter and one son.

Elisabeth was a German princess, daughter of the Catholic monarch Joachim I of Brandenburg. As was fashionable for daughters of the nobility in the 16th century, Elisabeth was given a thorough classical education, including several foreign languages and the fine arts. When she was 15, her father arranged a marriage for her to a German prince, the 55-year-old Duke Erich I of Braunschweig-Lüneburg. Elisabeth gave birth to two children, one daughter and one son, before Erich's death in 1540. As her son was still a small child on his father's death, Elisabeth, herself only 21, took over the governing of the duchy.

Although she had been raised in a Catholic family and lived in a Catholic region, Elisabeth was drawn to the ideas of the new Protestantism; now in power, she composed a treatise on the new religion, called *The Christian Epistle*, which she published and distributed to her subjects. She then turned her pen to other topics, completing a book of instruction for her daughter and a treatise on government for her son, as well as a book of consolation for other widows. Despite her influence, Elisabeth's son grew up to embrace Catholicism, causing immense conflict within their family and government. When her son took over power, he exiled Elisabeth and his sister to Hanover because of their religious beliefs. Suddenly deprived of the wealth and authority she had enjoyed, Elisabeth composed songs expressing her faith and her sorrow. She died in poverty a few years after her exile.

Laura York,
Anza, California

Braunschweig-Lüneburg, Sibylle Ursula von (1629–1671)

German writer and translator. *Name variations: Sibylle von Braunschweig-Luneburg; Sibylle of Brunswick-Luneburg. Born in 1629 in Braunschweig-Lüneburg (Germany); died in childbirth in 1671; daughter of August the Younger, duke of Braunschweig-Lüneburg; stepdaughter of* ****Sophie Elisabeth von Braunschweig-Lüneburg*** *(1613–1676); married in 1663; children: four.*

Sibylle Ursula was born into the ducal family of Braunschweig-Lüneburg, in modern Germany. She revealed an unusual talent for languages and scholarship at an early age, and was given a thorough classical education by her stepmother, the duchess Sophie Elisabeth. Sibylle Ursula, who did not marry until she was 34, devoted the years prior to marriage to composing poetry, translating foreign works into German, and writing plays. Among her more significant work is a novel, *Aramena*, which was completed after her death by her siblings. She also composed tracts on her Protestant religious beliefs and was recognized for her excellent translations of French literary works. Sibylle died in childbirth.

Laura York,
Anza, California

Braunschweig-Lüneburg, Sophie Elisabeth von (1613–1676)

German duchess, composer, and playwright. *Name variations: Sophie von Braunschweig-Luneburg. Born in 1613; died in 1676 in Braunschweig-Lüneburg (Germany); married August the Younger, duke of Braunschweig-Lüneburg, in 1635; children: many stepchildren, including* ****Sibylle Ursula von Braunschweig-Lüneburg*** *(1629–1671).*

Sophie Elisabeth was born into the German nobility and married August of Braunschweig-Lüneburg at age 22, becoming stepmother to his many children. The highly educated duchess promoted a lively, intellectual court and patronized baroque artists, for which she became known as the "Juno" of Braunschweig-Lüneburg, after the Roman goddess of myth. Sophie also contributed her own works to the art of her time, writing songs, plays, and librettos which were performed at court. In 1652, she completed a novel, *The Story of Dorinde*, based on French courtly literature. In addition, Sophie expressed her religious views in the prayers and various spiritual tracts she composed. She died about age 63.

Laura York,
Anza, California

Bray, Anna Eliza (1790–1883)

English novelist. *Name variations: Mrs. Bray. Born Anna Eliza Kempe at Newington, Surrey, on December 25, 1790; died in London, England, on January 21, 1883; daughter of J. Kempe; married Charles A. Stothard (an artist and son of artist R.A. Stothard), in 1818 (died 1821); married Reverend Edward Atkyns Bray, vicar of Tavistock, in 1823 (died 1857).*

Anna Bray wrote about a dozen, chiefly historical, novels. Considered perhaps the most valuable of her writings, *The Borders of the Tamar and the Tavy* (3 volumes, 1836), was an account of the traditions and superstitions of the neighborhood of Tavistock in the form of letters to Robert Southey, of whom she was a close friend. In 1818, she married artist Charles Alfred Stothard. Three years later, while working on his book *The Monumental Effigies of Great Britain*, Charles was making drawings of stained-glass windows when he fell from a ladder in the church at Beerferris and was killed. With the help of her brother Alfred John Kempe, Anna Bray completed the work. Among her writings are *De Foix* (1826), *Courtenay of Walreddon* (1844), *A Peep at the Pixies, or Legends of the West* (1854), *Life of Thomas Stothard* (1856), as well as *Trelawney of Trelawney*, *Branded*, *Good St. Louis and his Times*, and *White Hoods*. Her autobiography was published posthumously in 1884.

Brazil, Angela (1868–1947)

English author of immensely popular stories for girls. *Born on November 30, 1868, in Preston, Lancashire,*

England; died on March 14, 1947, in Coventry, England; fourth and youngest daughter of Clarence (manager of a cotton mill) and ***Angelica (McKinnell) Brazil****; sister of* ***Amy Brazil****; attended Miss Knowles' Select Ladies' School, Manchester High School, and Ellerslie College, Manchester; studied art at Heatherley's Art College, London; never married; no children.*

Selected works: The Fortunes of Philippa *(1906);* The Third Class at Miss Kaye's *(1908);* The Nicest Girl in the School *(1910);* A Fourth Form Friendship *(1912);* The Jolliest Term on Record *(1915);* The Madcap of the School *(1917);* Monitress Merle *(1922);* Captain Peggie *(1924);* My Own Schooldays *(1925);* The School on the Loch *(1946).*

Known as the English schoolgirl's favorite author, Angela Brazil did not begin writing professionally until she was 36. From 1906 until her death in 1947, she produced at least one book a year, over 50 titles in all.

The youngest of four children, Angela was raised primarily by her mother, who fostered in her a love of nature, literature, and art. During her formal education, Brazil experienced the first of the intense friendships that would later figure so prominently in her books. At 18, she rejected university study, opting to attend Heatherley's Art College in London, after which she worked as a governess. Following her father's death in 1899, she traveled to Europe and the Middle East with her sister Amy and her mother.

Angela Brazil

Her first work, *A Terrible Tom Boy* (1904), largely autobiographical, was followed by *The Fortunes of Philippa* (1906) which was based on her mother's school experiences. Brazil's early books were her most popular, including *The Third Class at Miss Kaye's* (1908), *The Nicest Girl in the School* (1910), *A Fourth Form Friendship* (1912), *The Jolliest Term on Record* (1915), *The Madcap of the School* (1917), *Monitress Merle* (1922), and *Captain Peggie* (1924). They appealed to largely upper- and middle-class fans. "Brazil's heroines," writes **Joanne Shattock**, "were characterized by their intense emotional attachments to those of the same sex, their notorious slang, which led to the books being banned in some schools, their respect for authority, and their devotion to games, especially hockey." During her career, Brazil also contributed to periodicals like *Little Folks* and *Our School Magazine*.

In her autobiography *My Own Schooldays*, written in 1925, Brazil recalls that her family holidays by the sea and in the countryside of Wales were as important an influence as any lessons learned in school. The location and adventures of these childhood outings often found their way into her stories. She also credited her early love of nature with providing "a capacity for inner happiness that is not affected by outside events."

Remaining single, Brazil lived with her unmarried brother and sister in Coventry. She never lost her passion for art, continuing to sketch and paint throughout her life. In 1925, she and her sister Amy mounted an exhibition at the Walker Gallery and, in 1929, over 300 of her flower studies were exhibited in Coventry. To the end of her life, Brazil continued writing a book a year, though her later work was produced to formula. Her last novel, *The School on the Loch*, was published in 1946, a year before her death.

SOURCES:

Saintbury, Elizabeth. "Angela Brazil: The Schoolgirl's Favourite Author," in *This England*. Spring 1985.

Shattock, Joanne. *The Oxford Guide to British Women Writers*. NY: Oxford University Press, 1993.

Barbara Morgan, Melrose, Massachusetts

Brazil, empress of.

See Leopoldina of Austria (1797–1826).
See Amelia of Leuchtenburg (1812–1873).

Bré, Ruth (1862–1911)

German feminist poet and author. Name variations: Bre; Elisabeth Bouness. Born Elisabeth Bouness in 1862; died in December 1911; daughter of unmarried parents.

Was an elementary school teacher and unsuccessful poet; founded Liga für Mutterschutz (League for the Protection of Mothers, 1904); for a brief period, the organization and its ideas helped the German feminist movement focus its ideas and influenced the development of feminist ideology throughout the Western world; eased out of the organization she had founded (1905).

During the first decade of the 20th century, poet and author Ruth Bré enjoyed a fleeting period of fame in Germany as a result of having founded the Liga für Mutterschutz (League for the Protection of Mothers; LPM) in 1904. Born in 1862 to unwed parents, Bré led a difficult and eccentric life on the fringes of respectable society, writing unsuccessful poetry and generally making a poor impression on members of the traditional establishment as well as on leaders of the emerging feminist movement. As an elementary school teacher, her social status was relatively low and economically she had barely entered into the lower rungs of the middle class.

Founded in Leipzig on November 12, 1904, the LPM was strongly influenced by ideas that Bré had already developed in previous writings. These included polemics calling for the cessation of the "capitalist rule of man" and the restoration of a matriarchal form of social organization. Strongly influenced by the ideas of Social Darwinism, she was impressed by some of the writings of the Swedish social reformer ***Ellen Key**, which had become available in German translations. In its first programmatic manifesto, the League announced that it was planning to found "mother-colonies" in the countryside, the purpose of which was to make it possible for unmarried mothers and their children to live a healthy life. Supported by state subsidies and the profits from moderately physical agricultural labor, the aim of these settlements would be the "improvement of the state of the nation through the breeding of the healthy." With this in mind, only healthy mothers would be accepted on these settlements.

Deeply concerned about illegitimate children, Bré noted ominously that there was an extremely high incidence of sickness, criminality and infant mortality among the illegitimate. She argued that if her plans could be extended to a high percentage of the 180,000 children born illegitimate in Germany every year, the "racial health" of the German Reich would quickly improve dramatically. Implicitly, this meant that the nation would be stronger, both in peace and in war. Bré's ideas were not original, resembling in many ways the anti-urbanist sentiments of the *völkisch* extreme Right publicists who since the 1880s had argued that Germany was becoming soft as a result of democracy, socialism, urbanism and humanitarian ideals. The racialist and Social Darwinist aspects of her ideas were also not original. What was new in Bré's writings was her feminist emphasis. The idea of an organization lobbying for the protection of mothers was regarded as eminently reasonable, and as a consequence the organization was maintained but its founder was eased out of power.

With the argument that her organization could be more effective with Berlin rather than Leipzig as its headquarters, Ruth Bré was persuaded in 1905 to resign the LPM presidency. Her advocacy of homes in the countryside, and the generally Utopian spirit of the organization, were also quickly discarded as a well-oiled machine of feminists took over. ***Helene Stoecker**, who thoroughly disapproved of Bré's notions, described her as a "totally undisciplined person" who was "a little crazy." The newly defined League now concentrated on more traditional welfare approaches within an urban setting. Outmaneuvered, Bré complained bitterly prior to resigning all of her offices in the League as a final act of protest:

> Instead of providing mothers and their children with a modest standard of life on a small country estate, instead of preparing a *home* for them, a home that the father or husband cannot or will not provide—instead of this, they are to be put in 'homes' with an *institutional* character, within city walls.—Instead of breeding human beings who are capable of work, they are bothering with the *inferior* once more.

Bré attempted to keep her original ideas alive by founding a renamed "*First* German League for the Protection of Mothers," but her organizational skills were weak and the effort faded. Politically skilled feminists like Helene Stöcker now dominated the field of maternal protection, and amateur enthusiasts like Ruth Bré slipped back into the obscurity from which they had briefly emerged. Deeply disillusioned with her brief experience with feminist politics, Ruth Bré died in December 1911.

SOURCES:

Allen, Ann Taylor. *Feminism and Motherhood in Germany, 1800–1914*. New Brunswick, NJ: Rutgers University Press, 1991.

———. "Mothers of the New Generation: Adele Schreiber, Helene Stöcker, and the Evolution of a German Idea of Motherhood, 1900–1914," in *Signs: Journal of Women in Culture and Society.* Vol. 10. No. 3. Spring, 1985, pp. 418–438.

Bouness, Elisabeth [Ruth Bré]. *Das Recht auf Mutterschaft: Ein Forderung zur Bekämpfung der Prostitution, der Frauen-und Geschlechtskrankheiten.* Leipzig: Frauen-Rundschau, 1903.

———. *Kaiserworte: Fürsorgegesetz und Lehrerschaft: Betrachtungen aus Liebe zum Vaterlande.* Leipzig: Frauen-Rundschau, 1903.

Bré, Ruth. *Staatskinder oder Mutterrecht? Versuche zur Erlösung aus dem sexuellen und wirtschaftlichen Elend.* Leipzig: Frauen-Rundschau, 1904.

Ehe? Zur Reform der sexuellen Moral, von Hedwig Dohm, Anita Ausgpurg, Helene Stöcker, Adele Schreiber, Käte Schirmacher, Grete Meisel-Hess, Ida Boy-Ed, Hans von Kahlenberg, Franziska Mann, Hermione von Preuschen, Elisabeth Dauthendey, Toni Schwabe, Ruth Bré. Berlin: Otto Beckmann Verlag, 1911.

Evans, Richard J. *The Feminist Movement in Germany 1894–1933.* Beverly Hills: SAGE Publications, 1976.

Hackett, Amy Kathleen. "The Politics of Feminism in Wilhelmine Germany, 1890–1933." Ph.D. dissertation, Columbia University, 1976.

Meyer, Alfred G. *The Feminism and Socialism of Lily Braun.* Bloomington: Indiana University Press, 1985.

Nowacki, Bernd. *Der Bund für Mutterschutz (1905–1933).* Husum: Matthiesen Verlag Ingwert Paulsen Jr., 1983.

Plothow, A. "Ruth Bré," in *Berliner Tageblatt.* December 15, 1911.

Schreiber, Adele. "Persönliches von Ruth Bré," in *Dresdner Neueste Nachrichten.* December 24, 1911.

Wickert, Christl. *Helene Stöcker, 1869–1943: Frauenrechtlerin, Sexualreformerin und Pazifistin. Eine Biographie.* Bonn: J. H. W. Dietz Verlag, 1991.

John Haag, Associate Professor, University of Georgia, Athens, Georgia

Breckinridge, Mary (1881–1965)

American nurse and midwife who founded the Frontier Nursing Service. *Born on February 17, 1881, in Memphis, Tennessee; died on May 16, 1965, in Hyden, Kentucky; first daughter and second of four children of Clifton Rodes (a cotton planter and commission merchant, U.S. congressional representative, and American minister to Russia, 1890s) and* ***Katherine (Carson) Breckinridge****; granddaughter of John Cabell Breckinridge (vice president under James Buchanan); attended Rosemont-Dézaley School, Lausanne, Switzerland, 1896–98; Low and Heywood School, Stamford, Connecticut; earned nursing degree, Saint Luke's Hospital School of Nursing, New York City, 1910; married Henry Ruffner Morrison, in 1904 (died 1906); married Richard Ryan Thompson, in 1912 (divorced 1920); children: (second marriage) Breckinridge (1914–1918); Mary (died in infancy).*

Born into a distinguished Southern family, Mary Breckinridge had just taken her place as a young society matron when a series of tragedies changed the course of her life. Following the devastating death of her first husband, a promising young lawyer, and the subsequent loss of her two young children by a second marriage, Breckinridge turned to nursing as an outlet for her grief and committed herself to saving the lives of young mothers and children in the remote mountains of southeastern Kentucky.

In 1918, after receiving her credentials as a registered nurse, Breckinridge left her second husband (they divorced in 1820) and volunteered for wartime duty with the American Red Cross, where she was eventually assigned to the American Committee for Devastated France, headed by ***Anne Morgan**. Breckinridge went to work in Vic-Sur-Aisne, caring for the infant victims of war as well as pregnant and nursing women. Through her work in France, and several trips to England, Breckinridge formulated a plan by which nurse-midwives could serve the needs of women and young children in rural America. Returning from France in 1921, she trained as a midwife in England and Scotland, and joined the Midwives Institute in 1924.

In 1925, with support from prominent citizens and capital inherited from her mother, Breckinridge founded the Kentucky Committee for Mothers and Babies, which in 1928 became the Frontier Nursing Service (FNS), modeled after the Highlands and Islands Medical and Nursing Service that Breckinridge had observed in Scotland. At the core of the operation was Hayden Hospital and Health Center, opened in June 1928, which would provide 12 beds and a physician for more serious medical emergencies. Flanking the hospital were six outpost nursing centers, each housing several nurses who traveled mostly by horseback to provide home care to the more remote rural families. In 1929, FNS became the American Association of Nurse-Midwives, from which Breckinridge established the Frontier Graduate School of Midwifery in 1939, a training program for nurse-midwives.

Breckinridge received many honors for her work, including the Harmon Fanton Prize for public health work in 1926 and the National League of Nursing ***Mary Adelaide Nutting** Award for Distinguished Service, in 1961. She remained director of FNS and editor of its quarterly bulletin until she died of leukemia and a stroke at the age of 84.

SOURCES:

McKown, Robin. *Heroic Nurses.* NY: Putnam, 1966.

Read, Phyllis J., and Bernard L. Witlieb. *The Book of Women's Firsts.* NY: Random House, 1992.

Sicherman, Barbara and Carol Hurd Green, eds. *Notable American Women: The Modern Period.* Cambridge, MA: the Belknap Press of Harvard University Press, 1980.

SUGGESTED READING:

Breckinridge, Mary. *Wide Neighborhoods: The Story of the Frontier Nursing Service.* (1952).

Barbara Morgan,
Melrose, Massachusetts

Breckinridge, Mary Martin (b. 1905)

American pioneering radio reporter during World War II. *Born in 1905 in Kentucky; graduated from Vassar College, 1927; studied at the New School for Social Research, New York; married a member of the American State Department.*

In the manner of pioneering print journalists ***Doris Fleeson** and ***Marguerite Higgins,** Mary Martin Breckinridge broke through the gender barrier in radio to become one of the first women to report the news during World War II. Beginning her career in Washington as a secretary for the Democratic National Committee and then for a member of Congress, Breckinridge went abroad in 1930 to work as a freelance photographer. In 1939, when World War II broke out, she was in London working for a photo syndicate. Edward R. Murrow, who was there covering the first bombing raids for CBS radio, put Breckinridge on the air to report events from a woman's point of view. Executives back home were so pleased with her performance that she became a regular. Breckinridge quickly moved from women's issues to broader war coverage. In December 1939, she broadcast first from the Netherlands and then temporarily replaced William L. Shirer in Berlin. Returning to Amsterdam, she continued reporting until forced to flee from the Nazi invasion. She took up her broadcasts again in Paris and later Italy.

Breckinridge gave up reporting to marry an American State Department employee who was involved in work with prisoners of war. After a three-day honeymoon, she and her new husband went to Berlin where they made prison-camp inspections. Although America was not yet officially at war with Germany, Breckinridge was not allowed to broadcast again because of her involvement with a member of the State Department. She lived most of the rest of her life abroad as a diplomat's wife, and she continued to publish photographs under her maiden name.

Barbara Morgan,
Melrose, Massachusetts

Breckinridge, Sophonisba Preston (1866–1948)

American social worker and educator. *Born in Lexington, Kentucky, on April 1, 1866; died in Chicago, Illinois, on July 30, 1948; daughter of William Campbell Preston Breckinridge (a lawyer who served in Congress) and Issas (Desha) Breckinridge; sister of Desha Breckinridge (editor of the* Lexington Herald*); sister-in-law of* ***Madeline McDowell Breckinridge*** *(1872–1920); graduated from Wellesley College, S.B., 1888; granted Ph.D. in political science and economics from University of Chicago, 1901, JD, 1904, LL.D, Oberlin, 1919, University of Kentucky, 1925.*

Selected publications: Legal Tender: A Study in American Monetary History *(1901); (with Edith Abbott)* The Delinquent Child and the Home *(1912); (with Marion Talbot)* The Modern Household *(1912); (with Edith Abbott)* Truancy *(1917);* New Homes for Old *(1921); (with sister-in-law Madeline McDowell Breckinridge)* A Leader in the New South *(1921);* Family Welfare Work in a Metropolitan Community *(1924);* Public Welfare Administration *(1927);* Marriage and the Civil Rights of Women *(1931);* Women in the Twentieth Century *(1933);* The Family and the State *and* Social Work and the Courts *(1934);* The Illinois Poor Law and Its Administration *(1939).*

After teaching high school in Washington D.C. (1888–94), Sophonisba Breckinridge clerked in her father's Lexington law office for a year and became the first woman in Kentucky admitted to the state bar (1895). Three years later, she entered the University of Chicago, where she was the first woman to receive a law degree in the college's history; she began instructing at the University in 1903. A champion of progressive reforms, Breckinridge founded the Chicago School of Civics and Philanthropy with ***Julia Lathrop** (1907), subsequently renamed the University of Chicago School of Social Service Administration (1920). She also founded the Immigrants' Protective League (1908), became vice-president of National Woman's Suffrage Association (1911), and was named delegate to the Women's Peace Conference at The Hague (1915). In 1912, Breckinridge co-authored *The Delinquent Child and the Home* with ***Edith Abbott** and *The Modern*

Household with **Marion Talbot**. She followed up her work with Abbott in 1917 with the report on *Truancy and Non-Attendance in the Chicago Schools*. At the University of Chicago School of Social Service Administration, Breckinridge was dean and professor of public welfare administration (1925–29), dean of College of Arts, Literature, and Science (1929–33), and professor emeritus of public welfare (1933–42). A pioneer in legislative social work and an early advocate for economic parity for women, she was also the founder of the *Social Service Review*, which she edited until her death in 1948.

SUGGESTED READING:

Fitzpatrick, Ellen. *Endless Crusade*. Oxford University Press, 1990.

Brécourt, Jeanne (b. 1837)

French courtesan and blackmailer. *Name variations: Jeanne de la Cour; Brecourt. Born Jeanne Amenaide Brécourt in 1837 in Paris, France; death date unknown; married a grocer named Gras, who deserted her.*

One of France's most infamous courtesans, Jeanne Brécourt destroyed a number of her paramours through blackmail and deceit, while feigning an aristocratic background. After plotting to have a wealthy lover blinded to guarantee his dependence, she was brought to trial in 1877 and defended by Charles Lachaud, who had also been the attorney for ***Marie Lafarge**. The trial, one of the more spectacular of its day, reportedly attracted the elite of Paris, including journalists, playwrights, and even members of the popular Comédie-Française.

Brécourt's early life included a troubled childhood and an abusive marriage. Born in poverty, she was adopted at age five by a wealthy baroness who sought to provide a home for the neglected child. When Brécourt was 11, her parents demanded her back to help support the family. At 18, after seven years on poverty row, she returned to the baroness. Soon after, she married impulsively, living in an abusive relationship for a number of years until her husband abandoned her. Brécourt then tried her hand at writing and acting, before adopting a new persona: she emerged as a beautiful courtesan named Jeanne de la Cour. Professing a devout hatred of all men, she proceeded to use and dismiss a cadre of wealthy lovers, many of whom became suicidal in her wake.

In 1873, Brécourt met Georges de Saint Pierre, a rich and handsome young man 16 years her junior. Faced with his family's disapproval and no marriage plans, Brécourt began to obsess about his fidelity. In a morbid plot, she convinced an old friend, Nathalis Gaudry, to blind Georges by throwing acid in his face, thus causing his dependence on her for the remainder of his life. The plan, which was carried out successfully after she and Georges returned home from a masked ball, eventually fell under the investigation of detective Gustave Macé, who would become one of France's most capable detectives. After months of sleuthing, during which time Brécourt tried to escape to Italy with Georges, Macé wore down Brécourt and located Gaudry. Further implicating Brécourt were letters she had hidden in order to blackmail Georges should he ever try to leave her.

The trial, during which Gaudry confessed to carrying out the crime because of his overwhelming love for Brécourt, culminated in the dramatic testimony of Georges de Saint Pierre, which ultimately clarified Brécourt's guilt. She was convicted and sentenced to 15 years in prison. Little is known of her final years, though by some accounts, she left prison haggard and old, and spent her last days peddling fruit, as she had as a child.

Barbara Morgan,
Melrose, Massachusetts

ACKNOWLEDGMENTS

Photographs and illustrations appearing in *Women in World History, Volume 2,* were received from the following sources:

Virgil Apger for Metro-Goldwyn-Mayer: **p. 662**; Courtesy of Atomium Books: From *A Tale of Two Germanys* (Wilimington, DE; text by Martyn Bond and photographs by Jons Michael Voss and Volker Doring), **p. 683**; Courtesy of Austrian Press and Information Service: **p. 15**; Courtesy of Beechcraft: **p. 347**; Berry College: **pp. 508, 510**; *Champaign-Urbana News Gazette,* photograph by Brian Johnson: **p. 598**; Courtesy of Columbia Records: **p. 53**; Commerce Graphics Ltd., Inc., photograph by Berenice Abbott: **p. 165**; Courtesy of Connecticut College: **p. 661**; Courtesy of the Metropolitan Opera, from a portrait by Simon Elwes: **p. 390**; Painting by Lucas Cranch the Elder: **p. 760**; Courtesy of Darrell Waters, Ltd. (Bedford House, London): **p. 665**; Engraving by Henry B. Hall, from a painting by John Hopper: **p. 13**; Photograph by John Engstead: **p. 475**; Courtesy of Fawcett Library: **p. 290**; Courtesy of G.E. Research and Development: **pp. 639, 640**; Courtesy of Halsman: **p. 829**; Oil by Francesco Hayez, c. 1840: **p. 369**; Courtesy of Historisches Museum der Stadtwien: **p. 486**; Compliments of the Speaker's Office Manager, House of Commons: **p. 759**; Courtesy of Moorland-Spingarn Research Center, Howard University (Washington, DC): **p. 432**; Courtesy of the International Institut voor Sociale Geschiedenis (Amsterdam): **p. 907**; Courtesy of the International Museum of Photography at the George Eastman House: **p. 777**; From the painting by Sir Thomas Lawrence: **p. 632**; Courtesy of the Library of Congress: **pp. 30, 69, 75, 170, 199, 278, 360, 371, 406, 500, 518, 543, 583, 586, 606, 619, 650, 711, 755, 867**; Courtesy of the Loreto House (Beaufort, Dublin): **p. 109**; Courtesy of Louisiana State University Press: **p. 735**; Courtesy of the Marguerite Bourgeoys Museum (Montreal, Canada): **p. 824, 826,** from an engraving by Massard, based on an engraving by Charles-Louis Simonneau (1722), **p. 820**; Portrait by Louise Marie Jeanne Mauduit, Madame Hersent (1806): **p. 710**; Courtesy of MCA: **p. 697**; Courtesy of the Metropolitan Museum of Art (New York City): Painting by Isabel Bishop, Arthur A. Hearn Fund, 1936 (36.27) **p. 566, p. 723**; Courtesy of Metro-Goldwyn-Mayer: **p. 43**; Courtesy of the Minerva Bernardino Foundation (Santo Domingo, Dominican Republic): **p. 494**; Courtesy of Bruno Monsaingeon, *Mademoiselle* (Paris: Editions van de Veloe): **p. 808**; Courtesy of Musee d'Orsay (Paris): **p. 214**; Courtesy of Musee National du Chateau de Fontainebleau: **p. 722**; Courtesy of Musee National de Louvre: **p. 420**; Courtesy of Musees Royaux des Beaux-Arts (Brussels), painting by Jan van Eyck: **p. 146**; Photographs by Nadar: **pp. 499, 746**; Courtesy of the National Film Archive (London): **p. 670**; Courtesy of the National Portrait Gallery: **p. 355**; Painting by Emily Osborn: **p. 676**; Courtesy of the Embassy of Pakistan: **p. 536**; Courtesy of Penguin Books: **p. 547**; Courtesy of the Pennsylvania Academy of Fine Arts, Henry Drinker Collection (Philadelphia): **p. 334**; Photograph by John Percival: **p. 659**; Detail of fresco by Pinturicchio: **p. 770**; Courtesy of Princeton University, Sylvia Beech Collection: **p. 288**; Courtesy of Radcliffe College, Schlesinger Library: **p. 349**; Photograph by Lettice Ramsey (1932): **p. 378**; Compliments of the Rank Organization: **p. 853**; Courtesy of the Royal Danish Embassy: **p. 127**; Courtesy of the Royal Danish Ministry of Foreign Affairs: **p. 356**; Courtesy of the Salvation Army, Heritage Museum (West Nyack, NY): **pp. 751, 785**; Photograph by Napoleon Sarony: **p. 269**; Courtesy of Sophia Smith College (Northampton, MA): **p. 206**; Courtesy of the South Dakota Historical Society: **p. 554**; Painting by Gilbert Stuart: **p. 554**; Courtesy of Swarthmore College, Peace Collection, Papers of Emily Greene Balch: **p. 100**; Courtesy of the Swedish Information Service (New York City): **p. 784**; Courtesy of the Swedish Institute (Box 7434, S-103 91, Stockholm): **p. 862**; Courtesy of the Theosophical

Publishing House: **p. 625**; Courtesy of the *Toledo Blade*: **p. 422**; Courtesy of the Toledo Museum of Art (Toledo, OH): **p. 336**; Effigy by Pietro Torrigiano, Westminster Abbey: **p. 324**; Courtesy of the U.S. House of Representatives: **pp. 74, 433, 637, 681, 699, 783, 851**; Courtesy of Underwood and Underwood: **p. 299**; Courtesy of United Artists: **p. 487**; Courtesy of United Press International: **p. 6**; Courtesy of Universal Press Syndicate: **p. 703**; Courtesy of Vassar College Libraries, Special Collections: **p. 559**; Courtesy of the Walker Art Gallery (Liverpool): **p. 310**; Courtesy of Warner Bros.: **p. 417**; Courtesy of Wellesley College Archives: **p. 235**; Courtesy of Wilson Sporting Goods: **p. 467**; Courtesy of WNBA Enterprises, LLC: **pp. 629, 701**.

ISBN 0-7876-4061-1
9 780787 640613
90000